NEW INTERNATIONAL VERSION

NIV

BIBLE
CONCORDANCE

NEW INTERNATIONAL VERSION

NIV

BIBLE
CONCORDANCE

JOHN R. KOHLENBERGER III

ZONDERVAN®

ZONDERVAN

NIV Bible Concordance
Copyright © 2012 by John R. Kohlenberger III

Adapted and updated from the *NIV Compact Concordance*
Copyright © 1993 by John R. Kohlenberger III

Requests for information should be addressed to:

Zondervan, 3900 Sparks Dr. SE, Grand Rapids, Michigan 49546

Library of Congress Cataloging-in-Publication Data

Kohlenberger, John R.
    NIV Bible concordance / John R. Kohlenberger III, editor.
      p. cm.
     ISBN 978-0-310-49490-4 (softcover)
   1. Bible—Concordances, English—New International. I. Title.
BS425.K6447 2012
  220.5'20813—dc23   2011049792

Cover photography: *Getty Images / Josef F. Stuefer*
Interior design: *John R. Kohlenberger III*

Printed in the United States of America

HB 12.20.2023

Dedication

To Peter Furler
with great respect and admiration

Sing to the LORD a new song;
    sing to the LORD, all the earth.
Sing to the LORD, praise his name;
    proclaim his salvation day after day.
Declare his glory among the nations,
    his marvelous deeds among all peoples.
Psalm 96:1–3 (NIV)

Contents

Acknowledgments

The NIV Bible Concordance is the product of the energies of many individuals in addition to the editor whose name is on the cover.

I must start with grateful thanks to God for allowing me the time and clarity to produce this book during my battle with advanced prostate cancer. My wife, Carolyn, and our children, Sarah and Josh, have been so precious and dear these past nine years. I have drawn great strength and support from my family, my *mishpachah*, my *ohana*, at Cascade View Covenant Church.

Stan Gundry, Executive Vice-President and Editor-in-Chief at Zondervan, has been a great friend who has walked with me through the process of making every concordance to the NIV. Verlyn Verbrugge, Senior Editor-at-Large, made many helpful suggestions and caught many mistakes and inconsistencies.

Brent Knopf created valuable programming to help me convert the previous edition of *The NIV Compact Concordance* into this revised edition. He often interrupted his work mixing the second CD for his excellent band, Ramona Falls, for which I am deeply grateful.

Introduction:
How to Use This Book

A concordance is an index to a book. It is usually arranged in alphabetical order and shows the location of key words in the book. In addition, it often supplies several words of the context in which each word is found.

The NIV Bible Concordance (NIVBC) is based on the best-selling NIV Compact Concordance (1993), fully revised for the 2011 edition of the New International Version (NIV). This is the first stand-alone concordance for the revised NIV. Two shorter concordances, for use within reference and study editions of the NIV, were introduced in 2011.

FEATURES OF THE NIV BIBLE CONCORDANCE

The NIVBC has four major features: (1) concordance entries, (2) key phrase indexes, (3) capsule biographies, and (4) KJV "See" references.

Concordance Entries

The NIVBC indexes 7,618 of the 14,408 words in the NIV from Aaron to Zuzites and numerals from 40 to 603,550. The 57,035 context lines represent 58,451 occurrences of these words. Below is a typical entry from the NIVBC:

> **AVENGES*** VENGEANCE
> 2Sa   22: 48   He is the God who **a** me, who puts
> Ps   9: 12   For he who **a** blood remembers;
>   18: 47   He is the God who **a** me,
>   94: 1   The LORD is a God who **a**. O God who **a**, shine forth.

Entries are arranged in alphabetical order. Numerals follow the letter Z. Entries index words exactly as they are spelled in the NIV. The asterisk (*) marks entries that index every occurrence of the word in the NIV; 2,442 entries are exhaustive, including frequently occurring words like "faith," "grace," and "love."

Related words, if any, follow the bold entry word in smaller, non-bolded print. Rather than listing all related words after each indexed word, the editor chose one indexed word to act as the "group heading." All related words are listed after the group heading, and each of the related word headings points back to the group heading. By looking up the related word, you can study additional texts containing other forms of the word and other members of the word's cognate "family." For example, VENGEANCE lists six additional terms you can study within the NIVBC to get a fuller biblical picture of revenge, both human and divine.

There are two entries for LORD and LORD'S. The proper name of God, "Yahweh," is represented in the NIV as LORD in small capital letters. The title "Lord" is capitalized when referring to God and in lower case when referring to a human being or false god. "Lord" and "lord" are indexed in the NIVBC under the heading

LORD and "Lord's" under the heading LORD'S. "LORD" is indexed under the heading LORD† and "LORD's" under the heading LORD'S†.

Contexts are organized in biblical order. A key to the abbreviations of the books of the Bible follows the introduction on page xii. Only the first appearance of a book's abbreviation is listed, as in the case of Ps (Psalms) in the example on page ix. The purpose of context lines in a concordance is simply to help the reader recognize or locate a specific verse in the Bible. For word study—or any kind of Bible study—the context offered by a concordance is rarely enough to go on. Nevertheless, sometimes a short sentence or a whole verse fits on one line, as in the case of John 11:35, "Jesus wept."

Taken by themselves, context lines can and do misrepresent the teaching of Scripture by taking statements out of the larger context. "There is no God" is a context taken straight from Psalm 14:1. Of course the Bible does not teach this; it is what "The fool says in his heart"! Similarly, a context for Leviticus 24:16 might read, "the LORD is to be put to death" while the text actually says, "anyone who blasphemes the name of the LORD is to be put to death."

Great care has been taken by the editor, programmer, and proofreaders of the *NIVBC* to create contexts that are informative and accurate. But the reader should always check word contexts by looking them up in the NIV itself. "The Wicked Bible," a KJV edition of 1631, accidentally omitted the word "not" from the seventh commandment, for which the printers were fined 300 pounds sterling! Though there are no longer such fines for misleading contexts, the editor and publisher are still deeply concerned that the *NIVBC* be used discerningly.

As noted in "A Word to the Reader," the translators' preface to the NIV:

> Mark 16:9–20 and John 7:53–8:11, although long accorded virtually equal status with the rest of the Gospels in which they stand, have a very questionable—and confused—standing in the textual history of the New Testament . . . A different typeface has now been chosen for these passages to indicate even more clearly their uncertain status.

Contexts to these verses in Mark and John are in italics, reflecting the formatting of the NIV.

Key Phrase Indexes
Following the entries for 193 highly frequent words are 250 key phrase indexes:

FEAR
...

FEAR OF THE LORD† 2Ch 17:10; 19:7, 9; Ps 19:9; 34:11; 111:10; Pr 1:7; 2:5; 9:10; 10:27; 14:27; 15:16; 16:6; 19:23; 22:4; 23:17; Isa 11:2, 3; 33:6

LORD†
...

FEAR OF THE LORD† See FEAR

These list biblical references to all occurrences of significant phrases—11,838 total references—but without contexts. Thus even in this smaller concordance, you can find every reference for such phrases as the FEAR OF THE LORD, HOLY SPIRIT, SON OF GOD, and SON OF MAN. Phrases are indexed at only one location; other words in the phrase are cross-referenced to the index. In the example above, FEAR OF THE LORD† is indexed under FEAR with a cross-reference at LORD†.

Capsule Biographies
Capsule biographies give significant information on 296 prominent individuals:

DEBORAH
1. Female prophet and judge who led Israel to victory over Canaanites (Jdg 4–5).
2. Rebekah's nurse (Ge 35:8).

It is easier to represent and to locate key events in an individual's life in such an entry, rather than by using context lines, especially in the entry on Jesus. As in the example above, different individuals of the same name are distinguished by separately numbered biographies. These entries index 3,879 biblical texts.

KJV "See" References
The King James, or Authorized, Version has been the dominant English Bible translation from the early seventeenth century to the latter half of the twentieth century. Because of this, the KJV has had profound impact on the language of both the church and English-speaking society. To help users familiar with KJV vocabulary find the proper NIV terms, 80 KJV words appear in 70 KJV "See" references, pointing to 112 NIV words and phrases. These include such headings as:

COMFORTER COMFORT (KJV, of the Holy Spirit,
   see ADVOCATE)

[HOLY] GHOST (KJV) See [HOLY] SPIRIT

Note that multiple-word "See" references, such as HOLY SPIRIT, do *not* refer to a multiple-word heading. Rather, they direct the user to look for that *combination* of words under the heading for *any* of the words in the multiple-word reference. Words translated in the KJV as "ghost" are usually translated in the NIV as "spirit," and the phrase "Holy Ghost" is always translated "Holy Spirit" in the NIV. In the case of this phrase, "Holy Spirit" is indexed exhaustively in the entry HOLY. But this is not the case for all multiple-word references.

Special NIV References
The 2011 edition of the NIV is about 95 percent indentical to the 1984 edition, but there are some noticeable differences in vocabulary that could affect users of the *NIVBC*. Some proper and place names are spelled differently. For example, the 1984 NIV "Abimelech" is "Abimelek" in the 2011 NIV. These words alphabetize similarly, but where spelling changes location of a proper name, it is cross referenced. This occurs in the case of 1984 NIV "Korazin," which references the 2011 NIV entry "Chorazin."

Two words common to English Bible translations are not used in the 2011 NIV: "saints" and "*Selah*." The Hebrew and Greek words translated "saints" in the 1984 edition of the NIV are now translated by a variety of words emphasizing God's people who are holy and faithful. "*Selah*" is explained in "A Word to the Reader":

Although *Selah*, used mainly in the Psalms, is probably a musical term, its meaning is uncertain. Since it may interrupt reading and distract the reader, this word has not been kept in the English text, but every occurrence has been signaled by a footnote.

Because the editor believes users want to know where "saints" was used in the 1984 edition of the NIV and how these texts are translated in the 2011 edition, a complete list of 2011 NIV translations and 1984 NIV references occurs in the entry SAINTS. Similarly, all 1984 NIV references to "*Selah*" are listed in the entry SELAH.

Abbreviations and Symbols

Other Abbreviations and Symbols

*	following entry head
=	exhaustive entry
LORD†	LORD
LORD'S†	LORD's
KJV	King James Version
NIV	New International Version
T	Psalm title

A

AARON

Genealogy of (Ex 6:16–20; Jos 21:4, 10; 1Ch 6:3–15).

Priesthood of (Ex 28:1; Nu 17; Heb 5:1–4; 7), garments (Ex 28; 39), consecration (Ex 29), ordination (Lev 8).

Spokesman for Moses (Ex 4:14–16, 27–31; 7:1–2). Supported Moses' hands in battle (Ex 17:8–13). Built golden calf (Ex 32; Dt 9:20). Talked against Moses (Nu 12). Priesthood opposed (Nu 16); staff budded (Nu 17). Forbidden to enter land (Nu 20:1–12). Death (Nu 20:22–29; 33:38–39).

AARON AND HIS SONS See SONS

SON OF AARON See SON

SONS OF AARON See SONS

AARON'S SONS See SONS

ABADDON*

Rev   9:11   whose name in Hebrew is **A**

ABANDON   ABANDONED

Dt   4:31   he will not **a** or destroy you
Jos   10: 6   "Do not **a** your servants.
1Ki   6:13   and will not **a** my people Israel."
2Ch 12: 5   I now **a** you to Shishak.' "
Ne   9:19   compassion you did not **a** them
         9:31   not put an end to them or **a** them,
Ps   16:10   because you will not **a** me
      138: 8   do not **a** the works of your hands.
Jer   12: 7   forsake my house, **a** my inheritance;
Ac   2:27   because you will not **a** me
1Ti   4: 1   in later times some will **a** the faith

ABANDONED   ABANDON

Ge   24:27   who has not **a** his kindness
Dt   29.25   because this people **a** the covenant
      32:15   They **a** the God who made them
Jdg   6:13   now the LORD has **a** us and given
1Ki   18:18   You have **a** the LORD's
Isa   54: 7   "For a brief moment I **a** you,
Ac   2:31   that he was not **a** to the realm
Ro   1:27   also **a** natural relations with women
2Co   4: 9   persecuted, but not **a**;

ABBA*

Mk   14:36   "**A**, Father," he said,
Ro   8:15   And by him we cry, "**A**, Father."
Gal   4: 6   the Spirit who calls out, "**A**,

ABDON

A judge of Israel (Jdg 12:13–15).

ABEDNEGO

Deported to Babylon with Daniel (Da 1:1–6). Name changed from Azariah (Da 1:7). Refused defilement by food (Da 1:8–20). Refused idol worship (Da 3:1–12); saved from furnace (Da 3:13–30).

ABEL

Second son of Adam (Ge 4:2). Offered proper sacrifice (Ge 4:4; Heb 11:4). Murdered by Cain (Ge 4:8; Mt 23:35; Lk 11:51; 1Jn 3:12).

ABHOR*

Lev   26:11   among you, and I will not **a** you.
      26:15   reject my decrees and **a** my laws
      26:30   of your idols, and I will **a** you.
      26:44   or **a** them so as to destroy them
Ps   26: 5   I **a** the assembly of evildoers
      139:21   **a** those who are in rebellion against
Am   6: 8   "I **a** the pride of Jacob and detest
Ro   2:22   You who **a** idols, do you rob

ABIATHAR

High priest in days of Saul and David (1Sa 22; 2Sa 15; 1Ki 1–2; Mk 2:26). Escaped Saul's slaughter of priests (1Sa 22:18–23). Supported David in Absalom's revolt (2Sa 15:24–29). Supported Adonijah (1Ki 1:7–42); deposed by Solomon (1Ki 2:22–35; cf. 1Sa 2:31–35).

ABIB   See AVIV

ABIGAIL

1. Sister of David (1Ch 2:16–17).
2. Wife of Nabal (1Sa 25:30); pled for his life with David (1Sa 25:14–35). Became David's wife after Nabal's death (1Sa 25:36–42); bore him Kileab (2Sa 3:3) also known as Daniel (1Ch 3:1).

ABIHU

Son of Aaron (Ex 6:23; 24:1, 9); killed for offering unauthorized fire (Lev 10; Nu 3:2–4; 1Ch 24:1–2).

ABIJAH

1. Second son of Samuel (1Ch 6:28); a corrupt judge (1Sa 8:1–5).
2. An Aaronic priest (1Ch 24:10; Lk 1:5).
3. Son of Jeroboam I of Israel; died as prophesied by Ahijah (1Ki 14:1–18).
4. Son of Rehoboam; king of Judah who fought Jeroboam I attempting to reunite the kingdom (1Ki 14:31 –15:8; 2Ch 12:1614:1; Mt 1:7).

ABILITY*   ABLE

Ge   47: 6   of any among them with special **a**,
Ex   31: 6   Also I have given **a** to all the skilled
      35:34   tribe of Dan, the **a** to teach others.
      36: 1   **a** to know how to carry out all
      36: 2   to whom the LORD had given **a**
Dt   8:18   for it is he who gives you the **a**
Ezr   2:69   According to their **a** they gave
Ecc   5:19   and the **a** to enjoy them, to accept
       6: 2   God does not grant them the **a**
Da   5:12   and also the **a** to interpret dreams,
Mt   25:15   one bag, each according to his **a**.
Ac   8:19   this **a** so that everyone on whom I
2Co   1: 8   far beyond our **a** to endure,
       8: 3   were able, and even beyond their **a**.

ABIMELEK

1. King of Gerar who took Abraham's wife Sarah, believing her to be his sister (Ge 20). Later made a covenant with Abraham (Ge 21:22–33).
2. King of Gerar who took Isaac's wife Rebekah,

believing her to be his sister (Ge 26:1–11). Later made a covenant with Isaac (Ge 26:12–31).

3. Son of Gideon (Jdg 8:31). Attempted to make himself king (Jdg 9).

ABIRAM
Sided with Dathan in rebellion against Moses and Aaron (Nu 16; 26:9; Dt 11:6).

ABISHAG
Shunammite virgin; attendant of David in his old age (1Ki 1:1–15; 2:17–22).

ABISHAI
Son of Zeruiah, David's sister (1Sa 26:6; 1Ch 2:16). One of David's chief warriors (1Ch 11:15–21): against Edom (1Ch 18:12–13), Ammon (2Sa 10), Absalom (2Sa 18), Sheba (2Sa 20). Wanted to kill Saul (1Sa 26), killed Abner (2Sa 2:18–27; 3:22–39), wanted to kill Shimei (2Sa 16:5–13; 19:16–23).

ABLAZE
Dt   5:23 while the mountain was a with fire,
Da   7: 9 with fire, and its wheels were all a.
Rev 8: 8 all a, was thrown into the sea.

ABLE ABILITY, DISABLED, ENABLE, ENABLED, ENABLES, ENABLING
Ge 13: 6 that they were not a to stay together.
Lev 26:37 So you will not be a to stand before
Nu 14:16 'The LORD was not a to bring
Jos 24:19 people, "You are not a to serve
1Sa 17:33 "You are not a to go out against
1Ki 3: 9 who is a to govern this great people
1Ch 29:14 that we should be a to give as
2Ch 2: 6 who is a to build a temple for him,
Job 41:10 Who then is a to stand against me?
Pr 17:16 they are not a to understand it?
Eze 7:19 gold will not be a to deliver them
Da 2:26 "Are you a to tell me what I saw
      3:17 the God we serve is a to deliver us
      4:37 walk in pride he is a to humble.
Hos 5:13 But he is not a to cure you, not a to heal your sores.
Mt 9:28 you believe that I am a to do this?"
    26:61 'I am a to destroy the temple of God
Lk 13:24 will try to enter and will not be a to.
    14:30 to build and wasn't a to finish.'
    21:15 your adversaries will be a to resist
    21:36 pray that you may be a to escape all
    21:36 you may be a to stand before
Ac 5:39 you will not be a to stop these men;
    11:29 as each one was a,
    15:10 we nor our ancestors have been a
    22:13 very moment I was a to see him.
Ro 8:39 will be a to separate us
    11:23 for God is a to graft them in again.
    14: 4 the Lord is a to make them stand.
    16:25 to him who is a to establish you
2Co 8: 3 they gave as much as they were a,
    9: 8 God is a to bless you abundantly,
Eph 3: 4 you will be a to understand my
    3:20 to him who is a to do immeasurably
    6:13 you may be a to stand your ground,

1Ti 3: 2 respectable, hospitable, a to teach,
2Ti 1:12 that he is a to guard what I have
    2:24 be kind to everyone, a to teach,
    3: 7 never a to come to a knowledge
    3:15 which are a to make you wise
Heb 2:18 he is a to help those who are being
    3:19 we see that they were not a to enter,
    5: 2 He is a to deal gently with those
    7:25 Therefore he is a to save completely
    9: 9 sacrifices being offered were not a
Jas 3: 2 a to keep their whole body in check.
    4:12 Judge, the one who is a to save
2Pe 1:15 my departure you will always be a
Jude 1:24 To him who is a to keep you
Rev 5: 5 He is a to open the scroll and its

ABNER
Cousin of Saul and commander of his army (1Sa 14:50; 17:55–57; 26). Made Ish-Bosheth king after Saul (2Sa 2:8–10), but later defected to David (2Sa 3:6–21). Killed Asahel (2Sa 2:18–32), for which he was killed by Joab and Abishai (2Sa 3:22–39).

ABODE*
Job 38:19 "What is the way to the a of light?
Isa 33:20 a peaceful a, a tent that will not be

ABOLISH* ABOLISHED
Da 11:31 and will a the daily sacrifice.
Hos 2:18 and battle I will a from the land,
Mt 5:17 think that I have come to a the Law
    5:17 I have not come to a them

ABOLISHED* ABOLISH
Da 12:11 the time that the daily sacrifice is a
Gal 5:11 the offense of the cross has been a.

ABOMINATION*
ABOMINATIONS
Da 9:27 set up an a that causes desolation,
    11:31 set up the a that causes desolation.
    12:11 the a that causes desolation is set
Mt 24:15 in the holy place 'the a that causes
Mk 13:14 "When you see 'the a that causes

ABOMINATIONS*
ABOMINATION
Pr 26:25 them, for seven a fill their hearts.
Isa 66: 3 ways, and they delight in their a;
Rev 17: 5 AND OF THE A OF THE EARTH.

ABOUND ABOUNDING,
ABOUNDS
Ps 72: 7 and prosperity a till the moon is no
    72:16 May grain a throughout the land;
2Co 9: 8 you will a in every good work.
Php 1: 9 that your love may a more and more

ABOUNDING* ABOUND
Ex 34: 6 to anger, a in love and faithfulness,
Nu 14:18 a in love and forgiving sin
Dt 33:23 "Naphtali is a with the favor
Ne 9:17 slow to anger and a in love.
Ps 86: 5 a in love to all who call to you.
    86:15 to anger, a in love and faithfulness.

Ps 103: 8 gracious, slow to anger, **a** in love.
Joel   2:13 slow to anger and **a** in love, and he
Jnh   4: 2 slow to anger and **a** in love, a God

ABOUNDS* ABOUND
Hab   1: 3 there is strife, and conflict **a.**
2Co   1: 5 also our comfort **a** through Christ.

ABOVE
Ge   3:14 "Cursed are you **a** all livestock
     28:13 There **a** it stood the LORD, and he
Lev 26:19 and make the sky **a** you like iron
Dt   4:39 that the LORD is God in heaven **a**
Ps   18:48 You exalted me **a** my foes;
     57: 5 Be exalted, O God, **a** the heavens;
     95: 3 great God, the great King **a** all gods.
    103:11 high as the heavens are **a** the earth,
Da   11:36 and magnify himself **a** every god
Mt   10:24 "The student is not **a** the teacher, nor
            a servant **a** his master.
Jn   3:31 The one who comes from **a** is **a** all;
      3:31 who comes from heaven is **a** all.
      8:23 "You are from below; I am from **a.**
Ro   12:10 Honor one another **a** yourselves.
Php   2: 9 him the name that is **a** every name,
Col   3: 2 Set your minds on things **a,**
1Ti   3: 2 the overseer is to be **a** reproach,
Jas   1:17 good and perfect gift is from **a,**
1Pe   4: 8 **A** all, love each other deeply,

ABRAHAM ABRAM
    Abram, son of Terah (Ge 11:26–27), husband of Sarah (Ge 11:29).
    Covenant relation with the LORD (Ge 12:1–3; 13:14–17; 15; 17; 22:15–18; Ex 2:24; Ne 9:8; Ps 105; Mic 7:20; Lk 1:68–75; Ro 4; Heb 6:13–15).
    Called from Ur, via Haran, to Canaan (Ge 12:1; Ac 7:2–4; Heb 11:8–10). Moved to Egypt, nearly lost Sarah to Pharoah (Ge 12:10–20). Divided the land with Lot; settled in Hebron (Ge 13). Saved Lot from four kings (Ge 14:1–16); blessed by Melchizedek (Ge 14:17–20; Heb 7:1–20). Declared righteous by faith (Ge 15:6; Ro 4:3; Gal 3:6–9). Fathered Ishmael by Hagar (Ge 16).
    Name changed from Abram (Ge 17:5; Ne 9:7). Circumcised (Ge 17; Ro 4:9–12). Entertained three visitors (Ge 18); promised a son by Sarah (Ge 18:9–15; 17:16). Questioned destruction of Sodom and Gomorrah (Ge 18:16–33). Moved to Gerar; nearly lost Sarah to Abimelek (Ge 20). Fathered Isaac by Sarah (Ge 21:1–7; Ac 7:8; Heb 11:11–12); sent away Hagar and Ishmael (Ge 21:8–21; Gal 4:22–30). Covenant with Abimelek (Ge 21:22–32). Tested by offering Isaac (Ge 22; Heb 11:17–19; Jas 2:21–24). Sarah died; bought field of Ephron for burial (Ge 23). Secured wife for Isaac (Ge 24). Fathered children by Keturah (Ge 25:1–6; 1Ch 1:32–33). Death (Ge 25:7–11).
    Called servant of God (Ge 26:24), friend of God (2Ch 20:7; Isa 41:8; Jas 2:23), prophet (Ge 20:7), father of Israel (Ex 3:15; Isa 51:2; Mt 3:9; Jn 8:39–58).

FATHER ABRAHAM See FATHER
GOD OF ABRAHAM See GOD

ABRAM ABRAHAM
Ge   17: 5 No longer will you be called **A**;

ABSALOM
    Son of David by Maacah (2Sa 3:3; 1Ch 3:2). Killed Amnon for rape of his sister Tamar; banished by David (2Sa 13). Returned to Jerusalem; received by David (2Sa 14). Rebelled against David (2Sa 15–17). Killed (2Sa 18).

ABSENT
Col   2: 5 For though I am **a** from you

ABSOLUTE*
1Ti   5: 2 women as sisters, with **a** purity.

ABSTAIN* ABSTAINS
Ex   19:15 **A** from sexual relations."
Nu   6: 3 they must **a** from wine and other
Ac   15:20 telling them to **a** from food polluted
     15:29 You are to **a** from food sacrificed
     21:25 they should **a** from food sacrificed
1Ti   4: 3 order them to **a** from certain foods,
1Pe   2:11 and exiles, to **a** from sinful desires,

ABSTAINS* ABSTAIN
Ro   14: 6 and whoever **a** does so to the Lord

ABUNDANCE ABUNDANT
Ge   41:29 great **a** are coming throughout
Job 36:31 the nations and provides food in **a.**
Ps   36: 8 They feast on the **a** of your house;
     66:12 but you brought us to a place of **a.**
Ecc   5:12 rich, their **a** permits them no sleep.
Isa 66:11 and delight in her overflowing **a.**
Jer   2:22 and use an **a** of cleansing powder,
Mt   13:12 given more, and they will have an **a.**
     25:29 given more, and they will have an **a.**
Lk   12:15 not consist in an **a** of possessions."
1Pe   1: 2 Grace and peace be yours in **a.**
2Pe   1: 2 yours in **a** through the knowledge
Jude 1: 2 peace and love be yours in **a.**

ABUNDANT ABUNDANCE, ABUNDANTLY
Dt   28:11 will grant you **a** prosperity—
     32: 2 grass, like **a** rain on tender plants.
Job 36:28 and **a** showers fall on mankind.
Ps   68: 9 You gave **a** showers, O God;
     78:15 gave them water as **a** as the seas;
    132:15 I will bless her with **a** provisions;
    145: 7 They celebrate your **a** goodness
Pr   12:11 work their land will have **a** food,
     28:19 work their land will have **a** food,
Jer 33: 9 will tremble at the **a** prosperity
Eze 17: 5 planted it like a willow by **a** water,
     31: 7 for its roots went down to **a** waters.
Joel 2:23 He sends you **a** showers,
Ro   5:17 who receive God's **a** provision

ABUNDANTLY ABUNDANT
Jos 17:14 and the LORD has blessed us **a.**"
1Ti   1:14 our Lord was poured out on me **a,**

ABUSE ABUSIVE
Pr   9: 7 rebukes the wicked incurs **a.**

1Pe   4: 4 wild living, and they heap **a** on you.
2Pe   2:10 afraid to heap **a** on celestial beings;
        2:11 do not heap **a** on such beings
Jude 1: 8 and heap **a** on celestial beings.

ABUSIVE* ABUSE
Ac   18: 6 they opposed Paul and became **a**,
2Ti   3: 2 proud, **a**, disobedient to their

ABYSS*
Lk   8:31 not to order them to go into the **A**.
Rev   9: 1 given the key to the shaft of the **A**.
        9: 2 When he opened the **A**, smoke rose
        9: 2 darkened by the smoke from the **A**.
        9:11 king over them the angel of the **A**,
       11: 7 up from the **A** will attack them,
       17: 8 yet will come up out of the **A** and go
       20: 1 having the key to the **A** and holding
       20: 3 He threw him into the **A**, and locked

ACACIA
Ex   25:10 them make an ark of **a** wood—
       25:23 "Make a table of **a** wood—
       26:15 "Make upright frames of **a** wood
       27: 1 "Build an altar of **a** wood,

ACCENT*
Mt   26:73 your **a** gives you away."

ACCEPT ACCEPTABLE,
ACCEPTANCE, ACCEPTED,
ACCEPTS
Ge   14:23 that I will **a** nothing belonging
Ex   23: 8 "Do not **a** a bribe, for a bribe blinds
Lev   26:23 things you do not **a** my correction
Dt   16:19 Do not **a** a bribe, for a bribe blinds
2Sa   24:23 the Lord your God **a** you."
Job   2:10 Shall we **a** good from God, and not
       42: 8 and I will **a** his prayer and not deal
Ps   119:108 **A**, Lord, the willing praise of my
Pr   4:10 my son, **a** what I say, and the years
       10: 8 The wise in heart **a** commands,
       19:20 Listen to advice and **a** discipline,
Eze   43:27 Then I will **a** you,
Zep   3: 7 you will fear me and **a** correction!'
Mal   1:10 "and I will **a** no offering from your
Mt   1:14 And if you are willing to **a** it, he is
       19:11 "Not everyone can **a** this word,
Jn   3:11 you people do not **a** our testimony.
        5:41 "I do not **a** glory from human
       14:17 The world cannot **a** him, because it
Ac   22:18 here will not **a** your testimony
Ro   14: 1 **A** the one whose faith is weak,
       15: 7 **A** one another, then, just as Christ
1Co   2:14 the Spirit does not **a** the things
Jas   1:21 humbly **a** the word planted in you,
1Jn   5: 9 We **a** human testimony, but God's

ACCEPTABLE ACCEPT
Pr   21: 3 just is more **a** to the Lord than
Isa   58: 5 call a fast, a day **a** to the Lord?
Php   4:18 a fragrant offering, an **a** sacrifice,
1Pe   2: 5 offering spiritual sacrifices **a** to God

ACCEPTANCE* ACCEPT
Ro   11:15 what will their **a** be but life
1Ti   1:15 saying that deserves full **a**:
        4: 9 saying that deserves full **a**.

ACCEPTED ACCEPT
Ge   4: 7 do what is right, will you not be **a**?
Lev   1: 4 it will be **a** on your behalf to make
        7:18 the one who offered it will not be **a**.
1Sa   8: 3 after dishonest gain and **a** bribes
Job   42: 9 and the Lord **a** Job's prayer.
Lk   4:24 "no prophet is **a** in his hometown.
Ac   2:41 Those who **a** his message were
Ro   10:16 all the Israelites **a** the good news.
       15: 7 then, just as Christ **a** you, in order
2Co   11: 4 different gospel from the one you **a**,
Gal   1: 9 you a gospel other than what you **a**,
1Th   2:13 us, you **a** it not as a human word,

ACCEPTS ACCEPT
Dt   27:25 "Cursed is anyone who **a** a bribe
Ps   6: 9 the Lord **a** my prayer.
Zep   3: 2 obeys no one, she **a** no correction.
Jn   3:32 heard, but no one **a** his testimony.
       13:20 whoever **a** anyone I send **a** me;
       13:20 whoever **a** me **a** the one who sent
Jas   1:27 that God our Father **a** as pure

ACCESS*
Est   1:14 Media who had special **a** to the king
Ro   5: 2 through whom we have gained **a**
Eph   2:18 through him we both have **a**

ACCLAIM*
Ps   89:15 those who have learned to **a** you,
Isa   24:14 from the west they **a** the Lord's

ACCOMPANIED ACCOMPANY
1Co   10: 4 from the spiritual rock that **a** them,
Jas   2:17 itself, if it is not **a** by action, is dead.

ACCOMPANIES* ACCOMPANY
Isa   40:10 him, and his recompense **a** him.
       62:11 and his recompense **a** him.' "
2Co   9:13 obedience that **a** your confession

ACCOMPANY ACCOMPANIED,
ACCOMPANIES
Dt   28: 2 **a** you if you obey the Lord your
Ecc   8:15 joy will **a** them in their toil all
Mk   16:17 *signs will a those who believe:*

ACCOMPLICES*
Pr   29:24 The **a** of thieves are their own

ACCOMPLISH ACCOMPLISHED
Dt   9: 5 to **a** what he swore to your fathers,
2Ki   19:31 of the Lord Almighty will **a** this.
Ecc   2: 2 And what does pleasure **a**?"
Isa   9: 7 of the Lord Almighty will **a** this.
       44:28 shepherd and will **a** all that I please;
       55:11 but will **a** what I desire and achieve

ACCOMPLISHED ACCOMPLISH
Isa   26:12 all that we have **a** you have done
Mt   5:18 from the Law until everything is **a**.

Eph   3:11 that he a in Christ Jesus our Lord.
Rev 10: 7 the mystery of God will be a, just as

ACCORD ACCORDANCE, ACCORDING
Nu 24:13 could not do anything of my own a,
Jn   10:18 me, but I lay it down of my own a.

ACCORDANCE ACCORD
Nu 14:19 In a with your great love,
2Ki 14:25 in a with the word of the LORD,
    23:25 in a with all the Law of Moses.
Ps 119:149 Hear my voice in a with your love;
Eze 35:11 I will treat you in a with the anger
Ac 24:14 everything that is in a with the Law
Ro   8: 5 those who live in a with the Spirit
    12: 6 then prophesy in a with your faith;
Eph 1: 5 in a with his pleasure and will—
2Th 2: 9 of the lawless one will be in a
Heb 10: 8 though they were offered in a

ACCORDING ACCORD
Ge   1:11 seed in it, a to their various kinds."
Ex 26:30 the tabernacle a to the plan shown
Dt 26:13 the widow, a to all you commanded.
2Ch 6:30 deal with everyone a to all they do,
Ps 18:24 a to the cleanness of my hands
    119: 9 By living a to your word.
Pr 12: 8 A person is praised a to their
Hos 12: 2 he will punish Jacob a to his ways and
         repay him a to his deeds.
Mt   9:29 "A to your faith let it be done
Jn 19: 7 a law, and a to that law he must die,
Ro   8: 4 who do not live a to the flesh but a to
         the Spirit.
Gal 3:29 seed, and heirs a to the promise.
2Ti 2: 5 except by competing a to the rules.
1Jn 5:14 that if we ask anything a to his will,
Rev 20:12 The dead were judged a to what

ACCOUNT ACCOUNTABLE, ACCOUNTING
Ge   2: 4 This is the a of the heavens
     5: 1 This is the written a of Adam's
     6: 9 This is the a of Noah and his
    10: 1 This is the a of Shem,
    11:10 This is the a of Shem's family line.
    11:27 This is the a of Terah's family line.
    25:12 This is the a of the family line
    25:19 This is the a of the family line
    36: 1 This is the a of the family line
    36: 9 This is the a of the family line
    37: 2 This is the a of Jacob's family line.
Dt 18:19 call to a anyone who does not listen
Jos 22:23 the LORD himself call us to a.
Mt 12:36 will have to give a on the day
    26:31 night you will all fall away on a
Lk 16: 2 Give an a of your management,
Ro 14:12 of us will give an a of ourselves
Heb 4:13 of him to whom we must give a.
1Jn 2:12 your sins have been forgiven on a

ACCOUNTABLE* ACCOUNT
Eze 3:18 I will hold you a for their blood.

Eze 3:20 I will hold you a for their blood.
    33: 6 I will hold the watchman a for their
    33: 8 I will hold you a for their blood.
    34:10 and will hold them a for my flock.
Da   6: 2 The satraps were made a to them so
Jnh 1:14 Do not hold us a for killing
Ro   3:19 and the whole world held a to God.

ACCOUNTING ACCOUNT
Ge   9: 5 lifeblood I will surely demand an a.
     9: 5 I will demand an a for the life

ACCREDITED* CREDIT
Ac   2:22 of Nazareth was a man a by God

ACCUMULATE* ACCUMULATED
Dt 17:17 He must not a large amounts

ACCUMULATED ACCUMULATE
2Ch 1:14 Solomon a chariots and horses;

ACCURATE ACCURATELY
Dt 25:15 You must have a and honest
Pr 11: 1 but a weights find favor with him.
Eze 45:10 You are to use a scales, an a ephah
         and an a bath.

ACCURATELY* ACCURATE
Ac 18:25 fervor and taught about Jesus a,

ACCURSED CURSE
2Pe 2:14 are experts in greed—an a brood!

ACCUSATION ACCUSE
Mic 6: 2 you mountains, the LORD's a;
Col 1:22 without blemish and free from a—
1Ti 5:19 not entertain an a against an elder

ACCUSATIONS ACCUSE
Ac 26: 2 I make my defense against all the a

ACCUSE ACCUSATION, ACCUSATIONS, ACCUSED, ACCUSER, ACCUSERS, ACCUSES, ACCUSING
Ps 103: 9 He will not always a, nor will he
Pr   3:30 Do not a anyone for no reason—
Zec 3: 1 standing at his right side to a him.
Lk   3:14 money and don't a people falsely—
1Pe 2:12 though they a you of doing wrong,

ACCUSED ACCUSE
Mk 15: 3 The chief priests a him of many
Ac 22:30 exactly why Paul was being a

ACCUSER* ACCUSE
Job 31:35 let my a put his indictment
Ps 109: 6 let an a stand at his right hand.
Isa 50: 8 Who is my a? Let him confront me!
Jn   5:45 Your a is Moses, on whom your
Rev 12:10 For the a of our brothers and sisters,

ACCUSERS ACCUSE
Ps 109:20 be the LORD's payment to my a,

ACCUSES* ACCUSE
Job 40: 2 Let him who a God answer him!"

Isa 54:17 will refute every tongue that **a** you.
Rev 12:10 who **a** them before our God day

ACCUSING ACCUSE
Ps 31:20 in your dwelling from **a** tongues.
Ro 2:15 their thoughts sometimes **a** them

ACHAN*
Sin at Jericho caused defeat at Ai; stoned (Jos 7; 22:20; 1Ch 2:7).

ACHE*
Pr 14:13 Even in laughter the heart may **a**,

ACHIEVE ACHIEVED, ACHIEVEMENT
Job 5:12 so that their hands **a** no success.
Ps 45:4 your right hand **a** awesome deeds.
Isa 55:11 **a** the purpose for which I sent it.

ACHIEVED ACHIEVE
Isa 63:5 so my own arm **a** salvation for me,

ACHIEVEMENT* ACHIEVE
Ecc 4:4 all **a** spring from one person's envy

ACHISH
King of Gath before whom David feigned insanity (1Sa 21:10–15). Later "ally" of David (2Sa 27–29).

ACHOR
Jos 7:26 called the Valley of **A** ever since.
Hos 2:15 will make the Valley of **A** a door

ACKNOWLEDGE ACKNOWLEDGED, ACKNOWLEDGES, ACKNOWLEDGMENT
1Ch 28:9 Solomon, **a** the God of your father,
Ps 79:6 on the nations that do not **a** you,
Isa 59:12 with us, and we **a** our iniquities:
Jer 3:13 Only **a** your guilt—
9:3 they do not **a** me,"
Da 4:25 you until you **a** that the Most High
Hos 6:3 Let us **a** the LORD; let us press on to **a** him.
Mt 10:32 also **a** before my Father in heaven.
Lk 12:8 will also **a** before the angels of God.
Jn 12:42 they would not openly **a** their faith
Ro 14:11 before me; every tongue will **a** God.' "
Php 2:11 every tongue **a** that Jesus Christ is
1Th 5:12 **a** those who work hard among you,
Heb 3:1 whom we **a** as our apostle and high
1Jn 4:3 spirit that does not **a** Jesus is not
2Jn 1:7 who do not **a** Jesus Christ as

ACKNOWLEDGED ACKNOWLEDGE
Lk 7:29 words, **a** that God's way was right,

ACKNOWLEDGES* ACKNOWLEDGE
Ps 91:14 will protect him, for he **a** my name.
Mt 10:32 "Whoever **a** me before others,

Lk 12:8 you, whoever publicly **a** me before
1Jn 2:23 whoever **a** the Son has the Father
4:2 Every spirit that **a** that Jesus Christ
4:15 If anyone **a** that Jesus is the Son

ACKNOWLEDGMENT* ACKNOWLEDGE
Hos 4:1 no love, no **a** of God in the land.
6:6 **a** of God rather than burnt offerings.

ACQUIRED ACQUIRES
Ge 12:16 sake, and Abram **a** sheep and cattle,
Ru 4:10 I have also **a** Ruth the Moabite,
Jer 48:36 The wealth they **a** is gone.

ACQUIRES* ACQUIRED
Pr 18:15 heart of the discerning **a** knowledge,

ACQUIT ACQUITTED, ACQUITTING
Ex 23:7 to death, for I will not **a** the guilty.

ACQUITTED* ACQUIT
Mt 12:37 For by your words you will be **a**,

ACQUITTING* ACQUIT
Dt 25:1 **a** the innocent and condemning
Pr 17:15 **A** the guilty and condemning

ACT ACTED, ACTION, ACTIONS, ACTIVE, ACTIVITY, ACTS
Nu 23:19 Does he speak and then not **a**?
1Ki 2:2 "So be strong, **a** like a man,
8:32 then hear from heaven and **a**.
8:39 Forgive and **a**; deal with everyone
Ps 106:3 Blessed are those who **a** justly,
119:126 It is time for you to **a**, LORD;
Isa 43:13 When I **a**, who can reverse it?"
52:13 See, my servant will **a** wisely;
Jn 8:4 *caught in the **a** of adultery.*

ACTED ACT
Ac 3:17 I know that you **a** in ignorance,
1Ti 1:13 I was shown mercy because I **a**

ACTION ACT
2Co 9:2 has stirred most of them to **a**.
Jas 2:17 if it is not accompanied by **a**,

ACTIONS ACT
Pr 20:11 small children are known by their **a**,
Gal 6:4 Each one should test their own **a**.
Titus 1:16 God, but by their **a** they deny him.

ACTIVE* ACT
Heb 4:12 For the word of God is alive and **a**.

ACTIVITY ACT
Ecc 3:1 for every **a** under the heavens:
3:17 for there will be a time for every **a**,

ACTS ACT
Ex 7:4 mighty **a** of judgment I will bring
1Ch 16:9 tell of all his wonderful **a**.
Ps 71:16 come and proclaim your mighty **a**,
71:24 tell of your righteous **a** all day long,
105:2 tell of all his wonderful **a**.

Ps 106: 2 Who can proclaim the mighty **a**
   145: 4 they tell of your mighty **a**.
   145:12 people may know of your mighty **a**
   150: 2 Praise him for his **a** of power;
Pr 12:10 but the kindest **a** of the wicked are
Isa 64: 6 all our righteous **a** are like filthy
Ro   1:27 Men committed shameful **a**
Gal   5:19 The **a** of the flesh are obvious:
Rev 15: 4 you, for your righteous **a** have been
    19: 8 for the righteous **a** of God's holy

ADAM
   1. First man (Ge 1:26—2:25; Ro 5:14; 1Ti 2:13). Sin of (Ge 3; Hos 6:7; Ro 5:12–21). Children of (Ge 4:15:5). Death of (Ge 5:5; Ro 5:12–21; 1Co 15:22).
   2. Town (Jos 3:16).

ADAR
   Month in which temple was rebuilt (Ezr 6:15); celebration of Purim (Est 3:7; 9:1–21).

ADD ADDED, ADDS
Dt   4: 2 Do not **a** to what I command you
   12:32 do not **a** to it or take away from it.
Pr   1: 5 wise listen and **a** to their learning,
   9: 9 and they will **a** to their learning.
   30: 6 Do not **a** to his words, or he will
Mt   6:27 you by worrying **a a** single hour
Lk 12:25 you by worrying can **a a** single hour
2Pe 1: 5 make every effort to **a** to your faith
Rev 22:18 them, God will **a** to that person

ADDED ADD
Pr   9:11 and years will be **a** to your life.
Ecc 3:14 nothing can be **a** to it and nothing
Ac   2:47 the Lord **a** to their number daily
   5:14 Lord and were **a** to their number.
Gal 3:19 It was **a** because of transgressions

ADDICTED*
Titus 2: 3 to be slanderers or **a** to much wine,

ADDS ADD
Pr 10:27 fear of the LORD **a** length to life,

ADMAH
Dt 29:23 and Gomorrah, **A** and Zeboyim,
Hos 11: 8 How can I treat you like **A**?

ADMINISTER ADMINISTRATION
1Ki 3:28 had wisdom from God to **a** justice.
Zec 7: 9 'A true justice;
2Co 8:19 which we **a** in order to honor

ADMINISTRATION* ADMINISTER
Eph 3: 2 heard about the **a** of God's grace
   3: 9 to everyone the **a** of this mystery,

ADMIRABLE*
Php 4: 8 whatever is lovely, whatever is **a**—

ADMIT
Job 27: 5 I will never **a** you are in the right;

ADMONISH* ADMONISHING
Col 3:16 and **a** one another with all wisdom
1Th 5:12 for you in the Lord and who **a** you.

ADMONISHING* ADMONISH
Col 1:28 **a** and teaching everyone with all

ADONIJAH
   1. Son of David by Haggith (2Sa 3:4; 1Ch 3:2). Attempted to be king after David; killed by Solomon's order (1Ki 1 2).
   2. Levite; teacher of the Law (2Ch 17:8).

ADOPTED* ADOPTION
Est   2:15 (the young woman Mordecai had **a**,
Ps 106:35 the nations and **a** their customs.

ADOPTION* ADOPTED
Ro   8:15 brought about your **a** to sonship.
   8:23 wait eagerly for our **a** to sonship,
   9: 4 Theirs is the **a** to sonship;
Gal   4: 5 that we might receive **a** to sonship.
Eph   1: 5 he predestined us for **a** to sonship

ADORE*
SS   1: 4 How right they are to **a** you!

ADORN ADORNED, ADORNMENT, ADORNS
Pr   1: 9 head and a chain to **a** your neck.
Isa 60: 7 and I will **a** my glorious temple.
Jer   4:30 You **a** yourself in vain.
1Pe 3: 5 hope in God used to **a** themselves.

ADORNED ADORN
Eze 16:11 I **a** you with jewelry: I put bracelets
Lk 21: 5 how the temple was **a** with beautiful

ADORNMENT* ADORN
1Pe 3: 3 should not come from outward **a**,

ADORNS* ADORN
Ps 93: 5 holiness **a** your house for endless
Pr 15: 2 tongue of the wise **a** knowledge,
Isa 61:10 as a bridegroom **a** his head like
   61:10 as a bride **a** herself with her jewels.

ADULLAM
1Sa 22: 1 Gath and escaped to the cave of **A**.
1Ch 11:15 David to the rock at the cave of **A**,

ADULTERER* ADULTERY
Lev 20:10 both the **a** and the adulteress are
Job 24:15 The eye of the **a** watches for dusk;
Heb 13: 4 for God will judge the **a** and all

ADULTERERS ADULTERY
Jer 23:10 The land is full of **a**;
Hos 7: 4 They are all **a**, burning like an oven
Mal 3: 5 against sorcerers, **a** and perjurers,
1Co 6: 9 nor idolaters nor **a** nor men who

ADULTERESS* ADULTERY
Lev 20:10 and the **a** are to be put to death.
Hos 3: 1 is loved by another man and is an **a**.
Ro   7: 3 still alive, she is called an **a**.
   7: 3 not an **a** if she marries another man.

ADULTERIES ADULTERY
Jer 3: 8 sent her away because of all her **a**.
Rev 14: 8 the maddening wine of her **a**."

Rev 19: 2 who corrupted the earth by her **a**.

ADULTEROUS ADULTERY

Pr 2:16 save you also from the **a** woman,
     5: 3 the lips of the **a** woman drip honey,
    23:27 for an **a** woman is a deep pit,
Eze 6: 9 have been grieved by their **a** hearts,
Hos 1: 2 for like an **a** wife this land is guilty
Mt 16: 4 and **a** generation looks for a sign,
Mk   8:38 and my words in this **a** and sinful
Jas 4: 4 You **a** people, don't you know

ADULTERY ADULTERER, ADULTERERS, ADULTERESS, ADULTERIES, ADULTEROUS

Ex 20:14 "You shall not commit **a**.
Dt   5:18 "You shall not commit **a**.
Ps 51: T *David had committed a with*
Pr   6:32 a man who commits **a** has no sense;
Eze 23:37 for they have committed **a** and
    23:37 They committed **a** with their idols;
Mt   5:27 was said, 'You shall not commit **a**.'
     5:28 lustfully has already committed **a**
     5:32 makes her the victim of **a**,
     5:32 a divorced woman commits **a**.
    15:19 murder, **a**, sexual immorality, theft,
    19: 9 another woman commits **a**."
    19:18 you shall not commit **a**, you shall
Mk 10:11 woman commits **a** against her.
    10:12 another man, she commits **a**."
    10:19 you shall not commit **a**, you shall
Lk 16:18 marries another woman commits **a**,
    16:18 a divorced woman commits **a**.
    18:20 'You shall not commit **a**, you shall
Jn   8: 3 *brought in a woman caught in a.*
Ro   2:22 that people should not commit **a**, do
          you commit **a**?
Jas 2:11 "You shall not commit **a**,"
     2:11 If you do not commit **a** but do
Rev 18: 3 of the earth committed **a** with her,

ADULTS*

1Co 14:20 be infants, but in your thinking be **a**.

ADVANCE ADVANCED

2Sa 22:30 your help I can **a** against a troop;
Ps 27: 2 When the wicked **a** against me
Ro   9:23 whom he prepared in **a** for glory—
Gal 3: 8 and announced the gospel in **a**
Eph 2:10 which God prepared in **a** for us
Php 1:12 has actually served to **a** the gospel.

ADVANCED ADVANCE

Job 32: 7 **a** years should teach wisdom.'

ADVANTAGE

Ex 22:22 "Do not take **a** of the widow
Lev 25:14 them, do not take **a** of each other.
Dt 24:14 Do not take **a** of a hired worker who
Ecc 6: 8 What **a** have the wise over fools?
     7:12 but the **a** of knowledge is this:
Ro   3: 1 What **a**, then, is there in being
2Co 11:20 or exploits you or takes **a** of you
1Th 4: 6 should wrong or take **a** of a brother
Jude 1:16 and flatter others for their own **a**.

ADVERSARIES ADVERSARY

Dt 32:41 I will take vengeance on my **a**
Ps 44: 7 enemies, you put our **a** to shame.
    56: 2 My **a** pursue me all day long;

ADVERSARY ADVERSARIES, ADVERSITY

Mt   5:25 with your **a** who is taking you
     5:25 or your **a** may hand you over
Lk 18: 3 'Grant me justice against my **a**.'

ADVERSITY* ADVERSARY

Pr 17:17 and a brother is born for a time of **a**.
Isa 30:20 the Lord gives you the bread of **a**

ADVICE ADVISERS

Nu 31:16 the ones who followed Balaam's **a**
2Sa 20:22 to all the people with her wise **a**,
2Ch 10:13 Rejecting the **a** of the elders,
    10:14 he followed the **a** of the young men
Pr   1:25 since you disregard all my **a** and do
    12: 5 but the **a** of the wicked is deceitful.
    12:15 to them, but the wise listen to **a**.
    19:20 Listen to **a** and accept discipline,
    20:18 Plans are established by seeking **a**;
    27: 9 friend springs from their heartfelt **a**.

ADVISERS ADVICE

Pr 11:14 but victory is won through many **a**.
    15:22 but with many **a** they succeed.
    24: 6 and victory is won through many **a**.

ADVOCATE*

Job 16:19 is in heaven; my **a** is on high.
Jn 14:16 he will give you another **a** to help
    14:26 But the **A**, the Holy Spirit,
    15:26 "When the **A** comes, whom I will
    16: 7 away, the **A** will not come to you;
1Jn 2: 1 sin, we have an **a** with the Father—

AENEAS*

Paralytic healed by Peter (Ac 9:33–34).

AFFAIRS

Ps 112: 5 who conduct their **a** with justice.
Pr 31:27 She watches over the **a** of her
1Co 7:32 is concerned about the Lord's **a**—
     7:33 about the **a** of this world—

AFFECTION

Dt 10:15 Yet the Lord set his **a** on your
2Co 6:12 We are not withholding our **a**
2Pe 1: 7 and to godliness, mutual **a**; and to
          mutual **a**, love.

AFFLICTED AFFLICTION

Jos 24: 5 and I **a** the Egyptians by what I did
Ru   1:21 The Lord has **a** me;
Job 2: 7 a Job with painful sores
    36: 6 alive but gives the **a** their rights.
Ps   9:12 he does not ignore the cries of the **a**.
     9:18 the hope of the **a** will never perish.
    34: 2 let the **a** hear and rejoice.
    73:14 All day long I have been **a**,
   119:67 Before I was **a** I went astray,
   119:71 me to be **a** so that I might learn your

Ps   119:75 that in faithfulness you have a me.
Isa   49:13 will have compassion on his a ones.
      53: 4 by God, stricken by him, and a.
      53: 7 He was oppressed and a, yet he did
Na   1:12 Although I have a you, Judah, I will

AFFLICTION AFFLICTED,
AFFLICTIONS
Dt   16: 3 the bread of a, because you left
Ps   107:41 he lifted the needy out of their a
Isa   30:20 of adversity and the water of a,
      48:10 have tested you in the furnace of a.
La   1: 9 on my a, for the enemy has
       3:33 For he does not willingly bring a
Ro   12:12 hope, patient in a, faithful in prayer.

AFFLICTIONS AFFLICTION
Lev   26:21 I will multiply your a seven times
Col   1:24 still lacking in regard to Christ's a,
Rev   2: 9 I know your a and your poverty—

AFRAID FEAR
Ge   3:10 and I was a because I was naked;
      26:24 Do not be a, for I am with you;
      50:19 Joseph said to them, "Don't be a.
Ex   2:14 Then Moses was a and thought,
       3: 6 because he was a to look at God.
      34:30 and they were a to come near him.
Lev   26: 6 down and no one will make you a.
Dt   1:21 Do not be a; do not be
       1:29 not be terrified; do not be a of them.
       2: 4 They will be a of you, but be very
      20: 3 Do not be fainthearted or a;
Jos   10:25 Joshua said to them, "Do not be a;
Ru   3:11 And now, my daughter, don't be a.
1Sa   15:24 I was a of the men and so I gave
      18:12 Saul was a of David,
1Ki   19: 3 Elijah was a and ran for his life.
2Ki   25:24 "Do not be a of the Babylonian
1Ch   13:12 David was a of God that day
Ne   2: 2 I was very much a,
Ps   27: 1 of my life—of whom shall I be a?
      56: 3 When I am a, I put my trust in you.
      56: 4 in God I trust and am not a.
Pr   3:24 you lie down, you will not be a;
Isa   12: 2 I will trust and not be a.
      44: 8 Do not tremble, do not be a.
Jer   1: 8 Do not be a of them, for I am
      30:10 and no one will make him a.
Eze   39:26 land with no one to make them a.
Da   4: 5 I had a dream that made me a.
Mt   8:26 little faith, why are you so a?"
      10:28 Do not be a of those who kill
      10:28 be a of the One who can destroy
      10:31 So don't be a; you are worth more
Mk   5:36 said, Jesus told him, "Don't be a;
Lk   9:34 and they were a as they entered
      12:32 "Do not be a, little flock, for your
Jn   14:27 hearts be troubled and do not be a.
Ac   27:24 and said, 'Do not be a, Paul.
Heb   13: 6 Lord is my helper; I will not be a.
2Pe   2:10 they are not a to heap abuse
Rev   2:10 Do not be a of what you are

AGABUS*
A Christian prophet (Ac 11:28; 21:10).

AGAG AGAGITE
King of Amalekites not killed by Saul (1Sa 15).

AGAGITE AGAG
Est   8: 3 end to the evil plan of Haman the A,

AGAIN
Mk   8:31 be killed and after three days rise a.
Jn   2:19 and I will raise it a in three days."
       3: 7 at my saying, 'You must be born a.'
Heb   6: 6 crucifying the Son of God all over a
Rev   7:16 'Never a will they hunger; never a

AGE AGE-OLD, AGED, AGES
Mt   13:39 The harvest is the end of the a,
Lk   18:30 many times as much in this a, and in
             the a to come eternal life."
Titus 2:12 and godly lives in this present a,

AGE-OLD AGE, OLD
Hab   3: 6 crumbled and the a hills collapsed—

AGED AGE
Job   12:12 Is not wisdom found among the a?
Pr   17: 6 children are a crown to the a,
      30:17 that scorns an a mother, will be

AGES AGE
Pr   8:23 I was formed long a ago, at the very
Ro   16:25 the mystery hidden for long a past,
Eph   3: 7 in the coming a he might show
       3: 9 for a past was kept hidden in God,
Col   1:26 that has been kept hidden for a
Heb   9:26 the culmination of the a to do away

AGO
Ps   74: 2 the nation you purchased long a,
      74:12 But God is my King from long a;
Jude   1: 4 about long a have secretly slipped

AGONY
Jer   4:19 Oh, the a of my heart!
Lk   16:24 because I am in a in this fire.'
Ac   2:24 freeing him from the a of death,
Rev   16:10 People gnawed their tongues in a

AGREE AGREEMENT, AGREES,
DISAGREEMENT
Mt   18:19 earth a about anything they ask for,
Mk   14:59 even then their testimony did not a.
Ro   7:16 want to do, I a that the law is good.

AGREEMENT AGREE
Da   11:23 After coming to an a with him,
2Co   6:16 What a is there between the temple
1Jn   5: 8 and the three are in a.

AGREES* AGREE
Ac   7:42 This a with what is written
1Co   4:17 Jesus, which a with what I teach

AGRIPPA*
Descendant of Herod; king before whom Paul
pled his case in Caesarea (Ac 25:13—26:32).

AHAB

1. Son of Omri; king of Israel (1Ki 16:28—22:40), husband of Jezebel (1Ki 16:31). Promoted Baal worship (1Ki 16:31-33); opposed by Elijah (1Ki 17:1; 18; 21), a prophet (1Ki 20:35-43), Micaiah (1Ki 22:1-28). Defeated Ben-Hadad (1Ki 20). Killed for failing to kill Ben-Hadad and for murder of Naboth (1Ki 20:3521:40).
2. A false prophet (Jer 29:21-22).

AHASUERUS See XERXES

AHAZ

Son of Jotham; king of Judah, (2Ki 16; 2Ch 28; Mt 1:9). Idolatry of (2Ki 16:3-4, 10-18; 2Ch 28:1-4, 22-25). Defeated by Aram and Israel (2Ki 16:5-6; 2Ch 28:5-15). Sought help from Assyria rather than the LORD (2Ki 16:7-9; 2Ch 28:16-21; Isa 7).

AHAZIAH

1. Son of Ahab; king of Israel (1Ki 22:51-2Ki 1:18; 2Ch 20:35-37). Made an unsuccessful alliance with Jehoshaphat (2Ch 20:35-37). Died for seeking Baal rather than the LORD (2Ki 1).
2. Son of Jehoram; king of Judah (2Ki 8:25-29; 9:14-29), also called Jehoahaz (2Ch 21:17—22:9; 25:23). Killed by Jehu while visiting Joram (2Ki 9:14-29; 2Ch 22:1-9).

AHEAD HEAD

1Co 11:21 of you go a with your own private
Php   3:13 and straining toward what is a,
1Ti   5:24 the place of judgment a of them;
Heb 11:26 because he was looking a to his
2Jn   1: 9 Anyone who runs a and does not

AHIJAH

1. Priest during Sauls reign (1Sa 14:3,18).
2. Prophet of Shiloh (1Ki 11:29-39; 14:1-18).

AHIKAM

Father of Gedaliah (2Ki 25:22), protector of Jeremiah (Jer 26:24).

AHIMAAZ

1. Father-in-law of Saul (1Sa 14:50).
2. Son of Zadok, the high priest, loyal to David (2Sa 15:27,36; 17:17-20; 18:19-33).

AHIMELEK

1. Priest who helped David in his flight from Saul (1Sa 21-22).
2. One of David's warriors (1Sa 26:6).

AHINOAM

1. Wife of Saul (1Sa 14:50).
2. Wife of David (1Sa 25:43; 30:5; 1Ch 3:1).

AHITHOPHEL

One of David's counselors who sided with Absalom (2Sa 15:12, 31-37; 1Ch 27:33-34); committed suicide when his advice was ignored (2Sa 16:15—17:23).

AI

Jos   7: 4 they were routed by the men of A,
        8:26 he had destroyed all who lived in A.

AID

Ge   50:25 "God will surely come to your a,
Ex   13:19 "God will surely come to your a,
Ru   1: 6 had come to the a of his people
Isa   38:14 Lord, come to my a!"
Php   4:16 you sent me a more than once

AIM* AIMLESSLY

Ps   21:12 turn their backs when you a at them
        64: 3 a cruel words like deadly arrows.
Ac   20:24 my only a is to finish the race
1Co   7:34 Her a is to be devoted to the Lord

AIMLESSLY* AIM

Pr   5: 6 her paths wander a, but she does not
1Co   9:26 do not run like someone running a;

AIR MIDAIR

1Co   9:26 not fight like a boxer beating the a.
        14: 9 You will just be speaking into the a.
Eph   2: 2 of the ruler of the kingdom of the a,
1Th   4:17 the clouds to meet the Lord in the a.
Rev   16:17 poured out his bowl into the a,

AKELDAMA* BLOOD, FIELD

Ac   1:19 called that field in their language A,

ALABASTER*

Mt   26: 7 him with an a jar of very expensive
Mk   14: 3 a woman came with an a jar of very
Lk   7:37 so she came there with an a jar

ALARM ALARMED

Joel   2: 1 sound the a on my holy hill.
2Co   7:11 indignation, what a, what longing,

ALARMED ALARM

Mk   13: 7 and rumors of wars, do not be a.
Ac   22:29 The commander himself was a
2Th   2: 2 or a by the teaching allegedly

ALERT*

Jos   8: 4 far from it. All of you be on the a.
Ps   17:11 me, with eyes a, to throw me
Isa   21: 7 on camels, let him be a, fully a."
Mk   13:33 Be a! You do not know
Eph   6:18 be a and always keep on praying
1Pe   1:13 with minds that are a and fully
        4: 7 Therefore be a and of sober mind so
        5: 8 Be a and of sober mind.

ALEXANDER

Ac   19:33 in the crowd pushed A to the front,
1Ti   1:20 Among them are Hymenaeus and A,
2Ti   4:14 A the metalworker did me a great

ALIEN* ALIENATED

Isa   28:21 and perform his task, his a task.

ALIENATED* ALIEN

Job   19:13 "He has a my family from me;
Gal   5: 4 by the law have been a from Christ;
Col   1:21 Once you were a from God

ALIVE LIVE
Ge   7: 3 their various kinds a throughout
Dt   6:24 might always prosper and be kept a,
1Sa 2: 6 LORD brings death and makes a;
Pr   1:12 let's swallow them a, like the grave,
Lk 24:23 vision of angels, who said he was a.
Ac   1: 3 convincing proofs that he was a.
Ro   6:11 to sin but a to God in Christ Jesus.
     7: 9 Once I was a apart from the law;
1Co 15:22 die, so in Christ all will be made a.
Col 2:13 flesh, God made you a with Christ.
1Th 4:17 we who are still a and are left will
Heb 4:12 For the word of God is a and active.
Rev 1:18 now look, I am a for ever and ever!

ALL
ALL ISRAEL See ISRAEL
ALL … HEART See HEART
ALL PEOPLE See PEOPLE
ALL PEOPLES See PEOPLES
ALL THE PEOPLE See PEOPLE
ALL THE PEOPLES See PEOPLES

ALLEGIANCE
Ro   6:17 that has now claimed your a.

ALLELUIA See HALLELUJAH

ALLIANCE ALLY
1Ki 3: 1 Solomon made an a with Pharaoh
Isa 30: 1 forming an a, but not by my Spirit,

ALLOTMENT ALLOTS, ALLOTTED
Dt 14:29 so that the Levites (who have no a
Eze 48:13 will have an a 25,000 cubits long

ALLOTS ALLOTMENT
Job 27:13 "Here is the fate God a

ALLOTTED ALLOTMENT
Nu 34: 2 will be a to you as an inheritance is
Da 12:13 rise to receive your a inheritance."

ALLOW ALLOWED
Ps 132: 4 I will a no sleep to my eyes
Pr   6: 4 A no sleep to your eyes, no slumber
Lk   4:41 and would not a them to speak,
Ac 16: 7 Spirit of Jesus would not a them to.

ALLOWED ALLOW
Ac 28:16 Paul was a to live by himself,
1Co 14:34 They are not a to speak, but must be
Rev 9: 5 They were not a to kill them
    16: 8 the sun was a to scorch people

ALLY ALLIANCE
Isa 48:14 The LORD's chosen a will carry

ALMIGHTY MIGHT
Ge 17: 1 to him and said, "I am God A;
Ex   6: 3 to Isaac and to Jacob as God A,
Nu 24: 4 who sees a vision from the A,
Ru   1:20 because the A has made my life
2Sa 7:26 'The LORD A is God over Israel!'
Job   6: 4 The arrows of the A are in me,

Job 11: 7 Can you probe the limits of the A?
    21:15 Who is the A, that we should serve
    33: 4 the breath of the A gives me life.
Ps 84: 3 LORD A, my King and my God.
    89: 8 Who is like you, LORD God A?
    91: 1 will rest in the shadow of the A.
Isa   6: 3 "Holy, holy, holy is the LORD A;
    47: 4 the LORD A is his name—
    48: 2 the LORD A is his name:
    51:15 the LORD A is his name—
    54: 5 the LORD A is his name—
Jer 11:17 The LORD A, who planted you,
Am   5:14 the LORD God A will be with you,
    5:15 the LORD God A will have mercy
Zec   8:22 to Jerusalem to seek the LORD A
Mal 3:10 says the LORD A, "and see if I
Rev 4: 8 holy is the Lord God A,' who was,
    19: 6 For our Lord God A reigns.

LORD† ALMIGHTY See LORD†
LORD† ALMIGHTY SAYS See LORD†
LORD† GOD ALMIGHTY See GOD

ALOFT*
Dt 32:11 to catch them and carries them a.

ALONE LONELY
Ge   2:18 "It is not good for the man to be a.
Ex 18:18 you cannot handle it a.
Dt   8: 3 that man does not live on bread a
Ne   9: 6 You a are the LORD.
Ps 16: 5 LORD, you a are my portion and
    76: 7 It is you a who are to be feared.
  148:13 LORD, for his name a is exalted;
Mt   4: 4 'Man shall not live on bread a,
Mk   2: 7 Who can forgive sins but God a?"
    10:18 "No one is good—except God a.
Jas   2:24 by what they do and not by faith a.
Rev 15: 4 For you a are holy. All nations will

ALPHA*
Rev 1: 8 "I am the A and the Omega,"
    21: 6 I am the A and the Omega,
    22:13 I am the A and the Omega, the First

ALREADY READY
Php 3:12 Not that I have a obtained all this,
2Th 2: 2 that the day of the Lord has a come.
    2: 7 power of lawlessness is a at work;
2Ti 2:18 the resurrection has a taken place,
1Jn 2: 8 and the true light is a shining.

ALTAR ALTARS
Ge   8:20 Noah built an a to the LORD and,
    12: 7 So he built an a there
    13:18 There he built an a to the LORD.
    22: 9 about, Abraham built an a there
    22: 9 his son Isaac and laid him on the a,
    26:25 Isaac built an a there and called
    33:20 There he set up an a and called it El
    35: 1 and build an a there to God,
Ex 17:15 Moses built an a and called it
    20:24 " 'Make an a of earth for me
    27: 1 "Build an a of acacia wood,
    30: 1 "Make an a of acacia wood

Ex 37:25 They made the **a** of incense
Dt 27: 5 Build there an **a** to the Lord your God, an **a** of stones.
Jos 8:30 on Mount Ebal an **a** to the Lord,
22:10 Manasseh built an imposing **a** there
Jdg 6:24 So Gideon built an **a** to the Lord
21: 4 the next day the people built an **a**
1Sa 7:17 he built an **a** there to the Lord.
14:35 Then Saul built an **a** to the Lord;
2Sa 24:25 David built an **a** to the Lord
1Ki 12:33 sacrifices on the **a** he had built
12:33 went up to the **a** to make offerings.
13: 2 he cried out against the **a**: "A, a!
16:32 He set up an **a** for Baal
18:30 he repaired the **a** of the Lord,
2Ki 16:10 He saw an **a** in Damascus and sent
1Ch 21:26 David built an **a** to the Lord
21:26 heaven on the **a** of burnt offering.
2Ch 4: 1 made a bronze **a** twenty cubits long,
4:19 the golden **a**; the tables
15: 8 He repaired the **a** of the Lord
32:12 'You must worship before one **a**
33:16 he restored the **a** of the Lord
Ezr 3: 2 began to build the **a** of the God
Isa 6: 6 he had taken with tongs from the **a**.
La 2: 7 The Lord has rejected his **a**
Eze 40:47 the **a** was in front of the temple.
Am 9: 1 I saw the Lord standing by the **a**,
Mal 1: 7 "By offering defiled food on my **a**.
Mt 5:24 your gift there in front of the **a**.
23:18 'If anyone swears by the **a**, it means
23:18 by the gift on the **a** is bound
Ac 17:23 worship, I even found an **a** with this
1Co 10:18 the sacrifices participate in the **a**?
Heb 13:10 We have an **a** from which those
Jas 2:21 he offered his son Isaac on the **a**?
Rev 6: 9 I saw under the **a** the souls of those

ALTARS ALTAR

Ex 34:13 Break down their **a**, smash their
Nu 23: 1 said, "Build me seven **a** here,
2Ch 33: 3 he also erected **a** to the Baals
34: 4 the **a** of the Baals were torn down;
34: 4 cut to pieces the incense **a** that were

ALTER* ALTERED

Ps 89:34 or **a** what my lips have uttered.

ALTERED* ALTER

Da 6: 8 it in writing so that it cannot be **a**—

ALWAYS

Dt 12:28 so that it may **a** go well with you
15:11 There will **a** be poor people
1Ch 16:11 and his strength; seek his face **a**.
Ps 16: 8 I keep my eyes **a** on the Lord.
51: 3 and my sin is **a** before me.
119:44 I will **a** obey your law, for ever
119:98 Your commands are **a** with me
Pr 6:21 Bind them **a** on your heart;
28:14 the one who **a** trembles before God,
Jer 12: 1 You are **a** righteous, Lord,
Hos 12: 6 justice, and wait for your God **a**.
Mt 26:11 The poor you will **a** have with you, but you will not **a** have me.

Mt 28:20 And surely I am with you **a**,
Jn 5:17 "My Father is **a** at his work to this
Ac 2:25 " 'I saw the Lord **a** before me.
7:51 You **a** resist the Holy Spirit!
1Co 13: 7 It **a** protects, **a** trusts, **a** hopes,
Eph 5:20 **a** giving thanks to God the Father
Php 4: 4 Rejoice in the Lord **a**. I will say it
Phm 1: 4 I **a** thank my God as I remember
Heb 7:25 because he **a** lives to intercede
1Pe 3:15 **A** be prepared to give an answer

AMALEK AMALEKITES

Ex 17:14 the name of **A** from under heaven."

AMALEKITES AMALEK

Ex 17: 8 The **A** came and attacked
Dt 25:17 Remember what the **A** did to you
1Sa 15: 3 attack the **A** and totally destroy all
15: 8 He took Agag king of the **A** alive,

AMASA

Nephew of David (1Ch 2:17). Commander of Absalom's forces (2Sa 17:24–27). Returned to David (2Sa 19:13). Killed by Joab (2Sa 20:4–13).

AMASSES*

Pr 28: 8 profit from the poor **a** it for another,

AMAZED AMAZEMENT

Mk 1:22 The people were **a** at his teaching,
6: 6 He was **a** at their lack of faith.
10:24 The disciples were **a** at his words.
Jn 7:21 did one miracle, and you are all **a**.
Ac 2: 7 Utterly **a**, they asked:
13:12 for he was **a** at the teaching

AMAZEMENT AMAZED, AMAZING

Lk 24:41 not believe it because of joy and **a**,

AMAZIAH

1. Son of Joash; king of Judah (2Ki 14; 2Ch 25). Defeated Edom (2Ki 14:7; 2Ch 25:5–13); defeated by Israel for worshiping Edom's gods (2Ki 14:8–14; 2Ch 25:14–24).

2. Idolatrous priest who opposed Amos (Am 7:10–17).

AMAZING* AMAZEMENT

Jos 3: 5 the Lord will do **a** things among
Jdg 13:19 the Lord did an **a** thing while
Pr 30:18 three things that are too **a** for me,

AMBASSADOR* AMBASSADORS

Eph 6:20 for which I am an **a** in chains.

AMBASSADORS AMBASSADOR

2Co 5:20 We are therefore Christ's **a**,

AMBITION*

Ro 15:20 It has always been my **a** to preach
2Co 12:20 jealousy, fits of rage, selfish **a**,
Gal 5:20 fits of rage, selfish **a**, dissensions,
Php 1:17 preach Christ out of selfish **a**,
2: 3 Do nothing out of selfish **a** or vain
1Th 4:11 to make it your **a** to lead a quiet life:

Jas   3:14 envy and selfish **a** in your hearts,
      3:16 where you have envy and selfish **a,**

AMBUSH

Hos   6: 9 As marauders lie in **a** for a victim,
Ac   23:21 of them are waiting in **a** for him.
      25: 3 they were preparing an **a** to kill him

AMEN

Dt   27:15 Then all the people shall say, "**A**!"
1Co 14:16 say "**A**" to your thanksgiving,
2Co   1:20 so through him the "**A**" is spoken
Rev   3:14 These are the words of the **A,**
      22:20 says, "Yes, I am coming soon." **A.**

AMENDS*

Job 20:10 His children must make a
Pr   14: 9 Fools mock at making **a** for sin,

AMMONITES

Ge   19:38 he is the father of the **A** of today.
Dt   2:19 When you come to the **A,** do not
      2:19 of any land belonging to the **A.**
Jdg 11: 4 the **A** were fighting against Israel,
1Ki 11: 5 Molek the detestable god of the **A.**
Jer   49: 6 I will restore the fortunes of the **A,**
Eze 25:10 Moab along with the **A** to the people
      25:10 that the **A** will not be remembered
Zep   2: 9 like Sodom, the **A** like Gomorrah—

AMNON

Firstborn of David (2Sa 3:2; 1Ch 3:1). Killed by
Absalom for raping his sister Tamar (2Sa 13).

AMON

1. Son of Manasseh; king of Judah (2Ki 21:18–
26; 1Ch 3:14; 2Ch 33:21–25).
2. Ruler of Samaria under Ahab (1Ki 22:26; 2Ch
18:25).

AMORITES

Ge   15:16 of the **A** has not yet reached its full
Nu   21:31 So Israel settled in the land of the **A.**
Jdg   6:10 do not worship the gods of the **A,**
Am   2: 9 "Yet I destroyed the **A** before them,

AMOS

1. Prophet from Tekoa (Am 1:1; 7:10–17).
2. Ancestor of Jesus (Lk 3:25).

ANAK ANAKITES

Nu 13:28 even saw descendants of **A** there.
Jos 15:13 (Arba was the forefather of **A.**)

ANAKITES ANAK

Dt   1:28 We even saw the **A** there.' "
      2:10 and numerous, and as tall as the **A.**
      9: 2 The people are strong and tall—**A**!
      9: 2 "Who can stand up against the **A**?"
Jos 11:22 No **A** were left in Israelite territory;

ANANIAS

1. Husband of Sapphira; died for lying to God
(Ac 5:1–11).
2. Disciple who baptized Saul (Ac 9:10–19).
3. High priest at Paul's arrest (Ac 22:30—24:1).

ANATHEMA (KJV: 1Co 16:22) See
CURSED

ANCESTORS ANCESTRY

Ex   13: 5 land he swore to your **a** to give you,
Dt   4:31 or forget the covenant with your **a,**
      5: 3 our **a** that the LORD made this
      10:15 LORD set his affection on your **a**
      30: 9 just as he delighted in your **a,**
      32:17 appeared, gods your **a** did not fear.
Jos 24:14 the gods your **a** worshiped beyond
1Ki   8:57 be with us as he was with our **a;**
      19: 4 I am no better than my **a.**"
Ezr   5:12 because our **a** angered the God
      10:11 the God of your **a,** and do his will.
Ne   9: 9 saw the suffering of our **a** in Egypt;
Ps   22: 4 In you our **a** put their trust;
Jer   7: 7 in the land I gave your **a** for ever
La   5: 7 Our **a** sinned and are no more,
Am   4: 4 gods, the gods their **a** followed,
Zec   1: 4 Do not be like your **a,** to whom
Lk   11:47 and it was your **a** who killed them.
Jn   4:20 Our **a** worshiped on this mountain,
      6:58 Your **a** ate manna and died,
Heb   1: 1 spoke to our **a** through the prophets
      8: 9 made with their **a** when I took them
1Pe   1:18 handed down to you from your **a,**
2Pe   3: 4 Ever since our **a** died,

GOD OF ... ANCESTORS See GOD

ANCESTRY ANCESTORS

Ro   9: 5 them is traced the human **a**

ANCHOR

Heb   6:19 We have this hope as an **a**

ANCIENT

Ps   68:33 the highest heavens, the **a** heavens,
    119:52 LORD, your **a** laws, and I find
Pr   22:28 not move an **a** boundary stone set
Isa   43:13 Yes, and from **a** days I am he.
      44: 7 since I established my **a** people,
Da   7: 9 and the **A** of Days took his seat.
      7:13 He approached the **A** of Days
      7:22 until the **A** of Days came
Rev 12: 9 that **a** serpent called the devil,
      20: 2 that **a** serpent, who is the devil,

ANDREW*

Apostle; brother of Simon Peter (Mt 4:18; 10:2;
Mk 1:16–18, 29; 3:18; 13:3; Lk 6:14; Jn 1:35–44;
6:8–9; 12:22; Ac 1:13).

ANGEL ANGELS, ARCHANGEL

Ge   16: 7 The **a** of the LORD found Hagar
      21:17 the **a** of God called to Hagar
      22:11 the **a** of the LORD called
      24: 7 he will send his **a** before you so
      31:11 The **a** of God said to me
      48:16 the **A** who has delivered me from all
Ex   3: 2 There the **a** of the LORD appeared
      14:19 Then the **a** of God, who had been
      23:20 I am sending an **a** ahead of you
      32:34 of, and my **a** will go before you.

Ex 33: 2 I will send an **a** before you
Nu 20:16 and sent an **a** and brought us
    22:22 and the **a** of the LORD stood
Jdg 2: 1 The **a** of the LORD went
    6:12 When the **a** of the LORD appeared
    6:22 that it was the **a** of the LORD,
    6:22 I have seen the **a** of the LORD
    13: 3 The **a** of the LORD appeared
1Sa 29: 9 pleasing in my eyes as an **a** of God;
2Sa 14:17 my lord the king is like an **a** of God
    19:27 My lord the king is like an **a**
    24:16 When the **a** stretched out his hand
    24:16 the **a** who was afflicting the people,
1Ki 13:18 an **a** said to me by the word
    19: 7 The **a** of the LORD came back
2Ki 1: 3 the **a** of the LORD said to Elijah
    19:35 That night the **a** of the LORD went
Job 33:23 Yet if there is an **a** at their side,
Ps 34: 7 The **a** of the LORD encamps
Da 3:28 who has sent his **a** and rescued his
    6:22 My God sent his **a**, and he shut
Hos 12: 4 He struggled with the **a**
Zec 1:11 to the **a** of the LORD who was
    3: 1 the high priest standing before the **a**
Mt 1:20 an **a** of the Lord appeared to him
    2:13 an **a** of the Lord appeared to Joseph
    28: 2 for an **a** of the Lord came down
Lk 1:11 an **a** of the Lord appeared to him,
    1:26 God sent the **a** Gabriel to Nazareth,
    2: 9 An **a** of the Lord appeared to them,
    22:43 An **a** from heaven appeared to him
Jn 12:29 others said an **a** had spoken to him.
Ac 5:19 during the night an **a** of the Lord
    6:15 his face was like the face of an **a**.
    7:30 an **a** appeared to Moses
    8:26 Now an **a** of the Lord said to Philip,
    10: 3 He distinctly saw an **a** of God,
    12: 7 Suddenly an **a** of the Lord appeared
    27:23 Last night an **a** of the God to whom
1Co 10:10 and were killed by the destroying **a**.
2Co 11:14 Satan himself masquerades as an **a**
Gal 1: 8 or an **a** from heaven should preach
    4:14 me as if I were an **a** of God, as if I
Rev 1: 1 by sending his **a** to his servant John,
    2: 1 "To the **a** of the church in Ephesus
    5: 2 I saw a mighty **a** proclaiming
    7: 2 I saw another **a** coming
    8: 3 Another **a**, who had a golden
    9:11 They had as king over them the **a**
    14: 6 I saw another **a** flying in midair,
    16: 2 The first **a** went and poured out his
    17: 3 the **a** carried me away in the Spirit
    19:17 And I saw an **a** standing in the sun,

ANGEL OF GOD Ge 21:17; 31:11; Ex 14:19;
Jdg 6:20; 13:6, 9; 1Sa 29:9; 2Sa 14:17, 20; 19:27; Ac
10:3; 27:23; Gal 4:14

ANGEL OF THE LORD Mt 1:20, 24; 2:13, 19;
28:2; Lk 1:11; 2:9; Ac 5:19; 8:26; 12:7, 23

ANGEL OF THE LORD† Ge 16:7, 9, 11; 22:11,
15; Ex 3:2; Nu 22:22, 23, 24, 25, 26, 27, 31, 32, 34,
35; Jdg 2:1, 4; 5:23; 6:11, 12, 21, 21, 22, 22; 13:3,
13, 15, 16, 16, 17, 20, 21, 21; 2Sa 24:16; 1Ki 19:7;

2Ki 1:3, 15; 19:35; 1Ch 21:12, 15, 16, 18, 30; Ps
34:7; 35:5, 6; Isa 37:36; Zec 1:11, 12; 3:1, 5, 6; 12:8

ANGELS ANGEL

Ge 19: 1 The two **a** arrived at Sodom
    28:12 and the **a** of God were ascending
    32: 1 his way, and the **a** of God met him.
Job 1: 6 One day the **a** came to present
Ps 8: 5 made them a little lower than the **a**
    78:25 Human beings ate the bread of **a**;
    91:11 will command his **a** concerning you
   103:20 you his **a**, you mighty ones who do
Mt 4: 6 will command his **a** concerning you,
    13:39 of the age, and the harvesters are **a**.
    18:10 that their **a** in heaven always see
    25:41 fire prepared for the devil and his **a**.
Mk 8:38 his Father's glory with the holy **a**."
    12:25 they will be like the **a** in heaven.
    13:32 knows, not even the **a** in heaven,
Lk 2:15 When the **a** had left them and gone
    4:10 will command his **a** concerning you
    12: 9 others will be disowned before the **a**
    16:22 and the **a** carried him to Abraham's
    20:36 for they are like the **a**.
Jn 1:51 and the **a** of God ascending
Ac 7:53 the law that was given through **a**
    23: 8 that there are neither **a** nor spirits,
Ro 8:38 death nor life, neither **a** nor demons,
1Co 4: 9 to **a** as well as to human beings.
    6: 3 you not know that we will judge **a**?
    11:10 her own head, because of the **a**.
    13: 1 speak in the tongues of men or of **a**,
Gal 3:19 The law was given through **a**
Col 2:18 and the worship of **a** disqualify you.
2Th 1: 7 in blazing fire with his powerful **a**.
1Ti 3:16 was seen by **a**, was preached among
    5:21 and Christ Jesus and the elect **a**,
Heb 1: 4 the **a** as the name he has inherited is
    1: 6 "Let all God's **a** worship him."
    1: 7 "He makes his **a** spirits, and his
    1:14 Are not all **a** ministering spirits sent
    2: 2 spoken through **a** was binding,
    2: 7 made them a little lower than the **a**;
    2: 9 who was made lower than the **a**
    12:22 thousands of **a** in joyful assembly,
    13: 2 hospitality to **a** without knowing it.
1Pe 1:12 Even **a** long to look into these
    3:22 with **a**, authorities and powers
2Pe 2: 4 if God did not spare **a** when they
Jude 1: 6 And the **a** who did not keep their
Rev 1:20 The seven stars are the **a**
    3: 5 name before my Father and his **a**.
    5:11 and heard the voice of many **a**,
    7: 1 this I saw four **a** standing at the four
    8: 2 I saw the seven **a** who stand before
    9:14 "Release the four **a** who are bound
    12: 7 and his **a** fought against the dragon,
    12: 7 the dragon and his **a** fought back.
    15: 1 seven **a** with the seven last
    21:12 and with twelve **a** at the gates.

ANGER ANGERED, ANGRY

Ex 4:14 Then the LORD's **a** burned against
    15: 7 You unleashed your burning **a**;

Ex	22:24	My a will be aroused, and I will kill
	32:10	so that my a may burn against them
	32:11	"why should your a burn against
	32:12	Turn from your fierce a;
	32:19	his a burned and he threw
	34: 6	slow to a, abounding in love
Lev	26:28	in my a I will be hostile toward you,
Nu	11: 1	he heard them his a was aroused.
	11:33	the a of the LORD burned against
	12: 9	The a of the LORD burned against
	14:18	'The LORD is slow to a,
	25:11	has turned my a away
	32:10	The LORD's a was aroused
Dt	6:15	God and his a will burn against you,
	9:19	I feared the a and wrath
	29:28	In furious a and in great wrath
Jos	7: 1	So the LORD's a burned against
	7:26	LORD turned from his fierce a.
Jdg	2:12	They aroused the LORD's a
	14:19	Burning with a, he returned to his
1Sa	20:30	Saul's a flared up at Jonathan
2Sa	12: 5	burned with a against the man
1Ki	16:13	they aroused the a of the LORD,
2Ki	22:13	Great is the LORD's a that burns
	24:20	of the LORD's a that all this
Ne	9:17	slow to a and abounding in love.
Ps	30: 5	For his a lasts only a moment,
	37: 8	Refrain from a and turn from wrath;
	78:38	Time after time he restrained his a
	86:15	slow to a, abounding in love
	90: 7	We are consumed by your a
	103: 8	slow to a, abounding in love.
	103: 9	nor will he harbor his a forever;
	145: 8	slow to a and rich in love.
Pr	15: 1	wrath, but a harsh word stirs up a.
	29: 8	up a city, but the wise turn away a.
	30:33	so stirring up a produces strife."
Ecc	7: 9	for a resides in the lap of fools.
Isa	63: 6	I trampled the nations in my a;
Da	9:16	turn away your a and your wrath
Joel	2:13	slow to a and abounding in love,
Jnh	3: 9	from his fierce a so that we will not
	4: 2	slow to a and abounding in love,
Na	1: 3	The LORD is slow to a but great
Mk	3: 5	He looked around at them in a and,
Eph	4:26	"In your a do not sin": Do not let
Col	3: 8	a, rage, malice, slander, and filthy
Jas	1:20	because human a does not produce

ANGER OF THE LORD† Nu 11:33; 12:9; Dt 9:7; Jdg 3:8; 2Sa 24:1; 1Ki 15:30; 16:13, 26, 33; 22:53; 2Ch 25:15; 28:25; 29:8; Jer 4:8; 23:20; 25:37; 30:24; 51:45

ANGERED ANGER

Ezr	5:12	because our ancestors a the God
Ps	78:58	They a him with their high places;
Pr	22:24	do not associate with one easily a,
1Co	13: 5	it is not easily a, it keeps no record

ANGRY ANGER

Ge	4: 5	So Cain was very a, and his face
Dt	4:21	The LORD was a with me because
Jdg	18:25	or some of the men may get a
Ps	2:12	he will be a and your way will lead

Ps	95:10	For forty years I was a
Pr	29:22	An a person stirs up conflict,
Isa	34: 2	The LORD is a with all nations;
Jer	3:12	the LORD, 'I will not be a forever.
Jnh	4: 1	very wrong, and he became a.
	4: 4	"Is it right for you to be a?"
Mic	7:18	You do not stay a forever
Mt	5:22	that anyone who is a with a brother
Lk	15:28	"The older brother became a
Jn	7:23	why are you a with me for healing
Heb	3:17	whom was he a for forty years?
Jas	1:19	to speak and slow to become a,
Rev	11:18	The nations were a, and your wrath

ANGUISH

1Sa	1:10	In her deep a Hannah prayed
Ps	6: 3	My soul is in deep a.
Pr	31: 6	wine for those who are in a!
Jer	4:19	Oh, my a, my a! I writhe in pain.
La	1: 4	women grieve, and she is in bitter a.
Zep	1:15	a day of distress and a, a day
Lk	21:25	nations will be in a and perplexity
	22:44	And being in a, he prayed more
Jn	16:21	is born she forgets the a because
Ro	9: 2	sorrow and unceasing a in my heart.

ANIMAL ANIMALS

Lev	20:15	man has sexual relations with an a,
	20:15	to death, and you must kill the a.
Dt	14: 6	You may eat any a that has
Ps	50:10	for every a of the forest is mine,
Da	8: 4	No a could stand against it,

ANIMALS ANIMAL

Ge	1:24	and the wild a, each according to its
	7:16	The a going in were male
	2:19	out of the ground all the wild a
Lev	11:46	are the regulations concerning a,
Dt	14: 4	These are the a you may eat:
Job	12; 7	"But ask the a, and they will teach
Ps	36: 6	preserve both people and a.
Ecc	3:19	human beings is like that of the a;
	3:19	humans have no advantage over a.
Isa	43:20	The wild a honor me, the jackals
Eze	34:28	nor will wild a devour them.
Jnh	3: 8	and a be covered with sackcloth.
Hab	2:17	destruction of a will terrify you.
Mal	1: 8	you offer blind a for sacrifice,
	1: 8	you sacrifice lame or diseased a,
Mk	1:13	He was with the wild a, and angels
Ac	11: 6	and saw four-footed a of the earth,
	15:20	from the meat of strangled a
2Pe	2:12	They are like unreasoning a,
	2:12	and like a they too will perish.

ANNA*

Female prophet who spoke about the child Jesus (Lk 2:36–38).

ANNALS

BOOK OF THE ANNALS 1Ki 11:41; 14:19, 29; 15:7, 23, 31; 16:5, 14, 20, 27; 22:39; 2Ki 1:18; 8:23; 10:34; 12:19; 13:8, 12; 14:15, 18, 28; 15:6, 11, 15, 21, 26, 31, 36; 16:19; 20:20; 21:17, 25; 23:28; 24:5; 1Ch 27:24; Ne 12:23; Est 2:23; 10:2

ANNAS

High priest A.D. 6–15 (Lk 3:2; Jn 18:13,24; Ac 4:6).

ANNIHILATE

Dt 9: 3 drive them out and a them quickly,
Est 3:13 to destroy, kill and a all the Jews—
8:11 a the armed men of any nationality
Da 11:44 a great rage to destroy and a many.

ANNOUNCE ANNOUNCED, ANNOUNCES

Mt 6: 2 the needy, do not a it with trumpets,

ANNOUNCED ANNOUNCE

Isa 48: 5 before they happened I a them
Gal 3: 8 faith, and a the gospel in advance
Heb 2: 3 which was first a by the Lord,
Rev 10: 7 just as he a to his servants

ANNOUNCES ANNOUNCE

Ps 68:11 The Lord a the word, and the women

ANNOYANCE*

Pr 12:16 Fools show their a at once,

ANNUAL*

Ex 30:10 This a atonement must be made
Jdg 21:19 there is the a festival of the Lord
1Sa 1:21 offer the a sacrifice to the Lord
2:19 her husband to offer the a sacrifice.
20: 6 because an a sacrifice is being made
2Ch 8:13 Moons and the three a festivals—
Heb 10: 3 those sacrifices are an a reminder

ANOINT ANOINTED, ANOINTING

Ex 30:26 Then use it to a the tent of meeting,
30:30 "A Aaron and his sons
Jdg 9:15 really want to a me king over you,
1Sa 9:16 A him ruler over my people Israel;
15: 1 to a you king over his people Israel;
1Ki 1:34 Nathan the prophet a him king over
19:16 a Jehu son of Nimshi king over
19:16 a Elisha son of Shaphat from Abel
2Ki 9: 3 I a you king over Israel.'
Ps 23: 5 You a my head with oil;
Ecc 9: 8 and always a your head with oil.
Da 9:24 and to a the Most Holy Place.
Mk 16: 1 that they might go to a Jesus' body.
Jas 5:14 a them with oil in the name

ANOINTED ANOINT

Ge 31:13 where you a a pillar and where you
Lev 7:36 On the day they were a, the Lord
1Sa 2:10 king and exalt the horn of his a."
10: 1 not the Lord a you ruler over his
16:13 oil and a him in the presence of his
24: 6 the Lord's a, or lay my hand
24: 6 for he is the a of the Lord."
2Sa 1:14 hand to destroy the Lord's a?"
2: 4 there they a David king over
5: 3 and they a David king over Israel.
19:21 He cursed the Lord's a."
1Ki 1:39 from the sacred tent and a Solomon.
1Ch 16:22 "Do not touch my a ones;

2Ch 6:42 God, do not reject your a one.
Ps 2: 2 the Lord and against his a,
105:15 "Do not touch my a ones;
Isa 61: 1 because the Lord has a me
Da 9:26 the A One will be put to death
Hab 3:13 your people, to save your a one.
Zec 4:14 "These are the two who are a
Lk 4:18 because he has a me to proclaim
Ac 4:26 the Lord and against his a one.'
10:38 how God a Jesus of Nazareth
2Co 1:21 you stand firm in Christ. He a us,

ANOINTED ONE 1Sa 2:35; 2Ch 6:42; Ps 28:8; 84:9; 89:38, 51; 132:10, 17; Da 9:25, 26; Hab 3:13; Ac 4:26

ANOINTING ANOINT

Ex 30:25 Make these into a sacred a oil,
30:25 It will be the sacred a oil.
Lev 8:12 He poured some of the a oil
1Ch 29:22 a him before the Lord to be ruler
Ps 45: 7 your companions by a you
Heb 1: 9 your companions by a you
1Jn 2:20 you have an a from the Holy One,
2:27 the a you received from him
2:27 as his a teaches you about all things and as that a is real,

ANOINTING OIL See OIL

ANOTHER

Lev 19:11 " 'Do not deceive one a.
Pr 27:17 iron, so one person sharpens a.
Ecc 4: 4 spring from one person's envy of a.
Isa 48:11 I will not yield my glory to a.
Lk 19:44 They will not leave one stone on a,
Jn 13:34 command I give you: Love one a.
13:34 loved you, so you must love one a.
Ro 12:10 Be devoted to one a in love.
12:10 Honor one a above yourselves.
1Co 16:20 Greet one a with a holy kiss.
Col 3:16 admonish one a with all wisdom
1Th 4:18 Therefore encourage one a
Heb 3:13 But encourage one a daily, as long
13: 1 Keep on loving one a as brothers
1Pe 3: 8 love one a, be compassionate
1Jn 3:23 to love one a as he commanded us.

ONE ANOTHER See ONE

ANSWER ANSWERED, ANSWERS

1Ki 18:26 "Baal, a us!" they shouted.
18:37 A me, Lord, a me, so these
Job 30:20 out to you, God, but you do not a;
40: 2 Let him who accuses God a him!"
Ps 38:15 you will a, Lord my God.
Pr 15: 1 A gentle a turns away wrath,
16: 1 the Lord comes the proper a
18:13 To a before listening—that is folly
24:26 An honest a is like a kiss
26: 5 A a fool according to his folly, or he
Ecc 10:19 and money is the a for everything.
Lk 23: 9 questions, but Jesus gave him no a.
1Pe 3:15 give an a to everyone who asks you

ANSWERED ANSWER

Ge 25:21 The Lord a his prayer, and his

1Ch 21:26 the LORD **a** him with fire
Ps   118:21 will give you thanks, for you **a** me;

ANSWERS ANSWER
1Ki 18:24 The god who **a** by fire—he is God."

ANT* ANTS
Pr   6: 6 Go to the **a**, you sluggard;

ANTICHRIST* ANTICHRISTS
1Jn   2:18 you have heard that the **a** is coming,
      2:22 Such a person is the **a**—
      4: 3 This is the spirit of the **a**, which you
2Jn   1: 7 person is the deceiver and the **a**.

ANTICHRISTS* ANTICHRIST
1Jn   2:18 even now many **a** have come.

ANTIOCH
Ac   11:26 he found him, he brought him to **A**.
     11:26 were called Christians first at **A**.
     13: 1 the church at **A** there were prophets
Gal   2:11 When Cephas came to **A**, I opposed

ANTIPAS* HEROD
Rev   2:13 in me, not even in the days of **A**,

ANTS* ANT
Pr   30:25 **A** are creatures of little strength,

ANXIETIES* ANXIOUS
Lk   21:34 drunkenness and the **a** of life,

ANXIETY ANXIOUS
Pr   12:25 **A** weighs down the heart, but a kind
Ecc 11:10 banish **a** from your heart and cast
1Pe   5: 7 Cast all your **a** on him because he

ANXIOUS ANXIETIES, ANXIETY
Php   4: 6 Do not be **a** about anything,

ANYTHING
Ge   18:14 Is **a** too hard for the LORD?
Pr   14:15 The simple believe **a**,
Jer 32:27 Is **a** too hard for me?
Mk   2:12 "We have never seen **a** like this!"
Ro   14: 2 person's faith allows them to eat **a**,
1Jn   2:15 not love the world or **a** in the world.
      3:22 and receive from him **a** we ask,

APART PART
Lev 20:26 I have set you **a** from the nations
Isa 45:21 And there is no God **a** from me,
Jn   15: 5 **a** from me you can do nothing.
Ro   1: 1 and set **a** for the gospel of God—
      3:21 But now **a** from the law
Gal   1:15 who set me **a** from my mother's

APOLLOS
   Christian from Alexandria, learned in the
Scriptures; instructed by Aquila and Priscilla (Ac
18:24–28). Ministered at Corinth (Ac 19:1; 1Co
1:12; 3; Titus 3:13).

APOLLYON*
Rev   9:11 Abaddon and in Greek is **A** (that is,

APOSTLE APOSTLES, APOSTLES',
   APOSTLESHIP, SUPER-APOSTLES
Ro   1: 1 called to be an **a** and set apart
     11:13 Inasmuch as I am the **a**
1Co   1: 1 called to be an **a** of Christ Jesus
      9: 1 Am I not an **a**? Have I not seen
     15: 9 not even deserve to be called an **a**,
2Co 12:12 among you the marks of a true **a**,
Gal   2: 8 in Peter as an **a** to the circumcised,
      2: 8 work in me as an **a** to the Gentiles.
1Ti   1: 1 Paul, an **a** of Christ Jesus
      2: 7 I was appointed a herald and an **a**—
2Ti   1:11 a herald and an **a** and a teacher.
Heb   3: 1 whom we acknowledge as our **a**
1Pe   1: 1 Peter, an **a** of Jesus Christ,

APOSTLES APOSTLE
   See also Andrew, Bartholomew, James, John,
Judas, Matthew, Matthias, Nathanael, Paul, Peter,
Philip, Simon, Thaddaeus, Thomas.
Mt   10: 2 are the names of the twelve **a**:
Lk   6:13 them, whom he also designated **a**:
     11:49 'I will send them prophets and **a**,
Ac   1:26 so he was added to the eleven **a**.
      2:43 and signs performed by the **a**.
      5:18 They arrested the **a** and put them
      8: 1 and all except the **a** were scattered
     14:14 when the **a** Barnabas and Paul heard
Ro   16: 7 They are outstanding among the **a**,
1Co 12:28 placed in the church first of all **a**,
     15: 9 For I am the least of the **a** and do
2Co 11:13 For such people are false **a**,
     11:13 masquerading as **a** of Christ.
Eph   2:20 built on the foundation of the **a**
      4:11 So Christ himself gave the **a**,
Rev   2: 2 have tested those who claim to be **a**
     21:14 names of the twelve **a** of the Lamb.

APOSTLES' APOSTLE
Ac   2:42 themselves to the **a** teaching
      4:35 and put it at the **a** feet, and it was
      8:18 at the laying on of the **a** hands,

APOSTLESHIP* APOSTLE
Ro   1: 5 and **a** to call all the Gentiles
1Co   9: 2 you are the seal of my **a** in the Lord.

APPALLED
Isa 52:14 Just as there were many who were **a**
Da   8:27 I was **a** by the vision; it was beyond

APPEAL
Ac   25:11 me over to them. I **a** to Caesar!"
2Co   5:20 God were making his **a** through us.
Phm   1: 9 yet I prefer to **a** to you on the basis
1Pe   5: 1 I **a** as a fellow elder and a witness

APPEAR APPEARANCE,
   APPEARANCES, APPEARED,
   APPEARING, APPEARS
Ge   1: 9 to one place, and let dry ground **a**."
Ex   23:15 is to **a** before me empty-handed.
Lev 16: 2 For I will **a** in the cloud over
Mt   24:30 will **a** the sign of the Son of Man

Mk 13:22 false prophets will **a** and perform
Lk 19:11 of God was going to **a** at once.
2Co 5:10 we must all **a** before the judgment
Col 3: 4 you also will **a** with him in glory.
Heb 9:24 now to **a** for us in God's presence.
9:28 and he will **a** a second time,

APPEARANCE APPEAR

1Sa 16: 7 "Do not consider his **a** or his
16: 7 People look at the outward **a**,
2Sa 14:25 for his handsome **a** as Absalom.
Isa 52:14 his **a** was so disfigured beyond
53: 2 in his **a** that we should desire him.
Eze 1:28 Like the **a** of a rainbow
1:28 This was the **a** of the likeness
Mt 28: 3 His **a** was like lightning, and his
Php 2: 8 And being found in **a** as a man,
Rev 4: 3 the one who sat there had the **a**

APPEARANCES* APPEAR

Jn 7:24 Stop judging by mere **a**, but instead
2Co 10: 7 You are judging by **a**. If anyone is

APPEARED APPEAR

Ge 12: 7 The LORD **a** to Abram and said,
12: 7 to the LORD, who had **a** to him.
26: 2 The LORD **a** to Isaac and said,
35: 9 God **a** to him again and blessed
Ex 3: 2 the angel of the LORD **a** to him
Nu 14:10 the glory of the LORD **a** at the tent
Jdg 6:12 angel of the LORD **a** to Gideon,
13: 3 The angel of the LORD **a** to her
1Ki 3: 5 Gibeon the LORD **a** to Solomon
Mt 1:20 an angel of the Lord **a** to him
Mk 1: 4 And so John the Baptist **a**
9: 4 And there **a** before them Elijah
Lk 2: 9 An angel of the Lord **a** to them,
24:34 Lord has risen and has **a** to Simon."
Jn 21:14 This was now the third time Jesus **a**
Ac 1: 3 He **a** to them over a period of forty
12: 7 Suddenly an angel of the Lord **a**
1Co 15: 5 and that he **a** to Cephas,
Titus 2:11 of God has **a** that offers salvation
Heb 9:26 But he has **a** once for all
1Jn 3: 8 The reason the Son of God **a** was

APPEARING APPEAR

1Ti 6:14 blame until the **a** of our Lord Jesus
2Ti 1:10 now been revealed through the **a**
4: 8 to all who have longed for his **a**.
Titus 2:13 the **a** of the glory of our great God

APPEARS APPEAR

Pr 14:12 There is a way that **a** to be right,
16:25 There is a way that **a** to be right,
SS 6:10 Who is this that **a** like the dawn,
Mal 3: 2 Who can stand when he **a**?
Col 3: 4 who is your life, **a**, then you
Jas 4:14 You are a mist that **a** for a little
1Pe 5: 4 And when the Chief Shepherd **a**,
1Jn 2:28 that when he **a** we may be confident
3: 2 But we know that when Christ **a**,

APPETITE

Pr 13: 2 but the unfaithful have an **a**

Pr 16:26 The **a** of laborers works for them;
Ecc 6: 7 mouth, yet their **a** is never satisfied.
Jer 50:19 their **a** will be satisfied on the hills

APPLE APPLES

Dt 32:10 he guarded him as the **a** of his eye,
Ps 17: 8 Keep me as the **a** of your eye;
Zec 2: 8 whoever touches you touches the **a**

APPLES* APPLE

Pr 25:11 Like **a** of gold in settings of silver is
SS 2: 5 refresh me with **a**, for I am faint
7: 8 the fragrance of your breath like **a**,

APPLICATION* APPLY

Heb 11:28 the Passover and the **a** of blood,

APPLIED APPLY

Ecc 1:13 I **a** my mind to study and to explore
1:17 I **a** myself to the understanding
1Co 4: 6 I have **a** these things to myself

APPLY APPLICATION, APPLIED, APPLYING

Pr 22:17 **a** your heart to what I teach,
23:12 **A** your heart to instruction and your

APPLYING APPLY

Pr 2: 2 and **a** your heart to understanding—

APPOINT APPOINTED

Nu 3:10 **A** Aaron and his sons to serve as
Dt 17:15 **a** over you a king the LORD your
1Sa 8: 5 now **a** a king to lead us, such as all
Ps 61: 7 **a** your love and faithfulness
1Th 5: 9 For God did not **a** us to suffer wrath
Titus 1: 5 and **a** elders in every town, as I
Rev 11: 3 And I will **a** my two witnesses,

APPOINTED APPOINT

Lev 23: 2 'These are my **a** festivals, the **a**
festivals of the LORD,
Dt 1:15 **a** them to have authority over you—
1Ki 1:35 I have **a** him ruler over Israel
Ezr 1: 2 he has **a** me to build a temple
Da 11:27 an end will still come at the **a** time.
Mic 6: 9 the rod and the One who **a** it.
Hab 2: 3 For the revelation awaits an **a** time;
Mk 3:16 These are the twelve he **a**:
Lk 1:20 will come true at their **a** time."
10: 1 this the Lord **a** seventy-two others
Jn 15:16 you and **a** you so that you might go
Ac 15: 2 So Paul and Barnabas were **a**,
Ro 9: 9 "At the **a** time I will return,
Heb 1: 2 Son, whom he **a** heir of all things,

APPOINTED FESTIVALS Lev 23:2, 2, 4, 37,
44; Nu 10:10; 29:39; 1Ch 23:31; 2Ch 2:4; 31:3;
Ezr 3:5; Ne 10:33; Isa 1:14; La 1:4; 2:6; Eze 36:38;
44:24; 45:17; 46:9, 11; Hos 2:11; 9:5; 12:9; Zep 3:18

APPOINTED TIME Ge 18:14; Ex 13:10; 23:15;
34:18; Nu 9:2, 3, 7, 13; 28:2; Ps 75:2; 102:13; Jer
33:20; Da 8:19; 11:27, 29, 35; Hab 2:3; Mt 8:29;
26:18; Lk 1:20; Ro 9:9; 1Co 4:5

APPROACH APPROACHING
Ex   24: 2 but Moses alone is to a the LORD;
Eph   3:12 in him we may a God with freedom
Heb   4:16 then a God's throne of grace

APPROACHING APPROACH
Heb 10:25 all the more as you see the Day a.
1Jn   5:14 is the confidence we have in a God:

APPROPRIATE*
Ge   49:28 giving each the blessing a to him.
Ecc   5:18 that it is a for a person to eat,
1Ti   2:10 deeds, a for women who profess
Titus 2: 1 must teach what is a to sound

APPROVAL APPROVE
Jdg 18: 6 Your journey has the LORD's a."
Jn   6:27 the Father has placed his seal of a."
Ro   14:18 to God and receives human a.
1Co 11:19 to show which of you have God's a.
Gal   1:10 trying to win the a of human beings,

APPROVE APPROVAL, APPROVED
Ro   1:32 also a of those who practice them.
       2:18 a of what is superior because you
      12: 2 to test and a what God's will is—

APPROVED* APPROVE
Ecc   9: 7 for God has already a what you do.
Ac   8: 1 And Saul a of their killing him.
2Co 10:18 who commends himself who is a,
1Th   2: 4 we speak as those a by God to be
2Ti   2:15 to present yourself to God as one a.

APPROVES* APPROVES
Ro   14:22 not condemn himself by what he a.

APT*
Pr   15:23 finds joy in giving an a reply—

AQUILA*
    Husband of Priscilla; co-worker with Paul, in-
structor of Apollos (Ac 18; Ro 16:3; 1Co 16:19;
2Ti 4:19).

ARABAH
Dt   4:49 included all the A east of the Jordan,
Zec 14:10 Jerusalem, will become like the A.

ARABIA ARABS
Isa 21:13 A prophecy against A:
Gal   1:17 before I was, but I went into A.
       4:25 Hagar stands for Mount Sinai in A

ARABS ARABIA
Ne   4: 7 the A, the Ammonites
Ac   2:11 Cretans and A—we hear them

ARAM ARAMAIC, ARAMEAN,
    PADDAN ARAM
Jdg 10: 6 and the gods of A, the gods
2Ki 13: 3 under the power of Hazael king of A
2Ch 16: 7 you relied on the king of A and not
      16: 7 the king of A has escaped from your

ARAMAIC ARAM
2Ki 18:26 "Please speak to your servants in A,

Ezr   4: 7 The letter was written in A script and
             in the A language.
Jn   19:20 and the sign was written in A,
Ac   21:40 were all silent, he said to them in A:
      26:14 I heard a voice saying to me in A,

ARAMEAN ARAM
Ge   31:20 Jacob deceived Laban the A by not
Dt   26: 5 "My father was a wandering A,

ARARAT
Ge   8: 4 came to rest on the mountains of A.

ARAUNAH
2Sa 24:16 the threshing floor of A the Jebusite.
1Ch 21:25 So David paid A six hundred
2Ch 3: 1 the threshing floor of A the Jebusite,

ARBITER*
Lk   12:14 me a judge or an a between you?"

ARCHANGEL* ANGEL
1Th   4:16 with the voice of the a
Jude   1: 9 But even the a Michael, when he

ARCHELAUS*
Mt   2:22 he heard that A was reigning

ARCHER ARCHERS
Ge   21:20 lived in the desert and became an a.
Pr   26:10 Like an a who wounds at random is

ARCHERS ARCHER
Ge   49:23 With bitterness a attacked him;
Job 16:13 his a surround me. Without pity,
Jer 50:29 "Summon a against Babylon,

ARCHIPPUS*
    Co-worker of Paul (Col 4:17; Phm 2).

ARCHITECT*
Heb 11:10 whose a and builder is God.

ARENA*
1Co   4: 9 those condemned to die in the a.

AREOPAGUS*
Ac   17:19 brought him to a meeting of the A,
      17:24 stood up in the meeting of the A
      17:34 a member of the A, also a woman

ARGUE ARGUING, ARGUMENT,
    ARGUMENTS
Job 13: 3 and to a my case with God.
      13: 8 Will you a the case for God?
Isa 43:26 for me, let us a the matter together;
Ac   6: 9 who began to a with Stephen.

ARGUING ARGUE
Ac   19: 8 a persuasively about the kingdom
Php   2:14 everything without grumbling or a,

ARGUMENT ARGUE
Lk   9:46 An a started among the disciples as
Heb   6:16 what is said and puts an end to all a.

ARGUMENTS ARGUE
Isa 41:21 "Set forth your a," says Jacob's

2Co 10: 5 We demolish a and every
Col   2: 4 deceive you by fine-sounding a.
2Ti   2:23 to do with foolish and stupid a,
Titus 3: 9 and genealogies and a and quarrels

ARIMATHEA

Mt 27:57 a rich man from A, named Joseph,
Jn 19:38 Joseph of A asked Pilate for the

ARISE RISE

2Ch 6:41 "Now a, LORD God, and come
Pr 31:28 Her children a and call her blessed;
SS   2:10 beloved spoke and said to me, "A,
Isa 60: 1 "A, shine, for your light has come,
Da 11: 3 Then a mighty king will a, who will

ARISTARCHUS*

Companion of Paul (Ac 19:29; 20:4; 27:2; Col 4:10; Phm 1:24).

ARK

Ge   6:14 So make yourself an a of cypress
Ex 25:10 "Have them make an a of acacia
    25:16 Then put in the a the tablets
    37: 1 Bezalel made the a of acacia wood—
Nu 10:35 Whenever the a set out, Moses said,
Dt 10: 2 Then you are to put them in the a."
    10: 5 put the tablets in the a I had made,
Jos 3: 3 you see the a of the covenant
1Sa 4:11 The a of God was captured,
     6: 3 "If you return the a of the god
     7: 2 The a remained at Kiriath Jearim
2Sa 6:17 They brought the a of the LORD
1Ki 8: 9 in the a except the two stone tablets
1Ch 13: 9 reached out his hand to steady the a,
2Ch 35: 3 "Put the sacred a in the temple
Lk 17:27 up to the day Noah entered the a.
Heb 9: 4 the gold-covered a of the covenant.
     9: 4 This contained the gold jar
    11: 7 in holy fear built an a to save his
Rev 11:19 within his temple was seen the a

ARK OF GOD 1Sa 3:3; 4:11, 13, 17, 18, 19, 21, 22; 5:1, 7, 8, 8, 8, 10, 10, 10, 11; 6:3; 14:18; 2Sa 6:2, 3, 4, 6, 7, 12, 12; 7:2; 15:24, 25, 29; 1Ch 13:3, 5, 6, 7, 12, 14; 15:1, 2, 15, 24; 16:1; 2Ch 1:4

ARK OF THE COVENANT Ex 25:22; 26:33, 34; 27:21; 30:6, 26, 36; 31:7; 39:35; 40:3, 5, 21; Lev 24:3; Nu 4:5; 7:89; 10:33; 17:4, 10; Dt 10:8; 31:9, 25, 26; Jos 3:3, 6, 8, 11, 14, 17; 4:7, 9, 16, 18; 6:6; 8:33; Jdg 20:27; 1Sa 4:4, 4; 2Sa 15:24; 1Ki 6:19; 1Ch 15:25, 26, 28, 29; 16:6, 37; 17:1; 22:19; 28:2, 18; Jer 3:16; Heb 9:4

ARK OF THE LORD† Jos 3:13; 4:5, 11; 6:7, 11, 12, 13, 13; 7:6; 1Sa 4:6; 5:3, 4; 6:1, 2, 8, 11, 15, 18, 19, 21; 7:1, 1; 2Sa 6:9, 10, 11, 13, 15, 16, 17; 1Ki 8:4; 1Ch 15:2, 3, 12, 14; 16:4; 2Ch 8:11

ARM ARMED, ARMIES, ARMOR, ARMOR-BEARER, ARMS, ARMY

Ex   6: 6 redeem you with an outstretched a
Nu 11:23 "Is the LORD's a too short?
Dt   4:34 mighty hand and an outstretched a,
     7:19 the mighty hand and outstretched a,
1Ki 8:42 hand and your outstretched a—

2Ch 32: 8 With him is only the a of flesh,
Job 40: 9 Do you have an a like God's,
Ps 44: 3 nor did their a bring them victory;
    44: 3 your a, and the light of your face,
    98: 1 his holy a have worked salvation
SS   8: 3 His left a is under my head and his
                  right a embraces me.
Isa 40:10 and he rules with a mighty a.
Jer 27: 5 and outstretched a I made the earth
1Pe 4: 1 a yourselves also with the same

ARMAGEDDON*

Rev 16:16 the place that in Hebrew is called A.

ARMED ARM

2Sa 22:40 You a me with strength for battle;
Mk 14:43 him was a crowd a with swords

ARMIES ARM

1Sa 17:10 "This day I defy the a of Israel!
    17:36 because he has defied the a
Lk 21:20 Jerusalem being surrounded by a,
Rev 19:14 The a of heaven were following

ARMOR ARM

1Ki 20:11 his a should not boast like one who
    22:34 Israel between the sections of his a.
1Ch 10:10 They put his a in the temple of their
Ps 35: 2 Take up shield and a;
Jer 46: 4 Polish your spears, put on your a!
Ro 13:12 darkness and put on the a of light.
Eph 6:11 Put on the full a of God, so that you
     6:13 Therefore put on the full a of God,

ARMOR-BEARER ARM

1Sa 14: 6 Jonathan said to his young a,
    31: 4 Saul said to his a, "Draw your
    31: 4 But his a was terrified and would

ARMS ARM

Ge 16: 5 I put my slave in your a, and now
Dt 33:27 underneath are the everlasting a.
Jdg 16:12 he snapped the ropes off his a as
Ps 18:32 It is God who a me with strength
Pr 31:17 her a are strong for her tasks.
    31:20 She opens her a to the poor
SS   5:14 His a are rods of gold set
Isa 40:11 He gathers the lambs in his a
Mk 10:16 And he took the children in his a,
Heb 12:12 strengthen your feeble a and weak

ARMY ARM

Ex 14:17 glory through Pharaoh and all his a,
Jos 5:14 of the a of the LORD I have now
Ps 33:16 king is saved by the size of his a;
Eze 37:10 and stood up on their feet—a vast a.
Joel 2: 2 a large and mighty a comes, such as
      2: 5 like a mighty a drawn up for battle.
      2:25 my great a that I sent among you.
Rev 19:19 the rider on the horse and his a.

ARNON

Nu 21:13 there and camped alongside the A,
    21:13 The A is the border of Moab,
Jer 48:20 by the A that Moab is destroyed.

AROMA

Ge   8:21 The LORD smelled the pleasing **a**
Ex 29:18 a pleasing **a**, a food offering
Lev   1: 9 an **a** pleasing to the LORD.
Nu 15: 3 as an **a** pleasing to the LORD—
2Co 2:14 us to spread the **a** of the knowledge
     2:15 God the pleasing **a** of Christ among
     2:16 one we are an **a** that brings death;
     2:16 to the other, an **a** that brings life.

AROMA PLEASING See PLEASING

PLEASING AROMA See PLEASING

AROUND

Jos   6: 4 day, march **a** the city seven times,
Ezr   3: 3 their fear of the peoples **a** them,
     9: 2 holy race with the peoples **a** them.
Ps   3: 3 are a shield **a** me, my glory, the One
  48:12 Walk about Zion, go **a** her,
Zec 2: 5 I myself will be a wall of fire **a** it,'
Lk   2: 9 the glory of the Lord shone **a** them,
1Pe 5: 8 the devil prowls **a** like a roaring lion

AROUSE ROUSE

Dt 31:29 and **a** his anger by what your hands
1Ki 16:33 and did more to **a** the anger
SS   2: 7 Do not **a** or awaken love until it so
Jer 25: 6 do not **a** my anger with what your
Eze 8:17 and continually **a** my anger?
Ro 11:14 I may somehow **a** my own people
1Co 10:22 we trying to **a** the Lord's jealousy?

AROUSED ROUSE

Ex 22:24 My anger will be **a**, and I will kill
Nu 11: 1 he heard them his anger was **a**.
Dt   9: 7 never forget how you **a** the anger
Jdg 2:12 They **a** the LORD's anger
2Ki 17:11 things that **a** the LORD's anger.
Ps 78:58 they **a** his jealousy with their idols.
Jer   8:19 "Why have they **a** my anger
Hos 11: 8 all my compassion is **a**.
Ro   7: 5 the sinful passions **a** by the law

ARRAYED*

Ps 110: 3 **A** in holy splendor, your young men
Isa 61:10 **a** me in a robe of his righteousness,

ARREST ARRESTED

Mt 10:19 But when they **a** you, do not worry
Mk 14: 1 were scheming to **a** Jesus secretly

ARRESTED ARREST

Mt 14: 3 Now Herod had **a** John and bound
  26:50 forward, seized Jesus and **a** him.
Ac   5:18 They **a** the apostles and put them
  12: 1 King Herod **a** some who belonged
  28:17 I was **a** in Jerusalem and handed

ARROGANCE ARROGANT,
ARROGANTLY

1Sa   2: 3 or let your mouth speak such **a**,
  15:23 and **a** like the evil of idolatry.
Pr   8:13 I hate pride and **a**, evil behavior
Jer 48:29 how great is her **a**!—
Hos 7:10 Israel's **a** testifies against him,

Mk   7:22 lewdness, envy, slander, **a** and folly.
2Co 12:20 slander, gossip, **a** and disorder.

ARROGANT ARROGANCE

Ne   9:16 became **a** and stiff-necked, and they
Ps   5: 5 The **a** cannot stand in your
  73: 3 For I envied the **a** when I saw
 119:78 May the **a** be put to shame
Pr 21:24 The proud and **a** person—
Hab 2: 5 he is **a** and never at rest.
Mal 3:15 But now we call the **a** blessed.
Ro   1:30 God-haters, insolent, **a** and boastful;
  11:20 Do not be **a**, but tremble.
1Co 4:18 Some of you have become **a**, as if I
1Ti 6:17 this present world not to be **a** nor
2Pe 2:10 Bold and **a**, they are not afraid

ARROGANTLY ARROGANCE

Mal 3:13 "You have spoken **a** against me,"

ARROW ARROWS

1Sa 20:36 boy ran, he shot an **a** beyond him.
Ps 91: 5 of night, nor the **a** that flies by day,
Pr 25:18 or a sharp **a** is one who gives false
Jer   9: 8 Their tongue is a deadly **a**;

ARROWS ARROW

Dt 32:42 I will make my **a** drunk with blood,
2Ki 13:15 "Get a bow and some **a**," and he
Job 6: 4 The **a** of the Almighty are in me,
Ps 38: 2 Your **a** have pierced me, and your
  64: 3 and aim cruel words like deadly **a**.
  64: 7 But God will shoot them with his **a**;
 127: 4 Like **a** in the hands of a warrior are
Pr 26:18 Like a maniac shooting flaming **a**
La   3:13 He pierced my heart with **a** from his
Eph 6:16 you can extinguish all the flaming **a**

ARTAXERXES

King of Persia; allowed rebuilding of temple under Ezra (Ezr 4; 7), and of walls of Jerusalem under his cupbearer Nehemiah (Ne 2; 5:14; 13:6).

ARTEMIS

Ac 19:27 of the great goddess **A** will be

ARTS

Ex   7:11 the same things by their secret **a**:
  8:18 to produce gnats by their secret **a**,
Rev 21: 8 those who practice magic **a**,
  22:15 those who practice magic **a**,

ASA

King of Judah (1Ki 15:8–24; 1Ch 3:10; 2Ch 14–16). Godly reformer (2Ch 15); in later years defeated Israel with help of Aram, not the LORD (1Ki 15:16–22; 2Ch 16).

ASAHEL

1. Nephew of David, one of his warriors (2Sa 23:24; 1Ch 2:16; 11:26; 27:7). Killed by Abner (2Sa 2); avenged by Joab (2Sa 3:22–39).
2. Levite; teacher (2Ch 17:8).

ASAPH

1. Recorder to Hezekiah (2Ki 18:18, 37; Isa 36:3, 22).

2. Levitical musician (1Ch 6:39; 15:17–19; 16:4–7, 37). Sons of (1Ch 25; 2Ch 5:12; 20:14; 29:13; 35:15; Ezr 2:41; 3:10; Ne 7:44; 11:17; 12:27–47). Psalms of (2Ch 29:30; Ps 50; 73–83).

ASCEND* ASCENDED, ASCENDING, ASCENTS

Dt 30:12 "Who will a into heaven to get it
Ps 24: 3 Who may a the mountain
Isa 14:13 your heart, "I will a to the heavens;
       14:14 I will a above the tops of the clouds;
Jn   6:62 of Man a to where he was before!
Ac   2:34 For David did not a to heaven,
Ro 10: 6 heart, 'Who will a into heaven?' "

ASCENDED ASCEND

Ps 47: 5 God has a amid shouts of joy,
      68:18 When you a on high, you took
Isa 37:24 many chariots I have a the heights
Eph 4: 8 "When he a on high, he took many
Heb 4:14 have a great high priest who has a

ASCENDING* ASCEND

Ge 28:12 and the angels of God were a
Eze 41: 7 the temple was built in a stages,
Jn   1:51 the angels of God a and descending
      20:17 them, 'I am a to my Father and your

ASCENTS* ASCEND

Fifteen songs of ascents (Ps 120–134).

ASCRIBE*

1Ch 16:28 A to the Lord, all you families
      16:28 a to the Lord glory and strength.
      16:29 A to the Lord the glory due his
Job 36: 3 I will a justice to my Maker.
Ps   29: 1 A to the Lord, you heavenly
      29: 1 a to the Lord glory and strength.
      29: 2 A to the Lord the glory due his
      96: 7 A to the Lord, all you families
      96: 7 a to the Lord glory and strength.
      96: 8 A to the Lord the glory due his

ASH ASHES

1Sa 2: 8 and lifts the needy from the a heap;
La   4: 5 in royal purple now lie on a heaps.

ASHAMED SHAME

Isa 29:22 "No longer will Jacob be a;
Jer 48:13 Then Moab will be a of Chemosh,
      48:13 as Israel was a when they trusted
Eze 43:10 that they may be a of their sins.
Mk 8:38 If anyone is a of me and my words
      8:38 the Son of Man will be a of them
Ro   1:16 For I am not a of the gospel,
      6:21 from the things you are now a of?
Php 1:20 and hope that I will in no way be a,
2Ti 1: 8 So do not be a of the testimony
      2:15 a worker who does not need to be a
Titus 2: 8 you may be a because they have
Heb 2:11 So Jesus is not a to call them
     11:16 Therefore God is not a to be called

ASHDOD

Jos 13: 3 the five Philistine rulers in Gaza, A,
1Sa 5: 1 they took it from Ebenezer to A.
Ne 13:23 who had married women from A,

ASHER

Son of Jacob by Zilpah (Ge 30:13; 35:26; 46:17; Ex 1:4; 1Ch 2:2). Tribe of blessed (Ge 49:20; Dt 33:24–25), numbered (Nu 1:40–41; 26:44–47), allotted land (Jos 10:24–31; Eze 48:2), failed to fully possess (Jdg 1:31–32), failed to support Deborah (Jdg 5:17), supported Gideon (Jdg 6:35; 7:23) and David (1Ch 12:36), 12,000 from (Rev 7:6).

ASHERAH ASHERAHS

Ex 34:13 stones and cut down their A poles.
Jdg 6:25 and cut down the A pole beside it.
1Ki 14:15 Lord's anger by making A poles.
      18:19 and the four hundred prophets of A,
2Ch 34: 4 smashed the A poles and the idols.

ASHERAHS* ASHERAH

Jdg 3: 7 God and served the Baals and the A.

ASHES ASH

Ge 18:27 though I am nothing but dust and a,
Est 4: 1 put on sackcloth and a, and went
Job 42: 6 myself and repent in dust and a."
Ps 102: 9 For I eat a as my food and mingle
Isa 61: 3 them a crown of beauty instead of a,
Mt 11:21 long ago in sackcloth and a.

ASHKELON

Jdg 1:18 also took Gaza, A and Ekron—
2Sa 1:20 proclaim it not in the streets of A,

ASHTORETH ASHTORETHS

1Ki 11: 5 He followed A the goddess

ASHTORETHS ASHTORETH

Jdg 2:13 him and served Baal and the A.
1Sa 7: 4 put away their Baals and A,

ASIA

Ac   2: 9 and Cappadocia, Pontus and A,
      16: 6 the word in the province of A.
Rev 1: 4 seven churches in the province of A:

ASK ASKED, ASKS

Ex 12:26 And when your children a you,
Dt 32: 7 A your father and he will tell you,
Ps 27: 4 One thing I a from the Lord,
Pr 30: 7 "Two things I a of you, Lord;
Isa 7:11 "A the Lord your God for a sign,
      65: 1 to those who did not a for me;
Mal 1: 2 "But you a, 'How have you loved
Mt 6: 8 what you need before you a him.
      7: 7 "A and it will be given to you;
Mk 11:24 you, whatever you a for in prayer,
Lk 11:13 Holy Spirit to those who a him!"
Jn 14:14 You may a me for anything in my
Eph 3:20 do immeasurably more than all we a
Jas 4: 3 When you a, you do not receive,
      4: 3 because you a with wrong motives,
1Jn 3:22 receive from him anything we a,

ASKED ASK
Ps 106:15 So he gave them what they a for,
Lk 22:31 Satan has a to sift all of you as
Jn 16:24 Until now you have not a

ASKS ASK
Lk 6:30 Give to everyone who a you,
   11:10 For everyone who a receives;
   11:29 It a for a sign, but none will be

ASLEEP SLEEP
Mk 5:39 The child is not dead but a."
   14:37 he said to Peter, "are you a?
Jn 11:11 "Our friend Lazarus has fallen a;
1Co 15:18 who have fallen a in Christ are lost.

ASPIRES*
1Ti 3: 1 Whoever a to be an overseer desires

ASSASSINATE ASSASSINATED
Est 6: 2 had conspired to a King Xerxes.

ASSASSINATED ASSASSINATE
2Ki 21:23 him and a the king in his palace.
   25:25 came with ten men and a Gedaliah

ASSEMBLE ASSEMBLED, ASSEMBLY
Ps 102:22 and the kingdoms a to worship
Zep 3: 8 I have decided to a the nations,

ASSEMBLED ASSEMBLE
Est 9:16 also a to protect themselves and get
1Co 5: 4 So when you are a and I am

ASSEMBLY ASSEMBLE
Nu 14:10 the whole a talked about stoning
   16:21 from this a so I can put an end
Dt 23: 1 or cutting may enter the a
2Ch 29:28 The whole a bowed in worship,
Ps 1: 5 nor sinners in the a of the righteous.
   22:22 in the a I will praise you,
   35:18 I will give you thanks in the great a;
   82: 1 God presides in the great a;
   149: 1 praise in the a of his faithful people.
Joel 1:14 Declare a holy fast; call a sacred a.
Heb 2:12 in the a I will sing your praises."
   12:22 thousands of angels in joyful a,

ASSERTED
1Th 2: 6 we could have a our authority.

ASSIGNED
1Ki 7:14 and did all the work a to him.
Isa 53: 9 He was a a grave with the wicked,
Mk 13:34 each with their a task, and tells
1Co 3: 5 as the Lord has a to each his task.
   7:17 whatever situation the Lord has a
2Co 10:13 of service God himself has a to us,

ASSIST
Nu 8:26 They may a their brothers
Ro 15:24 have you a me on my journey there,

ASSOCIATE
Jos 23: 7 Do not a with these nations
Ps 26: 4 deceitful, nor do I a with hypocrites.
Pr 22:24 do not a with one easily angered,

Jn 4: 9 Jews do not a with Samaritans.)
Ac 10:28 against our law for a Jew to a
Ro 12:16 be willing to a with people of low
1Co 5: 9 in my letter not to a with sexually
   5:11 you must not a with anyone who
2Th 3:14 Do not a with them, in order

ASSURANCE ASSURED
Job 24:22 established, they have no a of life.
1Ti 3:13 great a in their faith in Christ Jesus.
Heb 10:22 and with the full a that faith brings,
   11: 1 and a about what we do not see.

ASSURED ASSURANCE
Jos 2:14 the men a her. "If you don't tell
Col 4:12 the will of God, mature and fully a.

ASSYRIA ASSYRIANS
Ge 10:11 From that land he went to A,
2Ki 15:29 Tiglath-Pileser king of A came
   15:29 and deported the people to A.
   18:11 The king of A deported Israel to A
   19:10 into the hands of the king of A.'
Isa 30:31 voice of the LORD will shatter A;
Jer 50:18 his land as I punished the king of A.
Hos 14: 3 A cannot save us; we will not mount

KING OF ASSYRIA See KING

ASSYRIANS ASSYRIA
Isa 10:24 do not be afraid of the A, who beat
Eze 23: 5 she lusted after her lovers, the A—

ASTONISHED
Mt 22:33 this, they were a at his teaching.
Ac 4:13 they were a and they took note

ASTRAY STRAY
Nu 5:12 'If a man's wife goes a and is
Dt 17:17 wives, or his heart will be led a.
1Ki 11: 3 and his wives led him a.
2Ki 21: 9 Manasseh led them a, so that they
Ps 58: 3 Even from birth the wicked go a;
   119:67 Before I was afflicted I went a,
Pr 7:21 persuasive words she led him a;
   10:17 ignores correction leads others a.
   20: 1 whoever is led a by them is not
Isa 53: 6 have gone a, each of us has turned
Jer 50: 6 their shepherds have led them a
Am 2: 4 because they have been led a
Gal 2:13 hypocrisy even Barnabas was led a.
1Pe 2:25 For "you were like sheep going a,"
1Jn 3: 7 do not let anyone lead you a.
Rev 12: 9 Satan, who leads the whole world a.

ASTROLOGERS
Isa 47:13 Let your a come forward,
Da 2: 2 a to tell him what he had dreamed.

ATE EAT
Ge 3: 6 wisdom, she took some and a it.
   3: 6 who was with her, and he a it.
   3:13 serpent deceived me, and I a."
   27:25 Jacob brought it to him and he a;
Ex 16:35 The Israelites a manna forty years,
   16:35 they a manna until they reached

Nu 25: 2 The people **a** the sacrificial meal
Ru 2:14 She **a** all she wanted and had some
2Sa 9:11 So Mephibosheth **a** at David's table
2Ki 6:29 So we cooked my son and **a** him.
Ezr 10: 6 he **a** no food and drank no water,
Ps 78:25 Human beings **a** the bread
Jer 15:16 When your words came, I **a** them;
Eze 3: 3 So I **a** it, and it tasted as sweet as
Mt 14:20 They all **a** and were satisfied,
   15:37 They all **a** and were satisfied.
Mk 6:42 They all **a** and were satisfied,
Lk 9:17 They all **a** and were satisfied,
Jn 6:58 Your ancestors **a** manna and died,
1Co 10: 3 They all **a** the same spiritual food
Rev 10:10 from the angel's hand and **a** it.

ATHALIAH
Granddaughter of Omri; wife of Jehoram and mother of Ahaziah; encouraged their evil ways (2Ki 8:18, 27; 2Ch 22:2). At death of Ahaziah she made herself queen, killing all his sons but Joash (2Ki 11:1–3; 2Ch 22:10–12); killed six years later when Joash revealed (2Ki 11:4–16; 2Ch 23:1–15).

ATHENS
Ac 17:16 Paul was waiting for them in **A**,

ATHLETE*
2Ti 2: 5 competes as an **a** does not receive

ATONE* ATONEMENT
Ex 30:15 to the LORD to **a** for your lives.
2Ch 29:24 for a sin offering to **a** for all Israel,
Da 9:24 an end to sin, to **a** for wickedness,

ATONED* ATONEMENT
Dt 21: 8 Then the bloodshed will be **a** for,
1Sa 3:14 of Eli's house will never be **a**
Pr 16: 6 love and faithfulness sin is **a** for;
Isa 6: 7 is taken away and your sin **a** for."
   22:14 day this sin will not be **a** for,"
   27: 9 will Jacob's guilt be **a** for, and this

ATONEMENT ATONE, ATONED
Ex 25:17 "Make an **a** cover of pure gold—
   29:36 day as a sin offering to make **a**.
   29:36 Purify the altar by making **a** for it,
   30:10 Once a year Aaron shall make **a**
   30:10 This annual **a** must be made
   32:30 perhaps I can make **a** for your sin."
Lev 17:11 you to make **a** for yourselves
   17:11 blood that makes **a** for one's life.
   23:27 this seventh month is the Day of **A**.
Nu 25:13 God and made **a** for the Israelites."
1Ch 6:49 Holy Place, making **a** for Israel,
Ro 3:25 presented Christ as a sacrifice of **a**,
Heb 2:17 that he might make **a** for the sins

ATTACK ATTACKED, ATTACKS
1Sa 17:48 Philistine moved closer to **a** him,
   24: 7 and did not allow them to **a** Saul.
Ps 109: 3 they **a** me without cause.
Isa 54:15 If anyone does **a** you, it will not be
Ac 18:10 no one is going to **a** and harm you,
2Ti 4:18 will rescue me from every evil **a**

Rev 11: 7 up from the Abyss will **a** them,

ATTACKED ATTACK
Ge 4: 8 Cain **a** his brother Abel and killed
Ex 17: 8 and **a** the Israelites at Rephidim.
Est 8: 7 Jew, "Because Haman **a** the Jews,

ATTACKS ATTACK
Ex 21:15 "Anyone who **a** their father
Lk 11:22 But when someone stronger **a**
Jn 10:12 Then the wolf **a** the flock

ATTAIN* ATTAINED, ATTAINING
Ps 139: 6 for me, too lofty for me to **a**.
Pr 2:19 to her return or **a** the paths of life.
   11:19 Truly the righteous **a** life,

ATTAINED* ATTAIN
Pr 16:31 it is **a** in the way of righteousness.
   30: 3 nor have I **a** to the knowledge
Ro 9:31 righteousness, has not **a** their goal.
Php 3:16 live up to what we have already **a**.
Heb 7:11 could have been **a** through

ATTAINING* ATTAIN
Eph 4:13 **a** to the whole measure
Php 3:11 **a** to the resurrection from the dead.

ATTENDANTS ATTENDED
Ge 24:61 Rebekah and her **a** got ready
Est 2: 9 to her seven female **a** selected

ATTENDED ATTENDANTS
Da 7:10 Thousands upon thousands **a** him;
Mt 4:11 him, and angels came and **a** him.
Mk 1:13 the wild animals, and angels **a** him.

ATTENTION ATTENTIVE
Ex 4: 8 you or pay **a** to the first sign,
   15:26 if you pay **a** to his commands
   16:20 some of them paid no **a** to Moses;
Dt 28:13 If you pay **a** to the commands
1Ki 18:29 no one answered, no one paid **a**.
Ne 8:13 the teacher to give **a** to the words
Pr 4: 1 pay **a** and gain understanding.
   4:20 My son, pay **a** to what I say;
   5: 1 My son, pay **a** to my wisdom,
   17: 4 a liar pays **a** to a destructive tongue.
   22:17 Pay **a** and turn your ear
Ecc 7:21 Do not pay **a** to every word people
Isa 42:20 seen many things, but you pay no **a**;
Jer 44: 5 But they did not listen or pay **a**;
Titus 1:14 and will pay no **a** to Jewish myths
Heb 2: 1 We must pay the most careful **a**,
Jas 2: 3 If you show special **a** to the man
2Pe 1:19 and you will do well to pay **a** to it,
3Jn 1:10 I will call **a** to what he is doing,

ATTENTIVE ATTENTION
2Ch 6:40 your ears **a** to the prayers offered
Ne 1:11 let your ear be **a** to the prayer of this
1Pe 3:12 and his ears are **a** to their prayer,

ATTITUDE ATTITUDES
Ge 31: 2 Laban's **a** toward him was not what
1Ki 11:11 "Since this is your **a** and you have

Ezr   6:22 joy by changing the **a** of the king
Da   3:19 and his **a** toward them changed.
Eph   4:23 made new in the **a** of your minds;
1Pe   4: 1 yourselves also with the same **a**,

ATTITUDES* ATTITUDE
Heb   4:12 the thoughts and **a** of the heart.

ATTRACT* ATTRACTED, ATTRACTIVE
Isa   53: 2 no beauty or majesty to **a** us to him,

ATTRACTED ATTRACT
Est   2:17 Now the king was **a** to Esther more

ATTRACTIVE ATTRACT
Titus 2:10 teaching about God our Savior **a**.

AUDACITY*
Lk   11: 8 your shameless **a** he will surely get

AUDIENCE
2Ch   9:23 of the earth sought a **a** with Solomon
Pr   29:26 Many seek an **a** with a ruler, but it

AUGUSTUS*
Lk   2: 1 those days Caesar **A** issued a decree

AUTHOR*
Ac   3:15 You killed the **a** of life, but God

AUTHORITIES* AUTHORITY
Lk   12:11 rulers and **a**, do not worry
Jn   7:26 Have the **a** really concluded that he
Ac   16:19 into the marketplace to face the **a**.
Ro   13: 1 be subject to the governing **a**,
       13: 1 The **a** that exist have been
       13: 5 it is necessary to submit to the **a**,
       13: 6 for the **a** are God's servants,
Eph   3:10 rulers and **a** in the heavenly realms,
       6:12 against the **a**, against the powers
Col   1:16 thrones or powers or rulers or **a**;
       2:15 having disarmed the powers and **a**,
Titus 3: 1 people to be subject to rulers and **a**,
1Pe   3:22 **a** and powers in submission to him.

AUTHORITY AUTHORITIES
Jer   5:31 the priests rule by their own **a**,
Da   7: 6 heads, and it was given **a** to rule.
Mt   7:29 because he taught as one who had **a**,
       9: 6 the Son of Man has **a** on earth
      28:18 "All **a** in heaven and on earth has
Mk   1:27 A new teaching—and with **a**!
      10:42 high officials exercise **a** over them.
      11:28 what **a** are you doing these things?"
      11:28 "And who gave you **a** to do this?"
Lk   4:32 teaching, because his words had **a**.
       5:24 the Son of Man has **a** on earth
       7: 8 For I myself am a man under **a**,
Jn   10:18 I have **a** to lay it down and **a** to take
Ac   1: 7 the Father has set by his own **a**.
Ro   7: 1 the law has **a** over someone only as
      13: 1 for there is no **a** except
      13: 2 rebels against the **a** is rebelling
1Co   7: 4 wife does not have **a** over her own
       7: 4 does not have **a** over his own body

1Co 11:10 ought to have **a** over her own head,
      15:24 all dominion, **a** and power.
2Co 10: 8 freely about the **a** the Lord gave us
Col   2:10 is the head over every power and **a**.
1Ti   2: 2 for kings and all those in **a**, that we
       2:12 to teach or to assume **a** over a man;
Titus 2:15 Encourage and rebuke with all **a**.
Heb 13:17 your leaders and submit to their **a**,
1Pe   2:13 the Lord's sake to every human **a**:
       2:13 to the emperor, as the supreme **a**,
2Pe   2:10 desire of the flesh and despise **a**.
Jude 1: 6 did not keep their positions of **a**
Rev   2:27 just as I have received **a** from my
      12:10 our God, and the **a** of his Messiah.
      13: 4 the dragon because he had given **a**
      17:17 hand over to the beast their royal **a**,

AUTUMN*
Dt   11:14 its season, both **a** and spring rains,
Ps   84: 6 the **a** rains also cover it with pools.
Jer   5:24 who gives **a** and spring rains
Joel 2:23 has given you the **a** rains because he
       2:23 showers, both **a** and spring rains,
Jas   5: 7 crop, patiently waiting for the **a**
Jude 1:12 **a** trees, without fruit and uprooted—

AVENGE VENGEANCE
Lev 26:25 on you to **a** the breaking
Dt   32:35 It is mine to **a**; I will repay.
      32:43 people, for he will **a** the blood of his
1Sa 24:12 may the LORD **a** the wrongs you
2Ki   9: 7 I will **a** the blood of my servants
Est   8:13 on that day to **a** themselves on their
Ps   79:10 that you **a** the outpoured blood
Pr   20:22 for the LORD, and he will **a** you.
Jer   5: 9 "Should I not **a** myself on such
Ro   12:19 "It is mine to **a**; I will repay,"
Heb 10:30 him who said, "It is mine to **a**;
Rev   6:10 of the earth and **a** our blood?"

AVENGED VENGEANCE
Ge   4:24 If Cain is **a** seven times,
Eze   5:13 them will subside, and I will be **a**.
Rev 19: 2 He has **a** on her the blood of his

AVENGER VENGEANCE
Nu   35:12 will be places of refuge from the **a**,
Jos 20: 3 find protection from the **a** of blood.
Ps   8: 2 to silence the foe and the **a**.

AVENGES* VENGEANCE
2Sa 22:48 He is the God who **a** me, who puts
Ps   9:12 For he who **a** blood remembers;
      18:47 He is the God who **a** me,
      94: 1 The LORD is a God who **a**. O God
             who **a**, shine forth.

AVENGING* VENGEANCE
1Sa 25:26 and from **a** yourself with your own
      25:33 from **a** myself with my own hands.
Na   1: 2 The LORD is a jealous and **a** God;

AVIV*
     The month of the exodus and Passover (Ex 13:4; 23:15; 34:18; Dt 16:1).

AVOID AVOIDED, AVOIDS
Pr 4:15 **A** it, do not travel on it; turn from it
 15:12 resent correction, so they **a** the wise.
 20: 3 It is to one's honor to **a** strife,
 20:1p so **a** anyone who talks too much.
Ecc 7:18 fears God will **a** all extremes.
Ac 15:29 You will do well to **a** these things.
Gal 6:12 they do this is to **a** being persecuted
1Th 4: 3 you should **a** sexual immorality;
2Ti 2:16 **A** godless chatter, because those
Titus 3: 9 But **a** foolish controversies

AVOIDED* AVOID
Pr 16: 6 the fear of the LORD evil is **a**.

AVOIDS* AVOID
Pr 16:17 The highway of the upright **a** evil;

AWAIT WAIT
Jer 48:43 Terror and pit and snare **a** you,
Gal 5: 5 through the Spirit we eagerly **a**
Php 3:20 we eagerly **a** a Savior from there,

AWAITS WAIT
Ps 65: 1 Praise **a** you, our God, in Zion;
Pr 15:10 Stern discipline **a** anyone who
 28:22 are unaware that poverty **a** them.
Ecc 3:19 the same fate **a** them both:
Ob 1: 5 oh, what a disaster **a** you!—
Hab 2: 3 the revelation **a** an appointed time;

AWAKE WAKE
Ps 35:23 **A**, and rise to my defense!
 57: 8 **A**, my soul! **A**, harp and lyre!
Pr 6:22 when you **a**, they will speak to you.
 20:13 stay **a** and you will have food
Isa 51: 9 **A**, **a**, arm of the LORD,
 51: 9 **A**, as in days gone by,
 52: 1 **A**, a, Zion, clothe yourself
Da 12: 2 sleep in the dust of the earth will **a**:
1Th 5: 6 are asleep, but let us be **a** and sober.
 5:10 so that, whether we are **a** or asleep,
Rev 16:15 Blessed is the one who stays **a**

AWAKEN WAKE
Ps 108: 2 harp and lyre! I will **a** the dawn.
SS 8: 4 arouse or **a** love until it so desires.

AWARD*
2Ti 4: 8 Judge, will **a** to me on that day—

AWARE
Ex 34:29 he was not **a** that his face was
Nu 15:24 without the community being **a**
Mt 24:50 him and at an hour he is not **a** of.
Lk 12:46 him and at an hour he is not **a** of.
Gal 4:21 are you not **a** of what the law says?

AWAY
Ge 5:24 no more, because God took him **a**.
 30:23 "God has taken **a** my disgrace."
 31:49 me when we are **a** from each other.
Dt 9:12 They have turned **a** quickly
2Sa 12:13 "The LORD has taken **a** your sin.
Ezr 10:19 hands in pledge to put **a** their wives,
Job 1:21 gave and the LORD has taken **a**;

Ps 51: 2 Wash **a** all my iniquity and cleanse
 148: 6 a decree that will never pass **a**.
Pr 14: 7 Stay **a** from a fool, for you will not
 15: 1 A gentle answer turns **a** wrath,
Ecc 3: 6 time to keep and a time to throw **a**,
SS 8:14 Come **a**, my beloved, and be like
Eze 11:15 'They are far **a** from the LORD;
Jnh 1: 3 But Jonah ran **a** from the LORD
Na 1:12 they will be destroyed and pass **a**.
Zep 1: 2 "I will sweep **a** everything
 3:15 has taken **a** your punishment, he has
Mk 4:17 of the word, they quickly fall **a**.
 13:31 Heaven and earth will pass **a**, but my
  words will never pass **a**.
Lk 24: 2 They found the stone rolled **a**
Jn 1:29 who takes **a** the sin of the world!
 6:37 comes to me I will never drive **a**.
 14:28 'I am going **a** and I am coming back
1Co 7:31 in its present form is passing **a**.
2Co 3:16 turns to the Lord, the veil is taken **a**.
1Jn 2:17 The world and its desires pass **a**,
Rev 7:17 God will wipe **a** every tear

AWE* AWESOME, OVERAWED
Jos 4:14 they stood in **a** of him all the days
 4:14 just as they had stood in **a** of Moses.
1Sa 12:18 So all the people stood in **a**
1Ki 3:28 they held the king in **a**, because they
Job 25: 2 "Dominion **a** belong to God;
Ps 65: 8 The whole earth is filled with **a**
 119:120 I stand in **a** of your laws.
Isa 29:23 will stand in **a** of the God of Israel.
Jer 2:19 your God and have no **a** of me,"
 33: 9 they will be in **a** and will tremble
Hab 3: 2 I stand in **a** of your deeds, LORD.
Mal 2: 5 me and stood in **a** of my name.
Mt 9: 8 saw this, they were filled with **a**;
Lk 1:65 All the neighbors were filled with **a**,
 5:26 They were filled with **a** and said,
 7:16 They were all filled with **a**
Ac 2:43 Everyone was filled with **a**
Heb 12:28 acceptably with reverence and **a**,

AWESOME* AWE
Ge 28:17 and said, "How **a** is this place!
Ex 15:11 majestic in holiness, **a** in glory,
 34:10 among will see how **a** is the work
Dt 4:34 or by great and **a** deeds, like all
 7:21 is among you, is a great and **a** God.
 10:17 God, mighty and **a**, who shows no
 10:21 **a** wonders you saw with your own
 28:58 revere this glorious and **a** name—
 34:12 or performed the **a** deeds that Moses
Jdg 13: 6 looked like an angel of God, very **a**.
2Sa 7:23 **a** wonders by driving out nations
1Ch 17:21 **a** wonders by driving out nations
Ne 1: 5 the great and **a** God, who keeps his
 4:14 who is great and **a**, and fight
 9:32 God, mighty and **a**, who keeps his
Job 10:16 again display your **a** power against
 37:22 God comes in **a** majesty.
Ps 45: 4 let your right hand achieve **a** deeds.
 47: 2 For the LORD Most High is **a**,
 65: 5 You answer us with **a** and righteous

Ps   66: 3 to God, "How **a** are your deeds!
      66: 5 has done, his **a** deeds for mankind!
      68:35 You, God, are a **a** in your sanctuary;
      89: 7 he is more **a** than all who surround
      99: 3 them praise your great and **a** name—
     106:22 of Ham and **a** deeds by the Red Sea.
     111: 9 holy and **a** is his name.
     145: 6 tell of the power of your **a** works—
Isa   64: 3 you did **a** things that we did not
Eze   1:18 Their rims were high and **a**, and all
       1:22 a vault, sparkling like crystal, and **a**.
Da   2:31 dazzling statue, **a** in appearance.
       9: 4 the great and **a** God, who keeps his
Zep   2:11 The LORD will be **a** to them

AWFUL
Jdg   20: 3 us how this **a** thing happened."
Ne   9:18 they committed **a** blasphemies.
Jer   30: 7 How **a** that day will be!

AWL*
Ex   21: 6 and pierce his ear with an **a**.
Dt   15:17 take an **a** and push it through his

AWOKE WAKE
Ge   9:24 When Noah **a** from his wine
      28:16 When Jacob **a** from his sleep,
Jdg   16:20 He **a** from his sleep and thought,
1Ki   3:15 Then Solomon **a**—and he realized it
Ps   78:65 Then the Lord **a** as from sleep,

AX AXHEAD
Ecc   10:10 If the **a** is dull and its edge
Isa   10:15 Does the **a** raise itself
Mt   3:10 The **a** is already at the root

AXHEAD* AX
2Ki   6: 5 a tree, the iron **a** fell into the water.

AZARIAH
    1 King of Judah; see Uzziah (2Ki 15.1-7).
    2. Prophet (2Ch 15:1-8).
    3. Opponent of Jeremiah (Jer 43:2).
    4. Jewish exile; see Abednego (Da 1:6-19).

B

BAAL BAAL-BERITH, BAAL-ZEBUB, BAALS
Nu   25: 3 yoked themselves to the **B** of Peor.
Jdg   2:13 and served **B** and the Ashtoreths.
       6:31 If **B** really is a god, he can defend
1Ki   16:32 set up an altar for **B** in the temple
             of **B** that he built
      18:25 Elijah said to the prophets of **B**,
      19:18 knees have not bowed down to **B**
2Ki   3: 2 the sacred stone of **B** that his father
      10:28 So Jehu destroyed **B** worship
2Ch   23:17 the people went to the temple of **B**
      23:17 killed Mattan the priest of **B** in front
Jer   19: 5 They have built the high places of **B**
      19: 5 in the fire as offerings to **B**—
Hos   13: 1 he became guilty of **B** worship
Ro   11: 4 have not bowed the knee to **B**."

BAAL-BERITH BAAL
Jdg   8:33 They set up **B** as their god

BAAL-ZEBUB BAAL, BEELZEBUL
2Ki   1: 2 "Go and consult **B**, the god

BAALS BAAL
Jdg   3: 7 and served the **B** and the Asherahs.
      10:10 our God and serving the **B**."
1Sa   7: 4 So the Israelites put away their **B**
2Ch   17: 3 He did not consult the **B**
      34: 4 the altars of the **B** were torn down;

BAASHA
    King of Israel (1Ki 15:16—16:7; 2Ch 16:1-6).

BABBLER* BABBLING
Ac   17:18 "What is this **b** trying to say?"

BABBLING* BABBLER
Mt   6: 7 do not keep on **b** like pagans,

BABEL* BABYLON
Ge   11: 9 That is why it was called **B**—

BABIES* BABY
Ge   25:22 The **b** jostled each other within her,
Ex   2: 6 "This is one of the Hebrew **b**,"
Lk   18:15 bringing **b** to Jesus for him to place
Ac   7:19 their newborn **b** so that they would
1Pe   2: 2 Like newborn **b**, crave pure spiritual

BABY BABIES, BABY'S
Ex   2: 6 She opened it and saw the **b**.
       2: 9 "Take this **b** and nurse him for me,
       2: 9 So the woman took the **b** and nursed
1Ki   3:26 my lord, give her the living **b**!
Isa   49:15 "Can a mother forget the **b** at her
Lk   1:41 greeting, the **b** leaped in her womb,
       1:44 the **b** in my womb leaped for joy.
       1:57 time for Elizabeth to have her **b**,
       2: 6 the time came for the **b** to be born,
       2:12 You will find a **b** wrapped in cloths
       2:16 and the **b**, who was lying
Jn   16:21 her **b** is born she forgets the anguish

BABY'S* BABY
Ex   2: 8 the girl went and got the **b** mother.

BABYLON BABEL, BABYLONIANS
Ge   10:10 first centers of his kingdom were **B**,
1Ch   9: 1 were taken captive to **B** because
2Ch   36:18 He carried to **B** all the articles
      36:20 carried into exile to **B** the remnant,
Ps   137: 1 By the rivers of **B** we sat and wept
Isa   14: 4 up this taunt against the king of **B**:
      21: 9 '**B** has fallen, has fallen!
Jer   29:10 seventy years are completed for **B**,
      51:34 king of **B** has devoured us, he has
      51:37 **B** will be a heap of ruins, a haunt
Da   4:30 not this the great **B** I have built as
1Pe   5:13 She who is in **B**, chosen together
Rev   14: 8 Fallen is **B** the Great,' which made
      17: 5 on her forehead was a mystery: **B**
      18: 2 " 'Fallen! Fallen is **B** the Great!'

KING OF BABYLON See KING

BABYLONIANS BABYLON

Jer 32: 5 If you fight against the **B**, you will
    38: 2 goes over to the **B** will live.
Da 1: 4 the language and literature of the **B**.
Hab 1: 6 I am raising up the **B**, that ruthless

BACK BACKS, BACKSLIDING, BACKSLIDINGS

Ge 3:24 a flaming sword flashing **b** and forth
    19:26 But Lot's wife looked **b**, and she
Ex 22: 7 thief, if caught, must pay **b** double.
Ru 1:15 "your sister-in-law is going **b** to her
    1:15 and her gods. Go **b** with her."
    2: 6 "She is the Moabite who came **b**
1Sa 25:21 He has paid me **b** evil for good.
2Ki 20:11 made the shadow go **b** the ten steps
Ps 31:23 him, but the proud he pays **b** in full.
    51:13 so that sinners will turn **b** to you.
    90: 3 You turn people **b** to dust, saying,
SS 6:13 Come **b**, come **b**, O Shulammite;
Isa 38:17 have put all my sins behind your **b**.
Jer 29:14 will bring you **b** from captivity.
    29:14 will bring you **b** to the place
La 3:64 Pay them **b** what they deserve,
Mt 28: 2 rolled **b** the stone and sat on it.
Ro 9:20 a human being, to talk **b** to God?
Gal 4: 9 that you are turning **b** to those weak
Eph 4:14 tossed **b** and forth by the waves,
1Th 5:15 nobody pays **b** wrong for wrong,
Heb 6: 6 away, to be brought **b** to repentance.
    10:39 do not belong to those who shrink **b**

BACKBITING See SLANDER

BACKS BACK

Ex 23:27 make all your enemies turn their **b**
Ne 9:29 Stubbornly they turned their **b**
Pr 19:29 and beatings for the **b** of fools.
Isa 59:13 LORD, turning our **b** on our God,
2Pe 2:21 turn their **b** on the sacred command

BACKSLIDERS, -ING See also FAITHLESS, STUBBORN, UNFAITHFUL, WAYWARDNESS

BACKSLIDING* BACK

Jer 2:19 your **b** will rebuke you.
    3:22 I will cure you of **b**."
    15: 6 "You keep on **b**. So I will reach
Eze 37:23 save them from all their sinful **b**,

BACKSLIDINGS* BACK

Jer 5: 6 rebellion is great and their **b** many.

BAD

Ge 37: 2 he brought their father a **b** report
Ex 7:21 and the river smelled so **b**
Nu 13:32 among the Israelites a **b** report
Ecc 7:14 but when times are **b**, consider this:
Isa 5: 2 grapes, but it yielded only **b** fruit.
Jer 24: 2 the other basket had very **b** figs, so **b**
       they could not be eaten.
Mt 7:17 but a **b** tree bears **b** fruit.
    12:33 make a tree **b** and its fruit will be **b**,

BADGERS (KJV) See LEATHER

BAG

Mic 6:11 scales, with a **b** of false weights?
Mt 25:15 two bags, and to another one **b**,
Lk 10: 4 Do not take a purse or **b** or sandals;
Jn 12: 6 as keeper of the money **b**, he used

BAKED BAKER

Ex 12:39 they **b** loaves of unleavened bread.
Lev 6:17 It must not be **b** with yeast;
Da 2:33 partly of iron and partly of **b** clay.

BAKER BAKED

Ge 40: 1 the **b** of the king of Egypt offended

BALAAM

Prophet who attempted to curse Israel (Nu 22–24; Dt 23:4–5; 2Pe 2:15; Jude 11; Rev 2:14). Killed in Israel's vengeance on Midianites (Nu 31:8; Jos 13:22).

BALAK

Moabite king who hired Balaam to curse Israel (Nu 22–24; Jos 24:9).

BALANCE

Ps 62: 9 If weighed on a **b**, they are nothing;
Isa 40:12 on the scales and the hills in a **b**?

BALD BALDY

Lev 13:40 lost his hair and is **b** is clean.
Isa 3:17 LORD will make their scalps **b**."
Mic 1:16 make yourself as **b** as the vulture,

BALDY* BALD

2Ki 2:23 "Get out of here, **b**!" they said. "Get out of here, **b**!"

BALM

Jer 8:22 Is there no **b** in Gilead? Is there no

BAN*

1Ch 2: 7 by violating the **b** on taking devoted

BAND

Ps 2: 2 and the rulers **b** together against
Ac 4:26 and the rulers **b** together against

BANDAGED*

Isa 1: 6 not cleansed or **b** or soothed
Lk 10:34 He went to him and **b** his wounds,

BANDIT* BANDITS

Pr 23:28 Like a **b** she lies in wait

BANDITS* BANDIT

Ezr 8:31 from enemies and **b** along the way.
Hos 7: 1 into houses, **b** rob in the streets;
2Co 11:26 in danger from **b**, in danger

BANISH BANISHED

Ecc 11:10 **b** anxiety from your heart and cast
Jer 25:10 I will **b** from them the sounds of joy
Zec 13: 2 I will **b** the names of the idols

BANISHED BANISH

Ge 3:23 So the LORD God **b** him

Dt   30: 4 you have been **b** to the most distant
Jnh   2: 4 said, 'I have been **b** from your sight;

BANK BANKS
Ge   41:17 I was standing on the **b** of the Nile,
Ex   2: 3 put it among the reeds along the **b**
        7:15 Confront him on the **b** of the Nile,
2Ki   2:13 and stood on the **b** of the Jordan.
Mk   5: 1: rushed down the steep **b**

BANKS BANK
Eze   47:12 will grow on both **b** of the river.

BANNER
Ex   17:15 and called it The LORD is my **B**.
SS   2: 4 hall, and let him over me be love.
Isa   11:10 of Jesse will stand as a **b**

BANQUET BANQUETS
1Sa   25:36 in the house holding a **b** like
Est   1: 3 of his reign he gave a **b** for all his
        6:14 away to the **b** Esther had prepared.
        7: 1 Haman went to Queen Esther's **b**,
SS   2: 4 Let him lead me to the **b** hall,
Isa   25: 6 for all peoples, a **b** of aged wine—
Da   5: 1 King Belshazzar gave a great **b**
Mt   22: 4 Come to the wedding **b**.'
Lk   14:13 But when you give a **b**,

BANQUETS BANQUET
Mk   12:39 and the places of honor at **b**.

BAPTISM* BAPTIZE
Mt   21:25 John's **b**—where did it come from?
Mk   1: 4 preaching a **b** of repentance
       10:38 with the **b** I am baptized with?"
       10:39 with the **b** I am baptized with,
       11:30 John's **b**—was it from heaven,
Lk   3: 3 preaching a **b** of repentance
       12:50 But I have a **b** to undergo, and what
       20: 4 John's **b**—was it from heaven,
Ac   1:22 beginning from John's **b** to the time
       10:37 after the **b** that John preached—
       13:24 and **b** to all the people of Israel.
       18:25 though he knew only the **b** of John.
       19: 3 "Then what **b** did you receive?"
       19: 3 "John's **b**," they replied.
       19: 4 "John's **b** was a **b** of repentance.
Ro   6: 4 with him through **b** into death
Eph   4: 5 one Lord, one faith, one **b**;
Col   2:12 having been buried with him in **b**,
1Pe   3:21 this water symbolizes **b** that now

BAPTIST BAPTIZE
Mt   3: 1 In those days John the **B** came,
       11:11 anyone greater than John the **B**;
       14: 8 on a platter the head of John the **B**."
       16:14 replied, "Some say John the **B**;

BAPTIZE* BAPTISM, BAPTIST,
    BAPTIZED, BAPTIZING
Mt   3:11 "I **b** you with water for repentance.
        3:11 He will **b** you with the Holy Spirit
Mk   1: 8 I **b** you with water, but he will **b** you
Lk   3:16 them all, "I **b** you with water.
        3:16 He will **b** you with the Holy Spirit

Jn   1:25 do you **b** if you are not the Messiah,
        1:26 "I **b** with water," John replied,
        1:33 the one who sent me to **b** with water
        1:33 remain is the one who will **b**
1Co   1:14 that I did not **b** any of you except
        1:17 For Christ did not send me to **b**,

BAPTIZED* BAPTIZE
Mt   3: 6 they were **b** by him in the Jordan
        3:13 to the Jordan to be **b** by John.
        3:14 "I need to be **b** by you, and do you
        3:16 As soon as Jesus was **b**, he went
Mk   1: 5 they were **b** by him in the Jordan
        1: 9 and was **b** by John in the Jordan.
       10:38 be **b** with the baptism I am **b** with?"
       10:39 be **b** with the baptism I am **b** with,
       16:16 *believes and is **b** will be saved,*
Lk   3: 7 crowds coming out to be **b** by him,
        3:12 Even tax collectors came to be **b**.
        3:21 When all the people were being **b**,
             Jesus was **b** too.
        7:29 because they had been **b** by John.
        7:30 because they had not been **b**
Jn   3:22 spent some time with them, and **b**.
        3:23 people were coming and being **b**.
        4: 2 in fact it was not Jesus who **b**,
Ac   1: 5 For John **b** with water, but in a few
             days you will be **b**
        2:38 "Repent and be **b**, every one
        2:41 who accepted his message were **b**,
        8:12 they were **b**, both men and women.
        8:13 Simon himself believed and was **b**.
        8:16 they had simply been **b** in the name
        8:36 stand in the way of my being **b**?"
        8:38 into the water and Philip **b** him.
        9:18 He got up and was **b**,
       10:47 the way of their being **b** with water.
       10:48 ordered that they be **b** in the name
       11:16 'John **b** with water, but you will be **b**
             with the Holy Spirit.'
       16:15 members of her household were **b**,
       16:33 he and all his household were **b**.
       18: 8 heard Paul believed and were **b**.
       19: 5 they were **b** in the name of the Lord
       22:16 up, be **b** and wash your sins away,
Ro   6: 3 of us who were **b** into Christ Jesus
             were **b** into his death?
1Co   1:13 Were you **b** in the name of Paul?
        1:15 say that you were **b** in my name.
        1:16 I also **b** the household of Stephanas;
        1:16 don't remember if I **b** anyone else.)
       10: 2 They were all **b** into Moses
       12:13 we were all **b** by one Spirit so as
       15:29 those do who are **b** for the dead?
       15:29 at all, why are people **b** for them?
Gal   3:27 of you who were **b** into Christ have

BAPTIZING* BAPTIZE
Mt   3: 7 coming to where he was **b**, he said
       28:19 **b** them in the name of the Father
Jn   1:28 of the Jordan, where John was **b**.
        1:31 the reason I came with water was
        3:23 also was **b** at Aenon near Salim,
        3:26 he is **b**, and everyone is going

Jn   4: 1 and **b** more disciples than John—
      10:40 the place where John had been **b**

BAR BARRED
Jdg 16: 3 posts, and tore them loose, **b** and all.

BAR-JESUS*
Ac   13: 6 sorcerer and false prophet named **B**,

BARABBAS*
Prisoner released by Pilate instead of Jesus (Mt 27:16–26; Mk 15:7–15; Lk 23:18–19; Jn 18:40).

BARAK*
Judge who fought with Deborah against Canaanites (Jdg 4–5; 1Sa 12:11; Heb 11:32).

BARBARIAN*
Col   3:11 circumcised or uncircumcised, **b**,

BARBARIANS See FOREIGNER(S)

BARBS*
Nu   33:55 remain will become **b** in your eyes

BARE BAREFOOT, BARREN
Jdg 14: 6 his **b** hands as he might have torn
Isa 52:10 The LORD will lay **b** his holy arm
1Co 14:25 the secrets of their hearts are laid **b**.
Heb   4:13 and laid **b** before the eyes of him
2Pe   3:10 everything done in it will be laid **b**.

BAREFOOT BARE, FOOT
Isa 20: 3 gone stripped and **b** for three years,
Mic   1: 8 I will go about **b** and naked.

BARGAIN
Isa 36: 8 now, make a **b** with my master,

BARK
Ge   30:37 stripes on them by peeling the **b**
Ex   11: 7 among the Israelites not a dog will **b**

BARLEY
Ru   1:22 in Bethlehem as the **b** harvest was
2Ki   7: 1 two seahs of **b** for a shekel
Jn   6: 9 is a boy with five small **b** loaves
Rev   6: 6 six pounds of **b** for a day's wages,

BARN BARNS
Hag   2:19 Is there yet any seed left in the **b**?
Lk   3:17 and to gather the wheat into his **b**,

BARNABAS JOSEPH
Disciple, originally Joseph (Ac 4:36), prophet (Ac 13:1), apostle (Ac 14:14). Brought Paul to apostles (Ac 9:27), Antioch (Ac 11:22–29; Gal 2:1–13), on the first missionary journey (Ac 13–14). Together at Jerusalem Council, they separated over John Mark (Ac 15). Later co-workers (1Co 9:6; Col 4:10).

BARNS* BARN
Dt   28: 8 will send a blessing on your **b**
Ps 144:13 Our **b** will be filled with every kind
Pr   3:10 your **b** will be filled to overflowing,
Mt   6:26 not sow or reap or store away in **b**,
Lk   12:18 I will tear down my **b** and build

BARRED BAR
Jos   6: 1 Jericho were securely **b** because
Pr   18:19 disputes are like the **b** gates
Jnh   2: 6 the earth beneath **b** me in forever.

BARREN BARE
Ex   23:26 will miscarry or be **b** in your land.
1Sa   2: 5 She who was **b** has borne seven
Isa 54: 1 "Sing, **b** woman, you who never
Gal   4:27 "Be glad, **b** woman, you who never

BARRIER*
Jer   5:22 sea, an everlasting **b** it cannot cross.
Eph   2:14 groups one and has destroyed the **b**,

BARSABBAS*
Ac   1:23 Joseph called **B** (also known as
      15:22 They chose Judas (called **B**)

BARTER*
Job   6:27 fatherless and **b** away your friend.
      41: 6 Will traders **b** for it?
La   1:11 they **b** their treasures for food

BARTHOLOMEW*
Apostle (Mt 10:3; Mk 3:18; Lk 6:14; Ac 1:13). Possibly also called Nathanael (Jn 1:45–49; 21:2).

BARTIMAEUS*
Blind man healed by Jesus (Mk 10:46–52).

BARUCH
Jeremiah's secretary (Jer 32:12–16; 36; 43:1–6; 45:1–2).

BARZILLAI
1. Gileadite who aided David during Absalom's revolt (2Sa 17:27; 19:31–39).
2. Son-in-law of 1. (Ezr 2:61; Ne 7:63).

BASE BASING, BASIS
Ex   29:12 out the rest of it at the **b** of the altar.
Job 30: 8 A **b** and nameless brood, they were

BASHAN
Nu   21:33 went up along the road toward **B**,
      21:33 Og king of **B** and his whole army
Jos 13:30 including all of **B**, the entire realm of
                 Og king of **B**—
      22: 7 Moses had given land in **B**,
Ps   22:12 strong bulls of **B** encircle me.
Am   4: 1 you cows of **B** on Mount Samaria,

BASIN
Ex   30:18 "Make a bronze **b**, with its bronze
1Ki   7:30 and each had a **b** resting on four
Jn   13: 5 he poured water into a **b** and began

BASING BASE
Isa 36: 4 what are you **b** this confidence

BASIS BASE
Da   6: 5 said, "We will never find any **b**
Jn   18:38 "I find no **b** for a charge against
Phm   1: 9 to appeal to you on the **b** of love.

BASKET BASKETFULS, BASKETS
Ex   2: 3 she got a papyrus **b** for him
Dt 28: 5 Your **b** and your kneading trough
Isa 40:12 has held the dust of the earth in a **b**,
Am   8: 1 a **b** of ripe fruit.
Zec   5: 6 He replied, "It is a **b**."
Ac   9:25 him in a **b** through an opening
2Co 11:33 I was lowered in a **b** from a window

BASKETFULS BASKET
Mt 14:20 picked up twelve **b** of broken pieces
     15:37 picked up seven **b** of broken pieces
     16: 9 and how many **b** you gathered?

BASKETS BASKET
Mt 13:48 and collected the good fish in **b**,

BATCH*
Ro 11:16 is holy, then the whole **b** is holy;
1Co 5: 6 a little yeast leavens the whole **b**
     5: 7 you may be a new unleavened **b**—
Gal   5: 9 yeast works through the whole **b**

BATH BATHE
Eze 45:10 accurate ephah and an accurate **b**.
Jn 13:10 "Those who have had a **b** need only

BATHE BATH, BATHED, BATHING
Ex   2: 5 went down to the Nile to **b**, and her
Dt 33:24 and let him **b** his feet in oil.

BATHED BATHE
Isa 34: 6 sword of the LORD is **b** in blood,
Eze 16: 9 " 'I **b** you with water and washed

BATHING BATHE
2Sa 11: 2 From the roof he saw a woman **b**.

BATHSHEBA
Wife of Uriah who committed adultery with and became wife of David (2Sa 11; Ps 51), mother of Solomon (2Sa 12:24; 1Ki 1–2; 1Ch 3:5).

BATTLE BATTLEMENTS, BATTLES
Ex 13:18 went up out of Egypt ready for **b**.
Jos   4:13 **b** crossed over before the LORD
1Sa 17:47 for the **b** is the LORD's, and he
2Sa   1:25 "How the mighty have fallen in **b**!
    22:35 He trains my hands for **b**;
1Ki 22:30 "I will enter the **b** in disguise,
    22:30 disguised himself and went into **b**.
2Ch 20:15 For the **b** is not yours, but God's.
Ps 24: 8 mighty, the LORD mighty in **b**.
Ecc 9:11 to the swift or the **b** to the strong,
Isa 31: 4 come down to do **b** on Mount Zion
Eze 13: 5 it will stand firm in the **b** on the day
Hos 1: 7 bow, sword or **b**, or by horses
     2:18 and **b** I will abolish from the land,
Ob   1: 1 "Rise, let us go against her for **b**"—
Jas   4: 1 from your desires that **b** within you?
Rev 16:14 them for the **b** on the great day
    20: 8 and to gather them for **b**.

BATTLEMENTS* BATTLE
Isa 54:12 I will make your **b** of rubies,

BATTLES* BATTLE
1Sa 8:20 to go out before us and fight our **b**."
    18:17 and fight the **b** of the LORD."
    25:28 because you fight the LORD's **b**,
2Ch 32: 8 God to help us and to fight our **b**."

BEAM* BEAMS
Ezr 6:11 a **b** is to be pulled from their house

BEAMS BEAM
1Ki 6: 9 roofing it with **b** and cedar planks.
Ne 3: 3 They laid its **b** and put its doors
Jer 22: 7 they will cut up your fine cedar **b**
Zep 2:14 the **b** of cedar will be exposed.

BEAR BEARABLE, BEARING, BEARS, BIRTH, BIRTHRIGHT, BORE, BORN, BORNE, CHILDBEARING, CHILDBIRTH, FIRSTBORN, NATIVE-BORN, NEWBORN, REBIRTH
Ge 4:13 punishment is more than I can **b**.
    17:19 your wife Sarah will **b** you a son,
Ex 28:12 Aaron is to **b** the names on his
1Sa 17:36 has killed both the lion and the **b**;
Job 9: 9 He is the Maker of the **B** and Orion,
Ps 38: 4 me like a burden too heavy to **b**.
    92:14 They will still **b** fruit in old age,
Pr 17:12 meet a **b** robbed of her cubs than
Isa 11: 1 from his roots a Branch will **b** fruit.
    11: 7 The cow will feed with the **b**,
    53:11 many, and he will **b** their iniquities.
Jer 14: 9 us, LORD, and we **b** your name;
Eze 14:10 They will **b** their guilt—
Da 7: 5 second beast, which looked like a **b**.
Am 5:19 fled from a lion only to meet a **b**,
Mt 7:18 A good tree cannot **b** bad fruit,
    7:18 and a bad tree cannot **b** good fruit.
Lk 1:13 wife Elizabeth will **b** you a son,
    1:42 and blessed is the child you will **b**!
    21:13 And so you will **b** testimony to me.
Jn 15: 2 branch that does **b** fruit he prunes so
    15: 8 that you **b** much fruit,
    15:16 so that you might go and **b** fruit—
Ro 7: 4 order that we might **b** fruit for God.
    15: 1 We who are strong ought to **b**
1Co 10:13 be tempted beyond what you can **b**.
    15:49 man, so shall we **b** the image
Gal 6:17 for I **b** on my body the marks
Col 3:13 **B** with each other and forgive one
1Pe 4:16 but praise God that you **b** that name.
Rev 13: 2 but had feet like those of a **b**

BEARABLE BEAR
Mt 10:15 it will be more **b** for Sodom

BEARD
Lev 19:27 head or clip off the edges of your **b**.
Isa 50: 6 to those who pulled out my **b**;
Jer 48:37 head is shaved and every **b** cut off;

BEARING BEAR
Ge 1:12 plants **b** seed according to their kinds
     and trees **b** fruit with seed in it

Nu 13:23 cut off a branch **b** a single cluster
Pr 30:29 stride, four that move with stately **b**:
Joel 2:22 The trees are **b** their fruit;
Ro 2:15 their consciences also **b** witness,
Eph 4: 2 patient, **b** with one another in love.
Col 1: 6 the gospel is **b** fruit and growing
       1:10 **b** fruit in every good work,
Heb 13:13 the camp, **b** the disgrace he bore.
Rev 22: 2 tree of life, **b** twelve crops of fruit,

BEARS BEAR
Ge 49:21 a doe set free that **b** beautiful fawns.
1Ki 8:43 this house I have built **b** your Name.
2Ki 2:24 Then two **b** came out of the woods
Ps 68:19 Savior, who daily **b** our burdens.
Jer 7:11 which **b** my Name, become a den
Da 9:18 of the city that **b** your Name.
Gal 4:24 and **b** children who are to be slaves:
1Pe 2:19 if someone **b** up under the pain

BEAST BEASTS
Isa 35: 9 will be there, nor any ravenous **b**;
Da 7: 6 and there before me was another **b**,
       7: 6 This **b** had four heads, and it was
Rev 11: 7 the **b** that comes up from the Abyss
       13: 1 I saw a **b** coming out of the sea.
       13: 2 The **b** I saw resembled a leopard,
       13: 2 The dragon gave the **b** his power
       13:11 Then I saw a second **b**,
       13:18 calculate the number of the **b**, for it
       16: 2 people who had the mark of the **b**
       17: 3 on a scarlet **b** that was covered
       19:20 But the **b** was captured, and with it
       19:20 who had received the mark of the **b**
       20: 4 They had not worshiped the **b** or its

BEASTS BEAST
Lev 26: 6 I will remove wild **b** from the land,
Jer 12: 9 Go and gather all the wild **b**;
Eze 5:17 send famine and wild **b** against you,
Da 7: 3 Four great **b**, each different
1Co 15:32 If I fought wild **b** in Ephesus
Rev 6: 8 and by the wild **b** of the earth.

BEAT BEATEN, BEATING,
      BEATINGS, BEATS
Dt 24:20 When you **b** the olives from your
Ne 13:25 I **b** some of the men and pulled
Ps 78:66 He **b** back his enemies; he put them
Pr 23:35 They **b** me, but I don't feel it!
SS 5: 7 They **b** me, they bruised me;
Isa 2: 4 They will **b** their swords
Joel 3:10 **B** your plowshares into swords
Mic 4: 3 They will **b** their swords
Mt 7:25 blew and **b** against that house;
Ac 22:19 and **b** those who believe in you.

BEATEN BEAT
Ex 5:16 Your servants are being **b**,
Nu 22:32 him, "Why have you **b** your donkey
Jer 20: 2 he had Jeremiah the prophet **b**
Lk 12:48 deserving punishment will be **b**
Ac 16:22 them to be stripped and **b** with rods.
2Co 6: 9 yet we live on; **b**, and yet not killed;
       11:25 Three times I was **b** with rods,

BEATING BEAT
Ex 2:11 He saw an Egyptian **b** a Hebrew,
1Co 9:26 I do not fight like a boxer **b** the air.
1Pe 2:20 if you receive a **b** for doing wrong

BEATINGS BEAT
Pr 19:29 and **b** for the backs of fools.

BEATS* BEAT
Ex 21:20 "Anyone who **b** their male

BEAUTIFUL* BEAUTY
Ge 6: 2 the daughters of humans were **b**,
       12:11 "I know what a **b** woman you are.
       12:14 saw that Sarai was a very **b** woman.
       24:16 The woman was very **b**, a virgin;
       26: 7 of Rebekah, because she is **b**."
       29:17 had a lovely figure and was **b**.
       49:21 is a doe set free that bears **b** fawns.
Nu 24: 5 "How **b** are your tents, Jacob,
Dt 21:11 among the captives a **b** woman
Jos 7:21 I saw in the plunder a **b** robe
1Sa 25: 3 was an intelligent and **b** woman,
2Sa 11: 2 The woman was very **b**,
       13: 1 the **b** sister of Absalom son
       14:27 Tamar, and she became a **b** woman.
1Ki 1: 3 Israel for a **b** young woman
       1: 4 The woman was very **b**;
Est 2: 2 search be made for **b** young virgins
       2: 3 bring all these **b** young women
       2: 7 had a lovely figure and was **b**.
Job 42:15 there found women as **b** as Job's
Ps 48: 2 **B** in its loftiness, the joy
Pr 11:22 snout is a **b** woman who shows no
       24: 4 are filled with rare and **b** treasures.
Ecc 3:11 He has made everything **b** in its
SS 1: 8 you do not know, most **b** of women,
       1:10 Your cheeks are **b** with earrings,
       1:15 How **b** you are, my darling!
       1:15 Oh, how **b**! Your eyes are doves.
       2:10 my darling, my **b** one,
       2:13 my **b** one, come with me."
       4: 1 How **b** you are, my darling!
       4: 1 Oh, how **b**! Your eyes behind your
       4: 7 You are altogether **b**, my darling;
       5: 9 than others, most **b** of women?
       6: 1 beloved gone, most **b** of women?
       6: 4 You are as **b** as Tirzah, my darling,
       7: 1 How **b** your sandaled feet,
       7: 6 How **b** you are and how pleasing,
Isa 4: 2 the Branch of the LORD will be **b**
       28: 5 a **b** wreath for the remnant of his
       52: 7 How **b** on the mountains are the feet
Jer 3:19 land, the most **b** inheritance of any
       6: 2 Daughter Zion, so **b** and delicate.
       11:16 olive tree with fruit **b** in form.
       46:20 "Egypt is a **b** heifer, but a gadfly is
Eze 7:20 They took pride in their **b** jewelry
       16:12 ears and a **b** crown on your head.
       16:13 You became very **b** and rose to be
       20: 6 and honey, the most **b** of all lands.
       20:15 and honey, the most **b** of all lands—
       23:42 sister and **b** crowns on their heads.
       27:24 they traded with you **b** garments,

Eze 31: 3 with **b** branches overshadowing
31: 9 I made it **b** with abundant branches,
33:32 who sings love songs with a **b** voice
Da 4:12 Its leaves were **b**, its fruit abundant,
4:21 with **b** leaves and abundant fruit,
8: 9 to the east and toward the **B** Land.
11:16 will establish himself in the **B** Land
11:41 He will also invade the **B** Land.
11:45 the seas at the **b** holy mountain.
Zec 9:17 How attractive and **b** they will be!
Mt 23:27 which look **b** on the outside
26:10 She has done a **b** thing to me.
Mk 14: 6 She has done a **b** thing to me.
Lk 21: 5 temple was adorned with **b** stones
Ac 3: 2 carried to the temple gate called **B**,
3:10 begging at the temple gate called **B**,
Ro 10:15 "How **b** are the feet of those who

BEAUTIFULLY* BEAUTY

Rev 21: 2 prepared as a bride **b** dressed for her

BEAUTY* BEAUTIFUL,
BEAUTIFULLY

Est 1:11 order to display her **b** to the people
2: 3 let **b** treatments be given to them.
2: 9 provided her with her **b** treatments
2:12 months of **b** treatments prescribed
Ps 27: 4 to gaze on the **b** of the LORD
45:11 the king be enthralled by your **b**;
50: 2 Zion, perfect in **b**, God shines forth.
Pr 6:25 Do not lust in your heart after her **b**
31:30 is deceptive, and **b** is fleeting;
Isa 3:24 instead of **b**, branding.
28: 1 his glorious **b**, set on the head
28: 4 his glorious **b**, set on the head
33:17 Your eyes will see the king in his **b**
53: 2 He had no **b** or majesty to attract us
61: 3 them a crown of **b** instead of ashes,
La 2:15 that was called the perfection of **b**,
Eze 16:14 the nations on account of your **b**,
16:14 had given you made your **b** perfect,
16:15 you trusted in your **b** and used your
16:15 passed by and your **b** became his.
16:16 to him, and he possessed your **b**.
16:25 lofty shrines and degraded your **b**,
27: 3 say, Tyre, "I am perfect in **b**."
27: 4 your builders brought your **b**
27:11 they brought your **b** to perfection.
28: 7 draw their swords against your **b**
28:12 full of wisdom and perfect in **b**.
28:17 became proud on account of your **b**,
31: 7 It was majestic in **b**, with its
31: 8 the garden of God could match its **b**.
Jas 1:11 blossom falls and its **b** is destroyed.
1Pe 3: 3 Your **b** should not come
3: 4 the unfading **b** of a gentle and quiet

BECAME BECOME

Ge 2: 7 of life, and the man **b** a living being.
Ex 7:10 and his officials, and it **b** a snake.
15:25 water, and the water **b** fit to drink.
Lev 18:27 before you, and the land **b** defiled.
Jdg 8:27 and it **b** a snare to Gideon and his
2Ki 17:15 idols and themselves **b** worthless.

1Ch 11: 9 And David **b** more and more
2Ch 17:12 Jehoshaphat **b** more and more
26:16 But after Uzziah **b** powerful,
Jn 1:14 The Word **b** flesh and made his
1Co 9:20 To the Jews I **b** like a Jew, to win
9:20 under the law I **b** like one under
2Co 8: 9 yet for your sake he **b** poor,

BECOME BECAME

Ge 2:24 to his wife, and they **b** one flesh.
9:15 again will the waters **b** a flood
Dt 8:14 your heart will **b** proud and you will
Jdg 16: 7 I'll **b** as weak as any other man."
Ps 2: 7 today I have **b** your father.
Pr 13:20 Walk with the wise and **b** wise,
Lk 4: 3 of God, tell this stone to **b** bread."
Jn 1:12 he gave the right to **b** children
3:30 He must **b** greater; I must **b** less."
Ac 4:11 which has **b** the cornerstone.'
Rev 11:15 the world has **b** the kingdom of our

BED BEDS, SICKBED

Ge 39: 7 and said, "Come to **b** with me!"
48: 2 his strength and sat up on the **b**.
2Sa 13:11 her and said, "Come to **b** with me,
1Ki 1:47 the king bowed in worship on his **b**
Ps 41: 3 restores them from their **b** of illness.
Pr 26:14 hinges, so a sluggard turns on his **b**.
SS 1:16 And our **b** is verdant.
Isa 28:20 The **b** is too short to stretch out on,
Mt 8:14 Peter's mother-in-law lying in **b**
Lk 11: 7 and my children and I are in **b**.
17:34 night two people will be in one **b**;
Heb 13: 4 and the marriage **b** kept pure,
Rev 2:22 I will cast her on a **b** of suffering,

BEDS BED

Ps 36: 4 Even on their **b** they plot evil;
Mic 2: 1 to those who plot evil on their **b**!
Ac 5:15 laid them on **b** and mats so

BEELZEBUL* BAAL-ZEBUB

Mt 10:25 head of the house has been called **B**,
12:24 said, "It is only by **B**, the prince
12:27 And if I drive out demons by **B**,
Mk 3:22 said, "He is possessed by **B**!
Lk 11:15 said, "By **B**, the prince of demons,
11:18 claim that I drive out demons by **B**.
11:19 Now if I drive out demons by **B**,

BEER

1Sa 1:15 I have not been drinking wine or **b**;
Pr 20: 1 Wine is a mocker and **b** a brawler;
31: 4 drink wine, not for rulers to crave **b**,
31: 6 Let **b** be for those who are
Isa 24: 9 the **b** is bitter to its drinkers.
28: 7 stagger from wine and reel from **b**:
28: 7 and prophets stagger from **b** and are
29: 9 from wine, stagger, but not from **b**.
56:12 Let us drink our fill of **b**!
Mic 2:11 for you plenty of wine and **b**,'

BEERSHEBA

Ge 21:14 and wandered in the Desert of **B**.
21:33 planted a tamarisk tree in **B**,

Ge   22:19 and they set off together for **B**. And
            Abraham stayed in **B**.
      46: 1 and when he reached **B**, he offered
Jdg   20: 1 all Israel from Dan to **B**
1Sa   3:20 Dan to **B** recognized that Samuel
2Sa   3:10 Israel and Judah from Dan to **B**."
      17:11 Let all Israel, from Dan to **B**—
      24: 2 the tribes of Israel from Dan to **B**
      24:15 of the people from Dan to **B** died.
1Ki   4:25 from Dan to **B**, lived in safety,
1Ch 21: 2 count the Israelites from **B** to Dan.
2Ch 30: 5 throughout Israel, from **B** to Dan,
Am   8:14 'As surely as the god of **B** lives'—

BEES*
Dt   1:44 they chased you like a swarm of **b**
Jdg   14: 8 in it he saw a swarm of **b** and some
Ps   118:12 They swarmed around me like **b**,
Isa   7:18 and for **b** from the land of Assyria.

BEFORE BEFOREHAND
Ge   10: 9 was a mighty hunter **b** the LORD;
      18:22 remained standing **b** the LORD.
      24:15 **B** he had finished praying,
      27: 4 may give you my blessing **b** I die."
Ex   4:21 that you perform **b** Pharaoh all
       9:11 could not stand **b** Moses because
      20: 3 shall have no other gods **b** me.
      32: 1 make us gods who will go **b** us.
      33: 2 I will send an angel **b** you and drive
Lev   10: 2 them, and they died **b** the LORD.
Nu   17: 7 placed the staffs **b** the LORD
Dt   7:22 will drive out those nations **b** you,
      11:26 I am setting **b** you today a blessing
      30:15 I set **b** you today life and prosperity,
1Sa   4: 7 Nothing like this has happened **b**.
Ps   139: 4 **B** a word is on my tongue you,
Pr   16:18 Pride goes **b** destruction, a haughty
            spirit **b** a fall.
      18:12 **B** a downfall the heart is haughty, but
            humility comes **b** honor.
      18:13 To answer **b** listening—that is folly
Isa   43:10 **B** me no god was formed, nor will
      48: 5 **b** they happened I announced them
      65:24 **B** they call I will answer;
Mt   6: 8 what you need **b** you ask him.
      11:10 who will prepare your way **b** you.'
      24:38 For in the days **b** the flood,
Lk   22:34 Peter, **b** the rooster crows today,
Jn   8:58 answered, "**b** Abraham was born,
      13:19 "I am telling you now **b** it happens,
      17: 5 I had with you **b** the world began.
Col   1:17 He is **b** all things, and in him all
1Ti   5:20 you are to reprove **b** everyone,
Titus 1: 2 promised **b** the beginning of time,
1Pe   1:20 He was chosen **b** the creation

BEFOREHAND BEFORE
Mk   13:11 do not worry **b** about what to say.
Ac   4:28 will had decided **b** should happen.
Ro   1: 2 gospel he promised **b** through his

BEG BEGGAR, BEGGED, BEGGING
La   4: 4 the children **b** for bread, but no one
Lk   16: 3 to dig, and I'm ashamed to **b**—

Ac   3: 2 where he was put every day to **b**

BEGGAR* BEG
Lk   16:20 gate was laid a **b** named Lazarus,
      16:22 "The time came when the **b** died

BEGGED BEG
Mt   8:31 The demons **b** Jesus, "If you drive
Mk   6:56 They **b** him to let them touch even

BEGGING BEG
Ps   37:25 forsaken or their children **b** bread.
Ac   16: 9 of Macedonia standing and **b** him,

BEGINNING
Ge   1: 1 In the **b** God created the heavens
Ps   102:25 In the **b** you laid the foundations
     111:10 of the LORD is the **b** of wisdom;
Pr   1: 7 the LORD is the **b** of knowledge,
       4: 7 The **b** of wisdom is this:
       9:10 of the LORD is the **b** of wisdom,
Ecc   3:11 fathom what God has done from **b**
       7: 8 end of a matter is better than its **b**,
Isa   40:21 Has it not been told you from the **b**?
      46:10 I make known the end from the **b**,
Da   12: 1 from the **b** of nations until then.
Mt   19: 8 But it was not this way from the **b**.
      24: 8 All these are the **b** of birth pains.
      24:21 from the **b** of the world until now—
Mk   1: 1 The **b** of the good news about Jesus
Lk   1: 3 investigated everything from the **b**,
Jn   1: 1 In the **b** was the Word,
       8:44 He was a murderer from the **b**,
      15:27 you have been with me from the **b**.
Ac   1:22 **b** from John's baptism to the time
Gal   3: 3 After **b** by means of the Spirit,
Heb   7: 3 without **b** of days or end of life,
2Pe   2:20 at the end than they were at the **b**.
1Jn   1: 1 That which was from the **b**,
       3: 8 devil has been sinning from the **b**,
2Jn   1: 6 As you have heard from the **b**,
Rev   21: 6 and the Omega, the **B** and the End.
      22:13 and the Last, the **B** and the End.

BEGRUDGING*
Pr   23: 6 Do not eat the food of a **b** host,

BEHALF
Ge   25:21 to the LORD on **b** of his wife,
Lev   22:19 that it may be accepted on your **b**.
      22:20 it will not be accepted on your **b**.
1Sa   14: 6 the LORD will act in our **b**.
2Sa   24:25 LORD answered his prayer in **b**
Jn   8:14 "Even if I testify on my own **b**,
      16:26 that I will ask the Father on your **b**.

BEHAVE BEHAVIOR
Ro   13:13 Let us **b** decently, as in the daytime,

BEHAVIOR BEHAVE
Pr   1: 3 receiving instruction in prudent **b**,
Col   1:21 your minds because of your evil **b**.
1Pe   3: 1 words by the **b** of their wives,
       3:16 maliciously against your good **b**

BEHEADED
Lk   9: 9 But Herod said, "I **b** John.
Rev 20: 4 of those who had been **b** because

BEHEMOTH*
Job 40:15 "Look at **B**, which I made along

BEHIND
Mt   16:23 turned and said to Peter, "Get **b** me,
Mk 14:52 fled naked, leaving his garment **b**.
Lk   2:43 the boy Jesus stayed **b** in Jerusalem,
1Co 13:11 I put the ways of childhood **b** me.
Php   3:13 Forgetting what is **b** and straining
1Ti   5:24 the sins of others trail **b** them.

BEHOLD*
Nu 24:17 but not now; I **b** him, but not near.

BEING BEINGS
Ge   2: 7 life, and the man became a living **b**.
Job 10:19 If only I had never come into **b**,
Ps   103: 1 all my inmost **b**, praise his holy
       130: 5 my whole **b** waits, and in his word I
       139:13 For you created my inmost **b**;
Pr   23:16 my inmost **b** will rejoice when your
1Co 15:45 first man Adam became a living **b**";
Eph   3:16 through his Spirit in your inner **b**,
Php   2: 6 Who, **b** in very nature God, did not
2Pe   3: 5 God's word the heavens came into **b**
Rev   4:11 were created and have their **b**."

BEINGS BEING
Ps   78:25 Human **b** ate the bread of angels;
       89: 6 the LORD among the heavenly **b**?
      146: 3 in human **b**, who cannot save.
Ac   5: 4 You have not lied just to human **b**
       5:29 obey God rather than human **b**!
2Pe   2:10 afraid to heap abuse on celestial **b**;
       2:11 on such **b** when bringing judgment
Jude 1: 8 and heap abuse on celestial **b**.
Rev 18:13 and human **b** sold as slaves.

BEL
Isa   46: 1 **B** bows down, Nebo stoops low;

BELIAL*
2Co   6:15 is there between Christ and **B**?

BELIEVE BELIEVED, BELIEVER,
    BELIEVERS, BELIEVES, BELIEVING
Ex   4: 1 "What if they do not **b** me or listen
       4: 5 so that they may **b** that the LORD,
Nu   14:11 How long will they refuse to **b**
1Ki 10: 7 I did not **b** these things until I came
2Ch 32:15 Do not **b** him, for no god of any
Ps   78:32 spite of his wonders, they did not **b**.
Pr   14:15 The simple **b** anything,
Isa   43:10 so that you may know and **b** me
Hab   1: 5 in your days that you would not **b**,
Mt   9:28 "Do you **b** that I am able to do
       18: 6 those who **b** in me—
       21:22 If you **b**, you will receive whatever
       24:23 or, 'There he is!' do not **b** it.
       27:42 the cross, and we will **b** in him.
Mk   1:15 Repent and **b** the good news!"

Mk   5:36 told him, "Don't be afraid; just **b**."
       9:24 the boy's father exclaimed, "I do **b**;
       9:42 those who **b** in me—
      11:24 prayer, **b** that you have received it,
      15:32 the cross, that we may see and **b**."
      16:16 *does not **b** will be condemned.*
      16:17 *signs will accompany those who **b**:*
Lk   8:12 so that they may not **b** and be saved.
       8:13 They **b** for a while, but in the time
       8:50 just **b**, and she will be healed."
      22:67 "If I tell you, you will not **b** me,
      24:11 But they did not **b** the women,
      24:25 how slow to **b** all that the prophets
Jn   1: 7 so that through him all might **b**.
       3:12 of earthly things and you do not **b**;
       3:12 will you **b** if I speak of heavenly
       3:18 does not **b** stands condemned
       4:21 Jesus replied, "**b** me, a time is
       4:42 "We no longer **b** just because
       5:38 for you do not **b** the one he sent.
       5:47 since you do not **b** what he wrote,
       5:47 are you going to **b** what I say?"
       6:29 to **b** in the one he has sent."
       6:69 We have come to **b** and to know
       7: 5 even his own brothers did not **b**
       8:24 if you do not **b** that I am he,
       9:35 "Do you **b** in the Son of Man?"
       9:38 "Lord, I **b**," and he worshiped him.
      10:26 you do not **b** because you are not
      10:37 Do not **b** me unless I do the works
      10:38 even though you do not **b** me,
      11:27 "I **b** that you are the Messiah,
      11:40 "Did I not tell you that if you **b**,
      12:36 **B** in the light while you have the
      12:37 they still would not **b** in him.
      12:39 For this reason they could not **b**,
      12:44 in me does not **b** in me only,
      13:19 it does happen you will **b** that I am
      14: 1 You **b** in God; **b** also in me.
      14:10 Don't you **b** that I am in the Father,
      14:11 **B** me when I say that I am
      14:11 or at least **b** on the evidence
      14:29 that when it does happen you will **b**.
      16:30 This makes us **b** that you came
      16:31 "Do you now **b**?" Jesus replied.
      17:20 those who will **b** in me through their
      19:35 he testifies so that you also may **b**.
      20:27 into my side. Stop doubting and **b**."
      20:31 you may **b** that Jesus is the Messiah,
Ac   13:41 your days that you would never **b**,
      15: 7 the message of the gospel and **b**.
      16:31 They replied, "**B** in the Lord Jesus,
      19: 4 He told the people to **b** in the one
      22:19 and beat those who **b** in you.
      24:14 I **b** everything that is in accordance
      26:27 Agrippa, do you **b** the prophets?
      28:24 he said, but others would not **b**.
Ro   3:22 faith in Jesus Christ to all who **b**.
       4:11 he is the father of all who **b**
       6: 8 we **b** that we will also live with him.
      10:10 For it is with your heart that you **b**
      10:14 how can they **b** in the one of whom
1Co   1:21 was preached to save those who **b**.

2Co	4:13	faith, we also **b** and therefore speak,
Gal	3:22	might be given to those who **b**.
Eph	1:19	great power for us who **b**.
Php	1:29	of Christ not only to **b** in him,
1Th	2:13	is indeed at work in you who **b**.
	4:14	For we **b** that Jesus died and rose
	4:14	so we **b** that God will bring
2Th	2:11	delusion so that they will **b** the lie
1Ti	1:16	for those who would **b** in him
	4: 3	with thanksgiving by those who **b**
	4:10	and especially of those who **b**.
Titus	1: 6	a man whose children **b** and are not
Heb	11: 6	comes to him must **b** that he exists
Jas	1: 6	you ask, you must **b** and not doubt,
	2:19	You **b** that there is one God. Good! Even the demons **b** that—
1Pe	1: 8	you **b** in him and are filled
	2: 7	Now to you who **b**, this stone is
	2: 7	But to those who do not **b**,
	3: 1	if any of them do not **b** the word,
1Jn	3:23	to **b** in the name of his Son,
	4: 1	Dear friends, do not **b** every spirit,
	5:13	things to you who **b** in the name
Jude	1: 5	later destroyed those who did not **b**.

BELIEVED BELIEVE

Ge	15: 6	Abram **b** the LORD, and he
Ex	4:31	and they **b**. And when they heard
Ps	106:12	Then they **b** his promises and sang
Isa	53: 1	Who has **b** our message
Jnh	3: 5	The Ninevites **b** God. A fast was
Lk	1:45	Blessed is she who has **b**
Jn	1:12	to those who **b** in his name, he gave
	2:11	glory; and his disciples **b** in him.
	2:22	Then they **b** the scripture
	3:18	already because they have not **b**
	4:53	So he and his whole household **b**.
	5:46	If you **b** Moses, you would believe
	7:31	Still, many in the crowd **b** in him.
	7:39	whom those who **b** in him were
	7:48	rulers or of the Pharisees **b** in him?
	8:30	Even as he spoke, many **b** in him.
	8:31	To the Jews who had **b** him,
	10:42	And in that place many **b** in Jesus.
	11:45	had seen what Jesus did, **b** in him.
	12:38	who has **b** our message
	17: 8	you, and they **b** that you sent me.
	20: 8	also went inside. He saw and **b**.
	20:29	you have seen me, you have **b**;
	20:29	who have not seen and yet have **b**."
Ac	4: 4	But many who heard the message **b**;
	4: 4	the number of men who **b** grew
	5:14	more men and women **b** in the Lord
	8:12	they **b** Philip as he proclaimed
	9:42	and many people **b** in the Lord.
	11:17	them the same gift he gave us who **b**
	13:12	he **b**, for he was amazed
	13:48	were appointed for eternal life **b**.
	14: 1	great number of Jews and Greeks **b**.
	17:12	result, many of them **b**, as did
	18: 8	his entire household **b** in the Lord;
	18: 8	of the Corinthians who heard Paul **b**
	19: 2	the Holy Spirit when you **b**?"
	21:20	many thousands of Jews have **b**,

Ro	4: 3	"Abraham **b** God, and it was
	10:14	call on the one they have not **b** in?
	10:16	"Lord, who has **b** our message?"
1Co	15: 2	Otherwise, you have **b** in vain.
Gal	3: 6	So also Abraham "**b** God, and it
Eph	1:13	When you **b**, you were marked
2Th	1:10	at among all those who have **b**.
	1:10	because you **b** our testimony to you.
	2:12	condemned who have not **b** the truth
1Ti	3:16	the nations, was **b** on in the world,
2Ti	1:12	because I know whom I have **b**,
Heb	4: 3	Now we who have **b** enter that rest,
Jas	2:23	that says, "Abraham **b** God, and it
1Jn	5:10	they have not **b** the testimony God

BELIEVER BELIEVE

1Ki	18: 3	(Obadiah was a devout **b**
Ac	16: 1	a **b** but whose father was a Greek.
	16:15	you consider me a **b** in the Lord,"
1Co	7:17	each person should live as a **b** in
	7:12	brother has a wife who is not a **b**
	7:13	has a husband who is not a **b** and he
2Co	6:15	what does a **b** have in common
2Th	3: 6	keep away from every **b** who is idle
	3:15	but warn them as you would a fellow **b**.
1Ti	5:16	any woman who is a **b** has widows

BELIEVERS BELIEVE

Jn	4:41	of his words many more became **b**.
Ac	1:15	up among the **b** (a group numbering
	2:44	All the **b** were together and had
	4:32	All the **b** were one in heart
	5:12	all the **b** used to meet together
	9:41	Then he called for the **b**,
	10:45	The circumcised **b** who had come
	11: 2	the circumcised **b** criticized him
	15: 2	along with some other **b**, to go
	15: 5	some of the **b** who belonged
	15:23	To the Gentile **b** in Antioch,
	15:32	to encourage and strengthen the **b**.
	21:25	As for the Gentile **b**, we have
1Co	6: 5	to judge a dispute between **b**?
	14:22	a sign, not for **b** but for unbelievers;
	14:22	is not for unbelievers but for **b**.
2Co	11:26	and in danger from false **b**.
Gal	2: 4	because some false **b** had infiltrated
	6:10	those who belong to the family of **b**.
1Th	1: 7	a model to all the **b** in Macedonia
1Ti	4:12	set an example for the **b** in speech,
	6: 2	just because they are fellow **b**.
	6: 2	masters are dear to them as fellow **b**
Jas	2: 1	**b** in our glorious Lord Jesus Christ
1Pe	2:17	love the family of **b**, fear God,
3Jn	1:10	he even refuses to welcome other **b**.

BELIEVES* BELIEVE

Mk	9:23	is possible for one who **b**."
	11:23	**b** that what they say will happen,
	16:16	*Whoever **b** and is baptized*
Jn	3:15	everyone who **b** may have eternal
	3:16	whoever **b** in him shall not perish
	3:18	Whoever **b** in him is not
	3:36	Whoever **b** in the Son has eternal

Jn   5:24 **b** him who sent me has eternal life
     6:35 and whoever **b** in me will never be
     6:40 and **b** in him shall have eternal life,
     6:47 you, the one who **b** has eternal life.
     7:38 Whoever **b** in me, as Scripture has
    11:25 The one who **b** in me will live,
    12:44 "Whoever **b** in me does not believe in
    12:46 that no one who **b** in me should stay
    14:12 whoever **b** in me will do the works I
Ac 10:43 that everyone who **b** in him receives
    13:39 him everyone who **b** is set free
Ro   1:16 brings salvation to everyone who **b**:
     9:33 the one who **b** in him will never be
    10: 4 righteousness for everyone who **b**.
    10:11 "Anyone who **b** in him will never
1Jn 5: 1 Everyone who **b** that Jesus is
     5: 5 Only the one who **b** that Jesus is
     5:10 Whoever **b** in the Son of God

BELIEVING* BELIEVE

Jn 11:26 whoever lives by **b** in me will never
    12:11 Jews were going over to Jesus and **b**
    20:31 by **b** you may have life in his name.
Ac   9:26 not **b** that he really was a disciple.
1Co 7:14 sanctified through her **b** husband.
     9: 5 have the right to take a **b** wife along
Gal 3: 2 of the law, or by **b** what you heard?
     3: 5 law, or by your **b** what you heard?
1Ti 6: 2 Those who have **b** masters should

BELLIES* BELLY

Ps 17:14 stored up for the wicked fill their **b**;

BELLY BELLIES

Ge   3:14 You will crawl on your **b** and you
Jdg 3:21 and plunged it into the king's **b**.
2Sa 20:10 and Joab plunged it into his **b**,
Job 15: 2 fill their **b** with the hot east wind?
Da   2:32 of silver, its **b** and thighs of bronze,
Jnh 1:17 Jonah was in the **b** of the fish three
Mt 12:40 three nights in the **b** of a huge fish,

BELONG BELONGED, BELONGING, BELONGINGS, BELONGS

Ge 40: 8 "Do not interpretations **b** to God?
Ex 13:12 of your livestock **b** to the LORD.
Lev 25:55 for the Israelites **b** to me as servants.
Dt 10:14 LORD your God **b** the heavens,
    29:29 The secret things **b** to the LORD
    29:29 but the things revealed **b** to us
Job 12:13 "To God **b** wisdom and power;
    12:16 To him **b** strength and insight;
    25: 2 "Dominion and awe **b** to God;
Ps 47: 9 for the kings of the earth **b** to God;
    95: 4 and the mountain peaks **b** to him.
   115:16 The highest heavens **b**
Pr 16: 1 To humans **b** the plans of the heart,
SS   7:10 I **b** to my beloved, and his desire is
Isa 44: 5 Some will say, 'I **b** to the LORD';
Jer 5:10 for these people do not **b**
Jn   8:44 You **b** to your father, the devil,
     8:47 hear is that you do not **b** to God."
    15:19 As it is, you do not **b** to the world,

Ro   1: 6 those Gentiles who are called to **b**
     7: 4 that you might **b** to another, to him
     8: 9 of Christ, they do not **b** to Christ.
    14: 8 we live or die, we **b** to the Lord.
1Co 7:39 wishes, but he must **b** to the Lord.
     9:19 Though I am free and **b** to no one,
    12:15 not a hand, I do not **b** to the body,"
    15:23 when he comes, those who **b** to him.
2Co 10: 7 is confident that they **b** to Christ,
    10: 7 we **b** to Christ just as much as they
Gal 3:29 If you **b** to Christ, then you are
     5:24 Those who **b** to Christ Jesus have
     6:10 to those who **b** to the family
1Th 5: 5 We do not **b** to the night
     5: 8 But since we **b** to the day, let us be
1Jn 2:19 us, but they did not really **b** to us.
     3:19 how we know that we **b** to the truth

BELONGED BELONG

Jn 15:19 If you **b** to the world, it would love
Ac   9: 2 if he found any there who **b**
    12: 1 King Herod arrested some who **b**
1Jn 2:19 For if they had **b** to us, they would
     2:19 showed that none of them **b** to us.
     3:12 who **b** to the evil one and murdered

BELONGING BELONG

Ge 14:23 that I will accept nothing **b** to you,
Nu 16:26 Do not touch anything **b** to them,
Ru   2: 3 was working in a field **b** to Boaz,

BELONGINGS BELONG

Jer 46:19 Pack your **b** for exile, you who live
Eze 12: 4 bring out your **b** packed for exile.

BELONGS BELONG

Ex 34:19 offspring of every womb **b** to me,
Lev 27:30 from the trees, **b** to the LORD;
Dt   1:17 of anyone, for judgment **b** to God.
Job 41:11 Everything under heaven **b** to me.
Ps 22:28 for dominion **b** to the LORD
    89:18 Indeed, our shield **b** to the LORD,
   111:10 To him **b** eternal praise.
Jer 46:10 But that day **b** to the Lord,
Eze 18: 4 For everyone **b** to me, the parent as
Mt 19:14 of heaven **b** to such as these."
Jn   8:47 Whoever **b** to God hears what God
    16:15 All that **b** to the Father is mine.
Ro 12: 5 and each member **b** to all the others.
Col 3: 5 whatever **b** to your earthly nature:
Rev 7:10 "Salvation **b** to our God, who sits

BELOVED* LOVE

Dt 33:12 "Let the **b** of the LORD rest
SS   1:13 My **b** is to me a sachet of myrrh
     1:14 My **b** is to me a cluster of henna
     1:16 How handsome you are, my **b**!
     2: 3 the forest is my **b** among the young
     2: 8 Listen! My **b**! Look!
     2: 9 My **b** is like a gazelle or a young
     2:10 My **b** spoke and said to me, "Arise,
     2:16 My **b** is mine and I am his;
     2:17 my **b**, and be like a gazelle or like
     4:16 Let my **b** come into his garden
     5: 2 My **b** is knocking: "Open to me,

SS   5: 4 My **b** thrust his hand through
      5: 5 I arose to open for my **b**, and my
      5: 6 I opened for my **b**, but my **b** had
      5: 8 if you find my **b**, what will you tell
      5: 9 How is your **b** better than others,
      5: 9 How is your **b** better than others,
     5:10 My **b** is radiant and ruddy,
     5:16 This is my **b**, this is my friend,
     6: 1 Where has your **b** gone,
     6: 1 Which way did your **b** turn, that we
     6: 2 My **b** has gone down to his garden,
     6: 3 am my beloved's and my **b** is mine;
     7: 9 May the wine go straight to my **b**,
     7:10 I belong to my **b**, and his desire is
     7:11 my **b**, let us go to the countryside,
     7:13 that I have stored up for you, my **b**.
     8: 5 the wilderness leaning on her **b**?
     8:14 my **b**, and be like a gazelle or like
Jer   11:15 "What is my **b** doing in my temple

BELOVED'S* LOVE
SS   6: 3 I am my **b** and my beloved is mine;

BELOW
Dt   4:39 in heaven above and on the earth **b**.
Isa 37:31 kingdom of Judah will take root **b**
Jn   8:23 But he continued, "You are from **b**;
Ac   2:19 above and signs on the earth **b**,

BELSHAZZAR
King of Babylon in days of Daniel (Da 5).

BELT
Ex   12:11 with your cloak tucked into your **b**,
1Sa 18: 4 even his sword, his bow and his **b**.
1Ki 18:46 tucking his cloak into his **b**, he ran
2Ki   1: 8 had a leather **b** around his waist."
     4:29 "Tuck your cloak into your **b**,
     9: 1 "Tuck your cloak into your **b**,
Isa 11: 5 Righteousness will be his **b**
Jer 13: 1 buy a linen **b** and put it around your
Da 10: 5 with a **b** of fine gold from Uphaz
Mk   1: 6 with a leather **b** around his waist,
Eph 6:14 the **b** of truth buckled around your

BELTESHAZZAR DANIEL
Da   1: 7 to Daniel, the name **B**;

BEN HINNOM
2Ki 23:10 Topheth, which was in the Valley of **B**,
Jer   7:31 places of Topheth in the Valley of **B**

BEN-HADAD HADAD
1. King of Syria in time of Asa (1Ki 15:18–20; 2Ch 16:2–4).
2. King of Syria in time of Ahab (1Ki 20; 2Ki 5–7; 8:7–15).
3. King of Syria in time of Jehoahaz (2Ki 13:3, 24–25; Am 1:4).

BEN-ONI* BENJAMIN
Ge 35:18 she named her son **B**.

BENAIAH
A commander of Davids army (2Sa 8:18; 20:23; 23:20–30); loyal to Solomon (1Ki 1:8—2:46; 4:4).

BEND BENT
2Sa 22:35 my arms can **b** a bow of bronze.
Zec   9:13 I will **b** Judah as I **b** my bow and fill

BENEFICIAL* BENEFIT
1Co   6:12 but not everything is **b**.
    10:23 but not everything is **b**.

BENEFIT BENEFICIAL, BENEFITS
Job 22: 2 "Can a man be of **b** to God?
    22: 2 Can even a wise person **b** him?
Pr   11:17 Those who are kind **b** themselves,
Isa 38:17 my **b** that I suffered such anguish.
Jn   11:42 the **b** of the people standing here,
Ro   6:22 the **b** you reap leads to holiness,
2Co 1:15 you first so that you might **b** twice.
    4:15 All this is for your **b**,
Phm 1:20 that I may have some **b** from you

BENEFITS* BENEFIT
Dt   18: 8 He is to share equally in their **b**,
Ps 103: 2 my soul, and forget not all his **b**—
Ecc   7:11 thing and **b** those who see the sun.
Jn   4:38 and you have reaped the **b** of their

BENJAMIN BEN-ONI
Twelfth son of Jacob by Rachel (Ge 35:16–24; 46:19–21; 1Ch 2:2). Jacob refused to send him to Egypt, but relented (Ge 42–45). Tribe of blessed (Ge 49:27; Dt 33:12), numbered (Nu 1:37; 26:41), allotted land (Jos 18:11–28; Eze 48:23), failed to fully possess (Jdg 1:21), nearly obliterated (Jdg 20–21), sided with Ish-Bosheth (2Sa 2), but turned to David (1Ch 12:2, 29). 12,000 from (Rev 7:8).

BENT BEND
1Sa 24: 9 say, 'David is **b** on harming you'?
Ps   44:16 of the enemy, who is **b** on revenge.
    69:23 see, and their backs be **b** forever.
Isa 32: 6 folly, their hearts are **b** on evil:
Hos 11: 4 cheek, and I **b** down to feed them.
Lk   13:11 She was **b** over and could not
Jn   20: 5 He **b** over and looked in at the strips
Ro   11:10 see, and their backs be **b** forever."
Rev   6: 2 out as a conqueror **b** on conquest.

BERAKAH
2Ch 20:26 is why it is called the Valley of **B**

BEREA BEREAN
Ac   17:10 sent Paul and Silas away to **B**.

BEREAN* BEREA
Ac   17:11 Now the **B** Jews were of more noble

BEREAVE* BEREAVED, BEREAVEMENT, BEREAVES
Hos   9:12 children, I will **b** them of every one.

BEREAVED* BEREAVE
Ge   43:14 As for me, if I am **b**, I am **b**."
Ps   35:12 for good and leave me like one **b**.
Isa 49:21 I was **b** and barren; I was exiled

BEREAVEMENT* BEREAVE
Isa 49:20 born during your **b** will yet say

Jer   15: 7 I will bring **b** and destruction on my

BEREAVES* BEREAVE
La   1:20 Outside, the sword **b**; inside, there is

BESIDES
Dt   32:39 There is no god **b** me. I put to death
1Sa   2: 2 there is no one **b** you; there is no
2Sa 22:32 For who is God **b** the LORD?
Ps   18:31 For who is God **b** the LORD?
      73:25 earth has nothing I desire **b** you.
Isa   47: 8 'I am, and there is none **b** me.
      64: 4 no eye has seen any God **b** you,
Zep   2:15 And there is none **b** me."

BESIEGED SIEGE
La   3: 5 He has **b** me and surrounded me
Da   1: 1 Babylon came to Jerusalem and **b** it.
Zec   12: 2 Judah will be **b** as well as

BEST GOOD
Ge   45:18 I will give you the **b** of the land
      47: 6 your brothers in the **b** part
Ex   15: 4 The **b** of Pharaoh's officers are
Nu   18:29 as the LORD's portion the **b**
Dt   33:16 with the **b** gifts of the earth and its
Ps   90:10 yet the **b** of them are but trouble
SS   7: 9 and your mouth like the **b** wine.
Isa   48:17 who teaches you what is **b** for you,
Eze   44:30 The **b** of all the firstfruits and of all
Mic   7: 4 The **b** of them is like a brier,
Jn   2:10 but you have saved the **b** till now."
Php   1:10 you may be able to discern what is **b**
2Ti   2:15 Do your **b** to present yourself

BESTOW* BESTOWED,
BESTOWER, BESTOWING,
BESTOWS
Ps   31:19 you, that you **b** in the sight of all,
Isa   45: 4 name and **b** on you a title of honor,
      61: 3 to **b** on them a crown of beauty
      62: 2 that the mouth of the LORD will **b**.
Jer   23: 2 I will **b** punishment on you

BESTOWED BESTOW
1Ch 29:25 **b** on him royal splendor such as no

BESTOWER* BESTOW
Isa   23: 8 this against Tyre, the **b** of crowns,

BESTOWING* BESTOW
Pr   8:21 **b** a rich inheritance on those who

BESTOWS* BESTOW
Ps   84:11 the LORD **b** favor and honor;
      133: 3 For there the LORD **b** his blessing,

BETH AVEN
Hos   4:15 to Gilgal; do not go up to **B**.
      10: 5 Samaria fear for the calf-idol of **B**.

BETH SHAN
Jdg   1:27 Manasseh did not drive out the
           people of **B**
1Sa   31:10 fastened his body to the wall of **B**.

BETH SHEMESH
1Sa   6:14 cart came to the field of Joshua of **B**,

BETHANY
Mt   26: 6 While Jesus was in **B** in the home
Mk   11:12 next day as they were leaving **B**,
Jn   1:28 This all happened at **B** on the other

BETHEL EL BETHEL, LUZ
Ge   12: 8 he went on toward the hills east of **B**
      12: 8 with **B** on the west and Ai
      28:19 He called that place **B**,
      31:13 I am the God of **B**, where you
      35: 8 was buried under the oak outside **B**.
Jos   8: 9 and lay in wait between **B** and Ai,
Jdg   20:18 The Israelites went up to **B**
1Sa   7:16 went on a circuit from **B** to Gilgal
1Ki   12:29 One he set up in **B**, and the other
      13:11 a certain old prophet living in **B**,
2Ki   2: 2 the LORD has sent me to **B**."
       2: 2 So they went down to **B**.
      10:29 worship of the golden calves at **B**
      23:15 Even the altar at **B**, the high place
Am   4: 4 "Go to **B** and sin; go to Gilgal
       7:10 the priest of **B** sent a message

BETHESDA*
Jn   5: 2 which in Aramaic is called **B**

BETHLEHEM EPHRATH
Ge   35:19 on the way to Ephrath (that is, **B**).
Ru   1: 1 So a man from **B** in Judah,
       1:19 went on until they came to **B**.
       1:19 When they arrived in **B**, the whole
       4:11 in Ephrathah and be famous in **B**.
1Sa   16: 1 I am sending you to Jesse of **B**.
2Sa   23:15 from the well near the gate of **B**!"
Mic   5: 2 "But you, **B** Ephrathah, though you
Mt   2: 1 After Jesus was born in **B** in Judea,
       2: 6 " 'But you, **B**, in the land
       2:16 gave orders to kill all the boys in **B**
Lk   2:15 "Let's go to **B** and see this thing
Jn   7:42 David's descendants and from **B**,

BETHPHAGE
Mt   21: 1 came to **B** on the Mount of Olives,

BETHSAIDA
Mt   11:21 Woe to you, **B**! For if the miracles
Jn   12:21 Philip, who was from **B** in Galilee,

BETRAY BETRAYED, BETRAYER,
BETRAYING, BETRAYS
Ps   89:33 nor will I ever **b** my faithfulness.
Pr   16:10 and his mouth does not **b** justice.
      25: 9 do not **b** another's confidence,
Isa   24:16 The treacherous **b**!
      24:16 With treachery the treacherous **b**!"
Mt   10:21 "Brother will **b** brother to death,
      24:10 faith and will **b** and hate each other,
      26:21 I tell you, one of you will **b** me."
Jn   13:11 he knew who was going to **b** him,

BETRAYED BETRAY
La   1: 2 All her friends have **b** her;

Mt 27: 4 said, "for I have **b** innocent blood."
Lk 21:16 You will be **b** even by parents,
Jn 18: 2 Now Judas, who **b** him,

BETRAYER BETRAY
Isa 33: 1 Woe to you, **b**, you who have not
Mk 14:42 Let us go! Here comes my **b**!"

BETRAYING BETRAY
Lk 22:48 are you **b** the Son of Man

BETRAYS BETRAY
Pr 11:13 A gossip **b** a confidence,
    20:19 A gossip **b** a confidence;
Hab 2: 5 indeed, wine **b** him; he is arrogant
Mk 14:21 to that man who **b** the Son of Man!

BETROTH*
Hos 2:19 I will **b** you to me forever; I will **b** you
        in righteousness
    2:20 I will **b** you in faithfulness,

BETTER GOOD
Nu 11:18 We were **b** off in Egypt!"
1Sa 15:22 To obey is **b** than sacrifice,
    15:22 and to heed is **b** than the fat of rams.
Ps 37:16 **B** the little that the righteous have
    63: 3 Because your love is **b** than life,
    118: 8 It is **b** to take refuge in the LORD
Pr   8:19 My fruit is **b** than fine gold;
    12: 9 **B** to be a nobody and yet have
    15:16 **B** a little with the fear
    15:17 **B** a small serving of vegetables
    16: 8 **B** a little with righteousness than
    16:16 How much **b** to get wisdom than
    16:19 **B** to be lowly in spirit along
    16:32 **B** a patient person than a warrior,
    17: 1 **B** a dry crust with peace and quiet
    17:12 **B** to meet a bear robbed of her cubs
    19: 1 **B** the poor whose walk is blameless
    19:22 **b** to be poor than a liar.
    21: 9 **B** to live on a corner of the roof than
    21:19 **B** to live in a desert than
    22: 1 to be esteemed is **b** than silver
    27: 5 **B** is open rebuke than hidden love.
    28: 6 **B** the poor whose walk is blameless
Ecc 2:13 I saw that wisdom is **b** than folly,
    2:13 just as light is **b** than darkness.
    2:24 A person can do nothing **b** than
    3:12 there is nothing **b** for people than
    3:22 there is nothing **b** for a person than
    4: 3 **b** than both is the one who has never
    4: 6 **B** one handful with tranquillity than
    4: 9 Two are **b** than one, because they
    4:13 **B** a poor but wise youth than an old
    5: 5 It is **b** not to make a vow than
    6: 3 that a stillborn child is **b** off than he.
    6: 9 **B** what the eye sees than the roving
    7: 1 good name is **b** than fine perfume,
    7: 1 the day of death **b** than the day
    7: 2 It is **b** to go to a house of mourning
    7: 3 Frustration is **b** than laughter,
    7: 5 It is **b** to heed the rebuke of a wise
    7: 8 of a matter is **b** than its beginning,
    7: 8 and patience is **b** than pride.

Ecc 8:12 that it will go **b** with those who fear
    8:15 life, because there is nothing **b**
    9: 4 even a live dog is **b** off than a dead
    9:16 said, "Wisdom is **b** than strength."
    9:18 Wisdom is **b** than weapons of war,
SS   5: 9 How is your beloved **b** than others,
Jnh 4: 3 life, for it is **b** for me to die than
Mt   5:29 It is **b** for you to lose one part
    18: 6 it would be **b** for them to have
    26:24 It would be **b** for him if he had not
Lk   5:39 for they say, 'The old is **b**.' "
    10:42 Mary has chosen what is **b**, and it
1Co 7: 9 for it is **b** to marry than to burn
Eph 1:17 so that you may know him **b**.
Heb 6: 9 we are convinced of **b** things
    7:19 and a **b** hope is introduced,
    7:22 the guarantor of a **b** covenant.
    8: 6 is established on **b** promises.
    9:23 with **b** sacrifices than these.
    10:34 you knew that you yourselves had **b**
    11: 4 brought God a **b** offering than Cain
    11:16 they were longing for a **b** country—
    11:35 might gain an even **b** resurrection.
    11:40 since God had planned something **b**
    12:24 that speaks a **b** word than the blood
1Pe 3:17 For it is **b**, if it is God's will,
2Pe 2:21 It would have been **b** for them not

BETWEEN
Ge   3:15 And I will put enmity **b** you
    3:15 and **b** your offspring and hers;
    16: 5 May the LORD judge **b** you
    31:44 I, and let it serve as a witness **b** us."
Lev 10:10 that you can distinguish **b** the holy
    10:10 **b** the unclean and the clean,
1Sa 4: 4 who is enthroned **b** the cherubim.
Ro   10:12 For there is no difference **b** Jew
1Ti 2: 5 one mediator **b** God and mankind,

BEULAH*
Isa 62: 4 called Hephzibah, and your land **B**;

BEWARE*
2Ki 6: 9 "**B** of passing that place,
Job 36:21 **B** of turning to evil, which you seem
Isa 22:17 "**B**, the LORD is about to take
Jer 7:32 So **b**, the days are coming,
    9: 4 "**B** of your friends; do not trust
    19: 6 So **b**, the days are coming,
Lk   20:46 "**B** of the teachers of the law.

BEWITCHED* WITCHCRAFT
Gal 3: 1 Who has **b** you? Before your very

BEYOND
Dt   30:11 too difficult for you or **b** your reach.
Jos 24: 2 lived **b** the Euphrates River
Jdg 13:18 It is **b** understanding."
Job 36:26 great is God—**b** our understanding!
    37:23 The Almighty is **b** our reach
Ecc 7:23 to be wise"—but this was **b** me.
Jer 17: 9 above all things and **b** cure.
    30:12 is incurable, your injury **b** healing.
Ro   11:11 stumble so as to fall **b** recovery?
1Co 4: 6 "Do not go **b** what is written."

1Co 10:13 let you be tempted **b** what you can
2Co 1: 8 pressure, far **b** our ability to endure,
       10:16 the gospel in the regions **b** you.

BEZALEL
Judahite craftsman in charge of building the
tabernacle (Ex 31:1–11; 35:30—39:31).

BIDDING*
Ps 103:20 you mighty ones who do his **b**,
      148: 8 clouds, stormy winds that do his **b**,

BIER
Lk 7:14 touched the **b** they were carrying

BILDAD
One of Job's friends (Job 2:11; 8; 18; 25).

BILHAH
Servant of Rachel, mother of Jacob's sons Dan
and Naphtali (Ge 30:1–7; 35:25; 46:23–25).

BIND BINDING, BINDS, BOUND
Dt   6: 8 and **b** them on your foreheads.
Ne 10:29 and **b** themselves with a curse
Pr   3: 3 **b** them around your neck,
     6:21 **B** them always on your heart;
     7: 3 **B** them on your fingers;
Isa 8:16 **B** up this testimony of warning
     56: 6 foreigners who **b** themselves
     61: 1 He has sent me to **b**
Eze 34:16 I will **b** up the injured
Mt 16:19 whatever you **b** on earth will be
     18:18 whatever you **b** on earth will be

BINDING BIND
Heb 2: 2 spoken through angels was **b**,

BINDS BIND
Job 5:18 For he wounds, but he also **b** up;
Isa 30:26 when the LORD **b** up the bruises
Col 3:14 which **b** them all together in perfect

BIRD BIRDS
Ge   1:21 and every winged **b** according to its
     6:20 Two of every kind of **b**, of every
Dt 14:11 You may eat any clean **b**.
Ps 50:11 I know every **b** in the mountains,
Pr   6: 5 hunter, like a **b** from the snare
     7:23 liver, like a **b** darting into a snare,
     27: 8 Like a **b** that flees its nest is anyone
Ecc 10:20 because a **b** in the sky may carry
     10:20 a **b** on the wing may report what
Isa 46:11 From the east I summon a **b** of prey;

BIRDS BIRD
Jer   7:33 people will become food for the **b**
Da   4:12 and the **b** lived in its branches;
Mt   6:26 Look at the **b** of the air; they do not
     8:20 "Foxes have dens and **b** have nests,
     13: 4 path, and the **b** came and ate it up.
Mk   4:32 big branches that the **b** can perch
Rev 19:21 all the **b** gorged themselves on their

BIRTH BEAR
Ge   3:16 with painful labor you will give **b**
Lev 12: 7 for the woman who gives **b** to a boy

Dt 32:18 you forgot the God who gave you **b**.
1Sa 2:21 she gave **b** to three sons and two
Job 3: 1 mouth and cursed the day of his **b**.
Ps 51: 5 Surely I was sinful at **b**,
     58: 3 Even from **b** the wicked go astray;
     71: 6 From **b** I have relied on you;
Pr   8:24 I was given **b**, when there were no
Ecc 7: 1 of death better than the day of **b**.
Isa 7:14 will conceive and give **b** to a son,
     8: 3 she conceived and gave **b** to a son.
     26:18 in labor, but we gave **b** to wind.
Jer 2:27 and to stone, 'You gave me **b**.'
Mt 1:18 This is how the **b** of Jesus
     1:21 She will give **b** to a son, and you are
     24: 8 these are the beginning of **b** pains.
Lk 1:57 have her baby, she gave **b** to a son.
Jn 3: 6 Flesh gives **b** to flesh, but the Spirit
          gives **b** to spirit.
     9: 1 along, he saw a man blind from **b**.
Jas 1:15 has conceived, it gives **b** to sin;
     1:15 it is full-grown, gives **b** to death.
1Pe 1: 3 great mercy he has given us new **b**
Rev 12: 5 She gave **b** to a son, a male child,

BIRTHRIGHT BEAR
Ge 25:34 up and left. So Esau despised his **b**.

BIT BITE, BITS
Nu 21: 6 they **b** the people and many
2Ki 19:28 your nose and my **b** in your mouth,

BITE BIT, BITES, BITTEN
Am 5:19 the wall only to have a snake **b** him.

BITES BITE
Pr 23:32 In the end it **b** like a snake

BITS BIT
Jas 3: 3 When we put **b** into the mouths

BITTEN BITE
Nu 21: 8 anyone who is **b** can look at it

BITTER BITTERLY, BITTERNESS, EMBITTER
Ex   1:14 They made their lives **b** with harsh
     12: 8 along with **b** herbs, and bread made
Nu   5:19 may this **b** water that brings a curse
Ru   1:20 Almighty has made my life very **b**.
Pr   5: 4 but in the end she is **b** as gall,
     27: 7 hungry even what is **b** tastes sweet.
Rev 8:11 A third of the waters turned **b**,
     8:11 from the waters that had become **b**.

BITTERLY BITTER
1Sa 1:10 prayed to the LORD, weeping **b**.

BITTERNESS BITTER
Pr 14:10 Each heart knows its own **b**, and no
     17:25 and **b** to the mother who bore him.
Ro 3:14 mouths are full of cursing and **b**."
Eph 4:31 Get rid of all **b**, rage and anger,

BLACK
Zec 6: 6 the **b** horses is going toward
Mt 5:36 make even one hair white or **b**.

Rev 6: 5 and there before me was a **b** horse!
      6:12 The sun turned **b** like sackcloth

BLAME BLAMELESS, BLAMELESSLY
Ro   9:19 "Then why does God still **b** us?
1Ti 5: 7 so that no one may be open to **b**.
      6:14 or **b** until the appearing of our Lord

BLAMELESS* BLAME
Ge   6: 9 **b** among the people of his time,
     17: 1 walk before me faithfully and be **b**.
Dt 18:13 You must be **b** before the LORD
2Sa 22:24 I have been **b** before him and have
     22:26 to the **b** you show yourself **b**,
Job 1: 1 This man was **b** and upright;
      1: 8 he is **b** and upright, a man who fears
      2: 3 he is **b** and upright, a man who fears
      4: 6 and your **b** ways your hope?
      8:20 God does not reject one who is **b**
      9:20 if I were **b**, it would pronounce me
      9:21 "Although I am **b**, I have no
      9:22 say, 'He destroys both the **b**
     12: 4 though righteous and **b**!
     22: 3 would he gain if your ways were **b**?
     31: 6 and he will know that I am **b**—
Ps 15: 2 The one whose walk is **b**, who does
     18:23 I have been **b** before him and have
     18:25 to the **b** you show yourself **b**,
     19:13 Then I will be **b**, innocent of great
     26: 1 me, LORD, for I have led a **b** life;
     26:11 I lead a **b** life; deliver me and be
     37:18 The **b** spend their days under
     37:37 Consider the **b**, observe the upright;
     50:23 to the **b** I will show my salvation."
     84:11 from those whose walk is **b**.
    101: 2 I will be careful to lead a **b** life—
    101: 2 affairs of my house with a **b** heart.
    101: 6 one whose walk is **b** will minister
    119: 1 Blessed are those whose ways are **b**,
Pr   2: 7 is a shield to those whose walk is **b**,
      2:21 the land, and the **b** will remain in it;
     11: 5 of the **b** makes their paths straight,
     11:20 delights in those whose ways are **b**.
     19: 1 the poor whose walk is **b** than a fool
     20: 7 The righteous lead **b** lives;
     28: 6 poor whose walk is **b** than the rich
     28:10 trap, but the **b** will receive a good
     28:18 one whose walk is **b** is kept safe,
Eze 28:15 You were **b** in your ways
1Co 1: 8 so that you will be **b** on the day
Eph 1: 4 world to be holy and **b** in his sight.
      5:27 any other blemish, but holy and **b**.
Php 1:10 be pure and **b** for the day of Christ,
      2:15 so that you may become **b** and pure,
1Th 2:10 and **b** we were among you who
      3:13 your hearts so that you will be **b**
      5:23 body be kept **b** at the coming of our
Titus 1: 6 An elder must be **b**, faithful to his
      1: 7 God's household, he must be **b**—
Heb 7:26 one who is holy, **b**, pure, set apart
2Pe 3:14 spotless, **b** and at peace with him.
Rev 14: 5 found in their mouths; they are **b**.

BLAMELESSLY* BLAME
Lk   1: 6 Lord's commands and decrees **b**.

BLASPHEME* BLASPHEMED,
BLASPHEMER, BLASPHEMES,
BLASPHEMIES, BLASPHEMING,
BLASPHEMOUS, BLASPHEMY
Ex 22:28 "Do not **b** God or curse the ruler
Lev 24:16 when they **b** the Name they are
Ac 26:11 and I tried to force them to **b**.
1Ti 1:20 over to Satan to be taught not to **b**.
2Pe 2:12 these people **b** in matters they do
Rev 13: 6 It opened its mouth to **b** God,

BLASPHEMED* BLASPHEME
Lev 24:11 of the Israelite woman **b** the Name
1Sa 3:13 his sons **b** God, and he failed
2Ki 19: 6 of the king of Assyria have **b** me.
     19:22 Who is it you have ridiculed and **b**?
Isa 37: 6 of the king of Assyria have **b** me.
     37:23 Who is it you have ridiculed and **b**?
     52: 5 day long my name is constantly **b**.
Eze 20:27 also your ancestors **b** me by being
Ac 19:37 robbed temples nor **b** our goddess.
Ro   2:24 "God's name is **b** among

BLASPHEMER* BLASPHEME
Lev 24:14 "Take the **b** outside the camp.
     24:23 they took the **b** outside the camp
1Ti 1:13 Even though I was once a **b**

BLASPHEMES* BLASPHEME
Lev 24:16 anyone who **b** the name
Nu 15:30 **b** the LORD and must be cut off
Mk   3:29 whoever **b** against the Holy Spirit
Lk 12:10 but anyone who **b** against the Holy

BLASPHEMIES* BLASPHEME
Ne   9:18 or when they committed awful **b**.
      9:26 they committed awful **b**.
Rev 13: 5 a mouth to utter proud words and **b**

BLASPHEMING* BLASPHEME
Mt   9: 3 to themselves, "This fellow is **b**!"
Mk   2: 7 He's **b**! Who can forgive sins
Jas 2: 7 the ones who are **b** the noble name

BLASPHEMOUS* BLASPHEME
Ac   6:11 Stephen speak **b** words against
Rev 13: 1 horns, and on each head a **b** name.
     17: 3 beast that was covered with **b** names

BLASPHEMY* BLASPHEME
Mt 12:31 but **b** against the Spirit will not be
     12:31 but **b** against the Spirit will not be
     26:65 clothes and said, "He has spoken **b**!
     26:65 Look, now you have heard the **b**.
Mk 14:64 "You have heard the **b**.
Lk   5:21 "Who is this fellow who speaks **b**?
Jn 10:33 replied, "but for **b**, because you,
     10:36 you accuse me of **b** because I said,

BLAST* BLASTS
Ex 15: 8 By the **b** of your nostrils the waters
     19:13 sounds a long **b** may they approach

Ex 19:16 and a very loud trumpet **b**.
Nu 10: 5 When a trumpet **b** is sounded,
    10: 6 At the sounding of a second **b**,
    10: 6 The **b** will be the signal for setting
    10: 9 you, sound a **b** on the trumpets.
Jos 6: 5 you hear them sound a long **b**
     6:16 the priests sounded the trumpet **b**,
2Sa 22:16 at the **b** of breath from his nostrils.
Job 4: 9 the **b** of his anger they are no more.
    39:25 At the **b** of the trumpet it snorts,
Ps 18:15 at the **b** of breath from your nostrils.
    98: 6 and the **b** of the ram's horn—
   147:17 Who can withstand his icy **b**?
Isa 27: 8 with his fierce **b** he drives her out,
Eze 22:20 furnace to be melted with a fiery **b**,
Am   2: 2 war cries and the **b** of the trumpet.
Heb 12:19 to a trumpet **b** or to such a voice

BLASTS* BLAST
Lev 23:24 commemorated with trumpet **b**.
Rev 8:13 because of the trumpet **b** about to be

BLAZED BLAZING
Dt   4:11 of the mountain while it **b** with fire
2Sa 22: 9 his mouth, burning coals **b** out of it.
Jnh 4: 8 the sun **b** on Jonah's head so that he

BLAZING BLAZED
Ge 15:17 firepot with a **b** torch appeared
SS   8: 6 It burns like **b** fire, like a mighty
Isa 62: 1 dawn, her salvation like a **b** torch.
Eze 20:47 The **b** flame will not be quenched,
Da   3: 6 be thrown into a **b** furnace."
     7:11 destroyed and thrown into the **b** fire.
Mt 13:50 and throw them into the **b** furnace,
2Th 1: 7 heaven in **b** fire with his powerful
Rev 1:14 snow, and his eyes were like **b** fire.
     8:10 and a great star, **b** like a torch,
    19:12 His eyes are like **b** fire, and on his

BLEATING*
1Sa 15:14 then is this **b** of sheep in my ears?

BLEEDING BLOOD
Lev 12: 4 days to be purified from her **b**.
Lk   8:43 was there who had been subject to **b**

BLEMISH* BLEMISHED,
    BLEMISHES
Lev 22:21 without defect or **b** to be acceptable.
Nu 19: 2 you a red heifer without defect or **b**
2Sa 14:25 of his foot there was no **b** in him.
Eph 5:27 stain or wrinkle or any other **b**,
Col 1:22 in his sight, without **b** and free
1Pe 1:19 Christ, a lamb without **b** or defect.

BLEMISHED* BLEMISH
Mal 1:14 sacrifices a **b** animal to the Lord.

BLEMISHES* BLEMISH
2Pe 2:13 They are blots and **b**,
Jude 1:12 These people are **b** at your love

BLESS BLESSED, BLESSES,
    BLESSING, BLESSINGS
Ge 12: 3 I will **b** those who **b** you,

Ge 17:16 I will **b** her and will surely give you
    17:16 I will **b** her so that she will be
    22:17 I will surely **b** you and make your
    26: 3 I will be with you and will **b** you.
    26:24 I will **b** you and will increase
    27:29 and those who **b** you be blessed."
    27:34 cry and said to his father, "**B** me—
    28: 3 May God Almighty **b** you and make
    32:26 not let you go unless you **b** me."
    48: 9 them to me so I may **b** them."
Ex 12:32 have said, and go. And also **b** me."
    20:24 I will come to you and **b** you.
Nu   6:24 " ' "The LORD **b** you
    22: 6 know that whoever you **b** is blessed,
    23:20 I have received a command to **b**;
Dt   1:11 times and **b** you as he has promised!
     7:13 He will love you and **b** you
     7:13 He will **b** the fruit of your womb,
    14:29 the LORD your God may **b** you
    15: 4 inheritance, he will richly **b** you,
    16:15 the LORD your God will **b** you
    23:20 the LORD your God may **b** you
    24:19 the LORD your God may **b** you
    26:15 and **b** your people Israel
    27:12 on Mount Gerizim to **b** the people:
    33:11 **B** all his skills, LORD, and be
Jos 8:33 he gave instructions to **b** the people
Jdg 17: 2 "The LORD **b** you, my son!"
Ru   2: 4 "The LORD **b** you!"
     3:10 "The LORD **b** you,
1Sa 2:20 Eli would **b** Elkanah and his wife,
2Sa 2: 5 "The LORD **b** you for showing
    21: 3 so that you will **b** the LORD's
1Ch 4:10 that you would **b** me and enlarge
Ps   5:12 LORD, you **b** the righteous;
    28: 9 your people and **b** your inheritance;
    67: 1 May God be gracious to us and **b** us
    72: 5 pray for him and **b** him all day long.
   109:28 While they curse, may you **b**;
   115:12 remembers us and will **b** us:
   115:12 He will **b** his people Israel, he will **b**
           the house of Aaron,
   118:26 the house of the LORD we **b** you.
Pr 30:11 fathers and do not **b** their mothers;
Isa 19:25 The LORD Almighty will **b** them,
Jer 31:23 'The LORD **b** you, you prosperous
Hag 2:19 this day on I will **b** you.' "
Zec 4: 7 shouts of 'God **b** it! God **b** it!' "
Lk   6:28 **b** those who curse you,
Ro 12:14 **B** those who persecute you;
1Co 4:12 When we are cursed, we **b**;
2Co 9: 8 God is able to **b** you abundantly,
Heb 6:14 "I will surely **b** you and give you

BLESSED BLESS
Ge   1:22 God **b** them and said, "Be fruitful
     2: 3 Then God **b** the seventh day
     9: 1 Then God **b** Noah and his sons,
    14:19 he **b** Abram, saying, "**B** be
    22:18 all nations on earth will be **b**,
    28:14 on earth will be **b** through you
    39: 5 the LORD **b** the household
    47: 7 After Jacob **b** Pharaoh,
Ex 20:11 Therefore the LORD **b** the Sabbath

Ex 39:43 So Moses **b** them.
Lev 9:22 toward the people and **b** them.
Nu 24: 9 "May those who bless you be **b**
Dt 12: 7 the LORD your God has **b** you.
28: 3 You will be **b** in the city and **b**
Jos 22: 6 Then Joshua **b** them and sent them
Jdg 5:24 "Most **b** of women be Jael, the wife
5:24 most **b** of tent-dwelling women.
13:24 He grew and the LORD **b** him,
1Ch 17:27 have **b** it, and it will be **b**
Ne 9: 5 "B be your glorious name, and may
Job 5:17 "B is the one whom God corrects;
Ps 1: 1 B is the one who does not walk
2:12 B are all who take refuge in him.
32: 1 B is the one whose transgressions
33:12 B is the nation whose God is
40: 4 B is the one who trusts
41: 1 B are those who have regard
84: 5 B are those whose strength is
89:15 B are those who have learned
94:12 B is the one you discipline, LORD,
106: 3 B are those who act justly,
112: 1 B are those who fear the LORD,
118:26 B is he who comes in the name
119: 1 B are those whose ways are
119: 2 B are those who keep his statutes
127: 5 B is the man whose quiver is full
128: 1 B are all who fear the LORD,
144:15 B is the people of whom this is true;
144:15 b is the people whose God is
Pr 3:13 B are those who find wisdom,
8:34 B are those who listen to me,
22: 9 The generous will themselves be **b**,
28:20 A faithful person will be richly **b**,
29:18 b is the one who heeds wisdom's
31:28 Her children arise and call her **b**;
SS 6: 9 women saw her and called her **b**;
Isa 30:18 B are all who wait for him!
Mal 3:12 all the nations will call you **b**,
3:15 But now we call the arrogant **b**.
Mt 5: 3 "B are the poor in spirit, for theirs
5: 4 B are those who mourn, for they
5: 5 B are the meek, for they will inherit
5: 6 B are those who hunger and thirst
5: 7 B are the merciful, for they will be
5: 8 B are the pure in heart, for they will
5: 9 B are the peacemakers, for they will
5:10 B are those who are persecuted
5:11 "B are you when people insult you,
11: 6 B is anyone who does not stumble
Mk 11: 9 "B is he who comes in the name
Lk 1:42 "B are you among women, and **b** is
1:48 on all generations will call me **b**,
6:20 "B are you who are poor, for yours
6:21 B are you who hunger now, for you
6:21 B are you who weep now, for you
6:22 B are you when people hate you,
Jn 12:13 "B is he who comes in the name
12:13 "B is the king of Israel!"
13:17 things, you will be **b** if you do them.
Ac 20:35 'It is more **b** to give than
Ro 4: 7 "B are those whose transgressions
Gal 3: 8 nations will be **b** through you."

Eph 1: 3 who has **b** us in the heavenly realms
1Ti 6:15 God, the **b** and only Ruler, the King
Titus 2:13 while we wait for the **b** hope—
Heb 7: 7 without doubt the lesser is **b**
Jas 1:12 B is the one who perseveres under
5:11 we count as **b** those who have
1Pe 3:14 suffer for what is right, you are **b**.
Rev 1: 3 B is the one who reads aloud
1: 3 and **b** are those who hear it and take
14:13 B are the dead who die in the Lord
16:15 B is the one who stays awake
19: 9 B are those who are invited
20: 6 B and holy are those who share
22: 7 B is the one who keeps the words
22:14 "B are those who wash their robes,

BLESSES BLESS
Ps 29:11 the LORD **b** his people with peace.
Ro 10:12 all and richly **b** all who call on him,

BLESSING BLESS
Ge 12: 2 name great, and you will be a **b**.
27: 4 I may give you my **b** before I die."
48:20 name will Israel pronounce this **b**:
49:28 giving each the **b** appropriate
Dt 11:26 I am setting before you today a **b**
23: 5 but turned the curse into a **b** for you,
33: 1 This is the **b** that Moses the man
Ne 13: 2 however, turned the curse into a **b**.)
Pr 10:22 The **b** of the LORD brings wealth,
Eze 34:26 the places surrounding my hill a **b**.
34:26 there will be showers of **b**.
Joel 2:14 and relent and leave behind a **b**—
Zec 8:13 I will save you, and you will be a **b**.
Mal 3:10 out so much **b** that there will not be
Lk 24:51 While he was **b** them, he left them
Ro 15:29 the full measure of the **b** of Christ.
Gal 3:14 in order that the **b** given to Abraham
4:15 Where, then, is your **b** of me now?
Heb 12:17 when he wanted to inherit this **b**,
12:17 Even though he sought the **b**
1Pe 3: 9 repay evil with **b**, because to this
3: 9 called so that you may inherit a **b**.

BLESSINGS BLESS
Ge 49:26 Your father's **b** are greater than the **b**
Dt 11:29 proclaim on Mount Gerizim the **b**,
Jos 8:34 of the law—the **b** and the curses—
1Ch 23:13 to pronounce **b** in his name forever.
Pr 10: 6 B crown the head of the righteous,
Mal 2: 2 on you, and I will curse your **b**.
Ac 13:34 holy and sure **b** promised to David.'
Ro 15:27 have shared in the Jews' spiritual **b**,
15:27 to share with them their material **b**.

BLEW BLOW
Ex 15:10 But you **b** with your breath,
Jos 6: 9 of the priests who **b** the trumpets,
Hag 1: 9 What you brought home, I **b** away.
Mt 7:25 the winds **b** and beat against

BLIND BLINDED, BLINDNESS, BLINDS
Ex 4:11 gives them sight or makes them **b**?
Dt 27:18 is anyone who leads the **b** astray

2Sa 5: 8 and **b**' who are David's enemies."
　　　 5: 8 "The '**b** and lame' will not enter
Job 29:15 I was eyes to the **b** and feet
Ps 146: 8 the LORD gives sight to the **b**,
Isa 42:19 Who is **b** but my servant, and deaf
　　　42:19 Who is **b** like the one in covenant
　　　42:19 **b** like the servant of the LORD?
　　　56:10 Israel's watchmen are **b**, they all
Mt 9:27 there, two **b** men followed him,
　　　11: 5 The **b** receive sight, the lame walk,
　　　15:14 Leave them; they are **b** guides.
　　　15:14 If the **b** lead the **b**, both will fall
　　　23:16 "Woe to you, **b** guides! You say,
Mk 10:46 were leaving the city, a **b** man,
Lk 6:39 "Can the **b** lead the **b**?
Jn 9: 1 along, he saw a man **b** from birth.
　　　9:25 I do know. I was **b** but now I see!"
Ac 9: 9 For three days he was **b**, and did not
Ro 2:19 that you are a guide for the **b**, a light
2Pe 1: 9 not have them is nearsighted and **b**,
Rev 3:17 wretched, pitiful, poor, **b** and naked.

BLINDED* BLIND
Zec 11:17 withered, his right eye totally **b**!"
Jn 12:40 "He has **b** their eyes and hardened
Ac 22:11 the brilliance of the light had **b** me.
2Co 4: 4 god of this age has **b** the minds
1Jn 2:11 because the darkness has **b** them.

BLINDFOLDED
Mk 14:65 they **b** him, struck him with their

BLINDNESS* BLIND
Ge 19:11 with **b** so that they could not find
Dt 28:28 will afflict you with madness, **b** and
2Ki 6:18 LORD, "Strike this army with **b**."

BLINDS* BLIND
Ex 23: 8 a bribe **b** those who see and twists
Dt 16:19 for a bribe **b** the eyes of the wise

BLOCK
Isa 44:19 Shall I bow down to a **b** of wood?"
Eze 4: 1 son of man, take a **b** of clay, put it
　　　14: 7 a wicked stumbling **b** before their
Mt 16:23 You are a stumbling **b** to me;
Ro 11: 9 a stumbling **b** and a retribution
　　　14:13 mind not to put any stumbling **b**
1Co 1:23 a stumbling **b** to Jews
2Co 6: 3 We put no stumbling **b** in anyone's

BLOOD AKELDAMA, BLEEDING, BLOODSHED, BLOODSHOT, BLOODTHIRSTY, LIFEBLOOD
Ge 4:10 Your brother's **b** cries out to me
　　　9: 6 "Whoever sheds human **b**, by humans
　　　　　　shall their **b** be shed;
Ex 4:25 "Surely you are a bridegroom of **b**
　　　7:17 Nile, and it will be changed into **b**.
　　　12:13 The **b** will be a sign for you
　　　12:13 when I see the **b**, I will pass over
　　　24: 8 Moses then took the **b**, sprinkled it
　　　24: 8 "This is the **b** of the covenant
Lev 7:27 Anyone who eats **b** must be cut off
　　　16:15 and take its **b** behind the curtain

Lev 16:15 with it as he did with the bull's **b**:
　　　17:11 For the life of a creature is in the **b**,
　　　17:11 it is the **b** that makes atonement
　　　17:14 the life of every creature is its **b**.
　　　17:14 "You must not eat the **b** of any
Dt 12:23 But be sure you do not eat the **b**,
　　　　　　because the **b** is the life,
2Sa 7:12 to succeed you, your own flesh and **b**,
Ps 50:13 of bulls or drink the **b** of goats?
　　　59: 2 me from those who are after my **b**.
　　　72:14 for precious is their **b** in his sight.
　　106:38 They shed innocent **b**, the **b** of their
　　106:38 the land was desecrated by their **b**.
Pr 6:17 tongue, hands that shed innocent **b**,
Isa 1:11 I have no pleasure in the **b** of bulls
　　　9: 5 garment rolled in **b** will be destined
　　　34: 6 sword of the LORD is bathed in **b**,
　　　34: 6 the **b** of lambs and goats,
Eze 3:18 hold you accountable for their **b**.
Joel 2:31 the moon to **b** before the coming
　　　3:21 I leave their innocent **b** unavenged?
Na 3: 1 Woe to the city of **b**, full of lies,
Hab 2: 8 For you have shed human **b**;
Mt 23:30 in shedding the **b** of the prophets.'
　　　26:28 This is my **b** of the covenant,
　　　27: 6 the treasury, since it is **b** money."
　　　27: 8 why it has been called the Field of B
　　　27:24 "I am innocent of this man's **b**,"
Mk 14:24 "This is my **b** of the covenant,
Lk 22:44 his sweat was like drops of **b** falling
Jn 6:53 of the Son of Man and drink his **b**,
　　　19:34 bringing a sudden flow of **b**
Ac 2:20 the moon to **b** before the coming
　　　15:20 of strangled animals and from **b**.
　　　20:26 that I am innocent of the **b** of any
Ro 3:25 through the shedding of his **b**—
　　　5: 9 we have now been justified by his **b**,
1Co 11:25 cup is the new covenant in my **b**;
Eph 1: 7 we have redemption through his **b**,
　　　2:13 brought near by the **b** of Christ.
　　　6:12 struggle is not against flesh and **b**,
Col 1:20 by making peace through his **b**,
Heb 9: 7 year, and never without **b**, which he
　　　9:12 not enter by means of the **b** of goats
　　　9:12 Place once for all by his own **b**,
　　　9:20 said, "This is the **b** of the covenant,
　　　9:22 everything be cleansed with **b**,
　　　9:22 of **b** there is no forgiveness.
　　　12:24 the sprinkled **b** that speaks a better
1Pe 1:19 but with the precious **b** of Christ,
1Jn 1: 7 another, and the **b** of Jesus, his Son,
　　　5: 6 the one who came by water and **b**—
　　　5: 6 by water only, but by water and **b**.
Rev 1: 5 has freed us from our sins by his **b**,
　　　5: 9 with your **b** you purchased for God
　　　6:10 of the earth and avenge our **b**?"
　　　6:12 hair, the whole moon turned **b** red,
　　　7:14 them white in the **b** of the Lamb.
　　　8: 8 A third of the sea turned into **b**,
　　　12:11 over him by the **b** of the Lamb
　　　19:13 He is dressed in a robe dipped in **b**,

FLESH AND BLOOD See FLESH

BLOODSHED BLOOD
Nu	35:33	**B** pollutes the land, and atonement
Ps	51:14	Deliver me from the guilt of **b**, O God,
Isa	5: 7	he looked for justice, but saw **b**;
Jer	48:10	who keeps their sword from **b**!
Eze	35: 6	I will give you over to **b** and it will
	35: 6	Since you did not hate **b**, **b** will pursue you.
Hab	2:12	to him who builds a city with **b**

BLOODSHOT* BLOOD
Pr 23:29 Who has **b** eyes?

BLOODTHIRSTY* BLOOD
Ps	5: 6	The **b** and deceitful you, LORD,
	26: 9	my life with those who are **b**,
	55:23	the **b** and deceitful will not live
	139:19	Away from me, you who are **b**!
Pr	29:10	The **b** hate a person of integrity

BLOOM
SS	2:15	our vineyards that are in **b**.
Isa	35: 2	it will burst into **b**; it will rejoice

BLOSSOM
Isa	35: 1	the wilderness will rejoice and **b**.
Hos	14: 5	dew to Israel; he will **b** like a lily.

BLOT BLOTS, BLOTTED
Ex	17:14	because I will completely **b**
	32:32	then **b** me out of the book you have
Dt	9:14	**b** out their name from under heaven.
Ne	4: 5	or **b** out their sins from your sight,
Ps	51: 1	to your great compassion **b** out my
Jer	18:23	or **b** out their sins from your sight.
Rev	3: 5	I will never **b** out the name

BLOTS* BLOT
Isa	43:25	"I, even I, am he who **b** out your
2Pe	2:13	They are **b** and blemishes, reveling

BLOTTED BLOT
Dt 25: 6 so that his name will not be **b**

BLOW BLEW, BLOWN, BLOWS
Jer	14:17	a grievous wound, a crushing **b**.
Eze	33: 6	does not **b** the trumpet to warn
Joel	2: 1	**B** the trumpet in Zion;

BLOWN BLOW
Eph	4:14	and **b** here and there by every wind
Jas	1: 6	of the sea, **b** and tossed by the wind.
Jude	1:12	without rain, **b** along by the wind;

BLOWS BLOW
Pr	6:33	**B** and disgrace are his lot, and his
	20:30	**B** and wounds scrub away evil,
Isa	40: 7	the breath of the LORD **b** on them.
Jn	3: 8	The wind **b** wherever it pleases.

BLUE
Ex	24:10	of lapis lazuli, as bright **b** as the sky.
	26:31	"Make a curtain of **b**,
	28:31	of the ephod entirely of **b** cloth,
Rev	9:17	red, dark **b**, and yellow as sulfur.

BLUSH*
Jer	3: 3	you refuse to **b** with shame.
	6:15	they do not even know how to **b**.
	8:12	they do not even know how to **b**.

BOANERGES*
Mk 3:17 John (to them he gave the name **B**,

BOARDS
Ex	27: 8	Make the altar hollow, out of **b**.
1Ki	6:15	lined its interior walls with cedar **b**,

BOAST BOASTED, BOASTERS, BOASTFUL, BOASTING, BOASTS
1Ki	20:11	his armor should not **b** like one who
Ps	44: 8	In God we make our **b** all day long,
	52: 1	Why do you **b** of evil, you mighty
	52: 1	Why do you **b** all day long,
	75: 4	To the arrogant I say, 'B no more,'
	97: 7	put to shame, those who **b** in idols—
Pr	27: 1	Do not **b** about tomorrow, for you
Isa	45:25	and will make their **b** in him.
Jer	9:23	"Let not the wise **b** of their wisdom or the strong **b** of their strength or the rich **b** of their riches,
	9:24	let the one who boasts **b** about this:
Ro	2:17	if you rely on the law and **b** in God;
	2:23	You who **b** in the law, do you
	5: 2	And we **b** in the hope of the glory
1Co	1:31	"Let the one who boasts **b**
	13: 4	envy, it does not **b**, it is not proud.
2Co	10: 8	So even if I **b** somewhat freely
	10:17	"Let the one who boasts **b**
	11:30	If I must **b**, I will **b** of the things
Gal	6:14	May I never **b** except in the cross
Eph	2: 9	not by works, so that no one can **b**.
Php	2:16	then I will be able to **b** on the day
	3: 3	by his Spirit, who **b** in Christ Jesus,
Jas	3:14	do not **b** about it or deny the truth.
	4:16	is, you **b** in your arrogant schemes.

BOASTED BOAST
Est	5:11	Haman **b** to them about his vast
Ac	8: 9	He **b** that he was someone great,

BOASTERS* BOAST
Jer	48:45	of Moab, the skulls of the noisy **b**.
Zep	3:11	remove from you your arrogant **b**.

BOASTFUL* BOAST
Ps	12: 3	flattering lips and every **b** tongue—
Da	7:11	the **b** words the horn was speaking.
Ro	1:30	insolent, arrogant and **b**;
2Ti	3: 2	lovers of money, **b**, proud, abusive,
2Pe	2:18	For they mouth empty, **b** words and,

BOASTING BOAST
Php	1:26	you again your **b** in Christ Jesus
1Co	5: 6	Your **b** is not good. Don't you know
2Co	10:13	will confine our **b** to the sphere
Jas	4:16	All such **b** is evil.

BOASTS BOAST
Pr	20:14	goes off and **b** about the purchase.
Rev	18: 7	In her heart she **b**, 'I sit enthroned

BOAT BOATS

Mt	4:21 in a **b** with their father Zebedee,
	8:23 he got into the **b** and his disciples
	13: 2 around him that he got into a **b**
	14:13 he withdrew by **b** privately
	14:29 Then Peter got down out of the **b**,
Jn	21: 6 your net on the right side of the **b**

BOATS BOAT

Lk	5: 7 filled both **b** so full that they began

BOAZ

Wealthy Bethlehemite who showed favor to Ruth (Ru 2), married her (Ru 4). Ancestor of David (Ru 4:18–22; 1Ch 2:12–15), Jesus (Mt 1:5–16; Lk 3:23–32).

BODIES BODY

Lev	19:28 " 'Do not cut your **b** for the dead
Nu	14:29 In this wilderness your **b** will fall—
1Ch	10:12 men went and took the **b** of Saul
Isa	26:19 will live, LORD; their **b** will rise—
Da	3:27 that the fire had not harmed their **b**,
Lk	21:26 for the heavenly **b** will be shaken.
Ro	1:24 of their **b** with one another.
	12: 1 to offer your **b** as a living sacrifice,
1Co	6:15 not know that your **b** are members
	6:19 not know that your **b** are temples
	6:20 Therefore honor God with your **b**.
Eph	5:28 to love their wives as their own **b**.
Php	3:21 will transform our lowly **b** so
Heb	10:22 and having our **b** washed with pure
Jude	1: 8 ungodly people pollute their own **b**,

BODILY BODY

Col	2: 9 fullness of the Deity lives in **b** form,

BODY BODIES, BODILY, EMBODIMENT

Ps	139:16 Your eyes saw my unformed **b**;
Pr	14:30 A heart at peace gives life to the **b**,
Ecc	12:12 end, and much study wearies the **b**.
Zec	13: 6 'What are these wounds on your **b**?'
Mal	2:15 You belong to him in **b** and spirit.
Mt	10:28 not be afraid of those who kill the **b**
	10:28 can destroy both soul and **b** in hell.
	26:26 "Take and eat; this is my **b**."
	27:58 he asked for Jesus' **b**, and Pilate
Mk	14:22 saying, "Take it; this is my **b**."
Lk	11:34 Your eye is the lamp of your **b**.
	11:34 your whole **b** also is full of light.
	11:34 your **b** also is full of darkness.
	12: 4 not be afraid of those who kill the **b**
	22:19 "This is my **b** given for you;
Jn	13:10 their whole **b** is clean.
Ac	2:31 of the dead, nor did his **b** see decay.
Ro	12: 4 even though your **b** is subject
	12: 4 us has one **b** with many members,
1Co	6:13 The **b**, however, is not meant
	6:13 for the Lord, and the Lord for the **b**.
	6:18 a person commits are outside the **b**,
	7: 4 not have authority over her own **b**
	7: 4 not have authority over his own **b**
	9:27 I strike a blow to my **b** and make it

1Co	11:24 "This is my **b**, which is for you;
	12:12 Just as a **b**, though one, has many
	12:12 but all its many parts form one **b**,
	12:13 by one Spirit so as to form one **b**—
	12:24 But God has put the **b** together,
	15:44 it is sown a natural **b**, it is raised a spiritual **b**.
2Co	5: 8 would prefer to be away from the **b**
Gal	6:17 I bear on my **b** the marks of Jesus.
Eph	1:23 which is his **b**, the fullness of him
	4:25 for we are all members of one **b**.
	5:30 for we are members of his **b**.
Php	1:20 Christ will be exalted in my **b**,
Col	1:24 for the sake of his **b**, which is
1Th	4: 4 learn to control your own **b** in a way
Heb	10: 5 desire, but a **b** you prepared for me;
Jas	2:26 As the **b** without the spirit is dead,
1Pe	2:24 bore our sins" in his **b** on the cross,
Jude	1: 9 with the devil about the **b** of Moses,

BOILS

Ex	9: 9 festering **b** will break out on people
Dt	28:27 will afflict you with the **b** of Egypt

BOLD BOLDLY, BOLDNESS, EMBOLDENED

Pr	21:29 The wicked put up a **b** front,
	28: 1 but the righteous are as **b** as a lion.
2Co	3:12 we have such a hope, we are very **b**.
	10: 1 but "**b**" toward you when away!
Phm	1: 8 although in Christ I could be **b**

BOLDLY BOLD

Ex	14: 8 Israelites, who were marching out **b**.
Ac	4:31 Spirit and spoke the word of God **b**.
	9:28 speaking **b** in the name of the Lord.
	14: 3 time there, speaking **b** for the Lord,

BOLDNESS* BOLD

Ac	4:29 to speak your word with great **b**.
	28:31 with all **b** and without hindrance!

BOLTS

Job	38:35 Do you send the lightning **b** on their
Ps	18:14 great **b** of lightning he routed them.

BONDAGE

Ezr	9: 9 God has not forsaken us in our **b**.
Ro	8:21 will be liberated from its **b** to decay

BONE BONES

Ge	2:23 "This is now **b** of my bones
Pr	25:15 and a gentle tongue can break a **b**.
Eze	37: 7 the bones came together, **b** to **b**.

BONES BONE

Ge	50:25 you must carry my **b** up from this
Ex	12:46 Do not break any of the **b**.
Jos	24:32 And Joseph's **b**, which the Israelites
2Ki	13:21 When the body touched Elisha's **b**,
Ps	22:14 water, and all my **b** are out of joint.
	22:17 All my **b** are on display;
	34:20 he protects all his **b**, not one of them
Pr	14:30 life to the body, but envy rots the **b**.
	15:30 and good news gives health to the **b**.
Jer	20: 9 like a fire, a fire shut up in my **b**.

Eze 37: 4 "Prophesy to these **b** and say to them,
              'Dry **b**, hear the word
Mt   23:27 inside are full of the **b** of the dead
Jn   19:36 "Not one of his **b** will be broken,"
Heb 11:22 concerning the burial of his **b**.

BOOK BOOKS
Ex   24: 7 Then he took the **B** of the Covenant
     32:33 against me I will blot out of my **b**.
Dt   31:24 finished writing in a **b** the words
Jos   1: 8 Keep this **B** of the Law always
     23: 6 that is written in the **B** of the Law
2Ki 22: 8 "I have found the **B** of the Law
2Ch 34:15 "I have found the **B** of the Law
Ne   8: 8 They read from the **B** of the Law
Ps   69:28 they be blotted out of the **b** of life
Da   12: 1 name is found written in the **b**—
Jn   20:30 which are not recorded in this **b**.
Ac   1: 1 In my former **b**, Theophilus, I wrote
      8:28 in his chariot reading the **B** of Isaiah
Php   4: 3 whose names are in the **b** of life.
Rev   3: 5 of that person from the **b** of life,
     13: 8 been written in the Lamb's **b** of life,
     17: 8 have not been written in the **b** of life
     20:12 Another **b** was opened, which is the
            b of life.
     20:15 written in the **b** of life was thrown
     21:27 are written in the Lamb's **b** of life.

BOOK OF THE LAW See LAW

BOOK OF THE ANNALS See ANNALS

WRITTEN IN THE BOOK See WRITTEN

BOOKS* BOOK
Ecc 12:12 Of making many **b** there is no end,
Da   7:10 was seated, and the **b** were opened.
Jn   21:25 for the **b** that would be written.
Rev 20:12 the throne, and **b** were opened.
     20:12 they had done as recorded in the **b**.

BOOTH
Lk   5:27 the name of Levi sitting at his tax **b**.

BORDER BORDERS
2Ch   9:26 Philistines, as far as the **b** of Egypt.
Ps   78:54 them to the **b** of his holy land,

BORDERS BORDER
Ex   23:31 "I will establish your **b**
Mal   1: 5 even beyond the **b** of Israel!'

BORE BEAR
Isa 53: 4 up our pain and **b** our suffering,
     53:12 For he **b** the sin of many, and made
Mt   8:17 our infirmities and **b** our diseases."
Ro   7: 5 in us, so that we **b** fruit for death.
Heb 13:13 the camp, bearing the disgrace he **b**.
1Pe   2:24 "He himself **b** our sins" in his body
Rev 17: 6 of those who **b** testimony to Jesus.

BORN BEAR
Ge   17:17 himself, "Will a son be **b** to a man
Job 14: 1 "Mortals, **b** of woman, are of few
Ps   90: 2 Before the mountains were **b** or you
Pr   17:17 and a brother is **b** for a time
Ecc   3: 2 a time to be **b** and a time to die,

Isa   9: 6 For to us a child is **b**, to us a son is
     66: 8 Can a country be **b** in a day
Jer   1: 5 before you were **b** I set you apart;
Mt   2: 1 After Jesus was **b** in Bethlehem
Lk   1:35 one to be **b** will be called the Son
      2:11 of David a Savior has been **b** to you;
      7:28 among those **b** of women there is no
Jn   1:13 children **b** not of natural descent,
      1:13 or a husband's will, but **b** of God.
      3: 3 of God unless they are **b** again."
      3: 5 of God unless they are **b** of water
      3: 7 my saying, 'You must be **b** again.'
      3: 8 it is with everyone **b** of the Spirit."
      8:58 "before Abraham was **b**, I am!"
1Co 15: 8 to me also, as to one abnormally **b**.
Gal   4: 4 God sent his Son, **b** of a woman,
1Pe   1:23 For you have been **b** again,
1Jn   3: 9 No one who is **b** of God will
      3: 9 because they have been **b** of God.
      4: 7 Everyone who loves has been **b**
      5: 1 that Jesus is the Christ is **b** of God,
      5: 4 everyone **b** of God overcomes
      5:18 the One who was **b** of God keeps
Rev 12: 4 her child the moment he was **b**.

BORNE BEAR
Hos   5:15 my lair until they have **b** their guilt

BORROW BORROWER
Dt   15: 6 many nations but will **b** from none.
Ps   37:21 The wicked **b** and do not repay,
Mt   5:42 the one who wants to **b** from you.

BORROWER* BORROW
Ex   22:15 animal, the **b** will not have to pay.
Pr   22: 7 and the **b** is slave to the lender.
Isa 24: 2 as for buyer, for **b** as for lender,

BOTHER BOTHERING
Lk   8:49 "Don't **b** the teacher anymore."
     11: 7 one inside answers, 'Don't **b** me.

BOTHERING BOTHER
Lk   18: 5 yet because this widow keeps **b** me,

BOTTOM
Am   9: 3 from my eyes at the **b** of the sea,
Mk   15:38 was torn in two from top to **b**.

BOUGHS
Ps 118:27 With **b** in hand, join in the festal
Eze 31: 6 the birds of the sky nested in its **b**,

BOUGHT BUY
Ge   25:10 the field Abraham had **b**
Ex   15:16 until the people you **b** pass by.
2Sa 24:24 So David **b** the threshing floor
Ne   5: 8 we have **b** back our fellow Jews
Job 28:15 It cannot be **b** with the finest gold,
Mt   13:46 and sold everything he had and **b** it.
Ac   1:18 for his wickedness, Judas **b** a field;
     20:28 which he **b** with his own blood.
1Co   6:20 you were **b** at a price.
      7:23 You were **b** at a price;
2Pe   2: 1 the sovereign Lord who **b** them—

BOUND BIND

Ge	22: 9	He **b** his son Isaac and laid him
Pr	22:15	Folly is **b** up in the heart of a child,
Jer	39: 7	**b** him with bronze shackles to take
	40: 1	He had found Jeremiah **b** in chains
Mt	16:19	bind on earth will be **b** in heaven,
	18:18	bind on earth will be **b** in heaven,
Lk	13:16	whom Satan has kept **b** for eighteen
	13:16	the Sabbath day from what **b** her?"
Ro	7: 2	by law a married woman is **b** to her
1Co	7:15	brother or the sister is not **b** in such
	7:39	A woman is **b** to her husband as
Jude	1: 6	**b** with everlasting chains
Rev	9:14	"Release the four angels who are **b**
	20: 2	and **b** him for a thousand years.

BOUNDARIES BOUNDARY

Ps	74:17	It was you who set all the **b**
Ac	17:26	in history and the **b** of their lands.

BOUNDARY BOUNDARIES, BOUNDLESS, BOUNDS

Nu	34: 3	Your southern **b** will start in the east
Dt	19:14	move your neighbor's **b** stone set
Job	24: 2	There are those who move **b** stones;
Ps	16: 6	The **b** lines have fallen for me
	104: 9	You set a **b** they cannot cross;
Pr	15:25	but he sets the widow's **b** stones
	22:28	Do not move an ancient **b** stone set
Eze	47:15	"This is to be the **b** of the land:
Hos	5:10	are like those who move **b** stones.

BOUNDLESS BOUNDARY

Ps	119:96	a limit, but your commands are **b**.
Eph	3: 8	the Gentiles the **b** riches of Christ,

BOUNDS* BOUNDARY

Hos	4: 2	they break all **b**, and bloodshed
2Co	7: 4	all our troubles my joy knows no **b**.

BOUNTY*

Ge	49:26	than the **b** of the age-old hills.
Dt	28:12	the storehouse of his **b**, to send rain
1Ki	10:13	he had given her out of his royal **b**.
Ps	65:11	You crown the year with your **b**,
	68:10	settled in it, and from your **b**, God,
Jer	31:12	will rejoice in the **b** of the LORD—
	31:14	people will be filled with my **b**,"

BOYS

2Ki	2:24	and mauled forty-two of the **b**.

BOW BOWED, BOWS

Ge	27:29	sons of your mother **b** down to you.
Dt	5: 9	You shall not **b** down to them
Jos	23: 7	not serve them or **b** down to them.
2Sa	1:18	this lament of the **b** (it is written
	22:35	my arms can bend a **b** of bronze.
1Ki	22:34	But someone drew his **b** at random
Ps	5: 7	in reverence I **b** down toward your
	44: 6	I put no trust in my **b**, my sword
	95: 6	Come, let us **b** down in worship,
	138: 2	I will **b** down toward your holy
Isa	44:19	Shall I **b** down to a block
	45:23	Before me every knee will **b**;

Mt	4: 9	"if you will **b** down and worship
Ro	14:11	Lord, 'every knee will **b** before me;
Php	2:10	name of Jesus every knee should **b**,
Rev	6: 2	Its rider held a **b**, and he was given

BOWED BOW

Ge	18: 2	meet them and **b** low to the ground.
	37: 7	around mine and **b** down to it."
	42: 6	they **b** down to him with their faces
Ex	34: 8	Moses **b** to the ground at once
2Ch	33: 3	He **b** down to all the starry hosts
Ps	35:14	I **b** my head in grief as though
	38: 6	I am **b** down and brought very low;
	145:14	fall and lifts up all who are **b** down.
	146: 8	lifts up those who are **b** down,
Mt	2:11	and they **b** down and worshiped
Jn	19:30	he **b** his head and gave up his spirit.

BOWELS

2Ch	21:15	ill with a lingering disease of the **b**,

BOWL BOWLS

Mk	4:21	bring in a lamp to put it under a **b**
Rev	16: 2	and poured out his **b** on the land,

BOWLS BOWL

Rev	5: 8	they were holding golden **b** full
	16: 1	pour out the seven **b** of God's wrath

BOWS BOW

Ps	66: 4	All the earth **b** down to you;
Isa	44:15	he makes an idol and **b** down to it.
	46: 1	Bel **b** down, Nebo stoops low;

BOY BOY'S, BOYS

Ge	21:17	God heard the **b** crying,
	22:12	"Do not lay a hand on the **b**,"
Lev	12: 3	On the eighth day the **b** is to be
Jdg	13: 5	by a razor because the **b** is to be
1Sa	2:11	the **b** ministered before the LORD
	3: 8	that the LORD was calling the **b**.
Isa	7:16	for before the **b** knows enough
	8: 4	For before the **b** knows how to say
Mt	17:18	and it came out of the **b**, and he was
Lk	2:43	home, the **b** Jesus stayed behind

BOY'S BOY

1Ki	17:22	and the **b** life returned to him,
2Ki	4:34	out on him, the **b** body grew warm.

BOYS BOY

Ge	25:24	there were twin **b** in her womb.
	38:27	there were twin **b** in her womb.
Ex	1:18	Why have you let the **b** live?"
Mt	2:16	orders to kill all the **b** in Bethlehem

BRACE*

Job	38: 3	**B** yourself like a man; I will question
	40: 7	"**B** yourself like a man; I will question
Na	2: 1	watch the road, **b** yourselves,

BRACELETS

Ge	24:22	two gold **b** weighing ten shekels.
Eze	16:11	I put **b** on your arms and a necklace

BRAG*

Am	4: 5	**b** about your freewill offerings—

BRAIDS
Jdg 16:13 you weave the seven **b** of my head
16:13 Delilah took the seven **b** of his head,

BRANCH BRANCHES
Nu 13:23 they cut off a **b** bearing a single
Isa 4: 2 that day the **B** of the LORD will be
11: 1 from his roots a **B** will bear fruit.
14:19 out of your tomb like a rejected **b**;
Jer 23: 5 raise up for David a righteous **B**,
33:15 I will make a righteous **B** sprout
Zec 3: 8 going to bring my servant, the **B**.
6:12 is the man whose name is the **B**,
6:12 and he will **b** out from his place
Jn 15: 2 He cuts off every **b** in me that bears
15: 2 while every **b** that does bear fruit he
15: 4 No **b** can bear fruit by itself;

BRANCHES BRANCH
Ge 30:38 he placed the peeled **b** in all
Ex 25:32 Six **b** are to extend from the sides
Dt 24:20 do not go over the **b** a second time.
Eze 17: 6 Its **b** turned toward him, but its roots
17: 6 and produced **b** and put out leafy
Zec 4:12 are these two olive **b** beside the two
Lk 13:19 tree, and the birds perched in its **b**."
Jn 12:13 They took palm **b** and went
15: 5 "I am the vine; you are the **b**.
Ro 11:21 if God did not spare the natural **b**,
Rev 7: 9 were holding palm **b** in their hands.

BRAVE BRAVEST
2Sa 2: 7 then, be strong and **b**, for Saul your
13:28 you this order? Be strong and **b**."
1Ch 12: 8 They were **b** warriors,

BRAVEST* BRAVE
2Sa 17:10 Then even the **b** soldier,
Am 2:16 Even the **b** warriors will flee naked

BRAWLER*
Pr 20: 1 Wine is a mocker and beer a **b**;

BRAZEN*
Pr 7:13 him and with a **b** face she said:
Jer 3: 3 Yet you have the **b** look
Eze 16:30 things, acting like a **b** prostitute!

BREACH BREAK
Ps 106:23 stood in the **b** before him to keep his

BREACHING* BREAK
Ps 144:14 There will be no **b** of walls, no going
Pr 17:14 Starting a quarrel is like **b** a dam;

BREAD
Ex 12: 8 herbs, and **b** made without yeast.
12:17 the Festival of Unleavened **B**,
16: 4 "I will rain down **b** from heaven
23:15 the Festival of Unleavened **B**;
23:15 for seven days eat **b** made without
25:30 Put the **b** of the Presence on this
Dt 8: 3 that man does not live on **b** alone
16: 3 Do not eat it with **b** made
16: 3 for seven days eat unleavened **b**, the **b**
of affliction,

1Ki 17: 6 The ravens brought him **b** and meat
22:27 give him nothing but **b** and water
2Ch 4:19 on which was the **b** of the Presence;
Ne 9:15 their hunger you gave them **b**
Ps 37:25 forsaken or their children begging **b**.
41: 9 one who shared my **b**, has turned
78:25 Human beings ate the **b** of angels;
Pr 30: 8 riches, but give me only my daily **b**.
Isa 55: 2 Why spend money on what is not **b**,
Mt 4: 3 God, tell these stones to become **b**."
4: 4 'Man shall not live on **b** alone,
6:11 Give us today our daily **b**.
15:33 "Where could we get enough **b**
16: 5 lake, the disciples forgot to take **b**.
26:26 Jesus took **b**, and when he had given
Lk 11: 3 Give us each day our daily **b**.
22:19 And he took **b**, gave thanks
24:35 by them when he broke the **b**.
Jn 6:33 For the **b** of God is the **b** that comes
6:35 Jesus declared, "I am the **b** of life.
6:41 "I am the **b** that came down
6:48 I am the **b** of life.
6:51 I am the living **b** that came down
6:51 Whoever eats this **b** will live
6:51 This **b** is my flesh, which I will give
13:27 As soon as Judas took the **b**,
21:13 took the **b** and gave it to them,
Ac 2:42 to the breaking of **b** and to prayer.
1Co 10:16 And is not the **b** that we break
11:23 the night he was betrayed, took **b**,
11:26 For whenever you eat this **b**

THE FESTIVAL OF UNLEAVENED BREAD
See FESTIVAL

BREAK BREACH, BREACHING,
BREAKERS, BREAKING, BREAKS,
BROKE, BROKEN, BROKENNESS,
LAWBREAKER, LAWBREAKERS
Ex 12:46 Do not **b** any of the bones.
Nu 30: 2 he must not **b** his word but must do
Jos 22:16 'How could you **b** faith
Jdg 2: 1 'I will never **b** my covenant
Ps 2: 9 You will **b** them with a rod of iron;
Pr 25:15 and a gentle tongue can **b** a bone.
Isa 42: 3 A bruised reed he will not **b**,
Mt 12:20 A bruised reed he will not **b**,
15: 3 why do you **b** the command of God
Jn 19:33 dead, they did not **b** his legs.
Ac 20: 7 week we came together to **b** bread.
Ro 2:25 law, but if you **b** the law, you have
1Co 10:16 the bread that we **b** a participation
Rev 5: 2 "Who is worthy to **b** the seals

BREAKERS* BREAK
Ps 42: 7 waves and **b** have swept over me.
93: 4 mightier than the **b** of the sea—
Jnh 2: 3 all your waves and **b** swept over me.

BREAKING BREAK
Ex 32:19 **b** them to pieces at the foot
Lev 26:44 **b** my covenant with them. I am
Dt 31:20 rejecting me and **b** my covenant.
Jos 9:20 fall on us for **b** the oath we swore

Eze 16:59 despised my oath by **b** the covenant.
    17:18 despised the oath by **b** the covenant.
Zec 11:14 **b** the family bond between Judah
Ac   2:42 to the **b** of bread and to prayer.
Ro   2:23 do you dishonor God by **b** the law?
Jas 2:10 just one point is guilty of **b** all of it.

BREAKS BREAK
Ex   1:10 if war **b** out, will join our enemies,
Ps 29: 5 voice of the LORD **b** the cedars;
    76:12 He **b** the spirit of rulers; he is feared
Jer 23:29 "and like a hammer that **b** a rock
Da   2:40 for iron **b** and smashes everything—
1Jn 3: 4 Everyone who sins **b** the law;

BREAST BREASTPIECE, BREASTPLATE, BREASTPLATES, BREASTS
Ps 22: 9 trust in you, even at my mother's **b**.
Eze 21:12 Therefore beat your **b**.
Lk 18:13 but beat his **b** and said, 'God,

BREASTPIECE BREAST
Ex 28:15 "Fashion a **b** for making decisions—
    28:30 Urim and the Thummim in the **b**,

BREASTPLATE* BREAST
2Ch 18:33 hit the king of Israel between the **b**
Isa 59:17 He put on righteousness as his **b**,
Eph 6:14 with the **b** of righteousness in place,
1Th 5: 8 putting on faith and love as a **b**,

BREASTPLATES BREAST
Rev 9: 9 They had **b** like **b** of iron,

BREASTS BREAST
Pr   5:19 may her **b** satisfy you always,
SS   4: 5 Your **b** are like two fawns, like twin
La   4: 3 Even jackals offer their **b** to nurse
Na   2: 7 moan like doves and beat on their **b**.

BREATH BREATHED, BREATHING, GOD-BREATHED
Ge   1:30 everything that has the **b** of life
     2: 7 into his nostrils the **b** of life,
     6:17 every creature that has the **b** of life
Ex 15:10 But you blew with your **b**,
Nu 16:22 God who gives **b** to all living things,
    27:16 LORD, the God who gives **b** to all
2Sa 22:16 at the blast of **b** from his nostrils.
Job 27: 3 me, the **b** of God in my nostrils,
Ps 39: 5 Everyone is but a **b**, even those who
    150: 6 that has **b** praise the LORD.
Ecc 3:19 All have the same **b**;
La   4:20 our very life **b**, was caught in their
Eze 37: 8 them, but there was no **b** in them.
Ac 17:25 he himself gives everyone life and **b**
Rev 11:11 a half days the **b** of life from God
    13:15 given power to give **b** to the image

BREATHED BREATH
Ge   2: 7 **b** into his nostrils the breath of life,
Mk 15:37 With a loud cry, Jesus **b** his last.
Jn 20:22 with that he **b** on them and said,

BREATHING BREATH
Ac   9: 1 Saul was still **b** out murderous

BRIBE BRIBED, BRIBERY, BRIBES
Ex 23: 8 "Do not accept a **b**, for a **b** blinds
Dt 16:19 Do not accept a **b**, for a **b** blinds
    27:25 "Cursed is anyone who accepts a **b**
1Sa 12: 3 whose hand have I accepted a **b**
Pr   6:35 he will refuse a **b**, however great it
Ecc 7: 7 a fool, and a **b** corrupts the heart.
Isa 5:23 who acquit the guilty for a **b**,
Mic 3:11 Her leaders judge for a **b**, her priests
Ac 24:26 that Paul would offer him a **b**, so he

BRIBED* BRIBE
Ezr 4: 5 They **b** officials to work against

BRIBERY* BRIBE
2Ch 19: 7 is no injustice or partiality or **b**."

BRIBES BRIBE
Dt 10:17 no partiality and accepts no **b**.
1Sa 8: 3 accepted **b** and perverted justice.

BRICK BRICKS
Ge 11: 3 They used **b** instead of stone,
Ex   1:14 lives bitter with harsh labor in **b**

BRICKS BRICK
Ge 11: 3 "Come, let's make **b** and bake them

BRIDE BRIDE-PRICE
Ge 34:12 Make the price for the **b** and the gift
1Sa 18:25 for the **b** than a hundred Philistine
Ps 45: 9 at your right hand is the royal **b**
SS   4: 8 my **b**, come with me from Lebanon.
Isa 49:18 you will put them on, like a **b**.
    62: 5 as a bridegroom rejoices over his **b**,
Jer 2:32 a **b** her wedding ornaments?
Jn   3:29 The **b** belongs to the bridegroom.
Rev 19: 7 and his **b** has made herself ready.
    21: 2 prepared as a **b** beautifully dressed
    21: 9 I will show you the **b**, the wife
    22:17 The Spirit and the **b** say, "Come!"

BRIDE-PRICE* BRIDE
Ex 22:16 he must pay the **b**, and she shall be
    22:17 he must still pay the **b** for virgins.

BRIDEGROOM
Ex   4:25 "Surely you are a **b** of blood
Ps 19: 5 It is like a **b** coming out of his
Jer 25:10 the voices of bride and **b**, the sound
Mt 25: 1 lamps and went out to meet the **b**.
    25: 5 The **b** was a long time in coming,
Mk   2:20 will come when the **b** will be taken
Rev 18:23 The voice of **b** and bride will never

BRIDLE*
Ps 32: 9 but must be controlled by bit and **b**
Pr 26: 3 for the horse, a **b** for the donkey,

BRIEF*
Ezr 9: 8 for a **b** moment, the LORD our
Job 20: 5 that the mirth of the wicked is **b**,
Isa 54: 7 "For a **b** moment I abandoned you,

BRIER* BRIERS
Mic 7: 4 The best of them is like a **b**,

BRIERS BRIER
Isa 55:13 instead of **b** the myrtle will grow.
Lk   6:44 from thornbushes, or grapes from **b**.

BRIGHT BRIGHTENS, BRIGHTER, BRIGHTNESS
SS   6:10 dawn, fair as the moon, **b** as the sun,
Lk   9:29 his clothes became as **b** as a flash
Ac 22: 6 suddenly a **b** light from heaven
Rev 19: 8 Fine linen, **b** and clean, was given
     22:16 of David, and the **b** Morning Star."

BRIGHTENS* BRIGHT
Pr 16:15 When a king's face **b**, it means life;
Ecc 8: 1 A person's wisdom **b** their face

BRIGHTER BRIGHT
Pr   4:18 shining ever **b** till the full light
Ac 26:13 a light from heaven, **b** than the sun,

BRIGHTNESS* BRIGHT
2Sa 22:13 Out of the **b** of his presence bolts
     23: 4 like the **b** after rain that brings grass
Ps 18:12 Out of the **b** of his presence clouds
Isa 59: 9 for **b**, but we walk in deep shadows.
     60: 3 and kings to the **b** of your dawn.
     60:19 nor will the **b** of the moon shine
Da 12: 3 who are wise will shine like the **b**
Am   5:20 pitch-dark, without a ray of **b**?

BRILLIANCE* BRILLIANT
Ac 22:11 because the **b** of the light had
Rev 1:16 was like the sun shining in all its **b**.
     21:11 its **b** was like that of a very precious

BRILLIANT* BRILLIANCE
Ecc 9:11 or wealth to the **b** or favor
Eze 1: 4 lightning and surrounded by **b** light.
     1:27 and **b** light surrounded him.

BRIM*
Pr   3:10 and your vats will **b** over with new
Jn   2: 7 so they filled them to the **b**.

BRIMSTONE (KJV) See SULFUR

BRING BRINGING, BRINGS, BROUGHT
Ge   6:17 I am going to **b** floodwaters
     6:19 You are to **b** into the ark two of all
     28:15 and I will **b** you back to this land.
Ex   3: 8 to **b** them up out of that land
     6:26 "**B** the Israelites out of Egypt
     18:22 have them **b** every difficult case
     25: 2 the Israelites to **b** me an offering.
     32:12 do not **b** disaster on your people.
Nu 20: 5 Why did you **b** us up out of Egypt
Dt 24: 4 Do not **b** sin upon the land
     26:10 now I **b** the firstfruits of the soil
1Ki 21:21 'I am going to **b** disaster on you.
2Ki 22:16 I am going to **b** disaster on this
Pr   3: 8 This will **b** health to your body
     10: 4 but diligent hands **b** wealth.

Pr 11:17 but the cruel **b** ruin on themselves.
     18: 6 The lips of fools **b** them strife,
     29:11 rage, but the wise **b** calm in the end.
Isa 40: 9 You who **b** good news to Zion,
     40: 9 You who **b** good news to Jerusalem,
     52: 7 the feet of those who **b** good news,
     52: 7 proclaim peace, who **b** good tidings,
     54: 7 deep compassion I will **b** you back.
Jer 24: 6 and I will **b** them back to this land.
Eze 5:17 and I will **b** the sword against you.
Da   9:24 to **b** in everlasting righteousness,
Hos 4: 1 a charge to **b** against you who live
Lk 12:51 Do you think I came to **b** peace
Jn 10:16 this sheep pen. I must **b** them also.
Ro 10:15 feet of those who **b** good news!"
1Co 8: 8 But food does not **b** us near to God;
2Jn 1:10 to you and does not **b** this teaching,
Rev 15: 4 Lord, and **b** glory to your name?

BRINGING BRING
Ex 36: 5 "The people are **b** more than
Isa 1:13 Stop **b** meaningless offerings!
Mt 27:13 testimony they are **b** against you?"
Lk 18:15 **b** babies to Jesus for him to place
Heb 2:10 In **b** many sons and daughters

BRINGS BRING
Dt   6:10 the LORD your God **b** you
1Sa 2: 6 "The LORD **b** death and makes
     2: 6 he **b** down to the grave and raises
Pr 12:18 but the tongue of the wise **b** healing.
     15:20 A wise son **b** joy to his father,
Lk   6:45 A good man **b** good things
     6:45 an evil man **b** evil things
Ro   4:15 because the law **b** wrath.
2Co 7:10 Godly sorrow **b** repentance
     7:10 regret, but worldly sorrow **b** death.
Heb 1: 6 when God **b** his firstborn

BRITTLE*
Da   2:42 will be partly strong and partly **b**.

BROAD
2Sa 12:11 sleep with your wives in **b** daylight.
Isa 33:21 It will be like a place of **b** rivers
Mt   7:13 gate and **b** is the road that leads
2Pe 2:13 pleasure is to carouse in **b** daylight.

BROKE BREAK
Ex   9:10 and festering boils **b** out on people
     34: 1 on the first tablets, which you **b**.
2Ch 34: 4 These he **b** to pieces and scattered
     36:19 and **b** down the wall of Jerusalem;
Jer 31:32 Egypt, because they **b** my covenant,
Eze 44: 7 and blood, and you **b** my covenant.
Zec 11:10 took my staff called Favor and **b** it,
Mt 26:26 he **b** it and gave it to his disciples,
     27:52 and the tombs **b** open. The bodies
Mk 14:22 he **b** it and gave it to his disciples,
Ac   2:46 They **b** bread in their homes and ate
     20:11 he went upstairs again and **b** bread
1Co 11:24 had given thanks, he **b** it and said,
Rev 16: 2 festering sores **b** out on the people

BROKEN BREAK

1Sa	2:10	who oppose the LORD will be **b**.
	4:18	His neck was **b** and he died, for he
	5: 4	hands had been **b** off and were lying
Ne	1: 3	The wall of Jerusalem is **b** down,
Ps	34:20	his bones, not one of them will be **b**.
	51:17	My sacrifice, O God, is a **b** spirit;
	51:17	a **b** and contrite heart you, God,
Ecc	4:12	of three strands is not quickly **b**.
	12: 6	is severed, and the golden bowl is **b**;
	12: 6	spring, and the wheel **b** at the well,
Jer	2:13	**b** cisterns that cannot hold water.
Da	8: 8	its power the large horn was **b** off,
Hos	6: 7	at Adam, they have **b** the covenant;
Lk	20:18	on that stone will be **b** to pieces;
Jn	7:23	that the law of Moses may not be **b**,
	19:36	"Not one of his bones will be **b**,"
Ro	11:20	they were **b** off because of unbelief,

BROKENHEARTED* HEART

Ps	34:18	The LORD is close to the **b**
	109:16	the poor and the needy and the **b**.
	147: 3	He heals the **b** and binds up their
Isa	61: 1	He has sent me to bind up the **b**,

BROKENNESS* BREAK

Isa	65:14	of heart and wail in **b** of spirit.

BRONZE

Ge	4:22	forged all kinds of tools out of **b**
Ex	27: 2	piece, and overlay the altar with **b**.
	30:18	"Make a **b** basin, with its **b** stand,
Lev	26:19	and the ground beneath you like **b**.
Nu	21: 9	So Moses made a **b** snake and put it
Dt	28:23	The sky over your head will be **b**,
1Ki	7:15	He cast two **b** pillars, each eighteen
	7:27	also made ten movable stands of **b**;
2Ki	16:14	As for the **b** altar that stood before
	25:13	Babylonians broke up the **b** pillars,
	25:13	the **b** Sea that were at the temple
	25:13	and they carried the **b** to Babylon.
Ps	18:34	my arms can bend a bow of **b**.
Isa	48: 4	were iron, your forehead was **b**.
Da	2:32	of silver, its belly and thighs of **b**,
	10: 6	legs like the gleam of burnished **b**,
Zec	6: 1	mountains of **b**.
Rev	1:15	His feet were like **b** glowing
	1:18	and whose feet are like burnished **b**.

BROOD

Nu	32:14	"And here you are, a **b** of sinners,
Job	30: 8	A base and nameless **b**, they were
Isa	57: 4	Are you not a **b** of rebels,
Lk	3: 7	baptized by him, "You **b** of vipers!
2Pe	2:14	are experts in greed—an accursed **b**!

BROOK

1Ki	17: 4	You will drink from the **b**, and I
Ps	110: 7	will drink from a **b** along the way,

BROOM

1Ki	19: 4	He came to a **b** bush, sat down

BROTHER BROTHER'S, BROTHER-IN-LAW, BROTHERHOOD, BROTHERS

Ge	4: 8	Cain attacked his **b** Abel and killed
	20:13	say of me, "He is my **b**.' ' "
	27:41	then I will kill my **b** Jacob."
	42:20	you must bring your youngest **b**
	43:30	Deeply moved at the sight of his **b**,
	45: 4	"I am your **b** Joseph, the one you
Ex	7: 1	your **b** Aaron will be your prophet.
Dt	25: 5	Her husband's **b** shall take her
2Sa	13:12	"No, my **b**!" she said to him.
Pr	17:17	a **b** is born for a time of adversity.
	18:24	a friend who sticks closer than a **b**.
SS	8: 1	If only you were to me like a **b**,
Isa	19: 2	**b** will fight against **b**,
Ob	1:10	the violence against your **b** Jacob,
Mt	5:22	that anyone who is angry with a **b**
	5:22	anyone who says to a **b** or sister,
	10:21	"**B** will betray **b** to death,
	18:15	"If your **b** or sister sins,
Mk	3:35	Whoever does God's will is my **b**
Lk	15:28	"The older **b** became angry
	17: 3	"If your **b** or sister sins against you,
Ro	14:13	obstacle in the way of a **b** or sister.
	14:15	If your **b** or sister is distressed
	14:15	If your **b** or sister is distressed
	14:21	anything else that will cause your **b**
1Co	5:11	anyone who claims to be a **b** or sister
	6: 6	one **b** takes another to court—
	7:15	The **b** or the sister is not bound
	8:13	if what I eat causes my **b** or sister
Phm	1:16	but better than a slave, as a dear **b**.
	1:16	a fellow man and as a **b** in the Lord.
Jas	2:15	Suppose a **b** or a sister is without
	4:11	Anyone who speaks against a **b**
1Jn	2:10	who loves their **b** and sister lives in
	2:11	hates a **b** or sister is in the darkness
	3:10	who does not love their **b** and sister.
	3:15	who hates a **b** or sister is a murderer,
	3:17	and sees a **b** or sister in need but has
	4:20	claims to love God yet hates a **b**
	4:20	For whoever does not love their **b**
	4:21	loves God must also love their **b** and
	5:16	If you see any **b** or sister commit

BROTHER OR SISTER Nu 6:7; Mt 5:22, 22, 23; 18:15, 21, 35; Lk 17:3; Ro 14:10, 13, 15, 21; 1Co 5:11; 8:11, 13; 1Th 4:6; Jas 2:15; 4:11; 1Jn 2:9, 11; 3:15, 17; 4:20; 5:16

BROTHER'S BROTHER

Ge	4: 9	"Am I my **b** keeper?"
Dt	25: 7	does not want to marry his **b** wife,
	25: 7	to carry on his **b** name in Israel.
Mt	7: 5	to remove the speck from your **b** eye.
Mk	6:18	for you to have your **b** wife."

BROTHER-IN-LAW BROTHER

Ge	38: 8	your duty to her as a **b** to raise
Dt	25: 5	her and fulfill the duty of a **b** to her.

BROTHERHOOD* BROTHER

Am	1: 9	to Edom, disregarding a treaty of **b**,

BROTHERS BROTHER
Ge   9:25 of slaves will he be to his **b**."
      27:29 Be lord over your **b**, and may
      37:11 His **b** were jealous of him, but his
Jdg   9: 5 one stone murdered his seventy **b**,
2Ch 21:13 have also murdered your own **b**,
Hos 2: 1 "Say of your **b**, 'My people,'
Mt 12:49 "Here are my mother and my **b**.
      19:29 everyone who has left houses or **b**
      25:40 did for one of the least of these **b**
Mk   3:33 "Who are my mother and my **b**?"
      12:20 Now there were seven **b**.
Lk   21:16 even by parents, **b** and sisters,
      22:32 turned back, strengthen your **b**."
Jn   7: 5 For even his own **b** did not believe
Ro   8:29 be the firstborn among many **b**
Eph 6:23 Peace to the **b** and sisters, and love
Col   1: 2 the faithful **b** and sisters in Christ:
1Th 4:10 Yet we urge you, **b** and sisters, to do
2Th 3: 6 we command you, **b** and sisters,
1Ti   5: 1 Treat younger men as **b**,
Heb 2:11 Jesus is not ashamed to call them **b**
      13: 1 Keep on loving one another as **b**
1Jn   3:16 down our lives for our **b** and sisters.
Rev 12:10 For the accuser of our **b** and sisters,

BROTHERS AND SISTERS Jos 2:13; 6:23;
Job 42:11; Mt 25:40; Lk 14:26; 21:16; Ac 1:16; 6:3;
11:29; 12:17; 16:40; 18:18, 27; 21:7, 17; 28:14, 15;
Ro 1:13; 7:1, 4; 8:12, 29; 10:1; 11:25; 12:1; 15:14,
30; 16:14, 17; 1Co 1:10, 11, 26; 2:1; 3:1; 4:6; 6:8;
7:24, 29; 10:1; 11:33; 12:1; 14:6, 20, 26, 39; 15:1,
6, 50, 58; 16:15, 20; 2Co 1:8; 8:1; 13:11; Gal 1:2,
11; 3:15; 4:12, 28, 31; 5:11, 13; 6:1, 18; Eph 6:23;
Php 1:12, 14; 3:1, 13, 17; 4:1, 8, 21; Col 1:2; 4:15;
1Th 1:4; 2:1, 9, 14, 17; 3:7; 4:1, 10, 13; 5:1, 4, 12,
14, 25, 27; 2Th 1:3; 2:1, 13, 15; 3:1, 6, 13; 1Ti 4:6;
2Ti 4:21; Heb 2:11, 12; 3:1, 12; 10:19; 13:1, 22;
Jas 1:2, 16, 19; 2:1, 5, 14; 3:10, 12; 4:11; 5:7, 9, 10,
12, 19; 2Pe 1:10; 1Jn 3:13, 16; 3Jn 1:5; Rev 6:11;
12:10; 19:10

BROUGHT BRING
Ge   2:19 He **b** them to the man to see what he
      2:22 of the man, and he **b** her to the man.
      15: 7 LORD, who **b** you out of Ur
      21: 6 Sarah said, "God has **b** me laughter,
Ex   13: 9 For the LORD **b** you out of Egypt
      18:26 The difficult cases they **b** to Moses,
      32: 1 for this fellow Moses who **b** us
Nu 11:11 "Why have you **b** this trouble
      21: 5 said, "Why have you **b** us
Dt   8:15 He **b** you water out of hard rock.
Jdg   2: 1 "I **b** you up out of Egypt and led
1Ch 11:14 the LORD **b** about a great victory.
Ne   9:15 in their thirst you **b** them water
Ps   18:19 He **b** me out into a spacious place;
      30: 3 **b** me up from the realm of the dead;
Pr   8:22 "The LORD **b** me forth as the first
La   1: 5 The LORD has **b** her grief because
Eze 11: 1 **b** me to the gate of the house
      37: 1 and he **b** me out by the Spirit
Da   5:13 So Daniel was **b** before the king,
      5:13 the exiles my father the king **b**

Jnh   2: 6 my God, **b** my life up from the pit.
Mt 12:20 he has **b** justice through to victory.
Mk   6:28 and **b** back his head on a platter.
      8:22 and some people **b** a blind man
      12:16 They **b** the coin, and he asked them,
      15:22 They **b** Jesus to the place called
Ro   5:20 The law was **b** in so that the trespass
      6:13 God as those who have been **b**
2Co 3: 7 Now if the ministry that **b** death,
Eph 2:13 were far away have been **b** near
Col   2:10 Christ you have been **b** to fullness.
1Ti   6: 7 For we **b** nothing into the world,
Heb 6: 6 away, to be **b** back to repentance.
     11: 4 faith Abel **b** God a better offering

BROW
Ge   3:19 your **b** you will eat your food until

BROWN*
Zec   1: 8 him were red, **b** and white horses.

BRUISE* BRUISED, BRUISES
Ex   21:25 for burn, wound for wound, **b** for **b**.

BRUISED BRUISE
Isa   42: 3 A **b** reed he will not break,
Mt 12:20 A **b** reed he will not break,

BRUISES* BRUISE
Pr   23:29 Who has needless **b**?
Isa 30:26 LORD binds up the **b** of his people

BRUTAL* BRUTE
Eze 21:31 deliver you into the hands of **b** men,
2Ti   3: 3 without self-control, **b**, not lovers

BRUTE* BRUTAL, BRUTES
Ps   73:22 I was a **b** beast before you.
Pr   30: 2 Surely I am only a **b**, not a man;

BRUTES* BRUTE
Titus 1:12 always liars, evil **b**, lazy gluttons."

BUBBLING*
Isa 35: 7 a pool, the thirsty ground **b** springs.

BUCKET*
Isa 40:15 the nations are like a drop in a **b**;

BUCKLED*
Eph 6:14 belt of truth **b** around your waist,

BUD BUDDED
Isa 27: 6 Israel will **b** and blossom and fill all
Hab 3:17 Though the fig tree does not **b**

BUDDED BUD
Nu 17: 8 had not only sprouted but had **b**,
Eze 7:10 forth, the rod has **b**, arrogance has
Heb 9: 4 Aaron's staff that had **b**,

BUILD BUILDER, BUILDERS, BUILDING, BUILDINGS, BUILDS, BUILT, REBUILD, REBUILT
Ge   6:15 This is how you are to **b** it:
     11: 4 "Come, let us **b** ourselves a city,
Ex   27: 1 "**B** an altar of acacia wood,

Nu   23: 1 said, "**B** me seven altars here,
Dt   6:10 flourishing cities you did not **b**,
2Sa   7: 5 Are you the one to **b** me a house
1Ki   6: 1 he began to **b** the temple
Ezr   1: 3 and **b** the temple of the LORD,
Ps   51:18 Zion, to **b** up the walls of Jerusalem.
Ecc   3: 3 a time to tear down and a time to **b**,
Isa 57:14 "**B** up, **b** up, prepare the road!
     62:10 **B** up, **b** up the highway!
Mic   3:10 who **b** Zion with bloodshed,
Zep   1:13 Though they **b** houses, they will not
Hag   1: 8 bring down timber and **b** my house,
Mt   16:18 and on this rock I will **b** my church,
     23:29 You **b** tombs for the prophets
     27:40 the temple and **b** it in three days,
Jn   2:20 forty-six years to **b** this temple,
Ac   20:32 which can **b** you up and give you
Ro   15: 2 for their good, to **b** them up.
1Co   3:10 But each one should **b** with care.
     14:12 excel in those that **b** up the church.
1Th   5:11 one another and **b** each other up,

BUILDER* BUILD

Isa 62: 5 woman, so will your **B** marry you;
1Co   3:10 I laid a foundation as a wise **b**,
      3:14 the **b** will receive a reward.
      3:15 the **b** will suffer loss but yet will be
Heb   3: 3 just as the **b** of a house has greater
      3: 4 but God is the **b** of everything.
     11:10 whose architect and **b** is God.

BUILDERS BUILD

Ps 118:22 The stone the **b** rejected has become
    127: 1 builds the house, the **b** labor in vain.
Mt   21:42 " 'The stone the **b** rejected has
Mk   12:10 " 'The stone the **b** rejected has
Lk   20:17 " 'The stone the **b** rejected has
Ac   4:11 is " 'the stone you **b** rejected,
1Pe   2: 7 "The stone the **b** rejected has

BUILDING BUILD

Ge   11: 5 and the tower the people were **b**.
1Ki   9: 1 Solomon had finished **b** the temple
2Ki 25: 9 Every important **b** he burned down.
Ezr   4: 1 the exiles were **b** a temple
Ne   4:17 who were **b** the wall.
Mic   7:11 The day for **b** your walls will come,
Lk   6:48 They are like a man **b** a house,
Ro   15:20 I would not be **b** on someone else's
1Co   3: 9 you are God's field, God's **b**.
2Co   5: 1 is destroyed, we have a **b** from God,
     10: 8 authority the Lord gave us for **b** you
     13:10 the Lord gave me for **b** you up,
Eph   2:21 him the whole **b** is joined together
      4:29 only what is helpful for **b** others
Jude 1:20 by **b** yourselves up in your most

BUILDINGS BUILD

Mk   13: 1 What magnificent **b**!"

BUILDS BUILD

Ps 127: 1 Unless the LORD **b** the house,
    147: 2 The LORD **b** up Jerusalem;
Pr   14: 1 The wise woman **b** her house,
Jer 22:13 "Woe to him who **b** his palace

Hab   2: 9 "Woe to him who **b** his house
      2:12 "Woe to him who **b** a city
1Co   3:12 If anyone **b** on this foundation using
      8: 1 puffs up while love **b** up.
Eph   4:16 grows and **b** itself up in love,

BUILT BUILD

Ge   8:20 Noah **b** an altar to the LORD and,
     12: 7 So he **b** an altar there
     22: 9 about, Abraham **b** an altar there
     26:25 Isaac **b** an altar there and called
     35: 7 There he **b** an altar, and he called
Ex   17:15 Moses **b** an altar and called it
     24: 4 **b** an altar at the foot of the mountain
     32: 5 he **b** an altar in front of the calf
Jos   8:30 Joshua **b** on Mount Ebal an altar
     22:11 heard that they had **b** the altar
Jdg   6:24 So Gideon **b** an altar to the LORD
1Sa   7:17 he **b** an altar there to the LORD.
     14:35 Then Saul **b** an altar to the LORD;
2Sa 24:25 David **b** an altar to the LORD
1Ki   6:14 So Solomon **b** the temple
     12:31 Jeroboam **b** shrines on high places
2Ki 23:12 the altars Manasseh had **b** in the two
Ezr   3: 3 they **b** the altar on its foundation
Ps 122: 3 Jerusalem is **b** like a city that is
Pr   9: 1 Wisdom has **b** her house;
     24: 3 By wisdom a house is **b**,
Hos 10: 1 his fruit increased, he **b** more altars;
Zec   8: 9 strong so that the temple may be **b**.'
Mt   7:24 is like a wise man who **b** his house
Lk   6:49 practice is like a man who **b** a house
Ac   17:24 live in temples **b** by human hands.
1Co   3: 9 so that the church may be **b** up.
     14:26
2Co   5: 1 in heaven, not **b** by human hands.
Eph   2:20 **b** on the foundation of the apostles
      4:12 that the body of Christ may be **b**
Col   2: 7 rooted and **b** up in him,
Heb 11: 7 in holy fear **b** an ark to save his
1Pe   2: 5 are being **b** into a spiritual house
      3:20 of Noah while the ark was being **b**.

BULL BULLS

Ex   21:28 "If a **b** gores a man or woman to
            death, the **b** is to be stoned to death,
Lev   1: 5 to slaughter the young **b** before
      4: 3 LORD a young **b** without defect as
     16: 6 offer the **b** for his own sin offering
Ps   50: 9 I have no need of a **b** from your stall
    106:20 glorious God for an image of a **b**,
Isa 66: 3 whoever sacrifices a **b** is like one

BULLS BULL

Ex   24: 5 sacrificed young **b** as fellowship
Nu   23: 1 prepare seven **b** and seven rams
     29:11 a burnt offering of thirteen young **b**,
1Ki   7:25 The Sea stood on twelve **b**,
1Ch 29:21 a thousand **b**, a thousand rams
Ezr   6:17 of God they offered a hundred **b**,
Ps   22:12 Many **b** surround me; strong **b**
     50:13 Do I eat the flesh of **b** or drink
Jer 52:20 and the twelve bronze **b** under it,
Heb 10: 4 It is impossible for the blood of **b**

BURDEN BURDENED, BURDENS, BURDENSOME

Nu	11:14	the **b** is too heavy for me.
Ps	38: 4	overwhelmed me like a **b** too heavy
Ecc	1:13	What a heavy **b** God has laid
	3:10	I have seen the **b** God has laid
Isa	1:14	They have become a **b** to me;
	10:27	that day their **b** will be lifted
Mal	1:13	And you say, 'What a **b**!'
Mt	11:30	my yoke is easy and my **b** is light."
Ac	15:28	and to us not to **b** you with anything
2Co	11: 9	something, I was not a **b** to anyone,
	11: 9	kept myself from being a **b** to you
	12:14	and I will not be a **b** to you,
2Th	3: 8	so that we would not be a **b** to any
Heb	13:17	joy, not a **b**, for that would be of no
Rev	2:24	'I will not impose any other **b**

BURDENED* BURDEN

Isa	43:23	I have not **b** you with grain
	43:24	But you have **b** me with your sins
Mic	6: 3	How have I **b** you? Answer me.
Mt	11:28	all you who are weary and **b**, and I
2Co	5: 4	we groan and are **b**, because we do
Gal	5: 1	do not let yourselves be **b** again
1Ti	5:16	not let the church be **b** with them,

BURDENS BURDEN

Ps	68:19	our Savior, who daily bears our **b**.
Lk	11:46	down with **b** they can hardly carry,
Gal	6: 2	Carry each other's **b**, and in this

BURDENSOME* BURDEN

Isa	46: 1	images that are carried about are **b**,
1Jn	5: 3	And his commands are not **b**,

BURIAL BURY

Ge	23: 4	for a **b** site here so I can bury my
	49:30	the field as a **b** place from Ephron
Mt	26:12	body, she did it to prepare me for **b**.
	27: 7	to buy the potter's field as a **b** place

BURIED BURY

Ge	15:15	in peace and be **b** at a good old age.
Ru	1:17	die I will die, and there I will be **b**.
Ecc	8:10	Then too, I saw the wicked **b**—
Ro	6: 4	We were therefore **b** with him
1Co	15: 4	that he was **b**, that he was raised
Col	2:12	having been **b** with him in baptism,

BURIES* BURY

Pr	19:24	A sluggard **b** his hand in the dish;
	26:15	A sluggard **b** his hand in the dish;

BURN BURNED, BURNING, BURNT

Ex	3: 2	the bush was on fire it did not **b** up.
	21:25	**b** for **b**, wound for wound,
Dt	6:15	and his anger will **b** against you,
	7: 5	poles and **b** their idols in the fire.
	29:20	wrath and zeal will **b** against them.
Ps	79: 5	long will your jealousy **b** like fire?
	89:46	long will your wrath **b** like fire?
Jer	7:31	of Ben Hinnom to **b** their sons
Lk	3:17	barn, but he will **b** up the chaff

1Co	7: 9	to marry than to **b** with passion.
2Co	11:29	into sin, and I do not inwardly **b**?

BURNED BURN

Ex	4:14	the LORD's anger **b** against Moses
	32:19	his anger **b** and he threw the tablets
Nu	11: 3	the LORD had **b** among them.
Pr	6:27	his lap without his clothes being **b**?
Jer	36:23	until the entire scroll was **b**
1Co	3:15	If it is **b** up, the builder will suffer
Heb	6: 8	In the end it will be **b**.
Rev	8: 7	A third of the earth was **b** up, a third of the trees were **b** up, and all the green grass was **b** up.

BURNING BURN

Ex	27:20	so that the lamps may be kept **b**.
Lev	6: 9	the fire must be kept **b** on the altar.
Ps	18:28	You, LORD, keep my lamp **b**;
	118:12	consumed as quickly as **b** thorns;
Pr	25:22	you will heap **b** coals on his head,
Am	4:11	You were like a **b** stick snatched
Zec	3: 2	Is not this man a **b** stick snatched
Ac	7:30	the flames of a **b** bush in the desert
Ro	12:20	you will heap **b** coals on his head."
Rev	19:20	alive into the fiery lake of **b** sulfur.
	20:10	was thrown into the lake of **b** sulfur,
	21: 8	to the fiery lake of **b** sulfur.

BURNISHED*

1Ki	7:45	of the LORD were of **b** bronze.
Eze	1: 7	of a calf and gleamed like **b** bronze.
Da	10: 6	and legs like the gleam of **b** bronze,
Rev	2:18	and whose feet are like **b** bronze.

BURNT BURN

Ge	8:20	birds, he sacrificed **b** offerings on it.
	22: 2	Sacrifice him there as a **b** offering
Ex	10:25	**b** offerings to present to the LORD
	18:12	brought a **b** offering and other
	40: 6	"Place the altar of **b** offering
Lev	1: 3	the offering is a **b** offering
	6: 9	the regulations for the **b** offering:
	6: 9	The **b** offering is to remain
Jos	8:31	offered to the LORD **b** offerings
	22:26	but not for **b** offerings or sacrifices.'
Jdg	6:26	the second bull as a **b** offering."
	13:16	But if you prepare a **b** offering,
1Ki	3: 4	offered a thousand **b** offerings
	9:25	year Solomon sacrificed **b** offerings
	10: 5	and the **b** offerings he made
Ezr	3: 2	Israel to sacrifice **b** offerings on it,
	8:35	captivity sacrificed **b** offerings
	8:35	All this was a **b** offering
Job	1: 5	he would sacrifice a **b** offering
Ps	51:16	do not take pleasure in **b** offerings.
Isa	1:11	more than enough of **b** offerings,
	40:16	its animals enough for **b** offerings.
Eze	43:18	for sacrificing **b** offerings
Hos	6: 6	of God rather than **b** offerings.
Mic	6: 6	I come before him with **b** offerings,
Mk	12:33	more important than all **b** offerings
Heb	10: 6	with **b** offerings and sin offerings

BURNT OFFERING Ge 22:2, 3, 6, 7, 8, 13;

Ex 18:12; 29:18, 25, 42; 30:9, 28; 31:9; 35:16; 38:1;
40:6, 10, 29; Lev 1:3, 4, 6, 9, 10, 13, 14, 17; 3:5; 4:7,
10, 18, 24, 25, 29, 30, 33, 34; 5:7, 10; 6:9, 9, 10, 12,
25; 7:2, 8, 37; 8:18, 21, 28; 9:2, 3, 7, 12, 13, 14, 16,
17, 22, 24; 10:19; 12:6, 8; 14:13, 19, 22, 31; 15:15,
30; 16:3, 5, 24, 24; 17:8; 22:18; 23:12, 18; Nu 6:11,
14, 16; 7:15, 21, 27, 33, 39, 45, 51, 57, 63, 69, 75,
81, 87; 8:12; 15:5, 8, 24; 28:3, 6, 10, 10, 11, 13, 14,
15, 19, 23, 24, 27, 31; 29:2, 8, 11, 13, 16, 19, 22, 25,
28, 31, 34, 36, 38; Dt 13:16; Jdg 6:26; 11:31; 13:16,
23; 1Sa 6:14; 7:9, 10; 13:9, 9, 12; 2Sa 24:22; 2Ki
10:25; 16:13, 15, 15, 15; 1Ch 6:49; 16:40; 21:24, 26,
29; 22:1; 2Ch 7:1; 29:18, 24, 27, 28; Ezr 8:35; Job
1:5; 42:8; Eze 43:24; 45:23; 46:2, 4, 12, 12, 13, 15

BURNT OFFERINGS Ge 8:20; Ex 10:25; 20:24;
24:5; 32:6; 40:29; Lev 23:37; Nu 10:10; 15:3; 29:6,
39; Dt 12:6, 11, 13, 27; 27:6; 33:10; Jos 8:31; 22:23,
26, 27, 28, 29; Jdg 20:26; 21:4; 1Sa 6:15; 10:8;
15:22; 2Sa 6:17, 18; 24:24, 25; 1Ki 3:4, 15; 8:64, 64;
9:25; 10:5; 2Ki 5:17; 10:24; 16:15; 1Ch 16:1, 2, 40;
21:23, 26; 23:31; 29:21; 2Ch 1:6; 2:4; 4:6; 7:7, 7;
8:12; 9:4; 13:11; 23:18; 24:14, 14; 29:7, 31, 32, 32,
34, 35, 35; 30:15; 31:2, 3, 3; 35:12, 14, 16; Ezr 3:2,
3, 4, 5, 6; 6:9; 8:35; Ne 10:33; Ps 20:3; 40:6; 50:8;
51:16, 19; 66:13; Isa 1:11; 40:16; 43:23; 56:7; Jer
6:20; 7:21, 22; 14:12; 17:26; 33:18; Eze 40:38, 39,
42, 42; 43:18, 27; 44:11; 45:15, 17, 17, 25; Hos 6:6;
Am 5:22; Mic 6:6; Mk 12:33; Heb 10:6, 8

BURST
Ge   7:11 the springs of the great deep **b** forth,
Job 32:19 wine, like new wineskins ready to **b**.
Ps   60: 1 rejected us, God, and **b** upon us;
       98: 4 **b** into jubilant song with music;
Isa 35: 2 it will **b** into bloom; it will rejoice
     44:23 **B** into song, you mountains,
     49:13 **b** into song, you mountains!
     52: 9 **B** into songs of joy together,
     54: 1 **b** into song, shout for joy, you who
     55:12 hills will **b** into song before you,
Jer 23:19 the storm of the Lᴏʀᴅ will **b**
Eze   7:10 Doom has **b** forth, the rod has
Lk   5:37 the new wine will **b** the skins;
Ac   1:18 his body **b** open and all his

BURY BURIAL, BURIED, BURIES
Ge   23: 4 site here so I can **b** my dead."
     47:29 Do not **b** me in Egypt,
     50: 7 So Joseph went up to **b** his father.
Mt   8:22 and let the dead **b** their own dead."
Lk   9:60 "Let the dead **b** their own dead,

BUSH
Ex   3: 2 in flames of fire from within a **b**.
       3: 2 though the **b** was on fire it did not
Dt   33:16 of him who dwelt in the burning **b**.
Mk   12:26 in the account of the burning **b**,
Lk   20:37 But in the account of the burning **b**,
Ac   7:35 angel who appeared to him in the **b**.

BUSINESS
Ecc   4: 8 too is meaningless—a miserable **b**!
Da   8:27 got up and went about the king's **b**.
Ac   19:24 in a lot of **b** for the craftsmen there.

1Co   5:12 What **b** is it of mine to judge those
1Th   4:11 You should mind your own **b**
Jas   1:11 even while they go about their **b**.
       4:13 there, carry on **b** and make money."

BUSY* BUSYBODIES
1Ki 18:27 is deep in thought, or **b**, or traveling.
     20:40 While your servant was **b** here
Hag   1: 9 of you is **b** with your own house.
2Th   3:11 They are not **b**; they are busybodies.
Titus 2: 5 pure, to be **b** at home, to be kind,

BUSYBODIES* BUSY
2Th   3:11 They are not busy; they are **b**.
1Ti   5:13 idlers, but also **b** who talk nonsense,

BUY BOUGHT, BUYS
Ge   41:57 to Egypt to **b** grain from Joseph,
Ex   21: 2 "If you **b** a Hebrew servant, he is
Dt   28:68 slaves, but no one will **b** you.
Ru   4: 5 the day you **b** the land from Naomi,
2Sa 24:21 "To **b** your threshing floor,"
Pr   23:23 **B** the truth and do not sell it—
Isa 55: 1 have no money, come, **b** and eat!
     55: 1 **b** wine and milk without money
Jer 32: 7 and say, 'B my field at Anathoth,
     32: 7 it is your right and duty to **b** it.'
Mt   27: 7 **b** the potter's field as a burial place
Rev   3:18 I counsel you to **b** from me gold
     13:17 so that they could not **b** or sell

BUYS* BUY
Lev 22:11 But if a priest **b** a slave with money,
Pr   31:16 She considers a field and **b** it;
Rev 18:11 her because no one **b** their cargoes

BYWORD WORD
1Ki   9: 7 become a **b** and an object of ridicule
Job 17: 6 "God has made me a **b** to everyone,
Ps   44:14 made us a **b** among the nations;
Eze 23:10 She became a **b** among women,
Joel 2:17 of scorn, a **b** among the nations.

C

CAESAR
Mt   22:21 give back to **C** what is Caesar's,
Lk   2: 1 In those days **C** Augustus issued
       3: 1 year of the reign of Tiberius **C**—
Jn   19:12 this man go, you are no friend of **C**.
     19:12 claims to be a king opposes **C**."
Ac   25:11 me over to them. I appeal to **C**!"
     26:32 free if he had not appealed to **C**."

CAESAREA
Mt   16:13 came to the region of **C** Philippi,
Ac   10: 1 At **C** there was a man named
     12:19 Herod went from Judea to **C**
     25: 4 "Paul is being held at **C**, and I

CAIAPHAS*
     High priest at trial of Jesus (Mt 26:3, 57; Lk 3:2;
Jn 11:49; 18:13–28); at trial of disciples (Ac 4:6).

CAIN*
Firstborn of Adam (Ge 4:1), murdered brother Abel (Ge 4:1–25; Heb 11:4; 1Jn 3:12; Jude 11).

CAKES
Jer	7:18	and make c to offer to the Queen
	44:19	we were making c impressed
Hos	3: 1	gods and love the sacred raisin c."

CALAMITIES CALAMITY
Dt	31:17	disasters and c will come on them,
	31:21	many disasters and c come on them,
	32:23	"I will heap c on them and spend
1Sa	10:19	you out of all your disasters and c.
La	3:38	mouth of the Most High that both c

CALAMITY CALAMITIES
Ne	13:18	that our God brought all this c on us
Pr	21:23	tongues keep themselves from c.
	22: 8	Whoever sows injustice reaps c,
	24:16	the wicked stumble when c strikes.
Eze	7:26	C upon c will come, and rumor
Joel	2:13	love, and he relents from sending c.
Jnh	4: 2	a God who relents from sending c.

CALCULATE*
Rev	13:18	who has insight c the number

CALEB
Judahite who spied out Canaan (Nu 13:6); allowed to enter land because of faith (Nu 13:30—14:38; Dt 1:36). Given Hebron (Jos 14:6—15:19).

CALF CALF-IDOL, CALVES
Ex	32: 4	into an idol cast in the shape of a c,
Dt	9:16	an idol cast in the shape of a c.
Pr	15:17	love than a fattened c with hatred.
Isa	11: 6	the c and the lion and the yearling
Jer	31:18	disciplined me like an unruly c,
Lk	15:23	Bring the fattened c and kill it.
Ac	7:41	they made an idol in the form of a c.

CALF-IDOL* CALF, IDOL
Hos	8: 5	Samaria, throw out your c!
	10: 5	Samaria fear for the c of Beth Aven.

CALL CALLED, CALLING, CALLS, SO-CALLED
Ge	4:26	time people began to c on the name
	30:13	The women will c me happy."
Ex	3:15	the name you shall c me
Dt	4:26	I c the heavens and the earth as
Ru	1:20	"Don't c me Naomi," she told
	1:20	"C me Mara, because the Almighty
1Ki	18:24	you c on the name of your god,
	18:24	I will c on the name of the LORD.
Ps	4: 1	Answer me when I c to you,
	10:13	"He won't c me to account"?
	50:15	and c on me in the day of trouble;
	61: 2	the ends of the earth I c to you,
	86: 3	me, Lord, for I c to you all day long.
	116:13	and c on the name of the LORD.
	145:18	LORD is near to all who c on him, to all who c on him in truth.
Pr	1:28	"Then they will c to me but I will

Pr	8: 1	Does not wisdom c out?
	31:28	Her children arise and c her blessed;
Ecc	3:15	and God will c the past to account.
Isa	5:20	Woe to those who c evil good
	7:14	to a son, and will c him Immanuel.
	55: 6	c on him while he is near.
	65:24	Before they c I will answer;
Jer	33: 3	'C to me and I will answer you
La	3:21	Yet this I c to mind and therefore I
Hos	1: 4	said to Hosea, "C him Jezreel,
	2:16	"you will c me 'my husband';
	2:16	will no longer c me 'my master.'
Jnh	1: 6	Get up and c on your god!
	3: 8	Let everyone c urgently on God.
Zep	3: 9	all of them may c on the name
Zec	13: 9	They will c on my name and I will
Mal	3:12	all the nations will c you blessed,
Mt	1:23	they will c him Immanuel"
	9:13	I have not come to c the righteous,
Mk	10:18	"Why do you c me good?"
Lk	1:31	to a son, and you are to c him Jesus.
	6:46	"Why do you c me, 'Lord, Lord,'
Jn	13:13	"You c me 'Teacher' and 'Lord,'
	15:15	I no longer c you servants,
Ac	2:39	all whom the Lord our God will c."
	9:14	to arrest all who c on your name."
	10:15	"Do not c anything impure
Ro	10:12	and richly blesses all who c on him,
	11:29	gifts and his c are irrevocable.
1Co	1: 2	all those everywhere who c
1Th	4: 7	For God did not c us to be impure,
2Ti	2:22	along with those who c on the Lord
Heb	2:11	is not ashamed to c them brothers
Jas	5:14	Let them c the elders of the church

CALLED CALL
Ge	1: 5	God c the light "day," and the darkness he c "night."
	1: 8	God c the vault "sky."
	1:10	God c the dry ground "land,"
	1:10	the gathered waters he c "seas."
	2:19	and whatever the man c each living
	2:23	she shall be c 'woman,' for she was
	12: 8	and c on the name of the LORD.
	17: 5	No longer will you be c Abram;
	21:33	and there he c on the name
	26:25	and c on the name of the LORD.
Ex	3: 4	God c to him from within the bush,
	16:31	people of Israel c the bread manna.
	19: 3	and the LORD c to him
1Sa	3: 4	Then the LORD c Samuel.
2Ch	7:14	my people, who are c by my name,
Ne	13:25	them and c curses down on them.
Ps	34: 6	This poor man c, and the LORD
	116: 4	I c on the name of the LORD:
SS	6: 9	women saw her and c her blessed;
Isa	9: 6	he will be c Wonderful Counselor,
	49: 1	Before I was born the LORD c me;
	56: 7	for my house will be c a house
La	3:55	I c on your name, LORD,
Hos	11: 1	him, and out of Egypt I c my son.
Mt	1:16	of Jesus who is c the Messiah.
	2:15	"Out of Egypt I c my son."
	5: 9	for they will be c children of God.

Mt 21:13 " 'My house will be c a house
       21:16 Lord, have c forth your praise'?"
       23: 8 "But you are not to be c 'Rabbi,'
Lk   1:32 will be c the Son of the Most High.
       1:35 to be born will be c the Son of God.
       1:76 will be c a prophet of the Most
     23:46 Jesus c out with a loud voice,
Jn 10:35 If he c them 'gods,' to whom
    15:15 Instead, I have c you friends,
Ro   1: 1 c to be an apostle and set apart
       1: 6 are among those Gentiles who are c
       1: 7 by God and c to be his holy people:
       8:28 who have been c according to his
       8:30 And those he predestined, he also c;
                those he c, he also justified;
1Co   1: 1 c to be an apostle of Christ Jesus
       1: 2 Jesus and c to be his holy people,
       1: 9 who has c you into fellowship
       1:24 but to those whom God has c,
       1:26 of what you were when you were c.
       7:15 God has c us to live in peace.
       7:17 to them, just as God has c them.
Gal   1: 6 quickly deserting the one who c you
       1:15 womb and c me by his grace,
       5:13 and sisters, were c to be free.
Eph   1:18 the hope to which he has c you,
       4: 4 just as you were c to one hope when
                you were c;
Php 3:14 which God has c me heavenward
Col   3:15 of one body you were c to peace.
2Th 2:14 He c you to this through our gospel,
1Ti   6:12 you were c when you made your
2Ti   1: 9 has saved us and c us to a holy life—
Heb 9:15 that those who are c may receive
    11:16 is not ashamed to be c their God,
Jas   2:23 and he was c God's friend.
1Pe   1:15 But just as he who c you is holy,
       2: 9 the praises of him who c you
       3: 9 to this you were c so that you may
       5:10 who c you to his eternal glory
2Pe   1: 3 of him who c us by his own glory
1Jn   3: 1 we should be c children of God!
Jude 1: 1 To those who have been c, who are
Rev 12: 9 that ancient serpent c the devil,
    16:16 that in Hebrew is c Armageddon.
    17:14 and with him will be his c,
    19:11 whose rider is c Faithful and True.

CALLING CALL

1Sa   3: 8 that the LORD was c the boy.
Isa   6: 3 And they were c to one another:
    40: 3 A voice of one c:
    41: 2 east, c him in righteousness to his
Mt   3: 3 "A voice of one c in the wilderness,
Mk   1: 3 "a voice of one c in the wilderness,
    10:49 On your feet! He's c you."
Lk   3: 4 "A voice of one c in the wilderness,
Jn   1:23 the voice of one c in the wilderness,
Ac 22:16 your sins away, c on his name.'
Eph   4: 1 worthy of the c you have received.
2Th 1:11 God may make you worthy of his c,
Heb 3: 1 who share in the heavenly c,
2Pe   1:10 make every effort to confirm your c

CALLOUS* CALLOUSED

Ps 17:10 They close up their c hearts,
   73: 7 From their c hearts comes iniquity;
 119:70 Their hearts are c and unfeeling,

CALLOUSED* CALLOUS

Isa   6:10 Make the heart of this people c;
Mt 13:15 this people's heart has become c;
Ac 28:27 this people's heart has become c;

CALLS CALL

Ps 147: 4 the stars and c them each by name.
Pr   1:20 Out in the open wisdom c aloud,
Isa 40:26 and c forth each of them by name.
Hos 7: 7 fall, and none of them c on me.
Joel 2:32 everyone who c on the name
     2:32 the survivors whom the LORD c.
Mt 22:43 by the Spirit, c him 'Lord'?
Jn 10: 3 He c his own sheep by name
Ac   2:21 everyone who c on the name
Ro   9:12 not by works but by him who c—
   10:13 "Everyone who c on the name
1Th 2:12 who c you into his kingdom
     5:24 The one who c you is faithful,
Rev 2:20 Jezebel, who c herself a prophet.
   13:10 This c for patient endurance
   13:18 This c for wisdom. Let the person
   14:12 This c for patient endurance
   17: 9 "This c for a mind with wisdom.

CALM CALMED, CALMS

Ps 107:30 They were glad when it grew c,
Pr 29:11 rage, but the wise bring c in the end.
Isa   7: 4 careful, keep c and don't be afraid.
Eze 16:42 I will be c and no longer angry.
Jnh 1:11 to make the sea c down for us?"
Mk   4:39 died down and it was completely c.

CALMED* CALM

Ne   8:11 The Levites c all the people, saying,
Ps 131: 2 But I have c and quieted myself,

CALMS* CALM

Pr 15:18 the one who is patient c a quarrel.

CALVARY (KJV) See SKULL

CALVES CALF

2Ki 10:29 worship of the golden c at Bethel
Mal 4: 2 go out and frolic like well-fed c.
Heb 9:12 means of the blood of goats and c;

CAME COME

Ge   7: 6 when the floodwaters c on the earth.
    11: 5 the LORD c down to see the city
Ex 13: 3 this day, the day you c out of Egypt,
    34: 5 the LORD c down in the cloud
Lev 9:24 Fire c out from the presence
Nu 12: 5 the LORD c down in a pillar
    24: 2 by tribe, the Spirit of God c on him
Jdg 3:10 The Spirit of the LORD c on him,
    6:34 Spirit of the LORD c on Gideon,
  11:29 Spirit of the LORD c on Jephthah.
    14: 6 the LORD c powerfully upon him
   14:19 the LORD c powerfully upon him.
   15:14 Lehi, the Philistines c toward him

Jdg 15:14 the LORD c powerfully upon him.
1Sa 10:10 the Spirit of God c powerfully
 11: 6 the Spirit of God c powerfully
 16:13 of the LORD c powerfully
 16:23 the spirit from God c on Saul,
 18:10 an evil spirit from God c forcefully
 19: 9 the LORD c on Saul as he was
 19:20 the Spirit of God c on Saul's men,
 19:23 But the Spirit of God c even on him,
 19:23 walked along prophesying until he c
1Ch 12:18 Then the Spirit c on Amasai,
2Ch 15: 1 The Spirit of God c on Azariah son
 20:14 of the LORD c on Jahaziel son
 24:20 the Spirit of God c on Zechariah son
Eze 2: 2 the Spirit c into me and raised me
 3:24 Then the Spirit c into me and raised
 11: 5 the Spirit of the LORD c on me,
Ac 10:44 the Holy Spirit c on all who heard
 11:15 the Holy Spirit c on them as he had
 19: 6 on them, the Holy Spirit c on them,

WORD OF THE LORD† CAME See WORD

CAMEL CAMEL'S
Lev 11: 4 The c, though it chews the cud,
Mt 19:24 easier for a c to go through the eye
 23:24 strain out a gnat but swallow a c.
Mk 10:25 easier for a c to go through the eye
Lk 18:25 easier for a c to go through the eye

CAMEL'S CAMEL
Mk 1: 6 John wore clothing made of c hair,

CAMP CAMPED, ENCAMP, ENCAMPED, ENCAMPS
Ge 32: 2 he said, "This is the c of God!"
Ex 16:13 quail came and covered the c,
 16:13 was a layer of dew around the c.
 33: 7 it outside the c some distance away,
 33: 7 to the tent of meeting outside the c.
Nu 11:26 and Medad, had remained in the c.
 11:26 them, and they prophesied in the c.
Dt 23:14 about in your c to protect you
 23:14 Your c must be holy, so that he will
1Sa 4: 7 "A god has come into the c,"
 26: 5 Saul was lying inside the c,
Heb 13:13 go to him outside the c,

OUTSIDE THE CAMP Ex 29:14; 33:7, 7; Lev 4:12, 21; 6:11; 8:17; 9:11; 10:4, 5; 13:46; 14:3; 16:27; 24:14, 23; Nu 5:3, 4; 12:14, 15; 15:35, 36; 19:3, 9; 31:13, 19; Dt 23:10, 12; Jos 6:23; Heb 13:11, 13

CAMPED CAMP
Ex 19: 2 Israel c there in the desert in front
Nu 33:49 of Moab they c along the Jordan
Jos 3: 1 where they c before crossing over.

CAN CAN'T, CANNOT
Ge 4:13 punishment is more than I c bear.
 15: 5 if indeed you c count them."
 19: 5 out to us so that we c have sex
 41:15 a dream, and no one c interpret it.
 41:15 hear a dream you c interpret it."
Nu 23: 8 How c I curse those whom God has

Nu 23: 8 How c I denounce those whom
Dt 32:39 no one c deliver out of my hand.
Job 25: 4 c a mortal be righteous before God?
 25: 4 How c one born of woman be pure?
 40: 4 how c I reply to you?
Ps 49: 7 No one c redeem the life of another
 56: 4 What c mere mortals do to me?
 139: 7 Where c I go from your Spirit?
 139: 7 Where c I flee from your presence?
Pr 20: 6 but a faithful person who c find?
 31:10 wife of noble character who c find?
Ecc 2:24 A person c do nothing better than
 7:13 Who c straighten what he has made
Isa 22:22 what he opens no one c shut,
 22:22 and what he shuts no one c open.
 64: 5 How then c we be saved?
Jer 33:20 'If you c break my covenant
Eze 37: 3 "Son of man, c these bones live?"
Da 2: 9 I will know that you c interpret it
Hos 11: 8 "How c I give you up, Ephraim?
 11: 8 How c I hand you over, Israel?
Joel 2:11 it is dreadful. Who c endure it?
Mt 6:24 "No one c serve two masters.
Mk 2: 7 Who c forgive sins but God alone?"
Lk 3: 8 these stones God c raise up children
 18:26 this asked, "Who then c be saved?"
Jn 3: 4 "How c someone be born
 6:44 "No one c come to me unless
 15: 5 apart from me you c do nothing.
Ro 8:31 God is for us, who c be against us?
 10:14 how c they believe in the one
 10:14 how c they hear without someone
1Co 13: 2 prophecy and c fathom all mysteries
 13: 2 have a faith that c move mountains,
Php 4:13 I c do all this through him who
Heb 13: 6 What c mere mortals do to me?"
Jas 2:14 C such faith save them?
 3: 8 no human being c tame the tongue.
1Jn 4: 2 is how you c recognize the Spirit
Rev 3: 7 What he opens no one c shut,
 3: 7 and what he shuts no one c open.
 13: 4 Who c wage war against it?"

CAN'T CAN
Mt 27:42 they said, "but he c save himself!
Jn 13:37 "Lord, why c I follow you now?

CANA
Jn 2: 1 third day a wedding took place at C

CANAAN CANAANITE, CANAANITES
Ge 9:25 he said, "Cursed be C!
 13:12 Abram lived in the land of C,
 42: 5 was famine in the land of C also.
Ex 6: 4 them to give them the land of C,
Lev 14:34 "When you enter the land of C,
 25:38 of Egypt to give you the land of C
Nu 13: 2 some men to explore the land of C,
 33:51 'When you cross the Jordan into C,
Dt 32:49 and view C, the land I am giving
Jdg 4: 2 into the hands of Jabin king of C,
1Ch 16:18 C as the portion you will inherit."
Ps 106:38 they sacrificed to the idols of C,

Zep   2: 5 of the LORD is against you, C,
Ac   13:19 he overthrew seven nations in C,

CANAANITE CANAAN
Ge   10:18 Later the C clans scattered
      28: 1 "Do not marry a C woman.
Jos   5: 1 all the C kings along the coast heard
Jdg   1:32 lived among the C inhabitants
Zec 14:21 day there will no longer be a C
Mt   15:22 A C woman from that vicinity came

CANAANITES CANAAN
Ge   12: 6 At that time the C were in the land.
Ex   33: 2 before you and drive out the C,
Jdg   1: 1 go up first to fight against the C?"
      3: 5 The Israelites lived among the C,

CANCEL CANCELED, CANCELING
Dt   15: 1 every seven years you must c debts.
Ne   10:31 the land and will c all debts.

CANCELED CANCEL
Mt   18:27 on him, c the debt and let him go.
Col   2:14 having c the charge of our legal

CANCELING CANCEL
Dt   15: 2 for c debts has been proclaimed.
      31:10 in the year for c debts,

CANNOT CAN
Ex   19:23 "The people c come up Mount
      33:20 he said, "you c see my face, for no
Nu   11:14 I c carry all these people by myself;
2Sa   5: 6 thought, "David c get in here."
1Ki   8:27 the highest heaven, c contain you.
Job 12:14 What he tears down c be rebuilt;
      12:14 those he imprisons c be released.
Ps   5: 5 The arrogant c stand in your
      115: 5 mouths, but c speak, eyes, but c see.
Ecc   1:15 What is crooked c be straightened;
      1:15 what is lacking c be counted.
SS   8: 7 Many waters c quench love; rivers c
Isa 45:20 wood, who pray to gods that c save.
Da   6: 8 it in writing so that it c be altered—
      6: 8 and Persians, which c be repealed."
Mt   5:14 A town built on a hill c be hidden.
      16: 3 but you c interpret the signs
Mk   3:24 against itself, that kingdom c stand.
Lk   16:13 You c serve both God and money."
Ro   8: 8 the realm of the flesh c please God.
Jas   1:13 For God c be tempted by evil,
1Jn   5:18 safe, and the evil one c harm them.

CANOPY*
2Sa 22:12 made darkness his c around him—
2Ki 16:18 He took away the Sabbath c
Ps   18:11 his covering, his c around him—
Isa   4: 5 everything the glory will be a c.
      40:22 stretches out the heavens like a c,
Jer 43:10 he will spread his royal c

CAPERNAUM
Mt   4:13 he went and lived in C, which was
      11:23 And you, C, will you be lifted
Jn   6:59 teaching in the synagogue in C.

CAPITAL
Dt   21:22 someone guilty of a c offense is put

CAPSTONE* STONE; see also
   CORNERSTONE
Zec   4: 7 he will bring out the c to shouts
      4:10 they see the chosen c in the hand

CAPTAIN
2Ki   1: 9 sent to Elijah a c with his company
      1: 9 The c went up to Elijah, who was
Jnh   1: 6 The c went to him and said,
Rev 18:17 "Every sea c, and all who travel

CAPTIVATE* CAPTURE
Pr   6:25 or let her c you with her eyes.

CAPTIVE CAPTURE
Ge   14:14 that his relative had been taken c,
Ps   69:33 and does not despise his c people.
SS   7: 5 the king is held c by its tresses.
Isa 52: 2 your neck, Daughter Zion, now a c.
Jer 13:17 the LORD's flock will be taken c.
Eze 21:24 have done this, you will be taken c.
Ac   8:23 are full of bitterness and c to sin."
2Co 10: 5 we take c every thought to make it
Col   2: 8 no one takes you c through hollow
2Ti   2:26 who has taken them c to do his will.

CAPTIVES CAPTURE
Ps   68:18 ascended on high, you took many c;
Isa 14: 2 They will make c of their captors
      61: 1 to proclaim freedom for the c
Eph   4: 8 he took many c and gave gifts to his

CAPTIVITY CAPTURE
Dt   28:41 them, because they will go into c.
2Ki 25:21 So Judah went into c,
Ps   144:14 no going into c, no cry of distress
Jer 15: 2 those for c, to c.'
      30: 3 Judah back from c and restore them
      52:27 So Judah went into c,
Eze 29:14 I will bring them back from c
Rev 13:10 "If anyone is to go into c, into c

CAPTORS CAPTURE
1Ki   8:47 plead with you in the land of their c
      8:50 cause their c to show them mercy;
Ps   137: 3 for there our c asked us for songs,

CAPTURE CAPTIVATE, CAPTIVE,
   CAPTIVES, CAPTIVITY, CAPTORS,
   CAPTURED
1Sa   4:21 because of the c of the ark of God
      19:14 When Saul sent the men to c David,
      23:26 in on David and his men to c them,
Mt   26:55 out with swords and clubs to c me?

CAPTURED CAPTURE
1Sa   4:11 The ark of God was c, and Eli's two
2Sa   5: 7 David c the fortress of Zion—
2Ki 17: 6 the king of Assyria c Samaria
Rev 19:20 But the beast was c, and with it

CARAVAN
2Ch   9: 1 Arriving with a very great c—

CARCASS CARCASSES
Jdg 14: 9 taken the honey from the lion's c.
Mt 24:28 Wherever there is a c,

CARCASSES CARCASS
Dt 28:26 Your c will be food for all the birds
1Sa 17:46 This very day I will give the c
Jer 7:33 the c of this people will become

CARE CARED, CAREFREE,
CAREFUL, CAREFULLY,
CARELESSLY, CARES, CARING
Ge 2:15 of Eden to work it and take c of it.
Nu 3:25 for the c of the tabernacle and tent,
Dt 7:11 take c to follow the commands,
1Ki 1: 2 to serve the king and take c of him.
Ps 8: 4 human beings that you c for them?
65: 9 You c for the land and water it;
95: 7 of his pasture, the flock under his c.
144: 3 human beings that you c for them,
Pr 12:10 The righteous c for the needs
29: 7 The righteous c about justice
Jer 15:15 remember me and c for me.
Eze 34: 2 of Israel who only take c
34: 2 Should not shepherds take c
Zec 10: 3 the LORD Almighty will c for his
Mk 5:26 had suffered a great deal under the c
Lk 10:34 him to an inn and took c of him.
18: 4 fear God or c what people think,
Jn 21:16 Jesus said, "Take c of my sheep."
1Co 3:10 But each one should build with c.
4: 3 I c very little if I am judged by you
Eph 5:29 but they feed and c for their body,
1Ti 3: 5 family, how can he take c of God's
6:20 what has been entrusted to your c.
Heb 2: 6 a son of man that you c for him?
1Pe 5: 2 of God's flock that is under your c,
Rev 12: 6 where she might be taken c

CARED CARE
Hos 12:13 Egypt, by a prophet he c for him.
Mk 15:41 followed him and c for his needs.

CAREFREE* CARE
Eze 23:42 noise of a c crowd was around her;

CAREFUL* CARE
Ge 31:24 "Be c not to say anything to Jacob,
31:29 'Be c not to say anything to Jacob,
Ex 19:12 'Be c that you do not approach
23:13 "Be c to do everything I have said
34:12 Be c not to make a treaty with those
34:15 "Be c not to make a treaty
Lev 18: 4 laws and be c to follow my decrees.
25:18 decrees and be c to obey my laws,
26: 3 and are c to obey my commands,
Dt 2: 4 will be afraid of you, but be very c.
4: 9 Only be c, and watch yourselves
4:23 Be c not to forget the covenant
5:32 So be c to do what the LORD your
6: 3 be c to obey so that it may go well
6:12 be c that you do not forget
6:25 we are c to obey all this law before
7:12 these laws and are c to follow them,

Dt 8: 1 Be c to follow every command I am
8:11 Be c that you do not forget
11:16 Be c, or you will be enticed to turn
12: 1 laws you must be c to follow
12:13 Be c not to sacrifice your burnt
12:19 Be c not to neglect the Levites as
12:28 Be c to obey all these regulations I
12:30 be c not to be ensnared by inquiring
15: 5 are c to follow all these commands I
15: 9 Be c not to harbor this wicked
17:10 Be c to do everything they instruct
24: 8 be very c to do exactly as
Jos 1: 7 Be c to obey all the law my servant
1: 8 that you may be c to do everything
22: 5 be very c to keep the commandment
23: 6 be c to obey all that is written
23:11 So be very c to love the LORD
1Ki 8:25 if only your descendants are c in all
2Ki 10:31 Yet Jehu was not c to keep the law
17:37 You must always be c to keep
21: 8 only they will be c to do everything
1Ch 22:13 if you are c to observe the decrees
28: 8 Be c to follow all the commands
2Ch 6:16 if only your descendants are c in all
33: 8 only they will be c to do everything
Ezr 4:22 Be c not to neglect this matter.
Job 36:18 Be c that no one entices you
Ps 45:10 daughter, and pay c attention:
101: 2 I will be c to lead a blameless life—
Pr 4:26 Give c thought to the paths for your
13:24 the one who loves their children is c
21:28 a c listener will testify successfully.
27:23 give c attention to your herds;
Isa 7: 4 him, 'Be c, keep calm and don't be
Jer 17:21 Be c not to carry a load
17:24 But if you are c to obey me,
22: 4 For if you are c to carry out these
Eze 11:20 decrees and be c to keep my laws.
18:19 has been c to keep all my decrees,
20:19 decrees and be c to keep my laws.
20:21 they were not c to keep my laws,
36:27 decrees and be c to keep my laws.
37:24 laws and be c to keep my decrees.
Hag 1: 5 "Give c thought to your ways.
1: 7 "Give c thought to your ways.
2:15 " 'Now give c thought to this
2:18 give c thought to the day
2:18 temple was laid. Give c thought:
Mt 6: 1 "Be c not to practice your
16: 6 "Be c," Jesus said to them.
23: 3 So you must be c to do everything
Mk 8:15 "Be c," Jesus warned them.
Lk 21:34 "Be c, or your hearts will be
Ro 12:17 Be c to do what is right in the eyes
1Co 8: 9 Be c, however, that the exercise
10:12 firm, be c that you don't fall!
Eph 5:15 Be very c, then, how you live—
2Ti 4: 2 great patience and c instruction.
Titus 3: 8 God may be c to devote themselves
Heb 2: 1 We must pay the most c attention,
4: 1 let us be c that none of you be found

CAREFULLY CARE
Ex 15:26 "If you listen c to the LORD your

Dt   28:58 If you do not **c** follow all the words
Pr   12:26 The righteous choose their friends **c**,
Da   10:11 consider **c** the words I am
Mt   2: 8 "Go and search **c** for the child.

CARELESSLY* CARE
Lev   5: 4 any matter one might **c** swear

CARES* CARE
Dt   11:12 a land the LORD your God **c** for;
Job   39:16 she **c** not that her labor was in vain,
Ps   55:22 Cast your **c** on the LORD and he
     142: 4 no one **c** for my life.
Ecc   5: 3 comes when there are many **c**,
Jer   12:11 because there is no one who **c**.
      30:17 outcast, Zion for whom no one **c**.'
Na   1: 7 He **c** for those who trust in him,
Jn   10:13 hand and **c** nothing for the sheep.
1Th   2: 7 Just as a nursing mother **c** for her
1Pe   5: 7 on him because he **c** for you.

CARGO
Eze   27:25 with heavy **c** as you sail the sea.
Jnh   1: 5 And they threw the **c** into the sea
Ac   27:18 began to throw the **c** overboard

CARING* CARE
1Ti   5: 4 practice by **c** for their own family

CARMEL
1Sa   25: 5 "Go up to Nabal at **C** and greet him
1Ki   18:20 the prophets on Mount **C**.

CARNAL, CARNALLY (KJV) See
FLESH, MATERIAL, SINFUL,
UNSPIRITUAL, WORLDLY

CARNELIAN
Ex   28:17 The first row shall be **c**,

CAROUSE* CAROUSING
2Pe   2:13 of pleasure is to **c** in broad daylight.

CAROUSING* CAROUSE
Lk   21:34 hearts will be weighed down with **c**,
Ro   13:13 daytime, not in **c** and drunkenness,
1Pe   4: 3 orgies, **c** and detestable idolatry.

CARPENTER* CARPENTER'S,
CARPENTERS
Isa   44:13 The **c** measures with a line
Mk   6: 3 Isn't this the **c**? Isn't this Mary's

CARPENTER'S* CARPENTER
Mt   13:55 "Isn't this the **c** son?

CARPENTERS CARPENTER
1Ch   14: 1 and **c** to build a palace for him.
2Ch   24:12 **c** to restore the LORD's temple,
Ezr   3: 7 gave money to the masons and **c**,

CARRIED CARRY
Ge   14:12 also **c** off Abram's nephew Lot
      40:15 I was forcibly **c** off from the land
Ex   19: 4 and how I **c** you on eagles' wings
Dt   1:31 how the LORD your God **c** you,
      31: 9 who **c** the ark of the covenant

Dt   33:21 he **c** out the LORD's righteous
Jos   3:15 as the priests who **c** the ark reached
1Sa   5: 2 they **c** the ark into Dagon's temple
      17:34 and **c** off a sheep from the flock,
2Ki   24:14 He **c** all Jerusalem into exile:
Ezr   6:12 Let it be **c** out with diligence.
Est   2: 6 who had been **c** into exile
Ecc   8:11 for a crime is not quickly **c** out,
Isa   63: 9 up and **c** them all the days of old.
Jer   52:28 the people Nebuchadnezzar **c**
Jn   20:15 if you have **c** him away, tell me
Heb   13: 9 Do not be **c** away by all kinds
2Pe   1:21 God as they were **c** along
       3:17 you may not be **c** away by the error
Rev   17: 3 the angel **c** me away in the Spirit
      21:10 And he **c** me away in the Spirit

CARRIES CARRY
Nu   11:12 as a nurse **c** an infant, to the land
Dt   1:31 as a father **c** his son, all the way you
      32:11 to catch them and **c** them aloft.
Isa   40:11 arms and **c** them close to his heart;
      44:26 who **c** out the words of his servants

CARRY CARRIED, CARRIES,
CARRYING
Ge   47:30 **c** me out of Egypt and bury me
      50:25 you must **c** my bones up from this
Ex   13:19 you must **c** my bones up with you
Lev   16:22 The goat will **c** on itself all their
      26:15 and fail to **c** out all my commands
Dt   10: 8 of Levi to **c** the ark of the covenant
1Ch   15: 2 the Levites may **c** the ark of God,
      15: 2 the LORD chose them to **c** the ark
Isa   45:20 Ignorant are those who **c** about idols
      46: 4 I have made you and I will **c** you;
Jer   51:12 The LORD will **c** out his purpose,
Hos   11: 9 I will not **c** out my fierce anger,
Mt   3:11 whose sandals I am not worthy to **c**.
      27:32 and they forced him to **c** the cross.
Lk   14:27 whoever does not **c** their cross
2Co   4:10 We always **c** around in our body
Gal   6: 2 **C** each other's burdens, and in this
       6: 5 each one should **c** their own load.

CARRYING CARRY
Lk   5:18 Some men came **c** a paralyzed man
      22:10 a man **c** a jar of water will meet
Jn   19:17 **C** his own cross, he went
1Jn   5: 2 God and **c** out his commands.

CART
1Sa   6: 7 get a new **c** ready, with two cows
       6: 7 Hitch the cows to the **c**, but take
1Ch   13: 7 from Abinadab's house on a new **c**,

CARVED
Nu   33:52 Destroy all their **c** images and their
1Ki   6:32 olive-wood doors he **c** cherubim,
Ps   74: 6 They smashed all the **c** paneling
     144:12 our daughters will be like pillars **c**
Eze   41:18 were **c** cherubim and palm trees.
Hab   2:18 "Of what value is an idol **c**

CASE CASES

Ex	18:22	have them bring every difficult c
Jos	20: 4	state their c before the elders
2Sa	15: 4	a complaint or c could come to me
1Ki	15: 5	except in the c of Uriah the Hittite.
2Ki	8: 6	he assigned an official to her c
Job	13: 8	Will you argue the c for God?
Pr	22:23	for the LORD will take up their c
	23:11	he will take up their c against you.
Isa	1:17	plead the c of the widow.
	41:21	"Present your c," says the LORD.
Jer	12: 1	when I bring a c before you.
La	3:58	You, Lord, took up my c;
Mic	6: 1	plead my c before the mountains;
Ac	23:35	said, "I will hear your c when your
	25:14	Festus discussed Paul's c

CASES CASE

Ex	18:26	The difficult c they brought
1Co	6: 2	not competent to judge trivial c?

CAST CASTING, CASTS, DOWNCAST

Ex	32: 4	made it into an idol c in the shape
Lev	16: 8	He is to c lots for the two goats—
Jos	18: 8	I will c lots for you here at Shiloh
1Ki	7:15	He c two bronze pillars,
Est	3: 7	is, the lot) was c in the presence
	9:24	had c the pur (that is, the lot)
Ps	22:18	them and c lots for my garment.
	55:22	C your cares on the LORD and he
	71: 9	Do not c me away when I am old;
Pr	16:33	The lot is c into the lap, but its
Isa	14:12	You have been c down to the earth,
La	3:31	no one is c off by the Lord forever.
Joel	3: 3	They c lots for my people
Ob	1:11	his gates and c lots for Jerusalem,
Jnh	1: 7	let us c lots to find out who is
	1: 7	They c lots and the lot fell on Jonah.
Jn	19:24	them and c lots for my garment."
Ac	1:26	Then they c lots, and the lot fell
1Pe	5: 7	C all your anxiety on him because

CASTING* CAST

Jdg	20: 9	it in the order decided by c lots.
1Ch	24: 5	divided them impartially by c lots,
Pr	18:18	C the lot settles disputes and keeps
Eze	26: 3	you, like the sea c up its waves.
Mt	4:18	They were c a net into the lake,
	27:35	they divided up his clothes by c lots.
Mk	1:16	his brother Andrew c a net
Lk	23:34	they divided up his clothes by c lots.

CASTS CAST

Dt	18:11	or c spells, or who is a medium
Isa	40:19	a metalworker c it, and a goldsmith
	44:10	Who shapes a god and c an idol,

CATASTROPHE*

Ge	19:29	the c that overthrew the cities where
Isa	47:11	a c you cannot foresee will suddenly

CATCH CATCHES, CAUGHT

Mt	17:27	Take the first fish you c;
Lk	5: 4	and let down the nets for a c."

Lk	11:54	waiting to c him in something he
	20:20	They hoped to c Jesus in something

CATCHES CATCH

Job	5:13	He c the wise in their craftiness,
1Co	3:19	"He c the wise in their craftiness";

CATTLE

Ge	12:16	and Abram acquired sheep and c,
1Sa	15:14	What is this lowing of c that I
2Sa	12: 2	a very large number of sheep and c,
Ps	50:10	mine, and the c on a thousand hills.
	104:14	He makes grass grow for the c,
Hab	3:17	in the pen and no c in the stalls,
Jn	2:14	courts he found people selling c,

CAUGHT CATCH

Ge	22:13	in a thicket he saw a ram c by its
	39:12	She c him by his cloak and said,
Ex	22: 7	the thief, if c, must pay back double.
Dt	24: 7	If someone is c kidnapping a fellow
2Sa	18: 9	Absalom's hair got c in the tree.
Lk	5: 5	all night and haven't c anything.
Jn	8: 4	this woman was c in the act of
2Co	12: 2	Christ who fourteen years ago was c
Gal	6: 1	if someone is c in a sin, you who
1Th	4:17	are left will be c up together

CAUSE CAUSED, CAUSES

Ex	23:33	or they will c you to sin against me,
Dt	10:18	He defends the c of the fatherless
Jdg	6:31	"Are you going to plead Baal's c?
Ps	7:16	The trouble they c recoils on them;
	9: 4	you have upheld my right and my c,
	25: 3	who are treacherous without c.
	82: 3	uphold the c of the poor
	109: 3	they attack me without c.
	119:86	for I am being persecuted without c.
	119:154	Defend my c and redeem me;
Pr	24:28	against your neighbor without c—
Ecc	8: 3	Do not stand up for a bad c, for he
Isa	1:23	They do not defend the c
Jer	5:28	they do not defend the just c
	51:36	I will defend your c and avenge
La	3:59	wrong done to me. Uphold my c!
Mt	18: 7	the things that c people to stumble!
Lk	17: 2	tied around their neck than to c one
Ro	14:21	else that will c your brother or sister
	16:17	watch out for those who c divisions
1Co	8:13	so that I will not c them to fall.
	10:32	Do not c anyone to stumble,
Rev	13:15	and c all who refused to worship

CAUSED CAUSE

1Ki	14:16	and has c Israel to commit."
2Ki	23:15	of Nebat, who had c Israel to sin—

CAUSES CAUSE

Isa	8:14	he will be a stone that c people
Mt	5:29	If your right eye c you to stumble,
	5:30	if your right hand c you to stumble,
	18: 6	"If anyone c one of these little
	18: 8	hand or your foot c you to stumble,
Ro	14:20	eat anything that c someone else
1Co	8:13	if what I eat c my brother or sister

Jas   4: 1 What c fights and quarrels among
1Pe   2: 8 "A stone that c people to stumble

CAVE CAVERNS, CAVES
Ge   19:30 and his two daughters lived in a c.
     23: 9 so he will sell me the c
     25: 9 in the c of Machpelah near Mamre,
     49:29 my fathers in the c in the field
Jos   10:16 and hidden in the c at Makkedah.
1Sa   22: 1 and escaped to the c of Adullam.
     24: 3 a c was there, and Saul went
     24: 3 and his men were far back in the c.
1Ki   19: 9 There he went into a c and spent
Ps   57: T *had fled from Saul into the c.*
     142: T *When he was in the c.*

CAVERNS* CAVE
Isa   2:21 They will flee to c in the rocks

CAVES CAVE
1Ki   18: 4 prophets and hidden them in two c,
Isa   2:19 People will flee to c in the rocks
Heb 11:38 living in c and in holes
Rev   6:15 hid in c and among the rocks

CEASE
Ge   8:22 winter, day and night will never c."
Ps   46: 9 He makes wars c to the ends
1Co 13: 8 there are prophecies, they will c;

CEDAR CEDARS
2Sa   7: 2 living in a house of c, while the ark
1Ki   5:10 Solomon supplied with all the c
2Ch 25:18 sent a message to a c in Lebanon,
Ezr   3: 7 that they would bring c logs by sea
Job   40:17 Its tail sways like a c; the sinews
Ps   92:12 they will grow like a c of Lebanon;
SS   8: 9 we will enclose her with panels of c.
Eze   31: 3 Assyria, once a c in Lebanon,
Hos   14: 5 Like a c of Lebanon he will send

CEDARS CEDAR
Nu   24: 6 LORD, like c beside the waters.
Ps   29: 5 voice of the LORD breaks the c;
     29: 5 breaks in pieces the c of Lebanon.

CELEBRATE* CELEBRATED, CELEBRATING, CELEBRATION, CELEBRATIONS
Ex   10: 9 because we are to c a festival
     12:14 to come you shall c it as a festival
     12:17 "C the Festival of Unleavened
     12:17 C this day as a lasting ordinance
     12:47 community of Israel must c it.
     12:48 c the LORD's Passover must have
     23:14 times a year you are to c a festival
     23:15 "C the Festival of Unleavened
     23:16 "C the Festival of Harvest
     23:16 "C the Festival of Ingathering
     34:18 "C the Festival of Unleavened
     34:22 "C the Festival of Weeks
Lev   23:39 c the festival to the LORD
     23:41 C this as a festival to the LORD
     23:41 c it in the seventh month.
Nu   9: 2 "Have the Israelites c the Passover

Nu   9: 3 C it at the appointed time,
      9: 4 told the Israelites to c the Passover,
      9: 6 of them could not c the Passover
      9:10 are still to c the LORD's Passover,
      9:12 When they c the Passover,
      9:13 on a journey fails to c the Passover,
      9:14 also to c the LORD's Passover
     29:12 C a festival to the LORD for seven
Dt   16: 1 c the Passover of the LORD your
     16:10 Then c the Festival of Weeks
     16:13 C the Festival of Tabernacles
     16:15 For seven days c the festival
Jdg   16:23 to Dagon their god and to c, saying,
2Sa   6:21 I will c before the LORD.
2Ki   23:21 "C the Passover to the LORD
2Ch 30: 1 and c the Passover to the LORD,
     30: 2 Jerusalem decided to c the Passover
     30: 3 They had not been able to c it
     30: 5 and c the Passover to the LORD,
     30:13 in Jerusalem to c the Festival
     30:23 to c the festival seven more days;
Ne   8:12 of food and to c with great joy,
     12:27 to c joyfully the dedication
Est   9:21 have them c annually the fourteenth
Ps   2:11 fear and c his rule with trembling.
     89:16 day long; they c your righteousness.
    145: 7 They c your abundant goodness
Isa   30:29 as on the night you c a holy festival;
Hos   5: 7 they c their New Moon feasts,
Na   1:15 C your festivals, Judah, and fulfill
Zec   14:16 and to c the Festival of Tabernacles.
     14:18 up to c the Festival of Tabernacles.
     14:19 up to c the Festival of Tabernacles.
Mt   26:18 I am going to c the Passover
Lk   15:23 and kill it. Let's have a feast and c.
     15:24 and is found.' So they began to c.
     15:29 me even a young goat so I could c
     15:32 But we had to c and be glad,
Rev   11:10 will c by sending each other gifts,

CELEBRATED CELEBRATE
Jos   5:10 the Israelites c the Passover.
1Ki   8:65 They c it before the LORD our
2Ki   23:23 this Passover was c to the LORD
2Ch 30: 5 It had not been c in large numbers
     35: 1 Josiah c the Passover to the LORD
Ezr   3: 4 they c the Festival of Tabernacles
      6:19 month, the exiles c the Passover.
Ne   8:17 the Israelites had not c it like this.
Est   9:28 never fail to be c by the Jews—

CELEBRATING CELEBRATE
1Ch   15:29 she saw King David dancing and c,
Est   8:17 the Jews, with feasting and c.

CELEBRATION CELEBRATE
Est   9:22 and their mourning into a day of c.
Col   2:16 a New Moon c or a Sabbath day.

CELEBRATIONS* CELEBRATE
Hos   2:11 I will stop all her c:

CELESTIAL*
2Pe   2:10 afraid to heap abuse on c beings;
Jude   1: 8 and heap abuse on c beings.

CELL*
Jer 37:16 put into a vaulted c in a dungeon,
Ac 12: 7 appeared and a light shone in the c.
    16:24 he put them in the inner c

CENSER CENSERS
Lev 16:12 is to take a c full of burning coals
Nu 16:18 So each of them took his c,
2Ch 26:19 who had a c in his hand ready
Eze 8:11 Each had a c in his hand,
Rev 8: 3 who had a golden c, came and stood

CENSERS CENSER
Lev 10: 1 sons Nadab and Abihu took their c,
Nu 16:38 the c of the men who sinned
    16:38 Hammer the c into sheets to overlay

CENSUS
Ex 30:12 "When you take a c of the Israelites
Nu 1: 2 "Take a c of the whole Israelite
    26: 2 "Take a c of the whole Israelite
2Sa 24: 1 "Go and take a c of Israel
1Ch 21: 1 incited David to take a c of Israel.
Lk 2: 1 a decree that a c should be taken

CENTER
Eze 48: 8 the sanctuary will be in the c of it.
    48:15 The city will be in the c of it
Rev 4: 6 In the c, around the throne,
    5: 6 slain, standing at the c of the throne,
    7:17 at the c of the throne will be their

CENTS*
Mk 12:42 copper coins, worth only a few c.

CENTURION
Mt 8: 5 Capernaum, a c came to him,
    27:54 When the c and those with him who
Mk 15:39 And when the c, who stood there
Lk 7: 3 The c heard of Jesus and sent some
    23:47 The c, seeing what had happened,
Ac 10: 1 a c in what was known as the Italian
    22:25 Paul said to the c standing there,
    27: 1 handed over to a c named Julius,

CEPHAS PETER
Jn 1:42 You will be called C" (which,
1Co 1:12 another, "I follow C";
    3:22 Paul or Apollos or C or the world
    9: 5 and the Lord's brothers and C?
Gal 2:11 When C came to Antioch, I opposed

CEREMONIAL* CEREMONY
Lev 14: 2 at the time of their c cleansing,
    15:13 off seven days for his c cleansing;
Mk 7: 3 they give their hands a c washing,
Jn 2: 6 used by the Jews for c washing,
    3:25 Jew over the matter of c washing.
    11:55 for their c cleansing before
    18:28 to avoid c uncleanness they did not
Heb 9:10 and drink and various c washings—
    13: 9 not by eating c foods, which is of no

CEREMONIALLY* CEREMONY
Lev 4:12 outside the camp to a place c clean,
    5: 2 touch anything c unclean (whether

Lev 6:11 the camp to a place that is c clean.
    7:19 touches anything c unclean must not
    7:19 meat, anyone c clean may eat it.
    10:14 Eat them in a c clean place;
    11: 4 it is c unclean for you.
    12: 2 to a son will be c unclean for seven
    12: 7 she will be c clean from her flow
    13: 3 he shall pronounce them c unclean.
    14: 8 then they will be c clean.
    15:28 and after that she will be c clean.
    15:33 with a woman who is c unclean.
    17:15 they will be c unclean till evening;
    21: 1 must not make himself c unclean
    22: 3 of your descendants is c unclean
    27:11 they vowed is a c unclean animal—
Nu 5: 2 who is c unclean because of a dead
    6: 7 not make themselves c unclean
    8: 6 Israelites and make them c clean.
    9: 6 day because they were c unclean
    9:13 if anyone who is c clean and not
    18:11 household who is c clean may eat it.
    18:13 household who is c clean may eat it.
    19: 7 but he will be c unclean till evening.
    19: 9 in a c clean place outside the camp.
    19:18 a man who is c clean is to take some
Dt 12:15 Both the c unclean and the clean
    12:22 Both the c unclean and the clean
    14: 7 they are c unclean for you.
    15:22 Both the c unclean and the clean
1Sa 20:26 to David to make him c unclean—
2Ch 13:11 set out the bread on the c clean table
    30:17 for all those who were not c clean
Ezr 6:20 themselves and were all c clean.
Ne 12:30 Levites had purified themselves c,
Isa 66:20 of the LORD in c clean vessels.
Eze 22:10 period, when they are c unclean.
Ac 24:18 I was c clean when they found me
Heb 9:13 on those who are c unclean sanctify

CEREMONIES* CEREMONY
Heb 9:21 and everything used in its c.

CEREMONY* CEREMONIAL,
CEREMONIALLY, CEREMONIES
Ge 50:11 Egyptians are holding a solemn c
Ex 12:25 you as he promised, observe this c.
    12:26 'What does this c mean to you?'
    13: 5 are to observe this c in this month:

CERTAINTY*
Lk 1: 4 you may know the c of the things
Jn 17: 8 They knew with c that I came

CERTIFICATE* CERTIFIED
Dt 24: 1 her, and he writes her a c of divorce,
    24: 3 her and writes her a c of divorce,
Isa 50: 1 "Where is your mother's c
Jer 3: 8 I gave faithless Israel her c
Mt 5:31 divorces his wife must give her a c
    19: 7 a man give his wife a c of divorce
Mk 10: 4 a man to write a c of divorce

CERTIFIED* CERTIFICATE
Jn 3:33 Whoever has accepted it has c

CHAFF

Ps   1: 4 They are like c that the wind blows
      35: 5 May they be like c before the wind,
Isa 33:11 You conceive c, you give birth
Da   2:35 became like c on a threshing floor
Hos 13: 3 like c swirling from a threshing
Zep   2: 2 that day passes like windblown c,
Mt   3:12 up the c with unquenchable fire."

CHAIN CHAINED, CHAINS

Ge   41:42 and put a gold c around his neck.
Pr   1: 9 head and a c to adorn your neck.
Da   5: 7 and have a gold c placed around his
Mk   5: 3 him anymore, not even with a c.
Ac   28:20 Israel that I am bound with this c."
Rev 20: 1 and holding in his hand a great c.

CHAINED CHAIN

Mk   5: 4 For he had often been c hand
2Ti   2: 9 the point of being c like a criminal.
      2: 9 But God's word is not c.

CHAINS CHAIN

Ex   28:14 and two braided c of pure gold,
     28:14 and attach the c to the settings.
Ps   2: 3 "Let us break their c and throw off
Ecc   7:26 is a trap and whose hands are c.
La   3: 7 he has weighed me down with c.
Mk   5: 4 but he tore the c apart and broke
Ac   12: 7 and the c fell off Peter's wrists.
     16:26 open, and everyone's c came loose.
Eph   6:20 for which I am an ambassador in c.
Php   1: 7 whether I am in c or defending
Col   4:18 Remember my c. Grace be
2Ti   1:16 me and was not ashamed of my c.
Phm   1:10 became my son while I was in c.
Heb 11:36 and even c and imprisonment.
Jude 1: 6 with everlasting c for judgment

CHAIR

1Sa   4:18 Eli fell backward off his c

CHALDEA CHALDEAN,
CHALDEANS

Eze 23:16 and sent messengers to them in C.

CHALDEAN* CHALDEA

Ezr   5:12 the hands of Nebuchadnezzar the C,

CHALDEANS CHALDEA

Ge   11:31 from Ur of the C to go to Canaan.
Ne   9: 7 brought him out of Ur of the C

CHALLENGE CHALLENGED

Jer 49:19 Who is like me and who can c me?

CHALLENGED CHALLENGE

Jn   8:13 The Pharisees c him, "Here you
     18:26 whose ear Peter had cut off, c him,

CHAMBER CHAMBERS

Job 37: 9 The tempest comes out from its c,

CHAMBERS CHAMBER

Ps 104:13 the mountains from his upper c;
SS   1: 4 Let the king bring me into his c.

CHAMPION* CHAMPIONS

1Sa 17: 4 A c named Goliath, who was
     17:23 Goliath, the Philistine c from Gath,
Ps   19: 5 like a c rejoicing to run his course.
Isa 42:13 The LORD will march out like a c,

CHAMPIONS* CHAMPION

Isa   5:22 wine and c at mixing drinks,

CHANCE

1Sa   6: 9 us but that it happened to us by c."
Ecc   9:11 but time and c happen to them all.

CHANGE CHANGED, CHANGERS

Nu   23:19 being, that he should c his mind.
1Sa 15:29 of Israel does not lie or c his mind;
     15:29 being, that he should c his mind."
1Ki   8:47 if they have a c of heart in the land
Ps 110: 4 has sworn and will not c his mind:
Jer   7: 5 If you really c your ways and your
     13:23 Can an Ethiopian c his skin
Eze   1:17 the wheels did not c direction as
Mal   3: 6 "I the LORD do not c. So you,
Mt   18: 3 unless you c and become like little
Heb   7:21 has sworn and will not c his mind:
Jas   1:17 lights, who does not c like shifting

CHANGED CHANGE

1Sa 10: 9 to leave Samuel, God c Saul's heart,
Jer   2:11 Has a nation ever c its gods?
Da   3:19 and his attitude toward them c.
      6:15 edict that the king issues can be c."
Hos 11: 8 My heart is c within me;
Lk   9:29 the appearance of his face c, and his
1Co 15:51 not all sleep, but we will all be c—
Heb   1:12 like a garment they will be c.
      7:12 For when the priesthood is c, the law
           must be c also.

CHANGERS* CHANGE

Mt   21:12 overturned the tables of the money c
Mk   11:15 overturned the tables of the money c
Jn   2:15 scattered the coins of the money c

CHARACTER*

Ru   3:11 that you are a woman of noble c.
Pr   12: 4 of noble c is her husband's crown,
     31:10 A wife of noble c who can find?
Ac   17:11 were of more noble c than those
Ro   5: 4 perseverance, c; and c, hope.
1Co 15:33 "Bad company corrupts good c."

CHARGE CHARGED, CHARGES,
CHARGING

Ge   39: 4 Potiphar put him in c of his
     39:22 So the warden put Joseph in c of all
     41:40 You shall be in c of my palace,
Nu   4:16 is to have c of the oil for the light,
      4:16 is to be in c of the entire tabernacle
Dt   23:19 Do not c a fellow Israelite interest,
Job 34:13 Who put him in c of the whole
Ps   69:27 C them with crime upon crime;
SS   5: 8 Daughters of Jerusalem, I c you—
Hos 12: 2 The LORD has a c to bring against
Mt   24:47 you, he will put him in c of all his

Jn   13:29 Since Judas had **c** of the money,
     18:38 "I find no basis for a **c** against him.
Ro   8:33 will bring any **c** against those whom
1Co   9:18 the gospel I may offer it free of **c**,
2Co 11: 7 the gospel of God to you free of **c**?
Col   2:14 having canceled the **c** of our legal
2Ti   4: 1 and his kingdom, I give you this **c**:
Phm   1:18 or owes you anything, **c** it to me.
Rev 14:18 another angel, who had **c** of the fire,
     16: 5 I heard the angel in **c** of the waters

CHARGED CHARGE
Ro   5:13 sin is not **c** against anyone's account

CHARGES CHARGE
Job   4:18 if he **c** his angels with error,
Ps   50: 8 I bring no **c** against you concerning
Isa 50: 8 Who then will bring **c** against me?
Jer 25:31 the LORD will bring **c** against
Mt   12:10 a reason to bring **c** against Jesus,
Lk   23:14 no basis for your **c** against him.
Ac   24: 1 they brought their **c** against Paul

CHARGING CHARGE
Job   1:22 this, Job did not sin by **c** God

CHARIOT CHARIOTS
Ge   41:43 in a **c** as his second-in-command,
1Ki 22:34 The king told his **c** driver,
2Ki   2:11 suddenly a **c** of fire and horses
2Ch   1:17 They imported a **c** from Egypt
Ps 104: 3 He makes the clouds his **c** and rides
Zec   6: 2 The first **c** had red horses,
Ac   8:28 was sitting in his **c** reading the Book

CHARIOTS CHARIOT
Ex   14: 7 He took six hundred of the best **c**,
     14: 7 along with all the other **c** of Egypt,
     15:19 **c** and horsemen went into the sea,
Jos 11: 4 a large number of horses and **c**—
     17:18 though the Canaanites have **c** fitted
Jdg   4: 3 he had nine hundred **c** fitted
2Sa   8: 4 David captured a thousand of his **c**,
2Ki   6:17 and **c** of fire all around Elisha.
2Ch   1:14 Solomon accumulated **c** and horses;
      1:14 he had fourteen hundred **c**
Ps   20: 7 Some trust in **c** and some in horses,
     68:17 The **c** of God are tens of thousands
Na   2: 3 The metal on the **c** flashes
Hag   2:22 I will overthrow **c** and their drivers;
Rev   9: 9 horses and **c** rushing into battle.

CHARM* CHARMING, CHARMS
Pr   17: 8 A bribe is seen as a **c** by the one
     31:30 **C** is deceptive, and beauty is

CHARMING* CHARM
Pr   26:25 Though their speech is **c**, do not
SS   1:16 Oh, how **c**! And our bed is verdant.

CHARMS* CHARM
Isa   3:20 sashes, the perfume bottles and **c**,
Eze 13:18 the women who sew magic **c** on all
     13:20 I am against your magic **c**

CHASE CHASED, CHASING
Lev 26: 8 Five of you will **c** a hundred,
     26: 8 hundred of you will **c** ten thousand,
Dt   32:30 How could one man **c** a thousand,
Pr   12:11 those who **c** fantasies have no sense.
     28:19 those who **c** fantasies will have their
Hos   2: 7 She will **c** after her lovers but not

CHASED CHASE
Dt   1:44 they **c** you like a swarm of bees
Jos   7: 5 They **c** the Israelites from the city

CHASING CHASE
Ecc   1:14 are meaningless, a **c** after the wind.

CHASM*
Lk   16:26 you a great **c** has been set in place,

CHASTENED*
Job 33:19 someone may be **c** on a bed of pain
Ps 118:18 The LORD has **c** me severely,

CHATTER* CHATTERING
1Ti   6:20 Turn away from godless **c**
2Ti   2:16 Avoid godless **c**, because those who

CHATTERING* CHATTER
Pr   10: 8 but a **c** fool comes to ruin.
     10:10 grief, and a **c** fool comes to ruin.

CHEAPER*
Jn   2:10 the **c** wine after the guests have had

CHEAT* CHEATED, CHEATING
Lev   6: 2 stolen, or if they **c** their neighbor,
Mal   1:14 "Cursed is the **c** who has
1Co   6: 8 you yourselves **c** and do wrong,

CHEATED* CHEAT
Ge   31: 7 yet your father has **c** me
1Sa 12: 3 Whom have I **c**? Whom have I
     12: 4 "You have not **c** or oppressed us,"
Lk   19: 8 if I have **c** anybody out of anything,
1Co   6: 7 Why not rather be **c**?

CHEATING* CHEAT
Am   8: 5 price and **c** with dishonest scales,

CHEEK* CHEEKS
Job 16:10 they strike my **c** in scorn and unite
La   3:30 offer his **c** to one who would strike
Hos 11: 4 one who lifts a little child to the **c**,
Mic   5: 1 Israel's ruler on the **c** with a rod.
Mt   5:39 If anyone slaps you on the right **c**,
          turn to them the other **c** also.
Lk   6:29 If someone slaps you on one **c**,

CHEEKS* CHEEK
SS   1:10 Your **c** are beautiful with earrings,
      5:13 His **c** are like beds of spice yielding
Isa 50: 6 my **c** to those who pulled out my
La   1: 2 weeps at night, tears are on her **c**.

CHEER* CHEERFUL, CHEERFULLY, CHEERING, CHEERS
1Ki 21: 7 Get up and eat! **C** up. I'll get you
Mk   10:49 they called to the blind man, "**C** up!

CHEERFUL* CHEER
Pr   15:13 A happy heart makes the face c,
        15:15 but the c heart has a continual feast.
        17:22 A c heart is good medicine,
2Co   9: 7 compulsion, for God loves a c giver.

CHEERFULLY* CHEER
Ro   12: 8 if it is to show mercy, do it c.

CHEERING* CHEER
1Ki   1:45 From there they have gone up c,
2Ch 23:12 the people running and c the king,
Ecc   2: 3 I tried c myself with wine,

CHEERS* CHEER
Jdg   9:13 which c both gods and humans,
Pr   12:25 the heart, but a kind word c it up.

CHEMOSH
Nu   21:29 You are destroyed, people of C!
1Ki 11: 7 high place for C the detestable god
2Ki 23:13 for C the vile god of Moab,
Jer 48: 7 and C will go into exile,

CHERISH* CHERISHED,
  CHERISHES
Ps   83: 3 they plot against those you c.
Pr   4: 8 C her, and she will exalt you;

CHERISHED* CHERISH
Ps   66:18 If I had c sin in my heart, the Lord
Pr   4: 3 still tender, and c by my mother.
Hos   9:16 I will slay their c offspring."

CHERISHES* CHERISH
Pr   19: 8 one who c understanding will soon
        prosper.

CHERUB CHERUBIM
Ex   25:19 Make one c on one end and the
        second c on the other;
1Ki   6:26 The height of each c was ten cubits.
2Ch   3:11 of the first c was five cubits long
        3:11 touched the wing of the other c.
Eze 10:14 One face was that of a c, the second
        28:14 You were anointed as a guardian c,
        41:18 Each c had two faces:

CHERUBIM CHERUB
Ge   3:24 east side of the Garden of Eden c
Ex   25:18 make two c out of hammered gold
        26: 1 with c woven into them by a skilled
Nu   7:89 from between the two c
1Sa   4: 4 who is enthroned between the c.
2Sa   6: 2 who is enthroned between the c
        22:11 He mounted the c and flew;
1Ki   6:23 inner sanctuary he made a pair of c
2Ki 19:15 enthroned between the c, you alone
1Ch 13: 6 who is enthroned between the c—
2Ch   3: 7 gold, and he carved c on the walls.
Ps   18:10 He mounted the c and flew;
        80: 1 who sit enthroned between the c,
        99: 1 he sits enthroned between the c,
Isa 37:16 enthroned between the c, you alone
Eze   9: 3 of Israel went up from above the c,
        10: 1 that was over the heads of the c.

Eze 41:18 were carved c and palm trees.
        41:18 Palm trees alternated with c.
Heb   9: 5 the ark were the c of the Glory,

CHEST CHESTS
2Ki 12: 9 Jehoiada the priest took a c
        12: 9 entrance put into the c all the money
Da   2:32 pure gold, its c and arms of silver,
Rev   1:13 and with a golden sash around his c.

CHESTS* CHEST
Rev 15: 6 wore golden sashes around their c.

CHEW CHEWS
Lev 11: 4 are some that only c the cud or only
Dt   14: 7 of those that c the cud or that have
        14: 7 Although they c the cud, they do not

CHEWS CHEW
Lev 11: 3 a divided hoof and that c the cud.

CHICKS*
Mt   23:37 a hen gathers her c under her wings,
Lk   13:34 a hen gathers her c under her wings,

CHIEF CHIEFS
2Sa 23:13 of the thirty c warriors came down
Ezr   7: 5 the son of Aaron the c priest—
Da   10:13 one of the c princes, came to help
Mt   20:18 be delivered over to the c priests
        27: 6 The c priests picked up the coins
Mk   15: 3 The c priests accused him of many
Eph   2:20 Jesus himself as the c cornerstone.
1Pe   5: 4 And when the C Shepherd appears,

CHIEF PRIEST 2Ki 25:18; 2Ch 19:11; 24:6, 11;
26:20; 31:10; Ezr 7:5; Jer 52:24; Ac 19:14

CHIEF PRIESTS Mt 2:4; 16:21; 20:18; 21:15, 23,
45; 26:3, 14, 47, 59; 27:1, 3, 6, 12, 20, 41, 62; 28:11,
12; Mk 8:31; 10:33; 11:18, 27; 12:12; 14:1, 10, 43,
53, 55; 15:1, 3, 10, 11, 31; Lk 9:22; 19:47; 20:1,
19; 22:2, 4, 52, 66; 23:4, 10, 13; 24:20; Jn 7:32, 45;
11:47, 57; 12:10; 18:3, 35; 19:6, 15, 21; Ac 4:23;
5:24; 9:14, 21; 22:30; 23:14; 25:2, 15; 26:10, 12

CHIEFS CHIEF
1Ch 11:10 These were the c of David's mighty

CHILD CHILDHOOD, CHILDLESS,
  CHILDREN, CHILDREN'S,
  GRANDCHILDREN
Ge   4:25 "God has granted me another c
        17:17 Will Sarah bear a c at the age
Ex   2: 2 When she saw that he was a fine c,
Jdg 11:34 She was an only c. Except for her
Ru   4:16 Then Naomi took the c in her arms
1Sa   1:27 I prayed for this c, and the LORD
2Sa 12:16 David pleaded with God for the c.
1Ki   3: 7 I am only a little c and do not know
2Ch 22:11 she hid the c from Athaliah so she
Job   3:16 in the ground like a stillborn c,
Ps 131: 2 I am like a weaned c with its
        131: 2 like a weaned c I am content.
Pr   22:15 Folly is bound up in the heart of a c,
        23:13 Do not withhold discipline from a c;
        29:15 a c left undisciplined disgraces its

Ecc 6: 3 a stillborn c is better off than he.
Isa 9: 6 For to us a c is born, to us a son is
  11: 6 and a little c will lead them.
  54: 1 woman, you who never bore a c;
  65:20 a hundred will be thought a mere c;
  66:13 As a mother comforts her c, so will
Eze 18:20 The c will not share the guilt
  18:20 the parent share the guilt of the c.
Hos 11: 1 "When Israel was a c, I loved him,
Zec 12:10 for him as one mourns for an only c,
Mt 2:11 they saw the c with his mother
  18: 2 He called a little c to him, and placed
    the c among them.
Mk 5:39 The c is not dead but asleep."
  10:15 of God like a little c will never enter
Lk 1:42 and blessed is the c you will bear!
  1:80 And the c grew and became strong
Ac 13:10 "You are a c of the devil
1Co 13:11 When I was a c, I talked like a c, I
    thought like a c, I reasoned like a c.
Gal 4: 7 no longer a slave, but God's c;
  4: 7 his c, God has made you also an heir.
Heb 11:23 they saw he was no ordinary c,
1Jn 5: 1 loves the father loves his c as well.
Rev 12: 4 it might devour her c the moment he

CHILDBEARING* BEAR
Ge 3:16 make your pains in c very severe;
  18:11 old, and Sarah was past the age of c.
1Ti 2:15 women will be saved through c—
Heb 11:11 who was past c age, was enabled

CHILDBIRTH BEAR
Ro 8:22 as in the pains of c right
Gal 4:19 the pains of c until Christ is formed

CHILDHOOD CHILD
Ge 8:21 of the human heart is evil from c.
1Co 13:11 man, I put the ways of c behind me.

CHILDLESS CHILD
Ge 11:30 Now Sarai was c because she was
  15: 2 can you give me since I remain c
  25:21 of his wife, because she was c.
  29:31 to conceive, but Rachel remained c.
1Sa 15:33 your sword has made women c,
  15:33 your mother be c among women."
Ps 113: 9 He settles the c woman in her home
Lk 1: 7 they were c because Elizabeth was
  23:29 say, 'Blessed are the c women,

CHILDREN CHILD
Ge 3:16 labor you will give birth to c.
  21: 7 Abraham that Sarah would nurse c?
Ex 20: 5 punishing the c for the sin
Lev 20: 3 for by sacrificing his c to Molek,
Dt 4: 9 Teach them to your c and to their c
  6: 7 Impress them on your c.
  11:19 Teach them to your c,
  14: 1 You are the c of the LORD your
  24:16 are not to be put to death for their c,
  24:16 nor c put to death for their parents;
  29:29 belong to us and to our c forever,
  30:19 life, so that you and your c may live
  32:46 you may command your c to obey

Jos 4: 6 when your c ask you, 'What do
1Sa 2: 5 who was barren has borne seven c,
Ezr 10:44 some of them had c by these wives.
Ne 13:24 Half of their c spoke the language
Job 1: 5 "Perhaps my c have sinned
Ps 8: 2 Through the praise of c and infants
  37:25 forsaken or their c begging bread.
  78: 5 our ancestors to teach their c,
  103:13 As a father has compassion on his c,
  112: 2 Their c will be mighty in the land;
  127: 3 C are a heritage from the LORD,
Pr 13:24 spares the rod hates their c,
  13:24 the one who loves their c is careful
  14:26 and for their c it will be a refuge.
  17: 6 Children's c are a crown
  17: 6 and parents are the pride of their c.
  20: 7 blessed are their c after them.
  20:11 Even small c are known by their
  22: 6 Start c off on the way they should
  29:17 Discipline your c, and they will give
  31:28 Her c arise and call her blessed;
Isa 1: 4 of evildoers, c given to corruption!
  49:25 with you, and your c I will save.
  54:13 All your c will be taught
Jer 4:22 They are senseless c; they have no
  31:15 Rachel weeping for her c
La 4: 4 the c beg for bread, but no one gives
Eze 5:10 your midst parents will eat their c,
    and c will eat their parents.
  23:37 they even sacrificed their c,
Hos 1:10 they will be called 'c of the living
  2: 4 I will not show my love to her c,
    because they are the c of adultery.
Joel 1: 3 Tell it to your c, and let your c tell it
    to their c,
Zec 10: 7 Their c will see it and be joyful;
Mal 4: 6 the hearts of the parents to their c,
  4: 6 the hearts of the c to their parents;
Mt 2:18 Rachel weeping for her c
  3: 9 these stones God can raise up c
  5: 9 for they will be called c of God.
  7:11 how to give good gifts to your c,
  11:25 and revealed them to little c.
  18: 3 you change and become like little c,
  19:14 said, "Let the little c come to me,
  21:16 you hear what these c are saying?"
  21:16 " 'From the lips of c and infants
Mk 9:37 these little c in my name welcomes
  10:14 them, "Let the little c come to me,
  10:16 And he took the c in his arms,
  10:30 sisters, mothers, c and fields—
  13:12 C will rebel against their parents
Lk 6:35 and you will be c of the Most High,
  10:21 and revealed them to little c.
  18:16 But Jesus called the c to him
  18:16 said, "Let the little c come to me,
Jn 1:12 gave the right to become c of God—
  8:39 "If you were Abraham's c,"
  12:36 so that you may become c of light."
Ac 2:39 your c and for all who are far off—
Ro 8:14 the Spirit of God are the c of God.
  8:16 with our spirit that we are God's c.

Ro   9: 8 it is not the **c** by physical descent who
             are God's **c**,
      9: 8 it is the **c** of the promise who are
      9:26 there they will be called '**c**
1Co 14:20 and sisters, stop thinking like **c**.
2Co 12:14 **c** should not have to save up for their
             parents, but parents for their **c**.
Gal   3: 7 that those who have faith are **c**
      3:26 in Christ Jesus you are all **c** of God
      4:24 and bears **c** who are to be slaves:
Eph   5: 8 light in the Lord. Live as **c** of light
      6: 1 **C**, obey your parents in the Lord,
      6: 4 Fathers, do not exasperate your **c**;
Php   2:15 "**c** of God without fault in a warped
Col   3:20 **C**, obey your parents in everything,
      3:21 do not embitter your **c**, or they will
1Th   2: 7 we were like young **c** among you.
      2: 7 as a nursing mother cares for her **c**,
      5: 5 You are all **c** of the light and **c** of
             the day.
1Ti   3: 4 well and see that his **c** obey him,
      3:12 wife and must manage his **c** and his
      5:10 such as bringing up **c**,
      5:14 to have **c**, to manage their homes
Titus 1: 6 a man whose **c** believe and are not
      2: 4 to love their husbands and **c**,
Heb   2:13 am I, and the **c** God has given me."
     12: 7 God is treating you as his **c**. For
             what **c** are not disciplined
1Pe   1:14 As obedient **c**, do not conform
1Jn   3: 1 that we should be called **c** of God!
      3:10 This is how we know who the **c**
      3:10 are and who the **c** of the devil are:
      5:19 We know that we are **c** of God,
2Jn   1: 1 lady chosen by God and to her **c**,
3Jn   1: 4 to hear that my **c** are walking
Rev 21: 7 be their God and they will be my **c**.

CHILDREN'S CHILD
Pr   13:22 an inheritance for their **c** children,
     17: 6 **C** children are a crown to the aged,
Jer 31:29 and the **c** teeth are set on edge.'
Eze 18: 2 and the **c** teeth are set on edge'?
Mt   15:26 "It is not right to take the **c** bread

CHISEL CHISELED
Ex   34: 1 "**C** out two stone tablets like

CHISELED CHISEL
Dt   10: 3 **c** out two stone tablets like the first

CHOICE CHOICEST, CHOOSE,
CHOOSES, CHOSE, CHOSEN
1Ch 21:11 the LORD says: 'Take your **c**:
Pr   8:10 knowledge rather than **c** gold,
     10:20 tongue of the righteous is **c** silver,
     18: 8 words of a gossip are like **c** morsels;
SS   4:13 of pomegranates with **c** fruits,
      4:16 into his garden and taste its **c** fruits.
Jer   2:21 I had planted you like a **c** vine
Da   1:16 So the guard took away their **c** food
     10: 3 I ate no **c** food; no meat or wine
Ro   8:20 not by its own **c**, but by the will

CHOICEST CHOICE
Dt   33:15 with the **c** gifts of the ancient
Isa   5: 2 and planted it with the **c** vines.
     16: 8 have trampled down the **c** vines,

CHOIR* CHOIRS
Ne   12:38 The second **c** proceeded

CHOIRS CHOIR
1Ch 15:27 in charge of the singing of the **c**.
Ne   12:31 assigned two large **c** to give thanks.

CHOKE CHOKED
Mt   18:28 He grabbed him and began to **c** him.

CHOKED* CHOKE
Mt   13: 7 which grew up and **c** the plants.
Mk   4: 7 which grew up and **c** the plants,
Lk   8: 7 grew up with it and **c** the plants.
      8:14 go on their way they are **c** by life's

CHOOSE CHOICE
Nu   14: 4 "We should **c** a leader and go back
     17: 5 belonging to the man I **c** will sprout,
Dt   12:14 the place the LORD will **c** in one
     30:19 Now **c** life, so that you and your
Jos 24:15 **c** for yourselves this day whom you
2Ki 18:32 **C** life and not death!
Ps   65: 4 Blessed are those you **c** and bring
Pr   1:29 and did not **c** to fear the LORD.
      3:31 the violent or **c** any of their ways.
      8:10 **C** my instruction instead of silver,
Isa   7:15 to reject the wrong and **c** the right,
     14: 1 once again he will **c** Israel and will
Zec   2:12 land and will again **c** Jerusalem.
Jn   15:16 You did not **c** me, but I chose you
Ac   1:21 Therefore it is necessary to **c** one
      6: 3 **c** seven men from among you who
     15:14 God first intervened to **c** a people
2Co 12: 6 Even if I should **c** to boast, I would
Php   1:22 Yet what shall I **c**? I do not know!
1Pe   4: 3 the past doing what pagans **c** to do—

CHOOSES CHOICE
Nu   16: 7 The man the LORD **c** will be
Ps   68:16 the mountain where God **c** to reign,
Mt   11:27 to whom the Son **c** to reveal him.
Lk   10:22 to whom the Son **c** to reveal him."
Jn   7:17 Anyone who **c** to do the will of God
Jas   4: 4 anyone who **c** to be a friend

CHORAZIN*
Mt   11:21 "Woe to you, **C**! Woe to you,
Lk   10:13 "Woe to you, **C**! Woe to you,

CHOSE CHOICE
Ge   13:11 So Lot **c** for himself the whole plain
Dt   4:37 and **c** their descendants after them,
     10:15 and he **c** you, their descendants,
Jdg   5: 8 God **c** new leaders when war came
1Sa   2:28 I **c** your ancestor out of all the tribes
     17:40 hand, **c** five smooth stones
Ne   9: 7 who **c** Abram and brought him
Ps   33:12 the people he **c** for his inheritance.
     78:70 He **c** David his servant and took
Isa 65:12 sight and **c** what displeases me."

Eze 20: 5 On the day I **c** Israel, I swore
Lk 6:13 to him and **c** twelve of them,
Jn 15:16 but I **c** you and appointed you so
Ac 6: 5 They **c** Stephen, a man full of faith
15:22 They **c** Judas (called Barsabbas)
15:40 but Paul **c** Silas and left,
1Co 1:27 But God **c** the foolish things
1:27 God **c** the weak things of the world
Eph 1: 4 For he **c** us in him before
2Th 2:13 because God **c** you as firstfruits
Heb 11:25 He **c** to be mistreated along
Jas 1:18 He **c** to give us birth through

CHOSEN CHOICE

Ge 18:19 For I have **c** him, so that he will
Ex 31: 2 "See, I have **c** Bezalel son of Uri,
Lev 16:10 the goat **c** by lot as the scapegoat
Dt 7: 6 The Lord your God has **c** you
Jdg 10:14 and cry out to the gods you have **c**.
1Sa 8:18 for relief from the king you have **c**,
16: 1 I have **c** one of his sons to be king."
1Ki 8:44 Lord toward the city you have **c**
Ne 1: 9 the place I have **c** as a dwelling
Ps 89: 3 made a covenant with my **c** one,
105: 6 descendants of Abraham, his **c** ones,
119:30 I have **c** the way of faithfulness;
Isa 41: 8 whom I have **c**, you descendants
Am 3: 2 "You only have I **c** of all
Hag 2:23 ring, for I have **c** you,'
Zec 3: 2 who has **c** Jerusalem, rebuke you!
Mt 12:18 "Here is my servant whom I have **c**,
22:14 many are invited, but few are **c**."
Mk 13:20 whom he has **c**, he has shortened
Lk 9:35 "This is my Son, whom I have **c**;
10:42 Mary has **c** what is better, and it
23:35 if he is God's Messiah, the **C** One."
Jn 1:34 I testify that this is God's **C** One."
6:70 "Have I not **c** you, the Twelve?
15:19 but I have **c** you out of the world.
Ac 9:15 This man is my **c** instrument
Ro 8:33 against those whom God has **c**?
11: 5 the present time there is a remnant **c**
Eph 1:11 In him we were also **c**, having been
Col 3:12 as God's **c** people, holy and dearly
1Th 1: 4 loved by God, that he has **c** you,
Jas 2: 5 Has not God **c** those who are poor
1Pe 1:20 He was **c** before the creation
2: 4 rejected by humans but **c** by God
2: 9 But you are a **c** people, a royal
2Jn 1: 1 To the lady **c** by God and to her
Rev 17:14 his called, **c** and faithful followers."

CHRIST CHRIST'S, CHRISTIAN, CHRISTIANS, MESSIAH, MESSIAHS

Jn 1:17 and truth came through Jesus **C**.
1:41 found the Messiah" (that is, the **C**).
4:25 Messiah" (called **C**) "is coming.
Ac 3: 6 In the name of Jesus **C** of Nazareth,
4:10 by the name of Jesus **C** of Nazareth,
9:34 said to him, "Jesus **C** heals you.
Ro 1: 4 from the dead: Jesus **C** our Lord.
3:22 faith in Jesus **C** to all who believe.

Ro 5: 1 with God through our Lord Jesus **C**,
5: 6 powerless, **C** died for the ungodly.
5: 8 we were still sinners, **C** died for us.
5:11 in God through our Lord Jesus **C**,
5:17 life through the one man, Jesus **C**!
6: 4 just as **C** was raised from the dead
6:23 is eternal life in **C** Jesus our Lord.
7: 4 to the law through the body of **C**,
8: 1 for those who are in **C** Jesus,
8: 9 does not have the Spirit of **C**, they do
not belong to **C**.
8:17 heirs of God and co-heirs with **C**,
8:35 separate us from the love of **C**?
10: 4 **C** is the culmination of the law so
12: 5 so in **C** we, though many, form one
13:14 yourselves with the Lord Jesus **C**,
14: 9 **C** died and returned to life so that he
15: 3 even **C** did not please himself but,
15: 5 toward each other that **C** Jesus had,
15: 7 then, just as **C** accepted you,
16:18 people are not serving our Lord **C**,
1Co 1: 2 to those sanctified in **C** Jesus
1: 2 on the name of our Lord Jesus **C**—
1: 7 for our Lord Jesus **C** to be revealed.
1:13 Is **C** divided? Was Paul crucified
1:17 For **C** did not send me to baptize,
1:17 lest the cross of **C** be emptied of its
1:23 but we preach **C** crucified:
1:30 of him that you are in **C** Jesus,
2: 2 while I was with you except Jesus **C**
2:16 But we have the mind of **C**.
3:11 one already laid, which is Jesus **C**.
5: 7 For **C**, our Passover lamb, has been
6:15 bodies are members of **C** himself?
6:15 take the members of **C** and unite
8: 6 Jesus **C**, through whom all things
8:12 weak conscience, you sin against **C**.
10: 4 them, and that rock was **C**.
10: 9 We should not test **C**, as some
11: 1 as I follow the example of **C**.
11: 3 that the head of every man is **C**,
11: 3 is man, and the head of **C** is God.
12:27 Now you are the body of **C**,
15: 3 that **C** died for our sins according
15:14 And if **C** has not been raised,
15:22 die, so in **C** all will be made alive.
15:57 victory through our Lord Jesus **C**.
2Co 1: 5 abundantly in the sufferings of **C**,
1: 5 our comfort abounds through **C**.
3: 3 show that you are a letter from **C**,
3:14 because only in **C** is it taken away.
4: 4 gospel that displays the glory of **C**,
4: 5 but Jesus **C** as Lord, and ourselves
4: 6 glory displayed in the face of **C**.
5:10 before the judgment seat of **C**,
5:17 if anyone is in **C**, the new creation
6:15 What harmony is there between **C**
10: 1 the humility and gentleness of **C**,
11: 2 to **C**, so that I might present you as
11:13 masquerading as apostles of **C**.
Gal 1: 7 are trying to pervert the gospel of **C**.
2: 4 on the freedom we have in **C** Jesus
2:16 of the law, but by faith in Jesus **C**.

Gal 2:16 have put our faith in C Jesus that we
          may be justified by faith in C
     2:17 if, in seeking to be justified in C,
     2:17 that mean that C promotes sin?
     2:20 I have been crucified with C and I no
          longer live, but C lives in me.
     2:21 the law, C died for nothing!"
     3:13 C redeemed us from the curse
     3:16 meaning one person, who is C.
     3:26 So in C Jesus you are all children
     4:19 pains of childbirth until C is formed
     5: 1 is for freedom that C has set us free.
     5: 4 the law have been alienated from C;
     5:24 to C Jesus have crucified the flesh
     6:14 in the cross of our Lord Jesus C,
Eph 1: 3 God and Father of our Lord Jesus C,
     1: 3 with every spiritual blessing in C.
     1:10 in heaven and on earth under C.
     1:20 when he raised C from the dead
     2: 5 made us alive with C even when we
     2:10 created in C Jesus to do good
     2:12 that time you were separate from C,
     2:20 with C Jesus himself as the chief
     3: 8 Gentiles the boundless riches of C,
     3:17 so that C may dwell in your hearts
     4: 7 has been given as C apportioned it.
     4:13 whole measure of the fullness of C.
     4:15 of him who is the head, that is, C.
     4:32 other, just as in C God forgave you.
     5: 2 just as C loved us and gave himself
     5:21 one another out of reverence for C.
     5:23 the head of the wife as C is the head
     5:25 just as C loved the church and gave
Php 1: 6 completion until the day of C Jesus.
     1:18 false motives or true, C is preached.
     1:21 to me, to live is C and to die is gain.
     1:23 I desire to depart and be with C,
     1:27 a manner worthy of the gospel of C.
     1:29 on behalf of C not only to believe
     2: 5 have the same mindset as C Jesus:
     2:11 acknowledge that Jesus C is Lord,
     3: 7 now consider loss for the sake of C.
     3:10 I want to know C—yes, to know
     3:18 live as enemies of the cross of C.
     4:19 to the riches of his glory in C Jesus.
Col 1: 4 have heard of your faith in C Jesus
     1:27 which is C in you, the hope
     1:28 present everyone fully mature in C.
     2: 2 the mystery of God, namely, C,
     2: 6 as you received C Jesus as Lord,
     2: 9 For in C all the fullness of the Deity
     2:13 flesh, God made you alive with C.
     2:17 the reality, however, is found in C.
     3: 1 you have been raised with C,
     3: 1 hearts on things above, where C is,
     3: 3 your life is now hidden with C
     3:15 Let the peace of C rule in your
     3:16 of C dwell in you richly as you
1Th 4:16 and the dead in C will rise first.
     5: 9 salvation through our Lord Jesus C.
     5:18 this is God's will for you in C Jesus.
2Th 2: 1 the coming of our Lord Jesus C
     2:14 in the glory of our Lord Jesus C.

1Ti 1:12 I thank C Jesus our Lord, who has
     1:15 C Jesus came into the world to save
     1:16 C Jesus might display his immense
     2: 5 God and mankind, the man C Jesus,
     4: 6 will be a good minister of C Jesus,
     6:14 the appearing of our Lord Jesus C,
2Ti 1: 9 us in C Jesus before the beginning
     1:10 appearing of our Savior, C Jesus,
     2: 1 in the grace that is in C Jesus.
     2: 3 like a good soldier of C Jesus.
     2: 8 Remember Jesus C,
     2:10 the salvation that is in C Jesus,
     3:12 life in C Jesus will be persecuted,
     3:15 salvation through faith in C Jesus.
     4: 1 the presence of God and of C Jesus,
Titus 2:13 our great God and Savior, Jesus C,
Phm 1: 6 thing we share for the sake of C.
     1:20 in the Lord; refresh my heart in C.
Heb 3: 6 C is faithful as the Son over God's
     3:14 We have come to share in C,
     5: 5 C did not take on himself the glory
     6: 1 the elementary teachings about C
     9:11 when C came as high priest
     9:15 For this reason C is the mediator
     9:24 C did not enter a sanctuary made
     9:26 Otherwise C would have had
     9:28 so C was sacrificed once to take
    10:10 of the body of Jesus C once for all.
    11:26 for the sake of C as of greater value
    13: 8 Jesus C is the same yesterday
1Pe 1: 2 Spirit, to be obedient to Jesus C
     1: 3 and Father of our Lord Jesus C!
     1: 3 of Jesus C from the dead,
     1:11 the Spirit of C in them was pointing
     1:11 the Spirit of C in them was pointing
     1:19 but with the precious blood of C,
     2:21 called, because C suffered for you,
     3:15 But in your hearts revere C as Lord.
     3:18 For C also suffered once for sins,
     3:21 you by the resurrection of Jesus C,
     4: 1 since C suffered in his body,
     4:13 participate in the sufferings of C,
     4:14 insulted because of the name of C,
2Pe 1: 1 a servant and apostle of Jesus C,
     1: 1 Savior Jesus C have received a faith
     1:16 of our Lord Jesus C in power,
     3:18 of our Lord and Savior Jesus C.
1Jn 2: 1 Jesus C, the Righteous One.
     2:22 whoever denies that Jesus is the C.
     3:16 Jesus C laid down his life for us.
     3:23 Jesus C, and to love one another as
     4: 2 that Jesus C has come in the flesh is
     5: 1 believes that Jesus is the C is born
     5: 6 came by water and blood—Jesus C.
     5:20 is true by being in his Son Jesus C.
2Jn 1: 7 not acknowledge Jesus C as coming
     1: 9 teaching of C does not have God;
Jude 1: 1 a servant of Jesus C and a brother
     1: 1 the Father and kept for Jesus C:
     1: 4 deny Jesus C our only Sovereign
     1:17 of our Lord Jesus C foretold.
Rev 1: 1 The revelation from Jesus C,
     1: 5 and from Jesus C, who is

Rev 20: 4 reigned with C a thousand years.
20: 6 of C and will reign with him

CHRIST JESUS See JESUS

JESUS CHRIST See JESUS

LORD JESUS CHRIST See JESUS

CHRIST'S* CHRIST
1Co 7:22 was free when called is C slave.
9:21 God's law but am under C law),
2Co 2:14 captives in C triumphal procession
5:14 For C love compels us, because we
5:20 We are therefore C ambassadors,
5:20 We implore you on C behalf:
12: 9 so that C power may rest on me.
12:10 for C sake, I delight in weaknesses,
Col 1:22 by C physical body through death
1:24 lacking in regard to C afflictions,
2Th 3: 5 into God's love and C perseverance.
1Pe 5: 1 a witness of C sufferings who

CHRISTIAN* CHRIST
Ac 26:28 you can persuade me to be a C?"
1Pe 4:16 if you suffer as a C, do not be

CHRISTIANS* CHRIST
Ac 11:26 The disciples were called C first

CHRONICLES*
Est 6: 1 so he ordered the book of the c,

CHURCH CHURCHES
Mt 16:18 and on this rock I will build my c,
18:17 still refuse to listen, tell it to the c;
18:17 if they refuse to listen even to the c,
Ac 5:11 Great fear seized the whole c and all
8: 1 broke out against the c in Jerusalem,
8: 3 But Saul began to destroy the c.
12: 1 some who belonged to the c,
14:23 elders for them in each c and,
15: 4 they were welcomed by the c
20:28 Be shepherds of the c of God,
Ro 16: 5 also the c that meets at their house.
1Co 4:17 what I teach everywhere in every c.
5:12 mine to judge those outside the c?
6: 4 way of life is scorned in the c?
10:32 Jews, Greeks or the c of God—
11:18 that when you come together as a c,
12:28 God has placed in the c first of all
14: 4 one who prophesies edifies the c.
14:12 to excel in those that build up the c.
14:26 done so that the c may be built up.
14:35 for a woman to speak in the c.
15: 9 because I persecuted the c of God.
Gal 1:13 how intensely I persecuted the c
Eph 1:22 to be head over everything for the c,
3:10 through the c, the manifold wisdom
5:23 wife as Christ is the head of the c,
5:25 just as Christ loved the c and gave
Php 3: 6 as for zeal, persecuting the c;
Col 1:18 he is the head of the body, the c;
1:24 the sake of his body, which is the c.
1Ti 3: 5 how can he take care of God's c?)
5:16 not let the c be burdened with them,
5:16 the c can help those widows who

Heb 12:23 to the c of the firstborn,
Jas 5:14 the elders of the c to pray over them
3Jn 1: 9 I wrote to the c, but Diotrephes,

CHURCHES CHURCH
Ac 15:41 and Cilicia, strengthening the c.
16: 5 So the c were strengthened
1Co 7:17 is the rule I lay down in all the c.
11:16 nor do the c of God.
14:34 should remain silent in the c.
2Co 11: 8 I robbed other c by receiving
1Th 2:14 imitators of God's c in Judea,
2:14 the same things those c suffered
2Th 1: 4 among God's c we boast about your
Rev 1: 4 To the seven c in the province
1:20 stars are the angels of the seven c,
1:20 seven lampstands are the seven c.
2: 7 hear what the Spirit says to the c.
22:16 to give you this testimony for the c.

CHURNING
Pr 30:33 For as c cream produces butter,
Da 7: 2 winds of heaven c up the great sea.

CILICIA
Ac 21:39 from Tarsus in C, a citizen of no

CIRCLE CIRCLED, CIRCLING, CIRCUIT, CIRCULAR, ENCIRCLE, ENCIRCLED
Isa 40:22 enthroned above the c of the earth,
Mk 3:34 at those seated in a c around him

CIRCLED* CIRCLE
Jos 6:15 that day they c the city seven times.

CIRCLING* CIRCLE
Jos 6:11 carried around the city, c it once.

CIRCUIT* CIRCLE
1Sa 7:16 year he went on a c from Bethel
Ps 19: 6 and makes its c to the other;

CIRCULAR CIRCLE
2Ch 4: 2 the Sea of cast metal, c in shape,

CIRCULATED*
Mt 28:15 has been widely c among the Jews

CIRCUMCISE* CIRCUMCISED, CIRCUMCISION
Dt 10:16 C your hearts, therefore, and do not
30: 6 LORD your God will c your hearts
Jos 5: 2 knives and c the Israelites again."
Jer 4: 4 C yourselves to the LORD, c your hearts,
Lk 1:59 eighth day they came to c the child,
2:21 when it was time to c the child,
Jn 7:22 you c a boy on the Sabbath.
Ac 21:21 telling them not to c their children

CIRCUMCISED CIRCUMCISE
Ge 17:10 Every male among you shall be c.
17:26 his son Ishmael were both c
21: 4 was eight days old, Abraham c him,
Lev 12: 3 On the eighth day the boy is to be c.

Jos   5: 3 c the Israelites at Gibeath Haaraloth.
Ac   10:45 The c believers who had come
      11: 2 the c believers criticized him
      15: 1 "Unless you are c,
      16: 3 so he c him because of the Jews
Ro   2:26 those who are not c keep the law's
       2:26 he regarded as though they were c?
       4: 9 Is this blessedness only for the c,
1Co   7:18 Was a man already c when he was
       7:18 he was called? He should not be c.
Gal   2: 8 in Peter as an apostle to the c,
       5: 2 you that if you let yourselves be c,
       6:13 even those who are c keep the law,
       6:13 you to be c that they may boast
Col   2:11 c with a circumcision not performed
       2:11 put off when you were c by Christ,
       3:11 Gentile or Jew, c or uncircumcised,

CIRCUMCISION CIRCUMCISE
Ro   2:25 C has value if you observe the law,
       2:29 and c is c of the heart, by the Spirit,
1Co   7:19 C is nothing and uncircumcision is
Gal   2:12 those who belonged to the c group.
       5: 6 Jesus neither c nor uncircumcision
Php   3: 3 For it is we who are the c, we who
Col   2:11 circumcised with a c not performed
Titus 1:10 especially those of the c group.

CIRCUMSTANCES
1Co   7:15 or the sister is not bound in such c;
Php   4:11 to be content whatever the c.
1Th   5:18 give thanks in all c; for this is God's
Jas   1: 9 Believers in humble c ought to take

CISTERN CISTERNS
Ge   37:22 Throw him into this c here
2Ki   18:31 and drink water from your own c,
Pr   5:15 Drink water from your own c,
Jer   38: 6 and put him into the c of Malkijah,
      38: 6 Jeremiah by ropes into the c;

CISTERNS CISTERN
Ge   37:20 throw him into one of these c
Jer   2:13 and have dug their own c, broken c

CITADEL CITADELS
2Sa   12:26 and captured the royal c.
Ne   1: 1 year, while I was in the c of Susa,

CITADELS* CITADEL
Ps   48: 3 God is in her c; he has shown
      48:13 view her c, that you may tell
     122: 7 walls and security within your c."
Isa   34:13 Thorns will overrun her c,

CITIES CITY
Ge   13:12 while Lot lived among the c
      19:25 Thus he overthrew those c
      19:25 destroying all those living in the c—
      24:60 may your offspring possess the c
Nu   13:28 and the c are fortified and very
      21: 2 we will totally destroy their c."
      35:11 some towns to be your c of refuge,
Dt   6:10 flourishing c you did not build,
Jos   24:13 did not toil and c you did not build;

Ps   69:35 Zion and rebuild the c of Judah.
Isa   64:10 Your sacred c have become
Jer   4:16 raising a war cry against the c
Lk   19:17 small matter, take charge of ten c.'
      19:19 'You take charge of five c.'
2Pe   2: 6 if he condemned the c of Sodom
Rev   16:19 and the c of the nations collapsed.

CITIZEN CITIZENS, CITIZENSHIP
Ac   21:39 in Cilicia, a c of no ordinary city.
      22:25 to flog a Roman c who hasn't even

CITIZENS CITIZEN
Ac   16:38 that Paul and Silas were Roman c,
Eph   2:19 but fellow c with God's people

CITIZENSHIP* CITIZEN
Ac   22:28 to pay a lot of money for my c."
Eph   2:12 excluded from c in Israel
Php   3:20 But our c is in heaven.

CITY CITIES
Ge   4:17 Cain was then building a c, and he
      11: 4 let us build ourselves a c,
      18:24 are fifty righteous people in the c?
      19:14 LORD is about to destroy the c!"
Dt   28: 3 You will be blessed in the c
      28:16 You will be cursed in the c
Jos   6:16 the LORD has given you the c!
      18:28 Haeleph, the Jebusite c (that is,
Jdg   16: 3 took hold of the doors of the c gate,
2Sa   5: 9 fortress and called it the C of David.
1Ki   8:44 the LORD toward the c you have
1Ch   11: 7 and so it was called the C of David.
Ne   11: 1 the holy c, while the remaining nine
Ps   46: 4 river whose streams make glad the c
      48: 1 praise, in the c of our God, his holy
     122: 3 Jerusalem is built like a c that is
     127: 1 the LORD watches over the c,
Pr   8: 3 beside the gate leading into the c,
      11:10 the righteous prosper, the c rejoices;
      31:23 husband is respected at the c gate,
      31:31 works bring her praise at the c gate.
Isa   1:21 See how the faithful c has become
       1:26 Afterward you will be called the C
       1:26 of Righteousness, the Faithful C."
Jer   34: 2 to give this c into the hands
      34:22 and I will bring them back to this c.
La   1: 1 How deserted lies the c, once so full
Eze   4: 1 and draw the c of Jerusalem on it.
      11: 3 This c is a pot, and we are the meat
Da   9:24 your holy c to finish transgression,
Jnh   1: 2 "Go to the great c of Nineveh
       4:11 concern for the great c of Nineveh,
Hab   2:12 him who builds a c with bloodshed
Zep   2:15 This is the c of revelry that lived
Zec   14: 2 the c will be captured, the houses
      14: 2 Half of the c will go into exile,
Mt   4: 5 the devil took him to the holy c
Ac   18:10 I have many people in this c."
Heb   11:10 forward to the c with foundations,
      12:22 Zion, to the c of the living God,
      13:14 here we do not have an enduring c,
      13:14 we are looking for the c that is
Rev   2:13 who was put to death in your c—

Rev 3:12 and the name of the c of my God,
11: 2 trample on the holy c for 42 months.
16:19 The great c split into three parts,
17:18 The woman you saw is the great c
18:10 great c, you mighty c of Babylon!
20: 9 of God's people, the c he loves.
21: 2 I saw the Holy C, the new
22: 3 and of the Lamb will be in the c,

CITY OF DAVID 2Sa 5:7, 9; 6:10, 12, 16; 1Ki 2:10; 3:1; 8:1; 9:24; 11:27, 43; 14:31; 15:8; 22:50; 2Ki 8:24; 9:28; 12:21; 14:20; 15:7, 38; 16:20; 1Ch 11:5, 7; 13:13; 15:1, 29; 2Ch 5:2; 8:11; 9:31; 12:16; 14:1; 16:14; 21:1, 20; 24:16, 25; 27:9; 32:5, 30; 33:14; Ne 3:15; 12:37; Isa 22:9

HOLY CITY See HOLY

CIVILIAN*

2Ti 2: 4 a soldier gets entangled in c affairs,

CLAIM CLAIMED, CLAIMING, CLAIMS, RECLAIM

Job 41:11 Who has a c against me that I must
Pr 25: 6 and do not c a place among his great
Jn 9:41 but now that you c you can see,
10:33 you, a mere man, c to be God."
Titus 1:16 They c to know God, but by their
1Jn 1: 6 If we c to have fellowship with him
1: 8 If we c to be without sin,
1:10 If we c we have not sinned,
Rev 2: 2 you have tested those who c to be
3: 9 who c to be Jews though they are

CLAIMED CLAIM

Jn 19: 7 because he c to be the Son of God."
19:21 but that this man c to be king
Ro 1:22 Although they c to be wise,

CLAIMING CLAIM

Mk 13: 6 Many will come in my name, c,

CLAIMS CLAIM

Jas 2:14 if someone c to have faith but has
1Jn 2: 6 Whoever c to live in him must live
2: 9 Anyone who c to be in the light

CLAN CLANS

Ge 24:40 a wife for my son from my own c
Lev 25:10 family property and to your own c.
25:49 relative in their c may redeem them.
Nu 27: 4 from his c because he had no son?
1Sa 18:18 what is my family or my c in Israel,

CLANGING*

1Co 13: 1 a resounding gong or a c cymbal.

CLANS CLAN

Nu 1: 2 Israelite community by their c
Jos 14: 1 of the tribal c of Israel allotted
Mic 5: 2 though you are small among the c

CLAP* CLAPPED, CLAPS

Job 21: 5 c your hand over your mouth.
Ps 47: 1 C your hands, all you nations;
98: 8 Let the rivers c their hands,
Pr 30:32 evil, c your hand over your mouth!

Isa 55:12 trees of the field will c their hands.
La 2:15 All who pass your way c their hands
Na 3:19 the news about you c their hands

CLAPPED* CLAP

2Ki 11:12 and the people c their hands
Eze 25: 6 Because you have c your hands

CLAPS* CLAP

Job 27:23 It c its hands in derision and hisses
34:37 scornfully he c his hands among us

CLASPED* CLASPS

Mt 28: 9 him, c his feet and worshiped him.

CLASPS CLASPED

Ex 26: 6 make fifty gold c and use them

CLASSIFY*

2Co 10:12 We do not dare to c or compare

CLAUDIUS*

Ac 11:28 happened during the reign of C.)
18: 2 because C had ordered all Jews
23:26 C Lysias, To His Excellency,

CLAWS*

Da 4:33 and his nails like the c of a bird.
7:19 with its iron teeth and bronze c—

CLAY

Job 10: 9 that you molded me like c.
33: 6 in God's sight; I too am a piece of c.
Isa 29:16 potter were thought to be like the c!
41:25 as if he were a potter treading the c.
45: 9 Does the c say to the potter,
64: 8 We are the c, you are the potter;
Jer 18: 6 "Like c in the hand of the potter,
19: 1 "Go and buy a c jar from a potter.
La 4: 2 are now considered as pots of c,
Eze 4: 1 take a block of c, put it in front
Da 2:33 partly of iron and partly of baked c.
Ro 9:21 the same lump of c some pottery
2Co 4: 7 this treasure in jars of c to show
2Ti 2:20 and silver, but also of wood and c;

CLEAN CLEANNESS, CLEANSE, CLEANSED, CLEANSING

Ge 7: 2 pairs of every kind of c animal,
Lev 4:12 the camp to a place ceremonially c,
10:10 between the unclean and the c,
16:30 you will be c from all your sins.
Ps 24: 4 The one who has c hands and a pure
51: 7 me with hyssop, and I will be c;
Pr 20: 9 I am c and without sin"?
Ecc 9: 2 and the bad, the c and the unclean,
Eze 36:25 I will sprinkle c water on you, and you will be c;
Zec 3: 5 I said, "Put a c turban on his head."
3: 5 So they put a c turban on his head
Mt 8: 2 are willing, you can make me c."
12:44 swept c and put in order.
23:25 You c the outside of the cup
27:59 body, wrapped it in a c linen cloth,
Mk 7:19 this, Jesus declared all foods c.)

Jn   13:10   their whole body is c.
       13:10   And you are c, though not every one
       15: 3   You are already c because
Ac   10:15   impure that God has made c."
Ro   14:20   All food is c, but it is wrong
Rev   15: 6   They were dressed in c,
       19: 8   linen, bright and c, was given her
       19:14   dressed in fine linen, white and c.

CLEANNESS   CLEAN

2Sa   22:25   according to my c in his sight.
Ps   18:20   the c of my hands he has rewarded

CLEANSE   CLEAN

Ps   51: 2   my iniquity and c me from my sin.
       51: 7   C me with hyssop, and I will be
Zec   13: 1   to c them from sin and impurity.
Mt   10: 8   the dead, c those who have leprosy,
2Ti   2:21   Those who c themselves
Heb   9:14   c our consciences from acts
       10:22   having our hearts sprinkled to c us

CLEANSED   CLEAN

Jos   22:17   very day we have not c ourselves
2Ki   5:10   will be restored and you will be c."
Pr   30:12   eyes and yet are not c of their filth;
Isa   1: 6   not c or bandaged or soothed
Mt   8: 3   Immediately he was c of his
       11: 5   those who have leprosy are c,
Lk   4:27   prophet, yet not one of them was c—
       17:14   And as they went, they were c.
Heb   9:22   nearly everything be c with blood,
       10: 2   worshipers would have been c once
2Pe   1: 9   that they have been c from their past

CLEANSING   CLEAN

Mk   1:44   that Moses commanded for your c,
Eph   5:26   c her by the washing with water

CLEAR   CLEARED, CLEARLY

Lev   24: 2   to bring you c oil of pressed olives
Ne   8: 8   making it c and giving the meaning
Mt   3:12   and he will c his threshing floor,
1Co   4: 4   My conscience is c, but that does
1Ti   3: 9   of the faith with a c conscience.
2Ti   1: 3   with a c conscience, as night
Heb   13:18   are sure that we have a c conscience
1Pe   3:16   keeping a c conscience,
Rev   4: 6   like a sea of glass, c as crystal.
       21:11   jewel, like a jasper, c as crystal.
       22: 1   of the water of life, as c as crystal,

CLEARED   CLEAR

Ps   80: 9   You c the ground for it, and it took
Isa   5: 2   He dug it up and c it of stones

CLEARLY   CLEAR

Mk   8:25   restored, and he saw everything c.
Lk   6:42   you will see c to remove the speck
Ro   1:20   have been c seen, being understood

CLEFT*   CLEFTS

Ex   33:22   I will put you in a c in the rock

CLEFTS   CLEFT

SS   2:14   My dove in the c of the rock,

Ob   1: 3   you who live in the c of the rocks

CLEVER*

Isa   3: 3   skilled craftsman and c enchanter.
       5:21   own eyes and c in their own sight.

CLIMAX*

Eze   21:25   of punishment has reached its c,
       21:29   of punishment has reached its c.
       35: 5   time their punishment reached its c,

CLIMB   CLIMBED

1Sa   14:10   we will c up, because that will be
SS   7: 8   I said, "I will c the palm tree;
Am   9: 2   Though they c up to the heavens

CLIMBED   CLIMB

Lk   19: 4   c a sycamore-fig tree to see him,

CLING   CLUNG

Ps   31: 6   I hate those who c to worthless
       63: 8   I c to you; your right hand upholds
      137: 6   May my tongue c to the roof of my
Jnh   2: 8   "Those who c to worthless idols
Ro   12: 9   Hate what is evil; c to what is good.

CLOAK   CLOAKS

Ge   39:12   She caught him by his c and said,
       39:12   But he left his c in her hand and ran
Ex   4: 6   "Put your hand inside your c."
       4: 6   So Moses put his hand into his c,
       12:11   with your c tucked into your belt,
       22:26   take your neighbor's c as a pledge,
Dt   22:12   the four corners of the c you wear.
1Ki   11:30   hold of the new c he was wearing
       18:46   and, tucking his c into his belt,
2Ki   2: 8   Elijah took his c, rolled it
       2:13   picked up Elijah's c that had fallen
       4:29   "Tuck your c into your belt,
       9: 1   to him, "Tuck your c into your belt,
Mk   13:16   in the field go back to get their c.
Lk   8:44   him and touched the edge of his c,

CLOAKS   CLOAK

Mk   11: 8   Many people spread their c

CLOSE   CLOSED, CLOSER, ENCLOSE, ENCLOSED

1Sa   18: 9   time on Saul kept a c eye on David.
2Ki   11: 8   Stay c to the king wherever he
Ps   34:18   The LORD is c
       41: 9   Even my c friend, someone I
       55:13   myself, my companion, my c friend,
     148:14   of Israel, the people c to his heart.
Pr   16:28   and a gossip separates c friends.
       28:27   but those who c their eyes to them
Isa   40:11   arms and carries them c to his heart;
Jer   30:21   him near and he will come c to me—
       30:21   will devote himself to be c to me?'
Joel   2: 1   LORD is coming. It is c at hand—
Zec   13: 7   against the man who is c to me!"
Mt   6: 6   c the door and pray to your Father,
Rev   6: 8   Hades was following c behind him.

CLOSED   CLOSE

Ge   2:21   and then c up the place with flesh.

1Sa 1: 5 and the LORD had c her womb.
Jer 6:10 Their ears are c so they cannot hear.
Mt 13:15 ears, and they have c their eyes.
Ac 28:27 ears, and they have c their eyes.

CLOSER CLOSE
Ex 3: 5 "Do not come any c," God said.
Pr 18:24 a friend who sticks c than a brother.

CLOTH CLOTHS
Ex 28:31 robe of the ephod entirely of blue c,
Dt 22:17 shall display the c before the elders
2Ki 8:15 But the next day he took a thick c,
Mt 9:16 of unshrunk c on an old garment,
27:59 body, wrapped it in a clean linen c,

CLOTHE CLOTHED, CLOTHES, CLOTHING
Ps 45: 3 c yourself with splendor
132:16 I will c her priests with salvation,
132:18 I will c his enemies with shame,
Isa 52: 1 Zion, c yourself with strength!
Mt 25:43 clothes and you did not c me, I was
Lk 12:28 fire, how much more will he c you—
Ro 13:14 c yourselves with the Lord Jesus
1Co 15:53 the perishable must c itself
Col 3:12 c yourselves with compassion,
1Pe 5: 5 c yourselves with humility toward

CLOTHED CLOTHE
Ge 3:21 for Adam and his wife and c them.
2Ch 6:41 LORD God, be c with salvation,
Ps 30:11 my sackcloth and c me with joy,
104: 1 you are c with splendor
Pr 31:22 she is c in fine linen and purple.
31:25 She is c with strength and dignity;
Isa 61:10 For he has c me with garments
Zec 3: 5 clean turban on his head and c him,
Mt 25:36 I needed clothes and you c me,
Lk 24:49 the city until you have been c
Jn 19: 2 They c him in a purple robe
2Co 5: 2 longing to be c instead with our
Gal 3:27 into Christ have c yourselves
Rev 12: 1 a woman c with the sun,
16:15 one who stays awake and remains c,

CLOTHES CLOTHE
Dt 8: 4 Your c did not wear out and your
29: 5 wilderness, your c did not wear out,
Ps 22:18 They divide my c among them
Pr 6:27 his lap without his c being burned?
Jer 52:33 So Jehoiachin put aside his prison c
Hag 1: 6 You put on c, but are not warm.
Zec 3: 3 filthy c as he stood before the angel.
Mt 6:25 food, and the body more than c?
6:28 "And why do you worry about c?
17: 2 his c became as white as the light.
22:12 you get in here without wedding c,
25:36 I needed c and you clothed me,
27:35 they divided up his c by casting lots.
Jn 11:44 "Take off the grave c and let him
Ac 10:30 a man in shining c stood before me
1Ti 2: 9 or gold or pearls or expensive c,
Jas 2: 2 wearing a gold ring and fine c,
2: 2 and a poor man in filthy old c

1Pe 3: 3 wearing of gold jewelry or fine c.

CLOTHING CLOTHE
Ex 3:22 articles of silver and gold and for c,
12:35 articles of silver and gold and for c.
Dt 22: 5 A woman must not wear men's c,
22: 5 nor a man wear women's c,
Job 29:14 I put on righteousness as my c;
Ps 102:26 Like c you will change them
Da 7: 9 His c was as white as snow;
Mt 7:15 They come to you in sheep's c,
Mk 1: 6 John wore c made of camel's hair,
1Ti 6: 8 But if we have food and c, we will
Jude 1:23 hating even the c stained

CLOTHS* CLOTH
Eze 16: 4 rubbed with salt or wrapped in c.
Lk 2: 7 She wrapped him in c and placed
2:12 You will find a baby wrapped in c

CLOUD CLOUDS, THUNDERCLOUD
Ex 13:21 them in a pillar of c to guide them
19: 9 going to come to you in a dense c,
24:18 Moses entered the c as he went
40:34 the c covered the tent of meeting,
Nu 9:15 law, was set up, the c covered it.
9:15 evening till morning the c
1Ki 8:10 Place, the c filled the temple
18:44 "A c as small as a man's hand is
Ne 9:19 By day the pillar of c did not fail
Ps 105:39 He spread out a c as a covering,
Pr 16:15 his favor is like a rain c in spring.
Isa 19: 1 the LORD rides on a swift c and is
Eze 1: 4 an immense c with flashing
Mk 9: 7 Then a c appeared and covered them,
and a voice came from the c:
Lk 21:27 of Man coming in a c with power
Ac 1: 9 and a c hid him from their sight.
1Co 10: 2 all baptized into Moses in the c
Heb 12: 1 by such a great c of witnesses, let us
Rev 10: 1 He was robed in a c, with a rainbow
11:12 And they went up to heaven in a c,
14:14 and there before me was a white c,
14:14 seated on the c was one like a son

CLOUDS CLOUD
Ge 9:13 I have set my rainbow in the c,
Dt 33:26 you and on the c in his majesty.
1Ki 18:45 the sky grew black with c, the wind
Ps 68: 4 name, extol him who rides on the c;
104: 3 He makes the c his chariot and rides
Pr 8:28 when he established the c
25:14 Like c and wind without rain is one
Isa 14:14 will ascend above the tops of the c;
Eze 1:28 of a rainbow in the c on a rainy day,
Da 7:13 man, coming with the c of heaven.
Joel 2: 2 gloom, a day of c and blackness.
Na 1: 3 storm, and c are the dust of his feet.
Zep 1:15 gloom, a day of c and blackness—
Mt 24:30 of Man coming on the c of heaven,
26:64 and coming on the c of heaven."
1Th 4:17 them in the c to meet the Lord
Jude 1:12 They are c without rain,

Rev   1: 7 he is coming with the **c**,"

CLUB CLUBS
Pr   25:18 Like a **c** or a sword or a sharp arrow
Isa 10: 5 in whose hand is the **c** of my wrath!
Jer 51:20 "You are my war **c**, my weapon

CLUBS CLUB
Mk 14:43 a crowd armed with swords and **c**,

CLUNG* CLING
Ru   1:14 goodbye, but Ruth **c** to her.
2Ki 3: 3 Nevertheless he **c** to the sins
La   1: 9 Her filthiness **c** to her skirts;

CLUSTER
Nu 13:23 cut off a branch bearing a single **c**

CO-HEIRS* INHERIT
Ro   8:17 heirs of God and **c** with Christ,

CO-WORKERS* WORK
Ro   16: 3 and Aquila, my **c** in Christ Jesus.
1Co 3: 9 For we are **c** in God's service;
2Co 6: 1 As God's **c** we urge you not
Php 4: 3 with Clement and the rest of my **c**,
Col 4:11 are the only Jews among my **c**

COAL* COALS
2Sa 14: 7 out the only burning **c** I have left,
Isa 6: 6 flew to me with a live **c** in his hand,

COALS COAL
Nu 16:37 scatter the **c** some distance away,
Ps   11: 6 On the wicked he will rain fiery **c**
     18: 8 mouth, burning **c** blazed out of it.
Pr   6:28 walk on hot **c** without his feet being
     25:22 you will heap burning **c** on his head,
Eze 1:13 living creatures like burning **c**
     10: 2 burning **c** from among the cherubim
Ro   12:20 this, you will heap burning **c** on his

COARSE*
Eph 5: 4 foolish talk or **c** joking, which are

COAST
Nu 34: 6 western boundary will be the **c**

COAT COATED
Ge   6:14 rooms in it and **c** it with pitch inside
Dt   27: 4 you today, and **c** them with plaster.
1Sa 17: 5 wore a **c** of scale armor of bronze
Mt   5:40 your shirt, hand over your **c** as well.

COAT OF MANY COLOURS
(KJV) See ORNATE ROBE

COATED* COAT
Ex   2: 3 basket for him and **c** it with tar

COBRA* COBRA'S
Ps   58: 4 that of a **c** that has stopped its ears,
     91:13 You will tread on the lion and the **c**;

COBRA'S* COBRA
Isa 11: 8 The infant will play near the **c** den,

CODE*
Ro   2:27 even though you have the written **c**
     2:29 by the Spirit, not by the written **c**.
     7: 6 not in the old way of the written **c**.

COFFIN*
Ge   50:26 him, he was placed in a **c** in Egypt.

COILED* COILING
2Sa 22: 6 The cords of the grave **c** around me;
Ps   18: 5 The cords of the grave **c** around me;

COILING* COILED
Isa 27: 1 serpent, Leviathan the **c** serpent;

COIN* COINS
Mt   17:27 and you will find a four-drachma **c**.
     22:19 Show me the **c** used for paying
Mk   12:16 They brought the **c**, and he asked
Lk   15: 9 I have found my lost **c**.'

COINS COIN
Mt   18:28 who owed him a hundred silver **c**.
Lk   15: 8 suppose a woman has ten silver **c**
Jn   2:15 he scattered the **c** of the money

COLD
Ge   8:22 seedtime and harvest, **c** and heat,
Pr   25:25 Like **c** water to a weary soul is good
Zec 14: 6 there will be neither sunlight nor **c**,
Mt   10:42 anyone gives even a cup of **c** water
     24:12 the love of most will grow **c**,
Rev 3:16 neither hot nor **c**—I am about to spit

COLLAPSE COLLAPSED
Jos 6: 5 the wall of the city will **c**
Mt   15:32 hungry, or they may **c** on the way."

COLLAPSED COLLAPSE
Rev 11:13 earthquake and a tenth of the city **c**.
     16:19 parts, and the cities of the nations **c**.

COLLECT COLLECTED,
COLLECTION, COLLECTOR,
COLLECTORS
Ne   10:37 it is the Levites who **c** the tithes
Mk   12: 2 to the tenants to **c** from them some

COLLECTED COLLECT
Mt   13:48 down and **c** the good fish in baskets,
Heb 7: 6 yet he **c** a tenth from Abraham

COLLECTION* COLLECT
Isa 57:13 help, let your **c** of idols save you!
1Co 16: 1 about the **c** for the Lord's people:

COLLECTOR COLLECT
Da   11:20 out a tax **c** to maintain the royal
Mt   10: 3 Thomas and Matthew the tax **c**;
Lk   5:27 and saw a tax **c** by the name of Levi
     18:10 one a Pharisee and the other a tax **c**.
     19: 2 he was a chief tax **c** and was

TAX COLLECTOR See TAX

COLLECTORS COLLECT
Mt   5:46 Are not even the tax **c** doing that?

Mt   9:10 many tax **c** and sinners came
     11:19 a friend of tax **c** and sinners.'
     17:24 the **c** of the two-drachma temple tax
     21:32 but the tax **c** and the prostitutes did.

TAX COLLECTORS See TAX

COLONNADE*
1Ki   7: 6 He made a **c** fifty cubits long
Jn   10:23 courts walking in Solomon's **C**.
Ac   3:11 in the place called Solomon's **C**.
      5:12 to meet together in Solomon's **C**.

COLONY*
Ac   16:12 a Roman **c** and the leading city

COLT
Ge   49:11 a vine, his **c** to the choicest branch;
Zec   9: 9 donkey, on a **c**, the foal of a donkey.
Mt   21: 5 a donkey, and on a **c**, the foal
Jn   12:15 is coming, seated on a donkey's **c**."

COMB*
Pr   24:13 honey from the **c** is sweet to your
     27: 7 is full loathes honey from the **c**,

COME CAME, COMES, COMING
Ge   8:16 "**C** out of the ark, you and your
     15:16 your descendants will **c** back here,
     38:16 by the roadside and said, "**C** now,
     39: 7 and said, "**C** to bed with me!"
     50:24 But God will surely **c** to your aid
Ex   3: 5 "Do not **c** any closer," God said.
     19:11 that day the LORD will **c** down
     24: 1 to Moses, "**C** up to the LORD,
Nu   24:17 A star will **c** out of Jacob;
Dt   28: 2 All these blessings will **c** on you
     28:45 All these curses will **c** on you.
Jos 23:15 your God has promised you have **c**
Ru   1: 6 that the LORD had **c** to the aid
1Sa   4: 7 "A god has **c** into the camp,"
Ps   14: 7 salvation for Israel would **c**
     17: 2 Let my vindication **c** from you;
     24: 7 that the King of glory may **c** in.
     31: 2 ear to me, **c** quickly to my rescue;
     40:13 **c** quickly, LORD, to help me.
     88: 2 May my prayer **c** before you;
     90:10 Our days may **c** to seventy years,
     91:10 no disaster will **c** near your tent.
    119:41 May your unfailing love **c** to me,
    121: 1 where does my help **c** from?
    132: 8 and **c** to your resting place,
    144: 5 your heavens, LORD, and **c** down;
Pr   2: 6 from his mouth **c** knowledge
      9: 4 "Let all who are simple **c** to my
     10:28 hopes of the wicked **c** to nothing.
     24:34 poverty will **c** on you like a thief
Ecc   1: 4 Generations **c** and generations go,
      9:12 one knows when their hour will **c**:
     11: 8 Everything to **c** is meaningless.
SS   2:13 Arise, **c**, my darling;
      2:13 my beautiful one, **c** with me."
Isa   1:18 "**C** now, let us settle the matter,"
     37:32 out of Jerusalem will **c** a remnant,
     41:22 Or declare to us the things to **c**,
     59:20 "The Redeemer will **c** to Zion,

Jer 51:45 "**C** out of her, my people!
Eze   7: 6 The end has **c**! The end has **c**!
     36: 8 Israel, for they will soon **c** home.
     37: 5 enter you, and you will **c** to life.
Hos   1:11 the people of Israel will **c** together;
      3: 5 They will **c** trembling
Hab   2: 3 it will certainly **c** and will not delay.
Mal   3: 5 "So I will **c** to put you on trial.
Mt   2: 2 it rose and have **c** to worship him."
      4:19 "**C**, follow me," Jesus said, "and I
      6:10 your kingdom **c**, your will be done,
     10:34 suppose that I have **c** to bring peace
     10:34 I did not **c** to bring peace,
     12:28 the kingdom of God has **c** upon you.
     15:19 For out of the heart **c** evil thoughts—
     17:12 Elijah has already **c**, and they did
     19:14 "Let the little children **c** to me,
     20:28 Son of Man did not **c** to be served,
     24: 5 For many will **c** in my name,
     27:40 **C** down from the cross, if you are
Jn   2: 4 "My hour has not yet **c**."
      6:37 All those the Father gives me will **c**
     12:23 "The hour has **c** for the Son of Man
     14: 3 I will **c** back and take you to be
Ac   1:11 will **c** back in the same way you
1Co 16:22 let that person be cursed! **C**, Lord!
Gal   4: 4 But when the set time had fully **c**,
2Th   2: 2 the day of the Lord has already **c**.
Heb 10: 9 I am, I have **c** to do your will."
     12:22 But you have **c** to Mount Zion,
     12:22 You have **c** to thousands
Jas   4: 8 **C** near to God and he will **c** near
1Pe   2: 4 As you **c** to him, the living Stone—
2Pe   3: 9 but everyone to **c** to repentance.
1Jn   2:18 even now many antichrists have **c**.
      4: 2 that Jesus Christ has **c** in the flesh is
Rev   1: 4 and who is to **c**, and from the seven
      4: 8 who was, and is, and is to **c**."
     22:17 The Spirit and the bride say, "**C**!"
     22:17 let the one who hears say, "**C**!"
     22:17 let the one who is thirsty **c**;
     22:20 Amen. **C**, Lord Jesus.

DAYS TO COME See DAYS

COMES COME
1Ch 16:33 LORD, for he **c** to judge the earth.
     29:14 Everything **c** from you, and we have
     29:14 and we have given you only what **c**
Ps   3: 8 From the LORD **c** deliverance.
     96:13 for he **c**, he **c** to judge the earth.
    118:26 Blessed is he who **c** in the name
    121: 2 My help **c** from the LORD,
Pr   10: 8 but a chattering fool **c** to ruin.
     11: 2 When pride **c**, then **c** disgrace,
     11: 2 but with humility **c** wisdom.
     11:27 but evil **c** to one who searches for it.
     15:33 and humility **c** before honor.
Ecc   5:15 Everyone **c** naked from their
      5:15 and as everyone **c**, so they depart.
Isa 40:10 See, the Sovereign LORD **c**
Eze   7:10 See, it **c**! Doom has burst forth,
Jnh   2: 9 'Salvation **c** from the LORD.' "
Zec 14: 7 When evening **c**, there will be light.

Mt   12:43 "When an impure spirit c
      21: 5 'See, your king c to you,
Mk   11: 9 "Blessed is he who c in the name
Lk   18: 8 when the Son of Man c, will he find
Jn   3:31 The one who c from above is
       3:31 The one who c from heaven is
       6:33 God is the bread that c down
      10:10 The thief c only to steal and kill
      14: 6 No one c to the Father except
      15:26 "When the Advocate c, whom I
      16:13 the Spirit of truth, c, he will guide
Ac   1: 8 when the Holy Spirit c on you;
Ro   4:13 through the righteousness that c
1Co   11:12 But everything c from God.
2Co   3: 5 but our competence c from God.
Php   3: 9 of my own that c from the law,
       3: 9 the righteousness that c from God
1Jn   2:21 and because no lie c from the truth.
       4: 7 one another, for love c from God.
2Jn   1:10 If anyone c to you and does not
Rev   11: 5 them, fire c from their mouths
      11: 7 the beast that c up from the Abyss

COMFORT* COMFORTED, COMFORTER, COMFORTERS, COMFORTING, COMFORTS

Ge   5:29 said, "He will c us in the labor
      37:35 sons and daughters came to c him,
1Ch   7:22 and his relatives came to c him.
Job   2:11 and sympathize with him and c him.
       7:13 When I think my bed will c me
      16: 5 c from my lips would bring you
      36:16 to the c of your table laden
Ps   23: 4 your rod and your staff, they c me.
      71:21 my honor and c me once more.
     119:50 My c in my suffering is this:
     119:52 ancient laws, and I find c in them.
     119:76 May your unfailing love be my c,
     119:82 I say, "When will you c me?"
Isa   40: 1 C, c my people, says your God.
      51: 3 The LORD will surely c Zion
      51:19 come upon you—who can c you?—
      57:18 and restore c to Israel's mourners,
      61: 2 of our God, to c all who mourn,
      66:13 comforts her child, so will I c you;
Jer   16: 7 offer food to c those who mourn
      31:13 I will give them c and joy instead
La   1: 2 her lovers there is no one to c her.
       1: 9 there was none to c her.
       1:16 No one is near to c me, no one
       1:17 hands, but there is no one to c her.
       1:21 but there is no one to c me.
       2:13 that I may c you, Virgin Daughter
Eze   16:54 all you have done in giving them c.
Na   3: 7 Where can I find anyone to c you?"
Zec   1:17 the LORD will again c Zion
      10: 2 that are false, they give c in vain.
Lk   6:24 you have already received your c.
Jn   11:19 Mary to c them in the loss of their
1Co   14: 3 strengthening, encouraging and c.
2Co   1: 3 of compassion and the God of all c,
       1: 4 so that we can c those in any trouble
       1: 4 with the c we ourselves receive

2Co   1: 5 also our c abounds through Christ.
       1: 6 it is for your c and salvation;
       1: 6 it is for your c, which produces
       1: 7 so also you share in our c.
       2: 7 you ought to forgive and c him,
       7: 7 but also by the c you had given him.
Php   2: 1 Christ, if any c from his love, if any
Col   4:11 and they have proved a c to me.

COMFORTED* COMFORT

Ge   24:67 Isaac was c after his mother's death.
      37:35 comfort him, but he refused to be c.
2Sa   12:24 Then David c his wife Bathsheba,
Job   42:11 They c and consoled him over all
Ps   77: 2 hands, and I would not be c.
      86:17 LORD, have helped me and c me.
Isa   12: 1 has turned away and you have c me.
      52: 9 for the LORD has c his people,
      54:11 lashed by storms and not c, I will
      66:13 and you will be c over Jerusalem."
Jer   31:15 for her children and refusing to be c,
Mt   2:18 for her children and refusing to be c,
       5: 4 those who mourn, for they will be c.
Lk   16:25 but now he is c here and you are
Ac   20:12 man home alive and were greatly c.
2Co   1: 6 if we are c, it is for your comfort,
       7: 6 c us by the coming of Titus,

COMFORTER* COMFORT (KJV, of the Holy Spirit, see ADVOCATE)

Ecc   4: 1 and they have no c; power was
       4: 1 and they have no c.
Jer   8:18 You who are my C in sorrow,

COMFORTERS* COMFORT

Job   16: 2 you are miserable c, all of you!
Ps   69:20 was none, for c, but I found none.

COMFORTING* COMFORT

Isa   66:11 and be satisfied at her c breasts;
Zec   1:13 and c words to the angel who talked
Jn   11:31 been with Mary in the house, c her,
1Th   2:12 c and urging you to live lives

COMFORTS* COMFORT

Job   29:25 I was like one who c mourners.
Isa   49:13 For the LORD c his people
      51:12 "I, even I, am he who c you.
      66:13 As a mother c her child, so will I
2Co   1: 4 who c us in all our troubles,
       7: 6 But God, who c the downcast,

COMING COME

Ex   32: 1 Moses was so long in c down
Ecc   10:14 No one knows what is c—
Isa   13: 9 See, the day of the LORD is c—
Jer   7:32 the days are c, declares the LORD,
Eze   43: 2 of the God of Israel c from the east.
Da   7:13 of man, c with the clouds of heaven.
Joel   2: 1 for the day of the LORD is c.
Mic   1: 3 The LORD is c from his dwelling
Zep   1:14 near and c quickly.
Mk   13:26 will see the Son of Man c in clouds
1Th   1:10 who rescues us from the c wrath.
2Th   2: 1 Concerning the c of our Lord Jesus

Heb 10:37 he who is c will come and will not
Jas 5: 8 firm, because the Lord's c is near.
2Pe 1:16 about the c of our Lord Jesus Christ
3: 4 "Where is this 'c' he promised?
Jude 1:14 the Lord is c with thousands
Rev 1: 7 "Look, he is c with the clouds,"
3:11 I am c soon. Hold on to what you
13: 1 And I saw a beast c out of the sea.
19:15 C out of his mouth is a sharp sword
21: 2 c down out of heaven from God,
21:10 c down out of heaven from God.
22: 7 "Look, I am c soon! Blessed is

DAYS ARE COMING See DAYS

COMMAND COMMANDED,
COMMANDER, COMMANDING,
COMMANDMENT,
COMMANDMENTS, COMMANDS

Ex 7: 2 You are to say everything I c you,
34:11 Obey what I c you today.
Nu 14:41 are you disobeying the LORD's c?
24:13 to go beyond the c of the LORD—
Dt 4: 2 Do not add to what I c you and do
8: 1 to follow every c I am giving you
12:32 See that you do all I c you;
15:11 Therefore I c you to be openhanded
30:16 For I c you today to love
32:46 so that you may c your children
1Sa 13:14 you have not kept the LORD's c."
1Ki 11:10 did not keep the LORD's c.
Ps 91:11 he will c his angels concerning you
148: 5 for at his c they were created,
Pr 6:23 For this c is a lamp, this teaching is
8:29 the waters would not overstep his c,
13:13 whoever respects a c is rewarded.
Ecc 8: 2 Obey the king's c, I say,
Jer 1: 7 you to say whatever I c you.
1:17 and say to them whatever I c you.
7:23 but I gave them this c:
7:23 Walk in obedience to all I c you,
11: 4 me and do everything I c you,
26: 2 Tell them everything I c you;
La 1:18 yet I rebelled against his c.
Joel 2:11 mighty is the army that obeys his c.
Mt 4: 6 " 'He will c his angels concerning
15: 3 why do you break the c of God
Lk 4:10 " 'He will c his angels concerning
Jn 10:18 This c I received from my Father."
12:50 I know that his c leads to eternal
13:34 "A new c I give you:
15:12 My c is this: Love each other as I
15:14 are my friends if you do what I c.
15:17 This is my c: Love each other.
Ro 13: 9 whatever other c there may be, are
summed up in this one c:
1Co 14:37 I am writing to you is the Lord's c.
Gal 5:14 is fulfilled in keeping this one c:
1Ti 1: 5 The goal of this c is love,
1:18 I am giving you this c in keeping
6:14 to keep this c without spot or blame
6:17 C those who are rich in this present
Heb 9:19 Moses had proclaimed every c
11: 3 the universe was formed at God's c,

2Pe 2:21 on the sacred c that was passed
3: 2 and the c given by our Lord
1Jn 2: 7 I am not writing you a new c
2: 7 This old c is the message you have
3:23 And this is his c: to believe
4:21 And he has given us this c:
2Jn 1: 6 his c is that you walk in love.
Rev 3:10 Since you have kept my c to endure

COMMANDED COMMAND

Ge 2:16 And the LORD God c the man,
3:11 from the tree that I c you not to eat
7: 5 Noah did all that the LORD c him.
50:12 Jacob's sons did as he had c them:
Ex 7: 6 did just as the LORD c them.
19: 7 all the words the LORD had c him
Dt 4: 5 laws as the LORD my God c me,
6:24 The LORD c us to obey all these
18:20 in my name anything I have not c,
Jos 1: 9 Have I not c you? Be strong
1:16 "Whatever you have c us we will
2Sa 5:25 So David did as the LORD c him, ·
2Ki 17:13 entire Law that I c your ancestors
21: 8 be careful to do everything I c them
2Ch 33: 8 do everything I c them concerning
Ps 33: 9 came to be; he c, and it stood firm.
78: 5 which he c our ancestors to teach
Isa 13: 3 I have c those I prepared for battle;
Am 2:12 and c the prophets not to prophesy.
Jnh 2:10 And the LORD c the fish, and it
Mt 28:20 to obey everything I have c you.
Lk 8:29 For Jesus had c the impure spirit
Jn 12:49 the Father who sent me c me to say
14:31 exactly what my Father has c me.
Ac 10:42 He c us to preach to the people
1Co 9:14 way, the Lord has c that those who
1Jn 3:23 and to love one another as he c us.
2Jn 1: 4 in the truth, just as the Father c us.

AS THE LORD† … COMMANDED See
LORD†

COMMANDER COMMAND

Jos 5:15 The c of the LORD's army replied,
2Ki 18:17 king of Assyria sent his supreme c,
18:17 and his field c with a large army,
Da 8:11 to be as great as the c of the army

COMMANDING COMMAND

Dt 30:11 Now what I am c you today is not
2Ti 2: 4 rather tries to please his c officer.

COMMANDMENT* COMMAND

Jos 22: 5 be very careful to keep the c
Mt 22:36 which is the greatest c in the Law?"
22:38 This is the first and greatest c.
Mk 12:31 There is no c greater than these."
Lk 23:56 the Sabbath in obedience to the c.
Ro 7: 8 the opportunity afforded by the c,
7: 9 but when the c came, sin sprang
7:10 that the very c that was intended
7:11 the opportunity afforded by the c,
7:11 and through the c put me to death.
7:12 and the c is holy,
7:13 that through the c sin might become

Eph   6: 2   which is the first **c** with a promise—

COMMANDMENTS* COMMAND

Ex   20: 6   those who love me and keep my **c**.
    24:12   the law and **c** I have written for their
    34:28   words of the covenant—the Ten **C**.
Dt   4:13   the Ten **C**, which he commanded
    5:10   those who love me and keep my **c**.
    5:22   These are the **c** the Lord
    6: 6   These **c** that I give you today are
    7: 9   those who love him and keep his **c**.
    9:10   On them were all the **c** the Lord
   10: 4   the Ten **C** he had proclaimed to you
Ne   1: 5   those who love him and keep his **c**,
Pr   19:16   Whoever keeps **c** keeps their life,
Ecc 12:13   Fear God and keep his **c**, for this is
Da   9: 4   those who love him and keep his **c**,
Mt   19:17   you want to enter life, keep the **c**."
   22:40   the Prophets hang on these two **c**."
Mk 10:19   You know the **c**: 'You shall not
   12:28   "Of all the **c**, which is the most
Lk   18:20   You know the **c**: 'You shall not
Ro   13: 9   The **c**, "You shall not commit

COMMANDS COMMAND

Ge   26: 5   keeping my **c**, my decrees and my
Ex   25:22   give you all my **c** for the Israelites.
   34:32   gave them all the **c** the Lord had
Lev   4: 2   in any of the Lord's **c**—
   22:31   "Keep my **c** and follow them.
   26: 3   and are careful to obey my **c**,
   26:15   and fail to carry out all my **c** and so
Nu   15:39   so you will remember all the **c**
Dt   5:29   fear me and keep all my **c** always,
    7:11   take care to follow the **c**,
   11: 1   decrees, his laws and his **c** always.
   11:28   if you disobey the **c** of the Lord
   28: 1   carefully follow all his **c** I give you
   30:10   and keep his **c** and decrees that are
Jos   22: 5   to keep his **c**, to hold fast to him
Jdg   3: 4   they would obey the Lord's **c**,
1Sa 12:14   him and do not rebel against his **c**,
1Ki   2: 3   and keep his decrees and **c**, his laws
    8:58   in obedience to him and keep the **c**,
    8:61   live by his decrees and obey his **c**,
1Ch 28: 7   is unswerving in carrying out my **c**
   29:19   devotion to keep your **c**,
2Ch 31:21   in obedience to the law and the **c**,
Ezr   9:10   For we have forsaken the **c**
Ps   19: 8   The **c** of the Lord are radiant,
   78: 7   his deeds but would keep his **c**.
  112: 1   who find great delight in his **c**.
  119:10   do not let me stray from your **c**.
  119:32   I run in the path of your **c**, for you
  119:35   Direct me in the path of your **c**,
  119:47   in your **c** because I love them.
  119:48   I reach out for your **c**, which I love,
  119:73   me understanding to learn your **c**.
  119:86   All your **c** are trustworthy;
  119:96   a limit, but your **c** are boundless.
  119:98   Your **c** are always with me
 119:115   that I may keep the **c** of my God!
 119:127   I love your **c** more than gold,
 119:131   mouth and pant, longing for your **c**.

Ps 119:143   me, but your **c** give me delight.
  119:151   Lord, and all your **c** are true.
  119:172   word, for all your **c** are righteous.
  119:176   for I have not forgotten your **c**.
Pr   2: 1   words and store up my **c** within you,
    3: 1   but keep my **c** in your heart,
    7: 2   Keep my **c** and you will live;
   10: 8   The wise in heart accept **c**,
Isa 48:18   only you had paid attention to my **c**,
Jer   7:22   I did not just give them **c**
Mt   5:19   sets aside one of the least of these **c**
    5:19   teaches these **c** will be called great
Mk   7: 9   way of setting aside the **c** of God
Lk   1: 6   God, observing all the Lord's **c**
Jn   14:15   "If you love me, keep my **c**.
   14:21   Whoever has my **c** and keeps them
   15:10   If you keep my **c**, you will remain
   15:10   just as I have kept my Father's **c**
Ac   17:30   now he **c** all people everywhere
1Co   7:19   Keeping God's **c** is what counts.
Eph   2:15   aside in his flesh the law with its **c**
Col   2:22   are based on merely human **c**
1Jn   2: 3   come to know him if we keep his **c**.
    2: 4   but does not do what he **c** is a liar,
    3:22   because we keep his **c** and do what
    3:24   The one who keeps God's **c** lives
    5: 2   loving God and carrying out his **c**.
    5: 3   this is love for God: to keep his **c**.
        And his **c** are not burdensome,
2Jn   1: 6   that we walk in obedience to his **c**.
Rev 12:17   those who keep God's **c** and hold
   14:12   of the people of God who keep his **c**

COMMANDS OF THE LORD† Lev 4:22; Nu
15:39; Dt 4:2; 6:17; 8:6; 11:27, 28; 28:9, 13; 2Ki
17:16, 19; 1Ch 28:8; Ps 19:8

COMMEMORATE

Ex   12:14   "This is a day you are to **c**;

COMMEND* COMMENDABLE, COMMENDED, COMMENDS

Ecc   8:15   So I **c** the enjoyment of life,
Ro   16: 1   I **c** to you our sister Phoebe,
2Co   3: 1   we beginning to **c** ourselves again?
    4: 2   the truth plainly we **c** ourselves
    5:12   We are not trying to **c** ourselves
    6: 4   God we **c** ourselves in every way:
   10:12   with some who **c** themselves.
1Pe   2:14   wrong and to **c** those who do right.

COMMENDABLE* COMMEND

1Pe   2:19   For it is **c** if someone bears up under
    2:20   you endure it, this is **c** before God.

COMMENDED* COMMEND

Ne   11: 2   The people **c** all who volunteered
Job 29:11   of me, and those who saw me **c** me,
Lk   16: 8   "The master **c** the dishonest
Ac   15:40   **c** by the believers to the grace
Ro   13: 3   do what is right and you will be **c**.
2Co 12:11   I ought to have been **c** by you, for I
Heb 11: 2   This is what the ancients were **c** for.
   11: 4   By faith he was **c** as righteous,
   11: 5   he was **c** as one who pleased God.

Heb 11:39 These were all c for their faith,

COMMENDS* COMMEND

Ps 145: 4 One generation c your works
2Co 10:18 is not the one who c himself who is
       10:18 but the one whom the Lord c.

COMMISSION

Dt 3:28 But c Joshua, and encourage
Col 1:25 its servant by the c God gave me

COMMIT COMMITS, COMMITTED

Ex 20:14 "You shall not c adultery.
Dt   5:18 "You shall not c adultery.
1Sa 7: 3 and c yourselves to the LORD
1Ki 14:16 and has caused Israel to c."
2Ki 21:16 sin that he had caused Judah to c,
Ps 31: 5 Into your hands I c my spirit;
    37: 5 C your way to the LORD;
Pr 16: 3 C to the LORD whatever you do,
Mt   5:27 was said, 'You shall not c adultery.'
    19:18 you shall not c adultery, you shall
Mk 10:19 you shall not c adultery, you shall
Lk 18:20 'You shall not c adultery, you shall
    23:46 into your hands I c my spirit."
Ac 20:32 "Now I c you to God
Ro   2:22 that people should not c adultery, do
          you c adultery?
    13: 9 "You shall not c adultery,"
1Co 10: 8 We should not c sexual immorality,
Jas 2:11 "You shall not c adultery,"
     2:11 If you do not c adultery but do c
1Pe 4:19 to God's will should c themselves
1Jn 5:16 or sister c a sin that does not lead
Rev 2:22 I will make those who c adultery

COMMITS COMMIT

Lev 20:10 a man c adultery with another man's
Pr   6:32 a man who c adultery has no sense;
    29:22 a hot-tempered person c many sins.
Ecc 8:12 a wicked person who c a hundred
Eze 18:14 who sees all the sins his father c,
    22:11 you one man c a detestable offense
Mt   5:32 a divorced woman c adultery.
    19: 9 marries another woman c adultery."
Mk 10:11 another woman c adultery against
    10:12 another man, she c adultery."
Lk 16:18 marries another woman c adultery,
    16:18 a divorced woman c adultery.

COMMITTED COMMIT

Ge 50:17 the wrongs they c in treating you so
Ex 32:30 the people, "You have c a great sin.
Nu   5: 7 must confess the sin they have c.
Jdg 20: 6 because they c this lewd
1Ki 8:61 may your hearts be fully c
    15:14 Asa's heart was fully c
2Ch 16: 9 those whose hearts are fully c
Jer 2:13 "My people have c two sins:
     3: 9 the land and c adultery with stone
Eze 18:24 and because of the sins they have c,
Mt   5:28 lustfully has already c adultery
    11:27 "All things have been c to me
    27:23 What crime has he c?" asked Pilate.
Lk 10:22 "All things have been c to me

Ac 14:23 and fasting, c them to the Lord,
Ro   1:27 Men c shameful acts with other
     3:25 the sins c beforehand unpunished—
1Co 9:17 I am simply discharging the trust c
2Co 5:19 And he has c to us the message
1Pe 2:22 "He c no sin, and no deceit was
Rev 17: 2 her the kings of the earth c adultery,
    18: 3 of the earth c adultery with her,

COMMON

Ge 11: 1 had one language and a c speech.
Lev 10:10 between the holy and the c,
Pr 22: 2 Rich and poor have this in c:
    29:13 and the oppressor have this in c:
Ecc 9: 2 All share a c destiny—
Eze 22:26 between the holy and the c;
Ac   2:44 together and had everything in c.
Ro   9:21 special purposes and some for c use?
1Co 10:13 has overtaken you except what is c
    12: 7 of the Spirit is given for the c good.
2Co 6:14 and wickedness have in c?
     6:15 what does a believer have in c

COMMUNION (KJV) See
FELLOWSHIP, PARTICIPATION

COMMUNITY

Ge 28: 3 your numbers until you become a c
    35:11 a c of nations will come from you,
    48: 4 I will make you a c of peoples, and I
Ex 16: 2 desert the whole c grumbled against
Lev 4:13 " 'If the whole Israelite c sins
     4:13 even though the c is unaware
Nu 14:27 will this wicked c grumble against
Pr   6:19 person who stirs up conflict in the c.

COMPANION COMPANIONS

1Ki 20:35 of the prophets said to his c,
Job 30:29 a brother of jackals, a c of owls.
Ps 55:13 like myself, my c, my close friend,
    55:20 My c attacks his friends;
Pr 13:20 wise, for a c of fools suffers harm.
    28: 7 a c of gluttons disgraces his father.
    29: 3 but a c of prostitutes squanders his
Rev 1: 9 your brother and c in the suffering

COMPANIONS COMPANION

Ps 38:11 c avoid me because of my wounds;
    45: 7 you above your c by anointing you
Heb 1: 9 you above your c by anointing you

COMPANY

2Ki 2: 7 men from the c of the prophets went
     4:38 While the c of the prophets was
     6: 1 The c of the prophets said to Elisha,
Ps 14: 5 is present in the c of the righteous.
Pr 21:16 comes to rest in the c of the dead.
    24: 1 the wicked, do not desire their c;
Jer 15:17 I never sat in the c of revelers,
Lk   2:13 Suddenly a great c of the heavenly
1Co 15:33 "Bad c corrupts good character."

COMPARE* COMPARED,
COMPARING, COMPARISON

Job 28:17 Neither gold nor crystal can c

Job 28: 19 The topaz of Cush cannot **c** with it;
     39: 13 though they cannot **c** with the wings
Ps   40: 5 None can **c** with you; were I
     86: 8 no deeds can **c** with yours.
     89: 6 skies above can **c** with the LORD?
Pr   3: 15 nothing you desire can **c** with her.
      8: 11 nothing you desire can **c** with her.
Isa 40: 18 With whom, then, will you **c** God?
     40: 25 "To whom will you **c** me?
     46: 5 "With whom will you **c** me
La   2: 13 With what can I **c** you,
Eze 31: 8 nor could the plane trees **c** with its
Da   1: 13 **c** our appearance
Mt   11: 16 "To what can I **c** this generation?
Lk   7: 31 what, then, can I **c** the people of this
     13: 18 of God like? What shall I **c** it to?
     13: 20 "What shall I **c** the kingdom of God
2Co 10: 12 or **c** ourselves with some who
     10: 12 and **c** themselves with themselves,

COMPARED* COMPARE

Jdg   8: 2 "What have I accomplished **c**
      8: 3 What was I able to do **c** to you?"
Isa 46: 5 will you liken me that we may be **c**?
Eze 31: 2 " 'Who can be **c** with you
     31: 18 the trees of Eden can be **c** with you
Ro   5: 16 the gift of God be **c** with the result

COMPARING* COMPARE

Ro   8: 18 present sufferings are not worth **c**
2Co   8: 8 of your love by **c** it
Gal   6: 4 without **c** themselves to someone

COMPARISON* COMPARE

2Co   3: 10 was glorious has no glory now in **c**

COMPASSION*
COMPASSIONATE,
COMPASSIONS

Ex   33: 19 I will have **c** on whom I will have **c**.
Dt   13: 17 you mercy, and will have **c** on you.
     28: 54 man among you will have no **c**
     30: 3 your fortunes and have **c** on you
2Ki 13: 23 had **c** and showed concern for them
2Ch 30: 9 your children will be shown **c**
Ne   9: 19 of your great **c** you did not abandon
      9: 27 and in your great **c** you gave them
      9: 28 in your **c** you delivered them time
Ps   51: 1 to your great **c** blot out my
     77: 9 Has he in anger withheld his **c**?"
     90: 13 will it be? Have **c** on your servants.
    102: 13 You will arise and have **c** on Zion,
    103: 4 pit and crowns you with love and **c**,
    103: 13 As a father has **c** on his children,
    103: 13 so the LORD has **c** on those who
    116: 5 our God is full of **c**.
    119: 77 Let your **c** come to me that I may
    119:156 Your **c**, LORD, is great;
    135: 14 people and have **c** on his servants.
    145: 9 he has **c** on all he has made.
Isa 13: 18 infants, nor will they look with **c**
     14: 1 The LORD will have **c** on Jacob;
     27: 11 so their Maker has no **c** on them,
     30: 18 he will rise up to show you **c**.

Isa 49: 10 He who has **c** on them will guide
     49: 13 will have **c** on his afflicted ones.
     49: 15 and have no **c** on the child she has
     51: 3 and will look with **c** on all her ruins;
     54: 7 with deep **c** I will bring you back.
     54: 8 everlasting kindness I will have **c**
     54: 10 says the LORD, who has **c** on you.
     60: 10 you, in favor I will show you **c**.
     63: 7 Israel, according to his **c** and many
     63: 15 and **c** are withheld from us.
Jer 12: 15 I will again have **c** and will bring
     13: 14 or **c** to keep me from destroying
     21: 7 show them no mercy or pity or **c**.'
     30: 18 tents and have **c** on his dwellings;
     31: 20 I have great **c** for him,"
     33: 26 fortunes and have **c** on them.' "
     42: 12 I will show you **c** so that he will
             have **c** on you
La   3: 32 grief, he will show **c**, so great is his
Eze   9: 5 and kill, without showing pity or **c**.
     16: 5 or had **c** enough to do any of these
     39: 25 and will have **c** on all the people
Da   1: 9 to show favor and **c** to Daniel,
Hos   2: 19 and justice, in love and **c**.
     11: 8 all my **c** is aroused.
     13: 14 "I will have no **c**,
     14: 3 for in you the fatherless find **c**."
Jnh   3: 9 with **c** turn from his fierce anger so
Mic   7: 19 You will again have **c** on us;
Zec   7: 9 show mercy and **c** to one another.
     10: 6 I will restore them because I have **c**
Mal   3: 17 just as a father has **c** and spares his
Mt   9: 36 saw the crowds, he had **c** on them,
     14: 14 he had **c** on them and healed their
     15: 32 and said, "I have **c** for these people;
     20: 34 Jesus had **c** on them and touched
Mk   6: 34 a large crowd, he had **c** on them,
      8: 2 "I have **c** for these people;
Lk   15: 20 him and was filled with **c** for him;
Ro   9: 15 I will have **c** on whom I have **c**."
2Co   1: 3 the Father of **c** and the God of all
Php   2: 1 the Spirit, if any tenderness and **c**,
Col   3: 12 clothe yourselves with **c**, kindness,
Jas   5: 11 The Lord is full of **c** and mercy.

COMPASSIONATE*
COMPASSION

Ex   22: 27 cry out to me, I will hear, for I am **c**.
     34: 6 LORD, the **c** and gracious God,
2Ch 30: 9 LORD your God is gracious and **c**.
Ne   9: 17 gracious and **c**, slow to anger
Ps   86: 15 you, Lord, are a **c** and gracious God,
    103: 8 The LORD is **c** and gracious,
    111: 4 the LORD is gracious and **c**.
    112: 4 for those who are gracious and **c**
    145: 8 The LORD is gracious and **c**,
La   4: 10 their own hands **c** women have
Joel 2: 13 for he is gracious and **c**,
Jnh   4: 2 that you are a gracious and **c** God,
Eph   4: 32 Be kind and **c** to one another,
1Pe   3: 8 love one another, be **c** and humble.

COMPASSIONS* COMPASSION

La   3: 22 not consumed, for his **c** never fail.

COMPEL* COMPELLED, COMPELS, COMPULSION
Lk   14:23 lanes and **c** them to come in,
Gal   6:12 trying to **c** you to be circumcised.

COMPELLED COMPEL
Ac   20:22 "And now, **c** by the Spirit, I am
1Co   9:16 cannot boast, since I am **c** to preach.

COMPELS* COMPEL
Ex   3:19 you go unless a mighty hand **c** him.
Job   32:18 and the spirit within me **c** me;
2Co   5:14 For Christ's love **c** us, because we

COMPETENCE* COMPETENT
2Co   3: 5 but our **c** comes from God.

COMPETENT* COMPETENCE
Ro   15:14 and **c** to instruct one another.
1Co   6: 2 are you not **c** to judge trivial cases?
2Co   3: 5 Not that we are **c** in ourselves
          3: 6 He has made us **c** as ministers

COMPETES*
1Co   9:25 Everyone who **c** in the games goes
2Ti   2: 5 anyone who **c** as an athlete does not

COMPILED*
Pr   25: 1 **c** by the men of Hezekiah king

COMPLACENCY* COMPLACENT
Pr   1:32 and the **c** of fools will destroy them;
Eze   30: 9 ships to frighten Cush out of her **c**.

COMPLACENT* COMPLACENCY
Isa   32: 9 You women who are so **c**,
          32:11 Tremble, you **c** women;
Am   6: 1 Woe to you who are **c** in Zion,
Zep   1:12 lamps and punish those who are **c**,

COMPLAIN COMPLAINED, COMPLAINT, COMPLAINTS
Job   7:11 I will **c** in the bitterness of my soul.
Isa   29:24 those who **c** will accept
          40:27 Why do you **c**, Jacob? Why do you
La   3:39 Why should the living **c**

COMPLAINED COMPLAIN
Nu   11: 1 Now the people **c** about their

COMPLAINT COMPLAIN
Job   10: 1 I will give free rein to my **c**
Ps   64: 1 Hear me, my God, as I voice my **c**;
          142: 2 I pour out before him my **c**;
Hab   2: 1 what answer I am to give to this **c**.

COMPLAINTS* COMPLAIN
Nu   14:27 I have heard the **c** of these
Pr   23:29 Who has **c**? Who has needless

COMPLETE COMPLETED, COMPLETELY, COMPLETENESS, COMPLETION
Dt   16:15 your hands, and your joy will be **c**.
2Ki   12:15 because they acted with **c** honesty.
Jn   3:29 That joy is mine, and it is now **c**.

Jn   15:11 in you and that your joy may be **c**.
          16:24 will receive, and your joy will be **c**.
          17:23 that they may be brought to **c** unity.
Ac   20:24 **c** the task the Lord Jesus has given
2Co   7:16 I am glad I can have **c** confidence
          10: 6 once your obedience is **c**.
Php   2: 2 then make my joy **c** by being
Col   4:17 it that you **c** the ministry you have
Jas   1: 4 so that you may be mature and **c**,
          2:22 his faith was made **c** by what he did.
1Jn   1: 4 We write this to make our joy **c**.
          2: 5 for God is truly made **c** in them.
          4:12 in us and his love is made **c** in us.
          4:17 is how love is made **c** among us so
2Jn   1:12 to face, so that our joy may be **c**.

COMPLETED COMPLETE
Ge   2: 1 and the earth were **c** in all their vast
Ex   39:32 the tent of meeting, was **c**.
1Ki   6:14 Solomon built the temple and **c** it.
2Ch   36:21 until the seventy years were **c**
Ezr   6:15 The temple was **c** on the third day
Ne   6:15 So the wall was **c**
Isa   40: 2 her that her hard service has been **c**,
Jer   29:10 seventy years are **c** for Babylon,
Da   11:36 until the time of wrath is **c**, for what
          12: 7 broken, all these things will be **c**."
Lk   12:50 constraint I am under until it is **c**!
Rev   15: 1 because with them God's wrath is **c**.

COMPLETELY COMPLETE
Ex   11: 1 he does, he will drive you out **c**.
Nu   21: 3 They **c** destroyed them and their
Jos   17:13 labor but did not drive them out **c**.
Jdg   1:28 labor but never drove them out **c**.
1Sa   15: 9 they were unwilling to destroy **c**,
Ps   37:28 Wrongdoers will be **c** destroyed;
Jer   14:19 Have you rejected Judah **c**?
          30:11 'Though I **c** destroy all the nations
          30:11 scatter you, I will not **c** destroy you.
Mk   3: 5 it out, and his hand was **c** restored.
          4:39 wind died down and it was **c** calm.
Ac   3:16 through him that has **c** healed him,
2Pe   1:19 message as something **c** reliable,

COMPLETENESS* COMPLETE
1Co 13:10 but when **c** comes, what is in part

COMPLETION COMPLETE
Php   1: 6 on to **c** until the day of Christ Jesus.

COMPLIMENTS*
Pr   23: 8 eaten and will have wasted your **c**.

COMPREHEND* COMPREHENDED, COMPREHENDS
Ecc   8:17 No one can **c** what goes on under
          8:17 they know, they cannot really **c** it.

COMPREHENDED* COMPREHEND
Job   38:18 Have you **c** the vast expanses

COMPREHENDS* COMPREHEND
Job 28:13 No mortal **c** its worth; it cannot be

COMPULSION* COMPEL
1Co 7:37 who is under no **c** but has control
2Co 9: 7 not reluctantly or under **c**, for God

CONCEAL CONCEALED, CONCEALS
Ps 40:10 I do not **c** your love and your
Pr 25: 2 It is the glory of God to **c** a matter;
Isa 26:21 the earth will **c** its slain no longer.

CONCEALED CONCEAL
Isa 49: 2 arrow and **c** me in his quiver.
Jer 16:17 me, nor is their sin **c** from my eyes.
Mt 10:26 for there is nothing **c** that will not be
Mk 4:22 whatever is **c** is meant to be brought
Lk 8:17 nothing **c** that will not be known
12: 2 There is nothing **c** that will not be

CONCEALS* CONCEAL
Pr 10:11 the mouth of the wicked **c** violence.
10:18 Whoever **c** hatred with lying lips
28:13 Whoever **c** their sins does not

CONCEIT* CONCEITED
Isa 16: 6 of her **c**, her pride and her
Jer 48:29 her **c** and the haughtiness of her
Php 2: 3 out of selfish ambition or vain **c**.

CONCEITED* CONCEIT
1Sa 17:28 I know how **c** you are and how
Ro 11:25 so that you may not be **c**: Israel
12:16 people of low position. Do not be **c**.
2Co 12: 7 order to keep me from becoming **c**,
Gal 5:26 Let us not become **c**,
1Ti 3: 6 he may become **c** and fall under
6: 4 they are **c** and understand nothing.
2Ti 3: 4 rash, **c**, lovers of pleasure rather

CONCEIVE CONCEIVED, CONCEIVES, CONCEIVING
Ge 29:31 he enabled her to **c**, but Rachel
30:22 listened to her and enabled her to **c**.
Nu 11:12 Did I **c** all these people? Did I give
Job 15:35 They **c** trouble and give birth
Isa 33:11 You **c** chaff, you give birth to straw;

CONCEIVED CONCEIVE
Ps 51: 5 from the time my mother **c** me.
Isa 8: 3 and she **c** and gave birth to a son.
Mt 1:20 because what is **c** in her is
1Co 2: 9 and what no human mind has **c**" —
Jas 1:15 after desire has **c**, it gives birth

CONCEIVES* CONCEIVE
Ps 7:14 is pregnant with evil **c** trouble

CONCEIVING* CONCEIVE
Ge 20:18 household from **c** because

CONCERN* CONCERNED
Ge 39: 6 he did not **c** himself with anything
39: 8 "my master does not **c** himself
1Sa 23:21 LORD bless you for your **c** for me.

2Ki 13:23 showed **c** for them because of his
Job 9:21 blameless, I have no **c** for myself;
19: 4 my error remains my **c** alone.
Ps 131: 1 I do not **c** myself with great matters
Pr 29: 7 but the wicked have no such **c**.
Eze 36:21 I had **c** for my holy name,
Jnh 4:11 should I not have **c** for the great city
Ac 18:17 and Gallio showed no **c** whatever.
1Co 7:32 I would like you to be free from **c**.
12:25 that its parts should have equal **c**
2Co 7: 7 deep sorrow, your ardent **c** for me,
7:11 what **c**, what readiness to see justice
8:16 of Titus the same **c** I have for you.
11:28 of my **c** for all the churches.
Php 2:20 who will show genuine **c** for your
4:10 at last you renewed your **c** for me.

CONCERNED CONCERN
Ex 2:25 the Israelites and was **c** about them.
3: 7 and I am **c** about their suffering.
4:31 that the LORD was **c** about them
Ps 142: 4 at my right hand; no one is **c** for me.
Eze 36: 9 I am **c** for you and will look on you
Jnh 4:10 "You have been **c** about this plant,
1Co 7:32 An unmarried man is **c**
9: 9 Is it about oxen that God is **c**?
Php 4:10 Indeed, you were **c**, but you had no

CONCESSION*
1Co 7: 6 I say this as a **c**, not as a command.

CONCUBINE CONCUBINES
Ge 35:22 and slept with his father's **c** Bilhah,
Jdg 19: 9 the man, with his **c** and his servant,
2Sa 3: 7 had had a **c** named Rizpah daughter
3: 7 did you sleep with my father's **c**?"

CONCUBINES CONCUBINE
Ge 25: 6 he gave gifts to the sons of his **c**
2Sa 5:13 David took more **c** and wives
1Ki 11: 3 of royal birth and three hundred **c**,
Da 5: 3 wives and his **c** drank from them.

CONDEMN* CONDEMNATION, CONDEMNED, CONDEMNING, CONDEMNS, SELF-CONDEMNED
Job 9:20 innocent, my mouth would **c** me;
34:17 Will you **c** the just and mighty One?
34:29 if he remains silent, who can **c** him?
40: 8 Would you **c** me to justify yourself?
Ps 94:21 and **c** the innocent to death.
109: 7 guilty, and may his prayers **c** him.
109:31 lives from those who would **c** them.
Isa 50: 9 Who will **c** me? They will all wear
Mt 12:41 with this generation and **c** it;
12:42 with this generation and **c** it,
20:18 of the law. They will **c** him to death
Mk 10:33 They will **c** him to death and will
Lk 6:37 Do not **c**, and you will not be
11:31 of this generation and **c** them,
11:32 with this generation and **c** it,
Jn 3:17 Son into the world to **c** the world,
7:51 "Does our law **c** a man without first
8:11 *"Then neither do I **c** you,"*

Jn 12:48 words I have spoken will c them
Ro   2:27 yet obeys the law will c you who,
     14:22 is the one who does not c himself
2Co 7: 3 I do not say this to c you;
1Jn 3:20 If our hearts c us, we know that God
     3:21 if our hearts do not c us, we have
Jude 1: 9 did not himself dare to c him

CONDEMNATION* CONDEMN

Eze 33:12 former wickedness will not bring c.
Ro   3: 8 good may result"? Their c is just!
     5:16 followed one sin and brought c,
     5:18 just as one trespass resulted in c
     8: 1 there is now no c for those who are
2Co 3: 9 that brought c was glorious,
2Pe 2: 3 Their c has long been hanging over
Jude 1: 4 individuals whose c was written

CONDEMNED* CONDEMN

Dt 13:17 none of the c things are to be found
Job 32: 3 to refute Job, and yet had c him.
Ps 34:21 the foes of the righteous will be c.
    34:22 who takes refuge in him will be c.
    37:33 let them be c when brought to trial.
    79:11 your strong arm preserve those c
   102:20 and release those c to death."
Mt 12: 7 you would not have c the innocent.
    12:37 and by your words you will be c."
    23:33 How will you escape being c
    27: 3 saw that Jesus was c, he was seized
Mk 14:64 They all c him as worthy of death.
    16:16 whoever does not believe will be c.
Lk   6:37 not condemn, and you will not be c.
Jn   3:18 Whoever believes in him is not c,
     3:18 not believe stands c already because
     5:29 done what is evil will rise to be c.
     8:10 Has no one c you?"
    16:11 prince of this world now stands c.
Ac 25:15 against him and asked that he be c.
Ro   3: 7 glory, why am I still c as a sinner?"
     8: 3 And so he c sin in the flesh,
    14:23 whoever has doubts is c if they eat,
1Co 4: 9 like those c to die in the arena.
    11:32 that we will not be finally c
Gal 2:11 him to his face, because he stood c.
Col 2:14 which stood against us and c us;
2Th 2:12 all will be c who have not believed
Titus 2: 8 of speech that cannot be c,
Heb 11: 7 By his faith he c the world
Jas 5: 6 You have c and murdered
     5:12 Otherwise you will be c.
2Pe 2: 6 if he c the cities of Sodom
Rev 19: 2 He has c the great prostitute who

CONDEMNING* CONDEMN

Dt 25: 1 the innocent and c the guilty.
1Ki 8:32 c the guilty by bringing down
2Ch 6:23 c the guilty and bringing down
Pr 17:15 the guilty and c the innocent—
Ac 13:27 yet in c him they fulfilled the words
Ro   2: 1 you are c yourself, because you who

CONDEMNS* CONDEMN

Job 15: 6 Your own mouth c you, not mine;
Pr 12: 2 but he c those who devise wicked

Pr 14:34 exalts a nation, but sin c any people.
Ro   8:34 Who then is the one who c? No one.

CONDITION

Mt 12:45 the final c of that person is worse

CONDUCT CONDUCTED, SAFE-CONDUCT

Job 34:11 on them what their c deserves.
Ps 112: 5 who c their affairs with justice.
Pr 20:11 so is their c really pure and upright?
    21: 8 but the c of the innocent is upright.
Ecc 6: 8 how to c themselves before others?
Jer 4:18 "Your own c and actions have
     6:15 they ashamed of their detestable c?
    17:10 each person according to their c,
Eze 7: 3 I will judge you according to your c
Php 1:27 c yourselves in a manner worthy
1Ti 3:15 how people ought to c themselves
     4:12 the believers in speech, in c, in love,

CONDUCTED* CONDUCT

2Co 1:12 we have c ourselves in the world,

CONFESS* CONFESSED, CONFESSES, CONFESSING, CONFESSION

Lev 5: 5 they must c in what way they have
    16:21 goat and c over it all the wickedness
    26:40 if they will c their sins and the sins
Nu   5: 7 must c the sin they have committed.
Ne   1: 6 I c the sins we Israelites,
Ps 32: 5 "I will c my transgressions
    38:18 I c my iniquity; I am troubled by my
Jn   1:20 He did not fail to c, but confessed
Jas 5:16 Therefore c your sins to each other
1Jn 1: 9 If we c our sins, he is faithful

CONFESSED* CONFESS

1Sa 7: 6 day they fasted and there they c,
Ne   9: 2 stood in their places and c their sins
Da   9: 4 to the LORD my God and c:
Jn   1:20 confess, but c freely, "I am not
Ac 19:18 and openly c what they had done.

CONFESSES* CONFESS

Pr 28:13 whoever c and renounces them finds
2Ti 2:19 "Everyone who c the name

CONFESSING* CONFESS

Ezr 10: 1 While Ezra was praying and c,
Da   9:20 c my sin and the sin of my people
Mt   3: 6 C their sins, they were baptized
Mk   1: 5 C their sins, they were baptized

CONFESSION* CONFESS

Ne   9: 3 and spent another quarter in c
2Co 9:13 accompanies your c of the gospel
1Ti 6:12 when you made your good c
     6:13 Pontius Pilate made the good c,

CONFIDE* CONFIDES

Jdg 16:15 love you,' when you won't c in me?

CONFIDENCE* CONFIDENT

Jdg 9:26 and its citizens put their c in him.
2Ki 18:19 what are you basing this c of yours?
2Ch 32: 8 And the people gained c from what
    32:10 On what are you basing your c,
Job 4: 6 Should not your piety be your c
Ps 71: 5 LORD, my c since my youth.
Pr 3:32 but takes the upright into his c.
    11:13 A gossip betrays a c,
    20:19 A gossip betrays a c;
    25: 9 to court, do not betray another's c,
    31:11 Her husband has full c in her
Isa 32:17 will be quietness and c forever.
    36: 4 what are you basing this c of yours?
Jer 17: 7 in the LORD, whose c is in him.
    49:31 ease, which lives in c,"
Eze 29:16 will no longer be a source of c
Mic 7: 5 put no c in a friend.
2Co 2: 3 I had c in all of you, that you would
    3: 4 Such c we have through Christ
    7:16 I am glad I can have complete c
    8:22 so because of his great c in you.
Eph 3:12 approach God with freedom and c.
Php 3: 3 and who put no c in the flesh—
    3: 4 I myself have reasons for such c.
    3: 4 have reasons to put c in the flesh,
2Th 3: 4 We have c in the Lord that you are
Heb 3: 6 if indeed we hold firmly to our c
    4:16 God's throne of grace with c,
    10:19 since we have c to enter the Most
    10:35 So do not throw away your c;
    11: 1 Now faith is c in what we hope for
    13: 6 So we say with c, "The Lord is my
    13:17 Have c in your leaders and submit
1Jn 3:21 condemn us, we have c before God
    4:17 us so that we will have c on the day
    5:14 This is the c we have

CONFIDENT* CONFIDENCE

Job 6:20 distressed, because they had been c;
Ps 27: 3 against me, even then I will be c.
    27:13 I remain c of this: I will see
Lk 18: 9 To some who were c of their own
2Co 1:15 Because I was c of this, I wanted
    5: 6 Therefore we are always c
    5: 8 We are c, I say, and would prefer
    9: 4 be ashamed of having been so c.
    10: 7 If anyone is c that they belong
Gal 5:10 I am c in the Lord that you will take
Php 1: 6 being c of this, that he who began
    1:14 sisters have become c in the Lord
    2:24 I am c in the Lord that I myself will
Phm 1:21 C of your obedience, I write to you,
1Jn 2:28 that when he appears we may be c

CONFIDES* CONFIDE

Ps 25:14 The LORD c in those who fear

CONFINED

Ge 40: 3 same prison where Joseph was c.
Ps 88: 8 I am c and cannot escape;
Jer 32: 2 Jeremiah the prophet was c
    33: 1 While Jeremiah was still c
    39:15 While Jeremiah had been c

CONFIRM CONFIRMED, CONFIRMING

Ge 26: 3 will c the oath I swore to your father
Dt 29:13 to c you this day as his people,
Da 9:27 He will c a covenant with many
2Pe 1:10 make every effort to c your calling

CONFIRMED CONFIRM

Dt 4:31 which he c to them by oath.
Ps 105:10 He c it to Jacob as a decree, to Israel
Ac 14: 3 who c the message of his grace
Ro 15: 8 made to the patriarchs might be c
Heb 2: 3 was c to us by those who heard him.

CONFIRMING* CONFIRM

2Ki 23: 3 thus c the words of the covenant
1Co 1: 6 God thus c our testimony
Php 1: 7 or defending and c the gospel,

CONFLICT*

Pr 6:14 in his heart—he always stirs up c.
    6:19 a person who stirs up c in the
    10:12 Hatred stirs up c, but love covers over
    15:18 A hot-tempered person stirs up c,
    16:28 A perverse person stirs up c,
    28:25 The greedy stir up c, but those who
    29:22 An angry person stirs up c,
Hab 1: 3 there is strife, and c abounds.
Gal 5:17 They are in c with each other,
Heb 10:32 in a great c full of suffering.

CONFORM* CONFORMED, CONFORMITY, CONFORMS

Ro 12: 2 Do not c to the pattern of this world,
1Pe 1:14 do not c to the evil desires you had

CONFORMED* CONFORM

Eze 5: 7 You have not even c
    11:12 but have c to the standards
Ac 26: 5 that I c to the strictest sect of our
Ro 8:29 predestined to be c to the image

CONFORMITY* CONFORM

Eph 1:11 out everything in c with the purpose

CONFORMS* CONFORM

1Ti 1:11 that c to the gospel concerning

CONFRONT CONFRONTED, CONFRONTS

Ex 9:13 morning, c Pharaoh and say to him,
Job 9:32 that we might c each other in court.
Ps 17:13 LORD, c them, bring them down;
Eze 22: 2 Then c her with all her detestable

CONFRONTED CONFRONT

2Sa 22: 6 the snares of death c me.
Ps 18:18 They c me in the day of my disaster,

CONFRONTS* CONFRONT

Job 31:14 what will I do when God c me?

CONFUSE* CONFUSION

Ge 11: 7 and c their language so they will not

Ps 55: 9 Lord, c the wicked, confound their

CONFUSION CONFUSE
Ex 14:24 Egyptian army and threw it into c.
23:27 into c every nation you encounter.
Dt 7:23 into great c until they are destroyed.
28:28 madness, blindness and c of mind.
Jos 10:10 threw them into c before Israel,
1Sa 14:20 They found the Philistines in total c,
Ps 70: 2 take my life be put to shame and c;
Jer 51:34 us, he has thrown us into c, he has
Mic 7: 4 Now is the time of your c.
Gal 5:10 The one who is throwing you into c,

CONGREGATION*
CONGREGATIONS
Ps 26:12 the great c I will praise the LORD.
68:26 Praise God in the great c;
Ac 13:43 When the c was dismissed,

CONGREGATIONS*
CONGREGATION
1Co 14:33 as in all the c of the Lord's people.

CONNECTION
Col 2:19 They have lost c with the head,

CONQUER CONQUERED,
CONQUEROR, CONQUERORS
Rev 13: 7 God's holy people and to c them.

CONQUERED CONQUER
Jos 10:42 and their lands Joshua c in one
Heb 11:33 who through faith c kingdoms,

CONQUEROR* CONQUER
Mic 1:15 I will bring a c against you who live
Rev 6: 2 he rode out as a c bent on conquest.

CONQUERORS* CONQUER
Ro 8:37 are more than c through him who

CONSCIENCE* CONSCIENCE-
STRICKEN, CONSCIENCES,
CONSCIENTIOUS
Ge 20: 5 I have done this with a clear c
20: 6 I know you did this with a clear c,
1Sa 25:31 have on his c the staggering burden
Job 27: 6 my c will not reproach me as long
Ac 23: 1 to God in all good c to this day."
24:16 to keep my c clear before God
Ro 9: 1 my c confirms it through the Holy
13: 5 but also as a matter of c.
1Co 4: 4 My c is clear, but that does not
8: 7 a god, and since their c is weak, it is
8:10 if someone with a weak c sees you,
8:12 in this way and wound their weak c,
10:25 without raising questions of c,
10:27 you without raising questions of c.
10:28 who told you and for the sake of c.
10:29 am referring to the other person's c,
10:29 being judged by another's c?
2Co 1:12 Our c testifies that we have
4: 2 to everyone's c in the sight of God.
5:11 and I hope it is also plain to your c.

1Ti 1: 5 and a good c and a sincere faith.
1:19 holding on to faith and a good c,
3: 9 truths of the faith with a clear c.
2Ti 1: 3 with a clear c, as night and day I
Heb 9: 9 able to clear the c of the worshiper.
10:22 to cleanse us from a guilty c
13:18 We are sure that we have a clear c
1Pe 3:16 keeping a clear c, so that those who
3:21 the pledge of a clear c toward God.

CONSCIENCE-STRICKEN*
CONSCIENCE
1Sa 24: 5 David was c for having cut off
2Sa 24:10 David was c after he had counted

CONSCIENCES* CONSCIENCE
Ro 2:15 hearts, their c also bearing witness,
1Ti 4: 2 whose c have been seared as
Titus 1:15 their minds and c are corrupted.
Heb 9:14 cleanse our c from acts that lead

CONSCIENTIOUS* CONSCIENCE
2Ch 29:34 for the Levites had been more c

CONSCIOUS*
Ro 3:20 through the law we become c of our
1Pe 2:19 unjust suffering because they are c

CONSECRATE CONSECRATED
Ex 13: 2 "C to me every firstborn male.
19:10 "Go to the people and c them today
28:41 C them so they may serve me as
40: 9 c it and all its furnishings, and it
Lev 20: 7 " 'C yourselves and be holy,
25:10 C the fiftieth year and proclaim
Jos 7:13 "Go, c the people. Tell them,
1Ch 15:12 fellow Levites are to c yourselves
2Ch 29: 5 C yourselves now and c the temple

CONSECRATED CONSECRATE
Ex 29:43 and the place will be c by my glory.
Lev 8:30 So he c Aaron and his garments
Nu 15:40 and will be c to your God.
1Sa 21: 4 there is some c bread here—
2Ch 7:16 c this temple so that my Name may
Ps 50: 5 "Gather to me this c people,
Mk 2:26 house of God and ate the c bread,
Lk 2:23 male is to be c to the Lord"),
1Ti 4: 5 because it is c by the word of God

CONSENT
1Co 7: 5 other except perhaps by mutual c
Phm 1:14 want to do anything without your c,

CONSEQUENCES
Eze 16:58 You will bear the c of your

CONSIDER CONSIDERATE,
CONSIDERED, CONSIDERS
Dt 17:20 not c himself better than his fellow
1Sa 12:24 c what great things he has done
16: 7 "Do not c his appearance or his
2Ch 19: 6 them, "C carefully what you do,
Job 37:14 stop and c God's wonders.
Ps 5: 1 to my words, LORD, c my lament.
8: 3 When I c your heavens, the work

Ps 50:22 "**C** this, you who forget God, or I
    77:12 I will **c** all your works and meditate
    143: 5 and **c** what your hands have done.
Pr   6: 6 **c** its ways and be wise!
    20:25 and only later to **c** one's vows.
Ecc 2:12 I turned my thoughts to **c** wisdom,
     7:13 **C** what God has done:
Isa 47: 7 you did not **c** these things or reflect
Jer 2:31 **c** the word of the LORD:
La   1:11 LORD, and, **c**, for I am despised."
Mk   4:24 "**C** carefully what you hear,"
Lk 12:24 **C** the ravens: They do not sow
    12:27 "**C** how the wild flowers grow.
Ac 20:24 I **c** my life worth nothing to me;
Ro 11:22 **C** therefore the kindness
Php 2: 6 God, did not **c** equality with God
     3: 8 I **c** everything a loss because
     3: 8 I **c** them garbage, that I may gain
Heb 10:24 And let us **c** how we may spur one
    12: 3 **C** him who endured such opposition
Jas 1: 2 **C** it pure joy, my brothers
    1:26 Those who **c** themselves religious

CONSIDERATE* CONSIDER

Titus 3: 2 to be peaceable and **c**, and always
Jas 3:17 then peace-loving, **c**, submissive,
1Pe 2:18 only to those who are good and **c**,
     3: 7 the same way be **c** as you live

CONSIDERED CONSIDER

1Ki 16:31 He not only **c** it trivial to commit
Job 1: 8 "Have you **c** my servant Job?
     2: 3 "Have you **c** my servant Job?
    34: 6 Although I am right, I am **c** a liar;
Ps 44:22 we are **c** as sheep to be slaughtered.
Isa 53: 4 yet we **c** him punished by God,
Hos 9: 7 the prophet is **c** a fool, the inspired
Mt 14: 5 because they **c** John a prophet.
Ro   8:36 all day long; we are **c** as sheep to be
1Ti 1:12 that he **c** me trustworthy,
Heb 11:11 children because she **c** him faithful
Jas 2:21 not our father Abraham **c** righteous
    2:25 Rahab the prostitute **c** righteous

CONSIDERS CONSIDER

Pr 31:16 She **c** a field and buys it; out of her
Ro 14: 5 One person **c** one day more sacred
    14: 5 another **c** every day alike.

CONSIST CONSISTS

Lk 12:15 life does not **c** in an abundance

CONSISTS CONSIST

Eph 5: 9 fruit of the light **c** in all goodness,

CONSOLATION* CONSOLE

Job 6:10 Then I would still have this **c**—
    21: 2 let this be the **c** you give me.
Ps 94:19 within me, your **c** brought me joy.
Lk   2:25 He was waiting for the **c** of Israel,

CONSOLATIONS* CONSOLE

Job 15:11 Are God's **c** not enough for you,

CONSOLE* CONSOLATION, CONSOLATIONS

Job 21:34 "So how can you **c** me with your
Isa 22: 4 not try to **c** me over the destruction
    51:19 famine and sword—who can **c** you?
Jer 16: 7 anyone give them a drink to **c** them.

CONSORT*

Hos 4:14 because the men themselves **c**

CONSPIRACY CONSPIRE

Ps 64: 2 Hide me from the **c** of the wicked,
Isa 8:12 "Do not call **c** everything this people
                calls a **c**;

CONSPIRE CONSPIRACY

Ps   2: 1 Why do the nations **c**
    59: 3 Fierce men **c** against me for no
Mic 7: 3 they all **c** together.
Ac   4:27 to **c** against your holy servant Jesus,

CONSTANT CONSTANTLY

Dt 28:66 You will live in **c** suspense,
Pr 19:13 wife is like the **c** dripping of a leaky
Ac 27:33 "you have been in **c** suspense
Heb 5:14 by **c** use have trained themselves

CONSTANTLY CONSTANT

Pr   8:30 Then I was **c** at his side. I was filled
Ac   1:14 They all joined together **c** in prayer,

CONSTRAINT*

Lk 12:50 and what **c** I am under until it is

CONSTRUCTIVE*

1Co 10:23 but not everything is **c**.

CONSULT CONSULTED, CONSULTS

1Sa 28: 8 "**C** a spirit for me," he said,
2Ki 1: 2 "Go and **c** Baal-Zebub, the god
     8: 8 **C** the LORD through him;
2Ch 17: 3 He did not **c** the Baals
    25:15 "Why do you **c** this people's gods,
Isa 8:19 someone tells you to **c** mediums
     8:19 Why **c** the dead on behalf
    40:14 Whom did the LORD **c**
Eze 21:21 lots with arrows, he will **c** his idols,
Hos 4:12 My people **c** a wooden idol,
Gal 1:16 was not to **c** any human being.

CONSULTED CONSULT

1Ch 10:13 and even **c** a medium for guidance,

CONSULTS* CONSULT

Dt 18:11 or spiritist or who **c** the dead.
Eze 14:10 be as guilty as the one who **c** him.

CONSUME CONSUMED, CONSUMES, CONSUMING

Dt   5:25 This great fire will **c** us, and we will
Ps 21: 9 his wrath, and his fire will **c** them.
    59:13 **c** them in your wrath, **c** them till
Isa 26:11 reserved for your enemies **c** them.
Jer 17:27 that will **c** her fortresses.' "
Eze 15: 7 of the fire, the fire will yet **c** them.

Jn   2:17 "Zeal for your house will c me."
Heb 10:27 raging fire that will c the enemies

CONSUMED CONSUME
Lev 10: 2 presence of the LORD and c them,
Nu   11: 1 c some of the outskirts of the camp.
        16:35 c the 250 men who were offering
2Ki   1:10 fell from heaven and c the captain
2Ch   7: 1 heaven and c the burnt offering
Ps   37:20 they will be c, they will go
        90: 7 We are c by your anger and terrified
Ecc 10:12 but fools are c by their own lips.
La   3:22 LORD's great love we are not c,
Zep   3: 8 The whole world will be c
Zec   9: 4 on the sea, and she will be c by fire.
Rev 18: 8 She will be c by fire, for mighty is

CONSUMES CONSUME
Ps   69: 9 for zeal for your house c me,

CONSUMING CONSUME
Ex   24:17 the LORD looked like a c fire
Dt   4:24 For the LORD your God is a c fire,
2Sa   22: 9 c fire came from his mouth,
Heb 12:29 for our "God is a c fire."

CONSUMMATE*
Mt   1:25 he did not c their marriage until she

CONTAIN* CONTAINED,
   CONTAINS
1Ki   8:27 the highest heaven, cannot c you.
2Ch   2: 6 the highest heavens, cannot c him?
        6:18 the highest heavens, cannot c you.
Ecc   8: 8 one has power over the wind to c it,
2Pe   3:16 His letters c some things that are

CONTAINED* CONTAIN
Ac   10:12 It c all kinds of four-footed animals,
Heb   9: 4 This ark c the gold jar of manna,

CONTAINS CONTAIN
Pr   15: 6 of the righteous c great treasure,

CONTAMINATES*
2Co   7: 1 from everything that c body

CONTEMPLATE*
2Co   3:18 unveiled faces c the Lord's glory,

CONTEMPT CONTEMPTIBLE
Nu   14:11 will these people treat me with c?
Dt   17:12 Anyone who shows c for the judge
1Sa   2:17 the LORD's offering with c.
        25:39 Nabal for treating me with c.
Ps   123: 3 us, for we have endured no end of c.
Pr   14:31 oppresses the poor shows c for their
        17: 5 Whoever mocks the poor shows c
        18: 3 so does c, and with shame comes
Da   12: 2 others to shame and everlasting c.
Mal   1: 6 "It is you priests who show c
        1: 6 'How have we shown c for your
Ro   2: 4 do you show c for the riches of his
        14: 3 treat with c the one who does not,
Gal   4:14 you did not treat me with c or scorn.
1Th   5:20 Do not treat prophecies with c

CONTEMPTIBLE CONTEMPT
Pr   30:23 a c woman who gets married,
Da   11:21 "He will be succeeded by a c person

CONTEND CONTENDED,
   CONTENDING, CONTENDS,
   CONTENTIOUS
Ge   6: 3 "My Spirit will not c with humans
Jdg   6:32 day, saying, "Let Baal c with him."
Ps   35: 1 C, LORD, with those who c
Isa   49:25 I will c with those who c with you,
Jude 1: 3 urge you to c for the faith that was

CONTENDED* CONTEND
Dt   33: 8 you c with him at the waters
Php   4: 3 help these women since they have c

CONTENDING* CONTEND
Col   2: 1 to know how hard I am c for you

CONTENDS* CONTEND
Job   40: 2 "Will the one who c
Jer   15:10 whom the whole land strives and c!

CONTENT* CONTENTMENT
Ge   25:27 while Jacob was c to stay at home
Jos   7: 7 If only we had been c to stay
Ps   131: 2 like a weaned child I am c.
Pr   13:25 The righteous eat to their hearts' c,
        19:23 then one rests c,
Ecc   4: 8 toil, yet his eyes were not c with his
Lk   3:14 be c with your pay."
Php   4:11 to be c whatever the circumstances.
        4:12 learned the secret of being c in any
1Ti   6: 8 and clothing, we will be c with that.
Heb 13: 5 and be c with what you have,

CONTENTIOUS* CONTEND
1Co 11:16 If anyone wants to be c about this,

CONTENTMENT* CONTENT
Job   36:11 in prosperity and their years in c.
SS   8:10 in his eyes like one bringing c.
1Ti   6: 6 But godliness with c is great gain.

CONTINUAL CONTINUE
Pr   15:15 but the cheerful heart has a c feast.

CONTINUALLY CONTINUE
Lev 24: 2 the lamps may be kept burning c.
Nu   4: 7 the bread that is c there is to remain
Isa   27: 3 LORD, watch over it; I water it c.
Lk   24:53 And they stayed c at the temple,
1Th   5:17 pray c,
Heb 13:15 let us c offer to God a sacrifice

CONTINUE CONTINUAL,
   CONTINUALLY, CONTINUED,
   CONTINUES, CONTINUING
1Ch 17:27 that it may c forever in your sight;
2Ch   6:14 your servants who c wholeheartedly
Ps   36:10 C your love to those who know you,
        89:36 that his line will c forever and his
Jer   3: 5 Will your wrath c forever?'
Ac   13:43 urged them to c in the grace of God.

Ro 11:22 provided that you c in his kindness.
2Co 1:10 our hope that he will c to deliver us,
Gal 3:10 "Cursed is everyone who does not c
Php 2:12 c to work out your salvation
Col 1:23 if you c in your faith,
       2: 6 as Lord, c to live your lives in him,
1Ti 2:15 if they c in faith, love and holiness
2Ti 3:14 c in what you have learned and have
1Jn 2:28 dear children, c in him,
       3: 9 who is born of God will c to sin,
       5:18 born of God does not c to sin;
2Jn 1: 9 does not c in the teaching of Christ
Rev 22:11 Let the one who does wrong c to do
      22:11 let the vile person c to be vile;
      22:11 let the one who does right c to do
      22:11 let the holy person c to be holy."

CONTINUED CONTINUE
Jdg 1:29 the Canaanites c to live there among
Ps 78:17 But they c to sin against him,
Isa 64: 5 But when we c to sin against them,
Ac 14: 7 where they c to preach the gospel.

CONTINUES CONTINUE
Ps 100: 5 his faithfulness c through all
     119:90 Your faithfulness c through all
2Co 10:15 hope is that, as your faith c to grow,
1Jn 3: 6 No one who c to sin has either seen

CONTINUING CONTINUE
Ro 13: 8 except the c debt to love one

CONTRARY
Lev 10: 1 the LORD, c to his command.
2Ch 30:18 the Passover, c to what was written
Ac 18:13 worship God in ways c to the law."
Ro 11:24 and c to nature were grafted
Gal 5:17 For the flesh desires what is c
       5:17 and the Spirit what is c to the flesh.

CONTRIBUTION
   CONTRIBUTIONS
Ro 15:26 to make a c for the poor among

CONTRIBUTIONS
   CONTRIBUTION
2Ch 24:10 all the people brought their c gladly,
      31:12 they faithfully brought in the c,

CONTRITE*
Ps 51:17 a broken and c heart you, God,
Isa 57:15 with the one who is c and lowly
      57:15 and to revive the heart of the c.
      66: 2 who are humble and c in spirit,

CONTROL CONTROLLED,
   CONTROLS, SELF-CONTROL,
   SELF-CONTROLLED
Ex 32:25 that Aaron had let them get out of c
Jos 18: 1 country was brought under their c,
Ecc 2:19 Yet they will have c over all
Ro   6:20 free from the c of righteousness.
1Co 7: 9 But if they cannot c themselves,
       7:37 but has c over his own will,
1Th 4: 4 should learn to c your own body

1Jn 5:19 the whole world is under the c
Rev 16: 9 God, who had c over these plagues,

CONTROLLED CONTROL
Ps 32: 9 understanding but must be c by bit

CONTROLS* CONTROL
Job 37:15 Do you know how God c the clouds

CONTROVERSIAL*
   CONTROVERSIES
1Ti 1: 4 things promote c speculations rather

CONTROVERSIES*
   CONTROVERSIAL
Ac 26: 3 with all the Jewish customs and c.
1Ti 6: 4 They have an unhealthy interest in c
Titus 3: 9 But avoid foolish c and genealogies

CONVERSATION
Col 4: 6 Let your c be always full of grace,

CONVERT* CONVERTED,
   CONVERTS
Mt 23:15 over land and sea to win a single c,
      23:15 over land and sea to win a single c,
Ac   6: 5 from Antioch, a c to Judaism.
Ro 16: 5 who was the first c to Christ
1Ti 3: 6 He must not be a recent c, or he

CONVERTED* CONVERT
Ac 15: 3 told how the Gentiles had been c.

CONVERTS* CONVERT
Ac   2:11 (both Jews and c to Judaism);
      13:43 devout c to Judaism followed Paul
1Co 16:15 of Stephanas were the first c

CONVICT* CONVICTED,
   CONVICTION
Dt 19:15 is not enough to c anyone accused
2Sa 14:13 does he not c himself, for the king
Pr 24:25 go well with those who c the guilty,
Jude 1:15 to c all of them of all the ungodly

CONVICTED* CONVICT
1Co 14:24 they are c of sin and are brought
Jas 2: 9 and are c by the law as lawbreakers.

CONVICTION* CONVICT
Heb 3:14 indeed we hold our original c firmly
1Th 1: 5 with the Holy Spirit and deep c.

CONVINCED* CONVINCING
Ge 45:28 And Israel said, "I'm c!
Lk 16:31 they will not be c even if someone
Ac 19:26 hear how this fellow Paul has c
      26: 9 "I too was c that I ought to do all
      26:26 I am c that none of this has escaped
      28:24 Some were c by what he said,
Ro   2:19 if you are c that you are a guide
       8:38 I am c that neither death nor life,
      14: 5 them should be fully c in their own
      14:14 I am c, being fully persuaded
      15:14 I myself am c, my brothers
2Co 5:14 because we are c that one died

Php 1:25 **C** of this, I know that I will remain,
2Ti 1:12 am **c** that he is able to guard what I
3:14 have learned and have become **c** of,
Heb 6: 9 we are **c** of better things in your

CONVINCING* CONVINCED

Ac 1: 3 and gave many **c** proofs that he was

CONVULSION*

Mk 9:20 immediately threw the boy into a **c**.
Lk 9:42 threw him to the ground in a **c**.

COOK COOKED

Ex 23:19 "Do not **c** a young goat in its
Eze 24:10 **C** the meat well,

COOKED COOK

2Ki 6:29 So we **c** my son and ate him.
La 4:10 women have **c** their own children,

COOL*

Ge 3: 8 in the garden in the **c** of the day,
Jer 18:14 Do its **c** waters from distant sources
Lk 16:24 his finger in water and **c** my tongue,

COPIED* COPY

Eze 16:47 and **c** their detestable practices,

COPIES COPY

Heb 9:23 for the **c** of the heavenly things

COPPER

Mt 10: 9 or **c** to take with you in your belts—
Mk 12:42 and put in two very small **c** coins,

COPY COPIED, COPIES

Dt 17:18 himself on a scroll a **c** of this law,
Jos 8:32 Joshua wrote on stones a **c** of the law
2Ki 11:12 him with a **c** of the covenant
Heb 8: 5 They serve at a sanctuary that is a **c**
9:24 that was only a **c** of the true one;

CORBAN*

Mk 7:11 their father or mother is **C** (that is,

CORD CORDS

Ge 38:18 "Your seal and its **c**, and the staff
Nu 15:38 with a blue **c** on each tassel.
Jos 2:18 you have tied this scarlet **c**
Ecc 4:12 A **c** of three strands is not quickly

CORDS CORD

2Sa 22: 6 The **c** of the grave coiled around
Job 4:21 Are not the **c** of their tent pulled up,
Ps 129: 4 me free from the **c** of the wicked."
Pr 5:22 the **c** of their sins hold them fast.
Isa 54: 2 lengthen your **c**, strengthen your
Hos 11: 4 I led them with **c** of human
Jn 2:15 So he made a whip out of **c**,

CORINTH CORINTHIANS

Ac 18: 1 this, Paul left Athens and went to **C**.
1Co 1: 2 To the church of God in **C**, to those
2Co 1: 1 To the church of God in **C**,

CORINTHIANS* CORINTH

Ac 18: 8 of the **C** who heard Paul believed
2Co 6:11 We have spoken freely to you, **C**,

CORN [EARS OF] (KJV) See
GRAIN [HEADS OF], KERNEL

CORNELIUS*

Roman to whom Peter preached; first Gentile
Christian (Ac 10).

CORNER CORNERS,
CORNERSTONE

Ru 3: 9 "Spread the **c** of your garment over
1Sa 24: 4 and cut off a **c** of Saul's robe.
Pr 7:12 in the squares, at every **c** she lurks.)
21: 9 on a **c** of the roof than share a house
Eze 16: 8 I spread the **c** of my garment over
Ac 26:26 because it was not done in a **c**.

CORNERS CORNER

Dt 22:12 on the four **c** of the cloak you wear.
Isa 41: 9 from its farthest **c** I called you.
Eze 7: 2 come upon the four **c** of the land!
Mt 6: 5 on the street **c** to be seen by others.
22: 9 So go to the street **c** and invite
Ac 10:11 being let down to earth by its four **c**.
Rev 7: 1 standing at the four **c** of the earth,
20: 8 nations in the four **c** of the earth—

CORNERSTONE* CORNER,
STONE; see also CAPSTONE

Job 38: 6 its footings set, or who laid its **c**—
Ps 118:22 builders rejected has become the **c**;
Isa 28:16 a precious **c** for a sure foundation;
Jer 51:26 rock will be taken from you for a **c**,
Zec 10: 4 From Judah will come the **c**,
Mt 21:42 builders rejected has become the **c**;
Mk 12:10 builders rejected has become the **c**;
Lk 20:17 builders rejected has become the **c**'?
Ac 4:11 rejected, which has become the **c**.'
Eph 2:20 Christ Jesus himself as the chief **c**.
1Pe 2: 6 a chosen and precious **c**, and the one
2: 7 rejected has become the **c**,"

CORRECT* CORRECTED,
CORRECTING, CORRECTION,
CORRECTLY, CORRECTS

Job 6:26 Do you mean to **c** what I say,
40: 2 contends with the Almighty **c** him?
2Ti 4: 2 **c**, rebuke and encourage—

CORRECTED* CORRECT

Pr 29:19 Servants cannot be **c** by mere

CORRECTING* CORRECT

2Ti 3:16 **c** and training in righteousness,

CORRECTION* CORRECT

Lev 26:23 these things you do not accept my **c**
Job 36:10 He makes them listen to **c**
Pr 5:12 How my heart spurned **c**!
6:23 and **c** and instruction are the way
10:17 but whoever ignores **c** leads others
12: 1 but whoever hates **c** is stupid.
13:18 but whoever heeds **c** is honored.
15: 5 whoever heeds **c** shows prudence.
15:10 the one who hates **c** will die.

Pr   15:12 Mockers resent c, so they avoid
      15:31 Whoever heeds life-giving c will be
      15:32 who heeds c gains understanding.
Jer   2:30 they did not respond to c.
       5: 3 crushed them, but they refused c.
      7:28 Lord its God or responded to c.
Zep   3: 2 She obeys no one, she accepts no c.
       3: 7 you will fear me and accept c!'

CORRECTLY* CORRECT

Jdg 12: 6 he could not pronounce the word c,
Jer   1:12 to me, "You have seen c, for I am
Lk   7:43 "You have judged c," Jesus said.
    10:28 "You have answered c,"
Jn   7:24 appearances, but instead judge c."
2Ti   2:15 who c handles the word of truth.

CORRECTS* CORRECT

Job   5:17 "Blessed is the one whom God c;
Pr   9: 7 Whoever c a mocker invites insults;

CORRODED*

Jas   5: 3 Your gold and silver are c.

CORRUPT CORRUPTED, CORRUPTION, CORRUPTS

Ge   6:11 Now the earth was c in God's sight
Ex 32: 7 up out of Egypt, have become c.
Dt   4:16 so that you do not become c
Jdg   2:19 to ways even more c than those
Ps 14: 1 They are c, their deeds are vile;
    53: 3 has turned away, all have become c;
Pr   4:24 keep c talk far from your lips.
     6:12 who goes about with a c mouth,
   19:28 A c witness mocks at justice,
Da   6: 4 and neither c nor negligent.
Ac   2:40 yourselves from this c generation."

CORRUPTED CORRUPT

Eze 28:17 you c your wisdom because of your
2Co   7: 2 wronged no one, we have c no one,
Titus 1:15 but to those who are c and do not
     1:15 their minds and consciences are c.
Jude 1:23 even the clothing stained by c flesh.
Rev 19: 2 the great prostitute who c the earth

CORRUPTION CORRUPT

Ezr   9:11 land polluted by the c of its peoples.
Da   6: 4 They could find no c in him,
2Pe   1: 4 having escaped the c in the world
     2:20 they have escaped the c of the world

CORRUPTS* CORRUPT

Ecc   7: 7 into a fool, and a bribe c the heart.
1Co 15:33 "Bad company c good character."
Jas   3: 6 It c the whole body, sets the whole

COST COSTLY, COSTS

Nu 16:38 who sinned at the c of their lives.
Jos   6:26 the c of his firstborn son he will lay
     6:26 at the c of his youngest he will set
2Sa 24:24 burnt offerings that c me nothing."
1Ki 16:34 at the c of his firstborn son Abiram,
    16:34 at the c of his youngest son Segub,
Pr   4: 7 Though it c all you have,
     7:23 little knowing it will c him his life.

Isa 55: 1 milk without money and without c.
Lk 14:28 and estimate the c to see if you have
Rev 21: 6 thirsty I will give water without c

COSTLY COST

Ps 49: 8 the ransom for a life is c,
1Co   3:12 using gold, silver, c stones, wood,
Rev 18:12 every kind made of ivory, c wood,

COSTS COST

Pr   6:31 though it c him all the wealth of his

COULD

Ge 13:16 so that if anyone c count the dust,
    13:16 then your offspring c be counted.
Ex 40:35 Moses c not enter the tent
Nu 22:18 I c not do anything great or small
2Ch   7: 2 The priests c not enter the temple
   25:15 which c not save their own people
Eze 14:14 they c save only themselves by their
Mt 22:46 No one c say a word in reply,
Mk   6: 5 He c not do any miracles there,
Jn 12:39 For this reason they c not believe,
Rev 15: 8 no one c enter the temple until

COUNCIL COUNCILS

Job 15: 8 Do you listen in on God's c?
Ps 89: 7 the c of the holy ones God is greatly
  107:32 and praise him in the c of the elders.
Mk 15:43 a prominent member of the C,
Jn   3: 1 a member of the Jewish ruling c.
Ac 17:33 At that, Paul left the C.

COUNCILS COUNCIL

Mk 13: 9 will be handed over to the local c

COUNSEL COUNSELOR, COUNSELORS, COUNSELS

2Ch 18: 4 "First seek the c of the Lord."
    25:16 this and have not listened to my c."
Job 12:13 c and understanding are his.
Ps 73:24 You guide me with your c,
Pr   8:14 C and sound judgment are mine;
   15:22 Plans fail for lack of c,
Isa 11: 2 the Spirit of c and of might,
1Ti   5:14 So I c younger widows to marry,
Rev   3:18 I c you to buy from me gold refined

COUNSELOR COUNSEL

Isa   9: 6 And he will be called Wonderful C,
   40:13 or instruct the Lord as his c?
Ro 11:34 Or who has been his c?"

COUNSELORS COUNSEL

Ps 119:24 are my delight; they are my c.

COUNSELS* COUNSEL

Ps 16: 7 I will praise the Lord, who c me;

COUNT COUNTED, COUNTING, COUNTLESS, COUNTS

Ge 13:16 so that if anyone could c the dust,
   15: 5 up at the sky and c the stars—
   15: 5 if indeed you can c them."
   16:10 they will be too numerous to c."
Nu   1: 3 Aaron are to c according to their

Nu   23:10 Who can c the dust of Jacob
       31:26 community are to c all the people
Job 38:37 has the wisdom to c the clouds?
Ps   32: 2 the LORD does not c against them
       48:12 Zion, go around her, c her towers,
  139:18 Were I to c them, they would
Eze 33:12 person's former righteousness will c
Ro   4: 8 Lord will never c against them."
      6:11 c yourselves dead to sin but alive
Rev   7: 9 great multitude that no one could c,

COUNTED COUNT
Ge 13:16 dust, then your offspring could be c.
Nu   1:19 so he c them in the Desert of Sinai:
2Sa 24:10 after he had c the fighting men,
Hos   1:10 which cannot be measured or c.
Mt 26:15 So they c out for him thirty pieces
Ac   5:41 because they had been c worthy
2Th   1: 5 as a result you will be c worthy

COUNTERFEIT*
1Jn   2:27 and as that anointing is real, not c—

COUNTING COUNT
2Co   5:19 not c people's sins against them.

COUNTLESS COUNT
Nu 10:36 to the c thousands of Israel."
Heb 11:12 and as c as the sand on the seashore.

COUNTRIES COUNTRY
Dt 29:16 how we passed through the c
Isa 36:20 the gods of these c have been able
Eze 11:16 and scattered them among the c,
      11:16 in the c where they have gone.'
     20:34 you from the c where you have been
Da   9: 7 in all the c where you have scattered
Zec   8: 7 my people from the c of the east

COUNTRY COUNTRIES
Ge 12: 1 "Go from your c, your people
    15:13 will be strangers in a c not their own
Ex   1:10 fight against us and leave the c."
     6:11 to let the Israelites go out of his c."
Dt 28: 3 in the city and blessed in the c.
    28:16 in the city and cursed in the c.
Jos   9: 6 "We have come from a distant c;
    11:16 the hill c, all the Negev, the whole
Pr 28: 2 When a c is rebellious, it has many
    29: 4 By justice a king gives a c stability,
Isa 66: 8 Can a c be born in a day or a nation
Jer 17: 3 because of sin throughout your c.
Lk 15:13 had, set off for a distant c and there
Jn   4:44 prophet has no honor in his own c.)
2Co 11:26 in danger in the c, in danger at sea;
Heb 11:14 are looking for a c of their own.

HILL COUNTRY See HILL

COUNTS COUNT
Jn   6:63 the flesh c for nothing.
1Co 7:19 God's commands is what c.
Gal   5: 6 c is faith expressing itself through

COURAGE* COURAGEOUS
Jos   2:11 everyone's c failed because of you,

Jos   5: 1 they no longer had the c to face
2Sa   4: 1 he lost c, and all Israel became
     7:27 So your servant has found c to pray
1Ch 17:25 So your servant has found c to pray
2Ch 15: 8 son of Oded the prophet, he took c.
    19:11 Act with c, and may the LORD be
Ezr   7:28 I took c and gathered leaders
    10: 4 support you, so take c and do it."
Ps 107:26 in their peril their c melted away.
Eze 22:14 Will your c endure or your hands be
Da 11:25 and c against the king of the South.
Mt 14:27 immediately said to them: "Take c!
Mk   6:50 he spoke to them and said, "Take c!
Ac   4:13 When they saw the c of Peter
    23:11 stood near Paul and said, "Take c!
    27:22 now I urge you to keep up your c,
    27:25 So keep up your c, men, for I have
Php   1:20 will have sufficient c so that now as

COURAGEOUS* COURAGE
Dt 31: 6 Be strong and c. Do not be afraid
    31: 7 "Be strong and c, for you must go
    31:23 "Be strong and c, for you will bring
Jos   1: 6 Be strong and c, because you will
     1: 7 "Be strong and very c. Be careful
     1: 9 Be strong and c. Do not be afraid;
     1:18 put to death. Only be strong and c!"
    10:25 Be strong and c. This is what
1Ch 22:13 Be strong and c. Do not be afraid
    28:20 "Be strong and c, and do the work.
2Ch 26:17 eighty other c priests of the LORD
    32: 7 "Be strong and c. Do not be afraid
1Co 16:13 firm in the faith; be c; be strong.

COURSE
Ps 19: 5 a champion rejoicing to run his c.
Pr   2: 8 for he guards the c of the just
    15:21 understanding keeps a straight c.
    16: 9 In their hearts humans plan their c,
    17:23 in secret to pervert the c of justice.
Ecc   1: 6 it goes, ever returning on its c.
Jas   3: 6 sets the whole c of one's life on fire,

COURT COURTS, COURTYARD
Dt 25: 1 they are to take it to c
Jdg   4: 5 She held c under the Palm
Job   9:32 we might confront each other in c.
Pr 22:22 and do not crush the needy in c,
    25: 8 do not bring hastily to c, for what
    25: 9 If you take your neighbor to c,
    29: 9 a wise person goes to c with a fool,
Isa   3:13 The LORD takes his place in c;
Mt   5:25 adversary who is taking you to c.
Ac 25:10 am now standing before Caesar's c,
1Co   4: 3 judged by you or by any human c,
     6: 6 one brother takes another to c—
Jas   2: 6 ones who are dragging you into c?

COURTS COURT
Dt 17: 8 If cases come before your c that are
1Ch 28: 6 who will build my house and my c,
Ps 65: 4 and bring near to live in your c!
    84:10 in your c than a thousand elsewhere;
   100: 4 thanksgiving and his c with praise;
Isa   1:12 this of you, this trampling of my c?

Am 5:15 maintain justice in the **c**.
Zec 8:16 true and sound judgment in your **c**;
Lk   2:46 days they found him in the temple **c**,
    20: 1 teaching the people in the temple **c**
   22:53 day I was with you in the temple **c**,
Jn   2:14 the temple **c** he found people selling
Ac   5:42 in the temple **c** and from house

COURTYARD COURT
Ex 27: 9 "Make a **c** for the tabernacle.
1Ki 7: 9 from the outside to the great **c**
Mk 14:66 While Peter was below in the **c**,

COUSIN
Lev 25:49 or a **c** or any blood relative in their
Est   2: 7 Mordecai had a **c** named Hadassah,
Col   4:10 as does Mark, the **c** of Barnabas.

COVENANT COVENANTS
Ge   6:18 But I will establish my **c** with you,
    9: 9 "I now establish my **c** with you
  15:18 that day the LORD made a **c**
  17: 2 I will make my **c** between me
  31:44 now, let's make a **c**, you and I,
Ex   2:24 he remembered his **c** with Abraham,
    6: 5 and I have remembered my **c**.
  19: 5 if you obey me fully and keep my **c**,
  24: 7 he took the Book of the **C** and read
  34:28 on the tablets the words of the **c**—
Lev 26: 9 and I will keep my **c** with you.
Dt   4:13 He declared to you his **c**, the Ten
  29: 1 of the **c** the LORD commanded
  29: 1 addition to the **c** he had made
Jos   3: 6 "Take up the ark of the **c** and pass
Jdg   2: 1 'I will never break my **c** with you,
1Sa 20:16 So Jonathan made a **c**
  23:18 them made a **c** before the LORD.
1Ki 8: 1 ark of the LORD's **c** from Zion,
   8:21 which is the **c** of the LORD that he
   8:23 you who keep your **c** of love
2Ki 23: 2 all the words of the Book of the **C**,
1Ch 16:15 He remembers his **c** forever,
2Ch 34:30 all the words of the Book of the **C**,
Ne   1: 5 who keeps his **c** of love with those
Job 31: 1 "I made a **c** with my eyes not
Ps 78:37 him, they were not faithful to his **c**.
  105: 8 He remembers his **c** forever,
 132:12 If your sons keep my **c**
Pr   2:17 ignored the **c** she made before God.
Isa 42: 6 make you to be a **c** for the people
  42:19 Who is blind like the one in **c**
  61: 8 make an everlasting **c** with them.
Jer 11: 2 "Listen to the terms of this **c**
  31:31 I will make a new **c** with the people
  32:40 I will make an everlasting **c**
Eze 16:60 Yet I will remember the **c** I made
  16:60 I will establish an everlasting **c**
  37:26 I will make a **c** of peace with them;
  37:26 it will be an everlasting **c**.
Da   9:27 He will confirm a **c** with many
  11:28 heart will be set against the holy **c**.
Hos 6: 7 As at Adam, they have broken the **c**;
Mal 2:14 partner, the wife of your marriage **c**.
    3: 1 the messenger of the **c**, whom you

Mt 26:28 This is my blood of the **c**, which is
Mk 14:24 "This is my blood of the **c**, which is
Lk 22:20 "This cup is the new **c** in my blood,
Ro 11:27 this is my **c** with them when I take
1Co 11:25 "This cup is the new **c** in my blood;
2Co 3: 6 competent as ministers of a new **c**—
Gal 3:17 aside the **c** previously established
   4:24 One **c** is from Mount Sinai
Heb 7:22 become the guarantor of a better **c**.
   8: 8 I will make a new **c** with the people
   9:15 Christ is the mediator of a new **c**,
   9:15 the sins committed under the first **c**.
  12:24 to Jesus the mediator of a new **c**,
Rev 11:19 his temple was seen the ark of his **c**.

ARK OF THE COVENANT See ARK

COVENANT OF THE LORD† Nu 10:33; Dt
4:23; 10:8; 29:25; 31:9, 25, 26; Jos 3:3, 17; 4:7, 18;
6:6; 7:15; 8:33; 23:16; 1Sa 4:4; 1Ki 6:19; 8:21; 1Ch
15:25, 26, 28, 29; 16:37; 17:1; 22:19; 28:2, 18; 2Ch
6:11; Jer 3:16; 22:9

EVERLASTING COVENANT See
EVERLASTING

COVENANTS* COVENANT
Ro   9: 4 the **c**, the receiving of the law,
Gal 4:24 The women represent two **c**.
Eph 2:12 foreigners to the **c** of the promise,

COVER COVER-UP, COVERED, COVERING, COVERINGS, COVERS, GOLD-COVERED
Ex 25:17 "Make an atonement **c** of pure
  25:21 Place the **c** on top of the ark and put
  33:22 and **c** you with my hand until I have
Lev 16: 2 front of the atonement **c** on the ark,
  16: 2 in the cloud over the atonement **c**.
Nu   4: 6 Then they are to **c** the curtain
Ne   4: 5 Do not **c** up their guilt or blot
Ps 32: 5 to you and did not **c** up my iniquity.
  91: 4 He will **c** you with his feathers,
Jer 51:42 its roaring waves will **c** her.
Eze 13:10 is built, they **c** it with whitewash,
Hos 10: 8 will grow up and **c** their altars.
  10: 8 will say to the mountains, "**C** us!"
Hab 2:14 the LORD as the waters **c** the sea.
Lk 23:30 and to the hills, "**C** us!" '
1Co 11: 6 For if a woman does not **c** her head,
  11: 6 shaved, then she should **c** her head.
  11: 7 A man ought not to **c** his head,
Jas   5:20 death and **c** over a multitude of sins.

COVER-UP* COVER
1Pe 2:16 do not use your freedom as a **c**

COVERED COVER
Ge   7:20 **c** the mountains to a depth of more
  38:14 **c** herself with a veil to disguise
Ex 10:22 total darkness **c** all Egypt for three
  14:28 flowed back and **c** the chariots
  16:13 evening quail came and **c** the camp,
  19:18 Mount Sinai was **c** with smoke,
  24:15 up on the mountain, the cloud **c** it,
  40:34 the cloud **c** the tent of meeting,

Nu 9:15 law, was set up, the cloud c it.
Jdg 6:39 and let the ground be c with dew."
Ps 32: 1 are forgiven, whose sins are c.
85: 2 of your people and c all their sins.
Isa 6: 2 With two wings they c their faces,
6: 2 with two they c their feet,
51:16 c you with the shadow of my hand—
Da 9: 7 but this day we are c with shame—
Ob 1:10 Jacob, you will be c with shame;
Jnh 3: 8 and animals be c with sackcloth.
Mk 9: 7 Then a cloud appeared and c them,
Ro 4: 7 are forgiven, whose sins are c.
1Co 11: 4 with his head c dishonors his head.
Rev 4: 6 and they were c with eyes, in front
17: 3 that was c with blasphemous names

COVERING COVER
Ex 35:11 the tabernacle with its tent and its c,
1Co 11:15 For long hair is given to her as a c.

COVERINGS COVER
Ge 3: 7 together and made c for themselves.
Pr 31:22 She makes c for her bed;

COVERS COVER
Ex 22:15 money paid for the hire c the loss.
Pr 10:12 conflict, but love c over all wrongs.
17: 9 would foster love c over an offense.
Isa 25: 7 peoples, the sheet that c all nations;
2Co 3:15 Moses is read, a veil c their hearts.
1Pe 4: 8 because love c over a multitude

COVET* COVETED, COVETING
Ex 20:17 "You shall not c your neighbor's
20:17 "You shall not c your neighbor's
34:24 no one will c your land when you
Dt 5:21 "You shall not c your neighbor's
7:25 Do not c the silver and gold
Mic 2: 2 They c fields and seize them,
Ro 7: 7 had not said, "You shall not c."
13: 9 "You shall not c," and whatever
Jas 4: 2 You c but you cannot get what you

COVETED* COVET
Jos 7:21 shekels, I c them and took them.
Ac 20:33 I have not c anyone's silver or gold

COVETING* COVET
Ro 7: 7 not have known what c really was
7: 8 produced in me every kind of c.

COW COWS
Isa 11: 7 The c will feed with the bear,

COWARDLY* COWER
Rev 21: 8 But the c, the unbelieving, the vile,

COWER COWARDLY
Dt 33:29 Your enemies will c before you,

COWS COW
Ge 41: 2 of the river there came up seven c,
1Sa 6: 7 with two c that have calved
6: 7 Hitch the c to the cart, but take their
Job 21:10 their c calve and do not miscarry.
Am 4: 1 you c of Bashan on Mount Samaria,

CRAFT* CRAFTINESS, CRAFTS, CRAFTSMAN, CRAFTSMEN, CRAFTY
1Ch 28:21 person skilled in any c will help you

CRAFTINESS* CRAFT
Job 5:13 He catches the wise in their c,
1Co 3:19 "He catches the wise in their c";
Eph 4:14 and c of people in their deceitful

CRAFTS* CRAFT
Ex 31: 5 and to engage in all kinds of c.
35:33 to engage in all kinds of artistic c.

CRAFTSMAN CRAFT
Ex 39: 8 the work of a skilled c.
1Ki 7:14 from Tyre and a skilled c in bronze.
Jer 10: 3 and a c shapes it with his chisel.
10: 9 What the c and goldsmith have made

CRAFTSMEN CRAFT
Zec 1:20 the LORD showed me four c.

CRAFTY* CRAFT
Ge 3: 1 the serpent was more c than any
1Sa 23:22 They tell me he is very c.
Job 5:12 He thwarts the plans of the c,
15: 5 you adopt the tongue of the c.
Pr 7:10 like a prostitute and with c intent.
2Co 12:16 Yet, c fellow that I am, I caught you

CRAG CRAGS
Ps 78:16 he brought streams out of a rocky c

CRAGS CRAG
1Sa 24: 2 and his men near the C of the Wild

CRASH*
Zep 1:10 Quarter, and a loud c from the hills.
Mt 7:27 house, and it fell with a great c."

CRAVE* CRAVED, CRAVES, CRAVING, CRAVINGS
Nu 11: 4 with them began to c other food,
Dt 12:20 you, and you c meat and say,
Pr 21:10 The wicked c evil;
23: 3 Do not c his delicacies, for that food
23: 6 host, do not c his delicacies;
31: 4 drink wine, not for rulers to c beer,
Mic 7: 1 to eat, none of the early figs that I c.
1Pe 2: 2 babies, c pure spiritual milk,

CRAVED* CRAVE
Nu 11:34 the people who had c other food.
Ps 78:18 test by demanding the food they c.
78:29 he had given them what they c.
78:30 they turned from what they c,

CRAVES* CRAVE
Pr 21:26 All day long he c for more,

CRAVING* CRAVE
Job 20:20 he will have no respite from his c;
Ps 106:14 In the desert they gave in to their c;
Pr 10: 3 but he thwarts the c of the wicked.
21:25 The c of a sluggard will be the death

Jer   2:24 desert, sniffing the wind in her c—

CRAVINGS* CRAVE
Ps   10: 3 He boasts about the c of his heart;
Eph   2: 3 gratifying the c of our flesh

CRAWL*
Ge   3:14 You will c on your belly and you
Mic   7:17 like creatures that c on the ground.

CREAM
Pr   30:33 For as churning c produces butter,

CREATE* CREATED, CREATES,
CREATING, CREATION, CREATOR
Ps   51:10 C in me a pure heart, O God,
Isa   4: 5 the LORD will c over all of Mount
      45: 7 I form the light and c darkness,
      45: 7 I bring prosperity and c disaster;
      45:18 he did not c it to be empty,
      65:17 I will c new heavens and a new
      65:18 and rejoice forever in what I will c,
      65:18 for I will c Jerusalem to be a delight
Jer   31:22 The LORD will c a new thing
Mal   2:10 Did not one God c us? Why do we
Eph   2:15 His purpose was to c in himself one

CREATED* CREATE
Ge   1: 1 In the beginning God c the heavens
      1:21 So God c the great creatures
      1:27 So God c mankind in his own
      1:27 in the image of God he c them; male
             and female he c them.
      2: 4 and the earth when they were c,
      5: 1 When God c mankind, he made
      5: 2 He c them male and female
      5: 2 "Mankind" when they were c.
      6: 7 the earth the human race I have c—
Dt   4:32 the day God c human beings
Ps   89:12 You c the north and the south;
      89:47 futility you have c all humanity!
      102:18 a people not yet c may praise
      104:30 they are c, and you renew the face
      139:13 For you c my inmost being;
      148: 5 for at his command they were c,
Ecc   7:29 God c mankind upright, but they
Isa   40:26 to the heavens: Who c all these?
      41:20 that the Holy One of Israel has c it.
      43: 1 he who c you, Jacob, he who
      43: 7 my name, whom I c for my glory,
      45: 8 I, the LORD, have c it.
      45:12 made the earth and c mankind on it.
      45:18 he who c the heavens, he is God;
      48: 7 They are c now, and not long ago;
      54:16 it is I who c the blacksmith who
      54:16 it is I who have c the destroyer
      57:16 the very people I have c.
Eze   21:30 In the place where you were c,
      28:13 day you were c they were prepared.
      28:15 day you were c till wickedness was
Mk   13:19 when God c the world, until now—
Ro   1:25 and served c things rather than
1Co   11: 9 neither was man c for woman,
Eph   2:10 c in Christ Jesus to do good works,
       3: 9 hidden in God, who c all things.

Eph   4:24 the new self, c to be like God in true
Col   1:16 For in him all things were c:
       1:16 all things were c through him
1Ti   4: 3 which God c to be received
       4: 4 For everything God c is good,
Heb   12:27 that is, c things—so that what
Jas   1:18 be a kind of firstfruits of all he c.
Rev   4:11 for you c all things, and by your will
             they were c
      10: 6 who c the heavens and all that is

CREATES* CREATE
Am   4:13 the mountains, who c the wind,

CREATING* CREATE
Ge   2: 3 all the work of c that he had done.
Isa   57:19 c praise on their lips.

CREATION* CREATE
Ps   96:13 Let all c rejoice before the LORD,
Hab   2:18 who makes it trusts in his own c;
Mt   13:35 I will utter things hidden since the c
      25:34 for you since the c of the world.
Mk   10: 6 c God 'made them male and female.'
      16:15 and preach the gospel to all c.
Jn   17:24 because you loved me before the c
Ro   1:20 For since the c of the world God's
       8:19 For the c waits in eager expectation
       8:20 For the c was subjected
       8:21 that the c itself will be liberated
       8:22 the whole c has been groaning as
       8:39 nor anything else in all c, will be
2Co   5:17 is in Christ, the new c has come:
Gal   6:15 what counts is the new c.
Eph   1: 4 us in him before the c of the world
Col   1:15 God, the firstborn over all c.
Heb   4: 3 have been finished since the c
       4:13 Nothing in all c is hidden
       9:11 that is to say, is not a part of this c.
       9:26 suffer many times since the c
1Pe   1:20 He was chosen before the c
2Pe   3: 4 as it has since the beginning of c."
Rev   3:14 true witness, the ruler of God's c.
      13: 8 was slain from the c of the world.
      17: 8 the c of the world will be astonished

CREATOR* CREATE
Ge   14:19 Most High, C of heaven and earth.
      14:22 Most High, C of heaven and earth,
Dt   32: 6 your C, who made you and formed
Ecc   12: 1 Remember your C in the days
Isa   27:11 and their C shows them no favor.
      40:28 God, the C of the ends of the earth.
      42: 5 the LORD says—the C of the heavens,
      43:15 Holy One, Israel's C, your King."
Mt   19: 4 at the beginning the C 'made them
Ro   1:25 created things rather than the C—
Col   3:10 in knowledge in the image of its C.
1Pe   4:19 themselves to their faithful C

CREATURE CREATURES
Ge   1:28 over every living c that moves
       7: 4 earth every living c I have made."
Lev   11:42 to eat any c that moves along
      17:11 For the life of a c is in the blood,

Lev 17:14 the life of every **c** is its blood.
     17:14 must not eat the blood of any **c**,
     17:14 the life of every **c** is its blood;
Job 12:10 In his hand is the life of every **c**
Ps 136:25 He gives food to every **c**.
Eze 1:15 on the ground beside each **c** with its
Rev 4: 7 The first living **c** was like a lion,
     5:13 Then I heard every **c** in heaven

CREATURES CREATURE
Ge 1:20 "Let the water teem with living **c**,
     1:24 the land produce living **c** according
     1:24 the **c** that move along the ground,
     6:19 bring into the ark two of all living **c**,
     8:21 again will I destroy all living **c**, as I
     9:16 and all living **c** of every kind
Ps 104:24 the earth is full of your **c**.
Pr 30:25 Ants are **c** of little strength, yet they
Eze 1: 5 was what looked like four living **c**.
     10:15 These were the living **c** I had seen
     47: 9 living **c** will live wherever the river
Rev 4: 6 were four living **c**, and they were
     5: 6 encircled by the four living **c**
     8: 9 third of the living **c** in the sea died,
     19: 4 and the four living **c** fell down

CREDIT ACCREDITED, CREDITED, CREDITOR, CREDITORS, CREDITS
Lk 6:33 good to you, what **c** is that to you?
Ro 4:24 to whom God will **c** righteousness—
1Pe 2:20 it to your **c** if you receive a beating

CREDITED CREDIT
Ge 15: 6 and he **c** it to him as righteousness.
Ps 106:31 This was **c** to him as righteousness
Eze 18:20 of the righteous will be **c** to them,
Ro 4: 3 it was **c** to him as righteousness."
     4: 4 wages are not **c** as a gift but as
Gal 3: 6 it was **c** to him as righteousness."
Php 4:17 is that more be **c** to your account.
Jas 2:23 it was **c** to him as righteousness,"

CREDITOR CREDIT
Dt 15: 2 Every **c** shall cancel any loan they
Ps 109:11 May a **c** seize all he has;

CREDITORS* CREDIT
Isa 50: 1 Or to which of my **c** did I sell you?
Hab 2: 7 Will not your **c** suddenly arise?

CREDITS* CREDIT
Ro 4: 6 to whom God **c** righteousness apart

CRETANS* CRETE
Ac 2:11 converts to Judaism); **C** and Arabs—
Titus 1:12 "**C** are always liars, evil brutes,

CRETE CRETANS
Ac 27:12 This was a harbor in **C**, facing both
Titus 1: 5 The reason I left you in **C** was

CRIED CRY
Ex 2:23 groaned in their slavery and **c** out,
     14:10 terrified and **c** out to the LORD.
Nu 20:16 but when we **c** out to the LORD,
Jos 24: 7 But they **c** to the LORD for help,

Jdg 3: 9 But when they **c** out to the LORD,
     4: 3 they **c** to the LORD for help.
     6: 6 the Israelites that they **c**
     10:12 you and you **c** to me for help, did I
1Sa 7: 9 He **c** out to the LORD on Israel's
     12: 8 they **c** to the LORD for help,
     28:12 she **c** out at the top of her voice
Job 29:12 because I rescued the poor who **c**
Ps 18: 6 I **c** to my God for help.
     22: 5 To you they **c** out and were saved;
     107:13 Then they **c** to the LORD in their
Jnh 1: 5 and each **c** out to his own god.
     1:14 Then they **c** out to the LORD,
Mt 14:30 beginning to sink, **c** out, "Lord,
     27:46 three in the afternoon Jesus **c**
Rev 19: 4 And they **c**: "Amen, Hallelujah!"

CRIES CRY
Ge 4:10 Your brother's blood **c** out to me
Ps 22: 1 so far from my **c** of anguish?
Pr 8: 3 the city, at the entrance, she **c** aloud:

CRIME CRIMES, CRIMINAL, CRIMINALS
1Sa 20: 1 What is my **c**? How have I wronged
Ps 69:27 Charge them with **c** upon **c**;
Mk 15:14 "Why? What **c** has he committed?"
Ac 28:18 not guilty of any **c** deserving death.

CRIMES CRIME
Rev 18: 5 and God has remembered her **c**.

CRIMINAL* CRIME
Lk 23:40 But the other **c** rebuked him.
Jn 18:30 "If he were not a **c**," they replied,
2Ti 2: 9 the point of being chained like a **c**.
1Pe 4:15 or thief or any other kind of **c**,

CRIMINALS CRIME
Lk 23:32 both **c**, were also led out with him

CRIMSON
Isa 1:18 though they are red as **c**, they shall
     63: 1 with his garments stained **c**?

CRIPPLED
Mt 15:30 the **c**, the mute and many others,
Mk 9:45 to enter life **c** than to have two feet
Lk 14:13 invite the poor, the **c**, the lame,

CRISIS*
1Co 7:26 Because of the present **c**, I think

CRITICISM*
2Co 8:20 want to avoid any **c** of the way we

CROOKED*
Dt 32: 5 they are a warped and **c** generation.
Ps 125: 5 to **c** ways the LORD will banish
Pr 2:15 whose paths are **c** and who are
     8: 8 none of them is **c** or perverse.
     10: 9 whoever takes **c** paths will be found
Ecc 1:15 What is **c** cannot be straightened;
     7:13 can straighten what he has made **c**?
Isa 59: 8 They have turned them into **c** roads;
La 3: 9 he has made my paths **c**.

Lk   3: 5 The c roads shall become straight,
Php   2:15 fault in a warped and c generation."

CROP CROPS
Isa   5: 2 he looked for a c of good grapes,
Mt   13: 8 good soil, where it produced a c—
      21:41 his share of the c at harvest time."
Jn   4:36 and harvests a c for eternal life,

CROPS CROP
Ge   4:12 it will no longer yield its c for you.
Pr   3: 9 with the firstfruits of all your c;
      10: 5 He who gathers c in summer is
      28: 3 like a driving rain that leaves no c.
Eze 34:29 for them a land renowned for its c,
      36:30 of the trees and the c of the field,
Zec   8:12 the ground will produce its c,
2Ti   2: 6 the first to receive a share of the c.
Rev 22: 2 tree of life, bearing twelve c of fruit,

CROSS CROSSED, CROSSES, CROSSING, CROSSROADS
Dt   4:21 swore that I would not c the Jordan
      12:10 But you will c the Jordan and settle
      30:13 "Who will c the sea to get it
      31: 3 your God himself will c over ahead
      31: 3 also will c over ahead of you,
Jos   3.14 people broke camp to c the Jordan,
Ps   104: 9 You set a boundary they cannot c;
Jer   5:22 an everlasting barrier it cannot c.
      5:22 they may roar, but they cannot c it.
Mt   10:38 Whoever does not take up their c
      16:24 and take up their c and follow me.
Mk   15:21 and they forced him to carry the c.
      15:30 come down from the c and save
Jn   19:17 Carrying his own c, he went
      19:25 Near the c of Jesus stood his
Ac   2:23 him to death by nailing him to the c.
      5:30 you killed by hanging him on a c.
1Co   1:17 lest the c of Christ be emptied of its
      1:18 the message of the c is foolishness
Gal   5:11 offense of the c has been abolished.
      6:12 being persecuted for the c of Christ.
      6:14 in the c of our Lord Jesus Christ,
Eph   2:16 both of them to God through the c,
Php   2: 8 even death on a c!
      3:18 live as enemies of the c of Christ.
Col   1:20 through his blood, shed on the c.
      2:14 has taken it away, nailing it to the c.
      2:15 triumphing over them by the c.
Heb 12: 2 joy set before him he endured the c,
1Pe   2:24 bore our sins" in his body on the c,

CROSSED CROSS
Jos   4: 7 When it c the Jordan, the waters
2Ki   2: 8 and the two of them c over on dry
Jn   5:24 but has c over from death to life.

CROSSES CROSS
Jn   19:31 left on the c during the Sabbath,

CROSSING CROSS
Ge   48:14 and c his arms, he put his left hand
Dt   4:14 the land that you are c the Jordan

CROSSROADS* CROSS, ROAD
Jer   6:16 "Stand at the c and look;
Ob   1:14 at the c to cut down their fugitives,

CROUCHING
Ge   4: 7 what is right, sin is c at your door;

CROW* CROWED, CROWS
Jn   18:27 at that moment a rooster began to c.

CROWD CROWDING, CROWDS
Ex   23: 2 "Do not follow the c in doing
      23: 2 pervert justice by siding with the c,
Eze   7:12 for my wrath is on the whole c.
Mt   21: 8 A very large c spread their cloaks
Lk   9:13 we go and buy food for all this c."
Jn   7:31 Still, many in the c believed in him.

CROWDING CROWD
Mk   3: 9 him, to keep the people from c him.
      5:31 see the people c against you,"

CROWDS CROWD
Mt   9:36 When he saw the c, he had
Ac   8: 6 When the c heard Philip and saw
      17:13 agitating the c and stirring them up.

CROWED CROW
Mt   26:74 Immediately a rooster c.

CROWN CROWNED, CROWNS
Job 19: 9 and removed the c from my head.
      31:36 shoulder, I would put it on like a c.
Pr   4: 9 and present you with a glorious c."
      10: 6 Blessings c the head
      12: 4 noble character is her husband's c,
      14:24 The wealth of the wise is their c,
      16:31 Gray hair is a c of splendor;
      17: 6 Children's children are a c
      27:24 a c is not secure for all generations.
Isa 35:10 everlasting joy will c their heads.
      51:11 everlasting joy will c their heads.
      61: 3 on them a c of beauty instead
      62: 3 You will be a c of splendor
La   5:16 The c has fallen from our head.
Eze 16:12 ears and a beautiful c on your head.
Zec   9:16 sparkle in his land like jewels in a c.
Mt   27:29 then twisted together a c of thorns
Mk   15:17 then twisted together a c of thorns
Jn   19: 2 The soldiers twisted together a c
      19: 5 came out wearing the c of thorns
1Co   9:25 do it to get a c that will not last,
      9:25 do it to get a c that will last forever.
Php   4: 1 my joy and c, stand firm in the Lord
1Th   2:19 the c in which we will glory
2Ti   2: 5 not receive the victor's c except
      4: 8 store for me the c of righteousness,
Jas   1:12 that person will receive the c of life
1Pe   5: 4 you will receive the c of glory
Rev   2:10 will give you life as your victor's c.
      3:11 so that no one will take your c.
      6: 2 and he was given a c, and he rode
      12: 1 and a c of twelve stars on her head.
      14:14 of man with a c of gold on his head

CROWNED* CROWN

Ps   8: 5 the angels and c them with glory
Pr 14:18 the prudent are c with knowledge.
SS   3:11 which his mother c him on the day
Heb 2: 7 you c them with glory and honor
      2: 9 now c with glory and honor because

CROWNS CROWN

Ps 103: 4 life from the pit and c you with love
   149: 4 he c the humble with victory.
Isa 23: 8 the bestower of c, whose merchants
Jer 13:18 for your glorious c will fall
Rev 4: 4 and had c of gold on their heads.
      4:10 They lay their c before the throne
      9: 7 heads they wore something like c
    12: 3 ten horns and seven c on its heads.
    13: 1 with ten c on its horns, and on each
    19:12 fire, and on his head are many c.

CROWS CROW

Mt 26:34 night, before the rooster c, you will

CRUCIFIED* CRUCIFY

Mt 20:19 to be mocked and flogged and c.
    26: 2 Man will be handed over to be c."
    27:26 and handed him over to be c.
    27:35 When they had c him, they divided
    27:38 Two rebels were c with him,
    27:44 the same way the rebels who were c
    28: 5 are looking for Jesus, who was c.
Mk 15:15 and handed him over to be c.
    15:24 And they c him. Dividing up his
    15:25 in the morning when they c him.
    15:27 They c two rebels with him,
    15:32 Those c with him also heaped
    16: 6 for Jesus the Nazarene, who was c.
Lk 23:23 insistently demanded that he be c,
    23:33 called the Skull, they c him there,
    24: 7 be c and on the third day be raised
    24:20 sentenced to death, and they c him;
Jn 19:16 handed him over to them to be c.
    19:18 There they c him, and with him two
    19:20 where Jesus was c was near the city,
    19:23 When the soldiers c Jesus, they took
    19:32 the first man who had been c
    19:41 At the place where Jesus was c,
Ac   2:36 Jesus, whom you c, both Lord
    4:10 whom you c but whom God raised
Ro   6: 6 that our old self was c with him so
1Co 1:13 Was Paul c for you?
    1:23 but we preach Christ c:
    2: 2 you except Jesus Christ and him c.
    2: 8 they would not have c the Lord
2Co 13: 4 to be sure, he was c in weakness,
Gal 2:20 I have been c with Christ and I no
    3: 1 Christ was clearly portrayed as c.
    5:24 Christ Jesus have c the flesh with its
    6:14 which the world has been c to me,
Rev 11: 8 where also their Lord was c.

CRUCIFY* CRUCIFIED, CRUCIFYING

Mt 23:34 Some of them you will kill and c;
    27:22 They all answered, "C him!"

Mt 27:23 shouted all the louder, "C him!"
    27:31 Then they led him away to c him.
Mk 15:13 "C him!" they shouted.
    15:14 shouted all the louder, "C him!"
    15:20 Then they led him out to c him.
Lk 23:21 kept shouting, "C him! C him!"
Jn 19: 6 saw him, they shouted, "C! C!"
    19: 6 "You take him and c him.
    19:10 either to free you or to c you?"
    19:15 Take him away! C him!"
    19:15 "Shall I c your king?" Pilate asked.

CRUCIFYING* CRUCIFY

Heb 6: 6 their loss they are c the Son of God

CRUEL CRUELTY

Dt 28:33 but c oppression all your days.
Pr 11:17 but the c bring ruin on themselves.
    12:10 the kindest acts of the wicked are c.
    27: 4 Anger is c and fury overwhelming,
Isa 13: 9 a c day, with wrath and fierce

CRUELTY* CRUEL

Na   3:19 for who has not felt your endless c?

CRUMBS*

Mt 15:27 "Even the dogs eat the c that fall
Mk   7:28 the table eat the children's c."

CRUSH CRUSHED

Ge   3:15 he will c your head, and you will
Nu 24:17 He will c the foreheads of Moab,
Ps 68:21 Surely God will c the heads of his
Isa 53:10 it was the Lord's will to c him
Da   2:40 so it will c and break all the others.
Ro 16:20 peace will soon c Satan under your

CRUSHED CRUSH

Ps 34:18 and saves those who are c in spirit.
    51: 8 let the bones you have c rejoice.
Pr 17:22 but a c spirit dries up the bones.
    18:14 but a c spirit who can bear?
Isa 53: 5 he was c for our iniquities;
Jer   8:21 Since my people are c, I am c;
Eze 36: 3 c you from every side so that you
Da   7: 7 it c and devoured its victims
Mt 21:44 anyone on whom it falls will be c."
2Co 4: 8 pressed on every side, but not c;

CRY CRIED, CRIES, CRYING

Ex   2:23 and their c for help because of their
    3: 9 And now the c of the Israelites has
Nu 20:16 he heard our c and sent an angel
Jdg 10:14 c out to the gods you have chosen.
1Sa 9:16 people, for their c has reached me."
1Ki 17:22 The Lord heard Elijah's c,
Ps   5: 2 Hear my c for help, my King
    6: 9 The Lord has heard my c
    29: 9 And in his temple all c, "Glory!"
    34:15 and his ears are attentive to their c;
    40: 1 he turned to me and heard my c.
   130: 1 Out of the depths I c to you,
Pr   2: 3 and c aloud for understanding,
    21:13 their ears to the c of the poor will also c out

Isa   3: 7 But in that day he will **c** out,
Jer   4:31 I hear a **c** as of a woman in labor,
       4:31 the **c** of Daughter Zion gasping
   14:12 they fast, I will not listen to their **c**;
La   2:18 The hearts of the people **c**
Hos 7:14 They do not **c** out to me from their
Hab 2:11 The stones of the wall will **c** out,
Lk 19:40 keep quiet, the stones will **c** out."
Ro   8:15 by him we **c**, "*Abba*, Father."
Rev 18:10 they will stand far off and **c**:

CRYING CRY

Ge 21:17 God heard the boy **c**, and the angel
   21:17 has heard the boy **c** as he lies there.
Jn 20:11 Mary stood outside the tomb **c**.
Rev 21: 4 death' or mourning or **c** or pain,

CRYSTAL*

Job 28:17 Neither gold nor **c** can compare
Eze   1:22 sparkling like **c**, and awesome.
Rev 4: 6 looked like a sea of glass, clear as **c**.
   21:11 jewel, like a jasper, clear as **c**.
   22: 1 life, as clear as **c**,

CUBITS

Ge   6:15 ark is to be three hundred **c** long,
          fifty **c** wide and thirty **c** high.
1Sa 17: 4 His height was six **c** and a span.

CUBS

2Sa 17: 8 as a wild bear robbed of her **c**.
Pr 17:12 bear robbed of her **c** than a fool bent
Hos 13: 8 Like a bear robbed of her **c**, I will

CUCUMBER*

Isa   1: 8 vineyard, like a hut in a **c** field,
Jer 10: 5 Like a scarecrow in a **c** field,

CUD

Lev 11: 3 a divided hoof and that chews the **c**.
Dt 14: 6 a divided hoof and that chews the **c**.

CULMINATION*

Ro 10: 4 Christ is the **c** of the law so
1Co 10:11 whom the **c** of the ages has come.
Heb 9:26 all at the **c** of the ages to do away

CULTIVATE* CULTIVATED

Dt 28:39 You will plant vineyards and **c** them
Ps 104:14 cattle, and plants for people to **c**—

CULTIVATED CULTIVATE

Ro 11:24 were grafted into a **c** olive tree,

CUNNING*

Ps 64: 6 the human mind and heart are **c**.
   83: 3 **c** they conspire against your people;
2Co 11: 3 was deceived by the serpent's **c**,
Eph 4:14 by the **c** and craftiness of people

CUP CUPS

Ge 40:11 Pharaoh's **c** was in my hand,
   40:11 squeezed them into Pharaoh's **c** and
          put the **c** in his hand."
   44: 2 Then put my **c**, the silver one,
2Sa 12: 3 drank from his **c** and even slept
1Ki 7:26 and its rim was like the rim of a **c**,

Ps 23: 5 my head with oil; my **c** overflows.
   75: 8 of the Lᴏʀᴅ is a **c** full of foaming
Pr 23:31 when it sparkles in the **c**, when it
Isa 51:22 of your hand the **c** that made you
   51:22 from that **c**, the goblet of my wrath,
Jer 25:15 my hand this **c** filled with the wine
Eze 23:31 so I will put her **c** into your hand.
Mt 10:42 anyone gives even a **c** of cold water
   20:22 "Can you drink the **c** I am going
   23:25 You clean the outside of the **c**
   23:26 First clean the inside of the **c**
   26:27 Then he took a **c**, and when he had
   26:39 may this **c** be taken from me.
Mk 9:41 anyone who gives you a **c** of water
   10:38 "Can you drink the **c** I drink or be
   14:23 Then he took a **c**, and when he had
   14:36 Take this **c** from me.
Lk 11:39 Pharisees clean the outside of the **c**
   22:17 After taking the **c**, he gave thanks
   22:20 way, after the supper he took the **c**,
   22:20 "This **c** is the new covenant in my
   22:42 you are willing, take this **c** from me;
Jn 18:11 Shall I not drink the **c** the Father has
1Co 10:21 You cannot drink the **c** of the Lord
          and the **c** of demons too;
   11:25 after supper he took the **c**, saying,
          "This **c** is the new covenant in my
   11:27 or drinks the **c** of the Lord
Rev 14:10 full strength into the **c** of his wrath.
   16:19 gave her the **c** filled with the wine
   17: 4 She held a golden **c** in her hand,
   18: 6 a double portion from her own **c**.

CUPBEARER

Ge 40: 1 the **c** and the baker of the king
   41: 9 Then the chief **c** said to Pharaoh,
Ne   1:11 of this man." I was **c** to the king.

CUPS CUP

Ex 25:33 Three **c** shaped like almond flowers
Mk 7: 4 such as the washing of **c**,

CURDS

Ge 18: 8 He then brought some **c** and milk
Dt 32:14 with **c** and milk from herd and flock
Isa 7:15 He will be eating **c** and honey
Eze 34: 3 You eat the **c**, clothe yourselves

CURE CURED

2Ki 5: 3 He would **c** him of his leprosy."
Jer 17: 9 above all things and beyond **c**.
   30:15 wound, your pain that has no **c**?
Hos 5:13 But he is not able to **c** you, not able
Lk 9: 1 out all demons and to **c** diseases,

CURED CURE

Lk 6:18 troubled by impure spirits were **c**,
Jn 5: 9 At once the man was **c**;
Ac 19:12 their illnesses were **c** and the evil
   28: 9 sick on the island came and were **c**.

CURRENTS*

Jnh 2: 3 seas, and the **c** swirled about me;

CURSE ACCURSED, CURSED, CURSES, CURSING

Ge   4:11 Now you are under a c and driven
     8:21 again will I c the ground because
    12: 3 and whoever curses you I will c;
   27:13 him, "My son, let the c fall on me.
Ex 22:28 God or c the ruler of your people.
Lev 19:14 " 'Do not c the deaf or put
   24:11 blasphemed the Name with a c;
Nu   5:18 holds the bitter water that brings a c.
   22: 6 come and put a c on these people,
   22: 6 and whoever you c is cursed."
   22:12 You must not put a c on those
Dt 11:26 you today a blessing and a c—
   11:28 the c if you disobey the commands
   21:23 is hung on a pole is under God's c.
   23: 5 turned the c into a blessing for you,
Jos 9:23 You are now under a c:
   24: 9 son of Beor to put a c on you.
2Sa 16: 9 should this dead dog c my lord
2Ki 2:24 and called down a c on them
Ne 10:29 and bind themselves with a c
   13: 2 Balaam to call a c down on them.
   13: 2 turned the c into a blessing.)
Job 1:11 he will surely c you to your face."
   2: 5 he will surely c you to your face."
   2: 9 C God and die!"
Ps 62: 4 they bless, but in their hearts they c.
 109:28 While they c, may you bless;
Pr   3:33 The LORD's c is on the house
  30:11 "There are those who c their fathers
Isa 24: 6 Therefore a c consumes the earth;
Jer 24: 9 a c and an object of ridicule,
   42:18 You will be a c and an object
   42:18 a c and an object of reproach;
   44:12 They will become a c and an object
   44:12 a c and an object of reproach.
La   3:65 hearts, and may your c be on them!
Mal 2: 2 "I will send a c on you, and I will c
        your blessings.
Lk   6:28 bless those who c you,
Jn   7:49 of the law—there is a c on them."
Ro 12:14 bless and do not c.
Gal 1: 8 to you, let them be under God's c!
   1: 9 let them be under God's c!
   3:10 the works of the law are under a c,
   3:13 redeemed us from the c of the law by
        becoming a c for us,
Jas   3: 9 and with it we c human beings,
Rev 22: 3 No longer will there be any c.

CURSED CURSE

Ge   3:14 "C are you above all livestock
   3:17 "C is the ground because of you;
   9:25 he said, "C be Canaan!
  27:29 May those who curse you be c
Lev 20: 9 Because they have c their father
Nu 22: 6 and whoever you curse is c."
   23: 8 I curse those whom God has not c?
Dt 27:15 "C is anyone who makes an idol—
   27:16 "C is anyone who dishonors their
   27:17 "C is anyone who moves their
   27:18 "C is anyone who leads the blind

Dt 27:19 "C is anyone who withholds justice
   27:20 "C is anyone who sleeps with his
   27:21 "C is anyone who has sexual
   27:22 "C is anyone who sleeps with his
   27:23 "C is anyone who sleeps with his
   27:24 "C is anyone who kills their
   27:25 "C is anyone who accepts a bribe
   27:26 "C is anyone who does not uphold
   28:16 You will be c in the city and c
Jos 6:26 "C before the LORD is the one
1Sa 17:43 the Philistine c David by his gods.
2Sa 16: 7 As he c, Shimei said, "Get out,
   19:21 He c the LORD's anointed."
2Ki 9:34 "Take care of that c woman,"
Job 1: 5 sinned and c God in their hearts."
   3: 1 his mouth and c the day of his birth.
Pr 24:24 will be c by peoples and denounced
Jer 17: 5 "C is the one who trusts in man,
Mal 1:14 "C is the cheat who has
Mk 11:21 The fig tree you c has withered!"
Ro   9: 3 I could wish that I myself were c
1Co 4:12 When we are c, we bless;
   12: 3 "Jesus be c," and no one can say,
   16:22 love the Lord, let that person be c!
Gal 3:10 "C is everyone who does not
   3:13 "C is everyone who is hung
Heb 6: 8 and is in danger of being c.
Rev 16: 9 heat and they c the name of God,
   16:11 and c the God of heaven because
   16:21 they c God on account of the plague

CURSES CURSE

Ge 12: 3 you, and whoever c you I will curse;
Ex 21:17 "Anyone who c their father
Lev 20: 9 " 'Anyone who c their father
   24:15 'Anyone who c their God will be
Nu   5:23 priest is to write these c on a scroll
Dt 11:29 blessings, and on Mount Ebal the c.
   27:13 on Mount Ebal to pronounce c:
   28:15 all these c will come on you
Jos 8:34 the blessings and the c—just as it is
2Ch 34:24 all the c written in the book that has
Ne 13:25 them and called c down on them.
Pr 20:20 If someone c their father or mother,
   28:27 their eyes to them receive many c.
Mt 15: 4 and 'Anyone who c their father
Mk 14:71 He began to call down c, and he

CURSING CURSE

2Sa 16:10 If he is c because the LORD said
Ps 109:18 He wore c as his garment;
Hos 4: 2 There is only c, lying and murder,
Ro   3:14 "Their mouths are full of c
Jas   3:10 the same mouth come praise and c.

CURTAIN CURTAINS

Ex 26:31 "Make a c of blue,
   26:36 to the tent make a c of blue,
Mt 27:51 that moment the c of the temple was
Mk 15:38 the c of the temple was torn in two
Lk 23:45 the c of the temple was torn in two.
Heb 6:19 the inner sanctuary behind the c,
   9: 3 Behind the second c was a room
   10:20 way opened for us through the c,

CURTAINS CURTAIN
Ex 26: 1 with ten c of finely twisted linen
Nu 3:26 the c of the courtyard, the curtain

CUSH CUSHITE
Ge 2:13 winds through the entire land of C.
10: 6 C, Egypt, Put and Canaan.
Ps 7: T *sang to the LORD concerning C,*
Isa 20: 3 and portent against Egypt and C,

CUSHITE CUSH
Nu 12: 1 Moses because of his C wife, for he
had married a C.
2Sa 18:21 Then Joab said to a C, "Go,
18:21 The C bowed down before Joab
Jer 38: 7 a C, an official in the royal palace,

CUSTODY
Gal 3:23 we were held in c under the law,

CUSTOM CUSTOMS
Job 1: 5 This was Job's regular c.
Mk 10: 1 and as was his c, he taught them.
15: 6 Now it was the c at the festival
Lk 4:16 into the synagogue, as was his c.
Ac 15: 1 according to the c taught by Moses,
17: 2 As was his c, Paul went

CUSTOMS CUSTOM
Lev 18:30 the detestable c that were practiced
20:23 to the c of the nations I am going
Ps 106:35 with the nations and adopted their c.
Jn 19:40 in accordance with Jewish burial c.
Gal 2:14 force Gentiles to follow Jewish c?

CUT CUTS, CUTTING
Ge 15:10 him, c them in two and arranged
15:10 birds, however, he did not c in half.
17:14 flesh, will be c off from his people;
Ex 34:13 and c down their Asherah poles.
Lev 19:27 " 'Do not c the hair at the sides
19:28 " 'Do not c your bodies
21: 5 of their beards or c their bodies.
Dt 20:20 you may c down trees that you
Jos 4: 7 the Jordan was c off before the ark
4: 7 the waters of the Jordan were c off.
Jdg 21: 6 "Today one tribe is c off
1Sa 17:51 he c off his head with the sword.
24: 4 and c off a corner of Saul's robe.
2Sa 14:26 Whenever he c the hair of his head—
14:26 to c his hair once a year because it
1Ki 3:25 "C the living child in two and give
2Ch 15:16 Asa c it down, broke it
31: 1 and c down the Asherah poles.
34: 7 and c to pieces all the incense altars
Ps 31:22 said, "I am c off from your sight!"
118:10 name of the LORD I c them down.
Pr 2:22 the wicked will be c off
23:18 you, and your hope will not be c off.
Isa 9:14 So the LORD will c off from Israel
51: 1 to the rock from which you were c
53: 8 For he was c off from the land
Jer 34:18 I will treat like the calf they c in two
Eze 37:11 and our hope is gone; we are c off.'
Da 2:45 of the vision of the rock c

Mt 3:10 produce good fruit will be c down
24:22 "If those days had not been c short,
Mk 9:43 hand causes you to stumble, c it off.
15:46 placed it in a tomb c out of rock.
Jn 18:26 the man whose ear Peter had c off,
Ac 2:37 they were c to the heart and said
Ro 11:22 Otherwise, you also will be c off.
1Co 11: 6 might as well have her hair c off;

MUST BE CUT OFF See MUST

CUTS CUT
Jn 15: 2 He c off every branch in me

CUTTING CUT
Pr 26: 6 of a fool is like c off one's feet
Jn 18:10 priest's servant, c off his right ear.

CYMBAL* CYMBALS
1Co 13: 1 a resounding gong or a clanging c.

CYMBALS CYMBAL
2Sa 6: 5 lyres, timbrels, sistrums and c.
1Ch 15:16 lyres, harps and c.
2Ch 5:12 dressed in fine linen and playing c,
29:25 in the temple of the LORD with c,
Ezr 3:10 Levites (the sons of Asaph) with c,
Ne 12:27 and with the music of c,
Ps 150: 5 praise him with the clash of c, praise
him with resounding c.

CYPRESS
Ge 6:14 So make yourself an ark of c wood;

CYPRUS
Ac 4:36 a Levite from C, whom the apostles
13: 4 Seleucia and sailed from there to C.

CYRENE
Lk 23:26 they seized Simon from C, who was

CYRUS
Persian king who allowed exiles to return (2Ch
36:22—Ezr 1:8), to rebuild temple (Ezr 5:13—6:14),
as appointed by the LORD (Isa 44:28—45:13).

D

DAGON DAGON'S
Jdg 16:23 offer a great sacrifice to D their god
1Ch 10:10 hung up his head in the temple of D.

DAGON'S DAGON
1Sa 5: 2 they carried the ark into D temple

DAILY DAY
1Ki 4:22 Solomon's d provisions were thirty
2Ch 8:13 according to the d requirement
Job 23:12 of his mouth more than my d bread.
Ps 68:19 Savior, who d bears our burdens.
Pr 30: 8 but give me only my d bread.
Da 8:13 vision concerning the d sacrifice,
11:31 and will abolish the d sacrifice.
Mt 6:11 Give us today our d bread.
Lk 9:23 take up their cross d and follow me.
11: 3 Give us each day our d bread.

Jas   2:15 sister is without clothes and **d** food.

DAMASCUS

2Ki   8: 7 Elisha went to **D**, and Ben-Hadad
16:10 Then King Ahaz went to **D** to meet
16:10 He saw an altar in **D** and sent
Isa   7: 8 for the head of Aram is **D**, and the
head of **D** is only Rezin.
17: 1 A prophecy against **D**: "See, **D** will
Jer 49:23 Concerning **D**: "Hamath and Arpad
Am   1: 3 "For three sins of **D**, even for four,
Ac   9: 3 As he neared **D** on his journey,
22: 6 "About noon as I came near **D**,
Gal   1:17 Later I returned to **D**.

DAN

1. Son of Jacob by Bilhah (Ge 30:4–6; 35:25;
46:23). Tribe of blessed (Ge 49:16–17; Dt 33:22),
numbered (Nu 1:39; 26:43), allotted land (Jos
19:40–48; Eze 48:1), failed to fully possess (Jdg
1:34–35), failed to support Deborah (Jdg 5:17),
possessed Laish/Dan (Jdg 18).
2. Northernmost city in Israel (Ge 14:14; Jdg
18; 20:1).

DANCE DANCED, DANCES,
DANCING

Ecc   3: 4 a time to mourn and a time to **d**,
Jer 31: 4 and go out to **d** with the joyful.
31:13 young women will **d** and be glad,
Lk   7:32 the pipe for you, and you did not **d**;

DANCED* DANCE

1Sa 18: 7 As they **d**, they sang:
1Ki 18:26 they **d** around the altar they had
Mt   14: 6 of Herodias **d** for the guests
Mk   6:22 daughter of Herodias came in and **d**,

DANCES* DANCE

1Sa 21:11 he the one they sing about in their **d**:
29: 5 the David they sang about in their **d**:

DANCING DANCE

Ex   15:20 followed her, with timbrels and **d**.
32:19 the camp and saw the calf and the **d**,
Jdg 11:34 daughter, **d** to the sound of timbrels!
21:23 While the young women were **d**,
2Sa   6:14 David was **d** before the LORD
6:16 leaping and **d** before the LORD,
1Ch 15:29 when she saw King David **d**
Ps   30:11 You turned my wailing into **d**;
149: 3 Let them praise his name with **d**
La   5:15 our **d** has turned to mourning.

DANGER

Pr   22: 3 The prudent see **d** and take refuge,
27:12 The prudent see **d** and take refuge,
Mt   5:22 will be in **d** of the fire of hell.
Ac   19:40 is, we are in **d** of being charged
Ro   8:35 famine or nakedness or **d** or sword?
2Co 11:26 I have been in **d** from rivers, in **d**
from bandits, in **d** from my fellow
Jews, in **d** from Gentiles; in **d** in the
city, in **d** in the country, in **d** at sea;
Heb   6: 8 and is in **d** of being cursed.

DANIEL

1. Hebrew exile to Babylon, name changed to
Belteshazzar (Da 1:6–7). Refused to eat unclean
food (Da 1:8–21). Interpreted Nebuchadnezzar's dreams (Da 2; 4), writing on the wall (Da
5). Thrown into lion's den (Da 6). Visions of (Da
7–12).
2. Son of David (1Ch 3:1).

DARE DARED

Jn   9:34 sin at birth; how **d** you lecture us!"
Ac   7:32 with fear and did not **d** to look.
Ro   5: 7 person someone might possibly **d**

DARED DARE

Mk   12:34 then on no one **d** ask him any more
Jn   21:12 None of the disciples **d** ask him,

DARIUS

1. King of Persia (Ezr 4:5), allowed rebuilding of
temple (Ezr 5–6).
2. Mede who conquered Babylon (Da 5:31).

DARK DARKENED, DARKENS,
DARKEST, DARKNESS

2Sa 22:10 **d** clouds were under his feet.
2Ch   6: 1 that he would dwell in a **d** cloud;
Ps   35: 6 may their path be **d** and slippery,
139:12 even the darkness will not be **d**
Pr   2:13 the straight paths to walk in **d** ways,
SS   1: 5 **D** am I, yet lovely,
1: 5 Jerusalem, **d** like the tents of Kedar,
Isa 50:10 Let the one who walks in the **d**,
Jer   4:28 and the heavens above grow **d**,
Lk   12: 3 you have said in the **d** will be heard
Jn   12:35 the **d** does not know where they are
Ro   2:19 a light for those who are in the **d**,
Eph   6:12 against the powers of this **d** world
2Pe   1:19 it, as to a light shining in a **d** place,
Rev   8:12 so that a third of them turned **d**.

DARKENED DARK

SS   1: 6 am dark, because I am **d** by the sun.
Joel   2:10 the sun and moon are **d**,
Mt   24:29 of those days " 'the sun will be **d**,
Ro   1:21 and their foolish hearts were **d**.
Eph   4:18 They are **d** in their understanding
Rev   9: 2 sky were **d** by the smoke

DARKENS* DARK

Am   5: 8 into dawn and **d** day into night,

DARKEST* DARK

Ps   23: 4 though I walk through the **d** valley,
88   6 me in the lowest pit, in the **d** depths.

DARKNESS DARK

Ge   1: 2 **d** was over the surface of the deep,
1: 4 he separated the light from the **d**.
15:12 thick and dreadful **d** came over him.
Ex   10:22 total **d** covered all Egypt for three
14:20 the night the cloud brought **d**
20:21 approached the thick **d** where God
Dt   5:23 you heard the voice out of the **d**,
Jos 24: 7 and he put **d** between you

2Sa 22:29 the LORD turns my **d** into light.
Job 12:22 He reveals the deep things of **d** and
            brings utter **d** into the light.
Ps   18:11 He made **d** his covering, his canopy
     91: 6 the pestilence that stalks in the **d**,
     97: 2 Clouds and thick **d** surround him;
    107:10 Some sat in **d**, in utter **d**,
    112: 4 Even in **d** light dawns
    139:12 even the **d** will not be dark to you;
    139:12 like the day, for **d** is as light to you.
Pr   4:19 way of the wicked is like deep **d**;
Ecc   2:13 folly, just as light is better than **d**.
      5:17 All their days they eat in **d**,
Isa   5:20 who put **d** for light and light for **d**,
      9: 2 walking in **d** have seen a great light;
      9: 2 land of deep **d** a light has dawned.
     42:16 I will turn the **d** into light before
     45: 7 I form the light and create **d**, I bring
     58:10 then your light will rise in the **d**,
     61: 1 and release from **d** for the prisoners,
Jer 13:16 your God before he brings the **d**,
     13:16 he will turn it to utter **d** and change
Joel 2:31 The sun will be turned to **d**
Am   5:20 not the day of the LORD be **d**,
Na   1: 8 pursue his foes into the realm of **d**.
Zep   1:15 and ruin, a day of **d** and gloom,
Mt   4:16 living in **d** have seen a great light;
      6:23 your whole body will be full of **d**.
      6:23 If then the light within you is **d**, how
            great is that **d**!
     22:13 into the **d**, where there will be
Lk   11:34 your body also is full of **d**.
     23:44 **d** came over the whole land until
Jn   1: 5 The light shines in the **d**, and the **d**
      3:19 but people loved **d** instead of light
      8:12 follows me will never walk in **d**,
Ac   2:20 The sun will be turned to **d**
Ro   13:12 So let us put aside the deeds of **d**
2Co   4: 6 "Let light shine out of **d**," made his
      6:14 fellowship can light have with **d**?
Eph   5: 8 For you were once **d**, but now you
      5:11 to do with the fruitless deeds of **d**,
Col   1:13 rescued us from the dominion of **d**
1Th   5: 5 not belong to the night or to the **d**.
1Pe   2: 9 out of **d** into his wonderful light.
2Pe   2: 4 them in chains of **d** to be held
      2:17 Blackest **d** is reserved for them.
1Jn   1: 5 in him there is no **d** at all.
      2: 8 because the **d** is passing and the true
      2: 9 a brother or sister is still in the **d**.
Jude 1: 6 these he has kept in **d**,
      1:13 whom blackest **d** has been reserved
Rev 16:10 and its kingdom was plunged into **d**.

DARLING
SS   1:15 How beautiful you are, my **d**!
      2:10 me, "Arise, my **d**, my beautiful one,
      5: 2 me, my sister, my **d**, my dove,

DASH DASHED
2Ki   8:12 **d** their little children to the ground,
Ps   2: 9 you will **d** them to pieces like
Lk   19:44 They will **d** you to the ground,
Rev   2:27 will **d** them to pieces like pottery'—

DASHED DASH
Hos 10:14 when mothers were **d** to the ground
Na   3:10 Her infants were **d** to pieces

DATES*
2Sa   6:19 a cake of **d** and a cake of raisins
1Ch 16: 3 a cake of **d** and a cake of raisins
Ac   1: 7 or **d** the Father has set by his own
1Th   5: 1 **d** we do not need to write to you,

DATHAN*
    Involved in Korah's rebellion against Moses and
    Aaron (Nu 16:1–27; 26:9; Dt 11:6; Ps 106:17).

DAUGHTER DAUGHTER-IN-LAW, DAUGHTERS, DAUGHTERS-IN-LAW
Ge   19:31 One day the older **d** said
     24:24 him, "I am the **d** of Bethuel, the son
     29:10 Jacob saw Rachel **d** of his uncle
     34: 3 was drawn to Dinah **d** of Jacob;
     38: 2 There Judah met the **d**
Ex   2: 5 Pharaoh's **d** went down to the Nile
     21: 7 "If a man sells his **d** as a servant,
Lev 12: 5 If she gives birth to a **d**, for two
Nu   27: 8 no son, give his inheritance to his **d**.
Jdg 11:34 come out to meet him but his **d**,
     11:34 for her he had neither son nor **d**.
Ru   2: 2 said to her, "Go ahead, my **d**."
      3:10 bless you, my **d**," he replied.
1Sa 18:20 Now Saul's **d** Michal was in love
      ?Sa 6:16 Michal **d** of Saul watched
1Ki 11: 1 women besides Pharaoh's **d**—
Est   2: 7 had taken her as his own **d** when her
Ps   9:14 your praises in the gates of **D** Zion,
    137: 8 **D** Babylon, doomed to destruction,
Isa 47: 1 sit in the dust, Virgin **D** Babylon;
     52: 2 the chains on your neck, **D** Zion,
     62:11 "Say to **D** Zion, 'See, your Savior
Jer   6: 2 I will destroy **D** Zion, so beautiful
     46:11 and get balm, Virgin **D** Egypt.
Eze 16:45 You are a true **d** of your mother,
Mic   7: 6 a **d** rises up against her mother,
Zep   3:14 Sing, **D** Zion; shout aloud, Israel!
      3:14 with all your heart, **D** Jerusalem!
Zec   9: 9 Rejoice greatly, **D** Zion! Shout,
Mt   14: 6 Herod's birthday the **d** of Herodias
     15:28 her **d** was healed at that moment.
Mk   5:35 "Your **d** is dead," they said.
      7:29 the demon has left your **d**."
Lk   12:53 mother against **d** and **d** against

DAUGHTER JERUSALEM 2Ki 19:21; Isa
37:22; La 2:13, 15; Mic 4:8; Zep 3:14; Zec 9:9

DAUGHTER ZION 2Ki 19:21; Ps 9:14; Isa 1:8;
10:32; 16:1; 37:22; 52:2; 62:11; Jer 4:31; 6:2, 23; La
1:6; 2:1, 4, 8, 10, 13, 18; 4:22; Mic 1:13; 4:8, 10, 13;
Zep 3:14; Zec 2:10; 9:9; Mt 21:5; Jn 12:15

DAUGHTER-IN-LAW DAUGHTER
Ge   11:31 and his **d** Sarai, the wife of his son
     38:16 Not realizing that she was his **d**,
Lev 20:12 man has sexual relations with his **d**,
Ru   1:22 her **d**, arriving in Bethlehem as

1Ch 2: 4 Judah's **d** Tamar bore Perez
Mic 7: 6 a **d** against her mother-in-law—
Mt 10:35 a **d** against her mother-in-law—

DAUGHTERS DAUGHTER

Ge   6: 2 that the **d** of humans were beautiful,
     6: 4 of God went to the **d** of humans
    19:36 So both of Lot's **d** became pregnant
    29:16 Now Laban had two **d**; the name
Ex   2:16 Now a priest of Midian had seven **d**,
Nu 27: 1 The **d** of Zelophehad son of Hepher,
    27: 1 The names of the **d** were Mahlah,
    36:10 So Zelophehad's **d** did as
Dt   7: 3 Do not give your **d** to their sons
     7: 3 sons or take their **d** for your sons,
    12:31 and **d** in the fire as sacrifices to their
Ezr 9:12 do not give your **d** in marriage
     9:12 sons or take their **d** for your sons.
Job 42:15 women as beautiful as Job's **d**,
Ps 144:12 our **d** will be like pillars carved
Pr 30:15 "The leech has two **d**. 'Give!
SS   1: 5 yet lovely, **d** of Jerusalem, dark like
Eze 23: 2 two women, **d** of the same mother.
Joel 2:28 Your sons and **d** will prophesy,
Lk 23:28 and said to them, "**D** of Jerusalem,
Ac   2:17 Your sons and **d** will prophesy,
    21: 9 four unmarried **d** who prophesied.
2Co 6:18 and you will be my sons and **d**,
Heb 12: 8 not legitimate, not true sons and **d**
1Pe 3: 6 You are her **d** if you do what is right

DAUGHTERS OF JERUSALEM SS 1:5; 2:7;
3:5, 10; 5:8, 16; 8:4; Lk 23:28

DAUGHTERS-IN-LAW
DAUGHTER
Ru   1: 8 Then Naomi said to her two **d**,

DAVID

Son of Jesse (Ru 4:17–22; 1Ch 2:13–15), ancestor of Jesus (Mt 1:1–17; Lk 3:31). Wives and children (1Sa 18; 25:39–44; 2Sa 3:2–5; 5:13–16; 11:27; 1Ch 3:1–9).

Anointed king by Samuel (1Sa 16:1–13). Musician to Saul (1Sa 16:14–23; 18:10). Killed Goliath (1Sa 17). Relation with Jonathan (1Sa 18:1–4; 19–20; 23:16–18; 2Sa 1). Disfavor of Saul (1Sa 18:6—23:29). Spared Saul's life (1Sa 24; 26). Among Philistines (1Sa 21:10–14; 27–30). Lament for Saul and Jonathan (2Sa 1).

Anointed king of Judah (2Sa 2:1–11). Conflict with house of Saul (2Sa 2–4). Anointed king of Israel (2Sa 5:1–4; 1Ch 11:1–3). Conquered Jerusalem (2Sa 5:6–10; 1Ch 11:4–9). Brought ark to Jerusalem (2Sa 6; 1Ch 13; 15–16). The LORD promised eternal dynasty (2Sa 7; 1Ch 17; Ps 132). Showed kindness to Mephibosheth (2Sa 9). Adultery with Bathsheba, murder of Uriah (2Sa 11–12). Son Amnon raped daughter Tamar; killed by Absalom (2Sa 13). Absalom's revolt (2Sa 14–17); death (2Sa 18). Sheba's revolt (2Sa 20). Victories: Philistines (2Sa 5:17–25; 21:15–22; 1Ch 14:8–17; 20:4–8), Ammonites (2Sa 10; 1Ch 19), various (2Sa 8; 1Ch 18). Mighty men (2Sa 23:8–39; 1Ch 11–12). Punished for numbering army (2Sa 24; 1Ch 21). Ap-

pointed Solomon king (1Ki 1:28—2:9). Prepared for building of temple (1Ch 22–29). Last words (2Sa 23:1–7). Death (1Ki 2:10–12; 1Ch 29:28).

Psalmist (Mt 22:43–45), musician (Am 6:5), prophet (2Sa 23:2–7; Ac 1:16; 2:30).

Psalms of: 2 (Ac 4:25), 3–32, 34–41, 51–65, 68–70, 86, 95 (Heb 4:7), 101, 103, 108–110, 122, 124, 131, 133, 138–145.

CITY OF DAVID See CITY

HOUSE OF DAVID See HOUSE

SON OF DAVID See SON

DAWN DAWNED, DAWNS

Job 38:12 morning, or shown the **d** its place,
Ps 37: 6 righteous reward shine like the **d**,
    57: 8 harp and lyre! I will awaken the **d**.
   139: 9 If I rise on the wings of the **d**, if I
SS   6:10 Who is this that appears like the **d**,
Isa 14:12 heaven, morning star, son of the **d**!
    62: 1 her vindication shines out like the **d**,
Am   4:13 mankind, who turns **d** to darkness,
Mt 28: 1 at **d** on the first day of the week,

DAWNED DAWN

Isa 9: 2 land of deep darkness a light has **d**.
Mt   4:16 the shadow of death a light has **d**."

DAWNS* DAWN

Ps 65: 8 where morning **d**, where evening
   112: 4 in darkness light **d** for the upright,
Hos 10:15 When that day **d**, the king of Israel
2Pe 1:19 until the day **d** and the morning star

DAY DAILY, DAY'S, DAYBREAK, DAYLIGHT, DAYS, MIDDAY

Ge   1: 5 God called the light "**d**,"
     1: 5 and there was morning—the first **d**.
     1: 8 there was morning—the second **d**.
     1:13 and there was morning—the third **d**.
     1:19 there was morning—the fourth **d**.
     1:23 and there was morning—the fifth **d**.
     1:31 and there was morning—the sixth **d**.
     2: 2 the seventh **d** God had finished
     2: 2 so on the seventh **d** he rested
     8:22 **d** and night will never cease."
Ex 12:17 on this very **d** that I brought your
    12:17 Celebrate this **d** as a lasting
    13:21 By **d** the LORD went ahead
    13:21 so that they could travel by **d**
    16:30 the people rested on the seventh **d**.
    20: 8 "Remember the Sabbath **d**
    40: 2 on the first **d** of the first month.
Lev 12: 3 On the eighth **d** the boy is to be
    16:30 on this **d** atonement will be made
    23:28 Do not do any work on that **d**,
         because it is the **D** of Atonement,
Nu 14:14 before them in a pillar of cloud by **d**
Dt   1:33 in fire by night and in a cloud by **d**,
    24:15 their wages each **d** before sunset,
    30:19 This **d** I call the heavens
    34: 6 this **d** no one knows where his grave
Jos 1: 8 meditate on it **d** and night,
    10:14 has never been a **d** like it before

Jos 10:14 a **d** when the LORD listened
2Ki   7: 9 This is a **d** of good news and we are
     25:30 **D** by **d** the king gave Jehoiachin
1Ch 16:23 proclaim his salvation **d** after **d**.
Ne   8:10 This **d** is holy to our Lord.
      8:18 **D** after **d**, from the first **d** to the last,
      8:18 and on the eighth **d**, in accordance
Ps   1: 2 and who meditates on his law **d**
     19: 2 **D** after **d** they pour forth speech;
     37:13 for he knows their **d** is coming.
     50:15 and call on me in the **d** of trouble;
     84:10 Better is one **d** in your courts than
     96: 2 proclaim his salvation **d** after **d**.
    118:24 The LORD has done it this very **d**;
    119:97 I meditate on it all **d** long.
   119:164 Seven times a **d** I praise you
Pr   11: 4 is worthless in the **d** of wrath,
     27: 1 do not know what a **d** may bring.
Ecc   7: 1 the **d** of death better than the **d**
Isa   2:12 The LORD Almighty has a **d**
     13: 9 the **d** of the LORD is coming—
     13: 9 a cruel **d**, with wrath and fierce
     49: 8 in the **d** of salvation I will help you;
     60:19 sun will no more be your light by **d**,
     66: 8 Can a country be born in a **d**
Jer 17:22 but keep the Sabbath **d** holy, as I
     30: 7 How awful that **d** will be!
     46:10 But that **d** belongs to the Lord,
     46:10 a **d** of vengeance, for vengeance
     50:31 "for your **d** has come, the time
Eze   4: 6 you 40 days, a **d** for each year.
      7: 7 The time has come! The **d** is near!
     30: 2 and say, "Alas for that **d**!"
Da   6:13 He still prays three times a **d**."
Joel 1:15 Alas for that **d**! For the **d**
      2:31 great and dreadful **d** of the LORD.
Am   3:14 "On the **d** I punish Israel for her
      5:20 Will not the **d** of the LORD be
Ob   1:15 "The **d** of the LORD is near for all
Mic   7: 4 the **d** God visits you has come,
      7: 4 the **d** your watchmen sound
Hab   3:16 wait patiently for the **d** of calamity
Zep   1:14 The great **d** of the LORD is near—
      1:14 cry on the **d** of the LORD is bitter;
      3: 5 and every new **d** he does not fail,
Zec   2:11 be joined with the LORD in that **d**
     14: 1 A **d** of the LORD is coming,
     14: 7 It will be a unique **d**—a **d** known
     14: 7 with no distinction between **d**
Mal   3: 2 But who can endure the **d** of his
      4: 5 dreadful **d** of the LORD comes.
Mt   10:15 on the **d** of judgment than
     12:36 give account on the **d** of judgment
     20:19 On the third **d** he will be raised
     24:38 up to the **d** Noah entered the ark;
     25:13 because you do not know the **d**
     28: 1 at dawn on the first **d** of the week,
Lk   1:59 On the eighth **d** they came
      2:21 On the eighth **d**, when it was time
     11: 3 Give us each **d** our daily bread.
     17:24 in his **d** will be like the lightning,
     24:46 rise from the dead on the third **d**,
Jn   6:40 I will raise them up at the last **d**."

Ac   2: 1 When the **d** of Pentecost came,
      2:20 the great and glorious **d** of the Lord.
      2:46 Every **d** they continued to meet
      5:42 **D** after **d**, in the temple courts
     17:11 examined the Scriptures every **d**
     17:31 he has set a **d** when he will judge
Ro   2: 5 yourself for the **d** of God's wrath,
     14: 5 person considers one **d** more sacred
     14: 5 another considers every **d** alike.
1Co   5: 5 may be saved on the **d** of the Lord.
     15: 4 on the third **d** according
     15:31 I face death every **d**—yes, just as
2Co   4:16 inwardly we are being renewed **d**
      4:16 we are being renewed **d** by **d**.
      6: 2 in the **d** of salvation I helped you."
      6: 2 favor, now is the **d** of salvation.
     11:25 a night and a **d** in the open sea,
Eph   4:30 were sealed for the **d** of redemption.
      6:13 so that when the **d** of evil comes,
Php   1: 6 to completion until the **d** of Christ
1Th   5: 2 the **d** of the Lord will come like
      5: 8 But since we belong to the **d**, let us
2Th   2: 2 the **d** of the Lord has already come.
Heb   7:27 not need to offer sacrifices **d** after **d**,
2Pe   3: 8 With the Lord a **d** is like a thousand
      3: 8 and a thousand years are like a **d**.
      3:10 the **d** of the Lord will come like
1Jn   4:17 confidence on the **d** of judgment:
Jude 1: 6 chains for judgment on the great **D**.
Rev   1:10 On the Lord's **D** I was in the Spirit,
      6:17 the great **d** of their wrath has come,
      8:12 A third of the **d** was without light,
     16:14 on the great **d** of God Almighty.
     20:10 They will be tormented **d** and night
     21:25 On no **d** will its gates ever be shut,

DAY OF THE LORD Ac 2:20; 1Co 5:5; 2Co
1:14; 1Th 5:2; 2Th 2:2; 2Pe 3:10

DAY OF THE LORD† Isa 13:6, 9; Eze 13:5;
30:3; Joel 1:15; 2:1, 11, 31; 3:14; Am 5:18, 18, 20;
Ob 1:15; Zep 1:7, 14, 14; Zec 14:1; Mal 4:5

THIRD DAY Ge 1:13; 22:4; 31:22; 40:20; 42:18;
Ex 19:11, 15, 16; Lev 7:17, 18; 19:6, 7; Nu 7:24;
19:12; 29:20; Jos 9:17; Jdg 20:30; 1Sa 30:1; 2Sa 1:2;
1Ki 3:18; 2Ki 20:5, 8; Ezr 6:15; Est 5:1; Hos 6:2; Mt
16:21; 17:23; 20:19; 27:64; Lk 9:22; 13:32; 18:33;
24:7, 21, 46; Jn 2:1; Ac 10:40; 27:19; 1Co 15:4

DAY'S DAY
1Ki 19: 4 while he himself went a **d** journey
Ac   1:12 a Sabbath **d** walk from the city.

DAYBREAK DAY
Ge   32:24 and a man wrestled with him till **d**.
Ex   14:27 at **d** the sea went back to its place.
Lk   4:42 At **d**, Jesus went out to a solitary
     22:66 At **d** the council of the elders
Ac   5:21 At **d** they entered the temple courts,

DAYLIGHT DAY, LIGHT
2Sa 12:12 in broad **d** before all Israel.' "
Mt   10:27 I tell you in the dark, speak in the **d**;
Lk   12: 3 in the dark will be heard in the **d**,
2Pe   2:13 of pleasure is to carouse in broad **d**.

DAYS DAY

Ge   1:14 mark sacred times, and **d** and years,
      3:14 you will eat dust all the **d** of your
      3:17 food from it all the **d** of your life.
      7: 4 Seven **d** from now I will send rain
      7: 4 send rain on the earth for forty **d**
Ex 24:18 he stayed on the mountain forty **d**
    34:28 was there with the Lord forty **d**
Nu 13:25 At the end of forty **d** they returned
    14:34 the forty **d** you explored the land—
Dt 17:19 he is to read it all the **d** of his life so
    32: 7 Remember the **d** of old;
Jdg 17: 6 In those **d** Israel had no king;
    18: 1 In those **d** Israel had no king.
    18: 1 in those **d** the tribe of the Danites
    21:25 In those **d** Israel had no king;
1Sa 17:16 forty **d** the Philistine came forward
1Ki 19: 8 he traveled forty **d** and forty nights
Ps 21: 4 length of **d**, for ever and ever.
    23: 6 love will follow me all the **d** of my
    34:12 life and desires to see many good **d**,
    39: 5 You have made my **d** a mere
    90:10 Our **d** may come to seventy years,
    90:12 Teach us to number our **d**, that we
   128: 5 of Jerusalem all the **d** of your life.
Pr 9:11 For through wisdom your **d** will be
    31:12 good, not harm, all the **d** of her life.
Ecc 9: 9 all the **d** of this meaningless life
    12: 1 your Creator in the **d** of your youth,
    12: 1 before the **d** of trouble come
Isa 43:13 Yes, and from ancient **d** I am he.
    53:10 see his offspring and prolong his **d**,
Da 7: 9 and the Ancient of **D** took his seat.
    7:13 He approached the Ancient of **D**
    7:22 until the Ancient of **D** came
    12:11 is set up, there will be 1,290 **d**.
    12:12 and reaches the end of the 1,335 **d**.
Hos 3: 5 and to his blessings in the last **d**.
Joel 2:29 I will pour out my Spirit in those **d**.
Mt 4: 2 After fasting forty **d** and forty
Mk 1:13 he was in the wilderness forty **d**,
    10:34 Three **d** later he will rise."
Lk 4: 2 where for forty **d** he was tempted
    4: 2 He ate nothing during those **d**,
    19:43 The **d** will come upon you
Ac 1: 3 to them over a period of forty **d**
    2:17 " 'In the last **d**, God says, I will
Gal 4:10 You are observing special **d**
Eph 5:16 opportunity, because the **d** are evil.
2Ti 3: 1 will be terrible times in the last **d**.
Heb 1: 2 in these last **d** he has spoken to us
2Pe 3: 3 that in the last **d** scoffers will come,
Rev 11: 3 and they will prophesy for 1,260 **d**,
    11:11 a half **d** the breath of life from God
    12: 6 might be taken care of for 1,260 **d**.

DAYS ARE COMING Jer 7:32; 9:25; 16:14;
19:6; 23:5, 7; 30:3; 31:27, 31, 38; 33:14; 48:12; 49:2;
51:52; Am 8:11; 9:13; Heb 8:8

DAYS TO COME Ge 49:1; Ex 13:14; Nu 24:14;
Dt 31:29; Pr 31:25; Isa 27:6; 30:8; Jer 23:20; 30:24;
48:47; 49:39; Eze 38:16; Da 2:28

FORTY DAYS See FORTY

DAYSPRING (KJV) See DAWN, RISING SUN

DAZZLING*

Da 2:31 an enormous, **d** statue,
Mk 9: 3 His clothes became **d** white,

DEACON* DEACONS

Ro 16: 1 Phoebe, a **d** of the church in
           Cenchreae.
1Ti 3:12 A **d** must be faithful to his wife

DEACONS* DEACON

Php 1: 1 together with the overseers and **d**:
1Ti 3: 8 way, **d** are to be worthy of respect,
    3:10 against them, let them serve as **d**.

DEAD DIE

Ex 12:30 was not a house without someone **d**.
Lev 17:15 who eats anything found **d** or torn
    19:28 not cut your bodies for the **d** or put
Nu 16:48 stood between the living and the **d**,
Dt 18:11 or spiritist or who consults the **d**.
Ru 4: 5 the Moabite, the **d** man's widow,
    4: 5 name of the **d** with his property."
1Ch 10: 1 and many fell **d** on Mount Gilboa.
Job 26: 6 realm of the **d** is naked before God;
Ps 6: 5 Among the **d** no one proclaims your
  115:17 It is not the **d** who praise
Pr 2:18 and her paths to the spirits of the **d**.
Ecc 9: 4 a live dog is better off than a **d** lion!
Isa 8:19 Why consult the **d** on behalf
Mt 8:22 and let the **d** bury their own **d**."
    9:24 The girl is not **d** but asleep."
    10: 8 raise the **d**, cleanse those who have
    11: 5 the deaf hear, the **d** are raised,
    14: 2 he has risen from the **d**!
    23:27 inside are full of the bones of the **d**
    28: 7 'He has risen from the **d** and is
Mk 12:27 He is not the God of the **d**,
Lk 15:24 For this son of mine was **d** and is
    20:37 even Moses showed that the **d** rise,
    24: 5 look for the living among the **d**?
    24:46 and rise from the **d** on the third day,
Jn 5:21 For just as the Father raises the **d**
    11:44 The **d** man came out, his hands
    20: 9 that Jesus had to rise from the **d**.)
    21:14 after he was raised from the **d**.
Ac 2:24 But God raised him from the **d**,
Ro 6:11 count yourselves **d** to sin but alive
1Co 15:12 Christ has been raised from the **d**,
    15:12 there is no resurrection of the **d**?
    15:29 those do who are baptized for the **d**?
    15:29 If the **d** are not raised at all, why are
2Co 4:14 the Lord Jesus from the **d** will
Eph 2: 1 you were **d** in your transgressions
    5:14 rise from the **d**, and Christ will
Php 3:11 to the resurrection from the **d**.
Col 2:13 When you were **d** in your sins
1Th 4:16 and the **d** in Christ will rise first.
2Ti 4: 1 who will judge the living and the **d**,
Heb 11:19 that God could even raise the **d**,
Jas 2:26 As the body without the spirit is **d**, so
           faith without deeds is **d**.

1Pe	4: 5	ready to judge the living and the **d**.
Rev	1: 5	the firstborn from the **d**,
	1:18	I was **d**, and now look, I am alive
	11:18	time has come for judging the **d**,
	14:13	Blessed are the **d** who die
	20:12	And I saw the **d**, great and small,
	20:12	The **d** were judged according

DEAF

Ex	4:11	Who makes them **d** or mute?
Lev	19:14	" 'Do not curse the **d** or put
Pr	28: 9	If anyone turns a **d** ear to my
Isa	29:18	that day the **d** will hear the words
	35: 5	and the ears of the **d** unstopped.
	42:19	and **d** like the messenger I send?
Lk	7:22	leprosy are cleansed, the **d** hear,

DEAL DEALING, DEALT

Ex	8:22	day I will **d** differently with the land
2Ch	6:30	and **d** with everyone according to all
Heb	5: 2	He is able to **d** gently with those

DEALING DEAL

2Co	13 3	He is not weak in **d** with you, but is

DEALT DEAL

Ps	18:20	The Lord has **d** with me
1Th	2:11	you know that we **d** with each

DEAR* DEARER, DEARLY

2Sa	1:26	you were very **d** to me.
Ps	102:14	her stones are **d** to your servants;
Jer	31:20	Is not Ephraim my **d** son, the child
Ac	15:25	to you with our **d** friends Barnabas
Ro	12:19	Do not take revenge, my **d** friends,
	16: 5	Greet my **d** friend Epenetus,
	16: 8	Ampliatus, my **d** friend in the Lord.
	16: 9	in Christ, and my **d** friend Stachys.
	16:12	Greet my **d** friend Persis,
1Co	4:14	but to warn you as my **d** children.
	10:14	Therefore, my **d** friends,
	15:58	my **d** brothers and sisters,
2Co	7: 1	we have these promises, **d** friends,
	12:19	and everything we do, **d** friends,
Gal	4:19	My **d** children, for whom I am again
Eph	6:21	the **d** brother and faithful servant
Php	2:12	Therefore, my **d** friends, as you
	4: 1	in the Lord in this way, **d** friends!
Col	1: 7	Epaphras, our **d** fellow servant,
	4: 7	He is a **d** brother, a faithful minister
	4: 9	our faithful and **d** brother, who is
	4:14	Our **d** friend Luke, the doctor,
1Ti	6: 2	better because their masters are **d**
2Ti	1: 2	To Timothy, my **d** son:
Phm	1: 1	To Philemon our **d** friend
	1:16	better than a slave, as a **d** brother.
	1:16	He is very **d** to me but even dearer
Heb	6: 9	though we speak like this, **d** friends,
Jas	1:16	deceived, my **d** brothers and sisters.
	1:19	My **d** brothers and sisters, take note
	2: 5	Listen, my **d** brothers and sisters:
1Pe	2:11	**D** friends, I urge you, as foreigners
	4:12	**D** friends, do not be surprised
2Pe	3: 1	**D** friends, this is now my second
	3: 8	not forget this one thing, **d** friends:

2Pe	3:14	So then, **d** friends, since you are
	3:15	just as our **d** brother Paul also wrote
	3:17	Therefore, **d** friends, since you have
1Jn	2: 1	My **d** children, I write this to you so
	2: 7	**D** friends, I am not writing you
	2:12	I am writing to you, **d** children,
	2:14	I write to you, **d** children,
	2:18	**D** children, this is the last hour;
	2:28	And now, **d** children,
	3: 2	**D** friends, now we are children
	3: 7	**D** children, do not let anyone lead
	3:18	**D** children, let us not love
	3:21	**D** friends, if our hearts do not
	4: 1	**D** friends, do not believe every
	4: 4	You, **d** children, are from God
	4: 7	**D** friends, let us love one another,
	4:11	**D** friends, since God so loved us,
	5:21	**D** children, keep yourselves
2Jn	1: 5	And now, **d** lady, I am not writing
3Jn	1: 1	To my **d** friend Gaius, whom I love
	1: 2	**D** friend, I pray that you may enjoy
	1: 5	**D** friend, you are faithful in what
	1:11	**D** friend, do not imitate what is evil
Jude	1: 3	**D** friends, although I was very eager
	1:17	But, **d** friends, remember what
	1:20	But you, **d** friends, by building

DEARER* DEAR

Phm	1:16	is very dear to me but even **d** to you,

DEARLY* DEAR

Hos	4:18	their rulers **d** love shameful ways.
Eph	5: 1	therefore, as **d** loved children
Col	3:12	holy and **d** loved, clothe yourselves

DEATH DIE

Ex	21:12	with a fatal blow is to be put to **d**.
	21:15	father or mother is to be put to **d**.
	21:16	kidnaps someone is to be put to **d**,
	21:17	father or mother is to be put to **d**.
	22:19	with an animal is to be put to **d**.
	23: 7	an innocent or honest person to **d**,
	31:14	who desecrates it is to be put to **d**;
	31:15	on the Sabbath day is to be put to **d**.
Nu	35:16	the murderer is to be put to **d**.
Dt	13: 5	or dreamer must be put to **d**
	17: 6	witnesses a person is to be put to **d**,
	17: 6	is to be put to **d** on the testimony
	30:19	that I have set before you life and **d**,
	32:39	I put to **d** and I bring to life, I have
Ru	1:17	if even **d** separates you and me."
2Ki	4:40	of God, there is **d** in the pot!"
	19:35	put to **d** a hundred and eighty-five
2Ch	23:15	grounds, and there they put her to **d**.
	25: 4	he did not put their children to **d**,
	25: 4	"Parents shall not be put to **d**
	25: 4	nor children be put to **d** for their
Ps	18: 4	The cords of **d** entangled me;
	44:22	for your sake we face **d** all day long;
	89:48	Who can live and not see **d**, or who
	116:15	of the Lord is the **d** of his faithful
Pr	5: 5	Her feet go down to **d**;
	8:36	all who hate me love **d**."
	10: 2	but righteousness delivers from **d**.

Pr 11:19 but whoever pursues evil finds **d**.
    14:12 be right, but in the end it leads to **d**.
    15:11 **D** and Destruction lie open before
    16:25 be right, but in the end it leads to **d**.
    18:21 tongue has the power of life and **d**,
    19:18 do not be a willing party to their **d**.
    21:25 of a sluggard will be the **d** of him,
    23:14 with the rod and save them from **d**.
    27:20 **D** and Destruction are never
Ecc 7: 2 for **d** is the destiny of everyone;
SS 8: 6 for love is as strong as **d**,
Isa 25: 8 he will swallow up **d** forever.
    53:12 he poured out his life unto **d**,
Jer 15: 2 " 'Those destined for **d**, to **d**;
    26:16 man should not be sentenced to **d**!
Eze 18:23 any pleasure in the **d** of the wicked?
    18:32 take no pleasure in the **d** of anyone,
    33:11 no pleasure in the **d** of the wicked,
Hos 13:14 I will redeem them from **d**. Where,
        O **d**, are your plagues?
Mt 10:21 "Brother will betray brother to **d**,
    10:21 their parents and have them put to **d**.
    16:28 here will not taste **d** before they see
    26:66 "He is worthy of **d**,"
Jn 5:24 but has crossed over from **d** to life.
    8:51 obeys my word will never see **d**."
Ac 2:24 freeing him from the agony of **d**,
        because it was impossible for **d**
Ro 4:25 He was delivered over to **d** for our
    5:12 and **d** through sin, and in this way **d**
        came to all
    6: 3 Jesus were baptized into his **d**?
    6:23 For the wages of sin is **d**,
    7:24 from this body that is subject to **d**?
    8:13 the Spirit you put to **d** the misdeeds
    8:36 your sake we face **d** all day long;
1Co 15:21 For since **d** came through a man,
    15:26 The last enemy to be destroyed is **d**.
    15:31 I face **d** every day—yes, just as
    15:55 "Where, O **d**, is your victory?
    15:55 Where, O **d**, is your sting?"
2Co 4:10 around in our body the **d** of Jesus,
Php 2: 8 by becoming obedient to **d**—even **d**
        on a cross!
2Ti 1:10 Jesus, who has destroyed **d** and has
Heb 2:14 by his **d** he might break the power of
        him who holds the power of **d**—
Jas 5:20 of their way will save them from **d**
1Pe 3:18 He was put to **d** in the body
1Jn 3:14 that we have passed from **d** to life,
    3:14 who does not love remains in **d**.
    5:16 commit a sin that does not lead to **d**,
    5:16 those whose sin does not lead to **d**.
    5:16 There is a sin that leads to **d**.
Rev 1:18 And I hold the keys of **d** and Hades.
    2:11 not be hurt at all by the second **d**.
    6: 8 Its rider was named **D**, and Hades
    9: 6 those days people will seek **d**
    9: 6 long to die, but **d** will elude them.
    20: 6 The second **d** has no power over
    20:14 Then **d** and Hades were thrown
    20:14 The lake of fire is the second **d**.
    21: 4 There will be no more **d**'

Rev 21: 8 This is the second **d**."
PUT ... TO DEATH See PUT

DEBATE* DEBATED, DEBATING
Ac 15: 2 into sharp dispute and **d** with them.
    17:18 Stoic philosophers began to **d**
    18:28 his Jewish opponents in public **d**,

DEBATED* DEBATE
Ac 9:29 and **d** with the Hellenistic Jews,

DEBATING* DEBATE
Mk 12:28 of the law came and heard them **d**.

DEBAUCHERY*
Ro 13:13 not in sexual immorality and **d**,
2Co 12:21 and **d** in which they have indulged.
Gal 5:19 sexual immorality, impurity and **d**;
Eph 5:18 get drunk on wine, which leads to **d**.
1Pe 4: 3 living in **d**, lust, drunkenness,

DEBIR
Jos 12:13 the king of **D** one the king of Geder
Jdg 1:11 **D** (formerly called Kiriath Sepher).

DEBORAH
    1. Female prophet and judge who led Israel to victory over Canaanites (Jdg 4–5).
    2. Rebekah's nurse (Ge 35:8).

DEBT* DEBTOR, DEBTORS, DEBTS
Dt 15: 3 you must cancel any **d** your fellow
    24: 6 as security for a **d**,
1Sa 22: 2 or in **d** or discontented gathered
Job 24: 9 infant of the poor is seized for a **d**.
Mt 18:25 that he had be sold to repay the **d**.
    18:27 him, canceled the **d** and let him go.
    18:30 into prison until he could pay the **d**.
    18:32 said, 'I canceled all that **d** of yours
Lk 7:43 who had the bigger **d** forgiven."
Ro 13: 8 Let no **d** remain outstanding,
    13: 8 except the continuing **d** to love one

DEBTOR* DEBT
Isa 24: 2 as for lender, for **d** as for creditor.

DEBTORS* DEBT
Mt 6:12 as we also have forgiven our **d**.
Lk 16: 5 called in each one of his master's **d**.

DEBTS* DEBT
Dt 15: 1 seven years you must cancel **d**.
    15: 2 canceling **d** has been proclaimed.
    15: 9 the year for canceling **d**, is near,"
    31:10 in the year for canceling **d**,
2Ki 4: 7 "Go, sell the oil and pay your **d**.
Ne 10:31 the land and will cancel all **d**.
Pr 22:26 in pledge or puts up security for **d**;
Mt 6:12 And forgive us our **d**, as we
Lk 7:42 back, so he forgave the **d** of both.

DECAPOLIS*
Mt 4:25 from Galilee, the **D**, Jerusalem,
Mk 5:20 in the **D** how much Jesus had done
    7:31 Galilee and into the region of the **D**.

DECAY*

Ps   16:10 will you let your faithful one see **d**.
      49: 9 should live on forever and not see **d**.
      49:14 Their forms will **d** in the grave,
Ps   55:23 down the wicked into the pit of **d**;
Pr   12: 4 but a disgraceful wife is like **d** in his
Isa   5:24 so their roots will **d** and their
Hab   3:16 **d** crept into my bones, and my legs
Ac   2:27 you will not let your holy one see **d**.
      2:31 of the dead, nor did his body see **d**.
      13:34 so that he will never be subject to **d**.
      13:35 will not let your holy one see **d**.'
      13:37 raised from the dead did not see **d**.
Ro   8:21 be liberated from its bondage to **d**

DECEIT DECEIVE

Job   15:35 their womb fashions **d**."
Ps   32: 2 them and in whose spirit is no **d**.
      50:19 evil and harness your tongue to **d**.
      101: 7 No one who practices **d** will dwell
Pr   26:24 but in their hearts they harbor **d**.
Isa   53: 9 nor was any **d** in his mouth.
Jer   5:27 of birds, their houses are full of **d**;
Da   8:25 He will cause **d** to prosper, and he
Mk   7:22 greed, malice, **d**, lewdness, envy,
Jn   1:47 an Israelite in whom there is no **d**."
Ac   13:10 You are full of all kinds of **d**
Ro   1:29 envy, murder, strife, **d** and malice.
      3:13 their tongues practice **d**."
1Pe   2: 1 yourselves of all malice and all **d**,
      2:22 and no **d** was found in his mouth."

DECEITFUL DECEIVE

Ps   17: 1 it does not rise from **d** lips.
      26: 4 I do not sit with the **d**, nor do I
      43: 1 Rescue me from those who are **d**
      55:23 **d** will not live out half their days.
      119:29 Keep me from **d** ways;
Pr   12: 5 but the advice of the wicked is **d**.
      14:25 saves lives, but a false witness is **d**.
Jer   17: 9 The heart is **d** above all things
Hos 10: 2 Their heart is **d**, and now they must
2Co 11:13 people are false apostles, **d** workers,
Eph   4:14 of people in their **d** scheming.
      4:22 is being corrupted by its **d** desires;
1Pe   3:10 evil and their lips from **d** speech.
Rev 21:27 who does what is shameful or **d**,

DECEITFULLY DECEIVE

Zec 10: 2 The idols speak **d**, diviners see

DECEITFULNESS* DECEIVE

Mt   13:22 and the **d** of wealth choke the word,
Mk   4:19 the **d** of wealth and the desires
Heb   3:13 of you may be hardened by sin's **d**.

DECEIVE DECEIT, DECEITFUL,
DECEITFULLY, DECEITFULNESS,
DECEIVED, DECEIVER,
DECEIVERS, DECEIVES,
DECEIVING, DECEPTION,
DECEPTIVE

Lev 19:11 " 'Do not **d** one another.
Jos   9:22 said, "Why did you **d** us by saying,

1Sa 19:17 "Why did you **d** me like this
Job 13: 9 Could you **d** him as you might **d**
Pr   14: 5 An honest witness does not **d**,
Jer 29: 8 and diviners among you **d** you.
      37: 9 Do not **d** yourselves, thinking,
Zec 13: 4 garment of hair in order to **d**.
Mt   24: 5 am the Messiah,' and will **d** many.
      24:11 will appear and **d** many people.
      24:24 great signs and wonders to **d**,
Mk   13: 6 'I am he,' and will **d** many.
      13:22 and perform signs and wonders to **d**,
Ro   16:18 flattery they **d** the minds of naive
1Co   3:18 Do not **d** yourselves. If any of you
Gal   6: 3 they are not, they **d** themselves.
Eph   5: 6 Let no one **d** you with empty words,
Col   2: 4 no one may **d** you by fine-sounding
2Th   2: 3 Don't let anyone **d** you in any way,
Jas   1:22 to the word, and so **d** yourselves.
      1:26 rein on their tongues **d** themselves,
1Jn   1: 8 we **d** ourselves and the truth is not
Rev 20: 8 to **d** the nations in the four corners

DECEIVED DECEIVE

Ge   3:13 said, "The serpent **d** me, and I ate."
      31:20 Jacob **d** Laban the Aramean by not
Jer 20: 7 You **d** me, LORD, and I was **d**;
Hos   7:11 like a dove, easily **d** and senseless—
Ob   1: 3 The pride of your heart has **d** you,
Lk   21: 8 "Watch out that you are not **d**.
Jn   7:47 "You mean he has **d** you also?"
Ro   7:11 by the commandment, **d** me,
1Co   6: 9 Do not be **d**: Neither the sexually
2Co 11: 3 just as Eve was **d** by the serpent's
Gal   6: 7 Do not be **d**: God cannot be
1Ti   2:14 And Adam was not the one **d**; it was
          the woman who was **d**
2Ti   3:13 to worse, deceiving and being **d**.
Titus 3: 3 **d** and enslaved by all kinds
Jas   1:16 Don't be **d**, my dear brothers
Rev 13:14 it **d** the inhabitants of the earth.
      20:10 And the devil, who **d** them,

DECEIVER* DECEIVE

Job 12:16 both deceived and **d** are his.
Jer   9: 4 For every one of them is a **d**,
Mic   2:11 If a liar and **d** comes and says,
Mt   27:63 while he was still alive that **d** said,
2Jn   1: 7 Any such person is the **d**

DECEIVERS* DECEIVE

Job 11:11 Surely he recognizes **d**;
Ps   49: 5 when wicked **d** surround me—
2Jn   1: 7 I say this because many **d**, who do

DECEIVES* DECEIVE

Pr   26:19 is one who **d** their neighbor
Jer   9: 5 Friend **d** friend, and no one speaks
Mt   24: 4 "Watch out that no one **d** you.
Mk   13: 5 "Watch out that no one **d** you.
Jn   7:12 replied, "No, he **d** the people."
2Th   2:10 that wickedness **d** those who are

DECEIVING DECEIVE

Lev   6: 2 the LORD by **d** a neighbor
1Ki 22:23 the LORD has put a **d** spirit in the

1Ti 4: 1 the faith and follow **d** spirits
2Ti 3:13 bad to worse, **d** and being deceived.
Rev 20: 3 from **d** the nations anymore until

DECENCY* DECENTLY
1Ti 2: 9 modestly, with **d** and propriety,

DECENTLY* DECENCY
Ro 13:13 Let us behave **d**, as in the daytime,

DECEPTION* DECEIVE
Ps 12: 2 lips but harbor **d** in their hearts.
Pr 14: 8 ways, but the folly of fools is **d**.
26:26 malice may be concealed by **d**,
Jer 3:23 on the hills and mountains is a **d**;
9: 6 You live in the midst of **d**;
Hos 10:13 evil, you have eaten the fruit of **d**.
Mt 27:64 This last **d** will be worse than
2Co 4: 2 we do not use **d**, nor do we distort
Titus 1:10 full of meaningless talk and **d**,

DECEPTIVE* DECEIVE
Pr 11:18 A wicked person earns **d** wages,
23: 3 his delicacies, for that food is **d**.
31:30 Charm is **d**, and beauty is fleeting;
Jer 7: 4 Do not trust in **d** words and say,
7: 8 you are trusting in **d** words that are
15:18 You are to me like a **d** brook,
Mic 1:14 of Akzib will prove **d** to the kings
Col 2: 8 through hollow and **d** philosophy,

DECIDE DECIDED, DECISION, DECISIONS
Ex 18:16 me, and I **d** between the parties
1Sa 24:15 be our judge and **d** between us.
Isa 11: 3 or **d** by what he hears with his ears;
Eze 44:24 and **d** it according to my ordinances.
Jn 19:24 "Let's **d** by lot who will get it."
Ac 24:22 he said, "I will **d** your case."

DECIDED DECIDE
Ge 41:32 that the matter has been firmly **d**
Jdg 4: 5 up to her to have their disputes **d**.
20: 9 it in the order **d** by casting lots.
Jer 4:28 I have **d** and will not turn back."
Mt 27: 7 So they **d** to use the money to buy
Ac 4:28 and will had **d** beforehand should
2Co 9: 7 you should give what you have **d**

DECISION DECIDE
Ex 28:29 **d** as a continuing memorial before
Pr 16:33 but its every **d** is from the LORD.
Joel 3:14 multitudes in the valley of **d**!
3:14 LORD is near in the valley of **d**.
Jn 1:13 nor of human **d** or a husband's will,

DECISIONS DECIDE
Ex 28:15 a breastpiece for making **d**—
Nu 27:21 priest, who will obtain **d** for him
Isa 28: 7 they stumble when rendering **d**.
Jn 8:16 But if I do judge, my **d** are true,

DECLARE DECLARED, DECLARING
Ex 22: 9 whom the judges **d** guilty must pay
Dt 5: 1 and laws I **d** in your hearing today.
1Ch 16:24 **D** his glory among the nations,

Ps 5:10 **D** them guilty, O God!
19: 1 The heavens **d** the glory of God;
40: 5 deeds, they would be too many to **d**.
96: 3 **D** his glory among the nations,
Isa 42: 9 taken place, and new things I **d**;
Joel 1:14 **D** a holy fast; call a sacred
Ro 10: 9 If you **d** with your mouth, "Jesus is
Heb 2:12 "I will **d** your name to my brothers

DECLARED DECLARE
Dt 4:13 He **d** to you his covenant, the Ten
26:17 You have **d** this day
1Ki 8:53 just as you **d** through your servant
Mk 7:19 saying this, Jesus **d** all foods clean.)
Ro 2:13 the law who will be **d** righteous.
3:20 Therefore no one will be **d** righteous
Heb 3:11 So I **d** on oath in my anger,

DECLARES DECLARE
DECLARES THE LORD† See LORD†
DECLARES THE SOVEREIGN LORD† See
LORD†

DECLARING* DECLARE
Ps 22:31 **d** to a people yet unborn:
71: 8 praise, **d** your splendor all day long.
Jer 50:28 Babylon **d** in Zion how the LORD
Ac 2:11 we hear them **d** the wonders of God

DECREE DECREED, DECREES
1Ch 16:17 He confirmed it to Jacob as a **d**,
Ezr 5:13 King Cyrus issued a **d** to rebuild
Est 3: 9 let a **d** be issued to destroy them,
8: 8 Now write another **d** in the king's
Ps 2: 7 I will proclaim the LORD's **d**:
7: 6 Awake, my God; **d** justice.
81: 4 this is a **d** for Israel, an ordinance
148: 6 he issued a **d** that will never pass
Jer 51:12 his **d** against the people of Babylon.
Da 2:13 So the **d** was issued to put the wise
4:24 and this is the **d** the Most High has
6: 7 enforce the **d** that anyone who prays
6: 8 issue the **d** and put it in writing so
Lk 2: 1 days Caesar Augustus issued a **d**
Ro 1:32 they know God's righteous **d**

DECREED DECREE
1Ki 22:23 The LORD has **d** disaster
2Ki 8: 1 because the LORD has **d** a famine
Est 9:31 and Queen Esther had **d** for them,
Ps 78: 5 He **d** statutes for Jacob
Pr 31: 5 drink and forget what has been **d**,
Isa 10:22 Destruction has been **d**,
Jer 13:25 lot, the portion I have **d** for you,"
40: 2 LORD your God **d** this disaster
La 3:37 it happen if the Lord has not **d** it?
Da 9:24 "Seventy 'sevens' are **d** for your
Lk 22:22 Son of Man will go as it has been **d**.

DECREES DECREE
Ge 26: 5 my **d** and my instructions."
Ex 15:26 to his commands and keep all his **d**,
18:20 Teach them his **d** and instructions,
Lev 10:11 Israelites all the **d** the LORD has
18: 4 laws and be careful to follow my **d**.

Lev 18:26 you must keep my **d** and my laws.
     26: 3 " 'If you follow my **d** and are
     26:15 and if you reject my **d** and abhor my
Dt   4: 5 I have taught you **d** and laws as
Jos 24:25 Shechem he reaffirmed for them **d**
1Ki   6:12 if you follow my **d**, observe my
     11:33 nor kept my **d** and laws as David,
Ps   19: 9 The **d** of the LORD are firm, and all
    119:12 to you, LORD; teach me your **d**.
    119:16 I delight in your **d**; I will not neglect
    119:48 love, that I may meditate on your **d**.
    119:112 on keeping your **d** to the very end.
Pr   8:15 reign and rulers issue **d** that are just;
Isa 10: 1 to those who issue oppressive **d**,
Jer 31:35 who **d** the moon and stars to shine
Eze   5: 5 laws and **d** more than the nations
      5: 6 my laws and has not followed my **d**.
Zec   1: 6 But did not my words and my **d**,
Mal   4: 4 the **d** and laws I gave him at Horeb
Ac   17: 7 They are all defying Caesar's **d**,

DEDICATE DEDICATED,
DEDICATION, REDEDICATE

Lev 27: 2 makes a special vow to **d** a person
Pr   20:25 It is a trap to **d** something rashly

DEDICATED DEDICATE

Lev 21:12 it, because he has been **d**
Nu   18: 6 **d** to the LORD to do the work
Jdg 13: 5 a Nazirite, **d** to God from the womb.
2Sa   8:11 King David **d** these articles
1Ki   7:51 the things his father David had **d**—
      8:63 all the Israelites **d** the temple
2Ch 29:31 "You have now **d** yourselves
Ne   3: 1 They **d** it and set its doors in place,
      3: 1 which they **d**, and as far as
Lk   21: 5 stones and with gifts **d** to God.

DEDICATION DEDICATE

Nu   6: 2 vow, a vow of **d** to the LORD as
      6: 9 the hair that symbolizes their **d**,
      6:19 off the hair that symbolizes their **d**,
2Ch   7: 9 they had celebrated the **d** of the altar
Ezr   6:16 celebrated the **d** of the house of God
Ne   12:27 At the **d** of the wall of Jerusalem,
     12:27 celebrate joyfully the **d** with songs
Ps   30: T *For the **d** of the temple.*
Da   3: 2 to the **d** of the image he had set up.
Jn   10:22 came the Festival of **D** at Jerusalem.
1Ti   5:11 sensual desires overcome their **d**

DEED DEEDS

Ecc   3:17 activity, a time to judge every **d**."
     12:14 For God will bring every **d**
Jer 32:10 I signed and sealed the **d**, had it
Lk   24:19 powerful in word and **d** before God
Col   3:17 whether in word or **d**, do it all
2Th   2:17 strengthen you in every good **d**

DEEDS DEED

Dt   3:24 or on earth who can do the **d**
      4:34 or by great and awesome **d**, like all
     34:12 or performed the awesome **d**
1Sa   2: 3 knows, and by him **d** are weighed.
     24:13 'From evildoers come evil **d**,' so my

1Ch 16:24 his marvelous **d** among all peoples.
Ezr   9:13 to us is a result of our evil **d** and our
Job 34:25 Because he takes note of their **d**,
Ps   26: 7 and telling of all your wonderful **d**.
     28: 4 Repay them for their **d** and for their
     45: 4 your right hand achieve awesome **d**.
     65: 5 us with awesome and righteous **d**,
     66: 3 to God, "How awesome are your **d**!
     71:17 this day I declare your marvelous **d**.
     72:18 Israel, who alone does marvelous **d**,
     73:28 I will tell of all your **d**.
     75: 1 people tell of your wonderful **d**.
     77:11 I will remember the **d**
     77:12 and meditate on all your mighty **d**."
     78: 4 next generation the praiseworthy **d**
     78: 7 would not forget his **d** but would
     86: 8 no **d** can compare with yours.
     86:10 you are great and do marvelous **d**;
     88:12 or your righteous **d** in the land
     90:16 May your **d** be shown to your
     92: 4 For you make me glad by your **d**,
     96: 3 his marvelous **d** among all peoples.
    107: 8 and his wonderful **d** for mankind,
    107:15 and his wonderful **d** for mankind,
    107:21 and his wonderful **d** for mankind.
    107:24 his wonderful **d** in the deep.
    107:31 and his wonderful **d** for mankind.
    111: 3 Glorious and majestic are his **d**,
    141: 4 I take part in wicked **d** along
    145: 6 and I will proclaim your great **d**.
Pr   5:22 The evil **d** of the wicked ensnare
Isa   1:16 Take your evil **d** out of my sight;
Jer 32:19 purposes and mighty are your **d**.
     32:19 their conduct and as their **d** deserve.
Eze 22:28 Her prophets whitewash these **d**
Hos   5: 4 "Their **d** do not permit them
Ob   1:15 your **d** will return upon your own
Hab   3: 2 I stand in awe of your **d**, LORD.
Mt   5:16 that they may see your good **d**
     11:19 But wisdom is proved right by her **d**."
Lk   1:51 He has performed mighty **d** with his
     23:41 we are getting what our **d** deserve.
Jn   3:19 of light because their **d** were evil.
Ac   26:20 their repentance by their **d**.
1Ti   2:10 but with good **d**,
      5:10 and is well known for her good **d**,
      5:10 herself to all kinds of good **d**,
      6:18 good, to be rich in good **d**, and to be
Heb 10:24 another on toward love and good **d**,
Jas   2:14 claims to have faith but has no **d**?
      2:18 say, "You have faith; I have **d**."
      2:18 Show me your faith without **d**, and I
            will show you my faith by my **d**.
      2:26 is dead, so faith without **d** is dead.
1Pe   2:12 they may see your good **d**
Rev   2: 2 I know your **d**, your hard work
      2:19 I know your **d**, your love and faith,
      2:23 each of you according to your **d**.
      3: 1 I know your **d**; you have
      3: 2 I have found your **d** unfinished
      3: 8 I know your **d**. See, I have placed
      3:15 I know your **d**, that you are neither
     14:13 labor, for their **d** will follow them."

Rev 15: 3 "Great and marvelous are your **d,**

DEEP DEPTH, DEPTHS
Ge   1: 2 was over the surface of the **d,**
     2:21 caused the man to fall into a **d** sleep;
     7:11 the springs of the great **d** burst forth,
    15:12 Abram fell into a **d** sleep,
Ex 15: 5 The **d** waters have covered them;
1Sa 26:12 LORD had put them into a **d** sleep.
2Sa 22:17 he drew me out of **d** waters.
Job 34:22 There is no **d** shadow, no utter
Ps 36: 6 your justice like the great **d.**
    42: 7 **D** calls to **d** in the roar of your
Pr   4:19 of the wicked is like **d** darkness;
     9:18 that her guests are **d** in the realm
    22:14 of an adulterous woman is a **d** pit;
    25: 3 heavens are high and the earth is **d,**
Isa 29:10 has brought over you a **d** sleep:
La   2:13 Your wound is as **d** as the sea.
Eze 23:32 your sister's cup, a cup large and **d;**
Da   2:22 He reveals **d** and hidden things;
     8:18 I was in a **d** sleep, with my face
    10: 9 I fell into a **d** sleep, my face
Jnh 1: 5 he lay down and fell into a **d** sleep.
Lk   5: 4 "Put out into **d** water, and let down
Ac 20: 9 sinking into a **d** sleep as Paul talked
1Co 2:10 all things, even the **d** things of God.
1Ti 3: 9 They must keep hold of the **d** truths
Rev 2:24 learned Satan's so-called **d** secrets,

DEER
Ps 42: 1 As the **d** pants for streams of water,
Pr   5:19 A loving doe, a graceful **d**—
Hab 3:19 makes my feet like the feet of a **d,**

DEFAMED*
Isa 48:11 How can I let myself be **d?**

DEFEAT DEFEATED
Jdg 2:15 was against them to **d** them, just as
1Sa 4: 3 "Why did the LORD bring **d** on us
Ps 92:11 My eyes have seen the **d** of my

DEFEATED DEFEAT
Nu 14:42 You will be **d** by your enemies,
Jos 12: 1 the land whom the Israelites had **d**
1Co 6: 7 have been completely **d** already.

DEFECT
Lev 22:20 Do not bring anything with a **d,**
1Pe 1:19 Christ, a lamb without blemish or **d.**

DEFEND DEFENDED, DEFENDER,
   DEFENDING, DEFENDS, DEFENSE
Jdg 6:31 he can **d** himself when someone
Job 13:15 I will surely **d** my ways to his face.
Ps 72: 4 May he **d** the afflicted among
    74:22 Rise up, O God, and **d** your cause;
    82: 2 "How long will you **d** the unjust
   119:154 **D** my cause and redeem me;
Pr 31: 9 **d** the rights of the poor and needy.
Isa 1:17 seek justice. **D** the oppressed.
     1:23 They do not **d** the cause
Jer 5:28 they do not **d** the just cause
    51:36 I will **d** your cause and avenge you;

Lk 12:11 about how you will **d** yourselves
    21:14 how you will **d** yourselves.

DEFENDED DEFEND
Jer 22:16 He **d** the cause of the poor

DEFENDER DEFEND
Ex 22: 2 the **d** is not guilty of bloodshed;
Ps 68: 5 to the fatherless, a **d** of widows,
Pr 23:11 for their **D** is strong; he will take
Isa 19:20 he will send them a savior and **d,**

DEFENDING DEFEND
Ps 10:18 **d** the fatherless and the oppressed,
Ro   2:15 and at other times even **d** them.)
Php 1: 7 and, whether I am in chains or **d**

DEFENDS* DEFEND
Dt 10:18 He **d** the cause of the fatherless
    33: 7 With his own hands he **d** his cause.
Isa 51:22 says, your God, who **d** his people:

DEFENSE DEFEND
Ex 15: 2 LORD is my strength and my **d;**
Job 31:35 I sign now my **d**—let the Almighty
Ps 35:23 Awake, and rise to my **d!**
Isa 12: 2 himself, is my strength and my **d;**
Ac 22: 1 and fathers, listen now to my **d.**"
    25: 8 Then Paul made his **d:** "I have done
    26: 1 with his hand and began his **d:**
Php 1:16 I am put here for the **d** of the gospel.

DEFERRED*
Pr 13:12 Hope **d** makes the heart sick,

DEFIANT* DEFY
Pr   7:11 (She is unruly and **d,** her feet never
Jude 1:15 of all the **d** words ungodly sinners

DEFIED DEFY
1Sa 17:36 because he has **d** the armies
1Ki 13:26 is the man of God who **d** the word
Jer 48:26 drunk, for she has **d** the LORD.
Da   3:28 in him and **d** the king's command

DEFILE DEFILED, DEFILES
Ex 20:25 for you will **d** it if you use a tool
Lev 11:43 Do not **d** yourselves by any of these
    18:28 And if you **d** the land, it will vomit
Eze 20: 7 do not **d** yourselves with the idols
Da   1: 8 But Daniel resolved not to **d** himself
Mk   7:18 person from the outside can **d** them?
Rev 14: 4 are those who did not **d** themselves

DEFILED DEFILE
Ge 34: 5 that his daughter Dinah had been **d,**
Lev 18:25 Even the land was **d;** so I punished
Jos 22:19 If the land you possess is **d,**
Isa 24: 5 The earth is **d** by its people;
Jer 16:18 because they have **d** my land
Mal 1: 7 "By offering **d** food on my altar.
     1: 7 you ask, 'How have we **d** you?'

DEFILES DEFILE
Mt 15:11 their mouth, that is what **d** them."
Mk   7:15 comes out of a person that **d** them."

DEFRAUD FRAUD
Lev 19:13 " 'Do not **d** or rob your neighbor.
Mk 10:19 you shall not **d**, honor your father

DEFY DEFIANT, DEFIED
1Sa 17:10 "This day I **d** the armies of Israel!

DEITY*
Col   2: 9 Christ all the fullness of the **D** lives

DELAY DELAYED
Ps   40:17 you are my God, do not **d**.
Ecc   5: 4 a vow to God, do not **d** to fulfill it.
Isa 48: 9 my own name's sake I **d** my wrath;
Da   9:19 do not **d**, because your city and your
Hab   2: 3 it will certainly come and will not **d**.
Heb 10:37 coming will come and will not **d**."
Rev 10: 6 and said, "There will be no more **d**!

DELAYED DELAY
Jos 10:13 and **d** going down about a full day.
Isa 46:13 and my salvation will not be **d**.

DELIBERATE*
Ac   2:23 handed over to you by God's **d** plan

DELICACIES* DELICACY
Ge   49:20 he will provide **d** fit for a king.
Ps 141: 4 do not let me eat their **d**.
Pr   23: 3 Do not crave his **d**, for that food is
     23: 6 begrudging host, do not crave his **d**;
Jer 51:34 us and filled his stomach with our **d**,
La   4: 5 Those who once ate **d** are destitute

DELICACY* DELICACIES
SS   7:13 and at our door is every **d**, both new

DELICIOUS*
Pr   9:17 food eaten in secret is **d**!"

DELIGHT* DELIGHTED, DELIGHTFUL, DELIGHTING, DELIGHTS
Lev 26:31 and I will take no **d** in the pleasing
Dt   30: 9 The LORD will again **d** in you
1Sa   2: 1 enemies, for I **d** in your deliverance.
     15:22 "Does the LORD **d** in burnt
Ne   1:11 of your servants who **d** in revering
Job 22:26 then you will find **d** in the Almighty
     27:10 Will they find **d** in the Almighty?
Ps   1: 2 but whose **d** is in the law
     16: 3 noble ones in whom is all my **d**."
     35: 9 the LORD and **d** in his salvation.
     35:27 May those who **d** in my vindication
     37: 4 Take **d** in the LORD, and he will
     43: 4 of God, to God, my joy and my **d**.
     51:16 You do not **d** in sacrifice, or I would
     51:19 you will **d** in the sacrifices
     62: 4 my lofty place; they take **d** in lies.
     68:30 Scatter the nations who **d** in war.
    111: 2 are pondered by all who **d** in them.
    112: 1 who find great **d** in his commands.
    119:16 I **d** in your decrees; I will not
    119:24 Your statutes are my **d**; they are my
    119:35 your commands, for there I find **d**.

Ps 119:47 for I **d** in your commands because I
    119:70 and unfeeling, but I **d** in your law.
    119:77 I may live, for your law is my **d**.
    119:92 If your law had not been my **d**,
    119:143 me, but your commands give me **d**.
    119:174 LORD, and your law gives me **d**.
    147:10 nor his **d** in the legs of the warrior;
    149: 4 the LORD takes **d** in his people;
Pr   1:22 How long will mockers **d**
      2:14 who **d** in doing wrong and rejoice
      8:30 I was filled with **d** day after day,
     18: 2 but **d** in airing their own opinions.
     23:26 and let your eyes **d** in my ways,
Ecc   2:10 My heart took **d** in all my labor,
SS   1: 4 We rejoice and **d** in you;
      2: 3 I **d** to sit in his shade, and his fruit is
Isa 11: 3 he will **d** in the fear of the LORD.
     13:17 for silver and have no **d** in gold.
     32:14 wasteland forever, the **d** of donkeys,
     42: 1 my chosen one in whom I **d**;
     55: 2 and you will **d** in the richest of fare.
     58:13 if you call the Sabbath a **d**
     61:10 I **d** greatly in the LORD;
     62: 4 for the LORD will take **d** in you,
     65:18 for I will create Jerusalem to be a **d**
     65:19 Jerusalem and take **d** in my people;
     66: 3 and they **d** in their abominations;
     66:11 **d** in her overflowing abundance."
Jer   9:24 earth, for in these I **d**,"
     15:16 they were my joy and my heart's **d**,
     31:20 my dear son, the child in whom I **d**?
     49:25 abandoned, the town in which I **d**?
Eze 24:16 away from you the **d** of your eyes,
     24:21 you take pride, the **d** of your eyes,
     24:25 joy and glory, the **d** of their eyes,
Hos   7: 3 "They **d** the king with their
Mic   1:16 for the children in whom you **d**;
      7:18 angry forever but **d** to show mercy.
Zep   3:17 He will take great **d** in you;
Mt   12:18 chosen, the one I love, in whom I **d**;
Mk   12:37 large crowd listened to him with **d**.
Lk   1:14 He will be a joy and **d** to you,
Ro   7:22 in my inner being I **d** in God's law;
1Co 13: 6 Love does not **d** in evil but rejoices
2Co 12:10 for Christ's sake, I **d** in weaknesses,
Col   2: 5 and **d** to see how disciplined you are

DELIGHTED DELIGHT
Ex   18: 9 Jethro was **d** to hear about all
Dt   30: 9 just as he **d** in your ancestors,
2Sa 22:20 he rescued me because he **d** in me.
2Ch   9: 8 who has **d** in you and placed you
Est   5:14 This suggestion **d** Haman, and he
Isa   5: 7 of Judah are the vines he **d** in.
Lk   13:17 but the people were **d** with all
     22: 5 They were **d** and agreed to give him
2Th   2:12 the truth but have **d** in wickedness.

DELIGHTFUL* DELIGHT
Ps   16: 6 surely I have a **d** inheritance.
SS   1: 2 for your love is more **d** than wine.
      4:10 How **d** is your love, my sister,
Mal   3:12 for yours will be a **d** land,"

DELIGHTING* DELIGHT

Pr 8:31 his whole world and **d** in mankind.

DELIGHTS DELIGHT

Est 6: 6 for the man the king **d** to honor?"
Ps 22: 8 deliver him, since he **d** in him."
    35:27 who **d** in the well-being of his
    36: 8 them drink from your river of **d**.
    37:23 the steps of the one who **d** in him;
    147:11 the LORD **d** in those who fear
Pr 3:12 he loves, as a father the son he **d** in.
    10:23 of understanding **d** in wisdom.
    11:20 but he **d** in those whose ways are
    12:22 he **d** in people who are trustworthy.
    14:35 A king **d** in a wise servant,
    29:17 they will bring you the **d** you desire.
SS 7: 6 how pleasing, my love, with your **d**!
Col 2:18 Do not let anyone who **d** in false

DELILAH

Philistine woman who betrayed Samson (Jdg 16:4–22).

DELIVER DELIVERANCE, DELIVERED, DELIVERER, DELIVERS

Nu 21: 2 "If you will **d** these people into our
Dt 7:23 LORD your God will **d** them over
    32:39 and no one can **d** out of my hand.
Jos 8:18 for into your hand I will **d** the city."
2Ch 32:14 can your god **d** you from my hand?
Ps 6: 4 Turn, LORD, and **d** me;
    22: 8 Let him **d** him, since he delights
    31: 5 spirit; **d** me, LORD, my faithful God.
    50:15 I will **d** you, and you will honor
    51:14 **D** me from the guilt of bloodshed,
    72:12 For he will **d** the needy who cry out,
    109:21 of the goodness of your love, **d** me.
Isa 50: 2 Was my arm too short to **d** you?
Eze 7:19 gold will not be able to **d** them
Da 3:17 the God we serve is able to **d** us
Hos 13:14 "I will **d** this people from the power
Mt 6:13 but **d** us from the evil one.'
2Co 1:10 deadly peril, and he will **d** us again.
    1:10 hope that he will continue to **d** us,

DELIVERANCE DELIVER

Ge 45: 7 and to save your lives by a great **d**.
Ex 14:13 you will see the **d** the LORD will
1Sa 2: 1 my enemies, for I delight in your **d**.
Est 4:14 and **d** for the Jews will arise
Ps 3: 8 From the LORD comes **d**.
    32: 7 and surround me with songs of **d**.
    33:17 A horse is a vain hope for **d**;
    78:22 not believe in God or trust in his **d**.
Isa 45:24 me, 'In the LORD alone are **d**
Ob 1:17 But on Mount Zion will be **d**;
Php 1:19 to me will turn out for my **d**.

DELIVERED DELIVER

Ge 48:16 the Angel who has **d** me from all
Jos 6: 2 I have **d** Jericho into your hands,
Jdg 16:23 "Our god has **d** Samson,
Job 33:28 God has **d** me from going down

Ps 34: 4 he **d** me from all my fears.
    60: 5 hand, that those you love may be **d**.
    71:23 praise to you—I whom you have **d**.
    107: 6 and he **d** them from their distress.
    116: 8 LORD, have **d** me from death,
Isa 1:27 Zion will be **d** with justice,
Da 7:25 The holy people will be **d** into his
    12: 1 written in the book—will be **d**.
Ro 4:25 He was **d** over to death for our sins
2Th 3: 2 pray that we may be **d** from wicked

DELIVERER* DELIVER

Jdg 3: 9 he raised up for them a **d**,
    3:15 the LORD, and he gave them a **d**—
2Sa 22: 2 is my rock, my fortress and my **d**;
2Ki 13: 5 The LORD provided a **d** for Israel,
Ps 18: 2 is my rock, my fortress and my **d**;
    40:17 You are my help and my **d**;
    70: 5 You are my help and my **d**;
    140: 7 my strong **d**, you shield my head
    144: 2 my stronghold and my **d**, my shield,
Ac 7:35 be their ruler and **d** by God himself,
Ro 11:26 "The **d** will come from Zion;

DELIVERS DELIVER

Ps 34:17 he **d** them from all their troubles.
    34:19 the LORD **d** him from them all;
    37:40 The LORD helps them and **d** them;
    37:40 he **d** them from the wicked
Pr 10: 2 but righteousness **d** from death.

DELUDED* DELUSION

Pr 28:11 and discerning sees how **d** they are.
Isa 44:20 a **d** heart misleads him;
Rev 19:20 these signs he had **d** those who had

DELUSION* DELUDED, DELUSIONS

2Th 2:11 God sends them a powerful **d** so

DELUSIONS* DELUSION

Ps 4: 2 How long will you love **d** and seek
    119:118 decrees, for their **d** come to nothing.
Jer 14:14 and the **d** of their own minds.
    23:26 who prophesy the **d** of their own

DEMAND DEMANDED

Ge 9: 5 I will surely **d** an accounting.
    9: 5 I will **d** an accounting for the life
Lk 6:30 belongs to you, do not **d** it back.
1Co 1:22 Jews **d** signs and Greeks look

DEMANDED DEMAND

Lk 12:20 This very night your life will be **d**
    12:48 been given much, much will be **d**;

DEMAS*

Associate of Paul (Col 4:14; 2Ti 4:10; Phm 24).

DEMETRIUS

Ac 19:24 A silversmith named **D**, who made
3Jn 1:12 **D** is well spoken of by everyone—

DEMOLISH DEMOLISHED

Nu 33:52 idols, and **d** all their high places.
Hos 10: 2 The LORD will **d** their altars

2Co 10: 4 have divine power to **d** strongholds.

DEMOLISHED DEMOLISH
Jdg 6:28 there was Baal's altar, **d**,
2Ch 33: 3 places his father Hezekiah had **d**;

DEMON* DEMON-POSSESSED, DEMONIC, DEMONS
Mt   9:33 And when the **d** was driven out,
     11:18 drinking, and they say, 'He has a **d**.'
     17:18 Jesus rebuked the **d**, and it came
Mk   7:26 She begged Jesus to drive the **d**
      7:29 the **d** has left your daughter."
      7:30 lying on the bed, and the **d** gone.
Lk   4:33 there was a man possessed by a **d**,
      4:35 the **d** threw the man down before
      7:33 wine, and you say, 'He has a **d**.'
      8:29 driven by the **d** into solitary places.
      9:42 the **d** threw him to the ground
     11:14 was driving out a **d** that was mute.
     11:14 When the **d** left, the man who had
Jn   8:49 "I am not possessed by a **d**,"
     10:21 sayings of a man possessed by a **d**. Can a **d** open the eyes

DEMON-POSSESSED* DEMON, POSSESS
Mt   4:24 pain, the **d**, those having seizures,
      8:16 many who were **d** were brought
      8:28 two **d** men coming from the tombs
      8:33 what had happened to the **d** men.
      9:32 a man who was **d** and could not talk
     12:22 they brought him a **d** man who was
     15:22 My daughter is **d** and suffering
Mk   1:32 brought to Jesus all the sick and **d**.
      5:16 what had happened to the **d** man—
      5:18 the man who had been **d** begged
Lk   8:27 he was met by a **d** man
      8:36 the people how the **d** man had been
Jn   7:20 "You are **d**," the crowd answered.
      8:48 that you are a Samaritan and **d**?"
      8:52 "Now we know that you are **d**!
     10:20 them said, "He is **d** and raving mad.
Ac 19:13 Lord Jesus over those who were **d**.

DEMONIC* DEMON
Jas   3:15 heaven but is earthly, unspiritual, **d**.
Rev 16:14 They are **d** spirits that perform

DEMONS* DEMON
Mt   7:22 and in your name drive out **d**
      8:31 The **d** begged Jesus, "If you drive
      9:34 is by the prince of **d** that he drives out **d**."
     10: 8 those who have leprosy, drive out **d**.
     12:24 by Beelzebul, the prince of **d**, that this fellow drives out **d**."
     12:27 And if I drive out **d** by Beelzebul,
     12:28 the Spirit of God that I drive out **d**,
Mk   1:34 He also drove out many **d**, but he
      1:34 not let the **d** speak because they
      1:39 their synagogues and driving out **d**.
      3:15 and to have authority to drive out **d**.
      3:22 the prince of **d** he is driving out **d**."

Mk   5:12 The **d** begged Jesus, "Send us
      5:15 been possessed by the legion of **d**,
      6:13 They drove out many **d**
      9:38 "we saw someone driving out **d**
     16: 9 of whom he had driven seven **d**.
     16:17 In my name they will drive out **d**;
Lk   4:41 **d** came out of many people,
      8: 2 from whom seven **d** had come out;
      8:30 because many **d** had gone into him.
      8:32 The **d** begged Jesus to let them go
      8:33 When the **d** came out of the man,
      8:35 man from whom the **d** had gone out,
      8:38 The man from whom the **d** had gone
      9: 1 authority to drive out all **d**
      9:49 "we saw someone driving out **d**
     10:17 even the **d** submit to us in your
     11:15 the prince of **d**, he is driving out **d**."
     11:18 that I drive out **d** by Beelzebul.
     11:19 Now if I drive out **d** by Beelzebul,
     11:20 if I drive out **d** by the finger of God,
     13:32 'I will keep on driving out **d**
Ro   8:38 life, neither angels nor **d**
1Co 10:20 sacrifices of pagans are offered to **d**,
     10:20 want you to be participants with **d**.
     10:21 of the Lord and the cup of **d** too;
     10:21 the Lord's table and the table of **d**.
1Ti   4: 1 spirits and things taught by **d**.
Jas   2:19 Good! Even the **d** believe that—
Rev 9:20 they did not stop worshiping **d**,
     18: 2 She has become a dwelling for **d**

DEMONSTRATE* DEMONSTRATES, DEMONSTRATION
Ac 26:20 **d** their repentance by their deeds.
Ro   3:25 He did this to **d** his righteousness,
      3:26 he did it to **d** his righteousness

DEMONSTRATES* DEMONSTRATE
Ro   5: 8 God **d** his own love for us in this:

DEMONSTRATION* DEMONSTRATE
1Co 2: 4 but with a **d** of the Spirit's power,

DEN
Isa 11: 8 infant will play near the cobra's **d**,
Jer   7:11 become a **d** of robbers to you?
Da   6: 7 shall be thrown into the lions' **d**.
Na   2:11 Where now is the lions' **d**, the place
Mt 21:13 but you are making it 'a **d**
Mk 11:17 But you have made it 'a **d**
Lk 19:46 but you have made it 'a **d**

DENARII* DENARIUS
Lk   7:41 One owed him five hundred **d**,
     10:35 The next day he took out two **d**

DENARIUS DENARII
Mt 20: 2 agreed to pay them a **d** for the day
Mk 12:15 "Bring me a **d** and let me look
Lk 20:24 "Show me a **d**. Whose image

DENIED DENY
Ecc   2:10 I **d** myself nothing my eyes desired;
Mt   26:70 But he **d** it before them all.
Jn   18:25 He **d** it, saying, "I am not."
1Ti   5: 8 has **d** the faith and is worse than
Rev   3: 8 my word and have not **d** my name.

DENIES* DENY
Job   34: 5 innocent, but God **d** me justice.
1Jn   2:22 It is whoever **d** that Jesus is
       2:23 No one who **d** the Son has

DENOUNCE DENOUNCED
Nu   23: 7 'curse Jacob for me; come, **d** Israel.'

DENOUNCED DENOUNCE
Nu   23: 8 those whom the Lord has not **d**?

DENY DENIED, DENIES, DENYING, SELF-DENIAL
Ex   23: 6 "Do not **d** justice to your poor
Lev   16:29 month you must **d** yourselves
       23:27 a sacred assembly and **d** yourselves,
Job   27: 5 till I die, I will not **d** my integrity.
Isa   5:23 a bribe, but **d** justice to the innocent.
La   3:35 **d** people their rights before the Most
Am   2: 7 and **d** justice to the oppressed.
Mt   16:24 to be my disciple must **d** themselves
Mk   8:34 to be my disciple must **d** themselves
Lk   9:23 to be my disciple must **d** themselves
       22:34 you will **d** three times that you
Ac   4:16 a notable sign, and we cannot **d** it.
Titus   1:16 but by their actions they **d** him.
Jas   3:14 do not boast about it or **d** the truth.
Jude   1: 4 Jesus Christ our only Sovereign

DENYING* DENY
Eze   22:29 the foreigner, **d** them justice.
2Ti   3: 5 a form of godliness but **d** its power.
2Pe   2: 1 even **d** the sovereign Lord who
1Jn   2:22 **d** the Father and the Son.

DEPART DEPARTED, DEPARTS, DEPARTURE
Ge   49:10 The scepter will not **d** from Judah,
2Sa   12:10 the sword will never **d** from your
Job   1:21 mother's womb, and naked I will **d**.
Ecc   5:15 and as everyone comes, so they **d**.
Isa   52:11 **D**, **d**, go out from there!
Mt   25:41 say to those on his left, 'D from me,
Php   1:23 I desire to **d** and be with Christ,

DEPARTED DEPART
1Sa   4:21 "The Glory has **d** from Israel"—
       16:14 of the Lord had **d** from Saul,
       28:15 against me, and God has **d** from me.
Ps 119:102 I have not **d** from your laws, for you
La   1: 6 All the splendor has **d**
Eze   10:18 glory of the Lord **d** from over
2Ti   2:18 who have **d** from the truth.

DEPARTS* DEPART
Ps   146: 4 When their spirit **d**, they return
Ecc   6: 4 without meaning, it **d** in darkness,

DEPARTURE DEPART
Lk   9:31 They spoke about his **d**, which he
2Ti   4: 6 and the time for my **d** is near.
2Pe   1:15 after my **d** you will always be able

DEPEND DEPENDED, DEPENDING, DEPENDS
Ps   62: 7 salvation and my honor **d** on God;
Jer   49:11 Your widows too can **d** on me.' "
Ro   9:16 **d** on human desire or effort,

DEPENDED DEPEND
Hos   10:13 Because you have **d** on your own

DEPENDING DEPEND
2Ki   18:20 On whom are you **d**, that you rebel

DEPENDS* DEPEND
Ro   12:18 If it is possible, as far as it **d** on you,
Gal   3:18 For if the inheritance **d** on the law,
       3:18 then it no longer **d** on the promise;
Col   2: 8 which **d** on human tradition

DEPORTED
2Ki   15:29 and **d** the people to Assyria
       24:16 also **d** to Babylon the entire force

DEPOSES*
Da   2:21 he **d** kings and raises up others.

DEPOSIT DEPOSITED
Mt   25:27 you should have put my money on **d**
Lk   19:23 then didn't you put my money on **d**,
2Co   1:22 put his Spirit in our hearts as a **d**,
       5: 5 who has given us the Spirit as a **d**,
Eph   1:14 who is a **d** guaranteeing our
2Ti   1:14 Guard the good **d** that was entrusted

DEPOSITED* DEPOSIT
1Sa   10:25 a scroll and **d** it before the Lord.
Ezr   6: 5 they are to be **d** in the house of God.

DEPRAVED* DEPRAVITY
Eze   16:47 you soon became more **d** than they.
       23:11 she was more **d** than her sister.
Ro   1:28 so God gave them over to a **d** mind,
2Ti   3: 8 They are men of **d** minds, who,
2Pe   2: 2 Many will follow their **d** conduct
       2: 7 who was distressed by the **d** conduct

DEPRAVITY* DEPRAVED
Ro   1:29 of wickedness, evil, greed and **d**.
2Pe   2:19 they themselves are slaves of **d**—

DEPRIVE DEPRIVED
Dt   24:17 Do not **d** the foreigner
Pr   18: 5 and so **d** the innocent of justice.
       31: 5 **d** all the oppressed of their rights.
Isa   10: 2 to **d** the poor of their rights
       29:21 with false testimony **d** the innocent
La   3:36 to **d** them of justice—would not
Am   5:12 **d** the poor of justice in the courts.
Mal   3: 5 and **d** the foreigners among you
1Co   7: 5 Do not **d** each other except perhaps

DEPRIVED DEPRIVE
Jer   5:25 your sins have **d** you of good.

DEPTH DEEP

Ro   8:39 neither height nor **d**, nor anything
      11:33 the **d** of the riches of the wisdom
Php   1: 9 more in knowledge and **d** of insight,

DEPTHS DEEP

Ex   15: 5 they sank to the **d** like a stone.
Ps   69: 2 I sink in the miry **d**, where there is
     130: 1 Out of the **d** I cry to you, LORD;
Jnh   2: 3 You hurled me into the **d**, into the
Mt   18: 6 to be drowned in the **d** of the sea.

DERIDES* DERISION

Pr   11:12 Whoever **d** their neighbor has no

DERISION DERIDES

Eze 23:32 it will bring scorn and **d**, for it holds
Mic   6:16 over to ruin and your people to **d**;

DERIVES*

Eph   3:15 in heaven and on earth **d** its name.

DESCEND DESCENDANT,
DESCENDANTS, DESCENDED,
DESCENDING, DESCENT

Dt   32: 2 like rain and my words **d** like dew,
Ro   10: 7 "or 'Who will **d** into the deep?' "

DESCENDANT DESCEND

Ro   1: 3 to his earthly life was a **d** of David,

DESCENDANTS DESCEND

Ge   9: 9 with you and with your **d** after you
     15:18 "To your **d** I give this land,
Ex   12:24 ordinance for you and your **d**.
     28:43 ordinance for Aaron and his **d**.
Dt   4:37 and chose their **d** after them,
2Sa 22:51 to David and his **d** forever."
Ps 132:11 "One of your own **d** I will place
Jer 31:17 So there is hope for your **d**,"
Jn   7:42 Messiah will come from David's **d**
Ac   2:30 place one of his **d** on his throne.
      8:33 Who can speak of his **d**? For his life

DESCENDED DESCEND

Ex   19:18 because the LORD **d** on it in fire.
Lk   3:22 the Holy Spirit **d** on him in bodily
Eph   4: 9 except that he also **d** to the lower,
2Ti   2: 8 raised from the dead, **d** from David.
Heb   7:14 is clear that our Lord **d** from Judah,

DESCENDING DESCEND

Ge   28:12 of God were ascending and **d** on it.
Mt   3:16 saw the Spirit of God **d** like a dove
Mk   1:10 and the Spirit **d** on him like a dove.
Jn   1:51 and **d** on' the Son of Man."

DESCENT DESCEND

Jn   1:13 children born not of natural **d**,

DESECRATE DESECRATED,
DESECRATING

Eze   7:22 robbers will **d** the place I treasure.
Mt   12: 5 duty in the temple **d** the Sabbath
Ac   24: 6 and even tried to **d** the temple;

DESECRATED DESECRATE

Mal   2:11 Judah has **d** the sanctuary

DESECRATING* DESECRATE

Ne   13:17 you are doing—**d** the Sabbath day?
     13:18 against Israel by **d** the Sabbath."
Isa 56: 2 who keeps the Sabbath without **d** it,
     56: 6 who keep the Sabbath without **d** it
Eze 44: 7 **d** my temple while you offered me

DESERT DESERTED, DESERTING,
DESERTS

Pr   21:19 live in a **d** than with a quarrelsome
Isa 32:15 and the **d** becomes a fertile field,
     35: 6 the wilderness and streams in the **d**.
     40: 3 make straight in the **d** a highway

DESERTED DESERT

Dt   32:18 You **d** the Rock, who fathered you;
Isa 62: 4 No longer will they call you **D**,
La   1: 1 How **d** lies the city, once so full
Mt   26:56 all the disciples **d** him and fled.
2Ti   4:10 this world, has **d** me and has gone

DESERTING DESERT

Gal   1: 6 you are so quickly **d** the one who

DESERTS DESERT

Pr   19: 4 friend of the poor person **d** them.
Zec 11:17 shepherd, who **d** the flock!

DESERVE* DESERVED, DESERVES,
DESERVING

Ge   40:15 I have done nothing to **d** being put
Lev 26:21 seven times over, as your sins **d**.
Jdg 20:10 it can give them what they **d** for this
1Ki   2:26 You **d** to die, but I will not put you
Ps   28: 4 and bring back on them what they **d**.
     94: 2 pay back to the proud what they **d**.
    103.10 he does not treat us as our sins **d**
Ecc   8:14 who get what the wicked **d**,
      8:14 who get what the righteous **d**.
Isa 66: 6 repaying his enemies all they **d**.
Jer 14:16 out on them the calamity they **d**.
     17:10 according to what their deeds **d**."
     21:14 I will punish you as your deeds **d**,
     32:19 their conduct and as their deeds **d**.
     49:12 those who do not **d** to drink the cup
La   3:64 Pay them back what they **d**,
Eze 16:59 I will deal with you as you **d**,
Zec   1: 6 to us what our ways and practices **d**,
Mt   8: 8 I do not **d** to have you come under
     22: 8 those I invited did not **d** to come.
Lk   7: 6 I do not **d** to have you come under
     23:15 see, he has done nothing to **d** death.
     23:41 for we are getting what our deeds **d**.
Ro   1:32 those who do such things **d** death,
1Co 15: 9 and do not **d** to be called
     16:18 Such men **d** recognition.
2Co 11:15 end will be what their actions **d**.
Rev 16: 6 them blood to drink as they **d**."

DESERVED* DESERVE

2Sa 19:28 grandfather's descendants **d** nothing
Ezr   9:13 punished us less than our sins **d**

Job 33:27 is right, but I did not get what I **d**.
Ac 23:29 no charge against him that **d** death

DESERVES* DESERVE
Nu 35:31 the life of a murderer, who **d** to die.
Dt 25: 2 If the guilty person **d** to be beaten,
25: 2 the number of lashes the crime **d**,
Jdg 9:16 Have you treated him as he **d**?
Job 34:11 on them what their conduct **d**.
Jer 51: 6 he will repay her what she **d**.
Lk 7: 4 "This man **d** to have you do this,
10: 7 you, for the worker **d** his wages.
Ac 26:31 is not doing anything that **d** death
1Ti 1:15 saying that **d** full acceptance:
4: 9 saying that **d** full acceptance.
5:18 and "The worker **d** his wages."
Heb 10:29 severely do you think someone **d**

DESERVING DESERVE
Mt 10:13 If the home is **d**, let your peace rest
Ac 28:18 was not guilty of any crime **d** death.
Eph 2: 3 rest, we were by nature **d** of wrath.

DESIGNATE DESIGNATED
Ex 21:13 they are to flee to a place I will **d**.
Jos 20: 2 "Tell the Israelites to **d** the cities

DESIGNATED DESIGNATE
Lk 6:13 of them, whom he also **d** apostles:
Heb 5:10 was **d** by God to be high priest

DESIRABLE* DESIRE
Ge 3: 6 and also **d** for gaining wisdom,
Pr 22: 1 name is more **d** than great riches;

DESIRE* DESIRABLE, DESIRED, DESIRES
Ge 3:16 Your **d** will be for your husband,
Dt 5:21 You shall not set your **d** on your
1Sa 9:20 to whom is all the **d** of Israel turned,
2Sa 19:38 anything you **d** from me I will do
23: 5 salvation and grant me my every **d**.
2Ki 9:15 "If you **d** to make me king,
1Ch 28: 9 and understands every **d** and every
2Ch 1:11 "Since this is your heart's **d**
9: 8 and his **d** to uphold them forever,
Job 13: 3 But I **d** to speak to the Almighty
21:14 We have no **d** to know your ways.
Ps 10:17 Lord, hear the **d** of the afflicted;
20: 4 May he give you the **d** of your heart
21: 2 You have granted him his heart's **d**
27:12 turn me over to the **d** of my foes,
40: 6 and offering you did not **d**—
40: 8 I **d** to do your will, my God;
40:14 may all who **d** my ruin be turned
41: 2 give them over to the **d** of their foes.
70: 2 may all who **d** my ruin be turned
73:25 earth has nothing I **d** besides you.
Pr 3:15 nothing you **d** can compare
8:11 and nothing you **d** can compare
10:24 what the righteous **d** will be
11:23 The **d** of the righteous ends only
12:12 The wicked **d** the stronghold
19: 2 **D** without knowledge is not good—
24: 1 the wicked, do not **d** their company;

Pr 29:17 will bring you the delights you **d**.
Ecc 6: 2 that they lack nothing their hearts **d**,
12: 5 along and **d** no longer is stirred.
SS 6:12 it, my **d** set me among the royal
7:10 to my beloved, and his **d** is for me.
Isa 26: 8 and renown are the **d** of our hearts.
53: 2 appearance that we should **d** him.
55:11 but will accomplish what I **d**
Eze 24:25 their heart's **d**, and their sons
Hos 6: 6 For I **d** mercy, not sacrifice,
Mic 7: 3 the powerful dictate what they **d**—
Mal 3: 1 covenant, whom you **d**, will come,"
Mt 9:13 'I **d** mercy, not sacrifice.'
12: 7 what these words mean, 'I **d** mercy,
Ro 7:18 For I have the **d** to do what is good,
9:16 depend on human **d** or effort,
10: 1 my heart's **d** and prayer to God
1Co 12:31 Now eagerly **d** the greater gifts.
14: 1 and eagerly **d** gifts of the Spirit,
2Co 8:10 give but also to have the **d** to do so.
8:13 Our **d** is not that others might be
Php 1:23 I **d** to depart and be with Christ,
4:17 Not that I **d** your gifts; what I **d** is that more be credited
2Th 1:11 fruition your every **d** for goodness
Heb 10: 5 and offering you did not **d**,
10: 8 and sin offerings you did not **d**,
13:18 **d** to live honorably in every way.
Jas 1:14 dragged away by their own evil **d**
1:15 after **d** has conceived, it gives birth
4: 2 You **d** but do not have, so you kill.
2Pe 2:10 of those who follow the corrupt **d**

DESIRED DESIRE
1Ki 9: 1 and had achieved all he had **d** to do,
Ps 51: 6 Yet you **d** faithfulness even
Ecc 2:10 I denied myself nothing my eyes **d**;
Da 11:37 or for the one **d** by women, nor will
Hag 2: 7 what is **d** by all nations will come,
Lk 22:15 them, "I have eagerly **d** to eat this

DESIRES* DESIRE
Ge 4: 7 it **d** to have you, but you must rule
41:16 will give Pharaoh the answer he **d**."
2Sa 3:21 may rule over all that your heart **d**."
14:14 But that is not what God **d**;
1Ki 11:37 will rule over all that your heart **d**;
1Ch 29:18 keep these **d** and thoughts
Job 17:11 Yet the **d** of my heart
31:16 "If I have denied the **d** of the poor
Ps 34:12 life and **d** to see many good days,
37: 4 he will give you the **d** of your heart.
103: 5 who satisfies your **d** with good
140: 8 Do not grant the wicked their **d**,
145:16 satisfy the **d** of every living thing.
145:19 He fulfills the **d** of those who fear
Pr 11: 6 the unfaithful are trapped by evil **d**.
13: 4 but the **d** of the diligent are fully
19:22 What a person **d** is unfailing love;
SS 2: 7 arouse or awaken love until it so **d**.
3: 5 arouse or awaken love until it so **d**.
8: 4 arouse or awaken love until it so **d**.
Hab 2: 4 is puffed up; his **d** are not upright—
Mk 4:19 and the **d** for other things come

Jn   8:44 want to carry out your father's **d**.
Ro   1:24 over in the sinful **d** of their hearts
      6:12 body so that you obey its evil **d**.
      8: 5 their minds set on what the flesh **d**;
      8: 5 their minds set on what the Spirit **d**.
     13:14 how to gratify the **d** of the flesh.
Gal   5:16 and you will not gratify the **d**
      5:17 For the flesh **d** what is contrary
      5:24 the flesh with its passions and **d**.
Eph   2: 3 and following its **d** and thoughts.
      4:22 is being corrupted by its deceitful **d**;
Col   3: 5 lust, evil **d** and greed, which is
1Ti   3: 1 to be an overseer **d** a noble task.
      5:11 when their sensual **d** overcome their
      6: 9 harmful **d** that plunge people
2Ti   2:22 Flee the evil **d** of youth and pursue
      3: 6 are swayed by all kinds of evil **d**,
      4: 3 to suit their own **d**, they will gather
Jas   1:20 the righteousness that God **d**.
      4: 1 from your **d** that battle within you?
1Pe   1:14 do not conform to the evil **d** you had
      2:11 to abstain from sinful **d**,
      4: 2 their earthly lives for evil human **d**,
2Pe   1: 4 in the world caused by evil **d**.
      2:18 to the lustful **d** of the flesh,
      3: 3 and following their own evil **d**.
1Jn   2:17 The world and its **d** pass away,
Jude 1:16 they follow their own evil **d**;
      1:18 will follow their own ungodly **d**."

DESOLATE DESOLATION
Lev 26:34 years all the time that it lies **d**
Isa   1: 7 Your country is **d**, your cities
     54: 1 the children of the **d** woman than
Jer 50:23 How **d** is Babylon among
Da   9:17 look with favor on your **d** sanctuary.
Lk   13:35 Look, your house is left to you **d**.
Gal   4:27 the children of the **d** woman than

DESOLATION DESOLATE
2Ch 36:21 all the time of its **d** it rested,
Da   9:27 set up an abomination that causes **d**,
     11:31 up the abomination that causes **d**.
     12:11 abomination that causes **d** is set up,
Mt   24:15 'the abomination that causes **d**,'
Mk   13:14 causes **d**' standing where it does not
Lk   21:20 you will know that its **d** is near.

DESPAIR DESPAIRED, DESPAIRING
Isa 61: 3 of praise instead of a spirit of **d**.
2Co   4: 8 perplexed, but not in **d**;

DESPAIRED* DESPAIR
2Co   1: 8 to endure, so that we **d** of life itself.

DESPAIRING* DESPAIR
Dt   28:65 weary with longing, and a **d** heart.
Jer 14: 3 dismayed and **d**, they cover their

DESPERATE*
2Sa 12:18 He may do something **d**."
Job   6:26 say, and treat my **d** words as wind?
Ps   60: 3 have shown your people **d** times;
     79: 8 to meet us, for we are in **d** need.
    142: 6 Listen to my cry, for I am in **d** need;

DESPISE DESPISED, DESPISES
Ge   16: 4 she began to **d** her mistress.
Dt   23: 7 Do not **d** an Edomite,
     23: 7 Do not **d** an Egyptian, because you
2Sa 12: 9 Why did you **d** the word
Job   5:17 so do not **d** the discipline
     42: 6 Therefore I **d** myself and repent
Ps   51:17 contrite heart you, God, will not **d**.
    102:17 he will not **d** their plea.
Pr   1: 7 but fools **d** wisdom and instruction.
      3:11 do not **d** the LORD's discipline,
      6:30 People do not **d** a thief if he steals
     14:21 It is a sin to **d** one's neighbor,
     15:32 disregard discipline **d** themselves,
     23:22 do not **d** your mother when she is
Jer 14:21 the sake of your name do not **d** us;
Mic   3: 9 who **d** justice and distort all that is
Zec   4:10 "Who dares **d** the day of small
Mt   6:24 devoted to the one and **d** the other.
     18:10 you do not **d** one of these little ones.
Lk   16:13 devoted to the one and **d** the other.
1Co 11:22 Or do you **d** the church of God
Titus 2:15 Do not let anyone **d** you.
2Pe   2:10 desire of the flesh and **d** authority.

DESPISED DESPISE
Ge   25:34 up and left. So Esau **d** his birthright.
1Sa 17:42 health and handsome, and he **d** him.
2Sa   6:16 the LORD, she **d** him in her heart.
Ps   22: 6 by everyone, **d** by the people.
Pr   12: 8 and one with a warped mind is **d**.
Ecc   9:16 But the poor man's wisdom is **d**,
Isa 53: 3 He was **d** and rejected by mankind,
     53: 3 people hide their faces he was **d**,
1Co   1:28 of this world and the **d** things—

DESPISES DESPISE
Job 36: 5 "God is mighty, but **d** no one;
Pr   15:20 but a foolish man **d** his mother.

DESTINE* DESTINED, DESTINY, PREDESTINED
Isa 65:12 I will **d** you for the sword, and all

DESTINED DESTINE
Ps   49:14 They are like sheep and are **d** to die;
Jer 43:11 bringing death to those **d** for death,
     43:11 captivity to those **d** for captivity,
     43:11 the sword to those **d** for the sword.
Lk   2:34 "This child is **d** to cause the falling
1Co   2: 7 that God **d** for our glory before time
Col   2:22 things that are all **d** to perish
1Th   3: 3 quite well that we are **d** for them.
Heb   9:27 Just as people are **d** to die once,
1Pe   2: 8 which is also what they were **d** for.

DESTINY* DESTINE
Job   8:13 Such is the **d** of all who forget God;
Ps   73:17 then I understood their final **d**.
Ecc   7: 2 for death is the **d** of everyone;
      9: 2 All share a common **d**—
      9: 3 The same **d** overtakes all.
Isa 65:11 and fill bowls of mixed wine for **D**,
Php   3:19 Their **d** is destruction, their god is

DESTITUTE

Ps 102:17 will respond to the prayer of the **d**;
Pr   31: 8 for the rights of all who are **d**.
Heb 11:37 in sheepskins and goatskins, **d**,

DESTROY DESTROYED,
DESTROYER, DESTROYING,
DESTROYS, DESTRUCTION,
DESTRUCTIVE

Ge   6:13 I am surely going to **d** both them
       9:11 will there be a flood to **d** the earth."
      18:28 Will you **d** the whole city for lack
      18:28 there," he said, "I will not **d** it."
Ex   33: 3 and I might **d** you on the way."
Dt   6:15 he will **d** you from the face
       7: 2 them, then you must **d** them totally.
1Sa 15: 9 were unwilling to **d** completely,
1Ch 21:15 God sent an angel to **d** Jerusalem.
Est   3: 6 a way to **d** all Mordecai's people,
Ps   94:23 and **d** them for their wickedness;
      94:23 the LORD our God will **d** them.
Pr   1:32 complacency of fools will **d** them;
      11: 9 the godless **d** their neighbors,
Isa 65: 8 grapes and people say, 'Don't **d** it,
      65: 8 of my servants; I will not **d** them all.
Jer   4:27 though I will not **d** it completely.
Mt   10:28 of the One who can **d** both soul
Mk   14:58 say, 'I will **d** this temple made
Lk   4:34 Have you come to **d** us?
Jn   10:10 comes only to steal and kill and **d**;
Ac   8: 3 But Saul began to **d** the church.
Gal   1:13 the church of God and tried to **d** it.
Rev 11:18 destroying those who **d** the earth."

DESTROYED DESTROY

Ge   9:11 Never again will all life be **d**
      19:29 So when God **d** the cities
Dt   8:19 you today that you will surely be **d**.
Jos 24: 8 I **d** them from before you, and you
2Ki 10:28 So Jehu **d** Baal worship in Israel.
Est   7: 4 my people have been sold to be **d**,
Job 19:26 And after my skin has been **d**,
Ps   37: 9 For those who are evil will be **d**,
      37:38 But all sinners will be **d**;
Pr   6:15 he will suddenly be **d**—
      11: 3 but the unfaithful are **d** by their
      29: 1 many rebukes will suddenly be **d**—
Da   2:44 up a kingdom that will never be **d**,
       6:26 his kingdom will not be **d**,
       7:11 and its body **d** and thrown
Hos   4: 6 my people are **d** from lack
Lk   17:27 Then the flood came and **d** them all.
1Co   8:11 Christ died, is **d** by your knowledge.
      15:24 Father after he has **d** all dominion,
      15:26 The last enemy to be **d** is death.
2Co   4: 9 struck down, but not **d**.
       5: 1 if the earthly tent we live in is **d**,
Gal   5:15 out or you will be **d** by each other.
Eph   2:14 groups one and has **d** the barrier,
2Ti   1:10 who has **d** death and has brought
Heb 10:39 to those who shrink back and are **d**,
2Pe   2:12 born only to be caught and **d**,
       3:10 the elements will be **d** by fire,

Jude   1: 5 later **d** those who did not believe.

DESTROYER DESTROY

Ex   12:23 and he will not permit the **d** to enter
Jer   6:26 for suddenly the **d** will come
Heb 11:28 that the **d** of the firstborn would not

DESTROYING DESTROY

Ps   106:23 him to keep his wrath from **d** them.
Jer   23: 1 "Woe to the shepherds who are **d**
1Co 10:10 and were killed by the **d** angel.
Rev 11:18 for **d** those who destroy the earth."

DESTROYS DESTROY

Pr   6:32 whoever does so **d** himself.
      18: 9 in his work is brother to one who **d**.
      28:24 wrong," is partner to one who **d**.
Ecc   9:18 of war, but one sinner **d** much good.
Lk   12:33 no thief comes near and no moth **d**.
1Co   3:17 If anyone **d** God's temple, God will

DESTRUCTION DESTROY

Nu   32:15 you will be the cause of their **d**."
Dt   7:10 him he will repay to their face by **d**;
Ps   1: 6 the way of the wicked leads to **d**.
Pr   16:18 Pride goes before **d**, a haughty spirit
      17:19 builds a high gate invites **d**.
      24:22 for those two will send sudden **d**
      27:20 Death and **D** are never satisfied,
Isa 10:22 **D** has been decreed,
Hos 13:14 Where, O grave, is your **d**?
Hab   2:17 your **d** of animals will terrify you.
Mt   7:13 and broad is the road that leads to **d**,
Lk   6:49 collapsed and its **d** was complete."
Jn   17:12 lost except the one doomed to **d** so
Ro   9:22 of his wrath—prepared for **d**?
1Co   5: 5 over to Satan for the **d** of the flesh,
Gal   6: 8 flesh, from the flesh will reap **d**;
Php   3:19 Their destiny is **d**, their god is their
1Th   5: 3 **d** will come on them suddenly,
2Th   1: 9 will be punished with everlasting **d**
       2: 3 is revealed, the man doomed to **d**.
1Ti   6: 9 that plunge people into ruin and **d**.
2Pe   2: 1 bringing swift **d** on themselves.
       2: 3 and their **d** has not been sleeping.
       3: 7 of judgment and **d** of the ungodly.
       3:12 bring about the **d** of the heavens
       3:16 the other Scriptures, to their own **d**.
Rev 17: 8 up out of the Abyss and go to its **d**.
      17:11 to the seven and is going to his **d**.

DESTRUCTIVE DESTROY

Ex   12:13 No **d** plague will touch you when I
Pr   17: 4 a liar pays attention to a **d** tongue.
2Pe   2: 1 will secretly introduce **d** heresies,

DETERMINED DETERMINES

Jdg   1:27 for the Canaanites were **d** to live
       1:35 the Amorites were **d** also to hold
Ru   1:18 realized that Ruth was **d** to go
2Sa   17:14 the LORD had **d** to frustrate
Job 14: 5 A person's days are **d**;
Isa 14:26 This is the plan **d** for the whole
Da   11:36 for what has been **d** must take place.
1Co 15:38 But God gives it a body as he has **d**,

DETERMINES* DETERMINED
Ps 147: 4 He **d** the number of the stars
1Co 12:11 them to each one, just as he **d**.

DETEST DETESTABLE, DETESTED, DETESTS
Dt   7:26 Regard it as vile and utterly **d** it,
Job 19:19 All my intimate friends **d** me;
Ps   5: 6 and deceitful you, Lord, **d**.
    119:163 I hate and **d** falsehood but I love
Pr   8: 7 is true, for my lips **d** wickedness.
     13:19 soul, but fools **d** turning from evil.
     16:12 Kings **d** wrongdoing, for a throne is
     24: 9 folly are sin, and people **d** a mocker.
     29:27 The righteous **d** the dishonest;
     29:27 the wicked **d** the upright.
Am   5:10 and **d** the one who tells the truth.
      6: 8 pride of Jacob and **d** his fortresses;

DETESTABLE DETEST
Ge 46:34 for all shepherds are **d**
Dt   18: 9 to imitate the **d** ways of the nations
Pr   6:16 hates, seven that are **d** to him:
     21:27 The sacrifice of the wicked is **d**—
     28: 9 instruction, even their prayers are **d**.
Isa   1:13 Your incense is **d** to me.
     41:24 whoever chooses you is **d**.
     44:19 Shall I make a **d** thing from what is
Jer 44: 4 'Do not do this **d** thing that I hate!'
Eze   5: 9 Because of all your **d** idols, I will do
      8:13 doing things that are even more **d**."
Mal   2:11 A **d** thing has been committed
Lk   16:15 What people value highly is **d**
Titus 1:16 They are **d**, disobedient and unfit
1Pe   4: 3 orgies, carousing and **d** idolatry.
Rev 18: 2 for every unclean and **d** animal.

DETESTED* DETEST
Zec 11: 8 The flock **d** me, and I grew weary

DETESTS* DETEST
Dt   22: 5 the Lord your God **d** anyone who
     23:18 the Lord your God **d** them both.
     25:16 the Lord your God **d** anyone who
Pr   3:32 For the Lord **d** the perverse
     11: 1 The Lord **d** dishonest scales,
     11:20 The Lord **d** those whose hearts
     12:22 The Lord **d** lying lips, but he
     15: 8 The Lord **d** the sacrifice
     15: 9 The Lord **d** the way
     15:26 The Lord **d** the thoughts
     16: 5 The Lord **d** all the proud
     17:15 the Lord **d** them both.
     20:10 the Lord **d** them both.
     20:23 The Lord **d** differing weights,

DEVIATE*
2Ch 8:15 They did not **d** from the king's

DEVICES DEVISE
Ps   81:12 hearts to follow their own **d**.

DEVIL* DEVIL'S
Mt   4: 1 wilderness to be tempted by the **d**.
      4: 5 Then the **d** took him to the holy city

Mt   4: 8 Again, the **d** took him to a very high
      4:11 Then the **d** left him, and angels
     13:39 the enemy who sows them is the **d**.
     25:41 the eternal fire prepared for the **d**
Lk   4: 2 forty days he was tempted by the **d**.
      4: 3 The **d** said to him, "If you are
      4: 5 The **d** led him up to a high place
      4: 9 The **d** led him to Jerusalem and had
      4:13 the **d** had finished all this tempting,
      8:12 then the **d** comes and takes away
Jn   6:70 Yet one of you is a **d**!"
      8:44 the **d**, and you want to carry
     13: 2 the **d** had already prompted Judas,
Ac   10:38 who were under the power of the **d**,
     13:10 "You are a child of the **d**
Eph   4:27 and do not give the **d** a foothold.
1Ti   3: 6 under the same judgment as the **d**.
2Ti   2:26 and escape from the trap of the **d**,
Heb   2:14 the power of death—that is, the **d**—
Jas   4: 7 Resist the **d**, and he will flee
1Pe   5: 8 Your enemy the **d** prowls around
1Jn   3: 8 who does what is sinful is of the **d**,
      3: 8 because the **d** has been sinning
      3:10 and who the children of the **d** are:
Jude 1: 9 disputing with the **d** about the body
Rev   2:10 the **d** will put some of you in prison
     12: 9 that ancient serpent called the **d**,
     12:12 sea, because the **d** has gone down
     20: 2 serpent, who is the **d**, or Satan,
     20:10 And the **d**, who deceived them,

DEVIL'S* DEVIL
Eph   6:11 your stand against the **d** schemes.
1Ti   3: 7 fall into disgrace and into the **d** trap.
1Jn   3: 8 appeared was to destroy the **d** work.

DEVILS (KJV) See DEMONS, GOAT IDOLS

DEVIOUS* DEVISE
2Sa 22:27 to the **d** you show yourself shrewd.
Ps   18:26 to the **d** you show yourself shrewd.
Pr   2:15 and who are **d** in their ways.
     14: 2 those who despise him are **d** in their
     21: 8 The way of the guilty is **d**,

DEVISE DEVICES, DEVIOUS, DEVISED, DEVISES
Pr   12: 2 those who **d** wicked schemes.
Isa   8:10 **D** your strategy, but it will be

DEVISED DEVISE
Est   8: 5 **d** and wrote to destroy the Jews
Mt   28:12 met with the elders and **d** a plan,
2Pe   1:16 we did not follow cleverly **d** stories

DEVISES DEVISE
Pr   6:18 a heart that **d** wicked schemes,
     14:17 the one who **d** evil schemes is hated.
Na   1:11 the Lord and **d** wicked plans.

DEVOTE* DEVOTED, DEVOTING, DEVOTION, DEVOUT
1Ch 22:19 Now **d** your heart and soul
2Ch 31: 4 Levites so they could **d** themselves

Job   11:13 "Yet if you **d** your heart to him
Jer   30:21 who is he who will **d** himself to be
Mic   4:13 You will **d** their ill-gotten gains
1Co   7: 5 that you may **d** yourselves to prayer.
Col   4: 2 **D** yourselves to prayer,
1Ti   1: 4 or to **d** themselves to myths
        4:13 **d** yourself to the public reading
Titus   3: 8 God may be careful to **d** themselves
        3:14 people must learn to **d** themselves

DEVOTED DEVOTE

Jos   6:18 But keep away from the **d** things,
        7: 1 unfaithful in regard to the **d** things;
1Ki   11: 4 and his heart was not fully **d**
2Ch   17: 6 His heart was **d** to the ways
Ezr   7:10 For Ezra had **d** himself to the study
Ne   5:16 I **d** myself to the work on this wall.
Eze   20:16 For their hearts were **d** to their idols.
Mt   6:24 or you will be **d** to the one
Mk   7:11 is Corban (that is, **d** to God)—
Ac   2:42 They **d** themselves to the apostles'
       18: 5 Paul **d** himself exclusively
Ro   12:10 Be **d** to one another in love.
1Co   7:34 Her aim is to be **d** to the Lord
       16:15 and they have **d** themselves
2Co   7:12 for yourselves how **d** to us you are.

DEVOTING* DEVOTE

1Ti   5:10 **d** herself to all kinds of good deeds.

DEVOTION* DEVOTE

2Ki   20: 3 with wholehearted **d** and have done
1Ch   28: 9 serve him with wholehearted **d**
       29: 3 in my **d** to the temple of my God I
       29:19 son Solomon the wholehearted **d**
2Ch   32:32 his acts of **d** are written in the vision
       35:26 and his acts of **d** in accordance
Job   15: 4 piety and hinder **d** to God.
Isa   38: 3 with wholehearted **d** and have done
Jer   2: 2 " 'I remember the **d** of your
1Co   7:35 way in undivided **d** to the Lord.
2Co   11: 3 your sincere and pure **d** to Christ.

DEVOUR DEVOURED, DEVOURING, DEVOURS

Lev   26:38 the land of your enemies will **d** you.
Dt   28:38 little, because locusts will **d** it.
2Sa   2:26 to Joab, "Must the sword **d** forever?
1Ki   21:23 'Dogs will **d** Jezebel by the wall
2Ki   9:36 Jezreel dogs will **d** Jezebel's flesh.
Jer   5:17 They will **d** your harvests and food, **d**
              your sons and daughters;
       46:10 The sword will **d** till it is satisfied,
Mk   12:40 They **d** widows' houses
Gal   5:15 If you bite and **d** each other, watch
1Pe   5: 8 lion looking for someone to **d**.

DEVOURED DEVOUR

Isa   1:20 rebel, you will be **d** by the sword."
Jer   30:16 all who devour you will be **d**;
Rev   20: 9 down from heaven and **d** them.

DEVOURING DEVOUR

Mal   3:11 prevent pests from **d** your crops,

DEVOURS DEVOUR

2Sa   11:25 the sword **d** one as well as another.
Ps   50: 3 a fire **d** before him, and around him
Rev   11: 5 their mouths and **d** their enemies.

DEVOUT* DEVOTE

1Ki   18: 3 (Obadiah was a **d** believer
Isa   57: 1 the **d** are taken away, and no one
Lk   2:25 Simeon, who was righteous and **d**.
Ac   10: 2 He and all his family were **d**
       10: 7 and a **d** soldier who was one of his
       13:43 **d** converts to Judaism followed Paul
       22:12 He was a **d** observer of the law

DEW

Ge   27:28 May God give you heaven's **d**
Ex   16:13 was a layer of **d** around the camp.
Dt   32: 2 rain and my words descend like **d**,
Jdg   6:37 If there is **d** only on the fleece
Job   38:28 Who fathers the drops of **d**?
Pr   19:12 but his favor is like **d** on the grass.
Hos   6: 4 like the early **d** that disappears.
       14: 5 I will be like the **d** to Israel;
Hag   1:10 the heavens have withheld their **d**

DIADEM*

Isa   62: 3 a royal **d** in the hand of your God.

DIANA (KJV) See ARTEMIS

DICTATED

Jer   36: 4 while Jeremiah **d** all the words
       45: 1 the words Jeremiah the prophet **d**

DIDYMUS* THOMAS

Alternate name of the disciple Thomas (Jn 11:16; 20:24; 21:2).

DIE DEAD, DEATH, DIED, DIES, DYING

Ge   2:17 eat from it you will certainly **d**."
        3: 3 must not touch it, or you will **d**.' "
        3: 4 "You will not certainly **d**,"
Ex   11: 5 Every firstborn son in Egypt will **d**,
       14:11 you brought us to the desert to **d**?
Nu   23:10 Let me **d** the death of the righteous,
Dt   24:16 each will **d** for their own sin.
Ru   1:17 Where you **d** I will **d**, and there I
2Ki   14: 6 each will **d** for their own sin."
Job   2: 9 Curse God and **d**!"
Ps   37: 2 green plants they will soon **d** away.
      118:17 I will not **d** but live, and will
Pr   5:23 For lack of discipline they will **d**,
       10:21 many, but fools **d** for lack of sense.
       11: 7 placed in mortals **d** with them;
       15:10 the one who hates correction will **d**.
       23:13 them with the rod, they will not **d**.
Ecc   2:16 Like the fool, the wise too must **d**!
        3: 2 a time to be born and a time to **d**,
Isa   22:13 you say, "for tomorrow we **d**!"
       66:24 the worms that eat them will not **d**,
Jer   31:30 everyone will **d** for their own sin;
Eze   3:18 wicked person will **d** for their sin,
       18: 4 one who sins is the one who will **d**.
       18:31 Why will you **d**, people of Israel?

Eze 33: 8 wicked person will **d** for their sin,
Jnh 4: 8 He wanted to **d**, and said, "It would
          be better for me to **d** than to live."
Hab 1:12 my Holy One, you will never **d**.
Mt 26:35 "Even if I have to **d** with you, I will
    26:52 all who draw the sword will **d**
Mk   9:48 worms that eat them do not **d**,
Jn   6:50 which anyone may eat and not **d**.
     8:21 for me, and you will **d** in your sin.
    11:25 in me will live, even though they **d**;
    11:26 by believing in me will never **d**.
    21:23 did not say that he would not **d**;
Ro   5: 7 Very rarely will anyone **d** for a
     5: 7 someone might possibly dare to **d**.
    14: 8 and if we **d**, we **d** for the Lord.
    14: 8 whether we live or **d**, we belong
1Co 15:22 For as in Adam all **d**, so in Christ all
    15:32 eat and drink, for tomorrow we **d**."
Php 1:21 me, to live is Christ and to **d** is gain.
Heb 9:27 as people are destined to **d** once,
1Pe 2:24 so that we might **d** to sins and live
Rev 9: 6 they will long to **d**, but death will
    14:13 Blessed are the dead who **d**

MUST DIE See MUST

DIED DIE

Lev 10: 2 and they **d** before the LORD.
Nu   3: 4 **d** before the LORD when they
    14: 2 them, "If only we had **d** in Egypt!
    16:49 14,700 people **d** from the plague,
    16:49 those who had **d** because of Korah.
Jdg 16:30 more when he **d** than while he lived.
2Sa 24:15 people from Dan to Beersheba **d**.
1Ki 3:19 this woman's son **d** because she lay
1Ch 10:13 Saul **d** because he was unfaithful
Mk 15:39 of Jesus, saw how he **d**, he said,
Lk 16:22 "The time came when the beggar **d**
    16:22 The rich man also **d** and was buried.
Jn   6:58 Your ancestors ate manna and **d**,
Ro   5: 6 powerless, Christ **d** for the ungodly.
     5: 8 were still sinners, Christ **d** for us.
     6: 2 We are those who have **d** to sin;
     6: 8 Now if we **d** with Christ, we believe
     6:10 The death he **d**, he **d** to sin once
    14: 9 Christ **d** and returned to life so
1Co 8:11 for whom Christ **d**, is destroyed
    15: 3 that Christ **d** for our sins according
2Co 5:14 we are convinced that one **d** for all,
          and therefore all **d**.
     5:15 And he **d** for all, that those who live
     5:15 but for him who **d** for them and was
Gal 2:19 through the law I **d** to the law so
Col 2:20 Since you **d** with Christ
     3: 3 For you **d**, and your life is now
1Th 4:14 For we believe that Jesus **d** and rose
     5:10 He **d** for us so that, whether we are
2Ti 2:11 If we **d** with him, we will also live
Heb 9:15 now that he has **d** as a ransom to set
    11:13 still living by faith when they **d**.
Rev 2: 8 Last, who **d** and came to life again.
     8: 9 of the living creatures in the sea **d**,
     8:11 many people **d** from the waters
    16: 3 and every living thing in the sea **d**.

DIES DIE

Job 14:14 If someone **d**, will they live again?
Ecc 3:19 As one **d**, so **d** the other.
Jn 12:24 of wheat falls to the ground and **d**,
    12:24 But if it **d**, it produces many seeds.
Ro   7: 2 but if her husband **d**, she is released
    14: 7 none of us **d** for ourselves alone.
1Co 7:39 But if her husband **d**, she is free
    15:36 does not come to life unless it **d**.

DIFFERENCE* DIFFERENT

2Sa 19:35 Can I tell the **d** between what is
2Ch 12: 8 may learn the **d** between serving me
Eze 22:26 there is no **d** between the unclean
    44:23 my people the **d** between the holy
Ro   3:22 There is no **d** between Jew
    10:12 For there is no **d** between Jew
Gal 2: 6 whatever they were makes no **d**

DIFFERENCES* DIFFERENT

1Co 11:19 doubt there have to be **d** among you

DIFFERENT* DIFFERENCE,
DIFFERENCES, DIFFERENTLY,
DIFFERING, DIFFERS

Lev 19:19 " 'Do not mate **d** kinds
Nu 14:24 my servant Caleb has a **d** spirit
1Sa 10: 6 you will be changed into a **d** person.
Est 1: 7 of gold, each one **d** from the other,
     3: 8 Their customs are **d** from those
Da   7: 3 great beasts, each **d** from the others,
     7: 7 It was **d** from all the former beasts,
     7:19 which was **d** from all the others
     7:23 It will be **d** from all the other
     7:24 will arise, **d** from the earlier ones;
    11:29 this time the outcome will be **d**
Eze 15: 2 how is the wood of a vine **d**
Mk 16:12 *Jesus appeared in a **d** form to*
Ro 12: 6 We have **d** gifts,
1Co 4: 7 who makes you **d** from anyone else?
    12: 4 There are **d** kinds of gifts,
    12: 5 There are **d** kinds of service,
    12: 6 There are **d** kinds of working,
    12:10 to another speaking in **d** kinds
    12:28 guidance, and of **d** kinds of tongues.
2Co 11: 4 you receive a spirit from the Spirit
    11: 4 or a **d** gospel from the one you
Gal 1: 6 and are turning to a **d** gospel—
     4: 1 is underage, he is no **d** from a slave,
Heb 7:13 things are said belonged to a **d** tribe,
Jas 2:25 and sent them off in a **d** direction?

DIFFERENTLY* DIFFERENT

Ex   8:22 that day I will deal **d** with the land
Php 3:15 And if on some point you think **d**,

DIFFERING* DIFFERENT

Dt 25:13 Do not have two **d** weights in your
    25:14 Do not have two **d** measures in your
Pr 20:10 **D** weights and **d** measures—
    20:23 The LORD detests **d** weights,

DIFFERS* DIFFERENT

1Co 15:41 and star **d** from star in splendor.

DIFFICULT DIFFICULTIES

Ge 47: 9 My years have been few and **d**,
Ex 18:22 but have them bring every **d** case
Dt 30:11 commanding you today is not too **d**
2Ki 2:10 "You have asked a **d** thing,"
Da 2:11 What the king asks is too **d**.
    4: 9 and no mystery is too **d** for you.
Ac 15:19 that we should not make it **d**

DIFFICULTIES* DIFFICULT

2Co 12:10 in hardships, in persecutions, in **d**.

DIG DIGS, DUG

Dt 6:11 wells you did not **d**, and vineyards
Eze 8: 8 "Son of man, now **d** into the wall."
Am 9: 2 Though they **d** down to the depths

DIGNITY

Ex 28: 2 your brother Aaron to give him **d**
Pr 31:25 She is clothed with strength and **d**;

DIGS DIG

Pr 26:27 Whoever **d** a pit will fall into it;

DILIGENCE DILIGENT

Ezr 5: 8 The work is being carried on with **d**
Heb 6:11 to show this same **d** to the very end,

DILIGENT* DILIGENCE, DILIGENTLY

2Ch 24:13 men in charge of the work were **d**,
Pr 10: 4 poverty, but **d** hands bring wealth.
    12:24 **D** hands will rule, but laziness ends
    12:27 the **d** feed on the riches of the hunt.
    13: 4 desires of the **d** are fully satisfied.
    21: 5 The plans of the **d** lead to profit as
1Ti 4:15 Be **d** in these matters;

DILIGENTLY* DILIGENT

Zec 6:15 you **d** obey the LORD your God."
Jn 5:39 study the Scriptures **d** because you
Ro 12: 8 if it is to lead, do it **d**; if it is to show

DINAH*

Only daughter of Jacob, by Leah (Ge 30:21; 46:15). Raped by Shechem; avenged by Simeon and Levi (Ge 34).

DINE DINNER

Pr 23: 1 When you sit to **d** with a ruler,

DINNER DINE

Mk 2:15 While Jesus was having **d** at Levi's
Lk 14:12 "When you give a luncheon or **d**,

DIOTREPHES*

3Jn 1: 9 church, but **D**, who loves to be first,

DIP DIPPED, DIPPING, DIPS

Ps 58:10 when they **d** their feet in the blood

DIPPED DIP

2Ki 5:14 **d** himself in the Jordan seven times,
Mt 26:23 "The one who has **d** his hand
Rev 19:13 He is dressed in a robe **d** in blood,

DIPPING* DIP

Jn 13:26 Then, **d** the piece of bread, he gave

DIPS* DIP

Mk 14:20 "one who **d** bread into the bowl

DIRECT DIRECTED, DIRECTIVES, DIRECTOR, DIRECTS

Ge 18:19 so that he will **d** his children and his
Ps 119:35 **D** me in the path of your
    119:133 **D** my footsteps according to your
Jer 10:23 it is not for them to **d** their steps.
2Th 3: 5 May the Lord **d** your hearts
1Ti 5:17 The elders who **d** the affairs

DIRECTED DIRECT

Ge 24:51 master's son, as the LORD has **d**."
Nu 16:40 as the LORD **d** him through
Dt 2: 1 Red Sea, as the LORD had **d** me.
    6: 1 laws the LORD your God **d** me
Jos 11: 9 did to them as the LORD had **d**:
Pr 20:24 A person's steps are **d**
Jer 13: 2 as the LORD **d**, and put it around
Mt 26:19 disciples did as Jesus had **d** them
Ac 7:44 It had been made as God **d** Moses,
Titus 1: 5 elders in every town, as I **d** you.

DIRECTIVES* DIRECT

1Co 11:17 In the following **d** I have no praise

DIRECTOR DIRECT

FOR THE DIRECTOR OF MUSIC See MUSIC

DIRECTS* DIRECT

Ps 42: 8 By day the LORD **d** his love,
Isa 48:17 who **d** you in the way you should

DIRGE*

Mt 11:17 we sang a **d**, and you did not
Lk 7:32 we sang a **d**, and you did not cry.'

DISABLED* ABLE

2Sa 4: 4 to leave, he fell and became **d**.
Jn 5: 3 a great number of **d** people used
Heb 12:13 so that the lame may not be **d**,

DISAGREEMENT* AGREE

Ac 15:39 They had such a sharp **d** that they

DISAPPEAR DISAPPEARED, DISAPPEARS

Nu 27: 4 Why should our father's name **d**
Ru 4:10 his name will not **d** from among his
Mt 5:18 until heaven and earth **d**,
    5:18 by any means **d** from the Law until
Lk 16:17 earth to **d** than for the least stroke
Heb 8:13 is obsolete and outdated will soon **d**.
2Pe 3:10 The heavens will **d** with a roar;

DISAPPEARED* DISAPPEAR

Jdg 6:21 And the angel of the LORD **d**."
1Ki 20:40 busy here and there, the man **d**."
Lk 24:31 him, and he **d** from their sight.

DISAPPEARS* DISAPPEAR
Hos   6: 4 mist, like the early dew that **d**.
      13: 3 like the early dew that **d**, like chaff
1Co 13:10 comes, what is in part **d**.

DISAPPOINTED
Isa   49:23 who hope in me will not be **d**."

DISAPPROVE*
Pr   24:18 the LORD will see and **d** and turn

DISARMED* DISARMS
Col   2:15 And having **d** the powers

DISARMS* DISARMED
Job   12:21 on nobles and **d** the mighty.

DISASTER DISASTERS
Ex   32:12 and do not bring **d** on your people.
Dt   32:35 their day of **d** is near and their doom
Jos   24:20 he will turn and bring **d** on you
2Ch   7:22 that is why he brought all this **d**
Est   8: 6 how can I bear to see **d** fall on my
Ps   57: 1 of your wings until the **d** has passed.
Pr   1:26 turn will laugh when **d** strikes you;
       3:25 Have no fear of sudden **d**
       6:15 Therefore **d** will overtake him
      16: 4 even the wicked for a day of **d**.
      17: 5 whoever gloats over **d** will not go
      27:10 house when **d** strikes you—
Isa   3: 9 They have brought **d**
      45: 7 I bring prosperity and create **d**;
Jer   4:20 **D** follows **d**; the whole land lies
      17:17 you are my refuge in the day of **d**.
      18: 8 not inflict on it the **d** I had planned.
Eze   7: 5 the Sovereign LORD says: " '**D**!
Ob   1:13 of my people in the day of their **d**,

DISASTERS DISASTER
Dt   31:17 Many **d** and calamities will come
      31:17 ask, 'Have not these **d** come on us

DISCERN* DISCERNED,
DISCERNING, DISCERNMENT
Dt   32:29 this and **d** what their end will be!
Job   6:30 Can my mouth not **d** malice?
      34: 4 Let us **d** for ourselves what is right;
Ps   19:12 But who can **d** their own errors?
     139: 3 You **d** my going out and my lying
Php   1:10 you may be able to **d** what is best

DISCERNED* DISCERN
1Co   2:14 because they are **d** only through

DISCERNING* DISCERN
Ge   41:33 now let Pharaoh look for a **d**
      41:39 there is no one so **d** and wise as you.
2Sa   14:17 is like an angel of God in **d** good
1Ki   3: 9 So give your servant a **d** heart
       3:12 I will give you a wise and **d** heart,
Pr   1: 5 and let the **d** get guidance—
       8: 9 To the **d** all of them are right;
      10:13 is found on the lips of the **d**,
      14: 6 knowledge comes easily to the **d**,
      14:33 reposes in the heart of the **d**

Pr   15:14 The **d** heart seeks knowledge,
      16:21 The wise in heart are called **d**,
      17:10 A rebuke impresses a **d** person more
      17:24 A **d** person keeps wisdom in view,
      17:28 and **d** if they hold their tongues.
      18:15 heart of the **d** acquires knowledge,
      19:25 rebuke the **d**, and they will gain
      28: 7 A **d** son heeds instruction,
      28:11 and **d** sees how deluded they are.
Da   2:21 to the wise and knowledge to the **d**.
Hos   14: 9 Who is **d**? Let them understand.
1Co   11:29 drink without **d** the body of Christ
      11:31 if we were more **d** with regard

DISCERNMENT* DISCERN
Dt   32:28 without sense, there is no **d** in them.
1Ki   3:11 but for **d** in administering justice,
2Ch   2:12 endowed with intelligence and **d**,
Job   12:20 and takes away the **d** of elders.
Ps 119:125 give me **d** that I may understand
Pr   28: 2 but a ruler with **d** and knowledge

DISCHARGE DISCHARGED,
DISCHARGING
Lev   15: 2 any man has an unusual bodily **d**,
                  such a **d** is unclean.
2Ti   4: 5 **d** all the duties of your ministry.

DISCHARGED* DISCHARGE
Jdg   3:22 in after the blade, and his bowels **d**.
Ecc   8: 8 As no one is **d** in time of war,

DISCHARGING* DISCHARGE
1Co   9:17 I am simply **d** the trust committed

DISCIPLE DISCIPLES, DISCIPLES'
Mt   10:42 one of these little ones who is my **d**,
      13:52 of the law who has become a **d**
Lk   14:26 such a person cannot be my **d**.
      14:27 and follow me cannot be my **d**.
Jn   9:28 and said, "You are this fellow's **d**!
      13:23 of them, the **d** whom Jesus loved,
      18:15 and another **d** were following Jesus.
      18:15 Because this **d** was known
      19:26 and the **d** whom he loved standing
      19:38 Now Joseph was a **d** of Jesus,
      20: 2 to Simon Peter and the other **d**,
      21: 7 the **d** whom Jesus loved said
      21:20 that the **d** whom Jesus loved was
Ac   9:10 there was a **d** named Ananias.
      16: 1 where a **d** named Timothy lived,

DISCIPLES DISCIPLE
Mt   9:10 came and ate with him and his **d**.
      10: 1 Jesus called his twelve **d** to him
      26:56 Then all the **d** deserted him
      28:19 go and make **d** of all nations,
Mk   3: 7 withdrew with his **d** to the lake,
       6:29 John's **d** came and took his body
       7: 5 "Why don't your **d** live according
Lk   6:13 he called his **d** to him and chose
       9:46 An argument started among the **d** as
      11: 1 to pray, just as John taught his **d**."
Lk   14:33 you have cannot be my **d**.
Jn   2:11 and his **d** believed in him.

Jn   6:66 this time many of his **d** turned back
    8:31 to my teaching, you are really my **d**.
  12:16 At first his **d** did not understand all
  13:35 will know that you are my **d**, if you
  15: 8 showing yourselves to be my **d**.
  20:20 The **d** were overjoyed when they
Ac   6: 1 the number of **d** was increasing,
  11:26 The **d** were called Christians first
  14:22 strengthening the **d** and encouraging
  18:23 and Phrygia, strengthening all the **d**.

DISCIPLES'* DISCIPLE
Jn   13: 5 basin and began to wash his **d** feet,

DISCIPLINE* DISCIPLINED,
DISCIPLINES, SELF-DISCIPLINE
Dt   4:36 made you hear his voice to **d** you.
  11: 2 experienced the **d** of the LORD
  21:18 not listen to them when they **d** him,
Job   5:17 so do not despise the **d**
Ps   6: 1 in your anger or **d** me in your wrath.
  38: 1 in your anger or **d** me in your wrath.
  39:11 rebuke and **d** anyone for their sin,
  94:12 Blessed is the one you **d**, LORD,
Pr   3:11 do not despise the LORD's **d**,
  5:12 You will say, "How I hated **d**!
  5:23 For lack of **d** they will die,
  10:17 Whoever heeds **d** shows the way
  12: 1 Whoever loves **d** loves knowledge,
  13:18 Whoever disregards **d** comes
  13:24 their children is careful to **d** them.
  15: 5 A fool spurns a parent's **d**,
  15:10 Stern **d** awaits anyone who leaves
  15:32 who disregard **d** despise themselves,
  19:18 **D** your children, for in that there is
  19:20 Listen to advice and accept **d**,
  22:15 the rod of **d** will drive it far away.
  23:13 Do not withhold **d** from a child;
  29:17 **D** your children, and they will give
Jer   10:24 **D** me, LORD, but only in due
  17:23 would not listen or respond to **d**.
  30:11 I will **d** you but only in due
  32:33 would not listen or respond to **d**.
  46:28 I will **d** you but only in due
Hos   5: 2 I will **d** all of them.
1Co   4:21 Shall I come to you with a rod of **d**,
Heb   12: 5 do not make light of the Lord's **d**,
  12: 7 Endure hardship as **d**;
  12: 8 and everyone undergoes **d**—
  12:11 No **d** seems pleasant at the time,
Rev   3:19 Those whom I love I rebuke and **d**.

DISCIPLINED* DISCIPLINE
Isa   26:16 when you **d** them, they could barely
Jer   31:18 'You **d** me like an unruly calf, and I
    have been **d**.
1Co   11:32 we are being **d** so that we will not
Col   2: 5 delight to see how **d** you are
Titus   1: 8 self-controlled, upright, holy and **d**.
Heb   12: 7 For what children are not **d** by their
  12: 8 If you are not **d**—
  12: 9 all had human fathers who **d** us
  12:10 They **d** us for a little while as they

DISCIPLINES* DISCIPLINE
Dt   8: 5 your heart that as a man **d** his son, so
    the LORD your God **d** you.
Ps   94:10 Does he who **d** nations not punish?
Pr   3:12 because the LORD **d** those he
Heb   12: 6 because the Lord **d** the one he loves,
  12:10 but God **d** us for our good, in order

DISCLOSED
Mk   4:22 whatever is hidden is meant to be **d**,
Lk   12: 2 nothing concealed that will not be **d**,
Col   1:26 but is now **d** to the Lord's people.
Heb   9: 8 had not yet been **d** as long as

DISCORD*
Est   1:18 will be no end of disrespect and **d**.
2Co   12:20 I fear that there may be **d**, jealousy,
Gal   5:20 hatred, **d**, jealousy, fits of rage,

DISCOURAGE* DISCOURAGED,
DISCOURAGEMENT
Nu   32: 7 Why do you **d** the Israelites
Ezr   4: 4 set out to **d** the people of Judah

DISCOURAGED* DISCOURAGE
Nu   32: 9 they **d** the Israelites from entering
Dt   1:21 Do not be afraid; do not be **d**."
  31: 8 Do not be afraid; do not be **d**."
Jos   1: 9 do not be **d**, for the LORD your
  8: 1 "Do not be afraid; do not be **d**.
  10:25 "Do not be afraid; do not be **d**.
1Ch   22:13 Do not be afraid or **d**.
  28:20 Do not be afraid or **d**,
2Ch   20:15 or **d** because of this vast army.
  20:17 Do not be afraid; do not be **d**.
  32: 7 or **d** because of the king of Assyria
Job   4: 5 trouble comes to you, and you are **d**;
Isa   42: 4 or be **d** till he establishes justice
Eph   3:13 not to be **d** because of my sufferings
Col   3:21 children, or they will become **d**.

DISCOURAGEMENT*
DISCOURAGE
Ex   6: 9 not listen to him because of their **d**

DISCOVER DISCOVERED
Ecc   7:14 no one can **d** anything about their
  8:17 it out, no one can **d** its meaning.

DISCOVERED DISCOVER
Jdg   16: 9 the secret of his strength was not **d**.
2Ki   23:24 that Hilkiah the priest had **d**
Ecc   7:27 the Teacher, "this is what I have **d**:

DISCREDIT* DISCREDITED
Ne   6:13 would give me a bad name to **d** me.
Job   40: 8 "Would you **d** my justice?

DISCREDITED* DISCREDIT
Ac   19:27 the great goddess Artemis will be **d**;
2Co   6: 3 so that our ministry will not be **d**.

DISCREETLY* DISCRETION
Pr   26:16 than seven people who answer **d**.

DISCRETION* DISCREETLY

1Ch 22:12 May the Lord give you **d**
Pr   1: 4 knowledge and **d** to the young—
     2:11 **D** will protect you,
     3:21 preserve sound judgment and **d**;
     5: 2 that you may maintain **d** and your
     8:12 I possess knowledge and **d**.
    11:22 a beautiful woman who shows no **d**.

DISCRIMINATE* DISCRIMINATED

Ac 15: 9 He did not **d** between us and them,

DISCRIMINATED* DISCRIMINATE

Jas   2: 4 have you not **d** among yourselves

DISCUSSED DISCUSSION

Mk   8:16 They **d** this with one another
    11:31 They **d** it among themselves

DISCUSSING* DISCUSSION

Mk   9:10 **d** what "rising from the dead" meant.
Lk 24:17 "What are you **d** together as you

DISCUSSION DISCUSSED, DISCUSSING

Mk   8:17 Aware of their **d**, Jesus asked them:

DISEASE DISEASED, DISEASES

Dt   7:15 will keep you free from every **d**.
    28:22 will strike you with wasting **d**,
1Ki   8:37 whatever disaster or **d** may come,
Ps 106:15 but sent a wasting **d** among them.
Mt   4:23 healing every **d** and sickness among
     9:35 and healing every **d** and sickness.
    10: 1 and to heal every **d** and sickness.

DISEASED DISEASE

Mal   1: 8 you sacrifice lame or **d** animals,

DISEASES DISEASE

Dt   7:15 on you the horrible **d** you knew
    28:21 with **d** until he has destroyed you
Ps 103: 3 all your sins and heals all your **d**,
Mt   8:17 up our infirmities and bore our **d**."
Mk   3:10 those with **d** were pushing forward
Lk   9: 1 drive out all demons and to cure **d**,

DISFIGURE* DISFIGURED

Mt   6:16 for they **d** their faces to show others

DISFIGURED* DISFIGURE

Lev 21:18 is blind or lame, **d** or deformed;
Isa 52:14 his appearance was so **d** beyond

DISGRACE DISGRACED, DISGRACEFUL, DISGRACES

Ge 30:23 said, "God has taken away my **d**."
1Sa 17:26 and removes this **d** from Israel?
Ps 44:15 I live in **d** all day long, and my face
    52: 1 you who are a **d** in the eyes of God?
    74:21 Do not let the oppressed retreat in **d**;
Pr   6:33 Blows and **d** are his lot, and his
    11: 2 then comes **d**, but with humility
    19:26 is a child who brings shame and **d**.
Isa   4: 1 by your name. Take away our **d**!"
Eze 16:52 Bear your **d**, for you have furnished

Eze 16:52 be ashamed and bear your **d**, for you
    36:30 will no longer suffer **d** among
Mt   1:19 not want to expose her to public **d**,
Lk   1:25 and taken away my **d** among
Ac   5:41 worthy of suffering **d** for the Name.
1Co 11: 6 if it is a **d** for a woman to have her
    11:14 a man has long hair, it is a **d** to him,
1Ti   3: 7 so that he will not fall into **d**
Heb   6: 6 and subjecting him to public **d**.
    11:26 He regarded **d** for the sake of Christ
    13:13 the camp, bearing the **d** he bore.

DISGRACED DISGRACE

2Sa 13:22 because he had **d** his sister Tamar.
Ezr   9: 6 "I am too ashamed and **d**, my God,
Isa 45:17 you will never be put to shame or **d**,
Jer   2:26 "As a thief is **d** when he is caught,
     2:26 so the people of Israel are **d**—

DISGRACEFUL* DISGRACE

Pr 10: 5 sleeps during harvest is a **d** son.
    12: 4 a **d** wife is like decay in his bones.
    17: 2 servant will rule over a **d** son
Hos   4: 7 their glorious God for something **d**.
1Co 14:35 for it is **d** for a woman to speak

DISGRACES* DISGRACE

Lev 21: 9 a prostitute, she **d** her father;
Pr 28: 7 companion of gluttons **d** his father.
    29:15 child left undisciplined **d** its mother.

DISGUISE DISGUISED

Ge 38:14 herself with a veil to **d** herself,
2Ch 18:29 "I will enter the battle in **d**, but you
Pr 26:24 Enemies **d** themselves with their

DISGUISED DISGUISE

2Ch 35:22 **d** himself to engage him in battle.

DISH DISHES

Pr 19:24 A sluggard buries his hand in the **d**;
Mt 23:25 clean the outside of the cup and **d**,

DISHEARTENED HEART

1Th   5:14 encourage the **d**, help the weak,

DISHES DISH

Ex 25:29 make its plates and **d** of pure gold,
Ezr   1: 9 gold **d** 30 silver **d** 1,000 silver pans

DISHONEST*

Ex 18:21 trustworthy men who hate **d** gain—
Lev 19:35 " 'Do not use **d** standards
1Sa   8: 3 They turned aside after **d** gain
Pr 11: 1 The Lord detests **d** scales,
    13:11 **D** money dwindles away,
    20:23 and **d** scales do not please him.
    29:27 The righteous detest the **d**;
Jer 22:17 your heart are set only on **d** gain,
Eze 28:18 **d** trade you have desecrated your
Hos 12: 7 The merchant uses **d** scales
Am   8: 5 the price and cheating with **d** scales,
Mic   6:11 I acquit someone with **d** scales,
Lk 16: 8 commended the **d** manager because
    16:10 whoever is **d** with very little will also
         be **d** with much.

1Ti 3: 8 much wine, and not pursuing **d** gain.
Titus 1: 7 not violent, not pursuing **d** gain.
　　 1:11 and that for the sake of **d** gain.
1Pe 5: 2 not pursuing **d** gain, but eager

DISHONOR* DISHONORED, DISHONORS

Lev 18: 7 " 'Do not **d** your father by having
　　 18: 8 that would **d** your father.
　　 18:10 that would **d** you.
　　 18:14 " 'Do not **d** your father's brother
　　 18:16 that would **d** your brother.
　　 20:19 for that would **d** a close relative;
Dt 22:30 he must not **d** his father's bed.
Pr 30: 9 steal, and so **d** the name of my God.
Jer 14:21 do not **d** your glorious throne.
　　 20:11 their **d** will never be forgotten.
La 2: 2 its princes down to the ground in **d**.
Eze 22:10 are those who **d** their father's bed;
Jn 8:49 I honor my Father and you **d** me.
Ro 2:23 do you **d** God by breaking the law?
1Co 13: 5 It does not **d** others, it is not
　　 15:43 it is sown in **d**, it is raised in glory;
2Co 6: 8 through glory and **d**, bad report

DISHONORED* DISHONOR

Lev 20:11 his father's wife, he has **d** his father.
　　 20:17 He has **d** his sister and will be held
　　 20:20 with his aunt, he has **d** his uncle.
　　 20:21 act of impurity; he has **d** his brother.
Dt 21:14 her as a slave, since you have **d** her.
Ezr 4:14 not proper for us to see the king **d**,
1Co 4:10 You are honored, we are **d**!
Jas 2: 6 But you have **d** the poor. Is it not

DISHONORS* DISHONOR

Dt 27:16 is anyone who **d** their father
　　 27:20 wife, for he **d** his father's bed."
Job 20: 3 I hear a rebuke that **d** me, and my
Mic 7: 6 For a son **d** his father, a daughter
1Co 11: 4 with his head covered **d** his head.
　　 11: 5 her head uncovered **d** her head—

DISILLUSIONMENT*

Ps 7:14 trouble and gives birth to **d**.

DISMAYED

1Sa 17:11 and all the Israelites were **d**
Isa 41:10 do not be **d**, for I am your God.

DISOBEDIENCE* DISOBEY

Jos 22:22 in rebellion or **d** to the LORD,
Jer 43: 7 So they entered Egypt in **d**
Ro 5:19 just as through the **d** of the one man
　　 11:30 received mercy as a result of their **d**,
　　 11:32 has bound everyone over to **d** so
2Co 10: 6 be ready to punish every act of **d**,
Heb 2: 2 and **d** received its just punishment,
　　 4: 6 did not go in because of their **d**,
　　 4:11 by following their example of **d**.

DISOBEDIENT* DISOBEY

Ne 9:26 they were **d** and rebelled against
Lk 1:17 and the **d** to the wisdom
Ac 26:19 I was not **d** to the vision

Ro 10:21 long I have held out my hands to a **d**
　　 11:30 were at one time **d** to God have now
　　 11:31 so they too have now become **d**
Eph 2: 2 is now at work in those who are **d**.
　　 5: 6 wrath comes on those who are **d**.
　　 5:12 to mention what the **d** do in secret.
2Ti 3: 2 proud, abusive, **d** to their parents,
Titus 1: 6 to the charge of being wild and **d**.
　　 1:16 **d** and unfit for doing anything good.
　　 3: 3 At one time we too were foolish, **d**,
Heb 11:31 not killed with those who were **d**.
1Pe 3:20 to those who were **d** long ago

DISOBEY* DISOBEDIENCE, DISOBEDIENT, DISOBEYED, DISOBEYING, DISOBEYS

Dt 11:28 the curse if you **d** the commands
2Ch 24:20 'Why do you **d** the LORD's
Est 3: 3 "Why do you **d** the king's
Jer 42:13 and so **d** the LORD your God,
Ro 1:30 of doing evil; they **d** their parents;
1Pe 2: 8 because they **d** the message—

DISOBEYED* DISOBEY

Nu 14:22 in the wilderness but who **d** me
　　 27:14 Zin, both of you **d** my command
Jdg 2: 2 Yet you have **d** me. Why have you
Ne 9:29 arrogant and **d** your commands.
Isa 24: 5 they have **d** the laws,
Jer 43: 4 and all the people **d** the LORD's
Lk 15:29 for you and never **d** your orders.
Heb 3:18 enter his rest if not to those who **d**?

DISOBEYING* DISOBEY

Nu 14:41 said, "Why are you **d** the LORD's

DISOBEYS* DISOBEY

Eze 33:12 'If someone who is righteous **d**,

DISORDER*

Job 10:22 of utter darkness and **d**, where even
1Co 14:33 For God is not a God of **d**
2Co 12:20 slander, gossip, arrogance and **d**.
Jas 3:16 there you find **d** and every evil

DISOWN DISOWNED, DISOWNS

Pr 30: 9 I may have too much and **d** you
Mt 10:33 I will **d** before my Father in heaven.
　　 26:35 to die with you, I will never **d** you."
Mk 14:30 twice you yourself will **d** me three
2Ti 2:12 If we **d** him, he will also **d** us;

DISOWNED* DISOWN

Lk 12: 9 others will be **d** before the angels
Ac 3:13 and you **d** him before Pilate,
　　 3:14 You **d** the Holy and Righteous One

DISOWNS DISOWN

Lk 12: 9 whoever **d** me before others will be

DISPERSE DISPERSES

Eze 12:15 when I **d** them among the nations

DISPERSES* DISPERSE

Dt 30: 1 LORD your God **d** you among
Job 12:23 he enlarges nations, and **d** them.

DISPLACES*
Pr   30:23 and a servant who **d** her mistress.

DISPLAY DISPLAYED, DISPLAYS
Ps   22:17 All my bones are on **d**;
Isa   49: 3 in whom I will **d** my splendor."
Eze   28:22 and among you I will **d** my glory.
       39:21 "I will **d** my glory among
Ro   9:17 that I might **d** my power in you
1Co   4: 9 God has put us apostles on **d**
1Ti   1:16 Christ Jesus might **d** his immense

DISPLAYED DISPLAY
Ex   14:31 the LORD **d** against the Egyptians,
Jn   9: 3 the works of God might be **d** in him.

DISPLAYS* DISPLAY
Ps   7:11 a God who **d** his wrath every day.
Pr   14:29 one who is quick-tempered **d** folly.
Isa 42:23 Jacob, he **d** his glory in Israel.
2Co   4: 4 the gospel that **d** the glory of Christ,
2Th   2: 9 He will use all sorts of **d** of power

DISPLEASE DISPLEASED
Nu   11:11 What have I done to **d** you that you
1Th   2:15 They **d** God and are hostile

DISPLEASED DISPLEASE
2Sa 11:27 thing David had done **d** the LORD.
Isa 59:15 and was **d** that there was no justice.

DISPUTABLE* DISPUTE
Ro   14: 1 without quarreling over **d** matters.

DISPUTE DISPUTABLE, DISPUTES,
     DISPUTING
Job   9: 3 Though they wished to **d** with him,
Pr   17:14 the matter before a **d** breaks out.
Lk   22:24 A **d** also arose among them as
Ac   15: 2 Barnabas into sharp **d** and debate
1Co   6: 1 If any of you has a **d** with another,

DISPUTES DISPUTE
Pr   18:18 Casting the lot settles **d** and keeps
Isa   2: 4 and will settle **d** for many peoples.
1Co   6: 4 if you have **d** about such matters,

DISPUTING* DISPUTE
1Ti   2: 8 up holy hands without anger or **d**.
Jude 1: 9 when he was **d** with the devil

DISQUALIFIED* DISQUALIFY
1Co   9:27 I myself will not be **d** for the prize.

DISQUALIFY* DISQUALIFIED
Col   2:18 and the worship of angels **d** you.

DISREGARD* DISREGARDED,
     DISREGARDS
Pr   1:25 since you **d** all my advice and do
       8:33 instruction and be wise; do not **d** it.
      15:32 Those who **d** discipline despise

DISREGARDED* DISREGARD
Isa 40:27 my cause is **d** by my God"?

DISREGARDS* DISREGARD
Pr   13:18 Whoever **d** discipline comes

DISREPUTE*
2Pe   2: 2 will bring the way of truth into **d**.

DISRUPTING*
Titus 1:11 they are **d** whole households

DISSENSION* DISSENSIONS
Ro   13:13 debauchery, not in **d** and jealousy.

DISSENSIONS* DISSENSION
Gal   5:20 of rage, selfish ambition, **d**,

DISSOLVED*
Isa 34: 4 All the stars in the sky will be **d**

DISTANCE DISTANT
Ex   2: 4 at a **d** to see what would happen
       33: 7 it outside the camp some **d** away,
Dt   32:52 you will see the land only from a **d**;
Mk   14:54 Peter followed him at a **d**,
       15:40 women were watching from a **d**.
Heb 11:13 them and welcomed them from a **d**,

DISTANT DISTANCE
Jos   9: 6 "We have come from a **d** country;
Isa 49: 1 hear this, you **d** nations:
       66:19 to the **d** islands that have not heard
Jer   5:15 am bringing a **d** nation against you—
Zep   2:11 **D** nations will bow down to him,

DISTINCTION
Ex   8:23 I will make a **d** between my people

DISTINGUISH DISTINGUISHING
Lev 10:10 so that you can **d** between the holy
1Ki   3: 9 and to **d** between right and wrong.
Heb   5:14 have trained themselves to **d** good

DISTINGUISHING DISTINGUISH
1Co 12:10 to another **d** between spirits,

DISTORT*
Jer   23:36 So you **d** the words of the living
Mic   3: 9 despise justice and **d** all that is right;
Ac   20:30 **d** the truth in order to draw away
2Co   4: 2 nor do we **d** the word of God.
2Pe   3:16 ignorant and unstable people **d**,

DISTRACTED*
Lk   10:40 Martha was **d** by all the preparations

DISTRESS DISTRESSED,
     DISTRESSES
Jdg   2:15 They were in great **d**.
2Sa 22: 7 "In my **d** I called to the LORD;
2Ch 15: 4 in their **d** they turned to the LORD,
Ne   9:37 as they please. We are in great **d**.
Est   4: 4 about Mordecai, she was in great **d**.
Ps   18: 6 In my **d** I called to the LORD;
       77: 2 When I was in **d**, I sought the Lord;
       81: 7 In your **d** you called and I rescued
       86: 7 When I am in **d**, I call to you,
      107: 6 and he delivered them from their **d**.
      116: 3 I was overcome by **d** and sorrow.

Ps 120: 1 I call on the LORD in my **d**,
Jnh 2: 2 "In my **d** I called to the LORD,
Mt 24:21 For then there will be great **d**,
Jas 1:27 and widows in their **d** and to keep

DISTRESSED DISTRESS
Isa 63: 9 In all their distress he too was **d**,
Mk 14:33 and he began to be deeply **d**
Ro 14:15 sister is **d** because of what you eat,

DISTRESSES* DISTRESS
2Co 6: 4 in troubles, hardships and **d**;

DISTRIBUTE DISTRIBUTED, DISTRIBUTION
Nu 33:54 **D** the land by lot, according to your
33:54 **D** it according to your ancestral
Eze 47:21 are to **d** this land among yourselves

DISTRIBUTED DISTRIBUTE
Jos 18:10 there he **d** the land to the Israelites
Heb 2: 4 of the Holy Spirit **d** according to his

DISTRIBUTION* DISTRIBUTE
Ac 6: 1 overlooked in the daily **d** of food.

DISTURBANCE* DISTURBED
Ac 19:23 time there arose a great **d**
24:18 me, nor was I involved in any **d**.

DISTURBED DISTURBANCE
1Sa 28:15 "Why have you **d** me by bringing
Ps 42: 5 Why so **d** within me?
Da 7:15 that passed through my mind **d** me.
Ac 4: 2 They were greatly **d** because
15:24 without our authorization and **d** you,

DIVIDE DIVIDED, DIVIDING, DIVISION, DIVISIONS, DIVISIVE
Ex 14:16 hand over the sea to **d** the water so
Ps 22:18 They **d** my clothes among them
Isa 53:12 he will **d** the spoils with the strong,
Lk 12:13 tell my brother to **d** the inheritance
Jude 1:19 These are the people who **d** you,

DIVIDED DIVIDE
Ex 14:21 it into dry land. The waters were **d**,
Lev 11: 3 eat any animal that has a **d** hoof
Jos 14: 5 So the Israelites **d** the land, just as
2Ki 2: 8 The water **d** to the right
Ne 9:11 You **d** the sea before them,
Isa 63:12 hand, who **d** the waters before them,
Da 5:28 Your kingdom is **d** and given
Mt 12:25 "Every kingdom **d** against itself
12:25 or household **d** against itself will not
Lk 11:18 If Satan is **d** against himself,
23:34 they **d** up his clothes by casting lots.
1Co 1:13 Is Christ **d**? Was Paul crucified

DIVIDING DIVIDE
Jos 19:51 And so they finished **d** the land.
Jn 19:23 his clothes, **d** them into four shares,
Eph 2:14 the barrier, the **d** wall of hostility,
Heb 4:12 it penetrates even to **d** soul

DIVINATION DIVINATIONS, DIVINE, DIVINER, DIVINERS
Ge 44: 5 drinks from and also uses for **d**?
Lev 19:26 " 'Do not practice **d** or seek
Nu 23:23 There is no **d** against Jacob, no evil
Dt 18:10 the fire, who practices **d** or sorcery,
1Sa 15:23 For rebellion is like the sin of **d**,
Eze 13:23 see false visions or practice **d**.

DIVINATIONS DIVINATION
Jer 14:14 prophesying to you false visions, **d**,
Eze 13: 6 visions are false and their **d** a lie.

DIVINE DIVINATION
Isa 35: 4 with **d** retribution he will come
Ro 1:20 his eternal power and **d** nature—
9: 4 theirs the **d** glory, the covenants,
2Co 10: 4 they have **d** power to demolish
2Pe 1: 3 His **d** power has given us everything

DIVINER* DIVINATION
Isa 3: 2 and the prophet, the **d** and the elder,
Da 2:27 or **d** can explain to the king

DIVINERS DIVINATION
Isa 44:25 false prophets and makes fools of **d**,
Jer 29: 8 and **d** among you deceive you.
Zec 10: 2 deceitfully, **d** see visions that lie;

DIVISION DIVIDE
Lk 12:51 peace on earth? No, I tell you, but **d**.
1Co 12:25 there should be no **d** in the body,

DIVISIONS DIVIDE
Ex 12:41 day, all the LORD's **d** left Egypt.
Nu 1: 3 according to their **d** all the men
1Ch 23: 6 the Levites into **d** corresponding
Ro 16:17 to watch out for those who cause **d**
1Co 1:10 and that there be no **d** among you,
11:18 as a church, there are **d** among you,

DIVISIVE* DIVIDE
Titus 3:10 Warn a **d** person once,

DIVORCE* DIVORCED, DIVORCES
Dt 22:19 he must not **d** her as long as he
22:29 He can never **d** her as long as he
24: 1 and he writes her a certificate of **d**,
24: 3 her and writes her a certificate of **d**,
Isa 50: 1 is your mother's certificate of **d**
Jer 3: 8 faithless Israel her certificate of **d**
Mt 1:19 he had in mind to **d** her quietly.
5:31 must give her a certificate of **d**.'
19: 3 for a man to **d** his wife for any
19: 7 a man give his wife a certificate of **d**
19: 8 to **d** your wives because your hearts
Mk 10: 2 it lawful for a man to **d** his wife?"
10: 4 a man to write a certificate of **d**
1Co 7:11 And a husband must not **d** his wife.
7:12 to live with him, he must not **d** her.
7:13 to live with her, she must not **d** him.

DIVORCED* DIVORCE
Lev 21: 7 or **d** from their husbands,
21:14 not marry a widow, a **d** woman,
22:13 daughter becomes a widow or is **d**,

Nu 30: 9 or **d** woman will be binding on her.
Dt 24: 4 then her first husband, who **d** her,
1Ch 8: 8 after he had **d** his wives Hushim
Eze 44:22 not marry widows or **d** women;
Mt   5:32 who marries a **d** woman commits
Lk 16:18 who marries a **d** woman commits

DIVORCES* DIVORCE

Jer   3: 1 "If a man **d** his wife and she leaves
Mal   2:16 man who hates and **d** his wife,"
Mt   5:31 'Anyone who **d** his wife must give
      5:32 tell you that anyone who **d** his wife,
     19: 9 tell you that anyone who **d** his wife,
Mk 10:11 "Anyone who **d** his wife
     10:12 if she **d** her husband and marries
Lk 16:18 "Anyone who **d** his wife

DO DOES, DOING, DONE

Ge   4: 7 If you **d** what is right, will you not
     18:25 be it from you to **d** such a thing—
     18:25 the Judge of all the earth **d** right?"
Ex   19: 8 "We will **d** everything the LORD
     20:10 On it you shall not **d** any work,
Lev 18: 3 You must not **d** as they **d** in Egypt,
Nu   9:11 they are to **d** it on the fourteenth day
Jos   1: 8 be careful to **d** everything written
2Ki 17:15 ordered them, "**D** not **d** as they **d**."
Ps   37: 3 Trust in the LORD and **d** good;
    143:10 Teach me to **d** your will, for you are
Pr   4:23 for everything you **d** flows from it.
     16: 3 to the LORD whatever you **d**,
     31:29 "Many women **d** noble things,
Ecc   2:24 A person can **d** nothing better than
Jer 22: 3 **D** what is just and right.
     22: 3 **D** no wrong or violence
Eze 16:30 when you **d** all these things,
Mt   23: 3 careful to **d** everything they tell you.
     23: 3 But **d** not **d** what they **d**,
Mk   3: 4 to **d** good or to **d** evil, to save life
      6: 5 He could not **d** any miracles there,
Lk   6:31 **D** to others as you would have them **d**
Jn   6:28 "What must we **d** to **d** the works
      7:17 Anyone who chooses to **d** the will
Ac   16:30 "Sirs, what must I **d** to be saved?"
     22:10 " 'What shall I **d**, Lord?' I asked.
Ro   7:15 I **d** not understand what I **d**. For what
           I want to **d** I **d** not **d**,
Gal   6:10 let us **d** good to all people,
Eph   3:20 to **d** immeasurably more than all we
Col   3:17 And whatever you **d**,
      3:17 **d** it all in the name of the Lord
Heb   6: 9 things that have to **d** with salvation.
Jas   1:25 they will be blessed in what they **d**.
1Pe   3:11 must turn from evil and **d** good;

DO NOT FEAR See FEAR

DOCTOR

Mt   9:12 "It is not the healthy who need a **d**,
Col   4:14 the **d**, and Demas send greetings.

DOCTRINE* DOCTRINES

1Ti   1:10 else is contrary to the sound **d**
      4:16 Watch your life and **d** closely.
2Ti   4: 3 people will not put up with sound **d**.

Titus 1: 9 he can encourage others by sound **d**
       2: 1 what is appropriate to sound **d**.

DOCTRINES* DOCTRINE

1Ti   1: 3 not to teach false **d** any longer

DOE

Ge 49:21 "Naphtali is a **d** set free that bears
Pr   5:19 A loving **d**, a graceful deer—

DOEG*

Edomite; Saul's head shepherd; murdered 85 priests at Nob (1Sa 21:7; 22:6–23; Ps 52).

DOES DO

Dt   32: 4 A faithful God who **d** no wrong,
Ps   15: 5 Whoever **d** these things will never
    135: 6 The LORD **d** whatever pleases
    145:13 he promises and faithful in all he **d**.
Ecc   3:14 that everything God **d** will endure
Da   9:14 God is righteous in everything he **d**;
Zep   3: 5 her is righteous; he **d** no wrong.
Mk   3:35 Whoever **d** God's will is my brother
Jn   5:19 whatever the Father **d** the Son also **d**.
Ro   10: 5 "The person who **d** these things
Gal   3:12 "The person who **d** these things

DOG DOGS

Jdg   7: 5 their tongues as a **d** laps from those
1Sa 17:43 "Am I a **d**, that you come at me
Pr   26:11 As a **d** returns to its vomit, so fools
Ecc   9: 4 even a live **d** is better off than
2Pe   2:22 "A **d** returns to its vomit," and,

DOGS DOG

1Ki 21:19 In the place where **d** licked
     21:19 blood, **d** will lick up your blood—
2Ki   9:10 **d** will devour her on the plot
Ps   22:16 **D** surround me, a pack of villains
Isa 56:11 They are **d** with mighty appetites;
Mt   7: 6 "Do not give **d** what is sacred;
     15:26 bread and toss it to the **d**."
Php   3: 2 Watch out for those **d**,
Rev 22:15 Outside are the **d**, those who

DOING DO

Mk   11:28 authority are you **d** these things?"
1Pe   3:17 to suffer for **d** good than for **d** evil.

DOMINION

Job 25: 2 "**D** and awe belong to God;
Ps   22:28 for **d** belongs to the LORD and he
Da   4: 3 his **d** endures from generation
1Co 15:24 Father after he has destroyed all **d**,
Eph   1:21 power and **d**, and every name that is
Col   1:13 rescued us from the **d** of darkness

DONE DO

Ge   3:13 "What is this you have **d**?"
      4:10 LORD said, "What have you **d**?
Ex   18: 9 the good things the LORD had **d**
Est   6: 6 "What should be **d** for the man
Ps   46: 8 and see what the LORD has **d**,
     66: 5 Come and see what God has **d**,
     71:19 you who have **d** great things.
     98: 1 song, for he has **d** marvelous things;

Ps 105: 5 Remember the wonders he has **d**,
118:24 The Lᴏʀᴅ has **d** it this very day;
Pr 19:17 reward them for what they have **d**.
24:12 according to what they have **d**?
31:31 her for all that her hands have **d**,
Ecc 1: 9 what has been **d** will be **d** again;
8:17 then I saw all that God has **d**.
Isa 25: 1 you have **d** wonderful things,
Jer 50:29 for her deeds; do to her as she has **d**.
Eze 11:21 their own heads what they have **d**,
Joel 2:21 the Lᴏʀᴅ has **d** great things!
Ob 1:15 As you have **d**, it will be **d** to you;
Mic 6: 3 "My people, what have I **d** to you?
Mt 6:10 your will be **d**, on earth as it is
26:42 I drink it, may your will be **d**."
Lk 19:17 " 'Well **d**, my good servant!'
Jn 15: 7 you wish, and it will be **d** for you.
Ac 19:18 openly confessed what they had **d**.
Rev 16:17 from the throne, saying, "It is **d**!"
18: 6 her back double for what she has **d**.
20:12 what they had **d** as recorded
21: 6 He said to me: "It is **d**. I am

DONKEY DONKEY'S
Nu 22:30 The **d** said to Balaam, "Am I not your own **d**,
Zec 9: 9 lowly and riding on a **d**, on a colt, the foal of a **d**.
Mt 21: 5 gentle and riding on a **d**, and on a colt, the foal of a **d**.' "
2Pe 2:16 rebuked for his wrongdoing by a **d**—

DONKEY'S DONKEY
Nu 22:28 the Lᴏʀᴅ opened the **d** mouth,
Jdg 15:16 a **d** jawbone I have made donkeys

DOOMED
Ps 137: 8 Daughter Babylon, **d** to destruction,
Jn 17:12 None has been lost except the one **d**
2Th 2: 3 revealed, the man **d** to destruction.

DOOR DOORFRAME,
DOORFRAMES, DOORKEEPER,
DOORPOST, DOORS, DOORWAY
Ge 4: 7 is right, sin is crouching at your **d**;
19: 9 moved forward to break down the **d**.
Dt 15:17 it through his earlobe into the **d**,
Jdg 19:22 Pounding on the **d**, they shouted
Job 31:32 for my **d** was always open
Ps 141: 3 keep watch over the **d** of my lips.
Pr 5: 8 do not go near the **d** of her house,
9:14 She sits at the **d** of her house,
26:14 As a **d** turns on its hinges,
Mt 6: 6 close the **d** and pray to your Father,
7: 7 and the **d** will be opened to you.
Lk 13:24 effort to enter through the narrow **d**,
Ac 12:14 and exclaimed, "Peter is at the **d**!"
14:27 how he had opened a **d** of faith
1Co 16: 9 because a great **d** for effective work
2Co 2:12 that the Lord had opened a **d** for me,
Col 4: 3 God may open a **d** for our message,
Jas 5: 9 The Judge is standing at the **d**!
Rev 3: 8 I have placed before you an open **d**
3:20 I stand at the **d** and knock.

Rev 3:20 hears my voice and opens the **d**,
4: 1 before me was a **d** standing open

DOORFRAME DOOR, FRAME
Ex 12:23 sides of the **d** and will pass over

DOORFRAMES DOOR, FRAME
Dt 6: 9 Write them on the **d** of your houses

DOORKEEPER DOOR, KEEP
Ps 84:10 I would rather be a **d** in the house

DOORPOST DOOR, POSTS
Ex 21: 6 the **d** and pierce his ear with an awl.

DOORS DOOR
1Ki 6:31 to the inner sanctuary he made **d**
Ne 3: 1 dedicated it and set its **d** in place,
Ps 24: 7 you ancient **d**, that the King of glory
Mal 1:10 one of you would shut the temple **d**,
Jn 20:26 Though the **d** were locked,
Ac 5:19 of the Lord opened the **d** of the jail
16:26 At once all the prison **d** flew open,

DOORWAY DOOR, WAY
Ex 12:23 doorframe and will pass over that **d**,

DORCAS* TABITHA
Disciple, also known as Tabitha, whom Peter raised from the dead (Ac 9:36–43).

DOUBLE DOUBLE-EDGED,
DOUBLE-MINDED
Ex 22: 7 the thief, if caught, must pay back **d**.
1Sa 1: 5 he gave a **d** portion because he
2Ki 2: 9 "Let me inherit a **d** portion of your
Isa 40: 2 the Lᴏʀᴅ's hand **d** for all her sins.
61: 7 shame you will receive a **d** portion,
61: 7 so you will inherit a **d** portion
Hos 10:10 to put them in bonds for their **d** sin.
1Ti 5:17 church well are worthy of **d** honor,
Rev 18: 6 pay her back **d** for what she has
18: 6 Pour her a **d** portion from her own

DOUBLE-EDGED* DOUBLE,
EDGE
Jdg 3:16 Now Ehud had made a **d** sword
Ps 149: 6 and a **d** sword in their hands,
Pr 5: 4 is bitter as gall, sharp as a **d** sword.
Heb 4:12 Sharper than any **d** sword,
Rev 1:16 of his mouth was a sharp, **d** sword.
2:12 of him who has the sharp, **d** sword.

DOUBLE-MINDED* DOUBLE,
MIND
Ps 119:113 I hate **d** people, but I love your law.
Jas 1: 8 Such a person is **d** and unstable
4: 8 and purify your hearts, you **d**.

DOUBT DOUBTED, DOUBTING,
DOUBTS
Mt 14:31 faith," he said, "why did you **d**?"
21:21 if you have faith and do not **d**,
Mk 11:23 and does not **d** in their heart
Jas 1: 6 you must believe and not **d**,
Jude 1:22 Be merciful to those who **d**;

DOUBTED* DOUBT
Mt 28:17 they worshiped him; but some **d**.

DOUBTING* DOUBT
Jn 20:27 it into my side. Stop **d** and believe."

DOUBTS* DOUBT
Lk 24:38 and why do **d** rise in your minds?
Ro 14:23 whoever has **d** is condemned if they
Jas 1: 6 because the one who **d** is like

DOUGH
Ex 12:39 With the **d** the Israelites had brought
     12:39 The **d** was without yeast because
Lk 13:21 until it worked all through the **d**."
1Co 5: 6 yeast leavens the whole batch of **d**?
Gal 5: 9 through the whole batch of **d**."

DOVE DOVES
Ge 8: 8 he sent out a **d** to see if the water
Ps 55: 6 "Oh, that I had the wings of a **d**!
SS 5: 2 my darling, my **d**, my flawless one.
Hos 7:11 "Ephraim is like a **d**,
Mk 1:10 Spirit descending on him like a **d**.

DOVES DOVE
Lev 12: 8 she is to bring two **d** or two young
SS 4: 1 Your eyes behind your veil are **d**.
Isa 59:11 we moan mournfully like **d**.
Eze 7:16 Like **d** of the valleys, they will all
Mt 10:16 as snakes and as innocent as **d**.
     21:12 and the benches of those selling **d**.
Lk 2:24 "a pair of **d** or two young pigeons."

DOWN DOWNCAST, DOWNFALL
Ge 11: 5 the LORD came **d** to see the city
     18:21 that I will go **d** and see if what they
     46: 3 "Do not be afraid to go **d** to Egypt,
Ex 3: 8 So I have come **d** to rescue them
     19:11 that day the LORD will come **d**
     34: 5 the LORD came **d** in the cloud
Nu 11:25 the LORD came **d** in the cloud
2Sa 22:10 He parted the heavens and came **d**;
Ne 1: 3 The wall of Jerusalem is broken **d**,
     9:13 "You came **d** on Mount Sinai;
Ps 18:16 He reached **d** from on high and took
     23: 2 He makes me lie **d** in green
     113: 6 who stoops **d** to look on the heavens
Pr 5: 5 Her feet go **d** to death;
Ecc 3: 3 a time to tear **d** and a time to build,
Da 8:10 some of the starry host **d** to the earth
Mt 7:25 The rain came **d**, the streams rose,
Mk 6:40 So they sat **d** in groups of hundreds
     15:30 come **d** from the cross and save
Lk 4: 9 said, "throw yourself **d** from here.
Jn 6:41 bread that came **d** from heaven."
     10:11 The good shepherd lays **d** his life
Heb 1: 3 sins, he sat **d** at the right hand
     8: 1 who sat **d** at the right hand
     10:12 he sat **d** at the right hand of God,
     12: 2 sat **d** at the right hand of the throne
1Jn 3:16 Jesus Christ laid **d** his life for us.
     3:16 we ought to lay **d** our lives for our
Rev 3:12 which is coming **d** out of heaven
     12: 9 The great dragon was hurled **d**—

Rev 21: 2 coming **d** out of heaven from God,
     21:10 coming **d** out of heaven from God.

DOWNCAST DOWN, CAST
1Sa 1:18 and her face was no longer **d**.
Ps 42: 5 Why, my soul, are you **d**?
La 3:20 them, and my soul is **d** within me.
Lk 24:17 They stood still, their faces **d**.
2Co 7: 6 who comforts the **d**, comforted us

DOWNFALL DOWN, FALL
2Ch 28:23 But they were his **d** and the **d** of all
Pr 18:12 Before a **d** the heart is haughty,
Hos 14: 1 Your sins have been your **d**!

DRAGON
Rev 12: 3 an enormous red **d** with seven heads
     13: 2 The **d** gave the beast his power
     16:13 they came out of the mouth of the **d**,
     20: 2 He seized the **d**, that ancient

DRANK DRINK
Ge 9:21 When he **d** some of its wine,
Ex 24:11 they saw God, and they ate and **d**.
Dt 9: 9 I ate no bread and **d** no water.
Jer 51: 7 The nations **d** her wine;
Da 5: 4 As they **d** the wine, they praised
Ob 1:16 Just as you **d** on my holy hill, so all
Mk 14:23 it to them, and they all **d** from it.
1Co 10: 4 and **d** the same spiritual drink;
     10: 4 for they **d** from the spiritual rock

DRAW DRAWING, DRAWS
Ge 24:11 time the women go out to **d** water.
Ex 2:16 and they came to **d** water and fill
1Sa 31: 4 "**D** your sword and run me through,
Isa 12: 3 joy you will **d** water from the wells
Zep 3: 2 she does not **d** near to her God.
Mt 26:52 "for all who **d** the sword will die
Jn 2: 8 "Now **d** some out and take it
     4: 7 Samaritan woman came to **d** water,
     12:32 earth, will **d** all people to myself."
Heb 7:19 by which we **d** near to God.
     10:22 let us **d** near to God with a sincere

DRAWING DRAW
Lk 21:28 because your redemption is **d** near."

DRAWS DRAW
Isa 51: 5 My righteousness **d** near speedily,
Jer 17: 5 who **d** strength from mere flesh
Jn 6:44 the Father who sent me **d** them,

DREAD DREADED, DREADFUL
Ex 1:12 Egyptians came to **d** the Israelites
Nu 22: 3 Moab was filled with **d** because
Ps 53: 5 overwhelmed with **d**, where there was
     nothing to **d**.
Isa 8:13 to fear, he is the one you are to **d**.

DREADED DREAD
Dt 28:60 all the diseases of Egypt that you **d**,
Job 3:25 what I **d** has happened to me.

DREADFUL DREAD
Joel 2:11 day of the LORD is great; it is **d**.

Mal   4: 5 and **d** day of the LORD comes.
Mt   24:19 How **d** it will be in those days
Heb 10:31 It is a **d** thing to fall into the hands

DREAM DREAMED, DREAMER, DREAMS

Ge   20: 3 came to Abimelek in a **d** one night
       28:12 He had a **d** in which he saw
       31:11 angel of God said to me in the **d**,
       37: 5 Joseph had a **d**, and when he told it
       40: 5 had a **d** the same night, and each **d**
       41: 1 years had passed, Pharaoh had a **d**:
Jdg   7:13 as a man was telling a friend his **d**.
1Ki   3: 5 to Solomon during the night in a **d**,
Ecc   5: 3 A **d** comes when there are many
Jer   23:28 Let the prophet who has a **d** recount
              the **d**,
Da   2: 3 "I have had a **d** that troubles me
       4: 5 I had a **d** that made me afraid.
       7: 1 Daniel had a **d**, and visions passed
       7: 1 wrote down the substance of his **d**.
Joel   2:28 your old men will **d** dreams,
Mt   1:20 of the Lord appeared to him in a **d**
       2:12 having been warned in a **d** not to go
       2:13 the Lord appeared to Joseph in a **d**.
       2:19 the Lord appeared in a **d** to Joseph
       2:22 Having been warned in a **d**,
       27:19 a great deal today in a **d** because
Ac   2:17 visions, your old men will **d** dreams.

DREAMED* DREAM

Ps   126: 1 of Zion, we were like those who **d**.
Da   2: 2 to tell him what he had **d**.

DREAMER* DREAM

Ge   37:19 "Here comes that **d**!" they said
Dt   13: 3 to the words of that prophet or **d**.
      13: 5 **d** must be put to death for inciting
      13: 5 **d** tried to turn you from the way

DREAMS DREAM

Nu   12: 6 in visions, I speak to them in **d**.
Dt   13: 1 or one who foretells by **d**,
1Sa 28: 6 LORD did not answer him by **d**

DREGS*

Ps   75: 8 the earth drink it down to its very **d**.
Isa 51:17 who have drained to its **d** the goblet
Jer 48:11 like wine left on its **d**, not poured
Zep   1:12 who are like wine left on its **d**,

DRESS DRESSED

Ex   40:13 **d** Aaron in the sacred garments,
1Ti   2: 9 also want the women to **d** modestly,

DRESSED DRESS

Ex   20:25 do not build it with **d** stones, for you
1Sa 17:38 Then Saul **d** David in his own tunic.
Zec   3: 3 Now Joshua was **d** in filthy clothes
Lk   7:25 out to see? A man **d** in fine clothes?
      8:35 Jesus' feet, **d** and in his right mind;
      12:27 in all his splendor was **d** like one
Rev   3: 4 They will walk with me, **d** in white,
      4: 4 They were **d** in white and had
      15: 6 They were **d** in clean, shining linen

Rev 17: 4 The woman was **d** in purple
      19:13 He is **d** in a robe dipped in blood,
      21: 2 prepared as a bride beautifully **d**

DRIED DRY

Ge   8:13 the water had **d** up from the earth.
Jos   5: 1 coast heard how the LORD had **d**
Ps   22:15 My mouth is **d** up like a potsherd,
      106: 9 rebuked the Red Sea, and it **d** up;
Isa 51:10 Was it not you who **d** up the sea,
Rev 16:12 its water was **d** up to prepare

DRIFT*

Ac   27:32 held the lifeboat and let it **d** away.
Heb   2: 1 heard, so that we do not **d** away.

DRINK DRANK, DRINKING, DRINKS, DRUNK, DRUNKARD, DRUNKARD'S, DRUNKARDS, DRUNKENNESS

Ge   19:33 night they got their father to **d** wine,
Ex   15:23 they could not **d** its water because it
      15:25 and the water became fit to **d**.
      17: 1 was no water for the people to **d**.
Lev 10: 9 your sons are not to **d** wine or other
              fermented **d** whenever you go
Nu   4: 7 bowls, and the jars for **d** offerings;
      6: 3 from wine or other fermented **d**.
      6: 3 They must not **d** grape juice or eat
      20: 5 And there is no water to **d**!"
Jdg   7: 5 from those who kneel down to **d**."
      13: 4 Now see to it that you **d** no wine
2Sa 23:15 someone would get me a **d** of water
Ps   50:13 of bulls or **d** the blood of goats?
Pr   5:15 **D** water from your own cistern,
      7:18 let's **d** deeply of love till morning;
      23:20 not join those who **d** too much wine
Ecc   2:24 do nothing better than to eat and **d**
      9: 7 and **d** your wine with a joyful heart,
Jer   8:14 and given us poisoned water to **d**
      25:15 the nations to whom I send you **d** it.
Eze 23:32 "You will **d** your sister's cup, a cup
Da   1:12 but vegetables to eat and water to **d**.
Ob   1:16 they will **d** and **d** and be as if they
Mt   20:22 "Can you **d** the cup I am going to **d**?"
      26:27 them, saying, "**D** from it, all of you.
      27:34 There they offered Jesus wine to **d**,
      27:34 but after tasting it, he refused to **d** it.
Lk   12:19 eat, **d** and be merry.' '
Jn   7:37 who is thirsty come to me and **d**.
      18:11 Shall I not **d** the cup the Father has
1Co 10: 4 and drank the same spiritual **d**;
      10:21 You cannot **d** the cup of the Lord
      12:13 were all given the one Spirit to **d**.
Php   2:17 out like a **d** offering on the sacrifice
Col   2:16 judge you by what you eat or **d**,
2Ti   4: 6 being poured out like a **d** offering,
Heb   9:10 are only a matter of food and **d**
Rev 14: 8 all the nations **d** the maddening
      14:10 too, will **d** the wine of God's fury,
      16: 6 them blood to **d** as they deserve."

DRINK OFFERING Ge 35:14; Ex 29:40, 41;
30:9; Lev 23:13; Nu 6:17; 15:5, 7, 10, 24;

28:7, 7, 8, 9, 10, 14, 15, 24; 29:16, 22, 25, 28, 31,
34, 38; 2Ki 16:13, 15; Php 2:17; 2Ti 4:6

DRINK OFFERINGS Ex 37:16; Lev 23:18, 37;
Nu 4:7; 6:15; 28:31; 29:6, 11, 18, 19, 21, 24, 27, 30,
33, 37, 39; Dt 32:38; 1Ch 29:21; 2Ch 29:35; Ezr
7:17; Isa 57:6; Jer 7:18; 19:13; 32:29; 44:17, 18, 19,
19, 25; 52:19; Eze 20:28; 45:17; Joel 1:9, 13; 2:14

DRINKING DRINK
1Sa   1:15 I have not been **d** wine or beer;
Mt   11:19 The Son of Man came eating and **d**,
Lk   17:27 People were eating, **d**,
Ro   14:17 God is not a matter of eating and **d**,
1Ti   5:23 Stop **d** only water, and use a little

DRINKS DRINK
Isa   5:22 wine and champions at mixing **d**,
Am   4: 1 your husbands, "Bring us some **d**!"
Jn   4:13 "Everyone who **d** this water will be
        6:54 and **d** my blood has eternal life,
1Co 11:27 bread or **d** the cup of the Lord

DRIP* DRIPPING
Pr   5: 3 of the adulterous woman **d** honey,
Joel   3:18 day the mountains will **d** new wine,
Am   9:13 New wine will **d**

DRIPPING DRIP
Pr   19:13 wife is like the constant **d** of a leaky
      27:15 A quarrelsome wife is like the **d**

DRIVE DRIVEN, DRIVER, DRIVES,
DRIVING, DROVE
Ex   6: 1 my mighty hand he will **d** them
      23:30 little I will **d** them out before you,
Nu   33:52 **d** out all the inhabitants of the land
Dt   7:17 How can we **d** them out?"
Jos   13:13 But the Israelites did not **d**
      23:13 LORD your God will no longer **d**
Jdg   1:19 but they were unable to **d** the people
Pr   22:10 **D** out the mocker, and out goes
Isa   22:23 I will **d** him like a peg into a firm
Jer   49: 2 Israel will **d** out those who drove
Mt   10: 1 gave them authority to **d** out impure
Lk   11:19 Now if I **d** out demons
      11:19 do your followers **d** them out?
      19:45 he began to **d** out those who were
Jn   6:37 comes to me I will never **d** away.

DRIVEN DRIVE
Ex   12:39 yeast because they had been **d**
Dt   12:29 But when you have **d** them
Jn   12:31 prince of this world will be **d** out.

DRIVER DRIVE
Ex   15: 1 and **d** he has hurled into the sea.

DRIVES DRIVE
Mt   12:26 If Satan **d** out Satan, he is divided
1Jn   4:18 But perfect love **d** out fear,

DRIVING DRIVE
Ex   14:25 so that they had difficulty **d**.
Ac   26:24 great learning is **d** you insane."

DROP DROPS
Pr   17:14 so **d** the matter before a dispute
Isa   40:15 Surely the nations are like a **d**
Zec   8:12 and the heavens will **d** their dew.

DROPS DROP
Lk   22:44 his sweat was like **d** of blood falling

DROSS
Ps 119:119 of the earth you discard like **d**;
Pr   25: 4 Remove the **d** from the silver,
Isa   1:22 Your silver has become **d**,
Eze   22:18 of Israel have become **d** to me;

DROUGHT
Dt   28:22 with scorching heat and **d**,
Jer   17: 8 It has no worries in a year of **d**
Hag   1:11 I called for a **d** on the fields

DROVE DRIVE
Nu   11:31 LORD and **d** quail in from the sea.
Jos   24:18 the LORD **d** out before us all
Ps   44: 2 your hand you **d** out the nations
Jer   49: 2 will drive out those who **d** her out,"
Mt   8:16 and he **d** out the spirits with a word
      21:12 and **d** out all who were buying

DROWN DROWNED
Mk   4:38 "Teacher, don't you care if we **d**?"

DROWNED DROWN
Ex   15: 4 Pharaoh's officers are **d** in the Red
Mt   18: 6 and to be **d** in the depths of the sea.
Lk   8:33 steep bank into the lake and was **d**.
Heb 11:29 tried to do so, they were **d**.

DROWSINESS* DROWSY
Pr   23:21 poor, and **d** clothes them in rags.

DROWSY* DROWSINESS
Mt   25: 5 they all became **d** and fell asleep.

DRUNK DRINK
Ge   9:21 he became **d** and lay uncovered
Dt   32:42 I will make my arrows **d** with blood,
1Sa   1:13 Eli thought she was **d**
      25:36 He was in high spirits and very **d**.
2Sa   11:13 with him, and David made him **d**.
Isa   29: 9 be **d**, but not from wine, stagger,
Jer   51: 7 she made the whole earth **d**.
Na   3:11 You too will become **d**; you will go
Ac   2:15 These people are not **d**, as you
1Co 11:21 remains hungry and another gets **d**.
Eph   5:18 Do not get **d** on wine, which leads
Rev 17: 6 the woman was **d** with the blood
      18: 3 the nations have **d** the maddening

DRUNKARD DRINK
Isa   19:14 as a **d** staggers around in his vomit.
      24:20 The earth reels like a **d**, it sways
Mt   11:19 'Here is a glutton and a **d**, a friend
1Co   5:11 idolater or slanderer, a **d** or swindler.

DRUNKARD'S* DRINK
Pr   26: 9 a thornbush in a **d** hand is a proverb

DRUNKARDS DRINK

Pr 23:21 for **d** and gluttons become poor,
Isa 28: 1 the pride of Ephraim's **d**,
1Co 6:10 the greedy nor **d** nor slanderers nor

DRUNKENNESS* DRINK

Ecc 10:17 for strength and not for **d**.
Jer 13:13 fill with **d** all who live in this land,
Eze 23:33 You will be filled with **d**
Lk 21:34 **d** and the anxieties of life,
Ro 13:13 not in carousing and **d**, not in sexual
Gal 5:21 and envy; **d**, orgies, and the like.
1Ti 3: 3 not given to **d**, not violent
Titus 1: 7 not given to **d**, not violent,
1Pe 4: 3 living in debauchery, lust, **d**, orgies,

DRY DRIED

Ge 1: 9 place, and let **d** ground appear."
    7:22 Everything on **d** land that had
Ex 14:16 can go through the sea on **d** ground.
Jos 3:17 the Jordan and stood on **d** ground,
    3:17 completed the crossing on **d** ground.
Jdg 6:37 on the fleece and all the ground is **d**,
2Ki 2: 8 of them crossed over on **d** ground.
Ps 66: 6 He turned the sea into **d** land,
    95: 5 it, and his hands formed the **d** land.
Isa 53: 2 and like a root out of **d** ground.
Eze 17:24 I **d** up the green tree and make the **d**
    37: 4 bones and say to them, '**D** bones,
Jnh 2:10 and it vomited Jonah onto **d** land.
Heb 11:29 through the Red Sea as on **d** land;

DUE

Dt 32:35 In **d** time their foot will slip;
1Ch 16:29 to the LORD the glory **d** his name;
Ps 90:11 is as great as the fear that is your **d**.
Pr 3:27 good from those to whom it is **d**,
    11:31 If the righteous receive their **d**
Mal 1: 6 a father, where is the honor **d** me?
    1: 6 master, where is the respect **d** me?"
Ro 1:27 in themselves the **d** penalty for their
1Pe 5: 6 that he may lift you up in **d** time.

DUG DIG

Ps 57: 6 They **d** a pit in my path—
Isa 5: 2 He **d** it up and cleared it of stones
Jer 18:20 Yet they have **d** a pit for me.

DULL

Isa 6:10 make their ears **d** and close their
    59: 1 to save, nor his ear too **d** to hear.
Mk 7:18 "Are you so **d**?" he asked.
2Co 3:14 But their minds were made **d**,

DUNGEON

Ge 40:15 to deserve being put in a **d**."
Isa 42: 7 release from the **d** those who sit
Jer 37:16 was put into a vaulted cell in a **d**,

DUST

Ge 2: 7 a man from the **d** of the ground
    3:14 you will eat **d** all the days of your
    3:19 for **d** you are and to **d** you will
    13:16 I will make your offspring like the **d**
    13:16 so that if anyone could count the **d**,

Ge 28:14 Your descendants will be like the **d**
Nu 23:10 Who can count the **d** of Jacob
1Sa 2: 8 He raises the poor from the **d**
Job 42: 6 myself and repent in **d** and ashes."
Ps 22:15 you lay me in the **d** of death.
    103:14 he remembers that we are **d**.
Ecc 3:20 all come from **d**, and to **d** all return.
Isa 65:25 ox, and **d** will be the serpent's food.
Mt 10:14 town and shake the **d** off your feet.
Ac 13:51 So they shook the **d** off their feet as
1Co 15:47 first man was of the **d** of the earth;
Rev 18:19 They will throw **d** on their heads,

DUTIES DUTY

1Ki 3: 7 do not know how to carry out my **d**.
2Ti 4: 5 discharge all the **d** of your ministry.

DUTY DUTIES

Ge 38: 8 wife and fulfill your **d** to her as
Ecc 12:13 for this is the **d** of all mankind.
Ac 23: 1 I have fulfilled my **d** to God in all
1Co 7: 3 husband should fulfill his marital **d**

DWELL DWELLING, DWELLINGS, DWELLS, DWELT

Ex 25: 8 for me, and I will **d** among them.
2Sa 7: 5 the one to build me a house to **d** in?
1Ki 8:27 "But will God really **d** on earth?
Ezr 6:12 who has caused his Name to **d** there,
Ps 23: 6 I will **d** in the house of the LORD
    37: 3 **d** in the land and enjoy safe pasture.
    61: 4 I long to **d** in your tent forever
Pr 8:12 wisdom, **d** together with prudence;
Isa 26: 5 He humbles those who **d** on high,
    33:14 of us can **d** with the consuming fire?
    33:14 us can **d** with everlasting burning?"
    43:18 do not **d** on the past.
Jn 5:38 nor does his word **d** in you, for you
Ro 7:18 that good itself does not **d** in me,
Eph 3:17 Christ may **d** in your hearts through
Col 1:19 to have all his fullness **d** in him,
    3:16 of Christ **d** among you richly as you
Rev 12:12 heavens and you who **d** in them!

DWELLING DWELL

Lev 26:11 I will put my **d** place among you,
Dt 26:15 your holy **d** place, and bless your
1Ki 8:30 Hear from heaven, your **d** place,
Ps 90: 1 have been our **d** place throughout all
Isa 26:21 of his **d** to punish the people
La 2: 6 has laid waste his **d** like a garden;
Eze 37:27 My **d** place will be with them;
Mic 1: 3 LORD is coming from his **d** place;
Jn 1:14 flesh and made his **d** among us.
2Co 5: 2 clothed instead with our heavenly **d**,
Eph 2:22 built together to become a **d**
Rev 21: 3 God's **d** place is now among

DWELLINGS DWELL

Lk 16: 9 will be welcomed into eternal **d**.

DWELLS DWELL

Ps 46: 4 holy place where the Most High **d**.
    91: 1 Whoever **d** in the shelter
Isa 8:18 Almighty, who **d** on Mount Zion.

1Co   3:16 that God's Spirit **d** in your midst?
Joel 3:21 I will not." The Lᴏʀᴅ **d** in Zion!

DWELT DWELL
Dt   33:16 of him who **d** in the burning bush.
1Ch 17: 5 I have not **d** in a house from the day

DYING DIE
Jn   11:37 man have kept this man from **d**?"
Ro   7: 6 now, by **d** to what once bound us,
2Co   6: 9 **d**, and yet we live on;

DYNASTY*
1Sa 25:28 God will certainly make a lasting **d**
1Ki   2:24 and has founded a **d** for me as he
      11:38 I will build you a **d** as enduring as

E

EACH
Ge   1:24 animals, **e** according to its kind."
      49:28 giving **e** the blessing appropriate
Ex   12: 3 the tenth day of this month **e** man is
      12: 3 for his family, one for **e** household.
      25:20 The cherubim are to face **e** other,
Lev 25:14 do not take advantage of **e** other.
Nu   14:34 one year for **e** of the forty days you
1Sa 17:10 me a man and let us fight **e** other."
Eze 10:14 **E** of the cherubim had four faces:
Zec   7:10 Do not plot evil against **e** other.'
Mt   6:34 **E** day has enough trouble of its
      16:27 he will reward **e** person according to
Mk   9:50 and be at peace with **e** other."
Lk   11: 3 Give us **e** day our daily bread.
Jn   15:17 This is my command: Love **e** other.
Ac   2: 6 because **e** one heard their own
Ro   2: 6 God "will repay **e** person according to
      12: 5 **e** member belongs to all the others.
1Co   7: 7 But **e** of you has your own gift
      12: 7 Now to **e** one the manifestation
Gal   5:15 If you bite and devour **e** other,
      5:15 or you will be destroyed by **e** other.
      6: 2 Carry **e** other's burdens, and in this
Col   3: 9 Do not lie to **e** other, since you have
1Th   5:13 Live in peace with **e** other.
Jas   5:16 confess your sins to **e** other
      5:16 pray for **e** other so that you may be
1Pe   1:17 Father who judges **e** person's work
Rev   4: 8 **E** of the four living creatures had
      6:11 **e** of them was given a white robe,
      13: 1 and on **e** head a blasphemous name.
      20:13 and **e** person was judged according to
      22:12 I will give to **e** person according to

EAGER EAGERLY
Pr   31:13 and flax and works with **e** hands.
Zep   3: 7 they were still **e** to act corruptly
Ro   8:19 the creation waits in **e** expectation
1Co 14:12 Since you are **e** for gifts
      14:39 and sisters, be **e** to prophesy, and do
1Ti   6:10 Some people, **e** for money,
Titus 2:14 his very own, **e** to do what is good.
1Pe   3:13 to harm you if you are **e** to do good?
      5: 2 dishonest gain, but **e** to serve;

EAGERLY EAGER
Ro   8:23 groan inwardly as we wait **e** for our
1Co 12:31 Now **e** desire the greater gifts.
      14: 1 love and **e** desire gifts of the Spirit,
Php   3:20 And we **e** await a Savior from there,

EAGLE EAGLE'S, EAGLES, EAGLES'
Dt   14:12 the **e**, the vulture, the black vulture,
      32:11 like an **e** that stirs up its nest
Pr   30:19 the way of an **e** in the sky, the way
Jer 48:40 An **e** is swooping down,
Eze   1:10 each also had the face of an **e**.
      17: 3 A great **e** with powerful wings,
Da   7: 4 lion, and it had the wings of an **e**.
Hos   8: 1 An **e** is over the house
Ob   1: 4 Though you soar like the **e**
Hab   1: 8 fly like an **e** swooping to devour;
Rev   4: 7 man, the fourth was like a flying **e**.
      8:13 I heard an **e** that was flying
      12:14 given the two wings of a great **e**,

EAGLE'S* EAGLE
Ps 103: 5 your youth is renewed like the **e**.
Jer 49:16 you build your nest as high as the **e**,

EAGLES EAGLE
Isa 40:31 They will soar on wings like **e**;

EAGLES'* EAGLE
Ex   19: 4 how I carried you on **e** wings

EAR EARLOBE, EARS
Ex   21: 6 and pierce his **e** with an awl.
Lev   8:23 put it on the lobe of Aaron's right **e**,
2Ki 19:16 Give **e**, Lᴏʀᴅ, and hear;
Ne   1:11 let your **e** be attentive to the prayer
Job 12:11 Does not the **e** test words as
Ps   28: 1 Rock, do not turn a deaf **e** to me.
     116: 2 Because he turned his **e** to me, I will
Pr   2: 2 turning your **e** to wisdom
      25:12 of a wise judge to a listening **e**.
      28: 9 If anyone turns a deaf **e** to my
Ecc   1: 8 seeing, nor the **e** its fill of hearing.
Isa 59: 1 to save, nor his **e** too dull to hear.
      64: 4 one has heard, no **e** has perceived,
Da   9:18 Give **e**, our God, and hear;
Mk   14:47 of the high priest, cutting off his **e**.
Lk   22:51 he touched the man's **e** and healed
1Co   2: 9 eye has seen, what no **e** has heard,
      12:17 If the whole body were an **e**,

EARLIER EARLY
Zec   1: 4 to whom the **e** prophets proclaimed:
      7: 7 proclaimed through the **e** prophets
Heb 10:32 Remember those **e** days after you

EARLOBE* EAR
Dt   15:17 push it through his **e** into the door,

EARLY EARLIER
Ps 127: 2 In vain you rise **e** and stay up late,
Pr   27:14 loudly blesses their neighbor **e**
Isa   5:11 to those who rise **e** in the morning
Hos   6: 4 mist, like the **e** dew that disappears.
      9:10 it was like seeing the **e** fruit
Mic   7: 1 eat, none of the **e** figs that I crave.

Mt 27: 1 **E** in the morning, all the chief
Lk 24:22 went to the tomb **e** this morning

EARN EARNINGS, EARNS
Hag 1: 6 You **e** wages, only to put them
2Th 3:12 settle down and **e** the food they eat.

EARNEST* EARNESTLY,
EARNESTNESS
Rev 3:19 So be **e** and repent.

EARNESTLY EARNEST
Ps 63: 1 God, are my God, **e** I seek you;
Hos 5:15 their misery they will **e** seek me."
Ro 11: 7 of Israel sought so **e** they did not
Heb 11: 6 he rewards those who **e** seek him.
Jas 5:17 He prayed **e** that it would not rain,

EARNESTNESS EARNEST
2Co 7:11 what **e**, what eagerness to clear
8: 7 in complete **e** and in the love we

EARNINGS EARN
Pr 31:16 out of her **e** she plants a vineyard.

EARNS* EARN
Pr 11:18 A wicked person **e** deceptive wages,

EARRING* EARRINGS
Jdg 8:24 an **e** from your share of the plunder."
Pr 25:12 Like an **e** of gold or an ornament

EARRINGS EARRING
Ex 32: 2 them, "Take off the gold **e** that your
SS 1:10 Your cheeks are beautiful with **e**,
Isa 3:19 the **e** and bracelets and veils,
Eze 16:12 **e** on your ears and a beautiful crown

EARS EAR
Dt 29: 4 or eyes that see or **e** that hear.
Job 42: 5 My **e** had heard of you but now my
Ps 34:15 and his **e** are attentive to their cry;
40: 6 but my **e** you have opened—
115: 6 They have **e**, but cannot hear, noses,
Pr 20:12 **E** that hear and eyes that see—
21:13 Whoever shuts their **e** to the cry
26:17 dog by the **e** is someone who rushes
Isa 6:10 make their **e** dull and close their
6:10 hear with their **e**,
35: 5 and the **e** of the deaf unstopped.
Jer 6:10 Their **e** are closed so they cannot
Mt 11:15 Whoever has **e**, let them hear.
Mk 8:18 but fail to see, and **e** but fail to hear?
Ac 7:51 hearts and **e** are still uncircumcised.
28:27 they hardly hear with their **e**,
28:27 hear with their **e**,
2Ti 4: 3 to say what their itching **e** want
1Pe 3:12 his **e** are attentive to their prayer,
Rev 2: 7 Whoever has **e**, let them hear what

EARTH EARTH'S, EARTHLY
Ge 1: 1 God created the heavens and the **e**.
1: 2 Now the **e** was formless and empty,
4:12 be a restless wanderer on the **e**."
6:11 Now the **e** was corrupt in God's
6:17 on the **e** to destroy all life under

Ge 6:17 Everything on **e** will perish.
7:24 The waters flooded the **e**
9:13 the covenant between me and the **e**.
12: 3 on **e** will be blessed through you."
14:19 Most High, Creator of heaven and **e**.
24: 3 the God of heaven and the God of **e**,
28:14 will be like the dust of the **e**,
28:14 on **e** will be blessed through you
Ex 19: 5 Although the whole **e** is mine,
Nu 16:30 new, and the **e** opens its mouth
Jos 3:13 the Lord of all the **e**—set foot
1Ki 8:27 "But will God really dwell on **e**?
1Ch 16:23 Sing to the LORD, all the **e**;
16:30 Tremble before him, all the **e**!
Job 26: 7 he suspends the **e** over nothing.
Ps 8: 1 majestic is your name in all the **e**!
24: 1 The **e** is the LORD's,
46: 6 he lifts his voice, the **e** melts.
47: 2 the great King over all the **e**.
73:25 **e** has nothing I desire besides you.
97: 1 LORD reigns, let the **e** be glad;
102:25 you laid the foundations of the **e**,
108: 5 let your glory be over all the **e**.
Pr 8:26 its fields or any of the dust of the **e**.
Isa 6: 3 the whole **e** is full of his glory."
24:20 The **e** reels like a drunkard, it sways
37:16 God over all the kingdoms of the **e**.
You have made heaven and **e**.
40:22 enthroned above the circle of the **e**,
51: 6 the heavens, look at the **e** beneath;
51: 6 the **e** will wear out like a garment
55: 9 the heavens are higher than the **e**,
65:17 create new heavens and a new **e**.
66: 1 throne, and the **e** is my footstool.
Jer 10:10 When he is angry, the **e** trembles;
23:24 "Do not I fill heaven and **e**?"
33:25 the laws of heaven and **e**,
Da 2:39 bronze, will rule over the whole **e**.
12: 2 sleep in the dust of the **e** will awake:
Joel 2:30 in the heavens and on the **e**,
Am 9: 5 he touches the **e** and it melts, and all
Hab 2:20 let all the **e** be silent before him.
Zep 1:18 sudden end of all who live on the **e**.
Hag 2:21 to shake the heavens and the **e**.
Zec 14: 9 will be king over the whole **e**.
Mt 5: 5 the meek, for they will inherit the **e**.
5:13 "You are the salt of the **e**.
5:18 until heaven and **e** disappear,
5:35 or by the **e**, for it is his footstool;
6:10 will be done, on **e** as it is in heaven.
16:19 you bind on **e** will be bound
16:19 you loose on **e** will be loosed
24:35 Heaven and **e** will pass away,
28:18 and on **e** has been given to me.
Mk 4:31 is the smallest of all seeds on **e**.
Lk 12:4 on **e** peace to those on whom his
5:24 of Man has authority on **e** to forgive
Jn 12:32 when I am lifted up from the **e**,
Ac 2:19 above and signs on the **e** below,
4:24 the heavens and the **e** and the sea,
7:49 throne, and the **e** is my footstool.
1Co 10:26 for, "The **e** is the Lord's,
15:47 first man was of the dust of the **e**;

Eph   3:15   in heaven and on e derives its name.
Php   2:10   in heaven and on e and under the e,
Heb   1:10   you laid the foundations of the e,
2Pe   3:13   to a new heaven and a new e,
Rev   5: 3   one e or under the e could open
     8: 7   it was hurled down on the e. A third
          of the e was burned up,
    12:12   But woe to the e and the sea,
    20:11   The e and the heavens fled from his
    21: 1   I saw "a new heaven and a new e,"
    21: 1   and the first e had passed away,

ENDS OF THE EARTH Dt 28:49; 33:17; 1Sa 2:10; Job 28:24; 37:3; Ps 2:8; 22:27; 46:9; 48:10; 59:13; 61:2; 65:5; 67:7; 72:8; 98:3; 135:7; Pr 17:24; 30:4; Isa 5:26; 24:16; 40:28; 41:5, 9; 42:10; 43:6; 45:22; 48:20; 49:6; 52:10; 62:11; Jer 6:22; 10:13; 16:19; 25:31, 32; 31:8; 50:41; 51:16; Da 4:11; Mic 5:4; Zec 9:10; Mt 12:42; Mk 13:27; Lk 11:31; Ac 1:8; 13:47

HEAVEN AND ... EARTH Ge 14:19, 22; 24:3; Dt 4:39; Jos 2:11; 2Ki 19:15; 1Ch 21:16; 29:11; 2Ch 2:12; Ezr 5:11; Job 37:3; Ps 69:34; 73:9, 25; 115:15; 121:2; 124:8; 134:3; 146:6; Ecc 5:2; Isa 37:16; 55:10; 66:1; Jer 23:24; 33:25; 51:48; Da 4:35; Zec 5:9; Mt 5:18; 11:25; 16:19; 18:18; 24:30, 35; 28:18; Mk 13:31; Lk 2:14; 10:21; 16:17; 21:33; Ac 7:49; 17:24; Eph 1:10, 3.15; Php 2:10; Col 1:16; 2Pe 3:13; Rev 5:13; 21:1, 1

EARTH'S EARTH
Job   38: 4   you when I laid the e foundation?
Pr   3:19   the LORD laid the e foundations,

EARTHENWARE*
Pr   26:23   of silver dross on e are fervent lips

EARTHLY EARTH
Jn   3:12   I have spoken to you of e things
Ro   1: 3   as to his e life was a descendant
Eph   4: 9   descended to the lower, e regions?
Php   3:19   Their mind is set on e things.
Col   3: 2   on things above, not on e things.
     3: 5   whatever belongs to your e nature:
Jas   3:15   come down from heaven but is e,

EARTHQUAKE QUAKE
1Ki   19:11   After the wind there was an e, but the
          LORD was not in the e.
Isa   29: 6   will come with thunder and e
Eze   38:19   time there shall be a great e
Mt   28: 2   There was a violent e, for an angel
Ac   16:26   Suddenly there was such a violent e
Rev   6:12   There was a great e. The sun turned
    11:13   that very hour there was a severe e
    11:13   people were killed in the e,
    16:18   peals of thunder and a severe e.
    16:18   No e like it has ever occurred since

EARTHQUAKES QUAKE
Mt   24: 7   be famines and e in various places.

EASE EASIER, EASILY, EASY
Ru   2:13   have put me at e by speaking kindly
Pr   1:33   to me will live in safety and be at e,

EASIER EASE
Mt   9: 5   Which is e: to say, 'Your sins are
Lk   16:17   It is e for heaven and earth
    18:25   it is e for a camel to go through

EASILY EASE
Pr   22:24   do not associate with one e angered,
1Co   13: 5   it is not e angered, it keeps no
Heb   12: 1   and the sin that so e entangles.

EAST
Ge   2: 8   God had planted a garden in the e,
Ex   14:21   the sea back with a strong e wind
Ps   103:12   as far as the e is from the west,
Eze   43: 2   the God of Israel coming from the e.
Hos   13:15   An e wind from the LORD will
Jnh   4: 8   God provided a scorching e wind,
Mt   2: 1   Magi from the e came to Jerusalem
     8:11   you that many will come from the e
Rev   7: 2   another angel coming up from the e,

EASY EASE
2Ki   3:18   This is an e thing in the eyes
Mt   11:30   For my yoke is e and my burden is
Lk   12:19   Take life e; eat, drink and be

EAT ATE, EATEN, EATER, EATING, EATS
Ge   2:16   "You are free to e from any tree
     2:17   you must not e from the tree
     2:17   you e from it you will certainly
     3:19   brow you will e your food until you
Ex   12:11   This is how you are to e it:
    12:11   E it in haste; it is the LORD's
    12:20   E nothing made with yeast.
    12:20   live, you must e unleavened bread."
    16:12   'At twilight you will e meat,
    16:32   can see the bread I gave you to e
    32: 6   Afterward they sat down to e
Lev   11: 2   land, these are the ones you may e:
    17:12   "None of you may e blood,
    17:12   residing among you e blood."
Nu   11:13   wailing to me, 'Give us meat to e!'
Dt   8:16   He gave you manna to e
    14: 4   These are the animals you may e:
Jdg   14:14   "Out of the eater, something to e;
2Sa   9: 7   and you will always e at my table."
Ps   22:26   The poor will e and be satisfied;
    50:13   Do I e the flesh of bulls or drink
Pr   31:27   and does not e the bread of idleness.
Ecc   2:24   can do nothing better than to e,
     5:18   it is appropriate for a person to e,
Isa   11: 7   and the lion will e straw like the ox.
    55: 1   have no money, come, buy and e!
    65:25   and the lion will e straw like the ox,
Jer   19: 9   I will make them e the flesh of their
    19: 9   and they will e one another's flesh
La   2:20   Should women e their offspring,
Eze   3: 1   "Son of man, e what is before you, e
          this scroll;
Da   1:12   vegetables to e and water to drink.
Hag   1: 6   You e, but never have enough.
Mt   14:16   You give them something to e."
    15: 2   wash their hands before they e!"

Mt   25:35 and you gave me something to e,
      26:26 his disciples, saying, "Take and e;
Mk   2:26 which is lawful only for priests to e.
      14:14 where I may e the Passover with my
Lk   10: 8 welcomed, e what is offered to you.
      12:19 e, drink and be merry." '
      12:29 set your heart on what you will e
Jn   4:32 "I have food to e that you know
       6:31 them bread from heaven to e.' "
       6:53 unless you e the flesh of the Son
Ac   10:13 him, "Get up, Peter. Kill and e."
Ro   14: 2 faith allows them to e anything,
      14:15 is distressed because of what you e,
      14:20 a person to e anything that causes
      14:23 has doubts is condemned if they e,
1Co   5:11 Do not even e with such people.
       8:13 if what I e causes my brother
       8:13 I will never e meat again, so that I
      10:25 E anything sold in the meat market
      10:31 So whether you e or drink
      11:26 For whenever you e this bread
Col   2:16 let anyone judge you by what you e
2Th   3:10 is unwilling to work shall not e."
Rev   2: 7 I will give the right to e
       3:20 will come in and e with that person,
      10: 9 He said to me, "Take it and e it.

EATEN   EAT

Ge   3:11 Have you e from the tree that I
Jer   31:29 'The parents have e sour grapes,
Eze   4:14 I have never e anything found dead
Ac   10:14 "I have never e anything impure
      12:23 and he was e by worms and died.
Rev   10:10 but when I had e it, my stomach

EATER*   EAT

Jdg   14:14 "Out of the e, something to eat;
Isa   55:10 for the sower and bread for the e,
Na   3:12 the figs fall into the mouth of the e.

EATING   EAT

Ex   34:28 and forty nights without e bread
Isa   7:15 He will be e curds and honey
Mt   15:20 but e with unwashed hands does not
Lk   7:34 The Son of Man came e
Ro   14:15 Do not by your e destroy someone
      14:17 kingdom of God is not a matter of e
      14:23 eat, because their e is not from faith;
1Co   8: 4 about e food sacrificed to idols:
Heb   13: 9 not by e ceremonial foods, which is
Jude   1:12 e with you without the slightest

EATS   EAT

Lev   7:27 Anyone who e blood must be cut
1Sa   14:24 be anyone who e food before
Lk   15: 2 sinners and e with them."
Jn   6:51 Whoever e this bread will live
       6:54 Whoever e my flesh and drinks my
Ro   14: 2 faith is weak, e only vegetables.
      14: 6 Whoever e meat does so to the Lord,
1Co   11:27 whoever e the bread or drinks

EBAL

Dt   11:29 and on Mount E the curses.
Jos   8:30 Joshua built on Mount E an altar

EBED-MELEK*

A Cushite; saved Jeremiah from the cistern (Jer
38:1–13; 39:16).

EBENEZER*

1Sa   4: 1 The Israelites camped at E,
       5: 1 God, they took it from E to Ashdod.
       7:12 He named it E, saying, "Thus far

EBER

Ancestor of Abraham (Ge 11:14–17), of Jesus
(Lk 3:35).

EDEN

Ge   2: 8 planted a garden in the east, in E;
Eze   28:13 You were in E, the garden of God;

EDGE   DOUBLE-EDGED

Jos   3:15 and their feet touched the water's e,
Jer   31:29 the children's teeth are set on e.'
Mt   9:20 him and touched the e of his cloak.
      14:36 to let the sick just touch the e of his

EDICT

Est   4: 8 text of the e for their annihilation,
       8:11 The king's e granted the Jews
Da   6: 7 that the king should issue an e
Heb   11:23 they were not afraid of the king's e.

EDIFICATION*   EDIFIED, EDIFIES

Ro   14:19 what leads to peace and to mutual e.

EDIFIED*   EDIFICATION

1Co   14: 5 so that the church may be e.
      14:17 well enough, but no one else is e.

EDIFIES*   EDIFICATION

1Co   14: 4 who speaks in a tongue e themselves,
      14: 4 one who prophesies e the church.

EDOM   EDOMITE, EDOMITES, ESAU

Ge   25:30 (That is why he was also called E.)
      36: 1 the family line of Esau (that is, E).
Nu   20:18 But E answered: "You may not
1Ki   11:16 they had destroyed all the men in E.
Ps   60: 8 washbasin, on E I toss my sandal;
Isa   63: 1 Who is this coming from E,
Jer   49: 7 Concerning E: This is what
La   4:21 Daughter E, you who live
Eze   25:12 'Because E took revenge on Judah
Am   1:11 "For three sins of E, even for four,
Ob   1: 1 Sovereign LORD says about E—

EDOMITE   EDOM

Dt   23: 7 Do not despise an E,
1Sa   22: 9 But Doeg the E, who was standing
Ps   52: T *Doeg the E had gone to Saul*

EDOMITES   EDOM

Ge   36:43 line of Esau, the father of the E.
1Ch   18:13 all the E became subject to David.
Ps   60: T *Joab struck down twelve thousand E*
      137: 7 what the E did on the day Jerusalem

EDUCATED*

Ac   7:22 Moses was e in all the wisdom

EFFECT* EFFECTIVE
Job 41:26 The sword that reaches it has no e,
Isa 32:17 its e will be quietness
Zep 2: 2 before the decree takes e
1Co 15:10 his grace to me was not without e.
Eph 1:10 be put into e when the times reach
Heb 9:17 it never takes e while the one who
     9:18 was not put into e without blood.

EFFECTIVE* EFFECT
1Co 16: 9 a great door for e work has opened
Phm : 6 in the faith may be e in deepening
Jas 5:16 righteous person is powerful and e.

EFFORT* EFFORTS
Ecc 2:19 toil into which I have poured my e
Da 6:14 made every e until sundown to save
Lk 13:24 "Make every e to enter through
Ro 9:16 depend on human desire or e,
     14:19 Let us therefore make every e to do
Eph 4: 3 Make every e to keep the unity
1Th 2:16 in their e to keep us from speaking
     2:17 intense longing we made every e
Heb 4:11 make every e to enter that rest,
     12:14 Make every e to live in peace
2Pe 1: 5 make every e to add to your faith
     1:10 make every e to confirm your
     1:15 I will make every e to see
     3:14 make every e to be found spotless,

EFFORTS EFFORT
Gal 4:11 somehow I have wasted my e

EGG* EGGS
Lk 11:12 Or if he asks for an e, will give him

EGGS EGG
Dt 22: 6 is sitting on the young or on the e,
Isa 59: 5 They hatch the e of vipers and spin
     59: 5 Whoever eats their e will die,
Jer 17:11 that hatches it did not lay are those

EGLON
1. King of Moab killed by Ehud (Jdg 3:12–30).
2. City in Canaan (Jos 10).

EGYPT EGYPTIAN, EGYPTIANS
Ge 12:10 Abram went down to E to live there
     26: 2 and said, "Do not go down to E;
     37:28 the Ishmaelites, who took him to E.
     41:41 in charge of the whole land of E."
     42: 3 went down to buy grain from E.
     45: 9 God has made me lord of all E.
     45:20 the best of all E will be yours.' "
     46: 6 and all his offspring went to E,
     47:27 Now the Israelites settled in E
Ex 1: 8 meant nothing, came to power in E.
     3:11 and bring the Israelites out of E?"
     7: 3 my signs and wonders in E,
     11: 5 Every firstborn son in E will die,
     12:12 same night I will pass through E
     12:12 bring judgment on all the gods of E.
     12:40 people lived in E was 430 years.
     12:41 all the LORD's divisions left E.
     32: 1 Moses who brought us up out of E,

Nu 11:18 We were better off in E!"
     14: 4 choose a leader and go back to E."
     24: 8 "God brought them out of E;
Dt 6:21 "We were slaves of Pharaoh in E,
     6:21 us out of E with a mighty hand.
     16:12 that you were slaves in E,
Jos 15:47 as far as the Wadi of E
1Ki 4:30 greater than all the wisdom of E.
     10:28 horses were imported from E
     11:40 but Jeroboam fled to E, to Shishak
     14:25 king of E attacked Jerusalem.
2Ch 35:20 Necho king of E went up to fight
     36: 3 The king of E dethroned him
Ne 9:18 who brought you up out of E,'
Ps 80: 8 You transplanted a vine from E;
Isa 19: 1 A prophecy against E:
     19: 1 The idols of E tremble before him,
Jer 42:19 has told you, 'Do not go to E.'
     44: 1 all the Jews living in Lower E—
     46: 2 Concerning E: This is the message
     46: 2 army of Pharaoh Necho king of E,
La 5: 6 We submitted to E and Assyria
Eze 29: 2 your face against Pharaoh king of E
     30: 4 A sword will come against E,
Hos 11: 1 him, and out of E I called my son.
Mt 2:15 "Out of E I called my son."
Heb 11:22 the exodus of the Israelites from E
     11:27 By faith he left E, not fearing
Rev 11: 8 is figuratively called Sodom and E—

OUT OF EGYPT Ge 45:25; 47:30; Ex 3:10, 11,
12; 6:13, 26, 27; 12:17, 39, 42, 51; 13:3, 8, 9, 14, 16,
18; 14:11; 16:1, 6, 32; 17:3; 18:1; 20:2; 23:15; 29:46;
32:1, 4, 7, 8, 11, 23; 33:1; 34:18; Lev 11:45; 19:36;
22:33; 23:43; 25:38, 42, 55; 26:13, 45; Nu 1:1; 9:1;
15:41; 20:5, 16; 21:5; 22:5, 11; 23:22; 24:8; 26:4;
32:11; 33:1, 38; Dt 1:27; 4:20, 37, 45, 46; 5:6; 6:12,
21; 8:14; 9:12, 26; 13:5, 10; 16:1; 20:1; 23:4; 24:9;
25:17; 26:8; 29:25; Jos 2:10; 5:4; 24:6, 17; Jdg 2:1,
12; 6:8, 13; 11:13, 16; 19:30; 1Sa 8:8; 10:18; 12:6,
8; 15:6; 2Sa 7:6; 1Ki 6:1; 8:9, 16, 21, 51, 53; 9:9;
12:28; 2Ki 17:7, 36; 21:15; 1Ch 17:5; 2Ch 5:10; 6:5;
7:22; Ne 9:18; Ps 81:10; 114:1; Jer 2:6; 7:22; 11:4;
16:14; 23:7; 26:23; 31:32; 32:21; 34:13; 37:5; Eze
20:6, 9, 10; Da 9:15; Hos 2:15; 11:1; 12:9; 13:4; Am
2:10; 3:1; Mic 6:4; 7:15; Hag 2:5; Mt 2:15; Ac 7:36,
40; Heb 3:16; 8:9; Jude 1:5

KING OF EGYPT See KING

EGYPTIAN EGYPT
Ge 16: 1 she had an E slave named Hagar;
Ex 1:19 women are not like E women;
     2:11 He saw an E beating a Hebrew,
Dt 11: 4 what he did to the E army, to its
     23: 7 Do not despise an E, because you

EGYPTIANS EGYPT
Ex 1:12 so the E came to dread the Israelites
     3:22 And so you will plunder the E."
     12:36 had made the E favorably disposed
     12:36 so they plundered the E.
     14: 4 and the E will know that I am
     15:26 of the diseases I brought on the E,
Nu 14:13 "Then the E will hear about it!

EHUD
Left-handed judge who delivered Israel from Moabite king, Eglon (Jdg 3:12–30).

EIGHT EIGHTH
Ge	17:12	among you who is e days old must
	21: 4	When his son Isaac was e days old,
2Ki	22: 1	Josiah was e years old when he
1Pe	3:20	In it only a few people, e in all,

EIGHTEEN
Lk   13:11 been crippled by a spirit for e years.

EIGHTH EIGHT
Lev	12: 3	On the e day the boy is to be
	25:22	While you plant during the e year,
Lk	1:59	On the e day they came
	2:21	On the e day, when it was time
Php	3: 5	circumcised on the e day,
Rev	17:11	was, and now is not, is an e king.

EIGHTY
Ex	7: 7	Moses was e years old and Aaron
2Sa	19:35	I am now e years old. Can I tell
Ps	90:10	years, or e, if our strength endures;

EIGHTY-FIVE
Jos   14:10 So here I am today, e years old!

EITHER
Lk	16:13	E you will hate the one and love
Ro	11:21	branches, he will not spare you e.
Rev	3:15	I wish you were e one or the other!

EKRON
Jos	13: 3	to the territory of E on the north,
1Sa	5:10	So they sent the ark of God to E.
	6:17	Gaza, Ashkelon, Gath and E.
2Ki	1: 2	the god of E, to see if I will recover

EL BETHEL* BETHEL
Ge   35: 7 an altar, and he called the place E,

EL ELOHE ISRAEL* ISRAEL
Ge   33:20 he set up an altar and called it E.

ELAH
1. Son of Baasha; king of Israel (1Ki 16:6–14).
2. Valley in which David fought Goliath (1Sa 17:2, 19; 21:9).

ELAM
1Ch	1:17	E, Ashur, Arphaxad, Lud and Aram.
Jer	49:34	Jeremiah the prophet concerning E,

ELATION*
Pr   28:12 righteous triumph, there is great e;

ELDER* ELDERLY, ELDERS
Isa	3: 2	the prophet, the diviner and the e,
1Ti	5:19	accusation against an e unless it is
Titus	1: 6	An e must be blameless,
1Pe	5: 1	I appeal as a fellow e and a witness
2Jn	1: 1	The e, To the lady chosen by God
3Jn	1: 1	The e, To my dear friend Gaius,

ELDERLY* ELDER
Lev	19:32	show respect for the e and revere
2Ch	36:17	or young women, the e or the infirm.

ELDERS ELDER
Ex	3:16	assemble the e of Israel and say
	24: 1	and seventy of the e of Israel.
Dt	25: 7	she shall go to the e at the town gate
Jos	24: 1	He summoned the e, leaders,
Jdg	2: 7	of the e who outlived him and who
Ru	4: 2	Boaz took ten of the e of the town
2Ch	10:13	Rejecting the advice of the e,
Ps	105:22	he pleased and teach his e wisdom.
	119:100	have more understanding than the e,
Isa	3:14	enters into judgment against the e
La	5:14	The e are gone from the city gate;
Eze	8:11	of them stood seventy e of Israel,
Mt	15: 2	break the tradition of the e?
Mk	7: 3	holding to the tradition of the e.
Lk	9:22	things and be rejected by the e,
Ac	4: 5	the e and the teachers of the law met
	11:30	their gift to the e by Barnabas
	14:23	Barnabas appointed e for them
	15: 2	apostles and e about this question.
	15: 6	and e met to consider this question.
	15:23	The apostles and e, your brothers,
	16: 4	and e in Jerusalem for the people
	20:17	to Ephesus for the e of the church.
	21:18	James, and all the e were present.
	23:14	the chief priests and the e and said,
	24: 1	to Caesarea with some of the e
	25:15	the e of the Jews brought charges
1Ti	4:14	the body of e laid their hands
	5:17	The e who direct the affairs
Titus	1: 5	and appoint e in every town, as I
Jas	5:14	Let them call the e of the church
1Pe	5: 1	To the e among you, I appeal as
	5: 5	submit yourselves to your e.
Rev	4: 4	seated on them were twenty-four e.
	4:10	the twenty-four e fall down before
	5: 6	the four living creatures and the e.
	7:11	and around the e and the four living
	11:16	And the twenty-four e, who were
	14: 3	the four living creatures and the e.
	19: 4	The twenty-four e and the four

ELEAZAR
Third son of Aaron (Ex 6:23–25). Succeeded Aaron as high priest (Nu 20:26; Dt 10:6). Allotted land to tribes (Jos 14:1). Death (Jos 24:33).

ELECT* ELECTION
Mt	24:22	the e those days will be shortened.
	24:24	to deceive, if possible, even the e.
	24:31	they will gather his e from the four
Mk	13:20	But for the sake of the e, whom he
	13:22	to deceive, if possible, even the e.
	13:27	gather his e from the four winds,
Ro	11: 7	The e among them did,
1Ti	5:21	and Christ Jesus and the e angels,
2Ti	2:10	everything for the sake of the e,
Titus	1: 1	Christ to further the faith of God's e
1Pe	1: 1	Christ, To God's e, exiles scattered

ELECTION* ELECT
Ro   9:11 that God's purpose in **e** might stand:
     11:28 but as far as **e** is concerned, they are
2Pe 1:10 effort to confirm your calling and **e**.

ELEMENTAL* ELEMENTS
Gal 4: 3 slavery under the **e** spiritual forces
Col 2: 8 the **e** spiritual forces of this world
     2:20 Christ to the **e** spiritual forces

ELEMENTARY* ELEMENTS
Heb 5:12 to teach you the **e** truths of God's
     6: 1 let us move beyond the **e** teachings

ELEMENTS* ELEMENTAL,
ELEMENTARY
2Pe 3:10 the **e** will be destroyed by fire,
     3:12 fire, and the **e** will melt in the heat.

ELEVATE* ELEVATED
2Co 11: 7 in order to **e** you by preaching

ELEVATED* ELEVATE
Est 5:11 how he had **e** him above the other

ELEVEN
Ge 32:22 two female servants and his **e** sons
     37: 9 **e** stars were bowing down to me."
Ex 26: 8 All **e** curtains are to be the same
Dt   1: 2 (It takes **e** days to go from Horeb
Mt 28:16 Then the **e** disciples went to Galilee,
Lk 24: 9 they told all these things to the E
     24:33 There they found the E and those
Ac   1:26 so he was added to the **e** apostles.
     2:14 Then Peter stood up with the E,

ELI
1. High priest in youth of Samuel (1Sa 1–4).
Blessed Hannah (1Sa 1:12–18); raised Samuel (1Sa
2:11–26). Prophesied against because of wicked
sons (1Sa 2:27–36). Death of Eli and sons (1Sa
4:11–22).
2. Aramaic or Hebrew for "My God" in Jesus'
last words on the cross.
Mt 27:46 cried out in a loud voice, "**E, E,**

ELIAKIM JEHOIAKIM
1. Original name of king Jehoiakim (2Ki 23:34;
2Ch 36:4).
2. Hezekiah's palace administrator (2Ki 18:17–
37; 19:2; Isa 36:1–22; 37:2).

ELIASHIB
Ne   3: 1 E the high priest and his fellow

ELIEZER
1. Servant of Abraham (Ge 15:2).
2. Son of Moses (Ex 18:4; 1Ch 23:15–17).

ELIHU
A friend of Job (Job 32–37).

ELIJAH
Prophet; predicted famine in Israel (1Ki 17:1; Jas
5:17). Fed by ravens (1Ki 17:2–6). Raised Sidonian
widow's son (1Ki 17:7–24). Defeated prophets of
Baal at Carmel (1Ki 18:16–46). Ran from Jezebel

(1Ki 19:1–9). Prophesied death of Azariah (2Ki 1).
Succeeded by Elishah (1Ki 19:19–21; 2Ki 2:1–18).
Taken to heaven in whirlwind (2Ki 2:11–12).
Return prophesied (Mal 4:5–6); equated with
John the Baptist (Mt 17:9–13; Mk 9:9–13; Lk 1:17).
Appeared with Moses in transfiguration of Jesus
(Mt 17:1–8; Mk 9:1–8).

ELIM
Ex 15:27 Then they came to E, where there
Nu 33: 9 They left Marah and went to E,

ELIMELEK
Ru   1: 3 Now E, Naomi's husband, died,
     4: 9 from Naomi all the property of E,

ELIMINATE* ELIMINATED
Dt   7:22 will not be allowed to **e** them all

ELIMINATED* ELIMINATE
Dt   2:15 them until he had completely **e** them

ELIPHAZ
1. Firstborn of Esau (Ge 36).
2. A friend of Job (Job 4–5; 15; 22; 42:7, 9).

ELISHA
Prophet; successor of Elijah (1Ki 19:16–21); inherited his cloak (2Ki 2:1–18). Purified bad water
(2Ki 2:19–22). Cursed young men (2Ki 2:23–25).
Aided Israel's defeat of Moab (2Ki 3). Provided
widow with oil (2Ki 4:1–7). Raised Shunammite
woman's son (2Ki 4:8–37). Purified food (2Ki
4:38–41). Fed 100 men (2Ki 4:42–44). Healed
Naaman's leprosy (2Ki 5). Made axhead float (2Ki
6:1–7). Captured Arameans (2Ki 6:8–23). Political
adviser to Israel (2Ki 6:24—8:6; 9:1–3; 13:14–19),
Aram (2Ki 8:7–15). Death (2Ki 13:20).

ELIZABETH*
Mother of John the Baptist (Lk 1:5–58).

ELKANAH
Husband of Hannah, father of Samuel (1Sa
1–2).

ELOI*
Mk 15:34 cried out in a loud voice, "**E, E,**

ELON
Judge of Israel (Jdg 12:11–12).

ELOQUENCE* ELOQUENT
1Co 1:17 the gospel—not with wisdom and **e**,
     2: 1 not come with **e** or human wisdom

ELOQUENT* ELOQUENCE
Ex   4:10 I have never been **e**,
Pr 17: 7 E lips are unsuited to a godless

ELSE
Ex   4:13 Please send someone **e**."
Nu 12: 3 more humble than anyone **e**
Pr   4:23 Above all **e**, guard your heart,
     27: 2 Let someone **e** praise you, and not
Lk   7:19 or should we expect someone **e**?"
Jn   5:43 but if someone **e** comes in his own

Ac   4:12 Salvation is found in no one e,
Ro   8:39 depth, nor anything e in all creation,

ELYMAS
Ac   13: 8 E the sorcerer (for that is what his

EMASCULATE* EMASCULATED
Gal   5:12 go the whole way and e themselves!

EMASCULATED* EMASCULATE
Dt   23: 1 No one who has been e by crushing

EMBALMED*
Ge   50: 2 So the physicians e him,
         50:26 And after they e him, he was placed

EMBEDDED*
Ecc 12:11 sayings like firmly e nails—

EMBERS*
Ps 102: 3 my bones burn like glowing e.
Pr   26:21 As charcoal to e and as wood

EMBITTER* BITTER
Col   3:21 Fathers, do not e your children,

EMBLEM
Ex   39:30 the sacred e, out of pure gold

EMBODIMENT* BODY
Ro   2:20 have in the law the e of knowledge

EMBOLDENED* BOLD
Ps 138: 3 you answered me; you greatly e me.
1Co   8:10 person be e to eat what is sacrificed

EMBRACE EMBRACED,
EMBRACES, EMBRACING
Pr   5:20 Why e the bosom of a wayward
Ecc   3: 5 a time to e and a time to refrain

EMBRACED EMBRACE
Ge   48:10 his father kissed them and e them.
2Ch   7:22 and have e other gods,
Ac   20:37 They all wept as they e him

EMBRACES* EMBRACE
SS   2: 6 my head, and his right arm e me.
      8: 3 my head and his right arm e me.

EMBRACING* EMBRACE
Ecc   2: 3 myself with wine, and e folly—
      3: 5 embrace and a time to refrain from e,

EMBROIDERED EMBROIDERER
Ps   45:14 In e garments she is led to the king;
Eze 16:10 I clothed you with an e dress

EMBROIDERER EMBROIDERED
Ex   26:36 the work of an e.

EMERALD
Ex   28:18 shall be turquoise, lapis lazuli and e;
Rev   4: 3 shone like an e encircled the throne.
      21:19 the third agate, the fourth e,

EMMANUEL (KJV) See IMMANUEL
EMMAUS*
Lk   24:13 were going to a village called E,

EMPATHIZE*
Heb   4:15 have a high priest who is unable to e

EMPEROR*
Ac   25:25 made his appeal to the E I decided
1Pe   2:13 whether to the e, as the supreme
      2:17 of believers, fear God, honor the e.

EMPTIED EMPTY
Ne   5:13 such a person be shaken out and e!"
1Co   1:17 the cross of Christ be e of its power.

EMPTY EMPTIED, EMPTY-HANDED
Ge   1: 2 Now the earth was formless and e,
Ru   1:21 the LORD has brought me back e.
2Ki   4: 3 and ask all your neighbors for e jars.
Job 26: 7 out the northern skies over e space;
      35:16 So Job opens his mouth with e talk;
Isa 45:18 he did not create it to be e,
      55:11 It will not return to me e, but will
Jer   4:23 the earth, and it was formless and e;
Mt   12:36 for every e word they have spoken.
Lk   1:53 things but has sent the rich away e.
Eph   5: 6 no one deceive you with e words,
1Pe   1:18 you were redeemed from the e way
2Pe   2:18 For they mouth e, boastful words

EMPTY-HANDED EMPTY, HAND
Ge   31:42 would surely have sent me away e.
Ex   3:21 when you leave you will not go e.
      23:15 "No one is to appear before me e.
Dt   15:13 them, do not send them away e.
Ru   3:17 back to your mother-in-law e.' "
Mk   12: 3 him, beat him and sent him away e.

EN GEDI
1Sa 24: 1 "David is in the Desert of E."

ENABLE* ABLE
Lk   1:74 and to e us to serve him without fear
Ac   4:29 e your servants to speak your word

ENABLED* ABLE
Ge   29:31 was not loved, he e her to conceive,
      30:22 to her and e her to conceive.
Lev 26:13 e you to walk with heads held high.
Ru   4:13 her, the LORD e her to conceive,
1Ch 28:19 he e me to understand all the details
Jn   6:65 me unless the Father has e them."
Ac   2: 4 other tongues as the Spirit e them.
      7:10 and e him to gain the goodwill
Heb 11:11 was e to bear children because she

ENABLES* ABLE
Hab   3:19 he e me to tread on the heights.
Php   3:21 by the power that e him to bring

ENABLING* ABLE
Ac   14: 3 his grace by e them to perform signs

ENCAMP CAMP
Ex   14: 2 They are to e by the sea,

Zec   9: 8 I will e at my temple to guard it

ENCAMPED CAMP
Nu   9:23 At the LORD's command they e,
     24: 2 out and saw Israel e tribe by tribe,

ENCAMPS* CAMP
Ps   34: 7 the LORD e around those who fear

ENCHANTER ENCHANTERS
Isa   3: 3 skilled craftsman and clever e.
Da   2:27 "No wise man, e,

ENCHANTERS ENCHANTER
Da   1:20 and e in his whole kingdom.
       5: 7 The king summoned the e,

ENCIRCLE CIRCLE
Ps   22:12 strong bulls of Bashan e me.

ENCIRCLED CIRCLE
Rev   4: 3 shone like an emerald e the throne.
       5: 6 e by the four living creatures

ENCLOSE* CLOSE
SS   8: 9 we will e her with panels of cedar.

ENCLOSED CLOSE
SS   4:12 you are a spring e, a sealed

ENCOURAGE* ENCOURAGED,
  ENCOURAGEMENT,
  ENCOURAGES, ENCOURAGING
Dt   1:38 E him, because he will lead Israel
       3:28 Joshua, and e and strengthen him,
2Sa   11:25 and destroy it.' Say this to e Joab."
      19: 7 Now go out and e your men.
Job   16: 5 But my mouth would e you;
Ps   10:17 you e them, and you listen to their
      64: 5 They e each other in evil plans,
Jer   29: 8 to the dreams you e them to have.
Ac   15:32 said much to e and strengthen
Ro   12: 8 if it is to e, then give
2Co   13:11 for full restoration, e one another,
Eph   6:22 how we are, and that he may e you.
Col   4: 8 and that he may e your hearts.
1Th   3: 2 strengthen and e you in your faith,
       4:18 Therefore e one another with these
       5:11 Therefore e one another and build
       5:14 and disruptive, e the disheartened,
2Th   2:17 e your hearts and strengthen you
2Ti   4: 2 correct, rebuke and e—
Titus 1: 9 he can e others by sound doctrine
       2: 6 Similarly, e the young men to be
       2:15 E and rebuke with all authority.
Heb   3:13 But e one another daily, as long as it

ENCOURAGED* ENCOURAGE
Jdg   7:11 you will be e to attack the camp."
      20:22 But the Israelites e one another
2Ch   22: 3 his mother e him to act wickedly.
      32: 6 gate and e them with these words:
      35: 2 and e them in the service
Eze   13:22 and because you e the wicked not
Ac   9:31 of the Lord and e by the Holy Spirit,
      11:23 e them all to remain true to the Lord

Ac   16:40 the brothers and sisters and e them.
      18:27 the brothers and sisters e him
      27:36 They were all e and ate some food
      28:15 people Paul thanked God and was e.
Ro   1:12 I may be mutually e by each other's
1Co   14:31 everyone may be instructed and e.
2Co   7: 4 I am greatly e; in all our troubles
       7:13 By all this we are e. In addition
Col   2: 2 goal is that they may be e in heart
1Th   3: 7 persecution we were e about you
Heb   6:18 hope set before us may be greatly e.

ENCOURAGEMENT*
  ENCOURAGE
Ac   4:36 (which means "son of e"),
      20: 2 speaking many words of e
Ro   12: 8 if it is to encourage, then give e;
      15: 4 the e they provide we might have
      15: 5 e give you the same attitude of mind
2Co   7:13 In addition to our own e, we were
Php   2: 1 if you have any e from being united
2Th   2:16 by his grace gave us eternal e
Phm   1: 7 love has given me great joy and e,
Heb   12: 5 completely forgotten this word of e

ENCOURAGES* ENCOURAGE
Isa   41: 7 The metalworker e the goldsmith,

ENCOURAGING* ENCOURAGE
Ac   14:22 e them to remain true to the faith.
      15:31 it and were glad for its e message.
      20: 1 after e them, said goodbye and set
1Co   14: 3 their strengthening, e and comfort.
1Th   2:12 e, comforting and urging you to live
Heb   10:25 habit of doing, but e one another—
1Pe   5:12 e you and testifying that this is

ENCROACH
Pr   23:10 or e on the fields of the fatherless,

END ENDED, ENDLESS, ENDS,
  UNENDING
Ge   6:13 am going to put an e to all people,
Ex   12:41 At the e of the 430 years, to the very
Nu   16:21 this assembly so I can put an e
      23:10 and may my final e be like theirs!"
Dt   8:16 in the e it might go well with you.
      31:24 of this law from beginning to e,
Ne   9:31 great mercy you did not put an e
Job   19:25 in the e he will stand on the earth.
Ps   48:14 he will be our guide even to the e.
     119:33 that I may follow it to the e.
     119:112 keeping your decrees to the very e.
Pr   5: 4 but in the e she is bitter as gall,
       5:11 At the e of your life you will groan,
      14:12 right, but in the e it leads to death.
      14:13 ache, and rejoicing may e in grief.
      16:25 right, but in the e it leads to death.
      19:20 the e you will be counted among
      20:21 too soon will not be blessed at the e.
      23:32 In the e it bites like a snake
      25: 8 do in the e if your neighbor puts you
      28:23 the e gain favor rather than one who
Ecc   3:11 God has done from beginning to e.

Ecc 7: 8 The **e** of a matter is better than its
12:12 making many books there is no **e**,
Isa 9: 7 and peace there will be no **e**.
Eze 7: 2 " 'The **e**! The **e** has come upon
Da 4:34 At the **e** of that time, I,
6:26 his dominion will never **e**.
8:17 vision concerns the time of the **e**."
9:26 The **e** will come like a flood:
9:26 War will continue until the **e**,
12:13 "As for you, go your way till the **e**.
12:13 at the **e** of the days you will rise
Mt 10:22 stands firm to the **e** will be saved.
24:13 stands firm to the **e** will be saved.
24:14 nations, and then the **e** will come.
Lk 21: 9 but the **e** will not come right away."
Jn 13: 1 in the world, he loved them to the **e**.
1Co 15:24 Then the **e** will come, when he
2Co 3:13 seeing the **e** of what was passing
Heb 3:14 conviction firmly to the very **e**.
6: 8 In the **e** it will be burned.
1Pe 4: 7 The **e** of all things is near.
2Pe 2:20 are worse off at the **e** than they were
Rev 2:26 victorious and does my will to the **e**,
21: 6 Omega, the Beginning and the **E**.
22:13 the Last, the Beginning and the **E**.

ENDED *END*
Pr 10:19 Sin is not **e** by multiplying words,
22:10 quarrels and insults are **e**.
Rev 20: 3 until the thousand years were **e**.

ENDLESS *END*
Ps 106:31 as righteousness for **e** generations
Na 3:19 for who has not felt your **e** cruelty?

ENDOR
1Sa 28: 7 "There is one in **E**," they said.

ENDOW *ENDOWED*
Ps 72: 1 **E** the king with your justice, O God,

ENDOWED *ENDOW*
Isa 55: 5 for he has **e** you with splendor."

ENDS *END*
Ps 2: 8 the **e** of the earth your possession.
19: 4 their words to the **e** of the world.
67: 7 all the **e** of the earth will fear him.
Pr 20:17 but one **e** up with a mouth full
Isa 40:28 the Creator of the **e** of the earth.
49: 6 may reach to the **e** of the earth."
62:11 proclamation to the **e** of the earth:
Mic 5: 4 will reach to the **e** of the earth.
Lk 11:31 she came from the **e** of the earth
Ac 13:47 salvation to the **e** of the earth.' "
Ro 10:18 their words to the **e** of the world."

ENDS OF THE EARTH See EARTH

ENDURANCE* *ENDURE*
Ro 15: 4 so that through the **e** taught
15: 5 May the God who gives **e**
2Co 1: 6 you patient **e** of the same sufferings
6: 4 in great **e**; in troubles,
Col 1:11 might so that you may have great **e**
1Th 1: 3 your **e** inspired by hope in our Lord

1Ti 6:11 faith, love, **e** and gentleness.
2Ti 3:10 my purpose, faith, patience, love, **e**,
Titus 2: 2 and sound in faith, in love and in **e**.
Rev 1: 9 and patient **e** that are ours in Jesus,
13:10 This calls for patient **e**
14:12 This calls for patient **e** on the part

ENDURE ENDURANCE, ENDURED, ENDURES, ENDURING
1Sa 13:14 But now your kingdom will not **e**;
2Sa 7:16 your kingdom will **e** forever before
Job 20:21 his prosperity will not **e**.
Ps 37:18 and their inheritance will **e** forever.
49:12 despite their wealth, do not **e**;
72:17 May his name be forever;
89:29 his throne as long as the heavens **e**.
104:31 the glory of the LORD **e** forever;
Pr 12:19 Truthful lips **e** forever, but a lying
27:24 for riches do not **e** forever,
Ecc 3:14 everything God does will **e** forever;
Isa 55:13 sign, that will **e** forever."
66:22 earth that I make will **e** before me,"
66:22 will your name and descendants **e**.
Jer 44:22 could no longer **e** your wicked
Da 2:44 to an end, but it will itself **e** forever.
Joel 2:11 it is dreadful. Who can **e** it?
Na 1: 6 Who can **e** his fierce anger?
Mal 3: 2 who can **e** the day of his coming?
1Co 4:12 when we are persecuted, we **e** it;
10:13 a way out so that you can **e** it.
2Co 1: 8 far beyond our ability to **e**,
2Ti 2:10 Therefore I **e** everything
2:12 if we **e**, we will also reign with him.
4: 5 head in all situations, **e** hardship,
Heb 12: 7 **E** hardship as discipline;
1Pe 2:20 a beating for doing wrong and **e** it?
2:20 suffer for doing good and you **e** it,
Rev 3:10 kept my command to **e** patiently,

ENDURED* *ENDURE*
Ps 123: 3 for we have **e** no end of contempt.
123: 4 We have **e** no end of ridicule
Ac 13:18 forty years he **e** their conduct
2Ti 3:11 and Lystra, the persecutions I **e**.
Heb 10:32 when you **e** in a great conflict full
12: 2 joy set before him he **e** the cross,
12: 3 him who **e** such opposition
Rev 2: 3 and have **e** hardships for my name,

ENDURES *ENDURE*
Ge 8:22 "As long as the earth **e**,
1Ch 16:41 LORD, "for his love **e** forever."
Ps 102:12 your renown **e** through all
112: 9 poor, their righteousness **e** forever;
136: 1 *His love e forever.*
145:13 and your dominion **e** through all
Pr 12:12 but the root of the righteous **e**.
Isa 40: 8 but the word of our God **e** forever."
Da 9:15 yourself a name that **e** to this day,
Jn 6:27 but for food that **e** to eternal life,
2Co 9: 9 their righteousness **e** forever."
1Pe 1:25 but the word of the Lord **e** forever."

HIS LOVE ENDURES FOREVER See LOVE

ENDURING ENDURE

Ps   19: 9 of the LORD is pure, e forever.
2Th   1: 4 the persecutions and trials you are e.
Heb 13:14 For here we do not have an e city,
1Pe   1:23 the living and e word of God.

ENEMIES ENEMY

Ex   1:10 will join our e, fight against us
      23:22 I will be an enemy to your e
Lev 26:37 not be able to stand before your e.
Dt   6:19 thrusting out all your e before you,
      33:27 He will drive out your e before you,
Jos   5:13 "Are you for us or for our e?"
      21:44 Not one of their e withstood them;
      21:44 the LORD gave all their e
Jdg   2:14 into the hands of their e all around,
2Sa   7: 1 him rest from all his e around him,
Est   9: 5 The Jews struck down all their e
Job 19:11 he counts me among his e.
Ps   9: 6 Endless ruin has overtaken my e,
      23: 5 before me in the presence of my e.
      44: 7 but you give us victory over our e,
    110: 1 hand until I make your e a footstool
Pr   16: 7 he causes their e to make peace
      26:24 E disguise themselves with their
      29:24 of thieves are their own e;
Isa 59:18 so will he repay wrath to his e
Jer 12: 7 one I love into the hands of her e.
Da   4:19 if only the dream applied to your e
Mic   7: 6 a man's e are the members of his
Mt   5:44 love your e and pray for those who
      10:36 a man's e will be the members
Lk   6:35 But love your e, do good to them,
      20:43 until I make your e a footstool
Ro   5:10 if, while we were God's e, we were
1Co 15:25 he has put all his e under his feet.
Php   3:18 tears, many live as e of the cross
Col   1:21 were e in your minds because
Heb   1:13 hand until I make your e a footstool
      10:13 for his e to be made his footstool.
      10:27 fire that will consume the e of God.
Rev 11: 5 their mouths and devours their e.

ENEMY ENEMIES, ENMITY

Ex   15: 9 The e boasted, 'I will pursue, I will
      23:22 I will be an e to your enemies
2Sa 22:18 He rescued me from my powerful e,
Est   3:10 the Agagite, the e of the Jews.
      9:24 the Agagite, the e of all the Jews,
Ps   74:10 How long will the e mock you,
Pr   24:17 Do not gloat when your e falls;
      25:21 If your e is hungry, give him food
      27: 6 trusted, but an e multiplies kisses.
Jer 30:14 I have struck you as an e would
La   2: 5 The Lord is like an e;
Mic   2: 8 my people have risen up like an e.
Mt   13:39 the e who sows them is the devil.
Lk   10:19 to overcome all the power of the e;
Ro   12:20 "If your e is hungry, feed him;
1Co 15:26 The last e to be destroyed is death.
1Ti   5:14 and to give the e no opportunity
1Pe   5: 8 Your e the devil prowls around like

ENERGY*

Col   1:29 all the e Christ so powerfully works

ENGAGED

1Co   7:36 honorably toward the virgin he is e to,

ENGRAVE ENGRAVED, ENGRAVER

Ex   28:11 E the names of the sons of Israel
Zec   3: 9 and I will e an inscription on it,'

ENGRAVED ENGRAVE

Ex   32:16 the writing of God, e on the tablets.
Isa 49:16 I have e you on the palms of my
Jer 17: 1 "Judah's sin is e with an iron tool,
2Co   3: 7 which was e in letters on stone,

ENGRAVER* ENGRAVE

Ex   38:23 an e and designer,

ENHANCES*

Ro   3: 7 my falsehood e God's truthfulness

ENJOY JOY

Lev 26:34 the land will rest and e its sabbaths.
Nu   14:31 in to e the land you have rejected.
Dt   6: 2 you, and so that you may e long life.
Ps   37: 3 dwell in the land and e safe pasture.
Pr   28:16 ill-gotten gain will e a long reign.
Ecc   3:22 for a person than to e their work,
      5:19 and the ability to e them, to accept
      6: 2 not grant them the ability to e them,
              and strangers e them instead.
      9: 9 E life with your wife, whom you
Eph   6: 3 and that you may e long life
Heb 11:25 than to e the fleeting pleasures
3Jn   1: 2 I pray that you may e good health

ENJOYED JOY

2Ch 36:21 The land e its sabbath rests;

ENJOYMENT* JOY

Ecc   2:25 without him, who can eat or find e?
      4: 8 why am I depriving myself of e?"
      8:15 So I commend the e of life,
1Ti   6:17 us with everything for our e.

ENLARGE* LARGE

Ex   34:24 before you and e your territory,
1Ch   4:10 would bless me and e my territory!
Isa 54: 2 "E the place of your tent,
2Co   9:10 seed and will e the harvest of your

ENLARGED LARGE

Dt   12:20 your God has e your territory as he
Isa   9: 3 You have e the nation and increased
      26:15 You have e the nation, LORD;

ENLARGES LARGE

Dt   19: 8 LORD your God e your territory,

ENLIGHTEN* LIGHT

Isa 40:14 did the LORD consult to e him,

ENLIGHTENED* LIGHT

Eph   1:18 eyes of your heart may be e in order
Heb   6: 4 for those who have once been e,

ENMITY ENEMY
Ge 3:15 I will put **e** between you
Jas 4: 4 the world means **e** against God?

ENOCH
1. Son of Cain (Ge 4:17–18).
2. Descendant of Seth; walked with God and taken by him (Ge 5:18–24; Heb 11:5). Prophet (Jude 14).

ENOUGH
Dt 1: 6 "You have stayed long **e** at this
     9: 8 that he was angry **e** to destroy you.
2Sa 7:19 as if this were not **e** in your sight,
Ezr 9:14 Would you not be angry **e** with us
Pr 30:15 satisfied, four that never say, 'E!':
Ecc 1: 8 The eye never has **e** of seeing,
     5:10 Whoever loves money never has **e**;
Isa 7:13 Is it not **e** to try the patience
Joel 2:19 and olive oil, **e** to satisfy you fully;
Hag 1: 6 You eat, but never have **e**.

ENRICH* RICH
Ps 65: 9 and water it; you **e** it abundantly.
Pr 5:10 and your toil **e** the house of another.

ENRICHED RICH
1Co 1: 5 him you have been **e** in every way—
2Co 9:11 You will be **e** in every way so that you

ENSLAVE SLAVE
Jer 30: 8 no longer will foreigners **e** them.

ENSLAVED SLAVE
Ge 15:13 that they will be **e** and mistreated
Gal 4: 9 wish to be **e** by them all over again?
Titus 3: 3 and **e** by all kinds of passions

ENSLAVES* SLAVE
2Co 11:20 even put up with anyone who **e** you

ENSLAVING* SLAVE
Ex 6: 5 whom the Egyptians are **e**, and I

ENSNARE SNARE
Pr 5:22 evil deeds of the wicked **e** them;
Ecc 7:26 escape her, but the sinner she will **e**.

ENSNARED* SNARE
Dt 7:25 or you will be **e** by it, for it is
    12:30 be careful not to be **e** by inquiring
Ps 9:16 the wicked are **e** by the work
Pr 6: 2 said, **e** by the words of your mouth.
    22:25 learn their ways and get yourself **e**.

ENTANGLE* ENTANGLED, ENTANGLES
Ps 35: 8 may the net they hid **e** them,

ENTANGLED ENTANGLE
Ps 116: 3 The cords of death **e** me,
2Ti 2: 4 a soldier gets **e** in civilian affairs,
2Pe 2:20 Jesus Christ and are again **e** in it

ENTANGLES* ENTANGLE
Heb 12: 1 hinders and the sin that so easily **e**.

ENTER ENTERED, ENTERING, ENTERS, ENTRANCE
Ge 6:18 with you, and you will **e** the ark—
Ex 40:35 Moses could not **e** the tent
Nu 20:24 He will not **e** the land I give
Dt 1:37 and said, "You shall not **e** it, either.
Ps 95:11 'They shall never **e** my rest.' "
    100: 4 **E** his gates with thanksgiving
    118:20 through which the righteous may **e**.
Pr 2:10 For wisdom will **e** your heart,
Isa 26: 2 that the righteous nation may **e**,
    35:10 They will **e** Zion with singing;
    51:11 They will **e** Zion with singing;
Eze 37: 5 I will make breath **e** you, and you
Mt 5:20 you will certainly not **e** the kingdom
     7:13 "**E** through the narrow gate.
     7:21 will **e** the kingdom of heaven,
    18: 3 you will never **e** the kingdom
    18: 8 It is better for you to **e** life maimed
    19:17 If you want to **e** life,
Mk 10:15 like a little child will never **e** it."
    10:23 the rich to **e** the kingdom of God!"
Lk 13:24 effort to **e** through the narrow door,
    13:24 will try to **e** and will not be able to.
    24:26 these things and then **e** his glory?"
Jn 3: 5 no one can **e** the kingdom of God
Heb 3:11 'They shall never **e** my rest.' "
     4: 3 Now we who have believed **e**
     4:11 make every effort to **e** that rest,
     9:12 He did not **e** by means of the blood
    10:19 confidence to **e** the Most Holy Place
Rev 15: 8 no one could **e** the temple until
    21:27 Nothing impure will ever **e** it,

ENTERED ENTER
Ge 7: 9 came to Noah and **e** the ark, as God
Ex 24:18 Moses **e** the cloud as he went
Nu 7:89 When Moses **e** the tent of meeting
Dt 26: 1 you have **e** the land the LORD
2Ch 26:16 **e** the temple of the LORD to burn
Ps 73:17 till I **e** the sanctuary of God;
Isa 28:15 "We have **e** into a covenant
Eze 4:14 impure meat has ever **e** my mouth."
    37:10 commanded me, and breath **e** them;
    43: 4 of the LORD **e** the temple through
Lk 9:34 they were afraid as they **e** the cloud.
    22: 3 Then Satan **e** Judas, called Iscariot,
Jn 13:27 took the bread, Satan **e** into him.
Ac 11: 8 or unclean has ever **e** my mouth.'
Ro 5:12 just as sin **e** the world through one
Heb 6:20 Jesus, has **e** on our behalf.
     9:12 he **e** the Most Holy Place once
Rev 11:11 the breath of life from God **e** them,

ENTERING ENTER
Nu 32: 9 **e** the land the LORD had given
Mt 21:31 the prostitutes are **e** the kingdom
Lk 11:52 have hindered those who were **e**."
Heb 4: 1 the promise of **e** his rest still stands,

ENTERS ENTER
Mk 7:18 that nothing that **e** a person
Jn 10: 2 The one who **e** by the gate is
Heb 4:10 for anyone who **e** God's rest

ENTERTAIN* ENTERTAINMENT
Jdg 16:25 "Bring out Samson to **e** us."
Mt   9: 4 "Why do you **e** evil thoughts
1Ti 5:19 Do not **e** an accusation against

ENTERTAINMENT* ENTERTAIN
Da   6:18 without any **e** being brought to him.

ENTHRALLED*
Ps 45:11 Let the king be **e** by your beauty;

ENTHRONED* THRONE
1Sa 4: 4 who is **e** between the cherubim.
2Sa 6: 2 who is **e** between the cherubim
2Ki 19:15 of Israel, **e** between the cherubim,
1Ch 13: 6 who is **e** between the cherubim—
Ps   2: 4 The One **e** in heaven laughs;
     7: 7 while you sit **e** over them on high.
     9: 4 sitting **e** as the righteous judge.
     9:11 praises of the LORD, **e** in Zion;
    22: 3 Yet you are **e** as the Holy One;
    29:10 The LORD sits **e** over the flood;
    29:10 the LORD is **e** as King forever.
    55:19 God, who is **e** from of old,
    61: 7 May he be **e** in God's presence
    80: 1 You who sit **e** between
    99: 1 he sits **e** between the cherubim,
   102:12 But you, LORD, sit **e** forever;
   113: 5 God, the One who sits **e** on high,
   123: 1 to you, to you who sit **e** in heaven.
   132:14 here I will sit **e**, for I have desired it.
Isa 14:13 I will sit **e** on the mount
    37:16 of Israel, **e** between the cherubim,
    40:22 He sits **e** above the circle
    52: 2 rise up, sit **e**, Jerusalem.
Rev 18: 7 heart she boasts, 'I sit **e** as queen.

ENTHRONES* THRONE
Job 36: 7 he **e** them with kings and exalts

ENTHUSIASM*
2Co 8:17 but he is coming to you with much **e**
     9: 2 your **e** has stirred most of them

ENTICE ENTICED, ENTICES
2Ch 18:19 'Who will **e** Ahab king of Israel
Pr   1:10 if sinful men **e** you, do not give
2Pe 2:18 they **e** people who are just escaping
Rev 2:14 who taught Balak to **e** the Israelites

ENTICED* ENTICE
Nu 31:16 **e** the Israelites to be unfaithful
Dt   4:19 do not be **e** into bowing down
    11:16 or you will be **e** to turn away
2Ki 17:21 Jeroboam **e** Israel away
Job 31: 9 my heart has been **e** by a woman,
    31:27 so that my heart was secretly **e**
Eze 14: 9 the prophet is **e** to utter a prophecy,
    14: 9 I the LORD have **e** that prophet,
Jas 1:14 away by their own evil desire and **e**.

ENTICES* ENTICE
Dt 13: 6 or your closest friend secretly **e** you,
Job 36:18 careful that no one **e** you by riches;
Pr 16:29 A violent person **e** their neighbor

ENTIRE
Ex 14:28 the **e** army of Pharaoh that had
Dt   2:14 that **e** generation of fighting men
Jos 11:16 So Joshua took this **e** land:
Lk   2: 1 be taken of the **e** Roman world.
Ac 11:28 spread over the **e** Roman world.
    18: 8 and his **e** household believed
Gal 5:14 For the **e** law is fulfilled in keeping

ENTRANCE ENTER
Ex 26:36 "For the **e** to the tent make a curtain
    27:16 "For the **e** to the courtyard,
Mt 27:60 stone in front of the **e** to the tomb
Mk 15:46 he rolled a stone against the **e**
    16: 3 away from the **e** of the tomb?"
Jn 11:38 a cave with a stone laid across the **e**.
    20: 1 stone had been removed from the **e**.
Ac 12: 6 and sentries stood guard at the **e**.

ENTREAT ENTREATY
Zec 8:21 'Let us go at once to **e** the LORD

ENTREATY ENTREAT
2Ch 33:19 and how God was moved by his **e**,

ENTRUST TRUST
Jn   2:24 Jesus would not **e** himself to them,
2Ti 2: 2 many witnesses **e** to reliable people

ENTRUSTED TRUST
Ge 39: 4 and he **e** to his care everything he
2Ki 22: 7 account for the money **e** to them,
Jer 13:20 is the flock that was **e** to you,
Lk 12:48 the one who has been **e** with much,
Jn   5:22 but has **e** all judgment to the Son,
Ro   3: 2 the Jews have been **e** with the very
1Co 4: 1 as those **e** with the mysteries God
Gal 2: 7 that I had been **e** with the task
1Th 2: 4 by God to be **e** with the gospel.
1Ti 1:11 the blessed God, which he **e** to me.
     6:20 guard what has been **e** to your care.
2Ti 1:12 to guard what I have **e** to him until
     1:14 the good deposit that was **e** to you—
Titus 1: 3 light through the preaching **e** to me
1Pe 2:23 he **e** himself to him who judges
     5: 3 not lording it over those **e** to you,
Jude 1: 3 once for all **e** to God's holy people.

ENVELOPED*
Isa 42:25 It **e** them in flames, yet they did not

ENVIED ENVY
Ps 73: 3 For I **e** the arrogant when I saw

ENVIOUS ENVY
Dt 32:21 I will make them **e** by those who are
Ps 37: 1 evil or be **e** of those who do wrong;
Pr 24:19 of evildoers or be **e** of the wicked,
Ro 10:19 "I will make you **e** by those who
    11:11 to the Gentiles to make Israel **e**.

ENVOY
Pr 13:17 but a trustworthy **e** brings healing.

ENVY ENVIED, ENVIOUS, ENVYING

Pr   3:31 Do not **e** the violent or choose any
     14:30 life to the body, but **e** rots the bones.
     23:17 Do not let your heart **e** sinners,
     24: 1 Do not **e** the wicked, do not desire
Ecc   4: 4 from one person's **e** of another.
Mk   7:22 malice, deceit, lewdness, **e**, slander,
Ro   1:29 They are full of **e**, murder, strife,
    11:14 arouse my own people to **e** and save
1Co 13: 4 It does not **e**, it does not boast, it is
Gal   5:21 and **e**; drunkenness, orgies,
Php   1:15 true that some preach Christ out of **e**
1Ti   6: 4 quarrels about words that result in **e**,
Titus 3: 3 We lived in malice and **e**,
Jas   3:14 But if you harbor bitter **e** and selfish
     3:16 For where you have **e** and selfish
1Pe   2: 1 hypocrisy, **e**, and slander of every

ENVYING* ENVY

Gal   5:26 provoking and **e** each other.

EPAPHRAS*

Associate of Paul (Col 1:7; 4:12; Phm 23).

EPAPHRODITUS*

Associate of Paul (Php 2:25; 4:18).

EPHAH

Ex 16:36 (An omer is one-tenth of an **e**.)
Eze 45:10 an accurate **e** and an accurate bath.
Mic 6:10 and the short **e**, which is accursed?

EPHESIANS EPHESUS

Ac 19:28 "Great is Artemis of the **E**!"

EPHESUS EPHESIANS

Ac 18:19 They arrived at **E**, where Paul left
    19: 1 the interior and arrived at **E**.
    20:17 Paul sent to **E** for the elders
1Co 15:32 If I fought wild beasts in **E** with no
Eph 1: 1 God, To God's holy people in **E**,
Rev 2: 1 the angel of the church in **E** write:

EPHOD

Ex 28: 6 "Make the **e** of gold, and of blue,
Jdg 8:27 Gideon made the gold into an **e**,
    17: 5 he made an **e** and some household
1Sa 2:18 a boy wearing a linen **e**.
1Ch 15:27 David also wore a linen **e**.
Hos 3: 4 stones, without **e** or household gods.

EPHPHATHA*

Mk 7:34 a deep sigh said to him, *"E!"*

EPHRAIM

1. Second son of Joseph (Ge 41:52; 46:20). Blessed as firstborn by Jacob (Ge 48). Tribe of numbered (Nu 1:33; 26:37), blessed (Dt 33:17), allotted land (Jos 16:4–9; Eze 48:5), failed to fully possess (Jos 16:10; Jdg 1:29).

2. A term for the Northern Kingdom of Israel (Isa 7:17; Hos 5).

EPHRATH BETHLEHEM, EPHRATHAH

Ge 35:19 was buried on the way to **E** (that is,

EPHRATHAH EPHRATH

Ru 4:11 May you have standing in **E** and be
Mic 5: 2 Bethlehem **E**, though you are small

EPHRON

Hittite who sold Abraham a field (Ge 23).

EPICUREAN*

Ac 17:18 A group of **E** and Stoic philosophers

EPISTLE (KJV) See LETTER

EQUAL EQUALED, EQUALITY, EQUITY

Ge 44:18 though you are **e** to Pharaoh
Dt 33:25 and your strength will **e** your days.
1Ki 3:13 you will have no **e** among kings.
Isa 40:25 Or who is my **e**?" says the Holy
    46: 5 you compare me or count me **e**?
Da 1:19 and he found none **e** to Daniel,
Jn 5:18 Father, making himself **e** with God.
1Co 12:25 its parts should have **e** concern
2Co 2:16 And who is **e** to such a task?

EQUALED EQUAL

Mk 13:19 and never to be **e** again.

EQUALITY* EQUAL

2Co 8:13 pressed, but that there might be **e**.
    8:14 what you need. The goal is **e**,
Php 2: 6 God, did not consider **e** with God

EQUIP* EQUIPMENT, EQUIPPED

Eph 4:12 to **e** his people for works of service,
Heb 13:21 **e** you with everything good

EQUIPMENT EQUIP

Nu 3:36 all its **e**, and everything related
Zec 11:15 me, "Take again the **e** of a foolish

EQUIPPED EQUIP

2Ti 3:17 God may be thoroughly **e** for every

EQUITY* EQUAL

Ps   9: 8 and judges the peoples with **e**.
    58: 1 Do you judge people with **e**?
    67: 4 for you rule the peoples with **e**
    75: 2 it is I who judge with **e**.
    96:10 he will judge the peoples with **e**.
    98: 9 and the peoples with **e**.
    99: 4 you have established **e**; in Jacob you

ER

Ge 38: 6 Judah got a wife for **E**, his firstborn,

ERASTUS*

Associate(s) of Paul (Ac 19:22; Ro 16:23; 2Ti 4:20).

ERECT ERECTED

Dt 16:22 and do not **e** a sacred stone,

ERECTED ERECT
1Ki 7:21 He e the pillars at the portico
2Ki 21: 3 he also e altars to Baal and made

ERODES*
Job 14:18 "But as a mountain e and crumbles

ERRED* ERROR
Nu 15:28 for the one who e by sinning

ERROR ERRED, ERRORS
Job 4:18 if he charges his angels with e,
Isa 47:15 All of them go on in their e;
Mt 22:29 in e because you do not know
Ro 1:27 the due penalty for their e.
Jas 5:20 the e of their way will save them
2Pe 2:18 escaping from those who live in e.
     3:17 carried away by the e of the lawless
Jude 1:11 rushed for profit into Balaam's e;

ERRORS* ERROR
Ps 19:12 But who can discern their own e?

ESAU EDOM
Firstborn of Isaac, twin of Jacob (Ge 25:21–26).
Also called Edom (Ge 25:30). Sold Jacob his birthright (Ge 25:29–34); lost blessing (Gen 27). Married Hittites (Ge 26:34), Ishmaelites (Ge 28:6–9).
Reconciled to Jacob (Gen 33). Genealogy (Ge 36).
The LORD chose Jacob over Esau (Mal 1:2–3), but
gave Esau land (Dt 2:2–12). Descendants eventu-
ally obliterated (Ob 1–21; Jer 49:7–22).

ESCAPE ESCAPED, ESCAPES, ESCAPING
Ge 7: 7 wives entered the ark to e the waters
1Sa 19:10 That night David made good his e.
2Sa 15:14 or none of us will e from Absalom.
Job 11:20 will fail, and e will elude them;
Ps 68:20 the Sovereign LORD comes e
    89:48 who can e the power of the grave?
Pr 11: 9 through knowledge the righteous e.
    12:13 talk, and so the innocent e trouble.
Ecc 7:26 man who pleases God will e her,
Jer 11:11 on them a disaster they cannot e.
Eze 6: 9 those who e will remember me—
Mt 23:33 How will you e being condemned
Ro 2: 3 think you will e God's judgment?
1Th 5: 3 woman, and they will not e.
2Ti 2:26 and e from the trap of the devil,
Heb 2: 3 how shall we e if we ignore so great
    12:25 If they did not e when they refused

ESCAPED ESCAPE
1Sa 22: 1 Gath and e to the cave of Adullam.
Ps 124: 7 We have e like a bird
   124: 7 has been broken, and we have e.
La 2:22 day of the LORD's anger no one e
Jn 10:39 to seize him, but he e their grasp.
Heb 11:34 flames, and e the edge of the sword;
2Pe 1: 4 having e the corruption in the world
     2:20 If they have e the corruption

ESCAPES* ESCAPE
Ps 33:16 no warrior e by his great strength.

Joel 2: 3 a desert waste—nothing e them.

ESCAPING ESCAPE
1Co 3:15 only as one e through the flames.
2Pe 2:18 they entice people who are just e

ESHKOL
Nu 13:23 When they reached the Valley of E,

ESTABLISH ESTABLISHED, ESTABLISHES
Ge 6:18 But I will e my covenant with you,
     9: 9 "I now e my covenant with you
    17:21 But my covenant I will e with Isaac,
Ex 23:31 "I will e your borders from the Red
Dt 28: 9 The LORD will e you as his holy
2Sa 7:11 the LORD himself will e a house
1Ki 9: 5 I will e your royal throne over Israel
1Ch 28: 7 I will e his kingdom forever if he is
Ps 89: 4 'I will e your line forever and make
    90:17 e the work of our hands for us—yes, e
           the work of our hands.
Pr 16: 3 you do, and he will e your plans.
Isa 26:12 LORD, you e peace for us;
Eze 16:60 I will e an everlasting covenant
Ro 10: 3 of God and sought to e their own,
    10:25 Now to him who is able to e you
Heb 10: 9 sets aside the first to e the second.

ESTABLISHED ESTABLISH
Ge 9:17 the covenant I have e between me
Ex 6: 4 e my covenant with them to give
Dt 19:15 A matter must be e by the testimony
2Sa 7:16 your throne will be e forever.' "
1Ki 2:46 The kingdom was now e
Ps 8: 2 and infants you have e a stronghold
    78:69 like the earth that he e forever.
    93: 2 Your throne was e long ago;
    96:10 The world is firmly e, it cannot be
   103:19 The LORD has e his throne
   111: 8 They are e for ever and ever,
Pr 16:12 a throne is e through righteousness.
    20:18 Plans are e by seeking advice;
Isa 2: 2 temple will be e as the highest
    54:14 In righteousness you will be e:
Jer 33: 2 the LORD who formed it and e it—
    33:25 night and e the laws of heaven
Ro 13: 1 except that which God has e.
    13: 1 that exist have been e by God.
2Co 13: 1 "Every matter must be e
Gal 3:17 set aside the covenant previously e
Eph 3:17 that you, being rooted and e in love,
Col 1:23 continue in your faith, e and firm,
Heb 8: 6 one, since the new covenant is e
2Pe 1:12 are firmly e in the truth you now

ESTABLISHES ESTABLISH
Job 25: 2 he e order in the heights of heaven.
Pr 16: 9 course, but the LORD e their steps.
Isa 42: 4 or be discouraged till he e justice
    62: 7 give him no rest till he e Jerusalem

ESTATE
Ge 15: 2 one who will inherit my e is Eliezer
Ru 4: 6 I might endanger my own e.

Est   8: 7 Jews, I have given his **e** to Esther,
Ps 136:23 He remembered us in our low **e**
Lk   15:12 'Father, give me my share of the **e**.'

ESTEEM* ESTEEMED

Est   10: 3 in high **e** by his many fellow Jews,
Isa   2:22 Why hold them in **e**?
        53: 3 despised, and we held him in low **e**.
Gal   2: 6 for those who were held in high **e**—

ESTEEMED ESTEEM

Pr   22: 1 to be **e** is better than silver or gold.
Da   10:11 you who are highly **e**,

ESTHER HADASSAH

Jewess, originally named Hadassah, who lived
in Persia; cousin of Mordecai (Est 2:7). Chosen queen of Xerxes (Est 2:8–18). Persuaded by
Mordecai to foil Haman's plan to exterminate the
Jews (Est 3–4). Revealed Haman's plans to Xerxes, resulting in Haman's death (Est 7), the Jews'
preservation (Est 8–9), Mordecai's exaltation (Est
8:15; 9:4; 10). Decreed celebration of Purim (Est
9:18–32).

ETERNAL* ETERNITY

Ge   21:33 the name of the LORD, the E God.
Dt   33:27 The **e** God is your refuge,
1Ki   10: 9 of the LORD's **e** love for Israel,
Ps   16:11 with **e** pleasures at your right hand.
      111:10 To him belongs **e** praise.
      119:89 Your word, LORD, is **e**;
      119:160 all your righteous laws are **e**.
Ecc   12: 5 Then people go to their **e** home
Isa   26: 4 the LORD himself, is the Rock **e**.
       47: 7 said, 'I am forever—the **e** queen!'
Jer   10:10 he is the living God, the **e** King.
Da   4: 3 His kingdom is an **e** kingdom;
       4:34 His dominion is an **e** dominion;
Mt   18: 8 two feet and be thrown into **e** fire.
       19:16 good thing must I do to get **e** life?"
       19:29 times as much and will inherit **e** life.
       25:41 into the **e** fire prepared for the devil
       25:46 they will go away to **e** punishment,
       25:46 but the righteous to **e** life."
Mk   3:29 they are guilty of an **e** sin."
       10:17 "what must I do to inherit **e** life?"
       10:30 and in the age to come **e** life.
Lk   10:25 "what must I do to inherit **e** life?"
       16: 9 will be welcomed into **e** dwellings.
       18:18 what must I do to inherit **e** life?"
       18:30 age, and in the age to come **e** life."
Jn   3:15 who believes may have **e** life
       3:16 him shall not perish but have **e** life.
       3:36 believes in the Son has **e** life,
       4:14 of water welling up to **e** life."
       4:36 wage and harvests a crop for **e** life,
       5:24 believes in him who sent me has **e** life
       5:39 think that in them you have **e** life.
       6:27 but for food that endures to **e** life,
       6:40 and believes in him shall have **e** life,
       6:47 you, the one who believes has **e** life.
       6:54 flesh and drinks my blood has **e** life,
       6:68 You have the words of **e** life.
       10:28 I give them **e** life, and they shall

Jn   12:25 in this world will keep it for **e** life.
       12:50 that his command leads to **e** life.
       17: 2 he might give **e** life to all those you
       17: 3 Now this is **e** life: that they know
Ac   13:46 consider yourselves worthy of **e** life,
       13:48 were appointed for **e** life believed.
Ro   1:20 his **e** power and divine nature—
       2: 7 and immortality, he will give **e** life.
       5:21 bring **e** life through Jesus Christ our
       6:22 to holiness, and the result is **e** life.
       6:23 of God is **e** life in Christ Jesus our
       16:26 by the command of the **e** God,
2Co   4:17 for us an **e** glory that far outweighs
       4:18 temporary, but what is unseen is **e**.
       5: 1 from God, an **e** house in heaven,
Gal   6: 8 from the Spirit will reap **e** life.
Eph   3:11 according to his **e** purpose that he
2Th   2:16 his grace gave us **e** encouragement
1Ti   1:16 believe in him and receive **e** life.
       1:17 Now to the King **e**, immortal,
       6:12 Take hold of the **e** life to which you
2Ti   2:10 that is in Christ Jesus, with **e** glory.
Titus 1: 2 in the hope of **e** life, which God,
       3: 7 heirs having the hope of **e** life.
Heb   5: 9 he became the source of **e** salvation
       6: 2 of the dead, and **e** judgment.
       9:12 blood, thus obtaining **e** redemption.
       9:14 who through the **e** Spirit offered
       9:15 receive the promised **e** inheritance—
       13:20 of the **e** covenant brought back
1Pe   5:10 who called you to his **e** glory
2Pe   1:11 a rich welcome into the **e** kingdom
1Jn   1: 2 it, and we proclaim to you the **e** life,
       2:25 this is what he promised us—**e** life.
       3:15 no murderer has **e** life residing
       5:11 God has given us **e** life, and this life
       5:13 you may know that you have **e** life.
       5:20 He is the true God and **e** life.
Jude   1: 7 who suffer the punishment of **e** fire.
       1:21 Jesus Christ to bring you to **e** life.
Rev   14: 6 he had the **e** gospel to proclaim

ETERNAL LIFE Mt 19:16, 29; 25:46; Mk 10:17,
30; Lk 10:25; 18:18, 30; Jn 3:15, 16, 36; 4:14, 36;
5:24, 39; 6:27, 40, 47, 54, 68; 10:28; 12:25, 50; 17:2,
3; Ac 13:46, 48; Ro 2:7; 5:21; 6:22, 23; Gal 6:8; 1Ti
1:16; 6:12; Titus 1:2; 3:7; 1Jn 1:2; 2:25; 3:15; 5:11,
13, 20; Jude 1:21

ETERNITY* ETERNAL

Ps   93: 2 you are from all **e**.
Ecc   3:11 has also set **e** in the human heart;

ETHAN

1Ki   4:31 else, including E the Ezrahite—
1Ch   15:19 and E were to sound the bronze
Ps   89: T *A maskil of E the Ezrahite.*

ETHIOPIAN*

Jer   13:23 Can an E change his skin
Ac   8:27 and on his way he met an E eunuch,

EUNICE*

2Ti   1: 5 Lois and in your mother E and, I am

EUNUCH EUNUCHS
Est 2:14 the king's e who was in charge
Isa 56: 3 And let no e complain, "I am only
Ac   8:27 on his way he met an Ethiopian e,

EUNUCHS EUNUCH
2Ki 20:18 they will become e in the palace
Isa 56: 4 "To the e who keep my Sabbaths,
Mt   19:12 For there are e who were born
     19:12 there are e who have been made e
           by others—
     19:12 choose to live like e for the sake

EUODIA*
Php 4: 2 I plead with E and I plead

EUPHRATES
Ge   2:14 And the fourth river is the E.
     15:18 of Egypt to the great river, the E—
Dt   11:24 and from the E River
2Ki 24: 7 the Wadi of Egypt to the E River.
Rev 9:14 who are bound at the great river E."
     16:12 out his bowl on the great river E,

EUTYCHUS*
Ac   20: 9 window was a young man named E,

EVANGELIST* EVANGELISTS
Ac   21: 8 stayed at the house of Philip the e,
2Ti 4: 5 do the work of an e, discharge all

EVANGELISTS* EVANGELIST
Eph 4:11 the e, the pastors and teachers,

EVE*
Ge   3:20 Adam named his wife E,
      4: 1 Adam made love to his wife E,
2Co 11: 3 afraid that just as E was deceived
1Ti 2:13 For Adam was formed first, then E.

EVEN
Ru   1:17 if e death separates you and me."

EVEN-TEMPERED* TEMPER
Pr   17:27 and whoever has understanding is e.

EVENING EVENINGS
Ge   1: 5 And there was e, and there was
      8:11 the dove returned to him in the e,
     24:11 it was toward e, the time the women
Ps 102:11 My days are like the e shadow;
Ecc 11: 6 and at e let your hands not be idle,
Zec 14: 7 When e comes, there will be light.

EVENINGS* EVENING
Da   8:14 "It will take 2,300 e and mornings;
      8:26 "The vision of the e and mornings

EVENTS
2Ch 10:15 for this turn of e was from God,
Est 9:20 Mordecai recorded these e, and he
Lk   21:11 and fearful e and great signs
Ac   5:11 and all who heard about these e.

EVER EVERLASTING, FOREVER, FOREVERMORE
Ex   9:18 the worst hailstorm that has e fallen

Ex   11: 6 worse than there has e been or e will
     15:18 "The LORD reigns for e and e."
Dt   4:32 has anything like it e been heard of?
      8:19 you e forget the LORD your God
1Ki   3:12 anyone like you, nor will there e be.
2Ch 32:13 those nations e able to deliver their
Job   4: 7 being innocent, has e perished?
      4: 7 were the upright e destroyed?
Ps   5:11 you be glad; let them e sing for joy.
     10:16 The LORD is King for e and e;
     25: 3 one who hopes in you will e be put
     25:15 My eyes are e on the LORD,
     38:17 to fall, and my pain is e with me.
     45: 6 throne, O God, will last for e and e;
     45:17 nations will praise you for e and e.
     48:14 For this God is our God for e and e;
     49: 8 is costly, no payment is e enough—
     52: 8 in God's unfailing love for e and e.
     61: 8 I will e sing in praise of your name
     71: 6 I will e praise you.
     83:17 May they e be ashamed
     84: 4 they are e praising you.
     89:33 nor will I e betray my faithfulness.
    111: 8 They are established for e and e,
    132:12 will sit on your throne for e and e."
    145: 1 I will praise your name for e and e.
    145: 2 and extol your name for e and e.
    145:21 praise his holy name for e and e.
    148: 6 he established them for e and e—
Pr   4:18 shining e brighter till the full light
      5:19 may you e be intoxicated with her
Ecc   1: 6 it goes, e returning on its course.
Isa   6: 9 " 'Be e hearing, but never
      6: 9 be e seeing, but never perceiving.'
     66: 8 Who has e heard of such things?
     66: 8 Who has e seen things like this?
Jer   2:11 Has a nation e changed its gods?
      7: 7 I gave your ancestors for e and e.
     25: 5 you and your ancestors for e and e.
     31:36 "will Israel e cease being a nation
Da   2:20 to the name of God for e and e;
      7:18 possess it forever—yes, for e and e.'
     12: 3 like the stars for e and e.
Joel 2: 2 ancient times nor e will be in ages
Mic   4: 5 of the LORD our God for e and e.
Mt   9:33 "Nothing like this has e been seen
     13:14 " 'You will be e hearing but never
     13:14 you will be e seeing but never
Mk   11: 2 there, which no one has e ridden.
Jn   1:18 No one has e seen God, but the one
      3:13 No one has e gone into heaven
      7:46 "No one e spoke the way this man
Ac   28:26 "You will be e hearing but never
     28:26 you will be e seeing but never
Gal   1: 5 to whom be glory for e and e.
Eph   3:21 all generations, for e and e! Amen.
Php   4:20 God and Father be glory for e and e.
1Ti   1:17 God, be honor and glory for e and e.
2Ti   4:18 To him be glory for e and e. Amen.
Heb   1: 8 throne, O God, will last for e and e;
     13:21 to whom be glory for e and e.
1Pe   4:11 the glory and the power for e and e.
      5:11 To him be the power for e and e.

1Jn 4:12 No one has **e** seen God; but if we
Rev 1: 6 him be glory and power for **e** and **e**!
1:18 now look, I am alive for **e** and **e**!
4: 9 the throne and who lives for **e** and **e**,
7:12 strength be to our God for **e** and **e**.
10: 6 swore by him who lives for **e** and **e**,
11:15 and he will reign for **e** and **e**."
14:11 of their torment will rise for **e** and **e**.
20:10 tormented day and night for **e** and **e**.
21:27 Nothing impure will **e** enter it,
22: 5 And they will reign for **e** and **e**.

FOR EVER AND EVER Ex 15:18; Ps 9:5; 10:16;
21:4; 45:6, 17; 48:14; 52:8; 111:8; 119:44; 132:12,
14; 145:1, 2, 21; 148:6; Jer 7:7; 25:5; Da 2:20; 7:18;
12:3; Mic 4:5; Gal 1:5; Eph 3:21; Php 4:20; 1Ti
1:17; 2Ti 4:18; Heb 1:8; 13:21; 1Pe 4:11; 5:11; Rev
1:6, 18; 4:9, 10; 5:13; 7:12; 10:6; 11:15; 14:11; 15:7;
19:3; 20:10; 22:5

EVER-INCREASING* INCREASE
Ro 6:19 to impurity and to **e** wickedness,
2Co 3:18 into his image with **e** glory,

EVER-PRESENT* PRESENT
Ps 46: 1 and strength, an **e** help in trouble.

EVERLASTING* EVER
Ge 9:16 remember the **e** covenant between
17: 7 covenant as an **e** covenant between
17: 8 I will give as an **e** possession to you
17:13 in your flesh is to be an **e** covenant.
17:19 with him as an **e** covenant for his
48: 4 give this land as an **e** possession
Nu 18:19 It is an **e** covenant of salt before
Dt 33:15 and the fruitfulness of the **e** hills;
33:27 and underneath are the **e** arms.
2Sa 23: 5 have made with me an **e** covenant,
1Ch 16:17 a decree, to Israel as an **e** covenant:
16:36 the God of Israel, from **e** to **e**.
29:10 God of our father Israel, from **e** to **e**.
Ezr 9:12 your children as an **e** inheritance.'
Ne 9: 5 your God, who is from **e** to **e**."
Ps 41:13 the God of Israel, from **e** to **e**.
52: 5 God will bring you down to **e** ruin:
74: 3 your steps toward these **e** ruins,
78:66 he put them to **e** shame.
90: 2 world, from **e** to **e** you are God.
103:17 But from **e** to **e** the LORD's love is
105:10 a decree, to Israel as an **e** covenant:
106:48 the God of Israel, from **e** to **e**.
119:142 Your righteousness is **e** and your
139:24 in me, and lead me in the way **e**.
145:13 Your kingdom is an **e** kingdom,
Isa 9: 6 Mighty God, E Father,
24: 5 statutes and broken the **e** covenant.
30: 8 to come it may be an **e** witness.
33:14 of us can dwell with **e** burning?"
35:10 **e** joy will crown their heads.
40:28 The LORD is the **e** God,
45:17 by the LORD with an **e** salvation;
45:17 put to shame or disgraced, to ages **e**.
51:11 **e** joy will crown their heads.
54: 8 **e** kindness I will have compassion
55: 3 I will make an **e** covenant with you,

Isa 55:13 for an **e** sign, that will endure
56: 5 I will give them an **e** name that will
60:15 I will make you the **e** pride
60:19 for the LORD will be your **e** light,
60:20 the LORD will be your **e** light,
61: 7 your land, and **e** joy will be yours.
61: 8 and make an **e** covenant with them.
63:12 them, to gain for himself **e** renown,
Jer 5:22 the sea, an **e** barrier it cannot cross.
23:40 bring on you **e** disgrace—**e** shame
25: 9 of horror and scorn, and an **e** ruin.
31: 3 "I have loved you with an **e** love;
32:40 I will make an **e** covenant
50: 5 to the LORD in an **e** covenant
Eze 16:60 I will establish an **e** covenant
37:26 it will be an **e** covenant.
Da 7:14 His dominion is an **e** dominion
7:27 His kingdom will be an **e** kingdom,
9:24 to bring in **e** righteousness, to seal
12: 2 some to **e** life, others to shame and
e contempt.
Mic 6: 2 you **e** foundations of the earth.
Hab 1:12 LORD, are you not from **e**?
2Th 1: 9 will be punished with **e** destruction
Jude 1: 6 bound with **e** chains for judgment

EVERLASTING COVENANT Ge 9:16; 17:7,
13, 19; Nu 18:19; 2Sa 23:5; 1Ch 16:17; Ps 105:10;
Isa 24:5; 55:3; 61:8; Jer 32:40; 50:5; Eze 16:60;
37:26

EVERY EVERYONE, EVERYONE'S, EVERYTHING, EVERYWHERE
Ge 1:29 "I give you **e** seed-bearing plant
1:29 **e** tree that has fruit with seed in it.
6: 5 that **e** inclination of the thoughts
7: 4 of the earth **e** living creature I have
7:23 E living thing on the face
24: 1 LORD had blessed him in **e** way.
Ex 11: 5 E firstborn son in Egypt will die,
13: 2 "Consecrate to me **e** firstborn male.
Lev 17:14 the life of **e** creature is its blood.
Dt 7:15 will keep you free from **e** disease.
8: 1 follow **e** command I am giving you
8: 3 but on **e** word that comes
Jos 21:45 to Israel failed; **e** one was fulfilled.
23:14 E promise has been fulfilled;
1Ch 28: 9 for the LORD searches **e** heart and
understands **e** desire and **e** thought.
Ps 7:11 a God who displays his wrath **e** day.
50:10 for **e** animal of the forest is mine,
136:25 He gives food to **e** creature.
145: 2 E day I will praise you and extol
145:21 Let **e** creature praise his holy name
Pr 16:33 its **e** decision is from the LORD.
30: 5 "E word of God is flawless; he is
Ecc 3: 1 for **e** activity under the heavens:
12:14 For God will bring **e** deed into
judgment, including **e** hidden thing,
Isa 40: 4 E valley shall be raised up,
45:23 Before me **e** knee will bow; by me
e tongue
Jer 2:20 on **e** high hill and under **e** spreading
La 3:23 They are new **e** morning;

Eze 21: 7 E heart will melt with fear and
Mt 4: 4 but on e word that comes
 7:17 e good tree bears good fruit,
 12:25 "E kingdom divided against itself
 12:25 and e city or household divided
Jn 13:11 why he said not e one was clean.
 15: 2 He cuts off e branch in me
 15: 2 while e branch that does bear fruit
Ro 14:11 Lord, 'e knee will bow before me;
Php 2:10 name of Jesus e knee should bow,
1Th 5:22 reject e kind of evil.
1Jn 4: 1 do not believe e spirit, but test
Rev 1: 7 and "e eye will see him, even those
 7:17 God will wipe away e tear
 21: 4 'He will wipe e tear from their eyes.
 22: 2 of fruit, yielding its fruit e month.

EVERYONE EVERY, ONE
Dt 12: 8 here today, e doing as they see fit,
Jdg 17: 6 had no king; e did as they saw fit.
 21:25 had no king; e did as they saw fit.
1Ki 8:39 deal with e according to all they do,
Ps 11: 4 He observes e on earth;
 39: 5 E is but a breath, even those who
 53: 3 E has turned away, all have become
 62:12 "You reward e according to what
Pr 24:12 Will he not repay e according
Ecc 7: 2 for death is the destiny of e;
Jer 31:30 e will die for their own sin;
Joel 2:32 And e who calls on the name
Jnh 3: 8 Let e call urgently on God.
Mt 12:36 that e will have to give account
Lk 11: 4 also forgive e who sins against us.
 11:10 For e who asks receives;
Jn 3:15 e who believes may have eternal life
 13:35 By this e will know that you are my
Ac 2:21 e who calls on the name of the Lord
Ro 10:13 "E who calls on the name
1Co 10:33 as I try to please e in every way.
Heb 12:14 every effort to live in peace with e
1Pe 2:17 Show proper respect to e,
2Pe 3: 9 perish, but e to come to repentance.
1Jn 3: 4 E who sins breaks the law;
 4: 7 E who loves has been born of God
 5: 4 for e born of God overcomes

EVERYONE'S EVERY, ONE
Ac 1:24 prayed, "Lord, you know e heart.
2Co 4: 2 we commend ourselves to e conscience

EVERYTHING EVERY, THING
Ge 6:17 of life in it. E on earth will perish.
 39: 6 So Potiphar left e he had in Joseph's
Ex 7: 2 You are to say e I command you,
 19: 8 "We will do e the LORD has
 23:13 "Be careful to do e I have said
 24: 3 "E the LORD has said we will
Dt 15:18 your God will bless you in e you do.
 18:18 He will tell them e I command him.
 28:29 will be unsuccessful in e you do;
 29: 9 so that you may prosper in e you do.
1Ch 29:14 E comes from you, and we have
Ne 9: 6 You give life to e,

Job 1:11 out your hand and strike e he has,
Ps 24: 1 the LORD's, and e in it, the world,
 150: 6 Let e that has breath praise
Ecc 1: 2 E is meaningless."
 3: 1 There is a time for e, and a season
 3:11 He has made e beautiful in its time.
 3:14 that e God does will endure forever;
 10:19 and money is the answer for e.
Da 4:37 because e he does is right and all his
Mt 5:18 the Law until e is accomplished.
 28:20 to obey e I have commanded you.
Mk 9:23 "E is possible for one who
Lk 18:22 Sell e you have and give
Jn 14:26 will remind you of e I have said
Ac 2:44 were together and had e in common.
 3:22 you must listen to e he tells you.
 4:32 own, but they shared e they had.
1Co 6:12 but not e is beneficial.
 10:23 but not e is beneficial.
 10:23 but not e is constructive.
 15:27 For he "has put e under his feet."
 15:27 that "e" has been put under him,
 15:27 himself, who put e under Christ.
 16:14 Do e in love.
Gal 3:22 has locked up e under the control
1Ti 4: 4 For e God created is good,
2Pe 1: 3 power has given us e we need
Rev 21: 5 throne said, "I am making e new!"

EVERYWHERE EVERY, WHERE
Pr 15: 3 The eyes of the LORD are e,

EVIDENCE EVIDENT
Mk 14:55 were looking for e against Jesus so
Jn 14:11 on the e of the works themselves.
2Th 1: 5 All this is e that God's judgment is
Jas 2:20 do you want e that faith without

EVIDENT EVIDENCE
Php 4: 5 Let your gentleness be e to all.

EVIL EVILDOER, EVILDOERS, EVILS
Ge 2: 9 of the knowledge of good and e.
 3: 5 be like God, knowing good and e."
 6: 5 human heart was only e all the time.
 44: 4 'Why have you repaid good with e?
Ex 32:22 how prone these people are to e.
Nu 32:13 of those who had done e in his sight
Dt 1:35 this e generation shall see the good
 13: 5 You must purge the e from among
 28:20 ruin because of the e you have done
Jos 23:15 bring on you all the e things he has
Jdg 2:11 the Israelites did e in the eyes
 3: 7 The Israelites did e in the eyes
 3:12 Again the Israelites did e in the eyes
 3:12 they did this e the LORD gave
 4: 1 Again the Israelites did e in the eyes
 6: 1 The Israelites did e in the eyes
 10: 6 Again the Israelites did e in the eyes
 13: 1 Again the Israelites did e in the eyes
1Sa 12:20 "You have done all this e;
 16:14 and an e spirit from the LORD
 18:10 The next day an e spirit from God
 19: 9 an e spirit from the LORD came
1Ki 11: 6 So Solomon did e in the eyes

1Ki 16:25 But Omri did **e** in the eyes
2Ki 15:24 Pekahiah did **e** in the eyes
Job 1: 1 he feared God and shunned **e**.
1: 8 a man who fears God and shuns **e**."
2: 3 a man who fears God and shuns **e**.
15:35 conceive trouble and give birth to **e**;
28:28 and to shun **e** is understanding."
34:10 Far be it from God to do **e**,
36:21 Beware of turning to **e**, which you
Ps 5: 4 with you, **e** people are not welcome.
23: 4 I will fear no **e**, for you are with me;
28: 4 for their deeds and for their **e** work;
34:13 keep your tongue from **e** and your
34:14 Turn from **e** and do good;
34:16 LORD is against those who do **e**,
37: 1 not fret because of those who are **e**
37: 8 do not fret—it leads only to **e**.
37:27 Turn from **e** and do good;
49: 5 should I fear when **e** days come,
51: 4 and done what is **e** in your sight;
97:10 those who love the LORD hate **e**,
101: 4 have nothing to do with what is **e**.
141: 4 drawn to what is **e** so that I take part
Pr 3: 7 fear the LORD and shun **e**.
4:27 or the left; keep your foot from **e**.
8:13 To fear the LORD is to hate **e**;
8:13 **e** behavior and perverse speech.
11:19 but whoever pursues **e** finds death.
11:27 **e** comes to one who searches for it.
14:16 wise fear the LORD and shun **e**,
14:22 Do not those who plot **e** go astray?
16: 6 the fear of the LORD **e** is avoided.
17:13 **E** will never leave the house of one
who pays back **e** for good.
20:30 Blows and wounds scrub away **e**,
26:23 are fervent lips with an **e** heart.
Ecc 4: 3 who has not seen the **e** that is done
12:14 thing, whether it is good or **e**.
Isa 5:20 Woe to those who call **e** good and
good **e**,
13:11 I will punish the world for its **e**,
Jer 4:14 wash the **e** from your heart and be
18: 8 that nation I warned repents of its **e**,
18:10 if it does **e** in my sight and does not
Eze 3:18 dissuade them from their **e** ways
33:11 Turn from your **e** ways!
33:13 trust in their righteousness and do **e**,
33:13 will die for the **e** they have done.
33:15 decrees that give life, and do no **e**—
Hos 10:13 you have reaped **e**, you have eaten
Am 5:13 in such times, for the times are **e**.
5:14 Seek good, not **e**, that you may live.
Jnh 3: 8 Let them give up their **e** ways
Mic 3: 2 you who hate good and love **e**;
Hab 1:13 Your eyes are too pure to look on **e**;
Zec 8:17 do not plot **e** against each other,
Mal 2:17 "All who do **e** are good in the eyes
Mt 5:45 He causes his sun to rise on the **e**
6:13 but deliver us from the **e** one.'
7:11 though you are **e**, know how to give
12:35 an **e** man brings **e** things out of the **e**
13:38 weeds are the people of the **e** one,
15:19 out of the heart come **e** thoughts—

Mk 7:21 heart, that **e** thoughts come—
Lk 6: 9 to do good or to do **e**, to save life
11:13 though you are **e**, know how to give
Jn 3:19 of light because their deeds were **e**.
3:20 Everyone who does **e** hates
17:15 you protect them from the **e** one.
Ro 1:30 they invent ways of doing **e**;
2: 8 who reject the truth and follow **e**,
2: 9 for every human being who does **e**:
3: 8 "Let us do **e** that good may
6:12 body so that you obey its **e** desires.
7:19 to do, but the **e** I do not want to do—
7:21 to do good, **e** is right there with me.
12: 9 Hate what is **e**; cling to what is
12:17 Do not repay anyone **e** for **e**.
12:21 Do not be overcome by **e**, but
overcome **e** with good.
14:16 you know is good be spoken of as **e**.
16:19 good, and innocent about what is **e**.
1Co 10: 6 our hearts on **e** things as they did.
13: 6 Love does not delight in **e**
14:20 In regard to **e** be infants, but in your
Gal 1: 4 to rescue us from the present **e** age,
Eph 5:16 opportunity, because the days are **e**.
6:12 against the spiritual forces of **e**
6:16 all the flaming arrows of the **e** one.
Col 1:21 minds because of your **e** behavior.
3: 5 lust, **e** desires and greed, which is
1Th 5:22 reject every kind of **e**.
2Th 3: 3 you and protect you from the **e** one.
1Ti 6:10 of money is a root of all kinds of **e**.
2Ti 2:22 Flee the **e** desires of youth
3: 6 are swayed by all kinds of **e** desires,
Heb 5:14 to distinguish good from **e**.
Jas 1:13 For God cannot be tempted by **e**,
1:21 filth and the **e** that is so prevalent
2: 4 and become judges with **e** thoughts?
3: 6 a world of **e** among the parts
3: 8 It is a restless **e**, full of deadly
4:16 All such boasting is **e**.
1Pe 1:14 not conform to the **e** desires you had
2:16 your freedom as a cover-up for **e**;
3: 9 Do not repay **e** with **e** or insult
3: 9 the contrary, repay **e** with blessing,
3:10 days must keep their tongue from **e**
3:12 the Lord is against those who do **e**."
3:17 for doing good than for doing **e**.
2Pe 1: 4 in the world caused by **e** desires.
3: 3 and following their own **e** desires.
1Jn 2:13 you have overcome the **e** one.
2:14 and you have overcome the **e** one
3:12 Cain, who belonged to the **e** one
3:12 Because his own actions were **e**
5:18 and the **e** one cannot harm them.
5:19 is under the control of the **e** one.
3Jn 1:11 do not imitate what is **e** but what is
1:11 who does what is **e** has not seen
Jude 1:16 they follow their own **e** desires;

EVIL SPIRIT 1Sa 16:14, 15, 16, 23; 18:10; 19:9;
Ac 19:15, 16

EVIL SPIRITS Lk 7:21; 8:2; Ac 19:12, 13

EVIL IN THE EYES OF THE LORD† See
EYES

EVILDOER* EVIL

2Sa	3:39	the LORD repay the e according
Ps	10:15	call the e to account for his wickedness
	101: 8	I will cut off every e from the city
Pr	24:20	for the e has no future hope,
Mal	4: 1	arrogant and every e will be stubble,

EVILDOERS EVIL

1Sa	24:13	'From e come evil deeds,' so my
Job	8:20	or strengthen the hands of e.
	34: 8	He keeps company with e;
	34:22	no utter darkness, where e can hide.
Ps	14: 4	Do all these e know nothing?
	14: 6	You e frustrate the plans
	26: 5	I abhor the assembly of e and refuse
	36:12	See how the e lie fallen—
	53: 4	Do all these e know nothing?
	59: 2	Deliver me from e and save me
	64: 2	of the wicked, from the plots of e.
	92: 7	up like grass and all e flourish,
	92: 9	all e will be scattered.
	94: 4	all the e are full of boasting.
	94:16	will take a stand for me against e?
	119:115	from me, you e, that I may keep
	125: 5	the LORD will banish with the e.
	141: 4	deeds along with those who are e;
	141: 5	will still be against the deeds of e.
	141: 9	me safe from the traps set by e,
Pr	21:15	joy to the righteous but terror to e.
	24:19	Do not fret because of e or be
	28: 5	E do not understand what is right,
	29: 6	E are snared by their own sin,
Isa	1: 4	great, a brood of e, children given
	31: 2	nation, against those who help e.
Jer	23:14	They strengthen the hands of e,
Hos	10: 9	Will not war again overtake the e
Mal	3:15	Certainly e prosper, and even
Mt	7:23	Away from me, you e!'
Lk	13:27	Away from me, all you e!'
	18:11	robbers, e, adulterers—
2Ti	3:13	while e and impostors will go

EVILS* EVIL

Mk	7:23	All these e come from inside

EWE

2Sa	12: 3	except one little e lamb he had

EXACT*

Ge	43:21	us found his silver—the e weight—
Est	4: 7	including the e amount of money
Pr	22:23	up their case and will e life for life.
Mt	2: 7	from them the e time the star had
Jn	4:53	realized that this was the e time
Heb	1: 3	the e representation of his being,

EXALT* EXALTED, EXALTS

Ex	15: 2	my father's God, and I will e him.
Jos	3: 7	"Today I will begin to e you
1Sa	2:10	and e the horn of his anointed."
1Ch	25: 5	the promises of God to e him.

1Ch	29:12	power to e and give strength to all.
Job	19: 5	If indeed you would e yourselves
Ps	30: 1	I will e you, LORD, for you lifted
	34: 3	let us e his name together.
	35:26	may all who e themselves over me
	37:34	He will e you to inherit the land;
	38:16	e themselves over me when my feet
	75: 6	or from the desert can e themselves.
	89:17	and by your favor you e our horn.
	99: 5	E the LORD our God and worship
	99: 9	E the LORD our God and worship
	107:32	Let them e him in the assembly
	118:28	you are my God, and I will e you.
	145: 1	I will e you, my God the King;
Pr	4: 8	Cherish her, and she will e you;
	25: 6	Do not e yourself in the king's
	30:32	"If you play the fool and e yourself,
Isa	24:15	e the name of the LORD, the God
	25: 1	I will e you and praise your name,
Eze	29:15	will never again e itself
Da	4:37	praise and e and glorify the King
	11:36	He will e and magnify himself
	11:37	but will e himself above them all.
Hos	11: 7	High, I will by no means e them.
Mt	23:12	For those who e themselves will be
Lk	14:11	all those who e themselves will be
	18:14	all those who e themselves will be
2Th	2: 4	will e himself over everything

EXALTED* EXALT

Ex	15: 1	to the LORD, for he is highly e.
	15:21	to the LORD, for he is highly e.
Nu	24: 7	their kingdom will be e.
Jos	4:14	day the LORD e Joshua
2Sa	5:12	had e his kingdom for the sake
	22:47	E be my God, the Rock, my Savior!
	22:49	You e me above my foes;
	23: 1	of the man e by the Most High,
1Ch	14: 2	his kingdom had been highly e
	17:17	me as though I were the most e
	29:11	you are e as head over all.
	29:25	The LORD highly e Solomon
Ne	9: 5	and may it be e above all blessing
Job	24:24	For a little while they are e,
	36:22	"God is e in his power. Who is
	37:23	is beyond our reach and e in power;
Ps	18:46	to my Rock! E be God my Savior!
	18:48	You e me above my foes;
	21:13	Be e in your strength, LORD;
	27: 6	Then my head will be e
	35:27	"The LORD be e, who delights
	46:10	I will be e among the nations, I will be e in the earth."
	47: 9	earth belong to God; he is greatly e.
	57: 5	Be e, O God, above the heavens;
	57:11	Be e, O God, above the heavens;
	89:13	hand is strong, your right hand e.
	89:24	through my name his horn will be e.
	89:27	the most e of the kings of the earth.
	89:42	You have e the right hand of his
	92: 8	But you, LORD, are forever e.
	92:10	You have e my horn like
	97: 9	you are e far above all gods.
	99: 2	he is e over all the nations.

Ps 108: 5 Be **e**, O God, above the heavens;
113: 4 The LORD is **e** over all
138: 2 you have so **e** your solemn decree
138: 6 Though the LORD is **e**, he looks
148:13 the LORD, for his name alone is **e**;
Pr 11:11 blessing of the upright a city is **e**,
Isa 2: 2 it will be **e** above the hills, and all
2:11 the LORD alone will be **e**
2:12 for all that is **e** (and they will be
2:17 the LORD alone will be **e**
5:16 the LORD Almighty will be **e**
6: 1 high and **e**, seated on a throne;
12: 4 and proclaim that his name is **e**.
33: 5 The LORD is **e**, for he dwells
33:10 "Now will I be **e**; now will I be
52:13 be raised and lifted up and highly **e**.
57:15 is what the high and **e** One says—
Jer 17:12 throne, **e** from the beginning,
La 2:17 you, he has **e** the horn of your foes.
Eze 21:26 The lowly will be **e** and the **e** will be
brought low.
Hos 13: 1 he was **e** in Israel.
Mic 4: 1 it will be **e** above the hills,
6: 6 and bow down before the **e** God?
Mt 23:12 who humble themselves will be **e**.
Lk 14:11 who humble themselves will be **e**."
18:14 who humble themselves will be **e**."
Ac 2:33 **E** to the right hand of God, he has
5:31 God **e** him to his own right hand as
Php 1:20 now as always Christ will be **e**
2: 9 Therefore God **e** him to the highest
Heb 7:26 from sinners, **e** above the heavens.

EXALTS* EXALT
1Sa 2: 7 he humbles and he **e**.
Job 36: 7 them with kings and **e** them forever.
Ps 75: 7 He brings one down, he **e** another.
Pr 14:34 Righteousness **e** a nation, but sin

EXAMINE EXAMINED, EXAMINES
Job 34:23 God has no need to **e** people further,
Ps 11: 4 everyone on earth; his eyes **e** them.
17: 3 though you **e** me at night and test
26: 2 try me, **e** my heart and my mind;
Jer 17:10 search the heart and **e** the mind,
20:12 you who **e** the righteous and probe
La 3:40 Let us **e** our ways and test them,
1Co 11:28 to **e** themselves before they eat
2Co 13: 5 **E** yourselves to see whether you are

EXAMINED* EXAMINE
Job 5:27 "We have **e** this, and it is true.
13: 9 Would it turn out well if he **e** you?
Lk 23:14 I have **e** him in your presence
Ac 17:11 **e** the Scriptures every day to see
28:18 They **e** me and wanted to release

EXAMINES EXAMINE
Lev 13: 3 When the priest **e** that person,
Ps 11: 5 The LORD **e** the righteous,
Pr 5:21 the LORD, and he **e** all your paths.

EXAMPLE* EXAMPLES
2Ki 14: 3 everything he followed the **e** of his
Ecc 9:13 saw under the sun this **e** of wisdom

Eze 14: 8 and make them an **e** and a byword.
Jn 13:15 I have set you an **e** that you should
Ro 6:19 I am using an **e** from everyday life
7: 2 For **e**, by law a married woman is
1Co 11: 1 Follow my **e**, as I follow the
e of Christ.
Gal 3:15 let me take an **e** from everyday life.
Eph 5: 1 Follow God's **e**, therefore, as dearly
Php 3:17 Join together in following my **e**,
2Th 3: 7 how you ought to follow our **e**.
1Ti 1:16 his immense patience as an **e**
4:12 set an **e** for the believers in speech,
Titus 2: 7 everything set them an **e** by doing
Heb 4:11 following their **e** of disobedience.
Jas 3: 4 Or take ships as an **e**.
5:10 as an **e** of patience in the face
1Pe 2:21 leaving you an **e**, that you should
2Pe 2: 6 made them an **e** of what is going
Jude 1: 7 They serve as an **e** of those who

EXAMPLES* EXAMPLE
1Co 10: 6 Now these things occurred as **e**
10:11 These things happened to them as **e**
1Pe 5: 3 to you, but being **e** to the flock.

EXASPERATE*
Eph 6: 4 Fathers, do not **e** your children;

EXCEEDED
1Ki 10: 7 wealth you have far **e** the report I

EXCEL* EXCELLENT
Ge 49: 4 you will no longer **e**, for you went
1Co 14:12 try to **e** in those that build
2Co 8: 7 But since you **e** in everything—
8: 7 you also **e** in this grace of giving.

EXCELLENT EXCEL
Ps 45: 2 You are the most **e** of men and your
1Co 12:31 yet I will show you the most **e** way.
Php 4: 8 if anything is **e** or praiseworthy—
1Ti 3:13 have served well gain an **e** standing
Titus 3: 8 These things are **e** and profitable

EXCEPT
Nu 14:30 **e** Caleb son of Jephunneh
Dt 16: 6 **e** in the place he will choose as
2Sa 22:32 And who is the Rock **e** our God?
1Ki 15: 5 **e** in the case of Uriah the Hittite.
Hos 13: 4 no God but me, no Savior **e** me.
Mt 5:32 his wife, **e** for sexual immorality,
11:27 No one knows the Son **e** the Father,
11:27 no one knows the Father **e** the Son
19: 9 his wife, **e** for sexual immorality,
Mk 10:18 "No one is good—**e** God alone.
Lk 11:29 none will be given it **e** the sign
Jn 3:13 into heaven **e** the one who came
6:46 has seen the Father **e** the one who is
14: 6 comes to the Father **e** through me.
17:12 has been lost **e** the one doomed
1Co 10:13 has overtaken you **e** what is

EXCESSIVE
2Co 2: 7 not be overwhelmed by **e** sorrow.

EXCHANGE EXCHANGED, EXCHANGING
Mt   16:26 what can anyone give in **e** for their
Mk   8:37 what can anyone give in **e** for their
2Co   6:13 As a fair **e**—I speak as to my

EXCHANGED EXCHANGE
Ps 106:20 They **e** their glorious God
Jer   2:11 my people have **e** their glorious God
Hos   4: 7 they **e** their glorious God
Ro   1:23 **e** the glory of the immortal God
        1:25 They **e** the truth about God for a lie,
        1:26 Even their women **e** natural sexual

EXCHANGING* EXCHANGE
Jn   2:14 and others sitting at tables **e** money.

EXCLAIM
Ps   35:10 My whole being will **e**, "Who is

EXCLUDE* EXCLUDED
Isa   56: 3 "The LORD will surely **e** me
        66: 5 you, and **e** you because of my name,
Lk   6:22 when they **e** you and insult you
Rev 11: 2 But **e** the outer court;

EXCLUDED EXCLUDE
Eph   2:12 **e** from citizenship in Israel

EXCREMENT
2Ki 18:27 you, will have to eat their own **e**

EXCUSE* EXCUSES
Lk   14:18 I must go and see it. Please **e** me.'
        14:19 way to try them out. Please **e** me.'
Jn   15:22 but now they have no **e** for their sin.
Ro   1:20 made, so that people are without **e**.
        2: 1 have no **e**, you who pass judgment

EXCUSES* EXCUSE
Lk   14:18 "But they all alike began to make **e**.

EXECUTE EXECUTED
Isa   66:16 sword the LORD will **e** judgment
Eze 20:35 to face, I will **e** judgment upon you.
Da   2:24 had appointed to **e** the wise men
        2:24 "Do not **e** the wise men of Babylon.
Jn   18:31 we have no right to **e** anyone,"

EXECUTED EXECUTE
Mt   27:20 for Barabbas and to have Jesus **e**.

EXERTED*
Eph   1:20 he **e** when he raised Christ

EXHAUST* EXHAUSTED, EXHAUSTION
Jer   51:58 the peoples **e** themselves
Hab   2:13 that the nations **e** themselves

EXHAUSTED EXHAUST
Da   8:27 I lay **e** for several days.
Lk   22:45 found them asleep, **e** from sorrow.

EXHAUSTION* EXHAUST
Pr   6: 3 to the point of **e**—and give your

EXHORT* EXHORTATION
1Ti   5: 1 but **e** him as if he were your father.

EXHORTATION* EXHORT
Ac   13:15 you have a word of **e** for the people,
Heb 13:22 urge you to bear with my word of **e**,

EXILE EXILED, EXILES
2Ki 17:23 their homeland into **e** in Assyria,
        25:11 into **e** the people who remained
Ezr   6:21 who had returned from the **e** ate it,
Ne   1: 2 remnant that had survived the **e**,
Est   2: 6 who had been carried into **e**
Isa   5:13 Therefore my people will go into **e**
Jer   13:19 All Judah will be carried into **e**,
        48: 7 and Chemosh will go into **e**,
        49: 3 for Molek will go into **e**,
La   1: 3 harsh labor, Judah has gone into **e**.
Am   9:14 bring my people Israel back from **e**.

EXILED EXILE
Ne   1: 9 then even if your **e** people are

EXILES EXILE
Ezr   6:19 the **e** celebrated the Passover.
Ps 147: 2 he gathers the **e** of Israel.
Isa   56: 8 he who gathers the **e** of Israel:
Jer   24: 5 I regard as good the **e** from Judah,
Eze 11:25 I told the **e** everything the LORD
Zep   3:19 rescue the lame; I will gather the **e**.
1Pe   2:11 as foreigners and **e**, to abstain

EXISTS
Ecc   6:10 Whatever **e** has already been
Heb   2:10 and through whom everything **e**,
        11: 6 comes to him must believe that he **e**

EXODUS*
Heb 11:22 spoke about the **e** of the Israelites

EXPANSES*
Job 38:18 Have you comprehended the vast **e**

EXPECT EXPECTANTLY, EXPECTATION, EXPECTED, EXPECTING
Isa   64: 3 awesome things that we did not **e**,
Mt   11: 3 or should we **e** someone else?"
        24:44 at an hour when you do not **e** him.
Lk   12:40 at an hour when you do not **e** him."
Php   1:20 I eagerly **e** and hope that I will in no

EXPECTANTLY EXPECT
Ps   5: 3 my requests before you and wait **e**.

EXPECTATION* EXPECT
Eze 19: 5 her hope unfulfilled, her **e** gone,
Ro   8:19 waits in eager **e** for the children
Heb 10:27 but only a fearful **e** of judgment

EXPECTED EXPECT
Ge   48:11 "I never **e** to see your face again,
Hag   1: 9 "You **e** much, but see, it turned

EXPECTING EXPECT
Lk   6:35 to them without **e** to get anything

EXPEL* EXPELLED
1Co 5:13 "E the wicked person from among

EXPELLED* EXPEL
1Sa 28: 3 Saul had e the mediums
1Ki 15:12 He e the male shrine prostitutes
Ezr 10: 8 and would himself be e
Eze 28:16 God, and I e you, guardian cherub,
Ac 13:50 and e them from their region.

EXPENSE* EXPENSIVE
Lk 10:35 you for any extra e you may have.'
1Co 9: 7 serves as a soldier at his own e?

EXPENSIVE* EXPENSE
Mt 26: 7 an alabaster jar of very e perfume,
Mk 14: 3 an alabaster jar of very e perfume,
Lk 7:25 No, those who wear e clothes
Jn 12: 3 a pint of pure nard, an e perfume;
1Ti 2: 9 or gold or pearls or e clothes,

EXPERIENCE EXPERIENCED
Heb 11: 5 this life, so that he did not e death:

EXPERIENCED EXPERIENCE
Dt 11: 2 e the discipline of the LORD your
Jos 24:31 who had e everything the LORD
Gal 3: 4 Have you e so much in vain—

EXPERT EXPERTS
Mt 22:35 One of them, an e in the law,
Lk 10:25 one occasion an e in the law stood
  10:37 The e in the law replied, "The one

EXPERTS EXPERT
Lk 11:52 "Woe to you e in the law,

EXPLAIN EXPLAINED,
  EXPLAINING, EXPLAINS,
  EXPLANATION
Ge 41:24 but none of them could e it to me."
2Ch 9: 2 was too hard for him to e to her.
Job 15:17 "Listen to me and I will e to you;
Da 2: 6 if you tell me the dream and e it,
Mt 13:36 "E to us the parable of the weeds
  15:15 Peter said, "E the parable to us."
Jn 4:25 comes, he will e everything to us."
Rev 17: 7 I will e to you the mystery

EXPLAINED EXPLAIN
Jdg 14:17 She in turn e the riddle to her
1Sa 10:25 Samuel e to the people the rights
Mk 4:34 his own disciples, he e everything.
Lk 24:27 he e to them what was said in all
Ac 18:26 and e to him the way of God more

EXPLAINING* EXPLAIN
Jdg 14:15 your husband into e the riddle
Isa 28: 9 To whom is he e his message?
Ac 17: 3 e and proving that the Messiah had
  28:23 e about the kingdom of God,
1Co 2:13 the Spirit, e spiritual realities

EXPLAINS* EXPLAIN
Ac 8:31 said, "unless someone e it to me?"

EXPLANATION* EXPLAIN
Ecc 8: 1 Who knows the e of things?
Da 7:23 "He gave me this e:

EXPLOIT* EXPLOITED,
  EXPLOITING, EXPLOITS
Pr 22:22 Do not e the poor because they are
Isa 58: 3 you please and e all your workers.
2Co 12:17 Did I e you through any of the men
  12:18 Titus did not e you, did he?
2Pe 2: 3 their greed these teachers will e you

EXPLOITED* EXPLOIT
2Co 7: 2 corrupted no one, we have e no one.

EXPLOITING* EXPLOIT
Jas 2: 6 Is it not the rich who are e you?

EXPLOITS EXPLOIT
1Ch 11:19 Such were the e of the three mighty
2Co 11:20 anyone who enslaves you or e you

EXPLORE EXPLORED
Nu 13: 2 "Send some men to e the land
Jos 14: 7 from Kadesh Barnea to e the land.
Ecc 1:13 and to e by wisdom all that is done

EXPLORED EXPLORE
Nu 13:21 e the land from the Desert of Zin as

EXPOSE EXPOSED
Job 20:27 The heavens will e his guilt;
Pr 13:16 knowledge, but fools e their folly.
Mt 1:19 yet did not want to e her to public
1Co 4: 5 and will e the motives of the heart.
Eph 5:11 of darkness, but rather e them.

EXPOSED EXPOSE
Ex 20:26 or your private parts may be e.'
Pr 26:26 but their wickedness will be e
Eze 23:29 shame of your prostitution will be e.
Hab 2:16 Drink and let your nakedness be e!
Jn 3:20 for fear that their deeds will be e.
2Co 11:23 and been e to death again and again.
Eph 5:13 everything e by the light becomes
Heb 10:33 Sometimes you were publicly e
Rev 16:15 to go naked and be shamefully e."

EXPOUND*
Dt 1: 5 Moses began to e this law, saying:
Ps 49: 4 with the harp I will e my riddle:

EXPRESS EXPRESSING
2Sa 10: 2 sent a delegation to e his sympathy

EXPRESSING* EXPRESS
Gal 5: 6 counts is faith e itself through love.

EXTEND EXTENDED, EXTENDS,
  EXTENT
Ex 25:32 Six branches are to e from the sides
Dt 11:24 Your territory will e from the desert
Jos 1: 4 Your territory will e from the desert
Ps 110: 2 The LORD will e your mighty
Isa 66:12 "I will e peace to her like a river,
Zec 9:10 His rule will e from sea to sea

EXTENDED EXTEND
Ezr   7:28 and who has e his good favor to me
Est   8: 4 the king e the gold scepter to Esther

EXTENDS EXTEND
Pr   31:20 poor and e her hands to the needy.
Lk   1:50 His mercy e to those who fear him,

EXTENT* EXTEND
1Co 11:18 you, and to some e I believe it.
2Co   2: 5 he has grieved all of you to some e—

EXTERMINATE* EXTERMINATING
1Ki   9:21 whom the Israelites could not e—
Eze 25: 7 and e you from the countries.

EXTERMINATING* EXTERMINATE
Jos 11:20 them totally, e them without mercy,

EXTERNAL*
Heb   9:10 e regulations applying until the time

EXTINGUISH* EXTINGUISHED
Eph   6:16 you can e all the flaming arrows

EXTINGUISHED* EXTINGUISH
2Sa 21:17 the lamp of Israel will not be e."
Isa 43:17 never to rise again, e,

EXTOL*
1Ch 16: 4 the ark of the LORD, to e, thank,
Job 36:24 Remember to e his work,
Ps   34: 1 I will e the LORD at all times;
      68: 4 e him who rides on the clouds;
      95: 2 thanksgiving and e him with music
    109:30 mouth I will greatly e the LORD;
    111: 1 I will e the LORD with all my
    115:18 it is we who e the LORD,
    117: 1 e him, all you peoples.
    145: 2 praise you and e your name for ever
    145:10 your faithful people e you.
    147:12 E the LORD, Jerusalem;
Ro   15:11 let all the peoples e him."

EXTORT* EXTORTION
Eze 22:12 You e unjust gain from your
Lk   3:14 "Don't e money and don't accuse

EXTORTION EXTORT
Lev   6: 4 what they have stolen or taken by e,
Ps   62:10 Do not trust in e or put vain hope
Pr   28:16 A tyrannical ruler practices e,
Ecc   7: 7 E turns a wise person into a fool,
Isa 33:15 who reject gain from e and keep
Eze 22:29 The people of the land practice e
Hab   2: 6 and makes himself wealthy by e!

EXTRAORDINARY*
Ac   19:11 God did e miracles through Paul,

EXTREME
2Co   8: 2 and their e poverty welled up in rich

EYE EYES
Ge   2: 9 trees that were pleasing to the e
       3: 6 good for food and pleasing to the e,
Ex   21:24 e for e, tooth for tooth,

Lev 24:20 fracture for fracture, e for e,
Dt   19:21 life for life, e for e, tooth for tooth,
2Ki   9:30 heard about it, she put on e makeup,
Ezr   5: 5 But the e of their God was watching
Ps   17: 8 Keep me as the apple of your e;
      94: 9 Does he who formed the e not see?
Pr   7: 2 my teachings as the apple of your e.
      30:17 "The e that mocks a father,
Ecc   1: 8 The e never has enough of seeing,
Isa 64: 4 no e has seen any God besides you,
Am   9: 4 "I will keep my e on them for harm
Zec   2: 8 you touches the apple of his e—
      12: 4 will keep a watchful e over Judah,
Mt   5:29 If your right e causes you
       5:38 have heard that it was said, 'E for e,
       6:22 "The e is the lamp of the body.
       7: 3 speck of sawdust in your brother's e
       7: 3 to the plank in your own e?
      18: 9 if your e causes you to stumble,
      18: 9 to enter life with one e than to have
Mk   10:25 to go through the e of a needle than
1Co   2: 9 "What no e has seen, what no ear
      12:16 "Because I am not an e, I do not
      15:52 in the twinkling of an e, at the last
Eph   6: 6 to win their favor when their e is
Col   3:22 not only when their e is on you
Rev   1: 7 and "every e will see him,

EYES EYE
Ge   3: 7 the e of both of them were opened,
       6: 8 found favor in the e of the LORD.
      18: 3 "If I have found favor in your e,
Ex   15:26 God and do what is right in his e,
      34: 9 "if I have found favor in your e—
Nu   11:15 if I have found favor in your e—
      15:39 the lusts of your own hearts and e.
      22:31 the LORD opened Balaam's e,
      33:55 remain will become barbs in your e
Dt   11:12 the e of the LORD your God are
      12:25 what is right in the e of the LORD.
      16:19 for a bribe blinds the e of the wise
      34: 4 I have let you see it with your e,
Jos 23:13 on your backs and thorns in your e,
Jdg   16:28 on the Philistines for my two e."
1Sa 15:17 you were once small in your own e,
1Ki 10: 7 I came and saw with my own e.
2Ki   6:17 prayed, "Open his e, LORD,
       6:17 the LORD opened the servant's e,
2Ch 16: 9 For the e of the LORD range
Job 31: 1 "I made a covenant with my e not
      36: 7 does not take his e off the righteous;
      42: 5 of you but now my e have seen you.
Ps   13: 3 Give light to my e, or I will sleep
      19: 8 are radiant, giving light to the e.
      25:15 My e are ever on the LORD,
      36: 1 is no fear of God before their e.
      36: 2 their own e they flatter themselves
      66: 7 his power, his e watch the nations—
    101: 6 My e will be on the faithful
    115: 5 but cannot speak, e, but cannot see.
    118:23 this, and it is marvelous in our e.
    119:18 Open my e that I may see wonderful
    119:37 Turn my e away from worthless
    121: 1 I lift up my e to the mountains—

Ps 123: 1 I lift up my **e** to you, to you who sit
123: 2 As the **e** of slaves look to the hand
123: 2 so our **e** look to the LORD our
139:16 Your **e** saw my unformed body;
141: 8 But my **e** are fixed on you,
Pr 3: 7 Do not be wise in your own **e**;
4:25 Let your **e** look straight ahead;
6:17 haughty **e**, a lying tongue,
15: 3 The **e** of the LORD are
15:30 Light in a messenger's **e** brings joy
17:24 a fool's **e** wander to the ends
20: 8 he winnows out all evil with his **e**.
22:12 The **e** of the LORD keep watch
23:29 Who has bloodshot **e**?
26: 5 or he will be wise in his own **e**.
26:16 in his own **e** than seven people who
28:11 The rich are wise in their own **e**;
Ecc 2:10 denied myself nothing my **e** desired;
SS 4: 1 Your **e** behind your veil are doves.
Isa 1:15 in prayer, I hide my **e** from you;
6: 5 and my **e** have seen the King,
6:10 their ears dull and close their **e**.
6:10 they might see with their **e**,
11: 3 judge by what he sees with his **e**,
33:17 Your **e** will see the king in his
42: 7 to open **e** that are blind, to free
Jer 9: 1 water and my **e** a fountain of tears!
24: 6 My **e** will watch over them for their
La 3:48 from my **e** because my people are
Eze 1:18 four rims were full of **e** all around.
24:16 from you the delight of your **e**.
Da 7: 8 This horn had **e** like the **e**
10: 6 lightning, his **e** like flaming torches,
Hab 1:13 Your **e** are too pure to look on evil;
Zec 3: 9 There are seven **e** on that one stone,
4:10 since the seven **e** of the LORD
Mt 6:22 If your **e** are healthy, your whole
13:15 ears, and they have closed their **e**.
13:15 they might see with their **e**,
21:42 this, and it is marvelous in our **e**'?
Mk 8:25 Jesus put his hands on the man's **e**.
Then his **e** were opened,
Lk 10:23 "Blessed are the **e** that see what
16:15 justify yourselves in the **e** of others,
24:31 Then their **e** were opened and they
Jn 4:35 open your **e** and look at the fields!
9:10 "How then were your **e** opened?"
12:40 "He has blinded their **e** and
12:40 so they can neither see with their **e**,
Ac 1: 9 he was taken up before their very **e**,
4:19 replied, "Which is right in God's **e**:
9: 8 when he opened his **e** he could see
28:27 ears, and they have closed their **e**.
28:27 they might see with their **e**,
Ro 11:10 May their **e** be darkened so they
2Co 4:18 So we fix our **e** not on what is seen,
8:21 not only in the **e** of the Lord
8:21 of the Lord but also in the **e** of man.
Gal 4:15 you would have torn out your **e**
Eph 1:18 pray that the **e** of your heart may be
Php 3:17 keep your **e** on those who live as we
Heb 4:13 and laid bare before the **e** of him
12: 2 fixing our **e** on Jesus, the pioneer

Jas 2: 5 who are poor in the **e** of the world
1Pe 3:12 For the **e** of the Lord are
1Jn 1: 1 which we have seen with our **e**,
2:16 the lust of the **e**, and the pride
Rev 1:14 and his **e** were like blazing fire.
2:18 whose **e** are like blazing fire
4: 6 and they were covered with **e**,
5: 6 Lamb had seven horns and seven **e**,
7:17 away every tear from their **e**.' "
19:12 His **e** are like blazing fire,
21: 4 will wipe every tear from their **e**.

EVIL IN THE EYES OF THE LORD† Dt 4:25;
17:2; Jdg 2:11; 3:7, 12; 4:1; 6:1; 10:6; 13:1; 1Sa
15:19; 1Ki 11:6; 14:22; 15:26, 34; 16:19, 25, 30;
21:20, 25; 22:52; 2Ki 3:2; 8:18, 27; 13:2, 11; 14:24;
15:9, 18, 24, 28; 17:2, 17; 21:2, 6, 16, 20; 23:32, 37;
24:9, 19; 2Ch 21:6; 22:4; 29:6; 33:2, 6, 22; 36:5, 9,
12; Jer 52:2

FAVOR IN ... EYES Ge 6:8; 18:3; 19:19; 30:27;
32:5; 33:8, 10, 15; 34:11; 39:4, 21; 47:25, 29; 50:4;
Ex 34:9; Nu 11:15; 32:5; Jdg 6:17; Ru 2:10, 13; 1Sa
1:18; 20:3, 29; 27:5; 2Sa 14:22; 16:4

RIGHT IN THE EYES OF THE LORD† Dt
12:25, 28; 21:9; 1Ki 15:5, 11; 22:43; 2Ki 12:2; 14:3;
15:3, 34; 16:2; 18:3; 22:2; 2Ch 14:2; 20:32; 24:2;
25:2; 26:4; 27:2; 28:1; 29:2; 34:2

EYEWITNESSES* WITNESS
Lk 1: 2 by those who from the first were **e**
2Pe 1:16 but we were **e** of his majesty.

EZEKIEL
Priest called to be prophet to the exiles (Eze
1–3). Symbolically acted out destruction of Jerusalem (Eze 4–5; 12; 24).

EZION GEBER
1Ki 9:26 King Solomon also built ships at **E**,
22:48 set sail—they were wrecked at **E**.

EZRA
Priest and teacher of the Law who led a return
of exiles to Israel to reestablish temple and wor-
ship (Ezr 7–8). Corrected intermarriage of priests
(Ezr 9–10). Read Law at celebration of Festival of
Tabernacles (Ne 8). Participated in dedication of
Jerusalem's walls (Ne 12).

F

FACE FACED, FACEDOWN, FACES
Ge 4: 6 Why is your **f** downcast?
7: 4 from the **f** of the earth every living
11: 9 LORD scattered them over the **f**
32:30 "It is because I saw God **f** to **f**,
Ex 3: 6 Moses hid his **f**, because he was
33:11 would speak to Moses **f** to **f**, as one
33:20 "you cannot see my **f**, for no one
34:29 that his **f** was radiant because he had
Nu 6:25 the LORD make his **f** shine on you
12: 8 With him I speak **f** to **f**,
14:14 LORD, have been seen **f** to **f**,
Dt 5: 4 The LORD spoke to you **f** to **f**

Dt   31:17 I will hide my f from them, and they
      34:10 whom the LORD knew f to f,
Jdg   6:22 the angel of the LORD f to f!"
2Sa   14:24 he must not see my f."
      14:24 and did not see the f of the king.
2Ki   14: 8 let us f each other in battle."
1Ch   16:11 and his strength; seek his f always.
2Ch   7:14 and seek my f and turn from their
      25:17 let us f each other in battle."
      30: 9 He will not turn his f from you
Ezr   9: 6 to lift up my f to you, because our
Ne   2: 2 "Why does your f look so sad
Est   7: 8 mouth, they covered Haman's f.
Job   1:11 he will surely curse you to your f."
Ps   4: 6 Let the light of your f shine on us.
      10:11 he covers his f and never sees."
      13: 1 How long will you hide your f
      27: 8 My heart says of you, "Seek his f!"
      31:16 Let your f shine on your servant;
      44: 3 and the light of your f, for you loved
      44:22 your sake we f death all day long;
      51: 9 Hide your f from my sins and blot
      67: 1 bless us and make his f shine on us—
      80: 3 make your f shine on us, that we
     104:29 When you hide your f, they are
     105: 4 and his strength; seek his f always.
     119:135 Make your f shine on your servant
Pr   15:13 A happy heart makes the f cheerful,
Ecc   7: 3 because a sad f is good for the heart.
       8: 1 A person's wisdom brightens their f
SS   2:14 show me your f, let me hear your
       2:14 voice is sweet, and your f is lovely.
Isa   8:17 who is hiding his f
      50: 7 Therefore have I set my f like flint,
      50: 8 Let us f each other!
      54: 8 a surge of anger I hid my f from you
Jer   32: 4 will speak with him f to f and
      34: 3 he will speak with you f to f.
Eze   1:10 the four had the f of a human being,
       1:10 right side each had the f of a lion,
       1:10 on the left the f of an ox;
       1:10 each also had the f of an eagle.
      10:14 One f was that of a cherub,
      10:14 the second the f of a human being,
      10:14 the third the f of a lion,
      10:14 and the fourth the f of an eagle.
      39:23 So I hid my f from them and handed
      39:29 I will no longer hide my f
Da   10: 6 was like topaz, his f like lightning,
Hos   5:15 borne their guilt and seek my f—
Mt   17: 2 His f shone like the sun, and his
      18:10 in heaven always see the f of my
      26:67 they spit in his f and struck him
Lk   9:29 the appearance of his f changed,
Jn   19: 3 And they slapped him in the f.
Ac   6:15 they saw that his f was like the f
Ro   8:36 your sake we f death all day long;
1Co   13:12 mirror; then we shall see f to f.
2Co   3: 7 steadily at the f of Moses because
       4: 6 glory displayed in the f of Christ.
      10: 1 who am "timid" when f to f
Jas   1:23 who looks at his f in a mirror
1Pe   3:12 but the f of the Lord is against those

2Jn   1:12 visit you and talk with you f to f,
3Jn   1:14 you soon, and we will talk f to f.
Rev   1:16 His f was like the sun shining in all
       4: 7 ox, the third had a f like a man,
      10: 1 his f was like the sun, and his legs
      22: 4 They will see his f, and his name

FACED FACE
Ex   37: 9 The cherubim f each other,
Eze   1:17 of the four directions the creatures f;

FACEDOWN FACE
Ge   17: 3 Abram fell f, and God said to him,
Lev   9:24 it, they shouted for joy and fell f.
Nu   16: 4 When Moses heard this, he fell f.
Jos   5:14 Then Joshua fell f to the ground
       7: 6 fell f to the ground before the ark
Mt   17: 6 heard this, they fell f to the ground,

FACES FACE
1Ch   12: 8 Their f were the f of lions,
Ps   34: 5 their f are never covered
      83:16 Cover their f with shame, LORD,
Isa   6: 2 two wings they covered their f,
Eze   1: 6 but each of them had four f and four
      10:14 Each of the cherubim had four f:
      41:18 Each cherub had two f:
Mt   6:16 they disfigure their f to show others
2Co   3:18 unveiled f contemplate the Lord's
Rev   9: 7 and their f resembled human f.
      11:16 fell on their f and worshiped God,

FACT FACTS
Jn   4: 2 in f it was not Jesus who baptized,

FACTIONS*
1Ki   16:21 of Israel were split into two f;
Gal   5:20 rage, selfish ambition, dissensions, f

FACTS* FACT
Ac   19:36 since these f are undeniable,

FADE FADING
Dt   4: 9 or let them f from your heart as long
Ps   109:23 I f away like an evening shadow;
Jas   1:11 the rich will f away even while they
1Pe   1: 4 that can never perish, spoil or f.
       5: 4 of glory that will never f away.

FADING FADE
Isa   1:30 will be like an oak with f leaves,

FAIL FAILED, FAILING, FAILINGS,
    FAILS
Lev   26:15 and f to carry out all my commands
Nu   15:22 as a community unintentionally f
1Ki   2: 4 you will never f to have a successor
1Ch   28:20 He will not f you or forsake you
2Ch   34:33 they did not f to follow the LORD,
Ne   9:19 By day the pillar of cloud did not f
Ps   69: 3 My eyes f, looking for my God.
      89:28 my covenant with him will never f.
Pr   8:36 But those who f to find me harm
      15:22 Plans f for lack of counsel,
Isa   51: 6 my righteousness will never f.
      58:11 like a spring whose waters never f.

Jer 33:17 'David will never **f** to have a man
La 3:22 for his compassions never **f**.
Eze 2: 5 whether they listen or **f** to listen—
47:12 will not wither, nor will their fruit **f**.
Zep 3: 5 and every new day he does not **f**,
Mk 8:18 Do you have eyes but **f** to see, and
ears but **f** to hear?
Lk 1:37 For no word from God will ever **f**."
12:33 treasure in heaven that will never **f**,
22:32 Simon, that your faith may not **f**.
Ac 5:38 activity is of human origin, it will **f**.
2Co 13: 5 unless, of course, you **f** the test?

FAILED FAIL

Jos 21:45 LORD's good promises to Israel **f**;
23:14 LORD your God gave you has **f**.
23:14 has been fulfilled; not one has **f**.
1Ki 8:56 Not one word has **f** of all the good
15: 5 and had not **f** to keep any
Ne 9:17 and **f** to remember the miracles you
Ps 77: 8 Has his promise **f** for all time?
Ro 9: 6 is not as though God's word had **f**.
2Co 13: 6 discover that we have not **f** the test.

FAILING* FAIL

Ge 48:10 Now Israel's eyes were **f** because
Dt 8:11 God, **f** to observe his commands,
1Sa 12:23 I should sin against the LORD by **f**

FAILINGS* FAIL

Ro 15: 1 ought to bear with the **f** of the weak

FAILS FAIL

Ps 143: 7 me quickly, LORD; my spirit **f**.
Joel 1:10 new wine is dried up, the olive oil **f**.
Hab 3:17 though the olive crop **f**
1Co 13: 8 Love never **f**. But where there are

FAINT FAINTHEARTED, FAINTS

Job 26:14 how **f** the whisper we hear of him!
Ps 142: 3 When my spirit grows **f** within me,
SS 2: 5 me with apples, for I am **f** with love.
Isa 40:31 weary, they will walk and not be **f**.
Jer 31:25 refresh the weary and satisfy the **f**."
La 5:17 Because of this our hearts are **f**,

FAINTHEARTED* FAINT, HEART

Dt 20: 3 Do not be **f** or afraid; do not panic
20: 8 shall add, "Is anyone afraid or **f**?

FAINTS* FAINT

Ps 84: 2 even **f**, for the courts of the LORD;
119:81 My soul **f** with longing for your

FAIR FAIRLY, FAIRNESS

Job 26:13 By his breath the skies became **f**;
Pr 1: 3 doing what is right and just and **f**;
Hos 10:11 so I will put a yoke on her **f** neck.
Mt 16: 2 'It will be **f** weather, for the sky is
Col 4: 1 your slaves with what is right and **f**,

FAIRLY FAIR

Lev 19:15 the great, but judge your neighbor **f**.
Pr 31: 9 Speak up and judge **f**;
Eze 18: 8 and judges **f** between two parties.

FAIRNESS* FAIR

Pr 29:14 If a king judges the poor with **f**,

FAITH* FAITHFUL, FAITHFULLY, FAITHFULNESS, FAITHLESS

Ex 21: 8 because he has broken **f** with her.
Dt 32:51 because both of you broke **f** with me
Jos 22:16 'How could you break **f**
Jdg 9:16 good **f** by making Abimelek king?
9:19 in good **f** toward Jerub-Baal and his
1Sa 14:33 "You have broken **f**," he said.
2Ch 20:20 Have **f** in the LORD your God
20:20 have **f** in his prophets and you will
Isa 7: 9 If you do not stand firm in your **f**,
26: 2 may enter, the nation that keeps **f**.
Mt 6:30 more clothe you—you of little **f**?
8:10 anyone in Israel with such great **f**.
8:26 "You of little **f**, why are you so
9: 2 When Jesus saw their **f**, he said
9:22 he said, "your **f** has healed you."
9:29 "According to your **f** let it be done
13:58 there because of their lack of **f**.
14:31 "You of little **f**," he said, "why did
15:28 to her, "Woman, you have great **f**!
16: 8 "You of little **f**, why are you talking
17:20 "Because you have so little **f**.
17:20 if you have **f** as small as a mustard
21:21 you, if you have **f** and do not doubt,
24:10 time many will turn away from the **f**
Mk 2: 5 When Jesus saw their **f**, he said
4:40 Do you still have no **f**?"
5:34 "Daughter, your **f** has healed you.
6: 6 He was amazed at their lack of **f**.
10:52 said Jesus, "your **f** has healed you."
11:22 "Have **f** in God," Jesus answered.
16:14 *rebuked them for their lack of **f***
Lk 5:20 When Jesus saw their **f**, he said
7: 9 I have not found such great **f** even
7:50 the woman, "Your **f** has saved you;
8:25 "Where is your **f**?" he asked his
8:48 "Daughter, your **f** has healed you.
12:28 will he clothe you—you of little **f**!
17: 5 said to the Lord, "Increase our **f**!"
17: 6 "If you have **f** as small as a mustard
17:19 your **f** has made you well."
18: 8 comes, will he find **f** on the earth?"
18:42 your **f** has healed you."
22:32 you, Simon, that your **f** may not fail.
Jn 12:42 not openly acknowledge their **f**
Ac 3:16 By **f** in the name of Jesus, this man
3:16 the **f** that comes through him
6: 5 a man full of **f** and of the Holy
6: 7 of priests became obedient to the **f**.
11:24 full of the Holy Spirit and **f**,
13: 8 to turn the proconsul from the **f**.
14: 9 him, saw that he had **f** to be healed
14:22 them to remain true to the **f**.
14:27 how he had opened a door of **f**
15: 9 for he purified their hearts by **f**.
16: 5 churches were strengthened in the **f**
20:21 and have **f** in our Lord Jesus.
24:24 to him as he spoke about **f** in Christ
26:18 among those who are sanctified by **f**

Ac	27:25	men, for I have f in God that it will
Ro	1: 5	comes from f for his name's sake.
	1: 8	because your f is being reported all
	1:12	encouraged by each other's f.
	1:17	righteousness that is by f from first
	1:17	"The righteous will live by f."
	3:22	righteousness is given through f
	3:25	of his blood—to be received by f.
	3:26	one who justifies those who have f
	3:27	because of the law that requires f.
	3:28	a person is justified by f apart
	3:30	will justify the circumcised by f
	3:30	uncircumcised through that same f.
	3:31	we, then, nullify the law by this f?
	4: 5	their f is credited as righteousness.
	4: 9	that Abraham's f was credited
	4:11	f while he was still uncircumcised.
	4:12	of the f that our father Abraham had
	4:13	the righteousness that comes by f.
	4:14	f means nothing and the promise is
	4:16	the promise comes by f, so that it
	4:16	to those who have the f of Abraham.
	4:19	Without weakening in his f,
	4:20	was strengthened in his f and gave
	5: 1	we have been justified through f,
	5: 2	whom we have gained access by f
	9:30	it, a righteousness that is by f;
	9:32	Because they pursued it not by f
	10: 6	the righteousness that is by f says:
	10: 8	is, the message concerning f that we
	10:10	your mouth that you profess your f
	10:17	f comes from hearing the message,
	11:20	of unbelief, and you stand by f.
	12: 3	with the f God has distributed
	12: 6	prophesy in accordance with your f;
	14: 1	Accept the one whose f is weak,
	14: 2	One person's f allows them to eat
	14: 2	but another, whose f is weak,
	14:23	because their eating is not from f;
	14:23	that does not come from f is sin.
	16:26	to the obedience that comes from f—
1Co	2: 5	so that your f might not rest
	7:22	called to f in the Lord is the Lord's
	12: 9	to another f by the same Spirit,
	13: 2	I have a f that can move mountains,
	13:13	these three remain: f, hope and love.
	15:14	preaching is useless and so is your f.
	15:17	has not been raised, your f is futile;
	16:13	stand firm in the f; be courageous;
2Co	1:24	Not that we lord it over your f,
	1:24	because it is by f you stand firm.
	4:13	Since we have that same spirit of f,
	5: 7	For we live by f, not by sight.
	8: 7	in f, in speech, in knowledge,
	10:15	is that, as your f continues to grow,
	13: 5	to see whether you are in the f;
Gal	1:23	is now preaching the f he once tried
	2:16	of the law, but by f in Jesus Christ.
	2:16	have put our f in Christ Jesus
	2:16	we may be justified by f in Christ
	2:20	body, I live by f in the Son of God,
	3: 7	that those who have f are children
	3: 8	God would justify the Gentiles by f,

Gal	3: 9	who rely on f are blessed along with
		Abraham, the man of f.
	3:11	"the righteous will live by f."
	3:12	The law is not based on f;
	3:14	by f we might receive the promise
	3:22	being given through f in Jesus
	3:23	Before the coming of this f, we were
	3:23	law, locked up until the f that was
	3:24	came that we might be justified by f.
	3:25	Now that this f has come, we are no
	3:26	are all children of God through f,
	5: 5	eagerly await by f the righteousness
	5: 6	counts is f expressing itself through
Eph	1:15	heard about your f in the Lord Jesus
	2: 8	you have been saved, through f—
	3:12	through f in him we may approach
	3:17	may dwell in your hearts through f.
	4: 5	one Lord, one f, one baptism;
	4:13	until we all reach unity in the f
	6:16	take up the shield of f,
	6:23	and love with f from God the Father
Php	1:25	for your progress and joy in the f,
	1:27	as one for the f of the gospel
	2:17	and service coming from your f,
	3: 9	that which is through f in Christ—
	3: 9	comes from God on the basis of f.
Col	1: 4	have heard of your f in Christ Jesus
	1: 5	the f and love that spring
	1:23	if you continue in your f,
	2: 5	are and how firm your f in Christ is,
	2: 7	in the f as you were taught,
	2:12	him through your f in the working
1Th	1: 3	Father your work produced by f,
	1: 8	your f in God has become known
	3: 2	and encourage you in your f,
	3: 5	I sent to find out about your f.
	3: 6	has brought good news about your f
	3: 7	about you because of your f.
	3:10	and supply what is lacking in your f.
	5: 8	be sober, putting on f and love as
2Th	1: 3	because your f is growing more
	1: 4	and f in all the persecutions
	1:11	and your every deed prompted by f.
	3: 2	evil people, for not everyone has f.
1Ti	1: 2	To Timothy my true son in the f:
	1: 4	which is by f.
	1: 5	a good conscience and a sincere f.
	1:14	along with the f and love that are
	1:19	holding on to f and a good
	1:19	shipwreck with regard to the f.
	2:15	if they continue in f,
	3: 9	of the f with a clear conscience.
	3:13	assurance in their f in Christ Jesus.
	4: 1	later times some will abandon the f
	4: 6	nourished on the truths of the f
	4:12	conduct, in love, in f and in purity.
	5: 8	has denied the f and is worse than
	6:10	have wandered from the f
	6:11	righteousness, godliness, f, love,
	6:12	Fight the good fight of the f.
	6:21	so doing have departed from the f.
2Ti	1: 5	I am reminded of your sincere f,
	1:13	with f and love in Christ Jesus.

2Ti 2:18 and they destroy the f of some.
2:22 youth and pursue righteousness, f,
3: 8 who, as far as the f is concerned,
3:10 way of life, my purpose, f, patience,
3:15 salvation through f in Christ Jesus.
4: 7 finished the race, I have kept the f.
Titus 1: 1 Christ to further the f of God's elect
1: 4 Titus, my true son in our common f:
1:13 so that they will be sound in the f
2: 2 and sound in f, in love
3:15 Greet those who love us in the f.
Phm 1: 5 people and your f in the Lord Jesus.
1: 6 with us in the f may be effective
Heb 4: 2 because they did not share the f
4:14 us hold firmly to the f we profess.
6: 1 that lead to death, and of f in God,
6:12 to imitate those who through f
10:22 with the full assurance that f brings,
10:38 my righteous one will live by f.
10:39 but to those who have f and are saved.
11: 1 Now f is confidence in what we
11: 3 By f we understand that the universe
11: 4 f Abel brought God a better offering
11: 4 f he was commended as righteous,
11: 4 And by f Abel still speaks,
11: 5 By f Enoch was taken from this life,
11: 6 without f it is impossible to please
11: 7 By f Noah, when warned
11: 7 By his f he condemned the world
11: 7 that is in keeping with f.
11: 8 By f Abraham, when called to go
11: 9 By f he made his home
11:11 And by f even Sarah, who was past
11:13 these people were still living by f
11:17 By f Abraham, when God tested
11:20 By f Isaac blessed Jacob and Esau
11:21 By f Jacob, when he was dying,
11:22 By f Joseph, when his end was near,
11:23 By f Moses' parents hid him
11:24 By f Moses, when he had grown up,
11:27 By f he left Egypt, not fearing
11:28 By f he kept the Passover
11:29 f the people passed through the Red
11:30 By f the walls of Jericho fell,
11:31 By f the prostitute Rahab,
11:33 who through f conquered kingdoms,
11:39 were all commended for their f,
12: 2 Jesus, the pioneer and perfecter of f.
13: 7 their way of life and imitate their f.
Jas 1: 3 of your f produces perseverance.
2: 5 the eyes of the world to be rich in f
2:14 if someone claims to have f but has
2:14 Can such f save them?
2:17 In the same way, f by itself, if it is
2:18 But someone will say, "You have f;
2:18 Show me your f without deeds,
2:18 I will show you my f by my deeds.
2:20 that f without deeds is useless?
2:22 You see that his f and his actions
2:22 his f was made complete by what he
2:24 by what they do and not by f alone.
2:26 is dead, so f without deeds is dead.
5:15 in f will make the sick person well;

1Pe 1: 5 who through f are shielded by God's
1: 7 the proven genuineness of your f—
1: 9 receiving the end result of your f,
1:21 and so your f and hope are in God.
5: 9 standing firm in the f, because you
2Pe 1: 1 have received a f as precious as
1: 5 effort to add to your f goodness;
1Jn 5: 4 has overcome the world, even our f.
Jude 1: 3 contend for the f that was once
1:20 yourselves up in your most holy f
Rev 2:13 You did not renounce your f in me,
2:19 your love and f, your service

FAITHFUL* FAITH
Nu 12: 7 he is f in all my house.
Dt 7: 9 he is the f God, keeping his
32: 4 A f God who does no wrong,
33: 8 and Urim belong to your f servant.
1Sa 2: 9 will guard the feet of his f servants,
2:35 I will raise up for myself a f priest,
2Sa 20:19 We are the peaceful and f in Israel.
22:26 "To the f you show yourself f,
1Ki 3: 6 David, because he was f to you
2Ch 6:41 may your f people rejoice in your
31:18 For they were f in consecrating
31:20 and f before the LORD his God.
Ne 9: 8 You found his heart f to you,
Ps 4: 3 LORD has set apart his f servant
12: 1 LORD, for no one is f anymore;
16:10 will you let your f one see decay.
18:25 To the f you show yourself f,
25:10 and f toward those who keep
30: 4 of the LORD, you his f people;
31: 5 deliver me, LORD, my f God.
31:23 Love the LORD, all his f people!
32: 6 Therefore let all the f pray to you
33: 4 right and true; he is f in all he does.
37:28 just and will not forsake his f ones.
43: 3 Send me your light and your f care,
52: 9 you in the presence of your f people.
78: 8 whose spirits were not f to him.
78:37 him, they were not f to his covenant.
85: 8 peace to his people, his f servants—
86: 2 Guard my life, for I am f to you;
89:19 a vision, to your f people you said:
89:24 My f love will be with him,
89:37 the moon, the f witness in the sky."
97:10 for he guards the lives of his f ones
101: 6 My eyes will be on the f in the land,
111: 7 The works of his hands are f
116:15 is the death of his f servants.
132: 9 may your f people sing for joy.' "
132:16 her f people will ever sing for joy.
145:10 your f people extol you.
145:13 all he promises and f in all he does.
145:17 in all his ways and f in all he does.
146: 6 he remains f forever.
148:14 the praise of all his f servants,
149: 5 Let his f people rejoice in this honor
149: 9 this is the glory of all his f people.
Pr 2: 8 and protects the way of his f ones.
20: 6 love, but a f person who can find?
28:20 A f person will be richly blessed,
31:26 and f instruction is on her tongue.

Isa 1:21 See how the **f** city has become
      1:26 City of Righteousness, the **F** City."
     49: 7 who is **f**, the Holy One of Israel,
     55: 3 you, my **f** love promised to David.
Jer 3:12 for I am **f**, declares the LORD,
     42: 5 **f** witness against us if we do not act
Eze 43:11 so that they may be **f** to its design
    48:11 who were **f** in serving me and did
Hos 11:12 God, even against the **f** Holy One.
Joel 2:23 the autumn rains because he is **f**.
Mic 7: 2 The **f** have been swept
     7:20 You will be **f** to Jacob, and show
Zec 8: 3 Jerusalem will be called the **F** City,
     8: 8 I will be **f** and righteous to them as
Mt 1:19 Joseph her husband was **f** to the law,
   24:45 then is the **f** and wise servant,
   25:21 'Well done, good and **f** servant!
   25:21 You have been **f** with a few things;
   25:23 'Well done, good and **f** servant!
   25:23 You have been **f** with a few things;
Lk 12:42 then is the **f** and wise manager,
Ro 12:12 patient in affliction, **f** in prayer.
1Co 1: 9 God is **f**, who has called you
     4: 2 been given a trust must prove **f**.
     4:17 whom I love, who is **f** in the Lord.
  10:13 And God is **f**; he will not let you be
2Co 1:18 But as surely as God is **f**,
Eph 1: 1 in Ephesus, the **f** in Christ Jesus:
     6:21 brother and **f** servant in the Lord,
Col 1: 2 the **f** brothers and sisters in Christ,
     1: 7 who is a **f** minister of Christ on our
     4: 7 a **f** minister and fellow servant
     4: 9 Onesimus, our **f** and dear brother,
1Th 5:24 The one who calls you is **f**, and he
2Th 3: 3 But the Lord is **f**, and he will
1Ti 2: 7 a true and **f** teacher of the Gentiles.
     3: 2 to be above reproach, **f** to his wife,
     3:12 A deacon must be **f** to his wife
     5: 9 sixty, has been **f** to her husband,
2Ti 2:13 he remains **f**, for he cannot disown
Titus 1: 6 must be blameless, **f** to his wife,
Heb 2:17 and **f** high priest in service to God,
     3: 2 He was **f** to the one who appointed
     3: 2 just as Moses was **f** in all God's
     3: 5 "Moses was **f** as a servant in all
     3: 6 Christ is **f** as the Son over God's
     8: 9 because they did not remain **f** to my
  10:23 profess, for he who promised is **f**.
  11:11 she considered him **f** who had made
1Pe 4:10 as **f** stewards of God's grace in its
     4:19 themselves to their **f** Creator
     5:12 whom I regard as a **f** brother, I have
1Jn 1: 9 he is **f** and just and will forgive us
3Jn 1: 5 you are **f** in what you are doing
Rev 1: 5 who is the **f** witness, the firstborn
     2:10 Be **f**, even to the point of death,
     2:13 in the days of Antipas, my **f** witness,
     3:14 of the Amen, the **f** and true witness,
  14:12 commands and remain **f** to Jesus.
  17:14 his called, chosen and **f** followers."
  19:11 whose rider is called **F** and True.

FAITHFULLY FAITH

Dt 11:13 So if you **f** obey the commands I am

Jos 2:14 and **f** when the LORD gives us
1Sa 12:24 and serve him **f** with all your heart;
1Ki 2: 4 and if they walk **f** before me with all
2Ki 20: 3 how I have walked before you **f**
2Ch 19: 9 "You must serve **f**
   31:12 they **f** brought in the contributions,
   31:15 and Shekaniah assisted him **f**
   32: 1 all that Hezekiah had so **f** done,
   34:12 The workers labored **f**. Over them
Ne 9:33 you have acted **f**, while we acted
  13:14 what I have so **f** done for the house
Isa 38: 3 how I have walked before you **f**
Jer 23:28 the one who has my word speak it **f**.
Eze 18: 9 my decrees and **f** keeps my laws.

FAITHFULNESS* FAITH

Ge 24:27 his kindness and **f** to my master.
   24:49 show kindness and **f** to my master,
   32:10 and **f** you have shown your servant.
   47:29 you will show me kindness and **f**.
Ex 34: 6 to anger, abounding in love and **f**,
Jos 24:14 the LORD and serve him with all **f**.
1Sa 26:23 for their righteousness and **f**.
2Sa 2: 6 now show you kindness and **f**, and I
  15:20 LORD show you kindness and **f**."
Ps 26: 3 and have lived in reliance on your **f**.
   30: 9 Will it proclaim your **f**?
   36: 5 to the heavens, your **f** to the skies.
   40:10 I speak of your **f** and your saving
   40:10 and your **f** from the great assembly.
   40:11 your love and **f** always protect me.
   51: 6 Yet you desired **f** even in the womb;
   54: 5 in your **f** destroy them.
   57: 3 God sends forth his love and his **f**.
   57:10 your **f** reaches to the skies.
   61: 7 your love and **f** to protect him.
   71:22 praise you with the harp for your **f**,
   85:10 Love and **f** meet together;
   85:11 **f** springs forth from the earth,
   86:11 LORD, that I may rely on your **f**;
   86:15 to anger, abounding in love and **f**.
   88:11 in the grave, your **f** in Destruction?
   89: 1 will make your **f** known through all
   89: 2 that you have established your **f**
   89: 5 LORD, your **f** too, in the assembly
   89: 8 mighty, and your **f** surrounds you.
   89:14 love and **f** go before you.
   89:33 him, nor will I ever betray my **f**.
   89:49 in your **f** you swore to David?
   91: 4 his **f** will be your shield
   92: 2 in the morning and your **f** at night,
   96:13 and the peoples in his **f**.
   98: 3 his love and his **f** to Israel;
  100: 5 his **f** continues through all
  108: 4 your **f** reaches to the skies.
  111: 8 ever, enacted in **f** and uprightness.
  115: 1 glory, because of your love and **f**.
  117: 2 the **f** of the LORD endures forever.
  119:30 I have chosen the way of **f**;
  119:75 and that in **f** you have afflicted me.
  119:90 Your **f** continues through all
  138: 2 for your unfailing love and your **f**,
  143: 1 in your **f** and righteousness come
Pr 3: 3 Let love and **f** never leave you;

Pr 14:22 plan what is good find love and f.
16: 6 Through love and f sin is atoned for;
20:28 Love and f keep a king safe;
Isa 11: 5 belt and f the sash around his waist.
16: 5 in f a man will sit on it—
25: 1 perfect f you have done wonderful
38:18 to the pit cannot hope for your f.
38:19 tell their children about your f.
40: 6 all their f is like the flowers
42: 3 In f he will bring forth justice;
61: 8 In my f I will reward my people
La 3:23 new every morning; great is your f.
Hos 2:20 I will betroth you in f, and you will
4: 1 "There is no f, no love,
Hab 2: 4 righteous person will live by his f—
Mt 23:23 of the law—justice, mercy and f.
Ro 3: 3 their unfaithfulness nullify God's f?
Gal 5:22 forbearance, kindness, goodness, f,
3Jn 1: 3 testified about your f to the truth,
Rev 13:10 and f on the part of God's people.

FAITHLESS* FAITH

Ps 78:57 ancestors they were disloyal and f,
101: 3 I hate what f people do; I will have
119:158 I look on the f with loathing,
Pr 14:14 The f will be fully repaid for their
Jer 3: 6 you seen what f Israel has done?
3: 8 I gave f Israel her certificate
3:11 "F Israel is more righteous than
3:12 " 'Return, f Israel,'
3:14 "Return, f people,"
3:22 "Return, f people; I will cure you
12: 1 Why do all the f live at ease?
2Ti 2:13 if we are f, he remains faithful,

FALL DOWNFALL, FALLEN, FALLING, FALLS, FELL

Ge 2:21 LORD God caused the man to f
27:13 him, "My son, let the curse f on me.
Lev 26: 7 they will f by the sword before you.
Nu 14:29 this wilderness your bodies will f—
Dt 32: 2 Let my teaching f like rain and my
1Sa 3:19 of Samuel's words f to the ground.
1Ch 21:13 Let me f into the hands
21:13 do not let me f into human hands."
Ps 13: 4 and my foes will rejoice when I f.
37:24 he will not f, for the LORD
46: 5 God is within her, she will not f;
69: 9 of those who insult you f on me.
91: 7 A thousand may f at your side,
145:14 The LORD upholds all who f
Pr 11:28 who trust in their riches will f,
16:18 a haughty spirit before a f.
24:16 though the righteous f seven times,
Ecc 10: 8 Whoever digs a pit may f into it;
Isa 8:14 and a rock that makes them f.
40: 7 The grass withers and the flowers f,
40:30 and young men stumble and f;
65:12 and all of you will f in the slaughter;
Jer 6:15 So they will f among the fallen;
34:17 'freedom' to f by the sword,
La 1: 9 Her f was astounding;
Hos 10: 8 and to the hills, "F on us!"
Mt 7:25 yet it did not f, because it had its

Mt 13:21 of the word, they quickly f away.
Mk 4:17 of the word, they quickly f away.
13:25 the stars will f from the sky,
14:27 "You will all f away," Jesus told
Lk 10:18 "I saw Satan f like lightning
11:17 a house divided against itself will f.
23:30 say to the mountains, "F on us!"
Jn 16: 1 told you so that you will not f away.
Ro 3:23 and f short of the glory of God,
9:33 and a rock that makes them f,
11:11 stumble so as to f beyond recovery?
14: 4 own master, servants stand or f.
14:21 will cause your brother or sister to f.
1Co 8:13 my brother or sister to f into sin,
8:13 so that I will not cause them to f.
10:12 firm, be careful that you don't f!
Heb 10:31 It is a dreadful thing to f
1Pe 2: 8 and a rock that makes them f."
Rev 6:16 "F on us and hide us from the face

FALLEN FALL

1Sa 5: 3 f on his face on the ground before
2Sa 1:19 How the mighty have f!
Ps 36:12 See how the evildoers lie f—
Isa 14:12 How you have f from heaven,
21: 9 'Babylon has f, has f!
Am 9:11 "I will restore David's f shelter—
Jn 11:11 "Our friend Lazarus has f asleep;
Ac 15:16 return and rebuild David's f tent.
1Co 11:30 and a number of you have f asleep.
15: 6 living, though some have f asleep.
15:18 who have f asleep in Christ are lost.
15:20 of those who have f asleep.
Gal 5: 4 you have f away from grace.
1Th 4:15 precede those who have f asleep.
Heb 4: 1 of you be found to have f short of it.
6: 6 and who have f away, to be brought
Rev 9: 1 I saw a star that had f from the sky
14: 8 angel followed and said, " 'F!
17:10 Five have f, one is, the other has not
18: 2 " 'F! F is Babylon the Great!'

FALLING FALL

Lk 22:44 like drops of blood f to the ground.

FALLS FALL

Pr 11:14 For lack of guidance a nation f,
24:17 Do not gloat when your enemy f;
28:14 whoever hardens their heart f
Ecc 4:10 If either of them f down, one can
4:10 pity anyone who f and has no one
Lk 20:18 Everyone who f on that stone will
20:18 on whom it f will be crushed."
Jn 12:24 a kernel of wheat f to the ground
Heb 12:15 it that no one f short of the grace

FALSE FALSEHOOD, FALSELY

Ex 20:16 shall not give f testimony against
23: 1 "Do not spread f reports.
23: 7 Have nothing to do with a f charge
Dt 5:20 shall not give f testimony against
32:17 sacrificed to f gods, which are not
Job 36: 4 Be assured that my words are not f;
Ps 4: 2 you love delusions and seek f gods?

Ps 106:37 sons and their daughters to **f** gods.
Pr 12:17 the truth, but a **f** witness tells lies.
   13: 5 The righteous hate what is **f**,
   14: 5 but a **f** witness pours out lies.
   14:25 lives, but a **f** witness is deceitful.
   19: 5 A **f** witness will not go unpunished,
   21:28 A **f** witness will perish, but a careful
   25:18 one who gives **f** testimony against
Isa 44:25 who foils the signs of **f** prophets
Jer 14:14 are prophesying to you **f** visions,
   23:16 they fill you with **f** hopes.
   50:36 A sword against her **f** prophets!
Eze 13: 6 Their visions are **f** and their
Am 2: 4 they have been led astray by **f** gods,
Mt 7:15 "Watch out for **f** prophets.
   15:19 theft, **f** testimony, slander.
   24:11 and many **f** prophets will appear
   24:24 For **f** messiahs and **f** prophets will
Mk 10:19 you shall not give **f** testimony,
   13:22 For **f** messiahs and **f** prophets will
   14:57 gave this **f** testimony against him:
Lk 6:26 ancestors treated the **f** prophets.
   18:20 steal, you shall not give **f** testimony,
Ac 6:13 They produced **f** witnesses,
   13: 6 and **f** prophet named Bar-Jesus,
1Co 15:15 found to be **f** witnesses about God,
2Co 11:13 For such people are **f** apostles,
   11:26 and in danger from **f** believers.
Gal 2: 4 arose because some **f** believers had
Php 1:18 whether from **f** motives or true,
Col 2:18 anyone who delights in **f** humility
   2:23 their **f** humility and their harsh
1Ti 1: 3 not to teach **f** doctrines any longer
2Pe 2: 1 also **f** prophets among the people,
   2: 1 there will be **f** teachers among you.
1Jn 4: 1 because many **f** prophets have gone
Rev 16:13 out of the mouth of the **f** prophet.
   19:20 it the **f** prophet who had performed
   20:10 and the **f** prophet had been thrown.

FALSE PROPHET Ac 13:6; Rev 16:13; 19:20; 20:10

FALSE PROPHETS Isa 44:25; Jer 50:36; Hos 11:6; Mt 7:15; 24:11, 24; Mk 13:22; Lk 6:26; 2Pe 2:1; 1Jn 4:1

FALSEHOOD* FALSE

Job 21:34 is left of your answers but **f!**"
   31: 5 "If I have walked with **f** or my foot
Ps 52: 3 **f** rather than speaking the truth.
   119:163 hate and detest **f** but I love your law.
Pr 30: 8 Keep **f** and lies far from me;
Isa 28:15 our refuge and **f** our hiding place."
Ro 3: 7 my **f** enhances God's truthfulness
Eph 4:25 Therefore each of you must put off **f**
1Jn 4: 6 the Spirit of truth and the spirit of **f**.
Rev 22:15 everyone who loves and practices **f**.

FALSELY FALSE

Lev 19:12 " 'Do not swear **f** by my name
Isa 59: 3 Your lips have spoken **f**, and your
Da 6:24 men who had **f** accused Daniel were
Zec 5: 3 everyone who swears **f** will be

Mt 5:11 **f** say all kinds of evil against you
Mk 14:56 Many testified **f** against him,
Lk 3:14 money and don't accuse people **f**—
1Ti 6:20 ideas of what is **f** called knowledge,

FALTER* FALTERED, FALTERING

Pr 24:10 If you **f** in a time of trouble,
Isa 42: 4 he will not **f** or be discouraged till

FALTERED* FALTER

Ps 26: 1 in the LORD and have not **f**.
   105:37 from among their tribes no one **f**.

FALTERING* FALTER

Ex 6:12 to me, since I speak with **f** lips?"
   6:30 "Since I speak with **f** lips,
Job 4: 4 you have strengthened **f** knees.

FAME FAMOUS

Dt 26:19 **f** and honor high above all
Jos 9: 9 of the **f** of the LORD your God.
1Ch 14:17 So David's **f** spread throughout
2Ch 9: 1 of Sheba heard of Solomon's **f**,
Isa 66:19 islands that have not heard of my **f**
Hab 3: 2 LORD, I have heard of your **f**;

FAMILIAR

Isa 53: 3 a man of suffering, and **f** with pain.

FAMILIES FAMILY

Ex 1:21 God, he gave them **f** of their own.
Nu 1: 2 community by their clans and **f**,
   26: 2 whole Israelite community by **f**—
Ps 68: 6 God sets the lonely in **f**, he leads
   107:41 and increased their **f** like flocks.
Jer 31: 1 will be the God of all the **f** of Israel,
Am 3: 2 I chosen of all the **f** of the earth;

FAMILY FAMILIES

Ge 7: 1 ark, you and your whole **f**, because I
   24:38 go to my father's **f** and to my own
Dt 25: 9 not build up his brother's **f** line."
Jos 6:23 They brought out her entire **f**
Ru 3: 9 are a guardian-redeemer of our **f**."
   4:10 will not disappear from among his **f**
1Sa 18:18 what is my **f** or my clan in Israel,
2Ch 22:10 to destroy the whole royal **f**
Ezr 2:62 These searched for their **f** records,
Est 2:20 had kept secret her **f** background
Pr 31:15 she provides food for her **f**
Zec 11:14 breaking the **f** bond between Judah
Lk 9:61 go back and say goodbye to my **f**."
   12:52 in one **f** divided against each other,
Ac 10: 2 He and all his **f** were devout
Gal 6:10 who belong to the **f** of believers.
Eph 3:15 from whom every **f** in heaven
1Ti 3: 4 He must manage his own **f** well
   5: 4 practice by caring for their own **f**
Heb 11: 7 holy fear built an ark to save his **f**.
1Pe 2:17 love the **f** of believers, fear God,

FAMINE FAMINES

Ge 12:10 Now there was a **f** in the land,
   12:10 for a while because the **f** was severe.
   26: 1 Now there was a **f** in the land—
   26: 1 besides the previous **f** in Abraham's

Ge 41:27 They are seven years of **f**.
42: 5 for there was **f** in the land of Canaan
43: 1 Now the **f** was still severe
Dt 32:24 I will send wasting **f** against them,
Ru 1: 1 ruled, there was a **f** in the land.
1Ki 18: 2 Now the **f** was severe in Samaria,
2Ki 4:38 and there was a **f** in that region.
6:25 There was a great **f** in the city;
Ps 37:19 in days of **f** they will enjoy plenty.
Jer 14:15 'No sword or **f** will touch this land.'
14:15 prophets will perish by sword and **f**.
Eze 5:16 deadly and destructive arrows of **f**,
5:16 bring more and more **f** upon you
Am 8:11 I will send a **f** through the land—not
a **f** of food or a thirst for water, but a
f of hearing the words
Lk 4:25 was a severe **f** throughout the land.
Ac 11:28 a severe **f** would spread over
Ro 8:35 or persecution or **f** or nakedness
Rev 18: 8 death, mourning and **f**.

FAMINES FAMINE
Lk 21:11 **f** and pestilences in various places,

FAMOUS FAME
Ru 4:11 in Ephrathah and be **f** in Bethlehem.
2Sa 8:13 David became **f** after he returned
1Ki 1:47 Solomon's name more **f** than yours

FAN*
2Ti 1: 6 this reason I remind you to **f**

FANTASIES*
Ps 73:20 Lord, you will despise them as **f**.
Pr 12:11 those who chase **f** have no sense.
28:19 those who chase **f** will have their fill

FAR
Ge 18:25 **F** be it from you to do such a thing—
18:25 the wicked alike. **F** be it from you!
Nu 16: 3 said to them, "You have gone too **f**!
Jos 24:16 "**F** be it from us to forsake
1Sa 7:12 "Thus **f** the LORD has helped
12:23 me, **f** be it from me that I should sin
Ps 22: 1 Why are you so **f** from saving me, so **f**
from my cries of anguish?
103:12 as **f** as the east is from the west, so **f**
has he removed our
119:155 Salvation is **f** from the wicked,
Pr 31:10 She is worth **f** more than rubies.
Isa 29:13 lips, but their hearts are **f** from me.
57:19 peace, to those **f** and near,"
Jer 23:23 LORD, "and not a God **f** away?
Mk 7: 6 lips, but their hearts are **f** from me.
Rev 2: 5 Consider how **f** you have fallen!

FARMER
Mk 4: 3 A **f** went out to sow his seed.
2Ti 2: 6 The hardworking **f** should be
Jas 5: 7 See how the **f** waits for the land

FASHIONED FASHIONING
Ex 39: 8 They **f** the breastpiece—the work
Ps 94: 9 Does he who **f** the ear not hear?
Isa 37:19 wood and stone, **f** by human hands.

Isa 45:18 he who **f** and made the earth,

FASHIONING* FASHIONED, FASHIONS
Ex 32: 4 the shape of a calf, **f** it with a tool.

FASHIONS FASHIONING
Isa 44:15 But he also **f** a god and worships it;

FAST FASTED, FASTING
Dt 10:20 Hold **f** to him and take your oaths
11:22 to him and to hold **f** to him—
13: 4 serve him and hold **f** to him.
30:20 listen to his voice, and hold **f** to him.
Jos 22: 5 to hold **f** to him and to serve him
23: 8 to hold **f** to the LORD your God,
1Ki 11: 2 Solomon held **f** to them in love.
2Ki 18: 6 He held **f** to the LORD and did not
2Ch 20: 3 and he proclaimed a **f** for all Judah.
Ezr 8:21 I proclaimed a **f**, so that we might
Est 4:16 Jews who are in Susa, and **f** for me.
4:16 I and my attendants will **f** as you do.
Ps 119:31 I hold **f** to your statutes, LORD;
139:10 me, your right hand will hold me **f**.
Isa 56: 4 me and hold **f** to my covenant—
58: 5 Is this the kind of **f** I have chosen,
58: 5 Is that what you call a **f**, a day
Joel 1:14 Declare a holy **f**; call a sacred
Jnh 3: 5 A **f** was proclaimed, and all of them,
Mt 6:16 "When you **f**, do not look somber
9:14 it that we and the Pharisees **f** often,
but your disciples do not **f**?"
1Pe 5:12 the true grace of God. Stand **f** in it.

FASTED FAST
Isa 58: 3 'Why have we **f**,' they say, 'and you
Zec 7: 5 'When you **f** and mourned
7: 5 was it really for me that you **f**?
Ac 13: 3 So after they had **f** and prayed,

FASTING FAST
Ps 35:13 and humbled myself with **f**.
Isa 58: 6 not this the kind of **f** I have chosen:
Da 9: 3 in **f**, and in sackcloth and ashes.
Mt 4: 2 After **f** forty days and forty nights,
6:16 their faces to show others they are **f**.
Ac 13: 2 were worshiping the Lord and **f**,
14:23 with prayer and **f**, committed them

FAT FATTENED
Ge 4: 4 **f** portions from some of the firstborn
Lev 3:16 All the **f** is the LORD's.
Jdg 3:17 of Moab, who was a very **f** man.
Ps 66:15 I will sacrifice **f** animals to you
Eze 34:20 will judge between the **f** sheep

FATAL
Ex 21:12 who strikes a person with a **f** blow is
Na 3:19 can heal you; your wound is **f**.
Rev 13: 3 beast seemed to have had a **f** wound,
but the **f** wound had been healed.

FATE
Job 20:29 Such is the **f** God allots the wicked,
Ps 49:13 This is the **f** of those who trust
Ecc 2:14 that the same **f** overtakes them both.

FATHER ANCESTOR, FATHER'S, FATHER-IN-LAW, FATHERED, FATHERLESS, FATHERS, FOREFATHER, FOREFATHERS, PARENT

Ge   2:24 That is why a man leaves his **f**
      17: 4 You will be the **f** of many nations.
      19:32 Let's get our **f** to drink wine
      19:32 our family line through our **f**."
      26:24 "I am the God of your **f** Abraham.
      27:38 Esau said to his **f**, "Do you have only
             one blessing, my **f**? Bless me too,
             my **f**!"
      31: 5 the God of my **f** has been with me.
      46: 3 God, the God of your **f**," he said.
Ex   20:12 "Honor your **f** and your mother,
      21:15 "Anyone who attacks their **f**
      21:17 "Anyone who curses their **f**
      22:17 If her **f** absolutely refuses to give
Lev 18: 7 " 'Do not dishonor your **f**
      19: 3 you must respect your mother and **f**,
      20: 9 " 'Anyone who curses their **f**
Dt   1:31 carried you, as a **f** carries his son,
      5:16 "Honor your **f** and your mother,
      21:18 son who does not obey his **f**
      32: 6 Is he not your **F**, your Creator,
Jdg 17:10 with me and be my **f** and priest,
      18:19 with us, and be our **f** and priest.
Ru   4:22 Obed the **f** of Jesse, and Jesse the
             f of David.
2Sa   7:14 I will be his **f**, and he will be my
1Ki   2:12 sat on the throne of his **f** David,
1Ch 17:13 I will be his **f**, and he will be my
      22:10 will be my son, and I will be his **f**.
      28: 6 to be my son, and I will be his **f**.
      29:10 the God of our **f** Israel,
Job 38:28 Does the rain have a **f**?
Ps   2: 7 today I have become your **f**.
      27:10 Though my **f** and mother forsake
      68: 5 A **f** to the fatherless, a defender
      89:26 out to me, 'You are my **F**, my God,
      103:13 As a **f** has compassion on his
Pr   3:12 loves, as a **f** the son he delights in.
      10: 1 A wise son brings joy to his **f**,
      15:20 A wise son brings joy to his **f**,
      17:25 A foolish son brings grief to his **f**
      19:26 Whoever robs their **f** and drives
      20:20 If someone curses their **f** or mother,
      23:22 Listen to your **f**, who gave you life,
      23:24 The **f** of a righteous child has great
      28: 7 companion of gluttons disgraces his **f**.
      28:24 Whoever robs their **f** or mother
      29: 3 loves wisdom brings joy to his **f**,
Isa   8: 4 the boy knows how to say 'My **f**'
      9: 6 God, Everlasting **F**, Prince of Peace.
      43:27 Your first **f** sinned; those I sent
      45:10 Woe to the one who says to a **f**,
      63:16 But you are our **F**, though Abraham
      63:16 are our **F**, our Redeemer from of old
Jer   2:27 wood, 'You are my **f**,' and to stone,
      3:19 I thought you would call me '**F**'
      31: 9 because I am Israel's **f**, and Ephraim

Eze 18:19 the son not share the guilt of his **f**?'
Mic   7: 6 For a son dishonors his **f**, a daughter
Mal   1: 6 "A son honors his **f**, and a slave his
      1: 6 If I am a **f**, where is the honor due
      2:10 Do we not all have one **F**?
Mt   3: 9 'We have Abraham as our **f**.'
      5:16 deeds and glorify your **F** in heaven.
      6: 9 " 'Our **F** in heaven, hallowed be
      6:14 your heavenly **F** will also forgive
      6:15 your **F** will not forgive your sins.
      6:26 and yet your heavenly **F** feeds them.
      10:37 "Anyone who loves their **f**
      11:27 been committed to me by my **F**.
      11:27 No one knows the Son except the **F**,
      11:27 no one knows the **F** except the Son
      15: 4 said, 'Honor your **f** and mother'
      15: 4 and 'Anyone who curses their **f**
      18:10 see the face of my **F** in heaven.
      19: 5 this reason a man will leave his **f**
      19:19 honor your **f** and mother,' and 'love
      19:29 brothers or sisters or **f** or mother
      23: 9 And do not call anyone on earth '**f**,'
             for you have one **F**,
      28:19 baptizing them in the name of the **F**
Mk   14:36 "*Abba*, **F**," he said,
Lk   1:32 give him the throne of his **f** David,
      6:36 merciful, just as your **F** is merciful.
      9:59 first let me go and bury my **f**."
      11: 2 " '**F**, hallowed be your name,
      12:30 your **F** knows that you need them.
      12:53 **f** against son and son against **f**,
      14:26 me and does not hate **f** and mother,
      15:12 The younger one said to his **f**, '**F**,
      16:24 So he called to him, '**F** Abraham,
      18:20 honor your **f** and mother.' "
      23:34 Jesus said, "**F**, forgive them,
Jn   1:14 who came from the **F**, full of grace
      1:18 is in closest relationship with the **F**,
      3:35 The **F** loves the Son and has placed
      4:23 true worshipers will worship the **F**
      4:23 the kind of worshipers the **F** seeks.
      5:17 "My **F** is always at his work to this
      5:18 he was even calling God his own **F**,
      5:20 For the **F** loves the Son and shows
      6:44 me unless the **F** who sent me draws
      6:46 one has seen the **F** except the one
      6:46 is from God; only he has seen the **F**.
      8:19 they asked him, "Where is your **f**?"
      8:19 "You do not know me or my **F**,"
      8:19 me, you would know my **F** also."
      8:28 speak just what the **F** has taught me.
      8:41 are doing the works of your own **f**."
      8:41 "The only **F** we have is God
      8:44 You belong to your **f**, the devil,
      8:44 for he is a liar and the **f** of lies.
      10:17 The reason my **F** loves me is that I
      10:30 I and the **F** are one."
      10:38 and understand that the **F** is in me,
             and I in the **F**."
      12:27 '**F**, save me from this hour'?
      14: 6 comes to the **F** except through me.
      14: 9 who has seen me has seen the **F**.
      14: 9 How can you say, 'Show us the **F**'?

Jn   14:11 I am in the F and the F is in me;
        14:21 loves me will be loved by my F,
        14:28 be glad that I am going to the F, for
             the F is greater than I.
        15: 9 "As the F has loved me, so have I
        15:23 hates me hates my F as well.
        20:17 for I have not yet ascended to the F.
        20:17 ascending to my F and your F,
        20:21 As the F has sent me, I am sending
Ac   1: 4 but wait for the gift my F promised,
        13:33 today I have become your f.'
Ro   4:11 he is the f of all who believe
         4:16 He is the f of us all.
         8:15 And by him we cry, "Abba, F."
1Co 4:15 I became your f through the gospel.
2Co 1: 3 God and F of our Lord Jesus Christ,
         1: 3 the F of compassion and the God
         6:18 And, "I will be a F to you, and you
Gal   4: 6 Spirit who calls out, "Abba, F."
Eph 5:31 this reason a man will leave his f
         6: 2 "Honor your f and mother"—
Php 2:11 is Lord, to the glory of God the F.
1Th 2:11 of you as a f deals with his own
Heb 1: 5 today I have become your F"?
         1: 5 "I will be his F, and he will be my
        12: 7 are not disciplined by their f?
        12: 9 should we submit to the F of spirits
Jas   1:17 from the F of the heavenly lights,
1Jn   1: 3 our fellowship is with the F
         2:15 world, love for the F is not in them.
         2:22 denying the F and the Son.
         3: 1 what great love the F has lavished
2Jn   1: 9 in the teaching has both the F
Rev 2:27 have received authority from my F.
         3: 5 that name before my F and his
         3:21 sat down with my F on his throne.

FATHER ABRAHAM Ge 22:7; 26:3, 15, 18, 24;
28:13; 32:9; Jos 24:2, 3; Lk 1:73; 16:24, 30; Jn 8:53,
56; Ac 7:2; Ro 4:12; Jas 2:21

FATHER IN HEAVEN Mt 5:16, 45; 6:1, 9; 7:11;
10:32, 33; 12:50; 16:17; 18:10, 14, 19; Mk 11:25;
Lk 11:13

GOD AND FATHER See GOD

GOD OF ... FATHER See GOD

GOD THE FATHER See GOD

HEAVENLY FATHER Mt 5:48; 6:14, 26, 32;
15:13; 18:35

FATHER'S FATHER

Ge   12: 1 your f household to the land I will
        27:34 When Esau heard his f words,
        31:19 Rachel stole her f household gods.
        49: 4 for you went up onto your f bed,
Ex   15: 2 and I will praise him, my f God,
        18: 4 he said, "My f God was my helper;
2Sa 16:21 your f concubines whom he left
Est   4:14 you and your f family will perish.
Pr   4: 1 Listen, my sons, to a f instruction;
        13: 1 A wise son heeds his f instruction,
        13:13 A foolish child is a f ruin,
Eze 18:17 He will not die for his f sin;
Mt   16:27 come in his F glory with his angels,

Lk   2:49 know I had to be in my F house?"
Jn   2:16 Stop turning my F house
         5:43 I have come in my F name, and you
      10:29 can snatch them out of my F hand.
      14: 2 My F house has many rooms;
      15: 8 This is to my F glory, that you bear
Rev 14: 1 and his F name written on their

FATHER'S HOUSE See HOUSE

FATHER-IN-LAW FATHER

Ex   18: 8 Moses told his f about everything
Jn   18:13 Annas, who was the f of Caiaphas,

FATHERED* FATHER

Dt   32:18 deserted the Rock, who f you;

FATHERLESS FATHER

Ex   22:22 advantage of the widow or the f.
Dt   10:18 He defends the cause of the f
      14:29 the f and the widows who live
      24:17 the foreigner or the f of justice,
      24:19 the foreigner, the f and the widow,
      26:12 the foreigner, the f and the widow,
Ps   10:14 you are the helper of the f.
      68: 5 A father to the f, a defender
      82: 3 Defend the weak and the f;
Pr   23:10 or encroach on the fields of the f,
Isa   1:17 Take up the cause of the f;
Jer   5:28 do not promote the case of the f;
Hos 14: 3 for in you the f find compassion."
Mal   3: 5 who oppress the widows and the f,

FATHERS FATHER

Ex   3:15 'The LORD, the God of your f—
Isa 49:23 Kings will be your foster f, and their
Lk   11:11 "Which of you f, if your son asks
1Co 4:15 you do not have many f,
Eph 6: 4 F, do not exasperate your children,
Col   3:21 F, do not embitter your children,
1Ti   1: 9 for those who kill their f or mothers,
Heb 12: 9 all had human f who disciplined us
1Jn   2:13 I am writing to you, f, because you

GOD OF ... FATHERS See GOD

FATHOM* FATHOMED

Job   11: 7 "Can you f the mysteries of God?
Ps 145: 3 his greatness no one can f.
Ecc   3:11 yet no one can f what God has done
Isa 40:13 Who can f the Spirit of the LORD,
      40:28 and his understanding no one can f.
1Co 13: 2 of prophecy and can f all mysteries

FATHOMED* FATHOM

Job   5: 9 performs wonders that cannot be f,
       9:10 performs wonders that cannot be f,

FATTENED FAT

2Sa   6:13 he sacrificed a bull and a f calf.
Pr   15:17 with love than a f calf with hatred.
Isa   1:11 of rams and the fat of f animals;
Lk   15:23 Bring the f calf and kill it.
Jas   5: 5 You have f yourselves in the day

FAULT FAULTFINDERS, FAULTLESS, FAULTS, FAULTY

1Sa 29: 3 now, I have found no f in him."
Job 33:10 Yet God has found f with me;
Jer 2: 5 "What f did your ancestors find
Jnh 1:12 it is my f that this great storm has
Mt 18:15 sins, go and point out their f,
Php 2:15 of God without f in a warped
Jas 1: 5 generously to all without finding f,
     3: 2 Anyone who is never at f in what
Jude 1:24 his glorious presence without f

FAULTFINDERS* FAULT, FIND

Jude 1:16 These people are grumblers and f;

FAULTLESS* FAULT

Php 3: 6 righteousness based on the law, f.
Jas 1:27 Father accepts as pure and f is this:

FAULTS* FAULT

Job 10: 6 that you must search out my f
Ps 19:12 Forgive my hidden f.

FAULTY* FAULT

Ps 78:57 faithless, as unreliable as a f bow.
Hos 7:16 they are like a f bow.

FAVOR FAVORABLE, FAVORABLY, FAVORED, FAVORITISM, FAVORS

Ge   4: 4 The Lord looked with f on Abel
     6: 8 But Noah found f in the eyes
Ex 33:12 and you have found f with me.'
    34: 9 "if I have found f in your eyes,
Lev 26: 9 " 'I will look on you with f
Nu 11:15 if I have found f in your eyes—
Jdg 6:17 "If now I have found f in your eyes,
1Sa 2:26 in stature and in f with the Lord
2Sa 2: 6 you the same f because you have
2Ki 13: 4 Jehoahaz sought the Lord's f,
2Ch 33.12 In his distress he sought the f
Ezr 7:28 who has extended his good f to me
Ne   5:19 Remember me with f, my God,
    13:31 Remember me with f, my God.
Est 2:15 Esther won the f of everyone who
     7: 3 "If I have found f with you,
Ps 30: 5 a moment, but his f lasts a lifetime;
    77: 7 Will he never show his f again?
    90:17 May the f of the Lord our God rest
Pr   3:34 mockers but shows f to the humble
     8:35 life and receive f from the Lord.
    10:32 of the righteous know what finds f,
    11: 1 accurate weights find f with him.
    13:15 Good judgment wins f, but the way
    18:22 and receives f from the Lord.
    19: 6 Many curry f with a ruler,
Isa 49: 8 the time of my f I will answer you,
    61: 2 proclaim the year of the Lord's f
    66: 2 are the ones I look on with f:
Eze 36: 9 for you and will look on you with f;
Zec 11: 7 called one F and the other Union,
Lk   1:30 you have found f with God.
     2:14 peace to those on whom his f rests."
     2:52 stature, and in f with God and man.
     4:19 proclaim the year of the Lord's f."

Jn   5:32 is another who testifies in my f,
Ac   2:47 and enjoying the f of all the people.
2Co 6: 2 "In the time of my f I heard you,
     6: 2 now is the time of God's f, now is
1Pe 5: 5 proud but shows f to the humble."

FAVOR IN ... EYES See EYES

FAVORABLE FAVOR

Jer 42: 6 Whether it is f or unfavorable,

FAVORABLY FAVOR

Ex   3:21 the Egyptians f disposed toward this
    11: 3 the Egyptians f disposed toward

FAVORED FAVOR

Ps 30: 7 when you f me, you made my royal
Lk   1:28 "Greetings, you who are highly f!
     1:43 But why am I so f, that the mother

FAVORITISM* FAVOR

Ex 23: 3 do not show f to a poor person
Lev 19:15 to the poor or f to the great,
Ac 10:34 true it is that God does not show f
Ro   2:11 For God does not show f.
Gal 2: 6 God does not show f—
Eph 6: 9 heaven, and there is no f with him.
Col 3:25 for their wrongs, and there is no f.
1Ti 5:21 partiality, and to do nothing out of f.
Jas 2: 1 Lord Jesus Christ must not show f.
     2: 9 But if you show f, you sin and are

FAVORS FAVOR

Eze 16:15 You lavished your f on anyone who

FAWNS

Ge 49:21 a doe set free that bears beautiful f.
SS   4: 5 Your breasts are like two f, like twin f
         of a gazelle

FEAR AFRAID, FEARED, FEARFUL, FEARFULLY, FEARLESSLY, FEARS, FRIGHTEN, FRIGHTENED, GOD-FEARING

Ge   9: 2 The f and dread of you will fall
    22:12 Now I know that you f God,
    31:42 God of Abraham and the F of Isaac,
Ex   9:30 still do not f the Lord God."
    20:20 so that the f of God will be with you
Dt   2:25 and f of you on all the nations under
     6:13 F the Lord your God, serve him
    10:12 you but to f the Lord your God,
    31:12 learn to f the Lord your God
Jos 2:24 the people are melting in f because
     4:24 that you might always f the Lord
    24:14 "Now f the Lord and serve him
1Sa 12:14 If you f the Lord and serve
    12:24 be sure to f the Lord and serve
2Sa 23: 3 when he rules in the f of God,
1Ki 8:43 may know your name and f you,
2Ch 19: 7 Now let the f of the Lord be
    26: 5 who instructed him in the f of God.
Ezr 3: 3 Despite their f of the peoples around
Est 8:17 nationalities became Jews because f
Job 1: 9 "Does Job f God for nothing?"
     6:14 from a friend forsakes the f

Ps 2:11 Serve the LORD with f
3: 6 I will not f though tens of thousands
15: 4 but honors those who f the LORD;
19: 9 The f of the LORD is pure,
23: 4 the darkest valley, I will f no evil,
27: 1 and my salvation—whom shall I f?
33: 8 Let all the earth f the LORD;
34: 7 encamps around those who f him,
34: 9 F the LORD, you his holy people,
34: 9 for those who f him lack nothing.
34:11 I will teach you the f of the LORD.
46: 2 Therefore we will not f,
55:19 because they have no f of God.
67: 7 all the ends of the earth will f him.
86:11 heart, that I may f your name.
90:11 Your wrath is as great as the f that is
91: 5 You will not f the terror of night,
111:10 The f of the LORD is
112: 1 are those who f the LORD,
118: 4 Let those who f the LORD say:
119:63 I am a friend to all who f you, to all
128: 1 Blessed are all who f the LORD,
145:19 the desires of those who f him;
147:11 LORD delights in those who f him,
Pr 1: 7 The f of the LORD is
1:29 and did not choose to f the LORD.
1:33 and be at ease, without f of harm."
3: 7 f the LORD and shun evil.
8:13 To f the LORD is to hate evil;
9:10 The f of the LORD is
10:27 The f of the LORD adds length
14:16 The wise f the LORD and shun
14:27 The f of the LORD is a fountain
15:33 instruction is to f the LORD,
16: 6 through the f of the LORD evil is
19:23 The f of the LORD leads to life;
22: 4 Humility is the f of the LORD;
29:25 F of man will prove to be a snare,
31:21 she has no f for her household;
Ecc 3:14 does it so that people will f him.
5: 7 Therefore f God.
8:12 will go better with those who f God,
8:13 because the wicked do not f God,
12:13 of the matter: F God and keep his
Isa 8:12 do not f what they f, and do not
11: 3 will delight in the f of the LORD.
33: 6 the f of the LORD is the key to this
35: 4 fearful hearts, "Be strong, do not f;
41:10 So do not f, for I am with you;
41:13 right hand and says to you, Do not f;
43: 1 "Do not f, for I have redeemed you;
51: 7 Do not f the reproach of mere
54:14 you will have nothing to f.
Jer 5:22 Should you not f me?"
10: 7 Who should not f you,
17: 8 It does not f when heat comes;
Mic 6: 9 and to f your name is wisdom—
Zep 3:15 never again will you f any harm.
Lk 12: 5 I will show you whom you should f:
12: 5 into hell. Yes, I tell you, f him.
18: 4 'Even though I don't f God or care
Jn 12:42 their faith for f they would be put
20:19 the doors locked for f of the Jewish

Ac 5:11 Great f seized the whole church
Ro 8:15 slaves, so that you live in f again;
13: 3 want to be free from f of the one
2Co 5:11 we know what it is to f the Lord,
Gal 4:11 I f for you, that somehow I have
Php 1:14 to proclaim the gospel without f.
2:12 to work out your salvation with f
Heb 2:15 held in slavery by their f of death.
1Pe 1:17 time as foreigners here in reverent f.
3:14 "Do not f their threats; do not be
1Jn 4:18 There is no f in love.
4:18 But perfect love drives out f, because
f has to do
Jude 1:23 others show mercy, mixed with f—
Rev 14: 7 voice, "F God and give him glory,
15: 4 Who will not f you, Lord, and bring

DO NOT FEAR Ex 9:30; Ecc 8:13; Isa 8:12;
35:4; 41:10, 13, 14; 43:1; 51:7; 54:4; 57:11; Jer 10:5;
La 3:57; Zep 3:16; Hag 2:5; Mal 3:5; 1Pe 3:14

FEAR GOD Ge 22:12; 42:18; Ex 18:21; Job 1:9;
Ps 66:16; Ecc 5:7; 8:12, 13; 12:13; Lk 18:4; 23:40;
1Pe 2:17; Rev 14:7

FEAR OF GOD Ge 20:11; Ex 20:20; Dt 25:18;
2Sa 23:3; 2Ch 20:29; 26:5; Ps 36:1; 55:19; Ro 3:18;
1Pe 2:18

FEAR OF THE LORD† 2Ch 17:10; 19:7, 9; Ps
19:9; 34:11; 111:10; Pr 1:7; 2:5; 9:10; 10:27; 14:27;
15:16; 16:6; 19:23; 22:4; 23:17; Isa 11:2, 3; 33:6

FEAR THE LORD† Ex 9:30; Dt 6:2, 13, 24;
10:12, 20; 31:12, 13; Jos 4:24; 24:14; 1Sa 12:14, 24;
Ps 15:4; 22:23; 25:12; 27:1; 33:8; 34:9; 40:3; 112:1;
115:13; 118:4; 128:1; Pr 1:29; 3:7; 8:13; 14:16;
15:33; 24:21; Jer 5:24; 26:19

FEARED FEAR
Ex 1:21 And because the midwives f God,
14:31 the people f the LORD and put
Job 1: 1 he f God and shunned evil.
Ps 76: 7 It is you alone who are to be f.
89: 7 of the holy ones God is greatly f;
Jnh 1:16 this the men greatly f the LORD,
Hag 1:12 And the people f the LORD.
Mal 1:14 name is to be f among the nations.
3:16 those who f the LORD talked
3:16 concerning those who f the LORD
Mk 6:20 because Herod f John and protected
Jn 19:38 but secretly because he f the Jewish

FEARFUL FEAR
Heb 10:27 but only a f expectation of judgment

FEARFULLY* FEAR
Ps 139:14 I praise you because I am f

FEARLESSLY* FEAR
Ac 9:27 Damascus he had preached f
Eph 6:19 I will f make known the mystery
6:20 Pray that I may declare it f, as I

FEARS FEAR
Job 1: 8 a man who f God and shuns evil."
2: 3 a man who f God and shuns evil.
Ps 34: 4 he delivered me from all my f.

Pr   14:26 Whoever f the LORD has a secure
     31:30 a woman who f the LORD is to be
Ecc   7:18 Whoever f God will avoid all
2Co   7: 5 conflicts on the outside, f within.
1Jn   4:18 The one who f is not made perfect

FEAST FEASTING, FEASTS; see also
FESTIVAL

Pr   15:15 the cheerful heart has a continual f.
Ecc 10:19 A f is made for laughter,
Isa   25: 6 LORD Almighty will prepare a f
Mt   8:11 their places at the f with Abraham,
Lk   14: 8 someone invites you to a wedding f,
2Pe   2:13 in their pleasures while they f

FEASTING FEAST

Est   9:17 and made it a day of f and joy.
Job   1:13 daughters were f and drinking wine
Pr   17: 1 and quiet than a house full of f,
Zec   7: 6 were you not just f for yourselves?

FEASTS FEAST; see also FESTIVALS

Nu   10:10 festivals and New Moon f—
Job   1: 4 sons used to hold f in their homes
Jude 1:12 people are blemishes at your love f,

FEATHERS

Ps   91: 4 He will cover you with his f,
Eze 17: 3 long f and full plumage of varied
Da   4:33 heaven until his hair grew like the f

FEATURES

1Sa 16:12 a fine appearance and handsome f.

FED FEED, WELL-FED

Hos 13: 6 When I f them, they were satisfied;
Lk   6:25 Woe to you who are well f now,
Php   4:12 situation, whether well f or hungry,
Jas   2:16 keep warm and well f," but does

FEEBLE

Job   4: 3 how you have strengthened f hands.
Ps   38: 8 I am f and utterly crushed;
Isa   35: 3 Strengthen the f hands,
Heb 12:12 strengthen your f arms and weak

FEED FED, FEEDS

Isa   9:20 Each will f on the flesh of their own
     11: 7 The cow will f with the bear,
     65:25 wolf and the lamb will f together,
Eze 34:14 there they will f in a rich pasture
Hos 11: 4 cheek, and I bent down to f them.
Mic   3: 5 anyone who refuses to f them.
Mt   25:37 did we see you hungry and f you,
Mk   8: 4 get enough bread to f them?"
Jn   21:15 Jesus said, "F my lambs."
     21:17 Jesus said, "F my sheep.
Ro   12:20 "If your enemy is hungry, f him;
Jude 1:12 shepherds who f only themselves.

FEEDS FEED

Pr   15:14 but the mouth of a fool f on folly.
Isa 44:20 Such a person f on ashes;
Hos 12: 1 Ephraim f on the wind;
Mt   6:26 yet your heavenly Father f them.
Jn   6:57 so the one who f on me will live

FEEL FELT

Jdg 16:26 "Put me where I can f the pillars
Ps   115: 7 They have hands, but cannot f, feet,
2Co 11:29 Who is weak, and I do not f weak?

FEET FOOT

Ex   12:11 your sandals on your f and your
     24:10 Under his f was something like
     30:21 hands and f so that they will not die.
Dt   1:36 descendants the land he set his f on,
      8: 4 your f did not swell during these
Jos   3:15 and their f touched the water's edge,
Ru   3: 8 there was a woman lying at his f!
1Sa   2: 9 He will guard the f of his faithful
2Sa 22:34 He makes my f like the f of a deer;
Ps   8: 6 you put everything under their f:
     22:16 they pierce my hands and my f.
     40: 2 he set my f on a rock and gave me
     56:13 death and my f from stumbling,
     66: 9 lives and kept our f from slipping.
     73: 2 as for me, my f had almost slipped;
    110: 1 enemies a footstool for your f."
    115: 7 but cannot feel, f, but cannot walk,
   119:105 Your word is a lamp for my f,
Pr   4:26 thought to the paths for your f
      5: 5 Her f go down to death;
      6:18 f that are quick to rush into evil,
Isa   6: 2 with two they covered their f,
     52: 7 the mountains are the f of those who
Eze 34:18 the rest of your pasture with your f?
     34:18 also muddy the rest with your f?
Da   2:33 iron, its f partly of iron and partly
Na   1: 3 and clouds are the dust of his f.
      1:15 the f of one who brings good news,
Hab   3:19 he makes my f like the f of a deer,
Zec 14: 4 On that day his f will stand
Mt   7: 6 may trample them under their f,
     10:14 town and shake the dust off your f.
     22:44 put your enemies under your f." '
Lk   1:79 death, to guide our f into the path
      7:38 stood behind him at his f weeping,
      7:38 she began to wet his f with her tears.
      8:35 sitting at Jesus' f, dressed and in his
     24:39 Look at my hands and my f. It is I
Jn   13: 5 and began to wash his disciples' f,
Ac   2:35 enemies a footstool for your f." '
      4:35 and put it at the apostles' f, and it
Ro   3:15 "Their f are swift to shed blood;
     10:15 "How beautiful are the f of those
     16:20 will soon crush Satan under your f.
1Co 12:21 And the head cannot say to the f,
     15:25 has put all his enemies under his f.
Eph   1:22 God placed all things under his f
      6:15 with your f fitted with the readiness
1Ti   5:10 washing the f of the Lord's people,
Heb   1:13 enemies a footstool for your f"?
      2: 8 and put everything under their f."
     12:13 "Make level paths for your f,"
Rev   1:15 His f were like bronze glowing

FELIX

Governor before whom Paul was tried (Ac
23:23—24:27).

FELL FALL
Ge	7:12	And rain f on the earth forty days
	15:12	setting, Abram f into a deep sleep,
1Sa	4:18	Eli f backward off his chair
	31: 4	Saul took his own sword and f on it.
1Ki	18:38	the fire of the LORD f and burned
2Ki	1:10	Then fire f from heaven
Job	1:16	"The fire of God f from the heavens
Mt	25: 5	all became drowsy and f asleep.
Mk	4: 8	Still other seed f on good soil.
Jn	18: 6	they drew back and f to the ground.
Ac	5: 5	heard this, he f down and died.
Heb	11:30	By faith the walls of Jericho f,
Rev	1:17	him, I f at his feet as though dead.
	5:14	the elders f down and worshiped.
	6:13	and the stars in the sky f to earth,

FELLOW FELLOWSHIP
Lev	19:17	" 'Do not hate a f Israelite in your
Dt	10: 9	inheritance among their f Israelites;
	18:15	among you, from your f Israelites.
2Co	11:26	my f Jews, in danger from Gentiles;
Eph	2:19	but f citizens with God's people
2Th	3:15	them as you would a f believer.
1Pe	5: 1	I appeal as a f elder and a witness
Rev	22: 9	I am a f servant with you
	22: 9	with your f prophets and with all

FELLOWSHIP FELLOW
Ex	20:24	your burnt offerings and f offerings,
Lev	3: 1	" 'If your offering is a f offering,
Ac	2:42	to the apostles' teaching and to f,
1Co	1: 9	who has called you into f with his
	5: 2	your f the man who has been doing
2Co	6:14	what f can light have with darkness?
	13:14	the f of the Holy Spirit be with you
Gal	2: 9	Barnabas the right hand of f
1Jn	1: 3	so that you also may have f with us.
	1: 3	And our f is with the Father
	1: 6	If we claim to have f with him
	1: 7	light, we have f with one another,

FELLOWSHIP OFFERING Lev 3:1, 3, 6, 9;
4:10, 26, 31, 35; 7:11, 13, 14, 15, 18, 20, 21, 29, 33,
37; 9:4, 18, 22; 19:5; 22:21; 23:19; Nu 6:14, 17, 18;
7:17, 23, 29, 35, 41, 47, 53, 59, 65, 71, 77, 83, 88;
15:8; Pr 7:14

FELLOWSHIP OFFERINGS Ex 20:24; 24:5;
29:28; 32:6; Lev 6:12; 7:32, 34; 10:14; 17:5; Nu
10:10; 29:39; Dt 27:7; Jos 8:31; 22:23, 27; Jdg
20:26; 21:4; 1Sa 10:8; 11:15; 13:9; 2Sa 6:17, 18;
24:25; 1Ki 3:15; 8:63, 64, 64; 9:25; 2Ki 16:13; 1Ch
16:1, 2; 21:26; 2Ch 7:7; 29:35; 30:22; 31:2; 33:16;
Eze 43:27; 45:15, 17; 46:2, 12, 12; Am 5:22

FELT FEEL
Ex	10:21	darkness that can be f."
2Co	1: 9	we f we had received the sentence

FEMALE
Ge	1:27	male and f he created them.
	5: 2	He created them male and f
	6:19	male and f, to keep them alive
Mt	19: 4	the Creator 'made them male and f,'

Mk	10: 6	God 'made them male and f.'
Ac	16:16	met by a f slave who had a spirit
Gal	3:28	nor is there male and f, for you are

FERMENTED
Lev	10: 9	other f drink whenever you go
Nu	6: 3	abstain from wine and other f drink
	6: 3	made from wine or other f drink.
Dt	14:26	wine or other f drink, or anything
Lk	1:15	never to take wine or other f drink,

FEROCIOUS
Ge	37:33	Some f animal has devoured him.
Mt	7:15	but inwardly they are f wolves.

FERTILE FERTILIZE
Isa	5: 1	one had a vineyard on a f hillside.
	32:15	and the desert becomes a f field,
Jer	2: 7	I brought you into a f land to eat its

FERTILIZE* FERTILE
Lk	13: 8	year, and I'll dig around it and f it.

FERVENT* FERVOR
Pr	26:23	earthenware are f lips with an evil
Heb	5: 7	petitions with f cries and tears

FERVOR* FERVENT
Ac	18:25	and he spoke with great f and taught
Ro	12:11	but keep your spiritual f,

FESTIVAL FESTIVALS
Ex	5: 1	so that they may hold a f to me
	12:17	"Celebrate the F of Unleavened
	23:14	a year you are to celebrate a f to me.
	23:16	"Celebrate the F of Harvest
	23:16	"Celebrate the F of Ingathering
	34:18	"Celebrate the F of Unleavened
	34:22	"Celebrate the F of Weeks
	34:22	the F of Ingathering at the turn
Lev	23:34	the seventh month the LORD's F
Dt	16:14	Be joyful at your f—you, your sons
Ezr	3: 4	they celebrated the F of Tabernacles
Ne	8:18	They celebrated the f for seven
Zec	14:16	to celebrate the F of Tabernacles.
Mk	14: 2	"But not during the f," they said,
	15: 6	the f to release a prisoner whom
Lk	2:41	Jerusalem for the F of the Passover.
Jn	2:23	was in Jerusalem at the Passover F,
	7: 2	the Jewish F of Tabernacles was
	7:37	On the last and greatest day of the f,
	10:22	Then came the F of Dedication
	13: 1	It was just before the Passover F.
1Co	5: 8	Therefore let us keep the F,
Col	2:16	or with regard to a religious f,

FESTIVAL OF TABERNACLES Lev 23:34; Dt
16:13, 16; 31:10; 2Ch 8:13; Ezr 3:4; Zec 14:16, 18,
19; Jn 7:2

FESTIVAL OF UNLEAVENED BREAD Ex
12:17; 23:15; 34:18; Lev 23:6; Dt 16:16; 2Ch 8:13;
30:13, 21; 35:17; Ezr 6:22; Mt 26:17; Mk 14:1, 12;
Lk 22:1; Ac 12:3; 20:6

FESTIVALS FESTIVAL
Lev 23: 2 'These are my appointed f, the
           appointed f of the LORD,
2Ch 8:13 New Moons and the three annual f—
La   1: 4 for no one comes to her appointed f.
Hos 2:11 her yearly f, her New Moons,
     2:11 all her appointed f.
Am   5:21 "I hate, I despise your religious f;
Na   1:15 Celebrate your f, Judah, and fulfill
Zep 3:18 over the loss of your appointed f,

APPOINTED FESTIVALS See APPOINTED

FESTUS PORCIUS
Governor who sent Paul to Caesar (Ac 25–26).

FETTERS
Ps 149: 8 to bind their kings with f,

FEVER
Lev 26:16 and f that will destroy your sight
Job 30:30 my body burns with f.
Mk   1:30 mother-in-law was in bed with a f,
Lk   4:39 he bent over her and rebuked the f,
Jn   4:52 one in the afternoon, the f left him."
Ac 28: 8 bed, suffering from f and dysentery.

FEW FEWEST
Ge 47: 9 My years have been f and difficult,
Dt 26: 5 down into Egypt with a f people
1Ch 16:19 When they were but f in number,
Job 14: 1 are of f days and full of trouble.
Ecc 5: 2 are on earth, so let your words be f.
Mt   7:14 that leads to life, and only a f find it.
    22:14 many are invited, but f are chosen."
    25:21 have been faithful with a f things;
Lk 10: 2 is plentiful, but the workers are f.

FEWEST* FEW
Dt   7: 7 for you were the f of all peoples.

FIDELITY*
Ro   1:31 no understanding, no f, no love,
    16:10 whose f to Christ has stood the test.

FIELD AKELDAMA, FIELDS, GRAINFIELDS
Ge   4: 8 Abel, "Let's go out to the f." While
           they were in the f,
    23:17 So Ephron's f in Machpelah near
Lev 19: 9 not reap to the very edges of your f
    19:19 " 'Do not plant your f with two
Ru   2: 3 she was working in a f belonging
Ps 103:15 they flourish like a flower of the f;
Pr 24:30 I went past the f of a sluggard,
    31:16 She considers a f and buys it;
Isa 1: 8 like a hut in a cucumber f, like a city
     5: 8 and join f to f till no space is left
    40: 6 is like the flowers of the f.
Jer 10: 5 Like a scarecrow in a cucumber f,
    32: 7 you and say, 'Buy my f at Anathoth,
Mt   6:28 See how the flowers of the f grow.
     6:30 how God clothes the grass of the f,
    13:38 The f is the world, and the good
    13:44 heaven is like treasure hidden in a f.
    13:44 sold all he had and bought that f.

Mt 24:40 Two men will be in the f;
    27: 8 is why it has been called the F
Lk 14:18 'I have just bought a f, and I must
Ac   1:18 his wickedness, Judas bought a f;
1Co 3: 9 you are God's f, God's building.
1Pe 1:24 glory is like the flowers of the f;

FIELDS FIELD
Ex 23:10 "For six years you are to sow your f
Ru   2: 2 "Let me go to the f and pick
Ne   5: 3 "We are mortgaging our f,
Ps 50:11 and the insects in the f are mine.
    96:12 Let the f be jubilant, and everything
   144:13 by tens of thousands in our f;
Isa 32:12 Beat your breasts for the pleasant f,
Mic 2: 2 They covet f and seize them,
Lk   2: 8 shepherds living out in the f nearby,
Jn   4:35 open your eyes and look at the f!

FIERCE
Ge 49: 7 be their anger, so f, and their fury,
Ex 32:12 Turn from your f anger;
Nu 25: 4 the LORD's f anger may turn away
Jos 7:26 the LORD turned from his f anger.
Ps 85: 3 wrath and turned from your f anger.
Jer 30:24 The f anger of the LORD will not
Hos 11: 9 I will not carry out my f anger,
Jnh 3: 9 compassion turn from his f anger so
Na   1: 6 Who can endure his f anger?

FIERY FIRE
Ps 11: 6 On the wicked he will rain f coals
Eze 21:31 breathe out my f anger against you;
1Pe 4:12 do not be surprised at the f ordeal
Rev 10: 1 sun, and his legs were like f pillars.
    19:20 were thrown alive into the f lake
    21: 8 they will be consigned to the f lake

FIFTIETH FIFTY
Lev 25:11 The f year shall be a jubilee for you;

FIFTY FIFTIETH
Ge 18:24 What if there are f righteous people
    18:24 the sake of the f righteous people
Lev 23:16 Count off f days up to the day
Jn   8:57 "You are not yet f years old,"

FIG FIGS, SYCAMORE-FIG
Ge   3: 7 so they sewed f leaves together
Jdg 9:10 the trees said to the f tree,
1Ki 4:25 own vine and under their own f tree.
Pr 27:18 one who guards a f tree will eat its
Hos 9:10 seeing the early fruit on the f tree.
Mic 4: 4 own vine and under their own f tree,
Na   3:12 All your fortresses are like f trees
Hab 3:17 Though the f tree does not bud
Zec 3:10 to sit under your vine and f tree,'
Mt 21:19 Seeing a f tree by the road, he went
    24:32 learn this lesson from the f tree:
Lk 13: 6 "A man had a f tree growing in his
Jn   1:48 still under the f tree before Philip
Jas 3:12 and sisters, can a f tree bear olives,
Rev 6:13 as figs drop from a f tree

FIGHT FIGHTING, FIGHTS, FOUGHT

Ex 14:14 The Lord will f for you;
17: 9 men and go out to f the Amalekites.
Dt 1:30 is going before you, will f for you,
3:22 the Lord your God himself will f
Jdg 1: 1 first to f against the Canaanites?"
1Sa 17: 9 If he is able to f and kill me, we will
25:28 because you f the Lord's battles,
Ne 4:20 Our God will f for us!"
Ps 35: 1 f against those who f against me.
Jer 21: 5 I myself will f against you
Zec 14: 3 go out and f against those nations,
Jn 18:36 my servants would f to prevent my
1Co 9:26 I do not f like a boxer beating
2Co 10: 4 The weapons we f with are not
1Ti 1:18 them you may f the battle well,
6:12 F the good f of the faith.
2Ti 4: 7 I have fought the good f, I have
Rev 2:16 will f against them with the sword

FIGHTING FIGHT

Ex 2:13 he went out and saw two Hebrews f.
14:25 The Lord is f for them against
Jos 10:14 Surely the Lord was f for Israel!
Ac 5:39 find yourselves f against God."

FIGHTS FIGHT

Jos 23:10 because the Lord your God f
Jas 4: 1 What causes f and quarrels among

FIGS FIG

2Ki 20: 7 said, "Prepare a poultice of f."
Jer 24: 1 showed me two baskets of f placed
Mic 7: 1 eat, none of the early f that I crave.
Na 3:12 the f fall into the mouth of the eater.
Mk 11:13 because it was not the season for f.
Lk 6:44 People do not pick f
Jas 3:12 bear olives, or a grapevine bear f?
Rev 6:13 earth, as f drop from a fig tree

FIGURATIVELY* FIGURE

Jn 16:25 "Though I have been speaking f,
Gal 4:24 These things are being taken f:
Rev 11: 8 which is f called Sodom and Egypt—

FIGURE* FIGURATIVELY, FIGURES

Ge 29:17 but Rachel had a lovely f and was
1Sa 28:13 "I see a ghostly f coming
Est 2: 7 had a lovely f and was beautiful.
Eze 1:26 on the throne was a f like
8: 2 and I saw a f like that of a man.
Jn 7: 4 to become a public f acts in secret.
10: 6 Jesus used this f of speech,

FIGURES* FIGURE

2Ch 4: 3 the rim, f of bulls encircled it—
Eze 23:14 f of Chaldeans portrayed in red,
Jn 16:29 clearly and without f of speech.

FILL FILLED, FILLING, FILLS, FULL, FULLNESS, FULLY

Ge 1:28 f the earth and subdue it.
Lev 25:19 you will eat your f and live there
Dt 31:20 and when they eat their f and thrive,

Ps 16:11 you will f me with joy in your
81:10 wide your mouth and I will f it.
Pr 12:21 the wicked have their f of trouble.
28:19 who chase fantasies will have their f
Ecc 1: 8 seeing, nor the ear its f of hearing.
Isa 27: 6 and f all the world with fruit.
33: 5 he will f Zion with his justice
Jer 23:24 "Do not I f heaven and earth?"
Eze 10: 2 F your hands with burning coals
Hag 1: 6 You drink, but never have your f.
2: 7 and I will f this house with glory,'
Jn 2: 7 servants, "F the jars with water";
6:26 you ate the loaves and had your f.
Ac 2:28 you will f me with joy in your
Ro 15:13 May the God of hope f you with all
Eph 4:10 in order to f the whole universe.)
Col 1: 9 We continually ask God to f you
1:24 and I f up in my flesh what is still

FILLED FILL

Ge 6:13 the earth is f with violence because
Ex 1: 7 that the land was f with them.
31: 3 I have f him with the Spirit of God,
35:31 he has f him with the Spirit of God,
40:34 of the Lord f the tabernacle.
Lev 19:29 and be f with wickedness.
Dt 6:11 houses f with all kinds of good
34: 9 son of Nun was f with the spirit
1Ki 8:11 glory of the Lord f his temple.
2Ki 3:17 yet this valley will be f with water,
2Ch 5:14 the glory of the Lord f the temple
7: 1 glory of the Lord f the temple.
Ps 71: 8 My mouth is f with your praise,
72:19 may the whole earth be f with his
119:64 The earth is f with your love,
Pr 8:30 I was f with delight day after day,
Isa 6: 4 and the temple was f with smoke.
11: 9 for the earth will be f
Jer 25:15 my hand this cup f with the wine
Eze 10: 4 The cloud f the temple,
43: 5 glory of the Lord f the temple.
Da 2:35 mountain and f the whole earth.
Hab 2:14 For the earth will be f
3: 3 heavens and his praise f the earth.
Mt 5: 6 for righteousness, for they will be f.
Lk 1:15 and he will be f with the Holy Spirit
1:41 Elizabeth was f with the Holy Spirit.
1:67 His father Zechariah was f
2:40 he was f with wisdom, and the grace
Jn 12: 3 the house was f with the fragrance
Ac 2: 4 of them were f with the Holy Spirit
4: 8 Then Peter, f with the Holy Spirit,
4:31 they were all f with the Holy Spirit
5: 3 Satan has so f your heart that you
9:17 and be f with the Holy Spirit."
13: 9 called Paul, f with the Holy Spirit,
13:52 And the disciples were f with joy
Ro 15:14 f with knowledge and competent
Eph 5:18 Instead, be f with the Spirit,
Php 1:11 f with the fruit of righteousness
Rev 8: 5 censer, f it with fire from the altar,
12:12 He is f with fury, because he knows
15: 8 the temple was f with smoke
16:19 gave her the cup f with the wine

FILLING FILL
Eze 44: 4 the glory of the LORD f the temple

FILLS FILL
Nu 14:21 of the LORD f the whole earth,
Ps 107: 9 and f the hungry with good things.
Eph 1:23 him who f everything in every way.

FILTH FILTHINESS, FILTHY
Isa   4: 4 The Lord will wash away the f
Jas   1:21 get rid of all moral f and the evil
Rev 17: 4 things and the f of her adulteries.

FILTHINESS* FILTH
La   1: 9 Her f clung to her skirts; she did not

FILTHY* FILTH
Isa 64: 6 all our righteous acts are like f rags;
Zec   3: 3 in f clothes as he stood before
      3: 4 him, "Take off his f clothes."
Col   3: 8 and f language from your lips.
Jas   2: 2 and a poor man in f old clothes

FINAL FINALITY
Ps 73:17 then I understood their f destiny.
Isa 41:22 them and know their f outcome.
Lk 11:26 And the f condition of that person is

FINALITY* FINAL
Ro   9:28 on earth with speed and f."

FINANCIAL*
1Ti   6: 5 that godliness is a means to f gain.

FIND FAULTFINDERS, FINDING,
      FINDS, FOUND
Ge 18:26 "If I f fifty righteous people
Ex 33:13 and continue to f favor with you.
Nu 32:23 be sure that your sin will f you out.
Dt   4:29 you will f him if you seek him
     13: 3 LORD your God is testing you to f
1Sa 23:16 and helped him f strength in God.
     28: 7 "F me a woman who is a medium,
Job 23: 3 If only I knew where to f him;
Ps 62: 5 Yes, my soul, f rest in God;
     91: 4 under his wings you will f refuge;
    112: 1 LORD, who f great delight in his
    119:35 commands, for there I f delight.
    119:52 laws, and I f comfort in them.
    132: 5 till I f a place for the LORD,
Pr   2: 5 and f the knowledge of God.
      3:13 Blessed are those who f wisdom,
      4:22 for they are life to those who f them
      8:17 me, and those who seek me f me.
      8:35 For those who f me f life
      8:36 who fail to f me harm themselves;
     14:22 those who plan what is good f love
     20: 6 but a faithful person who can f?
     24:14 If you f it, there is a future hope
     31:10 wife of noble character who can f?
Ecc   2:24 and f satisfaction in their own toil.
     12:10 searched to f just the right words,
SS   3: 2 I looked for him but did not f him.
Isa 58:14 you will f your joy in the LORD,
Jer   6:16 it, and you will f rest for your souls.

Jer 29:13 and f me when you seek me with all
Da   6: 4 and the satraps tried to f grounds
      6: 4 They could f no corruption in him,
Hos 14: 3 in you the fatherless f compassion."
Mt   7: 7 seek and you will f;
     11:29 and you will f rest for your souls.
     16:25 loses their life for me will f it.
     22: 9 invite to the banquet anyone you f."
Lk   11: 9 seek and you will f;
     18: 8 comes, will he f faith on the earth?"
     23: 4 "I f no basis for a charge against
     24: 3 they did not f the body of the Lord
Jn   10: 9 come in and go out, and f pasture.
Ac   23: 9 "We f nothing wrong with this
Eph   5:10 and f out what pleases the Lord.

FINDING FIND
Ex 15:22 in the desert without f water.
Hos 9:10 it was like f grapes in the desert;

FINDS FIND
Ps 62: 1 Truly my soul f rest in God;
    119:162 promise like one who f great spoil.
Pr 10:23 A fool f pleasure in wicked
     11:19 but whoever pursues evil f death.
     11:27 Whoever seeks good f favor,
     14: 6 mocker seeks wisdom and f none,
     18:22 He who f a wife f what is good
Ecc   9:10 Whatever your hand f to do, do it
Mt   7: 8 the one who seeks f; and to the one
     10:39 Whoever f their life will lose it,
Lk   11:10 the one who seeks f; and to the one
     12:37 whose master f them watching
     15: 4 go after the lost sheep until he f it?
     15: 8 and search carefully until she f it?

FINE FINE-SOUNDING, FINEST
Ex   2: 2 When she saw that he was a f child,
Pr   8:19 My fruit is better than f gold;
Ecc   7: 1 good name is better than f perfume,
Da   10: 5 a belt of f gold from Uphaz around
Zec   3: 4 and I will put f garments on you."
Lk   7:25 A man dressed in f clothes?

FINE-SOUNDING* FINE, SOUND
Col   2: 4 may deceive you by f arguments.

FINEST FINE
Job 28:15 It cannot be bought with the f gold,
Ps 147:14 satisfies you with the f of wheat.
Isa 25: 6 the best of meats and the f of wines.

FINGER FINGERS
Ex   8:19 to Pharaoh, "This is the f of God."
     31:18 of stone inscribed by the f of God.
Lev   4: 6 He is to dip his f into the blood
Dt   9:10 tablets inscribed by the f of God.
2Ch 10:10 them, 'My little f is thicker than my
Mt   23: 4 not willing to lift a f to move them.
Lk   11:20 I drive out demons by the f of God,
     16:24 to dip the tip of his f in water
Jn   8: 6 *write on the ground with his f.*
     20:25 and put my f where the nails were,

FINGERS FINGER

Ps   8: 3 the work of your f, the moon
Pr   7: 3 Bind them on your f; write them
Da   5: 5 Suddenly the f of a human hand
Mk 7:33 Jesus put his f into the man's ears.

FINISH FINISHED, UNFINISHED

Ps 90: 9 we f our years with a moan.
Mt 10:23 you will not f going through
Jn   4:34 him who sent me and to f his work.
     5:36 that the Father has given me to f—
Ac 20:24 my only aim is to f the race
2Co 8:11 Now f the work, so that your eager
Gal 3: 3 are you now trying to f by means
Jas 1: 4 Let perseverance f its work so

FINISHED FINISH

Ge   2: 2 seventh day God had f the work he
  24:15 Before he had f praying,
Ex 40:33 And so Moses f the work.
Dt 32:45 Moses f reciting all these words
Jos 19:51 And so they f dividing the land.
1Ki 8:54 Solomon had f all these prayers
Ezr 6:14 They f building the temple
Jn 19:28 that everything had now been f,
  19:30 the drink, Jesus said, "It is f."
2Ti 4: 7 the good fight, I have f the race,
Heb 4: 3 works have been f since the creation
Rev 11: 7 when they have f their testimony,

FINS

Lev 11: 9 streams you may eat any that have f

FIRE FIERY, FIREPOT

Ex   3: 2 in flames of f from within a bush.
    3: 2 the bush was on f it did not burn up.
  13:21 in a pillar of f to give them light,
  19:18 the LORD descended on it in f.
  40:38 and f was in the cloud by night,
Lev 6:12 The f on the altar must be kept
   6:12 arrange the burnt offering on the f
   9:24 F came out from the presence
  10: 1 put f in them and added incense;
  10: 1 offered unauthorized f before
Nu 11: 1 f from the LORD burned among
  16:35 And f came out from the LORD
Dt 4:12 LORD spoke to you out of the f.
Jdg 6:21 F flared from the rock,
1Ki 18:38 Then the f of the LORD fell
  19:12 After the earthquake came a f, but the
      LORD was not in the f.
  19:12 after the f came a gentle whisper.
2Ki 1:10 Then f fell from heaven
   2:11 suddenly a chariot of f and horses
      of f appeared and
   6:17 and chariots of f all around Elisha.
  16: 3 and even sacrificed his son in the f,
  25: 9 He set f to the temple
Ne 1: 3 its gates have been burned with f."
Ps 50: 3 a f devours before him, and around
  89:46 long will your wrath burn like f?
Pr 6:27 Can a man scoop f into his lap
Isa 5:24 as tongues of f lick up straw and as
  10:17 The Light of Israel will become a f,

Isa 30:27 and his tongue is a consuming f.
  66:24 die, the f that burns them will not be
Jer 23:29 "Is not my word like f,"
  36:23 the entire scroll was burned in the f.
Eze 1:13 creatures was like burning coals of f
   1:13 F moved back and forth among
Da   3:25 four men walking around in the f,
   7: 9 His throne was flaming with f,
Am 4:11 a burning stick snatched from the f,
Zec 2: 5 myself will be like a wall of f around it,'
   3: 2 burning stick snatched from the f?"
Mal 3: 2 For he will be like a refiner's f
Mt 3:11 you with the Holy Spirit and f.
   5:22 will be in danger of the f of hell.
  18: 8 feet and be thrown into eternal f.
  25:41 the eternal f prepared for the devil
Mk 9:43 into hell, where the f never goes out.
   9:48 not die, and the f is not quenched.'
   9:49 Everyone will be salted with f.
Lk 3:16 you with the Holy Spirit and f.
  12:49 have come to bring f on the earth,
Jn 15: 6 up, thrown into the f and burned.
Ac 2: 3 to be tongues of f that separated
1Co 3:13 It will be revealed with f, and the f
2Th 1: 7 blazing f with his powerful angels.
Heb 10:27 of raging f that will consume
  12:29 for our "God is a consuming f."
Jas 3: 6 The tongue also is a f, a world
   3: 6 and is itself set on f by hell.
1Pe 1: 7 perishes even though refined by f—
2Pe 3:10 the elements will be destroyed by f,
Jude 1: 7 suffer the punishment of eternal f.
   1:23 others by snatching them from the f;
Rev 1:14 and his eyes were like blazing f.
   8: 7 came hail and f mixed with blood,
   9:17 and out of their mouths came f,
  11: 5 f comes from their mouths
  15: 2 a sea of glass glowing with f and,
  20:14 were thrown into the lake of f.
  20:14 The lake of f is the second death.

FIREPOT FIRE

Ge 15:17 a smoking f with a blazing torch

FIRM* FIRMLY

Ex 14:13 Stand f and you will see
2Ch 20:17 stand f and see the deliverance
Ezr 9: 8 giving us a f place in his sanctuary,
Job 11:15 you will stand f and without fear.
  36: 5 he is mighty, and f in his purpose.
  41:23 they are f and immovable.
Ps 19: 9 The decrees of the LORD are f,
  20: 8 and fall, but we rise up and stand f.
  30: 7 made my royal mountain stand f;
  33: 9 he commanded, and it stood f.
  33:11 plans of the LORD stand f forever,
  37:23 The LORD makes f the steps
  40: 2 rock and gave me a f place to stand.
  75: 3 quake, it is I who hold its pillars f.
  89: 2 that your love stands f forever,
  89: 4 and make your throne f through all
  93: 1 world is established, f and secure.
  93: 5 Your statutes, LORD, stand f;
 119:89 it stands f in the heavens.

Pr 10:25 but the righteous stand **f** forever.
      12: 7 the house of the righteous stands **f**.
Isa   7: 9 If you do not stand **f** in your faith,
      22:17 is about to take **f** hold of you
      22:23 drive him like a peg into a a **f** place;
      22:25 into the **f** place will give way;
Eze 13: 5 so that it will stand **f** in the battle
Zec   8:23 nations will take **f** hold of one Jew
Mt 10:22 the one who stands **f** to the end will
      24:13 the one who stands **f** to the end will
Mk 13:13 the one who stands **f** to the end will
Lk 21:19 Stand **f**, and you will win life.
1Co 1: 8 He will also keep you **f** to the end,
      10:12 if you think you are standing **f**,
      15:58 my dear brothers and sisters, stand **f**.
      16:13 on your guard; stand **f** in the faith;
2Co 1: 7 And our hope for you is **f**,
      1:21 both us and you stand **f** in Christ.
      1:24 because it is by faith you stand **f**.
Gal 5: 1 Stand **f**, then, and do not let
Eph 6:14 Stand **f** then, with the belt of truth
Php 1:27 that you stand **f** in the one Spirit,
      4: 1 stand **f** in the Lord in this way,
Col 1:23 established and **f**, and do not move
      2: 5 are and how **f** your faith in Christ is.
      4:12 that you may stand **f** in all the will
1Th 3: 8 since you are standing **f** in the Lord.
2Th 2:15 stand **f** and hold fast to the teachings
1Ti 2:19 themselves as a **f** foundation
2Ti 2:19 God's solid foundation stands **f**,
Heb 6:19 an anchor for the soul, **f** and secure.
Jas 5: 8 be patient and stand **f**,
1Pe 5: 9 Resist him, standing **f** in the faith,
      5:10 make you strong, **f** and steadfast.

FIRMLY FIRM

1Ch 16:30 The world is **f** established;
Ecc 12:11 sayings like **f** embedded nails—
1Co 15: 2 if you hold **f** to the word I preached
Heb 4:14 let us hold **f** to the faith we profess.

FIRST FIRSTBORN, FIRSTFRUITS

Ge 1: 5 and there was morning—the **f** day.
      13: 4 and where he had **f** built an altar.
Ex 12: 2 month is to be for you the **f** month,
          the **f** month of your year.
      34: 1 out two stone tablets like the **f** ones,
      34: 1 the words that were on the **f** tablets,
      34:19 "The **f** offspring of every womb
      40:17 set up on the **f** day of the **f** month
Nu 18:15 The **f** offspring of every womb,
      28:11 " 'On the **f** of every month,
1Ki 22: 5 of Israel, "**F** seek the counsel
Pr 8:22 LORD brought me forth as the **f**
      18:17 a lawsuit the **f** to speak seems right,
Isa 44: 6 I am the **f** and I am the last;
      48:12 I am he; I am the **f** and I am the last.
Da 7: 4 "The **f** was like a lion, and it had
Mt 5:24 **F** go and be reconciled to them;
      6:33 But seek **f** his kingdom and his
      7: 5 **f** take the plank out of your own
      8:21 **f** let me go and bury my father."
      19:30 But many who are **f** will be last,
      19:30 and many who are last will be **f**.

Mt 22:38 This is the **f** and greatest
Mk 9:11 law say that Elijah must come **f**?"
      9:35 wants to be **f** must be the very last,
      10:31 But many who are **f** will be last, and
          the last **f**."
      10:44 whoever wants to be **f** must be slave
      13:10 the gospel must **f** be preached to all
      16: 2 Very early on the **f** day of the week,
Lk 11:26 of that person is worse than the **f**."
Jn 8: 7 *is without sin be the **f** to throw*
Ac 11:26 disciples were called Christians **f**
Ro 1:16 **f** to the Jew, then to the Gentile.
      1:17 that is by faith from **f** to last, just as
1Co 12:28 in the church **f** of all apostles,
      15:45 "The **f** man Adam became a living
2Co 8: 5 They gave themselves **f** of all
Eph 1:12 who were the **f** to put our hope
      6: 2 which is the **f** commandment
1Th 4:16 and the dead in Christ will rise **f**.
1Ti 2:13 For Adam was formed **f**, then Eve.
Heb 8:13 he has made the **f** one obsolete;
      10: 9 He sets aside the **f** to establish
Jas 3:17 comes from heaven is **f** of all pure;
1Jn 4:19 We love because he **f** loved us.
3Jn 1: 9 who loves to be **f**, will not welcome
Rev 1:17 I am the **F** and the Last.
      2: 4 have forsaken the love you had at **f**.
      4: 7 The **f** living creature was like a lion,
      6: 1 I watched as the Lamb opened the **f**
      8: 7 The **f** angel sounded his trumpet,
      9:12 The **f** woe is past; two other woes
      13:12 all the authority of the **f** beast on its
      13:12 its inhabitants worship the **f** beast,
      20: 5 This is the **f** resurrection.
      21: 1 for the **f** heaven and the **f** earth had
      22:13 and the Omega, the **F** and the Last,

FIRSTBORN FIRST, BEAR

Ge 27:19 to his father, "I am Esau your **f**.
      48:18 "No, my father, this one is the **f**;
Ex 4:22 the LORD says: Israel is my **f** son,
      11: 5 Every **f** son in Egypt will die, from
          the **f** son of Pharaoh,
      11: 5 and all the **f** of the cattle as well.
      12:29 the LORD struck down all the **f**
      12:29 from the **f** of Pharaoh, who sat
      12:29 the **f** of all the livestock as well.
      13: 2 "Consecrate to me every **f** male.
      34:20 Redeem the **f** donkey with a lamb,
      34:20 Redeem all your **f** sons. "No one is
Nu 3:41 in place of all the **f** of the Israelites,
      3:41 place of all the **f** of the livestock
Jos 6:26 his **f** son he will lay its foundations;
1Ki 16:34 at the cost of his **f** son Abiram,
Ps 89:27 And I will appoint him to be my **f**,
Mic 6: 7 Shall I offer my **f** for my
Zec 12:10 for him as one grieves for a **f** son.
Lk 2: 7 and she gave birth to her **f**, a son.
Ro 8:29 might be the **f** among many brothers
Col 1:15 God, the **f** over all creation.
      1:18 and the **f** from among the dead,
Heb 1: 6 God brings his **f** into the world,
      12:23 to the church of the **f**, whose names
Rev 1: 5 faithful witness, the **f** from the dead,

FIRSTFRUITS FIRST, FRUIT
Ex   23:16 with the f of the crops you sow
      34:22 with the f of the wheat harvest,
Pr   3: 9 wealth, with the f of all your crops;
Ro   8:23 who have the f of the Spirit,
1Co 15:23 Christ, the f; then, when he comes,
Jas   1:18 that we might be a kind of f of all he
Rev 14: 4 mankind and offered as f to God

FISH FISHERMEN, FISHHOOK
Ge   1:26 they may rule over the f in the sea
Ex   7:18 The f in the Nile will die,
Nu 11: 5 We remember the f we ate in Egypt
Eze 47: 9 There will be large numbers of f,
Jnh   1:17 Now the Lord provided a huge f
      1:17 was in the belly of the f three days
      2: 1 From inside the f Jonah prayed
Mt   4:19 I will send you out to f for people."
      7:10 Or if he asks for a f, will give him
      12:40 three nights in the belly of a huge f,
      13:48 and collected the good f in baskets,
      14:17 five loaves of bread and two f,"
Mk   1:17 I will send you out to f for people."
      8: 7 They had a few small f as well;
Lk   5: 6 they caught such a large number of f
      5:10 from now on you will f for people."
Jn   6: 9 small barley loaves and two small f,
      21: 5 "Friends, haven't you any f?"
      21:11 It was full of large f, 153, but even

FISHERMEN FISH
Mk   1:16 a net into the lake, for they were f.

FISHHOOK* FISH, HOOK
Job 41: 1 "Can you pull in Leviathan with a f

FISTS
Isa 58: 4 in striking each other with wicked f.
Mt   26:67 his face and struck him with their f.

FIT FITTING
Dt   12: 8 today, everyone doing as they see f,
Jdg   17: 6 everyone did as they saw f.
      21:25 everyone did as they saw f.
Lk   9:62 and looks back is f for service

FITTING* FIT
Ps   33: 1 it is f for the upright to praise him.
      147: 1 how pleasant and f to praise him!
Pr   19:10 It is not f for a fool to live
      26: 1 in harvest, honor is not f for a fool.
1Co 14:40 everything should be done in a f
Col   3:18 to your husbands, as is f in the Lord.
Heb   2:10 to glory, it was f that God,

FIVE
Lev 26: 8 F of you will chase a hundred,
1Sa   6: 4 "F gold tumors and f gold rats,
      6:16 The f rulers of the Philistines saw
      17:40 chose f smooth stones
Isa 30:17 the threat of f you will all flee away,
Mt   14:19 Taking the f loaves and the two fish
      16: 9 Don't you remember the f loaves for
            the f thousand,

Mt   25: 2 F of them were foolish and
            f were wise.
      25:15 To one he gave f bags of gold,
Jn   4:18 is, you have had f husbands,
1Co 14:19 rather speak f intelligible words
Rev   9: 5 only to torture them for f months.
      17:10 F have fallen, one is, the other has

FIX* FIXED, FIXING
Dt   11:18 F these words of mine in your
Job 14: 3 Do you f your eye on them?
Pr   4:25 f your gaze directly before you.
2Co   4:18 So we f our eyes not on what is
Heb   3: 1 calling, f your thoughts on Jesus,

FIXED* FIX
2Ki   8:11 him with a f gaze until Hazael was
Job 38:10 when I f limits for it and set its
Ps   141: 8 But my eyes are f on you,
Pr   8:28 f securely the fountains of the deep,

FIXING* FIX
Heb 12: 2 f our eyes on Jesus, the pioneer

FLAME FLAMES, FLAMING
Jdg   13:20 As the f blazed up from the altar
      13:20 of the Lord ascended in the f.
Isa 10:17 become a fire, their Holy One a f;
2Ti   1: 6 you to fan into f the gift of God,

FLAMES FLAME
Ex   3: 2 Lord appeared to him in f of fire
Da   3:22 the f of the fire killed the soldiers
1Co   3:15 only as one escaping through the f.
Heb 11:34 quenched the fury of the f,

FLAMING FLAME
Ge   3:24 and a f sword flashing back
Da   7: 9 His throne was f with fire, and its
      10: 6 his eyes like f torches, his arms
Eph   6:16 you can extinguish all the f arrows

FLANK
Eze 34:21 Because you shove with f

FLASH FLASHED, FLASHES,
            FLASHING
Eze 21:10 polished to f like lightning!
Lk   9:29 his clothes became as bright as a f
1Co 15:52 in a f, in the twinkling of an eye,

FLASHED FLASH
Eze   1:13 was bright, and lightning f out of it.
Ac   9: 3 a light from heaven f around him.

FLASHES FLASH
Eze   1:14 back and forth like f of lightning.
Lk   17:24 which f and lights up the sky
Rev   4: 5 From the throne came f of lightning,
      8: 5 f of lightning and an earthquake.
      11:19 And there came f of lightning,
      16:18 Then there came f of lightning,

FLASHING FLASH
Ge   3:24 a flaming sword f back and forth
Dt   32:41 when I sharpen my f sword and my

FLASK*
1Sa 10: 1 Then Samuel took a f of olive oil
2Ki   9: 1 take this f of olive oil with you
      9: 3 take the f and pour the oil on his

FLATTER* FLATTERING, FLATTERY
Job 32:21 no partiality, nor will I f anyone;
Ps   12: 2 they f with their lips but harbor
     36: 2 their own eyes they f themselves too
     78:36 they would f him with their mouths,
Pr   29: 5 Those who f their neighbors are
Jude 1:16 f others for their own advantage.

FLATTERING* FLATTER
Ps   12: 3 May the LORD silence all f lips
Pr   26:28 it hurts, and a f mouth works ruin.
     28:23 rather than one who has a f tongue.
Eze 12:24 or f divinations among the people

FLATTERY* FLATTER
Job 32:22 for if I were skilled in f, my Maker
Da   11:32 f he will corrupt those who have
Ro   16:18 f they deceive the minds of naive
1Th   2: 5 You know we never used f, nor did

FLAW* FLAWLESS
Dt   15:21 or has any serious f, you must not
     17: 1 a sheep that has any defect or f in it,
SS   4: 7 there is no f in you.

FLAWLESS* FLAW
2Sa 22:31 The LORD's word is f;
Job   9:20 'My beliefs are f and I am pure
Ps   12: 6 And the words of the LORD are f,
     18:30 The LORD's word is f;
Pr   30: 5 "Every word of God is f; he is
SS   5: 2 my darling, my dove, my f one.

FLAX
Jos   2: 6 under the stalks of f she had laid

FLED FLEE
Ex   2:15 but Moses f from Pharaoh and went
1Sa 19:18 When David had f and made his
2Sa   4: 4 His nurse picked him up and f,
     19: 9 now he has f the country to escape
Ps   3: T he f from his son Absalom.
     57: T he had f from Saul into the
    114: 3 The sea looked and f, the Jordan
Mk   14:50 Then everyone deserted him and f.
Rev 20:11 and the heavens f from his presence,

FLEE FLED, FLEES
Ge   19:17 one of them said, "F for your lives!
     19:17 F to the mountains or you will be
Nu   35:11 killed someone accidentally may f.
Ps   68: 1 may his foes f before him.
    139: 7 Where can I f from your presence?
Pr   28: 1 The wicked f though no one
Isa 30:17 A thousand will f at the threat
     30:17 the threat of five you will all f away,
Jer 46: 6 "The swift cannot f nor the strong
     51: 6 "F from Babylon! Run for your
Jnh   1: 3 for Tarshish to f from the LORD.
Zec   2: 6 F from the land of the north,"
Lk   3: 7 Who warned you to f

1Co   6:18 F from sexual immorality.
     10:14 my dear friends, f from idolatry.
1Ti   6:11 man of God, f from all this,
2Ti   2:22 F the evil desires of youth
Jas   4: 7 the devil, and he will f from you.

FLEECE
Jdg   6:37 look, I will place a wool f
      6:37 If there is dew only on the f and all

FLEES FLEE
Dt   19: 4 kills a person and f there for safety—

FLEETING*
Job 14: 2 like f shadows, they do not endure.
Ps   39: 4 let me know how f my life is.
     89:47 Remember how f is my life.
    144: 4 their days are like a f shadow.
Pr   21: 6 made by a lying tongue is a f vapor
     31:30 Charm is deceptive, and beauty is f;
Heb 11:25 than to enjoy the f pleasures of sin.

FLESH
Ge   2:23 bone of my bones and f of my f;
      2:24 to his wife, and they become one f.
     15: 4 own f and blood will be your heir."
     17:13 My covenant in your f is to be
Lev 26:29 You will eat the f of your sons and
            the f of your daughters.
1Sa 17:44 "and I'll give your f to the birds
2Sa   7:12 succeed you, your own f and blood,
2Ch 32: 8 With him is only the arm of f,
Job 19:26 yet in my f I will see God;
Ps   50:13 Do I eat the f of bulls or drink
Jer   9:25 who are circumcised only in the f—
Eze 11:19 of stone and give them a heart of f.
     36:26 of stone and give you a heart of f.
     37: 6 to you and make f come upon you
Mt   19: 5 and the two will become one f'?
     26:41 spirit is willing, but the f is weak."
Lk   24:39 a ghost does not have f and bones,
Jn   1:14 The Word became f and made his
      3: 6 F gives birth to f, but the Spirit
      6:51 This bread is my f, which I will give
Ro   8: 4 do not live according to the f but
      8: 5 who live according to the f have their
            minds set on what the f desires;
      8: 8 the realm of the f cannot please God.
      8: 9 are not in the realm of the f but are
      8:13 live according to the f, you will die;
     13:14 how to gratify the desires of the f.
1Co   5: 5 to Satan for the destruction of the f,
      6:16 said, "The two will become one f."
     15:39 Not all f is the same:
     15:39 People have one kind of f,
2Co 12: 7 I was given a thorn in my f,
Gal   3: 3 trying to finish by means of the f?
      4:23 woman was born according to the f,
      4:29 the son born according to the f
      5:13 not use your freedom to indulge the f;
      5:16 will not gratify the desires of the f.
      5:19 The acts of the f are obvious: sexual
      5:24 have crucified the f with its passions
Eph   2: 3 gratifying the cravings of our f and
      2:15 setting aside in his f the law with its

Eph 5:31 and the two will become one **f**."
    6:12 For our struggle is not against **f**
Php 3: 2 evildoers, those mutilators of the **f**.
Col 1:24 fill up in my **f** what is still lacking
    2:11 Your whole self ruled by the **f** was put
    2:13 and in the uncircumcision of your **f**,
2Pe 2:18 to the lustful desires of the **f**,
1Jn 4: 2 that Jesus Christ has come in the **f** is
2Jn 1: 7 Jesus Christ as coming in the **f**,
Jude 1:23 the clothing stained by corrupted **f**.
Rev 19:18 so that you may eat the **f** of kings,
    19:18 and the **f** of all people,

FLESH AND BLOOD Ge 15:4; 29:14; 37:27;
Jdg 9:2; 2Sa 5:1; 7:12; 16:11; 19:12, 13; 1Ki 8:19;
2Ki 20:18; 1Ch 11:1; 2Ch 6:9; 32:21; Ne 5:5; Isa
39:7; 58:7; Mt 16:17; 1Co 15:50; Eph 6:12; Heb
2:14

FLEW FLY
Ps 18:10 He mounted the cherubim and **f**;
Isa 6: 6 one of the seraphim **f** to me

FLIES FLY
Ex 8:21 I will send swarms of **f** on you
    8:21 of the Egyptians will be full of **f**;
Ps 91: 5 of night, nor the arrow that **f** by day,
Isa 7:18 day the LORD will whistle for **f**

FLIGHT FLY
Dt 32:30 or two put ten thousand to **f**,
Mt 24:20 Pray that your **f** will not take place

FLINT
Ex 4:25 But Zipporah took a **f** knife, cut off
Jos 5: 2 "Make **f** knives and circumcise
Isa 50: 7 Therefore have I set my face like **f**,
Zec 7:12 They made their hearts as hard as **f**

FLIRTING*
Isa 3:16 outstretched necks, **f** with their eyes,

FLOAT* FLOATED
1Ki 5: 9 I will **f** them as rafts by sea
2Ki 6: 6 threw it there, and made the iron **f**.
2Ch 2:16 will **f** them as rafts by sea down

FLOATED* FLOAT
Ge 7:18 the ark **f** on the surface of the water.

FLOCK FLOCKS
Ex 2:17 to their rescue and watered their **f**.
    3: 1 Now Moses was tending the **f**
    3: 1 and he led the **f** to the far side
2Sa 7: 8 from tending the **f**, and appointed
Ps 77:20 You led your people like a **f**
    78:52 he brought his people out like a **f**;
    95: 7 of his pasture, the **f** under his care.
Isa 40:11 He tends his **f** like a shepherd:
Jer 10:21 prosper and all their **f** is scattered.
    23: 2 "Because you have scattered my **f**
    31:10 watch over his **f** like a shepherd.'
Eze 34: 2 not shepherds take care of the **f**?
Am 7:15 LORD took me from tending the **f**
Zec 11: 7 So I shepherded the **f** marked
    11: 7 particularly the oppressed of the **f**.

Mt 26:31 the sheep of the **f** will be scattered.'
Lk 12:32 little **f**, for your Father has been
Jn 10:16 and there shall be one **f** and one
Ac 20:28 all the **f** of which the Holy Spirit has
1Co 9: 7 Who tends a **f** and does not drink
1Pe 5: 2 of God's **f** that is under your care,
    5: 3 to you, but being examples to the **f**.

FLOCKS FLOCK
Ge 4: 2 Now Abel kept **f**, and Cain worked
Nu 32: 1 who had very large herds and **f**,
Lk 2: 8 keeping watch over their **f** at night.

FLOG FLOGGED, FLOGGING
Pr 19:25 **F** a mocker, and the simple will
Ac 22:25 As they stretched him out to **f** him,
    22:25 **f** a Roman citizen who hasn't even

FLOGGED FLOG
Dt 25: 3 the guilty party is **f** more than that,
Mt 10:17 councils and be **f** in the synagogues.
Jn 19: 1 Pilate took Jesus and had him **f**.
Ac 5:40 the apostles in and had them **f**.
    16:23 After they had been severely **f**,
    22:24 He directed that he be **f**
2Co 11:23 frequently, been **f** more severely,

FLOGGING* FLOG
Ps 89:32 with the rod, their iniquity with **f**;
Heb 11:36 Some faced jeers and **f**, and even

FLOOD FLOODGATES,
    FLOODWATERS
Ge 7: 7 the ark to escape the waters of the **f**.
    9:15 again will the waters become a **f**
Ps 29:10 LORD sits enthroned over the **f**;
Da 9:26 The end will come like a **f**:
Mal 2:13 You **f** the LORD's altar with tears.
Mt 24:38 For in the days before the **f**,
Lk 6:48 When a **f** came, the torrent struck
2Pe 2: 5 he brought the **f** on its ungodly

FLOODGATES FLOOD
Ge 7:11 the **f** of the heavens were opened.
Isa 24:18 The **f** of the heavens are opened,
Mal 3:10 I will not throw open the **f** of heaven

FLOODWATERS FLOOD
Ge 6:17 I am going to bring **f** on the earth
Isa 8: 7 bring against them the mighty **f**

FLOOR
Jdg 6:37 a wool fleece on the threshing **f**.
Ru 3: 3 Then go down to the threshing **f**,
1Ch 21:15 at the threshing **f** of Araunah
2Ch 3: 1 on the threshing **f** of Araunah
Hos 9: 1 of a prostitute at every threshing **f**.
Mt 3:12 and he will clear his threshing **f**,
Jas 2: 3 there" or "Sit on the **f** by my feet,"

FLOUR
Lev 2: 1 their offering is to be of the finest **f**.
Nu 7:13 the finest **f** mixed with olive oil as
1Ki 17:12 only a handful of **f** in a jar
2Ki 4:41 Elisha said, "Get some **f**." He put it
Lk 13:21 of **f** until it worked all through

FLOURISH FLOURISHING

Ps   72: 7 In his days may the righteous f
      92: 7 up like grass and all evildoers f,
      92:12 The righteous will f like a palm tree,
    103:15 they f like a flower of the field;
Pr   14:11 but the tent of the upright will f.
Isa   45: 8 spring up, let rightcousness f with it;
      55:10 the earth and making it bud and f,
Eze 17:24 green tree and make the dry tree f.
Ac   12:24 word of God continued to spread
        and f.

FLOURISHING FLOURISH

Ps   37:35 ruthless man f like a luxuriant native
     52: 8 I am like an olive tree f in the house
Hos 14: 8 I am like a f juniper;

FLOW FLOWED, FLOWING, FLOWS

Ex   14:26 that the waters may f back over
Nu 13:27 and it does f with milk and honey!
Ps   78:16 and made water f down like rivers.
   119:136 Streams of tears f from my eyes,
Ecc   1: 7 All streams f into the sea,
Joel 3:18 and the hills will f with milk;
    3:18 A fountain will f out of the LORD's
Am   9:13 mountains and f from all the hills,
Zec 14: 8 that day living water will f
Jn   7:38 of living water will f from within
    19:34 bringing a sudden f of blood

FLOWED FLOW

Ge   2:10 A river watering the garden f
Rev 14:20 and blood f out of the press,

FLOWER FLOWERS

Ps 103:15 they flourish like a f of the field;
Jas   1:10 they will pass away like a wild f.

FLOWERS FLOWER

Ex   25:33 Three cups shaped like almond f
1Ki   6:18 carved with gourds and open f.
Job 14: 2 They spring up like f and wither
Ps   37:20 the LORD's enemies are like the f
Isa   40: 6 all their faithfulness is like the f
    40: 7 The grass withers and the f fall,
Lk   12:27 "Consider how the wild f grow.
1Pe   1:24 and all their glory is like the f
     1:24 the grass withers and the f fall,

FLOWING FLOW

Ex   3: 8 land, a land f with milk and honey—
    33: 3 Go up to the land f with milk
Nu 16:14 brought us into a land f with milk
Jos   5: 6 us, a land f with milk and honey.
2Ki   4: 6 a jar left." Then the oil stopped f.
Ps 107:33 desert, f springs into thirsty ground,
Jer 32:22 a land f with milk and honey.
Eze 20: 6 them, a land f with milk and honey,
    32: 6 land with your f blood all the way
Da   7:10 A river of fire was f,
Rev 22: 1 f from the throne of God

LAND FLOWING WITH MILK AND HONEY Ex 3:8, 17; 13:5; 33:3; Lev 20:24;

Nu 14:8; 16:13, 14; Dt 6:3; 11:9; 26:9, 15; 27:3;
31:20; Jos 5:6; Jer 11:5; 32:22; Eze 20:6, 15

FLOWS FLOW

Pr   4:23 for everything you do f from it.
Eze 47: 9 will live wherever the river f.
    47: 9 because this water f there and makes

FLUTE

Da   3: 5 as you hear the sound of the horn, f,

FLY FLEW, FLIES, FLIGHT, FLYING

Ge   1:20 let birds f above the earth across
Pr   23: 5 and f off to the sky like an eagle.

FLYING FLY

Ge   8: 7 and it kept f back and forth until
Dt   14:19 All f insects are unclean to you;
Isa   6: 2 their feet, and with two they were f.
Zec   5: 1 and there before me was a f scroll.
Rev   4: 7 a man, the fourth was like a f eagle.
    8:13 an eagle that was f in midair call
    14: 6 I saw another angel f in midair,

FOAL*

Zec   9: 9 donkey, on a colt, the f of a donkey.
Mt   21: 5 and on a colt, the f of a donkey.' "

FOAM* FOAMING

Job 24:18 "Yet they are f on the surface
Ps   46: 3 though its waters roar and f

FOAMING* FOAM

Dt   32:14 You drank the f blood of the grape.
Ps   75: 8 is a cup full of f wine mixed
Mk   9:20 and rolled around, f at the mouth.
Jude 1:13 waves of the sea, f up their shame;

FOE FOES

Ps   8: 2 to silence the f and the avenger.
    61: 3 refuge, a strong tower against the f.

FOES FOE

2Sa 22:49 You exalted me above my f;
Ps   44: 5 your name we trample our f.
    97: 3 and consumes his f on every side.
  106:41 nations, and their f ruled over them.
Na   1: 2 LORD takes vengeance on his f

FOILS*

Ps   33:10 The LORD f the plans
Isa 44:25 who f the signs of false prophets

FOLD FOLDED, FOLDING, FOLDS

Ecc   4: 5 Fools f their hands and ruin

FOLDED FOLD

Ex   39: 9 long and a span wide—and f double.

FOLDING* FOLD

Pr   6:10 a little f of the hands to rest—
    24:33 a little f of the hands to rest—

FOLDS FOLD

Ne   5:13 shook out the f of my robe and said,

FOLLOW FOLLOWED, FOLLOWERS, FOLLOWING, FOLLOWS

Ex	16: 4	whether they will f my instructions.
	23: 2	"Do not f the crowd in doing
Lev	18: 4	laws and be careful to f my decrees.
Dt	4: 1	F them so that you may live
	5: 1	Learn them and be sure to f them.
	6:14	Do not f other gods, the gods
	17:19	f carefully all the words of this law
1Ki	11:10	forbidden Solomon to f other gods,
	18:21	If the LORD is God, f him; but if Baal is God, f him."
2Ch	34:33	they did not fail to f the LORD,
Ps	23: 6	love will f me all the days of my
	119:166	LORD, and I f your commands.
Jer	25: 6	Do not f other gods to serve
Eze	13: 3	the foolish prophets who f their own
Hos	11:10	They will f the LORD; he will roar
Mt	4:19	"Come, f me," Jesus said, "and I
	8:19	I will f you wherever you go."
	8:22	But Jesus told him, "F me, and let
	16:24	and take up their cross and f me.
	19:27	"We have left everything to f you!
Lk	9:23	take up their cross daily and f me.
	9:61	another said, "I will f you, Lord;
Jn	10: 4	his sheep f him because they know
	10: 5	But they will never f a stranger;
	10:27	I know them, and they f me.
	12:26	Whoever serves me must f me;
	13:36	you cannot f now, but you will f later."
	21:19	Then he said to him, "F me!"
1Co	1:12	One of you says, "I f Paul"; another, "I f Apollos"; another, "I f Cephas"; still another, "I f Christ."
	11: 1	F my example, as I f the example
	14: 1	F the way of love and eagerly desire
Gal	2:14	force Gentiles to f Jewish customs?
Eph	5: 1	F God's example, therefore,
1Ti	5:15	fact already turned away to f Satan.
1Pe	2:21	that you should f in his steps.
2Pe	1:16	we did not f cleverly devised stories
	2:15	and wandered off to f the way
Jude	1:18	will be scoffers who will f their own
Rev	14: 4	They f the Lamb wherever he goes.

FOLLOWED FOLLOW

Ex	14:23	and horsemen f them into the sea.
Nu	31:16	the ones who f Balaam's advice
	32:11	they have not f me wholeheartedly,
Dt	1:36	his feet on, because he f the LORD
Jos	14:14	ever since, because he f the LORD,
Jdg	2:12	They f and worshiped various gods
2Ki	17: 8	and f the practices of the nations
2Ch	10:14	he f the advice of the young men
Pr	7:22	All at once he f her like an ox going
Jer	9:14	they have f the stubbornness of their
	9:14	they have f the Baals, as their
Eze	16:47	You not only f their ways
Mt	9: 9	him, and Matthew got up and f him.
	26:58	But Peter f him at a distance,
Mk	1:18	once they left their nets and f him.
Lk	18:43	he received his sight and f Jesus,

Jn	6:66	turned back and no longer f him.
Eph	2: 2	to live when you f the ways of this
Rev	13: 3	filled with wonder and f the beast.

FOLLOWERS FOLLOW

Nu	16: 5	Then he said to Korah and all his f:
Ps	106:18	Fire blazed among their f;
Ac	17:34	of the people became f of Paul
Rev	17:14	be his called, chosen and faithful f."

FOLLOWING FOLLOW

Nu	32:15	If you turn away from f him, he will
2Sa	15:12	and Absalom's f kept on increasing.
Ps	119:14	in f your statutes as one rejoices
Php	3:17	Join together in f my example,
Heb	4:11	one will perish by f their example

FOLLOWS FOLLOW

Nu	14:24	spirit and f me wholeheartedly,
Jer	4:20	Disaster f disaster; the whole land
Eze	18: 9	He f my decrees and faithfully
Jn	8:12	Whoever f me will never walk

FOLLY FOOL

1Sa	25:25	means Fool, and f goes with him.
Pr	9:13	F is an unruly woman; she is simple
	13:16	knowledge, but fools expose their f.
	14:18	The simple inherit f, but the prudent
	14:24	but the f of fools yields f.
	14:29	who is quick-tempered displays f.
	16:22	but f brings punishment to fools.
	19: 3	A person's own f leads to their ruin,
	22:15	F is bound up in the heart of a child,
	26: 4	not answer a fool according to his f,
	26: 5	Answer a fool according to his f,
Ecc	2:13	I saw that wisdom is better than f,
	10: 1	so a little f outweighs wisdom
Mk	7:22	envy, slander, arrogance and f.
2Ti	3: 9	their f will be clear to everyone.

FOOD FOODS

Ge	1:30	I give every green plant for f."
	3: 6	the fruit of the tree was good for f
	3:19	you will eat your f until you return
	9: 3	and moves about will be f for you.
Lev	3:11	the altar as a f offering presented
	21: 8	they offer up the f of your God.
Nu	21: 5	And we detest this miserable f!"
Jos	5:12	after they ate this f from the land;
1Ki	17: 4	ravens to supply you with f there."
Ps	42: 3	My tears have been my f day
	78:18	test by demanding the f they craved.
	104:27	give them their f at the proper time.
Pr	12: 9	to be somebody and have no f.
	12:11	their land will have abundant f,
	20:13	awake and you will have f to spare.
	20:17	F gained by fraud tastes sweet,
	21:20	The wise store up choice f and olive
	22: 9	for they share their f with the poor.
	23: 3	his delicacies, for that f is deceptive.
	23: 6	Do not eat the f of a begrudging
	25:21	enemy is hungry, give him f to eat;
	31:14	ships, bringing her f from afar.
	31:15	she provides f for her family
Isa	58: 7	not to share your f with the hungry

Isa 65:25 ox, and dust will be the serpent's f.
Eze 18: 7 robbery but gives his f to the hungry
Da   1: 8 not to defile himself with the royal f
Mt   3: 4 His f was locusts and wild honey.
      6:25 Is not life more than f, and the body
Jn   4:32 them, "I have f to eat that you know
      4:34 "My f," said Jesus, "is to do
      6:27 Do not work for f that spoils,
      6:27 but for f that endures to eternal life,
      6:55 For my flesh is real f and my blood
Ac   15:20 to abstain from f polluted by idols,
1Co   3: 2 not solid f, for you were not yet
      6:13 "F for the stomach and the stomach
            and the stomach for f,
      8: 1 Now about f sacrificed to idols:
      8: 8 But f does not bring us near to God;
2Co 11:27 thirst and have often gone without f;
2Th   3:12 settle down and earn the f they eat.
1Ti   6: 8 But if we have f and clothing,
Heb   5:14 But solid f is for the mature,
Jas   2:15 sister is without clothes and daily f.

FOODS FOOD
Mk   7:19 this, Jesus declared all f clean.)
1Ti   4: 3 order them to abstain from certain f,

FOOL FOLLY, FOOL'S, FOOLISH, FOOLISHNESS, FOOLS
1Sa 25:25 his name means F, and folly goes
Ps   14: 1 The f says in his heart, "There is no
Pr   10:10 and a chattering f comes to ruin.
     10:18 lying lips and spreads slander is a f.
     14: 7 Stay away from a f, for you will not
     14:16 but a f is hotheaded and yet feels
     15: 5 A f spurns a parent's discipline,
     17:12 of her cubs than a f bent on folly.
     17:21 To have a f for a child brings grief;
     17:21 no joy for the parent of a godless f.
     19:10 It is not fitting for a f to live
     20: 3 strife, but every f is quick to quarrel.
     26: 4 Do not answer a f according to his
            folly,
     26: 5 Answer a f according to his folly,
     26: 7 is a proverb in the mouth of a f.
     26:12 is more hope for a f than for them.
     27:22 Though you grind a f in a mortar,
     29:20 There is more hope for a f than
Ecc   2:16 the wise, like the f, will not be long
      2:16 Like the f, the wise too must die!
      7: 7 Extortion turns a wise person into a f,
Hos   9: 7 the prophet is considered a f,
Mt   5:22 And anyone who says, 'You f!'
Lk   12:20 "But God said to him, 'You f!
2Co 11:21 I am speaking as a f—I also dare

FOOL'S FOOL
Pr   12:23 but a f heart blurts out folly.
     14: 3 A f mouth lashes out with pride,

FOOLISH FOOL
Pr   8: 5 you who are f, set your hearts on it.
     10: 1 a f son brings grief to his mother.
     14: 1 her own hands the f one tears hers
     15:20 but a f man despises his mother.

Pr   17:25 A f son brings grief to his father
     19:13 A f child is a father's ruin,
Jer   5:21 this, you f and senseless people,
Eze 13: 3 the f prophets who follow their own
Mt   7:26 practice is like a f man who built his
     25: 2 Five of them were f and five were
Lk   11:40 You f people! Did not the one who
     24:25 He said to them, "How f you are,
1Co   1:20 Has not God made f the wisdom
      1:27 God chose the f things of the world
Gal   3: 1 You f Galatians!
Eph   5: 4 be obscenity, f talk or coarse joking,
      5:17 Therefore do not be f,
2Ti   2:23 Don't have anything to do with f
Titus 3: 3 At one time we too were f,
      3: 9 But avoid f controversies

FOOLISHNESS* FOOL
2Sa 15:31 turn Ahithophel's counsel into f."
1Co   1:18 of the cross is f to those who are
      1:21 God was pleased through the f
      1:23 block to Jews and f to Gentiles,
      1:25 the f of God is wiser than human
      2:14 Spirit of God but considers them f,
      3:19 of this world is f in God's sight.
2Co 11: 1 you will put up with me in a little f.

FOOLS FOOL
Pr   1: 7 but f despise wisdom
      1:32 complacency of f will destroy them;
      3:35 inherit honor, but f get only shame.
     10:21 many, but f die for lack of sense.
     12:15 The way of f seems right to them,
     12:16 F show their annoyance at once,
     13:19 soul, but f detest turning from evil.
     13:20 for a companion of f suffers harm.
     14: 9 F mock at making amends for sin,
     14:24 crown, but the folly of f yields folly.
     16:22 but folly brings punishment to f.
     17:16 Why should f have money in hand
     17:28 Even f are thought wise if they keep
     18: 2 F find no pleasure in understanding
     18: 7 The mouths of f are their undoing,
     21:20 and olive oil, but f gulp theirs down.
     23: 9 Do not speak to f, for they will
     24: 7 Wisdom is too high for f;
     26:11 to its vomit, so f repeat their folly.
     28:26 Those who trust in themselves are f,
     29:11 F give full vent to their rage,
Ecc   4: 5 F fold their hands and ruin
      5: 4 He has no pleasure in f;
      7: 4 but the heart of f is in the house
      7: 5 person than to listen to the song of f.
      7: 6 under the pot, so is the laughter of f.
     10: 6 F are put in many high positions,
Mt   23:17 You blind f! Which is greater:
Ro   1:22 claimed to be wise, they became f
1Co   3:18 you should become "f" so that you
      4:10 We are f for Christ, but you are so
2Co 11:19 put up with f since you are so wise!

FOOT BAREFOOT, FEET, FOOTHOLD, UNDERFOOT
Ex   21:24 for tooth, hand for hand, f for f,

Ex 32:19 to pieces at the f of the mountain.
Dt 11:24 where you set your f will be yours:
Jos   1: 3 every place where you set your f,
Ps 91:12 will not strike your f against a stone.
    121: 3 He will not let your f slip—
Pr   1:15 them, do not set f on their paths;
     3:25 safety, and your f will not stumble.
     4:27 or the left; keep your f from evil.
    25:17 Seldom set f in your neighbor's
Isa   1: 6 the sole of your f to the top of your
Mt   4: 6 you will not strike your f against
     18: 8 or your f causes you to stumble,
Lk   4:11 you will not strike your f against
1Co 12:15 Now if the f should say, "Because I
Rev 10: 2 He planted his right f on the sea
     10: 2 on the sea and his left f on the land,

FOOTHOLD* FOOT
Ps 69: 2 the miry depths, where there is no f.
    73: 2 I had nearly lost my f.
Eph 4:27 and do not give the devil a f.

FOOTSTEPS STEP
Ps 119:133 Direct my f according to your word;
Ro   4:12 follow in the f of the faith that our

FOOTSTOOL
1Ch 28: 2 for the f of our God, and I made
Ps 99: 5 our God and worship at his f;
    110: 1 hand until I make your enemies a f
Isa 66: 1 is my throne, and the earth is my f.
La   2: 1 he has not remembered his f
Mt   5:35 or by the earth, for it is his f;
Ac   7:49 is my throne, and the earth is my f.
Heb 1:13 hand until I make your enemies a f
    10:13 for his enemies to be made his f.

FORBEARANCE*
Ro   2: 4 of his kindness, f and patience,
      3:25 his f he had left the sins committed
Gal   5:22 of the Spirit is love, joy, peace, f,

FORBID FORBIDDEN, FORBIDS
1Co 14:39 and do not f speaking in tongues.
1Ti   4: 3 They f people to marry and order

FORBIDDEN FORBID
1Ki 11:10 Although he had f Solomon

FORBIDS* FORBID
Nu 30: 5 But if her father f her when he hears
    30: 8 if her husband f her when he hears
Jn   5:10 the law f you to carry your mat."

FORCE FORCED, FORCEFUL,
FORCEFULLY, FORCES, FORCING
Ex 19:24 people must not f their way through
Jn   6:15 to come and make him king by f,
Ac 26:11 and I tried to f them to blaspheme.
Gal   2:14 that you f Gentiles to follow Jewish

FORCED FORCE
Ex   1:11 them to oppress them with f labor,
Jdg   1:28 pressed the Canaanites into f labor
1Ki   9:15 account of the f labor King Solomon
Mt 27:32 and they f him to carry the cross.

Phm 1:14 any favor you do would not seem f
Rev 13:16 It also f all people, great and small,

FORCEFUL* FORCE
2Co 10:10 "His letters are weighty and f,

FORCEFULLY* FORCE
1Sa 18:10 evil spirit from God came f on Saul.
2Sa 19:43 Judah pressed their claims even more f
Isa 28: 2 he will throw it f to the ground.

FORCES FORCE
Mt   5:41 If anyone f you to go one mile,
Gal   4: 3 under the elemental spiritual f
      4: 9 back to those weak and miserable f?
Eph   6:12 against the spiritual f of evil
Col   2: 8 and the elemental spiritual f of this
      2:20 to the elemental spiritual f of this

FORCING* FORCE
Lk 16:16 and everyone is f their way into it.
Ac   7:19 oppressed our ancestors by f them

FORDED* FORDS
Jos   2:23 f the river and came to Joshua son

FORDS FORDED
Jos   2: 7 road that leads to the f of the Jordan,

FOREFATHER FATHER
1Ki 15: 3 as the heart of David his f had been.
Ro   4: 1 our f according to the flesh,

FOREFATHERS* FATHER
Da 11:24 neither his fathers nor his f did.
Ac   7:12 he sent our f on their first visit.

FOREHEAD FOREHEADS
Ex 13: 9 a reminder on your f that this law
    28:38 It will be on Aaron's f, and he will
    28:38 will be on Aaron's f continually so
1Sa 17:49 and struck the Philistine on the f.
    17:49 The stone sank into his f, and he fell
Rev 14: 9 receives its mark on their f
    17: 5 written on her f was a mystery:

FOREHEADS FOREHEAD
Dt   6: 8 your hands and bind them on your f.
Rev 7: 3 we put a seal on the f of the servants
      9: 4 not have the seal of God on their f.
    13:16 on their right hands or on their f,
    14: 1 his Father's name written on their f.
    20: 4 had not received its mark on their f
    22: 4 face, and his name will be on their f.

FOREIGN FOREIGNER,
FOREIGNERS
Ge 35: 2 "Get rid of the f gods you have
Dt 32:12 no f god was with him.
Jos 24:23 "throw away the f gods that are
1Ki 11: 1 loved many f women besides
2Ch 14: 3 He removed the f altars and the high
    33:15 He got rid of the f gods
Ps 81: 9 You shall have no f god among you;
Isa 28:11 with f lips and strange tongues God

Jer   2:25 I love f gods, and I must go
Ac   17:18 seems to be advocating f gods."

FOREIGNER FOREIGN

Ex   22:21 "Do not mistreat or oppress a f,
Lev   19:10 Leave them for the poor and the f.
      24:22 are to have the same law for the f
Dt   23.20 You may charge a f interest, but not
1Ki   8:41 "As for the f who does not belong to
Ps   146: 9 The LORD watches over the f
Lk   17:18 to give praise to God except this f?"
1Co   14:11 I am a f to the speaker, and the
             speaker is a f to me.

FOREIGNERS FOREIGN

Ge   31:15 Does he not regard us as f?
Ex   21: 8 He has no right to sell her to f,
      23: 9 know how it feels to be f, because you
             were f in Egypt.
Jer   5:19 so now you will serve f in a land not
1Co   14:21 through the lips of f I will speak
Eph   2:12 f to the covenants of the promise,
       2:19 you are no longer f and strangers,
Heb   11:13 admitting that they were f
1Pe   2:11 I urge you, as f and exiles, to abstain

FOREKNEW* KNOW

Ro   8:29 For those God f he also predestined
      11: 2 did not reject his people, whom he f.

FOREKNOWLEDGE* KNOW

Ac   2:23 you by God's deliberate plan and f;
1Pe   1: 2 according to the f of God the Father,

FORESAW* FORESEE

Gal   3: 8 Scripture f that God would justify

FORESEE* FORESAW

Isa   47:11 you cannot f will suddenly come

FORESKIN* FORESKINS

Ex   4:25 cut off her son's f and touched

FORESKINS FORESKIN

1Sa   18:25 the bride than a hundred Philistine f,

FOREST

2Sa   18: 8 the f swallowed up more men
1Ki   7: 2 the F of Lebanon a hundred cubits
1Ch   16:33 Let the trees of the f sing, let them
Ps   50:10 for every animal of the f is mine,
Jas   3: 5 Consider what a great f is set on fire

FORETELL* FORETELLS,
   FORETOLD

Isa   44: 7 yes, let them f what will come.
      44: 8 I not proclaim this and f it long ago?

FORETELLS* FORETELL

Dt   13: 1 or one who f by dreams,

FORETOLD FORETELL

Ps   105:19 till what he f came to pass,
Isa   48: 3 I f the former things long ago,
Jude   1:17 apostles of our Lord Jesus Christ f.

FOREVER EVER

Ge   3:22 the tree of life and eat, and live f."
       6: 3 will not contend with humans f,
Ex   3:15 "This is my name f, the name you
      31:17 sign between me and the Israelites f,
Dt   29:29 belong to us and to our children f,
2Sa   7:13 the throne of his kingdom f.
       7:26 so that your name will be great f.
1Ki   2:33 head of Joab and his descendants f.
       2:33 there be the LORD's peace f."
       9: 3 built, by putting my Name there f.
1Ch   16:15 He remembers his covenant f,
      16:41 LORD, "for his love endures f."
      17:24 and that your name will be great f.
2Ch   5:13 "He is good; his love endures f."
      33: 7 of Israel, I will put my Name f.
Ezr   3:11 his love toward Israel endures f."
Ps   9: 7 The LORD reigns f;
      19: 9 of the LORD is pure, enduring f.
      23: 6 dwell in the house of the LORD f.
      28: 9 be their shepherd and carry them f.
      29:10 the LORD is enthroned as King f.
      33:11 plans of the LORD stand firm f,
      44: 8 and we will praise your name f.
      44:23 Rouse yourself! Do not reject us f.
      61: 4 I long to dwell in your tent f
      72:19 Praise be to his glorious name f;
      73:26 of my heart and my portion f.
      74:10 Will the foe revile your name f?
      77: 8 Has his unfailing love vanished f?
      79:13 of your pasture, will praise you f;
      81:15 and their punishment would last f.
      86:12 I will glorify your name f.
      89: 1 sing of the LORD's great love f;
      92: 8 But you, LORD, are f exalted.
     100: 5 is good and his love endures f;
     102:12 But you, LORD, sit enthroned f;
     104:31 the glory of the LORD endure f;
     107: 1 for he is good; his love endures f.
     110: 4 "You are a priest f, in the order
     111: 3 and his righteousness endures f.
     112: 6 they will be remembered f.
     117: 2 of the LORD endures f.
     118: 1 for he is good; his love endures f.
     119:111 Your statutes are my heritage f;
     119:152 that you established them to last f.
     136: 1 His love endures f.
     146: 6 he remains faithful f.
Pr   10:25 gone, but the righteous stand firm f.
      27:24 for riches do not endure f,
Ecc   3:14 everything God does will endure f;
Isa   25: 8 he will swallow up death f.
      26: 4 Trust in the LORD f,
      32:17 will be quietness and confidence f.
      40: 8 but the word of our God endures f."
      51: 6 But my salvation will last f,
      51: 8 But my righteousness will last f,
      57:15 he who lives f, whose name is holy:
      59:21 from this time on and f,"
Jer   3:12 the LORD, 'I will not be angry f.
      33:11 his love endures f."
La   5:19 You, LORD, reign f;
Eze   37:26 put my sanctuary among them f.

Da   2:44 to an end, but it will itself endure f.
      6:26 is the living God and he endures f;
Hos 2:19 I will betroth you to me f;
Jn   6:51 Whoever eats this bread will live f.
   14:16 to help you and be with you f—
Ro   9: 5 who is God over all, f praised!
  16:27 God be glory f through Jesus Christ!
1Co 9:25 do it to get a crown that will last f.
1Th 4:17 And so we will be with the Lord f.
Heb 5: 6 "You are a priest f, in the order
    7:17 "You are a priest f, in the order
    7:24 but because Jesus lives f, he has
    13: 8 the same yesterday and today and f.
1Pe 1:25 but the word of the Lord endures f."
1Jn 2:17 does the will of God lives f.
2Jn 1: 2 lives in us and will be with us f:

HIS LOVE ENDURES FOREVER See LOVE

FOREVERMORE EVER

Ps 125: 2 his people both now and f.
  131: 3 hope in the LORD both now and f.

FORFEIT

Mk 8:36 the whole world, yet f their soul?
Lk   9:25 and yet lose or f their very self?

FORGAVE* FORGIVE

Ps 32: 5 And you f the guilt of my sin.
   65: 3 by sins, you f our transgressions.
  78:38 he f their iniquities and did not
  85: 2 You f the iniquity of your people
Lk   7:42 him back, so he f the debts of both.
Eph 4:32 other, just as in Christ God f you.
Col 2:13 He f us all our sins,
   3:13 Forgive as the Lord f you.

FORGET FORGETS, FORGETTING, FORGOT, FORGOTTEN

Dt   4:23 Be careful not to f the covenant
   6:12 that you do not f the LORD,
2Ki 17:38 Do not f the covenant I have made
Job 8:13 Such is the destiny of all who f God;
Ps   9:17 the dead, all the nations that f God.
  10:12 hand, O God. Do not f the helpless.
  50:22 you who f God, or I will tear you
  78: 7 in God and would not f his deeds
 103: 2 my soul, and f not all his benefits—
 119:93 I will never f your precepts,
 137: 5 If I f you, Jerusalem, may my right
     hand f its skill.
Pr   3: 1 My son, do not f my teaching,
   4: 5 do not f my words or turn away
  31: 5 drink and f what has been decreed,
Isa 49:15 "Can a mother f the baby at her
  49:15 Though she may f, I will not f you!
  51:13 that you f the LORD your Maker,
Jer 2:32 Does a young woman f her jewelry,
  23:39 I will surely f you and cast you
Heb 6:10 he will not f your work and the love
  13: 2 Do not f to show hospitality
  13:16 And do not f to do good
2Pe 3: 8 But do not f this one thing,

FORGETS FORGET

Jn 16:21 is born she f the anguish because
Jas 1:24 immediately f what he looks like.

FORGETTING* FORGET

Php 3:13 F what is behind and straining
Jas 1:25 not f what they have heard,
2Pe 1: 9 f that they have been cleansed from

FORGIVE* FORGAVE, FORGIVEN, FORGIVENESS, FORGIVES, FORGIVING

Ge 50:17 I ask you to f your brothers the sins
  50:17 Now please f the sins of the servants
Ex 10:17 Now f my sin once more and pray
  23:21 he will not f your rebellion,
  32:32 But now, please f their sin—
  34: 9 f our wickedness and our sin,
Nu 14:19 great love, f the sin of these people,
Dt 29:20 will never be willing to f them;
Jos 24:19 He will not f your rebellion
1Sa 15:25 f my sin and come back with me,
  25:28 "Please f your servant's
1Ki 8:30 place, and when you hear, f.
   8:34 and f the sin of your people Israel
   8:36 and f the sin of your servants,
   8:39 F and act; deal with everyone
   8:50 And f your people, who have sinned
   8:50 f all the offenses they have
2Ki 5:18 may the LORD f your servant
   5:18 may the LORD f your servant
  24: 4 and the LORD was not willing to f.
2Ch 6:21 and when you hear, f.
   6:25 and f the sin of your people Israel
   6:27 and f the sin of your servants,
   6:30 F, and deal with everyone according
   6:39 And f your people, who have sinned
   7:14 and I will f their sin and will heal
Job 7:21 pardon my offenses and f my sins?
Ps 19:12 F my hidden faults.
  25:11 LORD, f my iniquity, though it is
  79: 9 and f our sins for your name's sake.
Isa 2: 9 do not f them.
Jer 5: 1 and seeks the truth, I will f this city.
   5: 7 "Why should I f you?
  18:23 Do not f their crimes or blot
  31:34 "For I will f their wickedness
  33: 8 and will f all their sins of rebellion
  36: 3 then I will f their wickedness
  50:20 for I will f the remnant I spare.
Da 9:19 Lord, f! Lord, hear and act!
Hos 1: 6 to Israel, that I should at all f them.
  14: 2 "F all our sins and receive us
Am 7: 2 I cried out, "Sovereign LORD, f!
Mt 6:12 And f us our debts, as we also have
   6:14 if you f other people when they sin
   6:14 heavenly Father will also f you.
   6:15 But if you do not f others their sins,
   6:15 your Father will not f your sins.
   9: 6 has authority on earth to f sins."
  18:21 how many times shall I f my brother
  18:35 of you unless you f your brother
Mk 2: 7 Who can f sins but God alone?"

Mk 2:10 has authority on earth to f sins."
    11:25 anything against anyone, f them,
    11:25 in heaven may f you your sins."
Lk 5:21 Who can f sins but God alone?"
    5:24 has authority on earth to f sins."
    6:37 F, and you will be forgiven.
    11: 4 F us our sins, for we also f everyone
    17: 3 and if they repent, f them.
    17: 4 saying 'I repent,' you must f them."
    23:34 "Father, f them, for they do not
Jn 20:23 If you f anyone's sins, their sins are
    20:23 if you do not f them, they are not
Ac 5:31 Israel to repentance and f their sins.
    8:22 that he may f you for having such
2Co 2: 7 you ought to f and comfort him,
    2:10 Anyone you f, I also f.
    2:10 if there was anything to f—
    12:13 a burden to you? F me this wrong!
Col 3:13 and f one another if any of you has
    3:13 F as the Lord forgave you.
Heb 8:12 For I will f their wickedness
1Jn 1: 9 just and will f us our sins and purify

FORGIVEN FORGIVE

Lev 4:20 the community, and they will be f.
Nu 14:20 "I have f them, as you asked.
Ps 32: 1 the one whose transgressions are f,
Mk 2: 9 man, 'Your sins are f,' or to say,
    3:29 the Holy Spirit will never be f;
Lk 7:47 tell you, her many sins have been f—
    7:47 But whoever has been f little loves
Ro 4: 7 are those whose transgressions are f,
Jas 5:15 If they have sinned, they will be f.

FORGIVENESS* FORGIVE

Ps 130: 4 But with you there is f, so that we
Mt 26:28 out for many for the f of sins.
Mk 1: 4 of repentance for the f of sins.
Lk 1;77 salvation through the f of their sins,
    3: 3 of repentance for the f of sins.
    24:47 for the f of sins will be preached
Ac 2:38 Jesus Christ for the f of your sins.
    10:43 in him receives f of sins through his
    13:38 that through Jesus the f of sins is
    26:18 so that they may receive f of sins
Eph 1: 7 through his blood, the f of sins,
Col 1:14 we have redemption, the f of sins.
Heb 9:22 the shedding of blood there is no f.

FORGIVES* FORGIVE

Ps 103: 3 who f all your sins and heals all
Mic 7:18 f the transgression of the remnant
Lk 7:49 "Who is this who even f sins?"

FORGIVING* FORGIVE

Ex 34: 7 and f wickedness, rebellion and sin.
Nu 14:18 abounding in love and f sin
Ne 9:17 But you are a f God,
Ps 86: 5 Lord, are f and good,
    99: 8 you were to Israel a f God,
Da 9: 9 The Lord our God is merciful and f,
Eph 4:32 to one another, f each other, just as

FORGOT FORGET

Dt 32:18 you f the God who gave you birth.

1Sa 12: 9 "But they f the LORD their God;
Ps 78:11 They f what he had done,
    106:21 They f the God who saved them,
Jer 23:27 just as their ancestors f my name

FORGOTTEN FORGET

Job 11: 6 God has even f some of your sin.
Ps 44:20 If we had f the name of our God
    77: 9 Has God f to be merciful? Has he
Isa 17:10 You have f God your Savior;
    49:14 forsaken me, the Lord has f me."
Jer 2:32 Yet my people have f me,
Hos 8:14 Israel has f their Maker and built
Lk 12: 6 Yet not one of them is f by God.
Heb 12: 5 have you completely f this word

FORM FORMED, FORMLESS, FORMS

Ex 20: 4 an image in the f of anything
Dt 4:15 You saw no f of any kind the day
Isa 52:14 and his f marred beyond human
Col 2: 9 of the Deity lives in bodily f,
2Ti 3: 5 having a f of godliness but denying

FORMED FORM

Ge 2: 7 the LORD God f a man
Dt 32: 6 Creator, who made you and f you?
Ps 94: 9 Does he who f the eye not see?
    103:14 for he knows how we are f,
Pr 8:23 I was f long ages ago, at the very
Ecc 11: 5 or how the body is f in a mother's
Isa 29:16 Shall what is f say to the one who f
    43:10 Before me no god was f, nor will
    45:18 be empty, but f it to be inhabited—
    49: 5 he who f me in the womb to be his
Jer 1: 5 "Before I f you in the womb I knew
    18: 4 so the potter f it into another pot,
Ro 9:20 "Shall what is f say to the one who f it,
Gal 4:19 of childbirth until Christ is f in you,
1Ti 2:13 For Adam was f first, then Eve.
Heb 11: 3 that the universe was f at God's
2Pe 3: 5 and the earth was f out of water

FORMER

Dt 4:32 Ask now about the f days,
Ezr 3:12 who had seen the f temple,
Ps 77: 5 I thought about the f days, the years
Isa 46: 9 Remember the f things,
Lk 11:42 latter without leaving the f undone.

FORMLESS* FORM

Ge 1: 2 Now the earth was f and empty,
Jer 4:23 at the earth, and it was f and empty;

FORMS FORM

Ps 33:15 he who f the hearts of all,
Am 4:13 He who f the mountains,
Zec 12: 1 and who f the human spirit within

FORSAKE FORSAKEN, FORSAKING

Dt 31: 6 he will never leave you nor f you."
Jos 1: 5 I will never leave you nor f you.
    24:16 us to f the LORD to serve other
2Ch 15: 2 but if you f him, he will f you.

Ps   27:10 Though my father and mother f me,
     37:28 just and will not f his faithful ones.
     94:14 he will never f his inheritance.
Pr   4: 6 Do not f wisdom, and she will
     27:10 Do not f your friend or a friend
Isa   1:28 those who f the LORD will perish.
     55: 7 Let the wicked f their ways
Jer 17:13 all who f you will be put to shame.
Heb 13: 5 will I leave you; never will I f you."

FORSAKEN FORSAKE

Ezr   9: 9 our God has not f us in our bondage.
      9:10 For we have f the commands
Ps   9:10 have never f those who seek you.
     22: 1 God, my God, why have you f me?
     37:25 yet I have never seen the righteous f
Isa 49:14 "The LORD has f me, the Lord
Mt   27:46 my God, why have you f me?").
Rev   2: 4 You have f the love you had at first.

FORSAKING FORSAKE

1Sa   8: 8 day, f me and serving other gods,

FORTH

Ge   3:24 f to guard the way to the tree of life.
Ps   19: 2 Day after day they pour f speech;
     50: 2 perfect in beauty, God shines f.
Eph   4:14 tossed back and f by the waves,

FORTIFIED FORTRESS

Nu   13:28 and the cities are f and very large.
Ne   9:25 They captured f cities and fertile
Pr   18:10 name of the LORD is a f tower;

FORTRESS FORTIFIED

2Sa   5: 7 David captured the f of Zion—
     22: 2 is my rock, my f and my deliverer;
Ps   28: 8 a f of salvation for his anointed one.
     31: 2 of refuge, a strong f to save me.
     46: 7 is with us; the God of Jacob is our f.
     59:17 are my f, my God on whom I can
     71: 3 me, for you are my rock and my f.
Pr   14:26 fears the LORD has a secure f,
Isa 17:10 not remembered the Rock, your f.
Jer 16:19 my strength and my f, my refuge

FORTUNE* FORTUNE-TELLING, FORTUNES

Ge   30:11 Then Leah said, "What good f!"
Job 31:25 wealth, the f my hands had gained,
Pr   21: 6 A f made by a lying tongue is
Isa 65:11 who spread a table for F and fill

FORTUNE-TELLING* FORTUNE

Ac   16:16 deal of money for her owners by f.

FORTUNES FORTUNE

Dt   30: 3 your God will restore your f
Ps 126: 1 the LORD restored the f of Zion,
Jer 32:44 Negev, because I will restore their f,
Hos   6:11 "Whenever I would restore the f
Mic   3:11 and her prophets tell f for money.

FORTY 40

Ge   7: 4 will send rain on the earth for f days
             and f nights,

Ge   18:29 "What if only f are found there?"
     18:29 "For the sake of f, I will not do it."
Ex   16:35 The Israelites ate manna f years,
     24:18 he stayed on the mountain f days
             and f nights.
Nu   14:34 For f years—one year for each of the f
             days you explored the land—
Dt   25: 3 must not impose more than f lashes.
Jos 14: 7 I was f years old when Moses
1Sa   4:18 He had led Israel f years.
2Sa   5: 4 became king, and he reigned f years.
1Ki 19: 8 he traveled f days and f nights until
2Ch   9:30 in Jerusalem over all Israel f years.
Ne   9:21 For f years you sustained them
Eze 29:12 cities will lie desolate f years among
Am   2:10 led you f years in the wilderness
Jnh   3: 4 "F more days and Nineveh will be
Mt   4: 2 After fasting f days and f nights,
Lk   4: 2 where for f days he was tempted
2Co 11:24 the Jews the f lashes minus one.
Heb   3:17 whom was he angry for f years?

FORTY DAYS Ge 7:4, 12, 17; 8:6; 50:3; Ex
24:18; 34:28; Nu 13:25; 14:34; Dt 9:9, 11, 18, 25;
10:10; 1Sa 17:16; 1Ki 19:8; Jnh 3:4; Mt 4:2; Mk
1:13; Lk 4:2; Ac 1:3

FORTY YEARS Ge 25:20; 26:34; Ex 16:35; Nu
14:33, 34; 32:13; Dt 2:7; 8:2, 4; 29:5; Jos 5:6; 14:7;
Jdg 3:11; 5:31; 8:28; 13:1; 1Sa 4:18; 2Sa 2:10; 5:4;
1Ki 2:11; 11:42; 2Ki 12:1; 1Ch 29:27; 2Ch 9:30;
24:1; Ne 9:21; Job 42:16; Ps 95:10; Eze 29:11, 12,
13; Am 2:10; 5:25; Ac 4:22; 7:23, 30, 36, 42; 13:18,
21; Heb 3:9, 17

FOSTER*

Pr   17: 9 Whoever would f love covers over
     17:11 Evildoers f rebellion against God;
Isa 49:23 Kings will be your f fathers,

FOUGHT FIGHT

Jos 10:42 the God of Israel, f for Israel.
1Co 15:32 If I f wild beasts in Ephesus with no
2Ti   4: 7 I have f the good fight, I have
Rev 12: 7 and his angels f against the dragon,
     12: 7 the dragon and his angels f back.

FOUND FIND

Ge   6: 8 But Noah f favor in the eyes
Ex   12:19 no yeast is to be f in your houses.
     33:12 and you have f favor with me.
1Sa   9: 2 a young man as could be f anywhere
2Ki 22: 8 "I have f the Book of the Law
1Ch 28: 9 If you seek him, he will be f by you;
2Ch 15:15 God eagerly, and he was f by them.
Ps   37:10 look for them, they will not be f.
Pr   10:13 Wisdom is f on the lips
     14: 9 but goodwill is f among the upright.
Isa 55: 6 Seek the LORD while he may be f;
     65: 1 I was f by those who did not seek
Jer 29:14 I will be f by you,"
Da   1:19 them, and he f none equal to Daniel,
      5:27 on the scales and f wanting.
     12: 1 everyone whose name is f written
Mt   1:18 she was f to be pregnant through
Lk   1:30 you have f favor with God.

Lk   7: 9 I have not f such great faith even
     15: 6 I have f my lost sheep.'
     15: 9 I have f my lost coin.'
     15:24 is alive again; he was lost and is f.'
Ac   4:12 Salvation is f in no one else,
Ro 10:20 "I was f by those who did not seek
Php 2: 8 And being f in appearance as a man,
Col   2:17 the reality, however, is f in Christ.
Heb 3: 3 Jesus has been f worthy of greater
Jas   2: 8 If you really keep the royal law f
Rev 5: 4 no one was f who was worthy
     20:15 whose name was not f written

FOUNDATION FOUNDATIONS, FOUNDED

1Ki 6:37 The f of the temple of the LORD
Ezr   3: 6 though the f of the LORD's temple
Job 38: 4 were you when I laid the earth's f?
Ps   97: 2 and justice are the f of his throne.
Isa 28:16 a precious cornerstone for a sure f;
Mt   7:25 fall, because it had its f on the rock.
Lk 14:29 For if you lay the f and are not able
Ro 15:20 not be building on someone else's f.
1Co 3:10 me, I laid a f as a wise builder,
     3:11 one can lay any f other than the one
Eph 2:20 built on the f of the apostles
1Ti 3:15 God, the pillar and f of the truth.
2Ti 2:19 God's solid f stands firm,
Heb 6: 1 not laying again the f of repentance
Rev 21:19 The first f was jasper, the second

FOUNDATIONS FOUNDATION

1Sa 2: 8 the f of the earth are the LORD's;
Ps 102:25 In the beginning you laid the f
   137: 7 they cried, "tear it down to its f!"
Pr   3:19 the LORD laid the earth's f,
Isa 48:13 My own hand laid the f of the earth,
Heb 1:10 Lord, you laid the f of the earth,
Rev 21:14 The wall of the city had twelve f,

FOUNDED FOUNDATION

Jer 10:12 he f the world by his wisdom

FOUNTAIN

Ps 36: 9 For with you is the f of life;
Pr   5:18 May your f be blessed, and may you
   14:27 The fear of the LORD is a f of life,
   18: 4 the f of wisdom is a rushing stream.
SS   4:12 are a spring enclosed, a sealed f.
Jer   9: 1 of water and my eyes a f of tears!
Joel 3:18 A f will flow out of the LORD's
Zec 13: 1 that day a f will be opened

FOUR FOURTH

Ge   2:10 it was separated into f headwaters.
1Ki 18:19 And bring the f hundred and fifty
   18:19 the f hundred prophets of Asherah,
Isa 11:12 of Judah from the f quarters
Eze 1: 5 what looked like f living creatures.
   10: 9 I saw beside the cherubim f wheels,
   10:14 Each of the cherubim had f faces:
Da   1:17 To these f young men God gave
   7: 3 F great beasts, each different
   8: 8 in its place f prominent horns grew
   8: 8 up toward the f winds of heaven.

Zec 1:20 the LORD showed me f craftsmen.
   6: 5 "These are the f spirits of heaven,
Mt 15:38 those who ate was f thousand men,
Mk 8:20 the seven loaves for the f thousand,
Rev 4: 6 the throne, were f living creatures,
   9:14 "Release the f angels who are

FOURTEEN

Mt 1:17 Thus there were f generations in all
   1:17 David, f from David to the exile
   1:17 and f from the exile to the Messiah.
2Co 12: 2 Christ who f years ago was caught
Gal 2: 1 Then after f years, I went up again

FOURTH FOUR

Ge 15:16 In the f generation your descendants
Ex 20: 5 f generation of those who hate me,

FOWLER* FOWLER'S

Pr   6: 5 like a bird from the snare of the f.

FOWLER'S* FOWLER

Ps 91: 3 he will save you from the f snare
  124: 7 escaped like a bird from the f snare;

FOX* FOXES

Ne   4: 3 even a f climbing up on it would
Lk 13:32 "Go tell that f, 'I will keep

FOXES FOX

Jdg 15: 4 and caught three hundred f and tied
SS   2:15 Catch for us the f, the little f
Lk   9:58 "F have dens and birds have nests,

FRACTURE*

Lev 24:20 f for f, eye for eye, tooth for tooth.

FRAGRANCE FRAGRANT

Ex 30:38 like it to enjoy its f must be cut off
SS   4:10 the f of your perfume more than any
Jn 12: 3 was filled with the f of the perfume.

FRAGRANT FRAGRANCE

Ex 25: 6 anointing oil and for the f incense;
   30: 7 "Aaron must burn f incense
Eph 5: 2 himself up for us as a f offering
Php 4:18 They are a f offering, an acceptable

FRAME DOORFRAME, DOORFRAMES, FRAMES

Ps 139:15 My f was not hidden from you

FRAMES FRAME

Ex 26:15 "Make upright f of acacia wood
Nu   3:36 take care of the f of the tabernacle,

FRANKINCENSE

Mt 2:11 him with gifts of gold, f and myrrh.

FRAUD* DEFRAUD

Pr 20:17 Food gained by f tastes sweet,
Jer 10:14 The images he makes are a f;
   51:17 The images he makes are a f;

FREE FREED, FREEDMEN, FREEDOM, FREELY

Ge 2:16 "You are f to eat from any tree

Ge   49:21 "Naphtali is a doe set **f** that bears
Ex   21: 2 year, he shall go **f**, without paying
Ps   73:12 always **f** of care, they go
     146: 7 The LORD sets prisoners **f**,
Pr   6: 3 to **f** yourself, since you have fallen
Isa 42: 7 to **f** captives from prison
Lk   13:12 you are set **f** from your infirmity."
Jn   8:32 truth, and the truth will set you **f**."
      8:36 So if the Son sets you **f**, you will be
             f indeed.
     19:12 on, Pilate tried to set Jesus **f**,
Ac   13:39 him everyone who believes is set **f**
Ro   6: 7 anyone who has died has been set **f**
      6:18 You have been set **f** from sin
      8: 2 Spirit who gives life has set you **f**
1Co   9:21 having the law (though I am not **f**
     12:13 Jews or Gentiles, slave or **f**—
Gal   3:28 neither slave nor **f**, nor is there male
      5: 1 for freedom that Christ has set us **f**.
1Pe   2:16 Live as **f** people, but do not use your
Rev 20: 3 he must be set **f** for a short time.
     22:17 the one who wishes take the **f** gift

FREED   FREE
Ps 116:16 you have **f** me from my chains.
Mk   5:34 and be **f** from your suffering."
1Co   7:22 in the Lord is the Lord's **f** person;
Rev   1: 5 has **f** us from our sins by his blood,

FREEDMEN*   FREE
Ac   6: 9 of the **F** (as it was called)—

FREEDOM   FREE
Ps 119:45 I will walk about in **f**, for I have
Isa 61: 1 to proclaim **f** for the captives
Lk   4:18 me to proclaim **f** for the prisoners
Ro   8:21 brought into the **f** and glory
1Co   7:21 although if you can gain your **f**,
     10:29 For why is my **f** being judged
2Co   3:17 the Spirit of the Lord is, there is **f**.
Gal   2: 4 spy on the **f** we have in Christ Jesus
      5: 1 It is for **f** that Christ has set us free.
      5:13 But do not use your **f** to indulge
Jas   1:25 into the perfect law that gives **f**,
1Pe   2:16 do not use your **f** as

FREELY   FREE
Isa 55: 7 and to our God, for he will **f** pardon.
Mt   10: 8 **F** you have received; **f** give.
Ro   3:24 and all are justified **f** by his grace
Eph   1: 6 which he has **f** given us in the One

FREEWILL   WILL
Ex   35:29 to the LORD **f** offerings for all
Ezr   1: 4 with **f** offerings for the temple
Ps   54: 6 I will sacrifice a **f** offering to you;

FRESH
Eze 47: 8 sea, the salty water there becomes **f**.
Jas   3:11 Can both **f** water and salt water flow

FRET*
Ps   37: 1 Do not **f** because of those who are
     37: 7 do not **f** when people succeed
     37: 8 do not **f**—it leads only to evil.

Pr   24:19 Do not **f** because of evildoers or be

FRICTION*
1Ti   6: 5 constant **f** between people of corrupt

FRIEND   FRIENDS, FRIENDSHIP
Ex   33:11 face to face, as one speaks to a **f**.
Dt   13: 6 your closest **f** secretly entices you,
2Sa 16:17 the love you show your **f**? If he's
             your **f**, why didn't you go
2Ch 20: 7 the descendants of Abraham your **f**?
Ps   41: 9 Even my close **f**, someone I trusted,
     88:18 You have taken from me **f** and
     88:18 darkness is my closest **f**.
Pr   17:17 A **f** loves at all times, and a brother
     18:24 there is a **f** who sticks closer than
     27: 6 Wounds from a **f** can be trusted,
     27:10 Do not forsake your **f** or a **f** of your
SS   5:16 this is my **f**, daughters of Jerusalem.
Isa 41: 8 you descendants of Abraham my **f**,
Jer   9: 5 **F** deceives **f**, and no one speaks
Mt   11:19 a **f** of tax collectors and sinners.'
Jn   19:12 this man go, you are no **f** of Caesar.
Jas   2:23 and he was called God's **f**.
      4: 4 to be a **f** of the world becomes

FRIENDS   FRIEND
Job   2:11 When Job's three **f**,
     42:10 After Job had prayed for his **f**,
Pr   16:28 and a gossip separates close **f**.
     17: 9 repeats the matter separates close **f**.
     18:24 who has unreliable **f** soon comes
La   1: 2 All her **f** have betrayed her;
Zec 13: 6 I was given at the house of my **f**.'
Jn   15:13 to lay down one's life for one's **f**.
     15:14 You are my **f** if you do what I

FRIENDSHIP   FRIEND
Dt   23: 6 Do not seek a treaty of **f** with them
Ezr   9:12 Do not seek a treaty of **f** with them
Lk   11: 8 and give you the bread because of **f**,
Jas   4: 4 don't you know that **f**

FRIGHTEN   FEAR
Dt   28:26 there will be no one to **f** them away.
Ne   6: 9 They were all trying to **f** us,

FRIGHTENED   FEAR
Php   1:28 without being **f** in any way by those
1Pe   3:14 not fear their threats; do not be **f**."

FROGS
Ex   8: 2 go, I will send a plague of **f** on your
Rev 16:13 impure spirits that looked like **f**;

FROLIC*
Ps 104:26 Leviathan, which you formed to **f** there.
Jer 50:11 you **f** like a heifer threshing grain
Mal   4: 2 go out and **f** like well-fed calves.

FRONT
Ex   14:19 God, who had been traveling in **f**
     14:19 moved from in **f** and stood behind
     32:15 inscribed on both sides, **f** and back.
Lev 19:14 or put a stumbling block in **f**

Mt   5:24 leave your gift there in f of the altar.

FROST FROSTY
Ex   16:14 thin flakes like f on the ground

FROSTY* FROST
Zec 14: 6 neither sunlight nor cold, f darkness.

FRUIT FIRSTFRUITS, FRUITFUL,
FRUITION, FRUITLESS
Ge   1:11 the land that bear f with seed in it,
       3: 3 'You must not eat f from the tree
Lev 19:23 plant any kind of f tree, regard its
           f as forbidden.
Dt   28: 4 The f of your womb will be blessed,
     28:53 you will eat the f of the womb,
Jdg   9:11 'Should I give up my f, so good
Ps   1: 3 which yields its f in season
Pr   8:19 My f is better than fine gold;
     11:30 The f of the righteous is a tree
     12:14 the f of their lips people are filled
     27:18 who guards a fig tree will eat its f,
Isa 11: 1 from his roots a Branch will bear f.
     27: 6 blossom and fill all the world with f.
     32:17 The f of that righteousness will be
Jer 17: 8 drought and never fails to bear f."
Eze 47:12 F trees of all kinds will grow
     47:12 will not wither, nor will their f fail.
     47:12 Their f will serve for food and their
Hos   9:10 it was like seeing the early f
     10:12 reap the f of unfailing love,
     14: 2 that we may offer the f of our lips.
Am   8: 1 a basket of ripe f.
Mt   3: 8 Produce f in keeping
       3:10 does not produce good f will be cut
       7:16 By their f you will recognize them.
       7:17 every good tree bears good f, but a
           bad tree bears bad f.
Lk   6:44 Each tree is recognized by its own f.
     13: 6 he went to look for f on it but did
Jn   15: 2 every branch in me that bears no f,
     15: 2 branch that does bear f he prunes so
     15:16 so that you might go and bear f—
Ro   7: 4 order that we might bear f for God.
Gal   5:22 But the f of the Spirit is love, joy,
Eph   5: 9 (for the f of the light consists in all
Php   1:11 filled with the f of righteousness
Col   1:10 bearing f in every good work,
Heb 13:15 the f of lips that openly profess his
Jas   3:17 full of mercy and good f,
Jude 1:12 trees, without f and uprooted—
Rev 22: 2 bearing twelve crops of f, yielding its
           f every month.

FRUITFUL FRUIT
Ge   1:22 "Be f and increase in number
       9: 1 "Be f and increase in number
     17: 6 I will make you very f; I will make
     35:11 be f and increase in number.
Ex   1: 7 the Israelites were exceedingly f;
Ps 105:24 The Lord made his people very f;
    128: 3 wife will be like a f vine within your
Isa 27: 2 "Sing about a f vineyard:
Jn   15: 2 prunes so that it will be even more f.

Php   1:22 body, this will mean f labor for me.

FRUITION FRUIT
2Th   1:11 he may bring to f your every desire

FRUITLESS* FRUIT
Eph   5:11 to do with the f deeds of darkness,

FRUSTRATE* FRUSTRATES,
FRUSTRATION
2Sa 17:14 had determined to f the good advice
Ezr   4: 5 f their plans during the entire reign
Ps   14: 6 You evildoers f the plans
1Co   1:19 of the intelligent I will f."

FRUSTRATES* FRUSTRATE
Ps 146: 9 but he f the ways of the wicked.
Pr   22:12 but he f the words of the unfaithful.

FRUSTRATION* FRUSTRATE
Ecc   5:17 with great f, affliction and anger.
       7: 3 F is better than laughter, because
Ro   8:20 For the creation was subjected to f,

FUEL
Isa 44:19 to say, "Half of it I used for f;
Eze 21:32 You will be f for the fire,

FULFILL FULFILLED,
FULFILLMENT, FULFILLS
Ge   38: 8 wife and f your duty to her as
Nu   23:19 Does he promise and not f?
Dt   25: 7 He will not f the duty
2Ch 10:15 f the word the Lord had spoken
     36:22 in order to f the word of the Lord
Ps   61: 8 name and f my vows day after day.
    116:14 I will f my vows to the Lord
Ecc   5: 5 a vow than to make one and not f it.
Isa 46:11 far-off land, a man to f my purpose.
Jer 11: 5 I will f the oath I swore to your
     33:14 I will f the good promise I made
Mt   1:22 f what the Lord had said through
       3:15 us to do this to f all righteousness."
       4:14 f what was said through the prophet
       5:17 come to abolish them but to f them.
       8:17 to f what was spoken through
     12:17 to f what was spoken through
     21: 4 to f what was spoken through
Jn   12:38 This was to f the word of Isaiah
     13:18 this is to f this passage of Scripture:
     15:25 this is to f what is written in their
1Co   7: 3 The husband should f his marital
Gal   6: 2 and in this way you will f the law

FULFILLED FULFILL
Jos 21:45 to Israel failed; every one was f.
     23:14 Every promise has been f;
2Ch   6:15 and with your hand you have f it—
Pr   13:12 sick, but a longing f is a tree of life.
     13:19 A longing f is sweet to the soul,
Jer 25:12 "But when the seventy years are f,
Da   12: 6 these astonishing things are f?"
Mt   2:15 And so was f what the Lord had said
       2:17 through the prophet Jeremiah was f:
       2:23 So was f what was said through

Mt   13:14 In them is f the prophecy of Isaiah:
      13:35 So was f what was spoken through
      26:54 would the Scriptures be f that say it
      26:56 of the prophets might be f."
      27: 9 by Jeremiah the prophet was f:
Mk   13: 4 sign that they are all about to be f?"
      14:49 But the Scriptures must be f."
Lk   1: 1 things that have been f among us,
       4:21 "Today this scripture is f in your
      18:31 about the Son of Man will be f.
      24:44 Everything must be f that is written
Jn   17:12 so that Scripture would be f.
      18: 9 words he had spoken would be f:
      19:24 the scripture might be f that said,
      19:28 and so that Scripture would be f,
      19:36 so that the scripture would be f:
Ac   1:16 the Scripture had to be f
       3:18 But this is how God f what he had
Ro   13: 8 whoever loves others has f the law.
Gal   5:14 the entire law is f in keeping this
Jas   2:23 And the scripture was f that says,
Rev   17:17 authority, until God's words are f.

FULFILLMENT FULFILL
2Ch   36:21 seventy years were completed in f
Lk   22:16 I will not eat it again until it finds f
Ro   13:10 Therefore love is the f of the law.
Eph   1:10 effect when the times reach their f—

FULFILLS* FULFILL
Ps   145:19 He f the desires of those who fear
Isa   44:26 f the predictions of his messengers,

FULL FILL
Ge   6:11 God's sight and was f of violence.
      15:16 has not yet reached its f measure."
2Ki   4: 6 When all the jars were f, she said
2Ch   24:10 them into the chest until it was f.
Job   14: 1 are of few days and f of trouble.
Ps   31:23 him, but the proud he pays back in f.
     116: 5 our God is f of compassion.
     127: 5 Blessed is the man whose quiver is f
Pr   27: 7 One who is f loathes honey
      31:11 Her husband has f confidence in her
Isa   1:15 Your hands are f of blood!
       6: 3 the whole earth is f of his glory."
Jer   51:56 he will repay in f.
La   1: 1 lies the city, once so f of people!
Eze   10:12 wings, were completely f of eyes,
Mt   12:34 mouth speaks what the heart is f of.
Lk   4: 1 Jesus, f of the Holy Spirit,
       6:45 mouth speaks what the heart is f of.
      11:34 your whole body also is f of light.
      11:34 your body also is f of darkness.
Jn   10:10 may have life, and have it to the f.
Ac   6: 3 who are known to be f of the Spirit
       6: 5 a man f of faith and of the Holy
       7:55 But Stephen, f of the Holy Spirit,
      11:24 man, f of the Holy Spirit and faith,
Ro   11:12 riches will their f inclusion bring!
Eph   4:19 of impurity, and they are f of greed.
       6:11 Put on the f armor of God,
1Ti   3: 4 so in a manner worthy of f respect.

FULL-GROWN* GROW
Jas   1:15 sin, when it is f, gives birth to death.

FULLNESS* FILL
Dt   33:16 its f and the favor of him who dwelt
Jn   1:16 of his f we have all received grace
Eph   1:23 the f of him who fills everything
       3:19 to the measure of all the f of God.
       4:13 the whole measure of the f of Christ.
Col   1:19 to have all his f dwell in him,
       1:25 to you the word of God in its f—
       2: 9 in Christ all the f of the Deity lives
       2:10 Christ you have been brought to f.

FULLY FILL
Ex   19: 5 Now if you obey me f and keep my
Dt   28: 1 If you f obey the LORD your God
1Ki   8:61 may your hearts be f committed
2Ch   16: 9 those whose hearts are f committed
Ps   119: 4 precepts that are to be f obeyed.
     119:138 they are f trustworthy.
Pr   13: 4 desires of the diligent are f satisfied.
Lk   6:40 everyone who is f trained will be
Ro   4:21 being f persuaded that God had
       8: 4 of the law might be f met in us,
      14: 5 them should be f convinced in their
1Co   13:12 then I shall know f, even as I am f
      15:58 Always give yourselves f
Gal   4: 4 But when the set time had f come,
2Ti   4:17 the message might be f proclaimed
2Jn   1: 8 for, but that you may be rewarded f.

FURIOUS FURY
Dt   29:28 In f anger and in great wrath
Jer   21: 5 a mighty arm in f anger and in great
      32:37 where I banish them in my f anger

FURNACE
Dt   4:20 you out of the iron-smelting f,
1Ki   8:51 of Egypt, out of that iron-smelting f.
Isa   48:10 have tested you in the f of affliction.
Jer   11: 4 of Egypt, out of the iron-smelting f.
Da   3: 6 be thrown into a blazing f."
Mal   4: 1 day is coming; it will burn like a f.
Mt   13:42 will throw them into the blazing f,
Rev   1:15 feet were like bronze glowing in a f,

FURNISHED FURNISHINGS
Mk   14:15 a large room upstairs, f and ready.

FURNISHINGS FURNISHED
Ex   25: 9 all its f exactly like the pattern I will
1Ki   7:48 also made all the f that were

FURTHER
Job   34:23 has no need to examine people f,

FURY FURIOUS
Isa   14: 6 in f subdued nations with relentless
Rev   12:12 He is filled with f, because he
      14:10 too, will drink the wine of God's f,
      16:19 with the wine of the f of his wrath.
      19:15 the winepress of the f of the wrath

FUTILE FUTILITY
Mal   3:14 have said, 'It is f to serve God.

Ro   1:21 but their thinking became **f** and their
1Co   3:20 that the thoughts of the wise are **f**."

FUTILITY FUTILE
Ps   78:33 So he ended their days in **f** and their
Eph   4:17 do, in the **f** of their thinking.

FUTURE
Dt   6:20 In the **f**, when your son asks you,
1Ch   17:17 have spoken about the **f** of the house
Ps   37:37 a **f** awaits those who seek peace.
Pr   23:18 There is surely a **f** hope for you,
      24:20 for the evildoer has no **f** hope,
Ecc   7:14 can discover anything about their **f**.
       8: 7 Since no one knows the **f**, who can
Jer   29:11 you, plans to give you hope and a **f**.
Da   8:26 vision, for it concerns the distant **f**."
Ro   8:38 neither the present nor the **f**, nor any
1Co   3:22 life or death or the present or the **f**—

G

GABBATHA*
Jn   19:13 Pavement (which in Aramaic is **G**).

GABRIEL*
   Angel who interpreted Daniel's visions (Da
8:16–26; 9:20–27); announced births of John (Lk
1:11–20), Jesus (Lk 1:26–38).

GAD
   1. Son of Jacob by Zilpah (Ge 30:9–11; 35:26;
1Ch 2:2). Tribe of blessed (Ge 49:19; Dt 33:20–21),
numbered (Nu 1:25; 26:18), allotted land east of
the Jordan (Nu 32; 34:14; Jos 18:7; 22), west (Eze
48:27–28), 12,000 from (Rev 7:5).
   2. Prophet; seer of David (1Sa 22:5; 2Sa 24:11–
19; 1Ch 29:29).

GADARENES*
Mt   8:28 the other side in the region of the **G**,

GAIN GAINED, GAINING, GAINS
Ge   15: 8 that I will **g** possession of it?"
Ex   14:17 And I will **g** glory through Pharaoh
1Sa   8: 3 They turned aside after dishonest **g**
Ps   60:12 With God we will **g** the victory,
      90:12 that we may **g** a heart of wisdom,
Pr   1:19 of all who go after ill-gotten **g**;
       3:13 those who **g** understanding,
       4: 1 pay attention and **g** understanding.
       8: 5 You who are simple, **g** prudence;
      16: 8 righteousness than much **g**
      28:16 who hates ill-gotten **g** will enjoy
      28:23 the end **g** favor rather than one who
      29:23 low, but the lowly in spirit **g** honor.
Ecc   1: 3 What do people **g** from all their
Isa   63:12 to **g** for himself everlasting renown,
Jer   17:11 it did not lay are those who **g** riches
Da   2: 8 certain that you are trying to **g** time,
Mt   16:26 for someone to **g** the whole world,
Mk   8:36 it for someone to **g** the whole world,
Lk   9:25 it for someone to **g** the whole world,
1Co   13: 3 but do not have love, I **g** nothing.

Php   1:21 me, to live is Christ and to die is **g**.
       3: 8 them garbage, that I may **g** Christ
1Ti   3: 8 wine, and not pursuing dishonest **g**.
       3:13 who have served well **g** an excellent
       6: 5 godliness is a means to financial **g**.
       6: 6 with contentment is great **g**.
2Ti   3: 6 and **g** control over gullible women,
Titus 1: 7 violent, not pursuing dishonest **g**.
1Pe   5: 2 not pursuing dishonest **g**, but eager

GAINED GAIN
Ps   30: 9 "What is **g** if I am silenced, if I go
Ecc   2:11 nothing was **g** under the sun.
Jer   32:20 have **g** the renown that is still yours.
Ro   5: 2 through whom we have **g** access
Gal   2:21 could be **g** through the law,
Heb   11:33 justice, and **g** what was promised;

GAINING GAIN
Ge   3: 6 and also desirable for **g** wisdom,
Pr   1: 2 for **g** wisdom and instruction;
Jn   4: 1 Pharisees had heard that he was **g**

GAINS* GAIN
Pr   11:16 A kindhearted woman **g** honor,
      11:24 gives freely, yet **g** even more;
      15:32 heeds correction **g** understanding.
Mic   4:13 You will devote their ill-gotten **g**
Php   3: 7 But whatever were **g** to me I now

GAIUS
Ro   16:23 **G**, whose hospitality I
3Jn   1: 1 To my dear friend **G**, whom I love

GALATIA GALATIANS
Ac   16: 6 the region of Phrygia and **G**,
Gal   1: 2 with me, To the churches in **G**:

GALATIANS* GALATIA
Gal   3: 1 You foolish **G**! Who has bewitched

GALILEAN* GALILEE
Mk   14:70 are one of them, for you are a **G**."
Lk   22:59 fellow was with him, for he is a **G**."
      23: 6 Pilate asked if the man was a **G**.
Ac   5:37 Judas the **G** appeared in the days

GALILEANS GALILEE
Lk   13: 1 the **G** whose blood Pilate had mixed
Jn   4:45 in Galilee, the **G** welcomed him.
Ac   2: 7 all these who are speaking **G**?

GALILEE GALILEAN, GALILEANS, TIBERIAS
Isa   9: 1 in the future he will honor **G**
Mt   3:13 Jesus came from **G** to the Jordan
       4:15 the Jordan, **G** of the Gentiles—
      21:11 the prophet from Nazareth in **G**."
      26:32 I will go ahead of you into **G**."
      28:10 Go and tell my brothers to go to **G**;
Lk   23:49 who had followed him from **G**,
Jn   2: 1 a wedding took place at Cana in **G**.
       7:41 can the Messiah come from **G**?

GALL
Ps   69:21 They put **g** in my food and gave me

Mt   27:34 Jesus wine to drink, mixed with **g**;

GALLIO*
Proconsul of Achaia, who refused to hear complaints against Paul (Ac 18:12–17).

GAMALIEL
Ac   5:34 But a Pharisee named **G**, a teacher
      22: 3 I studied under **G** and was

GAME GAMES
Ge   25:28 who had a taste for wild **g**,
      27: 3 country to hunt some wild **g** for me.

GAMES* GAME
1Co 9:25 who competes in the **g** goes

GANGRENE*
2Ti   2:17 Their teaching will spread like **g**.

GAP GAPS
Ne   6: 1 the wall and not a **g** was left in it—
Eze 22:30 stand before me in the **g** on behalf

GAPS* GAP
Ne   4: 7 and that the **g** were being closed,

GARBAGE*
1Co   4:13 of the earth, the **g** of the world—
Php   3: 8 I consider them **g**, that I may gain

GARDEN GARDENER, GARDENS
Ge   2: 8 the LORD God had planted a **g**
      2:15 put him in the **G** of Eden to work it
      3:23 banished him from the **G** of Eden
     13:10 watered, like the **g** of the LORD,
SS   4:12 You are a **g** locked up, my sister,
Isa 58:11 You will be like a well-watered **g**,
Jer 31:12 They will be like a well-watered **g**,
Eze 28:13 You were in Eden, the **g** of God;
      31: 9 all the trees of Eden in the **g** of God.
Mk   4:32 becomes the largest of all **g** plants,
Jn   18: 3 So Judas came to the **g**,
     19:41 there was a **g**, and in the **g** a new

GARDENER* GARDEN
Jn   15: 1 true vine, and my Father is the **g**.
     20:15 Thinking he was the **g**, she said,

GARDENS GARDEN
Am   4: 9 "Many times I struck your **g**

GARLAND*
Pr   1: 9 They are a **g** to grace your head
      4: 9 She will give you a **g** to grace your

GARMENT GARMENTS
Ge   9:23 Japheth took a **g** and laid it across
     25:25 his whole body was like a hairy **g**;
Ru   3: 9 the corner of your **g** over me,
2Ki   1: 8 "He had a **g** of hair and had
Ps 102:26 they will all wear out like a **g**.
Pr   25:20 Like one who takes away a **g**
Isa 50: 9 They will all wear out like a **g**;
     51: 6 the earth will wear out like a **g**
     61: 3 a **g** of praise instead of a spirit
Mt   9:16 patch of unshrunk cloth on an old **g**,

Mt   9:16 the patch will pull away from the **g**,
Mk   14:52 he fled naked, leaving his **g** behind.
Jn   19:23 This **g** was seamless, woven in one
     19:24 them and cast lots for my **g**."
Heb   1:11 they will all wear out like a **g**.

GARMENTS GARMENT
Ge   3:21 The LORD God made **g** of skin
Ex   28: 2 Make sacred **g** for your brother
Lev   8: 2 his sons, their **g**, the anointing oil,
     16: 4 These are sacred **g**; so he must
Job 31:19 of clothing, or the needy without **g**,
Pr   31:24 She makes linen **g** and sells them,
Isa 52: 1 Put on your **g** of splendor,
     61:10 For he has clothed me with **g**
     63: 1 Bozrah, with his **g** stained crimson?
Eze 16:10 linen and covered you with costly **g**.
Joel 2:13 Rend your heart and not your **g**.
Zec   3: 4 sin, and I will put fine **g** on you."

GATE GATES, GATEWAY
Dt   21:19 to the elders at the **g** of his town.
Jos   2: 5 when it was time to close the city **g**,
Ru   4:11 and all the people at the **g** said,
Est   2:19 Mordecai was sitting at the king's **g**.
Job 29: 7 "When I went to the **g** of the city
Ps   69:12 Those who sit at the **g** mock me,
    118:20 This is the **g** of the LORD through
Pr   31:23 husband is respected at the city **g**,
     31:31 works bring her praise at the city **g**.
Mt   7:13 "Enter through the narrow **g**. For
           wide is the **g** and broad
Jn   10: 2 who enters by the **g** is the shepherd.
     10: 7 I tell you, I am the **g** for the sheep.
     10: 9 I am the **g**; whoever enters through
Ac   3: 2 to the temple **g** called Beautiful,
Heb 13:12 suffered outside the city **g** to make
Rev 21:21 each **g** made of a single pearl.

GATES GATE
Dt   6: 9 of your houses and on your **g**.
Ne   1: 3 its **g** have been burned with fire."
Ps   24: 7 Lift up your heads, you **g**;
     87: 2 The LORD loves the **g** of Zion
    100: 4 Enter his **g** with thanksgiving
    118:19 Open for me the **g** of the righteous,
Isa 60:11 Your **g** will always stand open,
     60:18 walls Salvation and your **g** Praise.
     62:10 Pass through, pass through the **g**!
La   4:12 foes could enter the **g** of Jerusalem.
Eze 48:31 the **g** of the city will be named
     48:31 The three **g** on the north side will be
Mt   16:18 the **g** of Hades will not overcome it.
Rev 21:12 high wall with twelve **g**, and with
           twelve angels at the **g**.
     21:12 On the **g** were written the names
     21:21 The twelve **g** were twelve pearls,
     21:25 On no day will its **g** ever be shut,
     22:14 may go through the **g** into the city.

GATEWAY GATE, WAY
Ge   19: 1 Lot was sitting in the **g** of the city.
1Sa   9:18 Saul approached Samuel in the **g**
2Sa 19: 8 got up and took his seat in the **g**.
     19: 8 "The king is sitting in the **g**,"

GATH

1Sa   5: 8 of the god of Israel moved to **G**."
      17: 4 who was from **G**,
      21:10 Saul and went to Achish king of **G**.
2Sa   1:20 "Tell it not in **G**, proclaim it not
Mic   1:10 Tell it not in **G**; weep not at all.

GATHER GATHERED, GATHERS, INGATHERING

Ex   16: 4 each day and **g** enough for that day.
Lev   19: 9 or **g** the gleanings of your harvest.
Dt   30: 4 the LORD your God will **g** you
Ru   2: 7 and **g** among the sheaves behind
Ne   1: 9 I will **g** them from there and bring
Ps   106:47 and **g** us from the nations, that we
Isa   11:12 nations and **g** the exiles of Israel;
      34:16 and his Spirit will **g** them together.
Jer   3:17 all nations will **g** in Jerusalem
      23: 3 "I myself will **g** the remnant of my
      31:10 'He who scattered Israel will **g** them
Eze   39:28 I will **g** them to their own land,
Zep   2: 1 **G** together, **g** yourselves together,
       3:20 At that time I will **g** you;
Zec   14: 2 I will **g** all the nations to Jerusalem
Mt   12:30 and whoever does not **g** with me
      13:30 then **g** the wheat and bring it
      18:20 For where two or three **g** in my name,
      23:37 longed to **g** your children together,
      25:26 **g** where I have not scattered seed?
Mk   13:27 and **g** his elect from the four winds,
Lk   3:17 and to **g** the wheat into his barn,
      11:23 and whoever does not **g** with me
      13:34 longed to **g** your children together,
      17:37 body, there the vultures will **g**."
Rev   14:18 and **g** the clusters of grapes
      19:17 **g** together for the great supper
      20: 8 and to **g** them for battle.

GATHERED GATHER

Ge   1: 9 "Let the water under the sky be **g**
Ex   16:18 the one who **g** much did not have
      16:18 the one who **g** little did not have too
      16:18 Everyone had **g** just as much as they
Nu   11:32 day the people went out and **g** quail.
      11:32 No one **g** less than ten homers.
      16:19 When Korah had **g** all his followers
Ru   2:18 saw how much she had **g**.
Pr   30: 4 Whose hands have **g** up the wind?
Mt   16: 9 and how many basketfuls you **g**?
      25:32 All the nations will be **g** before him,
2Co   8:15 "The one who **g** much did not have
       8:15 the one who **g** little did not have too
2Th   2: 1 Jesus Christ and our being **g** to him,
Rev   14:19 **g** its grapes and threw them
      16:16 they **g** the kings together
      19:19 their armies **g** together to wage war

GATHERS GATHER

Ps   147: 2 he **g** the exiles of Israel.
Pr   10: 5 He who **g** crops in summer is
      13:11 but whoever **g** money little by little
Isa   40:11 He **g** the lambs in his arms
      56: 8 he who **g** the exiles of Israel:
Mt   23:37 as a hen **g** her chicks under her

GAUNT

Ge   41: 3 ugly and **g**, came up out of the Nile

GAVE GIVE

Ge   2:20 So the man **g** names to all
       3: 6 She also **g** some to her husband,
      14:20 Abram **g** him a tenth of everything.
      16:13 She **g** this name to the LORD who
      28: 4 the land God **g** to Abraham."
      35:12 The land I **g** to Abraham and Isaac I
      39:23 **g** him success in whatever he did.
      47:11 **g** them property in the best part
Ex   4:11 to him, "Who **g** human beings their
      31:18 he **g** him the two tablets
      34:32 and he **g** them all the commands
Nu   22:18 "Even if Balak **g** me all the silver
Dt   2:12 the land the LORD **g** them as their
       2:36 The LORD our God **g** us all
       3:12 I **g** the Reubenites and the Gadites
       8:16 He **g** you manna to eat
       9:10 The LORD **g** me two stone tablets
      26: 9 us to this place and **g** us this land,
      31: 9 law and **g** it to the Levitical priests,
      32: 8 the Most High **g** the nations their
Jos   11:23 he **g** it as an inheritance to Israel
      13:14 the tribe of Levi he **g** no inheritance,
      15:13 Joshua to Caleb son of Jephunneh
      19:49 the Israelites **g** Joshua son of Nun
      21:44 The LORD **g** them rest on every
      24:13 So I **g** you a land on which you did
Jdg   2:14 against Israel the LORD **g** them
       3: 6 **g** their own daughters to their sons,
1Sa   1: 5 But to Hannah he **g** a double portion
      27: 6 So on that day Achish **g** him Ziklag,
2Sa   8: 6 The LORD **g** David victory
      12: 8 I **g** your master's house to you,
      12: 8 I **g** you all Israel and Judah.
1Ki   4:29 God **g** Solomon wisdom and very
       5:12 The LORD **g** Solomon wisdom,
2Ch   36:17 God **g** them all into the hands
Ezr   2:69 to their ability they **g** to the treasury
Ne   9:15 their hunger you **g** them bread
       9:20 You **g** your good Spirit to instruct
       9:20 you **g** them water for their thirst.
       9:22 "You **g** them kingdoms
       9:27 compassion you **g** them deliverers,
Job   1:21 The LORD **g** and the LORD has
      42:10 and **g** him twice as much as he had
Ps   69:21 food and **g** me vinegar for my thirst.
     106:41 He **g** them into the hands
     135:12 he **g** their land as an inheritance,
Pr   8:29 he **g** the sea its boundary so
Ecc   12: 7 the spirit returns to God who **g** it.
Jer   3: 8 I **g** faithless Israel her certificate
Eze   3: 2 mouth, and he **g** me the scroll to eat.
Da   1: 7 The chief official **g** them new
       1:17 four young men God **g** knowledge
Mt   1:25 their marriage until she **g** birth
       1:25 And he **g** him the name Jesus.
       2:16 he **g** orders to kill all the boys
      25:35 and you **g** me something to eat,
      25:35 and you **g** me something to drink,
      25:42 hungry and you **g** me nothing to eat,

Mt   25:42   and you **g** me nothing to drink,
     26:26   he broke it and **g** it to his disciples,
     27:50   in a loud voice, he **g** up his spirit.
Mk   6: 7   and **g** them authority over impure
     11:28   who **g** you authority to do this?"
Jn   1:12   he **g** the right to become children
      3:16   so loved the world that he **g** his one
     17: 4   finishing the work you **g** me to do.
     17: 6   you **g** them to me and they have
     19:30   bowed his head and **g** up his spirit.
Ac   1: 3   **g** many convincing proofs that he
     11:17   if God **g** them the same gift he **g** us
Ro   1:24   Therefore God **g** them over
      1:26   God **g** them over to shameful lusts.
      1:28   so God **g** them over to a depraved
      8:32   own Son, but **g** him up for us all—
1Co   3: 2   I **g** you milk, not solid food, for you
2Co   5:18   **g** us the ministry of reconciliation:
      8: 3   they **g** as much as they were able,
      8: 5   They **g** themselves first of all
Gal   1: 4   who **g** himself for our sins to rescue
      2:20   who loved me and **g** himself for me.
Eph   4: 8   captives and **g** gifts to his people."
      4:11   So Christ himself **g** the apostles,
      5: 2   and **g** himself up for us as a fragrant
      5:25   the church and **g** himself up for her
Php   2: 9   **g** him the name that is above every
2Th   2:16   us and by his grace **g** us eternal
1Ti   2: 6   who **g** himself as a ransom for all
Titus 2:14   who **g** himself for us to redeem us
Heb   7: 2   and Abraham **g** him a tenth
1Jn   3:24   We know it by the Spirit he **g** us.
Rev 11:13   and **g** glory to the God of heaven.
     13: 2   The dragon **g** the beast his power
     16:19   **g** her the cup filled with the wine
     20:13   The sea **g** up the dead that were
     20:13   Hades **g** up the dead that were

GAVE THANKS See THANKS

GAZA

Jdg 16: 1   One day Samson went to **G**,
1Sa   6:17   one each for Ashdod, **G**, Ashkelon,
Am   1: 6   "For three sins of **G**, even for four,

GAZE GAZING

Ps   27: 4   to **g** on the beauty of the LORD
Pr   4:25   fix your **g** directly before you.
     23:31   Do not **g** at wine when it is red,
Rev 11: 9   and nation will **g** on their bodies

GAZELLE

2Sa   1:19   "A **g** lies slain on your heights,
      2:18   was as fleet-footed as a wild **g**.
SS   2: 9   My beloved is like a **g** or a young
      7: 3   two fawns, like twin fawns of a **g**.

GAZING* GAZE

SS   2: 9   our wall, **g** through the windows,
Da   10: 8   was left alone, **g** at this great vision;

GEDALIAH

Governor of Judah appointed by Nebuchadnezzar (2Ki 25:22–26; Jer 39–41).

GEHAZI*

Servant of Elisha (2Ki 4:12—5:27; 8:4–5).

GEMS

Ex   25: 7   other **g** to be mounted on the ephod

GENEALOGIES GENEALOGY

1Ch   9: 1   Israel was listed in the **g** recorded
1Ti   1: 4   themselves to myths and endless **g**.
Titus 3: 9   avoid foolish controversies and **g**

GENEALOGY GENEALOGIES

Mt   1: 1   This is the **g** of Jesus the Messiah
Heb   7: 3   without **g**, without beginning

GENERATION GENERATIONS

Ge   7: 1   I have found you righteous in this **g**.
     15:16   the fourth **g** your descendants will
Ex   1: 6   all his brothers and all that **g** died,
      3:15   name you shall call me from **g** to **g**.
     20: 5   and fourth **g** of those who hate me,
     34: 7   parents to the third and fourth **g**."
Nu   32:13   until the whole **g** of those who had
Dt   1:35   this evil **g** shall see the good land I
Jdg   2:10   another **g** grew up who knew
Job   8: 8   "Ask the former **g** and find
Ps   24: 6   Such is the **g** of those who seek
     48:13   you may tell of them to the next **g**.
     71:18   I declare your power to the next **g**,
     78: 4   will tell the next **g** the praiseworthy
    102:18   Let this be written for a future **g**,
    112: 2   the **g** of the upright will be blessed.
    145: 4   One **g** commends your works
Isa 34:17   forever and dwell there from **g** to **g**.
     53: 8   Yet who of his **g** protested?
La   5:19   your throne endures from **g** to **g**.
Da   4: 3   his dominion endures from **g** to **g**.
      4:34   his kingdom endures from **g** to **g**.
Joel 1: 3   and their children to the next **g**.
Mt   12:39   and adulterous **g** asks for a sign!
     17:17   "You unbelieving and perverse **g**,"
     23:36   tell you, all this will come on this **g**.
     24:34   this **g** will certainly not pass away
Mk   9:19   "You unbelieving **g**,"
     13:30   this **g** will certainly not pass away
Lk   1:50   to those who fear him, from **g** to **g**.
      7:31   can I compare the people of this **g**?
     11:29   Jesus said, "This is a wicked **g**.
     11:50   Therefore this **g** will be held
     21:32   this **g** will certainly not pass away
Ac   2:40   yourselves from this corrupt **g**."
Php   2:15   fault in a warped and crooked **g**."
Heb   3:10   That is why I was angry with that **g**;

GENERATIONS GENERATION

Ge   9:12   you, a covenant for all **g** to come:
     17: 7   after you for the **g** to come, to be
Ex   12:17   lasting ordinance for the **g** to come.
     30:21   his descendants for the **g** to come."
     31:13   me and you for the **g** to come,
     40:15   will continue throughout their **g**."
Dt   7: 9   a thousand **g** of those who love him
     32: 7   consider the **g** long past.
1Ch 16:15   promise he made, for a thousand **g**,
Ps   22:30   future **g** will be told about the Lord.

Ps	33:11	purposes of his heart through all **g**.
	45:17	your memory through all **g**;
	89: 1	faithfulness known through all **g**.
	90: 1	our dwelling place throughout all **g**.
	100: 5	faithfulness continues through all **g**.
	102:12	your renown endures through all **g**.
	105: 8	promise he made, for a thousand **g**,
	119:90	faithfulness continues through all **g**;
	135:13	renown, Lord, through all **g**.
	145:13	dominion endures through all **g**.
	146:10	forever, your God, O Zion, for all **g**.
Pr	27:24	and a crown is not secure for all **g**.
Ecc	1: 4	**G** come and **g** go, but the earth
Isa	41: 4	through, calling forth the **g**
	51: 8	my salvation through all **g**."
Mt	1:17	Thus there were fourteen **g** in all
Lk	1:48	now on all **g** will call me blessed,
Eph	3: 5	other **g** as it has now been revealed
	3:21	and in Christ Jesus throughout all **g**,
Col	1:26	has been kept hidden for ages and **g**,

GENEROSITY* GENEROUS

2Co	8: 2	extreme poverty welled up in rich **g**.
	9:11	and through us your **g** will result
	9:13	and for your **g** in sharing with them

GENEROUS* GENEROSITY, GENEROUSLY

Ps	37:26	They are always **g** and lend freely;
	112: 5	Good will come to those who are **g**
Pr	11:25	A **g** person will prosper;
	22: 9	The **g** will themselves be blessed,
Mt	20:15	are you envious because I am **g**?'
Lk	11:41	be **g** to the poor, and everything will
Ac	28: 7	showed us **g** hospitality for three
2Co	9: 5	for the **g** gift you had promised.
	9: 5	Then it will be ready as a **g** gift,
	9:11	that you can be **g** on every occasion,
1Ti	6:18	and to be **g** and willing to share

GENEROUSLY GENEROUS

Dt	15:10	Give **g** to them and do so without
1Ch	29:14	should be able to give as **g** as this?
Ps	37:21	not repay, but the righteous give **g**;
2Co	9: 6	whoever sows **g** will also reap **g**.
Jas	1: 5	who gives **g** to all without finding

GENITALS

Eze	16:26	your neighbors with large **g**,

GENTILE GENTILES

Ezr	6:21	practices of their **G** neighbors
Ne	5: 9	the reproach of our **G** enemies?
Ac	21:25	As for the **G** believers, we have
Ro	1:16	first to the Jew, then to the **G**.
	2: 9	first for the Jew, then for the **G**;
	2:10	first for the Jew, then for the **G**.
	10:12	no difference between Jew and **G**—
Gal	3:28	There is neither Jew nor **G**,
Col	3:11	Here there is no **G** or Jew,

GENTILES GENTILE

Isa	42: 6	for the people and a light for the **G**,
	49: 6	will also make you a light for the **G**,
Mt	4:15	the Jordan, Galilee of the **G**—

Lk	2:32	a light for revelation to the **G**,
	21:24	by the **G** until the times of the **G** are
	22:25	kings of the **G** lord it over them;
Ac	9:15	to proclaim my name to the **G**
	10:45	had been poured out even on **G**.
	11: 1	throughout Judea heard that the **G**
	11:18	to **G** God has granted repentance
	13:16	and you **G** who worship God,
	13:46	of eternal life, we now turn to the **G**.
	13:47	have made you a light for the **G**,
	14:27	had opened a door of faith to the **G**.
	15: 5	"The **G** must be circumcised
	15:19	it difficult for the **G** who are turning
	18: 6	From now on I will go to the **G**."
	22:21	send you far away to the **G**.' "
	26:20	and then to the **G**, I preached
	28:28	salvation has been sent to the **G**,
Ro	2:14	when **G**, who do not have the law,
	3: 9	**G** alike are all under the power
	3:29	Is he not the God of **G** too? Yes, of **G**
	9:24	from the Jews but also from the **G**?
	11:11	to the **G** to make Israel envious.
	11:12	their loss means riches for the **G**,
	11:13	I am talking to you **G**.
	11:13	as I am the apostle to the **G**, I take
	15: 9	that the **G** might glorify God for his
	15: 9	I will praise you among the **G**;
	15:27	For if the **G** have shared in the Jews'
1Co	1:23	block to Jews and foolishness to **G**,
	12:13	whether Jews or **G**, slave or free—
2Co	11:26	my fellow Jews, in danger from **G**;
Gal	1:16	I might preach him among the **G**,
	2: 2	gospel that I preach among the **G**.
	2: 8	at work in me as an apostle to the **G**.
	2:14	that you force **G** to follow Jewish
	3: 8	God would justify the **G** by faith,
	3:14	come to the **G** through Christ Jesus,
Eph	3: 6	the gospel the **G** are heirs together
	3: 8	preach to the **G** the boundless riches
	4:17	you must no longer live as the **G** do,
Col	1:27	known among the **G** the glorious
1Ti	2: 7	a true and faithful teacher of the **G**.
2Ti	4:17	and all the **G** might hear it.
Rev	11: 2	because it has been given to the **G**.

GENTLE* GENTLENESS, GENTLY

Dt	28:54	Even the most **g** and sensitive man
	28:56	The most **g** and sensitive woman
	28:56	and **g** that she would not venture
2Sa	18: 5	"Be **g** with the young man Absalom
1Ki	19:12	And after the fire came a **g** whisper.
Job	41: 3	Will it speak to you with **g** words?
Pr	15: 1	A **g** answer turns away wrath,
	25:15	and a **g** tongue can break a bone.
Jer	11:19	I had been like a **g** lamb led
Mt	11:29	me, for I am **g** and humble in heart,
	21: 5	to you, **g** and riding on a donkey,
Ac	27:13	When a **g** south wind began
1Co	4:21	I come in love and with a **g** spirit?
Eph	4: 2	Be completely humble and **g**;
1Ti	3: 3	not violent but **g**, not quarrelsome,
Titus	3: 2	always to be **g** toward everyone.
1Pe	3: 4	the unfading beauty of a **g** and quiet

GENTLENESS* GENTLE
2Co 10: 1 By the humility and **g** of Christ,
Gal 5:23 **g** and self-control.
Php 4: 5 Let your **g** be evident to all.
Col 3:12 kindness, humility, **g** and patience.
1Ti 6:11 faith, love, endurance and **g**.
1Pe 3:15 But do this with **g** and respect,

GENTLY GENTLE
Isa 40:11 he **g** leads those that have young.
Gal 6: 1 Spirit should restore that person **g**.
2Ti 2:25 Opponents must be **g** instructed,
Heb 5: 2 deal **g** with those who are ignorant

GENUINE* GENUINENESS
2Co 6: 8 **g**, yet regarded as impostors;
Php 2:20 who will show **g** concern for your

GENUINENESS* GENUINE
1Pe 1: 7 so that the proven **g** of your faith—

GERAHS
Eze 45:12 The shekel is to consist of twenty **g**.

GERAR
Ge 20: 2 Abimelek king of **G** sent for Sarah
26: 6 So Isaac stayed in **G**.

GERASENES
Lk 8:26 They sailed to the region of the **G**,

GERIZIM
Dt 27:12 on Mount **G** to bless the people:
Jos 8:33 people stood in front of Mount **G**

GERSHOM
Ex 2:22 and Moses named him **G**, saying,
1Ch 23:15 The sons of Moses: **G** and Eliezer.

GERSHON GERSHONITE, GERSHONITES
Ge 46:11 sons of Levi: **G**, Kohath and Merari.

GERSHONITE GERSHON
Nu 4:24 "This is the service of the **G** clans

GERSHONITES GERSHON
Nu 3:25 of meeting the **G** were responsible
1Ch 6:71 The **G** received the following:

GESHEM
Ne 6: 1 **G** the Arab and the rest of our

GESHUR
2Sa 13:38 After Absalom fled and went to **G**,

GET GETS, GOT, ILL-GOTTEN
Ge 24: 4 and **g** a wife for my son Isaac."
29:20 served seven years to **g** Rachel,
Nu 16:10 are trying to **g** the priesthood too.
Dt 30:12 will ascend into heaven to **g** it
Jdg 16:28 me with one blow **g** revenge
Pr 1: 5 and let the discerning **g** guidance—
3:35 honor, but fools **g** only shame.
4: 5 **G** wisdom, **g** understanding,
16:16 much better to **g** wisdom than gold,
to **g** insight rather than silver!

Pr 23: 4 Do not wear yourself out to **g** rich;
Eze 18:31 and **g** a new heart and a new spirit.
Mt 16:23 and said to Peter, "**G** behind me,
Mk 6: 2 did this man **g** these things?"
13:16 in the field go back to **g** their cloak.
Jn 19:24 "Let's decide by lot who will **g** it."
1Co 9:24 Run in such a way as to **g** the prize.

GETHSEMANE*
Mt 26:36 his disciples to a place called **G**,
Mk 14:32 They went to a place called **G**,

GETS GET
Pr 19: 8 The one who **g** wisdom loves life;
Ac 23:15 ready to kill him before he **g** here."

GEZER
Jos 16:10 dislodge the Canaanites living in **G**;
1Ch 14:16 army, all the way from Gibeon to **G**.

GHOST*
Mt 14:26 "It's a **g**," they said, and cried
Mk 6:49 on the lake, they thought he was a **g**.
Lk 24:37 and frightened, thinking they saw a **g**.
24:39 a **g** does not have flesh and bones,

[GIVE UP THE] GHOST (KJV) See BREATHED [HIS LAST], DIE, DIED, DYING, GAVE [UP HIS SPIRIT], PERISHED

[HOLY] GHOST (KJV) See [HOLY] SPIRIT

GIBEAH
Jdg 19:12 We will go on to **G**."
1Sa 10:26 Saul also went to his home in **G**,
2Sa 21: 6 exposed before the LORD at **G**
Hos 10: 9 again overtake the evildoers in **G**?

GIBEON GIBEONITES
Jos 10:12 "Sun, stand still over **G**, and you,
2Sa 2:13 out and met them at the pool of **G**.
1Ki 3: 5 At **G** the LORD appeared

GIBEONITES GIBEON
Jos 9:16 they made the treaty with the **G**,
2Sa 21: 1 it is because he put the **G** to death."

GIDEON JERUB-BAAL
Judge, also called Jerub-Baal; freed Israel from Midianites (Jdg 6–8; Heb 11:32). Given sign of fleece (Jdg 8:36–40).

GIFT GIFTED, GIFTS
Ge 30:20 has presented me with a precious **g**.
Nu 18: 7 the service of the priesthood as a **g**.
Dt 16:17 of you must bring a **g** in proportion
2Ch 9:24 everyone who came brought a **g**—
Pr 18:16 A **g** opens the way and ushers
21:14 A **g** given in secret soothes anger,
Ecc 3:13 in all their toil—this is the **g** of God.
5:19 in their toil—this is a **g** of God.
Mt 5:23 if you are offering your **g** at the altar
8: 4 and offer the **g** Moses commanded,
Jn 4:10 "If you knew the **g** of God and who

Ac   1: 4 wait for the **g** my Father promised,
      2:38 you will receive the **g** of the Holy
      8:20 you thought you could buy the **g**
    11:17 gave them the same **g** he gave us
Ro   1:11 to you some spiritual **g** to make you
     5:15 But the **g** is not like the trespass.
     5:15 the **g** that came by the grace
     6:23 the **g** of God is eternal life in Christ
    12: 6 If your **g** is prophesying,
1Co 7: 7 of you has your own **g** from God;
     7: 7 one has this **g**, another has that.
2Co 8:12 the **g** is acceptable according
     9:15 be to God for his indescribable **g**!
Eph 2: 8 from yourselves, it is the **g** of God—
1Ti 4:14 Do not neglect your **g**, which was
2Ti 1: 6 you to fan into flame the **g** of God,
Heb 6: 4 who have tasted the heavenly **g**,
Jas 1:17 good and perfect **g** is from above,
1Pe 3: 7 with you of the gracious **g** of life,
     4:10 you should use whatever **g** you have
Rev 22:17 the one who wishes take the free **g**

GIFTED* GIFT

1Co 14:37 prophet or otherwise **g** by the Spirit,

GIFTS GIFT

Nu   8:19 I have given the Levites as **g**
Dt 12: 6 your tithes and special **g**, what you
Ezr 1: 6 and with valuable **g**, in addition
Ps 68:18 you received **g** from people,
    76:11 let all the neighboring lands bring **g**
   112: 9 They have freely scattered their **g**
Pr 25:14 is one who boasts of **g** never given.
Mt   2:11 and presented him with **g** of gold,
     7:11 how to give good **g** to your children,
     7:11 in heaven give good **g** to those who
Lk 11:13 how to give good **g** to your children,
    21: 1 he saw the rich putting their **g**
Ac 10: 4 and **g** to the poor have come up as
Ro 11:29 for God's **g** and his call are
    12: 6 We have different **g**,
1Co 12: 1 Now about the **g** of the Spirit,
    12: 4 There are different kinds of **g**,
    12:28 then **g** of healing, of helping,
    12:30 Do all have **g** of healing?
    12:31 Now eagerly desire the greater **g**.
    14: 1 and eagerly desire **g** of the Spirit,
    14:12 Since you are eager for **g**
2Co 9: 9 "They have freely scattered their **g**
Eph 4: 8 captives and gave **g** to his people."
Php 4:17 Not that I desire your **g**;
Heb 2: 4 by **g** of the Holy Spirit distributed
     9: 9 indicating that the **g** and sacrifices

GIHON

Ge   2:13 name of the second river is the **G**;
2Ch 32:30 the upper outlet of the **G** spring

GILBOA

1Ch 10: 8 and his sons fallen on Mount **G**.

GILEAD GILEADITE, JABESH
GILEAD, RAMOTH GILEAD

Nu 32:29 the land of **G** as their possession.
Dt 34: 1 the whole land—from **G** to Dan,

Jdg 11: 1 His father was **G**; his mother was
2Sa 2: 9 He made him king over **G**,
1Ch 27:21 the half-tribe of Manasseh in **G**:
Jer 8:22 Is there no balm in **G**? Is there no
    46:11 "Go up to **G** and get balm,
Hos 6: 8 **G** is a city of evildoers,
Mic 7:14 Bashan and **G** as in days long ago.

GILEADITE GILEAD

Jdg 11: 1 Jephthah the **G** was a mighty
2Sa 19:31 Barzillai the **G** also came down

GILGAL

Jos 4:20 **G** the twelve stones they had taken
     5: 9 So the place has been called **G**
Jdg 2: 1 LORD went up from **G** to Bokim
1Sa 7:16 circuit from Bethel to **G** to Mizpah,

GIRD*

Ps 45: 3 **G** your sword on your side,

GIRGASHITES

Dt   7: 1 the Hittites, **G**, Amorites,

GIRL GIRLS

Ex   1:16 but if it is a **g**, let her live."
2Ki 5: 2 had taken captive a young **g**
Mk 5:41 (which means "Little **g**, I say
     6:22 The king said to the **g**, "Ask me

GIRLS GIRL

Joel 3: 3 they sold **g** for wine to drink.
Zec 8: 5 with boys and **g** playing there."

GIVE GAVE, GIVEN, GIVER, GIVES,
GIVING, LIFE-GIVING

Ge   1:29 "I **g** you every seed-bearing plant
     9: 3 plants, I now **g** you everything.
    12: 7 your offspring I will **g** this land."
    27: 4 I may **g** you my blessing before I
    28: 4 May he **g** you and your descendants
    28:22 that you **g** me I will **g** you a tenth."
Ex 13: 5 he swore to your ancestors to **g** you,
    17: 2 and said, "**G** us water to drink."
    20:16 "You shall not **g** false testimony
    30:15 are not to **g** more than a half shekel
    30:15 the poor are not to **g** less when you
Lev 18:21 " 'Do not **g** any of your children
Nu 6:26 toward you and **g** you peace." '
    11:13 wailing to me, '**G** us meat to eat!'
Dt   5:20 "You shall not **g** false testimony
    15:10 **G** generously to them and do so
    28: 1 all his commands I **g** you today,
Jos 1: 6 I swore to their ancestors to **g** them.
Jdg 6:17 eyes, **g** me a sign that it is really you
1Sa 1:11 forget your servant but **g** her a son,
     1:11 I will **g** him to the LORD for all
     1:28 So now I **g** him to the LORD.
     8: 6 they said, "**G** us a king to lead us,"
1Ki 3: 5 whatever you want me to **g** you."
    11:13 will **g** him one tribe for the sake
2Ch 1:10 **G** me wisdom and knowledge, that I
    15: 7 be strong and do not **g** up, for your
Ne   9: 6 You **g** life to everything,
Job 2: 4 "A man will **g** all he has for his

Ps   13: 3 **G** light to my eyes, or I will sleep
Pr   4:26 **G** careful thought to the paths
     21:26 but the righteous **g** without sparing.
     23:26 **g** me your heart and let your eyes
     25:21 enemy is hungry, **g** him food to eat;
     25:21 if he is thirsty, **g** him water to drink.
     25:26 well are the righteous who **g** way
     28:27 Those who **g** to the poor will lack
     30: 8 **g** me neither poverty nor riches,
     30: 8 but **g** me only my daily bread.
     30:15 "The leech has two daughters. 'G! G!'
Ecc   3: 6 a time to search and a time to **g** up,
SS   8: 7 one were to **g** all the wealth of one's
Isa   7:14 the Lord himself will **g** you a sign:
      7:14 will conceive and **g** birth to a son,
Eze 36:26 I will **g** you a new heart and put
     36:26 of stone and **g** you a heart of flesh.
Mt   6:11 **G** us today our daily bread.
      7: 6 "Do not **g** dogs what is sacred;
      7:11 know how to **g** good gifts to your
      7:11 your Father in heaven **g** good gifts
     10: 8 Freely you have received; freely **g**.
     16:19 I will **g** you the keys of the kingdom
     22:21 them, "So **g** back to Caesar what is
Mk   6:23 "Whatever you ask I will **g** you,
      8:37 what can anyone **g** in exchange
     10:19 you shall not **g** false testimony,
     10:45 to **g** his life as a ransom for many."
Lk   6:38 **G**, and it will be given to you.
     11: 3 **G** us each day our daily bread.
     11:13 know how to **g** good gifts to your
     11:13 Father in heaven **g** the Holy Spirit
     14:33 you who do not **g** up everything you
Jn   4:14 drinks the water I **g** them will never
      6:52 "How can this man **g** us his flesh
     10:28 I **g** them eternal life, and they shall
     13:34 "A new command I **g** you:
     14:16 he will **g** you another advocate
     14:27 I leave with you; my peace I **g** you.
     14:27 I do not **g** to you as the world gives.
     17: 2 people that he might **g** eternal life
Ac   2:45 possessions to **g** to anyone who had
      3: 6 have, but what I do have I **g** you.
     20:35 'It is more blessed to **g** than
Ro   2: 7 immortality, he will **g** eternal life.
      8:32 with him, graciously **g** us all things?
     12: 8 encourage, then **g** encouragement;
     12: 8 if it is giving, then **g** generously;
     13: 7 **G** to everyone what you owe them:
     14:12 then, each of us will **g** an account
1Co 13: 3 If I **g** all I possess to the poor and **g**
             over my body to
2Co   9: 7 you should **g** what you have decided
             in your heart to **g**,
Gal   2: 5 We did not **g** in to them
      6: 9 reap a harvest if we do not **g** up.
Eph   4:27 and do not **g** the devil a foothold.
Heb 13:17 as those who must **g** an account.
1Pe   3:15 Always be prepared to **g** an answer
Rev   2: 7 I will **g** the right to eat from the tree
      2:10 and I will **g** you life as your victor's
      2:17 I will **g** some of the hidden manna.
      2:17 also **g** that person a white stone

Rev   2:26 I will **g** authority over the nations—
      2:28 also **g** that one the morning star.
      3:21 I will **g** the right to sit with me
     14: 7 voice, "Fear God and **g** him glory,
     18: 6 **G** back to her as she has given;
     22:12 I will **g** to each person according

GIVE ... THANKS See THANKS

GIVEN GIVE

Ex   4:21 the wonders I have **g** you the power
     16:15 is the bread the LORD has **g** you
Nu   8:16 the Israelites who are to be **g** wholly
Dt   1:21 your God has **g** you the land.
     26:11 things the LORD your God has **g**
Job   3:23 Why is life **g** to a man whose way is
Ps   31: 8 You have not **g** me into the hands
    105:42 he remembered his holy promise **g**
    115:16 but the earth he has **g** to mankind.
    118:18 but he has not **g** me over to death.
Pr   25:11 of silver is a ruling rightly **g**.
Isa   9: 6 to us a son is **g**, and the government
La   2: 7 He has **g** the walls of her palaces
Am   9:15 from the land I have **g** them,"
Mt   6:33 all these things will be **g** to you as
      7: 7 "Ask and it will be **g** to you;
     22:30 people will neither marry nor be **g**
     25:29 For whoever has will be **g** more,
Mk   4:25 Whoever has will be **g** more;
      8:12 I tell you, no sign will be **g** to it."
Lk   6:38 Give, and it will be **g** to you.
      8:10 kingdom of God has been **g** to you,
     11: 9 Ask and it will be **g** to you;
     22:19 saying, "This is my body **g** for you;
Jn   1:16 grace in place of grace already **g**.
      1:17 For the law was **g** through Moses;
      3:27 can receive only what is **g** them
      6:39 lose none of all those he has **g** me,
     17:24 I want those you have **g** me to be
     17:24 glory you have **g** me because you
     18:11 drink the cup the Father has **g** me?"
Ac   5:32 whom God has **g** to those who obey
      7:53 the law that was **g** through angels
     20:24 the task the Lord Jesus has **g** me—
Ro   5: 5 Holy Spirit, who has been **g** to us.
     11:35 "Who has ever **g** to God, that God
1Co   4: 2 those who have been **g** a trust must
     11:24 and when he had **g** thanks, he broke
     12:13 and we were all **g** the one Spirit
2Co   5: 5 who has **g** us the Spirit as a deposit,
     12: 7 I was **g** a thorn in my flesh,
Gal   3:19 Why, then, was the law **g** at all?
      3:19 The law was **g** through angels
      3:22 being **g** through faith in Jesus
      3:22 might be **g** to those who believe.
      3:19 Why, then, was the law **g** at all?
Eph   1: 6 he has freely **g** us in the One he
      4: 7 one of us grace has been **g** as Christ
1Ti   4:14 which was **g** you through prophecy
1Pe   1: 3 great mercy he has **g** us new birth
2Pe   1: 3 divine power has **g** us everything
1Jn   4:13 he in us: He has **g** us of his Spirit.
      5:20 come and has **g** us understanding,
Rev   6: 2 and he was **g** a crown, and he rode

Rev 15: 2 They held harps **g** them by God
     20: 4 those who had been **g** authority

GIVER* GIVE
Pr 18:16 ushers the **g** into the presence
2Co 9: 7 for God loves a cheerful **g**.

GIVES GIVE
Ex   4:11 Who **g** them sight or makes them
Job 33: 4 breath of the Almighty **g** me life.
     35:10 Maker, who **g** songs in the night,
Ps 29:11 The LORD **g** strength to his
    119:130 unfolding of your words **g** light;
           it **g** understanding
    136:25 He **g** food to every creature.
Pr   2: 6 For the LORD **g** wisdom;
     11:24 One person **g** freely, yet gains even
     14:30 A heart at peace **g** life to the body,
     15:30 good news **g** health to the bones.
     19: 6 is the friend of one who **g** gifts.
     29: 4 justice a king **g** a country stability,
Ecc 2:26 who pleases him, God **g** wisdom,
      2:26 the sinner he **g** the task of gathering
Isa 40:29 He **g** strength to the weary
Hab 2:15 to him who **g** drink to his neighbors,
Mt 10:42 if anyone **g** even a cup of cold water
Jn   3:34 for God **g** the Spirit without limit.
      5:21 raises the dead and **g** them life,
      5:21 even so the Son **g** life to whom he is
      6:37 All those the Father **g** me will come
      6:63 The Spirit **g** life; the flesh counts
     14:27 I do not give to you as the world **g**.
1Co 15:57 He **g** us the victory through our
2Co 3: 6 the letter kills, but the Spirit **g** life.
1Th 4: 8 the very God who **g** you his Holy
Jas 1:25 into the perfect law that **g** freedom,
      4: 6 But he **g** us more grace. That is why
Rev 21:23 for the glory of God **g** it light,

GIVING GIVE
Ge 13:17 of the land, for I am **g** it to you."
Dt 11: 8 all the commands I am **g** you today,
Jos 1:13 give you rest by **g** you this land.'
Ne   8: 8 **g** the meaning so that the people
Est 9:19 a day for **g** presents to each other.
Ps 19: 8 LORD are right, **g** joy to the heart.
     19: 8 are radiant, **g** light to the eyes.
Pr   1: 4 for **g** prudence to those who are
     15:23 person finds joy in **g** an apt reply—
Mt   6: 4 so that your **g** may be in secret.
     24:38 marrying and **g** in marriage,
Ac 15: 8 accepted them by **g** the Holy Spirit
Ro 12: 8 if it is **g**, then give generously;
2Co 8: 7 you also excel in this grace of **g**.
Php 4:15 shared with me in the matter of **g**
Heb 10:25 not **g** up meeting together, as some

GLAD* GLADDENS, GLADNESS
Ex   4:14 you, and he will be **g** to see you.
Jos 22:33 They were **g** to hear the report
Jdg 8:25 "We'll be **g** to give them."
1Sa 19: 5 Israel, and you saw it and were **g**.
2Sa 1:20 the daughters of the Philistines be **g**,
1Ki 8:66 **g** in heart for all the good things
1Ch 16:31 heavens rejoice, let the earth be **g**;

2Ch 7:10 **g** in heart for the good things
Ps   5:11 let all who take refuge in you be **g**;
      9: 2 I will be **g** and rejoice in you;
     14: 7 let Jacob rejoice and Israel be **g**!
     16: 9 Therefore my heart is **g** and my
     21: 6 and made him **g** with the joy of your
     31: 7 I will be **g** and rejoice in your love,
     32:11 Rejoice in the LORD and be **g**,
     40:16 seek you rejoice and be **g** in you;
     45: 8 music of the strings makes you **g**.
     46: 4 river whose streams make **g** the city
     48:11 of Judah are **g** because of your
     53: 6 let Jacob rejoice and Israel be **g**!
     58:10 The righteous will be **g** when they
     67: 4 May the nations be **g** and sing
     68: 3 may the righteous be **g** and rejoice
     69:32 The poor will see and be **g**—
     70: 4 seek you rejoice and be **g** in you;
     90:14 sing for joy and be **g** all our days.
     90:15 Make us **g** for as many days as you
     92: 4 For you make me **g** by your deeds,
     96:11 heavens rejoice, let the earth be **g**;
     97: 1 LORD reigns, let the earth be **g**;
     97: 8 of Judah are **g** because of your
    105:38 Egypt was **g** when they left,
    107:30 They were **g** when it grew calm,
    118:24 let us rejoice today and be **g**.
    149: 2 people of Zion be **g** in their King.
Pr 23:15 then my heart will be **g** indeed;
     29: 6 righteous shout for joy and are **g**.
Ecc 8:15 sun than to eat and drink and be **g**.
Isa 25: 9 rejoice and be **g** in his salvation."
     35: 1 and the parched land will be **g**;
     65:18 be **g** and rejoice forever in what I
     66:10 with Jerusalem and be **g** for her,
Jer 20:15 who made him very **g**, saying,
     31:13 young women will dance and be **g**,
     41:13 who were with him, they were **g**.
     50:11 "Because you rejoice and are **g**,
La   4:21 Rejoice and be **g**, Daughter Edom,
Joel 2:21 land of Judah; be **g** and rejoice.
      2:23 Be **g**, people of Zion,
Hab 1:15 and so he rejoices and is **g**.
Zep 3:14 Be **g** and rejoice with all your heart,
Zec 2:10 "Shout and be **g**, Daughter Zion.
      8:19 will become joyful and **g** occasions
     10: 7 their hearts will be **g** as with wine.
Mt   5:12 Rejoice and be **g**, because great is
Lk 15:32 But we had to celebrate and be **g**,
Jn   4:36 and the reaper may be **g** together.
      8:56 he saw it and was **g**."
     11:15 for your sake I am **g** I was not there,
     14:28 you would be **g** that I am going
Ac   2:26 Therefore my heart is **g** and my
      2:46 and ate together with **g** and sincere
     11:23 he was **g** and encouraged them all
     13:48 they were **g** and honored the word
     15: 3 news made all the believers very **g**.
     15:31 were **g** for its encouraging message.
1Co 16:17 I was **g** when Stephanas,
2Co 2: 2 who is left to make me **g** but you
      7:16 I am **g** I can have complete
     13: 9 We are **g** whenever we are weak

Gal   4:27 "Be **g**, barren woman, you who
Php   2:17 I am **g** and rejoice with all of you.
      2:18 So you too should be **g** and rejoice
      2:28 you see him again you may be **g**
Rev 19: 7 rejoice and be **g** and give him glory!

GLADDENS* GLAD
Ps 104:15 wine that **g** human hearts,

GLADNESS* GLAD
2Ch 29:30 So they sang praises with **g**
Est   8:16 of happiness and joy, **g** and honor.
      8:17 was joy and **g** among the Jews,
Job   3:22 who are filled with **g** and rejoice
Ps   35:27 my vindication shout for joy and **g**;
     45:15 Led in with joy and **g**, they enter
     51: 8 Let me hear joy and **g**; let the bones
     65:12 the hills are clothed with **g**.
    100: 2 Worship the LORD with **g**;
Ecc   5:20 God keeps them occupied with **g**
      9: 7 eat your food with **g**, and drink your
Isa 16:10 **g** are taken away from the orchards;
     35:10 **G** and joy will overtake them,
     51: 3 Joy and **g** will be found in her,
     51:11 **G** and joy will overtake them,
Jer   7:34 an end to the sounds of joy and **g**
     16: 9 an end to the sounds of joy and **g**
     25:10 from them the sounds of joy and **g**,
     31:13 I will turn their mourning into **g**;
     33:11 the sounds of joy and **g**, the voices
     48:33 and **g** are gone from the orchards
Joel 1:16 and **g** from the house of our God?

GLASS*
Rev   4: 6 was what looked like a sea of **g**,
     15: 2 what looked like a sea of **g** glowing
     21:18 the city of pure gold, as pure as **g**.
     21:21 of gold, as pure as transparent **g**.

GLEAM* GLEAMED
Da   10: 6 legs like the **g** of burnished bronze,

GLEAMED* GLEAM
Eze   1: 7 a calf and **g** like burnished bronze.
Lk   24: 4 **g** like lightning stood beside them.

GLEAN GLEANED, GLEANINGS
Ru   2: 3 began to **g** behind the harvesters.

GLEANED* GLEAN
Ru   2:17 So Ruth **g** in the field until evening.

GLEANINGS GLEAN
Lev 19: 9 field or gather the **g** of your harvest.

GLIDE* GLIDED, GLIDING
Dt   32:24 venom of vipers that **g** in the dust.

GLIDED* GLIDE
Job   4:15 A spirit **g** past my face, and the hair

GLIDING* GLIDE
Job 26:13 his hand pierced the **g** serpent.
Isa 27: 1 Leviathan the **g** serpent,

GLOAT GLOATS
Ps   22:17 people stare and **g** over me.

Ps   30: 1 did not let my enemies **g** over me.
Pr   24:17 Do not **g** when your enemy falls;
Isa 14: 8 the cedars of Lebanon **g** over you
La   2:17 he has let the enemy **g** over you,
Rev 11:10 of the earth will **g** over them

GLOATS* GLOAT
Pr   17: 5 whoever **g** over disaster will not go

GLOOM
Isa   9: 1 there will be no more **g** for those
Joel 2: 2 a day of darkness and **g**, a day
Zep   1:15 a day of darkness and **g**, a day
Heb 12:18 to darkness, **g** and storm;

GLORIES* GLORY
1Pe   1:11 and the **g** that would follow.

GLORIFIED* GLORY
Isa 66: 5 'Let the LORD be **g**, that we may
Da   4:34 and **g** him who lives forever.
Jn   7:39 since Jesus had not yet been **g**.
     11: 4 God's Son may be **g** through it."
     12:16 after Jesus was **g** did they realize
     12:23 come for the Son of Man to be **g**.
     12:28 "I have **g** it, and will glorify it
     13:31 "Now the Son of Man is **g** and God
            is **g** in him.
     13:32 If God is **g** in him, God will glorify
     14:13 that the Father may be **g** in the Son.
Ac   3:13 our fathers, has **g** his servant Jesus.
Ro   1:21 they neither **g** him as God nor gave
      8:30 those he justified, he also **g**.
2Th   1:10 he comes to be **g** in his holy people
      1:12 of our Lord Jesus may be **g** in you,
1Pe   1:21 raised him from the dead and **g** him,

GLORIFIES* GLORY
Lk   1:46 "My soul **g** the Lord
Jn   8:54 as your God, is the one who **g** me.

GLORIFY* GLORY
Ps   34: 3 **G** the LORD with me; let us exalt
     63: 3 better than life, my lips will **g** you.
     69:30 song and **g** him with thanksgiving.
     86:12 I will **g** your name forever.
Isa 60:13 and I will **g** the place for my feet.
Da   4:37 and exalt and **g** the King of heaven,
Mt   5:16 deeds and **g** your Father in heaven.
Jn   8:54 "If I **g** myself, my glory means
     12:28 Father, **g** your name!" Then a voice
     12:28 glorified it, and will **g** it again."
     13:32 God will **g** the Son in himself, and
            will **g** him at once.
     16:14 He will **g** me because it is from me
     17: 1 **G** your Son, that your Son may **g** you.
     17: 5 **g** me in your presence
     21:19 death by which Peter would **g** God.
Ro   15: 6 one voice you may **g** the God
     15: 9 the Gentiles might **g** God for his
1Pe   2:12 and **g** God on the day he visits us.
Rev 16: 9 they refused to repent and **g** him.

GLORIFYING* GLORY
Lk   2:20 **g** and praising God for all the things

GLORIOUS* GLORY

Dt   28:58 do not revere this **g** and awesome
       33:29 shield and helper and your **g** sword.
1Ch   29:13 you thanks, and praise your **g** name.
Ne   9: 5 "Blessed be your **g** name, and may
Ps   45:13 All **g** is the princess within her
       66: 2 of his name; make his praise **g**.
       72:19 Praise be to his **g** name forever;
       87: 3 **G** things are said of you,
      106:20 They exchanged their **g** God
      111: 3 **G** and majestic are his deeds,
      145: 5 They speak of the **g** splendor
      145:12 and the **g** splendor of your kingdom.
Pr   4: 9 and present you with a **g** crown."
Isa   3: 8 the LORD, defying his **g** presence.
        4: 2 the LORD will be beautiful and **g**,
       11:10 him, and his resting place will be **g**.
       12: 5 LORD, for he has done **g** things;
       28: 1 to the fading flower, his **g** beauty,
       28: 4 That fading flower, his **g** beauty,
       28: 5 Almighty will be a **g** crown,
       42:21 to make his law great and **g**.
       60: 7 altar, and I will adorn my **g** temple.
       63:12 who sent his **g** arm of power to be
       63:14 to make for yourself a **g** name.
       63:15 from your lofty throne, holy and **g**.
       64:11 Our holy and **g** temple, where our
Jer   2:11 people have exchanged their **g** God
       13:18 for your **g** crowns will fall
       14:21 do not dishonor your **g** throne.
       17:12 A **g** throne,
       48:17 scepter, how broken the **g** staff!'
Hos   4: 7 they exchanged their **g** God
Zec   2: 8 the **G** One has sent me against
Mt   19:28 the Son of Man sits on his **g** throne,
       25:31 with him, he will sit on his **g** throne.
Lk   9:30 Moses and Elijah, appeared in **g**
              splendor,
Ac   2:20 of the great and **g** day of the Lord.
2Co   3: 8 of the Spirit be even more **g**?
        3: 9 that brought condemnation was **g**,
              how much more **g** is the ministry
        3:10 For what was **g** has no glory now
Eph   1: 6 to the praise of his **g** grace,
        1:17 our Lord Jesus Christ, the **g** Father,
        1:18 the riches of his **g** inheritance in his
        3:16 his **g** riches he may strengthen you
Php   3:21 so that they will be like his **g** body.
Col   1:11 power according to his **g** might so
        1:27 among the Gentiles the **g** riches
Jas   2: 1 in our **g** Lord Jesus Christ must not
1Pe   1: 8 with an inexpressible and **g** joy,
Jude   1:24 you before his **g** presence without

GLORY GLORIES, GLORIFIED,
GLORIFIES, GLORIFY,
GLORIFYING, GLORIOUS

Ex   14: 4 But I will gain **g** for myself through
       14:17 I will gain **g** through Pharaoh
       14:18 when I gain **g** through Pharaoh,
       15:11 awesome in **g**, working wonders?
       16: 7 in the morning you will see the **g**
       16:10 and there was the **g** of the LORD

Ex   24:16 and the **g** of the LORD settled
       24:17 the Israelites the **g** of the LORD
       29:43 place will be consecrated by my **g**.
       33:18 said, "Now show me your **g**."
       33:22 When my **g** passes by, I will put
       40:34 and the **g** of the LORD filled
       40:35 it, and the **g** of the LORD filled
Lev   9: 6 the **g** of the LORD may appear
        9:23 the **g** of the LORD appeared to all
Nu   14:10 the **g** of the LORD appeared
       14:21 and as surely as the **g** of the LORD
       14:22 not one of those who saw my **g**
       16:19 the **g** of the LORD appeared
       16:42 it and the **g** of the LORD appeared.
       20: 6 and the **g** of the LORD appeared
Dt   5:24 LORD our God has shown us his **g**
Jos   7:19 "My son, give **g** to the LORD,
1Sa   4:21 "The **G** has departed from Israel"—
        6: 5 country, and give **g** to Israel's god.
       15:29 He who is the **G** of Israel does not
1Ki   8:11 for the **g** of the LORD filled his
1Ch   16:10 **G** in his holy name; let the hearts
       16:24 Declare his **g** among the nations,
       16:28 ascribe to the LORD **g**
       29:11 the power and the **g** and the majesty
2Ch   5:14 for the **g** of the LORD filled
        7: 1 and the **g** of the LORD filled
Ps   3: 3 my **g**, the One who lifts my head
        4: 2 How long will you people turn my **g**
        8: 1 You have set your **g** in the heavens.
        8: 5 crowned them with **g** and honor.
       19: 1 The heavens declare the **g** of God;
       24: 7 that the King of **g** may come in.
       26: 8 live, the place where your **g** dwells.
       29: 1 beings, ascribe to the LORD **g**
       29: 3 the God of **g** thunders, the LORD
       29: 9 And in his temple all cry, "**G**!"
       34: 2 I will **g** in the LORD;
       57: 5 let your **g** be over all the earth.
       63: 2 and beheld your power and your **g**.
       66: 2 Sing the **g** of his name;
       72:19 the whole earth be filled with his **g**.
       73:24 afterward you will take me into **g**.
       85: 9 that his **g** may dwell in our land.
       89:17 For you are their **g** and strength,
       96: 3 Declare his **g** among the nations,
       96: 6 strength and **g** are in his sanctuary.
       96: 8 to the LORD the **g** due his name;
       97: 6 and all peoples see his **g**.
      102:15 kings of the earth will revere your **g**.
      104:31 May the **g** of the LORD endure
      108: 5 let your **g** be over all the earth.
      138: 5 for the **g** of the LORD is great.
      149: 9 this is the **g** of all his faithful
Pr   19:11 is to one's **g** to overlook an offense.
       20:29 The **g** of young men is their
       25: 2 It is the **g** of God to conceal
       25: 2 search out a matter is the **g** of kings.
Isa   4: 5 over everything the **g** will be
        6: 3 the whole earth is full of his **g**."
       24:16 "**G** to the Righteous One."
       24:23 and before its elders—with great **g**.
       26:15 You have gained **g** for yourself;

Isa	35: 2	The **g** of Lebanon will be given
	35: 2	they will see the **g** of the Lord,
	40: 5	And the **g** of the Lord will be
	42: 8	I will not yield my **g** to another
	42:12	Let them give **g** to the Lord
	43: 7	whom I created for my **g**, whom I
	44:23	Jacob, he displays his **g** in Israel.
	48:11	I will not yield my **g** to another.
	60:19	light, and your God will be your **g**.
	66:18	and they will come and see my **g**.
	66:19	not heard of my fame or seen my **g**.
	66:19	They will proclaim my **g** among
Eze	1:28	the likeness of the **g** of the Lord.
	3:23	the **g** of the Lord was standing
	3:23	like the **g** I had seen by the Kebar
	8: 4	there before me was the **g**
	9: 3	Now the **g** of the God of Israel went
	10: 4	Then the **g** of the Lord rose
	10: 4	the radiance of the **g** of the Lord.
	10:18	the **g** of the Lord departed
	11:23	The **g** of the Lord went
	39:13	and the day I display my **g** will be
	43: 2	and I saw the **g** of the God of Israel
	43: 2	and the land was radiant with his **g**.
	43: 5	and the **g** of the Lord filled
	44: 4	saw the **g** of the Lord filling
Hab	2:14	of the **g** of the Lord as the waters
	3: 3	His **g** covered the heavens and his
Hag	2: 7	and I will fill this house with **g**,'
Zec	2: 5	Lord, 'and I will be its **g** within.'
Mt	16:27	in his Father's **g** with his angels,
	24:30	of heaven, with power and great **g**.
	25:31	the Son of Man comes in his **g**,
Mk	8:38	in his Father's **g** with the holy
	10:37	the other at your left in your **g**."
	13:26	in clouds with great power and **g**.
Lk	2: 9	and the **g** of the Lord shone around
	2:14	"**G** to God in the highest heaven,
	2:32	and the **g** of your people Israel."
	9:26	of them when he comes in his **g**
	9:26	and in the **g** of the Father
	9:32	they saw his **g** and the two men
	19:38	in heaven and **g** in the highest!"
	21:27	in a cloud with power and great **g**.
	24:26	these things and then enter his **g**?"
Jn	1:14	We have seen his **g**, the **g** of the one
	2:11	through which he revealed his **g**;
	5:41	"I do not accept **g** from human
	5:44	can you believe since you accept **g**
	5:44	do not seek the **g** that comes
	7:18	own does so to gain personal **g**,
	7:18	he who seeks the **g** of the one who
	8:50	I am not seeking **g** for myself;
	8:54	glorify myself, my **g** means nothing.
	11: 4	it is for God's **g** so that God's Son
	11:40	believe, you will see the **g** of God?"
	12:41	said this because he saw Jesus' **g**
	15: 8	This is to my Father's **g**, that you
	17: 4	I have brought you **g** on earth
	17: 5	your presence with the **g** I had
	17:10	**g** has come to me through them.
	17:22	I have given them the **g** that you
	17:24	and to see my **g**, the **g** you have

Ac	7: 2	The God of **g** appeared to our father
	7:55	up to heaven and saw the **g** of God,
Ro	1:23	exchanged the **g** of the immortal
	2: 7	by persistence in doing good seek **g**,
	2:10	but **g**, honor and peace for everyone
	3: 7	truthfulness and so increases his **g**,
	3:23	and fall short of the **g** of God,
	4:20	in his faith and gave **g** to God,
	5: 2	boast in the hope of the **g** of God.
	8:17	that we may also share in his **g**.
	8:18	with the **g** that will be revealed
	8:21	and **g** of the children of God.
	9: 4	theirs the divine **g**, the covenants,
	9:23	to make the riches of his **g** known
	9:23	he prepared in advance for **g**—
	11:36	To him be the **g** forever! Amen.
	15:17	Therefore I **g** in Christ Jesus in my
	16:27	wise God be **g** forever through Jesus
1Co	2: 7	for our **g** before time began.
	2: 8	not have crucified the Lord of **g**.
	10:31	you do, do it all for the **g** of God.
	11: 7	since he is the image and **g** of God;
		but woman is the **g** of man.
	11:15	if a woman has long hair, it is her **g**?
	15:43	is sown in dishonor, it is raised in **g**;
2Co	1:20	is spoken by us to the **g** of God.
	3: 7	came with **g**, so that the Israelites
	3: 7	the face of Moses because of its **g**,
	3:10	was glorious has no **g** now in
		comparison with the surpassing **g**.
	3:11	if what was transitory came with **g**,
		how much greater is the **g**
	3:18	faces contemplate the Lord's **g**,
	3:18	his image with ever-increasing **g**,
	4: 4	gospel that displays the **g** of Christ,
	4: 6	the knowledge of God's **g** displayed
	4:15	to overflow to the **g** of God.
	4:17	us an eternal **g** that far outweighs
Gal	1: 5	to whom be **g** for ever and ever.
Eph	1:12	might be for the praise of his **g**.
	1:14	to the praise of his **g**.
	3:13	for you, which are your **g**.
	3:21	to him be **g** in the church
Php	1:11	to the **g** and praise of God.
	2:11	is Lord, to the **g** of God the Father.
	3:19	and their **g** is in their shame.
	4:19	to the riches of his **g** in Christ Jesus.
	4:20	To our God and Father be **g** for ever
Col	1:27	is Christ in you, the hope of **g**.
	3: 4	you also will appear with him in **g**.
1Th	2:12	calls you into his kingdom and **g**.
	2:19	which we will **g** in the presence
	2:20	Indeed, you are our **g** and joy.
2Th	1: 9	the Lord and from the **g** of his might
	2:14	in the **g** of our Lord Jesus Christ.
1Ti	1:11	to the gospel concerning the **g**
	1:17	be honor and **g** for ever and ever.
	3:16	on in the world, was taken up in **g**.
2Ti	2:10	is in Christ Jesus, with eternal **g**.
	4:18	To him be **g** for ever and ever.
Titus	2:13	appearing of the **g** of our great God
Heb	1: 3	The Son is the radiance of God's **g**
	2: 7	you crowned them with **g** and honor

Heb   2: 9 now crowned with **g** and honor
      2:10 many sons and daughters to **g**,
      3: 6 and the hope in which we **g**.
      5: 5 on himself the **g** of becoming a high
      9: 5 the ark were the cherubim of the **G**,
     13:21 to whom be **g** for ever and ever.
1Pe   1: 7 **g** and honor when Jesus Christ is
      1:24 all their **g** is like the flowers
      4:11 To him be the **g** and the power
      4:13 be overjoyed when his **g** is revealed.
      4:14 for the Spirit of **g** and of God rests
      5: 1 I will share in the **g** to be revealed:
      5: 4 you will receive the crown of **g**
      5:10 called you to his eternal **g** in Christ,
2Pe   1: 3 of him who called us by his own **g**
      1:17 and **g** from God the Father
      1:17 came to him from the Majestic **G**,
      3:18 To him be **g** both now and forever!
Jude 1:25 to the only God our Savior be **g**,
Rev   1: 6 to him be **g** and power for ever
      4: 9 the living creatures give **g**,
      4:11 to receive **g** and honor and power,
      5:12 and honor and **g** and praise!"
      5:13 praise and honor and **g** and power,
      7:12 Praise and **g** and wisdom and thanks
     11:13 and gave **g** to the God of heaven.
     14: 7 "Fear God and give him **g**,
     15: 4 Lord, and bring **g** to your name?
     15: 8 filled with smoke from the **g** of God
     18: 7 grief as the **g** and luxury she gave
     19: 1 Salvation and **g** and power belong
     19: 7 rejoice and be glad and give him **g**!
     21:11 It shone with the **g** of God, and its
     21:23 for the **g** of God gives it light,
     21:26 The **g** and honor of the nations will

GLORY OF ... GOD Ps 19:1; Pr 25:2; Eze 8:4;
9:3; 10:19; 11:22; 43:2; Jn 11:40; Ac 7:55; Ro 3:23;
5:2; 1Co 10.31, 11:7; 2Co 1:20; 4:15; Php 2:11;
Titus 2:13; Rev 15:8; 21:11, 23

GLORY OF THE LORD† Ex 16:7, 10; 24:16,
17; 40:34, 35; Lev 9:6, 23; Nu 14:10, 21; 16:19,
42; 20:6; 1Ki 8:11; 2Ch 5:14; 7:1, 2, 3; Ps 104:31;
138:5; Isa 35:2; 40:5; 58:8; 60:1; Eze 1:28; 3:12, 23;
10:4, 4, 18; 11:23; 43:4, 5; 44:4; Hab 2:14

GLOWING

1Sa 16:12 He was **g** with health and had a fine
Eze   1:27 his waist up he looked like **g** metal,
      8: 2 appearance was as bright as **g** metal.
Rev   1:15 His feet were like bronze **g**
     15: 2 like a sea of glass **g** with fire and,

GLUTTON* GLUTTONS,
GLUTTONY

Dt   21:20 not obey us. He is a **g** and a drunkard."
Mt   11:19 say, 'Here is a **g** and a drunkard,
Lk   7:34 say, 'Here is a **g** and a drunkard,

GLUTTONS* GLUTTON

Pr   23:21 for drunkards and **g** become poor,
     28: 7 companion of **g** disgraces his father.
Titus 1:12 always liars, evil brutes, lazy **g**."

GLUTTONY* GLUTTON

Pr   23: 2 to your throat if you are given to **g**.

GNASH* GNASHED, GNASHING

Ps   37:12 righteous and **g** their teeth at them;
    112:10 they will **g** their teeth and waste
La   2:16 they scoff and **g** their teeth and say,

GNASHED* GNASH

Ps   35:16 they **g** their teeth at me.
Ac   7:54 furious and **g** their teeth at him.

GNASHING* GNASH

Mt   8:12 will be weeping and **g** of teeth."
     13:42 there will be weeping and **g** of teeth.
     13:50 there will be weeping and **g** of teeth.
     22:13 will be weeping and **g** of teeth.'
     24:51 there will be weeping and **g** of teeth.
     25:30 will be weeping and **g** of teeth.'
Lk   13:28 there, and **g** of teeth, when you see

GNAT* GNATS

Mt   23:24 You strain out a **g** but swallow

GNATS GNAT

Ex   8:16 of Egypt the dust will become **g**."
Ps   105:31 and **g** throughout their country.

GO GOES, GOING, GONE

Ge   4: 8 Abel, "Let's **g** out to the field."
      7: 1 then said to Noah, "**G** into the ark,
     11: 7 let us **g** down and confuse their
     12: 1 to Abram, "**G** from your country,
     13:17 **G**, walk through the length
     18:21 that I will **g** down and see if what
     46: 4 I will **g** down to Egypt with you,
Ex   3:10 So now, **g**. I am sending you
      3:19 will not let you **g** unless a mighty
      5: 1 'Let my people **g**, so that they may
     12:31 **G**, worship the LORD as you have
     13:15 stubbornly refused to let us **g**,
     32: 1 make us gods who will **g** before us.
     33: 3 **G** up to the land flowing with milk
     33: 3 But I will not **g** with you,
     34: 9 eyes, then let the Lord **g** with us.
Nu   13:30 and said, "We should **g** up and take
     14: 3 better for us to **g** back to Egypt?"
Dt   1:26 But you were unwilling to **g** up;
      4:40 so that it may **g** well with you
Jos   1: 9 will be with you wherever you **g**."
Ru   1:16 Where you **g** I will **g**, and where
Ps   30: 9 I am silenced, if I **g** down to the pit?
     42: 4 how I used to **g** to the house of God
    122: 1 to me, "Let us **g** to the house
    139: 7 Where can I **g** from your Spirit?
Pr   6: 6 **G** to the ant, you sluggard;
     22: 6 off on the way they should **g**,
     31:18 her lamp does not **g** out at night.
Ecc 12: 5 Then people **g** to their eternal home
Isa   2: 3 let us **g** up to the mountain
      2: 3 The law will **g** out from Zion,
     55:12 You will **g** out in joy and be led
Jer   7:23 you, that it may **g** well with you.
Eze   1:12 Wherever the spirit would **g**, they
             would **g**, without turning

Mic 4: 2 let us **g** up to the mountain
      4: 2 The law will **g** out from Zion,
Zec 14: 3 Then the LORD will **g**
Mal 4: 2 And you will **g** out and frolic like
Mt   5:41 If anyone forces you to **g** one mile, **g**
              with them two miles.
      6: 6 when you pray, **g** into your room,
   28:19 Therefore **g** and make disciples
Mk 10:25 for a camel to **g** through the eye
Lk   9:57 will follow you wherever you **g**."
Jn   6:68 him, "Lord, to whom shall we **g**?
    8:21 Where I **g**, you cannot come."
   14: 3 if I **g** and prepare a place for you,
Rev 22:14 and may **g** through the gates

GOADS

Ecc 12:11 The words of the wise are like **g**,
Ac 26:14 hard for you to kick against the **g**.'

GOAL

Lk 13:32 on the third day I will reach my **g**.'
2Co 5: 9 So we make it our **g** to please him,
Php 3:14 on toward the **g** to win the prize
1Ti 1: 5 The **g** of this command is love,

GOAT   GOATS, SCAPEGOAT

Ge 15: 9 "Bring me a heifer, a **g** and a ram,
   30:32 and every spotted or speckled **g**.
   37:31 slaughtered a **g** and dipped the robe
Ex 26: 7 "Make curtains of **g** hair
Lev 16: 9 shall bring the **g** whose lot falls
   16:22 The **g** will carry on itself all their
   17: 7 of their sacrifices to the **g** idols
Nu   7:16 one male **g** for a sin offering;
Isa 11: 6 the leopard will lie down with the **g**,
Da   8: 5 suddenly a **g** with a prominent horn
   8:21 The shaggy **g** is the king of Greece,

GOATS   GOAT

Lev 16: 5 to take two male **g** for a sin offering
Nu   7:17 five male **g** and five male lambs
Ps 50:13 of bulls or drink the blood of **g**?
Eze 34:17 another, and between rams and **g**.
Mt 25:32 separates the sheep from the **g**.
Heb 9:12 not enter by means of the blood of **g**
   10: 4 of bulls and **g** to take away sins.

GOBLET   GOBLETS

Isa 51:22 from that cup, the **g** of my wrath,

GOBLETS   GOBLET

1Ki 10:21 All King Solomon's **g** were gold,
Da   5: 2 silver **g** that Nebuchadnezzar his

GOD   GOD'S, GOD-BREATHED, GOD-FEARING, GOD-HATERS, GODDESS, GODLESS, GODLESSNESS, GODLINESS, GODLY, GODS

Ge   1: 1 the beginning **G** created the heavens
    1: 2 of **G** was hovering over the waters.
    1: 3 And **G** said, "Let there be light,"
    1: 7 So **G** made the vault and separated
    1: 9 And **G** said, "Let the water under
    1:11 Then **G** said, "Let the land produce

Ge   1:21 So **G** created the great creatures
    1:21 And **G** saw that it was good.
    1:22 **G** blessed them and said,
    1:25 **G** made the wild animals according
    1:25 And **G** saw that it was good.
    1:26 Then **G** said, "Let us make
    1:27 So **G** created mankind in his own
    1:27 in the image of **G** he created them;
    1:28 **G** blessed them and said to them,
    1:31 **G** saw all that he had made, and it
    2: 3 Then **G** blessed the seventh day
    2: 4 when the LORD **G** made the earth
    2: 7 the LORD **G** formed a man
    2: 8 Now the LORD **G** had planted
    2:16 the LORD **G** commanded the man,
    2:22 the LORD **G** made a woman
    3: 1 to the woman, "Did **G** really say,
    3: 5 "For **G** knows that when you eat
    3: 5 and you will be like **G**,
    3: 8 of the LORD **G** as he was walking
    3: 8 from the LORD **G** among the trees
    3: 9 the LORD **G** called to the man,
    3:13 the LORD **G** said to the woman,
    3:14 So the LORD **G** said
    3:21 The LORD **G** made garments
    3:23 So the LORD **G** banished him
    5: 1 When **G** created mankind, he made
              them in the likeness of **G**.
    5:24 Enoch walked faithfully with **G**;
    5:24 no more, because **G** took him away.
    6: 2 the sons of **G** saw that the daughters
    6: 9 and he walked faithfully with **G**.
    6:12 **G** saw how corrupt the earth had
    8: 1 But **G** remembered Noah and all
    9: 1 Then **G** blessed Noah and his sons,
    9: 6 image of **G** has **G** made mankind.
    9:16 the everlasting covenant between **G**
  14:18 He was priest of **G** Most High,
  14:19 be Abram by **G** Most High,
  16:13 "You are the **G** who sees me,"
  17: 1 to him and said, "I am **G** Almighty;
  17: 7 to be your **G** and the **G** of your
  19:29 So when **G** destroyed the cities
  21: 2 the very time **G** had promised him.
  21: 6 said, "**G** has brought me laughter,
  21:17 **G** heard the boy crying,
  21:17 the angel of **G** called to Hagar
  21:20 **G** was with the boy as he grew up.
  21:22 "**G** is with you in everything you
  21:33 name of the LORD, the Eternal **G**.
  22: 1 Some time later **G** tested Abraham.
  22: 8 "**G** himself will provide the lamb
  22:12 Now I know that you fear **G**,
  25:11 death, **G** blessed his son Isaac,
  26:24 and said, "I am the **G** of your father
  28:12 the angels of **G** were ascending
  28:17 is none other than the house of **G**;
  30: 2 "Am I in the place of **G**, who has
  31:13 I am the **G** of Bethel, where you
  31:42 If the **G** of my father, the **G**
  31:42 But **G** has seen my hardship
  31:50 that **G** is a witness between you
  32: 1 way, and the angels of **G** met him.

Ge 32:28 because you have struggled with G
     32:30 "It is because I saw G face to face,
     33:11 for G has been gracious to me and I
     35: 1 Then G said to Jacob,
     35: 1 and build an altar there to G,
     35: 5 the terror of G fell on the towns all
     35:10 G said to him, "Your name is
     35:11 And G said to him, "I am G
     41:38 one in whom is the spirit of G?"
     41:51 said, "It is because G has made me
     41:52 said, "It is because G has made me
     46: 2 G spoke to Israel in a vision at night
     48:15 the G who has been my shepherd all
     50:19 Am I in the place of G?
     50:20 me, but G intended it for good
     50:24 But G will surely come to your aid
Ex   1:17 feared G and did not do what
     2:24 G heard their groaning and he
     3: 4 G called to him from within
     3: 5 "Do not come any closer," G said.
     3: 6 "I am the G of your father,
             the G of Abraham, the G of Isaac
             and the G of Jacob."
     3: 6 because he was afraid to look at G.
     3:12 And G said, "I will be with you.
     3:14 G said to Moses, "I AM WHO I AM.
     3:18 LORD, the G of the Hebrews,
     3:18 sacrifices to the LORD our G.'
     4:27 he met Moses at the mountain of G
     6: 7 own people, and I will be your G.
     6: 7 know that I am the LORD your G,
     7: 1 I have made you like G to Pharaoh,
     8:10 is no one like the LORD our G.
     8:19 Pharaoh, "This is the finger of G."
     10:16 sinned against the LORD your G
     13:19 "G will surely come to your aid,
     14:19 Then the angel of G, who had been
     15: 2 He is my G, and I will praise him,
     15: 2 my father's G, and I will exalt him.
     16:12 that I am the LORD your G.' "
     17: 9 with the staff of G in my hands."
     18: 4 "My father's G was my helper;
     18: 5 camped near the mountain of G.
     19: 3 Then Moses went up to G,
     20: 1 And G spoke all these words:
     20: 2 "I am the LORD your G,
     20: 5 the LORD your G, am a jealous G,
     20: 7 the name of the LORD your G,
     20:10 is a sabbath to the LORD your G.
     20:12 the LORD your G is giving you.
     20:19 But do not have G speak to us or we
     20:20 G has come to test you,
     20:20 that the fear of G will be with you
     22:20 any g other than the LORD must
     22:28 "Do not blaspheme G or curse
     23:19 to the house of the LORD your G.
     24:10 and saw the G of Israel.
     31:18 stone inscribed by the finger of G.
     34: 6 the compassionate and gracious G,
     34:14 Do not worship any other g,
     34:14 name is Jealous, is a jealous G.
Lev   2:13 the covenant of your G out of your
     11:44 I am the LORD your G;

Lev 18:21 not profane the name of your G.
     19: 2 I, the LORD your G, am holy.
     20: 7 because I am the LORD your G.
     21: 6 They must be holy to their G
     21: 6 not profane the name of their G.
     22:33 you out of Egypt to be your G.
     26:12 walk among you and be your G,
Nu   15:40 and will be consecrated to your G.
     16:22 "O G, the G who gives breath to all
     22: 9 G came to Balaam and asked,
     22:18 the command of the LORD my G.
     22:38 I must speak only what G puts
     23:19 G is not human, that he should lie,
     25:13 was zealous for the honor of his G
     27:16 the G who gives breath to all living
Dt   1:17 anyone, for judgment belongs to G.
     1:21 LORD, the G of your ancestors,
     1:32 did not trust in the LORD your G,
     3:22 the LORD your G himself will
     3:24 For what g is there in heaven
     4: 7 way the LORD our G is near us
     4:24 the LORD your G is a consuming fire,
             a jealous G.
     4:29 there you seek the LORD your G,
     4:31 the LORD your G is a merciful G;
     4:39 day that the LORD is G in heaven
     5: 9 the LORD your G, am a jealous G,
     5:11 the name of the LORD your G,
     5:12 the LORD your G has commanded
     5:14 is a sabbath to the LORD your G.
     5:15 the LORD your G brought you
     5:15 the LORD your G has commanded
     5:16 the LORD your G is giving you.
     5:24 a person can live even if G speaks
     5:26 voice of the living G speaking
     6: 2 fear the LORD your G as long as
     6: 4 The LORD our G, the LORD is
     6: 5 Love the LORD your G with all
     6:13 Fear the LORD your G, serve him
     6:16 Do not put the LORD your G
     7: 6 people holy to the LORD your G.
     7: 6 The LORD your G has chosen you
     7: 9 that the LORD your G is G; he is the
             faithful G,
     7:12 the LORD your G will keep his
     7:19 The LORD your G will do
     7:21 you, is a great and awesome G.
     8: 5 the LORD your G disciplines you.
     8:11 do not forget the LORD your G,
     8:18 But remember the LORD your G,
     9:10 tablets inscribed by the finger of G.
     10:12 what does the LORD your G ask
     10:12 you but to fear the LORD your G,
     10:12 to serve the LORD your G with all
     10:14 To the LORD your G belong
     10:17 For the LORD your G is G of gods
     10:21 he is your G, who performed
     11: 1 Love the LORD your G and keep
     11:13 to love the LORD your G
     12:12 rejoice before the LORD your G—
     12:28 in the eyes of the LORD your G.
     13: 3 The LORD your G is testing you
     13: 4 It is the LORD your G you must

Dt   14: 1 the children of the LORD your G.
      14: 2 people holy to the LORD your G.
      15: 6 the LORD your G will bless you
      15:19 the LORD your G every firstborn
      16:11 rejoice before the LORD your G
      16:17 the LORD your G has blessed you.
      16:22 for these the LORD your G hates.
      18:13 before the LORD your G.
      18:15 The LORD your G will raise
      19: 9 to love the LORD your G
      22: 5 the LORD your G detests anyone
      23: 5 the LORD your G would not listen
      23: 5 the LORD your G loves you.
      23:14 the LORD your G moves
      23:21 make a vow to the LORD your G,
      25:16 the LORD your G detests anyone
      26: 5 declare before the LORD your G:
      27: 5 there an altar to the LORD your G,
      28: 1 you fully obey the LORD your G
      28:15 you do not obey the LORD your G
      29:13 he may be your G as he promised
      29:29 things belong to the LORD our G,
      30: 2 return to the LORD your G
      30: 4 the LORD your G will gather you
      30: 6 The LORD your G will circumcise
      30:16 today to love the LORD your G,
      30:16 the LORD your G will bless you
      30:20 you may love the LORD your G,
      31: 6 the LORD your G goes with you;
      32: 3 Oh, praise the greatness of our G!
      32: 4 A faithful G who does no wrong,
      32:18 you forgot the G who gave you
      32:39 There is no g besides me. I put
      33:27 The eternal G is your refuge,
Jos   1: 9 the LORD your G will be with you
       1:13 'The LORD your G will give you
      14: 8 the LORD my G wholeheartedly.
      14:14 the LORD, the G of Israel,
      22: 5 to love the LORD your G, to walk
      22:22 "The Mighty One, G, the LORD!
      22:34 that the LORD is G.
      23: 3 the LORD your G has done to all
      23: 3 was the LORD your G who fought
      23: 8 to hold fast to the LORD your G,
      23:11 careful to love the LORD your G.
      23:14 the LORD your G gave you has
      23:15 the LORD your G has promised
      23:15 the LORD your G has destroyed
      24:19 He is a holy G; he is a jealous G.
Jdg   1: 7 Now G has paid me back for what I
       5: 5 before the LORD, the G of Israel.
       6:20 The angel of G said to him,
       6:31 If Baal really is a g, he can defend
       8:33 They set up Baal-Berith as their g
      13: 6 told him, "A man of G came to me.
      13: 6 He looked like an angel of G,
      16:23 a great sacrifice to Dagon their g
      16:23 "Our g has delivered Samson,
      16:28 Please, G, strengthen me just once
      20:27 ark of the covenant of G was there,
Ru   1:16 be my people and your G my G.
1Sa   2: 2 there is no Rock like our G.
       2: 3 for the LORD is a G who knows,

1Sa   2:25 G may mediate for the offender;
       3: 3 The lamp of G had not yet gone out,
       4:11 The ark of G was captured,
       5:11 the ark of the g of Israel away;
      10: 9 Samuel, G changed Saul's heart,
      10:26 men whose hearts G had touched.
      11: 6 the Spirit of G came powerfully
      12:12 the LORD your G was your king.
      14:15 It was a panic sent by G.
      16:15 evil spirit from G is tormenting you.
      17:36 defied the armies of the living G.
      17:45 the G of the armies of Israel,
      17:46 will know that there is a G in Israel.
      19:23 the Spirit of G came even on him,
      23:16 and helped him find strength in G.
      28:15 me, and G has departed from me.
      30: 6 found strength in the LORD his G.
2Sa   6: 7 therefore G struck him down,
       6: 7 he died there beside the ark of G.
       7:22 and there is no G but you, as we
       7:23 one nation on earth that G went
       7:27 "LORD Almighty, G of Israel,
      14:14 But that is not what G desires;
      14:17 lord the king is like an angel of G
      21:14 G answered prayer in behalf
      22: 3 my G is my rock, in whom I take
      22:31 "As for G, his way is perfect:
      22:32 For who is G besides the LORD?
      22:32 And who is the Rock except our G?
      22:33 It is G who arms me with strength
      22:47 Exalted be my G, the Rock,
1Ki   2: 3 what the LORD your G requires;
       4:29 G gave Solomon wisdom and very
       5: 5 for the Name of the LORD my G,
       8:23 there is no G like you in heaven
       8:27 "But will G really dwell on earth?
       8:60 may know that the LORD is G
       8:61 committed to the LORD our G,
      10:24 to hear the wisdom G had put in his
      11: 4 fully devoted to the LORD his G,
      11:33 Chemosh the g of the Moabites,
      11:33 and Molek the g of the Ammonites,
      15:30 of the LORD, the G of Israel.
      18:21 If the LORD is G, follow him;
      18:21 but if Baal is G, follow him."
      18:24 you call on the name of your g,
      18:24 The g who answers by fire—he is G."
      18:36 today that you are G in Israel
      18:39 and cried, "The LORD—he is G!
      20:28 Arameans think the LORD is a g of the
              hills and not a g of the valleys,
2Ki   1: 2 consult Baal-Zebub, the g of Ekron,
       5:15 there is no G in all the world except
      17: 7 sinned against the LORD their G,
      19: 4 has sent to ridicule the living G,
      19:15 you alone are G over all
      19:19 LORD our G, deliver us from his
1Ch   12:18 you, for your G will help you."
      13: 2 if it is the will of the LORD our G,
      16:35 Cry out, "Save us, G our Savior;
      17:20 and there is no G but you, as we
      17:24 Almighty, the G over Israel,
      21: 8 Then David said to G, "I have

1Ch 21:15 And **G** sent an angel to destroy
22: 1 of the Lord **G** is to be here,
22:19 soul to seeking the Lord your **G**.
28: 2 for the footstool of our **G**, and I
28: 9 acknowledge the **G** of your father,
28:20 for the Lord **G**, my **G**,
29: 1 the one whom **G** has chosen,
29: 1 not for man but for the Lord **G**.
29: 2 provided for the temple of my **G**—
29:10 Lord, the **G** of our father Israel,
29:13 Now, our **G**, we give you thanks,
29:18 the **G** of our fathers Abraham,
2Ch 1: 7 That night **G** appeared to Solomon
2: 4 for the Name of the Lord my **G**
2: 4 festivals of the Lord our **G**.
2: 5 because our **G** is greater than all
5:14 the Lord filled the temple of **G**.
6:14 there is no **G** like you in heaven
6:18 will **G** really dwell on earth
10:15 for this turn of events was from **G**,
13:12 **G** is with us; he is our leader.
15: 3 time Israel was without the true **G**,
15:12 Lord, the **G** of their ancestors,
15:15 They sought **G** eagerly, and he was
18:13 can tell him only what my **G** says."
19: 3 have set your heart on seeking **G**."
19: 7 with the Lord our **G** there is no
20: 6 are you not the **G** who is in heaven?
20:20 Have faith in the Lord your **G**
25: 8 **G** will overthrow you before
25: 8 for **G** has the power to help
26: 5 He sought **G** during the days
26: 5 who instructed him in the fear of **G**.
26: 5 the Lord, **G** gave him success.
30: 9 for the Lord your **G** is gracious
30:19 who sets their heart on seeking **G**—
31:21 he sought his **G** and worked
32:15 much less will your **g** deliver you
32:17 so the **g** of Hezekiah will not rescue
32:31 **G** left him to test him and to know
33:12 the favor of the Lord his **G**
33:19 how **G** was moved by his entreaty,
34:33 in Israel serve the Lord their **G**.
Ezr 1: 3 of Israel, the **G** who is in Jerusalem,
1: 3 and may their **G** be with them.
2:68 of the house of **G** on its site.
6:16 of the house of **G** with joy.
7: 9 the gracious hand of his **G** was
7:18 accordance with the will of your **G**.
7:23 for the temple of the **G** of heaven.
8:22 "The gracious hand of our **G** is
8:31 The hand of our **G** was on us,
9: 6 my **G**, to lift up my face to you,
9: 9 our **G** has not forsaken us in our
9: 9 life to rebuild the house of our **G**
10: 3 let us make a covenant before our **G**
10: 3 who fear the commands of our **G**.
Ne 1: 5 "Lord, the **G** of heaven,
4:20 Our **G** will fight for us!"
5:15 for **G** I did not act like that.
7: 2 feared **G** more than most people do.
8: 8 from the Book of the Law of **G**,
8:18 from the Book of the Law of **G**.

Ne 9: 5 up and praise the Lord your **G**,
9:17 But you are a forgiving **G**,
9:31 you are a gracious and merciful **G**.
9:32 "Now therefore, our **G**, the great **G**,
10:29 **G** given through Moses the servant
of **G**
10:39 not neglect the house of our **G**."
12:43 rejoicing because **G** had given them
13: 2 (Our **G**, however, turned the curse
13:11 is the house of **G** neglected?"
13:26 He was loved by his **G**, and **G** made
him king
13:31 Remember me with favor, my **G**.
Job 1: 1 he feared **G** and shunned evil.
1: 9 "Does Job fear **G** for nothing?"
1:22 sin by charging **G** with wrongdoing.
2:10 Shall we accept good from **G**,
4:17 a mortal be more righteous than **G**?
5:17 is the one whom **G** corrects;
8: 3 Does **G** pervert justice?
8:20 "Surely **G** does not reject one who
9: 2 prove their innocence before **G**?
11: 7 you fathom the mysteries of **G**?
12:13 "To **G** belong wisdom and power;
16: 7 Surely, **G**, you have worn me out;
19:26 yet in my flesh I will see **G**;
20:29 Such is the fate **G** allots the wicked,
21:19 'G stores up the punishment
21:22 anyone teach knowledge to **G**,
22:12 "Is not **G** in the heights of heaven?
22:13 Yet you say, 'What does **G** know?
22:21 "Submit to **G** and be at peace
25: 2 "Dominion and awe belong to **G**;
25: 4 can a mortal be righteous before **G**?
26: 6 realm of the dead is naked before **G**;
30:20 "I cry out to you, **G**, but you do not
31: 6 let **G** weigh me in honest scales
31:14 will I do when **G** confronts me?
32:13 let **G**, not a man, refute him.'
33:14 For **G** does speak—now one way,
33:26 that person can pray to **G** and find
34:10 Far be it from **G** to do evil,
34:23 **G** has no need to examine people
34:33 Should **G** then reward you on your
36: 5 "G is mighty, but despises no one;
36:26 How great is **G**—
40: 2 him who accuses **G** answer him!"
Ps 5: 2 my King and my **G**, for to you I
5: 4 you are not a **G** who is pleased
7:10 My shield is **G** Most High,
7:11 **G** is a righteous judge, a **G** who
displays his wrath
10:14 But you, **G**, see the trouble
14: 5 for **G** is present in the company
18: 2 my **G** is my rock, in whom I take
18:21 am not guilty of turning from my **G**.
18:28 my **G** turns my darkness into light.
18:30 As for **G**, his way is perfect:
18:31 For who is **G** besides the Lord?
18:31 And who is the Rock except our **G**?
18:32 It is **G** who arms me with strength
18:46 Exalted be **G** my Savior!
19: 1 The heavens declare the glory of **G**;

Ps 22: 1 My **G**, my **G**, why have you
22:10 womb you have been my **G**.
27: 9 me or forsake me, **G** my Savior.
29: 3 the **G** of glory thunders, the LORD
31: 5 deliver me, LORD, my faithful **G**.
31:14 I say, "You are my **G**."
33:12 the nation whose **G** is the LORD,
35:23 Contend for me, my **G** and Lord.
37:31 The law of their **G** is in their hearts;
40: 3 mouth, a hymn of praise to our **G**.
40: 8 I desire to do your will, my **G**;
42: 1 so my soul pants for you, my **G**.
42: 2 My soul thirsts for **G**, for the living **G**.
42: 5 Put your hope in **G**, for I will yet
42: 8 a prayer to the **G** of my life.
42:11 praise him, my Savior and my **G**.
43: 4 Then I will go to the altar of **G**, to **G**,
        my joy and my delight.
44: 8 **G** we make our boast all day long,
45: 6 O **G**, will last for ever and ever;
45: 7 therefore **G**, your **G**, has set you
46: 1 **G** is our refuge and strength,
46: 5 **G** is within her, she will not fall;
46:10 "Be still, and know that I am **G**;
47: 1 shout to **G** with cries of joy.
47: 6 Sing praises to **G**, sing praises;
47: 7 For **G** is the King of all the earth;
48: 9 O **G**, we meditate on your unfailing
48:14 For this **G** is our **G** for ever
49: 7 or give to **G** a ransom for them—
50: 2 perfect in beauty, **G** shines forth.
50: 3 Our **G** comes and will not be silent;
51: 1 O **G**, according to your unfailing
51:10 O **G**, and renew a steadfast spirit
51:17 sacrifice, O **G**, is a broken spirit;
53: 2 **G** looks down from heaven on all
53: 2 who understand, any who seek **G**.
54: 4 Surely **G** is my help; the Lord is
55:19 **G**, who is enthroned from of old,
56: 4 In **G**, whose word I praise—
        in **G** I trust
56:11 in **G** I trust and am not afraid.
56:13 that I may walk before **G** in the light
57: 3 **G** sends forth his love and his
57: 7 My heart, O **G**, is steadfast,
59:17 **G**, are my fortress, my **G**
62: 1 Truly my soul finds rest in **G**;
62: 7 and my honor depend on **G**;
62: 8 hearts to him, for **G** is our refuge.
62:11 "Power belongs to you, **G**,
63: 1 You, **G**, are my **G**, earnestly I seek
65: 5 and righteous deeds, **G** our Savior,
66: 1 Shout for joy to **G**, all the earth!
66: 3 Say to **G**, "How awesome are your
66: 5 Come and see what **G** has done,
66:16 Come and hear, all you who fear **G**;
66:20 Praise be to **G**, who has not rejected
68: 4 Sing to **G**, sing in praise of his
68: 6 **G** sets the lonely in families,
68:20 Our **G** is a **G** who saves;
68:26 Praise **G** in the great congregation;
68:35 You, **G**, are awesome in your
68:35 the **G** of Israel gives power

Ps 69: 5 You, **G**, know my folly; my guilt is
70: 1 Hasten, O **G**, to save me;
70: 5 come quickly to me, O **G**.
71:17 Since my youth, **G**, you have taught
71:18 my **G**, till I declare your power
71:19 Who is like you, **G**?
71:22 harp for your faithfulness, my **G**;
73:17 till I entered the sanctuary of **G**;
73:26 but **G** is the strength of my heart
76:11 Make vows to the LORD your **G**
77:13 What **g** is as great as our **G**?
77:14 You are the **G** who performs
78:19 They spoke against **G**;
78:59 When **G** heard them, he was
79: 9 Help us, **G** our Savior, for the glory
81: 1 Sing for joy to **G** our strength;
82: 1 **G** presides in the great assembly;
84: 2 my flesh cry out for the living **G**.
84:10 the house of my **G** than dwell
84:11 For the LORD **G** is a sun
86:12 you, Lord my **G**, with all my heart;
86:15 are a compassionate and gracious **G**,
87: 3 things are said of you, city of **G**:
89: 7 of the holy ones **G** is greatly feared;
90: 2 everlasting to everlasting you are **G**.
91: 2 fortress, my **G**, in whom I trust."
94: 1 O **G** who avenges, shine forth.
94:22 and my **G** the rock in whom I take
95: 3 For the LORD is the great **G**,
95: 7 for he is our **G** and we are
99: 8 you were to Israel a forgiving **G**,
99: 9 Exalt the LORD our **G**
99: 9 for the LORD our **G** is holy.
100: 3 Know that the LORD is **G**. It is he
106:21 They forgot the **G** who saved them,
106:33 they rebelled against the Spirit of **G**,
108: 1 My heart, O **G**, is steadfast;
108: 5 Be exalted, O **G**, above the heavens;
113: 5 Who is like the LORD our **G**,
115: 3 Our **G** is in heaven;
116: 5 our **G** is full of compassion.
123: 2 our eyes look to the LORD our **G**,
136: 2 Give thanks to the **G** of gods.
136:26 Give thanks to the **G** of heaven.
139:17 to me are your thoughts, **G**!
139:23 Search me, **G**, and know my heart;
143:10 to do your will, for you are my **G**;
144: 2 He is my loving **G** and my fortress,
145: 1 I will exalt you, my **G** the King;
147: 1 good it is to sing praises to our **G**,
150: 1 Praise **G** in his sanctuary;
Pr 2: 5 and find the knowledge of **G**.
3: 4 a good name in the sight of **G**
14:31 is kind to the needy honors **G**.
25: 2 It is the glory of **G** to conceal
28:14 one who always trembles before **G**,
30: 5 "Every word of **G** is flawless;
Ecc 1:13 What a heavy burden **G** has laid
2:26 who pleases him, **G** gives wisdom,
3:11 no one can fathom what **G** has done
3:13 in all their toil—this is the gift of **G**.
3:14 that everything **G** does will endure
3:14 **G** does it so that people will fear

Ecc 5: 2 heart to utter anything before **G**.
5: 4 When you make a vow to **G**, do not
5:19 when **G** gives someone wealth
5:19 in their toil—this is a gift of **G**.
7:18 Whoever fears **G** will avoid all
8:12 go better with those who fear **G**,
11: 5 cannot understand the work of **G**,
12: 7 the spirit returns to **G** who gave it.
12:13 of the matter: Fear **G** and keep his
Isa 5:16 the holy **G** will be proved holy
7:11 "Ask the LORD your **G** for a sign,
9: 6 Mighty **G**, Everlasting Father,
12: 2 Surely **G** is my salvation; I will trust
17:10 You have forgotten **G** your Savior;
25: 9 they will say, "Surely this is our **G**;
28:11 strange tongues **G** will speak to this
29:23 will stand in awe of the **G** of Israel.
30:18 For the LORD is a **G** of justice.
35: 4 your **G** will come, he will come
37:16 "LORD Almighty, the **G** of Israel,
37:16 you alone are **G** over all
40: 1 comfort my people, says your **G**.
40: 3 in the desert a highway for our **G**.
40: 8 the word of our **G** endures forever."
40:18 whom, then, will you compare **G**?
40:28 The LORD is the everlasting **G**,
41:10 not be dismayed, for I am your **G**.
41:13 the LORD your **G** who takes hold
43:10 Before me no **g** was formed,
44: 6 apart from me there is no **G**.
44:15 he also fashions a **g** and worships it;
45:18 he who created the heavens, he is **G**;
48:17 "I am the LORD your **G**,
49: 4 and my reward is with my **G**."
52: 7 who say to Zion, "Your **G** reigns!"
52:12 the **G** of Israel will be your rear
53: 4 we considered him punished by **G**,
55: 7 and to our **G**, for he will freely
57:21 says my **G**, "for the wicked."
59: 2 have separated you from your **G**;
60:19 light, and your **G** will be your glory.
61: 2 and the day of vengeance of our **G**,
61:10 my soul rejoices in my **G**.
62: 5 so will your **G** rejoice over you.
Jer 3:23 in the LORD our **G** is the salvation
7:23 I will be your **G** and you will be my
10:10 But the LORD is the true **G**;
10:10 he is the living **G**, the eternal King.
10:12 But **G** made the earth by his power;
23:23 "Am I only a **G** nearby,"
23:23 LORD, "and not a **G** far away?
23:36 distort the words of the living **G**,
31:33 I will be their **G**, and they will be
32:27 the LORD, the **G** of all mankind.
42: 6 we will obey the LORD our **G**,
42:13 and so disobey the LORD your **G**,
51:10 what the LORD our **G** has done.'
51:56 the LORD is a **G** of retribution;
Eze 1: 1 were opened and I saw visions of **G**.
11:20 be my people, and I will be their **G**.
28: 2 of your heart you say, "I am a **g**;
28: 2 you are a mere mortal and not a **g**,
28:13 You were in Eden, the garden of **G**;

Eze 34:31 and I am your **G**,
43: 2 the glory of the **G** of Israel coming
Da 2:19 Daniel praised the **G** of heaven
2:28 there is a **G** in heaven who reveals
3:17 the **G** we serve is able to deliver us
3:29 for no other **g** can save in this
6:12 days anyone who prays to any **g**
6:16 "May your **G**, whom you serve
9: 4 I prayed to the LORD my **G**
10:12 to humble yourself before your **G**,
11:32 who know their **G** will firmly resist
11:36 magnify himself above every **g**
11:36 things against the **G** of gods.
Hos 1: 9 not my people, and I am not your **G**.
1:10 be called 'children of the living **G**.'
4: 6 you have ignored the law of your **G**,
6: 6 of **G** rather than burnt offerings.
9: 8 and hostility in the house of his **G**.
12: 6 But you must return to your **G**;
13: 4 You shall acknowledge no **G**
Joel 2:13 Return to the LORD your **G**, for he
2:23 rejoice in the LORD your **G**, for he
Am 4:12 Israel, prepare to meet your **G**."
4:13 the LORD **G** Almighty is his
5:26 of your idols, the star of your **g**—
Jnh 1: 6 Get up and call on your **g**!
3: 5 The Ninevites believed **G**.
4: 2 are a gracious and compassionate **G**,
Mic 6: 8 and to walk humbly with your **G**.
7: 7 the LORD, I wait for **G** my Savior;
7:18 Who is a **G** like you, who pardons
Na 1: 2 is a jealous and avenging **G**;
Hab 1:11 whose own strength is their **g**."
3:18 I will be joyful in **G** my Savior.
Zep 3:17 The LORD your **G** is with you,
Hag 1:14 of the LORD Almighty, their **G**,
Zec 4: 7 shouts of '**G** bless it! **G** bless it!' "
12: 8 the house of David will be like **G**,
14: 5 Then the LORD my **G** will come,
Mal 2:10 Did not one **G** create us?
2:11 women who worship a foreign **g**.
3: 8 "Will a mere mortal rob **G**?
Mt 1:23 (which means "**G** with us").
4: 4 comes from the mouth of **G**.' "
4: 7 'Do not put the Lord your **G**
4:10 'Worship the Lord your **G**,
5: 8 pure in heart, for they will see **G**.
5: 9 for they will be called children of **G**.
6:24 You cannot serve both **G**
12:28 if it is by the Spirit of **G** that I drive
12:28 the kingdom of **G** has come
16:16 Messiah, the Son of the living **G**."
19: 6 Therefore what **G** has joined
19:26 but with **G** all things are possible."
22:21 Caesar's, and to **G** what is God's."
22:32 'I am the **G** of Abraham, the **G** of
Isaac, and the **G** of Jacob'?
22:32 He is not the **G** of the dead
22:37 " 'Love the Lord your **G** with all
27:40 the cross, if you are the Son of **G**!"
27:46 (which means "My **G**, my **G**,
27:54 "Surely he was the Son of **G**!"
Mk 1:24 who you are—the Holy One of **G**!"

Mk	2: 7	Who can forgive sins but **G** alone?"	Jn	8:47	belongs to **G** hears what **G** says.

Mk 2: 7 Who can forgive sins but **G** alone?"
7:13 Thus you nullify the word of **G**
10: 6 of creation **G** 'made them male
10: 9 Therefore what **G** has joined
10:18 "No one is good—except **G** alone.
10:24 hard it is to enter the kingdom of **G**!
10:27 is impossible, but not with **G**; all things are possible with **G**."
11:22 "Have faith in **G**," Jesus answered.
12:17 Caesar's and to **G** what is God's."
12:29 The Lord our **G**, the Lord is one.
12:30 Love the Lord your **G** with all your
15:34 (which means "My **G**, my **G**,
15:39 this man was the Son of **G**!"

Lk 1:19 I stand in the presence of **G**, and I
1:30 you have found favor with **G**.
1:35 be born will be called the Son of **G**.
1:37 For no word from **G** will ever fail."
1:47 my spirit rejoices in **G** my Savior,
2:14 "Glory to **G** in the highest heaven,
2:40 and the grace of **G** was on him.
2:52 and in favor with **G** and man.
3:38 Seth, the son of Adam, the son of **G**.
4: 3 "If you are the Son of **G**, tell this
4: 8 'Worship the Lord your **G** and serve
4:41 shouting, "You are the Son of **G**!"
5:21 Who can forgive sins but **G** alone?"
8:39 tell how much **G** has done for you."
10: 9 'The kingdom of **G** has come near
10:27 " 'Love the Lord your **G** with all
11:42 neglect justice and the love of **G**.
13:18 "What is the kingdom of **G** like?
18:13 but beat his breast and said, '**G**,
18:19 "No one is good—except **G** alone.
18:27 with man is possible with **G**."
20:25 Caesar's, and to **G** what is God's."
20:37 rise, for he calls the Lord 'the **G**
22:69 at the right hand of the mighty **G**."
22:70 "Are you then the Son of **G**?"

Jn 1: 1 and the Word was with **G**, and the Word was **G**.
1:12 the right to become children of **G**—
1:18 No one has ever seen **G**, but the one
1:18 who is himself **G** and is in closest
1:29 the Lamb of **G**, who takes away
1:49 "Rabbi, you are the Son of **G**;
3: 2 are a teacher who has come from **G**.
3: 2 signs you are doing if **G** were not
3:16 For **G** so loved the world that he
3:34 the one whom **G** has sent speaks the words of **G**,
3:34 for **G** gives the Spirit without limit.
4:24 **G** is spirit, and his worshipers must
5:18 even calling **G** his own Father, making himself equal with **G**.
5:44 glory that comes from the only **G**?
6:29 answered, "The work of **G** is this:
6:33 For the bread of **G** is the bread
6:69 that you are the Holy One of **G**."
7:17 do the will of **G** will find out whether my teaching comes from **G**
8:42 "If **G** were your Father, you would
8:42 not come on my own; **G** sent me.

Jn 8:47 belongs to **G** hears what **G** says.
11:40 you will see the glory of **G**?"
13: 3 that he had come from **G** and was returning to **G**;
13:31 glorified **G** and **G** is glorified in him.
14: 1 You believe in **G**;
17: 3 the only true **G**, and Jesus Christ,
20:17 Father, to my **G** and your **G**.' "
20:28 said to him, "My Lord and my **G**!"
20:31 the Son of **G**, and that by believing

Ac 1: 3 and spoke about the kingdom of **G**.
2:11 them declaring the wonders of **G**
2:22 was a man accredited by **G** to you
2:24 But **G** raised him from the dead,
2:33 Exalted to the right hand of **G**,
2:36 **G** has made this Jesus, whom you
3:15 life, but **G** raised him from the dead.
3:19 and turn to **G**, so that your sins may
4:31 and spoke the word of **G** boldly.
5: 4 lied to human beings but to **G**."
5:29 "We must obey **G** rather than
5:31 **G** exalted him to his own right hand
5:32 whom **G** has given to those who
5:39 find yourselves fighting against **G**."
6: 7 So the word of **G** spread.
7:55 to heaven and saw the glory of **G**,
7:55 standing at the right hand of **G**.
8:21 your heart is not right before **G**.
10:46 speaking in tongues and praising **G**.
11: 9 impure that **G** has made clean.'
12:24 the word of **G** continued to spread
13:32 What **G** promised our ancestors
14:22 to enter the kingdom of **G**,"
15:10 why do you try to test **G** by putting
17:23 UNKNOWN **G**. So you are ignorant
17:30 In the past **G** overlooked such
20:27 proclaim to you the whole will of **G**.
20:32 "Now I commit you to **G**
24:16 keep my conscience clear before **G**
28: 6 their minds and said he was a **g**.

Ro 1: 4 holiness was appointed the Son of **G**
1:16 because it is the power of **G**
1:17 the righteousness of **G** is revealed—
1:18 The wrath of **G** is being revealed
1:24 Therefore **G** gave them over
1:26 **G** gave them over to shameful lusts.
2:11 For **G** does not show favoritism.
2:16 **G** judges people's secrets through
3: 4 Let **G** be true, and every human
3:19 whole world held accountable to **G**.
3:23 and fall short of the glory of **G**,
3:29 Or is **G** the **G** of Jews only?
3:29 Is he not the **G** of Gentiles too?
4: 3 "Abraham believed **G**, and it was
4: 6 whom **G** credits righteousness apart
4:17 He is our father in the sight of **G**,
4:17 the **G** who gives life to the dead
4:24 whom **G** will credit righteousness—
5: 1 **G** through our Lord Jesus Christ,
5: 8 **G** demonstrates his own love for us
6:22 sin and have become slaves of **G**,
6:23 the gift of **G** is eternal life in Christ
7: 4 order that we might bear fruit for **G**.

Ro   8: 7 by the flesh is hostile to G;
     8: 8 realm of the flesh cannot please G.
     8:17 heirs of G and co-heirs with Christ,
     8:28 in all things G works for the good
     8:31 If G is for us, who can be against
     9:14 then shall we say? Is G unjust?
     9:18 Therefore G has mercy on whom he
     10: 9 in your heart that G raised him
     11: 2 G did not reject his people,
     11: 2 how he appealed to G against Israel:
     11:22 the kindness and sternness of G:
     11:32 For G has bound everyone over
     13: 1 except that which G has established.
     14:12 give an account of ourselves to G.
     16:20 The G of peace will soon crush
1Co 1:18 are being saved it is the power of G.
     1:20 Has not G made foolish the wisdom
     1:24 Christ the power of G and the
            wisdom of G.
     1:25 of G is wiser than human wisdom,
     1:25 G is stronger than human strength.
     1:27 G chose the foolish things
     1:27 G chose the weak things
     2: 9 the things G has prepared for those
     2:11 the thoughts of G except the Spirit
            of G.
     3: 6 it, but G has been making it grow.
     3:17 temple, G will destroy that person;
     6:20 Therefore honor G with your
     7: 7 of you has your own gift from G;
     7:15 G has called us to live in peace.
     7:20 they were in when G called them.
     7:24 as responsible to G, should remain
     7:24 they were in when G called them.
     8: 3 whoever loves G is known by G.
     8: 8 food does not bring us near to G;
     10:13 And G is faithful; he will not let you
     10:31 you do, do it all for the glory of G.
     12:24 But G has put the body together,
     14:25 they will fall down and worship G,
     14:25 "G is really among you!"
     14:33 For G is not a G of disorder
     15:24 over the kingdom to G the Father
     15:28 him, so that G may be all in all.
     15:34 are some who are ignorant of G—
     15:57 But thanks be to G! He gives us
2Co 1: 9 not rely on ourselves but on G,
     2:14 But thanks be to G, who always
     2:15 we are to G the pleasing aroma
     2:17 we do not peddle the word of G
     2:17 in Christ we speak before G with
            sincerity, as those sent from G.
     3: 5 but our competence comes from G.
     4: 2 nor do we distort the word of G.
     4: 4 The g of this age has blinded
     4: 4 of Christ, who is the image of G.
     4: 7 this all-surpassing power is from G
     5: 5 us for this very purpose is G,
     5:19 that G was reconciling the world
     5:20 as though G were making his appeal
     5:20 Be reconciled to G.
     5:21 G made him who had no sin to be
     5:21 become the righteousness of G.

2Co 6:16 we are the temple of the living G.
     6:16 and I will be their G, and they will
     9: 7 for G loves a cheerful giver.
     9: 8 G is able to bless you abundantly,
     10:13 of service G himself has assigned
Gal 2: 6 G does not show favoritism—
     3: 5 does G give you his Spirit and work
     3: 6 So also Abraham "believed G,
     3:11 on the law is justified before G,
     3:26 are all children of G through faith,
     4: 4 time had fully come, G sent his Son,
     6: 7 G cannot be mocked.
     6:16 follow this rule—to the Israel of G.
Eph 1:22 G placed all things under his feet
     2: 8 from yourselves, it is the gift of G—
     2:10 which G prepared in advance for us
     2:22 in which G lives by his Spirit.
     4: 6 one G and Father of all, who is over
     4:24 to be like G in true righteousness
     6: 6 doing the will of G from your heart.
Php 2: 6 being in very nature G, did not
            consider equality with G something
     2: 9 Therefore G exalted him
     2:13 for it is G who works in you to will
     3:14 which G has called me heavenward
     3:19 destruction, their g is their stomach,
     4: 7 And the peace of G,
     4:19 And my G will meet all your needs
Col 1:19 For G was pleased to have all his
     2:13 flesh, G made you alive with Christ.
     3: 1 is, seated at the right hand of G.
1Th 2: 4 we speak as those approved by G
     2: 4 not trying to please people but G,
     2:13 when you received the word of G,
     3: 9 How can we thank G enough
     4: 1 how to live in order to please G,
     4: 7 For G did not call us to be impure,
     4: 9 yourselves have been taught by G
     5: 9 For G did not appoint us to suffer
2Th 1: 8 punish those who do not know G
1Ti 1:17 the only G, be honor and glory
     2: 5 For there is one G and one mediator
            between G
     4: 4 For everything G created is good,
     5: 4 for this is pleasing to G.
2Ti 1: 6 you to fan into flame the gift of G,
Titus 1: 2 life, which G, who does not lie,
     2:13 of the glory of our great G
Heb 1: 1 In the past G spoke to our ancestors
     3: 4 but G is the builder of everything.
     4: 4 the seventh day G rested from all
     4:12 For the word of G is alive
     5: 5 But G said to him, "You are my
     6:10 G is not unjust; he will not forget
     6:18 G did this so that, by two
     6:18 which it is impossible for G to lie,
     7:19 by which we draw near to G.
     7:25 those who come to G through him,
     10: 7 come to do your will, my G.' "
     10:22 let us draw near to G with a sincere
     10:31 to fall into the hands of the living G.
     11: 5 because G had taken him away."
     11: 5 commended as one who pleased G.

Heb 11: 6 faith it is impossible to please **G**,
11:16 Therefore **G** is not ashamed to be called their **G**,
12: 7 **G** is treating you as his children.
12:10 but **G** disciplines us for our good,
12:29 for our "**G** is a consuming fire."
13:15 us continually offer to **G** a sacrifice

Jas 1:13 should say, "**G** is tempting me."
1:13 For **G** cannot be tempted by evil,
1:27 that **G** our Father accepts as pure
2:19 You believe that there is one **G**.
2:23 "Abraham believed **G**, and it was
4: 4 the world means enmity against **G**?
4: 6 "**G** opposes the proud but shows
4: 8 Come near to **G** and he will come

1Pe 1:21 Through him you believe in **G**,
1:21 and so your faith and hope are in **G**.
1:23 the living and enduring word of **G**.
2: 4 chosen by **G** and precious to him—
2:10 but now you are the people of **G**;
2:20 it, this is commendable before **G**.
3:18 the unrighteous, to bring you to **G**.
4: 2 desires, but rather for the will of **G**.
4:11 who speaks the very words of **G**.
4:11 do so with the strength **G** provides,
4:17 who do not obey the gospel of **G**?
5: 5 "**G** opposes the proud but shows

2Pe 1:21 from **G** as they were carried along
2: 4 if **G** did not spare angels when they

1Jn 1: 5 him and declare to you: **G** is light;
2: 5 love for **G** is truly made complete
2:14 and the word of **G** lives in you,
2:17 does the will of **G** lives forever.
3: 1 we should be called children of **G**!
3: 9 one who is born of **G** will continue
3: 9 because they have been born of **G**.
3:10 we know who the children of **G** are
3:17 how can the love of **G** be
3:20 that **G** is greater than our hearts,
4: 2 you can recognize the Spirit of **G**:
4: 2 has come in the flesh is from **G**,
4: 7 one another, for love comes from **G**.
4: 7 who loves has been born of **G** and knows **G**.
4: 8 does not love does not know **G**, because **G** is love.
4: 9 This is how **G** showed his love
4:11 Dear friends, since **G** so loved us,
4:12 No one has ever seen **G**; but if we
4:12 **G** lives in us and his love is made
4:15 that Jesus is the Son of **G**, **G** lives in them and they in **G**.
4:16 and rely on the love **G** has for us.
4:16 Whoever lives in love lives in **G**, and **G** in them.
4:20 claims to love **G** yet hates a brother
4:20 cannot love **G**, whom they have not
5: 2 that we love the children of **G**: by loving **G** and carrying out his
5: 3 In fact, this is love for **G**:
5: 4 born of **G** overcomes the world.
5:10 the Son of **G** accepts this testimony.
5:10 believed the testimony **G** has given

1Jn 5:11 **G** has given us eternal life, and this
5:14 we have in approaching **G**:
5:18 anyone born of **G** does not continue
5:18 who was born of **G** keeps them safe,

2Jn 1: 9 teaching of Christ does not have **G**;

3Jn 1:11 who does what is good is from **G**.
1:11 does what is evil has not seen **G**.

Jude 1: 4 the grace of our **G** into a license

Rev 2:18 are the words of the Son of **G**,
3: 1 who holds the seven spirits of **G**
4: 5 These are the seven spirits of **G**.
4: 8 holy is the Lord **G** Almighty,'
6: 9 been slain because of the word of **G**
7: 2 east, having the seal of the living **G**.
7:10 "Salvation belongs to our **G**,
7:12 strength be to our **G** for ever
7:17 **G** will wipe away every tear
11:16 seated on their thrones before **G**,
11:16 fell on their faces and worshiped **G**,
12: 5 her child was snatched up to **G**
13: 6 It opened its mouth to blaspheme **G**,
14: 7 voice, "Fear **G** and give him glory,
15: 3 are your deeds, Lord **G** Almighty.
15: 7 bowls filled with the wrath of **G**,
16:14 on the great day of **G** Almighty.
17:17 For **G** has put it into their hearts
18:20 Rejoice, you people of **G**!
18:20 For **G** has judged her
19: 1 glory and power belong to our **G**,
19: 6 For our Lord **G** Almighty reigns.
19: 9 "These are the true words of **G**."
19:13 and his name is the Word of **G**.
21: 3 and **G** himself will be with them and be their **G**.
21:11 It shone with the glory of **G**, and its
21:23 for the glory of **G** gives it light,
22: 5 for the Lord **G** will give them light.

ANGEL OF GOD See ANGEL

ARK OF GOD See ARK

FEAR GOD See FEAR

FEAR OF GOD See FEAR

GLORY OF ... GOD See GLORY

GOD AND FATHER Ro 15:6; 2Co 1:3; 11:31; Gal 1:4; Eph 1:3; 4:6; Php 4:20; 1Th 1:3; 3:11, 13; 1Pe 1:3; Rev 1:6

GOD OF ABRAHAM Ge 31:42, 53; Ex 3:6, 15, 16; 4:5; 1Ki 18:36; 2Ch 30:6; Ps 47:9; Mt 22:32; Mk 12:26; Lk 20:37; Ac 3:13; 7:32

GOD OF ... ANCESTORS Dt 1:11, 21; 4:1; 6:3; 12:1; 26:7; 27:3; 29:25; Jos 18:3; Jdg 2:12; 2Ki 21:22; 1Ch 5:25; 12:17; 2Ch 7:22; 11:16; 13:12, 18; 14:4; 15:12; 19:4; 20:6, 33; 21:10; 24:18, 24; 28:6, 9, 25; 29:5; 30:7, 19, 22; 33:12; 34:32, 33; 36:15; Ezr 7:27; 8:28; 10:11; Da 2:23; Ac 5:30; 22:14; 24:14

GOD OF HEAVEN Ge 24:3, 7; 2Ch 36:23; Ezr 1:2; 5:11, 12; 6:9, 10; 7:12, 21, 23, 23; Ne 1:4, 5; 2:4, 20; Ps 136:26; Da 2:18, 19, 37, 44; Jnh 1:9; Rev 11:13; 16:11

GOD OF ISRAEL Ex 5:1; 24:10; 32:27; 34:23; Nu 16:9; Jos 7:13, 19, 20; 8:30; 9:18, 19; 10:40, 42;

13:14, 33; 14:14; 22:16, 24; 24:2, 23; Jdg 4:6; 5:3,
5; 6:8; 11:21, 23; 21:3; Ru 2:12; 1Sa 1:17; 2:30; 5:7,
8, 8, 8, 10, 11; 6:3; 10:18; 14:41; 20:12; 23:10, 11;
25:32, 34; 2Sa 7:27; 12:7; 23:3; 1Ki 1:30, 48; 8:15,
17, 20, 23, 25, 26; 11:9, 31; 14:7, 13; 15:30; 16:13,
26, 33; 17:1, 14; 22:53; 2Ki 9:6; 10:31; 14:25; 18:5;
19:15, 20; 21:12; 22:15, 18; 1Ch 4:10; 5:26; 15:12,
14; 16:4, 36; 22:6; 23:25; 24:19; 28:4; 2Ch 2:12; 6:4,
7, 10, 14, 16, 17; 11:16; 13:5; 15:4, 13; 20:19; 29:7,
10; 30:1, 5; 32:17; 33:16, 18; 34:23, 26; 36:13; Ezr
1:3; 3:2; 4:1, 3; 5:1; 6:14, 21, 22; 7:6, 15; 8:35; 9:4,
15; Ps 41:13; 59:5; 68:8, 35; 69:6; 72:18; 106:48; Isa
17:6; 21:10, 17; 24:15; 29:23; 37:16, 21; 41:17; 45:3;
48:1, 2; 52:12; Jer 7:3, 21; 9:15; 11:3; 13:12; 16:9;
19:3, 15; 21:4; 23:2; 24:5; 25:15, 27; 27:4, 21; 28:2,
14; 29:4, 8, 21, 25; 30:2; 31:23; 32:14, 15, 36; 33:4;
34:2, 13; 35:13, 17, 18, 19; 37:7; 38:17; 39:16; 42:9,
15, 18; 43:10; 44:2, 7, 11, 25; 45:2; 46:25; 48:1;
50:18; 51:33; Eze 8:4; 9:3; 10:19, 20; 11:22; 43:2;
44:2; Zep 2:9; Mal 2:16; Mt 15:31; Lk 1:68

GOD OF JACOB Ex 3:6, 15; 4:5; 2Sa 23:1; Ps
20:1; 24:6; 46:7, 11; 75:9; 76:6; 81:1, 4; 84:8; 94:7;
114:7; 146:5; Isa 2:3; Mic 4:2; Mt 22:32; Mk 12:26;
Lk 20:37; Ac 7:46

GOD OF ... FATHER Ge 26:24; 28:13; 31:5,
29, 42, 53; 32:9, 9; 43:23; 46:1, 3; 50:17; Ex 3:6;
2Ki 20:5; 1Ch 28:9; 29:10; 2Ch 17:4; 21:12; 34:3;
Isa 38:5

GOD OF ... FATHERS Ex 3:13, 15, 16; 4:5;
1Ch 29:18, 20; Ac 3:13; 7:32

GOD THE FATHER Jn 6:27; 1Co 8:6; 15:24;
Gal 1:1; Eph 5:20; 6:23; Php 2:11; Col 1:3; 3:17;
1Th 1:1; 2Th 1:2; 1Ti 1:2; 2Ti 1:2; Titus 1:4; 1Pe
1:2; 2Pe 1:17; 2Jn 1:3; Jude 1:1

GRACE OF ... GOD See GRACE

HAND OF GOD See HAND

HOUSE OF ... GOD See HOUSE

KINGDOM OF GOD See KINGDOM

LIVING GOD Dt 5:26; Jos 3:10; 1Sa 17:26, 36;
2Ki 19:4, 16; Ps 42:2; 84:2; Isa 37:4, 17; Jer 10:10;
23:36; Da 6:20, 26; Hos 1:10; Mt 16:16; 26:63; Ac
14:15; Ro 9:26; 2Co 3:3; 6:16; 1Ti 3:15; 4:10; Heb
3:12; 9:14; 10:31; 12:22; Rev 7:2

LORD† GOD Ge 2:4, 5, 7, 8, 9, 15, 16, 18, 19,
21, 22; 3:1, 8, 8, 9, 13, 14, 21, 22, 23; 14:22; 24:12,
42; Ex 9:30; Jdg 21:3; 1Sa 23:10, 11; 2Sa 5:10; 7:25;
1Ki 19:10, 14; 1Ch 17:16, 17; 22:1, 19; 28:20; 29:1;
2Ch 1:9; 6:41, 41, 42; 26:5, 18; 32:16; Ne 9:7; Ps
59:5; 68:18; 72:18; 80:4, 19; 84:8, 11; 89:8; Jer 5:14;
15:16; 35:17; 38:17; 44:7; Hos 12:5; Am 3:13; 4:13;
5:14, 15, 16; 6:8, 14

LORD GOD Da 9:3; Lk 1:32; Rev 1:8; 4:8;
11:17; 15:3; 16:7; 18:8; 19:6; 21:22; 22:5

LORD† GOD ALMIGHTY 2Sa 5:10; 1Ki
19:10, 14; Ps 59:5; 80:4, 19; 84:8; 89:8; Jer 5:14;
15:16; 35:17; 38:17; 44:7; Hos 12:5; Am 3:13; 4:13;
5:14, 15, 16; 6:8, 14

**LORD† HIS/MY/OUR/THEIR/YOUR
GOD** See LORD†

MAN OF GOD See MAN

SON OF GOD See SON

SPIRIT OF GOD See SPIRIT

TEMPLE OF ... GOD See TEMPLE

WORD OF GOD See WORD

GOD'S GOD

Ge	6:11	the earth was corrupt in G sight
Dt	21:23	is hung on a pole is under G curse.
2Ch	20:15	For the battle is not yours, but G.
	36:19	They set fire to G temple and broke
Job	15: 8	Do you listen in on G council?
	33: 6	I am the same as you in G sight;
	37:14	stop and consider G wonders.
Ps	52: 8	I trust in G unfailing love for ever
	69:30	I will praise G name in song
Ecc	9: 1	and what they do are in G hands,
Mk	3:35	Whoever does G will is my brother
Lk	3: 6	all people will see G salvation.' "
	9:20	Peter answered, "G Messiah."
	20:25	is Caesar's, and to God what is G."
Jn	10:36	because I said, 'I am G Son'?
Ro	2: 3	think you will escape G judgment?
	2: 4	realizing that G kindness is intended
	3: 3	nullify G faithfulness?
	5: 5	because G love has been poured
	7:22	my inner being I delight in G law;
	8:16	our spirit that we are G children.
	9: 6	is not as though G word had failed.
	9:16	desire or effort, but on G mercy.
	11:29	for G gifts and his call are
	12: 2	to test and approve what G will is
	13: 6	for the authorities are G servants,
1Co	2: 7	we declare G wisdom, a mystery
	3: 9	For we are co-workers in G service;
	3: 9	you are G field, G building.
	3:16	that you yourselves are G temple
	3:16	that G Spirit dwells in your midst?
	7:19	Keeping G commands is what
	9:21	(though I am not free from G law
2Co	6: 2	now is the time of G favor, now is
Eph	1: 7	with the riches of G grace
	2:10	For we are G handiwork,
	5: 1	Follow G example, therefore,
1Th	4: 3	It is G will that you should be
	5:18	for this is G will for you in Christ
1Ti	6: 1	so that G name and our teaching
2Ti	2: 9	But G word is not chained.
	2:19	G solid foundation stands firm,
Titus	1: 7	an overseer manages G household,
Heb	1: 3	The Son is the radiance of G glory
	3: 6	is faithful as the Son over G house.
	9:24	now to appear for us in G presence.
	11: 3	was formed at G command,
Jas	2:23	and he was called G friend.
1Pe	2:15	For it is G will that by doing good
	3: 4	which is of great worth in G sight.
2Pe	3: 5	ago by G word the heavens came
1Jn	5: 9	G testimony is greater because it is
Rev	3:14	true witness, the ruler of G creation.
	11:19	G temple in heaven was opened,
	14:10	will drink the wine of G fury,

Rev 14:19 into the great winepress of **G** wrath.
   16: 1 the seven bowls of **G** wrath
   22:21 of the Lord Jesus be with **G** people.

GOD-BREATHED* BREATH, GOD
2Ti 3:16 All Scripture is **G** and is useful

GOD-FEARING* FEAR, GOD
Ac 2: 5 were staying in Jerusalem **G** Jews
   10: 2 all his family were devout and **G**;
   10:22 He is a righteous and **G** man, who is
   13:26 of Abraham and you **G** Gentiles,
   13:50 Jewish leaders incited the **G** women
   17: 4 as did a large number of **G** Greeks
   17:17 with both Jews and **G** Greeks,

GOD-HATERS* GOD, HATE
Ro 1:30 slanderers, **G**, insolent,

GODDESS GOD
1Ki 11: 5 He followed Ashtoreth the **g**
Ac 19:27 of the great **g** Artemis will be
   19:27 and the **g** herself, who is worshiped

GODHEAD (KJV) See DEITY, DIVINE

GODLESS GOD
Job 20: 5 the joy of the **g** lasts but a moment.
Pr 11: 9 their mouths the **g** destroy their
Jer 23:11 "Both prophet and priest are **g**;
1Ti 4: 7 Have nothing to do with **g** myths
   6:20 Turn away from **g** chatter
2Ti 2:16 Avoid **g** chatter, because those who
Heb 12:16 or is **g** like Esau, who for a single

GODLESSNESS* GOD
Ro 1:18 from heaven against all the **g**
   11:26 he will turn **g** away from Jacob.

GODLINESS* GOD
Ac 3:12 or **g** we had made this man walk?
1Ti 2: 2 and quiet lives in all **g** and holiness.
   3:16 from which true **g** springs is great:
   4: 8 value, but **g** has value for all things,
   6: 5 and who think that **g** is a means
   6: 6 **g** with contentment is great gain.
   6:11 and pursue righteousness, **g**, faith,
2Ti 3: 5 having a form of **g** but denying its
Titus 1: 1 of the truth that leads to **g**—
2Pe 1: 6 and to perseverance, **g**;
   1: 7 and to **g**, mutual affection;

GODLY* GOD
Mal 2:15 does the one God seek? **G** offspring.
Jn 9:31 to the **g** person who does his will.
Ac 8: 2 **G** men buried Stephen and mourned
2Co 1:12 you, with integrity and **g** sincerity.
   7:10 **G** sorrow brings repentance
   7:11 See what this **g** sorrow has
   11: 2 jealous for you with a **g** jealousy.
1Ti 4: 7 rather, train yourself to be **g**.
   6: 3 Lord Jesus Christ and to **g** teaching,
2Ti 3:12 live a **g** life in Christ Jesus will be
Titus 2:12 and **g** lives in this present age,
2Pe 1: 3 for a **g** life through our knowledge

2Pe 2: 9 how to rescue the **g** from trials
   3:11 You ought to live holy and **g** lives

GODS GOD
Ge 31:19 stole her father's household **g**.
   35: 4 Jacob all the foreign **g** they had
Ex 12:12 judgment on all the **g** of Egypt.
   15:11 Who among the **g** is like you,
   20: 3 shall have no other **g** before me.
   23:13 Do not invoke the names of other **g**;
   32: 4 they said, "These are your **g**, Israel,
Dt 5: 7 shall have no other **g** before me.
   7:25 The images of their **g** you are
   13: 2 us follow other **g**" (**g** you have not
   32:17 sacrificed to false **g**, which are not
Jos 24:14 Throw away the **g** your ancestors
Jdg 2:17 but prostituted themselves to other **g**
1Sa 17:43 the Philistine cursed David by his **g**.
1Ki 20:23 him, "Their **g** are **g** of the hills.
1Ch 16:26 For all the **g** of the nations are idols,
2Ch 2: 5 our God is greater than all other **g**.
Ps 82: 6 "I said, 'You are "**g**"'; you are all
   106:37 sons and their daughters to false **g**.
   135: 5 that our Lord is greater than all **g**.
Isa 45:20 who pray to **g** that cannot save.
Jer 2:11 Has a nation ever changed its **g**? (Yet
          they are not **g** at all.)
   10:11 'These **g**, who did not make
   16:20 Do people make their own **g**? Yes, but
          they are not **g**!"
Da 5: 4 they praised the **g** of gold and silver,
Hos 14: 3 We will never again say 'Our **g**'
Jn 10:34 Law, 'I have said you are "**g**"'?
Ac 19:26 He says that **g** made by human hands
          are no **g** at all.
1Co 8: 5 For even if there are so-called **g**,
   8: 5 earth (as indeed there are many "**g**"

GOES GO
Ex 12:23 the LORD **g** through the land
Nu 5:12 'If a man's wife **g** astray and is
Dt 31: 6 the LORD your God **g** with you;
2Ch 23: 7 close to the king wherever he **g**."
Pr 16:18 Pride **g** before destruction,
Da 9:25 From the time the word **g**
Rev 14: 4 follow the Lamb wherever he **g**.

GOG
Eze 38: 2 set your face against **G**, of the land
   38:18 When **G** attacks the land of Israel,
Rev 20: 8 of the earth—**G** and Magog—

GOING GO
Ge 6:17 I am **g** to bring floodwaters
Ps 144:14 of walls, no **g** into captivity, no cry
Pr 7:22 once he followed her like an ox **g**
Jn 13:21 you, one of you is **g** to betray me."
   13:36 him, "Lord, where are you **g**?"
   13:36 "Where I am **g**, you cannot follow
   14: 2 that I am **g** there to prepare a place
   16:10 because I am **g** to the Father,
1Pe 2:25 For "you were like sheep **g** astray,"

GOLD GOLD-COVERED, GOLDEN, GOLDSMITH

Ex	3:22 her house for articles of silver and **g**
	12:35 Egyptians for articles of silver and **g**
	20:23 gods of silver or gods of **g**.
	25:17 an atonement cover of pure **g**—
	25:31 "Make a lampstand of pure **g**.
	28: 6 "Make the ephod of **g**, and of blue,
	32:31 have made themselves gods of **g**.
Dt	17:17 large amounts of silver and **g**.
Jos	7:21 a bar of **g** weighing fifty shekels,
Jdg	8:27 Gideon made the **g** into an ephod,
1Sa	6: 4 "Five **g** tumors and five **g** rats,
1Ki	6:21 the inside of the temple with pure **g**,
	20: 3 'Your silver and **g** are mine,
2Ch	9:13 the **g** that Solomon received yearly
Ezr	1: 6 them with articles of silver and **g**,
Job	22:25 then the Almighty will be your **g**,
	23:10 tested me, I will come forth as **g**.
	28:15 cannot be bought with the finest **g**,
	31:24 "If I have put my trust in **g** or said to pure **g**,
Ps	19:10 They are more precious than **g**, than much pure **g**;
	115: 4 But their idols are silver and **g**,
	119:127 I love your commands more than **g**, more than pure **g**,
Pr	3:14 and yields better returns than **g**.
	8:19 My fruit is better than fine **g**;
	22: 1 esteemed is better than silver or **g**.
	25:11 Like apples of **g** in settings of silver
Isa	60:17 Instead of bronze I will bring you **g**,
Da	2:32 of the statue was made of pure **g**,
	3: 1 made an image of **g**, sixty cubits
Hag	2: 8 silver is mine and the **g** is mine,'
Zec	4: 2 "I see a solid **g** lampstand
	6:11 Take the silver and **g** and make
Mt	2:11 and presented him with gifts of **g**,
Ac	3: 6 "Silver or **g** I do not have, but what
1Pe	1: 7 of greater worth than **g**,
Rev	3:18 to buy from me **g** refined in the fire,
	4: 4 and had crowns of **g** on their heads.
	14:14 man with a crown of **g** on his head
	21:18 and the city of pure **g**, as pure as
	21:21 The great street of the city was of **g**,

GOLD-COVERED* GOLD, COVER

Heb	9: 4 and the **g** ark of the covenant.

GOLDEN GOLD

1Ki	12:28 advice, the king made two **g** calves.
Rev	1:12 I turned I saw seven **g** lampstands,
	1:13 and with a **g** sash around his chest.
	5: 8 they were holding **g** bowls full
	15: 7 seven angels seven **g** bowls filled

GOLDSMITH GOLD

Isa	46: 6 they hire a **g** to make it into a god,
Jer	10:14 every **g** is shamed by his idols.

GOLGOTHA*

Mt	27:33 a place called **G** (which means
Mk	15:22 to the place called **G** (which means
Jn	19:17 (which in Aramaic is called **G**).

GOLIATH

Philistine giant killed by David (1Sa 17; 21:9).

GOMER

Hos	1: 3 So he married **G** daughter

GOMORRAH

Ge	13:10 LORD destroyed Sodom and **G**.)
	18:20 against Sodom and **G** is so great
	19:24 burning sulfur on Sodom and **G**—
Dt	29:23 the destruction of Sodom and **G**,
Isa	1: 9 Sodom, we would have been like **G**.
Jer	23:14 the people of Jerusalem are like **G**."
Mt	10:15 **G** on the day of judgment than
Ro	9:29 we would have been like **G**."
2Pe	2: 6 and **G** by burning them to ashes,
Jude	1: 7 Sodom and **G** and the surrounding

GONE GO

Dt	34: 7 were not weak nor his strength **g**.
Jdg	4:14 Has not the LORD **g** ahead
Job	19: 4 If it is true that I have **g** astray,
Ps	90: 4 are like a day that has just **g** by,
Pr	30: 4 Who has **g** up to heaven and come
Isa	53: 6 like sheep, have **g** astray, each of us
La	1: 3 harsh labor, Judah has **g** into exile.
Mk	5:30 Jesus realized that power had **g**
Jn	2: 3 When the wine was **g**, Jesus' mother
2Co	5:17 The old has **g**, the new is here!
1Pe	3:22 who has **g** into heaven and is
1Jn	4: 1 because many false prophets have **g**
2Jn	1: 7 the flesh, have **g** out into the world.
Rev	12:12 sea, because the devil has **g** down

GONG*

1Co	13: 1 love, I am only a resounding **g**

GOOD BEST, BETTER, GOODNESS

Ge	1: 4 God saw that the light was **g**, and he
	1:10 And God saw that it was **g**.
	1:12 And God saw that it was **g**.
	1:18 And God saw that it was **g**.
	1:21 And God saw that it was **g**.
	1:25 And God saw that it was **g**.
	1:31 that he had made, and it was very **g**.
	2: 9 pleasing to the eye and **g** for food;
	2: 9 the tree of the knowledge of **g**
	2:17 from the tree of the knowledge of **g**
	2:18 "It is not **g** for the man to be alone.
	3: 6 the fruit of the tree was **g** for food
	3:22 like one of us, knowing **g** and evil.
	41:26 The seven **g** cows are seven years,
	50:20 God intended it for **g** to accomplish
Ex	3: 8 them up out of that land into a **g**
	18: 9 all the **g** things the LORD had
Nu	10:29 the LORD has promised **g** things
Dt	6:18 is right and **g** in the LORD's sight,
	6:18 and take over the **g** land the LORD
	10:13 giving you today for your own **g**?
Jos	21:45 of all the LORD's **g** promises
	23:15 just as all the **g** things the LORD
	23:15 from this **g** land he has given you.
1Sa	25:21 He has paid me back evil for **g**.
2Sa	14:17 like an angel of God in discerning **g**
1Ki	8:56 all the **g** promises he gave through

2Ch 7: 3 to the LORD, saying, "He is **g**;
   31:20 doing what was **g** and right
Ne 2:18 So they began this **g** work.
   9:20 You gave your **g** Spirit to instruct
Job 2:10 Shall we accept **g** from God,
Ps 14: 1 there is no one who does **g**.
   25: 7 me, for you, LORD, are **g**.
   34: 8 Taste and see that the LORD is **g**;
   34:14 Turn from evil and do **g**;
   37: 3 Trust in the LORD and do **g**;
   37:27 Turn from evil and do **g**;
   52: 9 in your name, for your name is **g**.
   73: 1 Surely God is **g** to Israel, to those
   84:11 no **g** thing does he withhold
   86: 5 are forgiving and **g**,
  100: 5 For the LORD is **g** and his love
  103: 5 your desires with **g** things so
  109: 5 They repay me evil for **g**, and hatred
  112: 5 **G** will come to those who are
  119:68 You are **g**, and what you do is **g**;
  133: 1 How **g** and pleasant it is
  145: 9 The LORD is **g** to all;
  147: 1 How **g** it is to sing praises to our
Pr 3: 4 and a **g** name in the sight of God
   3:27 Do not withhold **g** from those
  11:27 Whoever seeks **g** finds favor,
  13:21 are rewarded with **g** things.
  13:22 A **g** person leaves an inheritance
  14:22 those who plan what is **g** find love
  15: 3 watch on the wicked and the **g**.
  15:23 and how **g** is a timely word!
  15:30 **g** news gives health to the bones.
  17:22 A cheerful heart is **g** medicine,
  18:22 He who finds a wife finds what is **g**
  19: 2 Desire without knowledge is not **g**—
  22: 1 A **g** name is more desirable than
  31:12 She brings him **g**, not harm,
Ecc 3:12 happy and to do **g** while they live.
  12:14 hidden thing, whether it is **g** or evil.
Isa 1:19 you will eat the **g** things of the land;
  5: 4 When I looked for **g** grapes,
  5:20 Woe to those who call evil **g** and **g**
  40: 9 You who bring **g** news to Zion,
  52: 7 the feet of those who bring **g** news,
  61: 1 has anointed me to proclaim **g** news
Jer 6:16 ask where the **g** way is, and walk
  13:23 can you do **g** who are accustomed
  16:19 worthless idols that did them no **g**.
  24: 2 One basket had very **g** figs,
  33:14 I will fulfill the **g** promise I made
La 3:26 it is **g** to wait quietly
Eze 34:14 I will tend them in a **g** pasture,
  34:14 they will lie down in **g** grazing land,
Hos 8: 3 But Israel has rejected what is **g**;
Am 5:14 Seek **g**, not evil, that you may live.
Mic 6: 8 has shown you, O mortal, what is **g**.
Na 1:15 the feet of one who brings **g** news,
Zec 8:15 I have determined to do **g** again
Mt 5:13 It is no longer **g** for anything,
  5:45 his sun to rise on the evil and the **g**,
  7:11 know how to give **g** gifts to your
  7:11 heaven give **g** gifts to those who ask
  7:17 every **g** tree bears **g** fruit,

Mt 12:35 A **g** man brings **g** things out of the **g**
   stored up in him,
  13: 8 Still other seed fell on **g** soil,
  13:24 is like a man who sowed **g** seed
  13:48 and collected the **g** fish in baskets,
  25:21 'Well done, **g** and faithful servant!
Mk 1:15 Repent and believe the **g** news!"
  3: 4 to do **g** or to do evil, to save life
  4: 8 Still other seed fell on **g** soil.
  8:36 What **g** is it for someone to gain
  10:18 "Why do you call me **g**?"
  10:18 "No one is **g**—except God alone.
Lk 2:10 I bring you **g** news that will cause
  3: 9 does not produce **g** fruit will be cut
  6:27 do **g** to those who hate you,
  6:35 love your enemies, do **g** to them,
  6:43 "No **g** tree bears bad fruit, nor does a
   bad tree bear **g** fruit.
  7:22 and the **g** news is proclaimed
  8: 8 Still other seed fell on **g** soil.
  9:25 What **g** is it for someone to gain
  14:34 "Salt is **g**, but if it loses its
  18:19 "Why do you call me **g**?"
  18:19 "No one is **g**—except God alone.
  19:17 " 'Well done, my **g** servant!'
Jn 1:46 Can anything **g** come from there?"
  10:11 "I am the **g** shepherd. The **g**
  10:14 "I am the **g** shepherd; I know my
Ac 11:20 telling them the **g** news
Ro 3:12 there is no one who does **g**, not even
  7:12 is holy, righteous and **g**.
  7:16 want to do, I agree that the law is **g**.
  7:18 I know that **g** itself does not dwell
  7:18 For I have the desire to do what is **g**,
  8:28 for the **g** of those who love him,
  10:15 feet of those who bring **g** news!"
  12: 2 his **g**, pleasing and perfect will.
  12: 9 Hate what is evil; cling to what is **g**.
  12:21 by evil, but overcome evil with **g**.
  13: 4 is God's servant for your **g**.
  16:19 want you to be wise about what is **g**,
1Co 7: 1 "It is **g** for a man not to have sexual
  10:24 No one should seek their own **g**, but
   the **g** of others.
  10:33 For I am not seeking my own **g** but
   the **g** of many,
  15:33 company corrupts **g** character."
2Co 9: 8 you will abound in every **g** work.
Gal 4:18 provided the purpose is **g**, and to be
  5: 7 You were running a **g** race.
  6: 9 Let us not become weary in doing **g**,
  6:10 let us do **g** to all people,
Eph 2:10 in Christ Jesus to do **g** works,
  6: 8 each one for whatever **g** they do,
Php 1: 6 he who began a **g** work in you will
  2:13 act in order to fulfill his **g** purpose.
Col 1:10 bearing fruit in every **g** work,
1Th 5:15 strive to do what is **g** for each other
  5:21 test them all; hold on to what is **g**,
2Th 2:17 strengthen you in every **g** deed
  3:13 sisters, never tire of doing what is **g**.
1Ti 1: 5 a pure heart and a **g** conscience
  1: 8 the law is **g** if one uses it properly.

1Ti 3: 7 have a **g** reputation with outsiders,
4: 4 For everything God created is **g**,
6:12 Fight the **g** fight of the faith.
6:12 you made your **g** confession
6:18 Command them to do **g**, to be rich in **g** deeds,
2Ti 2: 3 like a **g** soldier of Christ Jesus.
3:17 equipped for every **g** work.
4: 7 I have fought the **g** fight, I have
Titus 1: 8 one who loves what is **g**, who is
2: 3 much wine, but to teach what is **g**.
2: 7 an example by doing what is **g**.
2:14 his very own, eager to do what is **g**.
Heb 5:14 to distinguish **g** from evil.
10: 1 law is only a shadow of the **g** things
10:24 another on toward love and **g** deeds,
12:10 but God disciplines us for our **g**,
13:16 do not forget to do **g** and to share
Jas 1:17 Every **g** and perfect gift is
4:17 knows the **g** they ought to do
1Pe 2: 3 you have tasted that the Lord is **g**.
2:12 Live such **g** lives among the pagans
2:12 they may see your **g** deeds
2:18 not only to those who are **g**
3:17 to suffer for doing **g** than for doing
3Jn 1: 2 I pray that you may enjoy **g** health
1:11 imitate what is evil but what is **g**.

GOOD NEWS 2Sa 4:10; 18:25, 26, 27, 31; 1Ki 1:42; 2Ki 7:9; Pr 15:30; 25:25; Isa 40:9, 9; 41:27; 52:7; 61:1; Na 1:15; Mt 4:23; 9:35; 11:5; Mk 1:1, 14, 15; Lk 1:19; 2:10; 3:18; 4:18, 43; 7:22; 8:1; 9:6; 16:16; 20:1; Ac 5:42; 8:12, 35; 10:36; 11:20; 13:32; 14:15; 17:18; 20:24; Ro 10:15, 16; 1Th 3:6; Heb 4:2, 6

GOODNESS GOOD
Ex 33:19 "I will cause all my **g** to pass
2Ch 6:41 faithful people rejoice in your **g**.
Ps 23: 6 Surely your **g** and love will follow
116:12 to the Lᴏʀᴅ for all his **g** to me?
Eph 5: 9 the fruit of the light consists in all **g**,
Heb 6: 5 who have tasted the **g** of the word
2Pe 1: 5 every effort to add to your faith **g**; and to **g**, knowledge;

GOODS
Ps 62:10 or put vain hope in stolen **g**;
Ecc 5:11 As **g** increase, so do those who
Hab 2: 6 to him who piles up stolen **g**

GOODWILL*
Est 9:30 words of **g** and assurance—
Pr 14: 9 but **g** is found among the upright.
Ac 7:10 him to gain the **g** of Pharaoh king
Php 1:15 and rivalry, but others out of **g**.

GOPHER [WOOD] (KJV) See CYPRESS

GORGE GORGED
Pr 23:20 wine or **g** themselves on meat,
Eze 32: 4 of the wild **g** themselves on you.

GORGED GORGE
Rev 19:21 all the birds **g** themselves on their

GOSHEN
Ge 45:10 You shall live in the region of **G**
Ex 8:22 deal differently with the land of **G**,

GOSPEL
Mt 24:14 And this **g** of the kingdom will be
Mk 13:10 the **g** must first be preached to all
Ac 14: 7 they continued to preach the **g**.
14:21 They preached the **g** in that city
Ro 1:16 For I am not ashamed of the **g**,
15:16 duty of proclaiming the **g** of God,
15:20 preach the **g** where Christ was not
1Co 1:17 me to baptize, but to preach the **g**—
9:12 anything rather than hinder the **g**
9:14 who preach the **g** should receive their living from the **g**.
9:16 Woe to me if I do not preach the **g**!
15: 1 to remind you of the **g** I preached
15: 2 By this **g** you are saved, if you hold
2Co 4: 3 And even if our **g** is veiled, it is
4: 4 light of the **g** that displays the glory
9:13 your confession of the **g** of Christ,
11: 4 or a different **g** from the one you
Gal 1: 6 and are turning to a different **g**—
1: 7 which is really no **g** at all.
1: 7 are trying to pervert the **g** of Christ.
3: 8 and announced the **g** in advance
Eph 3: 6 through the **g** the Gentiles are heirs
6:15 that comes from the **g** of peace.
Php 1: 7 or defending and confirming the **g**,
1:27 a manner worthy of the **g** of Christ.
1:27 together as one for the faith of the **g**
Col 1: 6 the **g** is bearing fruit and growing
1:23 from the hope held out in the **g**.
1:23 This is the **g** that you heard
1Th 2: 4 by God to be entrusted with the **g**.
2Th 1: 8 do not obey the **g** of our Lord Jesus.
2Ti 1: 8 join with me in suffering for the **g**,
Phm 1:13 me while I am in chains for the **g**.
Rev 14: 6 he had the eternal **g** to proclaim

GOSSIP* GOSSIPS
Pr 11:13 A **g** betrays a confidence, but a
16:28 and a **g** separates close friends.
18: 8 of a **g** are like choice morsels;
20:19 A **g** betrays a confidence;
26:20 without a **g** a quarrel dies down.
26:22 of a **g** are like choice morsels;
2Co 12:20 slander, **g**, arrogance and disorder.

GOSSIPS* GOSSIP
Ro 1:29 strife, deceit and malice. They are **g**,

GOT GET
Ex 32: 6 drink and **g** up to indulge in revelry.
1Co 10: 7 and **g** up to indulge in revelry."

GOUGE
Mt 5:29 stumble, **g** it out and throw it away.

GOURDS
1Ki 6:18 carved with **g** and open flowers.
2Ki 4:39 of its **g** as his garment could hold.

GOVERN GOVERNED, GOVERNING, GOVERNMENT, GOVERNOR, GOVERNORS

Ge   1:16 the greater light to **g** the day and the lesser light to **g** the night.
1Sa 9:17 to you about; he will **g** my people."
1Ki 3: 9 a discerning heart to **g** your people
2Ch 1:11 to **g** my people over whom I have
Job 34:17 Can someone who hates justice **g**?
Ps 136: 8 the sun to **g** the day,

GOVERNED GOVERN

Ro   8: 6 The mind **g** by the flesh is death, but the mind **g** by the Spirit

GOVERNING GOVERN

Ro 13: 1 be subject to the **g** authorities,

GOVERNMENT GOVERN

Isa 9: 6 and the **g** will be on his shoulders.

GOVERNOR GOVERN

Ge 42: 6 Now Joseph was the **g** of the land,
Ne   5:14 appointed to be their **g** in the land
    12:26 in the days of Nehemiah the **g**
Isa 60:17 I will make peace your **g**
Hag 2:21 "Tell Zerubbabel **g** of Judah that I
Mal 1: 8 Try offering them to your **g**!
Lk   3: 1 when Pontius Pilate was **g** of Judea,

GOVERNORS GOVERN

Mk 13: 9 of me you will stand before **g**

GRACE* GRACIOUS, GRACIOUSLY

Ps 45: 2 your lips have been anointed with **g**,
Pr   1: 9 They are a garland to **g** your head
     3:22 you, an ornament to **g** your neck.
     4: 9 give you a garland to **g** your head
    22:11 speaks with **g** will have the king
Isa 26:10 But when **g** is shown to the wicked,
Zec 12:10 inhabitants of Jerusalem a spirit of **g**
Lk   2:40 and the **g** of God was on him.
Jn   1:14 from the Father, full of **g** and truth.
     1:16 **g** in place of **g** already given.
     1:17 **g** and truth came through Jesus
Ac   4:33 God's **g** was so powerfully at work
     6: 8 a man full of God's **g** and power,
    11:23 saw what the **g** of God had done,
    13:43 them to continue in the **g** of God.
    14: 3 message of his **g** by enabling them
    14:26 had been committed to the **g** of God
    15:11 We believe it is through the **g** of our
    15:40 by the believers to the **g** of the Lord.
    18:27 to those who by **g** had believed.
    20:24 to the good news of God's **g**.
    20:32 you to God and to the word of his **g**,
Ro   1: 5 Through him we received **g**
     1: 7 **G** and peace to you from God our
     3:24 by his **g** through the redemption
     4:16 so that it may be by **g** and may be
     5: 2 by faith into this **g** in which we now
     5:15 how much more did God's **g**
     5:15 that came by the **g** of the one man,
     5:17 God's abundant provision of **g**

Ro   5:20 increased, **g** increased all the more,
     5:21 **g** might reign through righteousness
     6: 1 on sinning so that **g** may increase?
     6:14 are not under the law, but under **g**.
     6:15 are not under the law but under **g**?
    11: 5 time there is a remnant chosen by **g**.
    11: 6 And if by **g**, then it cannot be based
    11: 6 if it were, **g** would no longer be **g**.
    12: 3 by the **g** given me I say to every one
    12: 6 according to the **g** given to each
    15:15 because of the **g** God gave me
    16:20 The **g** of our Lord Jesus be
1Co 1: 3 **G** and peace to you from God our
     1: 4 you because of his **g** given you
     3:10 By the **g** God has given me, I laid
    15:10 But by the **g** of God I am what I am,
    15:10 his **g** to me was not without effect.
    15:10 but the **g** of God that was with me.
    16:23 The **g** of the Lord Jesus be
2Co 1: 2 **G** and peace to you from God our
     1:12 on worldly wisdom but on God's **g**.
     4:15 so that the **g** that is reaching more
     6: 1 you not to receive God's **g** in vain.
     8: 1 about the **g** that God has given
     8: 6 to completion this act of **g** on your
     8: 7 you also excel in this **g** of giving.
     8: 9 you know the **g** of our Lord Jesus
     9:14 the surpassing **g** God has given you.
    12: 9 to me, "My **g** is sufficient for you,
    13:14 May the **g** of the Lord Jesus Christ,
Gal 1: 3 **G** and peace to you from God our
     1: 6 called you to live in the **g** of Christ
     1:15 womb and called me by his **g**,
     2: 9 they recognized the **g** given to me.
     2:21 I do not set aside the **g** of God,
     3:18 but God in his **g** gave it to Abraham
     5: 4 you have fallen away from **g**.
     6:18 The **g** of our Lord Jesus Christ be
Eph 1: 2 **G** and peace to you from God our
     1: 6 to the praise of his glorious **g**,
     1: 7 with the riches of God's **g**
     2: 5 it is by **g** you have been saved.
     2: 7 the incomparable riches of his **g**,
     2: 8 For it is by **g** you have been saved,
     3: 2 of God's **g** that was given to me
     3: 7 of God's **g** given me through
     3: 8 Lord's people, this **g** was given me:
     4: 7 one of us **g** has been given as Christ
     6:24 **G** to all who love our Lord Jesus
Php 1: 2 **G** and peace to you from God our
     1: 7 all of you share in God's **g** with me.
     4:23 The **g** of the Lord Jesus Christ be
Col 1: 2 **G** and peace to you from God our
     1: 6 it and truly understood God's **g**
     4: 6 conversation be always full of **g**,
     4:18 **G** be with you.
1Th 1: 1 **G** and peace to you.
     5:28 The **g** of our Lord Jesus Christ be
2Th 1: 2 **G** and peace to you from God
     1:12 according to the **g** of our God
     2:16 his **g** gave us eternal encouragement
     3:18 The **g** of our Lord Jesus Christ be
1Ti 1: 2 **G**, mercy and peace from God

229   GRACIOUS–GRANT

1Ti   1:14 The **g** of our Lord was poured
     6:21 from the faith. **G** be with you all.
2Ti   1: 2 **G**, mercy and peace from God
     1: 9 because of his own purpose and **g**.
     1: 9 This **g** was given us in Christ Jesus
     2: 1 be strong in the **g** that is in Christ
     4:22 with your spirit. **G** be with you all.
Titus 1: 4 **G** and peace from God the Father
     2:11 For the **g** of God has appeared
     3: 7 having been justified by his **g**,
     3:15 us in the faith. **G** be with you all.
Phm   1: 3 **G** and peace to you from God our
     1:25 The **g** of the Lord Jesus Christ be
Heb   2: 9 by the **g** of God he might taste death
     4:16 approach God's throne of **g**
     4:16 find **g** to help us in our time of need.
   10:29 who has insulted the Spirit of **g**?
   12:15 no one falls short of the **g** of God
   13: 9 our hearts to be strengthened by **g**,
   13:25 **G** be with you all.
Jas   4: 6 But he gives us more **g**. That is why
1Pe   1: 2 **G** and peace be yours in abundance.
     1:10 who spoke of the **g** that was to come
     1:13 set your hope on the **g** to be brought
     4:10 of God's **g** in its various forms.
     5:10 And the God of all **g**, who called
     5:12 that this is the true **g** of God.
2Pe   1: 2 **G** and peace be yours in abundance
     3:18 grow in the **g** and knowledge of our
2Jn   1: 3 **G**, mercy and peace from God
Jude   1: 4 who pervert the **g** of our God
Rev   1: 4 **G** and peace to you from him who
   22:21 The **g** of the Lord Jesus be

GRACE AND PEACE Ro 1:7; 1Co 1:3; 2Co 1:2;
Gal 1:3; Eph 1:2; Php 1:2; Col 1:2; 1Th 1:1; 2Th
1:2; Titus 1:4; Phm 1:3; 1Pe 1:2; 2Pe 1:2; Rev 1:4

GRACE OF ... GOD Lk 2:40; Ac 11:23; 13:43;
14:26; 1Co 15:10, 10; Gal 2:21; 2Th 1:12; Titus
2:11; Heb 2:9; 12:15; 1Pe 5:12; Jude 1:4

GRACIOUS GRACE

Ge   21: 1 Now the Lord was **g** to Sarah as
Ex   34: 6 the compassionate and **g** God,
Nu   6:25 face shine on you and be **g** to you;
1Sa   2:21 And the Lord was **g** to Hannah;
2Ki 13:23 But the Lord was **g** to them
2Ch 30: 9 for the Lord your God is **g**
Ezr   7: 9 for the **g** hand of his God was
     8:22 king, "The **g** hand of our God is
Ne   2: 8 because the **g** hand of my God was
     9:17 God, **g** and compassionate,
     9:31 for you are a **g** and merciful God.
Ps   67: 1 May God be **g** to us and bless us
   86:15 are a compassionate and **g** God,
   103: 8 Lord is compassionate and **g**,
   145: 8 The Lord is **g**
Pr   16:21 and **g** words promote instruction.
   16:24 **G** words are a honeycomb,
Isa 30:18 the Lord longs to be **g** to you;
Joel   2:13 God, for he is **g** and compassionate,
Jnh   4: 2 I knew that you are a **g**
1Pe   3: 7 heirs with you of the **g** gift of life,

GRACIOUSLY GRACE

Hos 14: 2 all our sins and receive us **g**, that we

GRAFT* GRAFTED

Ro   11:23 for God is able to **g** them in again.

GRAFTED GRAFT

Ro   11:17 have been **g** in among the others

GRAIN GRAINS

Ge   41: 5 Seven heads of **g**, healthy and good,
Lev   2: 1 anyone brings a **g** offering
     2:13 Season all your **g** offerings
Dt   25: 4 an ox while it is treading out the **g**.
Ru   2: 2 up the leftover **g** behind anyone
Ps   78:24 eat, he gave them the **g** of heaven.
Ecc 11: 1 Ship your **g** across the sea;
Hos 14: 7 they will flourish like the **g**,
Joel   2:19 "I am sending you **g**, new wine
Mk   2:23 they began to pick some heads of **g**.
Lk   17:35 women will be grinding **g** together;
1Co   9: 9 an ox while it is treading out the **g**."
1Ti   5:18 an ox while it is treading out the **g**,"

GRAIN OFFERING Ex 29:41; 30:9; Lev 2:1,
3, 4, 5, 6, 7, 8, 9, 10, 11, 14, 15; 5:13; 6:14, 15, 20,
21, 23; 7:9, 10, 37; 9:4, 17; 10:12; 14:10, 20, 21, 31;
23:13; Nu 4:16; 5:15, 18, 25, 26; 6:17; 7:13, 19, 25,
31, 37, 43, 49, 55, 61, 67, 73, 79, 87; 8:8; 15:4, 6,
9, 24; 28:5, 8, 9, 12, 12, 13, 20, 28, 31; 29:3, 9, 11,
14, 16, 19, 22, 25, 28, 31, 34, 38; Jdg 13:19, 23; 2Ki
16:13, 15, 15, 15; 1Ch 21:23; Isa 66:3; Eze 45:24;
46:5, 5, 7, 11, 14, 14, 15, 20

GRAIN OFFERINGS Ex 40:29; Lev 2:13, 13;
23:18, 37; Nu 6:15; 29:6, 18, 21, 24, 27, 30, 33,
37, 39; Jos 22:23, 29; 1Ki 8:64, 64; 1Ch 23:29;
2Ch 7:7; Ezr 7:17; Ne 10:33; 13:5, 9; Isa 19:21;
43:23; 57:6; 66:20; Jer 14:12; 17:26; 33:18; 41:5;
Eze 42:13; 44:29; 45:15, 17, 17, 25; Joel 1:9, 13;
2:14; Am 5:22

GRAINFIELDS FIELD

Lk   6: 1 Jesus was going through the **g**,

GRAINS* GRAIN

Job 29:18 my days as numerous as the **g**
Ps   139:18 they would outnumber the **g**
Isa 48:19 your children like its numberless **g**;

GRANDCHILDREN CHILD

Ex   10: 2 and **g** how I dealt harshly
1Ti   5: 4 But if a widow has children or **g**,

GRANDMOTHER MOTHER

2Ti   1: 5 which first lived in your **g** Lois

GRANT GRANTED, GRANTS

Lev 26: 6 " 'I will **g** peace in the land,
Dt   28:11 The Lord will **g** you abundant
Est   7: 3 and if it pleases you, **g** me my life—
Ps   20: 5 May the Lord **g** all your
   51:12 salvation and **g** me a willing spirit,
   85: 7 Lord, and **g** us your salvation.
   140: 8 Do not **g** the wicked their desires,
Ecc   6: 2 God does not **g** them the ability
Isa 46:13 I will **g** salvation to Zion,

Hag 2: 9 'And in this place I will **g** peace,'
Mk 10:40 at my right or left is not for me to **g**.

GRANTED GRANT

1Sa 1:27 the LORD has **g** me what I asked
Est 7: 2 to half the kingdom, it will be **g**."
Ps 21: 6 Surely you have **g** him unending
Pr 10:24 what the righteous desire will be **g**
Mt 15:28 Your request is **g**."
Ac 11:18 Gentiles God has **g** repentance
Php 1:29 For it has been **g** to you on behalf

GRANTS* GRANT

Ps 127: 2 for he **g** sleep to those he loves.
  147:14 He **g** peace to your borders

GRAPE GRAPES

Nu 6: 3 They must not drink **g** juice or eat
Ob 1: 5 If **g** pickers came to you,

GRAPES GRAPE

Lev 19:10 or pick up the **g** that have fallen.
Nu 13:23 branch bearing a single cluster of **g**.
Dt 32:32 Their **g** are filled with poison,
Isa 5: 2 he looked for a crop of good **g**,
Jer 31:29 'The parents have eaten sour **g**,
Eze 18: 2 " 'The parents eat sour **g**,
Mic 6:15 you will crush **g** but not drink
Hab 3:17 bud and there are no **g** on the vines,
Mt 7:16 Do people pick **g** from thornbushes,
Rev 14:18 earth's vine, because its **g** are ripe."

GRASP GRASPED, GRASPING

Ecc 7:18 It is good to **g** the one and not let go
Jn 10:39 to seize him, but he escaped their **g**.

GRASPED GRASP

Hos 12: 3 In the womb he **g** his brother's heel;

GRASPING GRASP

Ge 25:26 out, with his hand **g** Esau's heel;

GRASS

Ps 37: 2 for like the **g** they will soon wither,
  103:15 The life of mortals is like **g**,
  104:14 He makes **g** grow for the cattle,
Pr 19:12 but his favor is like dew on the **g**.
Isa 40: 6 "All people are like **g**, and all their
Mt 6:30 that is how God clothes the **g**
1Pe 1:24 "All people are like **g**, and all their
  1:24 the **g** withers and the flowers fall,
Rev 8: 7 and all the green **g** was burned up.

GRASSHOPPERS

Nu 13:33 We seemed like **g** in our own eyes,
Isa 40:22 the earth, and its people are like **g**.

GRATIFY* GRATIFYING

Ro 13:14 how to **g** the desires of the flesh.
Gal 5:16 and you will not **g** the desires

GRATIFYING* GRATIFY

Eph 2: 3 time, **g** the cravings of our flesh

GRATITUDE

Col 3:16 to God with **g** in your hearts.

GRAVE GRAVES

Nu 19:16 who touches a human bone or a **g**,
Dt 34: 6 day no one knows where his **g** is.
Ps 5: 9 Their throat is an open **g**;
  6: 5 Who praises you from the **g**?
Pr 7:27 Her house is a highway to the **g**,
SS 8: 6 its jealousy unyielding as the **g**.
Hos 13:14 this people from the power of the **g**;
  13:14 Where, O **g**, is your destruction?
Jn 11:44 "Take off the **g** clothes and let him

GRAVES GRAVE

Ex 14:11 "Was it because there were no **g**
Eze 37:12 I am going to open your **g** and bring
Mt 23:29 and decorate the **g** of the righteous.
Lk 11:44 because you are like unmarked **g**,
Jn 5:28 are in their **g** will hear his voice
Ro 3:13 "Their throats are open **g**;

GRAY

Ps 71:18 Even when I am old and **g**, do not
Pr 16:31 **G** hair is a crown of splendor;
  20:29 **g** hair the splendor of the old.

GREAT GREATER, GREATEST, GREATLY, GREATNESS

Ge 1:16 God made two **g** lights—
  6: 5 LORD saw how **g** the wickedness
  12: 2 "I will make you into a **g** nation,
  12: 2 I will make your name **g**, and you
  15: 1 your shield, your very **g** reward."
  15:18 the Wadi of Egypt to the **g** river,
  46: 3 will make you into a **g** nation there.
Ex 32:10 I will make you into a **g** nation."
  32:11 brought out of Egypt with **g** power
Nu 14:19 In accordance with your **g** love,
Dt 4:32 Has anything so **g** as this ever
  7:21 you, is a **g** and awesome God.
  10:17 gods and Lord of lords, the **g** God,
  29:28 **g** wrath the LORD uprooted them
Jos 7: 9 will you do for your own **g** name?"
Jdg 16: 5 you the secret of his **g** strength
1Sa 18:14 everything he did he had **g** success,
2Sa 7: 9 Now I will make your name **g**,
  7:22 "How **g** you are,
  22:36 your help has made me **g**.
  24:14 of the LORD, for his mercy is **g**;
1Ch 16:25 For **g** is the LORD and most
  17:19 will, you have done this **g** thing
  17:19 made known all these **g** promises.
Ne 1: 5 of heaven, the **g** and awesome God,
  8: 6 praised the LORD, the **g** God;
Ps 18:35 your help has made me **g**.
  19:11 in keeping them there is **g** reward.
  25:11 forgive my iniquity, though it is **g**.
  36: 6 your justice like the **g** deep.
  40:16 always say, "The LORD is **g**!"
  47: 2 the **g** King over all the earth.
  48: 2 Mount Zion, the city of the **G** King.
  57:10 For **g** is your love,
  70: 4 always say, "The LORD is **g**!"
  89: 1 sing of the LORD's **g** love forever;
  95: 3 For the LORD is the **g** God, the **g** King
    above all gods.

Ps 103:11 so **g** is his love for those who fear
   108: 4 For **g** is your love, higher than
   117: 2 For **g** is his love toward us,
   119:165 G peace have those who love your
   145: 3 G is the LORD and most worthy
Pr 22: 1 is more desirable than **g** riches;
   23:24 father of a righteous child has **g** joy;
Isa 1: 4 a people whose guilt is **g**, a brood
   42:21 his righteousness to make his law **g**
Jer 10: 6 you are **g**, and your name is mighty
   27: 5 With my **g** power and outstretched
   32:19 **g** are your purposes and mighty are
La 3:23 **g** is your faithfulness.
Eze 17: 3 A **g** eagle with powerful wings,
Da 2:45 "The **g** God has shown the king
   7: 3 Four **g** beasts, each different
   9: 4 "Lord, the **g** and awesome God,
Joel 2:11 The day of the LORD is **g**;
   2:20 Surely he has done **g** things!
Na 1: 3 is slow to anger but **g** in power;
Zep 1:14 The **g** day of the LORD is near—
Mal 1:11 name will be **g** among the nations,
   4: 5 prophet Elijah to you before that **g**
Mt 4:16 in darkness have seen a **g** light;
   13:46 When he found one of **g** value,
   20:26 become **g** among you must be your
Mk 13:26 Man coming in clouds with **g** power
Lk 2:10 will cause **g** joy for all the people.
   6:23 because **g** is your reward in heaven.
   6:35 Then your reward will be **g**, and you
   21:23 There will be **g** distress in the land
   21:27 in a cloud with power and **g** glory.
Ac 8:10 man is rightly called the G Power
Eph 1:19 his incomparably **g** power for us
   2: 4 But because of his **g** love for us,
1Ti 3:16 which true godliness springs is **g**:
   6: 6 with contentment is **g** gain.
Titus 2:13 appearing of the glory of our **g** God
Heb 2: 3 If we ignore so **g** a salvation?
   10:21 since we have a **g** priest over
   12: 1 by such a **g** cloud of witnesses,
   13:20 Jesus, that **g** Shepherd of the sheep,
1Pe 1: 3 In his **g** mercy he has given us new
1Jn 3: 1 See what **g** love the Father has
Jude 1: 6 chains for judgment on the **g** Day.
Rev 6:17 For the **g** day of their wrath has
   7:14 have come out of the **g** tribulation;
   12: 9 The **g** dragon was hurled down—
   14: 8 Fallen is Babylon the G,'
   16:14 for the battle on the **g** day of God
   17: 1 the punishment of the **g** prostitute,
   18:10 Woe to you, **g** city, you mighty city
   20:11 I saw a **g** white throne and him who
   21:21 The **g** street of the city was of gold,

GREAT KING 2Ki 18:19, 28; Ezr 5:11; Ps 47:2;
48:2; 95:3; Isa 36:4, 13; Hos 5:13; 10:6; Mal 1:14;
Mt 5:35

GREATER GREAT

Ge 1:16 the **g** light to govern the day
Ex 18:11 the LORD is **g** than all other gods,
2Ch 2: 5 because our God is **g** than all other
Mt 11:11 has not risen anyone **g** than John

Mt 11:11 the kingdom of heaven is **g** than he.
   12: 6 something **g** than the temple is here.
Mk 12:31 is no commandment **g** than these."
Lk 11:31 now something **g** than Solomon is
   11:32 now something **g** than Jonah is here.
Jn 1:50 You will see **g** things than that."
   3:30 He must become **g**; I must become
   14:12 will do even **g** things than these,
   15:13 G love has no one than this:
1Co 12:31 Now eagerly desire the **g** gifts.
2Co 3:11 how much **g** is the glory
Heb 3: 3 worthy of **g** honor than Moses,
   7: 7 doubt the lesser is blessed by the **g**.
   11:26 as of **g** value than the treasures
1Pe 1: 7 of **g** worth than gold,
1Jn 3:20 know that God is **g** than our hearts,
   4: 4 is in you is **g** than the one who is

GREATEST GREAT

2Sa 7: 9 like the names of the **g** men
Mt 18: 4 of this child is the **g** in the kingdom
   22:38 is the first and **g** commandment.
   23:11 The **g** among you will be your
Lk 9:48 least among you all who is the **g**."
   22:24 of them was considered to be **g**.
Jn 7:37 On the last and **g** day of the festival,
1Co 13:13 But the **g** of these is love.

GREATLY GREAT

2Ch 33:12 humbled himself **g** before the God
Ezr 10:13 because we have sinned **g** in this
Ps 47: 9 earth belong to God; he is **g** exalted.
Isa 61:10 I delight **g** in the LORD;
Jnh 1:16 this the men **g** feared the LORD,

GREATNESS* GREAT

Ex 15: 7 "In the **g** of your majesty you threw
Dt 3:24 to show to your servant your **g**
   32: 3 Oh, praise the **g** of our God!
1Ch 29:11 is the **g** and the power and the glory
2Ch 9: 6 not even half the **g** of your wisdom
Est 10: 2 a full account of the **g** of Mordecai,
Ps 145: 3 his **g** no one can fathom.
   150: 2 praise him for his surpassing **g**.
Isa 9: 7 the **g** of his government and peace
   63: 1 forward in the **g** of his strength?
Eze 38:23 And so I will show my **g** and my
Da 4:22 your **g** has grown until it reaches
   5:18 Nebuchadnezzar sovereignty and **g**
   7:27 **g** of all the kingdoms under heaven
Mic 5: 4 his **g** will reach to the ends
Lk 9:43 were all amazed at the **g** of God.

GREECE GREEK, GREEKS

Da 8:21 The shaggy goat is the king of G,
   10:20 I go, the prince of G will come;

GREED GREEDY

Mk 7:22 adultery, **g**, malice, deceit,
Lk 12:15 on your guard against all kinds of **g**;
Ro 1:29 wickedness, evil, **g** and depravity.
Eph 4:19 of impurity, and they are full of **g**.
   5: 3 or of **g**, because these are improper
Col 3: 5 evil desires and **g**, which is idolatry.
2Pe 2: 3 In their **g** these teachers will exploit

2Pe 2:14 they are experts in **g**—

GREEDY GREED
Pr 15:27 The **g** bring ruin to their
  28:25 The **g** stir up conflict, but those who
Eze 33:31 but their hearts are **g** for unjust gain.
1Co 5:11 sister but is sexually immoral or **g**,
  6:10 thieves nor the **g** nor drunkards nor
Eph 5: 5 No immoral, impure or **g** person—

GREEK GREECE
Jn 19:20 written in Aramaic, Latin and G.
Ac 16: 1 a believer but whose father was a G.
  17:12 a number of prominent **G** women
    and many **G** men.
  21:37 "Do you speak G?" he replied.

GREEKS GREECE
Jn 12:20 there were some **G** among those
Ac 14: 1 number of Jews and **G** believed.
  18: 4 trying to persuade Jews and **G**.
  20:21 and **G** that they must turn to God
1Co 1:22 signs and **G** look for wisdom,

GREEN
Ge 1:30 I give every **g** plant for food."
  9: 3 Just as I gave you the **g** plants,
Ps 23: 2 makes me lie down in **g** pastures,
Jer 17: 8 its leaves are always **g**.
Mk 6:39 sit down in groups on the **g** grass.

GREET GREETED, GREETING, GREETINGS
Mt 5:47 And if you **g** only your own people,
1Co 16:20 **G** one another with a holy kiss.

GREETED GREET
Mt 23: 7 they love to be **g** with respect

GREETING GREET
Lk 1:29 what kind of **g** this might be.
1Co 16:21 I, Paul, write this **g** in my own hand.
Col 4:18 I, Paul, write this **g** in my own hand.
2Th 3:17 I, Paul, write this **g** in my own hand,

GREETINGS GREET
Mt 26:49 to Jesus, Judas said, "G, Rabbi!"
Lk 1:28 The angel went to her and said, "G,

GREW GROW
Ge 21:20 God was with the boy as he **g** up.
Jdg 13:24 He **g** and the LORD blessed him,
1Sa 2:21 the boy Samuel **g** up in the presence
  3:19 was with Samuel as he **g** up, and he
2Sa 3: 1 David **g** stronger and stronger,
  3: 1 while the house of Saul **g** weaker
Isa 53: 2 He **g** up before him like a tender
Lk 1:80 the child **g** and became strong
  2:40 And the child **g** and became strong;
  2:52 And Jesus **g** in wisdom and stature,
  13:19 It **g** and became a tree, and the birds
Ac 16: 5 in the faith and **g** daily in numbers.

GRIEF GRIEFS, GRIEVANCE, GRIEVE, GRIEVED, GRIEVES, GRIEVOUS
Ps 10:14 you consider their **g** and take it
Pr 10: 1 a foolish son brings **g** to his mother.
  14:13 ache, and rejoicing may end in **g**.
  17:21 To have a fool for a child brings **g**;
Ecc 1:18 the more knowledge, the more **g**.
La 3:32 Though he brings **g**, he will show
Jn 16:20 grieve, but your **g** will turn to joy.
1Pe 1: 6 may have had to suffer **g** in all kinds

GRIEFS* GRIEF
1Ti 6:10 pierced themselves with many **g**.

GRIEVANCE* GRIEF
Job 31:13 when they had a **g** against me,
Ac 19:38 craftsmen have a **g** against anybody,
Col 3:13 any of you has a **g** against someone.

GRIEVE GRIEF
2Sa 1:26 I **g** for you, Jonathan my brother;
Eph 4:30 do not **g** the Holy Spirit of God,
1Th 4:13 so that you do not **g** like the rest

GRIEVED GRIEF
Isa 63:10 they rebelled and **g** his Holy Spirit.

GRIEVES* GRIEF
Zec 12:10 for him as one **g** for a firstborn son.

GRIEVOUS GRIEF
Ge 18:20 is so great and their sin so **g**
Ecc 5:13 I have seen a **g** evil under the sun:
Jer 15:18 and my wound **g** and incurable?

GRIND GRINDING
Job 31:10 may my wife **g** another man's grain,

GRINDING GRIND
Jdg 16:21 they set him to **g** grain in the prison.
Lk 17:35 women will be **g** grain together;

GROAN GROANED, GROANING, GROANS
Pr 29: 2 when the wicked rule, the people **g**.
Ro 8:23 **g** inwardly as we wait eagerly
2Co 5: 2 Meanwhile we **g**, longing to be
  5: 4 in this tent, we **g** and are burdened,

GROANED* GROAN
Ex 2:23 The Israelites **g** in their slavery
Ps 77: 3 I remembered you, God, and I **g**;

GROANING GROAN
Ex 2:24 God heard their **g** and he
  6: 5 I have heard the **g** of the Israelites,
Jdg 2:18 their **g** under those who oppressed
Eze 21: 7 they ask you, 'Why are you **g**?'
Ro 8:22 the whole creation has been **g** as

GROANS GROAN
Ro 8:26 for us through wordless **g**.

GROPE
Dt 28:29 midday you will **g** about like a blind

La   4:14 Now they **g** through the streets as

GROUND GROUNDS
Ge   1:10 God called the dry **g** "land,"
       2: 7 formed a man from the dust of the **g**
       3:17 it,' "Cursed is the **g** because of you;
       4:10 blood cries out to me from the **g**.
Ex   3: 5 where you are standing is holy **g**."
      15:19 walked through the sea on dry **g**.
Jos   3:17 of the Jordan and stood on dry **g**,
       3:17 completed the crossing on dry **g**.
Jdg   6:37 on the fleece and all the **g** is dry,
1Sa   5: 3 his face on the **g** before the ark
2Ki   2: 8 two of them crossed over on dry **g**.
Job   3:16 away in the **g** like a stillborn child,
Ps   26:12 My feet stand on level **g**;
      73:18 you place them on slippery **g**;
     143:10 your good Spirit lead me on level **g**.
     147: 6 but casts the wicked to the **g**.
Ecc 12: 7 dust returns to the **g** it came from,
Isa 53: 2 shoot, and like a root out of dry **g**.
Ob   1: 3 'Who can bring me down to the **g**?'
Mt   10:29 to the **g** outside your Father's care.
      25:25 went out and hid your gold in the **g**.
Lk   22:44 like drops of blood falling to the **g**.
Jn   8: 6 *write on the **g** with his finger.*
      12:24 a kernel of wheat falls to the **g**
Eph   6:13 you may be able to stand your **g**,

GROUNDS GROUND
Da   6: 4 to find **g** for charges against Daniel
Lk   23:22 in him no **g** for the death penalty.

GROUP GROUPS
Nu   16: 3 They came as a **g** to oppose Moses

GROUPS GROUP
Mk   6:39 have all the people sit down in **g**

GROVE* GROVES
Ex   23:11 your vineyard and your olive **g**.
SS   6:11 I went down to the **g** of nut trees

GROVES GROVE
Dt   6:11 and olive **g** you did not plant—

GROW FULL-GROWN, GREW,
GROWING, GROWN, GROWS
Ge   2: 9 God made all kinds of trees **g**
Nu   6: 5 they must let their hair **g** long.
Jdg 16:22 on his head began to **g** again after it
1Sa   2:26 the boy Samuel continued to **g**
Ps   92:12 they will **g** like a cedar of Lebanon;
Pr   13:11 money little by little makes it **g**.
      20:13 not love sleep or you will **g** poor;
Isa 40:31 they will run and not **g** weary,
Eze 47:12 of all kinds will **g** on both banks
Jnh   4:10 you did not tend it or make it **g**.
Mt   6:28 See how the flowers of the field **g**.
1Co   3: 6 it, but God has been making it **g**.
2Co 10:15 as your faith continues to **g**,
1Pe   2: 2 so that by it you may **g** up in your
2Pe   3:18 But **g** in the grace and knowledge

GROWING GROW
Lk   13: 6 "A man had a fig tree **g** in his

Col   1: 6 and **g** throughout the whole world—
       1:10 work, **g** in the knowledge of God,
2Th   1: 3 so, because your faith is **g** more

GROWN GROW
Ex   2:11 after Moses had **g** up, he went
2Ch 10:10 The young men who had **g**
Heb 11:24 when he had **g** up, refused to be

GROWS GROW
Ps 142: 3 When my spirit **g** faint within me,
Mk   4:32 it **g** and becomes the largest of all
Eph   4:16 **g** and builds itself up in love,
Col   2:19 sinews, **g** as God causes it to grow.
Heb 12:15 and that no bitter root **g** up to cause

GRUDGE* GRUDGING,
GRUDGINGLY
Ge   27:41 Esau held a **g** against Jacob because
      50:15 if Joseph holds a **g** against us
Lev 19:18 bear a **g** against anyone among your
Mk   6:19 So Herodias nursed a **g** against John

GRUDGING* GRUDGE
Dt   15:10 to them and do so without a **g** heart;

GRUDGINGLY* GRUDGE
2Co   9: 5 a generous gift, not as one **g** given.

GRUMBLE GRUMBLED,
GRUMBLERS, GRUMBLING
Ex   16: 7 we, that you should **g** against us?"
Nu   14:27 wicked community **g** against me?
      16:11 that you should **g** against him?"
1Co 10:10 And do not **g**, as some of them did—
Jas   5: 9 Don't **g** against one another,

GRUMBLED GRUMBLE
Ex   15:24 So the people **g** against Moses,
      16: 2 whole community **g** against Moses
      17: 3 there, and they **g** against Moses.
Nu   14: 2 All the Israelites **g** against Moses
      16:41 whole Israelite community **g** against
Ps 106:25 They **g** in their tents and did not

GRUMBLERS* GRUMBLE
Jude 1:16 These people are **g** and faultfinders;

GRUMBLING GRUMBLE
Ex   16: 7 he has heard your **g** against him.
Nu   14:27 the complaints of these **g** Israelites.
      17: 5 of this constant **g** against you
Jn   6:43 "Stop **g** among yourselves,"
Php   2:14 Do everything without **g** or arguing,
1Pe   4: 9 hospitality to one another without **g**.

GUARANTEE* GUARANTEED,
GUARANTEEING, GUARANTOR
Ge   43: 9 I myself will **g** his safety;

GUARANTEED* GUARANTEE
Ge   44:32 Your servant **g** the boy's safety
Ro   4:16 and may be **g** to all Abraham's

GUARANTEEING* GUARANTEE
2Co   1:22 as a deposit, **g** what is to come.

2Co 5: 5 as a deposit, **g** what is to come.
Eph 1:14 is a deposit **g** our inheritance until

GUARANTOR* GUARANTEE
Heb 7:22 Jesus has become the **g** of a better

GUARD GUARDED, GUARDIAN,
GUARDIAN-REDEEMER,
GUARDIANS, GUARDING,
GUARDS, SAFEGUARD
Ge   3:24 forth to **g** the way to the tree of life.
1Sa   2: 9 He will **g** the feet of his faithful
     26:15 Why didn't you **g** your lord
Ne   4: 9 posted a **g** day and night to meet
Ps   25:20 **G** my life and rescue me; do not let
     91:11 his angels concerning you to **g** you
     141: 3 Set a **g** over my mouth, LORD;
Pr   2:11 you, and understanding will **g** you.
     4:13 let it go; **g** it well, for it is your life.
     4:23 Above all else, **g** your heart,
     7: 2 **g** my teachings as the apple of your
     13: 3 Those who **g** their lips preserve
     21:23 Those who **g** their mouths and their
Isa 52:12 God of Israel will be your rear **g**.
Mic 7: 5 embrace **g** the words of your lips.
Mal 2:15 So be on your **g**, and do not be
Mt   27:66 seal on the stone and posting the **g**.
Mk   13:33 Be on **g**! Be alert! You do not know
Lk   4:10 concerning you to **g** you carefully;
     12: 1 "Be on your **g** against the yeast
     12:15 Be on your **g** against all kinds
Ac   20:31 So be on your **g**!
1Co 16:13 Be on your **g**; stand firm
Php 4: 7 will **g** your hearts and your minds
1Ti   6:20 **g** what has been entrusted to your
2Ti   1:12 he is able to **g** what I have entrusted
     1:14 **G** the good deposit that was
     1:14 **g** it with the help of the Holy Spirit
2Pe   3:17 be on your **g** so that you may not be

GUARDED GUARD
Dt   32:10 he **g** him as the apple of his eye,
     33: 9 your word and **g** your covenant.
Eze 44:15 and who **g** my sanctuary

GUARDIAN GUARD
Eze 28:14 You were anointed as a **g** cherub,
Gal 3:24 So the law was our **g** until Christ
     3:25 has come, we are no longer under a **g**.

GUARDIAN-REDEEMER GUARD,
REDEEM
Ru   4:14 has not left you without a **g**.

GUARDIANS GUARD
1Co 4:15 if you had ten thousand **g** in Christ,
Gal 4: 2 The heir is subject to **g** and trustees

GUARDING GUARD
Lk   22:63 The men who were **g** Jesus began

GUARDS GUARD
Ne   4:22 so they can serve us as **g** by night
Ps   97:10 for he **g** the lives of his faithful ones
Mt   28: 4 The **g** were so afraid of him

GUEST GUESTS
Mk   14:14 Where is my **g** room, where I may
Lk   19: 7 has gone to be the **g** of a sinner."

GUESTS GUEST
Pr   9:18 that her **g** are deep in the realm
Mt   9:15 "How can the **g** of the bridegroom
Lk   14: 7 noticed how the **g** picked the places

GUIDANCE GUIDE
1Ch 10:13 and even consulted a medium for **g**,
Pr   1: 5 and let the discerning get **g**—
     11:14 For lack of **g** a nation falls,
Hab 2:19 Can it give **g**? It is covered

GUIDE GUIDANCE, GUIDED,
GUIDES
Ex   13:21 of cloud to **g** them on their way
     15:13 In your strength you will **g** them
Ne   9:19 cloud did not fail to **g** them on their
Ps   25: 5 **G** me in your truth and teach me,
     48:14 he will be our **g** even to the end.
     67: 4 equity and **g** the nations of the earth.
     73:24 You **g** me with your counsel,
     139:10 even there your hand will **g** me,
Pr   6:22 When you walk, they will **g** you;
Isa 9:16 Those who **g** this people mislead
     58:11 The LORD will **g** you always;
Lk   1:79 death, to **g** our feet into the path
Jn   16:13 he will **g** you into all the truth.

GUIDED GUIDE
Job 31:18 and from my birth I **g** the widow—
Ps   107:30 he **g** them to their desired haven.

GUIDES* GUIDE
Ps   23: 3 He **g** me along the right paths
     25: 9 He **g** the humble in what is right
Pr   11: 3 The integrity of the upright **g** them,
Isa 3:12 My people, your **g** lead you astray;
Mt   15:14 Leave them; they are blind **g**.
     23:16 "Woe to you, blind **g**! You say,
     23:24 You blind **g**! You strain out a gnat

GUILT GUILTLESS, GUILTY
Ge   44:16 God has uncovered your servants' **g**.
Lev 5:15 It is a **g** offering.
1Sa   6: 4 "What **g** offering should we send
Ezr 9: 6 our **g** has reached to the heavens.
Ps   32: 5 And you forgave the **g** of my sin.
     38: 4 My **g** has overwhelmed me like
Isa 1: 4 a people whose **g** is great, a brood
     6: 7 your **g** is taken away and your sin
Jer 2:22 stain of your **g** is still before me,"
Eze 18:19 'Why does the son not share the **g**
Hos 5:15 my lair until they have borne their **g**
Jn   9:41 claim you can see, your **g** remains.

GUILT OFFERING Lev 5:15, 16, 18, 19; 6:5,
6, 17; 7:1, 2, 5, 7, 37; 14:12, 13, 14, 17, 21, 24, 25,
28; 19:21, 22; Nu 6:12; 1Sa 6:3, 4, 8, 17; Ezr 10:19;
Eze 46:20

GUILT OFFERINGS Nu 18:9; 2Ki 12:16; Eze
40:39; 42:13; 44:29

GUILTLESS GUILT

Ex 20: 7 not hold anyone **g** who misuses his

GUILTY GUILT

Ex 23: 1 Do not help a **g** person by being
23: 7 to death, for I will not acquit the **g**.
34: 7 he does not leave the **g** unpunished;
Nu 14:18 he does not leave the **g** unpunished;
Job 10: 2 Do not declare me **g**, but tell me
Pr 21: 8 The way of the **g** is devious,
Isa 5:23 who acquit the **g** for a bribe,
Na 1: 3 will not leave the **g** unpunished.
Mk 3:29 they are **g** of an eternal sin."
Jn 8:46 Can any of you prove me **g** of sin?
19:11 over to you is **g** of a greater sin."
1Co 11:27 in an unworthy manner will be **g**
Heb 10: 2 would no longer have felt **g** for their
10:22 to cleanse us from a **g** conscience
Jas 2:10 at just one point is **g** of breaking all

GULLIBLE*

2Ti 3: 6 and gain control over **g** women,

GULP*

Pr 21:20 olive oil, but fools **g** theirs down.

GUSH* GUSHED, GUSHES

Isa 35: 6 Water will **g** forth in the wilderness

GUSHED* GUSH

Nu 20:11 Water **g** out, and the community
Ps 78:20 and water **g** out, streams flowed
105:41 opened the rock, and water **g** out;
Isa 48:21 he split the rock and water **g** out.

GUSHES* GUSH

Pr 15: 2 but the mouth of the fool **g** folly.
15:28 but the mouth of the wicked **g** evil.

H

HABAKKUK*

Prophet to Judah (Hab 1:1; 3:1).

HABIT

Nu 22:30 Have I been in the **h** of doing this
1Ti 5:13 they get into the **h** of being idle
Heb 10:25 as some are in the **h** of doing,

HAD HAVE

Ge 11: 1 the whole world **h** one language
Ex 36: 7 what they already **h** was more than
Nu 11: 4 and said, "If only we **h** meat to eat!
Jdg 1:19 because they **h** chariots fitted
1Sa 2:12 they **h** no regard for the LORD.
2Sa 12: 3 the poor man **h** nothing except one
2Ch 26:21 King Uzziah **h** leprosy until the day
Job 28:17 nor can it be **h** for jewels of gold.
42:10 him twice as much as he **h** before.
Ps 55: 6 "Oh, that I **h** the wings of a dove!
Isa 5: 1 My loved one **h** a vineyard
53: 2 He **h** no beauty or majesty to attract
Eze 1: 6 each of them **h** four faces and four
10:14 Each of the cherubim **h** four faces:
41:18 Each cherub **h** two faces:

Mt 7:29 he taught as one who **h** authority,
13:44 sold all he **h** and bought that field.
13:46 sold everything he **h** and bought it.
Mk 4: 6 withered because they **h** no root.
10:22 sad, because he **h** great wealth.
Jn 20: 9 Scripture that Jesus **h** to rise
Ac 1:16 the Scripture **h** to be fulfilled
2:13 "They have **h** too much wine."
2:45 to give to anyone who **h** need.
13:46 "We **h** to speak the word of God
14: 9 him, saw that he **h** faith to be healed
17: 3 proving that the Messiah **h** to suffer
Ro 4:21 fully persuaded that God **h** power
2Co 5:21 God made him who **h** no sin to be
Rev 4: 8 the four living creatures **h** six wings
5: 6 The Lamb **h** seven horns and seven
13: 1 It **h** ten horns and seven heads,
13: 3 seemed to have **h** a fatal wound,
14: 1 with him 144,000 who **h** his name

HADAD BEN-HADAD

Edomite adversary of Solomon (1Ki 11:14–25).

HADADEZER

2Sa 8: 3 David defeated **H** son of Rehob,

HADASSAH* ESTHER

Est 2: 7 Mordecai had a cousin named **H**,

HADES*

Mt 11:23 No, you will go down to **H**.
16:18 the gates of **H** will not overcome it.
Lk 10:15 No, you will go down there.
16:23 In **H**, where he was in torment,
Rev 1:18 And I hold the keys of death and **H**.
6: 8 **H** was following close behind him.
20:13 and **H** gave up the dead that were
20:14 **H** were thrown into the lake of fire.

HAGAR*

Servant of Sarah, wife of Abraham, mother of Ishmael (Ge 16:1–6; 25:12). Driven away by Sarah while pregnant (Ge 16:5–16); after birth of Isaac (Ge 21:9–21; Gal 4:21–31).

HAGGAI*

Post-exilic prophet who encouraged rebuilding of the temple (Ezr 5:1; 6:14; Hag 1–2).

HAGGITH

1Ki 1: 5 whose mother was **H**, put himself

HAIL HAILSTONES

Ex 9:19 because the **h** will fall on every
9:26 only place it did not **h** was the land
Ps 78:47 He destroyed their vines with **h**
147:17 He hurls down his **h** like pebbles.
Jn 19: 3 saying, "**H**, king of the Jews!"
Rev 8: 7 there came **h** and fire mixed
16:21 God on account of the plague of **h**,

HAILSTONES HAIL

Jos 10:11 the LORD hurled large **h** down
Eze 13:11 and I will send **h** hurtling down,
Rev 16:21 From the sky huge **h**, each weighing

HAIR HAIRS, HAIRSTYLES, HAIRY

Ex	26: 7	of goat **h** for the tent over
Lev	19:27	" 'Do not cut the **h** at the sides
Nu	6: 5	they must let their **h** grow long.
Jdg	16:19	shave off the seven braids of his **h**,
	16:22	But the **h** on his head began to grow
	20:16	of whom could sling a stone at a **h**
2Sa	14:26	to cut his **h** once a year because it
	18: 9	Absalom's **h** got caught in the tree.
2Ki	1: 8	"He had a garment of **h** and had
Pr	16:31	Gray **h** is a crown of splendor;
	20:29	gray **h** the splendor of the old.
SS	7: 5	Your **h** is like royal tapestry;
Isa	3:24	instead of well-dressed **h**, baldness;
Eze	8: 3	and took me by the **h** of my head.
Da	4:33	of heaven until his **h** grew like
	7: 9	the **h** of his head was white like
Mt	3: 4	clothes were made of camel's **h**,
Lk	7:44	her tears and wiped them with her **h**.
	21:18	But not a **h** of your head will perish.
Jn	11: 2	Lord and wiped his feet with her **h**.)
	12: 3	feet and wiped his feet with her **h**.
1Co	11: 6	she might as well have her **h** cut off;
	11:14	teach you that if a man has long **h**,
	11:15	but that if a woman has long **h**, it is
Rev	1:14	The **h** on his head was white like

HAIRS HAIR

Ps	40:12	They are more than the **h** of my
Mt	10:30	even the very **h** of your head are all
Lk	12: 7	the very **h** of your head are all

HAIRSTYLES* HAIR

1Ti	2: 9	not with elaborate **h** or gold
1Pe	3: 3	such as elaborate **h** and the wearing

HAIRY HAIR

Ge	27:11	brother Esau is a **h** man while I have

HALAH

2Ki	18:11	to Assyria and settled them in H,

HALF HALF-TRIBE, HALVES

Ge	15:10	birds, however, he did not cut in **h**.
Ex	24: 6	Moses took **h** of the blood and put it
	24: 6	the other **h** he splashed against
	30:13	This **h** shekel is an offering
Jos	8:33	**H** of the people stood in front
	8:33	**h** of them in front of Mount Ebal,
2Sa	10: 4	shaved off **h** of each man's beard,
1Ki	3:25	living child in two and give **h** to one
		and **h** to the other."
	10: 7	Indeed, not even **h** was told me;
Ne	4:16	day on, **h** of my men did the work,
	4:16	while the other **h** were equipped
	13:24	**H** of their children spoke
Est	5: 3	Even up to **h** the kingdom, it will be
Isa	44:19	to say, "**H** of it I used for fuel;
Eze	16:51	did not commit **h** the sins you did.
Da	7:25	hands for a time, times and **h** a time.
	12: 7	be for a time, times and **h** a time.
Mk	6:23	give you, up to **h** my kingdom."
Lk	19: 8	now I give **h** of my possessions
Rev	8: 1	in heaven for about **h** an hour.
	11:11	a **h** days the breath of life from God

Rev	12:14	time, times and **h** a time,

HALF-TRIBE HALF, TRIBE

Nu	32:33	the **h** of Manasseh son of Joseph
Jos	4:12	and the **h** of Manasseh crossed over,

HALL

1Ki	7: 7	He built the throne **h**, the **H**
SS	2: 4	Let him lead me to the banquet **h**,
Eze	41: 1	the man brought me to the main **h**
Da	5:10	his nobles, came into the banquet **h**.
Mt	22:10	and the wedding **h** was filled
Ac	19: 9	daily in the lecture **h** of Tyrannus.

HALLELUJAH* See also PRAISE THE LORD†

Rev	19: 1	multitude in heaven shouting: "**H**!
	19: 3	And again they shouted: "**H**!
	19: 4	And they cried: "Amen, **H**!"
	19: 6	peals of thunder, shouting: "**H**!

HALLOW, HALLOWED (KJV) See CONSECRATE, CONSECRATED, HOLY, SACRED, SET APART

HALLOWED* HOLY

Mt	6: 9	Father in heaven, **h** be your name,
Lk	11: 2	" 'Father, **h** be your name,

HALT

Job	38:11	here is where your proud waves **h**'?

HALVES HALF

Ge	15:10	arranged the **h** opposite each other;

HAM

Son of Noah (Ge 5:32; 1Ch 1:4), father of Canaan (Ge 9:18; 10:6–20; 1Ch 1:8–16). Saw Noah's nakedness (Ge 9:20–27).

HAMAN

Agagite nobleman honored by Xerxes (Est 3:1–2). Plotted to exterminate the Jews because of Mordecai (Est 3:3–15). Forced to honor Mordecai (Est 5–6). Plot exposed by Esther (Est 5:1–8; 7:1–8). Hanged (Est 7:9–10).

HAMATH LEBO HAMATH

2Sa	8: 9	Tou king of **H** heard that David had
2Ki	14:28	for Israel both Damascus and **H**,
	18:34	Where are the gods of **H**

HAMMER HAMMERED

Ex	25:31	**H** out its base and shaft, and make
Nu	16:38	**H** the censers into sheets to overlay
Jdg	4:21	a **h** and went quietly to him while he
Jer	10: 4	they fasten it with **h** and nails so it

HAMMERED HAMMER

Ex	25:18	cherubim out of **h** gold at the ends
2Ch	9:15	two hundred large shields of **h** gold;
	9:15	hundred small shields of **h** gold,

HAMOR

Ge	34: 2	When Shechem son of **H** the Hivite,

HAMPERED*
Pr   4:12 you walk, your steps will not be **h**;

HAMSTRING* HAMSTRUNG
Jos   11: 6 You are to **h** their horses and burn

HAMSTRUNG HAMSTRING
Jos   11: 9 He **h** their horses and burned their
1Ch 18: 4 He **h** all but a hundred of the chariot

HANAMEL
Jer   32: 7 **H** son of Shallum your uncle is

HANANEL
Ne   3: 1 and as far as the Tower of **H**.
Jer   31:38 the Tower of **H** to the Corner Gate.

HANANI
Ne   7: 2 charge of Jerusalem my brother **H**,

HANANIAH SHADRACH
1. False prophet; adversary of Jeremiah (Jer 28).
2. Original name of Shadrach (Da 1:6–19; 2:17).

HAND EMPTY-HANDED, HANDED, HANDFUL, HANDIWORK, HANDS, LEFT-HANDED, OPENHANDED, RIGHT-HANDED
Ge   3:22 not be allowed to reach out his **h**
        4:11 your brother's blood from your **h**.
       14:22 raised **h** I have sworn an oath
       16:12 his **h** will be against everyone and
             everyone's **h** against him,
       22:12 "Do not lay a **h** on the boy,"
       24: 2 he had, "Put your **h** under my thigh.
       25:26 out, with his **h** grasping Esau's heel;
       37:22 but don't lay a **h** on him."
       47:29 eyes, put your **h** under my thigh
       48:14 Israel reached out his right **h**
       48:14 he put his left **h** on Manasseh's
Ex   3:19 go unless a mighty **h** compels him.
        4: 6 "Put your **h** inside your cloak."
        6: 1 of my mighty **h** he will let them go;
       13: 3 you out of it with a mighty **h**.
       15: 6 Your right **h**, Lord, was majestic
       21:24 tooth for tooth, **h** for **h**, foot for foot,
       33:22 with my **h** until I have passed by.
Lev   1: 4 You are to lay your **h** on the head
        3: 2 You are to lay your **h** on the head
        4: 4 He is to lay his **h** on its head
Nu   14:30 with uplifted **h** to make your home,
Dt   3:24 your greatness and your strong **h**.
        4:34 by a mighty **h** and an outstretched
       12: 7 everything you have put your **h** to,
       19:21 tooth for tooth, **h** for **h**, foot for foot.
       32:39 and no one can deliver out of my **h**.
Jos   8: 7 your God will give it into your **h**.
Jdg   2:15 the **h** of the Lord was against
1Sa   17:50 his **h** he struck down the Philistine
       24:10 'I will not lay my **h** on my lord,
       26: 9 Who can lay a **h** on the Lord's

2Sa   1:14 lift your **h** to destroy the Lord's
       18:12 I would not lay a **h** on the king's
1Ki   8:24 with your **h** you have fulfilled it—
        8:42 your mighty **h** and your outstretched
       13: 4 he stretched out his **h** from the altar
       18:44 cloud as small as a man's **h** is rising
1Ch 21:17 let your **h** fall on me and my family,
       29:14 you only what comes from your **h**.
       29:16 Holy Name comes from your **h**,
2Ch   6:15 with your **h** you have fulfilled it—
       32:15 able to deliver his people from my **h**
             or the **h** of my predecessors.
       32:15 your god deliver you from my **h**!"
       32:22 from the **h** of Sennacherib king of
             Assyria and from the **h** of all others.
Ezr   7: 9 for the gracious **h** of his God was
Ne   2: 8 because the gracious **h** of my God
        4:17 materials did their work with one **h**
Job   40: 4 I put my **h** over my mouth.
Ps   10:12 Lift up your **h**, O God.
       16: 8 With him at my right **h**, I will not be
       32: 4 and night your **h** was heavy on me;
       37:24 the Lord upholds him with his **h**.
       44: 3 it was your right **h**, your arm,
       45: 9 at your right **h** is the royal bride
       63: 8 your right **h** upholds me.
       74:11 Why do you hold back your **h**, your
             right **h**?
       75: 8 In the **h** of the Lord is a cup full
       80:17 Let your **h** rest on the man at your
             right **h**,
       91: 7 ten thousand at your right **h**, but it
       95: 4 In his **h** are the depths of the earth,
       98: 1 his right **h** and his holy arm have
     109:31 he stands at the right **h** of the needy,
     110: 1 "Sit at my right **h** until I make your
     137: 5 may my right **h** forget its skill.
     139:10 even there your **h** will guide me, your
             right **h** will hold me fast.
     145:16 You open your **h** and satisfy
Pr   3:16 Long life is in her right **h**; in her left **h**
             are riches and honor.
       19:24 A sluggard buries his **h** in the dish;
       21: 1 the Lord's **h** the king's heart is
       27:16 the wind or grasping oil with the **h**.
Ecc   2:24 This too, I see, is from the **h** of God,
        9:10 Whatever your **h** finds to do, do it
Isa   1:25 I will turn my **h** against you;
        5:25 turned away, his **h** is still upraised.
       11: 8 child will put its **h** into the viper's
       40:12 the waters in the hollow of his **h**,
       40:12 of his **h** marked off the heavens?
       41:13 God who takes hold of your right **h**
       44: 5 still others will write on their **h**,
       48:13 My own **h** laid the foundations
       48:13 my right **h** spread out the heavens;
       53:10 of the Lord will prosper in his **h**.
       64: 8 we are all the work of your **h**.
Jer   22:24 were a signet ring on my right **h**,
       31:32 I took them by the **h** to lead them
       51: 7 was a gold cup in the Lord's **h**;
La   3: 3 he has turned his **h** against me again
Eze   1: 3 There the **h** of the Lord was

Eze 2: 9 and I saw a **h** stretched out to me.
20: 5 with uplifted **h** to the descendants
Da 3:17 deliver us from Your Majesty's **h**.
5: 5 the fingers of a human **h** appeared
10:10 A **h** touched me and set me
Am 7: 7 to plumb, with a plumb line in his **h**.
Jnh 4:11 people who cannot tell their right **h**
Hab 2:16 the LORD's right **h** is coming
3: 4 rays flashed from his **h**, where his
Mt 3:12 His winnowing fork is in his **h**,
5:30 And if your right **h** causes you
6: 3 not let your left **h** know what your
right **h** is doing,
12:10 a man with a shriveled **h** was there.
18: 8 If your **h** or your foot causes you
22:44 my right **h** until I put your enemies
26:64 at the right **h** of the Mighty One
Mk 1:31 to her, took her **h** and helped her up.
3: 1 a man with a shriveled **h** was there.
5:41 He took her by the **h** and said to her,
9:43 If your **h** causes you to stumble,
12:36 my right **h** until I put your enemies
14:62 at the right **h** of the Mighty One
Lk 5:13 Jesus reached out his **h** and touched
9:62 "No one who puts a **h** to the plow
20:42 said to my Lord: "Sit at my right **h**
22:69 at the right **h** of the mighty God."
Jn 7:30 but no one laid a **h** on him,
10:28 one will snatch them out of my **h**.
20:27 Reach out your **h** and put it into my
Ac 2:34 said to my Lord: "Sit at my right **h**
7:55 Jesus standing at the right **h** of God.
Ro 8:34 is at the right **h** of God and is
1Co 12:15 say, "Because I am not a **h**, I do not
Eph 1:20 at his right **h** in the heavenly realms,
Col 3: 1 is, seated at the right **h** of God.
Heb 1:13 "Sit at my right **h** until I make your
8: 1 sat down at the right **h** of the throne
10:12 he sat down at the right **h** of God,
1Pe 3:22 into heaven and is at God's right **h**—
Rev 1:16 In his right **h** he held seven stars,
5: 1 I saw in the right **h** of him who sat

HAND OF GOD 2Ch 30:12; Job 19:21; Ecc
2:24; Ac 2:33; 7:55, 56; Ro 8:34; Col 3:1; Heb 10:12

HAND OF THE LORD† Ex 9:3; 14:31; Jos
4:24; Jdg 2:15; 1Sa 7:13; 2Ki 3:15; Ezr 7:6, 28; Job
12:9; Ps 75:8; Isa 25:10; 41:20; 51:17; 66:14; Eze
1:3; 3:14, 22; 33:22; 37:1; 40:1

MIGHTY HAND Ex 3:19; 6:1, 1; 13:3, 9, 14, 16;
14:31; 32:11; Dt 4:34; 5:15; 6:21; 7:8, 19; 9:26; 11:2;
26:8; 1Ki 8:42; 2Ch 6:32; Ne 1:10; Ps 136:12; Jer
32:21; Eze 20:33, 34; Da 9:15; 1Pe 5:6

RIGHT HAND Ge 48:13, 14, 17, 18; Ex 15:6,
6, 12; Lev 8:23; 14:14, 17, 25, 28; Jdg 5:26; 16:29;
2Sa 20:9; 1Ki 2:19; 1Ch 6:39; Job 40:14; Ps 16:8,
11; 17:7; 18:35; 20:6; 21:8; 44:3; 45:4, 9; 48:10;
60:5; 63:8; 73:23; 74:11; 77:10; 78:54; 80:15, 17;
89:13, 25, 42; 91:7; 98:1; 108:6; 109:6, 31; 110:1,
5; 118:15, 16, 16; 121:5; 137:5; 138:7; 139:10;
142:4; Pr 3:16; Isa 41:10, 13; 44:20; 45:1; 48:13;
62:8; 63:12; Jer 22:24; La 2:3, 4; Eze 21:22; 39:3;
Da 12:7; Jnh 4:11; Hab 2:16; Mt 5:30; 6:3; 22:44;

26:64; 27:29; Mk 12:36; 14:62; Lk 6:6; 20:42; 22:69;
Ac 2:25, 33, 34; 3:7; 5:31; 7:55, 56; Ro 8:34; 2Co
6:7; Gal 2:9; Eph 1:20; Col 3:1; Heb 1:3, 13; 8:1;
10:12; 12:2; 1Pe 3:22; Rev 1:16, 17, 20; 2:1; 5:1,
7; 10:5

HANDED HAND
Mt 26: 2 Man will be **h** over to be crucified."
Mk 15:15 and **h** him over to be crucified.
Ac 3:13 You **h** him over to be killed,
1Ti 1:20 whom I have **h** over to Satan to be

HANDFUL HAND
Ecc 4: 6 Better one **h** with tranquillity than

HANDIWORK* HAND, WORK
Isa 19:25 people, Assyria my **h**, and Israel my
Eph 2:10 For we are God's **h**,

HANDKERCHIEFS*
Ac 19:12 so that even **h** and aprons that had

HANDLE HANDLES
Ex 18:18 you cannot **h** it alone.
Col 2:21 "Do not **h**! Do not taste!

HANDLES HANDLE
2Ti 2:15 who correctly **h** the word of truth.

HANDS HAND
Ge 5:29 painful toil of our **h** caused
27:22 Jacob, but the **h** are the **h** of Esau."
Ex 17:11 As long as Moses held up his **h**,
17:11 but whenever he lowered his **h**,
29:10 his sons shall lay their **h** on its head.
32:15 tablets of the covenant law in his **h**.
34: 4 the two stone tablets in his **h**.
Dt 6: 8 Tie them as symbols on your **h**
11:18 tie them as symbols on your **h**
23:25 you may pick kernels with your **h**,
Jos 24:11 but I gave them into your **h**.
Jdg 2:16 them out of the **h** of these raiders.
7: 6 of them drank from cupped **h**,
14: 6 his bare **h** as he might have torn
1Sa 5: 4 His head and **h** had been broken off
2Sa 24:14 Let us fall into the **h** of the LORD,
24:14 do not let me fall into human **h**."
2Ki 11:12 and the people clapped their **h**
22:19 by all the idols their **h** have made,
2Ch 6: 4 his **h** has fulfilled what he promised
Job 2: 6 "Very well, then, he is in your **h**;
Ps 22:16 they pierce my **h** and my feet.
24: 4 The one who has clean **h** and a pure
31: 5 Into your **h** I commit my spirit;
31:15 My times are in your **h**;
47: 1 Clap your **h**, all you nations;
63: 4 and in your name I will lift up my **h**.
90:17 establish the work of our **h** for us—
115: 7 They have **h**, but cannot feel, feet,
138: 8 do not abandon the works of your **h**.
Pr 10: 4 Lazy **h** make for poverty, but
diligent **h** bring wealth.
12:24 Diligent **h** will rule, but laziness
21:25 him, because his **h** refuse to work.
24:33 a little folding of the **h** to rest—

Pr	31:13	and flax and works with eager **h**.
	31:20	poor and extends her **h** to the needy.
Ecc	4: 5	Fools fold their **h** and ruin
	5:15	toil that they can carry in their **h**.
	10:18	because of idle **h**, the house leaks.
	11: 6	at evening let your **h** not be idle,
Isa	5:12	no respect for the work of his **h**.
	35: 3	Strengthen the feeble **h**,
	37:19	and stone, fashioned by human **h**.
	45:12	My own **h** stretched
	49:16	engraved you on the palms of my **h**;
	55:12	trees of the field will clap their **h**.
	65: 2	out my **h** to an obstinate people,
Jer	1:16	worshiping what their **h** have made.
	20:13	the needy from the **h** of the wicked.
	26:14	As for me, I am in your **h**;
La	3:41	hearts and our **h** to God in heaven,
Eze	1: 8	their four sides they had human **h**.
	10: 8	be seen what looked like human **h**.)
Da	2:45	of a mountain, but not by human **h**—
Hos	14: 3	gods' to what our own **h** have made,
Mic	7: 3	Both **h** are skilled in doing evil;
Zec	8:13	be afraid, but let your **h** be strong."
Mal	1:10	will accept no offering from your **h**.
Mk	7: 5	of eating their food with defiled **h**?"
	10:16	placed his **h** on them and blessed
	14:41	is delivered into the **h** of sinners.
Lk	23:46	into your **h** I commit my spirit."
	24:40	this, he showed them his **h** and feet.
Jn	20:27	"Put your finger here; see my **h**.
Ac	6: 6	prayed and laid their **h** on them.
	8:18	at the laying on of the apostles' **h**,
	13: 3	they placed their **h** on them and sent
	19: 6	When Paul placed his **h** on them,
	28: 8	placed his **h** on him and healed him.
Ro	10:21	have held out my **h** to a disobedient
1Co	15:24	when he **h** over the kingdom to God
1Th	4:11	own business and work with your **h**,
1Ti	2: 8	lifting up holy **h** without anger
	4:14	body of elders laid their **h** on you.
	5:22	not be hasty in the laying on of **h**,
2Ti	1: 6	you through the laying on of my **h**.
Heb	6: 2	the laying on of **h**, the resurrection
	10:31	to fall into the **h** of the living God.
1Jn	1: 1	looked at and our **h** have touched—
Rev	13:16	to receive a mark on their right **h**
	20: 4	mark on their foreheads or their **h**.

HANDSOME*

Ge	39: 6	Now Joseph was well-built and **h**,
1Sa	9: 2	as **h** a young man as could be found
	16:12	a fine appearance and **h** features.
	17:42	glowing with health and **h**, and he
2Sa	14:25	for his **h** appearance as Absalom.
1Ki	1: 6	also very **h** and was born next
SS	1:16	How **h** you are, my beloved!
Eze	23: 6	all of them **h** young men,
	23:12	horsemen, all **h** young men.
	23:23	Assyrians with them, **h** young men,
Da	1: 4	men without any physical defect, **h**,
Zec	11:13	the **h** price at which they valued me!

HANG HANGED, HANGING, HUNG

Mt	22:40	and the Prophets **h** on these two

HANGED* HANG

2Sa	17:23	house in order and then **h** himself.
Mt	27: 5	Then he went away and **h** himself.

HANGING HANG

Jos	10:26	they were left **h** on the poles until
2Sa	18: 9	He was left **h** in midair,
Ac	10:39	They killed him by **h** him

HANNAH

Wife of Elkanah, mother of Samuel (1Sa 1).
Prayer at dedication of Samuel (1Sa 2:1–10).
Blessed (1Sa 2:18–21).

HANUN

1Ch	19: 2	"I will show kindness to H son
	19: 2	David's envoys came to H

HAPPEN HAPPENED, HAPPENING, HAPPENS

Ge	49: 1	around so I can tell you what will **h**
Ecc	6:12	tell them what will **h** under the sun
Da	8:19	tell you what will **h** later in the time
	10:14	to you what will **h** to your people
Jnh	4: 5	to see what would **h** to the city.
Mk	10:32	told them what was going to **h**
Jn	13:19	when it does **h** you will believe
	14:29	that when it does **h** you will believe.
	18: 4	all that was going to **h** to him,
Ac	4:28	had decided beforehand should **h**.

HAPPENED HAPPEN

Dt	4:32	Has anything so great as this ever **h**,
1Sa	4: 7	Nothing like this has **h** before.
2Ki	24:20	anger that all this **h** to Jerusalem
Ezr	9:13	"What has **h** to us is a result of our
Ne	9:33	In all that has **h** to us, you have
Jer	40: 3	All this **h** because you people

HAPPENING HAPPEN

Lk	21:31	so, when you see these things **h**,
1Pe	4:12	as though something strange were **h**

HAPPENS HAPPEN

Jn	13:19	"I am telling you now before it **h**,
	14:29	I have told you now before it **h**,

HAPPIER* HAPPY

Ecc	4: 2	already died, are **h** than the living,
Mt	18:13	he is **h** about that one sheep than
1Co	7:40	she is **h** if she stays as she is—

HAPPINESS* HAPPY

Dt	24: 5	bring **h** to the wife he has married.
Est	8:16	For the Jews it was a time of **h**
Job	7: 7	my eyes will never see **h** again.
Ecc	2:26	knowledge and **h**, but to the sinner
Mt	25:21	Come and share your master's **h**!'
	25:23	Come and share your master's **h**!'

HAPPY* HAPPIER, HAPPINESS

Ge   30:13 Then Leah said, "How **h** I am! The
                  women will call me **h**."
1Ki   4:20 ate, they drank and they were **h**.
       10: 8 How **h** your people must be! How **h**
                  your officials,
2Ch   9: 7 How **h** your people must be! How **h**
                  your officials,
Est   5: 9 Haman went out that day **h**
Ps   68: 3 may they be **h** and joyful.
      113: 9 her home as a **h** mother of children.
      137: 8 **h** is the one who repays you
      137: 9 **H** is the one who seizes your infants
Pr   15:13 A **h** heart makes the face cheerful,
Ecc   3:12 better for people than to be **h**
        5:19 their lot and be **h** in their toil—
        7:14 When times are good, be **h**;
        11: 9 young, be **h** while you are young,
Jnh   4: 6 Jonah was very **h** about the plant.
Zec   8:19 occasions and **h** festivals for Judah.
1Co   7:30 those who are **h**, as if they were not;
2Co   7: 9 yet now I am **h**, not because you
        7:13 delighted to see how **h** Titus was,
Jas   5:13 Is anyone **h**? Let them sing songs

HARAN

Ge   11:26 the father of Abram, Nahor and **H**.
       11:27 the father of Abram, Nahor and **H**.
                  And **H** became the father of Lot.

HARASS* HARASSED

Dt   2: 9 "Do not **h** the Moabites or provoke
        2:19 do not **h** them or provoke them

HARASSED* HARASS

Mt   9:36 because they were **h** and helpless,
2Co   7: 5 rest, but we were **h** at every turn—

HARBOR

Dt   15: 9 careful not to **h** this wicked thought:
Job   36:13 "The godless in heart **h** resentment;
Ps   103: 9 nor will he **h** his anger forever;
Pr   26:24 lips, but in their hearts they **h** deceit.
Jas   3:14 But if you **h** bitter envy and selfish

HARD HARDEN, HARDENING, HARDENS, HARDER, HARDSHIP, HARDSHIPS

Ge   18:14 Is anything too **h** for the LORD?
Ex   7:13 Yet Pharaoh's heart became **h**
1Ki   10: 1 to test Solomon with **h** questions.
Pr   14:23 All **h** work brings a profit, but mere
Isa   40: 2 her **h** service has been completed,
Jer   32:17 Nothing is too **h** for you.
Zec   7:12 They made their hearts as **h** as flint
Mt   19:23 it is **h** for someone who is rich
Mk   10: 5 "It was because your hearts were **h**
Jn   6:60 disciples said, "This is a **h** teaching.
Ac   20:35 of **h** work we must help the weak,
        26:14 It is **h** for you to kick against
Ro   16:12 those women who work **h**
        16:12 woman who has worked very **h**
1Co   4:12 We work **h** with our own hands.
2Co   4: 8 We are **h** pressed on every side,

2Co   6: 5 in **h** work, sleepless nights
1Th   5:12 those who work **h** among you,
1Pe   4:18 "If it is **h** for the righteous to be
2Pe   3:16 things that are **h** to understand,
Rev   2: 2 your **h** work and your perseverance.

HARDEN HARD

Ex   4:21 I will **h** his heart so that he will not
       14:17 I will **h** the hearts of the Egyptians
1Sa   6: 6 Why do you **h** your hearts as
Ps   95: 8 "Do not **h** your hearts as you did
Ro   9:18 and he hardens whom he wants to **h**.
Heb   3: 8 do not **h** your hearts as you did
        4: 7 his voice, do not **h** your hearts."

HARDENED HARD

Ex   8:32 this time also Pharaoh **h** his heart
       10:20 But the LORD **h** Pharaoh's heart,
Jos   11:20 LORD himself who **h** their hearts
Mk   8:17 Are your hearts **h**?
Jn   12:40 blinded their eyes and **h** their hearts,
Ro   11: 7 them did, but the others were **h**,
Heb   3:13 you may be **h** by sin's deceitfulness.

HARDENING* HARD

Ro   11:25 Israel has experienced a **h** in part
Eph   4:18 in them due to the **h** of their hearts.

HARDENS* HARD

Pr   28:14 but whoever **h** their heart falls
Ro   9:18 and he **h** whom he wants to harden.

HARDER HARD

Jer   5: 3 They made their faces **h** than stone
1Co   15:10 No, I worked **h** than all of them—
2Co   11:23 I have worked much **h**,

HARDHEARTED* HEART

Dt   15: 7 do not be **h** or tightfisted toward

HARDSHIP HARD

Dt   15:18 Do not consider it a **h** to set your
Ne   9:32 do not let all this **h** seem trifling
Ro   8:35 Shall trouble or **h** or persecution
1Co   13: 3 give over my body to **h** that I may
2Ti   4: 5 endure **h**, do the work
Heb   12: 7 Endure **h** as discipline;

HARDSHIPS HARD

Nu   11: 1 about their **h** in the hearing
Ac   14:22 "We must go through many **h**
2Co   6: 4 in troubles, **h** and distresses;
       12:10 in insults, in **h**, in persecutions,
Rev   2: 3 and have endured **h** for my name,

HARDWORKING* WORK

2Ti   2: 6 The **h** farmer should be the first

HAREM

Est   2: 9 into the best place in the **h**.

HARLOT (KJV) See PROSTITUTE

HARLOTS*

Hos   4:14 the men themselves consort with **h**

HARM HARMED, HARMFUL, HARMING, HARMS

Ge 31: 7 God has not allowed him to **h** me.
    31:52 past this heap to your side to **h** you
    31:52 heap and pillar to my side to **h** me.
    48:16 who has delivered me from all **h**—
    50:20 You intended to **h** me, but God
1Sa 26:21 today, I will not try to **h** you again.
1Ch 16:22 do my prophets no **h**."
Ne   6: 2 But they were scheming to **h** me;
Ps 71:13 those who want to **h** me be covered
    121: 6 the sun will not **h** you by day,
Pr   3:29 Do not plot **h** against your neighbor,
     8:36 who fail to find me **h** themselves;
    12:21 No **h** overtakes the righteous,
    13:20 for a companion of fools suffers **h**.
    31:12 good, not **h**, all the days of her life.
Isa 11: 9 They will neither **h** nor destroy
Jer 7: 6 follow other gods to your own **h**,
    10: 5 they can do no **h** nor can they do
    29:11 to prosper you and not to **h** you,
Zep 3:15 never again will you fear any **h**.
Ac   9:13 all the **h** he has done to your holy
Ro 13:10 Love does no **h** to a neighbor.
1Co 11:17 your meetings do more **h** than good.
1Pe 3:13 Who is going to **h** you if you are
2Pe 2:13 They will be paid back with **h** for
          the **h** they have done.
1Jn 5:18 and the evil one cannot **h** them.
Rev 11: 5 If anyone tries to **h** them, fire comes
    11: 5 who wants to **h** them must die.

HARMED HARM

Da   3:27 that the fire had not **h** their bodies,

HARMFUL HARM

2Ki 4:41 And there was nothing **h** in the pot.

HARMING HARM

1Sa 25:34 who has kept me from **h** you, if you

HARMONY*

Zec 6:13 there will be **h** between the two.'
Ro 12:16 Live in **h** with one another.
2Co 6:15 What **h** is there between Christ

HARMS* HARM

Ge 26:11 "Anyone who **h** this man or his

HARP HARPIST, HARPISTS, HARPS

1Ch 25: 3 using the **h** in thanking and praising
Ps 33: 2 Praise the LORD with the **h**;
    98: 5 music to the LORD with the **h**,
    108: 2 Awake, **h** and lyre! I will awaken
    150: 3 praise him with the **h** and lyre,
Da   3: 5 lyre, **h**, pipe and all kinds of music,
Rev 5: 8 Each one had a **h** and they were

HARPIST* HARP

2Ki 3:15 But now bring me a **h**." While the
          h was playing,

HARPISTS* HARP

Rev 14: 2 like that of **h** playing their harps.
    18:22 The music of **h** and musicians,

HARPS HARP

1Sa 10: 5 and **h** being played before them,
1Ch 15:16 lyres, **h** and cymbals.
    25: 1 accompanied by **h**,
Ps 137: 2 There on the poplars we hung our **h**,
Rev 15: 2 They held **h** given them by God

HARSH HARSHLY

Ex   1:14 made their lives bitter with **h** labor
     6: 9 of their discouragement and **h** labor.
2Ch 10: 4 but now lighten the **h** labor
Pr 15: 1 wrath, but a **h** word stirs up anger.
2Co 13:10 I may not have to be **h** in my use
Col 2:23 and their **h** treatment of the body,
     3:19 wives and do not be **h** with them.
1Pe 2:18 but also to those who are **h**.

HARSHLY HARSH

Ge 42: 7 be a stranger and spoke **h** to them.
2Ch 10:13 The king answered them **h**.
1Ti 5: 1 Do not rebuke an older man **h**,

HARVEST HARVESTED, HARVESTERS, HARVESTS

Ge   8:22 seedtime and **h**, cold and heat,
Ex 23:16 "Celebrate the Festival of H
Lev 19: 9 or gather the gleanings of your **h**.
Dt 16:15 God will bless you in all your **h**
Pr 10: 5 who sleeps during **h** is a disgraceful
    20: 4 so at **h** time they look but find
Jer 8:20 "The **h** is past, the summer has
Joel 3:13 Swing the sickle, for the **h** is ripe.
Mic 6:15 You will plant but not **h**;
Mt   9:37 "The **h** is plentiful but the workers
    13:39 The **h** is the end of the age,
Lk 10: 2 He told them, "The **h** is plentiful,
    10: 2 Ask the Lord of the **h**, therefore, to
          send out workers into his **h** field.
Jn   4:35 'It's still four months until **h**'?
     4:35 at the fields! They are ripe for **h**.
1Co 9:11 if we reap a material **h** from you?
2Co 9:10 seed and will enlarge the **h** of your
Gal 6: 9 at the proper time we will reap a **h**
Heb 12:11 it produces a **h** of righteousness
Jas 3:18 in peace reap a **h** of righteousness.
Rev 14:15 come, for the **h** of the earth is ripe."

HARVESTED HARVEST

Hag 1: 6 You have planted much, but **h** little.
Rev 14:16 over the earth, and the earth was **h**.

HARVESTERS HARVEST

Ru   2: 3 and began to glean behind the **h**.
Mt 13:39 end of the age, and the **h** are angels.

HARVESTS HARVEST

Jer 5:17 They will devour your **h** and food,
Jn   4:36 a wage and **h** a crop for eternal life,

HAS HAVE

Ge 31:32 if you find anyone who **h** your gods,
Nu 14:24 my servant Caleb **h** a different spirit
Dt 21:15 If a man **h** two wives, and he loves
2Ch 25: 8 for God **h** the power to help
Job 1:12 everything he **h** is in your power,

Job   2: 4 "A man will give all he **h** for his
    11: 6 for true wisdom **h** two sides.
    42: 8 about me, as my servant Job **h**."
Ps 73:25 earth **h** nothing I desire besides you.
Pr 18:21 The tongue **h** the power of life
    23:29 Who **h** woe? Who **h** sorrow? Who **h**
        strife? Who **h** complaints? Who **h**
        needless bruises? Who **h** bloodshot
Ecc 5:10 loves money never **h** enough;
Isa 34: 8 For the LORD **h** a day
Jer 23:28 the prophet who **h** a dream recount
    23:28 let the one who **h** my word speak it
Eze 9: 6 not touch anyone who **h** the mark.
Mk 2:10 the Son of Man **h** authority on earth
    4: 9 said, "Whoever **h** ears to hear,
Lk 9:58 the Son of Man **h** no place to lay his
    12: 5 after your body **h** been killed,
Jn 3:36 believes in the Son **h** eternal life,
    4:44 prophet **h** no honor in his own
    15:13 Greater love **h** no one than this:
Ro 6: 9 death no longer **h** mastery over him.
1Co 7: 7 each of you **h** your own gift
    7: 7 one **h** this gift, another **h** that.
    7:13 a woman **h** a husband who is not
   11:14 teach you that if a man **h** long hair,
1Ti 4: 8 but godliness **h** value for all things,
1Jn 2:23 who denies the Son **h** the Father;
    2:23 acknowledges the Son **h** the Father
    5:12 Whoever **h** the Son **h** life;
Rev 20: 6 The second death **h** no power over

HASTE HASTEN, HASTILY, HASTY

Ex 12:11 Eat it in **h**; it is the LORD's
Dt 16: 3 because you left Egypt in **h**—
Pr 21: 5 lead to profit as surely as **h** leads
    29:20 you see someone who speaks in **h**?

HASTEN* HASTE

Ps 70: 1 **H**, O God, to save me;
  119:60 I will **h** and not delay to obey your
Isa 5:19 "Let God hurry; let him **h** his work so
    49:17 Your children **h** back, and those

HASTILY* HASTE

Pr 25: 8 do not bring **h** to court, for what

HASTY* HASTE

Pr 19: 2 how much more will **h** feet miss
Ecc 5: 2 do not be **h** in your heart to utter
1Ti 5:22 Do not be **h** in the laying

HATE GOD-HATERS, HATED, HATES, HATING, HATRED

Ex 18:21 men who **h** dishonest gain—
    20: 5 generation of those who **h** me,
Lev 19:17 " 'Do not **h** a fellow Israelite
Dt 7:10 those who **h** him he will repay
    7:10 repay to their face those who **h** him.
2Ch 18: 7 I **h** him because he never prophesies
Ps 5: 5 You **h** all who do wrong;
    36: 2 too much to detect or **h** their sin.
    45: 7 righteousness and **h** wickedness;
    97:10 those who love the LORD **h** evil,
  119:104 therefore I **h** every wrong path.
  119:163 I **h** and detest falsehood but I love

Ps 129: 5 May all who **h** Zion be turned back
  139:21 Do I not **h** those who **h** you,
Pr 1:22 in mockery and fools **h** knowledge?
    8:13 To fear the LORD is to **h** evil;
    9: 8 rebuke mockers or they will **h** you;
    13: 5 The righteous **h** what is false,
    25:17 too much of you, and they will **h** you.
    29:10 The bloodthirsty **h** a person
Ecc 3: 8 a time to love and a time to **h**,
Isa 61: 8 I **h** robbery and wrongdoing.
Jer 44: 4 not do this detestable thing that I **h**!'
Eze 35: 6 Since you did not **h** bloodshed,
Am 5:15 **H** evil, love good;
Mt 5:43 your neighbor and **h** your enemy.'
Lk 6:22 Blessed are you when people **h** you,
    6:27 do good to those who **h** you,
   14:26 and does not **h** father and mother,
   16:13 Either you will **h** the one and love
Jn 7: 7 The world cannot **h** you, but it hates
Ro 7:15 to do I do not do, but what I **h** I do.
    12: 9 **H** what is evil; cling to what is

HATED HATE

Ge 37: 4 they **h** him and could not speak
Est 9: 1 upper hand over those who **h** them.
Ecc 2:17 So I **h** life, because the work that is
Mal 1: 3 but Esau I have **h**, and I have turned
Mt 10:22 will be **h** by everyone because of me,
Jn 15:18 you, keep in mind that it **h** me first.
Ro 9:13 "Jacob I loved, but Esau I **h**."
Eph 5:29 all, no one ever **h** their own body,
Heb 1: 9 righteousness and **h** wickedness;

HATES HATE

Pr 6:16 There are six things the LORD **h**,
    12: 1 but whoever **h** correction is stupid.
    13:24 spares the rod **h** their children,
    15:27 but the one who **h** bribes will live.
    26:28 A lying tongue **h** those it hurts,
Mal 2:16 "The man who **h** and divorces his
Jn 3:20 Everyone who does evil **h** the light,
    12:25 while anyone who **h** their life in this
    15:19 That is why the world **h** you.
1Jn 2: 9 to be in the light but **h** a brother
    4:20 claims to love God yet **h** a brother

HATING* HATE

Titus 3: 3 being hated and **h** one another.
Jude 1:23 **h** even the clothing stained

HATRED HATE

Pr 10:12 **H** stirs up conflict, but love covers
    15:17 love than a fattened calf with **h**.
Gal 5:20 **h**, discord, jealousy, fits of rage,

HAUGHTY

Job 41:34 It looks down on all that are **h**;
Ps 18:27 bring low those whose eyes are **h**.
  131: 1 proud, LORD, my eyes are not **h**;
Pr 6:17 **h** eyes, a lying tongue,
    16:18 destruction, a **h** spirit before a fall.
    18:12 Before a downfall the heart is **h**,
Isa 13:11 put an end to the arrogance of the **h**
Zep 3:11 Never again will you be **h** on my

HAUNT

Jer	10:22	of Judah desolate, a **h** of jackals.
	51:37	be a heap of ruins, a **h** of jackals,
Rev	18: 2	a **h** for every impure spirit, a **h** for every unclean bird, a **h** for every

HAVE HAD, HAS, HAVING

Ge	18:10	and Sarah your wife will **h** a son."
	27:38	"Do you **h** only one blessing,
Ex	16:18	gathered much did not **h** too much,
	16:18	gathered little did not **h** too little.
	20: 3	"You shall **h** no other gods before
	33:19	I will **h** mercy on whom I will **h** mercy,
	33:19	I will **h** compassion on whom I will **h** compassion.
Dt	5: 7	"You shall **h** no other gods before
Jos	22:25	You **h** no share in the LORD.'
Ezr	4: 3	"You **h** no part with us in building
Job	40: 9	Do you **h** an arm like God's,
Ps	73:25	Whom **h** I in heaven but you?
	115: 5	They **h** mouths, but cannot speak,
	119:99	I **h** more insight than all my
Pr	4: 7	Though it cost all you **h**,
Ecc	6: 8	What advantage **h** the wise over
	7:12	Wisdom preserves those who **h** it.
Jer	2:28	**h** as many gods as you **h** towns.
	5:21	who **h** eyes but do not see, who **h** ears but do not hear:
Mal	2:10	Do we not all **h** one Father?
Mt	3: 9	'We **h** Abraham as our father.'
	21:21	you, if you **h** faith and do not doubt,
Mk	4:25	whoever does not **h**, even what they **h** will be taken
	10:21	sell everything you **h** and give
	10:21	and you will **h** treasure in heaven.
	14: 7	The poor you will always **h** with
	14: 7	But you will not always **h** me.
Lk	14:33	up everything you **h** cannot be my
	17: 6	you **h** faith as small as a mustard
Jn	3:16	shall not perish but **h** eternal life.
	4:32	"I **h** food to eat that you know
	5:39	think that in them you **h** eternal life.
	8:12	but will **h** the light of life."
	16:12	"I **h** much more to say to you,
	16:33	so that in me you may **h** peace.
	16:33	In this world you will **h** trouble.
Ac	3: 6	"Silver or gold I do not **h**, but what I do **h** I give you.
Ro	2:14	who do not **h** the law, do by nature
	2:14	even though they do not **h** the law.
	5: 1	we **h** peace with God through our
	8: 9	if anyone does not **h** the Spirit
	12: 6	We **h** different gifts,
1Co	2:16	But we **h** the mind of Christ.
	13: 2	If I **h** the gift of prophecy and can
	13: 2	and if I **h** a faith that can move
	13: 2	but do not **h** love, I am nothing.
2Co	4: 7	we **h** this treasure in jars of clay
	8:15	gathered much did not **h** too much,
	8:15	gathered little did not **h** too little."
Eph	1: 7	In him we **h** redemption through his
	2:18	through him we both **h** access
Heb	4:14	since we **h** a great high priest who

Heb	6:19	We **h** this hope as an anchor
Jas	2:14	if someone claims to **h** faith but has
1Jn	2:20	you **h** an anointing from the Holy
	3: 3	All who **h** this hope in him purify
	5:12	whoever does not **h** the Son of God does not **h** life.
Jude	1:19	instincts and do not **h** the Spirit.
Rev	22:14	that they may **h** the right to the tree

HAVEN

Ps	107:30	he guided them to their desired **h**.

HAVING HAVE

1Co	9:21	To those not **h** the law I became like
	9:21	so as to win those not **h** the law.
2Co	6:10	**h** nothing, and yet possessing
2Ti	3: 5	**h** a form of godliness but denying

HAVOC

Ac	9:21	"Isn't he the man who raised **h**

HAY

1Co	3:12	costly stones, wood, **h** or straw,

HAZAEL

1Ki	19:15	get there, anoint **H** king over Aram.
2Ki	8: 9	**H** went to meet Elisha,

HAZOR

Jos	11:11	breathed, and he burned **H** itself.
Jer	49:33	"**H** will become a haunt of jackals,

HEAD AHEAD, HEADS, HOTHEADED

Ge	3:15	he will crush your **h**, and you will
	28:18	the stone he had placed under his **h**
	48:18	put your right hand on his **h**."
Lev	1: 4	hand on the **h** of the burnt offering,
	19:27	cut the hair at the sides of your **h**
Nu	6: 5	no razor may be used on their **h**.
Dt	28:13	The LORD will make you the **h**,
Jdg	16:17	If my **h** were shaved, my strength
1Sa	1:11	razor will ever be used on his **h**."
	9: 2	he was a **h** taller than anyone else.
	17:51	him, he cut off his **h** with the sword.
Ps	23: 5	You anoint my **h** with oil;
	133: 2	is like precious oil poured on the **h**,
Pr	1: 9	They are a garland to grace your **h**
	10: 6	Blessings crown the **h**
	25:22	will heap burning coals on his **h**,
Isa	59:17	and the helmet of salvation on his **h**;
Jer	9: 1	that my **h** were a spring of water
Eze	8: 3	and took me by the hair of my **h**.
	33: 4	their blood will be on their own **h**.
Da	2:32	The **h** of the statue was made
	7: 9	hair of his **h** was white like wool.
Mt	8:20	of Man has no place to lay his **h**."
Mk	6:28	and brought back his **h** on a platter.
Jn	19: 2	crown of thorns and put it on his **h**.
Ro	12:20	will heap burning coals on his **h**."
1Co	11: 3	that the **h** of every man is Christ, and the **h** of the woman is man, and the **h** of Christ is God.
	11: 4	with his **h** covered dishonors his **h**.
	11: 5	her **h** uncovered dishonors her **h**—

1Co 11: 5 is the same as having her **h** shaved.
    12:21 And the **h** cannot say to the feet,
Eph 1:22 him to be **h** over everything
    5:23 husband is the **h** of the wife as Christ
        is the **h** of the church,
Col 1:18 And he is the **h** of the body,
2Ti 4: 5 you, keep your **h** in all situations,
Rev 1:14 hair on his **h** was white like wool,
    10: 1 a cloud, with a rainbow above his **h**;
    12: 1 a crown of twelve stars on her **h**.
    13: 1 and on each **h** a blasphemous name.
    14:14 man with a crown of gold on his **h**
    19:12 fire, and on his **h** are many crowns.

HEADLONG
Ac 1:18 there he fell **h**, his body burst open

HEADS HEAD
Ge 41: 5 Seven **h** of grain, healthy and good,
Lev 26:13 you to walk with **h** held high.
Ne 4: 4 their insults back on their own **h**.
Ps 7:16 comes down on their own **h**.
    22: 7 they hurl insults, shaking their **h**.
    24: 7 Lift up your **h**, you gates;
Isa 35:10 everlasting joy will crown their **h**.
    51:11 everlasting joy will crown their **h**.
Eze 11:21 on their own **h** what they have done,
Da 7: 6 This beast had four **h**, and it was
Mt 27:39 insults at him, shaking their **h**
Mk 2:23 they began to pick some **h** of grain.
Lk 21:28 stand up and lift up your **h**,
Ac 18: 6 "Your blood be on your own **h**!
Rev 4: 4 and had crowns of gold on their **h**.
    12: 3 enormous red dragon with seven **h**
    12: 3 ten horns and seven crowns on its **h**
    17: 9 The seven **h** are seven hills

HEAL* HEALED, HEALING, HEALS
Nu 12:13 the LORD, "Please, God, **h** her!"
Dt 32:39 I have wounded and I will **h**, and no
2Ki 20: 5 and seen your tears; I will **h** you.
    20: 8 the sign that the LORD will **h** me
2Ch 7:14 their sin and will **h** their land.
Job 5:18 he injures, but his hands also **h**.
Ps 6: 2 **h** me, LORD, for my bones are
    41: 4 **h** me, for I have sinned against
Ecc 3: 3 a time to kill and a time to **h**, a time
Isa 19:22 he will strike them and **h** them.
    19:22 respond to their pleas and **h** them.
    57:18 seen their ways, but I will **h** them;
    57:19 "And I will **h** them."
Jer 17:14 **H** me, LORD, and I will be healed;
    30:17 you to health and **h** your wounds,'
    33: 6 I will **h** my people and will let them
La 2:13 as deep as the sea. Who can **h** you?
Hos 5:13 to cure you, not able to **h** your sores.
    6: 1 torn us to pieces but he will **h** us;
    7: 1 whenever I would **h** Israel, the sins
    14: 4 "I will **h** their waywardness
Na 3:19 Nothing can **h** you; your wound is
Zec 11:16 or **h** the injured, or feed the healthy,
Mt 8: 7 to him, "Shall I come and **h** him?"
    10: 1 and to **h** every disease and sickness.
    10: 8 **H** the sick, raise the dead,

Mt 12:10 "Is it lawful to **h** on the Sabbath?"
    13:15 and turn, and I would **h** them.'
    17:16 but they could not **h** him."
Mk 3: 2 if he would **h** him on the Sabbath.
    6: 5 on a few sick people and **h** them.
Lk 4:23 'Physician, **h** yourself!'
    5:17 Lord was with Jesus to **h** the sick.
    6: 7 to see if he would **h** on the Sabbath.
    7: 3 him to come and **h** his servant.
    8:43 years, but no one could **h** her.
    9: 2 kingdom of God and to **h** the sick.
    10: 9 **H** the sick who are there and tell
    14: 3 "Is it lawful to **h** on the Sabbath
Jn 4:47 begged him to come and **h** his son,
    12:40 and I would **h** them."
Ac 4:30 Stretch out your hand to **h**
    28:27 and turn, and I would **h** them.'

HEALED* HEAL
Ge 20:17 and God **h** Abimelek, his wife
Ex 21:19 see that the victim is completely **h**.
Lev 13:37 grown in it, the affected person is **h**.
    14: 3 If they have been **h** of their defiling
Jos 5: 8 they were in camp until they were **h**.
1Sa 6: 3 Then you will be **h**, and you will
2Ki 2:21 'I have **h** this water.
2Ch 30:20 heard Hezekiah and **h** the people.
Ps 30: 2 to you for help, and you **h** me.
    107:20 He sent out his word and **h** them;
Isa 6:10 their hearts, and turn and be **h**."
    53: 5 him, and by his wounds we are **h**.
Jer 14:19 afflicted us so that we cannot be **h**?
    17:14 Heal me, LORD, and I will be **h**;
    51: 8 for her pain; perhaps she can be **h**.
    51: 9 " 'We would have **h** Babylon, but she
        cannot be **h**;
Eze 30:21 It has not been bound up to be **h**
    34: 4 strengthened the weak or **h** the sick
Hos 11: 3 did not realize it was I who **h** them.
Mt 4:24 and the paralyzed; and he **h** them.
    8: 8 the word, and my servant will be **h**.
    8:13 his servant was **h** at that moment.
    8:16 with a word and **h** all the sick.
    9:21 I only touch his cloak, I will be **h**."
    9:22 he said, "your faith has **h** you."
    9:22 the woman was **h** at that moment.
    12:15 him, and he **h** all who were ill.
    12:22 and Jesus **h** him, so that he could
    14:14 on them and **h** their sick.
    14:36 and all who touched it were **h**.
    15:28 her daughter was **h** at that moment.
    15:30 laid them at his feet; and he **h** them.
    17:18 boy, and he was **h** at that moment.
    19: 2 followed him, and he **h** them there.
    21:14 to him at the temple, and he **h** them.
Mk 1:34 and Jesus **h** many who had various
    3:10 For he had **h** many, so that those
    5:23 hands on her so that she will be **h**
    5:28 I just touch his clothes, I will be **h**."
    5:34 "Daughter, your faith has **h** you.
    6:13 sick people with oil and **h** them.
    6:56 and all who touched it were **h**.
    10:52 said Jesus, "your faith has **h** you."
Lk 4:40 his hands on each one, he **h** them.

Lk   5:15 him and to be **h** of their sicknesses.
      6:18 him and to be **h** of their diseases.
      7: 7 the word, and my servant will be **h**.
      8:47 and how she had been instantly **h**.
      8:48 "Daughter, your faith has **h** you.
      8:50 just believe, and she will be **h**."
      9:11 and **h** those who needed healing.
      9:42 **h** the boy and gave him back to his
     13:14 Indignant because Jesus had **h**
     13:14 So come and be **h** on those days,
     14: 4 he **h** him and sent him on his way.
     17:15 when he saw he was **h**, came back,
     18:42 your faith has **h** you."
     22:51 he touched the man's ear and **h** him.
Jn   5:10 said to the man who had been **h**,
      5:13 The man who was **h** had no idea
Ac   3:16 him that has completely **h** him,
      4: 9 and are being asked how he was **h**,
      4:10 that this man stands before you **h**.
      4:14 man who had been **h** standing there
      4:22 who was miraculously **h** was over
      5:16 spirits, and all of them were **h**.
      8: 7 who were paralyzed or lame were **h**.
     14: 9 at him, saw that he had faith to be **h**
     28: 8 placed his hands on him and **h** him.
Heb 12:13 may not be disabled, but rather **h**.
Jas   5:16 for each other so that you may be **h**.
1Pe   2:24 "by his wounds you have been **h**."
Rev 13: 3 but the fatal wound had been **h**.
     13:12 whose fatal wound had been **h**.

HEALING* HEAL

2Ch 28:15 sandals, food and drink, and **h** balm.
Pr   12:18 but the tongue of the wise brings **h**.
     13:17 but a trustworthy envoy brings **h**.
     16:24 sweet to the soul and **h** to the bones.
Isa 58: 8 and your **h** will quickly appear;
Jer   8:15 for a time of **h** but there is only
      8:22 is there no **h** for the wound of my
     14:19 for a time of **h** but there is only
     30:12 is incurable, your injury beyond **h**.
     30:13 remedy for your sore, no **h** for you.
     33: 6 I will bring health and **h** to it;
     46:11 there is no **h** for you.
Eze 47:12 for food and their leaves for **h**."
Mal   4: 2 righteousness will rise with **h** in its
Mt   4:23 and **h** every disease and sickness
      9:35 of the kingdom and **h** every disease
Lk   6:19 coming from him and **h** them all.
      9: 6 news and **h** people everywhere.
      9:11 and healed those who needed **h**.
     13:32 out demons and **h** people today
Jn   6: 2 he had performed by **h** the sick.
      7:23 me for **h** a man's whole body
Ac   10:38 **h** all who were under the power
1Co 12: 9 to another gifts of **h** by that one
     12:28 miracles, then gifts of **h**, of helping,
     12:30 Do all have gifts of **h**? Do all speak
Rev 22: 2 the tree are for the **h** of the nations.

HEALS* HEAL

Ex   15:26 for I am the Lᴏʀᴅ, who **h** you."
Lev 13:18 has a boil on their skin and it **h**,
Ps 103: 3 all your sins and **h** all your diseases,

Ps 147: 3 He **h** the brokenhearted and binds
Isa 30:26 and **h** the wounds he inflicted.
Ac   9:34 said to him, "Jesus Christ **h** you.

HEALTH* HEALTHIER, HEALTHY

1Sa 16:12 He was glowing with **h** and had
     17:42 boy, glowing with **h** and handsome,
     25: 6 Good **h** to you and your household!
     25: 6 And good **h** to all that is yours!
Ps   38: 3 your wrath there is no **h** in my body;
     38: 7 there is no **h** in my body.
Pr   3: 8 This will bring **h** to your body
      4:22 them and **h** to one's whole body.
     15:30 and good news gives **h** to the bones.
Isa 38:16 You restored me to **h** and let me
Jer 30:17 I will restore you to **h** and heal your
     33: 6 I will bring **h** and healing to it;
3Jn   1: 2 I pray that you may enjoy good **h**

HEALTHIER* HEALTH

Da   1:15 end of the ten days they looked **h**

HEALTHY* HEALTH

Ge   41: 5 Seven heads of grain, **h** and good,
     41: 7 of grain swallowed up the seven **h**,
Ps   73: 4 their bodies are **h** and strong.
Zec 11:16 or feed the **h**, but will eat the meat
Mt   6:22 If your eyes are **h**, your whole body
      9:12 "It is not the **h** who need a doctor,
Mk   2:17 "It is not the **h** who need a doctor,
Lk   5:31 "It is not the **h** who need a doctor,
     11:34 When your eyes are **h**, your whole

HEAP HEAPED, HEAPING

Ge   31:48 "This **h** is a witness between you
Dt   32:23 "I will **h** calamities on them
Jos   3:13 will be cut off and stand up in a **h**."
1Sa   2: 8 and lifts the needy from the ash **h**;
Pr   25:22 this, you will **h** burning coals on his
Ro   12:20 this, you will **h** burning coals on his
1Th   2:16 this way they always **h** up their sins
1Pe   4: 4 living, and they **h** abuse on you.

HEAPED HEAP

Mt   27:44 with him also **h** insults on him.

HEAPING* HEAP

Ps   39: 6 **h** up wealth without knowing whose
    110:16 **h** up the dead and crushing
Isa 30: 1 but not by my Spirit, **h** sin upon sin;

HEAR HEARD, HEARERS,
HEARING, HEARS

Ex   15:14 The nations will **h** and tremble;
     18: 9 Jethro was delighted to **h** about all
     22:27 I will **h**, for I am compassionate.
Nu   14:13 "Then the Egyptians will **h** about it!
Dt   1:17 too hard for you, and I will **h** it."
      4:36 heaven he made you **h** his voice
      5: 1 **H**, Israel, the decrees and laws I
      6: 3 **H**, Israel, and be careful to obey so
      6: 4 **H**, O Israel: The Lᴏʀᴅ our God,
      9: 1 **H**, Israel: You are now
     13:11 Then all Israel will **h** and be afraid,
     19:20 The rest of the people will **h** of this

Dt 20: 3 He shall say: "H, Israel:
31:13 law, must **h** it and learn to fear
Jos 7: 9 of the country will **h** about this
1Ki 8:30 **H** the supplication of your servant
8:30 **H** from heaven, your dwelling place, and when you **h**, forgive.
10: 8 before you and **h** your wisdom!
2Ki 19:16 Give ear, LORD, and **h**;
2Ch 7:14 then I will **h** from heaven, and I will
Job 5:27 So **h** it and apply it to yourself."
20: 3 I **h** a rebuke that dishonors me,
26:14 how faint the whisper we **h** of him!
31:35 ("Oh, that I had someone to **h** me!
Ps 5: 2 **H** my cry for help, my King and my
30:10 **H**, LORD, and be merciful to me;
51: 8 Let me **h** joy and gladness;
80: 1 **H** us, Shepherd of Israel, you who
94: 9 he who fashioned the ear not **h**?
95: 7 if only you would **h** his voice,
135:17 but cannot **h**, nor is there breath
Ecc 7:21 or you may **h** your servant cursing
Isa 1:10 **H** the word of the LORD,
21: 3 I am staggered by what I **h**, I am
29:18 day the deaf will **h** the words
30:21 your ears will **h** a voice behind you,
51: 7 "**H** me, you who know what is
59: 1 to save, nor his ear too dull to **h**.
65:24 while they are still speaking I will **h**.
Jer 5:21 **H** this, you foolish and senseless
5:21 not see, who have ears but do not **h**:
Eze 33: 7 so **h** the word I speak and give them
37: 4 bones, **h** the word of the LORD!
Da 3: 5 As soon as you **h** the sound
Mic 6: 2 "**H**, you mountains, the LORD's
Mt 11: 5 the deaf **h**, the dead are raised,
11:15 Whoever has ears, let them **h**.
13:17 and to **h** what you **h** but did not **h** it.
Mk 12:29 Jesus, "is this: '**H**, O Israel:
Lk 7:22 the deaf **h**, the dead are raised,
Jn 5:25 the dead will **h** the voice of the Son of God and those who **h** will live.
8:47 The reason you do not **h** is that you
Ac 13: 7 because he wanted to **h** the word
13:44 whole city gathered to **h** the word
17:32 "We want to **h** you again on this
Ro 2:13 is not those who **h** the law who are
10:14 how can they **h** without someone
2Ti 4: 3 what their itching ears want to **h**.
Heb 3: 7 "Today, if you **h** his voice,
Rev 1: 3 blessed are those who **h** it and take

HEARD HEAR

Ge 3: 8 his wife **h** the sound of the LORD
21:17 God **h** the boy crying, and the angel
Ex 2:24 God **h** their groaning and he
6: 5 I have **h** the groaning
16: 7 because he has **h** your grumbling
Nu 12: 2 And the LORD **h** this.
14:27 I have **h** the complaints of these
Dt 4:32 has anything like it ever been **h** of?
Jos 24:27 It has **h** all the words the LORD
2Sa 7:22 as we have **h** with our own ears.
1Ki 4:34 world, who had **h** of his wisdom.
10: 1 the queen of Sheba **h** about the fame

Ne 9:27 From heaven you **h** them,
Job 42: 5 My ears had **h** of you but now my
Ps 18: 6 From his temple he **h** my voice;
62:11 has spoken, two things I have **h**:
66:19 surely listened and has **h** my prayer.
78:59 When God **h** them, he was furious;
116: 1 love the LORD, for he **h** my voice; he **h** my cry for mercy.
Isa 40:21 Have you not **h**? Has it not been
40:28 Have you not **h**? The LORD is
66: 8 Who has ever **h** of such things?
Jer 18:13 Who has ever **h** anything like this?
La 3:56 You **h** my plea: "Do not close your
Eze 10: 5 the cherubim could be **h** as far away
Da 10:12 your words were **h**, and I have come
12: 8 I **h**, but I did not understand.
Hab 3:16 I **h** and my heart pounded, my lips
Mt 2: 3 King Herod **h** this he was disturbed,
5:21 "You have **h** that it was said
5:27 "You have **h** that it was said,
5:33 you have **h** that it was said
5:38 "You have **h** that it was said,
5:43 "You have **h** that it was said,
Mk 6: 2 and many who **h** him were amazed.
14:64 "You have **h** the blasphemy.
Lk 12: 3 in the dark will be **h** in the daylight,
Jn 6:45 Everyone who has **h** the Father
8:26 what I have **h** from him I tell
Ac 2: 6 because each one **h** their own
10:44 came on all who **h** the message.
Ro 10:14 in the one of whom they have not **h**?
1Co 2: 9 what no ear has **h**, and what no
2Co 12: 4 paradise and **h** inexpressible things,
Gal 3: 2 the law, or by believing what you **h**?
1Th 2:13 which you **h** from us, you accepted
2Ti 1:13 What you **h** from me, keep as
Heb 4: 2 the message they **h** was of no value
Jas 1:25 not forgetting what they have **h**,
2Pe 1:18 We ourselves **h** this voice that came
1Jn 1: 3 to you what we have seen and **h**,
3:11 this is the message you **h**
2Jn 1: 6 As you have **h** from the beginning,
Rev 1:10 I **h** behind me a loud voice like
22: 8 am the one who **h** and saw these

HEARERS* HEAR
1Ti 4:16 will save both yourself and your **h**.

HEARING HEAR
Nu 11: 1 hardships in the **h** of the LORD,
Dt 31:11 read this law before them in their **h**.
2Ch 34:30 He read in their **h** all the words
Isa 6: 9 " 'Be ever **h**, but never
Am 8:11 but a famine of **h** the words
Mt 13:14 " 'You will be ever **h** but never
Mk 4:12 and ever **h** but never understanding;
Lk 4:21 this scripture is fulfilled in your **h**."
Jn 7:51 condemn a man without first **h** him
Ac 28:26 say, "You will be ever **h** but never
Ro 10:17 faith comes from **h** the message,
1Co 12:17 eye, where would the sense of **h** be?

HEARS HEAR
Ps 69:33 The LORD **h** the needy and does

Pr 15:29 but he **h** the prayer of the righteous.
Isa 30:19 As soon as he **h**, he will answer you.
Mt 7:24 everyone who **h** these words
Lk 6:47 who comes to me and **h** my words
Jn 5:24 whoever **h** my word and believes
1Jn 5:14 according to his will, he **h** us.
Rev 3:20 If anyone **h** my voice and opens
 22:18 I warn everyone who **h** the words

HEART BROKENHEARTED, DISHEARTENED, FAINTHEARTED, HARDHEARTED, HEART'S, HEARTACHE, HEARTFELT, HEARTLESS, HEARTS, HEARTS', KINDHEARTED, WHOLEHEARTED, WHOLEHEARTEDLY

Ge 6: 5 of the human **h** was only evil all
 6: 6 and his **h** was deeply troubled.
 24:45 "Before I finished praying in my **h**,
Ex 4:21 I will harden his **h** so that he will
 7:13 Yet Pharaoh's **h** became hard
 7:22 arts, and Pharaoh's **h** became hard;
 8:15 he hardened his **h** and would not
 8:19 But Pharaoh's **h** was hard and he
 8:32 Pharaoh hardened his **h** and would
 9: 7 Yet his **h** was unyielding and he
 9:12 the LORD hardened Pharaoh's **h**
 9:35 So Pharaoh's **h** was hard and he
 10:20 the LORD hardened Pharaoh's **h**,
 10:27 the LORD hardened Pharaoh's **h**,
 11:10 the LORD hardened Pharaoh's **h**,
 14: 4 And I will harden Pharaoh's **h**,
 25: 2 everyone whose **h** prompts them
 28:30 may be over Aaron's **h** whenever he
 35:21 and whose **h** moved them came
Lev 19:17 not hate a fellow Israelite in your **h**.
Dt 4: 9 from your **h** as long as you live.
 4:29 him if you seek him with all your **h**
 6: 5 LORD your God with all your **h**
 8:14 then your **h** will become proud
 10:12 LORD your God with all your **h**
 11:13 and to serve him with all your **h**
 13: 3 you love him with all your **h**
 15:10 and do so without a grudging **h**;
 26:16 observe them with all your **h**
 29:18 you today whose **h** turns away
 30: 2 obey him with all your **h**
 30: 6 you may love him with all your **h**
 30:10 LORD your God with all your **h**
 30:14 and in your **h** so you may obey it.
Jos 22: 5 and to serve him with all your **h**
 23:14 You know with all your **h** and soul
1Sa 10: 9 God changed Saul's **h**, and all these
 12:20 serve the LORD with all your **h**.
 12:24 serve him faithfully with all your **h**;
 13:14 sought out a man after his own **h**
 14: 7 I am with you **h** and soul."
 16: 7 but the LORD looks at the **h**."
 17:32 "Let no one lose **h** on account
2Sa 6:16 LORD, she despised him in her **h**.
1Ki 2: 4 faithfully before me with all their **h**

1Ki 3: 9 So give your servant a discerning **h**
 8:17 had it in his **h** to build a temple
 8:48 they turn back to you with all their **h**
 9: 3 eyes and my **h** will always be there.
 9: 4 me faithfully with integrity of **h**
 10:24 the wisdom God had put in his **h**.
 11: 4 his wives turned his **h** after other
 11: 4 his **h** was not fully devoted
 14: 8 and followed me with all his **h**,
 15:14 Asa's **h** was fully committed
2Ki 22:19 Because your **h** was responsive
 23: 3 and decrees with all his **h** and all his
1Ch 28: 9 for the LORD searches every **h**
2Ch 6:38 they turn back to you with all their **h**
 7:16 eyes and my **h** will always be there.
 15:12 ancestors, with all their **h** and soul.
 15:17 Asa's **h** was fully committed
 17: 6 His **h** was devoted to the ways
 22: 9 sought the LORD with all his **h**."
 32:25 But Hezekiah's **h** was proud and he
 34:31 and decrees with all his **h** and all his
 36:13 hardened his **h** and would not turn
Ezr 1: 1 the LORD moved the **h** of Cyrus
 1: 5 everyone whose **h** God had moved—
Ne 4: 6 the people worked with all their **h**.
Job 19:27 How my **h** yearns within me!
 22:22 and lay up his words in your **h**.
 31: 7 if my **h** has been led by my eyes,
 37: 1 "At this my **h** pounds and leaps
Ps 7:10 High, who saves the upright in **h**.
 9: 1 to you, LORD, with all my **h**;
 14: 1 The fool says in his **h**, "There is no
 16: 9 Therefore my **h** is glad and my
 19:14 this meditation of my **h** be pleasing
 20: 4 he give you the desire of your **h**
 24: 4 who has clean hands and a pure **h**,
 26: 2 try me, examine my **h** and my mind;
 28: 7 my **h** trusts in him, and he helps me.
 37: 4 will give you the desires of your **h**.
 44:21 since he knows the secrets of the **h**?
 45: 1 My **h** is stirred by a noble theme as
 51:10 Create in me a pure **h**, O God,
 51:17 a broken and contrite **h** you, God,
 66:18 If I had cherished sin in my **h**,
 73: 1 to Israel, to those who are pure in **h**.
 73:26 My flesh and my **h** may fail,
 73:26 God is the strength of my **h** and my
 86:11 give me an undivided **h**, that I may
 90:12 that we may gain a **h** of wisdom.
 97:11 and joy on the upright in **h**.
 108: 1 My **h**, O God, is steadfast;
 109:22 and my **h** is wounded within me.
 111: 1 LORD with all my **h** in the council
 119: 2 and seek him with all their **h**—
 119:10 I seek you with all my **h**; do not let
 119:11 in my **h** that I might not sin against
 119:30 I have set my **h** on your laws.
 119:34 your law and obey it with all my **h**.
 119:36 Turn my **h** toward your statutes
 119:58 sought your face with all my **h**;
 119:69 I keep your precepts with all my **h**.
 119:111 they are the joy of my **h**.
 119:112 My **h** is set on keeping your decrees

Ps 119:145 I call with all my **h**;
119:161 but my **h** trembles at your word.
125: 4 good, to those who are upright in **h**.
138: 1 praise you, LORD, with all my **h**;
139:23 Search me, God, and know my **h**;
141: 4 Do not let my **h** be drawn to what is
148:14 of Israel, the people close to his **h**.
Pr 2: 2 applying your **h** to understanding—
3: 1 but keep my commands in your **h**,
3: 3 write them on the tablet of your **h**.
3: 5 Trust in the LORD with all your **h**
4: 4 hold of my words with all your **h**;
4:21 your sight, keep them within your **h**;
4:23 guard your **h**, for everything you do
6:14 who plots evil with deceit in his **h**—
6:21 Bind them always on your **h**;
6:25 not lust in your **h** after her beauty
7: 3 write them on the tablet of your **h**.
10: 8 The wise in **h** accept commands,
12:23 but a fool's **h** blurts out folly.
12:25 Anxiety weighs down the **h**,
13:12 Hope deferred makes the **h** sick,
14:13 Even in laughter the **h** may ache,
14:30 A **h** at peace gives life to the body,
15:13 A happy **h** makes the face cheerful,
15:15 the cheerful **h** has a continual feast.
15:28 The **h** of the righteous weighs its
15:30 eyes brings joy to the **h**, and good
16: 5 LORD detests all the proud of **h**.
17: 3 for gold, but the LORD tests the **h**.
17:20 One whose **h** is corrupt does not
17:22 A cheerful **h** is good medicine,
19:21 Many are the plans in a person's **h**,
20: 9 can say, "I have kept my **h** pure;
21: 1 hand the king's **h** is a stream
21: 2 right, but the LORD weighs the **h**.
22:11 One who loves a pure **h** and who
22:15 Folly is bound up in the **h** of a child,
22:17 apply your **h** to what I teach,
22:18 when you keep them in your **h**
23:15 if your **h** is wise, then my **h** will be
23:17 Do not let your **h** envy sinners,
23:19 and set your **h** on the right path:
23:26 give me your **h** and let your eyes
24:17 stumble, do not let your **h** rejoice,
27:19 the face, so one's life reflects the **h**.
Ecc 2:10 I refused my **h** no pleasure.
2:10 My **h** took delight in all my labor,
3:11 has also set eternity in the human **h**;
5: 2 your **h** to utter anything before God.
7: 7 a fool, and a bribe corrupts the **h**.
8: 5 and the wise **h** will know the proper
9: 7 and drink your wine with a joyful **h**,
11:10 banish anxiety from your **h** and cast
SS 3: 1 bed I looked for the one my **h** loves;
4: 9 You have stolen my **h**, my sister,
5: 2 I slept but my **h** was awake. Listen!
8: 6 Place me like a seal over your **h**,
Isa 6:10 Make the **h** of this people calloused;
40:11 arms and carries them close to his **h**;
51: 7 who have taken my instruction to **h**:
57:15 and to revive the **h** of the contrite.
66:14 this, your **h** will rejoice and you will

Jer 3:10 did not return to me with all her **h**,
3:15 give you shepherds after my own **h**,
4:14 wash the evil from your **h** and be
9:26 of Israel is uncircumcised in **h**."
17: 9 The **h** is deceitful above all things
17:10 "I the LORD search the **h**
20: 9 his word is in my **h** like a fire, a fire
24: 7 I will give them a **h** to know me,
24: 7 will return to me with all their **h**.
29:13 when you seek me with all your **h**.
32:39 I will give them singleness of **h**
32:41 plant them in this land with all my **h**
51:46 Do not lose **h** or be afraid
Eze 11:19 I will give them an undivided **h**
11:19 remove from them their **h** of stone
and give them a **h** of flesh.
18:31 and get a new **h** and a new spirit.
28: 2 " 'In the pride of your **h** you say,
36:26 I will give you a new **h** and put
36:26 remove from you your **h** of stone and
give you a **h** of flesh.
44: 7 foreigners uncircumcised in **h**
Hos 11: 8 My **h** is changed within me;
Joel 2:12 "return to me with all your **h**,
2:13 Rend your **h** and not your garments.
Ob 1: 3 pride of your **h** has deceived you,
Zep 3:14 Be glad and rejoice with all your **h**,
Mt 5: 8 Blessed are the pure in **h**, for they
5:28 adultery with her in his **h**.
6:21 treasure is, there your **h** will be also.
11:29 for I am gentle and humble in **h**,
12:34 mouth speaks what the **h** is full of.
13:15 For this people's **h** has become
15:18 a person's mouth come from the **h**,
15:19 out of the **h** come evil thoughts—
18:35 your brother or sister from your **h**."
22:37 the Lord your God with all your **h**
Mk 11:23 and does not doubt in their **h**
12:30 the Lord your God with all your **h**
12:33 To love him with all your **h**, with all
Lk 2:19 things and pondered them in her **h**.
2:51 treasured all these things in her **h**.
6:45 out of the good stored up in his **h**,
6:45 out of the evil stored up in his **h**.
6:45 mouth speaks what the **h** is full of.
8:15 for those with a noble and good **h**,
10:27 the Lord your God with all your **h**
12:34 treasure is, there your **h** will be also.
Ac 1:24 "Lord, you know everyone's **h**.
2:37 they were cut to the **h** and said
4:32 All the believers were one in **h**
5: 3 Satan has so filled your **h** that you
8:21 because your **h** is not right before
15: 8 who knows the **h**, showed that he
16:14 The Lord opened her **h** to respond
28:27 For this people's **h** has become
Ro 2:29 is circumcision of the **h**,
6:17 to obey from your **h** the pattern
10: 8 it is in your mouth and in your **h**,"
10: 9 in your **h** that God raised him
1Co 4: 5 will expose the motives of the **h**.
2Co 2: 4 anguish of **h** and with many tears,
4: 1 have this ministry, we do not lose **h**.

2Co 4:16 Therefore we do not lose **h**.
       9: 7 you have decided in your **h** to give,
Eph 1:18 eyes of your **h** may be enlightened
       5:19 music from your **h** to the Lord,
       6: 5 and with sincerity of **h**, just as you
       6: 6 doing the will of God from your **h**.
Php 1: 7 you, since I have you in my **h** and,
Col   2: 2 is that they may be encouraged in **h**
       3:22 with sincerity of **h** and reverence
       3:23 you do, work at it with all your **h**,
1Ti   1: 5 which comes from a pure **h**
2Ti   2:22 call on the Lord out of a pure **h**.
Phm 1:12 who is my very **h**—back to you.
       1:20 in the Lord; refresh my **h** in Christ.
Heb   3:12 unbelieving **h** that turns away
       4:12 the thoughts and attitudes of the **h**.
      10:22 draw near to God with a sincere **h**
      12: 5 do not lose **h** when he rebukes you,
1Pe   1:22 love one another deeply, from the **h**.
Rev 18: 7 In her **h** she boasts, 'I sit enthroned

ALL ... HEART Dt 4:29; 6:5; 10:12; 11:13; 13:3;
26:16; 30:2, 6, 10; Jos 22:5; 23:14; 1Sa 12:20, 24;
2Sa 3:21; 22:46; 1Ki 2:4; 8:48; 11:37; 14:8; 2Ki
10:31; 23:3, 25; 2Ch 6:38; 15:12; 22:9; 34:31; Ne
4:6; Job 37:24; Ps 9:1; 18:45; 64:10; 86:12; 94:15;
111:1; 119:2, 10, 34, 58, 69, 145; 138:1; Pr 3:5; 4:4;
16:5; Jer 3:10; 24:7; 29:13; 32:41; Joel 2:12; Zep
3:14; Mt 22:37; Mk 12:30, 33; Lk 10:27; Col 3:23

HEART'S* HEART

2Ch 1:11 "Since this is your **h** desire and you
Ps   21: 2 You have granted him his **h** desire
Jer 15:16 they were my joy and my **h** delight,
Eze 24:25 delight of their eyes, their **h** desire,
Ro   10: 1 my **h** desire and prayer to God

HEARTACHE* HEART

Pr   15:13 cheerful, but **h** crushes the spirit.

HEARTFELT* HEART

Pr   27: 9 a friend springs from their **h** advice.

HEARTLESS* HEART

La   4: 3 people have become **h** like ostriches

HEARTS HEART

Ex   9:34 and his officials hardened their **h**.
      14:17 I will harden the **h** of the Egyptians
Lev 26:36 I will make their **h** so fearful
      26:41 their uncircumcised **h** are humbled
Nu   15:39 chasing after the lusts of your own **h**
Dt   1:28 Our brothers have made our **h** melt
       5:29 that their **h** would be inclined to fear
       6: 6 I give you today are to be on your **h**.
      10:16 Circumcise your **h**, therefore,
      11:18 Fix these words of mine in your **h**
      30: 6 your God will circumcise your **h** and
             the **h** of your descendants,
Jos   5: 1 their **h** melted in fear and they no
       7: 5 At this the **h** of the people melted
      11:20 himself who hardened their **h**
      14: 8 me made the **h** of the people melt
      24:23 you and yield your **h** to the LORD,
1Sa   6: 6 you harden your **h** as the Egyptians
       7: 3 to the LORD with all your **h**,

1Sa 10:26 by valiant men whose **h** God had
2Sa 15: 6 so he stole the **h** of the people
1Ki   8:39 do, since you know their **h** (for you
       8:61 may your **h** be fully committed
      18:37 you are turning their **h** back again."
1Ch 29:18 and keep their **h** loyal to you.
      29:18 in the **h** of your people forever,
2Ch   6:30 do, since you know their **h** (for you
      11:16 Israel who set their **h** on seeking
      29:31 all whose **h** were willing brought
Job   1: 5 sinned and cursed God in their **h**."
Ps   4: 4 beds, search your **h** and be silent.
       7: 9 God who probes minds and **h**.
      33:15 he who forms the **h** of all,
      33:21 In him our **h** rejoice, for we trust
      37:31 The law of their God is in their **h**;
      62: 8 pour out your **h** to him, for God is
      78: 8 whose **h** were not loyal to God,
      81:12 their stubborn **h** to follow their own
      95: 8 "Do not harden your **h** as you did
     104:15 wine that gladdens human **h**,
     112: 7 their **h** are steadfast,
     112: 8 Their **h** are secure, they will have no
Pr   16:23 The **h** of the wise make their
Ecc   9: 3 madness in their **h** while they live,
Isa 26: 8 and renown are the desire of our **h**.
      29:13 lips, but their **h** are far from me.
      35: 4 say to those with fearful **h**,
      59:13 uttering lies our **h** have conceived.
      63:17 harden our **h** so we do not revere
      65:14 will sing out of the joy of their **h**,
Jer   4: 4 circumcise your **h**, you people
      12: 2 on their lips but far from their **h**.
      17: 1 on the tablets of their **h**
      31:33 their minds and write it on their **h**.
La   5:15 Joy is gone from our **h**;
Eze 14: 3 men have set up idols in their **h**
      20:16 For their **h** were devoted to their
Mal   4: 6 He will turn the **h** of the parents
       4: 6 the **h** of the children to their parents;
Mt   15: 8 lips, but their **h** are far from me.
      19: 8 wives because your **h** were hard.
Mk   6:52 their **h** were hardened.
       7: 6 lips, but their **h** are far from me.
Lk   1:17 to turn the **h** of the parents to their
      16:15 of others, but God knows your **h**.
      24:32 "Were not our **h** burning within us
Jn   5:42 not have the love of God in your **h**.
      12:40 their eyes and hardened their **h**,
      14: 1 "Do not let your **h** be troubled.
      14:27 Do not let your **h** be troubled and do
Ac   2:46 ate together with glad and sincere **h**,
       7:51 Your **h** and ears are still
      11:23 true to the Lord with all their **h**.
      15: 9 for he purified their **h** by faith.
      28:27 understand with their **h** and turn,
Ro   1:21 and their foolish **h** were darkened.
       2:15 of the law are written on their **h**,
       5: 5 into our **h** through the Holy Spirit,
       8:27 who searches our **h** knows the mind
1Co 14:25 the secrets of their **h** are laid bare.
2Co   1:22 put his Spirit in our **h** as a deposit,
       3: 2 written on our **h**, known and read

2Co 3: 3 of stone but on tablets of human **h**.
3:15 Moses is read, a veil covers their **h**.
4: 6 shine in our **h** to give us the light
6:11 and opened wide our **h** to you.
6:13 open wide your **h** also.
7: 2 Make room for us in your **h**.
Gal 4: 6 sent the Spirit of his Son into our **h**,
Eph 3:17 may dwell in your **h** through faith.
Php 4: 7 will guard your **h** and your minds
Col 3: 1 Christ, set your **h** on things above,
3:15 the peace of Christ rule in your **h**,
3:16 to God with gratitude in your **h**.
1Th 2: 4 people but God, who tests our **h**.
3:13 May he strengthen your **h** so
2Th 2:17 encourage your **h** and strengthen
Phm 1: 7 have refreshed the **h** of the Lord's
Heb 3: 8 do not harden your **h** as you did
8:10 minds and write them on their **h**.
10:16 I will put my laws in their **h**, and I
10:22 having our **h** sprinkled to cleanse us
13: 9 is good for our **h** to be strengthened
Jas 4: 8 you sinners, and purify your **h**,
1Pe 3:15 But in your **h** revere Christ as Lord.
2Pe 1:19 and the morning star rises in your **h**.
1Jn 3:20 If our **h** condemn us, we know that
God is greater than our **h**,
Rev 2:23 know that I am he who searches **h**
17:17 their **h** to accomplish his purpose

HEARTS'* HEART
Pr 13:25 The righteous eat to their **h** content,

HEAT
Ge 8:22 cold and **h**, summer and winter,
2Pe 3:12 and the elements will melt in the **h**.
Rev 16: 9 They were seared by the intense **h**

HEAVE [OFFERING] (KJV) See WAVE [OFFERING]

HEAVEN HEAVENLY, HEAVENS, HEAVENWARD
Ge 14:19 Most High, Creator of **h** and earth.
21:17 angel of God called to Hagar from **h**
22:11 LORD called out to him from **h**,
24: 3 the God of **h** and the God of earth,
28:12 with its top reaching to **h**,
Ex 16: 4 "I will rain down bread from **h**
20:22 that I have spoken to you from **h**:
Dt 3:24 For what god is there in **h**
26:15 Look down from **h**, your holy
30:12 It is not up in **h**, so that you have
30:12 "Who will ascend into **h** to get it
Jos 2:11 the LORD your God is God in **h**
1Ki 8:23 there is no God like you in **h**
8:27 even the highest **h**, cannot contain
8:30 Hear from **h**, your dwelling place,
22:19 multitudes of **h** standing around him
2Ki 1:10 fire fell from **h** and consumed
2: 1 take Elijah up to **h** in a whirlwind,
19:15 You have made **h** and earth.
1Ch 29:11 for everything in **h** and earth is
2Ch 6:14 there is no God like you in **h**
7:14 then I will hear from **h**, and I will

Ezr 7:12 teacher of the Law of the God of **h**:
Job 16:19 Even now my witness is in **h**;
41:11 Everything under **h** belongs to me.
Ps 2: 4 The One enthroned in **h** laughs;
73:25 Whom have I in **h** but you?
75: 5 Do not lift your horns against **h**;
115: 3 Our God is in **h**; he does whatever
121: 2 LORD, the Maker of **h** and earth.
Pr 30: 4 Who has gone up to **h** and come
Isa 14:12 How you have fallen from **h**,
66: 1 "H is my throne, and the earth is
Jer 23:24 "Do not I fill **h** and earth?"
Da 2:19 Then Daniel praised the God of **h**
7:13 man, coming with the clouds of **h**.
Mt 3: 2 the kingdom of **h** has come near."
3:16 At that moment **h** was opened,
4:17 the kingdom of **h** has come near."
5:12 because great is your reward in **h**,
5:19 be called least in the kingdom of **h**,
5:19 be called great in the kingdom of **h**.
6: 9 " 'Our Father in **h**, hallowed be
6:10 will be done, on earth as it is in **h**.
6:20 up for yourselves treasures in **h**,
7:21 will enter the kingdom of **h**,
7:21 the will of my Father who is in **h**.
16:19 you the keys of the kingdom of **h**;
16:19 bind on earth will be bound in **h**,
16:19 loose on earth will be loosed in **h**."
18: 3 will never enter the kingdom of **h**.
18:18 bind on earth will be bound in **h**,
18:18 loose on earth will be loosed in **h**.
19:14 the kingdom of **h** belongs to such as
19:21 and you will have treasure in **h**.
19:23 is rich to enter the kingdom of **h**.
23:13 the kingdom of **h** in people's faces.
24:30 the sign of the Son of Man in **h**.
24:35 H and earth will pass away, but my
26:64 and coming on the clouds of **h**."
28:18 "All authority in **h** and on earth has
Mk 1:10 he saw **h** being torn open
8:11 they asked him for a sign from **h**.
10:21 and you will have treasure in **h**.
11:30 was it from **h**, or of human origin?
13:31 H and earth will pass away, but my
14:62 and coming on the clouds of **h**."
Lk 3:21 as he was praying, **h** was opened
9:54 to call fire down from **h** to destroy
10:18 saw Satan fall like lightning from **h**.
10:20 that your names are written in **h**."
12:33 a treasure in **h** that will never fail,
15: 7 over one sinner who repents than
18:22 and you will have treasure in **h**.
19:38 "Peace in **h** and glory
21:33 H and earth will pass away, but my
24:51 left them and was taken up into **h**.
Jn 3:13 into **h** except the one who came from **h**—
6:31 'He gave them bread from **h**
6:38 I have come down from **h** not to do
12:28 Then a voice came from **h**, "I have
Ac 1:11 who has been taken from you into **h**,
7:49 " 'H is my throne, and the earth is
7:55 looked up to **h** and saw the glory

Ac	9: 3	a light from **h** flashed around him.
	11: 5	a large sheet being let down from **h**
	26:19	not disobedient to the vision from **h**.
Ro	10: 6	heart, 'Who will ascend into **h**?' "
1Co	15:47	of the earth; the second man is of **h**.
2Co	5: 1	an eternal house in **h**, not built
	12: 2	ago was caught up to the third **h**.
Gal	1: 8	**h** should preach a gospel other than
Eph	1:10	to bring unity to all things in **h**
Php	2:10	in **h** and on earth and under
	3:20	But our citizenship is in **h**.
Col	1: 5	from the hope stored up for you in **h**
	1:16	things in **h** and on earth,
	4: 1	that you also have a Master in **h**.
1Th	1:10	and to wait for his Son from **h**,
	4:16	himself will come down from **h**,
Heb	1: 3	at the right hand of the Majesty in **h**.
	4:14	high priest who has ascended into **h**,
	8: 5	a copy and shadow of what is in **h**.
	9:24	he entered **h** itself, now to appear
	12:23	whose names are written in **h**.
Jas	3:17	comes from **h** is first of all pure;
1Pe	1: 4	This inheritance is kept in **h** for you,
	3:22	who has gone into **h** and is at God's
2Pe	1:18	that came from **h** when we were
	3:13	we are looking forward to a new **h**
Rev	4: 1	me was a door standing open in **h**.
	5:13	I heard every creature in **h**
	11:19	God's temple in **h** was opened,
	12: 1	A great sign appeared in **h**:
	12: 7	Then war broke out in **h**.
	15: 5	I looked, and I saw in **h** the temple—
	19: 1	of a great multitude in **h** shouting:
	19:11	I saw **h** standing open and there
	19:14	armies of **h** were following him,
	21: 1	I saw "a new **h** and a new earth,"
	21: 1	for the first **h** and the first earth had
	21: 2	coming down out of **h** from God,
	21:10	coming down out of **h** from God.

GOD OF HEAVEN See GOD

HEAVEN AND ... EARTH See EARTH

KINGDOM OF HEAVEN See KINGDOM

HEAVENLY HEAVEN

Ps	11: 4	the LORD is on his **h** throne.
	29: 1	to the LORD, you **h** beings,
	89: 6	the LORD among the **h** beings?
	103:21	all his **h** hosts, you his servants who
Mt	5:48	as your **h** Father is perfect.
Mk	13:25	and the **h** bodies will be shaken.'
Lk	2:13	company of the **h** host appeared
2Co	5: 2	clothed instead with our **h** dwelling,
Eph	1: 3	who has blessed us in the **h** realms
	1:20	at his right hand in the **h** realms,
	6:12	forces of evil in the **h** realms.
2Ti	4:18	bring me safely to his **h** kingdom.
Heb	3: 1	who share in the **h** calling, fix your
	6: 4	who have tasted the **h** gift,
	9:23	for the copies of the **h** things to be
	9:23	the **h** things themselves with better
	12:22	of the living God, the **h** Jerusalem.

HEAVENS HEAVEN

Ge	1: 1	In the beginning God created the **h**
	2: 1	Thus the **h** and the earth were
	6:17	earth to destroy all life under the **h**,
	7:11	the floodgates of the **h** were opened.
	11: 4	with a tower that reaches to the **h**
Ex	20:11	in six days the LORD made the **h**
Dt	4:26	I call the **h** and the earth as
	10:14	the LORD your God belong the **h**,
		even the highest **h**,
	28:12	The LORD will open the **h**,
	31:28	and call the **h** and the earth to testify
	33:26	who rides across the **h** to help you
2Sa	22:10	He parted the **h** and came down;
1Ki	8:27	The **h**, even the highest heaven,
2Ch	2: 6	since the **h**, even the highest **h**,
Ezr	9: 6	and our guilt has reached to the **h**.
Ne	9: 6	You made the **h**, even the highest **h**,
Job	11: 8	They are higher than the **h** above—
	38:33	Do you know the laws of the **h**?
Ps	8: 3	When I consider your **h**, the work
	19: 1	The **h** declare the glory of God;
	33: 6	of the LORD the **h** were made,
	57: 5	Be exalted, O God, above the **h**;
	68:33	to him who rides across the highest **h**,
		the ancient **h**,
	71:19	righteousness, God, reaches to the **h**,
	102:25	the **h** are the work of your hands.
	103:11	as high as the **h** are above the earth,
	108: 4	great is your love, higher than the **h**;
	115:16	The highest **h** belong
	119:89	it stands firm in the **h**.
	135: 6	him, in the **h** and on the earth,
	136: 5	by his understanding made the **h**,
	139: 8	If I go up to the **h**, you are there;
	148: 1	Praise the LORD from the **h**;
Pr	3:19	understanding he set the **h** in place;
Ecc	3: 1	for every activity under the **h**
Isa	1: 2	Hear me, you **h**! Listen, earth!
	24: 4	the **h** languish with the earth.
	24:18	The floodgates of the **h** are opened,
	40:26	Lift up your eyes and look to the **h**:
	45: 8	"You **h** above, rain down my
	51: 6	the **h** will vanish like smoke,
	55: 9	"As the **h** are higher than the earth,
	65:17	I will create new **h** and a new earth.
Jer	10:11	who did not make the **h**
	31:37	if the **h** above can be measured
	32:17	you have made the **h** and the earth
Eze	1: 1	the **h** were opened and I saw visions
Da	12: 3	shine like the brightness of the **h**,
Joel	2:30	I will show wonders in the **h**
Hab	3:11	moon stood still in the **h** at the glint
Mt	11:23	Capernaum, will you be lifted to the **h**?
	24:31	from one end of the **h** to the other.
Mk	13:27	of the earth to the ends of the **h**.
Eph	4:10	who ascended higher than all the **h**,
Heb	7:26	from sinners, exalted above the **h**.
Jas	5:18	and the **h** gave rain, and the earth
2Pe	3: 5	God's word the **h** came into being
	3:10	The **h** will disappear with a roar,
Rev	6:14	The **h** receded like a scroll being
	14: 7	Worship him who made the **h**,

Rev 20:11 and the **h** fled from his presence,

HEAVENWARD* HEAVEN
Php 3:14 God has called me **h** in Christ Jesus.

HEAVIER HEAVY
2Ch 10:14 I will make it even **h**.
Pr 27: 3 a fool's provocation is **h** than both.

HEAVY HEAVIER
Ex 18:18 The work is too **h** for you;
Dt 25:13 in your bag—one **h**, one light.
1Ki 12: 4 "Your father put a **h** yoke on us,
Ecc 1:13 What a **h** burden God has laid
Isa 47: 6 on the aged you laid a very **h** yoke.
Mt 23: 4 They tie up **h**, cumbersome loads

HEBREW HEBREWS
Ge 14:13 and reported this to Abram the **H**.
41:12 Now a young **H** was there with us,
Ex 1:19 "**H** women are not like Egyptian
2: 6 "This is one of the **H** babies,"
2:11 He saw an Egyptian beating a **H**,
21: 2 "If you buy a **H** servant, he is
2Ki 18:26 speak to us in **H** in the hearing
Jer 34: 9 Everyone was to free their **H** slaves,
Jnh 1: 9 "I am a **H** and I worship
Php 3: 5 tribe of Benjamin, a **H** of Hebrews;

HEBREWS HEBREW
Ex 3:18 the God of the **H**, has met with us.
9: 1 the LORD, the God of the **H**, says:
2Co 11:22 Are they **H**? So am I.
Php 3: 5 tribe of Benjamin, a Hebrew of **H**;

HEBRON KIRIATH ARBA
Ge 13:18 near the great trees of Mamre at **H**,
23: 2 (that is, **H**) in the land of Canaan,
Jos 14:13 and gave him **H** as his inheritance.
20: 7 is, **H**) in the hill country of Judah.
21:13 Aaron the priest they gave **H** (a city
Jdg 16: 3 to the top of the hill that faces **H**.
2Sa 2:11 in **H** over Judah was seven years
3: 2 Sons were born to David in **H**:
1Ch 2:43 The sons of **H**:
11: 1 Israel came together to David at **H**

HEDGE* HEDGED
Job 1:10 "Have you not put a **h** around him
Isa 5: 5 I will take away its **h**, and it will be
Mic 7: 4 most upright worse than a thorn **h**.

HEDGED* HEDGE
Job 3:23 way is hidden, whom God has **h** in?

HEED HEEDS
1Sa 15:22 to **h** is better than the fat of rams.
Pr 16:20 Whoever gives **h** to instruction
Ecc 7: 5 It is better to **h** the rebuke of a wise

HEEDS* HEED
Pr 10:17 Whoever **h** discipline shows
13: 1 A wise son **h** his father's
13:18 whoever **h** correction is honored.
15: 5 but whoever **h** correction shows
15:31 Whoever **h** life-giving correction

Pr 15:32 but the one who **h** correction gains
28: 7 A discerning son **h** instruction,
29:18 the one who **h** wisdom's instruction.

HEEL*
Ge 3:15 head, and you will strike his **h**."
25:26 with his hand grasping Esau's **h**;
Job 18: 9 A trap seizes him by the **h**;
Hos 12: 3 the womb he grasped his brother's **h**;

HEGAI
Est 2: 3 them be placed under the care of **H**,

HEIFER
Ge 15: 9 "Bring me a **h**, a goat and a ram,
Nu 19: 2 to bring you a red **h** without defect
Jdg 14:18 "If you had not plowed with my **h**,
Heb 9:13 the ashes of a **h** sprinkled on those

HEIGHT HEIGHTS
Nu 23: 3 Then he went off to a barren **h**.
1Sa 16: 7 not consider his appearance or his **h**,
17: 4 His **h** was six cubits and a span.
Ro 8:39 neither **h** nor depth, nor anything

HEIGHTS HEIGHT
Dt 33:29 you, and you will tread on their **h**."
2Sa 1:19 "A gazelle lies slain on your **h**,
Job 22:12 "Is not God in the **h** of heaven?
Ps 18:33 he causes me to stand on the **h**.
148: 1 praise him in the **h** above.
Ob 1: 3 rocks and make your home on the **h**,
Mic 1: 3 and treads on the **h** of the earth.
Hab 3:19 he enables me to tread on the **h**.

HEIR INHERIT
Ge 15: 4 "This man will not be your **h**,
Lk 20:14 'This is the **h**,' they said.
Ro 4:13 that he would be **h** of the world,
Gal 4: 1 that as long as an **h** is underage,
4: 7 child, God has made you also an **h**.
Heb 1: 2 whom he appointed **h** of all things,
11: 7 became **h** of the righteousness

HEIRS INHERIT
Ro 4:14 those who depend on the law are **h**,
8:17 if we are children, then we are **h**—**h**
of God and co-heirs
Gal 3:29 and **h** according to the promise.
Eph 3: 6 gospel the Gentiles are **h** together
Titus 3: 7 we might become **h** having the hope
Heb 11: 9 who were **h** with him of the same
1Pe 3: 7 as **h** with you of the gracious gift

HELD HOLD
Ex 17:11 As long as Moses **h** up his hands,
Dt 4: 4 you who **h** fast to the LORD your
1Sa 7:17 and there he also **h** court for Israel.
1Ki 11: 2 Solomon **h** fast to them in love.
2Ki 18: 6 He **h** fast to the LORD and did not
Ps 17: 5 My steps have **h** to your paths;
SS 3: 4 I **h** him and would not let him go till
Isa 40:12 Who has **h** the dust of the earth
65: 2 All day long I have **h** out my hands
Ro 10:21 says, "All day long I have **h** out my
Gal 3:23 we were **h** in custody under the law,

Col 2:19 and **h** together by its ligaments
Rev 1:16 In his right hand he **h** seven stars,
     6: 2 Its rider **h** a bow, and he was given
    15: 2 They **h** harps given them by God
    17: 4 She **h** a golden cup in her hand,

HELDAI
Zec 6:14 The crown will be given to **H**,

HELL*
Mt   5:22 will be in danger of the fire of **h**.
     5:29 whole body to be thrown into **h**.
     5:30 for your whole body to go into **h**.
    10:28 can destroy both soul and body in **h**.
    18: 9 and be thrown into the fire of **h**.
    23:15 as much a child of **h** as you are.
    23:33 you escape being condemned to **h**?
Mk   9:43 than with two hands to go into **h**,
     9:45 have two feet and be thrown into **h**.
     9:47 have two eyes and be thrown into **h**,
Lk 12: 5 has authority to throw you into **h**.
Jas 3: 6 on fire, and is itself set on fire by **h**.
2Pe 2: 4 but sent them to **h**, putting them

HELLENISTIC*
Ac   6: 1 the **H** Jews among them complained
     9:29 talked and debated with the **H** Jews,

HELMET
Ps 108: 8 Ephraim is my **h**, Judah is my
Isa 59:17 and the **h** of salvation on his head;
Eph 6:17 Take the **h** of salvation
1Th 5: 8 and the hope of salvation as a **h**.

HELP HELPED, HELPER, HELPFUL,
HELPING, HELPLESS, HELPS
Ge   4: 1 the **h** of the LORD I have brought
Ex   2:23 and their cry for **h** because of their
     4:12 I will **h** you speak and will teach
    23: 5 be sure you **h** them with it.
Lev 25:35 **h** them as you would a foreigner
Dt   33:26 rides across the heavens to **h** you
Jos 24: 7 But they cried to the LORD for **h**,
2Sa 22:36 You make your saving **h** my shield;
    22:36 your **h** has made me great.
1Ch 12:22 Day after day men came to **h** David,
2Ch 16:12 in his illness he did not seek **h**
    28:16 sent to the kings of Assyria for **h**.
Ezr 4: 2 said, "Let us **h** you build because,
Ne   6:16 been done with the **h** of our God.
Job 29:12 I rescued the poor who cried for **h**,
Ps 18: 6 I cried to my God for **h**.
    22:24 him but has listened to his cry for **h**.
    30: 2 I called to you for **h**, and you healed
    33:20 he is our **h** and our shield.
    40:17 You are my **h** and my deliverer;
    46: 1 an ever-present **h** in trouble.
    72:12 the afflicted who have no one to **h**.
    79: 9 **H** us, God our Savior, for the glory
   108:12 enemy, for human **h** is worthless.
   109:21 **h** me for your name's sake;
   115: 9 he is their **h** and shield.
   121: 1 where does my **h** come from?
   146: 5 are those whose **h** is the God
Ecc 4:10 falls down, one can **h** the other up.

Ecc 4:10 falls and has no one to **h** them up.
Isa 41:10 I will strengthen you and **h** you;
    49: 8 in the day of salvation I will **h** you;
La   1: 7 hands, there was no one to **h** her.
Jnh 2: 2 the realm of the dead I called for **h**,
Mk   7:11 have been used to **h** their father
     9:24 **h** me overcome my unbelief!"
Lk 11:46 will not lift one finger to **h** them.
Ac 16: 9 over to Macedonia and **h** us."
    18:27 he was a great **h** to those who
    20:35 of hard work we must **h** the weak,
2Co 9: 2 For I know your eagerness to **h**,
1Th 5:14 the disheartened, **h** the weak,
1Ti 5:16 the church can **h** those widows who
Heb 2:18 to **h** those who are being tempted.
     4:16 and find grace to **h** us in our time

HELPED HELP
1Sa 7:12 "Thus far the LORD has **h** us."
Ps 118:13 about to fall, but the LORD **h** me.
Mk   1:31 to her, took her hand and **h** her up.
Lk   1:54 He has **h** his servant Israel,
Ac 26:22 But God has **h** me to this very day;
2Co 6: 2 and in the day of salvation I **h** you."

HELPER HELP
Ge   2:18 I will make a **h** suitable for him."
Ex 18: 4 said, "My father's God was my **h**;
Dt   33:29 He is your shield and your
Ps 10:14 you are the **h** of the fatherless.
   118: 7 The LORD is with me; he is my **h**.
Heb 13: 6 confidence, "The Lord is my **h**;

HELPFUL HELP
Eph 4:29 only what is **h** for building others

HELPING HELP
Lk   8: 3 These women were **h** to support
Ac   9:36 always doing good and **h** the poor.
1Co 12:28 gifts of healing, of **h**, of guidance,
1Ti 5:10 **h** those in trouble and devoting

HELPLESS HELP
Ps 10:12 hand, O God. Do not forget the **h**.
Pr 28:15 is a wicked ruler over a **h** people.
Mt   9:36 because they were harassed and **h**,

HELPS HELP
Ps 37:40 The LORD **h** them and delivers
Isa 50: 7 the Sovereign LORD **h** me, I will
Ro   8:26 the Spirit **h** us in our weakness.
Heb 2:16 For surely it is not angels he **h**,

HEM
1Sa 15:27 caught hold of the **h** of his robe,
Ps 139: 5 You **h** me in behind and before,
Hab 1: 4 The wicked **h** in the righteous,

HEMAN
1Ki 4:31 wiser than **H**, Kalkol and Darda,
1Ch 15:19 The musicians **H**, Asaph and Ethan
Ps 88: T *A maskil of **H** the Ezrahite.*

HEN
Mt 23:37 as a **h** gathers her chicks under her
Lk 13:34 as a **h** gathers her chicks under her

HEPHZIBAH
Isa   62: 4 But you will be called **H**, and your

HERALD
Hab   2: 2 tablets so that a **h** may run with it.
1Ti   2: 7 for this purpose I was appointed a **h**
2Ti   1:11 of this gospel I was appointed a **h**

HERBS
Ex   12: 8 along with bitter **h**, and bread made
Nu   9:11 with unleavened bread and bitter **h**.
La   3:15 He has filled me with bitter **h**

HERD   HERDERS, HERDS
Lev   27:32 Every tithe of the **h** and flock—
Mt   8:31 us out, send us into the **h** of pigs."

HERDERS   HERD
Ge   13: 7 quarreling arose between Abram's **h**
     26:20 the **h** of Gerar quarreled with those

HERDS   HERD
Nu   32: 1 who had very large **h** and flocks,
Dt   8:13 when your **h** and flocks grow large
     12: 6 the firstborn of your **h** and flocks.

HERE
Ge   3:12 "The woman you put **h** with me—
     22: 1 "**H** I am," he replied.
Ex   3: 4 And Moses said, "**H** I am."
1Sa   3: 4 Samuel answered, "**H** I am."
Ps   40: 7 Then I said, "**H** I am, I have come—
Isa   6: 8 And I said, "**H** am I. Send me!"
     40: 9 towns of Judah, "**H** is your God!"
Mt   12:42 greater than Solomon is **h**.
     24:23 to you, 'Look, **h** is the Messiah!'
Mk   14:42 Let us go! **H** comes my betrayer!"
     16: 6 He is not **h**. See the place where
Lk   24: 6 He is not **h**; he has risen!
Heb   10: 7 Then I said, '**H** I am—it is written
Rev   3:20 **H** I am! I stand at the door
     4: 1 "Come up **h**, and I will show you
     11:12 saying to them, "Come up **h**."

HERESIES*
2Pe   2: 1 will secretly introduce destructive **h**,

HERITAGE   INHERIT
Ps   61: 5 you have given me the **h** of those
     119:111 Your statutes are my **h** forever;
     127: 3 Children are a **h** from the LORD,
Isa   54:17 This is the **h** of the servants

HERMON
Dt   3: 8 the Arnon Gorge as far as Mount **H**.
Ps   133: 3 the dew of **H** were falling on Mount

HERO*   HEROES
1Sa   17:51 saw that their **h** was dead,
2Sa   23: 1 of Jacob, the **h** of Israel's songs:
Ps   52: 1 do you boast of evil, you mighty **h**?
Isa   3: 2 the **h** and the warrior, the judge

HEROD   ANTIPAS, HERODIANS
     1. King of Judea who tried to kill Jesus (Mt 2;
Lk 1:5).

     2. Son of 1. Tetrarch of Galilee who arrested and
beheaded John the Baptist (Mt 14:1–12; Mk 6:14–
29; Lk 3:1, 19–20; 9:7–9); tried Jesus (Lk 23:6–15).
     3. Grandson of 1. King of Judea who killed
James (Ac 12:2); arrested Peter (Ac 12:3–19).
Death (Ac 12:19–23).

HERODIANS*   HEROD
Mt   22:16 disciples to him along with the **H**.
Mk   3: 6 the **H** how they might kill Jesus.
     12:13 and **H** to Jesus to catch him in his

HERODIAS
     Wife of Herod the Tetrarch who persuaded her
daughter to ask for John the Baptist's head (Mt
14:1–12; Mk 6:14–29).

HEROES*   HERO
Ge   6: 4 They were the **h** of old, men of renown.
Ne   3:16 artificial pool and the House of the **H**.
Isa   5:22 to those who are **h** at drinking wine

HESHBON
Nu   21:26 **H** was the city of Sihon king
Dt   3: 6 we had done with Sihon king of **H**,

HESITATED
Ge   19:16 When he **h**, the men grasped his
Ac   20:27 For I have not **h** to proclaim to you

HEWN*
Isa   51: 1 the quarry from which you were **h**;

HEZEKIAH
     King of Judah. Restored the temple and worship
(2Ch 29–31). Sought the LORD for help against
Assyria (2Ki 18–19; 2Ch 32:1–23; Isa 36–37). Illness healed (2Ki 20:1–11; 2Ch 32:24–26; Isa 38).
Judged for showing Babylonians his treasures (2Ki
20:12–21; 2Ch 32:31; Isa 39).

HEZRON
Ru   4:18 Perez was the father of **H**,
Mt   1: 3 Perez the father of **H**, **H** the father

HID   HIDE
Ge   3: 8 they **h** from the LORD God among
Ex   2: 2 child, she **h** him for three months.
     3: 6 At this, Moses **h** his face,
Jos   6:17 because she **h** the spies we sent.
1Ki   18:13 I **h** a hundred of the LORD's
2Ch   22:11 she **h** the child from Athaliah so she
Isa   49: 2 in the shadow of his hand he **h** me;
     54: 8 In a surge of anger I **h** my face
Eze   39:23 So I **h** my face from them
Mt   13:44 When a man found it, he **h** it again,
     25:25 out and **h** your gold in the ground.
Heb   11:23 faith Moses' parents **h** him for three

HIDDEN   HIDE
Ge   4:14 and I will be **h** from your presence;
Jos   2: 6 **h** them under the stalks of flax she
     7:22 and there it was, **h** in his tent,
1Sa   10:22 "Yes, he has **h** himself among
2Ki   11: 3 He remained **h** with his nurse

Job 28:11 the rivers and bring **h** things to light.
Ps   19:12 Forgive my **h** faults.
     69: 5 my guilt is not **h** from you.
     119:11 I have **h** your word in my heart
     142: 3 where I walk people have **h** a snare
Pr   2: 4 and search for it as for **h** treasure,
     27: 5 Better is open rebuke than **h** love,
Ecc 12:14 including every **h** thing, whether it
Isa 40:27 "My way is **h** from the LORD;
     59: 2 your sins have **h** his face from you,
Da   2:22 He reveals deep and **h** things;
Mt   5:14 A town built on a hill cannot be **h**.
     10:26 or **h** that will not be made known.
     13:35 will utter things **h** since the creation
     13:44 heaven is like treasure **h** in a field.
Mk   4:22 For whatever is **h** is meant to be
Lk   10:21 because you have **h** these things
     18:34 Its meaning was **h** from them,
Ro   16:25 of the mystery **h** for long ages past,
1Co   2: 7 a mystery that has been **h**
      4: 5 bring to light what is **h** in darkness
Eph   3: 9 for ages past was kept **h** in God,
Col   1:26 that has been kept **h** for ages
      2: 3 in whom are **h** all the treasures
      3: 3 and your life is now **h** with Christ
Heb   4:13 in all creation is **h** from God's sight.
Rev   2:17 I will give some of the **h** manna.

HIDE HID, HIDDEN, HIDES, HIDING

Ge   18:17 "Shall I **h** from Abraham what I am
Ex   2: 3 when she could **h** him no longer,
Lev   4:11 But the **h** of the bull and all its flesh,
Nu   19: 5 Its **h**, flesh, blood and intestines.
Dt   31:17 I will **h** my face from them,
Ps   13: 1 How long will you **h** your face
     17: 8 **h** me in the shadow of your wings
     27: 5 he will **h** me in the shelter of his
     51: 9 **H** your face from my sins and blot
     143: 9 LORD, for I **h** myself in you.
Isa 53: 3 whom people **h** their faces he was
Eze 39:29 I will no longer **h** my face
Rev   6:16 **h** us from the face of him who sits

HIDES HIDE
Lk   8:16 lights a lamp and **h** it in a clay jar

HIDING HIDE
Ps   32: 7 You are my **h** place;
Pr   28:12 rise to power, people go into **h**.
Isa 45:15 are a God who has been **h** himself,

HIGH HIGHER, HIGHEST, HIGHLY
Ge   14:18 He was priest of God Most **H**,
     14:22 God Most **H**, Creator of heaven
Lev 16:32 to succeed his father as **h** priest is
     26:30 I will destroy your **h** places,
1Sa   2: 1 in the LORD my horn is lifted **h**.
1Ki   3: 2 were still sacrificing at the **h** places,
     11: 7 Solomon built a **h** place
     12:31 Jeroboam built shrines on **h** places
Ps   7: 7 you sit enthroned over them on **h**.
      7:10 My shield is God Most **H**,
     21: 7 of the Most **H** he will not be shaken.

Ps   46: 4 place where the Most **H** dwells.
     82: 6 you are all sons of the Most **H**.'
     103:11 For as **h** as the heavens are
     113: 5 the One who sits enthroned on **h**,
Pr   24: 7 Wisdom is too **h** for fools;
Isa 14:14 will make myself like the Most **H**."
Jer   2:20 on every **h** hill and under every
Eze   1:26 **h** above on the throne was a figure
Da   4:17 that the Most **H** is sovereign over all
Mt   4: 8 devil took him to a very **h** mountain
     17: 1 and led them up a **h** mountain
Mk   5: 7 me, Jesus, Son of the Most **H** God?
     14:53 They took Jesus to the **h** priest,
Jn   18:22 the way you answer the **h** priest?"
Ac   23: 4 dare you insult God's **h** priest!"
Eph   3:18 long and **h** and deep is the love
      4: 8 "When he ascended on **h**, he took
Heb   2:17 faithful **h** priest in service to God,
      7: 1 of Salem and priest of God Most **H**.
      7:26 Such a **h** priest truly meets our

HIGH PLACE 1Sa 9:12, 13, 14, 19, 25; 10:5, 13;
1Ki 3:4; 11:7; 2Ki 17:11; 23:15, 15, 15; 1Ch 16:39;
21:29; 2Ch 1:3, 13; Isa 16:12; Eze 20:29; Mic 1:5;
Lk 4:5

HIGH PLACES Lev 26:30; Nu 33:52; 1Ki 3:2,
3; 12:31, 32; 13:2, 32, 33, 33; 14:23; 15:14; 22:43;
2Ki 12:3; 14:4; 15:4, 35; 16:4; 17:9, 29, 32; 18:4,
22; 21:3; 23:5, 8, 9, 13, 19, 20; 2Ch 11:15; 14:3,
5; 15:17; 17:6; 20:33; 21:11; 28:4, 25; 31:1; 32:12;
33:3, 17, 19; 34:3; Ps 78:58; Isa 15:2; 36:7; Jer 7:31;
17:3; 19:5; 32:35; 48:35; Eze 6:3, 6; 16:16; Hos
10:8; Am 7:9

HIGH PRIEST Lev 16:32; 21:10; Nu 35:25, 28,
28, 32; Jos 20:6; 2Ki 12:10; 22:4, 8; 23:4; 2Ch 34:9;
Ne 3:1, 20; 13:28; Hag 1:1, 12, 14; 2:2, 4; Zec 3:1,
8; 6:11; Mt 26:3, 51, 57, 58, 62, 63, 65; Mk 2:26;
14:47, 53, 54, 60, 61, 63, 66; Lk 22:50, 54; Jn 11:49,
51; 18:13, 15, 16, 19, 22, 24; Ac 4:6; 5:17, 21, 27;
7:1; 9:1; 22:5; 23:2, 4, 5; 24:1; Heb 2:17; 3:1; 4:14,
15; 5:1, 5, 10; 6:20; 7:26; 8:1, 3; 9:7, 11, 25; 13:11

MOST HIGH Ge 14:18, 19, 20, 22; Nu 24:16;
Dt 32:8; 1Sa 2:10; 2Sa 22:14; 23:1; Ps 7:8, 10, 17;
9:2; 18:13; 21:7; 46:4; 47:2; 50:14; 57:2; 73:11;
77:10; 78:17, 35, 56; 82:6; 83:18; 87:5; 91:1, 9; 92:1;
97:9; 107:11; Isa 14:14; La 3:35, 38; Da 3:26; 4:2,
17, 24, 25, 32, 34; 5:18, 21; 7:18, 22, 25, 27; Hos
7:16; 11:7; Mk 5:7; Lk 1:32, 35, 76; 6:35; 8:28; Ac
7:48; 16:17; Heb 7:1

HIGHER HIGH
Dt   28:43 will rise above you **h** and **h**,
Ps   61: 2 lead me to the rock that is **h** than I.
     108: 4 is your love, **h** than the heavens;
Isa 55: 9 the heavens are **h** than the earth, so
              are my ways **h** than your ways

HIGHEST HIGH
1Ki   8:27 even the **h** heaven, cannot contain
Ps   115:16 The **h** heavens belong
Pr   9: 3 and she calls from the **h** point
Isa   2: 2 temple will be established as the **h**
Mt   4: 5 had him stand on the **h** point
     21: 9 "Hosanna in the **h** heaven!"

Lk   2:14 "Glory to God in the **h** heaven,
      19:38 in heaven and glory in the **h**!"
Php 2: 9 God exalted him to the **h** place

HIGHLY HIGH

Ex 15: 1 to the LORD, for he is **h** exalted.
1Ch 29:25 The LORD **h** exalted Solomon
Da 10:11 you who are **h** esteemed,
Lk   1:28 "Greetings, you who are **h** favored!
Ro 12: 3 of yourself more **h** than you ought,

HIGHWAY

Pr   7:27 Her house is a **h** to the grave,
     16:17 The **h** of the upright avoids evil;
Isa 40: 3 in the desert a **h** for our God.

HILKIAH

2Ki 22:10 king, "**H** the priest has given me
2Ch 34:14 **H** the priest found the Book

HILL HILLS

Ex 17: 9 on top of the **h** with the staff of God
1Sa 17: 3 The Philistines occupied one **h**
1Ki 16:24 He bought the **h** of Samaria
Isa 40: 4 every mountain and **h** made low;
Jer 26:18 the temple **h** a mound overgrown
Da   9:16 Jerusalem, your city, your holy **h**.
Mic   3:12 the temple **h** a mound overgrown
Mt   5:14 town built on a **h** cannot be hidden.
Lk   3: 5 in, every mountain and **h** made low.

HILL COUNTRY Ge 10:30; 14:6; 31:21, 23, 25,
54; 36:8, 9; Nu 13:17, 29; 14:40, 44, 45; Dt 1:7, 19,
20, 24, 41, 43; 2:1, 3, 5; 3:12, 25; Jos 9:1; 10:6, 40;
11:3, 16, 21, 21, 21; 12:8; 14:12; 15:48; 16:1; 17:15,
16, 18; 18:12; 19:50; 20:7, 7, 7; 21:11, 21; 24:4, 30,
33; Jdg 1:9, 19, 34; 2:9; 3:27; 4:5; 7:24; 10:1; 12:15;
17:1, 8; 18:2, 13; 19:1, 16, 18; 1Sa 1:1; 9:4; 13:2;
14:22; 2Sa 20:21; 1Ki 4:8; 12:25; 2Ki 5:22; 1Ch
4:42; 6:67; 2Ch 13:4; 19:4; 27:4; Ne 8:15; Ps 78:54;
Jer 17:26; 32:44; 33:13; Mal 1:3; Lk 1:39, 65

HOLY HILL See HOLY

HILLS HILL

1Ki 20:23 him, "Their gods are gods of the **h**.
2Ch 18:16 the **h** like sheep without a shepherd,
Ps   50:10 and the cattle on a thousand **h**.
     114: 6 leap like rams, you **h**, like lambs?
Pr   8:25 before the **h**, I was given birth,
Isa   2: 2 it will be exalted above the **h**,
Hos 10: 8 and to the **h**, "Fall on us!"
Joel 3:18 wine, and the **h** will flow with milk;
Am   9:13 mountains and flow from all the **h**,
Lk 23:30 and to the **h**, "Cover us!" '
Rev 17: 9 The seven heads are seven **h**

HINDER HINDERED, HINDERS, HINDRANCE

1Sa 14: 6 Nothing can **h** the LORD
Mt 19:14 and do not **h** them, for the kingdom
1Co 9:12 anything rather than **h** the gospel
1Pe 3: 7 so that nothing will **h** your prayers.

HINDERED* HINDER

Lk 11:52 and you have **h** those who were
Ro 15:22 This is why I have often been **h**

HINDERS* HINDER

Heb 12: 1 let us throw off everything that **h**

HINDRANCE* HINDER

Ac 28:31 with all boldness and without **h**!

HINGES*

Pr 26:14 As a door turns on its **h**,

HINT*

Eph 5: 3 you there must not be even a **h**

HIP

Ge 32:25 touched the socket of Jacob's **h** so that
            his **h** was wrenched as he wrestled

HIRAM

King of Tyre; helped David build his palace (2Sa
5:11–12; 1Ch 14:1); helped Solomon build the
temple (1Ki 5; 2Ch 2) and his navy (1Ki 9:10–27;
2Ch 8).

HIRE HIRED, HIRES

1Sa 2: 5 Those who were full **h** themselves
Mt 20: 1 in the morning to **h** workers for his

HIRED HIRE

Lev 19:13 the wages of a **h** worker overnight.
Dt 23: 4 and they **h** Balaam son of Beor
     24:14 of a **h** worker who is poor
Ne   6:13 He had been **h** to intimidate me so
Lk 15:15 and **h** himself out to a citizen
Jn 10:12 The **h** hand is not the shepherd

HIRES* HIRE

Pr 26:10 at random is one who **h** a fool

HISTORY

Ezr 4:19 that this city has a long **h** of revolt

HIT HITS

Ex 21:22 fighting and **h** a pregnant woman
Dt 19: 5 head may fly off and **h** his neighbor
Pr 23:35 "They **h** me," you will say,
Lk 22:64 "Who **h** you?"

HITS HIT

Ex 21:26 "An owner who **h** a male or female

HITTITE HITTITES

Ge 23:10 Ephron the **H** was sitting among his
     27:46 living because of these **H** women.
Jos   1: 4 all the **H** country—
2Sa 11: 3 Eliam and the wife of Uriah the **H**."
     11:17 moreover, Uriah the **H** died.

HITTITES HITTITE

Ge 25:10 Abraham had bought from the **H**.
Dt 20:17 the **H**, Amorites, Canaanites,
Ezr 9: 1 like those of the Canaanites, **H**,

HIVITES

Ex 23:28 hornet ahead of you to drive the **H**,
Jos   9: 7 The Israelites said to the **H**,

HOARDED* HOARDS

Ecc 5:13 wealth **h** to the harm of its owners,
Isa 23:18 they will not be stored up or **h**.

Jas   5: 3 You have **h** wealth in the last days.

HOARDS* HOARDED
Pr   11:26 People curse the one who **h** grain,

HOBAB
Nu   10:29 Now Moses said to **H** son of Reuel

HOLD HELD, HOLDING, HOLDS
Ex   4: 4 reached out and took **h** of the snake
       9: 2 go and continue to **h** them back,
       20: 7 Lord will not **h** anyone guiltless
Lev   19:13 " 'Do not **h** back the wages
Dt   5:11 Lord will not **h** anyone guiltless
       11:22 to him and to **h** fast to him—
       13: 4 serve him and **h** fast to him.
       30:20 listen to his voice, and **h** fast to him.
Jos   22: 5 to **h** fast to him and to serve him
2Sa   6: 6 out and took **h** of the ark of God,
2Ki   4:16 "you will **h** a son in your arms."
Ps   18:16 from on high and took **h** of me;
       73:23 you **h** me by my right hand.
      119:31 I **h** fast to your statutes, Lord;
Pr   3:18 of life to those who take **h** of her;
       3:18 those who **h** her fast will be blessed.
       4: 4 "Take **h** of my words with all your
       5:22 the cords of their sins **h** them fast.
       10:19 but the prudent **h** their tongues.
       17:28 discerning if they **h** their tongues.
Isa   22:17 is about to take firm **h** of you
       41:13 the Lord your God who takes **h**
       54: 2 tent curtains wide, do not **h** back;
Jer   6:11 of the Lord, and I cannot **h** it in.
Eze   3:18 I will **h** you accountable for their
       3:20 I will **h** you accountable for their
       33: 6 I will **h** the watchman accountable
Zec   8:23 nations will take firm **h** of one Jew
Mk   11:25 if you **h** anything against anyone,
Jn   8:31 "If you **h** to my teaching, you are
       20:17 Jesus said, "Do not **h** on to me,
Ac   2:24 for death to keep its **h** on him.
       7:60 do not **h** this sin against them."
1Co   15: 2 saved, if you **h** firmly to the word I
Php   2:16 as you **h** firmly to the word of life.
       3:12 I press on to take **h** of that for which
              Christ Jesus took **h** of me.
Col   1:17 and in him all things **h** together.
1Th   5:21 test them all; **h** on to what is good,
2Th   2:15 **h** fast to the teachings we passed
1Ti   3: 9 They must keep **h** of the deep truths
       6:12 Take **h** of the eternal life
       6:19 so that they may take **h** of the life
Titus 1: 9 He must **h** firmly to the trustworthy
Heb   3:14 indeed we **h** our original conviction
       4:14 God, let us **h** firmly to the faith we
       6:18 take **h** of the hope set before us may
       10:23 Let us **h** unswervingly to the hope
Rev   1:18 And I **h** the keys of death
       12:17 **h** fast their testimony about Jesus.
       19:10 sisters who **h** to the testimony

HOLDING HOLD
Ne   4:21 the work with half the men **h** spears,
Jer   15: 6 I am tired of **h** back.
Mk   7: 3 **h** to the tradition of the elders.

1Co   11: 2 and for **h** to the traditions just as I

HOLDS HOLD
2Th   2: 7 but the one who now **h** it back will
Heb   2:14 the power of him who **h** the power
Rev   2: 1 words of him who **h** the seven stars
       3: 1 of him who **h** the seven spirits
       3: 7 and true, who **h** the key of David.

HOLE HOLES
Ps   7:15 Whoever digs a **h** and scoops it out

HOLES HOLE
Hag   1: 6 to put them in a purse with **h** in it."

HOLIEST* HOLY
Nu   18:29 **h** part of everything given to you.'

HOLINESS* HOLY
Ex   15:11 majestic in **h**, awesome in glory,
Dt   32:51 you did not uphold my **h** among
1Ch   16:29 the Lord in the splendor of his **h**.
2Ch   20:21 the splendor of his **h** as they went
Ps   29: 2 the Lord in the splendor of his **h**.
       89:35 for all, I have sworn by my **h**—
       93: 5 **h** adorns your house for endless
       96: 9 the Lord in the splendor of his **h**;
Isa   29:23 they will acknowledge the **h**
       35: 8 it will be called the Way of **H**;
Eze   36:23 I will show the **h** of my great name,
       38:23 I will show my greatness and my **h**,
Am   4: 2 Lord has sworn by his **h**:
Lk   1:75 in **h** and righteousness before him
Ro   1: 4 Spirit of **h** was appointed the Son
       6:19 slaves to righteousness leading to **h**.
       6:22 the benefit you reap leads to **h**,
1Co   1:30 righteousness, **h** and redemption;
2Co   7: 1 perfecting **h** out of reverence
Eph   4:24 God in true righteousness and **h**
1Ti   2: 2 quiet lives in all godliness and **h**.
       2:15 in faith, love and **h** with propriety.
Heb   12:10 in order that we may share in his **h**.
       12:14 without **h** no one will see the Lord.

HOLLOW
Ex   27: 8 Make the altar **h**, out of boards.
Isa   40:12 the waters in the **h** of his hand,
Col   2: 8 no one takes you captive through **h**

HOLY HALLOWED, HOLIEST, HOLINESS
Ge   2: 3 the seventh day and made it **h**,
Ex   3: 5 you are standing is **h** ground."
       16:23 rest, a **h** sabbath to the Lord.
       19: 6 kingdom of priests and a **h** nation.'
       20: 8 the Sabbath day by keeping it **h**.
       26:33 curtain will separate the **H** Place from
              the Most **H** Place.
       28:36 on it as on a seal: **h to the Lord**.
       29:37 Then the altar will be most **h**, and
              whatever touches it will be **h**.
       30:10 It is most **h** to the Lord."
       30:29 whatever touches them will be **h**.
       31:13 I am the Lord, who makes you **h**.
       40: 9 all its furnishings, and it will be **h**.

Lev 10: 3 approach me I will be proved **h**;
10:10 you can distinguish between the **h**
11:44 consecrate yourselves and be **h**, because I am **h**.
11:45 therefore be **h**, because I am **h**.
19: 2 'Be **h** because I, the LORD your God, am **h**.
19: 8 they have desecrated what is **h**
19:24 the fourth year all its fruit will be **h**,
20: 3 sanctuary and profaned my **h** name.
20: 7 yourselves and be **h**, because I am
20: 8 I am the LORD, who makes you **h**.
20:26 You are to be **h** to me because I, the LORD, am **h**,
21: 6 They must be **h** to their God
21: 8 Consider them **h**, because I the LORD am **h**—I who make you **h**.
22: 9 am the LORD, who makes them **h**.
22:32 Do not profane my **h** name, for I must be acknowledged as **h**
22:32 I am the LORD, who made you **h**
25:12 it is a jubilee and is to be **h** for you;
27: 9 given to the LORD becomes **h**.
Nu 4:15 finished covering the **h** furnishings and all the **h** articles,
4:15 they must not touch the **h** things
6: 5 They must be **h** until the period
16: 7 chooses will be the one who is **h**.
20:12 enough to honor me as **h** in the sight
20:13 he was proved **h** among them.
Dt 5:12 the Sabbath day by keeping it **h**,
23:14 Your camp must be **h**, so that he
26:15 from heaven, your **h** dwelling place,
33: 2 myriads of **h** ones from the south,
Jos 5:15 place where you are standing is **h**."
24:19 He is a **h** God; he is a jealous God.
1Sa 2: 2 "There is no one **h** like the LORD;
6:20 of the LORD, this **h** God?
21: 5 The men's bodies are **h** even on missions that are not **h**.
2Ki 4: 9 often comes our way is a **h** man
1Ch 16:10 Glory in his **h** name; let the hearts
16:35 we may give thanks to your **h** name,
29: 3 I have provided for this **h** temple:
2Ch 3: 8 He built the Most **H** Place, its length
30:27 heaven, his **h** dwelling place.
Ezr 9: 2 have mingled the **h** race
Ne 8:10 This day is **h** to our Lord.
11: 1 them to live in Jerusalem, the **h** city,
Job 6:10 not denied the words of the **H** One.
Ps 2: 6 my king on Zion, my **h** mountain."
5: 7 I bow down toward your **h** temple.
11: 4 The LORD is in his **h** temple;
16: 3 the **h** people who are in the land,
22: 3 you are enthroned as the **H** One;
24: 3 Who may stand in his **h** place?
30: 4 praise his **h** name.
33:21 rejoice, for we trust in his **h** name.
47: 8 God is seated on his **h** throne.
77:13 Your ways, God, are **h**. What god is
78:54 them to the border of his **h** land,
89: 5 too, in the assembly of the **h** ones.
89:18 our king to the **H** One of Israel.

Ps 99: 3 great and awesome name—he is **h**.
99: 9 God and worship at his **h** mountain,
105: 3 Glory in his **h** name; let the hearts
111: 9 **h** and awesome is his name.
Pr 9:10 of the **H** One is understanding.
Isa 1: 4 they have spurned the **H** One
5:16 the **h** God will be proved **h** by his
6: 3 "**H, h, h** is the LORD Almighty;
6:13 so the **h** seed will be the stump
8:13 is the one you are to regard as **h**,
29:23 the holiness of the **H** One of Jacob,
40:25 who is my equal?" says the **H** One.
43: 3 your God, the **H** One of Israel,
52:10 The LORD will lay bare his **h** arm
54: 5 the **H** One of Israel is your
57:15 whose name is **h**: "I live in a high and **h** place,
58:13 doing as you please on my **h** day,
58:13 and the LORD's **h** day honorable,
Jer 2: 3 Israel was **h** to the LORD,
17:22 but keep the Sabbath day **h**, as I
Eze 20:41 I will be proved **h** through you
22:26 to my law and profane my **h** things;
22:26 do not distinguish between the **h**
28:22 and within you am proved to be **h**.
28:25 I will be proved **h** through them
36:20 nations they profaned my **h** name,
38:16 I am proved **h** through you before
44:23 people the difference between the **h**
Da 4:13 and there before me was a **h** one,
8:13 Then I heard a **h** one speaking,
9:24 your **h** city to finish transgression,
9:24 and to anoint the Most **H** Place.
11:28 will be set against the **h** covenant.
Jnh 2: 4 look again toward your **h** temple.'
Hab 2:20 The LORD is in his **h** temple;
Zec 8: 3 will be called the **H** Mountain."
14: 5 come, and all the **h** ones with him.
14:20 On that day H TO THE
Mt 1:18 to be pregnant through the **H** Spirit.
3:11 will baptize you with the **H** Spirit
4: 5 the devil took him to the **h** city
24:15 in the **h** place 'the abomination
27:52 many **h** people who had died were
28:19 and of the Son and of the **H** Spirit,
Mk 1:24 who you are—the **H** One of God!"
3:29 blasphemes against the **H** Spirit will
Lk 1:15 the **H** Spirit even before he is born.
1:35 "The **H** Spirit will come on you,
1:35 So the **h** one to be born will be
1:49 great things for me—**h** is his name.
3:22 the **H** Spirit descended on him
4: 1 full of the **H** Spirit, left the Jordan
10:21 full of joy through the **H** Spirit,
11:13 in heaven give the **H** Spirit to those
Jn 6:69 that you are the **H** One of God."
14:26 But the Advocate, the **H** Spirit,
20:22 and said, "Receive the **H** Spirit.
Ac 1: 5 will be baptized with the **H** Spirit."
2: 4 of them were filled with the **H** Spirit
2:27 will not let your **h** one see decay.
2:38 will receive the gift of the **H** Spirit.
4:27 against your **h** servant Jesus,

Ac   5: 3 that you have lied to the **H** Spirit
     8:15 that they might receive the **H** Spirit,
    10:44 the **H** Spirit came on all who heard
    13:35 will not let your **h** one see decay.'
    15: 8 them by giving the **H** Spirit to them,
    19: 2 "Did you receive the **H** Spirit
    19: 2 even heard that there is a **H** Spirit."
Ro   1: 2 his prophets in the **H** Scriptures
    7:12 the law is **h**, and the commandment
         is **h**,
    11:16 the dough offered as firstfruits is **h**,
         then the whole batch is **h**;
    11:16 if the root is **h**, so are the branches.
    12: 1 sacrifice, **h** and pleasing to God—
    15:16 to God, sanctified by the **H** Spirit.
    16:16 Greet one another with a **h** kiss.
1Co   1: 2 Jesus and called to be his **h** people,
    7:14 be unclean, but as it is, they are **h**.
Eph   1: 4 the creation of the world to be **h**
    2:21 to become a **h** temple in the Lord.
    3: 5 by the Spirit to God's **h** apostles
    4:30 do not grieve the **H** Spirit of God,
    5:26 to make her **h**, cleansing her
Col   1:22 death to present you **h** in his sight,
1Th   2:10 of how **h**, righteous and blameless
    3:13 Jesus comes with all his **h** ones.
    4: 7 us to be impure, but to live a **h** life.
2Th   1:10 comes to be glorified in his **h** people
1Ti   2: 8 lifting up **h** hands without anger
2Ti   1: 9 saved us and called us to a **h** life—
    2:21 made **h**, useful to the Master
    3:15 you have known the **H** Scriptures,
Titus 1: 8 upright, **h** and disciplined.
    3: 5 rebirth and renewal by the **H** Spirit,
Heb   2: 4 of the **H** Spirit distributed according
    2:11 Both the one who makes people **h**
    6: 4 who have shared in the **H** Spirit,
    7:26 one who is **h**, blameless, pure,
    9:12 he entered the Most **H** Place once
    10:10 we have been made **h** through
    10:14 forever those who are being made **h**.
    10:19 enter the Most **H** Place by the blood
    12:14 in peace with everyone and to be **h**;
    13:12 make the people **h** through his own
1Pe   1:15 But just as he who called you is **h**, so
         be **h** in all you do;
    1:16 "Be **h**, because I am **h**."
    2: 5 spiritual house to be a **h** priesthood,
    2: 9 a royal priesthood, a **h** nation,
    3: 5 this is the way the **h** women
2Pe   1:21 were carried along by the **H** Spirit.
    3:11 You ought to live **h** and godly lives
1Jn   2:20 have an anointing from the **H** One,
Jude 1:14 upon thousands of his **h** ones
    1:20 yourselves up in your most **h** faith
         and praying in the **H** Spirit,
Rev   3: 7 These are the words of him who is **h**
    4: 8 " '**H**, **h**, **h** is the Lord God
    11: 2 They will trample on the **h** city
    15: 4 For you alone are **h**. All nations will
    20: 6 **h** are those who share in the first
    21: 2 I saw the **H** City, the new
    21:10 high, and showed me the **H** City,

Rev 22:11 let the **h** person continue to be **h**."
    22:19 in the tree of life and in the **H** City,

HOLY CITY Ne 11:1, 18; Isa 48:2; 52:1; Da 9:24;
Mt 4:5; 27:53; Rev 11:2; 21:2, 10; 22:19

HOLY HILL Da 9:16, 20; Joel 2:1; 3:17; Ob 1:16;
Zep 3:11

HOLY MOUNTAIN Ps 2:6; 3:4; 15:1; 43:3;
48:1; 87:1; 99:9; Isa 11:9; 27:13; 56:7; 57:13; 65:11,
25; 66:20; Eze 20:40; Da 11:45; Zec 8:3

HOLY NAME Lev 20:3; 22:2, 32; 1Ch 16:10, 35;
29:16; Ps 30:4; 33:21; 97:12; 103:1; 105:3; 106:47;
145:21; Eze 20:39; 36:20, 21, 22; 39:7, 7, 25; 43:7,
8; Am 2:7

HOLY ONE 2Ki 19:22; Job 6:10; Ps 22:3; 71:22;
78:41; 89:18; Pr 9:10; 30:3; Isa 1:4; 5:19, 24; 10:17,
20; 12:6; 17:7; 29:19, 23; 30:11, 12, 15; 31:1; 37:23;
40:25; 41:14, 16, 20; 43:3, 14, 15; 45:11; 47:4;
48:17; 49:7, 7; 54:5; 55:5; 60:9, 14; Jer 50:29; 51:5;
Eze 39:7; Da 4:13, 23; 8:13, 13; Hos 11:9, 12; Hab
1:12; 3:3; Mk 1:24; Lk 1:35; 4:34; Jn 6:69; Ac 2:27;
13:35; 1Jn 2:20; Rev 16:5

HOLY ONES Dt 33:2, 3; Job 5:1; 15:15; Ps 89:5,
7; Da 4:17; Zec 14:5; 1Th 3:13; Jude 1:14

HOLY PLACE Ex 26:33, 33, 34; 28:29, 35, 43;
29:30; 31:11; Lev 6:30; 10:18; 16:2, 3, 16, 17, 20,
23, 27, 33; Jos 24:26; 1Ki 6:16; 7:50; 8:6, 8, 8, 10;
1Ch 6:49; 23:32; 2Ch 3:8, 10; 4:22; 5:7, 9, 11; 35:5;
Ps 24:3; 28:2; 46:4; Ecc 8:10; Isa 8:14; 57:15; 63:18;
Eze 41:4, 21, 23; 45:3, 4; Da 9:24; Mt 24:15; Ac
6:13; 21:28; Heb 9:2, 3, 8, 12, 25; 10:19; 13:11

HOLY SPIRIT Ps 51:11; Isa 63:10, 11; Mt 1:18,
20; 3:11; 12:32; 28:19; Mk 1:8; 3:29; 12:36; 13:11;
Lk 1:15, 35, 41, 67; 2:25, 26; 3:16, 22; 4:1; 10:21;
11:13; 12:10, 12; Jn 1:33; 14:26; 20:22; Ac 1:2, 5,
8, 16; 2:4, 33, 38; 4:8, 25, 31; 5:3, 32; 6:5; 7:51, 55;
8:15, 16, 17, 19; 9:17, 31; 10:38, 44, 45, 47; 11:15,
16, 24; 13:2, 4, 9, 52; 15:8, 28; 16:6; 19:2, 2, 6;
20:23, 28; 21:11; 28:25; Ro 5:5; 9:1; 14:17; 15:13,
16; 1Co 6:19; 12:3; 2Co 6:6; 13:14; Eph 1:13; 4:30;
1Th 1:5, 6; 4:8; 2Ti 1:14; Titus 3:5; Heb 2:4; 3:7;
6:4; 9:8; 10:15; 1Pe 1:12; 2Pe 1:21; Jude 1:20

HOLY TO THE LORD† Ex 28:36; 30:10, 37;
31:15; 39:30; Lev 19:8; 27:14, 23, 28, 30, 32; Dt
7:6; 14:2, 21; 26:19; Ne 8:9; Jer 2:3; 31:40; Eze
48:14; Zec 14:20, 21

MOST HOLY Ex 26:33, 34; 29:37; 30:10, 29, 36;
40:10; Lev 2:3, 10; 6:17, 25, 29; 7:1, 6; 10:12, 17;
14:13; 16:2, 3, 16, 17, 20, 23, 27, 33; 21:22; 24:9;
27:28; Nu 4:4, 19; 18:9, 9, 10; 1Ki 6:16; 7:50; 8:6;
1Ch 6:49; 23:13; 2Ch 3:8, 10; 4:22; 5:7; Ps 28:2;
Eze 41:4, 21, 23; 42:13, 13; 43:12; 44:13; 45:3;
48:12; Da 9:24; Heb 9:3, 8, 12, 25; 10:19; 13:11;
Jude 1:20

HOME HOMELAND, HOMELESS, HOMES

Nu 14:30 with uplifted hand to make your **h**,
Dt   6: 7 Talk about them when you sit at **h**
    11:19 talking about them when you sit at **h**
    20: 5 Let him go **h**, or he may die in battle

Dt 24: 5 one year he is to be free to stay at **h**
Jos 22: 7 When Joshua sent them **h**,
Ru   1:11 said, "Return **h**, my daughters.
2Sa 7:10 that they can have a **h** of their own
1Ch 16:43 David returned **h** to bless his family.
2Ch 10:16 So all the Israelites went **h**.
Ps 84: 3 Even the sparrow has found a **h**,
    113: 9 woman in her **h** as a happy mother
Pr   3:33 but he blesses the **h** of the righteous.
     7:11 and defiant, her feet never stay at **h**;
     27: 8 its nest is anyone who flees from **h**.
Ecc 12: 5 people go to their eternal **h**
Eze 36: 8 Israel, for they will soon come **h**.
Hag 1: 9 What you brought **h**, I blew away.
Mt   1:20 afraid to take Mary **h** as your wife,
    13:57 in his own town and in his own **h**."
Mk   2:11 get up, take your mat and go **h**."
     5:19 "Go **h** to your own people and tell
    10:29 "no one who has left **h** or brothers
Lk 10:38 woman named Martha opened her **h**
Jn   9: 7 and washed, and came **h** seeing.
    14:23 to them and make our **h** with them.
    19:27 on, this disciple took her into his **h**.
Ac 10:32 a guest in the **h** of Simon the tanner,
    16:15 baptized, she invited us to her **h**.
1Co 11:34 is hungry should eat something at **h**,
2Co 5: 8 the body and at **h** with the Lord.
Titus 2: 5 and pure, to be busy at **h**, to be kind,

HOMELAND HOME

Ge 30:25 way so I can go back to my own **h**.
Ru   2:11 and your **h** and came to live
2Ki 17:23 were taken from their **h** into exile
Ps 79: 7 Jacob and devastated his **h**.

HOMELESS* HOME

1Co 4:11 we are brutally treated, we are **h**.

HOMES HOME

Nu 32:18 will not return to our **h** until each
Jos 22: 6 them away, and they went to their **h**.
Ne   4:14 daughters, your wives and your **h**."
Isa 32:18 in secure **h**, in undisturbed places
Hos 11:11 I will settle them in their **h**,"
Mic 2: 2 They defraud people of their **h**,
Mk 10:30 **h**, brothers, sisters, mothers,
1Ti 5:14 to manage their **h** and to give
2Ti 3: 6 the kind who worm their way into **h**

HOMETOWN TOWN

Mt 13:54 Coming to his **h**, he began teaching
Lk   4:24 "no prophet is accepted in his **h**.

HOMOSEXUALITY*

1Ti 1:10 for those practicing **h**, for slave

HONEST HONESTLY, HONESTY

Ex 23: 7 put an innocent or **h** person to death,
Lev 19:36 Use **h** scales and weights, an **h**
           ephah and an **h** hin.
Dt 25:15 must have accurate and **h** weights
2Ki 22: 7 to them, because they are **h** in their
Job 31: 6 let God weigh me in **h** scales and he
Pr 12:17 An **h** witness tells the truth,

Pr 14: 5 An **h** witness does not deceive,
    16:11 **H** scales and balances belong
    17:26 surely to flog **h** officials is not right.

HONESTLY* HONEST

Jer 5: 1 one person who deals **h** and seeks

HONESTY* HONEST

Ge 30:33 And my **h** will testify for me
2Ki 12:15 because they acted with complete **h**.
Isa 59:14 in the streets, **h** cannot enter.

HONEY HONEYCOMB

Ex   3: 8 a land flowing with milk and **h**—
    16:31 and tasted like wafers made with **h**.
Lev 2:11 **h** in a food offering presented
Jdg 14: 8 he saw a swarm of bees and some **h**.
1Sa 14:26 woods, they saw the **h** oozing out;
Ps 19:10 they are sweeter than **h**, than **h**
   119:103 taste, sweeter than **h** to my mouth!
Pr   5: 3 lips of the adulterous woman drip **h**,
    24:14 also that wisdom is like **h** for you:
    25:16 If you find **h**, eat just enough—
SS   4:11 milk and **h** are under your tongue.
Isa 7:15 **h** when he knows enough to reject
Eze 3: 3 it tasted as sweet as **h** in my mouth.
Mt   3: 4 His food was locusts and wild **h**.
Rev 10: 9 mouth it will be as sweet as **h**.' "

HONEYCOMB* HONEY

1Sa 14:27 in his hand and dipped it into the **h**.
Ps 19:10 than honey, than honey from the **h**.
Pr 16:24 Gracious words are a **h**,
SS   4:11 Your lips drop sweetness as the **h**,
     5: 1 I have eaten my **h** and my honey;

HONOR HONORABLE, HONORABLY, HONORED, HONORS

Ex 12:42 to keep vigil to **h** the LORD
    20:12 "**H** your father and your mother,
Nu 20:12 in me enough to **h** me as holy
    25:13 he was zealous for the **h** of his God
Dt   5:16 "**H** your father and your mother,
Jdg 4: 9 are taking, the **h** will not be yours,
1Sa 2: 8 and has them inherit a throne of **h**.
     2:30 Those who **h** me I will **h**, but those
2Ki 10:20 "Call an assembly in **h** of Baal."
1Ch 29:12 Wealth and **h** come from you;
2Ch 1:11 possessions or **h**, nor for the death
    18: 1 Jehoshaphat had great wealth and **h**,
Ezr 10:11 Now **h** the LORD, the God of your
Est 6: 6 for the man the king delights to **h**?"
Ps   8: 5 and crowned them with glory and **h**.
    45:11 **h** him, for he is your lord.
    50:23 who sacrifice thank offerings **h** me,
    84:11 the LORD bestows favor and **h**;
   112: 9 their horn will be lifted high in **h**.
Pr   3: 9 **H** the LORD with your wealth,
     3:35 The wise inherit **h**, but fools get
    11:16 A kindhearted woman gains **h**,
    15:33 and humility comes before **h**.
    18:12 but humility comes before **h**.
    20: 3 It is to one's **h** to avoid strife,

Pr   22: 4 its wages are riches and **h** and life.
      29:23 low, but the lowly in spirit gain **h**.
      31:31 **H** her for all that her hands have
Ecc   10: 1 little folly outweighs wisdom and **h**.
Isa   9: 1 in the future he will **h** Galilee
      29:13 their mouth and **h** me with their lips,
Jer   33: 9 **h** before all nations on earth
Da   2:46 and paid him **h** and ordered
       5:23 you did not **h** the God who holds
Mal   1: 6 am a father, where is the **h** due me?
Mt   13:57 "A prophet is not without **h** except
      15: 4 'H your father and mother'
      15: 8 " 'These people **h** me with their
      19:19 **h** your father and mother,' and 'love
      23: 6 they love the place of **h** at banquets
Mk   6: 4 "A prophet is not without **h** except
Lk   14: 8 do not take the place of **h**,
Jn   4:44 that a prophet has no **h** in his own
       5:23 all may **h** the Son just as they
            h the Father.
       5:23 Whoever does not **h** the Son does
            not **h** the Father,
       8:49 Jesus, "but I **h** my Father and you
      12:26 My Father will **h** the one who
Ro   12:10 **H** one another above yourselves.
      13: 7 if respect, then respect; if **h**, then **h**.
1Co   6:20 Therefore **h** God with your bodies.
      12:23 honorable we treat with special **h**.
Eph   6: 2 "H your father and mother"—
1Ti   5:17 church well are worthy of double **h**,
Heb   2: 7 you crowned them with glory and **h**
       3: 3 worthy of greater **h** than Moses,
1Pe   1: 7 and **h** when Jesus Christ is revealed.
2Pe   1:17 He received **h** and glory from God
Rev   4: 9 **h** and thanks to him who sits
       4:11 to receive glory and **h** and power,
       5:12 and strength and **h** and glory
       7:12 wisdom and thanks and **h** and power
      13:14 an image in **h** of the beast who was
      21:26 **h** of the nations will be brought

HONORABLE HONOR
Pr   25:27 nor is it **h** to search out matters
1Th   4: 4 body in a way that is holy and **h**,

HONORABLY HONOR
Heb 13:18 and desire to live **h** in every way.

HONORED HONOR
Ex   20:24 Wherever I cause my name to be **h**,
Ps   12: 8 what is vile is **h** by the human race.
Pr   13:18 but whoever heeds correction is **h**.
      27:18 protects their master will be **h**.
Da   4:34 I **h** and glorified him who lives
Hag   1: 8 I may take pleasure in it and be **h**,"
Lk   14:10 you will be **h** in the presence of all
1Co   12:26 if one part is **h**, every part rejoices
Heb   13: 4 Marriage should be **h** by all,

HONORS* HONOR
Ps   15: 4 but **h** those who fear the LORD;
Pr   14:31 whoever is kind to the needy **h** God.
Mal   1: 6 "A son **h** his father, and a slave his
3Jn   1: 6 on their way in a manner that **h** God.

HOOF
Ex   10:26 not a **h** is to be left behind.
Lev   11: 3 eat any animal that has a divided **h**

HOOK FISHHOOK, HOOKS
2Ch   33:11 prisoner, put **h** in his nose,
Isa   37:29 I will put my **h** in your nose and my

HOOKS HOOK
Ex   26:37 Make gold **h** for this curtain
Isa   2: 4 and their spears into pruning **h**.
Joel   3:10 and your pruning **h** into spears.
Am   4: 2 you will be taken away with **h**,
Mic   4: 3 and their spears into pruning **h**.

HOPE HOPED, HOPELESS, HOPES
Ru   1:12 if I thought there was still **h** for me—
Ezr   10: 2 of this, there is still **h** for Israel.
Job   6: 8 that God would grant what I **h** for,
      13:15 he slay me, yet will I **h** in him;
      17:15 where then is my **h**—who can see
            any **h** for me?
Ps   9:18 the **h** of the afflicted will never
      31:24 heart, all you who **h** in the LORD.
      33:17 A horse is a vain **h** for deliverance;
      33:18 on those whose **h** is in his unfailing
      33:22 even as we put our **h** in you.
      37:34 **H** in the LORD and keep his way.
      39: 7 what do I look for? My **h** is in you.
      42: 5 Put your **h** in God, for I will yet
      52: 9 And I will **h** in your name, for your
      62: 5 rest in God; my **h** comes from him.
      65: 5 the **h** of all the ends of the earth
      71:14 As for me, I will always have **h**;
     119:43 for I have put my **h** in your laws.
     119:74 for I have put my **h** in your word.
     130: 5 waits, and in his word I put my **h**.
     130: 7 Israel, put your **h** in the LORD,
     146: 5 whose **h** is in the LORD their God.
     147:11 who put their **h** in his unfailing love.
Pr   13:12 **H** deferred makes the heart sick,
      23:18 There is surely a future **h** for you, and
            your **h** will not be cut off.
      24:14 there is a future **h** for you, and your **h**
            will not be cut off.
      26:12 There is more **h** for a fool than
Ecc   9: 4 who is among the living has **h**—
Isa   40:31 but those who **h** in the LORD will
      49:23 those who **h** in me will not be
Jer   14: 8 You who are the **h** of Israel,
      29:11 plans to give you **h** and a future.
La   3:21 call to mind and therefore I have **h**:
Eze   37:11 are dried up and our **h** is gone;
Mic   7: 7 for me, I watch in **h** for the LORD,
Zec   9:12 to your fortress, you prisoners of **h**;
Mt   12:21 name the nations will put their **h**."
Ac   2:26 my body also will rest in **h**,
      23: 6 because of the **h** of the resurrection
Ro   4:18 Against all **h**, Abraham in **h**
       5: 4 character; and character, **h**.
       5: 5 And **h** does not put us to shame,
       8:20 of the one who subjected it, in **h**
       8:24 For in this **h** we were saved.
       8:24 But **h** that is seen is no **h** at all.

Ro   8:25 if we **h** for what we do not yet have,
    12:12 Be joyful in **h**, patient in affliction,
    15: 4 they provide we might have **h**.
    15:12 in him the Gentiles will **h**."
    15:13 May the God of **h** fill you with all
    15:13 that you may overflow with **h**
1Co 13:13 these three remain: faith, **h** and love.
    15:19 for this life we have **h** in Christ,
2Co 1:10 him we have set our **h** that he will
Gal 5: 5 the righteousness for which we **h**.
Eph 1:12 were the first to put our **h** in Christ,
     2:12 without **h** and without God
     4: 4 to one **h** when you were called;
Col 1: 5 love that spring from the **h** stored
     1:23 do not move from the **h** held
     1:27 is Christ in you, the **h** of glory.
1Th 1: 3 your endurance inspired by **h** in our
     4:13 the rest of mankind, who have no **h**.
     5: 8 and the **h** of salvation as a helmet.
1Ti 1: 1 our Savior and of Christ Jesus our **h**,
     4:10 because we have put our **h**
     6:17 arrogant nor to put their **h** in wealth,
     6:17 but to put their **h** in God, who richly
Titus 1: 2 in the **h** of eternal life, which God,
     2:13 while we wait for the blessed **h**—
Heb 3: 6 and the **h** in which we glory.
     6:11 so that what you **h** for may be fully
     6:19 We have this **h** as an anchor
     7:19 and a better **h** is introduced,
    10:23 unswervingly to the **h** we profess,
    11: 1 faith is confidence in what we **h**
1Pe 1: 3 a living **h** through the resurrection
     1:21 and so your faith and **h** are in God.
     3: 5 the past who put their **h** in God used
     3:15 the reason for the **h** that you have.
1Jn 3: 3 All who have this **h** in him purify

HOPED HOPE
Job 30:26 Yet when I **h** for good, evil came;
Jer 8:15 We **h** for peace but no good has
Lk 20:20 They **h** to catch Jesus in something

HOPELESS* HOPE
Isa 57:10 but you would not say, 'It is **h**.'

HOPES* HOPE
2Ki 4:28 I tell you, 'Don't raise my **h**'?"
Ps 25: 3 No one who **h** in you will ever be
    119:116 do not let my **h** be dashed.
Pr 10:28 joy, but the **h** of the wicked come
    11: 7 **H** placed in mortals die with them;
Jer 23:16 they fill you with false **h**.
Jn   5:45 is Moses, on whom your **h** are set.
Ro   8:24 Who **h** for what they already have?
1Co 13: 7 trusts, always **h**, always perseveres.
    15:32 Ephesus with no more than human **h**,

HOPHNI*
A wicked priest (1Sa 1:3; 2:34; 4:4–17).

HOR
Nu 33:38 Aaron the priest went up Mount H,
Dt 32:50 brother Aaron died on Mount H

HOREB
Ex   3: 1 of the wilderness and came to H,
    17: 6 there before you by the rock at H.
Dt   5: 2 God made a covenant with us at H.
1Ki 19: 8 and forty nights until he reached H,
Ps 106:19 At H they made a calf

HORIZON*
Ne   1: 9 exiled people are at the farthest **h**,
Job 26:10 He marks out the **h** on the face
Pr   8:27 he marked out the **h** on the face

HORMAH
Nu 14:45 beat them down all the way to H.
    21: 3 so the place was named H.

HORN HORNS
Ex 19:13 the ram's **h** sounds a long blast may
    27: 2 Make a **h** at each of the four
1Sa 2: 1 in the LORD my **h** is lifted high.
    16: 1 Fill your **h** with oil and be on your
Ps 18: 2 my shield and the **h** of my salvation,
    92:10 You have exalted my **h** like
   148:14 he has raised up for his people a **h**,
La   2: 3 fierce anger he has cut off every **h**
Da   3: 5 soon as you hear the sound of the **h**,
     7: 8 This **h** had eyes like the eyes
     8: 5 with a prominent **h** between its eyes
Lk   1:69 He has raised up a **h** of salvation

HORNET*
Ex 23:28 I will send the **h** ahead of you
Dt   7:20 will send the **h** among them until
Jos 24:12 I sent the **h** ahead of you,

HORNS HORN
Ge 22:13 thicket he saw a ram caught by its **h**.
Ex 27: 2 so that the **h** and the altar are of one
Lev 4: 7 of the blood on the **h** of the altar
Jos 6: 4 carry trumpets of rams' **h** in front
Ps 75: 5 Do not lift your **h** against heaven;
Da   7: 7 the former beasts, and it had ten **h**.
     7:24 The ten **h** are ten kings who will
     8: 3 before me was a ram with two **h**,
Rev 5: 6 The Lamb had seven **h** and seven
     9:13 from the four **h** of the golden altar
    12: 3 ten **h** and seven crowns on its heads.
    13: 1 It had ten **h** and seven heads, with ten
          crowns on its **h**,
    13:11 It had two **h** like a lamb, but it
    17: 3 and had seven heads and ten **h**.

HORRIBLE HORROR
Dt   7:15 on you the **h** diseases you knew
Jer 5:30 "A **h** and shocking thing has
Hos 6:10 I have seen a **h** thing in Israel:

HORRIFIED*
Pr 25:23 which provokes a **h** look.
Jer 4: 9 heart, the priests will be **h**,

HORROR HORRIBLE
Dt 28:25 you will become a thing of **h** to all
2Ch 29: 8 made them an object of dread and **h**
Ps 55: 5 **h** has overwhelmed me.
Jer 2:12 and shudder with great **h**,"

Jer 25:18 a ruin and an object of **h** and scorn,
Eze 20:26 fill them with **h** so they would know

HORSE HORSEMAN, HORSEMEN, HORSES, HORSES'
Ex   15: 1 Both **h** and driver he has hurled
Est   6: 8 worn and a **h** the king has ridden,
Ps   32: 9 Do not be like the **h** or the mule,
     33:17 A **h** is a vain hope for deliverance;
    147:10 is not in the strength of the **h**,
Pr   26: 3 A whip for the **h**, a bridle
Jer 51:21 with you I shatter **h** and rider,
Zec   1: 8 me was a man mounted on a red **h**.
Rev   6: 2 and there before me was a white **h**!
      6: 4 Then another **h** came out, a fiery red
      6: 5 and there before me was a black **h**!
      6: 8 and there before me was a pale **h**!
     19:11 and there before me was a white **h**,

HORSEMAN HORSE, MAN
Am   2:15 and the **h** will not save his life.

HORSEMEN HORSE, MAN
Ex   14:28 and covered the chariots and **h**—
     15:19 chariots and **h** went into the sea,
2Ki   2:12 The chariots and **h** of Israel!"
     18:24 on Egypt for chariots and **h**?
Isa 31: 1 and in the great strength of their **h**,

HORSES HORSE
Ge   47:17 them food in exchange for their **h**,
Ex   14:23 and all Pharaoh's **h** and chariots
Dt   17:16 must not acquire great numbers of **h**
Jos 11: 6 You are to hamstring their **h**
1Ki   4:26 four thousand stalls for chariot **h**, and
            twelve thousand **h**.
     10:26 accumulated chariots and **h**;
2Ki   2:11 chariot of fire and of fire appeared
      6:17 saw the hills full of **h** and chariots
Ps   20: 7 trust in chariots and some in **h**,
Isa 31: 3 their **h** are flesh and not spirit.
Jer 12: 5 out, how can you compete with **h**?
Joel 2: 4 They have the appearance of **h**;
Zec   6: 2 The first chariot had red **h**,
Rev   9: 7 The locusts looked like **h** prepared
     19:14 riding on white **h** and dressed

HORSES' HORSE
Rev 14:20 rising as high as the **h** bridles

HOSANNA*
Mt   21: 9 shouted, "**H** to the Son of David!"
     21: 9 "**H** in the highest heaven!"
     21:15 courts, "**H** to the Son of David,"
Mk   11: 9 those who followed shouted, "**H**!"
     11:10 "**H** in the highest heaven!"
Jn   12:13 out to meet him, shouting, "**H**!"

HOSEA
Prophet whose wife and family pictured the unfaithfulness of Israel (Hos 1–3).

HOSHEA JOSHUA
1. Original name of Joshua (Nu 13:8, 16).
2. Last king of Israel (2Ki 15:30; 17:1–6).

HOSPITABLE* HOSPITALITY
1Ti   3: 2 respectable, **h**, able to teach,
Titus 1: 8 he must be **h**, one who loves what is

HOSPITALITY* HOSPITABLE
Ac   28: 7 and showed us generous **h** for three
Ro   12:13 people who are in need. Practice **h**.
     16:23 whose **h** I and the whole church
1Ti   5:10 showing **h**, washing the feet
Heb 13: 2 not forget to show **h** to strangers,
     13: 2 shown **h** to angels without knowing
1Pe   4: 9 Offer **h** to one another without
3Jn   1: 8 to show **h** to such people so that we

HOST HOSTS
Ne   9: 6 and all their starry **h**, the earth
Isa 34: 4 all the starry **h** will fall like
     40:26 brings out the starry **h** one by one
Da   8:10 of the starry **h** down to the earth
Lk   2:13 of the heavenly **h** appeared

HOSTILE HOSTILITY
Lev 26:21 " 'If you remain **h** toward me
Ro   8: 7 governed by the flesh is **h** to God;
1Th   2:15 displease God and are **h** to everyone

HOSTILITY HOSTILE
Ge   16:12 live in **h** toward all his brothers."
     25:18 in **h** toward all the tribes related
Hos   9: 8 paths, and **h** in the house of his God.
Eph   2:14 the barrier, the dividing wall of **h**,
      2:16 by which he put to death their **h**.

HOSTS HOST
2Ki 17:16 bowed down to all the starry **h**,
2Ch 33: 5 he built altars to all the starry **h**.
Ps 103:21 all his heavenly **h**, you his servants
    148: 2 praise him, all his heavenly **h**,
Isa 45:12 I marshaled their starry **h**.

HOT HOT-TEMPERED, HOTHEADED, HOTTER
Ex   11: 8 Then Moses, **h** with anger,
Ps   39: 3 my heart grew **h** within me.
Pr   6:28 on **h** coals without his feet being
Eze 38:18 Israel, my **h** anger will be aroused,
Da   3:22 the furnace so **h** that the flames
1Ti   4: 2 have been seared as with a **h** iron,
Rev   3:15 that you are neither cold nor **h**.

HOT-TEMPERED* HOT, TEMPER
Pr   15:18 A **h** person stirs up conflict,
     19:19 A **h** person must pay the penalty;
     22:24 not make friends with a **h** person,
     29:22 and a **h** person commits many sins.

HOTHEADED* HOT, HEAD
Pr   14:16 but a fool is **h** and yet feels secure.

HOTTER* HOT
Da   3:19 heated seven times **h** than usual

HOUNDED*
Ps 109:16 but **h** to death the poor

HOUR

Ecc	9:12	one knows when their **h** will come:
Mt	6:27	worrying add a single **h** to your life?
	24:36	about that day or **h** no one knows,
Mk	14:35	if possible the **h** might pass
	14:37	Couldn't you keep watch for one **h**?
Lk	12:40	an **h** when you do not expect him."
Jn	2: 4	"My **h** has not yet come."
	12:23	"The **h** has come for the Son
	12:27	'Father, save me from this **h**'?
	12:27	for this very reason I came to this **h**.
	17: 1	"Father, the **h** has come.
1Jn	2:18	Dear children, this is the last **h**;
Rev	3:10	keep you from the **h** of trial that is
	8: 1	in heaven for about half an **h**.
	14: 7	because the **h** of his judgment has
	17:12	one **h** will receive authority as kings
	18:10	In one **h** your doom has come!'

HOUSE HOUSEHOLD, HOUSEHOLDS, HOUSES, STOREHOUSE, STOREHOUSES

Ge	19: 2	turn aside to your servant's **h**.
	24:23	there room in your father's **h** for us
	28:17	This is none other than the the **h**
Ex	12:22	of the door of your **h** until morning.
	20:17	shall not covet your neighbor's **h**.
Lev	27:14	dedicates their **h** as something holy
Nu	12: 7	he is faithful in all my **h**.
Dt	5:21	set your desire on your neighbor's **h**
Jos	2: 1	entered the **h** of a prostitute named
	6:22	land, "Go into the prostitute's **h**
1Sa	1: 7	went up to the **h** of the LORD,
	3: 3	lying down in the **h** of the LORD,
2Sa	3: 1	The war between the **h** of Saul and the **h** of David lasted
	3: 1	while the **h** of Saul grew weaker
	7: 2	living in a **h** of cedar, while the ark
	7: 5	the one to build me a **h** to dwell in?
	7:11	LORD himself will establish a **h**
	23: 5	"If my **h** were not right with God,
1Ki	8:43	this **h** I have built bears your Name.
2Ki	15: 5	he died, and he lived in a separate **h**.
1Ch	9:23	the **h** called the tent of meeting.
	17:12	He is the one who will build a **h**
	22: 1	"The **h** of the LORD God is to be
Ezr	1: 5	up and build the **h** of the LORD
	3:11	of the **h** of the LORD was laid.
Ne	10:39	"We will not neglect the **h** of our
Ps	23: 6	in the **h** of the LORD forever.
	27: 4	in the **h** of the LORD all the days
	52: 8	tree flourishing in the **h** of God;
	69: 9	for zeal for your **h** consumes me,
	84:10	in the **h** of my God than dwell
	122: 1	"Let us go to the **h** of the LORD."
	127: 1	Unless the LORD builds the **h**,
Pr	7:27	Her **h** is a highway to the grave,
	9: 1	Wisdom has built her **h**; she has set
	9: 4	all who are simple come to my **h**!"
	14: 1	The wise woman builds her **h**,
	14:11	The **h** of the wicked will be
	21: 9	of the roof than share a **h**
Ecc	10:18	because of idle hands, the **h** leaks.

Isa	5: 8	Woe to you who add **h** to **h** and join
	7:13	said, "Hear now, you **h** of David!
	56: 7	for my **h** will be called a **h** of prayer
Jer	7:11	Has this **h**, which bears my Name,
	18: 2	"Go down to the potter's **h**,
	32:34	images in the **h** that bears my Name
Joel	3:18	will flow out of the LORD's **h**
Hab	2: 9	him who builds his **h** by unjust gain,
Hag	1: 4	while this **h** remains a ruin?"
	2: 7	and I will fill this **h** with glory,'
Zec	8: 9	for the **h** of the LORD Almighty.
	13: 6	I was given at the **h** of my friends.'
Mt	7:24	is like a wise man who built his **h**
	10:11	and stay at their **h** until you leave.
	12:29	can anyone enter a strong man's **h**
	21:13	" 'My **h** will be called a **h**
Mk	3:25	If a **h** is divided against itself, that **h** cannot stand.
	11:17	'My **h** will be called a **h** of prayer
Lk	6:48	They are like a man building a **h**,
	10: 7	Do not move around from **h** to **h**.
	11:17	a **h** divided against itself will fall.
	11:24	it says, 'I will return to the **h** I left.'
	15: 8	sweep the **h** and search carefully
	19: 9	salvation has come to this **h**,
Jn	2:16	Stop turning my Father's **h**
	2:17	for your **h** will consume me."
	12: 3	the **h** was filled with the fragrance
	14: 2	My Father's **h** has many rooms;
Ac	5:42	in the temple courts and from **h** to **h**,
	16:15	she said, "come and stay at my **h**."
	20:20	taught you publicly and from **h** to **h**.
	28:30	stayed there in his own rented **h**
Ro	16: 5	also the church that meets at their **h**.
2Co	5: 1	from God, an eternal **h** in heaven,
Heb	3: 2	Moses was faithful in all God's **h**.
	10:21	we have a great priest over the **h**
1Pe	2: 5	a spiritual **h** to be a holy priesthood,
2Jn	1:10	do not take them into your **h**

FATHER'S HOUSE Ge 24:23; Dt 22:21, 21; Jdg 11:7; Ps 45:10; Isa 3:6; Lk 2:49; Jn 2:16; 14:2

HOUSE OF DAVID 1Sa 20:16; 2Sa 3:1, 6; 1Ki 12:19, 20, 26; 13:2; 14:8; 2Ki 17:21; 2Ch 10:19; 21:7; Ps 122:5; Isa 7:2, 13; 16:5; 22:22; Jer 21:12; Zec 12:7, 8, 10, 12; 13:1

HOUSE OF ... GOD Ge 28:17; Ex 23:19; 34:26; Dt 23:18; Jos 9:23; Jdg 18:31; 1Ch 6:48; 9:11, 13, 26, 27; 22:1, 2, 11; 23:28; 25:6; 26:20; Ezr 2:68; 3:8, 9; 4:24; 5:2, 13, 14, 15, 16, 17; 6:5, 5, 7, 8, 16, 17, 22; 7:24; 8:17, 25, 30, 33, 36; 9:9; 10:1, 6, 9; Ne 6:10; 8:16; 10:32, 33, 34, 36, 37, 38, 39; 11:11, 16, 22; 12:40; 13:4, 7, 9, 11, 14; Ps 42:4; 52:8; 55:14; 84:10; 122:9; 135:2; Ecc 5:1; Da 1:2; Hos 9:8; Joel 1:13, 14, 16; Am 2:8; Mt 12:4; Mk 2:26; Lk 6:4; Heb 10:21

HOUSE OF THE LORD† Ex 23:19; 34:26; Dt 23:18; Jdg 19:18; 1Sa 1:7, 24; 3:3, 15; 2Sa 12:20; 1Ch 6:31; 9:23; 22:1, 11; Ezr 1:5; 2:68; 3:8, 11; 7:27; 8:29; Ne 10:35; Ps 23:6; 27:4; 92:13; 116:19; 118:26; 122:1, 9; 134:1; 135:2; Jer 17:26; 26:2, 7, 9, 10; 27:18, 21; 28:1, 5; 29:26; 33:11; 35:2, 4; 36:6;

41:5; La 2:7; Eze 8:14, 16; 11:1; Hos 8:1; Joel 1:9, 14; Hag 1:14; Zec 7:3; 8:9; 11:13; 14:21

HOUSEHOLD HOUSE

Ge	12: 1	and your father's **h** to the land I will
	15: 3	a servant in my **h** will be my heir."
	17:12	including those born in your **h**
	31:19	Rachel stole her father's **h** gods.
	39: 4	Potiphar put him in charge of his **h**,
Ex	12: 3	lamb for his family, one for each **h**.
Lev	16: 6	atonement for himself and his **h**.
Jos	24:15	But as for me and my **h**, we will
Jdg	18:14	some **h** gods and an image overlaid
Pr	31:21	it snows, she has no fear for her **h**;
	31:27	watches over the affairs of her **h**
Mic	7: 6	are the members of his own **h**.
Mt	10:36	will be the members of his own **h**.'
	12:25	or **h** divided against itself will not
Jn	4:53	So he and his whole **h** believed.
Ac	16:31	will be saved—you and your **h**."
	16:33	he and all his **h** were baptized.
Eph	2:19	people and also members of his **h**,
1Ti	3:12	manage his children and his **h** well.
	3:15	to conduct themselves in God's **h**,
	5: 8	and especially for their own **h**,
1Pe	4:17	for judgment to begin with God's **h**;

HOUSEHOLDS HOUSE

Nu	16:32	and swallowed them and their **h**,
Dt	11: 6	and swallowed them up with their **h**,
Pr	15:27	The greedy bring ruin to their **h**,
Titus	1:11	because they are disrupting whole **h**

HOUSES HOUSE

Ex	12: 7	of the **h** where they eat the lambs.
	12:27	who passed over the **h**
Dt	6: 9	them on the doorframes of your **h**
	11:20	them on the doorframes of your **h**
Ps	112: 3	Wealth and riches are in their **h**,
Isa	65:21	They will build **h** and dwell
Jer	29:28	Therefore build **h** and settle down;
Eze	11: 3	say, 'Haven't our **h** been recently
Mt	19:29	everyone who has left **h** or brothers
Mk	12:40	They devour widows' **h**
Ac	4:34	who owned land or **h** sold them,

HOVERING* HOVERS

Ge	1: 2	Spirit of God was **h** over the waters.
Isa	31: 5	Like birds **h** overhead, the LORD

HOVERS* HOVERING

Dt	32:11	up its nest and **h** over its young,

HOW HOWEVER, SOMEHOW

Ge	6:12	God saw **h** corrupt the earth had
	6:15	This is **h** you are to build it:
	28:17	and said, "H awesome is this place!
	39: 9	H then could I do such a wicked
Ex	12:11	This is **h** you are to eat it:
Nu	6:23	sons, 'This is **h** you are to bless
	23: 8	H can I curse those whom God has
Dt	31:27	**h** much more will you rebel after I
2Sa	1:19	H the mighty have fallen!
	7:22	"H great you are,
1Ki	3: 7	and do not know **h** to carry out my

2Ch	6:18	H much less this temple I have
	32:14	H then can your god deliver you
Job	2:13	to him, because they saw **h** great his
	25: 4	H then can a mortal be righteous
	40: 4	**h** can I reply to you?
Ps	6: 3	H long, LORD, **h** long?
	8: 1	**h** majestic is your name in all
	31:19	H abundant are the good things
	36: 7	H priceless is your unfailing love,
	92: 5	H great are your works, LORD,
	119: 9	H can a young person stay
	147: 1	**h** good it is to sing praises to our
Pr	15:23	and **h** good is a timely word!
SS	1:15	H beautiful you are, my darling!
	1:16	H handsome you are, my beloved!
Isa	1:21	See **h** the faithful city has become
	14:12	H you have fallen from heaven,
Jer	1: 6	I said, "I do not know **h** to speak;
	38:28	This is **h** Jerusalem was taken:
La	1: 1	H deserted lies the city, once so full
	1: 1	H like a widow is she, who once
Eze	33:10	H then can we live?" '
Hos	11: 8	"H can I give you up, Ephraim?
Mal	1: 2	you ask, 'H have you loved us?'
Mk	9:50	**h** can you make it salty again?
	10:23	"H hard it is for the rich to enter
Lk	12:27	"Consider **h** the wild flowers grow.
	20:44	H then can he be his son?"
Jn	3: 4	"H can someone be born when they
	7:15	"H did this man get such learning
Eph	5:15	Be very careful, then, **h** you live—
1Ti	3: 5	not know **h** to manage his own family, **h** can he take care of God's
Heb	2: 3	**h** shall we escape if we ignore so
2Pe	2: 9	then the Lord knows **h** to rescue

HOW LONG Ex 10:3, 7; 16:28; Nu 14:11, 11, 27; Jos 18:3; 1Sa 1:14; 16:1; 2Sa 2:26; 1Ki 18:21; Ne 2:6; Job 7.4, 8:2; 19:2; 29:2; Ps 4:2, 2; 6:3, 3; 13:1, 1, 2, 2; 35:17; 62:3; 74:9, 10; 79:5, 5; 80:4; 82:2; 89:46, 46; 90:13; 94:3, 3; 119:40, 84; Pr 1:22, 22; 6:9; Ecc 6:3; Isa 6:11; Jer 4:14, 21; 12:4; 13:27; 23:26; 31:22; 47:5, 6; Da 8:13; 12:6; Hos 8:5; Hab 1:2; 2:6; Zec 1:12; 2:2; Mt 17:17, 17; Mk 9:19, 19, 21; Lk 9:41; Jn 10:24; Php 1:8; Rev 6:10

HOW MUCH MORE Dt 31:27; 1Sa 21:5; 23:3; 2Sa 4:11; 16:11; 2Ki 5:13; Job 4:19; Pr 11:31; 15:11; 19:2, 7; 21:27; SS 4:10; Mt 7:11; 10:25; 12:12; Lk 11:13; 12:24, 28; Ro 5:9, 10, 15, 17; 11:24; 1Co 6:3; 2Co 3:9; Heb 9:14; 10:29; 12:9

HOWEVER HOW

Ex	16:20	H, some of them paid no attention
Dt	15: 4	H, there need be no poor people
	28:15	H, if you do not obey the LORD
Jos	14: 8	I, **h**, followed the LORD my God
Jer	34:14	Your ancestors, **h**, did not listen
Lk	18: 8	H, when the Son of Man comes,
Ro	9: 9	You, **h**, are not in the realm
1Pe	4:16	H, if you suffer as a Christian,

HUGE

2Sa	21:20	there was a **h** man with six fingers
	23:21	And he struck down a **h** Egyptian.

Da 2:35 the statue became a **h** mountain
Jnh 1:17 Now the LORD provided a **h** fish
Rev 8: 8 and something like a **h** mountain,
  16:21 From the sky **h** hailstones,

HULDAH

Female prophet consulted by Hilkiah the priest for King Josiah (2Ki 22; 2Ch 34:14–28).

HUMAN HUMANITY, HUMANS

Ge 6: 6 he had made **h** beings on the earth,
  6: 7 the earth the **h** race I have created—
  9: 6 "Whoever sheds **h** blood,
Ex 4:11 "Who gave **h** beings their mouths?
Lev 24:17 who takes the life of a **h** being is
  24:21 whoever kills a **h** being is to be put
Nu 19:16 anyone who touches a **h** bone
  23:19 God is not **h**, that he should lie,
  23:19 not a **h** being, that he should change
Jos 10:14 the LORD listened to a **h** being.
1Sa 15:29 for he is not a **h** being, that he
2Sa 7:19 Sovereign LORD, is for a mere **h**!
  7:14 with floggings inflicted by **h** hands.
1Ki 8:39 (for you alone know every **h** heart),
  13: 2 **h** bones will be burned on you.' "
2Ki 19:18 and stone, fashioned by **h** hands.
  23:14 and covered the sites with **h** bones.
1Ch 21:13 but do not let me fall into **h** hands."
2Ch 32:19 of the world—the work of **h** hands.
Ps 8: 4 **h** beings that you care for them?
  94:11 The LORD knows all **h** plans;
Ecc 3:11 has also set eternity in the **h** heart;
  3:19 Surely the fate of **h** beings is like
Isa 29:13 on merely **h** rules they have been
  37:19 and stone, fashioned by **h** hands.
  52:14 his form marred beyond **h** likeness—
Da 2:34 was cut out, but not by **h** hands.
  5: 5 the fingers of a **h** hand appeared
  7: 4 it stood on two feet like a **h** being,
  7: 4 and the mind of a **h** was given to it.
  8:25 be destroyed, but not by **h** power.
Hos 11: 4 I led them with cords of **h** kindness,
Hab 2: 8 For you have shed **h** blood;
  2:17 For you have shed **h** blood;
Mt 15: 9 teachings are merely **h** rules.' "
Mk 7: 7 their teachings are merely **h** rules.'
  11:30 was it from heaven, or of **h** origin?
  14:58 this temple made with **h** hands
Jn 1:13 nor of **h** decision or a husband's
  5:34 Not that I accept **h** testimony;
  8:15 You judge by **h** standards;
Ac 5:38 purpose or activity is of **h** origin,
  19:26 gods made by **h** hands are no gods
Ro 3: 4 be true, and every **h** being a liar.
  6:19 life because of your **h** limitations.
  9: 5 them is traced the **h** ancestry
  9:20 But who are you, a **h** being, to talk
1Co 1:25 of God is wiser than **h** wisdom,
  1:25 of God is stronger than **h** strength.
  1:26 of you were wise by **h** standards;
  2: 5 faith might not rest on **h** wisdom,
  2:13 not in words taught us by **h** wisdom
2Co 3: 3 of stone but on tablets of **h** hearts.
  5: 1 in heaven, not built by **h** hands.

Gal 1:10 to win the approval of **h** beings,
Php 2: 7 a servant, being made in **h** likeness.
Col 2: 8 which depends on **h** tradition
  2:22 are based on merely **h** commands
1Th 2:13 you accepted it not as a **h** word,
Heb 2:17 had to be made like them, fully **h**
  9:11 that is not made with **h** hands,
  9:24 enter a sanctuary made with **h** hands
Jas 5:17 Elijah was a **h** being, even as we
2Pe 1:21 never had its origin in the **h** will,
  1:21 though **h**, spoke from God as they
Rev 9: 7 and their faces resembled **h** faces.
  18:13 and **h** beings sold as slaves.

HUMANITY HUMAN, MAN

Eph 2:15 create in himself one new **h**
Heb 2:14 he too shared in their **h** so

HUMANS HUMAN

Ge 6: 3 will not contend with **h** forever,
Isa 2:22 Stop trusting in mere **h**, who have
1Co 3: 3 Are you not acting like mere **h**?

HUMBLE* HUMBLED, HUMBLES, HUMBLY, HUMILIATE, HUMILIATED, HUMILIATING, HUMILIATION, HUMILITY

Ex 10: 3 you refuse to **h** yourself before me?
Nu 12: 3 (Now Moses was a very **h** man,
  more **h** than anyone else on the face
Dt 8: 2 to **h** and test you in order to know
  8:16 to **h** and test you so that in the end it
2Sa 22:28 You save the **h**, but your eyes are
1Ki 11:39 I will **h** David's descendants
2Ch 7:14 will **h** themselves and pray and seek
  33:23 he did not **h** himself before
  36:12 did not **h** himself before Jeremiah
Ezr 8:21 we might **h** ourselves before our
Job 8: 7 Your beginnings will seem **h**,
  40:12 at all who are proud and **h** them,
Ps 18:27 You save the **h** but bring low those
  25: 9 He guides the **h** in what is right
  55:19 he will hear them and **h** them,
  147: 6 The LORD sustains the **h** but casts
  149: 4 he crowns the **h** with victory.
Pr 3:34 shows favor to the **h** and oppressed.
Isa 13:11 and will **h** the pride of the ruthless.
  23: 9 to **h** all who are renowned
  29:19 Once more the **h** will rejoice
  58: 5 a day for people to **h** themselves?
  66: 2 those who are **h** and contrite
Da 4:37 who walk in pride he is able to **h**.
  5:19 and those he wanted to **h**,
  10:12 and to **h** yourself before your God,
Zep 2: 3 the LORD, all you **h** of the land,
  3:12 leave within you the meek and **h**.
Mt 11:29 for I am gentle and **h** in heart,
  23:12 and those who **h** themselves will be
Lk 1:48 he has been mindful of the **h** state
  1:52 their thrones but has lifted up the **h**.
  14:11 and those who **h** themselves will be
  18:14 and those who **h** themselves will be
2Co 12:21 again my God will **h** me before you,
Eph 4: 2 Be completely **h** and gentle;

Jas 1: 9 Believers in **h** circumstances ought
     4: 6 the proud but shows favor to the **h**."
     4:10 **H** yourselves before the Lord,
1Pe 3: 8 another, be compassionate and **h**.
     5: 5 the proud but shows favor to the **h**."
     5: 6 **H** yourselves, therefore,

HUMBLED HUMBLE
Lev 26:41 their uncircumcised hearts are **h**
Dt   8: 3 He **h** you, causing you to hunger
1Ki 21:29 Because he has **h** himself, I will not
2Ch 12: 7 LORD saw that they **h** themselves,
    33:12 **h** himself greatly before the God
    34:27 because you **h** yourself before me
Ps 35:13 sackcloth and **h** myself with fasting.
    44: 9 But now you have rejected and **h** us;
   107:39 and they were **h** by oppression,
Isa 2: 9 be brought low and everyone **h**—
Jer 44:10 this day they have not **h** themselves
Da   5:22 son, have not **h** yourself, though you
Mt 23:12 who exalt themselves will be **h**,
Lk 14:11 who exalt themselves will be **h**,
Php 2: 8 he **h** himself by becoming obedient

HUMBLES* HUMBLE
1Sa 2: 7 he **h** and he exalts.
Isa 26: 5 He **h** those who dwell on high,

HUMBLY HUMBLE
Mic 6: 8 mercy and to walk **h** with your God.
Jas 1:21 **h** accept the word planted in you,

HUMILIATE* HUMBLE
Pr 25: 7 for him to **h** you before his nobles.

HUMILIATED HUMBLE
Isa 54: 4 not fear disgrace; you will not be **h**.
Jer 31:19 **h** because I bore the disgrace of my
Lk 13:17 all his opponents were **h**,
    14: 9 Then, **h**, you will have to take

HUMILIATING* HUMBLE
1Co 11:22 God by **h** those who have nothing?

HUMILIATION HUMBLE
Jas 1:10 rich should take pride in their **h**—

HUMILITY* HUMBLE
Ps 45: 4 in the cause of truth, **h** and justice;
Pr 11: 2 disgrace, but with **h** comes wisdom.
    15:33 LORD, and **h** comes before honor.
    18:12 haughty, but **h** comes before honor.
    22: 4 **H** is the fear of the LORD;
Zep 2: 3 Seek righteousness, seek **h**;
Ac 20:19 I served the Lord with great **h**
2Co 10: 1 By the **h** and gentleness of Christ,
Php 2: 3 in **h** value others above yourselves,
Col 2:18 let anyone who delights in false **h**
    2:23 their false **h** and their harsh
    3:12 kindness, **h**,
Jas 3:13 deeds done in the **h** that comes
1Pe 5: 5 with **h** toward one another, because,

HUNDRED HUNDREDFOLD
Ge   6: 3 their days will be a **h** and twenty
    15:13 four **h** years your descendants will

Ge 17:17 son be born to a man a **h** years old?
Lev 26: 8 Five of you will chase a **h**, and a **h**
1Ki 18:13 I hid a **h** of the LORD's prophets
Isa 65:20 at a **h** will be thought a mere child;
Mt 13:23 yielding a **h**, sixty or thirty times
    18:12 If a man owns a **h** sheep, and one
Lk   7:41 One owed him five **h** denarii,
Ac   1:15 (a group numbering about a **h**

HUNDREDFOLD* HUNDRED
Ge 26:12 land and the same year reaped a **h**,

HUNG HANG
Dt 21:23 because anyone who is **h** on a pole
Ps 137: 2 on the poplars we **h** our harps,
Mt 18: 6 a large millstone **h** around their
Mk   9:42 large millstone were **h** around their
Lk 19:48 do it, because all the people **h** on his
    23:39 of the criminals who **h** there hurled
Gal 3:13 "Cursed is everyone who is **h**

HUNGER HUNGRY
Dt   8: 3 causing you to **h** and then feeding
Ne   9:15 In their **h** you gave them bread
Pr   6:30 to satisfy his **h** when he is starving.
Isa 49:10 They will neither **h** nor thirst,
Mt   5: 6 Blessed are those who **h** and thirst
Lk   6:21 Blessed are you who **h** now, for you
2Co 6: 5 in hard work, sleepless nights and **h**;
    11:27 I have known **h** and thirst and have
Rev 7:16 'Never again will they **h**;

HUNGRY HUNGER
1Sa 2: 5 those who were **h** are **h** no more.
Job 24:10 carry the sheaves, but still go **h**.
Ps 50:12 If I were **h** I would not tell you,
   107: 9 and fills the **h** with good things.
   146: 7 oppressed and gives food to the **h**.
Pr 10: 3 does not let the righteous go **h**,
    19:15 deep sleep, and the shiftless go **h**.
    25:21 If your enemy is **h**, give him food
    27: 7 but to the **h** even what is bitter tastes
Isa 29: 8 as when a **h** person dreams of eating,
            but awakens **h** still;
    58: 7 it not to share your food with the **h**
Eze 18: 7 gives his food to the **h** and provides
Mt   4: 2 days and forty nights, he was **h**.
    12: 1 His disciples were **h** and began
    15:32 I do not want to send them away **h**,
    25:35 For I was **h** and you gave me
    25:42 For I was **h** and you gave me
Mk 11:12 were leaving Bethany, Jesus was **h**.
Lk   1:53 He has filled the **h** with good things
Jn   6:35 comes to me will never go **h**,
Ro 12:20 "If your enemy is **h**, feed him;
1Co 4:11 To this very hour we go **h**
    11:34 Anyone who is **h** should eat
Php 4:12 whether well fed or **h**,

HUNT HUNTED, HUNTER, HUNTS
Ge 27: 3 open country to **h** some wild game
Am   9: 3 there I will **h** them down and seize
Mic 7: 2 they **h** each other with nets.

HUNTED HUNT
La   3:52 enemies without cause **h** me like

HUNTER HUNT
Ge   10: 9 was a mighty **h** before the LORD;
     25:27 and Esau became a skillful **h**, a man

HUNTS HUNT
Lev 17:13 among you who **h** any animal
Ps   10: 2 the wicked man **h** down the weak,

HUR
Ex   17:12 Aaron and **H** held his hands up—

HURAM HURAM-ABI
1Ki   7:14 **H** was filled with wisdom,
2Ch   4:11 So **H** finished the work he had

HURAM-ABI* HURAM
2Ch   2:13 "I am sending you **H**, a man of great
     4:16 that **H** made for King Solomon

HURL HURLED
1Sa 25:29 of your enemies he will **h** away as
2Ch 26:15 and **h** large stones from the walls.
Ps   22: 7 they **h** insults, shaking their heads.
Mic   7:19 **h** all our iniquities into the depths

HURLED HURL
Ex   15: 1 and driver he has **h** into the sea.
Jos   10:11 the LORD **h** large hailstones down
1Sa 20:33 Saul **h** his spear at him to kill him.
La   2: 1 He has **h** down the splendor
Jnh   2: 3 You **h** me into the depths,
Mk   15:29 Those who passed by **h** insults
1Pe   2:23 When they **h** their insults at him,
Rev   8: 5 from the altar, and **h** it on the earth;
     12: 9 The great dragon was **h** down—
     12: 9 He was **h** to the earth, and his

HURRIED HURRY
Ge   18: 6 So Abraham **h** into the tent to Sarah.
     24:17 The servant **h** to meet her and said,
2Ki   5:21 So Gehazi **h** after Naaman.
Da   6:19 king got up and **h** to the lions' den.
Mt   28: 8 So the women **h** away
Lk   2:16 So they **h** off and found Mary

HURRIES* HURRY
Ecc   1: 5 sets, and **h** back to where it rises.

HURRY HURRIED, HURRIES
Ge   19:15 the angels urged Lot, saying, "**H**!
Ex   12:33 The Egyptians urged the people to **h**

HURT HURTS
Ecc   8: 9 lords it over others to his own **h**.
Da   6:22 They have not **h** me, because I was
Mk   16:18 poison, *it will not* **h** *them*
Jn   21:17 Peter was **h** because Jesus asked
2Co   7: 8 I see that my letter **h** you, but only
Rev   2:11 one who is victorious will not be **h**

HURTS* HURT
Ps   15: 4 who keeps an oath even when it **h**,
Pr   26:28 A lying tongue hates those it **h**,

HUSBAND HUSBAND'S, HUSBANDS
Ge   3: 6 She also gave some to her **h**,
     3:16 Your desire will be for your **h**,
     16: 3 and gave her to her **h** to be his wife.
Nu   30: 8 if her **h** forbids her when he hears
Dt   24: 4 then her first **h**, who divorced her,
Pr   7:19 My **h** is not at home; he has gone
     31:11 Her **h** has full confidence in her
     31:23 Her **h** is respected at the city gate,
     31:28 her **h** also, and he praises her:
Isa   54: 1 woman than of her who has a **h**,"
     54: 5 For your Maker is your **h**—
Jer   3:14 the LORD, "for I am your **h**.
     3:20 like a woman unfaithful to her **h**,
     31:32 though I was a **h** to them,"
Hos   2:16 LORD, "you will call me 'my **h**';
Mt   1:19 Because Joseph her **h** was faithful
     19:10 "If this is the situation between a **h**
Mk   10:12 if she divorces her **h** and marries
Jn   4:17 "I have no **h**," she replied.
     4:17 right when you say you have no **h**.
Ro   7: 2 bound to her **h** as long as he is alive,
     but if her **h** dies,
1Co   7: 2 and each woman with her own **h**.
     7: 3 The **h** should fulfill his marital duty
     to his wife, and likewise the wife to
     her **h**.
     7: 4 her own body but yields it to her **h**.
     7: 4 the **h** does not have authority over
     7:10 wife must not separate from her **h**.
     7:11 or else be reconciled to her **h**.
     7:11 And a **h** must not divorce his wife.
     7:14 For the unbelieving **h** has been
     7:14 sanctified through her believing **h**.
     7:39 is bound to her **h** as long as he lives.
     7:39 But if her **h** dies, she is free
2Co   11: 2 I promised you to one **h**, to Christ,
Gal   4:27 woman than of her who has a **h**."
Eph   5:23 For the **h** is the head of the wife as
     5:33 and the wife must respect her **h**.
1Ti   5: 9 sixty, has been faithful to her **h**,
Rev   21: 2 a bride beautifully dressed for her **h**.

HUSBAND'S HUSBAND
Dt   25: 5 Her **h** brother shall take her
Ru   2: 1 Naomi had a relative on her **h** side,
Pr   12: 4 of noble character is her **h** crown,
Jn   1:13 nor of human decision or a **h** will,

HUSBANDMAN (KJV) See FARMER, GARDENER

HUSBANDS HUSBAND
Jn   4:18 is, you have had five **h**, and the man
1Co   14:35 they should ask their own **h**
Eph   5:22 yourselves to your own **h** as you do
     5:25 **H**, love your wives, just as Christ
     5:28 **h** ought to love their wives as their
Col   3:18 submit yourselves to your **h**, as is
     3:19 **H**, love your wives and do not be
Titus   2: 4 the younger women to love their **h**
     2: 5 and to be subject to their **h**,
1Pe   3: 1 yourselves to your own **h** so that,

1Pe   3: 7 **H**, in the same way be considerate

HUSHAI
Wise man of David who frustrated Ahithophel's advice and foiled Absalom's revolt (2Sa 15:32–37; 16:15—17:16; 1Ch 27:33).

HUT*
Job   27:18 like a **h** made by a watchman.
Isa   1: 8 like a **h** in a cucumber field,
       24:20 it sways like a **h** in the wind;

HYMENAEUS*
A false teacher (1Ti 1:20; 2Ti 2:17).

HYMN* HYMNS
Ps   40: 3 my mouth, a **h** of praise to our God.
Mt   26:30 When they had sung a **h**, they went
Mk   14:26 When they had sung a **h**, they went
1Co   14:26 each of you has a **h**, or a word

HYMNS* HYMN
Ac   16:25 were praying and singing **h** to God,
Eph   5:19 to one another with psalms, **h**,
Col   3:16 with all wisdom through psalms, **h**,

HYPOCRISY* HYPOCRITE,
HYPOCRITES, HYPOCRITICAL
Mt   23:28 on the inside you are full of **h**
Mk   12:15 But Jesus knew their **h**.
Lk   12: 1 yeast of the Pharisees, which is **h**.
Gal   2:13 The other Jews joined him in his **h**,
       2:13 by their **h** even Barnabas was led
1Pe   2: 1 of all malice and all deceit, **h**, envy,

HYPOCRITE* HYPOCRISY
Mt   7: 5 You **h**, first take the plank
Lk   6:42 You **h**, first take the plank

HYPOCRITES* HYPOCRISY
Ps   26: 4 deceitful, nor do I associate with **h**.
Mt   6: 2 as the **h** do in the synagogue
       6: 5 do not be like the **h**, for they love
       6:16 do not look somber as the **h** do,
       15: 7 You **h**! Isaiah was right when he
       22:18 "You **h**, why are you trying to trap
       23:13 of the law and Pharisees, you **h**!
       23:15 of the law and Pharisees, you **h**!
       23:23 of the law and Pharisees, you **h**!
       23:25 of the law and Pharisees, you **h**!
       23:27 of the law and Pharisees, you **h**!
       23:29 of the law and Pharisees, you **h**!
       24:51 and assign him a place with the **h**,
Mk   7: 6 when he prophesied about you **h**;
Lk   12:56 **H**! You know how to interpret
       13:15 The Lord answered him, "You **h**!

HYPOCRITICAL* HYPOCRISY
1Ti   4: 2 teachings come through **h** liars,

HYSSOP
Ex   12:22 Take a bunch of **h**, dip it
Lev   14: 4 **h** be brought for the person to be
Nu   19: 6 **h** and scarlet wool and throw them
Ps   51: 7 Cleanse me with **h**, and I will be
Jn   19:29 the sponge on a stalk of the **h** plant,

Heb   9:19 scarlet wool and branches of **h**,

I

I AM
Ge   15: 1 **I am** your shield, your very great reward."
       17: 1 "**I am** God Almighty; walk before me
Ex   3:14 God said to Moses, "**I am** WHO **I am**.
       3:14 Israelites: '**I am** has sent me to you.' "
Ps   35: 3 Say to me, "**I am** your salvation."
       46:10 "Be still, and know that **I am** God;
Isa   41:10 So do not fear, for **I am** with you; do not be dismayed, for **I am** your God.
       43: 3 For **I am** the LORD your God,
       43:15 **I am** the LORD, your Holy One,
       44: 6 **I am** the first and **I am** the last;
       48:12 **I am** he; **I am** the first and **I am** the last.
Jer   3:14 the LORD, "for **I am** your husband.
       32:27 "**I am** the LORD, the God of all
Mt   16:15 he asked. "Who do you say **I am**?"
       28:20 And surely **I am** with you always,
Mk   8:29 he asked. "Who do you say **I am**?"
       14:62 "**I am**," said Jesus. "And you will see
Jn   6:35 Jesus declared, "**I am** the bread of life.
       6:41 "**I am** the bread that came down from heaven."
       6:48 **I am** the bread of life.
       6:51 **I am** the living bread that came down
       8:12 he said, "**I am** the light of the world.
       8:24 if you do not believe that **I am** he,
       8:28 then you will know that **I am** he
       8:58 "before Abraham was born, **I am**!"
       9: 5 While **I am** in the world, **I am** the light of the world."
       10: 7 I tell you, **I am** the gate for the sheep.
       10: 9 **I am** the gate; whoever enters
       10:11 "**I am** the good shepherd.
       10:14 "**I am** the good shepherd; I know my
       10:36 blasphemy because I said, '**I am** God's Son'?
       11:25 "**I am** the resurrection and the life.
       13:19 you will believe that **I am** who **I am**.
       14: 6 "**I am** the way and the truth and the life.
       14:10 you believe that **I am** in the Father,
       14:11 when I say that **I am** in the Father
       14:20 realize that **I am** in my Father, and you are in me, and **I am** in you.
       15: 1 "**I am** the true vine, and my Father
       15: 5 "**I am** the vine; you are the branches.
       18: 5 "**I am** he," Jesus said.
       18: 6 Jesus said, "**I am** he," they drew back
       18: 8 answered, "I told you that **I am** he.
Ac   9: 5 "**I am** Jesus, whom you are persecuting,"
       18:10 For **I am** with you, and no one is
       22: 8 '**I am** Jesus of Nazareth, whom you are persecuting,'
       26:15 '**I am** Jesus of Nazareth, whom you are persecuting,'

Rev 1: 8 "**I am** the Alpha and the Omega," says the Lord
1:17 **I am** the First and the Last.
1:18 **I am** the Living One; I was dead,
3:11 **I am** coming soon. Hold on to what
21: 6 **I am** the Alpha and the Omega, the Beginning
22: 7 "Look, **I am** coming soon! Blessed is
22:12 "Look, **I am** coming soon!
22:13 **I am** the Alpha and the Omega,
22:16 **I am** the Root and the Offspring of David,
22:20 "Yes, **I am** coming soon." Amen.

I AM THE LORD† Ge 15:7; 28:13; Ex 6:2, 6, 7, 8, 29; 7:5, 17; 10:2; 12:12; 14:4, 18; 15:26; 16:12; 20:2; 29:46, 46; 31:13; Lev 11:44, 45; 18:2, 4, 5, 6, 21, 30; 19:3, 4, 10, 12, 14, 16, 18, 25, 28, 30, 31, 32, 34, 36, 37; 20:7, 8, 24; 21:12, 15, 23; 22:2, 3, 8, 9, 16, 30, 31, 32, 33; 23:22, 43; 24:22; 25:17, 38, 55; 26:1, 2, 13, 44, 45; Nu 3:13, 41, 45; 10:10; 15:41, 41; Dt 5:6; 29:6; Jdg 6:10; 1Ki 20:13, 28; Ps 81:10; Isa 41:13; 42:8; 43:3, 11, 15; 44:24; 45:3, 5, 6, 18; 48:17; 49:23; 51:15; 60:22; Jer 9:24; 24:7; 32:27; Eze 6:7, 10, 13, 14; 7:4, 27; 11:10, 12; 12:15, 16, 20; 13:14, 21, 23; 14:8; 15:7; 16:62; 20:5, 7, 19, 20, 26, 38, 42, 44; 22:16; 24:27; 25:5, 7, 11, 17; 26:6; 28:22, 23, 26; 29:6, 9, 21; 30:8, 19, 25, 26; 32:15; 33:29; 34:27; 35:4, 9, 15; 36:11, 23, 38; 37:6, 13; 38:23; 39:6, 22, 28; Joel 2:27; Zec 10:6

I AM WITH YOU See WITH

IBZAN*
Judge of Israel (Jdg 12:8–10).

ICE ICY
Job 37:10 The breath of God produces **i**,

ICHABOD*
1Sa 4:21 She named the boy **I**, saying,

ICONIUM
Ac 14: 1 At **I** Paul and Barnabas went as
2Ti 3:11 to me in Antioch, **I** and Lystra,

ICY* ICE
Ps 147:17 Who can withstand his **i** blast?

IDDO
2Ch 9:29 **I** the seer concerning Jeroboam son
12:15 and of **I** the seer that deal
13:22 in the annotations of the prophet **I**.

IDEA IDEAS
Jn 18:34 "Is that your own **i**," Jesus asked,
2Pe 2:13 Their **i** of pleasure is to carouse

IDEAS IDEA
Ac 17:21 about and listening to the latest **i**.)

IDLE* IDLENESS, IDLERS
Dt 32:47 They are not just **i** words for you—
Job 11: 3 Will your **i** talk reduce others
Ecc 10:18 because of **i** hands, the house leaks.
11: 6 at evening let your hands not be **i**,
Isa 58:13 as you please or speaking **i** words,
Col 2:18 up with **i** notions by their unspiritual

1Th 5:14 warn those who are **i** and disruptive,
2Th 3: 6 away from every believer who is **i**
3: 7 We were not **i** when we were
3:11 We hear that some among you are **i**
1Ti 5:13 they get into the habit of being **i**

IDLENESS* IDLE
Pr 31:27 and does not eat the bread of **i**.

IDLERS* IDLE
1Ti 5:13 And not only do they become **i**,

IDOL CALF-IDOL, IDOL'S, IDOLATER, IDOLATERS, IDOLATRIES, IDOLATROUS, IDOLATRY, IDOLS
Ex 32: 4 made it into an **i** cast in the shape
Dt 27:15 is anyone who makes an **i**—
Ps 106:19 and worshiped an **i** cast from metal.
Isa 40:19 As for an **i**, a metalworker casts it,
41: 7 other nails down the **i** so it will not
44:15 he makes an **i** and bows down to it.
44:17 From the rest he makes a god, his **i**;
Eze 8: 3 court, where the **i** that provokes
Hos 4:12 My people consult a wooden **i**,
Hab 2:18 "Of what value is an **i** carved
1Co 8: 4 We know that "An **i** is nothing
10:19 food sacrificed to an **i** is anything, or that an **i** is anything?

IDOL'S* IDOL
1Co 8:10 eating in an **i** temple,

IDOLATER* IDOL
1Co 5:11 sexually immoral or greedy, an **i** or
Eph 5: 5 such a person is an **i**—

IDOLATERS* IDOL
1Co 5:10 or the greedy and swindlers, or **i**.
6: 9 immoral nor **i** nor adulterers nor
10: 7 Do not be **i**, as some of them were;
Rev 21: 8 magic arts, the **i** and all liars—
22:15 the **i** and everyone who loves

IDOLATRIES* IDOL
Jer 14:14 **i** and the delusions of their own

IDOLATROUS IDOL
2Ki 23: 5 away with the **i** priests appointed

IDOLATRY IDOL
1Sa 15:23 and arrogance like the evil of **i**.
Eze 23:49 the consequences of your sins of **i**.
1Co 10:14 my dear friends, flee from **i**.
Gal 5:20 **i** and witchcraft;
Col 3: 5 evil desires and greed, which is **i**.
1Pe 4: 3 orgies, carousing and detestable **i**.

IDOLS IDOL
Ex 34:17 "Do not make any **i**.
Lev 26:30 on the lifeless forms of your **i**, and **I**
Dt 7: 5 poles and burn their **i** in the fire.
32:16 angered him with their detestable **i**.
1Ki 15:12 of all the **i** his ancestors had made.
2Ki 17:15 They followed worthless **i**
1Ch 16:26 For all the gods of the nations are **i**,

Ps   31: 6 hate those who cling to worthless i;
      78:58 aroused his jealousy with their i.
     115: 4 But their i are silver and gold,
Isa   42: 8 glory to another or my praise to i.
      44: 9 All who make i are nothing,
Jer   10: 5 cucumber field, their i cannot speak;
      16:19 worthless i that did them no good.
Eze   14: 3 these men have set up i in their
      23:37 committed adultery with their i;
      23:39 sacrificed their children to their i,
Mic   5:13 I will destroy your i and your sacred
Hab   2:18 he makes i that cannot speak.
Zec   10: 2 The i speak deceitfully, diviners see
Ac   15:20 to abstain from food polluted by i,
      21:25 abstain from food sacrificed to i,
1Co   8: 1 Now about food sacrificed to i:
2Co   6:16 between the temple of God and i?
1Jn   5:21 children, keep yourselves from i.
Rev   2:14 so that they ate food sacrificed to i

IF
Ge   4: 7 I you do what is right, will you not
       4: 7 But i you do not do what is right,
Ex   19: 5 Now i you obey me fully and keep
      33:15 "I your Presence does not go
Dt   11:27 the blessing i you obey
      11:28 the curse i you disobey
1Ki   18:21 I the LORD is God, follow him;
      18:21 but i Baal is God, follow him."
1Ch   28: 9 I you seek him, he will be found
      28: 9 but i you forsake him, he will reject
Ps   95: 7 i only you would hear his voice,
Pr   17:28 are thought wise i they keep silent,
Jer   18: 7 that nation I warned repents of its
Eze   18:21 i a wicked person turns away
Mt   4: 3 and said, "I you are the Son of God,
      27:40 cross, i you are the Son of God!"
Mk   3:24 I a kingdom is divided against itself,
       5:28 thought, "I I just touch his clothes,
       8:38 I anyone is ashamed of me and my
Lk   6:32 "I you love those who love you,
Jn   13:17 you will be blessed i you do them.
      14:15 "I you love me, keep my
      15: 5 I you remain in me and I in you,
      15:10 I you keep my commands, you will
Ro   6: 8 Now i we died with Christ,
       8:31 I God is for us, who can be against
Heb   3: 7 "Today, i you hear his voice,
Jas   1: 5 I any of you lacks wisdom,
1Pe   4:16 i you suffer as a Christian, do not be
1Jn   1: 9 I we confess our sins, he is faithful
       3:20 I our hearts condemn us, we know
Rev   3:20 I anyone hears my voice and opens

IGNORANCE IGNORE
Ac   3:17 I know that you acted in i, as did
      17:30 In the past God overlooked such i,
1Ti   1:13 shown mercy because I acted in i
Heb   9: 7 sins the people had committed in i.

IGNORANT IGNORE
Isa   45:20 I are those who carry about idols
1Co   15:34 there are some who are i of God—
Heb   5: 2 to deal gently with those who are i

1Pe   2:15 good you should silence the i talk
2Pe   3:16 which i and unstable people distort,

IGNORE IGNORANCE, IGNORANT, IGNORED, IGNORES
Dt   22: 1 do not i it but be sure to take it back
Ps   9:12 he does not i the cries
Heb   2: 3 escape if we i so great a salvation?

IGNORED IGNORE
Hos   4: 6 because you have i the law of your
1Co   14:38 this, they will themselves be i.

IGNORES* IGNORE
Pr   10:17 whoever i correction leads others
1Co   14:38 But if anyone i this, they will

ILL ILLNESS, ILLNESSES
2Ch   32:24 In those days Hezekiah became i
Mt   4:24 to him all who were i with various

ILL-GOTTEN GET
Pr   1:19 the paths of all who go after i gain;
      10: 2 I treasures have no lasting value,
Mic   4:13 You will devote their i gains

ILLEGITIMATE*
Hos   5: 7 they give birth to i children.
Jn   8:41 "We are not i children,"

ILLNESS ILL
2Ki   8: 9 ask, 'Will I recover from this i?' "
2Ch   16:12 even in his i he did not seek help
Ps   41: 3 restores them from their bed of i.
Isa   38: 9 of Hezekiah king of Judah after his i
Gal   4:13 an i that I first preached the gospel

ILLNESSES* ILL
Dt   28:59 disasters, and severe and lingering i.
Ac   19:12 and their i were cured and the evil
1Ti   5:23 your stomach and your frequent i.

ILLUMINATED*
Eph   5:13 everything that is i becomes a light.
Rev   18: 1 and the earth was i by his splendor.

ILLUSIONS*
Isa   30:10 Tell us pleasant things, prophesy i.

ILLUSTRATION*
Heb   9: 9 This is an i for the present time,

IMAGE IMAGES
Ge   1:26 "Let us make mankind in our i,
       1:27 God created mankind in his own i, in
            the i of God he created them;
       9: 6 for in the i of God has God made
Ex   20: 4 make for yourself an i in the form
Lev   26: 1 or set up an i or a sacred stone
Ps   106:20 their glorious God for an i of a bull,
Isa   40:18 To what i will you liken him?
Da   3: 1 King Nebuchadnezzar made an i
Lk   20:24 Whose i and inscription are on it?"
Ro   8:29 to be conformed to the i of his Son,
1Co   11: 7 since he is the i and glory of God;
      15:49 just as we have borne the i of the
      15:49 so shall we bear the i of the heavenly

2Co 3:18 into his i with ever-increasing glory,
4: 4 glory of Christ, who is the i of God.
Col 1:15 The Son is the i of the invisible
3:10 in knowledge in the i of its Creator.
Rev 13:14 set up an i in honor of the beast who
14:11 who worship the beast and its i,
20: 4 or its i and had not received its mark

IMAGES IMAGE
Nu 33:52 Destroy all their carved i and their
Ps 97: 7 All who worship i are put to shame,
Isa 42:17 who say to i, 'You are our gods,'
Jer 10:14 The i he makes are a fraud;
Eze 5:11 my sanctuary with all your vile i
Ro 1:23 the immortal God for i made to look

IMAGINATION* IMAGINATIONS, IMAGINE
Eze 13: 2 who prophesy out of their own i:
13:17 who prophesy out of their own i.

IMAGINATIONS* IMAGINATION
Ps 73: 7 their evil i have no limits.
Isa 65: 2 not good, pursuing their own i—

IMAGINE IMAGINATION
Eph 3:20 more than all we ask or i,

IMITATE* IMITATED, IMITATORS
Dt 18: 9 do not learn to i the detestable ways
Eze 23:48 may take warning and not i you.
1Co 4:16 Therefore I urge you to i me.
2Th 3: 9 ourselves as a model for you to i.
Heb 6:12 but to i those who through faith
13: 7 of their way of life and i their faith.
3Jn 1:11 do not i what is evil but what is

IMITATED* IMITATE
2Ki 17:15 They i the nations around them

IMITATORS* IMITATE
1Th 1: 6 You became i of us and of the Lord,
2:14 became i of God's churches

IMMANUEL*
Isa 7:14 birth to a son, and will call him I.
8: 8 cover the breadth of your land, I!"
Mt 1:23 they will call him I" (which means

IMMEASURABLY* MEASURE
Eph 3:20 is able to do i more than all we ask

IMMENSE*
Eze 1: 4 an i cloud with flashing lightning and
1Ti 1:16 might display his i patience as

IMMORAL* IMMORALITY
1Co 5: 9 to associate with sexually i people—
5:10 the people of this world who are i,
5:11 or sister but is sexually i or greedy,
6: 9 Neither the sexually i nor idolaters
Eph 5: 5 No i, impure or greedy person—
1Ti 1:10 for the sexually i, for those
Heb 12:16 See that no one is sexually i, or is
13: 4 the adulterer and all the sexually i.
Rev 21: 8 the sexually i, those who practice

Rev 22:15 arts, the sexually i, the murderers,

IMMORALITY* IMMORAL
Nu 25: 1 in sexual i with Moabite women,
Jer 3: 9 Because Israel's i mattered so little
Mt 5:32 except for sexual i, makes her
15:19 adultery, sexual i, theft,
19: 9 except for sexual i, and marries
Mk 7:21 sexual i, theft, murder,
Ac 15:20 from sexual i, from the meat
15:29 strangled animals and from sexual i.
21:25 animals and from sexual i."
Ro 13:13 not in sexual i and debauchery,
1Co 5: 1 that there is sexual i among you,
6:13 is not meant for sexual i
6:18 Flee from sexual i. All other sins
7: 2 But since sexual i is occurring,
10: 8 We should not commit sexual i,
Gal 5:19 sexual i, impurity and debauchery;
Eph 5: 3 must not be even a hint of sexual i,
Col 3: 5 sexual i, impurity, lust, evil desires
1Th 4: 3 that you should avoid sexual i;
Jude 1: 4 grace of our God into a license for i
1: 7 gave themselves up to sexual i
Rev 2:14 to idols and committed sexual i.
2:20 misleads my servants into sexual i
2:21 given her time to repent of her i,
9:21 arts, their sexual i or their thefts.

IMMORTAL* IMMORTALITY
Ro 1:23 exchanged the glory of the i God
1Ti 1:17 Now to the King eternal, i,
6:16 who alone is i and who lives

IMMORTALITY* IMMORTAL
Pr 12:28 there is life; along that path is i.
Ro 2: 7 honor and i, he will give eternal life.
1Co 15:53 imperishable, and the mortal with i.
15:54 and the mortal with i,
2Ti 1:10 life and i to light through the gospel.

IMMOVABLE
Zec 12: 3 I will make Jerusalem an i rock

IMPALE* IMPALED
Ge 40:19 head and i your body on a pole.
Est 7: 9 The king said, "I him on it!"

IMPALED IMPALE
Ge 40:22 but he i the chief baker, just as
Jos 8:29 He i the body of the king of Ai
Est 2:23 the two officials were i on poles.
7:10 So they i Haman on the pole he had

IMPART*
Pr 29:15 A rod and a reprimand i wisdom,
Ro 1:11 I may i to you some spiritual gift
Gal 3:21 law had been given that could i life,

IMPARTIAL* IMPARTIALLY
Jas 3:17 mercy and good fruit, i and sincere.

IMPARTIALLY* IMPARTIAL
1Ch 24: 5 They divided them i by casting lots,
1Pe 1:17 who judges each person's work i,

IMPATIENT
Nu 21: 4 But the people grew i on the way;

IMPERISHABLE
1Co 15:42 is sown is perishable, it is raised i;
      15:50 nor does the perishable inherit the i.
1Pe 1:23 seed, but of i, through the living

IMPLORE*
2Co 5:20 We i you on Christ's behalf:

IMPORTANCE* IMPORTANT
1Co 15: 3 I passed on to you as of first i:

IMPORTANT IMPORTANCE
1Ki 3: 4 for that was the most i high place,
Jer 52:13 Every i building he burned down.
Mt 23:23 have neglected the more i matters
Mk 12:29 "The most i one," answered Jesus,
      12:33 as yourself is more i than all burnt
Lk 11:43 because you love the most i seats
Php 1:18 The i thing is that in every way,

IMPOSED
Rev 18:20 with the judgment she i on you."

IMPOSING*
Jos 22:10 of Manasseh built an i altar there
Da 7:20 the horn that looked more i than the
Pr 17:26 If i a fine on the innocent is not

IMPOSSIBLE
Ge 11: 6 they plan to do will be i for them.
Mt 17:20 Nothing will be i for you."
      19:26 "With man this is i, but with God
Mk 10:27 "With man this is i, but not
Lk 18:27 "What is i with man is possible
Ac 2:24 because it was i for death to keep its
Heb 6: 4 It is i for those who have once been
      6:18 things in which it is i for God to lie,
      10: 4 It is i for the blood of bulls
      11: 6 without faith it is i to please God,

IMPOSTORS*
2Co 6: 8 genuine, yet regarded as i;
2Ti 3:13 and i will go from bad to worse,

IMPRESS* IMPRESSED, IMPRESSES
Dt 6: 7 I them on your children.
Gal 6:12 Those who want to i people

IMPRESSED IMPRESS
Ecc 9:13 of wisdom that greatly i me:

IMPRESSES* IMPRESS
Pr 17:10 A rebuke i a discerning person more

IMPRISON* PRISON
Ac 22:19 from one synagogue to another to i

IMPRISONED PRISON
Jer 37:15 and i in the house of Jonathan
1Pe 3:19 made proclamation to the i spirits—

IMPRISONMENT* PRISON
Ezr 7:26 confiscation of property, or i.
Ac 23:29 against him that deserved death or i.

Ac 26:31 anything that deserves death or i."
Heb 11:36 and flogging, and even chains and i.

IMPRISONMENTS* PRISON
2Co 6: 5 in beatings, i and riots;

IMPROPER*
Eph 5: 3 because these are i for God's holy

IMPURE IMPURITIES, IMPURITY
Nu 5:14 he suspects his wife and she is i—
Mt 12:43 an i spirit comes out of a person,
Ac 10:15 "Do not call anything i that God
      11: 9 'Do not call anything i that God has
Eph 5: 5 No immoral, i or greedy person—
1Th 2: 3 not spring from error or i motives,
      4: 7 For God did not call us to be i,
Rev 16:13 three i spirits that looked like frogs;
      18: 2 demons and a haunt for every i spirit,
      21:27 Nothing i will ever enter it, nor will

IMPURE SPIRIT Mt 12:43; Mk 1:23, 26; 3:30;
5:2, 8; 7:25; 9:25; Lk 4:33; 8:29; 9:42; 11:24; Rev
18:2

IMPURE SPIRITS Mt 10:1; Mk 1:27; 3:11; 5:13;
6:7; Lk 4:36; 6:18; Ac 5:16; 8:7; Rev 16:13

IMPURITIES IMPURE
Isa 1:25 your dross and remove all your i.
Eze 36:25 I will cleanse you from all your i

IMPURITY IMPURE
Zec 13: 1 to cleanse them from sin and i.
Ro 1:24 hearts to sexual i for the degrading
      6:19 to offer yourselves as slaves to i
Gal 5:19 immorality, i and debauchery;
Eph 4:19 so as to indulge in every kind of i,
      5: 3 or of any kind of i, or of greed,
Col 3: 5 sexual immorality, i, lust,

INCENSE
Ex 30: 1 altar of acacia wood for burning i.
      40: 5 Place the gold altar of i in front
Lev 10: 1 put fire in them and added i;
Nu 16:17 is to take his censer and put i in it—
2Ch 26:16 the LORD to burn i on the altar of i.
Ps 141: 2 my prayer be set before you like i;
Isa 1:13 Your i is detestable to me.
Jer 1:16 me, in burning i to other gods
Hos 2:13 the days she burned i to the Baals;
Lk 1:10 the time for the burning of i came,
Heb 9: 4 which had the golden altar of i
Rev 5: 8 were holding golden bowls full of i,
      8: 4 The smoke of the i,

INCITED INCITING
1Sa 26:19 If the LORD has i you against me,
1Ch 21: 1 i David to take a census of Israel.

INCITING INCITED
Dt 13: 5 i rebellion against the LORD your

INCLINATION* INCLINATIONS,
       INCLINED, INCLINES
Ge 6: 5 that every i of the thoughts

Ge   8:21 even though every **i** of the human

INCLINATIONS* INCLINATION
Jer   7:24 they followed the stubborn **i** of their

INCLINED INCLINATION
Dt   5:29 their hearts would be **i** to fear me

INCLINES* INCLINATION
Ecc   10: 2 The heart of the wise **i** to the right,

INCOME
Ecc   5:10 wealth is never satisfied with their **i**.
1Co   16: 2 of money in keeping with your **i**,

INCOMPARABLE*
INCOMPARABLY
Eph   2: 7 ages he might show the **i** riches

INCOMPARABLY*
INCOMPARABLE
Eph   1:19 his **i** great power for us who believe.

INCREASE EVER-INCREASING, INCREASED, INCREASES, INCREASING
Ge   1:22 "Be fruitful and **i** in number and fill
      1:28 them, "Be fruitful and **i** in number;
      8:17 be fruitful and **i** in number on it."
     16:10 "I will **i** your descendants so much
Dt   1:11 **i** you a thousand times and bless
Ps   62:10 though your riches **i**, do not set your
Pr   22:16 oppresses the poor to **i** his wealth
Jer 23: 3 they will be fruitful and **i** in number.
Mt   24:12 Because of the **i** of wickedness,
Lk   17: 5 said to the Lord, "I our faith!"
Ro   5:20 in so that the trespass might **i**.
      6: 1 go on sinning so that grace may **i**?
1Th   3:12 May the Lord make your love **i**

INCREASED INCREASE
Ge   7:17 as the waters **i** they lifted the ark
Ex   1:20 the people **i** and became even more
Dt   1:10 your God has **i** your numbers so
Ac   6: 7 of disciples in Jerusalem **i** rapidly,
      9:31 by the Holy Spirit, it **i** in numbers.
Ro   5:20 But where sin **i**, grace **i** all the more,

INCREASES INCREASE
Isa 40:29 weary and **i** the power of the weak.

INCREASING INCREASE
Ac   6: 1 when the number of disciples was **i**,
2Th   1: 3 all of you have for one another is **i**.
2Pe   1: 8 possess these qualities in **i** measure,

INCREDIBLE*
Ac   26: 8 you consider it **i** that God raises

INCURABLE
2Ch 21:18 afflicted Jehoram with an **i** disease
Jer 10:19 My wound is **i**! Yet I said to myself,
Mic   1: 9 For Samaria's plague is **i**;

INDECENT
Dt   24: 1 to him because he finds something **i**

INDEPENDENT*
1Co 11:11 in the Lord woman is not **i** of man,
              nor is man **i** of woman.

INDESCRIBABLE*
2Co   9:15 Thanks be to God for his **i** gift!

INDESTRUCTIBLE*
Heb   7:16 the basis of the power of an **i** life.

INDIGNANT INDIGNATION
Mt   20:24 they were **i** with the two brothers.
Mk   1:41 Jesus was **i**. He reached out his hand
     10:14 When Jesus saw this, he was **i**.
Lk   13:14 **i** because Jesus had healed

INDIGNATION INDIGNANT
Ps   90: 7 your anger and terrified by your **i**.
Na   1: 6 Who can withstand his **i**?

INDISPENSABLE*
1Co 12:22 body that seem to be weaker are **i**,

INDULGE INDULGED, INDULGENCE, INDULGING, SELF-INDULGENCE
Ex   32: 6 and drink and got up to **i** in revelry.
Nu   25: 1 the men began to **i** in sexual
1Co 10: 7 drink and got up to **i** in revelry."
Gal   5:13 not use your freedom to **i** the flesh;

INDULGED* INDULGE
2Co 12:21 debauchery in which they have **i**.

INDULGENCE* INDULGE
Col   2:23 any value in restraining sensual **i**.

INDULGING* INDULGE
1Ti   3: 8 sincere, not **i** in much wine, and not

INEFFECTIVE*
2Pe   1: 8 they will keep you from being **i**

INEXPRESSIBLE*
2Co 12: 4 up to paradise and heard **i** things,
1Pe   1: 8 are filled with an **i** and glorious joy,

INFANCY* INFANT
2Ti   3:15 from **i** you have known the Holy

INFANT INFANCY, INFANTS
Nu   11:12 as a nurse carries an **i**, to the land
Isa 11: 8 The **i** will play near the cobra's den,
     65:20 in it an **i** who lives but a few days,

INFANTS INFANT
Ps   8: 2 **i** you have established a stronghold
Mt   21:16 the lips of children and you, Lord,
1Co   3: 1 are still worldly—mere **i** in Christ.
     14:20 In regard to evil be **i**, but in your
Eph   4:14 Then we will no longer be **i**,

INFILTRATED*
Gal   2: 4 some false believers had **i** our ranks

INFIRMITIES* INFIRMITY
Mt   8:17 "He took up our **i** and bore our

INFIRMITY* INFIRMITIES
Lk   13:12 you are set free from your i."

INFLAMED
Ro   1:27 and were i with lust for one another.

INFLICT INFLICTED
Dt   7:15 He will not i on you the horrible
       7:15 he will i them on all who hate you.
Ps 149: 7 to i vengeance on the nations
Jer 18: 8 not i on it the disaster I had planned.
      26: 3 and not i on them the disaster I was

INFLICTED INFLICT
Ge   12:17 the LORD i serious diseases
Isa 30:26 people and heals the wounds he i.

INFLUENCED* INFLUENTIAL
1Co 12: 2 or other you were i and led astray

INFLUENTIAL* INFLUENCED
1Co 1:26 not many were i; not many were

INGATHERING* GATHER
Ex   23:16 "Celebrate the Festival of I
      34:22 the Festival of I at the turn

INHABITANT INHABITANTS, INHABITED
Isa   6:11 the cities lie ruined and without i,
Jer   4: 7 towns will lie in ruins without i.

INHABITANTS INHABITANT
Lev 18:25 sin, and the land vomited out its i.
Nu   33:55 do not drive out the i of the land,
Jos   9:24 to wipe out all its i from before you.
Rev   6:10 until you judge the i of the earth
       8:13 Woe to the i of the earth,
      13: 8 All i of the earth will worship

INHABITED INHABITANT
Isa 45:18 to be empty, but formed it to be i—
Joel 3:20 Judah will be i forever
Zec 14:11 It will be i; never again will it be

INHERIT CO-HEIRS, HEIR, HEIRS, HERITAGE, INHERITANCE, INHERITED
Ge   15: 2 and the one who will i my estate is
Dt   1:38 because he will lead Israel to i it.
Jos   1: 6 these people to i the land I swore
2Ki   2: 9 "Let me i a double portion of your
Ps   37:11 the meek will i the land and enjoy
      37:29 The righteous will i the land
Pr   3:35 The wise i honor, but fools get only
      11:29 on their family will i only wind,
      14:18 The simple i folly, but the prudent
Isa 61: 7 so you will i a double portion
Zec   2:12 The LORD will i Judah as his
Mt   5: 5 the meek, for they will i the earth.
      19:29 times as much and will i eternal life.
Mk   10:17 "what must I do to i eternal life?"
Lk   10:25 "what must I do to i eternal life?"
      18:18 what must I do to i eternal life?"
1Co   6: 9 wrongdoers will not i the kingdom
      15:50 blood cannot i the kingdom of God,

Gal   5:21 live like this will not i the kingdom
Heb   1:14 to serve those who will i salvation?
Rev 21: 7 who are victorious will i all this,

INHERITANCE INHERIT
Ge   21:10 share in the i with my son Isaac."
Ex   34: 9 and our sin, and take us as your i."
Lev 20:24 I will give it to you as an i, a land
Nu   18:20 "You will have no i in their land,
Dt   4:20 to be the people of his i, as you now
      10: 9 the LORD is their i, as the LORD
Jos 14: 1 areas the Israelites received as an i
      14: 3 the Levites an i among the rest,
Ps   2: 8 and I will make the nations your i,
      16: 6 surely I have a delightful i.
      33:12 the people he chose for his i.
     136:21 and gave their land as an i,
Pr   13:22 A good person leaves an i for their
Jer   3:19 the most beautiful i of any nation.'
Da   12:13 will rise to receive your allotted i."
Joel 2:17 Do not make your i an object
Mt   25:34 take your i, the kingdom prepared
Lk   12:13 my brother to divide the i with me."
Gal   3:18 For if the i depends on the law,
       4:30 in the i with the free woman's son."
Eph   1:14 deposit guaranteeing our i until
       5: 5 has any i in the kingdom of Christ
Col   1:12 share in the i of his holy people
       3:24 you will receive an i from the Lord
Heb   9:15 may receive the promised eternal i—
1Pe   1: 4 and into an i that can never perish,
       1: 4 This i is kept in heaven for you,

INHERITED INHERIT
Heb   1: 4 as the name he has i is superior

INIQUITIES INIQUITY
Ps   78:38 he forgave their i and did not
      90: 8 You have set our i before you,
     103:10 or repay us according to our i.
Isa 53: 5 he was crushed for our i;
      53:11 many, and he will bear their i.
      59: 2 your i have separated you from your
Mic   7:19 hurl all our i into the depths

INIQUITY INIQUITIES
Ps   25:11 forgive my i, though it is great.
      32: 5 to you and did not cover up my i.
      38:18 I confess my i; I am troubled by my
      51: 2 Wash away all my i and cleanse me
      51: 9 from my sins and blot out all my i.
Isa 53: 6 has laid on him the i of us all.
Mic   2: 1 Woe to those who plan i, to those

INJURED INJURY
Isa   1: 5 Your whole head is i, your whole
Eze 34:16 I will bind up the i and strengthen
Zec 11:16 or heal the i, or feed the healthy,
Mal   1:13 "When you bring i,

INJURES INJURY
Lev 24:19 Anyone who i their neighbor is
Job   5:18 he i, but his hands also heal.

INJURY INJURED, INJURES
Ex 21:23 But if there is serious i, you are
Jer 30:12 is incurable, your i beyond healing.
Rev 9:19 heads with which they inflict i.

INJUSTICE
2Ch 19: 7 the LORD our God there is no i
Pr 13:23 for the poor, but i sweeps it away.
16: 8 than much gain with i.
Hab 2:12 and establishes a town by i!

INK*
Jer 36:18 and I wrote them in i on the scroll."
2Co 3: 3 written not with i but with the Spirit
2Jn 1:12 but I do not want to use paper and i.
3Jn 1:13 do not want to do so with pen and i.

INMOST INNER
Ps 139:13 For you created my i being;

INN*
Lk 10:34 brought him to an i and took care

INNER INMOST
2Sa 18:24 David was sitting between the i
1Ki 6:16 within the temple an i sanctuary,
Ro 7:22 in my i being I delight in God's law;

INNOCENCE INNOCENT
Job 27: 6 I will maintain my i and never let go
Ps 26: 6 I wash my hands in i, and go

INNOCENT INNOCENCE
Ex 23: 7 do not put an i or honest person
Dt 19:10 this so that i blood will not be shed
25: 1 acquitting the i and condemning
Job 34: 5 'I am i, but God denies me justice.
Ps 19:13 blameless, i of great transgression.
Pr 6:17 tongue, hands that shed i blood,
17:26 imposing a fine on the i is not good,
Isa 59: 7 they are swift to shed i blood.
Mt 10:16 shrewd as snakes and as i as doves.
12: 7 would not have condemned the i.
27: 4 said, "for I have betrayed i blood."
27:24 "I am i of this man's blood,"
Ac 18: 6 be on your own heads! I am i of it.
20:26 you today that I am i of the blood
Ro 16:19 is good, and i about what is evil.
1Co 4: 4 clear, but that does not make me i.

INQUIRE INQUIRED, INQUIRING
Jos 9:14 but did not i of the LORD.
1Sa 28: 7 medium, so I may go and i of her."
1Ch 10:14 and did not i of the LORD.
2Ch 20: 3 Jehoshaphat resolved to i
Isa 8:19 should not a people i of their God?
Eze 14: 3 Should I let them i of me at all?

INQUIRED INQUIRE
1Sa 22:10 Ahimelek i of the LORD for him;
28: 6 He i of the LORD, but the LORD

INQUIRING INQUIRE
Nu 27:21 for him by i of the Urim before
Dt 12:30 to be ensnared by i about their gods,

INSANE
1Sa 21:13 pretended to be i in their presence;
Ps 34: T *pretended to be i before Abimelek,*
Ac 26:24 great learning is driving you i."

INSCRIBE* INSCRIBED, INSCRIPTION
Isa 30: 8 on a tablet for them, i it on a scroll,

INSCRIBED INSCRIBE
Ex 31:18 the tablets of stone i by the finger
Dt 9:10 LORD gave me two stone tablets i
Zec 14:20 LORD will be i on the bells

INSCRIPTION INSCRIBE
Da 5:24 he sent the hand that wrote the i.
Mt 22:20 image is this? And whose i?"
2Ti 2:19 stands firm, sealed with this i:

INSECTS
Lev 11:20 " 'All flying i that walk on all
Dt 14:19 All flying i are unclean to you;

INSIDE
Ge 6:14 in it and coat it with pitch i and out.
Ex 4: 6 said, "Put your hand i your cloak."
12:46 "It must be eaten i the house;
1Ki 6:20 He overlaid the i with pure gold,
Mt 23:26 First clean the i of the cup and dish,
23:27 on the i are full of the bones
Mk 7:23 All these evils come from i
1Co 5:12 Are you not to judge those i?
Rev 5: 4 worthy to open the scroll or look i.

INSIGHT INSIGHTS
1Ki 4:29 Solomon wisdom and very great i,
Ps 119:99 I have more i than all my teachers,
Pr 5: 1 turn your ear to my words of i,
7: 4 and to i, "You are my relative."
16:16 than gold, to get i rather than silver!
20: 5 but one who has i draws them out.
21:30 no i, no plan that can succeed
23:23 wisdom, instruction and i as well.
Da 5:11 your father he was found to have i
9:22 I have now come to give you i
Eph 3: 4 to understand my i into the mystery
Php 1: 9 more in knowledge and depth of i,
2Ti 2: 7 the Lord will give you i into all this.
Rev 13:18 the person who has i calculate

INSIGHTS* INSIGHT
Job 15: 9 What i do you have that we do not

INSOLENT
Pr 29:21 from youth will turn out to be i.
Ro 1:30 God-haters, i, arrogant and boastful;

INSPIRE* INSPIRED, INSPIRES
Jer 32:40 and I will i them to fear me,
49:16 The terror you i and the pride of

INSPIRED* INSPIRE
2Sa 23: 1 "The i utterance of David son
Pr 30: 1 Agur son of Jakeh—an i utterance.
31: 1 an i utterance his mother taught
Hos 9: 7 a fool, the i person a maniac.

1Th 1: 3 and your endurance i by hope in our

INSPIRES* INSPIRE
Job 20: 3 and my understanding i me to reply.
Rev 22: 6 the God who i the prophets, sent his

INSTALLED
Ps 2: 6 "I have i my king on Zion, my holy

INSTANT INSTANTLY
Pr 6: 15 disaster will overtake him in an i;
Lk 4: 5 showed him in an i all the kingdoms

INSTANTLY* INSTANT
Lk 8: 47 him and how she had been i healed.
Ac 3: 7 up, and i the man's feet and ankles

INSTEAD
Ge 22: 13 sacrificed it as a burnt offering i
2Ch 28: 20 but he gave him trouble i of help.
Pr 8: 10 Choose my instruction i of silver,
Isa 60: 17 I of bronze I will bring you gold,
  61: 7 I of your shame you will receive
Jer 7: 24 i, they followed the stubborn
Jn 3: 19 but people loved darkness i of light
  15: 15 I, I have called you friends,

INSTINCT* INSTINCTS
2Pe 2: 12 creatures of i, born only to be
Jude 1: 10 things they do understand by i—

INSTINCTS* INSTINCT
Jude 1: 19 who follow mere natural i and do

INSTITUTED
Ro 13: 2 is rebelling against what God has i,

INSTRUCT INSTRUCTED, INSTRUCTION, INSTRUCTIONS, INSTRUCTOR, INSTRUCTS, WELL-INSTRUCTED
Dt 17: 10 to do everything they i you to do.
Ne 9: 20 gave your good Spirit to i them.
Ps 32: 8 I will i you and teach you
  105: 22 to i his princes as he pleased
Pr 9: 9 I the wise and they will be wiser
Isa 40: 13 or i the LORD as his counselor?
Da 11: 33 "Those who are wise will i many,
Ro 15: 14 and competent to i one another.
1Co 2: 16 mind of the Lord so as to i him?"
  14: 19 to i others than ten thousand words

INSTRUCTED INSTRUCT
2Ch 26: 5 who i him in the fear of God.
Isa 50: 4 my ear to listen like one being i.
Mt 21: 6 went and did as Jesus had i them.
Ac 18: 25 He had been i in the way
1Co 14: 31 in turn so that everyone may be i
2Ti 2: 25 Opponents must be gently i,

INSTRUCTION INSTRUCT
Ex 15: 25 issued a ruling and i for them
  24: 12 I have written for their i."
Pr 1: 2 for gaining wisdom and i;
  1: 3 for receiving i in prudent behavior,
  1: 7 but fools despise wisdom and i.

Pr 1: 8 to your father's i and do not forsake
  4: 1 Listen, my sons, to a father's i;
  4: 13 Hold on to i, do not let it go;
  6: 23 correction and i are the way to life,
  8: 10 Choose my i instead of silver,
  8: 33 Listen to my i and be wise;
  13: 1 A wise son heeds his father's i,
  13: 13 Whoever scorns i will pay for it,
  15: 33 Wisdom's i is to fear the LORD,
  16: 20 Whoever gives heed to i prospers,
  16: 21 and gracious words promote i.
  23: 12 Apply your heart to i and your ears
  23: 23 wisdom, i and insight as well.
  28: 9 If anyone turns a deaf ear to my i,
  29: 18 is the one who heeds wisdom's i.
  31: 26 and faithful i is on her tongue.
Isa 8: 20 Consult God's i and the testimony
  29: 24 those who complain will accept i."
1Co 14: 6 or prophecy or word of i?
  14: 26 a hymn, or a word of i, a revelation,
Gal 6: 6 the one who receives i in the word
Eph 6: 4 up in the training and i of the Lord.
1Th 4: 8 who rejects this i does not reject
2Th 3: 14 anyone who does not obey our i
1Ti 6: 3 the sound i of our Lord Jesus Christ
2Ti 4: 2 with great patience and careful i.

INSTRUCTIONS INSTRUCT
Ge 26: 5 commands, my decrees and my i."
Ex 12: 24 "Obey these i as a lasting ordinance
Jos 8: 33 when he gave i to bless the people
1Ki 3: 3 according to the i given him by his
Ac 1: 2 giving i through the Holy Spirit
1Ti 3: 14 I am writing you these i so that,

INSTRUCTOR* INSTRUCT
Mt 23: 10 for you have one I, the Messiah.
Ro 2: 20 an i of the foolish, a teacher of little
Gal 6: 6 share all good things with their i.

INSTRUCTS* INSTRUCT
Ps 16: 7 even at night my heart i me.
  25: 8 therefore he i sinners in his ways.
Isa 28: 26 His God i him and teaches him

INSTRUMENT* INSTRUMENTS
Eze 33: 32 beautiful voice and plays an i well,
Ac 9: 15 This man is my chosen i to proclaim
Ro 6: 13 to sin as an i of wickedness,
  6: 13 to him as an i of righteousness.

INSTRUMENTS INSTRUMENT
1Ch 15: 16 make a joyful sound with musical i:
  23: 5 with the musical i I have provided
2Ch 23: 13 with their i were leading the praises.
2Ti 2: 21 from the latter will be i for special

INSULT INSULTED, INSULTS
Ps 69: 9 the insults of those who i you fall
Pr 12: 16 once, but the prudent overlook an i.
Jer 20: 8 of the LORD has brought me i
Mt 5: 11 are you when people i you,
Lk 6: 22 when they exclude you and i you
  18: 32 mock him, i him and spit on him;
Heb 10: 33 you were publicly exposed to i

1Pe   3: 9 not repay evil with evil or i with i.

INSULTED INSULT
Heb 10:29 and who has i the Spirit of grace?
1Pe   4:14 If you are i because of the name

INSULTS INSULT
Ne   4: 4 Turn their i back on their own
Ps   22: 7 they hurl i, shaking their heads.
       69: 9 the i of those who insult you fall
Pr   9: 7 corrects a mocker invites i;
       22:10 quarrels and i are ended.
La   3:61 you have heard their i, all their plots
Mk 15:29 who passed by hurled i at him,
Jn   9:28 Then they hurled i at him and said,
Ro   15: 3 "The i of those who insult you have
2Co 12:10 in weaknesses, in i, in hardships,
1Pe   2:23 When they hurled their i at him,

INTEGRITY*
Dt   9: 5 your i that you are going in to take
1Ki   9: 4 you walk before me faithfully with i
1Ch 29:17 test the heart and are pleased with i.
Ne   7: 2 he was a man of i and feared God
Job   2: 3 And he still maintains his i,
       2: 9 "Are you still maintaining your i?
       6:29 reconsider, for my i is at stake.
      27: 5 till I die, I will not deny my i.
Ps   7: 8 according to my i, O Most High.
      25:21 May i and uprightness protect me,
      41:12 Because of my i you uphold me
      78:72 David shepherded them with i
Pr   10: 9 Whoever walks in i walks securely,
      11: 3 The i of the upright guides them,
      13: 6 guards the person of i,
      29:10 The bloodthirsty hate a person of i
Isa 45:23 my mouth has uttered in all i a word
      59: 4 no one pleads a case with i.
Mt   22:16 "we know that you are a man of i
Mk 12:14 we know that you are a man of i.
2Co   1:12 with you, with i and godly sincerity.
Titus 2: 7 In your teaching show i,

INTELLIGENCE INTELLIGENT
Isa 29:14 the i of the intelligent will vanish."
Da   5:11 he was found to have insight and i
1Co   1:19 the i of the intelligent I will

INTELLIGENT INTELLIGENCE
1Sa 25: 3 She was an i and beautiful woman,

INTELLIGIBLE*
1Co 14: 9 Unless you speak i words with your
      14:19 I would rather speak five i words

INTEND INTENDED, INTENT, INTENTIONAL, INTENTIONALLY, INTENTLY
1Ki   5: 5 I i, therefore, to build a temple
2Ch 29:10 Now I i to make a covenant

INTENDED INTEND
Ge   50:20 You i to harm me, but God i it
Jer 18:10 I will reconsider the good I had i
Ro   7:10 was i to bring life actually brought

INTENSE INTENSELY
1Th   2:17 our i longing we made every effort
Rev 16: 9 They were seared by the i heat

INTENSELY INTENSE
Gal   1:13 how i I persecuted the church

INTENT INTEND
Ex   32:12 with evil i that he brought them out,
Pr   7:10 like a prostitute and with crafty i.
Mt   22:18 But Jesus, knowing their evil i, said,

INTENTIONAL* INTEND
Nu   15:25 for it was not i and they have

INTENTIONALLY* INTEND
Ex   21:13 if it is not done i, but God lets it
Nu   35:20 throws something at them i so

INTENTLY* INTEND
Ac   1:10 They were looking i up into the sky
       6:15 the Sanhedrin looked i at Stephen,
Jas   1:25 whoever looks i into the perfect law
1Pe   1:10 you, searched i and with the greatest

INTERCEDE INTERCEDES, INTERCEDING, INTERCESSION, INTERCESSOR
1Sa   2:25 the LORD, who will i for them?"
Heb   7:25 him, because he always lives to i

INTERCEDES* INTERCEDE
Ro   8:26 the Spirit himself i for us through
       8:27 Spirit, because the Spirit i for God's

INTERCEDING* INTERCEDE
Ro   8:34 hand of God and is also i for us.

INTERCESSION* INTERCEDE
Isa 53:12 and made i for the transgressors.
1Ti   2: 1 i and thanksgiving be made for all

INTERCESSOR* INTERCEDE
Job 16:20 My i is my friend as my eyes pour

INTEREST INTERESTS, SELF-INTEREST
Lev 25:36 Do not take i or any profit
Dt   23:19 Do not charge a fellow Israelite i,
      23:20 You may charge a foreigner i,
Ne   5:10 But let us stop charging i!
Ps   15: 5 lends money to the poor without i;
Eze 18: 8 He does not lend to them at i or take
Lk   19:23 I could have collected it with i?'
1Ti   6: 4 They have an unhealthy i

INTERESTS INTEREST
1Co   7:34 and his i are divided.
Php   2: 4 not looking to your own i but each of
       you to the i of the others.
       2:21 everyone looks out for their own i,

INTERFERE
Ezr   6: 7 Do not i with the work on this

INTERMARRY* MARRY
Ge   34: 9 I with us; give us your daughters

Dt   7: 3 Do not i with them. Do not give
Jos   23:12 and if you i with them and associate
1Ki   11: 2 "You must not i with them,
Ezr   9:14 i with the peoples who commit such

INTERPRET INTERPRETATION, INTERPRETATIONS, INTERPRETER, INTERPRETS
Ge   41:15 "I had a dream, and no one can i it.
        41:15 you hear a dream you can i it."
Da   2: 6 tell me the dream and i it for me."
         4: 9 Here is my dream; i it for me.
Mt   16: 3 You know how to i the appearance
        16: 3 you cannot i the signs of the times.
1Co 12:30 Do all speak in tongues? Do all i?
        14:13 pray that they may i what they say.
        14:27 one at a time, and someone must i.

INTERPRETATION INTERPRET
Ge   40:16 that Joseph had given a favorable i,
Jdg   7:15 Gideon heard the dream and its i,
1Co 12:10 and to still another the i of tongues.
        14:26 a revelation, a tongue or an i.
2Pe   1:20 by the prophet's own i of things.

INTERPRETATIONS* INTERPRET
Ge   40: 8 to them, "Do not i belong to God?
Da   5:16 heard that you are able to give i

INTERPRETER INTERPRET
1Co 14:28 If there is no i, the speaker should

INTERPRETS* INTERPRET
Dt   18:10 divination or sorcery, i omens,
1Co 14: 5 unless someone i, so that the church

INTERVENED*
Ps   106:30 But Phinehas stood up and i, and
Ac   15:14 to us how God first i to choose

INTOXICATED*
Pr   5:19 may you ever be i with her love.
         5:20 son, be i with another man's wife?
Rev   17: 2 of the earth were i with the wine

INVADE INVADED, INVADING
Dt   12:29 you the nations you are about to i
Da   11:41 He will also i the Beautiful Land.
Na   1:15 No more will the wicked i you;

INVADED INVADE
2Ki   17: 5 king of Assyria i the entire land,
        24: 1 king of Babylon i the land,

INVADING INVADE
Hab   3:16 calamity to come on the nation i us.

INVENT*
Ro   1:30 they i ways of doing evil;

INVESTIGATED
Lk   1: 3 I myself have carefully i everything

INVISIBLE*
Ro   1:20 of the world God's i qualities—
Col   1:15 The Son is the image of the i God,
         1:16 visible and i, whether thrones

1Ti   1:17 eternal, immortal, i, the only God,
Heb   11:27 because he saw him who is i.

INVITE INVITED, INVITES
Pr   18: 6 strife, and their mouths i a beating.
Mt   22: 9 i to the banquet anyone you find.'
        25:38 we see you a stranger and i you in,
Lk   14:12 or dinner, do not i your friends,
        14:13 when you give a banquet, i the poor,

INVITED INVITE
Zep   1: 7 he has consecrated those he has i.
Mt   22:14 "For many are i, but few are
        25:35 I was a stranger and you i me in,
Lk   7:36 the Pharisees i Jesus to have dinner
        11:37 a Pharisee i him to eat with him;
        14:10 But when you are i, take the lowest
Rev   19: 9 Blessed are those who are i

INVITES INVITE
Pr   9: 7 corrects a mocker i insults;
        10:14 but the mouth of a fool i ruin.
1Co 10:27 If an unbeliever i you to a meal

INVOKE INVOKED
Ex   23:13 Do not i the names of other gods;
Ac   19:13 evil spirits tried to i the name

INVOKED* INVOKE
Hos   2:17 no longer will their names be i.
Eph   1:21 and every name that is i, not only

INWARDLY*
Mt   7:15 but i they are ferocious wolves.
Ro   2:29 No, a person is a Jew who is one i;
         8:23 groan i as we wait eagerly for our
2Co   4:16 yet i we are being renewed day
        11:29 led into sin, and I do not i burn?

IRON IRON-SMELTING
Ge   4:22 kinds of tools out of bronze and i.
Lev   26:19 make the sky above you like i
2Ki   6: 6 threw it there, and made the i float.
Ps   2: 9 You will break them with a rod of i;
Pr   27:17 As i sharpens i, so one person
Isa   60:17 you gold, and silver in place of i.
Da   2:33 its legs of i, its feet partly of i
         7: 7 It had large i teeth; it crushed
1Ti   4: 2 have been seared as with a hot i.
Rev   2:27 one 'will rule them with an i scepter
        12: 5 all the nations with an i scepter."
        19:15 will rule them with an i scepter."

IRON-SMELTING IRON
Dt   4:20 brought you out of the i furnace,

IRRATIONAL*
Jude   1:10 by instinct—as i animals do—

IRRELIGIOUS*
1Ti   1: 9 the unholy and i, for those who kill

IRREVOCABLE*
Ro   11:29 for God's gifts and his call are i.

ISAAC
Son of Abraham by Sarah (Ge 17:19; 21:1-7;

1Ch 1:28). Abrahamic covenant perpetuated through (Ge 17:21; 26:2–5). Offered up by Abraham (Ge 22; Heb 11:17–19). Rebekah taken as wife (Ge 24). Inherited Abraham's estate (Ge 25:5). Fathered Esau and Jacob (Ge 25:19–26; 1Ch 1:34). Nearly lost Rebekah to Abimelech (Ge 26:1–11). Covenant with Abimelech (Ge 26:12–31). Tricked into blessing Jacob (Ge 27). Death (Ge 35:27–29). Father of Israel (Ex 3:6; Dt 29:13; Ro 9:10).

ISAIAH

Prophet to Judah (Isa 1:1). Called by the LORD (Isa 6). Announced judgment to Ahaz (Isa 7), deliverance from Assyria to Hezekiah (2Ki 19; Isa 36–37), deliverance from death to Hezekiah (2Ki 20:1–11; Isa 38). Chronicler of Judah's history (2Ch 26:22; 32:32).

ISCARIOT JUDAS

Mt   10: 4 Simon the Zealot and Judas I,
Lk   22: 3 Judas, called I, one of the Twelve.

ISH-BOSHETH

Son of Saul who attempted to succeed him as king (2Sa 2:8—4:12; 1Ch 8:33).

ISHMAEL ISHMAELITES

Son of Abraham by Hagar (Ge 16; 1Ch 1:28). Blessed, but not son of covenant (Ge 17:18–21; Gal 4:21–31). Sent away by Sarah (Ge 21:8–21). Children (Ge 25:12–18; 1Ch 1:29–31). Death (Ge 25:17).

ISHMAELITES ISHMAEL

Ge   37:27 let's sell him to the I and not lay our

ISLAND ISLANDS

Rev   1: 9 was on the i of Patmos because
16:20 Every i fled away

ISLANDS ISLAND

Isa   42: 4 In his teaching the i will put their
66:19 to the distant i that have not heard

ISRAEL EL ELOHE ISRAEL, ISRAEL'S, ISRAELITE, ISRAELITES, JACOB

1. Name given to Jacob (Ge 32:28; 35:10; see JACOB).

2. Corporate name of Jacob's descendants; often specifically Northern Kingdom.

Ge   49:24 of the Shepherd, the Rock of I,
49:28 All these are the twelve tribes of I,
Ex   28:11 the sons of I on the two stones
28:29 of the sons of I over his heart
Nu   19:13 They must be cut off from I.
24:17 a scepter will rise out of I.
Dt   6: 4 Hear, O I: The LORD our God,
10:12 And now, I, what does the LORD
18: 1 no allotment or inheritance with I.
Jos   4:22 them, 'I crossed the Jordan on dry
24:31 I served the LORD throughout
Jdg   17: 6 In those days I had no king;
21: 3 one tribe be missing from I today?"
Ru   4:14 he become famous throughout I!

1Sa   3:20 And all I from Dan to Beersheba
4:21 "The Glory has departed from I"—
14:23 So on that day the LORD saved I,
15:26 has rejected you as king over I!"
17:46 will know that there is a God in I.
18:16 But all I and Judah loved David,
2Sa   5: 2 'You will shepherd my people I,
5: 3 they anointed David king over I.
7:26 LORD Almighty is God over I!'
14:25 all I there was not a man so highly
1Ki   1:35 I have appointed him ruler over I
8:25 to sit before me on the throne of I,
10: 9 and placed you on the throne of I.
10: 9 of the LORD's eternal love for I,
12: 1 for all I had gone there to make him
12:19 So I has been in rebellion against
18:17 "Is that you, you troubler of I?"
19:18 Yet I reserve seven thousand in I—
2Ki   5: 8 know that there is a prophet in I."
17:20 LORD rejected all the people of I;
1Ch   17:22 made your people I your very own
21: 1 incited David to take a census of I.
29:25 exalted Solomon in the sight of all I
2Ch   9: 8 of the love of your God for I and his
Ps   22: 3 you are the one I praises.
73: 1 Surely God is good to I, to those
78:21 Jacob, and his wrath rose against I,
81: 8 if you would only listen to me, I!
98: 3 his love and his faithfulness to I;
99: 8 you were to I a forgiving God,
125: 5 with the evildoers. Peace be on I.
Isa   1: 3 but I does not know, my people do
11:12 nations and gather the exiles of I;
27: 6 I will bud and blossom and fill all
44:21 Jacob, for you, I, are my servant.
44:21 I will not forget you.
46:13 salvation to Zion, my splendor to I.
Jer   2: 3 I was holy to the LORD,
23: 6 be saved and I will live in safety.
31: 2 I will come to give rest to I."
31:10 'He who scattered I will gather
31:31 a new covenant with the people of I
33:17 have a man to sit on the throne of I,
La   2: 5 he has swallowed up I.
Eze   3:17 you a watchman for the people of I;
33: 7 you a watchman for the people of I;
34: 2 prophesy against the shepherds of I;
36: 1 prophesy to the mountains of I
37:28 that I the LORD make I holy,
39:23 that the people of I went into exile
Da   9:20 the sin of my people I and making
Hos   7: 1 whenever I would heal I, the sins
11: 1 "When I was a child, I loved him,
Am   4:12 this is what I will do to you, I,
7:11 and I will surely go into exile,
8: 2 "The time is ripe for my people I;
9:14 I will bring my people I back
Mic   5: 2 for me one who will be ruler over I,
Zec   11:14 family bond between Judah and I.
Mal   1: 5 even beyond the borders of I!'
Mt   2: 6 who will shepherd my people I.' "
10: 6 Go rather to the lost sheep of I.
15:24 sent only to the lost sheep of I."

Mk 12:29 'Hear, O I: The Lord our God,
    15:32 this king of I, come down now
Lk   1:54 He has helped his servant I,
     2:34 the falling and rising of many in I,
    22:30 judging the twelve tribes of I.
Jn 12:13 "Blessed is the king of I!"
Ac   1: 6 going to restore the kingdom to I?"
     9:15 their kings and to the people of I.
Ro   9: 6 all who are descended from I are I.
     9:31 but the people of I, who pursued
    11: 7 of I sought so earnestly they did not
    11:26 and in this way all I will be saved.
Gal 6:16 follow this rule—to the I of God.
Eph 2:12 excluded from citizenship in I
     3: 6 Gentiles are heirs together with I,
Heb 8: 8 a new covenant with the people of I
Rev 7: 4 144,000 from all the tribes of I.
    21:12 the names of the twelve tribes of I.

ALL ISRAEL Ex 18:25; Dt 1:1; 5:1; 11:6; 13:11;
21:21; 27:9; 31:1, 7, 11; 32:45; 34:12; Jos 3:7, 17;
4:14; 7:24, 25; 8:15, 21; 10:15, 29, 31, 34, 36, 38,
43; 23:2; Jdg 8:27; 20:1; 1Sa 2:2; 3:20; 4:1, 5; 7:5;
10:20; 11:2; 12:1; 13:4, 20; 18:16; 19:5; 24:2; 25:1;
28:3, 4; 2Sa 2:9; 3:12, 21, 37; 4:1; 5:5; 6:5, 15; 8:15;
10:17; 12:8, 12; 14:25; 16:21, 22; 17:10, 11, 13; 1Ki
1:20; 2:15; 3:28; 4:1, 7; 5:13; 8:62, 65; 11:42; 12:1,
16, 18, 20; 14:13, 18; 15:27, 33; 18:20; 22:17; 2Ki
3:6; 9:14; 1Ch 9:1; 11:1, 10; 12:38; 13:5, 6; 14:8;
15:3, 28; 18:14; 19:17; 21:5; 28:4, 8; 29:21, 23, 25,
26; 2Ch 1:2; 7:8; 9:30; 10:1, 3, 16; 11:3; 12:1; 13:4,
15; 18:16; 24:5; 28:23; 29:24, 24; 30:1; 35:3; Ezr
6:17; 8:25, 35; 10:5; Ne 12:47; 13:26; Eze 5:4; 45:6;
Da 9:7, 11; Mal 4:4; Ac 2:36; Ro 11:26

CHILDREN OF ISRAEL (KJV) See
ISRAELITES

GOD OF ISRAEL See GOD

HOLY ONE OF ISRAEL 2Ki 19:22; Ps 71:22;
78:41; 89:18; Isa 1:4; 5:19, 24; 10:20; 12:6; 17:7;
29:19; 30:11, 12, 15; 31:1; 37:23; 41:14, 16, 20;
43:3, 14; 45:11; 47:4; 48:17; 49:7, 7; 54:5; 55:5;
60:9, 14; Jer 50:29; 51:5

ISRAEL AND JUDAH 1Sa 17:52; 18:16; 2Sa
3:10; 5:5; 11:11; 12:8; 21:2; 24:1; 1Ki 1:35; 2Ki
17:13; 1Ch 9:1; 2Ch 27:7; 30:1, 6; 31:6; 34:21;
35:27; 36:8; Isa 8:14; Jer 11:10, 17; 30:3, 4; 31:27;
32:30, 32; 33:14; 51:5; Eze 9:9

KING OF ISRAEL See KING

KINGS OF ISRAEL See KINGS

MEN OF ISRAEL Nu 26:51; Dt 29:10; Jos 10:24;
Jdg 20:33, 36, 48; 21:1; 1Sa 7:11; 11:8; 14:41; 17:19,
52; 2Sa 6:1; 16:15, 18; 17:14, 24; 19:41, 42, 43, 43;
20:2; 24:4; 1Ch 21:14; 2Ch 28:8; Ne 7:7; Ps 78:31;
Ac 5:35

PEOPLE OF ISRAEL Ex 16:31; 19:3; Lev 17:9;
Nu 15:30; 32:4; Dt 27:14; 32:52; Jos 4:7; 8:33; 1Sa
7:2; 10:17; 2Sa 15:6, 13; 1Ki 16:21; 2Ki 17:20,
23; 2Ch 6:11; 13:12; 30:6; 31:6; Ezr 2:2; 6:16; 9:1;
Ne 1:6; 10:39; Ps 103:7; Isa 46:3; Jer 2:26; 3:18,
21; 5:11, 15; 10:1; 13:11; 31:31, 33; 32:30, 30, 32;
33:14; 50:4, 33; Eze 3:1, 4, 5, 7, 17; 4:3, 4, 5, 13;
6:11; 9:9; 12:24; 13:5; 14:5, 6, 11; 18:29, 31; 20:13,

27, 39, 40, 44; 22:18; 24:21; 28:24, 25; 29:6, 16;
33:7, 11; 36:17, 21, 22, 32; 37:11; 39:22, 23, 25, 29;
40:4; 43:7, 10; 44:6, 12; 45:8; Hos 1:11; Joel 3:16;
Am 2:11; 3:1; 5:25; 6:1; 9:9; Mic 1:5; Mt 27:9; Lk
1:16; Ac 4:10, 27; 7:42; 9:15; 10:36; 13:17, 24; Ro
9:4, 31; 11:7; 1Co 10:18; Php 3:5; Heb 8:8, 10

TRIBES OF ISRAEL Ge 49:16, 28; Ex 24:4; Nu
30:1; 31:4; Dt 29:21; 33:5; Jos 3:12; 12:7; 22:14;
24:1; Jdg 18:1; 20:2, 10, 12; 21:5, 8, 15; 1Sa 2:28;
15:17; 2Sa 5:1; 15:2, 10; 19:9; 20:14; 24:2; 1Ki
11:32; 14:21; 2Ki 21:7; 1Ch 27:16, 22; 29:6; 2Ch
12:13; 33:7; Ezr 6:17; Ps 78:55; Eze 47:13, 21, 22;
48:19, 29, 31; Hos 5:9; Zec 9:1; Mt 19:28; Lk 22:30;
Rev 7:4; 21:12

ISRAEL'S ISRAEL

Jdg 10:16 he could bear I misery no longer.
2Sa 23: 1 God of Jacob, the hero of I songs:
Isa 44: 6 I King and Redeemer, the LORD
Jer   3: 9 Because I immorality mattered so
     31: 9 because I am I father, and Ephraim
Hos   5: 5 I arrogance testifies against them;
Jn   3:10 "You are I teacher," said Jesus,

ISRAELITE ISRAEL

Ex   16: 1 The whole I community set
     35:29 All the I men and women who were
Nu   8:16 male offspring from every I woman.
     20: 1 the whole I community arrived
     20:22 The whole I community set
Dt   23:19 Do not charge a fellow I interest,
Ne   9: 2 I descent had separated themselves
Jn   1:47 "Here truly is an I in whom there is
Ro   11: 1 I am an I myself, a descendant

ISRAELITES ISRAEL

Ex   1: 7 but the I were exceedingly fruitful;
      2:23 The I groaned in their slavery
      3: 9 now the cry of the I has reached me,
     12:35 The I did as Moses instructed
     12:37 The I journeyed from Rameses
     14:22 the I went through the sea on dry
     16:12 have heard the grumbling of the I.
     16:35 The I ate manna forty years,
     24:17 To the I the glory of the LORD
     28:30 for the I over his heart before
     29:45 I will dwell among the I and be their
     31:16 The I are to observe the Sabbath,
     33: 5 "Tell the I, 'You are a stiff-necked
     39:42 The I had done all the work just as
Lev 22:32 be acknowledged as holy by the I.
     25:46 rule over your fellow I ruthlessly.
     25:55 for the I belong to me as servants.
Nu   2:32 These are the I, counted according
      6:23 'This is how you are to bless the I.
      9: 2 "Have the I celebrate the Passover
      9:17 the I set out from the Desert of Sinai
     10:12 the I set out from the Desert of Sinai
     14: 2 All the I grumbled against Moses
     20:12 me as holy in the sight of the I,
     21: 6 they bit the people and many I died.
     26:65 had told those I they would surely
     27:12 and see the land I have given the I.
     33: 3 The I set out from Rameses

Nu 35:10 "Speak to the I and say to them:
Dt   4:44 is the law Moses set before the I.
     33: 1 on the I before his death.
Jos   1: 2 I am about to give to them—to the I.
      1:14 cross over ahead of your fellow I.
      5: 6 The I had moved
      7: 1 the I were unfaithful in regard
      8:32 in the presence of the I,
     18: 1 whole assembly of the I gathered
     21: 3 the I gave the Levites the following
     22: 9 of Manasseh left the I at Shiloh
Jdg   2:11 Then the I did evil in the eyes
      3:12 Again the I did evil in the eyes
      4: 1 Again the I did evil in the eyes
      6: 1 The I did evil in the eyes
     10: 6 because the I forsook the LORD
     13: 1 Again the I did evil in the eyes
1Sa   7: 4 So the I put away their Baals
     17: 2 Saul and the I assembled
1Ki   8:63 all the I dedicated the temple
      9:22 did not make slaves of any of the I;
     12:17 as for the I who were living
2Ki 17: 7 took place because the I had sinned
1Ch   9: 2 in their own towns were some I,
     10: 1 the I fled before them, and many
     11: 4 all the I marched to Jerusalem
     21: 2 count the I from Beersheba to Dan.
2Ch   7: 6 and all the I were standing.
Ezr   2:70 and the rest of the I settled in their
Ne   1: 6 I confess the sins we I,
      8:17 the I had not celebrated it like this.
Jer 16:14 who brought the I up out of Egypt,'
Hos   1:10 "Yet the I will be like the sand
      3: 1 Love her as the LORD loves the I,
Am   4: 5 you I, for this is what you love
Mic   5: 3 of his brothers return to join the I.
Ro   9:27 the number of the I be like the sand
     10: 1 to God for the I is that they may be
     10:16 not all the I accepted the good news.
2Co 11:22 So am I. Are they I? So am I.

ISSACHAR
Son of Jacob by Leah (Ge 30:18; 35:23; 1Ch 2:1).
Tribe of blessed (Ge 49:14–15; Dt 33:18–19), num-
bered (Nu 1:29; 26:25), allotted land (Jos 19:17–23;
Eze 48:25), assisted Deborah (Jdg 5:15), 12,000
from (Rev 7:7).

ISSUED ISSUES
Ex   15:25 There the LORD i a ruling
Lk   2: 1 days Caesar Augustus i a decree

ISSUES* ISSUED
Da   6:15 that the king i can be changed."

ITALIAN* ITALY
Ac   10: 1 what was known as the I Regiment.

ITALY ITALIAN
Ac   27: 1 decided that we would sail for I,
Heb 13:24 from I send you their greetings.

ITCHING*
2Ti   4: 3 to say what their i ears want to hear.

ITHAMAR
Son of Aaron (Ex 6:23; 1Ch 6:3). Duties at tabernacle (Ex 38:21; Nu 4:21–33; 7:8).

ITTAI
2Sa 15:19 The king said to I the Gittite,

IVORY
1Ki 10:22 silver and i, and apes and baboons.
     22:39 palace he built and adorned with i,
Am   3:15 adorned with i will be destroyed
Rev 18:12 and articles of every kind made of i,

J

JABBOK
Ge   32:22 sons and crossed the ford of the J.
Dt   3:16 the border) and out to the J River,

JABESH JABESH GILEAD
1Sa 11: 1 And all the men of J said to him,
     31:12 the wall of Beth Shan and went to J,
1Ch 10:12 and his sons and brought them to J.

JABESH GILEAD GILEAD, JABESH
2Sa   2: 4 the men from J who had buried Saul,

JABIN
Jos 11: 1 When J king of Hazor heard of this,
Jdg   4:23 day God subdued J king of Canaan

JACKALS
Ps   63:10 to the sword and become food for j.
Isa 13:21 will lie there, j will fill her houses;
     35: 7 In the haunts where j once lay,
Mal   1: 3 left his inheritance to the desert j."

JACOB ISRAEL
1. Second son of Isaac, twin of Esau (Ge
26:21–26; 1Ch 1:34). Bought Esau's birthright (Ge
26:29–34); tricked Isaac into blessing him (Ge
27:1–37). Fled to Haran (Ge 28:1–5). Abrahamic
covenant perpetuated through (Ge 28:13–15; Mal
1:2). Vision at Bethel (Ge 28:10–22). Served Laban for Rachel and Leah (Ge 29:1–30). Children
(Ge 29:31–30:24; 35:16–26; 1Ch 2–9). Flocks increased (Ge 30:25–43). Returned to Canaan (Ge
31). Wrestled with God; name changed to Israel
(Ge 32:22–32). Reconciled to Esau (Ge 33). Returned to Bethel (Ge 35:1–15). Favored Joseph
(Ge 37:3). Sent sons to Egypt during famine (Ge
42–43). Settled in Egypt (Ge 46). Blessed Ephraim
and Manasseh (Ge 48). Blessed sons (Ge 49:1–28;
Heb 11:21). Death (Ge 49:29–33). Burial (Ge
50:1–14).
2. Corporate name of Jacob's descendants; often
specifically Northern Kingdom.
Ps   53: 6 let J rejoice and Israel be glad!
     59:13 of the earth that God rules over J.
    135: 4 the LORD has chosen J to be his
Isa 44: 1 "But now listen, J, my servant,
Jer 30:10 do not be afraid, J my servant;
Eze 39:25 I will now restore the fortunes of J
Mic   7:20 You will be faithful to J, and show

Mal 1: 2 "Yet I have loved J,
Ro   9:13 "J I loved, but Esau I hated."

GOD OF JACOB See GOD

JAEL*
Woman who killed Canaanite general, Sisera (Jdg 4:17–22; 5:6, 24–27).

JAH (KJV: Ps 68:4) See LORD†

JAIL JAILER
Ac   4: 3 they put them in j until the next day.
     5:18 and put them in the public j.

JAILER JAIL
Ac 16:34 The j brought them into his house

JAIR
Judge from Gilead (Jdg 10:3–5).

JAIRUS*
Synagogue ruler whose daughter Jesus raised (Mk 5:22–43; Lk 8:41–56).

JAKIN
1Ki 7:21 The pillar to the south he named J

JAMBRES*
2Ti 3: 8 as Jannes and J opposed Moses,

JAMES
1. Apostle; brother of John (Mt 4:21–22; 10:2; Mk 3:17; Lk 5:1–10). At transfiguration (Mt 17:1–13; Mk 9:1–13; Lk 9:28–36). Killed by Herod (Ac 12:2).
2. Apostle; son of Alphaeus (Mt 10:3; Mk 3:18; Lk 6:15).
3. Brother of Jesus (Mt 13:55; Mk 6:3; Lk 24:10; Gal 1:19) and Judas (Jude 1). With believers before Pentecost (Ac 1:13). Leader of church at Jerusalem (Ac 12:17; 15; 21:18; Gal 2:9, 12.) Author of epistle (Jas 1:1).

JANNES*
2Ti 3: 8 Just as J and Jambres opposed

JAPHETH
Son of Noah (Ge 5:32; 1Ch 1:4–5). Blessed (Ge 9:18–28). Sons of (Ge 10:2–5).

JAR JARS
Ge 24:14 'Please let down your j that I may
Ex 16:33 "Take a j and put an omer of manna
1Ki 17:14 'The j of flour will not be used
Jer 19: 1 "Go and buy a clay j from a potter.
Mk 14: 3 She broke the j and poured
Lk   8:16 hides it in a clay j or puts it under
    22:10 city, a man carrying a j of water will
Heb 9: 4 This ark contained the gold j

JARS JAR
Jdg 7:19 broke the j that were in their hands.
Jn   2: 6 Nearby stood six stone water j,
2Co 4: 7 we have this treasure in j of clay

JASHAR*
Jos 10:13 as it is written in the Book of J.

2Sa 1:18 bow (it is written in the Book of J):

JASON
Ac 17: 7 and J has welcomed them into his

JASPER
Ex 28:20 row shall be topaz, onyx and j.
Eze 28:13 topaz, onyx and j, lapis lazuli,
Rev 4: 3 sat there had the appearance of j
    21:19 The first foundation was j,

JAVELIN
Jos 8:18 "Hold out toward Ai the j that is
1Sa 17:45 me with sword and spear and j, but I

JAWBONE
Jdg 15:15 Finding a fresh j of a donkey,

JAZER
Nu 21:32 After Moses had sent spies to J,
    32: 1 saw that the lands of J and Gilead

JEALOUS* JEALOUSLY, JEALOUSY
Ge 30: 1 children, she became j of her sister.
    37:11 His brothers were j of him, but his
Ex 20: 5 am a j God, punishing the children
    34:14 whose name is J, is a j God.
Nu   5:14 or if he is j and suspects her even
    11:29 replied, "Are you j for my sake?
Dt   4:24 God is a consuming fire, a j God.
     5: 9 am a j God, punishing the children
     6:15 is a j God and his anger will burn
    32:16 They made him j with their foreign
    32:21 They made me j by what is no god
Jos 24:19 He is a holy God; he is a j God.
1Ki 14:22 up his j anger more than those who
Isa 11:13 Ephraim will not be j of Judah,
Eze 16:38 vengeance of my wrath and j anger.
    16:42 my j anger will turn away from you;
    23:25 I will direct my j anger against you,
    36: 6 in my j wrath because you have
Joel 2:18 Then the LORD was j for his land
Na   1: 2 The LORD is a j and avenging
Zep 3: 8 consumed by the fire of my j anger.
Zec 1:14 'I am very j for Jerusalem and Zion,
     8: 2 "I am very j for Zion;
Ac   7: 9 "Because the patriarchs were j
    17: 5 But other Jews were j;
2Co 11: 2 I am j for you with a godly jealousy.

JEALOUSLY* JEALOUS
Jas 4: 5 says without reason that he j longs

JEALOUSY JEALOUS
Nu   5:14 feelings of j come over her husband
Ps 79: 5 How long will your j burn like fire?
Pr   6:34 For j arouses a husband's fury,
    27: 4 but who can stand before j?
SS   8: 6 death, its j unyielding as the grave.
Eze 8: 3 the idol that provokes to j stood.
    35:11 j you showed in your hatred of them
Zep 1:18 fire of his j the whole earth will be
Zec 8: 2 I am burning with j for her."
Ac   5:17 of the Sadducees, were filled with j.
    13:45 the crowds, they were filled with j.
Ro 13:13 debauchery, not in dissension and j.

1Co   3: 3 For since there is j and quarreling
     10:22 we trying to arouse the Lord's j?
2Co 11: 2 I am jealous for you with a godly j.
     12:20 I fear that there may be discord, j,
Gal   5:20 hatred, discord, j, fits of rage,

JEBUS JEBUSITE, JEBUSITES, JERUSALEM
1Ch 11: 4 marched to Jerusalem (that is, J).

JEBUSITE JEBUS
Jos 18:28 Zelah, Haeleph, the J city (that is,
2Sa 24:18 threshing floor of Araunah the J."
2Ch   3: 1 the threshing floor of Araunah the J,

JEBUSITES JEBUS
Ge 15:21 Canaanites, Girgashites and J."
Ex   3: 8 Amorites, Perizzites, Hivites and J.
Jos 15:63 Judah could not dislodge the J,
     15:63 to this day the J live there
2Sa   5: 6 The J said to David, "You will not

JECONIAH* JEHOIACHIN
A form of Jehoiachin (Mt 1:11–12).

JEDIDIAH* SOLOMON
2Sa 12:25 Nathan the prophet to name him J.

JEDUTHUN
1Ch 16:41 With them were Heman and J
2Ch 35:15 Heman and J the king's seer.
Ps 39: T For J. A psalm of David.
     62: T For J. A psalm of David.

JEER* JEERED, JEERS
Job 16:10 People open their mouths to j at me;

JEERED* JEER
2Ki   2:23 came out of the town and j at him.

JEERS* JEER
Heb 11:36 Some faced j and flogging,

JEHOAHAZ
1. Son of Jehu; king of Israel (2Ki 13:1–9).
2. Son of Josiah; king of Judah (2Ki 23:31–34; 2Ch 36:1–4).

JEHOASH JOASH
1. See JOASH.
2. Son of Jehoahaz; king of Israel. Defeat of Aram prophesied by Elisha (2Ki 13:10–25). Defeated Amaziah in Jerusalem (2Ki 14:1–16; 2Ch 25:17–24).

JEHOIACHIN JECONIAH
Son of Jehoiakim; king of Judah exiled by Nebuchadnezzar (2Ki 24:8–17; 2Ch 36:8–10; Jer 22:24–30; 24:1). Raised from prisoner status (2Ki 25:27–30; Jer 52:31–34).

JEHOIADA
Priest who sheltered Joash from Athaliah (2Ki 11–12; 2Ch 22:11—24:16).

JEHOIAKIM ELIAKIM
Son of Josiah; made king of Judah by Nebu-

chadnezzar (2Ki 23:34—24:6; 2Ch 36:4–8; Jer 22:18–23). Burned scroll of Jeremiah's prophecies (Jer 36).

JEHONADAB
Jer 35: 8 everything our forefather J son

JEHORAM JORAM
1. Son of Jehoshaphat; king of Judah (2Ki 8:16–24). Prophesied against by Elijah; killed by the LORD (2Ch 21).
2. See JORAM.

JEHOSHAPHAT
1. Son of Asa; king of Judah. Strengthened his kingdom (2Ch 17). Joined with Ahab against Aram (2Ki 22; 2Ch 18). Established judges (2Ch 19). Joined with Joram against Moab (2Ki 3; 2Ch 20).
2. Valley of judgment (Joel 3:2, 12).

JEHOVAH (KJV) See LORD†

JEHU
1. Prophet against Baasha (2Ki 16:1–7).
2. King of Israel. Anointed by Elijah to obliterate house of Ahab (1Ki 19:16–17); anointed by servant of Elisha (2Ki 9:1–13). Killed Joram and Ahaziah (2Ki 9:14–29; 2Ch 22:7–9), Jezebel (2Ki 9:30–37), relatives of Ahab (2Ki 10:1–17; Hos 1:4), ministers of Baal (2Ki 10:18–29). Death (2Ki 10:30–36).

JEPHTHAH
Judge from Gilead who delivered Israel from Ammon (Jdg 10:6—12:7). Made rash vow concerning his daughter (Jdg 11:30–40).

JEREMIAH
Prophet to Judah (Jer 1:1–3). Called by the LORD (Jer 1). Put in stocks (Jer 20:1–3). Threatened for prophesying (Jer 11:18–23; 26). Opposed by Hananiah (Jer 28). Scroll burned (Jer 36). Imprisoned (Jer 37). Thrown into cistern (Jer 38). Forced to Egypt with those fleeing Babylonians (Jer 43).

JERICHO
Nu 22: 1 along the Jordan across from J.
Dt 34: 3 whole region from the Valley of J,
Jos   5:10 camped at Gilgal on the plains of J,
      6: 2 I have delivered J into your hands,
      6:26 undertakes to rebuild this city, J:
1Ki 16:34 time, Hiel of Bethel rebuilt J.
2Ki 25: 5 and overtook him in the plains of J.
Lk 10:30 going down from Jerusalem to J,
     18:35 As Jesus approached J, a blind man
     19: 1 Jesus entered J and was passing
Heb 11:30 By faith the walls of J fell,

JEROBOAM
1. Official of Solomon; rebelled to become first king of Israel (1Ki 11:26–40; 12:1–20; 2Ch 10). Idolatry (1Ki 12:25–33); judgment for (1Ki 13–14; 2Ch 13).
2. Son of Jehoash; king of Israel (1Ki 14:23–29).

JERUB-BAAL GIDEON

Jdg   6:32 they gave him the name J that day,
1Sa 12:11 Then the LORD sent J, Barak,

JERUSALEM JEBUS

Jos 10: 1 Now Adoni-Zedek king of J heard
      15: 8 slope of the Jebusite city (that is, J).
Jdg   1: 8 The men of Judah attacked J
1Sa 17:54 Philistine's head and brought it to J;
2Sa   5: 5 in J he reigned over all Israel
      9:13 And Mephibosheth lived in J,
      11: 1 But David remained in J.
      15:29 took the ark of God back to J
      24:16 stretched out his hand to destroy J,
1Ki   3: 1 the LORD, and the wall around J.
      9:15 terraces, the wall of J, and Hazor,
      9:19 whatever he desired to build in J,
      10:26 chariot cities and also with him in J.
      10:27 silver as common in J as stones,
      11: 7 On a hill east of J, Solomon built
      11:13 my servant and for the sake of J,
      11:36 always have a lamp before me in J,
      11:42 in J over all Israel forty years.
      12:27 at the temple of the LORD in J,
      14:21 and he reigned seventeen years in J,
      14:25 Shishak king of Egypt attacked J.
      15: 2 and he reigned in J three years.
      15:10 and he reigned in J forty-one years.
      22:42 he reigned in J twenty-five years.
2Ki   8:17 and he reigned in J eight years.
      8:26 king, and he reigned in J one year.
      12: 1 and he reigned in J forty years.
      12:17 Then he turned to attack J.
      14: 2 he reigned in J twenty-nine years.
      14:13 Jehoash went to J and broke down
      15: 2 and he reigned in J fifty-two years.
      15: 2 name was Jekoliah; she was from J.
      15:33 and he reigned in J sixteen years.
      16: 2 and he reigned in J sixteen years.
      16: 5 Israel marched up to fight against J
      18: 2 he reigned in J twenty-nine years.
      18:17 from Lachish to King Hezekiah at J.
      18:35 can the LORD deliver J from my
      19:31 For out of J will come a remnant,
      21: 1 and he reigned in J fifty-five years.
      21: 4 said, "In J I will put my Name."
      21:12 am going to bring such disaster on J
      21:19 king, and he reigned in J two years.
      22: 1 and he reigned in J thirty-one years.
      23:27 and I will reject J, the city I chose,
      23:31 and he reigned in J three months.
      23:36 and he reigned in J eleven years.
      24: 8 and he reigned in J three months.
      24:10 king of Babylon advanced on J
      24:14 He carried all J into exile:
      24:18 and he reigned in J eleven years.
      24:20 anger that all this happened to J
      25: 1 Babylon marched against J with his
      25:10 broke down the walls around J.
1Ch 11: 4 all the Israelites marched to J
      21:16 sword in his hand extended over J.
2Ch   1: 4 he had pitched a tent for it in J.
      3: 1 the LORD in J on Mount Moriah,

2Ch   6: 6 now I have chosen J for my Name
      9: 1 she came to J to test him with hard
      20:15 and all who live in Judah and J!
      20:27 Judah and J returned joyfully to J,
      29: 8 LORD has fallen on Judah and J;
      36:19 and broke down the wall of J;
Ezr   1: 2 build a temple for him at J in Judah.
      2: 1 to Babylon (they returned to J
      3: 1 assembled together as one in J.
      4:12 up to us from you have gone to J
      4:24 of God in J came to a standstill until
      6:12 decree or to destroy this temple in J.
      7: 8 Ezra arrived in J in the fifth month
      9: 9 a wall of protection in Judah and J.
      10: 7 J for all the exiles to assemble in J.
Ne   1: 2 survived the exile, and also about J.
      1: 3 The wall of J is broken down,
      2:11 I went to J, and after staying there
      2:17 let us rebuild the wall of J, and we
      2:20 you have no share in J or any claim
      3: 8 They restored J as far as the Broad
      4: 8 fight against J and stir up trouble
      11: 1 the leaders of the people settled in J.
      12:27 At the dedication of the wall of J,
      12:43 in J could be heard far away.
Ps   51:18 Zion, to build up the walls of J.
      79: 1 they have reduced J to rubble.
      122: 2 feet are standing in your gates, J.
      122: 3 J is built like a city that is closely
      122: 6 Pray for the peace of J:
      125: 2 As the mountains surround J,
      128: 5 see the prosperity of J all the days
      137: 5 If I forget you, J, may my right
      147: 2 The LORD builds up J;
      147:12 Extol the LORD, J;
Ecc   1:12 Teacher, was king over Israel in J.
SS   6: 4 as lovely as J, as majestic as troops
Isa   1: 1 and J that Isaiah son of Amoz saw
      2: 1 Amoz saw concerning Judah and J:
      3: 1 is about to take from J and Judah
      3: 8 J staggers, Judah is falling;
      4: 3 are recorded among the living in J.
      8:14 for the people of J he will be a trap
      27:13 LORD on the holy mountain in J.
      31: 5 the LORD Almighty will shield J;
      33:20 your eyes will see J, a peaceful
      40: 2 Speak tenderly to J, and proclaim
      40: 9 You who bring good news to J,
      52: 1 Put on your garments of splendor, J,
      52: 2 rise up, sit enthroned, J.
      62: 6 posted watchmen on your walls, J;
      62: 7 give him no rest till he establishes J
      65:18 for I will create J to be a delight
      66:13 and you will be comforted over J."
Jer   2: 2 and proclaim in the hearing of J:
      3:17 all nations will gather in J to honor
      4: 5 in Judah and proclaim in J and say:
      4:14 J, wash the evil from your heart
      5: 1 "Go up and down the streets of J,
      6: 6 and build siege ramps against J.
      8: 5 Why does J always turn away?
      9:11 "I will make J a heap of ruins,
      13:27 Woe to you, J! How long will you

Jer 23:14 the people of J are like Gomorrah."
24: 1 carried into exile from J to Babylon
26:18 J will become a heap of rubble,
32: 2 of Babylon was then besieging J,
33:10 and the streets of J that are deserted,
39: 1 Babylon marched against J with his
51:50 a distant land, and call to mind J."
52:14 broke down all the walls around J.
La   1: 8 J has sinned greatly and so has
Eze 8: 3 in visions of God he took me to J,
14:21 I send against J my four dreadful
16: 2 man, confront J with her detestable
21: 2 set your face against J and preach
23: 4 is Samaria, and Oholibah is J.
Da   5: 3 taken from the temple of God in J,
6:10 the windows opened toward J.
9: 2 of J would last seventy years.
9:12 done like what has been done to J.
9:25 rebuild J until the Anointed One,
Joel 3: 1 I restore the fortunes of Judah and J,
3:16 roar from Zion and thunder from J;
3:17 J will be holy; never again will
Am   2: 5 will consume the fortresses of J."
Ob   1:11 entered his gates and cast lots for J,
Mic 1: 5 is Judah's high place? Is it not J?
4: 2 the word of the LORD from J.
Zep 3:16 On that day they will say to J,
Zec 1:14 'I am very jealous for J and Zion,
1:17 comfort Zion and choose J.' "
2: 2 me, "To measure J, to find out how
2: 4 man, 'J will be a city without walls
8: 3 J will be called the Faithful City,
8: 8 I will bring them back to live in J;
8:15 determined to do good again to J
8:22 powerful nations will come to J
9: 9 Shout, Daughter J! See, your king
9:10 Ephraim and the warhorses from J,
12: 3 I will make J an immovable rock
12:10 the inhabitants of J a spirit of grace
14: 2 I will gather all the nations to J
14: 8 living water will flow out from J,
14:16 nations that have attacked J will go
Mt   2: 1 Magi from the east came to J
16:21 to his disciples that he must go to J
20:18 "We are going up to J, and the Son
21:10 When Jesus entered J, the whole
23:37 "J, J, you who kill the prophets
Mk 10:33 "We are going up to J," he said,
15:41 had come up with him to J were
Lk   2:22 Mary took him to J to present him
2:41 Every year Jesus' parents went to J
2:43 the boy Jesus stayed behind in J,
4: 9 The devil led him to J and had him
9:31 about to bring to fulfillment at J.
9:51 Jesus resolutely set out for J.
13:34 "J, J, you who kill the prophets
18:31 them, "We are going up to J,
19:41 As he approached J and saw
21:20 "When you see J being surrounded
21:24 J will be trampled
23:28 "Daughters of J, do not weep
24:47 name to all nations, beginning at J.
Jn   1:19 the Jewish leaders in J sent priests

Jn   4:20 where we must worship is in J."
5: 1 Jesus went up to J for one
10:22 the Festival of Dedication at J.
Ac   1: 4 "Do not leave J, but wait
1: 8 and you will be my witnesses in J,
6: 7 of disciples in J increased rapidly,
9:13 has done to your holy people in J.
9:28 them and moved about freely in J,
11:27 some prophets came down from J
15: 2 to go up to J to see the apostles
20:22 I am going to J, not knowing what
21: 4 they urged Paul not to go on to J.
23:11 As you have testified about me in J,
Ro   15:19 So from J all the way around
Gal 1:17 to J to see those who were apostles
2: 1 I went up again to J, this time
4:25 corresponds to the present city of J,
4:26 But the J that is above is free,
Heb 12:22 of the living God, the heavenly J.
Rev 3:12 the new J, which is coming down
21: 2 the new J, coming down
21:10 and showed me the Holy City, J,

DAUGHTER JERUSALEM See DAUGHTER

DAUGHTERS OF JERUSALEM See
DAUGHTERS

PEOPLE OF JERUSALEM 2Ch 20:20; 21:11,
13; 22:1; 32:18, 22, 26, 33; 33:9; 34:32; 35:18; Isa
8:14; Jer 1:3; 8:1; 11:12; 19:3; 23:14; Eze 11:15; Zec
12:5; Mk 1:5; Jn 7:25; Ac 13:27

JESHUA
Ezr   2:36 (through the family of J) 973

JESSE
Father of David (Ru 4:17–22; 1Sa 16; 1Ch
2:12–17).

SON OF JESSE See SON

JESUS JESUS'; see also JUSTUS
LIFE: Genealogy (Mt 1:1–17; Lk 3:21–37).
Birth announced (Mt 1:18–25; Lk 1:26–45). Birth
(Mt 2:1–12; Lk 2:1–40). Escape to Egypt (Mt
2:13–23). As a boy in the temple (Lk 2:41–52).
Baptism (Mt 3:13–17; Mk 1:9–11; Lk 3:21–22; Jn
1:32–34). Temptation (Mt 4:1–11; Mk 1:12–13;
Lk 4:1–13). Ministry in Galilee (Mt 4:12—18:35;
Mk 1:14—9:50; Lk 4:14—13:9; Jn 1:35—2:11; 4; 6),
Transfiguration (Mt 17:1–8; Mk 9:2–8; Lk 9:28–
36), on the way to Jerusalem (Mt 19–20; Mk 10; Lk
13:10—19:27), in Jerusalem (Mt 21–25; Mk 11–13;
Lk 19:28—21:38; Jn 2:12—3:36; 5; 7–12). Last supper (Mt 26:17–35; Mk 14:12–31; Lk 22:1–38; Jn
13–17). Arrest and trial (Mt 26:36—27:31; Mk
14:43—15:20; Lk 22:39—23:25; Jn 18:1—19:16).
Crucifixion (Mt 27:32–66; Mk 15:21–47; Lk
23:26–55; Jn 19:28–42). Resurrection and appearances (Mt 28; Mk 16; Lk 24; Jn 20–21; Ac 1:1–11;
7:56; 9:3–6; 1Co 15:1–8; Rev 1:1–20).
MIRACLES. Healings: official's son (Jn 4:43–
54), demoniac in Capernaum (Mk 1:23–26; Lk
4:33–35), Peter's mother-in-law (Mt 8:14–17; Mk
1:29–31; Lk 4:38–39), leper (Mt 8:2–4; Mk 1:40–
45; Lk 5:12–16), paralytic (Mt 9:1–8; Mk 2:1–12;

Lk 5:17–26), cripple (Jn 5:1–9), shriveled hand (Mt 12:10–13; Mk 3:1–5; Lk 6:6–11), centurion's servant (Mt 8:5–13; Lk 7:1–10), widow's son raised (Lk 7:11–17), demoniac (Mt 12:22–23; Lk 11:14), Gadarene demoniacs (Mt 8:28–34; Mk 5:1–20; Lk 8:26–39), woman's bleeding and Jairus' daughter (Mt 9:18–26; Mk 5:21–43; Lk 8:40–56), blind man (Mt 9:27–31), mute man (Mt 9:32–33), Canaanite woman's daughter (Mt 15:21–28; Mk 7:24–30), deaf man (Mk 7:31–37), blind man (Mk 8:22–26), demoniac boy (Mt 17:14–18; Mk 9:14–29; Lk 9:37–43), ten lepers (Lk 17:11–19), man born blind (Jn 9:1–7), Lazarus raised (Jn 11), crippled woman (Lk 13:11–17), man with dropsy (Lk 14:1–6), two blind men (Mt 20:29–34; Mk 10:46–52; Lk 18:35–43), Malchus' ear (Lk 22:50–51). Other Miracles: water to wine (Jn 2:1–11), catch of fish (Lk 5:1–11), storm stilled (Mt 8:23–27; Mk 4:37–41; Lk 8:22–25), 5,000 fed (Mt 14:15–21; Mk 6:35–44; Lk 9:10–17; Jn 6:1–14), walking on water (Mt 14:25–33; Mk 6:48–52; Jn 6:15–21), 4,000 fed (Mt 15:32–39; Mk 8:1–9), money from fish (Mt 17:24–27), fig tree cursed (Mt 21:18–22; Mk 11:12–14), catch of fish (Jn 21:1–14).

MAJOR TEACHING: Sermon on the Mount (Mt 5–7; Lk 6:17–49), to Nicodemus (Jn 3), to Samaritan woman (Jn 4), Bread of Life (Jn 6:22–59), at Festival of Tabernacles (Jn 7–8), woes to Pharisees (Mt 23; Lk 11:37–54), Good Shepherd (Jn 10:1–18), Olivet Discourse (Mt 24–25; Mk 13; Lk 21:5–36), Upper Room Discourse (Jn 13–16).

PARABLES: Sower (Mt 13:3–23; Mk 4:3–25; Lk 8:5–18), seed's growth (Mk 4:26–29), wheat and weeds (Mt 13:24–30, 36–43), mustard seed (Mt 13:31–32; Mk 4:30–32), yeast (Mt 13:33; Lk 13:20–21), hidden treasure (Mt 13:44), valuable pearl (Mt 13:45–46), net (Mt 13:47–51), house owner (Mt 13:52), good Samaritan (Lk 10:25–37), unmerciful servant (Mt 18:15–35), lost sheep (Mt 18:10–14; Lk 15:4–7), lost coin (Lk 15:8–10), prodigal son (Lk 15:11–32), dishonest manager (Lk 16:1–13), rich man and Lazarus (Lk 16:19–31), persistent widow (Lk 18:1–8), Pharisee and tax collector (Lk 18:9–14), payment of workers (Mt 20:1–16), tenants and the vineyard (Mt 21:28–46; Mt 12:1–12; Lk 20:9–19), wedding banquet (Mt 22:1–14), faithful servant (Mt 24:45–51), ten virgins (Mt 25:1–13), talents (Mt 25:1–30; Lk 19:12–27).

DISCIPLES: Call (Jn 1:35–51; Mt 4:18–22; 9:9; Mk 1:16–20; 2:13–14; Lk 5:1–11, 27–28). Named Apostles (Mk 3:13–19; Lk 6:12–16). Twelve sent out (Mt 10; Mk 6:7–11; Lk 9:1–5). Seventy sent out (Lk 10:1–24). Defection of (Jn 6:60–71; Mt 26:56; Mk 14:50–52). Final commission (Mt 28:16–20; Jn 21:15–23; Ac 1:3–8).See also APOSTLES.

Ac   2:32 God has raised this J to life, and we
      9: 5 Saul asked. "I am J, whom you are
      9:34 said to him, "J Christ heals you.
     15:11 of our Lord J that we are saved,
     16:31 "Believe in the Lord J, and you will
     20:24 the task the Lord J has given me—
Ro   3:24 redemption that came by Christ J.
      5:17 life through the one man, J Christ!

Ro   8: 1 for those who are in Christ J,
1Co   1: 7 for our Lord J Christ to be revealed.
      2: 2 I was with you except J Christ
      6:11 in the name of the Lord J Christ
      8: 6 and there is but one Lord, J Christ,
     12: 3 Spirit of God says, "J be cursed,"
     12: 3 and no one can say, "J is Lord,"
2Co   4: 5 but J Christ as Lord, and ourselves
     13: 5 Do you not realize that Christ J is
Gal   2:16 of the law, but by faith in J Christ.
      2:16 in Christ J that we may be justified
      3:28 for you are all one in Christ J.
      5: 6 in Christ J neither circumcision nor
      6:17 I bear on my body the marks of J.
Eph   1: 5 to sonship through J Christ,
      2:10 in Christ J to do good works,
      2:20 with Christ J himself as the chief
Php   1: 6 completion until the day of Christ J.
      2: 5 have the same mindset as Christ J:
      2:10 name of J every knee should bow,
Col   3:17 do it all in the name of the Lord J,
1Th   1:10 J, who rescues us from the coming
      4:14 For we believe that J died and rose
      4:14 with J those who have fallen asleep
      5:23 at the coming of our Lord J Christ.
2Th   1: 7 happen when the Lord J is revealed
      2: 1 the coming of our Lord J Christ
1Ti   1:15 Christ J came into the world to save
2Ti   1:10 Christ J, who has destroyed death
      2: 3 like a good soldier of Christ J.
      3:12 life in Christ J will be persecuted,
Titus 2:13 our great God and Savior, J Christ,
Heb   2: 9 But we do see J, who was made
      2:11 So J is not ashamed to call them
      3: 1 fix your thoughts on J, whom we
      3: 3 J has been found worthy of greater
      4:14 into heaven, J the Son of God, let us
      6:20 where our forerunner, J, has entered
      7:22 J has become the guarantor
      7:24 but because J lives forever, he has
      8: 6 fact the ministry J has received is as
     12: 2 fixing our eyes on J, the pioneer
     12:24 to J the mediator of a new covenant,
     13: 8 J Christ is the same yesterday
1Pe   1: 3 through the resurrection of J Christ
2Pe   1:16 of our Lord J Christ in power,
1Jn   1: 7 another, and the blood of J, his Son,
      2: 1 J Christ, the Righteous One.
      2: 6 to live in him must live as J did.
      4:15 acknowledges that J is the Son
Rev   1: 1 The revelation from J Christ,
     12:17 hold fast their testimony about J.
     17: 6 of those who bore testimony to J.
     22:16 "I, J, have sent my angel to give
     22:20 Amen. Come, Lord J.

CHRIST JESUS Ac 24:24; Ro 1:1; 3:24; 6:3, 11, 23; 8:1, 2, 34, 39; 15:5, 16, 17; 16:3; 1Co 1:1, 2, 4, 30; 4:15, 17; 15:31; 16:24; 2Co 1:1; 13:5; Gal 2:4, 16; 3:14, 26, 28; 4:14; 5:6, 24; Eph 1:1, 1; 2:6, 7, 10, 13, 20; 3:1, 6, 11, 21; Php 1:1, 1, 6, 8, 26; 2:5; 3:3, 8, 12, 14; 4:7, 19, 21; Col 1:1, 4; 2:6; 4:12; 1Th 2:14; 5:18; 1Ti 1:1, 1, 2, 12, 14, 15, 16; 2:5; 3:13; 4:6;

5:21; 6:13; 2Ti 1:1, 1, 2, 9, 10, 13; 2:1, 3, 10; 3:12, 15; 4:1; Titus 1:4; Phm 1:1, 9, 23

JESUS CHRIST Jn 1:17; 17:3; Ac 2:38; 3:6; 4:10; 8:12; 9:34; 10:36, 48; 11:17; 15:26; 16:18; 28:31; Ro 1:4, 6, 7, 8; 2:16; 3:22; 5:1, 11, 15, 17, 21; 7:25; 13:14; 15:6, 30; 16:25, 27; 1Co 1:2, 3, 7, 8, 9, 10; 2:2; 3:11; 6:11; 8:6; 15:57; 2Co 1:2, 3, 19; 4:5; 8:9; 13:14; Gal 1:1, 3, 12; 2:16; 3:1, 22; 6:14, 18; Eph 1:2, 3, 5, 17; 5:20; 6:23, 24; Php 1:2, 11, 19; 2:11, 21; 3:20; 4:23; Col 1:3; 1Th 1:1, 3; 5:9, 23, 28; 2Th 1:1, 2, 12; 2:1, 14, 16; 3:6, 12, 18; 1Ti 6:3, 14; 2Ti 2:8; Titus 1:1; 2:13; 3:6; Phm 1:3, 25; Heb 10:10; 13:8, 21; Jas 1:1; 2:1; 1Pe 1:1, 2, 3, 3, 7, 13; 2:5; 3:21; 4:11; 2Pe 1:1, 1, 8, 11, 14, 16; 2:20; 3:18; 1Jn 1:3; 2:1; 3:16, 23; 4:2; 5:6, 20; 2Jn 1:3, 7; Jude 1:1, 1, 4, 17, 21, 25; Rev 1:1, 2, 5

JESUS ... MESSIAH Mt 1:1, 16, 18; 27:17, 22; Mk 1:1; Jn 9:22; 20:31; Ac 5:42; 9:22; 18:5, 28

JESUS OF NAZARETH Mt 26:71; Mk 1:24; 10:47; Lk 4:34; 18:37; 24:19; Jn 1:45; 18:5, 7; Ac 2:22; 6:14; 10:38; 22:8; 26:9

LORD JESUS Mk 16:19; Lk 24:3; Ac 1:21; 4:33; 7:59; 8:16; 11:17, 20; 15:11, 26; 16:31; 19:5, 13, 17; 20:21, 24, 35; 21:13; 28:31; Ro 1:7; 5:1, 11; 13:14; 14:14; 15:6, 30; 16:20; 1Co 1:2, 3, 7, 8, 10; 5:3, 4; 6:11; 8:6; 11:23; 15:57; 16:23; 2Co 1:2, 3, 14; 4:14; 8:9; 11:31; 13:14; Gal 1:3; 6:14, 18; Eph 1:2, 3, 15, 17; 5:20; 6:23, 24; Php 1:2; 2:19; 3:20; 4:23; Col 1:3; 3:17; 1Th 1:1, 3; 2:15, 19; 3:11, 13; 4:1, 2; 5:9, 23, 28; 2Th 1:1, 2, 7, 8, 12, 12; 2:1, 8, 14, 16; 3:6, 12, 18; 1Ti 6:3, 14; Phm 1:3, 5, 25; Heb 13:20; Jas 1:1; 2:1; 1Pe 1:3; 2Pe 1:8, 14, 16; Jude 1:17, 21; Rev 22:20, 21

LORD JESUS CHRIST Ac 11:17; 15:26; 28:31; Ro 1:7; 5:1, 11; 13:14; 15:6, 30; 1Co 1:2, 3, 7, 8, 10; 6:11; 15:57; 2Co 1:2, 3; 8:9; 13:14; Gal 1:3; 6:14, 18; Eph 1:2, 3, 17; 5:20; 6:23, 24; Php 1:2; 3:20; 4:23; Col 1:3; 1Th 1:1, 3; 5:9, 23, 28; 2Th 1:1, 2, 12; 2:1, 14, 16; 3:6, 12, 18; 1Ti 6:3, 14; Phm 1:3, 25; Jas 1:1; 2:1; 1Pe 1:3; 2Pe 1:8, 14, 16; Jude 1:17, 21

NAME OF JESUS See NAME

JESUS' JESUS
Mt   27:58 he asked for J body, and Pilate
Lk   8:35 sitting at J feet, dressed and in his
Jn   12:41 said this because he saw J glory
     19:34 of the soldiers pierced J side
Ac   3:16 It is J name and the faith
2Co   4: 5 as your servants for J sake.

JETHRO*
Father-in-law and adviser of Moses (Ex 3:1; 4:18; 18). Also known as Reuel (Ex 2:18).

JEW JEWISH, JEWS, JEWS', JUDAISM
Est   2: 5 the citadel of Susa of the tribe
     10: 3 Mordecai the J was second in rank
Zec   8:23 take firm hold of one J by the hem
Jn   4: 9 "You are a J and I am a Samaritan
     18:35 "Am I a J?" Pilate replied.

Ac   21:39 "I am a J, from Tarsus in Cilicia,
Ro   1:16 first to the J, then to the Gentile.
      2: 9 first for the J, then for the Gentile;
      2:29 a person is a J who is one inwardly;
     10:12 For there is no difference between J
1Co   9:20 To the Jews I became like a J,
Gal   2:14 "You are a J, yet you live like a Gentile and not like a J.
      3:28 There is neither J nor Gentile,
Col   3:11 Here there is no Gentile or J,

JEWEL* JEWELRY, JEWELS
Pr   20:15 that speak knowledge are a rare j.
SS   4: 9 eyes, with one j of your necklace.
Isa 13:19 Babylon, the j of kingdoms,
Rev 21:11 was like that of a very precious j,

JEWELRY JEWEL
Ex   35:22 and brought gold j of all kinds:
Jer   2:32 Does a young woman forget her j,
Eze 16:11 I adorned you with j: I put bracelets
1Pe   3: 3 the wearing of gold j or fine clothes.

JEWELS JEWEL
Job 28:17 it, nor can it be had for j of gold.
Isa 54:12 your gates of sparkling j, and all
     61:10 as a bride adorns herself with her j.
Zec   9:16 sparkle in his land like j in a crown.

JEWISH JEW
Ezr   6: 7 the J elders rebuild this house
Ne   1: 2 them about the J remnant that had
Jn   3: 1 a member of the J ruling council.
     11:51 Jesus would die for the J nation,
Ac   13: 6 There they met a J sorcerer
     16: 1 whose mother was J and a believer
     24:24 with his wife Drusilla, who was J.
Gal   2:14 force Gentiles to follow J customs?

JEWS JEW
Ezr   5: 5 watching over the elders of the J,
Ne   4: 1 He ridiculed the J,
Est   3:13 kill and annihilate all the J—
      4:14 deliverance for the J will arise
     10: 3 preeminent among the J, and held
     10: 3 spoke up for the welfare of all the J.
Da   3: 8 came forward and denounced the J.
Mt   2: 2 who has been born king of the J?
     27:11 him, "Are you the king of the J?"
     27:37 THIS IS JESUS, THE KING OF THE J.
Jn   4: 9 (For J do not associate
      4:22 do know, for salvation is from the J.
     19: 3 saying, "Hail, king of the J!"
     19:21 "Do not write 'The King of the J,'
     19:21 man claimed to be king of the J."
Ac   17: 4 Some of the J were persuaded
     20:21 I have declared to both J
     21:20 many thousands of J have believed,
Ro   3:29 Or is God the God of J only?
      9:24 not only from the J
     15:27 they owe it to the J to share
1Co   1:22 J demand signs and Greeks look
      9:20 To the J I became like a Jew, to win the J.
     12:13 whether J or Gentiles,

1Th 2:14 those churches suffered from the J
Rev 2: 9 slander of those who say they are J
     3: 9 claim to be J though they are not,

KING OF THE JEWS See KING

JEWS'* JEW
Ro 15:27 shared in the J spiritual blessings,

JEZEBEL*
Sidonian wife of Ahab (1Ki 16:31). Promoted Baal worship (1Ki 16:32–33). Killed prophets of the LORD (1Ki 18:4, 13). Opposed Elijah (1Ki 19:1–2). Had Naboth killed (1Ki 21). Death prophesied (1Ki 21:17–24). Killed by Jehu (2Ki 9:30–37). Metaphor of immorality (Rev 2:20).

JEZREEL JEZREELITE
1Ki 21:23 devour Jezebel by the wall of J.'
2Ki 9:36 J dogs will devour Jezebel's flesh.
    10: 7 baskets and sent them to Jehu in J.
Hos 1: 4 house of Jehu for the massacre at J,
     1:11 land, for great will be the day of J.
     2:22 olive oil, and they will respond to J.

JEZREELITE JEZREEL
1Ki 21: 1 vineyard belonging to Naboth the J.
2Ki 9:25 field that belonged to Naboth the J.

JOAB
Nephew of David (1Ch 2:16). Commander of his army (2Sa 8:16). Victorious over Ammon (2Sa 10; 1Ch 19), Rabbah (2Sa 11; 1Ch 20), Jerusalem (1Ch 11:6), Absalom (2Sa 18), Sheba (2Sa 20). Killed Abner (2Sa 3:22–39), Amasa (2Sa 20:1–13). Numbered David's army (2Sa 24; 1Ch 21). Sided with Adonijah (1Ki 1:17, 19). Killed by Benaiah (1Ki 2:5–6, 28–35).

JOANNA*
Lk 8: 3 J the wife of Chuza, the manager
   24:10 It was Mary Magdalene, J,

JOASH JEHOASH
1. Son of Ahaziah; king of Judah. Sheltered from Athaliah by Jehoiada (2Ki 11; 2Ch 22:10—23:21). Repaired temple (2Ki 12; 2Ch 24).
2. See JEHOASH.

JOB
Wealthy man from Uz; feared God (Job 1:1–5). Integrity tested by disaster (Job 1:6–22), personal affliction (Job 2). Maintained innocence in debate with three friends (Job 3–31), Elihu (Job 32–37). Rebuked by the LORD (Job 38–41). Vindicated and restored to greater stature by the LORD (Job 42). Example of righteousness (Eze 14:14, 20).

JOCHEBED*
Mother of Moses and Aaron (Ex 6:20; Nu 26:59).

JOEL
1. Son of Samuel (1Sa 8:2; 1Ch 6:28).
2. Prophet (Joel 1:1; Ac 2:16).

JOHANAN
1. First high priest in Solomon's temple (1Ch 6:9–10).
2. Jewish leader who tried to save Gedaliah from assassination (Jer 40:13–14); took Jews, including Jeremiah, to Egypt (Jer 40–43).

JOHN
1. Son of Zechariah and Elizabeth (Lk 1). Called the Baptist (Mt 3:1–12; Mk 1:2–8). Witness to Jesus (Mt 3:11–12; Mk 1:7–8; Lk 3:15–18; Jn 1:6–35; 3:27–30; 5:33–36). Doubts about Jesus (Mt 11:2–6; Lk 7:18–23). Arrest (Mt 4:12; Mk 1:14). Execution (Mt 14:1–12; Mk 6:14–29; Lk 9:7–9). Ministry compared to Elijah (Mt 11:7–19; Mk 9:11–13; Lk 7:24–35).
2. Apostle; brother of James (Mt 4:21–22; 10:2; Mk 3:17; Lk 5:1–10). At transfiguration (Mt 17:1–13; Mk 9:1–13; Lk 9:28–36). Desire to be greatest (Mk 10:35–45). Leader of church at Jerusalem (Ac 4:1–3; Gal 2:9). Elder who wrote epistles (2Jn 1; 3Jn 1). Prophet who wrote Revelation (Rev 1:1; 22:8).
3. Cousin of Barnabas, co-worker with Paul, (Ac 12:12—13:13; 15:37; see MARK).

JOIN JOINED, JOINS
Ex   1:10 war breaks out, will j our enemies,
Ne 10:29 all these now j their fellow Israelites
Pr 23:20 Do not j those who drink too much
   24:21 do not j with rebellious officials,
Jer 3:18 the people of Judah will j the people
Eze 37:17 J them together into one stick so
Da 11:34 who are not sincere will j them.
Ac   5:13 No one else dared j them,
     9:26 he tried to j the disciples, but they
Ro 15:30 to j me in my struggle by praying
2Ti 1: 8 j with me in suffering
     2: 3 J with me in suffering, like a good
1Pe 4: 4 you do not j them in their reckless,

JOINED JOIN
1Sa 10:10 him, and he j in their prophesying.
Hos 4:17 Ephraim is j to idols;
Zec 2:11 "Many nations will be j
Mt 19: 6 Therefore what God has j together,
Mk 10: 9 Therefore what God has j together,
Ac   1:14 They all j together constantly
Eph 2:21 him the whole building is j together
     4:16 body, j and held together by every

JOINS* JOIN
Hos 7: 5 and he j hands with the mockers
1Co 16:16 to everyone who j in the work

JOINT* JOINTS
Job 31:22 shoulder, let it be broken off at the j.
Ps 22:14 water, and all my bones are out of j.

JOINTS* JOINT
Heb 4:12 soul and spirit, j and marrow;

JOKING*
Ge 19:14 his sons-in-law thought he was j.
Pr 26:19 neighbor and says, "I was only j!"

Eph   5: 4 foolish talk or coarse j, which are

JONADAB   See also JEHONADAB
2Sa 13: 3 J was a very shrewd man.

JONAH
Prophet in days of Jeroboam II (2Ki 14:25). Called to Nineveh; fled to Tarshish (Jnh 1:1–3). Cause of storm; thrown into sea (Jnh 1:4–16). Swallowed by fish (Jnh 1:17). Prayer (Jnh 2). Preached to Nineveh (Jnh 3). Attitude reproved by the LORD (Jnh 4). Sign of (Mt 12:39–41; Lk 11:29–32).

JONATHAN
Son of Saul (1Sa 13:16; 1Ch 8:33). Valiant warrior (1Sa 13–14). Relation to David (1Sa 18:1–4; 19–20; 23:16–18). Killed at Gilboa (1Sa 31). Mourned by David (2Sa 1).

JOPPA
2Ch   2:16 float them as rafts by sea down to J.
Ezr   3: 7 logs by sea from Lebanon to J,
Jnh   1: 3 He went down to J, where he found
Ac   9:43 Peter stayed in J for some time

JORAM
1. Son of Ahab; king of Israel. With Jehoshaphat fought against Moab (2Ki 3). Killed with Ahaziah by Jehu (2Ki 8:25–29; 9:14–26; 2Ch 22:5–9).

2. See JEHORAM.

JORDAN
Ge   13:10 the J toward Zoar was well watered,
Nu   22: 1 and camped along the J across
        34:12 boundary will go down along the J
Dt   1: 1 in the wilderness east of the J—
        3:27 you are not going to cross this J.
Jos   1: 2 cross the J River into the land I am
        3:11 all the earth will go into the J ahead
        3:17 stopped in the middle of the J
        4: 8 stones from the middle of the J,
        4:22 'Israel crossed the J on dry ground.'
        23: 4 between the J
2Ki   2: 7 and Elisha had stopped at the J.
        2:13 back and stood on the bank of the J.
        5:10 wash yourself seven times in the J,
        6: 4 They went to the J and began to cut
Ps 114: 3 looked and fled, the J turned back;
Isa   9: 1 the Way of the Sea, beyond the J—
Jer 12: 5 you manage in the thickets by the J?
Mt   3: 6 were baptized by him in the J River.
        4:15 the Sea, beyond the J,
Mk   1: 9 and was baptized by John in the J.
Jn   1:28 Bethany on the other side of the J,

JOSEPH   BARNABAS, JUSTUS
1. Son of Jacob by Rachel (Ge 30:24; 1Ch 2:2). Favored by Jacob, hated by brothers (Ge 37:3–4). Dreams (Ge 37:5–11). Sold by brothers (Ge 37:12–36). Served Potiphar; imprisoned by false accusation (Ge 39). Interpreted dreams of Pharaoh's servants (Ge 40), of Pharaoh (Ge 41:4–40). Made greatest in Egypt (Ge 41:41–57). Sold grain to brothers (Ge 42–45). Brought Jacob and sons

to Egypt (Ge 46–47). Sons Ephraim and Manasseh blessed (Ge 48). Blessed (Ge 49:22–26; Dt 33:13–17). Death (Ge 50:22–26; Ex 13:19; Heb 11:22). 12,000 from (Rev 7:8).

2. Husband of Mary mother of Jesus (Mt 1:16–24; 2:13–19; Lk 1:27; 2; Jn 1:45).

3. Disciple from Arimathea, who gave his tomb for Jesus' burial (Mt 27:57–61; Mk 15:43–47; Lk 23:50–52).

4. Disciple, also known as Barsabbas and Justus, proposed as a replacement for Judas (Ac 1:23).

5. Original name of Barnabas (Ac 4:36).

JOSHUA   HOSHEA
1. Son of Nun; name changed from Hoshea (Nu 13:8, 16; 1Ch 7:27). Fought Amalekites under Moses (Ex 17:9–14). Servant of Moses on Sinai (Ex 24:13; 32:17). Spied Canaan (Nu 13). With Caleb, allowed to enter land (Nu 14:6, 30). Succeeded Moses (Dt 1:38; 31:1–8; 34:9).

Charged Israel to conquer Canaan (Jos 1). Crossed Jordan (Jos 3–4). Circumcised sons of wilderness wanderings (Jos 5). Conquered Jericho (Jos 6), Ai (Jos 7–8), five kings at Gibeon (Jos 10:1–28), southern Canaan (Jos 10:29–43), northern Canaan (Jos 11–12). Defeated at Ai (Jos 7). Deceived by Gibeonites (Jos 9). Renewed covenant (Jos 8:30–35; 24:1–27). Divided land among tribes (Jos 13–22). Last words (Jos 23). Death (Jos 24:28–31).

2. High priest during rebuilding of temple (Hag 1–2; Zec 3:1–9; 6:11).
Ezr   4: 3 J and the rest of the heads
        10:18 the descendants of J son of Jozadak,
Ne   12: 1 son of Shealtiel and with J:

JOSIAH
Son of Amon; king of Judah (2Ki 21:26; 1Ch 3:14). Prophesied (1Ki 13:2). Book of the Law discovered during his reign (2Ki 22; 2Ch 34:14–31). Reforms (2Ki 23:1–25; 2Ch 34:1–13; 35:1–19). Killed by Pharaoh Neco (2Ki 23:29–30; 2Ch 35:20–27).

JOTHAM
1. Son of Gideon (Jdg 9).

2. Son of Azariah (Uzziah); king of Judah (2Ki 15:32–38; 2Ch 26:21—27:9).

JOURNEY
Ge   24:21 LORD had made his j successful.
Ex   3:18 Let us take a three-day j
Nu   33: 1 the stages in the j of the Israelites
Dt   1:33 who went ahead of you on your j,
        2: 7 has watched over your j through this
Jdg 18: 6 Your j has the LORD's approval."
Ezr   8:21 ask him for a safe j for us and our
Isa 35: 8 The unclean will not j on it;
Mt   25:14 it will be like a man going on a j,
Lk   9: 3 "Take nothing for the j—
Ac   9:27 how Saul on his j had seen the Lord
Ro   15:24 to have you assist me on my j there,

JOY* ENJOY, ENJOYED,
ENJOYMENT, JOYFUL, JOYFULLY,
JOYOUS, OVERJOYED, REJOICE,
REJOICED, REJOICES, REJOICING

Ge	31:27	so I could send you away with j
Lev	9:24	saw it, they shouted for j and fell
Dt	16:15	hands, and your j will be complete.
Jdg	9:19	may Abimelek be your j, and may
1Ch	12:40	and sheep, for there was j in Israel.
	16:27	and j are in his dwelling place.
	16:33	them sing for j before the LORD,
	29:17	j how willingly your people who are
	29:22	drank with great j in the presence
2Ch	30:26	There was great j in Jerusalem,
Ezr	3:12	while many others shouted for j.
	3:13	of the shouts of j from the sound
	6:16	of the house of God with j.
	6:22	they celebrated with j the Festival
	6:22	the LORD had filled them with j
Ne	8:10	for the j of the LORD is your
	8:12	of food and to celebrate with great j,
	8:17	And their j was very great.
	12:43	because God had given them great j.
Est	8:16	it was a time of happiness and j,
	8:17	there was j and gladness among
	9:17	and made it a day of feasting and j.
	9:18	and made it a day of feasting and j.
	9:19	of the month of Adar as a day of j
	9:22	when their sorrow was turned into j
	9:22	the days as days of feasting and j
Job	3:7	may no shout of j be heard in it.
	6:10	my j in unrelenting pain—that I had
	8:21	and your lips with shouts of j.
	9:25	fly away without a glimpse of j.
	10:20	from me so I can have a moment's j
	20:5	brief, the j of the godless lasts
	33:26	will see God's face and shout for j;
	38:7	and all the angels shouted for j?
Ps	4:7	Fill my heart with j when their grain
	5:11	you be glad; let them ever sing for j.
	16:11	you will fill me with j in your
	19:8	are right, giving j to the heart.
	20:5	we shout for j over your victory
	21:1	How great is his j in the victories
	21:6	glad with the j of your presence.
	27:6	tent I will sacrifice with shouts of j;
	28:7	My heart leaps for j, and with my
	30:11	my sackcloth and clothed me with j,
	33:3	play skillfully, and shout for j.
	35:27	delight in my vindication shout for j
	42:4	of the Mighty One with shouts of j
	43:4	God, to God, my j and my delight.
	45:7	by anointing you with the oil of j.
	45:15	Led in with j and gladness,
	47:1	shout to God with cries of j.
	47:5	God has ascended amid shouts of j,
	48:2	its loftiness, the j of the whole earth,
	51:8	Let me hear j and gladness;
	51:12	Restore to me the j of your salvation
	65:8	fades, you call forth songs of j.
	65:13	they shout for j and sing.
	66:1	Shout for j to God, all the earth!

Ps	67:4	the nations be glad and sing for j,
	71:23	My lips will shout for j when I sing
	81:1	Sing for j to God our strength;
	86:4	Bring j to your servant, Lord, for I
	89:12	and Hermon sing for j at your name.
	90:14	that we may sing for j and be glad
	92:4	I sing for j at what your hands have
	94:19	me, your consolation brought me j.
	95:1	let us sing for j to the LORD;
	96:12	all the trees of the forest sing for j.
	97:11	and j on the upright in heart.
	98:4	Shout for j to the LORD,
	98:6	shout for j before the LORD,
	98:8	let the mountains sing together for j;
	100:1	Shout for j to the LORD,
	105:43	his chosen ones with shouts of j;
	106:5	I may share in the j of your nation
	107:22	and tell of his works with songs of j.
	118:15	Shouts of j and victory resound
	119:111	they are the j of my heart.
	126:2	our tongues with songs of j.
	126:3	for us, and we are filled with j.
	126:5	with tears will reap with songs of j.
	126:6	will return with songs of j,
	132:9	your faithful people sing for j.' "
	132:16	faithful people will ever sing for j.
	137:3	tormentors demanded songs of j;
	137:6	not consider Jerusalem my highest j.
	149:5	honor and sing for j on their beds.
Pr	10:1	A wise son brings j to his father,
	10:28	The prospect of the righteous is j,
	11:10	wicked perish, there are shouts of j.
	12:20	those who promote peace have j.
	14:10	and no one else can share its j.
	15:20	A wise son brings j to his father,
	15:21	Folly brings j to one who has no
	15:23	A person finds j in giving an apt
	15:30	in a messenger's eyes brings j
	17:21	there is no j for the parent
	21:15	it brings j to the righteous but terror
	23:24	of a righteous child has great j;
	27:9	and incense bring j to the heart,
	27:11	my son, and bring j to my heart;
	29:3	A man who loves wisdom brings j
	29:6	but the righteous shout for j and are
Ecc	8:15	j will accompany them in their toil
	11:9	let your heart give you j in the days
Isa	9:3	the nation and increased their j;
	12:3	With j you will draw water
	12:6	Shout aloud and sing for j,
	16:9	shouts of j over your ripened fruit
	16:10	J and gladness are taken away
	22:13	But see, there is j and revelry,
	24:11	all j turns to gloom, all joyful
	24:14	raise their voices, they shout for j;
	26:19	in the dust wake up and shout for j—
	35:2	will rejoice greatly and shout for j.
	35:6	and the mute tongue shout for j.
	35:10	everlasting j will crown their heads.
	35:10	Gladness and j will overtake them,
	42:11	Let the people of Sela sing for j;
	44:23	Sing for j, you heavens,
	48:20	Announce this with shouts of j

Isa 49:13 Shout for j, you heavens;
     51: 3 J and gladness will be found in her,
     51:11 everlasting j will crown their heads.
     51:11 Gladness and j will overtake them,
     52: 8 together they shout for j.
     52: 9 Burst into songs of j together,
     54: 1 shout for j, you who were never
     55:12 You will go out in j and be led forth
     56: 7 give them j in my house of prayer.
     58:14 you will find your j in the LORD,
     60: 5 heart will throb and swell with j;
     60:15 pride and the j of all generations.
     61: 3 the oil of j instead of mourning,
     61: 7 land, and everlasting j will be yours.
     65:14 will sing out of the j of their hearts,
     65:18 to be a delight and its people a j.
     66: 5 glorified, that we may see your j!'
Jer   7:34 I will bring an end to the sounds of j
     15:16 they were my j and my heart's
     16: 9 I will bring an end to the sounds of j
     25:10 banish from them the sounds of j
     31: 7 "Sing with j for Jacob;
     31:12 shout for j on the heights of Zion;
     31:13 comfort and j instead of sorrow.
     33: 9 this city will bring me renown, j,
     33:11 the sounds of j and gladness,
     48:33 J and gladness are gone
     48:33 no one treads them with shouts of j.
     48:33 are shouts, they are not shouts of j.
     51:48 them will shout for j over Babylon,
La   2:15 of beauty, the j of the whole earth?"
      5:15 J is gone from our hearts;
Eze   7: 7 is panic, not j, on the mountains.
     24:25 their stronghold, their j and glory,
Joel 1:12 Surely the people's j is withered
      1:16 j and gladness from the house of our
Mt   13:20 word and at once receives it with j.
     13:44 in his j went and sold all he had
     28: 8 afraid yet filled with j, and ran
Mk   4:16 word and at once receive it with j.
Lk   1:14 He will be a j and delight to you,
      1:44 the baby in my womb leaped for j.
      1:58 great mercy, and they shared her j.
      2:10 will cause great j for all the people.
      6:23 "Rejoice in that day and leap for j,
      8:13 ones who receive the word with j
     10:17 The seventy-two returned with j
     10:21 full of j through the Holy Spirit,
     24:41 still did not believe it because of j
     24:52 returned to Jerusalem with great j.
Jn   3:29 and is full of j when he hears
      3:29 That j is mine, and it is now
     15:11 told you this so that my j may be
     15:11 and that your j may be complete.
     16:20 grieve, but your grief will turn to j.
     16:21 because of her j that a child is born
     16:22 and no one will take away your j.
     16:24 receive, and your j will be complete.
     17:13 full measure of my j within them.
Ac   2:28 you will fill me with j in your
      8: 8 So there was great j in that city.
     13:52 the disciples were filled with j
     14:17 of food and fills your hearts with j."

Ac   16:34 filled with j because he had come
Ro   14:17 peace and j in the Holy Spirit,
     15:13 the God of hope fill you with all j
     15:32 so that I may come to you with j,
2Co   1:24 but we work with you for your j,
      2: 3 you, that you would all share my j.
      7: 4 our troubles my j knows no bounds.
      7: 7 so that my j was greater than ever.
      8: 2 trial, their overflowing j and their
Gal   4:27 shout for j and cry aloud, you who
      5:22 But the fruit of the Spirit is love, j,
Php   1: 4 for all of you, I always pray with j
      1:25 for your progress and j in the faith,
      2: 2 then make my j complete by being
      2:29 him in the Lord with great j,
      4: 1 I love and long for, my j and crown,
1Th   1: 6 severe suffering with the j given
      2:19 our j, or the crown in which we will
      2:20 Indeed, you are our glory and j.
      3: 9 in return for all the j we have
2Ti   1: 4 you, so that I may be filled with j.
Phm   1: 7 Your love has given me great j
Heb   1: 9 by anointing you with the oil of j."
     12: 2 the j set before him he endured
     13:17 this so that their work will be a j,
Jas   1: 2 Consider it pure j, my brothers
      4: 9 to mourning and your j to gloom.
1Pe   1: 8 with an inexpressible and glorious j,
1Jn   1: 4 write this to make our j complete.
2Jn   1: 4 It has given me great j to find some
      1:12 face, so that our j may be complete.
3Jn   1: 3 It gave me great j when some
      1: 4 I have no greater j than to hear
Jude 1:24 without fault and with great j—

JOYFUL* JOY

Dt   16:14 Be j at your festival—
1Sa 18: 6 with j songs and with timbrels
1Ki   8:66 j and glad in heart for all the good
1Ch 15:16 to make a j sound with musical
2Ch   7:10 j and glad in heart for the good
Ps   68: 3 may they be happy and j.
    100: 2 come before him with j songs.
Pr   23:25 may she who gave you birth be j!
Ecc   9: 7 and drink your wine with a j heart,
Isa 24: 8 The j timbrels are stilled, the noise
     24: 8 has stopped, the j harp is silent.
     24:11 all j sounds are banished from the
Jer 31: 4 and go out to dance with the j.
Hab   3:18 I will be j in God my Savior.
Zec   8:19 tenth months will become j and glad
     10: 7 Their children will see it and be j;
Ro   12:12 Be j in hope, patient in affliction,
Col   1:12 and giving j thanks to the Father,
Heb 12:22 thousands of angels in j assembly,

JOYFULLY* JOY

Dt   28:47 not serve the LORD your God j
2Ch 20:27 Jerusalem returned j to Jerusalem,
     30:23 seven days they celebrated j.
Ne   12:27 to celebrate j the dedication
Job 39:13 "The wings of the ostrich flap j,
Ps   33: 1 Sing j to the LORD, you righteous;
    145: 7 and j sing of your righteousness.

Lk   15: 5 finds it, he **j** puts it on his shoulders
      19:37 of disciples began **j** to praise God
Heb 10:34 **j** accepted the confiscation of your

JOYOUS* JOY
Est   8:15 the city of Susa held a **j** celebration.

JOZABAD
2Ki 12:21 who murdered him were **J** son
Ezr   8:33 so were the Levites **J** son of Jeshua

JOZADAK
1Ch   6:15 **J** was deported when the LORD
Hag   1:12 Joshua son of **J**, the high priest,

JUBILANT*
1Ch 16:32 let the fields be **j**, and everything
Ps   94: 3 how long will the wicked be **j**?
       96:12 Let the fields be **j**, and everything
       98: 4 earth, burst into **j** song with music;
Hos   9: 1 do not be **j** like the other nations.

JUBILEE
Lev   25:11 The fiftieth year shall be a **j** for you;
       27:17 a field during the Year of **J**,
Nu   36: 4 When the Year of **J** for the Israelites

JUDAH JUDEA, JUDEAN
   1. Son of Jacob by Leah (Ge 29:35; 35:23; 1Ch
2:1). Did not want to kill Joseph (Ge 37:26–27).
Among Canaanites, fathered Perez by Tamar (Ge
38). Tribe of blessed as ruling tribe (Ge 49:8–12;
Dt 33:7), numbered (Nu 1:27; 26:22), allotted land
(Jos 15; Eze 48:7), failed to fully possess (Jos 15:63;
Jdg 1:1–20).
   2. Name used for people and land of Southern
Kingdom.
Ru   1: 7 take them back to the land of **J**.
2Sa   2: 4 David king over the tribe of **J**.
        5: 5 he reigned over **J** seven years
        5. 5 all Israel and **J** thirty-three years.
       24: 1 and take a census of Israel and **J**."
1Ch 28: 4 He chose **J** as leader,
       28: 4 the tribe of **J** he chose my family,
Ne   6: 7 'There is a king in **J**!'
Isa   1: 1 The vision concerning **J**
        3: 8 Jerusalem staggers, **J** is falling;
Jer   2:28 For you, **J**, have as many gods as
       13:19 All **J** will be carried into exile,
       30: 3 Israel and **J** back from captivity
       31:31 of Israel and with the people of **J**.
La   1: 3 harsh labor, **J** has gone into exile.
Hos   1: 7 Yet I will show love to **J**; and I will
Joel   3: 1 when I restore the fortunes of **J**
Mic   5: 2 you are small among the clans of **J**,
Zec   1:19 are the horns that scattered **J**,
        8:15 to do good again to Jerusalem and **J**.
       10: 4 From **J** will come the cornerstone,
       11:14 breaking the family bond between **J**
Mal   2:11 **J** has been unfaithful.
        2:11 **J** has desecrated the sanctuary
Mt   2: 6 in the land of **J**, are by no means least
             among the rulers of **J**;
Heb   7:14 that our Lord descended from **J**,
        8: 8 of Israel and with the people of **J**.

Rev   5: 5 the Lion of the tribe of **J**, the Root

ISRAEL AND JUDAH See ISRAEL

KING OF JUDAH See KING

KINGS OF JUDAH See KINGS

MEN OF JUDAH Jdg 1:3, 8, 17, 19; 2Sa 2:4;
19:14, 15, 16, 41, 42, 43, 43; 20:2, 4; 2Ki 25:25;
2Ch 13:15; 14:13; 16:6; 20:13, 24, 27; 23:8; Ezr
10:9; Ne 13:23; Jer 17:25; 41:3

PEOPLE OF JUDAH Nu 2:3; Jos 14:6; 15:12,
63; 18:14; Jdg 1:16; 15:10; 2Sa 1:18; 2:7; 1Ki 4:20;
2Ki 14:21; 16:6; 23:2; 1Ch 2:10; 4:27; 2Ch 13:18;
20:4, 18; 25:5; 26:1; 32:9; 34:9, 30; Ezr 4:4, 6; Ne
4:16; 11:25; 13:16; Isa 5:3, 7; 11:12; 22:21; Jer 3:18;
4:3, 4; 5:11; 7:2, 30; 11:2, 9; 12:14; 13:11; 17:20;
18:11; 25:1, 2; 26:18; 31:31; 32:32; 35:13; 36:3, 6,
31; 44:24; 50:4, 33; Eze 4:6; 8:17; 25:3; Da 9:7; Hos
1:11; 5:12; Joel 3:6, 8, 19; Ob 1:12; Zep 2:7; Zec
10:3; Heb 8:8

TRIBE OF JUDAH Ex 31:2; 35:30; 38:22; Nu
1:27; 7:12; 13:6; 34:19; Jos 7:1, 18; 15:1, 20, 21; 2Sa
2:4, 10; 1Ki 12:20; 2Ki 17:18; 1Ch 4:18; 28:4; 2Ch
19:11; Ps 78:68; Rev 5:5; 7:5

JUDAISM* JEW
Ac   2:11 (both Jews and converts to **J**);
        6: 5 from Antioch, a convert to **J**.
       13:43 devout converts to **J** followed Paul
Gal   1:13 of my previous way of life in **J**,
        1:14 I was advancing in **J** beyond many

JUDAS ISCARIOT
   1. Apostle; son of James (Lk 6:16; Jn 14:22; Ac
1:13). Probably also called Thaddaeus (Mt 10:3;
Mk 3:18).
   2. Brother of James and Jesus (Mt 13:55; Mk
6:3), also called Jude (Jude 1).
   3. Christian prophet (Ac 15:22–32).
   4. Apostle, also called Iscariot, who betrayed
Jesus (Mt 10:4; 26:14–56; Mk 3:19; 14:10–50; Lk
6:16; 22:3–53; Jn 6:71; 12:4; 13:2–30; 18:2–11). Suicide of (Mt 27:3–5; Ac 1:16–25).

JUDE*
Jude   1: 1 **J**, a servant of Jesus Christ

JUDEA JUDAH
Mt   2: 1 Jesus was born in Bethlehem in **J**,
        3: 1 preaching in the wilderness of **J**
Mt   24:16 let those who are in **J** flee
Mk   3: 8 many people came to him from **J**,
Lk   1: 5 king of **J** there was a priest named
        3: 1 Pontius Pilate was governor of **J**,
        7:17 about Jesus spread throughout **J**
Ac   1: 8 and in all **J** and Samaria,
        8: 1 apostles were scattered throughout **J**
        9:31 Then the church throughout **J**,
1Th   2:14 imitators of God's churches in **J**,

JUDEAN JUDAH
Mk   1: 5 The whole **J** countryside and all

JUDGE JUDGE'S, JUDGED, JUDGES, JUDGING, JUDGMENT, JUDGMENTS

Ge	16: 5	May the LORD j between you
	18:25	Will not the J of all the earth do
	19: 9	and now he wants to play the j!
	31:53	God of their father, j between us."
Ex	2:14	made you ruler and j over us?
	18:14	Why do you alone sit as j, while all
Lev	19:15	the great, but j your neighbor fairly.
Dt	1:16	between your people and j fairly,
	17: 9	to the j who is in office at that time.
Jdg	2:18	the LORD raised up a j for them,
	2:18	he was with the j and saved them
	11:27	the J, decide the dispute this day
1Sa	2:10	the LORD will j the ends
	3:13	I would j his family forever because
	24:12	May the LORD j between you
1Ki	8:32	J between your servants,
1Ch	16:33	LORD, for he comes to j the earth.
2Ch	6:23	J between your servants,
	19: 7	J carefully, for with the LORD our
Job	9:15	only plead with my J for mercy.
Ps	7: 8	Let the LORD j the peoples.
	7:11	God is a righteous j, a God who
	9: 4	sitting enthroned as the righteous j.
	51: 4	verdict and justified when you j.
	75: 2	it is I who j with equity.
	76: 9	rose up to j, to save all the afflicted
	82: 8	up, O God, j the earth, for all
	94: 2	Rise up, J of the earth; pay back
	96:10	he will j the peoples with equity.
	96:13	he comes, he comes to j the earth.
	96:13	He will j the world in righteousness
	98: 9	LORD, for he comes to j the earth.
	98: 9	He will j the world in righteousness
	110: 6	He will j the nations,
Pr	31: 9	Speak up and j fairly;
Isa	2: 4	He will j between the nations
	3:13	he rises to j the people.
	11: 3	He will not j by what he sees
	33:22	For the LORD is our j, the LORD
Jer	11:20	who j righteously and test the heart
Eze	7: 3	I will j you according to your
	7:27	by their own standards I will j them.
	18:30	I will j each of you according
	20:36	Egypt, so I will j you,
	22: 2	Will you j this city of bloodshed?
	33:20	But I will j each of you according
	34:17	I will j between one sheep
Joel	3:12	there I will sit to j all the nations
Mic	3:11	Her leaders j for a bribe, her priests
	4: 3	He will j between many peoples
Mt	7: 1	"Do not j, or you too will be
Lk	6:37	"Do not j, and you will not be
	12:14	who appointed me a j or an arbiter
	18: 2	there was a j who neither feared
	19:22	'I will j you by your own words,
Jn	5:27	authority to j because he is the Son
	5:30	I j only as I hear, and my judgment
	7:24	but instead j correctly."
	8:16	But if I do j, my decisions are true,
	12:47	keep them, I do not j that person.
Jn	12:47	For I did not come to j the world,
	12:48	There is a j for the one who rejects
	18:31	and j him by your own law."
Ac	7:27	'Who made you ruler and j over us?
	10:42	is the one whom God appointed as j
	17:31	set a day when he will j the world
Ro	2: 1	for at whatever point you j another,
	3: 4	you speak and prevail when you j."
	3: 6	so, how could God j the world?
	14:10	why do you j your brother or sister?
1Co	4: 3	indeed, I do not even j myself.
	4: 5	Therefore j nothing before
	5:12	mine to j those outside the church?
	5:12	Are you not to j those inside?
	6: 2	the Lord's people will j the world?
	6: 3	you not know that we will j angels?
Col	2:16	Therefore do not let anyone j you
2Ti	4: 1	who will j the living and the dead,
	4: 8	the righteous J, will award to me
Heb	10:30	"The Lord will j his people."
	12:23	You have come to God, the J of all,
	13: 4	for God will j the adulterer and all
Jas	4:12	There is only one Lawgiver and J,
	4:12	who are you to j your neighbor?
	5: 9	The J is standing at the door!
1Pe	4: 5	to him who is ready to j the living
Jude	1:15	to j everyone, and to convict all
Rev	6:10	until you j the inhabitants
	20: 4	who had been given authority to j.

JUDGE'S* JUDGE

Mt	27:19	Pilate was sitting on the j seat,
Jn	19:13	and sat down on the j seat at a place

JUDGED JUDGE

Ps	9:19	let the nations be j in your presence.
Eze	20:36	As I j your ancestors
	24:14	You will be j according to your
Mt	7: 1	"Do not judge, or you too will be j.
Jn	5:24	will not be j but has crossed over
Ro	2:12	all who sin under the law will be j
1Co	4: 3	I care very little if I am j by you
	10:29	For why is my freedom being j
Jas	2:12	who are going to be j by the law
	3: 1	we who teach will be j more strictly.
	5: 9	brothers and sisters, or you will be j.
Rev	18:20	God has j her with the judgment she
	20:12	The dead were j according to what

JUDGES JUDGE

The Judges of Israel

Judge	Oppressor	Peace	Text
Othniel	Aram	40 years	Jdg 3:7–11
Ehud	Moab	80 years	Jdg 3:12–30
Shamgar	Philistia		Jdg 3:31
Deborah	Canaan	40 years	Jdg 4–5
Gideon	Midian	40 years	Jdg 6–8
Tola		23 years	Jdg 10:1–2
Jair		22 years	Jdg 10:3–5
Jephthah	Ammon	6 years	Jdg 10:6—12:7
Ibzan		7 years	Jdg 12:8–10
Elon		10 years	Jdg 12:11–12

| Abdon | | 8 years | Jdg 12:13–15 |
| Samson | Philistia | 20 years | Jdg 13–16 |

See also each judge by name

Jdg	2:16	Then the LORD raised up j,
Ru	1: 1	In the days when the j ruled,
Job	9:24	of the wicked, he blindfolds its j.
Ps	9: 8	and j the peoples with equity.
	58:11	there is a God who j the earth."
	75: 7	It is God who j: He brings one
Pr	29:14	If a king j the poor with fairness,
Lk	11:19	So then, they will be your j.
Jn	5:22	Moreover, the Father j no one,
Ac	4:19	to you, or to him? You be the j!
Ro	2:16	God j people's secrets through Jesus
1Co	4: 4	It is the Lord who j me.
Heb	4:12	it j the thoughts and attitudes
Jas	4:11	or j them speaks against the law and
		j it.
1Pe	1:17	a Father who j each person's work
	2:23	himself to him who j justly.
Rev	18: 8	mighty is the Lord God who j her.
	19:11	With justice he j and wages war.

JUDGING JUDGE

Dt	1:17	Do not show partiality in j;
Pr	24:23	To show partiality in j is not good:
Isa	16: 5	one who in j seeks justice
Mt	19:28	thrones, j the twelve tribes of Israel.
Jn	7:24	Stop j by mere appearances,
2Co	10: 7	You are j by appearances.
Rev	11:18	The time has come for j the dead,

JUDGMENT JUDGE

Ex	6: 6	arm and with mighty acts of j.
	12:12	and I will bring j on all the gods
Nu	33: 4	the LORD had brought j on their
Dt	1:17	of anyone, for j belongs to God.
	32:41	sword and my hand grasps it in j,
1Sa	25:33	May you be blessed for your good j
Job	24: 1	the Almighty not set times for j?
Ps	1: 5	the wicked will not stand in the j,
	9: 7	he has established his throne for j.
	76: 8	From heaven you pronounced j,
	82: 1	he renders j among the "gods":
	119:66	Teach me knowledge and good j,
	122: 5	There stand the thrones for j,
	143: 2	Do not bring your servant into j,
Pr	3:21	preserve sound j and discretion;
	8:14	Counsel and sound j are mine;
	18: 1	against all sound j starts quarrels.
Ecc	3:17	will bring into j both the righteous
	11: 9	things God will bring you into j.
	12:14	God will bring every deed into j,
Isa	3:14	enters into j against the elders
	28: 6	of justice to the one who sits in j,
	53: 8	oppression and j he was taken away.
	66:16	his sword the LORD will execute j
Jer	2:35	But I will pass j on you because you
	25:31	he will bring j on all mankind
	51:18	when their j comes, they will perish.
Eze	11:10	and I will execute j on you
Da	7:22	pronounced j in favor of the holy

Am	7: 4	Sovereign LORD was calling for j
Hab	1:12	have appointed them to execute j;
Zec	8:16	true and sound j in your courts;
Mt	5:21	who murders will be subject to j.'
	5:22	brother or sister will be subject to j.
	10:15	Gomorrah on the day of j than
	11:24	on the day of j than for you."
	12:36	the day of j for every empty word
	12:41	stand up at the j with this generation
Jn	5:22	but has entrusted all j to the Son,
	5:30	and my j is just, for I seek not
	8:26	"I have much to say in j of you.
	9:39	"For j I have come into this world,
	12:31	Now is the time for j on this world;
	16: 8	about sin and righteousness and j:
	16:11	and about j, because the prince
Ac	24:25	self-control and the j to come,
Ro	2: 1	you who pass j on someone else,
	2: 1	because you who pass j do the same
	2: 2	God's j against those who do such
	5:16	The j followed one sin and brought
	12: 3	rather think of yourself with sober j,
	14:10	will all stand before God's j seat.
	14:13	Therefore let us stop passing j
1Co	7:40	In my j, she is happier if she stays
	11:29	eat and drink j on themselves.
	14:24	of sin and are brought under j by all,
2Co	5:10	we must all appear before the j seat
2Th	1: 5	this is evidence that God's j is right,
1Ti	3: 6	fall under the same j as the devil.
	5:12	Thus they bring j on themselves,
Heb	6: 2	of the dead, and eternal j.
	9:27	to die once, and after that to face j,
	10:27	only a fearful expectation of j
Jas	2:13	because j without mercy will be
	2:13	Mercy triumphs over j.
	4:11	not keeping it, but sitting in j on it.
1Pe	4:17	For it is time for j to begin
2Pe	2: 4	chains of darkness to be held for j;
	2: 9	for punishment on the day of j.
	3: 7	fire, being kept for the day of j
1Jn	4:17	have confidence on the day of j:
Jude	1: 6	everlasting chains for j on the great
Rev	14: 7	because the hour of his j has come.

JUDGMENTS JUDGE

1Ch	16:14	his j are in all the earth.
Jer	1:16	I will pronounce my j on my people
Eze	14:21	Jerusalem my four dreadful j—
Da	9:11	and sworn j written in the Law
Hos	6: 5	then my j go forth like the sun.
Ro	11:33	How unsearchable his j, and his
1Co	2:15	the Spirit makes j about all things,
	2:15	is not subject to merely human j,
Rev	16: 5	"You are just in these j, O Holy
	16: 7	Almighty, true and just are your j."
	19: 2	for true and just are his j.

JUG

| 1Sa | 26:12 | spear and water j near Saul's head, |
| 1Ki | 17:12 | in a jar and a little olive oil in a j. |

JUICE

| Nu | 6: 3 | They must not drink grape j or eat |

JUMPED* JUMPING

Mk 10:50 he j to his feet and came to Jesus.
Jn   21: 7 taken it off) and j into the water.
Ac   3: 8 He j to his feet and began to walk.
     14:10 the man j up and began to walk.
     19:16 the man who had the evil spirit j

JUMPING* JUMPED

Ac   3: 8 walking and j, and praising God.

JUNIA*

Ro   16: 7 Andronicus and J, my fellow Jews

JUNIPER

1Ki   5: 8 in providing the cedar and j logs.
Isa 60:13 to you, the j, the fir and the cypress
Hos 14: 8 I am like a flourishing j;

JUPITER (KJV) See ZEUS

JUST JUSTICE, JUSTIFICATION, JUSTIFIED, JUSTIFIES, JUSTIFY, JUSTIFYING, JUSTLY

Ge   18:19 by doing what is right and j,
Dt   32: 4 are perfect, and all his ways are j.
     32: 4 does no wrong, upright and j is he.
     32:47 They are not j idle words for you—
2Sa   8:15 doing what was j and right for all
1Ch 18:14 doing what was j and right for all
2Ch 12: 6 and said, "The Lord is j."
Ne   9:13 and laws that are j and right,
Job 34:17 Will you condemn the j and mighty
     35: 2 "Do you think this is j? You say,
Ps   37:28 For the Lord loves the j and will
     37:30 and their tongues speak what is j.
     99: 4 in Jacob you have done what is j
     111: 7 of his hands are faithful and j;
     119:121 I have done what is righteous and j;
Pr   1: 3 doing what is right and j and fair;
      2: 8 for he guards the course of the j
      2: 9 will understand what is right and j
      8: 8 All the words of my mouth are j;
      8:15 and rulers issue decrees that are j;
     12: 5 The plans of the righteous are j,
     21: 3 j is more acceptable to the Lord
Isa 32: 7 even when the plea of the needy is j.
     58: 2 They ask me for j decisions
Jer   4: 2 j and righteous way you swear,
     22: 3 Do what is j and right.
     22:15 He did what was right and j, so all
     23: 5 do what is j and right in the land.
     33:15 he will do what is j and right
Eze 18: 5 a righteous man who does what is j
     18:19 Since the son has done what is j
     18:21 decrees and does what is j and right,
     18:25 say, 'The way of the Lord is not j.'
     18:27 and does what is j and right,
     18:29 say, 'The way of the Lord is not j.'
     33:14 their sin and do what is j and right—
     33:16 They have done what is j and right;
     33:17 'The way of the Lord is not j.' But it is
            their way that is not j.
     33:19 and does what is j and right,
     33:20 say, 'The way of the Lord is not j.'

Eze 45: 9 and do what is j and right.
Da   4:37 does is right and all his ways are j.
Lk   8:50 j believe, and she will be healed."
Jn   5:30 and my judgment is j, for I seek not
Ro   3: 8 Their condemnation is j!
      3:26 time, so as to be j and the one who
2Th   1: 6 God is j: He will pay back trouble
Heb   2: 2 received its j punishment,
1Jn   1: 9 he is faithful and j and will forgive
Rev 15: 3 J and true are your ways,
     16: 5 "You are j in these judgments,
     16: 7 true and j are your judgments."
     19: 2 for true and j are his judgments.

JUSTICE* JUST

Ge   49:16 "Dan will provide j for his people
Ex   23: 2 do not pervert j by siding
     23: 6 "Do not deny j to your poor people
Lev 19:15 " 'Do not pervert j; do not show
Dt   16:19 Do not pervert j or show partiality.
     16:20 Follow j and j alone, so that you
     24:17 the foreigner or the fatherless of j,
     27:19 "Cursed is anyone who withholds j;
1Sa   8: 3 and accepted bribes and perverted j.
2Sa 15: 4 and I would see that they receive j."
     15: 6 who came to the king asking for j,
1Ki   3:11 for discernment in administering j,
      3:28 wisdom from God to administer j.
      7: 7 hall, the Hall of J, where he was
     10: 9 he has made you king to maintain j
2Ch   9: 8 to maintain j and righteousness."
Ezr   7:25 to administer j to all the people
Est   1:13 experts in matters of law and j,
Job   8: 3 Does God pervert j?
      9:19 And if it is a matter of j, who can
     19: 7 though I call for help, there is no j.
     27: 2 who has denied me j, the Almighty,
     29:14 j was my robe and my turban.
     31:13 "If I have denied j to any of my
     34: 5 am innocent, but God denies me j.
     34:12 that the Almighty would pervert j.
     34:17 Can someone who hates j govern?
     36: 3 I will ascribe j to my Maker.
     36:17 and j have taken hold of you.
     37:23 in his j and great righteousness,
     40: 8 "Would you discredit my j?
Ps   7: 6 Awake, my God; decree j.
      9:16 Lord is known by his acts of j;
     11: 7 the Lord is righteous, he loves j;
     33: 5 Lord loves righteousness and j;
     36: 6 your j like the great deep.
     45: 4 in the cause of truth, humility and j;
     45: 6 a scepter of j will be the scepter
     50: 6 righteousness, for he is a God of j.
     72: 1 Endow the king with your j, O God,
     72: 2 your afflicted ones with j.
     89:14 j are the foundation of your throne;
     97: 2 j are the foundation of his throne.
     99: 4 The King is mighty, he loves j—
     101: 1 I will sing of your love and j;
     103: 6 and j for all the oppressed.
     112: 5 who conduct their affairs with j.
     140:12 the Lord secures j for the poor
Pr   8:20 righteousness, along the paths of j,

Pr 16:10 and his mouth does not betray j.
    17:23 in secret to pervert the course of j.
    18: 5 and so deprive the innocent of j.
    19:28 A corrupt witness mocks at j,
    21:15 When j is done, it brings joy
    29: 4 By j a king gives a country stability,
    29: 7 The righteous care about j
    29:26 is from the LORD that one gets j.
Ecc 3:16 was there, in the place of j—
     5: 8 in a district, and j and rights denied,
Isa 1:17 Learn to do right; seek j.
     1:21 She once was full of j;
     1:27 Zion will be delivered with j,
     5: 7 And he looked for j, but saw
     5:16 Almighty will be exalted by his j,
     5:23 a bribe, but deny j to the innocent.
     9: 7 and upholding it with j
    10: 2 withhold j from the oppressed of my
    11: 4 with j he will give decisions
    16: 5 one who in judging seeks j
    28: 6 He will be a spirit of j to the one
    28:17 I will make j the measuring line
    29:21 testimony deprive the innocent of j.
    30:18 For the LORD is a God of j.
    32: 1 and rulers will rule with j.
    32:16 The LORD's j will dwell
    33: 5 he will fill Zion with his j
    42: 1 and he will bring j to the nations.
    42: 3 In faithfulness he will bring forth j;
    42: 4 be discouraged till he establishes j
    51: 4 my j will become a light
    51: 5 my arm will bring j to the nations.
    56: 1 "Maintain j and do what is right,
    59: 4 No one calls for j; no one pleads
    59: 8 there is no j in their paths.
    59: 9 So j is far from us,
    59:11 We look for j, but find none;
    59:14 So j is driven back,
    59:15 was displeased that there was no j.
    61: 8 "For I, the LORD, love j;
Jer 5:28 have no limit; they do not seek j.
     9:24 j and righteousness on earth,
    12: 1 would speak with you about your j:
    21:12 " 'Administer j every morning;
La   3:36 to deprive them of j—would not
Eze 22:29 the foreigner, denying them j.
    34:16 I will shepherd the flock with j.
Hos 2:19 betroth you in righteousness and j,
    12: 6 maintain love and j, and wait
Am   2: 7 ground and deny j to the oppressed.
     5: 7 There are those who turn j
     5:10 hate the one who upholds j in court
     5:12 deprive the poor of j in the courts.
     5:15 maintain j in the courts.
     5:24 But let j roll on like a river,
     6:12 But you have turned j into poison
Mic 3: 1 Should you not embrace j,
     3: 8 and with j and might, to declare
     3: 9 who despise j and distort all that is
Hab 1: 4 is paralyzed, and j never prevails.
     1: 4 the righteous, so that j is perverted.
Zep 3: 5 by morning he dispenses his j,
Zec 7: 9 'Administer true j; show mercy

Mal 2:17 them" or "Where is the God of j?"
     3: 5 the foreigners among you of j,
Mt 12:18 he will proclaim j to the nations.
    12:20 out, till he has brought j through
    23:23 j, mercy and faithfulness.
Lk 11:42 you neglect j and the love of God.
    18: 3 'Grant me j against my adversary.'
    18: 5 I will see that she gets j, so that she
    18: 7 will not God bring about j for his
    18: 8 you, he will see that they get j,
Ac   8:33 humiliation he was deprived of j.
    17:31 he will judge the world with j
    28: 4 the goddess J has not allowed him
2Co 7:11 what readiness to see j done.
Heb 1: 8 a scepter of j will be the scepter
    11:33 administered j, and gained what was
Rev 19:11 With j he judges and wages war.

JUSTIFICATION* JUST
Eze 16:52 you have furnished some j for your
Ac 13:39 sin, a j you were not able to obtain
Ro   4:25 sins and was raised to life for our j.
     5:16 many trespasses and brought j.
     5:18 one righteous act resulted in j

JUSTIFIED* JUST
Ps 51: 4 your verdict and j when you judge.
Lk 18:14 the other, went home j before God.
Ro   3:24 all are j freely by his grace through
     3:28 that a person is j by faith apart
     4: 2 in fact, Abraham was j by works,
     5: 1 since we have been j through faith,
     5: 9 Since we have now been j by his
     8:30 those he called, he also j; those he j,
    10:10 heart that you believe and are j,
1Co 6:11 you were j in the name of the Lord
Gal 2:16 that a person is not j by the works
     2:16 Jesus that we may be j by faith
     2:16 works of the law no one will be j.
     2:17 in seeking to be j in Christ, we Jews
     3:11 relies on the law is j before God,
     3:24 came that we might be j by faith.
     5: 4 be j by the law have been alienated
Titus 3: 7 so that, having been j by his grace,

JUSTIFIES* JUST
Ro   3:26 the one who j those who have faith
     4: 5 but trusts God who j the ungodly,
     8:33 God has chosen? It is God who j.

JUSTIFY* JUST
Est 7: 4 such distress would j disturbing
Job 40: 8 you condemn me to j yourself?
Isa 53:11 my righteous servant will j many,
Lk 10:29 But he wanted to j himself, so he
    16:15 "You are the ones who j yourselves
Ro   3:30 who will j the circumcised by faith
Gal 3: 8 that God would j the Gentiles

JUSTIFYING* JUST
Job 32: 2 Job for j himself rather than God.

JUSTLY* JUST
Ps 58: 1 Do you rulers indeed speak j?
   106: 3 Blessed are those who act j,

Jer   7: 5 actions and deal with each other j,
Mic   6: 8 To act j and to love mercy
Lk   23:41 We are punished j, for we are
1Pe   2:23 himself to him who judges j.

JUSTUS* JOSEPH

Ac   1:23 (also known as J) and Matthias.
      18: 7 next door to the house of Titius J,
Col   4:11 Jesus, who is called J, also sends

K

KADESH KADESH BARNEA, MERIBAH KADESH

Nu   20: 1 Desert of Zin, and they stayed at K.
Dt   1:46 And so you stayed in K many days—

KADESH BARNEA KADESH

Nu   32: 8 from K to look over the land.

KEBAR

Eze   1: 1 among the exiles by the K River,
       3:23 the glory I had seen by the K River,
      43: 3 visions I had seen by the K River,

KEDESH

Jos   12:22 the king of K one the king
Jdg   4: 6 son of Abinoam from K in Naphtali

KEDORLAOMER

Ge   14:17 Abram returned from defeating K

KEEP DOORKEEPER, KEEPER, KEEPING, KEEPS, KEPT

Ge   6:19 female, to k them alive with you.
      17: 9 for you, you must k my covenant,
      31:49 "May the LORD k watch between
Ex   15:26 his commands and k all his decrees,
      19: 5 obey me fully and k my covenant,
      20: 6 love me and k my commandments.
Lev   15:31 " 'You must k the Israelites
Nu   6:24 LORD bless you and k you;
Dt   4: 2 k the commands of the LORD your
       5:10 love me and k my commandments.
       6:17 Be sure to k the commands
       7: 9 love him and k his commandments.
       7:12 your God will k his covenant
      11: 1 your God and k his requirements,
      13: 4 K his commands and obey him;
      30:10 your God and k his commands
      30:16 and to k his commands,
Jos   1: 8 K this Book of the Law always
      22: 5 to k his commands, to hold fast
2Sa   7:25 k forever the promise you have
1Ki   8:25 k for your servant David my father
       8:58 to him and k the commands,
2Ki   17:19 even Judah did not k the commands
      23: 3 the LORD and k his commands,
1Ch   29:18 and k their hearts loyal to you.
2Ch   6:14 you who k your covenant of love
      34:31 the LORD and k his commands,
Ne   1: 5 love him and k his commandments,
Job   14:16 my steps but not k track of my sin.
Ps   18:28 You, LORD, k my lamp burning;

Ps   19:13 K your servant also from willful
      37:34 Hope in the LORD and k his way.
      78:10 they did not k God's covenant
     119: 2 Blessed are those who k his statutes
     121: 7 The LORD will k you from all
     141: 3 k watch over the door of my lips.
Pr   4:21 sight, k them within your heart;
       4:24 K your mouth free of perversity;
       7: 2 K my commands and you will live;
       7: 5 They will k you from the adulterous
      12:23 The prudent k their knowledge
      17:28 are thought wise if they k silent,
      30: 8 K falsehood and lies far from me;
Ecc   3: 6 up, a time to k and a time to throw
      12:13 Fear God and k his commandments,
Isa   26: 3 You will k in perfect peace those
      33:15 k their hands from accepting bribes,
      42: 6 I will k you and will make you to be
      46: 8 "Remember this, k it in mind,
      58:13 "If you k your feet from breaking
Jer   16:11 forsook me and did not k my law.
Eze   20:19 decrees and be careful to k my laws.
Da   9: 4 love him and k his commandments,
Am   5:13 Therefore the prudent k quiet
       9: 4 "I will k my eye on them for harm
Mt   10:10 a staff, for the worker is worth his k.
      19:17 to enter life, k the commandments."
Lk   12:35 service and k your lamps burning,
      17:33 tries to k their life will lose it,
Jn   9:16 for he does not k the Sabbath."
      10:24 saying, "How long will you k us
      12:25 in this world will k it for eternal life.
      14:15 "If you love me, k my commands.
      15:10 If you k my commands, you will
Ac   2:24 for death to k its hold on him.
      15: 5 required to k the law of Moses."
      18: 9 k on speaking, do not be silent.
Ro   7:19 not want to do—this I k on doing.
      12:11 but k your spiritual fervor,
      14:22 these things k between yourself
      16:17 K away from them.
1Co   1: 8 He will also k you firm to the end,
2Co   12: 7 in order to k me from becoming
Gal   5:25 let us k in step with the Spirit.
Eph   4: 3 Make every effort to k the unity
2Th   3: 6 to k away from every believer who
1Ti   5:22 the sins of others. K yourself pure.
2Ti   1:13 k as the pattern of sound teaching,
       4: 5 you, k your head in all situations,
Heb   9:20 God has commanded you to k."
      10:26 If we deliberately k on sinning
      13: 1 K on loving one another as brothers
      13: 5 K your lives free from the love
Jas   1:26 and yet do not k a tight rein on their
       2: 8 If you really k the royal law found
       3: 2 able to k their whole body in check.
1Pe   3:10 see good days must k their tongue
2Pe   1: 8 measure, they will k you from being
1Jn   5: 3 is love for God: to k his commands.
       5:21 children, k yourselves from idols.
Jude   1: 6 angels who did not k their positions
       1:21 k yourselves in God's love as you
       1:24 To him who is able to k you

Rev 3:10 **k** you from the hour of trial that is
12:17 those who **k** God's commands
14:12 people of God who **k** his commands
22: 9 and with all who **k** the words of this

KEEPER KEEP
Ge 4: 9 "Am I my brother's **k**?"
Jn 12: 6 as **k** of the money bag, he used

KEEPING KEEP
Ex 20: 8 the Sabbath day by **k** it holy.
Dt 5:12 the Sabbath day by **k** it holy,
6: 2 long as you live by **k** all his decrees
13:18 your God by **k** all his commands
Ps 19:11 in **k** them there is great reward.
119:112 My heart is set on **k** your decrees
Pr 6:24 **k** you from your neighbor's wife,
15: 3 **k** watch on the wicked and the good.
Mt 3: 8 Produce fruit in **k** with repentance.
Lk 2: 8 **k** watch over their flocks at night.
3: 8 Produce fruit in **k** with repentance.
1Co 7:19 **K** God's commands is what counts.
16: 2 of money in **k** with your income,
Jas 4:11 law, you are not **k** it, but sitting
1Pe 3:16 **k** a clear conscience, so that those
2Pe 3: 9 Lord is not slow in **k** his promise,
3:13 in **k** with his promise we are looking

KEEPS KEEP
Ne 1: 5 who **k** his covenant of love
9:32 who **k** his covenant of love, do not
Ps 15: 4 who **k** an oath even when it hurts,
Pr 11:13 but a trustworthy person **k** a secret.
15:21 has understanding **k** a straight
17:24 A discerning person **k** wisdom
19:16 Whoever **k** commandments
k their life,
Isa 56: 2 it fast, who **k** the Sabbath without
56: 2 **k** their hands from doing any evil."
Da 9. 4 who **k** his covenant of love
Jn 7:19 Yet not one of you **k** the law.
14:21 and **k** them is the one who loves me.
1Co 13: 5 angered, it **k** no record of wrongs.
Jas 2:10 For whoever **k** the whole law
1Jn 3: 6 one who lives in him **k** on sinning.
3:24 The one who **k** God's commands
Rev 22: 7 Blessed is the one who **k** the words

KEILAH
1Sa 23: 5 So David and his men went to **K**,
23: 5 and saved the people of **K**.

KENITE
Jdg 1:16 the **K**, went up from the City
4:17 the wife of Heber the **K**,

KEPT KEEP
Ge 4: 2 Now Abel **k** flocks, and Cain
7:17 forty days the flood **k** coming
20:18 for the LORD had **k** all the women
37:11 but his father **k** the matter in mind.
Ex 12:42 Because the LORD **k** vigil
16:33 LORD to be **k** for the generations
Lev 6: 9 the fire must be **k** burning
Nu 17:10 to be **k** as a sign to the rebellious.

Dt 7: 8 you and **k** the oath he swore to your
2Sa 22:22 For I have **k** the ways
2Ki 18: 6 he **k** the commands the LORD had
Ne 9: 8 You have **k** your promise because
Ps 130: 3 LORD, **k** a record of sins, Lord,
Pr 28:18 whose walk is blameless is **k** safe,
28:26 who walk in wisdom are **k** safe.
29:25 trusts in the LORD is **k** safe.
Isa 38:17 In your love you **k** me from the pit
Mt 19:20 "All these I have **k**," the young
2Co 11: 9 I have **k** myself from being a burden
2Ti 4: 7 finished the race, I have **k** the faith.
Heb 13: 4 all, and the marriage bed **k** pure,
1Pe 1: 4 This inheritance is **k** in heaven
2Pe 3: 7 being **k** for the day of judgment
Rev 3: 8 yet you have **k** my word and have
3:10 Since you have **k** my command
9:15 four angels who had been **k** ready

KERNEL* KERNELS
Mk 4:28 the head, then the full **k** in the head.
Jn 12:24 you, unless a **k** of wheat falls

KERNELS KERNEL
Dt 23:25 you may pick **k** with your hands,
Lk 6: 1 them in their hands and eat the **k**.

KETTLES*
Mk 7: 4 the washing of cups, pitchers and **k**.)

KETURAH*
Wife of Abraham (Ge 25:1-4; 1Ch 1:32-33).

KEY KEYS
Isa 22:22 on his shoulder the **k** to the house
33: 6 the LORD is the **k** to this treasure.
Lk 11:52 because you have taken away the **k**
Rev 3: 7 and true, who holds the **k** of David.
9: 1 the star was given the **k** to the shaft
20: 1 having the **k** to the Abyss

KEYS* KEY
Mt 16:19 I will give you the **k** of the kingdom
Rev 1:18 And I hold the **k** of death

KICK*
Ac 26:14 hard for you to **k** against the goads.'

KIDNAPPER* KIDNAPS
Dt 24: 7 them as a slave, the **k** must die.

KIDNAPS* KIDNAPPER
Ex 21:16 "Anyone who **k** someone is to be

KIDRON
2Sa 15:23 The king also crossed the **K** Valley,
Jn 18: 1 disciples and crossed the **K** Valley.

KILION
Ru 1: 5 both Mahlon and **K** also died,

KILL KILLED, KILLING, KILLS
Ge 4:14 and whoever finds me will **k** me."
12:12 they will **k** me but will let you live.
20:11 they will **k** me because of my wife.'
26: 7 of this place might **k** me on account
37:18 reached them, they plotted to **k** him.

Ex	2:15	he tried to **k** Moses, but Moses fled
	4:19	who wanted to **k** you are dead."
	4:23	so I will **k** your firstborn son.' "
1Sa	19: 1	and all the attendants to **k** David.
	20:33	hurled his spear at him to **k** him.
	20:33	that his father intended to **k** David.
1Ki	11:40	Solomon tried to **k** Jeroboam,
Pr	1:32	of the simple will **k** them,
Ecc	3: 3	a time to **k** and a time to heal, a time
Mt	2:13	to search for the child to **k** him."
	10:28	afraid of those who **k** the body but cannot **k** the soul.
	14: 5	Herod wanted to **k** John, but he was
	17:23	They will **k** him, and on the third day
Mk	9:31	They will **k** him, and after three days
	14: 1	to arrest Jesus secretly and **k** him.
Jn	10:10	The thief comes only to steal and **k**
Rev	6: 4	and to make people **k** each other.

KILLED KILL

Ge	4: 8	attacked his brother Abel and **k** him.
Ex	2:12	he **k** the Egyptian and hid him
	13:15	the LORD **k** the firstborn of both
Nu	35:11	who has **k** someone accidentally
1Sa	17:50	down the Philistine and **k** him.
Ne	9:26	They **k** your prophets, who had
Hos	6: 5	I **k** you with the words of my
Mk	8:31	and that he must be **k** and after three
Lk	11:48	they **k** the prophets, and you build
Ac	3:15	You **k** the author of life, but God
	23:12	to eat or drink until they had **k** Paul.
2Co	6: 9	we live on; beaten, and yet not **k**;
Rev	9:18	mankind was **k** by the three plagues
	19:21	The rest were **k** with the sword

KILLING KILL

1Ki	18: 4	While Jezebel was **k** off
Est	3: 6	the idea of **k** only Mordecai.
Ac	8: 1	And Saul approved of their **k** him.

KILLS KILL

Ge	4:15	anyone who **k** Cain will suffer
Lev	24:21	Whoever **k** an animal must make
	24:21	whoever **k** a human being is to be
2Co	3: 6	for the letter **k**, but the Spirit gives

KIND KINDEST, KINDHEARTED, KINDNESS, KINDNESSES, KINDS

Ge	1:24	animals, each according to its **k**."
	6:20	Two of every **k** of bird, of every **k** of animal and of every **k** of creature that
	7: 2	pairs of every **k** of clean animal,
	7: 2	pair of every **k** of unclean animal,
Ex	1:20	So God was **k** to the midwives
2Ch	10: 7	"If you will be **k** to these people
Pr	11:17	Those who are **k** benefit themselves,
	12:25	the heart, but a **k** word cheers it up.
	14:21	blessed is the one who is **k**
	14:31	whoever is **k** to the needy honors
	19:17	Whoever is **k** to the poor lends
Isa	58: 5	Is this the **k** of fast I have chosen,
Da	4:27	by being **k** to the oppressed.
Zec	1:13	So the LORD spoke **k**
Mt	8:27	and asked, "What **k** of man is this?

Lk	6:35	because he is **k** to the ungrateful
Jn	4:23	for they are the **k** of worshipers
1Co	13: 4	Love is patient, love is **k**. It does not
	15:35	what **k** of body will they come?"
Eph	4:32	Be **k** and compassionate to one
2Ti	2:24	but must be **k** to everyone,
Titus	2: 5	to be **k**, and to be subject to their
2Pe	3:11	what **k** of people ought you to be?

KINDEST* KIND

Pr	12:10	the **k** acts of the wicked are cruel.

KINDHEARTED* KIND, HEART

Pr	11:16	A **k** woman gains honor,

KINDLE KINDLED

Jer	15:14	my anger will **k** a fire that will burn

KINDLED KINDLE

Dt	32:22	For a fire will be **k** by my wrath,
Lk	12:49	and how I wish it were already **k**!

KINDNESS KIND

Ge	19:19	you have shown great **k** to me
	21:23	a foreigner the same **k** I have shown
	24:12	and show **k** to my master Abraham.
	24:27	who has not abandoned his **k**
	32:10	I am unworthy of all the **k**
	39:21	he showed him **k** and granted him
	40:14	you, remember me and show me **k**;
	47:29	promise that you will show me **k**
Jos	2:12	that you will show **k** to my family,
	2:12	because I have shown **k** to you.
Ru	1: 8	May the LORD show you **k**, as you have shown **k** to your dead
	2:20	"He has not stopped showing his **k**
1Sa	15: 6	for you showed **k** to all the Israelites
	20: 8	As for you, show **k** to your servant,
	20:14	But show me unfailing **k** like the LORD's **k** as long as
2Sa	2: 6	May the LORD now show you **k**
	9: 3	to whom I can show God's **k**?"
	22:51	he shows unfailing **k** to his
Job	6:14	"Anyone who withholds **k**
Ps	141: 5	that is a **k**; let him rebuke me—
Isa	54: 8	everlasting **k** I will have compassion
Jer	9:24	who exercises **k**,
	31: 3	I have drawn you with unfailing **k**.
Hos	11: 4	I led them with cords of human **k**,
Ac	14:17	He has shown **k** by giving you rain
Ro	2: 4	contempt for the riches of his **k**,
	2: 4	realizing that God's **k** is intended
	11:22	Consider therefore the **k** and
	11:22	but **k** to you, provided that you continue in his **k**.
2Co	6: 6	understanding, patience and **k**;
Gal	5:22	peace, forbearance, **k**, goodness,
Eph	2: 7	expressed in his **k** to us in Christ
Col	3:12	yourselves with compassion, **k**,
Titus	3: 4	But when the **k** and love of God our

KINDNESSES* KIND

Ps	106: 7	they did not remember your many **k**,
Isa	63: 7	I will tell of the **k** of the LORD,
	63: 7	to his compassion and many **k**.

KINDS KIND

Ge	1:11	in it, according to their various **k**."
	1:21	in it, according to their **k**, and every
	1:24	living creatures according to their **k**:
Lev	19:19	" 'Do not mate different **k** of
	19:19	plant your field with two **k** of seed.
	19:19	clothing woven of two **k** of material.
Dt	12:31	they do all **k** of detestable things
Jer	15: 3	"I will send four **k** of destroyers
Da	3: 5	pipe and all **k** of music, you must
Mt	5:11	falsely say all **k** of evil against you
1Co	12: 4	There are different **k** of gifts,
1Ti	6:10	of money is a root of all **k** of evil.
Jas	1: 2	whenever you face trials of many **k**,
1Pe	1: 6	had to suffer grief in all **k** of trials.

KING KING'S, KINGDOM, KINGDOMS, KINGS, KINGSHIP

The Kings of the United Kingdom

Name	Ruled	Dates B.C.
1. Saul	40 years	1050-1010
2. David	40 years	1010-970
3. Solomon	40 years	970-930

The Kings of Israel

Name	Ruled	Dates B.C.
1. Jeroboam I	22 years	930-909
2. Nadab	2 years	909-908
3. Baasha	24 years	908-886
4. Elah	2 years	886-885
5. Zimri	7 days	885
6. Omri	12 years	885-874
7. Ahab	22 years	874-853
8. Ahaziah	2 years	853-852
9. Joram	12 years	852-841
10. Jehu	28 years	841-814
11. Jehoahaz	17 years	814-798
12. Jehoash	16 years	798-782
13. Jeroboam II	41 years	793-753
14. Zechariah	6 months	753
15. Shallum	1 month	752
16. Menahem	10 years	752-742
17. Pekahiah	2 years	742-740
18. Pekah	20 years	752-732
19. Hoshea	9 years	732-722

The Kings (and Queen) of Judah

Name	Ruled	Dates B.C.
1. Rehoboam	17 years	930-913
2. Abijah	3 years	913-910
3. Asa	41 years	910-869
4. Jehoshaphat	25 years	872-848
5. Jehoram	8 years	848-841
6. Ahaziah	1 year	841
7. Queen Athaliah	6 years	841-835
8. Joash	40 years	835-796
9. Amaziah	29 years	796-767
10. Uzziah / Azariah	52 years	792-740
11. Jotham	16 years	750-735
12. Ahaz	16 years	732-715
13. Hezekiah	29 years	715-686
14. Manasseh	55 years	697-642
15. Amon	2 years	642-640
16. Josiah	31 years	640-609
17. Jehoahaz	3 months	609
18. Jehoiakim	11 years	609-598
19. Jehoiachin	3 months	598-597
20. Zedekiah / Mattaniah	11 years	597-586

See also each king by name.

Ge	14:18	Melchizedek **k** of Salem brought
	20: 2	Abimelek **k** of Gerar sent for Sarah
	26: 8	Abimelek **k** of the Philistines looked
Ex	1: 8	Then a new **k**, to whom Joseph
Nu	21:26	the city of Sihon **k** of the Amorites,
	21:33	and Og **k** of Bashan and his whole
	22:10	"Balak son of Zippor, **k** of Moab,
	23:21	the shout of the **K** is among them.
Dt	17:14	"Let us set a **k** over us like all
Jdg	9: 8	said to the olive tree, 'Be our **k**.'
	17: 6	In those days Israel had no **k**;
	18: 1	In those days Israel had no **k**.
	19: 1	In those days Israel had no **k**.
	21:25	In those days Israel had no **k**;
1Sa	8: 5	now appoint a **k** to lead us, such as
	11:15	made Saul **k** in the presence
	12:12	'No, we want a **k** to rule over us'—
	12:12	the LORD your God was your **k**.
	15:11	"I regret that I have made Saul **k**,
	16: 1	I have rejected him as **k** over Israel?
	16: 1	chosen one of his sons to be **k**."
2Sa	2: 4	they anointed David **k** over the tribe
1Ki	1:30	Solomon your son shall be **k**
Ps	2: 6	"I have installed my **k** on Zion,
	10:16	The LORD is **K** for ever and ever;
	24: 7	that the **K** of glory may come in.
	33:16	No **k** is saved by the size of his
	44: 4	You are my **K** and my God,
	47: 7	For God is the **K** of all the earth;
	48: 2	Mount Zion, the city of the Great **K**.
Isa	6: 5	and my eyes have seen the **K**,
	32: 1	a **k** will reign in righteousness
	43:15	One, Israel's Creator, your **K**."
Jer	10:10	he is the living God, the eternal **K**.
	30: 9	their God and David their **k**, whom I
Eze	37:24	servant David will be **k** over them,
Da	2: 4	Then the astrologers answered the **k**,
Hos	3: 5	their God and David their **k**.
Mic	2:13	Their **K** will pass through before
Zep	3:15	The LORD, **k** of Israel,
Zec	9: 9	See, your **k** comes to you,
	14: 9	LORD will be **k** over the whole
Mal	1:14	For I am a great **k**,"
Mt	2: 2	is the one who has been born **k**
	21: 5	'See, your **k** comes to you,
	27:11	him, "Are you the **k** of the Jews?"
	27:37	THIS IS JESUS, THE **K** OF THE JEWS.
Mk	15:32	Let this Messiah, this **k** of Israel,
Lk	19:38	"Blessed is the **k** who comes
	23: 3	Jesus, "Are you the **k** of the Jews?"
Jn	1:49	you are the **k** of Israel."
	12:13	"Blessed is the **k** of Israel!"

Jn 18:37 "You are a **k**, then!" said Pilate.
18:37 answered, "You say that I am a **k**.
19:15 "Shall I crucify your **k**?"
19:15 "We have no **k** but Caesar,"
19:21 "Do not write 'The **K** of the Jews,'
19:21 man claimed to be **k** of the Jews."
Ac 17: 7 saying that there is another **k**,
1Ti 1:17 Now to the **K** eternal, immortal,
6:15 the **K** of kings and Lord of lords,
Heb 7: 1 This Melchizedek was **k** of Salem
Rev 15: 3 true are your ways, **K** of the nations.
17:14 he is Lord of lords and **K** of kings—
19:16 thigh he has this name written: κ

GREAT KING See GREAT

KING OF ASSYRIA 2Ki 15:19, 20, 20, 29; 16:7,
8, 9, 10, 18; 17:3, 4, 4, 5, 6, 24, 26, 27; 18:7, 9, 11,
13, 14, 14, 16, 17, 19, 23, 28, 30, 31, 33; 19:4, 6, 8,
10, 20, 32, 36; 20:6; 23:29; 1Ch 5:6, 26, 26; 2Ch
28:20, 21; 32:1, 7, 9, 10, 11, 22; 33:11; Ezr 4:2;
6:22; Isa 7:17, 20; 8:4, 7; 10:12; 20:1, 4, 6; 36:1, 2,
4, 8, 13, 15, 16, 18; 37:4, 6, 8, 10, 21, 33, 37; 38:6;
Jer 50:17, 18; Na 3:18

KING OF BABYLON 2Ki 20:12, 18; 24:1, 7,
10, 12, 16, 20; 25:1, 6, 8, 8, 11, 20, 22, 23, 24, 27;
2Ch 36:6; Ezr 2:1; 5:12, 13; Ne 7:6; 13:6; Est 2:6;
Isa 14:4; 39:1, 7; Jer 20:4; 21:2, 4, 7, 10; 22:25; 24:1;
25:1, 9, 11, 12; 27:6, 8, 9, 11, 12, 13, 14, 17, 20;
28:2, 3, 4, 11, 14; 29:21, 22; 32:2, 3, 4, 28, 36; 34:1,
2, 3, 7, 21; 35:11; 36:29; 37:1, 17, 19; 38:3, 17, 18,
22, 23; 39:1, 3, 3, 5, 6, 11, 13; 40:5, 7, 9, 11; 41:2,
18; 42:11; 43:10; 44:30; 46:2, 13, 26; 49:28, 30;
50:17, 18, 43; 51:31, 34; 52:3, 4, 9, 10, 12, 12, 15,
26, 31, 34; Eze 17:12; 19:9; 21:19, 21; 24:2; 26:7;
29:18, 19; 30:10, 24, 25, 25; 32:11; Da 1:1; 7:1

KING OF EGYPT Ge 40:1, 1, 5; 41:46; Ex 1:15,
17, 18; 2:23; 3:18, 19; 5:4; 6:11, 13, 27, 29; 14:5, 8;
Dt 7:8; 11:3; 1Ki 3:1; 9:16; 11:18; 14:25; 2Ki 17:4,
7; 18:21; 23:29; 24:7; 2Ch 12:2, 9; 35:20; 36:3, 4;
Isa 36:6; Jer 25:19; 44:30; 46:2, 17; Eze 29:2, 3;
30:21, 22; 31:2; 32:2; Ac 7:10

KING OF ISRAEL 1Sa 24:14; 26:20; 29:3; 2Sa
6:20; 1Ki 15:9, 16, 17, 19, 25, 32; 16:8, 23, 29; 20:2,
4, 7, 11, 13, 21, 22, 28, 31, 32, 40, 41, 43; 21:18;
22:2, 3, 4, 5, 6, 8, 9, 10, 18, 26, 29, 30, 30, 31, 32,
33, 34, 41, 44, 51; 2Ki 3:1, 4, 5, 9, 10, 11, 12, 13,
13; 5:5, 6, 7, 8; 6:9, 10, 11, 12, 21, 26; 7:6; 8:16, 25,
26; 9:21; 13:1, 10, 14, 16; 14:1, 8, 9, 11, 13, 17, 23;
15:1, 8, 17, 23, 27, 29, 32; 16:5, 7; 17:1; 18:1, 9, 10;
21:3; 23:13; 24:13; 1Ch 5:17; 2Ch 8:11; 16:1, 3;
18:3, 4, 5, 7, 8, 9, 17, 19, 25, 28, 29, 29, 30, 31, 32,
33, 34; 20:35; 21:2; 22:5; 25:17, 18, 21, 23, 25; 28:5,
19; 29:27; 30:26; 35:3, 4; Ezr 3:10; 5:11; Ne 13:26;
Pr 1:1; Isa 7:1; Jer 41:9; Hos 1:1; 10:15; Am 1:1;
7:10; Zep 3:15; Mt 27:42; Mk 15:32; Jn 1:49; 12:13

KING OF JUDAH 1Ki 12:23, 27; 15:1, 9, 17,
25, 28, 33; 16:8, 10, 15, 23, 29; 22:2, 10, 29, 41, 51;
2Ki 1:17; 3:1, 7, 9, 14; 8:16, 16, 25, 29; 9:16, 21, 27,
29; 10:13; 12:18; 13:1, 10, 12; 14:1, 9, 11, 13, 15,
17, 23; 15:1, 8, 13, 17, 23, 27, 32; 16:1; 17:1; 18:1,
14, 14, 16; 19:10; 21:11; 22:16, 18; 24:12; 25:27, 27;
1Ch 4:41; 5:17; 2Ch 11:3; 13:1; 16:1, 7; 18:3, 9, 28;
19:1; 20:31, 35; 21:12; 22:1, 6; 25:17, 18, 21, 23, 25;

30:24; 32:8, 9, 23; 34:24, 26; 35:21; Est 2:6; Pr 25:1;
Isa 7:1; 37:10; 38:9; Jer 1:2, 3, 3; 15:4; 21:7; 22:1,
2, 6, 11, 18, 24; 24:1, 8; 25:1, 3; 26:1, 18, 19; 27:1,
3, 12, 18, 20, 21; 28:1, 4; 29:3; 32:1, 3, 4; 34:2, 4, 6,
21; 35:1; 36:1, 9, 28, 29, 30, 32; 37:1, 7; 38:22; 39:1,
4; 44:30; 45:1; 46:2; 49:34; 51:59; 52:31, 31; Da 1:1,
2; Am 1:1; Zep 1:1; Zec 14:5

KING OF KINGS Ezr 7:12; Eze 26:7; Da 2:37;
1Ti 6:15; Rev 17:14; 19:16

KING OF THE JEWS Mt 2:2; 27:11, 29, 37; Mk
15:2, 9, 12, 18, 26; Lk 23:3, 37, 38; Jn 18:33, 39;
19:3, 19, 21, 21

LORD THE KING See KING

KING'S KING

Nu 20:17 We will travel along the **K** Highway
1Sa 18:18 I should become the **k** son-in-law?"
2Sa 9:13 because he always ate at the **k** table;
Pr 21: 1 the LORD's hand the **k** heart is
Ecc 8: 2 Obey the **k** command, I say,
Jer 52:33 his life ate regularly at the **k** table.
Heb 11:23 they were not afraid of the **k** edict.

KINGDOM KING

Ex 19: 6 you will be for me a **k** of priests
Dt 17:18 When he takes the throne of his **k**,
1Sa 13:14 But now your **k** will not endure;
28:17 The LORD has torn the **k**
2Sa 7:12 and blood, and I will establish his **k**.
1Ki 11:31 'See, I am going to tear the **k**
1Ch 17:11 own sons, and I will establish his **k**.
29:11 Yours, LORD, is the **k**;
Ps 45: 6 justice will be the scepter of your **k**.
103:19 in heaven, and his **k** rules over all.
145:13 Your **k** is an everlasting **k**, and your
Isa 9: 7 on David's throne and over his **k**,
Jer 18: 7 that a nation or **k** is to be uprooted,
Eze 29:14 There they will be a lowly **k**.
Da 2:39 "After you, another **k** will arise,
2:39 Next, a third **k**, one of bronze,
2:44 up a **k** that will never be destroyed,
4: 3 His **k** is an eternal **k**;
5:28 Your **k** is divided and given
7:18 of the Most High will receive the **k**
7:27 His **k** will be an everlasting **k**,
Ob 1:21 And the **k** will be the LORD's.
Mt 3: 2 for the **k** of heaven has come near."
4:17 for the **k** of heaven has come near."
4:23 proclaiming the good news of the **k**,
5: 3 spirit, for theirs is the **k** of heaven.
5:10 for theirs is the **k** of heaven.
5:19 be called least in the **k** of heaven,
5:19 be called great in the **k** of heaven.
5:20 you will certainly not enter the **k**
6:10 your **k** come, your will be done,
6:33 But seek first his **k** and his
7:21 Lord,' will enter the **k** of heaven,
8:12 of the **k** will be thrown outside,
9:35 proclaiming the good news of the **k**
10: 7 'The **k** of heaven has come near.'
11:11 in the **k** of heaven is greater than he.
11:12 the **k** of heaven has been subjected
12:25 "Every **k** divided against itself will

Mt	12:28	the **k** of God has come upon you.
	13:11	of the **k** of heaven has been given
	13:19	hears the message about the **k**
	13:24	"The **k** of heaven is like a man who
	13:31	"The **k** of heaven is like a mustard
	13:33	"The **k** of heaven is like yeast
	13:38	seed stands for the people of the **k**.
	13:44	"The **k** of heaven is like treasure
	13:45	the **k** of heaven is like a merchant
	13:47	the **k** of heaven is like a net that was
	13:52	in the **k** of heaven is like the owner
	16:19	you the keys of the **k** of heaven;
	16:28	the Son of Man coming in his **k**."
	18: 1	is the greatest in the **k** of heaven?"
	18: 3	you will never enter the **k** of heaven.
	18: 4	is the greatest in the **k** of heaven.
	18:23	the **k** of heaven is like a king who
	19:12	for the sake of the **k** of heaven.
	19:14	for the **k** of heaven belongs to such
	19:23	who is rich to enter the **k** of heaven.
	20: 1	the **k** of heaven is like a landowner
	20:21	and the other at your left in your **k**."
	21:31	the prostitutes are entering the **k**
	21:43	that the **k** of God will be taken away
	22: 2	"The **k** of heaven is like a king who
	23:13	You shut the door of the **k** of heaven
	24:14	this gospel of the **k** will be preached
	25: 1	time the **k** of heaven will be like ten
	25:34	the **k** prepared for you since
	26:29	it new with you in my Father's **k**."
Mk	1:15	"The **k** of God has come near.
	3:24	If a **k** is divided against itself, that **k** cannot stand.
	4:11	of the **k** of God has been given
	4:26	"This is what the **k** of God is like.
	6:23	I will give you, up to half my **k**."
	9: 1	they see that the **k** of God has come
	9:47	you to enter the **k** of God with one
	10:14	for the **k** of God belongs to such as
	10:15	anyone who will not receive the **k**
	10:23	for the rich to enter the **k** of God!"
	10:24	how hard it is to enter the **k** of God!
	11:10	"Blessed is the coming **k** of our
	12:34	are not far from the **k** of God."
	13: 8	rise against nation, and **k** against **k**.
	14:25	I drink it new in the **k** of God."
	15:43	himself waiting for the **k** of God,
Lk	1:33	his **k** will never end."
	4:43	the good news of the **k** of God
	6:20	are poor, for yours is the **k** of God.
	7:28	in the **k** of God is greater than he."
	8: 1	the good news of the **k** of God.
	8:10	of the **k** of God has been given
	9: 2	them out to proclaim the **k** of God
	9:11	spoke to them about the **k** of God,
	9:27	not taste death before they see the **k**
	9:60	you go and proclaim the **k** of God."
	9:62	is fit for service in the **k** of God."
	10: 9	'The **k** of God has come near
	10:11	The **k** of God has come near.'
	11: 2	be your name, your **k** come.
	11:18	himself, how can his **k** stand?"
	11:20	the **k** of God has come upon you.

Lk	12:31	But seek his **k**, and these things will
	12:32	has been pleased to give you the **k**.
	13:18	asked, "What is the **k** of God like?
	13:29	places at the feast in the **k** of God.
	14:15	eat at the feast in the **k** of God."
	16:16	of the **k** of God is being preached,
	17:20	when the **k** of God would come,
	17:21	is,' because the **k** of God is in your
	18:16	for the **k** of God belongs to such as
	18:24	is for the rich to enter the **k** of God!
	18:29	children for the sake of the **k** of God
	19:11	thought that the **k** of God was going
	21:31	you know that the **k** of God is near.
	22:16	it finds fulfillment in the **k** of God."
	22:18	the vine until the **k** of God comes."
	22:29	And I confer on you a **k**, just as my
	22:30	drink at my table in my **k** and sit
	23:42	me when you come into your **k**."
	23:51	was waiting for the **k** of God.
Jn	3: 3	no one can see the **k** of God unless
	3: 5	no one can enter the **k** of God unless
	18:36	said, "My **k** is not of this world.
Ac	1: 3	days and spoke about the **k** of God.
	1: 6	going to restore the **k** to Israel?"
	8:12	the good news of the **k** of God
	14:22	hardships to enter the **k** of God,"
	19: 8	persuasively about the **k** of God.
	20:25	preaching the **k** will ever see me
	28:23	explaining about the **k** of God,
	28:31	He proclaimed the **k** of God
Ro	14:17	For the **k** of God is not a matter
1Co	4:20	For the **k** of God is not a matter
	6: 9	wrongdoers will not inherit the **k**
	15:24	when he hands over the **k** to God
	15:50	blood cannot inherit the **k** of God,
Gal	5:21	live like this will not inherit the **k**
Eph	2: 2	and of the ruler of the **k** of the air,
	5: 5	any inheritance in the **k** of Christ
Col	1:12	of his holy people in the **k** of light.
	1:13	us into the **k** of the Son he loves,
	4:11	my co-workers for the **k** of God.
1Th	2:12	who calls you into his **k** and glory.
2Th	1: 5	be counted worthy of the **k** of God,
2Ti	4: 1	in view of his appearing and his **k**,
	4:18	bring me safely to his heavenly **k**.
Heb	1: 8	justice will be the scepter of your **k**.
	12:28	since we are receiving a **k**
Jas	2: 5	inherit the **k** he promised those who
2Pe	1:11	into the eternal **k** of our Lord
Rev	1: 6	has made us to be a **k** and priests
	1: 9	companion in the suffering and **k**
	5:10	You have made them to be a **k**
	11:15	"The **k** of the world has become the **k** of our Lord
	12:10	and the power and the **k** of our God,
	16:10	and its **k** was plunged into darkness.
	17:12	kings who have not yet received a **k**,

KINGDOM OF GOD Mt 12:28; 19:24; 21:31, 43; Mk 1:15; 4:11, 26, 30; 9:1, 47; 10:14, 15, 23, 24, 25; 12:34; 14:25; 15:43; Lk 4:43; 6:20; 7:28; 8:1, 10; 9:2, 11, 27, 60, 62; 10:9, 11; 11:20; 13:18, 20, 28, 29; 14:15; 16:16; 17:20, 20, 21; 18:16, 17, 24, 25, 29; 19:11; 21:31; 22:16, 18; 23:51; Jn 3:3, 5; Ac 1:3;

8:12; 14:22; 19:8; 28:23, 31; Ro 14:17; 1Co 4:20; 6:9, 10; 15:50; Gal 5:21; Col 4:11; 2Th 1:5

KINGDOM OF HEAVEN Mt 3:2; 4:17; 5:3, 10, 19, 19, 20; 7:21; 8:11; 10:7; 11:11, 12; 13:11, 24, 31, 33, 44, 45, 47, 52; 16:19; 18:1, 3, 4, 23; 19:12, 14, 23; 20:1; 22:2; 23:13; 25:1

KINGDOMS KING

Dt   3:21 to all the **k** over there where you are
1Ki   4:21 Solomon ruled over all the **k**
2Ki   19:15 you alone are God over all the **k**
      19:19 that all the **k** of the earth may know
2Ch 20: 6 You rule over all the **k**
Ps   68:32 Sing to God, you **k** of the earth,
Isa   37:16 you alone are God over all the **k**
      37:20 that all the **k** of the earth may know
Jer   33:24 has rejected the two **k** he chose'?
Eze   37:22 nations or be divided into two **k**.
Da   2:44 It will crush all those **k** and bring
       4:17 Most High is sovereign over all **k**
Zep   3: 8 to gather the **k** and to pour out my
Lk   4: 5 in an instant all the **k** of the world.
Heb 11:33 who through faith conquered **k**,

KINGS KING

Ge   14: 9 king of Ellasar—four **k** against five.
      17: 6 of you, and **k** will come from you.
Jos   12: 1 These are the **k** of the land whom
2Sa   11: 1 at the time when **k** go off to war,
1Ki   10:23 wisdom than all the other **k**
Ps   2: 2 The **k** of the earth rise
      47: 9 for the **k** of the earth belong to God;
      68:29 at Jerusalem **k** will bring you gifts.
      72:11 May all **k** bow down to him and all
      89:27 most exalted of the **k** of the earth.
     110: 5 he will crush **k** on the day of his
     138: 4 May all the **k** of the earth praise
     149: 8 to bind their **k** with fetters,
Pr   8:15 By me **k** reign and rulers issue
      16:12 **K** detest wrongdoing, for a throne is
      31: 4 it is not for **k** to drink wine,
Isa   24:21 above and the **k** on the earth below.
      52:15 **k** will shut their mouths because
      60:11 their **k** led in triumphal procession.
Da   2:21 he deposes **k** and raises up others.
       2:47 God of **k** and a revealer
       7:17 'The four great beasts are four **k**
       7:24 ten horns are ten **k** who will come
       7:24 he will subdue three **k**.
Lk   10:24 and **k** wanted to see what you see
      21:12 you will be brought before **k**
Ac   4:26 The **k** of the earth rise
1Ti   2: 2 for **k** and all those in authority,
       6:15 the King of **k** and Lord of lords,
Rev   1: 5 and the ruler of the **k** of the earth.
      16:16 they gathered the **k** together
      17: 2 her the **k** of the earth committed
      17:12 you saw are ten **k** who have not yet
      17:14 he is Lord of lords and King of **k**—
      19:16 this name written: KING OF **K** AND
      19:19 I saw the beast and the **k** of the earth
      21:24 the **k** of the earth will bring their

KING OF KINGS See KING

KINGS OF ISRAEL 1Ki 14:19; 15:31; 16:5, 14, 20, 27, 33; 20:31; 22:39; 2Ki 1:18; 8:18; 10:34; 13:8, 12, 13; 14:15, 16, 28, 29; 15:11, 15, 21, 26, 31; 16:3; 17:2, 8; 23:19, 22; 1Ch 9:1; 2Ch 20:34; 21:6, 13; 27:7; 28:2, 27; 33:18; 35:18, 27; 36:8; Mic 1:14

KINGS OF JUDAH 1Sa 27:6; 1Ki 14:29; 15:7, 23; 22:45; 2Ki 8:23; 12:18, 19; 14:18; 15:6, 36; 16:19; 18:5; 20:20; 21:17, 25; 23:5, 11, 12, 22, 28; 24:5; 2Ch 16:11; 25:26; 28:26; 32:32; 34:11; Isa 1:1; Jer 1:18; 17:19, 20; 19:3, 4, 13; 20:5; Hos 1:1; Mic 1:1

KINGS OF THE EARTH 1Ki 10:23; 2Ch 9:22, 23; Ps 2:2; 47:9; 76:12; 89:27; 102:15; 138:4; 148:11; La 4:12; Eze 27:33; Mt 17:25; Ac 4:26; Rev 1:5; 6:15; 17:2, 18; 18:3, 9; 19:19; 21:24

KINGSHIP KING

1Sa   10:25 the people the rights and duties of **k**.
1Ch   11:10 gave his **k** strong support to extend
Mic   4: 8 **k** will come to Daughter

KIRIATH ARBA HEBRON

Ge   23: 2 She died at **K** (that is, Hebron)
      35:27 Isaac in Mamre, near **K** (that is,
Jos   21:11 They gave them **K** (that is, Hebron),

KIRIATH JEARIM

1Sa   7: 1 men of **K** came and took up the ark
1Ch   13: 5 to bring the ark of God from **K**.

KISH

1Sa   10:21 Finally Saul son of **K** was taken.

KISHON

Jdg   5:21 The river **K** swept them away,
Ps   83: 9 to Sisera and Jabin at the river **K**,

KISS KISSED, KISSES, KISSING

Ge   27:26 "Come here, my son, and **k** me."
      31:28 even let me **k** my grandchildren
1Ki   19:20 "Let me **k** my father and mother
Ps   2:12 **K** his son, or he will be angry
      85:10 and peace **k** each other.
Pr   24:26 An honest answer is like a **k**
SS   1: 2 Let him **k** me with the kisses of his
       8: 1 I would **k** you, and no one would
Hos   13: 2 They **k** calf-idols!"
Mt   26:48 "The one I **k** is the man;
Lk   7:45 You did not give me a **k**, but this
      22:48 the Son of Man with a **k**?"
Ro   16:16 Greet one another with a holy **k**.
1Co   16:20 Greet one another with a holy **k**.
2Co   13:12 Greet one another with a holy **k**.
1Th   5:26 all God's people with a holy **k**.
1Pe   5:14 Greet one another with a **k** of love.

KISSED KISS

Ge   29:11 Then Jacob **k** Rachel and began
      33: 4 his arms around his neck and **k** him.
      45:15 And he **k** all his brothers and wept
      50: 1 father and wept over him and **k** him.
Ex   4:27 at the mountain of God and **k** him.
Ru   1: 9 Then she **k** them goodbye and they
1Sa   10: 1 poured it on Saul's head and **k** him,
      20:41 Then they **k** each other and wept

1Ki 19:18 and whose mouths have not **k** him."
Pr 7:13 She took hold of him and **k** him
Mk 14:45 Judas said, "Rabbi!" and **k** him.
Lk 7:38 hair, **k** them and poured perfume

KISSES* KISS
Pr 27: 6 trusted, but an enemy multiplies **k**.
SS 1: 2 kiss me with the **k** of his mouth—

KISSING* KISS
Lk 7:45 I entered, has not stopped **k** my feet.

KNEADING
Dt 28: 5 and your **k** trough will be blessed.
28:17 and your **k** trough will be cursed.

KNEE* KNEES
Isa 45:23 Before me every **k** will bow;
Ro 11: 4 thousand who have not bowed the **k**
14:11 Lord, 'every **k** will bow before me;
Php 2:10 name of Jesus every **k** should bow,

KNEEL KNELT
Est 3: 2 Mordecai would not **k** down or pay
Ps 95: 6 let us **k** before the Lord our
Eph 3:14 For this reason I **k** before the Father,

KNEES KNEE
Jdg 7: 6 the rest got down on their **k** to drink.
1Ki 19:18 all whose **k** have not bowed down
Isa 35: 3 hands, steady the **k** that give way;
Da 6:10 times a day he got down on his **k**
Lk 5: 8 saw this, he fell at Jesus' **k** and said,
Heb 12:12 your feeble arms and weak **k**.

KNELT* KNEEL
2Ch 6:13 **k** down before the whole assembly
7: 3 they **k** on the pavement with their
29:29 everyone present with him **k** down
Est 3: 2 officials at the king's gate **k** down
Mt 8: 2 with leprosy came and **k** before him
9:18 leader came and **k** before him
15:25 The woman came and **k** before him.
17:14 approached Jesus and **k** before him.
27:29 Then they **k** in front of him
Lk 22:41 beyond them, **k** down and prayed,
Ac 20:36 he **k** down with all of them
21: 5 and there on the beach we **k** to pray.

KNEW KNOW
Dt 34:10 whom the Lord **k** face to face,
Jdg 2:10 who **k** neither the Lord nor what
2Ch 33:13 Manasseh **k** that the Lord is God.
Job 23: 3 If only I **k** where to find him;
Pr 24:12 say, "But we **k** nothing about this,"
Jer 1: 5 I formed you in the womb I **k** you,
19: 4 nor the kings of Judah ever **k**,
Jnh 4: 2 I **k** that you are a gracious
Mt 7:23 tell them plainly, 'I never **k** you.
12:25 Jesus **k** their thoughts and said
Lk 4:41 because they **k** he was the Messiah.
Jn 2:24 himself to them, for he **k** all people.
4:10 "If you **k** the gift of God and who it
8:19 "If you **k** me, you would know my
13: 1 Jesus **k** that the hour had come
13:11 For he **k** who was going to betray

Ro 1:21 For although they **k** God,

KNIFE KNIVES
Ge 22:10 hand and took the **k** to slay his son.
Ex 4:25 But Zipporah took a flint **k**, cut off
Pr 23: 2 and put a **k** to your throat if you are

KNIT*
Job 10:11 flesh and **k** me together with bones
Ps 139:13 you **k** me together in my mother's

KNIVES KNIFE
Jos 5: 2 "Make flint **k** and circumcise

KNOCK* KNOCKING, KNOCKS
Mt 7: 7 **k** and the door will be opened
Lk 11: 9 **k** and the door will be opened
Rev 3:20 I stand at the door and **k**.

KNOCKING* KNOCK
SS 5: 2 My beloved is **k**: "Open to me,
Da 5: 6 became weak and his knees were **k**.
Lk 13:25 door, you will stand outside **k**
Ac 12:16 But Peter kept on **k**, and when they

KNOCKS KNOCK
Mt 7: 8 and to the one who **k**, the door will
Lk 11:10 and to the one who **k**, the door will
12:36 and **k** they can immediately open

KNOW FOREKNEW, FOREKNOWLEDGE, KNEW, KNOWING, KNOWLEDGE, KNOWN, KNOWS, WELL-KNOWN
Ge 15: 8 Lord, how can I **k** that I will gain
22:12 Now I **k** that you fear God,
Ex 3:19 I **k** that the king of Egypt will not let
6: 7 you will **k** that I am the Lord
7: 5 the Egyptians will **k** that I am
14: 4 the Egyptians will **k** that I am
18:11 Now I **k** that the Lord is greater
33:12 said, 'I **k** you by name and you have
33:12 teach me your ways so I may **k** you
Nu 16:28 "This is how you will **k**
Dt 7: 9 **K** therefore that the Lord your
8: 2 in order to **k** what was in your heart,
18:21 "How can we **k** when a message
Jos 3: 7 so they may **k** that I am with you as
4:24 of the earth might **k** that the hand
23:14 You **k** with all your heart and soul
1Sa 17:46 the whole world will **k** that there is
1Ki 8:39 since you **k** their hearts (for you
alone **k** every human heart),
Job 11: 6 **K** this: God has even forgotten some
19:25 I **k** that my redeemer lives,
42: 2 "I **k** that you can do all things;
42: 3 things too wonderful for me to **k**.
Ps 9:10 Those who **k** your name trust
14: 4 Do all these evildoers **k** nothing?
36:10 your love to those who **k** you,
46:10 says, "Be still, and **k** that I am God;
73:11 They say, "How would God **k**?
73:11 Does the Most High **k** anything?"
100: 3 **K** that the Lord is God. It is he

Ps	139: 1	me, LORD, and you k me.
	139:23	Search me, God, and k my heart;
	139:23	test me and k my anxious thoughts.
	145:12	that all people may k of your mighty
Pr	27: 1	you do not k what a day may bring.
	30: 4	the name of his son? Surely you k!
Ecc	8: 5	the wise heart will k the proper time
	8:16	I applied my mind to k wisdom
	8:17	Even if the wise claim they k,
Isa	1: 3	but Israel does not k, my people do
	29:15	think, "Who sees us? Who will k?"
	29:16	say to the potter, "You k nothing"?
	40:21	Do you not k? Have you not heard?
	44: 8	there is no other Rock; I k not one."
Jer	4:22	people are fools; they do not k me.
	4:22	they k not how to do good."
	6:15	they do not even k how to blush.
	9:24	have the understanding to k me,
	22:16	Is that not what it means to k me?"
	24: 7	I will give them a heart to k me,
	31:34	say to one another, 'K the LORD,'
	31:34	because they will all k me,
	33: 3	unsearchable things you do not k.'
Eze	2: 5	they will k that a prophet has been
	6:10	they will k that I am the LORD;
Da	11:32	but the people who k their God will
Mt	6: 3	let your left hand k what your right
	7:11	k how to give good gifts to your
	9: 6	I want you to k that the Son of Man
	22:29	because you do not k the Scriptures
	24:42	because you do not k on what day
	26:74	to them, "I don't k the man!"
Mk	12:24	because you do not k the Scriptures
Lk	1: 4	so that you may k the certainty
	11:13	k how to give good gifts to your
	12:48	the one who does not k and does
	13:25	'I don't k you or where you come
	18:20	You k the commandments:
	21:31	you k that the kingdom of God is
	22:34	deny three times that you k me."
	23:34	they do not k what they are doing."
Jn	1:26	among you stands one you do not k.
	3:11	you, we speak of what we k, and we
	4:22	worship what you do not k; we
		worship what we do k,
	4:42	and we k that this man really is
	6:69	to k that you are the Holy One
	7:28	"Yes, you k me, and you k where I
	7:28	sent me is true. You do not k him,
	8:14	valid, for I k where I came
	8:19	"You do not k me or my Father,"
	8:19	me, you would k my Father also."
	8:32	Then you will k the truth,
	8:55	Though you do not k him, I k him.
	8:55	but I do k him and obey his word.
	9:25	he is a sinner or not, I don't k.
	9:25	One thing I do k. I was blind
	10: 4	follow him because they k his voice.
	10:14	I k my sheep and my sheep k me—
	10:27	I k them, and they follow me.
	12:35	the dark does not k where they are
	13:17	Now that you k these things,
	13:35	this everyone will k that you are my

Jn	14: 7	If you really k me, you will k my
	14: 7	you do k him and have seen him."
	14:17	But you k him, for he lives with you
	15:21	they do not k the one who sent me.
	16:30	we can see that you k all things
	17: 3	that they k you, the only true God,
	17:23	the world will k that you sent me
	21:15	he said, "you k that I love you."
	21:24	We k that his testimony is true.
Ac	1: 7	"It is not for you to k the times
	1:24	"Lord, you k everyone's heart.
Ro	3:17	the way of peace they do not k."
	6: 3	don't you k that all of us who were
	6: 6	we k that our old self was crucified
	6:16	Don't you k that when you offer
	7: 1	speaking to those who k the law—
	7:14	We k that the law is spiritual;
	7:18	I k that good itself does not dwell
	8:22	We k that the whole creation has
	8:26	We do not k what we ought to pray
	8:28	we k that in all things God works
	11: 2	Don't you k what Scripture says
1Co	1:21	through its wisdom did not k him,
	2: 2	I resolved to k nothing while I was
	3:16	Don't you k that you yourselves are
	5: 6	Don't you k that a little yeast
	6: 2	do you not k that the Lord's people
	6:15	Do you not k that your bodies are
	6:16	Do you not k that he who unites
	6:19	Do you not k that your bodies are
	7:16	How do you k, wife, whether you
	7:16	Or, how do you k, husband,
	8: 2	who think they k something do not
		yet k as they ought to k.
	8: 4	We k that "An idol is nothing at all
	9:13	Don't you k that those who serve
	9:24	Do you not k that in a race all
	12: 2	You k that when you were pagans,
	13: 9	For we k in part and we prophesy
	13:12	Now I k in part; then I shall k fully,
	14: 9	how will anyone k what you are
	14:16	since they do not k what you are
	15:58	because you k that your labor
2Co	4:14	because we k that the one who
	5: 1	For we k that if the earthly tent we
	5: 6	k that as long as we are at home
	5:11	we k what it is to fear the Lord,
	8: 9	For you k the grace of our Lord
	12: 2	I k a man in Christ who fourteen
	12: 2	body or out of the body I do not k—
Gal	1:11	I want you to k, brothers and sisters,
	2:16	k that a person is not justified
	4: 9	But now that you k God—
Eph	1:17	so that you may k him better.
	1:18	in order that you may k the hope
	3:19	and to k this love that surpasses
	6: 8	because you k that the Lord will
Php	3:10	I want to k Christ—yes, to k
	4:12	I k what it is to be in need, and I k
		what it is to have plenty.
Col	2: 2	order that they may k the mystery
	4: 1	because you k that you also have
	4: 6	you may k how to answer everyone.

1Th 3: 3 For you **k** quite well that we are
     5: 2 for you **k** very well that the day
2Th 1: 8 will punish those who do not **k** God
     2: 6 And now you **k** what is holding him
1Ti 1: 7 they do not **k** what they are talking
     3: 5 anyone does not **k** how to manage
     3: 15 you will **k** how people ought
2Ti 1: 12 because I **k** whom I have believed,
     2: 23 because you **k** they produce
     3: 14 of, because you **k** those from whom
Titus 1: 16 They claim to **k** God, but by their
Heb 8: 11 or say to one another, 'K the Lord,'
     8: 11 because they will all **k** me,
     11: 8 though he did not **k** where he was
Jas 1: 3 because you **k** that the testing
     3: 1 because you **k** that we who teach
     4: 4 don't you **k** that friendship
     4: 14 you do not even **k** what will happen
1Pe 1: 18 For you **k** that it was not
2Pe 1: 12 even though you **k** them and are
1Jn 2: 3 We **k** that we have come to **k** him
     2: 4 Whoever says, "I **k** him," but does
     2: 5 This is how we **k** we are in him:
     2: 11 They do not **k** where they are going,
     2: 18 This is how we **k** it is the last hour.
     2: 20 Holy One, and all of you **k** the truth.
     2: 29 If you **k** that he is righteous, you **k**
              that everyone who does
     3: 1 reason the world does not **k** us is that
              it did not **k** him.
     3: 2 But we **k** that when Christ appears,
     3: 10 This is how we **k** who the children
     3: 14 We **k** that we have passed
     3: 16 This is how we **k** what love is:
     3: 19 This is how we **k** that we belong
     3: 24 this is how we **k** that he lives in us:
     3: 24 We **k** it by the Spirit he gave us.
     4: 8 does not love does not **k** God,
     4: 13 This is how we **k** that we live in him
     4: 16 so we **k** and rely on the love God
     5: 2 This is how we **k** that we love
     5: 13 you may **k** that you have eternal life.
     5: 15 And if we **k** that he hears us—
     5: 15 we **k** that we have what we asked
     5: 18 We **k** that anyone born of God does
     5: 20 We **k** also that the Son of God has
     5: 20 so that we may **k** him who is true.
2Jn 1: 1 I only, but also all who **k** the truth—
3Jn 1: 12 and you **k** that our testimony is true.
Jude 1: 5 Though you already **k** all this,
Rev 2: 2 I **k** your deeds, your hard work
     2: 2 I **k** that you cannot tolerate wicked
     2: 9 I **k** your afflictions and your
     2: 9 I **k** about the slander of those who
     2: 13 I **k** where you live—
     2: 19 I **k** your deeds, your love and faith,
     3: 3 you will not **k** at what time I will
     3: 8 I **k** your deeds. See, I have placed
     3: 8 I **k** that you have little strength,
     3: 15 I **k** your deeds, that you are neither

KNOW THAT I AM THE LORD† Ex 6:7; 7:5,
17; 10:2; 14:4, 18; 16:12; 29:46; 31:13; Dt 29:6; 1Ki
20:13, 28; Isa 45:3; 49:23; Eze 6:7, 10, 13, 14; 7:4,

27; 11:10, 12; 12:15, 16, 20; 13:14, 21, 23; 14:8;
15:7; 16:62; 20:20, 26, 38, 42, 44; 22:16; 24:27;
25:5, 7, 11, 17; 26:6; 28:22, 23, 26; 29:6, 9, 21; 30:8,
19, 25, 26; 32:15; 33:29; 34:27; 35:4, 9, 15; 36:11,
23, 38; 37:6, 13; 38:23; 39:6, 22, 28

KNOW THAT I THE LORD† Ex 8:22; Isa
49:26; 60:16; Eze 5:13; 17:21, 24; 20:12; 21:5;
22:22; 34:30; 35:12; 36:36; 37:14, 28; 39:7; Joel 3:17

KNOW THAT THE LORD† Ex 11:7; 18:11;
Nu 16:28; Dt 4:35; Jos 2:9; 22:31; Jdg 16:20; 17:13;
1Ki 8:60; 2Ki 2:3, 5; 2Ch 13:5; Ps 4:3; 100:3; 135:5;
140:12; Zec 2:9, 11; 4:9; 6:15

KNOWING KNOW

Ge 3: 5 will be like God, **k** good and evil."
     3: 22 like one of us, **k** good and evil.
Pr 7: 23 little **k** it will cost him his life.
Mt 22: 18 But Jesus, **k** their evil intent, said,
Lk 9: 47 Jesus, **k** their thoughts, took a little
Jn 18: 4 **k** all that was going to happen
     19: 28 **k** that everything had now been
Php 3: 8 worth of **k** Christ Jesus my Lord,
Phm 1: 21 **k** that you will do even more than I
Heb 13: 2 hospitality to angels without **k** it.

KNOWLEDGE KNOW

Ge 2: 9 the tree of the **k** of good and evil.
     2: 17 eat from the tree of the **k** of good
Nu 24: 16 who has **k** from the Most High,
2Ch 1: 10 Give me wisdom and **k**, that I may
Job 21: 22 "Can anyone teach **k** to God,
     38: 2 my plans with words without **k**?
     42: 3 that obscures my plans without **k**?'
Ps 19: 2 night after night they reveal **k**.
     94: 10 he who teaches mankind lack **k**?
     119: 66 Teach me **k** and good judgment,
     139: 6 Such **k** is too wonderful for me,
Pr 1: 4 **k** and discretion to the young—
     1: 7 of the LORD is the beginning of **k**,
     1: 29 since they hated **k** and did not
     2: 5 the LORD and find the **k** of God.
     2: 6 from his mouth come **k**
     2: 10 and **k** will be pleasant to your soul.
     3: 20 by his **k** the watery depths were
     8: 10 of silver, **k** rather than choice gold,
     8: 12 I possess **k** and discretion.
     9: 10 **k** of the Holy One is understanding.
     10: 14 The wise store up **k**, but the mouth
     11: 9 but through **k** the righteous escape.
     12: 1 Whoever loves discipline loves **k**,
     12: 23 The prudent keep their **k**
     13: 16 All who are prudent act with **k**,
     14: 6 but **k** comes easily to the discerning.
     15: 7 The lips of the wise spread **k**,
     15: 14 The discerning heart seeks **k**,
     17: 27 The one who has **k** uses words
     18: 15 heart of the discerning acquires **k**,
     19: 2 Desire without **k** is not good—
     19: 25 the discerning, and they will gain **k**.
     20: 15 but lips that speak **k** are a rare jewel.
     21: 11 attention to the wise they get **k**.
     23: 12 and your ears to words of **k**.
     24: 4 through **k** its rooms are filled

Pr   24: 5 and those who have **k** muster their
Ecc   1:18 the more **k**, the more grief.
       2:26 God gives wisdom, **k** and happiness,
       7:12 but the advantage of **k** is this:
Isa   11: 2 the Spirit of the **k** and fear
      11: 9 the **k** of the LORD as the waters
      40:14 Who was it that taught him **k**,
      53:11 by his **k** my righteous servant will
Jer   3:15 heart, who will lead you with **k**
      10:14 is senseless and without **k**;
Da   1:17 these four young men God gave **k**
Hos   4: 6 people are destroyed from lack of **k**.
       4: 6 "Because you have rejected **k**,
Hab   2:14 will be filled with the **k** of the glory
Mal   2: 7 lips of a priest ought to preserve **k**,
Mt   13:11 "Because the **k** of the secrets
Lk   1:77 to give his people the **k** of salvation
       8:10 He said, "The **k** of the secrets
      11:52 you have taken away the key to **k**.
Ac   18:24 with a thorough **k** of the Scriptures.
Ro   1:28 it worthwhile to retain the **k** of God,
       2:20 have in the law the embodiment of **k**
      10: 2 God, but their zeal is not based on **k**.
      11:33 riches of the wisdom and **k** of God!
      15:14 filled with **k** and competent
1Co   8: 1 We know that "We all possess **k**."
       8: 1 But **k** puffs up while love builds up.
       8:10 with all your **k**, eating in an idol's
       8:11 Christ died, is destroyed by your **k**.
      12: 8 to another a message of **k** by means
      13: 2 can fathom all mysteries and all **k**,
      13: 8 where there is **k**, it will pass away.
2Co   2:14 aroma of the **k** of him everywhere.
       4: 6 of the **k** of God's glory displayed
       8: 7 in **k**, in complete earnestness,
      10: 5 sets itself up against the **k** of God,
      11: 6 as a speaker, but I do have **k**.
Eph   3:19 to know this love that surpasses **k**—
       4:13 faith and in the **k** of the Son of God
Php   1: 9 and more in **k** and depth of insight,
Col   1:10 work, growing in the **k** of God,
       2: 3 all the treasures of wisdom and **k**.
       3:10 is being renewed in **k** in the image
1Ti   2: 4 and to come to a **k** of the truth.
       6:20 ideas of what is falsely called **k**,
2Ti   2:25 leading them to a **k** of the truth,
       3: 7 able to come to a **k** of the truth.
Heb   10:26 we have received the **k** of the truth,
2Pe   1: 3 for a godly life through our **k** of him
       1: 5 and to goodness, **k**;
       3:18 grow in the grace and **k** of our Lord

KNOWN KNOW

Ex   6: 3 I did not make myself fully **k**
Dt   13: 2 other gods" (gods you have not **k**)
Ps   9:16 The LORD is **k** by his acts
      16:11 You make **k** to me the path of life;
      67: 2 that your ways may be **k** on earth,
      89: 1 make your faithfulness **k** through all
      98: 2 LORD has made his salvation **k**
     105: 1 make **k** among the nations what he
     119:168 for all my ways are **k** to you.
Pr   20:11 Even small children are **k** by their
Isa   12: 4 make **k** among the nations what he

Isa   46:10 I make **k** the end
      61: 9 descendants will be **k** among
Jer   7: 9 follow other gods you have not **k**,
Eze   38:23 I will make myself **k** in the sight
      39: 7 " 'I will make **k** my holy name
Zec   14: 7 a day **k** only to the LORD—
Mt   10:26 or hidden that will not be made **k**.
      24:43 of the house had **k** at what time
Mk   6:14 for Jesus' name had become well **k**.
Lk   19:42 had only **k** on this day what would
Jn   1:18 with the Father, has made him **k**.
      15:15 my Father I have made **k** to you.
      16:14 he will receive what he will make **k**
      17:26 I have made you **k** to them, and will
            continue to make you **k** in order
Ac   2:28 You have made **k** to me the paths
Ro   1:19 since what may be **k** about God is
       3:21 of God has been made **k**,
       7: 7 I would not have **k** what sin was had
       7: 7 I would not have **k** what coveting
       9:22 his wrath and make his power **k**,
      11:34 "Who has **k** the mind of the Lord?
      15:20 the gospel where Christ was not **k**,
      16:26 and made **k** through the prophetic
1Co   2:16 "Who has **k** the mind of the Lord so
       8: 3 But whoever loves God is **k** by God.
      13:12 know fully, even as I am fully **k**.
2Co   3: 2 our hearts, **k** and read by everyone.
       6: 9 **k**, yet regarded as unknown;
Gal   4: 9 or rather are **k** by God—how is it
Eph   1: 9 he made **k** to us the mystery of his
       3: 3 that is, the mystery made **k** to me
       6:19 I will fearlessly make **k** the mystery
2Ti   3:15 from infancy you have **k** the Holy
Heb   3:10 and they have not **k** my ways.'
2Pe   2:21 for them not to have **k** the way
       2:21 than to have **k** it and then to turn
1Jn   3: 2 we will be has not yet been made **k**.
Rev   1: 1 He made it **k** by sending his angel

KNOWS KNOW

Ge   3: 5 "For God **k** that when you eat
1Sa   2: 3 for the LORD is a God who **k**,
Est   4:14 who **k** but that you have come
Job   23:10 But he **k** the way that I take;
Ps   44:21 since he **k** the secrets of the heart?
      94:11 The LORD **k** all human plans; he **k**
     103:14 for he **k** how we are formed,
Pr   9:13 she is simple and **k** nothing.
      14:10 Each heart **k** its own bitterness,
Ecc   2:19 who **k** whether that person will be
       8: 7 Since no one **k** the future, who can
       9:12 no one **k** when their hour will come:
Mt   6: 8 your Father **k** what you need before
       6:32 and your heavenly Father **k** that you
      11:27 No one **k** the Son except the Father,
      11:27 no one **k** the Father except the Son
      24:36 about that day or hour no one **k**,
Lk   12:47 "The servant who **k** the master's
      16:15 of others, but God **k** your hearts.
Ac   15: 8 God, who **k** the heart,
Ro   8:27 who searches our hearts **k** the mind
1Co   2:11 who **k** a person's thoughts except
       2:11 the same way no one **k** the thoughts

1Co 3:20 "The Lord **k** that the thoughts
2Ti 2:19 "The Lord **k** those who are his,"
Jas 4:17 **k** the good they ought to do
2Pe 2: 9 the Lord **k** how to rescue the godly
1Jn 4: 6 and whoever **k** God listens to us;
        4: 7 has been born of God and **k** God.
Rev 19:12 a name written on him that no one **k**

KOHATH KOHATHITE, KOHATHITES

Ge 46:11 Gershon, **K** and Merari.
Nu 26:58 (**K** was the forefather of Amram;
1Ch 23: 6 Gershon, **K** and Merari.

KOHATHITE KOHATH

Nu 3:29 The **K** clans were to camp

KOHATHITES KOHATH

Nu 3:28 The **K** were responsible for the care
      4:15 The **K** are to carry those things
1Ch 9:32 Some of the **K**, their fellow Levites,

KORAH

1. Levite who led rebellion against Moses and Aaron (Nu 16; Jude 11).
2. Psalms of the sons of Korah: Pss 42; 44-49; 84; 85; 87; 88

SONS OF KORAH See SONS

KORAZIN (NIV 1984) See CHORAZIN

KOUM*

Mk 5:41 and said to her, *"Talitha k!"*

L

LABAN

Brother of Rebekah (Ge 24:29), father of Rachel and Leah (Ge 29:16). Received Abraham's servant (Ge 24:29–51). Provided daughters as wives for Jacob in exchange for Jacob's service (Ge 29:1–30). Provided flocks for Jacob's service (Ge 30:25–43). After Jacob's departure, pursued and covenanted with him (Ge 31).

LABOR LABORER, LABORERS, LABORING, LABORS

Ex   1:11 them to oppress them with forced **l**,
        6: 9 of their discouragement and harsh **l**.
       20: 9 Six days you shall **l** and do all your
Dt   5:13 Six days you shall **l** and do all your
Jdg 1:30 did subject them to forced **l**.
        1:35 they too were pressed into forced **l**.
1Ki 12: 4 but now lighten the harsh **l**
Ps 48: 6 there, pain like that of a woman in **l**.
    107:12 So he subjected them to bitter **l**;
    127: 1 the house, the builders **l** in vain.
    128: 2 You will eat the fruit of your **l**;
Pr 12:24 rule, but laziness ends in forced **l**.
Ecc 2:10 My heart took delight in all my **l**,
        5:18 their toilsome **l** under the sun during
Isa 26:18 writhed in **l**, but we gave birth to
       54: 1 for joy, you who were never in **l**;

Isa 55: 2 and your **l** on what does not satisfy?
Jer 51:58 the nations' **l** is only fuel
Hab 2:13 that the people's **l** is only fuel
Mt   6:28 They do not **l** or spin.
Jn   4:38 have reaped the benefits of their **l**."
1Co 3: 8 rewarded according to their own **l**.
      15:58 know that your **l** in the Lord is not
Gal 4:27 cry aloud, you who were never in **l**;
Php 2:16 Christ that I did not run or **l** in vain.
Rev 14:13 "they will rest from their **l**, for their

LABORER* LABOR

Job 7: 2 or a hired **l** waiting to be paid,
       14: 6 he has put in his time like a hired **l**.
Ecc 5:12 The sleep of a **l** is sweet, whether

LABORERS LABOR

Ne   4:10 "The strength of the **l** is giving out,
Pr 16:26 The appetite of **l** works for them;
Mal 3: 5 against those who defraud **l** of their

LABORING* LABOR

2Th 3: 8 **l** and toiling so that we would not be

LABORS* LABOR

Ecc 1: 3 do people gain from all their **l**
1Co 16:16 who joins in the work and **l** at it.
1Th 3: 5 that our **l** might have been in vain.

LACHISH

Jos 10:32 The LORD gave **L** into Israel's
2Ch 25:27 him in Jerusalem and he fled to **L**,
Mic 1:13 You who live in **L**, harness fast

LACK LACKED, LACKING, LACKS

Dt   8: 9 not be scarce and you will **l** nothing;
Ps 23: 1 LORD is my shepherd, I **l** nothing.
       34: 9 for those who fear him **l** nothing.
       94:10 who teaches mankind **l** knowledge?
Pr   5:23 For **l** of discipline they will die,
       10:21 many, but fools die for **l** of sense.
       11:14 For **l** of guidance a nation falls,
       15:22 Plans fail for **l** of counsel,
       28:27 who give to the poor will **l** nothing,
Ecc 10: 3 they **l** sense and show everyone how
Isa 5:13 go into exile for **l** of understanding;
Hos 4: 6 my people are destroyed from **l**
Zec 10: 2 wander like sheep oppressed for **l**
Mt 13:58 there because of their **l** of faith.
Mk   6: 6 He was amazed at their **l** of faith.
       16:14 *rebuked them for their l of faith*
Lk 18:22 said to him, "You still **l** one thing.
1Co 1: 7 you do not **l** any spiritual gift as you
        7: 5 because of your **l** of self-control.
Col 2:23 but they **l** any value in restraining

LACKED LACK

Dt   2: 7 you, and you have not **l** anything.
Ne   9:21 they **l** nothing, their clothes did not
1Co 12:24 greater honor to the parts that **l** it,

LACKING LACK

Ecc 1:15 what is **l** cannot be counted.
Ro 12:11 Never be **l** in zeal, but keep your
Col 1:24 in my flesh what is still **l** in regard
Jas 1: 4 and complete, not **l** anything.

LACKS LACK
Pr   25:28   is a person who l self-control.
      31:11   in her and l nothing of value.
Eze   34: 8   because my flock l a shepherd
Jas   1: 5   If any of you l wisdom, you should

LADY*
2Jn   1: 1   To the l chosen by God and to her
      1: 5   dear l, I am not writing you a new

LAID LAY
Ge   22: 9   his son Isaac and l him on the altar,
Nu   27:23   Then he l his hands on him
Dt   34: 9   because Moses had l his hands
1Ki   6:37   the LORD was l in the fourth year,
Ezr   3:11   of the house of the LORD was l.
Job   38: 4   you when I l the earth's foundation?
Ps   18:15   of the earth l bare at your rebuke,
    102:25   the beginning you l the foundations
Pr   3:19   By wisdom the LORD l the earth's
Ecc   1:13   What a heavy burden God has l
Isa   14: 8   "Now that you have been l low,
    44:28   "Let its foundations be l." '
    53: 6   and the LORD has l on him
Eze   24: 2   of Babylon has l siege to Jerusalem
Zec   4: 9   of Zerubbabel have l the foundation
Mk   6:29   and took his body and l it in a tomb.
    16: 6   See the place where they l him.
Lk   6:48   deep and l the foundation on rock.
Jn   11:38   with a stone l across the entrance.
    19:42   tomb was nearby, they l Jesus there.
Ac   6: 6   prayed and l their hands on them.
    7:58   the witnesses l their coats at the feet
1Co   3:11   other than the one already l,
    14:25   the secrets of their hearts are l bare.
1Ti   4:14   the body of elders l their hands
Heb   1:10   you l the foundations of the earth,
    4:13   and l bare before the eyes of him
2Pe   3:10   everything done in it will be l bare.
1Jn   3:16   Jesus Christ l down his life for us.

LAKE
Mt   4:18   They were casting a net into the l,
    8:24   a furious storm came up on the l,
    14:25   went out to them, walking on the l.
Mk   4: 1   Again Jesus began to teach by the l.
Lk   8:33   down the steep bank into the l
Jn   6:25   found him on the other side of the l,
Rev   19:20   into the fiery l of burning sulfur,
    20:10   thrown into the l of burning sulfur,
    20:14   Hades were thrown into the l of fire.
    20:14   The l of fire is the second death.

LAMB LAMB'S, LAMBS
Ge   22: 8   "God himself will provide the l
    30:32   every dark-colored l and every
Ex   12:21   and slaughter the Passover l.
Lev   3: 7   If you offer a l, you are to present it
    4:32   someone brings a l as their sin
    5: 7   who cannot afford a l is to bring two
Nu   9:11   They are to eat the l,
2Sa   12: 6   must pay for that l four times over,
Isa   11: 6   The wolf will live with the l,
    53: 7   he was led like a l to the slaughter,

Isa   65:25   wolf and the l will feed together,
Jer   11:19   I had been like a gentle l led
Mk   14:12   to sacrifice the Passover l,
Jn   1:29   "Look, the L of God, who takes
Ac   8:32   and as a l before its shearer is silent,
1Co   5: 7   our Passover l, has been sacrificed.
1Pe   1:19   a l without blemish or defect.
Rev   5: 6   Then I saw a L, looking as if it had
    5: 6   The L had seven horns and seven
    5:12   "Worthy is the L, who was slain,
    6: 1   I watched as the L opened the first
    7:14   them white in the blood of the L.
    12:11   over him by the blood of the L
    13: 8   of life, the L who was slain
    14: 1   and there before me was the L,
    15: 3   God's servant Moses and of the L:
    17:14   They will wage war against the L, but
        the L will triumph over them
    19: 7   For the wedding of the L has come,
    21: 9   you the bride, the wife of the L."
    21:14   of the twelve apostles of the L.
    21:23   gives it light, and the L is its lamp.
    22: 1   from the throne of God and of the L

LAMB'S* LAMB
Rev   13: 8   have not been written in the L book
    21:27   names are written in the L book

LAMBS LAMB
Ex   29:38   regularly each day: two l a year old.
Ps   114: 4   leaped like rams, the hills like l.
Isa   40:11   He gathers the l in his arms
Lk   10: 3   you out like l among wolves.
Jn   21:15   Jesus said, "Feed my l."

LAME
2Sa   4: 4   of Saul had a son who was l in both
    5: 6   blind and the l can ward you off."
    9: 3   he is l in both feet."
Isa   33:23   even the l will carry off plunder.
    35: 6   Then will the l leap like a deer,
Mic   4: 6   the LORD, "I will gather the l;
Zep   3:19   I will rescue the l; I will gather
Mal   1: 8   When you sacrifice l or diseased
Mt   11: 5   The blind receive sight, the l walk,
    15:31   the l walking and the blind seeing.
Lk   14:13   poor, the crippled, the l, the blind,
Ac   3: 2   Now a man who was l from birth
    4: 9   kindness shown to a man who was l
    14: 8   In Lystra there sat a man who was l.

LAMECH
Ge   4:19   L married two women, one named

LAMENT LAMENTATION, LAMENTS
2Sa   1:17   took up this l concerning Saul
    3:33   The king sang this l for Abner:
Ps   5: 1   my words, LORD, consider my l.
Eze   19: 1   "Take up a l concerning the princes

LAMENTATION LAMENT
La   2: 5   mourning and l for Daughter Judah.

LAMENTS LAMENT

2Ch 35:25 Jeremiah composed l for Josiah,
     35:25 in Israel and are written in the L.

LAMP LAMPS, LAMPSTAND, LAMPSTANDS

1Sa 3: 3 The l of God had not yet gone out,
2Sa 22:29 You, LORD, are my l;
1Ki 11:36 may always have a l before me
     15: 4 the LORD his God gave him a l
2Ki 8:19 promised to maintain a l for David
Job 18: 5 "The l of a wicked man is snuffed
Ps 18:28 You, LORD, keep my l burning;
   119:105 Your word is a l for my feet, a light
   132:17 and set up a l for my anointed one.
Pr   6:23 For this command is a l,
   20:27 The human spirit is the l
   31:18 and her l does not go out at night.
Mt 5:15 Neither do people light a l and put it
   6:22 "The eye is the l of the body.
Lk 8:16 "No one lights a l and hides it
Jn 5:35 John was a l that burned and gave
Rev 21:23 gives it light, and the Lamb is its l.
  22: 5 They will not need the light of a l

LAMPS LAMP

Ex 27:21 are to keep the l burning before
Mt 25: 1 be like ten virgins who took their l
Lk 12:35 for service and keep your l burning,
Rev 4: 5 of the throne, seven l were blazing.

LAMPSTAND LAMP

Ex 25:31 "Make a l of pure gold.
Nu 3:31 ark, the table, the l, the altars,
Zec 4: 2 "I see a solid gold l with a bowl
   4:11 on the right and the left of the l?"
Heb 9: 2 In its first room were the l
Rev 2: 5 and remove your l from its place.

LAMPSTANDS LAMP

2Ch 4: 7 He made ten gold l according
Rev 1:12 when I turned I saw seven golden l,
   1:20 the seven l are the seven churches.
  11: 4 "the two olive trees" and the two l,

LAND LANDOWNER, LANDS, WASTELAND, WASTELANDS

Ge 1:10 God called the dry ground "l,"
   1:11 said, "Let the l produce vegetation:
   1:24 "Let the l produce living creatures
   7:22 on dry l that had the breath of life
  12: 1 household to the l I will show you.
  12: 7 your offspring I will give this l."
  12:10 Now there was a famine in the l,
  13:15 All the l that you see I will give
  15:18 "To your descendants I give this l,
  17: 8 The whole l of Canaan, where you
  24: 7 your offspring I will give this l'—
  26: 1 Now there was a famine in the l—
  28:15 and I will bring you back to this l.
  31:13 and go back to your native l.' "
  40:15 off from the l of the Hebrews,
  41:30 and the famine will ravage the l.
  42: 6 Joseph was the governor of the l,

Ge 50:24 of this l to the l he promised on oath
Ex 1: 7 so numerous that the l was filled
   3: 8 of that l into a good and spacious l,
        a l flowing with milk and honey—
   6: 8 I will bring you to the l I swore
   8:22 that I, the LORD, am in this l.
  20: 2 out of Egypt, out of the l of slavery.
  20:12 the l the LORD your God is giving
  34:12 live in the l where you are going,
Lev 18:25 Even the l was defiled;
  18:25 and the l vomited out its inhabitants.
  25: 5 The l is to have a year of rest.
  25:23 because the l is mine and you reside
       in my l as foreigners
  26:34 will enjoy its sabbath years all
Nu 13: 2 men to explore the l of Canaan,
  13:30 go up and take possession of the l,
  14: 9 not be afraid of the people of the l,
  14:23 them will ever see the l I promised
  26:55 Be sure that the l is distributed
  35:33 not pollute the l where you are.
  35:33 Bloodshed pollutes the l,
Dt 1: 8 See, I have given you this l.
   8: 7 God is bringing you into a good l—
  11:10 take over is not like the l of Egypt,
  28:21 you from the l you are entering
  29:24 has the LORD done this to this l?
  34: 1 LORD showed him the whole l—
Jos 1: 6 these people to inherit the l I swore
   2: 1 "Go, look over the l," he said,
   5:12 after they ate this food from the l;
  11:23 So Joshua took the entire l, just as
  11:23 Then the l had rest from war.
  13: 2 "This is the l that remains:
  14: 4 Levites received no share of the l
  14: 9 me, 'The l on which your feet have
Jdg 1:27 were determined to live in that l.
Ru 1: 1 ruled, there was a famine in the l.
2Sa 21:14 answered prayer in behalf of the l.
  24:25 his prayer in behalf of the l,
1Ki 8:34 bring them back to the l you gave
  17: 7 there had been no rain in the l.
2Ki 17: 5 king of Assyria invaded the entire l,
  24: 1 king of Babylon invaded the l,
  25:21 went into captivity, away from her l.
1Ch 14:17 fame spread throughout every l,
2Ch 7:14 their sin and will heal their l.
   7:20 then I will uproot Israel from my l,
  32:21 withdrew to his own l in disgrace.
  36:21 The l enjoyed its sabbath rests;
Ezr 9:11 'The l you are entering to possess is
       a l polluted
Ne 9:36 the l you gave our ancestors so they
Ps 25:13 their descendants will inherit the l.
  37:11 the meek will inherit the l and enjoy
  37:29 The righteous will inherit the l
  44: 3 by their sword that they won the l,
  65: 9 You care for the l and water it;
 136:21 and gave their l as an inheritance,
 142: 5 my portion in the l of the living."
Pr 2:21 For the upright will live in the l,
  12:11 who work their l will have abundant
Isa 2: 8 Their l is full of idols;

Isa	6:13	And though a tenth remains in the l,
	6:13	seed will be the stump in the l."
	9: 2	in the l of deep darkness a light has
	53: 8	was cut off from the l of the living;
Jer	2: 7	you into a fertile l to eat its fruit
	2: 7	came and defiled my l and made my
	22:29	O l, l, l, hear the word
	31:17	children will return to their own l.
Eze	7:23	For the l is full of bloodshed,
	36:24	and bring you back into your own l.
	39:28	I will gather them to their own l,
	43: 2	and the l was radiant with his glory.
Da	11:41	He will also invade the Beautiful L.
Hos	2:23	I will plant her for myself in the l;
Zec	3: 9	the sin of this l in a single day.
Mal	4: 6	strike the l with total destruction."
Mt	4:16	those living in the l of the shadow
Mk	15:33	came over the whole l until three
Lk	21:23	There will be great distress in the l
Jas	5:17	it did not rain on the l for three
Rev	7: 3	"Do not harm the l or the sea
	16: 2	and poured out his bowl on the l,

**LAND FLOWING WITH MILK AND
HONEY** See FLOWING

LANDOWNER* LAND

Mt	20: 1	of heaven is like a l who went
	20:11	they began to grumble against the l.
	21:33	There was a l who planted

LANDS LAND

Ge	26: 3	descendants I will give all these l
Ps	106:27	and scatter them throughout the l.
	107: 3	those he gathered from the l,
	111: 6	giving them the l of other nations.
Isa	36:18	of any nations ever delivered their l
Eze	20: 6	honey, the most beautiful of all l.
Hab	2: 8	you have destroyed l and cities
	2:17	you have destroyed l and cities
Zec	10: 9	in distant l they will remember me.

LANGUAGE LANGUAGES

Ge	11: 1	Now the whole world had one l
	11: 9	there the LORD confused the l
Dt	28:49	down, a nation whose l you will not
Ne	13:24	their children spoke the l of Ashdod
	13:24	know how to speak the l of Judah.
Jer	5:15	a people whose l you do not know,
Jn	8:44	he speaks his native l, for he is a liar
Ac	2: 6	one heard their own l being spoken.
Col	3: 8	slander, and filthy l from your lips.
Rev	5: 9	God persons from every tribe and l
	7: 9	people and l, standing before
	13: 7	every tribe, people, l and nation.
	14: 6	to every nation, tribe, l and people.

LANGUAGES LANGUAGE

Isa	66:18	the people of all nations and l,
Zec	8:23	"In those days ten people from all l

LANTERNS*

Jn	18: 3	carrying torches, l and weapons.

LAODICEA

Col	4:16	you in turn read the letter from L.

Rev	3:14	the angel of the church in L write:

LAP

Jdg	7: 5	"Separate those who l the water
Pr	6:27	into his l without his clothes being
	16:33	The lot is cast into the l, but its
Lk	6:38	over, will be poured into your l.

LAPIS LAZULI

Ex	24:10	like a pavement made of l lazuli,
	28:18	be turquoise, l lazuli and emerald;
Eze	1:26	what looked like a throne of l lazuli,
	10: 1	a throne of l lazuli above the vault

LARGE ENLARGE, ENLARGED, ENLARGES, LARGER, LARGEST

Nu	13:28	the cities are fortified and very l.
Dt	6:10	a land with l, flourishing cities you
	17:17	He must not accumulate l amounts
Jos	10:11	LORD hurled l hailstones down
Eze	23:32	your sister's cup, a cup l and deep;
Da	2:31	there before you stood a l statue—
	4:11	The tree grew l and strong and its
	7: 7	It had l iron teeth; it crushed
	8:21	the l horn between its eyes is
Mk	14:15	He will show you a l room upstairs,
Gal	6:11	See what l letters I use as I write
Rev	6: 4	To him was given a l sword.
	18:21	up a boulder the size of a l millstone

LARGER LARGE

Nu	33:54	To a l group give a l inheritance,
Dt	11:23	you will dispossess nations l

LARGEST* LARGE

Mt	13:32	it is the l of garden plants,
Mk	4:32	becomes the l of all garden plants,

LASHES

Dt	25: 3	must not impose more than forty l.
Pr	17:10	person more than a hundred l a fool.
2Co	11:24	from the Jews the forty l minus one.

LAST LASTING, LASTS, LATTER

Ex	14:24	During the l watch of the night
2Sa	23: 1	These are the l words of David:
1Ch	23:27	According to the l instructions
Ps	45: 6	O God, will l for ever and ever;
	119:152	you established them to l forever.
Isa	2: 2	In the l days the mountain
	41: 4	the first of them and with the l—
	44: 6	I am the first and I am the l;
	48:12	I am the first and I am the l.
	51: 6	But my salvation will l forever,
Da	9: 2	of Jerusalem would l seventy years.
Hos	3: 5	and to his blessings in the l days.
Mic	4: 1	In the l days the mountain
Mt	19:30	But many who are first will be l, and many who are l will be first.
	20: 8	beginning with the l ones hired
	21:37	L of all, he sent his son to them.
	27:64	This l deception will be worse than
Mk	9:35	wants to be first must be the very l,
	10:31	But many who are first will be l, and the l first."

Mk   15:37 a loud cry, Jesus breathed his l.
Jn   6:40 I will raise them up at the l day."
      7:37 On the l and greatest day
     11:24 in the resurrection at the l day."
     15:16 fruit that will l—and so
Ac   2:17 " 'In the l days, God says, I will
Ro   1:17 that is by faith from first to l, just as
1Co   9:25 it to get a crown that will l forever.
     15: 8 and l of all he appeared to me also,
     15:26 The l enemy to be destroyed is
     15:52 twinkling of an eye, at the l trumpet.
2Ti   3: 1 will be terrible times in the l days.
Heb   1: 2 in these l days he has spoken to us
      1: 8 O God, will l for ever and ever;
1Pe   1: 5 is ready to be revealed in the l time.
2Pe   3: 3 that in the l days scoffers will come,
1Jn   2:18 Dear children, this is the l hour;
Jude 1:18 "In the l times there will be scoffers
Rev   1:17 I am the First and the L.
      2: 8 of him who is the First and the L,
     15: 1 angels with the seven l plagues—l,
     21: 9 full of the seven l plagues came
     22:13 the First and the L, the Beginning

LASTING LAST

Ex   12:14 to the LORD—a l ordinance.
     28:43 is to be a l ordinance for Aaron
Lev 24: 8 of the Israelites, as a l covenant.
Nu   25:13 have a covenant of a l priesthood,
Heb 10:34 had better and l possessions.

A LASTING ORDINANCE Ex 12:14, 17, 24;
27:21; 28:43; 29:9; 30:21; Lev 3:17; 10:9; 16:29, 31,
34; 17:7; 23:14, 21, 31, 41; 24:3; Nu 10:8; 15:15;
18:23; 19:10, 21; 2Ch 2:4; Eze 46:14

LASTS LAST

Job 20: 5 is brief, the joy of the godless l
Ps   30: 5 For his anger l only a moment, but his
                favor l a lifetime;
Pr   12:19 but a lying tongue l only a moment.
2Co   3:11 greater is the glory of that which l!

LATE LATER

Ps 127: 2 In vain you rise early and stay up l,

LATER LATE

Mk   10:34 Three days l he will rise."
Jn   13: 7 doing, but l you will understand."
Gal   3:17 introduced 430 years l, does not set
1Ti   4: 1 l times some will abandon the faith
Rev   1:19 is now and what will take place l.

LATIN*

Jn   19:20 written in Aramaic, L and Greek.

LATTER LAST

Job 42:12 The LORD blessed the l part
Mt   23:23 You should have practiced the l,
Php   1:16 The l do so out of love,

LAUD (KJV) See SING ... PRAISE, SING ... PRAISES

LAUGH LAUGHED, LAUGHINGSTOCK, LAUGHS, LAUGHTER

Ge   18:13 "Why did Sarah l and say, 'Will I
     21: 6 hears about this will l with me."
Ps   59: 8 But you l at them, LORD;
Pr   31:25 she can l at the days to come.
Ecc   3: 4 a time to weep and a time to l,
Lk   6:21 you who weep now, for you will l.
      6:25 Woe to you who l now, for you will

LAUGHED LAUGH

Ge   17:17 he l and said to himself, "Will a son
     18:12 So Sarah l to herself as she thought,
La   1: 7 at her and l at her destruction.
Lk   8:53 They l at him, knowing that she was

LAUGHINGSTOCK LAUGH

La   3:14 I became the l of all my people;

LAUGHS LAUGH

Ps   2: 4 The One enthroned in heaven l;
     37:13 but the Lord l at the wicked, for he

LAUGHTER LAUGH

Ge   21: 6 said, "God has brought me l,
Ps 126: 2 Our mouths were filled with l,
Pr   14:13 Even in l the heart may ache,
Ecc   7: 3 Frustration is better than l,
     10:19 A feast is made for l, wine makes
Jas   4: 9 Change your l to mourning and your

LAUNDERER'S

Mal   3: 2 be like a refiner's fire or a l soap.

LAVER (KJV) See BASIN

LAVISHED

Eph   1: 8 that he l on us. With all wisdom
1Jn   3: 1 See what great love the Father has l

LAW LAW'S, LAWFUL, LAWGIVER, LAWS, LAWSUITS

Ex   16:34 with the tablets of the covenant l,
     25:16 the ark the tablets of the covenant l,
     31:18 the two tablets of the covenant l,
Lev 24:22 to have the same l for the foreigner
Nu   5:29 is the l of jealousy when a woman
      6:13 " 'Now this is the l of the Nazirite
Dt   1: 5 Moses began to expound this l,
      6:25 to obey all this l before the LORD
     17:18 himself on a scroll a copy of this l,
     27:26 of this l by carrying them out."
     31: 9 So Moses wrote down this l
     31:11 you shall read this l before them
     31:26 "Take this Book of the L and place
Jos   1: 7 to obey all the l my servant Moses
      1: 8 Keep this Book of the L always
      8:32 on stones a copy of the l of Moses.
     22: 5 the l that Moses the servant
2Ki 22: 8 the Book of the L in the temple
2Ch   6:16 walk before me according to my l,

2Ch 17: 9 the Book of the L of the LORD;
    34:14 the Book of the L of the LORD
Ezr 7: 6 well versed in the L of Moses,
Ne 8: 2 the priest brought the L before
    8: 8 read from the Book of the L of God,
Ps 1: 2 delight is in the l of the LORD,
    1: 2 and who meditates on his l day
   19: 7 The l of the LORD is perfect,
   37:31 The l of their God is in their hearts;
   40: 8 your l is within my heart."
   89:30 "If his sons forsake my l and do not
 119:18 may see wonderful things in your l.
 119:70 unfeeling, but I delight in your l.
 119:72 The l from your mouth is more
 119:77 I may live, for your l is my delight.
 119:97 Oh, how I love your l! I meditate
 119:142 is everlasting and your l is true.
 119:163 detest falsehood but I love your l.
 119:165 peace have those who love your l,
Isa 2: 3 The l will go out from Zion,
   42:21 his righteousness to make his l great
Jer 2: 8 deal with the l did not know me;
   8: 8 for we have the l of the LORD,"
   31:33 "I will put my l in their minds
La 2: 9 among the nations, the l is no more,
Da 9:11 All Israel has transgressed your l
Hos 4: 6 because you have ignored the l
Mic 4: 2 The l will go out from Zion,
Hab 1: 4 Therefore the l is paralyzed,
   1: 7 they are a l to themselves
Zec 7:12 would not listen to the l
Mal 2: 9 partiality in matters of the l."
Mt 5:17 that I have come to abolish the L
   7:12 you, for this sums up the L
   22:36 greatest commandment in the L?"
   22:40 All the L and the Prophets hang
   23:23 the more important matters of the l—
Lk 2:23 (as it is written in the L of the Lord,
   2:39 required by the L of the Lord,
   10:26 "What is written in the L?"
   11:52 "Woe to you experts in the l,
   16:17 stroke of a pen to drop out of the L.
   24:44 written about me in the L of Moses,
Jn 1:17 For the l was given through Moses;
   7:19 Has not Moses given you the l?
   7:19 Yet not one of you keeps the l.
   18:31 and judge him by your own l."
Ac 6:13 this holy place and against the l.
   13:39 able to obtain under the l of Moses.
   15: 5 required to keep the l of Moses."
   28:23 from the L of Moses
Ro 2:12 All who sin apart from the l will also
       perish apart from the l,
   2:12 who sin under the l will be judged by
       the l.
   2:15 the requirements of the l are written
   2:20 you have in the l the embodiment
   2:25 has value if you observe the l, but if
       you break the l,
   3:19 that whatever the l says, it says to
       those who are under the l,
   3:20 through the l we become conscious
   3:21 apart from the l the righteousness

Ro 3:28 faith apart from the works of the l.
   3:31 we, then, nullify the l by this faith?
   3:31 Not at all! Rather, we uphold the l.
   4:13 It was not through the l
   4:15 because the l brings wrath.
   4:15 And where there is no l there is no
   5:13 in the world before the l was given,
   5:13 anyone's account where there is no l.
   5:20 The l was brought in so
   6:14 because you are not under the l,
   6:15 sin because we are not under the l
   7: 1 the l has authority over someone
   7: 4 died to the l through the body
   7: 5 passions aroused by the l were
   7: 6 we have been released from the l so
   7: 7 Is the l sinful? Certainly not!
   7: 8 For apart from the l, sin was dead.
   7: 9 Once I was alive apart from the l;
   7:12 So then, the l is holy,
   7:14 We know that the l is spiritual;
   7:22 my inner being I delight in God's l;
   7:25 in my mind am a slave to God's l,
   7:25 sinful nature a slave to the l of sin.
   8: 2 through Christ Jesus the l of the Spirit
   8: 2 has set you free from the l of sin
   8: 3 For what the l was powerless to do
   8: 4 of the l might be fully met in us,
   8: 7 it does not submit to God's l,
   9: 4 the receiving of the l, the temple
   9:31 who pursued the l as the way
   10: 4 Christ is the culmination of the l so
   13: 8 loves others has fulfilled the l.
   13:10 love is the fulfillment of the l.
1Co 9: 9 For it is written in the L of Moses:
   9:20 under the l I became like one under
       the l (though I myself am not under
       the l), so as to win those under the l.
   9:21 those not having the l I became like
       one not having the l (though I am
       not free from God's l but am under
       Christ's l), so as to win those not
       having the l.
   15:56 is sin, and the power of sin is the l.
Gal 2:16 is not justified by the works of the l,
   2:16 Christ and not by the works of the l,
   2:16 of the l no one will be justified.
   2:19 "For through the l I died to the l so
   3: 2 the Spirit by the works of the l,
   3: 5 among you by the works of the l,
   3:10 the works of the l are under a curse,
   3:11 on the l is justified before God,
   3:13 curse of the l by becoming a curse
   3:19 Why, then, was the l given at all?
   3:19 The l was given through angels
   3:21 would certainly have come by the l.
   3:23 we were held in custody under the l,
   3:24 So the l was our guardian until
   4: 4 born of a woman, born under the l,
   4:21 you not aware of what the l says?
   5: 3 he is obligated to obey the whole l.
   5: 4 by the l have been alienated
   5:14 For the entire l is fulfilled
   5:18 the Spirit, you are not under the l.

Gal	6: 2	in this way you will fulfill the l
Eph	2:15	in his flesh the l with its commands
Php	3: 5	in regard to the l, a Pharisee;
	3: 6	as for righteousness based on the l,
	3: 9	of my own that comes from the l,
1Ti	1: 8	We know that the l is good if one
Titus	3: 9	arguments and quarrels about the l,
Heb	7:12	the l must be changed also.
	7:19	(for the l made nothing perfect),
	10: 1	The l is only a shadow of the good
Jas	1:25	into the perfect l that gives freedom,
	2: 8	you really keep the royal l found
	2:10	For whoever keeps the whole l
	4:11	judges them speaks against the l
	4:11	When you judge the l, you are not
1Jn	3: 4	Everyone who sins breaks the l;
Rev	15: 5	is, the tabernacle of the covenant l—

BOOK OF THE LAW Dt 28:61; 29:21; 30:10; 31:26; Jos 1:8; 8:31, 34; 23:6; 24:26; 2Ki 14:6; 22:8, 11; 2Ch 17:9; 34:14, 15; Ne 8:1, 3, 8, 18; 9:3; Gal 3:10

LAW OF MOSES Jos 8:31, 32; 23:6; 1Ki 2:3; 2Ki 14:6; 23:25; 2Ch 23:18; 30:16; Ezr 3:2; 7:6; Ne 8:1; Da 9:11, 13; Lk 2:22; 24:44; Jn 7:23; Ac 13:39; 15:5, 21; 28:23; 1Co 9:9; Heb 10:28

LAW OF THE LORD† Ex 13:9; 2Ki 10:31; 1Ch 16:40; 22:12; 2Ch 12:1; 17:9; 19:8; 31:3, 4; 34:14; 35:26; Ezr 7:10; Ne 9:3; Ps 1:2; 19:7; 119:1; Isa 5:24; Jer 8:8; Am 2:4

TEACHER OF THE LAW Ezr 7:11, 12, 21; Ne 8:1, 4, 9; 12:26, 36; Mt 8:19; 13:52; Ac 5:34; 1Co 1:20

TEACHERS OF THE LAW Mt 2:4; 5:20; 7:29; 9:3; 12:38; 15:1; 16:21; 17:10; 20:18; 21:15; 23:2, 13, 15, 23, 25, 27, 29; 26:57; 27:41; Mk 1:22; 2:6, 16; 3:22; 7:1, 5; 8:31; 9:11, 14; 10:33; 11:18, 27; 12:12, 28, 35, 38; 14:1, 43, 53; 15:1, 31; Lk 5:17, 21, 30, 6:7, 11; 9:22; 11:53; 15:2; 19:47; 20:1, 19, 39, 46; 22:2, 66; 23:10; Ac 4:5; 6:12; 23:9; 1Ti 1:7

LAW'S* LAW

Ro	2:26	keep the l requirements, will they

LAWBREAKER* BREAK

Ro	2:27	code and circumcision, are a l.
Gal	2:18	then I really would be a l.
Jas	2:11	murder, you have become a l.

LAWBREAKERS* BREAK

1Ti	1: 9	the righteous but for l and rebels,
Jas	2: 9	and are convicted by the law as l.

LAWFUL LAW

Mt	12:12	Therefore it is l to do good
	19: 3	"Is it l for a man to divorce his wife
Mk	2:26	which is l only for priests to eat.
Lk	14: 3	"Is it l to heal on the Sabbath

LAWGIVER* LAW

Isa	33:22	the LORD is our l, the LORD is
Jas	4:12	There is only one L and Judge,

LAWLESS LAWLESSNESS

2Th	2: 8	And then the l one will be revealed,

Heb	10:17	l acts I will remember no more."
2Pe	3:17	be carried away by the error of the l

LAWLESSNESS* LAWLESS

2Th	2: 3	occurs and the man of l is revealed,
	2: 7	the secret power of l is already
1Jn	3: 4	sins breaks the law; in fact, sin is l.

LAWS LAW

Ex	21: 1	"These are the l you are to set
Lev	25:18	decrees and be careful to obey my l,
	26:43	their sins because they rejected my l
Dt	4: 1	and I l I am about to teach you.
	30:16	keep his commands, decrees and l;
Jos	24:25	reaffirmed for them decrees and l.
1Ki	11:33	nor kept my decrees and l as David,
Ezr	7:10	teaching its decrees and l in Israel.
Job	38:33	Do you know the l of the heavens?
Ps	18:22	All his l are before me; I have not
	119:30	I have set my heart on your l.
	119:43	for I have put my hope in your l.
	119:120	fear of you; I stand in awe of your l.
	119:164	I praise you for your righteous l.
	119:175	you, and may your l sustain me.
	147:20	they do not know his l.
Isa	10: 1	Woe to those who make unjust l,
Eze	5: 6	She has rejected my l and has not
	36:27	decrees and be careful to keep my l.
Heb	8:10	I will put my l in their minds
	10:16	I will put my l in their hearts, and I

LAWSUITS* LAW

Ex	23: 6	justice to your poor people in their l.
Dt	17: 8	judge—whether bloodshed, l or
Hos	10: 4	therefore l spring up like poisonous
1Co	6: 7	you have l among you means you

LAY LAID, LAYING, LAYS

Ge	22:12	"Do not l a hand on the boy,"
Ex	7: 4	Then I will l my hand on Egypt
	29:10	his sons shall l their hands on its
Lev	1: 4	You are to l your hand on the head
	4:15	the community are to l their hands
Nu	8:10	the Israelites are to l their hands
	27:18	leadership, and l your hand on him.
Dt	9:25	I l prostrate before the LORD
1Sa	26: 9	Who can l a hand on the LORD's
Job	1:12	the man himself do not l a finger."
	22:22	and l up his words in your heart.
Ecc	10: 4	calmness can l great offenses
Isa	28:16	"See, I l a stone in Zion, a tested
Mt	8:20	of Man has no place to l his head."
	28: 6	Come and see the place where he l.
Mk	6: 5	except l his hands on a few sick
Lk	9:58	of Man has no place to l his head."
Jn	10:15	and I l down my life for the sheep.
	10:18	but I l it down of my own accord.
	10:18	I have authority to l it down
	13:37	I will l down my life for you."
	15:13	to l down one's life for one's
Ac	8:19	whom I l my hands may receive
Ro	9:33	I l in Zion a stone that causes people
1Co	3:11	no one can l any foundation other
	7:17	This is the rule I l down in all

1Ti	6:19	In this way they will l up treasure
1Pe	2: 6	"See, I l a stone in Zion, a chosen
1Jn	3:16	we ought to l down our lives for our
Rev	4:10	They l their crowns before

LAYING LAY

Lk	4:40	and l his hands on each one,
Ac	8:18	the Spirit was given at the l
1Ti	5:22	Do not be hasty in the l on of hands,
2Ti	1: 6	is in you through the l on of my
Heb	6: 1	not l again the foundation
	6: 2	cleansing rites, the l on of hands,

LAYS LAY

Jn	10:11	The good shepherd l down his life

LAZARUS*

1. Poor man in Jesus' parable (Lk 16:19–31).
2. Brother of Mary and Martha whom Jesus raised from the dead (Jn 11:1—12:19).

LAZINESS* LAZY

Pr	12:24	will rule, but l ends in forced labor.
	19:15	L brings on deep sleep,
Ecc	10:18	Through l, the rafters sag;

LAZULI LAPIS

Job	28: 6	lapis l comes from its rocks, and its
SS	5:14	ivory decorated with lapis l.
Isa	54:11	your foundations with lapis l.
La	4: 7	rubies, their appearance like lapis l.

LAZY* LAZINESS

Ex	5: 8	They are l; that is why they are
	5:17	Pharaoh said, "L, that's what you
		are—l!
Pr	10: 4	L hands make for poverty,
	12:27	The l do not roast any game,
	26:15	he is too l to bring it back to his
Mt	25:26	replied, 'You wicked, l servant!
Titus	1:12	always liars, evil brutes, l gluttons."
Heb	6:12	We do not want you to become l,

LEAD LEADER, LEADERS, LEADERSHIP, LEADING, LEADS, LED

Ex	15:13	love you will l the people you have
	32:34	l the people to the place I spoke of,
Nu	14: 8	with us, he will l us into that land,
Dt	31: 2	old and I am no longer able to l you.
Jos	1: 6	because you will l these people
1Sa	8: 5	now appoint a king to l us, such as
2Ch	1:10	that I may l this people, for who is
	8:14	and the Levites to l the praise
Ps	27:11	l me in a straight path because
	43: 3	your faithful care, let them l me;
	61: 2	l me to the rock that is higher than I.
	139:24	me, and l me in the way everlasting.
	143:10	may your good Spirit l me on level
Pr	4:11	and l you along straight paths.
	5: 5	her steps l straight to the grave.
	20: 7	The righteous l blameless lives;
	21: 5	of the diligent l to profit as surely as
Ecc	5: 6	Do not let your mouth l you
Isa	3:12	people, your guides l you astray;

Isa	11: 6	and a little child will l them.
	49:10	and l them beside springs of water.
Jer	31: 9	I will l them beside streams of water
Da	12: 3	those who l many to righteousness,
Mt	6:13	And l us not into temptation,
	15:14	If the blind l the blind, both will fall
Lk	6:39	"Can the blind l the blind?
	11: 4	And l us not into temptation.' "
Ro	2: 4	God's kindness is intended to l you
	12: 8	if it is to l, do it diligently; if it is
1Th	4:11	it your ambition to l a quiet life:
1Jn	2:26	those who are trying to l you astray.
	3: 7	do not let anyone l you astray.
	5:16	a sin that does not l to death,
Rev	7:17	'he will l them to springs of living

LEADER LEAD

Lev	4:22	" 'When a l sins unintentionally
1Sa	7: 6	Now Samuel was serving as l
	7:15	continued as Israel's l all the days
	12: 2	Now you have a king as your l.
1Ch	28: 4	He chose Judah as l,
Lk	8:41	a synagogue l, came and fell

LEADERS LEAD

Nu	1:16	the l of their ancestral tribes.
	7:10	the l brought their offerings for its
1Sa	8: 1	he appointed his sons as Israel's l.
1Ch	29: 9	at the willing response of their l,
Isa	3:14	the elders and l of his people:
Jer	25:34	roll in the dust, you l of the flock.
Mic	3: 1	"Listen, you l of Jacob, you rulers
Jn	7:13	publicly about him for fear of the l.
	9:22	they were afraid of the Jewish l,
1Co	3:21	no more boasting about human l!
Heb	13: 7	Remember your l, who spoke
	13:17	Have confidence in your l

LEADERSHIP* LEAD

Nu	33: 1	by divisions under the l of Moses
	27:18	a man in whom is the spirit of l,
Ps	109: 8	may another take his place of l.
Ac	1:20	another take his place of l.'

LEADING LEAD

Dt	1:15	So I took the l men of your tribes,
Mk	14:48	"Am I l a rebellion," said Jesus,
Ro	6:19	slaves to righteousness l to holiness.
2Ti	2:25	will grant them repentance l them

LEADS LEAD

Dt	27:18	is anyone who l the blind astray
Ps	23: 2	he l me beside quiet waters,
	37: 8	do not fret—it l only to evil.
	68: 6	he l out the prisoners with singing;
Pr	2:18	Surely her house l down to death
	10:17	ignores correction l others astray.
	12:26	the way of the wicked l them astray.
	14:12	be right, but in the end it l to death.
	14:23	but mere talk l only to poverty.
	16:25	be right, but in the end it l to death.
	19:23	The fear of the LORD l to life;
	21: 5	profit as surely as haste l to poverty.
Isa	40:11	he gently l those that have young.
Mt	7:13	gate and broad is the road that l

Mt 7:14 and narrow the road that l to life,
Jn 10: 3 own sheep by name and l them out.
Ro 6:16 are slaves to sin, which l to death,
    6:16 which l to righteousness?
    6:22 the benefit you reap l to holiness,
    14:19 every effort to do what l to peace
2Co 2:14 God, who always l us as captives
     7:10 sorrow brings repentance that l
Titus 1: 1 of the truth that l to godliness—
1Jn 5:16 There is a sin that l to death.
Rev 12: 9 Satan, who l the whole world astray.

LEAF LEAVES
Ge 8:11 beak was a freshly plucked olive l!
Ps 1: 3 and whose l does not wither—
Pr 11:28 righteous will thrive like a green l.

LEAH
Wife of Jacob (Ge 29:16–30); bore six sons and one daughter (Ge 29:31—30:21; 34:1; 35:23).

LEAN LEANED, LEANING
Ge 41:20 The l, ugly cows ate up the seven
Pr 3: 5 l not on your own understanding;

LEANED LEAN
Ge 47:31 Israel worshiped as he l on the top
Jn 21:20 one who had l back against Jesus
Heb 11:21 worshiped as he l on the top of his

LEANING LEAN
Jn 13:25 L back against Jesus, he asked him,

LEAP LEAPED, LEAPS
Ps 29: 6 He makes Lebanon l like a calf,
Isa 35: 6 Then will the lame l like a deer,
Lk 6:23 "Rejoice in that day and l for joy,

LEAPED LEAP
Ps 114: 4 the mountains l like rams, the hills
Lk 1:41 greeting, the baby l in her womb,

LEAPS* LEAP
Job 37: 1 heart pounds and l from its place.
Ps 28: 7 My heart l for joy, and with my

LEARN LEARNED, LEARNING
Dt 4:10 they may l to revere me as long as
    5: 1 L them and be sure to follow them.
    18: 9 do not l to imitate the detestable
    31:12 and l to fear the LORD your God
Ps 119: 7 heart as l l your righteous laws.
Pr 19:25 and the simple will l prudence;
Isa 1:17 L to do right; seek justice.
    26: 9 people of the world l righteousness.
Jer 35:13 'Will you not l a lesson and obey
Mt 11:29 my yoke upon you and l from me,
Mk 13:28 "Now l this lesson from the fig
Jn 14:31 that the world may l that I love
1Th 4: 4 of you should l to control your own
1Ti 2:11 A woman should l in quietness
    5: these should l first of all to put their
Titus 3:14 Our people must l to devote
Rev 14: 3 No one could l the song except

LEARNED LEARN
Ps 119:152 Long ago I l from your statutes
Pr 24:32 and l a lesson from what I saw:
Ecc 1:17 and folly, but I l that this, too,
    9:11 to the brilliant or favor to the l;
Mt 11:25 these things from the wise and l,
Jn 6:45 Father and l from him comes to me.
    15:15 that l l from my Father I have made
Eph 4:20 however, is not the way of life you l
Php 4: 9 Whatever you have l or received
    4:11 I have l to be content whatever
2Ti 3:14 continue in what you have l
    3:14 you know those from whom you l it,
Heb 5: 8 he was, he l obedience from what he
Rev 2:24 have not l Satan's so-called deep

LEARNING LEARN
Pr 1: 5 let the wise listen and add to their l,
    4: 2 I give you sound l, so do not forsake
    9: 9 and they will add to their l.
Isa 44:25 who overthrows the l of the wise
Jn 7:15 man get such l without having been
Ac 26:24 "Your great l is driving you
2Ti 3: 7 always l but never able to come

LEAST LESS
1Sa 9:21 is not my clan the l of all the clans
Isa 60:22 The l of you will become
Mt 5:18 letter, not the l stroke of a pen,
    5:19 one of the l of these commands
    5:19 others accordingly will be called l
    25:40 did for one of the l of these brothers
Lk 7:28 yet the one who is l in the kingdom
    9:48 the one who is l among you all who
1Co 15: 9 For I am the l of the apostles and do
2Co 11: 5 I do not think I am in the l inferior
Eph 3: 8 Although I am less than the l of all

LEATHER
Ex 25: 5 red and another type of durable l;
Lev 13:48 wool, any l or anything made of l—
Nu 4: 6 to cover the curtain with a durable l,
2Ki 1: 8 and had a l belt around his waist."
Mt 3: 4 and he had a l belt around his waist.

LEAVE LEAVES
Ex 12:10 Do not l any of it till morning;
    12:33 people to hurry and l the country.
    34: 7 he does not l the guilty unpunished;
Lev 19:10 L them for the poor
Nu 11:20 did we ever l Egypt?" ' "
Dt 31: 6 he will never l you nor forsake
Jos 1: 5 I will never l you nor forsake you.
Ru 1:16 "Don't urge me to l you or to turn
Mk 10: 7 this reason a man will l his father
Jn 8:11 *"Go now and l your life of sin."*
    14:18 I will not l you as orphans;
    14:27 Peace I l with you; my peace I give
Eph 5:31 this reason a man will l his father
Heb 13: 5 God has said, "Never will I l you;

LEAVEN (KJV) See YEAST

LEAVENS*
1Co 5: 6 that a little yeast l the whole batch

LEAVES LEAF, LEAVE

Ge 2:24 That is why a man l his father
3: 7 so they sewed fig l together
Pr 13:22 A good person l an inheritance
15:10 awaits anyone who l the path;
Jer 17: 8 its l are always green.
Eze 47:12 Their l will not wither, nor will their
47:12 for food and their l for healing."
Mk 11:13 it, he found nothing but l, because it
1Co 7:15 But if the unbeliever l, let it be so.
Rev 22: 2 the l of the tree are for the healing

LEBANON

Dt 11:24 will extend from the desert to L,
1Ki 4:33 from the cedar of L to the hyssop
5: 6 that cedars of L be cut for me.
2Ki 14: 9 "A thistle in L sent a message to a
cedar in L,
Ps 29: 6 He makes L leap like a calf,
92:12 they will grow like a cedar of L;
Isa 40:16 L is not sufficient for altar fires,
Hab 2:17 have done to L will overwhelm you,

LEBBAEUS (KJV) See THADDAEUS

LEBO HAMATH HAMATH

Nu 34: 8 and from Mount Hor to L.
2Ki 14:25 the boundaries of Israel from L to

LECTURE*

Jn 9:34 in sin at birth; how dare you l us!"
Ac 19: 9 had discussions daily in the l hall

LED LEAD

Ex 3: 1 he l the flock to the far side
32:21 you, that you l them into such great
Dt 8: 2 the LORD your God l you all
17:17 wives, or his heart will be l astray.
1Ki 11: 3 and his wives l him astray.
2Ki 21: 9 Manasseh l them astray, so that they
2Ch 26:16 powerful, his pride l to his downfall.
Ne 13:26 but even he was l into sin by foreign
Job 31: 7 if my heart has been l by my eyes,
Ps 77:19 Your path l through the sea,
78:52 he l them like sheep through
Pr 7:21 persuasive words she l him astray;
20: 1 whoever is l astray by them is not
Isa 53: 7 he was l like a lamb
55:12 go out in joy and be l forth in peace;
Jer 11:19 I had been like a gentle lamb l
50: 6 their shepherds have l them astray
Hos 11: 4 I l them with cords of human
Am 2:10 l you forty years in the wilderness
Mt 4: 1 Jesus was l by the Spirit
27:31 they l him away to crucify him.
Lk 4: 1 and was l by the Spirit
4: 5 The devil l him up to a high place
4: 9 The devil l him to Jerusalem
Ac 8:32 "He was l like a sheep
Ro 8:14 For those who are l by the Spirit
2Co 7: 9 but because your sorrow l you
Gal 5:18 But if you are l by the Spirit,

LEECH*

Pr 30:15 "The l has two daughters. 'Give!

LEEKS*

Nu 11: 5 melons, l, onions and garlic.

LEFT LEFT-HANDED, LEFTOVER

Ge 7:23 Only Noah was l, and those
13: 9 If you go to the l, I'll go to the right;
Ex 12:41 all the LORD's divisions l Egypt.
Nu 26:65 one of them was l except Caleb son
Dt 28:14 to the right or to the l,
Jos 1: 7 turn from it to the right or to the l
23: 6 turning aside to the right or to the l.
Jdg 3: 4 They were l to test the Israelites
2Ki 22: 2 turning aside to the right or to the l.
Pr 4:27 Do not turn to the right or the l;
Isa 30:21 you turn to the right or to the l,
Mt 6: 3 do not let your l hand know what
25:33 on his right and the goats on his l.
Mk 8: 8 of broken pieces that were l over.
10:28 "We have l everything to follow
10:40 my right or l is not for me to grant.
Lk 17:34 one will be taken and the other l.
1Th 4:15 who are l until the coming
Heb 10:26 of the truth, no sacrifice for sins is l,
2Pe 2:15 They have l the straight way

LEFT-HANDED* HAND, LEFT

Jdg 3:15 Ehud, a l man, the son of Gera
20:16 hundred select troops who were l,
1Ch 12: 2 or to sling stones right-handed or l;

LEFTOVER* LEFT

Ru 2: 2 pick up the l grain behind anyone

LEGAL

Col 2:14 the charge of our l indebtedness,

LEGION LEGIONS

Mk 5: 9 "My name is L," he replied,

LEGIONS* LEGION

Mt 26:53 at my disposal more than twelve l

LEGITIMATE*

Heb 12: 8 then you are not l, not true sons

LEGS

Ps 147:10 his delight in the l of the warrior;
Da 2:33 its l of iron, its feet partly of iron
10: 6 and l like the gleam of burnished
Jn 19:33 dead, they did not break his l.
Rev 10: 1 sun, and his l were like fiery pillars.

LEMA*

Mt 27:46 *"Eli, Eli, l sabachthani?"*
Mk 15:34 *"Eloi, Eloi, l sabachthani?"*

LEMUEL*

Pr 31: 1 The sayings of King L—
31: 4 It is not for kings, L—it is not

LEND LENDER, LENDS,
MONEYLENDER

Ex 22:25 "If you l money to one of my
Lev 25:37 You must not l them money
Dt 15: 8 freely l them whatever they need.
28:12 You will l to many nations but will

Dt   28:44 They will l to you, but you will not l
Ps   37:26 are always generous and l freely;
       112: 5 those who are generous and l freely,
Eze   18: 8 He does not l to them at interest
Lk   6:34 Even sinners l to sinners,

LENDER* LEND
Pr   22: 7 and the borrower is slave to the l.
Isa   24: 2 for borrower as for l, for debtor as

LENDS* LEND
Ps   15: 5 who l money to the poor without
Pr   19:17 is kind to the poor l to the LORD,
Eze   18:13 He l at interest and takes a profit.

LENGTH LONG
Ge   13:17 walk through the l and breadth
Pr   10:27 fear of the LORD adds l to life,

LENGTHY* LONG
Mk   12:40 and for a show make l prayers.
Lk   20:47 and for a show make l prayers.

LEOPARD
Isa   11: 6 the l will lie down with the goat,
Jer   13:23 change his skin or a l its spots?
Da   7: 6 beast, one that looked like a l.
Rev   13: 2 The beast I saw resembled a l,

LEPROSY LEPROUS
2Ki   5: 1 was a valiant soldier, but he had l.
        7: 3 Now there were four men with l
2Ch   26:21 King Uzziah had l until the day he
Mt   8: 3 he was cleansed of his l.
       11: 5 those who have l are cleansed,
Lk   4:27 many in Israel with l in the time
       17:12 village, ten men who had l met him.

LEPROUS LEPROSY
Ex   4: 6 when he took it out, the skin was l—
Nu   12:10 the tent, Miriam's skin was l—

LESS LEAST
Ex   30:15 give l when you make the offering
2Ch   6:18 How much l this temple I have
       32:15 How much l will your god deliver
Ezr   9:13 you have punished us l than our sins
Jn   3:30 I must become l."

LESSON
Mk   13:28 "Now learn this l from the fig tree:

LEST
Pr   31: 5 l they drink and forget what has
1Co   1:17 l the cross of Christ be emptied

LET
Ge   1: 3 And God said, "L there be light,"
        1: 6 "L there be a vault between
        1: 9 place, and l dry ground appear."
        1:11 "L the land produce vegetation:
        1:14 "L there be lights in the vault
        1:20 said, "L the water teem with living
        1:24 "L the land produce living creatures
        1:26 "L us make mankind in our image,
       11: 7 l us go down and confuse their
Ex   1:16 but if it is a girl, l her live."

Ex   5: 1 'L my people go, so that they may
        5: 2 LORD and I will not l Israel go."
       13:17 When Pharaoh l the people go,
Ps   22: 8 they say, "l the LORD rescue him.
       25: 2 do not l me be put to shame, nor l
       33: 8 L all the earth fear the LORD;
       95: 1 l us sing for joy to the LORD;
      118:24 l us rejoice today and be glad.
Jer   9:24 but l the one who boasts boast
La   3:40 them, and l us return to the LORD.
Joel   3:10 L the weakling say, "I am strong!"
Mt   27:43 L God rescue him now if he wants
Mk   4: 9 has ears to hear, l them hear."
       10: 9 joined together, l no one separate."
Jn   7:37 "L anyone who is thirsty come
       14: 1 "Do not l your hearts be troubled.
Ro   3: 4 L God be true, and every human
2Co   10:17 "L the one who boasts boast
Eph   4:26 Do not l the sun go down while you
Col   3:15 L the peace of Christ rule in your
        3:16 L the message of Christ dwell
Heb   10:22 l us draw near to God with a sincere
1Jn   4: 7 Dear friends, l us love one another,
Rev   22:17 L the one who is thirsty come;

LETTER LETTERS
Mt   5:18 not the smallest l, not the least
2Co   3: 2 You yourselves are our l,
        3: 6 not of the l but of the Spirit; for the
               l kills,
2Th   3:14 not obey our instruction in this l.

LETTERS LETTER
2Ch   32:17 also wrote l ridiculing the LORD,
2Co   3: 7 which was engraved in l on stone,
       10:10 "His l are weighty and forceful,
Gal   6:11 See what large l I use as I write
2Th   3:17 the distinguishing mark in all my l.
2Pe   3:16 He writes the same way in all his l,

LEVEL
Ps   143:10 good Spirit lead me on l ground.
Isa   26: 7 The path of the righteous is l;
       40: 4 the rough ground shall become l,
       45: 2 before you and will l the mountains;
Jer   31: 9 a l path where they will not stumble,
Lk   6:17 with them and stood on a l place.
Heb   12:13 "Make l paths for your feet,"

LEVI LEVITE, LEVITES, LEVITICAL
    1. Son of Leah (Ge 29:34; 46:11; 1Ch 2:1). With Simeon avenged rape of Dinah (Ge 34). Tribe of blessed (Ge 49:5–7; Dt 33:8–11), chosen as priests (Nu 3–4), numbered (Nu 3:39; 26:62), given cities, but not land (Nu 18; 35; Dt 10:9; Jos 13:14; 21), land (Eze 48:8–22), 12,000 from (Rev 7:7).
    2. See MATTHEW.

LEVIATHAN*
Job   3: 8 day, those who are ready to rouse L.
       41: 1 "Can you pull in L with a fishhook
Ps   74:14 was you who crushed the heads of L
      104:26 and L, which you formed to frolic
Isa   27: 1 L the gliding serpent, L the coiling

LEVITE LEVI
Nu   3:20 These were the L clans,
Dt 26:12 tithe, you shall give it to the L,
Jdg 19: 1 Now a L who lived in a remote area
Ac   4:36 Joseph, a L from Cyprus,

LEVITES LEVI
Ex 32:26 And all the L rallied to him.
Nu   1:53 The L, however, are to set up their
       1:53 The L are to be responsible
       3:12 The L are mine,
       8: 6 "Take the L from among all
    16: 7 You L have gone too far!"
    18:21 "I give to the L all the tithes
    35: 7 must give the L forty-eight towns,
Jos 14: 4 The L received no share of the land
1Ch 15: 2 but the L may carry the ark of God,
    23: 6 David separated the L into divisions
2Ch 31: 2 to their duties as priests or L—
Ezr   6:18 the L in their groups for the service
Ne   8: 9 and the L who were instructing
Mal   3: 3 he will purify the L and refine them

PRIESTS AND LEVITES See PRIESTS

LEVITICAL LEVI
Heb   7:11 attained through the L priesthood—

LEVY
Am   5:11 You l a straw tax on the poor

LEWD LEWDNESS
Jdg 20: 6 because they committed this l

LEWDNESS LEWD
Eze 16:58 will bear the consequences of your l
    23:48 "So I will put an end to l
Mk   7:22 malice, deceit, l, envy, slander,

LIAR* LIE
Dt 19:18 and if the witness proves to be a l,
Job 34: 6 I am right, I am considered a l;
Ps 116:11 my alarm I said, "Everyone is a l."
Pr   17: 4 a l pays attention to a destructive
    19:22 better to be poor than a l.
    30: 6 will rebuke you and prove you a l.
Mic   2:11 If a l and deceiver comes and says,
Jn   8:44 for he is a l and the father of lies.
    8:55 not, I would be a l like you, but I do
Ro   3: 4 be true, and every human being a l.
1Jn   1:10 we make him out to be a l and his
    2: 4 does not do what he commands is a l,
    2:22 Who is the l? It is whoever denies
    4:20 yet hates a brother or sister is a l.
    5:10 God has made him out to be a l,

LIARS* LIE
Ps 63:11 the mouths of l will be silenced.
Isa 57: 4 a brood of rebels, the offspring of l?
Mic   6:12 your inhabitants are l and their
1Ti   1:10 for slave traders and l
    4: 2 come through hypocritical l,
Titus 1:12 "Cretans are always l, evil brutes,
Rev   3: 9 Jews though they are not, but are l—
    21: 8 magic arts, the idolaters and all l—

LIBATIONS*
Ps 16: 4 I will not pour out l of blood to such

LIBERAL* LIBERALLY
2Co   8:20 of the way we administer this l gift.

LIBERALLY* LIBERAL
Dt 15:14 Supply them l from your flock,

LIBERATED* LIBERTY
Ro   8:21 the creation itself will be l from its

LIBERTY* LIBERATED
Lev 25:10 proclaim l throughout the land to all

LICE* (KJV) See also GNATS
Jer 43:12 shepherd picks his garment clean of l,

LICENSE*
Jude   1: 4 of our God into a l for immorality

LICK
Ps 72: 9 him and his enemies l the dust.
Isa 49:23 they will l the dust at your feet.
Mic   7:17 They will l dust like a snake,

LIE LIAR, LIARS, LIED, LIES, LYING
Lev   6: 3 find lost property and l about it,
    19:11 " 'Do not l. " 'Do not deceive
Nu 23:19 that he should l, not a human being,
Dt   6: 7 when you l down and when you get
    11:19 when you l down and when you get
Ru   3: 4 go and uncover his feet and l down.
1Sa 15:29 who is the Glory of Israel does not l
Ps   4: 8 In peace I will l down and sleep,
    23: 2 He makes me l down in green
    38:12 all day long they scheme and l.
    89:35 and I will not l to David—
Pr   3:24 when you l down, your sleep will be
Isa 11: 6 the leopard will l down
    28:15 for we have made a l our refuge
Jer   9: 5 They have taught their tongues to l;
    23:14 They commit adultery and live a l.
Eze 13: 6 are false and their divinations a l.
    34:14 There they will l down in good
Zep   3:13 They will eat and l down and no one
Ro   1:25 the truth about God for a l,
Col   3: 9 Do not l to each other, since you
2Th   2: 9 signs and wonders that serve the l,
    2:11 so that they will believe the l
Titus 1: 2 who does not l, promised before
Heb   6:18 which it is impossible for God to l,
1Jn   1: 6 we l and do not live out the truth.
    2:21 because no l comes from the truth.
Rev 14: 5 No l was found in their mouths;

LIED LIE
Ge 18:15 Sarah was afraid, so she l and said,
Jer   5:12 They have l about the LORD;
Ac   5: 4 You have not l just to human beings

LIES LIE
Job 27: 4 and my tongue will not utter l.
Ps   5: 6 you destroy those who tell l.
    5: 9 with their tongues they tell l.
    10: 7 His mouth is full of l and threats;

Ps	12: 2	Everyone l to their neighbor;
	34:13	evil and your lips from telling l.
	58: 3	they are wayward, spreading l.
	144: 8	whose mouths are full of l,
Pr	6:19	a false witness who pours out l
	12:17	the truth, but a false witness tells l.
	19: 5	whoever pours out l will not go free.
	19: 9	and whoever pours out l will perish.
	29:12	If a ruler listens to l, all his officials
	30: 8	Keep falsehood and l far from me;
Jer	5:31	The prophets prophesy l, the priests
	9: 3	their tongue like a bow, to shoot l;
	14:14	"The prophets are prophesying l
La	1: 1	How deserted l the city, once so full
Eze	13:22	the righteous with your l, when I
Hos	11:12	Ephraim has surrounded me with l,
Na	3: 1	of blood, full of l, full of plunder,
Hab	2:18	Or an image that teaches l?
Zep	3:13	will do no wrong; they will tell no l.
Jn	8:44	When he l, he speaks his native
	8:44	for he is a liar and the father of l.

LIFE LIVE

Ge	1:30	that has the breath of l in it—
	2: 7	into his nostrils the breath of l,
	2: 9	of the garden were the tree of l
	6:17	to destroy all l under the heavens,
	9: 5	for the l of another human being.
	9:11	Never again will all l be destroyed
Ex	21: 6	Then he will be his servant for l.
	21:23	injury, you are to take l for l,
	23:26	I will give you a full l span.
Lev	17:14	because the l of every creature is its
	24:17	" 'Anyone who takes the l
	24:18	must make restitution—l for l.
Nu	35:31	a ransom for the l of a murderer,
Dt	4:42	one of these cities and save their l.
	12:23	because the blood is the l, and you
		must not eat the l with the meat
	19:21	l for l, eye for eye, tooth for tooth,
	30:15	See, I set before you today l
	30:19	have set before you l and death,
	30:19	Now choose l, so that you and your
	30:20	For the LORD is your l, and he
	32:39	I put to death and I bring to l, I have
	32:47	idle words for you—they are your l.
1Sa	19: 5	He took his l in his hands when he
Ne	9: 6	You give l to everything,
Job	2: 4	will give all he has for his own l.
	2: 6	but you must spare his l."
	10: 1	"I loathe my very l; therefore I will
	33: 4	breath of the Almighty gives me l.
	33:30	the light of l may shine on them.
	42:12	of Job's l more than the former part.
Ps	16:11	make known to me the path of l;
	17:14	this world whose reward is in this l.
	23: 6	will follow me all the days of my l,
	27: 1	LORD is the stronghold of my l—
	34:12	Whoever of you loves l and desires
	36: 9	For with you is the fountain of l;
	49: 7	No one can redeem the l of another
	49: 8	the ransom for a l is costly,
	63: 3	Because your love is better than l,
	69:28	they be blotted out of the book of l

Ps	91:16	With long l I will satisfy him
	103:15	The l of mortals is like grass,
	104:33	I will sing to the LORD all my l;
	119:25	preserve my l according to your
Pr	1:19	it takes away the l of those who get
	3: 2	they will prolong your l many years
	3:16	Long l is in her right hand;
	3:18	She is a tree of l to those who take
	6:23	and instruction are the way to l,
	6:26	man's wife preys on your very l.
	7:23	little knowing it will cost him his l.
	8:35	For those who find me find l
	10:11	of the righteous is a fountain of l,
	10:27	fear of the LORD adds length to l,
	11:30	fruit of the righteous is a tree of l,
	13:12	but a longing fulfilled is a tree of l.
	13:14	of the wise is a fountain of l,
	14:27	of the LORD is a fountain of l,
	15: 4	The soothing tongue is a tree of l,
	16:22	Prudence is a fountain of l
	18:21	The tongue has the power of l
	19: 8	The one who gets wisdom loves l;
	19:23	The fear of the LORD leads to l;
	21:21	righteousness and love finds l,
	22: 5	who would preserve their l stay far
Ecc	2:17	So I hated l, because the work
	9: 9	Enjoy l with your wife, whom you
	9: 9	of this meaningless l that God has
	9: 9	For this is your lot in l and in your
	10:19	wine makes l merry, and money is
Isa	53:10	the LORD makes his l an offering
	53:11	he will see the light of l and be
	53:12	he poured out his l unto death,
La	3:58	up my case; you redeemed my l.
Eze	18:27	just and right, they will save their l.
	37: 5	enter you, and you will come to l.
Da	12: 2	some to everlasting l,
Jnh	2: 6	God, brought my l up from the pit.
Mal	2: 5	with him, a covenant of l and peace,
Mt	6:25	do not worry about your l, what you
	6:25	Is not l more than food,
	7:14	and narrow the road that leads to l,
	10:39	finds their l will lose it, and whoever
		loses their l for my sake
	16:21	and on the third day be raised to l.
	16:25	wants to save their l will lose it, but
		whoever loses their l for me
	18: 8	It is better for you to enter l maimed
	19:16	thing must I do to get eternal l?"
	19:29	as much and will inherit eternal l.
	20:28	to give his l as a ransom for many."
	25:46	but the righteous to eternal l."
Mk	3: 4	or to do evil, to save l or to kill?"
	8:35	wants to save their l will lose it, but
		whoever loses their l for me
	9:43	you to enter l maimed than with two
	10:17	must I do to inherit eternal l?"
	10:30	and in the age to come eternal l.
	10:45	to give his l as a ransom for many."
Lk	6: 9	do evil, to save l or to destroy it?"
	9:22	and on the third day be raised to l."
	9:24	wants to save their l will lose it, but
		whoever loses their l for me will

Lk 12:15 l does not consist in an abundance
    12:22 do not worry about your l, what you
    12:25 can add a single hour to your l?
    14:26 yes, even their own l—
    17:33 tries to keep their l will lose it,
    17:33 whoever loses their l will preserve
    21:19 Stand firm, and you will win l.
Jn 1: 4 In him was l, and that l was the light
    3:15 who believes may have eternal l
    3:36 believes in the Son has eternal l,
    3:36 rejects the Son will not see l,
    4:14 of water welling up to eternal l."
    5:21 raises the dead and gives them l, even
         so the Son gives l to whom he
    5:24 him who sent me has eternal l
    5:24 but has crossed over from death to l.
    5:26 For as the Father has l in himself,
    5:26 the Son also to have l in himself.
    5:39 that in them you have eternal l.
    5:40 you refuse to come to me to have l.
    6:27 for food that endures to eternal l,
    6:33 heaven and gives l to the world."
    6:35 Jesus declared, "I am the bread of l.
    6:40 believes in him shall have eternal l,
    6:47 the one who believes has eternal l.
    6:48 I am the bread of l.
    6:51 I will give for the l of the world."
    6:53 his blood, you have no l in you.
    6:63 The Spirit gives l; the flesh counts
    6:63 they are full of the Spirit and l.
    6:68 You have the words of eternal l.
    8:12 but will have the light of l."
    10:10 I have come that they may have l,
    10:11 The good shepherd lays down his l
    10:15 and I lay down my l for the sheep.
    10:28 I give them eternal l, and they shall
    11:25 "I am the resurrection and the l.
    12:25 who loves their l will lose it, while
          anyone who hates their l
    12:50 that his command leads to eternal l.
    13:37 I will lay down my l for you."
    14: 6 am the way and the truth and the l.
    15:13 lay down one's l for one's friends.
    17: 2 he might give eternal l to all those
    17: 3 Now this is eternal l: that they know
    20:31 by believing you may have l in his
Ac 2:28 made known to me the paths of l;
    2:32 God has raised this Jesus to l,
    3:15 You killed the author of l, but God
    11:18 granted repentance that leads to l."
    13:48 appointed for eternal l believed.
Ro 2: 7 immortality, he will give eternal l.
    4:25 was raised to l for our justification.
    5:10 shall we be saved through his l!
    5:18 in justification and l for all people.
    5:21 bring eternal l through Jesus Christ
    6: 4 the Father, we too may live a new l.
    6:13 have been brought from death to l;
    6:22 holiness, and the result is eternal l.
    6:23 God is eternal l in Christ Jesus our
    7:10 to bring l actually brought death.
    8: 2 of the Spirit who gives l has set you
    8: 6 the mind governed by the Spirit is l

Ro 8:11 give l to your mortal bodies because
    8:38 convinced that neither death nor l,
1Co 15:19 If only for this l we have hope
    15:36 does not come to l unless it dies.
2Co 2:16 to the other, an aroma that brings l.
    3: 6 the letter kills, but the Spirit gives l.
    4:10 so that the l of Jesus may also be
    5: 4 is mortal may be swallowed up by l.
Gal 2:20 The l I now live in the body, I live
    3:21 had been given that could impart l,
    6: 8 from the Spirit will reap eternal l.
Eph 4: 1 to live a l worthy of the calling you
    6: 3 you may enjoy long l on the earth."
Php 2:16 as you hold firmly to the word of l.
    4: 3 whose names are in the book of l.
Col 1:10 may live a l worthy of the Lord
    3: 3 your l is now hidden with Christ
1Th 4:12 your daily l may win the respect
1Ti 1:16 believe in him and receive eternal l.
    4: 8 promise for both the present l and
         the l to come.
    4:16 Watch your l and doctrine closely.
    6:12 Take hold of the eternal l
    6:19 may take hold of the l that is truly l.
2Ti 1: 9 saved us and called us to a holy l—
    1:10 and has brought l and immortality
    3:12 live a godly l in Christ Jesus will be
Titus 1: 2 in the hope of eternal l, which God,
    3: 7 heirs having the hope of eternal l.
Heb 7:16 of the power of an indestructible l.
Jas 1:12 person will receive the crown of l
    3:13 Let them show it by their good l,
1Pe 3: 7 with you of the gracious gift of l,
    3:10 "Whoever would love l and see
2Pe 1: 3 for a godly l through our knowledge
1Jn 1: 1 proclaim concerning the Word of l.
    2:25 is what he promised us—eternal l.
    3:14 that we have passed from death to l,
    3:16 Jesus Christ laid down his l for us.
    5:11 God has given us eternal l, and this l
    5:20 He is the true God and eternal l.
Jude 1:21 Christ to bring you to eternal l.
Rev 2: 7 the right to eat from the tree of l,
    2: 8 Last, who died and came to l again.
    2:10 and I will give you l as your victor's
    3: 5 of that person from the book of l.
    11:11 a half days the breath of l from God
    13: 8 written in the Lamb's book of l,
    17: 8 in the book of l from the creation
    20: 4 They came to l and reigned
    20:12 was opened, which is the book of l.
    20:15 in the book of l was thrown
    21: 6 from the spring of the water of l.
    21:27 are written in the Lamb's book of l.
    22: 1 me the river of the water of l,
    22: 2 side of the river stood the tree of l,
    22:14 may have the right to the tree of l
    22:17 take the free gift of the water of l.
    22:19 that person any share in the tree of l

ETERNAL LIFE Mt 19:16, 29; 25:46; Mk 10:17,
30; Lk 10:25; 18:18, 30; Jn 3:15, 16, 36; 4:14, 36;
5:24, 39; 6:27, 40, 47, 54, 68; 10:28; 12:25, 50; 17:2,
3; Ac 13:46, 48; Ro 2:7; 5:21; 6:22, 23; Gal 6:8;

1Ti 1:16; 6:12; Titus 1:2; 3:7; 1Jn 1:2; 2:25; 3:15;
5:11, 13, 20; Jude 1:21

LIFE'S* LIVE
Ps   39: 4 my l end and the number of my
Lk   8:14 way they are choked by l worries,

LIFE-GIVING* GIVE
Pr   15:31 Whoever heeds l correction will be
1Co 15:45 the last Adam, a l spirit.

LIFEBLOOD BLOOD
Ge   9: 4 not eat meat that has its l still in it.

LIFELESS LIVE
Ps 106:28 and ate sacrifices offered to l gods;
Jer 16:18 defiled my land with the l forms
Hab   2:19 Or to l stone, 'Wake up!'

LIFETIME LIVE
1Ki   3:13 that in your l you will have no equal
Ps   30: 5 a moment, but his favor lasts a l;
Lk   16:25 in your l you received your good

LIFT LIFTED, LIFTING, LIFTS,
UPLIFTED
Dt   32:40 I l my hand to heaven and solemnly
Ps   24: 7 L up your heads, you gates;
      28: 2 as I l up my hands toward your
      63: 4 in your name I will l up my hands.
      91:12 they will l you up in their hands,
     121: 1 I l up my eyes to the mountains—
     123: 1 I l up my eyes to you, to you who
     134: 2 L up your hands in the sanctuary
Isa   40: 9 l up your voice with a shout, l it up,
La   2:19 L up your hands to him for the lives
       3:41 Let us l up our hearts and our hands
Mt   4: 6 they will l you up in their hands,
Lk   11:46 you yourselves will not l one finger
      21:28 place, stand up and l up your heads,
Jas   4:10 the Lord, and he will l you up.
1Pe   5: 6 that he may l you up in due time.

LIFTED LIFT
Ex   17:16 "Because hands were l up against
Nu   9:21 whenever the cloud l, they set out.
1Sa   2: 1 in the Lord my horn is l high.
Ne   8: 6 and all the people l their hands
Ps   30: 1 for you l me out of the depths
      40: 2 He l me out of the slimy pit,
      93: 3 The seas have l up, Lord,
     112: 9 their horn will be l high in honor.
     118:16 The Lord's right hand is l high;
Isa   52:13 he will be raised and l up and highly
      63: 9 he l them up and carried them all
Eze   3:12 Then the Spirit l me up, and I heard
       8: 3 The Spirit l me up between earth
      11: 1 Then the Spirit l me up and brought
Mt   11:23 will you be l to the heavens?
Lk   24:50 he l up his hands and blessed them.
Jn   3:14 Just as Moses l up the snake
       3:14 so the Son of Man must be l up,
       8:28 "When you have l up the Son
      12:32 I, when I am l up from the earth,
      12:34 'The Son of Man must be l up'?

LIFTING LIFT
Ps 141: 2 may the l up of my hands be like
1Ti   2: 8 l up holy hands without anger

LIFTS LIFT
1Sa   2: 8 and l the needy from the ash heap;
Ps   3: 3 glory, the One who l my head high.
     113: 7 and l the needy from the ash heap;
     145:14 and l up all who are bowed down.

LIGAMENT* LIGAMENTS
Eph   4:16 held together by every supporting l,

LIGAMENTS* LIGAMENT
Col   2:19 held together by its l and sinews,

LIGHT DAYLIGHT, ENLIGHTEN,
ENLIGHTENED, LIGHTEN,
LIGHTENED, LIGHTS, TWILIGHT
Ge   1: 3 "Let there be l," and there was l.
       1: 5 God called the l "day,"
       1:16 the greater l to govern the day and the
             lesser l to govern the night.
Ex   13:21 in a pillar of fire to give them l,
      25:37 on it so that they l the space in front
Dt   25:13 in your bag—one heavy, one l.
2Sa   22:29 Lord turns my darkness into l.
Ezr   9: 8 and so our God gives l to our eyes
Job   3:20 "Why is l given to those in misery,
      38:19 "What is the way to the abode of l?
Ps   4: 6 Let the l of your face shine on us.
      18:28 my God turns my darkness into l.
      19: 8 are radiant, giving l to the eyes.
      27: 1 The Lord is my l and my
      36: 9 fountain of life; in your l we see l.
      56:13 walk before God in the l of life.
      76: 4 You are radiant with l,
      89:15 who walk in the l of your presence,
     104: 2 The Lord wraps himself in l as
     119:105 a lamp for my feet, a l on my path.
     119:130 unfolding of your words gives l;
     139:12 the day, for darkness is as l to you.
Pr   4:18 shining ever brighter till the full l
      13: 9 The l of the righteous shines
      15:30 L in a messenger's eyes brings joy
Ecc   2:13 just as l is better than darkness.
Isa   2: 5 let us walk in the l of the Lord.
       9: 2 in darkness have seen a great l;
      42: 6 the people and a l for the Gentiles,
      45: 7 I form the l and create darkness,
      49: 6 also make you a l for the Gentiles,
      53:11 he will see the l of life and be
      58:10 then your l will rise in the darkness,
      60: 1 for your l has come, and the glory
      60:19 The sun will no more be your l
      60:19 Lord will be your everlasting l,
Eze   1:27 and brilliant l surrounded him.
Am   5:18 That day will be darkness, not l.
Mic   7: 8 darkness, the Lord will be my l.
Mt   4:16 in darkness have seen a great l;
       5:14 "You are the l of the world.
       5:16 way, let your l shine before others,
       6:22 your whole body will be full of l.
      11:30 yoke is easy and my burden is l."

Mt	17: 2	his clothes became as white as the l.
	24:29	and the moon will not give its l;
Mk	13:24	and the moon will not give its l;
Lk	2:32	a l for revelation to the Gentiles,
	8:16	those who come in can see the l.
	11:33	those who come in may see the l.
Jn	1: 4	that life was the l of all mankind.
	1: 5	The l shines in the darkness,
	1: 7	witness to testify concerning that l,
	1: 9	The true l that gives l to everyone
	3:19	L has come into the world,
	3:20	Everyone who does evil hates the l,
	5:35	you chose for a time to enjoy his l.
	8:12	he said, "I am the l of the world.
	8:12	but will have the l of life."
	9: 5	the world, I am the l of the world."
	12:35	Walk while you have the l,
	12:46	I have come into the world as a l,
Ac	9: 3	suddenly a l from heaven flashed
	13:47	" 'I have made you a l
Ro	13:12	darkness and put on the armor of l.
1Co	3:13	is, because the Day will bring it to l.
2Co	4: 6	made his l shine in our hearts
	4:17	For our l and momentary troubles
	6:14	Or what fellowship can l have
	11:14	masquerades as an angel of l.
Eph	5: 8	but now you are l in the Lord. Live as children of l
	5: 9	(for the fruit of the l consists in all
Col	1:12	his holy people in the kingdom of l.
1Th	5: 5	You are all children of the l
1Ti	6:16	and who lives in unapproachable l,
Heb	12: 5	son, do not make l of the Lord's
1Pe	2: 9	out of darkness into his wonderful l.
2Pe	1:19	it, as to a l shining in a dark place,
1Jn	1: 5	God is l; in him there is no darkness
	1: 7	But if we walk in the l, as he is in the l, we have fellowship
	2: 8	and the true l is already shining.
	2: 9	Anyone who claims to be in the l
Rev	8:12	A third of the day was without l,
	21:23	for the glory of God gives it l,
	22: 5	They will not need the l of a lamp or the l of the sun, for the Lord God will give them l.

LIGHTEN LIGHT

2Ch	10: 9	'L the yoke your father put on us'?"
Jnh	1: 5	the cargo into the sea to l the ship.

LIGHTENED* LIGHT

Ac	27:38	they l the ship by throwing the grain

LIGHTNING

Ex	9:23	and l flashed down to the ground.
	19:16	third day there was thunder and l,
	20:18	the people saw the thunder and l
2Sa	22:15	with great bolts of l he routed them.
Job	37:15	the clouds and makes his l flash?
Ps	18:12	with hailstones and bolts of l.
	97: 4	His l lights up the world;
Jer	10:13	He sends l with the rain and brings
Eze	1:13	it was bright, and l flashed out of it.
Da	10: 6	his face like l, his eyes like flaming

Mt	24:27	For as l that comes from the east is
	28: 3	His appearance was like l, and his
Lk	9:29	became as bright as a flash of l.
	10:18	replied, "I saw Satan fall like l
Rev	4: 5	From the throne came flashes of l,
	8: 5	flashes of l and an earthquake.
	11:19	And there came flashes of l,
	16:18	Then there came flashes of l,

LIGHTS LIGHT

Ge	1:14	"Let there be l in the vault
	1:16	God made two great l—
Ps	136: 7	who made the great l—
Lk	8:16	"No one l a lamp and hides it
Jas	1:17	from the Father of the heavenly l,

LIKE LIKE-MINDED, LIKENESS

Ge	3: 5	and you will be l God,
	3:22	"The man has now become l one
	13:16	I will make your offspring l the dust
	28:14	Your descendants will be l the dust
Ex	7: 1	I have made you l God to Pharaoh,
	8:10	there is no one l the Lord our
	15:11	Who among the gods is l you,
	24:17	of the Lord looked l a consuming
	34: 1	out two stone tablets l the first ones,
Nu	11: 7	The manna was l coriander seed and looked l resin.
	13:33	We seemed l grasshoppers in our
Dt	8:20	L the nations the Lord destroyed
	18:15	for you a prophet l me from among
	32:31	For their rock is not l our Rock,
	33:29	Who is l you, a people saved
1Sa	2: 2	is no one holy l the Lord;
	25:25	He is just l his name—
2Sa	7:22	There is no one l you, and there is
1Ki	8:23	there is no God l you in heaven
	14: 8	have not been l my servant David,
	21:25	(There was never anyone l Ahab,
1Ch	17:21	And who is l your people Israel—
Job	1: 8	There is no one on earth l him;
	9:32	"He is not a mere mortal l me that I
	40: 9	Do you have an arm l God's,
Ps	1: 3	That person is l a tree planted
	1: 4	They are l chaff that the wind blows
	18:33	He makes my feet l the feet
	22:14	I am poured out l water, and all my
	35:10	exclaim, "Who is l you, Lord?
	48:10	L your name, O God, your praise
	86: 8	Among the gods there is none l you,
	103:15	The life of mortals is l grass,
	113: 5	Who is l the Lord our God,
	114: 4	leaped l rams, the hills l lambs.
Pr	7:22	once he followed her l an ox going
	11:22	L a gold ring in a pig's snout is
	25:11	L apples of gold in settings of silver
Ecc	2:16	L the fool, the wise too must die!
	12:11	The words of the wise are l goads,
SS	2: 2	L a lily among thorns is my darling
	8: 6	Place me l a seal over your heart,
Isa	1: 9	we would have become l Sodom,
	1:18	"Though your sins are l scarlet,
	11: 7	and the lion will eat straw l the ox.

Isa   40: 6 "All people are l grass, and all their
                faithfulness is l the flowers
       46: 9 I am God, and there is none l me.
       53: 2 grew up before him l a tender shoot,
       53: 6 We all, l sheep, have gone astray,
       64: 6 our righteous acts are l filthy rags;
Jer   10: 6 No one is l you, LORD;
       23:29 "Is not my word l fire,"
La   1:12 Is any suffering l my suffering
        2: 5 The Lord is l an enemy;
Eze   1: 4 of the fire looked l glowing metal,
        1:10 Their faces looked l this:
        1:26 heads was what looked l a throne
        8: 2 and I saw a figure l that of a man.
Da   3:25 and the fourth looks l a son
        7: 4 "The first was l a lion, and it had
        7:13 there before me was one l a son
      10: 6 His body was l topaz, his face l
      10: 6 his voice l the sound of a multitude.
Hos   1:10 "Yet the Israelites will be l the sand
        6: 4 Your love is l the morning mist,
      14: 5 I will be l the dew to Israel;
Mic   7:18 Who is a God l you, who pardons
Na   1: 6 His wrath is poured out l fire;
Zec   1: 4 Do not be l your ancestors, to whom
      13: 9 I will refine them l silver and test
Mt   9:36 l sheep without a shepherd.
      10:16 you out l sheep among wolves.
Lk   6:48 They are l a man building a house,
      13:18 "What is the kingdom of God l?
      22:26 But you are not to be l that.
      22:26 the one who rules l the one who
Ac   3:22 for you a prophet l me from among
Ro   5:15 But the gift is not l the trespass.
       9:29 we would have become l Sodom,
1Co   9:20 To the Jews I became l a Jew,
      13:11 I was a child, I talked l a child, I
               thought l a child, I reasoned l a child.
1Pe   1:24 "All people are l grass, and all their
2Pe   3: 8 the Lord a day is l a thousand years,
               and a thousand years are l a day.
       3:10 day of the Lord will come l a thief.
Rev   1:13 the lampstands was someone l a son
       2:18 whose eyes are l blazing fire
       3: 3 I will come l a thief, and you will
       4: 7 The first living creature was l a lion,
               the second was l an ox, the third
               had a face l a man, the fourth was l a
               flying eagle.
      10: 1 his face was l the sun, and his legs
               were l fiery pillars.
      13: 4 and asked, "Who is l the beast?
      16:15 "Look, I come l a thief!
      19:12 His eyes are l blazing fire,

LIKE-MINDED* LIKE, MIND
Php   2: 2 make my joy complete by being l,
1Pe   3: 8 all of you, be l, be sympathetic,

LIKENESS LIKE
Ge   1:26 in our l, so that they may rule over
       5: 1 he made them in the l of God.
Ps   17:15 I will be satisfied with seeing your l.
Isa   52:14 his form marred beyond human l—

Ro   8: 3 his own Son in the l of sinful flesh
Php   2: 7 of a servant, being made in human l.
Jas   3: 9 who have been made in God's l.

LILIES LILY
1Ki   7:22 on top were in the shape of l.
SS   2:16 I am his; he browses among the l.

LILY LILIES
2Ch   4: 5 the rim of a cup, like a l blossom.
SS   2: 1 a rose of Sharon, a l of the valleys.
        2: 2 Like a l among thorns is my darling
Hos   14: 5 he will blossom like a l.

LIMIT LIMITS
Ps   147: 5 his understanding has no l.
Jer   5:28 Their evil deeds have no l;
Jn   3:34 for God gives the Spirit without l.

LIMITS LIMIT
Ex   19:23 'Put l around the mountain and set it
Job   11: 7 Can you probe the l
2Co   10:13 will not boast beyond proper l,

LIMP
Isa   13: 7 all hands will go l, every heart will
Zep   3:16 do not let your hands hang l.

LINE
Ge   19:32 preserve our family l through our
Dt   25: 9 not build up his brother's family l."
Ru   4: 4 it except you, and I am next in l."
Ps   89:29 I will establish his l forever,
Isa   28:17 I will make justice the measuring l
               and righteousness the plumb l;
Jer   33:15 Branch sprout from David's l;
Mt   17:27 go to the lake and throw out your l.
Lk   2: 4 to the house and l of David.

LINEN
Ex   26: 1 with ten curtains of finely twisted l
      28:39 "Weave the tunic of fine l and make
               the turban of fine l.
Lev   16: 4 He is to put on the sacred l tunic,
      16: 4 around him and put on the l turban.
Pr   31:22 she is clothed in fine l and purple.
      31:24 She makes l garments and sells
Jer   13: 1 buy a l belt and put it around your
Eze   9: 2 clothed in l who had a writing kit
Da   10: 5 before me was a man dressed in l,
Mk   15:46 So Joseph bought some l cloth,
Jn   20: 6 He saw the strips of l lying there,
Rev   15: 6 shining l and wore golden sashes
      19: 8 (Fine l stands for the righteous acts

LINGER
Pr   23:30 Those who l over wine, who go
Hab   2: 3 Though it l, wait for it;

LION LION'S, LIONS, LIONS'
Ge   49: 9 Like a l he crouches and lies down,
Jdg   14: 6 that he tore the l apart with his bare
1Sa   17:34 When a l or a bear came and carried
Ps   91:13 You will tread on the l
Ecc   9: 4 a live dog is better off than a dead l!
Isa   11: 7 and the l will eat straw like the ox.

Isa 65:25 and the l will eat straw like the ox,
Jer 4: 7 A l has come out of his lair;
  25:38 Like a l he will leave his lair,
Eze 1:10 right side each had the face of a l,
  10:14 the third the face of a l,
Da 7: 4 "The first was like a l, and it had
Hos 13: 7 So I will be like a l to them,
1Pe 5: 8 around like a roaring l looking
Rev 4: 7 The first living creature was like a l,
  5: 5 See, the L of the tribe of Judah,
  13: 2 a bear and a mouth like that of a l.

LION'S LION
Ge 49: 9 You are a l cub, Judah;
2Ti 4:17 I was delivered from the l mouth.

LIONS LION
Ps 22:21 Rescue me from the mouth of the l;
Da 6:20 able to rescue you from the l?"

LIONS' LION
Da 6: 7 shall be thrown into the l den.
Na 2:11 Where now is the l den, the place

LIPS
Ex 6:12 me, since I speak with faltering l?"
Dt 23:23 Whatever your l utter you must be
Ps 34: 1 his praise will always be on my l.
  40: 9 I do not seal my l, LORD, as you
  63: 3 than life, my l will glorify you.
  119:171 May my l overflow with praise,
  140: 3 the poison of vipers is on their l.
  141: 3 keep watch over the door of my l.
Pr 5: 3 the l of the adulterous woman drip
  10:13 is found on the l of the discerning,
  10:18 conceals hatred with lying l
  10:21 The l of the righteous nourish many,
  10:32 The l of the righteous know what
  12:22 The LORD detests lying l, but he
  13: 3 who guard their l preserve their
  14: 7 will not find knowledge on their l.
  15: 7 The l of the wise spread knowledge,
  24:26 honest answer is like a kiss on the l.
  26:23 on earthenware are fervent l
  27: 2 an outsider, and not your own l.
Ecc 10:12 fools are consumed by their own l.
SS 4:11 Your l drop sweetness as
Isa 6: 5 I am a man of unclean l, and I live
      among a people of unclean l,
  28:11 with foreign l and strange tongues
  29:13 mouth and honor me with their l,
Jer 12: 2 You are always on their l but far
Hos 14: 2 that we may offer the fruit of our l.
Mal 2: 7 "For the l of a priest ought
Mt 15: 8 people honor me with their l,
  21:16 read, " 'From the l of children
Lk 4:22 gracious words that came from his l.
Ro 3:13 "The poison of vipers is on their l."
1Co 14:21 and through the l of foreigners I will
Col 3: 8 and filthy language from your l.
Heb 13:15 the fruit of l that openly profess his
1Pe 3:10 and their l from deceitful speech.

LIPS
Jos 1: 8 Book of the Law always on your l;

LIQUOR (KJV)

LIST LISTED
1Ch 11:11 this is the l
  27: 1 This is the
Ezr 2: 2 The l of th
Ne 7: 7 The l of th
Ps 56: 8 l my tears
1Ti 5: 9 the l of wi

LISTED LIST
Nu 1:18 years old

LISTEN LISTEN
LISTENS
Ex 4: 1 if they do
  6:30 lips, why
  7:13 hard and
  15:26 "If you l
  23:22 If you l c
Lev 26:14 if you wil
Dt 18:15 You mus
  30:20 LORD yo
1Ki 4:34 From all
2Ki 17:40 They wo
  21: 9 But the
Ps 5: 1 L to my
  34:11 Come, n
  55: 1 L to my
  143: 1 my pray
Pr 1: 5 let the
  4: 1 L, my s
  8:33 L to my
  8:34 Blessed
  12:15 to them
Ecc 5: 1 Go nea
Isa 44: 1 "But n
Jer 7:24 But the
Eze 2: 5 And w
  40: 4 look ca
Zec 7:13 " 'Whe
Mt 12:42 the ear
Mk 9: 7 is my
Jn 10:27 My sh
Ac 3:22 you m
Jas 1:19 Every
  1:22 Do n
1Jn 4: 6 is not

LISTENED l
Ge 3:17 "Beca
  30:17 God l
  30:22 he l t
Nu 21: 3 The l
Dt 9:19 But a
  10:10 the L
  34: 9 So th
Ne 8: 3 all th
Isa 66: 4 answ
Da 9: 6 We l

LISTENING
1Sa 3:10 said
Pr 18:13 To a

Isa 40: 6 "All people are l grass, and all their faithfulness is l the flowers
46: 9 I am God, and there is none l me.
53: 2 grew up before him l a tender shoot,
53: 6 We all, l sheep, have gone astray,
64: 6 our righteous acts are l filthy rags;
Jer 10: 6 No one is l you, LORD;
23:29 "Is not my word l fire,"
La 1:12 Is any suffering l my suffering
2: 5 The Lord is l an enemy;
Eze 1: 4 of the fire looked l glowing metal,
1:10 Their faces looked l this:
1:26 heads was what looked l a throne
8: 2 and I saw a figure l that of a man.
Da 3:25 and the fourth looks l a son
7: 4 "The first was l a lion, and it had
7:13 there before me was one l a son
10: 6 His body was l topaz, his face l
10: 6 his voice l the sound of a multitude.
Hos 1:10 "Yet the Israelites will be l the sand
6: 4 Your love is l the morning mist,
14: 5 I will be l the dew to Israel;
Mic 7:18 Who is a God l you, who pardons
Na 1: 6 His wrath is poured out l fire;
Zec 1: 4 Do not be l your ancestors, to whom
13: 9 I will refine them l silver and test
Mt 9:36 l sheep without a shepherd.
10:16 you out l sheep among wolves.
Lk 6:48 They are l a man building a house,
13.18 "What is the kingdom of God l?
22:26 But you are not to be l that.
22:26 the one who rules l the one who
Ac 3:22 for you a prophet l me from among
Ro 5:15 But the gift is not l the trespass.
9:29 we would have become l Sodom,
1Co 9:20 To the Jews I became l a Jew,
13:11 I was a child, I talked l a child, I thought l a child, I reasoned l a child.
1Pe 1:24 "All people are l grass, and all their
2Pe 3: 8 the Lord a day is l a thousand years, and a thousand years are l a day.
3:10 day of the Lord will come l a thief.
Rev 1:13 the lampstands was someone l a son
2:18 whose eyes are l blazing fire
3: 3 I will come l a thief, and you will
4: 7 The first living creature was l a lion, the second was l an ox, the third had a face l a man, the fourth was l a flying eagle.
10: 1 his face was l the sun, and his legs were l fiery pillars.
13: 4 and asked, "Who is l the beast?
16:15 "Look, I come l a thief!
19:12 His eyes are l blazing fire,

LIKE-MINDED* LIKE, MIND
Php 2: 2 make my joy complete by being l,
1Pe 3: 8 all of you, be l, be sympathetic,

LIKENESS LIKE
Ge 1:26 in our l, so that they may rule over
5: 1 he made them in the l of God.
Ps 17:15 I will be satisfied with seeing your l.
Isa 52:14 his form marred beyond human l—

Ro 8: 3 his own Son in the l of sinful flesh
Php 2: 7 of a servant, being made in human l.
Jas 3: 9 who have been made in God's l.

LILIES LILY
1Ki 7:22 on top were in the shape of l.
SS 2:16 I am his; he browses among the l.

LILY LILIES
2Ch 4: 5 the rim of a cup, like a l blossom.
SS 2: 1 a rose of Sharon, a l of the valleys.
2: 2 Like a l among thorns is my darling
Hos 14: 5 he will blossom like a l.

LIMIT LIMITS
Ps 147: 5 his understanding has no l.
Jer 5:28 Their evil deeds have no l;
Jn 3:34 for God gives the Spirit without l.

LIMITS LIMIT
Ex 19:23 'Put l around the mountain and set it
Job 11: 7 Can you probe the l
2Co 10:13 will not boast beyond proper l,

LIMP
Isa 13: 7 all hands will go l, every heart will
Zep 3:16 do not let your hands hang l.

LINE
Ge 19:32 preserve our family l through our
Dt 25: 9 not build up his brother's family l."
Ru 4: 4 it except you, and I am next in l."
Ps 89:29 I will establish his l forever,
Isa 28:17 I will make justice the measuring l and righteousness the plumb l;
Jer 33:15 Branch sprout from David's l;
Mt 17:27 go to the lake and throw out your l.
Lk 2: 4 to the house and l of David.

LINEN
Ex 26: 1 with ten curtains of finely twisted l
28:39 "Weave the tunic of fine l and make the turban of fine l.
Lev 16: 4 He is to put on the sacred l tunic,
16: 4 around him and put on the l turban.
Pr 31:22 she is clothed in fine l and purple.
31:24 She makes l garments and sells
Jer 13: 1 buy a l belt and put it around your
Eze 9: 2 clothed in l who had a writing kit
Da 10: 5 before me was a man dressed in l,
Mk 15:46 So Joseph bought some l cloth,
Jn 20: 6 He saw the strips of l lying there,
Rev 15: 6 shining l and wore golden sashes
19: 8 (Fine l stands for the righteous acts

LINGER
Pr 23:30 Those who l over wine, who go
Hab 2: 3 Though it l, wait for it;

LION LION'S, LIONS, LIONS'
Ge 49: 9 Like a l he crouches and lies down,
Jdg 14: 6 that he tore the l apart with his bare
1Sa 17:34 When a l or a bear came and carried
Ps 91:13 You will tread on the l
Ecc 9: 4 a live dog is better off than a dead l!
Isa 11: 7 and the l will eat straw like the ox.

Isa 65:25 and the l will eat straw like the ox,
Jer 4: 7 A l has come out of his lair;
25:38 Like a l he will leave his lair,
Eze 1:10 right side each had the face of a l,
10:14 the third the face of a l,
Da 7: 4 "The first was like a l, and it had
Hos 13: 7 So I will be like a l to them,
1Pe 5: 8 around like a roaring l looking
Rev 4: 7 The first living creature was like a l,
5: 5 See, the L of the tribe of Judah,
13: 2 a bear and a mouth like that of a l.

LION'S LION
Ge 49: 9 You are a l cub, Judah;
2Ti 4:17 I was delivered from the l mouth.

LIONS LION
Ps 22:21 Rescue me from the mouth of the l;
Da 6:20 able to rescue you from the l?"

LIONS' LION
Da 6: 7 shall be thrown into the l den.
Na 2:11 Where now is the l den, the place

LIPS
Ex 6:12 me, since I speak with faltering l?"
Dt 23:23 Whatever your l utter you must be
Ps 34: 1 his praise will always be on my l.
40: 9 I do not seal my l, LORD, as you
63: 3 than life, my l will glorify you.
119:171 May my l overflow with praise,
140: 3 the poison of vipers is on their l.
141: 3 keep watch over the door of my l.
Pr 5: 3 the l of the adulterous woman drip
10:13 is found on the l of the discerning,
10:18 conceals hatred with lying l
10:21 The l of the righteous nourish many,
10:32 The l of the righteous know what
12:22 The LORD detests lying l, but he
13: 3 who guard their l preserve their
14: 7 will not find knowledge on their l.
15: 7 The l of the wise spread knowledge,
24:26 honest answer is like a kiss on the l.
26:23 on earthenware are fervent l
27: 2 an outsider, and not your own l.
Ecc 10:12 fools are consumed by their own l.
SS 4:11 Your l drop sweetness as
Isa 6: 5 I am a man of unclean l, and I live
among a people of unclean l,
28:11 with foreign l and strange tongues
29:13 mouth and honor me with their l,
Jer 12: 2 You are always on their l but far
Hos 14: 2 that we may offer the fruit of our l.
Mal 2: 7 "For the l of a priest ought
Mt 15: 8 people honor me with their l,
21:16 read, " 'From the l of children
Lk 4:22 gracious words that came from his l.
Ro 3:13 "The poison of vipers is on their l."
1Co 14:21 and through the l of foreigners I will
Col 3: 8 and filthy language from your l.
Heb 13:15 the fruit of l that openly profess his
1Pe 3:10 and their l from deceitful speech.

LIPS
Jos 1: 8 Book of the Law always on your l;

LIQUOR (KJV) See JUICE, WINE

LIST LISTED
1Ch 11:11 this is the l of David's mighty
27: 1 This is the l of the Israelites—
Ezr 2: 2 The l of the men of the people
Ne 7: 7 The l of the men of Israel:
Ps 56: 8 l my tears on your scroll—
1Ti 5: 9 the l of widows unless she is over

LISTED LIST
Nu 1:18 years old or more were l by name,

LISTEN LISTENED, LISTENING, LISTENS
Ex 4: 1 if they do not believe me or l to me
6:30 lips, why would Pharaoh l to me?"
7:13 hard and he would not l to them,
15:26 "If you l carefully to the LORD
23:22 If you l carefully to what he says
Lev 26:14 if you will not l to me and carry
Dt 18:15 You must l to him.
30:20 LORD your God, l to his voice,
1Ki 4:34 From all nations people came to l
2Ki 17:40 They would not l, however,
21: 9 But the people did not l.
Ps 5: 1 L to my words, LORD,
34:11 Come, my children, l to me;
55: 1 L to my prayer, O God, do not
143: 1 my prayer, l to my cry for mercy;
Pr 1: 5 let the wise l and add to their
4: 1 L, my sons, to a father's instruction;
8:33 L to my instruction and be wise;
8:34 Blessed are those who l to me,
12:15 to them, but the wise l to advice.
Ecc 5: 1 Go near to l rather than to offer
Isa 44: 1 "But now l, Jacob, my servant,
Jer 7:24 But they did not l or pay attention;
Eze 2: 5 And whether they l or fail to l—
40: 4 look carefully and l closely and pay
Zec 7:13 " 'When I called, they did not l;
Mt 12:42 the earth to l to Solomon's wisdom,
Mk 9: 7 is my Son, whom I love. L to him!"
Jn 10:27 My sheep l to my voice;
Ac 3:22 you must l to everything he tells
Jas 1:19 Everyone should be quick to l,
1:22 Do not merely l to the word, and so
1Jn 4: 6 is not from God does not l to us.

LISTENED LISTEN
Ge 3:17 "Because you l to your wife and ate
30:17 God l to Leah, and she became
30:22 he l to her and enabled her
Nu 21: 3 The LORD l to Israel's plea
Dt 9:19 But again the LORD l to me.
10:10 the LORD l to me at this time also.
34: 9 So the Israelites l to him and did
Ne 8: 3 all the people l attentively
Isa 66: 4 answered, when I spoke, no one l.
Da 9: 6 We have not l to your servants

LISTENING LISTEN
1Sa 3:10 said, "Speak, for your servant is l."
Pr 18:13 To answer before l—that is folly

Lk 10:39 at the Lord's feet l to what he said.

LISTENS LISTEN

Pr 1:33 whoever l to me will live in safety
17: 4 A wicked person l to deceitful lips;
Lk 10:16 "Whoever l to you l to me;
Jn 18:37 on the side of truth l to me."
1Jn 4: 6 and whoever knows God l to us;

LITTLE

Ex 16:18 the one who gathered l did not have
16:18 who gathered l did not have too l.
23:30 L by l I will drive them out before
1Ki 17:12 in a jar and a l olive oil in a jug.
Ps 8: 5 have made them a l lower than
Pr 6:10 A l sleep, a l slumber, a l folding
13:11 but whoever gathers money l by l
15:16 Better a l with the fear
16: 8 Better a l with righteousness than
Ecc 10: 1 so a l folly outweighs wisdom
Isa 11: 6 and a l child will lead them.
Mt 6:30 more clothe you—you of l faith?
8:26 "You of l faith, why are you so
14:31 "You of l faith," he said, "why did
16: 8 "You of l faith, why are you talking
17:20 "Because you have so l faith.
19:14 "Let the l children come to me,
Mk 9:37 welcomes one of these l children
Lk 7:47 has been forgiven l loves l."
18:17 of God like a l child will never enter
1Co 5: 6 a l yeast leavens the whole batch
2Co 8:15 the one who gathered l did not have
8:15 who gathered l did not have too l."
Gal 5: 9 "A l yeast works through the whole
1Ti 5:23 and use a l wine because of your
Heb 2: 7 You made them a l lower than
Rev 3: 8 I know that you have l strength,
10: 2 He was holding a l scroll, which lay

LIVE ALIVE, LIFE, LIFE'S, LIFELESS, LIFETIME, LIVED, LIVES, LIVING

Ge 3:22 tree of life and eat, and l forever."
12:12 they will kill me but will let you l.
Ex 1:16 but if it is a girl, let her l."
20:12 that you may l long in the land
33:20 face, for no one may see me and l."
Lev 23:42 All native-born Israelites are to l
Nu 21: 8 who is bitten can look at it and l."
Dt 4: 1 Follow them so that you may l
5:24 a person can l even if God speaks
6: 2 LORD your God as long as you l
8: 3 that man does not l on bread alone
30: 6 heart and with all your soul, and l.
Jdg 1:27 the Canaanites were determined to l
Job 14:14 If someone dies, will they l again?
Ps 15: 1 Who may l on your holy mountain?
24: 1 in it, the world, and all who l in it;
26: 8 I love the house where you l,
63: 4 I will praise you as long as I l,
119:175 Let me l that I may praise you,
Pr 2:21 For the upright will l in the land,
4: 4 keep my commands, and you will l.
15:27 but the one who hates bribes will l.
21: 9 Better to l on a corner of the roof

Pr 21:19 Better to l in a desert than
Ecc 3:12 happy and to do good while they l.
9: 4 even a l dog is better off than a dead
Isa 6: 5 I l among a people of unclean lips,
11: 6 The wolf will l with the lamb,
26:19 But your dead will l, LORD;
55: 3 come to me; listen, that you may l.
65:20 or an old man who does not l out his
Eze 18: 9 he will surely l,
18:32 Repent and l!
20:11 the person who obeys them will l.
37: 3 "Son of man, can these bones l?"
Am 5: 6 Seek the LORD and l, or he will
Jnh 4: 3 it is better for me to die than to l."
4: 8 be better for me to die than to l."
Hab 2: 4 the righteous person will l by his
Zec 2:11 I will l among you and you will
10:12 in his name they will l securely,"
Mt 4: 4 'Man shall not l on bread alone,
Lk 10:28 "Do this and you will l."
Jn 6:51 eats this bread will l forever.
6:58 feeds on this bread will l forever."
11:25 The one who believes in me will l,
14:19 Because I l, you also will l.
Ac 17:24 does not l in temples built by human
17:28 'For in him we l and move and have
Ro 1:17 "The righteous will l by faith."
6: 8 believe that we will also l with him.
8: 4 who do not l according to the flesh
14: 8 If we l, we l for the Lord;
14: 8 So, whether we l or die, we belong
1Co 7:17 each person should l as a believer
8: 6 all things came and for whom we l;
2Co 5: 7 For we l by faith, not by sight.
5:15 that those who l should no longer l
6:16 "I will l with them and walk among
Gal 2:20 with Christ and I no longer l,
3:11 because "the righteous will l
3:12 person who does these things will l
5:25 Since we l by the Spirit, let us keep
Eph 4: 1 I urge you to l a life worthy
4:17 you must no longer l as the Gentiles
5: 8 in the Lord. L as children of light
Php 1:21 me, to l is Christ and to die is gain.
3:17 your eyes on those who l as we do.
Col 1:10 so that you may l a life worthy
1Th 4: 1 we instructed you how to l in order
5:13 L in peace with each other.
1Ti 2: 2 that we may l peaceful and quiet
2Ti 3:12 everyone who wants to l a godly life
Titus 2:12 and to l self-controlled,
Heb 10:38 my righteous one will l by faith.
12:14 Make every effort to l in peace
1Pe 1:17 l out your time as foreigners here
2:12 L such good lives among the pagans
2Pe 3:11 You ought to l holy and godly lives

AS I LIVE Nu 14:21, 28; Dt 32:40; 1Sa 20:14; Job 27:6; Ps 63:4; 104:33; 116:2; 146:2; Isa 49:18; Jer 22:24; 46:18; Eze 5:11; 14:16, 18, 20; 16:48; 17:16, 19; 18:3; 20:3, 31, 33; 33:11, 27; 34:8; 35:6, 11; Zep 2:9; Ro 14:11; 2Pe 1:13

LIVED LIVE

Ex   12:40   time the Israelite people l in Egypt
Dt   26: 5   Egypt with a few people and l there
Jos   24: 2   l beyond the Euphrates River
    24: 7   you l in the wilderness for a long
Jdg   1:30   so these Canaanites l among them,
    3: 5   The Israelites l among
Lk   1:80   and he l in the wilderness until he
Col   3: 7   in these ways, in the life you once l.
Titus   3: 3   We l in malice and envy,

LIVES LIVE

Ge   9: 3   Everything that l and moves
    45: 7   save your l by a great deliverance.
    50:20   being done, the saving of many l.
Ex   1:14   They made their l bitter with harsh
    30:16   making atonement for your l."
Job   19:25   I know that my redeemer l,
Ps   18:46   The Lord l! Praise be to my
Pr   11:30   and the one who is wise saves l.
    13: 3   guard their lips preserve their l,
    14:25   A truthful witness saves l,
Isa   57:15   he who l forever, whose name is
Jer   10:23   that people's l are not their own;
Da   3:28   to give up their l rather than serve
    4:34   and glorified him who l forever.
    12: 7   him swear by him who l forever,
Jn   11:26   whoever l by believing in me will
    14:17   for he l with you and will be in you.
Ro   6:10   but the life he l, he l to God.
    8: 9   if indeed the Spirit of God l in you.
    14: 7   For none of us l for ourselves alone,
Gal   2:20   I no longer live, but Christ l in me.
Eph   2:22   in which God l by his Spirit.
Col   2: 9   of the Deity l in bodily form,
1Th   2: 8   the gospel of God but our l as well.
    2:12   urging you to live l worthy of God,
1Ti   2: 2   peaceful and quiet l in all godliness
    6:16   and who l in unapproachable light,
2Ti   1:14   help of the Holy Spirit who l in us.
Titus   2:12   and godly l in this present age,
Heb   7:24   but because Jesus l forever, he has
    7:25   because he always l to intercede
    13: 5   Keep your l free from the love
1Pe   3: 2   the purity and reverence of your l.
    4: 2   rest of their earthly l for evil human
2Pe   3:11   You ought to live holy and godly l
1Jn   2:10   brother and sister l in the light,
    2:14   and the word of God l in you,
    2:17   does the will of God l forever.
    3:24   one who keeps God's commands l
    3:24   is how we know that he l in us:
    3:16   to lay down our l for our brothers
    4:16   Whoever l in love l in God,
Rev   4: 9   sits on the throne and who l for ever
    4:10   and worship him who l for ever
    10: 6   he swore by him who l for ever
    15: 7   of God, who l for ever and ever.

AS SURELY AS THE LORD† ... LIVES See
LORD†

LIVESTOCK

Ge   1:25   kinds, the l according to their kinds,

Ge   2:20   So the man gave names to all the l,
    3:14   "Cursed are you above all l and all
Ex   34:19   all the firstborn males of your l,

LIVING LIVE

Ge   2: 7   life, and the man became a l being.
    3:20   become the mother of all the l.
    6:19   into the ark two of all l creatures,
    8:21   again will I destroy all l creatures,
Nu   16:22   God who gives breath to all l things,
Dt   5:26   the voice of the l God speaking
Jos   3:10   know that the l God is among you
1Sa   17:26   defy the armies of the l God?"
2Ki   19: 4   has sent to ridicule the l God,
Ps   84: 2   and my flesh cry out for the l God.
    119: 9   By l according to your word.
    142: 5   my portion in the land of the l."
Ecc   9: 4   who is among the l has hope—
Isa   53: 8   was cut off from the land of the l;
Jer   2:13   the spring of l water, and have dug
    10:10   he is the l God, the eternal King.
    17:13   the Lord, the spring of l water.
Eze   1: 5   what looked like four l creatures.
    10:17   the spirit of the l creatures was
Da   6:26   "For he is the l God and he endures
Hos   1:10   be called 'children of the l God.'
Zec   14: 8   On that day l water will flow
Mt   4:16   the people l in darkness have seen
    16:16   the Messiah, the Son of the l God."
    22:32   the God of the dead but of the l."
Jn   4:10   he would have given you l water."
    6:51   I am the l bread that came down
    7:38   said, rivers of l water will flow
Ro   8:11   Jesus from the dead is l in you,
    9:26   called 'children of the l God.' "
    12: 1   to offer your bodies as a l sacrifice,
    14: 9   the Lord of both the dead and the l.
1Co   9:14   the gospel should receive their l
2Co   6:16   For we are the temple of the l God.
1Ti   4:10   we have put our hope in the l God,
2Ti   4: 1   who will judge the l and the dead,
Heb   10:20   and l way opened for us through
    10:31   to fall into the hands of the l God.
    11:13   All these people were still l by faith
1Pe   1:23   through the l and enduring word
    2: 4   As you come to him, the l Stone—
Rev   1:18   I am the L One; I was dead,
    4: 6   were four l creatures, and they were
    7:17   will lead them to springs of l water.'

LIVING GOD See GOD

LIVING WATER Jer 2:13; 17:13; Zec 14:8; Jn
4:10, 11; 7:38; Rev 7:17

LOAD LOADED, LOADS

Ne   13:19   gates so that no l could be brought
Jer   17:24   bring no l through the gates of this
Lk   11:46   because you l people down
Gal   6: 5   each one should carry their own l.

LOADED LOAD

2Ti   3: 6   who are l down with sins and are

LOADS LOAD

Mt   23: 4   cumbersome l and put them

LOAF LOAVES
Jdg 7:13 "A round l of barley bread came
1Ki 17:13 first make a small l of bread for me
Pr   6:26 can be had for a l of bread,
Hos 7: 8 Ephraim is a flat l not turned over.
1Co 10:17 one body, for we all share the one l.

LOAN
Dt 15: 2 shall cancel any l they have made
    24:10 When you make a l of any kind

LOAVES LOAF
Ex 12:39 they baked l of unleavened bread.
Nu 11: 8 cooked it in a pot or made it into l.
Mk   6:41 he gave thanks and broke the l.
     8: 6 When he had taken the seven l
     8:19 When I broke the five l for the five
     8:20 when I broke the seven l for the four
Lk 11: 5 'Friend, lend me three l of bread;

LOCKED
SS   4:12 You are a garden l up, my sister,
Lk   3:20 to them all: He l John up in prison.
Jn 20:19 with the doors l for fear
    20:26 Though the doors were l,
Ac   5:23 "We found the jail securely l,
Gal 3:22 Scripture has l up everything under
     3:23 l up until the faith that was to come
Rev 20: 3 Abyss, and l and sealed it over him,

LOCUSTS
Ex 10: 4 go, I will bring l into your country
2Ch 7:13 or command l to devour the land
Joel 2:25 you for the years the l have eaten—
Mt   3: 4 His food was l and wild honey.
Rev 9: 3 of the smoke l came down

LOFTY
Ps 138: 6 though l, he sees them from afar.
   139: 6 for me, too l for me to attain.
Isa 26: 5 dwell on high, he lays the l city low;
Eze 16:24 and made a l shrine in every public

LOGS
2Ch 2: 3 "Send me cedar l as you did for my
Ezr 3: 7 that they would bring cedar l by sea

LOIS*
2Ti 1: 5 first lived in your grandmother L

LONELY* ALONE
Ps 25:16 to me, for I am l and afflicted.
    68: 6 God sets the l in families, he leads
Mk   1:45 but stayed outside in l places.
Lk   5:16 Jesus often withdrew to l places

LONG LENGTH, LENGTHY,
LONGED, LONGER, LONGING,
LONGINGS, LONGS
Ex 17:11 As l as Moses held up his hands,
    20:12 so that you may live l in the land
Nu   6: 5 they must let their hair grow l.
    14:11 How l will they refuse to believe
Dt   6: 2 and so that you may enjoy l life.
1Ki 18:21 "How l will you waver between

2Ch 1:11 since you have not asked for a l life
Ps 40:16 may those who l for your saving
    70: 4 may those who l for your saving
    93: 2 Your throne was established l ago;
   116: 2 me, I will call on him as l as I live.
   119:97 I meditate on it all day l.
   119:174 I l for your salvation, LORD.
Pr   3:16 L life is in her right hand; in her left
Isa 48: 3 I foretold the former things l ago,
Jer 44:14 to which they l to return and live;
La   5:20 Why do you forsake us so l?
Hos 7:13 I l to redeem them but they speak
Am   5:18 Woe to you who l for the day
Mt 25: 5 The bridegroom was a l time
Lk 10:13 they would have repented l ago,
Jn   9: 4 As l as it is day, we must do
1Co 11:14 teach you that if a man has l hair,
    11:15 but that if a woman has l hair, it is
Eph 3:18 to grasp how wide and l and high
Php 1: 8 God can testify how I l for all
1Pe 1:12 Even angels l to look into these
Rev 6:10 voice, "How l, Sovereign Lord,

HOW LONG See HOW

LONG-SUFFERING* SUFFER
Jer 15:15 You are l—do not take me away;

LONGED LONG
Mt 13:17 righteous people l to see what you
    23:37 how often I have l to gather your
Lk 13:34 how often I have l to gather your
2Ti 4: 8 to all who have l for his appearing.

LONGER LONG
Ge 17: 5 No l will you be called Abram;
    17:15 wife, you are no l to call her Sarai;
    32:28 "Your name will no l be Jacob,
Lev 26:13 that you would no l be slaves
Isa 29:22 "No l will Jacob be ashamed;
    62:12 After, the City No L Deserted.
Eze 14:11 of Israel will no l stray from me,
    39:29 I will no l hide my face from them,
Mt   5:13 It is no l good for anything,
Mk   8: 8 So they ate no l two, but one flesh.
Jn 13:33 I will be with you only a little l.
Ro   6: 6 that we should no l be slaves to sin—
Gal 2:20 crucified with Christ and I no l live,
     4: 7 So you are no l a slave, but God's
Eph 2:19 you are no l foreigners
     4:14 Then we will no l be infants,
Heb 8:11 No l will they teach their neighbor,
Rev 21: 1 away, and there was no l any sea.
    22: 3 No l will there be any curse.

LONGING* LONG
Dt 28:65 eyes weary with l, and a despairing
Job 7: 2 Like a slave l for the evening
Ps 119:20 My soul is consumed with l for your
   119:81 My soul faints with l for your
   119:131 and pant, l for your commands.
Pr 13:12 sick, but a l fulfilled is a tree of life.
    13:19 A l fulfilled is sweet to the soul,
Eze 23:27 will not look on these things with l
Lk 16:21 and l to eat what fell from the rich

Ro   15:23 since I have been l for many years
2Co   5: 2 l to be clothed instead with our
      7: 7 He told us about your l for me,
      7:11 what alarm, what l, what concern,
1Th   2:17 our intense l we made every effort
Heb 11:16 they were l for a better country—

LONGINGS* LONG

Ps   38: 9 All my l lie open before you, Lord;
    112:10 the l of the wicked will come

LONGS* LONG

Ps   63: 1 for you, my whole being l for you,
Isa 26: 9 in the morning my spirit l for you.
     30:18 Yet the LORD l to be gracious
Php   2:26 For he l for all of you and is
Jas   4: 5 he jealously l for the spirit he has

LONGSUFFERING (KJV) See PATIENCE

LOOK LOOKED, LOOKING, LOOKS

Ge   13:14 "L around from where you are,
     15: 5 said, "L up at the sky and count
     19:17 Don't l back, and don't stop
Ex   3: 6 because he was afraid to l at God.
Nu   21: 8 anyone who is bitten can l at it
     32: 8 Kadesh Barnea to l over the land.
Dt   3:27 L at the land with your own eyes,
     26:15 L down from heaven, your holy
Jos   2: 1 "Go, l over the land," he said,
1Sa 16: 7 The LORD does not l at the things
                 people l at.
     16: 7 People l at the outward appearance,
1Ch 16:11 L to the LORD and his strength;
Job 31: 1 my eyes not to l lustfully at a young
Ps   34: 5 Those who l to him are radiant;
     80:14 L down from heaven and see!
    105: 4 L to the LORD and his strength;
    113: 6 who stoops down to l
    123: 2 so our eyes l to the LORD our
Pr   1:28 they will l for me but will not find
      4:25 Let your eyes l straight ahead;
Isa   3: 9 The l on their faces testifies against
     17: 7 that day people will l to their Maker
     31: 1 do not l to the Holy One of Israel,
     40:26 up your eyes and l to the heavens:
     42:18 l, you blind, and see!
     60: 5 Then you will l and be radiant,
Jer   3: 3 Yet you have the brazen l
      6:16 "Stand at the crossroads and l;
Eze   5:11 I will not l on you with pity or spare
     34:11 for my sheep and l after them.
     34:12 them, so will I l after my sheep.
Da   9:17 Lord, l with favor on your desolate
Hab   1:13 Your eyes are too pure to l on evil;
Zec 12:10 They will l on me, the one they
Mt   6:26 L at the birds of the air; they do not
     18:12 go to l for the one that wandered
     23:27 which l beautiful on the outside
Mk   8:24 they l like trees walking around."
     13:21 is the Messiah!' or, 'L, there he is!'
Lk   6:41 "Why do you l at the speck

Lk   24:39 L at my hands and my feet. It is I
Jn   1:36 by, he said, "L, the Lamb of God!"
      4:35 open your eyes and l at the fields!
      7:34 You will l for me, but you will not
     13:33 You will l for me, and just as I told
     19:37 "They will l on the one they have
1Ti   4:12 Don't let anyone l down on you
Jas   1:27 to l after orphans and widows
1Pe   1:12 Even angels long to l into these
2Pe   3:12 as you l forward to the day of God
Rev   1:18 and now l, I am alive for ever
     16:15 "L, I come like a thief!
     22: 7 "L, I am coming soon!
     22:12 "L, I am coming soon!

LOOKED LOOK

Ge   4: 4 The LORD l with favor on Abel
     19:26 But Lot's wife l back, and she
Ex   2:25 So God l on the Israelites and was
     24:17 the LORD l like a consuming fire
1Sa   6:19 to death because they l into the ark
Ps 102:19 "The LORD l down from his
SS   3: 1 I l for him but did not find him.
Eze   1: 5 the fire was what l like four living
      1:26 their heads was what l like a throne
     10: 1 I l, and I saw the likeness
     22:30 "I l for someone among them who
     34: 6 and no one searched or l for them.
     37: 8 I l, and tendons and flesh appeared
     44: 4 I l and saw the glory of the LORD
Da   7: 2 "In my vision at night I l, and there
      7: 9 "As I l, "thrones were set in place,
      8: 3 I l up, and there before me was
     10: 5 I l up and there before me was
Hab   3: 6 he l, and made the nations tremble.
Zec   1:18 Then I l up, and there before me
      2: 1 Then I l up, and there before me
      5: 1 I l again, and there before me was
      5: 9 Then I l up—and there before me
      6: 1 I l up again, and there before me
Mt   25:36 I was sick and you l after me, I was
Mk   10:21 Jesus l at him and loved him.
Lk   18: 9 and l down on everyone else,
     22:61 Lord turned and l straight at Peter.
Ac   7:55 l up to heaven and saw the glory
1Jn   1: 1 which we have l at and our hands
Rev   4: 1 After this I l, and there before me
      5:11 I l and heard the voice of many
      6: 2 I l, and there before me was a white
      7: 9 After this I l, and there before me
     14: 1 Then I l, and there before me was
     15: 2 And I saw what l like a sea of glass

LOOKING LOOK

Ps   69: 3 My eyes fail, l for my God.
    119:82 My eyes fail, l for your promise;
    119:123 My eyes fail, l for your salvation,
Mk   3: 2 Some of them were l for a reason
     16: 6 "You are l for Jesus the Nazarene,
Ac   1:10 They were l intently up into the sky
Php   2: 4 not l to your own interests but each
1Th   2: 6 We were not l for praise
Heb 11:26 Egypt, because he was l ahead to his
     13:14 we are l for the city that is to come.

1Pe 5: 8 prowls around like a roaring lion l
2Pe 3:13 his promise we are l forward
Rev 5: 6 saw a Lamb, l as if it had been slain,

LOOKINGGLASSES (KJV) See
MIRROR

LOOKS LOOK
1Sa 16: 7 but the Lord l at the heart."
Ezr 8:22 God is on everyone who l to him,
Ps 14: 2 The Lord l down from heaven
     33:13 From heaven the Lord l down
     85:11 righteousness l down from heaven.
    104:32 he who l at the earth, and it
    138: 6 is exalted, he l kindly on the lowly;
Mt   5:28 anyone who l at a woman lustfully
     16: 4 adulterous generation l for a sign,
Lk   9:62 and l back is fit for service
Jn   6:40 is that everyone who l to the Son
     12:45 The one who l at me is seeing
Php 2:21 For everyone l out for their own
Jas 1:25 whoever l intently into the perfect

LOOSE
Jdg 16: 3 posts, and tore them l, bar and all.
Isa 33:23 Your rigging hangs l: The mast is
Mt 16:19 and whatever you l on earth will be
    18:18 and whatever you l on earth will be
Ac 16:26 open, and everyone's chains came l.

LOOT
Isa 42:24 handed Jacob over to become l,
Eze 39:10 them and l those who looted them,

LORD LORD'S, LORDED,
LORDING, LORDS; see also
LORD† (Yahweh)
Ge 18:27 been so bold as to speak to the L,
     45: 8 l of his entire household and ruler
Ex   4:10 Lord, "Pardon your servant, L.
     15:17 the sanctuary, L, your hands
     34: 9 your eyes, then let the L go with us.
Nu 12:11 my l, I ask you not to hold against
     16:13 now you also want to l it over us!
Dt 10:17 God is God of gods and L of lords,
Jos 3:11 of the L of all the earth will go
1Sa 24:10 'I will not lay my hand on my l,
1Ki 3:10 The L was pleased that Solomon
Ne   1:11 L, let your ear be attentive
     4:14 Remember the L, who is great
    10:29 and decrees of the Lord our L.
Job 28:28 human race, "The fear of the L—
Ps   2: 4 the L scoffs at them.
     8: 1 our L, how majestic is your name
     12: 4 will defend us—who is l over us?"
     16: 2 say to the Lord, "You are my L;
     30: 8 to the L I cried for mercy:
     35:23 Contend for me, my God and L.
     37:13 but the L laughs at the wicked,
     38:22 to help me, my L and my Savior.
     40:17 may the L think of me.
     54: 4 the L is the one who sustains me.
     57: 9 I will praise you, L,
     62:12 and with you, L, is unfailing love";

Ps 68:11 The L announces the word, and the
    69: 6 L, the Lord Almighty, may those
    86: 5 You, L, are forgiving and good,
    86: 8 the gods there is none like you, L;
    97: 5 before the L of all the earth.
   110: 1 The Lord says to my l:
   135: 5 that our L is greater than all gods.
   136: 3 Give thanks to the L of lords:
   147: 5 Great is our L and mighty in power;
Isa 6: 1 died, I saw the L, high and exalted,
     7:14 Therefore the L himself will give
    49:14 me, the L has forgotten me."
Jer 46:10 But that day belongs to the L,
La   3:31 no one is cast off by the L forever.
Eze 18:25 say, 'The way of the L is not just.'
Da   2:47 the God of gods and the L of kings
     5:23 yourself up against the L of heaven.
     9: 3 So I turned to the L God
     9: 7 "L, you are righteous, but this day
     9: 9 The L our God is merciful
     9:19 L, listen! L, forgive! L, hear and act!
Am   9: 1 I saw the L standing by the altar,
Mic 1: 2 you, the L from his holy temple.
Mal 3: 1 suddenly the L you are seeking will
Mt   1:20 an angel of the L appeared to him
     3: 3 'Prepare the way for the L,
     4: 7 'Do not put the L your God
     4:10 'Worship the L your God, and serve
     7:21 "Not everyone who says to me, 'L, L,'
     9:38 Ask the L of the harvest, therefore,
    12: 8 Son of Man is L of the Sabbath."
    20:25 rulers of the Gentiles l it over them,
    21: 9 who comes in the name of the L!"
    21:42 the L has done this, and it is
    22:37 " 'Love the L your God with all
    22:44 " 'The L said to my L: "Sit at my
    23:39 comes in the name of the L.' "
Mk   1: 3 'Prepare the way for the L,
     5:19 tell them how much the L has done
    12:11 the L has done this, and it is
    12:29 The L our God, the L is one.
    12:30 Love the L your God with all your
    12:37 David himself calls him 'L.'
Lk   1:11 an angel of the L appeared to him,
     1:32 The L God will give him the throne
     1:46 "My soul glorifies the L
     2: 9 An angel of the L appeared to them,
     2: 9 glory of the L shone around them,
     2:11 he is the Messiah, the L.
     4:18 "The Spirit of the L is on me,
     5:12 to the ground and begged him, "L,
     5:17 the power of the L was with Jesus
     6: 5 Son of Man is L of the Sabbath."
     6:46 "Why do you call me, 'L, L,'
    10:21 you, Father, L of heaven and earth,
    10:27 " 'Love the L your God with all
    19:31 say, 'The L needs it.' "
    19:38 who comes in the name of the L!"
    24:34 The L has risen and has appeared
Jn   1:23 straight the way for the L.' "
     9:38 Then the man said, "L, I believe,"
    13:13 "You call me 'Teacher' and 'L,'
    20:18 with the news: "I have seen the L!"

Jn 20:28 said to him, "My L and my God!"
21:17 He said, "L, you know all things;
Ac 2:21 on the name of the L will be saved.'
2:34 yet he said, " 'The L said to my L:
2:36 you crucified, both L and Messiah."
4:26 rulers band together against the L
5:19 an angel of the L opened the doors
7:59 Stephen prayed, "L Jesus,
8:16 baptized in the name of the L Jesus.
9: 5 "Who are you, L?" Saul asked.
9:31 Living in the fear of the L,
10:36 Jesus Christ, who is L of all.
11:23 true to the L with all their hearts.
16:31 "Believe in the L Jesus, and you
22:10 " 'What shall I do, L?' I asked.
Ro 4:24 him who raised Jesus our L
5: 1 God through our L Jesus Christ,
6:23 is eternal life in Christ Jesus our L.
8:39 of God that is in Christ Jesus our L.
10: 9 "Jesus is L," and believe in your
10:12 the same L is L of all and richly
10:13 the name of the L will be saved."
12:11 your spiritual fervor, serving the L.
13:14 yourselves with the L Jesus Christ,
14: 4 for the L is able to make them stand.
14: 8 If we live, we live for the L; and if we
die, we die for the L.
14: 8 we live or die, we belong to the L.
14: 9 he might be the L of both the dead
1Co 1:31 the one who boasts boast in the L."
2: 8 they would not have crucified the L
2:16 has known the mind of the L so as
3: 5 as the L has assigned to each his
4: 4 It is the L who judges me.
6:13 for sexual immorality but for the L,
and the L for the body.
6:14 his power God raised the L
7:10 this command (not I, but the L):
7:12 To the rest I say this (I, not the L):
7:25 I have no command from the L,
7:32 how he can please the L.
7:34 to be devoted to the L in both body
7:39 wishes, but he must belong to the L.
8: 6 and there is but one L, Jesus Christ,
10:21 You cannot drink the cup of the L
11:23 The L Jesus, on the night he was
11:27 against the body and blood of the L.
12: 3 "Jesus is L," except by the Holy
15:57 victory through our L Jesus Christ.
15:58 your labor in the L is not in vain.
16:22 If anyone does not love the L,
2Co 1:24 Not that we I it over your faith,
2:12 found that the L had opened a door
3:17 Now the L is the Spirit, and where the
Spirit of the L is,
4: 5 but Jesus Christ as L, and ourselves
5: 8 the body and at home with the L.
8: 5 gave themselves first of all to the L,
10:17 the one who boasts boast in the L."
10:18 but the one whom the L commends.
13:10 the authority the L gave me
Gal 6:14 in the cross of our L Jesus Christ,
Eph 2:21 to become a holy temple in the L.

Eph 4: 5 one L, one faith, one baptism;
5: 8 but now you are light in the L.
5:10 and find out what pleases the L.
5:19 music from your heart to the L,
5:22 own husbands as you do to the L.
6: 1 obey your parents in the L, for this
6: 8 that the L will reward each one
6:10 be strong in the L and in his mighty
Php 2:11 acknowledge that Jesus Christ is L,
3: 1 brothers and sisters, rejoice in the L!
3: 8 of knowing Christ Jesus my L,
4: 1 stand firm in the L in this way,
4: 4 Rejoice in the L always. I will say it
4: 5 be evident to all. The L is near.
Col 1:10 you may live a life worthy of the L
2: 6 as you received Christ Jesus as L,
3:13 Forgive as the L forgave you.
3:17 do it all in the name of the L Jesus,
3:18 your husbands, as is fitting in the L.
3:20 in everything, for this pleases the L.
3:23 as working for the L, not for human
3:24 inheritance from the L as a reward.
4:17 you have received in the L."
1Th 1: 6 became imitators of us and of the L,
3: 8 since you are standing firm in the L.
3:12 May the L make your love increase
4: 1 urge you in the L Jesus to do this
4: 6 The L will punish all those who
4:15 are left until the coming of the L,
4:17 the clouds to meet the L in the air.
4:17 so we will be with the L forever.
5: 2 day of the L will come like a thief
5:23 at the coming of our L Jesus Christ.
2Th 1: 7 happen when the L Jesus is revealed
1:12 of our L Jesus may be glorified
2: 1 the coming of our L Jesus Christ
2: 8 whom the L Jesus will overthrow
3: 3 But the L is faithful, and he will
3: 5 May the L direct your hearts
1Ti 1:14 The grace of our L was poured
6:14 the appearing of our L Jesus Christ,
6:15 the King of kings and L of lords,
2Ti 1: 8 of the testimony about our L
2:19 "The L knows those who are his,"
4: 8 which the L, the righteous Judge,
4:17 But the L stood at my side and gave
Phm 1:25 The grace of the L Jesus Christ be
Heb 1:10 "In the beginning, L, you laid
8: 2 the true tabernacle set up by the L,
8:11 'Know the L,' because they will all
10:30 "The L will judge his people."
12: 6 because the L disciplines the one he
12:14 holiness no one will see the L.
13: 6 confidence, "The L is my helper;
Jas 1: 7 to receive anything from the L.
1:12 crown of life that the L has promised
3: 9 With the tongue we praise our L
4:10 Humble yourselves before the L,
5:11 The L is full of compassion
5:15 the L will raise them up.
1Pe 1:25 the word of the L endures forever."
2: 3 you have tasted that the L is good.
3:12 the L is against those who do evil."

1Pe	3:15 in your hearts revere Christ as L.
2Pe	1:11 into the eternal kingdom of our L
	1:16 the coming of our L Jesus Christ
	2: 1 the sovereign L who bought them—
	2: 9 then the L knows how to rescue
	3: 9 The L is not slow in keeping his
	3:10 day of the L will come like a thief.
	3:18 and knowledge of our L and Savior
Jude	1: 4 Christ our only Sovereign and L.
	1:14 the L is coming with thousands
Rev	4: 8 holy is the L God Almighty,'
	6:10 long, Sovereign L, holy and true,
	11: 8 where also their L was crucified.
	11:15 has become the kingdom of our L
	11:17 thanks to you, L God Almighty,
	14:13 who die in the L from now on."
	15: 4 Who will not fear you, L, and bring
	17:14 triumph over them because he is L
	19: 6 For our L God Almighty reigns.
	19:16 KING OF KINGS AND L OF LORDS.
	21:22 because the L God Almighty
	22: 5 for the L God will give them light.
	22:20 Amen. Come, L Jesus.

ANGEL OF THE LORD See ANGEL

LORD GOD Da 9:3; Lk 1:32; Rev 1:8; 4:8;
11:17; 15:3; 16:7; 18:8; 19:6; 21:22; 22:5

LORD JESUS See JESUS

LORD JESUS CHRIST See JESUS

LORD THE KING 1Sa 24:8; 26:15, 15, 17, 19;
29:8, 2Sa 3:21; 4:8; 9:11; 13:33; 14:9, 12, 15, 17, 17,
18, 19, 19, 22; 15:15, 21, 21; 16:4, 9; 18:28, 31, 32;
19:19, 20, 26, 27, 27, 28, 30, 35, 37; 24:3, 3, 21, 22;
1Ki 1:2, 13, 18, 20, 20, 21, 24, 27, 27, 36, 37; 2:38;
20:4, 9; 2Ki 6:12, 26; 8:5; 1Ch 21:3, 23; Jer 37:20;
38:9; Da 1:10; 4:24

LORD THE LORD† ALMIGHTY Ps 69:6;
Isa 1:24; 3:1, 15; 10:16, 23, 24, 33; 19:4; 22:5, 12,
14, 15; 28:22; Jer 2:19; 46:10, 10; 49:5; 50:31; Am
3:13; 5:16; 9:5

NAME OF THE LORD See NAME

LORD'S LORD; see also LORD'S†
(Yahweh's)

Nu	14:17 "Now may the L strength be
Mal	1:12 it by saying, 'The L table is defiled,'
Lk	1:38 "I am the L servant,"
	1:66 For the L hand was with him.
	4:19 proclaim the year of the L favor."
	10:39 who sat at the L feet listening
Ac	11:21 The L hand was with them,
	21:14 up and said, "The L will be done."
Ro	12:13 Share with the L people who are
1Co	7:32 is concerned about the L affairs
	10:21 have a part in both the L table
	10:22 we trying to arouse the L jealousy?
	10:26 "The earth is the L, and everything
	11:20 it is not the L Supper you eat,
	11:26 you proclaim the L death until he
2Co	3:18 faces contemplate the L glory,
Gal	1:19 only James, the L brother.
Eph	5:17 but understand what the L will is.

2Ti	2:24 And the L servant must not be
Heb	12: 5 not make light of the L discipline,
Jas	4:15 "If it is the L will, we will live
	5: 8 firm, because the L coming is near.
1Pe	2:13 Submit yourselves for the L sake
2Pe	3:15 that our L patience means salvation,
Rev	1:10 On the L Day I was in the Spirit,

LORD† (Yahweh) LORD'S† (Yahweh's); see also LORD

Ge	2: 4 when the L God made the earth
	2: 7 the L God formed a man
	2:16 the L God commanded the man,
	2:22 the L God made a woman
	3: 9 But the L God called to the man,
	3:13 Then the L God said to the woman,
	3:14 So the L God said to the serpent,
	3:23 So the L God banished him
	4: 4 The L looked with favor on Abel
	4:15 the L put a mark on Cain so that no
	4:26 began to call on the name of the L.
	6: 6 The L regretted that he had made
	6: 8 found favor in the eyes of the L.
	7:16 Then the L shut him in.
	8:20 Noah built an altar to the L and,
	9:26 said, "Praise be to the L, the God
	10: 9 was a mighty hunter before the L;
	11: 9 there the L scattered them over
	12: 1 The L had said to Abram,
	12: 7 So he built an altar there to the L.
	13: 4 Abram called on the name of the L.
	15: 6 Abram believed the L, and he
	15:18 that day the L made a covenant
	17: 1 old, the L appeared to him and said,
	18: 1 The L appeared to Abraham near
	18:14 Is anything too hard for the L?
	18:19 way of the L by doing what is right
	19:14 because the L is about to destroy
	21: 1 Now the L was gracious to Sarah as
	22:14 that place The L Will Provide.
	24: 1 the L had blessed him in every way.
	25:21 Isaac prayed to the L on behalf
	26: 2 The L appeared to Isaac and said,
	26:25 and called on the name of the L.
	28:16 "Surely the L is in this place, and I
	31:49 "May the L keep watch between
	39: 2 The L was with Joseph so that he
	39:23 because the L was with Joseph
Ex	3: 2 There the angel of the L appeared
	3:15 'The L, the God of your fathers—
	4:11 makes them blind? Is it not I, the L?
	4:31 they heard that the L was concerned
	5: 2 I do not know the L and I will not
	6: 2 also said to Moses, "I am the L.
	6: 7 will know that I am the L your God,
	8:10 there is no one like the L our God.
	9:12 But the L hardened Pharaoh's heart
	9:30 still do not fear the L God."
	10:16 have sinned against the L your God
	10:20 But the L hardened Pharaoh's heart,
	10:27 But the L hardened Pharaoh's heart,
	11:10 but the L hardened Pharaoh's heart,
	12:27 'It is the Passover sacrifice to the L,

Ex 12:29 midnight the L struck down all
13: 9 For the L brought you out of Egypt
13:12 give over to the L the first offspring
13:21 By day the L went ahead of them
14: 8 The L hardened the heart of Pharaoh
14:13 the deliverance the L will bring you
14:18 that I am the L when I gain glory
14:30 That day the L saved Israel
15: 3 The L is a warrior; the L is
15:11 Who among the gods is like you, L?
15:26 for I am the L, who heals you."
16:12 know that I am the L your God.' "
16:29 the L has given you the Sabbath;
17: 7 saying, "Is the L among us or not?"
17:15 and called it The L is my Banner.
18:10 "Praise be to the L, who rescued
19: 8 will do everything the L has said."
19:20 The L descended to the top
20: 2 "I am the L your God, who brought
20: 5 for I, the L your God, am a jealous
20: 7 misuse the name of the L your God,
20: 7 the L will not hold anyone guiltless
20:10 day is a sabbath to the L your God.
20:11 in six days the L made the heavens
20:11 Therefore the L blessed the Sabbath
20:12 in the land the L your God is giving
23:25 Worship the L your God, and his
24: 3 "Everything the L has said we will
24:12 The L said to Moses,
24:16 the glory of the L settled on Mount
24:16 on the seventh day the L called
25: 1 The L said to Moses,
28:36 on it as on a seal: HOLY TO THE L.
30:11 Then the L said to Moses,
31:13 so you may know that I am the L,
31:18 When the L finished speaking
32:11 sought the favor of the L his God.
33: 9 while the L spoke with Moses.
34: 5 Then the L came down in the cloud
34: 5 him and proclaimed his name, the L.
34: 6 proclaiming, "The L, the L,
34:10 work that I, the L, will do for you.
34:14 for the L, whose name is Jealous,
34:29 because he had spoken with the L.
40:34 glory of the L filled the tabernacle.
40:38 of the L was over the tabernacle
Lev 1: 2 you brings an offering to the L,
1: 9 offering, an aroma pleasing to the L.
8:36 did everything the L commanded
9:23 the glory of the L appeared to all
10: 2 them, and they died before the L.
19: 2 'Be holy because I, the L your God,
20: 8 I am the L, who makes you holy.
20:26 to me because I, the L, am holy,
23:40 rejoice before the L your God
24:16 blasphemes the name of the L is
Nu 6:24 " ' "The L bless you and keep
8: 5 The L said to Moses:
10:29 for the place about which the L said,
10:29 for the L has promised good things
11: 1 hardships in the hearing of the L,
11: 1 fire from the L burned among them
14:14 have already heard that you, L,

Nu 14:14 with these people and that you, L,
14:18 'The L is slow to anger,
14:21 glory of the L fills the whole earth,
16: 7 and incense in them before the L.
16: 7 The man the L chooses will be
20:13 the Israelites quarreled with the L
21: 6 the L sent venomous snakes among
21:14 the Book of the Wars of the L says:
22:31 Then the L opened Balaam's eyes,
22:31 he saw the angel of the L standing
23:12 "Must I not speak what the L puts
30: 2 When a man makes a vow to the L
32:12 followed the L wholeheartedly.'
Dt 1:21 the L your God has given you
1:21 and take possession of it as the L,
2: 7 The L your God has blessed you
2: 7 forty years the L your God has been
4:29 from there you seek the L your God,
4:39 to heart this day that the L is God
5: 6 "I am the L your God, who brought
5: 9 for I, the L your God, am a jealous
5:11 misuse the name of the L your God,
5:14 day is a sabbath to the L your God.
6: 4 The L our God, the L is one.
6: 5 Love the L your God with all your
6:16 Do not put the L your God
6:25 all this law before the L our God,
7: 1 When the L your God brings you
7: 6 are a people holy to the L your God.
7: 8 it was because the L loved you
7: 9 that the L your God is God; he is
7:12 then the L your God will keep his
7:22 The L your God will drive out those
8: 5 so the L your God disciplines you.
9:10 The L gave me two stone tablets
9:10 commandments the L proclaimed
10:12 what does the L your God ask of you
but to fear the L your God,
10:12 to serve the L your God with all
10:14 the L your God belong the heavens,
10:17 For the L your God is God of gods
10:20 Fear the L your God and serve him.
10:22 now the L your God has made you
11: 1 Love the L your God and keep his
11:13 to love the L your God and to serve
13: 3 The L your God is testing you
14: 1 are the children of the L your God.
16: 1 the Passover of the L your God,
17:15 you a king the L your God chooses.
18: 2 the L is their inheritance, as he
18:15 The L your God will raise
28: 1 If you fully obey the L your God
28: 1 the L your God will set you high
28:15 if you do not obey the L your God
29: 1 covenant the L commanded Moses
29:29 things belong to the L our God,
30: 4 there the L your God will gather
30: 6 The L your God will circumcise
30:10 if you obey the L your God
30:10 turn to the L your God with all your
30:16 you today to love the L your God,
30:16 the L your God will bless you
30:20 that you may love the L your God,

Dt	30:20	For the L is your life, and he will
	31: 6	for the L your God goes with you;
	34: 5	the servant of the L died there
	34: 5	there in Moab, as the L had said.
Jos	1:13	Moses the servant of the L gave you
	1:13	'The L your God will give you rest
	2:11	for the L your God is God in heaven
	7:20	I have sinned against the L, the God
	10:14	since, a day when the L listened
	10:14	Surely the L was fighting for Israel!
	21:44	The L gave them rest on every side,
	21:44	the L gave all their enemies
	22: 5	to love the L your God, to walk
	22:22	"The Mighty One, God, the L!
	22:34	that the L is God.
	23:11	very careful to love the L your God.
	24:15	if serving the L seems undesirable
	24:15	household, we will serve the L."
	24:18	the L drove out before us all
	24:18	We too will serve the L, because he
Jdg	2:12	They forsook the L, the God of their
	3: 9	But when they cried out to the L,
Ru	1: 8	May the L show you kindness,
	4:13	her, the L enabled her to conceive,
1Sa	1:11	give him to the L for all the days
	1:19	Hannah, and the L remembered her.
	1:28	So now I give him to the L.
	2: 2	"There is no one holy like the L;
	2:25	but if anyone sins against the L,
	2:26	in favor with the L and with people.
	3: 1	ministered before the L under Eli.
	3: 1	days the word of the L was rare;
	3: 8	A third time the L called,
	3: 8	that the L was calling the boy.
	3:19	The L was with Samuel as he grew
	4: 3	"Why did the L bring defeat on us
	5: 3	the ground before the ark of the L!
	7:12	"Thus far the L has helped us."
	10: 1	"Has not the L anointed you ruler
	11:15	Saul king in the presence of the L.
	11:15	fellowship offerings before the L.
	12: 5	"The L is witness against you,
	12:18	all the people stood in awe of the L
	12:22	his great name the L will not reject
	12:24	be sure to fear the L and serve him
	13:14	the L has sought out a man after his
	14: 6	Perhaps the L will act in our behalf.
	14: 6	Nothing can hinder the L
	15:22	"Does the L delight in burnt
	15:22	as much as in obeying the L?
	15:28	"The L has torn the kingdom
	16:13	the Spirit of the L came powerfully
	17:45	you in the name of the L Almighty,
2Sa	5:10	because the L God Almighty was
	6:14	David was dancing before the L
	7:22	"How great you are, Sovereign L!
	8: 6	The L gave David victory wherever
	12:13	"I have sinned against the L."
	12:13	"The L has taken away your sin.
	22: 2	"The L is my rock, my fortress
	22:29	You, L, are my lamp; the L turns
	24:14	Let us fall into the hands of the L,
1Ki	1:30	day what I swore to you by the L,

1Ki	2: 3	and observe what the L your God
	3: 3	love for the L by walking according
	5: 5	for the Name of the L my God,
	5:12	The L gave Solomon wisdom,
	8:11	the glory of the L filled his temple.
	8:23	"L, the God of Israel, there is no
	8:61	fully committed to the L our God,
	9: 3	The L said to him: "I have heard
	10: 9	Praise be to the L your God,
	11: 4	not fully devoted to the L his God,
	15:14	fully committed to the L all his life.
	18:21	If the L is God, follow him;
	18:36	"L, the God of Abraham,
	18:39	fell prostrate and cried, "The L—he is
		God! The L—he is God!"
	19:11	for the L is about to pass by."
	19:11	but the L was not in the wind.
	19:11	but the L was not in the earthquake.
	21:23	also concerning Jezebel the L says:
	22: 5	"First seek the counsel of the L."
2Ki	3:18	is an easy thing in the eyes of the L;
	13:23	But the L was gracious to them
	17:20	Therefore the L rejected all
	18: 5	Hezekiah trusted in the L, the God
	19: 1	and went into the temple of the L.
	19:31	of the L Almighty will accomplish
	20:11	the L made the shadow go back
	21:12	Therefore this is what the L,
	22: 2	what was right in the eyes of the L
	22: 8	of the Law in the temple of the L."
	23: 3	covenant in the presence of the L—
	23:21	the Passover to the L your God, as it
	23:25	him who turned to the L as he did—
	24: 2	The L sent Babylonian, Aramean,
	24: 2	the word of the L proclaimed by his
	24: 4	and the L was not willing to forgive.
	25: 9	He set fire to the temple of the L,
1Ch	10:13	because he was unfaithful to the L; he
		did not keep the word of the L
	11: 3	as the L had promised through
	11: 9	because the L Almighty was
	13: 6	up from there the ark of God the L,
	16: 8	Give praise to the L, proclaim his
	16:11	Look to the L and his strength;
	16:23	Sing to the L, all the earth;
	17: 1	covenant of the L is under a tent."
	17:20	"There is no one like you, L,
	21:24	will not take for the L what is yours,
	22: 1	"The house of the L God is to be
	22:11	build the house of the L your God,
	22:13	and laws that the L gave Moses
	22:16	the work, and the L be with you."
	22:19	and soul to seeking the L your God.
	22:19	to build the sanctuary of the L God,
	22:19	the ark of the covenant of the L
	25: 7	and skilled in music for the L—
	28: 9	for the L searches every heart
	28:20	for the L God, my God, is with you.
	28:20	of the temple of the L is finished.
	29: 1	is not for man but for the L God.
	29:11	Yours, L, is the greatness
	29:11	Yours, L, is the kingdom;
	29:25	The L highly exalted Solomon

2Ch	1: 1	for the L his God was with him
	2:11	"Because the L loves his people,
	5:14	the glory of the L filled the temple
	6:17	And now, L, the God of Israel,
	7: 1	the glory of the L filled the temple.
	7:12	the L appeared to him at night
	7:21	'Why has the L done such a thing
	9: 8	Praise be to the L your God,
	9: 8	as king to rule for the L your God.
	13:12	do not fight against the L, the God
	14: 6	those years, for the L gave him rest.
	15:15	So the L gave them rest on every
	16: 9	of the L range throughout the earth
	17: 9	them the Book of the Law of the L;
	18:15	but the truth in the name of the L?"
	19: 6	for mere mortals but for the L,
	19: 9	wholeheartedly in the fear of the L.
	20:15	This is what the L says to you:
	20:20	Have faith in the L your God
	21: 7	the L was not willing to destroy
	26: 5	As long as he sought the L,
	26:16	He was unfaithful to the L his God,
	26:16	the temple of the L to burn incense
	29:31	now dedicated yourselves to the L.
	29:31	offerings to the temple of the L."
	30: 9	If you return to the L, then your
	30: 9	for the L your God is gracious
	31:20	and faithful before the L his God.
	32: 8	with us is the L our God to help us
	33:13	the L was moved by his entreaty
	33:13	Manasseh knew that the L is God.
	34:14	been taken into the temple of the L,
	34:14	of the L that had been given through
	34:31	to follow the L and keep his
	36:22	fulfill the word of the L spoken
	36:22	the L moved the heart of Cyrus king
Ezr	3:10	foundation of the temple of the L,
	3:10	took their places to praise the L,
	7: 6	the hand of the L his God was
	7:10	and observance of the Law of the L,
	9: 5	hands spread out to the L my God
	9: 8	the L our God has been gracious
Ne	1: 5	"L, the God of heaven, the great
	8: 1	which the L had commanded
	8:10	the joy of the L is your strength."
	9: 6	You alone are the L. You made
Job	1: 6	to present themselves before the L,
	1:21	The L gave and the L has taken
	1:21	may the name of the L be praised."
	38: 1	the L spoke to Job out of the storm.
	42:12	The L blessed the latter part of Job's
Ps	1: 2	whose delight is in the law of the L,
	1: 6	For the L watches over the way
	2: 2	rulers band together against the L
	3: 8	From the L comes deliverance.
	4: 6	Many, L, are asking, "Who will
	5: 3	In the morning, L, you hear my
	6: 1	L, do not rebuke me in your anger
	7: 1	L my God, I take refuge in you;
	8: 1	L, our Lord, how majestic is your
	9: 9	The L is a refuge for the oppressed,
	9:19	Arise, L, do not let mortals triumph;
	10:16	The L is King for ever and ever;

Ps	11: 5	The L examines the righteous,
	12: 6	And the words of the L are flawless,
	13: 1	How long, L? Will you forget me
	14: 6	of the poor, but the L is their refuge.
	15: 4	but honors those who fear the L;
	16: 2	I say to the L, "You are my Lord;
	16: 8	I keep my eyes always on the L.
	17: 1	Hear me, L, my plea is just;
	18: 1	I love you, L, my strength.
	18: 6	In my distress I called to the L;
	18:31	For who is God besides the L?
	19: 7	The law of the L is perfect,
	19: 7	statutes of the L are trustworthy,
	19:14	heart be pleasing in your sight, L,
	20: 5	May the L grant all your requests.
	20: 7	trust in the name of the L our God.
	21:13	Be exalted in your strength, L;
	22: 8	"He trusts in the L," they say, "let
		the L rescue him.
	23: 1	The L is my shepherd, I lack
	23: 6	dwell in the house of the L forever.
	24: 3	may ascend the mountain of the L?
	24: 8	The L strong and mighty, the L
	25:10	All the ways of the L are loving
	26: 2	Test me, L, and try me, examine my
	27: 1	The L is my light and my
	27: 1	The L is the stronghold of my life—
	27: 4	One thing I ask from the L, this only
	27: 4	to gaze on the beauty of the L
	27: 6	I will sing and make music to the L.
	28: 7	The L is my strength and my shield;
	29: 1	Ascribe to the L, you heavenly
	29: 1	ascribe to the L glory and strength.
	29: 4	The voice of the L is powerful;
	30: 4	Sing the praises of the L, you his
	31: 5	deliver me, L, my faithful God.
	32: 2	one whose sin the L does not count
	33: 1	Sing joyfully to the L,
	33: 6	of the L the heavens were made,
	33:12	is the nation whose God is the L,
	33:20	We wait in hope for the L; he is our
	34: 1	I will extol the L at all times;
	34: 4	I sought the L, and he answered me;
	34: 7	of the L encamps around those who
	34: 8	Taste and see that the L is good;
	34: 9	Fear the L, you his holy people,
	34:15	The eyes of the L are
	34:18	The L is close to the brokenhearted
	35:10	will exclaim, "Who is like you, L?
	36: 6	You, L, preserve both people
	37: 4	Take delight in the L, and he will
	37: 5	Commit your way to the L;
	38:21	L, do not forsake me; do not be far
	40: 1	I waited patiently for the L;
	40:13	Be pleased to save me, L;
	41:10	But may you have mercy on me, L;
	46: 7	The L Almighty is with us;
	47: 2	For the L Most High is awesome,
	48: 1	Great is the L, and most worthy
	50: 1	the L, speaks and summons
	55:22	Cast your cares on the L and he will
	59: 8	But you laugh at them, L;
	68: 4	his name is the L.

Ps   68:20 from the Sovereign L comes escape
     69:31 This will please the L more than
     70: 5 and my deliverer; L, do not delay.
     71: 1 In you, L, I have taken refuge;
     73:28 made the Sovereign L my refuge;
     75: 8 In the hand of the L is a cup full
     78: 4 the praiseworthy deeds of the L,
     81:10 I am the L your God, who brought
     83:18 that you, whose name is the L—
     84:11 For the L God is a sun and shield;
     85: 7 Show us your unfailing love, L,
     86:11 Teach me your way, L, that I may
     87: 2 The L loves the gates of Zion more
     88: 1 L, you are the God who saves me;
     89: 6 above can compare with the L?
     91: 2 I will say of the L, "He is my
     92: 1 It is good to praise the L and make
     92: 4 you make me glad by your deeds, L;
     93: 1 The L reigns, he is robed in majesty;
     93: 5 Your statutes, L, stand firm;
     94: 1 The L is a God who avenges.
     94:12 Blessed is the one you discipline, L,
     94:18 your unfailing love, L,
     95: 1 Come, let us sing for joy to the L;
     95: 3 For the L is the great God, the great
     96: 1 Sing to the L a new song;
     96: 5 idols, but the L made the heavens.
     96: 9 Worship the L in the splendor of his
     97: 1 The L reigns, let the earth be glad;
     97:10 Let those who love the L hate evil,
     98: 2 The L has made his salvation known
     99: 1 The L reigns, let the nations
     99: 5 Exalt the L our God and worship
    100: 2 Worship the L with gladness;
    101: 1 to you, L, I will sing praise.
    102:12 But you, L, sit enthroned forever;
    103: 1 Praise the L, my soul; all my inmost
    103: 8 The L is compassionate
    103:19 The L has established his throne
    104: 1 Praise the L, my soul. L my God,
    104:24 How many are your works, L!
    104:33 I will sing to the L all my life;
    105: 4 Look to the L and his strength;
    105:24 The L made his people very fruitful;
    106:47 Save us, L our God, and gather us
    107: 1 Give thanks to the L, for he is good;
    107: 8 thanks to the L for his unfailing love
    107:43 ponder the loving deeds of the L.
    108: 3 I will praise you, L,
    109:26 Help me, L my God;
    110: 1 The L says to my lord: "Sit at my
    110: 4 The L has sworn and will not
    111: 2 Great are the works of the L;
    111: 4 the L is gracious
    111:10 The fear of the L is the beginning
    112: 1 Praise the L. Blessed are those who
    113: 1 Praise the L. Praise the L, you
    113: 5 Who is like the L our God, the One
    115: 1 Not to us, L, not to us but to your
    115:18 it is we who extol the L, both now
    116: 5 The L is gracious and righteous;
    116:12 I return to the L for all his goodness
    116:15 the sight of the L is the death of his

Ps 117: 1 Praise the L, all you nations;
    118: 7 The L is with me; he is my helper.
    118: 8 to take refuge in the L than to trust
    118:18 The L has chastened me severely,
    118:24 The L has done it this very day;
    118:26 he who comes in the name of the L.
    119: 1 walk according to the law of the L.
    119:64 The earth is filled with your love, L;
    119:89 Your word, L, is eternal;
    119:126 It is time for you to act, L;
    119:159 preserve my life, L, in accordance
    120: 1 I call on the L in my distress, and he
    121: 2 My help comes from the L,
    121: 5 The L watches over you—the L is
    122: 1 "Let us go to the house of the L."
    123: 2 so our eyes look to the L our God,
    124: 1 If the L had not been on our side—
    124: 8 Our help is in the name of the L,
    125: 2 so the L surrounds his people both
    126: 3 The L has done great things for us,
    127: 1 Unless the L builds the house,
    127: 1 Unless the L watches over the city,
    127: 3 Children are a heritage from the L,
    128: 1 Blessed are all who fear the L,
    129: 4 But the L is righteous; he has cut me
    130: 3 If you, L, kept a record of sins,
    130: 5 I wait for the L, my whole being
    131: 3 put your hope in the L both now
    132: 1 L, remember David and all his
    132:13 For the L has chosen Zion, he has
    133: 3 For there the L bestows his blessing,
    134: 3 May the L bless you from Zion,
    135: 3 Praise the L, for the L is good;
    135: 6 The L does whatever pleases him,
    136: 1 Give thanks to the L, for he is good.
    137: 4 can we sing the songs of the L while
    138: 1 I will praise you, L, with all my
    138: 8 The L will vindicate me;
    138: 8 your love, L, endures forever—
    139: 1 You have searched me, L, and you
    140: 1 Rescue me, L, from evildoers;
    141: 1 I call to you, L, come quickly to me;
    141: 3 Set a guard over my mouth, L;
    142: 5 I cry to you, L; I say, "You are my
    143: 9 Rescue me from my enemies, L,
    144: 3 L, what are human beings that you
    145: 3 Great is the L and most worthy
    145: 8 The L is gracious
    145: 9 The L is good to all;
    145:17 The L is righteous in all his ways
    145:18 The L is near to all who call on him,
    146: 5 whose hope is in the L their God.
    146: 7 The L sets prisoners free,
    147: 2 The L builds up Jerusalem;
    147: 7 Sing to the L with grateful praise;
    148: 1 Praise the L. Praise the L
    148: 7 Praise the L from the earth,
    149: 4 For the L takes delight in his
    150: 1 Praise the L. Praise God in his
    150: 6 has breath praise the L. Praise the L.
Pr   1: 7 The fear of the L is the beginning
      1:29 and did not choose to fear the L.
      2: 5 you will understand the fear of the L

Pr 2: 6 For the L gives wisdom;
3: 5 Trust in the L with all your heart
3: 7 fear the L and shun evil.
3: 9 Honor the L with your wealth,
3:12 because the L disciplines those he
3:19 By wisdom the L laid the earth's
5:21 your ways are in full view of the L,
6:16 There are six things the L hates,
8:13 To fear the L is to hate evil;
8:35 life and receive favor from the L.
9:10 The fear of the L is the beginning
10:22 The blessing of the L brings wealth,
10:27 The fear of the L adds length to life,
10:29 The way of the L is a refuge
11: 1 The L detests dishonest scales,
12: 2 people obtain favor from the L,
12:22 The L detests lying lips, but he
14: 2 fears the L walks uprightly,
14:16 The wise fear the L and shun evil,
14:26 Whoever fears the L has a secure
14:27 The fear of the L is a fountain
15: 3 The eyes of the L are everywhere,
15:16 the fear of the L than great wealth
15:29 The L is far from the wicked, but he
15:33 instruction is to fear the L,
16: 1 from the L comes the proper answer
16: 2 but motives are weighed by the L.
16: 3 Commit to the L whatever you do,
16: 4 The L works out everything to its
16: 5 The L detests all the proud of heart.
16: 6 the fear of the L evil is avoided.
16: 9 but the L establishes their steps.
16:20 is the one who trusts in the L.
16:33 but its every decision is from the L.
17: 3 for gold, but the L tests the heart.
18:10 name of the L is a fortified tower;
18:22 good and receives favor from the L.
19:14 but a prudent wife is from the L.
19:17 is kind to the poor lends to the L,
19:23 The fear of the L leads to life;
20:10 the L detests them both.
20:12 the L has made them both.
20:22 Wait for the L, and he will avenge
20:23 The L detests differing weights,
20:24 person's steps are directed by the L.
20:27 is the lamp of the L that sheds light
21: 2 are right, but the L weighs the heart.
21: 3 acceptable to the L than sacrifice.
21:30 plan that can succeed against the L.
21:31 battle, but victory rests with the L.
22: 2 The L is the Maker of them all.
22: 4 Humility is the fear of the L;
22:12 the L keep watch over knowledge,
22:19 So that your trust may be in the L,
22:23 for the L will take up their case
23:17 be zealous for the fear of the L.
24:21 Fear the L and the king, my son,
25:22 his head, and the L will reward you.
28: 5 who seek the L understand it fully.
28:25 who trust in the L will prosper.
29:25 whoever trusts in the L is kept safe.
29:26 it is from the L that one gets justice.
31:30 a woman who fears the L is to be

Isa 1: 4 They have forsaken the L;
1:18 let us settle the matter," says the L.
2: 3 us go up to the mountain of the L,
2: 3 the word of the L from Jerusalem.
2:11 the L alone will be exalted
2:11 the L Almighty will be exalted
3:13 The L takes his place in court;
4: 2 the Branch of the L will be beautiful
5: 7 of the L Almighty is the nation
5:16 the L Almighty will be exalted
6: 3 holy, holy is the L Almighty;
7:11 "Ask the L your God for a sign,
9: 7 of the L Almighty will accomplish
11: 2 The Spirit of the L will rest on him—
11: 2 of the knowledge and fear of the L—
11: 9 of the L as the waters cover the sea.
12: 2 The L, the L himself, is my strength
13: 9 See, the day of the L is coming—
18: 7 will be brought to the L Almighty
18: 7 of the Name of the L Almighty.
24: 1 the L is going to lay waste the earth
25: 1 L, you are my God; I will exalt you
25: 6 this mountain the L Almighty will
25: 8 The Sovereign L will wipe away
25: 8 all the earth. The L has spoken.
26: 4 Trust in the L forever, for the L, the L
        himself, is the Rock
26: 8 Yes, L, walking in the way of your
26:13 L our God, other lords besides you
26:21 the L is coming out of his dwelling
27: 1 the L will punish with his sword—
27:12 that day the L will thresh
28: 5 In that day the L Almighty will be
29: 6 the L Almighty will come
29:15 to hide their plans from the L,
29:19 the humble will rejoice in the L;
30:18 Yet the L longs to be gracious
30:18 For the L is a God of justice.
30:26 when the L binds up the bruises
30:30 The L will cause people to hear his
33: 2 L, be gracious to us; we long
33: 6 the fear of the L is the key to this
33:22 For the L is our judge, the L is our
        lawgiver, the L is our king;
34: 2 The L is angry with all nations;
35: 2 they will see the glory of the L,
35:10 those the L has rescued will return.
37:15 And Hezekiah prayed to the L:
40: 3 prepare the way for the L;
40: 5 the glory of the L will be revealed,
40: 5 For the mouth of the L has spoken."
40: 7 because the breath of the L blows
40:10 the Sovereign L comes with power,
40:14 Whom did the L consult
40:27 "My way is hidden from the L;
40:28 The L is the everlasting God,
40:31 in the L will renew their strength.
41:14 declares the L, your Redeemer,
41:20 that the hand of the L has done this,
42: 8 "I am the L; that is my name!
42:10 Sing to the L a new song, his praise
42:13 The L will march out like
42:21 It pleased the L for the sake of his
43: 3 For I am the L your God, the Holy

Isa 43:11 am the **L**, and apart from me there is
44: 6 and Redeemer, the **L** Almighty:
44:23 heavens, for the **L** has done this;
44:23 for the **L** has redeemed Jacob,
45: 5 I am the **L**, and there is no other;
45: 7 I, the **L**, do all these things.
45:17 the **L** with an everlasting salvation;
45:21 Was it not I, the **L**? And there is no
48:17 "I am the **L** your God, who teaches
49: 7 because of the **L**, who is faithful,
49:14 Zion said, "The **L** has forsaken me,
50: 5 The Sovereign **L** has opened my
50:10 Who among you fears the **L**
50:10 trust in the name of the **L** and rely
51: 1 righteousness and who seek the **L**:
51:11 Those the **L** has rescued will return.
51:15 For I am the **L** your God, who stirs
51:15 the **L** Almighty is his name.
52:10 The **L** will lay bare his holy arm
53: 1 has the arm of the **L** been revealed?
53: 6 the **L** has laid on him the iniquity
53:10 and though the **L** makes his life
53:10 the will of the **L** will prosper in his
54: 5 the **L** Almighty is his name—
55: 6 Seek the **L** while he may be found;
55: 7 Let them turn to the **L**, and he will
56: 6 bind themselves to the **L** to minister
56: 6 to love the name of the **L**, and to be
58: 5 a fast, a day acceptable to the **L**?
58:11 The **L** will guide you always;
59: 1 the arm of the **L** is not too short
59:19 people will fear the name of the **L**,
59:19 that the breath of the **L** drives along.
60: 1 the glory of the **L** rises upon you.
60:19 the **L** will be your everlasting light,
61: 1 Spirit of the Sovereign **L** is on me,
　　　　because the **L** has anointed me
61: 3 a planting of the **L** for the display
61: 8 "For I, the **L**, love justice;
61:10 I delight greatly in the **L**;
62: 4 for the **L** will take delight in you,
63: 7 I will tell of the kindnesses of the **L**,
63: 7 according to all the **L** has done
64: 8 Yet you, **L**, are our Father.
65:23 will be a people blessed by the **L**,
66:15 See, the **L** is coming with fire,
Jer 1: 9 Then the **L** reached out his hand
2:19 when you forsake the **L** your God
3:12 declares the **L**, 'I will frown on you
3:12 declares the **L**, 'I will not be angry
3:25 have sinned against the **L** our God,
3:25 have not obeyed the **L** our God."
4: 4 Circumcise yourselves to the **L**,
6:10 The word of the **L** is offensive
8: 7 not know the requirements of the **L**.
9:24 in these I delight," declares the **L**.
10: 6 No one is like you, **L**; you are great,
10:10 But the **L** is the true God; he is
10:21 and do not inquire of the **L**;
12: 1 You are always righteous, **L**, when I
14: 7 us, do something, **L**, for the sake
14:20 acknowledge our wickedness, **L**,
16:19 **L**, my strength and my fortress,

Jer 17: 7 is the one who trusts in the **L**,
17:10 "I the **L** search the heart
17:13 **L**, you are the hope of Israel;
17:13 because they have forsaken the **L**,
20:11 But the **L** is with me like a mighty
23: 6 The **L** Our Righteous Savior.
24: 7 a heart to know me, that I am the **L**.
28: 9 as one truly sent by the **L** only if his
31:11 For the **L** will deliver Jacob
31:22 The **L** will create a new thing
31:34 'Know the **L**,' because they will all
32:27 "I am the **L**, the God of all
33:16 The **L** Our Righteous Savior.'
36: 6 of the **L** that you wrote as I dictated.
40: 3 And now the **L** has brought it about;
42: 3 the **L** your God will tell us where
42: 4 pray to the **L** your God as you have
42: 4 I will tell you everything the **L** says
42: 6 we will obey the **L** our God,
50: 4 go in tears to seek the **L** their God.
51:10 " 'The **L** has vindicated us;
51:56 For the **L** is a God of retribution;
La 1: 5 The **L** has brought her grief because
3:24 to myself, "The **L** is my portion;
3:25 The **L** is good to those whose hope
3:26 quietly for the salvation of the **L**.
3:40 test them, and let us return to the **L**.
Eze 1: 3 the word of the **L** came to Ezekiel
1: 3 There the hand of the **L** was on him.
1:28 of the likeness of the glory of the **L**.
3:23 glory of the **L** was standing there,
4:14 Then I said, "Not so, Sovereign **L**!
10: 4 the glory of the **L** rose from above
10: 4 of the radiance of the glory of the **L**.
10:18 the glory of the **L** departed
15: 7 them, you will know that I am the **L**.
30: 3 is near, the day of the **L** is near—
34:24 I the **L** will be their God, and my
36:23 nations will know that I am the **L**,
37: 4 'Dry bones, hear the word of the **L**!
43: 4 the **L** entered the temple through
44: 4 the glory of the **L** filling the temple of
　　　　the **L**,
48:35 time on will be: THE **L** IS THERE."
Da 9: 2 the word of the **L** given to Jeremiah
9:14 The **L** did not hesitate to bring
9:14 for the **L** our God is righteous
Hos 1: 7 but I, the **L** their God, will save
2:13 but me she forgot," declares the **L**.
2:20 and you will acknowledge the **L**.
3: 1 her as the **L** loves the Israelites.
3: 5 will return and seek the **L** their God
4: 1 because the **L** has a charge to bring
6: 1 "Come, let us return to the **L**.
6: 3 Let us acknowledge the **L**;
10:12 for it is time to seek the **L**, until he
12: 5 the **L** God Almighty, the **L** is his
14: 1 Return, Israel, to the **L** your God.
Joel 1:15 For the day of the **L** is near;
2:11 The **L** thunders at the head of his
2:11 The day of the **L** is great;
2:13 Return to the **L** your God, for he is
2:21 Surely the **L** has done great things!

Joel 2:23 rejoice in the **L** your God, for he has
    2:31 the great and dreadful day of the **L**.
    2:32 on the name of the **L** will be saved;
    2:32 the survivors whom the **L** calls.
    3:14 the day of the **L** is near in the valley
    3:16 The **L** will roar from Zion
    3:16 the **L** will be a refuge for his people,
Am 1: 2 "The **L** roars from Zion
    4:13 the **L** God Almighty is his name.
    5: 6 Seek the **L** and live, or he will
    5:15 Perhaps the **L** God Almighty will
    5:18 do you long for the day of the **L**?
    7:15 But the **L** took me from tending
    8:11 of hearing the words of the **L**.
    9: 5 The Lord, the **L** Almighty—
Ob 1:15 "The day of the **L** is near for all
Jnh 1: 3 But Jonah ran away from the **L**
    1: 3 for Tarshish to flee from the **L**.
    1: 4 the **L** sent a great wind on the sea,
    1:17 Now the **L** provided a huge fish
    2: 9 'Salvation comes from the **L**.' "
    4: 2 He prayed to the **L**, "Isn't this what
    4: 6 the **L** God provided a leafy plant
Mic 1:12 disaster has come from the **L**,
    4: 2 us go up to the mountain of the **L**,
    4: 2 the word of the **L** from Jerusalem.
    5: 4 his flock in the strength of the **L**,
    5: 4 of the name of the **L** his God.
    6: 2 the **L** has a case against his people;
    6: 8 what does the **L** require of you?
    7: 7 I watch in hope for the **L**, I wait
Na 1: 2 The **L** is a jealous and avenging
    1: 3 The **L** is slow to anger but great
    1: 3 the **L** will not leave the guilty
Hab 1:12 **L**, are you not from everlasting?
    1:12 You, **L**, have appointed them
    2:14 of the **L** as the waters cover the sea.
    2:20 The **L** is in his holy temple;
    3: 2 **L**, I have heard of your fame;
    3: 2 I stand in awe of your deeds, **L**.
Zep 1: 7 Be silent before the Sovereign **L**, for
        the day of the **L** is near.
    1:14 The great day of the **L** is near—
    1:14 The cry on the day of the **L** is bitter;
    3:17 The **L** your God is with you,
Hag 1:12 obeyed the voice of the **L** their God
    1:12 And the people feared the **L**.
    2:23 declares the **L**, 'and I will make you
Zec 1: 2 "The **L** was very angry with your
    1:17 and the **L** will again comfort Zion
    3: 1 standing before the angel of the **L**,
    3: 2 The **L** said to Satan, "The **L** rebuke
    3: 2 The **L**, who has chosen Jerusalem,
    4: 6 by my Spirit,' says the **L** Almighty.
    6:12 place and build the temple of the **L**.
    8:21 'Let us go at once to entreat the **L**
    9:16 The **L** their God will save his people
   14: 5 Then the **L** my God will come,
   14: 7 a day known only to the **L**—
   14: 9 The **L** will be king over the whole
   14: 9 On that day there will be one **L**,
   14:20 **L** will be inscribed on the bells
Mal 1: 2 "I have loved you," says the **L**.

Mal 1: 2 declares the **L**. "Yet I have loved
    3: 6 "I the **L** do not change. So you,
    4: 5 and dreadful day of the **L** comes.

ANGEL OF THE LORD† See ANGEL

ANGER OF THE LORD† See ANGER

ARK OF THE LORD† See ARK

AS SURELY AS THE LORD† ... LIVES Jdg
8:19; Ru 3:13; 1Sa 14:39, 45; 19:6; 20:3, 21; 25:26;
26:10, 16; 28:10; 29:6; 2Sa 4:9; 12:5; 14:11; 15:21;
1Ki 1:29; 2:24; 17:12; 18:10; 22:14; 2Ki 2:2, 4, 6;
3:14; 4:30; 5:16, 20; 2Ch 18:13; Jer 4:2; 5:2; 12:16;
16:14, 15; 23:7, 8; 38:16; 44:26; Hos 4:15

AS THE LORD† ... COMMANDED Ex 7:6,
10, 20; 16:34; 17:1; 34:4; 36:1; 39:1, 5, 7, 21, 26, 29,
31, 32, 42, 43; 40:16, 19, 21, 23, 25, 27, 29, 32; Lev
8:4, 9, 13, 17, 21, 29; 9:7, 10; 10:15; 16:34; 24:23;
Nu 1:19, 54; 2:33; 3:42; 4:49; 8:3, 20, 22; 9:5; 15:36;
17:11; 20:27; 26:4; 27:11, 22; 31:7, 31, 41, 47;
36:10; Dt 1:19, 41; 4:5; 10:5; Jos 11:15, 20; 14:2, 5;
19:50; 21:3, 8; 2Sa 5:25; 24:19; Ps 106:34

COMMANDS OF THE LORD† See
COMMANDS

COVENANT OF THE LORD† See
COVENANT

DAY OF THE LORD† See DAY

DECLARES THE LORD† Ge 22:16; Nu 14:28;
2Ki 9:26, 26; 19:33; 22:19; 2Ch 34:27; Isa 14:22,
22, 23; 17:3, 6; 22:25; 30:1; 31:9; 37:34; 41:14;
43:10, 12; 49:18; 52:5, 5; 54:17; 55:8; 59:20; 66:2,
17, 22; Jer 1:8, 15, 19; 2:3, 9, 12, 29; 3:1, 10, 12,
12, 13, 14, 16, 20; 4:1, 9, 17; 5:9, 11, 15, 18, 22, 29;
6:12; 7:11, 13, 19, 30, 32; 8:1, 3, 13, 17; 9:3, 6, 9,
24, 25; 12:17; 13:11, 14, 25; 15:3, 6, 9, 20; 16:5, 11,
14, 16; 17:24; 18:6; 19:6, 12; 21:7, 10, 13, 14; 22:5,
16, 24; 23:1, 2, 4, 5, 7, 11, 12, 23, 24, 24, 28, 29, 30,
31, 32, 32, 33; 25:7, 9, 12, 29, 31; 27:8, 11, 15, 22;
28:4; 29:9, 11, 14, 14, 19, 19, 23, 32; 30:3, 8, 10, 11,
17, 21; 31:1, 14, 16, 17, 20, 27, 28, 31, 32, 33, 34,
36, 37, 38; 32:5, 30, 44; 33:14; 34:5, 17, 22; 35:13;
39:17, 18; 42:11; 44:29; 45:5; 46:5, 23, 26, 28;
48:12, 25, 30, 35, 38, 43, 44, 47; 49:2, 6, 13, 16, 26,
30, 31, 32, 37, 38, 39; 50:4, 10, 20, 21, 30, 35, 40;
51:24, 25, 26, 39, 48, 52, 53; Eze 16:58; 37:14; Hos
2:13, 16, 21; 11:11; Joel 2:12; Am 2:11, 16; 3:10,
15; 4:3, 6, 8, 9, 10, 11; 9:7, 8, 12, 13; Ob 1:4, 8; Mic
4:6; 5:10; Na 2:13; 3:5; Zep 1:2, 3, 10; 2:9; 3:8; Hag
1:9, 13; 2:4, 4, 8, 9, 14, 17, 23, 23, 23; Zec 1:3, 4,
16; 2:5, 6, 6, 10; 3:10; 8:6, 11, 17; 10:12; 11:6; 12:4;
13:2, 7, 8; Mal 1:2

DECLARES THE SOVEREIGN LORD† Jer
2:22; Eze 5:11; 11:8, 21; 12:25, 28; 13:8, 16; 14:11,
14, 16, 18, 20, 23; 15:8; 16:8, 14, 19, 23, 30, 43,
48, 63; 17:16; 18:3, 9, 23, 30, 32; 20:3, 31, 33, 36,
40, 44; 21:7, 13; 22:12, 31; 23:34; 24:14; 25:14;
26:5, 14, 21; 28:10; 29:20; 30:6; 31:18; 32:8, 14,
16, 31, 32; 33:11; 34:8, 15, 30, 31; 35:6, 11; 36:14,
15, 23, 32; 38:18, 21; 39:5, 8, 10, 13, 20, 29; 43:19,
27; 44:12, 15, 27; 45:9, 15; 47:23; 48:29; Am 4:5;
8:3, 9, 11

EVIL IN THE EYES OF THE LORD† See EYES

FEAR OF THE LORD† See FEAR

FEAR THE LORD† See FEAR

GIVE THANKS TO THE LORD† 1Ch 16:34, 41; 2Ch 20:21; Ps 7:17; 9:1; 106:1; 107:1, 8, 15, 21, 31; 118:1, 19, 29; 136:1; Jer 33:11

GLORY OF THE LORD† See GLORY

HAND OF THE LORD† See HAND

HOLY TO THE LORD† See HOLY

HOUSE OF THE LORD† See HOUSE

I AM THE LORD† See I AM

KNOW THAT I AM THE LORD† See KNOW

KNOW THAT I THE LORD† See KNOW

KNOW THAT THE LORD† See KNOW

LAW OF THE LORD† See LAW

LORD THE LORD† ALMIGHTY See LORD

LORD† ALMIGHTY 1Sa 1:3, 11; 4:4; 15:2; 17:45; 2Sa 6:2, 18; 7:8, 26, 27; 1Ki 18:15; 2Ki 3:14; 19:31; 1Ch 11:9; 17:7, 24; Ps 24:10; 46:7, 11; 48:8; 69:6; 84:1, 3, 12; Isa 1:9, 24; 2:12; 3:1, 15; 5:7, 9, 16, 24; 6:3, 5; 8:13, 18; 9:7, 13, 19; 10:16, 23, 24, 26, 33; 13:4, 13; 14:22, 23, 24, 27; 17:3; 18:7, 7; 19:4, 12, 16, 17, 18, 20, 25; 21:10; 22:5, 12, 14, 14, 15, 25; 23:9; 24:23; 25:6; 28:5, 22, 29; 29:6; 31:4, 5; 37:16, 32; 39:5; 44:6; 45:13; 47:4; 48:2; 51:15; 54:5; Jer 2:19; 6:6, 9; 7:3, 21; 8:3; 9:7, 15, 17; 10:16; 11:17, 20, 22; 16:9; 19:3, 11, 15; 20:12; 23:15, 16, 36; 25:8, 27, 28, 29, 32; 26:18; 27:4, 18, 19, 21; 28:2, 14; 29:4, 8, 17, 21, 25; 30:8; 31:23, 35; 32:14, 15, 18; 33:11, 12; 35:13, 18, 19; 39:16; 42:15, 18; 43:10; 44:2, 11, 25; 46:10, 10, 18, 25; 48:1, 15; 49:5, 7, 26, 35; 50:18, 25, 31, 33, 34; 51:5, 14, 19, 33, 57, 58; Am 9:5; Mic 4:4; Na 2:13; 3:5; Hab 2:13; Zep 2:9, 10; Hag 1:2, 5, 7, 9, 14; 2:4, 6, 7, 8, 9, 9, 11, 23, 23; Zec 1:3, 3, 3, 4, 6, 12, 14, 16, 17; 2:8, 9, 11; 3:7, 9, 10; 4:6, 9; 5:4; 6:12, 15; 7:3, 4, 9, 12, 12, 13; 8:1, 2, 3, 4, 6, 6, 7, 9, 9, 11, 14, 14, 18, 19, 20, 21, 22, 23; 9:15; 10:3; 12:5; 13:2, 7; 14:16, 17, 21, 21; Mal 1:4, 6, 8, 9, 10, 11, 13, 14; 2:2, 4, 7, 8, 12, 16; 3:1, 5, 7, 10, 11, 12, 14, 17; 4:1, 3

LORD† ALMIGHTY SAYS 1Sa 15:2; 2Sa 7:8; 1Ch 17:7; Isa 10:24; 22:15; Jer 6:6, 9; 9:7, 17; 11:22; 19:11; 23:15, 16; 25:8, 28, 32; 26:18; 27:19; 29:17; 33:12; 49:7, 35; 50:33; 51:58; Hag 1:2, 5, 7; 2:6, 11; Zec 1:3, 4, 14, 17; 2:8; 3:7; 6:12; 8:2, 4, 6, 7, 9, 14, 19, 20, 23; Mal 1:4

LORD† GOD Ge 2:4, 5, 7, 8, 9, 15, 16, 18, 19, 21, 22; 3:1, 8, 8, 9, 13, 14, 21, 22, 23; 14:22; 24:12, 42; Ex 9:30; Jdg 21:3; 1Sa 23:10, 11; 2Sa 5:10; 7:25; 1Ki 19:10, 14; 1Ch 17:16, 17; 22:1, 19; 28:20; 29:1; 2Ch 1:9; 6:41, 41, 42; 26:5, 18; 32:16; Ne 9:7; Ps 59:5; 68:18; 72:18; 80:4, 19; 84:8, 11; 89:8; Jer 5:14; 15:16; 35:17; 38:17; 44:7; Hos 12:5; Am 3:13; 4:13; 5:14, 15, 16; 6:8, 14; Jnh 4:6

LORD† GOD ALMIGHTY 2Sa 5:10; 1Ki 19:10, 14; Ps 59:5; 80:4, 19; 84:8; 89:8; Jer 5:14;

15:16; 35:17; 38:17; 44:7; Hos 12:5; Am 3:13; 4:13; 5:14, 15, 16; 6:8, 14

LORD† HIS GOD Ex 32:11; Lev 4:22; Dt 17:19; 18:7; 1Sa 30:6; 2Sa 14:11; 1Ki 5:3; 11:4; 15:3, 4; 2Ki 5:11; 16:2; 2Ch 1:1; 14:2, 11; 15:9; 26:16; 27:6; 28:5; 31:20; 33:12; 34:8; 36:5, 12; Ezr 7:6; Hos 7:10; Jnh 2:1; Mic 5:4

LORD† MY GOD Nu 22:18; Dt 4:5; 26:14; Jos 14:8, 9; 2Sa 24:24; 1Ki 3:7; 5:4, 5; 8:28; 17:20, 21; 1Ch 21:17; 22:7; 2Ch 2:4; 6:19; Ezr 7:28; 9:5; Ps 7:1, 3; 13:3; 25:1; 30:2, 12; 35:24; 40:5; 104:1; 109:26; Jer 31:18; Da 9:4, 20; Jnh 2:6; Zec 11:4; 14:5

LORD† OUR GOD Ex 3:18; 5:3; 8:10, 26, 27; 10:25, 26; Dt 1:6, 19, 20, 25, 41; 2:29, 33, 36, 37; 3:3; 4:7; 5:2, 24, 25, 27, 27; 6:4, 20, 24, 25; 18:16; 29:15, 18, 29; Jos 18:6; 22:19, 29; 24:17, 24; Jdg 11:24; 1Sa 7:8; 1Ki 8:57, 59, 61, 65; 2Ki 18:22; 19:19; 1Ch 13:2; 15:13; 16:14; 29:16; 2Ch 2:4; 13:11; 14:7, 11; 19:7; 29:6; 32:8, 11; Ezr 9:8; Ne 10:34; Ps 20:7; 94:23; 99:5, 8, 9, 9; 105:7; 106:47; 113:5; 122:9; 123:2; Isa 26:13; 36:7; 37:20; Jer 3:22, 23, 25, 25; 5:19, 24; 8:14; 14:22; 16:10; 26:16; 31:6; 37:3; 42:6, 6, 20; 43:2; 50:28; 51:10; Da 9:10, 13, 14; Mic 4:5; 7:17

LORD† THEIR GOD Ex 10:7; 29:46, 46; Lev 26:44; Nu 23:21; Jdg 3:7; 8:34; 1Sa 12:9; 1Ki 9:9; 2Ki 17:7, 9, 14, 16, 19; 18:12; 2Ch 31:6; 33:17; 34:33; 36:23; Ne 9:3, 3, 4; Ps 146:5; Jer 3:21; 22:9; 30:9; 43:1; 50:4; Eze 28:26; 34:30; 39:22, 28; Hos 1:7; 3:5; Zep 2:7; Hag 1:12, 12; Zec 9:16; 10:6

LORD† YOUR GOD Ge 27:20; Ex 6:7; 8:28; 10:8, 16, 17; 15:26; 16:12; 20:2, 5, 7, 10, 12; 23:19, 25; 34:24, 26; Lev 11:44; 18:2, 4, 30; 19:2, 3, 4, 10, 25, 31, 34, 36; 20:7, 24; 23:22, 28, 40, 43; 24:22; 25:17, 38, 55; 26:1, 13; Nu 10:9, 10; 15:41, 41; Dt 1:10, 21, 26, 30, 31, 32; 2:7, 7, 30; 3:18, 20, 21, 22; 4:2, 3, 4, 10, 19, 21, 23, 23, 24, 25, 29, 30, 31, 34, 40; 5:6, 9, 11, 12, 14, 15, 15, 16, 16, 32, 33; 6:1, 2, 5, 10, 13, 15, 16, 17; 7:1, 2, 6, 6, 9, 12, 16, 18, 19, 19, 20, 21, 22, 23, 25; 8:2, 5, 6, 7, 10, 11, 14, 18, 19, 20; 9:3, 4, 5, 6, 7, 16, 23; 10:9, 12, 12, 12, 14, 17, 20, 22; 11:1, 2, 12, 12, 13, 22, 25, 27, 28, 29, 31; 12:4, 5, 7, 7, 9, 10, 11, 12, 15, 18, 18, 18, 20, 21, 27, 27, 28, 29, 31; 13:3, 4, 5, 5, 10, 12, 16, 18; 14:1, 2, 21, 23, 23, 24, 25, 26, 29; 15:4, 5, 6, 7, 10, 14, 15, 18, 19, 20, 21; 16:1, 2, 5, 7, 8, 10, 10, 11, 15, 15, 16, 17, 18, 20, 21, 22; 17:1, 2, 8, 12, 14, 15; 18:5, 9, 12, 13, 14, 15, 16; 19:1, 2, 3, 8, 9, 10, 14; 20:1, 4, 13, 14, 16, 17, 18; 21:1, 5, 10, 23; 22:5; 23:5, 5, 14, 18, 18, 20, 21, 21, 23; 24:4, 9, 13, 18, 19; 25:15, 16, 19; 26:1, 2, 3, 4, 5, 10, 11, 13, 16, 19; 27:2, 3, 5, 6, 6, 7, 9, 10; 28:1, 1, 2, 8, 9, 13, 15, 45, 47, 52, 53, 58, 62; 29:6, 10, 12; 30:1, 2, 3, 4, 6, 7, 9, 10, 10, 16, 16, 20; 31:3, 6, 11, 12, 13, 26; Jos 1:9, 11, 13, 15, 17; 2:11; 3:3, 9; 4:5, 23, 23, 24; 8:7; 9:9, 24; 10:19; 22:3, 4, 5; 23:3, 3, 5, 5, 8, 10, 11, 13, 13, 14, 15, 15, 16; Jdg 6:10, 26; 1Sa 12:12, 14, 19; 13:13; 15:15, 21, 30; 25:26, 28, 29, 31; 2Sa 14:17; 18:28; 24:3, 23; 1Ki 1:17; 2:3; 10:9; 13:6, 21; 17:12; 18:10; 2Ki 17:39; 19:4, 4; 23:21; 1Ch 11:2; 22:11, 12, 18, 19; 28:8; 29:20; 2Ch 9:8, 8; 16:7; 20:20; 28:10; 30:8, 9;

35:3; Ne 8:9; 9:5; Ps 76:11; 81:10; Isa 7:11; 37:4, 4; 41:13; 43:3; 48:17; 51:15; 55:5; 60:9; Jer 2:17, 19; 3:13; 13:16; 26:13; 40:2; 42:2, 3, 4, 5, 13, 20, 21; Eze 20:5, 7, 19, 20; Hos 12:9; 13:4; 14:1; Joel 1:14; 2:13, 14, 23, 26, 27; 3:17; Am 9:15; Mic 7:10; Zep 3:17; Zec 6:15

LOVE THE LORD† See LOVE

NAME OF THE LORD† See NAME

PRAISE BE TO THE LORD† See PRAISE

PRAISE THE LORD† See PRAISE

PRESENCE OF THE LORD† See PRESENCE

SAYS THE LORD† 2Ki 18:30, 32; 20:17; 2Ch 32:11; Ps 12:5; 91:14; Isa 1:11, 18; 33:10; 36:15, 18; 39:6; 41:21; 45:13; 48:22; 54:1, 8, 10; 57:19; 59:21, 21; 65:7, 25; 66:9, 20, 21, 23; Jer 6:15; 8:12; 24:8; 30:3; 33:11, 13; 44:26; 49:2, 18; Am 1:5, 15; 2:3; 5:17, 27; 9:15; Zep 3:20; Hag 1:8; 2:7, 9; Zec 1:3; 3:9; 4:6; 7:13; 8:14; Mal 1:2, 6, 8, 9, 10, 11, 13, 13, 14; 2:2, 4, 8, 16, 16; 3:1, 5, 7, 10, 11, 12, 13, 17; 4:1, 3

SERVANT OF THE LORD† See SERVANT

SOVEREIGN LORD† Ge 15:2, 8; Ex 23:17; 34:23; Dt 3:24; 9:26; Jos 7:7; Jdg 6:22; 16:28; 2Sa 7:18, 19, 19, 20, 22, 28, 29; 1Ki 2:26; 8:53; Ps 68:20; 71:5, 16; 73:28; 109:21; 140:7; 141:8; Isa 7:7; 25:8; 28:16; 30:15; 40:10; 48:16; 49:22; 50:4, 5, 7, 9; 51:22; 52:4; 56:8; 61:1, 11; 65:13, 15; Jer 1:6; 2:22; 4:10; 7:20; 14:13; 32:17, 25; 44:26; 50:25; Eze 2:4; 3:11, 27; 4:14; 5:5, 7, 8, 11; 6:3, 3, 11; 7:2, 5; 8:1; 9:8; 11:7, 8, 13, 16, 17, 21; 12:10, 19, 23, 25, 28, 28; 13:3, 8, 8, 9, 13, 16, 18, 20; 14:4, 6, 11, 14, 16, 18, 20, 21, 23; 15:6, 8; 16:3, 8, 14, 19, 23, 30, 36, 43, 48, 59, 63; 17:3, 9, 16, 19, 22; 18:3, 9, 23, 30, 32; 20:3, 3, 5, 27, 30, 31, 33, 36, 39, 40, 44, 47, 49; 21:7, 13, 24, 26, 28; 22:3, 12, 19, 28, 31; 23:22, 28, 32, 34, 35, 46, 49; 24:3, 6, 9, 14, 21, 24; 25:3, 3, 6, 8, 12, 13, 14, 15, 16; 26:3, 5, 7, 14, 15, 19, 21; 27:3; 28:2, 6, 10, 12, 22, 24, 25; 29:3, 8, 13, 16, 19, 20; 30:2, 6, 10, 13, 22; 31:10, 15, 18; 32:3, 8, 11, 14, 16, 31, 32; 33:11, 25, 27; 34:2, 8, 10, 11, 15, 17, 20, 30, 31; 35:3, 6, 11, 14; 36:2, 3, 4, 4, 5, 6, 7, 13, 14, 15, 22, 23, 32, 33, 37; 37:3, 5, 9, 12, 19, 21; 38:3, 10, 14, 17, 18, 21; 39:1, 5, 8, 10, 13, 17, 20, 25, 29; 43:18, 19, 27; 44:6, 9, 12, 15, 27; 45:9, 9, 15, 18; 46:1, 16; 47:13, 23; 48:29; Am 1:8; 3:7, 8, 11; 4:2, 5; 5:3; 6:8; 7:1, 2, 4, 4, 5, 6; 8:1, 3, 9, 11; 9:8; Ob 1:1; Mic 1:2; Hab 3:19; Zep 1:7; Zec 9:14

SPIRIT OF THE LORD† See SPIRIT

TEMPLE OF THE LORD† See TEMPLE

VOICE OF THE LORD† See VOICE

WHAT THE LORD† SAYS Ex 4:22; 7:17; 8:1, 20; 11:4; Nu 24:13; 1Sa 2:27; 2Sa 7:5; 12:11; 24:12; 1Ki 12:24; 13:2, 21; 20:13, 14, 28, 42; 21:19, 19; 22:11; 2Ki 1:4, 6, 16; 2:21; 3:16, 17; 4:43; 7:1; 9:3, 12; 19:6, 32; 20:1; 22:16; 1Ch 17:4; 21:10, 11; 2Ch 11:4; 12:5; 18:10; 20:15; 34:24; Isa 8:11; 18:4; 31:4; 37:6, 33; 38:1; 43:1, 14, 16; 44:2, 6, 24; 45:1, 11, 14, 18; 48:17; 49:7, 8, 25; 50:1; 52:3; 56:1, 4; 65:8; 66:1, 12; Jer 2:2, 5; 4:3, 27; 6:16, 21, 22; 8:4; 9:23; 10:1, 2, 18; 11:11, 21; 12:14; 13:9, 13; 14:10, 15; 15:2,

19; 16:3, 5; 17:5, 21; 18:11, 13; 19:1; 20:4; 21:8, 12; 22:1, 3, 6, 11, 18, 30; 23:38; 26:2, 4; 27:16; 28:11, 13, 16; 29:10, 16, 31, 32; 30:5, 12, 18; 31:2, 7, 15, 16, 35, 37; 32:3, 28, 42; 33:2, 10, 17, 20, 25; 34:2, 4, 17; 36:29, 30; 37:9; 38:2, 3; 44:30; 45:4; 47:2; 48:40; 49:1, 12, 28; 51:1, 36; Eze 11:5; 21:3; 30:6; Am 1:3, 6, 9, 11, 13; 2:1, 4, 6; 3:12; 5:4; 7:17; Mic 3:5; 6:1; Na 1:12; Zec 1:16; 8:3

WHAT THE SOVEREIGN LORD† SAYS Isa 7:7; 28:16; 49:22; 52:4; 65:13; Jer 7:20; Eze 2:4; 3:11, 27; 5:5, 7, 8; 6:3, 11; 7:2, 5; 11:7, 16, 17; 12:10, 19, 23, 28; 13:3, 8, 13, 18, 20; 14:4, 6, 21; 15:6; 16:3, 36, 59; 17:3, 9, 19, 22; 20:3, 5, 27, 30, 39, 47; 21:24, 26, 28; 22:3, 19, 28; 23:22, 28, 32, 35, 46; 24:3, 6, 9, 21; 25:3, 6, 8, 12, 13, 15, 16; 26:3, 7, 15, 19; 27:3; 28:2, 6, 12, 22, 25; 29:3, 8, 13, 19; 30:2, 10, 13, 22; 31:10, 15; 32:3, 11; 33:25, 27; 34:2, 10, 11, 17, 20; 35:3, 14; 36:2, 3, 4, 5, 6, 7, 13, 22, 33, 37; 37:5, 9, 12, 19, 21; 38:3, 10, 14, 17; 39:1, 17, 25; 43:18; 44:6, 9; 45:9, 18; 46:1, 16; 47:13; Am 3:11; 5:3; Ob 1:1

WORD OF THE LORD† See WORD

LORD'S† (Yahweh's) LORD† (Yahweh); see also LORD'S

Ex	4:14	the L anger burned against Moses
	9:29	may know that the earth is the L.
	12:11	Eat it in haste; it is the L Passover.
	24: 3	told the people all the L words
	34:34	whenever he entered the L presence
Lev	23: 4	are the L appointed festivals,
Nu	9:23	At the L command they encamped,
	9:23	and at the L command they set out.
	11:23	Moses, "Is the L arm too short?
	14:41	are you disobeying the L command?
	31: 3	they may carry out the L vengeance
	32:13	The L anger burned against Israel
Dt	6:18	is right and good in the L sight,
	10:13	and to observe the L commands
	32: 9	For the L portion is his people,
	33:21	he carried out the L righteous will,
Jos	21:45	Not one of all the L good promises
Jdg	2:12	They aroused the L anger
	3: 4	they would obey the L commands,
1Sa	2:25	for it was the L will to put them
	4: 3	us bring the ark of the L covenant
	13:14	you have not kept the L command."
	17:47	for the battle is the L, and he will
	24:10	lord, because he is the L anointed.'
2Sa	22:31	The L word is flawless;
1Ki	10: 9	Because of the L eternal love
Ps	24: 1	The earth is the L, and everything
	32:10	the L unfailing love surrounds
	89: 1	will sing of the L great love forever;
	103:17	to everlasting the L love is
	118:15	"The L right hand has done mighty
Pr	3:11	do not despise the L discipline,
	3:33	The L curse is on the house
	19:21	but it is the L purpose that prevails.
	21: 1	In the L hand the king's heart is
Isa	2: 2	the L temple will be established as
	24:14	the west they acclaim the L majesty.
	30: 9	to listen to the L instruction.

Isa 38: 7 " 'This is the L sign to you
    40: 2 has received from the L hand double
    49: 4 Yet what is due me is in the L hand,
    53:10 Yet it was the L will to crush him
    55:13 This will be for the L renown,
    61: 2 to proclaim the year of the L favor
    62: 3 a crown of splendor in the L hand,
Jer 13:17 because the L flock will be taken
    25:17 So I took the cup from the L hand
    48:10 who is lax in doing the L work!
    51: 6 It is time for the L vengeance;
La   3:22 of the L great love we are not
Eze 7:19 them in the day of the L wrath.
Joel 3:18 will flow out of the L house and will
Ob   1:21 And the kingdom will be the L.
Mic 4: 1 the L temple will be established as
    6: 2 you mountains, the L accusation;
Hab 2:16 the L right hand is coming around
Zep 2: 3 sheltered on the day of the L anger.
Zec 14:20 the L house will be like the sacred

LORDED* LORD

Ne 5:15 assistants also l it over the people.

LORDING* LORD

1Pe 5: 3 not l it over those entrusted to you,

LORDS LORD

Dt 10:17 God is God of gods and Lord of l,
Ps 136: 3 Give thanks to the Lord of l:
Isa 26:13 other l besides you have ruled over
1Co 8: 5 are many "gods" and many "l"),
Rev 17:14 over them because he is Lord of l
    19:16 KING OF KINGS AND LORD OF L.

LOSE LOSES, LOSS, LOST

Ge 26: 9 I thought I might l my life
1Sa 17:32 "Let no one l heart on account
Isa 7: 4 Do not l heart because of these two
Mt 10:39 Whoever finds their life will l it,
Mk 8:35 wants to save their life will l it,
Lk 9:25 and yet l or forfeit their very self?
Jn 6:39 that I shall l none of all those he has
    12:25 Anyone who loves their life will l it,
2Co 4: 1 this ministry, we do not l heart.
    4:16 Therefore we do not l heart.
Heb 12: 3 you will not grow weary and l heart.
    12: 5 do not l heart when he rebukes you,
2Jn 1: 8 you do not l what we have worked

LOSES LOSE

Mt 5:13 But if the salt l its saltiness,
Mk 8:35 but whoever l their life for me
Lk 15: 4 a hundred sheep and l one of them.
    15: 8 has ten silver coins and l one.

LOSS LOSE

Ro 11:12 their l means riches for the Gentiles,
1Co 3:15 the builder will suffer l but yet will
Php 3: 8 I consider everything a l because
Heb 6: 6 their l they are crucifying the Son

LOST LOSE

Nu 17:12 "We will die! We are l, we are all l!
Ps 73: 2 I had nearly l my foothold.

Ps 119:176 I have strayed like a l sheep.
Jer 50: 6 "My people have been l sheep;
Eze 34: 4 back the strays or searched for the l.
    34:16 I will search for the l and bring back
Mt 10: 6 Go rather to the l sheep of Israel.
    15:24 "I was sent only to the l sheep
Lk 15: 4 go after the l sheep until he finds it?
    15: 6 I have found my l sheep.'
    15: 9 I have found my l coin.'
    15:24 he was l and is found.'
    19:10 came to seek and to save the l."
Jn 17:12 None has been l except the one
    18: 9 "I have not l one of those you gave
Php 3: 8 for whose sake I have l all things.
Col 2:19 They have l connection

LOT LOT'S, LOTS, PUR

Nephew of Abraham (Ge 11:27; 12:5). Chose to live in Sodom (Ge 13). Rescued from four kings (Ge 14). Rescued from Sodom (Ge 19:1–29; 2Pe 2:7). Fathered Moab and Ammon by his daughters (Ge 19:30–38).

Lev 16: 9 shall bring the goat whose l falls
Nu 33:54 Distribute the land by l,
1Sa 14:42 said, "Cast the l between me
Est 3: 7 is, the l) was cast in the presence
    9:24 the l) for their ruin and destruction.
Job 31: 2 For what is our l from God above,
Ps 16: 5 and my cup; you make my l secure.
Pr 16:33 The l is cast into the lap, but its
    18:18 Casting the l settles disputes
Ecc 3:22 their work, because that is their l.
    5:19 to accept their l and be happy
Jnh 1: 7 cast lots and the l fell on Jonah.
Ac 1:26 cast lots, and the l fell to Matthias;

LOT'S* LOT

Ge 13: 7 arose between Abram's herders and L.
    19:26 But L wife looked back, and she
    19:36 of L daughters became pregnant
Ps 83: 8 them to reinforce L descendants.
Lk 17:32 Remember L wife!

LOTS LOT

Lev 16: 8 He is to cast l for the two goats—
Jos 18:10 then cast l for them in Shiloh
1Ch 25: 8 as student, cast l for their duties.
Ps 22:18 them and cast l for my garment.
Joel 3: 3 They cast l for my people
Ob 1:11 his gates and cast l for Jerusalem,
Mt 27:35 divided up his clothes by casting l.
Ac 1:26 Then they cast l, and the lot fell

LOUD

Ex 12:30 and there was l wailing in Egypt,
    19:16 and a very l trumpet blast.
Jos 6: 5 have the whole army give a l shout;
Eze 9: 1 I heard him call out in a l voice,
Da 4:14 He called in a l voice:
Mk 15:34 Jesus cried out in a l voice, "Eloi,
Jn 11:43 Jesus called in a l voice, "Lazarus,
Rev 1:10 I heard behind me a l voice like
    21: 3 I heard a l voice from the throne

LOVE* BELOVED, BELOVED'S, LOVED, LOVELY, LOVER, LOVERS, LOVES, LOVING

Ge	4: 1	Adam made l to his wife Eve,
	4:17	Cain made l to his wife, and she
	4:25	Adam made l to his wife again,
	20:13	'This is how you can show your l
	22: 2	son, your only son, whom you l—
	29:18	Jacob was in l with Rachel and said,
	29:20	days to him because of his l for her.
	29:21	and I want to make l to her.'
	29:23	to Jacob, and Jacob made l to her.
	29:30	Jacob made l to Rachel also, and his l
		for Rachel was greater than his l
	29:32	Surely my husband will l me now."
	38: 2	He married her and made l to her;
Ex	15:13	In your unfailing l you will lead
	20: 6	showing l to a thousand generations
		of those who l me
	21: 5	'I l my master and my wife
	34: 6	abounding in l and faithfulness,
	34: 7	maintaining l to thousands,
Lev	19:18	but l your neighbor as yourself.
	19:34	L them as yourself, for you were
Nu	14:18	abounding in l and forgiving sin
	14:19	In accordance with your great l,
Dt	5:10	showing l to a thousand generations
		of those who l me
	6: 5	L the LORD your God with all
	7: 9	his covenant of l to a thousand
		generations of those who l him
	7:12	God will keep his covenant of l
	7:13	He will l you and bless you
	10:12	to l him, to serve the LORD your
	10:19	are to l those who are foreigners,
	11: 1	L the LORD your God and keep
	11:13	to l the LORD your God
	11:22	to l the LORD your God, to walk
	13: 3	out whether you l him with all your
	13: 6	or the wife you l, or your closest
	19: 9	to l the LORD your God
	21:15	is the son of the wife he does not l,
	21:16	the son of the wife he does not l.
	30: 6	you may l him with all your heart
	30:16	today to l the LORD your God,
	30:20	you may l the LORD your God,
	33: 3	Surely it is you who l the people;
Jos	22: 5	to l the LORD your God, to walk
	23:11	careful to l the LORD your God.
Jdg	5:31	may all who l you be like the sun
	14:16	You don't really l me.
	16: 4	he fell in l with a woman
	16:15	"How can you say, 'I l you,'
Ru	4:13	When he made l to her, the LORD
1Sa	1:19	Elkanah made l to his wife Hannah,
	18:20	Saul's daughter Michal was in l
	18:22	you, and his attendants all l you;
	20:17	reaffirm his oath out of l for him,
2Sa	1:26	Your l for me was wonderful,
	7:15	my l will never be taken away
	11:11	and drink and make l to my wife?
2Sa	12:24	he went to her and made l to her.
	13: 1	son of David fell in l with Tamar,

2Sa	13: 4	said to him, "I'm in l with Tamar,
	16:17	"So this is the l you show your
	19: 6	You l those who hate you and hate
		those who l you.
1Ki	3: 3	Solomon showed his l
	3:26	deeply moved out of l for her son
	8:23	you who keep your covenant of l
	10: 9	of the LORD's eternal l for Israel,
	11: 2	Solomon held fast to them in l.
1Ch	2:21	He made l to her, and she bore him
	7:23	Then he made l to his wife again,
	16:34	for he is good; his l endures forever.
	16:41	"for his l endures forever."
	17:13	I will never take my l away
2Ch	5:13	his l endures forever."
	6:14	you who keep your covenant of l
	6:42	Remember the great l promised
	7: 3	his l endures forever."
	7: 6	saying, "His l endures forever."
	9: 8	Because of the l of your God
	19: 2	and l those who hate the LORD?
	20:21	LORD, for his l endures forever."
Ezr	3:11	his l toward Israel endures forever."
Ne	1: 5	who keeps his covenant of l with
		those who l him
	9:17	slow to anger and abounding in l.
	9:32	who keeps his covenant of l, do not
	13:22	to me according to your great l.
Job	15:34	the tents of those who l bribes.
	19:19	those I l have turned against me.
	37:13	or to water his earth and show his l.
Ps	4: 2	How long will you l delusions
	5: 7	by your great l, can come into your
	5:11	those who l your name may rejoice
	6: 4	save me because of your unfailing l.
	11: 5	those who l violence, he hates
	13: 5	But I trust in your unfailing l;
	17: 7	me the wonders of your great l,
	18: 1	I l you, LORD, my strength.
	18:50	he shows unfailing l to his anointed,
	21: 7	through the unfailing l of the Most
	23: 6	l will follow me all the days of my
	25: 6	your great mercy and l, for they are
	25: 7	according to your l remember me,
	26: 3	been mindful of your unfailing l
	26: 8	I l the house where you live,
	31: 7	I will be glad and rejoice in your l,
	31:16	save me in your unfailing l.
	31:21	me the wonders of his l when I was
	31:23	L the LORD, all his faithful
	32:10	LORD's unfailing l surrounds
	33: 5	the earth is full of his unfailing l.
	33:18	whose hope is in his unfailing l,
	33:22	May your unfailing l be with us,
	36: 5	Your l, LORD,
	36: 7	How priceless is your unfailing l,
	36:10	Continue your l to those who know
	40:10	I do not conceal your l and your
	40:11	may your l and faithfulness always
	42: 8	By day the LORD directs his l,
	44:26	us because of your unfailing l.
	45: 7	You l righteousness and hate
	48: 9	we meditate on your unfailing l.

Ps 51: 1 God, according to your unfailing l;
52: 3 You l evil rather than good,
52: 4 You l every harmful word,
52: 8 I trust in God's unfailing l for ever
57: 3 God sends forth his l and his
57:10 For great is your l,
59:16 in the morning I will sing of your l;
60: 5 that those you l may be delivered.
61: 7 appoint your l and faithfulness
62:12 and with you, Lord, is unfailing l";
63: 3 Because your l is better than life,
66:20 prayer or withheld his l from me!
69:13 in your great l, O God, answer me
69:16 out of the goodness of your l;
69:36 and those who l his name will dwell
77: 8 his unfailing l vanished forever?
85: 7 Show us your unfailing l, Lord,
85:10 L and faithfulness meet together;
86: 5 abounding in l to all who call
86:13 For great is your l toward me;
86:15 abounding in l and faithfulness.
88:11 Is your l declared in the grave,
89: 1 sing of the Lord's great l forever;
89: 2 that your l stands firm forever,
89:14 l and faithfulness go before you.
89:24 My faithful l will be with him,
89:28 I will maintain my l to him forever,
89:33 but I will not take my l from him,
89:49 where is your former great l,
90:14 the morning with your unfailing l,
92: 2 proclaiming your l in the morning
94:18 slipping," your unfailing l, Lord,
97:10 Let those who l the Lord hate
98: 3 He has remembered his l and his
100: 5 is good and his l endures forever;
101: 1 I will sing of your l and justice;
103: 4 crowns you with l and compassion,
103: 8 slow to anger, abounding in l.
103:11 so great is his l for those who fear
103:17 to everlasting the Lord's l is
106: 1 for he is good; his l endures forever.
106:45 and out of his great l he relented.
107: 1 for he is good; his l endures forever.
107: 8 to the Lord for his unfailing l
107:15 to the Lord for his unfailing l
107:21 to the Lord for his unfailing l
107:31 to the Lord for his unfailing l
108: 4 For great is your l, higher than
108: 6 that those you l may be delivered.
109:21 out of the goodness of your l,
109:26 me according to your unfailing l.
115: 1 because of your l and faithfulness.
116: 1 I l the Lord, for he heard my
117: 2 For great is his l toward us,
118: 1 for he is good; his l endures forever.
118: 2 "His l endures forever."
118: 3 "His l endures forever."
118: 4 "His l endures forever."
118:29 for he is good; his l endures forever.
119:41 May your unfailing l come to me,
119:47 in your commands because I l them.
119:48 which I l, that I may meditate
119:64 The earth is filled with your l,

Ps 119:76 May your unfailing l be my
119:88 In your unfailing l preserve my life,
119:97 Oh, how I l your law! I meditate
119:113 people, but I l your law.
119:119 therefore I l your statutes.
119:124 your servant according to your l
119:127 Because I l your commands more
119:132 do to those who l your name.
119:149 my voice in accordance with your l;
119:159 See how I l your precepts;
119:159 Lord, in accordance with your l.
119:163 detest falsehood but I l your law.
119:165 peace have those who l your law,
119:167 your statutes, for I l them greatly.
122: 6 "May those who l you be secure.
130: 7 for with the Lord is unfailing l
136: 1 *His l endures forever.*
136: 2 *His l endures forever.*
136: 3 *His l endures forever.*
136: 4 *His l endures forever.*
136: 5 *His l endures forever.*
136: 6 *His l endures forever.*
136: 7 *His l endures forever.*
136: 8 *His l endures forever.*
136: 9 *His l endures forever.*
136:10 *His l endures forever.*
136:11 *His l endures forever.*
136:12 *His l endures forever.*
136:13 *His l endures forever.*
136:14 *His l endures forever.*
136:15 *His l endures forever.*
136:16 *His l endures forever.*
136:17 *His l endures forever.*
136:18 *His l endures forever.*
136:19 *His l endures forever.*
136:20 *His l endures forever.*
136:21 *His l endures forever.*
136:22 *His l endures forever.*
136:23 *His l endures forever.*
136:24 *His l endures forever.*
136:25 *His l endures forever.*
136:26 *His l endures forever.*
138: 2 your name for your unfailing l
138: 8 your l, Lord, endures forever—
143: 8 bring me word of your unfailing l,
143:12 In your unfailing l, silence my
145: 8 slow to anger and rich in l.
145:20 Lord watches over all who l him,
147:11 who put their hope in his unfailing l.
Pr 1:22 who are simple l your simple ways?
3: 3 Let l and faithfulness never leave
4: 6 l her, and she will watch over you.
5:19 you ever be intoxicated with her l.
7:18 let's drink deeply of l till morning;
7:18 let's enjoy ourselves with l!
8:17 I l those who l me, and those who
8:21 a rich inheritance on those who l me
8:36 all who hate me l death."
9: 8 rebuke the wise and they will l you.
10:12 but l covers over all wrongs.
14:22 those who plan what is good find l
15:17 with l than a fattened calf
16: 6 Through l and faithfulness sin is

Pr 17: 9 Whoever would foster l covers over
    18:21 and those who l it will eat its fruit.
    19:22 What a person desires is unfailing l;
    20: 6 Many claim to have unfailing l,
    20:13 Do not l sleep or you will grow
    20:28 L and faithfulness keep a king safe;
    20:28 through l his throne is made secure.
    21:21 righteousness and l finds life,
    27: 5 Better is open rebuke than hidden l.
Ecc 3: 8 a time to l and a time to hate, a time
     9: 1 but no one knows whether l or hate
     9: 6 Their l, their hate and their jealousy
     9: 9 whom you l, all the days of this
SS   1: 2 your l is more delightful than wine.
     1: 3 No wonder the young women l you!
     1: 4 will praise your l more than wine.
     1: 7 you whom I l, where you graze your
     2: 4 hall, and let his banner over me be l.
     2: 5 with apples, for I am faint with l.
     2: 7 or awaken l until it so desires.
     3: 5 or awaken l until it so desires.
     3:10 with purple, its interior inlaid with l.
     4:10 How delightful is your l, my sister,
     4:10 more pleasing is your l than wine,
     5: 1 drink your fill of l.
     5: 8 Tell him I am faint with l.
     7: 6 pleasing, my l, with your delights!
     7:12 there I will give you my l.
     8: 4 or awaken l until it so desires.
     8: 6 for l is as strong as death,
     8: 7 Many waters cannot quench l;
     8: 7 all the wealth of one's house for l,
Isa 1:23 they all l bribes and chase
     5: 1 sing for the one I l a song about his
     8: 3 Then I made l to the prophetess,
    16: 5 In l a throne will be established;
    38:17 In your l you kept me from the pit
    43: 4 and because I l you, I will give
    54:10 yet my unfailing l for you will not
    55: 3 my faithful l I promised to David.
    56: 6 to him, to l the name of the LORD,
    56:10 around and dream, they l to sleep.
    57: 8 a pact with those whose beds you l,
    61: 8 "For I, the LORD, l justice;
    63: 9 In his l and mercy he redeemed
    66:10 be glad for her, all you who l her;
Jer 2:25 I l foreign gods, and I must go
     2:33 How skilled you are at pursuing l!
     5:31 and my people l it this way.
    12: 7 I will give the one I l l into the hands
    14:10 "They greatly l to wander;
    16: 5 my l and my pity from this people,"
    31: 3 loved you with an everlasting l;
    32:18 You show l to thousands but bring
    33:11 his l endures forever."
La   3:22 of the LORD's great l we are not
     3:32 so great is his unfailing l.
Eze 16: 8 saw that you were old enough for l,
    23:17 to the bed of l, and in their lust they
    33:31 Their mouths speak of l, but their
    33:32 more than one who sings l songs
Da   9: 4 who keeps his covenant of l with
           those who l him

Hos 1: 6 for I will no longer show l to Israel,
     1: 7 Yet I will show l to Judah;
     2: 4 I will not show my l to her children,
     2:19 and justice, in l and compassion.
     2:23 I will show my l to the one I called
     3: 1 show your l to your wife again,
     3: 1 L her as the LORD loves
     3: 1 gods and l the sacred raisin cakes."
     4: 1 no l, no acknowledgment of God
     4:18 their rulers dearly l shameful ways.
     6: 4 Your l is like the morning mist,
     9: 1 you l the wages of a prostitute
     9:15 I will no longer l them;
    10:12 reap the fruit of unfailing l,
    11: 4 of human kindness, with ties of l.
    12: 6 maintain l and justice, and wait
    14: 4 waywardness and l them freely,
Joel 2:13 slow to anger and abounding in l,
Am   4: 5 for this is what you l to do,"
     5:15 Hate evil, l good; maintain justice
Jnh 2: 8 turn away from God's l for them.
     4: 2 slow to anger and abounding in l,
Mic 3: 2 you who hate good and l evil;
     6: 8 to l mercy and to walk humbly
     7:20 and show l to Abraham, as you
Zep 3:17 his l he will no longer rebuke you,
Zec 8:17 other, and do not l to swear falsely.
     8:19 Therefore l truth and peace."
Mt   3:17 said, "This is my Son, whom I l;
     5:43 said, 'L your neighbor and hate your
     5:44 l your enemies and pray for those
     5:46 If you l those who l you,
     6: 5 for they l to pray standing
     6:24 will hate the one and l the other,
    12:18 the one I l, in whom I delight;
    17: 5 said, "This is my Son, whom I l;
    19:19 'l your neighbor as yourself.' "
    22:37 " 'L the Lord your God with all
    22:39 'L your neighbor as yourself.'
    23: 6 they l the place of honor at banquets
    23: 7 they l to be greeted with respect
    24:12 the l of most will grow cold,
Mk   1:11 "You are my Son, whom I l;
     9: 7 "This is my Son, whom I l.
    12:30 L the Lord your God with all your
    12:31 'L your neighbor as yourself.'
    12:33 To l him with all your heart, with all
    12:33 l your neighbor as yourself is more
Lk   3:22 "You are my Son, whom I l;
     6:27 L your enemies, do good to those
     6:32 "If you l those who l you,
     6:32 Even sinners l those who l them.
     6:35 But l your enemies, do good
     7:42 which of them will l him more?"
     7:47 as her great l has shown.
    10:27 " 'L the Lord your God with all
    10:27 'L your neighbor as yourself.' "
    11:42 you neglect justice and the l of God.
    11:43 because you l the most important
    16:13 will hate the one and l the other,
    20:13 I will send my son, whom I l;
    20:46 l to be greeted with respect
Jn   5:42 that you do not have the l of God

Jn	8:42	you would l me, for I have come
	11: 3	Jesus, "Lord, the one you l is sick."
	13:34	command I give you: L one another.
	13:34	you, so you must l one another.
	13:35	my disciples, if you l one another."
	14:15	"If you l me, keep my commands.
	14:21	I too will l them and show myself
	14:23	My Father will l them, and we will
	14:24	Anyone who does not l me will not
	14:31	world may learn that I l the Father
	15: 9	I loved you. Now remain in my l.
	15:10	you will remain in my l, just as I
	15:10	commands and remain in his l.
	15:12	L each other as I have loved you.
	15:13	Greater l has no one than this:
	15:17	This is my command: L each other.
	15:19	the world, it would l you as its own.
	17:26	order that the l you have for me may
	21:15	do you l me more than these?"
	21:15	he said, "you know that I l you."
	21:16	"Simon son of John, do you l me?"
	21:16	Lord, you know that I l you."
	21:17	"Simon son of John, do you l me?"
	21:17	him the third time, "Do you l me?"
	21:17	you know that I l you."
Ro	1:31	no fidelity, no l, no mercy.
	5: 5	because God's l has been poured
	5: 8	God demonstrates his own l for us
	8:28	for the good of those who l him,
	8:35	separate us from the l of Christ?
	8:39	separate us from the l of God that is
	12: 9	L must be sincere. Hate what is evil;
	12:10	Be devoted to one another in l.
	13: 8	the continuing debt to l one another,
	13: 9	"L your neighbor as yourself."
	13:10	L does no harm to a neighbor.
	13:10	Therefore l is the fulfillment
	14:15	eat, you are no longer acting in l.
	15:30	Christ and by the l of the Spirit,
1Co	2: 9	has prepared for those who l him—
	4:17	my son whom I l, who is faithful
	4:21	shall I come in l and with a gentle
	8: 1	puffs up while l builds up.
	13: 1	but do not have l, I am only
	13: 2	but do not have l, I am nothing.
	13: 3	but do not have l, I gain nothing.
	13: 4	L is patient, l is kind.
	13: 6	L does not delight in evil
	13: 8	L never fails. But where there are
	13:13	these three remain: faith, hope and l.
		But the greatest of these is l.
	14: 1	Follow the way of l and eagerly
	16:14	Do everything in l.
	16:22	If anyone does not l the Lord,
	16:24	My l to all of you in Christ Jesus.
2Co	2: 4	you know the depth of my l for you.
	2: 8	therefore, to reaffirm your l for him.
	5:14	For Christ's l compels us,
	6: 6	in the Holy Spirit and in sincere l;
	8: 7	in the l we have kindled in you—
	8: 8	sincerity of your l by comparing it
	8:24	show these men the proof of your l
	11:11	Because I do not l you?

2Co	12:15	If I l you more, will you l me less?
	13:11	the God of l and peace will be
	13:14	and the l of God, and the fellowship
Gal	5: 6	is faith expressing itself through l.
	5:13	serve one another humbly in l.
	5:14	"L your neighbor as yourself."
	5:22	But the fruit of the Spirit is l, joy,
Eph	1: 4	holy and blameless in his sight. In l
	1:15	and your l for all God's people,
	2: 4	But because of his great l for us,
	3:17	being rooted and established in l,
	3:18	and high and deep is the l of Christ,
	3:19	and to know this l that surpasses
	4: 2	bearing with one another in l.
	4:15	speaking the truth in l, we will grow
	4:16	grows and builds itself up in l,
	5: 2	and walk in the way of l, just as
	5:25	Husbands, l your wives, just as
	5:28	to l their wives as their own bodies.
	5:33	must l his wife as he loves himself,
	6:23	and l with faith from God the Father
	6:24	to all who l our Lord Jesus Christ
	6:24	Lord Jesus Christ with an undying l.
Php	1: 9	that your l may abound more
	1:16	The latter do so out of l,
	2: 1	if any comfort from his l, if any
	2: 2	having the same l, being one
	4: 1	sisters, you whom I l and long for,
Col	1: 4	and of the l you have for all God's
	1: 5	l that spring from the hope stored
	1: 8	also told us of your l in the Spirit.
	2: 2	encouraged in heart and united in l,
	3:14	And over all these virtues put on l,
	3:19	l your wives and do not be harsh
1Th	1: 3	your labor prompted by l, and your
	3: 6	good news about your faith and l.
	3:12	May the Lord make your l increase
	4: 9	your l for one another we do not
	4: 9	been taught by God to l each other.
	4:10	in fact, you do l all of God's family
	5: 8	on faith and l as a breastplate,
	5:13	in the highest regard in l because
2Th	1: 3	the l all of you have for one another
	2:10	because they refused to l the truth
	3: 5	Lord direct your hearts into God's l
1Ti	1: 5	The goal of this command is l,
	1:14	faith and l that are in Christ Jesus.
	2:15	faith, l and holiness with propriety.
	4:12	conduct, in l, in faith and in purity.
	6:10	For the l of money is a root of all
	6:11	faith, l, endurance and gentleness.
2Ti	1: 7	us power, l and self-discipline.
	1:13	with faith and l in Christ Jesus.
	2:22	faith, l and peace, along with those
	3: 3	without l, unforgiving, slanderous,
	3:10	faith, patience, l, endurance,
Titus	2: 2	in faith, in l and in endurance.
	2: 4	younger women to l their husbands
	3: 4	and l of God our Savior appeared,
	3:15	Greet those who l us in the faith.
Phm	1: 5	about your l for all his holy people
	1: 7	Your l has given me great joy
	1: 9	to appeal to you on the basis of l.

Heb	6:10	the l you have shown him as you
	10:24	may spur one another on toward l
	13: 5	your lives free from the l of money
Jas	1:12	has promised to those who l him.
	2: 5	he promised those who l him?
	2: 8	"L your neighbor as yourself,"
1Pe	1: 8	you have not seen him, you l him;
	1:22	you have sincere l for each other, l
		one another deeply,
	2:17	everyone, l the family of believers,
	3: 8	be sympathetic, l one another,
	3:10	For, "Whoever would l life and see
	4: 8	Above all, l each other deeply,
	4: 8	because l covers over a multitude
	5:14	Greet one another with a kiss of l.
2Pe	1: 7	and to mutual affection, l.
	1:17	saying, "This is my Son, whom I l;
1Jn	2: 5	l for God is truly made complete
	2:15	Do not l the world or anything
	2:15	l for the Father is not in them.
	3: 1	See what great l the Father has
	3:10	anyone who does not l their brother
	3:11	We should l one another.
	3:14	to life, because we l each other.
	3:14	Anyone who does not l remains
	3:16	This is how we know what l is:
	3:17	how can the l of God be
	3:18	let us not l with words or speech
	3:23	l one another as he commanded us.
	4: 7	Dear friends, let us l one another,
	4: 7	one another, for l comes from God.
	4: 8	Whoever does not l does not know
		God, because God is l.
	4: 9	is how God showed his l among us:
	4:10	This is l: not that we loved God,
	4:11	us, we also ought to l one another.
	4:12	if we l one another, God lives in us
		and his l is made complete
	4:16	and rely on the l God has for us.
	4:16	God is l. Whoever lives in l lives
	4:17	This is how l is made complete
	4:18	There is no fear in l. But perfect l
		drives out fear,
	4:18	who fears is not made perfect in l.
	4:19	We l because he first loved us.
	4:20	claims to l God yet hates a brother
	4:20	For whoever does not l their brother
	4:20	whom they have seen, cannot l God,
	4:21	loves God must also l their brother
	5: 2	how we know that we l the children
	5: 3	In fact, this is l for God: to keep his
2Jn	1: 1	her children, whom I l in the truth—
	1: 3	Son, will be with us in truth and l.
	1: 5	I ask that we l one another.
	1: 6	And this is l: that we walk
	1: 6	his command is that you walk in l.
3Jn	1: 1	friend Gaius, whom I l in the truth.
	1: 6	have told the church about your l.
Jude	1: 2	peace and l be yours in abundance.
	1:12	are blemishes at your l feasts,
	1:21	yourselves in God's l as you wait
Rev	2: 4	You have forsaken the l you had
	2:19	I know your deeds, your l and faith,

Rev	3:19	Those whom I l l rebuke
	12:11	they did not l their lives so much as

HIS LOVE ENDURES FOREVER 1Ch 16:34, 41; 2Ch 5:13; 7:3, 6; 20:21; Ps 100:5; 106:1; 107:1; 118:1, 2, 3, 4, 29; 136:1, 2, 3, 4, 5, 6, 7, 8, 9, 10, 11, 12, 13, 14, 15, 16, 17, 18, 19, 20, 21, 22, 23, 24, 25, 26; Jer 33:11

LOVE THE LORD† Dt 6:5; 11:1, 13, 22; 19:9; 30:16, 20; Jos 22:5; 23:11; Ps 31:23; 97:10; 116:1

LOVE YOUR NEIGHBOR Lev 19:18; Mt 5:43; 19:19; 22:39; Mk 12:31, 33; Lk 10:27; Ro 13:9; Gal 5:14; Jas 2:8

UNFAILING LOVE Ex 15:13; Ps 6:4; 13:5; 18:50; 21:7; 26:3; 31:16; 32:10; 33:5, 18, 22; 36:7; 44:26; 48:9; 51:1; 52:8; 62:12; 77:8; 85:7; 90:14; 94:18; 107:8, 15, 21, 31; 109:26; 119:41, 76, 88; 130:7; 138:2; 143:8, 12; 147:11; Pr 19:22; 20:6; Isa 54:10; La 3:32; Hos 10:12

LOVED* LOVE

Ge	24:67	she became his wife, and he l her;
	25:28	had a taste for wild game, l Esau, but
		Rebekah l Jacob.
	29:31	the LORD saw that Leah was not l,
	29:33	the LORD heard that I am not l,
	34: 3	he l the young woman and spoke
	37: 3	Now Israel l Joseph more than any
	37: 4	that their father l him more than any
Dt	4:37	Because he l your ancestors
	7: 8	it was because the LORD l you
	10:15	on your ancestors and l them,
1Sa	1: 5	a double portion because he l her,
	18: 1	with David, and he l him as himself.
	18: 3	David because he l him as himself.
	18:16	But all Israel and Judah l David,
	18:28	that his daughter Michal l David,
	20:17	because he l him as he l himself.
2Sa	1:23	in life they were l and admired,
	12:24	The LORD l him;
	12:25	and because the LORD l him,
	13:15	he hated her more than he had l her.
1Ki	11: 1	l many foreign women besides
2Ch	11:21	Rehoboam l Maakah daughter
	26:10	in the fertile lands, for he l the soil.
Ne	13:26	He was l by his God, and God made
Ps	44: 3	light of your face, for you l them.
	47: 4	us, the pride of Jacob, whom he l.
	78:68	of Judah, Mount Zion, which he l.
	109:17	He l to pronounce a curse—
Isa	5: 1	My l one had a vineyard on a fertile
Jer	2: 2	youth, how as a bride you l me
	8: 2	which they have l and served
	31: 3	"I have l you with an everlasting
Eze	16:37	those you l as well as those you
Hos	2: 1	(which means "not l"), for I will no
	2: 1	and of your sisters, 'My l one.'
	2:23	to the one I called 'Not my l one.'
	3: 1	though she is l by another man
	9:10	became as vile as the thing they l.
	11: 1	"When Israel was a child, I l him,
Mal	1: 2	"I have l you," says the LORD.
	1: 2	"But you ask, 'How have you l us?'

Mal 1: 2 "Yet I have l Jacob,
Mk 10:21 Jesus looked at him and l him.
   12: 6 one left to send, a son, whom he l.
Lk 16:14 The Pharisees, who l money,
Jn 3:16 For God so l the world that he gave
   3:19 people l darkness instead of light
  11: 5 Now Jesus l Martha and her sister
  11:36 the Jews said, "See how he l him!"
  12:43 for they l human praise more than
  13: 1 Having l his own who were in the
       world, he l them to the end.
  13:23 the disciple whom Jesus l,
  13:34 As I have l you, so you must love
  14:21 The one who loves me will be l
  14:28 If you l me, you would be glad
  15: 9 "As the Father has l me, so have I
       l you.
  15:12 Love each other as I have l you.
  16:27 loves you because you have l me
  17:23 have l them even as you have l me.
  17:24 me because you l me before
  19:26 disciple whom he l standing nearby,
  20: 2 disciple, the one Jesus l, and said,
  21: 7 the disciple whom Jesus l said
  21:20 whom Jesus l was following them.
Ro 1: 7 To all in Rome who are l by God
  8:37 conquerors through him who l us.
  9:13 "Jacob I l, but Esau I hated."
  9:25 l will call her 'my l one' who is not
       my l one,"
  11:28 they are l on account
Gal 2:20 who l me and gave himself for me.
Eph 5: 1 therefore, as dearly l children
   5: 2 just as Christ l us and gave himself
   5:25 just as Christ l the church and gave
Col 3:12 holy and dearly l, clothe yourselves
1Th 1: 4 brothers and sisters l by God,
   2: 8 Because we l you so much, we were
2Th 2:13 brothers and sisters l by the Lord,
   2:16 who l us and by his grace gave us
2Ti 4:10 for Demas, because he l this world,
Heb 1: 9 You have l righteousness and hated
2Pe 2:15 who l the wages of wickedness.
1Jn 4:10 not that we l God, but that he l us
   4:11 since God so l us, we also ought
   4:19 We love because he first l us.
Jude 1: 1 who are l in God the Father
Rev 3: 9 and acknowledge that I have l you.

LOVELY* LOVE

Ge 29:17 but Rachel had a l figure and was
Est 1:11 and nobles, for she was l to look at.
   2: 7 had a l figure and was beautiful.
Ps 84: 1 How l is your dwelling place,
SS 1: 5 am I, yet l, daughters of Jerusalem,
   2:14 voice is sweet, and your face is l.
   4: 3 a scarlet ribbon; your mouth is l.
   5:16 is sweetness itself; he is altogether l.
   6: 4 my darling, as l as Jerusalem,
Am 8:13 "In that day "the l young women
Php 4: 8 is pure, whatever is l, whatever is

LOVER* LOVE

Isa 47: 8 listen, you l of pleasure,

1Ti 3: 3 not quarrelsome, not a l of money.

LOVERS* LOVE

Jer 3: 1 lived as a prostitute with many l—
   3: 2 the roadside you sat waiting for l,
   4:30 Your l despise you; they want to kill
La 1: 2 Among all her l there is no one
Eze 16:33 gifts, but you give gifts to all your l,
  16:36 in your promiscuity with your l,
  16:37 I am going to gather all your l,
  16:39 deliver you into the hands of your l,
  16:41 and you will no longer pay your l.
  23: 5 and she lusted after her l,
  23: 9 delivered her into the hands of her l,
  23:20 There she lusted after her l,
  23:22 I will stir up your l against you,
Hos 2: 5 'I will go after my l, who give me
   2: 7 She will chase after her l but not
   2:10 lewdness before the eyes of her l;
   2:12 she said were her pay from her l,
   2:13 and went after her l, but me she
   8: 9 Ephraim has sold herself to l.
2Ti 3: 2 People will be l of themselves,
       l of money,
   3: 3 brutal, not l of the good,
   3: 4 l of pleasure rather than l of God—

LOVES* LOVE

Ge 44:20 sons left, and his father l him.'
Dt 10:18 l the foreigner residing among you,
  15:16 because he l you and your family
  21:15 and he l one but not the other,
  21:16 son of the wife he l in preference
  23: 5 the LORD your God l you.
  28:54 or the wife he l or his surviving
  28:56 will begrudge the husband she l
  33:12 one the LORD l rests between his
Ru 4:15 who l you and who is better to you
2Ch 2:11 "Because the LORD l his people,
Ps 11: 7 LORD is righteous, he l justice;
  33: 5 The LORD l righteousness
  34:12 Whoever of you l life and desires
  37:28 For the LORD l the just and will
  87: 2 The LORD l the gates of Zion
  91:14 "Because he l me,"
  99: 4 The King is mighty, he l justice—
 119:140 tested, and your servant l them.
  127: 2 for he grants sleep to those he l.
  146: 8 down, the LORD l the righteous.
Pr 3:12 the LORD disciplines those he l,
  12: 1 Whoever l discipline l knowledge,
  13:24 but the one who l their children is
  15: 9 wicked, but he l those who pursue
  17:17 A friend l at all times, and a brother
  17:19 Whoever l a quarrel l sin;
  19: 8 The one who gets wisdom l life;
  21:17 Whoever l pleasure will become
  21:17 whoever l wine and olive oil will
  22:11 One who l a pure heart and who
  29: 3 A man who l wisdom brings joy
Ecc 5:10 Whoever l money never has
   5:10 whoever l wealth is never satisfied
SS 3: 1 bed I looked for the one my heart l;
   3: 2 I will search for the one my heart l.

SS   3: 3 you seen the one my heart l?"
        3: 4 when I found the one my heart l.
Hos 3: 1 her as the LORD l the Israelites,
     10:11 Ephraim is a trained heifer that l
     12: 7 dishonest scales and l to defraud.
Mal 2:11 the sanctuary the LORD l
Mt 10:37 "Anyone who l their father
     10:37 anyone who l their son or daughter
Lk   7: 5 because he l our nation and has built
     7:47 has been forgiven little l little."
Jn   3:35 The Father l the Son and has placed
     5:20 For the Father l the Son and shows
    10:17 The reason my Father l me is that I
    12:25 Anyone who l their life will lose it,
    14:21 and keeps them is the one who l me.
    14:21 The one who l me will be loved
    14:23 "Anyone who l me will obey my
    16:27 the Father himself l you because
Ro 13: 8 for whoever l others has fulfilled
1Co 8: 3 whoever l God is known by God.
2Co 9: 7 for God l a cheerful giver.
Eph 1: 6 has freely given us in the One he l.
    5:28 He who l his wife l himself.
    5:33 must love his wife as he l himself,
Col 1:13 us into the kingdom of the Son he l,
Titus 1: 8 hospitable, one who l what is good,
Heb 12: 6 the Lord disciplines the one he l,
1Jn 2:10 Anyone who l their brother
    2:15 If anyone l the world, love for
    4: 7 Everyone who l has been born
    4:21 Anyone who l God must also love
    5: 1 everyone who l the father l his child
3Jn .1: 9 but Diotrephes, who l to be first,
Rev 1: 5 To him who l us and has freed us
    20: 9 camp of God's people, the city he l.
    22:15 and everyone who l and practices

LOVING* LOVE
Ps 25:10 All the ways of the LORD are l
    32: 8 I will counsel you with my l eye
  107:43 ponder the l deeds of the LORD.
  144: 2 He is my l God and my fortress,
Pr   5:19 A l doe, a graceful deer—
Heb 13: 1 Keep on l one another as brothers
1Jn 5: 2 by l God and carrying out his

LOVINGKINDNESS (KJV) See
UNFAILING LOVE

LOW BELOW, LOWER, LOWERED, LOWEST, LOWLY
2Sa 22:28 are on the haughty to bring them l.
Job 40:11 all who are proud and bring them l,
Ps 116: 6 when I was brought l, he saved me.
  136:23 remembered us in our l estate
Pr 29:23 Pride brings a person l,
Isa 2:11 and human pride brought l;
    40: 4 up, every mountain and hill made l;
Lk   3: 5 in, every mountain and hill made l.
Ro 12:16 associate with people of l position.

LOWER LOW
Dt 28:43 but you will sink l and l.
Ps   8: 5 made them a little l than the angels

2Co 11: 7 it a sin for me to l myself in order
Eph 4: 9 that he also descended to the l,
Heb 2: 7 made them a little l than the angels;

LOWERED LOW
Ex 17:11 but whenever he l his hands,
Jer 38: 6 They l Jeremiah by ropes
Mk 2: 4 then l the mat the man was lying on.
Ac 9:25 and l him in a basket through
2Co 11:33 I was l in a basket from a window

LOWEST LOW
Ge 9:25 The l of slaves will he be to his
Ps 88: 6 You have put me in the l pit,
Lk 14:10 take the l place, so that when your

LOWING
1Sa 15:14 What is this l of cattle that I hear?"

LOWLY* LOW
Job 5:11 The l he sets on high, and those who
Ps 119:141 Though I am l and despised, I do
  138: 6 is exalted, he looks kindly on the l;
Pr 16:19 Better to be l in spirit along
   29:23 low, but the l in spirit gain honor.
Isa 57:15 one who is contrite and l in spirit,
   57:15 to revive the spirit of the l
Eze 21:26 The l will be exalted and the exalted
   29:14 There they will be a l kingdom.
Zec 9: 9 victorious, l and riding on a donkey,
Mt 18: 4 takes the l position of this child
1Co 1:28 God chose the l things of this world
Php 3:21 will transform our l bodies so

LOYAL LOYALTY
1Ki 12:20 of Judah remained l to the house
1Ch 29:18 and keep their hearts l to you.
Ps 78: 8 whose hearts were not l to God,

LOYALTY* LOYAL
Jdg 8:35 failed to show any l to the family
1Ch 12:33 to help David with undivided l—

LUCIFER (KJV) See MORNING STAR

LUCRE (KJV) See DISHONEST GAIN, MONEY

LUKE*
    Associate of Paul (Col 4:14; 2Ti 4:11; Phm 24).

LUKEWARM* WARM
Rev 3:16 So, because you are l—

LUMP*
Ro 9:21 of the same l of clay some pottery

LURK* LURKED, LURKS
Ps 56: 6 they l, they watch my steps,
Pr 24:15 Do not l like a thief near the house
Hos 13: 7 like a leopard I will l by the path.

LURKED* LURK
Job 31: 9 or if I have l at my neighbor's door,

LURKS* LURK
Pr   7:12 the squares, at every corner she l.)

LUST* LUSTED, LUSTFUL,
LUSTFULLY, LUSTS
Pr   6:25 Do not l in your heart after her
Isa 57: 5 You burn with l among the oaks
     57: 8 looked with l on their naked bodies.
Eze 16:36 Because you poured out your l
   20:30 did and l after their vile images?
   23: 8 bosom and poured out their l on her.
   23:11 yet in her l and prostitution she was
   23:17 love, and in their l they defiled her.
Na   3: 4 of the wanton l of a prostitute,
Ro   1:27 and were inflamed with l for one
Col   3: 5 impurity, l, evil desires and greed,
1Th 4: 5 not in passionate l like the pagans,
1Pe 4: 3 living in debauchery, l,
1Jn 2:16 the l of the flesh, the l of the eyes,

LUSTED LUST
Eze   6: 9 eyes, which have l after their idols.
   23: 5 and she l after her lovers,

LUSTFUL* LUST
Jer 13:27 your adulteries and l neighings,
2Pe 2:18 by appealing to the l desires

LUSTFULLY* LUST
Job 31: 1 not to look l at a young woman.
Mt   5:28 at a woman l has already committed

LUSTS* LUST
Nu 15:39 after the l of your own hearts
Ro   1:26 God gave them over to shameful l.

LUXURY
Pr 19:10 is not fitting for a fool to live in l—
Lk 16:19 fine linen and lived in l every day
Jas   5: 5 You have lived on earth in l
Rev 18: 7 as the glory and l she gave herself.

LUZ BETHEL
Ge 28:19 though the city used to be called L.
   48: 3 appeared to me at L in the land

LYDDA
Ac   9:32 the Lord's people who lived in L.

LYDIA LYDIA'S
Jer 46: 9 men of L who draw the bow.
Ac 16:14 from the city of Thyatira named L,

LYDIA'S* LYDIA
Ac 16:40 they went to L house, where they

LYING LIE
Ge 28:13 the land on which you are l.
Ex 14:30 Israel saw the Egyptians l dead
Jdg 16:13 making a fool of me and l to me.
Ru   3: 8 and there was a woman l at his feet!
1Sa 3: 3 Samuel was l down in the house
    5: 4 off and were l on the threshold;
   26: 5 Saul was l inside the camp,
Ps 31:18 Let their l lips be silenced,
  120: 2 from l lips and from deceitful

Pr   6:17 haughty eyes, a l tongue,
   12:19 but a l tongue lasts only a moment.
   12:22 The LORD detests l lips, but he
   21: 6 by a l tongue is a fleeting vapor
   26:28 A l tongue hates those it hurts,
Jer 23:26 in the hearts of these l prophets,
Eze 13: 9 false visions and utter l divinations.
Da   4:10 These are the visions I saw while l
Hos 4: 2 There is only cursing, l and murder,
Mt   8:14 he saw Peter's mother-in-law l
Mk   2: 4 lowered the mat the man was l on.
    7:30 and found her child l on the bed,
Lk   2:12 in cloths and l in a manger."
Jn   5: 6 When Jesus saw him l there
   20: 6 He saw the strips of linen l there,
Ro   9: 1 I am not l, my conscience confirms

LYRE LYRES
1Sa 16:23 David would take up his l and play.
   18:10 while David was playing the l, as he
   19: 9 While David was playing the l,
Job 30:31 My l is tuned to mourning, and my
Ps 33: 2 music to him on the ten-stringed l.
   57: 8 Awake, harp and l! I will awaken
  150: 3 praise him with the harp and l,
Da   3: 7 flute, zither, l, harp and all kinds

LYRES LYRE
1Sa 10: 5 down from the high place with l,
   18: 6 songs and with timbrels and l.
1Ch 15:16 l, harps and cymbals.
2Ch 20:28 of the LORD with harps and l

LYSTRA
Ac 14: 8 In L there sat a man who was lame.
2Ti 3:11 Iconium and L, the persecutions I

M

MAAKAH
2Sa 3: 3 Absalom the son of M daughter
1Ki 15: 2 His mother's name was M daughter
   15:10 name was M daughter

MACEDONIA
Ac 16: 9 had a vision of a man of M standing
   18: 5 Silas and Timothy came from M,
   20: 3 he decided to go back through M.

MACHPELAH
Ge 23: 9 so he will sell me the cave of M,
   49:30 the cave in the field of M,
   50:13 him in the cave in the field of M,

MAD MADDENING, MADMAN,
MADMEN, MADNESS
Dt 28:34 The sights you see will drive you m.
Jer 51: 7 therefore they have now gone m.
Jn 10:20 is demon-possessed and raving m.

MADDENING* MAD
Rev 14: 8 all the nations drink the m wine
   18: 3 the nations have drunk the m wine

MADE MAKE

Ge   1: 7 So God **m** the vault and separated
     1:16 God **m** two great lights—
     1:16 He also **m** the stars.
     1:25 God **m** the wild animals according
     1:31 God saw all that he had **m**, and it
     2: 3 the seventh day and **m** it holy,
     2:22 the LORD God **m** a woman
     3:21 The LORD God **m** garments
     6: 6 that he had **m** human beings
     9: 6 image of God has God **m** mankind.
    15:18 day the LORD **m** a covenant
    24:21 not the LORD had **m** his journey
    45: 9 God has **m** me lord of all Egypt.
Ex   1:14 They **m** their lives bitter with harsh
     2:14 "Who **m** you ruler and judge over
     7: 1 I have **m** you like God to Pharaoh,
    12: 8 herbs, and bread **m** without yeast.
    12:36 The LORD had **m** the Egyptians
    20:11 six days the LORD **m** the heavens
    24: 8 that the LORD has **m** with you
    32: 4 **m** it into an idol cast in the shape
    36: 8 among the workers **m** the tabernacle
    37: 1 Bezalel **m** the ark of acacia wood—
    37:10 They **m** the table of acacia wood—
    37:17 They **m** the lampstand of pure gold.
    37:25 They **m** the altar of incense
    37:29 They also **m** the sacred anointing oil
    38: 9 Next they **m** the courtyard.
    39: 1 also **m** sacred garments for Aaron,
Lev 16:34 Atonement is to be **m** once a year
Nu 14:36 **m** the whole community grumble
    21: 2 Israel **m** this vow to the LORD:
    21: 9 So Moses **m** a bronze snake and put
Dt   1:28 Our brothers have **m** our hearts melt
    5: 2 The LORD our God **m** a covenant
   32: 6 who **m** you and formed you?
   32:21 They **m** me jealous by what is no
Jos 24:25 that day Joshua **m** a covenant
Jdg 11:30 Jephthah **m** a vow to the LORD:
1Sa   1:11 And she **m** a vow, saying,
    15:11 "I regret that I have **m** Saul king,
    20:16 So Jonathan **m** a covenant
2Sa 23: 5 surely he would not have **m** with me
1Ki 12:28 the king **m** two golden calves.
2Ki 17:38 Do not forget the covenant I have **m**
    18: 4 the bronze snake Moses had **m**,
    19:15 You have **m** heaven and earth.
1Ch 22: 5 So David **m** extensive preparations
2Ch   2:12 of Israel, who **m** heaven and earth!
    3:10 the Most Holy Place he **m** a pair
    4:19 **m** all the furnishings that were
Ne   9: 6 You **m** the heavens,
    9:10 You **m** a name for yourself,
Job   7:20 Why have you **m** me your target?
    31: 1 "I **m** a covenant with my eyes not
    33: 4 The Spirit of God has **m** me;
Ps   8: 5 You have **m** them a little lower than
    33: 6 of the LORD the heavens were **m**,
    73:28 I have **m** the Sovereign LORD my
    95: 5 for he **m** it, and his hands formed
    96: 5 but the LORD **m** the heavens.
    98: 2 The LORD has **m** his salvation

Ps 100: 3 It is he who **m** us, and we are his;
   136: 7 who **m** the great lights—
   139:14 I am fearfully and wonderfully **m**;
Pr   8:26 before he **m** the world or its fields
Ecc   3:11 He has **m** everything beautiful in its
    7:13 straighten what he has **m** crooked?
Isa 22:11 did not look to the One who **m** it,
    43: 7 my glory, whom I formed and **m**."
    44:21 I have **m** you, you are my servant;
    45:12 It is I who **m** the earth and created
    53:12 **m** intercession for the transgressors.
    66: 2 Has not my hand **m** all these things,
Jer 10:12 But God **m** the earth by his power;
    25: 6 anger with what your hands have **m**.
    27: 5 outstretched arm I **m** the earth
    31:32 It will not be like the covenant I **m**
    33: 2 LORD says, he who **m** the earth,
    51:15 "He **m** the earth by his power;
La   3:12 and **m** me the target for his arrows.
Eze   3:17 I have **m** you a watchman
   16:60 I will remember the covenant I **m**
   33: 7 I have **m** you a watchman
Da   2:38 he has **m** you ruler over them all.
    3: 1 King Nebuchadnezzar **m** an image
Hos 14: 3 to what our own hands have **m**,
Am   5: 8 He who **m** the Pleiades and Orion,
Jnh   1: 9 who **m** the sea and the dry land."
Mt   5:33 to the Lord the vows you have **m**.'
Mk   1: 6 John wore clothing **m** of camel's
    2:27 them, "The Sabbath was **m** for man,
    15: 5 But Jesus still **m** no reply, and Pilate
Lk 17:19 your faith has **m** you well."
   19:46 but you have **m** it 'a den
Jn   1: 3 all things were **m**; without him
        nothing was **m** that has been **m**.
    1:18 with the Father, has **m** him known.
    9: 6 **m** some mud with the saliva,
Ac   2:36 God has **m** this Jesus, whom you
   10:15 impure that God has **m** clean."
   17:24 "The God who **m** the world
Ro   1:19 because God has **m** it plain to them.
1Co   1:20 Has not God **m** foolish the wisdom
   12:14 Even so the body is not **m** up of one
   15:22 die, so in Christ all will be **m** alive.
   15:28 the Son himself will be **m** subject
2Co   3: 6 He has **m** us competent as ministers
    5:21 God **m** him who had no sin to be sin
   12: 9 you, for my power is **m** perfect
Eph   2: 5 **m** us alive with Christ even
    2:14 who has **m** the two groups one
Php   2: 7 servant, being **m** in human likeness.
Heb   1: 2 whom also he **m** the universe.
    2: 7 You **m** them a little lower than
    8: 9 It will not be like the covenant I **m**
Jas   2:22 his faith was **m** complete by what he
    3: 9 who have been **m** in God's likeness.
1Jn   2: 5 for God is truly **m** complete in them.
Rev   5:10 You have **m** them to be a kingdom
    14: 7 Worship him who **m** the heavens,
    19: 7 and his bride has **m** herself ready.

MADMAN* MAD

1Sa 21:13 was in their hands he acted like a **m**,

MADMEN MAD
1Sa 21:15 Am I so short of **m** that you have

MADNESS MAD
Dt   28:28 The LORD will afflict you with **m**,
Ecc   7:25 of wickedness and the **m** of folly.
       9: 3 there is **m** in their hearts while they

MAGDALENE
Mt   27:56 Among them were Mary **M**,
Mk   16: 1 Mary **M**, Mary the mother of James,
Lk   8: 2 Mary (called **M**) from whom seven
Jn   20: 1 Mary **M** went to the tomb and saw

MAGI
Mt   2: 1 **M** from the east came to Jerusalem
      2:16 that he had been outwitted by the **M**,

MAGIC* MAGICIAN, MAGICIANS
Isa 47:12 with your **m** spells and with your
Eze 13:18 to the women who sew **m** charms
     13:20 I am against your **m** charms
Rev   9:21 repent of their murders, their **m** arts,
     18:23 your **m** spell all the nations were led
     21: 8 those who practice **m** arts,
     22:15 dogs, those who practice **m** arts,

MAGICIAN* MAGIC
Da   2:10 ever asked such a thing of any **m**
      2:27 **m** or diviner can explain to the king

MAGICIANS MAGIC
Ge   41: 8 so he sent for all the **m** and wise
Ex   7:11 the Egyptian **m** also did the same
      7:22 the Egyptian **m** did the same things
      8: 7 the **m** did the same things by their
      8:18 when the **m** tried to produce gnats
      9:11 The **m** could not stand before Moses
Da   2: 2 So the king summoned the **m**,
      5:11 appointed him chief of the **m**,

MAGNIFICENCE* MAGNIFY
1Ch 22: 5 for the LORD should be of great **m**

MAGNIFICENT* MAGNIFY
1Ki   8:13 I have indeed built a **m** temple
2Ch   2: 9 temple I build must be large and **m**.
      6: 2 I have built a **m** temple for you,
Isa 28:29 is wonderful, whose wisdom is **m**.
Mk   13: 1 What **m** buildings!"

MAGNIFY* MAGNIFICENCE,
MAGNIFICENT
Da   11:36 and **m** himself above every god

MAGOG
Eze 38: 2 of the land of **M**, the chief prince
     39: 6 I will send fire on **M** and on those
Rev 20: 8 Gog and **M**—and to gather them

MAHANAIM
Ge   32: 2 So he named that place **M**.
2Sa 17:24 David went to **M**, and Absalom

MAHER-SHALAL-HASH-BAZ
Isa   8: 3 LORD said to me, "Name him **M**.

MAHLON MAHLON'S
Ru   1: 5 both **M** and Kilion also died,

MAHLON'S* MAHLON
Ru   4:10 Ruth the Moabite, **M** widow, as my

MAIMED
Mk   9:43 to enter life **m** than with two hands

MAIN
1Ki   7:50 for the doors of the **m** hall

MAINTAIN MAINTAINED,
MAINTAINING, MAINTAINS
Ru   4: 5 in order to **m** the name of the dead
1Ki 10: 9 he has made you king to **m** justice
2Ki   8:19 He had promised to **m** a lamp
Isa 56: 1 "**M** justice and do what is right,
Hos 12: 6 **m** love and justice, and wait
Am   5:15 **m** justice in the courts.
Ro   3:28 For we **m** that a person is justified

MAINTAINED* MAINTAIN
Rev   6: 9 God and the testimony they had **m**.

MAINTAINING* MAINTAIN
Ex   34: 7 **m** love to thousands, and forgiving
Job   2: 9 "Are you still **m** your integrity?

MAINTAINS MAINTAIN
Job   2: 3 And he still **m** his integrity,

MAJESTIC* MAJESTY
Ex   15: 6 hand, LORD, was **m** in power.
     15:11 **m** in holiness, awesome in glory,
Job 37: 4 he thunders with his **m** voice.
Ps   8: 1 how **m** is your name in all the earth!
      8: 9 how **m** is your name in all the earth!
     29: 4 the voice of the LORD is **m**.
     68:15 Mount Bashan, **m** mountain,
     76: 4 more **m** than mountains rich
    111: 3 Glorious and **m** are his deeds,
SS   6: 4 as **m** as troops with banners.
      6:10 sun, **m** as the stars in procession?
Isa 30:30 cause people to hear his **m** voice
Eze 31: 7 It was **m** in beauty, with its
2Pe   1:17 came to him from the **M** Glory,

MAJESTY MAJESTIC
Ex   15: 7 your **m** you threw down those who
Dt   5:24 has shown us his glory and his **m**,
     11: 2 his **m**, his mighty hand,
     33:17 In **m** he is like a firstborn bull;
     33:26 help you and on the clouds in his **m**.
1Ch 16:27 Splendor and **m** are before him;
     29:11 glory and the **m** and the splendor,
Est   1: 4 and the splendor and glory of his **m**.
      7: 3 you, Your **M**, and if it pleases you,
Job 37:22 God comes in awesome **m**.
     40:10 and clothe yourself in honor and **m**.
Ps   21: 5 bestowed on him splendor and **m**.
     45: 3 clothe yourself with splendor and **m**.
     45: 4 In your **m** ride forth victoriously
     68:34 of God, whose **m** is over Israel,
     93: 1 LORD reigns, he is robed in **m**;
     96: 6 Splendor and **m** are before him;

Ps 104: 1 are clothed with splendor and **m**.
 145: 5 of the glorious splendor of your **m**—
Isa 2:10 LORD and the splendor of his **m**!
 2:19 LORD and the splendor of his **m**,
 2:21 LORD and the splendor of his **m**,
 24:14 west they acclaim the LORD's **m**.
 26:10 do not regard the **m** of the LORD.
 53: 2 no beauty or **m** to attract us to him,
Eze 31: 2 can be compared with you in **m**?
 31:18 with you in splendor and **m**?
Da 4:30 power and for the glory of my **m**?"
Mic 5: 4 in the **m** of the name of the LORD
Zec 6:13 he will be clothed with **m** and will
Ac 19:27 will be robbed of her divine **m**."
 25:26 to write to His **M** about him.
Heb 1: 3 at the right hand of the **M** in heaven.
 8: 1 of the throne of the **M** in heaven,
2Pe 1:16 but we were eyewitnesses of his **m**.
Jude 1:25 only God our Savior be glory, **m**,

MAKE MADE, MAKER, MAKERS, MAKES, MAKING, MAN-MADE

Ge 1:26 "Let us **m** mankind in our image,
 2:18 I will **m** a helper suitable for him."
 3:16 "I will **m** your pains in childbearing
 6:14 So **m** yourself an ark of cypress
 11: 4 so that we may **m** a name
 12: 2 "I will **m** you into a great nation,
 12: 2 I will **m** your name great, and you
 13:16 I will **m** your offspring like the dust
 17: 2 I will **m** my covenant between me
 17: 6 I will **m** you very fruitful; I will **m**
 21:18 I will **m** him into a great nation."
 22:17 **m** your descendants as numerous as
 24:40 you and **m** your journey a success,
 26: 4 I will **m** your descendants as
 28: 3 bless you and **m** you fruitful
 32: 9 relatives, and I will **m** you prosper,'
 46: 3 for I will **m** you into a great nation
 48: 4 'I am going to **m** you fruitful
Ex 6: 3 I did not **m** myself fully known
 9: 4 But the LORD will **m** a distinction
 20: 4 "You shall not **m** for yourself
 20:23 Do not **m** any gods to be alongside
 22: 3 steals must certainly **m** restitution,
 25: 9 **M** this tabernacle and all its
 25:10 "Have them **m** an ark of acacia
 25:23 "**M** a table of acacia wood—
 25:31 "**M** a lampstand of pure gold.
 25:40 See that you **m** them according
 28: 2 **M** sacred garments for your brother
 32: 1 **m** us gods who will go before us.
 32:10 I will **m** you into a great nation."
 34:17 "Do not **m** any idols.
Lev 1: 4 your behalf to **m** atonement for you.
 4:20 this way the priest will **m** atonement
 8:15 So he consecrated it to **m** atonement
 20:25 must therefore **m** a distinction
Nu 6:25 the LORD **m** his face shine on you
 21: 8 "**M** a snake and put it up on a pole;
Dt 7: 2 **M** no treaty with them, and show
 30: 9 LORD your God will **m** you most
Jos 9: 7 us, so how can we **m** a treaty

2Sa 7: 9 Now I will **m** your name great,
 22:36 You **m** your saving help my shield;
Ezr 10: 3 Now let us **m** a covenant before our
Job 7:17 is mankind that you **m** so much
Ps 4: 8 LORD, **m** me dwell in safety.
 20: 4 heart and **m** all your plans succeed.
 27: 6 sing and **m** music to the LORD.
 80: 7 **m** your face shine on us, that we
 108: 1 sing and **m** music with all my soul.
 110: 1 right hand until I **m** your enemies
 115: 8 Those who **m** them will be like
 119:165 and nothing can **m** them stumble.
Pr 3: 6 and he will **m** your paths straight.
 10: 4 Lazy hands **m** for poverty,
 13: 5 the wicked **m** themselves a stench
 16: 7 he causes their enemies to **m** peace
 16:23 of the wise **m** their mouths prudent.
Ecc 5: 4 When you **m** a vow to God, do not
Isa 6:10 **M** the heart of this people calloused;
 14:14 I will **m** myself like the Most
 29:16 formed it, "You did not **m** me"?
 40: 3 **m** straight in the desert a highway
 44: 9 All who **m** idols are nothing,
 49: 6 also **m** you a light for the Gentiles,
 49: 8 will **m** you to be a covenant
 55: 3 I will **m** an everlasting covenant
 61: 8 and **m** an everlasting covenant
 66:22 that I **m** will endure before me,"
Jer 10:11 who did not **m** the heavens
 16:20 Do people **m** their own gods?
 30:10 and no one will **m** him afraid.
 31:31 "when I will **m** a new covenant
 32:40 I will **m** an everlasting covenant
 33:15 time I will **m** a righteous Branch
Eze 34:25 " 'I will **m** a covenant of peace
 37: 5 I will **m** breath enter you, and you
 37:26 I will **m** a covenant of peace
 39: 7 " 'I will **m** known my holy name
Hos 2:18 day I will **m** a covenant for them
Jnh 2: 9 What I have vowed I will **m** good.
Mt 3: 3 Lord, **m** straight paths for him.' "
 27:65 **m** the tomb as secure as you know
 28:19 go and **m** disciples of all nations,
Lk 1:17 to **m** ready a people prepared
 13:24 "**M** every effort to enter through
Jn 1:23 '**M** straight the way
Ac 2:35 until I **m** your enemies a footstool
Ro 9:20 'Why did you **m** me like this?' "
 14: 4 for the Lord is able to **m** them stand.
 14:19 Let us therefore **m** every effort to do
1Co 9:27 **m** it my slave so that after I have
2Co 5: 9 So we **m** it our goal to please him,
Eph 4: 3 **M** every effort to keep the unity
 5:19 and **m** music from your heart
Col 4: 5 **m** the most of every opportunity.
1Th 4:11 to **m** it your ambition to lead a quiet
2Th 1:11 our God may **m** you worthy of his
2Ti 3:15 are able to **m** you wise for salvation
Heb 1:13 right hand until I **m** your enemies
 2:17 he might **m** atonement for the sins
 4:11 **m** every effort to enter that rest,
 8: 8 when I will **m** a new covenant
 12: 5 son, do not **m** light of the Lord's

Heb 12:14 **M** every effort to live in peace
2Pe 1: 5 **m** every effort to add to your faith
1:10 **m** every effort to confirm your
3:14 **m** every effort to be found spotless,
1Jn 1:10 we **m** him out to be a liar and his

MAKER* MAKE
Job 4:17 man be more pure than his **M**?
9: 9 He is the **M** of the Bear and Orion,
32:22 my **M** would soon take me away.
35:10 'Where is God my **M**, who gives
36: 3 I will ascribe justice to my **M**.
40:19 yet its **M** can approach it with his
Ps 95: 6 us kneel before the LORD our **M**;
115:15 LORD, the **M** of heaven and earth.
121: 2 LORD, the **M** of heaven and earth.
124: 8 LORD, the **M** of heaven and earth.
134: 3 he who is the **M** of heaven
146: 6 He is the **M** of heaven and earth,
149: 2 Let Israel rejoice in their **M**;
Pr 14:31 poor shows contempt for their **M**,
17: 5 poor shows contempt for their **M**;
22: 2 The LORD is the **M** of them all.
Ecc 11: 5 work of God, the **M** of all things.
Isa 17: 7 that day people will look to their **M**
27:11 so their **M** has no compassion
44:24 I am the LORD, the **M** of all things,
45: 9 to those who quarrel with their **M**,
45:11 the Holy One of Israel, and its **M**:
51:13 that you forget the LORD your **M**,
54: 5 For your **M** is your husband—
Jer 10:16 these, for he is the **M** of all things,
51:19 these, for he is the **M** of all things,
Hos 8:14 Israel has forgotten their **M**

MAKERS* MAKE
Isa 45:16 All the **m** of idols will be put

MAKES MAKE
Ex 4:11 Who **m** them deaf or mute?
11: 7 the LORD **m** a distinction between
Lev 20: 8 I am the LORD, who **m** you holy.
Dt 27:15 "Cursed is anyone who **m** an idol—
1Sa 2: 6 LORD brings death and **m** alive;
2Sa 22:34 He **m** my feet like the feet of a deer;
Ps 18:33 He **m** my feet like the feet of a deer;
23: 2 He **m** me lie down in green pastures,
Pr 13:12 Hope deferred **m** the heart sick,
15:13 A happy heart **m** the face cheerful,
Ecc 10:19 for laughter, wine **m** life merry,
Isa 8:14 stumble and a rock that **m** them fall.
53:10 and though the LORD **m** his life
Mk 7:37 "He even **m** the deaf hear
Ro 9:33 stumble and a rock that **m** them fall,
1Co 3: 7 but only God, who **m** things grow.
1Pe 2: 8 and a rock that **m** them fall."

MAKING MAKE
Ne 8: 8 it clear and giving the meaning so
Ps 19: 7 are trustworthy, **m** wise the simple.
Ecc 12:12 Of **m** many books there is no end,
Isa 43:19 I am **m** a way in the wilderness
Mt 21:13 you are **m** it 'a den of robbers.' "
Mk 2:21 from the old, **m** the tear worse.
Jn 5:18 Father, **m** himself equal with God.

1Co 3: 6 it, but God has been **m** it grow.
Eph 5:16 **m** the most of every opportunity,
Col 1:20 by **m** peace through his blood,
Rev 21: 5 said, "I am **m** everything new!"

MALACHI*
Mal 1: 1 of the LORD to Israel through **M**.

MALE MALES
Ge 1:27 **m** and female he created them.
5: 2 He created them **m** and female
6:19 all living creatures, **m** and female,
17:10 Every **m** among you shall be
Ex 13: 2 to me every firstborn **m**.
20:10 nor your **m** or female servant,
Nu 8:16 the first **m** offspring from every
Dt 5:14 nor your **m** or female servant,
2Ki 23: 7 quarters of the **m** shrine prostitutes
Mt 19: 4 the Creator 'made them **m** and
Lk 2:23 Lord, "Every firstborn **m** is to be
Gal 3:28 nor free, nor is there **m** and female,
Rev 12: 5 She gave birth to a son, a **m** child,

MALES MALE
Ex 12:48 Passover must have all the **m** in his
34:19 including all the firstborn **m** of your

MALICE MALICIOUS
Nu 35:20 with **m** aforethought shoves another
Dt 4:42 a neighbor without **m** aforethought.
Mk 7:22 adultery, greed, **m**, deceit, lewdness,
Ro 1:29 envy, murder, strife, deceit and **m**.
1Co 5: 8 with the old bread leavened with **m**
Eph 4:31 slander, along with every form of **m**.
Col 3: 8 anger, rage, **m**, slander, and filthy
Titus 3: 3 We lived in **m** and envy,
1Pe 2: 1 rid yourselves of all **m** and all

MALICIOUS MALICE
Ex 23: 1 guilty person by being a **m** witness.
Dt 19:16 If a **m** witness takes the stand
1Ti 3:11 not **m** talkers but temperate
6: 4 envy, strife, **m** talk, evil suspicions

MALIGN*
Ps 12: 5 them from those who **m** them."
Titus 2: 5 that no one will **m** the word of God.

MAMMON (KJV) See MONEY, WEALTH

MAMRE
Ge 13:18 to live near the great trees of **M**
25: 9 in the cave of Machpelah near **M**,

MALLOW*
Job 6: 6 is there flavor in the sap of the **m**?

MAN HORSEMAN, HORSEMEN, HUMANITY, MAN-MADE, MAN'S, MANKIND, MEN, MEN'S, PEOPLE, PERSON
Ge 2: 7 the LORD God formed a **m**
2: 7 and the **m** became a living being.
2:15 The LORD God took the **m**
2:18 is not good for the **m** to be alone.

Ge   2:20 So the **m** gave names to all
        2:23 for she was taken out of **m**."
        3: 9 the LORD God called to the **m**,
        3:22 "The **m** has now become like one
        4: 1 LORD I have brought forth a **m**."
        32:24 a **m** wrestled with him till daybreak.
Lev   20:10 " 'If a **m** commits adultery
        20:13 " 'If a **m** has sexual relations with a **m**
              as one does with
Nu   1: 2 families, listing every **m** by name,
Dt   8: 3 that **m** does not live on bread alone
        22: 5 nor a **m** wear women's clothing,
        32:30 How could one **m** chase a thousand,
Jdg   8:21 'As is the **m**, so is his strength.' "
        16: 7 become as weak as any other **m**."
1Sa   13:14 sought out a **m** after his own heart
1Ch   29: 1 this palatial structure is not for **m**
Est   6: 7 "For the **m** the king delights
Job   2: 4 "A **m** will give all he has for his
         4:17 **m** be more pure than his Maker?
         5: 7 Yet **m** is born to trouble as surely as
        38: 3 Brace yourself like a **m**; I will
        40: 7 "Brace yourself like a **m**; I will
Ps   127: 5 Blessed is the **m** whose quiver is
Pr   6:32 a **m** who commits adultery has no
        30:19 way of a **m** with a young woman.
Isa   53: 3 by mankind, a **m** of suffering,
Jer   17: 5 "Cursed is the one who trusts in **m**,
Da   7:13 before me was one like a son of **m**,
Hos   11: 9 I am God, and not a **m**—the Holy
Zec   6:12 'Here is the **m** whose name is
Mt   4: 4 "'M shall not live on bread alone,
        9: 6 the Son of **M** has authority on earth
        19: 5 this reason a **m** will leave his father
        19:26 "With **m** this is impossible, but with
Mk   2:27 "The Sabbath was made for **m**, not **m**
              for the Sabbath.
        9:12 that the Son of **M** must suffer much
Lk   2:52 stature, and in favor with God and **m**.
         4: 4 'M shall not live on bread alone.' "
         6: 5 them, "The Son of **M** is Lord
Jn   9:35 "Do you believe in the Son of **M**?"
Ac   3:11 While the **m** held on to Peter
         7:56 the Son of **M** standing at the right
        10:26 he said, "I am only a **m** myself."
        16: 9 vision of a **m** of Macedonia standing
Ro   5:12 entered the world through one **m**,
1Co   7: 1 "It is good for a **m** not to have
         7: 2 each **m** should have sexual relations
        11: 3 that the head of every **m** is Christ,
              and the head of the woman is **m**,
        11: 7 A **m** ought not to cover his head,
        11: 7 but woman is the glory of **m**.
        11:14 teach you that if a **m** has long hair,
        13:11 When I became a **m**, I put the ways
        15:21 For since death came through a **m**,
        15:47 The first **m** was of the dust
        15:47 the second **m** is of heaven.
        15:49 borne the image of the earthly **m**,
        15:49 bear the image of the heavenly **m**.
2Co   8:21 of the Lord but also in the eyes of **m**.
        12: 2 I know a **m** in Christ who fourteen
Eph   5:31 this reason a **m** will leave his father

Php   2: 8 being found in appearance as a **m**,
Heb   2: 6 a son of **m** that you care for him?
1Ti   2: 5 and mankind, the **m** Christ Jesus,
Rev   1:13 was someone like a son of **m**,
         4: 7 ox, the third had a face like a **m**,
        13:18 beast, for it is the number of a **m**.
        14:14 on the cloud was one like a son of **m**

MAN OF GOD Dt 33:1; Jos 14:6; Jdg 13:6, 8;
1Sa 2:27; 9:6, 7, 8, 10; 1Ki 12:22; 13:1, 3, 4, 5, 6, 6,
7, 8, 11, 12, 14, 14, 16, 19, 21, 23, 26, 29, 31; 17:18,
24; 20:28; 2Ki 1:9, 10, 11, 12, 13; 4:7, 9, 16, 21, 22,
25, 25, 27, 27, 40, 42; 5:8, 14, 15, 20; 6:6, 9, 10, 15;
7:2, 17, 18, 19, 19; 8:2, 4, 7, 8, 11; 13:19; 23:16, 17;
1Ch 23:14; 2Ch 8:14; 11:2; 25:7, 9, 9; 30:16; Ezr
3:2; Ne 12:24, 36; Jer 35:4; 1Ti 6:11

SON OF MAN See SON

MAN-MADE* MAKE, MAN
Dt   4:28 you will worship **m** gods of wood

MAN'S MAN
Ge   2:21 he took one of the **m** ribs

MANAGE* MANAGER, MANAGES
Jer   12: 5 how will you **m** in the thickets
1Ti   3: 4 He must **m** his own family well
         3: 5 not know how to **m** his own family,
         3:12 to his wife and must **m** his children
         5:14 to **m** their homes and to give

MANAGER MANAGE
Lk   12:42 then is the faithful and wise **m**,
        16: 1 a rich man whose **m** was accused

MANAGES* MANAGE
Titus   1: 7 an overseer **m** God's household,

MANASSEH
   1. Firstborn of Joseph (Ge 41:51; 46:20).
Blessed by Jacob but not as firstborn (Ge 48).
Tribe of blessed (Dt 33:17), numbered (Nu 1:35;
26:34), half allotted land east of Jordan (Nu 32;
Jos 13:8–33), half west (Jos 16; Eze 48:4), failed to
fully possess (Jos 17:12–13; Jdg 1:27), 12,000 from
(Rev 7:6).
   2. Son of Hezekiah; king of Judah (2Ki 21:1–18;
2Ch 33:1–20). Judah exiled for his detestable sins
(2Ki 21:10–15). Repentance (2Ch 33:12–19).

MANDRAKES
Ge   30:14 give me some of your son's **m**."
SS   7:13 The **m** send out their fragrance,

MANGER
Isa   1: 3 the donkey its owner's **m**, but Israel
Lk   2:12 in cloths and lying in a **m**."

MANIFESTATION*
1Co   12: 7 each one the **m** of the Spirit is given

MANKIND MAN
Ge   1:26 said, "Let us make **m** in our image,
         5: 2 named them "M" when they were
Dt   32: 8 he divided all **m**, he set up boundaries
Ps   8: 4 what is **m** that you are mindful of
        33:13 the LORD looks down and sees all **m**;

Ps   66: 5 has done, his awesome deeds for **m**!
    107: 8 love and his wonderful deeds for **m**,
Pr   8:31 whole world and delighting in **m**.
Ecc   1:13 a heavy burden God has laid on **m**!
       7:29 God created **m** upright, but they have
      12:13 for this is the duty of all **m**.
Isa   45:12 made the earth and created **m** on it.
Jer   32:27 "I am the LORD, the God of all **m**.
Zec   2:13 Be still before the LORD, all **m**,
Jn   1: 4 that life was the light of all **m**.
       2:25 did not need any testimony about **m**,
Heb   2: 6 "What is **m** that you are mindful of
1Ti   2: 5 one mediator between God and **m**,
Rev   9:15 were released to kill a third of **m**.

MANNA
Ex   16:31 people of Israel called the bread **m**.
Nu   11: 6 we never see anything but this **m**!"
Dt   8:16 He gave you **m** to eat
Jos   5:12 The **m** stopped the day after they ate
Ps   78:24 he rained down **m** for the people
Jn   6:49 Your ancestors ate the **m**
Heb   9: 4 This ark contained the gold jar of **m**,
Rev   2:17 I will give some of the hidden **m**.

MANNER
1Co   11:27 in an unworthy **m** will be guilty
Php   1:27 conduct yourselves in a **m** worthy
Heb   11:19 a **m** of speaking he did receive Isaac

MANOAH*
Father of Samson (Jdg 13:2–21; 16:31).

MANSIONS*
Ps   49:14 the grave, far from their princely **m**.
Isa   5: 9 the fine **m** left without occupants.
Am   3:15 and the **m** will be demolished,"
       5:11 though you have built stone **m**,

MANY
Ge   17: 4 You will be the father of **m** nations.
      50:20 being done, the saving of **m** lives.
Dt   15: 6 you will lend to **m** nations but will
      15: 6 You will rule over **m** nations
      17:17 He must not take **m** wives, or his
Jdg   16:30 Thus he killed **m** more when he died
1Ki   8: 5 sacrificing so **m** sheep and cattle
      11: 1 loved **m** foreign women besides
Ps   32:10 **M** are the woes of the wicked,
      34:12 life and desires to see **m** good days,
     104:24 How **m** are your works, LORD!
Pr   3: 2 they will prolong your life **m** years
       9:11 wisdom your days will be **m**,
      11:14 victory is won through **m** advisers.
      15:22 but with **m** advisers they succeed.
      31:29 "**M** women do noble things,
Ecc   5: 3 **m** words mark the speech of a fool.
      12:12 Of making **m** books there is no end,
SS   8: 7 **M** waters cannot quench love;
Isa   52:14 as there were **m** who were appalled
      52:15 so he will sprinkle **m** nations,
      53:11 my righteous servant will justify **m**,
      53:12 For he bore the sin of **m**, and made
Jer   11:13 have as **m** gods as you have towns;
Da   9:27 He will confirm a covenant with **m**

Da   12: 3 those who lead **m** to righteousness,
Mt   10:31 are worth more than **m** sparrows.
      18:21 how **m** times shall I forgive my
      22:14 "For **m** are invited, but few are
      24: 5 the Messiah,' and will deceive **m**.
      26:28 poured out for **m** for the forgiveness
Mk   10:31 But **m** who are first will be last,
      10:45 to give his life as a ransom for **m**."
Lk   2:34 the falling and rising of **m** in Israel,
      10:41 worried and upset about **m** things,
Jn   20:30 Jesus performed **m** other signs
      21:25 Jesus did **m** other things as well.
Ac   1: 3 gave **m** convincing proofs that he
       5:12 The apostles performed **m** signs
      14:22 "We must go through **m** hardships
Ro   5:19 one man the **m** were made sinners,
       5:19 man the **m** will be made righteous.
      12: 5 we, though **m**, form one body,
1Co   1:26 Not **m** of you were wise by human
       1:26 not **m** were of noble birth.
      12:12 though one, has **m** parts, but all its **m**
            parts form one body,
Heb   2:10 In bringing **m** sons and daughters
       9:28 once to take away the sins of **m**;
Jas   1: 2 whenever you face trials of **m** kinds,
       3: 1 Not **m** of you should become
1Jn   2:18 even now **m** antichrists have come.
2Jn   1: 7 I say this because **m** deceivers,
Rev   5:11 and heard the voice of **m** angels,
      19:12 fire, and on his head are **m** crowns.

MAON
1Sa   23:24 his men were in the Desert of M,

MARA*
Ru   1:20 "Call me **M**, because the Almighty

MARAH
Ex   15:23 (That is why the place is called M.)

MARANATHA (KJV) Translated "Come, Lord!" in 1Co 16:22.

MARCH MARCHED, MARCHING
Jos   6: 4 day, **m** around the city seven times,
Isa   42:13 The LORD will **m** out like

MARCHED MARCH
Nu   33: 3 They **m** out defiantly in full view

MARCHING MARCH
Ex   14: 8 Israelites, who were **m** out boldly.
Jos   6:13 **m** before the ark of the LORD
2Sa   5:24 As soon as you hear the sound of **m**

MARITAL* MARRY
Ex   21:10 of her food, clothing and **m** rights.
1Co   7: 3 husband should fulfill his **m** duty

MARK MARKED, MARKS
Cousin of Barnabas (Ac 12:12; 15:37–39; Col
4:10; 2Ti 4:11; Phm 24; 1Pe 5:13), see JOHN.
Ge   1:14 serve as signs to **m** sacred times,
       4:15 the LORD put a **m** on Cain so
Eze   9: 6 do not touch anyone who has the **m**.
Rev   13:16 to receive a **m** on their right hands

Rev 14: 9 and receives its **m** on their forehead
16: 2 on the people who had the **m**
19:20 those who had received the **m**
20: 4 and had not received its **m** on their

MARKED MARK
Job 38: 5 Who **m** off its dimensions?
Pr 8:27 when he **m** out the horizon
Ac 17:26 he **m** out their appointed times
Eph 1:13 you were **m** in him with a seal,
Heb 12: 1 with perseverance the race **m**

MARKET MARKETPLACE, MARKETPLACES
Jn 2:16 my Father's house into a **m**!"

MARKETPLACE MARKET
Lk 7:32 are like children sitting in the **m**

MARKETPLACES MARKET
Mt 23: 7 to be greeted with respect in the **m**

MARKS MARK
Lev 19:28 dead or put tattoo **m** on yourselves.
Jn 20:25 "Unless I see the nail **m** in his
Gal 6:17 I bear on my body the **m** of Jesus.

MARRED*
Isa 52:14 and his form **m** beyond human
Jer 18: 4 from the clay was **m** in his hands;

MARRIAGE MARRY
Ge 29:26 daughter in **m** before the older one.
Dt 23: 2 one born of a forbidden **m** nor any
Jdg 3: 6 They took their daughters in **m**
Ezr 9:12 do not give your daughters in **m**
Ne 13:25 to give your daughters in **m** to their
13:25 to take their daughters in **m** for your
Mt 22:30 neither marry nor be given in **m**;
24:38 marrying and giving in **m**,
Heb 13: 4 **M** should be honored by all, and
the **m** bed kept pure,

MARRIAGES* MARRY
Ne 13:26 Was it not because of **m** like these

MARRIED MARRY
Ge 4:19 Lamech **m** two women, one named
Dt 24: 5 If a man has recently **m**, he must not
Ezr 10:10 you have **m** foreign women,
Pr 30:23 a contemptible woman who gets **m**,
Isa 62: 4 in you, and your land will be **m**.
Mt 1:18 was pledged to be **m** to Joseph,
Mk 12:23 be, since the seven were **m** to her?"
Lk 1:27 to be **m** to a man named Joseph,
Ro 7: 2 by law a **m** woman is bound to her
1Co 7:10 the **m** I give this command (not I,
7:33 But a **m** man is concerned
7:36 is not sinning. They should get **m**.

MARRIES MARRY
Dt 24: 1 If a man **m** a woman who becomes
Jer 3: 1 she leaves him and **m** another man,
Mt 5:32 anyone who **m** a divorced woman
19: 9 and **m** another woman commits
Mk 10:11 **m** another woman commits adultery

Lk 16:18 wife and **m** another woman commits
16:18 the man who **m** a divorced woman
Ro 7: 3 an adulteress if she **m** another man.
1Co 7:28 and if a virgin **m**, she has not

MARROW
Heb 4:12 soul and spirit, joints and **m**;

MARRY INTERMARRY, MARITAL, MARRIAGE, MARRIAGES, MARRIED, MARRIES, MARRYING
Dt 25: 5 his widow must not **m** outside
Jdg 11:37 friends, because I will never **m**."
Hos 1: 2 **m** a promiscuous woman and have
Mt 19:10 and wife, it is better not to **m**."
22:30 people will neither **m** nor be given
Mk 12:19 the man must **m** the widow
1Co 7: 9 they should **m**, for it is better to **m**
7:28 But if you do **m**, you have not
1Ti 4: 3 They forbid people to **m** and order
5:14 So I counsel younger widows to **m**,

MARRYING* MARRY
Ezr 10: 2 our God by **m** foreign women
Ne 13:27 to our God by **m** foreign women?"
Mal 2:11 by **m** women who worship a foreign
Mt 24:38 drinking, **m** and giving in marriage,
Lk 17:27 **m** and being given in marriage

MARS' (KJV) See AREOPAGUS

MARTHA*
Sister of Mary and Lazarus (Lk 10:38–42; Jn 11; 12:2).

MARTYR*
Ac 22:20 blood of your **m** Stephen was shed,

MARVELED* MARVELOUS
Lk 2:33 mother **m** at what was said
2Th 1:10 to be **m** at among all those who have

MARVELING* MARVELOUS
Lk 9:43 While everyone was **m** at all

MARVELOUS* MARVELED, MARVELING
1Ch 16:24 his **m** deeds among all peoples.
Job 37: 5 God's voice thunders in **m** ways;
Ps 71:17 to this day I declare your **m** deeds.
72:18 of Israel, who alone does **m** deeds.
86:10 For you are great and do **m** deeds;
96: 3 his **m** deeds among all peoples.
98: 1 new song, for he has done **m** things;
118:23 done this, and it is **m** in our eyes.
Zec 8: 6 "It may seem **m** to the remnant
8: 6 time, but will it seem **m** to me?"
Mt 21:42 done this, and it is **m** in our eyes'?
Mk 12:11 done this, and it is **m** in our eyes'?"
Rev 15: 1 in heaven another great and **m** sign:
15: 3 "Great and **m** are your deeds,

MARY
1. Mother of Jesus (Mt 1:16–25; Lk 1:27–56; 2:1–40). With Jesus at temple (Lk 2:41–52), at the wedding in Cana (Jn 2:1–5), questioning his san-

ity (Mk 3:21), at the cross (Jn 19:25–27). Among disciples after Ascension (Ac 1:14).

2. Magdalene; former demoniac (Lk 8:2). Helped support Jesus' ministry (Lk 8:1–3). At the cross (Mt 27:56; Mk 15:40; Jn 19:25), burial (Mt 27:61; Mk 15:47). Saw angel after resurrection (Mt 28:1–10; Mk 16:1–9; Lk 24:1–12); also Jesus (Jn 20:1–18).

3. Sister of Martha and Lazarus (Jn 11). Washed Jesus' feet (Jn 12:1–8).

4. Mother of James and Joses; witnessed crucifixion (Mt 27:56; Mk 15:40) and empty tomb (Mk 16:1; Lk 24:10).

MASONS
1Ch	22:15	stonecutters, **m** and carpenters,
2Ch	24:12	They hired **m** and carpenters
Ezr	3: 7	Then they gave money to the **m**

MASQUERADE* MASQUERADES, MASQUERADING
2Co 11:15 also **m** as servants of righteousness.

MASQUERADES* MASQUERADE
2Co 11:14 for Satan himself **m** as an angel

MASQUERADING* MASQUERADE
2Co 11:13 workers, **m** as apostles of Christ.

MASSAH
Ex	17: 7	he called the place **M** and Meribah
Dt	33: 8	You tested him at **M**;
Ps	95: 8	did that day at **M** in the wilderness,

MASTER MASTER'S, MASTERED, MASTERS, MASTERY
Ge	24:12	show kindness to my **m** Abraham.
Ex	21: 5	'I love my **m** and my wife
Pr	25:13	he refreshes the spirit of his **m**.
Isa	1: 3	The ox knows its **m**, the donkey its
Hos	2:16	you will no longer call me 'my **m**.'
Mal	1: 6	If I am a **m**, where is the respect due
Mt	10:24	teacher, nor a servant above his **m**.
	24:46	servant whose **m** finds him doing so
	25:21	"His **m** replied, 'Well done,
	25:23	"His **m** replied, 'Well done,
Jn	13:16	no servant is greater than his **m**,
	15:20	'A servant is not greater than his **m**.'
Ro	6:14	For sin shall no longer be your **m**,
	14: 4	To their own **m**, servants stand
Eph	6: 9	know that he who is both their **M**
Col	4: 1	that you also have a **M** in heaven.
2Ti	2:21	useful to the **M** and prepared to do

MASTER'S MASTER
Mt	25:21	Come and share your **m** happiness!'
Lk	12:47	"The servant who knows the **m** will

MASTERED* MASTER
1Co	6:12	but I will not be **m** by anything.
2Pe	2:19	are slaves to whatever has **m** them."

MASTERS MASTER
Ex 1:11 So they put slave **m** over them

Mt	6:24	"No one can serve two **m**.
Lk	16:13	"No one can serve two **m**.
Eph	6: 5	obey your earthly **m** with respect
	6: 9	And **m**, treat your slaves in the same
Col	3:22	obey your earthly **m** in everything;
	4: 1	**M**, provide your slaves with what is
1Ti	6: 1	should consider their **m** worthy
	6: 2	who have believing **m** should not
Titus	2: 9	be subject to their **m** in everything,
1Pe	2:18	God submit yourselves to your **m**,

MASTERY* MASTER
Ro 6: 9 death no longer has **m** over him.

MAT MATS
Mk	2: 9	'Get up, take your **m** and walk'?
Jn	5: 8	Pick up your **m** and walk."
Ac	9:34	Get up and roll up your **m**."

MATCHED*
2Co 8:11 do it may be **m** by your completion

MATERIAL
Ro	15:27	share with them their **m** blessings.
1Co	9:11	if we reap a **m** harvest from you?
1Jn	3:17	If anyone has **m** possessions

MATS* MAT
Mk	6:55	carried the sick on **m** to wherever
Ac	5:15	**m** so that at least Peter's shadow

MATTANIAH ZEDEKIAH
Original name of King Zedekiah (2Ki 24:17).

MATTER MATTERS
Dt	19:15	A **m** must be established
Ecc	12:13	here is the conclusion of the **m**:
Mt	18:16	so that 'every **m** may be established
2Co	13: 1	"Every **m** must be established

MATTERS MATTER
Mt 23:23 neglected the more important **m**

MATTHEW
Apostle; former tax collector (Mt 9:9–13; 10:3; Mk 3:18; Lk 6:15; Ac 1:13). Also called Levi (Mk 2:14–17; Lk 5:27–32).

MATTHIAS*
Disciple chosen to replace Judas (Ac 1:23–26).

MATURE* MATURITY, PREMATURELY
Lk	8:14	and pleasures, and they do not **m**.
1Co	2: 6	a message of wisdom among the **m**,
Eph	4:13	of the Son of God and become **m**,
	4:15	in every respect the **m** body of him
Php	3:15	who are **m** should take such a view
Col	1:28	we may present everyone fully **m**
	4:12	will of God, **m** and fully assured.
Heb	5:14	But solid food is for the **m**,
Jas	1: 4	finish its work so that you may be **m**

MATURITY* MATURE
Heb 6: 1 Christ and be taken forward to **m**,

MEAL

Lk 11:38 did not first wash before the **m**.
1Co 10:27 If an unbeliever invites you to a **m**
Heb 12:16 a single **m** sold his inheritance rights

MEAN MEANING, MEANINGLESS, MEANS

Ex 12:26 you, 'What does this ceremony **m**
Jos 4: 6 ask you, 'What do these stones **m**?'
Da 5:26 "Here is what these words **m**:
Mt 12: 7 you had known what these words **m**,

MEANING MEAN

Ne 8: 8 and giving the **m** so that the people
Ecc 6:11 the less the **m**, and how does

MEANINGLESS MEAN

Ecc 1: 2 "**M**! **M**!" says the Teacher. "Utterly **m**!
Everything is **m**."
2:11 everything was **m**, a chasing
12: 8 "**M**! **M**!" says the Teacher.
"Everything is **m**!"
1Ti 1: 6 these and have turned to **m** talk.

MEANS MEAN

Ge 40:12 "This is what it **m**," Joseph said
Da 2:25 tell the king what his dream **m**."
4:18 tell me what it **m**, for none
5:17 for the king and tell him what it **m**.
Mt 13:18 to what the parable of the sower **m**:
1Co 9:22 by all possible **m** I might save some.
Heb 9:12 He did not enter by **m** of the blood
2Pe 3:15 our Lord's patience **m** salvation,

MEASURE IMMEASURABLY, MEASURED, MEASURES

Ge 15:16 has not yet reached its full **m**."
Jer 10:24 me, LORD, but only in due **m**—
30:11 discipline you but only in due **m**;
46:28 discipline you but only in due **m**;
Eze 45: 3 **m** off a section 25,000 cubits long
Zec 2: 2 "To **m** Jerusalem, to find out how
Mk 4:24 "With the **m** you use, it will be
Lk 6:38 For with the **m** you use, it will be
Eph 3:19 be filled to the **m** of all the fullness
4:13 to the whole **m** of the fullness
2Pe 1: 8 these qualities in increasing **m**,
Rev 11: 1 "Go and **m** the temple of God

MEASURED MEASURE

Isa 40:12 Who has **m** the waters in the hollow
Jer 31:37 if the heavens above can be **m**
Mk 4:24 you use, it will be **m** to you—

MEASURES MEASURE

Dt 25:14 Do not have two differing **m** in your
Pr 20:10 Differing weights and differing **m**—

MEAT

Ge 9: 4 "But you must not eat **m** that has its
Ex 16:12 'At twilight you will eat **m**,
Nu 11:13 wailing to me, 'Give us **m** to eat!'
Pr 23:20 wine or gorge themselves on **m**,
Ac 15:20 from the **m** of strangled animals
Ro 14: 6 Whoever eats **m** does so to the Lord,

Ro 14:21 It is better not to eat **m** or drink
1Co 8:13 I will never eat **m** again, so that I
10:25 sold in the **m** market without raising

MEDAD

Nu 11:27 **M** are prophesying in the camp."

MEDDLER*

1Pe 4:15 kind of criminal, or even as a **m**.

MEDE MEDIA

Da 5:31 and Darius the **M** took over

MEDES MEDIA

Da 5:28 and given to the **M** and Persians."
6: 8 in accordance with the law of the **M**
Ac 2: 9 Parthians, **M** and Elamites;

MEDIA MEDE, MEDES

Ezr 6: 2 of Ecbatana in the province of **M**,
Da 8:20 you saw represents the kings of **M**

MEDIATE* MEDIATOR

1Sa 2:25 God may **m** for the offender;
Job 9:33 there were someone to **m** between us,

MEDIATOR* MEDIATE

Gal 3:19 through angels and entrusted to a **m**.
3:20 A **m**, however, implies more than one
1Ti 2: 5 is one God and one **m** between God
Heb 8: 6 which he is **m** is superior to the old
9:15 this reason Christ is the **m** of a new
12:24 to Jesus the **m** of a new covenant,

MEDICINE*

Pr 17:22 A cheerful heart is good **m**,

MEDITATE* MEDITATED, MEDITATES, MEDITATION

Ge 24:63 out to the field one evening to **m**,
Jos 1: 8 **m** on it day and night, so that you
Ps 48: 9 God, we **m** on your unfailing love.
77:12 and **m** on all your mighty deeds."
119:15 I **m** on your precepts and consider
119:23 your servant will **m** on your decrees.
119:27 I may **m** on your wonderful deeds.
119:48 love, that I may **m** on your decrees.
119:78 but I will **m** on your precepts.
119:97 I **m** on it all day long.
119:99 teachers, for I **m** on your statutes.
119:148 that I may **m** on your promises.
143: 5 I **m** on all your works and consider
145: 5 I will **m** on your wonderful works.

MEDITATED* MEDITATE

Ps 39: 3 While I **m**, the fire burned;
77: 3 I **m**, and my spirit grew faint.
77: 6 My heart **m** and my spirit asked:

MEDITATES* MEDITATE

Ps 1: 2 and who **m** on his law day

MEDITATION* MEDITATE

Ps 19:14 this **m** of my heart be pleasing
49: 3 the **m** of my heart will give you
104:34 May my **m** be pleasing to him, as I

MEDITERRANEAN
Ex   23:31 from the Red Sea to the M Sea,

MEDIUM* MEDIUMS
Lev 20:27 or woman who is a m or spiritist
Dt   18:11 or who is a m or spiritist or who
1Sa 28: 7 "Find me a woman who is a m, so I
1Ch 10:13 even consulted a m for guidance,

MEDIUMS MEDIUM
Lev 19:31 " 'Do not turn to m or seek
2Ki 21: 6 and consulted m and spiritists.
     23:24 Josiah got rid of the m and spiritists,
Isa   8:19 someone tells you to consult m

MEEK*
Ps   37:11 But the m will inherit the land
Zep   3:12 I will leave within you the m
Mt   5: 5 Blessed are the m, for they will

MEET MEETING, MEETINGS, MEETS, MET
Ex   19:17 out of the camp to m with God,
     30:36 meeting, where I will m with you.
Ps   42: 2 When can I go and m with God?
     79: 8 your mercy come quickly to m us,
     85:10 Love and faithfulness m together;
Pr   7:10 Then out came a woman to m him,
Am   4:12 Israel, prepare to m your God."
Ac   2:46 day they continued to m together
      5:12 all the believers used to m together
1Co 11:34 you m together it may not result
1Th   4:17 the clouds to m the Lord in the air.

MEETING MEET
Ex   27:21 In the tent of m, outside the curtain
     29:44 "So I will consecrate the tent of m
     33: 7 away, calling it the "tent of m."
     40:34 the cloud covered the tent of m,
Jos 18: 1 and set up the tent of m there.
Heb 10:25 not giving up m together, as some

TENT OF MEETING See TENT

MEETINGS* MEET
1Co 11:17 for your m do more harm than good.

MEETS MEET
Ro   16: 5 the church that m at their house.
1Co 16:19 so does the church that m at their
Phm   1: 2 to the church that m in your home:
Heb   7:26 a high priest truly m our need—

MEGIDDO
Jos 12:21 of Taanach one the king of M one
Jdg   1:27 Ibleam or M and their surrounding

MELCHIZEDEK
Ge   14:18 M king of Salem brought out bread
Ps 110: 4 a priest forever, in the order of M."
Heb   5:10 to be high priest in the order of M.
      6:20 priest forever, in the order of M.
      7: 1 This M was king of Salem
      7:11 one in the order of M,

MELONS*
Nu   11: 5 also the cucumbers, m, leeks,

MELT MELTED, MELTS
Ex   15:15 the people of Canaan will m away;
Dt   1:28 brothers have made our hearts m
Jos 14: 8 the hearts of the people m in fear.
Mic   1: 4 The mountains m beneath him
Na   1: 5 before him and the hills m away.
2Pe   3:12 and the elements will m in the heat.

MELTED MELT
Jos   2:11 our hearts m in fear and everyone's

MELTS MELT
Ps 147:18 He sends his word and m them;
Am   9: 5 he touches the earth and it m,

MEMBER MEMBERS
Mk   15:43 a prominent m of the Council,
Jn   3: 1 named Nicodemus who was a m
Ac   17:34 Dionysius, a m of the Areopagus,
Ro   12: 5 and each m belongs to all the others.

MEMBERS MEMBER
Mic   7: 6 a man's enemies are the m of his
Mt   10:36 a man's enemies will be the m of his
Ro   12: 4 of us has one body with many m,
1Co   6:15 your bodies are m of Christ himself?
Eph   2:19 people and also m of his household,
      3: 6 with Israel, m together of one body,
      4:25 for we are all m of one body.
      5:30 for we are m of his body.
Col   3:15 since as m of one body you were

MEMORABLE* MEMORY
Eze 39:13 I display my glory will be a m day

MEMORIAL MEMORY
Ex   28:12 the ephod as m stones for the sons
Lev   2: 2 burn this as a m portion on the altar,
Jos   4: 7 stones are to be a m to the people

MEMORIES* MEMORY
1Th   3: 6 you always have pleasant m of us

MEMORY MEMORABLE, MEMORIAL, MEMORIES
Mt   26:13 done will also be told, in m of her."

MEN MAN
Ge   6: 4 the heroes of old, m of renown.
     18: 2 up and saw three m standing nearby.
Nu   1:44 These were the m counted by Moses
     13: 2 "Send some m to explore the land
     16:29 If these m die a natural death
     26:51 of the m of Israel was 601,730.
Dt   16:16 year all your m must appear before
Jdg 15:15 it and struck down a thousand m.
2Sa 18: 8 up more m that day than the sword.
     23: 8 his spear against eight hundred m,
     24: 2 Beersheba and enroll the fighting m,
1Ki 12:10 The young m who had grown
2Ki   4:43 can I set this before a hundred m?"
1Ch 17:17 I were the most exalted of m.
Pr   11:16 but ruthless m gain only wealth.
Da   1:17 To these four young m God gave
      3:25 I see four m walking around
Mk   6:44 of the m who had eaten was five

Lk 9:30 Two **m**, Moses and Elijah,
Ac 4: 4 the number of **m** who believed grew
    4:13 ordinary **m**, they were astonished
Ro 1:27 **m** also abandoned natural relations
    1:27 **M** committed shameful acts with
        other **m**,
1Co 6: 9 nor **m** who have sex with **m**
    13: 1 in the tongues of **m** or of angels,
    16:18 Such **m** deserve recognition.
Gal 1: 1 Paul, an apostle—sent not from **m**
1Ti 2: 8 Therefore I want the **m** everywhere
Titus 2: 2 Teach the older **m** to be temperate,
    2: 6 encourage the young **m** to be
Heb 7:28 the law appoints as high priests **m**

MEN OF ISRAEL See ISRAEL

MEN OF JUDAH See JUDAH

MEN'S MAN
Dt 22: 5 A woman must not wear **m** clothing,

MENAHEM*
King of Israel (2Ki 15:14–23).

MEND*
Ps 60: 2 **m** its fractures, for it is quaking.
Ecc 3: 7 a time to tear and a time to **m**,

MENE*
Da 5:25 the inscription that was written: M, M,
    5:26 is what these words mean: *M*:

MENTION
Eph 5:12 even to **m** what the disobedient do

MEPHIBOSHETH
Son of Jonathan shown kindness by David (2Sa 4:4; 9; 21:7). Accused of siding with Absalom (2Sa 16:1–4; 19:24–30).

MERAB*
Daughter of Saul (1Sa 14:49; 18:17–19; 2Sa 21:8).

MERARI MERARITE, MERARITES
Ge 46:11 Gershon, Kohath and **M**.
Jos 21: 7 The descendants of **M**,
1Ch 6:19 The sons of **M**: Mahli and Mushi.
2Ch 34:12 Levites descended from **M**,

MERARITE MERARI
Nu 3:20 The **M** clans: Mahli and Mushi.
    4:45 the total of those in the **M** clans.

MERARITES MERARI
Nu 3:36 The **M** were appointed to take care

MERCHANDISE
Ne 10:31 the neighboring peoples bring **m**
Mk 11:16 carry **m** through the temple courts.

MERCHANT MERCHANTS
Pr 31:14 She is like the **m** ships, bringing her
Hos 12: 7 The **m** uses dishonest scales and
Mt 13:45 heaven is like a **m** looking for fine

MERCHANTS MERCHANT
Ge 37:28 So when the Midianite **m** came by,

Ps 107:23 they were **m** on the mighty waters.
Na 3:16 your **m** till they are more numerous
Rev 18:11 "The **m** of the earth will weep

MERCIFUL* MERCY
Ge 19:16 city, for the LORD was **m** to them.
Dt 4:31 the LORD your God is a **m** God;
1Ki 20:31 heard that the kings of Israel are **m**.
Ne 9:31 for you are a gracious and **m** God.
Ps 26:11 deliver me and be **m** to me.
    27: 7 be **m** to me and answer me.
    30:10 Hear, LORD, and be **m** to me;
    31: 9 Be **m** to me, LORD, for I am
    56: 1 Be **m** to me, my God, for my
    77: 9 Has God forgotten to be **m**?
    78:38 Yet he was **m**; he forgave their
Da 9: 9 The Lord our God is **m**
Mt 5: 7 Blessed are the **m**, for they will be
Lk 1:54 servant Israel, remembering to be **m**
    6:36 Be **m**, just as your Father is **m**.
Heb 2:17 in order that he might become a **m**
Jas 2:13 to anyone who has not been **m**.
Jude 1:22 Be **m** to those who doubt;

MERCY* MERCIFUL
Ge 43:14 Almighty grant you **m** before
Ex 33:19 I will have **m** on whom I will have **m**,
Dt 7: 2 with them, and show them no **m**.
    13:17 will show you **m**, and will have
Jos 11:20 exterminating them without **m**,
2Sa 24:14 of the LORD, for his **m** is great;
1Ki 8:28 servant's prayer and his plea for **m**,
    8:50 cause their captors to show them **m**;
1Ch 21:13 the LORD, for his **m** is very great;
2Ch 6:19 servant's prayer and his plea for **m**.
Ne 9:31 your great **m** you did not put an end
    13:22 and show **m** to me according to your
Est 4: 8 the king's presence to beg for **m**
Job 9:15 only plead with my Judge for **m**.
    27:22 against him without **m** as he flees
    41: 3 Will it keep begging you for **m**?
Ps 4: 1 have **m** on me and hear my prayer.
    6: 2 Have **m** on me, LORD, for I am
    6: 9 LORD has heard my cry for **m**;
    9:13 Have **m** and lift me
    25: 6 LORD, your great **m** and love,
    28: 2 Hear my cry for **m** as I call to you
    28: 6 for he has heard my cry for **m**.
    30: 8 to the Lord I cried for **m**:
    31:22 Yet you heard my cry for **m** when I
    40:11 Do not withhold your **m** from me,
    41: 4 I said, "Have **m** on me, LORD;
    41:10 But may you have **m** on me,
    51: 1 Have **m** on me, O God,
    57: 1 Have **m** on me, my God, have **m**
    59: 5 show no **m** to wicked traitors.
    69:16 in your great **m** turn to me.
    79: 8 may your **m** come quickly to meet
    86: 3 have **m** on me, Lord, for I call
    86: 6 listen to my cry for **m**.
    86:16 Turn to me and have **m** on me;
    106:46 held them captive to show them **m**.
    116: 1 he heard my cry for **m**.
    119:132 Turn to me and have **m** on me,

Ps 123: 2 our God, till he shows us his **m**.
123: 3 Have **m** on us, LORD, have **m**
130: 2 ears be attentive to my cry for **m**.
140: 6 Hear, LORD, my cry for **m**.
142: 1 up my voice to the LORD for **m**.
143: 1 my prayer, listen to my cry for **m**;
Pr 6:34 he will show no **m** when he takes
18:23 The poor plead for **m**, but the rich
21:10 their neighbors get no **m** from them.
28:13 and renounces them finds **m**.
Isa 13:18 they will have no **m** on infants,
47: 6 hand, and you showed them no **m**.
55: 7 and he will have **m** on them,
63: 9 his love and **m** he redeemed them;
Jer 6:23 they are cruel and show no **m**.
13:14 I will allow no pity or **m**
21: 7 he will show them no **m** or pity
50:42 they are cruel and without **m**.
Da 2:18 them to plead for **m** from the God
9:18 but because of your great **m**.
Hos 6: 6 For I desire **m**, not sacrifice,
Am 5:15 LORD God Almighty will have **m**
Mic 6: 8 to love **m** and to walk humbly
7:18 angry forever but delight to show **m**.
Hab 1:17 net, destroying nations without **m**?
3: 2 in wrath remember **m**.
Zec 1:12 how long will you withhold **m**
1:16 'I will return to Jerusalem with **m**,
7: 9 show **m** and compassion to one
Mt 5: 7 merciful, for they will be shown **m**.
9:13 'I desire **m**, not sacrifice.'
9:27 calling out, "Have **m** on us,
12: 7 mean, 'I desire **m**, not sacrifice,'
15:22 Son of David, have **m** on me!
17:15 "Lord, have **m** on my son," he said.
18:33 Shouldn't you have had **m** on your
20:30 Son of David, have **m** on us!"
20:31 Son of David, have **m** on us!"
23:23 justice, **m** and faithfulness.
Mk 5:19 and how he has had **m** on you."
10:47 Son of David, have **m** on me!"
10:48 "Son of David, have **m** on me!"
Lk 1:50 His **m** extends to those who fear
1:58 the Lord had shown her great **m**,
1:72 to show **m** to our ancestors
1:78 because of the tender **m** of our God,
10:37 "The one who had **m** on him."
18:13 said, 'God, have **m** on me, a sinner.'
18:38 Son of David, have **m** on me!"
18:39 "Son of David, have **m** on me!"
Ro 1:31 no fidelity, no love, no **m**.
9:15 "I will have **m** on whom I have **m**,
9:16 desire or effort, but on God's **m**.
9:18 Therefore God has **m** on whom he
wants to have **m**,
9:23 glory known to the objects of his **m**,
11:30 have now received **m** as a result
11:31 may now receive **m** as a result of
God's **m** to you.
11:32 so that he may have **m** on them all.
12: 1 in view of God's **m**, to offer your
12: 8 if it is to show **m**, do it cheerfully.
15: 9 might glorify God for his **m**. As it is

1Co 7:25 who by the Lord's **m** is trustworthy.
2Co 4: 1 since through God's **m** we have this
Gal 6:16 and **m** to all who follow this rule—
Eph 2: 4 love for us, God, who is rich in **m**,
Php 2:27 But God had **m** on him, and not
1Ti 1: 2 **m** and peace from God the Father
1:13 I was shown **m** because I acted
1:16 very reason I was shown **m** so
2Ti 1: 2 **m** and peace from God the Father
1:16 May the Lord show **m**
1:18 that he will find **m** from the Lord
Titus 3: 5 we had done, but because of his **m**.
Heb 4:16 so that we may receive **m** and find
10:28 law of Moses died without **m**
Jas 2:13 because judgment without **m** will be
2:13 **M** triumphs over judgment.
3:17 submissive, full of **m** and good fruit,
5:11 Lord is full of compassion and **m**.
1Pe 1: 3 In his great **m** he has given us new
2:10 once you had not received **m**, but
now you have received **m**.
2Jn 1: 3 **m** and peace from God the Father
Jude 1: 2 **M**, peace and love be yours
1:21 for the **m** of our Lord Jesus Christ
1:23 to others show **m**, mixed with fear—

MERCY SEAT, MERCYSEAT (KJV)
See ATONEMENT COVER

MERELY
Ro 2:28 nor is circumcision **m** outward
Jas 1:22 Do not **m** listen to the word, and so

MERIBAH   MERIBAH KADESH
Ex 17: 7 **M** because the Israelites quarreled
Nu 20:13 These were the waters of **M**,
Dt 33: 8 with him at the waters of **M**.
Ps 95: 8 harden your hearts as you did at **M**,
106:32 of **M** they angered the LORD,

MERIBAH KADESH   KADESH, MERIBAH
Nu 27:14 (These were the waters of **M**,

MERRY
Ecc 10:19 wine makes life **m**, and money is
Lk 12:19 eat, drink and be **m**." '

MESHACH*   MISHAEL
Hebrew exiled to Babylon; name changed from Mishael (Da 1:6–7). Refused defilement by food (Da 1:8–20). Refused to worship idol (Da 3:1–18); saved from furnace (Da 3:19–30).

MESHEK
Ge 10: 2 Madai, Javan, Tubal, **M** and Tiras.
10:23 Uz, Hul, Gether and **M**.
Ps 120: 5 Woe to me that I dwell in **M**, that I
Eze 38: 3 Gog, chief prince of **M** and Tubal.
39: 1 Gog, chief prince of **M** and Tubal.

MESOPOTAMIA*
Ac 2: 9 residents of **M**,
7: 2 Abraham while he was still in **M**,

MESSAGE MESSENGER, MESSENGERS

Nu 23: 7 Then Balaam spoke his **m**:
Dt 18:22 is a **m** the LORD has not spoken.
2Ch 25:18 in Lebanon sent a **m** to a cedar
Ps 36: 1 I have a **m** from God in my heart
Isa 9: 8 Lord has sent a **m** against Jacob;
28: 9 To whom is he explaining his **m**?
53: 1 Who has believed our **m**
Jer 23:21 yet they have run with their **m**;
23:33 'What is the **m** from the LORD?'
49:14 I have heard a **m** from the LORD;
Da 10: 1 Its **m** was true and it concerned
Mt 10: 7 As you go, proclaim this **m**:
Jn 12:38 who has believed our **m**
17:20 will believe in me through their **m**,
Ac 2:41 who accepted his **m** were baptized,
4: 4 many who heard the **m** believed;
10:36 You know the **m** God sent
15:31 were glad for its encouraging **m**.
17:11 for they received the **m** with great
Ro 10:16 "Lord, who has believed our **m**?"
10:17 faith comes from hearing the **m**,
1Co 1:18 For the **m** of the cross is foolishness
2: 4 My **m** and my preaching were not
12: 8 through the Spirit a **m** of wisdom, to
another a **m** of knowledge
2Co 5:19 to us the **m** of reconciliation.
Col 3:16 Let the **m** of Christ dwell among
2Th 3: 1 that the **m** of the Lord may spread
Titus 1: 9 to the trustworthy **m** as it has been
Heb 4: 2 the **m** they heard was of no value
1Pe 2: 8 because they disobey the **m**—
2Pe 1:19 have the prophetic **m** as something
1Jn 1: 5 This is the **m** we have heard
3:11 For this is the **m** you heard

MESSENGER MESSAGE

Isa 41:27 to Jerusalem a **m** of good news.
42:19 servant, and deaf like the **m** I send?
Da 4:13 a **m**, coming down from heaven.
Hag 1:13 the LORD's **m**, gave this message
Mal 2: 7 because he is the **m** of the LORD
3: 1 the **m** of the covenant, whom you
Mt 11:10 " 'I will send my **m** ahead of you,
Jn 13:16 nor is a **m** greater than the one who
2Co 12: 7 a thorn in my flesh, a **m** of Satan,

MESSENGERS MESSAGE

2Sa 15:10 sent secret **m** throughout the tribes
2Ch 36:15 word to them through his **m** again
Ps 104: 4 He makes winds his **m**,
Isa 44:26 and fulfills the predictions of his **m**,

MESSIAH CHRIST, MESSIAHS

Mt 1: 1 genealogy of Jesus the **M** the son
1:16 mother of Jesus who is called the **M**.
16:16 "You are the **M**, the Son
22:42 "What do you think about the **M**?
23:10 for you have one Instructor, the **M**.
24: 5 'I am the **M**,' and will deceive
Mk 1: 1 of the good news about Jesus the **M**,
8:29 Peter answered, "You are the **M**."
14:61 him, "Are you the **M**, the Son

Lk 2:11 born to you; he is the **M**, the Lord.
9:20 Peter answered, "God's **M**."
23:39 insults at him: "Aren't you the **M**?
Jn 1:20 confessed freely, "I am not the **M**."
1:41 "We have found the **M**" (that is,
4:25 that **M**" (called Christ) "is coming.
7:41 Others said, "He is the **M**."
20:31 you may believe that Jesus is the **M**,
Ac 2:36 you crucified, both Lord and **M**."
5:42 the good news that Jesus is the **M**.
8: 5 and proclaimed the **M** there.
9:22 by proving that Jesus is the **M**.
17: 3 and proving that the **M** had to suffer
18:28 the Scriptures that Jesus was the **M**.
26:23 that the **M** would suffer and,
Ro 9: 5 traced the human ancestry of the **M**,
Rev 11:15 kingdom of our Lord and of his **M**,

MESSIAHS* MESSIAH

Mt 24:24 For false **m** and false prophets will
Mk 13:22 For false **m** and false prophets will

MET MEET

Ge 32: 1 way, and the angels of God **m** him.
Ex 3:18 God of the Hebrews, has **m** with us.
5: 3 God of the Hebrews has **m** with us.
Mt 28: 9 Suddenly Jesus **m** them.
Jn 18: 2 because Jesus had often **m** there

METAL METALWORKER

Lev 19: 4 or make **m** gods for yourselves.
1Ki 14: 9 other gods, idols made of **m**;
2Ch 4: 2 He made the Sea of cast **m**,
Ps 106:19 and worshiped an idol cast from **m**.
Isa 48: 5 image and **m** god ordained them.'
Eze 1:27 waist up he looked like glowing **m**,
8: 2 was as bright as glowing **m**.

METALWORKER METAL, WORK

Isa 40:19 As for an idol, a **m** casts it,
Hos 8: 6 This calf—a **m** has made it; it is not
2Ti 4:14 Alexander the **m** did me a great deal

METHUSELAH

Ge 5:27 **M** lived a total of 969 years,

MICAH

1. Idolater from Ephraim (Jdg 17–18).
2. Prophet from Moresheth (Jer 26:18–19; Mic 1:1).

MICAIAH

Prophet of the LORD who spoke against Ahab (1Ki 22:1–28; 2Ch 18:1–27).

MICHAEL

Archangel (Jude 9); warrior in angelic realm, protector of Israel (Da 10:13, 21; 12:1; Rev 12:7).

MICHAL*

Daughter of Saul, wife of David (1Sa 14:49; 18:20–28). Warned David of Saul's plot (1Sa 19). Saul gave her to Paltiel (1Sa 25:44); David retrieved her (2Sa 3:13–16). Criticized David for dancing before the ark (2Sa 6:16–23; 1Ch 15:29).

MIDAIR* AIR

2Sa 18: 9 He was left hanging in **m**,
Rev   8:13 eagle that was flying in **m** call
      14: 6 I saw another angel flying in **m**,
      19:17 voice to all the birds flying in **m**,

MIDDAY DAY

Dt   28:29 At **m** you will grope about like
Isa 59:10 At **m** we stumble as if it were

MIDDLE MIDST

Ge   2: 9 In the **m** of the garden were the tree
Jos   3:17 stopped in the **m** of the Jordan
      4: 3 stones from the **m** of the Jordan,
     10:13 The sun stopped in the **m** of the sky
Jdg 16: 3 Samson lay there only until the **m**
Ru   3: 8 In the **m** of the night something
Da   9:27 the **m** of the 'seven' he will put
Jn   19:18 one on each side and Jesus in the **m**.

MIDIAN MIDIANITE, MIDIANITES

Ex   2:15 from Pharaoh and went to live in **M**,
     18: 1 the priest of **M** and father-in-law
Jdg   7: 2 I cannot deliver **M** into their hands,
Ps   83: 9 Do to them as you did to **M**, as you

MIDIANITE MIDIAN

Ge   37:28 So when the **M** merchants came by,
Nu   25: 6 the camp a **M** woman right before

MIDIANITES MIDIAN

Ge   37:36 the **M** sold Joseph in Egypt
Nu   31: 2 on the **M** for the Israelites.
Jdg   6.16 and you will strike down all the **M**,

MIDNIGHT NIGHT

Ex   11: 4 **m** I will go throughout Egypt.
     12:29 **m** the LORD struck down all
Ps 119:62 At **m** I rise to give you thanks
Ac   16:25 About **m** Paul and Silas were

MIDST MIDDLE

Ps 135: 9 his signs and wonders into your **m**,
    136:14 brought Israel through the **m** of it,

MIDWIVES

Ex   1:17 The **m**, however, feared God

MIGHT ALMIGHTY, MIGHTIER, MIGHTY

Ex   9:16 that I **m** show you my power
     33: 3 and I **m** destroy you on the way."
Dt   5:29 so that it **m** go well with them
Jos   4:24 you **m** always fear the LORD your
Jdg 16:30 Then he pushed with all his **m**,
2Sa   6: 5 with all their **m** before the LORD,
      6:14 before the LORD with all his **m**,
2Ch   6:41 place, you and the ark of your **m**.
     20: 6 Power and **m** are in your hand,
Ps   21:13 we will sing and praise your **m**.
     54: 1 vindicate me by your **m**.
     59:11 In your **m** uproot them and bring
     80: 2 Awaken your **m**; come and save us.
    119:11 heart that I **m** not sin against you.
    119:71 so that I **m** learn your decrees.
    119:101 path so that I **m** obey your word.

Ecc   9:10 do, do it with all your **m**,
Isa 11: 2 the Spirit of counsel and of **m**,
     63:15 Where are your zeal and your **m**?
Jer 16:21 I will teach them my power and **m**.
Mic   3: 8 and with justice and **m**, to declare
Zec   4: 6 'Not by **m** nor by power, but by my
Mt   13:15 Otherwise they **m** see with their
Mk   14:35 possible the hour **m** pass from him.
Lk   22: 4 with them how he **m** betray Jesus.
Jn   1: 7 so that through him all **m** believe.
Ac   28:27 Otherwise they **m** see with their
1Co   9:22 all possible means I **m** save some.
2Co   8: 9 through his poverty **m** become rich.
Col   1:11 his glorious **m** so that you may have
1Ti   6:16 To him be honor and **m** forever.
2Th   1: 9 the Lord and from the glory of his **m**
1Pe   2:24 so that we **m** die to sins and live
1Jn   3: 5 so that he **m** take away our sins.

MIGHTIER* MIGHT

Ps   93: 4 **M** than the thunder of the great
     93: 4 **m** than the breakers of the sea—

MIGHTY MIGHT

Ge   10: 9 a **m** hunter before the LORD."
     49:24 of the hand of the **M** One of Jacob,
Ex   6: 1 of my **m** hand he will let them go;
      7: 4 with **m** acts of judgment I will bring
     13: 3 brought you out of it with a **m** hand.
Dt   3:24 do the deeds and **m** works you do?
      5:15 you out of there with a **m** hand
      7: 8 he brought you out with a **m** hand
     10:17 the great God, **m** and awesome,
     34:12 no one has ever shown the **m** power
Jos 22:22 "The **M** One, God, the LORD!
2Sa   1:19 How the **m** have fallen!
     23: 8 the names of David's **m** warriors:
2Ch 14:11 to help the powerless against the **m**.
Ne   9:32 the great God, **m** and awesome,
Job 36: 5 "God is **m**, but despises no one;
Ps   24: 8 The LORD strong and **m**, the LORD
            m in battle.
     45: 3 sword on your side, you **m** one;
     50: 1 The **M** One, God, the LORD,
     62: 7 he is my **m** rock, my refuge.
     68:33 who thunders with **m** voice.
     71:16 will come and proclaim your **m** acts,
     77:12 and meditate on all your **m** deeds."
     77:15 your **m** arm you redeemed your
     89: 8 are **m**, and your faithfulness
     93: 4 the LORD on high is **m**.
     99: 4 The King is **m**, he loves justice—
    106: 2 Who can proclaim the **m** acts
    110: 2 LORD will extend your **m** scepter
    118:15 right hand has done **m** things!
    136:12 with a **m** hand and outstretched arm;
    145: 4 they tell of your **m** acts.
    145:12 all people may know of your **m** acts
    147: 5 Great is our Lord and **m** in power;
    150: 1 praise him in his **m** heavens.
SS   8: 6 like blazing fire, like a **m** flame.
Isa   9: 6 Wonderful Counselor, **M** God,
     33:21 the LORD will be our **M** One.
     49:26 Redeemer, the **M** One of Jacob."

Isa 60:16 Redeemer, the **M** One of Jacob.
      63: 1 I, proclaiming victory, **m** to save."
Jer 10: 6 great, and your name is **m** in power.
      20:11 LORD is with me like a **m** warrior;
      32:18 Great and **m** God, whose name is
      32:19 purposes and **m** are your deeds.
Eze 20:33 I will reign over you with a **m** hand
Da   4: 3 are his signs, how **m** his wonders!
      11: 3 Then a **m** king will arise, who will
Zep   3:17 with you, the **M** Warrior who saves.
Mk   14:62 at the right hand of the **M** One
Lk   1:49 for the **M** One has done great things
Eph   1:19 power is the same as the **m** strength
      6:10 in the Lord and in his **m** power.
1Pe   5: 6 under God's **m** hand, that he may
Rev 18: 8 **m** is the Lord God who judges her.

MIGHTY HAND See HAND

MIGHTY ONE Ge 49:24; Jos 22:22, 22; Job
34:17; Ps 42:4; 45:3; 50:1; 132:2, 5; Isa 1:24; 10:13,
34; 33:21; 49:26; 60:16; Mt 26:64; Mk 14:62; Lk
1:49

MILDEW

Dt   28:22 with blight and **m**, which will
2Ch   6:28 to the land, or blight or **m**,
Am   4: 9 destroying them with blight and **m**.

MILE*

Mt   5:41 If anyone forces you to go one **m**,

MILETUS

2Ti   4:20 and I left Trophimus sick in **M**.

MILK

Ex   3: 8 a land flowing with **m** and honey—
      23:19 cook a young goat in its mother's **m**.
SS   4:11 **m** and honey are under your tongue.
Isa   55: 1 buy wine and **m** without money
Joel 3:18 wine, and the hills will flow with **m**;
1Co   3: 2 I gave you **m**, not solid food,
Heb   5:12 You need **m**, not solid food!
1Pe   2: 2 crave pure spiritual **m**, so that by it

**LAND FLOWING WITH MILK AND
HONEY** See FLOWING

MILKAH

Ge   11:29 the name of Nahor's wife was **M**;

MILL

Mt   24:41 will be grinding with a hand **m**;

MILLSTONE STONE

Jdg   9:53 a woman dropped an upper **m** on his
Lk   17: 2 with a **m** tied around their neck than

MILLSTONES STONE

Dt   24: 6 Do not take a pair of **m**—

MIND DOUBLE-MINDED, LIKE-
MINDED, MINDFUL, MINDS,
MINDSET

Ge   37:11 but his father kept the matter in **m**.
Nu   23:19 being, that he should change his **m**.
Dt   28:65 LORD will give you an anxious **m**,
      29: 4 the LORD has not given you a **m**

1Sa 15:29 does not lie or change his **m**;
1Ch 28: 9 devotion and with a willing **m**,
2Ch 30:12 to give them unity of **m** to carry
Ps   26: 2 me, examine my heart and my **m**;
      110: 4 sworn and will not change his **m**:
Ecc   2: 3 my **m** still guiding me with wisdom.
Jer 17:10 search the heart and examine the **m**,
La   3:21 Yet this I call to **m** and therefore I
Da   4:16 let him be given the **m** of an animal,
      7: 4 the **m** of a human was given to it.
Mt   1:19 he had in **m** to divorce her quietly.
      22:37 all your soul and with all your **m**.'
Mk   3:21 for they said, "He is out of his **m**."
      5:15 there, dressed and in his right **m**;
      12:30 with all your **m** and with all your
Lk   10:27 your strength and with all your **m**';
Ac   4:32 believers were one in heart and **m**.
Ro   1:28 gave them over to a depraved **m**,
      7:25 then, I myself in my **m** am a slave
      8: 6 The **m** governed by the flesh is
      8: 6 the **m** governed by the Spirit is life
      8: 7 The **m** governed by the flesh is
      11:34 "Who has known the **m**
      12: 2 by the renewing of your **m**.
      14:13 make up your **m** not to put any
      15: 6 so that with one **m** and one voice
1Co   1:10 but that you be perfectly united in **m**
      2: 9 what no human **m** has conceived"—
      2:16 "Who has known the **m** of the Lord
      2:16 But we have the **m** of Christ.
      14:14 spirit prays, but my **m** is unfruitful.
2Co   5:13 If we are "out of our **m**," as some
      5:13 if we are in our right **m**, it is for you.
      13:11 another, be of one **m**, live in peace.
Php   2: 2 being one in spirit and of one **m**.
      3:19 Their **m** is set on earthly things.
Col   2:18 idle notions by their unspiritual **m**.
1Th   4:11 You should **m** your own business
Heb   7:21 sworn and will not change his **m**:
1Pe   4: 7 of sober **m** so that you may pray.
Rev 17: 9 "This calls for a **m** with wisdom.

MINDFUL* MIND

Ps   8: 4 is mankind that you are **m** of them,
      26: 3 for I have always been **m** of your
Lk   1:48 he has been **m** of the humble state
Heb   2: 6 is mankind that you are **m** of them,

MINDS MIND

Dt   11:18 words of mine in your hearts and **m**;
Ps   7: 9 the righteous God who probes **m**
Isa 26: 3 peace those whose **m** are steadfast,
Jer 23:16 speak visions from their own **m**,
      31:33 "I will put my law in their **m**
Lk   24:38 and why do doubts rise in your **m**?
      24:45 he opened their **m** so they could
Ro   8: 5 to the flesh have their **m** set on what
      8: 5 the Spirit have their **m** set on what
2Co   3:14 But their **m** were made dull,
      4: 4 god of this age has blinded the **m**
Eph   4:23 made new in the attitude of your **m**;
Php   4: 7 hearts and your **m** in Christ Jesus.
Col   3: 2 Set your **m** on things above,

Heb   8:10 I will put my laws in their **m**
     10:16 and I will write them on their **m**."
1Pe   1:13 with **m** that are alert and fully sober,
Rev   2:23 I am he who searches hearts and **m**,

MINDSET* MIND
Php   2: 5 have the same **m** as Christ Jesus:

MINE
Ex   19: 5 Although the whole earth is **m**,
Nu   3:12 The Levites are **m**,
      3:13 for all the firstborn are **m**.
Dt   32:35 It is **m** to avenge; I will repay.
Job 28: 1 There is a **m** for silver and a place
Ps   50:10 for every animal of the forest is **m**,
Pr   8:14 Counsel and sound judgment are **m**;
SS   2:16 My beloved is **m** and I am his;
Isa   who carry out plans that are not **m**,
Hag   2: 8 'The silver is **m** and the gold is **m**,'
Mt   7:24 who hears these words of **m**
     25:40 of these brothers and sisters of **m**,
Jn   16:15 All that belongs to the Father is **m**.
Ro   12:19 for it is written: "It is **m** to avenge;
Heb 10:30 him who said, "It is **m** to avenge;

MINGLED*
Ezr   9: 2 and have **m** the holy race
Ps 106:35 but they **m** with the nations

MINISTER MINISTERED,
MINISTERING, MINISTERS,
MINISTRY
Nu   16: 9 the community and **m** to them?
Dt   10: 8 to stand before the LORD to **m**
1Ch 15: 2 and to **m** before him forever."
Ps 101: 6 one whose walk is blameless will **m**
     135: 2 you who **m** in the house
Ro   15:16 to be a **m** of Christ Jesus
1Ti   4: 6 you will be a good **m** of Christ

MINISTERED* MINISTER
1Sa   2:11 the boy **m** before the LORD under
      3: 1 The boy Samuel **m** before
1Ch   6:32 They **m** with music before

MINISTERING MINISTER
1Ch 24: 3 for their appointed order of **m**.
Heb   1:14 Are not all angels **m** spirits sent

MINISTERS* MINISTER
Ex   28:35 Aaron must wear it when he **m**.
Isa 61: 6 you will be named **m** of our God.
2Co   3: 6 He has made us competent as **m**

MINISTRY MINISTER
Lk   3:23 years old when he began his **m**.
Ac   1:17 our number and shared in our **m**."
      6: 4 to prayer and the **m** of the word."
Ro   11:13 to the Gentiles, I take pride in my **m**
2Co   3: 7 Now if the **m** that brought death,
      4: 1 God's mercy we have this **m**, we do
      5:18 and gave us the **m** of reconciliation:
      6: 3 so that our **m** will not be discredited.
2Ti   4: 5 discharge all the duties of your **m**.
Heb   8: 6 in fact the **m** Jesus has received is as

MIRACLE* MIRACLES,
MIRACULOUS
Ex   7: 9 'Perform a **m**,' then say to Aaron,
Mk   9:39 no one who does a **m** in my name
Jn   7:21 them, "I did one **m**, and you are all

MIRACLES* MIRACLE
1Ch 16:12 done, his **m**, and the judgments he
Ne   9:17 to remember the **m** you performed
Job   5: 9 fathomed, **m** that cannot be counted.
      9:10 fathomed, **m** that cannot be counted.
Ps   77:11 I will remember your **m** of long ago.
     77:14 You are the God who performs **m**;
     78:12 He did **m** in the sight of their
     105: 5 done, his **m**, and the judgments he
     106: 7 they gave no thought to your **m**;
     106:22 **m** in the land of Ham and awesome
Mt   7:22 in your name perform many **m**?'
     11:20 most of his **m** had been performed,
     11:21 if the **m** that were performed in you
     11:23 if the **m** that were performed in you
     13:58 he did not do many **m** there because
Mk   6: 2 What are these remarkable **m** he is
      6: 5 He could not do any **m** there,
Lk   10:13 if the **m** that were performed in you
     19:37 voices for all the **m** they had seen:
Ac   2:22 man accredited by God to you by **m**,
      8:13 by the great signs and **m** he saw.
     19:11 did extraordinary **m** through Paul,
1Co 12:28 then **m**, then gifts of healing,
     12:29 Are all teachers? Do all work **m**?
2Co 12:12 including signs, wonders and **m**.
Gal   3: 5 work **m** among you by the works
Heb   2: 4 wonders and various **m**, and by gifts

MIRACULOUS MIRACLE
Mt   13:54 this wisdom and these **m** powers?"
1Co 12:10 to another **m** powers, to another

MIRE
Ps   40: 2 the slimy pit, out of the mud and **m**;
Isa 57:20 whose waves cast up **m** and mud.

MIRIAM
Sister of Moses and Aaron (Nu 26:59); with them a leader of Israel (Mic 6:4). Prophet who led singing and dancing at Red Sea (Ex 15:20–21). Struck with leprosy for criticizing Moses (Nu 12). Death (Nu 20:1).

MIRROR*
Job 37:18 skies, hard as a **m** of cast bronze?
1Co 13:12 we see only a reflection as in a **m**;
Jas   1:23 who looks at his face in a **m**

MISCARRY
Ex   23:26 and none will **m** or be barren in your

MISDEEDS*
Ps   99: 8 God, though you punished their **m**.
Ro   8:13 you put to death the **m** of the body,

MISERABLE MISERY
Gal   4: 9 back to those weak and **m** forces?

MISERY MISERABLE

Ex   3: 7 "I have indeed seen the **m** of my
Nu 23:21 in Jacob, no **m** observed in Israel.
Jdg 10:16 he could bear Israel's **m** no longer.
Ps   44:24 and forget our **m** and oppression?
      56: 8 Record my **m**; list my tears on your
Ecc   8: 6 person may be weighed down by **m**.
Hos   5:15 in their **m** they will earnestly seek
Ro   3:16 ruin and **m** mark their ways,
Jas   5: 1 wail because of the **m** that is coming

MISFORTUNE

Nu 23:21 "No **m** is seen in Jacob, no misery
Ob   1:12 your brother in the day of his **m**,

MISHAEL MESHACH

Original name of Meshach (Da 1:6–19; 2:17).

MISLEAD MISLEADS, MISLED

Pr   24:28 would you use your lips to **m**?
Isa   9:16 who guide this people **m** them,
    47:10 knowledge **m** you when you say

MISLEADS* MISLEAD

Isa 44:20 a deluded heart **m** him;
Rev   2:20 her teaching she **m** my servants

MISLED MISLEAD

1Co 15:33 Do not be **m**:

MISS* MISSES, MISSING

Jdg 20:16 sling a stone at a hair and not **m**.
Pr   19: 2 more will hasty feet **m** the way!

MISSES* MISS

1Sa 20: 6 If your father **m** me at all, tell him,

MISSING MISS

Jdg 21: 3 Why should one tribe be **m**
Isa 40:26 strength, not one of them is **m**.

MISSION

Isa 48:15 him, and he will succeed in his **m**.
Ac   12:25 and Saul had finished their **m**,

MIST* MISTS

Isa 44:22 cloud, your sins like the morning **m**.
Hos   6: 4 Your love is like the morning **m**,
    13: 3 they will be like the morning **m**,
Ac   13:11 Immediately **m** and darkness came
Jas   4:14 You are a **m** that appears for a little

MISTAKE

Ecc   5: 6 messenger, "My vow was a **m**."

MISTREAT MISTREATED

Ex   22:21 "Do not **m** or oppress a foreigner,
Eze 22:29 poor and needy and **m** the foreigner,
Lk   6:28 you, pray for those who **m** you.

MISTREATED MISTREAT

Ge 15:13 they will be enslaved and **m** there.
    16: 6 Then Sarai **m** Hagar; so she fled
Nu   20:15 The Egyptians **m** us and our
Eze 22: 7 the foreigner and **m** the fatherless
Heb 11:25 He chose to be **m** along
    11:37 destitute, persecuted and **m**—

Heb 13: 3 and those who are **m** as if you

MISTRESS

Ge 16: 4 she began to despise her **m**.
Ps 123: 2 slave look to the hand of her **m**,

MISTS* MIST

2Pe   2:17 water and **m** driven by a storm.

MISUSE* MISUSES

Ex   20: 7 "You shall not **m** the name
Dt   5:11 "You shall not **m** the name
Ps 139:20 your adversaries **m** your name.

MISUSES* MISUSE

Ex   20: 7 anyone guiltless who **m** his name.
Dt   5:11 anyone guiltless who **m** his name.

MITE(S) (KJV) See PENNY, SMALL COPPER [COINS]

MIXED MIXES, MIXING, MIXTURE, WELL-MIXED

Ex   29: 2 yeast and with olive oil **m** in,
Lev   7:10 whether **m** with olive oil or dry,
Ps   75: 8 full of foaming wine **m** with spices;
Pr   9: 5 food and drink the wine I have **m**.
Da   2:41 it, even as you saw iron **m** with clay.
Mk 15:23 Then they offered him wine **m**
Jude 1:23 to others show mercy, **m** with fear—
Rev   8: 7 came hail and fire **m** with blood,

MIXES* MIXED

Da   2:43 any more than iron **m** with clay.
Hos   7: 8 "Ephraim **m** with the nations;

MIXING MIXED

Isa   5:22 wine and champions at **m** drinks,

MIXTURE* MIXED

Da   2:43 so the people will be a **m** and will
Jn   19:39 Nicodemus brought a **m** of myrrh

MIZPAH

Ge 31:49 It was also called **M**, because he
1Sa   7: 6 was serving as leader of Israel at **M**.
Jer   41: 1 to Gedaliah son of Ahikam at **M**.

MOAB MOABITE, MOABITES

Ge 19:37 had a son, and she named him **M**;
Nu   22: 3 **M** was terrified because there were
Dt   34: 5 of the LORD died there in **M**,
Jdg   3:12 Eglon king of **M** power over Israel.
Ru   1: 1 live for a while in the country of **M**.
1Sa 22: 4 So he left them with the king of **M**,
2Ki   1: 1 death, **M** rebelled against Israel.
    23:13 for Chemosh the vile god of **M**,
Isa   15: 1 A prophecy against **M**: Ar in **M** is
Jer   48: 1 Concerning **M**: This is what
    48:16 "The fall of **M** is at hand;
Eze 25: 8 'Because **M** and Seir said, "Look,
Am   2: 1 "For three sins of **M**, even for four,
Zep   2: 9 "surely **M** will become like Sodom,

MOABITE MOAB

Nu 25: 1 sexual immorality with **M** women,
Dt   23: 3 No Ammonite or **M** or any of their

Ru   1:22   Moab accompanied by Ruth the **M**,
Ne   13: 1   **M** should ever be admitted

MOABITES   MOAB
Ge   19:37   he is the father of the **M** of today.

MOAN
Ps   90: 9   we finish our years with a **m**.
Isa   59:11   we **m** mournfully like doves.

MOCK   MOCKED, MOCKER, MOCKERS, MOCKERY, MOCKING, MOCKS
Ps   22: 7   All who see me **m** me;
    74:22   remember how fools **m** you all day
   119:51   The arrogant **m** me unmercifully,
Pr   1:26   I will **m** when calamity overtakes
    14: 9   Fools **m** at making amends for sin,
La   3:63   standing, they **m** me in their songs.
Hab   1:10   They **m** kings and scoff at rulers.
Mk   10:34   who will **m** him and spit on him,

MOCKED   MOCK
2Ch   36:16   But they **m** God's messengers,
Ps   74:18   how the enemy has **m** you, LORD,
    89:51   have **m**, with which they have **m**
Mt   27:29   knelt in front of him and **m** him.
    27:41   of the law and the elders **m** him.
Lk   23:11   his soldiers ridiculed and **m** him.
Gal   6: 7   not be deceived: God cannot be **m**.

MOCKER   MOCK
Pr   9: 7   corrects a **m** invites insults;
    9:12   if you are a **m**, you alone will suffer.
    20: 1   Wine is a **m** and beer a brawler;
    22:10   Drive out the **m**, and out goes strife;
    24: 9   folly are sin, and people detest a **m**.

MOCKERS   MOCK
Ps   1: 1   take or sit in the company of **m**,
Pr   3:34   He mocks proud **m** but shows favor
    29: 8   **M** stir up a city, but the wise turn

MOCKERY*   MOCK
Pr   1:22   How long will mockers delight in **m**
Jer   10:15   are worthless, the objects of **m**;
    51:18   are worthless, the objects of **m**;

MOCKING   MOCK
Isa   50: 6   I did not hide my face from **m**
Lk   22:63   who were guarding Jesus began **m**

MOCKS   MOCK
Pr   17: 5   Whoever **m** the poor shows
    19:28   A corrupt witness **m** at justice,
    30:17   "The eye that **m** a father,

MODEL*
Php   3:17   and just as you have us as a **m**,
1Th   1: 7   And so you became a **m** to all
2Th   3: 9   to offer ourselves as a **m** for you

MODESTLY*   MODESTY
1Ti   2: 9   I also want the women to dress **m**,

MODESTY*   MODESTLY
1Co   12:23   are treated with special **m**,

MOLDED*
Job   10: 9   Remember that you **m** me like clay.

MOLDY
Jos   9: 5   of their food supply was dry and **m**.

MOLEK
Lev   20: 2   any of his children to **M** is to be put
1Ki   11:33   and **M** the god of the Ammonites,
2Ki   23:10   son or daughter in the fire to **M**.
Jer   32:35   their sons and daughters to **M**,

MOMENT   MOMENTARY
Ex   33: 5   I were to go with you even for a **m**,
Nu   4:20   even for a **m**, or they will die."
Job   20: 5   the joy of the godless lasts but a **m**.
Ps   2:12   for his wrath can flare up in a **m**.
    30: 5   For his anger lasts only a **m**, but his
Pr   12:19   but a lying tongue lasts only a **m**.
Isa   54: 7   "For a brief **m** I abandoned you,
    66: 8   or a nation be brought forth in a **m**?
Mt   8:13   And his servant was healed at that **m**.
    9:22   the woman was healed at that **m**.
Jn   18:27   at that **m** a rooster began to crow.
Ac   5:10   At that **m** she fell down at his feet
Gal   2: 5   We did not give in to them for a **m**,

MOMENTARY*   MOMENT
2Co   4:17   **m** troubles are achieving for us

MONEY
Ex   22:25   "If you lend **m** to one of my people
    30:16   Receive the atonement **m**
2Ki   12: 4   "Collect all the **m** that is brought as
    12: 4   and the **m** brought voluntarily
Ps   15: 5   who lends **m** to the poor without
Pr   13:11   Dishonest **m** dwindles away, but
      whoever gathers **m** little by little
Ecc   5:10   Whoever loves **m** never has enough;
    7:12   is a shelter as **m** is a shelter,
    10:19   and **m** is the answer for everything.
Isa   55: 1   and you who have no **m**, come,
Mic   3:11   and her prophets tell fortunes for **m**.
Mt   6:24   You cannot serve both God and **m**.
    27: 5   So Judas threw the **m**
Lk   3:14   "Don't extort **m** and don't accuse
    9: 3   bag, no bread, no **m**, no extra shirt.
    16:13   You cannot serve both God and **m**."
Jn   2:14   sitting at tables exchanging **m**.
    12: 6   as keeper of the **m** bag, he used
Ac   5: 2   kept back part of the **m** for himself,
1Co   16: 2   you should set aside a sum of **m**
1Ti   3: 3   not quarrelsome, not a lover of **m**.
    6:10   the love of **m** is a root of all kinds
2Ti   3: 2   of themselves, lovers of **m**, boastful,
Heb   13: 5   your lives free from the love of **m**

MONEYLENDER*   LEND
Lk   7:41   people owed money to a certain **m**.

MONOPOLY*
Job   15: 8   Do you have a **m** on wisdom?

MONSTER*
Job   7:12   or the **m** of the deep, that you put
Ps   74:13   the heads of the **m** in the waters.

Isa 27: 1 he will slay the **m** of the sea.
51: 9 pieces, who pierced that **m** through?
Eze 29: 3 you great **m** lying among your
32: 2 you are like a **m** in the seas

MONTH MONTHLY, MONTHS

Ex 12: 2 "This **m** is to be for you the first **m**,
40: 2 on the first day of the first **m**.
Lev 23:24 first day of the seventh **m** you are
23:27 day of this seventh **m** is the Day
23:34 the seventh **m** the LORD's Festival
25: 9 on the tenth day of the seventh **m**;
Nu 3:15 Count every male a **m** old or more."
11:21 them meat to eat for a whole **m**!'
Ezr 6:19 On the fourteenth day of the first **m**,
Ne 8: 2 day of the seventh **m** Ezra the priest
Est 9:21 and fifteenth days of the **m** of Adar
Eze 47:12 Every **m** they will bear fruit,
Rev 9:15 day and **m** and year were released
22: 2 of fruit, yielding its fruit every **m**.

MONTHLY MONTH

Lev 15:19 of her **m** period will last seven days,
Nu 28:14 This is the **m** burnt offering to be

MONTHS MONTH

Ex 2: 2 a fine child, she hid him for three **m**.
Jdg 11:37 "Give me two **m** to roam the hills
1Sa 6: 1 been in Philistine territory seven **m**,
1Ch 13:14 in his house for three **m**,
Jn 4:35 'It's still four **m** until harvest'?
Gal 4:10 are observing special days and **m**
Rev 9: 5 but only to torture them for five **m**.
11: 2 trample on the holy city for 42 **m**.
13: 5 its authority for forty-two **m**.

MOON MOONS

Ge 37: 9 this time the sun and **m** and eleven
Nu 28:14 at each new **m** during the year.
Dt 17: 3 sun or the **m** or the stars in the sky,
Jos 10:13 and the **m** stopped, till the nation
Ps 8: 3 of your fingers, the **m** and the stars,
72: 7 abound till the **m** is no more.
74:16 you established the sun and **m**.
89:37 be established forever like the **m**,
104:19 He made the **m** to mark the seasons,
121: 6 you by day, nor the **m** by night.
136: 9 the **m** and stars to govern the night;
148: 3 Praise him, sun and **m**;
SS 6:10 fair as the **m**, bright as the sun,
Isa 13:10 and the **m** will not give its light.
Jer 31:35 who decrees the **m** and stars to shine
Eze 32: 7 and the **m** will not give its light.
Joel 2:31 the **m** to blood before the coming
Hab 3:11 **m** stood still in the heavens
Mt 24:29 and the **m** will not give its light;
Ac 2:20 the **m** to blood before the coming
1Co 15:41 the **m** another and the stars another;
Col 2:16 a New **M** celebration or a Sabbath
Rev 6:12 hair, the whole **m** turned blood red,
8:12 a third of the **m**, and a third
12: 1 sun, with the **m** under her feet
21:23 need the sun or the **m** to shine on it,

MOONS MOON

2Ch 8:13 the New **M** and the three annual
31: 3 at the New **M** and at the appointed
Isa 1:13 New **M**,

MORAL*

Jas 1:21 get rid of all **m** filth and the evil

MORDECAI

Benjamite exile who raised Esther (Est 2:5–15).
Exposed plot to kill Xerxes (Est 2:19–23). Refused
to honor Haman (Est 3:1–6; 5:9–14). Charged Es-
ther to foil Haman's plot against the Jews (Est 4).
Xerxes forced Haman to honor Mordecai (Est 6).
Mordecai exalted (Est 8–10). Established Purim
(Est 9:18–32).

MORE MUCH

Ge 3: 1 the serpent was **m** crafty than any
4:13 "My punishment is **m** than I can
5:24 then he was no **m**, because God took
37: 3 Now Israel loved Joseph **m** than any
Ex 1:12 But the **m** they were oppressed, the **m**
they multiplied and spread;
Nu 1:18 years old or **m** were listed by name,
3:15 every male a month old or **m**."
12: 3 **m** humble than anyone else
Dt 7:14 will be blessed **m** than any other
Jos 10:11 **m** of them died from the hail than
Jdg 16:30 Thus he killed many **m** when he
2Sa 1:26 **m** wonderful than that of women.
18: 8 the forest swallowed up **m** men
1Ki 16:33 and did **m** to arouse the anger
2Ki 2:12 And Elisha saw him no **m**.
1Ch 11: 9 David became **m** and **m** powerful,
Job 4:17 a mortal be **m** righteous than God?
42:12 of Job's life **m** than the former part.
Ps 19:10 They are **m** precious than gold,
37:10 while, and the wicked will be no **m**;
69:31 please the LORD **m** than an ox,
71:14 I will praise you **m** and **m**.
119:127 I love your commands **m** than
gold, **m** than pure gold,
130: 6 for the Lord **m** than watchmen wait
Pr 3:14 for she is **m** profitable than silver
8:11 wisdom is **m** precious than rubies,
21: 3 just is **m** acceptable to the LORD
22: 1 good name is **m** desirable than great
31:10 She is worth far **m** than rubies.
Ecc 1:18 the **m** knowledge, the **m** grief.
SS 1: 2 your love is **m** delightful than wine.
Isa 54: 1 because **m** are the children
60:19 The sun will no **m** be your light
Jer 31:34 and will remember their sins no **m**."
La 5: 7 Our ancestors sinned and are no **m**,
Hos 13: 2 Now they sin **m** and **m**;
Jnh 3: 4 "Forty **m** days and Nineveh will be
Na 1:15 No **m** will the wicked invade you;
Mt 2:18 comforted, because they are no **m**."
6:25 Is not life **m** than food, and the
body **m** than clothes?
Mk 4:25 Whoever has will be given **m**;
12:43 this poor widow has put **m**
Lk 3:16 one who is **m** powerful than I will

Lk 12:23 For life is **m** than food, and the
           body **m** than clothes.
Jn 16:12 "I have much **m** to say to you,
   16:16 a little while you will see me no **m**,
   21:15 do you love me **m** than these?"
Ac 17:11 of **m** noble character than those
Ro 5: 9 how much **m** shall we be saved
    8:37 things we are **m** than conquerors
   14: 5 considers one day **m** sacred than
2Co 3: 9 how much **m** glorious is
Heb 8:12 and will remember their sins no **m**."
   10:17 lawless acts I will remember no **m**."
Jas 4: 6 But he gives us **m** grace.
Rev 10: 6 said, "There will be no **m** delay!
   21: 4 There will be no **m** death'
   22: 5 There will be no **m** night.

HOW MUCH MORE See HOW

MORIAH*
Ge 22: 2 Isaac—and go to the region of **M**.
2Ch 3: 1 LORD in Jerusalem on Mount **M**,

MORNING MORNINGS
Ge 1: 5 was evening, and there was **m**—
Ex 12:10 Do not leave any of it till **m**;
   16:12 and in the **m** you will be filled
   29:39 Offer one in the **m** and the other
Dt 28:67 In the **m** you will say, "If only it
2Sa 23: 4 he is like the light of **m** at sunrise
Ezr 3: 3 both the **m** and evening sacrifices.
Job 38: 7 while the **m** stars sang together
Ps 5: 3 In the **m**, LORD, you hear my
     5: 3 the **m** I lay my requests before you
   30: 5 night, but rejoicing comes in the **m**.
   130: 6 more than watchmen wait for the **m**,
Pr 27:14 their neighbor early in the **m**, it will
Ecc 11: 6 Sow your seed in the **m**,
Isa 14:12 you have fallen from heaven, **m** star,
   50: 4 He wakens me **m** by **m**, wakens my
La 3:23 They are new every **m**; great is your
Hos 6: 4 Your love is like the **m** mist,
   13: 3 they will be like the **m** mist,
Zep 3: 5 **M** by **m** he dispenses his justice,
Lk 24: 1 very early in the **m**, the women took
   24:22 They went to the tomb early this **m**
Ac 2:15 It's only nine in the **m**!
2Pe 1:19 and the **m** star rises in your hearts.
Rev 2:28 I will also give that one the **m** star.
   22:16 of David, and the bright **M** Star."

MORNINGS* MORNING
Da 8:14 "It will take 2,300 evenings and **m**;
    8:26 **m** that has been given you is true,

MORTAL MORTALS
Ge 6: 3 humans forever, for they are **m**;
Dt 5:26 For what **m** has ever heard the voice
Job 4:17 'Can a **m** be more righteous than
    9:32 "He is not a mere **m** like me that I
   10: 4 Do you see as a **m** sees?
   13: 9 deceive you as you might deceive a **m**?
Ps 9:20 let the nations know they are only **m**.

Mic 6: 8 He has shown you, O **m**, what is good.
Mal 3: 8 "Will a mere **m** rob God?
Ro 1:23 made to look like a **m** human being
    6:12 not let sin reign in your **m** body so
    8:11 give life to your **m** bodies because
1Co 15:53 and the **m** with immortality.
2Co 5: 4 so that what is **m** may be swallowed

MORTALS MORTAL
Job 14: 1 "**M**, born of woman, are of few
Ps 56: 4 What can mere **m** do to me?
   103:15 The life of **m** is like grass,
   144: 3 mere **m** that you think of them?
Isa 51:12 Who are you that you fear mere **m**,
Heb 13: 6 afraid. What can mere **m** do to me?"

MORTGAGING*
Ne 5: 3 were saying, "We are **m** our fields,

MOSES
Levite; brother of Aaron (Ex 6:20; 1Ch 6:3). Put in basket into Nile; discovered and raised by Pharaoh's daughter (Ex 2:1–10). Fled to Midian after killing Egyptian (Ex 2:11–15). Married to Zipporah, fathered Gershom (Ex 2:16–22).

Called by the LORD to deliver Israel (Ex 3–4). Pharaoh's resistance (Ex 5). Ten plagues (Ex 7–11). Passover and Exodus (Ex 12–13). Led Israel through Red Sea (Ex 14). Song of deliverance (Ex 15:1–21). Brought water from rock (Ex 17:1–7). Raised hands to defeat Amalekites (Ex 17:8–16). Delegated judges (Ex 18; Dt 1:9–18).

Received Law at Sinai (Ex 19–23; 25–31; Jn 1:17). Announced Law to Israel (Ex 19:7–8; 24; 35). Broke tablets of golden calf (Ex 32; Dt 9). Saw glory of the LORD (Ex 33–34). Supervised building of tabernacle (Ex 36–40). Set apart Aaron and priests (Lev 8–9). Numbered tribes (Nu 1–4; 26). Opposed by Aaron and Miriam (Nu 12). Sent spies into Canaan (Nu 13). Announced forty years of wandering for failure to enter land (Nu 14). Opposed by Korah (Nu 16). Forbidden to enter land for striking rock (Nu 20:1–13; Dt 1:37). Lifted bronze snake for healing (Nu 21:4–9; Jn 3:14). Final address to Israel (Dt 1–33). Succeeded by Joshua (Nu 27:12–23; Dt 34). Death and burial by God (Dt 34:5–12).

"Law of Moses" (1Ki 2:3; Ezr 3:2; Mk 12:26; Lk 24:44). "Book of Moses" (2Ch 25:12; Ne 13:1). "Song of Moses" (Ex 15:1–21; Rev 15:3). "Prayer of Moses" (Ps 90).

LAW OF MOSES See LAW

MOST INMOST, MUCH
Ge 14:18 He was priest of God **M** High,
Ex 26:33 Holy Place from the **M** Holy Place.
Nu 4: 4 the care of the **m** holy things.
   24:16 has knowledge from the **M** High,
Jdg 5:24 "**M** blessed of women be Jael,
1Ki 3: 4 that was the **m** important high place,
1Ch 16:25 the LORD and **m** worthy of praise;
Ps 7:10 My shield is God **M** High,
   46: 4 place where the **M** High dwells.

Ps 48: 1 and **m** worthy of praise, in the city
 78:35 God **M** High was their Redeemer.
 91: 1 the shelter of the **M** High will rest
SS 1: 8 do not know, **m** beautiful of women,
Isa 14:14 will make myself like the **M** High."
Jer 3:19 the **m** beautiful inheritance of any
Eze 20: 6 honey, the **m** beautiful of all lands.
Da 4:17 the **M** High is sovereign over all
 7:25 He will speak against the **M** High
Mk 5: 7 me, Jesus, Son of the **M** High God?
 12:28 which is the **m** important?"
Lk 1:32 be called the Son of the **M** High.
 1:76 be called a prophet of the **M** High;
 20:47 men will be punished **m** severely."
Eph 5:16 making the **m** of every opportunity,
Col 4: 5 make the **m** of every opportunity
Jude 1:20 yourselves up in your **m** holy faith

MOST HIGH See HIGH

MOST HOLY See HOLY

MOTH MOTHS
Ps 39:11 you consume their wealth like a **m**—
Isa 51: 8 For the **m** will eat them up like
Lk 12:33 thief comes near and no **m** destroys.

MOTHER GRANDMOTHER,
MOTHER'S, MOTHER-IN-LAW,
MOTHERS
Ge 2:24 why a man leaves his father and **m**
 3:20 because she would become the **m**
 17:16 so that she will be the **m** of nations;
Ex 20:12 "Honor your father and your **m**,
 21:15 father or **m** is to be put to death.
 21:17 father or **m** is to be put to death.
Lev 18: 7 having sexual relations with your **m**.
 19: 3 of you must respect your **m**
 20: 9 they have cursed their father or **m**,
Dt 5:16 "Honor your father and your **m**,
 21:18 who does not obey his father and **m**
 22: 6 do not take the **m** with the young.
 27:16 who dishonors their father or **m**."
Jdg 5: 7 arose, until I arose, a **m** in Israel.
1Sa 2:19 Each year his **m** made him a little
2Sa 20:19 to destroy a city that is a **m** in Israel.
1Ki 19:20 me kiss my father and **m** goodbye,"
Ps 27:10 my father and **m** forsake me,
 51: 5 from the time my **m** conceived me.
 113: 9 her home as a happy **m** of children.
Pr 10: 1 a foolish son brings grief to his **m**.
 15:20 but a foolish man despises his **m**.
 20:20 If someone curses their father or **m**,
 23:22 do not despise your **m** when she is
 23:25 May your father and **m** rejoice;
 29:15 left undisciplined disgraces its **m**.
 30:17 that scorns an aged **m**, will be
 31: 1 inspired utterance his **m** taught him.
SS 6: 9 the only daughter of her **m**,
Isa 8: 4 how to say 'My father' or 'My **m**,'
 49:15 "Can a **m** forget the baby at her
 66:13 As a **m** comforts her child, so will I
Jer 20:17 with my **m** as my grave, her womb
Hos 2: 2 "Rebuke your **m**, rebuke her,
Mic 7: 6 a daughter rises up against her **m**,

Mt 1:16 and Mary was the **m** of Jesus who is
 2:11 they saw the child with his **m** Mary,
 10:35 father, a daughter against her **m**,
 10:37 or **m** more than me is not worthy
 12:48 "Who is my **m**, and who are my
 19: 5 a man will leave his father and **m**
 19:19 honor your father and **m**,' and 'love
Mk 7:10 'Honor your father and **m**,' and,
 10:19 honor your father and **m**.' "
Lk 11:27 "Blessed is the **m** who gave you
 12:53 **m** against daughter and daughter
 against **m**,
 14:26 me and does not hate father and **m**,
 18:20 honor your father and **m**.' "
Jn 19:27 to the disciple, "Here is your **m**."
Gal 4:26 is above is free, and she is our **m**.
Eph 5:31 a man will leave his father and **m**
 6: 2 "Honor your father and **m**"—
1Th 2: 7 Just as a nursing **m** cares for her
2Ti 1: 5 Lois and in your **m** Eunice and, I am
Heb 7: 3 Without father or **m**,
Rev 17: 5 THE GREAT THE **M** OF PROSTITUTES

MOTHER'S MOTHER
Ex 23:19 not cook a young goat in its **m** milk.
Job 1:21 "Naked I came from my **m** womb,
Ps 22:10 my **m** womb you have been my
Pr 1: 8 and do not forsake your **m** teaching.
 6:20 and do not forsake your **m** teaching.
Ecc 5:15 comes naked from their **m** womb,
 11: 5 the body is formed in a **m** womb,
Isa 50: 1 "Where is your **m** certificate
Jn 3: 4 a second time into their **m** womb

MOTHER-IN-LAW MOTHER
Dt 27:23 is anyone who sleeps with his **m**."
Ru 2:11 done for your **m** since the death
Mic 7: 6 a daughter-in-law against her **m**—
Mt 10:35 a daughter-in-law against her **m**—
Mk 1:30 Simon's **m** was in bed with a fever,

MOTHERS MOTHER
Pr 30:11 fathers and do not bless their **m**;
Hos 10:14 when **m** were dashed to the ground
Mk 13:17 for pregnant women and nursing **m**!
1Ti 1: 9 for those who kill their fathers or **m**,
 5: 2 older women as **m**, and younger

MOTHS MOTH
Mt 6:19 earth, where **m** and vermin destroy,
Jas 5: 2 rotted, and **m** have eaten your clothes.

MOTIONED
Jn 13:24 Simon Peter **m** to this disciple
Ac 12:17 Peter **m** with his hand for them to be
 13:16 up, Paul **m** with his hand and said:
 19:33 He **m** for silence in order to make
 26: 1 So Paul **m** with his hand and began

MOTIVES*
Pr 16: 2 but **m** are weighed by the LORD.
1Co 4: 5 and will expose the **m** of the heart.
Php 1:18 way, whether from false **m** or true,
1Th 2: 3 not spring from error or impure **m**,
Jas 4: 3 because you ask with wrong **m**,

MOUND
Jer 26:18 the temple hill a **m** overgrown
Mic 3:12 the temple hill a **m** overgrown

MOUNT MOUNTAIN, MOUNTAINS, MOUNTAINSIDE, MOUNTAINTOPS, MOUNTED
Ex 19:20 descended to the top of **M** Sinai
34:29 Moses came down from **M** Sinai
Nu 33:39 years old when he died on **M** Hor.
Dt 11:29 on **M** Gerizim the blessings, and
on **M** Ebal the curses.
34: 1 Moses climbed **M** Nebo
Jos 8:30 Joshua built on **M** Ebal an altar
1Ch 10: 8 and his sons fallen on **M** Gilboa.
2Ch 3: 1 LORD in Jerusalem on **M** Moriah,
Ps 78:68 he chose the tribe of Judah, **M** Zion,
89: 9 when its waves **m** up, you still them.
Isa 14:13 on the utmost heights of **M** Zaphon.
Eze 28:14 You were on the holy **m** of God;
Ob 1:17 But on **M** Zion will be deliverance;
Mic 4: 7 will rule over them in **M** Zion
Zec 14: 4 the **M** of Olives will be split in two
Mk 13: 3 the **M** of Olives opposite the temple,
Gal 4:24 One covenant is from **M** Sinai
Heb 12:22 But you have come to **M** Zion,
Rev 14: 1 standing on **M** Zion, and with him

MOUNT OF OLIVES 2Sa 15:30; Zec 14:4, 4; Mt 21:1; 24:3; 26:30; Mk 11:1; 13:3; 14:26; Lk 19:29, 37; 21:37; 22:39; Ac 1:12

MOUNT SINAI Ex 19:11, 18, 20, 23; 24:16; 31:18; 34:2, 4, 29, 32; Lev 7:38; 25:1; 26:46; 27:34; Nu 3:1; 28:6; Ne 9:13; Ac 7:30, 38; Gal 4:24, 25

MOUNT ZION 2Ki 19:31; Ps 48:2, 11; 74:2; 78:68; 125:1; 133:3; Isa 4:5; 8:18; 10:12; 18:7; 24:23; 29:8; 31:4; 37:32; La 5:18; Joel 2:32; Ob 1:17, 21; Mic 4:7; Heb 12:22; Rev 14:1

MOUNTAIN MOUNT
Ge 22:14 "On the **m** of the LORD it will be
Ex 3: 1 and came to Horeb, the **m** of God.
19: 2 there in the desert in front of the **m**.
19:20 called Moses to the top of the **m**.
24:18 he stayed on the **m** forty days
32:19 them to pieces at the foot of the **m**.
Dt 5: 4 face to face out of the fire on the **m**.
1Ki 19: 8 he reached Horeb, the **m** of God.
Job 14:18 "But as a **m** erodes and crumbles
Ps 15: 1 Who may live on your holy **m**?
24: 3 Who may ascend the **m**
48: 1 in the city of our God, his holy **m**.
68:16 you rugged **m**, at the **m** where God
Isa 2: 2 the last days the **m** of the LORD's
11: 9 harm nor destroy on all my holy **m**,
40: 4 up, every **m** and hill made low;
65:25 nor destroy on all my holy **m**,"
Da 2:45 the vision of the rock cut out of a **m**,
Mic 4: 1 the last days the **m** of the LORD's
Zec 14: 4 with half of the **m** moving north
Mt 4: 8 the devil took him to a very high **m**
17:20 you can say to this **m**,
Mk 9: 2 with him and led them up a high **m**,

Lk 3: 5 filled in, every **m** and hill made low.
Jn 4:21 the Father neither on this **m** nor
2Pe 1:18 we were with him on the sacred **m**.
Rev 6:14 every **m** and island was removed
8: 8 and something like a huge **m**,
21:10 me away in the Spirit to a **m** great

HOLY MOUNTAIN See HOLY

MOUNTAINS MOUNT
Ge 7:20 covered the **m** to a depth of more
8: 4 ark came to rest on the **m** of Ararat.
Ps 36: 6 righteousness is like the highest **m**,
46: 2 the **m** fall into the heart of the sea,
90: 2 Before the **m** were born or you
97: 5 The **m** melt like wax before
98: 8 let the **m** sing together for joy;
121: 1 I lift up my eyes to the **m**—
125: 2 As the **m** surround Jerusalem,
Isa 2: 2 established as the highest of the **m**;
52: 7 How beautiful on the **m** are the feet
54:10 Though the **m** be shaken
55:12 the **m** and hills will burst into song
Eze 34: 6 My sheep wandered over all the **m**
39: 4 On the **m** of Israel you will fall,
Hos 10: 8 Then they will say to the **m**,
Mic 4: 1 established as the highest of the **m**;
Na 1:15 there on the **m**, the feet of one who
Mk 13:14 those who are in Judea flee to the **m**.
Lk 23:30 Then " 'they will say to the **m**,
1Co 13: 2 if I have a faith that can move **m**,
Rev 6:16 They called to the **m** and the rocks,
16:20 away and the **m** could not be found.

MOUNTAINSIDE MOUNT
Mt 5: 1 he went up on a **m** and sat down.
Mk 6:46 them, he went up on a **m** to pray.

MOUNTAINTOPS MOUNT
Isa 42:11 let them shout from the **m**.
Eze 6:13 on every high hill and on all the **m**,

MOUNTED MOUNT
Ex 25: 7 other gems to be **m** on the ephod
2Sa 22:11 He **m** the cherubim and flew;
SS 5:12 washed in milk, **m** like jewels.

MOURN MOURNED, MOURNING, MOURNS
Ge 23: 2 and Abraham went to **m** for Sarah
Ezr 10: 6 to **m** over the unfaithfulness
Ne 8: 9 Do not **m** or weep."
Ecc 3: 4 a time to **m** and a time to dance,
Isa 61: 2 of our God, to comfort all who **m**,
Zec 12:10 they will **m** for him as one mourns
Mt 5: 4 Blessed are those who **m**, for they
9:15 of the bridegroom **m** while he is
Lk 6:25 now, for you will **m** and weep.
Ro 12:15 **m** with those who **m**.
1Co 7:30 those who **m**, as if they did not;
Rev 1: 7 on earth "will **m** because of him."
18: 7 I am not a widow; I will never **m**.'

MOURNED MOURN
Nu 14:39 to all the Israelites, they **m** bitterly.
Ne 1: 4 For some days I **m** and fasted

Da   10: 2 time I, Daniel, **m** for three weeks.
Lk   23:27 including women who **m** and wailed
Ac   8: 2 Stephen and **m** deeply for him.

MOURNING MOURN

Est   4: 3 there was great **m** among the Jews,
       9:22 their **m** into a day of celebration.
Ecc   7: 2 to go to a house of **m** than to go
Isa   61: 3 the oil of joy instead of **m**,
Jer   31:13 I will turn their **m** into gladness;
La   5:15 our dancing has turned to **m**.
Rev   21: 4 There will be no more death' or **m**

MOURNS MOURN

Zec   12:10 for him as one **m** for an only child,

MOUTH MOUTHS

Nu   16:30 the earth opens its **m** and swallows
      22:38 only what God puts in my **m**."
Dt   8: 3 comes from the **m** of the LORD.
      18:18 and I will put my words in his **m**.
      30:14 it is in your **m** and in your heart so
2Ki   4:34 the bed and lay on the boy, **m** to **m**,
Job   23:12 of his **m** more than my daily bread.
      40: 4 I put my hand over my **m**.
Ps   10: 7 His **m** is full of lies and threats;
      17: 3 my **m** has not transgressed.
      19:14 May these words of my **m** and this
      40: 3 He put a new song in my **m**, a hymn
      71: 8 My **m** is filled with your praise,
      78: 2 I will open my **m** with a parable;
     119:103 taste, sweeter than honey to my **m**!
     141: 3 Set a guard over my **m**, LORD;
Pr   2: 6 from his **m** come knowledge
       4:24 Keep your **m** free of perversity;
       8: 7 My **m** speaks what is true, for my
      10:11 The **m** of the righteous is a fountain
      10:31 the **m** of the righteous comes
      14: 3 A fool's **m** lashes out with pride,
      15: 2 but the **m** of the fool gushes folly.
      26:28 hurts, and a flattering **m** works ruin.
      27: 2 praise you, and not your own **m**;
Ecc   5: 2 Do not be quick with your **m**, do not
       6: 7 Everyone's toil is for their **m**,
SS   1: 2 kiss me with the kisses of his **m**—
       5:16 His **m** is sweetness itself;
Isa   29:13 come near to me with their **m**
      40: 5 the **m** of the LORD has spoken."
      45:23 my **m** has uttered in all integrity
      48: 3 my **m** announced them and I made
      49: 2 He made my **m** like a sharpened
      51:16 I have put my words in your **m**
      53: 7 afflicted, yet he did not open his **m**;
      55:11 my word that goes out from my **m**:
      59:21 I have put in your **m** will always be
Jer   1: 9 "I have put my words in your **m**.
Eze   3: 2 So I opened my **m**, and he gave me
Da   7: 8 being and a **m** that spoke boastfully.
Hos   6: 5 killed you with the words of my **m**—
Mal   2: 7 people seek instruction from his **m**.
Mt   4: 4 that comes from the **m** of God.' "
      12:34 the **m** speaks what the heart is full
      15:11 someone's **m** does not defile them,
            but what comes out of their **m**,

Lk   6:45 the **m** speaks what the heart is full
Ac   8:32 is silent, so he did not open his **m**.
Ro   10: 8 it is in your **m** and in your heart,"
      10: 9 If you declare with your **m**,
2Th   2: 8 overthrow with the breath of his **m**
Jas   3:10 Out of the same **m** come praise
1Pe   2:22 and no deceit was found in his **m**."
Rev   1:16 coming out of his **m** was a sharp,
       2:16 them with the sword of my **m**.
       3:16 I am about to spit you out of my **m**.
      10:10 It tasted as sweet as honey in my **m**,
      13: 6 It opened its **m** to blaspheme God,
      19:15 out of his **m** is a sharp sword

MOUTHS MOUTH

Ex   4:11 "Who gave human beings their **m**?
Ps   37:30 The **m** of the righteous utter
      73: 9 Their **m** lay claim to heaven,
      78:36 they would flatter him with their **m**,
     115: 5 They have **m**, but cannot speak,
     135:17 hear, nor is there breath in their **m**.
Pr   16:23 of the wise make their **m** prudent,
      18: 7 The **m** of fools are their undoing,
Isa   52:15 kings will shut their **m** because
Eze   33:31 Their **m** speak of love, but their
Da   6:22 and he shut the **m** of the lions.
Ro   3:14 "Their **m** are full of cursing
Eph   4:29 talk come out of your **m**, but only
Jas   3: 3 we put bits into the **m** of horses
Rev   9:17 and out of their **m** came fire,
      11: 5 fire comes from their **m** and devours
      14: 5 No lie was found in their **m**;

MOVE MOVED, MOVES

Ge   1:24 creatures that **m** along the ground,
Lev   11:29 the animals that **m** along the ground,
Nu   1:51 Whenever the tabernacle is to **m**,
Dt   19:14 Do not **m** your neighbor's boundary
Job   24: 2 are those who **m** boundary stones;
Pr   23:10 Do not **m** an ancient boundary stone
Isa   46: 7 From that spot it cannot **m**.
Mt   17:20 mountain, 'M from here to there,' and
            it will **m**.
Ac   17:28 'For in him we live and **m** and have
1Co   13: 2 I have a faith that can **m** mountains,
      15:58 Let nothing **m** you.
Col   1:23 do not **m** from the hope held

MOVED MOVE

Ge   7:21 Every living thing that **m** on land
Ex   35:21 and whose heart **m** them came
1Ki   3:26 whose son was alive was deeply **m**
1Ch   16:30 is firmly established; it cannot be **m**.
2Ch   33:19 and how God was **m** by his entreaty,
      36:22 the LORD **m** the heart of Cyrus
Ezr   1: 5 everyone whose heart God had **m**—
Isa   33:20 abode, a tent that will not be **m**;
Eze   1:19 When the living creatures **m**, the
            wheels beside them **m**;
Jn   11:33 he was deeply **m** in spirit

MOVES MOVE

Ge   9: 3 and **m** about will be food for you.
Lev   11:41 creature that **m** along the ground is
Dt   23:14 For the LORD your God **m**

Dt 27:17 is anyone who **m** their neighbor's

MUCH MORE, MOST

Ex 16:18 one who gathered **m** did not have
           too **m**,
     16:18 gathered just as **m** as they needed.
Dt 28:38 You will sow **m** seed in the field
1Ki 8:27 How **m** less this temple I have built!
Job 7:17 and gave him twice as **m** as he had
Ps 19:10 than gold, than **m** pure gold;
Pr 16:16 How **m** better to get wisdom than
     23:20 not join those who drink too **m** wine
Ecc 1:18 with **m** wisdom comes **m** sorrow;
     9:18 but one sinner destroys **m** good.
    12:12 end, and **m** study wearies the body.
Hag 1: 9 "You expected **m**, but see, it turned
Mt 6:26 Are you not **m** more valuable than
     23:15 you make them twice as **m** a child
Mk 9:12 that the Son of Man must suffer **m**
Lk 12:48 one who has been entrusted
          with **m**, **m** more will be asked.
     16:10 little will also be dishonest with **m**.
Jn 8:26 "I have **m** to say in judgment
     15: 5 and I in you, you will bear **m** fruit;
     16:12 "I have **m** more to say to you,
Ac 2:13 said, "They have had too **m** wine."
2Co 3:11 how **m** greater is the glory
     8:15 one who gathered **m** did not have
          too **m**,
1Ti 3: 8 not indulging in **m** wine, and not
Titus 2: 3 be slanderers or addicted to **m** wine,
Heb 1: 4 So he became as **m** superior
Rev 12:11 they did not love their lives so **m** as
     18: 7 Give her as **m** torment and grief as

HOW MUCH MORE See HOW

MUD MUDDIED

Ps 40: 2 the slimy pit, out of the **m** and mire;
Isa 57:20 whose waves cast up mire and **m**.
Jer 38: 6 and Jeremiah sank down into the **m**.
Jn 9: 6 made some **m** with the saliva,
2Pe 2:22 returns to her wallowing in the **m**."

MUDDIED* MUD

Pr 25:26 Like a **m** spring or a polluted well
Eze 32:13 of man or **m** by the hooves of cattle.
     34:19 drink what you have **m** with your

MULBERRY*

Lk 17: 6 seed, you can say to this **m** tree,

MULE

2Sa 18: 9 He was riding his **m**, and as the **m**
1Ki 1:38 Solomon mount King David's **m**,
Ps 32: 9 Do not be like the horse or the **m**,

MULTIPLIED MULTIPLY

Ex 1: 7 they **m** greatly,
     11: 9 my wonders may be **m** in Egypt."

MULTIPLIES MULTIPLY

Pr 27: 6 be trusted, but an enemy **m** kisses.

MULTIPLY MULTIPLIED, MULTIPLIES, MULTIPLYING

Ge 9: 7 **m** on the earth and increase
Ex 7: 3 heart, and though I **m** my signs
Lev 26:21 I will **m** your afflictions seven times
Ecc 10:14 and fools **m** words. No one knows

MULTIPLYING* MULTIPLY

Pr 10:19 Sin is not ended by **m** words,
Mk 4: 8 and produced a crop, some **m** thirty,

MULTITUDE MULTITUDES

Isa 31: 1 who trust in the **m** of their chariots
Da 10: 6 and his voice like the sound of a **m**.
Jas 5:20 death and cover over a **m** of sins.
1Pe 4: 8 because love covers over a **m**
Rev 7: 9 there before me was a great **m**
     19: 6 I heard what sounded like a great **m**,

MULTITUDES MULTITUDE

1Ki 22:19 throne with all the **m** of heaven
Ne 9: 6 and the **m** of heaven worship you.
Da 12: 2 **M** who sleep in the dust of the earth
Joel 3:14 **M**, **m** in the valley of decision!

MURDER MURDERED, MURDERER, MURDERERS, MURDEROUS, MURDERS

Ex 20:13 "You shall not **m**.
Nu 35:12 of **m** may not die before they stand
Dt 5:17 "You shall not **m**.
Hos 4: 2 lying and **m**, stealing and adultery;
Mt 5:21 'You shall not **m**, and anyone who
     15:19 **m**, adultery, sexual immorality,
Mk 10:19 'You shall not **m**, you shall not
Ro 1:29 They are full of envy, **m**, strife,
     13: 9 "You shall not **m**," "You shall not
Jas 2:11 also said, "You shall not **m**,"
1Jn 3:12 And why did he **m** him?

MURDERED MURDER

Jdg 9:18 You have **m** his seventy sons
Mt 23:31 of those who **m** the prophets.
Ac 7:52 now you have betrayed and **m** him—
1Jn 3:12 to the evil one and **m** his brother.

MURDERER MURDER

Nu 35:16 is a **m**; the **m** is to be put to death.
     35:31 accept a ransom for the life of a **m**,
Jn 8:44 He was a **m** from the beginning,
Ac 3:14 asked that a **m** be released to you.
1Jn 3:15 who hates a brother or sister is a **m**,
     3:15 that no **m** has eternal life residing

MURDERERS MURDER

1Ti 1: 9 kill their fathers or mothers, for **m**,
Rev 21: 8 vile, the **m**, the sexually immoral,
     22:15 the **m**, the idolaters and everyone

MURDEROUS* MURDER

Ac 9: 1 out **m** threats against the Lord's

MURDERS MURDER

Mt 5:21 anyone who **m** will be subject
Rev 9:21 Nor did they repent of their **m**,

MUSHI
Nu   3:20 The Merarite clans: Mahli and **M**.

MUSIC MUSICAL, MUSICIAN, MUSICIANS
Ge   31:27 and singing to the **m** of timbrels
1Ch   6:31 charge of the **m** in the house
       6:32 with **m** before the tabernacle,
        25: 6 their father for the **m** of the temple
        25: 7 and skilled in **m** for the LORD—
Ne   12:27 and with the **m** of cymbals,
Job 21:12 They sing to the **m** of timbrel
Ps   27: 6 sing and make **m** to the LORD.
       33: 2 make **m** to him on the ten-stringed
       45: 8 ivory the **m** of the strings makes you
       57: 7 I will sing and make **m**.
       81: 2 Begin the **m**, strike the timbrel,
       87: 7 As they make **m** they will sing,
       92: 1 LORD and make **m** to your name,
       92: 3 to the **m** of the ten-stringed lyre
       95: 2 and extol him with **m** and song.
       98: 4 burst into jubilant song with **m**;
       98: 5 make **m** to the LORD
      108: 1 sing and make **m** with all my soul.
      144: 9 the ten-stringed lyre I will make **m**
      147: 7 make **m** to our God on the harp.
      149: 3 and make **m** to him with timbrel
Isa   30:32 club will be to the **m** of timbrels
La   5:14 young men have stopped their **m**.
Eze 26:13 the **m** of your harps will be heard no
Da   3: 5 pipe and all kinds of **m**, you must
       3: 7 lyre, harp and all kinds of **m**,
       3:10 all kinds of **m** must fall down
       3:15 pipe and all kinds of **m**, if you are
Am   5:23 not listen to the **m** of your harps.
Lk   15:25 the house, he heard **m** and dancing.
Eph   5:19 make **m** from your heart to the Lord,
Rev   18:22 The **m** of harpists and musicians,

FOR THE DIRECTOR OF MUSIC Ps 4:T;
5:T; 6:T; 8:T; 9:T; 11:T; 12:T; 13:T; 14:T; 18:T;
19:T; 20:T; 21:T; 22:T; 31:T; 36:T; 39:T; 40:T; 41:T;
42:T; 44:T; 45:T; 46:T; 47:T; 49:T; 51:T; 52:T; 53:T;
54:T; 55:T; 56:T; 57:T; 58:T; 59:T; 60:T; 61:T; 62:T;
64:T; 65:T; 66:T; 67:T; 68:T; 69:T; 70:T; 75:T; 76:T;
77:T; 80:T; 81:T; 84:T; 85:T; 88:T; 109:T; 139:T;
140:T; Hab 3:19

MUSICAL* MUSIC
1Ch 15:16 a joyful sound with **m** instruments:
       23: 5 the **m** instruments I have provided
2Ch   7: 6 with the LORD's **m** instruments,
       34:12 skilled in playing **m** instruments—
Ne   12:36 with **m** instruments prescribed
Am   6: 5 and improvise on **m** instruments.

MUSICIAN* MUSIC
1Ch   6:33 Heman, the **m**, the son of Joel,

MUSICIANS MUSIC
1Ki 10:12 to make harps and lyres for the **m**.
1Ch   9:33 Those who were **m**, heads of Levite
       15:16 appoint their fellow Levites as **m**
       15:19 The **m** Heman, Asaph and Ethan
2Ch   5:12 All the Levites who were **m**—

2Ch   9:11 to make harps and lyres for the **m**.
       35:15 The **m**, the descendants of Asaph,
Ezr   2:70 the **m**, the gatekeepers
Ps   68:25 are the singers, after them the **m**;
Rev   18:22 The music of harpists and **m**,

MUST
Ge   2:17 you **m** not eat from the tree
       3: 1 'You **m** not eat from any tree
       4: 7 have you, but you **m** rule over it."
       9: 4 "But you **m** not eat meat that has its
       17:12 is eight days old **m** be circumcised,
Ex   22: 3 they **m** be sold to pay for their theft.
Dt   7: 2 then you **m** destroy them totally.
       13: 4 the LORD your God you **m** follow, and
              him you **m** revere.
       18:13 You **m** be blameless before
1Sa   26:16 you and your men **m** die,
2Sa   12: 5 lives, the man who did this **m** die!
Ps   119:84 How long **m** your servant wait?
Pr   19:19 A hot-tempered person **m** pay
Hos   12: 6 But you **m** return to your God;
Mt   16:21 that he **m** be killed and on the third
Mk   8:34 be my disciple **m** deny themselves
       10:17 "what **m** I do to inherit eternal
       13: 7 Such things **m** happen, but the end
       14:49 But the Scriptures **m** be fulfilled."
Lk   9:22 and he **m** be killed and on the third
Jn   3: 7 my saying, 'You **m** be born again.'
       3:14 so the Son of Man **m** be lifted up,
       4:24 and his worshipers **m** worship
       13:34 you, so you **m** love one another.
       15: 4 it **m** remain in the vine.
Ac   20:21 Greeks that they **m** turn to God
Ro   12: 9 Love **m** be sincere. Hate what is
1Co   7:10 A wife **m** not separate from her
       7:11 a husband **m** not divorce his wife.
2Co   5:10 we **m** all appear before the judgment
Eph   5:33 **m** love his wife as he loves himself,
              and the wife **m** respect her husband.
1Ti   3:12 A deacon **m** be faithful to his wife
              and **m** manage his children
Titus 1: 6 An elder **m** be blameless,
Heb   11: 6 anyone who comes to him **m** believe
Rev   4: 1 I will show you what **m** take place
       22: 6 the things that **m** soon take place."

MUST BE CUT OFF Ex 12:15, 19; 30:33, 38;
31:14; Lev 7:20, 21, 25, 27; 17:4, 9, 14; 18:29; 19:8;
22:3; 23:29; Nu 9:13; 15:30; 19:13, 20

MUST DIE Nu 15:35; Dt 22:22; 24:7; Jdg 6:30;
1Sa 14:39, 43; 20:31; 26:16; 2Sa 12:5; 14:14; Ecc
2:16; Jer 26:8; Zec 13:3; Jn 19:7; Rev 11:5

MUST NOT EAT Ge 2:17; 3:1, 3, 17; 9:4; Lev
3:17; 7:24, 26; 11:4, 8, 11; 17:14; 22:6, 8; 23:14;
Nu 6:4; Dt 12:16, 17, 23, 24; 15:23; Jdg 13:14; 1Ki
13:9, 17; Eze 44:31

MUST PURGE Dt 13:5; 17:7, 12; 19:13, 19;
21:21; 22:21, 22, 24; 24:7

MUST WASH Lev 6:27; 11:25, 28, 40, 40; 13:6,
34; 14:8, 9, 47; 15:5, 6, 7, 8, 10, 11, 13, 21, 22, 27;
16:26, 28; 17:15; Nu 19:7, 19

MUSTARD*
Mt   13:31 kingdom of heaven is like a **m** seed,
     17:20 you have faith as small as a **m** seed,
Mk   4:31 It is like a **m** seed, which is
Lk   13:19 It is like a **m** seed, which a man took
     17: 6 you have faith as small as a **m** seed,

MUSTER
Pr   24: 5 have knowledge **m** their strength.

MUTE
Ex   4:11 Who makes them deaf or **m**?
Isa 35: 6 and the **m** tongue shout for joy.
Mt   9:33 out, the man who had been **m** spoke.
Mk   7:37 the deaf hear and the **m** speak."
1Co 12: 2 influenced and led astray to **m** idols.

MUTILATORS*
Php   3: 2 those evildoers, those **m** of the flesh.

MUTTER
Isa   8:19 who whisper and **m**, should not

MUTUAL* MUTUALLY
Ro   14:19 leads to peace and to **m** edification.
1Co   7: 5 other except perhaps by **m** consent
2Pe   1: 7 and to godliness, **m** affection; and
          to **m** affection, love.

MUTUALLY* MUTUAL
Ro   1:12 and I may be **m** encouraged by each

MUZZLE*
Dt   25: 4 Do not **m** an ox while it is treading
Ps   39: 1 I will put a **m** on my mouth while
1Co   9: 9 "Do not **m** an ox while it is treading
1Ti   5:18 "Do not **m** an ox while it is treading

MYRRH
Ps   45: 8 All your robes are fragrant with **m**
SS   1.13 of **m** resting between my breasts.
Mt   2:11 gifts of gold, frankincense and **m**.
Mk   15:23 offered him wine mixed with **m**,
Jn   19:39 Nicodemus brought a mixture of **m**
Rev 18:13 of incense, **m** and frankincense,

MYRTLE
Isa 55:13 instead of briers the **m** will grow.
Zec   1: 8 He was standing among the **m** trees

MYSTERIES* MYSTERY
Job 11: 7 "Can you fathom the **m** of God?
Da   2:28 is a God in heaven who reveals **m**.
      2:29 of **m** showed you what is going
      2:47 Lord of kings and a revealer of **m**,
1Co   4: 1 with the **m** God has revealed.
     13: 2 can fathom all **m** and all knowledge,
     14: 2 they utter **m** by the Spirit.

MYSTERY* MYSTERIES
Da   2:18 God of heaven concerning this **m**,
      2:19 During the night the **m** was revealed
      2:27 the king the **m** he has asked about,
      2:30 me, this **m** has been revealed to me,
      2:47 for you were able to reveal this **m**."
      4: 9 and no **m** is too difficult for you.

Ro   11:25 want you to be ignorant of this **m**,
     16:25 the revelation of the **m** hidden
1Co   2: 7 a **m** that has been hidden
     15:51 Listen, I tell you a **m**: We will not
Eph   1: 9 to us the **m** of his will according
      3: 3 that is, the **m** made known to me
      3: 4 my insight into the **m** of Christ,
      3: 6 This **m** is that through the gospel
      3: 9 the administration of this **m**,
      5:32 This is a profound **m**—but I am
      6:19 I will fearlessly make known the **m**
Col   1:26 the **m** that has been kept hidden
      1:27 the glorious riches of this **m**,
      2: 2 that they may know the **m** of God,
      4: 3 we may proclaim the **m** of Christ,
1Ti   3:16 the **m** from which true godliness
Rev   1:20 The **m** of the seven stars that you
     10: 7 the **m** of God will be accomplished,
     17: 5 written on her forehead was a **m**:
     17: 7 explain to you the **m** of the woman

MYTHS*
1Ti   1: 4 or to devote themselves to **m**
      4: 7 Have nothing to do with godless **m**
2Ti   4: 4 from the truth and turn aside to **m**.
Titus 1:14 will pay no attention to Jewish **m**

N

NAAMAN
Aramean general whose leprosy was cleansed by Elisha (2Ki 5; Lk 4:27).

NABAL
Wealthy Carmelite the LORD killed for refusing to help David (1Sa 25). David married Abigail, his widow (1Sa 25.39–42).

NABOTH*
Jezreelite killed by Jezebel for his vineyard (1Ki 21). Ahab's family destroyed for this (1Ki 21:17–24; 2Ki 9:21–37).

NADAB
1. Firstborn of Aaron (Ex 6:23); killed with Abihu for offering unauthorized fire (Lev 10; Nu 3:4).
2. Son of Jeroboam I; king of Israel (1Ki 15:25–32).

NAGGING*
Jdg 16:16 With such **n** she prodded him day
Pr   21:19 than with a quarrelsome and **n** wife.

NAHASH
1Sa 11: 1 **N** the Ammonite went

NAHOR
Ge   11:26 the father of Abram, **N** and Haran.
     22:23 eight sons to Abraham's brother **N**.
     24:15 the wife of Abraham's brother **N**.

NAHUM
Prophet against Nineveh (Na 1:1).

NAIL* NAILING, NAILS
Jn 20:25 "Unless I see the **n** marks in his

NAILING* NAIL
Ac 2:23 him to death by **n** him to the cross.
Col 2:14 has taken it away, **n** it to the cross.

NAILS NAIL
Ecc 12:11 sayings like firmly embedded **n**—
Isa 41: 7 The other **n** down the idol so it will
Jn 20:25 and put my finger where the **n** were,

NAIOTH
1Sa 19:18 Samuel went to **N** and stayed there.

NAIVE*
Ro 16:18 they deceive the minds of **n** people.

NAKED NAKEDNESS
Ge 2:25 Adam and his wife were both **n**,
9:22 the father of Canaan, saw his father **n**
Job 1:21 "**N** I came from my mother's womb,
and **n** I will depart.
Ecc 5:15 Everyone comes **n** from their
Isa 58: 7 when you see the **n**, to clothe them,
Eze 16: 7 had grown, yet you were stark **n**.
16: 8 over you and covered your **n** body.
23:29 They will leave you stark **n**,
Mk 14:52 he fled **n**, leaving his garment
2Co 5: 3 are clothed, we will not be found **n**.
11:27 I have been cold and **n**.
Rev 3:17 wretched, pitiful, poor, blind and **n**.

NAKEDNESS NAKED
Ro 8:35 persecution or famine or **n** or danger
Rev 3:18 so you can cover your shameful **n**;

NAME NAME'S, NAMED, NAMES
Ge 2:19 man to see what he would **n** them;
4:26 to call on the **n** of the LORD.
11: 4 that we may make a **n** for ourselves;
12: 2 I will make your **n** great, and you
12: 8 and called on the **n** of the LORD.
13: 4 called on the **n** of the LORD.
16:13 She gave this **n** to the LORD who
17: 5 your **n** will be Abraham, for I have
17:15 call her Sarai; her **n** will be Sarah.
21:33 he called on the **n** of the LORD,
26:25 and called on the **n** of the LORD.
32:28 "Your **n** will no longer be Jacob,
32:29 Jacob said, "Please tell me your **n**."
Ex 3:15 "This is my **n** forever, the **n** you
6: 3 by my **n** the LORD I did not make
17:14 completely blot out the **n** of Amalek
20: 7 "You shall not misuse the **n**
33:17 with you and I know you by **n**."
33:19 you, and I will proclaim my **n**,
34: 5 with him and proclaimed his **n**,
34:14 for the LORD, whose **n** is Jealous,
Lev 19:12 " 'Do not swear falsely by my **n** and
so profane the **n** of your God.
24:11 Israelite woman blasphemed the **N**
Nu 1: 2 listing every man by **n**, one by one.
17: 2 Write the **n** of each man on his staff.

Dt 5:11 "You shall not misuse the **n**
10: 8 and to pronounce blessings in his **n**,
12:11 will choose as a dwelling for his **N**—
18: 5 minister in the LORD's **n** always.
25: 6 carry on the **n** of the dead brother so
28:58 this glorious and awesome **n**—
Jos 7: 9 and wipe out our **n** from the earth.
Jdg 13:17 "What is your **n**, so that we may
Ru 4: 5 order to maintain the **n** of the dead
1Sa 12:22 of his great **n** the LORD will not
17:45 in the **n** of the LORD Almighty,
25:25 He is just like his **n**—his **n** means
2Sa 6: 2 which is called by the **N**, the **n**
7: 9 Now I will make your **n** great,
1Ki 5: 5 will build the temple for my **N**.'
8:29 you said, 'My **N** shall be there,'
18:24 Then you call on the **n** of your god,
18:24 I will call on the **n** of the LORD.
1Ch 17: 8 I will make your **n** like the names
2Ch 7:14 people, who are called by my **n**,
Ezr 6:12 who has caused his **N** to dwell there,
Ne 9:10 You made a **n** for yourself,
Ps 5:11 those who love your **n** may rejoice
8: 1 how majestic is your **n** in all
9: 5 you have blotted out their **n** for ever
9:10 Those who know your **n** trust
20: 7 in the **n** of the LORD our God.
29: 2 to the LORD the glory due his **n**;
34: 3 let us exalt his **n** together.
44:20 If we had forgotten the **n** of our God
54: 1 Save me, O God, by your **n**;
66: 2 Sing the glory of his **n**;
68: 4 his **n** is the LORD.
74:10 Will the foe revile your **n** forever?
74:21 the poor and needy praise your **n**.
79: 9 our Savior, for the glory of your **n**;
96: 8 to the LORD the glory due his **n**;
103: 1 my inmost being, praise his holy **n**.
113: 1 praise the **n** of the LORD.
115: 1 not to us but to your **n** be the glory,
124: 8 Our help is in the **n** of the LORD,
138: 2 will praise your **n** for your unfailing
145: 1 I will praise your **n** for ever
147: 4 the stars and calls them each by **n**.
149: 3 Let them praise his **n** with dancing
Pr 3: 4 and a good **n** in the sight of God
10: 7 but the **n** of the wicked will rot.
18:10 The **n** of the LORD is a fortified
22: 1 A good **n** is more desirable than
30: 4 What is his **n**, and what is the **n**
Ecc 7: 1 A good **n** is better than
SS 1: 3 your **n** is like perfume poured out.
Isa 12: 4 and proclaim that his **n** is exalted.
26: 8 your **n** and renown are the desire
40:26 and calls forth each of them by **n**.
42: 8 "I am the LORD; that is my **n**!
50:10 trust in the **n** of the LORD and rely
56: 5 I will give them an everlasting **n**
57:15 who lives forever, whose **n** is holy:
63:14 to make for yourself a glorious **n**.
Jer 7:11 which bears my **N**, become a den
10: 6 and your **n** is mighty in power.
14: 7 LORD, for the sake of your **n**.

Jer 15:16 for I bear your **n**, LORD God
27:15 'They are prophesying lies in my **n**.
Eze 20: 9 it to keep my **n** from being profaned
20:14 of my **n** I did what would keep it
20:22 of my **n** I did what would keep it
36:22 but for the sake of my holy **n**,
48:35 the **n** of the city from that time
Da 2:20 "Praise be to the **n** of God for ever
12: 1 everyone whose **n** is found written
Hos 12: 5 God Almighty, the LORD is his **n**!
Joel 2:32 the **n** of the LORD will be saved;
Am 9:12 and all the nations that bear my **n**,"
Mic 5: 4 of the **n** of the LORD his God.
6: 9 and to fear your **n** is wisdom—
Zep 3: 9 may call on the **n** of the LORD
Zec 6:12 is the man whose **n** is the Branch,
13: 9 They will call on my **n** and I will
14: 9 one LORD, and his **n** the only **n**.
Mal 1: 6 who show contempt for my **n**.
4: 2 But for you who revere my **n**,
Mt 1:21 and you are to give him the **n** Jesus,
6: 9 in heaven, hallowed be your **n**,
7:22 did we not prophesy in your **n** and in
your **n** drive out demons
12:21 In his **n** the nations will put their
18:20 where two or three gather in my **n**,
24: 5 For many will come in my **n**,
28:19 baptizing them in the **n** of the Father
Mk 9:41 water in my **n** because you belong
11: 9 who comes in the **n** of the Lord!"
Lk 11: 2 hallowed be your **n**, your kingdom
19:38 who comes in the **n** of the Lord!"
Jn 1:12 to those who believed in his **n**,
5:43 I have come in my Father's **n**,
10: 3 He calls his own sheep by **n**
12:28 Father, glorify your **n**!"
14:13 I will do whatever you ask in my **n**,
15:16 in my **n** the Father will give you.
16:23 give you whatever you ask in my **n**.
16:24 not asked for anything in my **n**.
17:11 power of your **n**, the **n** you gave me,
20:31 believing you may have life in his **n**.
Ac 2:21 on the **n** of the Lord will be saved.'
3:16 By faith in the **n** of Jesus, this man
4:12 is no other **n** under heaven given
4:17 no longer to anyone in this **n**."
5:40 them not to speak in the **n** of Jesus,
15:17 all the Gentiles who bear my **n**,
Ro 10:13 on the **n** of the Lord will be saved."
1Co 6:11 in the **n** of the Lord Jesus Christ
Eph 1:21 and every **n** that is invoked, not only
3:15 in heaven and on earth derives its **n**.
Php 2: 9 gave him the **n** that is above every **n**,
2:10 at the **n** of Jesus every knee should
Col 3:17 do it all in the **n** of the Lord Jesus,
2Ti 2:19 "Everyone who confesses the **n**
Heb 1: 4 the angels as the **n** he has inherited
13:15 of lips that openly profess his **n**.
Jas 5:14 them with oil in the **n** of the Lord.
1Pe 4:16 but praise God that you bear that **n**.
1Jn 2:12 been forgiven on account of his **n**.
3:23 to believe in the **n** of his Son,
5:13 you who believe in the **n** of the Son

Rev 2: 3 have endured hardships for my **n**,
2:13 Yet you remain true to my **n**.
2:17 stone with a new **n** written on it,
3: 5 I will never blot out the **n** of that
3: 5 acknowledge that **n** before my Father
3: 8 my word and have not denied my **n**.
3:12 will write on them the **n** of my God
3:12 I will also write on them my new **n**.
11:18 and your people who revere your **n**,
13: 1 and on each head a blasphemous **n**.
13:17 which is the **n** of the beast or the
number of its **n**.
14: 1 144,000 who had his **n** and his
Father's **n** written on their
16: 9 heat and they cursed the **n** of God,
17: 5 The **n** written on her forehead was a
mystery:
19:12 He has a **n** written on him that no
19:13 blood, and his **n** is the Word of God.
19:16 on his thigh he has this **n** written:
20:15 whose **n** was not found written
22: 4 and his **n** will be on their foreheads.

HOLY NAME See HOLY

NAME OF JESUS Ac 2:38; 3:6, 16; 4:10, 18;
5:40; 8:12; 9:27; 10:48; 16:18; 19:13; 26:9; Php 2:10

NAME OF THE LORD Mt 21:9; 23:39; Mk
11:9; Lk 13:35; 19:38; Jn 12:13; Ac 2:21; 8:16; 9:28;
19:5, 13, 17; 21:13; Ro 10:13; 1Co 6:11; Col 3:17;
2Th 3:6; 2Ti 2:19; Jas 5:10, 14

NAME OF THE LORD† Ge 4.26; 12:8; 13:4;
21:33; 26:25; Ex 20:7; Lev 24:11, 16; Dt 5:11; 18:7,
22; 21:5; 28:10; 32:3; 1Sa 17:45; 20:42; 2Sa 6:2, 18;
1Ki 3:2; 5:3, 5; 8:17, 20; 18:24, 32; 22:16; 2Ki 2:24;
5:11; 1Ch 16:2; 21:19; 22:7, 19; 2Ch 2:1, 4; 6:7, 10;
18:15; 33:18; Job 1:21; Ps 7:17; 20:7; 102:15, 21;
113:1, 2, 3; 116:4, 13, 17; 118:10, 11, 12, 26; 122:4;
124:8; 129:8; 135:1; 148:5, 13; Pr 18:10; Isa 18:7;
24:15; 30:27; 48:1; 50:10; 56:6; 59:19; Jer 3:17;
11:21; 26:16, 20; 44:16; Joel 2:26, 32; Am 6:10; Mic
4:5; 5:4; Zep 3:9, 12

NAME'S NAME

Ps 23: 3 along the right paths for his **n** sake.
79: 9 and forgive our sins for your **n** sake.
106: 8 Yet he saved them for his **n** sake,
Eze 20:44 when I deal with you for my **n** sake

NAMED NAME

Ge 3:20 Adam **n** his wife Eve, because she
5: 2 he **n** them "Mankind" when they
were
5:29 He **n** him Noah and said, "He will
27:36 said, "Isn't he rightly **n** Jacob?
Ex 2:10 She **n** him Moses, saying, "I drew
1Sa 4:21 She **n** the boy Ichabod, saying,
7:12 He **n** it Ebenezer, saying, "Thus far
Lk 2:21 he was **n** Jesus, the name the angel

NAMES NAME

Ge 2:20 So the man gave **n** to all
Ex 28: 9 engrave on them the **n** of the sons
Dt 7:24 wipe out their **n** from under heaven.

2Sa   7: 9 like the **n** of the greatest men
Hos   2:17 I will remove the **n** of the Baals
Mt   10: 2 These are the **n** of the twelve
Lk   10:20 but rejoice that your **n** are written
Php   4: 3 whose **n** are in the book of life.
Heb 12:23 whose **n** are written in heaven.
Rev 17: 3 was covered with blasphemous **n**
      17: 8 of the earth whose **n** have not been
      21:12 the gates were written the **n**
      21:14 on them were the **n** of the twelve
      21:27 only those whose **n** are written

NAOMI
Wife of Elimelech, mother-in-law of Ruth (Ru 1:2, 4). Left Bethlehem for Moab during famine (Ru 1:1). Returned a widow, with Ruth (Ru 1:6–22). Advised Ruth to seek marriage with Boaz (Ru 2:17—3:4). Cared for Ruth's son Obed (Ru 4:13–17).

NAPHTALI NAPHTALITES
Son of Jacob by Bilhah (Ge 30:8; 35:25; 1Ch 2:2). Tribe of blessed (Ge 49:21; Dt 33:23), numbered (Nu 1:43; 26:50), allotted land (Jos 19:32–39; Eze 48:3), failed to fully possess (Jdg 1:33), supported Deborah (Jdg 4:10; 5:18), David (1Ch 12:34), 12,000 from (Rev 7:6).

NAPHTALITES* NAPHTALI
Jdg   1:33 the **N** too lived among the Canaanite

NARD
Jn   12: 3 Mary took about a pint of pure **n**,

NARROW
Nu   22:24 in a **n** path through the vineyards,
Mt   7:13 "Enter through the **n** gate.
Lk   13:24 effort to enter through the **n** door,

NATHAN
Prophet and chronicler of Israel's history (1Ch 29:29; 2Ch 9:29). Announced the Davidic covenant (2Sa 7; 1Ch 17). Denounced David's sin with Bathsheba (2Sa 12). Supported Solomon (1Ki 1).

NATHANAEL*
Apostle (Jn 1:45–49; 21:2). Probably also called Bartholomew (Mt 10:3).

NATION NATIONAL,
NATIONALITY, NATIONS
Ge   12: 2 "I will make you into a great **n**,
      15:14 But I will punish the **n** they serve as
      35:11 A **n** and a community of nations
Ex   19: 6 a kingdom of priests and a holy **n**.'
      32:10 I will make you into a great **n**."
Nu   14:12 I will make you into a **n** greater
Dt   4: 7 What other **n** is so great as to have
Jos   4: 1 the whole **n** had finished crossing
       5: 8 the whole **n** had been circumcised,
2Sa   7:23 the one **n** on earth that God went
2Ki 18:33 god of any **n** ever delivered his land
1Ch 16:20 they wandered from **n** to **n**,
Ps   33:12 Blessed is the **n** whose God is
     147:20 He has done this for no other **n**;
Pr   11:14 For lack of guidance a **n** falls,

Pr   14:34 Righteousness exalts a **n**, but sin
Isa   2: 4 **N** will not take up sword against **n**,
       9: 3 You have enlarged the **n**
      26: 2 gates that the righteous **n** may enter,
             the **n** that keeps faith.
      60:12 For the **n** or kingdom that will not
      65: 1 To a **n** that did not call on my name,
      66: 8 a **n** be brought forth in a moment?
Jer   2:11 Has a **n** ever changed its gods?
      18: 8 if that **n** I warned repents of its evil,
Eze 37:22 I will make them one **n** in the land,
Mic   4: 3 **N** will not take up sword against **n**,
Mal   3: 9 your whole **n**—because you are
Mt   24: 7 **N** will rise against **n**, and kingdom
Jn   11:50 than that the whole **n** perish."
1Pe   2: 9 a holy **n**, God's special possession,
Rev   5: 9 and language and people and **n**.
       7: 9 could count, from every **n**, tribe,
      14: 6 to every **n**, tribe,

NATIONAL* NATION
2Ki 17:29 each **n** group made its own gods

NATIONALITY NATION
Est   2:10 Esther had not revealed her **n**

NATIONS NATION
Ge   17: 4 You will be the father of many **n**.
      18:18 and all **n** on earth will be blessed
      22:18 through your offspring all **n** on earth
Ex   19: 5 out of all **n** you will be my treasured
      34:24 I will drive out **n** before you
Lev 18:28 out the **n** that were before you.
      20:26 you apart from the **n** to be my own.
Dt   7: 1 seven **n** larger and stronger than
      15: 6 and you will lend to many **n** but will
      15: 6 You will rule over many **n** but none
      32:43 Rejoice, you **n**, with his people,
Jos 23: 7 with these **n** that remain among you;
Jdg   3: 1 These are the **n** the Lᴏʀᴅ left
1Sa   8:20 Then we will be like all the other **n**,
1Ki   4:34 From all **n** people came to listen
2Ki 17:15 They imitated the **n** around them
2Ch 20: 6 rule over all the kingdoms of the **n**.
Ne   1: 8 I will scatter you among the **n**,
Ps   2: 1 Why do the **n** conspire
       2: 8 I will make the **n** your inheritance,
       9: 5 You have rebuked the **n**
      22:28 the Lᴏʀᴅ and he rules over the **n**.
      33:10 The Lᴏʀᴅ foils the plans of the **n**;
      46:10 I will be exalted among the **n**, I will
      47: 8 God reigns over the **n**; God is seated
      66: 7 by his power, his eyes watch the **n**—
      67: 2 earth, your salvation among all **n**.
      68:30 Scatter the **n** who delight in war.
      72:17 all **n** will be blessed through him,
      96: 5 For all the gods of the **n** are idols,
      99: 2 he is exalted over all the **n**.
     106:35 they mingled with the **n** and adopted
     110: 6 He will judge the **n**,
     113: 4 Lᴏʀᴅ is exalted over all the **n**,
Isa   2: 2 the hills, and all **n** will stream to it.
       5:26 lifts up a banner for the distant **n**,
      11:10 the **n** will rally to him, and his

Isa 12: 4 known among the **n** what he has
40:15 Surely the **n** are like a drop
42: 1 and he will bring justice to the **n**.
49:22 I will beckon to the **n**, I will lift
51: 4 justice will become a light to the **n**.
52:15 so he will sprinkle many **n**,
56: 7 called a house of prayer for all **n**."
60: 3 **N** will come to your light, and kings
66:18 and gather the people of all **n**
Jer 1: 5 you as a prophet to the **n**."
3:17 and all **n** will gather in Jerusalem
31:10 the word of the LORD, you **n**;
33: 9 honor before all **n** on earth that hear
46:28 completely destroy all the **n** among
La 1: 1 who once was great among the **n**!
Eze 22: 4 make you an object of scorn to the **n**
34:13 I will bring them out from the **n**
36:23 Then the **n** will know that I am
37:22 they will never again be two **n** or be
39:21 will display my glory among the **n**,
Hos 7: 8 "Ephraim mixes with the **n**;
Joel 2:17 of scorn, a byword among the **n**.
3: 2 scattered my people among the **n**
Am 9:12 and all the **n** that bear my name,"
Ob 1:15 day of the LORD is near for all **n**.
Zep 3: 8 I have decided to assemble the **n**,
Hag 2: 7 what is desired by all **n** will come,
Zec 8:13 have been a curse among the **n**, so I
8:23 **n** will take firm hold of one Jew
9:10 He will proclaim peace to the **n**.
14: 2 I will gather all the **n** to Jerusalem
Mal 1:11 My name will be great among the **n**,
3:12 all the **n** will call you blessed,
Mt 12:18 and he will proclaim justice to the **n**.
24: 9 you will be hated by all **n** because
24:14 whole world as a testimony to all **n**,
25:32 All the **n** will be gathered before
28:19 go and make disciples of all **n**,
Mk 11:17 called a house of prayer for all **n**'?
Ac 4:25 " 'Why do the **n** rage
17:26 From one man he made all the **n**,
Ro 4:18 and so became the father of many **n**,
15:12 who will arise to rule over the **n**;
Gal 3: 8 "All **n** will be blessed through
1Ti 3:16 was preached among the **n**,
Rev 2:26 I will give authority over the **n**—
12: 5 who "will rule all the **n** with an iron
15: 3 true are your ways, King of the **n**.
15: 4 All **n** will come and worship before
18:23 magic spell all the **n** were led astray.
19:15 with which to strike down the **n**.
20: 8 to deceive the **n** in the four corners
21:24 The **n** will walk by its light,
22: 2 the tree are for the healing of the **n**.

NATIVE NATIVE-BORN
Jn 8:44 he speaks his **n** language, for he is
Ac 2: 8 of us hears them in our **n** language?

NATIVE-BORN BEAR, NATIVE
Ex 12:49 The same law applies both to the **n**

NATURAL NATURE
Nu 16:29 If these men die a **n** death and suffer

Jn 1:13 children born not of **n** descent,
Ro 1:26 their women exchanged **n** sexual
11:21 if God did not spare the **n** branches,
1Co 15:44 it is sown a **n** body, it is raised

NATURE NATURAL; for SINFUL NATURE see also FLESH
Ro 1:20 his eternal power and divine **n**—
7:18 dwell in me, that is, in my sinful **n**.
7:25 in my sinful **n** a slave to the law
Eph 2: 3 we were by **n** deserving of wrath.
Php 2: 6 Who, being in very **n** God, did not
Col 3: 5 whatever belongs to your earthly **n**:
2Pe 1: 4 you may participate in the divine **n**,

NAZARENE* NAZARETH
Mt 2:23 that he would be called a **N**.
Mk 14:67 "You also were with that **N**,
16: 6 "You are looking for Jesus the **N**,
Ac 24: 5 He is a ringleader of the **N** sect

NAZARETH NAZARENE
Mt 2:23 went and lived in a town called **N**.
Mk 1:24 do you want with us, Jesus of **N**?
Lk 1:26 God sent the angel Gabriel to **N**,
4:16 He went to **N**, where he had been
Jn 1:46 "**N**! Can anything good come
19:19 It read: JESUS OF **N** THE KING
Ac 2:22 Jesus of **N** was a man accredited
10:38 how God anointed Jesus of **N**

JESUS OF NAZARETH See JESUS

NAZIRITE NAZIRITES
Nu 6: 2 of dedication to the LORD as a **N**,
Jdg 13: 5 a razor because the boy is to be a **N**,

NAZIRITES NAZIRITE
Am 2:12 you made the **N** drink wine

NEAR NEARBY, NEARER, NEARSIGHTED
Dt 4: 7 have their gods **n** them the way our
God is **n** us whenever we pray
30:14 No, the word is very **n** you; it is
Ps 69:18 Come **n** and rescue me;
73:28 as for me, it is good to be **n** God.
85: 9 his salvation is **n** those who fear
145:18 The LORD is **n** to all who call
Isa 11: 8 infant will play **n** the cobra's den,
55: 6 call on him while he is **n**.
Eze 7: 7 The day is **n**! There is panic,
Joel 1:15 For the day of the LORD is **n**;
Zep 1: 7 for the day of the LORD is **n**.
Mk 1:15 "The kingdom of God has come **n**.
Lk 10: 9 of God has come **n** to you.'
21:28 your redemption is drawing **n**."
Ro 10: 8 "The word is **n** you; it is in your
1Co 10: 8 food does not bring us **n** to God;
Php 4: 5 be evident to all. The Lord is **n**.
Heb 10:22 let us draw **n** to God with a sincere
Jas 4: 8 Come **n** to God and he will come **n**
1Pe 4: 7 The end of all things is **n**.
Rev 1: 3 written in it, because the time is **n**.
22:10 of this scroll, because the time is **n**.

NEARBY NEAR
Jer   23:23 "Am I only a God **n**,"

NEARER* NEAR
Ro   13:11 because our salvation is **n** now than

NEARSIGHTED* NEAR, SEE
2Pe   1: 9 whoever does not have them is **n**

NEBO
Dt   34: 1 Moses climbed Mount **N**
Isa   46: 1 Bel bows down, **N** stoops low;

NEBUCHADNEZZAR
Babylonian king. Subdued and exiled Judah (2Ki 24–25; 2Ch 36; Jer 39). Dreams interpreted by Daniel (Da 2; 4). Worshiped God (Da 3:28–29; 4:34–37).

NEBUZARADAN
2Ki   25: 8 **N** commander of the imperial guard,
Jer   52:12 **N** commander of the imperial guard,

NECESSARY*
Ac   1:21 Therefore it is **n** to choose one
Ro   13: 5 it is **n** to submit to the authorities,
2Co   9: 5 So I thought it **n** to urge the brothers
Php   1:24 it is more **n** for you that I remain
       2:25 I think it is **n** to send back to you
Heb   8: 3 and so it was **n** for this one
       9:16 it is **n** to prove the death of the one
       9:23 It was **n**, then, for the copies
       10:18 sacrifice for sin is no longer **n**.

NECHO
Pharaoh who killed Josiah (2Ki 23:29–30; 2Ch 35:20–22), deposed Jehoahaz (2Ki 23:33–35; 2Ch 36:3–4).

NECK NECKS, STIFF-NECKED
Ge   27:16 part of his **n** with the goatskins.
Pr   1: 9 head and a chain to adorn your **n**.
       3:22 you, an ornament to grace your **n**.
       6:21 fasten them around your **n**.
SS   7: 4 Your **n** is like an ivory tower.
Jer   28:10 Hananiah took the yoke off the **n**
Hos   10:11 so I will put a yoke on her fair **n**.
Mt   18: 6 large millstone hung around their **n**

NECKS NECK
Isa   3:16 walking along with outstretched **n**,

NEED NEEDED, NEEDS, NEEDY
Ex   14:14 you **n** only to be still."
       16:16 is to gather as much as they **n**.
Dt   15: 8 freely lend them whatever they **n**.
1Ki   8:59 Israel according to each day's **n**,
Job   34:23 God has no **n** to examine people
Ps   50: 9 I have no **n** of a bull from your stall
       79: 8 meet us, for we are in desperate **n**.
       142: 6 to my cry, for I am in desperate **n**;
Mt   3:14 saying, "I **n** to be baptized by you,
       6: 8 knows what you **n** before you ask
Mk   2:17 is not the healthy who **n** a doctor,
Lk   12:30 your Father knows that you **n** them.
       15:14 country, and he began to be in **n**.

Jn   2:25 He did not **n** any testimony
       13:10 "Those who have had a bath **n** only
Ac   2:45 to give to anyone who had **n**.
       4:35 distributed to anyone who had **n**.
Ro   12:13 with the Lord's people who are in **n**.
1Co   12:21 say to the hand, "I don't **n** you!"
2Co   8:14 your plenty will supply what they **n**,
Eph   4:28 something to share with those in **n**.
1Th   5: 1 dates we do not **n** to write to you,
1Ti   5: 3 to those widows who are really in **n**.
2Ti   2:15 a worker who does not **n** to be
Heb   4:16 grace to help us in our time of **n**.
       7:26 a high priest truly meets our **n**—
2Pe   1: 3 power has given us everything we **n**
1Jn   2:27 you do not **n** anyone to teach you.
       3:17 sister in **n** but has no pity on them,
Rev   21:23 The city does not **n** the sun
       22: 5 They will not **n** the light of a lamp

NEEDED NEED
Ex   16:18 had gathered just as much as they **n**.
Mt   25:36 I **n** clothes and you clothed me,
Ac   17:25 human hands, as if he **n** anything.

NEEDLE
Lk   18:25 to go through the eye of a **n** than

NEEDS NEED
Pr   12:10 care for the **n** of their animals,
Isa   58:11 he will satisfy your **n**
Mk   15:41 followed him and cared for his **n**.
Eph   4:29 others up according to their **n**, that it
Php   2:25 whom you sent to take care of my **n**.
       4:19 God will meet all your **n** according
Titus   3:14 in order to provide for urgent **n**
Jas   2:16 does nothing about their physical **n**,

NEEDY NEED
Ex   22:25 of my people among you who is **n**,
Dt   15:11 who are poor and **n** in your land.
1Sa   2: 8 and lifts the **n** from the ash heap;
Job   29:16 I was a father to the **n**; I took
Ps   9:18 But God will never forget the **n**;
       35:10 and **n** from those who rob them."
       69:33 The LORD hears the **n** and does
       70: 5 But as for me, I am poor and **n**;
       72:12 he will deliver the **n** who cry out,
       74:21 the poor and **n** praise your name.
       113: 7 and lifts the **n** from the ash heap;
       140:12 poor and upholds the cause of the **n**.
Pr   14:21 is the one who is kind to the **n**.
       14:31 is kind to the **n** honors God.
       22:22 poor and do not crush the **n** in court,
       31: 9 defend the rights of the poor and **n**.
       31:20 poor and extends her hands to the **n**.
Isa   11: 4 righteousness he will judge the **n**,
Am   8: 4 you who trample the **n** and do away
Mt   6: 2 "So when you give to the **n**, do not

NEGEV
Ge   13: 1 went up from Egypt to the **N**,
       24:62 Roi, for he was living in the **N**.
Jos   11:16 all the **N**, the whole region
Ps   126: 4 LORD, like streams in the **N**.

NEGLECT* NEGLECTED

Dt   12:19 to **n** the Levites as long as you live
     14:27 do not **n** the Levites living in your
Ezr   4:22 Be careful not to to **n** this matter.
Ne   10:39 "We will not **n** the house of our
Est   6:10 Do not **n** anything you have
Ps 119:16 I will not **n** your word.
SS   1: 6 my own vineyard I had to **n**.
Lk   11:42 but you **n** justice and the love
Ac   6: 2 for us to **n** the ministry of the word
1Ti   4:14 Do not **n** your gift, which was given

NEGLECTED* NEGLECT

Ne   13:11 "Why is the house of God **n**?"
Mt   23:23 But you have **n** the more important

NEHEMIAH

Cupbearer of Artaxerxes (Ne 2:1); governor of Israel (Ne 8:9). Returned to Jerusalem to rebuild walls (Ne 2–6). With Ezra, reestablished worship (Ne 8). Prayer confessing nation's sin (Ne 9). Dedicated wall (Ne 12).

NEHUSHTAN*

2Ki 18: 4 incense to it. (It was called **N**.)

NEIGHBOR NEIGHBOR'S, NEIGHBORS

Ex   20:16 give false testimony against your **n**.
     20:17 or anything that belongs to your **n**."
Lev 19:13 " 'Do not defraud or rob your **n**.
     19:17 Rebuke your **n** frankly so you will
     19:18 people, but love your **n** as yourself.
Dt   4:42 killed a **n** without malice
      5:20 give false testimony against your **n**.
     19:11 assaults and kills a **n**, and then flees
2Ch   6:22 "When anyone wrongs their **n**
Ps   15: 3 who does no wrong to a **n**,
Pr   3:29 Do not plot harm against your **n**,
     11:12 derides their **n** has no sense,
     14:21 It is a sin to despise one's **n**,
     16:29 A violent person entices their **n**
     24:28 against your **n** without cause—
     25:18 gives false testimony against a **n**.
     27:10 better a **n** nearby than a relative far
     27:14 anyone loudly blesses their **n** early
Isa 19: 2 fight against brother, **n** against **n**,
Jer 31:34 No longer will they teach their **n**,
Mt   5:43 'Love your **n** and hate your enemy.'
     19:19 and 'love your **n** as yourself.' "
Mk   12:31 'Love your **n** as yourself.'
Lk   10:27 and, 'Love your **n** as yourself.' "
     10:29 asked Jesus, "And who is my **n**?"
Ro   13: 9 "Love your **n** as yourself."
     13:10 Love does no harm to a **n**.
Gal   5:14 "Love your **n** as yourself."
Eph   4:25 and speak truthfully to your **n**,
Heb   8:11 No longer will they teach their **n**,
Jas   2: 8 "Love your **n** as yourself," you are

LOVE YOUR NEIGHBOR See LOVE

NEIGHBOR'S NEIGHBOR

Ex   20:17 "You shall not covet your **n** house.
     20:17 You shall not covet your **n** wife,

Ex   22:26 If you take your **n** cloak as a pledge,
Lev 19:16 anything that endangers your **n** life.
Dt   5:21 "You shall not covet your **n** wife.
      5:21 not set your desire on your **n** house
     19:14 not move your **n** boundary stone set
     27:17 moves their **n** boundary stone."
Pr   25:17 Seldom set foot in your **n** house—

NEIGHBORS NEIGHBOR

Ex   11: 2 alike are to ask their **n** for articles
1Sa 15:28 and has given it to one of your **n**—
2Ki   4: 3 and ask all your **n** for empty jars.
Ezr   1: 6 All their **n** assisted them
      6:21 practices of their Gentile **n** in order
Ps   79: 4 We are objects of contempt to our **n**,
     79:12 our **n** seven times the contempt they
Pr   29: 5 who flatter their **n** are spreading
Ro   15: 2 of us should please our **n** for their

NEPHEW*

Ge   12: 5 He took his wife Sarai, his **n** Lot,
     14:12 carried off Abram's **n** Lot and his

NEST NESTED, NESTING, NESTS

Dt   22: 6 across a bird's **n** beside the road,
Isa 11: 8 will put its hand into the viper's **n**.
Ob   1: 4 and make your **n** among the stars,
Hab   2: 9 setting his **n** on high to escape

NESTED* NEST

Eze 31: 6 the birds of the sky **n** in its boughs,

NESTING* NEST

Da   4:21 having **n** places in its branches

NESTS NEST

Mt   8:20 "Foxes have dens and birds have **n**,

NET NETS

Ps   35: 8 may the **n** they hid entangle them,
Pr   1:17 spread a **n** where every bird can see
La   1:13 He spread a **n** for my feet
Hab   1:15 he catches them in his **n**, he gathers
Mt   13:47 heaven is like a **n** that was let down
Mk   1:16 his brother Andrew casting a **n**
Jn   21: 6 were unable to haul the **n** in because

NETS NET

Ps 141:10 Let the wicked fall into their own **n**,
Mt   4:20 At once they left their **n**
Lk   5: 4 and let down the **n** for a catch."

NEVER

Ge   8:21 And **n** again will I destroy all living
Dt   9: 7 **n** forget how you aroused the anger
     31: 6 he will **n** leave you nor forsake
Jdg   1:28 but **n** drove them out completely.
2Sa   7:15 my love will **n** be taken away
1Ki   2: 4 you will **n** fail to have a successor
      8:25 'You shall **n** fail to have a successor
      9: 5 'You shall **n** fail to have a successor
2Ch 18: 7 because he **n** prophesies anything
Ps   9:18 But God will **n** forget the needy;
     14: 4 they **n** call on the LORD.
     30: 6 secure, I said, "I will **n** be shaken."
     89:28 my covenant with him will **n** fail.

Ps   95:11 'They shall **n** enter my rest.' "
Pr   3: 3 love and faithfulness **n** leave you;
      13: 4 A sluggard's appetite is **n** filled,
      30:15 are three things that are **n** satisfied,
            four that **n** say, 'Enough!':
Ecc   1: 8 The eye **n** has enough of seeing,
       5:10 loves money **n** has enough; whoever
            loves wealth is **n** satisfied
Isa   6: 9 ever hearing, but **n** understanding;
      28:16 who relies on it will **n** be stricken
      51: 6 my righteousness will **n** fail.
Jer   33:17 'David will **n** fail to have a man
La   3:22 for his compassions **n** fail.
Da   2:44 a kingdom that will **n** be destroyed,
       6:26 destroyed, his dominion will **n** end.
Hos   14: 3 We will **n** again say 'Our gods'
Mk   3:29 the Holy Spirit will **n** be forgiven;
       4:12 be ever seeing but **n** perceiving,
Lk   21:33 but my words will **n** pass away.
Jn   4:14 the water I give them will **n** thirst.
       6:35 comes to me will **n** go hungry,
       8:51 obeys my word will **n** see death."
      10:28 eternal life, and they shall **n** perish;
      11:26 lives by believing in me will **n** die.
Ro   9:33 who believes in him will **n** be put
1Co   13: 8 Love **n** fails. But where there are
Gal   6:14 May I **n** boast except in the cross
2Th   3:13 sisters, **n** tire of doing what is good.
Heb   3:11 'They shall **n** enter my rest.' "
       4: 3 'They shall **n** enter my rest.' "
      13: 5 God has said, "**N** will I leave you;
1Pe   1: 4 into an inheritance that can **n** perish,
       2: 6 one who trusts in him will **n** be put
       5: 4 of glory that will **n** fade away.
2Pe   1:10 do these things, you will **n** stumble,
Rev   7:16 'N again will they hunger; **n** again

NEVER-FAILING*

Am   5:24 river, righteousness like a **n** stream!

NEW

Ex   1: 8 Then a **n** king, to whom Joseph
Jdg   5: 8 God chose **n** leaders when war came
Ezr   9: 9 He has granted us **n** life to rebuild
Ne   13: 5 **n** wine and olive oil prescribed
Ps   33: 3 Sing to him a **n** song;
      40: 3 He put a **n** song in my mouth,
      98: 1 Sing to the Lord a **n** song, for he
Pr   3:10 vats will brim over with **n** wine.
Ecc   1: 9 there is nothing **n** under the sun.
Isa   42: 9 taken place, and **n** things I declare;
      42:10 Sing to the Lord a **n** song,
      43:19 See, I am doing a **n** thing!
      62: 2 you will be called by a **n** name
      65:17 create **n** heavens and a **n** earth.
      66:22 the **n** heavens and the **n** earth
Jer   31:31 I will make a **n** covenant
La   3:23 They are **n** every morning;
Eze   11:19 heart and put a **n** spirit in them;
      18:31 and get a **n** heart and a **n** spirit.
      36:26 I will give you a **n** heart and put a
            n spirit in you;
Joel   3:18 day the mountains will drip **n** wine,
Am   9:13 **N** wine will drip from the mountains

Zep   3: 5 and every **n** day he does not fail,
Mt   9:17 they pour **n** wine into **n** wineskins,
      13:52 his storeroom **n** treasures as well as
Mk   1:27 A **n** teaching—and with authority!
Lk   5:39 after drinking old wine wants the **n**,
      22:20 "This cup is the **n** covenant in my
Jn   13:34 "A **n** command I give you:
Ac   5:20 tell the people all about this **n** life."
      17:19 we know what this **n** teaching is
Ro   6: 4 the Father, we too may live a **n** life.
1Co   5: 7 you may be a **n** unleavened batch—
      11:25 "This cup is the **n** covenant in my
2Co   3: 6 as ministers of a **n** covenant—
       5:17 is in Christ, the **n** creation has come:
       5:17 The old has gone, the **n** is here!
Gal   6:15 what counts is the **n** creation.
Eph   2:15 in himself one **n** humanity
       4:23 to be made **n** in the attitude of your
       4:24 and to put on the **n** self,
Col   3:10 and have put on the **n** self, which is
Heb   8: 8 I will make a **n** covenant
       9:15 is the mediator of a **n** covenant,
      10:20 by a **n** and living way opened for us
      12:24 Jesus the mediator of a **n** covenant,
1Pe   1: 3 great mercy he has given us **n** birth
2Pe   3:13 are looking forward to a **n** heaven and
            a **n** earth,
1Jn   2: 7 I am not writing you a **n** command
2Jn   1: 5 I am not writing you a **n** command
Rev   2:17 a white stone with a **n** name written
       3:12 the city of my God, the **n** Jerusalem,
       3:12 will also write on them my **n** name.
       5: 9 And they sang a **n** song, saying:
      14: 3 they sang a **n** song before the throne
      21: 1 I saw "a **n** heaven and a **n** earth,"
      21: 2 saw the Holy City, the **n** Jerusalem,
      21: 5 said, "I am making everything **n**!"

NEW MOON Nu 10:10; 28:14; 1Sa 20:5, 18, 24;
2Ki 4:23; 1Ch 23:31; Ezr 3:5; Ne 10:33; Ps 81:3; Isa
1:14; 66:23; Eze 46:1, 6; Hos 5:7; Am 8:5; Col 2:16

NEW WINE Ge 27:28, 37; Nu 18:12; Dt 7:13;
11:14; 12:17; 14:23; 18:4; 28:51; 33:28; 2Ki 18:32;
2Ch 31:5; 32:28; Ne 5:11; 10:37, 39; 13:5, 12; Ps
4:7; Pr 3:10; Isa 24:7; 36:17; 62:8; Jer 31:12; Hos
2:8, 9, 22; 4:11; 7:14; 9:2; Joel 1:5, 10; 2:19, 24;
3:18; Am 9:13; Hag 1:11; Zec 9:17; Mt 9:17, 17;
Mk 2:22, 22; Lk 5:37, 37, 38

NEWBORN BEAR

1Pe   2: 2 Like **n** babies, crave pure spiritual

NEWS

2Ki   7: 9 This is a day of good **n** and we are
Ps   112: 7 They will have no fear of bad **n**;
Pr   15:30 good **n** gives health to the bones.
      25:25 to a weary soul is good **n**
Isa   40: 9 You who bring good **n** to Jerusalem,
      52: 7 the feet of those who bring good **n**,
      61: 1 me to proclaim good **n** to the poor.
Na   1:15 the feet of one who brings good **n**,
Mt   4:23 proclaiming the good **n**
       9:35 proclaiming the good **n**
      11: 5 and the good **n** is proclaimed

Mk   1: 1 the good **n** about Jesus the Messiah,
    1:15 Repent and believe the good **n**!"
Lk   1:19 to you and to tell you this good **n**.
    2:10 I bring you good **n** that will cause
    3:18 and proclaimed the good **n** to them.
    4:43 "I must proclaim the good **n**
    8: 1 proclaiming the good **n**
    9: 6 proclaiming the good **n** and healing
   16:16 the good **n** of the kingdom of God is
Jn   20:18 went to the disciples with the **n**:
Ac   5:42 proclaiming the good **n** that Jesus is
  10:36 announcing the good **n** of peace
  17:18 Paul was preaching the good **n**
Ro   10:15 feet of those who bring good **n**!"

GOOD NEWS See GOOD

NEXT
Ge   18:10 return to you about this time **n** year,
Ps   78: 4 we will tell the **n** generation

NICODEMUS*
Pharisee who visted Jesus at night (Jn 3). Argued for fair treatment of Jesus (Jn 7:50–52). With Joseph, prepared Jesus for burial (Jn 19:38–42).

NICOLAITANS*
Rev   2: 6 You hate the practices of the **N**,
  2:15 who hold to the teaching of the **N**.

NIGER*
Ac   13: 1 Simeon called **N**, Lucius of Cyrene,

NIGHT MIDNIGHT, NIGHTS, OVERNIGHT
Ge   1: 5 and the darkness he called "**n**."
  1:16 and the lesser light to govern the **n**.
  8:22 winter, day and **n** will never cease."
Ex   13:21 by **n** in a pillar of fire to give them
  40:38 and fire was in the cloud by **n**,
Dt   28:66 filled with dread both **n** and day,
Jos   1: 8 meditate on it day and **n**, so that you
Job   35:10 Maker, who gives songs in the **n**,
Ps   1: 2 who meditates on his law day and **n**.
  16: 7 even at **n** my heart instructs me.
  19: 2 **n** after **n** they reveal knowledge.
  42: 8 his love, at **n** his song is with me—
  63: 6 of you through the watches of the **n**.
  74:16 day is yours, and yours also the **n**;
  77: 6 I remembered my songs in the **n**.
  90: 4 gone by, or like a watch in the **n**.
  91: 5 You will not fear the terror of **n**,
  119:55 In the **n**, LORD, I remember your
  121: 6 you by day, nor the moon by **n**.
  136: 9 the moon and stars to govern the **n**;
Pr   31:15 She gets up while it is still **n**;
  31:18 and her lamp does not go out at **n**.
Ecc   2:23 even at **n** their minds do not rest.
Isa   21:11 "Watchman, what is left of the **n**?
  58:10 and your **n** will become like
Jer   33:20 the day and my covenant with the **n**,
Zec   14: 7 no distinction between day and **n**.
Mt   24:43 time of **n** the thief was coming,
Lk   2: 8 keeping watch over their flocks at **n**.
  6:12 and spent the **n** praying to God.

Jn   3: 2 He came to Jesus at **n** and said,
  9: 4 **N** is coming, when no one can
  11:10 when a person walks at **n** that they
1Th   5: 2 Lord will come like a thief in the **n**.
  5: 5 We do not belong to the **n**
Rev   8:12 light, and also a third of the **n**.
  20:10 will be tormented day and **n** for ever
  21:25 be shut, for there will be no **n** there.
  22: 5 There will be no more **n**.

NIGHTS NIGHT
Ge   7:12 on the earth forty days and forty **n**.
Ex   24:18 the mountain forty days and forty **n**.
1Ki   19: 8 and forty **n** until he reached Horeb,
Jnh   1:17 of the fish three days and three **n**.
Mt   4: 2 After fasting forty days and forty **n**,
  12:40 three **n** in the belly of a huge fish,
  12:40 and three **n** in the heart of the earth.
2Co   6: 5 hard work, sleepless **n** and hunger;

NILE
Ex   1:22 is born you must throw into the **N**,
  2: 5 went down to the **N** to bathe,
  7:17 hand I will strike the water of the **N**,

NIMROD
Ge   10: 9 "Like **N**, a mighty hunter before

NINE NINTH
Jos   13: 7 as an inheritance among the **n** tribes
Ac   2:15 It's only **n** in the morning!

NINETY
Ge   17:17 Sarah bear a child at the age of **n**?"

NINETY-NINE
Ge   17: 1 When Abram was **n** years old,
Lk   15: 4 Doesn't he leave the **n** in the open

NINEVEH NINEVITES
Jnh   1: 2 "Go to the great city of **N**
Na   1: 1 A prophecy concerning **N**.
Mt   12:41 The men of **N** will stand

NINEVITES* NINEVEH
Jnh   3: 5 The **N** believed God. A fast was
Lk   11:30 For as Jonah was a sign to the **N**,

NINTH NINE
Jer   52: 6 By the **n** day of the fourth month

NO NONE, NOTHING
Ex   20: 3 "You shall have **n** other gods
Dt   4:35 besides him there is **n** other.
  5: 7 "You shall have **n** other gods
  15: 4 there need be **n** poor people among
  32: 4 A faithful God who does **n** wrong,
1Ki   8:23 there is **n** God like you in heaven
Pr   6:32 who commits adultery has **n** sense;
  9: 4 To those who have **n** sense she says,
  11:12 derides their neighbor has **n** sense,
  12:11 who chase fantasies has **n** sense.
  15:21 brings joy to one who has **n** sense,
  17:18 One who has **n** sense shakes hands
  24:30 of someone who has **n** sense;
Ecc   12:12 making many books there is **n** end,

Isa 43:11 and apart from me there is **n** savior.
Jer 31:34 will remember their sins **n** more."
Eze 13:10 when there is **n** peace, and because,
Zec 14: 7 with **n** distinction between day
Mt 5:37 need to say is simply 'Yes' or '**N**';
24:36 about that day or hour **n** one knows,
Mk 8:12 tell you, **n** sign will be given to it."
10:18 "**N** one is good—except God alone.
Lk 1:37 For **n** word from God will ever
16:13 "**N** one can serve two masters.
Jn 1:18 **N** one has ever seen God,
4:44 a prophet has **n** honor in his own
Ro 8: 1 there is now **n** condemnation
Jas 5:12 to say is a simple "Yes" or "**N**."
Rev 21: 1 and there was **n** longer any sea.
21: 4 There will be **n** more death'
22: 3 **N** longer will there be any curse.
22: 5 There will be **n** more night.

NOAH
Righteous man (Eze 14:14, 20) called to build ark (Ge 6–8; Heb 11:7; 1Pe 3:20; 2Pe 2:5). God's covenant with (Ge 9:1–17). Drunkenness of (Ge 9:18–23). Blessed sons, cursed Canaan (Ge 9:24–27).

NOB
1Sa 21: 1 David went to **N**, to Ahimelek

NOBLE
Ru 3:11 that you are a woman of **n** character.
Ps 16: 3 "They are the **n** ones in whom is all
45: 1 by a **n** theme as I recite my verses
Pr 12: 4 **n** character is her husband's crown,
31:10 A wife of **n** character who can find?
31:29 "Many women do **n** things, but you
Isa 32: 8 But the **n** make **n** plans, and by **n**
deeds they stand.
Lk 8:15 good soil stands for those with a **n**
Ac 17:11 were of more **n** character than those
1Co 1:26 not many were of **n** birth.
Php 4: 8 whatever is **n**, whatever is right,
1Ti 3: 1 to be an overseer desires a **n** task.
Jas 2: 7 who are blaspheming the **n** name

NOBODY
Jn 9:32 **N** has ever heard of opening
1Th 5:15 Make sure that **n** pays back wrong

NOISE
Ex 32:17 Joshua heard the **n** of the people
Isa 13: 4 Listen, a **n** on the mountains,
29: 6 thunder and earthquake and great **n**,

NOMINATED*
Ac 1:23 they **n** two men: Joseph called
Barsabbas

NONE NO
Dt 15: 6 nations but will borrow from **n**.
15: 6 nations but **n** will rule over you.
1Sa 3:19 he let **n** of Samuel's words fall
Ps 86: 8 Among the gods there is **n** like you,
Pr 2:19 **N** who go to her return or attain
Isa 46: 9 I am God, and there is **n** like me.

Isa 47: 8 'I am, and there is **n** besides me.
Mt 12:39 **n** will be given it except the sign
16: 4 **n** will be given it except the sign
Jn 6:39 that I shall lose **n** of all those he has
17:12 **N** has been lost except the one

NONSENSE
3Jn 1:10 spreading malicious **n** about us.

NOON
Mk 15:33 At **n**, darkness came over the whole

NORTH
Ge 13:14 where you are, to the **n** and south,
Nu 34: 9 This will be your boundary on the **n**.
Ps 89:12 You created the **n** and the south;
Isa 41:25 "I have stirred up one from the **n**,
Jer 4: 6 I am bringing disaster from the **n**,
Eze 1: 4 a windstorm coming out of the **n**—
Da 11: 6 king of the **N** to make an alliance,
Zec 2: 6 Come! Flee from the land of the **n**,"
14: 4 with half of the mountain moving **n**

NOSE NOSES
2Ki 19:28 I will put my hook in your **n** and my
2Ch 33:11 put a hook in his **n**, bound him

NOSES* NOSE
Ps 115: 6 but cannot hear, **n**, but cannot smell.
Eze 23:25 They will cut off your **n** and your

NOSTRILS
Ge 2: 7 breathed into his **n** the breath of life,
7:22 had the breath of life in its **n** died.
Ex 15: 8 blast of your **n** the waters piled up.
Ps 18:15 at the blast of breath from your **n**.
Isa 2:22 who have but a breath in their **n**.

NOTABLE*
Am 6: 1 you **n** men of the foremost nation,
Ac 4:16 they have performed a **n** sign,

NOTE
Ac 4:13 they took **n** that these men had been

NOTHING NO, THING
Ge 14:23 I will accept **n** belonging to you,
Ex 1: 8 to whom Joseph meant **n**,
2Sa 24:24 burnt offerings that cost me **n**."
2Ch 9: 2 was too hard for him to explain
Ne 9:21 they lacked **n**, their clothes did not
Job 1: 9 "Does Job fear God for **n**?"
Ps 34: 9 for those who fear him lack **n**.
73:25 earth has **n** I desire besides you.
82: 5 "The 'gods' know **n**, they
understand.
Pr 8:11 **n** you desire can compare with her.
9:13 she is simple and knows **n**.
10:28 the hopes of the wicked come to **n**.
28:27 who give to the poor will lack **n**,
Ecc 1: 9 there is **n** new under the sun.
3:22 there is **n** better for a person than
8:15 life, because there is **n** better
Isa 44: 9 All who make idols are **n**,
53: 2 **n** in his appearance that we should
Jer 32:17 **N** is too hard for you.

Da   9:26 will be put to death and will have **n**.
Mt   17:20 **N** will be impossible for you."
Lk   23:15 see, he has done **n** to deserve death.
Jn   5:30 By myself I can do **n**; I judge only
          15: 5 apart from me you can do **n**.
Ro   14:14 Jesus, that **n** is unclean in itself.
1Co   8: 4 We know that "An idol is **n** at all
          13: 2 but do not have love, I am **n**.
Gal   2:21 through the law, Christ died for **n**!"
Php   2: 7 he made himself **n** by taking
1Ti   6: 7 For we brought **n** into the world, and
                    we can take **n** out of it.
Heb   4:13 **N** in all creation is hidden
          7:19 (for the law made **n** perfect),

NOTICE
Ps   10:11 says to himself, "God will never **n**;

NOURISH NOURISHED,
NOURISHING, NOURISHMENT
Pr   10:21 The lips of the righteous **n** many,

NOURISHED NOURISH
Dt   32:13 He **n** him with honey from the rock,
Da   1:15 better **n** than any of the young men

NOURISHING* NOURISH
Ro   11:17 and now share in the **n** sap

NOURISHMENT* NOURISH
Pr   3: 8 to your body and **n** to your bones.

NOW
Ge   22:12 **N** I know that you fear God,
Ezr   9: 8 "But **n**, for a brief moment,
Ps   20: 6 **N** this I know: The LORD gives
        131: 3 put your hope in the LORD both **n**
Hab   2:16 instead of glory. **N** it is your turn!
Zec   1: 5 Where are your ancestors **n**?
Mt   12:42 **n** something greater than Solomon
Lk   1:48 From **n** on all generations will call
Jn   2:10 but you have saved the best till **n**."
          5:25 has **n** come when the dead will hear
          9:25 I do know. I was blind but **n** I see!"
        13:19 am telling you **n** before it happens,
        13:36 you cannot follow **n**, but you will
        16:12 to you, more than you can **n** bear.
Ro   3:21 But **n** apart from the law
          5: 9 Since we have **n** been justified
          8: 1 there is **n** no condemnation for those
        13:11 our salvation is nearer **n** than
1Co   13:13 And **n** these three remain:
2Co   6: 2 you, **n** is the time of God's favor,
Gal   4: 9 But **n** that you know God—
Eph   2: 2 the spirit who is **n** at work in those
          3: 5 generations as it has **n** been revealed
Col   1:26 is **n** disclosed to the Lord's people.
1Pe   1: 8 even though you do not see him **n**,
          2:10 but **n** you have received mercy.
1Jn   2:18 even **n** many antichrists have come.
Rev   1:19 what is **n** and what will take place
          21: 3 dwelling place is **n** among

NULLIFY
Nu   30:13 husband may confirm or **n** any vow
Mt   15: 6 Thus you **n** the word of God
Ro   3: 3 Will their unfaithfulness **n** God's
          3:31 Do we, then, **n** the law by this faith?

NUMBER NUMBERED,
NUMBERING, NUMBERLESS,
NUMBERS, NUMEROUS,
OUTNUMBER
Ge   1:22 increase in **n** and fill the water
          1:28 "Be fruitful and increase in **n**;
          9: 1 and increase in **n** and fill the earth.
Nu   26:51 The total **n** of the men of Israel was
Dt   32: 8 according to the **n** of the sons
1Ki   3: 8 people, too numerous to count or **n**.
1Ch   21: 5 Joab reported the **n** of the fighting
Ps   90:12 Teach us to **n** our days, that we may
        105:12 When they were but few in **n**,
        147: 4 He determines the **n** of the stars
Jer   23: 3 will be fruitful and increase in **n**.
Mt   14:21 The **n** of those who ate was
        15:38 The **n** of those who ate was four
Jn   21: 6 net in because of the large **n** of fish.
Ac   2:47 their **n** daily those who were being
          5:14 the Lord and were added to their **n**.
          6: 1 the **n** of disciples was increasing,
        11:21 and a great **n** of people believed
Ro   11:25 part until the full **n** of the Gentiles
Rev   6:11 until the full **n** of their fellow
          7: 4 I heard the **n** of those who were
        13:18 who has insight calculate the **n** of
                    the beast, for it is the **n** of a man.
                    That **n** is 666.
        20: 8 In **n** they are like the sand

NUMBERED NUMBER
Ex   1: 5 The descendants of Jacob **n** seventy
Nu   25: 9 who died in the plague **n** 24,000.
Lk   12: 7 the very hairs of your head are all **n**.
        22:37 he was **n** with the transgressors';

NUMBERING* NUMBER
1Ch   21: 6 include Levi and Benjamin in the **n**,
          27:24 came on Israel on account of this **n**,
Ac   1:15 group **n** about a hundred and twenty)
Rev   5:11 angels, **n** thousands upon thousands,

NUMBERLESS* NUMBER
Isa   48:19 sand, your children like its **n** grains;

NUMBERS NUMBER
Ge   17: 2 and will greatly increase your **n**."
          28: 3 increase your **n** until you become
          48: 4 you fruitful and increase your **n**.
Lev   26: 9 you fruitful and increase your **n**,
Dt   1:10 your God has increased your **n** so

NUMEROUS NUMBER
Ge   16:10 that they will be too **n** to count."
          22:17 your descendants as **n** as the stars
Ex   1: 9 Israelites have become far too **n**
          23:29 and the wild animals too **n** for you.

Dt   1:10   you are as **n** as the stars in the sky.
Ne   9:23   made their children as **n** as the stars
Zec   10: 8   they will be as **n** as before.
Heb 11:12   came descendants as **n** as the stars

NURSE   NURSED, NURSING
Ge   21: 7   that Sarah would **n** children?
Ex   2: 7   of the Hebrew women to **n** the baby
Nu   11:12   in my arms, as a **n** carries an infant,
2Sa   4: 4   His **n** picked him up and fled, but as
2Ki   11: 1   hidden with his **n** at the temple
Isa   66:11   For you will **n** and be satisfied

NURSED   NURSE
Ex   2: 9   the woman took the baby and **n** him.
Lk   11:27   who gave you birth and **n** you."

NURSING   NURSE
Isa   49:23   and their queens your **n** mothers.
Lk   21:23   for pregnant women and **n** mothers!
1Th   2: 7   Just as a **n** mother cares for her

O

OAK   OAKS
Ge   35: 4   Jacob buried them under the **o**
2Sa   18:10   saw Absalom hanging in an **o** tree."
Eze   6:13   spreading tree and every leafy **o**—

OAKS   OAK
Ps   29: 9   voice of the LORD twists the **o**
Isa   57: 5   You burn with lust among the **o**

OATH   OATHS
Ge   21:31   the two men swore an **o** there.
          24: 7   spoke to me and promised me on **o**,
          26: 3   will confirm the **o** I swore to your
Ex   13:11   as he promised on **o** to you and your
          33: 1   go up to the land I promised on **o**
Nu   30: 2   takes an **o** to obligate himself
Dt   6:18   land the LORD promised on **o**
          7: 8   you and kept the **o** he swore to your
          29:12   you this day and sealing with an **o**,
Jos   2:17   "This **o** you made us swear will not
          6:22   in accordance with your **o** to her."
1Sa   14:24   had bound the people under an **o**,
          24:22   So David gave his **o** to Saul.
Ezr   10: 5   and all Israel under **o** to do what had
Ne   13:25   I made them take an **o** in God's
Ps   15: 4   who keeps an **o** even when it hurts,
          95:11   So I declared on **o** in my anger,
          119:106 I have taken an **o** and confirmed it,
          132:11 The LORD swore an **o** to David,
Ecc   8: 2   because you took an **o** before God.
Mt   5:33   'Do not break your **o**, but fulfill
Heb   4: 3   "So I declared on **o** in my anger,
          7:20   And it was not without an **o**!

OATHS   OATH
Dt   6:13   only and take your **o** in his name.

OBADIAH
     1. Believer who sheltered 100 prophets from
Jezebel (1Ki 18:1-16).

2. Prophet against Edom (Ob 1).

OBED
Ru   4:22   **O** the father of Jesse, and Jesse
Lk   3:32   Jesse, the son of **O**, the son of Boaz,

OBED-EDOM
2Sa   6:10   took it to the house of **O** the Gittite.
1Ch   26: 5   (For God had blessed **O**.)

OBEDIENCE   OBEY
Ge   49:10   and the **o** of the nations shall be his.
Dt   10:12   to walk in **o** to him, to love him,
          26:17   and that you will walk in **o** to him,
          30:16   to walk in **o** to him, and to keep his
Jos   22: 5   to walk in **o** to him, to keep his
1Ki   8:58   to walk in **o** to him and keep
1Ch   21:19   So David went up in **o** to the word
2Ch   31:21   of God's temple and in **o** to the law
Lk   23:56   rested on the Sabbath in **o**
Ac   21:24   you yourself are living in **o**
Ro   1: 5   all the Gentiles to the **o** that comes
          5:19   through the **o** of the one man
          6:16   to death, or to **o**, which leads
          16:19   Everyone has heard about your **o**,
          16:26   might come to the **o** that comes
2Co   9:13   God for the **o** that accompanies your
          10: 6   once your **o** is complete.
Phm   1:21   Confident of your **o**, I write to you,
Heb   5: 8   he learned **o** from what he suffered
2Jn   1: 6   that we walk in **o** to his commands.

OBEDIENT*   OBEY
Dt   30:17   heart turns away and you are not **o**,
Jdg   2:17   who had been **o** to the LORD's
                   commands.
Isa   1:19   If you are willing and **o**, you will
Lk   2:51   with them and was **o** to them.
Ac   6: 7   of priests became **o** to the faith.
Ro   6:16   yourselves to someone as **o** slaves,
2Co   2: 9   the test and be **o** in everything.
          7:15   he remembers that you were all **o**,
          10: 5   every thought to make it **o** to Christ.
Php   2: 8   himself by becoming **o** to death—
Titus   3: 1   to be **o**, to be ready to do whatever
1Pe   1: 2   to be **o** to Jesus Christ and sprinkled
          1:14   As **o** children, do not conform

OBEY   OBEDIENCE, OBEDIENT, OBEYED, OBEYING, OBEYS
Ex   12:24   "**O** these instructions as a lasting
          19: 5   Now if you **o** me fully and keep my
          24: 7   the LORD has said; we will **o**."
Lev   18: 4   You must **o** my laws and be careful
          25:18   decrees and be careful to **o** my laws,
Nu   15:40   remember to **o** all my commands
Dt   4:30   to the LORD your God and **o** him.
          5:27   We will listen and **o**."
          6: 3   and be careful to **o** so that it may go
          6:24   commanded us to **o** all these decrees
          11:13   you faithfully **o** the commands I am
          11:27   the blessing if you **o** the commands
          12:28   **o** all these regulations I am giving
          13: 4   Keep his commands and **o** him;
          21:18   son who does not **o** his father

Dt   28: 1 If you fully **o** the LORD your God
        28:15 you do not **o** the LORD your God
        30: 2 God and **o** him with all your heart
        30:10 if you **o** the LORD your God
        30:14 and in your heart so you may **o** it.
        32:46 children to **o** carefully all the words
Jos   1: 7 **o** all the law my servant Moses gave
        24:24 the LORD our God and **o** him."
Jdg   3: 4 whether they would **o** the LORD's
1Sa   12:14 serve and **o** him and do not rebel
        15:22 To **o** is better than sacrifice,
1Ki   8:61 by his decrees and **o** his commands,
2Ki   17:13 I commanded your ancestors to **o**
2Ch   34:31 and to **o** the words of the covenant
Ps   103:18 and remember to **o** his precepts.
       103:20 do his bidding, who **o** his word.
       119:17 while I live, that I may **o** your word.
       119:34 your law and **o** it with all my heart.
       119:57 I have promised to **o** your words.
       119:67 went astray, but now I **o** your word.
       119:100 the elders, for I **o** your precepts.
       119:129 therefore I **o** them.
       119:167 I **o** your statutes, for I love them
Pr   5:13 I would not **o** my teachers or turn
Jer   7:23 **O** me, and I will be your God
        11: 4 I said, 'O me and do everything I
        11: 7 again and again, saying, "O me."
        18:10 evil in my sight and does not **o** me,
        42: 6 for we will **o** the LORD our God."
Mt   8:27 the winds and the waves **o** him!"
        28:20 to **o** everything I have commanded
Lk   11:28 hear the word of God and **o** it."
Jn   14:24 not love me will not **o** my teaching.
Ac   5:29 "We must **o** God rather than human
        5:32 God has given to those who **o** him."
Ro   2:13 it is those who **o** the law who will
        6:12 body so that you **o** its evil desires.
        6:16 you are slaves of the one you **o**—
        6:17 you have come to **o** from your heart
        15:18 in leading the Gentiles to **o** God
Gal   5: 3 he is obligated to **o** the whole law.
Eph   6: 1 **o** your parents in the Lord, for this
        6: 5 **o** your earthly masters with respect
        6: 5 of heart, just as you would **o** Christ.
Col   3:20 **o** your parents in everything,
        3:22 Slaves, **o** your earthly masters
2Th   3:14 who does not **o** our instruction
1Ti   3: 4 well and see that his children **o** him,
Heb   5: 9 eternal salvation for all who **o** him
1Pe   4:17 for those who do not **o** the gospel

OBEYED OBEY

Ge   22:18 blessed, because you have **o** me."
        26: 5 because Abraham **o** me and did
Jos   1:17 Just as we fully **o** Moses, so we will
2Ki   18:12 they had not **o** the LORD their
Ps   119: 4 down precepts that are to be fully **o**.
Jer   3:13 and have not **o** me,' "
Da   9:10 we have not **o** the LORD our God
Jnh   3: 3 Jonah **o** the word of the LORD
Mic   5:15 on the nations that have not **o** me."
Jn   15:20 If they **o** my teaching, they will
        17: 6 to me and they have **o** your word.
Ac   7:53 through angels but have not **o** it."

Php   2:12 dear friends, as you have always **o**—
Heb   11: 8 as his inheritance, **o** and went,
1Pe   3: 6 who **o** Abraham and called him her

OBEYING* OBEY

Dt   8:20 for not **o** the LORD your God.
1Sa   15:22 as much as in **o** the LORD?
1Ki   11:38 is right in my eyes by **o** my decrees
Ps   119: 5 were steadfast in **o** your decrees!
Jer   16:12 of your evil hearts instead of **o** me.
Gal   5: 7 you to keep you from **o** the truth?
1Pe   1:22 purified yourselves by **o** the truth so

OBEYS OBEY

Lev   18: 5 for the person who **o** them will live
Ne   9:29 'The person who **o** them will live
Eze   20:11 the person who **o** them will live.
Jn   8:51 whoever **o** my word will never see
Ro   2:27 and yet **o** the law will condemn you
1Jn   2: 5 But if anyone **o** his word,

OBJECT OBJECTS

Jer   18:16 Their land will be an **o** of horror

OBJECTS OBJECT

Ro   9:23 glory known to the **o** of his mercy,

OBLATION(S) (KJV) See GIFT(S), OFFERING(S), PORTION, SACRIFICE

OBLIGATE* OBLIGATED, OBLIGATION, OBLIGATIONS

Nu   30: 2 or takes an oath to **o** himself

OBLIGATED OBLIGATE

Ro   1:14 I am **o** both to Greeks
Gal   5: 3 that he is **o** to obey the whole law.

OBLIGATION OBLIGATE

Ro   8:12 brothers and sisters, we have an **o**—

OBLIGATIONS* OBLIGATE

Nu   3: 8 fulfilling the **o** of the Israelites
1Ki   9:25 them, and so fulfilled the temple **o**.

OBSCENITY*

Eph   5: 4 Nor should there be **o**, foolish talk

OBSCURES*

Job   38: 2 "Who is this that **o** my plans
        42: 3 **o** my plans without knowledge?'

OBSERVANCE* OBSERVE

Ex   13: 9 This **o** will be for you like a sign
Ezr   7:10 and **o** of the Law of the LORD,

OBSERVE OBSERVANCE, OBSERVED, OBSERVER, OBSERVES, OBSERVING

Ex   31:13 'You must **o** my Sabbaths.
Lev   25: 2 the land itself must **o** a sabbath
Dt   4: 6 **O** them carefully, for this will show
        5:12 "O the Sabbath day by keeping it
        8: 6 **O** the commands of the LORD
        11:22 you carefully **o** all these commands

Dt   26:16 carefully o them with all your heart
Ps   37:37 the blameless, o the upright;
Mk   7: 9 in order to o your own traditions!
Ro   2:25 has value if you o the law,

OBSERVED
Lk   17:20 God is not something that can be o,

OBSERVER* OBSERVE
Ac   22:12 He was a devout o of the law

OBSERVES* OBSERVE
Ps   11: 4 He o everyone on earth;

OBSERVING* OBSERVE
1Sa 20:29 because our family is o a sacrifice
2Ch 13:11 are o the requirements of the LORD
Lk   1: 6 righteous in the sight of God, o all
Gal   4:10 You are o special days and months

OBSOLETE*
Heb   8:13 he has made the first one o; and what
            is o and outdated will soon

OBSTACLE* OBSTACLES
Ro   14:13 block or o in the way of a brother

OBSTACLES* OBSTACLE
Isa 57:14 Remove the o out of the way of my
Jer   6:21 "I will put o before this people.
Ro   16:17 put o in your way that are contrary

OBSTINATE
Isa 65: 2 held out my hands to an o people,
Eze   3: 7 all the Israelites are hardened and o.
Ro   10:21 to a disobedient and o people."

OBTAIN OBTAINED, OBTAINING
Pr   12: 2 Good people o favor
Ro   11: 7 sought so earnestly they did not o.
2Ti   2:10 they too may o the salvation that is

OBTAINED OBTAIN
Ro   9:30 not pursue righteousness, have o it,
Php   3:12 Not that I have already o all this,

OBTAINING* OBTAIN
Heb   9:12 blood, thus o eternal redemption.

OBVIOUS*
Mt   6:18 so that it will not be o to others
Gal   5:19 The acts of the flesh are o:
1Ti   5:24 The sins of some are o,
      5:25 good deeds are o, and even those that
            are not o cannot remain hidden

OCCASIONS*
Zec   8:19 and glad o and happy festivals
Eph   6:18 the Spirit on all o with all kinds

ODED
2Ch 28: 9 of the LORD named O was there,

ODOR*
Jn   11:39 "by this time there is a bad o, for he

OFFEND* OFFENDED, OFFENDER, OFFENSE, OFFENSES, OFFENSIVE
Job 34:31 'I am guilty but will o no more.
Jn   6:61 said to them, "Does this o you?

OFFENDED OFFEND
Mt   15:12 that the Pharisees were o when they

OFFENDER OFFEND
Ex   21:22 the o must be fined whatever

OFFENSE OFFEND
Dt   19:15 or o they may have committed.
     21:22 someone guilty of a capital o is put
Pr   17: 9 would foster love covers over an o,
     19:11 it is to one's glory to overlook an o.
Mt   17:27 "But so that we may not cause o,
Mk   6: 3 And they took o at him.
Gal   5:11 that case the o of the cross has been

OFFENSES OFFEND
Job   7:21 Why do you not pardon my o
Ecc 10: 4 calmness can lay great o to rest.
Isa 44:22 swept away your o like a cloud,
     59:12 For our o are many in your sight,
Eze 18:30 Turn away from all your o;
     33:10 "Our o and sins weigh us down,

OFFENSIVE OFFEND
Ps 139:24 See if there is any o way in me,

OFFER OFFERED, OFFERING, OFFERINGS, OFFERS
Ex   29:38 "This is what you are to o
Dt   12:14 O them only at the place
Ps   4: 5 O the sacrifices of the righteous
Isa   1:15 even when you o many prayers,
Jer   7:16 pray for this people nor o any plea
Hos 14: 2 that we may o the fruit of our lips.
Mic   6: 7 Shall I o my firstborn for my
Mt   5:24 then come and o your gift.
Ro   6:13 Do not o any part of yourself to sin
      6:13 rather o yourselves to God as those
     12: 1 o your bodies as a living sacrifice,
Heb   9:25 he enter heaven to o himself again
     13:15 let us continually o to God

OFFERED OFFER
Lev 10: 1 they o unauthorized fire before
1Sa 13: 9 And Saul o up the burnt offering.
1Ki   3: 4 and Solomon o a thousand burnt
Ps 106:28 and ate sacrifices o to lifeless gods;
Isa 50: 6 I o my back to those who beat me,
Mt   27:34 There they o Jesus wine to drink,
1Co   9:13 altar share in what is o on the altar?
     10:20 of pagans are o to demons,
Heb   7:27 sins once for all when he o himself.
      9:14 eternal Spirit o himself unblemished
     11:17 tested him, o Isaac as a sacrifice.
Jas   5:15 the prayer o in faith will make

OFFERING OFFER
Ge   4: 4 with favor on Abel and his o,
     22: 2 Sacrifice him there as a burnt o
     22: 8 provide the lamb for the burnt o,

Ex 29:14 outside the camp. It is a sin o.
       29:18 It is a burnt o to the LORD,
       29:18 a food o presented to the LORD.
       29:24 before the LORD as a wave o.
       29:40 quarter of a hin of wine as a drink o.
Lev   1: 3 " 'If the o is a burnt o
        2: 1 anyone brings a grain o
        3: 1 " 'If your o is a fellowship o,
        4: 3 young bull without defect as a sin o
        5:15 the sanctuary shekel. It is a guilt o.
        7:37 the regulations for the burnt o, the
              grain o, the sin o, the guilt o, the
              ordination o and the fellowship o,
        9:24 consumed the burnt o and the fat
1Sa 13: 9 And Saul offered up the burnt o.
1Ch 21:26 from heaven on the altar of burnt o.
2Ch 7: 1 and consumed the burnt o
Ezr   6:17 lambs and, as a sin o for all Israel,
Ps   40: 6 Sacrifice and o you did not desire—
   116:17 I will sacrifice a thank o to you
Isa 53:10 the LORD makes his life an o
Mt   5:23 if you are o your gift at the altar
Ro   8: 3 likeness of sinful flesh to be a sin o.
Eph 5: 2 himself up for us as a fragrant o
Php 2:17 out like a drink o on the sacrifice
        4:18 They are a fragrant o, an acceptable
2Ti   4: 6 being poured out like a drink o,
Heb 10: 5 "Sacrifice and o you did not desire,
      11: 4 God a better o than Cain did.
1Pe   2: 5 o spiritual sacrifices acceptable

BURNT OFFERING See BURNT

DRINK OFFERING See DRINK

FELLOWSHIP OFFERING See FELLOWSHIP

GRAIN OFFERING See GRAIN

GUILT OFFERING See GUILT

SIN OFFERING See SIN

WAVE OFFERING See WAVE

OFFERINGS OFFER
Ge   8:20 birds, he sacrificed burnt o on it.
Ex 40:29 offered on it burnt o and grain o,
1Sa 15:22 the LORD delight in burnt o
Ps 40: 6 burnt o and sin o you did not
    50:14 "Sacrifice thank o to God,
Isa   1:13 Stop bringing meaningless o!
Jer   6:20 Your burnt o are not acceptable;
Hos 6: 6 of God rather than burnt o.
Mal 3: 8 we robbing you?' "In tithes and o.
Mk 12:33 is more important than all burnt o
Heb 10: 6 with burnt o and sin o you were not

BURNT OFFERINGS See BURNT

DRINK OFFERINGS See DRINK

FELLOWSHIP OFFERINGS See
FELLOWSHIP

GRAIN OFFERINGS See GRAIN

GUILT OFFERINGS See GUILT

SIN OFFERINGS See SIN

OFFERS OFFER
Titus 2:11 God has appeared that o salvation

Heb 10:11 and again he o the same sacrifices,

OFFICER OFFICERS, OFFICIALS
2Ti   2: 4 tries to please his commanding o.

OFFICERS OFFICER
Ex 15: 4 best of Pharaoh's o are drowned

OFFICIALS OFFICER
Ex   5:21 his o and have put a sword in their
      9:20 Those o of Pharaoh who feared
Ezr   4: 5 They bribed o to work against them
Pr 17:26 surely to flog honest o is not right.
    29:12 to lies, all his o become wicked.
Jer 52:10 he also killed all the o of Judah.
Mk 10:42 their high o exercise authority over

OFFSPRING
Ge   3:15 and between your o and hers;
    12: 7 "To your o I will give this land."
    13:16 dust, then your o could be counted.
    26: 4 through your o all nations on earth
    28:14 be blessed through you and your o.
Ex 13:12 to the LORD the first o of every
Ru   4:12 Through the o the LORD gives
2Sa 7:12 will raise up your o to succeed you,
Isa 44: 3 I will pour out my Spirit on your o,
    53:10 sin, he will see his o and prolong his
Mal 2:15 Godly o. So be on your guard,
Ac   3:25 'Through your o all peoples
    17:28 own poets have said, 'We are his o'
    17:29 "Therefore since we are God's o,
Ro   4:18 said to him, "So shall your o be."
     9: 8 who are regarded as Abraham's o
Rev 22:16 I am the Root and the O of David,

OFTEN
Lk 13:34 how o I have longed to gather your
Jn 18: 2 because Jesus had o met there

OG
Nu 21:33 and O king of Bashan and his whole
Dt 31: 4 to them what he did to Sihon and O,
Ps 136:20 and O king of Bashan—

OHOLIAB*
Craftsman who worked on the tabernacle (Ex
31:6; 35:34; 36:1-2; 38:23).

OIL
Ge 28:18 as a pillar and poured o on top of it.
    35:14 he also poured o on it.
Ex 25: 6 olive o for the light;
    25: 6 spices for the anointing o
    29: 7 Take the anointing o and anoint him
    30:25 It will be the sacred anointing o.
Dt 14:23 grain, new wine and olive o,
1Sa 10: 1 Samuel took a flask of olive o
    16:13 So Samuel took the horn of o
1Ki 17:16 up and the jug of o did not run dry,
2Ki 4: 6 Then the o stopped flowing.
Ps 23: 5 You anoint my head with o;
    45: 7 by anointing you with the o of joy.
  104:15 hearts, o to make their faces shine,
  133: 2 It is like precious o poured
Pr   5: 3 and her speech is smoother than o;

Pr   21:17 wine and olive **o** will never be rich.
Isa   1: 6 bandaged or soothed with olive **o**.
      61: 3 the **o** of joy instead of mourning,
Joel   2:24 will overflow with new wine and **o**.
Mt   25: 3 but did not take any **o** with them.
Heb   1: 9 by anointing you with the **o** of joy."
Jas   5:14 anoint them with **o** in the name

ANOINTING OIL Ex 25:6; 29:7, 21; 30:25, 25, 31; 31:11; 35:8, 15, 28; 37:29; 39:38; 40:9; Lev 8:2, 10, 12, 30; 10:7; 21:10, 12; Nu 4:16

OLIVE OIL Ex 25:6; 29:2, 2, 23; 30:24; 35:8, 28; 39:37; Lev 2:1, 4, 4, 7; 5:11; 6:15; 7:10, 12; 8:26; 9:4; 14:10, 21; 23:13; Nu 4:9; 5:15; 6:15, 15; 7:13, 19, 25, 31, 37, 43, 49, 55, 61, 67, 73, 79; 8:8; 11:8; 15:4, 6, 9; 18:12; 28:9; 29:3; Dt 7:13; 8:8; 11:14; 12:17; 14:23; 18:4; 28:51; 1Sa 10:1; 1Ki 5:11; 17:12; 2Ki 4:2; 9:1; 20:13; 1Ch 9:29; 12:40; 27:28; 2Ch 2:10, 15; 11:11; 31:5; 32:28; Ezr 3:7; 6:9; 7:22; Ne 5:11; 10:37, 39; 13:5, 12; Job 29:6; Pr 21:17, 20; Isa 1:6; 39:2; 57:9; Jer 31:12; 40:10; 41:8; Eze 16:13, 19; 23:41; 27:17; 45:14, 24; 46:5; Hos 2:5, 22; 12:1; Joel 1:10; 2:19; Mic 6:7; Hag 1:11; 2:12; Lk 16:6; Rev 18:13

OLD AGE-OLD, OLDER
Ge   17:12 is eight days **o** must be circumcised,
      17:17 be born to a man a hundred years **o**?
      21: 7 have borne him a son in his **o** age."
Nu   1: 3 in Israel who are twenty years **o**
      14:29 every one of you twenty years **o**
Dt   32: 7 Remember the days of **o**;
Ps   71: 9 Do not cast me away when I am **o**;
Pr   20:29 gray hair the splendor of the **o**.
      22: 6 when they are **o** they will not turn
La   5:21 renew our days as of **o**
Joel   2:28 your **o** men will dream dreams,
Mic   5: 2 whose origins are from of **o**,
Mk   2:22 pours new wine into **o** wineskins.
Jn   3: 4 someone be born when they are **o**?"
Ac   2:17 your **o** men will dream dreams.
Ro   4:19 he was about a hundred years **o**—
1Co   5: 7 Get rid of the **o** yeast, so that you
2Co   5:17 The **o** has gone, the new is here!
Eph   4:22 to put off your **o** self, which is being
Heb   8: 6 is mediator is superior to the **o** one,
1Jn   2: 7 you a new command but an **o** one,
Rev   21: 4 for the **o** order of things has passed

OLDER OLD
1Ti   5: 1 Do not rebuke an **o** man harshly,
       5: 2 **o** women as mothers, and younger
Titus 2: 2 Teach the **o** men to be temperate,
       2: 3 teach the **o** women to be reverent

OLIVE OLIVES
Ge   8:11 beak was a freshly plucked **o** leaf!
Ex   25: 6 **o** oil for the light;
Jdg   9: 8 They said to the **o** tree, 'Be our
Ps   52: 8 I am like an **o** tree flourishing
Jer   11:16 LORD called you a thriving **o** tree
Hab   3:17 though the **o** crop fails
Zec   4: 3 Also there are two **o** trees by it,
Ro   11:17 though a wild **o** shoot, have been
      11:24 were cut out of an **o** tree that is wild

Ro   11:24 were grafted into a cultivated **o** tree,
Rev   11: 4 They are "the two **o** trees"

OLIVE OIL See OIL

OLIVES OLIVE
Dt   24:20 you beat the **o** from your trees,
Zec   14: 4 the Mount of **O** will be split in two
Mt   24: 3 Jesus was sitting on the Mount of **O**,
Jas   3:12 can a fig tree bear **o**, or a grapevine

MOUNT OF OLIVES See MOUNT

OMEGA*
Rev   1: 8 "I am the Alpha and the **O**,"
      21: 6 I am the Alpha and the **O**,
      22:13 I am the Alpha and the **O**, the First

OMENS
Dt   18:10 interprets **o**, engages in witchcraft,

OMIT*
Jer   26: 2 I command you; do not **o** a word.

OMNIPOTENT (KJV) See ALMIGHTY

OMRI
King of Israel (1Ki 16:21-26).

ONAN
Ge   38: 8 Then Judah said to **O**,
      46:12 **O** had died in the land of Canaan).

ONCE ONE
Ge   18:32 angry, but let me speak just **o** more.
Ex   30:10 **O** a year Aaron shall make
Job   40: 5 I spoke **o**, but I have no answer—
La   1: 1 lies the city, **o** so full of people!
Ro   6:10 he died, he died to sin **o** for all;
       7: 9 **O** I was alive apart from the law;
Eph   5: 8 For you were **o** darkness, but now
Heb   7:27 He sacrificed for their sins **o** for all
       9:12 he entered the Most Holy Place **o**
       9:27 Just as people are destined to die **o**,
1Pe   2:10 **o** you had not received mercy,
       3:18 For Christ also suffered **o** for sins,

ONE EVERYONE, ONCE, ONES
Ge   2:24 his wife, and they become **o** flesh.
Ex   12: 3 for his family, **o** for each household.
      33:11 face to face, as **o** speaks to a friend.
Nu   1: 2 listing every man by name, **o** by **o**.
Dt   6: 4 LORD our God, the LORD is **o**.
Jos   23:10 **O** of you routs a thousand,
Ps   14: 3 no **o** who does good, not even **o**.
Ecc   4: 9 Two are better than **o**, because they
Isa   30:17 thousand will flee at the threat of **o**;
Eze   18: 4 The **o** who sins is the **o** who will
      34:23 I will place over them **o** shepherd,
      37:22 I will make them **o** nation
      37:22 There will be **o** king over all
Zec   14: 9 On that day there will be **o** LORD,
Mal   2:10 Do we not all have **o** Father? Did not **o** God create us?
Mk   10: 8 and the two will become **o** flesh.'
      10: 9 joined together, let no **o** separate."

Mk 10:21 "**O** thing you lack," he said.
    12:29 The Lord our God, the Lord is **o.**
Lk 10:42 or indeed only **o.**
Jn   1:14 the glory of the **o** and only Son,
     1:18 No **o** has ever seen God, but the **o**
     3:16 loved the world that he gave his **o**
    10:16 be **o** flock and **o** shepherd.
    10:30 I and the Father are **o.**"
Ro   3:10 no **o** righteous, not even **o;**
     5:15 died by the trespass of the **o** man,
     5:15 that came by the grace of the **o** man,
    13: 9 are summed up in this **o** command:
1Co 6:16 with a prostitute is **o** with her
     8: 4 and that "There is no God but **o.**"
    10:17 Because there is **o** loaf, we, who are
           many, are **o** body,
    10:24 No **o** should seek their own good,
    12:12 as a body, though **o,** has many parts,
           but all its many parts form **o** body,
    12:13 were all baptized by **o** Spirit so as to
           form **o** body—
    12:13 and we were all given the **o** Spirit
Gal 5:14 fulfilling in keeping this **o** command:
Eph 4: 5 **o** Lord, **o** faith, **o** baptism;
1Ti 2: 5 For there is **o** God and **o** mediator
2Pe 3: 8 But do not forget this **o** thing,

ANOINTED ONE See ANOINTED

HOLY ONE See HOLY

MIGHTY ONE See MIGHTY

ONE ANOTHER Ge 42:21; Lev 19:11; 26:37;
Jdg 19:30; 20:22; 2Ki 7:6; 2Ch 20:23; Est 9:22; Job
41:17; Isa 6:3; 9:19; Jer 9:20; 22:8; 23:27, 30, 31:34;
Zec 7:9; 14:13; Mal 2:10; Mk 8:16; 12:7; 14:4; Lk
2:15; 6:11; 8:25; 12:1; Jn 5:44; 7:35; 11:56; 12:19;
13:22, 34, 34, 35; 16:17, 19; 19:24; Ac 2:12; 26:31;
Ro 1:24, 27; 12:10, 10, 16; 13:8; 14:13; 15:7, 14;
16:16; 1Co 1:10; 16:20; 2Co 13:11, 12; Gal 5:13;
Eph 4:2, 32; 5:19, 21; Php 2:5; Col 3:13, 16; 1Th
4:9, 18; 5:11; 2Th 1:3; Titus 3:3; Heb 3:13; 8:11;
10:24, 25; 13:1; Jas 4:11; 5:9; 1Pe 1:22; 3:8; 4:9; 5:5,
14; 1Jn 1:7; 3:11, 23; 4:7, 11, 12; 2Jn 1:5

ONES ONE

Dt 33: 3 all the holy **o** are in your hand.
1Ch 28:21 his chosen **o,** the children of Jacob.
Ps 17:14 there be leftovers for their little **o.**
    37:28 and will not forsake his faithful **o.**
   105:15 "Do not touch my anointed **o;**
Mt 18: 6 anyone causes one of these little **o**—
1Th 3:13 Jesus comes with all his holy **o.**
Jude 1:14 upon thousands of his holy **o**

HOLY ONES See HOLY

ONESIMUS*

Col 4: 9 He is coming with **O,** our faithful
Phm 1:10 that I appeal to you for my son **O,**

ONESIPHORUS*

2Ti 1:16 show mercy to the household of **O,**
     4:19 and Aquila and the household of **O.**

ONIONS*

Nu 11: 5 melons, leeks, **o** and garlic.

ONLY

Ge   6: 5 of the human heart was **o** evil all
     7:23 **O** Noah was left, and those
    22: 2 "Take your son, your **o** son,
Nu 11: 4 and said, "If **o** we had meat to eat!
    14: 2 them, "If **o** we had died in Egypt!
    20: 3 said, "If **o** we had died when our
Dt 15: 5 if **o** you fully obey the LORD your
1Ki 18:22 "I am the **o** one of the LORD's
Job 23: 3 If **o** I knew where to find him;
Ps 30: 5 For his anger lasts **o** a moment,
Pr 30: 8 but give me **o** my daily bread.
Jer 23:23 "Am I **o** a God nearby,"
Mt   4:10 your God, and serve him **o.**' "
     7:14 that leads to life, and **o** a few find it.
Mk 13:32 nor the Son, but **o** the Father.
Jn   1:14 the glory of the one and **o** Son,
     1:18 God, but the one and **o** Son, who is
     3:16 that he gave his one and **o** Son,
Ro   3:29 Or is God the God of Jews **o?**
1Ti 1:17 invisible, the **o** God, be honor
1Jn 4: 9 **o** Son into the world that we might

ONYX

Ex 28: 9 "Take two **o** stones and engrave
    28:20 row shall be topaz, **o** and jasper.

OPEN OPENED, OPENHANDED,
OPENING, OPENS

Dt 28:12 The LORD will **o** the heavens,
Ps 78: 2 I will **o** my mouth with a parable,
   118:19 **O** for me the gates of the righteous;
   145:16 You **o** your hand and satisfy
Pr 15:11 and Destruction lie **o** before
    27: 5 Better is **o** rebuke than hidden love.
SS   5: 2 "**O** to me, my sister, my darling,
Isa 42: 7 to **o** eyes that are blind, to free
    53: 7 afflicted, yet he did not **o** his mouth;
Mal 3:10 I will not throw **o** the floodgates
Mt 13:35 "I will **o** my mouth in parables,
    17:27 **o** its mouth and you will find
Mk   1:10 he saw heaven being torn **o**
Ac   7:56 "I see heaven **o** and the Son of Man
Rev 3: 8 I have placed before you an **o** door
     4: 1 before me was a door standing **o**
     5: 2 to break the seals and **o** the scroll?"
    19:11 I saw heaven standing **o** and there

OPENED OPEN

Ge   3: 7 the eyes of both of them were **o,**
Nu 16:32 and the earth **o** its mouth
Ne   8: 5 Ezra **o** the book. All the people
Ps 40: 6 but my ears you have **o**—
   105:41 He **o** the rock, and water gushed
Isa 35: 5 will the eyes of the blind be **o**
    50: 5 Sovereign LORD has **o** my ears;
Da   7:10 was seated, and the books were **o.**
Zec 13: 1 day a fountain will be **o** to the house
Mt   3:16 At that moment heaven was **o,**
Lk 11: 9 knock and the door will be **o** to you.
    24:45 Then he **o** their minds so they could
Ac 10:11 He saw heaven **o** and something
Heb 10:20 and living way **o** for us through
Rev 6: 1 I watched as the Lamb **o** the first

Rev 11:19 God's temple in heaven was **o**,
    20:12 before the throne, and books were **o**.

OPENHANDED* HAND, OPEN
Dt 15: 8 be **o** and freely lend them whatever
    15:11 to be **o** toward your fellow Israelites

OPENING OPEN
Mk 2: 4 they made an **o** in the roof

OPENS OPEN
Isa 22:22 what he **o** no one can shut, and what
Rev 3: 7 What he **o** no one can shut,
    3:20 hears my voice and **o** the door,

OPHIR
1Ki 10:11 ships brought gold from **O**;
Isa 13:12 gold, more rare than the gold of **O**.

OPINIONS*
1Ki 18:21 long will you waver between two **o**?
Pr 18: 2 but delight in airing their own **o**.

OPPONENTS* OPPOSE
Ps 127: 5 they contend with their **o** in court.
Pr 18:18 disputes and keeps strong **o** apart.
Lk 13:17 said this, all his **o** were humiliated,
Jn 10:31 Again his Jewish **o** picked up stones
Ac 18:28 he vigorously refuted his Jewish **o** in
    20:19 testing by the plots of my Jewish **o**.
2Ti 2:25 **O** must be gently instructed,

OPPORTUNE* OPPORTUNITY
Mk 6:21 Finally the **o** time came.
Lk 4:13 he left him until an **o** time.

OPPORTUNITY OPPORTUNE
Mt 26:16 watched for an **o** to hand him over.
Ac 25:16 have had an **o** to defend themselves
Ro 7: 8 sin, seizing the **o** afforded
2Co 5:12 are giving you an **o** to take pride
    11:12 under those who want an **o** to be
Gal 6:10 as we have **o**, let us do good to all
Eph 5:16 making the most of every **o**,
Php 4:10 but you had no **o** to show it.
Col 4: 5 make the most of every **o**.
1Ti 5:14 to give the enemy no **o** for slander.
Heb 11:15 they would have had **o** to return.

OPPOSE OPPONENTS, OPPOSED, OPPOSES, OPPOSING, OPPOSITION
Ex 23:22 enemies and will **o** those who **o** you.
Nu 16: 3 They came as a group to **o** Moses
1Sa 2:10 those who **o** the LORD will be
Job 23:13 stands alone, and who can **o** him?
Ps 55:18 me, even though many **o** me.
2Ti 3: 8 so also these teachers **o** the truth.
Titus 1: 9 doctrine and refute those who **o** it.
    2: 8 those who **o** you may be ashamed

OPPOSED OPPOSE
Gal 2:11 came to Antioch, I **o** him to his face,
    3:21 therefore, **o** to the promises of God?
2Ti 3: 8 as Jannes and Jambres **o** Moses,

OPPOSES* OPPOSE
Mk 3:26 if Satan **o** himself and is divided,
Lk 23: 2 He **o** payment of taxes to Caesar
Jn 19:12 who claims to be a king **o** Caesar."
Jas 4: 6 "God **o** the proud but shows favor
1Pe 5: 5 "God **o** the proud but shows favor

OPPOSING OPPOSE
1Ti 6:20 the **o** ideas of what is falsely called

OPPOSITION OPPOSE
Nu 16:42 the assembly gathered in **o** to Moses
    20: 2 the people gathered in **o** to Moses
Heb 12: 3 Consider him who endured such **o**

OPPRESS OPPRESSED, OPPRESSES, OPPRESSION, OPPRESSOR, OPPRESSORS
Ex 1:11 slave masters over them to **o** them
    22:21 "Do not mistreat or **o** a foreigner,
1Ch 17: 9 people will not **o** them anymore,
Ps 105:14 He allowed no one to **o** them;
Isa 3: 5 People will **o** each other—
Eze 22:29 they **o** the poor and needy
Da 7:25 the Most High and **o** his holy people
Am 5:12 There are those who **o** the innocent
Zec 7:10 Do not **o** the widow
Mal 3: 5 wages, who **o** the widows

OPPRESSED OPPRESS
Ex 1:12 But the more they were **o**, the more
Jdg 2:18 of their groaning under those who **o**
Ne 9:27 hands of their enemies, who **o** them.
Ps 9: 9 The LORD is a refuge for the **o**,
    82: 3 the cause of the poor and the **o**.
    103: 6 and justice for all the **o**.
    146: 7 He upholds the cause of the **o**
Pr 16:19 spirit along with the **o** than to share
    31: 5 and deprive all the **o** of their rights.
Isa 1:17 Defend the **o**. Take up the cause
    53: 7 He was **o** and afflicted, yet he did
    58:10 and satisfy the needs of the **o**,
Zep 3:19 time I will deal with all who **o** you.
Zec 10: 2 the people wander like sheep **o**
Lk 4:18 sight for the blind, to set the **o** free,

OPPRESSES* OPPRESS
Pr 14:31 Whoever **o** the poor shows
    22:16 who **o** the poor to increase his wealth
    28: 3 A ruler who **o** the poor is like
Eze 18:12 He **o** the poor and needy.

OPPRESSION OPPRESS
Dt 26: 7 and saw our misery, toil and **o**.
Ps 72:14 He will rescue them from **o**
    119:134 Redeem me from human **o**, that I
Isa 53: 8 By **o** and judgment he was taken
    58: 9 "If you do away with the yoke of **o**,
Eze 45: 9 Give up your violence and **o** and do

OPPRESSOR OPPRESS
Ps 72: 4 of the needy; may he crush the **o**.
Isa 51:13 For where is the wrath of the **o**?
Jer 22: 3 Rescue from the hand of the **o** the

OPPRESSORS OPPRESS
Jdg   6: 9 you from the hand of all your o;
Zep   3: 1 Woe to the city of o,

ORACLE*
Pr   16:10 The lips of a king speak as an o,

ORDAIN ORDAINED, ORDINATION
Ex   29: 9 you shall o Aaron and his sons.

ORDAINED ORDAIN
Ps 111: 9 he o his covenant forever—
     139:16 all the days o for me were written
Isa   37:26 Long ago I o it. In days of old I
Eze   28:14 as a guardian cherub, for so I o you.
Hab   1:12 my Rock, have o them to punish.

ORDEAL*
1Pe   4:12 at the fiery o that has come on you

ORDER ORDERED, ORDERLY, ORDERS
Nu   9:23 They obeyed the LORD's o,
Dt   8: 2 test you in o to know what was
2Ch   36:22 Persia, in o to fulfill the word
Ps 110: 4 forever, in the o of Melchizedek."
Mk   7: 9 of God in o to observe your own
Ro   7: 4 in o that we might bear fruit
Heb   5:10 high priest in the o of Melchizedek.
      9:10 applying until the time of the new o.
Rev   21: 4 for the old o of things has passed

ORDERED ORDER
2Ki   17:15 although the LORD had o them,

ORDERLY* ORDER
Lk   1: 3 to write an o account for you,
1Co   14:40 be done in a fitting and o way.

ORDERS ORDER
Mk   1:27 He even gives o to impure spirits
      3:12 But he gave them strict o not to tell
      9: 9 Jesus gave them o not to tell anyone
Ac   5:28 "We gave you strict o not to teach

ORDINANCE ORDINANCES
Ex   12:17 Celebrate this day as a lasting o
     29: 9 priesthood is theirs by a lasting o.

A LASTING ORDINANCE See LASTING

ORDINANCES* ORDINANCE
Ne   9:29 They sinned against your o, of which
Eze   44:24 decide it according to my o.

ORDINARY
Ac   4:13 that they were unschooled, o men,
Heb   11:23 because they saw he was no o child,

ORDINATION ORDAIN
Ex   29:22 (This is the ram for the o.)

OREB
Jdg   7:25 the Midianite leaders, O and Zeeb.
Ps   83:11 Make their nobles like O and Zeeb,

ORGIES*
Gal   5:21 drunkenness, o, and the like.
1Pe   4: 3 lust, drunkenness, o,

ORIGIN ORIGINAL, ORIGINATE, ORIGINS
Est   6:13 is of Jewish o, you cannot stand
Ac   5:38 purpose or activity is of human o,
2Pe   1:21 For prophecy never had its o

ORIGINAL* ORIGIN
2Ch   24:13 of God according to its o design
Heb   3:14 we hold our o conviction firmly

ORIGINATE* ORIGIN
1Co   14:36 Or did the word of God o with you?

ORIGINS* ORIGIN
Mic   5: 2 over Israel, whose o are from of old,

ORION
Job   9: 9 He is the Maker of the Bear and O,

ORNAMENT* ORNAMENTS
Pr   3:22 life for you, an o to grace your neck.
     25:12 an o of fine gold is the rebuke

ORNAMENTS ORNAMENT
Ex   33: 6 So the Israelites stripped off their o

ORNATE
Ge   37: 3 and he made an o robe for him.
2Sa   13:18 She was wearing an o robe, for this

ORPAH
Ru   1: 4 one named O and the other Ruth.

ORPHANS*
Jn   14:18 I will not leave you as o;
Jas   1:27 to look after o and widows in their

OTHER OTHER'S, OTHERS, OTHERWISE
Ge   28:17 This is none o than the house
Ex   20: 3 shall have no o gods before me.
     23:13 Do not invoke the names of o gods;
Dt   4:35 besides him there is no o.
Jdg   2:19 following o gods and serving
1Sa   8:20 we will be like all the o nations,
1Ki   11: 4 wives turned his heart after o gods,
2Ki   17: 7 They worshiped o gods
2Ch   2: 5 our God is greater than all o gods.
Ps 147:20 He has done this for no o nation;
Ecc   4:10 falls down, one can help the o up.
Isa   44: 8 No, there is no o Rock; I know not
     45: 5 I am the LORD, and there is no o;
Jer   7: 6 if you do not follow o gods to your
Da   3:29 for no o god can save in this way."
Zec   8:17 do not plot evil against each o,
Mt   6:14 if you forgive o people when they sin
      6:24 you will hate the one and love the o,
      6:24 to the one and despise the o.
Lk   17:34 one will be taken and the o left.
Jn   20:30 Jesus performed many o signs
     21:25 Jesus did many o things as well.
1Co   14:21 "With o tongues and through

1Pe 1:22 you have sincere love for each **o**,
      4: 8 all, love each **o** deeply, because love
2Pe 3:16 as they do the **o** Scriptures, to their
1Jn 3:14 to life, because we love each **o**.
Rev 3:15 I wish you were either one or the **o**!

NO OTHER Ex 20:3; Nu 5:19; Dt 4:35, 39; 5:7;
1Sa 18:25; 1Ki 8:60; 1Ch 23:17; Ps 147:20; Isa
44:8; 45:5, 6, 14, 14, 18, 22; 46:9; Jer 30:7; Eze
31:14, 14; Da 3:29; Joel 2:27; Mk 12:32; Ac 4:12;
1Co 11:16; Gal 5:10

OTHER GODS Ex 18:11; 20:3; 23:13; Dt 5:7;
6:14; 7:4; 8:19; 11:16, 28; 13:2, 6, 13; 17:3; 18:20;
28:14, 36, 64; 29:26; 30:17; 31:18, 20; Jos 23:16;
24:2, 16; Jdg 2:17, 19; 10:13; 1Sa 8:8; 26:19; 1Ki
9:6, 9; 11:4, 10; 14:9; 2Ki 17:7, 35, 37, 38; 22:17;
2Ch 2:5; 7:19, 22; 28:25; 34:25; Ps 16:4; Jer 1:16;
7:6, 9, 18; 11:10; 13:10; 16:11, 13; 19:13; 22:9; 25:6;
32:29; 35:15; 44:3, 5, 8, 15; Hos 3:1

OTHER'S* OTHER
Ro   1:12 encouraged by each **o** faith.
Gal 6: 2 Carry each **o** burdens, and in this

OTHERS OTHER
Ps 15: 3 a neighbor, and casts no slur on **o**;
Pr 10:17 ignores correction leads **o** astray.
SS   5: 9 How is your beloved better than **o**,
Da 12: 2 life, **o** to shame and everlasting
Mt   7: 2 For in the same way you judge **o**,
     7:12 to **o** what you would have them do
Lk   6:31 Do to **o** as you would have them do
Ro 13: 8 for whoever loves **o** has fulfilled
2Co 5:11 fear the Lord, we try to persuade **o**.
Php 2: 3 humility value **o** above yourselves,

OTHERWISE OTHER
Isa 6:10 **O** they might see with their eyes,
Mt 13:15 **O** they might see with their eyes,
Ac 28:27 **O** they might see with their eyes,
1Ti 6: 3 If anyone teaches **o** and does not

OTHNIEL
Nephew of Caleb (Jos 15:15-19; Jdg 1:12-15).
Judge who freed Israel from Aram (Jdg 3:7-11).

OUGHT
Ro   1:28 that they do what **o** not to be done.
    12: 3 of yourself more highly than you **o**,
Jas 4:17 knows the good they **o** to do
2Pe 3:11 what kind of people **o** you to be?
1Jn 3:16 we **o** to lay down our lives for our
3Jn 1: 8 We **o** therefore to show hospitality

OUTCOME
Isa 41:22 them and know their final **o**.
Da 12: 8 lord, what will the **o** of all this be?"
Heb 13: 7 Consider the **o** of their way of life
1Pe 4:17 what will the **o** be for those who do

OUTNUMBER NUMBER
Ps 139:18 they would **o** the grains of sand—

OUTPOURED* POUR
Ps 79:10 that you avenge the **o** blood of your
Eze 20:33 outstretched arm and with **o** wrath.

Eze 20:34 outstretched arm and with **o** wrath.

OUTPOURING* POUR
Eze 9: 8 of Israel in this **o** of your wrath

OUTRAGEOUS
Jdg 19:23 is my guest, don't do this **o** thing.

OUTSIDE OUTSIDERS
Pr 22:13 sluggard says, "There's a lion **o**!
Mt 22:13 and throw him **o**, into the darkness,
Lk 11:39 you Pharisees clean the **o** of the cup
    13:33 no prophet can die **o** Jerusalem!
1Co 5:13 God will judge those **o**.
Heb 13:12 suffered **o** the city gate to make
Rev 22:15 **O** are the dogs, those who practice

OUTSIDE THE CAMP See CAMP

OUTSIDERS* OUTSIDE
Col 4: 5 wise in the way you act toward **o**;
1Th 4:12 daily life may win the respect of **o**
1Ti 3: 7 also have a good reputation with **o**,

OUTSTANDING
SS   5:10 and ruddy, **o** among ten thousand.
Ro 13: 8 Let no debt remain **o**,

OUTSTRETCHED STRETCH
Ex   6: 6 I will redeem you with an **o** arm
Dt   4:34 by a mighty hand and an **o** arm,
1Ki 8:42 your mighty hand and your **o** arm—
Ps 136:12 with a mighty hand and **o** arm;
Isa 3:16 walking along with **o** necks,
Jer 27: 5 power and **o** arm I made the earth
    32:17 by your great power and **o** arm,
Eze 20:33 with a mighty hand and an **o** arm

OUTSTRETCHED ARM Ex 6:6; Dt 4:34; 5:15;
7:19; 9:29; 11:2; 26:8; 1Ki 8:42; 2Ki 17:36; 2Ch
6:32; Ps 136:12; Jer 27:5; 32:17, 21; Eze 20:33, 34

OUTWARD* OUTWARDLY
1Sa 16: 7 People look at the **o** appearance,
Ro   2:28 nor is circumcision merely **o**
1Pe 3: 3 should not come from **o** adornment,

OUTWARDLY* OUTWARD
Ro   2:28 is not a Jew who is one only **o**,
2Co 4:16 Though **o** we are wasting away,
Heb 9:13 sanctify them so that they are **o** clean.

OUTWEIGHS* WEIGH
Ecc 10: 1 so a little folly **o** wisdom and honor.
2Co 4:17 an eternal glory that far **o** them all.

OUTWIT* OUTWITTED
2Co 2:11 in order that Satan might not **o** us.

OUTWITTED* OUTWIT
Mt   2:16 that he had been **o** by the Magi,

OVER
Ex 12:13 I see the blood, I will pass **o** you.
    12:23 and will pass **o** that doorway, and he
Ps   1: 6 the LORD watches **o** the way
     8: 6 You made them rulers **o** the works
   113: 4 LORD is exalted **o** all the nations,

Ps 145:20 The Lord watches o all who love
Isa 31: 5 it, he will 'pass o' it and will rescue
Mk 15:15 and handed him o to be crucified.

OVERAWED* AWE
Ps 49:16 Do not be o when others grow rich,

OVERBEARING*
Titus 1: 7 not o, not quick-tempered, not given

OVERCAME OVERCOME
Hos 12: 4 struggled with the angel and o him;

OVERCOME OVERCAME, OVERCOMES
Ge 32:28 God and with humans and have o."
Mt 16:18 and the gates of Hades will not o it.
Mk   9:24 help me o my unbelief!"
Lk 10:19 and to o all the power of the enemy;
Jn   1: 5 and the darkness has not o it.
    16:33 But take heart! I have o the world."
Ro 12:21 Do not be o by evil, but o evil
1Ti 5:11 sensual desires o their dedication
2Pe 2:20 are again entangled in it and are o,
1Jn 2:13 because you have o the evil one.
     4: 4 are from God and have o them,
     5: 4 is the victory that has o the world,

OVERCOMES* OVERCOME
1Jn 5: 4 everyone born of God o the world.
     5: 5 Who is it that o the world?

OVERFLOW OVERFLOWING, OVERFLOWS
Ps 65:11 and your carts o with abundance.
   119:171 May my lips o with praise, for you
La   1:16 I weep and my eyes o with tears.
Ro   5:15 man, Jesus Christ, o to the many!
    15:13 so that you may o with hope
2Co 4:15 people may cause thanksgiving to o
1Th 3:12 love increase and o for each other

OVERFLOWING OVERFLOW
Pr   3:10 then your barns will be filled to o,
     8:24 there were no springs o with water;
2Co 8: 2 trial, their o joy and their extreme
     9:12 o in many expressions of thanks
Col 2: 7 taught, and o with thankfulness.

OVERFLOWS* OVERFLOW
Ps 23: 5 anoint my head with oil; my cup o.

OVERJOYED* JOY
Da   6:23 The king was o and gave orders
Mt   2:10 they saw the star, they were o.
Jn 20:20 The disciples were o when they saw
Ac 12:14 she was so o she ran back without
1Pe 4:13 that you may be o when his glory is

OVERLOOK* OVERLOOKED, OVERLOOKS
Dt   9:27 O the stubbornness of this people,
    24:19 in your field and you o a sheaf,
Pr 12:16 at once, but the prudent o an insult.
    19:11 it is to one's glory to o an offense.

OVERLOOKED* OVERLOOK
Ac   6: 1 because their widows were being o
    17:30 In the past God o such ignorance,

OVERLOOKS OVERLOOK
2Ch 20:24 came to the place that o the desert

OVERNIGHT NIGHT
Lev 19:13 back the wages of a hired worker o.
Jnh 4:10 It sprang up o and died o.

OVERPOWER POWER
Ge 32:25 man saw that he could not o him,
Rev 11: 7 attack them, and o and kill them.

OVERRIGHTEOUS* RIGHTEOUS
Ecc 7:16 Do not be o, neither be overwise—

OVERSEER OVERSEERS
Pr   6: 7 It has no commander, no o or ruler,
1Ti 3: 1 to be an o desires a noble task.
     3: 2 Now the o is to be above reproach,
Titus 1: 7 Since an o manages God's
1Pe 2:25 the Shepherd and O of your souls.

OVERSEERS OVERSEER
Ex   5:15 the Israelite o went and appealed
Ac 20:28 the Holy Spirit has made you o.
Php 1: 1 together with the o and deacons:

OVERSHADOW* OVERSHADOWING
1Ch 28:18 and o the ark of the covenant
Lk   1:35 power of the Most High will o you.

OVERSHADOWING OVERSHADOW
Ex 25:20 upward, o the cover with them.
Heb 9: 5 of the Glory, o the atonement cover.

OVERTAKE OVERTAKES
Ps 91:10 no harm will o you, no disaster will

OVERTAKES OVERTAKE
Pr 12:21 No harm o the righteous,

OVERTHREW OVERTHROW
Ge 19:25 Thus he o those cities and the entire
Jer 50:40 As I o Sodom and Gomorrah along

OVERTHROW OVERTHREW, OVERTHROWN, OVERTHROWS
2Th 2: 8 whom the Lord Jesus will o

OVERTHROWN OVERTHROW
Isa 13:19 will be o by God like Sodom

OVERTHROWS OVERTHROW
Pr 13: 6 but wickedness o the sinner.
Isa 44:25 who o the learning of the wise

OVERTURNED
Mk 11:15 He o the tables of the money

OVERWHELMED OVERWHELMING
2Sa 22: 5 the torrents of destruction o me.

1Ki 10: 5 temple of the LORD, she was o.
Ps 38: 4 My guilt has o me like a burden too
65: 3 When we were o by sins,
Mt 26:38 "My soul is o with sorrow
Mk 7:37 People were o with amazement.
9:15 they were o with wonder and ran
2Co 2: 7 so that he will not be o by excessive

OVERWHELMING
OVERWHELMED
Pr 27: 4 Anger is cruel and fury o, but who
Isa 10:22 has been decreed, o and righteous.
28:15 When an o scourge sweeps by,
Na 1: 8 with an o flood he will make an end

OVERWICKED* WICKED
Ecc 7:17 Do not be o, and do not be a fool—

OVERWISE* WISE
Ecc 7:16 not be overrighteous, neither be o—

OWE OWES
Ro 13: 7 Give to everyone what you o them: If
you o taxes, pay taxes;
Phm 1:19 that you o me your very self.

OWES* OWE
Dt 15: 3 any debt your fellow Israelite o you.
Phm 1:18 you any wrong or o you anything,

OWN OWNER, OWNER'S, OWNERSHIP, OWNS
Ge 1:27 created mankind in his o image,
15: 4 a son who is your o flesh and blood
Ex 6: 7 I will take you as my o people, and I
32:13 to whom you swore by your o self:
Dt 24:16 each will die for their o sin.
1Sa 13:14 sought out a man after his o heart
Pr 3: 7 Do not be wise in your o eyes;
26:12 see a person wise in their o eyes?
Isa 48:11 For my o sake, for my o sake, I do
53: 6 each of us has turned to our o way;
Jer 10:23 that people's lives are not their o;
31:30 everyone will die for their o sin;
Eze 33: 4 their blood will be on their o head.
Jn 1:11 He came to that which was his o, but
his o did not receive him.
7:16 "My teaching is not my o.
10:12 shepherd and does not o the sheep.
10:18 but I lay it down of my o accord.
12:49 For I did not speak on my o,
Ro 8:32 He who did not spare his o Son,
1Co 6:19 You are not your o;
7: 7 of you has your o gift from God;
Gal 6: 5 each one should carry their o load.
Php 2: 4 not looking to your o interests

OWNER OWN
Mt 21:40 when the o of the vineyard comes,
24:43 If the o of the house had known

OWNER'S OWN
Isa 1: 3 the donkey its o manger, but Israel

OWNERSHIP* OWN
2Co 1:22 set his seal of o on us, and put his

OWNS OWN
Mt 18:12 If a man o a hundred sheep, and one

OX OXEN
Ex 20:17 or female servant, his o or donkey,
Dt 22:10 Do not plow with an o and a donkey
25: 4 Do not muzzle an o while it is
Pr 7:22 he followed her like an o going
Isa 11: 7 and the lion will eat straw like the o.
65:25 and the lion will eat straw like the o.
Eze 1:10 lion, and on the left the face of an o;
Lk 13:15 of you on the Sabbath untie your o
1Co 9: 9 "Do not muzzle an o while it is
1Ti 5:18 "Do not muzzle an o while it is
Rev 4: 7 the second was like an o, the third

OXEN OX
1Ki 19:20 then left his o and ran after Elijah.
Lk 14:19 'I have just bought five yoke of o,
1Co 9: 9 Is it about o that God is concerned?

P

PADDAN ARAM ARAM
Ge 28: 2 Go at once to P, to the house of
35: 9 After Jacob returned from P,

PAGAN PAGANS
Isa 2: 6 Philistines and embrace p customs.
57: 8 you have put your p symbols.
Mt 18:17 treat them as you would a p or a tax
Lk 12:30 For the p world runs after all such

PAGANS* PAGAN
Mt 5:47 Do not even p do that?
6: 7 do not keep on babbling like p,
6:32 For the p run after all these things,
1Co 5: 1 of a kind that even p do not tolerate:
10:20 but the sacrifices of p are offered
12: 2 You know that when you were p,
1Th 4: 5 not in passionate lust like the p,
1Pe 2:12 such good lives among the p that,
4: 3 the past doing what p choose to do—
3Jn 1: 7 out, receiving no help from the p.

PAID PAY
Jdg 1: 7 Now God has p me back for what I
1Sa 25:21 He has p me back evil for good.
Ne 9:30 Yet they p no attention, so you gave
Isa 40: 2 that her sin has been p for, that she
Zec 11:12 So they p me thirty pieces of silver.
2Pe 2:13 They will be p back with harm

PAIN PAINFUL, PAINS
Job 6:10 my joy in unrelenting p—that I had
33:19 on a bed of p with constant distress
Isa 53: 4 Surely he took up our p and bore
Jer 4:19 I writhe in p. Oh, the agony of my
15:18 Why is my p unending and my
Mt 4:24 those suffering severe p,
Jn 16:21 to a child has p because her time has
1Pe 2:19 up under the p of unjust suffering
Rev 21: 4 death' or mourning or crying or p,

PAINFUL PAIN

Ge   3:17 through **p** toil you will eat food
       5:29 **p** toil of our hands caused
Job   6:25 How **p** are honest words!
Eze 28:24 neighbors who are **p** briers
2Co 2: 1 I would not make another **p** visit
Heb 12:11 seems pleasant at the time, but **p**.

PAINS PAIN

Ge   3:16 "I will make your **p** in childbearing
Mk 13: 8 These are the beginning of birth **p**.
Ro   8:22 as in the **p** of childbirth right
Gal   4:19 in the **p** of childbirth until Christ is
1Th   5: 3 as labor **p** on a pregnant woman,

PAIRS

Ge   7: 8 **P** of clean and unclean animals,

PALACE PALACES

2Sa 5:11 and they built a **p** for David.
1Ki   7: 2 He built the **P** of the Forest
       9: 1 of the Lord and the royal **p**,
Est   9: 4 Mordecai was prominent in the **p**;
Jer 22:13 "Woe to him who builds his **p**
    52:13 the royal **p** and all the houses
Jn 18:28 to the **p** of the Roman governor.
Ac 23:35 be kept under guard in Herod's **p**.

PALACES PALACE

Hos 8:14 forgotten their Maker and built **p**;
Lk   7:25 and indulge in luxury are in **p**.

PALE

Isa 29:22 no longer will their faces grow **p**.
Jer 30: 6 labor, every face turned deathly **p**?
Da 10: 8 my face turned deathly **p** and I was
Rev 6: 8 and there before me was a **p** horse!

PALESTINE (KJV) See PHILISTIA, PHILISTINE

PALM PALMS

Ex 15:27 twelve springs and seventy **p** trees,
Jdg   4: 5 She held court under the **P**
1Ki   6:29 cherubim, **p** trees and open flowers.
Ps 92:12 righteous will flourish like a **p** tree,
Jn 12:13 They took **p** branches and went
Rev 7: 9 and were holding **p** branches in their

PALMS PALM

Lev 23:40 from **p**, willows and other leafy
Ne   8:15 and from myrtles, **p** and shade trees,
Isa 49:16 engraved you on the **p** of my hands;

PAMPERED*

Pr 29:21 A servant **p** from youth will turn

PANELED PANELING

Hag 1: 4 to be living in your **p** houses,

PANELING* PANELED

1Ki 6:15 **p** them from the floor of the temple
Ps 74: 6 They smashed all the carved **p**

PANIC

Dt 20: 3 do not **p** or be terrified by them.
1Sa 14:15 It was a **p** sent by God.

Isa 28:16 on it will never be stricken with **p**.
Eze 7: 7 There is **p**, not joy,
Zec 14:13 by the Lord with great **p**.

PANTS*

Ps 42: 1 As the deer **p** for streams of water, so
         my soul **p** for you,

PAPER*

2Jn 1:12 but I do not want to use **p** and ink.

PAPYRUS

Ex   2: 3 she got a **p** basket for him

PARABLE PARABLES

Ps 78: 2 I will open my mouth with a **p**;
Eze 17: 2 and tell it to the Israelites as a **p**.
Mt 13:18 to what the **p** of the sower means:
    15:15 Peter said, "Explain the **p** to us."
    21:33 "Listen to another **p**: There was
Lk 20:19 he had spoken this **p** against them.

PARABLES PARABLE

See also JESUS: PARABLES
Mt 13:35 "I will open my mouth in **p**, I will
Lk   8:10 but to others I speak in **p**, so that,

PARADISE*

Lk 23:43 today you will be with me in **p**."
2Co 12: 4 was caught up to **p** and heard
Rev 2: 7 tree of life, which is in the **p** of God.

PARALYZED

Hab 1: 4 Therefore the law is **p**, and justice
Mt   9: 2 Some men brought to him a **p** man,
Mk   2: 3 bringing to him a **p** man,
Jn   5: 3 the blind, the lame, the **p**.
Ac   9:33 who was **p** and had been bedridden

PARAN

Ge 21:21 he was living in the Desert of **P**,
Nu 10:12 came to rest in the Desert of **P**.
Hab 3: 3 the Holy One from Mount **P**.

PARCHED

Ps 143: 6 I thirst for you like a **p** land.
Isa 41:18 and the **p** ground into springs.

PARCHMENTS*

2Ti 4:13 and my scrolls, especially the **p**.

PARDON PARDONED, PARDONS

2Ch 30:18 Lord, who is good, **p** everyone
Job 7:21 Why do you not **p** my offenses
Isa 55: 7 and to our God, for he will freely **p**.

PARDONED* PARDON

Nu 14:19 just as you have **p** them

PARDONS* PARDON

Mic 7:18 like you, who **p** sin and forgives

PARENT FATHER, PARENT'S, PARENTS

Pr 17:21 is no joy for the **p** of a godless fool.

PARENT'S* PARENT

Pr 15: 5 A fool spurns a **p** discipline,

PARENTS PARENT

Ex	20: 5	for the sin of the **p** to the third
Dt	24:16	**P** are not to be put to death for their
	24:16	nor children put to death for their **p**;
Pr	17: 6	and **p** are the pride of their children.
	19:14	and wealth are inherited from **p**,
Jer	31:29	say, 'The **p** have eaten sour grapes,
Eze	18: 2	" 'The **p** eat sour grapes,
Mal	4: 6	the hearts of the **p** to their children,
	4: 6	the hearts of the children to their **p**;
Mk	13:12	Children will rebel against their **p**
Lk	1:17	the hearts of the **p** to their children
	2:27	When the **p** brought in the child
	18:29	sisters or **p** or children for the sake
	21:16	You will be betrayed even by **p**,
Jn	9: 3	this man nor his **p** sinned,"
Ro	1:30	of doing evil; they disobey their **p**;
2Co	12:14	not have to save up for their **p**, but **p** for their children.
Eph	6: 1	Children, obey your **p** in the Lord,
Col	3:20	Children, obey your **p** in everything,
1Ti	5: 4	family and so repaying their **p**
2Ti	3: 2	disobedient to their **p**, ungrateful,

PARSIN* PERES

Da   5:25 MENE, MENE, TEKEL, **P**

PART APART, PARTED, PARTLY, PARTS

Nu	18:29	and holiest **p** of everything given
2Sa	20: 1	share in David, no **p** in Jesse's son!
1Ki	12:16	in David, what **p** in Jesse's son?
Job	42:12	The LORD blessed the latter **p** of Job's life more than the former **p**.
Ps	144: 5	**P** your heavens, LORD, and come
Mt	5:29	you to lose one **p** of your body than
Jn	13: 8	wash you, you have no **p** with me."
1Co	12:14	so the body is not made up of one **p**
	13: 9	know in **p** and we prophesy in **p**,
	13:10	comes, what is in **p** disappears.

PARTED PART

Ge	13:11	The two men **p** company:
2Sa	22:10	He **p** the heavens and came down;
Ac	15:39	disagreement that they **p** company.

PARTIAL* PARTIALITY

Pr   18: 5 It is not good to be **p** to the wicked

PARTIALITY* PARTIAL

Lev	19:15	do not show **p** to the poor
Dt	1:17	Do not show **p** in judging;
	10:17	who shows no **p** and accepts no
	16:19	Do not pervert justice or show **p**.
2Ch	19: 7	our God there is no injustice or **p**
Job	13: 8	Will you show him **p**?
	13:10	to account if you secretly showed **p**.
	32:21	I will show no **p**, nor will I flatter
	34:19	who shows no **p** to princes and does
Ps	82: 2	unjust and show **p** to the wicked?
Pr	24:23	To show **p** in judging is not good:
	28:21	To show **p** is not good—
Mal	2: 9	but have shown **p** in matters
Lk	20:21	that you do not show **p** but teach

1Ti   5:21 to keep these instructions without **p**,

PARTICIPANTS* PARTICIPATE

1Co 10:20 not want you to be **p** with demons.

PARTICIPATE* PARTICIPANTS, PARTICIPATION

1Co	10:18	not those who eat the sacrifices **p**
1Pe	4:13	But rejoice inasmuch as you **p**
2Pe	1: 4	that through them you may **p**

PARTICIPATION* PARTICIPATE

1Co	10:16	we give thanks a **p** in the blood
	10:16	bread that we break a **p** in the body
Php	3:10	resurrection and **p** in his sufferings,

PARTLY PART

Da   2:33 its feet **p** of iron and **p** of baked

PARTNER PARTNERS, PARTNERSHIP

Pr	2:17	who has left the **p** of her youth
Mal	2:14	though she is your **p**, the wife
1Pe	3: 7	them with respect as the weaker **p**

PARTNERS PARTNER

Eph   5: 7 Therefore do not be **p** with them.

PARTNERSHIP* PARTNER

Php	1: 5	because of your **p** in the gospel
Phm	1: 6	I pray that your **p** with us

PARTS PART

Pr	18: 8	they go down to the inmost **p**.
1Co	12:20	is, there are many **p**, but one body.

PASHHUR

Priest; opponent of Jeremiah (Jer 20:1–6).

PASS PASSED, PASSER-BY, PASSES, PASSING

Ex	12:13	I see the blood, I will **p** over you.
	12:23	and will **p** over that doorway,
	33:19	"I will cause all my goodness to **p**
Nu	20:17	Please let us **p** through your
	21:22	"Let us **p** through your country.
1Ki	9: 8	All who **p** by will be appalled
	19:11	for the LORD is about to **p** by."
Ps	90:10	for they quickly **p**, and we fly away.
	105:19	till what he foretold came to **p**,
Ecc	6:12	days they **p** through like a shadow?
Isa	31: 5	he will '**p** over' it and will rescue
	43: 2	When you **p** through the waters,
	62:10	**P** through, **p** through the gates!
Jer	22: 8	many nations will **p** by this city
La	1:12	it nothing to you, all you who **p** by?
Da	7:14	dominion that will not **p** away,
Am	5:17	for I will **p** through your midst,"
Mt	24:35	Heaven and earth will **p** away, but my words will never **p** away.
Mk	14:35	possible the hour might **p** from him.
Ro	2: 1	you who **p** judgment on someone
1Co	13: 8	there is knowledge, it will **p** away.
Jas	1:10	since they will **p** away like a wild
1Jn	2:17	The world and its desires **p** away,

PASSED PASS
Ge 15:17 appeared and **p** between the pieces.
Ex 12:27 who **p** over the houses
33:22 you with my hand until I have **p** by.
34: 6 And he **p** in front of Moses,
Nu 33: 8 **p** through the sea into the desert,
Jos 3:17 while all Israel **p** by until the whole
2Ch 21:20 He **p** away, to no one's regret,
Ps 37:36 he soon **p** away and was no more;
57: 1 your wings until the disaster has **p**.
Lk 10:32 and saw him, **p** by on the other side.
1Co 15: 3 For what I received I **p** on to you as
Heb 11:29 faith the people **p** through the Red
1Jn 3:14 We know that we have **p** from death
Rev 21: 1 and the first earth had **p** away,
21: 4 the old order of things has **p** away."

PASSER-BY* PASS
Pr 26:10 is one who hires a fool or any **p**.

PASSES PASS
Ex 33:22 When my glory **p** by, I will put you
Zep 2: 2 that day **p** like windblown chaff,

PASSING PASS
Ro 14:13 Therefore let us stop **p** judgment
1Co 7:31 world in its present form is **p** away.
2Co 3:13 seeing the end of what was **p** away.
1Jn 2: 8 because the darkness is **p**

PASSION* PASSIONATE, PASSIONS
Ps 11: 5 love violence, he hates with a **p**.
Hos 7: 6 Their **p** smolders all night,
1Co 7: 9 better to marry than to burn with **p**.

PASSIONATE* PASSION
1Th 4: 5 not in **p** lust like the pagans, who do

PASSIONS* PASSION
Ro 7: 5 the sinful **p** aroused by the law were
1Co 7:36 if his **p** are too strong and he feels
Gal 5:24 have crucified the flesh with its **p**
Titus 2:12 to ungodliness and worldly **p**,
3: 3 and enslaved by all kinds of **p**

PASSOVER
Ex 12:11 Eat it in haste; it is the LORD's **P**.
Lev 23: 5 The LORD's **P** begins at twilight
Nu 9: 2 "Have the Israelites celebrate the **P**
Dt 16: 1 celebrate the **P** of the LORD your
Jos 5:10 the Israelites celebrated the **P**.
2Ki 23:21 "Celebrate the **P** to the LORD
2Ch 30: 1 and celebrate the **P** to the LORD,
Ezr 6:19 month, the exiles celebrated the **P**.
Mk 14:12 customary to sacrifice the **P** lamb,
14:12 preparations for you to eat the **P**?"
Lk 22: 8 preparations for us to eat the **P**."
1Co 5: 7 For Christ, our **P** lamb, has been
Heb 11:28 By faith he kept the **P**

PAST
Ge 18:11 Sarah was **p** the age of childbearing.
Ecc 3:15 and God will call the **p** to account.
Isa 43:18 do not dwell on the **p**.

Isa 65:16 For the **p** troubles will be forgotten
Ac 14:16 In the **p**, he let all nations go their
17:30 In the **p** God overlooked such
Ro 15: 4 was written in the **p** was written
16:25 the mystery hidden for long ages **p**,
Eph 3: 9 for ages **p** was kept hidden in God,
Heb 1: 1 In the **p** God spoke to our ancestors
11:11 Sarah, who was **p** childbearing age,
1Pe 3: 5 women of the **p** who put their hope
2Pe 1: 9 been cleansed from their **p** sins.

PASTORS*
Eph 4:11 the evangelists, the **p** and teachers,

PASTURE PASTURELANDS, PASTURES
Ps 37: 3 dwell in the land and enjoy safe **p**.
79:13 the sheep of your **p**, will praise you
95: 7 God and we are the people of his **p**,
100: 3 are his people, the sheep of his **p**.
Jer 23: 1 and scattering the sheep of my **p**!"
50: 7 their verdant **p**, the LORD,
Eze 34:13 I will **p** them on the mountains
Jn 10: 9 will come in and go out, and find **p**.

PASTURELANDS PASTURE
Nu 35: 2 And give them **p** around the towns.

PASTURES PASTURE
Ps 23: 2 He makes me lie down in green **p**,

PATCH
Mk 2:21 "No one sews a **p** of unshrunk cloth

PATH PATHS
Nu 22:24 in a narrow **p** through the vineyards,
2Sa 22:37 You provide a broad **p** for my feet,
Ne 9:19 did not fail to guide them on their **p**,
Job 16:22 years will pass before I take the **p**
Ps 16:11 make known to me the **p** of life;
27:11 me in a straight **p** because of my
119: 9 young person stay on the **p** of purity?
119:32 I run in the **p** of your commands,
119:105 a lamp for my feet, a light on my **p**.
Pr 2: 9 and just and fair—every good **p**.
5: 8 Keep to a **p** far from her, do not go
12:28 along that **p** is immortality.
15:10 awaits anyone who leaves the **p**;
15:19 the **p** of the upright is a highway.
15:24 The **p** of life leads upward
21:16 strays from the **p** of prudence comes
Isa 26: 7 The **p** of the righteous is level;
Jer 31: 9 on a level **p** where they will not
Mt 13: 4 some fell along the **p**, and the birds
Lk 1:79 guide our feet into the **p** of peace."
2Co 6: 3 no stumbling block in anyone's **p**,

PATHS PATH
Ps 17: 5 My steps have held to your **p**;
23: 3 He guides me along the right **p**
25: 4 ways, LORD, teach me your **p**.
Pr 1:19 Such are the **p** of all who go
2:13 who have left the straight **p** to walk
2:18 and her **p** to the spirits of the dead.
3: 6 and he will make your **p** straight.

Pr 4:11 and lead you along straight **p**.
4:26 careful thought to the **p** for your feet
5:21 and he examines all your **p**.
8:20 righteousness, along the **p** of justice,
22: 5 In the **p** of the wicked are snares
Isa 2: 3 so that we may walk in his **p**."
Jer 6:16 ask for the ancient **p**, ask where
Mic 4: 2 so that we may walk in his **p**."
Mt 3: 3 Lord, make straight **p** for him.' "
Ac 2:28 made known to me the **p** of life;
Ro 11:33 and his **p** beyond tracing out!
Heb 12:13 "Make level **p** for your feet,"

PATIENCE* PATIENT

Pr 19:11 A person's wisdom yields **p**; it is
25:15 Through **p** a ruler can be persuaded,
Ecc 7: 8 and **p** is better than pride.
Isa 7:13 not enough to try the **p** of humans?
7:13 Will you try the **p** of my God also?
Ro 2: 4 forbearance and **p**, not realizing
9:22 bore with great **p** the objects of his
2Co 6: 6 understanding, **p** and kindness;
Col 1:11 may have great endurance and **p**,
3:12 humility, gentleness and **p**.
1Ti 1:16 might display his immense **p** as
2Ti 3:10 of life, my purpose, faith, **p**, love,
4: 2 with great **p** and careful instruction.
Heb 6:12 **p** inherit what has been promised.
Jas 5:10 as an example of **p** in the face
2Pe 3:15 that our Lord's **p** means salvation,

PATIENT* PATIENCE, PATIENTLY

Ne 9:30 many years you were **p** with them.
Job 6:11 What prospects, that I should be **p**?
Pr 14:29 Whoever is **p** has great
15:18 the one who is **p** calms a quarrel.
16:32 Better a **p** person than a warrior,
Mt 18:26 'Be **p** with me,' he begged, 'and I
18:29 and begged him, 'Be **p** with me,
Ro 12:12 Be joyful in hope, **p** in affliction,
1Co 13: 4 Love is **p**, love is kind. It does not
2Co 1: 6 produces in you **p** endurance
Eph 4: 2 be **p**, bearing with one another
1Th 5:14 help the weak, be **p** with everyone.
Jas 5: 7 Be **p**, then, brothers and sisters,
5: 8 You too, be **p** and stand firm,
2Pe 3: 9 Instead he is **p** with you,
Rev 1: 9 **p** endurance that are ours in Jesus,
13:10 This calls for **p** endurance
14:12 This calls for **p** endurance

PATIENTLY* PATIENT

Ps 37: 7 the Lord and wait **p** for him;
40: 1 I waited **p** for the Lord;
Isa 38:13 I waited **p** till dawn, but like a lion
Hab 3:16 Yet I will wait **p** for the day
Ac 26: 3 I beg you to listen to me **p**.
Ro 8:25 we do not yet have, we wait for it **p**.
Heb 6:15 And so after waiting **p**,
Jas 5: 7 **p** waiting for the autumn and spring
1Pe 3:20 ago when God waited **p** in the days
Rev 3:10 have kept my command to endure **p**,

PATMOS*

Rev 1: 9 the island of **P** because of the word

PATRIARCH* PATRIARCHS

Ac 2:29 confidently that the **p** David died
7: 8 Jacob became the father of the twelve **p**.
Heb 7: 4 Even the **p** Abraham gave him

PATRIARCHS PATRIARCH

Jn 7:22 but from the **p**), you circumcise
Ro 9: 5 Theirs are the **p**, and from them is
15: 8 made to the **p** might be confirmed

PATTERN

Ex 25:40 them according to the **p** shown you
Nu 8: 4 exactly like the **p** the Lord had
Ro 5:14 who is a **p** of the one to come.
12: 2 not conform to the **p** of this world,
2Ti 1:13 me, keep as the **p** of sound teaching,
Heb 8: 5 according to the **p** shown you

PAUL SAUL

Also called Saul (Ac 13:9). Pharisee from Tarsus (Ac 9:11; Php 3:5). Apostle (Gal 1). At stoning of Stephen (Ac 8:1). Persecuted Church (Ac 9:1–2; Gal 1:13). Vision of Jesus on road to Damascus (Ac 9:4–9; 26:12–18). In Arabia (Gal 1:17). Preached in Damascus; escaped death through the wall in a basket (Ac 9:19–25). In Jerusalem; sent back to Tarsus (Ac 9:26–30).

Brought to Antioch by Barnabas (Ac 11:22–26). First missionary journey to Cyprus and Galatia (Ac 13–14). Stoned at Lystra (Ac 14:19–20). At Jerusalem council (Ac 15). Split with Barnabas over Mark (Ac 15:36–41).

Second missionary journey with Silas (Ac 16–20). Called to Macedonia (Ac 16:6–10). Freed from prison in Philippi (Ac 16:16–40). In Thessalonica (Ac 17:1–9). Speech in Athens (Ac 17:16–33). In Corinth (Ac 18). In Ephesus (Ac 19). Return to Jerusalem (Ac 20). Farewell to Ephesian elders (Ac 20:13–38). Arrival in Jerusalem (Ac 21:1–26). Arrested (Ac 21:27–36). Addressed crowds (Ac 22), Sanhedrin (Ac 23:1–11). Sent to Caesarea (Ac 23:12–35). Trial before Felix (Ac 24), Festus (Ac 25:1–12). Before Agrippa (Ac 25:13—26:32). Voyage to Rome; shipwreck (Ac 27). Arrival in Rome (Ac 28).

Letters: Romans, 1 and 2 Corinthians, Galatians, Ephesians, Philippians, Colossians, 1 and 2 Thessalonians, 1 and 2 Timothy, Titus, Philemon.

PAVEMENT

Ex 24:10 feet was something like a **p** made
Jn 19:13 seat at a place known as the Stone **P**

PAW*

1Sa 17:37 rescued me from the **p** of the lion and the **p** of the bear will rescue

PAY PAID, PAYING, PAYMENT, PAYS, REPAID, REPAY, REPAYING

Ge 23:13 I will **p** the price of the field.
Ex 4: 8 you or **p** attention to the first sign,
15:26 if you **p** attention to his commands
22: 3 they must be sold to **p** for their
22: 4 they must **p** back double.

Ex   30:12 them, each one must **p** the LORD
Lev   26:43 They will **p** for their sins because
Dt   7:12 If you **p** attention to these laws
Ps   94: 2 **p** back to the proud what they
Pr   4: 1 **p** attention and gain understanding.
       4:20 My son, **p** attention to what I say;
       5: 1 My son, **p** attention to my wisdom,
       6:31 he must **p** sevenfold, though it costs
      19:19 person must **p** the penalty;
      22:17 **P** attention and turn your ear
      24:29 I'll **p** them back for what they did."
Jer   7:24 they did not listen or **p** attention;
Eze   40: 4 **p** attention to everything I am going
Zec   11:12 "If you think it best, give me my **p**;
Mt   20: 4 and I will **p** you whatever is right.'
      22:16 because you **p** no attention to who
      22:17 Is it right to **p** the imperial tax
Lk   3:14 be content with your **p**."
      19: 8 I will **p** back four times
Ro   13: 6 This is also why you **p** taxes,
2Th   1: 6 He will **p** back trouble to those who
2Pe   1:19 you will do well to **p** attention to it,
Rev   18: 6 **p** her back double for what she has

PAYING PAY
1Ch   21:24 "No, I insist on **p** the full price.
Mt   22:19 me the coin used for **p** the tax."

PAYMENT PAY
Ps   49: 8 a life is costly, no **p** is ever enough—
Isa   65: 7 their laps the full **p** for their former
Php   4:18 I have received full **p** and have

PAYS PAY
Ps   31:23 him, but the proud he **p** back in full.
Pr   17:13 the house of one who **p** back evil
1Th   5:15 sure that nobody **p** back wrong

PEACE PEACE-LOVING,
PEACEABLE, PEACEFUL,
PEACEMAKERS
Lev   26: 6 " 'I will grant **p** in the land,
Nu   6:26 toward you and give you **p**." '
      25:12 him I am making my covenant of **p**
Dt   20:10 a city, make its people an offer of **p**.
Jos   9:15 Joshua made a treaty of **p** with them
      11:19 not one city made a treaty of **p**
Jdg   3:11 So the land had **p** for forty years,
       3:30 and the land had **p** for eighty years.
       5:31 Then the land had **p** forty years.
       6:24 there and called it The LORD Is **P**.
       8:28 lifetime, the land had **p** forty years.
1Sa   1:17 "Go in **p**, and may the God of Israel
       7:14 And there was **p** between Israel
      20:42 David, "Go in **p**, for we have sworn
2Sa   10:19 they made **p** with the Israelites
1Ki   2:33 there be the LORD's **p** forever."
2Ki   9:17 and ask, 'Do you come in **p**?' "
1Ch   19:19 they made **p** with David and became
      22: 9 have a son who will be a man of **p**
2Ch   14: 1 his days the country was at **p** for ten
      20:30 kingdom of Jehoshaphat was at **p**,
Job   3:26 I have no **p**, no quietness; I have no
      22:21 to God and be at **p** with him;

Ps   29:11 LORD blesses his people with **p**.
      34:14 and do good; seek **p** and pursue it.
      37:11 the land and enjoy **p** and prosperity.
      37:37 a future awaits those who seek **p**.
      85: 8 he promises **p** to his people,
      85:10 righteousness and **p** kiss each other.
     119:165 Great **p** have those who love your
      120: 7 I am for **p**; but when I speak,
      122: 6 Pray for the **p** of Jerusalem:
      147:14 He grants **p** to your borders
Pr   3:17 ways, and all her paths are **p**.
      12:20 but those who promote **p** have joy.
      14:30 A heart at **p** gives life to the body,
      16: 7 their enemies to make **p** with them.
      17: 1 Better a dry crust with **p** and quiet
Ecc   3: 8 a time for war and a time for **p**.
Isa   9: 6 Everlasting Father, Prince of **P**.
      14: 7 All the lands are at rest and at **p**;
      26: 3 in perfect **p** those whose minds are
      32:17 fruit of that righteousness will be **p**;
      48:18 your **p** would have been like a river,
      48:22 "There is no **p**," says the LORD,
      52: 7 who proclaim **p**, who bring good
      53: 5 that brought us **p** was on him,
      54:10 nor my covenant of **p** be removed,"
      55:12 go out in joy and be led forth in **p**;
      57: 2 who walk uprightly enter into **p**;
      57:19 **P, p**, to those far and near,"
      57:21 "There is no **p**," says my God,
      59: 8 The way of **p** they do not know;
      59: 8 who walks along them will know **p**.
      66:12 "I will extend **p** to her like a river,
Jer   6:14 '**P, p**,' they say, when there is no **p**.
       8:11 "**P, p**," they say, when there is no **p**.
      30:10 Jacob will again have **p**
      33: 6 will let them enjoy abundant **p**
      46:27 Jacob will again have **p**
La   3:17 I have been deprived of **p**;
Eze   13:10 saying, "**P**," when there is no **p**,
      34:25 " 'I will make a covenant of **p**
      37:26 I will make a covenant of **p**
Mic   5: 5 he will be our **p** when the Assyrians
Na   1:15 brings good news, who proclaims **p**!
Hag   2: 9 'And in this place I will grant **p**,'
Zec   8:19 Therefore love truth and **p**."
       9:10 He will proclaim **p** to the nations.
Mal   2: 5 a covenant of life and **p**, and I gave
       2: 6 He walked with me in **p**
Mt   10:13 is deserving, let your **p** rest on it;
      10:34 I have come to bring **p** to the earth.
      10:34 I did not come to bring **p**,
Mk   9:50 and be at **p** with each other."
Lk   1:79 to guide our feet into the path of **p**."
       2:14 and on earth **p** to those on whom his
       7:50 faith has saved you; go in **p**."
      10: 6 If someone who promotes **p** is there,
      10: 6 your **p** will rest on them;
      19:38 "**P** in heaven and glory
      19:42 this day what would bring you **p**—
Jn   14:27 **P** I leave with you; my **p** I give you.
      16:33 so that in me you may have **p**.
Ac   10:36 news of **p** through Jesus Christ,
Ro   2:10 and **p** for everyone who does good:

Ro 3:17 the way of **p** they do not know."
    5: 1 we have **p** with God through our
    8: 6 governed by the Spirit is life and **p**.
    12:18 on you, live at **p** with everyone.
    14:19 every effort to do what leads to **p**
    16:20 **p** will soon crush Satan under your
1Co 7:15 God has called us to live in **p**.
    14:33 is not a God of disorder but of **p**—
2Co 13:11 another, be of one mind, live in **p**.
Gal 5:22 Spirit is love, joy, **p**, forbearance,
    6:16 **P** and mercy to all who follow this
Eph 2:14 For he himself is our **p**, who has
    2:15 out of the two, thus making **p**,
    2:17 preached **p** to you who were far away
      and **p** to those who were near.
    4: 3 of the Spirit through the bond of **p**.
    6:15 that comes from the gospel of **p**.
Php 4: 7 And the **p** of God, which transcends
Col 1:20 by making **p** through his blood,
    3:15 Let the **p** of Christ rule in your
    3:15 of one body you were called to **p**.
1Th 5: 3 people are saying, "**P** and safety,"
    5:13 Live in **p** with each other.
    5:23 the God of **p**, sanctify you through
2Th 3:16 the Lord of **p** himself give you **p**
2Ti 2:22 love and **p**, along with those who
Heb 7: 2 of Salem" means "king of **p**."
    12:11 **p** for those who have been trained
    12:14 effort to live in **p** with everyone
    13:20 Now may the God of **p**,
Jas 3:18 who sow in **p** reap a harvest
1Pe 3:11 they must seek **p** and pursue it.
2Pe 3:14 blameless and at **p** with him.
Rev 6: 4 given power to take **p** from the earth
GRACE AND PEACE See GRACE

PEACE-LOVING* PEACE, LOVE
Jas 3:17 then **p**, considerate, submissive,

PEACEABLE* PEACE
Titus 3: 2 no one, to be **p** and considerate,

PEACEFUL PEACE
1Ti 2: 2 that we may live **p** and quiet lives

PEACEMAKERS* PEACE
Mt 5: 9 Blessed are the **p**, for they will be
Jas 3:18 **P** who sow in peace reap a harvest

PEARL* PEARLS
Rev 21:21 pearls, each gate made of a single **p**.

PEARLS PEARL
Mt 7: 6 do not throw your **p** to pigs.
    13:45 is like a merchant looking for fine **p**.
1Ti 2: 9 or gold or **p** or expensive clothes,
Rev 21:21 The twelve gates were twelve **p**,

PEBBLE*
2Sa 17:13 until not so much as a **p** is left."
Am 9: 9 and not a **p** will reach the ground.

PEDDLE*
2Co 2:17 we do not **p** the word of God

PEG
Jdg 4:21 She drove the **p** through his temple
Isa 22:23 I will drive him like a **p** into a firm
Zec 10: 4 from him the tent **p**, from him

PEKAH
King of Israel (2Ki 15:25–31; 2Ch 28:6; Isa 7:1).

PEKAHIAH*
Son of Menahem; king of Israel (2Ki 15:22–26).

PELETHITES
2Sa 20: 7 and the Kerethites and **P** and all
1Ch 18:17 was over the Kerethites and **P**;

PELTED*
2Sa 16: 6 He **p** David and all the king's
2Co 11:25 with rods, once I was **p** with stones,

PEN PENS
Ps 45: 1 my tongue is the **p** of a skillful
Isa 8: 1 and write on it with an ordinary **p**:
Hab 3:17 though there are no sheep in the **p**
Mt 5:18 not the least stroke of a **p**,
Jn 10: 1 who does not enter the sheep **p**
3Jn 1:13 I do not want to do so with **p**

PENALTIES* PENALTY
Pr 19:29 **P** are prepared for mockers,

PENALTY PENALTIES
Lev 5: 6 As a **p** for the sin they have
Pr 19:19 person must pay the **p**;
Eze 23:49 You will suffer the **p** for your
Lk 23:22 in him no grounds for the death **p**.
Ro 1:27 themselves the due **p** for their error.

PENETRATES*
Heb 4:12 it **p** even to dividing soul and spirit,

PENIEL
Ge 32:30 So Jacob called the place **P**, saying,

PENINNAH
1Sa 1: 2 **P** had children, but Hannah had none.

PENITENT* REPENT
Isa 1:27 her **p** ones with righteousness.

PENNIES* PENNY
Lk 12: 6 not five sparrows sold for two **p**?

PENNY* PENNIES
Mt 5:26 out until you have paid the last **p**.
    10:29 Are not two sparrows sold for a **p**?
Lk 12:59 out until you have paid the last **p**."

PENS PEN
Ps 50: 9 your stall or of goats from your **p**,
    78:70 and took him from the sheep **p**;

PENTECOST*
Ac 2: 1 When the day of **P** came, they were
    20:16 if possible, by the day of **P**.
1Co 16: 8 I will stay on at Ephesus until **P**,

PEOPLE PEOPLE'S, PEOPLES
Ge 4:26 At that time **p** began to call

Ge	6:13	"I am going to put an end to all **p**,
	11: 6	said, "If as one **p** speaking the same
	12: 1	your **p** and your father's household
	18:24	sake of the fifty righteous **p** in it?
Ex	3:10	Pharaoh to bring my **p** the Israelites
	5: 1	'Let my **p** go, so that they may hold
	6: 7	I will take you as my own **p**, and I
	8:23	distinction between my **p** and your **p**.
	13:17	When Pharaoh let the **p** go, God did
	15:13	will lead the **p** you have redeemed.
	15:24	So the **p** grumbled against Moses,
	19: 8	The **p** all responded together,
	24: 3	told the **p** all the Lord's words
	32: 1	When the **p** saw that Moses was so
	32: 9	"and they are a stiff-necked **p**.
	32:12	and do not bring disaster on your **p**.
	33:13	that this nation is your **p**."
Lev	9: 7	atonement for yourself and the **p**;
	16:24	atonement for himself and for the **p**.
	26:12	be your God, and you will be my **p**.
Nu	11:11	put the burden of all these **p** on me?
	14:11	"How long will these **p** treat me
	14:19	forgive the sin of these **p**, just as
	20: 2	and the **p** gathered in opposition
	21: 7	So Moses prayed for the **p**.
	22: 5	"A **p** has come out of Egypt;
Dt	4: 6	is a wise and understanding **p**."
	4:20	to be the **p** of his inheritance, as you
	5:28	"I have heard what this **p** said
	7: 6	you are a **p** holy to the Lord your
	26:18	declared this day that you are his **p**,
	31: 7	must go with this **p** into the land
	31:16	and these **p** will soon prostitute
	32: 9	For the Lord's portion is his **p**,
	32:43	with his **p**, for he will avenge
	32:43	make atonement for his land and **p**.
	33:29	like you, a **p** saved by the Lord?
Jos	1: 6	because you will lead these **p**
	3:16	So the **p** crossed over opposite
	24: 6	When I brought your **p**
	24:25	Joshua made a covenant for the **p**,
Jdg	2: 7	The **p** served the Lord
	2:19	the **p** returned to ways even more
Ru	1:16	Your **p** will be my **p** and your God
1Sa	2:26	favor with the Lord and with **p**.
	8: 7	to all that the **p** are saying to you;
	10:24	is no one like him among all the **p**."
	12:22	the Lord will not reject his **p**,
	16: 7	Lord does not look at the things **p**
2Sa	5: 2	'You will shepherd my **p** Israel,
	7:10	Wicked **p** will not oppress them
	7:23	out to redeem as a **p** for himself,
	24:17	angel who was striking down the **p**,
1Ki	3: 8	here among the **p** you have chosen,
	4:34	From all nations **p** came to listen
	8:30	and of your **p** Israel when they pray
	8:56	to his **p** Israel just as he promised.
	18:39	When all the **p** saw this, they fell
2Ki	17:23	So the **p** of Israel were taken
	23: 3	all the **p** pledged themselves
	25:11	into exile the **p** who remained
1Ch	17:21	went out to redeem a **p** for himself,
	29:17	how willingly your **p** who are here

2Ch	2:11	"Because the Lord loves his **p**,
	6:41	may your faithful **p** rejoice in your
	7: 5	and all the **p** dedicated the temple
	7:14	if my **p**, who are called by my
	30: 6	"**P** of Israel, return to the Lord,
	36:16	Lord was aroused against his **p**
Ezr	2: 1	Now these are the **p** of the province
	3: 1	the **p** assembled together as one
Ne	1:10	"They are your servants and your **p**,
	4: 6	for the **p** worked with all their heart.
	4:14	the officials and the rest of the **p**,
	8: 1	all the **p** came together as one
Est	3: 6	a way to destroy all Mordecai's **p**,
	7: 3	And spare my **p**—this is my request.
Job	12: 2	you are the only **p** who matter,
	34:23	has no need to examine **p** further,
Ps	3: 8	May your blessing be on your **p**.
	22:22	I will declare your name to my **p**;
	29:11	The Lord gives strength to his **p**;
	30: 4	of the Lord, you his faithful **p**;
	31:23	Love the Lord, all his faithful **p**!
	33:12	the **p** he chose for his inheritance.
	34: 9	you his holy **p**, for those who fear
	36: 7	**P** take refuge in the shadow of your
	50: 4	the earth, that he may judge his **p**:
	53: 6	When God restores his **p**, let Jacob
	81:13	"If my **p** would only listen to me,
	90: 3	You turn **p** back to dust, saying,
	94:14	For the Lord will not reject his **p**;
	95: 7	God and we are the **p** of his pasture,
	95:10	said, 'They are a **p** whose hearts go
	125: 2	Lord surrounds his **p** both now
	133: 1	it is when God's **p** live together
	135:14	For the Lord will vindicate his **p**
	144:15	blessed is the **p** whose God is
	149: 1	in the assembly of his faithful **p**.
	149: 4	the Lord takes delight in his **p**;
	149: 5	Let his faithful **p** rejoice in this
	149: 9	this is the glory of all his faithful **p**.
Pr	12:22	delights in **p** who are trustworthy.
	14:34	a nation, but sin condemns any **p**.
	29: 2	the righteous thrive, the **p** rejoice;
	29: 2	when the wicked rule, the **p** groan.
	29:18	is no revelation, **p** cast off restraint;
Jer	31:31	a new covenant with the **p** of Israel
		and with the **p** of Judah.
Ecc	3:12	there is nothing better for **p** than
Isa	1: 3	not know, my **p** do not understand."
	1: 4	nation, a **p** whose guilt is great,
	5:13	Therefore my **p** will go into exile
	6:10	Make the heart of this **p** calloused;
	9: 2	The **p** walking in darkness have
	19:25	"Blessed be Egypt my **p**,
	29:13	"These **p** come near to me
	40: 1	comfort my **p**, says your God.
	40: 5	and all **p** will see it together.
	40: 6	"All **p** are like grass, and all their
	40: 7	Surely the **p** are grass.
	42: 6	make you to be a covenant for the **p**
	49: 8	make you to be a covenant for the **p**,
	49:13	For the Lord comforts his **p**
	51: 4	"Listen to me, my **p**; hear me,
	52: 6	Therefore my **p** will know my

Isa 53: 3 whom **p** hide their faces he was
53: 8 of my **p** he was punished.
60:21 Then all your **p** will be righteous
62:12 They will be called the Holy **P**,
65: 2 held out my hands to an obstinate **p**,
65:23 for they will be a **p** blessed
Jer 2:11 my **p** have exchanged their glorious
2:13 "My **p** have committed two sins:
2:32 Yet my **p** have forgotten me,
3:18 In those days the **p** of Judah will join
the **p** of Israel,
4:22 "My **p** are fools; they do not know
5:14 and these **p** the wood it consumes.
5:31 authority, and my **p** love it this way.
6:27 a tester of metals and my **p** the ore,
7:16 not pray for this **p** nor offer any plea
7:23 be your God and you will be my **p**.
16:20 Do **p** make their own gods?
18:15 Yet my **p** have forgotten me;
23: 2 to the shepherds who tend my **p**:
30: 3 'when I will bring my **p** Israel
31:33 be their God, and they will be my **p**.
50: 6 "My **p** have been lost sheep;
La 1: 1 lies the city, once so full of **p**!
Eze 2: 8 Do not rebel like that rebellious **p**;
12: 2 you are living among a rebellious **p**.
13:23 I will save my **p** from your hands.
33: 7 you a watchman for the **p** of Israel;
36: 8 branches and fruit for my **p** Israel,
36:28 you will be my **p**, and I will be your
36:38 cities to be filled with flocks of **p**.
37:11 these bones are the **p** of Israel.
37:13 you, my **p**, will know that I am
38:14 day, when my **p** Israel are living
39: 7 my holy name among my **p** Israel.
39:29 pour out my Spirit on the **p** of Israel,
Da 7:18 But the holy **p** of the Most High will
7:21 was waging war against the holy **p**
7:27 over to the holy **p** of the Most High.
8:24 those who are mighty, the holy **p**.
9:19 city and your **p** bear your Name."
9:24 'sevens' are decreed for your **p**
9:26 The **p** of the ruler who will come
10:14 will happen to your **p** in the future,
11:32 but the **p** who know their God will
12: 1 great prince who protects your **p**,
Hos 1:10 'You are not my **p**,' they will be
2:23 will say to those called 'Not my **p**,'
'You are my **p**';
4:14 a **p** without understanding will
Joel 2:18 for his land and took pity on his **p**.
3:16 LORD will be a refuge for his **p**,
Am 9:14 I will bring my **p** Israel back
Jnh 4:11 twenty thousand **p** who cannot tell
Mic 3: 5 the prophets who lead my **p** astray,
6: 2 the LORD has a case against his **p**;
7:14 Shepherd your **p** with your staff,
Zep 2: 9 remnant of my **p** will plunder them;
Hag 1:12 And the **p** feared the LORD.
Zec 2:11 in that day and will become my **p**.
8: 7 "I will save my **p** from the
13: 9 'They are my **p**,' and they will say,
Mt 1:21 because he will save his **p**

Mt 2: 6 who will shepherd my **p** Israel.' "
4:16 the **p** living in darkness have seen
4:19 I will send you out to fish for **p**."
5:47 And if you greet only your own **p**,
13:38 stands for the **p** of the kingdom.
13:38 The weeds are the **p** of the evil one,
23: 5 "Everything they do is done for **p**
Mk 5:19 "Go home to your own **p** and tell
7: 6 " 'These **p** honor me with their
8:27 asked them, "Who do **p** say I am?"
Lk 1:17 to make ready a **p** prepared
1:68 because he has come to his **p**
2:10 will cause great joy for all the **p**.
3: 6 all **p** will see God's salvation.' "
6:22 Blessed are you when **p** hate you,
13:23 "Lord, are only a few **p** going to be
21:23 in the land and wrath against this **p**.
Jn 2:24 himself to them, for he knew all **p**.
3:19 but **p** loved darkness instead of light
7:43 Thus the **p** were divided because
11:50 one man die for the **p** than
12:32 earth, will draw all **p** to myself."
18:14 be good if one man died for the **p**.
Ac 2:17 I will pour out my Spirit on all **p**.
2:47 and enjoying the favor of all the **p**.
3:22 like me from among your own **p**;
5:13 they were highly regarded by the **p**.
9:13 done to your holy **p** in Jerusalem.
15:14 to choose a **p** for his name
18:10 because I have many **p** in this city."
Ro 1:18 the godlessness and wickedness of **p**,
5:12 and in this way death came to all **p**,
5:18 resulted in condemnation for all **p**,
5:18 in justification and life for all **p**.
8:27 for God's **p** in accordance
9: 3 off from Christ for the sake of my **p**,
9: 4 the **p** of Israel. Theirs is
9:25 call them 'my **p**' who are not my **p**;
11: 1 I ask then: Did God reject his **p**?
15:10 you Gentiles, with his **p**."
1Co 6: 2 the Lord's **p** will judge the world?
9:22 I have become all things to all **p** so
2Co 6:16 their God, and they will be my **p**."
Eph 1:15 Jesus and your love for all God's **p**,
1:18 glorious inheritance in his holy **p**,
2:19 but fellow citizens with God's **p**
4: 8 captives and gave gifts to his **p**."
5: 3 these are improper for God's holy **p**.
6:18 keep on praying for all the Lord's **p**.
Col 1:12 of his holy **p** in the kingdom
1:26 but is now disclosed to the Lord's **p**.
3:12 as God's chosen **p**, holy and dearly
1Th 2: 4 We are not trying to please **p**
2:14 You suffered from your own **p** the
5:26 Greet all God's **p** with a holy kiss.
1Ti 2: 4 who wants all **p** to be saved
2: 6 gave himself as a ransom for all **p**.
4:10 God, who is the Savior of all **p**,
5:10 washing the feet of the Lord's **p**,
6: 9 desires that plunge **p** into ruin
2Ti 2: 2 entrust to reliable **p** who will also be
Titus 1:10 For there are many rebellious **p**,
2:11 that offers salvation to all **p**.

Titus 2:14 himself a **p** that are his very own,
Phm 1: 7 refreshed the hearts of the Lord's **p**.
Heb 2:17 atonement for the sins of the **p**.
  4: 9 a Sabbath-rest for the **p** of God;
  5: 1 priest is selected from among the **p**
  5: 3 sins, as well as for the sins of the **p**.
  8: 8 new covenant with the **p** of Israel and
       with the **p** of Judah.
  8:10 be their God, and they will be my **p**.
  9:27 Just as **p** are destined to die once,
  10:30 again, "The Lord will judge his **p**."
  11:13 All these **p** were still living by faith
  13:12 to make the **p** holy through his own
1Pe 1:24 For, "All **p** are like grass, and all
  2: 8 "A stone that causes **p** to stumble
  2: 9 But you are a chosen **p**, a royal
  2:10 Once you were not a **p**, but now you
       are the **p** of God;
2Pe 2: 1 also false prophets among the **p**,
  3:11 what kind of **p** ought you to be?
Jude 1: 3 for all entrusted to God's holy **p**.
Rev 5: 8 which are the prayers of God's **p**.
  8: 3 with the prayers of all God's **p**,
  13: 4 **P** worshiped the dragon because he
  13: 7 to wage war against God's holy **p**
  14:12 part of the **p** of God who keep his
  16: 6 have shed the blood of your holy **p**
  17: 6 with the blood of God's holy **p**,
  18: 4 my **p**,' so that you will not share
  18:20 Rejoice, you **p** of God!
  19: 8 the righteous acts of God's holy **p**.)
  21: 3 dwelling place is now among the **p**,
  22:21 of the Lord Jesus be with God's **p**.

ALL PEOPLE Ge 6:13; Job 37:7; Ps 64:9; 65:2;
145:12; Isa 40:5, 6; 66:16; Jer 17:20; 45:5; Eze 21:5;
Joel 2:28; Zep 1:17; Zec 9:1; 10:1; Lk 3:6; Jn 2:24;
12:32; 17:2; Ac 2:17; 17:30; 22:15; Ro 5:12, 18, 18;
1Co 9:22; 15:19; Gal 6:10; 1Ti 2:1, 4, 6; 4:10; Titus
2:11; 1Pe 1:24; Rev 13:16; 19:18

ALL THE PEOPLE Ge 6:12; 26:11; 29:22; 35:6;
Ex 11:8; 18:21; 19:11; 32:3; 33:8; Lev 9:23, 24;
10:3; Nu 13:32; 15:26; 24:17; 31:26; Dt 13:9; 17:7,
13; 20:11; 27:14, 15, 16, 17, 18, 19, 20, 21, 22, 23,
24, 25, 26; Jos 2:24; 5:5, 5; 8:25; 11:14; 24:2, 27;
Jdg 9:49, 51; 16:30; 20:2; Ru 3:11; 4:9, 11; 1Sa 2:23;
7:2; 10:24, 24; 11:15; 12:18; 2Sa 3:31, 32, 34, 36,
37; 6:19; 15:17, 23, 23, 24, 30; 16:14; 17:2, 3, 3, 16,
22; 19:9, 39; 20:22; 1Ki 1:39, 40; 4:30; 12:12; 18:24,
30, 39; 2Ki 10:9, 18; 11:14, 18, 19, 20; 14:21; 16:15;
17:20; 23:2, 3, 21; 25:26; 1Ch 13:4; 16:36, 43;
28:21; 2Ch 7:4, 5; 10:12; 20:18; 23:13, 17, 20, 21;
24:10; 26:1; 29:36; 32:9; 34:9, 30; 35:13; Ezr 3:11;
7:25; 10:9; Ne 4:16; 8:1, 3, 5, 6, 9, 11, 12; 9:10; Est
1:5; Job 1:3; Ps 33:8; 106:48; Ecc 4:16; Isa 9:9; Jer
13:11, 11; 19:14; 25:1, 2; 26:2, 7, 8, 8, 9, 11, 12, 16,
18; 28:1, 5, 7, 11; 29:16, 25; 34:8, 19; 36:6, 9, 10;
38:1, 4; 41:13, 14, 16; 42:1, 8; 43:4; 44:15, 20, 24;
Eze 20:40; 38:20; 39:13, 25; 45:16, 22; Da 9:6; Am
9:1; Zec 7:5; Mal 2:9; Mt 12:23; 13:2; 22:10; 27:25;
Mk 1:5; 4:1; 5:20; 6:39; 9:15; Lk 2:10; 3:21; 4:28,
36; 7:29; 8:37, 47, 52; 18:43; 19:7, 48; 20:6, 45;
21:38; 23:48; 24:19; Ac 2:47; 3:9, 11; 4:10, 21; 5:34;
8:9, 10; 10:41; 13:24; Heb 9:19, 19

PEOPLE OF ISRAEL See ISRAEL
PEOPLE OF JERUSALEM See JERUSALEM
PEOPLE OF JUDAH See JUDAH

PEOPLE'S PEOPLE

2Ch 25:15 "Why do you consult this **p** gods,
Isa 25: 8 he will remove his **p** disgrace
Jer 10:23 know that **p** lives are not their own;
Mt 13:15 this **p** heart has become calloused;
  23: 4 and put them on other **p** shoulders,
Ac 28:27 this **p** heart has become calloused;
2Co 5:19 not counting **p** sins against them.

PEOPLES PEOPLE

Ge 12: 3 and all **p** on earth will be blessed
  17:16 kings of **p** will come from her."
  25:23 and two **p** from within you will be
  27:29 serve you and **p** bow down to you.
  28: 3 until you become a community of **p**.
  48: 4 I will make you a community of **p**,
Dt 4:27 will scatter you among the **p**,
  7: 7 for you were the fewest of all **p**.
  14: 2 of all the **p** on the face of the earth,
  28:10 all the **p** on earth will see that you
Jos 4:24 all the **p** of the earth might know
Jdg 2:12 various gods of the **p** around them.
1Ki 8:43 all the **p** of the earth may know your
2Ch 7:20 an object of ridicule among all **p**.
Ezr 3: 3 their fear of the **p** around them,
  10: 2 women from the **p** around us.
Ne 10:30 in marriage to the **p** around us
Ps 2: 1 conspire and the **p** plot in vain?
  9: 8 and judges the **p** with equity.
  67: 3 May the **p** praise you, God;
  87: 6 will write in the register of the **p**:
  96:10 he will judge the **p** with equity.
  117: 1 all you nations; extol him, all you **p**.
Isa 2: 4 and will settle disputes for many **p**
  11:10 will stand as a banner for the **p**;
  17:12 Woe to the **p** who roar—
  25: 6 prepare a feast of rich food for all **p**,
  34: 1 pay attention, you **p**!
  49:22 I will lift up my banner to the **p**;
  55: 4 I have made him a witness to the **p**,
Jer 10: 3 the practices of the **p** are worthless;
Da 7:14 **p** of every language worshiped him.
Mic 4: 1 the hills, and **p** will stream to it.
  5: 7 the midst of many **p** like dew
Zep 3: 9 "Then I will purify the lips of the **p**,
  3:20 praise among all the **p** of the earth
Zec 8:20 "Many **p** and the inhabitants
  12: 2 sends all the surrounding **p** reeling.
Ac 3:25 'Through your offspring all **p**
  4:25 nations rage and the **p** plot in vain?
Rev 1: 7 all **p** on earth "will mourn because
  10:11 must prophesy again about many **p**,

ALL PEOPLES Ge 12:3; 28:14; Dt 7:7; 1Ki 9:7;
1Ch 16:24; 2Ch 7:20; Ps 66:8; 96:3; 97:6; Isa 25:6,
7; Ac 3:25; Rev 1:7

ALL THE PEOPLES Dt 7:6, 16, 19; 14:2; 28:10,
37; Jos 4:24; 1Ki 8:43, 60; 2Ch 6:33; 32:13; Ps 67:3,
5; Jer 1:15; 25:9; Da 4:35; Hab 2:5; Zep 3:20; Mt
24:30; Ro 15:11

PEOR
Nu 25: 3 yoked themselves to the Baal of P.
Dt 4: 3 who followed the Baal of P,
Jos 22:17 Was not the sin of P enough for us?

PERCEIVE PERCEIVED, PERCEIVING
Ps 139: 2 you **p** my thoughts from afar.
Pr 24:12 not he who weighs the heart **p** it?

PERCEIVED* PERCEIVE
Isa 64: 4 no ear has **p**, no eye has seen any

PERCEIVING* PERCEIVE
Isa 6: 9 be ever seeing, but never **p**.'
Mt 13:14 you will be ever seeing but never **p**.
Mk 4:12 may be ever seeing but never **p**,
Ac 28:26 will be ever seeing but never **p**."

PERCH
Ge 8: 9 **p** because there was water over all

PERES* PARSIN
Da 5:28 P: Your kingdom is divided

PEREZ
Ge 38:29 And he was named P.
Ru 4:12 may your family be like that of P,
Mt 1: 3 Judah the father of P and Zerah,

PERFECT* PERFECTER, PERFECTING, PERFECTION
Dt 32: 4 his works are **p**, and all his ways are
2Sa 22:31 "As for God, his way is **p**:
Job 36: 4 one who has **p** knowledge is
37:16 of him who has **p** knowledge?
Ps 18:30 As for God, his way is **p**:
19: 7 The law of the LORD is **p**,
50: 2 From Zion, **p** in beauty, God shines
64: 6 say, "We have devised a **p** plan!"
SS 6: 9 but my dove, my **p** one, is unique,
Isa 25: 1 for in **p** faithfulness you have done
26: 3 in **p** peace those whose minds are
Eze 16:14 had given you made your beauty **p**,
27: 3 say, Tyre, "I am **p** in beauty."
28:12 full of wisdom and **p** in beauty.
Mt 5:48 Be **p**, therefore, as your heavenly Father is **p**.
19:21 answered, "If you want to be **p**, go,
Ro 12: 2 his good, pleasing and **p** will.
2Co 12: 9 my power is made **p** in weakness."
Col 3:14 binds them all together in **p** unity.
Heb 2:10 of their salvation **p** through what he
5: 9 once made **p**, he became the source
7:19 (for the law made nothing **p**),
7:28 Son, who has been made **p** forever.
9:11 more **p** tabernacle that is not made
10: 1 make **p** those who draw near
10:14 he has made **p** forever those who
11:40 with us would they be made **p**.
12:23 the spirits of the righteous made **p**,
Jas 1:17 good and **p** gift is from above,
1:25 looks intently into the **p** law
3: 2 never at fault in what they say is **p**,
1Jn 4:18 But **p** love drives out fear,

1Jn 4:18 The one who fears is not made **p**

PERFECTER* PERFECT
Heb 12: 2 on Jesus, the pioneer and **p** of faith.

PERFECTING* PERFECT
2Co 7: 1 **p** holiness out of reverence for God.

PERFECTION* PERFECT
Ps 119:96 To all **p** I see a limit, but your
La 2:15 city that was called the **p** of beauty,
Eze 27: 4 builders brought your beauty to **p**.
27:11 they brought your beauty to **p**.
28:12 " 'You were the seal of **p**,
43:10 Let them consider its **p**,
Heb 7:11 **p** could have been attained through

PERFORM PERFORMED, PERFORMS
Ex 3:20 wonders that I will **p** among them.
2Sa 7:23 to **p** great and awesome wonders
1Ki 8:11 the priests could not **p** their service
Jer 21: 2 Perhaps the LORD will **p** wonders
Mk 13:22 prophets will appear and **p** signs
Jn 3: 2 For no one could **p** the signs you are

PERFORMED PERFORM
Ex 4:30 also **p** the signs before the people,
Nu 14:11 all the signs I have **p** among them?
Dt 11: 3 the signs he **p** and the things he did
Ne 9:17 the miracles you **p** among them.
Mt 11:21 that were **p** in you had been **p**
Jn 10:41 "Though John never **p** a sign,
Ac 5:12 The apostles **p** many signs
Rev 13:13 And it **p** great signs, even causing
19:20 false prophet who had **p** the signs

PERFORMS PERFORM
Ps 77:14 You are the God who **p** miracles;

PERFUME
Ex 30:33 Whoever makes **p** like it and puts it
Ecc 7: 1 A good name is better than fine **p**,
SS 1: 3 your name is like **p** poured out.
Mk 14: 3 an alabaster jar of very expensive **p**,
Jn 12: 7 she should save this **p** for the day

PERGAMUM*
Rev 1:11 to Ephesus, Smyrna, P, Thyatira,
2:12 the angel of the church in P write:

PERIL
2Co 1:10 delivered us from such a deadly **p**,

PERISH PERISHABLE, PERISHED, PERISHES, PERISHING
Ge 6:17 life in it. Everything on earth will **p**.
Lev 26:38 You will **p** among the nations;
Jos 23:13 until you **p** from this good land,
Est 4:16 is against the law. And if I **p**, I **p**."
Ps 37:20 But the wicked will **p**:
73:27 Those who are far from you will **p**;
102:26 They will **p**, but you remain;
Pr 11:10 when the wicked **p**, there are shouts
19: 9 and whoever pours out lies will **p**.
21:28 A false witness will **p**, but a careful

Pr   28:28 but when the wicked **p**,
Isa   1:28 who forsake the LORD will **p**.
      29:14 the wisdom of the wise will **p**,
      60:12 that will not serve you will **p**;
Jer   51:18 their judgment comes, they will **p**.
Jnh   1: 6 notice of us so that we will not **p**."
      3: 9 fierce anger so that we will not **p**."
Zec   11: 9 the dying die, and the perishing **p**.
Mt   18:14 any of these little ones should **p**.
Lk   13: 3 unless you repent, you too will all **p**.
      13: 5 you repent, you too will all **p**."
      21:18 But not a hair of your head will **p**.
Jn   3:16 whoever believes in him shall not **p**
      10:28 eternal life, and they shall never **p**;
      11:50 than that the whole nation **p**."
Ac   8:20 "May your money **p** with you,
Ro   2:12 law will also **p** apart from the law,
Col   2:22 that are all destined to **p** with use,
2Th   2:10 They **p** because they refused to love
Heb   1:11 They will **p**, but you remain;
1Pe   1: 4 into an inheritance that can never **p**,
2Pe   3: 9 you, not wanting anyone to **p**,

PERISHABLE PERISH
1Co 15:42 The body that is sown is **p**, it is
1Pe   1:18 was not with **p** things such as silver
      1:23 not of **p** seed, but of imperishable,

PERISHED PERISH
Ge   7:21 living thing that moved on land **p**—
Dt   2:14 fighting men had **p** from the camp,
Job   4: 7 Who, being innocent, has ever **p**?
Ps   119:92 I would have **p** in my affliction.
Jer   7:28 Truth has **p**; it has vanished

PERISHES PERISH
Job   8:13 so **p** the hope of the godless.
1Pe   1: 7 which **p** even though refined

PERISHING PERISH
Ecc   7:15 the righteous **p** in their
1Co   1:18 is foolishness to those who are **p**,
2Co   2:15 being saved and those who are **p**.
      4: 3 it is veiled to those who are **p**.

PERIZZITES
Ge   13: 7 The Canaanites and **P** were
Ex   3: 8 Amorites, **P**, Hivites and Jebusites.
Jos   24:11 you, as did also the Amorites, **P**,

PERJURERS* PERJURY
Mal   3: 5 adulterers and **p**, against those who
1Ti   1:10 for slave traders and liars and **p**—

PERJURY* PERJURERS
Jer   7: 9 commit adultery and **p**, burn incense

PERMANENT* PERMANENTLY
Lev   25:34 not be sold; it is their **p** possession.
Jos   8:28 Ai and made it a **p** heap of ruins,
Jn   8:35 Now a slave has no **p** place
Heb   7:24 lives forever, he has a **p** priesthood.

PERMANENTLY PERMANENT
Lev   25:23 " 'The land must not be sold **p**,

PERMIT* PERMITTED
Ex   12:23 he will not **p** the destroyer to enter
Hos   5: 4 "Their deeds do not **p** them
Ac   24:23 and **p** his friends to take care of his
1Ti   2:12 I do not **p** a woman to teach

PERMITTED PERMIT
Mt   19: 8 "Moses **p** you to divorce your
2Co   12: 4 things, things that no one is **p** to tell.

PERPETUAL
Ex   29:28 to be the **p** share from the Israelites

PERPLEXED
2Co   4: 8 **p**, but not in despair;

PERSECUTE PERSECUTED,
PERSECUTING, PERSECUTION,
PERSECUTIONS, PERSECUTORS
Dt   30: 7 your enemies who hate and **p** you.
Mt   5:11 **p** you and falsely say all kinds
       5:44 and pray for those who **p** you,
Lk   11:49 they will kill and others they will **p**.'
      21:12 this, they will seize you and **p** you.
Jn   15:20 persecuted me, they will **p** you also.
Ac   9: 4 "Saul, Saul, why do you **p** me?"
      22: 7 Saul! Why do you **p** me?'
Ro   12:14 Bless those who **p** you; bless and do

PERSECUTED PERSECUTE
Ps   119:86 me, for I am being **p** without cause.
Mt   5:10 Blessed are those who are **p** because
       5:12 same way they **p** the prophets who
Jn   15:20 If they **p** me, they will persecute
Ac   22: 4 I **p** the followers of this Way to their
1Co   4:12 when we are **p**, we endure it;
      15: 9 because I **p** the church of God.
2Co   4: 9 **p**, but not abandoned;
Gal   1.13 how intensely I **p** the church of God
1Th   3: 4 kept telling you that we would be **p**.
2Ti   3:12 godly life in Christ Jesus will be **p**,
Heb   11:37 destitute, **p** and mistreated—

PERSECUTING* PERSECUTE
Ac   9: 5 Jesus, whom you are **p**," he replied.
      22: 8 whom you are **p**,' he replied.
      26:11 I was so obsessed with **p** them that I
      26:15 whom you are **p**,' the Lord replied.
Php   3: 6 as for zeal, **p** the church;

PERSECUTION PERSECUTE
Mt   13:21 or **p** comes because of the word,
Ac   8: 1 day a great **p** broke out against
Ro   8:35 trouble or hardship or **p** or famine
Heb   10:33 publicly exposed to insult and **p**;

PERSECUTIONS* PERSECUTE
Mk   10:30 along with **p**—and in the age
2Co   12:10 in hardships, in **p**, in difficulties.
2Th   1: 4 faith in all the **p** and trials you are
2Ti   3:11 **p**, sufferings—what kinds of things
      3:11 Iconium and Lystra, the **p** I endured.

PERSECUTORS PERSECUTE
Ps   119:84 When will you punish my **p**?

Jer 15:15 Avenge me on my **p**.

PERSEVERANCE* PERSEVERE

Ro 5: 3 we know that suffering produces **p**;
5: 4 **p**, character; and character, hope.
2Th 1: 4 churches we boast about your **p**
3: 5 into God's love and Christ's **p**.
Heb 12: 1 let us run with **p** the race marked
Jas 1: 3 the testing of your faith produces **p**.
1: 4 Let **p** finish its work so that you
5:11 You have heard of Job's **p** and have
2Pe 1: 6 to self-control, **p**; and to **p**,
Rev 2: 2 deeds, your hard work and your **p**.
2:19 your service and **p**, and that you are

PERSEVERE* PERSEVERANCE, PERSEVERED, PERSEVERES, PERSEVERING

1Ti 4:16 **P** in them, because if you do,
Heb 10:36 You need to **p** so that when you

PERSEVERED* PERSEVERE

2Co 12:12 I **p** in demonstrating among you
Heb 11:27 he **p** because he saw him who is
Jas 5:11 count as blessed those who have **p**.
Rev 2: 3 You have **p** and have endured

PERSEVERES* PERSEVERE

1Co 13: 7 trusts, always hopes, always **p**.
Jas 1:12 is the one who **p** under trial because,

PERSEVERING* PERSEVERE

Lk 8:15 retain it, and by **p** produce a crop.

PERSIA PERSIANS

Ezr 1: 1 heart of Cyrus king of **P** to make
Da 8:20 the kings of Media and **P**.
10:20 to fight against the prince of **P**,

PERSIANS PERSIA

Da 6:15 law of the Medes and **P** no decree

PERSIST PERSISTENCE

Isa 1: 5 Why do you **p** in rebellion?
Ro 11:23 And if they do not **p** in unbelief,

PERSISTENCE* PERSIST

Ro 2: 7 those who by **p** in doing good seek

PERSON PERSON'S

Ex 23: 7 put an innocent or honest **p** to death,
Lev 18: 5 the **p** who obeys them will live by
Pr 11:25 A generous **p** will prosper;
12: 8 A **p** is praised according to their
26:12 you see a **p** wise in their own eyes?
28:20 A faithful **p** will be richly blessed,
Eze 20:11 which the **p** who obeys them will live.
Mt 12:12 more valuable is a **p** than a sheep!
Ro 10: 5 "The **p** who does these things will live
1Co 2:15 The **p** with the Spirit makes

PERSON'S PERSON

Pr 16: 2 All a **p** ways seem pure to them,
20:24 A **p** steps are directed
1Co 3:13 will test the quality of each **p** work.
2:11 For who knows a **p** thoughts except

1Pe 1:17 who judges each **p** work impartially,

PERSUADE PERSUADED, PERSUASIVE

Ac 18: 4 trying to **p** Jews and Greeks.
26:28 in such a short time you can **p** me
28:23 from the Prophets he tried to **p** them
2Co 5:11 to fear the Lord, we try to **p** others.

PERSUADED PERSUADE

Mt 27:20 and the elders **p** the crowd to ask
Ro 4:21 being fully **p** that God had power

PERSUASIVE* PERSUADE

Pr 7:21 With **p** words she led him astray;
1Co 2: 4 were not with wise and **p** words,

PERVERSE PERVERT

Dt 32:20 for they are a **p** generation,
Pr 3:32 For the LORD detests the **p**
15: 4 but a **p** tongue crushes the spirit.
17:20 one whose tongue is **p** falls
Lk 9:41 unbelieving and **p** generation,"

PERVERSION* PERVERT

Lev 18:23 sexual relations with it; that is a **p**.
20:12 What they have done is a **p**;
Jude 1: 7 up to sexual immorality and **p**.

PERVERT* PERVERSE, PERVERSION, PERVERTED, PERVERTING

Ex 23: 2 do not **p** justice by siding
Lev 19:15 " 'Do not **p** justice; do not show
Dt 16:19 Do not **p** justice or show partiality.
Job 8: 3 Does God **p** justice?
8: 3 Does the Almighty **p** what is right?
34:12 that the Almighty would **p** justice.
Pr 17:23 in secret to **p** the course of justice.
Gal 1: 7 are trying to **p** the gospel of Christ.
Jude 1: 4 who **p** the grace of our God

PERVERTED PERVERT

1Sa 8: 3 and accepted bribes and **p** justice.
Jer 3:21 because they have **p** their ways

PERVERTING* PERVERT

Ac 13:10 Will you never stop **p** the right ways

PESTILENCE PESTILENCES

Dt 32:24 consuming **p** and deadly plague;
Ps 91: 6 nor the **p** that stalks in the darkness,

PESTILENCES* PESTILENCE

Lk 21:11 famines and **p** in various places,

PETER CEPHAS, SIMON

Apostle, brother of Andrew, also called Simon (Mt 10:2; Mk 3:16; Lk 6:14; Ac 1:13), and Cephas (Jn 1:42). Confession of Christ (Mt 16:13–20; Mk 8:27–30; Lk 9:18–27). At transfiguration (Mt 17:1–8; Mk 9:2–8; Lk 9:28–36; 2Pe 1:16–18). Caught fish with coin (Mt 17:24–27). Denial of Jesus predicted (Mt 26:31–35; Mk 14:27–31; Lk 22:31–34; Jn 13:31–38). Denied Jesus (Mt 26:69–75; Mk 14:66–

72; Lk 22:54–62; Jn 18:15–27). Commissioned by Jesus to shepherd his flock (Jn 21:15–23).
  Speech at Pentecost (Ac 2). Healed beggar (Ac 3:1–10). Speech at temple (Ac 3:11–26), before Sanhedrin (Ac 4:1–22). In Samaria (Ac 8:14–25). Sent by vision to Cornelius (Ac 10). Announced salvation of Gentiles in Jerusalem (Ac 11; 15). Freed from prison (Ac 12). Inconsistency at Antioch (Gal 2:11–21). At Jerusalem Council (Ac 15). Letters: 1–2 Peter.

PETITION PETITIONS
Est 7: 3 you, grant me my life—this is my **p.**
Jer 7:16 nor offer any plea or **p** for them;
Da   9: 3 pleaded with him in prayer and **p,**
Php 4: 6 by prayer and **p,** with thanksgiving,

PETITIONS* PETITION
Da   9:17 the prayers and **p** of your servant.
1Ti 2: 1 then, first of all, that **p,** prayers,
Heb 5: 7 up prayers and **p** with fervent cries

PHANTOM*
Ps 39: 6 everyone goes around like a mere **p;**

PHARAOH PHARAOH'S
Ge 12:15 they praised her to **P,** and she was
    41:14 So **P** sent for Joseph, and he was
    47:10 Jacob blessed **P** and went
Ex   1:22 **P** gave this order to all his people:
     2:15 Moses fled from **P** and went to live
     3:11 "Who am I that I should go to **P**
     5: 2 **P** said, "Who is the Lᴏʀᴅ, that I
    11: 1 "I will bring one more plague on **P**
    14:17 I will gain glory through **P** and all
Dt   7: 8 from the power of **P** king of Egypt.
Isa 36: 6 Such is **P** king of Egypt to all who
Ro   9:17 For Scripture says to **P:**

PHARAOH'S PHARAOH
Ex   2: 5 **P** daughter went down to the Nile
     7: 3 But I will harden **P** heart,
     7:13 Yet **P** heart became hard and he
     7:22 arts, and **P** heart became hard;
     8:19 But **P** heart was hard and he would
     9:12 the Lᴏʀᴅ hardened **P** heart and he
     9:35 So **P** heart was hard and he would
    10:20 But the Lᴏʀᴅ hardened **P** heart,
    10:27 But the Lᴏʀᴅ hardened **P** heart,
    11:10 But the Lᴏʀᴅ hardened **P** heart,
    14: 4 And I will harden **P** heart, and he
1Ki 11: 1 foreign women besides **P** daughter—
Heb 11:24 be known as the son of **P** daughter.

PHARISEE PHARISEES
Lk 11:37 a **P** invited him to eat with him;
Jn   3: 1 Now there was a **P,** a man named
Ac   5:34 But a **P** named Gamaliel, a teacher
    23: 6 I am a **P,** descended from Pharisees.
Php 3: 5 in regard to the law, a **P;**

PHARISEES PHARISEE
Mt   5:20 surpasses that of the **P**
    16: 6 guard against the yeast of the **P**
    23:13 you, teachers of the law and **P,**

Mk   2:18 disciples and the **P** were fasting.
Lk 11:42 "Woe to you **P,** because you give
Ac 23: 7 a dispute broke out between the **P**

PHILADELPHIA*
Rev 1:11 Thyatira, Sardis, **P** and Laodicea."
     3: 7 the angel of the church in **P** write:

PHILEMON*
Phm 1: 1 To **P** our dear friend and fellow

PHILIP
  1. Apostle (Mt 10:3; Mk 3:18; Lk 6:14; Jn 1:43–48; 14:8; Ac 1:13).
  2. Deacon (Ac 6:1–7); evangelist in Samaria (Ac 8:4–25), to Ethiopian (Ac 8:26–40).
  3. Herod Philip I (Mt 14:3; Mk 6:17).
  4. Herod Philip II (Lk 3:1).

PHILIPPI
Mt 16:13 came to the region of Caesarea **P,**
Ac 16:12 From there we traveled to **P,**
Php 1: 1 holy people in Christ Jesus at **P,**

PHILISTIA PHILISTINE
Ex 15:14 anguish will grip the people of **P.**
Ps 60: 8 over **P** I shout in triumph."

PHILISTINE PHILISTIA, PHILISTINES
Jos 13: 3 held by the five **P** rulers in Gaza,
1Sa 6: 1 been in **P** territory seven months,
    14: 1 let's go over to the **P** outpost
    17:23 Goliath, the **P** champion from Gath,
    17:37 rescue me from the hand of this **P."**

PHILISTINES PHILISTINE
Ge 21:34 in the land of the **P** for a long time.
    26: 1 to Abimelek king of the **P** in Gerar.
Jdg 10: 7 He sold them into the hands of the **P**
    13: 1 the hands of the **P** for forty years.
    16: 5 The rulers of the **P** went to her
    16:30 said, "Let me die with the **P!"**
1Sa 4: 1 went out to fight against the **P.**
     5: 1 After the **P** had captured the ark
    13:20 to the **P** to have their plow points,
    17: 1 Now the **P** gathered their forces
    17:51 When the **P** saw that their hero was
    23: 1 the **P** are fighting against Keilah
    27: 1 do is to escape to the land of the **P.**
    31: 1 Now the **P** fought against Israel;
2Sa 5:17 When the **P** heard that David had
     8: 1 David defeated the **P** and subdued
    21:15 with his men to fight against the **P,**
2Ki 18: 8 he defeated the **P,** as far as Gaza
Isa 14:31 Melt away, all you **P!** A cloud
Jer 47: 4 Lᴏʀᴅ is about to destroy the **P,**
Eze 25:16 to stretch out my hand against the **P,**
Am   1: 8 till the last of the **P** are dead,"

PHILOSOPHER* PHILOSOPHY
1Co 1:20 Where is the **p** of this age?

PHILOSOPHERS* PHILOSOPHY
Ac 17:18 Stoic **p** began to debate with him.

PHILOSOPHY* PHILOSOPHER, PHILOSOPHERS

Col   2: 8 through hollow and deceptive **p**,

PHINEHAS

1. Grandson of Aaron (Ex 6:25; Jos 22:30–32). Zeal for the LORD stopped plague (Nu 25:7–13; Ps 106:30).

2. Son of Eli; a wicked priest (1Sa 1:3; 2:12–17; 4:1–19).

PHOEBE*

Ro   16: 1 I commend to you our sister **P**,

PHYLACTERIES*

Mt   23: 5 They make their **p** wide

PHYSICAL*

Da   1: 4 young men without any **p** defect,
Ro   2:28 circumcision merely outward and **p**.
       9: 8 not the children by **p** descent who are
Col   1:22 by Christ's **p** body through death
1Ti   4: 8 For **p** training is of some value,
Jas   2:16 does nothing about their **p** needs,

PHYSICIAN* PHYSICIANS

Jer   8:22 Is there no **p** there? Why then is
Lk   4:23 proverb to me: 'P, heal yourself!'

PHYSICIANS PHYSICIAN

Job   13: 4 you are worthless **p**, all of you!

PICK PICKED

Lev   19:10 or **p** up the grapes that have fallen.
Dt   23:25 you may **p** kernels with your hands,
Ru   2:16 and leave them for her to **p** up,
Mk   2:23 they began to **p** some heads
Jn   5: 8 P up your mat and walk."

PICKED PICK

Lk   14: 7 noticed how the guests **p** the places
Jn   5: 9 he **p** up his mat and walked.
       8:59 this, they **p** up stones to stone him,

PIECE PIECES

Ex   15:25 and the LORD showed him a **p**
1Sa   24:11 look at this **p** of your robe in my
1Ki   17:11 bring me, please, a **p** of bread."
Mk   2:21 the new **p** will pull away
Jn   13:26 to whom I will give this **p** of bread
      19:23 woven in one **p** from top to bottom.

PIECES PIECE

Ge   15:17 appeared and passed between the **p**.
Ex   32:19 breaking them to **p** at the foot
Jdg   20: 6 cut her into **p** and sent one piece
1Ki   11:30 wearing and tore it into twelve **p**.
2Ki   18: 4 into **p** the bronze snake Moses had
Ps   2: 9 will dash them to **p** like pottery."
Jer   34:18 two and then walked between its **p**.
Hos   6: 5 Therefore I cut you in **p** with my
Mic   1: 7 All her idols will be broken to **p**;
Zec   11:12 So they paid me thirty **p** of silver.
Mt   14:20 of broken **p** that were left over.
      15:37 of broken **p** that were left over.
Lk   20:18 on that stone will be broken to **p**;

Rev   2:27 will dash them to **p** like pottery' —

PIERCE PIERCED

Ex   21: 6 doorpost and **p** his ear with an awl.
Ps   22:16 they **p** my hands and my feet.
Pr   12:18 words of the reckless **p** like swords,
Lk   2:35 a sword will **p** your own soul too."

PIERCED PIERCE

Isa   53: 5 But he was **p** for our transgressions,
Zec   12:10 the one they have **p**, and they will
Jn   19:37 the one they have **p**."
Rev   1: 7 see him, even those who **p** him";

PIG* PIG'S, PIGS

Lev   11: 7 And the **p**, though it has a divided
Dt   14: 8 The **p** is also unclean;

PIG'S* PIG

Pr   11:22 a **p** snout is a beautiful woman who
Isa   66: 3 is like one who presents **p** blood,

PIGEONS

Lev   5: 7 or two young **p** to the LORD as
      12: 8 to bring two doves or two young **p**,
Lk   2:24 "a pair of doves or two young **p**."

PIGS PIG

Isa   66:17 among those who eat the flesh of **p**,
Mt   7: 6 do not throw your pearls to **p**.
Mk   5:11 A large herd of **p** was feeding
Lk   15:16 with the pods that the **p** were eating,

PILATE PONTIUS

Governor of Judea. Questioned Jesus (Mt 27:1–26; Mk 15:15; Lk 22:66—23:25; Jn 18:28—19:16); sent him to Herod (Lk 23:6–12); consented to his crucifixion when crowds chose Barabbas (Mt 27:15–26; Mk 15:6–15; Lk 23:13–25; Jn 19:1–10).

PILGRIMS (KJV) See STRANGERS

PILLAR PILLARS

Ge   19:26 back, and she became a **p** of salt.
      28:18 set it up as a **p** and poured oil on top
      31:52 and this **p** is a witness, that I will
Ex   13:21 them in a **p** of cloud to guide them
      13:21 by night in a **p** of fire to give them
Nu   14:14 you go before them in a **p** of cloud by
           day and a **p** of fire by night.
1Ti   3:15 the **p** and foundation of the truth.
Rev   3:12 make a **p** in the temple of my God.

PILLARS PILLAR

Ex   24: 4 up twelve stone **p** representing
Jdg   16:29 reached toward the two central **p**
1Ki   7:15 He cast two bronze **p**, each eighteen
2Ki   25:13 Babylonians broke up the bronze **p**,
Ps   75: 3 quake, it is I who hold its **p** firm.
     144:12 our daughters will be like **p** carved
Pr   9: 1 she has set up its seven **p**.
SS   5:15 His legs are **p** of marble set on bases
Gal   2: 9 those esteemed as **p**, gave me
Rev   10: 1 sun, and his legs were like fiery **p**.

PINE*

Isa   19: 8 throw nets on the water will **p** away.

Isa 44:14 or planted a **p**, and the rain made it

PIONEER*
Heb 2:10 should make the **p** of their salvation
12: 2 Jesus, the **p** and perfecter of faith.

PIPE PIPERS, PIPES
Ps 150: 4 praise him with the strings and **p**,
Da 3: 5 harp, **p** and all kinds of music,
Mt 11:17 " 'We played the **p** for you,
1Co 14: 7 make sounds, such as the **p** or harp,

PIPERS* PIPE
Rev 18:22 and musicians, **p** and trumpeters,

PIPES PIPE
Ge 4:21 play stringed instruments and **p**.

PISGAH
Dt 3:27 Go up to the top of **P** and look west

PIT
Ex 21:33 "If anyone uncovers a **p** or digs one
Ps 7:15 out falls into the **p** they have made.
35: 8 may they fall into the **p**, to their
40: 2 He lifted me out of the slimy **p**,
103: 4 who redeems your life from the **p**
Pr 23:27 an adulterous woman is a deep **p**,
26:27 Whoever digs a **p** will fall into it;
Isa 24:17 Terror and **p** and snare await you,
38:17 kept me from the **p** of destruction;
Eze 19: 4 him, and he was trapped in their **p**.
Jnh 2: 6 God, brought my life up from the **p**.
Mt 15:14 the blind, both will fall into a **p**."

PITCH
Ge 6:14 it and coat it with **p** inside and out.
Ex 2: 3 for him and coated it with tar and **p**.

PITIED* PITY
1Co 15:19 we are of all people most to be **p**.

PITIFUL* PITY
Rev 3:17 not realize that you are wretched, **p**,

PITY PITIED, PITIFUL
Dt 7:16 Do not look on them with **p** and do
2Ch 36:15 because he had **p** on his people
Ps 72:13 He will take **p** on the weak
Ecc 4:10 But **p** anyone who falls and has no
Eze 7: 4 I will not look on you with **p**;
Lk 10:33 when he saw him, he took **p** on him.
1Jn 3:17 sister in need but has no **p** on them,

PLACE PLACED, PLACES
Ge 22:14 that **p** The LORD Will Provide.
28:16 "Surely the LORD is in this **p**,
50:19 Am I in the **p** of God?
Ex 3: 5 the **p** where you are standing is holy
26:33 The curtain will separate the Holy **P**
from the Most Holy **P**.
32:34 lead the people to the **p** I spoke of,
Lev 16: 3 Aaron is to enter the Most Holy **P**:
26:11 will put my dwelling **p** among you,
Dt 12: 5 to seek the **p** the LORD your God
Jos 5:15 for the **p** where you are standing is
1Ki 8:13 you, a **p** for you to dwell forever."

2Ki 17:11 every high **p** they burned incense,
2Ch 6:21 Hear from heaven, your dwelling **p**;
Ezr 9: 8 giving us a firm **p** in his sanctuary,
Est 4:14 the Jews will arise from another **p**,
Ps 24: 3 Who may stand in his holy **p**?
26: 8 live, the **p** where your glory dwells.
32: 7 You are my hiding **p**;
84: 1 How lovely is your dwelling **p**,
118: 5 he brought me into a spacious **p**.
132:14 "This is my resting **p** for ever
Pr 8:27 there when he set the heavens in **p**,
Ecc 6: 6 Do not all go to the same **p**?
SS 8: 6 **P** me like a seal over your heart,
Isa 8:14 He will be a holy **p**; for both Israel
42: 9 the former things have taken **p**,
Eze 37:27 My dwelling **p** will be with them;
Da 7: 9 "thrones were set in **p**,
Hag 2: 9 'And in this **p** I will grant peace,'
Mt 8:20 of Man has no **p** to lay his head."
27:33 They came to a **p** called Golgotha
(which means "the **p** of the skull").
Lk 18:15 for him to **p** his hands on them.
Jn 14: 2 going there to prepare a **p** for you?
Ac 18:12 brought him to the **p** of judgment.
Php 2: 9 God exalted him to the highest **p**
2Pe 1:19 it, as to a light shining in a dark **p**,
Rev 1: 1 his servants what must soon take **p**.
20:11 and there was no **p** for them.
22: 6 the things that must soon take **p**."

HIGH PLACE See HIGH

HOLY PLACE See HOLY

PLACED PLACE
Mk 15:46 and **p** it in a tomb cut out of rock.
Lk 2: 7 in cloths and **p** him in a manger,
Jn 6:27 him God the Father has **p** his seal
1Co 12:18 fact God has **p** the parts in the body,
12:28 God has **p** in the church first of all
Eph 1:22 And God **p** all things under his feet

PLACES PLACE
1Ki 3: 2 were still sacrificing at the high **p**,
2Ki 18: 4 He removed the high **p**,
Ps 78:58 They angered him with their high **p**;
Jer 19: 5 They have built the high **p** of Baal
Mt 13: 5 Some fell on rocky **p**, where it did

HIGH PLACES See HIGH

PLAGUE PLAGUED, PLAGUES
Ex 11: 1 Moses, "I will bring one more **p**
32:35 struck the people with a **p** because
Nu 11:33 and he struck them with a severe **p**.
14:37 and died of a **p** before the LORD.
16:48 and the dead, and the **p** stopped.
25: 8 Then the **p** against the Israelites was
Dt 28:21 The LORD will **p** you
2Sa 24:13 Or three days of **p** in your land?
2Ch 6:28 famine or **p** comes to the land,
Ps 91: 6 nor the **p** that destroys at midday.
Jer 14:12 with the sword, famine and **p**."
Zec 14:12 This is the **p** with which the LORD
Rev 11: 6 kind of **p** as often as they want.

Rev 16:21 God on account of the **p** of hail,
because the **p** was so terrible.

PLAGUED* PLAGUE

Ps 73: 5 they are not **p** by human ills.

PLAGUES PLAGUE

Hos 13:14 Where, O death, are your **p**?
Rev 9:18 was killed by the three **p** of fire,
15: 1 seven angels with the seven last **p**—
21: 9 bowls full of the seven last **p** came
22:18 person the **p** described in this scroll.

PLAIN PLAINS

Ge 13:12 Lot lived among the cities of the **p**
19:29 God destroyed the cities of the **p**,
Isa 40: 4 become level, the rugged places a **p**.
Ro 1:19 known about God is **p** to them,
because God has made it **p** to them.

PLAINS PLAIN

Dt 34: 8 Moses in the **p** of Moab thirty days,
1Ki 20:23 But if we fight them on the **p**,

PLAN PLANNED, PLANS

Ge 11: 6 then nothing they **p** to do will be
Ex 26:30 according to the **p** shown you
Est 8: 3 to the evil **p** of Haman the Agagite,
Pr 14:22 those who **p** what is good find love
21:30 no **p** that can succeed against
Isa 8:10 propose your **p**, but it will not stand,
28:29 Almighty, whose **p** is wonderful,
Am 3: 7 does nothing without revealing his **p**
Ac 2:23 over to you by God's deliberate **p**
Eph 1:11 to the **p** of him who works

PLANK

Mt 7: 3 attention to the **p** in your own eye?
Lk 6:42 first take the **p** out of your eye,

PLANNED PLAN

Ps 17: 3 you will find that I have **p** no evil;
40: 5 have done, the things you **p** for us.
Isa 14:24 "Surely, as I have **p**, so it will be,
23: 9 The Lord Almighty **p** it, to bring
46:11 what I have **p**, that I will do.
La 2:17 The Lord has done what he **p**;
Heb 11:40 since God had **p** something better

PLANS PLAN

Ps 20: 4 heart and make all your **p** succeed.
33:11 But the **p** of the Lord stand firm
94:11 The Lord knows all human **p**;
107:11 despised the **p** of the Most High.
Pr 12: 5 The **p** of the righteous are just,
15:22 **P** fail for lack of counsel,
16: 3 you do, and he will establish your **p**.
19:21 Many are the **p** in a person's heart,
20:18 **P** are established by seeking advice;
Isa 29:15 to hide their **p** from the Lord,
30: 1 those who carry out **p** that are not
32: 8 But the noble make noble **p**,
Jer 29:11 For I know the **p** I have for you,"
29:11 "**p** to prosper you and not to harm
Mk 15: 1 the whole Sanhedrin, made their **p**.
2Co 1:17 do I make my **p** in a worldly manner

PLANT PLANTED, PLANTING, PLANTS, REPLANTED

Ge 1:29 "I give you every seed-bearing **p**
Ex 15:17 and **p** them on the mountain of your
Lev 19:19 " 'Do not **p** your field with two
Ecc 3: 2 die, a time to **p** and a time to uproot,
Eze 16: 7 I made you grow like a **p**
Hos 2:23 I will **p** her for myself in the land;
Am 9:15 I will **p** Israel in their own land,
Jnh 4: 6 the Lord God provided a leafy **p**
Mt 15:13 "Every **p** that my heavenly Father
1Co 15:37 you do not **p** the body that will be,

PLANTED PLANT

Ge 2: 8 the Lord God had **p** a garden
Ps 1: 3 person is like a tree **p** by streams
92:13 **p** in the house of the Lord,
Isa 60:21 They are the shoot I have **p**,
Jer 17: 8 They will be like a tree **p**
18: 9 or kingdom is to be built up and **p**,
Mt 15:13 Father has not **p** will be pulled
21:33 was a landowner who **p** a vineyard.
1Co 3: 6 I **p** the seed, Apollos watered it,
Jas 1:21 humbly accept the word **p** in you,

PLANTING PLANT

Isa 61: 3 a **p** of the Lord for the display

PLANTS PLANT

Ge 1:11 seed-bearing **p** and trees on the land
9: 3 Just as I gave you the green **p**, I now
Ps 144:12 youth will be like well-nurtured **p**,
Pr 31:16 out of her earnings she **p** a vineyard.
Mk 4:32 becomes the largest of all garden **p**,
1Co 3: 7 neither the one who **p** nor the one
9: 7 Who **p** a vineyard and does not eat

PLASTER

Dt 27: 2 large stones and coat them with **p**.
Da 5: 5 and wrote on the **p** of the wall,

PLATE PLATES, PLATTER

Ex 28:36 "Make a **p** of pure gold

PLATES PLATE

Ex 25:29 make its **p** and dishes of pure gold,

PLATFORM*

2Ch 6:13 He stood on the **p** and then knelt
Ne 8: 4 on a high wooden **p** built

PLATTER PLATE

Mk 6:25 head of John the Baptist on a **p**."

PLAY PLAYED, PLAYING

Ge 19: 9 and now he wants to **p** the judge!
1Sa 16:23 David would take up his lyre and **p**.
Ps 33: 3 **p** skillfully, and shout for joy.
Isa 11: 8 The infant will **p** near the cobra's

PLAYED PLAY

Mt 11:17 " 'We **p** the pipe for you, and you
1Co 14: 7 what tune is being **p** unless there is

PLAYING PLAY

1Sa 18:10 while David was **p** the lyre, as he

1Sa 19: 9 While David was **p** the lyre,
Zec 8: 5 filled with boys and girls **p** there."
Rev 14: 2 like that of harpists **p** their harps.

PLEA PLEAD, PLEADED, PLEADS, PLEAS

1Ki 8:28 prayer and his **p** for mercy,
 9: 3 and **p** you have made before me;
Ps 17: 1 Hear me, LORD, my **p** is just;
 102:17 he will not despise their **p**.
Jer 7:16 pray for this people nor offer any **p**
La 3:56 You heard my **p**: "Do not close

PLEAD PLEA

2Ch 6:37 and **p** with you in the land of their
Ps 43: 1 **p** my cause against an unfaithful
Isa 1:17 **p** the case of the widow.
Jer 30:13 There is no one to **p** your cause,
Mic 6: 1 up, **p** my case before the mountains;
Mal 1: 9 "Now **p** with God to be gracious to us.

PLEADED PLEA

Dt 3:23 At that time I **p** with the LORD:
Est 8: 3 Esther again **p** with the king,
Da 9: 3 Lord God and **p** with him in prayer
2Co 12: 8 Three times I **p** with the Lord

PLEADS PLEA

Job 16:21 of a man he **p** with God as one **p**

PLEAS* PLEA

2Ch 6:39 hear their prayer and their **p**,
Job 13: 6 listen to the **p** of my lips.
Isa 19:22 he will respond to their **p** and heal

PLEASANT PLEASE

Ge 49:15 resting place and how **p** is his land,
Ps 16: 6 lines have fallen for me in **p** places;
 106:24 Then they despised the **p** land,
 133: 1 and **p** it is when God's people live
 135: 3 sing praise to his name, for that is **p**.
 147: 1 how **p** and fitting to praise him!
Pr 2:10 knowledge will be **p** to your soul.
 3:17 Her ways are **p** ways, and all her
Isa 30:10 Tell us **p** things, prophesy illusions.
Jer 3:19 my children and give you a **p** land,
Heb 12:11 No discipline seems **p** at the time,

PLEASANTNESS* PLEASE

Pr 27: 9 the **p** of a friend springs from their

PLEASE PLEASANT, PLEASANTNESS, PLEASED, PLEASES, PLEASING, PLEASURE, PLEASURES

Ex 21: 8 If she does not **p** the master who has
Dt 12:13 burnt offerings anywhere you **p**.
Job 10: 3 Does it **p** you to oppress me,
Ps 69:31 This will **p** the LORD more than
Pr 20:23 and dishonest scales do not **p** him.
 21: 1 he channels toward all who **p** him.
Isa 44:28 and will accomplish all that I **p**;
 46:10 will stand, and I will do all that I **p**.'
Jer 6:20 your sacrifices do not **p** me."

Jer 27: 5 are on it, and I give it to anyone I **p**.
Hos 10:10 When I **p**, I will punish them;
Jn 5:30 for I seek not to **p** myself but him
Ro 8: 8 the realm of the flesh cannot **p** God.
 15: 1 of the weak and not to **p** ourselves.
 15: 2 Each of us should **p** our neighbors
1Co 7:32 how he can **p** the Lord.
 7:33 how he can **p** his wife—
 10:33 even as I try to **p** everyone in every
2Co 5: 9 So we make it our goal to **p** him,
Gal 1:10 Or am I trying to **p** people? If I were
 6: 8 Whoever sows to **p** their flesh,
 6: 8 whoever sows to **p** the Spirit,
Col 1:10 of the Lord and **p** him in every way:
1Th 2: 4 We are not trying to **p** people
 4: 1 you how to live in order to **p** God,
2Ti 2: 4 tries to **p** his commanding officer.
Titus 2: 9 to try to **p** them, not to talk back
Heb 11: 6 faith it is impossible to **p** God,

PLEASED PLEASE

Ex 33:13 If you are **p** with me, teach me your
Nu 14: 8 If the LORD is **p** with us, he will
 24: 1 Balaam saw that it **p** the LORD
Dt 28:63 Just as it **p** the LORD to make you
Jdg 18:20 The priest was very **p**. He took
1Sa 12:22 because the LORD was **p** to make
1Ki 3:10 The Lord was **p** that Solomon had
1Ch 29:17 the heart and are **p** with integrity.
Ps 5: 4 For you are not a God who is **p**
 40:13 Be **p** to save me, LORD;
Isa 42:21 It **p** the LORD for the sake of his
Eze 18:23 am I not **p** when they turn from their
Da 8: 4 It did as it **p** and became great.
Mic 6: 7 Will the LORD be **p**
Mal 1:10 I am not **p** with you,"
Mt 3:17 with him I am well **p**."
 17: 5 whom I love; with him I am well **p**.
Mk 1:11 with you I am well **p**."
Lk 3:22 with you I am well **p**."
 10:21 for this is what you were **p** to do.
Jn 5:21 gives life to whom he is **p** to give it.
1Co 1:21 God was **p** through the foolishness
 10: 5 God was not **p** with most of them;
Col 1:19 God was **p** to have all his fullness
Heb 10: 6 and sin offerings you were not **p**.
 10: 8 desire, nor were you **p** with them"—
 11: 5 was commended as one who **p** God.
 13:16 for with such sacrifices God is **p**.
2Pe 1:17 with him I am well **p**."

PLEASES PLEASE

Job 23:13 He does whatever he **p**.
Ps 115: 3 he does whatever **p** him.
 135: 6 The LORD does whatever **p** him,
Pr 15: 8 but the prayer of the upright **p** him.
Ecc 2:26 To the person who **p** him, God gives
 2:26 hand it over to the one who **p** God.
 7:26 The man who **p** God will escape
Isa 56: 4 who choose what **p** me and hold fast
Da 4:35 He does as he **p** with the powers
 11: 3 with great power and do as he **p**.
 11:36 "The king will do as he **p**.
Jn 3: 8 The wind blows wherever it **p**.

Jn   8:29 alone, for I always do what **p** him."
Eph   5:10 and find out what **p** the Lord.
Col   3:20 in everything, for this **p** the Lord.
1Ti   2: 3 This is good, and **p** God our Savior,
1Jn   3:22 his commands and do what **p** him.

PLEASING PLEASE

Ge   2: 9 trees that were **p** to the eye
    8:21 The LORD smelled the **p** aroma
Ex 29:18 offering to the LORD, a **p** aroma,
Lev   1: 9 offering, an aroma **p** to the LORD.
Ezr   6:10 they may offer sacrifices **p**
Ps 19:14 of my heart be **p** in your sight,
   104:34 May my meditation be **p** to him, as I
SS   1: 3 **P** is the fragrance of your perfumes;
    4:10 How much more **p** is your love than
    7: 6 How beautiful you are and how **p**,
Ro 12: 1 living sacrifice, holy and **p** to God—
   14:18 serves Christ in this way is **p** to God
Php   4:18 an acceptable sacrifice, **p** to God.
1Ti   5: 4 grandparents, for this is **p** to God.
Heb 13:21 may he work in us what is **p** to him,

AROMA PLEASING Lev 1:9, 13, 17; 2:2, 9; 3:5;
4:31; 6:15, 21; 17:6; 23:18; Nu 15:3, 7, 10, 13, 14,
24; 18:17; 28:2, 8, 24, 27; 29:2, 8, 13, 36

PLEASING AROMA Ge 8:21; Ex 29:18, 25, 41;
Lev 2:12; 3:16; 8:21, 28; 23:13; 26:31; Nu 28:6, 13;
29:6; 2Co 2:15

PLEASURE PLEASE

Ge 18:12 lord is old, will I now have this **p**?"
Ps 51:16 you do not take **p** in burnt offerings.
   147:10 His **p** is not in the strength
Pr 10:23 A fool finds **p** in wicked schemes,
    16: 7 the LORD takes **p** in anyone's
    18: 2 Fools find no **p** in understanding
    21:17 Whoever loves **p** will become poor;
Ecc   2: 2 And what does **p** accomplish?"
    7: 4 heart of fools is in the house of **p**.
Isa   1:11 I have no **p** in the blood of bulls
Jer   6:10 they find no **p** in it.
Eze 18:32 For I take no **p** in the death
   33:11 I take no **p** in the death
Hag   1: 8 so that I may take **p** in it and be
Eph   1: 5 in accordance with his **p** and will—
    1: 9 of his will according to his good **p**,
1Ti   5: 6 for **p** is dead even while she lives.
2Ti   3: 4 lovers of **p** rather than lovers
Heb 10:38 I take no **p** in the one who shrinks
2Pe   2:13 Their idea of **p** is to carouse

PLEASURES* PLEASE

Ps 16:11 with eternal **p** at your right hand.
Lk   8:14 riches and **p**, and they do not
Titus 3: 3 by all kinds of passions and **p**.
Heb 11:25 than to enjoy the fleeting **p** of sin.
Jas   4: 3 may spend what you get on your **p**.
2Pe   2:13 reveling in their **p** while they feast

PLEDGE PLEDGED

Ge 38:17 me something as a **p** until you send
Ex 22:26 take your neighbor's cloak as a **p**,
Nu 30: 2 an oath to obligate himself by a **p**,
Dt 24:17 take the cloak of the widow as a **p**.

Pr   6: 1 if you have shaken hands in **p**
    22:26 not be one who shakes hands in **p**
Eze 18: 7 returns what he took in **p** for a loan.
1Pe   3:21 the **p** of a clear conscience toward

PLEDGED PLEDGE

Mt   1:18 His mother Mary was **p** to be
Lk   1:27 to a virgin **p** to be married to a man
1Co   7:27 Are you **p** to a woman? Do not seek

PLEIADES

Job 38:31 "Can you bind the chains of the **P**?
Am   5: 8 He who made the **P** and Orion,

PLENTIFUL PLENTY

Mt   9:37 "The harvest is **p** but the workers
Lk 10: 2 "The harvest is **p**, but the workers

PLENTY PLENTIFUL

Mic   2:11 'I will prophesy for you **p** of wine
2Co   8:14 the present time your **p** will supply
Php   4:12 whether living in **p** or in want.

PLOT PLOTS, PLOTTED

Ne   4:15 heard that we were aware of their **p**
Est   2:22 Mordecai found out about the **p**
Ps   2: 1 conspire and the peoples **p** in vain?
    64: 6 They **p** injustice and say, "We have
Pr   3:29 Do not **p** harm against your
    14:22 Do not those who **p** evil go astray?
Jer 11:18 the LORD revealed their **p** to me,
Na   1: 9 Whatever they **p** against
Zec   8:17 do not **p** evil against each other,
Mk   3: 6 began to **p** with the Herodians how
Ac   4:25 rage and the peoples **p** in vain?
    23:16 son of Paul's sister heard of this **p**,

PLOTS PLOT

Pr   6:14 who **p** evil with deceit in his heart—
Na   1:11 come forth who **p** evil against

PLOTTED PLOT

Est   9:24 had **p** against the Jews to destroy
Jn 11:53 that day on they **p** to take his life.

PLOW PLOWED, PLOWMAN, PLOWMEN, PLOWS, PLOWSHARES

Dt 22:10 Do not **p** with an ox and a donkey
1Sa 13:20 the Philistines to have their **p** points,
Pr 20: 4 Sluggards do not **p** in season;
Lk   9:62 "No one who puts a hand to the **p**

PLOWED PLOW

Jdg 14:18 "If you had not **p** with my heifer,

PLOWMAN* PLOW

Am   9:13 the reaper will be overtaken by the **p**

PLOWMEN* PLOW

Ps 129: 3 **P** have plowed my back and made

PLOWS PLOW

1Co   9:10 because whoever **p** and threshes

PLOWSHARES* PLOW

Isa   2: 4 They will beat their swords into **p**

Joel 3:10 Beat your **p** into swords and your
Mic   4: 3 They will beat their swords into **p**

PLUCK*
Ps   52: 5 you up and **p** you from your tent;
Mk   9:47 eye causes you to stumble, **p** it out.

PLUMB
2Ki 21:13 the **p** line used against the house
Isa 28:17 line and righteousness the **p** line;
Am   7: 8 I am setting a **p** line among my

PLUNDER PLUNDERED
Ex   3:22 And so you will **p** the Egyptians."
Nu   14:31 that you said would be taken as **p**,
Dt   20:14 the city, you may take these as **p**
Jos   7:21 I saw in the **p** a beautiful robe
Est   3:13 month of Adar, and to **p** their goods.
      8:11 to **p** the property of their enemies.
      9:10 did not lay their hands on the **p**.
Isa   3:14 the **p** from the poor is in your
Jer 30:16 Those who **p** you will be plundered;
Eze 39:10 they will **p** those who plundered
Mk   3:27 he can **p** the strong man's house.
Hab   2: 8 the peoples who are left will **p** you.
Zep   2: 9 remnant of my people will **p** them;

PLUNDERED PLUNDER
Ex   12:36 so they **p** the Egyptians.
Jdg   2:14 the hands of raiders who **p** them.
Ps   12: 5 "Because the poor are **p**
Eze 34: 8 so has been **p** and has become food

PLUNGE
1Ti   6: 9 harmful desires that **p** people

POCKET*
1Sa 25:29 hurl away as from the **p** of a sling.

PODS*
2Ki   6:25 of a cab of seed **p** for five shekels.
Lk   15:16 with the **p** that the pigs were eating,

POETS*
Nu   21:27 That is why the **p** say:
Ac   17:28 As some of your own **p** have said,

POINT
Pr   9: 3 calls from the highest **p** of the city,
Mt   4: 5 stand on the highest **p** of the temple.
     26:38 with sorrow to the **p** of death.
Ro   2: 1 for at whatever **p** you judge another,
Heb 12: 4 to the **p** of shedding your blood.
Jas   2:10 yet stumbles at just one **p** is guilty
Rev   2:10 even to the **p** of death, and I will

POISON
Dt   32:32 Their grapes are filled with **p**,
Ps 140: 3 the **p** of vipers is on their lips.
Am   6:12 you have turned justice into **p**
Mk   16:18 *and when they drink deadly p,*
Ro   3:13 "The **p** of vipers is on their lips."
Jas   3: 8 It is a restless evil, full of deadly **p**.

POLE POLES
Nu   21: 8 "Make a snake and put it up on a **p**;
Dt   16:21 any wooden Asherah **p** beside

Dt   21:23 is hung on a **p** is under God's curse.
Jdg   6:25 cut down the Asherah **p** beside it.
1Ki 16:33 made an Asherah **p** and did more
Est   7:10 impaled Haman on the **p** he had set
Gal   3:13 is everyone who is hung on a **p**."

POLES POLE
Ex   25:13 Then make **p** of acacia wood
Dt   12: 3 and burn their Asherah **p** in the fire;
2Ki 17:10 and Asherah **p** on every high hill
Est   9:13 ten sons be impaled on **p**."

POLISHED
Isa 49: 2 he made me into a **p** arrow
Eze 21:11 " 'The sword is appointed to be **p**,

POLLUTE* POLLUTED, POLLUTES
Nu   35:33 " 'Do not **p** the land where you
Jude 1: 8 these ungodly people **p** their own

POLLUTED* POLLUTE
Ezr   9:11 possess is a land **p** by the corruption
Pr   25:26 a **p** well are the righteous who give
Ac   15:20 to abstain from food **p** by idols,
Jas   1:27 oneself from being **p** by the world.

POLLUTES* POLLUTE
Nu   35:33 Bloodshed **p** the land,

POMEGRANATES
Ex   28:33 Make **p** of blue, purple and scarlet
Dt   8: 8 vines and fig trees, **p**, olive oil
1Ki   7:18 He made **p** in two rows encircling
SS   8: 2 wine to drink, the nectar of my **p**.

PONDER PONDERED
Ps   64: 9 of God and **p** what he has done.
    107:43 **p** the loving deeds of the LORD.
    119:95 me, but I will **p** your statutes.

PONDERED PONDER
Ps 111: 2 they are **p** by all who delight
Ecc 12: 9 He **p** and searched out and set
Lk   2:19 these things and **p** them in her heart.

PONTIUS PILATE
Lk   3: 1 when **P** Pilate was governor

POOL POOLS
2Sa   2:13 and met them at the **p** of Gibeon.
1Ki 22:38 chariot at a **p** in Samaria (where
Ps 114: 8 who turned the rock into a **p**,
Jn   5: 2 Jerusalem near the Sheep Gate a **p**,
      9: 7 the **P** of Siloam" (this word means

POOLS POOL
Ps 107:35 He turned the desert into **p** of water

POOR POOREST, POVERTY
Ex   23: 3 not show favoritism to a **p** person
     23: 6 not deny justice to your **p** people
Lev 19:10 Leave them for the **p**
     23:22 Leave them for the **p**
     27: 8 anyone making the vow is too **p**
Dt   15: 4 need be no **p** people among you,
     15: 7 If anyone is **p** among your fellow
     15:11 There will always be **p** people

Dt   24:12 If the neighbor is **p**, do not go
       24:14 of a hired worker who is **p**
1Sa   2: 8 He raises the **p** from the dust
2Sa 12: 1 town, one rich and the other **p**.
Job   5:16 So the **p** have hope, and injustice
       24: 4 and force all the **p** of the land
       30:25 Has not my soul grieved for the **p**?
Ps   14: 6 frustrate the plans of the **p**,
       34: 6 This **p** man called, and the LORD
       35:10 You rescue the **p** from those too
       40:17 But as for me, I am **p** and needy;
       68:10 God, you provided for the **p**.
       69:32 The **p** will see and be glad—
       82: 3 uphold the cause of the **p**
     112: 9 freely scattered their gifts to the **p**,
     113: 7 He raises the **p** from the dust
     140:12 the LORD secures justice for the **p**
Pr   13: 7 another pretends to be **p**, yet has
       14:20 The **p** are shunned even by their
       14:31 oppresses the **p** shows contempt
       17: 5 mocks the **p** shows contempt
       19: 1 Better the **p** whose walk is
       19:17 Whoever is kind to the **p** lends
       19:22 better to be **p** than a liar.
       20:13 not love sleep or you will grow **p**;
       21:13 their ears to the cry of the **p** will
       21:17 loves pleasure will become **p**;
       22: 2 Rich and **p** have this in common:
       22: 9 for they share their food with the **p**.
       22:22 not exploit the **p** because they are **p**
       28: 6 Better the **p** whose walk is
       28:27 who give to the **p** will lack nothing,
       29: 7 care about justice for the **p**,
       31: 9 defend the rights of the **p** and needy.
       31:20 She opens her arms to the **p**
Ecc   4:13 Better a **p** but wise youth than
Isa   3:14 the plunder from the **p** is in your
       10: 2 to deprive the **p** of their rights
       14:30 poorest of the **p** will find pasture,
       25: 4 You have been a refuge for the **p**,
       32: 7 schemes to destroy the **p** with lies,
       61: 1 me to proclaim good news to the **p**.
Jer 22:16 He defended the cause of the **p**
Eze 18:12 He oppresses the **p** and needy.
Am   2: 7 on the heads of the **p** as on the dust
       4: 1 you women who oppress the **p**
       5:11 You levy a straw tax on the **p**
Zec   7:10 the fatherless, the foreigner or the **p**.
Mt   5: 3 "Blessed are the **p** in spirit,
       11: 5 good news is proclaimed to the **p**.
Mk 10:21 you have and give to the **p**, and you
       12:42 But a **p** widow came and put in two
       14: 7 The **p** you will always have
Lk   4:18 me to proclaim good news to the **p**.
       6:20 "Blessed are you who are **p**,
       11:41 be generous to the **p**, and everything
       14:13 a banquet, invite the **p**, the crippled,
       19: 8 give half of my possessions to the **p**,
       21: 2 also saw a **p** widow put in two very
Jn 12: 8 will always have the **p** among you,
Ac   9:36 doing good and helping the **p**.
       10: 4 and gifts to the **p** have come up as
       24:17 to bring my people gifts for the **p**

Ro 15:26 for the **p** among the Lord's people
1Co 13: 3 If I give all I possess to the **p**
2Co 6:10 **p**, yet making many rich;
       8: 9 yet for your sake he became **p**,
       9: 9 freely scattered their gifts to the **p**;
Gal   2:10 should continue to remember the **p**,
Jas   2: 2 and a **p** man in filthy old clothes
       2: 5 not God chosen those who are **p**
Rev   3:17 pitiful, **p**, blind and naked.

POOREST POOR

2Ki 24:14 Only the **p** people of the land were
Jer 52:16 left behind the rest of the **p** people

POPULATION*

Pr 14:28 A large **p** is a king's glory,

PORCIUS* FESTUS

Ac 24:27 Felix was succeeded by **P** Festus,

PORTENT*

Isa 20: 3 as a sign and **p** against Egypt

PORTICO

1Ki 6: 3 The **p** at the front of the main hall
1Ch 28:11 the plans for the **p** of the temple,

PORTION PORTIONS

Lev   2: 2 and burn this as a memorial **p**
       5:12 take a handful of it as a memorial **p**
Nu 18:29 present as the LORD's **p** the best
Dt 32: 9 For the LORD's **p** is his people,
Jos 18: 7 do not get a **p** among you,
1Sa   1: 5 he gave a double **p** because he loved
2Ki   2: 9 "Let me inherit a double **p** of your
Ps 16: 5 you alone are my **p** and my cup;
       73:26 of my heart and my **p** forever.
     119:57 You are my **p**, LORD;
     142: 5 my **p** in the land of the living."
Isa 53:12 I will give him a **p** among the great,
       61: 7 shame you will receive a double **p**,
Jer 10:16 He who is the **P** of Jacob is not like
La   3:24 to myself, "The LORD is my **p**;
Zec   2:12 LORD will inherit Judah as his **p**
Rev 18: 6 Pour her a double **p** from her own

PORTIONS PORTION

Ge   4: 4 fat **p** from some of the firstborn
Lev   9:24 offering and the fat **p** on the altar.
Jos 19:49 dividing the land into its allotted **p**,

PORTRAYED

Gal   3: 1 Christ was clearly **p** as crucified.

POSITION POSITIONS

Est   4:14 to your royal **p** for such a time as
Da   2:48 the king placed Daniel in a high **p**
Ro 12:16 to associate with people of low **p**.
2Pe   3:17 lawless and fall from your secure **p**.

POSITIONS POSITION

2Ch 20:17 Take up your **p**; stand firm and see
Ecc 10: 6 Fools are put in many high **p**,
Jude 1: 6 the angels who did not keep their **p**

POSSESS DEMON-POSSESSED, POSSESSED, POSSESSING, POSSESSION, POSSESSIONS

Lev 20:24 said to you, "You will **p** their land;
Nu 33:53 for I have given you the land to **p**.
Dt   4:14 you are crossing the Jordan to **p**.
       28:21 from the land you are entering to **p**.
Ezr   9:11 are entering to **p** is a land polluted
Pr   8:12 I **p** knowledge and discretion.
Isa 60:21 and they will **p** the land forever.
Da   7:18 the kingdom and will **p** it forever—
1Co 13: 3 If I give all I **p** to the poor and give
2Pe   1: 8 if you **p** these qualities in increasing

POSSESSED POSSESS

Jer 16:19 "Our ancestors **p** nothing but false
Mk   3:22 said, "He is **p** by Beelzebul!
Lk   4:33 the synagogue there was a man **p**
Jn   8:49 "I am not **p** by a demon,"
      10:21 the sayings of a man **p** by a demon.

POSSESSING* POSSESS

2Co   6:10 nothing, and yet **p** everything.

POSSESSION POSSESS

Ge   15: 7 give you this land to take **p** of it."
      17: 8 I will give as an everlasting **p** to you
Ex   6: 8 I will give it to you as a **p**. I am
      19: 5 nations you will be my treasured **p**.
Nu   13:30 should go up and take **p** of the land,
Dt   1: 8 take **p** of the land the LORD swore
      7: 6 to be his people, his treasured **p**.
Jos   1:11 take **p** of the land the LORD your
      21:43 and they took **p** of it and settled
Ps   2: 8 the ends of the earth your **p**.
     135: 4 his own, Israel to be his treasured **p**.
Isa 14: 2 And Israel will take **p** of the nations
Eze 44:28 You are to give them no **p** in Israel; I
           will be their **p**.
Mal   3:17 "they will be my treasured **p**.
Eph   1:14 of those who are God's **p**—
1Pe   2: 9 God's special **p**, that you may

POSSESSIONS POSSESS

Ge   15:14 they will come out with great **p**.
Ecc   5:19 God gives someone wealth and **p**,
Mt   19:21 go, sell your **p** and give to the poor,
Lk   11:21 his own house, his **p** are safe.
      12:15 not consist in an abundance of **p**."
      19: 8 now I give half of my **p** to the poor,
Ac   4:32 that any of their **p** was their own,
2Co 12:14 because what I want is not your **p**
Heb 10:34 yourselves had better and lasting **p**.
1Jn   3:17 If anyone has material **p** and sees

POSSIBLE

Mt   19:26 but with God all things are **p**."
      26:39 if it is **p**, may this cup be taken
Mk   9:23 "Everything is **p** for one who
      10:27 all things are **p** with God."
      14:35 if **p** the hour might pass from him.
Lk   18:27 with man is **p** with God."
Ro   12:18 If it is **p**, as far as it depends on you,
1Co   9:19 to everyone, to win as many as **p**.

1Co   9:22 by all **p** means I might save some.

POSTS

Ex   27:17 All the **p** around the courtyard are
Jdg 16: 3 together with the two **p**, and tore

POT POTSHERD, POTSHERDS, POTTER, POTTER'S, POTTERY

2Ki   4:40 of God, there is death in the **p**!"
Isa 29:16 Can the **p** say to the potter,
Jer   1:13 "I see a **p** that is boiling,"
      18: 4 the potter formed it into another **p**,
Eze 11: 3 This city is a **p**, and we are the meat

POTIPHAR*

Egyptian who bought Joseph (Ge 37:36), set him over his house (Ge 39:1–6), sent him to prison (Ge 39:7–30).

POTSHERD POT

Ps   22:15 My mouth is dried up like a **p**,

POTSHERDS POT

Isa 45: 9 but **p** among the **p** on the ground.

POTTER POT

Isa 29:16 Can the pot say to the **p**,
      45: 9 Does the clay say to the **p**,
      64: 8 We are the clay, you are the **p**;
Jer 18: 6 "Like clay in the hand of the **p**,
Zec 11:13 said to me, "Throw it to the **p**"—
Ro   9:21 Does not the **p** have the right

POTTER'S POT

Jer 18: 2 "Go down to the **p** house, and there
Mt   27: 7 to buy the **p** field as a burial place

POTTERY POT

Ps   2: 9 will dash them to pieces like **p**."
Ro   9:21 of clay some **p** for special purposes
Rev   2:27 will dash them to pieces like **p**'—

POUR OUTPOURED, OUTPOURING, POURED, POURING, POURS

Lev   4: 7 of the bull's blood he shall **p**
Nu   20: 8 their eyes and it will **p** out its water.
Dt   12:16 **p** it out on the ground like water.
2Ki   4: 4 **P** oil into all the jars, and as each is
Ps   19: 2 Day after day they **p** forth speech;
      62: 8 **p** out your hearts to him, for God is
      79: 6 **P** out your wrath on the nations
Isa 44: 3 I will **p** out my Spirit on your
Eze 20: 8 So I said I would **p** out my wrath
      39:29 for I will **p** out my Spirit
Joel 2:28 I will **p** out my Spirit on all people.
Zec 12:10 I will **p** out on the house of David
Mal   3:10 **p** out so much blessing that there
Mt   9:17 Neither do people **p** new wine
Ac   2:17 I will **p** out my Spirit on all people.
Rev 16: 1 **p** out the seven bowls of God's
      18: 6 **P** her a double portion from her

POURED POUR

Ge   28:18 it up as a pillar and **p** oil on top of it.

Ge 35:14 and he **p** out a drink offering on it; he also **p** oil on it.
Lev 8:12 He **p** some of the anointing oil
2Sa 23:16 he **p** it out before the LORD.
2Ch 34:25 my anger will be **p** out on this place
Ps 22:14 I am **p** out like water, and all my
133: 2 It is like precious oil **p** on the head,
SS 1: 3 your name is like perfume **p** out.
Isa 19:14 The LORD has **p** into them a spirit
32:15 till the Spirit is **p** on us
La 4:11 he has **p** out his fierce anger.
Mt 26:28 which is **p** out for many
Mk 14: 3 jar and **p** the perfume on his head.
Lk 6:38 over, will be **p** into your lap.
22:20 in my blood, which is **p** out for you.
Ac 2:33 and has **p** out what you now see
10:45 the Holy Spirit had been **p** out even
Ro 5: 5 because God's love has been **p**
Php 2:17 even if I am being **p** out like a drink
1Ti 1:14 The grace of our Lord was **p**
2Ti 4: 6 I am already being **p** out like a drink
Titus 3: 6 whom he **p** out on us generously
Rev 14:10 which has been **p** full strength
16: 2 went and **p** out his bowl on the land,

POURING POUR

1Sa 1:15 I was **p** out my soul to the LORD.
2Ki 4: 5 the jars to her and she kept **p**.
Lk 10:34 his wounds, **p** on oil and wine.

POURS POUR

Pr 14: 5 but a false witness **p** out lies.
Lk 5:37 And no one **p** new wine into old

POVERTY* POOR

Dt 28:48 in nakedness and dire **p**, you will
1Sa 2: 7 The LORD sends **p** and wealth;
Pr 6:11 and **p** will come on you like a thief
10: 4 Lazy hands make for **p**, but diligent
10:15 city, but **p** is the ruin of the poor.
11:24 withholds unduly, but comes to **p**.
13:18 disregards discipline comes to **p**
14:23 profit, but mere talk leads only to **p**.
21: 5 profit as surely as haste leads to **p**.
22:16 gifts to the rich—both come to **p**.
24:34 and **p** will come on you like a thief
28:19 fantasies will have their fill of **p**.
28:22 and are unaware that **p** awaits them.
30: 8 give me neither **p** nor riches,
31: 7 forget their **p** and remember their
Ecc 4:14 been born in **p** within his kingdom.
Mk 12:44 she, out of her **p**, put in everything—
Lk 21: 4 she out of her **p** put in all she had
2Co 8: 2 their extreme **p** welled up in rich
8: 9 you through his **p** might become
Rev 2: 9 I know your afflictions and your **p**—

POWDER

Ex 32:20 then he ground it to **p**, scattered it
2Ki 23:15 the high place and ground it to **p**,
Job 9:30 and my hands with cleansing **p**,

POWER OVERPOWER, POWERFUL, POWERFULLY, POWERLESS, POWERS

Ex 9:16 that I might show you my **p**
15: 6 hand, LORD, was majestic in **p**.
32:11 brought out of Egypt with great **p**
Dt 8:17 "My **p** and the strength of my
34:12 no one has ever shown the mighty **p**
1Ki 18:46 The **p** of the LORD came on Elijah
1Ch 29:11 greatness and the **p** and the glory
2Ch 20: 6 **P** and might are in your hand,
32: 7 for there is a greater **p** with us than
Job 1:12 everything he has is in your **p**,
9: 4 wisdom is profound, his **p** is vast.
12:13 "To God belong wisdom and **p**;
36:22 "God is exalted in his **p**. Who is
37:23 beyond our reach and exalted in **p**;
Ps 20: 6 the victorious **p** of his right hand.
37:17 the **p** of the wicked will be broken,
62:11 "**P** belongs to you, God,
63: 2 and beheld your **p** and your glory.
66: 3 So great is your **p** that your enemies
68:34 Proclaim the **p** of God,
77:14 you display your **p** among
89:13 Your arm is endowed with **p**;
145: 6 of the **p** of your awesome works—
147: 5 Great is our Lord and mighty in **p**;
150: 2 Praise him for his acts of **p**;
Pr 3:27 it is due, when it is in your **p** to act.
8:14 I have insight, I have **p**.
18:21 The tongue has the **p** of life
24: 5 The wise prevail through great **p**,
28:12 but when the wicked rise to **p**,
Ecc 8: 8 As no one has **p** over the wind
Isa 40:10 Sovereign LORD comes with **p**,
40:26 Because of his great **p** and mighty
40:29 and increases the **p** of the weak.
63:12 who sent his glorious arm of **p** to be
Jer 10: 6 great, and your name is mighty in **p**.
10:12 But God made the earth by his **p**;
27: 5 With my great **p** and outstretched
32:17 and the earth by your great **p**
Da 2:20 wisdom and **p** are his.
6:27 Daniel from the **p** of the lions."
11: 3 who will rule with great **p** and do as
Hos 13:14 this people from the **p** of the grave;
Mic 3: 8 I am filled with **p**, with the Spirit
Na 1: 3 is slow to anger but great in **p**;
Zec 4: 6 'Not by might nor by **p**, but by my
Mt 22:29 know the Scriptures or the **p** of God.
24:30 of heaven, with **p** and great glory.
Mk 9: 1 kingdom of God has come with **p**."
13:26 Man coming in clouds with great **p**
Lk 1:17 in the spirit and **p** of Elijah, to turn
1:35 you, and the **p** of the Most High will
4:14 to Galilee in the **p** of the Spirit,
6:19 because **p** was coming from him
8:46 I know that **p** has gone
9: 1 he gave them **p** and authority
10:19 to overcome all the **p** of the enemy;
21:27 of Man coming in a cloud with **p**
24:49 until you have been clothed with **p**
Jn 19:11 "You would have no **p** over me if it

Ac   1: 8 you will receive **p** when the Holy
      4:28 They did what your **p** and will had
      4:33 With great **p** the apostles continued
      8:10 man is rightly called the Great **P**
   10:38 Nazareth with the Holy Spirit and **p**,
   26:18 and from the **p** of Satan to God,
Ro   1:16 because it is the **p** of God
      1:20 his eternal **p** and divine nature—
      4:21 that God had **p** to do what he had
      9:17 that I might display my **p** in you
   15:13 hope by the **p** of the Holy Spirit.
   15:19 by the **p** of signs and wonders,
   15:19 through the **p** of the Spirit of God.
1Co 1:17 cross of Christ be emptied of its **p**.
      1:18 us who are being saved it is the **p**
      1:24 Christ the **p** of God and the wisdom
      2: 4 a demonstration of the Spirit's **p**,
      6:14 By his **p** God raised the Lord
   15:24 all dominion, authority and **p**.
   15:56 is sin, and the **p** of sin is the law.
2Co 4: 7 this all-surpassing **p** is from God
      6: 7 truthful speech and in the **p** of God;
   10: 4 they have divine **p** to demolish
   12: 9 for you, for my **p** is made perfect
   12: 9 so that Christ's **p** may rest on me.
   13: 4 weakness, yet he lives by God's **p**.
   13: 4 yet by God's **p** we will live
Eph 1:19 his incomparably great **p** for us who
      1:19 **p** is the same as the mighty strength
      1:21 rule and authority, **p** and dominion,
      3:16 you with **p** through his Spirit
      3:20 according to his **p** that is at work
      6:10 in the Lord and in his mighty **p**.
Php 3:10 to know the **p** of his resurrection
      3:21 by the **p** that enables him to bring
Col   1:11 strengthened with all **p** according
      2:10 He is the head over every **p**
1Th 1: 5 simply with words but also with **p**,
2Th 2: 7 For the secret **p** of lawlessness is
2Ti   1: 7 us timid, but gives us **p**,
      3: 5 form of godliness but denying its **p**.
Heb 2:14 by his death he might break the **p** of
            him who holds the **p** of death—
      7:16 of the **p** of an indestructible life.
1Pe   1: 5 by God's **p** until the coming
2Pe 1: 3 His divine **p** has given us everything
      1:16 of our Lord Jesus Christ in **p**,
Jude 1:25 majesty, **p** and authority,
Rev 4:11 to receive glory and honor and **p**,
      5:12 to receive **p** and wealth and wisdom
      6: 4 Its rider was given **p** to take peace
      6: 8 They were given **p** over a fourth
      7: 2 four angels who had been given **p**
   11:17 because you have taken your great **p**
   12:10 the **p** and the kingdom of our God,
   13: 2 The dragon gave the beast his **p**
   19: 1 and glory and **p** belong to our God,
   20: 6 second death has no **p** over them,

POWERFUL POWER

Ge 18:18 surely become a great and **p** nation,
Nu 13:28 But the people who live there are **p**,
Jos   4:24 that the hand of the LORD is **p**
1Ch 11: 9 David became more and more **p**,

2Ch 26:16 But after Uzziah became **p**,
     27: 6 Jotham grew **p** because he walked
Est   9: 4 and he became more and more **p**.
Ps   29: 4 The voice of the LORD is **p**;
Ecc 7:19 wise person more **p** than ten rulers
Zec 8:22 **p** nations will come to Jerusalem
Mk   1: 7 me comes the one more **p** than I,
Lk 24:19 **p** in word and deed before God
Ac   9:22 more **p** and baffled the Jews living
2Th 1: 7 in blazing fire with his **p** angels.
Heb 1: 3 sustaining all things by his **p** word.
Jas   5:16 prayer of a righteous person is **p**

POWERFULLY POWER

Jdg 14:19 the Spirit of the LORD came **p** upon
   15:14 The Spirit of the LORD came **p** upon
1Sa 10:10 the Spirit of God came **p** upon him,
   11: 6 the Spirit of God came **p** upon him,
   16:13 the Spirit of the LORD came **p** upon

POWERLESS POWER

2Ch 14:11 you to help the **p** against the mighty.
Ro   5: 6 when we were still **p**, Christ died
     8: 3 what the law was **p** to do because it

POWERS POWER

Isa 24:21 day the LORD will punish the **p**
Da   4:35 as he pleases with the **p** of heaven
Mt 13:54 wisdom and these miraculous **p**?"
Ro   8:38 the present nor the future, nor any **p**,
1Co 12:10 to another miraculous **p**, to another
Eph 6:12 against the **p** of this dark world
Col   1:16 whether thrones or **p** or rulers
     2:15 And having disarmed the **p**
Heb 6: 5 of God and the **p** of the coming age
1Pe 3:22 and **p** in submission to him.

PRACTICE PRACTICED, PRACTICES

Lev 19:26 " 'Do not **p** divination or seek
Ps 119:56 This has been my **p**: I obey your
Jer   6:13 and priests alike, all **p** deceit.
Eze 13:23 see false visions or **p** divination.
   33:31 but they do not put them into **p**.
Mt   7:24 **p** is like a wise man who built his
   23: 3 for they do not **p** what they preach.
Lk   8:21 hear God's word and put it into **p**."
Ro 12:13 who are in need. **P** hospitality.
Php 4: 9 me, or seen in me—put it into **p**.
1Ti 5: 4 to put their religion into **p** by caring
Rev 21: 8 immoral, those who **p** magic arts,
   22:15 the dogs, those who **p** magic arts,

PRACTICED PRACTICE

Lev 18:30 that were **p** before you came and do
Mt 23:23 You should have **p** the latter,
Ac   8: 9 a man named Simon had **p** sorcery
   19:19 number who had **p** sorcery brought

PRACTICES PRACTICE

Ex 23:24 or worship them or follow their **p**.
Lev 18: 3 Do not follow their **p**.
Jdg   2:19 They refused to give up their evil **p**
2Ki 17: 8 followed the **p** of the nations
Ps 101: 7 No one who **p** deceit will dwell
Pr 28:16 A tyrannical ruler **p** extortion,

Jer 10: 3 the **p** of the peoples are worthless;
Eze   7: 3 repay you for all your detestable **p.**
Mt   5:19 but whoever **p** and teaches these
Col   3: 9 taken off your old self with its **p**
Rev 22:15 who loves and **p** falsehood.

PRAETORIUM*

Mt   27:27 soldiers took Jesus into the **P**
Mk   15:16 the **P**) and called together the whole

PRAISE PRAISED, PRAISES,
PRAISEWORTHY, PRAISING

Ge   9:26 He also said, "**P** be to the LORD,
Ex   15: 2 and I will **p** him, my father's God,
Lev 19:24 an offering of **p** to the LORD.
Dt   10:21 He is the one you **p**; he is your God,
     26:19 declared that he will set you in **p**,
     32: 3 Oh, **p** the greatness of our God!
Ru   4:14 "**P** be to the LORD, who this day
2Sa 22: 4 who is worthy of **p**, and have been
     22:47 **P** be to my Rock!
1Ki   8:33 to you and give **p** to your name,
      8:35 this place and give **p** to your name
1Ch 16: 7 associates to give **p** to the LORD
     16: 8 Give **p** to the LORD, proclaim his
     16:25 the LORD and most worthy of **p**;
     23: 5 four thousand are to **p** the LORD
     29:10 saying, "**P** be to you, LORD,
2Ch   5:13 musicians joined in unison to give **p**
      6:24 turn back and give **p** to your name,
      6:26 this place and give **p** to your name
     20:21 and to **p** him for the splendor of his
     29:30 ordered the Levites to **p** the LORD
Ezr   3:10 took their places to **p** the LORD,
Ne   9: 5 be exalted above all blessing and **p.**
Ps   8: 2 Through the **p** of children
     16: 7 I will **p** the LORD, who counsels
     22:23 You who fear the LORD, **p** him!
     26: 7 proclaiming aloud your **p**
     28: 7 for joy, and with my song I **p** him.
     30: 4 his faithful people; **p** his holy name.
     30:12 my God, I will **p** you forever.
     33: 1 it is fitting for the upright to **p** him.
     34: 1 his **p** will always be on my lips.
     40: 3 my mouth, a hymn of **p** to our God.
     42: 5 for I will yet **p** him, my Savior
     43: 5 for I will yet **p** him, my Savior
     45:17 therefore the nations will **p** you
     47: 7 sing to him a psalm of **p.**
     48: 1 and most worthy of **p**, in the city
     51:15 and my mouth will declare your **p.**
     56: 4 In God, whose word I **p**—in God I
     57: 9 I will **p** you, Lord,
     63: 4 I will **p** you as long as I live,
     65: 1 **P** awaits you, our God, in Zion;
     66: 2 of his name; make his **p** glorious.
     66: 8 **P** our God, all peoples, let the sound
     68:19 **P** be to the Lord, to God our Savior,
     68:26 **P** God in the great congregation;
     69:30 I will **p** God's name in song
     69:34 Let heaven and earth **p** him, the seas
     71: 8 My mouth is filled with your **p**,
     71:14 I will **p** you more and more.
     71:22 I will **p** you with the harp for your

Ps   74:21 the poor and needy **p** your name.
     75: 1 We **p** you, God, we **p** you, for your
     86:12 I will **p** you, Lord my God, with all
     89: 5 The heavens **p** your wonders,
     92: 1 It is good to **p** the LORD and make
     96: 2 Sing to the LORD, **p** his name;
    100: 4 thanksgiving and his courts with **p**;
    100: 4 give thanks to him and **p** his name.
    101: 1 to you, LORD, I will sing **p.**
    102:18 not yet created may **p** the LORD:
    103: 1 **P** the LORD, my soul;
    103:20 **P** the LORD, you his angels,
    104: 1 **P** the LORD, my soul.
    105: 2 Sing to him, sing **p** to him; tell of
    106: 2 the LORD or fully declare his **p**?
    108: 3 I will **p** you, LORD,
    111:10 To him belongs eternal **p.**
    113: 1 **p** the name of the LORD.
    117: 1 **P** the LORD, all you nations;
    119:175 Let me live that I may **p** you,
    135: 1 **p** him, you servants of the LORD,
    135:20 you who fear him, **p** the LORD.
    138: 1 I will **p** you, LORD, with all my
    139:14 I **p** you because I am fearfully
    144: 1 **P** be to the LORD my Rock,
    145: 3 the LORD and most worthy of **p**;
    145:10 All your works **p** you, LORD;
    145:21 Let every creature **p** his holy name
    146: 1 **P** the LORD. **P** the LORD,
    147: 1 how pleasant and fitting to **p** him!
    148: 1 **P** the LORD. **P** the LORD
    148: 1 **p** him in the heights above.
    148:13 Let them **p** the name of the LORD,
    149: 1 his **p** in the assembly of his faithful
    149: 6 May the **p** of God be in their mouths
    150: 2 **P** him for his acts of power; **p** him
    150: 6 that has breath **p** the LORD.
Pr   27: 2 Let someone else **p** you, and not
     27:21 but people are tested by their **p.**
     31:31 let her works bring her **p** at the city
SS   1: 4 we will **p** your love more than wine.
Isa 12: 1 "I will **p** you, LORD.
     38:18 For the grave cannot **p** you, death
            cannot sing your **p**;
     42:10 his **p** from the ends of the earth,
     61: 3 a garment of **p** instead of a spirit
Jer 33: 9 **p** and honor before all nations
Da   2:20 "**P** be to the name of God for ever
      4:37 **p** and exalt and glorify the King
Jnh   2: 9 But I, with shouts of grateful **p**,
Hab   3: 3 heavens and his **p** filled the earth.
Mt   21:16 Lord, have called forth your **p**'?"
Lk   19:37 disciples began joyfully to **p** God
Jn   12:43 for they loved human **p** more than
            p from God.
Ac   12:23 because Herod did not give **p**
Ro   2:29 Such a person's **p** is not from other
     15: 7 you, in order to bring **p** to God.
     15:11 And again, "**P** the Lord, all you
1Co   4: 5 time each will receive their **p**
2Co   1: 3 **P** be to the God and Father of our
Eph   1: 6 to the **p** of his glorious grace,
      1:12 might be for the **p** of his glory.

Eph 1:14 to the **p** of his glory.
1Th 2: 6 We were not looking for **p**
Heb 13:15 offer to God a sacrifice of **p**—
Jas 3: 9 With the tongue we **p** our Lord
5:13 Let them sing songs of **p**.
1Pe 4:16 but **p** God that you bear that name.
Rev 5:13 and to the Lamb be **p** and honor
7:12 **P** and glory and wisdom and thanks
19: 5 "**P** our God, all you his servants,

PRAISE BE TO THE LORD† Ge 9:26; 24:27;
Ex 18:10; Ru 4:14; 1Sa 25:32, 39; 2Sa 18:28; 1Ki
1:48; 5:7; 8:15, 56; 10:9; 1Ch 16:36; 2Ch 2:12; 6:4;
9:8; Ezr 7:27; Ps 28:6; 31:21; 41:13; 72:18; 89:52;
106:48; 124:6; 135:21; 144:1

PRAISE THE LORD† Ge 29:35; Dt 8:10; Jdg
5:2, 3, 9; 1Ch 16:4, 36; 23:5, 30; 29:20; 2Ch 29:30;
Ezr 3:10; Ne 9:5; Ps 16:7; 26:12; 33:2; 68:26; 92:1;
102:18; 103:1, 2, 20, 21, 22, 22; 104:1, 35, 35;
105:45; 106:1, 48; 111:1; 112:1; 113:1, 1, 9; 115:17,
18; 116:19; 117:1, 2; 134:1, 2; 135:1, 3, 19, 19, 20,
20, 21; 146:1, 1, 2, 10; 147:1, 20; 148:1, 1, 7, 14;
149:1, 9; 150:1, 6, 6; Isa 62:9; Zec 11:5

SING ... PRAISE 1Ch 16:9, 9; 2Ch 20:22; Ps
13:6; 21:13; 47:7; 59:17; 61:8; 66:4; 68:4, 4, 32;
71:22, 23; 75:9; 96:2; 101:1; 104:33; 105:2, 2; 135:3;
138:1; 146:2; Isa 38:18; Jer 20:13; Jas 5:13

PRAISED PRAISE

Ge 12:15 saw her, they **p** her to Pharaoh,
Jdg 16:24 people saw him, they **p** their god,
2Sa 14:25 there was not a man so highly **p**
1Ch 29:10 David **p** the LORD in the presence
Ne 8: 6 Ezra **p** the LORD, the great God;
Job 1:21 may the name of the LORD be **p**."
Ps 113: 2 Let the name of the LORD be **p**,
Pr 12: 8 A person is **p** according to their
31:30 who fears the LORD is to be **p**.
Isa 63: 7 the deeds for which he is to be **p**,
Da 2:19 Then Daniel **p** the God of heaven
4:34 Then I **p** the Most High;
5: 4 they **p** the gods of gold and silver,
Lk 18:43 the people saw it, they also **p** God.
23:47 what had happened, **p** God and said,
Ro 1:25 than the Creator—who is forever **p**.
9: 5 who is God over all, forever **p**!
Gal 1:24 And they **p** God because of me.
1Pe 4:11 God may be **p** through Jesus Christ.

PRAISES PRAISE

2Sa 22:50 I will sing the **p** of your name.
2Ch 23:13 their instruments were leading the **p**.
29:30 So they sang **p** with gladness
31: 2 and to sing **p** at the gates
Ps 6: 5 Who **p** you from the grave?
9:11 Sing the **p** of the LORD,
9:14 I may declare your **p** in the gates
18:49 I will sing the **p** of your name.
35:28 righteousness, your **p** all day long.
47: 6 Sing **p** to God, sing **p**; sing **p** to our
King, sing **p**.
147: 1 How good it is to sing **p** to our God,
Pr 31:28 her husband also, and he **p** her:
Jer 31: 7 Make your **p** heard, and say,

Ro 15: 9 I will sing the **p** of your name."
Heb 2:12 in the assembly I will sing your **p**."
1Pe 2: 9 you may declare the **p** of him who

SING ... PRAISES 2Sa 22:50; 2Ch 31:2; Ps 7:17;
9:2, 11; 18:49; 30:4, 12; 47:6, 6, 6, 6; 66:4; 147:1;
Ro 15:9; Heb 2:12

PRAISEWORTHY* PRAISE

Ps 78: 4 tell the next generation the **p** deeds
Php 4: 8 if anything is excellent or **p**—

PRAISING PRAISE

1Ch 25: 3 harp in thanking and **p** the LORD.
2Ch 7: 6 David had made for **p** the LORD
Lk 2:13 with the angel, **p** God and saying,
2:20 **p** God for all the things they had
24:53 continually at the temple, **p** God.
Ac 2:47 **p** God and enjoying the favor of all
3: 8 walking and jumping, and **p** God.
10:46 speaking in tongues and **p** God.
1Co 14:16 when you are **p** God in the Spirit,

PRAY PRAYED, PRAYER, PRAYERS, PRAYING, PRAYS

Ex 8: 9 setting the time for me to **p** for you
Nu 21: 7 **P** that the LORD will take
Dt 4: 7 our God is near us whenever we **p**
1Sa 12:23 the LORD by failing to **p** for you.
1Ki 8:30 when they **p** toward this place.
2Ch 6:32 they come and **p** toward this temple,
6:38 **p** toward the land you gave their
7:14 will humble themselves and **p**
Ezr 6:10 and **p** for the well-being of the king
Job 42: 8 My servant Job will **p** for you, and I
Ps 5: 2 King and my God, for to you I **p**.
32: 6 Therefore let all the faithful **p**
122: 6 **P** for the peace of Jerusalem:
Isa 37: 4 Therefore **p** for the remnant that still
45:20 who **p** to gods that cannot save.
Jer 7:16 "So do not **p** for this people nor
29: 7 **P** to the LORD for it, because if it
29:12 call on me and come and **p** to me,
42: 3 **P** that the LORD your God will
Da 9:23 As soon as you began to **p**, a word
Mt 5:44 and **p** for those who persecute you,
6: 5 "And when you **p**, do not be like
6: 9 "This, then, is how you should **p**:
14:23 on a mountainside by himself to **p**.
19:13 his hands on them and **p** for them.
26:36 here while I go over there and **p**."
Lk 5:33 "John's disciples often fast and **p**,
6:28 you, **p** for those who mistreat you.
11: 1 teach us to **p**, just as John taught his
18: 1 them that they should always **p**
18:10 men went up to the temple to **p**,
22:40 them, "**P** that you will not fall
Jn 17:20 I **p** also for those who will believe
Ro 8:26 do not know what we ought to **p** for,
1Co 11:13 Is it proper for a woman to **p** to God
14:13 in a tongue should **p** that they may
14:15 I will **p** with my spirit, but I will
also **p** with my understanding;
Eph 1:18 I **p** that the eyes of your heart may
3:16 I **p** that out of his glorious riches he

Eph 6:18 **p** in the Spirit on all occasions
1Th 5:17 **p** continually,
2Th 1:11 in mind, we constantly **p** for you,
1Ti 2: 8 I want the men everywhere to **p**,
5: 5 day to **p** and to ask God for help.
Jas 5:13 Let them **p**. Is anyone happy?
5:16 **p** for each other so that you may be
1Pe 4: 7 of sober mind so that you may **p**.
1Jn 5:16 saying that you should **p** about that.

PRAYED PRAY

Ge 20:17 Then Abraham **p** to God, and God
24:12 Then he **p**, "LORD, God of my
25:21 Isaac **p** to the LORD on behalf
Nu 11: 2 he **p** to the LORD and the fire died
21: 7 So Moses **p** for the people.
Jdg 16:28 Then Samson **p** to the LORD,
1Sa 1:27 I **p** for this child, and the LORD
1Ki 18:36 Elijah stepped forward and **p**:
19: 4 under it and **p** that he might die.
2Ki 6:17 And Elisha **p**, "Open his eyes,
2Ch 30:18 But Hezekiah **p** for them, saying,
Ne 1: 4 and **p** before the God of heaven.
4: 9 But we **p** to our God and posted
Job 42:10 After Job had **p** for his friends,
Da 6:10 day he got down on his knees and **p**,
9: 4 I **p** to the LORD my God
Jnh 2: 1 From inside the fish Jonah **p**
Mt 26:39 with his face to the ground and **p**,
Mk 1:35 off to a solitary place, where he **p**.
14:35 and **p** that if possible the hour might
Lk 5:16 withdrew to lonely places and **p**.
18:11 Pharisee stood by himself and **p**:
22:41 beyond them, knelt down and **p**,
Jn 17: 1 he looked toward heaven and **p**:
Ac 4:31 After they had **p**, the place where they
6: 6 who **p** and laid their hands on them.
8:15 they **p** for the new believers there
13: 3 So after they had fasted and **p**,
Jas 5:17 He earnestly that it would not

PRAYER PRAY

Ge 25:21 The LORD answered his **p**, and his
2Sa 21:14 God answered **p** in behalf
24:25 Then the LORD answered his **p**
1Ki 8:49 place, hear their **p** and their plea,
2Ch 7:12 "I have heard your **p** and have
30:27 for their **p** reached heaven, his holy
33:19 His **p** and how God was moved
Ezr 8:23 about this, and he answered our **p**.
Job 42: 8 I will accept his **p** and not deal
Ps 4: 1 have mercy on me and hear my **p**.
6: 9 the LORD accepts my **p**.
17: 1 Hear my **p**—it does not rise
55: 1 Listen to my **p**, O God, do not
65: 2 You who answer **p**, to you all
66:20 God, who has not rejected my **p**
86: T **A p of David.**
Pr 15: 8 but the **p** of the upright pleases him.
15:29 but he hears the **p** of the righteous.
Isa 56: 7 my house will be called a house of **p**
Hab 3: 1 **A p of Habakkuk the prophet.**
Mt 21:13 house will be called a house of **p**,'
21:22 receive whatever you ask for in **p**."

Mk 9:29 kind can come out only by **p**."
11:24 whatever you ask for in **p**,
Jn 17:15 My **p** is not that you take them
Ac 1:14 all joined together constantly in **p**,
2:42 to the breaking of bread and to **p**.
6: 4 will give our attention to **p**
10:31 God has heard your **p**
16:13 we expected to find a place of **p**.
Ro 10: 1 and **p** to God for the Israelites is
12:12 patient in affliction, faithful in **p**.
1Co 7: 5 you may devote yourselves to **p**.
2Co 13: 9 and our **p** is that you may be fully
Php 1: 9 And this is my **p**: that your love
4: 6 in every situation, by **p** and petition,
Col 4: 2 Devote yourselves to **p**,
1Ti 4: 5 by the word of God and **p**.
Jas 5:15 the **p** offered in faith will make
5:16 The **p** of a righteous person is
1Pe 3:12 and his ears are attentive to their **p**,

PRAYERS PRAY

1Ch 5:20 He answered their **p**, because they
Ps 35:13 When my **p** returned to me
Isa 1:15 even when you offer many **p**, I am
Mk 12:40 and for a show make lengthy **p**.
2Co 1:11 as you help us by your **p**.
Eph 6:18 on all occasions with all kinds of **p**
1Ti 2: 1 that petitions, **p**,
Heb 5: 7 he offered up **p** and petitions
1Pe 3: 7 so that nothing will hinder your **p**.
Rev 5: 8 which are the **p** of God's people,
8: 3 with the **p** of all God's people,

PRAYING PRAY

Ge 24:45 "Before I finished **p** in my heart,
1Sa 1:13 Hannah was **p** in her heart, and her
2Ch 7: 1 When Solomon finished **p**,
Da 6:11 found Daniel **p** and asking God
Mk 11:25 And when you stand **p**, if you hold
Lk 3:21 And as he was **p**, heaven was
6:12 pray, and spent the night **p** to God.
9:29 As he was **p**, the appearance of his
Jn 17: 9 I am not **p** for the world,
Ac 9:11 from Tarsus named Saul, for he is **p**.
16:25 Silas were **p** and singing hymns
Ro 15:30 join me in my struggle by **p** to God
Eph 6:18 always keep on **p** for all the Lord's
Jude 1:20 holy faith and **p** in the Holy Spirit,

PRAYS PRAY

Da 6: 7 that anyone who **p** to any god
1Co 11: 4 Every man who **p** or prophesies
14:14 tongue, my spirit **p**, but my mind is

PREACH PREACHED, PREACHER, PREACHING

Mt 4:17 From that time on Jesus began to **p**,
23: 3 for they do not practice what they **p**.
Ac 9:20 At once he began to **p**
16:10 God had called us to **p** the gospel
Ro 1:15 is why I am so eager to **p** the gospel
10:15 how can anyone **p** unless they are
15:20 to **p** the gospel where Christ was not
1Co 1:17 me to baptize, but to **p** the gospel—

1Co 1:23 but we **p** Christ crucified:
      9:14 that those who **p** the gospel should
      9:16 For when I **p** the gospel, I cannot
      9:16 Woe to me if I do not **p** the gospel!
2Co 4: 5 For what we **p** is not ourselves,
    10:16 so that we can **p** the gospel
Gal 1: 8 heaven should **p** a gospel other than
Php 1:15 It is true that some **p** Christ
2Ti 4: 2 **P** the word; be prepared in season

PREACHED PREACH
Jer 28:16 you have **p** rebellion against
Mk   6:12 out and **p** that people should repent.
    13:10 And the gospel must first be **p** to all
    14: 9 the gospel is **p** throughout
Lk 24:47 of sins will be **p** in his name to all
Ac   8: 4 who had been scattered **p** the word
    15:21 of Moses has been **p** in every city
1Co 9:27 slave so that after I have **p** to others,
    15: 1 remind you of the gospel I **p** to you,
    15:12 if it is **p** that Christ has been raised
2Co 11: 4 a Jesus other than the Jesus we **p**,
Gal 1: 8 a gospel other than the one we **p**
Eph 2:17 **p** peace to you who were far away
Php 1:18 false motives or true, Christ is **p**.
1Ti 3:16 by angels, was **p** among the nations,
1Pe 1:25 this is the word that was **p** to you.

PREACHER* PREACH
1Co 9:18 of my rights as a **p** of the gospel.
2Pe 2: 5 Noah, a **p** of righteousness,

PREACHING PREACH
Ezr 6:14 prosper under the **p** of Haggai
Am   7:16 stop **p** against the descendants
Mt 12:41 for they repented at the **p** of Jonah,
Ac 18: 5 devoted himself exclusively to **p**,
Ro 10:14 can they hear without someone **p**
1Co 2: 4 and my **p** were not with wise
    9:18 in **p** the gospel I may offer it free
Gal 1: 9 anybody is **p** to you a gospel other
1Ti 4:13 of Scripture, to **p** and to teaching.
    5:17 especially those whose work is **p**

PRECEDE*
1Th 4:15 will certainly not **p** those who have

PRECEPTS*
Dt 33:10 He teaches your **p** to Jacob and your
Ps 19: 8 The **p** of the LORD are right,
   103:18 and remember to obey his **p**.
   105:45 that they might keep his **p**
   111: 7 all his **p** are trustworthy.
   111:10 all who follow his **p** have good
   119: 4 You have laid down **p** that are to be
   119:15 I meditate on your **p** and consider
   119:27 me to understand the way of your **p**,
   119:40 How I long for your **p**!
   119:45 for I have sought out your **p**.
   119:56 has been my practice: I obey your **p**.
   119:63 fear you, to all who follow your **p**.
   119:69 lies, I keep your **p** with all my heart.
   119:78 but I will meditate on your **p**.
   119:87 but I have not forsaken your **p**.
   119:93 I will never forget your **p**,

Ps 119:94 I have sought out your **p**.
   119:100 than the elders, for I obey your **p**.
   119:104 I gain understanding from your **p**;
   119:110 but I have not strayed from your **p**.
   119:128 because I consider all your **p** right,
   119:134 oppression, that I may obey your **p**.
   119:141 and despised, I do not forget your **p**.
   119:159 See how I love your **p**;
   119:168 I obey your **p** and your statutes,
   119:173 help me, for I have chosen your **p**.

PRECIOUS
Ex 28:17 mount four rows of **p** stones on it.
1Sa 26:21 you considered my life **p** today,
2Ch 3: 6 adorned the temple with **p** stones.
Ps 19:10 They are more **p** than gold,
    35:17 ravages, my **p** life from these lions.
    72:14 for **p** is their blood in his sight.
   116:15 **P** in the sight of the LORD is
   119:72 your mouth is more **p** to me than
   139:17 How **p** to me are your thoughts,
Pr   3:15 She is more **p** than rubies;
    8:11 for wisdom is more **p** than rubies,
Isa 28:16 stone, a **p** cornerstone for a sure
Eze 28:13 every **p** stone adorned you:
1Pe 1:19 but with the **p** blood of Christ,
    2: 4 but chosen by God and **p** to him—
    2: 6 a chosen and **p** cornerstone,
2Pe 1: 1 have received a faith as **p** as ours:
    1: 4 us his very great and **p** promises,
Rev 21:11 was like that of a very **p** jewel,
    21:19 with every kind of **p** stone.

PREDESTINED* DESTINE
Ro 8:29 **p** to be conformed to the image
    8:30 And those he **p**, he also called;
Eph 1: 5 he **p** us for adoption to sonship
    1:11 having been **p** according to the plan

PREDICTED* PREDICTION
1Sa 28:17 has done what he **p** through me.
Ac   7:52 even killed those who **p** the coming
    11:28 through the Spirit **p** that a severe
    16:16 a spirit by which she **p** the future.
1Pe 1:11 pointing when he **p** the sufferings

PREDICTING* PREDICTION
1Ki 22:13 without exception are **p** success
2Ch 18:12 without exception are **p** success

PREDICTION* PREDICTED,
PREDICTING, PREDICTIONS
Jer 28: 9 LORD only if his **p** comes true."

PREDICTIONS* PREDICTION
Isa 44:26 and fulfills the **p** of his messengers,
    47:13 those stargazers who make **p** month

PREGNANT
Ge 19:36 Lot's daughters became **p** by their
    21: 2 Sarah became **p** and bore a son
    25:21 and his wife Rebekah became **p**.
Ex 21:22 hit a **p** woman and she gives birth
Ps   7:14 Whoever is **p** with evil conceives
Mt 24:19 it will be in those days for **p** women

1Th 5: 3 as labor pains on a **p** woman,
Rev 12: 2 She was **p** and cried out in pain as

PREMATURELY* MATURE
Ex 21:22 and she gives birth **p** but there is no

PREPARATION PREPARE
Mt 27:62 the one after **P** Day, the chief priests
Jn 19:14 It was the day of **P** of the Passover;

PREPARATIONS PREPARE
1Ch 22: 5 David made extensive **p** before his
Mk 14:12 to go and make **p** for you to eat

PREPARE PREPARATION,
PREPARATIONS, PREPARED
Ps 23: 5 You **p** a table before me
Isa 25: 6 the LORD Almighty will **p** a feast
40: 3 "In the wilderness **p** the way
Am 4:12 to you, Israel, **p** to meet your God."
Mal 3: 1 who will **p** the way before me.
Mt 3: 3 wilderness, 'P the way for the Lord,
11:10 who will **p** your way before you.'
26:12 body, she did it to **p** me for burial.
Jn 14: 2 that I am going there to **p** a place

PREPARED PREPARE
Ex 23:20 to bring you to the place I have **p**.
1Ch 15: 1 he **p** a place for the ark of God
2Ch 1: 4 Jearim to the place he had **p** for it,
Pr 19:29 Penalties are **p** for mockers,
Mt 20:23 for whom they have been **p** by my
25:34 the kingdom **p** for you since
Lk 1:17 to make ready a people **p**
Ro 9:23 whom he **p** in advance for glory—
1Co 2: 9 the things God has **p** for those who
Eph 2:10 which God **p** in advance for us
2Ti 2:21 Master and **p** to do any good work.
4: 2 be **p** in season and out of season;
Heb 10: 5 not desire, but a body you **p** for me;
11:16 God, for he has **p** a city for them.
1Pe 3:15 Always be **p** to give an answer
Rev 12: 6 the wilderness to a place **p** for her
21: 2 **p** as a bride beautifully dressed

PRESBYTERY (KJV) See ELDERS

PRESCRIBED
1Ch 24:19 to the regulations **p** for them
2Ch 29:25 and lyres in the way **p** by David
Ezr 3: 4 of burnt offerings **p** for each day.
3:10 as **p** by David king of Israel.
7:23 Whatever the God of heaven has **p**,
Ne 12:24 as **p** by David the man of God.
Heb 8: 4 already priests who offer the gifts **p**

PRESENCE PRESENT
Ex 18:12 father-in-law in the **p** of God.
25:30 Put the bread of the **P** on this table
33:14 replied, "My **P** will go with you,
34:34 he entered the LORD's **p** to speak
Lev 9:24 came out from the **p** of the LORD
10: 2 came out from the **p** of the LORD
Nu 4: 7 "Over the table of the **P** they are
Dt 4:37 brought you out of Egypt by his **P**
1Sa 2:21 grew up in the **p** of the LORD.

1Sa 6:20 can stand in the **p** of the LORD,
21: 6 of the **P** that had been removed
2Sa 22:13 of the brightness of his **p** bolts
2Ki 17:23 LORD removed them from his **p**,
23:27 also from my **p** as I removed Israel,
24:20 in the end he thrust them from his **p**.
Ezr 9:15 not one of us can stand in your **p**."
Job 1:12 went out from the **p** of the LORD.
2: 7 went out from the **p** of the LORD
Ps 5: 5 The arrogant cannot stand in your **p**.
16:11 you will fill me with joy in your **p**,
21: 6 him glad with the joy of your **p**.
23: 5 before me in the **p** of my enemies.
31:20 the shelter of your **p** you hide them
41:12 me and set me in your **p** forever.
51:11 Do not cast me from your **p** or take
52: 9 you in the **p** of your faithful people.
89:15 who walk in the light of your **p**,
90: 8 our secret sins in the light of your **p**.
114: 7 the **p** of the Lord, at the **p** of the God
139: 7 Where can I flee from your **p**?
Isa 26:17 pain, so were we in your **p**, LORD.
63: 9 and the angel of his **p** saved them.
Jer 5:22 "Should you not tremble in my **p**?
Eze 38:20 of the earth will tremble at my **p**.
Da 7:13 of Days and was led into his **p**.
Hos 6: 2 restore us, that we may live in his **p**.
Na 1: 5 The earth trembles at his **p**,
Mal 3:16 his **p** concerning those who feared
Jn 8:38 what I have seen in the Father's **p**,
17: 5 me in your **p** with the glory I had
Ac 2:28 you will fill me with joy in your **p**.'
1Th 2:19 will glory in the **p** of our Lord Jesus
3:13 holy in the **p** of our God and Father
2Th 1: 9 shut out from the **p** of the Lord
Heb 9:24 now to appear for us in God's **p**.
1Jn 3:19 we set our hearts at rest in his **p**:
Jude 1:24 before his glorious **p** without fault
Rev 14:10 sulfur in the **p** of the holy angels
20:11 and the heavens fled from his **p**,

LORD'S† PRESENCE Ge 4:16; Ex 29:11; 34:34;
Nu 17:9; 20:9

PRESENCE OF THE LORD† Ge 27:7; Ex
28:30; Lev 9:24; 10:2; Dt 12:7, 18; 14:23, 26; 15:20;
18:7; 19:17; 27:7; 29:10, 15; Jos 18:6, 8, 10; 19:51;
1Sa 2:21; 6:20; 11:15; 12:3; 26:20; 1Ki 19:11; 2Ki
23:3; 1Ch 29:22; 2Ch 34:31; Job 1:12; 2:7; Isa 2:10,
19, 21; Eze 44:3; 46:3

PRESENT EVER-PRESENT,
PRESENCE, PRESENTED
Lev 18:23 A woman must not **p** herself
Nu 16:17 Aaron are to **p** your censers also."
18:29 You must **p** as the LORD's portion
Ezr 6: 3 be rebuilt as a place to **p** sacrifices,
Job 1: 6 to **p** themselves before the LORD,
2: 1 to **p** themselves before the LORD,
Ps 14: 5 for God is **p** in the company
Isa 41:21 "P your case," says the LORD.
Mk 10:30 times as much in this **p** age:
Lk 2:22 to Jerusalem to **p** him to the Lord
Ro 8:18 that our **p** sufferings are not worth
8:38 demons, neither the **p** nor the future,

1Co 3:22 life or death or the **p** or the future—
7:26 Because of the **p** crisis, I think
7:31 world in its **p** form is passing away.
2Co 11: 2 that I might **p** you as a pure virgin
Gal 1: 4 sins to rescue us from the **p** evil age,
Eph 1:21 not only in the **p** age
5:27 and to **p** her to himself as a radiant
Col 1:22 body through death to **p** you holy
1Ti 4: 8 holding promise for both the **p** life
2Ti 2:15 Do your best to **p** yourself to God as
Titus 2:12 upright and godly lives in this **p** age,
2Pe 3: 7 By the same word the **p** heavens
Jude 1:24 **p** you before his glorious presence

PRESENTED PRESENT
Mt 2:11 and **p** him with gifts of gold,
Ac 1: 3 he **p** himself to them and gave many
9:41 the widows, and **p** her to them alive.
Ro 3:25 God **p** Christ as a sacrifice

PRESERVE PRESERVES
Ge 19:32 and **p** our family line through our
Ps 36: 6 LORD, **p** both people and animals.
119:25 **p** my life according to your word.
Pr 3:21 **p** sound judgment and discretion;
5: 2 and your lips may **p** knowledge.
22: 5 those who would **p** their life stay far
Eze 7:13 not one of them will **p** their life.
Lk 17:33 whoever loses their life will **p** it.

PRESERVES* PRESERVE
Ps 31:23 The LORD **p** those who are true
41: 2 The LORD protects and **p** them—
119:50 Your promise **p** my life.
Ecc 7:12 Wisdom **p** those who have it.

PRESS PRESSED, PRESSURE
Php 3:12 I **p** on to take hold
3:14 I **p** on toward the goal to win

PRESSED PRESS
Ps 118: 5 When hard **p**, I cried to the LORD;
Lk 6:38 A good measure, **p** down,
2Co 4: 8 We are hard **p** on every side, but not

PRESSURE PRESS
2Co 1: 8 We were under great **p**, far beyond
11:28 I face daily the **p** of my concern

PRESUMES* PRESUMPTION, PRESUMPTUOUSLY
Dt 18:20 But a prophet who **p** to speak in my

PRESUMPTION* PRESUMES
Nu 14:44 in their **p** they went up toward
1Sa 25:28 "Please forgive your servant's **p**.

PRESUMPTUOUSLY* PRESUMES
Dt 18:22 That prophet has spoken **p**, so do

PRETENDED PRETENSION
Ge 42: 7 but he **p** to be a stranger and spoke
1Sa 21:13 So he **p** to be insane in their

PRETENSION* PRETENDED
2Co 10: 5 every **p** that sets itself up against

PREVAIL PREVAILS
2Ch 14:11 not let mere mortals **p** against you."
Isa 54:17 weapon forged against you will **p**,
Ro 3: 4 you speak and **p** when you judge."

PREVAILS* PREVAIL
1Sa 2: 9 "It is not by strength that one **p**;
Pr 19:21 it is the LORD's purpose that **p**.
Hab 1: 4 is paralyzed, and justice never **p**.

PREY PREYS
Ge 15:11 Then birds of **p** came down
Na 2:13 I will leave you no **p** on the earth.
Hab 2: 7 Then you will become their **p**.

PREYS* PREY
Pr 6:26 another man's wife **p** on your very

PRICE PRICELESS
Ge 23: 9 for the full **p** as a burial site among
Lev 25:50 The **p** for their release is to be based
1Ch 21:22 Sell it to me at the full **p**."
Job 28:18 the **p** of wisdom is beyond rubies.
Zec 11:13 the handsome **p** at which they
Mt 27: 9 the **p** set on him by the people
Ac 5: 8 is this the **p** you and Ananias got
1Co 6:20 you were bought at a **p**.
7:23 You were bought at a **p**;

PRICELESS* PRICE
Ps 36: 7 How **p** is your unfailing love,

PRIDE PROUD
Lev 26:19 I will break down your stubborn **p**
2Ch 26:16 powerful, his **p** led to his downfall.
32:26 repented of the **p** of his heart, as did
Ps 47: 4 inheritance for us, the **p** of Jacob,
Pr 8:13 I hate **p** and arrogance,
11: 2 When **p** comes, then comes
13:10 there is **p**, but wisdom is found
14: 3 A fool's mouth lashes out with **p**,
16:18 **P** goes before destruction, a haughty
17: 6 parents are the **p** of their children.
29:23 **P** brings a person low, but the lowly
Ecc 7: 8 and patience is better than **p**.
Isa 2:11 humbled and human **p** brought low;
25:11 will bring down their **p** despite
60:15 I will make you the everlasting **p**
Eze 28: 2 " 'In the **p** of your heart you say,
Da 4:37 those who walk in **p** he is able
Am 8: 7 sworn by himself, the **P** of Jacob:
2Co 5:12 you an opportunity to take **p** in us,
7: 4 I take great **p** in you.
Gal 6: 4 they can take **p** in themselves alone,
Jas 1: 9 to take **p** in their high position.
1Jn 2:16 **p** of life—comes not from the Father

PRIEST PRIEST'S, PRIESTHOOD, PRIESTLY, PRIESTS
Ge 14:18 He was **p** of God Most High,
Ex 2:16 Now a **p** of Midian had seven
18: 1 the **p** of Midian and father-in-law
28: 3 so he may serve me as **p**.
Lev 4: 3 " 'If the anointed **p** sins,
4:20 this way the **p** will make atonement

Lev 5: 6 the **p** shall make atonement for them
     5:13 this way the **p** will make atonement
Nu   5:10 give to the **p** will belong to the **p**.'"
Jdg 17:10 with me and be my father and **p**,
1Sa   2:11 before the LORD under Eli the **p**.
     2:35 will raise up for myself a faithful **p**,
     21: 6 So the **p** gave him the consecrated
2Ch 13: 9 seven rams may become a **p** of what
Ne   8: 9 Ezra the **p** and teacher of the Law,
Ps 110: 4 "You are a **p** forever, in the order
Jer 23:11 "Both prophet and **p** are godless;
Eze   1: 3 the LORD came to Ezekiel the **p**,
Zec   6:13 And he will be a **p** on his throne.
Mk 14:63 The high **p** tore his clothes.
Heb 2:17 faithful high **p** in service to God,
     3: 1 as our apostle and high **p**.
     4:14 a great high **p** who has ascended
     4:15 do not have a high **p** who is unable
     5: 6 "You are a **p** forever, in the order
     6:20 He has become a high **p** forever,
     7: 3 Son of God, he remains a **p** forever.
     7:15 another **p** like Melchizedek appears,
     7:26 Such a high **p** truly meets our need—
     8: 1 We do have such a high **p**, who sat
     9:11 Christ came as high **p** of the good
   10:21 we have a great **p** over the house
   13:11 The high **p** carries the blood

HIGH PRIEST See HIGH

PRIEST'S PRIEST

Lev   6:29 Any male in a **p** family may eat it;
     21: 9 " 'If a **p** daughter defiles herself
    22:10 one outside a **p** family may eat

PRIESTHOOD PRIEST

Ex   29: 9 The **p** is theirs by a lasting
Nu 16:10 now you are trying to get the **p** too.
   25:13 will have a covenant of a lasting **p**,
Ezr   2:62 excluded from the **p** as unclean.
Heb 7:24 lives forever, he has a permanent **p**.
1Pe   2: 5 into a spiritual house to be a holy **p**,
     2: 9 people, a royal **p**, a holy nation,

PRIESTLY PRIEST

Jos 18: 7 because the **p** service of the LORD
Ro 15:16 He gave me the **p** duty

PRIESTS PRIEST

Ex   19: 6 you will be for me a kingdom of **p**
   28: 1 Ithamar, so they may serve me as **p**.
   40:15 father, so they may serve me as **p**.
Lev 21: 7 because **p** are holy to their God.
Dt   31: 9 law and gave it to the Levitical **p**,
Jos   3:15 as soon as the **p** who carried the ark
    6: 4 Have seven **p** carry trumpets
1Sa 22:17 "Turn and kill the **p** of the LORD,
2Ch   5: 7 The **p** then brought the ark
   31: 2 Hezekiah assigned the **p** and Levites
   34: 5 the bones of the **p** on their altars,
Ezr   6:20 The **p** and Levites had purified
   10: 5 up and put the leading **p** and Levites
Ne   3:28 the Horse Gate, the **p** made repairs,
   13:30 So I purified the **p** and the Levites
Ps   99: 6 and Aaron were among his **p**,

Isa 28: 7 **P** and prophets stagger from beer
Jer   5:31 the **p** rule by their own authority,
Eze 22:26 Her **p** do violence to my law
   44:28 be the only inheritance the **p** have.
Hos   4: 6 I also reject you as my **p**;
Mic   3:11 for a bribe, her **p** teach for a price,
Mal   1: 6 "It is you **p** who show contempt
Mt 20:18 will be delivered over to the chief **p**
   27: 3 thirty pieces of silver to the chief **p**
Mk   2:26 which is lawful only for **p** to eat.
   15: 3 The chief **p** accused him of many
Ac   6: 7 large number of **p** became obedient
Heb 7:27 Unlike the other high **p**, he does not
Rev   1: 6 a kingdom and **p** to serve his God
    5:10 a kingdom and **p** to serve our God,
   20: 6 but they will be **p** of God

CHIEF PRIESTS See CHIEF

PRIESTS AND LEVITES 1Ki 8:4; 1Ch 13:2;
15:14; 23:2; 24:6, 31; 28:13, 21; 2Ch 11:13; 23:4, 6;
24:5; 29:4; 30:15, 25, 27; 31:2, 4, 9; 34:30; 35:8; Ezr
1:5; 3:8, 12; 6:20; 7:13; 8:29, 30; 9:1; 10:5; Ne 8:13;
11:20; 12:1, 30, 44, 44; 13:30; Isa 66:21; Jn 1:19

PRINCE PRINCES, PRINCESS

Ge 49:26 brow of the **p** among his brothers.
Dt   33:16 brow of the **p** among his brothers.
Isa   9: 6 God, Everlasting Father, **P** of Peace.
Eze 34:24 David will be **p** among them.
   37:25 my servant will be their **p** forever.
   45:17 the **p** to provide the burnt offerings,
   46: 8 When the **p** enters, he is to go
Da   8:25 and take his stand against the **P**
   10:20 to fight against the **p** of Persia,
   10:20 I go, the **p** of Greece will come;
   10:21 them except Michael, your **p**.
   11:22 it and a **p** of the covenant will be
   12: 1 the great **p** who protects your
Lk 11:15 "By Beelzebul, the **p** of demons,
Jn 12:31 now the **p** of this world will be
   14:30 for the **p** of this world is coming.
   16:11 because the **p** of this world now
Ac   5:31 him to his own right hand as **P**

PRINCES PRINCE

Jdg   5: 9 My heart is with Israel's **p**,
1Sa   2: 8 he seats them with **p** and has them
Job 34:19 who shows no partiality to **p**
Ps 113: 8 he seats them with **p**, with the
   118: 9 in the LORD than to trust in **p**.
   146: 3 Do not put your trust in **p**, in human
   148:11 you **p** and all rulers on earth,
Pr   8:16 by me **p** govern, and nobles—
Isa 40:23 He brings **p** to naught and reduces
Eze 19: 1 a lament concerning the **p** of Israel
Da   8:25 his stand against the Prince of **p**.
   10:13 one of the chief **p**, came to help me,
Rev   6:15 of the earth, the **p**, the generals,

PRINCESS* PRINCE

Ps 45:13 All glorious is the **p** within her

PRISCILLA

Wife of Aquila; co-worker with Paul (Ac 18;

Ro 16:3; 1Co 16:19; 2Ti 4:19); instructor of Apollos (Ac 18:24–28).

PRISON IMPRISON, IMPRISONED, IMPRISONMENT, IMPRISONMENTS, PRISONER, PRISONERS

Ge 39:20 But while Joseph was there in the p,
Jdg 16:25 So they called Samson out of the p,
2Ki 25:29 Jehoiachin put aside his p clothes
Ps 66:11 You brought us into p and laid
    142: 7 Set me free from my p, that I may
Isa 42: 7 blind, to free captives from p
Mt 4:12 heard that John had been put in p,
    14:10 and had John beheaded in the p.
    25:36 me, I was in p and you came to visit
Lk 22:33 I am ready to go with you to p
Ac 8: 3 men and women and put them in p.
    12: 5 So Peter was kept in p,
    16:26 At once all the p doors flew open,
2Co 11:23 been in p more frequently,
Heb 13: 3 remember those in p as if you were
        together with them in p,
Rev 2:10 put some of you in p to test you,
    20: 7 Satan will be released from his p

PRISONER PRISON

Jdg 15:10 have come to take Samson p,"
2Ki 24:12 of Babylon, he took Jehoiachin p.
2Ch 33:11 who took Manasseh p, put a hook
Mk 15: 6 to release a p whom the people
Ro 7:23 making me a p of the law of sin
Eph 3: 1 the p of Christ Jesus for the sake

PRISONERS PRISON

Ps 68: 6 he leads out the p with singing;
    79:11 groans of the p come before you;
    107:10 darkness, p suffering in iron chains,
    146: 7 The LORD sets p free,
Isa 51:14 The cowering p will soon be set
    61: 1 and release from darkness for the p,
Zec 9:12 to your fortress, you p of hope;
Lk 4:18 me to proclaim freedom for the p
Ac 9: 2 women, he might take them as p

PRIVATE

Ex 20:26 or your p parts may be exposed.'
Mt 17:19 the disciples came to Jesus in p
Lk 9:18 Once when Jesus was praying in p

PRIVILEGE*

2Co 8: 4 us for the p of sharing in this service

PRIZE*

1Co 9:24 runners run, but only one gets the p?
    9:24 Run in such a way as to get the p.
    9:27 will not be disqualified for the p.
Php 3:14 on toward the goal to win the p

PROBE PROBES

Job 11: 7 Can you p the limits
Ps 17: 3 Though you p my heart, though you
Jer 20:12 the righteous and p the heart

PROBES* PROBE

Ps 7: 9 the righteous God who p minds

PROBLEMS*

Dt 1:12 But how can I bear your p and your
Da 5:12 explain riddles and solve difficult p.
    5:16 and to solve difficult p. If you can

PROCEDURE* PROCESSION

Ecc 8: 5 will know the proper time and p.
    8: 6 proper time and p for every matter,

PROCESSION PROCEDURE

1Sa 10:10 at Gibeah, a p of prophets met him;
Ne 12:36 the teacher of the Law led the p.
Ps 68:24 Your p, God, has come into view,
    118:27 join in the festal p up to the horns
Isa 60:11 their kings led in triumphal p.
1Co 4: 9 on display at the end of the p,
2Co 2:14 as captives in Christ's triumphal p

PROCLAIM PROCLAIMED, PROCLAIMING, PROCLAIMS, PROCLAMATION

Ex 33:19 and I will p my name, the LORD,
Lev 25:10 p liberty throughout the land to all
Dt 30:12 it and p it to us so we may obey it?"
    32: 3 I will p the name of the LORD.
2Sa 1:20 p it not in the streets of Ashkelon,
1Ch 16: 8 Give praise to the LORD, p his name;
    16:23 p his salvation day after day.
Ne 8:15 and that they should p this word
Ps 2: 7 I will p the LORD's decree:
    9:11 p among the nations what he has
    19: 1 the skies p the work of his hands.
    22:31 They will p his righteousness,
    30: 9 Will it p your faithfulness?
    40: 9 I p your saving acts in the great
    50: 6 the heavens p his righteousness,
    64: 9 they will p the works of God
    68:11 women who p it are a mighty throng:
    68:34 P the power of God, whose majesty
    71:16 I will come and p your mighty acts,
    79:13 to generation we will p your praise.
    96: 2 p his salvation day after day.
    97: 6 The heavens p his righteousness,
    105: 1 Give praise to the LORD, p his name;
    106: 2 Who can p the mighty acts
    118:17 will p what the LORD has done.
    145: 6 and I will p your great deeds.
Isa 12: 4 praise to the LORD, p his name;
    40: 2 p to her that her hard service has
    42:12 and p his praise in the islands.
    43:21 myself that they may p my praise.
    44: 8 Did I not p this and foretell it long
    52: 7 who bring good news, who p peace,
    61: 1 has anointed me to p good news
    61: 1 to p freedom for the captives
    66:19 They will p my glory among
Jer 7: 2 house and there p this message:
    50: 2 and p among the nations,
Hos 5: 9 tribes of Israel I p what is certain.
Jnh 3: 2 and p to it the message I give you."
Mic 3: 5 astray, they p 'peace' if they have

Zec   9:10 He will p peace to the nations.
Mt   10: 7 As you go, p this message:
      10:27 in your ear, p from the roofs.
      12:18 and he will p justice to the nations.
Lk   4:18 he has anointed me to p good news
      4:19 to p the year of the Lord's favor."
      9:60 you go and p the kingdom of God."
Ac   17:23 this is what I am going to p to you.
      20:27 I have not hesitated to p to you
Ro   10: 8 message concerning faith that we p:
      16:25 the message I p about Jesus Christ,
1Co 11:26 cup, you p the Lord's death until he
Php   1:14 more to p the gospel without fear.
Col   1:28 He is the one we p,
       4: 4 Pray that I may p it clearly, as I
1Jn   1: 1 this we p concerning the Word
Rev 14: 6 and he had the eternal gospel to p

PROCLAIMED PROCLAIM
Ex   9:16 my name might be p in all the earth.
      34: 5 there with him and p his name,
Dt   10: 4 the Ten Commandments he had p
Isa 43: 9 this and p to us the former things?
      43:12 I have revealed and saved and p—
Lk   7:22 and the good news is p to the poor.
      16:16 and the Prophets were p until John.
Ac   28:31 He p the kingdom of God
Ro   9:17 that my name might be p in all
      15:19 I have fully p the gospel of Christ.
Col   1:23 has been p to every creature under
2Ti   4:17 me the message might be fully p

PROCLAIMING PROCLAIM
Ex   34: 6 And he passed in front of Moses, p,
Ps   26: 7 p aloud your praise and telling of all
      92: 2 p your love in the morning and your
      92:15 p, "The LORD is upright;
Mk   1:14 Galilee, p the good news of God.
Lk   9: 6 p the good news and healing people
Ac   4: 2 p in Jesus the resurrection
       5:42 p the good news that Jesus is
      17: 3 "This Jesus I am p to you is
2Th   2: 4 God's temple, p himself to be God.

PROCLAIMS* PROCLAIM
Dt   18:22 If what a prophet p in the name
Ps   6: 5 the dead no one p your name.
Na   1:15 brings good news, who p peace!

PROCLAMATION PROCLAIM
Ezr   1: 1 to make a p throughout his realm
Isa 62:11 The LORD has made p to the ends
1Pe   3:19 made p to the imprisoned spirits—

PROCONSUL
Ac   13:12 the p saw what had happened,

PRODUCE PRODUCED,
    PRODUCES
Ge   1:11 said, "Let the land p vegetation:
       1:24 "Let the land p living creatures
       3:18 It will p thorns and thistles for you,
Dt   14:22 of all that your fields p each year.
Jos   5:11 they ate some of the p of the land:
Eze 36: 8 will p branches and fruit for my

Mt   3: 8 P fruit in keeping with repentance.
Lk   3: 9 that does not p good fruit will be cut
Jas   3:12 can a salt spring p fresh water.

PRODUCED PRODUCE
Nu   17: 8 budded, blossomed and p almonds.
Mk   4: 8 It came up, grew and p a crop,

PRODUCES PRODUCE
Pr   30:33 and as twisting the nose p blood, so
            stirring up anger p strife."
Mt   13:23 This is the one who p a crop,
Jn   12:24 But if it dies, it p many seeds.
Ro   5: 3 know that suffering p perseverance;
2Co   1: 6 which p in you patient endurance
Heb   6: 8 But land that p thorns and thistles is
      12:11 it p a harvest of righteousness

PROFANE PROFANED
Lev 18:21 for you must not p the name of your
      19:12 and so p the name of your God.
      22:32 Do not p my holy name, for I must
Eze 20:39 and no longer p my holy name
Zep   3: 4 Her priests p the sanctuary and do
Mal   2:10 Why do we p the covenant of our

PROFANED PROFANE
Jer 34:16 have turned around and p my name;
Eze 20: 9 my name from being p in the eyes
      36:20 the nations they p my holy name,
      39: 7 no longer let my holy name be p,

PROFESS* PROFESSED
Ro   10:10 your mouth that you p your faith
1Ti   2:10 for women who p to worship God.
Heb   4:14 let us hold firmly to the faith we p.
      10:23 hold unswervingly to the hope we p,
      13:15 fruit of lips that openly p his name.

PROFESSED* PROFESS
1Ti   6:21 which some have p and in so doing

PROFIT PROFITABLE
Lev 25:37 at interest or sell them food at a p.
Pr   14:23 All hard work brings a p, but mere
      21: 5 lead to p as surely as haste leads
Isa 44:10 casts an idol, which can p nothing?
Eze 18: 8 at interest or take a p from them.
2Co   2:17 not peddle the word of God for p.

PROFITABLE* PROFIT
Pr   3:14 for she is more p than silver
      31:18 She sees that her trading is p,
Titus 3: 8 are excellent and p for everyone.

PROFOUND*
Job   9: 4 His wisdom is p, his power is vast.
Ps   92: 5 LORD, how p your thoughts!
Ecc   7:24 exists is far off and most p—
Ac   24: 3 acknowledge this with p gratitude.
Eph   5:32 This is a p mystery—but I am

PROGRESS*
Ezr   5: 8 and is making rapid p under their
Jn   13: 2 The evening meal was in p,
Php   1:25 continue with all of you for your p

1Ti   4:15 so that everyone may see your **p**.

PROLONG*

Dt   5:33 **p** your days in the land that you will
Ps   85: 5 Will you **p** your anger through all
Pr   3: 2 for they will **p** your life many years
Isa 53:10 will see his offspring and **p** his days,
La   4:22 he will not **p** your exile.

PROMINENT

Est   9: 4 Mordecai was **p** in the palace;
Da   8: 5 with a **p** horn between its eyes came
Mk 15:43 a **p** member of the Council,
Lk   14: 1 to eat in the house of a **p** Pharisee,
Ac   17: 4 Greeks and quite a few **p** women.
     17:12 a number of **p** Greek women

PROMISCUITY PROMISCUOUS

Eze 16:25 increasing **p** to anyone who passed
     23:29 Your lewdness and **p**

PROMISCUOUS* PROMISCUITY

Dt   22:21 in Israel by being **p** while still in her
Eze 23:19 more **p** as she recalled the days
Hos   1: 2 marry a **p** woman and have children

PROMISE PROMISED, PROMISES

Nu   23:19 Does he **p** and not fulfill?
     30: 6 after her lips utter a rash **p**
Jos   9:21 So the leaders' **p** to them was kept.
     23:14 Every **p** has been fulfilled;
2Sa   7:25 keep forever the **p** you have made
1Ki   6:12 will fulfill through you the **p** I gave
     8:20 LORD has kept the **p** he made:
     8:24 You have kept your **p** to your
Ne   5:13 anyone who does not keep this **p**.
     9: 8 have kept your **p** because you are
Ps   77: 8 Has his **p** failed for all time?
   105:42 he remembered his holy **p** given
   106:24 they did not believe his **p**.
   119:41 your salvation, according to your **p**;
   119:50 Your **p** preserves my life.
   119:58 gracious to me according to your **p**.
   119:162 in your **p** like one who finds great
Pr   11: 7 all the **p** of their power comes
Ac   2:39 The **p** is for you and your children
     26: 7 This is the **p** our twelve tribes are
Ro   4:13 his offspring received the **p** that he
     4:20 through unbelief regarding the **p**
     9: 8 of the **p** who are regarded as
Gal   3:14 faith we might receive the **p**
Eph   2:12 foreigners to the covenants of the **p**,
     6: 2 is the first commandment with a **p**—
1Ti   4: 8 holding **p** for both the present life
2Ti   1: 1 in keeping with the **p** of life that is
Heb   4: 1 since the **p** of entering his rest still
     6:13 When God made his **p** to Abraham,
   11:11 him faithful who had made the **p**.
2Pe   2:19 They **p** them freedom, while they
     3: 9 Lord is not slow in keeping his **p**,
     3:13 with his **p** we are looking forward

PROMISED PROMISE

Ge   18:19 for Abraham what he has **p** him."
     21: 1 did for Sarah what he had **p**.

Ge   24: 7 who spoke to me and **p** me on oath,
     28:15 I have done what I have **p** you."
Ex   3:17 I have **p** to bring you up out of your
     32:13 descendants all this land I **p** them,
Nu   10:29 for the LORD has **p** good things
     14:23 of them will ever see the land I **p**
Dt   15: 6 your God will bless you as he has **p**,
     26:18 his treasured possession as he **p**,
     34: 4 him, "This is the land I **p** on oath
Jos   23: 5 as the LORD your God **p** you.
2Sa   7:28 and you have **p** these good things
1Ki   8:15 his own hand has fulfilled what he **p**
     9: 5 as I **p** David your father when I
2Ch   6:15 with your mouth you have **p**
Ps   119:57 I have **p** to obey your words.
Isa   55: 3 you, my faithful love **p** to David.
Mk   6:23 And he **p** her with an oath,
Lk   24:49 to send you what my Father has **p**;
Ac   1: 4 but wait for the gift my Father **p**,
     2:33 from the Father the **p** Holy Spirit
     13:23 to Israel the Savior Jesus, as he **p**.
     13:32 What God **p** our ancestors
Ro   4:21 God had power to do what he had **p**.
2Co 11: 2 I **p** you to one husband, to Christ,
Eph   1:13 in him with a seal, the **p** Holy Spirit,
Titus 1: 2 lie, **p** before the beginning of time,
Heb   6:15 Abraham received what was **p**.
   10:23 we profess, for he who **p** is faithful.
   10:36 you will receive what he has **p**.
   11:13 They did not receive the things **p**;
Jas   1:12 the Lord has **p** to those who love
     2: 5 the kingdom he **p** those who love
2Pe   3: 4 say, "Where is this 'coming' he **p**?
1Jn   2:25 And this is what he **p** us—

PROMISES PROMISE

Jos   21:45 of all the LORD's good **p** to Israel
     23:14 all the good **p** the LORD your God
1Ki   8:56 all the good **p** he gave through his
1Ch 17:19 and made known all these great **p**.
Ps   85: 8 he **p** peace to his people, his faithful
   106:12 they believed his **p** and sang his
   119:140 Your **p** have been thoroughly tested,
   119:148 that I may meditate on your **p**.
   145:13 LORD is trustworthy in all he **p**
Ro   9: 4 law, the temple worship and the **p**.
2Co   1:20 matter how many **p** God has made,
     7: 1 since we have these **p**, dear friends,
Gal   3:21 therefore, opposed to the **p** of God?
Heb   8: 6 covenant is established on better **p**.
2Pe   1: 4 us his very great and precious **p**,

PROMOTE PROMOTES

Pr   12:20 but those who **p** peace have joy.
     16:21 and gracious words **p** instruction.
1Ti   1: 4 Such things **p** controversial

PROMOTES* PROMOTE

Lk   10: 6 If someone who **p** peace is there,
Gal   2:17 doesn't that mean that Christ **p** sin?

PROMPTED*

Mt   14: 8 **P** by her mother, she said,
Jn   13: 2 and the devil had already **p** Judas,
1Th   1: 3 by faith, your labor **p** by love,

2Th 1:11 and your every deed **p** by faith.

PRONE*
Ex 32:22 "You know how **p** these people are

PRONOUNCE PRONOUNCED
Ge 48:20 name will Israel **p** this blessing:
Dt 10: 8 and to **p** blessings in his name,
Jdg 12: 6 he could not **p** the word correctly,
1Ch 23:13 to **p** blessings in his name forever.
Ps 109:17 He loved to **p** a curse—may it come
Jer 1:16 I will **p** my judgments on my people

PRONOUNCED PRONOUNCE
1Ch 16:12 miracles, and the judgments he **p**,
Ps 76: 8 From heaven you **p** judgment,
Da 7:22 and **p** judgment in favor of the holy

PROOF PROVE
Dt 22:14 I did not find **p** of her virginity,"
Ac 17:31 He has given **p** of this to everyone
2Co 8:24 Therefore show these men the **p**

PROOFS* PROVE
Ac 1: 3 gave many convincing **p** that he was

PROPER PROPERLY
Ps 104:27 give them their food at the **p** time.
145:15 give them their food at the **p** time.
Ecc 8: 5 the wise heart will know the **p** time
Mt 3:15 it is **p** for us to do this to fulfill all
24:45 give them their food at the **p** time?
1Co 11:13 Is it **p** for a woman to pray to God
2Co 10:13 will not boast beyond **p** limits,
Gal 6: 9 at the **p** time we will reap a harvest
2Th 2: 6 he may be revealed at the **p** time.
1Ti 2: 6 now been witnessed to at the **p** time.
5: 3 Give **p** recognition to those widows
1Pe 2:17 Show **p** respect to everyone,

PROPERLY* PROPER
1Ti 1: 8 that the law is good if one uses it **p**.

PROPERTY
Ge 23: 4 Sell me some **p** for a burial site here
Lev 25:10 of you is to return to your family **p**
Ru 4: 5 the name of the dead with his **p**."
Lk 15:12 So he divided his **p** between them.
Ac 5: 1 Sapphira, also sold a piece of **p**.
Heb 10:34 accepted the confiscation of your **p**,

PROPHECIES PROPHESY
La 2:14 The **p** they gave you were false
1Co 13: 8 But where there are **p**, they will
1Th 5:20 Do not treat **p** with contempt

PROPHECY PROPHESY
2Ki 9:25 Lᴏʀᴅ spoke this **p** against him:
Eze 14: 9 if the prophet is enticed to utter a **p**,
Da 9:24 to seal up vision and **p** and to anoint
1Co 12:10 powers, to another **p**, to another
13: 2 If I have the gift of **p** and can
14: 1 gifts of the Spirit, especially **p**.
14: 6 or knowledge or **p** or word
14:22 **p**, however, is not for unbelievers
2Th 2: 2 whether by a **p** or by word of mouth

2Pe 1:20 that no **p** of Scripture came
Rev 1: 3 who reads aloud the words of this **p**,
19:10 the Spirit of **p** who bears testimony
22: 7 keeps the words of the **p** written
22:18 the words of the **p** of this scroll:

PROPHESIED PROPHESY
Nu 11:25 the Spirit rested on them, they **p**—
1Sa 19:24 and he too **p** in Samuel's presence.
Jer 2: 8 The prophets **p** by Baal,
26:11 because he has **p** against this city.
Mt 11:13 Prophets and the Law **p** until John.
Mk 7: 6 when he **p** about you hypocrites;
Jn 11:51 that year he **p** that Jesus would die
Ac 19: 6 and they spoke in tongues and **p**.
21: 9 four unmarried daughters who **p**.
Jude 1:14 seventh from Adam, **p** about them:

PROPHESIES PROPHESY
2Ch 18: 7 because he never **p** anything good
Jer 28: 9 But the prophet who **p** peace will be
Eze 12:27 and he **p** about the distant future.'
1Co 11: 4 **p** with his head covered dishonors
14: 3 one who **p** speaks to people for

PROPHESY PROPHECIES, PROPHECY, PROPHESIED, PROPHESIES, PROPHESYING, PROPHET, PROPHET'S, PROPHETESS, PROPHETIC, PROPHETS
1Sa 10: 6 upon you, and you will **p** with them;
Isa 30:10 Tell us pleasant things, **p** illusions.
Jer 5:31 The prophets **p** lies, the priests rule
Eze 13: 2 **p** against the prophets of Israel who
13:17 who **p** out of their own imagination. **P** against them
34: 2 **p** against the shepherds of Israel;
37: 4 "**P** to these bones and say to them,
Joel 2:28 Your sons and daughters will **p**,
Am 2:12 commanded the prophets not to **p**.
7:16 say, " 'Do not **p** against Israel,
Mic 2: 6 "Do not **p**," their prophets say.
Mt 7:22 did we not **p** in your name
Lk 22:64 blindfolded him and demanded, "**P**!
Ac 2:17 Your sons and daughters will **p**,
Ro 12: 6 **p** in accordance with your faith;
1Co 13: 9 we know in part and we **p** in part,
14: 5 but I would rather have you **p**.
14:39 be eager to **p**, and do not forbid
Rev 11: 3 and they will **p** for 1,260 days,

PROPHESYING PROPHESY
1Sa 10:13 After Saul stopped **p**, he went
19:20 they saw a group of prophets **p**,
1Ki 18:29 continued their frantic **p** until
1Ch 25: 1 and Jeduthun for the ministry of **p**,
Jer 14:14 me, "The prophets are **p** lies in my
Ro 12: 6 If your gift is **p**, then prophesy
1Co 14:24 comes in while everyone is **p**,
Rev 11: 6 not rain during the time they are **p**;

PROPHET PROPHESY
Ex 7: 1 your brother Aaron will be your **p**.

Ex	15:20	Then Miriam the **p**, Aaron's sister,
Nu	12: 6	"When there is a **p** among you,
Dt	13: 1	If a **p**, or one who foretells
	18:18	for them a **p** like you from among
	18:22	That **p** has spoken presumptuously,
	34:10	no **p** has risen in Israel like Moses,
Jdg	4: 4	Deborah, a **p**, the wife of Lappidoth,
1Sa	3:20	Samuel was attested as a **p**
	9: 9	because the **p** of today used to be
1Ki	1: 8	Nathan the **p**, Shimei and Rei
	18:36	the **p** Elijah stepped forward
	22: 7	asked, "Is there no longer a **p**
2Ki	5: 8	know that there is a **p** in Israel."
	6:12	"but Elisha, the **p** who is in Israel,
	20: 1	The **p** Isaiah son of Amoz went
	22:14	went to speak to the **p** Huldah,
2Ch	35:18	since the days of the **p** Samuel;
	36:12	himself before Jeremiah the **p**,
Ezr	5: 1	Haggai the **p** and Zechariah the **p**,
	6:14	under the preaching of Haggai the **p**
Ne	6:14	remember also the **p** Noadiah
Ps	51: T	*When the p Nathan came to him*
Jer	1: 5	I appointed you as a **p**
	23:11	"Both **p** and priest are godless;
	28: 1	Judah, the **p** Hananiah son of Azzur,
Eze	2: 5	know that a **p** has been among them.
	33:33	that a **p** has been among them."
Da	9: 2	the LORD given to Jeremiah the **p**,
Hos	9: 7	so great, the **p** is considered a fool,
Am	7:14	"I was neither a **p** nor the son of a **p**,
Hab	1: 1	that Habakkuk the **p** received.
Hag	1: 1	LORD came through the **p** Haggai
Zec	1: 1	came to the **p** Zechariah son
	13: 4	"On that day every **p** will be ashamed
Mal	4: 5	"See, I will send the **p** Elijah to you
Mt	10:41	Whoever welcomes a **p** as a **p** will
	11: 9	A **p**? Yes, I tell you, and more than a **p**.
	12:39	it except the sign of the **p** Jonah.
Mk	6: 4	"A **p** is not without honor except in
Lk	1:76	will be called a **p** of the Most High;
	2:36	There was also a **p**, Anna,
	4:24	"no **p** is accepted in his hometown.
	7:16	"A great **p** has appeared among
	20: 6	are persuaded that John was a **p**."
	24:19	"He was a **p**, powerful in word
Jn	1:21	"Are you the **P**?"
	7:40	said, "Surely this man is the **P**."
Ac	7:37	for you a **p** like me from your own
	13: 6	and false **p** named Bar-Jesus,
	21:10	a **p** named Agabus came down
1Co	14:37	If anyone thinks they are a **p** or
Rev	2:20	Jezebel, who calls herself a **p**.
	16:13	and out of the mouth of the false **p**.
	19:20	it the false **p** who had performed
	20:10	and the false **p** had been thrown.

FALSE PROPHET See FALSE

PROPHET'S PROPHESY

2Pe	1:20	about by the **p** own interpretation

PROPHETESS* PROPHESY

Isa	8: 3	Then I made love to the **p**, and she

PROPHETIC PROPHESY

2Pe	1:19	have the **p** message as something

PROPHETS PROPHESY

Nu	11:29	that all the LORD's people were **p**
1Sa	10:11	Is Saul also among the **p**?"
	19:24	say, "Is Saul also among the **p**?"
	28: 6	answer him by dreams or Urim or **p**.
1Ki	18: 4	was killing off the LORD's **p**,
	18:40	them, "Seize the **p** of Baal.
	19:10	put your **p** to death with the sword.
2Ki	17:23	through all his servants the **p**.
1Ch	16:22	do my **p** no harm."
2Ch	18:22	in the mouths of these **p** of yours.
Ne	9:30	you warned them through your **p**.
Ps	105:15	do my **p** no harm."
Isa	44:25	who foils the signs of false **p**
Jer	5:13	The **p** are but wind and the word is
	14:14	"The **p** are prophesying lies in my
	23: 9	Concerning the **p**: My heart is
	23:30	"I am against the **p** who steal
La	2: 9	her **p** no longer find visions
Eze	13: 2	prophesy against the **p** of Israel who
Hos	6: 5	I cut you in pieces with my **p**,
Mic	3: 6	The sun will set for the **p**,
Zep	3: 4	Her **p** are unprincipled;
Zec	1: 5	And the **p**, do they live forever?
Mt	5:17	come to abolish the Law or the **P**;
	7:12	for this sums up the Law and the **P**.
	7:15	"Watch out for false **p**.
	22:40	Law and the **P** hang on these two
	24:24	messiahs and false **p** will appear
Lk	6:23	is how their ancestors treated the **p**.
	10:24	For I tell you that many **p** and kings
	11:49	'I will send them **p** and apostles,
	16:29	'They have Moses and the **P**;
	24:25	believe all that the **p** have spoken!
	24:44	of Moses, the **P** and the Psalms."
Ac	3:24	all the **p** who have spoken have
	10:43	All the **p** testify about him
	13: 1	the church at Antioch there were **p**
	26:22	saying nothing beyond what the **p**
	28:23	and from the **P** he tried to persuade
Ro	1: 2	promised beforehand through his **p**
	3:21	to which the Law and the **P** testify.
	11: 3	they have killed your **p** and torn
1Co	12:28	apostles, second **p**, third teachers,
	12:29	Are all **p**? Are all teachers?
	14:32	The spirits of **p** are subject to the control of **p**.
Eph	2:20	the foundation of the apostles and **p**,
	3: 5	Spirit to God's holy apostles and **p**.
	4:11	the apostles, the **p**, the evangelists,
1Th	2:15	killed the Lord Jesus and the **p**
Heb	1: 1	our ancestors through the **p** at many
1Pe	1:10	the **p**, who spoke of the grace
2Pe	2: 1	were also false **p** among the people,
	3: 2	spoken in the past by the holy **p**
1Jn	4: 1	because many false **p** have gone
Rev	11:10	because these two **p** had tormented
	16: 6	of your holy people and your **p**,
	18:20	Rejoice, apostles and **p**!
	22: 6	the God who inspires the **p**, sent his

FALSE PROPHETS See FALSE

PROPORTION

Dt 16:10 giving a freewill offering in **p**
     16:17 you must bring a gift in **p** to the way

PROPOSE* PROPOSED

Dt   1:14 me, "What you **p** to do is good."
Isa   8:10 **p** your plan, but it will not stand,

PROPOSED PROPOSE

Ezr 10:16 So the exiles did as was **p**.

PROPRIETY*

1Ti   2: 9 with decency and **p**,
     2:15 in faith, love and holiness with **p**.

PROSELYTE(S) (KJV) See CONVERT(S)

PROSPECT*

Pr 10:28 The **p** of the righteous is joy,

PROSPER PROSPERED, PROSPERITY, PROSPEROUS, PROSPERS

Ge 32: 9 relatives, and I will make you **p**,'
Dt   5:33 you, so that you may live and **p**
   28:63 pleased the LORD to make you **p**
    29: 9 you may **p** in everything you do.
1Ki   2: 3 this so that you may **p** in all you do
Ezr   6:14 **p** under the preaching of Haggai
Ps 51:18 May it please you to **p** Zion,
Pr 11:10 When the righteous **p**, the city
   11:25 A generous person will **p**;
   17:20 whose heart is corrupt does not **p**;
   19: 8 cherishes understanding will soon **p**.
   28:13 conceals their sins does not **p**,
   28:25 who trust in the LORD will **p**.
Isa 53:10 of the LORD will **p** in his hand.
Jer 12: 1 Why does the way of the wicked **p**?
   29:11 "plans to **p** you and not to harm

PROSPERED* PROSPER

Ge 39: 2 was with Joseph so that he **p**, and he
1Ch 29:23 He **p** and all Israel obeyed him.
2Ch 14: 7 on every side." So they built and **p**.
   31:21 And so he **p**.
Da   6:28 So Daniel **p** during the reign
    8:12 It **p** in everything it did, and truth
Hos 10: 1 as his land **p**, he adorned his sacred

PROSPERITY PROSPER

Dt 28:11 LORD will grant you abundant **p**—
   30:15 I set before you today life and **p**,
Job 21:16 their **p** is not in their own hands,
   36:11 will spend the rest of their days in **p**
Ps 25:13 They will spend their days in **p**,
    73: 3 when I saw the **p** of the wicked.
  122: 9 LORD our God, I will seek your **p**.
  128: 2 blessings and **p** will be yours.
Pr   3: 2 years and bring you peace and **p**.
    8:18 and honor, enduring wealth and **p**.
   21:21 and love finds life, **p** and honor.
Ecc 6: 6 twice over but fails to enjoy his **p**.

Isa 45: 7 I bring **p** and create disaster;
La   3:17 I have forgotten what **p** is.

PROSPEROUS PROSPER

Dt 30: 9 your God will make you most **p**
   30: 9 delight in you and make you **p**,
Jos   1: 8 Then you will be **p** and successful.
Ps 10: 5 His ways are always **p**;

PROSPERS PROSPER

Ps   1: 3 whatever they do **p**.
Pr 16:20 gives heed to instruction **p**,

PROSTITUTE PROSTITUTED, PROSTITUTES, PROSTITUTION

Ge 34:31 he have treated our sister like a **p**?"
   38:15 he thought she was a **p**, for she had
Ex 34:15 for when they **p** themselves to their
Lev 19:29 your daughter by making her a **p**,
   20: 6 and spiritists to **p** themselves
Nu 15:39 not **p** yourselves by chasing
Dt 23:17 or woman is to become a shrine **p**.
Jos   2: 1 the house of a **p** named Rahab
    6:25 But Joshua spared Rahab the **p**,
Pr   6:26 For a **p** can be had for a loaf
    7:10 him, dressed like a **p** and with crafty
Isa   1:21 the faithful city has become a **p**!
Jer   3: 3 Yet you have the brazen look of a **p**;
Eze 16:15 and used your fame to become a **p**.
   23: 7 She gave herself as a **p** to all
Hos 3: 3 you must not be a **p** or be intimate
Na   3: 4 because of the wanton lust of a **p**,
1Co 6:15 of Christ and unite them with a **p**?
    6:16 who unites himself with a **p** is one
Heb 11:31 By faith the **p** Rahab, because she
Jas   2:25 Rahab the **p** considered righteous
Rev 17: 1 you the punishment of the great **p**,
   19: 2 the great **p** who corrupted the earth

PROSTITUTED PROSTITUTE

Jdg 2:17 but **p** themselves to other gods
Ps 106:39 by their deeds they **p** themselves.

PROSTITUTES PROSTITUTE

1Ki 3:16 Now two **p** came to the king
   14:24 There were even male shrine **p**
   15:12 He expelled the male shrine **p**
Pr 29: 3 of **p** squanders his wealth.
Isa 57: 3 you offspring of adulterers and **p**!
Joel 3: 3 my people and traded boys for **p**;
Mic 1: 7 her gifts from the wages of **p**,
Mt 21:31 the **p** are entering the kingdom
Lk 15:30 your property with **p** comes home,
Rev 17: 5 THE MOTHER OF **P** AND OF THE

PROSTITUTION PROSTITUTE

Lev 19:29 the land will turn to **p** and be filled
Jer 3: 2 have defiled the land with your **p**
Eze 16:16 places, where you carried on your **p**.
   23: 3 engaging in **p** from their youth.
Hos 4:10 they will engage in **p** but not
    4:12 A spirit of **p** leads them astray;
Na   3: 4 who enslaved nations by her **p**

PROSTRATE PROSTRATING
Dt   9:18 again I fell **p** before the LORD
1Ki 18:39 saw this, they fell **p** and cried,
Da   2:46 King Nebuchadnezzar fell **p** before
      8:17 standing, I was terrified and fell **p**.

PROSTRATING PROSTRATE
Ge   43:28 down, **p** themselves before him.

PROTECT PROTECTED,
PROTECTION, PROTECTS
Dt   23:14 moves about in your camp to **p** you
Est   9:16 assembled to **p** themselves and get
Ps   12: 7 will **p** us forever from the wicked,
     20: 1 the name of the God of Jacob **p** you.
     25:21 May integrity and uprightness **p** me,
     32: 7 you will **p** me from trouble
     40:11 love and faithfulness always **p** me.
     61: 7 your love and faithfulness to **p** him.
     91:14 I will **p** him, for he acknowledges
    140: 1 **p** me from the violent,
Pr   2:11 Discretion will **p** you,
      4: 6 forsake wisdom, and she will **p** you;
     14: 3 but the lips of the wise **p** them.
Mal   2:16 "does violence to the one he should **p**,"
Jn   17:11 **p** them by the power of your name,
     17:15 that you **p** them from the evil one.
2Th   3: 3 you and **p** you from the evil one.

PROTECTED* PROTECT
Jos 24:17 He **p** us on our entire journey
1Sa 30:23 He has **p** us and delivered into our
Ezr   8:31 on us, and he **p** us from enemies
Job   5:21 You will be **p** from the lash
Mk   6:20 Herod feared John and **p** him,
Jn   17:12 I **p** them and kept them safe
2Pe   2: 5 people, but **p** Noah, a preacher

PROTECTION PROTECT
Ge   19: 8 they have come under the **p** of my
Jos 20: 3 find **p** from the avenger of blood.
Ezr   9: 9 he has given us a wall of **p** in Judah
Ps   5:11 Spread your **p** over them, that those

PROTECTS PROTECT
Ps   34:20 he **p** all his bones, not one of them
     41: 2 The LORD **p** and preserves them—
    116: 6 The LORD **p** the unwary;
Pr   2: 8 and **p** the way of his faithful ones.
     27:18 and whoever **p** their master will be
Da   12: 1 the great prince who **p** your people,
1Co 13: 7 It always **p**, always trusts,

PROTEST
Ac   18: 6 he shook out his clothes in **p**

PROUD PRIDE
Dt   8:14 your heart will become **p** and you
2Ch 32:25 Hezekiah's heart was **p** and he did
Ps   31:23 him, but the **p** he pays back in full.
     94: 2 pay back to the **p** what they deserve.
    101: 5 has haughty eyes and a **p** heart,
    131: 1 My heart is not **p**, LORD, my eyes
Pr   3:34 He mocks **p** mockers but shows

Pr   16: 5 The LORD detests all the **p**
     16:19 than to share plunder with the **p**.
     21: 4 Haughty eyes and a **p** heart—
Isa   2:12 has a day in store for all the **p**
Eze 28:17 Your heart became **p** on account
Hos 13: 6 they were satisfied, they became **p**;
Ro   12:16 Do not be **p**, but be willing
1Co 13: 4 envy, it does not boast, it is not **p**.
2Ti   3: 2 of money, boastful, **p**, abusive,
Jas   4: 6 "God opposes the **p** but shows
1Pe   5: 5 "God opposes the **p** but shows
Rev 13: 5 was given a mouth to utter **p** words

PROVE PROOF, PROOFS,
PROVED, PROVEN, PROVING
Ge   44:16 How can we **p** our innocence?
Pr   29:25 Fear of man will **p** to be a snare,
Hab   2: 3 of the end and will not **p** false.
Jn   2:18 can you show us to **p** your authority
      8:46 Can any of you **p** me guilty of sin?
     16: 8 he will **p** the world to be
1Co   4: 2 been given a trust must **p** faithful.

PROVED PROVE
Dt   13:14 and it has been **p** that this detestable
     17: 4 and it has been **p** that this detestable
Job 32:12 But not one of you has **p** Job wrong;
Ps 105:19 the word of the LORD **p** him true.
Isa   5:16 the holy God will be **p** holy by his
Eze 28:25 I will be **p** holy through them
Mt   11:19 wisdom is **p** right by her deeds."
Ro   3: 4 you may be **p** right when you speak

PROVEN* PROVE
1Pe   1: 7 the **p** genuineness of your faith—

PROVERB PROVERBS
Ps   49: 4 I will turn my ear to a **p**;
Pr   26: 7 one who is lame is a **p** in the mouth
     26: 9 in a drunkard's hand is a **p**
Eze 18: 3 you will no longer quote this **p**
Lk   4:23 "Surely you will quote this **p** to me:

PROVERBS PROVERB
1Ki   4:32 He spoke three thousand **p** and his
Pr   1: 1 The **p** of Solomon son of David,
     10: 1 The **p** of Solomon: A wise son
     25: 1 These are more **p** of Solomon,
Ecc 12: 9 out and set in order many **p**.

PROVIDE PROVIDED, PROVIDES,
PROVISION, PROVISIONS
Ge   22: 8 "God himself will **p** the lamb
     22:14 that place The LORD Will **P**.
1Ch 22: 1 I have taken great pains to **p**
Isa 43:20 because I **p** water in the wilderness
     61: 3 and **p** for those who grieve in Zion—
Ac   27: 3 to his friends so they might **p** for his
1Co 10:13 **p** a way out so that you can endure
1Ti   5: 8 Anyone who does not **p** for their
Titus 3:14 in order to **p** for urgent needs

PROVIDED PROVIDE
Ge   22:14 of the LORD it will be **p**."

1Ki 8:21 I have **p** a place there for the ark,
1Ch 29: 2 all my resources I have **p**
Ps 68:10 bounty, God, you **p** for the poor.
111: 9 He **p** redemption for his people;
Jnh 1:17 Now the LORD **p** a huge fish
4: 6 the LORD God **p** a leafy plant
4: 7 at dawn the next day God **p** a worm,
4: 8 rose, God **p** a scorching east wind,
Ro 11:22 **p** that you continue in his kindness.
Gal 4:18 to be zealous, **p** the purpose is good,
Heb 1: 3 After he had **p** purification for sins,

PROVIDES PROVIDE
Job 5:10 He **p** rain for the earth; he sends
Ps 111: 5 He **p** food for those who fear him;
147: 9 He **p** food for the cattle
Pr 31:15 she **p** food for her family
Eze 18: 7 hungry and **p** clothing for the naked.
1Ti 6:17 who richly **p** us with everything
1Pe 4:11 do so with the strength God **p**,

PROVING* PROVE
Ac 9:22 in Damascus by **p** that Jesus is
17: 3 and **p** that the Messiah had to suffer
18:28 **p** from the Scriptures that Jesus was

PROVISION PROVIDE
Ps 144:13 will be filled with every kind of **p**.
Ro 5:17 those who receive God's abundant **p**

PROVISIONS PROVIDE
Ps 132:15 I will bless her with abundant **p**;
Pr 6: 8 yet it stores its **p** in summer

PROVOCATION* PROVOKE
Pr 27: 3 but a fool's **p** is heavier than both.

PROVOKE PROVOCATION,
PROVOKED, PROVOKES
Dt 2: 5 Do not **p** them to war, for I will not

PROVOKED* PROVOKE
1Sa 1: 7 her rival **p** her till she wept
Ecc 7: 9 Do not be quickly **p** in your spirit,
Jer 32:32 Judah have **p** me by all the evil they

PROVOKES* PROVOKE
Pr 25:23 which **p** a horrified look.
Eze 8: 3 where the idol that **p** to jealousy

PROWLS
1Pe 5: 8 enemy the devil **p** around like

PRUDENCE* PRUDENT
Pr 1: 4 giving **p** to those who are simple,
8: 5 You who are simple, gain **p**;
8:12 "I, wisdom, dwell together with **p**;
12: 8 is praised according to their **p**,
15: 5 whoever heeds correction shows **p**.
16:22 **P** is a fountain of life to the prudent,
19:25 mocker, and the simple will learn **p**;
21:16 from the path of **p** comes to rest

PRUDENT PRUDENCE
Pr 1: 3 receiving instruction in **p** behavior,
10:19 words, but the **p** hold their tongues.

Pr 12:16 at once, but the **p** overlook an insult.
12:23 The **p** keep their knowledge
13:16 All who are **p** act with knowledge,
14: 8 The wisdom of the **p** is to give
14:15 but the **p** give thought to their steps.
14:18 the **p** are crowned with knowledge.
19:14 but a **p** wife is from the LORD.
22: 3 The **p** see danger and take refuge,
27:12 The **p** see danger and take refuge,
Jer 49: 7 Has counsel perished from the **p**?
Am 5:13 Therefore the **p** keep quiet in such

PRUNES* PRUNING
Jn 15: 2 does bear fruit he **p** so that it will be

PRUNING PRUNES
Isa 2: 4 and their spears into **p** hooks.
Joel 3:10 and your **p** hooks into spears.

PSALM PSALMS
Ps 47: 7 sing to him a **p** of praise.
Ac 13:33 As it is written in the second **P**:

PSALMS* PSALM
Lk 20:42 himself declares in the Book of **P**:
24:44 of Moses, the Prophets and the **P**."
Ac 1:20 "it is written in the Book of **P**:
Eph 5:19 speaking to one another with **p**,
Col 3:16 another with all wisdom through **p**,

PUBLIC PUBLICLY
Pr 1:20 she raises her voice in the **p** square;
Eze 16:24 a lofty shrine in every **p** square.
Mt 1:19 want to expose her to **p** disgrace,
Lk 20:26 him in what he had said there in **p**.
Col 2:15 he made a **p** spectacle of them,
1Ti 4:13 devote yourself to the **p** reading
Heb 6: 6 and subjecting him to **p** disgrace.

PUBLICAN (KJV) See PAGANS, TAX
COLLECTOR

PUBLICLY PUBLIC
Lk 1:80 the wilderness until he appeared **p**
Jn 7:13 no one would say anything **p**
Ac 20:20 have taught you **p** and from house
Heb 10:33 Sometimes you were **p** exposed

PUFFED* PUFFS
1Co 4: 6 Then you will not be **p** up in being
Col 2:18 they are **p** up with idle notions
Hab 2: 4 "See, the enemy is **p** up;

PUFFS* PUFFED
1Co 8: 1 knowledge **p** up while love builds

PUL TIGLATH-PILESER
2Ki 15:19 **P** king of Assyria invaded the land,

PULL PULLED, PULLING
Ru 2:16 Even **p** out some stalks for her
Mk 2:21 the new piece will **p** away

PULLED PULL
Ge 19:10 out and **p** Lot back into the house
37:28 his brothers **p** Joseph
Ezr 9: 3 **p** hair from my head and beard

Ne   13:25   of the men and **p** out their hair.
Mt   15:13   Father has not planted will be **p**

PULLING* PULL

Mt   13:29   'because while you are **p** the weeds,

PUNISH PUNISHED, PUNISHES, PUNISHING, PUNISHMENT

Ge   15:14   But I will **p** the nation they serve as
Ex   32:34   when the time comes for me to **p**, I
            will **p** them for their sin."
Lev   26:18   me, I will **p** you for your sins seven
2Sa   7:14   I will **p** him with a rod wielded
Pr   23:13   if you **p** them with the rod, they will
Isa   13:11   I will **p** the world for its evil,
Jer   2:19   Your wickedness will **p** you;
        21:14   I will **p** you as your deeds deserve,
Hos   10:10   When I please, I will **p** them;
Zep   1:12   and **p** those who are complacent,
Ac   4:21   could not decide how to **p** them,
        7: 7   But I will **p** the nation they serve as
1Th   4: 6   The Lord will **p** all those who
2Th   1: 8   He will **p** those who do not know
1Pe   2:14   by him to **p** those who do wrong

PUNISHED PUNISH

Ge   19:15   be swept away when the city is **p**."
Ezr   9:13   you have **p** us less than our sins
Ps   99: 8   God, though you **p** their misdeeds.
Isa   53: 8   of my people he was **p**.
La   3:39   should the living complain when **p**
Mk   12:40   men will be **p** most severely."
Lk   23:41   We are **p** justly, for we are getting
2Th   1: 9   They will be **p** with everlasting
Heb   10:29   to be **p** who has trampled the Son

PUNISHES PUNISH

Ex   34: 7   he **p** the children and their children
Nu   14:18   he **p** the children for the sin

PUNISHING PUNISH

Ex   20: 5   God, **p** the children for the sin
Dt   5: 9   God, **p** the children for the sin

PUNISHMENT PUNISH

Ge   4:13   "My **p** is more than I can bear.
Ps   91: 8   eyes and see the **p** of the wicked.
Pr   16:22   prudent, but folly brings **p** to fools.
Isa   53: 5   the **p** that brought us peace was
Jer   4:18   This is your **p**. How bitter it is!
La   4: 6   The **p** of my people is greater than
Eze   39:21   all the nations will see the **p** I inflict
Hos   9: 7   The days of **p** are coming, the days
Zep   3:15   The Lord has taken away your **p**,
Mt   25:46   they will go away to eternal **p**,
Lk   12:48   and does things deserving **p** will be
        21:22   this is the time of **p** in fulfillment
Ro   13: 4   wrath to bring **p** on the wrongdoer.
Heb   2: 2   and disobedience received its just **p**,
2Pe   2: 9   to hold the unrighteous for **p**
1Jn   4:18   fear, because fear has to do with **p**.
Jude   1: 7   of those who suffer the **p** of eternal
Rev   17: 1   I will show you the **p** of the great

PUR LOT, PURIM

Est   3: 7   the **p** (that is, the lot)

PURCHASED

Ps   74: 2   the nation you **p** long ago,
Rev   5: 9   your blood you **p** for God persons
       14: 4   They were **p** from among mankind

PURE PURIFICATION, PURIFIED, PURIFIES, PURIFY, PURITY

Ex   25:11   Overlay it with **p** gold, both inside
       25:31   "Make a lampstand of **p** gold.
       37: 6   the atonement cover of **p** gold—
2Sa   22:27   to the **p** you show yourself **p**,
1Ki   6:21   the inside of the temple with **p** gold,
2Ki   2:22   the water has remained **p** to this
Job   4:17   man be more **p** than his Maker?
       14: 4   Who can bring what is **p**
Ps   19: 9   The fear of the Lord is **p**,
       19:10   than gold, than much **p** gold;
       24: 4   who has clean hands and a **p** heart,
       51:10   Create in me a **p** heart, O God,
Pr   15:26   gracious words are **p** in his sight.
       16: 2   All a person's ways seem **p** to them,
       20: 9   can say, "I have kept my heart **p**;
       20:11   so is their conduct really **p**
Isa   52:11   Come out from it and be **p**, you who
Hab   1:13   Your eyes are too **p** to look on evil;
Mt   5: 8   Blessed are the **p** in heart, for they
2Co   11: 2   I might present you as a **p** virgin
Php   1:10   may be **p** and blameless for the day
       2:15   you may become blameless and **p**,
       4: 8   whatever is **p**, whatever is lovely,
1Ti   1: 5   which comes from a **p** heart
       5:22   the sins of others. Keep yourself **p**.
2Ti   2:22   call on the Lord out of a **p** heart.
Titus   1:15   To the **p**, all things are **p**,
       2: 5   to be self-controlled and **p**, to be
Heb   7:26   blameless, **p**, set apart from sinners,
       10:22   our bodies washed with **p** water.
       13: 4   all, and the marriage bed kept **p**,
Jas   1:27   that God our Father accepts as **p**
       3:17   comes from heaven is first of all **p**;
1Jn   3: 3   purify themselves, just as he is **p**.
Rev   21:18   and the city of **p** gold, as **p** as glass.

PURGE

Dt   13: 5   You must **p** the evil from among
       19:19   You must **p** the evil from among
Pr   20:30   and beatings **p** the inmost being.

MUST PURGE See MUST

PURIFICATION PURE

Lev   12: 6   the days of her **p** for a son
Lk   2:22   time came for the **p** rites required
Ac   21:24   join in their **p** rites and pay their
Heb   1: 3   After he had provided **p** for sins,

PURIFIED PURE

Ezr   6:20   Levites had **p** themselves and were
Ne   12:30   and Levites had **p** themselves
            ceremonially, they **p** the people,
Ps   12: 6   flawless, like silver **p** in a crucible,
Da   12:10   Many will be **p**, made spotless

Ac   15: 9 them, for he **p** their hearts by faith.
1Pe   1:22 you have **p** yourselves by obeying

PURIFIES* PURE
1Jn   1: 7 of Jesus, his Son, **p** us from all sin.

PURIFY PURE
Ex   29:36 **P** the altar by making atonement
Nu   19:12 They must **p** themselves
Zep   3: 9 I will **p** the lips of the peoples,
2Co   7: 1 let us **p** ourselves from everything
Titus 2:14 to **p** for himself a people that are his
Jas   4: 8 you sinners, and **p** your hearts,
1Jn   1: 9 and **p** us from all unrighteousness.
      3: 3 have this hope in him **p** themselves,

PURIM PUR
Est   9:26 (Therefore these days were called **P**,

PURITY* PURE
Ps 119: 9 young person stay on the path of **p**?
Hos   8: 5 long will they be incapable of **p**?
2Co   6: 6 in **p**, understanding,
1Ti   4:12 in conduct, in love, in faith and in **p**.
      5: 2 women as sisters, with absolute **p**.
1Pe   3: 2 when they see the **p** and reverence

PURPLE
Ex   25: 4 **p** and scarlet yarn and fine linen;
Pr   31:22 she is clothed in fine linen and **p**.
Da   5:29 Daniel was clothed in **p**, a gold
Mk   15:17 They put a **p** robe on him,
Rev 17: 4 The woman was dressed in **p**
     18:16 dressed in fine linen, **p** and scarlet,

PURPOSE PURPOSED, PURPOSES
Ex   9:16 I have raised you up for this very **p**,
Job 36: 5 he is mighty, and firm in his **p**.
     42: 2 no **p** of yours can be thwarted.
Pr   19:21 it is the LORD's **p** that prevails.
Isa 46:10 I say, 'My **p** will stand, and I will
     55:11 and achieve the **p** for which I sent it.
Jer 51:12 The LORD will carry out his **p**,
Ro   8:28 have been called according to his **p**.
      9:11 that God's **p** in election might stand:
      9:17 "I raised you up for this very **p**,
1Co   3: 8 and the one who waters have one **p**,
2Co   5: 5 fashioned us for this very **p** is God,
Gal   4:18 be zealous, provided the **p** is good,
Eph   1:11 in conformity with the **p** of his will,
      2:15 His **p** was to create in himself one
      3:11 to his eternal **p** that he accomplished
Php   2:13 to act in order to fulfill his good **p**.
2Ti   1: 9 but because of his own **p** and grace.
Heb   6:17 nature of his **p** very clear
Rev 17:17 to accomplish his **p** by agreeing

PURPOSED* PURPOSE
Isa 14:24 and as I have **p**, so it will happen.
     14:27 For the LORD Almighty has **p**,
Jer 49:20 what he has **p** against those who
     50:45 what he has **p** against the land
Eph   1: 9 good pleasure, which he **p** in Christ,

PURPOSES PURPOSE
Ps   33:10 he thwarts the **p** of the peoples.

Pr   20: 5 The **p** of a person's heart are deep
Jer 23:20 until he fully accomplishes the **p**
     32:19 great are your **p** and mighty are
Ro   9:21 of clay some pottery for special **p**
2Ti   2:20 some are for special **p** and some

PURSE PURSES
Hag   1: 6 to put them in a **p** with holes in it."
Lk   10: 4 Do not take a **p** or bag or sandals;
     22:36 "But now if you have a **p**, take it,

PURSES PURSE
Lk   12:33 Provide **p** for yourselves that will

PURSUE PURSUED, PURSUES, PURSUING, PURSUIT
Lev 26: 7 You will **p** your enemies, and they
Dt   19: 6 of blood might **p** him in a rage,
Ps   34:14 and do good; seek peace and **p** it.
Pr   15: 9 he loves those who **p** righteousness.
Isa 51: 1 you who **p** righteousness and who
Jer   9:16 I will **p** them with the sword until I
Eze   5: 2 For I will **p** them with drawn sword.
Ro   9:30 who did not **p** righteousness,
1Ti   6:11 this, and **p** righteousness, godliness,
2Ti   2:22 of youth and **p** righteousness, faith,
1Pe   3:11 they must seek peace and **p** it.

PURSUED PURSUE
Ex   14:23 The Egyptians **p** them, and all
Ps   18:37 I **p** my enemies and overtook them;
Ro   9:32 Because they **p** it not by faith but as

PURSUES PURSUE
Pr   11:19 but whoever **p** evil finds death.
     13:21 Trouble **p** the sinner,
     21:21 Whoever **p** righteousness and love
     28: 1 The wicked flee though no one **p**,

PURSUING PURSUE
Lev 26:17 will flee even when no one is **p** you.
Hos   5:11 in judgment, intent on **p** idols.
1Ti   3: 8 wine, and not **p** dishonest gain.
Titus 1: 7 not violent, not **p** dishonest gain.
1Pe   5: 2 not **p** dishonest gain, but eager

PURSUIT PURSUE
Jos 20: 5 If the avenger of blood comes in **p**,
1Sa 23:28 Then Saul broke off his **p** of David
Ps   56: 1 God, for my enemies are in hot **p**;

PUSH
Dt   15:17 and **p** it through his earlobe

PUT PUTS, PUTTING
Ge   2:15 and **p** him in the Garden of Eden
      3:12 "The woman you **p** here with me—
      3:15 And I will **p** enmity between you
      4:15 the LORD **p** a mark on Cain so
      6:13 Noah, "I am going to **p** an end to all
     24: 2 had, "**P** your hand under my thigh.
     47:29 **p** your hand under my thigh
Ex   4: 6 "**P** your hand inside your cloak."
     16:34 Aaron **p** the manna with the tablets
Nu   14:15 If you **p** all these people to death,
     17:10 "**P** back Aaron's staff in front

Nu 21: 8 a snake and **p** it up on a pole;
22: 6 come and **p** a curse on these people,
Dt 32:39 I **p** to death and I bring to life,
1Sa 5: 3 Dagon and **p** him back in his place.
7: 4 So the Israelites **p** away their Baals
1Ki 11:36 city where I chose to **p** my Name.
2Ch 10: 4 "Your father **p** a heavy yoke on us,
33: 7 of Israel, I will **p** my Name forever.
Job 40: 4 I **p** my hand over my mouth.
Ps 22: 4 In you our ancestors **p** their trust;
25: 1 you, Lord my God, I **p** my trust.
25: 2 do not let me be **p** to shame, nor let
33:22 even as we **p** our hope in you.
40: 3 He **p** a new song in my mouth,
40: 3 the Lord and **p** their trust in him.
42: 5 **P** your hope in God, for I will yet
78:18 They willfully **p** God to the test
119:43 for I have **p** my hope in your laws.
143: 8 love, for I have **p** my trust in you.
Isa 8:17 I will **p** my trust in him.
11: 8 the young child will **p** its hand
42: 1 I will **p** my Spirit on him, and he
59:17 He **p** on righteousness as his
Jer 1: 9 "I have **p** my words in your mouth.
32:14 **p** them in a clay jar so they will last
38: 6 **p** him into the cistern of Malkijah,
Eze 36:27 And I will **p** my Spirit in you
37:14 I will **p** my Spirit in you and you
Da 9:26 the Anointed One will be **p** to death
Mal 3:15 even when they **p** God to the test,
Mt 4: 7 'Do not **p** the Lord your God
12:18 I will **p** my Spirit on him, and he
Mk 12:44 out of her poverty, **p** in everything—
Jn 20:25 **p** my finger where the nails were,
and **p** my hand into his side,
Ro 7:11 through the commandment **p** me
8:13 if by the Spirit you **p** to death
9·33 in him will never be **p** to shame."
10:11 in him will never be **p** to shame."
1Co 4: 9 to me that God has **p** us apostles
12:24 But God has **p** the body together,
13:11 I **p** the ways of childhood behind
15:25 reign until he has **p** all his enemies
2Co 1:22 us, and **p** his Spirit in our hearts as
Eph 4:24 and to **p** on the new self,
6:11 **P** on the full armor of God,
Php 3: 3 who **p** no confidence in the flesh—
Col 2:11 the flesh was **p** off when you were
3:14 And over all these virtues **p** on love,
Heb 2: 8 and **p** everything under their feet."
Rev 7: 3 or the trees until we **p** a seal

PUT ... TO DEATH Ge 26:11; 38:7, 10; 42:37;
Ex 19:12; 21:12, 14, 15, 16, 17, 29; 22:19; 31:14,
15; 35:2; Lev 19:20; 20:2, 4, 9, 10, 11, 12, 13, 15,
16, 27; 24:16, 16, 17, 21; 27:29; Nu 1:51; 3:10,
38; 14:15; 18:7; 25:5, 15; 35:16, 17, 18, 19, 19, 21,
21, 30, 30, 31; Dt 9:28; 13:5, 9; 17:6, 6, 12; 18:20;
21:22; 24:16, 16; 32:39; Jos 1:18; 10:26; 11:17; Jdg
6:31; 20:13; 21:5; 1Sa 2:25; 11:12, 13; 14:45; 15:3,
33; 19:6; 20:32; 2Sa 4:10; 8:2; 14:7, 32; 19:21, 22;
21:1, 4, 9; 1Ki 1:51; 2:8, 24, 26; 18:9; 19:10, 14, 17,
17; 2Ki 11:8, 15, 16; 14:6, 6; 16:9; 19:35; 1Ch 2:3;
10:14; 2Ch 15:13; 22:9; 23:7, 14, 15; 25:4, 4, 4;

Est 4:11; 9:15; Ps 78:31; Isa 37:36; 65:15; Jer 18:21;
26:15, 19, 21, 24; 29:21; 38:4; Eze 18:13; Da 2:13,
13, 14; 5:19, 19; 9:26; Mt 10:21; 15:4; 24:9; 26:59;
Mk 7:10; 13:12; 14:55; Lk 21:16; Ac 2:23; 5:33;
12:2; 26:10; Ro 7:11; 8:13; Eph 2:16; Col 3:5; Heb
11:37; 1Pe 3:18; Rev 2:13

PUT ... TO THE SWORD Nu 21:24; Dt 13:15;
20:13; Jos 8:24; 10:28, 30, 32, 35, 37, 39; 11:10, 11,
12, 14; 13:22; 19:47; Jdg 1:8, 25; 20:37, 48; 21:10;
1Sa 22:19; 2Sa 15:14; 1Ki 1:51; 2:8; 19:10, 14, 17,
17; 2Ki 11:15; 2Ch 21:4; 23:14; Job 1:15, 17; Ps
78:64; Jer 15:9; 20:4; 21:7; 25:31; Ac 12:2

PUTS PUT

Nu 23:12 I not speak what the Lord **p**
Mt 7:24 **p** them into practice is like a wise
Lk 9:62 "No one who **p** a hand to the plow

PUTTING PUT

1Ki 9: 3 built, by **p** my Name there forever.
1Th 5: 8 **p** on faith and love as a breastplate,
Heb 2: 8 In **p** everything under them,
2Pe 2: 4 **p** them in chains of darkness to be

Q

QUAIL*

Ex 16:13 That evening **q** came and covered
Nu 11:31 and drove **q** in from the sea.
11:32 the people went out and gathered **q**.
Ps 105:40 They asked, and he brought them **q**;

QUAKE EARTHQUAKE, EARTHQUAKES, QUAKED

Ps 46: 3 the mountains **q** with their surging.
75: 3 When the earth and all its people **q**,
Na 1: 5 The mountains **q** before him
Rev 16:18 on earth, so tremendous was the **q**.

QUAKED* QUAKE

Jdg 5: 5 The mountains **q** before
2Sa 22: 8 The earth trembled and **q**,
Ps 18: 7 The earth trembled and **q**,
77:18 the earth trembled and **q**.

QUALIFIED

Col 1:12 who has **q** you to share
2Ti 2: 2 who will also be **q** to teach others.

QUALITIES* QUALITY

Da 6: 3 by his exceptional **q** that the king
Ro 1:20 of the world God's invisible **q**—
2Pe 1: 8 if you possess these **q** in increasing

QUALITY QUALITIES

1Co 3:13 and the fire will test the **q** of each

QUARREL QUARRELED, QUARRELING, QUARRELS, QUARRELSOME

Pr 15:18 but the one who is patient calms a **q**.
17:14 Starting a **q** is like breaching a dam;
17:19 Whoever loves a **q** loves sin;
20: 3 strife, but every fool is quick to **q**.

Pr 26:17 who rushes into a **q** not their own.
26:20 without a gossip a **q** dies down.
Isa 45: 9 to those who **q** with their Maker,
Mt 12:19 He will not **q** or cry out; no one will
Jas 4: 2 what you want, so you **q** and fight.

QUARRELED QUARREL
Ex 17: 7 Meribah because the Israelites **q**
Nu 20: 3 They **q** with Moses and said,

QUARRELING QUARREL
Ge 13: 7 **q** arose between Abram's herders
Ro 14: 1 without **q** over disputable matters.
1Co 3: 3 there is jealousy and **q** among you,
2Ti 2:14 Warn them before God against **q**

QUARRELS QUARREL
1Ti 6: 4 **q** about words that result in envy,
2Ti 2:23 because you know they produce **q**.
Titus 3: 9 and arguments and **q** about the law,
Jas 4: 1 causes fights and **q** among you?

QUARRELSOME QUARREL
Pr 19:13 a **q** wife is like the constant dripping
21: 9 than share a house with a **q** wife.
21:19 to live in a desert than with a **q**
26:21 so is a **q** person for kindling strife.
1Ti 3: 3 gentle, not **q**, not a lover of money.
2Ti 2:24 the Lord's servant must not be **q**

QUEEN
1Ki 10: 1 When the **q** of Sheba heard
2Ch 9: 1 When the **q** of Sheba heard
15:16 from her position as **q** mother,
Est 1:12 **Q** Vashti refused to come.
2:17 and made her **q** instead of Vashti.
Isa 47: 7 said, 'I am forever—the eternal **q**!'
Jer 7:18 cakes to offer to the **Q** of Heaven.
La 1: 1 She who was **q** among the provinces
Eze 16:13 very beautiful and rose to be a **q**.
Mt 12:42 The **Q** of the South will rise
Ac 8:27 means "**q** of the Ethiopians").
Rev 18: 7 she boasts, 'I sit enthroned as **q**.

QUENCH QUENCHED
SS 8: 7 Many waters cannot **q** love;
Isa 1:31 together, with no one to **q** the fire."
Jer 4: 4 burn with no one to **q** it.
1Th 5:19 Do not **q** the Spirit.

QUENCHED QUENCH
2Ki 22:17 against this place and will not be **q**.'
Isa 66:24 fire that burns them will not be **q**,
Jer 7:20 and it will burn and not be **q**.
Mk 9:48 do not die, and the fire is not **q**.'
Heb 11:34 **q** the fury of the flames,

QUESTION QUESTIONS
Job 38: 3 I will **q** you, and you shall answer
40: 7 I will **q** you, and you shall answer
Mt 22:35 in the law, tested him with this **q**:
Mk 11:29 Jesus replied, "I will ask you one **q**,
Jn 8: 6 *were using this **q** as a trap,*

QUESTIONS QUESTION
2Ch 9: 1 to Jerusalem to test him with hard **q**.

Mt 22:46 no one dared to ask him any more **q**.
1Co 10:25 the meat market without raising **q**

QUICK QUICK-TEMPERED, QUICKLY
Pr 6:18 feet that are **q** to rush into evil,
20: 3 strife, but every fool is **q** to quarrel.
Ecc 5: 2 Do not be **q** with your mouth,
Jas 1:19 Everyone should be **q** to listen,

QUICK, QUICKEN (KJV) See also GIVE LIFE, LIVING

QUICK-TEMPERED* QUICK, TEMPER
Pr 14:17 A **q** person does foolish things,
14:29 but one who is **q** displays folly.
Titus 1: 7 not **q**, not given to drunkenness,

QUICKLY QUICK
Dt 4:26 that you will **q** perish from the land
Jos 23:16 and you will **q** perish from the good
Jdg 2:17 They **q** turned from the ways
Ps 22:19 are my strength; come **q** to help me.
69:17 answer me **q**, for I am in trouble.
71:12 come **q**, God, to help me.
90:10 for they **q** pass, and we fly away.
Ecc 4:12 of three strands is not **q** broken.
7: 9 Do not be **q** provoked in your spirit,
8:11 for a crime is not **q** carried out,
Jn 13:27 "What you are about to do, do **q**."
Gal 1: 6 you are so **q** deserting the one who

QUIET QUIETED, QUIETLY, QUIETNESS
Ps 23: 2 he leads me beside **q** waters,
Pr 17: 1 and **q** than a house full of feasting,
Ecc 9:17 The **q** words of the wise are more
Isa 62: 1 sake I will not remain **q**, till her
Am 5:13 Therefore the prudent keep **q**
Mk 4:39 the wind and said to the waves, "**Q**!
6:31 with me by yourselves to a **q** place
Lk 19:40 "if they keep **q**, the stones will cry
1Th 4:11 it your ambition to lead a **q** life:
1Ti 2: 2 peaceful and **q** lives in all godliness
2:12 authority over a man; she must be **q**.
1Pe 3: 4 beauty of a gentle and **q** spirit,

QUIETED QUIET
Ps 131: 2 But I have calmed and **q** myself,

QUIETLY QUIET
La 3:26 it is good to wait **q** for the salvation
Mt 1:19 he had in mind to divorce her **q**.

QUIETNESS* QUIET
Job 3:26 I have no peace, no **q**; I have no
Isa 30:15 in **q** and trust is your strength,
32:17 its effect will be **q** and confidence
1Ti 2:11 A woman should learn in **q** and full

QUIRINIUS*
Lk 2: 2 took place while **Q** was governor

QUIVER
Ps 127: 5 Blessed is the man whose **q** is full

Isa   49: 2 arrow and concealed me in his **q**.

QUOTE
Eze 16:44 quotes proverbs will **q** this proverb
      18: 3 you will no longer **q** this proverb
Lk   4:23 "Surely you will **q** this proverb

R

RABBI RABBONI
Mt   23: 8 "But you are not to be called 'R,'
      26:49 Jesus, Judas said, "Greetings, R!"
Jn   1:38 "R" (which means "Teacher"),

RABBONI* RABBI
Jn   20:16 him and cried out in Aramaic, "R!"

RACE
Ezr   9: 2 have mingled the holy **r**
Ecc   9:11 The **r** is not to the swift or the battle
Ac   20:24 my only aim is to finish the **r**
Ro   9: 3 of my people, those of my own **r**,
1Co   9:24 know that in a **r** all the runners run,
Gal   2: 2 had not been running my **r** in vain.
      5: 7 You were running a good **r**.
2Ti   4: 7 I have finished the **r**, I have kept
Heb 12: 1 with perseverance the **r** marked

RACHEL
   Daughter of Laban (Ge 29:16); wife of Jacob
(Ge 29:28); bore two sons (Ge 30:22 24; 35:16–
24; 46:19). Stole Laban's gods (Ge 31:19, 32–35).
Death (Ge 35:19–20).

RADIANCE* RADIANT
Job 31:26 if I have regarded the sun in its **r**
Eze   1:28 rainy day, so was the **r** around him.
      10: 4 court was full of the **r** of the glory
Heb   1: 3 The Son is the **r** of God's glory

RADIANT RADIANCE
Ex   34:29 that his face was **r** because he had
Ps   19: 8 The commands of the LORD are **r**,
      34: 5 Those who look to him are **r**;
      76: 4 You are **r** with light, more majestic
     132:18 head will be adorned with a **r** crown."
SS   5:10 My beloved is **r** and ruddy,
Isa 60: 5 Then you will look and be **r**,
Eze 43: 2 and the land was **r** with his glory.
Eph   5:27 present her to himself as a **r** church,

RAGE RAGING
Dt   19: 6 of blood might pursue him in a **r**,
Job 15:13 so that you vent your **r** against God
Pr   29:11 Fools give full vent to their **r**,
Isa 41:11 "All who **r** against you will surely
Ac   4:25 " 'Why do the nations **r**
2Co 12:20 may be discord, jealousy, fits of **r**,
Gal   5:20 jealousy, fits of **r**, selfish ambition,
Eph   4:31 Get rid of all bitterness, **r** and anger,
Col   3: 8 anger, **r**, malice, slander, and filthy

RAGING RAGE
Jnh   1:15 overboard, and the **r** sea grew calm.
Lk   8:24 rebuked the wind and the **r** waters;

RAGS
Isa 64: 6 our righteous acts are like filthy **r**;
Jer 38:12 "Put these old **r**

RAHAB
   Prostitute of Jericho who hid Israelite spies (Jos
2; 6.22–25; Heb 11:31; Jas 2:25). Mother of Boaz
(Mt 1:5).

RAIDERS
Jdg   2:14 the hands of **r** who plundered them.

RAIN RAINBOW, RAINED, RAINS
Ge   2: 5 the LORD God had not sent **r**
      7: 4 from now I will send **r** on the earth
Ex   16: 4 "I will **r** down bread from heaven
Lev 26: 4 I will send you **r** in its season,
Dt   11:14 then I will send **r** on your land in its
1Ki 17: 1 there will be neither dew nor **r**
      18: 1 and I will send **r** on the land."
2Ch   6:26 there is no **r** because your people
Job 38:28 Does the **r** have a father?
Ps 147: 8 he supplies the earth with **r**
Isa 45: 8 above, **r** down my righteousness;
Jer 14:22 idols of the nations bring **r**?
Zec 14:17 Almighty, they will have no **r**.
Mt   5:45 and sends **r** on the righteous
      7:25 The **r** came down, the streams rose,
Jas   5:17 prayed earnestly that it would not **r**,
Jude 1:12 They are clouds without **r**,
Rev 11: 6 it will not **r** during the time they are

RAINBOW RAIN
Ge   9:13 I have set my **r** in the clouds, and it
Eze   1:28 the appearance of a **r** in the clouds
Rev   4: 3 A **r** that shone like an emerald
      10: 1 in a cloud, with a **r** above his head;

RAINED* RAIN
Ge   19:24 the LORD **r** down burning sulfur
Ex   9:23 So the LORD **r** hail on the land
Ps   78:24 he **r** down manna for the people
      78:27 He **r** meat down on them like dust,
Eze 22:24 or **r** on in the day of wrath.'
Lk   17:29 fire and sulfur **r** down from heaven

RAINS RAIN
Dt   11:14 both autumn and spring **r**,
Jer   5:24 autumn and spring **r** in season,
Joel 2:23 both autumn and spring **r**, as before.
Jas   5: 7 waiting for the autumn and spring **r**.

RAISE RISE
Dt   18:15 The LORD your God will **r**
1Sa   2:35 I will **r** up for myself a faithful
Pr   8: 1 Does not understanding **r** her voice?
Isa 11:12 He will **r** a banner for the nations
      14:13 I will **r** my throne above the stars
Mt   3: 9 these stones God can **r** up children
Jn   2:19 and I will **r** it again in three days."
      6:39 me, but **r** them up at the last day.
Ac   3:22 'The Lord your God will **r**
1Co   6:14 from the dead, and he will **r** us also.
2Co   4:14 the dead will also **r** us with Jesus
Heb 11:19 that God could even **r** the dead,

RAISED RISE
Ex 9:16 But I have **r** you up for this very
Jdg 2:18 Whenever the LORD **r** up a judge
Ps 89:19 I have **r** up a young man
Isa 40: 4 Every valley shall be **r** up,
52:13 he will be **r** and lifted up and highly
Mt 17:23 the third day he will be **r** to life."
Lk 7:22 the dead are **r**, and the good news is
Ac 2:24 But God **r** him from the dead,
10:40 but God **r** him from the dead
13:30 But God **r** him from the dead,
13:34 God **r** him from the dead so that he
Ro 4:25 was **r** to life for our justification.
6: 4 just as Christ was **r** from the dead
8:11 of him who **r** Jesus from the dead is
9:17 "I **r** you up for this very purpose,
10: 9 your heart that God **r** him
1Co 15: 4 he was **r** on the third day according
15:20 Christ has indeed been **r**
2Co 5:15 who died for them and was **r** again.
Eph 2: 6 And God **r** us up with Christ
Col 2:12 of God, who **r** him from the dead.

RAISES RISE
1Sa 2: 8 He **r** the poor from the dust and lifts
Ps 113: 7 He **r** the poor from the dust and lifts
Jn 5:21 For just as the Father **r** the dead

RAISINS
Nu 6: 3 drink grape juice or eat grapes or **r**.
SS 2: 5 Strengthen me with **r**, refresh me

RALLY*
Isa 11:10 the nations will **r** to him, and his

RAM RAMS, RAMS'
Ge 22:13 in a thicket he saw a **r** caught by its
Ex 25: 5 **r** skins dyed red and another type
29:22 (This is the **r** for the ordination.)
Lev 8:22 He then presented the other **r**, the **r**
for the ordination,
Da 8: 3 there before me was a **r** with two

RAMAH
Jer 31:15 "A voice is heard in **R**,
Mt 2:18 "A voice is heard in **R**,

RAMESES
Ex 1:11 and **R** as store cities for Pharaoh.

RAMOTH GILEAD GILEAD
1Ki 22: 6 "Shall I go to war against **R**,

RAMPART* RAMPARTS
Ps 91: 4 will be your shield and **r**.

RAMPARTS RAMPART
Ps 48:13 consider well her **r**, view her
Hab 2: 1 watch and station myself on the **r**;

RAMS RAM
1Sa 15:22 to heed is better than the fat of **r**.
Ps 114: 4 the mountains leaped like **r**, the hills
Mic 6: 7 be pleased with thousands of **r**,

RAMS'* RAM
Jos 6: 4 priests carry trumpets of **r** horns
1Ch 15:28 with the sounding of **r** horns

RAN RUN
Ge 39:12 in her hand and **r** out of the house.
1Ki 18:46 he **r** ahead of Ahab all the way
19: 3 Elijah was afraid and **r** for his life.
Jnh 1: 3 But Jonah **r** away from the LORD

RANGE
2Ch 16: 9 the LORD **r** throughout the earth
Zec 4:10 **r** throughout the earth will rejoice

RANK RANKS
1Sa 18: 5 Saul gave him a high **r** in the army.
Est 10: 3 Mordecai the Jew was second in **r**

RANKS RANK
Gal 2: 4 false believers had infiltrated our **r**

RANSOM RANSOMED
Nu 35:31 " 'Do not accept a **r** for the life
Ps 49: 8 the **r** for a life is costly, no payment
Mt 20:28 to give his life as a **r** for many."
Mk 10:45 to give his life as a **r** for many."
1Ti 2: 6 who gave himself as a **r** for all
Heb 9:15 he has died as a **r** to set them free

RANSOMED RANSOM
Lev 19:20 but who has not been **r** or given her

RARE
1Sa 3: 1 days the word of the LORD was **r**;
Pr 20:15 that speak knowledge are a **r** jewel.

RASH RASHLY
Nu 30: 6 or after her lips utter a **r** promise
Ps 106:33 and **r** words came from Moses' lips.

RASHLY* RASH
Pr 13: 3 those who speak **r** will come to ruin.
20:25 It is a trap to dedicate something **r**

RATHER
Job 32: 2 for justifying himself **r** than God.
Mt 10: 6 Go **r** to the lost sheep of Israel.
Mk 7:15 **R**, it is what comes out of a person
Ac 5:29 "We must obey God **r** than human
1Co 9:12 anything **r** than hinder the gospel
14: 5 but I would **r** have you prophesy.
14:19 in the church I would **r** speak five
1Pe 4: 2 desires, but **r** for the will of God.

RAVEN RAVENS
Ge 8: 7 and sent out a **r**, and it kept flying
Job 38:41 food for the **r** when its young cry

RAVENS RAVEN
1Ki 17: 6 The **r** brought him bread and meat
Ps 147: 9 and for the young **r** when they call.
Lk 12:24 Consider the **r**: They do not sow

RAW
Ex 12: 9 Do not eat the meat **r** or boiled
1Sa 2:15 boiled meat from you, but only **r**."

RAYS
Mal 4: 2 will rise with healing in its r.

RAZOR
Nu   6: 5 no r may be used on their head.
Jdg 16:17 "No r has ever been used on my
1Sa   1:11 no r will ever be used on his head."

REACH REACHES
Dt 30:11 difficult for you or beyond your r.
Job 37:23 The Almighty is beyond our r
Ps 144: 7 R down your hand from on high;
Isa 11:11 day the Lord will r out his hand
Mic   5: 4 his greatness will r to the ends
Rev 12:14 half a time, out of the serpent's r.

REACHES REACH
Ge   11: 4 with a tower that r to the heavens,
Ps 57:10 your faithfulness r to the skies.
      71:19 God, r to the heavens, you who
Da 12:12 for and r the end of the 1,335 days.

READ READER, READING, READS
Ex   24: 7 the Covenant and r it to the people.
Dt   17:19 he is to r it all the days of his life so
Jos   8:34 Joshua r all the words of the law—
2Ki 23: 2 He r in their hearing all the words
Ne   8: 8 They r from the Book of the Law
        8: 8 understood what was being r.
Isa 34:16 in the scroll of the LORD and r:
Jer 36: 6 r to the people from the scroll
        36:23 Whenever Jehudi had r three or four
Da   5:16 If you can r this writing and tell me
Mk 12:10 Haven't you r this passage
Lk   4:16 as was his custom. He stood up to r,
2Co   3: 2 hearts, known and r by everyone.
        3:15 Even to this day when Moses is r,

READER* READ
Mt 24:15 let the r understand—
Mk 13:14 let the r understand—then let those

READINESS* READY
2Co   7:11 concern, what r to see justice done.
Eph   6:15 feet fitted with the r that comes

READING READ
Ac   8:30 you understand what you are r?"
1Ti   4:13 yourself to the public r of Scripture,

READS* READ
Da   5: 7 "Whoever r this writing and tells
Rev   1: 3 is the one who r aloud the words

READY ALREADY, READINESS
Ps 119:173 May your hand be r to help me,
Mt 24:44 So you also must be r,
      25:10 The virgins who were r went
Lk   1:17 to make r a people prepared
      12:38 servants whose master finds them r,
1Pe   1: 5 the salvation that is r to be revealed
Rev   9:15 the four angels who had been kept r
      19: 7 and his bride has made herself r.

REAFFIRM
2Co   2: 8 therefore, to r your love for him.

REAL* REALITIES, REALITY, REALLY
Jn   6:55 For my flesh is r food and my blood
              is r drink.
1Jn   2:27 all things and as that anointing is r,

REALITIES* REAL
1Co   2:13 the Spirit, explaining spiritual r
Heb 10: 1 not the r themselves.

REALITY* REAL
Col   2:17 the r, however, is found in Christ.

REALIZE REALIZED
Hos   7: 2 but they do not r that I remember all
Jn   12:16 Jesus was glorified did they r
      13: 7 "You do not r now what I am
      20:14 but she did not r that it was Jesus.
      21: 4 but the disciples did not r that it was

REALIZED REALIZE
Ge   3: 7 opened, and they r they were naked;
Jdg   6:22 When Gideon r that it was the angel
      13:21 Manoah r that it was the angel
1Sa   3: 8 Eli r that the LORD was calling
      18:28 When Saul r that the LORD was
1Ki   3:15 and he r it had been a dream.
Mk   5:30 At once Jesus r that power had gone

REALLY REAL
Ge   3: 1 "Did God r say, 'You must not eat
Jdg   6:31 If Baal r is a god, he can defend
1Ki   8.27 "But will God r dwell on earth?
Jn   13:38 "Will you r lay down your life
1Jn   2:19 us, but they did not r belong to us.

REALM REALMS
Nu   16:30 go down alive into the r of the dead,
Ps   9:17 go down to the r of the dead,
      16:10 not abandon me to the r of the dead,
      49:15 redeem me from the r of the dead;
Isa 14:15 brought down to the r of the dead,
Ac   2:27 not abandon me to the r of the dead,
Ro   7: 5 when we were in the r of the flesh,

REALMS* REALM
Eph   1: 3 the heavenly r with every spiritual
        1:20 at his right hand in the heavenly r,
        2: 6 in the heavenly r in Christ Jesus,
        3:10 and authorities in the heavenly r,
        6:12 forces of evil in the heavenly r.

REAP REAPER, REAPS
Lev 19: 9 do not r to the very edges of your
Job   4: 8 evil and those who sow trouble r it.
Ps 126: 5 sow with tears will r with songs
Hos   8: 7 sow the wind and r the whirlwind.
      10:12 r the fruit of unfailing love,
Lk   12:24 They do not sow or r, they have no
Jn   4:38 to r what you have not worked for.
Ro   6:22 the benefit you r leads to holiness,
1Co   9:11 too much if we r a material harvest
2Co   9: 6 sows sparingly will also r sparingly,
        9: 6 generously will also r generously.
Gal   6: 8 from the flesh will r destruction;
        6: 8 from the Spirit will r eternal life.
Rev 14:15 because the time to r has come,

REAPER REAP
Am 9:13 "when the r will be overtaken
Jn 4:36 and the r may be glad together.

REAPS* REAP
Pr 11:18 one who sows righteousness r a sure
    22: 8 Whoever sows injustice r calamity,
Jn 4:36 one who r draws a wage and harvests
    4:37 'One sows and another r' is true.
Gal 6: 7 A man r what he sows.

REAR
Nu 10:25 as the r guard for all the units,
Jos 6: 9 and the r guard followed the ark.
Isa 52:12 God of Israel will be your r guard.

REASON REASONED,
UNREASONING
Ps 38:19 hate me without r are numerous.
Mt 19: 5 this r a man will leave his father
Lk 6: 7 were looking for a r to accuse Jesus,
Jn 12:27 it was for this very r I came to this
    15:25 'They hated me without r.'
    18:37 the r I was born and came
1Pe 3:15 asks you to give the r for the hope
2Pe 1: 5 For this very r, make every effort
1Jn 3: 8 The r the Son of God appeared was

REASONED REASON
Ac 17:17 So he r in the synagogue with both
1Co 13:11 thought like a child, I r like a child.

REBEKAH
Sister of Laban, secured as bride for Isaac (Ge 24). Mother of Esau and Jacob (Ge 25:19–26). Taken by Abimelech as sister of Isaac; returned (Ge 26:1–11). Encouraged Jacob to trick Isaac out of blessing (Ge 27:1–17).

REBEL REBELLED, REBELLING,
REBELLION, REBELLIOUS, REBELS
Ex 23:21 Do not r against him; he will not
Nu 14: 9 Only do not r against the LORD.
Jos 22:18 you r against the LORD today,
1Sa 12:14 and do not r against his commands,
Mk 13:12 Children will r against their parents

REBELLED REBEL
Nu 20:24 both of you r against my command
Dt 1:26 you r against the command
Ne 9:26 were disobedient and r against you;
Ps 78:56 the test and r against the Most High;
   106:33 for they r against the Spirit of God,
Isa 63:10 Yet they r and grieved his Holy
Jer 14: 7 For we have often r; we have sinned

REBELLING REBEL
Ro 13: 2 the authority is r against what God

REBELLION REBEL
Ex 23:21 he will not forgive your r, since my
    34: 7 and forgiving wickedness, r and sin.
Nu 14:18 in love and forgiving r and r.
Jos 24:19 He will not forgive your r and your
1Sa 15:23 For r is like the sin of divination,

Da 8:13 the r that causes desolation,
Mk 14:48 "Am I leading a r," said Jesus,
2Th 2: 3 day will not come until the r occurs
Heb 3: 8 your hearts as you did in the r,

REBELLIOUS REBEL
Dt 21:18 r son who does not obey his father
Ps 25: 7 the sins of my youth and my r ways;
Pr 24:21 son, and do not join with r officials,
Eze 2: 5 for they are a r people—

REBELS REBEL
Jos 1:18 Whoever r against your word
Mk 15:27 They crucified two r with him,
Ro 13: 2 whoever r against the authority is
1Ti 1: 9 righteous but for lawbreakers and r,

REBIRTH* BEAR
Titus 3: 5 saved us through the washing of r

REBUILD BUILD
Jos 6:26 one who undertakes to r this city,
Ezr 5: 2 set to work to r the house of God
Ne 2:17 let us r the wall of Jerusalem,
Ps 102:16 For the LORD will r Zion
Isa 58:12 Your people will r the ancient ruins
Ezr 5: 3 authorized you to r this temple
Da 9:25 r Jerusalem until the Anointed One,
Am 9:14 "They will r the ruined cities
Hag 1: 2 come to r the LORD's house.' "
Mt 26:61 of God and r it in three days.' "
Ac 15:16 will return and r David's fallen tent.

REBUILT BUILD
2Ch 24:13 They r the temple of God according
Ezr 6: 3 Let the temple be r as a place
Ne 7: 1 After the wall had been r and I had
Eze 36:36 that I the LORD have r what was
Zec 1:16 and there my house will be r.

REBUKE REBUKED, REBUKES,
REBUKING
Lev 19:17 R your neighbor frankly so you will
Ps 6: 1 do not r me in your anger
   119:21 You r the arrogant, who are
   141: 5 let him r me—that is oil on my
Pr 3:11 discipline, and do not resent his r,
    9: 8 r the wise and they will love you.
   17:10 A r impresses a discerning person
   19:25 r the discerning, and they will gain
   25:12 of fine gold is the r of a wise judge
   27: 5 Better is open r than hidden love.
   30: 6 he will r you and prove you a liar.
Ecc 7: 5 to heed the r of a wise person than
Isa 54: 9 with you, never to r you again.
Jer 2:19 your backsliding will r you.
Hos 2: 2 "R your mother, r her, for she is not
Zep 3:17 in his love he will no longer r you,
Zec 3: 2 Satan, "The LORD r you, Satan!
Mk 8:32 took him aside and began to r him.
Lk 17: 3 or sister sins against you, r them;
1Ti 5: 1 Do not r an older man harshly,
2Ti 4: 2 correct, r and encourage—
Titus 1:13 Therefore r them sharply,
    2:15 Encourage and r with all authority.

Jude 1: 9 slander but said, "The Lord **r** you!"
Rev   3:19 Those whom I love I **r**

REBUKED REBUKE

Ps 106: 9 He **r** the Red Sea, and it dried up;
Mt   8:26 he got up and **r** the winds
      17:18 Jesus **r** the demon, and it came
Lk   3:19 John **r** Herod the tetrarch because
      4:39 So he bent over her and **r** the fever,
2Pe 2:16 he was **r** for his wrongdoing

REBUKES REBUKE

Job 22: 4 "Is it for your piety that he **r** you
Ps   2: 5 He **r** them in his anger and terrifies
Pr 28:23 Whoever **r** a person will in the end
    29: 1 many **r** will suddenly be destroyed—
Heb 12: 5 and do not lose heart when he **r** you,

REBUKING REBUKE

2Ti 3:16 and is useful for teaching, **r**,

RECALL* RECALLED, RECALLING

2Pe 3: 2 I want you to **r** the words spoken

RECALLED* RECALL

Isa 63:11 Then his people **r** the days of old,
Eze 23:19 more promiscuous as she **r** the days
Jn   2:22 his disciples **r** what he had said.

RECALLING RECALL

1Ti 1:18 by **r** them you may fight the battle

RECEDED

Ge   8: 3 The water **r** steadily from the earth.
Rev 6:14 The heavens **r** like a scroll being

RECEIVE RECEIVED, RECEIVES, RECEIVING

Ge   4:11 its mouth to **r** your brother's blood
Nu 18:23 They will **r** no inheritance among
Dt   9: 9 on the mountain to **r** the tablets
Ps   24: 5 They will **r** blessing
    27:10 forsake me, the LORD will **r** me.
Pr 28:10 trap, but the blameless will **r** a good
Isa 61: 7 shame you will **r** a double portion,
Da 12:13 rise to **r** your allotted inheritance."
Hos 14: 2 all our sins and **r** us graciously,
Mt 10:41 a prophet will **r** a prophet's reward,
Mk 10:15 anyone who will not **r** the kingdom
    10:30 fail to **r** a hundred times as much
Lk   7:22 The blind **r** sight, the lame walk,
Jn   1:11 his own, but his own did not **r** him.
    1:12 Yet to all who did **r** him, to those
   16:24 Ask and you will **r**, and your joy
   20:22 them and said, "**R** the Holy Spirit.
Ac   1: 8 But you will **r** power when the Holy
    2:38 you will **r** the gift of the Holy Spirit.
   19: 2 "Did you **r** the Holy Spirit
   20:35 more blessed to give than to **r**.' "
Ro 11:31 that they too may now **r** mercy as
1Co 4: 5 time each will **r** their praise
    9:14 the gospel should **r** their living
2Co 1: 4 the comfort we ourselves **r**
    6:17 no unclean thing, and I will **r** you."
Gal 3:14 faith we might **r** the promise
1Ti 1:16 believe in him and **r** eternal life.

Heb 4:16 so that we may **r** mercy and find
   11:13 They did not **r** the things promised;
Jas   1: 7 should not expect to **r** anything
    1:12 that person will **r** the crown of life
1Pe 5: 4 you will **r** the crown of glory
2Pe 1:11 you will **r** a rich welcome
1Jn 3:22 and **r** from him anything we ask,
Rev 4:11 to **r** glory and honor and power,
    5:12 to **r** power and wealth and wisdom
   13:16 to **r** a mark on their right hands
   18: 4 you will not **r** any of her plagues;

RECEIVED RECEIVE

Nu 23:20 I have **r** a command to bless;
Jos 14: 1 are the areas the Israelites **r** as
    14: 4 The Levites **r** no share of the land
Mt   6: 2 you, they have **r** their reward in full.
    10: 8 Freely you have **r**; freely give.
Mk 11:24 believe that you have **r** it, and it will
Jn   1:16 of his fullness we have all **r** grace
Ac   8:17 on them, and they **r** the Holy Spirit.
   10:47 They have **r** the Holy Spirit just as
Ro   8:15 The Spirit you **r** does not make you
   11:30 to God have now **r** mercy as a result
1Co 2:12 What we have **r** is not the spirit
   11:23 For I **r** from the Lord what I
Eph 4: 1 worthy of the calling you have **r**.
Col   2: 6 just as you **r** Christ Jesus as Lord,
    4:17 complete the ministry you have **r**
1Ti 4: 4 rejected if it is **r** with thanksgiving,
Heb 8: 6 ministry Jesus has **r** is as superior
1Pe 2:10 once you had not **r** mercy, but now
           you have **r** mercy.
    4:10 should use whatever gift you have **r**
2Pe 1: 1 Savior Jesus Christ have **r** a faith as
    1:17 He **r** honor and glory from God
Rev 2:27 just as I have **r** authority from my
   19:20 deluded those who had **r** the mark
   20: 4 had not **r** its mark on their foreheads

RECEIVES RECEIVE

Pr 18:22 good and **r** favor from the LORD.
Lk 11:10 For everyone who asks **r**;
Ac 10:43 who believes in him **r** forgiveness
Rev 14:11 or for anyone who **r** the mark of its

RECEIVING RECEIVE

Pr   1: 3 for **r** instruction in prudent
Ro   9: 4 the covenants, the **r** of the law,
1Pe 1: 9 for you are **r** the end result of your
3Jn 1: 7 went out, **r** no help from the pagans.

RECENT*

1Ti 3: 6 He must not be a **r** convert, or he

RECITE RECITED, RECITING

Dt 27:14 The Levites shall **r** to all the people
Ps 45: 1 a noble theme as I **r** my verses

RECITED* RECITE

Dt 31:30 Moses **r** the words of this song

RECITING* RECITE

Dt 32:45 Moses finished **r** all these words

RECKLESS
Pr 12:18 words of the **r** pierce like swords,

RECKONED RECKONING
Ge 21:12 Isaac that your offspring will be **r**.
Ro 9: 7 Isaac that your offspring will be **r**."
Heb 11:18 Isaac that your offspring will be **r**."

RECKONING* RECKONED
Isa 10: 3 What will you do on the day of **r**,
Hos 5: 9 will be laid waste on the day of **r**.
 9: 7 coming, the days of **r** are at hand.

RECLAIM* CLAIM
Isa 11:11 time to **r** the surviving remnant

RECLINED* RECLINING
Lk 7:36 Pharisee's house and **r** at the table.
 11:37 so he went in and **r** at the table.
 22:14 Jesus and his apostles **r** at the table.

RECLINING RECLINED
Est 7: 8 on the couch where Esther was **r**.
Jn 13:23 Jesus loved, was **r** next to him.

RECOGNITION* RECOGNIZE
Est 6: 3 **r** has Mordecai received for this?"
1Co 16:18 and yours also. Such men deserve **r**.
1Ti 5: 3 Give proper **r** to those widows who

RECOGNIZE RECOGNITION,
RECOGNIZED, RECOGNIZING
Ge 42: 8 his brothers, they did not **r** him.
Job 2:12 a distance, they could hardly **r** him;
Mt 7:16 By their fruit you will **r** them.
Lk 19:44 because you did not **r** the time
Jn 1:10 him, the world did not **r** him.
1Jn 4: 2 This is how you can **r** the Spirit
 4: 6 This is how we **r** the Spirit of truth

RECOGNIZED RECOGNIZE
Mt 12:33 be bad, for a tree is **r** by its fruit.
Lk 24:31 eyes were opened and they **r** him,
Ac 12:14 When she **r** Peter's voice, she was
Ro 7:13 in order that sin might be **r** as sin,

RECOGNIZING* RECOGNIZE
Lk 24:16 but they were kept from **r** him.

RECOMMENDATION*
2Co 3: 1 letters of **r** to you or from you?

RECOMPENSE*
Isa 40:10 him, and his **r** accompanies him.
 62:11 and his **r** accompanies him.' "

RECONCILE* RECONCILED,
RECONCILIATION, RECONCILING
Ac 7:26 He tried to **r** them by saying, 'Men,
Eph 2:16 and in one body to **r** both of them
Col 1:20 and through him to **r** to himself all

RECONCILED* RECONCILE
Mt 5:24 First go and be **r** to them;
Lk 12:58 try hard to be **r** on the way, or your
Ro 5:10 we were **r** to him through the death
 5:10 having been **r**, shall we be saved

1Co 7:11 or else be **r** to her husband.
2Co 5:18 who **r** us to himself through Christ
 5:20 you on Christ's behalf: Be **r** to God.
Col 1:22 But now he has **r** you by Christ's

RECONCILIATION* RECONCILE
Ro 5:11 whom we have now received **r**.
 11:15 For if their rejection brought **r**
2Co 5:18 Christ and gave us the ministry of **r**:
 5:19 committed to us the message of **r**.

RECONCILING* RECONCILE
2Co 5:19 that God was **r** the world to himself

RECORD RECORDED, RECORDS
Ps 56: 8 **R** my misery; list my tears on your
 130: 3 you, LORD, kept a **r** of sins, Lord,
Hos 13:12 is stored up, his sins are kept on **r**.
1Co 13: 5 angered, it keeps no **r** of wrongs.

RECORDED RECORD
Nu 33: 2 command Moses **r** the stages
Jos 24:26 Joshua **r** these things in the Book
1Ch 9: 1 in the genealogies **r** in the book
Est 9:20 Mordecai **r** these events, and he sent
Job 19:23 that my words were **r**, that they
Jn 20:30 which are not **r** in this book.
Rev 20:12 to what they had done as **r**

RECORDS RECORD
1Ch 4:22 (These **r** are from ancient times.)
Ezr 2:62 These searched for their family **r**,
Ne 7:64 These searched for their family **r**,

RECOUNT*
Ps 119:13 With my lips I **r** all the laws
Jer 23:28 prophet who has a dream **r** the dream,

RECOVER RECOVERY
Isa 38: 1 are going to die; you will not **r**."

RECOVERY RECOVER
Isa 38: 9 king of Judah after his illness and **r**:
Ro 11:11 they stumble so as to fall beyond **r**?

RED
Ge 25:25 The first to come out was **r**, and his
Ex 15: 4 officers are drowned in the **R** Sea.
 25: 5 ram skins dyed **r** and another type
Nu 19: 2 bring you a **r** heifer without defect
2Ki 3:22 across the way, the water looked **r**—
Ps 106: 9 He rebuked the **R** Sea, and it dried
Pr 23:31 Do not gaze at wine when it is **r**,
Isa 1:18 though they are **r** as crimson,
Zec 1: 8 was a man mounted on a **r** horse.
 6: 2 The first chariot had **r** horses,
Mt 16: 3 for the sky is **r** and overcast.'
Heb 11:29 people passed through the **R** Sea as
Rev 6: 4 horse came out, a fiery **r** one.
 6:12 the whole moon turned blood **r**,
 9:17 Their breastplates were fiery **r**,
 12: 3 an enormous **r** dragon with seven

REDEDICATE* DEDICATE
Nu 6:12 They must **r** themselves

REDEEM GUARDIAN-REDEEMER, REDEEMED, REDEEMER, REDEEMS, REDEMPTION

Ex   6: 6 and I will r you with an outstretched
     13:13 R with a lamb every firstborn
     13:13 R every firstborn among your sons.
Lev 25:25 to come and r what they have sold.
Ru   4: 6 "Then I cannot r it because I might
2Sa   7:23 out to r as a people for himself,
Ps   49: 7 No one can r the life of another
     49:15 God will r me from the realm
    130: 8 He himself will r Israel from all
Hos 13:14 I will r them from death.
Lk   24:21 the one who was going to r Israel.
Gal   4: 5 to r those under the law, that we
Titus 2:14 for us to r us from all wickedness

REDEEMED REDEEM

Ex   15:13 you will lead the people you have r.
Dt   15:15 and the LORD your God r you.
Ne   1:10 whom you r by your great strength
Ps 107: 2 those he r from the hand of the foe,
Isa 35: 9 But only the r will walk there,
     44:22 Return to me, for I have r you."
     63: 9 In his love and mercy he r them;
Lk   1:68 has come to his people and r them.
Gal   3:13 Christ r us from the curse of the law
1Pe   1:18 that you were r from the empty way
Rev 14: 3 except the 144,000 who had been r

REDEEMER REDEEM

Job 19:25 I know that my r lives,
Ps   19:14 sight, LORD, my Rock and my R.
     78:35 that God Most High was their R.
Isa 44: 6 Israel's King and R, the LORD
     48:17 your R, the Holy One of Israel:
     59:20 "The R will come to Zion, to those

REDEEMS* REDEEM

Ps 103: 4 who r your life from the pit

REDEMPTION REDEEM

Ru   4: 7 for the r and transfer of property
Ps 130: 7 unfailing love and with him is full r.
Lk   2:38 forward to the r of Jerusalem.
     21:28 because your r is drawing near."
Ro   3:24 by his grace through the r that came
      8:23 to sonship, the r of our bodies.
1Co   1:30 is, our righteousness, holiness and r.
Eph   1: 7 In him we have r through his blood,
      1:14 our inheritance until the r of those
      4:30 you were sealed for the day of r.
Col   1:14 in whom we have r, the forgiveness
Heb   9:12 own blood, thus obtaining eternal r.

REDUCE REDUCED

2Ki 10:32 days the LORD began to r the size
Jer 10:24 anger, or you will r me to nothing.

REDUCED REDUCE

Ps   79: 1 they have r Jerusalem to rubble.
Eze 16:27 against you and r your territory;

REED REEDS

2Ki 18:21 that splintered r of a staff,

Isa 42: 3 A bruised r he will not break,
Mt   12:20 A bruised r he will not break,
Lk   7:24 A r swayed by the wind?

REEDS REED

Ex   2: 3 put it among the r along the bank

REEL* REELED, REELING, REELS

Isa 28: 7 stagger from wine and r from beer:

REELED* REEL

Ps 107:27 They r and staggered like

REELING* REEL

Zec 12: 2 sends all the surrounding peoples r.

REELS* REEL

Isa 24:20 The earth r like a drunkard, it sways

REFINE* REFINED, REFINER

Jer   9: 7 "See, I will r and test them,
Zec 13: 9 I will r them like silver and test
Mal   3: 3 the Levites and r them like gold

REFINED REFINE

Job 28: 1 silver and a place where gold is r.
Ps   12: 6 a crucible, like gold r seven times.
Isa 48:10 I have r you, though not as silver;
Da   12:10 made spotless and r, but the wicked
1Pe   1: 7 perishes even though r by fire—

REFINER* REFINE

Mal   3: 3 He will sit as a r and purifier

REFLECT REFLECTION, REFLECTS

Ecc   5:20 They seldom r on the days of their

REFLECTION* REFLECT

1Co 13:12 now we see only a r as in a mirror;

REFLECTS* REFLECT

Pr   27:19 As water r the face, so one's life
              r the heart.

REFORM

Jer 18:11 and r your ways and your actions.'

REFRAIN

Ps   37: 8 R from anger and turn from wrath;
Ecc   3: 5 and a time to r from embracing,

REFRESH REFRESHED, REFRESHES, REFRESHING

Jer 31:25 I will r the weary and satisfy
Phm   1:20 in the Lord; r my heart in Christ.

REFRESHED REFRESH

Ps   68: 9 you r your weary inheritance.
Pr   11:25 whoever refreshes others will be r.

REFRESHES REFRESH

Ps   23: 3 he r my soul. He guides me along

REFRESHING* REFRESH

Ps   19: 7 of the LORD is perfect, r the soul.
Ac   3:19 times of r may come from the Lord,

REFUGE

Nu   35:11 some towns to be your cities of r,

Dt   33:27 The eternal God is your r,
Jos 20: 2 Israelites to designate the cities of r,
Ru   2:12 wings you have come to take r."
2Sa 22: 3 stronghold, my r and my savior—
      22:31 he shields all who take r in him.
Ps   2:12 Blessed are all who take r in him.
      5:11 let all who take r in you be glad;
      9: 9 The LORD is a r
      11: 1 In the LORD I take r.
      16: 1 safe, my God, for in you I take r.
      17: 7 your right hand those who take r
      31: 2 be my rock of r, a strong fortress
      34: 8 blessed is the one who takes r
      36: 7 People take r in the shadow of your
      46: 1 God is our r and strength,
      59:16 fortress, my r in times of trouble.
      62: 8 your hearts to him, for God is our r.
      71: 1 In you, LORD, I have taken r;
      91: 2 "He is my r and my fortress,
     118: 8 better to take r in the LORD than
     144: 2 in whom I take r, who subdues
Pr   14:26 and for their children it will be a r.
     14:32 in death the righteous seek r in God.
     30: 5 a shield to those who take r in him.
Isa 25: 4 You have been a r for the poor, a r
Jer 16:19 my fortress, my r in time of distress,
Na   1: 7 is good, a r in times of trouble.

REFUSE REFUSED
Ex   8: 2 If you r to let them go, I will send
Lev 26:21 toward me and r to listen to me,
Nu   14:11 How long will they r to believe
Eze   3:27 and whoever will r let them r;
Jn   5:40 yet you r to come to me to have life.
Heb 12:25 it that you do not r him who speaks.

REFUSED REFUSE
Ex   13:15 Pharaoh stubbornly r to let us go,
Jdg   2:19 They r to give up their evil practices
Jer   5: 3 crushed them, but they r correction.
2Th   2:10 They perish because they r to love
Heb 12:25 when they r him who warned them
Rev 16: 9 but they r to repent and glorify him.

REFUTE REFUTED
Job 32: 3 they had found no way to r Job,
Titus 1: 9 doctrine and r those who oppose it.

REFUTED* REFUTE
Ac   18:28 For he vigorously r his Jewish

REGARD REGARDED, REGARDS
1Sa   2:12 they had no r for the LORD.
Ps   41: 1 Blessed are those who have r
     74:20 Have r for your covenant,
Isa   8:13 is the one you are to r as holy, he is
1Co 14:20 In r to evil be infants, but in your
1Th   5:13 in the highest r in love because

REGARDED REGARD
Ex   11: 3 and Moses himself was highly r
Isa 40:17 they are r by him as worthless
Ac   5:13 even though they were highly r
2Co   5:16 Though we once r Christ in this
Heb 11:26 He r disgrace for the sake of Christ

REGARDS REGARD
Ro   14: 6 Whoever r one day as special does
     14:14 if anyone r something as unclean,

REGIONS
2Co 10:16 the gospel in the r beyond you.
Eph   4: 9 descended to the lower, earthly r?

REGISTER
Lk   2: 5 He went there to r with Mary,

REGRET REGRETTED
1Sa 15:11 "I r that I have made Saul king,
2Co   7:10 leads to salvation and leaves no r,

REGRETTED* REGRET
Ge   6: 6 The LORD r that he had made
1Sa 15:35 the LORD r that he had made Saul

REGULAR
Nu   28: 3 as a r burnt offering each day.
2Ki 25:30 gave Jehoiachin a r allowance as

REGULATION REGULATIONS
Heb   7:18 The former r is set aside because it

REGULATIONS REGULATION
Ex   12:43 "These are the r for the Passover
Lev 26:46 the r that the LORD established
Dt   12:28 to obey all these r I am giving you,
Col   2:23 Such r indeed have an appearance
Heb   9:10 external r applying until the time

REHOBOAM
Son of Solomon (1Ki 11:43; 1Ch 3:10). Harsh treatment of subjects caused divided kingdom (1Ki 12:1–24; 14:21–31; 2Ch 10–12).

REIGN REIGNED, REIGNS
Dt   17:20 his descendants will r a long time
1Sa   8:11 the king who will r over you will
Ps   68:16 mountain where God chooses to r,
Pr   8:15 By me kings r and rulers issue
Isa   9: 7 He will r on David's throne
     24:23 for the LORD Almighty will r
     32: 1 a king will r in righteousness
Jer 23: 5 a King who will r wisely and do
La   5:19 You, LORD, r forever;
Eze 20:33 I will r over you with a mighty hand
Lk   1:33 he will r over Jacob's descendants
Ro   6:12 Therefore do not let sin r in your
1Co   4: 8 you really had begun to r so that we
           also might r with you!
     15:25 For he must r until he has put all his
2Ti   2:12 we endure, we will also r with him.
Rev   5:10 God, and they will r on the earth."
     11:15 and he will r for ever and ever."
     11:17 great power and have begun to r.
     20: 6 will r with him for a thousand years.
     22: 5 And they will r for ever and ever.

REIGNED REIGN
Ro   5:21 so that, just as sin r in death,
Rev 20: 4 and r with Christ a thousand years.

REIGNS REIGN

Ex   15:18 "The Lord r for ever and ever."
Ps   9: 7 The Lord r forever;
      47: 8 God r over the nations;
      93: 1 The Lord r, he is robed
     96:10 the nations, "The Lord r."
      97: 1 The Lord r, let the earth be glad;
      99: 1 The Lord r, let the nations
   146:10 The Lord r forever, your God,
Isa   52: 7 who say to Zion, "Your God r!"
Lk   22:53 is your hour—when darkness r."
Rev 19: 6 For our Lord God Almighty r.

REIN

Jas   1:26 and yet do not keep a tight r on their

REJECT REJECTED, REJECTION, REJECTS

Lev 26:15 if you r my decrees and abhor my
1Sa 12:22 the Lord will not r his people,
2Ch   7:20 will r this temple I have consecrated
Ps   44:23 Rouse yourself! Do not r us forever.
     94:14 the Lord will not r his people;
Isa   31: 7 day every one of you will r the idols
Hos   4: 6 I also r you as my priests;
Ro   11: 1 I ask then: Did God r his people?
1Th   4: 8 this instruction does not r a human
      5:22 r every kind of evil.

REJECTED REJECT

Nu 11:20 because you have r the Lord,
Dt   32:15 them and r the Rock their Savior.
1Sa   8: 7 it is not you they have r, but they
         have r me as their king.
    15:23 Because you have r the word of the
         Lord, he has r you as king."
1Ki 12: 8 Rehoboam r the advice the elders
    19:10 The Israelites have r your covenant,
2Ki 17:15 They r his decrees and the covenant
    17:20 Therefore the Lord r all
Ps   60: 1 You have r us, God, and burst
    66:20 to God, who has not r my prayer
   118:22 stone the builders r has become
Isa   5:24 for they have r the law
    41: 9 chosen you and have not r you.
    53: 3 He was despised and r by mankind,
Jer   8: 9 Since they have r the word
    14:19 Have you r Judah completely?
Hos   8: 3 But Israel has r what is good;
Zec 10: 6 will be as though I had not r them,
Mt   21:42 stone the builders r has become
Mk   9:12 of Man must suffer much and be r?
Ac   4:11 is " 'the stone you builders r,
1Ti   4: 4 nothing is to be r if it is received
Heb 10:28 Anyone who r the law of Moses
1Pe   2: 4 r by humans but chosen by God
     2: 7 stone the builders r has become

REJECTION* REJECT

Ro   11:15 if their r brought reconciliation

REJECTS* REJECT

Lk 10:16 listens to me; whoever r you r me;
    10:16 whoever r me r him who sent me."

Jn   3:36 whoever r the Son will not see life,
    12:48 is a judge for the one who r me
1Th   4: 8 anyone who r this instruction does

REJOICE JOY

Dt   12: 7 shall r in everything you have put
    32:43 R, you nations, with his people,
1Ch 16:10 of those who seek the Lord r.
    16:31 Let the heavens r, let the earth be
2Ch   6:41 may your faithful people r in your
Ps   5:11 those who love your name may r
     9:14 Zion, and there r in your salvation.
    14: 7 let Jacob r and Israel be glad!
    31: 7 I will be glad and r in your love,
    34: 2 let the afflicted hear and r.
    51: 8 let the bones you have crushed r.
    63:11 But the king will r in God;
    64:10 The righteous will r in the Lord
    66: 6 come, let us r in him.
    68: 3 righteous be glad and r before God;
    89:16 They r in your name all day long;
    97: 1 let the distant shores r.
   104:31 may the Lord r in his works—
   105: 3 of those who seek the Lord r.
   118:24 let us r today and be glad.
   119:14 I r in following your statutes as one
  119:162 I r in your promise like one who
   149: 2 Let Israel r in their Maker;
Pr   5:18 may you r in the wife of your youth.
    23:25 May your father and mother r;
    24:17 stumble, do not let your heart r,
    29: 2 the righteous thrive, the people r;
Isa   9: 3 they r before you as people r
    29:19 Once more the humble will r
    35: 1 the wilderness will r and blossom.
    61: 7 of disgrace you will r in your
    62: 5 bride, so will your God r over you.
Jer   31:12 they will r in the bounty
Hab   3:18 yet I will r in the Lord, I will be
Zep   3:17 but will r over you with singing."
Zec   9: 9 R greatly, Daughter Zion!
Lk   6:23 "R in that day and leap for joy,
    10:20 do not r that the spirits submit
    10:20 but r that your names are written
    15: 6 together and says, 'R with me;
    15: 9 together and says, 'R with me;
Ro   12:15 R with those who r;
    16:19 obedience, so I r because of you;
Php   2:17 I am glad and r with all of you.
    3: 1 brothers and sisters, r in the Lord!
    4: 4 R in the Lord always. I will say it
         again: R!
1Th   5:16 R always,
1Pe   4:13 r inasmuch as you participate
Rev 18:20 "R over her, you heavens! R,
    18:20 R, apostles and prophets!
    19: 7 Let us r and be glad and give him

REJOICED JOY

1Ch 29: 9 The people r at the willing response
    29: 9 David the king also r greatly.
Job 31:25 if I have r over my great wealth,
Ps 122: 1 I r with those who said to me,
Jn   8:56 Your father Abraham r

REJOICES JOY

1Sa	2: 1	"My heart r in the LORD;
Ps	13: 5	my heart r in your salvation.
	16: 9	my heart is glad and my tongue r;
Pr	11:10	the righteous prosper, the city r;
	23:24	a man who fathers a wise son r
Isa	61:10	my soul r in my God.
	62: 5	as a bridegroom r over his bride,
Lk	1:47	and my spirit r in God my Savior,
Ac	2:26	my heart is glad and my tongue r;
1Co	12:26	part is honored, every part r with it.
	13: 6	delight in evil but r with the truth.

REJOICING JOY

2Sa	6:12	to the City of David with r.
Ne	12:43	The sound of r in Jerusalem could
Ps	30: 5	night, but r comes in the morning.
Pr	8:30	after day, r always in his presence,
	14:13	may ache, and r may end in grief.
Lk	15: 7	the same way there will be more r
Ac	5:41	r because they had been counted
2Co	6:10	sorrowful, yet always r;

REKAB

Jer 35: 6 son of R gave us this command:

REKABITES

Jer 35: 3 the whole family of the R.

RELATE*

Ps 71:15 I know not how to r them all.

RELATIONS

Ex	22:19	"Anyone who has sexual r
Lev	18: 6	any close relative to have sexual r.
	18:22	" 'Do not have sexual r
	20:13	" a man has sexual r with a man as
Ro	1:26	women exchanged natural sexual r
1Co	7: 1	to have sexual r with a woman."

RELATIONSHIP

Jn 1:18 and is in closest r with the Father,

RELATIVE RELATIVES

Lev	18: 6	approach any close r to have sexual
	25:25	their nearest r is to come
Ru	2:20	added, "That man is our close r;
	3: 2	you have worked, is a r of ours.
Pr	7: 4	and to insight, "You are my r."
	27:10	a neighbor nearby than a r far away.

RELATIVES RELATIVE

Lev	25:48	One of their r may redeem them:
Pr	19: 7	The poor are shunned by all their r—
Mk	6: 4	among his r and in his own home."
Lk	21:16	brothers and sisters, r and friends,
1Ti	5: 8	who does not provide for their r,

RELEASE RELEASED

Isa	61: 1	r from darkness for the prisoners,
Mt	27:15	the festival to r a prisoner chosen

RELEASED RELEASE

Lev	25:54	their children are to be r in the Year
	27:21	When the field is r in the Jubilee,
2Ki	25:27	he r Jehoiachin king of Judah

Mk	15:15	crowd, Pilate r Barabbas to them.
Ac	3:14	asked that a murderer be r to you.
Ro	7: 2	she is r from the law that binds her
	7: 6	we have been r from the law so
1Co	7:27	Do not seek to be r. Are you free
Rev	20: 7	over, Satan will be r from his prison

RELENT RELENTED, RELENTS

Ex	32:12	r and do not bring disaster on your
Dt	32:36	r concerning his servants when he
Jer	18: 8	then I will r and not inflict on it
	26: 3	I will r and not inflict on them
Joel	2:14	He may turn and r and leave behind
Am	1:11	Edom, even for four, I will not r.
Jnh	3: 9	God may yet r and with compassion

RELENTED* RELENT

Ex	32:14	the LORD r and did not bring
Jdg	2:18	for the LORD r because of their
2Sa	24:16	the LORD r concerning
1Ch	21:15	saw it and r concerning the disaster
Ps	106:45	and out of his great love he r.
Jer	42:10	for I have r concerning the disaster I
Am	7: 3	So the LORD r. "This will not
	7: 6	So the LORD r. "This will not
Jnh	3:10	he r and did not bring on them

RELENTS* RELENT

Joel	2:13	and he r from sending calamity.
Jnh	4: 2	a God who r from sending calamity.

RELIABLE RELY

2Ti	2: 2	entrust to r people who will also be
2Pe	1:19	message as something completely r,

RELIANCE* RELY

Ps	26: 3	have lived in r on your faithfulness.
Pr	25:19	a lame foot is r on the unfaithful

RELIED RELY

2Ch	13:18	were victorious because they r
	16: 8	Yet when you r on the LORD,
Ps	71: 6	From birth I have r on you;

RELIEF

1Sa	8:18	cry out for r from the king you have
Est	4:14	r and deliverance for the Jews will
	9:22	the Jews got r from their enemies,
Job	35: 9	they plead for r from the arm
Ps	94:13	you grant them r from days
	143: 1	and righteousness come to my r.
La	3:49	will flow unceasingly, without r,
	3:56	not close your ears to my cry for r."
2Th	1: 7	and give r to you who are troubled,

RELIES* RELY

Isa	28:16	the one who r on it will never be
Gal	3:11	no one who r on the law is justified

RELIGION* RELIGIOUS

Ac	25:19	dispute with him about their own r
	26: 5	to the strictest sect of our r,
1Ti	5: 4	of all to put their r into practice
Jas	1:26	themselves, and their r is worthless.
	1:27	R that God our Father accepts as

RELIGIOUS RELIGION

Am	5:21	"I hate, I despise your **r** festivals;
Col	2:16	or with regard to a **r** festival, a New
Jas	1:26	Those who consider themselves **r**

RELY RELIABLE, RELIANCE, RELIED, RELIES

2Ch	14:11	for we **r** on you, and in your name
Ps	59:10	my God on whom I can **r.**
	59:17	fortress, my God on whom I can **r.**
Isa	50:10	of the Lord and **r** on their God.
Eze	33:26	You **r** on your sword, you do
Ro	2:17	if you **r** on the law and boast
2Co	1: 9	that we might not **r** on ourselves
Gal	3:10	For all who **r** on the works
1Jn	4:16	and **r** on the love God has for us.

REMAIN REMAINED, REMAINS

Nu	33:55	you allow to **r** will become barbs
Jos	23: 7	with these nations that **r** among you;
Jdg	2:23	had allowed those nations to **r;**
2Ch	33: 4	said, "My Name will **r** in Jerusalem
Ps	102:27	But you **r** the same, and your years
Jn	1:32	heaven as a dove and **r** on him.
	15: 4	**R** in me, as I also **r** in you.
	15: 4	fruit by itself; it must **r** in the vine.
	15: 5	If you **r** in me and I in you, you will
	15: 7	If you **r** in me and my words **r**
	15: 9	have I loved you. Now **r** in my love.
Ro	13: 8	Let no debt **r** outstanding,
1Co	7:20	Each person should **r**
	13:13	And now these three **r:**
Heb	1:11	They will perish, but you **r;**
1Jn	2:27	just as it has taught you, **r** in him.
Rev	2:13	Yet you **r** true to my name.
	14:12	commands and **r** faithful to Jesus.

REMAINED REMAIN

2Sa	11: 1	But David **r** in Jerusalem.
Mk	14:61	But Jesus **r** silent and gave no
1Jn	2:19	to us, they would have **r** with us;
Rev	14: 4	with women, for they **r** virgins.

REMAINS REMAIN

Dt	24:20	Leave what **r** for the foreigner,
Jos	13: 2	"This is the land that **r:**
Ps	146: 6	he **r** faithful forever.
Hag	2: 5	And my Spirit **r** among you.
Jn	3:36	see life, for God's wrath **r** on them.
	6:56	flesh and drinks my blood **r** in me,
2Co	3:14	to this day the same veil **r**
2Ti	2:13	if we are faithless, he **r** faithful,
Heb	7: 3	Son of God, he **r** a priest forever.
1Jn	3: 9	sin, because God's seed **r** in them;

REMARKABLE*

Mk	6: 2	What are these **r** miracles he is
Lk	5:26	"We have seen **r** things today."
Jn	9:30	The man answered, "Now that is **r**!

REMEDY*

2Ch	36:16	his people and there was no **r.**
Pr	6:15	suddenly be destroyed—without **r.**
	29: 1	suddenly be destroyed—without **r.**
Isa	3: 7	day he will cry out, "I have no **r.**

Jer	30:13	plead your cause, no **r** for your sore,
Mic	2:10	is defiled, it is ruined, beyond all **r.**

REMEMBER REMEMBERED, REMEMBERS, REMEMBRANCE

Ge	9:15	I will **r** my covenant between me
Ex	20: 8	"**R** the Sabbath day by keeping it
	33:13	**R** that this nation is your people."
Lev	26:42	I will **r** my covenant with Jacob
Dt	5:15	**R** that you were slaves in Egypt
	8:18	But **r** the Lord your God, for it is
Jos	1:13	"**R** the command that Moses
1Ch	16:12	**R** the wonders he has done,
Ne	5:19	**R** me with favor, my God, for all I
	13:31	**R** me with favor, my God.
Job	10: 9	**R** that you molded me like clay.
	36:24	**R** to extol his work, which people
Ps	25: 6	**R**, Lord, your great mercy
	63: 6	On my bed I **r** you; I think of you
	74: 2	**R** the nation you purchased long
	77:11	I will **r** the deeds of the Lord;
Ecc	12: 1	**R** your Creator in the days of your
Isa	46: 8	"**R** this, keep it in mind, take it
	64: 9	do not **r** our sins forever.
Jer	31:34	and will **r** their sins no more."
La	1: 1	**R**, Lord, what has happened
Eze	36:31	Then you will **r** your evil ways
Hos	7: 2	realize that I **r** all their evil deeds.
Hab	3: 2	in wrath **r** mercy.
Mk	8:18	but fail to hear? And don't you **r?**
Lk	1:72	and to **r** his holy covenant,
	17:32	**R** Lot's wife!
	23:42	**r** me when you come into your
Gal	2:10	we should continue to **r** the poor,
Php	1: 3	I thank my God every time I **r** you.
2Ti	2: 8	**R** Jesus Christ, raised from the dead,
Heb	8:12	and will **r** their sins no more."
Jas	5:20	**r** this. Whoever turns a sinner
Rev	3: 3	**R**, therefore, what you have

REMEMBERED REMEMBER

Ge	8: 1	But God **r** Noah and all the wild
	19:29	cities of the plain, he **r** Abraham,
	30:22	Then God **r** Rachel; he listened
Ex	2:24	he **r** his covenant with Abraham,
	6: 5	and I have **r** my covenant.
1Sa	1:19	wife Hannah, and the Lord **r** her.
Ps	78:35	They **r** that God was their Rock,
	98: 3	He has **r** his love and his
	106:45	for their sake he **r** his covenant
	111: 4	He has caused his wonders to be **r;**
	136:23	He **r** us in our low estate,
Isa	17:10	you have not **r** the Rock,
	65:17	The former things will not be **r**,
Eze	18:22	committed will be **r** against them.
	33:13	that person has done will be **r;**
Mt	26:75	Peter **r** the word Jesus had spoken:
Jn	2:17	His disciples **r** that it is written:
Rev	16:19	God **r** Babylon the Great and gave
	18: 5	heaven, and God has **r** her crimes.

REMEMBERS REMEMBER

1Ch	16:15	He **r** his covenant forever,
Ps	103:14	are formed, he **r** that we are dust.

Ps 111: 5 he **r** his covenant forever.
Isa 43:25 own sake, and **r** your sins no more.

REMEMBRANCE REMEMBER
Lk 22:19 given for you; do this in **r** of me."
1Co 11:24 is for you; do this in **r** of me."

REMIND REMINDER
Jn 14:26 will **r** you of everything I have said
2Pe 1:12 So I will always **r** you of these

REMINDER REMIND
Ex 13: 9 a **r** on your forehead that this law
Heb 10: 3 those sacrifices are an annual **r**

REMISSION (KJV) See
FORGIVENESS

REMNANT
Ge 45: 7 you to preserve for you a **r** on earth
2Ki 19:31 For out of Jerusalem will come a **r**,
2Ch 36:20 carried into exile to Babylon the **r**,
Ezr 9: 8 has been gracious in leaving us a **r**
Ne 1: 2 the Jewish **r** that had survived
Isa 10:21 A **r** will return, a **r** of Jacob will
         11:11 reclaim the surviving **r** of his people
Jer 23: 3 "I myself will gather the **r** of my
         50:20 for I will forgive the **r** I spare.
Zec 8:12 inheritance to the **r** of this people.
Ro 9:27 by the sea, only the **r** will be saved.
         11: 5 the present time there is a **r** chosen

REMOTE
Lev 16:22 on itself all their sins to a **r** place;

REMOVAL* REMOVE
Isa 27: 9 be the full fruit of the **r** of his sin:
1Pe 3:21 not the **r** of dirt from the body

REMOVE REMOVAL, REMOVED
Ex 12:15 the first day **r** the yeast from your
Job 9:34 someone to **r** God's rod from me,
Ps 39:10 **R** your scourge from me;
         119:22 **R** from me their scorn
Isa 1:25 your dross and **r** all your impurities.
Eze 36:26 I will **r** from you your heart of stone
Zec 3: 9 'and I will **r** the sin of this land
Lk 6:42 you will see clearly to **r** the speck

REMOVED REMOVE
2Ki 17:18 Israel and **r** them from his presence.
Ps 30:11 you **r** my sackcloth and clothed me
         103:12 so far has he **r** our transgressions
Jn 20: 1 that the stone had been **r**
2Co 3:14 It has not been **r**, because only
Rev 6:14 and island was **r** from its place.

REND*
Isa 64: 1 that you would **r** the heavens
Joel 2:13 **R** your heart and not your garments.

RENEW RENEWAL, RENEWED,
RENEWING
Ps 51:10 and **r** a steadfast spirit within me.
Isa 40:31 in the LORD will **r** their strength.
La 5:21 we may return; **r** our days as of old

RENEWAL* RENEW
Job 14:14 service I will wait for my **r** to come.
Isa 57:10 You found **r** of your strength,
Mt 19:28 at the **r** of all things, when the Son
Titus 3: 5 of rebirth and **r** by the Holy Spirit,

RENEWED RENEW
2Ch 34:31 **r** the covenant in the presence
Ps 103: 5 that your youth is **r** like the eagle's.
2Co 4:16 yet inwardly we are being **r** day
Col 3:10 which is being **r** in knowledge

RENEWING* RENEW
Ro 12: 2 transformed by the **r** of your mind.

RENOUNCE* RENOUNCED,
RENOUNCES
Eze 14: 6 and **r** all your detestable practices!
Da 4:27 **R** your sins by doing what is right,
Rev 2:13 You did not **r** your faith in me,

RENOUNCED* RENOUNCE
Ps 89:39 You have **r** the covenant with your
2Co 4: 2 we have **r** secret and shameful

RENOUNCES* RENOUNCE
Pr 28:13 confesses and **r** them finds mercy.

RENOWN*
Ge 6: 4 were the heroes of old, men of **r**.
Ps 102:12 your **r** endures through all
         135:13 endures forever, your **r**, LORD,
Isa 26: 8 and **r** are the desire of our hearts.
         55:13 This will be for the LORD's **r**,
         63:12 to gain for himself everlasting **r**,
Jer 13:11 'to be my people for my **r**
         32:20 have gained the **r** that is still yours.
         33: 9 Then this city will bring me **r**, joy,
         49:25 the city of **r** not been abandoned,
Eze 26:17 city of **r**, peopled by men of the sea!

REPAID PAY
Pr 14:14 The faithless will be fully **r** for their
Jer 18:20 Should good be **r** with evil?
Lk 6:34 to sinners, expecting to be **r** in full.
         14:14 you will be **r** at the resurrection
Col 3:25 Anyone who does wrong will be **r**

REPAIR REPAIRED, REPAIRER,
REPAIRING
2Ch 24: 5 Israel, to **r** the temple of your God.
Ezr 9: 9 the house of our God and **r** its ruins,
Am 9:11 I will **r** its broken walls and restore

REPAIRED REPAIR
2Ch 15: 8 He **r** the altar of the LORD
         29: 3 temple of the LORD and **r** them.
Ne 3: 4 son of Hakkoz, **r** the next section.
Jer 19:11 jar is smashed and cannot be **r**.

REPAIRER* REPAIR
Isa 58:12 you will be called **R** of Broken

REPAIRING REPAIR
2Ki 12: 7 but hand it over for **r** the temple."
Ezr 4:12 the walls and **r** the foundations.

REPAY PAY

Dt   7:10 he will not be slow to **r** to their face
    32: 6 Is this the way you **r** the LORD,
    32:35 It is mine to avenge; I will **r**.
Ru   2:12 May the LORD **r** you for what you
Ps   28: 4 **R** them for their deeds and for their
    35:12 They **r** me evil for good and leave
  103:10 or **r** us according to our iniquities.
Isa   59:18 so will he **r** wrath to his enemies
Jer   25:14 I will **r** them according to their
    51:56 God of retribution; he will **r** in full.
Eze   7: 3 and **r** you for all your detestable
Joel   2:25 "I will **r** you for the years
Ro   12:17 Do not **r** anyone evil for evil.
    12:19 I will **r**," says the Lord.
Heb 10:30 I will **r**," and again, "The Lord will
1Pe   3: 9 Do not **r** evil with evil or insult
    3: 9 the contrary, **r** evil with blessing,
Rev   2:23 and I will **r** each of you according

REPAYING PAY

1Ti   5: 4 own family and so **r** their parents

REPEALED

Est   1:19 which cannot be **r**, that Vashti is
Da   6: 8 and Persians, which cannot be **r**."

REPEAT REPEATS, REPEATED

Pr   26:11 to its vomit, so fools **r** their folly.
Hab   3: 2 **R** them in our day, in our time make

REPEATED REPEAT

Heb 10: 1 the same sacrifices **r** endlessly year

REPEATS* REPEAT

Pr   17: 9 whoever **r** the matter separates close

REPENT PENITENT, REPENTANCE, REPENTED, REPENTS

1Ki   8:47 and **r** and plead with you in the land
Job 36:10 commands them to **r** of their evil.
    42: 6 I despise myself and **r** in dust
Isa   59:20 those in Jacob who **r** of their sins,"
Jer   8: 6 None of them **r** of their wickedness,
    15:19 "If you **r**, I will restore you that you
Eze 18:32 the Sovereign LORD. **R** and live!
Mt   3: 2 and saying, "**R**, for the kingdom
    4:17 time on Jesus began to preach, "**R**,
Mk   6:12 and preached that people should **r**.
Lk   13: 3 But unless you **r**, you too will all
    17: 3 and if they **r**, forgive them.
Ac   2:38 Peter replied, "**R** and be baptized,
    3:19 **R**, then, and turn to God,
    17:30 all people everywhere to **r**.
    26:20 I preached that they should **r**
Rev   2: 5 If you do not **r**, I will come to you
    2:21 I have given her time to **r** of her
    9:20 by these plagues still did not **r**
    16: 9 they refused to **r** and glorify him.

REPENTANCE REPENT

Isa   30:15 "In **r** and rest is your salvation,
Mt   3: 8 Produce fruit in keeping with **r**.
Mk   1: 4 preaching a baptism of **r**
Lk   3: 8 Produce fruit in keeping with **r**.

Lk   5:32 call the righteous, but sinners to **r**."
    24:47 **r** for the forgiveness of sins will be
Ac   5:31 that he might bring Israel to **r**
    11:18 to Gentiles God has granted **r**
    20:21 that they must turn to God in **r**
    26:20 demonstrate their **r** by their deeds.
Ro   2: 4 is intended to lead you to **r**?
2Co   7:10 Godly sorrow brings **r** that leads
2Ti   2:25 God will grant them **r** leading them
Heb   6: 1 not laying again the foundation of **r**
2Pe   3: 9 to perish, but everyone to come to **r**.

REPENTED REPENT

2Ch 32:26 Hezekiah **r** of the pride of his heart,
Zec   1: 6 "Then they **r** and said,
Mt   11:21 they would have **r** long ago
Lk   11:32 for they **r** at the preaching of Jonah;

REPENTS* REPENT

Eze 33:12 And if someone who is wicked **r**,
Jer   18: 8 if that nation I warned **r** of its evil,
Lk   15: 7 over one sinner who **r** than over
    15:10 of God over one sinner who **r**."

REPHAITES

Ge   15:20 Hittites, Perizzites, **R**,
Dt   2:11 they too were considered **R**,
1Ch 20: 4 one of the descendants of the **R**,

REPLANTED* PLANT

Eze 36:36 and have **r** what was desolate.

REPLY

Pr   15:23 person finds joy in giving an apt **r**—
Mt   27:14 But Jesus made no **r**, not even

REPORT REPORTS

Ge   37: 2 he brought their father a bad **r**
Nu   13:32 spread among the Israelites a bad **r**
1Ki 10: 7 you have far exceeded the **r** I heard.
Lk   7:22 and **r** to John what you have seen

REPORTS REPORT

Ex   23: 1 "Do not spread false **r**. Do not help
Mt   14: 1 time Herod the tetrarch heard the **r**
Ac   9:13 "I have heard many **r** about this

REPOSES*

Pr   14:33 Wisdom **r** in the heart

REPRESENT REPRESENTATION

Da   8:22 was broken off **r** four kingdoms
Gal   4:24 The women **r** two covenants.
Heb   5: 1 and is appointed to **r** the people

REPRESENTATION* REPRESENT

Heb   1: 3 glory and the exact **r** of his being,

REPRIMAND*

Ru   2:15 among the sheaves and don't **r** her.
Pr   29:15 A rod and a **r** impart wisdom,

REPROACH

Jos   5: 9 "Today I have rolled away the **r**
Job 27: 6 my conscience will not **r** me as long
Isa   51: 7 Do not fear the **r** of mere mortals
Jer   20: 8 brought me insult and **r** all day long.

1Ti 3: 2 Now the overseer is to be above r,

REPROVE*
1Ti 5:20 you are to r before everyone,

REPUTATION
1Ti 3: 7 also have a good r with outsiders,
Rev 3: 1 you have a r of being alive, but you

REQUEST REQUESTS
Est 7: 3 And spare my people—this is my r.
Ps 21: 2 have not withheld the r of his lips.

REQUESTS REQUEST
Ps 20: 5 May the LORD grant all your r.
Php 4: 6 thanksgiving, present your r to God.

REQUIRE REQUIRED, REQUIREMENT, REQUIREMENTS, REQUIRES
Ps 40: 6 and sin offerings you did not r.
Mic 6: 8 what does the LORD r of you?

REQUIRED REQUIRE
Ac 15: 5 and r to keep the law of Moses."
Ro 2:14 do by nature things r by the law,
1Co 4: 2 Now it is r that those who have

REQUIREMENT REQUIRE
Ro 8: 4 the righteous r of the law might be

REQUIREMENTS REQUIRE
Dt 11: 1 LORD your God and keep his r,
2Ki 23:24 did to fulfill the r of the law written
Jer 8: 7 my people do not know the r
Ro 2:15 that the r of the law are written

REQUIRES REQUIRE
1Ki 2: 3 what the LORD your God r:
Jn 6:28 we do to do the works God r?"
Heb 9:22 the law r that nearly everything be

RESCUE RESCUED, RESCUES
Ge 37:21 he tried to r him from their hands.
Ex 3: 8 So I have come down to r them
Dt 28:29 and robbed, with no one to r you.
1Sa 17:37 of the bear will r me from the hand
Job 5:19 From six calamities he will r you;
Ps 22: 8 they say, "let the LORD r him.
31: 2 ear to me, come quickly to my r;
34:22 The LORD will r his servants;
35:10 You r the poor from those too
44:26 r us because of your unfailing love.
69:14 R me from the mire, do not let me
82: 4 R the weak and the needy;
91:14 says the LORD, "I will r him;
143: 9 R me from my enemies, LORD,
Isa 31: 5 he will 'pass over' it and will r it."
Jer 1: 8 for I am with you and will r you,"
Eze 34:10 I will r my flock from their mouths,
Da 6:20 been able to r you from the lions?"
Mt 27:43 Let God r him now if he wants him,
Ro 7:24 Who will r me from this body
Gal 1: 4 our sins to r us from the present evil
2Pe 2: 9 the Lord knows how to r the godly

RESCUED RESCUE
Ex 18:10 who r the people from the hand
1Sa 11:13 this day the LORD has r Israel."
17:37 The LORD who r me
Ps 18:17 He r me from my powerful enemy,
81: 7 your distress you called and I r you,
Pr 11: 8 The righteous person is r
Isa 35:10 those the LORD has r will return.
51:11 Those the LORD has r will return.
Da 3:28 sent his angel and r his servants!
6:27 He has r Daniel from the power
Ac 12:11 and r me from Herod's clutches
Col 1:13 For he has r us from the dominion

RESCUES* RESCUE
1Sa 14:39 as the LORD who r Israel lives,
Ps 55:18 He r me unharmed from the battle
Pr 12: 6 but the speech of the upright r them.
Jer 20:13 He r the life of the needy
Da 6:27 He r and he saves;
Am 3:12 a shepherd r from the lion's mouth
1Th 1:10 who r us from the coming wrath.

RESEMBLED* RESEMBLING
Rev 9: 7 gold, and their faces r human faces.
9:17 The heads of the horses r the heads
13: 2 The beast I saw r a leopard, but had

RESEMBLING* RESEMBLED
Heb 7: 3 or end of life, r the Son of God,

RESENT* RESENTFUL, RESENTMENT
Pr 3:11 discipline, and do not r his rebuke,
15:12 Mockers r correction, so they avoid

RESENTFUL* RESENT
2Ti 2:24 to everyone, able to teach, not r.

RESENTMENT RESENT
Job 5: 2 R kills a fool, and envy slays
36:13 "The godless in heart harbor r;

RESERVE RESERVED
1Ki 19:18 Yet I r seven thousand in Israel—

RESERVED RESERVE
Ge 27:36 "Haven't you r any blessing
Ro 11: 4 "I have r for myself seven thousand
2Pe 2:17 Blackest darkness is r for them.
3: 7 heavens and earth are r for fire,

RESETTLE* SETTLE
1Ch 9: 2 Now the first to r on their own
Eze 36:33 all your sins, I will r your towns,

RESIDED
Ex 6: 4 Canaan, where they r as foreigners.

RESIST RESISTED
Jdg 2:14 whom they were no longer able to r.
Pr 28: 4 but those who heed it r them.
Da 11:32 know their God will firmly r him.
Mt 5:39 I tell you, do not r an evil person.
Lk 21:15 of your adversaries will be able to r
Ac 7:51 You always r the Holy Spirit!

Ro   9:19 For who is able to **r** his will?"
Jas   4: 7 **R** the devil, and he will flee
1Pe   5: 9 **R** him, standing firm in the faith,

RESISTED* RESIST
Job   9: 4 Who has **r** him and come
Da   10:13 Persian kingdom **r** me twenty-one
Heb 12: 4 you have not yet **r** to the point

RESOLVE* RESOLVED
Mal   2: 2 if you do not **r** to honor my name,"

RESOLVED* RESOLVE
2Ch 20: 3 Jehoshaphat **r** to inquire
Da   1: 8 Daniel **r** not to defile himself
Mal   2: 2 because you have not **r** to honor me.
1Co   2: 2 For I **r** to know nothing while I was

RESOUND RESOUNDED, RESOUNDING
Ps   98: 7 Let the sea **r**, and everything in it,
    118:15 joy and victory **r** in the tents

RESOUNDED* RESOUND
2Sa 22:14 the voice of the Most High **r**.
Ps   18:13 the voice of the Most High **r**.
     77:17 water, the heavens **r** with thunder;

RESOUNDING* RESOUND
2Ch 30:21 day with **r** instruments dedicated
Ps 150: 5 cymbals, praise him with **r** cymbals.
1Co 13: 1 I am only a **r** gong or a clanging

RESPECT RESPECTABLE, RESPECTED, RESPECTS
Lev 19: 3 of you must **r** your mother
     19:32 show **r** for the elderly and revere
Mal   1: 6 a master, where is the **r** due me?"
Mk   12: 6 of all, saying, 'They will **r** my son.'
Ro   13: 7 If revenue, then revenue; if **r**, then **r**;
Eph   5:33 and the wife must **r** her husband.
      6: 5 obey your earthly masters with **r**
1Th   4:12 that your daily life may win the **r**
1Ti   3: 4 do so in a manner worthy of full **r**.
      3: 8 way, deacons are to be worthy of **r**,
      3:11 the women are to be worthy of **r**,
      6: 1 their masters worthy of full **r**,
Titus 2: 2 worthy of **r**, self-controlled,
1Pe   2:17 Show proper **r** to everyone,
      3: 7 them with **r** as the weaker partner

RESPECTABLE* RESPECT
1Ti   3: 2 self-controlled, **r**, hospitable,

RESPECTED RESPECT
Dt   1:13 and **r** men from each of your tribes,
Pr   31:23 Her husband is **r** at the city gate,
Heb 12: 9 disciplined us and we **r** them for it.

RESPECTS RESPECT
Pr   13:13 whoever **r** a command is rewarded.

RESPOND RESPONSE
2Ch 32:25 he did not **r** to the kindness shown
Ps 102:17 He will **r** to the prayer
Pr   13: 1 but a mocker does not **r** to rebukes.

Isa 19:22 and he will **r** to their pleas and heal
Jer   2:30 they did not **r** to correction.
     17:23 would not listen or **r** to discipline.
Hos   2:21 "I will **r** to the skies, and they will **r**
Ac   16:14 The Lord opened her heart to **r**

RESPONSE RESPOND
1Ki 18:26 But there was no **r**;
1Ch 29: 9 at the willing **r** of their leaders,

RESPONSIBILITIES RESPONSIBLE
Nu   8:26 are to assign the **r** of the Levites."

RESPONSIBILITY RESPONSIBLE
Mt   27:24 blood," he said. "It is your **r**!"

RESPONSIBLE RESPONSIBILITIES, RESPONSIBILITY
Nu   1:53 The Levites are to be **r** for the care
     14:37 these men who were **r** for spreading
Jnh   1: 8 who is **r** for making all this trouble
Lk   11:50 this generation will be held **r**
1Co   7:24 each person, as **r** to God,

REST RESTED, RESTING, RESTLESS, RESTS, SABBATH-REST
Ge   8: 4 the seventh month the ark came to **r**
Ex   16:23 is to be a day of sabbath **r**, a holy
     31:15 seventh day is a day of sabbath **r**,
     33:14 go with you, and I will give you **r**."
Lev 23:24 you are to have a day of sabbath **r**,
     25: 4 land is to have a year of sabbath **r**,
     25: 5 The land is to have a year of **r**.
Nu   10:36 Whenever it came to **r**, he said,
Dt   12:10 and he will give you **r** from all your
Jos   1:13 LORD your God will give you **r**
     11:23 Then the land had **r** from war.
     14:15 Then the land had **r** from war.
     21:44 The LORD gave them **r** on every
2Sa   7:11 give you **r** from all your enemies.
1Ki   5: 4 the LORD my God has given me **r**
1Ch 22: 9 who will be a man of peace and **r**, and
            I will give him **r** from all
     28: 2 build a house as a place of **r**
Job   3:17 and there the weary are at **r**.
Ps   16: 9 my body also will **r** secure,
     62: 1 Truly my soul finds **r** in God;
     62: 5 Yes, my soul, find **r** in God;
     90:17 favor of the Lord our God **r** on us;
     91: 1 the Most High will **r** in the shadow
     95:11 'They shall never enter my **r**.' "
Pr   6:10 a little folding of the hands to **r**—
Isa 11: 2 Spirit of the LORD will **r** on him—
     30:15 repentance and **r** is your salvation,
     32:18 homes, in undisturbed places of **r**.
     44:17 From the **r** he makes a god, his idol;
     57:20 which cannot **r**, whose waves cast
Jer 16:16 it, and you will find **r** for your souls.
     47: 6 of the LORD, how long till you **r**?
Mt   11:28 and burdened, and I will give you **r**.
Mk   6:31 to a quiet place and get some **r**."
1Co   2: 5 your faith might not **r** on human
2Co 12: 9 so that Christ's power may **r** on me.
1Th   4:13 that you do not grieve like the **r**

Heb 3:11 'They shall never enter my r.' "
  4: 3 we who have believed enter that r,
  4:10 for anyone who enters God's r
Rev 14:11 There will be no r day or night
  14:13 Spirit, "they will r from their labor,

RESTED REST
Ge 2: 2 on the seventh day he r from all his
Ex 16:30 So the people r on the seventh day.
  20:11 in them, but he r on the seventh day.
  31:17 seventh day he r and was refreshed.' "
Nu 11:25 When the Spirit r on them,
2Ch 36:21 all the time of its desolation it r,
Heb 4: 4 the seventh day God r from all his

RESTING REST
2Ki 2:15 spirit of Elijah is r on Elisha."
Ps 132: 8 and come to your r place,
Isa 11:10 and his r place will be glorious.
  28:12 "This is the r place, let the weary

RESTITUTION
Ex 22: 3 who steals must certainly make r,
Lev 6: 5 They must make r in full, add a fifth
Nu 5: 8 the r belongs to the LORD

RESTLESS REST
Ge 4:12 You will be a r wanderer
Jas 3: 8 It is a r evil, full of deadly poison.

RESTORATION RESTORE
2Co 13:11 Strive for full r, encourage one

RESTORE RESTORATION,
  RESTORED, RESTORES
Dt 30: 3 your God will r your fortunes
2Ch 24: 4 later Joash decided to r the temple
Ne 4: 2 Will they r their wall?
Ps 51:12 R to me the joy of your salvation
  80: 3 R us, O God; make your face shine
  126: 4 R our fortunes, LORD,
Isa 49: 6 to be my servant to r the tribes
Jer 15:19 I will r you that you may serve me;
  31:18 R me, and I will return, because you
La 5:21 R us to yourself, LORD, that we
Da 9:25 the time the word goes out to r
Hos 6: 2 on the third day he will r us, that we
Am 9:11 "In that day "I will r David's fallen
Na 2: 2 The LORD will r the splendor
Zec 9:12 announce that I will r twice as much
Mt 17:11 Elijah comes and will r all things.
Ac 1: 6 this time going to r the kingdom
  15:16 ruins I will rebuild, and I will r it,
Gal 6: 1 by the Spirit should r that person
1Pe 5:10 will himself r you and make you

RESTORED RESTORE
Ex 4: 7 it was r, like the rest of his flesh.
2Ki 5:10 your flesh will be r and you will be
Job 42:10 the LORD r his fortunes and gave
Ps 85: 1 you r the fortunes of Jacob.
Eze 21:27 The crown will not be r until he
Mk 3: 5 out, and his hand was completely r.
  8:25 opened, his sight was r, and he saw

2Co 13: 9 prayer is that you may be fully r.

RESTORES* RESTORE
Ps 14: 7 When the LORD r his people,
  41: 3 and r them from their bed of illness.
  53: 6 When God r his people, let Jacob
Mk 9:12 does come first, and r all things.

RESTRAIN RESTRAINED,
  RESTRAINING, RESTRAINT
Job 9:13 God does not r his anger;

RESTRAINED RESTRAIN
Ps 78:38 Time after time he r his anger
2Pe 2:16 voice and r the prophet's madness.

RESTRAINING* RESTRAIN
Pr 27:16 r her is like r the wind or
Col 2:23 any value in r sensual indulgence.

RESTRAINT RESTRAIN
Pr 17:27 has knowledge uses words with r,
  29:18 is no revelation, people cast off r;

RESTS REST
Dt 33:12 one the LORD loves r between his
2Ch 28:11 for the LORD's fierce anger r
  36:21 The land enjoyed its sabbath r;
Pr 19:23 then one r content,
Lk 2:14 to those on whom his favor r."
1Pe 4:14 Spirit of glory and of God r on you.

RESULT RESULTED
Nu 25:18 when the plague came as a r
Ezr 9:13 to us is a r of our evil deeds and our
Ro 6:22 to holiness, and the r is eternal life.
  11:31 too may now receive mercy as a r
2Co 3: 3 from Christ, the r of our ministry,
2Th 1: 5 as a r you will be counted worthy
1Pe 1: 7 may r in praise, glory and honor
  1: 9 you are receiving the end r of your

RESULTED* RESULT
Ro 5:18 as one trespass r in condemnation
  5:18 one righteous act r in justification

RESURRECTION*
Mt 22:23 who say there is no r, came to him
  22:28 at the r, whose wife will she be
  22:30 the r people will neither marry nor
  22:31 But about the r of the dead—
  27:53 came out of the tombs after Jesus' r
Mk 12:18 who say there is no r, came to him
  12:23 At the r whose wife will she be,
Lk 14:14 be repaid at the r of the righteous."
  20:27 who say there is no r, came to Jesus
  20:33 at the r whose wife will she be,
  20:35 in the r from the dead will neither
  20:36 since they are children of the r.
Jn 11:24 rise again in the r at the last day."
  11:25 said to her, "I am the r and the life.
Ac 1:22 become a witness with us of his r."
  2:31 he spoke of the r of the Messiah,
  4: 2 in Jesus the r of the dead.
  4:33 to testify to the r of the Lord Jesus.
  17:18 good news about Jesus and the r.

Ac   17:32 they heard about the **r** of the dead,
     23: 6 of the hope of the **r** of the dead."
     23: 8 Sadducees say that there is no **r**,
     24:15 that there will be a **r** of both
     24:21 'It is concerning the **r** of the dead
Ro   1: 4 in power by his **r** from the dead:
      6: 5 be united with him in a **r** like his.
1Co 15:12 say that there is no **r** of the dead?
     15:13 If there is no **r** of the dead, then not
     15:21 the **r** of the dead comes also through
     15:29 Now if there is no **r**, what will those
     15:42 So will it be with the **r** of the dead.
Php   3:10 yes, to know the power of his **r**
      3:11 attaining to the **r** from the dead.
2Ti   2:18 that the **r** has already taken place,
Heb   6: 2 on of hands, the **r** of the dead,
     11:35 they might gain an even better **r**.
1Pe   1: 3 a living hope through the **r** of Jesus
      3:21 It saves you by the **r** of Jesus Christ,
Rev 20: 5 This is the first **r**.
     20: 6 are those who share in the first **r**.

RETAIN
Lk   8:15 who hear the word, **r** it,

RETALIATE*
1Pe   2:23 their insults at him, he did not **r**;

RETIRE*
Nu   8:25 fifty, they must **r** from their regular

RETREAT
Ps   44:10 You made us **r** before the enemy,
     74:21 Do not let the oppressed **r**

RETRIBUTION*
Ps   69:22 may it become **r** and a trap.
Isa 34: 8 a year of **r**, to uphold Zion's cause.
     35: 4 with divine **r** he will come to save
     59:18 to his enemies and **r** to his foes,
Jer 51:56 For the LORD is a God of **r**;
Ro   11: 9 a stumbling block and a **r** for them.

RETURN RETURNED, RETURNS
Ge   3:19 you are and to dust you will **r**."
     18:10 "I will surely **r** to you about this
     29:18 for you seven years in **r** for your
Lev 25:10 you is to **r** to your family property
Nu   10:36 came to rest, he said, "**R**, LORD,
Dt   30: 2 your children **r** to the LORD your
2Sa 12:23 go to him, but he will not **r** to me."
2Ch 30: 9 If you **r** to the LORD, then your
Ne   1: 9 but if you **r** to me and obey my
Job 10:21 before I go to the place of no **r**,
     16:22 pass before I take the path of no **r**.
     22:23 If you **r** to the Almighty, you will
Ps   80:14 **R** to us, God Almighty!
     90: 3 saying, "**R** to dust, you mortals."
    116:12 What shall I **r** to the LORD for all
    126: 6 to sow, will **r** with songs of joy,
Pr   2:19 None who go to her **r** or attain
Ecc   3:20 all come from dust, and to dust all **r**.
Isa 10:21 A remnant will **r**, a remnant
     35:10 the LORD has rescued will **r**.
     44:22 **R** to me, for I have redeemed you."

Isa 55:11 It will not **r** to me empty, but will
Jer   3:12 " '**R**, faithless Israel,'
      4: 1 Israel, will **r**, then **r** to me,"
     24: 7 for they will **r** to me with all their
     31: 8 a great throng will **r**.
     31:22 the woman will **r** to the man."
La   3:40 them, and let us **r** to the LORD.
Hos   5: 4 deeds do not permit them to **r**
      6: 1 "Come, let us **r** to the LORD.
     12: 6 But you must **r** to your God;
     14: 1 **R**, Israel, to the LORD your God.
Joel 2:12 "**r** to me with all your heart,
Zec   1: 3 '**R** to me,' declares the LORD
             Almighty, 'and I will **r** to you,'
     10: 9 will survive, and they will **r**.
Mal   3: 7 **R** to me, and I will **r** to you,"
Ro   9: 9 "At the appointed time I will **r**,

RETURNED RETURN
Ge   8: 9 so it **r** to Noah in the ark.
Nu   13:25 forty days they **r** from exploring
1Ki 17:22 and the boy's life **r** to him, and he
Ezr   2: 1 to Babylon (they **r** to Jerusalem
Ps   35:13 my prayers **r** to me unanswered,
Am   4: 6 town, yet you have not **r** to me,"
Mt   27: 3 **r** the thirty pieces of silver
Ro   14: 9 **r** to life so that he might be the Lord
1Pe   2:25 but now you have **r** to the Shepherd

RETURNS RETURN
Pr   3:14 silver and yields better **r** than gold.
     26:11 As a dog **r** to its vomit, so fools
Ecc 12: 7 and the spirit **r** to God who gave it.
Isa 52: 8 When the LORD **r** to Zion,
Mt   24:46 finds him doing so when he **r**.
2Pe   2:22 "A dog **r** to its vomit," and,
      2:22 that is washed **r** to her wallowing

REUBEN REUBENITES
Firstborn of Jacob by Leah (Ge 29:32; 46:8; 1Ch 2:1). Attempted to rescue Joseph (Ge 37:21–30). Lost birthright for sleeping with Bilhah (Ge 35:22; 49:4). Tribe of blessed (Ge 49:3–4; Dt 33:6), numbered (Nu 1:21; 26:7), allotted land east of Jordan (Nu 32; 34:14; Jos 13:15), west (Eze 48:6), failed to help Deborah (Jdg 5:15–16), supported David (1Ch 12:37), 12,000 from (Rev 7:5).

REUBENITES REUBEN
Nu   32: 1 The **R** and Gadites, who had very
Dt   29: 8 gave it as an inheritance to the **R**,
Jos 13: 8 the **R** and the Gadites had received

REUEL See JETHRO

REVEAL REVEALED, REVEALS, REVELATION, REVELATIONS
Nu   12: 6 **r** myself to them in visions, I speak
Ps   19: 2 night after night they **r** knowledge.
Da   2:11 No one can **r** it to the king except
Mt   11:27 to whom the Son chooses to **r** him.
Gal   1:16 to **r** his Son in me so that I might

REVEALED REVEAL
Dt   29:29 but the things **r** belong to us

Est 2:10 Esther had not r her nationality
Isa 40: 5 the glory of the LORD will be r,
43:12 I have r and saved and proclaimed—
53: 1 has the arm of the LORD been r?
65: 1 "I r myself to those who did not ask
Da 2:19 During the night the mystery was r
Mt 11:25 and r them to little children.
16:17 for this was not r to you by flesh
Lk 17:30 this on the day the Son of Man is r.
Jn 2:11 signs through which he r his glory;
12:38 has the arm of the Lord been r?"
17: 6 "I have r you to those whom you
Ro 1:17 the righteousness of God is r—
8:18 with the glory that will be r in us.
10:20 I r myself to those who did not ask
16:26 now r and made known through
1Co 2:10 these are the things God has r to us
3:13 It will be r with fire, and the fire
2Co 4:11 may also be r in our mortal body.
Eph 3: 5 generations as it has now been r
2Th 1: 7 the Lord Jesus is r from heaven
2: 3 and the man of lawlessness is r,
1Pe 1: 7 and honor when Jesus Christ is r.
1:20 but was r in these last times for your
4:13 be overjoyed when his glory is r.
Rev 15: 4 your righteous acts have been r."

REVEALS* REVEAL
Nu 23: 3 Whatever he r to me I will tell
Job 12:22 He r the deep things of darkness
Da 2:22 He r deep and hidden things;
2:28 is a God in heaven who r mysteries.
Am 4:13 and who r his thoughts to mankind,

REVELATION* REVEAL
2Sa 7:17 David all the words of this entire r.
1Ch 17:15 David all the words of this entire r.
Pr 29:18 Where there is no r, people cast off
Da 10: 1 a r was given to Daniel (who was
Hab 2: 2 "Write down the r and make it
2: 3 For the r awaits an appointed time;
Lk 2:32 a light for r to the Gentiles,
Ro 16:25 with the r of the mystery hidden
1Co 14: 6 to you, unless I bring you some r
14:26 a r, a tongue or an interpretation.
14:30 And if a r comes to someone who is
Gal 1:12 I received it by r from Jesus Christ.
2: 2 I went in response to a r and,
Eph 1:17 give you the Spirit of wisdom and r,
3: 3 mystery made known to me by r,
Rev 1: 1 The r from Jesus Christ, which God

REVELATIONS* REVEAL
2Co 12: 1 on to visions and r from the Lord.
12: 7 of these surpassingly great r.

REVELED* REVELRY
Ne 9:25 they r in your great goodness.
Ac 7:41 r in what their own hands had made.

REVELING REVELRY
2Pe 2:13 r in their pleasures while they feast

REVELRY REVELED, REVELING
Ex 32: 6 and drink and got up to indulge in r.

1Co 10: 7 drink and got up to indulge in r."
Zep 2:15 This is the city of r that lived

REVENGE VENGEANCE
Lev 19:18 " 'Do not seek r or bear a grudge
Jdg 16:28 one blow get r on the Philistines
Ro 12:19 Do not take r, my dear friends,

REVENUE
Ro 13: 7 owe taxes, pay taxes; if r, then r;

REVERE* REVERED, REVERENCE, REVERENT, REVERING
Lev 19:32 for the elderly and r your God.
Dt 4:10 learn to r me as long as they live
13: 4 must follow, and him you must r.
14:23 to r the LORD your God always.
17:19 may learn to r the LORD his God
28:58 book, and do not r this glorious
Job 37:24 Therefore, people r him, for does he
Ps 22:23 R him, all you descendants
33: 8 let all the people of the world r him.
102:15 kings of the earth will r your glory.
Isa 25: 3 cities of ruthless nations will r you.
59:19 of the sun, they will r his glory.
63:17 our hearts so we do not r you?
Hos 10: 3 because we did not r the LORD.
Mal 4: 2 But for you who r my name, the sun
1Pe 3:15 But in your hearts r Christ as Lord.
Rev 11:18 and your people who r your name,

REVERED REVERE
Mal 2: 5 called for reverence and he r me

REVERENCE REVERE
Lev 19:30 and have r for my sanctuary.
Ne 5:15 of r for God I did not act like that.
Ps 5: 7 in r I bow down toward your holy
Jer 44:10 not humbled themselves or shown r,
Da 6:26 must fear and r the God of Daniel.
2Co 7: 1 perfecting holiness out of r for God.
Eph 5:21 to one another out of r for Christ.
Col 3:22 sincerity of heart and r for the Lord.
1Pe 3: 2 see the purity and r of your lives.

REVERENT* REVERE
Ecc 8:12 fear God, who are r before him.
Titus 2: 3 women to be r in the way they live,
Heb 5: 7 heard because of his r submission.
1Pe 1:17 time as foreigners here in r fear.
2:18 in r fear of God submit yourselves

REVERING* REVERE
Dt 8: 6 in obedience to him and r him.
Ne 1:11 who delight in r your name.

REVERSE*
Isa 43:13 When I act, who can r it?"

REVILE
Ps 10:13 Why does the wicked man r God?
74:10 Will the foe r your name forever?

REVIVE*
Ps 80:18 r us, and we will call on your name.
85: 6 Will you not r us again, that your

Isa 57:15 to **r** the spirit of the lowly and to **r** the
               heart of the contrite.
Hos   6: 2 After two days he will **r** us;

REVOKE* REVOKED, REVOKING
Ps 132:11 to David, a sure oath he will not **r**:

REVOKED* REVOKE
Est   8: 8 and sealed with his ring can be **r**."
Isa 45:23 integrity a word that will not be **r**:
Zec 11:11 It was **r** on that day, and so

REVOKING* REVOKE
Zec 11:10 **r** the covenant I had made with all

REWARD REWARDED, REWARDING, REWARDS
Ge   15: 1 am your shield, your very great **r**."
1Sa 24:19 May the LORD **r** you well
Ps   17:14 of this world whose **r** is in this life.
     19:11 in keeping them there is great **r**.
     62:12 "You **r** everyone according to what
    127: 3 the LORD, offspring a **r** from him.
Pr   9:12 are wise, your wisdom will **r** you;
     11:18 sows righteousness reaps a sure **r**.
     12:14 work of their hands brings them **r**.
     19:17 he will **r** them for what they have
     25:22 head, and the LORD will **r** you.
Isa 40:10 See, his **r** is with him, and his
     49: 4 hand, and my **r** is with my God."
     61: 8 my faithfulness I will **r** my people
     62:11 See, his **r** is with him, and his
Jer 17:10 to **r** each person according to their
     32:19 you **r** each person according to their
Mt   5:12 because great is your **r** in heaven,
      6: 1 you will have no **r** from your Father
      6: 5 they have received their **r** in full.
     10:41 a prophet will receive a prophet's **r**,
     10:41 will receive a righteous person's **r**
     16:27 he will **r** each person according
Lk   6:23 because great is your **r** in heaven.
      6:35 Then your **r** will be great, and you
1Co   3:14 the builder will receive a **r**.
      9:17 If I preach voluntarily, I have a **r**;
Eph   6: 8 that the Lord will **r** each one
Col   3:24 an inheritance from the Lord as a **r**.
Heb 11:26 he was looking ahead to his **r**.
Rev 22:12 My **r** is with me, and I will give

REWARDED REWARD
Ru   2:12 May you be richly **r** by the LORD,
2Sa 22:21 cleanness of my hands he has **r** me.
2Ch 15: 7 give up, for your work will be **r**."
Ps   18:24 The LORD has **r** me according
Pr   13:13 whoever respects a command is **r**.
     13:21 the righteous are **r** with good things.
     14:14 their ways, and the good **r** for theirs.
Jer 31:16 for your work will be **r**,"
1Co   3: 8 and they will each be **r** according
Heb 10:35 it will be richly **r**.
2Jn   1: 8 for, but that you may be **r** fully.

REWARDING* REWARD
Rev 11:18 for **r** your servants the prophets

REWARDS REWARD
1Sa 26:23 The LORD **r** everyone for their
Heb 11: 6 he **r** those who earnestly seek him.

REZIN
Isa   7: 1 King **R** of Aram and Pekah son

RHODA*
Ac   12:13 a servant named **R** came to answer

RIB* RIBS
Ge   2:22 a woman from the **r** he had taken

RIBLAH
2Ki 25: 6 taken to the king of Babylon at **R**,

RIBS* RIB
Ge   2:21 he took one of the man's **r**
Da   7: 5 it had three **r** in its mouth between

RICH ENRICH, ENRICHED, RICHES, RICHEST, RICHLY
Ge   26:13 The man became **r**, and his wealth
2Sa 12: 1 town, one **r** and the other poor.
Job 34:19 does not favor the **r** over the poor,
Ps   21: 3 came to greet him with **r** blessings
     49:16 be overawed when others grow **r**,
    145: 8 slow to anger and **r** in love.
Pr   13: 7 One person pretends to be **r**, yet has
     21:17 wine and olive oil will never be **r**.
     22: 2 **R** and poor have this in common:
     23: 4 Do not wear yourself out to get **r**;
     28: 6 blameless than the **r** whose ways are
     28:20 to get **r** will not go unpunished.
     28:22 The stingy are eager to get **r** and are
Ecc   5:12 but as for the **r**, their abundance
Isa 33: 6 a **r** store of salvation and wisdom
     53: 9 and with the **r** in his death,
Jer   9:23 or the **r** boast of their riches,
Eze 34:14 there they will feed in a **r** pasture
Mt   19:23 for someone who is **r** to enter
Lk   1:53 but has sent the **r** away empty.
      6:24 "But woe to you who are **r**, for you
     12:21 but is not **r** toward God."
     16: 1 "There was a **r** man whose manager
     16:19 "There was a **r** man who was
     21: 1 he saw the **r** putting their gifts
2Co   6:10 poor, yet making many **r**;
      8: 2 poverty welled up in **r** generosity.
      8: 9 that though he was **r**, yet for your
Eph   2: 4 love for us, God, who is **r** in mercy,
1Ti   6: 9 Those who want to get **r** fall
      6:17 Command those who are **r** in this
      6:18 to be **r** in good deeds, and to be
Jas   1:10 But the **r** should take pride in their
      2: 5 the eyes of the world to be **r** in faith
      5: 1 Now listen, you **r** people,
2Pe   1:11 you will receive a **r** welcome
Rev   2: 9 and your poverty—yet you are **r**!
      3:17 You say, 'I am **r**; I have acquired
      3:18 in the fire, so you can become **r**;

RICHES RICH
1Ki 10:23 King Solomon was greater in **r**
Job 36:18 careful that no one entices you by **r**;

Ps 49: 6 wealth and boast of their great **r**?
62:10 though your **r** increase, do not set
119:14 statutes as one rejoices in great **r**.
Pr 3:16 in her left hand are **r** and honor.
11:28 Those who trust in their **r** will fall,
22: 1 name is more desirable than great **r**;
27:24 for **r** do not endure forever,
30: 8 give me neither poverty nor **r**,
Isa 10: 3 Where will you leave your **r**?
60: 5 you the **r** of the nations will come.
Jer 9:23 strength or the rich boast of their **r**,
Lk 8:14 by life's worries, **r** and pleasures,
Ro 9:23 to make the **r** of his glory known
11:12 if their transgression means **r**
11:12 how much greater **r** will their full
11:33 the depth of the **r** of the wisdom
Eph 2: 7 he might show the incomparable **r**
3: 8 to the Gentiles the boundless **r**
Col 1:27 among the Gentiles the glorious **r**
2: 2 they may have the full **r** of complete

RICHEST RICH
Isa 55: 2 and you will delight in the **r** of fare.

RICHLY RICH
Pr 28:20 A faithful person will be **r** blessed,
Ro 10:12 and **r** blesses all who call on him,
Col 3:16 dwell among you **r** as you teach
1Ti 6:17 who **r** provides us with everything

RID
Ge 21:10 "Get **r** of that slave woman and her
35: 2 "Get **r** of the foreign gods you have
Jdg 10:16 Then they got **r** of the foreign gods
1Sa 7: 3 **r** yourselves of the foreign gods
Lk 22: 2 for some way to get **r** of Jesus,
1Co 5: 7 Get **r** of the old yeast, so that you
Gal 4:30 "Get **r** of the slave woman and her
Eph 4:31 Get **r** of all bitterness,
Col 3: 8 **r** yourselves of all such things as
Jas 1:21 get **r** of all moral filth and the evil
1Pe 2: 1 **r** yourselves of all malice and all

RIDDLE RIDDLES
Jdg 14:12 "Let me tell you a **r**," Samson said
Ps 49: 4 with the harp I will expound my **r**:

RIDDLES* RIDDLE
Nu 12: 8 face to face, clearly and not in **r**;
Pr 1: 6 the sayings and **r** of the wise.
Da 5:12 dreams, explain **r** and solve difficult

RIDE RIDER, RIDERS, RIDES, RIDING, RODE
Ps 45: 4 In your majesty **r** forth victoriously

RIDER RIDE
Rev 6: 2 Its **r** held a bow, and he was given
19:11 whose **r** is called Faithful and True.

RIDERS RIDE
Rev 9:17 and **r** I saw in my vision looked like

RIDES* RIDE
Dt 33:26 who **r** across the heavens to help
Ps 68: 4 extol him who **r** on the clouds;

Ps 68:33 to him who **r** across the highest
104: 3 and **r** on the wings of the wind.
Isa 19: 1 the LORD **r** on a swift cloud and is
Rev 17: 7 of the woman and of the beast she **r**,

RIDICULE RIDICULED
2Ki 19: 4 has sent to **r** the living God,
Ps 123: 4 We have endured no end of **r**
Isa 37:17 has sent to **r** the living God.

RIDICULED RIDICULE
2Ki 19:22 Who is it you have **r**
Jer 20: 7 I am **r** all day long;
Lk 23:11 and his soldiers **r** and mocked him.

RIDING RIDE
Zec 9: 9 lowly and **r** on a donkey, on a colt,
Mt 21: 5 gentle and **r** on a donkey,
Rev 19:14 **r** on white horses and dressed

RIGGING*
Pr 23:34 the high seas, lying on top of the **r**.
Isa 33:23 Your **r** hangs loose: The mast is not

RIGHT RIGHTFULLY, RIGHTS
Ge 4: 7 If you do what is **r**, will you not be
4: 7 But if you do not do what is **r**, sin is
13: 9 If you go to the left, I'll go to the **r**;
18:19 of the LORD by doing what is **r**
18:25 not the Judge of all the earth do **r**?"
48:13 on his **r** toward Israel's left hand
48:13 on his left toward Israel's **r** hand,
Ex 14:22 with a wall of water on their **r**
15: 6 Your **r** hand, LORD, was majestic
15:26 God and do what is **r** in his eyes,
Dt 5:32 do not turn aside to the **r**
6:18 Do what is **r** and good
13:18 and doing what is **r** in his eyes.
28:14 you today, to the **r** or to the left,
Jos 1: 7 do not turn from it to the **r**
1Sa 12:23 you the way that is good and **r**.
1Ki 3: 9 to distinguish between **r** and wrong.
8:36 Teach them the **r** way to live,
15: 5 David had done what was **r**
2Ki 7: 9 other, "What we're doing is not **r**.
Ne 9:13 and laws that are just and **r**,
Job 40:14 that your own **r** hand can save you.
Ps 16: 8 With him at my **r** hand, I will not be
16:11 eternal pleasures at your **r** hand.
17: 7 your **r** hand those who take refuge
18:35 shield, and your **r** hand sustains me;
19: 8 The precepts of the LORD are **r**,
23: 3 He guides me along the **r** paths
25: 9 He guides the humble in what is **r**
33: 4 For the word of the LORD is **r**
44: 3 it was your **r** hand, your arm,
45: 4 let your **r** hand achieve awesome
51: 4 so you are **r** in your verdict
63: 8 your **r** hand upholds me.
73:23 you hold me by my **r** hand.
80:17 hand rest on the man at your **r** hand,
89:13 hand is strong, your **r** hand exalted.
91: 7 ten thousand at your **r** hand, but it
106: 3 act justly, who always do what is **r**.
110: 1 "Sit at my **r** hand until I make your

Ps   110: 5 The Lord is at your r hand;
     118:15 "The LORD's r hand has done
     137: 5 may my r hand forget its skill.
     139:10 me, your r hand will hold me fast.
Pr   1: 3 doing what is r and just and fair;
       3:16 Long life is in her r hand; in her left
       4:27 Do not turn to the r or the left;
       8: 9 To the discerning all of them are r;
      12:15 The way of fools seems r to them,
      14:12 There is a way that appears to be r,
      16:13 value the one who speaks what is r.
      16:25 There is a way that appears to be r,
      18:17 a lawsuit the first to speak seems r,
      21: 2 may think their own ways are r,
      28: 5 do not understand what is r,
Ecc   7:20 no one who does what is r
SS   1: 4 How r they are to adore you!
Isa   1:17 Learn to do r; seek justice.
       7:15 to reject the wrong and choose the r,
      30:10 us no more visions of what is r!
      30:21 Whether you turn to the r
      41:10 you with my righteous r hand.
      41:13 God who takes hold of your r hand
      48:13 my r hand spread out the heavens;
      64: 5 to the help of those who gladly do r,
Jer   22: 3 Do what is just and r.
      23: 5 and do what is just and r in the land.
Eze   1:10 on the r side each had the face
      18: 5 man who does what is just and r.
      18:21 decrees and does what is just and r,
      33:14 their sin and do what is just and r—
Hos   14: 9 The ways of the LORD are r;
Am   3:10 "They do not know how to do r,"
Jnh   4:11 people who cannot tell their r hand
Zec   3: 1 and Satan standing at his r side
Mt   5:29 If your r eye causes you to stumble,
       6: 3 know what your r hand is doing,
      22:44 my r hand until I put your enemies
      25:33 He will put the sheep on his r
Mk   7:27 "for it is not r to take the children's
      14:62 of Man sitting at the r hand
Jn   1:12 he gave the r to become children
Ac   2:34 said to my Lord: "Sit at my r hand
       7:55 Jesus standing at the r hand of God.
Ro   3: 4 that you may be proved r when you
       8:34 is at the r hand of God and is
       9:21 Does not the potter have the r
      12:17 careful to do what is r in the eyes
1Co   6:12 "I have the r to do anything,"
       7:35 but that you may live in a r way
       9: 4 Don't we have the r to food
      10:23 "I have the r to do anything,"
2Co   8:21 we are taking pains to do what is r,
Eph   1:20 and seated him at his r hand
       6: 1 parents in the Lord, for this is r.
Php   4: 8 whatever is r, whatever is pure,
Col   3: 1 is, seated at the r hand of God.
Heb   1: 3 he sat down at the r hand
       1:13 "Sit at my r hand until I make your
      10:12 he sat down at the r hand of God,
Jas   2: 8 as yourself," you are doing r.
1Pe   3:14 if you should suffer for what is r,
       3:22 into heaven and is at God's r hand—

1Jn   2:29 who does what is r has been born
       3: 7 one who does what is r is righteous,
Rev   1:16 In his r hand he held seven stars,
       2: 7 I will give the r to eat from the tree
       3:21 I will give the r to sit with me
      22:11 one who does r continue to do r;
      22:14 that they may have the r to the tree

RIGHT HAND See HAND

RIGHT IN THE EYES OF THE LORD† See EYES

RIGHT-HANDED* HAND
1Ch   12: 2 or to sling stones r or left-handed;

RIGHTEOUS OVERRIGHTEOUS, RIGHTEOUSLY, RIGHTEOUSNESS
Ge   6: 9 Noah was a r man,
      18:23 "Will you sweep away the r
      38:26 said, "She is more r than I, since I
Nu   23:10 Let me die the death of the r,
Dt   4: 8 is so great as to have such r decrees
1Sa   24:17 "You are more r than I," he said.
Ne   9: 8 your promise because you are r.
       9:33 to us, you have remained r;
Job   4:17 'Can a mortal be more r than God?
      36: 7 He does not take his eyes off the r;
Ps   1: 5 nor sinners in the assembly of the r.
       4: 5 Offer the sacrifices of the r and trust
       5:12 Surely, LORD, you bless the r;
       7:11 God is a r judge, a God who
       9: 4 sitting enthroned as the r judge.
      11: 7 For the LORD is r, he loves
      15: 2 who does what is r, who speaks
      34:15 eyes of the LORD are on the r,
      37: 6 will make your r reward shine like
      37:16 little that the r have than the wealth
      37:21 not repay, but the r give generously;
      37:25 yet I have never seen the r forsaken
      37:30 The mouths of the r utter wisdom,
      55:22 he will never let the r be shaken.
      64:10 The r will rejoice in the LORD
      65: 5 us with awesome and r deeds,
      68: 3 But may the r be glad and rejoice
      71:15 My mouth will tell of your r deeds,
      72: 7 In his days may the r flourish
     112: 4 gracious and compassionate and r.
     116: 5 The LORD is gracious and r;
     118:19 Open for me the gates of the r;
     118:20 through which the r may enter.
     119: 7 upright heart as I learn your r laws.
     119:137 You are r, LORD, and your laws
     119:144 Your statutes are always r;
     140:13 Surely the r will praise your name,
     143: 2 for no one living is r before you.
     145:17 The LORD is r in all his ways
     146: 8 down, the LORD loves the r.
Pr   3:33 but he blesses the home of the r.
       4:18 path of the r is like the morning sun,
      10: 6 Blessings crown the head of the r,
      10: 7 The name of the r is used
      10:11 The mouth of the r is a fountain
      10:16 The wages of the r is life,
      10:20 The tongue of the r is choice silver,

Pr 10:24 what the r desire will be granted.
10:28 The prospect of the r is joy,
10:32 lips of the r know what finds favor,
11: 9 but through knowledge the r escape.
11:23 The desire of the r ends only
11:30 The fruit of the r is a tree of life,
12:10 The r care for the needs of their
12:21 No harm overtakes the r,
13: 5 The r hate what is false,
13: 9 The light of the r shines brightly,
14:32 even in death the r seek refuge
15:28 heart of the r weighs its answers,
15:29 but he hears the prayer of the r.
18:10 the r run to it and are safe.
20: 7 The r lead blameless lives;
21:15 it brings joy to the r but terror
23:24 The father of a r child has great joy;
24:16 for though the r fall seven times,
28: 1 but the r are as bold as a lion.
29: 2 When the r thrive, the people
29: 6 but the r shout for joy and are glad.
29: 7 The r care about justice
29:27 The r detest the dishonest;
Ecc 7:15 the r perishing in their
7:20 there is no one on earth who is r,
8:14 the r who get what the wicked
8:14 wicked who get what the r deserve.
Isa 5:16 will be proved holy by his r acts.
26: 7 The path of the r is level;
41:10 uphold you with my r right hand.
45:21 from me, a r God and a Savior;
53:11 by his knowledge my r servant will
64: 6 and all our r acts are like filthy rags;
Jer 12: 1 You are always r, Lord, when I
23: 5 I will raise up for David a r Branch,
23: 6 The Lord Our R Savior.
33:15 time I will make a r Branch sprout
33:16 The Lord Our R Savior.'
La 1:18 "The Lord is r, yet I rebelled
Eze 3:20 when a r person turns from their
18: 5 "Suppose there is a r man who does
18:20 of the r will be credited to them,
33:12 'If someone who is r disobeys,
33:12 The r person who sins will not be
Da 9:14 us, for the Lord our God is r
Hab 2: 4 but the r person will live by his
Zep 3: 5 The Lord within her is r;
Zec 9: 9 king comes to you, r and victorious,
Mal 3:18 see the distinction between the r
Mt 5:45 and sends rain on the r
13:43 the r will shine like the sun
13:49 and separate the wicked from the r
25:37 "Then the r will answer him, 'Lord,
25:46 but the r to eternal life."
Mk 2:17 I have not come to call the r,
Lk 23:47 said, "Surely this was a r man."
Ac 3:14 You disowned the Holy and R One
24:15 will be a resurrection of both the r
Ro 1:17 "The r will live by faith."
2: 5 his r judgment will be revealed.
2:13 obey the law who will be declared r.
3:10 "There is no one r, not even one;
3:20 Therefore no one will be declared r

Ro 5:18 one r act resulted in justification
5:19 one man the many will be made r.
7:12 commandment is holy, r and good.
8: 4 order that the r requirement
Gal 3:11 because "the r will live by faith."
1Ti 1: 9 that the law is made not for the r
2Ti 4: 8 which the Lord, the r Judge,
Titus 3: 5 because of r things we had done,
Heb 10:38 "But my r one will live by faith.
Jas 2:21 our father Abraham considered r
2:25 Rahab the prostitute considered r
2:24 is considered r by what they do
5:16 The prayer of a r person is powerful
1Pe 3:12 For the eyes of the Lord are on the r
3:18 for sins, the r for the unrighteous,
4:18 "If it is hard for the r to be saved,
1Jn 2: 1 Jesus Christ, the R One.
3: 7 The one who does what is right is r,
just as he is r.
Rev 15: 4 for your r acts have been revealed."
19: 8 (Fine linen stands for the r acts

RIGHTEOUSLY* RIGHTEOUS

Isa 33:15 Those who walk r and speak what is
Jer 11:20 who judge r and test the heart

RIGHTEOUSNESS RIGHTEOUS

Ge 15: 6 and he credited it to him as r.
Dt 6:25 commanded us, that will be our r."
9: 4 of this land because of my r."
1Sa 26:23 rewards everyone for their r
1Ki 10: 9 you king to maintain justice and r."
Job 37:23 in his justice and great r, he does
Ps 7:17 to the Lord because of his r;
9: 8 He rules the world in r and judges
18:20 dealt with me according to my r;
22:31 They will proclaim his r,
33: 5 The Lord loves r and justice;
35:24 Vindicate me in your r, Lord my
35:28 My tongue will proclaim your r,
36: 6 Your r is like the highest
45: 7 You love r and hate wickedness;
48:10 your right hand is filled with r.
50: 6 And the heavens proclaim his r,
71: 2 In your r, rescue me and deliver me;
71:19 Your r, God,
72: 2 May he judge your people in r,
85:10 r and peace kiss each other.
89:14 R and justice are the foundation
96:13 He will judge the world in r
98: 2 and revealed his r to the nations.
98: 9 He will judge the world in r
103: 6 The Lord works r and justice
103:17 his r with their children's children—
106:31 to him as r for endless generations
111: 3 his deeds, and his r endures forever.
132: 9 your priests be clothed with your r;
145: 7 and joyfully sing of your r.
Pr 8:20 I walk in the way of r,
10: 2 value, but r delivers from death.
11: 5 The r of the blameless makes their
11: 6 The r of the upright delivers them,
11:18 but the one who sows r reaps a sure
12:28 In the way of r there is life;

Pr 13: 6 **R** guards the person of integrity,
14:34 **R** exalts a nation, but sin condemns
15: 9 but he loves those who pursue **r**.
16:12 for a throne is established through **r**.
16:31 it is attained in the way of **r**.
21:21 Whoever pursues **r** and love finds
Ecc 7:15 the righteous perishing in their **r**,
Isa 1:26 you will be called the City of **R**,
9: 7 with justice and **r** from that time
11: 4 but with **r** he will judge the needy,
11: 5 **R** will be his belt and faithfulness
16: 5 justice and speeds the cause of **r**.
26: 9 the people of the world learn **r**.
28:17 measuring line and **r** the plumb line;
32: 1 a king will reign in **r** and rulers will
32:17 The fruit of that **r** will be peace;
33: 5 will fill Zion with his justice and **r**.
42: 6 the LORD, have called you in **r**;
42:21 sake of his **r** to make his law great
45: 8 heavens above, rain down my **r**;
46:13 I am bringing my **r** near, it is not far
51: 5 My **r** draws near speedily,
51: 6 last forever, my **r** will never fail.
51: 8 But my **r** will last forever,
56: 1 and my **r** will soon be revealed.
58: 8 then your **r** will go before you,
59:17 He put on **r** as his breastplate,
61:10 and arrayed me in a robe of his **r**,
Jer 9:24 justice and **r** on earth, for in these I
Eze 3:20 a righteous person turns from their **r**
14:20 save only themselves by their **r**.
18:20 The **r** of the righteous will be
33:12 that person's former **r** will count
Da 9:24 to bring in everlasting **r**, to seal
12: 3 and those who lead many to **r**,
Hos 2:19 I will betroth you in **r** and justice,
10:12 Sow **r** for yourselves, reap the fruit
10:12 he comes and showers his **r** on you.
Am 5:24 a river, **r** like a never-failing stream!
Mic 7: 9 me out into the light; I will see his **r**.
Zep 2: 3 Seek **r**, seek humility;
Mal 4: 2 the sun of **r** will rise with healing
Mt 3:15 for us to do this to fulfill all **r**."
5: 6 those who hunger and thirst for **r**,
5:10 who are persecuted because of **r**,
5:20 you that unless your **r** surpasses
6: 1 not to practice your **r** in front
6:33 But seek first his kingdom and his **r**,
Jn 16: 8 to be in the wrong about sin and **r**
Ac 24:25 As Paul talked about **r**,
Ro 1:17 a **r** that is by faith from first to last,
3: 5 brings out God's **r** more clearly,
3:22 This **r** is given through faith
3:25 He did this to demonstrate his **r**,
3:26 to demonstrate his **r** at the present
4: 3 and it was credited to him as **r**."
4: 5 ungodly, their faith is credited as **r**.
4: 6 to whom God credits **r** apart
4: 9 faith was credited to him as **r**.
4:13 through the **r** that comes by faith.
4:22 why "it was credited to him as **r**."
6:13 to him as an instrument of **r**.
6:16 or to obedience, which leads to **r**?

Ro 6:18 sin and have become slaves to **r**.
6:19 yourselves as slaves to **r** leading
8:10 the Spirit gives life because of **r**.
9:30 who did not pursue **r**, have obtained
it, a **r** that is by faith;
10: 3 they did not submit to God's **r**.
10: 4 there may be **r** for everyone who
14:17 but of **r**, peace and joy in the Holy
1Co 1:30 is, our **r**, holiness and redemption.
2Co 3: 9 is the ministry that brings **r**!
5:21 him we might become the **r** of God.
6: 7 with weapons of **r** in the right hand
6:14 For what do **r** and wickedness have
9: 9 their **r** endures forever."
9:10 will enlarge the harvest of your **r**.
11:15 also masquerade as servants of **r**.
Gal 2:21 if **r** could be gained through the law,
3: 6 and it was credited to him as **r**."
3:21 **r** would certainly have come
Eph 4:24 created to be like God in true **r**
5: 9 consists in all goodness, **r** and truth)
6:14 with the breastplate of **r** in place,
Php 1:11 the fruit of **r** that comes through
3: 6 as for **r** based on the law, faultless.
3: 9 him, not having a **r** of my own
1Ti 6:11 all this, and pursue **r**, godliness.
2Ti 2:22 evil desires of youth and pursue **r**,
3:16 correcting and training in **r**,
4: 8 is in store for me the crown of **r**,
Heb 5:13 with the teaching about **r**.
7: 2 Melchizedek means "king of **r**";
11: 7 and became heir of the **r** that is
12:11 it produces a harvest of **r** and peace
Jas 2:23 and it was credited to him as **r**,"
3:18 sow in peace reap a harvest of **r**.
1Pe 2:24 we might die to sins and live for **r**;
2Pe 2:21 not to have known the way of **r**,
3:13 and a new earth, where **r** dwells

RIGHTFULLY* RIGHT
Eze 21:27 he to whom it **r** belongs shall come;

RIGHTS RIGHT
Ex 21: 9 his son, he must grant her the **r**
21:10 of her food, clothing and marital **r**.
Dt 21:16 sons, he must not give the **r**
Job 36: 6 alive but gives the afflicted their **r**.
Pr 31: 8 for the **r** of all who are destitute.
Isa 10: 2 to deprive the poor of their **r**
La 3:35 deny people their **r** before the Most
1Co 9:15 But I have not used any of these **r**.
Heb 12:16 sold his inheritance **r** as the oldest

RING
Ge 41:42 Pharaoh took his signet **r** from his
Est 3:12 himself and sealed with his own **r**.
8:10 dispatches with the king's signet **r**,
Pr 11:22 Like a gold **r** in a pig's snout is
Jer 22:24 were a signet **r** on my right hand,
Da 6:17 king sealed it with his own signet **r**
Hag 2:23 I will make you like my signet **r**,
Lk 15:22 Put a **r** on his finger and sandals

RIOT RIOTS
Mk 14: 2 they said, "or the people may **r**."

Ac 17: 5 a mob and started a **r** in the city.

RIOTS* RIOT

Ac 24: 5 **r** among the Jews all over the world.
2Co 6: 5 in beatings, imprisonments and **r**;

RIPE

Joel 3:13 the sickle, for the harvest is **r**.
Am 8: 2 "The time is **r** for my people Israel;
Na 3:12 like fig trees with their first **r** fruit;
Mk 4:29 As soon as the grain is **r**, he puts
Jn 4:35 at the fields! They are **r** for harvest.
Rev 14:15 for the harvest of the earth is **r**."

RISE ARISE, RAISE, RAISED, RAISES, RISEN, RISES, RISING, ROSE

Nu 10:35 out, Moses said, "**R** up, LORD!
      24:17 a scepter will **r** out of Israel.
Ps 7: 6 **r** up against the rage of my enemies.
      27:12 for false witnesses **r** up against me,
      74:22 **R** up, O God, and defend your
      94: 2 **R** up, Judge of the earth;
      139: 9 If I **r** on the wings of the dawn, if I
Isa 26:19 their bodies will **r**—let those who
      30:18 therefore he will **r** up to show you
Da 7:17 four kings that will **r** from the earth.
      12:13 the days you will **r** to receive your
Am 8:14 they will fall, never to **r** again."
Mal 4: 2 of righteousness will **r** with healing
Mt 5:45 He causes his sun to **r** on the evil
      27:63 'After three days I will **r** again.'
Mk 8:31 killed and after three days **r** again.
      13: 8 Nation will **r** against nation,
Lk 18:33 On the third day he will **r** again."
Jn 5:29 who have done what is good will **r**
      5:29 who have done what is evil will **r**
      20: 9 that Jesus had to **r** from the dead.)
Ac 17: 3 had to suffer and **r** from the dead.
Eph 5:14 sleeper, **r** from the dead, and Christ
1Th 4:16 and the dead in Christ will **r** first.

RISEN RISE

Dt 34:10 then, no prophet has **r** in Israel like
Mt 28: 6 is not here; he has **r**, just as he said.
Mk 16: 6 He has **r**! He is not here.
Lk 24:34 The Lord has **r** and has appeared

RISES RISE

Ecc 1: 5 The sun **r** and the sun sets,
Isa 2:19 when he **r** to shake the earth.
      60: 1 the glory of the LORD **r** upon you.
Lk 16:31 if someone **r** from the dead.' "
2Pe 1:19 the morning star **r** in your hearts.

RISING RISE

Ps 113: 3 From the **r** of the sun to the place
Mk 9:10 discussing what "**r** from the dead"
Lk 2:34 the falling and **r** of many in Israel,

RITES

Heb 6: 2 instruction about cleansing **r**,

RIVAL RIVALRY

1Sa 1: 7 her **r** provoked her till she wept

RIVALRY* RIVAL

Php 1:15 preach Christ out of envy and **r**,

RIVER RIVERS

Ge 2:10 A **r** watering the garden flowed
      15:18 the Wadi of Egypt to the great **r**,
      41: 2 of the **r** there came up seven cows,
Dt 1: 7 as far as the great **r**, the Euphrates.
      11:24 and from the Euphrates **R**
Jos 1: 2 cross the Jordan **R** into the land I am
      24: 2 lived beyond the Euphrates **R**
Ps 46: 4 There is a **r** whose streams make
      78:44 He turned their **r** into blood;
Isa 48:18 peace would have been like a **r**,
      66:12 "I will extend peace to her like a **r**,
La 2:18 let your tears flow like a **r** day
Eze 47:12 will grow on both banks of the **r**.
Da 7:10 A **r** of fire was flowing,
Am 5:24 But let justice roll on like a **r**,
Mt 3: 6 baptized by him in the Jordan **R**.
Rev 12:15 the serpent spewed water like a **r**,
      22: 1 the angel showed me the **r**

RIVERS RIVER

Ps 78:16 and made water flow down like **r**.
      137: 1 By the **r** of Babylon we sat
Jn 7:38 **r** of living water will flow
Rev 8:10 fell from the sky on a third of the **r**
      16: 4 angel poured out his bowl on the **r**

ROAD CROSSROADS, ROADS

Nu 22:22 stood in the **r** to oppose him.
Mt 7:13 gate and broad is the **r** that leads
Mk 11: 8 people spread their cloaks on the **r**,

ROADS ROAD

Lk 3: 5 The crooked **r** shall become

ROAR ROARING, ROARS

Ps 46: 3 though its waters **r** and foam
Isa 17:13 Although the peoples **r** like the **r**
Jer 25:30 " 'The LORD will **r** from on high;
Hos 11:10 he will **r** like a lion.
Joel 3:16 The LORD will **r** from Zion
2Pe 3:10 The heavens will disappear with a **r**;
Rev 10: 3 he gave a loud shout like the **r**
      14: 2 heaven like the **r** of rushing waters
      19: 6 like the **r** of rushing waters and like

ROARING ROAR

Ps 65: 7 who stilled the **r** of the seas, the **r** of
      their waves,
1Pe 5: 8 prowls around like a **r** lion looking

ROARS ROAR

Hos 11:10 When he **r**, his children will come
Am 1: 2 "The LORD **r** from Zion

ROB ROBBER, ROBBERS, ROBBERY, ROBS

Lev 19:13 not defraud or **r** your neighbor.
Mal 3: 8 "Will a mere mortal **r** God?

ROBBER* ROB

Jn 10: 1 some other way, is a thief and a **r**.

ROBBERS ROB
Jer   7:11 Name, become a den of r to you?
Mt 21:13 you are making it 'a den of r.' "
Lk 10:30 Jericho, when he was attacked by r.
     19:46 you have made it 'a den of r.' "
Jn   10: 8 come before me are thieves and r,

ROBBERY ROB
Isa 61: 8 I hate r and wrongdoing.
Eze 22:29 practice extortion and commit r;

ROBE ROBED, ROBES
Ge 37: 3 and he made an ornate r for him.
Ex 28: 4 an ephod, a r, a woven tunic,
Jos   7:21 in the plunder a beautiful r
1Sa 2:19 year his mother made him a little r
     15:27 caught hold of the hem of his r,
     24: 4 and cut off a corner of Saul's r.
2Sa 13:18 She was wearing an ornate r,
Isa   6: 1 the train of his r filled the temple.
     61:10 me in a r of his righteousness,
Zec   8:23 hold of one Jew by the hem of his r
Lk 15:22 Bring the best r and put it on him.
Jn 19: 5 crown of thorns and the purple r,
Heb 1:12 You will roll them up like a r;
Rev 1:13 dressed in a r reaching down to his
     6:11 each of them was given a white r,
     19:13 He is dressed in a r dipped in blood,

ROBED* ROBE
Est   6:11 He r Mordecai, and led him
Ps 93: 1 LORD reigns, he is r in majesty;
    93: 1 the LORD is r in majesty
Isa 63: 1 Who is this, r in splendor,
Rev 10: 1 He was r in a cloud, with a rainbow

ROBES ROBE
Ps 45: 8 All your r are fragrant with myrrh
Mk 12:38 like to walk around in flowing r
Rev   7:13 asked me, "These in white r—
    22:14 are those who wash their r, that they

ROBS* ROB
Pr 19:26 Whoever r their father and drives
    28:24 Whoever r their father or mother

ROCK ROCKS, ROCKY
Ge 49:24 of the Shepherd, the R of Israel,
Ex 17: 6 Strike the r, and water will come
    33:22 I will put you in a cleft in the r
Nu 20: 8 Speak to that r before their eyes
Dt 32: 4 He is the R, his works are perfect,
    32:13 him with honey from the r,
    32:15 and rejected the R their Savior.
    32:31 For their r is not like our R,
1Sa 2: 2 there is no R like our God.
2Sa 22: 2 "The LORD is my r, my fortress
Ps 18: 2 The LORD is my r, my fortress
    19:14 LORD, my R and my Redeemer.
    27: 5 tent and set me high upon a r.
    40: 2 he set my feet on a r and gave me
    61: 2 lead me to the r that is higher than I.
    62: 2 Truly he is my r and my salvation;
    92:15 he is my R, and there is no
Isa 26: 4 LORD himself, is the R eternal.

Isa 44: 8 No, there is no other R; I know not
    48:21 he split the r and water gushed out.
    51: 1 Look to the r from which you were
Da   2:34 you were watching, a r was cut out,
Zec 12: 3 make Jerusalem an immovable r
Mt   7:24 man who built his house on the r.
    16:18 and on this r I will build my church,
Mk 15:46 and placed it in a tomb cut out of r.
Ro   9:33 and a r that makes them fall,
1Co 10: 4 the spiritual r that accompanied
      them, and that r was Christ.
1Pe   2: 8 and a r that makes them fall."

ROCKS ROCK
Ps 78:15 He split the r in the wilderness
   137: 9 and dashes them against the r.
Isa   2:19 People will flee to caves in the r
Ob   1: 3 you who live in the clefts of the r
Na   1: 6 the r are shattered before him.
Mt 27:51 The earth shook, the r split
Rev   6:15 and among the r of the mountains.

ROCKY ROCK
Mk   4: 5 Some fell on r places, where it did

ROD RODS
2Sa   7:14 I will punish him with a r wielded
Ps   2: 9 will break them with a r of iron;
    23: 4 your r and your staff, they comfort
Pr 13:24 Whoever spares the r hates their
    22:15 the r of discipline will drive it far
    23:13 if you punish them with the r,
    29:15 A r and a reprimand impart
Isa 11: 4 the earth with the r of his mouth;
Hos   4:12 and a diviner's r speaks to them.

RODE RIDE
Hab   3: 8 the sea when you r your horses
Rev   6: 2 and he r out as a conqueror bent

RODS ROD
2Co 11:25 Three times I was beaten with r,

ROLL ROLLED
Da 12: 4 Daniel, r up and seal the words
Am   5:24 But let justice r on like a river,
Mk 16: 3 "Who will r the stone away
Heb 1:12 You will r them up like a robe;

ROLLED ROLL
Jos   5: 9 "Today I have r away the reproach
Da 12: 9 because the words are r up and sealed
Lk 24: 2 They found the stone r away
Rev   6:14 receded like a scroll being r up,

ROMAN ROME
Ac 16:37 even though we are R citizens,
    22:25 to flog a R citizen who hasn't even

ROMANS ROME
Jn 11:48 then the R will come and take away

ROME ROMAN, ROMANS
Ac 18: 2 had ordered all Jews to leave R.
    28:14 And so we came to R.
Ro   1:15 the gospel also to you who are in R.

ROOF ROOFS
Ge 19: 8 under the protection of my r."
Jos 2: 6 of flax she had laid out on the r.)
2Sa 11: 2 the r he saw a woman bathing.
Ps 22:15 tongue sticks to the r of my mouth;
Pr 21: 9 a corner of the r than share a house
Mt 8: 8 to have you come under my r.
Mk 2: 4 an opening in the r above Jesus
Ac 10: 9 city, Peter went up on the r to pray.

ROOFS ROOF
Mt 10:27 in your ear, proclaim from the r.

ROOM ROOMS, STOREROOM
Mt 6: 6 go into your r, close the door
Mk 14:15 He will show you a large r upstairs,
Lk 2: 7 there was no guest r available
Jn 8:37 because you have no r for my word.
    21:25 the whole world would not have r
Ro 12:19 but leave r for God's wrath, for it is
2Co 7: 2 Make r for us in your hearts.

ROOMS ROOM
Mt 24:26 is, in the inner r,' do not believe it.
Lk 12: 3 ear in the inner r will be proclaimed
Jn 14: 2 My Father's house has many r;

ROOSTER
Mt 26:34 before the r crows, you will disown
    26:75 "Before the r crows, you will

ROOT ROOTED, ROOTS
Pr 12:12 but the r of the righteous endures.
Isa 11:10 day the R of Jesse will stand as
    53: 2 and like a r out of dry ground.
Mt 3:10 ax is already at the r of the trees,
    13:21 But since they have no r, they last
Ro 11:16 if the r is holy, so are the branches.
    15:12 "The R of Jesse will spring up,
1Ti 6:10 the love of money is a r of all kinds
Rev 5: 5 the tribe of Judah, the R of David,
    22:16 I am the R and the Offspring

ROOTED* ROOT
Eph 3:17 you, being r and established in love,
Col 2: 7 r and built up in him,

ROOTS ROOT
Isa 11: 1 from his r a Branch will bear fruit.
Jer 17: 8 that sends out its r by the stream.
Eze 17: 9 many people to pull it up by the r.
Hos 14: 5 of Lebanon he will send down his r;
Mt 15:13 planted will be pulled up by the r.

ROSE RISE
Ge 7:18 The waters r and increased greatly
1Ch 21: 1 Satan r up against Israel and incited
SS 2: 1 I am a r of Sharon, a lily
Eze 1:19 the living creatures r from the
        ground, the wheels also r.
Mt 2: 2 We saw his star when it r and have
    7:25 the streams r, and the winds blew
Ac 10:41 with him after he r from the dead.
1Th 4:14 believe that Jesus died and r again,

ROT ROTS, ROTTED
Pr 10: 7 but the name of the wicked will r.
Hos 5:12 like r to the people of Judah.
Zec 14:12 Their flesh will r while they are still

ROTS* ROT
Pr 14:30 to the body, but envy r the bones.

ROTTED* ROT
Jas 5: 2 Your wealth has r, and moths have

ROUGH* ROUGHER
Isa 40: 4 the r ground shall become level,
    42:16 them and make the r places smooth.
Lk 3: 5 become straight, the r ways smooth.
Jn 6:18 was blowing and the waters grew r.

ROUGHER* ROUGH
Jnh 1:11 The sea was getting r and r.

ROUND
Ecc 1: 6 r and r it goes, ever returning

ROUSE AROUSE, AROUSED
Job 3: 8 those who are ready to r Leviathan.
Ps 59: 5 r yourself to punish all the nations;

ROUTED ROUTS
Ps 18:14 great bolts of lightning he r them.
Heb 11:34 in battle and r foreign armies.

ROUTS* ROUTED
Jos 23:10 One of you r a thousand,

ROW
Jnh 1:13 the men did their best to r back

ROYAL
Jos 11:12 Joshua took all these r cities
1Ki 9: 5 I will establish your r throne over
2Ch 22:10 to destroy the whole r family
Ps 45: 9 your right hand is the r bride in gold
Isa 62: 3 a r diadem in the hand of your God.
Da 1: 8 not to defile himself with the r food
Jas 2: 8 If you really keep the r law found
1Pe 2: 9 are a chosen people, a r priesthood,
Rev 17:17 over to the beast their r authority,

RUBBLE
Jer 26:18 Jerusalem will become a heap of r,
Mic 3:12 Jerusalem will become a heap of r,
2Ch 7:21 temple will become a heap of r.

RUBIES RUBY
Job 28:18 the price of wisdom is beyond r.
Pr 3:15 She is more precious than r;
    8:11 for wisdom is more precious than r,
    31:10 She is worth far more than r.

RUBY* RUBIES
Rev 4: 3 had the appearance of jasper and r.
    21:20 fifth onyx, the sixth r, the seventh

RUDDER*
Jas 3: 4 by a very small r wherever the pilot

RUDDY
SS 5:10 My beloved is radiant and r,

RUGGED
Ps   68:16 why gaze in envy, you r mountain,
Isa   40: 4 become level, the r places a plain.

RUIN RUINED, RUINS
Dt   28:20 and come to sudden r because
Job 22:19 The righteous see their r
Pr   10: 8 but a chattering fool comes to r.
      10:14 but the mouth of a fool invites r.
      10:29 but it is the r of those who do evil.
      11:17 but the cruel bring r on themselves.
      11:29 Whoever brings r on their family
      15:27 The greedy bring r to their
      18:24 unreliable friends soon comes to r,
      19: 3 person's own folly leads to their r,
      19:13 A foolish child is a father's r,
      26:28 and a flattering mouth works r.
Ecc   4: 5 fold their hands and r themselves.
SS   2:15 the little foxes that r the vineyards,
Isa 25: 2 the fortified town a r, the foreigners'
Eze 21:27 A r! A r! I will make it a r!
Hos 4:14 understanding will come to r!
Mic   6:13 you, to r you because of your sins.
Zep   1:15 a day of trouble and r, a day
Hag   1: 4 while this house remains a r?"
1Ti   6: 9 desires that plunge people into r
Rev 18:19 one hour she has been brought to r!'

RUINED RUIN
Ex   10: 7 you not yet realize that Egypt is r?"
Isa   3:14 "It is you who have r my vineyard;
      6: 5 "I am r! For I am a man of unclean
Jer   4:27 "The whole land will be r, though I
Mt 12:25 divided against itself will be r,
Mk   2:22 wine and the wineskins will be r.

RUINS RUIN
Ezr   9: 9 house of our God and repair its r,
Ne   2.17 Jerusalem lies in r, and its gates
Isa 51: 3 look with compassion on all her r;
Jer   9:11 "I will make Jerusalem a heap of r,
Am   9:11 its broken walls and restore its r—
Ac 15:16 Its r I will rebuild, and I will restore
2Ti   2:14 value, and only r those who listen.

RULE RULER, RULER'S, RULERS, RULES, RULING
Ge   1:26 so that they may r over the fish
      3:16 husband, and he will r over you."
      4: 7 have you, but you must r over it."
      37: 8 Will you actually r us?"
Dt 15: 6 You will r over many nations but
            none will r over you.
Jdg   8:22 said to Gideon, "R over us—
1Sa 12:12 'No, we want a king to r over us'—
2Ch 6: 6 David to r my people Israel.'
Ps 67: 4 for you r the peoples with equity
  119:133 to your word; let no sin r over me.
Pr 12:24 Diligent hands will r, but laziness
      17: 2 A prudent servant will r over
Isa 28:10 a r for this, a r for that;
      32: 1 and rulers will r with justice.
Mic   4: 7 The LORD will r over them
Zec   6:13 and will sit and r on his throne.

Zec   9:10 His r will extend from sea to sea
Ro 15:12 who will arise to r over the nations;
1Co   7:17 This is the r I lay down in all
Gal   6:16 and mercy to all who follow this r—
Eph   1:21 far above all r and authority,
Col   3:15 the peace of Christ r in your hearts,
2Th 3:10 were with you, we gave you this r:
Rev 2:27 that one 'will r them with an iron
      12: 5 who "will r all the nations
      19:15 "He will r them with an iron

RULER RULE
Ex   2:14 "Who made you r and judge over
1Sa 10: 1 the LORD anointed you r over his
      13:14 and appointed him r of his people,
2Sa 7: 8 and appointed you r over my people
Ps 82: 7 you will fall like every other r."
Pr 19: 6 Many curry favor with a r,
      23: 1 When you sit to dine with a r,
      25:15 Through patience a r can be
      29:12 If a r listens to lies, all his officials
      29:26 Many seek an audience with a r,
Ecc   9:17 than the shouts of a r of fools.
Isa 60:17 governor and well-being your r.
Da   5:29 was proclaimed the third highest r
      9:25 the Anointed One, the r, comes,
Mic   5: 2 me one who will be r over Israel,
Mt   2: 6 will come a r who will shepherd my
Ac   7:27 'Who made you r and judge over
Eph   2: 2 of the r of the kingdom of the air,
1Ti   6:15 the blessed and only R, the King
Rev 1: 5 and the r of the kings of the earth.
      3:14 witness, the r of God's creation.

RULER'S RULE
Ge 49:10 nor the r staff from between his

RULERS RULE
Jdg 16: 5 The r of the Philistines went to her
Job 12:17 He leads r away stripped and makes
Ps   2: 2 and the r band together against
      8: 6 You made them r over the works
  119:161 R persecute me without cause,
Pr   8:15 and r issue decrees that are just;
      31: 4 drink wine, not for r to crave beer,
Isa   1:10 of the LORD, you r of Sodom;
      32: 1 and r will rule with justice.
      40:23 and reduces the r of this world
Da   7:27 and all r will worship and obey
Mt   2: 6 by no means least among the r
      20:25 that the r of the Gentiles lord it over
Ac   4:26 the r band together against the Lord
      13:27 and their r did not recognize Jesus,
Ro 13: 3 For r hold no terror for those who
1Co   2: 6 of this age or of the r of this age,
Eph   3:10 God should be made known to the r
      6:12 blood, but against the r,
Col   1:16 or powers or r or authorities;

RULES RULE
Nu 15:15 is to have the same r for you
2Sa 23: 3 when he r in the fear of God,
Ps 22:28 LORD and he r over the nations.
      66: 7 He r forever by his power, his eyes
  103:19 heaven, and his kingdom r over all.

Isa 29:13 on merely human r they have been
40:10 power, and he r with a mighty arm.
Mk 7: 7 their teachings are merely human r.'
Lk 22:26 and the one who r like the one who
Col 2:20 to the world, do you submit to its r:
2Ti 2: 5 by competing according to the r.
Rev 17:18 is the great city that r over the kings

RULING RULE
Ex 15:25 There the LORD issued a r
Pr 25:11 settings of silver is a r rightly given.
Jn 3: 1 a member of the Jewish r council.

RUMOR RUMORS
Eze 7:26 calamity will come, and r upon r.
Jn 21:23 the r spread among the believers

RUMORS RUMOR
Jer 51:46 or be afraid when r are heard
Mt 24: 6 You will hear of wars and r of wars,

RUN RAN, RUNNERS, RUNNING, RUNS
1Sa 31: 4 your sword and r me through,
Ps 19: 5 champion rejoicing to r his course.
119:32 I r in the path of your commands,
Pr 4:12 when you r, you will not stumble.
18:10 the righteous r to it and are safe.
Isa 10: 3 To whom will you r for help?
40:31 they will r and not grow weary,
Jer 51:45 my people! R for your lives!
Joel 3:18 ravines of Judah will r with water.
Hab 2: 2 so that a herald may r with it.
Mt 6:32 the pagans r after all these things,
1Co 9:24 R in such a way as to get the prize.
Php 2:16 on the day of Christ that I did not r
Heb 12: 1 let us r with perseverance the race

RUNNERS* RUN
1Co 9:24 not know that in a race all the r run,

RUNNING RUN
Ps 133: 2 on the head, r down on the beard,
Pr 5:15 cistern, r water from your own well.
Jnh 1:10 (They knew he was r away
Lk 17:23 Do not go r off after them.
1Co 9:26 do not run like someone r aimlessly;
Gal 2: 2 and had not been r my race in vain.
5: 7 You were r a good race. Who cut

RUNS RUN
Jn 10:12 he abandons the sheep and r away.
2Jn 1: 9 Anyone who r ahead and does not

RUSH RUSHES, RUSHING
Pr 1:16 for their feet r into evil, they are
6:18 feet that are quick to r into evil,
Isa 59: 7 Their feet r into sin; they are swift

RUSHES RUSH
Pr 26:17 by the ears is someone who r

RUSHING RUSH
Pr 18: 4 fountain of wisdom is a r stream.
Eze 1:24 like the roar of r waters,
43: 2 voice was like the roar of r waters,

Rev 1:15 was like the sound of r waters.
14: 2 heaven like the roar of r waters
19: 6 like the roar of r waters and like

RUTH
Moabitess; widow who went to Bethlehem with mother-in-law Naomi (Ru 1). Gleaned in field of Boaz; shown favor (Ru 2). Proposed marriage to Boaz (Ru 3). Married (Ru 4:1–12); bore Obed, ancestor of David (Ru 4:13–22), Jesus (Mt 1:5).

RUTHLESS RUTHLESSLY
Ps 37:35 r man flourishing like a luxuriant
Pr 11:16 honor, but r men gain only wealth.
Isa 29:20 The r will vanish, the mockers will

RUTHLESSLY RUTHLESS
Ex 1:14 labor the Egyptians worked them r.
Lev 25:43 Do not rule over them r, but fear

S

SABACHTHANI*
Mt 27:46 voice, *"Eli, Eli, lema s?"*
Mk 15:34 voice, *"Eloi, Eloi, lema s?"*

SABAOTH (KJV) See ALMIGHTY

SABBATH SABBATHS
Ex 16:23 'Tomorrow is to be a day of s rest, a holy s to the LORD.
20: 8 "Remember the S day by keeping it
31:14 " 'Observe the S, because it is
Lev 23:16 up to the day after the seventh S,
25: 2 the land itself must observe a s
Nu 15:32 found gathering wood on the S day.
Dt 5:12 "Observe the S day by keeping it
2Ch 36:21 The land enjoyed its s rests;
Ne 13:17 desecrating the S day?
Ps 92: T *A song. For the S day.*
Isa 56: 2 who keeps the S without desecrating
58:13 keep your feet from breaking the S
Jer 17:21 not to carry a load on the S day
Mt 12: 1 through the grainfields on the S.
Mk 2:28 Son of Man is Lord even of the S."
Lk 6: 9 ask you, which is lawful on the S:
13:10 On a S Jesus was teaching in one
14: 3 law, "Is it lawful to heal on the S
Col 2:16 a New Moon celebration or a S day.

SABBATH-REST* REST
Heb 4: 9 then, a S for the people of God;

SABBATHS SABBATH
Ex 31:13 Israelites, 'You must observe my S.
Lev 26:34 the land will rest and enjoy its s.
Eze 20:12 I gave them my S as a sign between

SACKCLOTH
1Ch 21:16 elders, clothed in s, fell facedown.
Ps 30:11 you removed my s and clothed me
Da 9: 3 in fasting, and in s and ashes.
Joel 1:13 Put on s, you priests, and mourn;
Jnh 3: 5 the greatest to the least, put on s.
Mt 11:21 would have repented long ago in s

SACRED

Ge	1:14	serve as signs to mark s times,
Ex	12:16	On the first day hold a s assembly,
	23:24	and break their s stones to pieces.
	28: 2	Make s garments for your brother
	30:31	'This is to be my s anointing oil
Lev	23: 2	you are to proclaim as s assemblies.
Ps	15: 1	Lord, who may dwell in your s tent?
Isa	1:29	be ashamed because of the s oaks
Hos	3: 4	prince, without sacrifice or s stones,
Joel	1:14	a holy fast; call a s assembly.
Mt	7: 6	"Do not give dogs what is s;
Ro	14: 5	one day more s than another;
1Co	3:17	for God's temple is s, and you
2Pe	1:18	were with him on the s mountain.
	2:21	turn their backs on the s command

SACRIFICE SACRIFICED, SACRIFICES

Ge	22: 2	S him there as a burnt offering
Ex	5:17	'Let us go and s to the Lord.'
	12:27	'It is the Passover s to the Lord,
Jdg	11:31	and I will s it as a burnt offering."
1Sa	2:13	any of the people offered a s,
	15:22	To obey is better than s, and to heed
1Ki	18:38	the Lord fell and burned up the s,
1Ch	21:24	or s a burnt offering that costs me
Ps	40: 6	S and offering you did not desire—
	50:14	"S thank offerings to God,
	50:23	Those who s thank offerings honor
	51:16	You do not delight in s, or I would
	51:17	My s, O God, is a broken spirit;
	54: 6	I will s a freewill offering to you;
	107:22	Let them s thank offerings and tell
	141: 2	of my hands be like the evening s.
Pr	15: 8	The Lord detests the s
	21: 3	acceptable to the Lord than s.
	21:27	The s of the wicked is detestable—
Eze	20:26	the s of every firstborn—
Da	8:13	the vision concerning the daily s,
	9:27	of the 'seven' he will put an end to s
	12:11	the time that the daily s is abolished
Hos	6: 6	not s, and acknowledgment of God
Zep	1: 7	The Lord has prepared a s;
Mt	9:13	'I desire mercy, not s.'
Ro	3:25	God presented Christ as a s
	12: 1	to offer your bodies as a living s,
Eph	5: 2	as a fragrant offering and s to God.
Php	2:17	out like a drink offering on the s
	4:18	an acceptable s, pleasing to God.
Heb	9:26	away with sin by the s of himself.
	10: 5	"S and offering you did not desire,
	10:10	have been made holy through the s
	10:14	one s he has made perfect forever
	10:18	s for sin is no longer necessary.
	11:17	God tested him, offered Isaac as a s.
	13:15	offer to God a s of praise—
1Jn	2: 2	He is the atoning s for our sins,
	4:10	sent his Son as an atoning s for our

SACRIFICED SACRIFICE

Ge	8:20	birds, he s burnt offerings on it.
	22:13	s it as a burnt offering instead of his

Lev	18:21	of your children to be s to Molek,
2Ki	17:17	They s their sons and daughters
Lk	22: 7	the Passover lamb had to be s.
Ac	15:29	are to abstain from food s to idols,
1Co	5: 7	our Passover lamb, has been s.
	8: 1	Now about food s to idols:
Heb	7:27	He s for their sins once for all
	9:28	so Christ was s once to take away
Rev	2:14	to sin so that they ate food s to idols
	2:20	and the eating of food s to idols.

SACRIFICES SACRIFICE

Ex	3:18	to offer s to the Lord our God.'
	22:20	"Whoever s to any god other than
Lev	17: 7	offer any of their s to the goat idols
Dt	12:31	in the fire as s to their gods.
Jos	22:26	but not for burnt offerings or s.'
2Ch	7: 1	the burnt offering and the s,
	7:12	place for myself as a temple for s.
Ezr	6: 3	be rebuilt as a place to present s,
Ps	4: 5	Offer the s of the righteous and trust
	50: 8	against you concerning your s
Isa	1:11	"The multitude of your s—
	56: 7	and s will be accepted on my altar;
Jer	6:20	your s do not please me."
Am	5:25	"Did you bring me s and offerings
Mk	12:33	than all burnt offerings and s."
1Co	10:20	but the s of pagans are offered
Heb	7:27	he does not need to offer s day
	9:23	themselves with better s than these.
	13:16	for with such s God is pleased.
1Pe	2: 5	offering spiritual s acceptable

SAD SADDENED

Ne	2: 1	I had not been s in his presence
Ecc	7: 3	because a s face is good
Lk	18:23	he became very s, because he was

SADDENED* SAD

Mk	14:19	They were s, and one by one they

SADDUCEES

Mt	16: 1	The Pharisees and S came to Jesus
	16: 6	the yeast of the Pharisees and S."
	22:34	that Jesus had silenced the S,
Mk	12:18	Then the S, who say there is no
Ac	23: 7	out between the Pharisees and the S,

SAFE SAVE

2Sa	18:29	"Is the young man Absalom s?"
Ezr	8:21	and ask him for a s journey for us
Job	21: 9	Their homes are s and free
Ps	12: 7	will keep the needy s and will
	16: 1	Keep me s, my God, for in you I
	27: 5	of trouble he will keep me s in his
	37: 3	in the land and enjoy s pasture.
Pr	18:10	the righteous run to it and are s.
	28:18	whose walk is blameless is kept s,
	28:26	who walk in wisdom are kept s.
	29:25	trusts in the Lord is kept s.
Jer	12: 5	If you stumble in s country,
Lk	15:27	calf because he has him back s
Jn	17:12	kept them s by that name you gave
1Jn	5:18	who was born of God keeps them s,

SAFE-CONDUCT* CONDUCT
Ne   2: 7 they will provide me s until I arrive

SAFEGUARD* GUARD
Php   3: 1 to you again, and it is a s for you.

SAFELY SAVE
Ge   19:16 and led them s out of the city,
     28:21 I return s to my father's household,
Lev 25:18 laws, and you will live s in the land.
1Ki 22:28 "If you ever return s, the LORD

SAFETY SAVE
Dt   12:10 you so that you will live in s.
Ps   4: 8 alone, LORD, make me dwell in s.
     141:10 their own nets, while I pass by in s.
Pr   3:23 Then you will go on your way in s,
Isa 14:30 and the needy will lie down in s.
Jer 33:16 saved and Jerusalem will live in s.
Eze 34:28 They will live in s, and no one will
Hos   2:18 land, so that all may lie down in s.
1Th   5: 3 "Peace and s," destruction will

SAIL SAILED, SAILORS
2Ch 20:37 and were not able to set s to trade.

SAILED SAIL
Jnh   1: 3 and s for Tarshish to flee
Lk   8:23 As they s, he fell asleep.

SAILORS SAIL
Jnh   1: 5 All the s were afraid and each cried

SAINT(S)
     Translated in the NIV as "faithful," "faithful
people," "faithful servants," "God's people," "godly,"
"his people," "holy people," "Lord's people," "his
own people," "people of God," "your people."
     Following are all NIV 1984 references to "saints":
1Sa 2:9; 2Ch 6:41; Ps 16:3; 30:4; 31:23; 34:9; 52:9;
79:2; 85:8; 116:15; 132:9, 16; 145:10; 148:14; 149:1,
5, 9; Da 7:18, 21, 22, 25, 25, 27; 8:12; Ac 9:13, 32;
26:10; Ro 1:7; 8:27; 15:25, 26, 31; 16:2, 15; 1Co 6:1,
2; 14:33; 16:15; 2Co 1:1; 8:4; 9:1; 13:13; Eph 1:1, 15,
18; 3:18; 6:18; Php 1:1; 4:21, 22; Col 1:4, 12, 26; 1Ti
5:10; Phm 1:5, 7; Jude 1:3; Rev 5:8; 8:3, 4; 11:18;
13:7, 10; 14:12; 16:6; 17:6; 18:20, 24; 19:8

SAKE
Ge   12:16 He treated Abram well for her s,
     18:24 the s of the fifty righteous people
Lev 26:45 their s I will remember the covenant
Jos 23: 3 done to all these nations for your s;
1Sa 12:22 the s of his great name the LORD
1Ki 11:12 for the s of David your father, I will
Ps   23: 3 the right paths for his name's s.
     25:11 For the s of your name, LORD,
     44:22 your s we face death all day long;
     69: 7 For I endure scorn for your s,
     106: 8 Yet he saved them for his name's s,
     109:21 LORD, help me for your name's s;
     132:10 For the s of your servant David,
Isa 42:21 for the s of his righteousness
     43:25 for my own s, and remembers your
     48: 9 my own name's s I delay my wrath;
     48:11 For my own s, for my own s, I do

Isa 62: 1 For Zion's s I will not keep silent,
Jer 14: 7 LORD, for the s of your name.
     14:21 the s of your name do not despise
Eze 20: 9 But for the s of my name, I brought
     20:14 the s of my name I did what would
     20:22 the s of my name I did what would
     36:32 that I am not doing this for your s,
Da   9:17 For your s, Lord, look with favor
Mt   10:39 loses their life for my s will find it.
     19:29 my s will receive a hundred times as
Ro   8:36 your s we face death all day long;
      9: 3 from Christ for the s of my people,
     14:20 the work of God for the s of food.
1Co   9:23 I do all this for the s of the gospel,
2Co   4:11 given over to death for Jesus' s,
      8: 9 yet for your s he became poor,
     12:10 is why, for Christ's s, I delight
Php   3: 7 consider loss for the s of Christ.
Heb 11:26 disgrace for the s of Christ as
1Pe   2:13 for the Lord's s to every human
3Jn   1: 7 It was for the s of the Name

SALE SELL
Dt   28:68 you will offer yourselves for s
Ps   44:12 gaining nothing from their s.

SALEM
Ge   14:18 Melchizedek king of S brought
Heb   7: 2 also, "king of S" means "king

SALIVA*
1Sa 21:13 and letting s run down his beard.
Jn   9: 6 made some mud with the s, and put

SALT SALTED, SALTINESS, SALTY
Ge   19:26 back, and she became a pillar of s.
Lev   2:13 all your grain offerings with s. Do not
              leave the s of the covenant
Nu   18:19 covenant of s before the LORD
2Ki   2:20 bowl," he said, "and put s in it."
Mt   5:13 "You are the s of the earth.
      5:13 But if the s loses its saltiness,
Mk   9:50 "S is good, but if it loses its
Col   4: 6 seasoned with s, so that you may
Jas   3:11 s water flow from the same spring?

SALTED* SALT
Ex   30:35 It is to be s and pure and sacred.
Mk   9:49 Everyone will be s with fire.

SALTINESS SALT
Lk   14:34 but if it loses its s, how can it be

SALTY SALT
Mt   5:13 how can it be made s again? It is no

SALVATION* SAVE
Ex   15: 2 he has become my s.
2Sa 22: 3 my shield and the horn of my s.
     23: 5 he would not bring to fruition my s
1Ch 16:23 proclaim his s day after day.
2Ch   6:41 be clothed with s, may your faithful
Ps   9:14 Zion, and there rejoice in your s.
     13: 5 my heart rejoices in your s.
     14: 7 that s for Israel would come
     18: 2 my shield and the horn of my s,

Ps 27: 1 The LORD is my light and my s—
    28: 8 a fortress of s for his anointed one.
    35: 3 Say to me, "I am your s."
    35: 9 in the LORD and delight in his s.
    37:39 The s of the righteous comes
    50:23 to the blameless I will show my s."
    51:12 Restore to me the joy of your s
    53: 6 that s for Israel would come
    62: 1 rest in God; my s comes from him.
    62: 2 Truly he is my rock and my s;
    62: 6 Truly he is my rock and my s;
    62: 7 My s and my honor depend on God;
    67: 2 on earth, your s among all nations.
    69:13 O God, answer me with your sure s.
    69:27 do not let them share in your s.
    69:29 may your s, God, protect me.
    74:12 he brings s on the earth.
    85: 7 love, LORD, and grant us your s.
    85: 9 Surely his s is near those who fear
    91:16 satisfy him and show him my s."
    95: 1 us shout aloud to the Rock of our s.
    96: 2 proclaim his s day after day.
    98: 1 his holy arm have worked s for him.
    98: 2 The LORD has made his s known
    98: 3 of the earth have seen the s of our
   116:13 I will lift up the cup of s and call
   118:14 he has become my s.
   118:21 you have become my s.
   119:41 your s, according to your promise;
   119:81 soul faints with longing for your s,
   119:123 looking for your s, looking for your
   119:155 S is far from the wicked, for they do
   119:166 I wait for your s, LORD, and I
   119:174 I long for your s, LORD, and your
   132:16 I will clothe her priests with s,
Isa 12: 2 Surely God is my s; I will trust
    12: 2 he has become my s."
    12: 3 will draw water from the wells of s
    25: 9 let us rejoice and be glad in his s."
    26: 1 God makes s its walls and ramparts.
    26:18 We have not brought s to the earth,
    30:15 "In repentance and rest is your s,
    33: 2 morning, our s in time of distress.
    33: 6 a rich store of s and wisdom
    45: 8 the earth open wide, let s spring up,
    45:17 the LORD with an everlasting s;
    46:13 and my s will not be delayed.
    46:13 I will grant s to Zion, my splendor
    49: 6 that my s may reach to the ends
    49: 8 and in the day of s I will help you;
    51: 5 near speedily, my s is on the way,
    51: 6 But my s will last forever,
    51: 8 my s through all generations."
    52: 7 who proclaim s, who say to Zion,
    52:10 the earth will see the s of our God.
    56: 1 for my s is close at hand and my
    59: 16 so his own arm achieved s for him,
    59:17 and the helmet of s on his head;
    60:18 you will call your walls S and your
    61:10 has clothed me with garments of s
    62: 1 the dawn, her s like a blazing torch.
    63: 5 so my own arm achieved s for me,
Jer 3:23 in the LORD our God is the s

La 3:26 wait quietly for the s of the LORD.
Jnh 2: 9 'S comes from the LORD.' "
Lk 1:69 He has raised up a horn of s for us
    1:71 s from our enemies
    1:77 of s through the forgiveness of their
    2:30 For my eyes have seen your s,
    3: 6 all people will see God's s.' "
   19: 9 "Today s has come to this house,
Jn 4:22 we do know, for s is from the Jews.
Ac 4:12 S is found in no one else, for there is
   13:26 that this message of s has been sent.
   13:47 that you may bring s to the ends
   28:28 know that God's s has been sent
Ro 1:16 brings s to everyone who believes:
   11:11 s has come to the Gentiles to make
   13:11 because our s is nearer now than
2Co 1: 6 it is for your comfort and s;
    6: 2 and in the day of s I helped you."
    6: 2 of God's favor, now is the day of s.
    7:10 brings repentance that leads to s
Eph 1:13 of truth, the gospel of your s.
    6:17 Take the helmet of s and the sword
Php 2:12 to work out your s with fear
1Th 5: 8 and the hope of s as a helmet.
    5: 9 to receive s through our Lord Jesus
2Ti 2:10 that they too may obtain the s that is
    3:15 make you wise for s through faith
Titus 2:11 appeared that offers s to all people.
Heb 1:14 to serve those who will inherit s?
    2: 3 we escape if we ignore so great a s?
    2: 3 This s, which was first announced
    2:10 of their s perfect through what he
    5: 9 of eternal s for all who obey him
    6: 9 the things that have to do with s.
    9:28 to bring s to those who are waiting
1Pe 1: 5 the coming of the s that is ready
    1: 9 of your faith, the s of your souls.
    1:10 Concerning this s, the prophets,
    2: 2 by it you may grow up in your s,
2Pe 3:15 that our Lord's patience means s,
Jude 1: 3 to write to you about the s we share,
Rev 7:10 "S belongs to our God, who sits
   12:10 "Now have come the s
   19: 1 S and glory and power belong to our

SAMARIA SAMARITAN, SAMARITANS

1Ki 16:24 the hill, calling it S, after Shemer,
   16:32 the temple of Baal that he built in S.
   20:43 of Israel went to his palace in S.
2Ki 17: 6 the king of Assyria captured S
Isa 7: 9 The head of Ephraim is S,
   36:19 Have they rescued S from my hand?
Eze 23: 4 Oholah is S, and Oholibah is
Hos 8: 5 S, throw out your calf-idol!
Am 6: 1 to you who feel secure on Mount S,
Mic 1: 6 "Therefore I will make S a heap
Jn 4: 4 Now he had to go through S.
Ac 1: 8 and in all Judea and S,
   8: 1 scattered throughout Judea and S.
   8:14 that S had accepted the word of God,
       they sent Peter and John to S.

SAMARITAN SAMARIA

Lk 10:33 But a S, as he traveled, came where
     17:16 and thanked him—and he was a S.
Jn   4: 7 When a S woman came to draw
     8:48 we right in saying that you are a S
Ac   8:25 the gospel in many S villages.

SAMARITANS SAMARIA

Jn   4: 9 (For Jews do not associate with S.)

SAME

Ge 11: 6 people speaking the s language they
Ex   5: 8 to make the s number of bricks as
     7:11 did the s things by their secret arts:
     7:22 Egyptian magicians did the s things
     8: 7 the magicians did the s things
    34:16 they will lead your sons to do the s.
Dt   7:19 The LORD your God will do the s
1Sa 2:34 they will both die on the s day.
Ps 102:27 But you remain the s, and your
Ecc 2:14 that the s fate overtakes them both.
     9: 3 The s destiny overtakes all.
Mt   5:12 for in the s way they persecuted
     7: 2 For in the s way you judge others,
Ac   1:11 in the s way you have seen him go
    11:17 God gave them the s gift he gave us
Ro   2: 1 who pass judgment on the s things.
    10:12 the s Lord is Lord of all and richly
    12: 4 do not all have the s function,
    15: 5 give you the s attitude of mind
1Co 10: 3 They all ate the s spiritual food
    12: 4 but the s Spirit distributes them.
    12: 5 kinds of service, but the s Lord.
Php 2: 5 have the s mindset as Christ Jesus:
     4: 2 to be of the s mind in the Lord.
1Ti 3: 6 and fall under the s judgment as
Heb 1:12 But you remain the s, and your
    13: 8 Jesus Christ is the s yesterday

SAMSON*

Danite judge. Birth promised (Jdg 13). Married to Philistine, but wife given away (Jdg 14). Vengeance on the Philistines (Jdg 15). Betrayed by Delilah (Jdg 16:1–22). Death (Jdg 16:23–31). Feats of strength: killed lion (Jdg 14:6), 30 Philistines (Jdg 14:19), 1,000 Philistines with jawbone (Jdg 15:13–17), carried off gates of Gaza (Jdg 16:3), pushed down temple of Dagon (Jdg 16:25–30; Heb 11:32).

SAMUEL

Ephraimite judge and prophet (Heb 11:32). Birth prayed for (1Sa 1:10–18). Dedicated to temple by Hannah (1Sa 1:21–28). Raised by Eli (1Sa 2:11, 18–26). Called as prophet (1Sa 3). Led Israel to victory over Philistines (1Sa 7). Asked by Israel for a king (1Sa 8). Anointed Saul as king (1Sa 9–10). Farewell speech (1Sa 12). Rebuked Saul for sacrifice (1Sa 13). Announced rejection of Saul (1Sa 15). Anointed David as king (1Sa 16). Protected David from Saul (1Sa 19:18–24). Death (1Sa 25:1). Returned from dead to condemn Saul (1Sa 28).

SANBALLAT

Led opposition to Nehemiah's rebuilding of Jerusalem (Ne 2:10, 19; 4; 6).

SANCTIFIED* SANCTIFY

Jn   17:19 myself, that they too may be truly s.
Ac   20:32 among all those who are s.
     26:18 a place among those who are s
Ro   15:16 to God, s by the Holy Spirit.
1Co 1: 2 to those s in Christ Jesus and called
     6:11 you were s, you were justified
     7:14 husband has been s through his
     7:14 wife has been s through her
1Th 4: 3 It is God's will that you should be s:
Heb 10:29 blood of the covenant that s them,

SANCTIFY* SANCTIFIED, SANCTIFYING

Jn   17:17 S them by the truth; your word is
     17:19 For them I s myself, that they too
1Th 5:23 peace, s you through and through.
Heb 9:13 are ceremonially unclean s them so

SANCTIFYING* SANCTIFY

2Th 2:13 be saved through the s work
1Pe 1: 2 through the s work of the Spirit,

SANCTUARIES SANCTUARY

Lev 26:31 into ruins and lay waste your s,

SANCTUARY SANCTUARIES

Ex   15:17 made for your dwelling, the s, Lord,
     25: 8 "Then have them make a s for me,
Lev 10:13 Eat it in the s area, because it is
     19:30 and have reverence for my s.
Nu   3:28 responsible for the care of the s.
     18: 1 for offenses connected with the s,
1Ki 6:19 He prepared the inner s within
1Ch 22:19 to build the s of the LORD God,
Ezr 9: 8 and giving us a firm place in his s,
Ps   20: 2 May he send you help from the s
     60: 6 God has spoken from his s:
     63: 2 I have seen you in the s and beheld
     68:24 of my God and King into the s.
     68:35 You, God, are awesome in your s;
     73:17 till I entered the s of God;
     74: 7 They burned your s to the ground;
    102:19 looked down from his s on high,
    114: 2 Judah became God's s, Israel his
    134: 2 Lift up your hands in the s
    150: 1 Praise God in his s; praise him
La   1:10 she saw pagan nations enter her s—
Eze 5:11 because you have defiled my s
     37:26 I will put my s among them forever.
Da   8:11 and his s was thrown down.
     9:26 come will destroy the city and the s.
Heb 6:19 enters the inner s behind the curtain,
     8: 2 and who serves in the s, the true
     8: 5 They serve at a s that is a copy
     9:24 Christ did not enter a s made

SAND

Ge   22:17 the sky and as the s on the seashore.
     32:12 make your descendants like the s
     41:49 of grain, like the s of the sea;

Ex   2:12 the Egyptian and hid him in the s.
1Ki   4:20 Israel were as numerous as the s
Jer   33:22 and as measureless as the s
Hos   1:10 "Yet the Israelites will be like the s
Mt   7:26 man who built his house on s.
Ro   9:27 of the Israelites be like the s
Heb 11:12 sky and as countless as the s
Rev 20: 8 In number they are like the s

SANDAL SANDALS

Ge   14:23 not even a thread or the strap of a s,
Ru   4: 7 one party took off his s and gave it

SANDALS SANDAL

Ex   3: 5 "Take off your s, for the place
     12:11 your s on your feet and your staff
Dt   25: 9 take off one of his s, spit in his face
     29: 5 wear out, nor did the s on your feet.
Jos   5:15 "Take off your s, for the place
Mt   3:11 I, whose s I am not worthy to carry.

SANG SING

Ex   15: 1 and the Israelites s this song
     15:21 Miriam s to them:
Nu   21:17 Then Israel s this song:
Jdg   5: 1 Barak son of Abinoam s this song:
1Sa 18: 7 As they danced, they s:
     29: 5 Isn't this the David they s
2Sa   3:33 The king s this lament for Abner:
     22: 1 David s to the LORD the words
2Ch   5:13 in praise to the LORD and s:
     29:30 So they s praises with gladness
Ezr   3:11 thanksgiving they s to the LORD:
Ne   12:42 The choirs s under the direction
Job 38: 7 while the morning stars s together
Ps 106:12 his promises and s his praise.
Mt   11:17 we s a dirge, and you did not
Rev   5: 9 And they s a new song, saying:
     14: 3 they s a new song before the throne
     15: 3 s the song of God's servant Moses

SANHEDRIN

Mt   26:59 the whole S were looking for false
Jn   11:47 Pharisees called a meeting of the S.
Ac   4:15 them to withdraw from the S
      5:21 arrived, they called together the S—
      6:12 and brought him before the S.

SANK SINK

Ex   15: 5 they s to the depths like a stone.
1Sa 17:49 The stone s into his forehead,
Jer 38: 6 and Jeremiah s down into the mud.
Jnh   2: 6 the roots of the mountains I s down;

SAP

Hos   7: 9 Foreigners s his strength, but he
Ro   11:17 the nourishing s from the olive root,

SAPPHIRA*

Ac   5: 1 together with his wife S, also sold

SAPPHIRE*

Rev 21:19 jasper, the second s, the third agate,

SARAH SARAI

Wife of Abraham, originally named Sarai; bar-

ren (Ge 11:29–31; 1Pe 3:6). Taken by Pharaoh as Abraham's sister; returned (Ge 12:10–20). Gave Hagar to Abraham; sent her away in pregnancy (Ge 16). Name changed; Isaac promised (Ge 17:15–21; 18:10–15; Heb 11:11). Taken by Abimelech as Abraham's sister; returned (Ge 20). Isaac born; Hagar and Ishmael sent away (Ge 21:1–21; Gal 4:21–31). Death (Ge 23).

SARAI SARAH

Ge   17:15 "As for S your wife, you are no longer
            to call her S;

SARDIS

Rev   3: 1 the angel of the church in S write:

SASH SASHES

Ex   28: 4 a woven tunic, a turban and a s.
Isa 11: 5 faithfulness the s around his waist.
Rev   1:13 with a golden s around his chest.

SASHES SASH

Rev 15: 6 wore golden s around their chests.

SAT SIT

Ge   48: 2 his strength and s up on the bed.
Ex   2:15 Midian, where he s down by a well.
Jdg 19:15 They went and s in the city square,
Ru   4: 1 gate and s down there just as
1Ki 19: 4 s down under it and prayed that he
Ne   1: 4 these things, I s down and wept.
Ps 137: 1 By the rivers of Babylon we s
Mt   5: 1 up on a mountainside and s down.
     13: 2 that he got into a boat and s in it,
     28: 2 rolled back the stone and s on it.
Lk   7:15 The dead man s up and began
     10:39 who s at the Lord's feet listening
Jn   4: 6 the journey, s down by the well.
     12:14 found a young donkey and s on it,
Heb   1: 3 he s down at the right hand
      8: 1 who s down at the right hand
     10:12 he s down at the right hand of God,
     12: 2 and s down at the right hand
Rev   3:21 and s down with my Father on his
      4: 3 And the one who s there had
      5: 1 of him who s on the throne a scroll

SATAN

1Ch 21: 1 S rose up against Israel and incited
Job   1: 6 and S also came with them.
      2: 1 and S also came with them
Zec   3: 2 The LORD said to S, "The LORD
            rebuke you, S!
Mt   4:10 said to him, "Away from me, S!
     12:26 If S drives out S, he is divided
     16:23 said to Peter, "Get behind me, S!
Mk   4:15 it, S comes and takes away the word
Lk   10:18 "I saw S fall like lightning
     22: 3 Then S entered Judas,
Jn   13:27 took the bread, S entered into him.
Ac   5: 3 is it that S has so filled your heart
     26:18 and from the power of S to God,
Ro   16:20 will soon crush S under your feet.
1Co   5: 5 hand this man over to S
      7: 5 so that S will not tempt you because

2Co 2:11 in order that **S** might not outwit us.
11:14 **S** himself masquerades as an angel
12: 7 a messenger of **S**, to torment me.
2Th 2: 9 be in accordance with how **S** works.
1Ti 1:20 whom I have handed over to **S** to be
5:15 already turned away to follow **S**.
Rev 2: 9 are not, but are a synagogue of **S**.
2:13 where **S** has his throne.
3: 9 who are of the synagogue of **S**,
12: 9 or **S**, who leads the whole world
20: 2 or **S**, and bound him for a thousand
20: 7 **S** will be released from his prison

SATISFACTION SATISFY
Ecc 2:24 drink and find **s** in their own toil.
3:13 drink, and find **s** in all their toil—

SATISFIED SATISFY
Lev 26:26 You will eat, but you will not be **s**.
Dt 6:11 then when you eat and are **s**,
Ps 17:15 I will be **s** with seeing your likeness.
22:26 The poor will eat and be **s**;
63: 5 I will be fully **s** as with the richest
104:28 hand, they are **s** with good things.
Pr 13: 4 the desires of the diligent are fully **s**.
18:20 the harvest of their lips they are **s**.
27:20 Death and Destruction are never **s**,
30:15 are three things that are never **s**,
Ecc 5:10 whoever loves wealth is never **s**
Isa 53:11 he will see the light of life and be **s**;
Hos 13: 6 When I fed them, they were **s**;
Mt 14:20 They all ate and were **s**,
15:37 They all ate and were **s**.
Lk 6:21 who hunger now, for you will be **s**.

SATISFIES* SATISFY
Ps 103: 5 who **s** your desires with good things
107: 9 for he **s** the thirsty and fills
147:14 and **s** you with the finest of wheat.

SATISFY SATISFACTION, SATISFIED, SATISFIES
Ps 90:14 **S** us in the morning with your
91:16 With long life I will **s** him and show
132:15 her poor I will **s** with food.
145:16 **s** the desires of every living thing.
Pr 5:19 may her breasts **s** you always,
6:30 he steals to **s** his hunger when he is
Isa 55: 2 and your labor on what does not **s**?
58:10 and **s** the needs of the oppressed,
Jer 31:25 refresh the weary and **s** the faint."
Joel 2:19 and olive oil, enough to **s** you fully;

SAUL PAUL
1. Benjamite; anointed by Samuel as first king of Israel (1Sa 9–10). Defeated Ammonites (1Sa 11). Rebuked for offering sacrifice (1Sa 13:1–15). Defeated Philistines (1Sa 14). Rejected as king for failing to annihilate Amalekites (1Sa 15). Soothed from evil spirit by David (1Sa 16:14–23). Sent David against Goliath (1Sa 17). Jealousy and attempted murder of David (1Sa 18:1–11). Gave David Michal as wife (1Sa 18:12–30). Second attempt to kill David (1Sa 19). Anger at Jonathan (1Sa 20:26–34). Pursued David: killed priests at

Nob (1Sa 22), went to Keilah and Ziph (1Sa 23), life spared by David at En Gedi (1Sa 24) and in his tent (1Sa 26). Rebuked by Samuel's spirit for consulting medium at Endor (1Sa 28). Wounded by Philistines; took his own life (1Sa 31; 1Ch 10). Lamented by David (2Sa 1:17–27). Children (1Sa 14:49–51; 1Ch 8).
2. See PAUL

SAVAGE*
Eze 34:25 rid the land of **s** beasts so that they
Ac 20:29 **s** wolves will come in among you

SAVE SAFE, SAFELY, SAFETY, SALVATION, SAVED, SAVES, SAVING, SAVIOR
Ge 45: 5 because it was to **s** lives that God
Dt 4:42 one of these cities and **s** their life.
2Sa 22:28 You **s** the humble, but your eyes are
1Ch 16:35 Cry out, "**S** us, God our Savior;
Job 40:14 that your own right hand can **s** you.
Ps 6: 4 **s** me because of your unfailing love.
17: 7 you who **s** by your right hand those
18:27 You **s** the humble but bring low
28: 9 **S** your people and bless your
31:16 **s** me in your unfailing love.
69:35 for God will **s** Zion and rebuild
71: 2 turn your ear to me and **s** me.
72:13 needy and **s** the needy from death.
86: 2 **s** your servant who trusts in you.
91: 3 Surely he will **s** you
109:31 to **s** their lives from those who
146: 3 in human beings, who cannot **s**.
Pr 2:12 Wisdom will **s** you from the ways
2:16 Wisdom will **s** you
Isa 33:22 is our king; it is he who will **s** us.
35: 4 retribution he will come to **s** you."
36:20 have been able to **s** their lands
38:20 The LORD will **s** me, and we will
45:20 who pray to gods that cannot **s**.
46: 7 it cannot **s** them from their troubles.
59: 1 of the LORD is not too short to **s**,
63: 1 proclaiming victory, mighty to **s**."
Jer 15:20 I am with you to rescue and **s** you,"
17:14 **s** me and I will be saved, for you are
La 4:17 for a nation that could not **s** us.
Eze 3:18 evil ways in order to **s** their life,
14:14 it, they could **s** only themselves
34:22 I will **s** my flock, and they will no
Hos 1: 7 and I will **s** them—not by bow,
Zep 1:18 nor their gold will be able to **s** them
Zec 8: 7 "I will **s** my people
Mt 1:21 because he will **s** his people
16:25 wants to **s** their life will lose it,
27:42 they said, "but he can't **s** himself!
Lk 6: 9 to do evil, to **s** life or to destroy it?"
19:10 came to seek and to **s** the lost."
23:37 the king of the Jews, **s** yourself."
Jn 3:17 but to **s** the world through him.
12:27 'Father, **s** me from this hour'?
12:47 judge the world, but to **s** the world.
Ac 2:40 "**S** yourselves from this corrupt
Ro 11:14 people to envy and **s** some of them.

1Co 7:16 whether you will s your husband?
     7:16 whether you will s your wife?
     9:22 all possible means I might s some.
1Ti 1:15 came into the world to s sinners—
Heb 7:25 to s completely those who come
Jas 2:14 Can such faith s them?
     5:20 of their way will s them from death
Jude 1:23 s others by snatching them

SAVED SAVE

Ex   14:30 day the LORD s Israel
Dt   33:29 like you, a people s by the LORD?
Jdg   2:16 who s them out of the hands
1Sa 14:23 So on that day the LORD s Israel,
2Ch 32:22 So the LORD s Hezekiah
Ps   18: 3 and I have been s from my enemies.
     22: 5 To you they cried out and were s;
     33:16 No king is s by the size of his army;
     34: 6 he s him out of all his troubles.
    106: 8 Yet he s them for his name's sake,
    106:21 They forgot the God who s them,
    116: 6 when I was brought low, he s me.
Isa 25: 9 we trusted in him, and he s us.
     45:17 Israel will be s by the LORD
     45:22 "Turn to me and be s, all you ends
     64: 5 How then can we be s?
Jer   4:14 the evil from your heart and be s.
      8:20 has ended, and we are not s."
     17:14 save me and I will be s, for you are
Eze   3:19 but you will have s yourself.
     33: 5 they would have s themselves.
Joel 2:32 the name of the LORD will be s;
Mt   10:22 who stands firm to the end will be s.
     19:25 and asked, "Who then can be s?"
     24:13 who stands firm to the end will be s.
Mk   15:31 "He s others," they said, "but he
Lk   7:50 the woman, "Your faith has s you;
     13:23 only a few people going to be s?"
Jn   10. 9 enters through me will be s.
Ac   2:21 on the name of the Lord will be s.'
      2:47 daily those who were being s.
      4:12 mankind by which we must be s."
     15:11 of our Lord Jesus that we are s,
     16:30 "Sirs, what must I do to be s?"
Ro   5: 9 how much more shall we be s
      8:24 For in this hope we were s.
      9:27 the sea, only the remnant will be s.
     10: 1 the Israelites is that they may be s.
     10: 9 him from the dead, you will be s.
     10:13 on the name of the Lord will be s."
     11:26 and in this way all Israel will be s.
1Co   1:18 to us who are being s it is the power
      3:15 will suffer loss but yet will be s—
      5: 5 so that his spirit may be s on the day
     10:33 of many, so that they may be s.
     15: 2 By this gospel you are s, if you hold
Eph   2: 5 it is by grace you have been s.
      2: 8 For it is by grace you have been s,
2Th   2:10 refused to love the truth and so be s.
      2:13 to be s through the sanctifying work
1Ti   2: 4 who wants all people to be s
      2:15 will be s through childbearing—
2Ti   1: 9 He has s us and called us to a holy
Titus 3: 5 he s us, not because of righteous

Titus 3: 5 He s us through the washing
Heb 10:39 to those who have faith and are s.
1Pe   4:18 it is hard for the righteous to be s,

SAVES SAVE

1Sa 17:47 sword or spear that the LORD s;
Ps   7:10 High, who s the upright in heart.
     34:18 s those who are crushed in spirit.
     55:16 I call to God, and the LORD s me.
     68:20 Our God is a God who s;
    145:19 he hears their cry and s them.
Pr   11:30 and the one who is wise s lives.
     14:25 A truthful witness s lives, but
Zep   3:17 you, the Mighty Warrior who s.
1Pe   3:21 baptism that now s you also—
      3:21 It s you by the resurrection of Jesus

SAVING SAVE

Ge   50:20 being done, the s of many lives.
1Sa 14: 6 can hinder the LORD from s,
Ps   40: 9 I proclaim your s acts in the great
     40:10 of your faithfulness and your s help.
     40:16 long for your s help always say,
     70: 4 long for your s help always say,
     71:15 deeds, of your s acts all day long—

SAVIOR* SAVE

Dt   32:15 them and rejected the Rock their S.
2Sa 22: 3 stronghold, my refuge and my s—
     22:47 be my God, the Rock, my S!
1Ch 16:35 Cry out, "Save us, God our S;
Ps   18:46 to my Rock! Exalted be God my S!
     24: 5 and vindication from God their S.
     25: 5 for you are God my S, and my hope
     27: 9 reject me or forsake me, God my S.
     38:22 to help me, my Lord and my S.
     42: 5 yet praise him, my S and my God.
     42:11 yet praise him, my S and my God.
     43: 5 yet praise him, my S and my God.
     51:14 you who are God my S, and my
     65: 5 God our S, the hope of all the ends
     68:19 to God our S, who daily bears our
     79: 9 us, God our S, for the glory of your
     85: 4 God our S, and put away your
     89:26 Father, my God, the Rock my S.'
Isa 17:10 You have forgotten God your S;
     19:20 he will send them a s and defender,
     43: 3 God, the Holy One of Israel, your S;
     43:11 and apart from me there is no s.
     45:15 himself, the God and S of Israel.
     45:21 from me, a righteous God and a S;
     49:26 am your S, your Redeemer,
     60:16 am your S, your Redeemer,
     62:11 Daughter Zion, 'See, your S comes!
     63: 8 and so he became their S.
Jer 14: 8 of Israel, its S in times of distress,
     23: 6 The LORD Our Righteous S
     33:16 The LORD Our Righteous S.'
Hos 13: 4 no God but me, no S except me.
Mic   7: 7 the LORD, I wait for God my S;
Hab   3:18 I will be joyful in God my S.
Lk   1:47 and my spirit rejoices in God my S,
      2:11 the town of David a S has been born
Jn   4:42 that this man really is the S

Ac 5:31 and S that he might bring Israel
13:23 has brought to Israel the S Jesus,
Eph 5:23 his body, of which he is the S.
Php 3:20 we eagerly await a S from there,
1Ti 1: 1 Jesus by the command of God our S
2: 3 This is good, and pleases God our S,
4:10 God, who is the S of all people,
2Ti 1:10 through the appearing of our S,
Titus 1: 3 me by the command of God our S,
1: 4 the Father and Christ Jesus our S.
2:10 teaching about God our S attractive.
2:13 of the glory of our great God and S,
3: 4 and love of God our S appeared,
3: 6 through Jesus Christ our S,
2Pe 1: 1 S Jesus Christ have received a faith
1:11 of our Lord and S Jesus Christ.
2:20 our Lord and S Jesus Christ and are
3: 2 Lord and S through your apostles.
3:18 of our Lord and S Jesus Christ.
1Jn 4:14 his Son to be the S of the world.
Jude 1:25 to the only God our S be glory,

SAW SEE
Ge 1: 4 God s that the light was good,
1:31 God s all that he had made, and it
3: 6 When the woman s that the fruit
6: 2 the sons of God s that the daughters
6:12 God s how corrupt the earth had
22:13 there in a thicket he s a ram caught
Ex 2: 2 When she s that he was a fine child,
2: 5 She s the basket among the reeds
2:11 He s an Egyptian beating a Hebrew,
3: 2 Moses s that though the bush was
24:10 and s the God of Israel.
34:35 they s that his face was radiant.
Nu 22:23 When the donkey s the angel
Dt 4:15 You s no form of any kind the day
32:19 The LORD s this and rejected
2Sa 11: 2 the roof he s a woman bathing.
Ps 31: 7 for you s my affliction and knew
73: 3 the arrogant when I s the prosperity
139:16 Your eyes s my unformed body;
Ecc 2:13 I s that wisdom is better than folly,
8:17 then I s all that God has done.
Isa 6: 1 that King Uzziah died, I s the Lord,
Eze 1: 1 were opened and I s visions of God.
Da 2:26 able to tell me what I s in my dream
4:10 These are the visions I s while lying
8: 2 my vision I s myself in the citadel
10: 7 was the only one who s the vision;
Am 9: 1 I s the Lord standing by the altar,
Mt 2: 2 We s his star when it rose and have
3:16 he s the Spirit of God descending
9: 2 When Jesus s their faith, he said
Mk 1:10 he s heaven being torn open
3:11 Whenever the impure spirits s him,
15:39 in front of Jesus, s how he died,
Lk 9:32 they s his glory and the two men
Jn 1:29 The next day John s Jesus coming
19:35 The man who s it has given
20: 1 s that the stone had been removed
20: 8 also went inside. He s and believed.
Ac 2: 3 They s what seemed to be tongues
7:55 up to heaven and s the glory of God,

Ac 10:11 He s heaven opened and something
11:23 s what the grace of God had done,
Heb 11:27 persevered because he s him who is
Rev 1: 2 who testifies to everything he s—
1:12 And when I turned I s seven golden
5: 6 Then I s a Lamb, looking as if it had
21: 1 Then I s "a new heaven and a new
22: 8 one who heard and s these things.

SAY SAYING, SAYINGS, SAYS
Ge 3: 1 "Did God really s, 'You must not
12:19 Why did you s, 'She is my sister,'
18:13 "Why did Sarah laugh and s,
26: 9 Why did you s, 'She is my sister'?"
Ex 7: 2 are to s everything I command you,
Job 40: 5 twice, but I will s no more."
Pr 4:10 accept what I s, and the years
5: 7 do not turn aside from what I s.
8: 6 for I have trustworthy things to s;
Mt 5:37 All you need to s is simply 'Yes'
10:19 do not worry about what to s or how
to s it.
10:19 time you will be given what to s,
16:15 he asked. "Who do you s I am?"
Mk 2: 9 to s to this paralyzed man,
8:27 them, "Who do people s I am?"
Lk 11:54 catch him in something he might s.
Jn 8:26 "I have much to s in judgment
8:43 you are unable to hear what I s.
12:49 who sent me commanded me to s all
16:12 "I have much more to s to you,
18:37 answered, "You s that I am a king.
1Co 15:12 of you s that there is no resurrection
Titus 2:12 It teaches us to s "No"
Jas 5:12 All you need to s is a simple "Yes"
Rev 22:17 The Spirit and the bride s,

SAYING SAY
1Ti 1:15 Here is a trustworthy s that deserves
3: 1 Here is a trustworthy s:
4: 9 This is a trustworthy s that deserves
2Ti 2:11 Here is a trustworthy s: If we died
Titus 3: 8 This is a trustworthy s. And I want
Rev 5:12 In a loud voice they were s:
5:13 on the sea, and all that is in them, s:

SAYINGS SAY
Pr 1: 6 the s and riddles of the wise.
22:17 turn your ear to the s of the wise;
Ecc 12:11 goads, their collected s like firmly
Jn 10:21 said, "These are not the s of a man

SAYS SAY
Ex 23:22 If you listen carefully to what he s
1Sa 9: 6 and everything he s comes true.
Ps 14: 1 The fool s in his heart, "There is no
53: 1 The fool s in his heart, "There is no
Ac 19:26 He s that gods made by human
Ro 3:19 we know that whatever the law s, it s
to those who are under the law,
Jas 1:23 not do what it s is like someone who

WHAT THE SOVEREIGN LORD† SAYS
See LORD†

WHAT THE LORD† SAYS See LORD†

LORD† ALMIGHTY SAYS See LORD†
SAYS THE LORD† See LORD†

SCALE SCALES
1Sa 17: 5 wore a coat of **s** armor of bronze
Ps 18:29 with my God I can **s** a wall.

SCALES SCALE
Lev 11: 9 may eat any that have fins and **s**.
    19:36 Use honest **s** and honest weights,
Pr 11: 1 The LORD detests dishonest **s**,
    16:11 Honest **s** and balances belong
Da 5:27 You have been weighed on the **s**
Ac 9:18 something like **s** fell from Saul's
Rev 6: 5 Its rider was holding a pair of **s**

SCAPEGOAT GOAT
Lev 16:10 sending it into the wilderness as a **s**.

SCARECROW*
Jer 10: 5 Like a **s** in a cucumber field,

SCARLET
Ge 38:28 so the midwife took a **s** thread
Ex 25: 4 purple and **s** yarn and fine linen;
Lev 14: 4 **s** yarn and hyssop be brought
Nu 19: 6 hyssop and **s** wool and throw them
Jos 2:21 she tied the **s** cord in the window.
Isa 1:18 "Though your sins are like **s**,
Mt 27:28 him and put a **s** robe on him,
Heb 9:19 **s** wool and branches of hyssop,
Rev 17: 3 I saw a woman sitting on a **s** beast

SCATTER SCATTERED,
SCATTERING, SCATTERS
Lev 26:33 I will **s** you among the nations
Dt 4:27 The LORD will **s** you among
Ne 1: 8 I will **s** you among the nations,
Ecc 3: 5 a time to **s** stones and a time
Jer 9:16 I will **s** them among nations
    30:11 all the nations among which I **s** you,
Zec 10: 9 Though I **s** them among the peoples,

SCATTERED SCATTER
Ge 11: 4 otherwise we will be **s** over the face
Nu 10:35 May your enemies be **s**;
Dt 30: 3 from all the nations where he **s** you.
2Ch 18:16 "I saw all Israel **s** on the hills like
Ps 89:10 strong arm you **s** your enemies.
    112: 9 They have freely **s** their gifts
Isa 11:12 he will assemble the **s** people
Jer 31:10 'He who **s** Israel will gather them
La 4:16 The LORD himself has **s** them;
Eze 34:12 As a shepherd looks after his **s** flock
Zec 1:19 "These are the horns that **s** Judah,
    2: 6 "for I have **s** you to the four winds
    13: 7 and the sheep will be **s**, and I will
Mt 26:31 and the sheep of the flock will be **s**.'
Jn 11:52 but also for the **s** children of God,
Ac 8: 1 apostles were **s** throughout Judea
    8: 4 who had been **s** preached the word
2Co 9: 9 "They have freely **s** their gifts
Jas 1: 1 To the twelve tribes **s** among
1Pe 1: 1 exiles **s** throughout the provinces

SCATTERING SCATTER
Jer 23: 1 and **s** the sheep of my pasture!"
Mk 4: 4 As he was **s** the seed, some fell

SCATTERS SCATTER
Mt 12:30 whoever does not gather with me **s**.
Jn 10:12 the wolf attacks the flock and **s** it.

SCEPTER
Ge 49:10 The **s** will not depart from Judah,
Nu 24:17 a **s** will rise out of Israel.
Est 4:11 unless the king extends the gold **s**
Ps 45: 6 a **s** of justice will be the **s** of your
    125: 3 The **s** of the wicked will not remain
Heb 1: 8 a **s** of justice will be the **s** of your
Rev 2:27 one 'will rule them with an iron **s**
    12: 5 rule all the nations with an iron **s**."
    19:15 "He will rule them with an iron **s**."

SCHEME SCHEMES, SCHEMING
Est 9:25 that the evil **s** Haman had devised
Ecc 7:27 another to discover the **s** of things—

SCHEMES SCHEME
Ex 21:14 But if anyone **s** and kills someone
Ps 21:11 against you and devise wicked **s**,
Pr 6:18 a heart that devises wicked **s**,
    24: 9 The **s** of folly are sin, and people
2Co 2:11 For we are not unaware of his **s**.
Eph 6:11 take your stand against the devil's **s**.

SCHEMING* SCHEME
Ne 6: 2 But they were **s** to harm me;
Mk 14: 1 **s** to arrest Jesus secretly and kill him,
Eph 4:14 of people in their deceitful **s**.

SCOFF SCOFFED, SCOFFERS,
SCOFFS
Ps 59: 8 you **s** at all those nations.
La 2:15 they **s** and shake their heads

SCOFFED* SCOFF
2Ch 36:16 **s** at his prophets until the wrath

SCOFFERS SCOFF
Isa 28:14 you **s** who rule this people
2Pe 3: 3 that in the last days **s** will come,

SCOFFS* SCOFF
Ps 2: 4 the Lord **s** at them.
Pr 29: 9 the fool rages and **s**, and there is no

SCOOP* SCOOPS
Pr 6:27 Can a man **s** fire into his lap without

SCOOPS* SCOOP
Ps 7:15 **s** it out falls into the pit they have

SCORCH* SCORCHED,
SCORCHING
Rev 16: 8 and the sun was allowed to **s** people

SCORCHED SCORCH
Ge 41:27 heads of grain **s** by the east wind:
Pr 6:28 hot coals without his feet being **s**?
Da 3:27 their robes were not **s**, and there was
Mk 4: 6 the plants were **s**, and they withered

SCORCHING SCORCH
Jnh   4: 8 God provided a s east wind,
Jas   1:11 For the sun rises with s heat

SCORN SCORNED, SCORNING, SCORNS
Ps   39: 8 do not make me the s of fools.
      69: 7 For I endure s for your sake,
      69:20 S has broken my heart and has left
      89:41 he has become the s of his
    109:25 I am an object of s to my accusers;
    119:22 Remove from me their s
Isa   43:28 Jacob to destruction and Israel to s.
Eze 36: 7 around you will also suffer s.
Mic   6:16 you will bear the s of the nations."

SCORNED SCORN
Ps   22: 6 worm and not a man, s by everyone,
SS   8: 7 house for love, it would be utterly s.

SCORNING* SCORN
Heb 12: 2 he endured the cross, s its shame,

SCORNS* SCORN
Pr   13:13 Whoever s instruction will pay
     30:17 that s an aged mother, will be

SCORPION SCORPIONS
Lk   11:12 asks for an egg, will give him a s?
Rev   9: 5 of the sting of a s when it strikes.

SCORPIONS SCORPION
1Ki 12:11 I will scourge you with s.' "
Rev   9:10 like s, and in their tails they had

SCOUNDREL SCOUNDRELS
Pr   16:27 A s plots evil, and on their lips
Isa   32: 5 noble nor the s be highly respected.

SCOUNDRELS SCOUNDREL
1Sa   2:12 Eli's sons were s; they had no
1Ki 21:10 But seat two s opposite him
Isa   32: 7 S use wicked methods, they make

SCOURGE
Ps   39:10 Remove your s from me;
Isa   28:15 an overwhelming s sweeps by,
     28:18 the overwhelming s sweeps by,

SCREAM*
Ge   39:15 When he heard me s for help, he left
Dt   22:24 was in a town and did not s for help,

SCRIBE SCRIBE'S
Jer   36:32 and gave it to the s Baruch son

SCRIBE'S* SCRIBE
Jer   36:23 the king cut them off with a s knife

SCRIPTURE SCRIPTURES
Mk 12:10 Haven't you read this passage of S:
Lk   4:21 "Today this s is fulfilled in your
Jn   2:22 they believed the s and the words
     7:42 Does not S say that the Messiah will
   10:35 and S cannot be set aside—
Ac   1:16 the S had to be fulfilled
     8:32 of S the eunuch was reading:

1Ti   4:13 yourself to the public reading of S,
2Ti   3:16 All S is God-breathed and is useful
2Pe   1:20 that no prophecy of S came

SCRIPTURES SCRIPTURE
Da   9: 2 understood from the S,
Mt   22:29 error because you do not know the S
Mk 14:49 But the S must be fulfilled."
Lk   24:27 said in all the S concerning himself.
    24:45 so they could understand the S.
Jn   5:39 You study the S diligently because
     5:39 These are the very S that testify
Ac   17:11 examined the S every day to see
    18:28 the S that Jesus was the Messiah.
1Co 15: 3 died for our sins according to the S,
    15: 4 on the third day according to the S,
2Ti   3:15 infancy you have known the Holy S,
2Pe   3:16 as they do the other S, to their own

SCROLL SCROLLS
Ex   17:14 "Write this on a s as something
Dt   17:18 for himself on a s a copy of this law,
1Sa 10:25 He wrote them down on a s
Ps   40: 7 it is written about me in the s.
Isa   8: 1 "Take a large s and write on it
    29:11 is nothing but words sealed in a s.
    34: 4 and the heavens rolled up like a s;
Jer   36: 4 to him, Baruch wrote them on the s.
    45: 1 a s the words Jeremiah the prophet
Eze   3: 1 eat what is before you, eat this s;
Da   12: 4 seal the words of the s until the time
Zec   5: 1 and there before me was a flying s.
Mal   3:16 A s of remembrance was written
Lk   4:17 and the s of the prophet Isaiah was
Heb 10: 7 it is written about me in the s—
Rev   1:11 "Write on a s what you see
     5: 2 to break the seals and open the s?"
    6:14 receded like a s being rolled up,
   10: 8 take the s that lies open in the hand
   22:18 the words of the prophecy of this s:

SCROLLS* SCROLL
Ac   19:19 sorcery brought their s together
    19:19 they calculated the value of the s,
2Ti   4:13 and my s, especially the parchments.

SCUM*
La   3:45 You have made us s and refuse
1Co   4:13 We have become the s of the earth,

SEA SEAS, SEASHORE
Ge   1:26 they may rule over the fish in the s
    32:12 descendants like the sand of the s,
    41:49 of grain, like the sand of the s;
Ex   14:16 the Israelites can go through the s
    14:27 stretched out his hand over the s,
    14:27 the LORD swept them into the s.
    15: 1 and driver he has hurled into the s.
Nu   11:31 and drove quail in from the s.
    34: 6 be the coast of the Mediterranean S.
Dt   11:24 River to the Mediterranean S.
    30:13 Nor is it beyond the s, so that you
1Ki   7:23 He made the S of cast metal,
2Ki 25:13 the bronze S that were at the temple
Ne   9:11 You divided the s before them,

Job 11: 9 than the earth and wider than the **s**.
Ps   46: 2 fall into the heart of the **s**,
     74:13 It was you who split open the **s**
     93: 4 mightier than the breakers of the **s**—
     95: 5 The **s** is his, for he made it, and his
     106: 7 rebelled by the **s**, the Red **S**.
     139: 9 if I settle on the far side of the **s**,
Ecc   1: 7 All streams flow into the **s**, yet the **s**
     11: 1 Ship your grain across the **s**;
Isa 10:22 people be like the sand by the **s**,
     48:18 well-being like the waves of the **s**.
     57:20 the wicked are like the tossing **s**,
Da   7: 3 the others, came up out of the **s**.
Jnh   1: 4 LORD sent a great wind on the **s**,
Mic   7:19 iniquities into the depths of the **s**.
Hab   2:14 LORD as the waters cover the **s**.
Zec   9:10 His rule will extend from **s** to **s**
Mt   18: 6 to be drowned in the depths of the **s**.
Mk   11:23 throw yourself into the **s**,' and does
1Co 10: 1 that they all passed through the **s**.
Heb 11:29 people passed through the Red **S** as
Jas   1: 6 who doubts is like a wave of the **s**,
Jude 1:13 They are wild waves of the **s**,
Rev   4: 6 there was what looked like a **s**
      8: 8 was thrown into the **s**. A third of the **s**
             turned into blood,
     10: 2 He planted his right foot on the **s**
     13: 1 dragon stood on the shore of the **s**.
     13: 1 I saw a beast coming out of the **s**.
     15: 2 I saw what looked like a **s** of glass
     20:13 the **s** gave up the dead that were
     21: 1 and there was no longer any **s**.

SEAL SEALED, SEALS
Ex   28:21 each engraved like a **s**
Est   8: 8 and **s** it with the king's signet ring—
Ps   40: 9 I do not **s** my lips, LORD, as you
SS   8: 6 Place me like a **s** over your heart,
Isa   8:16 **s** up God's instruction among my
Eze 28:12 " 'You were the **s** of perfection,
Da   8:26 but **s** up the vision, for it concerns
      9:24 to **s** up vision and prophecy
     12: 4 **s** the words of the scroll until
Mt   27:66 secure by putting a **s** on the stone
Jn   6:27 him God the Father has placed his **s**
1Co   9: 2 For you are the **s** of my apostleship
2Co   1:22 set his **s** of ownership on us, and put
Eph   1:13 you were marked in him with a **s**,
Rev   6: 3 the Lamb opened the second **s**,
      6: 5 When the Lamb opened the third **s**,
      6: 7 the Lamb opened the fourth **s**,
      6: 9 When he opened the fifth **s**, I saw
      6:12 I watched as he opened the sixth **s**.
      7: 2 east, having the **s** of the living God.
      7: 3 or the trees until we put a **s**
      8: 1 When he opened the seventh **s**,
      9: 4 those people who did not have the **s**
     10: 4 "**S** up what the seven thunders have
     22:10 me, "Do not **s** up the words

SEALED SEAL
Isa 29:11 is nothing but words **s** in a scroll.
Da   6:17 the king **s** it with his own signet ring
     12: 9 up and **s** until the time of the end.

Eph   4:30 with whom you were **s** for the day
2Ti   2:19 stands firm, **s** with this inscription:
Rev   5: 1 on both sides and **s** with seven seals.
      7: 4 the number of those who were **s**:
     20: 3 and locked and **s** it over him,

SEALS SEAL
Rev   5: 2 "Who is worthy to break the **s**
      6: 1 opened the first of the seven **s**.

SEAMLESS*
Jn   19:23 This garment was **s**, woven in one

SEARCH SEARCHED, SEARCHES,
   SEARCHING
Ezr   5:17 let a **s** be made in the royal archives
Est   2: 2 "Let a **s** be made for beautiful
Ps   4: 4 beds, **s** your hearts and be silent.
     139:23 **S** me, God, and know my heart;
Pr   2: 4 and **s** for it as for hidden treasure,
     25: 2 to **s** out a matter is the glory
     25:27 nor is it honorable to **s** out matters
Ecc   3: 6 a time to **s** and a time to give up,
SS   3: 2 I will **s** for the one my heart loves.
Jer 17:10 "I the LORD **s** the heart
Eze 34:11 I myself will **s** for my sheep
     34:16 I will **s** for the lost and bring back
Mt   2: 8 "Go and **s** carefully for the child.
Lk   15: 8 and **s** carefully until she finds it?

SEARCHED SEARCH
1Sa 23:14 Day after day Saul **s** for him,
Ps   139: 1 You have **s** me, LORD, and you
Ecc 12:10 The Teacher **s** to find just the right
1Pe   1:10 **s** intently and with the greatest care,

SEARCHES SEARCH
1Ch 28: 9 for the LORD **s** every heart
Pr   11:27 but evil comes to one who **s** for it.
Ro   8:27 he who **s** our hearts knows the mind
1Co   2:10 The Spirit **s** all things, even the deep
Rev   2:23 will know that I am he who **s** hearts

SEARCHING SEARCH
Jdg   5:15 Reuben there was much **s** of heart.
Am   8:12 east, **s** for the word of the LORD,
Lk   2:49 "Why were you **s** for me?"

SEARED*
1Ti   4: 2 whose consciences have been **s** as
Rev 16: 9 They were **s** by the intense heat

SEAS SEA
Ge   1:10 the gathered waters he called "**s**."
Ps   65: 7 who stilled the roaring of the **s**,
     93: 3 The **s** have lifted up, LORD, the **s**
Jnh   2: 3 into the very heart of the **s**,

SEASHORE SEA
Ge   22:17 in the sky and as the sand on the **s**.
Jos 11: 4 as numerous as the sand on the **s**.
1Ki   4:20 as numerous as the sand on the **s**;
      4:29 as measureless as the sand on the **s**.
Jer 33:22 as the sand on the **s**.' "
Hos   1:10 will be like the sand on the **s**,
Heb 11:12 as countless as the sand on the **s**.

Rev 20: 8 they are like the sand on the s.

SEASON SEASONED, SEASONS

Lev 2:13 S all your grain offerings with salt.
     26: 4 I will send you rain in its s,
Dt   28:12 to send rain on your land in s
Ps   1: 3 which yields its fruit in s and whose
Pr   20: 4 Sluggards do not plow in s;
Ecc   3: 1 and a s for every activity under
2Ti   4: 2 be prepared in s and out of s;
Titus 1: 3 at his appointed s he has brought

SEASONED* SEASON

Col   4: 6 be always full of grace, s with salt,

SEASONS SEASON

Ps 104:19 He made the moon to mark the s,
Gal   4:10 days and months and s and years!

SEAT SEATED, SEATS

Ex   18:13 The next day Moses took his s
2Ki 25:28 gave him a s of honor higher than
Pr   31:23 he takes his s among the elders
Da   7: 9 and the Ancient of Days took his s.
Mt   23: 2 and the Pharisees sit in Moses' s.
Lk   14: 9 to you, 'Give this person your s.'
Ro   14:10 all stand before God's judgment s.
2Co   5:10 all appear before the judgment s

SEATED SEAT

Ps   47: 8 God is s on his holy throne.
Isa   6: 1 high and exalted, s on a throne;
Lk   22:69 of Man will be s at the right hand
Jn   12:15 is coming, s on a donkey's colt."
     20:12 s where Jesus' body had been,
Eph   1:20 and s him at his right hand
      2: 6 and s us with him in the heavenly
Col   3: 1 Christ is, s at the right hand of God.
Rev   4: 4 s on them were twenty-four elders.
     11:16 who were s on their thrones before
     14:14 s on the cloud was one like a son
     19: 4 God, who was s on the throne.
     20: 4 were s those who had been given
     20:11 throne and him who was s on it.
     21: 5 He who was s on the throne said,

SEATS SEAT

1Sa   2: 8 he s them with princes and has them
Ps 113: 8 he s them with princes,
Lk   11:43 you love the most important s

SECLUSION*

Lk   1:24 and for five months remained in s.

SECOND TWO

Ge   22:15 to Abraham from heaven a s time
     41: 5 fell asleep again and had a s dream:
Ex   4: 8 first sign, they may believe the s.
Lev 19:10 not go over your vineyard a s time
Nu   9:11 the fourteenth day of the s month
Dt   24:20 not go over the branches a s time
1Ki   9: 2 LORD appeared to him a s time,
Est   10: 3 Mordecai the Jew was s in rank
Eze 10:14 the s the face of a human being,
Da   7: 5 "And there before me was a s beast,
Jnh   3: 1 the LORD came to Jonah a s time:

Hag   2:20 came to Haggai a s time
Zec 11:14 I broke my s staff called Union,
Mt   22:39 And the s is like it:
Jn   3: 4 "Surely they cannot enter a s time
1Co 12:28 first of all apostles, s prophets,
     15:47 of the earth; the s man is of heaven.
Titus 3:10 once, and then warn them a s time.
Heb   9:28 and he will appear a s time,
Rev   2:11 will not be hurt at all by the s death.
      4: 7 was like a lion, the s was like an ox,
      6: 3 When the Lamb opened the s seal,
      8: 8 The s angel sounded his trumpet,
     11:14 The s woe has passed; the third woe
     16: 3 The s angel poured out his bowl
     20: 6 The s death has no power over
     20:14 The lake of fire is the s death.
     21: 8 This is the s death."

SECRET SECRETLY, SECRETS

Ex   7:11 did the same things by their s arts:
     7:22 did the same things by their s arts,
     8: 7 did the same things by their s arts;
     8:18 tried to produce gnats by their s arts,
Dt   29:29 The s things belong to the LORD
Jdg   16: 6 "Tell me the s of your great
Est   2:20 But Esther had kept s her family
Ps   51: 6 taught me wisdom in that s place.
     90: 8 you, our s sins in the light of your
   139:15 you when I was made in the s place,
Pr   9:17 food eaten in s is delicious!"
     11:13 but a trustworthy person keeps a s.
     21:14 A gift given in s soothes anger,
Jer   23:24 Who can hide in s places so that I
Mt   6: 4 so that your giving may be in s.
      6: 4 who sees what is done in s,
      6: 6 who sees what is done in s,
      6:18 who sees what is done in s,
Mk   4:11 "The s of the kingdom of God has
2Co   4: 2 we have renounced s and shameful
Eph   5:12 what the disobedient do in s.
Php   4:12 I have learned the s of being content
2Th   2: 7 For the s power of lawlessness is

SECRETLY SECRET

Dt   13: 6 or your closest friend s entices you,
2Ki 17: 9 The Israelites s did things against
Mt   2: 7 Herod called the Magi s and found
     26: 4 schemed to arrest Jesus s and kill him.
Mk   14: 1 scheming to arrest Jesus s and kill him.
Jn   19:38 but s because he feared the Jewish
2Pe   2: 1 They will s introduce destructive
Jude   1: 4 long ago have s slipped in among

SECRETS SECRET

Ps   44:21 it, since he knows the s of the heart?
Mt   13:11 knowledge of the s of the kingdom
Ro   2:16 God judges people's s through Jesus
1Co 14:25 as the s of their hearts are laid bare.
Rev   2:24 not learned Satan's so-called deep s,

SECT

Ac   24: 5 He is a ringleader of the Nazarene s
     26: 5 to the strictest s of our religion,

SECURE SECURELY, SECURES, SECURITY

Dt	33:12	beloved of the LORD rest s in him,
2Sa	22:33	with strength and keeps my way s.
1Ki	2:45	throne will remain s before
Ps	16: 5	and my cup; you make my lot s.
	16: 9	my body also will rest s,
	18:32	with strength and keeps my way s.
	112: 8	Their hearts are s, they will have no
	122: 6	"May those who love you be s.
Pr	14:16	a fool is hotheaded and yet feels s.
	14:26	fears the LORD has a s fortress,
Am	6: 1	you who feel s on Mount Samaria,
Zec	1:15	angry with the nations that feel s.
Mt	27:64	to be made s until the third day.
Heb	6:19	as an anchor for the soul, firm and s.
2Pe	3:17	and fall from your s position.

SECURELY SECURE

Pr   10: 9   Whoever walks in integrity walks s,

SECURES* SECURE

Ps   140:12   the LORD s justice for the poor

SECURITY SECURE

Dt	24: 6	as s for a debt, because that would be taking a person's livelihood as s.
Job	31:24	or said to pure gold, 'You are my s,'
Ps	122: 7	walls and s within your citadels."
Pr	17:18	pledge and puts up s for a neighbor.
	22:26	in pledge or puts up s for debts;
Jer	30:10	Jacob will again have peace and s,

SEDUCE* SEDUCED, SEDUCES, SEDUCTIVE

2Pe   2:14   they s the unstable;

SEDUCED* SEDUCE

Pr   7:21   she s him with her smooth talk.

SEDUCES* SEDUCE

Ex   22:16   a man s a virgin who is not pledged

SEDUCTIVE* SEDUCE

Pr   2:16   wayward woman with her s words,
      7: 5   wayward woman with her s words.

SEE NEARSIGHTED, SAW, SEEING, SEEN, SEES, SIGHT

Ge	2:19	man to s what he would name them;
	8: 8	a dove to s if the water had receded
	9:16	clouds, I will s it and remember
	13:15	All the land that you s I will give
Ex	12:13	and when I s the blood, I will pass
	14:13	and you will s the deliverance
	14:13	The Egyptians you s today you will never s again.
	16: 4	and s whether they will follow my
	33:20	he said, "you cannot s my face, for no one may s me and live."
Nu	14:23	them will ever s the land I promised
Dt	12: 8	today, everyone doing as they s fit,
	34: 4	I have let you s it with your eyes,
Jdg	2:22	s whether they will keep the way
Job	7:20	you who s everything we do?

Job	19:26	yet in my flesh I will s God;
Ps	11: 7	the upright will s his face.
	16:10	you let your faithful one s decay.
	34: 8	and s that the LORD is good;
	115: 5	but cannot speak, eyes, but cannot s.
Isa	40: 5	and all people will s it together.
	53:10	he will s his offspring and prolong
	53:11	he will s the light of life and be
	65:17	"S, I will create new heavens
Eze	8:12	say, 'The LORD does not s us;
Da	3:25	I s four men walking around
Joel	2:28	your young men will s visions.
Mic	7: 9	I will s his righteousness.
Mt	5: 8	pure in heart, for they will s God.
	7: 5	you will s clearly to remove
	13:16	are your eyes because they s,
Mk	8:18	Do you have eyes but fail to s,
	14:62	you will s the Son of Man sitting
	16: 6	S the place where they laid him.
Lk	3: 6	people will s God's salvation.' "
Jn	9:25	I was blind but now I s!"
	14:19	the world will not s me anymore, but you will s me.
	16:16	a little while you will s me no more,
	16:16	after a little while you will s me."
Ac	2:17	your young men will s visions,
	2:27	will not let your holy one s decay.
1Co	13:12	For now we s only a reflection as
	13:12	then we shall s face to face.
2Co	13: 5	yourselves to s whether you are
Heb	12:14	holiness no one will s the Lord.
1Jn	3: 2	like him, for we shall s him as he is.
	5:16	If you s any brother or sister
Rev	1: 7	and "every eye will s him,
	22: 4	They will s his face, and his name

SEED SEED-BEARING, SEEDS, SEEDTIME

Ge	1:11	the land that bear fruit with s in it,
Lev	19:19	plant your field with two kinds of s.
Ecc	11: 6	Sow your s in the morning,
Isa	6:13	so the holy s will be the stump
	55:10	so that it yields s for the sower
Mt	13: 3	"A farmer went out to sow his s.
	13:31	of heaven is like a mustard s,
	17:20	have faith as small as a mustard s,
Mk	4:31	It is like a mustard s, which is
Lk	8:11	The s is the word of God.
Jn	12:24	and dies, it remains only a single s.
1Co	3: 6	I planted the s, Apollos watered it,
	9:11	have sown spiritual s among you,
2Co	9:10	Now he who supplies s to the sower
Gal	3:16	spoken to Abraham and to his s.
	3:29	then you are Abraham's s, and heirs
1Pe	1:23	again, not of perishable s,
1Jn	3: 9	because God's s remains in them;

SEED-BEARING* SEED

Ge   1:11   s plants and trees on the land
      1:29   "I give you every s plant

SEEDS SEED

Jn   12:24   But if it dies, it produces many s.
Gal   3:16   Scripture does not say "and to s,"

SEEDTIME* SEED
Ge   8:22 as the earth endures, s and harvest,

SEEING SEE
Isa   6: 9 be ever s, but never perceiving.'
Mt   13:14 you will be ever s but never
      15:31 the lame walking and the blind s.
Jn   8:56 rejoiced at the thought of s my day;
2Co   3:13 prevent the Israelites from s the end

SEEK SEEKING, SEEKS, SELF-SEEKING, SOUGHT
Ex   18:15 people come to me to s God's will.
Lev 19:18 " 'Do not s revenge or bear
     19:31 turn to mediums or s out spiritists,
Dt   4:29 you will find him if you s him
     23: 6 Do not s a treaty of friendship
1Ki 22: 5 of Israel, "First s the counsel
1Ch 28: 9 If you s him, he will be found
2Ch   7:14 pray and s my face and turn
     15: 2 If you s him, he will be found
Ezr   9:12 Do not s a treaty of friendship
Ps   4: 2 you love delusions and s false gods?
      9:10 never forsaken those who s you.
     24: 6 the generation of those who s him,
     34:10 but those who s the LORD lack no
     63: 1 God, are my God, earnestly I s you;
     105: 3 of those who s the LORD rejoice.
     105: 4 and his strength; s his face always.
     119: 2 and s him with all their heart—
     119:10 I s you with all my heart; do not let
     119:176 S your servant, for I have not
Pr   8:17 me, and those who s me find me.
     18:15 for the ears of the wise s it out.
     28: 5 those who s the LORD understand
Isa   1:17 Learn to do right; s justice.
     55: 6 S the LORD while he may be
     65: 1 found by those who did not s me.
Jer 29:13 You will s me and find me
Hos 10:12 for it is time to s the LORD,
Am   5: 6 S the LORD and live, or he will
Zep   2: 3 S the LORD, all you humble
      2: 3 S righteousness, s humility;
Mt   6:33 But s first his kingdom and his
      7: 7 be given to you; s and you will find;
Lk   12:31 But s his kingdom, and these things
     19:10 For the Son of Man came to s
Jn   5:30 for I s not to please myself but him
      5:44 do not s the glory that comes
Ac   15:17 the rest of mankind may s the Lord,
Ro   10:20 found by those who did not s me;
1Co   7:27 Do not s to be released.
     10:24 No one should s their own good,
Heb 11: 6 rewards those who earnestly s him.
1Pe   3:11 they must s peace and pursue it.

SEEKING SEEK
1Ch 22:19 and soul to s the LORD your God.
2Ch 30:19 who sets their heart on s God—
Pr   20:18 Plans are established by s advice;
Mal   3: 1 the Lord you are s will come to his
Jn   8:50 I am not s glory for myself;
1Co 10:33 For I am not s my own good

SEEKS SEEK
Pr   11:27 Whoever s good finds favor,
     14: 6 The mocker s wisdom and finds
     15:14 The discerning heart s knowledge,
Mt   7: 8 the one who s finds; and to the one
Jn   4:23 the kind of worshipers the Father s.
Ro   3:11 there is no one who s God.

SEEM SEEMED, SEEMS
Pr   16: 2 All a person's ways s pure to them,
Zec   8: 6 "It may s marvelous to the remnant
      8: 6 but will it s marvelous to me?"

SEEMED SEEM
Ge   29:20 they s like only a few days to him
Nu   13:33 We s like grasshoppers in our own
Ac   2: 3 They saw what s to be tongues
Rev 13: 3 of the beast s to have had a fatal

SEEMS SEEM
Jos 24:15 serving the LORD s undesirable
Pr   12:15 The way of fools s right to them,
Heb 12:11 No discipline s pleasant at the time,

SEEN SEE
Ge   16:13 "I have now s the One who sees
Ex   3: 7 "I have indeed s the misery of my
     33:23 but my face must not be s."
Nu   14:14 LORD, have been s face to face,
Dt   4: 9 forget the things your eyes have s
Jos 23: 3 yourselves have s everything
Jdg   6:22 I have s the angel of the LORD
     13:22 said to his wife. "We have s God!"
Ezr   3:12 heads, who had s the former temple,
Ps   37:25 old, yet I have never s the righteous
     37:35 I have s a wicked and ruthless man
     98: 3 the earth have s the salvation of our
Ecc   1:14 I have s all the things that are done
Isa   6: 5 and my eyes have s the King,
      9: 2 in darkness have s a great light;
     64: 4 no eye has s any God besides you,
Mt   2: 9 the star they had s when it rose went
      4:16 in darkness have s a great light;
Lk   2:30 For my eyes have s your salvation,
Jn   1:14 We have s his glory, the glory
      1:18 No one has ever s God, but the one
      6:46 No one has s the Father except
     14: 9 who has s me has s the Father.
     20:25 told him, "We have s the Lord!"
     20:29 blessed are those who have not s
Ro   8:24 But hope that is s is no hope at all.
1Co   2: 9 "What no eye has s, what no ear
Php   4: 9 or heard from me, or s in me—
1Ti   3:16 by the Spirit, was s by angels,
1Pe   1: 8 Though you have not s him,
1Jn   1: 3 We proclaim to you what we have s
      4:12 No one has ever s God; but if we
3Jn   1:11 does what is evil has not s God.
Rev   1:19 what you have s, what is now

SEER SEERS
1Sa   9: 9 of today used to be called a s.)
      9:19 "I am the s," Samuel replied.
2Sa 24:11 come to Gad the prophet, David's s:
1Ch 29:29 in the records of Samuel the s,

1Ch 29:29 and the records of Gad the **s**,
2Ch 9:29 Iddo the **s** concerning Jeroboam son
29:30 words of David and of Asaph the **s**.
Am 7:12 said to Amos, "Get out, you **s**!

SEERS SEER

2Ki 17:13 through all his prophets and **s**:
Mic 3: 7 The **s** will be ashamed

SEES SEE

Ge 16:13 "You are the God who **s** me,"
Nu 24: 3 of one whose eye **s** clearly,
24:15 of one whose eye **s** clearly,
Ps 33:13 looks down and **s** all mankind;
Isa 11: 3 judge by what he **s** with his eyes,
47:10 and have said, 'No one **s** me.'
Mt 6: 4 Father, who **s** what is done in secret,
6: 6 Father, who **s** what is done in secret,
6:18 Father, who **s** what is done in secret,
Jn 5:19 do only what he **s** his Father doing,
1Jn 3:17 material possessions and **s** a brother

SEIR

Ge 32: 3 to his brother Esau in the land of **S**,
Dt 2: 4 descendants of Esau, who live in **S**.
Eze 35: 2 man, set your face against Mount **S**;

SELAH

The Hebrew word for "Selah" is not translated in the NIV, but is indicated in the notes to Psalms and Habakkuk.

Following is a list of all occurrences of "Selah" in the NIV 1984: Ps 3:2, 4, 8; 4:2, 4; 7:5; 9:16, 20; 20:3; 21:2; 24:6, 10; 32:4, 5, 7; 39:5, 11; 44:8; 46:3, 7, 11; 47:4; 48:8; 49:13, 15; 50:6; 52:3, 5; 54:3; 55:7, 19; 57:3, 6; 59:5, 13; 60:4; 61:4; 62:4, 8; 66:4, 7, 15; 67:1, 4; 68:7, 19, 32; 75:3; 76:3, 9; 77:3, 9, 15; 81:7; 82:2; 83:8; 84:4, 8; 85:2; 87:3, 6; 88:7, 10; 89:4, 37, 45, 48; 140:3, 5, 8; 143:6; Hab 3:3, 9, 13

SELECT SELECTED

Ex 12:21 and **s** the animals for your families
18:21 **s** capable men from all the people—
Nu 35:11 **s** some towns to be your cities
Isa 66:21 And I will **s** some of them also to be

SELECTED SELECT

Nu 18: 6 I myself have **s** your fellow Levites

SELF SELFISH

Lk 9:25 and yet lose or forfeit their very **s**?
Ro 6: 6 know that our old **s** was crucified
Eph 4:22 to put off your old **s**, which is being
Col 3:10 and have put on the new **s**, which is
1Pe 3: 4 it should be that of your inner **s**,

SELF-CONDEMNED* CONDEMN

Titus 3:11 are warped and sinful; they are **s**.

SELF-CONTROL* CONTROL

Pr 16:32 with **s** than one who takes a city.
25:28 through is a person who lacks **s**.
Ac 24:25 **s** and the judgment to come,
1Co 7: 5 tempt you because of your lack of **s**.
Gal 5:23 gentleness and **s**.
2Ti 3: 3 slanderous, without **s**, brutal,

2Pe 1: 6 and to knowledge, **s**; and to **s**,

SELF-CONTROLLED* CONTROL

1Ti 3: 2 his wife, temperate, **s**, respectable,
Titus 1: 8 what is good, who is **s**, upright,
2: 2 worthy of respect, **s**, and sound
2: 5 to be **s** and pure, to be busy
2: 6 encourage the young men to be **s**.
2:12 and to live **s**, upright and godly lives

SELF-DENIAL* DENY

Ps 132: 1 remember David and all his **s**.

SELF-DISCIPLINE* DISCIPLINE

2Ti 1: 7 but gives us power, love and **s**.

SELF-INDULGENCE* INDULGE

Mt 23:25 inside they are full of greed and **s**.
Jas 5: 5 have lived on earth in luxury and **s**.

SELF-INTEREST INTEREST

Mt 27:18 out of **s** that they had handed Jesus

SELF-SEEKING* SEEK

Ro 2: 8 for those who are **s** and who reject
1Co 13: 5 it is not **s**, it is not easily angered,

SELFISH* SELF

Ps 119:36 your statutes and not toward **s** gain.
Pr 18: 1 An unfriendly person pursues **s** ends
2Co 12:20 fits of rage, **s** ambition, slander,
Gal 5:20 fits of rage, **s** ambition, dissensions,
Php 1:17 preach Christ out of **s** ambition,
2: 3 Do nothing out of **s** ambition,
Jas 3:14 envy and **s** ambition in your hearts,
3:16 you have envy and **s** ambition,

SELL SALE, SELLING, SELLS, SOLD

Ge 23: 9 so he will **s** me the cave
25:31 "First **s** me your birthright."
Lev 25:14 " 'If you **s** land to any of your
Pr 23:23 Buy the truth and do not **s** it—
Mk 10:21 **s** everything you have and give
Rev 13:17 buy or **s** unless they had the mark,

SELLING SELL

Ge 25:33 to him, **s** his birthright to Jacob.
Mk 11:15 those who were buying and **s** there.
Lk 17:28 buying and **s**, planting and building.
Jn 2:14 courts he found people **s** cattle,

SELLS SELL

Pr 31:24 makes linen garments and **s** them,

SEND SENDING, SENDS, SENT

Ge 7: 4 from now I will **s** rain on the earth
Ex 23:27 "I will **s** my terror ahead of you
33: 2 I will **s** an angel before you
Lev 16:21 He shall **s** the goat away
Dt 11:14 then I will **s** rain on your land in its
28:20 The LORD will **s** on you curses,
1Sa 5:11 said, "**S** the ark of the god of Israel
Ps 43: 3 **S** me your light and your faithful
104:30 When you **s** your Spirit, they are
Isa 6: 8 the Lord saying, "Whom shall I **s**?
6: 8 And I said, "Here am I. **S** me!"
Mal 3: 1 "I will **s** my messenger, who will

Mal 4: 5 I will **s** the prophet Elijah to you
Mt 9:38 to **s** out workers into his harvest
11:10 " 'I will **s** my messenger ahead
24:31 And he will **s** his angels with a loud
Mk 1: 2 "I will **s** my messenger ahead
1:17 I will **s** you out to fish for people."
6: 7 he began to **s** them out two by two
10: 4 of divorce and **s** her away."
Lk 11:49 'I will **s** them prophets and apostles,
20:13 I will **s** my son, whom I love;
Jn 3:17 God did not **s** his Son into the world
14:26 whom the Father will **s** in my name,
15:26 whom I will **s** to you
16: 7 but if I go, I will **s** him to you.
Ac 3:20 and that he may **s** the Messiah,
1Co 1:17 For Christ did not **s** me to baptize,

SENDING SEND
Ex 3:10 I am **s** you to Pharaoh to bring my
23:20 I am **s** an angel ahead of you
Joel 2:13 love, and he relents from **s** calamity.
Jnh 4: 2 a God who relents from **s** calamity.
Mt 10:16 "I am **s** you out like sheep among
Jn 20:21 the Father has sent me, I am **s** you."
Ro 8: 3 God did by **s** his own Son

SENDS SEND
Ps 57: 3 He **s** from heaven and saves me,
Mt 5:45 and **s** rain on the righteous

SENNACHERIB
Assyrian king whose siege of Jerusalem was overthrown by the LORD following prayer of Hezekiah and Isaiah (2Ki 18:13—19:37; 2Ch 32:1–21; Isa 36–37).

SENSE SENSES, SENSITIVE, SENSITIVITY
Dt 32:28 They are a nation without **s**, there is
Pr 6:32 who commits adultery has no **s**;
7: 7 young men, a youth who had no **s**.
9: 4 To those who have no **s** she says,
10:21 many, but fools die for lack of **s**.
11:12 derides their neighbor has no **s**,
12:11 those who chase fantasies have no **s**.
15:21 brings joy to one who has no **s**,
17:18 One who has no **s** shakes hands
Ecc 10: 3 they lack **s** and show everyone how

SENSES* SENSE
Lk 15:17 "When he came to his **s**, he said,
1Co 15:34 Come back to your **s** as you ought,
2Ti 2:26 that they will come to their **s**

SENSITIVE SENSE
Dt 28:56 gentle and **s** woman among you—

SENSITIVITY* SENSE
Eph 4:19 Having lost all **s**, they have given

SENSUAL* SENSUALITY
Col 2:23 value in restraining **s** indulgence.
1Ti 5:11 when their **s** desires overcome their

SENSUALITY* SENSUAL
Eph 4:19 given themselves over to **s** so as

SENT SEND
Ge 2: 5 the LORD God had not **s** rain
8: 8 he **s** out a dove to see if the water
45: 5 to save lives that God **s** me ahead
Ex 3:14 'I AM has **s** me to you.' "
Nu 13:17 When Moses **s** them to explore
16:29 then the LORD has not **s** me.
21: 6 the LORD **s** venomous snakes
Jos 2: 1 son of Nun secretly **s** two spies
24:12 I **s** the hornet ahead of you,
1Sa 14:15 It was a panic **s** by God.
2Sa 24:15 So the LORD **s** a plague on Israel
2Ki 14: 9 "A thistle in Lebanon **s** a message
Ps 107:20 He **s** out his word and healed them;
Isa 55:11 achieve the purpose for which I **s** it.
61: 1 He has **s** me to bind
Jer 3: 8 and **s** her away because of all her
28: 9 will be recognized as one truly **s**
44: 4 again I **s** my servants the prophets,
Eze 39:28 though I **s** them into exile among
Da 3:28 who has **s** his angel and rescued his
6:22 My God **s** his angel, and he shut
Mt 10:40 me welcomes the one who **s** me.
Mk 1:12 At once the Spirit **s** him
Lk 1:26 God **s** the angel Gabriel
4:18 He has **s** me to proclaim freedom
9: 2 and he **s** them out to proclaim
10:16 rejects me rejects him who **s** me."
13:34 prophets and stone those **s** to you,
Jn 1: 6 There was a man **s** from God whose
3:28 the Messiah but am **s** ahead of him.'
4:34 "is to do the will of him who **s** me
5:24 believes him who **s** me has eternal
8:16 I stand with the Father, who **s** me.
9: 4 must do the works of him who **s** me.
16: 5 now I am going to him who **s** me.
17: 3 and Jesus Christ, whom you have **s**.
17:18 As you **s** me into the world, I have **s**
them into the world.
20:21 As the Father has **s** me, I am
Ro 10:15 anyone preach unless they are **s**?
Gal 4: 4 time had fully come, God **s** his Son,
1Jn 4:10 **s** his Son as an atoning sacrifice
Rev 22:16 have **s** my angel to give you this

SENTENCE SENTENCED
Ecc 8:11 the **s** for a crime is not quickly
Ac 13:28 no proper ground for a death **s**,
2Co 1: 9 we felt we had received the **s**

SENTENCED SENTENCE
Jer 26:16 "This man should not be **s** to death!
Lk 24:20 handed him over to be **s** to death,

SEPARATE SEPARATED, SEPARATES
Ex 26:33 The curtain will **s** the Holy Place
Mt 19: 6 has joined together, let no one **s**."
Ro 8:35 Who shall **s** us from the love
1Co 7:10 A wife must not **s** from her
2Co 6:17 "Come out from them and be **s**,
Eph 2:12 at that time you were **s** from Christ,

SEPARATED SEPARATE
Ge 1: 4 and he **s** the light from the darkness.

Ge 1: 7 s the water under the vault
Isa 59: 2 your iniquities have s you from your
Eph 4: 18 s from the life of God because

SEPARATES SEPARATE
Pr 16: 28 and a gossip s close friends.
17: 9 repeats the matter s close friends.
Mt 25: 32 another as a shepherd s the sheep

SEPULCHRE(S) (KJV) See GRAVE(S), TOMB(S)

SERAPHIM*
Isa 6: 2 Above him were s, each with six wings:
6: 6 of the s flew to me with a live coal

SERIOUS SERIOUSNESS
Ex 21: 23 But if there is s injury, you are
Jer 6: 14 my people as though it were not s.

SERIOUSNESS* SERIOUS
Titus 2: 7 In your teaching show integrity, s

SERPENT SERPENT'S
Ge 3: 1 Now the s was more crafty than any
3: 13 woman said, "The s deceived me,
Isa 27: 1 Leviathan the gliding s, Leviathan the coiling s;
Rev 12: 9 that ancient s called the devil,
20: 2 that ancient s, who is the devil,

SERPENT'S SERPENT
Isa 65: 25 the ox, and dust will be the s food.
2Co 11: 3 Eve was deceived by the s cunning,

SERVANT SERVE
Ge 35: 25 The sons of Rachel's s Bilhah:
35: 26 The sons of Leah's s Zilpah.
Ex 14: 31 their trust in him and in Moses his s.
21: 2 "If you buy a Hebrew s, he is
Nu 12: 7 But this is not true of my s Moses;
Dt 5: 14 nor your male or female s, nor your
1Sa 3: 10 "Speak, for your s is listening."
2Sa 7: 19 the future of the house of your s—
1Ki 3: 7 you have made your s king in place
8: 56 he gave through his s Moses.
8: 66 LORD had done for his s David
20: 40 While your s was busy here
Job 1: 8 "Have you considered my s Job?
2: 3 "Have you considered my s Job?
42: 8 My s Job will pray for you, and I
Ps 19: 11 By them your s is warned;
19: 13 Keep your s also from willful sins;
31: 16 Let your face shine on your s;
78: 70 He chose David his s and took him
89: 3 one, I have sworn to David my s,
105: 26 He sent Moses his s, and Aaron,
Pr 11: 29 and the fool will be s to the wise.
14: 35 A king delights in a wise s, but a shameful s arouses his fury.
17: 2 A prudent s will rule over
Isa 24: 2 for the master as for his s, for the mistress as for her s,
41: 8 Israel, my s, Jacob, whom I have
42: 1 "Here is my s, whom I uphold,

Isa 43: 10 "and my s whom I have chosen,
44: 1 Jacob, my s, Israel, whom I have
45: 4 For the sake of Jacob my s, of Israel
48: 20 LORD has redeemed his s Jacob."
49: 3 said to me, "You are my s, Israel,
52: 13 See, my s will act wisely; he will be
53: 11 my righteous s will justify many,
Jer 30: 10 do not be afraid, Jacob my s;
33: 21 my covenant with David my s—
Eze 34: 24 my s David will be prince among
Zec 3: 8 I am going to bring my s,
Mt 8: 13 his s was healed at that moment.
20: 26 great among you must be your s,
24: 45 then is the faithful and wise s,
25: 21 'Well done, good and faithful s!
Lk 1: 38 "I am the Lord's s,"
1: 54 He has helped his s Israel,
1: 69 for us in the house of his s David
Jn 12: 26 and where I am, my s also will be.
Ac 3: 13 our fathers, has glorified his s Jesus.
12: 13 a s named Rhoda came to answer
Ro 1: 1 Paul, a s of Christ Jesus, called to be
13: 4 authority is God's s for your good.
14: 4 are you to judge someone else's s?
Php 2: 7 by taking the very nature of a s,
Col 1: 23 of which I, Paul, have become a s.
2Ti 2: 24 And the Lord's s must not be
3: 17 the s of God may be thoroughly
Heb 3: 5 "Moses was faithful as a s in all
Rev 15: 3 sang the song of God's s Moses
19: 10 I am a fellow s with you

SERVANT OF THE LORD† Dt 34:5; Jos 1:1, 13, 15; 8:31, 33; 11:12; 12:6, 6; 13:8; 14:7; 18:7; 22:2, 4, 5; 24:29; Jdg 2:8; 2Ki 18:12; 2Ch 24:6; Isa 42:19

SERVANT'S SERVE
1Sa 1: 11 you will only look on your s misery
2Ki 6: 17 Then the LORD opened the s eyes,
2Ch 6: 19 give attention to your s prayer
Ps 119: 122 Ensure your s well-being; do not let

SERVANTS SERVE
Lev 25: 55 for the Israelites belong to me as s.
Dt 32: 36 relent concerning his s when he sees
1Sa 2: 9 will guard the feet of his faithful s,
25: 42 attended by her five female s,
2Ki 10: 19 in order to destroy the s of Baal.
17: 23 through all his s the prophets.
Ezr 5: 11 "We are the s of the God of heaven
Job 4: 18 If God places no trust in his s, if he
Ps 34: 22 The LORD will rescue his s;
90: 13 Have compassion on your s.
103: 21 hosts, you his s who do his will.
104: 4 his messengers, flames of fire his s.
113: 1 Praise the LORD, you his s;
Pr 31: 15 and portions for her female s.
Isa 44: 26 who carries out the words of his s
65: 8 in it,' so will I do in behalf of my s;
65: 14 My s will sing out of the joy of their
Jer 7: 25 again I sent you my s the prophets.
Da 9: 6 not listened to your s the prophets,
Lk 17: 10 do, should say, 'We are unworthy s;
Jn 15: 15 I no longer call you s,

Ac   4:29 enable your s to speak your word
Ro   13: 6 for the authorities are God's s,
1Co   3: 5 Only s, through whom you came
2Co 11:15 if his s also masquerade as s
Heb   1: 7 spirits, and his s flames of fire."
Rev   7: 3 the foreheads of the s of our God."
      19: 2 avenged on her the blood of his s."
      22: 3 in the city, and his s will serve him.

SERVE SERVANT, SERVANT'S, SERVANTS, SERVED, SERVES, SERVICE, SERVING

Ge   1:14 let them s as signs to mark sacred
     15:14 punish the nation they s as slaves,
     25:23 and the older will s the younger."
Ex   28: 1 so they may s me as priests.
Nu   1: 3 or more and able to s in the army.
Dt   6:13 s him only and take your oaths
     10:12 to s the LORD your God with all
     11:13 God and to s him with all your heart
     13: 4 s him and hold fast to him.
     28:47 you did not s the LORD your God
Jos 22: 5 him and to s him with all your heart
     24:14 and s him with all faithfulness.
     24:15 this day whom you will s,
     24:15 household, we will s the LORD."
     24:18 We too will s the LORD,
1Sa   7: 3 to the LORD and s him only,
     12:20 s the LORD with all your heart.
     12:24 s him faithfully with all your heart;
2Ki 17:35 to them, s them or sacrifice to them.
2Ch 19: 9 "You must s faithfully
Ne   9:35 they did not s you or turn from their
Job 36:11 If they obey and s him, they will
Ps   2:11 S the LORD with fear
Isa 60:12 that will not s you will perish;
Jer   2:20 you said, 'I will not s you!'
     25: 6 Do not follow other gods to s
Da   3:17 the God we s is able to deliver us
Mt   4:10 Lord your God, and s him only.' "
      6:24 "No one can s two masters.
      6:24 You cannot s both God and money.
Mk   10:45 but to s, and to give his life as
Lk   16:13 "No one can s two masters.
     16:13 You cannot s both God
Ro   12: 7 if it is serving, then s; if it is
Gal   5:13 s one another humbly in love.
Eph   6: 7 S wholeheartedly, as if you were
1Th   1: 9 to God from idols to s the living
1Ti   6: 2 they should s them even better
Heb   9:14 so that we may s the living God!
1Pe   4:10 gift you have received to s others,
      5: 2 dishonest gain, but eager to s;
Rev   1: 6 and priests to s his God and Father—
      5:10 a kingdom and priests to s our God,
      7:15 the throne of God and s him day

SERVED SERVE

Ge   29:20 So Jacob s seven years to get
Jos 24:15 gods your ancestors s beyond
Jdg   2:13 they forsook him and s Baal
Jer   5:19 s foreign gods in your own land,
Mt   20:28 Son of Man did not come to be s,

Jn   12: 2 Martha s, while Lazarus was among
Ac   17:25 And he is not s by human hands,
Ro   1:25 and s created things rather than
1Ti   3:13 Those who have s well gain

SERVES SERVE

Lk   22:26 one who rules like the one who s.
Jn   12:26 Whoever s me must follow me;
     12:26 Father will honor the one who s me.
Ro   14:18 because anyone who s Christ in this
1Pe   4:11 If anyone s, they should do so

SERVICE SERVE

Nu   8:25 they must retire from their regular s
     18: 7 I am giving you the s
2Ch   5:14 could not perform their s because
Job   7: 1 "Do not mortals have hard s
Lk   9:62 and looks back is fit for s
     12:35 "Be dressed ready for s and keep
Ro   15:17 in Christ Jesus in my s to God.
1Co 12: 5 There are different kinds of s,
     16:15 to the s of the Lord's people.
2Co   9:12 This s that you perform is not only
     10:13 of s God himself has assigned to us,
Eph   4:12 to equip his people for works of s,
Rev   2:19 and faith, your s and perseverance,

SERVING SERVE

Jos 24:15 if s the LORD seems undesirable
Jdg   2:19 following other gods and s
2Ch 12: 8 learn the difference between s me
                 and s the kings of other lands."
Pr   15:17 Better a small s of vegetables
Ro   12: 7 if it is s, then serve; if it is teaching,
     12:11 your spiritual fervor, s the Lord.
     16:18 people are not s our Lord Christ,
Eph   6: 7 as if you were s the Lord,
Col   3:24 It is the Lord Christ you are s.
2Ti   2: 4 No one s as a soldier gets entangled
1Pe   1:12 that they were not s themselves

SET SETS, SETTING, SETTINGS

Ge   9:13 I have s my rainbow in the clouds,
     28:18 under his head and s it up as a pillar
     31:45 took a stone and s it up as a pillar.
     35:14 Jacob s up a stone pillar at the place
Ex   24: 4 and s up twelve stone pillars
     26:30 "S up the tabernacle according
     40:18 When Moses s up the tabernacle,
Lev 20:26 I have s you apart from the nations
Nu   8:17 in Egypt, I s them apart for myself.
      9:23 the LORD's command they s out.
Dt   10:15 Yet the LORD s his affection
     16:21 Do not s up any wooden Asherah
     27: 2 you, s up some large stones and coat
     28: 1 LORD your God will s you high
     30:15 See, I s before you today life
Jos   4: 9 Joshua s up the twelve stones
1Sa   5: 2 temple and s it beside Dagon.
2Ki 25: 9 He s fire to the temple
Ps   4: 3 the LORD has s apart his faithful
      8: 1 You have s your glory
    142: 7 S me free from my prison, that I
Pr   8: 5 who are foolish, s your hearts on it.
      9: 1 she has s up its seven pillars.

Isa 50: 7 Therefore have I s my face like
Eze 14: 4 any of the Israelites s up idols
Da   9:27 And at the temple he will s
     11:28 his heart will be s against the holy
Mk 15:17 a crown of thorns and s it on him.
Lk   4:18 the blind, to s the oppressed free,
     16:26 and you a great chasm has been s
Jn   8:32 truth, and the truth will s you free."
     10:35 and Scripture cannot be s aside—
Ac   1: 7 or dates the Father has s by his own
Ro   8: 2 Spirit who gives life has s you free
2Co 1:22 s his seal of ownership on us,
Gal 5: 1 for freedom that Christ has s us free.
Col 3: 1 s your hearts on things above,
Heb 4: 7 God again s a certain day, calling it

SETH
Ge   4:25 birth to a son and named him S,

SETS SET
2Ch 30:19 who s their heart on seeking God—
Job 5:11 The lowly he s on high, and those
Ps 68: 6 God s the lonely in families,
    146: 7 The LORD s prisoners free,
Ecc 1: 5 The sun rises and the sun s,
Mt   5:19 Therefore anyone who s aside one
2Th 2: 4 so that he s himself up in God's
Heb 10: 9 He s aside the first to establish

SETTING SET
Dt 11:26 I am s before you today a blessing
Jer 21: 8 I am s before you the way of life
Mk   7: 9 a fine way of s aside the commands
Eph 2:15 by s aside in his flesh the law

SETTINGS SET
Pr 25:11 gold in s of silver is a ruling rightly

SETTLE RESETTLE, SETTLED,
   SETTLES
Ge 47: 4 So now, please let your servants s
Nu 33:53 possession of the land and s in it,
Isa 1:18 "Come now, let us s the matter," says
     2: 4 will s disputes for many peoples.
Jer 29: 5 "Build houses and s down;
Eze 37:14 and I will s you in your own land.
Mt   5:25 "S matters quickly with your
2Th 3:12 in the Lord Jesus Christ to s down

SETTLED SETTLE
Ex 24:16 of the LORD s on Mount Sinai.
     40:35 meeting because the cloud had s
Dt 19: 1 driven them out and s in their towns
2Ki 18:11 to Assyria and s them in Halah,

SETTLES SETTLE
Ps 113: 9 He s the childless woman in her
Pr 18:18 Casting the lot s disputes and keeps

SEVEN SEVENS, SEVENTH
Ge   4:15 will suffer vengeance s times over."
     7: 2 Take with you s pairs of every kind
     21:28 Abraham set apart s ewe lambs
     29:18 "I'll work for you s years in return
     41: 2 of the river there came up s cows,
     41: 5 S heads of grain, healthy and good,

Ex   2:16 a priest of Midian had s daughters,
     12:15 For s days you are to eat bread
     25:37 make its s lamps and set them
     29:35 you, taking s days to ordain them.
Lev 4: 6 of it s times before the LORD,
     12: 2 be ceremonially unclean for s days,
     15:19 her monthly period will last s days,
     15:24 him, he will be unclean for s days;
     23:15 offering, count off s full weeks.
     23:42 in temporary shelters for s days:
     25: 8 " 'Count off s sabbath years—
     26:18 you for your sins s times over.
Nu 23: 1 said, "Build me s altars here,
Dt   7: 1 s nations larger and stronger than
     15: 1 every s years you must cancel debts.
Jos 6: 4 Have s priests carry trumpets
     6: 4 march around the city s times,
Jdg 16:13 Delilah took the s braids of his
1Sa 2: 5 was barren has borne s children,
1Ki 19:18 Yet I reserve s thousand in Israel—
2Ki 5:10 wash yourself s times in the Jordan,
Ps 79:12 our neighbors s times the contempt
    119:164 S times a day I praise you for your
Pr   6:16 hates, s that are detestable to him:
     9: 1 she has set up its s pillars.
     24:16 for though the righteous fall s times,
     26:25 for s abominations fill their hearts.
Isa 4: 1 that day s women will take hold
Da   3:19 the furnace heated s times hotter
     4:16 animal, till s times pass by for him.
     9:25 comes, there will be s 'sevens,'
Zec 3: 9 There are s eyes on that one stone,
     4: 2 a bowl at the top and s lamps on it,
Mt 18:22 not s times, but seventy-seven times.
Mk 12:20 Now there were s brothers.
     16: 9 of whom he had driven s demons.
Lk 11:26 takes s other spirits more wicked
Ro 11: 4 for myself s thousand who have not
Rev 1: 4 To the s churches in the province
     1: 4 from the s spirits before his throne,
     1:12 I turned I saw s golden lampstands,
     1:16 In his right hand he held s stars,
     3: 1 him who holds the s spirits of God
            and the s stars.
     4: 5 of the throne, s lamps were blazing.
     4: 5 These are the s spirits of God.
     5: 1 both sides and sealed with s seals.
     6: 1 Lamb opened the first of the s seals.
     8: 2 I saw the s angels who stand before
     8: 2 and s trumpets were given to them.
     10: 4 And when the s thunders spoke,
     12: 3 enormous red dragon with s heads
     12: 3 ten horns and s crowns on its heads.
     15: 1 s angels with the s last plagues—
     15: 7 to the s angels s golden bowls filled
     16: 1 the temple saying to the s angels,
     16: 1 pour out the s bowls of God's wrath
     17: 9 The s heads are s hills

SEVENS* SEVEN
Da   9:24 "Seventy 's' are decreed for your
     9:25 will be seven 's,' and sixty-two 's.'
     9:26 After the sixty-two 's,' the Anointed

SEVENTH SEVEN

Ge 2: 2 the s day God had finished the work
2: 2 so on the s day he rested from all
Ex 16:30 So the people rested on the s day.
20:10 the s day is a sabbath to the LORD
23:11 but during the s year let the land lie
23:12 but on the s day do not work,
Lev 16:29 day of the s month you must deny
23:16 up to the day after the s Sabbath,
23:24 the first day of the s month you are
23:27 tenth day of this s month is the Day
23:34 the s month the LORD's Festival
25: 4 in the s year the land is to have
Jos 6:16 The s time around, when the priests
Heb 4: 4 "On the s day God rested from all
Rev 8: 1 When he opened the s seal,
11:15 The s angel sounded his trumpet,
16:17 The s angel poured out his bowl

SEVENTY

Ge 46:27 which went to Egypt, were s in all.
Ex 24: 1 Abihu, and s of the elders of Israel.
Nu 11:25 on him and put it on the s elders.
2Ch 36:21 until the s years were completed
Ps 90:10 Our days may come to s years,
Jer 25:12 "But when the s years are fulfilled,
Da 9: 2 of Jerusalem would last s years.
9:24 "S 'sevens' are decreed for your

SEVENTY-SEVEN

Ge 4:24 seven times, then Lamech s times."
Mt 18:22 you, not seven times, but s times.

SEVENTY-TWO

Lk 10: 1 this the Lord appointed s others

SEVERE

Ge 3:16 your pains in childbearing very s;
12:10 a while because the famine was s.
41:57 the famine was s everywhere.
Nu 11:33 and he struck them with a s plague.
1Ki 18: 2 Now the famine was s in Samaria,
2Ki 25: 3 the city had become so s that there
Lk 4:25 there was a s famine throughout
15:14 there was a s famine in that whole
Ac 11:28 a s famine would spread over
2Co 8: 2 In the midst of a very s trial,
1Th 1: 6 the midst of s suffering with the joy

SEWED SEWS

Ge 3: 7 so they s fig leaves together

SEWS SEWED

Mt 9:16 "No one s a patch of unshrunk

SEX* SEXUAL, SEXUALLY

Ge 19: 5 so that we can have s with them."
Jdg 19:22 to your house so we can have s
1Co 6: 9 nor men who have s with men

SEXUAL SEX

Ex 22:19 "Anyone who has s relations
Lev 18: 6 close relative to have s relations.
20:15 " 'If a man has s relations
Nu 25: 1 to indulge in s immorality
Mt 5:32 except for s immorality, makes her

Mt 15:19 adultery, s immorality, theft,
19: 9 except for s immorality, and marries
Ac 15:20 from s immorality, from the meat
Ro 1:24 of their hearts to s impurity
13:13 not in s immorality and debauchery,
1Co 5: 1 there is s immorality among you,
6:13 is not meant for s immorality.
6:18 Flee from s immorality.
10: 8 should not commit s immorality,
2Co 12:21 s sin and debauchery in which they
Gal 5:19 s immorality,
Eph 5: 3 not be even a hint of s immorality,
Col 3: 5 s immorality, impurity, lust,
1Th 4: 3 that you should avoid s immorality;
Jude 1: 7 gave themselves up to s immorality
Rev 2:14 idols and committed s immorality.
2:20 my servants into s immorality
9:21 their s immorality or their thefts.

SEXUALLY* SEX

1Co 5: 9 to associate with s immoral people—
5:11 or sister but is s immoral or greedy,
6: 9 Neither the s immoral nor idolaters
6:18 but whoever sins s, sins against
1Ti 1:10 for the s immoral, for those
Heb 12:16 See that no one is s immoral, or is
13: 4 the adulterer and all the s immoral.
Rev 21: 8 the murderers, the s immoral,
22:15 practice magic arts, the s immoral,

SHACKLES

2Ch 33:11 bound him with bronze s and took
36: 6 him with bronze s to take him
Ps 2: 3 their chains and throw off their s."
Na 1:13 your neck and tear your s away."

SHADE

Ps 121: 5 the LORD is your s at your right
SS 2: 3 I delight to sit in his s, and his fruit
Isa 25: 4 the storm and a s from the heat.
Eze 31: 6 all the great nations lived in its s.
Jnh 4: 6 over Jonah to give s for his head
Mk 4:32 that the birds can perch in its s."

SHADOW SHADOWS

2Ki 20:11 the LORD made the s go back
1Ch 29:15 Our days on earth are like a s,
Ps 17: 8 hide me in the s of your wings
36: 7 take refuge in the s of your wings.
57: 1 the s of your wings until the disaster
63: 7 help, I sing in the s of your wings.
91: 1 will rest in the s of the Almighty.
Isa 49: 2 in the s of his hand he hid me;
51:16 covered you with the s of my hand—
Mt 4:16 the s of death a light has dawned."
Lk 1:79 in darkness and in the s of death,
Ac 5:15 at least Peter's s might fall on some
Col 2:17 These are a s of the things that were
Heb 8: 5 is a copy and s of what is in heaven.
10: 1 The law is only a s of the good

SHADOWS SHADOW

Job 14: 2 like fleeting s, they do not endure.
Jas 1:17 who does not change like shifting s.

SHADRACH HANANIAH
Hebrew exiled to Babylon; name changed from
Hananiah (Da 1:6–7). Refused defilement by food
(Da 1:8–20). Refused to worship idol (Da 3:1–18);
saved from furnace (Da 3:19–30).

SHAGGY*
Da   8:21 The s goat is the king of Greece,

SHAKE SHAKEN, SHAKES, SHAKING, SHOOK
Ps 10: 6 himself, "Nothing will ever s me."
     64: 8 all who see them will s their heads
     99: 1 the cherubim, let the earth s.
Isa   2:19 when he rises to s the earth.
Hag 2: 6 I will once more s the heavens
      2:21 that I am going to s the heavens
Mk   6:11 and s the dust off your feet as
Heb 12:26 "Once more I will s not only

SHAKEN SHAKE
Ps 15: 5 does these things will never be s.
    16: 8 at my right hand, I will not be s.
    30: 6 secure, I said, "I will never be s."
    55:22 he will never let the righteous be s.
    62: 2 he is my fortress, I will never be s.
   112: 6 Surely the righteous will never be s;
Isa 54:10 Though the mountains be s
    54:10 you will not be s nor my covenant
Mt 24:29 and the heavenly bodies will be s.'
Lk   6:38 down, s together and running over,
Ac   2:25 is at my right hand, I will not be s.
Heb 12:28 a kingdom that cannot be s, let us be

SHAKES SHAKE
Ps 29: 8 voice of the LORD s the desert;
Pr 22:26 Do not be one who s hands
Isa 30:28 He s the nations in the sieve

SHAKING* SHAKE
Ps 22: 7 they hurl insults, s their heads.
Mt 27:39 hurled insults at him, s their heads
Mk 15:29 at him, s their heads and saying,

SHALLOW
Mt 13: 5 up quickly, because the soil was s.

SHALLUM
King of Israel (2Ki 15:10–16).

SHALMANESER*
King of Assyria; conquered and deported Israel
(2Ki 17:3–4; 18:9).

SHAME ASHAMED, SHAMED, SHAMEFUL
Ge 2:25 were both naked, and they felt no s.
Ps   4: 2 you people turn my glory into s?
    22: 5 they trusted and were not put to s.
    25: 3 hopes in you will ever be put to s,
         but s will come on those who are
    34: 5 their faces are never covered with s.
    69: 6 seek you not be put to s because
    97: 7 who worship images are put to s,
Pr   3:35 inherit honor, but fools get only s.

Pr 13: 5 a stench and bring s on themselves.
    13:18 discipline comes to poverty and s,
    18:13 that is folly and s.
Isa 30: 5 everyone will be put to s because
    45:17 you will never be put to s
    61: 7 of your s you will receive a double
Jer   8: 9 The wise will be put to s;
     8:12 No, they have no s at all;
Eze 39:26 They will forget their s and all
Da   9: 7 but this day we are covered with s—
    12: 2 life, others to s and everlasting
Ro   5: 5 And hope does not put us to s,
     9:33 in him will never be put to s."
   10:11 in him will never be put to s."
1Co 1:27 things of the world to s the wise;
Php 3:19 and their glory is in their s.
Heb 12: 2 scorning its s, and sat down
1Pe 2: 6 trusts in him will never be put to s."

SHAMED SHAME
Jer 10:14 every goldsmith is s by his idols.
Joel 2:26 never again will my people be s.

SHAMEFUL SHAME
Jer   3:24 our youth s gods have consumed
Ro   1:26 this, God gave them over to s lusts.
     1:27 Men committed s acts with other
2Co 4: 2 have renounced secret and s ways;
Eph 5:12 It is s even to mention what
Rev 21:27 nor will anyone who does what is s

SHAMGAR*
Judge; killed 600 Philistines (Jdg 3:31; 5:6).

SHAPE SHAPED, SHAPES, SHAPING
Ex 32: 4 it into an idol cast in the s of a calf,
2Ki 17:16 two idols cast in the s of calves,
Job 38:14 The earth takes s like clay under

SHAPED SHAPE
Job 10: 8 "Your hands s me and made me.

SHAPES SHAPE
Isa 44:10 Who s a god and casts an idol,
Jer 10: 3 and a craftsman s it with his chisel.

SHAPHAN
2Ki 22: 8 high priest said to S the secretary,

SHAPING* SHAPE
Jer 18: 4 the pot he was s from the clay was
    18: 4 pot, s it as seemed best to him.

SHARE SHARED, SHARERS, SHARES, SHARING
Ge 21:10 that woman's son will never s
Lev 6:18 come it is his perpetual s of the food
     6:22 It is the LORD's perpetual s and is
    19:17 neighbor frankly so you will not s
Nu 18:20 I am your s and your inheritance
Dt 10: 9 That is why the Levites have no s
Jos 14: 4 The Levites received no s
    22:25 You have no s in the LORD.'
2Sa 20: 1 shouted, "We have no s in David,
2Ch 10:16 "What s do we have in David,

Ne   2:20 you have no **s** in Jerusalem or any
Ps   69:27 do not let them **s** in your salvation.
Pr   22: 9 for they **s** their food with the poor.
Ecc   9: 2 All **s** a common destiny—
Eze 18:20 The child will not **s** the guilt
     18:20 nor will the parent **s** the guilt
Mt 25:21 and **s** your master's happiness!'
Lk   3:11 who has two shirts should **s**
     15:12 'Father, give me my **s** of the estate.'
Ac   8:21 have no part or **s** in this ministry,
Ro   8:17 if indeed we **s** in his sufferings
      8:17 that we may also **s** in his glory.
     12:13 **S** with the Lord's people who are
     15:27 it to the Jews to **s** with them their
1Co 10:17 one body, for we all **s** the one loaf.
2Co   1: 7 that just as you **s** in our sufferings,
      1: 7 so also you **s** in our comfort.
Gal   4:30 the slave woman's son will never **s**
      6: 6 in the word should **s** all good things
Eph   4:28 they may have something to **s**
Col   1:12 who has qualified you to **s**
2Th   2:14 that you might **s** in the glory of our
1Ti   5:22 and do not **s** in the sins of others.
      6:18 and to be generous and willing to **s**.
2Ti   2: 6 the first to receive a **s** of the crops.
Phm 1: 6 every good thing we **s** for the sake
Heb   3:14 We have come to **s** in Christ,
     12:10 order that we may **s** in his holiness.
     13:16 to do good and to **s** with others,
1Pe   5: 1 will **s** in the glory to be revealed:
Rev 18: 4 so that you will not **s** in her sins,
     20: 6 those who **s** in the first resurrection.
     22:19 that person any **s** in the tree of life

SHARED SHARE
Ps   41: 9 I trusted, one who **s** my bread,
Jn   13:18 'He who **s** my bread has turned
Ac   1:17 our number and **s** in our ministry."
      4:32 own, but they **s** everything they had.
Heb   2:14 he too **s** in their humanity so
      6: 4 gift, who have **s** in the Holy Spirit,

SHARERS* SHARE
Eph   3: 6 **s** together in the promise in Christ

SHARES SHARE
2Jn   1:11 Anyone who welcomes them **s**

SHARING SHARE
1Co   9:10 do so in the hope of **s** in the harvest.
2Co   9:13 for your generosity in **s** with them
Php   2: 1 if any common **s** in the Spirit, if any

SHARON
SS   2: 1 I am a rose of **S**, a lily

SHARP SHARPENED, SHARPENS,
   SHARPER
Pr   5: 4 as gall, **s** as a double-edged sword.
Isa   5:28 Their arrows are **s**, all their bows
Ac   15:39 They had such a **s** disagreement
Rev   1:16 coming out of his mouth was a a **s**,
      2:12 are the words of him who has the **s**,
     14:14 his head and a **s** sickle in his hand.
     19:15 out of his mouth is a a **s** sword

SHARPENED SHARP
Isa 49: 2 He made my mouth like a a **s** sword,
Eze 21: 9 sword, a sword, **s** and polished—

SHARPENS* SHARP
Pr   27:17 As iron **s** iron, so one person
           s another.

SHARPER* SHARP
Heb   4:12 **S** than any double-edged sword,

SHATTER SHATTERED, SHATTERS
Isa 30:31 voice of the LORD will **s** Assyria;
Jer 51:20 with you I **s** nations, with you I
Hag   2:22 and **s** the power of the foreign

SHATTERED SHATTER
Ex   15: 6 right hand, LORD, **s** the enemy.
1Ki 19:11 and **s** the rocks before the LORD,
Job 16:12 All was well with me, but he **s** me;
     17:11 days have passed, my plans are **s**.
Ecc 12: 6 before the pitcher is **s** at the spring,
Isa   7: 8 years Ephraim will be too **s** to be
Na   1: 6 the rocks are **s** before him.

SHATTERS SHATTER
Ps   46: 9 He breaks the bow and **s** the spear;

SHAVE SHAVED
Nu   6:18 the Nazirite must **s** off the hair
Dt   14: 1 or **s** the front of your heads
Jdg 16:19 someone to **s** off the seven braids

SHAVED SHAVE
Nu   6:19 the Nazirite has **s** off the hair
Jdg 16:17 If my head were **s**, my strength
Ac   21:24 so that they can have their heads **s**.
1Co 11: 5 it is the same as having her head **s**.

SHEAF SHEAVES
Ge   37: 7 the field when suddenly my **s** rose
Lev 23:11 wave the **s** before the LORD so it
Dt   24:19 in your field and you overlook a **s**,

SHEAR SHEARER, SHEARERS
Dt   15:19 do not **s** the firstborn of your sheep.

SHEARER* SHEAR
Ac   8:32 and as a lamb before its **s** is silent,

SHEARERS SHEAR
Isa 53: 7 and as a sheep before its **s** is silent,

SHEATH
Eze 21: 3 I will draw my sword from its **s**
Jer 47: 6 Return to your **s**; cease and be still.'

SHEAVES SHEAF
Ge   37: 7 while your **s** gathered around mine
Ru   2:15 "Let her gather among the **s**
Ps 126: 6 songs of joy, carrying **s** with them.

SHEBA
   1. Benjamite; rebelled against David (2Sa 20).
   2. Queen of Sheba (1Ki 10; 2Ch 9).

SHECHEM

1. Raped Jacob's daughter Dinah; killed by Simeon and Levi (Ge 34).
2. City where Joshua renewed the covenant (Jos 24). Abimelech as king (Jdg 9).

SHED SHEDDING, SHEDS

Ge   9: 6 by humans shall their blood be s;
Nu 35:33 the land on which blood has been s,
Dt   19:10 innocent blood will not be s in your
2Ki 21:16 s so much innocent blood that he
Ps 106:38 They s innocent blood, the blood
Pr   6:17 tongue, hands that s innocent blood,
Isa   59: 7 they are swift to s innocent blood.
Eze 22:12 people who accept bribes to s blood;
Hab   2: 8 For you have s human blood;
        2:17 For you have s human blood;
Mt   23:35 blood that has been s on earth,
Ro   3:15 "Their feet are swift to s blood;
Col   1:20 through his blood, s on the cross.
Rev 16: 6 for they have s the blood of your

SHEDDING SHED

Heb   9:22 without the s of blood there is no
       12: 4 resisted to the point of s your blood.

SHEDS* SHED

Ge   9: 6 "Whoever s human blood,
Pr   20:27 of the LORD that s light on one's
Eze 18:10 who s blood or does any of these

SHEEP SHEEP'S, SHEEPSKINS

Lev   1:10 flock, from either the s or the goats,
Nu   27:17 not be like s without a shepherd."
Dt   17: 1 God an ox or a s that has any defect
1Sa 15:14 then is this bleating of s in my ears?
       17:35 it and rescued the s from its mouth.
2Sa 12: 4 from taking one of his own s
1Ki 22:17 the hills like s without a shepherd,
Ps   44:22 we are considered as s to be
       74: 1 your anger smolder against the s
       78:52 he led them like s through
       78:70 and took him from the s pens;
      100: 3 are his people, the s of his pasture.
     119:176 I have strayed like a lost s.
SS   4: 2 teeth are like a flock of s just shorn,
Isa   13:14 gazelle, like s without a shepherd,
       53: 6 We all, like s, have gone astray,
       53: 7 as a s before its shearers is silent,
Jer   23: 1 and scattering the s of my pasture!"
       50: 6 "My people have been lost s;
Eze 34:15 I myself will tend my s and have
Zec 13: 7 and the s will be scattered, and I
Mt   9:36 helpless, like s without a shepherd.
       10: 6 Go rather to the lost s of Israel.
       10:16 you out like s among wolves.
       12:11 "If any of you has a s and it falls
       25:32 as a shepherd separates the s
Lk   15: 4 go after the lost s until he finds it?
Jn   10: 1 anyone who does not enter the s pen
       10: 3 He calls his own s by name
       10: 7 I tell you, I am the gate for the s.
       10:11 lays down his life for the s.
       10:15 and I lay down my life for the s.

Jn   10:27 My s listen to my voice;
       21:17 Jesus said, "Feed my s.
Ac   8:32 "He was led like a s
Ro   8:36 we are considered as s to be
Heb 13:20 Jesus, that great Shepherd of the s,
1Pe   2:25 For "you were like s going astray,"

SHEEP'S* SHEEP

Mt   7:15 They come to you in s clothing,

SHEEPSKINS* SHEEP

Heb 11:37 They went about in s and goatskins,

SHEET SHEETS

Isa   25: 7 the s that covers all nations;
Ac   10:11 like a large s being let down to earth

SHEETS* SHEET

Ex   39: 3 They hammered out thin s of gold
Nu   16:38 Hammer the censers into s

SHEKEL SHEKELS

Ex   30:13 according to the sanctuary s,
       30:13 This half s is an offering

SHEKELS SHEKEL

Ge   37:28 sold him for twenty s of silver
Lev   27: 3 twenty and sixty at fifty s of silver,
       27: 4 a female, set her value at thirty s;
1Ch 21:25 David paid Araunah six hundred s
Hos   3: 2 I bought her for fifteen s of silver

SHELAH

Ge   38:11 until my son S grows up."
       46:12 Onan, S, Perez and Zerah (but Er

SHELTER SHELTERED, SHELTERS

Ps   27: 5 hide me in the s of his sacred tent
       31:20 In the s of your presence you hide
       55: 8 I would hurry to my place of s,
       61: 4 take refuge in the s of your wings.
       91: 1 in the s of the Most High will rest
Ecc   7:12 Wisdom is a s as money is a s,
Isa   1: 8 Daughter Zion is left like a s
        4: 6 It will be a s and shade
       25: 4 a s from the storm and a shade
       32: 2 Each one will be like a s
       58: 7 provide the poor wanderer with s—
Am   9:11 "I will restore David's fallen s—
Jnh   4: 5 There he made himself a s, sat in its
Rev   7:15 he who sits on the throne will s them

SHELTERED* SHELTER

Zep   2: 3 perhaps you will be s on the day

SHELTERS SHELTER

Lev   23:42 Live in temporary s for seven days:
Ne   8:14 in temporary s during the festival
Mk   9: 5 Let us put up three s—one for you,

SHEM

Son of Noah (Ge 5:32; 6:10). Blessed (Ge 9:26). Descendants (Ge 10:21–31; 11:10–32; Lk 3:36).

SHEMAIAH

1Ki 12:22 of God came to S the man of God:
2Ch 12: 5 the prophet S came to Rehoboam

Jer 29:31 Because **S** has prophesied to you,

SHEMER
1Ki 16:24 of Samaria from **S** for two talents

SHEPHERD SHEPHERDED, SHEPHERDS
Ge 48:15 God who has been my **s** all my life
49:24 because of the **S**, the Rock of Israel,
Nu 27:17 will not be like sheep without a **s**."
1Sa 21: 7 Doeg the Edomite, Saul's chief **s**.
2Sa   7: 7 I commanded to **s** my people Israel,
1Ki 22:17 on the hills like sheep without a **s**,
1Ch 11: 2 you, 'You will **s** my people Israel,
Ps 23: 1 The LORD is my **s**, I lack nothing.
28: 9 be their **s** and carry them forever.
78:71 him to be the **s** of his people Jacob,
80: 1 Hear us, **S** of Israel, you who lead
Ecc 12:11 given by one **s**.
Isa 40:11 He tends his flock like a **s**:
Jer 31:10 will watch over his flock like a **s**.'
Eze 34: 5 scattered because there was no **s**,
34:12 As a **s** looks after his scattered flock
Mic   5: 4 and **s** his flock in the strength
Zec 10: 2 like sheep oppressed for lack of a **s**.
11: 4 "**S** the flock marked for slaughter.
11: 9 and said, "I will not be your **s**.
11:17 "Woe to the worthless **s**,
13: 7 "Strike the **s**, and the sheep will be
Mt   2: 6 come a ruler who will **s** my people
25:32 another as a **s** separates the sheep
26:31 " 'I will strike the **s**, and the sheep
Mk   6:34 they were like sheep without a **s**.
Jn 10:11 "I am the good **s**. The good **s** lays
10:14 "I am the good **s**; I know my sheep
10:16 there shall be one flock and one **s**.
Heb 13:20 Jesus, that great **S** of the sheep,
1Pe   2:25 now you have returned to the **S**
5: 4 And when the Chief **S** appears,
Rev   7:17 center of the throne will be their **s**;

SHEPHERDED* SHEPHERD
Ps 78:72 David **s** them with integrity of heart;
Zec 11: 7 So I **s** the flock marked
11: 7 the other Union, and I **s** the flock.

SHEPHERDS SHEPHERD
Ge 46:34 for all **s** are detestable
Ex   2:19 Egyptian rescued us from the **s**.
Nu 14:33 Your children will be **s** here
Isa 13:20 there no **s** will rest their flocks.
56:11 They are **s** who lack understanding;
Jer   3:15 I will give you **s** after my own heart,
23: 1 "Woe to the **s** who are destroying
50: 6 their **s** have led them astray
Eze 34: 2 prophesy against the **s** of Israel;
34: 2 Should not **s** take care of the flock?
Zec 10: 3 "My anger burns against the **s**,
Lk   2: 8 there were **s** living out in the fields
Ac 20:28 Be **s** of the church of God, which he
1Pe   5: 2 Be **s** of God's flock that is under
Jude 1:12 **s** who feed only themselves.

SHESHBAZZAR
Ezr   1: 8 them out to **S** the prince of Judah.

Ezr   5:16 "So this **S** came and laid

SHEWBREAD (KJV) See BREAD OF THE PRESENCE

SHIBBOLETH* SIBBOLETH
Jdg 12: 6 they said, "All right, say '**S**.' "

SHIELD SHIELDED, SHIELDS
Ge 15: 1 I am your **s**, your very great
Ex 40: 3 in it and **s** the ark with the curtain.
Dt 33:29 He is your **s** and helper and your
2Sa 22:36 You make your saving help my **s**;
Ps   3: 3 you, LORD, are a **s** around me,
5:12 them with your favor as with a **s**.
7:10 My **s** is God Most High, who saves
18: 2 my **s** and the horn of my salvation,
28: 7 LORD is my strength and my **s**;
33:20 he is our help and our **s**.
84:11 For the LORD God is a sun and **s**;
91: 4 his faithfulness will be your **s**
115: 9 he is their help and **s**.
119:114 You are my refuge and my **s**;
144: 2 my **s**, in whom I take refuge,
Pr   2: 7 he is a **s** to those whose walk is
30: 5 he is a **s** to those who take refuge
Isa 31: 5 LORD Almighty will **s** Jerusalem;
Zec   9:15 the LORD Almighty will **s** them.
Eph   6:16 take up the **s** of faith,

SHIELDED SHIELD
Dt 32:10 He **s** him and cared for him;
1Pe   1: 5 who through faith are **s** by God's

SHIELDS SHIELD
Dt 33:12 for he **s** him all day long,

SHIFTING*
Jas   1:17 does not change like **s** shadows.

SHIFTLESS*
Pr 19:15 on deep sleep, and the **s** go hungry.

SHILOH
Jos 18: 1 of the Israelites gathered at **S**
1Sa   1:24 to the house of the LORD at **S**.
Ps 78:60 He abandoned the tabernacle of **S**,

SHIMEI
Cursed David (2Sa 16:5–14); spared (2Sa 19:16–23). Killed by Solomon (1Ki 2:8–9, 36–46).

SHINAR
Ge 11: 2 they found a plain in **S** and settled

SHINE SHINES, SHINING, SHONE
Nu   6:25 the LORD make his face **s** on you
Job 33:30 that the light of life may **s** on them.
Ps   4: 6 Let the light of your face **s** on us.
37: 6 your righteous reward **s** like
67: 1 bless us and make his face **s** on us—
80: 1 between the cherubim, **s** forth
94: 1 O God who avenges, **s** forth.
118:27 and he has made his light **s** on us.
Isa 60: 1 "Arise, **s**, for your light has come,
Da 12: 3 are wise will **s** like the brightness

Mt   5:16 let your light s before others,
      13:43 the righteous will s like the sun
Lk   1:79 to s on those living in darkness
2Co   4: 6 said, "Let light s out of darkness,"
            made his light s in our hearts to give
Eph   5:14 the dead, and Christ will s on you."
Php   2:15 you will s among them like stars
Rev 21:23 need the sun or the moon to s on it,

SHINES* SHINE
Ps   50: 2 Zion, perfect in beauty, God s forth.
     97:11 Light s on the righteous and joy
Pr   13: 9 The light of the righteous s brightly,
Isa 62: 1 till her vindication s out like
Lk   11:36 of light as when a lamp s its light
Jn   1: 5 The light s in the darkness,

SHINING SHINE
Pr   4:18 s ever brighter till the full light
Lk   23:45 for the sun stopped s.
2Pe   1:19 as to a light s in a dark place,
1Jn   2: 8 and the true light is already s.
Rev   1:16 His face was like the sun s in all its

SHIP SHIPS, SHIPWRECK, SHIPWRECKED
Ecc 11: 1 S your grain across the sea;
Jnh   1: 4 storm arose that the s threatened
Ac   27:22 only the s will be destroyed.

SHIPS SHIP
1Ki   9:26 also built s at Ezion Geber, which is
     22:48 built a fleet of trading s to go
Ps 107:23 Some went out on the sea in s;
Pr   31:14 She is like the merchant s,
Jas   3: 4 Or take s as an example.

SHIPWRECK* SHIP
Eze 27:27 heart of the sea on the day of your s.
1Ti   1·19 so have suffered s with regard

SHIPWRECKED* SHIP
2Co 11:25 three times I was s, I spent a night

SHIRT SHIRTS
Lk   6:29 do not withhold your s from them.
      9: 3 bag, no bread, no money, no extra s.

SHIRTS* SHIRT
Lk   3:11 who has two s should share

SHISHAK
2Ch 12: 2 S king of Egypt attacked Jerusalem

SHOCKED* SHOCKING
Ge   34: 7 They were s and furious,
Eze 16:27 who were s by your lewd conduct.

SHOCKING* SHOCKED
Jer   5:30 s thing has happened in the land:

SHOE(S) (KJV) See SANDAL(S)

SHONE SHINE
Mt   17: 2 His face s like the sun, and his
Lk   2: 9 the glory of the Lord s around them,
Rev 21:11 It s with the glory of God, and its

SHOOK SHAKE
Ps   18: 7 the foundations of the mountains s;
Isa   6: 4 and thresholds s and the temple was
Mt   27:51 The earth s, the rocks split
Ac   13:51 So they s the dust off their feet as
      18: 6 he s out his clothes in protest

SHOOT SHOOTS
Isa 11: 1 A s will come up from the stump
     53: 2 grew up before him like a tender s,
     60:21 They are the s I have planted,
Ro   11:17 though a wild olive s, have been

SHOOTS SHOOT
Ps 128: 3 be like olive s around your table.
Hos 14: 6 his young s will grow.

SHORE SHORES
Ex   14:30 the Egyptians lying dead on the s.
Lk   5: 3 asked him to put out a little from s.
Rev 13: 1 dragon stood on the s of the sea.

SHORES SHORE
Ps   72:10 and of distant s bring tribute to him.
     97: 1 let the distant s rejoice.

SHORT SHORTENED
Nu   11:23 Moses, "Is the LORD's arm too s?
Isa 50: 2 Was my arm too s to deliver you?
     59: 1 of the LORD is not too s to save,
Mt   13:21 have no root, they last only a s time,
     24:22 "If those days had not been cut s,
Lk   19: 3 because he was s he could not see
Jn   7:33 "I am with you for only a s time,
Ac   26:28 such a s time you can persuade me
Ro   3:23 and fall s of the glory of God,
1Co   7:29 and sisters, is that the time is s.
Heb   4. 1 you be found to have fallen s of it.
Rev 12:12 he knows that his time is s."
     20: 3 that, he must be set free for a s time.

SHORTENED* SHORT
Mt   24:22 of the elect those days will be s.
Mk   13:20 whom he has chosen, he has s them.

SHOULD
Mt   23:23 You s have practiced the latter,
Lk   18: 1 show them that they s always pray
Php   2:10 the name of Jesus every knee s bow,
Jas   3: 1 Not many of you s become teachers,

SHOULDER SHOULDERS
Isa 22:22 I will place on his s the key
Zep   3: 9 of the LORD and serve him s to s.

SHOULDERS SHOULDER
Ex   28:12 on his s as a memorial before
Dt   33:12 LORD loves rests between his s."
Ps   81: 6 "I removed the burden from their s;
Isa   9: 4 the bar across their s, the rod
      9: 6 and the government will be on his s.
Mt   23: 4 and put them on other people's s,
Lk   15: 5 finds it, he joyfully puts it on his s

SHOUT SHOUTED, SHOUTING, SHOUTS

Nu 23:21 the **s** of the King is among them.
Jos 6:16 Joshua commanded the army, "S!
Ezr 3:11 And all the people gave a great **s**
Ps 20: 5 May we **s** for joy over your victory
35:27 delight in my vindication **s** for joy
47: 1 **s** to God with cries of joy.
66: 1 **S** for joy to God, all the earth!
95: 1 let us **s** aloud to the Rock of our
98: 4 **S** for joy to the LORD,
100: 1 **S** for joy to the LORD,
Isa 12: 6 **S** aloud and sing for joy,
26:19 in the dust wake up and **s** for joy—
35: 6 deer, and the mute tongue **s** for joy.
40: 9 lift up your voice with a **s**, lift it up,
42: 2 He will not **s** or cry out, or raise his
44:23 **s** aloud, you earth beneath.
54: 1 burst into song, **s** for joy, you who
Jer 31:12 and **s** for joy on the heights of Zion;
Zec 9: 9 **S**, Daughter Jerusalem!
Rev 10: 3 he gave a loud **s** like the roar

SHOUTED SHOUT

Lev 9:24 it, they **s** for joy and fell facedown.
1Sa 17: 8 stood and **s** to the ranks of Israel,
Job 38: 7 together and all the angels **s** for joy?
Mk 15:13 "Crucify him!" they **s**.
Rev 18: 2 With a mighty voice he **s**:
19: 3 And again they **s**: "Hallelujah!

SHOUTING SHOUT

Mt 21:15 the children **s** in the temple courts,
Jn 12:13 and went out to meet him, **s**,

SHOUTS SHOUT

2Sa 6:15 up the ark of the LORD with **s**
Ps 27: 6 his sacred tent I will sacrifice with **s**
47: 5 God has ascended amid **s** of joy,
Ecc 9:17 to be heeded than the **s** of a ruler

SHOW SHOWED, SHOWING, SHOWN, SHOWS

Ge 12: 1 household to the land I will **s** you.
22: 2 on a mountain I will **s** you."
24:12 **s** kindness to my master Abraham.
Ex 9:16 that I might **s** you my power
18:20 and **s** them the way they are to live
25: 9 exactly like the pattern I will **s** you.
33:18 said, "Now **s** me your glory."
Dt 1:17 Do not **s** partiality in judging;
4: 6 for this will **s** your wisdom
7: 2 with them, and **s** them no mercy.
Jos 2:12 you will **s** kindness to my family,
Ru 1: 8 May the LORD **s** you kindness,
1Sa 20:14 But **s** me unfailing kindness like
2Sa 9: 1 Saul to whom I can **s** kindness
22:26 the faithful you **s** yourself faithful,
Ezr 2:59 they could not **s** that their families
Ps 17: 7 **S** me the wonders of your great
18:26 to the pure you **s** yourself pure,
18:26 the devious you **s** yourself shrewd.
25: 4 **S** me your ways, LORD, teach me
39: 4 "**S** me, LORD, my life's end

Ps 85: 7 **S** us your unfailing love, LORD,
102:13 Zion, for it is time to **s** favor to her;
143: 8 **S** me the way I should go, for to you
Ecc 10: 3 and **s** everyone how stupid they are.
SS 2:14 the mountainside, **s** me your face,
Isa 30:18 he will rise up to **s** you compassion.
Jer 32:18 You **s** love to thousands but bring
La 3:32 he will **s** compassion, so great is his
Hos 1: 6 for I will no longer **s** love to Israel,
2:23 I will **s** my love to the one I called
Joel 2:30 I will **s** wonders in the heavens
Mic 7:20 and **s** love to Abraham, as you
Zec 7: 9 **s** mercy and compassion to one
Mt 22:19 **S** me the coin used for paying
Mk 12:40 and for a **s** make lengthy prayers.
Jn 2:18 "What sign can you **s** us to prove
14: 8 **s** us the Father and that will be
Ac 2:19 I will **s** wonders in the heavens
10:34 it is that God does not **s** favoritism
Ro 2:11 For God does not **s** favoritism.
1Co 12:31 yet I will **s** you the most excellent
2Co 11:30 of the things that **s** my weakness.
Gal 2: 6 God does not **s** favoritism—
Eph 2: 7 ages he might **s** the incomparable
Titus 2: 7 In your teaching **s** integrity,
Jas 2:18 **S** me your faith without deeds, and I
will **s** you my faith by my deeds.
1Pe 2:17 **S** proper respect to everyone,
Jude 1:23 to others **s** mercy, mixed with fear—
Rev 1: 1 **s** his servants what must soon take
4: 1 I will **s** you what must take place
17: 1 I will **s** you the punishment
21: 9 "Come, I will **s** you the bride,

SHOWED SHOW

Ge 39:21 he **s** him kindness and granted him
Dt 34: 1 There the LORD **s** him the whole
1Ki 3: 3 Solomon **s** his love for the LORD
Mt 4: 8 **s** him all the kingdoms of the world
Lk 24:40 this, he **s** them his hands and feet.
Jn 20:20 this, he **s** them his hands and side.
1Jn 4: 9 This is how God **s** his love among
Rev 21:10 and **s** me the Holy City, Jerusalem,
22: 1 the angel **s** me the river of the water

SHOWERS

Dt 32: 2 like dew, like **s** on new grass,
Ps 68: 9 You gave abundant **s**, O God;
Jer 3: 3 Therefore the **s** have been withheld,
Eze 34:26 there will be **s** of blessing.
Hos 10:12 and **s** his righteousness on you.

SHOWING SHOW

Ex 20: 6 **s** love to a thousand generations
Dt 5:10 **s** love to a thousand generations
Jn 15: 8 **s** yourselves to be my disciples.

SHOWN SHOW

Ex 25:40 the pattern **s** you on the mountain.
Dt 4:35 You were **s** these things so that you
1Ki 3: 6 "You have **s** great kindness to your
Ps 78:11 done, the wonders he had **s** them.
Mic 6: 8 He has **s** you, O mortal, what is
Mt 5: 7 merciful, for they will be **s** mercy.
Jn 10:32 "I have **s** you many good works

1Co 3:13 their work will be s for what it is,

SHOWS SHOW
Dt 10:17 who s no partiality and accepts no
Ps 123: 2 our God, till he s us his mercy.
Pr 3:34 mockers but s favor to the humble
10:17 Whoever heeds discipline s the way
15: 5 heeds correction s prudence.
1Pe 5: 5 proud but s favor to the humble."

SHREWD SHREWDLY
2Sa 22:27 to the devious you show yourself s.
Mt 10:16 Therefore be as s as snakes and as

SHREWDLY* SHREWD
Ex 1:10 we must deal s with them or they
Lk 16: 8 manager because he had acted s.

SHRINE SHRINES
Ge 38:21 "Where is the s prostitute who was
Dt 23:17 woman is to become a s prostitute.
1Ki 14:24 There were even male s prostitutes
Hos 4:14 and sacrifice with s prostitutes—

SHRINES SHRINE
1Ki 12:31 Jeroboam built s on high places
Eze 16:25 street corner you built your lofty s

SHRINK* SHRINKS
Heb 10:39 do not belong to those who s back
Rev 12:11 not love their lives so much as to s

SHRINKS* SHRINK
Heb 10:38 no pleasure in the one who s back."

SHRIVEL SHRIVELED
Isa 64: 6 we all s up like a leaf, and like

SHRIVELED SHRIVEL
1Ki 13: 4 stretched out toward the man s up,
Mk 3: 1 and a man with a s hand was there.

SHUDDER
Eze 32:10 and their kings will s with horror
Jas 2:19 the demons believe that—and s.

SHUHITE
Job 2:11 Bildad the S and Zophar

SHULAMMITE*
SS 6:13 Come back, come back, O S;
6:13 Why would you gaze on the S as

SHUN* SHUNNED, SHUNS
Job 28:28 and to s evil is understanding."
Pr 3: 7 fear the LORD and s evil.
14:16 wise fear the LORD and s evil,

SHUNAMMITE
1Ki 1: 3 a S, and brought her to the king.
2Ki 4:12 to his servant Gehazi, "Call the S."

SHUNNED* SHUN
Job 1: 1 he feared God and s evil.
Pr 14:20 The poor are s even by their
19: 7 The poor are s by all their

SHUNS* SHUN
Job 1: 8 a man who fears God and s evil."
2: 3 a man who fears God and s evil.
Isa 59:15 and whoever s evil becomes a prey.

SHUT SHUTS
Ge 7:16 Then the LORD s him in.
19: 6 them and s the door behind him
Dt 11:17 he will s up the heavens so that it
2Ch 6:26 "When the heavens are s
Isa 22:22 what he opens no one can s,
52:15 kings will s their mouths because
60:11 they will never be s, day or night,
Da 6:22 and he s the mouths of the lions.
Mt 23:13 You s the door of the kingdom
Heb 11:33 who s the mouths of lions,
Rev 3: 7 What he opens no one can s,
11: 6 They have power to s
21:25 On no day will its gates ever be s,

SHUTS SHUT
Isa 22:22 and what he s no one can open.
Rev 3: 7 and what he s no one can open.

SIBBOLETH* SHIBBOLETH
Jdg 12: 6 If he said, "S," because he could

SICK SICKBED, SICKNESS
Pr 13:12 Hope deferred makes the heart s,
Eze 34: 4 healed the s or bound up the injured.
Mt 8:16 with a word and healed all the s.
9:12 who need a doctor, but the s.
10: 8 Heal the s, raise the dead,
25:36 I was s and you looked after me,
Jn 11: 1 Now a man named Lazarus was s.
Ac 19:12 touched him were taken to the s,
1Co 11:30 many among you are weak and s,
2Ti 4:20 and I left Trophimus s in Miletus.
Jas 5:14 Is anyone among you s?

SICKBED* BED, SICK
Ps 41: 3 LORD sustains them on their s

SICKLE
Joel 3:13 Swing the s, for the harvest is ripe.
Rev 14:14 his head and a sharp s in his hand.

SICKNESS SICK
Ex 23:25 I will take away s from among you,
Mt 4:23 disease and s among the people.
Jn 11: 4 said, "This s will not end in death.

SIDE SIDES
1Ch 22: 9 rest from all his enemies on every s.
2Ch 15:15 LORD gave them rest on every s.
20:30 God had given him rest on every s.
Ps 91: 7 A thousand may fall at your s,
124: 1 the LORD had not been on our s—
Pr 3:26 for the LORD will be at your s
8:30 Then I was constantly at his s.
Jer 20:10 whispering, "Terror on every s!
Eze 1:10 on the right s each had the face
4: 4 lie on your left s and put the sin
Joel 3:12 to judge all the nations on every s.
Zec 3: 1 standing at his right s to accuse him.
Jn 18:37 Everyone on the s of truth listens

Jn 19:18 one on each s and Jesus
   19:34 the soldiers pierced Jesus' s
   20:20 he showed them his hands and s.
2Ti 4:17 the Lord stood at my s and gave me
Heb 10:33 at other times you stood s by s
Rev 22: 2 On each s of the river stood the tree

SIDES SIDE

Ex 12: 7 and put it on the s and tops
   29:16 splash it against the s of the altar.
Nu 33:55 in your eyes and thorns in your s.
Job 11: 6 wisdom, for true wisdom has two s.
Eze 2:10 On both s of it were written words
Da 7: 5 It was raised up on one of its s,
Rev 5: 1 a scroll with writing on both s

SIDON

Jdg 1:31 drive out those living in Akko or S
1Ki 17: 9 once to Zarephath in the region of S
Eze 28:21 of man, set your face against S;
Mt 11:21 had been performed in Tyre and S,
Mk 7:31 vicinity of Tyre and went through S,
Lk 4:26 in Zarephath in the region of S.

SIEGE BESIEGED

Dt 28:52 They will lay s to all the cities
2Ki 6:25 the s lasted so long that a donkey's
   18: 9 against Samaria and laid s to it.
   24:10 on Jerusalem and laid s to it,
Ps 31:21 love when I was in a city under s.

SIEVE*

Isa 30:28 the nations in the s of destruction;
Am 9: 9 the nations as grain is shaken in a s,

SIFT*

Lk 22:31 Satan has asked to s all of you as

SIGH* SIGHED, SIGHING

Mk 7:34 and with a deep s said to him,

SIGHED* SIGH

Mk 8:12 He s deeply and said, "Why does

SIGHING SIGH

Isa 35:10 and sorrow and s will flee away.

SIGHT SEE

Ge 6:11 the earth was corrupt in God's s
Ex 3: 3 will go over and see this strange s—
   4:11 Who gives them s or makes them
Nu 20:12 me as holy in the s of the Israelites,
Ps 19:14 of my heart be pleasing in your s,
   51: 4 and done what is evil in your s;
   72:14 for precious is their blood in his s.
   90: 4 years in your s are like a day
   116:15 in the s of the LORD is the death
Pr 3: 4 a good name in the s of God
Jer 18:10 if it does evil in my s and does not
Mt 11: 5 The blind receive s, the lame walk,
Ac 1: 9 and a cloud hid him from their s.
1Co 3:19 this world is foolishness in God's s.
2Co 5: 7 For we live by faith, not by s.
Eph 1: 4 to be holy and blameless in his s.
1Pe 3: 4 which is of great worth in God's s.

SIGN SIGNS

Ge 9:12 "This is the s of the covenant I am
   17:11 and it will be the s of the covenant
Ex 3:12 this will be the s to you that it is I
   4: 8 you or pay attention to the first s,
   12:13 The blood will be a s for you
   13:16 And it will be like a s on your hand
Nu 16:38 Let them be a s to the Israelites."
   17:10 to be kept as a s to the rebellious.
Dt 13: 1 and announces to you a s or wonder,
Jdg 6:17 eyes, give me a s that it is really you
1Ki 13: 3 the man of God gave a s: "This is
        the s the LORD
Ps 71: 7 I have become a s to many;
Isa 7:14 the Lord himself will give you a s:
   55:13 for an everlasting s, that will endure
Eze 20:12 my Sabbaths as a s between us,
   24:24 Ezekiel will be a s to you;
Mt 12:38 we want to see a s from you."
   12:39 adulterous generation asks for a s!
   16: 1 him to show them a s from heaven.
   24: 3 what will be the s of your coming
   24:30 will appear the s of the Son of Man
Mk 8:12 I tell you, no s will be given to it."
Lk 2:12 This will be a s to you:
   11:29 It asks for a s, but none will be given
        it except the s
   23: 8 to see him perform a s of some sort.
Jn 2:18 "What s can you show us to prove
   6:14 people saw the s Jesus performed,
   10:41 "Though John never performed a s,
Ac 4:16 they have performed a notable s,
Ro 4:11 he received circumcision as a s,
1Co 14:22 are a s, not for believers
Rev 12: 1 A great s appeared in heaven:
   12: 3 Then another s appeared in heaven:
   15: 1 another great and marvelous s:

SIGNAL

Mk 14:44 Now the betrayer had arranged a s

SIGNET

Ge 41:42 Pharaoh took his s ring from his
Est 3:10 So the king took his s ring from his
   8: 2 The king took off his s ring,
Jer 22:24 were a s ring on my right hand,
Da 6:17 king sealed it with his own s ring
Hag 2:23 'and I will make you like my s ring,

SIGNS SIGN

Ge 1:14 let them serve as s to mark sacred
Ex 4: 9 if they do not believe these two s
   7: 3 though I multiply my s and wonders
Nu 14:11 of all the s I have performed among
Dt 4:34 by testings, by s and wonders,
   34:11 who did all those s and wonders
Ps 74: 9 We are given no s from God;
   78:43 the day he displayed his s in Egypt,
   105:27 They performed his s among them,
Isa 8:18 We are s and symbols in Israel
   44:25 who foils the s of false prophets
Da 6:27 he performs s and wonders
Mt 16: 3 but you cannot interpret the s
   24:24 and perform great s and wonders

Mk 13:22 perform s and wonders to deceive,
Jn 2:11 Galilee was the first of the s through
2:23 people saw the s he was performing
3: 2 could perform the s you are doing
4:48 "Unless you people see s
7:31 he perform more s than this man?"
9:16 can a sinner perform such s?"
12:37 Jesus had performed so many s
20:30 Jesus performed many other s
Ac 2:19 above and s on the earth below,
2:43 and s performed by the apostles.
5:12 The apostles performed many s
14: 3 grace by enabling them to perform s
Ro 15:19 by the power of s and wonders,
1Co 1:22 Jews demand s and Greeks look
2Co 12:12 including s, wonders and miracles.
2Th 2: 9 sorts of displays of power through s
Heb 2: 4 God also testified to it by s,
Rev 13:13 And it performed great s,
16:14 are demonic spirits that perform s,
19:20 these s he had deluded those who

SIGNS AND WONDERS Ex 7:3; Dt 4:34;
6:22; 7:19; 26:8; 34:11; Ne 9:10; Ps 135:9; Jer 32:20,
21; Da 4:2; 6:27; Mt 24:24; Mk 13:22; Jn 4:48; Ac
4:30; 5:12; 14:3; 15:12; Ro 15:19; 2Th 2:9

SIHON
Nu 21:21 to say to S king of the Amorites:
Dt 31: 4 will do to them what he did to S
Ps 136:19 S king of the Amorites

SILAS*
Prophet (Ac 15:22–32); co-worker with Paul on
second missionary journey (Ac 16–18; 2Co 1:19).
Co-writer with Paul (1Th 1:1; 2Th 1:1); Peter (1Pe
5:12).

SILENCE SILENCED, SILENT
Ps 8: 2 to s the foe and the avenger.
1Pe 2:15 good you should s the ignorant talk
Rev 8: 1 there was s in heaven for about half

SILENCED SILENCE
Ps 63:11 while the mouths of liars will be s.
Pr 10:31 but a perverse tongue will be s.
Mt 22:34 that Jesus had s the Sadducees,
Ro 3:19 so that every mouth may be s
Titus 1:11 They must be s, because they are

SILENT SILENCE
Est 4:14 For if you remain s at this time,
Ps 30:12 may sing your praises and not be s.
32: 3 When I kept s, my bones wasted
39: 2 So I remained utterly s, not even
50: 3 Our God comes and will not be s;
83: 1 O God, do not remain s; do not turn
Pr 17:28 are thought wise if they keep s,
Ecc 3: 7 a time to be s and a time to speak,
Isa 53: 7 as a sheep before its shearers is s,
62: 1 For Zion's sake I will not keep s,
Jer 4:19 pounds within me, I cannot keep s.
Hab 2:20 let all the earth be s before him.
Zep 1: 7 Be s before the Sovereign LORD,
Mk 14:61 But Jesus remained s and gave no
Ac 8:32 and as a lamb before its shearer is s,

1Co 14:34 Women should remain s

SILOAM
Jn 9: 7 of S" (this word means "Sent").

SILVER
Ge 37:28 him for twenty shekels of s
Ex 11: 2 ask their neighbors for articles of s
20:23 not make for yourselves gods of s
25: 3 gold, s and bronze;
Dt 17:17 not accumulate large amounts of s
Jos 7:21 two hundred shekels of s and a bar
2Ch 1:15 The king made s and gold as
Ps 12: 6 like s purified in a crucible,
66:10 God, tested us; you refined us like s.
115: 4 But their idols are s and gold,
Pr 2: 4 if you look for it as for s and search
3:14 for she is more profitable than s
8:10 Choose my instruction instead of s,
22: 1 to be esteemed is better than s
25: 4 Remove the dross from the s,
25:11 of s is a ruling rightly given.
Isa 48:10 I have refined you, though not as s;
Eze 22:18 They are but the dross of s.
Da 2:32 its chest and arms of s, its belly
5: 4 they praised the gods of gold and s,
Hag 2: 8 'The s is mine and the gold is
Zec 11:12 So they paid me thirty pieces of s.
13: 9 I will refine them like s and test
Mal 3: 3 and refine them like gold and s.
Mt 26:15 out for him thirty pieces of s.
Ac 3: 6 Peter said, "S or gold I do not have,
1Co 3:12 on this foundation using gold, s,
2Ti 2:20 are articles not only of gold and s,
1Pe 1:18 not with perishable things such as s

SILVERSMITH
Ac 19:24 A s named Demetrius, who made

SIMEON
Son of Jacob by Leah (Ge 29:33; 35:23; 1Ch 2:1).
With Levi killed Shechem for rape of Dinah (Ge
34:25–29). Held hostage by Joseph in Egypt (Ge
42:24—43:23). Tribe of blessed (Ge 49:5–7), numbered (Nu 1:23; 26:14), allotted land (Jos 19:1–9;
Eze 48:24), 12,000 from (Rev 7:7).

SIMON PETER
1. See PETER.
2. Apostle, called the Zealot (Mt 10:4; Mk 3:18;
Lk 6:15; Ac 1:13).
3. Samaritan sorcerer (Ac 8:9–24).

SIMPLE
Ex 18:22 the s cases they can decide
Ps 19: 7 are trustworthy, making wise the s.
119:130 it gives understanding to the s.
Pr 1:22 long will you who are s love your s
8: 5 You who are s, gain prudence;
14:15 The s believe anything,

SIN SIN'S, SINFUL, SINNED, SINNER, SINNER'S, SINNERS, SINNING, SINS
Ge 4: 7 is right, s is crouching at your door;

Ex   20: 5 the children for the s of the parents
     32:32 But now, please forgive their s—
     34: 7 wickedness, rebellion and s.
Lev   4: 3 bull without defect as a s offering
      5: 6 goat from the flock as a s offering;
Nu   5: 7 and must confess the s they have
     14:18 love and forgiving s and rebellion.
     32:23 be sure that your s will find you out.
Dt   24:16 each will die for their own s.
1Sa 12:23 that I should s against the LORD
     15:23 rebellion is like the s of divination,
1Ki   8:46 for there is no one who does not s—
     13:34 This was the s of the house
2Ki 14: 6 each will die for their own s."
2Ch   7:14 I will forgive their s and will heal
Ne   13:26 even he was led into s by foreign
Job   1:22 Job did not s by charging God
      2:10 this, Job did not s in what he said.
Ps   4: 4 Tremble and do not s; when you are
     32: 2 is the one whose s the LORD does
     32: 5 Then I acknowledged my s to you
     32: 5 And you forgave the guilt of my s.
     36: 2 too much to detect or hate their s.
     38:18 I am troubled by my s.
     39: 1 ways and keep my tongue from s;
     51: 2 iniquity and cleanse me from my s.
     66:18 If I had cherished s in my heart,
    119:11 heart that I might not s against you.
    119:133 to your word; let no s rule over me.
Pr   10:19 S is not ended by multiplying
     14: 9 Fools mock at making amends for s,
     14:21 It is a s to despise one's neighbor,
     16: 6 love and faithfulness s is atoned for;
     17:19 Whoever loves a quarrel loves s;
     20: 9 I am clean and without s"?
     29: 6 Evildoers are snared by their own s,
Ecc   5: 6 not let your mouth lead you into s.
Isa   3: 9 they parade their s like Sodom;
      6: 7 taken away and your s atoned for."
     53:10 makes his life an offering for s,
     53:12 For he bore the s of many,
     64: 5 we continued to s against them,
Jer 16:18 for their wickedness and their s,
     31:30 everyone will die for their own s;
Eze   3:18 wicked person will die for their s,
     18:26 their righteousness and commits s,
     18:26 the s they have committed they will
     33: 8 wicked person will die for their s,
Da   9:20 confessing my s and the s of my
Hos 13: 2 Now they s more and more;
Mic   6: 7 of my body for the s of my soul?
      7:18 you, who pardons s and forgives
Zec   3: 4 I have taken away your s, and I will
Mt   6:14 people when they s against you,
Mk   3:29 they are guilty of an eternal s."
Jn   1:29 who takes away the s of the world!
      8: 7 who is without s be the first to
      8:34 everyone who sins is a slave to s.
      8:46 any of you prove me guilty of s?
     16: 9 about s, because people do not
Ac   7:60 do not hold this s against them."
Ro   2:12 All who s apart from the law will
      2:12 and all who s under the law will be

Ro   4: 8 is the one whose s the Lord will
      5:12 just as s entered the world through
      5:12 and death through s, and in this way
      5:20 But where s increased,
      6: 2 We are those who have died to s;
      6:11 count yourselves dead to s but alive
      6:14 s shall no longer be your master,
      6:23 For the wages of s is death,
      7: 7 not have known what s was had it
      7:25 sinful nature a slave to the law of s.
      8: 2 has set you free from the law of s
     14:23 that does not come from faith is s.
1Co   8:12 conscience, you s against Christ.
     15:56 The sting of death is s, and the power
           of s is the law.
2Co   5:21 God made him who had no s to be s
Gal   2:17 that mean that Christ promotes s?
      6: 1 if someone is caught in a s, you who
Eph   4:26 "In your anger do not s":
Heb   4:15 just as we are—yet he did not s.
      9:26 to do away with s by the sacrifice
     10:18 for s is no longer necessary.
     11:25 to enjoy the fleeting pleasures of s.
     12: 1 and the s that so easily entangles.
Jas   1:15 has conceived, it gives birth to s;
      4:17 do and doesn't do it, it is s for them.
1Pe   2:22 "He committed no s, and no deceit
1Jn   1: 7 Jesus, his Son, purifies us from all s.
      1: 8 If we claim to be without s,
      2: 1 so that you will not s. But if anybody
           does s, we have
      3: 4 in fact, s is lawlessness.
      3: 5 away our sins. And in him is no s.
      3: 6 continues to s has either seen him
      3: 9 is born of God will continue to s,
      5:16 sister commit a s that does not lead
      5:16 There is a s that leads to death.
      5:17 All wrongdoing is s, and there is s
           that does not lead

SIN OFFERING Ex 29:14, 36; 30:10; Lev 4:3, 8,
14, 20, 21, 24, 25, 29, 32, 33, 34; 5:6, 7, 8, 9, 9, 11,
11, 12; 6:17, 25, 25, 30; 7:7, 37; 8:2, 14; 9:2, 3, 7, 8,
10, 15, 15, 22; 10:16, 17, 19, 19; 12:6, 8; 14:13, 13,
19, 22, 31; 15:15, 30; 16:3, 5, 6, 9, 11, 11, 15, 25;
23:19; Nu 6:11, 14, 16; 7:16, 22, 28, 34, 40, 46, 52,
58, 64, 70, 76, 82, 87; 8:8, 12; 15:24, 25, 27; 28:15,
22; 29:5, 11, 11, 16, 19, 22, 25, 28, 31, 34, 38; 2Ch
29:21, 23, 24, 24; Ezr 6:17; 8:35; Eze 43:19, 21, 22,
25; 44:27; 45:19, 22, 23; 46:20; Ro 8:3; Heb 13:11

SIN OFFERINGS Lev 16:27; 2Ki 12:16; Ne
10:33; Ps 40:6; Eze 40:39; 42:13; 44:29; 45:17, 25;
Hos 8:11; Heb 10:6, 8

SIN'S* SIN
Heb   3:13 may be hardened by s deceitfulness.

SINAI
Ex   19: 1 they came to the Desert of S.
     19:20 descended to the top of Mount S
     31:18 speaking to Moses on Mount S,
Lev 27:34 Moses at Mount S for the Israelites.
Nu   1:19 he counted them in the Desert of S:
Ps   68:17 the Lord has come from S into his

Gal   4:24 One covenant is from Mount **S**
MOUNT SINAI See MOUNT

SINCERE* SINCERELY, SINCERITY
Da   11:34 many who are not **s** will join them.
Lk   20:20 sent spies, who pretended to be **s**.
Ac   2:46 ate together with glad and **s** hearts,
Ro   12: 9 Love must be **s**. Hate what is evil;
2Co   6: 6 in the Holy Spirit and in **s** love;
     11: 3 somehow be led astray from your **s**
1Ti   1: 5 and a good conscience and a **s** faith.
      3: 8 are to be worthy of respect, **s**,
2Ti   1: 5 I am reminded of your **s** faith,
Heb 10:22 us draw near to God with a **s** heart
Jas   3:17 and good fruit, impartial and **s**.
1Pe   1:22 that you have **s** love for each other,

SINCERELY SINCERE
Job 33: 3 my lips **s** speak what I know.

SINCERITY* SINCERE
1Co   5: 8 with the unleavened bread of **s**
2Co   1:12 with you, with integrity and godly **s**.
      2:17 Christ we speak before God with **s**,
      8: 8 I want to test the **s** of your love
Eph   6: 5 fear, and with **s** of heart, just as you
Col   3:22 but with **s** of heart and reverence

SINEWS
Col   2:19 held together by its ligaments and **s**,

SINFUL SIN; for SINFUL NATURE
see also FLESH
Ps   51: 5 Surely I was **s** at birth,
Pr   1:10 if **s** men entice you, do not give
Isa   1: 4 Woe to the **s** nation, a people whose
Eze 37:23 them from all their **s** backsliding,
Lk   5: 8 from me, Lord; I am a **s** man!"
      7:37 town who lived a **s** life learned
Ro   7: 5 the **s** passions aroused by the law
      7:18 dwell in me, that is, in my **s** nature.
      7:25 in my **s** nature a slave to the law
      8: 3 in the likeness of **s** flesh to be a sin
Heb   3:12 and sisters, that none of you has a **s**,
1Pe   2:11 to abstain from **s** desires,
1Jn   3: 8 The one who does what is **s** is

SING SANG, SINGERS, SINGING, SINGS, SONG, SONGS, SUNG
Ex   15: 1 "I will **s** to the LORD, for he is
Dt   31:19 to the Israelites and have them **s** it,
Jdg   5: 3 I, even I, will **s** to the LORD;
1Sa 21:11 Isn't he the one they **s** about in their
Ps   5:11 you be glad; let them ever **s** for joy.
     13: 6 I will **s** the LORD's praise, for he
     30: 4 **S** the praises of the LORD, you his
     30:12 that my heart may **s** your praises
     33: 1 **S** joyfully to the LORD,
     33: 3 **S** to him a new song;
     47: 6 **S** praises to God, **s** praises; **s** praises
     57: 7 I will **s** and make music.
     59:16 in the morning I will **s** of your love;
     63: 7 I **s** in the shadow of your wings.
     66: 2 **S** the glory of his name;

Ps   68: 4 **S** to God, **s** in praise of his name,
     89: 1 I will **s** of the LORD's great love
     95: 1 let us **s** for joy to the LORD;
     96: 1 **S** to the LORD a new song;
     98: 1 **S** to the LORD a new song, for he
    101: 1 I will **s** of your love and justice;
    108: 1 I will **s** and make music with all my
    119:172 May my tongue **s** of your word,
    137: 3 "**S** us one of the songs of Zion!"
    147: 1 How good it is to **s** praises to our
    149: 1 **S** to the LORD a new song,
Isa   5: 1 I will **s** for the one I love a song
     27: 2 "**S** about a fruitful vineyard:
     54: 1 "**S**, barren woman, you who never
Jer 31: 7 "**S** with joy for Jacob;
1Co 14:15 I will **s** with my spirit, but I will also **s**
            with my understanding.
Eph   5:19 **S** and make music from your heart
Jas   5:13 Let them **s** songs of praise.

SING ... PRAISE See PRAISE

SING ... PRAISES See PRAISES

SINGED*
Da   3:27 nor was a hair of their heads **s**;

SINGERS SING
Ps   68:25 In front are the **s**, after them

SINGING SING
Ex   32:18 it is the sound of **s** that I hear."
Ps   63: 5 **s** lips my mouth will praise you.
     68: 6 he leads out the prisoners with **s**;
     98: 5 with the harp and the sound of **s**,
SS   2:12 the season of **s** has come, the cooing
Isa 35:10 They will enter Zion with **s**;
     51:11 They will enter Zion with **s**;
Zep   3:17 but will rejoice over you with **s**."
Ac   16:25 were praying and **s** hymns to God,
Col   3:16 **s** to God with gratitude in your

SINGLE SINGLED
Ex   23:29 I will not drive them out in a **s** year,
Nu   13:23 cut off a branch bearing a **s** cluster
Zec   3: 9 the sin of this land in a **s** day.
Mt   6:27 worrying add a **s** hour to your life?
Jn   12:24 and dies, it remains only a **s** seed.
Heb 12:16 a **s** meal sold his inheritance rights
Rev 21:21 pearls, each gate made of a **s** pearl.

SINGLED* SINGLE
1Ki   8:53 For you **s** them out from all

SINGS SING
Eze 33:32 more than one who **s** love songs

SINK SANK
Dt   28:43 but you will **s** lower and lower.
Ps   69: 2 I **s** in the miry depths, where there is
Jer 51:64 'So will Babylon **s** to rise no more

SINNED SIN
Lev   5: 5 confess in what way they have **s**.
Nu   14:40 Surely we have **s**!"
1Sa 15:24 Saul said to Samuel, "I have **s**.
2Sa 12:13 "I have **s** against the LORD."

2Sa 24:10 "I have s greatly in what I have
2Ch 6:37 'We have s, we have done wrong
Job 1: 5 "Perhaps my children have s
33:27 'I have s, I have perverted what is
Ps 51: 4 have I s and done what is evil
Jer 2:35 you because you say, 'I have not s.'
14:20 we have indeed s against you.
La 5: 7 Our ancestors s and are no more,
Da 9: 5 we have s and done wrong.
Mic 7: 9 Because I have s against him, I will
Mt 27: 4 "I have s," he said, "for I have
Lk 15:18 I have s against heaven and against
Jn 9: 2 who s, this man or his parents,
Ro 3:23 for all have s and fall short
5:12 came to all people, because all s—
Jas 5:15 If they have s, they will be forgiven.
2Pe 2: 4 did not spare angels when they s,
1Jn 1:10 If we claim we have not s, we make

SINNER SIN

Pr 13: 6 but wickedness overthrows the s.
Ecc 9:18 war, but one s destroys much good.
Lk 15: 7 heaven over one s who repents than
18:13 said, 'God, have mercy on me, a s.'
Jn 9:16 "How can a s perform such signs?"
Jas 5:20 Whoever turns a s from the error
1Pe 4:18 become of the ungodly and the s?"

SINNER'S* SIN

Pr 13:22 but a s wealth is stored

SINNERS SIN

Ps 1: 1 stand in the way that s take or sit
25: 8 therefore he instructs s in his ways.
37:38 But all s will be destroyed;
51:13 so that s will turn back to you.
Pr 23:17 Do not let your heart envy s,
Isa 1:28 rebels and s will both be broken,
Mt 9:13 come to call the righteous, but s."
Mk 14:41 Man is delivered into the hands of s.
Lk 15: 2 "This man welcomes s and eats
24: 7 be delivered over to the hands of s,
Ro 5: 8 While we were still s, Christ died
Gal 2:17 find ourselves also among the s,
1Ti 1:15 came into the world to save s—
Heb 7:26 set apart from s,
12: 3 endured such opposition from s,

SINNING SIN

Ge 13:13 were s greatly against the LORD.
Ex 20:20 be with you to keep you from s."
Ps 78:32 In spite of all this, they kept on s;
Ro 6: 1 Shall we go on s so that grace may
1Co 15:34 senses as you ought, and stop s;
1Ti 5:20 those elders who are s you are
Heb 10:26 If we deliberately keep on s after we
1Jn 3: 6 No one who lives in him keeps on s.
3: 8 because the devil has been s

SINS SIN

Lev 4: 2 'When anyone s unintentionally
4: 3 " 'If the anointed priest s,
5: 1 anyone s because they do not speak
16:30 you will be clean from all your s.

Lev 26:40 if they will confess their s and the s of
their ancestors
Nu 15:30 " 'But anyone who s defiantly,
1Sa 2:25 but if anyone s against the LORD,
2Ki 17:22 persisted in all the s of Jeroboam
Ezr 9: 6 because our s are higher than our
9:13 punished us less than our s deserved
Ne 9: 2 confessed their s and the s of their
Ps 19:13 your servant also from willful s;
32: 1 are forgiven, whose s are covered.
51: 9 Hide your face from my s and blot
79: 9 forgive our s for your name's sake.
85: 2 your people and covered all their s.
103: 3 who forgives all your s and heals all
103:10 he does not treat us as our s deserve
130: 3 LORD, kept a record of s, Lord,
Pr 5:22 the cords of their s hold them fast.
28:13 Whoever conceals their s does not
29:22 person commits many s.
Ecc 7:20 who does what is right and never s.
Isa 1:18 "Though your s are like scarlet,
38:17 have put all my s behind your back.
40: 2 LORD's hand double for all her s.
43:25 and remembers your s no more.
59: 2 your s have hidden his face
64: 6 like the wind our s sweep us away.
Jer 31:34 will remember their s no more."
La 3:39 complain when punished for their s?
Eze 18: 4 The one who s is the one who will
33:10 offenses and s weigh us down,
36:33 day I cleanse you from all your s,
Hos 14: 1 Your s have been your downfall!
14: 2 "Forgive all our s and receive us
Mic 7:19 you will tread our s underfoot
Mt 1:21 will save his people from their s."
6:15 if you do not forgive others their s,
your Father will not forgive your s.
9: 6 has authority on earth to forgive s."
18:15 "If your brother or sister s,
26:28 for many for the forgiveness of s.
Mk 1: 5 Confessing their s, they were
Lk 5:24 has authority on earth to forgive s."
11: 4 Forgive us our s, for we also forgive
everyone who s against us.
17: 3 your brother or sister s against you,
Jn 8:24 you that you would die in your s;
20:23 If you forgive anyone's s, their s are
forgiven;
Ac 2:38 Christ for the forgiveness of your s.
3:19 so that your s may be wiped out,
10:43 forgiveness of s through his name."
22:16 be baptized and wash your s away,
26:18 they may receive forgiveness of s
Ro 4: 7 are forgiven, whose s are covered.
4:25 delivered over to death for our s
1Co 6:18 but whoever s sexually, s against their
own body.
15: 3 Christ died for our s according
2Co 5:19 counting people's s against them.
Gal 1: 4 gave himself for our s to rescue us
Eph 1: 7 the forgiveness of s, in accordance
2: 1 dead in your transgressions and s,
Col 2:13 When you were dead in your s

Col 2:13 He forgave us all our **s**,
1Ti 5:22 and do not share in the **s** of others.
Heb 1: 3 he had provided purification for **s**,
     2:17 atonement for the **s** of the people.
     7:27 He sacrificed for their **s** once for all
     8:12 will remember their **s** no more."
     9:28 once to take away the **s** of many;
    10: 4 of bulls and goats to take away **s**.
    10:12 for all time one sacrifice for **s**,
    10:26 of the truth, no sacrifice for **s** is left,
Jas 5:16 Therefore confess your **s** to each
    5:20 and cover over a multitude of **s**.
1Pe 2:24 so that we might die to **s** and live
    3:18 For Christ also suffered once for **s**,
    4: 8 love covers over a multitude of **s**.
1Jn 1: 9 If we confess our **s**, he is faithful
    1: 9 will forgive us our **s** and purify us
    2: 2 He is the atoning sacrifice for our **s**,
    3: 5 so that he might take away our **s**.
    4:10 Son as an atoning sacrifice for our **s**.
Rev 1: 5 freed us from our **s** by his blood,

SION (KJV) See ZION

SISERA
Jdg 4: 2 **S**, the commander of his army,
    5:26 She struck **S**, she crushed his head,

SISTER SISTERS
Ge 12:13 Say you are my **s**, so that I will be
   20: 2 of his wife Sarah, "She is my **s**."
   26: 7 "She is my **s**," because he was
Lev 18: 9 have sexual relations with your **s**,
Pr 7: 4 "You are my **s**," and to insight,
SS 4: 9 stolen my heart, my **s**, my bride;
Jer 3: 7 and her unfaithful **s** Judah saw it.
Eze 16:46 Your older **s** was Samaria,
Mk 3:35 does God's will is my brother and **s**
Lk 10:40 don't you care that my **s** has left me
Jn 11: 5 loved Martha and her **s** and Lazarus.
Ro 16: 1 I commend to you our **s** Phoebe,
1Co 7:15 brother or the **s** is not bound in such
2Jn 1:13 The children of your **s**, who is

SISTERS SISTER
Mt 19:29 left houses or brothers or **s** or father
Mk 6: 3 Aren't his **s** here with us?"
1Ti 5: 2 and younger women as **s**,

SIT SAT, SITS, SITTING
Ex 18:14 Why do you alone **s** as judge,
Dt 6: 7 about them when you **s** at home
   11:19 about them when you **s** at home
1Ki 8:25 have a successor to **s** before me
Ps 1: 1 or **s** in the company of mockers,
   26: 5 and refuse to **s** with the wicked.
   80: 1 You who **s** enthroned between
  110: 1 "**S** at my right hand until I make
  139: 2 You know when I **s** and when I rise;
SS 2: 3 I delight to **s** in his shade, and his
Isa 14:13 I will **s** enthroned on the mount
   16: 5 in faithfulness a man will **s** on it—
Jer 33:17 fail to have a man to **s** on the throne
Eze 28: 2 I **s** on the throne of a god
Mic 4: 4 Everyone will **s** under their own

Mal 3: 3 He will **s** as a refiner and purifier
Mt 20:23 but to **s** at my right or left is not
   22:44 "**S** at my right hand until I put your
   23: 2 and the Pharisees **s** in Moses' seat.
Mk 14:32 his disciples, "**S** here while I pray."
Lk 22:30 in my kingdom and **s** on thrones,
Jn 6:10 said, "Have the people **s** down."
Ac 2:34 to my Lord: "**S** at my right hand
Heb 1:13 "**S** at my right hand until I make
Rev 3:21 I will give the right to **s** with me
   18: 7 she boasts, 'I **s** enthroned as queen.

SITS SIT
Ps 29:10 The Lᴏʀᴅ **s** enthroned over
   99: 1 he **s** enthroned between
  113: 5 the One who **s** enthroned on high,
Isa 28: 6 to the one who **s** in judgment,
   40:22 He **s** enthroned above the circle
Mt 19:28 Son of Man **s** on his glorious throne,
Rev 4: 9 thanks to him who **s** on the throne
   5:13 "To him who **s** on the throne
   6:16 the face of him who **s** on the throne
   17: 1 prostitute, who **s** by many waters

SITTING SIT
2Ch 18:18 I saw the Lᴏʀᴅ **s** on his throne
Est 2:19 Mordecai was **s** at the king's gate.
Mt 26:64 the Son of Man **s** at the right hand
Lk 8:35 had gone out, **s** at Jesus' feet,
Rev 4: 2 in heaven with someone **s** on it.
   17: 3 There I saw a woman **s** on a scarlet

SITUATION SITUATIONS
1Co 7:24 should remain in the **s** they were
Php 4:12 of being content in any and every **s**,

SITUATIONS* SITUATION
2Ti 4: 5 you, keep your head in all **s**,

SIX SIXTH
Ex 20: 9 **S** days you shall labor and do all
1Sa 17: 4 His height was **s** cubits and a span.
1Ch 20: 6 there was a huge man with **s** fingers
Pr 6:16 There are **s** things the Lᴏʀᴅ
Isa 6: 2 were seraphim, each with **s** wings:
Rev 4: 8 the four living creatures had **s** wings

SIXTH SIX
Lev 25:21 you such a blessing in the **s** year
Rev 6:12 I watched as he opened the **s** seal.
   16:12 The **s** angel poured out his bowl

SIXTY
Mt 13: 8 **s** or thirty times what was sown.

SIZE
2Ki 10:32 began to reduce the **s** of Israel.
Ps 33:16 king is saved by the **s** of his army;

SKIES SKY
Ps 19: 1 the **s** proclaim the work of his
   36: 5 heavens, your faithfulness to the **s**.
   89: 6 For who in the **s** above can compare
  108: 4 your faithfulness reaches to the **s**.
Jer 51: 9 for her judgment reaches to the **s**,

SKILL SKILLED, SKILLFUL, SKILLFULLY, SKILLS

Ps 137: 5 may my right hand forget its s.
Ecc 10:10 is needed, but s will bring success.

SKILLED SKILL

Ex 35:10 "All who are s among you are
1Ch 28:21 every willing person s in any craft
Pr 22:29 Do you see someone s in their
Jer 4:22 They are s in doing evil;
Mic 7: 3 Both hands are s in doing evil;

SKILLFUL SKILL

Ps 45: 1 my tongue is the pen of a s writer.
78:72 with s hands he led them.

SKILLFULLY SKILL

Ps 33: 3 play s, and shout for joy.

SKILLS SKILL

Ex 31: 3 knowledge and with all kinds of s—
35:31 knowledge and with all kinds of s—

SKIN SKINS

Ge 3:21 LORD God made garments of s
Job 2: 4 "S for s!" Satan replied.
19:20 escaped only by the s of my teeth.
19:26 And after my s has been destroyed,
Jer 13:23 Can an Ethiopian change his s

SKINS SKIN

Ex 25: 5 ram s dyed red and another type
26:14 tent a covering of ram s dyed red,
Lk 5:37 the new wine will burst the s;

SKIRTS

Isa 47: 2 Lift up your s, bare your legs,
La 1: 9 Her filthiness clung to her s;

SKULL

2Ki 9:35 they found nothing except her s,
Mt 27:33 (which means "the place of the s").
Lk 23:33 they came to the place called the S,

SKY SKIES

Ge 1: 8 God called the vault "s."
22:17 as numerous as the stars in the s
26: 4 as numerous as the stars in the s
Ex 24:10 lapis lazuli, as bright blue as the s.
Lev 26:19 and make the s above you like iron
Dt 1:10 are as numerous as the stars in the s.
Ps 89:37 moon, the faithful witness in the s."
Pr 30:19 the way of an eagle in the s, the way
Isa 34: 4 the stars in the s will be dissolved
Jer 33:22 me as countless as the stars in the s
Mt 16: 3 to interpret the appearance of the s,
Mk 13:25 the stars will fall from the s,
Ac 1:10 up into the s as he was going,
Php 2:15 shine among them like stars in the s
Rev 6:13 and the stars in the s fell to earth,
12: 4 swept a third of the stars out of the s

SLACK*

Pr 18: 9 One who is s in his work is brother

SLAIN SLAY

1Sa 18: 7 "Saul has s his thousands,
21:11 " 'Saul has s his thousands,
29: 5 " 'Saul has s his thousands,
Pr 7:26 her s are a mighty throng.
Eze 37: 9 four winds and breathe into these s,
Da 7:11 I kept looking until the beast was s
Rev 5: 6 looking as if it had been s,
5:12 who was s, to receive power
6: 9 those who had been s because
13: 8 life, the Lamb who was s

SLANDER SLANDERED, SLANDERER, SLANDERERS, SLANDEROUS, SLANDEROUSLY, SLANDERS

Lev 19:16 spreading s among your people.
Ps 15: 3 whose tongue utters no s, who does
54: 5 Let evil recoil on those who s me;
Pr 10:18 lying lips and spreads s is a fool.
Mt 15:19 immorality, theft, false testimony, s.
Mk 3:28 all their sins and every s they utter,
2Co 12:20 of rage, selfish ambition, s, gossip,
Eph 4:31 brawling and s, along with every
Col 3: 8 malice, s, and filthy language
1Ti 5:14 give the enemy no opportunity for s.
Titus 3: 2 to s no one, to be peaceable
Jas 4:11 and sisters, do not s one another.
1Pe 2: 1 envy, and s of every kind.
3:16 in Christ may be ashamed of their s.
Jude 1: 9 himself dare to condemn him for s
Rev 13: 6 to s his name and his dwelling place

SLANDERED SLANDER

1Co 4:13 when we are s, we answer kindly.
1Ti 6: 1 and our teaching may not be s.

SLANDERER* SLANDER

Jer 9: 4 is a deceiver, and every friend a s.
1Co 5:11 immoral or greedy, an idolater or s,

SLANDERERS* SLANDER

Ps 140:11 May s not be established
Eze 22: 9 In you are s who are bent
Ro 1:30 s, God-haters, insolent,
1Co 6:10 nor drunkards nor s nor swindlers
Titus 3: 3 live, not to be s or addicted to much

SLANDEROUS* SLANDER

2Ti 3: 3 unforgiving, s, without self-control,

SLANDEROUSLY* SLANDER

Ro 3: 8 as some s claim that we say—

SLANDERS* SLANDER

Dt 22:14 and s her and gives her a bad name,
Ps 101: 5 Whoever s their neighbor in secret,

SLAPPED SLAPS

2Ch 18:23 went up and s Micaiah in the face.
Mt 26:67 him with their fists. Others s him
Jn 18:22 one of the officials nearby s him

SLAPS* SLAPPED

Mt 5:39 If anyone s you on the right cheek,

Lk   6:29 If someone s you on one cheek,
2Co 11:20 or puts on airs or s you in the face.

SLAUGHTER SLAUGHTERED

Ex   12: 6 of Israel must s them at twilight.
     29:11 S it in the LORD's presence
Lev   1: 5 s the young bull before the LORD,
      3: 2 and s it at the entrance to the tent
Dt   12:15 you may s your animals in any
Pr   7:22 her like an ox going to the s,
Isa 53: 7 he was led like a lamb to the s,
Jer 11:19 been like a gentle lamb led to the s;
Zec 11: 4 "Shepherd the flock marked for s.
Ac   8:32 "He was led like a sheep to the s,

SLAUGHTERED SLAUGHTER

Nu   11:22 if flocks and herds were s for them?
     14:16 so he s them in the wilderness.'
Ps   44:22 we are considered as sheep to be s.
Ro   8:36 we are considered as sheep to be s."

SLAVE ENSLAVE, ENSLAVED, ENSLAVES, ENSLAVING, SLAVERY, SLAVES

Ge   9:26 May Canaan be the s of Shem.
     16: 1 she had an Egyptian s named Hagar;
     16: 5 I put my s in your arms, and now that
     21:10 "Get rid of that s woman and her
     21:13 make the son of the s into a nation
     39:19 "This is how your s treated me,"
Ex   1:11 So they put s masters over them
      3: 7 crying out because of their s drivers,
     21:26 destroys it must let the s go free
Ps 123: 2 eyes of a female s look to the hand
Pr   22: 7 and the borrower is s to the lender.
Mal   1: 6 honors his father, and a s his master.
Mk 10:44 wants to be first must be s of all.
Jn   8:34 you, everyone who sins is a s to sin.
Ac   7: 9 they sold him as a s into Egypt.
Ro   7:14 I am unspiritual, sold as a s to sin.
1Co   7:21 Were you a s when you were
      9:19 I have made myself a s to everyone,
     12:13 whether Jews or Gentiles, s or free—
Gal   3:28 Jew nor Gentile, neither s nor free,
      4: 7 you are no longer a s, but God's child;
      4:30 "Get rid of the s woman and her
      4:30 the s woman's son will never share
Eph   6: 8 they do, whether they are s or free.
Col   3:11 Scythian, s or free, but Christ is all,
1Ti   1:10 for s traders and liars and perjurers—
Phm   1:16 no longer as a s, but better than a s,
Rev 13:16 free and s, to receive a mark

SLAVERY SLAVE

Ex   2:23 The Israelites groaned in their s
     20: 2 out of Egypt, out of the land of s.
Dt   7: 8 redeemed you from the land of s,
Ne   5: 5 subject our sons and daughters to s.
Gal   4: 3 in s under the elemental spiritual
1Ti   6: 1 of s should consider their masters

SLAVES SLAVE

Ge   9:25 The lowest of s will he be to his

Ge   15:14 punish the nation they serve as s,
Ex   6: 6 I will free you from being s to them,
Dt   5:15 Remember that you were s in Egypt
     16:12 that you were s in Egypt, and follow
1Ki   9:22 Solomon did not make s of any
Ps 123: 2 As the eyes of s look to the hand
Ecc 10: 7 I have seen s on horseback,
Jer 34: 9 was to free their Hebrew s,
Jn   8:33 and have never been s of anyone.
Ro   6: 6 we should no longer be s to sin—
      6:16 to someone as obedient s, you are s of
            the one you obey—
      6:19 so now offer yourselves as s
      6:22 from sin and have become s of God,
      8:15 you received does not make you s,
1Co   7:23 do not become s of human beings.
Gal   2: 4 in Christ Jesus and to make us s.
      4: 8 you were s to those who by nature
Eph   6: 5 S, obey your earthly masters
Col   3:22 S, obey your earthly masters
      4: 1 provide your s with what is right
Titus 2: 9 Teach s to be subject to their
2Pe   2:19 for "people are s to whatever has

SLAY SLAIN, SLAYS

Ge   22:10 hand and took the knife to s his son.
Job 13:15 Though he s me, yet will I hope
Ps   34:21 Evil will s the wicked; the foes
Isa 11: 4 of his lips he will s the wicked.

SLAYS* SLAY

Job   5: 2 kills a fool, and envy s the simple.

SLEEK

Ge   41: 4 ugly and gaunt ate up the seven s,
Dt   32:15 with food, they became heavy and s.

SLEEP ASLEEP, SLEEPER, SLEEPING, SLEEPLESS, SLEEPS, SLEPT

Ge   2:21 caused the man to fall into a deep s;
     15:12 Abram fell into a deep s, and a thick
     28:11 it under his head and lay down to s.
Ex   22:27 What else can they s in?
Dt   24:13 so that your neighbor may s in it.
1Sa 26:12 LORD had put them into a deep s.
Ps   4: 8 In peace I will lie down and s,
     13: 3 light to my eyes, or I will s in death,
     76: 5 lie plundered, they s their last s;
     78:65 Then the Lord awoke as from s,
    121: 4 Israel will neither slumber nor s.
    127: 2 for he grants s to those he loves.
    132: 4 I will allow no s to my eyes
Pr   6: 9 When will you get up from your s?
      6:10 A little s, a little slumber, a little
Ecc   5:12 The s of a laborer is sweet,
Isa 29:10 has brought over you a deep s:
Da   8:18 I was in a deep s, with my face
     10: 9 I fell into a deep s, my face
     12: 2 Multitudes who s in the dust
Jnh   1: 5 he lay down and fell into a deep s.
Ac   20: 9 sinking into a deep s as Paul talked
1Co 15:51 We will not all s, but we will all be
1Th   4:13 about those who s in death,
      5: 7 For those who s, s at night,

SLEEPER* SLEEP
Eph 5:14 "Wake up, s, rise from the dead,

SLEEPING SLEEP
1Ki 18:27 Maybe he is s and must be
Mt 26:40 to his disciples and found them s.
Mk 13:36 suddenly, do not let him find you s.

SLEEPLESS* SLEEP
2Co 6: 5 in hard work, s nights and hunger;

SLEEPS SLEEP
Dt 27:20 "Cursed is anyone who s with his
Pr 6:29 So is he who s with another man's
10: 5 son, but he who s during harvest is

SLEPT SLEEP
SS 5: 2 I s but my heart was awake. Listen!

SLIMY*
Ps 40: 2 He lifted me out of the s pit,

SLING
Jdg 20:16 each of whom could s a stone
1Sa 17:50 over the Philistine with a s
1Ch 12: 2 or to s stones right-handed
Pr 26: 8 tying a stone in a s is the giving

SLIP SLIPPED, SLIPPERY, SLIPPING
Dt 32:35 In due time their foot will s;
Ps 37:31 is in their hearts; their feet do not s.
121: 3 He will not let your foot s—

SLIPPED SLIP
Ps 73: 2 But as for me, my feet had almost s;
Jn 5:13 for Jesus had s away into the crowd
2Co 11:33 in the wall and s through his hands.

SLIPPERY* SLIP
Ps 35: 6 may their path be dark and s,
73:18 Surely you place them on s ground;
Jer 23:12 their path will become s;

SLIPPING SLIP
Ps 66: 9 our lives and kept our feet from s.
94:18 "My foot is s," your unfailing love,

SLOW
Ex 4:10 I am s of speech and tongue."
34: 6 and gracious God, s to anger,
Nu 14:18 'The Lord is s to anger,
Dt 7:10 he will not be s to repay to their
Ne 9:17 s to anger and abounding in love.
Ps 86:15 and gracious God, s to anger,
103: 8 and gracious, s to anger,
145: 8 s to anger and rich in love.
Joel 2:13 s to anger and abounding in love,
Jnh 4: 2 s to anger and abounding in love,
Na 1: 3 The Lord is s to anger but great
Lk 24:25 are, and how s to believe all
Jas 1:19 s to speak and s to become angry,
2Pe 3: 9 The Lord is not s in keeping his

SLUGGARD SLUGGARD'S,
SLUGGARDS
Pr 6: 6 Go to the ant, you s;
6: 9 How long will you lie there, you s?

Pr 21:25 The craving of a s will be the death
26:14 its hinges, so a s turns on his bed.
26:15 A s buries his hand in the dish;

SLUGGARD'S* SLUGGARD
Pr 13: 4 A s appetite is never filled,

SLUGGARDS* SLUGGARD
Pr 10:26 smoke to the eyes, so are s to
20: 4 S do not plow in season;

SLUMBER
Ps 121: 3 he who watches over you will not s;
121: 4 over Israel will neither s nor sleep.
Pr 6:10 a little s, a little folding of the hands
Ro 13:11 for you to wake up from your s,

SLUR*
Ps 15: 3 a neighbor, and casts no s on others;

SLY*
Pr 25:23 unexpected rain is a s tongue—

SMALL SMALLEST
1Ki 18:44 "A cloud as s as a man's hand is
2Ki 4: 2 she said, "except a s jar of olive oil."
Isa 49: 6 "It is too s a thing for you to be my
Mic 5: 2 though you are s among the clans
Mt 7:14 But s is the gate and narrow
17:20 if you have faith as s as a mustard
Mk 12:42 and put in two very s copper coins,
Lk 19:17 been trustworthy in a very s matter,
Jas 3: 5 the tongue is a s part of the body,

SMALLEST SMALL
Mt 5:18 not the s letter, not the least stroke
Mk 4:31 which is the s of all seeds on earth.

SMASH SMASHED
Ex 34:13 s their sacred stones and cut down
Dt 12: 3 s their sacred stones and burn their

SMASHED SMASH
2Ki 11:18 They s the altars and idols to pieces
18: 4 s the sacred stones and cut down
Jer 19:11 this city just as this potter's jar is s
Da 2:34 its feet of iron and clay and s them.

SMELL
Dt 4:28 which cannot see or hear or eat or s.
Ps 115: 6 but cannot hear, noses, but cannot s.
Ecc 10: 1 As dead flies give perfume a bad s,
Da 3:27 and there was no s of fire on them.

SMOKE SMOKING
Ex 19:18 Mount Sinai was covered with s,
Ps 68: 2 May you blow them away like s—
104:32 touches the mountains, and they s.
Isa 6: 4 and the temple was filled with s.
Joel 2:30 blood and fire and billows of s.
Ac 2:19 blood and fire and billows of s.
Rev 8: 4 The s of the incense,
9: 2 darkened by the s from the Abyss.
15: 8 the temple was filled with s

SMOKING* SMOKE
Ge 15:17 a s firepot with a blazing torch

SMOLDER* SMOLDERING
Ps　74: 1　does your anger s against the sheep
　　80: 4　will your anger s against the prayers

SMOLDERING SMOLDER
Isa　42: 3　and a s wick he will not snuff out.
Mt　12:20　and a s wick he will not snuff out,

SMOOTH
1Sa　17:40　chose five s stones from the stream,
Ps　55:21　His talk is s as butter, yet war is
Pr　6:24　wife, from the s talk of a wayward
　　7:21　she seduced him with her s talk.
Isa　42:16　them and make the rough places s.
Lk　3: 5　become straight, the rough ways s.

SMYRNA
Rev　2: 8　the angel of the church in S write:

SNAKE SNAKES
Ex　4: 3　it on the ground and it became a s,
　　7:10　and his officials, and it became a s.
Nu　21: 8　"Make a s and put it up on a pole;
2Ki　18: 4　into pieces the bronze s Moses had
Pr　23:32　In the end it bites like a s
Mic　7:17　They will lick dust like a s,
Mt　7:10　he asks for a fish, will give him a s?
Jn　3:14　lifted up the s in the wilderness,
Ac　28: 5　But Paul shook the s off into the fire

SNAKES SNAKE
Nu　21: 6　sent venomous s among them;
Mt　10:16　Therefore be as shrewd as s and as
Lk　10:19　given you authority to trample on s
1Co　10: 9　of them did—and were killed by s.
Rev　9:19　for their tails were like s,

SNARE ENSNARE, ENSNARED,
　SNARED, SNARES
Ex　23:33　of their gods will certainly be a s
Dt　7:16　gods, for that will be a s to you.
Ps　69:22　table set before them become a s;
　　91: 3　he will save you from the fowler's s
　　142: 3　where I walk people have hidden a s
Pr　6: 5　like a bird from the s of the fowler.
　　29:25　Fear of man will prove to be a s,
Ro　11: 9　"May their table become a s

SNARED SNARE
Pr　3:26　will keep your foot from being s.
　　29: 6　Evildoers are s by their own sin,

SNARES SNARE
Jos　23:13　they will become s and traps
Jdg　2: 3　you, and their gods will become s
Ps　18: 5　the s of death confronted me.
Pr　13:14　turning a person from the s of death.

SNATCH SNATCHED, SNATCHES,
　SNATCHING
Jn　10:28　no one will s them out of my hand.

SNATCHED SNATCH
Am　4:11　You were like a burning stick s
Zec　3: 2　Is not this man a burning stick s

SNATCHES SNATCH
Mt　13:19　and s away what was sown in their

SNATCHING* SNATCH
Jude　1:23　save others by s them from the fire;

SNEER
Ps　35:21　They s at me and say, "Aha! Aha!

SNEEZED*
2Ki　4:35　The boy s seven times and opened

SNIFF*
Mal　1:13　and you s at it contemptuously,"

SNOUT*
Pr　11:22　a pig's s is a beautiful woman who

SNOW SNOW-COOLED, SNOWS
Ex　4: 6　it had become as white as s.
Nu　12:10　it became as white as s.
2Ki　5:27　it had become as white as s.
Ps　51: 7　me, and I will be whiter than s.
Isa　1:18　scarlet, they shall be as white as s;
Da　7: 9　His clothing was as white as s;
Mt　28: 3　and his clothes were white as s.
Rev　1:14　as white as s, and his eyes were like

SNOW-COOLED* SNOW
Pr　25:13　Like a s drink at harvest time is

SNOWS* SNOW
Pr　31:21　When it s, she has no fear for her

SNUFF SNUFFED
Isa　42: 3　a smoldering wick he will not s out.
Mt　12:20　a smoldering wick he will not s out,

SNUFFED SNUFF
Job　21:17　is the lamp of the wicked s out?
Pr　13: 9　but the lamp of the wicked is s out.

SO-CALLED* CALL
1Co　8: 5　For even if there are s gods,
Rev　2:24　not learned Satan's s deep secrets,

SOAKED
Jn　19:29　was there, so they s a sponge in it,

SOAP*
Job　9:30　Even if I washed myself with s
Jer　2:22　Although you wash yourself with s
Mal　3: 2　a refiner's fire or a launderer's s.

SOAR SOARED
Isa　40:31　They will s on wings like eagles;
Jer　49:22　An eagle will s and swoop down,
Ob　1: 4　Though you s like the eagle

SOARED* SOAR
2Sa　22:11　he s on the wings of the wind.
Ps　18:10　he s on the wings of the wind.

SOBER
Ro　12: 3　think of yourself with s judgment,
1Th　5: 6　asleep, but let us be awake and s.
　　5: 8　let us be s, putting on faith and love
1Pe　1:13　with minds that are alert and fully s,

1Pe 4: 7 and of **s** mind so that you may pray.
5: 8 Be alert and of **s** mind.

SOCKET
Ge 32:25 he touched the **s** of Jacob's hip so

SODOM
Ge 13:12 plain and pitched his tents near **S.**
13:13 Now the people of **S** were wicked
18:20 said, "The outcry against **S**
19:24 rained down burning sulfur on **S**
Isa 1: 9 we would have become like **S,**
Eze 16:49 this was the sin of your sister **S:**
Lk 10:12 on that day for **S** than for that town.
Ro 9:29 we would have become like **S,**
Jude 1: 7 way, **S** and Gomorrah
Rev 11: 8 which is figuratively called **S**

SODOMITE(S) (KJV) See SHRINE PROSTITUTE(S)

SOIL
Ge 4: 2 kept flocks, and Cain worked the **s.**
9:20 a man of the **s,** proceeded to plant
Ex 23:19 the firstfruits of your **s** to the house
Mt 13:23 the seed falling on good **s** refers

SOLD SELL
Ge 37:28 **s** him for twenty shekels of silver
Ex 22: 3 they must be **s** to pay for their theft.
Lev 25:23 land must not be **s** permanently,
Dt 32:30 unless their Rock had **s** them,
Jdg 4: 2 So the LORD **s** them
10: 7 He **s** them into the hands
1Ki 21:25 who **s** himself to do evil in the eyes
Mt 10:29 Are not two sparrows **s** for a penny?
13:44 in his joy went and **s** all he had
13:46 went away and **s** everything he had
Ac 5: 1 Sapphira, also **s** a piece of property.
Ro 7:14 I am unspiritual, **s** as a slave to sin.
1Co 10:25 Eat anything **s** in the meat market
Heb 12:16 a single meal **s** his inheritance rights

SOLDIER SOLDIERS
1Co 9: 7 Who serves as a **s** at his own
2Ti 2: 3 like a good **s** of Christ Jesus.

SOLDIERS SOLDIER
Mt 27:27 the governor's **s** took Jesus
28:12 plan, they gave the **s** a large sum
Jn 19:23 When the **s** crucified Jesus,
19:34 one of the **s** pierced Jesus' side

SOLE
Dt 28:65 resting place for the **s** of your foot.
Isa 1: 6 From the **s** of your foot to the top

SOLEMN
Jos 6:26 time Joshua pronounced this **s** oath:
Eze 16: 8 I gave you my **s** oath and entered

SOLID
1Co 3: 2 I gave you milk, not **s** food, for you
2Ti 2:19 God's **s** foundation stands firm,
Heb 5:14 But **s** food is for the mature,

SOLITARY
Mk 1:35 the house and went off to a **s** place,
6:32 by themselves in a boat to a **s** place.

SOLOMON JEDIDIAH
Son of David by Bathsheba; king of Judah (2Sa 12:24; 1Ch 3:5, 10). Appointed king by David (1Ki 1); adversaries Adonijah, Joab, Shimei killed by Benaiah (1Ki 2). Asked for wisdom (1Ki 3; 2Ch 1). Judged between two prostitutes (1Ki 3:16–28). Built temple (1Ki 5–7; 2Ch 2–5); prayer of dedication (1Ki 8; 2Ch 6). Visited by Queen of Sheba (1Ki 10; 2Ch 9). Wives turned his heart from God (1Ki 11:1–13). Jeroboam rebelled against (1Ki 11:26–40). Death (1Ki 11:41–43; 2Ch 9:29–31).
Proverbs of (1Ki 4:32; Pr 1:1; 10:1; 25:1); psalms of (Ps 72; 127); song of (SS 1:1).

SOMBER*
Mt 6:16 do not look **s** as the hypocrites do,

SOME SOMEHOW, SOMEONE, SOMETHING
Ge 3: 6 She also gave **s** to her husband,
Mk 4:15 **S** people are like seed along
8:28 replied, "**S** say John the Baptist;
1Co 9:22 all possible means I might save **s.**
1Ti 4: 1 later times **s** will abandon the faith
2Pe 3:16 His letters contain **s** things that are

SOMEHOW HOW, SOME
Ro 11:14 that I may **s** arouse my own people
Gal 4:11 that **s** I have wasted my efforts
Php 3:11 and so, **s,**

SOMEONE ONE, SOME
Ex 4:13 Please send **s** else."
12:30 was not a house without **s** dead.
Nu 35:11 who has killed **s** accidentally may
Job 14:14 If **s** dies, will they live again?
Pr 26:17 by the ears is **s** who rushes
Eze 22:30 for **s** among them who would build
Lk 7:19 come, or should we expect **s** else?"
16:31 will not be convinced even if **s** rises
Ro 10:14 can they hear without **s** preaching

SOMETHING SOME, THING
Ex 24:10 his feet was **s** like a pavement made
Nu 16:30 LORD brings about **s** totally new,
Dt 8:16 **s** your ancestors had never known,
Mt 25:35 hungry and you gave me **s** to eat,
Ac 3: 5 expecting to get **s** from them.
9:18 **s** like scales fell from Saul's eyes,
Php 2: 6 equality with God **s** to be used to his
Rev 8: 8 and **s** like a huge mountain,
9: 7 their heads they wore **s** like crowns

SON SONS, SONS', SONSHIP; see also CHILD
Ge 5: 3 he had a **s** in his own likeness, in his
15: 4 but a **s** who is your own flesh
17:19 your wife Sarah will bear you a **s,**
21: 2 bore a **s** to Abraham in his old age,
21:10 rid of that slave woman and her **s,**
21:10 in the inheritance with my **s** Isaac."

Ge 22: 2 "Take your **s**, your only **s**,
    22:12 have not withheld from me your **s**,
           your only **s**."
    25:11 God blessed his **s** Isaac,
Ex   4:23 so I will kill your firstborn **s**.' "
    11: 5 Every firstborn **s** in Egypt will die,
Nu 18:15 you must redeem every firstborn **s**
Dt   1:31 as a father carries his **s**, all the way
     6:20 In the future, when your **s** asks you,
     8: 5 heart that as a man disciplines his **s**,
    18:10 among you who sacrifices their **s**
    21:18 rebellious **s** who does not obey his
2Sa 7:14 be his father, and he will be my **s**.
1Ki 3:23 'My **s** is alive and your **s** is dead,'
     8:19 but your **s**, your own flesh
2Ki 6:29 So we cooked my **s** and ate him.
1Ch 22:10 He will be my **s**, and I will be his
Ps   2: 7 He said to me, "You are my **s**;
     2:12 Kiss his **s**, or he will be angry
    80:15 planted, the **s** you have raised
Pr   3: 1 My **s**, do not forget my teaching,
     3:12 as a father the **s** he delights in.
     4: 3 For I too was a **s** to my father,
     6:20 My **s**, keep your father's command
    10: 1 A wise **s** brings joy to his father, but a
           foolish **s** brings grief to his mother.
Isa 7:14 will conceive and give birth to a **s**,
     8: 3 she conceived and gave birth to a **s**.
     9: 6 is born, to us a **s** is given,
Jer 31:20 Is not Ephraim my dear **s**, the child
Da   3:25 and the fourth looks like a **s**
     7:13 there before me was one like a **s**
Hos 11: 1 him, and out of Egypt I called my **s**.
Am   7:14 a prophet nor the **s** of a prophet,
Mal 1: 6 "A **s** honors his father, and a slave
Mt   1: 1 Jesus the Messiah the **s** of David, the **s**
           of Abraham:
     1:23 will conceive and give birth to a **s**,
     2:15 "Out of Egypt I called my **s**."
     3:17 said, "This is my **S**, whom I love;
     4: 3 "If you are the **S** of God, tell these
     8:20 the **S** of Man has no place to lay his
    11:27 one knows the **S** except the Father,
    11:27 one knows the Father except the **S**
    12: 8 For the **S** of Man is Lord
    12:32 who speaks a word against the **S**
    12:40 so the **S** of Man will be three days
    13:55 "Isn't this the carpenter's **s**?
    14:33 "Truly you are the **S** of God."
    16:16 Messiah, the **S** of the living God."
    16:27 For the **S** of Man is going to come
    17: 5 said, "This is my **S**, whom I love;
    19:28 when the **S** of Man sits on his
    20:18 the **S** of Man will be delivered over
    20:28 just as the **S** of Man did not come
    21: 9 "Hosanna to the **S** of David!"
    22:42 about the Messiah? Whose **s** is he?"
    22:42 "The **s** of David," they replied.
    24:27 will be the coming of the **S** of Man.
    24:30 will appear the sign of the **S** of Man
    24:44 because the **S** of Man will come
    25:31 "When the **S** of Man comes in his
    26:63 you are the Messiah, the **S** of God."

Mt 27:54 "Surely he was the **S** of God!"
    28:19 and of the **S** and of the Holy Spirit,
Mk   1: 1 Jesus the Messiah, the **S** of God,
     1:11 "You are my **S**, whom I love;
     2:28 So the **S** of Man is Lord even
     8:38 the **S** of Man will be ashamed
     9: 7 "This is my **S**, whom I love.
    10:45 For even the **S** of Man did not come
    13:32 nor the **S**, but only the Father.
    14:62 you will see the **S** of Man sitting
    15:39 said, "Surely this man was the **S**
Lk   1:32 and will be called the **S** of the Most
     1:35 be born will be called the **S** of God.
     2: 7 she gave birth to her firstborn, a **s**.
     3:22 "You are my **S**, whom I love;
     9:35 saying, "This is my **S**, whom I have
     9:58 the **S** of Man has no place to lay his
    12: 8 the **S** of Man will also acknowledge
    15:21 longer worthy to be called your **s**.'
    18: 8 when the **S** of Man comes, will he
    18:31 about the **S** of Man will be fulfilled.
    19:10 For the **S** of Man came to seek
    20:44 How then can he be his **s**?"
Jn   1:49 "Rabbi, you are the **S** of God;
     3:14 so the **S** of Man must be lifted up,
     3:16 that he gave his one and only **S**,
     3:36 believes in the **S** has eternal life,
     3:36 whoever rejects the **S** will not see
     5:19 the **S** can do nothing by himself;
     6:40 is that everyone who looks to the **S**
    11: 4 God's **S** may be glorified through
    12:34 'The **S** of Man must be lifted up'?
    13:31 "Now the **S** of Man is glorified
    17: 1 Glorify your **S**, that your **S** may
Ac   7:56 the **S** of Man standing at the right
    13:33 " 'You are my **s**; today I have
Ro   1: 4 holiness was appointed the **S** of God
     5:10 to him through the death of his **S**,
     8: 3 by sending his own **S** in the likeness
     8:29 be conformed to the image of his **S**,
     8:32 He who did not spare his own **S**,
1Co 15:28 the **S** himself will be made subject
Gal 2:20 I live by faith in the **S** of God,
     4: 4 God sent his **S**, born of a woman,
     4:30 rid of the slave woman and her **s**,
Col 1:13 into the kingdom of the **S** he loves,
1Th 1:10 and to wait for his **S** from heaven,
Heb 1: 2 days he has spoken to us by his **S**,
     1: 5 did God ever say, "You are my **S**;
     4:14 into heaven, Jesus the **S** of God,
     5: 5 God said to him, "You are my **S**;
     7:28 appointed the **S**, who has been made
    10:29 be punished who has trampled the **S**
    12: 6 chastens everyone he accepts as his **s**."
Jas 2:21 he offered his **s** Isaac on the altar?
2Pe 1:17 saying, "This is my **S**, whom I love;
1Jn 1: 3 is with the Father and with his **S**,
     1: 7 Jesus, his **S**, purifies us from all sin.
     2:23 one who denies the **S** has the Father;
     2:23 acknowledges the **S** has the Father
     3: 8 The reason the **S** of God appeared
     4: 9 only **S** into the world that we might
     4:14 the Father has sent his **S** to be

1Jn 5: 5 believes that Jesus is the **S** of God.
 5:11 eternal life, and this life is in his **S**.
Rev 1:13 lampstands was someone like a **s**
 2:18 are the words of the **S** of God,
 12: 5 She gave birth to a **s**, a male child,
 14:14 on the cloud was one like a **s** of man

MY SON Ge 21:10; 22:7, 8; 24:3, 4, 6, 7, 8, 37, 38, 40; 27:1, 8, 13, 18, 20, 21, 21, 24, 25, 26, 27, 37, 43; 34:8; 37:35; 38:11, 26; 42:38; 43:29; 45:28; 48:19; 49:9; Ex 4:23; Jos 7:19; Jdg 8:23; 17:2, 3; 1Sa 3:6, 16; 4:16; 10:2; 14:39, 40, 41, 42; 22:8, 8; 24:16; 26:17, 21, 25; 2Sa 7:14; 13:25; 14:11, 16; 16:11; 18:22, 33, 33, 33, 33, 33; 19:4, 4, 4; 1Ki 1:21, 33; 3:20, 21, 22, 23; 17:12, 18; 2Ki 6:28, 29; 14:9; 1Ch 17:13; 22:5, 7, 10, 11; 28:5, 6, 9; 29:1, 19; 2Ch 25:18; Ps 2:7; Pr 1:8, 10, 15; 2:1; 3:1, 11, 21; 4:10, 20; 5:1, 20; 6:1, 3, 20; 7:1; 19:27; 23:15, 19, 26; 24:13, 21; 27:11; 31:2, 2; Ecc 12:12; Hos 11:1; Mt 2:15; 3:17; 17:5, 15; 21:37; Mk 1:11; 9:7, 17; 12:6; Lk 3:22; 9:35, 38; 15:31; 20:13; Ac 13:33; 1Co 4:17; 1Ti 1:18; 2Ti 2:1; Phm 1:10, 10; Heb 1:5, 5; 5:5; 12:5; 1Pe 5:13; 2Pe 1:17

SON OF AARON Ex 6:25; 38:21; Lev 7:33; Nu 3:32; 4:16, 28, 33; 7:8; 16:37; 25:7, 11; 26:1; Jos 24:33; Jdg 20:28; Ezr 7:5

SON OF DAVID 2Sa 13:1, 1; 1Ch 29:22; 2Ch 1:1; 13:6; 30:26; 35:3; Pr 1:1; Ecc 1:1; Mt 1:1, 20; 9:27; 12:23; 15:22; 20:30, 31; 21:9, 15; 22:42; Mk 10:47, 48; 12:35; Lk 3:31; 18:38, 39; 20:41

SON OF GOD Mt 4:3, 6; 8:29; 14:33; 26:63; 27:40, 43, 54; Mk 1:1; 3:11; 15:39; Lk 1:35; 3:38; 4:3, 9, 41; 22:70; Jn 1:49; 5:25; 11:27; 19:7; 20:31; Ac 9:20; Ro 1:4; 2Co 1:19; Gal 2:20; Eph 4:13; Heb 4:14; 6:6; 7:3; 10:29; 1Jn 3:8; 4:15; 5:5, 10, 12, 13, 20; Rev 2:18

SON OF JESSE 1Sa 16:18; 20:27, 30, 31; 22:7, 8, 9, 13; 25:10; 2Sa 23:1; 1Ch 10:14; 12:18; 29:26; Ps 72:20; Lk 3:32; Ac 13:22

SON OF MAN Ps 80:17; Eze 2:1, 3, 6, 8; 3:1, 3, 4, 10, 17, 25; 4:1, 16; 5:1; 6:2; 7:2; 8:5, 6, 8, 12, 15, 17; 11:2, 4, 15; 12:2, 3, 9, 18, 22, 27; 13:2, 17; 14:3, 13; 15:2; 16:2; 17:2; 20:3, 4, 27, 46; 21:2, 6, 9, 12, 14, 19, 28; 22:2, 18, 24; 23:2, 36; 24:2, 16, 25; 25:2; 26:2; 27:2; 28:2, 12, 21; 29:2, 18; 30:2, 21; 31:2; 32:2, 18; 33:2, 7, 10, 12, 24, 30; 34:2; 35:2; 36:1, 17; 37:3, 9, 11, 16; 38:2, 14; 39:1, 17; 40:4; 43:7, 10, 18; 44:5; 47:6; Da 7:13; 8:17; Mt 8:20; 9:6; 10:23; 11:19; 12:8, 32, 40; 13:37, 41; 16:13, 27, 28; 17:9, 12, 22; 19:28; 20:18, 28; 24:27, 30, 30, 37, 39, 44; 25:31; 26:2, 24, 24, 45, 64; Mk 2:10, 28; 8:31, 38; 9:9, 12, 31; 10:33, 45; 13:26; 14:21, 21, 41, 62; Lk 5:24; 6:5, 22; 7:34; 9:22, 26, 44, 58; 11:30; 12:8, 10, 40; 17:22, 24, 26, 30; 18:8, 31; 19:10; 21:27, 36; 22:22, 48, 69; 24:7; Jn 1:51; 3:13, 14; 5:27; 6:27, 53, 62; 8:28; 9:35; 12:23, 34, 34; 13:31; Ac 7:56; Heb 2:6; Rev 1:13; 14:14

SONG SING
Dt 31:21 this **s** will testify against them,
 32:44 all the words of this **s** in the hearing
Jdg 5: 1 Barak son of Abinoam sang this **s**:
Ps 33: 3 Sing to him a new **s**;

Ps 40: 3 He put a new **s** in my mouth,
 69:30 I will praise God's name in **s**
 96: 1 Sing to the LORD a new **s**;
 98: 4 burst into jubilant **s** with music;
 119:54 the theme of my **s** wherever I lodge.
 149: 1 Sing to the LORD a new **s**,
Isa 5: 1 sing for the one I love a **s** about his
 49:13 burst into **s**, you mountains!
 54: 1 burst into **s**, shout for joy, you who
 55:12 hills will burst into **s** before you,
Rev 5: 9 And they sang a new **s**, saying:
 14: 3 they sang a new **s** before the throne
 15: 3 sang the **s** of God's servant Moses

SONGS SING
2Sa 23: 1 God of Jacob, the hero of Israel's **s**:
1Ki 4:32 and his **s** numbered a thousand
Ne 12:46 for the **s** of praise and thanksgiving
Job 35:10 my Maker, who gives **s** in the night,
Ps 77: 6 I remembered my **s** in the night.
 100: 2 come before him with joyful **s**.
 126: 6 to sow, will return with **s** of joy,
 137: 3 for there our captors asked us for **s**,
 137: 3 "Sing us one of the **s** of Zion!"
Eph 5:19 hymns, and **s** from the Spirit.
Col 3:16 and **s** from the Spirit,
Jas 5:13 Let them sing **s** of praise.

SONS SON; see also CHILDREN
Ge 6: 2 the **s** of God saw that the daughters
 9: 1 Then God blessed Noah and his **s**,
 10:32 These are the clans of Noah's **s**,
 35:22 heard of it. Jacob had twelve **s**:
Ex 13:15 and redeem each of my firstborn **s**.'
 28: 9 on them the names of the **s** of Israel
Nu 18: 7 and your **s** may serve as priests
Dt 7: 3 not give your daughters to their **s** or
 take their daughters for your **s**,
Ru 4:15 who is better to you than seven **s**,
Ps 82: 6 you are all **s** of the Most High.'
 89:30 "If his **s** forsake my law and do not
 132:12 their **s** will sit on your throne
Joel 2:28 Your **s** and daughters will prophesy,
Ac 2:17 Your **s** and daughters will prophesy,
2Co 6:18 and you will be my **s** and daughters,
Heb 2:10 In bringing many **s** and daughters
 12: 8 legitimate, not true **s** and daughters

AARON AND HIS SONS Ex 27:21; 28:4, 41, 43; 29:4, 9, 9, 10, 15, 19, 20, 24, 27, 28, 32, 35, 44; 30:19, 30; 39:27; 40:12, 31; Lev 2:3, 10; 6:9, 16, 20, 25; 7:31, 35; 8:2, 6, 14, 18, 22, 27, 31, 31, 36; 9:1; 10:6; 17:2; 21:24; 22:2, 18; 24:9; Nu 3:9, 10, 38, 48, 51; 4:5, 15, 19, 27; 6:23; 8:13, 19, 22

AARON'S SONS Ex 28:40; Lev 1:5, 8, 11; 2:2; 3:2, 5, 8, 13; 6:14; 8:13, 24; 10:1; Nu 3:3

SONS OF AARON Lev 1:7; 7:10; 16:1; 21:1; Nu 3:2; 10:8; 1Ch 6:3; 24:1; 2Ch 13:9, 10

SONS OF KORAH Ex 6:24; Ps 42:T; 44:T; 45:T; 46:T; 47:T; 48:T; 49:T; 84:T; 85:T; 87:T; 88:T

SONS' SON
Ge 6:18 wife and your **s** wives with you.
Lev 10:13 your **s** share of the food offerings

SONSHIP* SON
Ro   8:15 brought about your adoption to s.
       8:23 we wait eagerly for our adoption to s,
       9: 4 Theirs is the adoption to s;
Gal   4: 5 that we might receive adoption to s.
Eph   1: 5 adoption to s through Jesus Christ,

SOON
Ps   37: 2 for like the grass they will s wither,
     106:13 But they s forgot what he had done
Pr   5:14 And I was s in serious trouble
Isa 56: 1 my righteousness will s be revealed.
Da   9:23 As s as you began to pray, a word
Ro   16:20 peace will s crush Satan under your
Rev   1: 1 his servants what must s take place.
      3:11 I am coming s. Hold on to what you
     22: 7 "Look, I am coming s!
     22:12 "Look, I am coming s!
     22:20 things says, "Yes, I am coming s."

SOOTHING
Pr   15: 4 The s tongue is a tree of life,

SORCERER SORCERY
Ac   13: 6 There they met a Jewish s and false

SORCERERS SORCERY
Ex   7:11 then summoned wise men and s,
Jer 27: 9 mediums or your s who tell you,
Da   2: 2 s and astrologers to tell him what he

SORCERESS* SORCERY
Ex   22:18 "Do not allow a s to live.
Isa 57: 3 you—come here, you children of a s,

SORCERIES SORCERY
Isa 47: 9 in spite of your many s and all your
Na   3: 4 the mistress of s, who enslaved

SORCERY SORCERER,
   SORCERERS, SORCERESS,
   SORCERIES
Dt   18:10 fire, who practices divination or s,
Ac   8: 9 a man named Simon had practiced s
      8:11 them for a long time with his s.
     19:19 who had practiced s brought their

SORE SORES
Jer 30:13 no remedy for your s, no healing

SOREK*
Jdg 16: 4 of S whose name was Delilah.

SORES SORE
Job   2: 7 Job with painful s from the soles
Hos   5:13 to cure you, not able to heal your s.
Rev 16: 2 festering s broke out on the people

SORROW SORROWFUL
Ps   6: 7 My eyes grow weak with s;
     90:10 best of them are but trouble and s,
     116: 3 I was overcome by distress and s.
Pr   23:29 Who has s? Who has strife?
Ecc   1:18 with much wisdom comes much s;
Isa 35:10 and s and sighing will flee away.
     51:11 and s and sighing will flee away.

Isa 60:20 light, and your days of s will end.
Jer 31:12 garden, and they will s no more.
Mk   14:34 "My soul is overwhelmed with s
Ro   9: 2 I have great s and unceasing
2Co   7:10 Godly s brings repentance that leads
      7:10 but worldly s brings death.

SORROWFUL SORROW
2Co   6:10 s, yet always rejoicing;

SORT SORTS
Lk   23: 8 to see him perform a sign of some s.

SORTS SORT
1Co 14:10 Undoubtedly there are all s
2Th   2: 9 He will use all s of displays

SOUGHT SEEK
Ex   32:11 Moses s the favor of the LORD his
1Sa 13:14 the LORD has s out a man after his
2Ch 26: 5 As long as he s the LORD,
     31:21 he s his God and worked
Ps   34: 4 I s the LORD, and he answered
     119:45 for I have s out your precepts.
     119:58 I have s your face with all my heart;
Isa   9:13 them, nor have they s the LORD
Ro   11: 7 of Israel s so earnestly they did not

SOUL SOULS
Dt   6: 5 and with all your s and with all your
     10:12 all your heart and with all your s,
     30: 6 all your heart and with all your s,
Jos 22: 5 all your heart and with all your s."
2Ki 23:25 and with all his s and with all his
Ps   19: 7 LORD is perfect, refreshing the s.
     23: 3 he refreshes my s. He guides me
     42: 1 of water, so my s pants for you,
     42:11 Why, my s, are you downcast?
     62: 5 Yes, my s, find rest in God;
     103: 1 Praise the LORD, my s;
     108: 1 sing and make music with all my s.
     116: 7 my s, for the LORD has been good
Pr   13:19 A longing fulfilled is sweet to the s,
     16:24 sweet to the s and healing
La   3:20 and my s is downcast within me.
Mic   6: 7 fruit of my body for the sin of my s?
Mt   10:28 kill the body but cannot kill the s.
     10:28 of the One who can destroy both s
     16:26 the whole world, yet forfeit their s?
     22:37 and with all your s and with all your
Mk   8:36 the whole world, yet forfeit their s?
Lk   1:46 "My s glorifies the Lord
      2:35 sword will pierce your own s too."
Jn   12:27 "Now my s is troubled, and what
1Th   5:23 s and body be kept blameless
Heb   4:12 it penetrates even to dividing s
      6:19 this hope as an anchor for the s,
1Pe   2:11 which wage war against your s.
3Jn   1: 2 even as your s is getting along well.

SOULS SOUL
Jer   6:16 and you will find rest for your s.
Mt   11:29 and you will find rest for your s.
1Pe   2:25 Shepherd and Overseer of your s.
Rev   6: 9 I saw under the altar the s of those

Rev 20: 4 I saw the s of those who had been

SOUND FINE-SOUNDING, SOUNDED, SOUNDING

Ge 3: 8 his wife heard the s of the LORD
Ex 32:18 "It is not the s of victory, it is not the s of defeat;
Dt 4:12 You heard the s of words but saw
Ps 66: 8 let the s of his praise be heard;
115: 7 nor can they utter a s with their
Pr 3:21 preserve s judgment and discretion;
8:14 Counsel and s judgment are mine;
Isa 6: 4 the s of their voices the doorposts
Eze 3:12 me a loud rumbling s as the glory
Joel 2: 1 s the alarm on my holy hill.
Jn 3: 8 You hear its s, but you cannot tell
Ac 2: 2 Suddenly a s like the blowing
1Co 14: 8 if the trumpet does not s a clear call,
15:52 For the trumpet will s, the dead will
1Ti 1:10 else is contrary to the s doctrine
6: 3 does not agree to the s instruction
2Ti 1:13 keep as the pattern of s teaching,
4: 3 will not put up with s doctrine.
Titus 1: 9 can encourage others by s doctrine
2: 1 what is appropriate to s doctrine.
Rev 1:15 his voice was like the s of rushing

SOUNDED SOUND

Rev 6: 6 I heard what s like a voice among
19: 6 Then I heard what s like a great

SOUNDING SOUND

Ps 47: 5 the LORD amid the s of trumpets.
150: 3 Praise him with the s of the trumpet,

SOUR

Jer 31:29 'The parents have eaten s grapes,
Eze 18: 2 " 'The parents eat s grapes,
Rev 10: 9 It will turn your stomach s,

SOURCE

Heb 5: 9 he became the s of eternal salvation

SOUTH

Ge 13:14 to the north and s, to the east
Ps 89:12 You created the north and the s;
Da 11: 5 king of the S will become strong,
Zec 14: 4 moving north and half moving s.
Mt 12:42 The Queen of the S will rise

SOVEREIGN SOVEREIGNTY

Ge 15: 2 But Abram said, "S LORD,
Ex 23:17 are to appear before the S LORD.
2Sa 7:18 "Who am I, S LORD, and what is
7:22 "How great you are, S LORD!
Ps 71: 5 you have been my hope, S LORD,
71:16 your mighty acts, S LORD;
140: 7 S LORD, my strong deliverer,
Isa 25: 8 The S LORD will wipe away
40:10 the S LORD comes with power,
50: 4 The S LORD has given me
61: 1 The Spirit of the S LORD is
61:11 to grow, so the S LORD will make
Jer 32:17 "Ah, S LORD, you have made
Da 4:25 Most High is s over all kingdoms

Hab 3:19 The S LORD is my strength;
Zep 1: 7 Be silent before the S LORD,
2Pe 2: 1 even denying the s Lord who
Jude 1: 4 deny Jesus Christ our only S
Rev 6:10 "How long, S Lord, holy and true,

DECLARES THE SOVEREIGN LORD† See LORD†

SOVEREIGN LORD† See LORD†

WHAT THE SOVEREIGN LORD† SAYS See LORD†

SOVEREIGNTY SOVEREIGN

Da 7:27 Then the s, power and greatness

SOW SOWED, SOWER, SOWN, SOWS

Ex 23:10 six years you are to s your fields
Dt 28:38 You will s much seed in the field
Job 4: 8 evil and those who s trouble reap it.
Ps 126: 5 Those who s with tears will reap
Ecc 11: 6 S your seed in the morning,
Hos 8: 7 "They s the wind and reap
10:12 S righteousness for yourselves,
Mt 6:26 they do not s or reap or store away
13: 3 "A farmer went out to s his seed.
1Co 15:36 What you s does not come to life
Jas 3:18 Peacemakers who s in peace reap
2Pe 2:22 "A s that is washed returns to her

SOWED SOW

Mt 13:24 is like a man who s good seed in his

SOWER SOW

Isa 55:10 so that it yields seed for the s
Mt 13:18 to what the parable of the s means:
Jn 4:36 so that the s and the reaper may be
2Co 9:10 Now he who supplies seed to the s

SOWN SOW

Mt 13: 8 sixty or thirty times what was s.
Mk 4:15 along the path, where the word is s.
1Co 9:11 we have s spiritual seed among you,
15:42 The body that is s is perishable, it is

SOWS SOW

Pr 11:18 the one who s righteousness reaps
22: 8 Whoever s injustice reaps calamity,
Mt 13:39 the enemy who s them is the devil.
Mk 4:14 The farmer s the word.
2Co 9: 6 Whoever s sparingly will also reap
9: 6 whoever s generously will also reap
Gal 6: 7 A man reaps what he s.

SPACIOUS

Ex 3: 8 of that land into a good and s land,
Ps 18:19 He brought me out into a s place;

SPAN

Ex 23:26 I will give you a full life s.

SPARE SPARED, SPARES, SPARING

Ge 18:24 not s the place for the sake
Est 7: 3 And s my people—this is my
Jer 50:20 for I will forgive the remnant I s.
Eze 6: 8 " 'But I will s some, for some

Zec 11: 5 Their own shepherds do not **s** them.
Ro   8:32 He who did not **s** his own Son,
     11:21 God did not **s** the natural branches,
           he will not **s** you either.
2Pe 2: 4 if God did not **s** angels when they
     2: 5 if he did not **s** the ancient world

SPARED SPARE
Ge 12:13 my life will be **s** because of you."
    19:20 Then my life will be **s**."
Jos 6:25 But Joshua **s** Rahab the prostitute,
Ps 30: 3 you **s** me from going down

SPARES* SPARE
Est 4:11 scepter to them and **s** their lives.
Pr 13:24 Whoever **s** the rod hates their
Mal 3:17 and **s** his son who serves him.

SPARING SPARE
Pr 21:26 but the righteous give without **s**.

SPARKLE*
Zec 9:16 They will **s** in his land like jewels

SPARROW SPARROWS
Ps 84: 3 Even the **s** has found a home,

SPARROWS SPARROW
Hos 11:11 come from Egypt, trembling like **s**,
Mt 10:29 Are not two **s** sold for a penny?
Lk 12: 7 you are worth more than many **s**.

SPEAK SPEAKER, SPEAKING, SPEAKS, SPOKE, SPOKEN
Ge 18:27 I have been so bold as to **s**
    37: 4 and could not **s** a kind word to him.
Ex   4:12 I will help you **s** and will teach you
     6:30 "Since I **s** with faltering lips,
    33:11 The LORD would **s** to Moses face
Nu 12: 8 to **s** against my servant Moses?"
    20: 8 S to that rock before their eyes
    22:35 the men, but **s** only what I tell you."
Dt 18:20 a prophet who presumes to **s** in my
1Sa 3: 9 and if he calls you, say, 'S, LORD,
2Ki 18:26 Don't **s** to us in Hebrew
Job 13: 3 But I desire to **s** to the Almighty
Ps 49: 3 My mouth will **s** words of wisdom;
    75: 5 against heaven; do not **s** so defiantly.' "
   135:16 have mouths, but cannot **s**, eyes,
Pr 18:17 a lawsuit the first to **s** seems right,
    20:15 that **s** knowledge are a rare jewel.
    23: 9 Do not **s** to fools, for they will scorn
    31: 8 S up for those who cannot **s**
Ecc 3: 7 a time to be silent and a time to **s**,
Isa 28:11 strange tongues God will **s** to this
    40: 2 S tenderly to Jerusalem,
Jer 10: 5 cucumber field, their idols cannot **s**;
Eze 3:18 or **s** out to dissuade them from their
Da   7:25 He will **s** against the Most High
Zec 10: 2 The idols **s** deceitfully, diviners see
Mt 13:13 This is why I **s** to them in parables:
Mk   7:37 the deaf hear and the mute **s**."
Jn 12:49 For I did not **s** on my own,
Ac   2: 4 began to **s** in other tongues as

Ac   4:18 commanded them not to **s** or teach
1Co 12:30 Do all **s** in tongues?
     14: 2 in a tongue does not **s** to people
     14: 5 every one of you to **s** in tongues,
     14:19 I would rather **s** five intelligible
Jas 1:19 slow to **s** and slow to become angry,

SPEAKER SPEAK
1Co 14:11 I am a foreigner to the **s**, and the **s** is a
          foreigner to me.

SPEAKING SPEAK
Dt   5:26 the voice of the living God **s**
Mt 10:20 not be you **s**, but the Spirit of your
          Father **s** through you.
Mk 12:36 David himself, **s** by the Holy Spirit,
Ac 10:46 For they heard them **s** in tongues
1Co 12:10 to another **s** in different kinds
Eph 4:15 Instead, **s** the truth in love, we will
     5:19 **s** to one another with psalms,

SPEAKS SPEAK
Ex 33:11 face to face, as one **s** to a friend.
Dt   5:24 can live even if God **s** with them.
    18:19 that the prophet **s** in my name.
Ps 15: 2 who **s** the truth from their heart;
Pr   8: 7 My mouth **s** what is true, for my
    22:11 who **s** with grace will have the king
    31:26 She **s** with wisdom, and faithful
Mt 12:32 but anyone who **s** against the Holy
Lk   6:45 the mouth **s** what the heart is full of.
1Co 14: 3 the one who prophesies **s** to people
Heb 11: 4 And by faith Abel still **s**,
    12:25 it that you do not refuse him who **s**.

SPEAR SPEARS
1Sa 17: 7 His **s** shaft was like a weaver's rod,
    19:10 to pin him to the wall with his **s**,
    20:33 Saul hurled his **s** at him to kill him.
Ps 46: 9 breaks the bow and shatters the **s**;
Jn 19:34 soldiers pierced Jesus' side with a **s**,

SPEARS SPEAR
Isa 2: 4 and their **s** into pruning hooks.
Joel 3:10 and your pruning hooks into **s**.
Mic 4: 3 and their **s** into pruning hooks.

SPECIAL
Nu   6: 2 or woman wants to make a **s** vow,
Dt 12: 6 your tithes and **s** gifts, what you
Ro   9:21 some pottery for **s** purposes and some
    14: 6 regards one day as **s** does so
Gal 4:10 You are observing **s** days
2Ti 2:20 some are for **s** purposes and some
Jas 2: 3 If you show **s** attention to the man

SPECK
Mt   7: 4 'Let me take the **s** out of your eye,'

SPECTACLE
1Co 4: 9 We have been made a **s** to the whole
Col 2:15 he made a public **s** of them,

SPEECH
Ge 11: 1 had one language and a common **s**.
Ex   4:10 I am slow of **s** and tongue."

Ps 19: 2 Day after day they pour forth s;
    19: 3 They have no s, they use no words;
Jn 10: 6 Jesus used this figure of s,
2Co 8: 7 in faith, in s, in knowledge,
1Ti 4:12 set an example for the believers in s,
1Jn 3:18 let us not love with words or s but

SPEED* SPEEDILY
Ro   9:28 out his sentence on earth with s
2Pe 3:12 to the day of God and s its coming.

SPEEDILY SPEED
Isa 51: 5 My righteousness draws near s,

SPELL* SPELLS
Rev 18:23 your magic s all the nations were

SPELLS SPELL
Dt 18:11 or casts s, or who is a medium
Mic 5:12 and you will no longer cast s.

SPEND SPENT
Ge 19: 2 "we will s the night in the square."
Jdg 19:20 Only don't s the night
Pr 31: 3 Do not s your strength on women,
Isa 55: 2 Why s money on what is not bread,
2Co 12:15 So I will very gladly s for you

SPENT SPEND
Pr   5:11 when your flesh and body are s.
Mk   5:26 many doctors and had s all she had,
Lk   6:12 and s the night praying to God.
    15:14 After he had s everything, there was

SPICES
Ex 25: 6 s for the anointing oil
1Ki 10:10 large quantities of s, and precious
Mt 23:23 You give a tenth of your s—
Jn 19:40 it, with the s, in strips of linen.

SPIED SPY
Jos 6:22 the two men who had s out the land,

SPIES SPY
Ge 42: 9 them and said to them, "You are s!
Jos 6:17 because she hid the s we sent.
Heb 11:31 because she welcomed the s,
Jas 2:25 did when she gave lodging to the s

SPIN
Mt   6:28 They do not labor or s.

SPIRIT SPIRIT'S, SPIRITIST,
SPIRITISTS, SPIRITS, SPIRITUAL
Ge   1: 2 the S of God was hovering over
     6: 3 said, "My S will not contend
Ex 31: 3 I have filled him with the S of God,
Nu 11:25 the power of the S that was on him
    11:25 When the S rested on them,
    24: 2 by tribe, the S of God came on him
Dt 34: 9 the s of wisdom because Moses had
Jdg 6:34 Then the S of the LORD came
    11:29 Then the S of the LORD came
    13:25 the S of the LORD began to stir
    14: 6 The S of the LORD came
    15:14 The S of the LORD came

1Sa 10: 6 The S of the LORD will come
    16:13 day on the S of the LORD came
    16:14 Saul, and an evil s from the LORD
    16:15 an evil s from God is tormenting
    28: 8 "Consult a s for me," he said,
2Sa 23: 2 "The S of the LORD spoke
2Ki 2: 9 inherit a double portion of your s,"
     2:15 said, "The s of Elijah is resting
2Ch 18:21 be a deceiving s in the mouths of all
Ne   9:20 You gave your good S to instruct
Job 33: 4 The S of God has made me;
Ps 31: 5 Into your hands I commit my s;
    34:18 saves those who are crushed in s.
    51:10 and renew a steadfast s within me.
    51:11 or take your Holy S from me.
    51:17 My sacrifice, O God, is a broken s;
   106:33 they rebelled against the S of God,
   139: 7 Where can I go from your S?
   143:10 may your good S lead me on level
Pr 16:18 a haughty s before a fall.
    20:27 The human s is the lamp
    29:23 low, but the lowly in s gain honor.
Ecc 12: 7 the s returns to God who gave it.
Isa 11: 2 The S of the LORD will rest on
         him—the S of wisdom
    30: 1 but not by my S, heaping sin
    32:15 till the S is poured on us
    40:13 Who can fathom the S
    42: 1 I will put my S on him, and he will
    44: 3 pour out my S on your offspring,
    48:16 has sent me, endowed with his S.
    57:15 one who is contrite and lowly in s,
    59:21 "My S, who is on you, will not
    61: 1 The S of the Sovereign LORD is
    63:10 rebelled and grieved his Holy S.
Eze 3:12 Then the S lifted me up, and I heard
    11:19 heart and put a new s in them;
    13: 3 prophets who follow their own s
    36:26 a new heart and put a new s in you;
Da   4: 8 and the s of the holy gods is in him.)
Joel 2:28 I will pour out my S on all people.
Zec 4: 6 but by my S,' says the LORD
Mt   1:18 to be pregnant through the Holy S.
     3:11 He will baptize you with the Holy S
     3:16 he saw the S of God descending like
     4: 1 was led by the S into the wilderness
     5: 3 "Blessed are the poor in s, for theirs
    10:20 but the S of your Father speaking
    12:31 blasphemy against the S will not be
    26:41 The s is willing, but the flesh is
    28:19 and of the Son and of the Holy S,
Mk   1: 8 will baptize you with the Holy S."
Lk   1:15 the Holy S even before he is born.
     1:35 "The Holy S will come on you,
     1:80 child grew and became strong in s;
     3:16 He will baptize you with the Holy S
     4: 1 was led by the S into the wilderness,
     4:18 "The S of the Lord is on me,
    11:13 in heaven give the Holy S to those
    23:46 into your hands I commit my s."
Jn   1:33 on whom you see the S come down
     1:33 who will baptize with the Holy S.'
     3: 5 they are born of water and the S.

Jn	3: 6	to flesh, but the S gives birth to s.
	3:34	for God gives the S without limit.
	4:24	God is s, and his worshipers must worship in the S
	6:63	The S gives life; the flesh counts
	7:39	By this he meant the S, whom those
	7:39	that time the S had not been given,
	14:17	the S of truth. The world cannot
	14:26	the Holy S, whom the Father will
	15:26	the S of truth who goes
	16:13	But when he, the S of truth, comes,
	20:22	and said, "Receive the Holy S.
Ac	1: 5	will be baptized with the Holy S."
	1: 8	when the Holy S comes on you;
	2: 4	of them were filled with the Holy S
	2: 4	other tongues as the S enabled them.
	2:17	I will pour out my S on all people.
	2:38	will receive the gift of the Holy S.
	4:31	they were all filled with the Holy S
	5: 3	that you have lied to the Holy S
	6: 3	who are known to be full of the S
	7:51	You always resist the Holy S!
	8:15	that they might receive the Holy S,
	9:17	and be filled with the Holy S."
	11:16	will be baptized with the Holy S.'
	13: 2	the Holy S said, "Set apart for me
	19: 2	"Did you receive the Holy S
	19: 2	even heard that there is a Holy S."
Ro	1: 9	in my s in preaching the gospel
	7: 6	we serve in the new way of the S,
	8: 4	to the flesh but according to the S.
	8: 5	with the S have their minds set on what the S desires.
	8: 9	flesh but are in the realm of the S,
	8: 9	if anyone does not have the S
	8:13	but if by the S you put to death
	8:15	The S you received does not make
	8:16	The S himself testifies with our s
	8:23	who have the firstfruits of the S,
	8:26	way, the S helps us in our weakness.
	8:26	but the S himself intercedes for us
1Co	2:10	God has revealed to us by his S.
	2:10	The S searches all things,
	2:14	are discerned only through the S.
	3: 1	as people who live by the S but as
	5: 3	present, I am with you in s.
	6:17	with the Lord is one with him in s.
	6:19	bodies are temples of the Holy S,
	12: 1	Now about the gifts of the S,
	12: 4	but the same S distributes them.
	12:13	we were all baptized by one S so as
	14: 1	and eagerly desire gifts of the S,
	14:37	prophet or otherwise gifted by the S,
2Co	1:22	put his S in our hearts as a deposit,
	3: 3	ink but with the S of the living God,
	3: 6	the letter kills, but the S gives life.
	3:17	Now the Lord is the S, and where the S of the Lord is,
	5: 5	who has given us the S as a deposit,
	7: 1	that contaminates body and s,
Gal	3: 2	Did you receive the S by the works
	3:14	might receive the promise of the S.
	5:16	say, walk by the S, and you will not

Gal	5:22	But the fruit of the S is love, joy,
	5:25	Since we live by the S, let us keep in step with the S.
	6: 1	you who live by the S should restore
	6: 8	whoever sows to please the S, from the S will reap eternal life.
Eph	1:13	with a seal, the promised Holy S,
	2:18	have access to the Father by one S.
	2:22	in which God lives by his S.
	4: 3	the unity of the S through the bond
	4: 4	There is one body and one S, just as
	4:30	do not grieve the Holy S of God,
	5:18	Instead, be filled with the S,
	5:19	hymns, and songs from the S.
	6:17	of salvation and the sword of the S,
Php	2: 2	being one in s and of one mind.
Col	1: 9	and understanding that the S gives,
	2: 5	body, I am present with you in s
	3:16	and songs from the S,
1Th	5:19	Do not quench the S.
	5:23	May your whole s, soul and body be
2Th	2:13	the sanctifying work of the S
1Ti	3:16	was vindicated by the S, was seen
2Ti	1: 7	the S God gave us does not make us
	4:22	The Lord be with your s.
Heb	2: 4	of the Holy S distributed according
	4:12	even to dividing soul and s,
	6: 4	gift, who have shared in the Holy S,
	10:29	and who has insulted the S of grace?
1Pe	1: 2	the sanctifying work of the S, to be
	3: 4	beauty of a gentle and quiet s,
2Pe	1:21	were carried along by the Holy S.
1Jn	3:24	We know it by the S he gave us.
	4: 1	do not believe every s, but test
	4:13	he in us: He has given us of his S.
Jude	1:20	holy faith and praying in the Holy S,
Rev	1.10	On the Lord's Day I was in the S,
	2: 7	let them hear what the S says
	4: 2	At once I was in the S, and there

EVIL SPIRIT See EVIL

HOLY SPIRIT See HOLY

IMPURE SPIRIT See IMPURE

MY SPIRIT Ge 6:3; 2Ki 5:26; Job 6:4; 7:11; 10:12; 17:1; Ps 31:5; 73:21; 77:3, 6; 142:3; 143:4, 7; Isa 26:9; 30:1; 38:16; 42:1; 44:3; 59:21; La 1:16; Eze 3:14; 36:27; 37:14; 39:29; Joel 2:28, 29; Hag 2:5; Zec 4:6; 6:8; Mt 12:18; Lk 1:47; 23:46; Ac 2:17, 18; 7:59; Ro 1:9; 1Co 14:14, 15, 15; 16:18

SPIRIT OF GOD Ge 1:2; 41:38; Ex 31:3; 35:31; Nu 24:2; 1Sa 10:10; 11:6; 19:20, 23; 2Ch 15:1; 24:20; Job 33:4; Ps 106:33; Eze 11:24; Mt 3:16; 12:28; Ro 8:9, 14; 15:19; 1Co 2:11, 14; 6:11; 7:40; 12:3; Eph 4:30; 1Jn 4:2

SPIRIT OF THE LORD† Jdg 3:10; 6:34; 11:29; 13:25; 14:6, 19; 15:14; 1Sa 10:6; 16:13, 14; 2Sa 23:2; 1Ki 18:12; 2Ki 2:16; 2Ch 20:14; Isa 11:2; 40:13; 63:14; Eze 11:5; 37:1; Mic 3:8

SPIRIT'S* SPIRIT

1Co	2: 4	a demonstration of the S power,

SPIRITIST* SPIRIT
Lev 20:27 s among you must be put to death.
Dt 18:11 or who is a medium or s or who

SPIRITISTS SPIRIT
Lev 19:31 not turn to mediums or seek out s,
1Sa 28: 3 the mediums and s from the land.
2Ki 23:24 Josiah got rid of the mediums and s,

SPIRITS SPIRIT
Ru 3: 7 and drinking and was in good s,
Ps 78: 8 whose s were not faithful to him.
Mt 12:45 it seven other s more wicked than
Lk 4:36 power he gives orders to impure s
Ac 8: 7 shrieks, impure s came out of many,
1Co 12:10 to another distinguishing between s,
14:32 The s of prophets are subject
Heb 1: 7 "He makes his angels s, and his
12: 9 should we submit to the Father of s
1Pe 3:19 proclamation to the imprisoned s—
1Jn 4: 1 but test the s to see whether they are
Rev 1: 4 from the seven s before his throne,
16:13 I saw three impure s that looked like

EVIL SPIRITS See EVIL

IMPURE SPIRITS See SPIRITS

SPIRITUAL SPIRIT
Ro 1:11 to you some s gift to make you
7:14 We know that the law is s; but I am
12:11 but keep your s fervor,
15:27 have shared in the Jews' s blessings,
1Co 2:13 the Spirit, explaining s realities
9:11 If we have sown s seed among you,
10: 3 They all ate the same s food
15:44 a natural body, it is raised a s body.
Eph 1: 3 realms with every s blessing
6:12 against the s forces of evil
1Pe 2: 2 crave pure s milk, so that by it you
2: 5 are being built into a s house to be
2: 5 offering s sacrifices acceptable

SPIT
Dt 25: 9 of his sandals, s in his face and say,
Mt 27:30 They s on him, and took the staff
Mk 14:65 Then some began to s at him;
Lk 18:32 mock him, insult him and s on him;
Rev 3:16 I am about to s you out of my

SPLASH
Ex 29:16 and s it against the sides of the altar.

SPLENDOR
1Ch 16:29 the LORD in the s of his holiness.
29:11 the glory and the majesty and the s,
Job 37:22 of the north he comes in golden s;
Ps 21: 5 you have bestowed on him s
29: 2 the LORD in the s of his holiness.
45: 3 clothe yourself with s and majesty.
96: 5 S and majesty are before him;
96: 9 the LORD in the s of his holiness;
104: 1 you are clothed with s and majesty.
110: 3 Arrayed in holy s, your young men
145: 5 of the glorious s of your majesty—
145:12 and the glorious s of your kingdom.

Ps 148:13 his s is above the earth
Pr 16:31 Gray hair is a crown of s;
20:29 strength, gray hair the s of the old.
Isa 2:10 LORD and the s of his majesty!
49: 3 in whom I will display my s."
55: 5 for he has endowed you with s."
60:21 my hands, for the display of my s.
61: 3 the LORD for the display of his s.
62: 3 You will be a crown of s
63: 1 robed in s, striding forward
Hos 14: 6 His s will be like an olive tree,
Hab 3: 4 His s was like the sunrise;
Mt 6:29 in all his s was dressed like one
Lk 9:30 and Elijah, appeared in glorious s,
2Th 2: 8 and destroy by the s of his coming.
Rev 21:24 of the earth will bring their s into it.

SPLINTERED
2Ki 18:21 on Egypt, that s reed of a staff,

SPLIT
Nu 16:31 this, the ground under them s apart
1Ki 13: 3 The altar will be s apart
16:21 of Israel were s into two factions;
Ps 74:13 It was you who s open the sea
Zec 14: 4 the Mount of Olives will be s in two
Mt 27:51 The earth shook, the rocks s
Rev 16:19 The great city s into three parts,

SPOIL SPOILS
Ps 119:162 promise like one who finds great s.
1Pe 1: 4 that can never perish, s or fade.

SPOILS SPOIL
Ex 15: 9 I will divide the s; I will gorge
Nu 31:27 Divide the s equally between
Isa 53:12 he will divide the s with the strong,
Jn 6:27 Do not work for food that s,

SPOKE SPEAK
Ge 16:13 name to the LORD who s to her:
39:10 though she s to Joseph day
Ex 20: 1 And God s all these words:
Nu 3: 1 at the time the LORD s to Moses
23: 7 Then Balaam s his message:
Dt 4:12 the LORD s to you out of the fire.
5: 4 The LORD s to you face to face
1Ki 4:32 He s three thousand proverbs
4:33 He s about plant life, from the cedar
Job 42: 3 Surely I s of things I did not
Ps 99: 7 He s to them from the pillar
Jer 35:17 I s to them, but they did not listen;
Mt 9:33 out, the man who had been mute s.
Mk 4:33 similar parables Jesus s the word
Jn 8:30 Even as he s, many believed in him.
Heb 1: 1 In the past God s to our ancestors
13: 7 who s the word of God to you.
2Pe 1:21 s from God as they were carried

SPOKEN SPEAK
Ex 34:29 face was radiant because he had s
Nu 12: 2 "Has the LORD s only through
Dt 18:22 That prophet has s presumptuously,
Ezr 1: 1 word of the LORD s by Jeremiah,
Job 42: 7 because you have not s the truth

Ps   60: 6 God has **s** from his sanctuary:
Isa 45:19 I have not **s** in secret,
Lk   20:19 knew he had **s** this parable against
Jn   2:21 the temple he had **s** of was his body.
Ac   2: 6 heard their own language being **s**.
Heb   1: 2 in these last days he has **s** to us

SPONGE

Mk   15:36 ran, filled a **s** with wine vinegar,
Jn   19:29 so they soaked a **s** in it, put the **s** on a
            stalk of the hyssop

SPOT SPOTLESS, SPOTS, SPOTTED

Isa 28: 8 and there is not a **s** without filth.
     46: 7 From that **s** it cannot move.
1Ti   6:14 to keep this command without **s**

SPOTLESS* SPOT

Da   11:35 and made **s** until the time of the end,
     12:10 will be purified, made **s** and refined,
2Pe   3:14 make every effort to be found **s**,

SPOTS SPOT

Lev 13:38 man or woman has white **s** on the skin,
Jer 13:23 change his skin or a leopard its **s**?

SPOTTED SPOT

Ge   30:32 them every speckled or **s** sheep,
     30:32 lamb and every **s** or speckled goat.

SPRANG* SPRING

Jnh   4:10 It **s** up overnight and died overnight.
Mt   13: 5 It **s** up quickly, because the soil was
Mk   4: 5 It **s** up quickly, because the soil was
Ro   7: 9 came, sin **s** to life and I died.

SPREAD SPREADING, SPREADS

Ge   10:32 these the nations **s** out over the earth
Ex   23: 1 "Do not **s** false reports. Do not help
     37: 9 cherubim had their wings **s** upward,
1Ch 14:17 So David's fame **s** throughout every
Ps   5:11 **S** your protection over them,
     78:19 "Can God really **s** a table
    143: 6 I **s** out my hands to you; I thirst
Pr   15: 7 The lips of the wise **s** knowledge,
Isa 48:13 my right hand **s** out the heavens;
Lk   19:36 people **s** their cloaks on the road.
Jn   21:23 the rumor **s** among the believers
Ac   6: 7 So the word of God **s**.
     12:24 the word of God continued to **s**
     13:49 of the Lord **s** through the whole
     19:20 way the word of the Lord **s** widely
2Co   2:14 and uses us to **s** the aroma
2Th   3: 1 message of the Lord may **s** rapidly
2Ti   2:17 Their teaching will **s** like gangrene.

SPREADING SPREAD

1Sa   2:24 report I hear **s** among the LORD's
1Ki   8:38 and **s** out their hands toward this
Pr   29: 5 who flatter their neighbors are **s** nets
Jer   2:20 under every **s** tree you lay down as
     17: 2 Asherah poles beside the **s** trees
Eze   1:11 They each had two wings **s**
1Th   3: 2 in God's service in **s** the gospel

SPREADS SPREAD

Job 36:29 Who can understand how he **s**
Pr   10:18 lying lips and **s** slander is a fool.

SPRING SPRANG, SPRINGS, SPRINGTIME

Ge   16: 7 the LORD found Hagar near a **s**
Dt   11:14 both autumn and **s** rains, so that you
Ecc   4: 4 all achievement **s** from one person's
Isa 45: 8 let salvation **s** up, let righteousness
     58:11 like a **s** whose waters never fail.
Jer   2:13 forsaken me, the **s** of living water,
      9: 1 that my head were a **s** of water
     17:13 the LORD, the **s** of living water.
Jn   4:14 become in them a **s** of water welling
Ro   15:12 "The Root of Jesse will **s** up,
Jas   3:12 can a salt **s** produce fresh water.
Rev 21: 6 without cost from the **s** of the water

SPRINGS SPRING

Ge   7:11 day all the **s** of the great deep burst
Dt   8: 7 deep **s** gushing out into the valleys
Ps   114: 8 a pool, the hard rock into **s** of water.
Pr   5:16 Should your **s** overflow
Isa 49:10 and lead them beside **s** of water.
2Pe   2:17 These people are **s** without water
Rev   7:17 'he will lead them to **s** of living

SPRINGTIME* SPRING

Zec 10: 1 Ask the LORD for rain in the **s**;

SPRINKLE SPRINKLED

Lev 16:14 he shall **s** some of it with his finger
Nu   8: 7 **S** the water of cleansing on them;
Isa 52:15 so he will **s** many nations, and kings
Eze 36:25 I will **s** clean water on you, and you

SPRINKLED SPRINKLE

Heb 10:22 having our hearts **s** to cleanse us
1Pe   1: 2 to Jesus Christ and **s** with his blood:

SPROUT

Nu   17: 5 to the man I choose will **s**, and I will
Pr   23: 5 for they will surely **s** wings and fly
Jer 33:15 I will make a righteous Branch **s**

SPUR*

Heb 10:24 consider how we may **s** one another

SPURNED SPURNS

Pr   1:30 accept my advice and **s** my rebuke,
Isa   1: 4 they have **s** the Holy One of Israel
La   2: 6 his fierce anger he has **s** both king

SPURNS* SPURNED

Pr   15: 5 A fool **s** a parent's discipline,

SPY SPIED, SPIES, SPYING

Dt   1:22 "Let us send men ahead to **s**
Jos   2: 2 have come here tonight to **s**
Gal   2: 4 had infiltrated our ranks to **s**

SPYING SPY

Ge   42:30 treated us as though we were **s**

SQUANDERED SQUANDERS

Lk   15:13 and there **s** his wealth in wild living.

SQUANDERS* SQUANDERED
Pr 29: 3 of prostitutes **s** his wealth.

SQUARE SQUARES
Ge 19: 2 "we will spend the night in the **s**."
Ex 27: 1 it is to be **s**, five cubits long and five
28: 16 It is to be **s**—a span long and a span
30: 2 It is to be **s**, a cubit long and a cubit
Jdg 19: 20 don't spend the night in the **s**."
Ne 8: 1 one in the **s** before the Water Gate.
Pr 1: 20 she raises her voice in the public **s**;
Rev 21: 16 The city was laid out like a **s**,

SQUARES SQUARE
Pr 7: 12 now in the **s**, at every corner she

STABILITY*
Pr 29: 4 By justice a king gives a country **s**,

STAFF STAFFS
Ge 38: 25 seal and cord and **s** these are."
49: 10 nor the ruler's **s** from between his
Ex 4: 4 it turned back into a **s** in his hand.
7: 12 Aaron's **s** swallowed up their staffs.
14: 16 Raise your **s** and stretch out your
Nu 17: 6 and Aaron's **s** was among them.
20: 11 and struck the rock twice with his **s**.
Ps 23: 4 your rod and your **s**, they comfort
Mic 7: 14 Shepherd your people with your **s**,
Zec 11: 10 I took my **s** called Favor and broke
Mt 27: 48 put it on a **s**, and offered it to Jesus
Mk 15: 19 they struck him on the head with a **s**
Heb 9: 4 manna, Aaron's **s** that had budded,

STAFFS STAFF
Ex 7: 12 Aaron's staff swallowed up their **s**.
Nu 17: 7 Moses placed the **s** before

STAGES
Nu 33: 1 Here are the **s** in the journey

STAGGER STAGGERED, STAGGERS
Ps 60: 3 have given us wine that makes us **s**.
Isa 28: 7 Priests and prophets **s** from beer
28: 7 they **s** when seeing visions,
29: 9 but not from wine, **s**, but not
Jer 25: 16 they will **s** and go mad because
Am 8: 12 People will **s** from sea to sea

STAGGERED STAGGER
Ps 107: 27 They reeled and **s** like drunkards;

STAGGERS STAGGER
Isa 3: 8 Jerusalem **s**, Judah is falling;

STAIN* STAINED
Jer 2: 22 the **s** of your guilt is still before
Eph 5: 27 without **s** or wrinkle or any other

STAINED STAIN
Isa 63: 1 with his garments **s** crimson?
Jude 1: 23 hating even the clothing **s**

STAIRWAY
Ge 28: 12 he saw a **s** resting on the earth,
2Ki 20: 11 it had gone down on the **s** of Ahaz.

STAKES
Isa 54: 2 your cords, strengthen your **s**.

STALK STALKS
Ge 41: 5 good, were growing on a single **s**.
Jn 19: 29 sponge on a **s** of the hyssop plant,

STALKS* STALK
Jos 2: 6 hidden them under the **s** of flax she
Ru 2: 16 Even pull out some **s** for her
Ps 91: 6 nor the pestilence that **s**

STALL STALLS
Ps 50: 9 I have no need of a bull from your **s**

STALLS STALL
1Ki 4: 26 Solomon had four thousand **s**
Hab 3: 17 in the pen and no cattle in the **s**,

STAND STANDING, STANDS, STOOD
Ex 9: 11 magicians could not **s** before Moses
14: 13 **S** firm and you will see
Lev 19: 32 " 'S up in the presence
26: 37 be able to **s** before your enemies.
Nu 30: 4 which she obligated herself will **s**.
Dt 10: 8 to **s** before the LORD to minister
11: 25 No one will be able to **s** against you.
Jos 3: 8 waters, go and **s** in the river.' "
10: 12 "Sun, **s** still over Gibeon, and you,
2Ch 20: 17 **s** firm and see the deliverance
Job 19: 25 that in the end he will **s** on the earth.
Ps 1: 1 or **s** in the way that sinners take
1: 5 Therefore the wicked will not **s**
10: 1 Why, LORD, do you **s** far off?
24: 3 Who may **s** in his holy place?
33: 11 plans of the LORD **s** firm forever,
40: 2 rock and gave me a firm place to **s**.
76: 7 Who can **s** before you when you are
78: 13 he made the water **s** up like a wall.
93: 5 Your statutes, LORD, **s** firm;
119: 120 fear of you; I **s** in awe of your laws.
130: 3 a record of sins, Lord, who could **s**?
Pr 10: 25 but the righteous **s** firm forever.
Isa 7: 9 If you do not **s** firm in your faith, you
will not **s** at all.' "
11: 10 the Root of Jesse will **s** as a banner
29: 23 will **s** in awe of the God of Israel.
Jer 15: 1 and Samuel were to **s** before me,
Eze 22: 30 **s** before me in the gap on behalf
Mic 5: 4 He will **s** and shepherd his flock
Hab 3: 2 I **s** in awe of your deeds, LORD.
Zec 14: 4 that day his feet will **s** on the Mount
Mal 3: 2 Who can **s** when he appears?
Mt 12: 25 divided against itself will not **s**.
Lk 4: 9 had him **s** on the highest point
21: 19 **S** firm, and you will win life.
Ac 11: 17 think that I could **s** in God's way?"
Ro 5: 2 into this grace in which we now **s**.
14: 4 their own master, servants **s** or fall.
14: 4 for the Lord is able to make them **s**.
14: 10 we will all **s** before God's judgment
1Co 15: 58 my dear brothers and sisters, **s** firm.
16: 13 on your guard; **s** firm in the faith;

2Co 1:24 joy, because it is by faith you **s** firm.
Gal   5: 1 **S** firm, then, and do not let
Eph   6:11 can take your **s** against the devil's
Col   4:12 that you may **s** firm in all the will
2Th   2:15 **s** firm and hold fast to the teachings
Jas   5: 8 be patient and **s** firm,
Rev   3:20 I **s** at the door and knock.

STANDARD STANDARDS
Nu   1:52 in their own camp under their **s**.

STANDARDS STANDARD
Lev 19:35 " 'Do not use dishonest **s**
Nu   2:34 way they encamped under their **s**,
Eze   7:27 by their own **s** I will judge them.

STANDING STAND
Ge   18:22 but Abraham remained **s** before
Ex   3: 5 where you are **s** is holy ground."
Nu   22:23 angel of the LORD **s** in the road
Jos   4:10 who carried the ark remained **s**
      5:15 the place where you are **s** is holy."
Ru   2: 1 side, a man of **s** from the clan
      4:11 May you have **s** in Ephrathah
2Ch 18:18 multitudes of heaven **s** on his right
Eze   3:23 the glory of the LORD was **s** there,
Am   7: 7 The Lord was **s** by a wall that had
      9: 1 I saw the Lord **s** by the altar, and he
Zec   1: 8 He was **s** among the myrtle trees
      3: 1 the high priest **s** before the angel
      3: 1 Satan **s** at his right side to accuse
Mt   6: 5 love to pray **s** in the synagogues
Lk   9:32 glory and the two men **s** with him.
Ac   7:55 and Jesus **s** at the right hand of God.
1Co 10:12 So, if you think you are **s** firm,
1Ti   3:13 have served well gain an excellent **s**
Jas   5: 9 The Judge is **s** at the door!
1Pe   5: 9 Resist him, **s** firm in the faith,
Rev   7: 9 **s** before the throne and before
      20:12 great and small, **s** before the throne,

STANDS STAND
1Ki   7:27 also made ten movable **s** of bronze;
2Ki   25:13 the movable **s** and the bronze Sea
Ps   89: 2 that your love **s** firm forever,
      119:89 it **s** firm in the heavens.
Pr   12: 7 the house of the righteous **s** firm.
Mt   10:22 the one who **s** firm to the end will
Jn   1:26 among you **s** one you do not know.
      16:11 of this world now **s** condemned.
2Ti   2:19 God's solid foundation **s** firm,
Heb   4: 1 promise of entering his rest still **s**,

STAR STARGAZERS, STARRY, STARS
Nu   24:17 A **s** will come out of Jacob;
Isa   14:12 heaven, morning **s**, son of the dawn!
Mt   2: 2 We saw his **s** when it rose and have
2Pe   1:19 the morning **s** rises in your hearts.
Rev   2:28 also give that one the morning **s**.
      8:11 the name of the **s** is Wormwood.
      9: 1 I saw a **s** that had fallen
      9: 1 The **s** was given the key to the shaft
      22:16 David, and the bright Morning **S**."

STARGAZERS* STAR
Isa   47:13 those **s** who make predictions

STARRY STAR
2Ki   17:16 They bowed down to all the **s** hosts,
Isa   40:26 He who brings out the **s** host one
Da   8:10 it threw some of the **s** host down

STARS STAR
Ge   1:16 He also made the **s**.
      15: 5 up at the sky and count the **s**—
      37: 9 eleven **s** were bowing down to me."
Dt   1:10 today you are as numerous as the **s**
Job   38: 7 while the morning **s** sang together
Ps   148: 3 praise him, all you shining **s**.
Isa   14:13 raise my throne above the **s** of God;
Da   12: 3 like the **s** for ever and ever.
Joel 2:10 darkened, and the **s** no longer shine.
Mk   13:25 the **s** will fall from the sky,
Php   2:15 you will shine among them like **s**
Rev   1:16 In his right hand he held seven **s**,
      6:13 and the **s** in the sky fell to earth,
      8:12 and a third of the **s**, so that a third
      12: 1 a crown of twelve **s** on her head.
      12: 4 Its tail swept a third of the **s**

START
Ne   2:18 replied, "Let us **s** rebuilding."
Pr   22: 6 **S** children off on the way they

STARVE STARVING
Ex   16: 3 this desert to **s** this entire assembly

STARVING STARVE
Pr   6:30 to satisfy his hunger when he is **s**.
Lk   15:17 to spare, and here I am **s** to death!

STATE STATEMENTS
Job   23: 4 I would **s** my case before him
Isa   43:26 **s** the case for your innocence.
Lk   1:48 of the humble **s** of his servant.

STATEMENTS* STATE
Mk   14:56 him, but their **s** did not agree.

STATUE
Da   2:31 there before you stood a large **s**—

STATURE*
1Sa   2:26 boy Samuel continued to grow in **s**
SS   7: 7 Your **s** is like that of the palm,
Lk   2:52 And Jesus grew in wisdom and **s**,

STATUTES
Ps   19: 7 The **s** of the LORD are
      93: 5 Your **s**, LORD, stand firm;
      119: 2 Blessed are those who keep his **s**
      119:14 in following your **s** as one rejoices
      119:24 Your **s** are my delight; they are my
      119:36 Turn my heart toward your **s**
      119:99 teachers, for I meditate on your **s**.
      119:111 Your **s** are my heritage forever;
      119:125 that I may understand your **s**.
      119:129 Your **s** are wonderful;
      119:138 The **s** you have laid down are
      119:152 your **s** that you established them

Ps 119:167 I obey your **s**, for I love them
Isa 24: 5 laws, violated the **s** and broken

STAY STAYED
Ge 13: 6 that they were not able to **s** together.
Ex 16:29 Everyone is to **s** where they are
Ps 119: 9 young person **s** on the path of purity?
Pr 7:11 defiant, her feet never **s** at home;
14: 7 S away from a fool, for you will not
Mic 7:18 You do not **s** angry forever
Mk 14:34 "S here and keep watch."

STAYED STAY
Ex 24:18 And he **s** on the mountain forty days
Nu 9:18 as the cloud **s** over the tabernacle,
Lk 2:43 the boy Jesus **s** behind in Jerusalem,

STEADFAST* STEADFASTLY
Ps 51:10 God, and renew a **s** spirit within me.
57: 7 My heart, O God, is **s**, my heart is **s**;
108: 1 My heart, O God, is **s**; I will sing
112: 7 their hearts are **s**,
119: 5 my ways were **s** in obeying your
Pr 4:26 your feet and be **s** in all your ways.
Isa 26: 3 peace those whose minds are **s**,
1Pe 5:10 and make you strong, firm and **s**.

STEADFASTLY* STEADFAST
2Ch 27: 6 because he walked **s** before

STEADY
Ex 17:12 that his hands remained **s** till sunset.
1Ch 13: 9 reached out his hand to **s** the ark,
Isa 35: 3 hands, **s** the knees that give way;

STEAL STEALING, STEALS, STOLE, STOLEN
Ex 20:15 "You shall not **s**.
Lev 19:11 " 'Do not **s**. " 'Do not lie.
Dt 5:19 "You shall not **s**.
Jer 23:30 "I am against the prophets who **s**
Mt 6:19 and where thieves break in and **s**.
19:18 you shall not **s**, you shall not give
Jn 10:10 The thief comes only to **s** and kill
Ro 13: 9 "You shall not **s**," "You shall not
Eph 4:28 has been stealing must **s** no longer,

STEALING STEAL
Ro 2:21 You who preach against **s**, do you

STEALS STEAL
Ex 22: 3 "Anyone who **s** must certainly
Pr 6:30 a thief if he **s** to satisfy his hunger

STEEL (KJV) See BRONZE

STEERED*
Jas 3: 4 they are **s** by a very small rudder

STEP FOOTSTEPS, STEPS
Ps 1: 1 is the one who does not walk in **s**
Job 34:21 he sees their every **s**.
Gal 5:25 let us keep in **s** with the Spirit.

STEPHEN*
Deacon (Ac 6:5). Arrested (Ac 6:8–15). Speech

to Sanhedrin (Ac 7). Stoned (Ac 7:54–60; 8:2; 11:19; 22:20).

STEPS STEP
Ex 20:26 And do not go up to my altar on **s**,
2Ki 20: 9 Shall the shadow go forward ten **s**, or shall it go back ten **s**?"
Ps 37:23 The LORD makes firm the **s**
Pr 5: 5 her **s** lead straight to the grave.
14:15 the prudent give thought to their **s**.
16: 9 but the LORD establishes their **s**.
20:24 A person's **s** are directed
Jer 10:23 it is not for them to direct their **s**.
1Pe 2:21 that you should follow in his **s**.

STERN STERNNESS
Pr 15:10 S discipline awaits anyone who

STERNNESS* STERN
Ro 11:22 therefore the kindness and **s** of God: **s** to those who fell,

STEW
Ge 25:29 when Jacob was cooking some **s**,
2Ki 4:39 he cut them up into the pot of **s**,

STEWARDS
1Pe 4:10 as faithful **s** of God's grace in its

STICK STICKS
2Ki 6: 6 Elisha cut a **s** and threw it there,
Eze 37:16 take a **s** of wood and write on it,
Am 4:11 You were like a burning **s** snatched
Zec 3: 2 Is not this man a burning **s** snatched

STICKS STICK
Pr 18:24 there is a friend who **s** closer than

STIFF-NECKED NECK
Ex 32: 9 to Moses, "and they are a **s** people.
34: 9 Although this is a **s** people,
2Ki 17:14 and were as **s** as their ancestors,
Pr 29: 1 Whoever remains **s** after many
Ac 7:51 "You **s** people! Your hearts

STILL STILLED
Ge 9: 4 eat meat that has its lifeblood **s** in it.
Ex 14:14 you need only to be **s**."
Lev 19:26 eat any meat with the blood **s** in it.
Jos 10:13 So the sun stood **s**, and the moon
Ps 37: 7 Be **s** before the LORD and wait
46:10 "Be **s**, and know that I am God;
89: 9 its waves mount up, you **s** them.
Da 11:35 it will **s** come at the appointed time.
Hab 3:11 moon stood **s** in the heavens
Zec 2:13 Be **s** before the LORD,
Mk 4:39 Be **s**!" Then the wind died down
8:17 Do you **s** not see or understand?
Jn 12:37 they **s** would not believe in him.
Ro 5: 8 While we were **s** sinners,
Heb 11: 4 And by faith Abel **s** speaks,

STILLED STILL
Ps 65: 7 who **s** the roaring of the seas,

STIMULATE*
2Pe 3: 1 of them as reminders to **s** you

STING
1Co 15:55 Where, O death, is your s?"
Rev 9: 5 that of the s of a scorpion when it

STINGY*
Pr 28:22 The s are eager to get rich and are

STIPULATIONS
Dt   6:20 you, "What is the meaning of the s,
Jer 44:23 his law or his decrees or his s,

STIR STIRRED, STIRRING, STIRS
Pr 28:25 The greedy s up conflict, but those

STIRRED STIR
1Ki 14:22 the sins they committed they s
Ps 45: 1 My heart is s by a noble theme as I
Hag 1:14 So the LORD s up the spirit
Ac 13:50 They s up persecution against Paul

STIRRING STIR
Pr 30:33 so s up anger produces strife."
Ac 17:13 agitating the crowds and s them up.

STIRS STIR
Pr   6.19 a person who s up conflict
    10:12 Hatred s up conflict, but love covers
    15: 1 wrath, but a harsh word s up anger.
    15:18 A hot-tempered person s
    16:28 A perverse person s up conflict,
    29:22 An angry person s up conflict,
Lk 23: 5 "He s up the people all over Judea

STOIC*
Ac 17:18 S philosophers began to debate

STOLE STEAL
Ge 31:19 Rachel s her father's household
2Sa 15: 6 so he s the hearts of the people
Mt 28:13 s him away while we were asleep.'

STOLEN STEAL
Ex 22: 4 If the s animal is found alive in their
Lev 6: 4 they must return what they have s
Ps 62:10 or put vain hope in s goods;
Pr   9:17 "S water is sweet; food eaten
SS   4: 9 You have s my heart, my sister,
Eze 33:15 return what they have s,

STOMACH
Eze 3: 3 giving you and fill your s with it."
Mk   7:19 go into their heart but into their s,
1Co 6:13 "Food for the s and the s for food,
Php 3:19 their god is their s, and their glory is
1Ti 5:23 use a little wine because of your s
Rev 10: 9 It will turn your s sour, but 'in your

STONE CAPSTONE,
   CORNERSTONE, MILLSTONE,
   MILLSTONES, STONED, STONES,
   STONING
Ge 28:18 Jacob took the s he had placed
    31:45 So Jacob took a s and set it up as
    35:14 Jacob set up a s pillar at the place
Ex 17: 4 They are almost ready to s me."
    24: 4 up twelve s pillars representing

Ex 28:10 six names on one s
    31:18 law, the tablets of s inscribed
    34: 1 out two s tablets like the first ones,
Lev 26: 1 image or a sacred s for yourselves,
Dt   4:13 then wrote them on two s tablets.
    16:22 and do not erect a sacred s, for these
    19:14 your neighbor's boundary s set
    28:36 other gods, gods of wood and s.
1Sa 7:12 Then Samuel took a s and set it
    17:50 the Philistine with a sling and a s;
2Ki 10:27 They demolished the sacred s
Ps 91:12 will not strike your foot against a s.
    118:22 The s the builders rejected has
Isa 8:14 and Judah he will be a s that causes
    28:16 "See, I lay a s in Zion, a tested s,
Jer 3: 9 and committed adultery with s
Eze 11:19 remove from them their heart of s
    36:26 remove from you your heart of s
Zec 3: 9 There are seven eyes on that one s,
Mt   4: 6 not strike your foot against a s.' "
     7: 9 asks for bread, will give him a s?
    23:37 the prophets and s those sent to you,
    24: 2 you, not one s here will be left
Mk 12:10 " 'The s the builders rejected has
    16: 3 "Who will roll the s away
Lk   4: 3 God, tell this s to become bread."
    20:18 on that s will be broken to pieces;
Jn   8: 7 the first to throw a s at her."
     8:59 they picked up stones to s him,
    10:32 For which of these do you s me?"
    19:13 at a place known as the S Pavement
Ac   4:11 Jesus is " 'the s you builders
Ro   9:32 They stumbled over the stumbling s.
2Co 3: 3 not on tablets of s but on tablets
1Pe 2: 4 As you come to him, the living S—
     2: 6 "See, I lay a s in Zion, a chosen
Rev 2:17 person a white s with a new name
    21:19 with every kind of precious s.

STONED STONE
Lev 24:23 outside the camp and s him.
Nu 15:36 outside the camp and s him to death,
Jos 7:25 Then all Israel s him, and after they
1Ki 21:13 outside the city and s him to death.
2Ch 24:21 order of the king they s him to death
Ac 14:19 They s Paul and dragged him

STONES STONE
Ex 23:24 and break their sacred s to pieces.
    28: 9 "Take two onyx s and engrave
    28:21 There are to be twelve s,
Dt 27: 2 set up some large s and coat them
Jos 4: 3 take up twelve s from the middle
1Sa 17:40 hand, chose five smooth s
1Ki 18:31 Elijah took twelve s, one for each
2Ki 17:10 They set up sacred s and Asherah
    18: 4 smashed the sacred s and cut down
Ps 102:14 For her s are dear to your servants;
Ecc 3: 5 a time to scatter s and a time
Mt   3: 9 of these s God can raise up children
     4: 3 God, tell these s to become bread."
Mk 13: 1 What massive s!
Lk 19:40 they keep quiet, the s will cry out."
1Co 3:12 silver, costly s, wood, hay or straw,

1Pe 2: 5 like living s, are being built

STONING* STONE
Nu 14:10 assembly talked about s them.
1Sa 30: 6 the men were talking of s him;
Jn 10:33 "We are not s you for any good
Ac 7:59 While they were s him,
Heb 11:37 They were put to death by s;

STOOD STAND
Ge 28:13 There above it s the LORD, and he
Ex 15: 8 The surging waters s up like a wall;
Dt 5: 5 that time I s between the LORD
Jos 3:17 of the Jordan and s on dry ground,
 10:13 So the sun s still, and the moon
Zec 3: 5 while the angel of the LORD s by.
Lk 10:25 occasion an expert in the law s
 18:11 The Pharisee s by himself
 22:28 You are those who have s by me
Jn 19:25 Near the cross of Jesus s his mother,
 20:19 Jesus came and s among them
Ro 16:10 fidelity to Christ has s the test.
2Ti 4:17 But the Lord s at my side and gave
Jas 1:12 trial because, having s the test,
Rev 22: 2 each side of the river s the tree

STOOP STOOPS
Mk 1: 7 sandals I am not worthy to s down

STOOPS STOOP
Ps 113: 6 who s down to look on the heavens

STOP STOPPED
Job 37:14 s and consider God's wonders.
Isa 1:13 S bringing meaningless offerings!
 1:16 out of my sight; s doing wrong.
 2:22 S trusting in mere humans,
Jer 32:40 I will never s doing good to them,
Mk 9:39 "Do not s him," Jesus said.
Jn 2:16 S turning my Father's house
 5:14 S sinning or something worse may
 6:43 "S grumbling among yourselves,"
 7:24 S judging by mere appearances,
 20:27 S doubting and believe."
Ac 5:39 you will not be able to s these men;
Ro 14:13 Therefore let us s passing judgment
1Co 14:20 and sisters, s thinking like children.
Rev 4: 8 Day and night they never s saying:

STOPPED STOP
Nu 16:48 and the dead, and the plague s.
Jos 3:16 the water from upstream s flowing.
 10:13 The sun s in the middle of the sky
2Sa 24:25 land, and the plague on Israel was s.
2Ki 4: 6 a jar left." Then the oil s flowing.
Mk 5:29 Immediately her bleeding s and she
Lk 23:45 for the sun s shining.

STORE STORED, STORES,
 STORING
Pr 2: 1 and s up my commands within you,
 2: 7 He holds success in s
 7: 1 and s up my commands within you.
 10:14 The wise s up knowledge,
 21:20 The wise s up choice food and olive

Isa 2:12 LORD Almighty has a day in s
 33: 6 a rich s of salvation and wisdom
Mt 6:19 "Do not s up for yourselves
 6:26 not sow or reap or s away in barns,
2Ti 4: 8 Now there is in s for me the crown

STORED STORE
Pr 13:22 but a sinner's wealth is s
Lk 6:45 out of the good s up in his heart,
 6:45 out of the evil s up in his heart.
Col 1: 5 spring from the hope s up for you

STOREHOUSE HOUSE
Dt 28:12 the heavens, the s of his bounty,
Mal 3:10 Bring the whole tithe into the s,

STOREHOUSES HOUSE
Job 38:22 "Have you entered the s of the snow
 or seen the s of the hail,
Ps 33: 7 sea into jars; he puts the deep into s.
 135: 7 and brings out the wind from his s.
Isa 39: 2 showed them what was in his s—

STOREROOM* ROOM
Mt 13:52 his s new treasures as well as old."
Lk 12:24 sow or reap, they have no s or barn;

STORES STORE
Pr 6: 8 yet it s its provisions in summer
Lk 12:21 it will be with whoever s up things

STORIES*
2Pe 1:16 we did not follow cleverly devised s
 2: 3 will exploit you with fabricated s.

STORING* STORE
Ecc 2:26 s up wealth to hand it over
Ro 2: 5 you are s up wrath against yourself

STORM
Ex 9:24 It was the worst s in all the land
Job 38: 1 LORD spoke to Job out of the s.
 40: 6 LORD spoke to Job out of the s:
Ps 107:29 He stilled the s to a whisper;
Isa 25: 4 a shelter from the s and a shade
Jer 30:23 the s of the LORD will burst
Jnh 1:12 is my fault that this great s has come
Na 1: 3 way is in the whirlwind and the s,
Lk 8:24 the s subsided, and all was calm.

STRAIGHT STRAIGHTEN,
 STRAIGHTENED
Ps 27:11 lead me in a s path because of my
 107: 7 He led them by a s way to a city
Pr 2:13 who have left the s paths to walk
 3: 6 him, and he will make your paths s.
 4:11 wisdom and lead you along s paths
 4:25 Let your eyes look s ahead;
 5: 5 her steps lead s to the grave.
 11: 5 the blameless makes their paths s,
 15:21 has understanding keeps a s course.
Isa 40: 3 make s in the desert a highway
Mt 3: 3 the Lord, make s paths for him.' "
Lk 3: 5 The crooked roads shall become s,
Jn 1:23 'Make s the way for the Lord.' "
2Pe 2:15 They have left the s way

STRAIGHTEN STRAIGHT
Ecc 7:13 Who can s what he has made

STRAIGHTENED STRAIGHT
Ecc 1:15 What is crooked cannot be s;
Lk 13:13 her, and immediately she s

STRAIN* STRAINING
Ex 18:23 you will be able to stand the s,
Mt 23:24 You s out a gnat but swallow

STRAINING STRAIN
Php 3:13 behind and s toward what is ahead,

STRANGE STRANGER, STRANGER'S, STRANGERS
Ex 3: 3 "I will go over and see this s sight—
Isa 28:11 and s tongues God will speak to this
Eze 3: 5 of obscure speech and s language,
Heb 13: 9 away by all kinds of s teachings.

STRANGER STRANGE
Ge 23: 4 "I am a foreigner and s among you.
Ps 119:19 I am a s on earth; do not hide your
Mt 25:35 I was a s and you invited me in,
Jn 10: 5 But they will never follow a s;
Heb 11: 9 in the promised land like a s

STRANGER'S* STRANGE
Jn 10: 5 they do not recognize a s voice."

STRANGERS STRANGE
Ge 15:13 years your descendants will be s
Lev 25:23 in my land as foreigners and s.
1Ch 16:19 in number, few indeed, and s in it,
Pr 5:17 alone, never to be shared with s.
Heb 11:13 they were foreigners and s on earth.
13: 2 not forget to show hospitality to s,
3Jn 1: 5 even though they are s to you.

STRAPS
Mk 1: 7 the s of whose sandals I am not worthy

STRAW
Ex 5:10 'I will not give you any more s.
Isa 11: 7 and the lion will eat s like the ox.
1Co 3:12 silver, costly stones, wood, hay or s,

STRAY ASTRAY, STRAYED, STRAYS
Ps 119:10 do not let me s from your
Pr 7:25 turn to her ways or s into her paths.
Eze 14:11 of Israel will no longer s from me,

STRAYED STRAY
Ps 44:18 our feet had not s from your path.
119:176 I have s like a lost sheep.
Jer 31:19 After I s, I repented; after I came

STRAYS STRAY
Pr 21:16 Whoever s from the path
Eze 34:16 for the lost and bring back the s.

STREAM STREAMS
1Sa 17:40 chose five smooth stones from the s,
Isa 2: 2 the hills, and all nations will s to it.
Am 5:24 righteousness like a never-failing s!

Mic 4: 1 the hills, and peoples will s to it.

STREAMS STREAM
Ge 2: 6 but s came up from the earth
Dt 10: 7 to Jotbathah, a land with s of water.
Job 6:15 as undependable as intermittent s,
Ps 1: 3 person is like a tree planted by s
42: 1 As the deer pants for s of water,
46: 4 is a river whose s make glad the city
126: 4 Lord, like s in the Negev.
Ecc 1: 7 All s flow into the sea, yet the sea is
Isa 35: 6 in the wilderness and s in the desert.
44: 4 like poplar trees by flowing s.
La 3:48 S of tears flow from my eyes
Mt 7:27 The rain came down, the s rose,

STREET STREETS
Mt 6: 5 and on the s corners to be seen
22: 9 So go to the s corners and invite
Rev 21:21 The great s of the city was of gold,
22: 2 the middle of the great s of the city.

STREETS STREET
Ps 144:14 captivity, no cry of distress in our s.
Zec 8: 5 The city s will be filled with boys
Mt 12:19 no one will hear his voice in the s.

STRENGTH STRONG
Ex 15: 2 "The Lord is my s and my
Nu 14:17 may the Lord's s be displayed,
Dt 4:37 by his Presence and his great s,
6: 5 all your soul and with all your s.
33:25 and your s will equal your days.
Jdg 7: 2 me, 'My own s has saved me.'
16:15 told me the secret of your great s."
1Sa 2: 9 "It is not by s that one prevails;
2Sa 22:33 It is God who arms me with s
2Ki 23:25 with all his soul and with all his s,
1Ch 16:11 Look to the Lord and his s;
16:28 ascribe to the Lord glory and s.
29:12 In your hands are s and power
Ne 8:10 the joy of the Lord is your s."
Ps 18: 1 I love you, Lord, my s.
21:13 Be exalted in your s, Lord;
28: 7 The Lord is my s and my shield;
29:11 The Lord gives s to his people;
33:17 despite all its great s it cannot save.
46: 1 God is our refuge and s,
59: 9 You are my s, I watch for you;
59:17 You are my s, I sing praise to you;
65: 6 having armed yourself with s,
73:26 but God is the s of my heart and my
84: 5 Blessed are those whose s is in you,
84: 7 They go from s to s, till each
96: 7 ascribe to the Lord glory and s.
105: 4 Look to the Lord and his s;
118:14 The Lord is my s and my
147:10 pleasure is not in the s of the horse,
Pr 24: 5 who have knowledge muster their s.
30:25 Ants are creatures of little s,
31:25 She is clothed with s and dignity;
Ecc 9:16 I said, "Wisdom is better than s."
Isa 12: 2 himself, is my s and my defense;
31: 1 and in the great s of their horsemen,
40:26 of his great power and mighty s,

Isa 40:31 in the LORD will renew their s.
63: 1 forward in the greatness of his s?
Jer 9:23 the strong boast of their s or the rich
Mic 5: 4 his flock in the s of the LORD,
Hab 3:19 The Sovereign LORD is my s;
Mk 12:30 all your mind and with all your s.'
1Co 1:25 of God is stronger than human s.
Eph 1:19 power is the same as the mighty s
Php 4:13 all this through him who gives me s.
2Ti 4:17 stood at my side and gave me s,
Heb 11:34 whose weakness was turned to s;
1Pe 4:11 do so with the s God provides,
Rev 3: 8 I know that you have little s,
5:12 wealth and wisdom and s and honor
7:12 power and s be to our God for ever

STRENGTHEN STRONG
Jdg 16:28 God, s me just once more, and let
2Ch 16: 9 to s those whose hearts are fully
Ps 89:21 surely my arm will s him.
119:28 s me according to your word.
Isa 35: 3 S the feeble hands, steady the knees
41:10 I will s you and help you;
Eze 34:16 bind up the injured and s the weak,
Zec 10:12 I will s them in the LORD
Lk 22:32 have turned back, s your brothers."
Ac 15:32 to encourage and s the believers.
Eph 3:16 of his glorious riches he may s you
1Th 3:13 May he s your hearts so that you
2Th 2:17 hearts and s you in every good deed
Heb 12:12 s your feeble arms and weak knees.

STRENGTHENED STRONG
Job 4: 3 many, how you have s feeble hands.
Eze 34: 4 You have not s the weak or healed
Lk 22:43 heaven appeared to him and s him.
Ac 16: 5 So the churches were s in the faith
Col 1:11 being s with all power according
2: 7 s in the faith as you were taught,
Heb 13: 9 good for our hearts to be s by grace,

STRENGTHENING STRONG
1Co 14: 3 speaks to people for their s,

STRENUOUSLY*
Col 1:29 To this end I s contend with all

STRETCH OUTSTRETCHED, STRETCHED, STRETCHES
Ex 3:20 So I will s out my hand and strike
14:16 and s out your hand over the sea
Ps 138: 7 You s out your hand against
Zep 1: 4 "I will s out my hand against Judah
Mk 3: 5 said to the man, "S out your hand."
Ac 4:30 S out your hand to heal and perform

STRETCHED STRETCH
Ex 14:21 Moses s out his hand over the sea,
2Sa 24:16 When the angel s out his hand
1Ki 13: 4 the hand he s out toward the man
Isa 45:12 My own hands s out the heavens;
Jer 10:12 and s out the heavens by his

STRETCHES STRETCH
Ps 104: 2 he s out the heavens like a tent

Zec 12: 1 The LORD, who s out the heavens,

STRICKEN STRIKE
Isa 53: 4 him punished by God, s by him,

STRICT STRICTEST, STRICTLY
Mk 3:12 But he gave them s orders not to tell
Ac 5:28 "We gave you s orders not to teach
1Co 9:25 in the games goes into s training.

STRICTEST* STRICT
Ac 26: 5 that I conformed to the s sect of our

STRICTLY* STRICT
Lk 9:21 Jesus s warned them not to tell this
Jas 3: 1 who teach will be judged more s.

STRIFE STRIVE
Pr 13:10 Where there is s, there is pride,
17: 1 than a house full of feasting, with s.
18: 6 The lips of fools bring them s,
20: 3 It is to one's honor to avoid s,
22:10 out the mocker, and out goes s;
23:29 Who has s? Who has complaints?
30:33 so stirring up anger produces s."
Ro 1:29 envy, murder, s, deceit and malice.
1Ti 6: 4 about words that result in envy, s,

STRIKE STRICKEN, STRIKES, STROKE, STRUCK
Ge 3:15 your head, and you will s his heel."
Ex 3:20 s the Egyptians with all the wonders
12:12 and s down every firstborn of both
17: 6 S the rock, and water will come
Ps 91:12 you will not s your foot against
Isa 11: 4 He will s the earth with the rod
Zec 13: 7 "S the shepherd, and the sheep will
Mal 4: 6 s the land with total destruction."
Mt 4: 6 you will not s your foot against
Mk 14:27 " 'I will s the shepherd,
1Co 9:27 I s a blow to my body and make it
Rev 11: 6 and to s the earth with every kind
19:15 with which to s down the nations.

STRIKES STRIKE
Ex 21:12 "Anyone who s a person

STRINGED
Ge 4:21 father of all who play s instruments

STRIPPED STRIPS
Ge 37:23 his brothers, they s him of his robe—
Ex 33: 6 So the Israelites s off their
Isa 20: 3 as my servant Isaiah has gone s
Mt 27:28 They s him and put a scarlet robe
Ac 16:22 the magistrates ordered them to be s

STRIPS STRIPPED
Jn 11:44 and feet wrapped with s of linen,
20: 5 in at the s of linen lying there

STRIVE* STRIFE, STRIVING
Ac 24:16 So I s always to keep my
2Co 13:11 S for full restoration, encourage one
1Ti 4:10 That is why we labor and s,
1Th 5:15 always s to do what is good for each

STRIVING STRIVE
Php   1:27   s together as one for the faith

STROKE STRIKE
Mt   5:18   letter, not the least s of a pen,
Lk   16:17   than for the least s of a pen to drop

STRONG STRENGTH,
STRENGTHEN, STRENGTHENED, STRENGTHENING, STRONGER
Nu   24:18   be conquered, but Israel will grow s.
Dt   3:24   your greatness and your s hand.
      31: 6   Be s and courageous. Do not be
Jos   1: 6   Be s and courageous, because you
      10:25   Be s and courageous.
      23: 6   "Be very s; be careful to obey all
Jdg   5:21   March on, my soul; be s!
2Sa   10:12   Be s, and let us fight bravely for our
1Ki   2: 2   "So be s, act like a man,
1Ch   22:13   Be s and courageous.
      28:20   his son, "Be s and courageous,
2Ch   32: 7   "Be s and courageous. Do not be
Ps   24: 8   The LORD s and mighty,
      31: 2   of refuge, a s fortress to save me.
      35:10   the poor from those too s for them,
      140: 7   Sovereign LORD, my s deliverer,
Pr   31:17   her arms are s for her tasks.
Ecc   9:11   not to the swift or the battle to the s,
SS   8: 6   for love is as s as death, its jealousy
Isa   35: 4   fearful hearts, "Be s, do not fear;
      53:12   he will divide the spoils with the s,
Jer   9:23   or the s boast of their strength
      50:34   Yet their Redeemer is s;
Eze   3:14   with the s hand of the LORD
Da   2:40   will be a fourth kingdom, s as iron—
Joel   3:10   Let the weakling say, "I am s!"
Hag   2: 4   But now be s, Zerubbabel,'
      2: 4   'Be s, Joshua son of Jozadak,
      2: 4   Be s, all you people of the land,'
Zec   8: 9   'Let your hands be s so
Mt   12:29   can anyone enter a s man's house
      12:29   unless he first ties up the s man?
Lk   1:80   child grew and became s in spirit;
      2:40   And the child grew and became s;
Ro   15: 1   We who are s ought to bear
1Co   1:27   things of the world to shame the s.
      16:13   in the faith; be courageous; be s.
2Co   12:10   For when I am weak, then I am s.
Eph   6:10   be s in the Lord and in his mighty
2Ti   2: 1   be s in the grace that is in Christ
1Pe   5:10   himself restore you and make you s,

STRONGER STRONG
Nu   14:12   a nation greater and s than they."
Dt   7: 1   nations larger and s than you—
2Sa   3: 1   David grew s and s, while the house
1Co   1:25   of God is s than human strength.

STRONGHOLD STRONGHOLDS
1Sa   22: 4   him as long as David was in the s.
Ps   9: 9   oppressed, a s in times of trouble.
      18: 2   and the horn of my salvation, my s.
      27: 1   The LORD is the s of my life—
      52: 7   man who did not make God his s

Ps   144: 2   my fortress, my s and my deliverer,
Pr   12:12   The wicked desire the s of evildoers,

STRONGHOLDS STRONGHOLD
Zep   3: 6   their s are demolished.
2Co   10: 4   have divine power to demolish s.

STRUCK STRIKE
Ex   12:29   midnight the LORD s down all
Nu   20:11   and s the rock twice with his staff.
1Sa   17:49   and s the Philistine on the forehead.
Ps   78:20   True, he s the rock, and water
Da   2:34   It s the statue on its feet of iron
Zec   13: 8   "two-thirds will be s down
Mk   14:65   him, s him with their fists, and said,
Ac   23: 3   law by commanding that I be s!"

STRUCTURE
1Ch   29: 1   because this palatial s is not for man

STRUGGLE STRUGGLED
Ro   15:30   join me in my s by praying to God
Eph   6:12   For our s is not against flesh
Heb   12: 4   In your s against sin, you have not

STRUGGLED STRUGGLE
Ge   32:28   because you have s with God
Hos   12: 3   as a man he s with God.

STUBBLE
Ob   1:18   Esau will be s, and they will set him
Na   1:10   they will be consumed like dry s.
Mal   4: 1   and every evildoer will be s,

STUBBORN STUBBORNLY, STUBBORNNESS
Lev   26:19   I will break down your s pride
Ps   78: 8   a s and rebellious generation,
Mk   3: 5   deeply distressed at their s hearts,

STUBBORNLY STUBBORN
Ex   13:15   When Pharaoh s refused to let us

STUBBORNNESS STUBBORN
Dt   9:27   Overlook the s of this people,
Jer   3:17   No longer will they follow the s
Ro   2: 5   But because of your s and your

STUDENT* STUDY
1Ch   25: 8   teacher as well as s, cast lots
Mt   10:24   "The s is not above the teacher,
Lk   6:40   The student is not above the teacher,

STUDENTS* STUDY
Mt   10:25   It is enough for s to be like their

STUDIED* STUDY
Ac   22: 3   I s under Gamaliel and was

STUDY* STUDENT, STUDENTS, STUDIED
Ezr   7:10   Ezra had devoted himself to the s
Ecc   1:13   I applied my mind to s
      12:12   end, and much s wearies the body.
Jn   5:39   You s the Scriptures diligently

STUMBLE STUMBLED, STUMBLES, STUMBLING

Ps 37:24 though he may s, he will not fall,
   119:165 law, and nothing can make them s.
Pr   3:23 in safety, and your foot will not s.
     24:17 when they s, do not let your heart
Isa   8:14 be a stone that causes people to s
Jer 13:16 before your feet s on the darkening
     31: 9 a level path where they will not s,
Eze   7:19 for it has caused them to s into sin.
Da   11:35 Some of the wise will s, so that they
Hos 14: 9 them, but the rebellious s in them.
Mal   2: 8 teaching have caused many to s;
Mt   5:29 If your right eye causes you to s,
     11: 6 Blessed is anyone who does not s
     18: 6 to s, it would be better for them
Mk   9:43 If your hand causes you to s, cut it
Lk   17: 1 that cause people to s are bound
Jn   11: 9 who walks in the daytime will not s,
     11:10 a person walks at night that they s,
Ro   9:33 Zion a stone that causes people to s
     11:11 Did they s so as to fall beyond
     14:20 that causes someone else to s.
1Co 10:32 Do not cause anyone to s,
Jas   3: 2 We all s in many ways.
1Pe   2: 8 "A stone that causes people to s
      2: 8 They s because they disobey
2Pe   1:10 do these things, you will never s,
1Jn   2:10 is nothing in them to make them s.

STUMBLED STUMBLE

Ps   17: 5 to your paths; my feet have not s.
Ro   9:32 They s over the stumbling stone.

STUMBLES STUMBLE

Jas   2:10 yet s at just one point is guilty

STUMBLING STUMBLE

Lev 19:14 or put a s block in front of the blind,
Ps   56:13 me from death and my feet from s,
Eze 14: 3 and put wicked s blocks before their
Mt   16:23 You are a s block to me; you do not
Ro   9:32 They stumbled over the s stone.
     11: 9 a s block and a retribution for them.
     14:13 up your mind not to put any s block
1Co   1:23 a s block to Jews and foolishness
      8: 9 rights does not become a s block
2Co   6: 3 We put no s block in anyone's path,
Jude 1:24 him who is able to keep you from s

STUMP

Isa   6:13 so the holy seed will be the s
     11: 1 will come up from the s of Jesse;

STUPID STUPIDITY

Pr   12: 1 but whoever hates correction is s.
Ecc 10: 3 and show everyone how s they are.
2Ti   2:23 to do with foolish and s arguments,

STUPIDITY* STUPID

Ecc   7:25 to understand the s of wickedness

STUPOR

Ro   11: 8 "God gave them a spirit of s,

SUBDUE SUBDUED, SUBDUES

Ge   1:28 fill the earth and s it.
1Ch 17:10 I will also s all your enemies.

SUBDUED SUBDUE

Jos 10:40 So Joshua s the whole region,
Ps   47: 3 He s nations under us,

SUBDUES SUBDUE

Ps   18:47 me, who s nations under me,

SUBJECT SUBJECTED

Dt   20:11 people in it shall be s to forced labor
Jdg   1:30 Zebulun did s them to forced labor.
Mt   5:22 or sister will be s to judgment.
      9:20 then a woman who had been s
1Co 14:32 of prophets are s to the control
     15:28 the Son himself will be made s
Titus 2: 5 and to be s to their husbands,
      2: 9 Teach slaves to be s to their masters
      3: 1 Remind the people to be s to rulers
Heb   2: 8 left nothing that is not s to them.

SUBJECTED SUBJECT

Ro   8:20 For the creation was s to frustration,
Heb   2: 5 to angels that he has s the world

SUBMISSION SUBMIT

1Co 14:34 but must be in s, as the law says.
1Ti   2:11 should learn in quietness and full s.
Heb   5: 7 was heard because of his reverent s.

SUBMISSIVE* SUBMIT

Jas   3:17 considerate, s, full of mercy

SUBMIT SUBMISSION, SUBMISSIVE, SUBMITS, SUBMITTED

2Ch 30: 8 s to the LORD.
Ps   81:11 Israel would not s to me.
Pr   3: 6 in all your ways s to him, and he
Lk   10:17 even the demons s to us in your
Ro   8: 7 it does not s to God's law, nor can it
     13: 5 it is necessary to s to the authorities,
1Co 16:16 to s to such people and to everyone
Eph   5:21 S to one another out of reverence
Col   3:18 s yourselves to your husbands, as is
Heb 12: 9 How much more should we s
     13:17 your leaders and s to their authority,
Jas   4: 7 S yourselves, then, to God.
1Pe   2:13 S yourselves for the Lord's sake
      3: 1 the same way s yourselves to your
      5: 5 s yourselves to your elders.

SUBMITS* SUBMIT

Eph   5:24 Now as the church s to Christ,

SUBMITTED SUBMIT

1Pe   3: 5 They s themselves to their own

SUBTRACT*

Dt   4: 2 command you and do not s from it,

SUCCEED SUCCESS, SUCCESSFUL, SUCCESSOR

2Sa   7:12 will raise up your offspring to s you,

1Ki 22:22 " 'You will s in enticing him,'
Ps 20: 4 heart and make all your plans s.
Pr 15:22 but with many advisers they s.
    21:30 plan that can s against the LORD.
Ecc 11: 6 for you do not know which will s,

SUCCESS SUCCEED

Ge 39:23 and gave him s in whatever he did.
1Sa 18:14 In everything he did he had great s,
1Ch 12:18 S, s to you, and s to those who help
    22:13 you will have s if you are careful
2Ch 26: 5 the LORD, God gave him s.
Ne   2:20 "The God of heaven will give us s.
Ps 118:25 LORD, grant us s!
Pr   2: 7 He holds s in store for the upright,
Ecc 10:10 is needed, but skill will bring s.

SUCCESSFUL SUCCEED

Ge 24:12 make me s today, and show
Jos 1: 7 that you may be s wherever you go.
2Ki 18: 7 he was s in whatever he undertook.
2Ch 20:20 in his prophets and you will be s."

SUCCESSOR SUCCEED

1Ki 2: 4 never fail to have a s on the throne
     8:25 fail to have a s to sit before me
     9: 5 never fail to have a s on the throne

SUCH

Ex 32:21 that you led them into s great sin?"
Lev 25:21 I will send you s a blessing
Ps 139: 6 S knowledge is too wonderful
Jer 5: 9 avenge myself on s a nation as this?
Mt   8:10 anyone in Israel with s great faith.
Mk 13: 7 S things must happen, but the end is
Lk 12:30 pagan world runs after all s things,
Jn   9:16 can a sinner perform s signs?"
1Co 9:24 Run in s a way as to get the prize.
2Co 3: 4 S confidence we have through
Heb 7:26 S a high priest truly meets our
    12: 3 him who endured s opposition
1Jn 2:22 S a person is the antichrist—
2Jn 1: 7 Any s person is the deceiver
3Jn 1: 8 show hospitality to s people so

SUDDEN SUDDENLY

Lev 26:16 I will bring on you s terror,
Dt 28:20 come to s ruin because of the evil
Pr   3:25 Have no fear of s disaster

SUDDENLY SUDDEN

Ps 73:19 How s are they destroyed,
Mal 3: 1 s the Lord you are seeking will
Mt 28: 9 S Jesus met them.
Mk 13:36 If he comes s, do not let him find
Ac   9: 3 s a light from heaven flashed around
1Th 5: 3 destruction will come on them s,

SUE*

Mt   5:40 if anyone wants to s you and take

SUFFER LONG-SUFFERING,
SUFFERED, SUFFERING,
SUFFERINGS, SUFFERS

Job 36:15 But those who s he delivers in their

Ps 16: 4 who run after other gods will s more
Pr   9:12 you are a mocker, you alone will s.
Isa 53:10 to crush him and cause him to s,
Mk   8:31 the Son of Man must s many things
Lk 22:15 this Passover with you before I s.
    24:26 the Messiah have to s these things
    24:46 The Messiah will s and rise
Ac   3:18 saying that his Messiah would s.
1Co 3:15 the builder will s loss but yet will be
2Co 1: 6 of the same sufferings we s.
Php 1:29 believe in him, but also to s for him,
Heb 9:26 to s many times since the creation
1Pe 3:17 to s for doing good than for doing
     4:16 if you s as a Christian, do not be
Rev 2:10 you will s persecution for ten days.

SUFFERED SUFFER

Isa 53:11 After he has s, he will see the light
Mk   5:26 She had s a great deal under the care
Heb 2: 9 glory and honor because he s death,
     2:10 salvation perfect through what he s.
     2:18 Because he himself s when he was
     5: 8 learned obedience from what he s
1Pe 2:21 called, because Christ s for you,
     4: 1 since Christ s in his body,

SUFFERING SUFFER

Ex   3: 7 and I am concerned about their s.
Job 2:13 they saw how great his s was.
Ps 22:24 or scorned the s of the afflicted one;
    119:50 My comfort in my s is this:
Isa 53: 3 a man of s, and familiar with pain.
La   1:12 Is any s like my s that was inflicted
Mt   4:24 diseases, those s severe pain,
     8: 6 lies at home paralyzed, s terribly."
    15:22 is demon-possessed and s terribly."
    17:15 "He has seizures and is s greatly.
Ac   5:41 been counted worthy of s disgrace
Ro   5: 3 know that s produces perseverance;
2Ti 1: 8 join with me in s for the gospel,
     2: 3 Join with me in s, like a good
Heb 13: 3 as if you yourselves were s.
Jas 5:10 example of patience in the face of s,

SUFFERINGS SUFFER

Ro   5: 3 but we also glory in our s,
     8:18 that our present s are not worth
2Co 1: 5 share abundantly in the s of Christ,
     1: 7 know that just as you share in our s,
Php 3:10 and participation in his s,
1Pe 1:11 he predicted the s of the Messiah
     4:13 as you participate in the s of Christ,
     5: 9 is undergoing the same kind of s.

SUFFERS* SUFFER

Job 15:20 his days the wicked man s torment,
Pr 13:20 for a companion of fools s harm.
1Co 12:26 If one part s, every part s with it;
1Pe 4: 1 whoever s in the body is done with sin.

SUFFICIENT

2Co 12: 9 said to me, "My grace is s for you,

SUITABLE

Ge   2:18 I will make a helper s for him."

SUKKOTH
Ge 33:17 That is why the place is called S.
Jdg 8:16 and taught the men of S a lesson

SULFUR
Ge 19:24 the LORD rained down burning s
Ps 11: 6 will rain fiery coals and burning s;
Lk 17:29 fire and s rained down from heaven
Rev 9:17 mouths came fire, smoke and s.
14:10 with burning s in the presence
19:20 alive into the fiery lake of burning s.
20:10 thrown into the lake of burning s,
21: 8 to the fiery lake of burning s.

SUMMED* SUMS
Ro 13: 9 be, are s up in this one command:

SUMMER
Pr 6: 8 yet it stores its provisions in s
Mk 13:28 come out, you know that s is near.

SUMMON SUMMONS
Ps 68:28 S your power, God; show us your
Isa 45: 4 I s you by name and bestow on you

SUMMONS SUMMON
Ps 50: 1 s the earth from the rising of the sun
Isa 45: 3 God of Israel, who s you by name.

SUMS* SUMMED
Mt 7:12 to you, for this s up the Law

SUN SUNLIGHT, SUNRISE, SUNSET
Jos 10:13 So the s stood still, and the moon
Jdg 5:31 may all who love you be like the s
Ps 72: 5 May he endure as long as the s,
84:11 For the LORD God is a s
113: 3 of the s to the place where it sets,
121: 6 the s will not harm you by day,
136: 8 the s to govern the day,
148: 3 Praise him, s and moon;
Pr 4:18 the righteous is like the morning s,
Ecc 1: 9 there is nothing new under the s.
SS 6:10 bright as the s, majestic as the stars
Isa 60:19 The s will no more be your light
Joel 2:31 The s will be turned to darkness
3:15 The s and moon will be darkened,
Mic 3: 6 The s will set for the prophets,
Mal 4: 2 the s of righteousness will rise
Mt 5:45 He causes his s to rise on the evil
13:43 the righteous will shine like the s
17: 2 His face shone like the s, and his
Mk 13:24 distress, " 'the s will be darkened,
Lk 1:78 which the rising s will come to us
23:45 for the s stopped shining.
Ac 2:20 The s will be turned to darkness
7:42 them over to the worship of the s,
Eph 4:26 Do not let the s go down while you
Rev 1:16 His face was like the s shining in all
8:12 and a third of the s was struck,
9: 2 The s and sky were darkened
10: 1 his face was like the s, and his legs
12: 1 a woman clothed with the s,
21:23 The city does not need the s

Rev 22: 5 light of a lamp or the light of the s,

UNDER THE SUN Ecc 1:3, 9, 14; 2:11, 17, 18, 19, 20, 22; 3:16; 4:1, 3, 7, 15; 5:13, 18; 6:1, 12; 8:9, 15, 15, 17; 9:3, 6, 9, 9, 11, 13; 10:5

SUNG SING
Mt 26:30 When they had s a hymn, they went

SUNLIGHT SUN
Zec 14: 6 day there will be neither s nor cold,

SUNRISE SUN
2Sa 23: 4 light of morning at s on a cloudless
Hab 3: 4 His splendor was like the s;

SUNSET SUN
Ex 17:12 that his hands remained steady till s.
22:26 cloak as a pledge, return it by s,
Dt 24:15 them their wages each day before s,

SUPER-APOSTLES* APOSTLE
2Co 11: 5 in the least inferior to those "s."
12:11 not in the least inferior to the "s,"

SUPERIOR*
Da 8:25 and he will consider himself s.
Ro 2:18 what is s because you are instructed
11:18 to be s to those other branches.
Heb 1: 4 So he became as much s
1: 4 as the name he has inherited is s
8: 6 ministry Jesus has received is as s
8: 6 he is mediator is s to the old one,

SUPERSTITIONS*
Isa 2: 6 They are full of s from the East;

SUPPER
Lk 22:20 after the s he took the cup, saying,
1Co 11:25 way, after s he took the cup, saying,
Rev 19: 9 to the wedding s of the Lamb!"

SUPPLICATION SUPPLICATIONS
1Ki 8:30 Hear the s of your servant
2Ch 6:24 making s before you in this temple,
Zec 12:10 of Jerusalem a spirit of grace and s.

SUPPLICATIONS* SUPPLICATION
1Ki 8:54 these prayers and s to the LORD,
2Ch 6:21 Hear the s of your servant

SUPPLIED SUPPLY
Ac 20:34 hands of mine have s my own needs
Php 4:18 I am amply s, now that I have

SUPPLIES SUPPLY
Ps 147: 8 he s the earth with rain and makes
2Co 9:10 Now he who s seed to the sower

SUPPLY SUPPLIED, SUPPLIES, SUPPLYING
Lev 26:26 When I cut off your s of bread,
Ps 78:20 Can he s meat for his people?"
2Co 8:14 your plenty will s what they need,
1Th 3:10 and s what is lacking in your faith.

SUPPLYING* SUPPLY
2Co 9:12 you perform is not only s the needs

SUPPORT SUPPORTED, SUPPORTING, SUPPORTS
Jdg 16:26 can feel the pillars that s the temple,
Ps   18:18 disaster, but the LORD was my s.
Ro   11:18 You do not s the root, but the root
1Co   9:12 others have this right of s from you,

SUPPORTED SUPPORT
Ps   94:18 your unfailing love, LORD, s me.
Col   2:19 s and held together by its ligaments

SUPPORTING SUPPORT
Ezr   5: 2 of God were with them, s them.
Eph   4:16 held together by every s ligament,

SUPPORTS SUPPORT
Ro   11:18 support the root, but the root s you.

SUPPRESS*
Ro   1:18 who s the truth by their wickedness,

SUPREMACY* SUPREME
Col   1:18 in everything he might have the s.

SUPREME SUPREMACY
Isa   20: 1 In the year that the s commander,

SURE SURELY
Nu   28:31 Be s the animals are without defect.
     32:23 you may be s that your sin will find
Dt   6:17 Be s to keep the commands
     14:22 Be s to set aside a tenth of all
     23:23 your lips utter you must be s to do,
     29:18 make s there is no root among you
Jos   23:13 you may be s that the LORD your
1Sa 12:24 But be s to fear the LORD
Ps   69:13 answer me with your s salvation.
    132:11 David, a s oath he will not revoke:
Pr   27:23 Be s you know the condition
Isa 28:16 cornerstone for a s foundation;
Eph   5: 5 For of this you can be s:

SURELY SURE
Ge   6:13 I am s going to destroy both them
     18:18 Abraham will s become a great
     22:17 I will s bless you and make your
     28:16 "S the LORD is in this place,
     50:24 But God will s come to your aid
Ex   13:19 said, "God will s come to your aid,
Nu   26:65 told those Israelites they would s die
Jos 10:14 S the LORD was fighting
Job   1:11 he will s curse you to your face."
      2: 5 he will s curse you to your face."
Ps   5:12 S, LORD, you bless the righteous;
     23: 6 S your goodness and love will
     54: 4 S God is my help; the Lord is
     73: 1 S God is good to Israel, to those
     85: 9 S his salvation is near those who
Pr   23:18 There is s a future hope for you,
Isa 12: 2 S God is my salvation; I will trust
     53: 4 S he took up our pain and bore our
Eze 33:15 that person will s live; they will not
Mt   28:20 And s I am with you always,
Mk   14:19 to him, "S you don't mean me?"
     15:39 "S this man was the Son of God!"

Lk   23:47 said, "S this was a righteous man."
2Co   1:18 But as s as God is faithful,

SURFACE
Ge   1: 2 darkness was over the s of the deep,
      7:18 the ark floated on the s of the water.

SURGING
Ex   15: 8 The s waters stood up like a wall;
Ps   89: 9 You rule over the s sea;
Zec 10:11 the s sea will be subdued and all

SURPASS* SURPASSED, SURPASSES, SURPASSING
Pr   31:29 noble things, but you s them all."

SURPASSED* SURPASS
Jn   1:15 me has s me because he was before
      1:30 me has s me because he was before

SURPASSES* SURPASS
Ps 138: 2 solemn decree that it s your fame.
Pr   8:19 what I yield s choice silver.
Mt   5:20 that unless your righteousness s
Eph   3:19 to know this love that s knowledge—

SURPASSING* SURPASS
Ps 150: 2 praise him for his s greatness.
2Co   3:10 now in comparison with the s glory.
      9:14 of the s grace God has given you.
Php   3: 8 a loss because of the s worth

SURPRISE SURPRISED
Ps   35: 8 may ruin overtake them by s—
1Th   5: 4 this day should s you like a thief.

SURPRISED SURPRISE
Jn   3: 7 You should not be s at my saying,
1Pe   4: 4 They are s that you do not join them
      4:12 do not be s at the fiery ordeal
1Jn   3:13 Do not be s, my brothers and sisters,

SURRENDER SURRENDERED
Jer 38:21 But if you refuse to s, this is what

SURRENDERED SURRENDER
Lk   23:25 asked for, and s Jesus to their will.

SURROUND SURROUNDED, SURROUNDING, SURROUNDS
Ps   5:12 you s them with your favor as
     22:12 Many bulls s me; strong bulls
     22:16 Dogs s me, a pack of villains
     32: 7 and s me with songs of deliverance.
     89: 7 more awesome than all who s him.
     97: 2 Clouds and thick darkness s him;
    125: 2 As the mountains s Jerusalem,

SURROUNDED SURROUND
Ge   19: 4 both young and old—s the house.
Jdg 19:22 wicked men of the city s the house.
Eze   1:27 and brilliant light s him.
Lk   21:20 you see Jerusalem being s
Heb 12: 1 since we are s by such a great cloud
Rev 20: 9 and s the camp of God's people,

SURROUNDING SURROUND
Rev   4: 4 S the throne were twenty-four other

SURROUNDS* SURROUND
Ps   32:10 LORD's unfailing love s the one
     89: 8 mighty, and your faithfulness s you.
    125: 2 so the LORD s his people both

SURVEYED*
Ecc   2:11 Yet when I s all that my hands had

SURVIVE SURVIVED, SURVIVES, SURVIVORS
Dt   4:27 few of you will s among the nations
Am   7: 2 How can Jacob s? He is so small!"
      7: 5 How can Jacob s? He is so small!"
Mk   13:20 short those days, no one would s.

SURVIVED SURVIVE
Ex   14:28 into the sea. Not one of them s.
Nu   14:38 Nun and Caleb son of Jephunneh s.
Ne   1: 2 Jewish remnant that had s the exile,

SURVIVES SURVIVE
Isa 37: 4 pray for the remnant that still s."
1Co   3:14 If what has been built s, the builder

SURVIVORS SURVIVE
Isa   1: 9 Almighty had left us some s,
Eze 14:22 Yet there will be some s—

SUSA
Ezr   4: 9 and Babylon, the Elamites of S,
Ne   1: 1 year, while I was in the citadel of S,
Est   1: 2 his royal throne in the citadel of S,

SUSPECTS SUSPICIONS
Nu   5:14 over her husband and he s his wife

SUSPENDS*
Job 26: 7 he s the earth over nothing.

SUSPENSE
Jn   10:24 "How long will you keep us in s?

SUSPICIONS* SUSPECTS
1Ti   6: 4 in envy, strife, malicious talk, evil s

SUSTAIN SUSTAINED, SUSTAINING, SUSTAINS
Ru   4:15 your life and s you in your old age.
Ps   51:12 grant me a willing spirit, to s me.
     55:22 on the LORD and he will s you;
Isa 46: 4 I am he, I am he who will s you.
     46: 4 I will s you and I will rescue you.

SUSTAINED SUSTAIN
Ne   9:21 For forty years you s them

SUSTAINING* SUSTAIN
Heb   1: 3 s all things by his powerful word.

SUSTAINS SUSTAIN
Ps   18:35 shield, and your right hand s me;
    146: 9 the foreigner and s the fatherless
    147: 6 The LORD s the humble but casts
Isa 50: 4 to know the word that s the weary.

SWADDLED, SWADDLING, SWADDLINGBAND (KJV) See WRAPPED IN CLOTHS

SWALLOW SWALLOWED
Nu   16:34 "The earth is going to s us too!"
Ps   21: 9 The LORD will s them up in his
     84: 3 and the s a nest for herself,
Isa 25: 8 he will s up death forever.
Jnh   1:17 provided a huge fish to s Jonah,
Mt   23:24 You strain out a gnat but s a camel.

SWALLOWED SWALLOW
Ge   41: 7 of grain s up the seven healthy,
Nu   16:32 earth opened its mouth and s them
Ps 106:17 The earth opened up and s Dathan;
1Co 15:54 "Death has been s up in victory."
2Co   5: 4 so that what is mortal may be s

SWAYED
Mt   11: 7 A reed s by the wind?
     22:16 You aren't s by others, because you
2Ti   3: 6 and are s by all kinds of evil desires,

SWEAR SWEARING, SWEARS, SWORE, SWORN
Ge   22:16 and said, "I s by myself,
Lev 19:12 " 'Do not s falsely by my name
Jos   2:12 please s to me by the LORD
     23: 7 names of their gods or s by them.
Ps   24: 4 trust in an idol or s by a false god.
Isa 45:23 by me every tongue will s.
Mt   5:34 I tell you, do not s an oath at all:
Heb   6:13 was no one greater for him to s by,
Jas   5:12 my brothers and sisters, do not s—

SWEARING* SWEAR
Jer   5: 2 lives,' still they are s falsely."

SWEARS SWEAR
Zec   5: 3 everyone who s falsely will be
Mt   23:16 'If anyone s by the temple, it means
     23:16 but anyone who s by the gold

SWEAT*
Ge   3:19 the s of your brow you will eat your
Lk   22:44 his s was like drops of blood falling

SWEEP SWEEPS, SWEPT
Ge   18:23 "Will you s away the righteous
Ps   90: 5 Yet you s people away in the sleep
SS   8: 7 rivers cannot s it away.
Lk   15: 8 s the house and search carefully

SWEEPS SWEEP
Pr   1:27 disaster s over you like a whirlwind,
Isa 40:24 a whirlwind s them away like chaff.

SWEET SWEETER, SWEETNESS
Job 20:12 "Though evil is s in his mouth
Ps 119:103 How s are your words to my taste,
Pr   9:17 "Stolen water is s; food eaten
     13:19 A longing fulfilled is s to the soul,
     16:24 s to the soul and healing
     20:17 Food gained by fraud tastes s,
Ecc   5:12 The sleep of a laborer is s,

Isa 5:20 who put bitter for s and s for bitter.
Eze 3: 3 it tasted as s as honey in my mouth.
Rev 10:10 It tasted as s as honey in my mouth,

SWEETER* SWEET
Jdg 14:18 said to him, "What is s than honey?
Ps 19:10 they are s than honey, than honey
    119:103 my taste, s than honey to my mouth!

SWEETNESS* SWEET
SS 4:11 Your lips drop s as the honeycomb,
    5:16 His mouth is s itself;

SWELL
Dt 8: 4 feet did not s during these forty

SWEPT SWEEP
Ge 19:15 you will be s away when the city is
Ex 14:27 and the LORD s them into the sea.
Ps 58: 9 the wicked will be s away.
Mt 12:44 s clean and put in order.
Hos 10: 7 s away like a twig on the surface
Rev 12: 4 Its tail s a third of the stars

SWIFT SWIFTLY
Pr 1:16 into evil, they are s to shed blood.
Ecc 9:11 The race is not to the s or the battle
Isa 59: 7 they are s to shed innocent blood.
Jer 46: 6 "The s cannot flee nor the strong
Ro 3:15 "Their feet are s to shed blood;
2Pe 2: 1 bringing s destruction

SWIFTLY SWIFT
Ps 147:15 to the earth; his word runs s.
Isa 60:22 in its time I will do this s."

SWINDLER* SWINDLERS
1Co 5:11 or slanderer, a drunkard or s.

SWINDLERS* SWINDLERS
1Co 5:10 or the greedy and s, or idolaters.
    6:10 nor slanderers nor s will inherit

SWINE (KJV) See PIG

SWING
Joel 3:13 S the sickle, for the harvest is ripe.

SWIRLED*
2Sa 22: 5 The waves of death s about me;
Jnh 2: 3 seas, and the currents s about me;

SWORD SWORDS
Ge 3:24 and a flaming s flashing back
Ex 18: 4 saved me from the s of Pharaoh."
Lev 26: 7 they will fall by the s before you.
Nu 14: 3 this land only to let us fall by the s?
Dt 32:41 when I sharpen my flashing s
Jos 5:13 of him with a drawn s in his hand.
1Sa 17:45 "You come against me with s
    17:47 here will know that it is not by s
    31: 4 Saul took his own s and fell on it.
2Sa 12:10 the s will never depart from your
1Ch 21:30 he was afraid of the s of the angel
Ne 4:18 the builders wore his s at his side as
Ps 22:20 Deliver me from the s, my precious
    44: 3 by their s that they won the land,

Ps 44: 6 my s does not bring me victory;
    45: 3 Gird your s on your side,
    149: 6 and a double-edged s in their hands,
Pr 5: 4 as gall, sharp as a double-edged s.
Isa 2: 4 will not take up s against nation,
    49: 2 made my mouth like a sharpened s,
Jer 15: 2 those for the s, to the s;
La 1:20 Outside, the s bereaves;
Eze 5: 2 For I will pursue them with drawn s.
Hos 2:18 Bow and s and battle I will abolish
Mic 4: 3 will not take up s against nation,
Mt 10:34 did not come to bring peace, but a s.
    26:52 all who draw the s will die by the s.
Lk 2:35 a s will pierce your own soul too."
Ac 12: 2 of John, to death with the s.
Ro 13: 4 for rulers do not bear the s for no
Eph 6:17 of salvation and the s of the Spirit,
Heb 4:12 Sharper than any double-edged s,
    11:34 and escaped the edge of the s;
    11:37 they were killed by the s.
Rev 1:16 mouth was a sharp, double-edged s.
    6: 4 To him was given a large s.
    13:14 the beast who was wounded by the s
    19:15 of his mouth is a sharp s

PUT ... TO THE SWORD See PUT

SWORDS SWORD
Pr 12:18 words of the reckless pierce like s,
Ps 37:15 their s will pierce their own hearts,
    57: 4 arrows, whose tongues are sharp s.
    64: 3 They sharpen their tongues like s
Isa 2: 4 They will beat their s
Joel 3:10 Beat your plowshares into s
Mk 14:48 "that you have come out with s

SWORE SWEAR
Ge 26: 3 and will confirm the oath I s to your
Ex 6: 8 to the land I s with uplifted hand
    32:13 to whom you s by your own self:
Nu 14:30 of you will enter the land I s
Dt 6:10 into the land he s to your fathers,
Ps 89:49 in your faithfulness you s to David?
    132:11 The LORD s an oath to David,
Lk 1:73 the oath he s to our father Abraham:
Heb 6:13 him to swear by, he s by himself,
Rev 10: 6 And he s by him who lives for ever

SWORN SWEAR
Jos 21:43 gave Israel all the land he had s
Ps 89:35 for all, I have s by my holiness—
    110: 4 The LORD has s and will not
Jer 32:22 You gave them this land you had s
Eze 20:42 the land I had s with uplifted hand
Heb 7:21 "The Lord has s and will not

SYCAMORE-FIG FIG
Am 7:14 and I also took care of s trees.
Lk 19: 4 and climbed a s tree to see him,

SYCHAR*
Jn 4: 5 came to a town in Samaria called S,

SYMBOL* SYMBOLIC,
SYMBOLIZES, SYMBOLS
Ex 13:16 and a s on your forehead

Nu   6: 7 because the s of their dedication

SYMBOLIC* SYMBOL
Zec   3: 8 who are men s of things to come:

SYMBOLIZES* SYMBOL
Nu   6: 9 the hair that s their dedication,
       6:18 off the hair that s their dedication.
       6:19 off the hair that s their dedication,
1Pe   3:21 this water s baptism that now saves

SYMBOLS* SYMBOL
Dt   6: 8 Tie them as s on your hands
      11:18 tie them as s on your hands and bind
Isa   8:18 and s in Israel from the LORD
      57: 8 you have put your pagan s.

SYMPATHETIC* SYMPATHY
1Pe   3: 8 like-minded, be s, love one another,

SYMPATHIZE* SYMPATHY
Job   2:11 by agreement to go and s with him

SYMPATHY SYMPATHETIC, SYMPATHIZE
Ps   69:20 I looked for s, but there was none,

SYNAGOGUE SYNAGOGUES
Mt   13:54 began teaching the people in their s,
Lk   4:16 the Sabbath day he went into the s,
       8:41 a man named Jairus, a s leader,
Jn   16: 2 They will put you out of the s;
Ac   13:14 On the Sabbath they entered the s
      14: 1 went as usual into the Jewish s.
      17: 2 Paul went into the s, and on three
      18: 4 Every Sabbath he reasoned in the s,
      18:26 He began to speak boldly in the s.
Rev   2: 9 and are not, but are a s of Satan.
       3: 9 those who are of the s of Satan,

SYNAGOGUES SYNAGOGUE
Mt   4:23 teaching in their s,
       6: 2 as the hypocrites do in the s
      10:17 councils and be flogged in the s.
Lk   12:11 "When you are brought before s,
Jn   18:20 "I always taught in s
Ac   13: 5 the word of God in the Jewish s.

SYNTYCHE*
Php   4: 2 and I plead with S to be of the same

SYRIA SYRIAN
Mt   4:24 News about him spread all over S,
Gal   1:21 Then I went to S and Cilicia.

SYRIAN* SYRIA
Mk   7:26 was a Greek, born in S Phoenicia.
Lk   4:27 only Naaman the S."

SWORE SWEAR
Ge   26: 3 and will confirm the oath I s to your
Ex   6: 8 to the land I s with uplifted hand
      32:13 to whom you s by your own self:
Nu   14:30 of you will enter the land I s
Dt   6:10 into the land he s to your fathers,
Ps   89:49 in your faithfulness you s to David?
     132:11 The LORD s an oath to David,

Lk   1:73 the oath he s to our father Abraham:
Heb   6:13 him to swear by, he s by himself,
Rev 10: 6 And he s by him who lives for ever

SWORN SWEAR
Jos 21:43 gave Israel all the land he had s
Ps   89:35 for all, I have s by my holiness—
     110: 4 The LORD has s and will not
Jer 32:22 You gave them this land you had s
Eze 20:42 the land I had s with uplifted hand
Heb   7:21 "The Lord has s and will not

SYCAMORE-FIG FIG
Am   7:14 and I also took care of s trees.
Lk   19: 4 and climbed a s tree to see him,

SYCHAR*
Jn   4: 5 came to a town in Samaria called S,

SYMBOL* SYMBOLIC, SYMBOLIZES, SYMBOLS
Ex   13:16 and a s on your forehead
Nu   6: 7 because the s of their dedication

SYMBOLIC* SYMBOL
Zec   3: 8 who are men s of things to come:

SYMBOLIZES* SYMBOL
Nu   6: 9 the hair that s their dedication,
       6:18 off the hair that s their dedication.
       6:19 off the hair that s their dedication,
1Pe   3:21 this water s baptism that now saves

SYMBOLS* SYMBOL
Dt   6: 8 Tie them as s on your hands
      11:18 tie them as s on your hands and bind
Isa   8:18 and s in Israel from the LORD
      57: 8 you have put your pagan s.

SYMPATHETIC* SYMPATHY
1Pe   3: 8 like-minded, be s, love one another,

SYMPATHIZE* SYMPATHY
Job   2:11 by agreement to go and s with him

SYMPATHY SYMPATHETIC, SYMPATHIZE
Ps   69:20 I looked for s, but there was none,

SYNAGOGUE SYNAGOGUES
Mt   13:54 began teaching the people in their s,
Lk   4:16 the Sabbath day he went into the s,
       8:41 a man named Jairus, a s leader,
Jn   16: 2 They will put you out of the s;
Ac   13:14 On the Sabbath they entered the s
      14: 1 went as usual into the Jewish s.
      17: 2 Paul went into the s, and on three
      18: 4 Every Sabbath he reasoned in the s,
      18:26 He began to speak boldly in the s.
Rev   2: 9 and are not, but are a s of Satan.
       3: 9 those who are of the s of Satan,

SYNAGOGUES SYNAGOGUE
Mt   4:23 teaching in their s,
       6: 2 as the hypocrites do in the s
      10:17 councils and be flogged in the s.
Lk   12:11 "When you are brought before s,

Jn   18:20 "I always taught in s
Ac   13: 5 the word of God in the Jewish s.

SYNTYCHE*
Php   4: 2 and I plead with S to be of the same

SYRIA SYRIAN
Mt   4:24 News about him spread all over S,
Gal   1:21 Then I went to S and Cilicia.

SYRIAN* SYRIA
Mk   7:26 was a Greek, born in S Phoenicia.
Lk   4:27 only Naaman the S."

T

TABERNACLE TABERNACLES
Ex   25: 9 Make this t and all its furnishings
      38:21 of the materials used for the t, the t
      40:18 When Moses set up the t, he put
      40:34 the glory of the LORD filled the t.
Nu   1:50 They are to carry the t and all its
Heb   8: 2 the true t set up by the Lord,
       9:11 more perfect t that is not made
Rev   15: 5 that is, the t of the covenant law—

TABERNACLES TABERNACLE
Lev   23:34 the LORD's Festival of T begins,
Dt   16:16 of Weeks and the Festival of T.
Zec   14:16 and to celebrate the Festival of T.
Jn   7: 2 the Jewish Festival of T was near,

TABITHA* DORCAS
Disciple, also known as Dorcas, whom Peter
raised from the dead (Ac 9:36–42).

TABLE TABLES
Ex   25:23 "Make a t of acacia wood—
Nu   3:31 care of the ark, the t, the lampstand,
Ps   23: 5 You prepare a t before me
      78:19 "Can God really spread a t
1Co   10:21 have a part in both the Lord's t and
           the t of demons.

TABLES TABLE
Mk   11:15 He overturned the t of the money
Jn   2:15 changers and overturned their t.
Ac   6: 2 word of God in order to wait on t.

TABLET* TABLETS
Pr   3: 3 write them on the t of your heart.
       7: 5 write them on the t of your heart.
Isa   30: 8 write it on a t for them, inscribe it
Lk   1:63 He asked for a writing t,

TABLETS TABLET
Ex   31:18 the t of stone inscribed by the finger
      32:19 and he threw the t out of his hands,
Dt   10: 5 and put the t in the ark I had made,
2Co   3: 3 not on t of stone but on t of human

TAIL TAILS
Dt   28:13 will make you the head, not the t.
Jdg   15: 4 and tied them t to t in pairs.
Rev   12: 4 Its t swept a third of the stars

TAILS* TAIL
Jdg   15: 4 fastened a torch to every pair of t,
Rev   9:10 They had t with stingers,
       9:10 in their t they had power to torment
       9:19 was in their mouths and in their t;
       9:19 for their t were like snakes,

TAKE TAKEN, TAKES, TAKING, TOOK
Ge   15: 7 give you this land to t possession
      22: 2 Then God said, "T your son,
      22:17 Your descendants will t possession
Ex   3: 5 "T off your sandals, for the place
       6: 7 I will t you as my own people, and I
      21:23 injury, you are to t life for life,
      22:22 "Do not t advantage of the widow
      34: 9 sin, and t us as your inheritance."
Lev   10:17 to you to t away the guilt
      25:14 do not t advantage of each other.
Nu   1: 2 "T a census of the whole Israelite
      13:30 go up and t possession of the land,
Dt   1: 8 t possession of the land the LORD
      12:32 do not add to it or t away from it.
      31:26 "T this Book of the Law and place
1Sa   8:11 He will t your sons and make them
1Ki   11:34 I will not t the whole kingdom
      19: 4 "T my life; I am no better than my
1Ch   17:13 I will never t my love away
Job   23:10 But he knows the way that I t;
Ps   2:12 Blessed are all who t refuge in him.
      25:18 my distress and t away all my sins.
      27:14 be strong and t heart and wait
      31:24 Be strong and t heart, all you who
      36: 7 People t refuge in the shadow
      49:17 for they will t nothing with them
      51:11 or t your Holy Spirit from me.
      73:24 afterward you will t me into glory.
      89:33 but I will not t my love from him,
     118: 8 It is better to t refuge in the LORD
     119:43 Never t your word of truth from my
Pr   4: 4 "T hold of my words with all your
      22:23 for the LORD will t up their case
Isa   62: 4 for the LORD will t delight in you,
Jer   51:11 The LORD will t vengeance,
Eze   3:10 t to heart all the words I speak
      33:11 I t no pleasure in the death
Da   8:13 "How long will it t for the vision
      11:36 has been determined must t place.
Hos   14: 2 T words with you and return
Mic   4: 3 Nation will not t up sword against
Mt   1:20 afraid to t Mary home as your wife,
       2:13 "t the child and his mother
       2:20 trying to t the child's life are dead."
       7: 5 first t the plank out of your own
      11:29 T my yoke upon you and learn
      16:24 deny themselves and t up their cross
      17:27 T it and give it to them for my tax
      26:26 to his disciples, saying, "T and eat;
Mk   2: 9 say, 'Get up, t your mat and walk'?
       8:34 deny themselves and t up their cross
      14:36 T this cup from me.
Lk   21: 7 sign that they are about to t place?"
Ac   1:20 and, " 'May another t his place

Ro 12:19 Do not t revenge, my dear friends,
2Co 12: 8 with the Lord to t it away from me.
Eph 6:11 that you can t your stand against
1Ti 3: 5 how can he t care of God's church?)
6:12 T hold of the eternal life
Heb 9:28 sacrificed once to t away the sins
Rev 1: 1 his servants what must soon t place.
4: 1 I will show you what must t place
5: 9 "You are worthy to t the scroll
22:17 let the one who wishes t the free gift

TAKEN TAKE
Ge 2:23 for she was t out of man."
27:36 and now he's t my blessing!"
Lev 6: 4 they have stolen or t by extortion,
Nu 8:16 I have t them as my own in place
19: 3 it is to be t outside the camp
Jos 7:11 They have t some of the devoted
1Sa 10:21 Finally Saul son of Kish was t.
2Sa 7:15 my love will never be t away
12:13 "The LORD has t away your sin.
Ps 31: 1 In you, LORD, I have t refuge;
Ecc 3:14 be added to it and nothing t from it.
Isa 6: 7 your guilt is t away and your sin
Jer 13:17 LORD's flock will be t captive.
38:28 This is how Jerusalem was t:
Da 5: 2 Nebuchadnezzar his father had t
Zec 3: 4 "See, I have t away your sin, and I
Mt 13:12 even what they have will be t
24:40 one will be t and the other left.
26:39 possible, may this cup be t from me.
Lk 24:51 left them and was t up into heaven.
Jn 20:13 "They have t my Lord away,"
Ac 1: 9 he was t up before their very eyes,
Php 3:13 consider myself yet to have t hold
1Ti 3:16 on in the world, was t up in glory.
Heb 11: 5 By faith Enoch was t from this life,
11: 5 because God had t him away."

TAKES TAKE
Lev 24:17 " 'Anyone who t the life
1Ki 20:11 not boast like one who t it off.' "
Ps 34: 8 blessed is the one who t refuge
149: 4 the LORD t delight in his people;
Isa 57: 1 perish, and no one t it to heart;
Na 1: 2 The LORD t vengeance on his foes
Mk 4:15 t away the word that was sown
Lk 6:30 and if anyone t what belongs to you,
Jn 1:29 who t away the sin of the world!
10:18 No one t it from me, but I lay it
Rev 22:19 if anyone t words away from this

TAKING TAKE
Php 2: 7 himself nothing by t the very nature

TALEBEARER (KJV) See GOSSIP, SPREADING SLANDER

TALENT TALENTS
Ex 25:39 A t of pure gold is to be used

TALENTS TALENT
Est 3: 9 I will give ten thousand t of silver

TALES*
1Ti 4: 7 with godless myths and old wives' t;

TALK TALKED, TALKING, TALKS
Dt 6: 7 T about them when you sit at home
Pr 12:13 are trapped by their sinful t, and so
Ro 9:20 a human being, to t back to God?

TALKED TALK
Ge 35:14 the place where God had t with him,
1Co 13:11 When I was a child, I t like a child,

TALKING TALK
Mt 17: 3 them Moses and Elijah, t with Jesus.
Jn 4:27 to find him t with a woman.

TALKS* TALK
Pr 20:19 so avoid anyone who t too much.

TALL TALLER
1Ch 11:23 an Egyptian who was five cubits t.

TALLER TALL
1Sa 9: 2 he was a head t than anyone else.

TAMAR
1. Wife of Judah's sons Er and Onan (Ge 38:1–10). Tricked Judah into fathering children when he refused her his third son (Ge 38:11–30; Mt 1:3).
2. Daughter of David, raped by Amnon (2Sa 13).

TAMARISK
Ge 21:33 Abraham planted a t tree

TAME*
Jas 3: 8 no human being can t the tongue.

TANNER
Ac 9:43 some time with a t named Simon.

TAR
Ge 14:10 Valley of Siddim was full of t pits,

TARES (KJV) See WEEDS

TARGET
Job 16:12 He has made me his t;
La 3:12 and made me the t for his arrows.

TARSHISH
Ps 48: 7 them like ships of T shattered
Isa 60: 9 in the lead are the ships of T,
Jnh 1: 3 from the LORD and headed for T.

TARSUS
Ac 9:11 ask for a man from T named Saul,
11:25 Barnabas went to T to look for Saul,

TASK TASKS
1Ch 29: 1 The t is great, because this palatial
Mk 13:34 each with their assigned t, and tells
Ac 20:24 complete the t the Lord Jesus has
20:24 the t of testifying to the good news
1Co 3: 5 the Lord has assigned to each his t.
2Co 2:16 And who is equal to such a t?
1Ti 3: 1 to be an overseer desires a noble t.

TASKS TASK
Pr   31:17 her arms are strong for her t.

TASSELS
Dt   22:12 Make t on the four corners
Mt   23: 5 and the t on their garments long;

TASTE TASTED, TASTY
Ps   34: 8 T and see that the LORD is good;
119:103 How sweet are your words to my t,
Pr   24:13 from the comb is sweet to your t.
SS   2: 3 shade, and his fruit is sweet to my t.
Mt   16:28 here will not t death before they see
Col   2:21 Do not t! Do not touch!"?
Heb   2: 9 God he might t death for everyone.

TASTED TASTE
Eze   3: 3 it t as sweet as honey in my mouth.
Heb   6: 4 who have t the heavenly gift,
1Pe   2: 3 you have t that the Lord is good.
Rev 10:10 It t as sweet as honey in my mouth,

TASTY TASTE
Ge   27: 4 Prepare me the kind of t food I like

TATTOO*
Lev 19:28 dead or put t marks on yourselves.

TAUGHT TEACH
Dt   4: 5 I have t you decrees and laws as
31:22 that day and t it to the Israelites.
2Ki 17:28 t them how to worship the LORD.
2Ch 17: 9 They t throughout Judah,
Ps 119:102 laws, for you yourself have t me.
Pr   4: 4 Then he t me, and he said to me,
31: 1 inspired utterance his mother t him.
Isa 29:13 human rules they have been t.
40:14 him, and who t him the right way?
54:13 All your children will be t
Hos 11: 3 It was I who t Ephraim to walk,
Mt   7:29 because he t as one who had
Mk   4: 2 He t them many things by parables,
Jn   6:45 'They will all be t by God.'
7:15 learning without having been t?"
Ac   20:20 to you but have t you publicly
1Co   2:13 not in words t us by human wisdom
but in words t by the Spirit,
Gal   1:12 it from any man, nor was I t it;
1Ti   1:20 to Satan to be t not to blaspheme.
4: 1 spirits and things t by demons.
1Jn   2:27 just as it has t you, remain in him.

TAUNT TAUNTS
1Ki 18:27 At noon Elijah began to t them.
Ps 102: 8 All day long my enemies t me;

TAUNTS TAUNT
Ps 119:42 then I can answer anyone who t me,
Eze 36:15 No longer will I make you hear the t

TAX TAXES
2Ch 24: 6 Jerusalem the t imposed by Moses
Mt   5:46 not even the t collectors doing that?
11:19 a friend of t collectors and sinners.'
17:24 your teacher pay the temple t?"
22:17 right to pay the imperial t to Caesar

Lk   18:10 Pharisee and the other a t collector.

TAX COLLECTOR
Da 11:20; Mt 10:3; 18:17; Lk 5:27; 18:10, 11, 13; 19:2

TAX COLLECTORS
Mt 5:46; 9:10, 11; 11:19; 21:31, 32; Mk 2:15, 16, 16; Lk 3:12; 5:29, 30; 7:29, 34; 15:1

TAXES TAX
Ro   13: 7 you owe them: If you owe t, pay t;

TEACH TAUGHT, TEACHER, TEACHERS, TEACHES, TEACHING, TEACHINGS
Ex   4:12 speak and will t you what to say."
18:20 T them his decrees and instructions,
33:13 t me your ways so I may know you
Lev 10:11 and so you can t the Israelites all
Dt   4: 9 T them to your children and to their
6: 1 your God directed me to t you
8: 3 to t you that man does not live
11:19 T them to your children,
1Sa 12:23 I will t you the way that is good
1Ki   8:36 T them the right way to live,
Job   6:24 "T me, and I will be quiet;
21:22 "Can anyone t knowledge to God,
Ps   25: 4 ways, LORD, t me your paths.
32: 8 and t you in the way you should go;
34:11 I will t you the fear of the LORD.
51:13 I will t transgressors your ways,
78: 5 our ancestors to t their children,
90:12 T us to number our days, that we
143:10 T me to do your will, for you are my
Pr   9: 9 t the righteous and they will add
22:17 apply your heart to what I t,
Jer 31:34 No longer will they t their neighbor,
Mic   4: 2 He will t us his ways, so that we
Mt   5: 2 and he began to t them. He said:
Lk   11: 1 "Lord, t us to pray, just as John
12:12 for the Holy Spirit will t you
Jn   14:26 will t you all things and will remind
Ac   5:28 "We gave you strict orders not to t
Ro   2:21 who t others, do you not t
12: 7 if it is teaching, then t;
15: 4 in the past was written to t us,
Col   3:16 dwell among you richly as you t
1Ti   1: 3 not to t false doctrines any longer
2:12 I do not permit a woman to t
3: 2 respectable, hospitable, able to t,
2Ti   2: 2 will also be qualified to t others.
2:24 to everyone, able to t, not resentful.
Titus 2: 1 must t what is appropriate to sound
2:15 then, are the things you should t.
Heb   5:12 to t you the elementary truths
8:11 No longer will they t their neighbor,
Jas   3: 1 that we who t will be judged more
1Jn   2:27 you do not need anyone to t you.

TEACHER TEACH
Ezr   7: 6 He was a t well versed in the Law
Ne   8: 1 They told Ezra the t of the Law
12:36 Ezra the t of the Law led
Ecc   1: 1 The words of the T, son of David,
12: 9 Not only was the T wise, but he

Mt   10:24 "The student is not above the t,
      13:52 "Therefore every t of the law who
      22:36 "T, which is the greatest
      23: 8 called 'Rabbi,' for you have one T,
Lk   6:40 The student is not above the t,
Jn   1:38 said, "Rabbi" (which means "T"),
       3: 2 know that you are a t who has come
      13:14 your Lord and T, have washed your
1Co   1:20 Where is the t of the law?

TEACHER OF THE LAW See LAW

TEACHERS TEACH

Ps   119:99 I have more insight than all my t,
Pr   5:13 I would not obey my t or turn my
Mt   7:29 and not as their t of the law.
Mk   12:38 "Watch out for the t of the law.
Lk   20:46 "Beware of the t of the law.
1Co   12:28 prophets, third t, then miracles,
Eph   4:11 the evangelists, the pastors and t,
2Ti   4: 3 around them a great number of t
Heb   5:12 by this time you ought to be t,
Jas   3: 1 Not many of you should become t,
2Pe   2: 1 as there will be false t among you.
       2: 3 their greed these t will exploit you

TEACHERS OF THE LAW See LAW

TEACHES TEACH

Ps   25: 9 in what is right and t them his way.
      94:10 Does he who t mankind lack
Isa   48:17 God, who t you what is best for you,
Hab   2:18 Or an image that t lies? For the one
Mt   5:19 and t these commands will be called
1Ti   6: 3 If anyone t otherwise and does not
Titus 2:12 It t us to say "No" to ungodliness
1Jn   2:27 But as his anointing t you about all

TEACHING TEACH

Ezr   7:10 to t its decrees and laws in Israel.
Ps   78: 1 My people, hear my t;
Pr   1: 8 and do not forsake your mother's t.
       3: 1 son, do not forget my t, but keep my
       6:23 command is a lamp, this t is a light,
      13:14 The t of the wise is a fountain
Mt   28:20 t them to obey everything I have
Mk   1:27 A new t—and with authority!
      11:18 whole crowd was amazed at his t.
Lk   4:15 He was t in their synagogues,
      19:47 Every day he was t at the temple.
Jn   7:17 out whether my t comes from God
       8:31 "If you hold to my t, you are really
      14:23 who loves me will obey my t.
Ac   2:42 devoted themselves to the apostles' t
       5:42 to house, they never stopped t
Ro   12: 7 if it is t, then teach;
Eph   4:14 there by every wind of t
Col   1:28 and t everyone with all wisdom,
2Th   3: 6 live according to the t you received
1Ti   4:13 of Scripture, to preaching and to t.
       5:17 whose work is preaching and t.
       6: 3 our Lord Jesus Christ and to godly t,
2Ti   2:17 Their t will spread like gangrene.
       3:16 is God-breathed and is useful for t,
Titus 1:11 by t things they ought not to teach—
       2: 7 In your t show integrity,

Heb   5:13 with the t about righteousness.
2Jn   1: 9 in the t has both the Father
       1:10 to you and does not bring this t,
Rev   2:20 By her t she misleads my servants

TEACHINGS TEACH

Pr   7: 2 guard my t as the apple of your eye.
Mt   15: 9 their t are merely human rules.' "
Col   2:22 on merely human commands and t.
2Th   2:15 hold fast to the t we passed
Heb   6: 1 let us move beyond the elementary t
      13: 9 away by all kinds of strange t.

TEAR TEARING, TEARS, TORE, TORN

1Ki   11:13 Yet I will not t the whole kingdom
Ecc   3: 3 a time to t down and a time to build,
Mt   7: 6 feet, and turn and t you to pieces.
Mk   2:21 from the old, making the t worse.
Rev   7:17 God will wipe away every t
      21: 4 'He will wipe every t from their

TEARING TEAR

2Co   10: 8 you up rather than t you down,

TEARS TEAR

Job   12:14 What he t down cannot be rebuilt;
Ps   42: 3 My t have been my food day
     126: 5 Those who sow with t will reap
Pr   15:25 The LORD t down the house
Isa   25: 8 LORD will wipe away the t
Jer   9: 1 water and my eyes a fountain of t!
      31:16 from weeping and your eyes from t,
      50: 4 of Judah together will go in t to seek
La   1:16 I weep and my eyes overflow with t.
Lk   7:38 she began to wet his feet with her t.
2Co   2: 4 anguish of heart and with many t,
Php   3:18 and now tell you again even with t,
Heb   5: 7 and t to the one who could save him

TEETH TOOTH

Nu   11:33 the meat was still between their t
Job   19:20 escaped only by the skin of my t.
Ps   3: 7 break the t of the wicked.
      35:16 they gnashed their t at me.
Jer   31:29 and the children's t are set on edge.'
Da   7: 7 It had large iron t; it crushed
Mt   8:12 will be weeping and gnashing of t."
Ac   7:54 furious and gnashed their t at him.
Rev   9: 8 and their t were like lions' t.

TEKEL*

Da   5:25 MENE, MENE, T, PARSIN
       5:27 T: You have been weighed

TEKOA

2Sa   14: 4 the woman from T went to the king,
Am   1: 1 Amos, one of the shepherds of T—

TELL TELLING, TELLS, TOLD

Ex   6:11 t Pharaoh king of Egypt to let
Nu   22:35 men, but speak only what I t you."
Dt   18:18 He will t them everything I
Jdg   14:12 "Let me t you a riddle,"
Ru   3: 4 He will t you what to do."
1Sa   3:15 He was afraid to t Eli the vision,

2Ch 18:15 I make you swear to **t** me nothing
Ps   5: 6 you destroy those who **t** lies.
     50:12 If I were hungry I would not **t** you,
     66:16 let me **t** you what he has done
     78: 4 we will **t** the next generation
   105: 2 **t** of all his wonderful acts.
Isa 41:23 **t** us what the future holds, so we
Eze 40: 4 **T** the people of Israel everything
Da   2: 4 **T** your servants the dream, and we
Jnh   4:11 people who cannot **t** their right hand
Mt   4: 3 **t** these stones to become bread."
    12:16 He warned them not to **t** others
Jn 20:15 away, **t** me where you have put him,
Ac 13:32 "We **t** you the good news:
1Co 15:51 Listen, I **t** you a mystery:

TRULY I TELL YOU See TRULY

TELLING TELL
Jn 13:19 "I am **t** you now before it happens,

TELLS TELL
Pr 12:17 An honest witness **t** the truth, but a
           false witness **t** lies.
Mt 24:26 "So if anyone **t** you, 'There he is,
Jn 19:35 He knows that he **t** the truth, and he

TEMANITE
Job   2:11 Eliphaz the **T**, Bildad the Shuhite

TEMPER* EVEN-TEMPERED, HOT-TEMPERED, QUICK-TEMPERED
1Sa 20: 7 But if he loses his **t**, you can be sure

TEMPERANCE (KJV) See SELF-CONTROL

TEMPERATE*
1Ti   3: 2 reproach, faithful to his wife, **t**,
      3:11 not malicious talkers but **t**
Titus 2: 2 Teach the older men to be **t**,

TEMPEST
Ps 50: 3 him, and around him a **t** rages.
    55: 8 shelter, far from the **t** and storm."

TEMPLE TEMPLES
Jdg   4:21 She drove the peg through his **t**
    16:30 and down came the **t** on the rulers
1Sa   5: 2 they carried the ark into Dagon's **t**
1Ki   6: 1 began to build the **t** of the LORD.
     6:38 the **t** was finished in all its details
     8:11 the glory of the LORD filled his **t**.
     8:27 How much less this **t** I have built!
2Ki 25: 9 He set fire to the **t** of the LORD,
2Ch 24: 4 to restore the **t** of the LORD.
    36:23 appointed me to build a **t** for him
Ezr   3:12 who had seen the former **t**,
     5: 3 authorized you to rebuild this **t**
     6:15 The **t** was completed on the third
Ps 27: 4 the LORD and to seek him in his **t**.
    30: **T** For the dedication of the **t**.
Isa   6: 1 and the train of his robe filled the **t**.
Jer   7:14 bears my Name, the **t** you trust in,
Eze 10: 4 The cloud filled the **t**, and the court
    43: 4 LORD entered the **t** through

Da   5: 2 had taken from the **t** in Jerusalem,
     9:27 And at the **t** he will set
Mic   4: 1 the LORD's **t** will be established
Hab 2:20 The LORD is in his holy **t**;
Zec   4: 9 have laid the foundation of this **t**;
Mt   4: 5 stand on the highest point of the **t**.
    12: 6 something greater than the **t** is here.
    23:35 whom you murdered between the **t**
    26:61 'I am able to destroy the **t** of God
    27:51 moment the curtain of the **t** was torn
Mk 15:38 The curtain of the **t** was torn in two
Lk 21: 5 about how the **t** was adorned
Jn   2:14 the **t** courts he found people selling
     2:21 the **t** he had spoken of was his body.
Ac   2:46 to meet together in the **t** courts.
     5:42 in the **t** courts and from house
1Co 3:16 that you yourselves are God's **t**
2Co 6:16 For we are the **t** of the living God.
Eph 2:21 rises to become a holy **t** in the Lord.
2Th 2: 4 so that he sets himself up in God's **t**,
Rev 3:12 make a pillar in the **t** of my God.
   11:19 Then God's **t** in heaven was opened,
   11:19 within his **t** was seen the ark of his
   21:22 Almighty and the Lamb are its **t**.

TEMPLE OF ... GOD Jdg 9:27; 2Ki 19:37; 1Ch 28:12, 21; 29:2, 3, 3, 7; 2Ch 3:3; 4:11; 5:14; 7:5; 15:18; 22:12; 23:3, 9; 24:5, 7, 13, 18, 27; 25:24; 28:24; 29:5; 31:13; 32:21; 33:7; 34:8, 9; 36:18; Ezr 1:3, 4, 7; 5:8; 6:3, 7; 7:16, 17, 19, 20, 23; Isa 2:3; 37:38; Da 1:2, 2; 5:3; Mic 4:2; Mt 26:61; 2Co 6:16, 16; Rev 3:12; 11:1

TEMPLE OF THE LORD† 1Ki 3:1; 6:1, 37; 7:12, 40, 45, 51; 8:10, 63, 64; 9:1, 10; 10:5, 12; 12:27; 14:26; 15:15; 2Ki 11:3, 4, 4, 10, 13, 15, 18, 19; 12:4, 9, 9, 10, 11, 12, 13, 16, 18; 14:14; 15:35; 16:8, 14, 18; 18:15, 16; 19:1, 14; 20:5, 8; 21:4, 5; 22:3, 4, 5, 8, 9; 23:2, 2, 4, 6, 7, 11, 12, 24; 24:13, 13; 25:9, 13, 16; 1Ch 6:32; 22:14; 23:4, 24, 28, 32; 24:19; 25:6; 26:12, 22, 27; 28:12, 13, 20; 29:8; 2Ch 3:1; 4:16; 5:1, 13; 7:2, 7, 11, 11; 8:1, 16, 16; 9:4, 11; 12:9; 20:5, 28; 23:5, 6, 12, 14, 18, 20; 24:4, 8, 12, 14, 18; 26:16, 21; 27:2, 3; 28:21; 29:3, 5, 15, 16, 17, 18, 20, 25, 31, 35; 30:1, 15; 31:10, 11, 16; 33:4, 5, 15; 34:8, 14, 15, 17, 30, 30; 36:7, 10, 14; Ezr 1:3, 7; 3:10; Isa 37:1, 14; 38:20, 22; 66:20; Jer 7:4, 4, 4; 20:1; 24:1; 38:14; 52:13, 17, 20; Eze 8:16; 44:4, 5; Hos 9:4; Zec 6:12, 13, 14, 15

TEMPLES TEMPLE
Ac 17:24 does not live in **t** built by human
1Co 6:19 your bodies are **t** of the Holy Spirit,

TEMPORARY
2Co 4:18 since what is seen is **t**, but what is

TEMPT* TEMPTATION, TEMPTED, TEMPTER, TEMPTING
1Co 7: 5 Satan will not **t** you because of your
Jas   1:13 by evil, nor does he **t** anyone;

TEMPTATION* TEMPT
Mt   6:13 And lead us not into **t**, but deliver us
   26:41 pray so that you will not fall into **t**.
Mk 14:38 pray so that you will not fall into **t**.

Lk 11: 4 And lead us not into t.' "
22:40 "Pray that you will not fall into t."
22:46 pray so that you will not fall into t."
1Co 10:13 No t has overtaken you except what
1Ti 6: 9 who want to get rich fall into t

TEMPTED* TEMPT
Mt 4: 1 the wilderness to be t by the devil.
Mk 1:13 forty days, being t by Satan.
Lk 4: 2 for forty days he was t by the devil.
1Co 10:13 not let you be t beyond what you
10:13 But when you are t, he will
Gal 6: 1 yourselves, or you also may be t.
1Th 3: 5 in some way the tempter had t you
Heb 2:18 he himself suffered when he was t,
2:18 able to help those who are being t.
4:15 but we have one who has been t
Jas 1:13 When t, no one should say, "God is
1:13 For God cannot be t by evil,
1:14 but each person is t when they are

TEMPTER* TEMPT
Mt 4: 3 The t came to him and said, "If you
1Th 3: 5 in some way the t had tempted you

TEMPTING* TEMPT
Lk 4:13 the devil had finished all this t,
Jas 1:13 no one should say, "God is t me."

TEN TENS, TENTH, TITHE, TITHES
Ge 18:32 "For the sake of t, I will not destroy
Ex 34:28 the T Commandments.
Lev 26: 8 of you will chase t thousand,
Dt 4:13 his covenant, the T Commandments,
10: 4 the T Commandments he had
1Sa 1: 8 I mean more to you than t sons?"
2Ki 20: 9 Shall the shadow go forward t steps,
or shall it go back t steps?"
Ps 91: 7 side, t thousand at your right hand,
Da 1:12 test your servants for t days:
7:24 The t horns are t kings who will
Mt 25: 1 will be like t virgins who took their
25:28 give it to the one who has t bags.
Lk 15: 8 suppose a woman has t silver coins
Rev 5:11 and t thousand times t thousand.
12: 3 dragon with seven heads and t horns
17:12 "The t horns you saw are t kings

TENANTS
Mt 21:34 servants to the t to collect his fruit.

TEND TENDING, TENDS
Jer 23: 2 to the shepherds who t my people:
Eze 34:14 I will t them in a good pasture,

TENDER TENDERLY, TENDERNESS
Isa 53: 2 grew up before him like a t shoot,
Lk 1:78 because of the t mercy of our God,

TENDERLY* TENDER
Ge 34: 3 young woman and spoke t to her.
Isa 40: 2 Speak t to Jerusalem, and proclaim
Hos 2:14 the wilderness and speak t to her.

TENDERNESS* TENDER
Isa 63:15 Your t and compassion are withheld

Php 2: 1 the Spirit, if any t and compassion,

TENDING TEND
Ex 3: 1 Now Moses was t the flock
1Sa 16:11 "He is t the sheep."

TENDS TEND
Isa 40:11 He t his flock like a shepherd:

TENS TEN
1Sa 18: 7 and David his t of thousands."
Ps 3: 6 I will not fear though t of thousands

TENT TENTMAKER, TENTS
Ex 27:21 In the t of meeting,
33: 7 to the t of meeting outside the camp.
40: 2 up the tabernacle, the t of meeting,
2Sa 7: 2 the ark of God remains in a t."
20: 1 Every man to his t, Israel!"
Ps 15: 1 who may dwell in your sacred t?
61: 4 I long to dwell in your t forever
Isa 33:20 abode, a t that will not be moved;
54: 2 "Enlarge the place of your t,
Ac 15:16 return and rebuild David's fallen t.
2Co 5: 1 that if the earthly t we live in is
2Pe 1:13 as long as I live in the t of this body,

TENT OF MEETING Ex 27:21; 28:43; 29:4, 10,
11, 30, 32, 42, 44; 30:16, 18, 20, 26, 36; 31:7; 33:7,
7; 35:21; 38:8, 30; 39:32, 40; 40:2, 6, 7, 12, 22, 24,
26, 29, 30, 32, 34, 35; Lev 1:1, 3, 5; 3:2, 8, 13; 4:4,
5, 7, 7, 14, 16, 18, 18; 6:16, 26, 30; 8:3, 4, 31, 33,
35; 9:5, 23; 10:7, 9; 12:6; 14:11, 23; 15:14, 29; 16:7,
16, 17, 20, 23, 33; 17:4, 5, 6, 9; 19:21; 24:3; Nu
1:1; 2:2, 17; 3:7, 8, 25, 25, 38; 4:3, 4, 15, 23, 25, 25,
28, 30, 33, 35, 37, 39, 41, 43, 47; 6:10, 13, 18; 7:5,
89; 8:9, 15, 19, 22, 24, 26; 10:3; 11:16; 12:4; 14:10;
16:18, 19, 42, 43, 50; 17:4; 18:4, 6, 21, 22, 23, 31;
19:4; 20:6; 25:6; 27:2; 31:54; Dt 31:14, 14; Jos 18:1;
19:51; 1Sa 2:22; 1Ki 8:4; 1Ch 6:32; 9:21, 23; 23:32;
2Ch 1:3, 6, 13; 5:5

TENTH TEN
Ge 14:20 Abram gave him a t of everything.
Nu 18:26 you must present a t of that tithe as
Dt 14:22 Be sure to set aside a t of all
1Sa 8:15 He will take a t of your grain
Isa 6:13 And though a t remains in the land,
Lk 11:42 because you give God a t of your
18:12 a week and give a t of all I get.'
Heb 7: 4 the patriarch Abraham gave him a t

TENTMAKER* TENT
Ac 18: 3 and because he was a t as they were,

TENTS TENT
Ge 13:12 plain and pitched his t near Sodom.
Nu 1:52 are to set up their t by divisions,
Ps 84:10 than dwell in the t of the wicked.

TERAH
Ge 11:27 T became the father of Abram,

TEREBINTH
Isa 6:13 as the t and oak leave stumps

TERMS
Dt   29: 1 These are the t of the covenant
Jer   11: 3 is the one who does not obey the t

TERRIBLE TERROR
2Ti   3: 1 There will be t times in the last

TERRIFIED TERROR
Dt   7:21 Do not be t by them, for the LORD
      20: 3 do not panic or be t by them.
Est   7: 6 Then Haman was t before the king
Ps   90: 7 anger and t by your indignation.
Jer   1:17 Do not be t by them, or I will terrify
Eze   2: 6 of what they say or be t by them,
Mt   14:26 walking on the lake, they were t.
      17: 6 they fell facedown to the ground, t.
      27:54 they were t, and exclaimed,
Mk   4:41 They were t and asked each other,

TERRIFYING TERROR
Heb 12:21 The sight was so t that Moses said,

TERRITORY
Ex   34:24 before you and enlarge your t,
Jos   1: 4 Your t will extend from the desert
1Ch   4:10 would bless me and enlarge my t!
2Co 10:16 already done in someone else's t.

TERROR TERRIBLE, TERRIFIED,
TERRIFYING, TERRORS
Ex   23:27 "I will send my t ahead of you
Dt   2:25 very day I will begin to put the t
      28:67 of the t that will fill your hearts
Job   9:34 his t would frighten me no more.
Ps   31:13 whispering, "T on every side!"
      91: 5 You will not fear the t of night,
Pr   21:15 to the righteous but t to evildoers.
Isa 13: 8 T will seize them, pain and anguish
      24:17 T and pit and snare await you,
      51:13 live in constant t every day because
      54:14 T will be far removed; it will not
Jer 20:10 many whispering, "T on every side!
Lk   21:26 People will faint from t,
Ro   13: 3 rulers hold no t for those who do

TERRORS TERROR
Ps   55: 4 the t of death have fallen on me.
La   2:22 so you summoned against me t

TERTIUS*
Ro   16:22 I, T, who wrote down this letter,

TEST TESTED, TESTER, TESTING,
TESTINGS, TESTS
Ex   16: 4 In this way I will t them and see
Dt   6:16 your God to the t as you did
      8: 2 t you in order to know what was
Jdg   3: 4 They were left to t the Israelites
      6:39 Allow me one more t
1Ki 10: 1 she came to t Solomon with hard
1Ch 29:17 that you t the heart and are pleased
Ps   26: 2 T me, LORD, and try me,
      78:18 to the t by demanding the food they
      106:14 the wilderness they put God to the t.
      139:23 t me and know my anxious

Jer   9: 7 I will refine and t them, for what
      11:20 judge righteously and t the heart
Mal   3:10 T me in this," says the LORD
Lk   4:12 put the Lord your God to the t.' "
      10:25 expert in the law stood up to t Jesus.
Ac   5: 9 could you conspire to t the Spirit
Ro   12: 2 you will be able to t and approve
      16:10 fidelity to Christ has stood the t.
1Co   3:13 and the fire will t the quality of each
      10: 9 We should not t Christ, as some
2Co 13: 5 you are in the faith; t yourselves.
      13: 5 unless, of course, you fail the t?
Gal   6: 4 Each one should t their own actions.
1Th   5:21 but t them all; hold on to what is
Jas   1:12 having stood the t, that person will
1Jn   4: 1 t the spirits to see whether they are
Rev   2:10 put some of you in prison to t you,
      3:10 the whole world to t the inhabitants

TESTED TEST
Ge   22: 1 Some time later God t Abraham.
Ex   17: 7 because they t the LORD saying,
Nu   14:22 disobeyed me and t me ten times—
Job 23:10 when he has t me, I will come forth
      34:36 that Job might be t to the utmost
Ps   66:10 For you, God, t us; you refined us
Pr   27:21 but people are t by their praise.
Ecc   7:23 All this I t by wisdom and I said,
Isa 28:16 I lay a stone in Zion, a t stone,
      48:10 I have t you in the furnace
Da   1:14 to this and t them for ten days.
Lk   11:16 Others t him by asking for a sign
1Ti   3:10 They must first be t;
Heb 11:17 when God t him, offered Isaac as

TESTER* TEST
Jer   6:27 "I have made you a t of metals

TESTIFIED TESTIFY
Mk   14:56 Many t falsely against him, but their
Jn   5:37 me has himself t concerning me.
Heb   2: 4 God also t to it by signs,

TESTIFIES TESTIFY
Jn   5:32 There is another who t in my favor,
      19:35 truth, and he t so that you also may
      21:24 This is the disciple who t to these
Ro   8:16 The Spirit himself t with our spirit
Rev   1: 2 who t to everything he saw—
      22:20 He who t to these things says,

TESTIFY TESTIFIED, TESTIFIES,
TESTIMONY
Dt   31:21 them, this song will t against them,
Pr   24:28 Do not t against your neighbor
Isa 59:12 your sight, and our sins t against us.
Jer 14: 7 Although our sins t against us,
Jn   1: 7 came as a witness to t concerning
      1:34 I t that this is God's Chosen One."
      5:39 These are the very Scriptures that t
      7: 7 it hates me because I t that its works
      15:26 from the Father—he will t about me.
Ac   4:33 power the apostles continued to t
      10:43 All the prophets t about him
Ro   3:21 which the Law and the Prophets t.

1Jn 4:14 t that the Father has sent his Son
5: 7 For there are three that t:

TESTIMONY TESTIFY

Ex 20:16 shall not give false t against your
Nu 35:30 murderer only on the t of witnesses.
Dt 19:18 a liar, giving false t against a fellow
Isa 8:20 instruction and the t of warning.
Mt 15:19 immorality, theft, false t, slander.
24:14 the whole world as a t to all nations,
Mk 14:59 Yet even then their t did not agree.
Lk 21:13 And so you will bear t to me.
22:71 said, "Why do we need any more t?
Jn 2:25 He did not need any t
8:17 that the t of two witnesses is true.
21:24 We know that his t is true.
2Ti 1: 8 be ashamed of the t about our Lord
1Jn 5: 9 We accept human t, but God's t is
greater because it is the t of God,
Rev 1: 9 the word of God and the t of Jesus.
12:11 the Lamb and by the word of their t;
19:10 sisters who hold to the t of Jesus.

ARK OF THE TESTIMONY See ARK OF THE
COVENANT

TESTING* TEST

Dt 13: 3 The LORD your God is t you
Eze 21:13 " 'T will surely come.
Lk 8:13 but in the time of t they fall away.
Ac 20:19 the midst of severe t by the plots
Heb 3: 8 rebellion, during the time of t
Jas 1: 3 that the t of your faith produces

TESTINGS* TEST

Dt 4:34 nation, by t, by signs and wonders,

TESTS TEST

Pr 17: 3 for gold, but the LORD t the heart.
1Th 2: 4 people but God, who t our hearts.

TETRARCH

Mt 14: 1 time Herod the t heard the reports
Lk 3:19 John rebuked Herod the t because

THADDAEUS

Apostle (Mt 10:3; Mk 3:18); probably also
known as Judas son of James (Lk 6:16; Ac 1:13).

THANK THANKFUL,
THANKFULNESS, THANKING,
THANKS, THANKSGIVING

Lev 22:29 you sacrifice a t offering
2Ch 29:31 brought sacrifices and t offerings,
Ps 50:14 "Sacrifice t offerings to God,
116:17 I will sacrifice a t offering to you
Da 2:23 I t and praise you, God of my
Lk 18:11 'God, I t you that I am not like other
Jn 11:41 I t you that you have heard me.
1Co 10:30 because of something I t God for?
Php 1: 3 I t my God every time I remember
1Th 3: 9 How can we t God enough for you

THANKFUL* THANK

Col 3:15 you were called to peace. And be t.
4: 2 to prayer, being watchful and t.

Heb 12:28 let us be t, and so worship God

THANKFULNESS* THANK

Lev 7:12 they offer it as an expression of t,
1Co 10:30 If I take part in the meal with t,
Col 2: 7 were taught, and overflowing with t.

THANKING* THANK

1Ch 25: 3 using the harp in t and praising

THANKS THANK

Ne 12:31 assigned two large choirs to give t.
Ps 7:17 I will give t to the LORD because
9: 1 I will give t to you, LORD, with all
35:18 I will give you t in the great
107: 1 Give t to the LORD, for he is
136: 2 Give t to the God of gods.
Mt 14:19 he gave t and broke the loaves.
Ro 1:21 glorified him as God nor gave t
1Co 11:24 and when he had given t, he broke it
15:57 But t be to God! He gives us
2Co 2:14 But t be to God, who always leads
9:15 T be to God for his indescribable
1Th 5:18 give t in all circumstances;
Rev 4: 9 and t to him who sits on the throne
7:12 glory and wisdom and t and honor
11:17 "We give t to you, Lord God

GAVE THANKS 2Ch 7:3, 6; Ne 12:40; Mt 14:19;
Mk 6:41; 8:7; Lk 2:38; 9:16; 22:17, 19; 24:30; Jn
6:11; Ac 27:35; Ro 1:21

GIVE ... THANKS 1Ch 16:34, 35, 41; 29:13;
2Ch 5:13; 20:21; 31:2; Ne 12:31; Ps 7:17; 9:1;
35:18; 100:4; 106:1, 47; 107:1, 8, 15, 21, 31; 118:1,
19, 21, 29; 119:62; 136:1, 2, 3, 26; Jer 33:11; Ro
14:6; 1Co 10:16; 2Co 1:11; 1Th 5:18; Rev 4:9;
11:17

THANKSGIVING THANK

Ezr 3:11 and t they sang to the LORD:
Ne 12:27 the dedication with songs of t
Ps 95: 2 Let us come before him with t
100: 4 Enter his gates with t and his courts
1Co 10:16 Is not the cup of t for which we give
2Co 9:11 us your generosity will result in t
Php 4: 6 with t, present your requests to God.
1Ti 4: 3 to be received with t by those who

THEFT* THIEF

Ex 22: 3 they must be sold to pay for their t.
Mt 15:19 adultery, sexual immorality, t,
Mk 7:21 sexual immorality, t, murder,

THEFTS* THIEF

Rev 9:21 their sexual immorality or their t.

THEME*

Ps 22:25 From you comes the t of my praise
45: 1 by a noble t as I recite my verses
119:54 Your decrees are the t of my song

THEOPHILUS*

Lk 1: 3 account for you, most excellent T,
Ac 1: 1 In my former book, T, I wrote

THESSALONIANS*
THESSALONICA
1Th 1: 1 church of the **T** in God the Father
2Th 1: 1 church of the **T** in God our Father

THESSALONICA THESSALONIANS
Ac 17: 1 they came to **T**, where there was
   17:11 noble character than those in **T**,
Php 4:16 for even when I was in **T**, you sent

THICK
Ge 15:12 a **t** and dreadful darkness came over
Ex 19:16 with a **t** cloud over the mountain,
Ps 97: 2 and **t** darkness surround him;

THIEF THEFT, THEFTS, THIEVES
Pr 6:11 poverty will come on you like a **t**
   6:30 People do not despise a **t** if he steals
Lk 12:39 at what hour the **t** was coming,
Jn 10:10 The **t** comes only to steal and kill
1Th 5: 2 of the Lord will come like a **t**
1Pe 4:15 it should not be as a murderer or **t**
Rev 16:15 "Look, I come like a **t**!

THIEVES THIEF
Mt 6:19 and where **t** break in and steal.
Jn 10: 8 All who have come before me are **t**
1Co 6:10 nor **t** nor the greedy nor drunkards

THIGH THIGHS
Ge 24: 2 he had, "Put your hand under my **t**.
   47:29 eyes, put your hand under my **t**
Rev 19:16 on his **t** he has this name written:

THIGHS THIGH
Da 2:32 of silver, its belly and **t** of bronze,

THIN
Ge 41: 7 The **t** heads of grain swallowed
Ex 16:14 **t** flakes like frost on the ground
Jdg 7: 4 and I will **t** them out for you there.

THING EVERYTHING, NOTHING, SOMETHING, THINGS
Ge 1:21 every living **t** with which the water
   7:21 Every living **t** that moved on land
   19: 7 Don't do this wicked **t**.
Jdg 19:24 don't do such an outrageous **t**."
2Sa 13:12 Don't do this wicked **t**.
2Ki 3:18 This is an easy **t** in the eyes
Ps 27: 4 One **t** I ask from the LORD,
   84:11 no good **t** does he withhold
Isa 43:19 See, I am doing a new **t**!
Jer 31:22 The LORD will create a new **t**
Mt 19:16 what good **t** must I do to get eternal
Mk 10:21 "One **t** you lack," he said.
Jn 9:25 not, I don't know. One **t** I do know.
Php 3:13 But one **t** I do: Forgetting what is

THINGS THING
Nu 10:29 the LORD has promised good **t**
2Sa 7:28 you have promised these good **t**
Ps 15: 5 Whoever does these **t** will never be
   71:19 heavens, you who have done great **t**.
  118:15 right hand has done mighty **t**!

Pr 6:16 There are six **t** the LORD hates,
   31:29 "Many women do noble **t**, but you
Isa 66: 2 Has not my hand made all these **t**,
Jer 10:16 these, for he is the Maker of all **t**,
Joel 2:21 Surely the LORD has done great **t**!
Mt 19:26 but with God all **t** are possible."
Mk 11:33 what authority I am doing these **t**."
Lk 6:45 A good man brings good **t**
   6:45 an evil man brings evil **t**
   9:22 Son of Man must suffer many **t**
  10:42 but few **t** are needed—
Jn 1: 3 Through him all **t** were made;
   1:50 You will see greater **t** than that."
  14:12 will do even greater **t** than these,
  21:25 Jesus did many other **t** as well.
1Co 2:10 these are the **t** God has revealed
   2:10 The Spirit searches all **t**, even the deep **t** of God.
Eph 1:22 And God placed all **t** under his feet
Col 1:17 He is before all **t**, and in him all **t**
1Pe 4: 7 The end of all **t** is near.
Rev 4:11 for you created all **t**, and by your
   21: 4 the old order of **t** has passed away."
   22: 6 to show his servants the **t** that must

THINK THINKING, THINKS, THOUGHT, THOUGHTS
Ps 40:17 may the Lord **t** of me.
   63: 6 I **t** of you through the watches
  144: 3 mere mortals that you **t** of them?
Isa 44:19 No one stops to **t**, no one has
Eze 28: 2 though you **t** you are as wise as
Mt 22:42 "What do you **t** about the Messiah?
Jn 5:39 Scriptures diligently because you **t**
Ro 12: 3 Do not **t** of yourself more highly
1Co 8: 2 Those who **t** they know something
   10:12 if you **t** you are standing firm,
Php 4: 8 **t** about such things.

THINKING THINK
Pr 23: 7 of person who is always **t**
Lk 5:22 Jesus knew what they were **t**
1Co 14:20 and sisters, stop **t** like children.
   14:20 be infants, but in your **t** be adults.
2Pe 3: 1 to stimulate you to wholesome **t**.

THINKS THINK
Job 24:15 he **t**, 'No eye will see me,' and he
1Co 14:37 If anyone **t** they are a prophet

THIRD THREE
Eze 5:12 A **t** of your people will die
   5:12 a **t** will fall by the sword outside
   5:12 and a **t** I will scatter to the winds
   10:14 being, the **t** the face of a lion,
Da 5: 7 he will be made the **t** highest ruler
Hos 6: 2 on the **t** day he will restore us,
Mk 14:41 Returning the **t** time, he said
Lk 18:33 On the **t** day he will rise again."
Jn 21:17 because Jesus asked him the **t** time,
Ac 20: 9 he fell to the ground from the **t** story
2Co 12: 2 ago was caught up to the **t** heaven.
Rev 4: 7 an ox, the **t** had a face like a man,
   6: 5 When the Lamb opened the **t** seal,

Rev 8:10 fell from the sky on a **t** of the rivers
12: 4 Its tail swept a **t** of the stars
THIRD DAY See DAY

THIRST THIRSTS, THIRSTY
Ps 69:21 food and gave me vinegar for my **t**.
Mt   5: 6 who hunger and **t** for righteousness,
Jn   4:14 the water I give them will never **t**.
2Co 11:27 I have known hunger and **t** and have
Rev 7:16 never again will they **t**.

THIRSTS* THIRST
Ps 42: 2 My soul **t** for God, for the living

THIRSTY THIRST
Ex 17: 3 the people were **t** for water there,
Ps 107: 9 for he satisfies the **t** and fills
Pr 25:21 if he is **t**, give him water to drink.
Isa 55: 1 all you who are **t**,
Mt 25:35 I was **t** and you gave me something
Jn   6:35 believes in me will never be **t**.
7:37 "Let anyone who is **t** come to me
19:28 be fulfilled, Jesus said, "I am **t**."
Ro 12:20 if he is **t**, give him something
Rev 21: 6 the **t** I will give water without cost
22:17 Let the one who is **t** come;

THIRTY
Ge 41:46 Joseph was **t** years old when he
Lev 27: 4 a female, set her value at **t** shekels;
2Sa 23:24 Among the **T** were:
Pr 22:20 Have I not written **t** sayings for you,
Mt 13: 8 sixty or **t** times what was sown.
Lk   3:23 Jesus himself was about **t** years old

THISTLE THISTLES
2Ki 14: 9 "A **t** in Lebanon sent a message

THISTLES THISTLE
Ge   3:18 It will produce thorns and **t** for you,
Heb 6: 8 produces thorns and **t** is worthless

THOMAS* DIDYMUS
Apostle, also called Didymus (Mt 10:3; Mk 3:18;
Lk 6:15; Jn 11:16; 14:5; 21:2; Ac 1:13). Doubted
resurrection (Jn 20:24–28).

THORN* THORNBUSH,
    THORNBUSHES, THORNS
Mic 7: 4 most upright worse than a **t** hedge.
2Co 12: 7 I was given a **t** in my flesh,

THORNBUSH THORN
Jdg 9:14 "Finally all the trees said to the **t**,
Isa 55:13 of the **t** will grow the juniper,

THORNBUSHES THORN
Lk   6:44 People do not pick figs from **t**,

THORNS THORN
Ge   3:18 It will produce **t** and thistles for you,
Nu 33:55 in your eyes and **t** in your sides.
Jer 12:13 They will sow wheat but reap **t**;
Mt 13: 7 Other seed fell among **t**, which grew
Jn 19: 2 twisted together a crown of **t**
Heb 6: 8 land that produces **t** and thistles is

THOROUGH THOROUGHLY
Ac 18:24 man, with a **t** knowledge

THOROUGHLY THOROUGH
Ps 119:140 Your promises have been **t** tested,
Ac 22: 3 and was **t** trained in the law of our
2Ti 3:17 of God may be **t** equipped for every

THOUGH
Job 13:15 **T** he slay me, yet will I hope in him;
Ps 17: 3 **T** you probe my heart, **t** you
27:10 **T** my father and mother forsake me,
37:24 **t** he may stumble, he will not fall,
Isa 1:18 "**T** your sins are like scarlet,
Hab 2: 3 **T** it linger, wait for it;
3:17 **T** the fig tree does not bud and there
Lk   8:10 **t** hearing, they may not understand.'
Jn 11:25 in me will live, even **t** they die;
Ro   8:10 even **t** your body is subject to death
9: 6 It is not as **t** God's word had failed.

THOUGHT THINK
1Sa 1:13 was not heard. Eli **t** she was drunk
1Ch 28: 9 every desire and every **t**. If you seek
Ps 106: 7 they gave no **t** to your miracles;
Pr 14:15 but the prudent give **t** to their steps.
21:29 but the upright give **t** to their ways.
1Co 13:11 I talked like a child, I **t** like a child,
2Co 10: 5 we take captive every **t** to make it

THOUGHTS THINK
Ge   6: 5 of the **t** of the human heart was only
Ps 92: 5 LORD, how profound your **t**!
139:23 test me and know my anxious **t**.
Pr 15:26 The LORD detests the **t**
Isa 55: 8 "For my **t** are not your **t**,
Mt   9: 4 Knowing their **t**, Jesus said,
15:19 For out of the heart come evil **t**—
Ro   2:15 and their **t** sometimes accusing them
1Co 2:11 knows a person's **t** except their own
Heb 3: 1 calling, fix your **t** on Jesus,
4:12 it judges the **t** and attitudes

THOUSAND THOUSANDS
Dt   7: 9 love to a **t** generations of those who
32:30 How could one man chase a **t**, or two
put ten **t** to flight,
Jos 23:10 One of you routs a **t**,
Jdg 15:16 jawbone I have killed a **t** men."
Ps 50:10 is mine, and the cattle on a **t** hills.
84:10 in your courts than a **t** elsewhere;
90: 4 A **t** years in your sight are like a day
91: 7 A **t** may fall at your side, ten **t**
105: 8 he made, for a **t** generations,
SS   5:10 and ruddy, outstanding among ten **t**.
Mt 14:21 those who ate was about five **t** men,
15:38 of those who ate was four **t** men,
Mk   8: 9 About four **t** were present.
2Pe 3: 8 With the Lord a day is like a **t** years,
and a **t** years are like a day.
Rev 5:11 thousands, and ten **t** times ten **t**.
20: 4 and reigned with Christ a **t** years.

THOUSANDS THOUSAND
Ex 34: 7 maintaining love to **t**, and forgiving

1Sa 18: 7 "Saul has slain his t, and David his
          tens of t."
Ps 68:17 The chariots of God are tens of t
          and t of t;
Da   7:10 T upon t attended him;
Heb 12:22 You have come to t upon t of angels
Jude 1:14 the Lord is coming with t upon t
Rev 5:11 of many angels, numbering t upon t,

THREAT THREATENED, THREATS
Isa 30:17 A thousand will flee at the t of one;

THREATENED THREAT
Ex 32:14 on his people the disaster he had t.
Isa 38:14 I am being t; Lord, come to my
Jnh   3:10 on them the destruction he had t.

THREATS THREAT
Ac   4:21 After further t they let them go.
      9: 1 out murderous t against the Lord's

THREE THIRD
Ge   6:10 Noah had t sons: Shem,
     18: 2 up and saw t men standing nearby.
Ex 23:14 "'T' times a year you are to celebrate
Dt 14:28 At the end of every t years, bring all
     19:15 the testimony of two or t witnesses.
1Sa 31: 8 his t sons fallen on Mount Gilboa.
2Sa 23: 9 As one of the t mighty warriors,
Job   2:11 When Job's t friends,
Pr   30:15 "There are t things that are never
     30:18 "There are t things that are too
     30:21 "Under t things the earth trembles,
     30:29 "There are t things that are stately
Ecc   4:12 of t strands is not quickly broken.
Da   3:24 "Weren't there t men that we tied
      7: 5 it had t ribs in its mouth between its
Am   1: 3 "For t sins of Damascus,
Jnh   1:17 belly of the fish t days and t nights.
Mt 12:40 For as Jonah was t days and t nights
     12:40 so the Son of Man will be t days and t
          nights in the heart of the earth.
     17: 4 If you wish, I will put up t shelters—
     18:20 where two or t gather in my name,
     26:34 you will disown me t times."
     26:75 you will disown me t times."
     27:46 About t in the afternoon Jesus cried
     27:63 said, 'After t days I will rise again.'
Mk   8:31 be killed and after t days rise again.
     14:30 yourself will disown me t times."
Jn   2:19 and I will raise it again in t days."
1Co 13:13 And now these t remain:
     14:27 or at the most t—should speak,
2Co 12: 8 T times I pleaded with the Lord
     13; 1 testimony of two or t witnesses."
1Jn   5: 7 For there are t that testify:

THRESH THRESHED, THRESHES, THRESHING
Mic   4:13 "Rise and t, Daughter Zion, for I

THRESHED THRESH
Ru   2:17 she t the barley she had gathered,

THRESHES* THRESH
1Co   9:10 whoever plows and t should be able to

THRESHING THRESH
Ru   3: 3 Then go down to the t floor,
2Sa 24:18 altar to the LORD on the t floor
Hos   9: 1 of a prostitute at every t floor.
Lk   3:17 fork is in his hand to clear his t floor

THRESHOLD
1Sa   5: 4 broken off and were lying on the t;
Eze 10:18 from over the t of the temple
     47: 1 under the t of the temple toward
Zep   1: 9 all who avoid stepping on the t,

THREW THROW
Ex   7:10 Aaron t his staff down in front
     15:25 He t it into the water, and the water
     32:19 and he t the tablets out of his hands,
2Ki   6: 6 Elisha cut a stick and t it there,
Da   3:24 that we tied up and t into the fire?"
      6:16 Daniel and t him into the lions' den.
Jnh   1:15 took Jonah and t him overboard,
Mt 27: 5 So Judas t the money
Rev 20: 3 He t him into the Abyss, and locked

THRIVE
Pr   11:28 the righteous will t like a green leaf.
     29: 2 When the righteous t, the people
     29:16 When the wicked t, so does sin,

THROAT THROATS
Ps   5: 9 Their t is an open grave;
Pr   23: 2 put a knife to your t if you are given

THROATS THROAT
Ro   3:13 "Their t are open graves;

THROB*
Isa 60: 5 your heart will t and swell with joy;

THRONE ENTHRONED, ENTHRONES, THRONES
Ex   17:16 up against the t of the LORD,
2Sa   7:13 I will establish the t of his kingdom
1Ch 17:12 and I will establish his t forever.
Ps   11: 4 the LORD is on his heavenly t.
     45: 6 Your t, O God, will last for ever
     47: 8 God is seated on his holy t.
     89:14 justice are the foundation of your t;
Pr   20:28 through love his t is made secure.
Isa   6: 1 high and exalted, seated on a t;
     66: 1 "Heaven is my t, and the earth is
Jer 33:21 have a descendant to reign on his t.
Eze   1:26 above on the t was a figure like
     28: 2 I sit on the t of a god in the heart
Da   7: 9 His t was flaming with fire, and its
Mt   5:34 either by heaven, for it is God's t;
     19:28 Son of Man sits on his glorious t,
Lk   1:32 The Lord God will give him the t
Ac   7:49 " 'Heaven is my t, and the earth is
Heb   1: 8 the Son he says, "Your t, O God,
      4:16 then approach God's t of grace
     12: 2 at the right hand of the t of God.

Rev 2:13 where Satan has his t.
      3:21 give the right to sit with me on my t,
      3:21 sat down with my Father on his t.
      4: 2 there before me was a t in heaven
      4:10 They lay their crowns before the t
      5:13 "To him who sits on the t
    20:11 I saw a great white t and him who
    22: 3 The t of God and of the Lamb will

THRONES THRONE
Mt 19:28 me will also sit on twelve t,
Col 1:16 whether t or powers or rulers
Rev 4: 4 the throne were twenty-four other t,
    20: 4 I saw t on which were seated those

THRONG
Ps 42: 4 joy and praise among the festive t.
Jer 31: 8 a great t will return.

THROUGH
Ge 12: 3 on earth will be blessed t you."
    21:12 you, because it is t Isaac that your
    22:18 t your offspring all nations on earth
Ex 14:22 the Israelites went t the sea on dry
Ps 72:17 all nations will be blessed t him,
Pr 16: 6 T love and faithfulness sin is atoned
Isa 43: 2 When you pass t the waters, I will
Mt 1:18 to be pregnant the Holy Spirit.
Jn 10: 9 whoever enters t me will be saved.
    14: 6 comes to the Father except t me.
Ro 5: 1 since we have been justified t faith,
1Co 8: 6 t whom all things came and t whom
          we live.
Eph 2: 8 grace you have been saved, t faith—

THROW THREW, THROWN
Ex 1:22 that is born you must t into the Nile,
    4: 3 LORD said, "T it on the ground."
Jos 24:23 "t away the foreign gods that are
Zec 11:13 said to me, "T it to the potter"—
Mt 5:30 to stumble, cut it off and t it away.
    7: 6 do not t your pearls to pigs.
Jn 8: 7 *the first to t a stone at her.*"
Heb 10:35 So do not t away your confidence;
    12: 1 let us t off everything that hinders

THROWN THROW
Da 3:21 and t into the blazing furnace.
    6:12 would be t into the lions' den?"
Rev 19:20 them were t alive into the fiery lake
    20:10 was t into the lake of burning sulfur,
    20:14 Hades were t into the lake of fire.

THRUST
2Ki 17:20 until he t them from his presence.
Isa 8:22 they will be t into utter darkness.

THUMMIM
Ex 28:30 Urim and the T in the breastpiece,
Ezr 2:63 ministering with the Urim and T.

THUNDER THUNDERED, THUNDERS
Ex 9:23 the sky, the LORD sent t and hail,
    20:18 When the people saw the t
Job 40: 9 and can your voice t like his?

Ps 93: 4 Mightier than the t of the great
Joel 3:16 from Zion and t from Jerusalem;
Mk 3:17 which means "sons of t"),
Rev 4: 5 lightning, rumblings and peals of t.
    6: 1 living creatures say in a voice like t,
    16:18 peals of t and a severe earthquake.

THUNDERCLOUD* CLOUD
Ps 81: 7 you, I answered you out of a t;

THUNDERED THUNDER
Ps 18:13 The LORD t from heaven;
Jn 12:29 was there and heard it said it had t;

THUNDERS THUNDER
Job 37: 5 God's voice t in marvelous ways;
Ps 29: 3 the God of glory t, the LORD t
Jer 10:13 When he t, the waters
Rev 10: 3 the voices of the seven t spoke.

THWART* THWARTED, THWARTS
Isa 14:27 has purposed, and who can t him?

THWARTED* THWART
Job 42: 2 no purpose of yours can be t.
Isa 8:10 your strategy, but it will be t;

THWARTS THWART
Ps 33:10 he t the purposes of the peoples.

THYATIRA
Ac 16:14 from the city of T named Lydia,
Rev 2:18 the angel of the church in T write:

TIBERIAS GALILEE
Jn 6: 1 Sea of Galilee (that is, the Sea of T),

TIBERIUS*
Lk 3: 1 year of the reign of T Caesar—

TIBNI*
King of Israel (1Ki 16:21–22).

TIDINGS*
Isa 52: 7 who bring good t, who proclaim

TIE TIED, TIES, TYING
Dt 6: 8 T them as symbols on your hands
    11:18 t them as symbols on your hands
Mt 23: 4 They t up heavy, cumbersome loads

TIED TIE
Ge 38:28 a scarlet thread and t it on his wrist
Jos 2:21 she t the scarlet cord in the window.
Lk 19:30 you will find a colt t there, which no

TIES TIE
Hos 11: 4 of human kindness, with t of love.
Mt 12:29 unless he first t up the strong man?

TIGHT* TIGHTFISTED
Jas 1:26 and yet do not keep a t rein on their

TIGHTFISTED* TIGHT
Dt 15: 7 not be hardhearted or t toward them.

TIGLATH-PILESER PUL
2Ki 16: 7 to say to T king of Assyria, "I am
1Ch 5: 6 whom T king of Assyria took

TIGRIS*

Ge   2:14 The name of the third river is the T;
Da 10: 4 on the bank of the great river, the T,

TILES*

Lk   5:19 his mat through the t into the middle

TIMBREL TIMBRELS

Ex 15:20 Aaron's sister, took a t in her hand,
Ps 150: 4 praise him with t and dancing,

TIMBRELS TIMBREL

Jdg 11:34 daughter, dancing to the sound of t!
Isa 24: 8 The joyful t are stilled, the noise
Jer 31: 4 Again you will take up your t

TIME TIMES

Ge   4:26 At that t people began to call
      6: 5 human heart was only evil all the t.
Dt 32:35 In due t their foot will slip;
Ne   9:28 you delivered them t after t.
Est   4:14 royal position for such a t as this?"
Ps 119:126 It is t for you to act, LORD;
Ecc   3: 1 There is a t for everything,
      3:11 made everything beautiful in its t.
      8: 5 wise heart will know the proper t
Da   7:25 be delivered into his hands for a t,
            times and half a t.
     12: 1 There will be a t of distress such as
     12: 7 "It will be for a t, times and half a t.
Hos 10:12 for it is t to seek the LORD,
Lk 21: 8 'I am he,' and, 'The t is near.'
Ro   5: 6 at just the right t, when we were still
      9: 9 "At the appointed t I will return,
1Co   4: 5 that t each will receive their praise
      7:29 and sisters, is that the t is short.
2Co   6: 2 tell you, now is the t of God's favor,
Gal   4: 4 But when the set t had fully come,
2Ti   1: 9 Jesus before the beginning of t,
Titus 1: 2 promised before the beginning of t,
Heb   9:28 and he will appear a second t,
     10:12 had offered for all t one sacrifice
1Pe   4:17 For it is t for judgment to begin
Rev   1: 3 is written in it, because the t is near.
      2:21 I have given her t to repent of her
      3: 3 will not know at what t I will come
     12:14 she would be taken care of for a t,
            times and half a t,
     22:10 of this scroll, because the t is near.

APPOINTED TIME See APPOINTED

TIMES TIME

Ge   1:14 serve as signs to mark sacred t,
      4:15 will suffer vengeance seven t over."
Ex 23:14 "Three t a year you are to celebrate
Jos   6: 4 march around the city seven t,
Ps   9: 9 a stronghold in t of trouble.
     31:15 My t are in your hands;
     62: 8 Trust in him at all t, you people;
Pr 17:17 A friend loves at all t, and a brother
     24:16 for though the righteous fall seven t,
Isa 46:10 from ancient t, what is still to come.
Da   7:25 hands for a time, t and half a time.

Am   5:13 the prudent keep quiet in such t, for
            the t are evil.
Mt 16: 3 cannot interpret the signs of the t.
     18:22 not seven t, but seventy-seven t.
Mk   4: 8 some sixty, some a hundred t."
     14:30 yourself will disown me three t."
Lk 17: 4 they sin against you seven t in a day
Ac   1: 7 "It is not for you to know the t
1Ti   4: 1 later t some will abandon the faith
2Ti   3: 1 There will be terrible t in the last
Rev   5:11 and ten thousand t ten thousand.
     12:14 care of for a time, t and half a time,

TIMID*

2Co 10: 1 who am "t" when face to face
2Ti   1: 7 God gave us does not make us t,

TIMOTHY

Believer from Lystra (Ac 16:1). Joined Paul on
second missionary journey (Ac 16–20). Sent to
settle problems at Corinth (1Co 4:17; 16:10). Led
church at Ephesus (1Ti 1:3). Co-writer with Paul
(1Th 1:1; 2Th 1:1; Phm 1).

TIP

Job 33: 2 my words are on the t of my tongue.

TIRE TIRED

2Th   3:13 never t of doing what is good.

TIRED TIRE

Ex 17:12 When Moses' hands grew t,
Isa 40:28 He will not grow t or weary, and his
Jn   4: 6 Jesus, t as he was from the journey,

TIRZAH

1Ki 15:33 became king of all Israel in T,

TISHBITE

1Ki 17: 1 Now Elijah the T, from Tishbe
2Ki   1: 8 king said, "That was Elijah the T."

TITHE TEN

Lev 27:30 " 'A t of everything
Nu 18:26 of that t as the LORD's offering.
Dt 12:17 your own towns the t of your grain
Ne 10:37 we will bring a t of our crops
Mal   3:10 Bring the whole t

TITHES TEN

Nu 18:21 the Levites all the t in Israel as their
Ne 10:37 it is the Levites who collect the t
Mal   3: 8 "In t and offerings.

TITLE*

Isa 45: 4 and bestow on you a t of honor,

TITUS*

Gentile co-worker of Paul (Gal 2:1–3; 2Ti 4:10);
sent to Corinth (2Co 2:13; 7–8; 12:18), Crete (Titus 1:4–5).

TOBIAH

Enemy of Nehemiah and the exiles (Ne 2:10–
19; 4; 6; 13:4–9).

TOBIJAH
Zec   6:14 crown will be given to Heldai, T,

TODAY
Ex   14:13 Egyptians you see t you will never
       34:11 Obey what I command you t.
Dt   5: 3 with all of us who are alive here t.
       30:15 I set before you t life and prosperity,
Ps   2: 7 t I have become your father.
       95: 7 T, if only you would hear his voice,
Mt   6:11 Give us t our daily bread.
Lk   2:11 T in the town of David a Savior has
       4:21 "T this scripture is fulfilled in your
       19: 9 him, "T salvation has come to this
       23:43 t you will be with me in paradise."
Ac   13:33 t I have become your father.'
Heb   1: 5 t I have become your Father"?
       3: 7 "T, if you hear his voice,
       3:13 as long as it is called "T,"
       4: 7 "T, if you hear his voice, do not
       13: 8 Christ is the same yesterday and t

TOES
Da   2:42 As the t were partly iron and partly

TOGETHER
Ge   3: 7 so they sewed fig leaves t and made
Dt   22:10 with an ox and a donkey yoked t.
Ne   8: 1 all the people came t as one
Ps   2: 2 the rulers band t against the LORD
       85:10 Love and faithfulness meet t;
       133: 1 when God's people live t in unity!
       139:13 you knit me t in my mother's
Isa   11: 6 calf and the lion and the yearling t;
       65:25 The wolf and the lamb will feed t,
Eze   37: 7 and the bones came t, bone to bone.
Mt   19: 6 Therefore what God has joined t,
Ac   2:44 All the believers were t and had
       4:26 the rulers band t against the Lord
       5:12 to meet t in Solomon's Colonnade.
2Co   6:14 Do not be yoked t with unbelievers.
Eph   3: 6 the gospel the Gentiles are heirs t
              with Israel, members t of one body,
              and sharers t in the promise in Christ
Rev 16:16 they gathered the kings t

TOIL TOILED, TOILING
Ge   3:17 through painful t you will eat food
       5:29 painful t of our hands caused
Ecc   2:24 and find satisfaction in their own t.
       3:13 and find satisfaction in all their t—
       4: 4 I saw that all t and all achievement
       5:19 their lot and be happy in their t—
       6: 7 Everyone's t is for their mouth,

TOILED TOIL
2Co 11:27 I have labored and t and have often

TOILING TOIL
2Th   3: 8 t so that we would not be a burden

TOLA
A judge of Israel (Jdg 10:1–2).

TOLD TELL
Ge   3:11 "Who t you that you were naked?

Ge   22: 9 the place God had t him about,
Dt   1:18 time I t you everything you were
Jdg 16:17 So he t her everything.
1Ki 10: 7 Indeed, not even half was t me;
Ps   44: 1 our ancestors have t us what you did
Isa 48: 5 Therefore I t you these things long
Lk   2:20 which were just as they had been t.
Jn   14:29 I have t you now before it happens,
Ac   11: 4 Peter t them the whole story:

TOLERATE
Hab   1:13 you cannot t wrongdoing.
Rev   2: 2 that you cannot t wicked people,

TOMB TOMBS
Mt   27:65 make the t as secure as you know
Mk   15:46 and placed it in a t cut out of rock.
Lk   24: 2 the stone rolled away from the t,

TOMBS TOMB
Mt   23:29 You build t for the prophets
       27:52 and the t broke open. The bodies

TOMORROW
Pr   27: 1 Do not boast about t, for you do not
Isa 22:13 drink," you say, "for t we die!"
Mt   6:34 do not worry about t, for t
1Co 15:32 "Let us eat and drink, for t we die."
Jas   4:14 not even know what will happen t.

TONGUE TONGUES
Ex   4:10 I am slow of speech and t."
Job 33: 2 my words are on the tip of my t.
Ps   34:13 keep your t from evil and your lips
       39: 1 my ways and keep my t from sin;
       51:14 Savior, and my t will sing of your
       52: 4 every harmful word, you deceitful t!
       71:24 My t will tell of your righteous acts
       119:172 May my t sing of your word, for all
       137: 6 May my t cling to the roof of my
       139: 4 Before a word is on my t you,
Pr   6:17 a lying t, hands that shed innocent
       11:12 who has understanding holds their t.
       12:18 but the t of the wise brings healing.
       15: 4 The soothing t is a tree of life, but a
              perverse t crushes the spirit.
       18:21 The t has the power of life
       25:15 and a gentle t can break a bone.
       26:28 A lying t hates those it hurts,
       28:23 than one who has a flattering t.
       31:26 and faithful instruction is on her t.
SS   4:11 milk and honey are under your t.
Isa 32: 4 and the stammering t will be fluent
       45:23 by me every t will swear.
       50: 4 has given me a well-instructed t,
       59: 3 and your t mutters wicked things.
Mk   7:33 he spit and touched the man's t.
Lk   16:24 of his finger in water and cool my t,
Ro   14:11 every t will acknowledge God.' "
1Co 14: 2 who speaks in a t does not speak
       14: 4 speaks in a t edifies themselves,
       14: 9 speak intelligible words with your t,
       14:13 one who speaks in a t should pray
       14:19 than ten thousand words in a t.
       14:26 a revelation, a t or an interpretation.

1Co 14:27 If anyone speaks in a t, two—
Php 2:11 and every t acknowledge that Jesus
Jas 3: 5 the t is a small part of the body,
     3: 8 but no human being can tame the t.

TONGUES TONGUE

Jdg 7: 5 the water with their t as a dog laps
Ps   5: 9 with their t they tell lies.
    12: 4 who say, "By our t we will prevail;
    37:30 and their t speak what is just.
   126: 2 laughter, our t with songs of joy.
Pr 10:19 words, but the prudent hold their t.
    17:28 and discerning if they hold their t.
Isa 28:11 and strange t God will speak to this
Jer 23:31 the prophets who wag their own t
Ac   2: 3 saw what seemed to be t of fire
     2: 4 in other t as the Spirit enabled them.
    10:46 For they heard them speaking in t
    19: 6 and they spoke in t and prophesied.
Ro   3:13 their t practice deceit."
1Co 12:10 speaking in different kinds of t,
    12:10 still another the interpretation of t.
    12:28 guidance, and of different kinds of t.
    12:30 Do all speak in t? Do all interpret?
    13: 1 If I speak in the t of men
    13: 8 where there are t, they will be
    14: 5 like every one of you to speak in t,
    14: 5 greater than the one who speaks in t,
    14:18 I speak in t more than all of you.
    14:21 "With other t and through the lips
    14:39 and do not forbid speaking in t.
Jas 1:26 rein on their t deceive themselves,

TOOK TAKE

Ge   2:21 he t one of the man's ribs
     3: 6 wisdom, she t some and ate it.
     5:24 no more, because God t him away.
Jos 11:16 So Joshua t this entire land:
Ps 68:18 on high, you t many captives;
    78:70 and t him from the sheep pens;
Isa 53: 4 Surely he t up our pain and bore our
Da   7: 9 and the Ancient of Days t his seat.
Mt   4: 5 Then the devil t him to the holy city
     4: 8 Again, the devil t him to a very high
     8:17 "He t up our infirmities and bore
    26:26 they were eating, Jesus t bread,
    26:27 Then he t a cup, and when he had
1Co 11:23 the night he was betrayed, t bread,
    11:25 after supper he t the cup, saying,
Eph 4: 8 he t many captives and gave gifts
Php 3:12 for which Christ Jesus t hold of me.

TOOTH TEETH

Ex 21:24 eye for eye, t for t, hand for hand,
Lev 24:20 for fracture, eye for eye, t for t.
Mt   5:38 was said, 'Eye for eye, and t for t.'

TOP TOPS

Ge 28:12 earth, with its t reaching to heaven,
Ex 19:20 Moses to the t of the mountain.
Dt 28:13 you will always be at the t,
Isa 1: 6 foot to the t of your head there is no
Mt 27:51 was torn in two from t to bottom.
Jn 19:23 in one piece from t to bottom.

TOPHETH

2Ki 23:10 He desecrated T, which was
Jer 19:12 I will make this city like T.

TOPPLE

Isa 40:20 to set up an idol that will not t.

TOPS TOP

Ex 12: 7 t of the doorframes of the houses

TORCH TORCHES

Ge 15:17 firepot with a blazing t appeared
Isa 62: 1 dawn, her salvation like a blazing t.
Rev 8:10 blazing like a t, fell from the sky

TORCHES TORCH

Eze 1:13 like burning coals of fire or like t.
Da 10: 6 his eyes like flaming t, his arms

TORE TEAR

Ge 37:34 Then Jacob t his clothes,
Jos 7: 6 Then Joshua t his clothes and fell
1Ki 14: 8 I t the kingdom away
Mt 26:65 the high priest t his clothes and said,

TORMENT TORMENTED, TORMENTORS

Job 15:20 his days the wicked man suffers t,
Lk 16:28 not also come to this place of t.'
2Co 12: 7 flesh, a messenger of Satan, to t me.
Rev 18: 7 Give her as much t and grief as

TORMENTED TORMENT

1Sa 16:14 evil spirit from the LORD t him.
Rev 11:10 two prophets had t those who live
    20:10 They will be t day and night

TORMENTORS* TORMENT

Ps 137: 3 songs, our t demanded songs of joy;
Isa 51:23 I will put it into the hands of your t,

TORN TEAR

Ge 37:33 Joseph has surely been t to pieces."
Lev 22: 8 found dead or t by wild animals,
1Sa 28:17 The LORD has t the kingdom away
Mk   1:10 he saw heaven being t open
Lk 23:45 curtain of the temple was t in two.
Gal 4:15 you would have t out your eyes
Php 1:23 I am t between the two: I desire

TORTURE TORTURED

Mt   8:29 to t us before the appointed time?"

TORTURED* TORTURE

Mt 18:34 him over to the jailers to be t,
Heb 11:35 There were others who were t,

TOSS TOSSED, TOSSING

Mt 15:26 bread and t it to the dogs."

TOSSED TOSS

Eph 4:14 t back and forth by the waves,
Jas 1: 6 of the sea, blown and t by the wind.

TOSSING TOSS

Isa 57:20 But the wicked are like the t sea,

TOTAL TOTALLY
Ex 38:26 old or more, a t of 603,550 men.
Nu 26:51 The t number of the men of Israel

TOTALLY TOTAL
Nu 16:30 brings about something t new,
Dt 7: 2 them, then you must destroy them t.
Am 9: 8 I will not t destroy the descendants

TOUCH TOUCHED, TOUCHES
Ge 3: 3 and you must not t it, or you will
Ex 19:12 the mountain or t the foot of it.
Nu 4:15 But they must not t the holy things
Job 5:19 in seven no harm will t you.
Ps 105:15 "Do not t my anointed ones;
Isa 52:11 out from there! T no unclean thing!
Eze 9: 6 do not t anyone who has the mark.
Mt 9:21 "If I only t his cloak, I will be
Lk 24:39 T me and see; a ghost does not have
2Co 6:17 T no unclean thing, and I will
Col 2:21 Do not taste! Do not t!"?
Heb 11:28 firstborn would not t the firstborn

TOUCHED TOUCH
Ge 32:25 he t the socket of Jacob's hip so
1Sa 10:26 valiant men whose hearts God had t.
Isa 6: 7 and said, "See, this has t your lips;
Jer 1: 9 out his hand and t my mouth
Da 10:16 who looked like a man t my lips,
Mt 8: 3 reached out his hand and t the man.
   14:36 cloak, and all who t it were healed.
Mk 5:30 and asked, "Who t my clothes?"
Ac 19:12 aprons that had t him were taken
1Jn 1: 1 looked at and our hands have t—

TOUCHES TOUCH
Ex 19:12 Whoever t the mountain is to be put
Ps 104:32 it trembles, who t the mountains,
Am 9: 5 he t the earth and it melts, and all
Zec 2: 8 for whoever t you t the apple of his

TOWER WATCHTOWER
Ge 11: 4 with a t that reaches to the heavens,
Ps 61: 3 refuge, a strong t against the foe.
Pr 18:10 name of the LORD is a fortified t;
Lk 14:28 one of you wants to build a t.

TOWN HOMETOWN, TOWNS
Ezr 2: 1 and Judah, each to their own t,
Ne 7: 6 and Judah, each to his own t,
Mt 2:23 and lived in a t called Nazareth.
   5:14 A t built on a hill cannot be hidden.
   13:57 not without honor except in his own t
Mk 6: 4 without honor except in his own t,
Lk 2: 3 went to their own t to register.
   2:11 in the t of David a Savior has been

TOWNS TOWN
Nu 35: 2 Israelites to give the Levites t to live
   35:15 These six t will be a place of refuge
Jos 14: 4 of the land but only t to live in,
Jer 11:13 have as many gods as you have t;
Mt 9:35 Jesus went through all the t
   10:23 will not finish going through the t

TRACE TRACED, TRACING
Heb 7: 6 did not t his descent from Levi,

TRACED* TRACE
Ro 9: 5 from them is t the human ancestry

TRACING* TRACE
Ro 11:33 and his paths beyond t out!

TRACK
Job 14:16 my steps but not keep t of my sin.

TRADE TRADED, TRADERS, TRADING
Ge 42:34 you, and you can t in the land.' "
Isa 23:17 will ply her t with all the kingdoms
Rev 18:22 worker of any t will ever be found

TRADED TRADE
Joel 3: 3 people and t boys for prostitutes;

TRADERS TRADE
1Ti 1:10 for slave t and liars and perjurers—

TRADING TRADE
1Ki 10:22 The king had a fleet of t ships at sea
Pr 31:18 She sees that her t is profitable,

TRADITION TRADITIONS
Mt 15: 2 "Why do your disciples break the t
Mk 7:13 your t that you have handed down.
Col 2: 8 which depends on human t

TRADITIONS TRADITION
Mk 7: 8 and are holding on to human t."
Gal 1:14 zealous for the t of my fathers.

TRAIL
1Ti 5:24 the sins of others t behind them.

TRAIN* TRAINED, TRAINING, TRAINS, UNTRAINED
Isa 2: 4 nor will they t for war anymore.
   6: 1 the t of his robe filled the temple.
Mic 4: 3 nor will they t for war anymore.
1Ti 4: 7 rather, t yourself to be godly.

TRAINED TRAIN
Lk 6:40 everyone who is fully t will be like
Ac 22: 3 was thoroughly t in the law of our
Heb 5:14 by constant use have t themselves
   12:11 for those who have been t by it.

TRAINING* TRAIN
1Co 9:25 in the games goes into strict t.
Eph 6: 4 instead, bring them up in the t
1Ti 4: 8 For physical t is of some value,
2Ti 3:16 correcting and t in righteousness,

TRAINS* TRAIN
2Sa 22:35 He t my hands for battle;
Ps 18:34 He t my hands for battle;
   144: 1 my Rock, who t my hands for war,

TRAITOR TREASON
Lk 6:16 and Judas Iscariot, who became a t.
Jn 18: 5 Judas the t was standing there

TRAITORS TREASON
Ps   59:   5   show no mercy to wicked **t**.

TRAMPLE TRAMPLED
Ps   44:   5   through your name we **t** our foes.
Joel   3:13   Come, **t** the grapes,
Am   2:   7   They **t** on the heads of the poor as
     8:   4   you who **t** the needy and do away
Mt   7:   6   do, they may **t** them under their feet,
Lk   10:19   I have given you authority to **t**
Rev   11:   2   They will **t** on the holy city for 42

TRAMPLED TRAMPLE
2Ki   9:33   the horses as they **t** her underfoot.
Isa   63:   6   I **t** the nations in my anger;
Da   7:   7   and **t** underfoot whatever was left.
     8:   7   knocked it to the ground and **t** on it,
     8:10   down to the earth and **t** on them.
Mt   5:13   to be thrown out and **t** underfoot.
Lk   21:24   Jerusalem will be **t**
Heb   10:29   to be punished who has **t** the Son
Rev   14:20   They were **t** in the winepress

TRANCE*
Ac   10:10   was being prepared, he fell into a **t**.
     11:   5   praying, and in a **t** I saw a vision.
     22:17   praying at the temple, I fell into a **t**

TRANQUILLITY*
Ecc   4:   6   handful with **t** than two handfuls

TRANSACTION* TRANSACTIONS
Jer   32:25   silver and have the **t** witnessed.' "

TRANSACTIONS* TRANSACTION
Ru   4:   7   the method of legalizing **t** in Israel.)

TRANSCENDS*
Php   4:   7   God, which **t** all understanding,

TRANSFER*
Ru   4:   7   and **t** of property to become final,
2Sa   3:10   and **t** the kingdom from the house

TRANSFIGURED*
Mt   17:   2   There he was **t** before them.
Mk   9:   2   There he was **t** before them.

TRANSFORM* TRANSFORMED
Php   3:21   will **t** our lowly bodies so that they

TRANSFORMED TRANSFORM
Ro   12:   2   be **t** by the renewing of your mind.
2Co   3:18   are being **t** into his image

TRANSGRESSED*
TRANSGRESSION
Ps   17:   3   my mouth has not **t**.
Da   9:11   All Israel has **t** your law and turned

TRANSGRESSION*
TRANSGRESSED,
TRANSGRESSIONS,
TRANSGRESSORS
Ps   19:13   be blameless, innocent of great **t**.
Isa   53:   8   the **t** of my people he was punished.

Da   9:24   people and your holy city to finish **t**,
Mic   1:   5   All this is because of Jacob's **t**,
     1:   5   What is Jacob's **t**? Is it not Samaria?
     3:   8   to declare to Jacob his **t**, to Israel his
     6:   7   Shall I offer my firstborn for my **t**,
     7:18   forgives the **t** of the remnant of his
Ro   4:15   where there is no law there is no **t**.
     11:11   because of their **t**, salvation has
     11:12   if their **t** means riches for the world,

TRANSGRESSIONS*
TRANSGRESSION
Ps   32:   1   is the one whose **t** are forgiven,
     32:   5   I said, "I will confess my **t**
     39:   8   Save me from all my **t**; do not make
     51:   1   great compassion blot out my **t**.
     51:   3   For I know my **t**, and my sin is
     65:   3   by sins, you forgave our **t**.
     103:12   so far has he removed our **t** from us.
Isa   43:25   am he who blots out your **t**, for my
     50:   1   your **t** your mother was sent away.
     53:   5   But he was pierced for our **t**, he was
Mic   1:13   for the **t** of Israel were found in you.
Ro   4:   7   are those whose **t** are forgiven,
Gal   3:19   added because of **t** until the Seed
Eph   2:   1   you were dead in your **t** and sins,
     2:   5   even when we were dead in **t**—

TRANSGRESSORS*
TRANSGRESSION
Ps   51:13   Then I will teach **t** your ways,
Isa   53:12   death, and was numbered with the **t**.
     53:12   and made intercession for the **t**.
Lk   22:37   'And he was numbered with the **t**';

TRANSITORY*
2Co   3:   7   because of its glory, **t** though it was,
     3:11   And if what was **t** came with glory,

TRANSPARENT*
Rev   21:21   city was of gold, as pure as **t** glass.

TRAP TRAPPED, TRAPS
Ps   31:   4   Keep me free from the **t** that is set
     69:22   may it become retribution and a **t**.
Pr   20:25   It is a **t** to dedicate something rashly
     28:10   evil path will fall into their own **t**,
Isa   8:14   people of Jerusalem he will be a **t**
Mt   22:15   and laid plans to **t** him in his words.
Lk   21:34   will close on you suddenly like a **t**.
Ro   11:   9   their table become a snare and a **t**,
1Ti   3:   7   into disgrace and into the devil's **t**.
     6:   9   and a **t** and into many foolish
2Ti   2:26   and escape from the **t** of the devil,

TRAPPED TRAP
Pr   6:   2   you have been **t** by what you said,
     11:   6   the unfaithful are **t** by evil desires.
     12:13   Evildoers are **t** by their sinful talk,

TRAPS TRAP
Jos   23:13   will become snares and **t** for you,
Jdg   2:   3   they will become **t** for you, and their
La   4:20   life breath, was caught in their **t**.

TRAVEL TRAVELED, TRAVELER

Ex 13:21 so that they could t by day or night.
Pr 4:15 Avoid it, do not t on it; turn from it
Mt 23:15 You t over land and sea to win

TRAVELED TRAVEL

Ge 12: 6 Abram t through the land as far as
Ex 15:22 For three days they t in the desert
1Ki 19: 8 he t forty days and forty nights until

TRAVELER TRAVEL

Job 31:32 my door was always open to the t—
Jer 14: 8 like a t who stays only a night?

TREACHEROUS TREASON

Ps 25: 3 on those who are t without cause.
Isa 24:16 Woe to me! The t betray!
Zep 3: 4 unprincipled; they are t people.
Hab 1:13 Why then do you tolerate the t?
2Ti 3: 4 t, rash, conceited, lovers of pleasure

TREACHERY TREASON

Isa 59:13 rebellion and t against the LORD,

TREAD TREADING, TREADS

Dt 33:29 and you will t on their heights."
Ps 91:13 You will t on the lion and the cobra;
Mic 7:19 you will t our sins underfoot
Hab 3:19 he enables me to t on the heights.

TREADING TREAD

Dt 25: 4 Do not muzzle an ox while it is t
1Co 9: 9 "Do not muzzle an ox while it is t
1Ti 5:18 "Do not muzzle an ox while it is t

TREADS TREAD

Am 4:13 and t on the heights of the earth—
Rev 19:15 He t the winepress of the fury

TREASON TRAITOR, TRAITORS, TREACHEROUS, TREACHERY

2Ki 11:14 her robes and called out, "T! T!"

TREASURE TREASURED, TREASURES, TREASURIES, TREASURY

Pr 2: 4 and search for it as for hidden t,
Isa 33: 6 of the LORD is the key to this t.
Eze 7:22 robbers will desecrate the place I t.
Mt 6:21 For where your t is, there your heart
13:44 of heaven is like t hidden in a field.
19:21 poor, and you will have t in heaven.
Lk 12:33 a t in heaven that will never fail,
2Co 4: 7 But we have this t in jars of clay
1Ti 6:19 In this way they will lay up t

TREASURED* TREASURE

Ex 19: 5 nations you will be my t possession.
Dt 7: 6 to be his people, his t possession.
14: 2 chosen you to be his t possession.
26:18 his t possession as he promised,
Job 23:12 I have t the words of his mouth
Ps 135: 4 own, Israel to be his t possession.
Isa 64:11 fire, and all that we t lies in ruins.
Mal 3:17 "they will be my t possession.
Lk 2:19 But Mary t up all these things

Lk 2:51 his mother t all these things in her

TREASURES TREASURE

Dt 33:19 seas, on the t hidden in the sand."
2Ki 20:13 and everything found among his t.
24:13 Nebuchadnezzar removed the t
1Ch 29: 3 my God I now give my personal t
Pr 10: 2 Ill-gotten t have no lasting value,
Isa 45: 3 I will give you hidden t,
Mt 2:11 they opened their t and presented
6:19 store up for yourselves t on earth,
13:52 his storeroom new t as well as old."
Col 2: 3 in whom are hidden all the t
Heb 11:26 of greater value than the t of Egypt,

TREASURIES TREASURE

2Ch 16: 2 out of the t of the LORD's temple
Pr 8:21 who love me and making their t full.

TREASURY TREASURE

Ezr 2:69 to the t for this work 61,000 darics
Mt 27: 6 against the law to put this into the t,
Mk 12:43 more into the t than all the others.

TREAT TREATED, TREATING, TREATMENT

Lev 22: 2 his sons to t with respect the sacred
Nu 14:11 "How long will these people t me
Ps 103:10 he does not t us as our sins deserve
Mt 18:17 t them as you would a pagan
18:35 how my heavenly Father will t each
Jn 15:21 They will t you this way because
Ro 14:10 why do you t them with contempt?
Eph 6: 9 t your slaves in the same way.
1Th 5:20 Do not t prophecies with contempt
1Ti 5: 1 T younger men as brothers,
1Pe 3: 7 t them with respect as the weaker

TREATED TREAT

Ge 12:16 He t Abram well for her sake,
Ex 18:11 those who had t Israel arrogantly."
Lev 19:34 you must be t as your native-born.
25:40 They are to be t as hired workers
1Sa 24:17 "You have t me well, but I have t
Lk 6:23 how their ancestors t the prophets.
Heb 10:29 who has t as an unholy thing

TREATING TREAT

Ge 18:25 t the righteous and the wicked alike.
Heb 12: 7 God is t you as his children.

TREATMENT TREAT

Col 2:23 and their harsh t of the body,

TREATY

Ex 34:12 not to make a t with those who live
Dt 7: 2 Make no t with them, and show
23: 6 Do not seek a t of friendship
Jos 9: 6 make a t with us."
Am 1: 9 disregarding a t of brotherhood,

TREE TREES

Ge 1:29 every t that has fruit with seed in it.
2: 9 of the garden were the t of life and
the t of the knowledge of good
3: 1 not eat from any t in the garden'?"

Ge   3:24 to guard the way to the t of life.
2Sa 18: 9 Absalom's hair got caught in the t.
1Ki 14:23 hill and under every spreading t.
.·Ps   1: 3 person is like a t planted by streams
      52: 8 I am like an olive t flourishing
      92:12 righteous will flourish like a palm t,
Pr   3:18 She is a t of life to those who take
      11:30 fruit of the righteous is a t of life,
      27:18 who guards a fig t will eat its fruit,
Isa   65:22 For as the days of a t, so will be
Jer   17: 8 They will be like a t planted
Eze   17:24 I the LORD bring down the tall t and
             make the low t grow tall.
      17:24 I dry up the green t and make the
             dry t flourish.
Da   4:10 and there before me stood a t
Hos   9:10 seeing the early fruit on the fig t.
      14: 6 His splendor will be like an olive t,
Mic   4: 4 own vine and under their own fig t,
Hab   3:17 Though the fig t does not bud
Zec   3:10 to sit under your vine and fig t,'
Mt   3:10 every t that does not produce good
      12:33 "Make a t good and its fruit will be
      12:33 or make a t bad and its fruit will be
      12:33 for a t is recognized by its fruit.
Mk   11:13 Seeing in the distance a fig t in leaf,
Lk   19: 4 climbed a sycamore-fig t to see him,
Ro   11:24 of an olive t that is wild by nature,
      11:24 grafted into a cultivated olive t,
Jas   3:12 sisters, can a fig t bear olives,
Rev   2: 7 the right to eat from the t of life,
      22: 2 side of the river stood the t of life,
      22: 2 the leaves of the t are for the healing
      22.14 may have the right to the t of life
      22:19 that person any share in the t of life

TREES TREE

Ge   1:11 and t on the land that bear fruit
      3: 2 eat fruit from the t in the garden,
Dt   20:19 do not destroy its t by putting an ax
Jdg   9: 8 One day the t went out to anoint
1Ch   14:15 marching in the tops of the poplar t,
Ps   96:12 let all the t of the forest sing for joy.
Isa   55:12 all the t of the field will clap their
Eze   47:12 Fruit t of all kinds will grow on both
Zec   4:11 "What are these two olive t
Mt   3:10 The ax is already at the root of the t,
Mk   8:24 they look like t walking around."
Jude 1:12 autumn t, without fruit
Rev   8: 7 a third of the t were burned up,
      11: 4 They are "the two olive t"

TREMBLE TREMBLED, TREMBLES,
TREMBLING

Ex   15:14 The nations will hear and t;
1Ch   16:30 T before him, all the earth!
Ps   4: 4 T and do not sin; when you are
      99: 1 LORD reigns, let the nations t;
      114: 7 T, earth, at the presence of the Lord,
Isa   66: 2 in spirit, and who t at my word.
Jer   5:22 "Should you not t in my presence?
Eze   38:20 of the earth will t at my presence.
Joel 2: 1 Let all who live in the land t,
Hab   3: 6 he looked, and made the nations t.

Ro   11:20 Do not be arrogant, but t.

TREMBLED TREMBLE

Ex   19:16 Everyone in the camp t.
      20:18 mountain in smoke, they t with fear.
2Sa   22: 8 they t because he was angry.
Ac   7:32 Moses t with fear and did not dare

TREMBLES TREMBLE

Ps   97: 4 up the world; the earth sees and t.
      104:32 and it t, who touches the mountains,
      119:161 cause, but my heart t at your word.
Jer   10:10 When he is angry, the earth t;
Na   1: 5 The earth t at his presence,

TREMBLING TREMBLE

Ps   2:11 fear and celebrate his rule with t.
Da   10:10 me and set me t on my hands
Mk   16: 8 T and bewildered, the women went
Php   2:12 out your salvation with fear and t,
Heb   12:21 that Moses said, "I am t with fear."

TRENCH

1Ki   18:38 and also licked up the water in the t.
Da   9:25 It will be rebuilt with streets and a t,

TRESPASS* TRESPASSES

Ro   5:15 But the gift is not like the t.
      5:15 many died by the t of the one man,
      5:17 if, by the t of the one man,
      5:18 just as one t resulted
      5:20 in so that the t might increase.

TRESPASSES* TRESPASS

Ro   5:16 but the gift followed many t

TRIAL TRIALS

Nu   35:12 die before they stand t before
Ps   37:33 be condemned when brought to t.
Joel 3: 2 I will put them on t for what they did
Mal   3: 5 "So I will come to put you on t.
Mk   13:11 you are arrested and brought to t,
2Co   8: 2 In the midst of a very severe t,
Jas   1:12 one who perseveres under t because,
Rev   3:10 you from the hour of t that is going

TRIALS* TRIAL

Dt   7:19 saw with your own eyes the great t,
      29: 3 own eyes you saw those great t,
Lk   22:28 who have stood by me in my t.
1Th   3: 3 one would be unsettled by these t.
2Th   1: 4 persecutions and t you are enduring.
Jas   1: 2 whenever you face t of many kinds,
1Pe   1: 6 had to suffer grief in all kinds of t.
2Pe   2: 9 how to rescue the godly from t

TRIBAL TRIBE

Jos   11:23 Israel according to their t divisions.

TRIBE HALF-TRIBE, TRIBAL, TRIBES

Nu   1: 4 One man from each t, each of them
      17: 3 staff for the head of each ancestral t.
      36: 9 each Israelite t is to keep the land it
Jos   13:14 the t of Levi he gave no inheritance,
Jdg   21: 6 grieved for the t of Benjamin,

2Sa   2:10 The **t** of Judah, however, remained
            loyal
1Ki 11:13 will give him one **t** for the sake
Ps   78:68 but he chose the **t** of Judah,
Heb   7:13 that **t** has ever served at the altar.
Rev   5: 5 the Lion of the **t** of Judah, the Root
        5: 9 for God persons from every **t**
      11: 9 half days some from every people, **t**,
      14: 6 to every nation, **t**,

TRIBE OF JUDAH See JUDAH

TRIBES TRIBE

Ge   49:28 All these are the twelve **t** of Israel,
Ex   24: 4 pillars representing the twelve **t**
      39:14 the name of one of the twelve **t**.
1Ki 11:31 Solomon's hand and give you ten **t**.
      18:31 each of the **t** descended from Jacob,
Ps 122: 4 That is where the **t** go up—the **t**
Isa   49: 6 my servant to restore the **t** of Jacob
Mt   19:28 judging the twelve **t** of Israel.
Jas   1: 1 To the twelve **t** scattered among
Rev 21:12 the names of the twelve **t** of Israel.

TRIBES OF ISRAEL See ISRAEL

TRIBULATION*

Rev   7:14 who have come out of the great **t**;

TRIBUTE

Nu   31:28 set apart as **t** for the LORD one
1Ki   4:21 These countries brought **t** and were

TRICK* TRICKERY

1Th   2: 3 motives, nor are we trying to **t** you.

TRICKERY* TRICK

Ac   13:10 are full of all kinds of deceit and **t**.
2Co 12:16 fellow that I am, I caught you by **t**!

TRIED TRY

Ge   37:21 he **t** to rescue him from their hands.
Ex   2:15 heard of this, he **t** to kill Moses,
      8:18 the magicians **t** to produce gnats
Dt   4:34 Has any god ever **t** to take
Ps   73:16 When I **t** to understand all this,
      95: 9 they **t** me, though they had seen
Jn   5:18 For this reason they **t** all the more
     19:12 then on, Pilate **t** to set Jesus free,
Gal   1:23 is now preaching the faith he once **t**
Heb   3: 9 your ancestors tested and **t** me,

TRIES TRY

Lk   17:33 Whoever **t** to keep their life will

TRIMMED

Mt   25: 7 virgins woke up and **t** their lamps.

TRIUMPH TRIUMPHAL,
TRIUMPHANT, TRIUMPHED,
TRIUMPHING, TRIUMPHS

Ps   9:19 Arise, LORD, do not let mortals **t**;
      25: 2 nor let my enemies **t** over me.
      54: 7 and my eyes have looked in **t** on my
    112: 8 the end they will look in **t** on their
    118: 7 I look in **t** on my enemies.
Pr   28:12 When the righteous **t**, there is great

Isa   42:13 cry and will **t** over his enemies.
Rev 17:14 the Lamb will **t** over them because

TRIUMPHAL* TRIUMPH

Isa   60:11 their kings led in **t** procession.
2Co   2:14 as captives in Christ's **t** procession

TRIUMPHANT* TRIUMPH

Da   11:12 thousands, yet he will not remain **t**.

TRIUMPHED TRIUMPH

Dt   32:27 and say, 'Our hand has **t**;
Rev   5: 5 of Judah, the Root of David, has **t**.
     12:11 They **t** over him by the blood

TRIUMPHING* TRIUMPH

Col   2:15 of them, **t** over them by the cross.

TRIUMPHS* TRIUMPH

Jas   2:13 Mercy **t** over judgment.

TRIVIAL*

1Ki 16:31 He not only considered it **t**
Eze   8:17 Is it a **t** matter for the people
1Co   6: 2 you not competent to judge **t** cases?

TROOPS

Ex   14: 9 and chariots, horsemen and **t**—
Ps 110: 3 Your **t** will be willing on your day
Rev   9:16 of the mounted **t** was twice ten

TROPHIMUS

2Ti   4:20 Corinth, and I left **T** sick in Miletus.

TROUBLE TROUBLED,
TROUBLEMAKERS, TROUBLER,
TROUBLES

Ge   41:51 God has made me forget all my **t**
Nu   11:11 "Why have you brought this **t**
Jos   7:25 The LORD will bring **t** on you
1Ki 18:18 "I have not made **t** for Israel,"
Job   2:10 accept good from God, and not **t**?"
      5: 7 to **t** as surely as sparks fly upward.
     14: 1 are of few days and full of **t**.
     42:11 him over all the **t** the LORD had
Ps   7:14 is pregnant with evil conceives **t**
      7:16 The **t** they cause recoils on them;
      9: 9 a stronghold in times of **t**.
     10:14 you, God, see the **t** of the afflicted;
     22:11 for **t** is near and there is no one
     27: 5 the day of **t** he will keep me safe
     32: 7 you will protect me from **t**
     37:39 he is their stronghold in time of **t**.
     41: 1 LORD delivers them in times of **t**.
     46: 1 strength, an ever-present help in **t**.
     50:15 and call on me in the day of **t**;
     59:16 my fortress, my refuge in times of **t**.
     66:14 my mouth spoke when I was in **t**.
     90:10 yet the best of them are but **t**
     91:15 I will be with him in **t**, I will deliver
   107: 6 cried out to the LORD in their **t**,
  119:143 **T** and distress have come upon me,
   138: 7 Though I walk in the midst of **t**,
   143:11 righteousness, bring me out of **t**.
Pr   11: 8 righteous person is rescued from **t**,
     12:13 talk, and so the innocent escape **t**.

Pr   12:21 but the wicked have their fill of t.
     13:21 T pursues the sinner,
     19:23 one rests content, untouched by t.
     24:10 If you falter in a time of t,
     25:19 on the unfaithful in a time of t.
     28:14 hardens their heart falls into t.
Ecc 12: 1 before the days of t come
Jer 30: 7 It will be a time of t for Jacob,
Da   9:25 and a trench, but in times of t.
Jnh   1: 8 for making all this t for us?
Na   1: 7 is good, a refuge in times of t.
Zep   1:15 and anguish, a day of t and ruin,
Mt   6:34 Each day has enough t of its own.
     13:21 When t or persecution comes
Jn   16:33 In this world you will have t.
Ro   8:35 Shall t or hardship or persecution
2Co   1: 4 any t with the comfort we ourselves
2Th   1: 6 He will pay back t to those who t
Jas   5:13 Is anyone among you in t?

TROUBLED TROUBLE
Ge   6: 6 the earth, and his heart was deeply t.
Ps   38:18 I am t by my sin.
Mk   14:33 began to be deeply distressed and t.
Lk   1:29 Mary was greatly t at his words
Jn   14: 1 "Do not let your hearts be t.
     14:27 Do not let your hearts be t and do
2Th   1: 7 and give relief to you who are t,

TROUBLEMAKER* TROUBLE
2Sa 20: 1 Now a t named Sheba son of Bikri,
Pr   6:12 A t and a villain, who goes about
Ac   24: 5 "We have found this man to be a t.

TROUBLEMAKERS* TROUBLE
Dt   13:13 that t have arisen among you and
1Sa 30:22 and t among David's followers said,

TROUBLER* TROUBLE
1Ki 18:17 him, "Is that you, you t of Israel?"

TROUBLES TROUBLE
Ps   34: 6 he saved him out of all his t.
     34:17 he delivers them from all their t.
     34:19 righteous person may have many t,
     40:12 For t without number surround me;
     54: 7 have delivered me from all my t,
Isa 46: 7 it cannot save them from their t.
1Co   7:28 those who marry will face many t
2Co   1: 4 who comforts us in all our t,
      4:17 momentary t are achieving for us
      6: 4 in t, hardships and distresses;
      7: 4 all our t my joy knows no bounds.
Php   4:14 it was good of you to share in my t.

TRUE TRULY, TRUTH
Nu   11:23 not what I say will come t for you."
     12: 7 this is not t of my servant Moses;
Dt   18:22 does not take place or come t, that is
1Sa   9: 6 and everything he says comes t.
1Ki 10: 6 achievements and your wisdom is t.
2Ch   6:17 your servant David come t.
     15: 3 time Israel was without the t God,
Job 11: 6 wisdom, for t wisdom has two sides.

Ps   33: 4 word of the LORD is right and t;
    119:142 is everlasting and your law is t.
    119:151 and all your commands are t.
    119:160 All your words are t;
    144:15 is the people of whom this is t;
Pr   8: 7 My mouth speaks what is t, for my
Ecc 12:10 what he wrote was upright and t.
Isa 65:16 land will swear by the one t God.
Jer 10:10 But the LORD is the t God;
     28: 9 only if his prediction comes t."
Eze 33:33 "When all this comes t—
Lk   1:20 which will come t at their appointed
     16:11 who will trust you with t riches?
Jn   1: 9 The t light that gives light
      4:23 the t worshipers will worship
      5:32 that his testimony about me is t.
      6:32 Father who gives you the t bread
      7:28 authority, but he who sent me is t.
      8:16 my decisions are t, because I am not
     15: 1 "I am the t vine, and my Father is
     17: 3 the only t God, and Jesus Christ,
     19:35 testimony, and his testimony is t.
     21:24 We know that his testimony is t.
Ac   10:34 "I now realize how t it is that God
     11:23 them all to remain t to the Lord
     14:22 them to remain t to the faith.
     17:11 day to see if what Paul said was t.
Ro   3: 4 Let God be t, and every human
     12: 1 this is your t and proper worship.
Eph   4:24 to be like God in t righteousness
Php   4: 8 whatever is t, whatever is noble,
Col   1: 5 have already heard in the t message
1Th   1: 9 idols to serve the living and t God,
Titus 1:13 This saying is t. Therefore rebuke
1Jn   2: 8 and the t light is already shining.
      5:20 so that we may know him who is t
      5:20 He is the t God and eternal life.
3Jn   1:12 you know that our testimony is t.
Rev   2:13 Yet you remain t to my name.
      3: 7 the words of him who is holy and t,
      3:14 the faithful and t witness, the ruler
      6:10 Lord, holy and t, until you judge
     15: 3 Just and t are your ways,
     16: 7 t and just are your judgments."
     19: 2 for t and just are his judgments.
     19: 9 "These are the t words of God."
     19:11 whose rider is called Faithful and T.
     21: 5 these words are trustworthy and t."
     22: 6 "These words are trustworthy and t.

TRULY TRUE
Col   1: 6 it and t understood God's grace.

TRULY I TELL YOU Mt 5:18, 26; 6:2, 5, 16;
8:10; 10:15, 23, 42; 11:11; 13:17; 16:28; 17:20; 18:3,
13, 18, 19; 19:23, 28; 21:21, 31; 23:36; 24:2, 34, 47;
25:12, 40, 45; 26:13, 21, 34; Mk 3:28; 8:12; 9:1, 41;
10:15, 29; 11:23; 12:43; 13:30; 14:9, 18, 25, 30; Lk
4:24; 9:27; 12:37, 44; 18:17, 29; 21:3, 32; 23:43; Jn
1:51; 3:3, 5, 11; 5:19, 24, 25; 6:26, 32, 47, 53; 8:34,
51, 58; 10:1, 7; 12:24; 13:16, 20, 21, 38; 14:12; 16:7,
20, 23; 21:18

TRUMPET TRUMPETERS, TRUMPETS

Ex 19:16 mountain, and a very loud t blast.
Lev 23:24 commemorated with t blasts.
    25: 9 sound the t throughout your land.
Nu 10: 5 When a t blast is sounded, the tribes
Isa 27:13 And in that day a great t will sound.
Eze 33: 5 Since they heard the sound of the t
Joel 2:15 Blow the t in Zion, declare a holy
Zec 9:14 Sovereign LORD will sound the t;
Mt 24:31 send his angels with a loud t call,
1Co 14: 8 if the t does not sound a clear call,
    15:52 the twinkling of an eye, at the last t.
1Th 4:16 archangel and with the t call of God,
Rev 1:10 behind me a loud voice like a t,
    8: 7 The first angel sounded his t,

TRUMPETERS TRUMPET

2Ch 5:13 The t and musicians joined

TRUMPETS TRUMPET

Nu 10: 2 "Make two t of hammered silver,
    29: 1 It is a day for you to sound the t.
Jos 6: 8 carrying the seven t before
Jdg 7:19 They blew their t and broke the jars
Ps 47: 5 the LORD amid the sounding of t.
Mt 6: 2 do not announce it with t,
Rev 8: 2 and seven t were given to them.

TRUST* ENTRUST, ENTRUSTED, TRUSTED, TRUSTFULLY, TRUSTING, TRUSTS, TRUSTWORTHY

Ex 14:31 the LORD and put their t in him
    19: 9 and will always put their t in you."
Nu 20:12 "Because you did not t in me
Dt 1:32 you did not t in the LORD your
    9:23 You did not t him or obey him.
    28:52 walls in which you t fall down.
Jdg 11:20 did not t Israel to pass through his
2Ki 17:14 who did not t in the LORD their
    18:30 not let Hezekiah persuade you to t
1Ch 9:22 to their positions of t by David
Job 4:18 If God places no t in his servants,
    8:14 What they t in is fragile;
    15:15 If God places no t in his holy ones,
    31:24 "If I have put my t in gold or said
    39:12 Can you t it to haul in your grain
Ps 4: 5 the righteous and t in the LORD.
    9:10 Those who know your name t
    13: 5 But I t in your unfailing love;
    20: 7 Some t in chariots and some
    20: 7 we t in the name of the LORD our
    22: 4 In you our ancestors put their t;
    22: 9 you made me t in you, even at my
    24: 4 who does not t in an idol or swear
    25: 1 In you, LORD my God, I put my t.
    25: 2 I t in you; do not let me be put
    31: 6 as for me, I t in the LORD.
    31:14 But I t in you, LORD; I say,
    33:21 rejoice, for we t in his holy name.
    37: 3 T in the LORD and do good;
    37: 5 t in him and he will do this:

Ps 40: 3 the LORD and put their t in him.
    44: 6 I put no t in my bow, my sword
    49: 6 those who t in their wealth
    49:13 fate of those who t in themselves,
    52: 8 I t in God's unfailing love for ever
    55:23 But as for me, I t in you.
    56: 3 When I am afraid, I put my t in you.
    56: 4 in God I t and am not afraid.
    56:11 in God I t and am not afraid.
    62: 8 T in him at all times, you people;
    62:10 Do not t in extortion or put vain
    78: 7 Then they would put their t in God
    78:22 in God or t in his deliverance.
    86: 4 servant, Lord, for I put my t in you.
    91: 2 my fortress, my God, in whom I t."
    115: 8 them, and so will all who t in them.
    115: 9 All you Israelites, t in the LORD—
    115:10 House of Aaron, t in the LORD—
    115:11 who fear him, t in the LORD—
    118: 8 in the LORD than to t in humans.
    118: 9 in the LORD than to t in princes.
    119:42 who taunts me, for I t in your word.
    119:66 judgment, for I t your commands.
    125: 1 Those who t in the LORD are like
    135:18 them, and so will all who t in them.
    143: 8 love, for I have put my t in you.
    146: 3 Do not put your t in princes,
Pr 3: 5 T in the LORD with all your heart
    11:28 Those who t in their riches will fall,
    21:22 the stronghold in which they t.
    22:19 So that your t may be
    23: 4 do not t your own cleverness.
    28:25 but those who t in the LORD will
    28:26 Those who t in themselves are
Isa 8:17 I will put my t in him.
    12: 2 I will t and not be afraid.
    26: 3 are steadfast, because they t in you.
    26: 4 T in the LORD forever,
    30:15 in quietness and t is your strength,
    31: 1 who t in the multitude of their
    36:15 not let Hezekiah persuade you to t
    42:17 But those who t in idols, who say
    50:10 t in the name of the LORD
Jer 2:37 the LORD has rejected those you t;
    5:17 the fortified cities in which you t.
    7: 4 Do not t in deceptive words and say,
    7:14 the temple you t in, the place I gave
    9: 4 do not t anyone in your clan.
    12: 6 Do not t them, though they speak
    28:15 you have persuaded this nation to t
    29:31 and has persuaded you to t in lies,
    39:18 with your life, because you t in me,
    48: 7 Since you t in your deeds
    49: 4 you t in your riches and say,
Eze 33:13 but then they t in their righteousness
Mic 7: 5 Do not t a neighbor;
Na 1: 7 He cares for those who t in him,
Zep 3: 2 She does not t in the LORD,
    3:12 remnant of Israel will t in the name
Lk 16:11 who will t you with true riches?
Ac 14:23 Lord, in whom they had put their t.
Ro 15:13 all joy and peace as you t in him,
1Co 4: 2 been given a t must prove faithful.

1Co 9:17 simply discharging the t committed
2Co 13: 6 I t that you will discover that we
Heb 2:13 again, "I will put my t in him."

TRUSTED* TRUST

1Sa 27:12 Achish t David and said to himself,
2Ki 18: 5 Hezekiah t in the LORD, the God
1Ch 5:20 their prayers, because they t in him.
Job 12:20 He silences the lips of t advisers
Ps   5: 9 a word from their mouth can be t;
    22: 4 they t and you delivered them.
    22: 5 in you they t and were not put
    26: 1 I have t in the LORD and have not
    41: 9 someone I t, one who shared my
    52: 7 stronghold but t in his great wealth
   116:10 I t in the LORD when I said,
Pr 27: 6 Wounds from a friend can be t,
Isa 20: 5 Those who t in Cush and boasted
    25: 9 we t in him, and he saved us.
    25: 9 This is the LORD, we t in him;
    47:10 You have t in your wickedness
Jer 13:25 forgotten me and t in false gods.
    38:22 those t friends of yours.
    48:13 was ashamed when they t in Bethel.
Eze 16:15 " 'But you t in your beauty
Da   3:28 They t in him and defied the king's
     6:23 on him, because he had t in his God.
Lk 11:22 away the armor in which the man t
    16:10 "Whoever can be t with very little can
          also be t with much,
Ac 12:20 a t personal servant of the king,
Titus 2:10 but to show that they can be fully t,
     3: 8 those who have t in God may be

TRUSTFULLY* TRUST

Pr   3:29 your neighbor, who lives t near you.

TRUSTING* TRUST

Job 15:31 himself by t what is worthless,
Ps 112: 7 hearts are steadfast, t in the LORD.
Isa 2:22 Stop t in mere humans, who have
Jer 7: 8 you are t in deceptive words that are

TRUSTS* TRUST

Ps 21: 7 For the king t in the LORD;
    22: 8 "He t in the LORD," they say,
    28: 7 my heart t in him, and he helps me.
    32:10 love surrounds the one who t
    40: 4 Blessed is the one who t in the LORD,
    84:12 blessed is the one who t in you.
    86: 2 save your servant who t in you.
Pr 16:20 and blessed is the one who t
    29:25 but whoever t in the LORD is kept
Jer 17: 5 "Cursed is the one who t in man,
    17: 7 "But blessed is the one who t
Hab 2:18 who makes it t in its own creation;
Mt 27:43 He t in God. Let God rescue him
Ro   4: 5 but t God who justifies the ungodly,
1Co 13: 7 protects, always t, always hopes,
1Pe 2: 6 the one who t in him will never be

TRUSTWORTHY* TRUST

Ex 18:21 t men who hate dishonest gain—
2Sa 7:28 Your covenant is t, and you have
Ne 13:13 because they were considered t.

Ps 19: 7 The statutes of the LORD are t,
   111: 7 all his precepts are t.
   119:86 All your commands are t;
   119:138 down are righteous; they are fully t.
   145:13 The LORD is t in all he promises
Pr   8: 6 Listen, for I have t things to say;
    11:13 but a t person keeps a secret.
    12:22 but he delights in people who are t.
    13:17 but a t envoy brings healing.
    25:13 harvest time is a t messenger
Da   2:45 is true and its interpretation is t."
     6: 4 because he was t and neither corrupt
Lk 16:11 if you have not been t in handling
    16:12 if you have not been t with someone
    19:17 'Because you have been t in a very
Jn   8:26 But he who sent me is t, and what I
1Co 7:25 as one who by the Lord's mercy is t.
1Ti 1:12 that he considered me t,
     1:15 Here is a t saying that deserves full
     3: 1 Here is a t saying:
     3:11 but temperate and t in everything.
     4: 9 This is a t saying that deserves full
2Ti 2:11 Here is a t saying: If we died
Titus 1: 9 the t message as it has been taught,
     3: 8 This is a t saying. And I want you
Rev 21: 5 for these words are t and true."
    22: 6 to me, "These words are t and true.

TRUTH* TRUE, TRUTHFUL, TRUTHFULLY, TRUTHFULNESS, TRUTHS

Ge 42:16 tested to see if you are telling the t.
1Ki 17:24 LORD from your mouth is the t."
    22:16 the t in the name of the LORD?"
2Ch 18:15 the t in the name of the LORD?"
Job 42: 7 you have not spoken the t about me,
    42: 8 You have not spoken the t about me,
Ps 15: 2 who speaks the t from their heart;
    25: 5 Guide me in your t and teach me,
    45: 4 forth victoriously in the cause of t,
    52: 3 falsehood rather than speaking the t.
   119:43 Never take your word of t from my
   145:18 on him, to all who call on him in t.
Pr 12:17 An honest witness tells the t,
    22:21 you to be honest and to speak the t,
    23:23 Buy the t and do not sell it—
Isa 45:19 I, the LORD, speak the t;
    48: 1 but not in t or righteousness—
    59:14 t has stumbled in the streets,
    59:15 T is nowhere to be found,
Jer 5: 1 who deals honestly and seeks the t,
     5: 3 do not your eyes look for t?
     7:28 T has perished; it has vanished
     9: 3 it is not by t that they triumph
     9: 5 friend, and no one speaks the t.
    26:15 in t the LORD has sent me to you
Da   8:12 did, and t was thrown to the ground.
     9:13 sins and giving attention to your t.
    10:21 what is written in the Book of T.
    11: 2 "Now then, I tell you the t:
Am   5:10 and detest the one who tells the t.
Zec 8:16 Speak the t to each other, and render
     8:19 Therefore love t and peace."

Mt	22:16	of God in accordance with the t.
Mk	5:33	with fear, told him the whole t.
	12:14	of God in accordance with the t.
Lk	20:21	of God in accordance with the t.
Jn	1:14	from the Father, full of grace and t.
	1:17	and t came through Jesus Christ.
	3:21	whoever lives by the t comes
	4:23	the Father in the Spirit and in t,
	4:24	must worship in the Spirit and in t."
	5:33	to John and he has testified to the t.
	7:18	the one who sent him is a man of t;
	8:32	you will know the t, and the t will set you free."
	8:40	a man who has told you the t that I
	8:44	not holding to the t, for there is no t in him.
	8:45	Yet because I tell the t, you do not
	8:46	If I am telling the t, why don't you
	9:24	glory to God by telling the t,"
	14:6	"I am the way and the t and the life.
	14:17	the Spirit of t. The world cannot
	15:26	the Spirit of t who goes
	16:13	But when he, the Spirit of t, comes, he will guide you into all the t.
	17:17	Sanctify them by the t; your word is t.
	18:23	But if I spoke the t, why did you
	18:37	into the world is to testify to the t.
	18:37	on the side of t listens to me."
	18:38	"What is t?" retorted Pilate.
	19:35	He knows that he tells the t, and he
Ac	20:30	distort the t in order to draw away
	21:24	everyone will know there is no t
	21:34	could not get at the t because
	24:8	to learn the t about all these charges
	28:25	"The Holy Spirit spoke the t
Ro	1:18	people, who suppress the t by their
	1:25	They exchanged the t about God
	2:2	who do such things is based on t.
	2:8	and who reject the t and follow evil,
	2:20	embodiment of knowledge and t—
	9:1	I speak the t in Christ—I am not
	15:8	of the Jews on behalf of God's t,
1Co	5:8	unleavened bread of sincerity and t.
	13:6	in evil but rejoices with the t.
2Co	4:2	by setting forth the t plainly we
	11:10	As surely as the t of Christ is in me,
	12:6	because I would be speaking the t.
	13:8	we cannot do anything against the t, but only for the t.
Gal	2:5	so that the t of the gospel might be
	2:14	in line with the t of the gospel,
	4:16	your enemy by telling you the t?
	5:7	you to keep you from obeying the t?
Eph	1:13	when you heard the message of t,
	4:15	Instead, speaking the t in love,
	4:21	in accordance with the t that is
	5:9	in all goodness, righteousness and t)
	6:14	belt of t buckled around your waist,
2Th	2:10	because they refused to love the t
	2:12	who have not believed the t
	2:13	the Spirit and through belief in the t.
1Ti	2:4	and to come to a knowledge of the t.
	2:7	I am telling the t, I am not lying—

1Ti	3:15	the pillar and foundation of the t.
	4:3	who believe and who know the t.
	6:5	who have been robbed of the t
2Ti	2:15	who correctly handles the word of t.
	2:18	who have departed from the t.
	2:25	them to a knowledge of the t,
	3:7	to come to a knowledge of the t.
	3:8	so also these teachers oppose the t.
	4:4	will turn their ears away from the t
Titus	1:1	their knowledge of the t that leads
	1:14	commands of those who reject the t.
Heb	10:26	received the knowledge of the t,
Jas	1:18	give us birth through the word of t,
	3:14	do not boast about it or deny the t.
	5:19	one of you should wander from the t
1Pe	1:22	by obeying the t so that you have
2Pe	1:12	established in the t you now have.
	2:2	and will bring the way of t
1Jn	1:6	we lie and do not live out the t.
	1:8	ourselves and the t is not in us.
	2:4	a liar, and the t is not in that person.
	2:8	its t is seen in him and in you,
	2:20	One, and all of you know the t.
	2:21	you because you do not know the t,
	2:21	and because no lie comes from the t.
	3:18	or speech but with actions and in t.
	3:19	we know that we belong to the t
	4:6	is how we recognize the Spirit of t
	5:6	testifies, because the Spirit is the t.
2Jn	1:1	her children, whom I love in the t—
	1:1	I only, but also all who know the t—
	1:2	because of the t, which lives in us
	1:3	Son, will be with us in t and love.
	1:4	of your children walking in the t,
3Jn	1:1	friend Gaius, whom I love in the t.
	1:3	about your faithfulness to the t,
	1:4	my children are walking in the t.
	1:8	that we may work together for the t.
	1:12	and even by the t itself.

TRUTHFUL* TRUTH

Pr	12:19	T lips endure forever, but a lying
	14:25	A t witness saves lives, but a false
	22:21	you bring back t reports to those
Jer	4:2	and if in a t, just and righteous way
Jn	3:33	it has certified that God is t.
2Co	6:7	in t speech and in the power of God;

TRUTHFULLY* TRUTH

Eph	4:25	and speak t to your neighbor, for we

TRUTHFULNESS* TRUTH

Ro	3:7	"If my falsehood enhances God's t

TRUTHS* TRUTH

1Ti	3:9	keep hold of the deep t of the faith
	4:6	nourished on the t of the faith
Heb	5:12	teach you the elementary t of God's

TRY TRIED, TRIES, TRYING

Ps	26:2	and t me, examine my heart and my
Isa	7:13	Will you t the patience of my God
Lk	12:58	t hard to be reconciled on the way,
	13:24	will t to enter and will not be able
Ac	15:10	why do you t to test God by putting

1Co 10:33 even as I t to please everyone
     14:12 t to excel in those that build
2Co 5:11 the Lord, we t to persuade others.
Titus 2: 9 in everything, to t to please them,

TRYING TRY

Nu 16:10 now you are t to get the priesthood
Da 8:15 the vision and t to understand it,
Mt 2:20 those who were t to take the child's
2Co 5:12 We are not t to commend ourselves
Gal 1:10 Or am I t to please people? If I were
     3: 3 are you now t to finish by means
1Th 2: 4 We are not t to please people
1Pe 1:11 t to find out the time
1Jn 2:26 those who are t to lead you astray.

TUCK TUCKED, TUCKING

2Ki 4:29 "T your cloak into your belt,
     9: 1 him, "T your cloak into your belt,

TUCKED* TUCK

Ex 12:11 with your cloak t into your belt,

TUCKING* TUCK

1Ki 18:46 Elijah and, t his cloak into his belt,

TUMORS

1Sa 5: 6 on them and afflicted them with t.
     6: 4 "Five gold t and five gold rats,

TUNE TUNED

1Co 14: 7 anyone know what t is being played

TUNED* TUNE

Job 30:31 My lyre is t to mourning, and my

TUNIC TUNICS

Ex 28: 4 robe, a woven t, a turban and a sash.

TUNICS TUNIC

Ex 29: 8 Bring his sons and dress them in t

TUNNEL*

2Ki 20:20 the t by which he brought water
Job 28:10 They t through the rock;

TURBAN

Ex 28: 4 robe, a woven tunic, a t and a sash.
Zec 3: 5 I said, "Put a clean t on his head."

TURMOIL

Ps 65: 7 their waves, and the t of the nations.
Pr 15:16 LORD than great wealth with t.

TURN TURNED, TURNING, TURNS

Ex 23:27 make all your enemies t their backs
     32:12 T from your fierce anger;
Lev 19: 4 " 'Do not t to idols or make metal
Nu 32:15 If you t away from following him,
Dt   5:32 do not t aside to the right
     28:14 Do not t aside from any
     30:10 t to the LORD your God with all
Jos 1: 7 do not t from it to the right
1Ki 8:58 May he t our hearts to him, to walk
2Ch 7:14 face and t from their wicked ways,
     30: 9 He will not t his face from you
Ne   9:29 in order to t them back to your law,

Job 33:30 to t them back from the pit,
Ps   4: 2 long will you people t my glory
     6: 4 T, LORD, and deliver me;
     25:16 T to me and be gracious to me, for I
     28: 1 my Rock, do not t a deaf ear to me.
     34:14 T from evil and do good;
     51:13 so that sinners will t back to you.
     78: 6 they in t would tell their children.
    119:36 T my heart toward your statutes
    119:132 T to me and have mercy on me,
Pr   4: 5 my words or t away from them.
     4:27 Do not t to the right or the left;
     7:25 Do not let your heart t to her ways
     22: 6 they are old they will not t from it.
Isa 6:10 their hearts, and t and be healed."
     17: 7 and t their eyes to the Holy One
     28: 6 to those who t back the battle
     29:16 You t things upside down,
     30:21 Whether you t to the right
     41:18 I will t the desert into pools
     45:22 "T to me and be saved, all you ends
     55: 7 Let them t to the LORD, and he
     56:11 they all t to their own way,
Jer 18:11 So t from your evil ways, each one
     31:13 I will t their mourning
Eze 33: 9 you do warn the wicked person to t
     33:11 they t from their ways and live. T!
Joel 2:14 He may t and relent and leave
Jnh   3: 9 compassion t from his fierce anger
Mal 4: 6 He will t the hearts of the parents
Mt   5:39 t to them the other cheek also.
     10:35 to t " 'a man against his father,
Lk   1:17 to t the hearts of the parents to their
Jn 12:40 understand with their hearts, nor t—
     16:20 grieve, but your grief will t to joy.
Ac   3:19 and t to God, so that your sins may
     26:18 and t them from darkness to light,
1Co 14:31 For you can all prophesy in t so
     15:23 But each in t: Christ, the firstfruits;
1Ti 6:20 T away from godless chatter
2Ti 4: 4 They will t their ears away from the
            truth and t aside to myths.
Heb 12:25 if we t away from him who warns
1Pe 3:11 They must t from evil and do good;
Rev 10: 9 It will t your stomach sour,

TURNED TURN

Ex   4: 4 and it t back into a staff in his hand.
Dt 23: 5 t the curse into a blessing for you,
1Sa 7: 2 all the people of Israel t back
1Ki 11: 4 old, his wives t his heart after other
2Ch 15: 4 their distress they t to the LORD,
Est 9: 1 now the tables were t and the Jews
     9:22 when their sorrow was t into joy
Ps 14: 3 All have t away, all have become
     30:11 You t my wailing into dancing;
     40: 1 he t to me and heard my cry.
     41: 9 shared my bread, has t against me.
     66: 6 He t the sea into dry land,
    114: 3 looked and fled, the Jordan t back;
Ecc 2:12 I t my thoughts to consider wisdom,
Isa 9:12 his anger is not t away, his hand is
     53: 6 each of us has t to our own way;
Hos 7: 8 Ephraim is a flat loaf not t over.

Joel 2:31 The sun will be t to darkness
Jnh 3:10 and how they t from their evil ways,
Zec 7:11 stubbornly they t their backs
Lk 22:32 And when you have t back,
Jn 2: 9 the water that had been t into wine.
13:18 shared my bread has t against me.'
Ro 3:12 All have t away, they have together
Rev 6:12 The sun t black like sackcloth
6:12 the whole moon t blood red,
10:10 I had eaten it, my stomach t sour.

TURNING TURN
2Ki 21:13 dish, wiping it and t it upside down.
Pr 2: 2 t your ear to wisdom and applying
14:27 t a person from the snares of death.
Gal 4: 9 it that you are t back to those weak

TURNS TURN
Dt 30:17 if your heart t away and you are not
2Sa 22:29 the LORD t my darkness
Pr 15: 1 A gentle answer t away wrath,
Ecc 7: 7 Extortion t a wise person into a fool,
Isa 44:25 of the wise and t it into nonsense,
Eze 18:21 a wicked person t away from all
33:18 If a righteous person t from their
2Co 3:16 But whenever anyone t to the Lord,
Jas 5:20 Whoever t a sinner from the error

TURTLE(S), TURTLEDOVE (KJV)
See DOVE(S)

TWELVE 12,000, 144,000
Ge 35:22 Israel heard of it. Jacob had t sons:
49:28 All these are the t tribes of Israel,
Ex 24: 4 t stone pillars representing the t
28:21 There are to be t stones,
28:21 with the name of one of the t tribes.
Jos 4: 3 to take up t stones from the middle
1Ki 11:30 wearing and tore it into t pieces.
18:31 Elijah took t stones, one for each
Mt 10: 1 Jesus called his t disciples to him
Mk 3:14 He appointed t that they might be
Lk 9:17 the disciples picked up t basketfuls
Jas 1: 1 To the t tribes scattered among
Rev 12: 1 and a crown of t stars on her head.
21:12 wall with t gates, and with t
21:12 written the names of the t tribes
21:14 wall of the city had t foundations,
21:14 were the names of the t apostles
21:21 The t gates were t pearls,
22: 2 tree of life, bearing t crops of fruit,

TWENTY
Nu 1: 3 the men in Israel who are t years old

TWICE TWO
Ex 16: 5 is to be t as much as they gather
Nu 20:11 and struck the rock t with his staff.
1Ki 11: 9 Israel, who had appeared to him t.
Mk 14:30 the rooster crows t you yourself will

TWILIGHT LIGHT
Ex 12: 6 of Israel must slaughter them at t.
16:12 'At t you will eat meat,
Lev 23: 5 The LORD's Passover begins at t

TWIN TWINS
Ge 25:24 there were t boys in her womb.
SS 4: 2 Each has its t; not one of them is
Ac 28:11 figurehead of the t gods Castor and Pollux.

TWINKLING*
1Co 15:52 a flash, in the t of an eye, at the last

TWINS* TWIN
Ro 9:11 before the t were born or had done

TWIST* TWISTED, TWISTING, TWISTS
Ps 56: 5 All day long they t my words;

TWISTED TWIST
Ex 26: 1 with ten curtains of finely t linen
Mt 27:29 then t together a crown of thorns

TWISTING* TWIST
Pr 30:33 and as t the nose produces blood,

TWISTS TWIST
Ex 23: 8 see and t the words of the innocent.

TWO SECOND, TWICE
Ge 1:16 God made t great lights—
4:19 Lamech married t women,
6:19 into the ark t of all living creatures,
Ex 31:18 he gave him the t tablets
34: 1 out t stone tablets like the first ones,
Lev 16: 8 He is to cast lots for the t goats—
Dt 4:13 then wrote them on t stone tablets.
17: 6 On the testimony of t or three
22: 9 Do not plant t kinds of seed in your
25:13 Do not have t differing weights
1Ki 3:16 Now t prostitutes came to the king
Ps 62:11 has spoken, t things I have heard:
Pr 30: 7 "T things I ask of you, LORD;
30:15 "The leech has t daughters. 'Give!
Ecc 4: 9 T are better than one, because they
Isa 6: 2 t wings they covered their faces,
with t they covered their feet, and
with t they were flying.
Eze 1:11 They each had t wings spreading
1:11 each had t other wings covering its
Da 8: 3 before me was a ram with t horns,
Zec 4:11 "What are these t olive trees
14: 4 of Olives will be split in t from east
Mt 6:24 "No one can serve t masters.
18:16 be established by the testimony of t
19: 5 and the t will become one flesh'?
Mk 6: 7 he began to send them out t by t
12:42 and put in t very small copper coins,
15:27 They crucified t rebels with him,
Lk 9:30 T men, Moses and Elijah,
17:35 T women will be grinding grain
18:10 "T men went up to the temple
1Co 6:16 "The t will become one flesh."
Gal 4:24 The women represent t covenants.
Eph 2:14 who has made the t groups one
Rev 11: 3 And I will appoint my t witnesses,
19:20 The t of them were thrown alive

TWO-EDGED (KJV) See DOUBLE-EDGED

TYCHICUS*
Companion of Paul (Ac 20:4; Eph 6:21; Col 4:7; 2Ti 4:12; Titus 3:12).

TYRANNICAL*
Pr   28:16 A t ruler practices extortion, but one

TYRANNUS*
Ac   19: 9 daily in the lecture hall of T.

TYRE
1Ki   5: 1 Hiram king of T heard that Solomon
Ps   45:12 The city of T will come with a gift,
Isa   23: 1 For T is destroyed and left without
Eze   27: 2 man, take up a lament concerning T.
     28:12 a lament concerning the king of T
Mt   11:22 it will be more bearable for T

U

UGLY
Ge   41: 3 seven other cows, u and gaunt,

UNAPPROACHABLE*
1Ti   6:16 is immortal and who lives in u light,

UNASHAMED*
1Jn   2:28 and u before him at his coming.

UNAUTHORIZED
Lev   10: 1 and they offered u fire before

UNAVENGED*
Joel   3:21 I leave their innocent blood u?

UNAWARE
Lev   4:13 even though the community is u
     5: 2 they are u that they have become
2Co   2:11 For we are not u of his schemes.

UNBELIEF* UNBELIEVER, UNBELIEVERS, UNBELIEVING
Mk   9:24 help me overcome my u!"
Ro   4:20 not waver through u regarding
     11:20 they were broken off because of u,
     11:23 And if they do not persist in u,
1Ti   1:13 because I acted in ignorance and u.
Heb   3:19 not able to enter, because of their u.

UNBELIEVER* UNBELIEF
1Co   7:15 But if the u leaves, let it be so.
     10:27 If an u invites you to a meal
     14:24 if an u or an inquirer comes in while
2Co   6:15 believer have in common with an u?
1Ti   5: 8 the faith and is worse than an u.

UNBELIEVERS* UNBELIEF
Lk   12:46 and assign him a place with the u.
Ro   15:31 be kept safe from the u in Judea
1Co   6: 6 and this in front of u!
     14:22 a sign, not for believers but for u;
     14:22 is not for u but for believers.

1Co   14:23 and inquirers or u come in, will they
2Co   4: 4 this age has blinded the minds of u,
     6:14 Do not be yoked together with u.

UNBELIEVING* UNBELIEF
Mt   17:17 "You u and perverse generation,"
Mk   9:19 "You u generation," Jesus replied,
Lk   9:41 "You u and perverse generation,"
1Co   7:14 the u husband has been sanctified
     7:14 and the u wife has been sanctified
Heb   3:12 u heart that turns away
Rev   21: 8 But the cowardly, the u, the vile,

UNBLEMISHED*
Heb   9:14 the eternal Spirit offered himself u

UNCEASING UNCEASINGLY
Ro   9: 2 sorrow and u anguish in my heart.

UNCEASINGLY* UNCEASING
La   3:49 My eyes will flow u, without relief,

UNCERTAIN*
1Ti   6:17 which is so u, but to put their hope

UNCHANGEABLE* UNCHANGING
Heb   6:18 that, by two u things in which it is

UNCHANGING* UNCHANGABLE
Heb   6:17 to make the u nature of his purpose

UNCIRCUMCISED UNCIRCUMCISION
Ex   12:48 in the land. No u male may eat it.
Lev   26:41 when their u hearts are humbled
1Sa   17:26 Who is this u Philistine that he
Jer   9:26 For all these nations are really u,
     9:26 whole house of Israel is u in heart."
Ac   7:51 Your hearts and ears are still u.
Ro   3:30 and the u through that same faith.
     4:11 he had by faith while he was still u.
1Co   7:18 Was a man u when he was called?
Col   3:11 or Jew, circumcised or u, barbarian,

UNCIRCUMCISION* UNCIRCUMCISED
1Co   7:19 is nothing and u is nothing.
Gal   5: 6 neither circumcision nor u has any
     6:15 circumcision nor u means anything;
Col   2:13 your sins and in the u of your flesh,

UNCLEAN UNCLEANNESS
Ge   7: 2 one pair of every kind of u animal,
Lev   10:10 between the u and the clean,
     11:11 since you are to regard them as u,
     17:15 will be ceremonially u till evening;
     20:25 between clean and u animals
     20:25 that I have set apart as u for you.
Ezr   6:21 themselves from the u practices
Isa   6: 5 For I am a man of u lips, and I live
           among a people of u lips,
     52:11 Touch no u thing! Come out from it
La   1:17 has become an u thing among them.
Ac   10:14 never eaten anything impure or u."

Ro 14:14 Jesus, that nothing is **u** in itself.
14:14 if anyone regards something as **u**,
then for that person it is **u**.
2Co 6:17 Touch no **u** thing, and I will receive

UNCLEANNESS UNCLEAN
Eze 36:29 I will save you from all your **u**.
Jn 18:28 to avoid ceremonial **u** they did not

UNCLOTHED*
2Co 5: 4 because we do not wish to be **u**

UNCONCERNED*
Eze 16:49 were arrogant, overfed and **u**;

UNCOVER UNCOVERED
Ru 3: 4 Then go and **u** his feet and lie down.

UNCOVERED UNCOVER
Ge 9:21 drunk and lay **u** inside his tent.
Ru 3: 7 quietly, **u** his feet and lay down.
1Co 11: 5 her head **u** dishonors her head—
11:13 to pray to God with her head **u**?
Heb 4:13 Everything is **u** and laid bare before

UNDER
Ge 4:11 Now you are **u** a curse and driven
24: 2 he had, "Put your hand **u** my thigh.
47:29 eyes, put your hand **u** my thigh
Ex 6: 7 from **u** the yoke of the Egyptians.
1Ki 4:25 everyone **u** their own vine and
Ps 8: 6 you put everything **u** their feet:
91: 4 **u** his wings you will find refuge;
95: 7 of his pasture, the flock **u** his care.
Jer 3:13 foreign gods **u** every spreading tree,
Mic 4: 4 Everyone will sit **u** their own vine
Mt 5:15 light a lamp and put it **u** a bowl.
22:44 I put your enemies **u** your feet." '
Lk 13:34 hen gathers her chicks **u** her wings,
Jn 13: 3 had put all things **u** his power,
Ac 4:12 is no other name **u** heaven given
Ro 6:14 because you are not **u** the law, but
u grace.
1Co 9:21 God's law but am **u** Christ's law),
15:27 he "has put everything **u** his feet."
15:27 who put everything **u** Christ.
Gal 1: 8 to you, let them be **u** God's curse!
1: 9 accepted, let them be **u** God's curse!
4: 5 to redeem those **u** the law, that we
Rev 6: 9 I saw **u** the altar the souls of those

UNDER THE SUN See SUN

UNDERFOOT FOOT
Heb 10:29 who has trampled the Son of God **u**,

UNDERGOES* UNDERGOING
Heb 12: 8 and everyone **u** discipline—

UNDERGOING* UNDERGOES
1Pe 5: 9 the world is **u** the same kind

UNDERNEATH
Dt 33:27 and **u** are the everlasting arms.

UNDERSTAND
UNDERSTANDING,
UNDERSTANDS, UNDERSTOOD
Ge 11: 7 so they will not **u** each other."
Job 38: 4 Tell me, if you **u**.
42: 3 Surely I spoke of things I did not **u**,
Ps 14: 2 to see if there are any who **u**,
73:16 When I tried to **u** all this, it troubled
119:27 Cause me to **u** the way of your
119:125 that I may **u** your statutes.
Pr 2: 5 you will **u** the fear of the LORD
2: 9 Then you will **u** what is right
30:18 amazing for me, four that I do not **u**:
Ecc 7:25 So I turned my mind to **u**,
11: 5 so you cannot **u** the work of God,
Isa 1: 3 not know, my people do not **u**."
6:10 with their ears, **u** with their hearts,
44:18 their minds closed so they cannot **u**.
52:15 they have not heard, they will **u**.
Jer 17: 9 and beyond cure. Who can **u** it?
31:19 after I came to **u**, I beat my breast.
Da 1:17 Daniel could **u** visions and dreams
9:25 "Know and **u** this: From the time
Hos 14: 9 Let them **u**. The ways
Mt 13:15 ears, **u** with their hearts and turn,
24:15 let the reader **u**—
Mk 4:13 How then will you **u** any parable?
Lk 24:45 so they could **u** the Scriptures.
Jn 13: 7 I am doing, but later you will **u**."
Ac 8:30 "Do you **u** what you are reading?"
Ro 7:15 I do not **u** what I do. For what I
15:21 those who have not heard will **u**."
1Co 2:12 that we may **u** what God has freely
2:14 and cannot **u** them because they are
Eph 5:17 but **u** what the Lord's will is.
Heb 5:11 you because you no longer try to **u**.
11: 3 By faith we **u** that the universe was
1Ti 6: 4 they are conceited and **u** nothing.
2Pe 1:20 all, you must **u** that no prophecy
3: 3 all, you must **u** that in the last days
3:16 some things that are hard to **u**,

UNDERSTANDING
UNDERSTAND
Dt 4: 6 your wisdom and **u** to the nations,
1Ki 4:29 of **u** as measureless as the sand
Job 12:12 Does not long life bring **u**?
28:12 Where does **u** dwell?
28:28 is wisdom, and to shun evil is **u**."
32: 8 of the Almighty, that gives them **u**.
36:26 How great is God—beyond our **u**!
37: 5 he does great things beyond our **u**.
Ps 49:20 lack **u** are like the beasts that perish.
111:10 follow his precepts have good **u**.
119:32 for you have broadened my **u**.
119:34 Give me **u**, so that I may keep your
119:100 I have more **u** than the elders, for I
119:104 I gain **u** from your precepts;
119:130 it gives **u** to the simple.
136: 5 who by his **u** made the heavens,
147: 5 mighty in power; his **u** has no limit.
Pr 1: 6 for **u** proverbs and parables,
2: 2 and applying your heart to **u**—

Pr   2: 6 his mouth come knowledge and **u**.
      3: 5 heart and lean not on your own **u**;
      3:13 who find wisdom, those who gain **u**,
      4: 5 Get wisdom, get **u**; do not forget my
      4: 7 Though it cost all you have, get **u**.
      9:10 knowledge of the Holy One is **u**.
     10:23 a person of **u** delights in wisdom.
     11:12 one who has **u** holds their tongue.
     14:29 Whoever is patient has great **u**,
     15:21 but whoever has **u** keeps a straight
     15:32 one who heeds correction gains **u**.
     17:27 whoever has **u** is even-tempered.
     18: 2 Fools find no pleasure in **u**
     19: 8 the one who cherishes **u** will soon
Ecc   1:17 I applied myself to the **u** of wisdom,
Isa   6: 9 " 'Be ever hearing, but never **u**;
     11: 2 the Spirit of wisdom and of **u**,
     40:14 or showed him the path of **u**?
     40:28 weary, and his **u** no one can fathom.
     56:11 They are shepherds who lack **u**;
Jer   3:15 will lead you with knowledge and **u**.
      9:24 that they have the **u** to know me,
     10:12 stretched out the heavens by his **u**.
Da   1:17 and **u** of all kinds of literature
      5:12 a keen mind and knowledge and **u**,
     10:12 day that you set your mind to gain **u**
Hos   4:11 and new wine take away their **u**.
Mk   4:12 and ever hearing but never **u**;
     12:33 with all your **u** and with all your
Lk   2:47 who heard him was amazed at his **u**
Ac   28:26 will be ever hearing but never **u**;
Ro   10:19 angry by a nation that has no **u**."
2Co   6: 6 in purity, **u**, patience and kindness;
Eph   1: 8 With all wisdom and **u**,
Php   4: 7 which transcends all **u**, will guard
Col   1: 9 wisdom and **u** that the Spirit gives,
      2: 2 have the full riches of complete **u**,
Jas   3:13 Who is wise and **u** among you?
1Jn   5:20 God has come and has given us **u**,

UNDERSTANDS* UNDERSTAND

Dt   29: 4 has not given you a mind that **u**
1Ch 28: 9 every heart and **u** every desire
Job 28:23 God **u** the way to it and he alone
Isa 57: 1 no one **u** that the righteous are taken
Mt   13:23 who hears the word and **u** it.
Ro   3:11 there is no one who **u**; there is no
1Co 14: 2 Indeed, no one **u** them;

UNDERSTOOD UNDERSTAND

Ne   8: 8 the people **u** what was being read.
      8:12 because they now **u** the words
Ps   73:17 then I **u** their final destiny.
Isa 40:21 Have you not **u** since the earth was
Da   9: 2 I, Daniel, **u** from the Scriptures,
Ro   1:20 being **u** from what has been made,

UNDERTAKEN

Lk   1: 1 Many have **u** to draw up an account

UNDESIRABLE*

Jos 24:15 serving the LORD seems **u** to you,

UNDIVIDED*

1Ch 12:33 to help David with **u** loyalty—

Ps   86:11 give me an **u** heart, that I may fear
Eze 11:19 I will give them an **u** heart and put
1Co   7:35 in a right way in **u** devotion

UNDOING UNDONE

Pr   18: 7 The mouths of fools are their **u**,

UNDONE UNDOING

Lk   11:42 latter without leaving the former **u**.

UNDYING*

Eph   6:24 Lord Jesus Christ with an **u** love.

UNENDING* END

Ps   21: 6 you have granted him **u** blessings
Jer 15:18 Why is my pain **u** and my wound

UNEQUALED*

Mt   24:21 **u** from the beginning of the world
Mk   13:19 of distress **u** from the beginning,

UNFADING*

1Pe   3: 4 the **u** beauty of a gentle and quiet

UNFAILING*

Ex   15:13 your **u** love you will lead the people
1Sa 20:14 But show me **u** kindness like
2Sa 22:51 he shows **u** kindness to his anointed,
Ps   6: 4 save me because of your **u** love.
     13: 5 But I trust in your **u** love;
     18:50 he shows **u** love to his anointed,
     21: 7 through the **u** love of the Most High
     26: 3 always been mindful of your **u** love
     31:16 save me in your **u** love.
     32:10 the LORD's **u** love surrounds
     33: 5 the earth is full of his **u** love.
     33:18 those whose hope is in his **u** love,
     33:22 May your **u** love be with us,
     36: 7 How priceless is your **u** love,
     44:26 rescue us because of your **u** love.
     48: 9 O God, we meditate on your **u** love.
     51: 1 O God, according to your **u** love;
     52: 8 I trust in God's **u** love for ever
     62:12 and with you, Lord, is **u** love";
     77: 8 Has his **u** love vanished forever?
     85: 7 Show us your **u** love, LORD,
     90:14 us in the morning with your **u** love,
     94:18 "My foot is slipping," your **u** love,
    107: 8 thanks to the LORD for his **u** love
    107:15 thanks to the LORD for his **u** love
    107:21 thanks to the LORD for his **u** love
    107:31 thanks to the LORD for his **u** love
    109:26 save me according to your **u** love.
    119:41 May your **u** love come to me,
    119:76 May your **u** love be my comfort,
    119:88 In your **u** love preserve my life,
    130: 7 for with the LORD is **u** love
    138: 2 praise your name for your **u** love
    143: 8 bring me word of your **u** love, for I
    143:12 In your **u** love, silence my enemies;
    147:11 who put their hope in his **u** love.
Pr   19:22 What a person desires is **u** love;
     20: 6 Many claim to have **u** love,
Isa 54:10 yet my **u** love for you will not be
Jer 31: 3 I have drawn you with **u** kindness.

La 3:32 compassion, so great is his **u** love.
Hos 10:12 reap the fruit of **u** love, and break

UNFAILING LOVE See LOVE

UNFAITHFUL UNFAITHFULNESS
Lev 6: 2 is **u** to the LORD by deceiving
Nu 5: 6 and so is **u** to the LORD is guilty
5:12 wife goes astray and is **u** to him
1Ch 10:13 Saul died because he was **u**
Ezr 10: 2 "We have been **u** to our God
Pr 11: 6 but the **u** are trapped by evil desires.
13: 2 the **u** have an appetite for violence.
13:15 but the way of the **u** leads to their
22:12 but he frustrates the words of the **u**.
23:28 and multiplies the **u** among men.
25:19 foot is reliance on the **u** in a time
Jer 3:20 But like a woman **u** to her husband,
3:20 Israel, have been **u** to me,"
Eze 20:27 blasphemed me by being **u** to me:
Hos 5: 7 They are **u** to the LORD;
Mal 2:10 ancestors by being **u** to one another?
2:11 Judah has been **u**. A detestable thing
2:14 You have been **u** to her, though she
2:15 and do not be **u** to the wife of your
2:16 be on your guard, and do not be **u**.

UNFAITHFULNESS UNFAITHFUL
Nu 14:33 suffering for your **u**, until the last
1Ch 9: 1 to Babylon because of their **u**.
Eze 18:24 Because of the **u** they are guilty
Hos 1: 2 wife this land is guilty of **u**
Ro 3: 3 Will their **u** nullify God's

UNFINISHED* FINISH
Titus 1: 5 might put in order what was left **u**
Rev 3: 2 for I have found your deeds **u**

UNFIT*
Titus 1:16 and **u** for doing anything good.

UNFOLDING*
Ps 119:130 The **u** of your words gives light;

UNFORGIVING*
2Ti 3: 3 without love, **u**, slanderous,

UNFORMED*
Ps 139:16 Your eyes saw my **u** body;

UNFRIENDLY*
Pr 18: 1 An **u** person pursues selfish ends

UNFRUITFUL
Mk 4:19 in and choke the word, making it **u**.
1Co 14:14 my spirit prays, but my mind is **u**.

UNGODLINESS* UNGODLY
Isa 32: 6 They practice **u** and spread error
Jer 23:15 Jerusalem **u** has spread throughout
Titus 2:12 It teaches us to say "No" to **u**
Jude 1:15 acts they have committed in their **u**,

UNGODLY UNGODLINESS
Pr 11:31 earth, how much more the **u**
Ro 4: 5 but trusts God who justifies the **u**,
5: 6 still powerless, Christ died for the **u**.

1Ti 1: 9 and rebels, the **u** and sinful,
2Ti 2:16 in it will become more and more **u**.
2Pe 2: 6 of what is going to happen to the **u**;
Jude 1:15 all the **u** acts they have committed

UNGRATEFUL*
Lk 6:35 because he is kind to the **u**
2Ti 3: 2 disobedient to their parents, **u**,

UNHARMED
Da 3:25 unbound and **u**, and the fourth looks

UNHEARD-OF*
Eze 7: 5 " 'Disaster! U disaster!
Da 11:36 will say **u** things against the God

UNHOLY*
1Ti 1: 9 and sinful, the **u** and irreligious,
2Ti 3: 2 to their parents, ungrateful, **u**,
Heb 10:29 has treated as an **u** thing the blood

UNINFORMED
1Th 4:13 you to be **u** about those who sleep

UNINTENTIONALLY
Lev 4: 2 'When anyone sins **u** and does what
Nu 15:22 if you as a community **u** fail to keep
Dt 4:42 they had **u** killed a neighbor without

UNION UNITE
Zec 11:14 I broke my second staff called U,

UNIT
Ex 36:18 to fasten the tent together as a **u**.

UNITE UNION, UNITED, UNITES, UNITY
1Co 6:15 Christ and **u** them with a prostitute?

UNITED UNITE
Ge 2:24 and mother and is **u** to his wife,
Mt 19: 5 and mother and be **u** to his wife,
Ro 6: 5 be **u** with him in a resurrection like
1Co 1:10 that you be perfectly **u** in mind
6:17 whoever is **u** with the Lord is one
Eph 5:31 and mother and be **u** to his wife,
Php 2: 1 from being **u** with Christ, if any
Col 2: 2 encouraged in heart and **u** in love,

UNITES* UNITE
1Co 6:16 he who **u** himself with a prostitute is

UNITY* UNITE
2Ch 30:12 the people to give them **u** of mind
Ps 133: 1 God's people live together in **u**!
Jn 17:23 they may be brought to complete **u**.
Eph 1:10 to bring **u** to all things in heaven
4: 3 keep the **u** of the Spirit through
4:13 until we all reach **u** in the faith
Col 3:14 binds them all together in perfect **u**.

UNIVERSE*
1Co 4: 9 made a spectacle to the whole **u**,
Eph 4:10 in order to fill the whole **u**.)
Heb 1: 2 through whom also he made the **u**.
11: 3 understand that the **u** was formed

UNJUST

Eze 18:25 Hear, you Israelites: Is my way **u**? Is it
not your ways that are **u**?
Lk 18: 6 "Listen to what the **u** judge says.
Ro 3: 5 That God is **u** in bringing his wrath
9:14 shall we say? Is God **u**? Not at all!
Heb 6:10 God is not **u**; he will not forget your
1Pe 2:19 pain of **u** suffering because they are

UNKNOWN

Ps 81: 5 I heard an **u** voice say:
Ac 17:23 with this inscription: TO AN **U** GOD.

UNLAWFUL

Mt 12: 2 Your disciples are doing what is **u**
Ac 16:21 by advocating customs **u** for us

UNLEAVENED

Ex 12:17 "Celebrate the Festival of U Bread,
Dt 16:16 at the Festival of U Bread,
Mt 26:17 first day of the Festival of U Bread,

THE FESTIVAL OF UNLEAVENED BREAD
See FESTIVAL

UNLESS

Ps 94:17 U the LORD had given me help,
127: 1 U the LORD builds the house,
La 5:22 **u** you have utterly rejected us
Lk 13: 3 But **u** you repent, you too will all
Jn 3: 3 of God **u** they are born again."
4:48 "U you people see signs
12:24 you, **u** a kernel of wheat falls
Ac 8:31 "**u** someone explains it to me?"
Rev 13:17 not buy or sell **u** they had the mark,

UNLIKE

2Co 2:17 U so many, we do not peddle
Heb 7:27 U the other high priests, he does not

UNLOVED*

Dt 21:17 the son of his **u** wife as the firstborn

UNMARRIED

1Co 7: 8 It is good for them to stay **u**, as I do.
7:32 An **u** man is concerned

UNNATURAL*

Ro 1:26 natural sexual relations for **u** ones.

UNPLOWED

Ex 23:11 the seventh year let the land lie **u**
Jer 4: 3 "Break up your **u** ground and do
Hos 10:12 love, and break up your **u** ground;

UNPRINCIPLED*

Zep 3: 4 Her prophets are **u**;

UNPRODUCTIVE

Titus 3:14 for urgent needs and not live **u** lives.
2Pe 1: 8 **u** in your knowledge of our Lord

UNPROFITABLE*

Isa 30: 6 humps of camels, to that **u** nation,
Titus 3: 9 because these are **u** and useless.

UNPUNISHED

Ex 34: 7 Yet he does not leave the guilty **u**;

Nu 14:18 Yet he does not leave the guilty **u**;
Pr 6:29 no one who touches her will go **u**.
11:21 The wicked will not go **u**, but those
19: 5 A false witness will not go **u**,
28:20 one eager to get rich will not go **u**.
Na 1: 3 LORD will not leave the guilty **u**.
Ro 3:25 the sins committed beforehand **u**—

UNQUENCHABLE

Lk 3:17 will burn up the chaff with **u** fire."

UNREASONING* REASON

2Pe 2:12 They are like **u** animals,

UNREPENTANT*

Ro 2: 5 your stubbornness and your **u** heart,

UNRIGHTEOUS*
UNRIGHTEOUSNESS

Isa 55: 7 their ways and the **u** their thoughts.
Zep 3: 5 not fail, yet the **u** know no shame.
Mt 5:45 rain on the righteous and the **u**.
1Pe 3:18 the righteous for the **u**, to bring you
2Pe 2: 9 to hold the **u** for punishment

UNRIGHTEOUSNESS
UNRIGHTEOUS

1Jn 1: 9 us our sins and purify us from all **u**.

UNRULY

Pr 9:13 Folly is an **u** woman; she is simple

UNSCHOOLED*

Ac 4:13 John and realized that they were **u**,

UNSEARCHABLE

Ro 11:33 How **u** his judgments, and his paths

UNSEEN*

Mt 6: 6 and pray to your Father, who is **u**.
6:18 but only to your Father, who is **u**;
2Co 4:18 but on what is **u**, since what is seen
4:18 temporary, but what is **u** is eternal.

UNSETTLED*

1Th 3: 3 no one would be **u** by these trials.
2Th 2: 2 not to become easily **u** or alarmed

UNSHRUNK

Mt 9:16 "No one sews a patch of **u** cloth

UNSPIRITUAL*

Ro 7:14 but I am **u**, sold as a slave to sin.
Col 2:18 up with idle notions by their **u** mind.
Jas 3:15 down from heaven but is earthly, **u**,

UNSTABLE*

Jas 1: 8 double-minded and **u** in all they do.
2Pe 2:14 they seduce the **u**; they are experts
3:16 which ignorant and **u** people distort,

UNSWERVINGLY*

Heb 10:23 Let us hold **u** to the hope we

UNTHINKABLE*

Job 34:12 It is **u** that God would do wrong,

UNTIE
Mk 1: 7 am not worthy to stoop down and **u**.
Lk 13:15 of you on the Sabbath **u** your ox

UNTRAINED* TRAIN
2Co 11: 6 I may indeed be **u** as a speaker, but I

UNVEILED*
2Co 3:18 with **u** faces contemplate the Lord's

UNWARY*
Ps 116: 6 The LORD protects the **u**;

UNWASHED*
Mt 15:20 with **u** hands does not defile them."
Mk 7: 2 hands that were defiled, that is, **u**.

UNWHOLESOME*
Eph 4:29 Do not let any **u** talk come

UNWISE*
Dt 32: 6 LORD, you foolish and **u** people?
Eph 5:15 how you live—not as **u** but as wise,

UNWORTHY*
Ge 32:10 I am **u** of all the kindness
Job 40: 4 "I am **u**—how can I reply to you?
Lk 17:10 do, should say, 'We are **u** servants;
1Co 11:27 Lord in an **u** manner will be guilty

UNYIELDING
Ex 7:14 to Moses, "Pharaoh's heart is **u**;
Pr 18:19 wronged is more **u** than a fortified

UPHELD UPHOLD
Ps 9: 4 For you have **u** my right and my

UPHOLD UPHELD, UPHOLDING, UPHOLDS
Ps 41:12 Because of my integrity you **u** me
82: 3 **u** the cause of the poor
Isa 41:10 I will **u** you with my righteous right
42: 1 whom I **u**, my chosen one in whom
Ro 3:31 Not at all! Rather, we **u** the law.

UPHOLDING* UPHOLD
Isa 9: 7 establishing and **u** it with justice

UPHOLDS UPHOLD
Ps 37:17 but the LORD **u** the righteous.
37:24 for the LORD **u** him with his hand.
63: 8 I cling to you; your right hand **u** me.
140:12 poor and **u** the cause of the needy.
145:14 The LORD **u** all who fall and lifts
146: 7 He **u** the cause of the oppressed

UPLIFTED LIFT
Ex 6: 8 the land I swore with **u** hand to give
Ps 106:26 to them with **u** hand that he would

UPPER
Eze 42: 5 Now the **u** rooms were narrower,

UPRIGHT UPRIGHTLY, UPRIGHTNESS
Ge 37: 7 suddenly my sheaf rose and stood **u**,
Dt 32: 4 who does no wrong, **u** and just is he.

Job 1: 1 This man was blameless and **u**;
1: 8 he is blameless and **u**, a man who
2: 3 he is blameless and **u**, a man who
33: 3 My words come from an **u** heart;
Ps 7:10 High, who saves the **u** in heart.
11: 7 the **u** will see his face.
25: 8 Good and **u** is the LORD;
33: 1 it is fitting for the **u** to praise him.
64:10 all the **u** in heart will glory in him!
92:15 proclaiming, "The LORD is **u**;
97:11 righteous and joy on the **u** in heart.
112: 4 in darkness light dawns for the **u**,
119: 7 an **u** heart as I learn your righteous
Pr 2: 7 He holds success in store for the **u**,
2:21 For the **u** will live in the land,
3:32 but takes the **u** into his confidence.
11: 3 The integrity of the **u** guides them,
15: 8 but the prayer of the **u** pleases him.
21:29 but the **u** give thought to their ways.
Isa 26: 7 you, the **U** One, make the way
Mic 2: 7 good to the one whose ways are **u**?
Titus 1: 8 who is self-controlled, **u**,
2:12 **u** and godly lives in this present age,

UPRIGHTLY* UPRIGHT
Pr 14: 2 Whoever fears the LORD walks **u**,
Isa 57: 2 Those who walk **u** enter into peace;

UPRIGHTNESS UPRIGHT
Ps 25:21 May integrity and **u** protect me,
111: 8 ever, enacted in faithfulness and **u**.

UPRISINGS*
Lk 21: 9 When you hear of wars and **u**,

UPROOT UPROOTED
2Ch 7:20 then I will **u** Israel from my land,
Ecc 3: 2 die, a time to plant and a time to **u**,
Jer 1:10 and kingdoms to **u** and tear down,

UPROOTED UPROOT
Dt 28:63 You will be **u** from the land you are
Pr 10:30 The righteous will never be **u**,
Jer 18: 7 that a nation or kingdom is to be **u**,
31:40 The city will never again be **u**
Lk 17: 6 tree, 'Be **u** and planted in the sea,'
Jude 1:12 autumn trees, without fruit and **u**—

UPSET
Lk 10:41 worried and **u** about many things,

UPWARD
Ex 37: 9 cherubim had their wings spread **u**,
Eze 1:11 each had two wings spreading out **u**,

UR
Ge 15: 7 you out of **U** of the Chaldeans
Ne 9: 7 him out of **U** of the Chaldeans

URGE URGED, URGENTLY, URGING
Ru 1:16 "Don't **u** me to leave you or to turn
Ro 12: 1 Therefore, I **u** you,
1Co 4:16 Therefore I **u** you to imitate me.
Titus 2: 4 they can **u** the younger women
Jude 1: 3 **u** you to contend for the faith

URGED URGE

Ge 19:15 of dawn, the angels **u** Lot, saying,
Ex 12:33 The Egyptians **u** the people to hurry

URGENTLY URGE

Jnh 3: 8 Let everyone call **u** on God.

URGING URGE

Ru 1:18 to go with her, she stopped **u** her.
1Th 2:12 **u** you to live lives worthy of God,

URIAH

Hittite husband of Bathsheba, killed by David's order (2Sa 11).

URIM

Ex 28:30 put the U and the Thummim
1Sa 28: 6 did not answer him by dreams or U
Ezr 2:63 was a priest ministering with the U

USE USED, USEFUL, USELESS, USES

Lev 19:35 " 'Do not **u** dishonest standards
Jdg 2:22 I will **u** them to test Israel and see
Mt 7: 2 and with the measure you **u**, it will
1Co 9:18 make full **u** of my rights as a preacher
Gal 5:13 do not **u** your freedom to indulge
1Ti 5:23 and **u** a little wine because of your
1Pe 4:10 you should **u** whatever gift you have

USED USE

Mt 22:19 Show me the coin **u** for paying
Jn 10: 6 Jesus **u** this figure of speech,
Php 2: 6 to be **u** to his own advantage;
1Co 9:15 But I have not **u** any of these rights.

USEFUL USE

Eph 4:28 doing something **u** with their own
2Ti 2:21 **u** to the Master and prepared to do
     3:16 God-breathed and is **u** for teaching,
Phm 1:11 now he has become **u** both to you

USELESS USE

1Sa 12:21 Do not turn away after **u** idols.
1Co 15:14 our preaching is **u** and so is your
Titus 3: 9 these are unprofitable and **u**.
Phm 1:11 Formerly he was **u** to you, but now
Heb 7:18 set aside because it was weak and **u**
Jas 2:20 that faith without deeds is **u**?

USES USE

1Ti 1: 8 the law is good if one **u** it properly.

UTMOST

Job 34:36 to the **u** for answering like a wicked

UTTER UTTERANCE, UTTERED, UTTERLY

Dt 23:23 Whatever your lips **u** you must be
Ps 37:30 mouths of the righteous **u** wisdom,
    78: 2 I will **u** hidden things, things from
  115: 7 nor can they **u** a sound with their
Mt 13:35 I will **u** things hidden since
1Co 14: 2 they **u** mysteries by the Spirit.
Rev 13: 5 was given a mouth to **u** proud words

UTTERANCE UTTER

2Sa 23: 1 "The inspired **u** of David son

UTTERED UTTER

Ps 89:34 or alter what my lips have **u**.
Jer 29:23 and in my name they have **u** lies—

UTTERLY UTTER

Ps 119: 8 do not **u** forsake me.
Ecc 1: 2 says the Teacher. "U meaningless!
SS 8: 7 for love, it would be **u** scorned.
Ro 7:13 sin might become **u** sinful.

UZ

Job 1: 1 of U there lived a man whose name

UZZAH

2Sa 6: 6 U reached out and took hold
1Ch 13: 9 U reached out his hand to steady

UZZIAH AZARIAH

Son of Amaziah; king of Judah also known as Azariah (2Ki 15:1-7; 1Ch 6:24; 2Ch 26). Struck with leprosy because of pride (2Ch 26:16-23).

V

VAIN

Lev 26:20 Your strength will be spent in **v**,
Ps 2: 1 conspire and the peoples plot in **v**?
    33:17 A horse is a **v** hope for deliverance;
    73:13 in **v** I have kept my heart pure
  127: 1 the house, the builders labor in **v**
Isa 65:23 They will not labor in **v**, nor will
La 4:17 eyes failed, looking in **v** for help;
Eze 6:10 I did not threaten in **v** to bring this
Mt 15: 9 They worship me in **v**;
Ac 4:25 rage and the peoples plot in **v**?
1Co 15: 2 Otherwise, you have believed in **v**.
    15:58 your labor in the Lord is not in **v**.
2Co 6: 1 you not to receive God's grace in **v**.
Gal 2: 2 had not been running my race in **v**.
    3: 4 you experienced so much in **v**—if it
            really was in **v**?
Php 2: 3 out of selfish ambition or **v** conceit.

VALIANT

1Sa 10:26 by **v** men whose hearts God had
    31:12 all their **v** men marched through

VALID

Jn 8:14 my testimony is **v**, for I know where

VALLEY VALLEYS

Jos 7:26 that place has been called the V
    10:12 you, moon, over the V of Aijalon."
Jdg 16: 4 in the V of Sorek whose name was
1Sa 17: 3 another, with the **v** between them.
2Ki 23:10 which was in the V of Ben Hinnom,
2Ch 33: 6 in the fire in the V of Ben Hinnom,
Ps 23: 4 though I walk through the darkest **v**,
Isa 22: 1 A prophecy against the V of Vision:
    40: 4 Every **v** shall be raised up,
Eze 37: 2 many bones on the floor of the **v**,
Hos 2:15 will make the V of Achor a door

Joel   3:14   LORD is near in the **v** of decision.
Lk   3: 5   Every **v** shall be filled in,

VALLEYS VALLEY
Dt   8: 7   deep springs gushing out into the **v**
SS   2: 1   I am a rose of Sharon, a lily of the **v**.

VALUABLE VALUE
Lk   12:24   And how much more **v** you are than

VALUE VALUABLE, VALUED
Lev   27: 3   set the **v** of a male between the ages
1Ki   10:21   of little **v** in Solomon's days.
Pr   10: 2   treasures have no lasting **v**,
    16:13   they **v** the one who speaks what is
    31:11   in her and lacks nothing of **v**.
Mt   13:46   When he found one of great **v**,
Lk   16:15   What people **v** highly is detestable
Ro   3: 1   or what **v** is there in circumcision?
Php   2: 3   Rather, in humility **v** others
1Ti   4: 8   For physical training is of some **v**, but
        godliness has **v** for all things,
Heb   4: 2   they heard was of no **v** to them,
    11:26   as of greater **v** than the treasures

VALUED VALUE
Lk   7: 2   whom his master **v** highly, was sick

VANISH VANISHED, VANISHES
Ps   104:35   But may sinners **v** from the earth

VANISHED VANISH
Ps   12: 1   those who are loyal have **v**
    77: 8   Has his unfailing love **v** forever?

VANISHES VANISH
Jas   4:14   appears for a little while and then **v**.

VANITIES, VANITY (KJV) See
BREATH, DECEIT, DELUSIONS,
DESTRUCTION, DISHONEST,
EMPTY, EVIL, FALSE, FALSEHOOD,
FLEETING, FRUSTRATION,
FUTILE, FUTILITY, LIES,
MEANINGLESS, WORTHLESS
IDOLS

VARIOUS
Ge   1:11   in it, according to their **v** kinds."
Jdg   2:12   and worshiped **v** gods of the peoples
Mk   1:34   healed many who had **v** diseases.
Heb   1: 1   at many times and in **v** ways,
1Pe   4:10   of God's grace in its **v** forms.

VASHTI*
Queen of Persia replaced by Esther (Est 1–2).

VAST
Ge   2: 1   were completed in all their **v** array.
Dt   1:19   of the Amorites through all that **v**
    8:15   He led you through the **v**
Ps   139:17   How **v** is the sum of them!

VATS
Pr   3:10   and your **v** will brim over with new
Joel   2:24   the **v** will overflow with new wine

VAULT
Ge   1: 6   there be a **v** between the waters
    1: 8   God called the **v** "sky."
    1:14   there be lights in the **v** of the sky
Eze   1:22   was what looked something like a **v**,
    10: 1   above the **v** that was over the heads

VEGETABLES
Pr   15:17   Better a small serving of **v** with love
Da   1:12   Give us nothing but **v** to eat
Ro   14: 2   whose faith is weak, eats only **v**.

VEGETATION
Ge   1:11   God said, "Let the land produce **v**:

VEIL VEILED
Ex   34:33   to them, he put a **v** over his face.
La   3:65   Put a **v** over their hearts, and may
2Co   3:13   who would put a **v** over his face
    3:15   is read, a **v** covers their hearts.

VEILED VEIL
2Co   4: 3   if our gospel is **v**, it is **v** to those who
        are perishing.

VENGEANCE AVENGE, AVENGED,
AVENGER, AVENGES, AVENGING,
REVENGE
Ge   4:15   kills Cain will suffer **v** seven times
Nu   31: 3   carry out the LORD's **v** on them.
Isa   34: 8   For the LORD has a day of **v**,
    61: 2   favor and the day of **v** of our God,
Jer   50:15   Since this is the **v** of the LORD, take
        v on her;
Na   1: 2   The LORD takes **v** on his foes

VENOM VENOMOUS
Dt   32:33   Their wine is the **v** of serpents,
Ps   58: 4   Their **v** is like the **v** of a snake,

VENOMOUS VENOM
Nu   21: 6   the LORD sent **v** snakes among
Jer   8:17   I will send **v** snakes among you,

VENT
Pr   29:11   Fools give full **v** to their rage,
La   4:11   The LORD has given full **v** to his
Da   11:30   **v** his fury against the holy covenant.

VERDANT
Jer   50: 7   against the LORD, their **v** pasture,

VERDICT
1Ki   3:28   all Israel heard the **v** the king had
Jn   3:19   This is the **v**: Light has come

VERMIN
Mt   6:19   on earth, where moths and **v** destroy,

VERSED*
Ezr   7: 6   He was a teacher well **v** in the Law

VERY
Ge   1:31   that he had made, and it was **v** good.
    15: 1   your shield, your **v** great reward."
    17: 6   I will make you **v** fruitful;
Dt   30:14   No, the word is **v** near you; it is

Jos   23:11 So be **v** careful to love the LORD
1Ki 19:10 "I have been **v** zealous
Ps 104: 1 LORD my God, you are **v** great;
Mt   4: 8 devil took him to a **v** high mountain

VICTIM VICTIMS

Mt   5:32 makes her the **v** of adultery, and

VICTIMS VICTIM

Ps 10:10 His **v** are crushed, they collapse;
     10:14 The **v** commit themselves to you;
Pr   7:26 Many are the **v** she has brought
Na   3: 1 full of plunder, never without **v**!

VICTOR'S* VICTORY

2Ti   2: 5 does not receive the **v** crown except
Rev 2:10 I will give you life as your **v** crown.

VICTORIES* VICTORY

Jdg   5:11 They recite the **v** of the LORD, the **v** of
            his villagers in Israel.
2Sa 22:51 "He gives his king great **v**;
Ps 18:50 He gives his king great **v**;
     21: 1 great is his joy in the **v** you give!
     21: 5 Through the **v** you gave, his glory is
     44: 4 my God, who decrees **v** for Jacob.

VICTORIOUS VICTORY

Zec   9: 9 king comes to you, righteous and **v**,
Rev 2: 7 To the one who is **v**, I will give
     2:11 The one who is **v** will not be hurt
     2:17 To the one who is **v**, I will give
     2:26 To the one who is **v** and does my
     3: 5 The one who is **v** will, like them,
     3:12 The one who is **v** I will make
     3:21 To the one who is **v**, I will give
     15: 2 those who had been **v** over the beast
     21: 7 Those who are **v** will inherit all this,

VICTORIOUSLY* VICTORY

Ps 45: 4 In your majesty ride forth **v**

VICTORY VICTOR'S, VICTORIES, VICTORIOUS, VICTORIOUSLY

Ex 32:18 "It is not the sound of **v**, it is not
2Sa   8: 6 LORD gave David **v** wherever he
Ps 20: 5 May we shout for joy over your **v**
     44: 6 bow, my sword does not bring me **v**;
     60:12 With God we will gain the **v**, and he
   129: 2 they have not gained the **v** over me.
   149: 4 he crowns the humble with **v**.
Pr 11:14 but **v** is won through many advisers.
     21:31 battle, but **v** rests with the LORD.
     24: 6 **v** is won through many advisers.
Isa 63: 1 I, proclaiming **v**, mighty to save."
1Co 15:54 has been swallowed up in **v**."
     15:57 He gives us the **v** through our Lord
1Jn   5: 4 This is the **v** that has overcome

VIEW

Pr   5:21 ways are in full **v** of the LORD,
     17:24 person keeps wisdom in **v**,
2Ti   4: 1 and in **v** of his appearing and his

VILE VILEST

2Ki 23:13 for Ashtoreth the **v** goddess
     23:13 for Chemosh the **v** god of Moab,
Ps 12: 8 what is **v** is honored by the human
     15: 4 who despises a **v** person but honors
   101: 3 with approval on anything that is **v**.
Eze   5:11 my sanctuary with all your **v** images
Rev 21: 8 unbelieving, the **v**, the murderers,

VILEST* VILE

1Ki 21:26 He behaved in the **v** manner

VILLAGE

Mt 10:11 Whatever town or **v** you enter,
Mk   6: 6 Jesus went around teaching from **v**
            to **v**.

VINDICATE VINDICATED, VINDICATES, VINDICATION

Dt 32:36 The LORD will **v** his people
Ps 26: 1 **V** me, LORD, for I have led
     35:24 **V** me in your righteousness,
     54: 1 by your name; **v** me by your might.
   135:14 For the LORD will **v** his people
   138: 8 The LORD will **v** me;

VINDICATED VINDICATE

Job 13:18 my case, I know I will be **v**.
Ps 17:15 I will be **v** and will see your face;
Jer 51:10 " 'The LORD has **v** us;
1Ti   3:16 in the flesh, was **v** by the Spirit,

VINDICATES* VINDICATE

Ps 57: 2 God Most High, to God, who **v** me.
Isa 50: 8 He who **v** me is near. Who then will

VINDICATION VINDICATE

Ps 24: 5 and **v** from God their Savior.
     37: 6 dawn, your **v** like the noonday sun.
Isa 54:17 and this is their **v** from me,"
     62: 1 till her **v** shines out like the dawn,

VINE VINES, VINEYARD, VINEYARDS

Ge 49:22 "Joseph is a fruitful **v**, a fruitful **v**
Dt 32:32 Their **v** comes from the **v** of Sodom
1Ki   4:25 everyone under their own **v**
Ps 80: 8 You transplanted a **v** from Egypt;
   128: 3 like a fruitful **v** within your house;
Isa 36:16 you will eat fruit from your own **v**
Jer   2:21 I had planted you like a choice **v**
     2:21 against me into a corrupt, wild **v**?
Eze 17: 6 and became a low, spreading **v**.
Hos 10: 1 Israel was a spreading **v**;
Mk 14:25 from the fruit of the **v** until that day
Jn 15: 1 "I am the true **v**, and my Father is
Rev 14:18 clusters of grapes from the earth's **v**,

VINEGAR

Nu   6: 3 must not drink **v** made from wine
Pr 10:26 As **v** to the teeth and smoke
Mk 15:36 filled a sponge with wine **v**, put it

VINES VINE

Dt 24:21 do not go over the **v** again.

Hab 3:17 and there are no grapes on the **v**,

VINEYARD VINE
Ge   9:20 of the soil, proceeded to plant a **v**.
Dt   22: 9 plant two kinds of seed in your **v**;
1Ki 21: 1 The **v** was in Jezreel,
Pr   31:16 out of her earnings she plants a **v**.
SS   1: 6 my own **v** I had to neglect.
Isa   5: 1 for the one I love a song about his **v**:
         My loved one had a **v** on a fertile
     27: 2 "Sing about a fruitful **v**:
Mt   21:33 he rented the **v** to some farmers
1Co   9: 7 Who plants a **v** and does not eat its

VINEYARDS VINE
Lev 25: 3 and for six years prune your **v**
SS   2:15 foxes that ruin the **v**, our **v**

VIOLATE VIOLATED, VIOLATION
Lev 26:15 commands and so **v** my covenant,
Ps   89:31 if they **v** my decrees and fail to keep

VIOLATED VIOLATE
Jos   7:11 they have **v** my covenant, which I
Jdg   2:20 this nation has **v** the covenant I
Da   11:32 those who have **v** the covenant,

VIOLATION VIOLATE
Heb   2: 2 every **v** and disobedience received

VIOLENCE VIOLENT
Ge   6:11 in God's sight and was full of **v**.
Ps   7:16 their **v** comes down on their own
Isa 53: 9 though he had done no **v**, nor was
     60:18 No longer will **v** be heard in your
Eze 22:26 Her priests do **v** to my law
     45: 9 Give up your **v** and oppression
Joel 3:19 because of **v** done to the people
Ob   1:10 of the **v** against your brother Jacob,
Jnh   3: 8 give up their evil ways and their **v**.
Hab   2:17 The **v** you have done to Lebanon
Zep   3: 4 the sanctuary and do **v** to the law.
Mal   2:16 "does **v** to the one he should protect,"
Mt   11:12 of heaven has been subjected to **v**,

VIOLENT VIOLENCE
2Sa 22: 3 from **v** people you save me.
Pr   3:31 Do not envy the **v** or choose any
Eze 18:10 "Suppose he has a **v** son, who sheds
Mt   11:12 and **v** people have been raiding it.
     28: 2 There was a **v** earthquake,
1Ti   1:13 and a persecutor and a **v** man, I was
      3: 3 to drunkenness, not **v** but gentle,
Titus 1: 7 not **v**, not pursuing dishonest gain.

VIPER VIPER'S, VIPERS
Pr   23:32 like a snake and poisons like a **v**.
Ac   28: 3 the fire, a **v**, driven out by the heat,

VIPER'S* VIPER
Isa 11: 8 will put its hand into the **v** nest.

VIPERS VIPER
Ps 140: 3 the poison of **v** is on their lips.
Lk   3: 7 baptized by him, "You brood of **v**!
Ro   3:13 "The poison of **v** is on their lips."

VIRGIN VIRGINS
Dt   22:15 at the gate proof that she was a **v**.
1Ki   1: 2 look for a young **v** to serve the king
Isa   7:14 The **v** will conceive and give birth
Jer 31:21 Return, **V** Israel, return to your
Mt   1:23 "The **v** will conceive and give birth
Lk   1:34 asked the angel, "since I am a **v**?"
1Co   7:28 and if a **v** marries, she has not
2Co 11: 2 I might present you as a pure **v**

VIRGINS VIRGIN
Mt   25: 1 will be like ten **v** who took their
1Co   7:25 Now about **v**: I have no command
Rev 14: 4 with women, for they remained **v**.

VIRTUES*
Col   3:14 And over all these **v** put on love,

VISIBLE
Eph   5:13 exposed by the light becomes **v**—
Col   1:16 heaven and on earth, **v** and invisible,
Heb 11: 3 was not made out of what was **v**.

VISION VISIONS
Ge   15: 1 the LORD came to Abram in a **v**:
     46: 2 God spoke to Israel in a **v** at night
Nu   24: 4 who sees a **v** from the Almighty,
1Sa   3:15 He was afraid to tell Eli the **v**,
Ps   89:19 Once you spoke in a **v**, to your
Isa 22: 1 A prophecy against the Valley of **V**:
Da   2:45 the meaning of the **v** of the rock cut
      7: 2 "In my **v** at night I looked,
      8: 1 had a **v**, after the one that had
      8:26 but seal up the **v**, for it concerns
      9:24 to seal up **v** and prophecy
     10: 7 was the only one who saw the **v**;
Zec   1: 8 During the night I had a **v**, and there
Lk   1:22 They realized he had seen a **v**
Ac   9:10 The Lord called to him in a **v**,
     10:17 about the meaning of the **v**, the men
     16: 9 During the night Paul had a **v**
     26:19 disobedient to the **v** from heaven.
Rev   9:17 riders I saw in my **v** looked like this:

VISIONS VISION
Nu   12: 6 reveal myself to them in **v**, I speak
1Sa   3: 1 there were not many **v**.
Isa 30:10 say to the seers, "See no more **v**!"
Jer 23:16 They speak **v** from their own minds,
Eze   1: 1 were opened and I saw **v** of God.
Da   1:17 And Daniel could understand **v**
Joel 2:28 dreams, your young men will see **v**.
Ac   2:17 your young men will see **v**, your old

VISIT VISITS
Mt   25:36 in prison and you came to **v** me.'

VISITS* VISIT
Mic   7: 4 The day God **v** you has come,
1Pe   2:12 and glorify God on the day he **v** us.

VOICE VOICES
Ex   19:19 and the **v** of God answered him.
Dt   4:33 Has any other people heard the **v**
     30:20 listen to his **v**, and hold fast to him.
Job 40: 9 and can your **v** thunder like his?

Ps   19: 4 Yet their **v** goes out into all
      27: 7 Hear my **v** when I call, LORD;
      29: 3 The **v** of the LORD is over
      95: 7 Today, if only you would hear his **v**,
Pr   1: 20 she raises her **v** in the public square;
       8: 1 Does not understanding raise her **v**?
Isa   30: 21 your ears will hear a **v** behind you,
     40: 3 A **v** of one calling:
Jer   31: 15 "A **v** is heard in Ramah,
Eze   1: 24 waters, like the **v** of the Almighty,
Mt   2: 18 "A **v** is heard in Ramah,
      3: 17 And a **v** from heaven said, "This is
Mk   1: 3 "a **v** of one calling
Jn   1: 23 "I am the **v** of one calling
      5: 25 the dead will hear the **v** of the Son
    10: 3 him, and the sheep listen to his **v**.
    12: 28 Then a **v** came from heaven,
Ro   10: 18 "Their **v** has gone out into all
    15: 6 and one **v** you may glorify the God
1Th   4: 16 with the **v** of the archangel
Heb   3: 7 "Today, if you hear his **v**,
2Pe   1: 17 God the Father when the **v** came
Rev   3: 20 If anyone hears my **v** and opens

VOICE OF THE LORD† Dt 5:25; 18:16; Ps
29:3, 4, 4, 5, 7, 8, 9; Isa 30:31; Hag 1:12

VOICES VOICE

Nu   14: 1 of the community raised their **v**
Rev 10: 3 the **v** of the seven thunders spoke.
    11: 15 and there were loud **v** in heaven,

VOLUNTARILY VOLUNTARY

1Co 9: 17 If I preach **v**, I have a reward; if not **v**,
            I am simply discharging

VOLUNTARY* VOLUNTARILY, VOLUNTEERED

Phm 1: 14 not seem forced but would be **v**.

VOLUNTEERED VOLUNTARY

1Ch 12: 38 All these were fighting men who **v**
Ne   11: 2 The people commended all who **v**

VOMIT VOMITED

Lev 18: 28 it will **v** you out as it vomited
Pr   26: 11 As a dog returns to its **v**, so fools
Isa   28: 8 All the tables are covered with **v**
2Pe   2: 22 "A dog returns to its **v**," and,

VOMITED VOMIT

Lev 18: 25 and the land **v** out its inhabitants.
Jnh   2: 10 fish, and it **v** Jonah onto dry land.

VOW VOWED, VOWS

Ge   28: 20 Then Jacob made a **v**, saying,
Nu   6: 2 woman wants to make a special **v**,
    21: 2 Israel made this **v** to the LORD:
    30: 2 a man makes a **v** to the LORD
Dt   23: 21 If you make a **v** to the LORD your
Jdg 11: 30 Jephthah made a **v** to the LORD:
1Sa   1: 11 And she made a **v**, saying,
Ecc   5: 4 no pleasure in fools; fulfill your **v**.
      5: 5 not to make a **v** than to make one
Ac   18: 18 because of a **v** he had taken.

VOWED VOW

Dt   12: 6 what you have **v** to give and your
Jdg 11: 39 father, and he did to her as he had **v**.
Jnh   2: 9 What I have **v** I will make good.

VOWS VOW

Nu   6: 21 the Nazirite who **v** offerings
    30: 4 all her **v** and every pledge
    30: 5 it, none of her **v** or the pledges
Ps   22: 25 who fear you I will fulfill my **v**.
    50: 14 God, fulfill your **v** to the Most High,
   116: 14 I will fulfill my **v** to the LORD
Pr   20: 25 and only later to consider one's **v**.
Jnh   1: 16 to the LORD and made **v** to him.
Mt   5: 33 to the Lord the **v** you have made.'

VULTURE VULTURES

Lev 11: 13 unclean: the eagle, the **v**, the black **v**,

VULTURES VULTURE

Mt   24: 28 is a carcass, there the **v** will gather.

W

WADI

Nu   34: 5 join the **W** of Egypt and end
2Ki 24: 7 territory, from the **W** of Egypt

WAGE WAGED, WAGES, WAGING

Mic   3: 5 **w** war against anyone who refuses
2Co 10: 3 we do not **w** war as the world does.
Rev 17: 14 They will **w** war against the Lamb,
    19. 19 to **w** war against the rider on the

WAGED WAGE

Jos 11: 18 Joshua **w** war against all these kings

WAGES WAGE

Lev 19: 13 " 'Do not hold back the **w**
Pr   10: 16 The **w** of the righteous is life,
Mic   1: 7 her gifts from the **w** of prostitutes,
Mal   3: 5 who defraud laborers of their **w**,
Lk   10: 7 you, for the worker deserves his **w**.
Jn   6: 7 take more than half a year's **w**
    12: 5 It was worth a year's **w**."
Ro   4: 4 **w** are not credited as a gift but as
     6: 23 For the **w** of sin is death, but the gift
1Ti   5: 18 and "The worker deserves his **w**."
2Pe   2: 15 who loved the **w** of wickedness.

WAGING WAGE

Da   7: 21 this horn was **w** war against the holy
Ro   7: 23 **w** war against the law of my mind

WAIL WAILED, WAILING

Isa   13: 6 **W**, for the day of the LORD is
Mic   1: 8 Because of this I will weep and **w**;

WAILED WAIL

Nu   11: 18 The LORD heard you when you **w**,

WAILING WAIL

Ex   12: 30 and there was loud **w** in Egypt,
Nu   11: 4 again the Israelites started **w**
Ps   30: 11 You turned my **w** into dancing;

WAIST

2Ki	1: 8	had a leather belt around his w."
2Ch	10:10	finger is thicker than my father's w.
Isa	11: 5	faithfulness the sash around his w.
Jer	13: 1	linen belt and put it around your w,
Mt	3: 4	he had a leather belt around his w.
Jn	13: 4	and wrapped a towel around his w.
Eph	6:14	belt of truth buckled around your w,

WAIT AWAIT, AWAITS, WAITED, WAITING, WAITS

Ps	27:14	W for the LORD; be strong
	33:20	We w in hope for the LORD;
	119:166	I w for your salvation, LORD,
	130: 5	I w for the LORD, my whole being
	130: 6	I w for the Lord more than
Pr	1:18	These men lie in w for their own
Isa	30:18	Blessed are all who w for him!
La	3:26	it is good to w quietly
Hab	2: 3	Though it linger, w for it;
	3:16	Yet I will w patiently for the day
Ac	1: 4	w for the gift my Father promised,
Ro	8:23	groan inwardly as we w eagerly
1Th	1:10	and to w for his Son from heaven,
Titus	2:13	while we w for the blessed hope—

WAITED WAIT

Ps	40: 1	I w patiently for the LORD;
Jnh	4: 5	w to see what would happen

WAITING WAIT

Heb	9:28	to those who are w for him.

WAITS WAIT

Da	12:12	Blessed is the one who w
Ro	8:19	the creation w in eager expectation

WAKE AWAKE, AWAKEN, AWOKE, WAKENS, WOKE

Isa	26:19	let those who dwell in the dust w
Ro	13:11	has already come for you to w
Eph	5:14	"W up, sleeper, rise from the dead,
Rev	3: 2	W up! Strengthen what remains

WAKENS* WAKE

Isa	50: 4	He w me morning by morning, w my ear to listen

WALK WALKED, WALKING, WALKS

Ge	17: 1	w before me faithfully and be
Lev	26:12	I will w among you and be your
Dt	5:33	W in obedience to all
	6: 7	and when you w along the road,
	10:12	your God, to w in obedience to him,
	11:19	and when you w along the road,
	11:22	to w in obedience to him and to hold
	26:17	that you will w in obedience to him,
	28: 9	God and w in obedience to him.
Jos	22: 5	your God, to w in obedience to him,
1Ki	2: 3	W in obedience to him, and keep his
Ps	1: 1	Blessed is the one who does not w
	15: 2	The one whose w is blameless,
	23: 4	Even though I w through the darkest
	84:11	from those whose w is blameless.

Ps	89:15	who w in the light of your presence,
	115: 7	but cannot w, nor can they utter
	119:45	I will w about in freedom, for I have
Pr	4:12	When you w, your steps will not be
	6:22	When you w, they will guide you;
	9: 6	w in the way of insight."
	13:20	W with the wise and become wise,
	28:26	but those who w in wisdom are kept
Isa	2: 3	so that we may w in his paths."
	2: 5	let us w in the light of the LORD.
	30:21	saying, "This is the way; w in it."
	33:15	Those who w righteously and speak
	40:31	weary, they will w and not be faint.
	43: 2	When you w through the fire,
	57: 2	Those who w uprightly enter
Jer	6:16	and w in it, and you will find rest
Da	4:37	those who w in pride he is able
Am	3: 3	Do two w together unless they have
Mic	4: 5	All the nations may w in the name
	4: 5	but we will w in the name
	6: 8	and to w humbly with your God.
Mk	2: 9	say, 'Get up, take your mat and w'?
Jn	8:12	Whoever follows me will never w
Ac	3: 8	jumped to his feet and began to w.
Gal	5:16	So I say, w by the Spirit, and you
1Jn	1: 6	with him and yet w in the darkness,
	1: 7	But if we w in the light, as he is
2Jn	1: 6	his command is that you w in love.
3Jn	1: 3	telling how you continue to w in it.
Rev	9:20	idols that cannot see or hear or w.
	21:24	The nations will w by its light,

WALKED WALK

Ge	5:24	Enoch w faithfully with God;
	24:40	before whom I have w faithfully,
Jos	14: 9	which your feet have w will be your
Mt	14:29	w on the water and came toward

WALKING WALK

Dt	8: 6	w in obedience to him and revering
1Ki	3: 3	the LORD by w according
Da	3:25	I see four men w around in the fire,
Mt	14:26	the disciples saw him w on the lake,
Ac	3: 8	the temple courts, w and jumping,
2Jn	1: 4	some of your children w in the truth,
3Jn	1: 4	that my children are w in the truth.

WALKS WALK

Pr	10: 9	Whoever w in integrity w securely,
Ecc	2:14	while the fool w in the darkness;
Jn	11: 9	Anyone who w in the daytime will

WALL WALLS

Ex	14:22	with a w of water on their right
Jos	2:15	she lived in was part of the city w.
	6:20	gave a loud shout, the w collapsed;
2Ki	25: 4	the city w was broken through,
Ne	1: 3	The w of Jerusalem is broken down,
	2:17	let us rebuild the w of Jerusalem,
	12:27	dedication of the w of Jerusalem,
Da	5: 5	and wrote on the plaster of the w,
Zec	2: 5	I myself will be a w of fire around
Ac	9:25	basket through an opening in the w.
2Co	11:33	in a basket from a window in the w
Eph	2:14	barrier, the dividing w of hostility,

Rev 21:12 a great, high **w** with twelve gates,

WALLOWING
2Pe 2:22 returns to her **w** in the mud."

WALLS WALL
Dt 1:28 are large, with **w** up to the sky.
Ne 2:13 Gate, examining the **w** of Jerusalem,
Ps 51:18 to build up the **w** of Jerusalem.
    122: 7 May there be peace within your **w**
Pr 25:28 a city whose **w** are broken through
Isa 26: 1 God makes salvation its **w**
    54:12 and all your **w** of precious stones.
    58:12 be called Repairer of Broken **W**,
    60:18 you will call your **w** Salvation
Jer 52:14 down all the **w** around Jerusalem.
Heb 11:30 By faith the **w** of Jericho fell,

WANDER WANDERED,
WANDERER, WANDERING
Nu 32:13 he made them **w** in the wilderness
Pr 5: 6 her paths **w** aimlessly, but she does
Jas 5:19 one of you should **w** from the truth

WANDERED WANDER
1Ch 16:20 they **w** from nation to nation,
Ps 107: 4 Some **w** in desert wastelands,
Eze 34: 6 My sheep **w** over all the mountains
Mt 18:12 go to look for the one that **w** off?
1Ti 6:10 have **w** from the faith and pierced

WANDERER WANDER
Ge 4:12 You will be a restless **w**

WANDERING WANDER
Dt 26: 5 "My father was a **w** Aramean,

WANT WANTED, WANTING,
WANTS
Lev 26: 5 you will eat all the food you **w**
1Sa 8:19 they said. "We **w** a king over us.
1Ki 3: 5 whatever you **w** me to give you."
Mt 8:29 "What do you **w** with us,
    19:21 "If you **w** to be perfect, go,
Lk 18:41 "Lord, I **w** to see," he replied.
    19:14 say, 'We don't **w** this man to be our
Ro 7:15 For what I **w** to do I do not do,
    13: 3 Do you **w** to be free from fear
2Co 12:14 to you, because what I **w** is not your
Gal 4:21 me, you who **w** to be under the law,
Php 3:10 I **w** to know Christ—yes, to know
    4:12 whether living in plenty or in **w**.

WANTED WANT
Ex 4:19 for all those who **w** to kill you are
Jnh 4: 8 He **w** to die, and said, "It would be
Mt 14: 5 Herod **w** to kill John, but he was
    21:31 of the two did what his father **w**?"
1Co 12:18 of them, just as he **w** them to be.
Heb 6:17 Because God **w** to make

WANTING WANT
Da 5:27 weighed on the scales and found **w**.
2Pe 3: 9 with you, not **w** anyone to perish,

WANTS WANT
Mt 5:42 away from the one who **w** to borrow
    20:26 whoever **w** to become great among
Mk 8:35 For whoever **w** to save their life will
    10:43 whoever **w** to become great among
Ro 9:18 on whom he **w** to have mercy,
    9:18 he hardens whom he **w** to harden.
1Ti 2: 4 who **w** all people to be saved
2Ti 3:12 everyone who **w** to live a godly life
1Pe 5: 2 you are willing, as God **w** you to be;

WAR WARRIOR, WARS
Ex 17:16 will be at **w** against the Amalekites
    32:17 "There is the sound of **w**
Jos 11:23 Then the land had rest from **w**.
1Sa 11:23 wage **w** against them until you have
2Sa 11: 1 at the time when kings go off to **w**,
Ps 68:30 Scatter the nations who delight in **w**.
    120: 7 but when I speak, they are for **w**.
    144: 1 who trains my hands for **w**,
Ecc 3: 8 a time for **w** and a time for peace.
    9:18 is better than weapons of **w**, but one
Isa 2: 4 nor will they train for **w** anymore.
Da 7:21 horn was waging **w** against the holy
    9:26 **W** will continue until the end,
Ro 7:23 me, waging **w** against the law of my
2Co 10: 3 we do not wage **w** as the world
1Pe 2:11 which wage **w** against your soul.
Rev 12: 7 Then **w** broke out in heaven.
    17:14 They will wage **w** against the Lamb,
    19:11 With justice he judges and wages **w**.

WARM LUKEWARM, WARMS,
WARMTH
Ecc 4:11 lie down together, they will keep **w**.
        But how can one keep **w** alone?
Hag 1: 6 You put on clothes, but are not **w**.
Jas 2:16 keep **w** and well fed," but does

WARMS WARM
Isa 44:15 some of it he takes and **w** himself,

WARMTH WARM
Ps 19: 6 nothing is deprived of its **w**.

WARN* WARNED, WARNING,
WARNINGS, WARNS
Ex 19:21 **w** the people so they do not force
Nu 24:14 let me **w** you of what this people
1Sa 8: 9 but **w** them solemnly and let them
1Ki 2:42 swear by the LORD and **w** you,
2Ch 19:10 you are to **w** them not to sin against
Ps 81: 8 **w** me, my people, and I will **w** you—
Jer 42:19 Be sure of this: I **w** you today
Eze 3:18 you do not **w** them or speak
    3:19 if you do **w** the wicked person
    3:20 Since you did not **w** them, they will
    3:21 if you do **w** the righteous person not
    33: 3 blows the trumpet to **w** the people,
    33: 6 blow the trumpet to **w** the people
    33: 9 if you do **w** the wicked person
Lk 16:28 Let him **w** them, so that they will
Ac 4:17 we must **w** them to speak no longer
1Co 4:14 but to **w** you as my dear children.

Gal 5:21 I w you, as I did before, that those
1Th 5:14 w those who are idle and disruptive,
2Th 3:15 but w them as you would a fellow
2Ti 2:14 W them before God against
Titus 3:10 W a divisive person once, and then w
              them a second time.
Rev 22:18 I w everyone who hears the words

WARNED WARN

2Ki 17:13 The LORD w Israel and Judah
Ne   9:29 "You w them in order to turn them
     9:30 By your Spirit you w them through
     9:34 or the statutes you w them to keep.
Ps   2:10 be w, you rulers of the earth.
    19:11 By them your servant is w;
Jer 18: 8 if that nation I w repents of its evil,
    22:21 I w you when you felt secure,
Mt   2:12 having been w in a dream not to go
     2:22 Having been w in a dream,
     3: 7 Who w you to flee from the coming
1Th 4: 6 as we told you and w you before.
Heb 11: 7 when w about things not yet seen,
    12:25 they refused him who w them

WARNING WARN

Jer 6: 8 Take w, Jerusalem, or I will turn
Eze 33: 5 If they had heeded the w,
Ac 13:51 shook the dust off their feet as a w
1Ti 5:20 so that the others may take w.

WARNINGS WARN

1Co 10:11 and were written down as w for us,

WARNS WARN

Heb 12:25 from him who w us from heaven?

WARPED

Dt 32: 5 to their shame they are a w

WARRIOR WAR

Ex 15: 3 The LORD is a w; the LORD is
1Ch 28: 3 because you are a w and have shed
Pr 16:32 Better a patient person than a w,
Jer 20:11 LORD is with me like a mighty w;

WARS WAR

Nu 21:14 Book of the W of the LORD says:
Ps 46: 9 He makes w cease to the ends
Mt 24: 6 You will hear of w and rumors of w,

WASH WASHED, WASHING,
WHITEWASH, WHITEWASHED

Ex 40:31 his sons used it to w their hands
2Ki 5:10 "Go, w yourself seven times
Ps 51: 7 me, and I will be whiter than
Jer 4:14 w the evil from your heart and be
Lk 11:38 did not first w before the meal.
Jn   9: 7 "w in the Pool of Siloam" (this
    13: 5 and began to w his disciples' feet,
Ac 22:16 be baptized and w your sins away,
Jas 4: 8 W your hands, you sinners,
Rev 22:14 are those who w their robes,

MUST WASH See MUST

WASHED WASH

Ps 73:13 and have w my hands in innocence.

Jn   9:11 So I went and w, and then I could
1Co 6:11 But you were w, you were
Heb 10:22 and having our bodies w with pure
2Pe 2:22 and, "A sow that is w returns to her
Rev 7:14 they have w their robes and made

WASHING WASH

Ex 30:18 basin, with its bronze stand, for w.
2Ch 4: 6 was to be used by the priests for w.
Jn   2: 6 used by the Jews for ceremonial w,
Eph 5:26 the w with water through the word,
1Ti 5:10 w the feet of the Lord's people,
Titus 3: 5 He saved us through the w of rebirth

WASTE WASTED, WASTING

Isa 24:16 But I said, "I w away, I w away!
Jer 2:15 They have laid w his land;
Eze 4:17 will w away because of their sin.
Mk 14: 4 another, "Why this w of perfume?

WASTED WASTE

Jn   6:12 are left over. Let nothing be w."

WASTELAND LAND

Isa 43:19 the wilderness and streams in the w.

WASTELANDS LAND

Ps 107: 4 Some wandered in desert w,

WASTING WASTE

2Co 4:16 Though outwardly we are w away,

WATCH WATCHED, WATCHES,
WATCHFUL, WATCHING,
WATCHMAN, WATCHMEN

Ge 31:49 the LORD keep w between you
Dt   4:15 Therefore w yourselves very
Ps 39: 1 "I will w my ways and keep my
    59: 9 You are my strength, I w for you;
    90: 4 gone by, or like a w in the night.
   141: 3 keep w over the door of my lips.
Pr   4: 6 love her, and she will w over you.
     6:22 you sleep, they will w over you;
Jer 31:10 them and will w over his flock like
Mic 7: 7 for me, I w in hope for the LORD,
Mt   7:15 "W out for false prophets.
    24:42 "Therefore keep w, because you do
    26:41 "W and pray so that you will not
Mk 13:35 "Therefore keep w because you do
Lk   2: 8 keeping w over their flocks at night.
Php 3: 2 W out for those dogs,
1Ti 4:16 W your life and doctrine closely.
Heb 13:17 because they keep w over you as
2Jn 1: 8 W out that you do not lose what we

WATCHED WATCH

Mt 26:16 on Judas w for an opportunity

WATCHES* WATCH

Nu 19: 5 While he w, the heifer is to be
Job 24:15 The eye of the adulterer w for dusk;
Ps   1: 6 For the LORD w over the way
    33:14 his dwelling place he w all who live
    63: 6 of you through the w of the night.
   119:148 My eyes stay open through the w
   121: 3 he who w over you will not

Ps 121: 4 he who w over Israel will neither
121: 5 The LORD w over you—
127: 1 Unless the LORD w over the city,
145:20 The LORD w over all who love
146: 9 The LORD w over the foreigner
Pr 31:27 She w over the affairs of her
Ecc 11: 4 Whoever w the wind will not plant;
La 2:19 night, as the w of the night begin;
4:16 he no longer w over them.

WATCHFUL WATCH
Col 4: 2 to prayer, being w and thankful.

WATCHING WATCH
Jer 1:12 for I am w to see that my word is
44:27 For I am w over them for harm,
Mk 15:40 Some women were w
Lk 12:37 servants whose master finds them w
1Pe 5: 2 is under your care, w over them—

WATCHMAN WATCH
Eze 3:17 I have made you a w for the people
33: 6 but I will hold the w accountable

WATCHMEN WATCH
Ps 130: 6 more than w wait for the morning.
Isa 56:10 Israel's w are blind, they all lack
Mic 7: 4 the day your w sound the alarm.

WATCHTOWER TOWER
Isa 21: 8 after day, my lord, I stand on the w;

WATER WATERED, WATERING, WATERS, WELL-WATERED
Ge 1: 6 the waters to separate w from w."
1:20 said, "Let the w teem with living
7:18 ark floated on the surface of the w.
Ex 7:20 all the w was changed into blood.
15:25 He threw it into the w, and the w
17: 1 but there was no w for the people
Nu 5:19 may this bitter w that brings a curse
20: 2 Now there was no w
21: 5 There is no w! And we detest this
2Ki 2: 8 rolled it up and struck the w with it.
2: 8 The w divided to the right
6: 5 tree, the iron axhead fell into the w.
Ps 1: 3 like a tree planted by streams of w,
22:14 I am poured out like w, and all my
42: 1 As the deer pants for streams of w,
Pr 5:15 Drink w from your own cistern,
9:17 "Stolen w is sweet; food eaten
25:21 if he is thirsty, give him w to drink.
Isa 12: 3 joy you will draw w from the wells
30:20 of adversity and the w of affliction,
32: 2 like streams of w in the desert
49:10 and lead them beside springs of w.
Jer 2:13 the spring of living w, and have dug
2:13 broken cisterns that cannot hold w.
17: 8 a tree planted by the w that sends
31: 9 I will lead them beside streams of w
Eze 36:25 I will sprinkle clean w on you,
Zec 14: 8 On that day living w will flow
Mt 14:29 walked on the w and came toward
Mk 1: 8 I baptize you with w, but he will
9:41 anyone who gives you a cup of w

Lk 5: 4 "Put out into deep w, and let down
Jn 2: 9 of the banquet tasted the w that had
3: 5 of God unless they are born of w
4:10 he would have given you living w."
7:38 rivers of living w will flow
19:34 a sudden flow of blood and w.
Eph 5:26 washing with w through the word,
Heb 10:22 our bodies washed with pure w.
Jas 3:11 Can both fresh w and salt w flow
1Pe 3:21 this w symbolizes baptism that now
2Pe 2:17 These people are springs without w
1Jn 5: 6 This is the one who came by w
5: 6 He did not come by w only, but by
w and blood.
Rev 7:17 lead them to springs of living w."
21: 6 the thirsty I will give w without cost
21: 6 cost from the spring of the w of life.
22: 1 showed me the river of the w of life,
22:17 take the free gift of the w of life.

WATERED WATER
Ps 104:16 The trees of the LORD are well w,
1Co 3: 6 I planted the seed, Apollos w it,

WATERING WATER
Ge 2:10 A river w the garden flowed
Isa 55:10 not return to it without w the earth

WATERS WATER
Ge 1: 2 of God was hovering over the w.
1:10 the gathered w he called "seas."
7: 7 the ark to escape the w of the flood.
Ex 14:21 it into dry land. The w were divided,
Jos 4: 7 the w of the Jordan were cut off.
Ps 18:16 he drew me out of deep w.
23: 2 he leads me beside quiet w,
106:32 the w of Meribah they angered
SS 8: 7 Many w cannot quench love;
Isa 11: 9 the LORD as the w cover the sea.
43: 2 When you pass through the w, I will
55: 1 you who are thirsty, come to the w;
58:11 like a spring whose w never fail.
Hab 2:14 the LORD as the w cover the sea.
1Co 3: 7 nor the one who w is anything,
Rev 8:11 A third of the w turned bitter,

WAVE WAVES
Ex 29:24 before the LORD as a w offering.
Lev 23:11 w the sheaf before the LORD so it
Jas 1: 6 the one who doubts is like a w

WAVE OFFERING Ex 29:24, 26; 35:22; 38:24, 29; Lev 7:30; 8:27, 29; 9:21; 10:15; 14:12, 24; 17, 20; Nu 6:20; 8:11, 13, 15, 21; 18:18

WAVER*
1Ki 18:21 "How long will you w between two
Ro 4:20 Yet he did not w through unbelief

WAVES WAVE
2Sa 22: 5 The w of death swirled about me;
Ps 89: 9 when its w mount up, you still them.
Isa 57:20 rest, whose w cast up mire and mud.
Mt 8:27 the winds and the w obey him!"
Eph 4:14 tossed back and forth by the w,
Jude 1:13 They are wild w of the sea,

WAX

Ps 22:14 My heart has turned to w;
97: 5 mountains melt like w before

WAY DOORWAY, GATEWAY, WAYS

Ge 3:24 forth to guard the w to the tree
Ex 13:21 of cloud to guide them on their w
18:20 show them the w they are to live
Dt 1:33 to show you the w you should go.
32: 6 Is this the w you repay the LORD,
1Sa 12:23 I will teach you the w that is good
2Sa 22:31 "As for God, his w is perfect:
1Ki 8:23 continue wholeheartedly in your w.
8:36 Teach them the right w to live,
2Ch 6:27 Teach them the right w to live,
Job 23:10 But he knows the w that I take;
Ps 1: 1 stand in the w that sinners take or sit
1: 6 the LORD watches over the w
1: 6 but the w of the wicked leads
18:30 As for God, his w is perfect:
32: 8 teach you in the w you should go;
37: 5 Commit your w to the LORD;
86:11 Teach me your w, LORD, that I
139:24 if there is any offensive w in me,
139:24 and lead me in the w everlasting.
Pr 4:11 I instruct you in the w of wisdom
12:15 The w of fools seems right to them,
14:12 There is a w that appears to be right,
16: 7 takes pleasure in anyone's w,
19: 2 more will hasty feet miss the w!
22: 6 off on the w they should go,
30:19 the w of a man with a young woman.
Isa 30:21 behind you, saying, "This is the w;
35: 8 it will be called the W of Holiness;
40: 3 the wilderness prepare the w
48:17 directs you in the w you should go.
53: 6 each of us has turned to our own w;
Jer 5:31 and my people love it this w.
21: 8 I am setting before you the w of life
and the w of death.
Mal 3: 1 who will prepare the w before me.
Mt 3: 3 'Prepare the w for the Lord,
5:12 in the same w they persecuted
Lk 7:27 will prepare your w before you.'
Jn 14: 6 "I am the w and the truth
Ac 1:11 in the same w you have seen him go
9: 2 any there who belonged to the W,
19: 9 and publicly maligned the W.
22: 4 followers of this W to their death,
24:14 our ancestors as a follower of the W,
1Co 9:24 Run in such a w as to get the prize.
10:13 also provide a w out so that you can
12:31 will show you the most excellent w.
14: 1 Follow the w of love and eagerly
Col 1:10 the Lord and please him in every w:
Titus 2:10 every w they will make the teaching
Heb 2:17 fully human in every w, in order
4:15 who has been tempted in every w,
9: 8 the w into the Most Holy Place had
10:20 living w opened for us through
13:18 desire to live honorably in every w.
Jas 5:20 the error of their w will save them
2Pe 2:21 have known the w of righteousness,

WAYS WAY

Ge 6:12 on earth had corrupted their w.
Ex 33:13 teach me your w so I may know you
Dt 32: 4 are perfect, and all his w are just.
2Ki 17:13 "Turn from your evil w.
2Ch 11:17 years, following the w of David
Job 34:21 "His eyes are on the w of mortals;
Ps 25: 4 Show me your w, LORD, teach me
25:10 All the w of the LORD are loving
37: 7 fret when people succeed in their w,
51:13 I will teach transgressors your w,
77:13 Your w, God, are holy. What god is
119:59 I have considered my w and have
139: 3 you are familiar with all my w.
145:17 The LORD is righteous in all his w
Pr 2:12 save you from the w of wicked men,
3: 6 in all your w submit to him, and he
3:17 Her w are pleasant w, and all her
4:26 feet and be steadfast in all your w.
5:21 For your w are in full view
6: 6 consider its w and be wise!
7:25 Do not let your heart turn to her w
16: 2 All a person's w seem pure to them,
16:17 who guard their w preserve their
21: 2 may think their own w are right,
Isa 2: 3 He will teach us his w, so that we
42:24 For they would not follow his w;
55: 7 Let the wicked forsake their w
55: 8 neither are your w my w,"
Jer 10: 2 "Do not learn the w of the nations
18:11 So turn from your evil w, each one
Eze 16:47 You not only followed their w
28:15 in your w from the day you were
33: 8 out to dissuade them from their w,
Da 4:37 does is right and all his w are just.
Hos 14: 9 The w of the LORD are right;
Jnh 3:10 how they turned from their evil w,
Hag 1: 5 "Give careful thought to your w.
Lk 3: 5 straight, the rough w smooth.
Ro 1:30 they invent w of doing evil;
1Co 13:11 I put the w of childhood behind me.
Col 3: 7 You used to walk in these w,
Jas 3: 2 We all stumble in many w.
Rev 15: 3 Just and true are your w,

WAYWARD WAYWARDNESS

Pr 2:16 woman, from the w woman with her
6:24 from the smooth talk of a w woman.
23:27 pit, and a w wife is a narrow well.

WAYWARDNESS* WAYWARD

Pr 1:32 the w of the simple will kill them,
Hos 14: 4 "I will heal their w and love them

WEAK WEAKENED, WEAKER, WEAKLING, WEAKNESS, WEAKNESSES

Jdg 16: 7 I'll become as w as any other man."
Ps 41: 1 are those who have regard for the w;
72:13 He will take pity on the w
82: 3 Defend the w and the fatherless;
82: 4 Rescue the w and the needy;
Eze 34: 4 You have not strengthened the w
Mt 26:41 spirit is willing, but the flesh is w."

Ac 20:35 of hard work we must help the w,
Ro 14: 1 Accept the one whose faith is w,
     15: 1 to bear with the failings of the w
1Co 1:27 God chose the w things of the world
      8: 9 become a stumbling block to the w.
      9:22 To the w I became w, to win the w.
     11:30 That is why many among you are w
2Co 12:10 For when I am w, then I am strong.
Gal   4: 9 that you are turning back to those w
1Th   5:14 help the w, be patient
Heb   7:18 is set aside because it was w
     12:12 your feeble arms and w knees.

WEAKENED WEAK
Ro   8: 3 to do because it was w by the flesh,

WEAKER* WEAK
2Sa   3: 1 the house of Saul grew w and w.
1Co 12:22 that seem to be w are indispensable,
1Pe   3: 7 them with respect as the w partner

WEAKLING* WEAK
Joel 3:10 Let the w say, "I am strong!"

WEAKNESS⁺ WEAK
La   1: 6 w they have fled before the pursuer.
Ro   8:26 way, the Spirit helps us in our w.
1Co 1:25 the w of God is stronger than human
      2: 3 I came to you in w with great fear
     15:43 it is sown in w, it is raised in power;
2Co 11:30 boast of the things that show my w.
     12: 9 my power is made perfect in w."
     13: 4 he was crucified in w, yet he lives
Heb   5: 2 since he himself is subject to w.
      7:28 as high priests men in all their w;
     11:34 whose w was turned to strength;

WEAKNESSES* WEAK
2Co 12: 5 about myself, except about my w.
     12: 9 all the more gladly about my w,
     12:10 sake, I delight in w, in insults,
Heb   4:15 is unable to empathize with our w,

WEALTH WEALTHY
Dt   8:18 gives you the ability to produce w,
1Sa   2: 7 The LORD sends poverty and w;
1Ki   3:13 not asked for—both w and honor—
2Ch   1:11 desire and you have not asked for w,
Ps   37:16 that the righteous have than the w
     39: 6 up w without knowing whose it will
     49: 6 those who trust in their w and boast
     49:10 perish, leaving their w to others.
     49:12 despite their w, do not endure;
Pr   3: 9 Honor the LORD with your w,
     10: 4 poverty, but diligent hands bring w.
     10:22 blessing of the LORD brings w,
     11: 4 W is worthless in the day of wrath,
     13: 7 pretends to be poor, yet has great w.
     13:22 but a sinner's w is stored
     15:16 of the LORD than great w
Ecc   5:10 whoever loves w is never satisfied
      5:13 w hoarded to the harm of its owners,
SS   8: 7 to give all the w of one's house
Ob   1:13 nor seize their w in the day of their
Mt   13:22 deceitfulness of w choke the word,

Mk   10:22 away sad, because he had great w.
     12:44 They all gave out of their w;
Lk   15:13 and there squandered his w in wild
     16:11 trustworthy in handling worldly w,
1Ti   6:17 arrogant nor to put their hope in w,
Jas   5: 2 Your w has rotted, and moths have
      5: 3 You have hoarded w in the last
Rev   3:17 I have acquired w and do not need
      5:12 to receive power and w and wisdom

WEALTHY WEALTH
Ge   13: 2 Abram had become very w
Lk   19: 2 was a chief tax collector and was w.

WEANED
Ps 131: 2 like a w child I am content.

WEAPON WEAPONS
Ne   4:17 one hand and held a w in the other,
Isa 54:17 no w forged against you will

WEAPONS WEAPON
Ecc   9:18 Wisdom is better than w of war,
Isa 13: 5 the LORD and the w of his wrath—
Jn   18: 3 carrying torches, lanterns and w.
2Co   6: 7 with w of righteousness in the right
     10: 4 The w we fight with are not the w

WEAR WEARING, WORE, WORN
Lev 19:19 " 'Do not w clothing woven
Dt   8: 4 Your clothes did not w out and your
     22: 5 woman must not w men's clothing,
     22: 5 nor a man w women's clothing,
     29: 5 your clothes did not w out, nor did
Ps 102:26 they will all w out like a garment.
Pr   23: 4 Do not w yourself out to get rich;
Isa 51: 6 the earth will w out like a garment
Mt   6:31 or 'What shall we w?'
Heb   1:11 they will all w out like a garment
Rev   3:18 and white clothes to w, so you can
     19: 8 and clean, was given her to w."

WEARIED WEARY
Isa 43:22 you have not w yourselves for me,
     43:24 sins and w me with your offenses.
Mal   2:17 You have w the LORD with your

WEARIES* WEARY
Ecc 10:15 The toil of fools w them;
     12:12 no end, and much study w the body.

WEARING WEAR
Ge   37:23 the ornate robe he was w—
1Sa 18: 4 Jonathan took off the robe he was w
2Sa 13:18 She was w an ornate robe, for this
1Ki 11:30 took hold of the new cloak he was w
Jn   19: 5 Jesus came out w the crown
Jas   2: 3 attention to the man w fine clothes
1Pe   3: 3 hairstyles and the w of gold jewelry
Rev   7: 9 They were w white robes and were

WEARY WEARIED, WEARIES
Ps   68: 9 you refreshed your w inheritance.
Isa   1:14 I am w of bearing them.
     40:28 He will not grow tired or w, and his
     40:31 they will run and not grow w,

Isa 50: 4 know the word that sustains the **w**.
Jer 9: 5 they **w** themselves with sinning.
Mt 11:28 all you who are **w** and burdened,
Gal 6: 9 Let us not become **w** in doing good,
Heb 12: 3 so that you will not grow **w** and lose
Rev 2: 3 my name, and have not grown **w**.

WEDDING
Ps 45: T *A maskil. A **w** song.*
Mt 22: 2 a king who prepared a **w** banquet
22:11 who was not wearing **w** clothes.
Rev 19: 7 For the **w** of the Lamb has come,

WEED* WEEDS
Mt 13:41 and they will **w** out of his kingdom

WEEDS WEED
Mt 13:25 and sowed **w** among the wheat,

WEEK WEEKS
Mt 28: 1 at dawn on the first day of the **w**,
Lk 18:12 I fast twice a **w** and give a tenth
1Co 16: 2 On the first day of every **w**,

WEEKS WEEK
Ex 34:22 "Celebrate the Festival of **W**
Lev 23:15 offering, count off seven full **w**.

WEEP WEEPING, WEPT
Ps 69:10 When I **w** and fast, I must endure
Ecc 3: 4 a time to **w** and a time to laugh,
La 1:16 "This is why I **w** and my eyes
Lk 6:21 Blessed are you who **w** now, for you
23:28 of Jerusalem, do not **w** for me;

WEEPING WEEP
Ne 8: 9 people had been **w** as they listened
Ps 6: 8 for the Lᴏʀᴅ has heard my **w**.
30: 5 **w** may stay for the night,
126: 6 Those who go out **w**, carrying seed
Jer 31:15 mourning and great **w**, Rachel **w**
Mt 2:18 Rachel **w** for her children
8:12 where there will be **w** and gnashing
13:42 where there will be **w** and gnashing
22:13 where there will be **w** and gnashing
24:51 where there will be **w** and gnashing
25:30 where there will be **w** and gnashing

WEIGH OUTWEIGHS, WEIGHED, WEIGHS, WEIGHTIER, WEIGHTS
1Co 14:29 the others should **w** carefully what

WEIGHED WEIGH
1Sa 2: 3 knows, and by him deeds are **w**.
Job 28:15 nor can its price be **w** out in silver.
Ecc 8: 6 though a person may be **w** down
Da 5:27 You have been **w** on the scales
Lk 21:34 or your hearts will be **w** down

WEIGHS WEIGH
Pr 12:25 Anxiety **w** down the heart,
15:28 heart of the righteous **w** its answers,
21: 2 right, but the Lᴏʀᴅ **w** the heart.
24:12 not he who **w** the heart perceive it?

WEIGHTIER* WEIGH
Jn 5:36 "I have testimony **w** than

WEIGHTS WEIGH
Lev 19:36 Use honest scales and honest **w**,
Dt 25:13 Do not have two differing **w** in your
Pr 11: 1 but accurate **w** find favor with him.
20:23 The Lᴏʀᴅ detests differing **w**,

WELCOME WELCOMED, WELCOMES
Mt 10:14 If anyone will not **w** you or listen
Mk 9:37 welcomes me does not **w** me
2Pe 1:11 you will receive a rich **w**
2Jn 1:10 them into your house or **w** them.
3Jn 1:10 he even refuses to **w** other believers.

WELCOMED WELCOME
Lk 10: 8 "When you enter a town and are **w**,

WELCOMES WELCOME
Mt 10:40 "Anyone who **w** you **w** me, and
anyone who **w** me **w** the one
18: 5 whoever **w** one such child in my
name **w** me.
2Jn 1:11 Anyone who **w** them shares in their

WELL WELLED, WELLING, WELLS
Ge 12:16 He treated Abram **w** for her sake,
Dt 5:16 and that it may go **w** with you
6: 3 to obey so that it may go **w** with you
12:28 so that it may always go **w** with you
2Ch 6: 8 'You did **w** to have it in your heart
Ps 105:40 he fed them **w** with the bread
Pr 5:15 running water from your own **w**.
23:27 and a wayward wife is a narrow **w**.
Isa 3:10 Tell the righteous it will be **w**
Jer 32:39 that all will then go **w** for them
Mt 3:17 with him I am **w** pleased."
15:31 the crippled made **w**, the lame
17: 5 with him I am **w** pleased.
25:21 "His master replied, '**W** done,
Lk 14: 5 falls into a **w** on the Sabbath day,
17:19 your faith has made you **w**."
Jn 4: 6 Jacob's **w** was there, and Jesus,
Ac 15:29 You will do **w** to avoid these things.
Eph 6: 3 "so that it may go **w** with you
1Ti 1:18 them you may fight the battle **w**,
Jas 5:15 in faith will make the sick person **w**;
2Pe 1:17 with him I am **w** pleased."
3Jn 1: 2 and that all may go **w** with you, even
as your soul is getting along **w**.

WELL-BEING
Ezr 6:10 pray for the **w** of the king and his
Ps 35:27 delights in the **w** of his servant."

WELL-FED* FED
Jer 5: 8 They are **w**, lusty stallions,
Mal 4: 2 will go out and frolic like **w** calves.

WELL-INSTRUCTED* INSTRUCT
Isa 50: 4 Sovereign Lᴏʀᴅ has given me a **w**
tongue,

WELL-KNOWN* KNOW
Nu   16: 2 w community leaders who had been
Mt   27:16 they had a w prisoner whose name

WELL-MIXED* MIXED
Lev   6:21 bring it w and present the grain

WELL-WATERED WATER
Isa   58:11 You will be like a w garden,
Jer   31:12 They will be like a w garden,

WELLED* WELL
2Co   8: 2 their extreme poverty w up in rich

WELLING* WELL
Jn   4:14 in them a spring of water w

WELLS WELL
Dt   6:11 did not provide, w you did not dig,
Ne   9:25 kinds of good things, w already dug,
Isa   12: 3 draw water from the w of salvation.

WENT
Hos 11: 2 the more they w away from me.

WEPT WEEP
Nu   14: 1 raised their voices and w aloud.
Ezr   3:12 temple, w aloud when they saw
Ps 137: 1 and w when we remembered Zion.
Isa   38: 3 And Hezekiah w bitterly.
Lk   19:41 and saw the city, he w over it
     22:62 And he went outside and w bitterly.
Jn   11:35 Jesus w.
Rev   5: 4 I w and w because no one was found

WEST WESTERN
Ge   13:14 north and south, to the east and w.
Ps 103:12 as far as the east is from the w,
     107: 3 from east and w, from north
Isa   43: 5 the east and gather you from the w.
Zec 14: 4 will be split in two from east to w,
     14: 8 of it w to the Mediterranean Sea,

WESTERN WEST
Nu   34: 6 " 'Your w boundary will be

WET
Lk   7:38 she began to w his feet with her

WHALE(S) (KJV) See CREATURES, HUGE FISH, MONSTER

WHAT WHATEVER
Ex   3:13 and they ask me, 'W is his name?'
Dt   10:12 w does the LORD your God ask
     30:11 Now w I am commanding you today
Eze 24: 6 this is w the Sovereign LORD
Mic   6: 8 has shown you, O mortal, w is good.
      6: 8 w does the LORD require of you?

WHATEVER WHAT
2Ch   1: 7 "Ask for w you want me to give
Ps   1: 3 w they do prospers.
     135: 6 The LORD does w pleases him,
Eze 24: 6 piece by piece in w order it comes.
Mt   16:19 w you bind on earth will be bound
     16:19 w you loose on earth will be loosed

Mt   18:18 w you bind on earth will be bound
     18:18 w you loose on earth will be loosed
Mk   11:24 I tell you, w you ask in prayer,
Jn   14:13 I will do w you ask in my name,
     15:16 so that w you ask in my name
     16:23 my Father will give you w you ask
Php   4: 8 w is true, w is noble, w is right, w is
                 pure, w is lovely, w is admirable—
1Jn   5:15 know that he hears us—w we ask—

WHEAT
Ex   34:22 with the firstfruits of the w harvest,
Mt   3:12 gathering his w into the barn
     13:25 and sowed weeds among the w,
Lk   22:31 has asked to sift all of you as w.
Jn   12:24 you, unless a kernel of w falls

WHEEL WHEELS
Eze   1:16 to be made like a w intersecting a w.

WHEELS WHEEL
Ex   14:25 He jammed the w of their chariots
Eze   1:16 appearance and structure of the w:
Da   7: 9 with fire, and its w were all ablaze.

WHENEVER
Dt   4: 7 our God is near us w we pray
1Co 11:26 For w you eat this bread and drink
2Co   3:16 But w anyone turns to the Lord,
Jas   1: 2 w you face trials of many kinds,

WHERE EVERYWHERE, WHEREVER
Ex   3: 5 the place w you are standing is holy
Dt   11:24 Every place w you set your foot will
     32:37 "Now w are their gods, the rock
Job 28:12 But w can wisdom be found?
     28:23 to it and he alone knows w it dwells,
Ps   26: 8 I love the house w you live, the
                 place w your glory dwells.
     42: 3 me all day long, "W is your God?"
     121: 1 w does my help come from?
     139: 7 W can I go from your Spirit?
Hos 13:14 W, O death, are your plagues?
Mal   1: 6 am a father, w is the honor due me?
      1: 6 a master, w is the respect due me?"
Mt   6:21 For w your treasure is, there your
     28: 6 Come and see the place w he lay.
1Co 15:55 "W, O death, is your victory?
Col   3: 1 hearts on things above, w Christ is,
2Pe   3: 4 "W is this 'coming' he promised?

WHEREVER WHERE
Jos   1: 7 you may be successful w you go.
1Ch 18: 6 gave David victory w he went.
Mk   14: 9 w the gospel is preached throughout
Lk   9:57 him, "I will follow you w you go."
Rev 14: 4 They follow the Lamb w he goes.

WHETHER
Ro   14: 8 So, w we live or die, we belong
1Co 12:13 w Jews or Gentiles, slave or free—
Php   4:12 situation, w well fed or hungry,
Col   3:17 you do, w in word or deed, do it all
1Jn   4: 1 but test the spirits to see w they are

WHILE

Ps   32: 6 pray to you **w** you may be found;
Isa   55: 6 Seek the LORD **w** he may be
      65:24 **w** they are still speaking I will hear.
Da   9:21 **w** I was still in prayer, Gabriel,
Jn   12:35 Walk **w** you have the light,
      16:16 after a little **w** you will see me."
Ro   5: 8 **W** we were still sinners, Christ died
2Co   5: 4 For **w** we are in this tent, we groan
Titus 2:13 **w** we wait for the blessed hope—
1Pe   5:10 after you have suffered a little **w**,

WHIP WHIPS

Jn   2:15 So he made a **w** out of cords,

WHIPS WHIP

Jos 23:13 **w** on your backs and thorns in your

WHIRLWIND WIND

2Ki   2:11 and Elijah went up to heaven in a **w**.
Ps   77:18 Your thunder was heard in the **w**,
Hos   8: 7 "They sow the wind and reap the **w**.
Na   1: 3 His way is in the **w** and the storm,

WHISPER WHISPERED

1Ki 19:12 And after the fire came a gentle **w**.
Job 26:14 how faint the **w** we hear of him!
Ps 107:29 He stilled the storm to a **w**;

WHISPERED WHISPER

Mt 10:27 what is **w** in your ear,

WHITE WHITER

Isa   1:18 scarlet, they shall be as **w** as snow;
Da   7: 9 His clothing was as **w** as snow;
      7: 9 hair of his head was **w** like wool.
Zec   1: 8 him were red, brown and **w** horses.
      6: 3 the third **w**, and the fourth dappled—
Mt   5:36 you cannot make even one hair **w**
     28: 3 and his clothes were **w** as snow.
Ac   1:10 dressed in **w** stood beside them.
Rev   1:14 hair on his head was **w** like wool, as
          w as snow,
     2:17 person a **w** stone with a new name
     3: 4 dressed in **w**, for they are worthy.
     6: 2 and there before me was a **w** horse!
     7:13 asked me, "These in **w** robes—
   14:14 and there before me was a **w** cloud,
   19:11 and there before me was a **w** horse,
   20:11 I saw a great **w** throne and him who

WHITER WHITE

Ps   51: 7 wash me, and I will be **w** than snow.
Mk   9: 3 **w** than anyone in the world could

WHITEWASH WASH

Eze 13:10 wall is built, they cover it with **w**,
     22:28 Her prophets **w** these deeds for them

WHITEWASHED WASH

Mt 23:27 You are like **w** tombs, which look
Ac   23: 3 "God will strike you, you **w** wall!

WHOEVER

Pr   10: 9 **W** walks in integrity walks securely,
Mt 10:32 "**W** acknowledges me before

Mt 12:50 For **w** does the will of my Father
Mk   3:29 but **w** blasphemes against the Holy
     8:35 For **w** wants to save their life will
     8:35 but **w** loses their life for me
     9:40 for **w** is not against us is for us.
Jn   3:36 **W** believes in the Son has eternal
     3:36 **w** rejects the Son will not see life,
1Jn   4:16 **W** lives in love lives in God,

WHOLE WHOLEHEARTED, WHOLEHEARTEDLY, WHOLLY

Ge   11: 1 Now the **w** world had one language
    18:28 Will you destroy the **w** city for lack
Ex   12:47 The **w** community of Israel must
    19: 5 Although the **w** earth is mine,
Lev 16:17 and the **w** community of Israel.
Nu 14:21 of the LORD fills the **w** earth,
    32:13 until the **w** generation of those who
Dt   13:16 all its plunder as a **w** burnt offering
    19: 8 gives you the **w** land he promised
Jos   2: 3 have come to spy out the **w** land."
1Sa   1:28 For his **w** life he will be given over
    17:46 the **w** world will know that there is
1Ki 10:24 The **w** world sought audience
2Ki 21: 8 will keep the **w** Law that my servant
Ps   48: 2 the joy of the **w** earth,
    72:19 may the **w** earth be filled with his
Pr   4:22 them and health to one's **w** body.
    8:31 rejoicing in his **w** world
Isa   1: 5 Your **w** head is injured, your **w** heart
    6: 3 the **w** earth is full of his glory."
   14:26 the plan determined for the **w** world;
La   2:15 of beauty, the joy of the **w** earth?"
Eze 34: 6 were scattered over the **w** earth,
Da   2:35 mountain and filled the **w** earth.
Zep   1:18 of his jealousy the **w** earth will be
Zec 14: 9 will be king over the **w** earth.
Mal   3:10 Bring the **w** tithe
Mt   5:29 your body than for your **w** body
    6:22 your **w** body will be full of light.
   16:26 be for someone to gain the **w** world,
   24:14 in the **w** world as a testimony to all
Mk 15:33 came over the **w** land until three
Lk   21:35 who live on the face of the **w** earth.
Jn   12:19 Look how the **w** world has gone
    13:10 their **w** body is clean.
    21:25 even the **w** world would not have
Ac   17:26 that they should inhabit the **w** earth;
    20:27 proclaim to you the **w** will of God.
Ro   3:19 and the **w** world held accountable
    8:22 the **w** creation has been groaning as
1Co   4: 9 made a spectacle to the **w** universe,
    5: 6 a little yeast leavens the **w** batch
   12:17 If the **w** body were an eye,
Gal   5: 3 he is obligated to obey the **w** law.
Eph   2:21 In him the **w** building is joined
    4:10 in order to fill the **w** universe.)
    4:13 attaining to the **w** measure
1Th   5:23 May your **w** spirit, soul and body be
Titus 1:11 they are disrupting **w** households
Jas   2:10 For whoever keeps the **w** law
1Jn   2: 2 but also for the sins of the **w** world.
    5:19 that the **w** world is under the control

Rev　3:10　to come on the **w** world to test
　　　6:12　hair, the **w** moon turned blood red,
　　　12:　9　Satan, who leads the **w** world astray.
　　　13:　3　The **w** world was filled with wonder

WHOLEHEARTED* HEART, WHOLE

2Ki　20:　3　and with **w** devotion and have done
1Ch　28:　9　serve him with **w** devotion
　　　29:19　my son Solomon the **w** devotion
Isa　38:　3　and with **w** devotion and have done

WHOLEHEARTEDLY* HEART, WHOLE

Nu　14:24　a different spirit and follows me **w**,
　　　32:11　they have not followed me **w**,
　　　32:12　for they followed the LORD **w**.'
Dt　　1:36　he followed the LORD **w**."
Jos　14:　8　followed the LORD my God **w**.
　　　14:　9　followed the LORD my God **w**.'
　　　14:14　the LORD, the God of Israel, **w**.
1Ki　　8:23　your servants who continue **w**
1Ch　29:　9　given freely and **w** to the LORD.
2Ch　　6:14　your servants who continue **w**
　　　15:15　oath because they had sworn it **w**.
　　　19:　9　and **w** in the fear of the LORD.
　　　25:　2　the eyes of the LORD, but not **w**.
　　　31:21　he sought his God and worked **w**.
Ps　119:80　May I **w** follow your decrees,
Eph　6:　7　Serve **w**, as if you were serving

WHOLESOME*

2Pe　3:　1　to stimulate you to **w** thinking.

WHOLLY* WHOLE

Nu　3:　9　who are to be given **w** to him.
　　　8:16　who are to be given **w** to me.
1Ti　4:15　give yourself **w** to them,

WHORE(S) (KJV) See PROMISCUOUS, PROSTITUTE(S), PROSTITUTION, UNFAITHFUL

WHOREDOM (KJV) See ADULTERY, PROSTITUTION, UNFAITHFULNESS

WHY

Ge　　4:　6　said to Cain, "**W** are you angry?
　　　12:19　**W** did you say, 'She is my sister,'
　　　32:29　replied, "**W** do you ask my name?"
Jdg　13:18　replied, "**W** do you ask my name?
Job　24:　1　"**W** does the Almighty not set times
Ps　　2:　1　**W** do the nations conspire
　　　10:　1　**W**, LORD, do you stand far off?
　　　22:　1　my God, **w** have you forsaken me?
　　　42:　5　**W**, my soul, are you downcast?
　　　79:10　**W** should the nations say,
Isa　　1:　5　**W** do you persist in rebellion?
　　　40:27　**W** do you complain, Jacob? **W** do
La　　5:20　**W** do you always forget us? **W** do
Am　　5:18　**W** do you long for the day
Mt　　9:11　"**W** does your teacher eat with tax
　　　17:19　"**W** couldn't we drive it out?"

Mt　27:46　God, **w** have you forsaken me?").
Mk　10:18　"**W** do you call me good?"
Ac　　9:　4　Saul, **w** do you persecute me?"

WICK

Isa　42:　3　a smoldering **w** he will not snuff
Mt　12:20　a smoldering **w** he will not snuff

WICKED OVERWICKED, WICKEDLY, WICKEDNESS

Ge　13:13　Now the people of Sodom were **w**
　　　18:23　away the righteous with the **w**?
　　　39:　9　could I do such a **w** thing and sin
Nu　14:35　things to this whole **w** community,
Dt　15:　9　careful not to harbor this **w** thought:
Jdg　19:22　some of the **w** men of the city
1Sa　15:18　completely destroy those **w** people,
　　　25:17　He is such a **w** man that no one can
2Sa　13:12　Don't do this **w** thing.
2Ki　17:11　They did **w** things that aroused
2Ch　7:14　my face and turn from their **w** ways,
　　　19:　2　"Should you help the **w** and love
Ne　13:17　them, "What is this **w** thing you are
Job　15:20　his days the **w** man suffers torment,
　　　20:29　Such is the fate God allots the **w**,
　　　27:　4　my lips will not say anything **w**,
　　　27:13　is the fate God allots to the **w**,
Ps　　1:　1　does not walk in step with the **w**
　　　1:　5　Therefore the **w** will not stand
　　　7:　9　to an end the violence of the **w**
　　　10:13　Why does the **w** man revile God?
　　　11:　6　On the **w** he will rain fiery coals
　　　26:　5　and refuse to sit with the **w**.
　　　32:10　Many are the woes of the **w**,
　　　36:　1　concerning the sinfulness of the **w**:
　　　37:13　but the Lord laughs at the **w**, for he
　　　37:40　he delivers them from the **w**
　　　49:　5　when **w** deceivers surround me—
　　　50:16　But to the **w** person, God says:
　　　58:　3　Even from birth the **w** go astray;
　　　73:　3　when I saw the prosperity of the **w**.
　　　82:　2　unjust and show partiality to the **w**?
　　112:10　The **w** will see and be vexed,
　　119:61　Though the **w** bind me with ropes,
　119:155　Salvation is far from the **w**, for they
　　140:　8　Do not grant the **w** their desires,
　　141:10　Let the **w** fall into their own nets,
　　146:　9　but he frustrates the ways of the **w**.
Pr　　2:12　save you from the ways of **w** men,
　　　4:14　Do not set foot on the path of the **w**
　　　5:22　evil deeds of the **w** ensnare them;
　　　6:18　a heart that devises **w** schemes,
　　　9:　7　rebukes the **w** incurs abuse.
　　　10:20　the heart of the **w** is of little value.
　　　10:28　the hopes of the **w** come to nothing.
　　　11:　5　but the **w** are brought down by their
　　　11:10　when the **w** perish, there are shouts
　　　11:21　The **w** will not go unpunished,
　　　12:　5　but the advice of the **w** is deceitful.
　　　12:10　the kindest acts of the **w** are cruel.
　　　10:23　A fool finds pleasure in **w** schemes,
　　　14:19　the **w** at the gates of the righteous.
　　　15:　3　keeping watch on the **w**
　　　15:26　detests the thoughts of the **w**,

Pr 21:10 The **w** crave evil;
21:29 The **w** put up a bold front,
24: 1 Do not envy the **w**, do not desire
28: 1 The **w** flee though no one pursues,
28: 4 forsake instruction praise the **w**,
29: 7 but the **w** have no such concern.
29:16 When the **w** thrive, so does sin,
29:27 the **w** detest the upright.
Ecc 7:15 and the **w** living long in their
8:14 the **w** who get what the righteous
Isa 11: 4 breath of his lips he will slay the **w**.
13:11 for its evil, the **w** for their sins.
26:10 But when grace is shown to the **w**,
48:22 says the LORD, "for the **w**."
53: 9 He was assigned a grave with the **w**,
55: 7 Let the **w** forsake their ways
57:20 But the **w** are like the tossing sea,
Jer 12: 1 Why does the way of the **w** prosper?
35:15 of you must turn from your **w** ways
Eze 3:18 that **w** person will die for their sin,
13:22 because you encouraged the **w** not
14: 7 put a **w** stumbling block before their
18:21 if a **w** person turns away from all
18:23 any pleasure in the death of the **w**?
21:25 profane and **w** prince of Israel,
33: 8 that **w** person will die for their sin,
33:11 no pleasure in the death of the **w**,
33:19 if a **w** person turns away from their
Da 12:10 but the **w** will continue to be **w**.
Na 1:15 No more will the **w** invade you;
Mt 12:39 "A **w** and adulterous generation
12:45 other spirits more **w** than itself,
Lk 6:35 he is kind to the ungrateful and **w**.
Ac 2:23 with the help of **w** men, put him
1Co 5:13 "Expel the **w** person from among
2Jn 1:11 them shares in their **w** work.
Rev 2: 2 that you cannot tolerate **w** people,

WICKEDLY WICKED
2Ch 6:37 we have done wrong and acted **w**';
Ne 1: 7 We have acted very **w** toward you.

WICKEDNESS WICKED
Ge 6: 5 The LORD saw how great the **w**
Ex 34: 7 and forgiving **w**, rebellion and sin.
Lev 16:21 and confess over it all the **w**
19:29 to prostitution and be filled with **w**.
Dt 9: 4 on account of the **w** of these nations
Ps 45: 7 You love righteousness and hate **w**;
92:15 Rock, and there is no **w** in him."
Pr 11: 5 are brought down by their own **w**.
13: 6 but **w** overthrows the sinner.
Ecc 3:16 **w** was there, in the place of justice—
Jer 3: 2 land with your prostitution and **w**.
8: 6 None of them repent of their **w**,
14:20 We acknowledge our **w**, LORD,
31:34 "For I will forgive their **w** and will
Eze 18:20 the **w** of the wicked will be charged
28:15 you were created till **w** was found
33:19 person turns away from their **w**
Da 4:27 and your **w** by being kind
9:24 end to sin, to atone for **w**, to bring
Hos 9: 9 God will remember their **w**
Jnh 1: 2 it, because its **w** has come up before

Mt 24:12 Because of the increase of **w**,
Lk 11:39 inside you are full of greed and **w**.
Ac 1:18 the payment he received for his **w**,
Ro 1:18 who suppress the truth by their **w**,
1Co 5: 8 bread leavened with malice and **w**,
2Co 6:14 and **w** have in common?
2Ti 2:19 the Lord must turn away from **w**."
Titus 2:14 for us to redeem us from all **w**
Heb 1: 9 loved righteousness and hated **w**;
8:12 For I will forgive their **w** and will
2Pe 2:15 of Bezer, who loved the wages of **w**.

WIDE
Ps 81:10 Open **w** your mouth and I will fill it.
Isa 54: 2 stretch your tent curtains **w**, do not
Mt 7:13 For **w** is the gate and broad is
23: 5 They make their phylacteries **w**
2Co 6:13 open **w** your hearts also.
Eph 3:18 to grasp how **w** and long and high

WIDOW WIDOW'S, WIDOWHOOD, WIDOWS, WIDOWS'
Ex 22:22 "Do not take advantage of the **w**
Dt 10:18 cause of the fatherless and the **w**,
25: 5 his brother's **w** shall go up to him
Ru 4: 5 the dead man's **w**, in order
Ps 146: 9 sustains the fatherless and the **w**,
Isa 1:17 plead the case of the **w**.
La 1: 1 How like a **w** is she, who once was
Mk 12:19 the man must marry the **w** and raise
Lk 2:37 was a **w** until she was eighty-four.
18: 3 there was a **w** in that town who kept
21: 3 "this poor **w** has put in more than
1Ti 5: 4 if a **w** has children or grandchildren,
Rev 18: 7 I am not a **w**; I will never mourn.'

WIDOW'S WIDOW
Ge 38:14 she took off her **w** clothes,
Job 29:13 I made the **w** heart sing.
Pr 15:25 but he sets the **w** boundary stones

WIDOWHOOD WIDOW
Isa 54: 4 no more the reproach of your **w**.

WIDOWS WIDOW
Dt 14:29 the **w** who live in your towns may
Ps 68: 5 a defender of **w**, is God in his holy
Mal 3: 5 wages, who oppress the **w**
Lk 4:25 you that there were many **w** in Israel
Ac 6: 1 Jews because their **w** were being
1Co 7: 8 to the unmarried and the **w** I say:
1Ti 5: 3 to those who are really in need.
Jas 1:27 after orphans and **w** in their distress

WIDOWS' WIDOW
Mk 12:40 They devour **w** houses

WIFE WIVES, WIVES'
Ge 2:24 and mother and is united to his **w**,
3:20 Adam named his **w** Eve,
12:18 didn't you tell me she was your **w**?
19:26 But Lot's **w** looked back, and she
20:11 they will kill me because of my **w**.'
24:67 So she became his **w**, and he loved

Ex 20:17 shall not covet your neighbor's w,
Lev 18: 8 relations with your father's w;
20:10 adultery with another man's w—
Nu 5:12 'If a man's w goes astray and is
Dt 5:21 shall not covet your neighbor's w.
21:15 is the son of the w he does not love,
24: 5 happiness to the w he has married.
Ru 4:13 took Ruth and she became his w.
2Sa 12:10 took the w of Uriah the Hittite to be
Ps 128: 3 Your w will be like a fruitful vine
Pr 5:18 you rejoice in the w of your youth.
6:24 you from your neighbor's w,
6:26 another man's w preys on your very
12: 4 A w of noble character is her
12: 4 a disgraceful w is like decay in his
18:22 He who finds a w finds what is good
19:13 a quarrelsome w is like the constant
19:14 but a prudent w is from the LORD.
31:10 A w of noble character who can
Ecc 9: 9 Enjoy life with your w, whom you
Hos 1: 2 for like an adulterous w this land is
Mal 2:14 you and the w of your youth.
Mt 1:20 afraid to take Mary home as your w,
5:32 you that anyone who divorces his w,
19: 3 for a man to divorce his w for any
Mk 6:18 for you to have your brother's w."
10: 2 lawful for a man to divorce his w?"
12:23 At the resurrection whose w will she
Lk 17:32 Remember Lot's w!
18:29 "no one who has left home or w
1Co 7: 2 sexual relations with his own w,
7:11 a husband must not divorce his w.
7:33 how he can please his w—
Eph 5:23 head of the w as Christ is the head
5:28 He who loves his w loves himself.
5:33 must love his w as he loves himself,
5:33 and the w must respect her husband.
1Ti 3: 2 faithful to his w, temperate,
3:12 A deacon must be faithful to his w
Titus 1: 6 faithful to his w, a man whose
Rev 21: 9 you the bride, the w of the Lamb."

WILD WILDERNESS

Ge 1:25 God made the w animals according
8: 1 all the w animals and the livestock
Ex 32:25 saw that the people were running w
Lev 26:22 I will send w animals against you,
Mk 1: 6 and he ate locusts and w honey.
1:13 He was with the w animals,
Lk 15:13 squandered his wealth in w living.
Ro 11:17 and you, though a w olive shoot,
1Co 15:32 If I fought w beasts in Ephesus
Titus 1: 6 not open to the charge of being w
1Pe 4: 4 join them in their reckless, w living,
Jude 1:13 They are w waves of the sea,

WILDERNESS WILD

Ex 3: 1 led the flock to the far side of the w
4:27 "Go into the w to meet Moses."
16:32 eat in the w when I brought you
Nu 14:29 In this w your bodies will fall—
32:13 them wander in the w forty years,
Dt 8:16 He gave you manna to eat in the w,
29: 5 years that I led you through the w,

Ne 9:21 years you sustained them in the w;
Ps 68: 7 when you marched through the w,
78:15 He split the rocks in the w and gave
78:19 God really spread a table in the w?
78:52 led them like sheep through the w.
106:14 in the w they put God to the test.
Isa 40: 3 "In the w prepare the way
Eze 20:13 Israel rebelled against me in the w.
Hos 2:14 I will lead her into the w and speak
13: 5 I cared for you in the w, in the land
Am 2:10 years in the w to give you the land
Mk 1: 3 "a voice of one calling in the w,
1:13 and he was in the w forty days,
Jn 6:31 ancestors ate the manna in the w;
Heb 3: 8 during the time of testing in the w,
Rev 12: 6 fled into the w to a place prepared
17: 3 me away in the Spirit into a w.

WILL FREEWILL, WILLFUL, WILLFULLY, WILLING, WILLINGLY, WILLINGNESS

Ex 18:15 people come to me to seek God's w.
Dt 10:10 It was not his w to destroy you.
33:21 out the LORD's righteous w,
1Sa 2:25 it was the LORD's w to put them
2Sa 7:21 your word and according to your w,
1Ch 13: 2 if it is the w of the LORD our God,
Ezr 7:18 accordance with the w of your God.
10:11 of your ancestors, and do his w.
Ps 40: 8 I desire to do your w, my God;
103:21 you his servants who do his w.
143:10 Teach me to do your w, for you are
Isa 53:10 Yet it was the LORD's w to crush
53:10 the w of the LORD w prosper
Eze 12:25 But I the LORD w speak what I w,
Mt 6:10 kingdom come, your w be done,
7:21 only the one who does the w of my
10:29 Yet not one of them w fall
26:39 Yet not as I w, but as you w."
Mk 3:35 Whoever does God's w is my
14:36 Yet not what I w, but what you w."
Lk 22:42 yet not my w, but yours be done."
23:25 and surrendered Jesus to their w.
Jn 1:13 human decision or a husband's w,
4:34 "is to do the w of him who sent me
6:38 down from heaven not to do my w
6:38 but to do the w of him who sent me.
7:17 chooses to do the w of God w find
9:31 to the godly person who does his w.
10:28 no one w snatch them out of my
Ac 4:28 w had decided beforehand should
20:27 to you the whole w of God.
21:14 and said, "The Lord's w be done."
Ro 2:18 if you know his w and approve
9:19 For who is able to resist his w?"
12: 2 test and approve what God's w is—his
good, pleasing and perfect w.
1Co 7:37 but has control over his own w,
Eph 1: 5 with his pleasure and w—
1: 9 us the mystery of his w according
1:11 with the purpose of his w,
5:17 but understand what the Lord's w is.
6: 6 doing the w of God from your heart.

Php 2:13 for it is God who works in you to w
Col 1: 9 of his w through all the wisdom
4:12 may stand firm in all the w of God,
1Th 4: 3 It is God's w that you should be
5:18 for this is God's w for you in Christ
2Ti 2:26 has taken them captive to do his w.
Heb 2: 4 Spirit distributed according to his w.
10: 7 I have come to do your w,
13:21 everything good for doing his w,
Jas 4:15 "If it is the Lord's w, we w live
1Pe 2:15 For it is God's w that by doing good
3:17 if it is God's w, to suffer for doing
4: 2 desires, but rather for the w of God.
4:19 God's w should commit themselves
2Pe 1:21 never had its origin in the human w,
1Jn 2:17 whoever does the w of God lives
5:14 we ask anything according to his w,
Rev 2:26 and does my w to the end, I w give

WILLFUL WILL
Ps 19:13 Keep your servant also from w sins;

WILLFULLY* WILL
Ps 78:18 They w put God to the test

WILLING WILL
Ex 10:27 and he was not w to let them go.
35: 5 Everyone who is w is to bring
2Ki 8:19 the LORD was not w to destroy
24: 4 the LORD was not w to forgive.
1Ch 28: 9 devotion and with a w mind,
29: 5 who is w to consecrate themselves
Ps 51:12 salvation and grant me a w spirit,
Da 3:28 were w to give up their lives rather
Mt 8: 3 "I am w," he said.
18:14 Father in heaven is not w that any
23: 4 they themselves are not w to lift
23:37 her wings, and you were not w.
26:41 The spirit is w, but the flesh is
Lk 22:42 if you are w, take this cup from me;
Ro 12:16 be w to associate with people of low
1Ti 6:18 and to be generous and w to share.
1Pe 5: 2 must, but because you are w, as God

WILLINGLY WILL
Jdg 5: 2 the people w offer themselves—
1Ch 29:17 All these things I have given w
La 3:33 For he does not w bring affliction

WILLINGNESS* WILL
2Co 8:11 so that your eager w to do it may be
8:12 For if the w is there, the gift is

WIN WINNING, WINS, WON
Pr 3: 4 you will w favor and a good name
Mt 23:15 land and sea to w a single convert,
Lk 21:19 Stand firm, and you will w life.
1Co 9:19 everyone, to w as many as possible.
Gal 1:10 Am I now trying to w the approval
Php 3:14 on toward the goal to w the prize
1Th 4:12 your daily life may w the respect

WIND WHIRLWIND, WINDS
1Ki 19:11 but the LORD was not in the w.
Ps 1: 4 like chaff that the w blows away.

Ps 18:10 he soared on the wings of the w.
104: 3 and rides on the wings of the w.
Pr 11:29 on their family will inherit only w,
30: 4 hands have gathered up the w?
Ecc 1:14 meaningless, a chasing after the w.
8: 8 As no one has power over the w
Eze 5: 2 And scatter a third to the w.
Hos 8: 7 "They sow the w and reap
Jnh 1: 4 the LORD sent a great w
4: 8 God provided a scorching east w,
Mk 4:41 Even the w and the waves obey
Jn 3: 8 The w blows wherever it pleases.
Ac 2: 2 of a violent w came from heaven
Eph 4:14 there by every w of teaching
Jas 1: 6 the sea, blown and tossed by the w.

WINDOW
Jos 2:21 she tied the scarlet cord in the w.
1Sa 19:12 Michal let David down through a w,
Ac 20: 9 in a w was a young man named
2Co 11:33 in a basket from a w in the wall

WINDS WIND
Ps 104: 4 He makes w his messengers,
Mt 7:25 and the w blew and beat against
8:27 Even the w and the waves obey
24:31 will gather his elect from the four w,

WINE
Ge 9:21 When he drank some of its w,
19:32 Let's get our father to drink w
Nu 6: 3 they must abstain from w and other
Dt 7:13 your grain, new w and olive oil—
Jdg 13: 4 Now see to it that you drink no w or
1Sa 1:15 I have not been drinking w or beer;
Ne 13:12 grain, new w and olive oil
Ps 4: 7 when their grain and new w abound.
75: 8 is a cup full of foaming w mixed
104:15 w that gladdens human hearts,
Pr 3:10 vats will brim over with new w.
9: 2 prepared her meat and mixed her w;
20: 1 W is a mocker and beer a brawler;
23:20 join those who drink too much w
23:31 Do not gaze at w when it is red,
31: 4 it is not for kings to drink w,
31: 6 w for those who are in anguish!
Ecc 2: 3 I tried cheering myself with w,
9: 7 drink your w with a joyful heart,
10:19 for laughter, w makes life merry,
SS 1: 2 your love is more delightful than w.
7: 9 and your mouth like the best w.
Isa 5:22 those who are heroes at drinking w
28: 7 stagger from w and reel from beer:
51:21 one, made drunk, but not with w.
55: 1 buy w and milk without money
Da 1: 8 himself with the royal food and w,
Joel 2:24 the vats will overflow with new w
3:18 day the mountains will drip new w,
Am 2:12 you made the Nazirites drink w
Mic 2:11 'I will prophesy for you plenty of w
Mt 9:17 Neither do people pour new w
9:17 No, they pour new w into new
27:34 There they offered Jesus w to drink,
Lk 23:36 They offered him w vinegar

Jn   2: 3 When the **w** was gone,
     2: 9 water that had been turned into **w**.
Ac   2:13 said, "They have had too much **w**."
Ro 14:21 drink **w** or to do anything else
Eph 5:18 Do not get drunk on **w**, which leads
1Ti 3: 8 not indulging in much **w**, and not
     5:23 and use a little **w** because of your
Rev 14: 8 the nations drink the maddening **w**
    14:10 too, will drink the **w** of God's fury,
    16:19 the cup filled with the **w** of the fury
    18: 3 have drunk the maddening **w** of her

WINEPRESS

Dt 15:14 your threshing floor and your **w**.
Isa 63: 2 like those of one treading the **w**?
La   1:15 his **w** the Lord has trampled Virgin
Rev 14:19 into the great **w** of God's wrath.
    19:15 He treads the **w** of the fury

WINESKINS

Job 32:19 wine, like new **w** ready to burst.
Mt   9:17 do people pour new wine into old **w**.
     9:17 they pour new wine into new **w**,

WING WINGED, WINGS

2Ch 3:11 One **w** of the first cherub was five
     3:11 touched the **w** of the other cherub.

WINGED WING

Ge   1:21 every **w** bird according to its kind.

WINGS WING

Ex 19: 4 how I carried you on eagles' **w**
    37: 9 had their **w** spread upward,
Ru   2:12 under whose **w** you have come
1Ki 8: 7 cherubim spread their **w** over
Ps 17: 8 hide me in the shadow of your **w**
    91: 4 under his **w** you will find refuge;
Isa 6: 2 were seraphim, each with six **w**:
    40:31 They will soar on **w** like eagles;
Eze 1: 6 of them had four faces and four **w**.
    10:21 Each had four faces and four **w**,
Zec 5: 9 women, with the wind in their **w**!
Lk 13:34 hen gathers her chicks under her **w**,
Rev 4: 8 the four living creatures had six **w**

WINNING* WIN

Ex 17:11 the Israelites were **w**, but whenever
    17:11 his hands, the Amalekites were **w**.

WINNOW WINNOWING, WINNOWS

Isa 41:16 You will **w** them, the wind will pick
Jer 15: 7 I will **w** them with a winnowing

WINNOWING WINNOW

Mt   3:12 His **w** fork is in his hand, and he

WINNOWS* WINNOW

Pr 20: 8 he **w** out all evil with his eyes.
    20:26 A wise king **w** out the wicked;

WINS* WIN

Pr 13:15 Good judgment **w** favor,

WINTER

Ge   8:22 summer and **w**, day and night will
Ps 74:17 you made both summer and **w**.
Mk 13:18 that this will not take place in **w**,

WIPE WIPED

Ge   7: 4 I will **w** from the face of the earth
Ex 32:12 to **w** them off the face of the earth'?
1Ki 21:21 I will **w** out your descendants
Isa 14:22 "I will **w** out Babylon's name
    25: 8 Sovereign LORD will **w** away
Rev 7:17 God will **w** away every tear
    21: 4 'He will **w** every tear from their

WIPED WIPE

Ge   7:23 on the face of the earth was **w** out;
Ps 119:87 They almost **w** me from the earth,
Lk   7:38 Then she **w** them with her hair,
Ac   3:19 so that your sins may be **w** out,

WISDOM WISE

Ge   3: 6 and also desirable for gaining **w**,
Ex 28: 3 to whom I have given **w** in such
Dt   4: 6 for this will show your **w**
1Ki 4:29 God gave Solomon **w** and very great
    10: 6 achievements and your **w** is true.
2Ch 1:10 Give me **w** and knowledge, that I
Job 9: 4 His **w** is profound, his power is vast.
    11: 6 and disclose to you the secrets of **w**,
        for true **w** has two sides.
    12:13 "To God belong **w** and power;
    28:12 But where can **w** be found?
    28:28 that is **w**, and to shun evil is
Ps 37:30 The mouths of the righteous utter **w**,
    51: 6 you taught me **w** in that secret place.
   111:10 the LORD is the beginning of **w**;
Pr   1: 7 but fools despise **w** and instruction.
     1:20 Out in the open **w** calls aloud,
     2: 6 For the LORD gives **w**;
     3:13 Blessed are those who find **w**,
     4: 5 Get **w**, get understanding;
     4: 7 The beginning of **w** is this: Get **w**.
     8:11 for **w** is more precious than rubies,
     9: 1 **W** has built her house; she has set
     9:10 the LORD is the beginning of **w**,
    11: 2 but with humility comes **w**.
    13:10 **w** is found in those who take advice.
    19: 8 The one who gets **w** loves life;
    23:23 **w**, instruction and insight as well.
    29: 3 A man who loves **w** brings joy
    29:15 A rod and a reprimand impart **w**,
    31:26 She speaks with **w**, and faithful
Ecc 1:13 explore by **w** all that is done under
     2: 3 my mind still guiding me with **w**.
     2:13 I saw that **w** is better than folly,
     7:12 **W** is a shelter as money is a shelter,
     7:12 **W** preserves those who have it.
     9:18 **W** is better than weapons of war,
    10: 1 so a little folly outweighs **w**
Isa 11: 2 rest on him—the Spirit of **w**
    28:29 wonderful, whose **w** is magnificent.
Jer 9:23 "Let not the wise boast of their **w**
    10:12 he founded the world by his **w**
Eze 28:12 full of **w** and perfect in beauty.

Da 2:14 Daniel spoke to him with w
5:14 intelligence and outstanding w.
Mic 6: 9 and to fear your name is w—
Mt 11:19 w is proved right by her deeds."
12:42 the earth to listen to Solomon's w,
13:54 "Where did this man get this w
Lk 2:40 he was filled with w, and the grace
2:52 And Jesus grew in w and stature,
Ac 6: 3 known to be full of the Spirit and w.
Ro 11:33 the depth of the riches of the w
1Co 1:17 not with w and eloquence,
1:19 "I will destroy the w of the wise;
1:20 Has not God made foolish the w
1:30 has become for us w from God—
2: 7 we declare God's w, a mystery
3:19 the w of this world is foolishness
12: 8 through the Spirit a message of w,
Eph 1:17 may give you the Spirit of w
Col 1: 9 of his will through all the w
1:28 and teaching everyone with all w,
2: 3 are hidden all the treasures of w
2:23 indeed have an appearance of w,
Jas 1: 5 If any of you lacks w, you should
3:13 in the humility that comes from w.
3:17 But the w that comes from heaven is
Rev 5:12 and wealth and w and strength
7:12 Praise and glory and w and thanks
13:18 This calls for w. Let the person who
17: 9 "This calls for a mind with w.

WISDOM'S WISE
Pr 15:33 W instruction is to fear the LORD,

WISE OVERWISE, WISDOM, WISDOM'S, WISELY, WISER
Ge 41:39 no one so discerning and w as you.
Ex 7:11 Pharaoh then summoned w men
Dt 4: 6 "Surely this great nation is a w
16:19 for a bribe blinds the eyes of the w
1Ki 3:12 I will give you a w and discerning
Job 5:13 He catches the w in their craftiness,
32: 9 It is not only the old who are w,
Ps 2:10 Therefore, you kings, be w;
19: 7 trustworthy, making w the simple.
94: 8 fools, when will you become w?
107:43 the one who is w heed these things
Pr 3: 7 Do not be w in your own eyes;
6: 6 consider its ways and be w!
9: 9 Instruct the w and they will be wiser
10: 1 A w son brings joy to his father,
10:14 The w store up knowledge,
11:30 and the one who is w saves lives.
13: 1 A w son heeds his father's
13:20 Walk with the w and become w,
14:16 The w fear the LORD and shun
16:23 of the w make their mouths prudent,
17:28 Even fools are thought w if they
23:15 if your heart is w, then my heart will
24: 5 The w prevail through great power,
26: 5 or he will be w in his own eyes.
29:11 but the w bring calm in the end.
Ecc 2:14 The w have eyes in their heads,
7:19 Wisdom makes one w person more
9:17 The quiet words of the w are more

Ecc 12:11 The words of the w are like goads,
Isa 29:14 the wisdom of the w will perish,
Jer 8: 9 The w will be put to shame;
9:23 "Let not the w boast of their
Eze 28: 6 " 'Because you think you are w, as
w as a god,
Da 2:21 He gives wisdom to the w
11:35 Some of the w will stumble,
12: 3 Those who are w will shine like
Mt 11:25 have hidden these things from the w
25: 2 them were foolish and five were w.
Lk 12:42 then is the faithful and manager,
Ro 1:22 Although they claimed to be w,
16:27 to the only w God be glory forever
1Co 1:19 will destroy the wisdom of the w;
1:26 of you were w by human standards;
3:10 I laid a foundation as a w builder,
3:18 If any of you think you are w
3:18 "fools" so that you may become w.
3:19 "He catches the w in their
Eph 5:15 not as unwise but as w,
Col 4: 5 Be w in the way you act toward
2Ti 3:15 to make you w for salvation through
Jas 3:13 Who is w and understanding among

WISELY WISE
Isa 52:13 See, my servant will act w;
Jer 23: 5 a King who will reign w and do

WISER WISE
1Ki 4:31 He was w than anyone else,
Pr 9: 9 the wise and they will be w still;
26:16 A sluggard is w in his own eyes
1Co 1:25 of God is w than human wisdom,

WISH WISHED, WISHES
Job 11: 5 Oh, how I w that God would speak,
Jn 15: 7 ask whatever you w, and it will be
Ro 9: 3 I could w that I myself were cursed
Gal 4: 9 Do you w to be enslaved by them all
Rev 3:15 I w you were either one or the other!

WISHED WISH
Mt 17:12 have done to him everything they w.

WISHES WISH
Da 4:25 and gives them to anyone he w.
Rev 22:17 the one who w take the free gift of

WITCH (KJV) See MEDIUM, SORCERESS, SORCERY

WITCHCRAFT* BEWITCHED
Dt 18:10 interprets omens, engages in w,
2Ki 9:22 w of your mother Jezebel abound?"
2Ch 33: 6 practiced divination and w,
Mic 5:12 I will destroy your w and you will
Na 3: 4 prostitution and peoples by her w.
Gal 5:20 idolatry and w;

WITH
I AM WITH YOU Ge 26:24; 28:15; Jos 3:7; 1Sa
14:7; 2Ki 10:15; Isa 41:10; 43:5; Jer 1:8, 19; 15:20;
30:11; 42:11; 46:28; Hag 1:13; 2:4; Mt 28:20; Jn
7:33; Ac 18:10; 1Co 5:3, 4; Gal 4:18

I WILL BE WITH YOU Ge 26:3; 31:3; Ex 3:12;
Jos 1:5; Jdg 6:16; 1Ki 11:38; Isa 43:2; Jn 13:33

WITHER WITHERED, WITHERS

Ps   1: 3 season and whose leaf does not w—
       37:19 In times of disaster they will not w;

WITHERED WITHER

Ge   41:23 w and thin and scorched by the east
Zec   11:17 May his arm be completely w,
Mt   13: 6 they w because they had no root.
       21:19 Immediately the tree w.

WITHERS WITHER

Ps   129: 6 roof, which w before it can grow;
Isa   40: 7 The grass w and the flowers fall,
Jn   15: 6 a branch that is thrown away and w;
1Pe   1:24 the grass w and the flowers fall,

WITHHELD WITHHOLD

Ge   22:12 because you have not w from me
Ps   66:20 my prayer or w his love from me!
       77: 9 he in anger w his compassion?"
Hag   1:10 of you the heavens have w their dew

WITHHOLD WITHHELD, WITHHOLDS

Ne   9:20 You did not w your manna
Ps   40:11 Do not w your mercy from me,
       84:11 no good thing does he w from those
Pr   23:13 Do not w discipline from a child;

WITHHOLDS WITHHOLD

Dt   27:19 "Cursed is anyone who w justice
Eze   18:17 He w his hand from mistreating

WITHIN

Ex   3: 2 him in flames of fire from w a bush.
Ps   40: 8 your law is w my heart."
       42: 5 Why so disturbed w me?
       46: 5 God is w her, she will not fall;
       51:10 and renew a steadfast spirit w me.
      122: 7 May there be peace w your walls
      142: 3 When my spirit grows faint w me,
Pr   2: 1 and store up my commands w you,
       4:21 your sight, keep them w your heart;
Zep   3: 5 The LORD w her is righteous;
       3:12 But I will leave w you the meek
Zec   2: 5 LORD, 'and I will be its glory w.'
Mt   6:23 If then the light w you is darkness,
Mk   7:21 For it is from w, out of a person's
Jn   7:38 water will flow from w them."
1Co   2:11 except their own spirit w them?
Rev   11:19 w his temple was seen the ark of his

WITHOUT

Ex   12:15 you are to eat bread made w yeast.
       34:28 days and forty nights w eating bread
Lev   1: 3 you are to offer a male w defect.
Nu   27:17 not be like sheep w a shepherd."
2Ch   15: 3 long time Israel was w the true God,
               w a priest to teach and w the law.
       18:16 on the hills like sheep w a shepherd,
Ps   69: 4 many are my enemies w cause,

Pr   6:27 his lap w his clothes being burned?
       19: 2 Desire w knowledge is not good—
Isa   13:14 gazelle, like sheep w a shepherd,
       52: 3 w money you will be redeemed."
       55: 1 buy wine and milk w money and
Mt   9:36 helpless, like sheep w a shepherd.
       23:23 the latter, w neglecting the former.
Jn   3:34 for God gives the Spirit w limit.
       8: 7 who is w sin be the first to
Eph   2:12 w hope and w God in the world.
Php   2:14 Do everything w grumbling
Col   1:22 his sight, w blemish and free
1Th   2: 1 our visit to you was not w results.
Heb   9:22 w the shedding of blood there is no
Jas   2:18 Show me your faith w deeds, and I
1Pe   1:19 Christ, a lamb w blemish or defect.
Rev   21: 6 the thirsty I will give water w cost

WITHSTAND

Jos   10: 8 one of them will be able to w you."
       23: 9 day no one has been able to w you.
Na   1: 6 Who can w his indignation?

WITNESS EYEWITNESSES, WITNESSES

Ge   31:44 and let it serve as a w between us."
Nu   35:30 on the testimony of only one w.
Dt   19:15 One w is not enough to convict
Jos   22:27 it is to be a w between us and you
Jdg   11:10 replied, "The LORD is our w;
1Sa   12: 5 "The LORD is w against you,
       20:42 'The LORD is w between you
Job   16:19 Even now my w is in heaven;
Pr   12:17 An honest w tells the truth, but a
               false w tells lies.
       14:25 A truthful w saves lives, but a false w
               is deceitful.
       19: 9 A false w will not go unpunished,
       21:28 A false w will perish, but a careful
Jn   1: 8 he came only as a w to the light.
Ro   2:15 their consciences also bearing w,
1Pe   5: 1 and a w of Christ's sufferings who
Rev   1: 5 who is the faithful w, the firstborn
       2:13 my faithful w, who was put to death
       3:14 the faithful and true w, the ruler

WITNESSES WITNESS

Dt   17: 6 or three w a person is to be put
       19:15 by the testimony of two or three w.
       30:19 and the earth as w against you that I
Jos   24:22 "You are w against yourselves
Ru   4:10 Today you are w!"
Ps   27:12 foes, for false w rise up against me,
Isa   43:10 "You are my w,"
Mt   18:16 by the testimony of two or three w.'
       26:60 though many false w came forward.
Mk   14:63 "Why do we need any more w?"
Ac   1: 8 and you will be my w in Jerusalem,
       2:32 Jesus to life, and we are all w of it.
       6:13 They produced false w,
Heb   12: 1 by such a great cloud of w, let us
Rev   11: 3 And I will appoint my two w,

WIVES WIFE

Ge   6:18 wife and your sons' w with you.
Dt 17:17 He must not take many w, or his
     21:15 If a man has two w, and he loves
1Ki 11: 3 He had seven hundred w of royal
     11: 3 and his w led him astray.
1Ch 14: 3 In Jerusalem David took more w
Ezr 10:11 you and from your foreign w."
Mt 19: 8 divorce your w because your hearts
Eph 5:22 W, submit yourselves to your own
     5:25 love your w, just as Christ loved
Col 3:18 W, submit yourselves to your
1Pe 3: 1 W, in the same way submit
     3: 1 words by the behavior of their w,
     3: 7 considerate as you live with your w,

WIVES'* WIFE

1Ti 4: 7 with godless myths and old w tales;

WIZARD (KJV) See SPIRITIST

WOE WOES

Job 10:15 If I am guilty—w to me! Even if I
Pr 23:29 Who has w? Who has sorrow?
Isa   3:11 W to the wicked! Disaster is
     5: 8 W to you who add house to house
     5:20 W to those who call evil good
     6: 5 "W to me!" I cried. "I am ruined!
Jer 13:27 in the fields. W to you, Jerusalem!
    23: 1 "W to the shepherds who are
La   5:16 W to us, for we have sinned!
Hos 9:12 W to them when I turn away
Am 5:18 W to you who long for the day
Na   3: 1 W to the city of blood, full of lies,
Hab 2:19 W to him who says to wood,
Zec 11:17 "W to the worthless shepherd,
Mt 18: 7 W to the world because of the things
    18: 7 w to the person through whom they
    23:13 "W to you, teachers of the law
    23:16 "W to you, blind guides!
Mk 14:21 w to that man who betrays the Son
Lk   6:24 "But w to you who are rich, for you
    11:42 "W to you Pharisees, because you
    11:52 "W to you experts in the law,
1Co 9:16 W to me if I do not preach
Jude 1:11 W to them! They have taken
Rev 8:13 call out in a loud voice: "W! W!
    18:10 will stand far off and cry: " 'W!

WOES* WOE

Ps 32:10 Many are the w of the wicked,
Rev 9:12 two other w are yet to come.

WOKE WAKE

Ge 41: 7 Then Pharaoh w up; it had been
Mt   1:24 When Joseph w up, he did what
    25: 7 "Then all the virgins w

WOLF WOLVES

Isa 11: 6 The w will live with the lamb,
    65:25 The w and the lamb will feed
Jn 10:12 Then the w attacks the flock

WOLVES WOLF

Eze 22:27 her are like w tearing their prey;

Zep 3: 3 her rulers are evening w, who leave
Mt 7:15 but inwardly they are ferocious w.
    10:16 you out like sheep among w.
Ac 20:29 savage w will come in among you

WOMAN WOMEN, WOMEN'S

Ge 2:22 the LORD God made a w
    2:23 she shall be called 'w,' for she was
    3: 6 When the w saw that the fruit
    3:12 "The w you put here with me—
    3:15 put enmity between you and the w,
    3:16 To the w he said, "I will make your
  12:11 "I know what a beautiful w you are.
  20: 3 she is a married w."
  21:10 "Get rid of that slave w and her
  24:16 The w was very beautiful, a virgin;
  24:43 If a young w comes out to draw
Ex 3:22 Every w is to ask her neighbor
  21:10 If he marries another w, he must not
  21:22 hit a pregnant w and she gives birth
Lev 12: 2 'A w who becomes pregnant
  15:19 " 'When a w has her regular flow
  18:17 have sexual relations with both a w
  18:22 with a man as one does with a w;
  20:13 with a man as one does with a w,
Nu 5:29 of jealousy when a w goes astray
  30: 3 "When a young w still living in her
  30:10 "If a w living with her husband
Dt 4:16 whether formed like a man or a w,
  20: 7 Has anyone become pledged to a w
  21:11 among the captives a beautiful w
  22: 5 A w must not wear men's clothing,
  24: 1 If a man marries a w who becomes
Jdg 4: 9 Sisera into the hands of a w."
  9:54 they can't say, 'A w killed him.' "
  14: 2 "I have seen a Philistine w
  16: 4 love with a w in the Valley of Sorek
Ru 3:11 that you are a w of noble character.
1Sa 1:15 "I am a w who is deeply troubled.
  25: 3 was an intelligent and beautiful w,
  28: 7 "Find me a w who is a medium,
2Sa 11: 2 From the roof he saw a w bathing.
  13:17 "Get this w out of my sight and bolt
  14: 2 had a wise w brought from there.
  20:16 a wise w called from the city,
1Ki 3:18 was born, this w also had a baby.
  17:24 Then the w said to Elijah, "Now I
2Ki 4: 8 And a well-to-do w was there,
  8: 1 to the w whose son he had restored
  9:34 "Take care of that cursed w,"
Ezr 10:14 who has married a foreign w come
Job 2:10 "You are talking like a foolish w.
  14: 1 born of w, are of few days and full
  31: 1 not to look lustfully at a young w.
Ps 113: 9 He settles the childless w in her
Pr 6:24 the smooth talk of a wayward w.
  9:13 Folly is an unruly w; she is simple
  11:16 A kindhearted w gains honor,
  11:22 snout is a beautiful w who shows no
  14: 1 The wise w builds her house,
  30:19 the way of a man with a young w.
  30:23 a contemptible w who gets married,
  31:30 a w who fears the LORD is to be
Isa 54: 1 barren w, you who never bore

Isa   62: 5 As a young man marries a young **w**,
Jer   2:32 Does a young **w** forget her jewelry,
      51:22 with you I shatter man and **w**,
Mt   5:28 a **w** lustfully has already committed
       9:20 then a **w** who had been subject
      15:22 A Canaanite **w** from that vicinity
      19: 9 and marries another **w** commits
      26: 7 a **w** came to him with an alabaster
Mk   7:25 him, a **w** whose little daughter was
Lk   7:37 A **w** in that town who lived a sinful
      10:38 a village where a **w** named Martha
      13:12 her forward and said to her, "**W**,
      15: 8 suppose a **w** has ten silver coins
Jn   2: 4 "**W**, why do you involve me?"
       4: 7 a Samaritan **w** came to draw water,
       8: 4 this **w** was caught in the act
      19:26 he said to her, "**W**, here is your
      20:15 He asked her, "**W**, why are you
Ac   9:40 Turning toward the dead **w**, he said,
      16:14 of those listening was a **w**
      17:34 also a **w** named Damaris,
Ro   7: 2 by law a married **w** is bound to her
      16:12 another **w** who has worked very
1Co   7: 2 and each **w** with her own husband.
       7:34 An unmarried **w** or virgin is
       7:34 a married **w** is concerned
       7:39 A **w** is bound to her husband as long
      11: 3 and the head of the **w** is man,
      11: 6 For if a **w** does not cover her head,
      11: 6 for a **w** to have her hair cut off
      11: 7 but **w** is the glory of man.
Gal   4: 4 born of a **w**, born under the law,
       4:27 barren **w**, you who never bore
       4:30 "Get rid of the slave **w** and her son,
       4:31 we are not children of the slave **w**, but
             of the free **w**.
1Ti   2:11 A **w** should learn in quietness
       5:16 any **w** who is a believer has widows
Rev   2.20 You tolerate that **w** Jezebel.
      12: 1 a **w** clothed with the sun,
      12: 4 in front of the **w** who was
      12:13 he pursued the **w** who had given
      17: 3 There I saw a **w** sitting on a scarlet
      17:18 The **w** you saw is the great city

WOMB

Ge   25:23 "Two nations are in your **w**,
Ex   13: 2 of every **w** among the Israelites
Dt   7:13 He will bless the fruit of your **w**,
Jdg   13: 5 dedicated to God from the **w**.
1Sa   1: 5 and the LORD had closed her **w**.
Job   1:21 I came from my mother's **w**,
Ps   22: 9 Yet you brought me out of the **w**;
     139:13 knit me together in my mother's **w**.
Pr   31: 2 Listen, son of my **w**!
Ecc   11: 5 the body is formed in a mother's **w**,
Jer   1: 5 I formed you in the **w** I knew you,
Lk   1:44 the baby in my **w** leaped for joy.
Jn   3: 4 into their mother's **w** to be born!"
Ro   4:19 and that Sarah's **w** was also dead.
Gal   1:15 who set me apart from my mother's **w**

WOMEN WOMAN

Ge   4:19 Lamech married two **w**, one named

Nu   25: 1 sexual immorality with Moabite **w**,
Jdg   5:24 "Most blessed of **w** be Jael,
       5:24 most blessed of tent-dwelling **w**.
Ezr   10: 2 God by marrying foreign **w**
Ne   13:26 he was led into sin by foreign **w**.
Ps   68:25 them are the young **w** playing
      78:63 and their young **w** had no wedding
SS   1: 3 No wonder the young **w** love you!
       1: 8 most beautiful of **w**,
       2: 2 is my darling among the young **w**.
Isa   3:12 my people, **w** rule over them.
La   2:21 young **w** have fallen by the sword.
Zec   5: 9 and there before me were two **w**,
Mal   2:11 marrying **w** who worship a foreign
Mt   11:11 **w** there has not risen anyone greater
      24:41 Two **w** will be grinding with a hand
      28: 5 The angel said to the **w**, "Do not be
Mk   15:41 In Galilee these **w** had followed him
      15:41 Many other **w** who had come
Lk   1:42 "Blessed are you among **w**,
       8: 2 some **w** who had been cured of evil
      23:27 him, including **w** who mourned
      23:55 The **w** who had come with Jesus
      24:11 But they did not believe the **w**,
Ac   1:14 along with the **w** and Mary
       2:18 both men and **w**, I will pour out my
       8:12 were baptized, both men and **w**.
      16:13 to the **w** who had gathered there.
      17: 4 and quite a few prominent **w**.
Ro   1:26 Even their **w** exchanged natural
      16:12 those **w** who work hard in the Lord.
1Co   14:34 **W** should remain silent
Gal   4:24 The **w** represent two covenants.
Php   4: 3 help these **w** since they have
1Ti   2: 9 I also want the **w** to dress modestly,
       2:15 But **w** will be saved through
       3:11 the **w** are to be worthy of respect,
       5: 2 older **w** as mothers, and younger **w**
2Ti   3: 6 and gain control over gullible **w**,
Titus 2: 3 teach the older **w** to be reverent
       2: 4 they can urge the younger **w** to love
Heb   11:35 **W** received back their dead,
1Pe   3: 5 this is the way the holy **w** of the past

WOMEN'S* WOMAN

Dt   22: 5 nor a man wear **w** clothing,
Rev   9: 8 Their hair was like **w** hair, and their

WON WIN

1Sa   19: 5 The LORD **w** a great victory
Est   2:15 Esther the favor of everyone who
Ps   44: 3 by their sword that they **w** the land,
Pr   11:14 victory is **w** through many advisers.
Mt   18:15 listen to you, you have **w** them over.
1Pe   3: 1 they may be **w** over without words

WONDER WONDERED, WONDERFUL, WONDERFULLY, WONDERING, WONDERS

Dt   13: 1 and announces to you a sign or **w**,
SS   1: 3 No **w** the young women love you!
Isa   29:14 these people with **w** upon **w**;
Rev   13: 3 The whole world was filled with **w**

WONDERED* WONDER

Lk	1:29	w what kind of greeting this might
	1:66	Everyone who heard this w about it,

WONDERFUL* WONDER

2Sa	1:26	Your love for me was w, more w than that of women.
1Ch	16: 9	praise to him; tell of all his w acts.
Job	42: 3	things too w for me to know.
Ps	9: 1	I will tell of all your w deeds.
	26: 7	and telling of all your w deeds.
	75: 1	people tell of your w deeds.
	105: 2	praise to him; tell of all his w acts.
	107: 8	love and his w deeds for mankind,
	107:15	love and his w deeds for mankind,
	107:21	love and his w deeds for mankind.
	107:24	LORD, his w deeds in the deep.
	107:31	love and his w deeds for mankind.
	119:18	that I may see w things in your law.
	119:27	I may meditate on your w deeds.
	119:129	Your statutes are w; therefore I obey
	131: 1	great matters or things too w for me.
	139: 6	Such knowledge is too w for me,
	139:14	your works are w, I know that full
	145: 5	I will meditate on your w works.
Isa	9: 6	And he will be called W Counselor,
	25: 1	faithfulness you have done w things,
	28:29	whose plan is w, whose wisdom is
Mt	21:15	of the law saw the w things he did
Lk	13:17	with all the w things he was doing.
1Pe	2: 9	you out of darkness into his w light.

WONDERFULLY* WONDER

Ps	139:14	because I am fearfully and w made;

WONDERING WONDER

Ac	10:17	While Peter was w

WONDERS WONDER

Ex	3:20	all the w that I will perform among
	11:10	all these w before Pharaoh,
	15:11	awesome in glory, working w?
Dt	10:21	awesome w you saw with your own
2Sa	7:23	awesome w by driving out nations
1Ch	16:12	Remember the w he has done,
Job	37:14	stop and consider God's w.
Ps	17: 7	Show me the w of your great love,
	31:21	for he showed me the w of his love
	65: 8	earth is filled with awe at your w;
	78:32	in spite of his w, they did not
	89: 5	The heavens praise your w,
	136: 4	to him who alone does great w,
Da	4: 3	are his signs, how mighty his w!
Joel	2:30	I will show w in the heavens
Mt	24:24	great signs and w to deceive,
Jn	4:48	you people see signs and w,"
Ac	2:11	we hear them declaring the w
	2:19	I will show w in the heavens
2Co	12:12	including signs, w and miracles.
2Th	2: 9	signs and w that serve the lie,
Heb	2: 4	it by signs, w and various miracles,

WOOD WOODEN, WOODS

Ge	6:14	make yourself an ark of cypress w;
	22: 9	altar there and arranged the w on it.

Ex	15:25	LORD showed him a piece of w.
	25:10	them make an ark of acacia w—
	25:13	make poles of acacia w and overlay
	25:23	"Make a table of acacia w—
	26:15	of acacia w for the tabernacle.
	27: 1	"Build an altar of acacia w,
Lev	14: 4	live clean birds and some cedar w,
Dt	28:64	gods of w and stone, which neither
1Ki	18:23	put it on the w but not set fire to it.
Isa	44:19	Shall I bow down to a block of w?"
	60:17	Instead of w I will bring you bronze,
Eze	20:32	the world, who serve w and stone."
	37:16	take a stick of w and write on it,
Hab	2:19	Woe to him who says to w,
1Co	3:12	costly stones, w, hay or straw,

WOODEN WOOD

Dt	16:21	any w Asherah pole beside the altar
Ne	8: 4	stood on a high w platform built
Isa	48: 5	my w image and metal god ordained
Hos	4:12	My people consult a w idol,

WOODS WOOD

2Ki	2:24	two bears came out of the w

WOOL

Nu	19: 6	scarlet w and throw them onto
Dt	18: 4	the first w from the shearing of your
	22:11	Do not wear clothes of w and linen
Pr	31:13	She selects w and flax and works
Isa	1:18	red as crimson, they shall be like w.
Da	7: 9	hair of his head was white like w.
Rev	1:14	hair on his head was white like w,

WORD BYWORD, WORDLESS, WORDS

Ge	15: 1	the w of the LORD came to Abram
	37: 4	could not speak a kind w to him.
Nu	23: 5	The LORD put a w in Balaam's
	23: 5	back to Balak and give him this w."
	30: 2	he must not break his w but must do
Dt	8: 3	but on every w that comes
	30:14	No, the w is very near you; it is
Jos	1:18	Whoever rebels against your w
1Sa	3: 1	those days the w of the LORD was
2Sa	22:31	The LORD's w is flawless;
1Ki	8:56	Not one w has failed of all the good
	17: 2	the w of the LORD came to Elijah:
1Ch	17: 3	But that night the w of God came
2Ch	36:22	fulfill the w of the LORD spoken
Ps	33: 4	For the w of the LORD is right
	56: 4	In God, whose w I praise—in God I
	56:10	in the LORD, whose w I praise—
	107:20	He sent out his w and healed them;
	119: 9	By living according to your w.
	119:11	I have hidden your w in my heart
	119:42	who taunts me, for I trust in your w.
	119:74	for I have put my hope in your w.
	119:89	Your w, LORD, is eternal;
	119:105	Your w is a lamp for my feet, a light
	119:172	May my tongue sing of your w,
	139: 4	Before a w is on my tongue you,
Pr	12:25	the heart, but a kind w cheers it up.
	15: 1	wrath, but a harsh w stirs up anger.

Pr 15:23 and how good is a timely **w**!
30: 5 "Every **w** of God is flawless; he is
Isa 1:10 Hear the **w** of the LORD,
40: 8 the **w** of our God endures forever."
55:11 so is my **w** that goes out from my
Jer 5:13 but wind and the **w** is not in them;
23:29 "Is not my **w** like fire,"
Da 9: 2 to the **w** of the LORD given
9:23 as you began to pray, a **w** went out,
9:23 consider the **w** and understand
Mt 4: 4 but on every **w** that comes
12:36 every empty **w** they have spoken.
15: 6 Thus you nullify the **w** of God
Mk 4:14 The farmer sows the **w**.
Lk 1: 2 eyewitnesses and servants of the **w**.
Jn 1: 1 In the beginning was the **W**, and the
W was with God, and the **W** was God.
1:14 The **W** became flesh and made his
8:37 you have no room for my **w**.
17:17 them by the truth; your **w** is truth.
Ac 4:31 and spoke the **w** of God boldly.
6: 4 prayer and the ministry of the **w**."
Ro 9: 6 is not as though God's **w** had failed.
10: 8 "The **w** is near you; it is in your
2Co 2:17 we do not peddle the **w** of God
4: 2 nor do we distort the **w** of God.
Eph 6:17 of the Spirit, which is the **w** of God.
Php 2:16 as you hold firmly to the **w** of life.
2Ti 2:15 and who correctly handles the **w**
Heb 1: 3 all things by his powerful **w**.
4:12 For the **w** of God is alive and active.
6: 5 tasted the goodness of the **w** of God
Jas 1:21 humbly accept the **w** planted in you,
1:22 Do not merely listen to the **w**,
1Pe 1:23 the living and enduring **w** of God.
2Pe 3: 5 ago by God's **w** the heavens came
1Jn 2: 5 But if anyone obeys his **w**,
Rev 3: 8 yet you have kept my **w** and have
12:11 and by the **w** of their testimony,
19:13 and his name is the **W** of God.
20: 4 Jesus and because of the **w** of God.

WORD OF GOD 1Ki 12:22; 1Ch 17:3; Pr
30:5; Mt 15:6; Mk 7:13; Lk 3:2; 5:1; 8:11; 11:28;
Jn 10:35; Ac 4:31; 6:2, 7; 8:14; 11:1; 12:24; 13:5,
7, 46; 17:13; 18:11; 1Co 14:36; 2Co 2:17; 4:2; Eph
6:17; Col 1:25; 1Th 2:13, 13; 1Ti 4:5; Titus 2:5;
Heb 4:12; 6:5; 13:7; 1Pe 1:23; 1Jn 2:14; Rev 1:2, 9;
6:9; 19:13; 20:4

WORD OF THE LORD† Ge 15:1, 4; Ex 9:20,
21; Nu 3:16, 51; Dt 5:5; 1Sa 3:1, 7; 15:10, 23, 26;
2Sa 7:4; 12:9; 24:11; 1Ki 6:11; 12:24; 13:1, 2, 5, 9,
17, 18, 20, 21, 26, 26, 32; 15:29; 16:1, 7, 12, 34;
17:2, 8, 16, 24; 18:1, 31; 19:9; 20:35; 21:17, 28;
22:19, 38; 2Ki 1:17; 3:12; 4:44; 7:1; 9:26, 36; 10:17;
14:25; 15:12; 20:4, 16, 19; 23:16; 24:2; 1Ch 10:13;
15:15; 22:8; 2Ch 11:2; 12:7; 18:18; 29:15; 30:12;
34:21; 36:12, 21, 22; Ezr 1:1; Ps 33:4, 6; 105:19; Isa
1:10; 2:3; 28:13, 14; 38:4; 39:5, 8; 66:5; Jer 1:2, 4,
11, 13; 2:1, 4, 31; 6:10; 7:2; 8:9; 9:20; 13:3, 8; 14:1;
16:1; 17:15, 20; 18:5; 19:3; 20:8; 21:11; 22:2, 29;
24:4; 25:3; 27:18; 28:12; 29:20, 30; 31:10; 32:6, 8,
26; 33:1, 19, 23; 34:12; 35:12; 36:27; 37:6; 39:15;
42:7, 15; 43:8; 44:24, 26; 46:1; 47:1; 49:34; Eze 1:3;

3:16; 6:1; 7:1; 11:14; 12:1, 8, 17, 21, 26; 13:1, 2;
14:2, 12; 15:1; 16:1, 35; 17:1, 11; 18:1; 20:2, 45, 47;
21:1, 8, 18; 22:1, 17, 23; 23:1; 24:1, 15, 20; 25:1;
26:1; 27:1; 28:1, 11, 20; 29:1, 17; 30:1, 20; 31:1;
32:1, 17; 33:1, 23; 34:1, 7, 9; 35:1; 36:1, 16; 37:4,
15; 38:1; Da 9:2; Hos 1:1; 4:1; Joel 1:1; Am 7:16;
8:12; Jnh 1:1; 3:1, 3; Mic 1:1; 4:2; Zep 1:1; 2:5; Hag
1:1, 3; 2:1, 10, 20; Zec 1:1, 7; 4:6, 8; 6:9; 7:1, 4, 8;
8:1, 18; 9:1; 11:11; 12:1; Mal 1:1

WORD OF THE LORD† CAME Ge 15:1, 4;
1Sa 15:10; 2Sa 7:4; 1Ki 6:11; 13:20; 16:1, 7; 17:2,
8; 18:1; 19:9; 21:17, 28; 2Ki 20:4; 1Ch 22:8; 2Ch
11:2; 12:7; Isa 38:4; Jer 1:2, 4, 11, 13; 2:1; 13:3, 8;
16:1; 18:5; 24:4; 28:12; 29:30; 32:6, 26; 33:1, 19,
23; 34:12; 35:12; 36:27; 37:6; 39:15; 42:7; 43:8; Eze
1:3; 3:16; 6:1; 7:1; 11:14; 12:1, 8, 17, 21, 26; 13:1;
14:2, 12; 15:1; 16:1; 17:1, 11; 18:1; 20:2, 45; 21:1, 8,
18; 22:1, 17, 23; 23:1; 24:1, 15, 20; 25:1; 26:1; 27:1;
28:1, 11, 20; 29:1, 17; 30:1, 20; 31:1; 32:1, 17; 33:1,
23; 34:1; 35:1; 36:16; 37:15; 38:1; Jnh 1:1; 3:1; Hag
1:1, 3; 2:1, 10, 20; Zec 1:1, 7; 4:8; 6:9; 7:1, 8

WORDLESS* WORD
Ro 8:26 intercedes for us through **w** groans.

WORDS WORD
Ex 20: 1 And God spoke all these **w**:
24: 3 told the people all the LORD's **w**
34:28 the tablets the **w** of the covenant—
Dt 11:18 Fix these **w** of mine in your hearts
13: 3 you must not listen to the **w**
18:19 to my **w** that the prophet speaks
31:24 writing in a book the **w** of this law
32:45 Moses finished reciting all these **w**
32:47 They are not just idle **w** for you—
Jos 8:34 Joshua read all the **w** of the law—
2Sa 23: 1 These are the last **w** of David:
Ps 5: 1 Listen to my **w**, LORD,
12: 6 the **w** of the LORD are flawless,
19: 3 have no speech, they use no **w**;
19: 4 their **w** to the ends of the world.
19:14 May these **w** of my mouth and this
49: 3 My mouth will speak **w** of wisdom;
64: 3 and aim cruel **w** like deadly arrows.
119:103 How sweet are your **w** to my taste,
119:130 The unfolding of your **w** gives light;
119:160 All your **w** are true;
Pr 2: 1 if you accept my **w** and store up my
2:16 woman with her seductive **w**,
7:21 persuasive **w** she led him astray;
10:19 Sin is not ended by multiplying **w**,
12:18 The **w** of the reckless pierce like
16:24 Gracious **w** are a honeycomb,
26:22 The **w** of a gossip are like choice
30: 6 Do not add to his **w**, or he will
Ecc 5: 2 are on earth, so let your **w** be few.
10:14 and fools multiply **w**. No one knows
12:11 The **w** of the wise are like goads,
Jer 15:16 When your **w** came, I ate them;
Da 9:12 have fulfilled the **w** spoken against
Hos 6: 5 killed you with the **w** of my mouth—
Zec 1: 6 But did not my **w** and my decrees,
Mt 7:24 everyone who hears these **w** of mine
12:37 For by your **w** you will be acquitted,

Mt 12:37 by your **w** you will be condemned."
    24:35 but my **w** will never pass away.
Mk 12:13 to Jesus to catch him in his **w**.
Lk 4:32 because his **w** had authority.
    6:47 and hears my **w** and puts them
Jn 6:68 You have the **w** of eternal life.
    15: 7 in me and my **w** remain in you,
Ac 2:40 With many other **w** he warned them;
1Co 2:13 speak, not in **w** taught us by human
    2:13 but in **w** taught by the Spirit,
  14:19 rather speak five intelligible **w**
1Pe 3: 1 they may be won over without **w**
1Jn 3:18 let us not love with **w** or speech
Rev 1: 3 is the one who reads aloud the **w**
  19: 9 "These are the true **w** of God."
  22: 6 "These **w** are trustworthy and true.
  22:19 if anyone takes **w** away from this

WORE WEAR

Mk 1: 6 John **w** clothing made of camel's
Rev 9: 7 their heads they **w** something like
  15: 6 **w** golden sashes around their chests.

WORK CO-WORKERS, HANDIWORK, HARDWORKING, METALWORKER, WORKED, WORKER, WORKERS, WORKING, WORKS

Ge 2: 2 God had finished the **w** he had been
    2: 2 seventh day he rested from all his **w**.
    2:15 him in the Garden of Eden to **w** it
    4:12 When you **w** the ground, it will no
Ex 20:10 On it you shall not do any **w**,
  23:12 but on the seventh day do not **w**,
  32:16 The tablets were the **w** of God;
  40:33 And so Moses finished the **w**.
Lev 25:40 they are to **w** for you until the Year
Nu 8:11 be ready to do the **w** of the LORD.
Dt 5:14 On it you shall not do any **w**,
  27:15 the LORD, the **w** of skilled hands—
1Ch 22:16 Now begin the **w**, and the LORD
2Ch 2: 7 a man skilled to **w** in gold
    8:16 All Solomon's **w** was carried out,
Ezr 4: 5 bribed officials to **w** against them
    4:24 Thus the **w** on the house of God
    6: 7 interfere with the **w** on this temple
Ne 2:18 So they began this good **w**.
Job 1:10 You have blessed the **w** of his
Ps 8: 3 your heavens, the **w** of your fingers,
  19: 1 the skies proclaim the **w** of his
  90:17 establish the **w** of our hands for us—
Pr 14:23 All hard **w** brings a profit, but mere
  21:25 him, because his hands refuse to **w**.
  31:17 She sets about her **w** vigorously;
Ecc 11: 5 so you cannot understand the **w**
Isa 2: 8 bow down to the **w** of their hands,
  64: 8 we are all the **w** of your hand.
Jer 48:10 who is lax in doing the LORD's **w**!
Lk 13:14 people, "There are six days for **w**.
Jn 5:17 is always at his **w** to this very day,
    6:27 Do not **w** for food that spoils,
    6:29 answered, "The **w** of God is this:
    9: 4 is coming, when no one can **w**.

Jn 17: 4 by finishing the **w** you gave me
Ac 13: 2 and Saul for the **w** to which I have
Ro 4: 5 to the one who does not **w** but trusts
  14:20 Do not destroy the **w** of God
  16:12 those women who **w** hard
1Co 3:13 test the quality of each person's **w**.
    4:12 We **w** hard with our own hands.
  12:11 All these are the **w** of one
Gal 2: 8 who was at **w** in Peter as an apostle
    2: 8 also at **w** in me as an apostle
Eph 3:20 to his power that is at **w** within us,
    4:16 up in love, as each part does its **w**.
Php 1: 6 he who began a good **w** in you will
    2:12 continue to **w** out your salvation
Col 3:23 you do, **w** at it with all your heart,
1Th 4:11 business and **w** with your hands,
    5:12 those who **w** hard among you,
2Th 2: 7 of lawlessness is already at **w**;
    3:10 is unwilling to **w** shall not eat."
1Ti 5:17 those whose **w** is preaching
2Ti 2:21 and prepared to do any good **w**.
    3:17 equipped for every good **w**.
Heb 6:10 he will not forget your **w**
  13:17 Do this so that their **w** will be a joy,
1Pe 1:17 judges each person's **w** impartially,
1Jn 3: 8 was to destroy the devil's **w**.
2Jn 1:11 them shares in their wicked **w**.
3Jn 1: 8 that we may **w** together for the truth.
Rev 2: 2 your hard **w** and your perseverance.
    9:20 not repent of the **w** of their hands;

WORKED WORK

Ge 4: 2 kept flocks, and Cain **w** the soil.
  29:30 he **w** for Laban another seven years.
Ex 1:13 and **w** them ruthlessly.
Ps 98: 1 his holy arm have **w** salvation
Jn 4:38 to reap what you have not **w** for.
1Co 15:10 No, I **w** harder than all of them—
2Th 3: 8 the contrary, we **w** night and day,
2Jn 1: 8 you do not lose what we have **w** for,

WORKER WORK

Lk 10: 7 for the **w** deserves his wages.
1Ti 5:18 and "The **w** deserves his wages."
2Ti 2:15 a **w** who does not need to be
Rev 18:22 No **w** of any trade will ever be

WORKERS WORK

Ex 31: 6 all the skilled **w** to make everything
  36: 8 were skilled among the **w** made
1Ki 5:18 Hiram and **w** from Byblos cut
2Ki 12:14 it was paid to the **w**, who used it
Ne 4:22 guards by night and as **w** by day."
Ecc 3: 9 What do **w** gain from their toil?
Mt 9:37 is plentiful but the **w** are few.
  20: 1 morning to hire **w** for his vineyard.
Lk 10: 2 is plentiful, but the **w** are few.
  10: 2 to send out **w** into his harvest field.
2Co 11:13 deceitful **w**, masquerading as

WORKING WORK

Ex 15:11 awesome in glory, **w** wonders?
Jn 5:17 to this very day, and I too am **w**."
1Co 12: 6 There are different kinds of **w**,
Col 3:23 all your heart, as **w** for the Lord,

Jas   2:22 and his actions were **w** together,

WORKS WORK

Dt   3:24 do the deeds and mighty **w** you do?
      32: 4 He is the Rock, his **w** are perfect,
Ps   8: 6 You made them rulers over the **w**
      92: 5 How great are your **w**, LORD,
     103: 6 The LORD **w** righteousness
     138: 8 do not abandon the **w** of your hands.
     145: 6 of the power of your awesome **w**—
Pr   8:22 me forth as the first of his **w**,
      31:31 let her **w** bring her praise at the city
Jn   7: 3 there may see the **w** you do.
      10:25 The **w** I do in my Father's name
      10:32 "I have shown you many good **w**
      10:38 believe the **w**, that you may know
      14:11 the evidence of the **w** themselves.
      15:24 done among them the **w** no one else
Ro   3:20 in God's sight by the **w** of the law;
       3:27 The law that requires **w**?
       4: 6 credits righteousness apart from **w**:
       8:28 in all things God **w** for the good
Gal   2:16 not justified by the **w** of the law,
       2:16 not by the **w** of the law, because by
             the **w** of the law no one
       3: 2 receive the Spirit by the **w** of the law,
       3: 5 the **w** of the law, or by your believing
       3:10 on the **w** of the law are under a curse,
Eph   1:11 plan of him who **w** out everything
       2: 9 not by **w**, so that no one can boast.
       2:10 in Christ Jesus to do good **w**,
       4:12 to equip his people for **w** of service,
Php   2:13 for it is God who **w** in you to will
Col   1:29 the energy Christ so powerfully **w**
2Th   2: 9 be in accordance with how Satan **w**.
Heb   4: 4 day God rested from all his **w**."

WORLD WORLDLY

Ge   11: 1 Now the whole **w** had one language
      11: 9 the language of the whole **w**.
      41:57 all the **w** came to Egypt to buy grain
2Ki   5:15 no God in all the **w** except in Israel.
1Ch   16:30 The **w** is firmly established;
Ps   9: 8 He rules the **w** in righteousness
      19: 4 their words to the ends of the **w**.
      50:12 for the **w** is mine, and all that is
      90: 2 or you brought forth the whole **w**,
      96:13 He will judge the **w** in righteousness
Pr   8:23 beginning, when the **w** came to be.
Isa   13:11 I will punish the **w** for its evil,
Mt   4: 8 him all the kingdoms of the **w**
       5:14 "You are the light of the **w**.
      16:26 be for someone to gain the whole **w**,
Jn   1:10 He was in the **w**, and though the **w**
       1:10 the **w** did not recognize him.
       1:29 who takes away the sin of the **w**!
       3:16 God so loved the **w** that he gave his
       3:17 Son into the **w** to condemn the **w**, but
             to save the **w** through him.
       8:12 he said, "I am the light of the **w**.
       9: 5 While I am in the **w**, I am the light of
             the **w**."
      15:19 If you belonged to the **w**, it would
      15:19 but I have chosen you out of the **w**.

Jn   15:19 That is why the **w** hates you.
      16:33 In this **w** you will have trouble.
      16:33 I have overcome the **w**."
      17: 5 I had with you before the **w** began.
      17:18 As you sent me into the **w**, I have sent
             them into the **w**.
      18:36 said, "My kingdom is not of this **w**.
Ac   17:31 he will judge the **w** with justice
Ro   3:19 and the whole **w** held accountable
       5:12 sin entered the **w** through one man,
      10:18 their words to the ends of the **w**."
1Co   1:27 things of the **w** to shame the wise;
       3:19 the wisdom of this **w** is foolishness
       6: 2 the Lord's people will judge the **w**?
2Co   5:19 that God was reconciling the **w**
      10: 3 we do not wage war as the **w** does.
1Ti   1:15 came into the **w** to save sinners—
       6: 7 For we brought nothing into the **w**,
Heb   1: 6 God brings his firstborn into the **w**
      11: 7 By his faith he condemned the **w**
      11:38 the **w** was not worthy of them.
Jas   1:27 from being polluted by the **w**.
       4: 4 the **w** means enmity against God?
1Pe   1:20 chosen before the creation of the **w**,
1Jn   2: 2 but also for the sins of the whole **w**.
       2:15 Do not love the **w** or anything in
             the **w**.
       5: 4 born of God overcomes the **w**.
       5: 4 the victory that has overcome the **w**,
Rev   11:15 of the **w** has become the kingdom
      13: 8 was slain from the creation of the **w**.

WORLDLY WORLD

Lk   16:11 trustworthy in handling **w** wealth,
1Co   3: 1 Spirit but as people who are still **w**—
Titus 2:12 to ungodliness and **w** passions,

WORM WORMS

Ps   22: 6 But I am a **w** and not a man,
Isa   41:14 Do not be afraid, you **w** Jacob,

WORMS WORM

Mk   9:48 where " 'the **w** that eat them do
Ac   12:23 and he was eaten by **w** and died.

WORMWOOD*

Rev   8:11 the name of the star is **W**. A third

WORN WEAR

Ge   18:12 "After I am **w** out and my lord is

WORRIED WORRY

Lk   10:41 "you are **w** and upset about many

WORRIES WORRY

Lk   8:14 way they are choked by life's **w**,

WORRY WORRIED, WORRIES, WORRYING

Mt   6:25 I tell you, do not **w** about your life,
       6:34 Therefore do not **w** about tomorrow,
             for tomorrow will **w** about itself.
      10:19 do not **w** about what to say or how

WORRYING WORRY

Mt   6:27 you by **w** add a single hour to your

WORSE WORST

Mt 12:45 of that person is **w** than the first.
Jn   5:14 something **w** may happen to you."
1Ti 5: 8 faith and is **w** than an unbeliever.
2Pe 2:20 they are **w** off at the end than they

WORSHIP WORSHIPED, WORSHIPERS, WORSHIPING, WORSHIPS

Ex   4:23 "Let my son go, so he may **w** me."
    20: 5 not bow down to them or **w** them;
    34:14 Do not **w** any other god,
Dt 12: 4 You must not **w** the LORD your
Jos 22:27 that we will **w** the LORD at his
2Ki 17:37 wrote for you. Do not **w** other gods.
1Ch 16:29 **W** the LORD in the splendor of his
Ps 95: 6 let us bow down in **w**, let us kneel
    97: 7 All who **w** images are put to shame,
   100: 2 **W** the LORD with gladness;
Jer 23:27 forgot my name through Baal **w**.
Da   3:28 or **w** any god except their own God.
Jnh 1: 9 am a Hebrew and I **w** the LORD,
Zec 14:17 go up to Jerusalem to **w** the King,
Mt   2: 2 it rose and have come to **w** him."
     4: 9 "if you will bow down and **w** me."
Lk   4: 8 'W the Lord your God and serve
Jn   4:24 his worshipers must **w** in the Spirit
Ro 12: 1 this is your true and proper **w**.
Heb 10: 1 perfect those who draw near to **w**.
Rev 4:10 throne and **w** him who lives for ever
    13:12 and its inhabitants **w** the first beast,
    14: 7 **W** him who made the heavens,

WORSHIPED WORSHIP

Ex 12:27 the people bowed down and **w**.
Dt 29:26 They went off and **w** other gods
Jos 24: 2 Euphrates River and **w** other gods.
2Ch 24:18 and **w** Asherah poles and idols.
    29:30 gladness and bowed down and **w**.
Mt 28: 9 to him, clasped his feet and **w** him.
Rev 5:14 and the elders fell down and **w**.
    13: 4 People **w** the dragon because he had
    13: 4 and they also **w** the beast and asked,
    20: 4 They had not **w** the beast or its

WORSHIPERS WORSHIP

Jn   4:24 and his **w** must worship in the Spirit

WORSHIPING WORSHIP

Jdg 2:19 other gods and serving and **w** them.
Ac 13: 2 While they were **w** the Lord
Rev 9:20 they did not stop **w** demons,

WORSHIPS WORSHIP

Isa 44:15 But he also fashions a god and **w** it;

WORST WORSE

1Ti 1:16 so that in me, the **w** of sinners,

WORTH WORTHLESS, WORTHY

Job 28:13 No mortal comprehends its **w**;
Pr 31:10 She is **w** far more than rubies.
Mt 10:31 you are **w** more than many
Jn 12: 5 It was **w** a year's wages."
Ro   8:18 sufferings are not **w** comparing

Php 3: 8 the surpassing **w** of knowing Christ
1Pe 1: 7 of greater **w** than gold,
     3: 4 which is of great **w** in God's sight.

WORTHLESS WORTH

Ge 41:27 so are the seven **w** heads of grain
Dt 32:21 and angered me with their **w** idols.
Ps 31: 6 I hate those who cling to **w** idols;
    60:11 the enemy, for human help is **w**.
Pr 11: 4 Wealth is **w** in the day of wrath,
Jer 2: 5 They followed **w** idols and became **w** themselves.
Zec 11:17 "Woe to the **w** shepherd,
Mt 25:30 And throw that **w** servant outside,
Heb 6: 8 and thistles is **w** and is in danger
Jas 1:26 themselves, and their religion is **w**.

WORTHY WORTH

1Ch 16:25 is the LORD and most **w** of praise;
Ps 18: 3 to the LORD, who is **w** of praise,
   145: 3 is the LORD and most **w** of praise;
Mt   3:11 whose sandals I am not **w** to carry.
    10:37 or mother more than me is not **w**
    10:38 cross and follow me is not **w** of me.
Lk   3:16 whose sandals I am not **w** to untie.
    15:19 I am no longer **w** to be called your
Ro 16: 2 in the Lord in a way **w** of his people
Eph 4: 1 live a life **w** of the calling you have
Php 1:27 in a manner **w** of the gospel
Col 1:10 you may live a life **w** of the Lord
1Ti 3: 8 way, deacons are to be **w** of respect,
     3:11 the women are to be **w** of respect,
Titus 2: 2 men to be temperate, **w** of respect,
Heb 3: 3 Jesus has been found **w** of greater
    11:38 the world was not **w** of them.
Rev 3: 4 me, dressed in white, for they are **w**.
     4:11 "You are **w**, our Lord and God,
     5: 2 "Who is **w** to break the seals
     5:12 "W is the Lamb, who was slain,

WOUND WOUNDS

Ex 21:25 burn for burn, **w** for **w**,
Pr 25:20 or like vinegar poured on a **w**, is one
Jer 10:19 of my injury! My **w** is incurable!
La   2:13 Your **w** is as deep as the sea.
Na   3:19 can heal you; your **w** is fatal.
1Co 8:12 way and **w** their weak conscience,
Rev 13: 3 beast seemed to have had a fatal **w**,
          but the fatal **w** had been healed.

WOUNDS WOUND

Job 5:18 For he **w**, but he also binds up;
Ps 147: 3 brokenhearted and binds up their **w**.
Pr 27: 6 **W** from a friend can be trusted,
Isa 53: 5 on him, and by his **w** we are healed.
Zec 13: 6 'What are these **w** on your body?'
1Pe 2:24 "by his **w** you have been healed."

WOVEN

Ex 28: 4 a robe, a **w** tunic, a turban
Jn 19:23 **w** in one piece from top to bottom.

WRAPPED WRAPS

Mk 15:46 down the body, **w** it in the linen,
Lk   2: 7 She **w** him in cloths and placed him

Jn   13: 4 and **w** a towel around his waist.
     20: 7 that had been **w** around Jesus' head.

WRAPS WRAPPED
Ps 104: 2 The LORD **w** himself in light as

WRATH
Nu 16: 46 **W** has come out from the LORD;
Dt   32: 22 For a fire will be kindled by my **w**,
2Sa   6: 8 because the LORD's **w** had broken
1Ch 27: 24 God's **w** came on Israel on account
2Ch 36: 16 at his prophets until the **w**
Ps   2: 5 his anger and terrifies them in his **w**,
      6: 1 anger or discipline me in your **w**.
     37: 8 Refrain from anger and turn from **w**;
     76: 10 Surely your **w** against mankind
Pr   15: 1 A gentle answer turns away **w**,
Isa 13: 13 at the **w** of the LORD Almighty,
     51: 17 of the LORD the cup of his **w**,
Jer   6: 11 I am full of the **w** of the LORD,
     25: 15 cup filled with the wine of my **w**
La   4: 11 LORD has given full vent to his **w**;
Eze   5: 13 and my **w** against them will subside,
     20: 8 said I would pour out my **w** on them
Na   1: 2 and vents his **w** against his enemies.
Zep   1: 15 That day will be a day of **w**—
Mt   3: 7 you to flee from the coming **w**?
Jn   3: 36 life, for God's **w** remains on them.
Ro   1: 18 The **w** of God is being revealed
      2: 5 are storing up **w** against yourself for
              the day of God's **w**,
      5: 9 saved from God's **w** through him!
      9: 22 great patience the objects of his **w**—
Eph   2: 3 we were by nature deserving of **w**.
1Th   1: 10 who rescues us from the coming **w**.
      5: 9 God did not appoint us to suffer **w**
Rev   6: 17 the great day of their **w** has come,
     15: 1 with them God's **w** is completed.
     19: 15 the fury of the **w** of God Almighty.

WRESTLED WRESTLING
Ge   32: 24 and a man **w** with him till daybreak.

WRESTLING* WRESTLED
Col   4: 12 He is always **w** in prayer for you,

WRETCHED
Ro   7: 24 What a **w** man I am!
Rev   3: 17 you do not realize that you are **w**,

WRINKLE*
Eph   5: 27 without stain or **w** or any other

WRIST WRISTS
Ge   38: 28 thread and tied it on his **w** and said,

WRISTS WRIST
Ac   12: 7 and the chains fell off Peter's **w**.

WRITE WRITER, WRITES,
WRITING, WRITTEN, WROTE
Ex   17: 14 "**W** this on a scroll as something
     34: 27 to Moses, "**W** down these words,
Nu   17: 2 **W** the name of each man on his
Dt   6: 9 **W** them on the doorframes of your
     10: 2 I will **w** on the tablets the words

Dt   17: 18 he is to **w** for himself on a scroll
     27: 8 And you shall **w** very clearly all
Pr   3: 3 **w** them on the tablet of your heart.
      7: 3 **w** them on the tablet of your heart.
Jer 31: 33 their minds and **w** it on their hearts.
Lk   1: 3 too decided to **w** an orderly account
Jn   8: 6 *started to **w** on the ground*
Heb   8: 10 minds and **w** them on their hearts.
1Jn   2: 1 I **w** this to you so that you will not
Rev   1: 19 "**W**, therefore, what you have seen,
      3: 12 I will **w** on them the name of my
      3: 12 I will also **w** on them my new name.
     21: 5 Then he said, "**W** this down,

WRITER* WRITE
Ps   45: 1 my tongue is the pen of a skillful **w**.

WRITES WRITE
Dt   24: 1 and he **w** her a certificate of divorce,

WRITING WRITE
Ex   32: 16 the **w** was the **w** of God,
Dt   31: 24 Moses finished **w** in a book
Da   5: 7 "Whoever reads this **w** and tells me
1Co 14: 37 what I am **w** to you is the Lord's
1Jn   2: 7 I am not **w** you a new command
2Jn   1: 5 I am not **w** you a new command
Rev   5: 1 the throne a scroll with **w** on both

WRITTEN WRITE
Ex   32: 32 me out of the book you have **w**."
Dt   28: 58 which are **w** in this book, and do not
Jos   1: 8 be careful to do everything **w** in it.
     23: 6 obey all that is **w** in the Book
1Ki   2: 3 as **w** in the Law of Moses.
2Ki 23: 21 God, as it is **w** in this Book
Ne   8: 14 They found **w** in the Law,
Ps   40: 7 it is **w** about me in the scroll.
Pr   22: 20 Have I not **w** thirty sayings for you,
Da   12: 1 everyone whose name is found **w**
Mal   3: 16 remembrance was **w** in his presence
Mt   26: 24 of Man will go just as it is **w**
     27: 37 they placed the **w** charge against
Lk   10: 20 that your names are **w** in heaven."
     24: 44 must be fulfilled that is **w** about me
Jn   20: 31 these are **w** that you may believe
     21: 25 If every one of them were **w** down,
Ro   2: 15 of the law are **w** on their hearts,
     15: 4 that was **w** in the past was **w**
1Co   4: 6 "Do not go beyond what is **w**."
     10: 11 were **w** down as warnings for us,
2Co   3: 3 **w** not with ink but with the Spirit
Heb 10: 7 it is **w** about me in the scroll—
     12: 23 whose names are **w** in heaven.
Rev   2: 17 stone with a new name **w** on it,
     13: 8 all whose names have not been **w**
     14: 1 and his Father's name **w** on their
     17: 5 The name **w** on her forehead was
     19: 12 He has a name **w** on him that no one
     20: 15 whose name was not found **w**
     21: 12 the gates were **w** the names
     21: 27 only those whose names are **w**

IT IS ... WRITTEN Jos 8:34; 10:13; 2Sa 1:18;
2Ki 23:21; 2Ch 35:12; Ne 8:15; 10:34, 36; Ps 40:7;

Da 9:13; Mt 4:4, 6, 7, 10; 11:10; 21:13; 26:24, 31; Mk 1:2; 7:6; 9:13; 14:21, 27; Lk 2:23; 3:4; 4:4, 8, 10, 17; 7:27; 19:46; 22:37; Jn 2:17; 6:31, 45; 8:17; 12:14; Ac 1:20; 13:33; 15:15; 23:5; Ro 1:17; 2:24; 3:4, 10; 4:17; 8:36; 9:13, 33; 10:15; 11:8, 26; 12:19; 14:11; 15:3, 9, 21; 1Co 1:19, 31; 2:9; 3:19; 9:9; 10:7; 14:21; 15:45; 2Co 4:13; 8:15; 9:9; Gal 3:10, 13; 4:22, 27; Heb 10:7; 1Pe 1:16

WRITTEN IN THE ... BOOK

Jos 8:31, 34; 10:13; 23:6; 2Sa 1:18; 1Ki 11:41; 14:19, 29; 15:7, 23, 31; 16:5, 14, 20, 27; 22:39, 45; 2Ki 1:18; 8:23; 10:34; 12:19; 13:8, 12; 14:6, 15, 18, 28; 15:6, 11, 15, 21, 26, 31, 36; 16:19; 20:20; 21:17, 25; 22:16; 23:24, 28; 24:5; 2Ch 16:11; 25:4, 26; 27:7; 28:26; 34:24; 35:12, 27; 36:8; Ezr 6:18; Est 10:2; Da 10:21; 12:1; Lk 3:4; Ac 1:20; 7:42; Gal 3:10; Rev 13:8; 17:8; 20:15; 21:27

WRONG WRONGDOER, WRONGDOERS, WRONGDOING, WRONGED, WRONGS

Ex 23: 2 not follow the crowd in doing w.
Nu 5: 7 restitution for the w they have done,
Dt 32: 4 A faithful God who does no w,
1Sa 26:21 a fool and have been terribly w."
1Ki 8:47 we have done w, we have acted
Job 34:12 is unthinkable that God would do w,
Ps 5: 5 You hate all who do w;
119:128 precepts right, I hate every w path.
Isa 7:15 he knows enough to reject the w
Da 9: 5 we have sinned and done w.
Zep 3: 5 her is righteous; he does no w.
3:13 They will do no w; they will tell no
Lk 23:41 But this man has done nothing w."
Jn 16: 8 the world to be in the w about sin
Ac 23: 9 "We find nothing w with this
Ro 13: 4 But if you do w, be afraid, for rulers
Col 3:25 Anyone who does w will be repaid
1Th 5:15 that nobody pays back w for w,
Rev 22:11 who does w continue to do w;

WRONGDOER* WRONG

Nu 5: 8 which atonement is made for the w.
Ro 13: 4 wrath to bring punishment on the w.

WRONGDOERS WRONG

1Co 6: 9 that w will not inherit the kingdom

WRONGDOING WRONG

Job 1:22 did not sin by charging God with w.
Hab 1:13 look on evil; you cannot tolerate w.
1Jn 5:17 All w is sin, and there is sin

WRONGED WRONG

Nu 5: 7 give it all to the person they have w.
Pr 18:19 A brother w is more unyielding than
1Co 6: 7 Why not rather be w?

WRONGS WRONG

Ge 50:15 pays us back for all the w we did
Pr 10:12 conflict, but love covers over all w.
1Co 13: 5 angered, it keeps no record of w.

WROTE WRITE

Ex 24: 4 w down everything the LORD had
34:28 he w on the tablets the words
Dt 10: 4 The LORD w on these tablets what
2Ch 32:17 also w letters ridiculing the LORD,
Da 5: 5 and w on the plaster of the wall,
Jn 1:45 "We have found the one Moses w
5:46 believe me, for he w about me.
8: 8 *down and w on the ground.*
Ac 1: 1 I w about all that Jesus began to do

X

XERXES*

1. The father of Darius the Mede (Da 9:1).
2. King of Persia (Ezr 4:6; Est 1–3; 6–10); husband of Esther (Est 2:16; 7:5; 8:1, 7). Deposed Vashti; replaced her with Esther (Est 1–2). Sealed Haman's edict to annihilate the Jews (Est 3). Received Esther without having called her (Est 5:1–8). Honored Mordecai (Est 6). Hanged Haman (Est 7). Issued edict allowing Jews to defend themselves (Est 8). Exalted Mordecai (Est 8:1–2, 15; 9:4; 10:1–3).

Y

YAHWEH See LORD†

YARN

Ex 25: 4 purple and scarlet y and fine linen;
2Ch 2: 7 crimson and blue y, and experienced

YEAR YEAR'S, YEARS

Ge 17:21 bear to you by this time next y."
Ex 23:14 "Three times a y you are
34:23 Three times a y all your men are
Lev 16:34 to be made once a y for all the sins
25: 4 in the seventh y the land is to have a y of sabbath rest,
25:11 The fiftieth y shall be a jubilee
Nu 14:34 one y for each of the forty days you
Dt 1: 3 In the fortieth y, on the first day
1Sa 1: 3 Y after y this man went up from his
7:16 From y to y he went on a circuit
1Ki 10:25 Y after y, everyone who came
2Ki 4:16 "About this time next y,"
Ne 10:31 Every seventh y we will forgo
Isa 6: 1 In the y that King Uzziah died,
34: 8 day of vengeance, a y of retribution,
61: 2 to proclaim the y of the LORD's
63: 4 the y for me to redeem had come.
Zec 14:16 go up y after y to worship the King,
Lk 2:41 Every y Jesus' parents went
13: 8 'leave it alone for one more y,
Jn 11:49 who was high priest that y,
18:13 of Caiaphas, the high priest that y.
Heb 9: 7 and that only once a y, and never
10: 1 same sacrifices repeated endlessly y after y,

YEAR'S YEAR
Mk   6:37 take more than half a **y** wages!
Jn   6: 7 take more than half a **y** wages

YEARNS*
Job 19:27 How my heart **y** within me!
Ps   84: 2 My soul **y**, even faints,
Isa   26: 9 My soul **y** for you in the night;
Jer 31:20 Therefore my heart **y** for him;

YEARS YEAR
Ge   1:14 mark sacred times, and days and **y**,
     25: 8 old age, an old man and full of **y**;
     35:29 to his people, old and full of **y**.
     41:26 The seven good cows are seven **y**,
     41:30 seven **y** of famine will follow them.
     47: 9 My **y** have been few and difficult,
Ex 12:40 people lived in Egypt was 430 **y**.
     16:35 The Israelites ate manna forty **y**,
Lev 25: 8 " 'Count off seven sabbath **y**—seven
           times seven **y**—
Nu   1: 3 men in Israel who are twenty **y** old
     14:34 For forty **y**—one year for each
Dt   2: 7 These forty **y** the Lord your God
     8: 4 did not swell during these forty **y**.
2Sa 21: 1 was a famine for three successive **y**;
2Ch 36:21 until the seventy **y** were completed
Ezr   5:11 temple that was built many **y** ago,
Ne   9:21 For forty **y** you sustained them
Job 36:26 number of his **y** is past finding out.
Ps   90: 4 A thousand **y** in your sight are like
     90:10 Our days may come to seventy **y**,
     95:10 For forty **y** I was angry
Pr   3: 2 they will prolong your life many **y**
     9:11 and **y** will be added to your life.
     10:27 but the **y** of the wicked are cut short.
Ecc   6: 6 if he lives a thousand **y** twice over
Jer 25:12 when the seventy **y** are fulfilled,
Da   9: 2 of Jerusalem would last seventy **y**,
Joel 2.25 for the **y** the locusts have eaten—
Mt   2:16 its vicinity who were two **y** old
     9:20 to bleeding for twelve **y** came
Lk   3:23 Jesus himself was about thirty **y** old
     13:16 has kept bound for eighteen long **y**,
Jn   2:20 "It has taken forty-six **y** to build
2Pe   3: 8 the Lord a day is like a thousand **y**,
          and a thousand **y** are like a day.
Rev 20: 2 and bound him for a thousand **y**.

YEAST
Ex 12:15 you are to eat bread made without **y**.
     12:15 whoever eats anything with **y** in it
     12:20 Eat nothing made with **y**.
Lev   2:11 must be made without **y**, for you are
          not to burn any **y**
Mt 16: 6 on your guard against the **y**
1Co   5: 6 a little **y** leavens the whole batch
Gal   5: 9 "A little **y** works through the whole

YES
Mt   5:37 All you need to say is simply '**Y**'
2Co   1:17 in the same breath I say both "**Y**,
     1:20 has made, they are "**Y**" in Christ.
Jas   5:12 All you need to say is a simple "**Y**"

YESTERDAY
Heb 13: 8 Jesus Christ is the same **y** and today

YET
Job 13:15 he slay me, **y** will I hope in him;
     19:26 **y** in my flesh I will see God;
Ps   42: 5 for I will **y** praise him, my Savior
Pr 30:24 small, **y** they are extremely wise:
     30:25 **y** they store up their food
Ecc   1: 7 into the sea, **y** the sea is never full.
Am   4: 6 **y** you have not returned to me,"
Hab   3:16 **Y** I will wait patiently for the day
Mal   1: 2 "**Y** I have loved Jacob,
Mt   6:26 **y** your heavenly Father feeds them.
Mk   8:36 whole world, **y** forfeit their soul?
Jn   2: 4 "My hour has not **y** come."
     6:70 **Y** one of you is a devil!"
     7: 6 told them, "My time is not **y** here;
     7: 8 my time has not **y** fully come."
     7:39 since Jesus had not **y** been glorified.
     8:20 **Y** no one seized him, because his
          hour had not **y** come.
     20:29 have not seen and **y** have believed."
Ro   8:25 we hope for what we do not **y** have,
Heb 12: 4 you have not **y** resisted to the point
Rev   9:12 two other woes are **y** to come.
     17:10 one is, the other has not **y** come;

YIELD YIELDED, YIELDING
Ge   4:12 it will no longer **y** its crops for you.
Lev 25:19 Then the land will **y** its fruit,
Pr   8:19 what I **y** surpasses choice silver.
Isa 42: 8 I will not **y** my glory to another

YIELDED* YIELD
Ps 107:37 vineyards that **y** a fruitful harvest;
Isa   5: 2 good grapes, but it **y** only bad fruit.
Lk   8: 8 It came up and **y** a crop, a hundred
     12:16 rich man **y** an abundant harvest.

YIELDING YIELD
Rev 22: 2 of fruit, **y** its fruit every month.

YOKE YOKED
Ex   6: 6 from under the **y** of the Egyptians.
Dt 28:48 He will put an iron **y** on your neck
1Ki 12: 4 "Your father put a heavy **y** on us,
Mt 11:29 Take my **y** upon you and learn
     11:30 For my **y** is easy and my burden is
Gal   5: 1 be burdened again by a **y** of slavery.

YOKED YOKE
Dt 22:10 with an ox and a donkey **y** together.
Ps 106:28 They **y** themselves to the Baal
2Co   6:14 Do not be **y** together

YOUNG YOUNGER, YOUNGEST, YOUTH, YOUTHS
Ex 23:19 "Do not cook a **y** goat in its
Lev   1:14 are to offer a dove or a **y** pigeon.
     5: 7 or two **y** pigeons to the Lord as
     14:22 and two doves or two **y** pigeons,
Nu 30: 3 "When a **y** woman still living in her
Dt 22: 6 do not take the mother with the **y**.
     32:25 The **y** men and **y** women will perish,

Ru   2: 5 does that y woman belong to?"
1Sa   2:17 This sin of the y men was very great
2Ch 10:14 he followed the advice of the y men
      36:17 did not spare y men or y women,
Ps   37:25 I was y and now I am old, yet I have
      78:63 Fire consumed their y men,
     119: 9 How can a y person stay on the path
Pr   7: 7 I noticed among the y men, a youth
      20:29 The glory of y men is their strength,
Isa 11: 8 the y child will put its hand
      40:11 he gently leads those that have y.
Jer   1: 6 know how to speak; I am too y."
La   1:18 My y men and y women have gone
Da   1: 4 y men without any physical defect,
      1:17 To these four y men God gave
Joel 2:28 dreams, your y men will see visions.
Mk   14:51 A y man, wearing nothing
      16: 5 they saw a y man dressed in a white
Lk   2:24 "a pair of doves or two y pigeons."
Ac   2:17 your y men will see visions,
      7:58 at the feet of a y man named Saul.
      20: 9 in a window was a y man named
1Ti   4:12 down on you because you are y,
Titus 2: 6 encourage the y men to be
1Jn   2:13 I am writing to you, y men,

YOUNGER YOUNG

Ge   19:35 and the y daughter went in and slept
      25:23 and the older will serve the y."
      29:27 we will give you the y one also,
Ro   9:12 told, "The older will serve the y."
1Ti   5: 1 Treat y men as brothers,
      5:14 So I counsel y widows to marry,
Titus 2: 4 they can urge the y women to love
1Pe   5: 5 you who are y, submit yourselves

YOUNGEST YOUNG

Ge   9:24 found out what his y son had done
      42:20 you must bring your y brother
Jos   6:26 at the cost of his y he will set up its
1Sa 17:14 David was the y. The three oldest
1Ki 16:34 gates at the cost of his y son Segub,
Lk   22:26 among you should be like the y,

YOUTH YOUNG

Nu   11:28 who had been Moses' aide since y,
1Sa 17:33 he has been a warrior from his y."
Ps   71: 5 LORD, my confidence since my y.
     103: 5 your y is renewed like the eagle's.
     144:12 in their y will be like well-nurtured
Pr   2:17 who has left the partner of her y
      5:18 you rejoice in the wife of your y.
      7: 7 young men, a y who had no sense.
Ecc   4:13 Better a poor but wise y than an old
      11:10 for y and vigor are meaningless.
      12: 1 your Creator in the days of your y,
Eze 16:60 with you in the days of your y, and I
Mal   2:14 between you and the wife of your y.
2Ti   2:22 Flee the evil desires of y and pursue

YOUTHS YOUNG

Isa 40:30 Even y grow tired and weary,

Z

ZACCHAEUS

Lk   19: 2 A man was there by the name of Z;

ZADOK ZADOKITES

2Sa 15:27 The king also said to Z the priest,
1Ki   1:26 and Z the priest, and Benaiah son
Ne   13:13 Shelemiah the priest, Z the scribe,

ZADOKITES* ZADOK

Eze 48:11 the Z, who were faithful in serving

ZALMON

Jdg   9:48 and all his men went up Mount Z.
Ps   68:14 it was like snow fallen on Mount Z.

ZALMUNNA

Jdg   8: 5 and I am still pursuing Zebah and Z,
Ps   83:11 all their princes like Zebah and Z,

ZAPHON

Jos 13:27 Z with the rest of the realm of Sihon
Ps   48: 2 like the heights of Z is Mount Zion,

ZAREPHATH

1Ki 17: 9 "Go at once to Z in the region
Lk   4:26 but to a widow in Z in the region

ZEAL ZEALOUS, ZEALOUSLY

Nu   25:11 I did not put an end to them in my z.
Dt   29:20 wrath and z will burn against them.
2Ki 10:16 me and see my z for the LORD."
      19:31 "The z of the LORD Almighty
Ps   69: 9 for z for your house consumes me,
     119:139 My z wears me out, for my enemies
Isa 37:32 The z of the LORD Almighty will
      59:17 wrapped himself in z as in a cloak.
Eze   5:13 I the LORD have spoken in my z.
Jn   2:17 "Z for your house will consume
Ro   10: 2 their z is not based on knowledge.
      12:11 Never be lacking in z, but keep your

ZEALOUS ZEAL

Nu   25:13 because he was z for the honor
1Ki 19:10 "I have been very z for the LORD
      19:14 "I have been very z for the LORD
Pr   23:17 but always be z for the fear
Eze 39:25 and I will be z for my holy name.
Ac   21:20 and all of them are z for the law.
Ro   10: 2 about them that they are z for God,
Gal   1:14 was extremely z for the traditions
      4:17 Those people are z to win you over,
      4:18 It is fine to be z,

ZEALOUSLY* ZEAL

Ne   3:20 of Zabbai z repaired another section,

ZEBAH

Jdg   8: 5 I am still pursuing Z and Zalmunna,
Ps   83:11 Zeeb, all their princes like Z

ZEBEDEE ZEBEDEE'S

Mt   4:21 James son of Z and his brother John.
      26:37 the two sons of Z along with him,

Mk   1:20 they left their father **Z** in the boat
     10:35 John, the sons of **Z**, came to him.
Lk   5:10 the sons of **Z**, Simon's partners.

ZEBEDEE'S* ZEBEDEE

Mt   20:20 the mother of **Z** sons came to Jesus
     27:56 Joseph, and the mother of **Z** sons.

ZEBOYIM

Dt   29:23 Admah and **Z**, which the LORD
Hos 11: 8 How can I make you like **Z**?

ZEBUL

Jdg   9:30 When **Z** the governor of the city

ZEBULUN

Son of Jacob by Leah (Ge 30:20; 35:23; 1Ch 2:1).
Tribe of blessed (Ge 49:13; Dt 33:18–19), numbered (Nu 1:31; 26:27), allotted land (Jos 19:10–16;
Eze 48:26), failed to fully possess (Jdg 1:30), supported Deborah (Jdg 4:6–10; 5:14, 18), David (1Ch
12:33), 12,000 from (Rev 7:8).

ZECHARIAH

1. Son of Jeroboam II; king of Israel (2Ki
15:8–12).
2. Post-exilic prophet who encouraged rebuilding of temple (Ezr 5:1; 6:14; Zec 1:1).

ZEDEKIAH MATTANIAH

1. False prophet (1Ki 22:11–24; 2Ch 18:10–23).
2. Mattaniah, son of Josiah (1Ch 3:15), made
king of Judah by Nebuchadnezzar (2Ki 24:17—
25:7; 2Ch 36:10–14; Jer 37–39; 52:1–11).

ZEEB

Jdg   7:25 the Midianite leaders, Oreb and **Z**.
Ps   83:11 Make their nobles like Oreb and **Z**,

ZELOPHEHAD ZELOPHEHAD'S

Nu   26.33 (**Z** son of Hepher had no sons;
Jos 17: 3 Now **Z** son of Hepher, the son

ZELOPHEHAD'S ZELOPHEHAD

Nu   36: 6 LORD commands for **Z** daughters:

ZEPHANIAH

Prophet; descendant of Hezekiah (Zep 1:1).

ZERUBBABEL

Descendant of David (1Ch 3:19; Mt 1:3). Led
return from exile (Ezr 2:2; Ne 7:7). Governor of
Israel; helped rebuild altar and temple (Ezr 3; Hag
1–2; Zec 4).

ZERUIAH ZERUIAH'S

2Sa   2:18 The three sons of **Z** were there:

ZERUIAH'S* ZERUIAH

1Ch   2:16 **Z** three sons were Abishai,

ZEUS

Ac   14:12 Barnabas they called **Z**, and Paul

ZIBA

2Sa   9: 2 of Saul's household named **Z**.
      16: 1 summit, there was **Z**, the steward
      19:26 But **Z** my servant betrayed me.

ZIKLAG

1Sa 27: 6 So on that day Achish gave him **Z**,
     30: 1 They had attacked **Z** and burned it,
     30:26 When David reached **Z**, he sent

ZILPAH

Servant of Leah, mother of Jacob's sons Gad and
Asher (Ge 30:9–12; 35:26, 46:16–18).

ZIMRI

King of Israel (1Ki 16:9–20).

ZIN

Nu   13:21 the Desert of **Z** as far as Rehob,

ZION

2Sa   5: 7 David captured the fortress of **Z**—
2Ki 19:31 out of Mount **Z** a band of survivors.
Ps   2: 6 "I have installed my king on **Z**,
      9:11 of the LORD, enthroned in **Z**;
     14: 7 for Israel would come out of **Z**!
     48: 2 the heights of Zaphon is Mount **Z**,
     50: 2 From **Z**, perfect in beauty,
     65: 1 Praise awaits you, our God, in **Z**;
     74: 2 Mount **Z**, where you dwelt.
     78:68 of Judah, Mount **Z**, which he loved.
     87: 2 **Z** more than all the other dwellings
     87: 5 "This one was born in **Z**."
    102:13 arise and have compassion on **Z**,
    137: 3 "Sing us one of the songs of **Z**!"
SS   3:11 out, and look, you daughters of **Z**.
Isa   1:27 **Z** will be delivered with justice,
      2: 3 The law will go out from **Z**,
     14:32 "The LORD has established **Z**,
     28:16 I lay a stone in **Z**, a tested stone,
     40: 9 You who bring good news to **Z**,
     51: 3 The LORD will surely comfort **Z**
     51:11 They will enter **Z** with singing;
     52: 1 awake, **Z**, clothe yourself
     52: 8 When the LORD returns to **Z**,
Jer 50: 5 They will ask the way to **Z** and turn
La   2:13 comfort you, Virgin Daughter **Z**?
Joel 2: 1 Blow the trumpet in **Z**;
      3:21 The LORD dwells in **Z**!
Am   1: 2 "The LORD roars from **Z**
      6: 1 to you who are complacent in **Z**,
Mic   3:12 of you, **Z** will be plowed like a field,
      4: 2 The law will go out from **Z**,
Zec   1:17 the LORD will again comfort **Z**
      9: 9 Rejoice greatly, Daughter **Z**!
Mt   21: 5 "Say to Daughter **Z**, 'See, your king
Ro   9:33 I lay in **Z** a stone that causes people
     11:26 "The deliverer will come from **Z**;
Heb 12:22 But you have come to Mount **Z**,
1Pe   2: 6 I lay a stone in **Z**, a chosen
Rev 14: 1 standing on Mount **Z**, and with him

DAUGHTER ZION See DAUGHTER

MOUNT ZION See MOUNT

ZIPH ZIPHITES

1Sa 23:14 and in the hills of the Desert of **Z**.

ZIPHITES* ZIPH

1Sa 23:19 The **Z** went up to Saul at Gibeah

1Sa 26: 1 The **Z** went to Saul at Gibeah
Ps 54: T *When the **Z** had gone to Saul*

ZIPPOR
Nu 22: 4 So Balak son of **Z**, who was king

ZIPPORAH
Daughter of Reuel; wife of Moses (Ex 2:21–22; 4:20–26; 18:1–6).

ZITHER
Da 3: 7 the sound of the horn, flute, **z**, lyre,

ZIV
1Ki 6: 1 Israel, in the month of **Z**, the second

ZOAN
Ps 78:43 his wonders in the region of **Z**.

ZOAR
Ge 19:22 (That is why the town was called **Z**.)
19:30 for he was afraid to stay in **Z**.

ZOBAH
1Sa 14:47 the kings of **Z**, and the Philistines.
1Ch 18: 3 defeated Hadadezer king of **Z**,

ZOPHAR*
One of Job's friends (Job 2:11; 11; 20; 42:9).

ZORAH
Jdg 13: 2 A certain man of **Z**, named Manoah,

NUMERALS

40* FORTY
Eze 4: 6 I have assigned you **40** days, a day

42
Rev 11: 2 on the holy city for **42** months.

153*
Jn 21:11 It was full of large fish, **153**,

666*
1Ki 10:14 received yearly was **666** talents,
2Ch 9:13 received yearly was **666** talents,
Ezr 2:13 of Adonikam **666**
Rev 13:18 number of a man. That number is **666**.

1,260*
Rev 11: 3 they will prophesy for **1,260** days.
12: 6 be taken care of for **1,260** days.

1,290*
Da 12:11 is set up, there will be **1,290** days.

1,335*
Da 12:12 reaches the end of the **1,335** days.

12,000*
Rev 7: 5 tribe of Judah **12,000** were sealed,
7: 5 from the tribe of Reuben **12,000**,
7: 5 from the tribe of Gad **12,000**,
7: 6 from the tribe of Asher **12,000**,
7: 6 from the tribe of Naphtali **12,000**,
7: 6 from the tribe of Manasseh **12,000**,
7: 7 from the tribe of Simeon **12,000**,
7: 7 from the tribe of Levi **12,000**,
7: 7 from the tribe of Issachar **12,000**,
7: 8 from the tribe of Zebulun **12,000**,
7: 8 from the tribe of Joseph **12,000**,
7: 8 from the tribe of Benjamin **12,000**.
21:16 and found it to be **12,000** stadia

144,000*
Rev 7: 4 **144,000** from all the tribes of Israel.
14: 1 with him **144,000** who had his name
14: 3 song except the **144,000** who had

601,730*
Nu 26:51 of the men of Israel was **601,730**.

603,550*
Ex 38:26 old or more, a total of **603,550** men.
Nu 1:46 The total number was **603,550**.
2:32 by their divisions, number **603,550**.